A book that contains all prime
numbers up to ten million...
(or else, learning Python and trying to produce
the fastest algorithm!)

By Dr Evangelos Himonides
(September 2009)

```
   2    3    5    7   11   13   17   19   23   29   31   37   41   43   47   53   59   61   67   71   73   79   83   89   97  101  103
 107  109  113  127  131  137  139  149  151  157  163  167  173  179  181  191  193  197  199  211
 223  227  229  233  239  241  251  257  263  269  271  277  281  283  293  307  311  313  317  331
 337  347  349  353  359  367  373  379  383  389  397  401  409  419  421  431  433  439  443  449
 457  461  463  467  479  487  491  499  503  509  521  523  541  547  557  563  569  571  577  587
 593  599  601  607  613  617  619  631  641  643  647  653  659  661  673  677  683  691  701  709
 719  727  733  739  743  751  757  761  769  773  787  797  809  811  821  823  827  829  839  853
 857  859  863  877  881  883  887  907  911  919  929  937  941  947  953  967  971  977  983  991
 997 1009 1013 1019 1021 1031 1033 1039 1049 1051 1061 1063 1069 1087 1091 1093
1097 1103 1109 1117 1123 1129 1151 1153 1163 1171 1181 1187 1193 1201 1213 1217
1223 1229 1231 1237 1249 1259 1277 1279 1283 1289 1291 1297 1301 1303 1307 1319
1321 1327 1361 1367 1373 1381 1399 1409 1423 1427 1429 1433 1439 1447 1451 1453
1459 1471 1481 1483 1487 1489 1493 1499 1511 1523 1531 1543 1549 1553 1559 1567
1571 1579 1583 1597 1601 1607 1609 1613 1619 1621 1627 1637 1657 1663 1667 1669
1693 1697 1699 1709 1721 1723 1733 1741 1747 1753 1759 1777 1783 1787 1789 1801
1811 1823 1831 1847 1861 1867 1871 1873 1877 1879 1889 1901 1907 1913 1931 1933
1949 1951 1973 1979 1987 1993 1997 1999 2003 2011 2017 2027 2029 2039 2053 2063
2069 2081 2083 2087 2089 2099 2111 2113 2129 2131 2137 2141 2143 2153 2161 2179
2203 2207 2213 2221 2237 2239 2243 2251 2267 2269 2273 2281 2287 2293 2297 2309
2311 2333 2339 2341 2347 2351 2357 2371 2377 2381 2383 2389 2393 2399 2411 2417
2423 2437 2441 2447 2459 2467 2473 2477 2503 2521 2531 2539 2543 2549 2551 2557
2579 2591 2593 2609 2617 2621 2633 2647 2657 2659 2663 2671 2677 2683 2687 2689
2693 2699 2707 2711 2713 2719 2729 2731 2741 2749 2753 2767 2777 2789 2791 2797
2801 2803 2819 2833 2837 2843 2851 2857 2861 2879 2887 2897 2903 2909 2917 2927
2939 2953 2957 2963 2969 2971 2999 3001 3011 3019 3023 3037 3041 3049 3061 3067
3079 3083 3089 3109 3119 3121 3137 3163 3167 3169 3181 3187 3191 3203 3209 3217
3221 3229 3251 3253 3257 3259 3271 3299 3301 3307 3313 3319 3323 3329 3331 3343
3347 3359 3361 3371 3373 3389 3391 3407 3413 3433 3449 3457 3461 3463 3467 3469
3491 3499 3511 3517 3527 3529 3533 3539 3541 3547 3557 3559 3571 3581 3583 3593
3607 3613 3617 3623 3631 3637 3643 3659 3671 3673 3677 3691 3697 3701 3709 3719
3727 3733 3739 3761 3767 3769 3779 3793 3797 3803 3821 3823 3833 3847 3851 3853
3863 3877 3881 3889 3907 3911 3917 3919 3923 3929 3931 3943 3947 3967 3989 4001
4003 4007 4013 4019 4021 4027 4049 4051 4057 4073 4079 4091 4093 4099 4111 4127
4129 4133 4139 4153 4157 4159 4177 4201 4211 4217 4219 4229 4231 4241 4243 4253
4259 4261 4271 4273 4283 4289 4297 4327 4337 4339 4349 4357 4363 4373 4391 4397
4409 4421 4423 4441 4447 4451 4457 4463 4481 4483 4493 4507 4513 4517 4519 4523
4547 4549 4561 4567 4583 4591 4597 4603 4621 4637 4639 4643 4649 4651 4657 4663
4673 4679 4691 4703 4721 4723 4729 4733 4751 4759 4783 4787 4789 4793 4799 4801
4813 4817 4831 4861 4871 4877 4889 4903 4909 4919 4931 4933 4937 4943 4951 4957
4967 4969 4973 4987 4993 4999 5003 5009 5011 5021 5023 5039 5051 5059 5077 5081
5087 5099 5101 5107 5113 5119 5147 5153 5167 5171 5179 5189 5197 5209 5227 5231
5233 5237 5261 5273 5279 5281 5297 5303 5309 5323 5333 5347 5351 5381 5387 5393
5399 5407 5413 5417 5419 5431 5437 5441 5443 5449 5471 5477 5479 5483 5501 5503
5507 5519 5521 5527 5531 5557 5563 5569 5573 5581 5591 5623 5639 5641 5647 5651
5653 5657 5659 5669 5683 5689 5693 5701 5711 5717 5737 5741 5743 5749 5779 5783
5791 5801 5807 5813 5821 5827 5839 5843 5849 5851 5857 5861 5867 5869 5879 5881
5897 5903 5923 5927 5939 5953 5981 5987 6007 6011 6029 6037 6043 6047 6053 6067
6073 6079 6089 6091 6101 6113 6121 6131 6133 6143 6151 6163 6173 6197 6199 6203
6211 6217 6221 6229 6247 6257 6263 6269 6271 6277 6287 6299 6301 6311 6317 6323
6329 6337 6343 6353 6359 6361 6367 6373 6379 6389 6397 6421 6427 6449 6451 6469
6473 6481 6491 6521 6529 6547 6551 6553 6563 6569 6571 6577 6581 6599 6607 6619
6637 6653 6659 6661 6673 6679 6689 6691 6701 6703 6709 6719 6733 6737 6761 6763
6779 6781 6791 6793 6803 6823 6827 6829 6833 6841 6857 6863 6869 6871 6883 6899
6907 6911 6917 6947 6949 6959 6961 6967 6971 6977 6983 6991 6997 7001 7013 7019
7027 7039 7043 7057 7069 7079 7103 7109 7121 7127 7129 7151 7159 7177 7187 7193
7207 7211 7213 7219 7229 7237 7243 7247 7253 7283 7297 7307 7309 7321 7331 7333
7349 7351 7369 7393 7411 7417 7433 7451 7457 7459 7477 7481 7487 7489 7499 7507
7517 7523 7529 7537 7541 7547 7549 7559 7561 7573 7577 7583 7589 7591 7603 7607
7621 7639 7643 7649 7669 7673 7681 7687 7691 7699 7703 7717 7723 7727 7741 7753
7757 7759 7789 7793 7817 7823 7829 7841 7853 7867 7873 7877 7879 7883 7901 7907
7919 7927 7933 7937 7949 7951 7963 7993 8009 8011 8017 8039 8053 8059 8069 8081
8087 8089 8093 8101 8111 8117 8123 8147 8161 8167 8171 8179 8191 8209 8219 8221
8231 8233 8237 8243 8263 8269 8273 8287 8291 8293 8297 8311 8317 8329 8353 8363
8369 8377 8387 8389 8419 8423 8429 8431 8443 8447 8461 8467 8501 8513 8521 8527
8537 8539 8543 8563 8573 8581 8597 8599 8609 8623 8627 8629 8641 8647 8663 8669
8677 8681 8689 8693 8699 8707 8713 8719 8731 8737 8741 8747 8753 8761 8779 8783
8803 8807 8819 8821 8831 8837 8839 8849 8861 8863 8867 8887 8893 8923 8929 8933
8941 8951 8963 8969 8971 8999 9001 9007 9011 9013 9029 9041 9043 9049 9059 9067
9091 9103 9109 9127 9133 9137 9151 9157 9161 9173 9181 9187 9199 9203 9209 9221
9227 9239 9241 9257 9277 9281 9283 9293 9311 9319 9323 9337 9341 9343 9349 9371
9377 9391 9397 9403 9413 9419 9421 9431 9433 9437 9439 9461 9463 9467 9473 9479
9491 9497 9511 9521 9533 9539 9547 9551 9587 9601 9613 9619 9623 9629 9631 9643
9649 9661 9677 9679 9689 9697 9719 9721 9733 9739 9743 9749 9767 9769 9781 9787
9791 9803 9811 9817 9829 9833 9839 9851 9857 9859 9871 9883 9887 9901 9907 9923
9929 9931 9941 9949 9967 9973 10007 10009 10037 10039 10061 10067 10069 10079
10091 10093 10099 10103 10111 10133 10139 10141 10151 10159 10163 10169 10177
10181 10193 10211 10223 10243 10247 10253 10259 10267 10271 10273 10289 10301
10303 10313 10321 10331 10333 10337 10343 10357 10369 10391 10399 10427 10429
10433 10453 10457 10459 10463 10477 10487 10499 10501 10513 10529 10531 10559
10567 10589 10597 10601 10607 10613 10627 10631 10639 10651 10657 10663 10667
10687 10691 10709 10711 10723 10729 10733 10739 10753 10771 10781 10789 10799
10831 10837 10847 10853 10859 10861 10867 10883 10889 10891 10903 10909 10937
10939 10949 10957 10973 10979 10987 10993 11003 11027 11047 11057 11059 11069
11071 11083 11087 11093 11113 11117 11119 11131 11149 11159 11161 11171 11173
11177 11197 11213 11239 11243 11251 11257 11261 11273 11279 11287 11299 11311
11317 11321 11329 11351 11353 11369 11383 11393 11399 11411 11423 11437 11443
11447 11467 11471 11483 11489 11491 11497 11503 11519 11527 11549 11551 11579
11587 11593 11597 11617 11621 11633 11657 11677 11681 11689 11699 11701 11717
11719 11731 11743 11777 11779 11783 11789 11801 11807 11813 11821 11827 11831
```

```
11833  11839  11863  11867  11887  11897  11903  11909  11923  11927  11933  11939  11941
11953  11959  11969  11971  11981  11987  12007  12011  12037  12041  12043  12049  12071
12073  12097  12101  12107  12109  12113  12119  12143  12149  12157  12161  12163  12197
12203  12211  12227  12239  12241  12251  12253  12263  12269  12277  12281  12289  12301
12323  12329  12343  12347  12373  12377  12379  12391  12401  12409  12413  12421  12433
12437  12451  12457  12473  12479  12487  12491  12497  12503  12511  12517  12527  12539
12541  12547  12553  12569  12577  12583  12589  12601  12611  12613  12619  12637  12641
12647  12653  12659  12671  12689  12697  12703  12713  12721  12739  12743  12757  12763
12781  12791  12799  12809  12821  12823  12829  12841  12853  12889  12893  12899  12907
12911  12917  12919  12923  12941  12953  12959  12967  12973  12979  12983  13001  13003
13007  13009  13033  13037  13043  13049  13063  13093  13099  13103  13109  13121  13127
13147  13151  13159  13163  13171  13177  13183  13187  13217  13219  13229  13241  13249
13259  13267  13291  13297  13309  13313  13327  13331  13337  13339  13367  13381  13397
13399  13411  13417  13421  13441  13451  13457  13463  13469  13477  13487  13499  13513
13523  13537  13553  13567  13577  13591  13597  13613  13619  13627  13633  13649  13669
13679  13681  13687  13691  13693  13697  13709  13711  13721  13723  13729  13751  13757
13759  13763  13781  13789  13799  13807  13829  13831  13841  13859  13873  13877  13879
13883  13901  13903  13907  13913  13921  13931  13933  13963  13967  13997  13999  14009
14011  14029  14033  14051  14057  14071  14081  14083  14087  14107  14143  14149  14153
14159  14173  14177  14197  14207  14221  14243  14249  14251  14281  14293  14303  14321
14323  14327  14341  14347  14369  14387  14389  14401  14407  14411  14419  14423  14431
14437  14447  14449  14461  14479  14489  14503  14519  14533  14537  14543  14549  14551
14557  14561  14563  14591  14593  14621  14627  14629  14633  14639  14653  14657  14669
14683  14699  14713  14717  14723  14731  14737  14741  14747  14753  14759  14767  14771
14779  14783  14797  14813  14821  14827  14831  14843  14851  14867  14869  14879  14887
14891  14897  14923  14929  14939  14947  14951  14957  14969  14983  15013  15017  15031
15053  15061  15073  15077  15083  15091  15101  15107  15121  15131  15137  15139  15149
15161  15173  15187  15193  15199  15217  15227  15233  15241  15259  15263  15269  15271
15277  15287  15289  15299  15307  15313  15319  15329  15331  15349  15359  15361  15373
15377  15383  15391  15401  15413  15427  15439  15443  15451  15461  15467  15473  15493
15497  15511  15527  15541  15551  15559  15569  15581  15583  15601  15607  15619  15629
15641  15643  15647  15649  15661  15667  15671  15679  15683  15727  15731  15733  15737
15739  15749  15761  15767  15773  15787  15791  15797  15803  15809  15817  15823  15859
15877  15881  15887  15889  15901  15907  15913  15919  15923  15937  15959  15971  15973
15991  16001  16007  16033  16057  16061  16063  16067  16069  16073  16087  16091  16097
16103  16111  16127  16139  16141  16183  16187  16189  16193  16217  16223  16229  16231
16249  16253  16267  16273  16301  16319  16333  16339  16349  16361  16363  16369  16381
16411  16417  16421  16427  16433  16447  16451  16453  16477  16481  16487  16493  16519
16529  16547  16553  16561  16567  16573  16603  16607  16619  16631  16633  16649  16651
16657  16661  16673  16691  16693  16699  16703  16729  16741  16747  16759  16763  16787
16811  16823  16829  16831  16843  16871  16879  16883  16889  16901  16903  16921  16927
16931  16937  16943  16963  16979  16981  16987  16993  17011  17021  17027  17029  17033
17041  17047  17053  17077  17093  17099  17107  17117  17123  17137  17159  17167  17183
17189  17191  17203  17207  17209  17231  17239  17257  17291  17293  17299  17317  17321
17327  17333  17341  17351  17359  17377  17383  17387  17389  17393  17401  17417  17419
17431  17443  17449  17467  17471  17477  17483  17489  17491  17497  17509  17519  17539
17551  17569  17573  17579  17581  17597  17599  17609  17623  17627  17657  17659  17669
17681  17683  17707  17713  17729  17737  17747  17749  17761  17783  17789  17791  17807
17827  17837  17839  17851  17863  17881  17891  17903  17909  17911  17921  17923  17929
17939  17957  17959  17971  17977  17981  17987  17989  18013  18041  18043  18047  18049
18059  18061  18077  18089  18097  18119  18121  18127  18131  18133  18143  18149  18169
18181  18191  18199  18211  18217  18223  18229  18233  18251  18253  18257  18269  18287
18289  18301  18307  18311  18313  18329  18341  18353  18367  18371  18379  18397  18401
18413  18427  18433  18439  18443  18451  18457  18461  18481  18493  18503  18517  18521
18523  18539  18541  18553  18583  18587  18593  18617  18637  18661  18671  18679  18691
18701  18713  18719  18731  18743  18749  18757  18773  18787  18793  18797  18803  18839
18859  18869  18899  18911  18913  18917  18919  18947  18959  18973  18979  19001  19009
19013  19031  19037  19051  19069  19073  19079  19081  19087  19121  19139  19141  19157
19163  19181  19183  19207  19211  19213  19219  19231  19237  19249  19259  19267  19273
19289  19301  19309  19319  19333  19373  19379  19381  19387  19391  19403  19417  19421
19423  19427  19429  19441  19447  19457  19463  19469  19471  19477  19483  19489
19501  19507  19531  19541  19543  19553  19559  19571  19577  19583  19597  19603  19609
19661  19681  19687  19697  19699  19709  19717  19727  19739  19751  19753  19759  19763
19777  19793  19801  19813  19819  19841  19843  19853  19861  19867  19889  19891  19913
19919  19927  19937  19949  19961  19963  19973  19979  19991  19993  19997  20011  20021
20023  20029  20047  20051  20063  20071  20089  20101  20107  20113  20117  20123  20129
20143  20147  20149  20161  20173  20177  20183  20201  20219  20231  20233  20249  20261
20269  20287  20297  20323  20327  20333  20341  20347  20353  20357  20359  20369  20389
20393  20399  20407  20411  20431  20441  20443  20477  20479  20483  20507  20509  20521
20533  20543  20549  20551  20563  20593  20599  20611  20627  20639  20641  20663  20681
20693  20707  20717  20719  20731  20743  20747  20749  20753  20759  20771  20773  20789
20807  20809  20849  20857  20873  20879  20887  20897  20899  20903  20921  20929  20939
20947  20959  20963  20981  20983  21001  21011  21013  21017  21019  21023  21031  21059
21061  21067  21089  21101  21107  21121  21139  21143  21149  21157  21163  21169  21179
21187  21191  21193  21211  21221  21227  21247  21269  21277  21283  21313  21317  21319
21323  21341  21347  21377  21379  21383  21391  21397  21401  21407  21419  21433  21467
21481  21487  21491  21493  21499  21503  21517  21521  21523  21529  21557  21559  21563
21569  21577  21587  21589  21599  21601  21611  21613  21617  21647  21649  21661  21673
21683  21701  21713  21727  21737  21739  21751  21757  21767  21773  21787  21799  21803
21817  21821  21839  21841  21851  21859  21863  21871  21881  21893  21911  21929  21937
21943  21961  21977  21991  21997  22003  22013  22027  22031  22037  22039  22051  22063
22067  22073  22079  22091  22093  22109  22111  22123  22129  22133  22147  22153  22157
22159  22171  22189  22193  22229  22247  22259  22271  22273  22277  22279  22283  22291
22303  22307  22343  22349  22367  22369  22381  22391  22397  22409  22433  22441  22447
22453  22469  22481  22483  22501  22511  22531  22541  22543  22549  22567  22571  22573
22613  22619  22621  22637  22639  22643  22651  22669  22679  22691  22697  22699  22709
22717  22721  22727  22739  22741  22751  22769  22777  22783  22787  22807  22811  22817
22853  22859  22861  22871  22877  22901  22907  22921  22937  22943  22961  22963  22973
22993  23003  23011  23017  23021  23027  23029  23039  23041  23053  23057  23059  23063
```

```
23071 23081 23087 23099 23117 23131 23143 23159 23167 23173 23189 23197 23201
23203 23209 23227 23251 23269 23279 23291 23293 23297 23311 23321 23327 23333
23339 23357 23369 23371 23399 23417 23431 23447 23459 23473 23497 23509 23531
23537 23539 23549 23557 23561 23563 23567 23581 23593 23599 23603 23609 23623
23627 23629 23633 23663 23669 23671 23677 23687 23689 23719 23741 23743 23747
23753 23761 23767 23773 23789 23801 23813 23819 23827 23831 23833 23857 23869
23873 23879 23887 23893 23899 23909 23911 23917 23929 23957 23971 23977 23981
23993 24001 24007 24019 24023 24029 24043 24049 24061 24071 24077 24083 24091
24097 24103 24107 24109 24113 24121 24133 24137 24151 24169 24179 24181 24197
24203 24223 24229 24239 24247 24251 24281 24317 24329 24337 24359 24371 24373
24379 24391 24407 24413 24419 24421 24439 24443 24469 24473 24481 24499 24509
24517 24527 24533 24547 24551 24571 24593 24611 24623 24631 24659 24671 24677
24683 24691 24697 24709 24733 24749 24763 24767 24781 24793 24799 24809 24821
24841 24847 24851 24859 24877 24889 24907 24917 24919 24923 24943 24953 24967
24971 24977 24979 24989 25013 25031 25033 25037 25057 25073 25087 25097 25111
25117 25121 25127 25147 25153 25163 25169 25171 25183 25189 25219 25229 25237
25243 25247 25253 25261 25301 25303 25307 25309 25321 25339 25343 25349 25357
25367 25373 25391 25409 25411 25423 25439 25447 25453 25457 25463 25469 25471
25523 25537 25541 25561 25577 25579 25583 25589 25601 25603 25609 25621 25633
25639 25643 25657 25667 25673 25679 25693 25703 25717 25733 25741 25747 25759
25763 25771 25793 25799 25801 25819 25841 25847 25849 25867 25873 25889 25903
25913 25919 25931 25933 25939 25943 25951 25969 25981 25997 25999 26003 26017
26021 26029 26041 26053 26083 26099 26107 26111 26113 26119 26141 26153 26161
26171 26177 26183 26189 26203 26209 26227 26237 26249 26251 26261 26263 26267
26293 26297 26309 26317 26321 26339 26347 26357 26371 26387 26393 26399 26407
26417 26423 26431 26437 26449 26459 26479 26489 26497 26501 26513 26539 26557
26561 26573 26591 26597 26627 26633 26641 26647 26669 26681 26683 26687 26693
26699 26701 26711 26713 26717 26723 26729 26731 26737 26759 26777 26783 26801
26813 26821 26833 26839 26849 26861 26863 26879 26881 26891 26893 26903 26921
26927 26947 26951 26953 26959 26981 26987 26993 27011 27017 27031 27043 27059
27061 27067 27073 27077 27091 27103 27107 27109 27127 27143 27179 27191 27197
27211 27239 27241 27253 27259 27271 27277 27281 27283 27299 27329 27337 27361
27367 27397 27407 27409 27427 27431 27437 27449 27457 27479 27481 27487 27509
27527 27529 27539 27541 27551 27581 27583 27611 27617 27631 27647 27653 27673
27689 27691 27697 27701 27733 27737 27739 27743 27749 27751 27763 27767 27773
27779 27791 27793 27799 27803 27809 27817 27823 27827 27847 27851 27883 27893
27901 27917 27919 27941 27943 27947 27953 27961 27967 27983 27997 28001 28019
28027 28031 28051 28057 28069 28081 28087 28097 28099 28109 28111 28123 28151
28163 28181 28183 28201 28211 28219 28229 28277 28279 28283 28289 28297 28307
28309 28319 28349 28351 28387 28393 28403 28409 28411 28429 28433 28439 28447
28463 28477 28493 28499 28513 28517 28537 28541 28547 28549 28559 28571 28573
28579 28591 28597 28603 28607 28619 28621 28627 28631 28643 28649 28657 28661
28663 28669 28687 28697 28703 28711 28723 28729 28751 28753 28759 28771 28789
28793 28807 28813 28817 28843 28859 28867 28871 28879 28901 28909 28921
28927 28933 28949 28961 28979 29009 29017 29021 29023 29027 29033 29059 29063
29077 29101 29123 29129 29131 29137 29147 29153 29167 29173 29179 29191 29201
29207 29209 29221 29231 29243 29251 29269 29287 29297 29303 29311 29327 29333
29339 29347 29363 29383 29387 29389 29399 29401 29411 29423 29429 29437 29443
29453 29473 29483 29501 29527 29531 29537 29567 29569 29573 29581 29587 29599
29611 29629 29633 29641 29663 29669 29671 29683 29717 29723 29741 29753 29759
29761 29789 29803 29819 29833 29837 29851 29863 29867 29873 29879 29881 29917
29921 29927 29947 29959 29983 29989 30011 30013 30029 30047 30059 30071 30089
30091 30097 30103 30109 30113 30119 30133 30137 30139 30161 30169 30181 30187
30197 30203 30211 30223 30241 30253 30259 30269 30271 30293 30307 30313 30319
30323 30341 30347 30367 30389 30391 30403 30427 30431 30449 30467 30469 30491
30493 30497 30509 30517 30529 30539 30553 30557 30559 30577 30593 30631 30637
30643 30649 30661 30671 30677 30689 30697 30703 30707 30713 30727 30757 30763
30773 30781 30803 30809 30817 30829 30839 30841 30851 30853 30859 30869 30871
30881 30893 30911 30931 30937 30941 30949 30971 30977 30983 31013 31019 31033
31039 31051 31063 31069 31079 31081 31091 31121 31123 31139 31147 31151 31153
31159 31177 31181 31183 31189 31193 31219 31223 31231 31237 31247 31249 31253
31259 31267 31271 31277 31307 31319 31321 31327 31333 31337 31357 31379 31387
31391 31393 31397 31469 31477 31481 31489 31511 31513 31517 31531 31541 31543
31547 31567 31573 31583 31601 31607 31627 31643 31649 31657 31663 31667 31687
31699 31721 31723 31727 31729 31741 31751 31769 31771 31793 31799 31817 31847
31849 31859 31873 31883 31891 31907 31957 31963 31973 31981 31991 32003 32009
32027 32029 32051 32057 32059 32063 32069 32077 32083 32089 32099 32117 32119
32141 32143 32159 32173 32183 32189 32191 32203 32213 32233 32237 32251 32257
32261 32297 32299 32303 32309 32321 32323 32327 32341 32353 32359 32363 32369
32371 32377 32381 32401 32411 32413 32423 32429 32441 32443 32467 32479 32491
32497 32503 32507 32531 32533 32537 32561 32563 32569 32573 32579 32587 32603
32609 32611 32621 32633 32647 32653 32687 32693 32707 32713 32717 32719 32749
32771 32779 32783 32789 32797 32801 32803 32831 32833 32839 32843 32869 32887
32909 32911 32917 32933 32939 32941 32957 32969 32971 32983 32987 32993 32999
33013 33023 33029 33037 33049 33053 33071 33073 33083 33091 33107 33113 33119
33149 33151 33161 33179 33181 33191 33199 33203 33211 33223 33247 33287 33289
33301 33311 33317 33329 33331 33343 33347 33349 33353 33359 33377 33391 33403
33409 33413 33427 33457 33461 33469 33479 33487 33493 33503 33521 33529 33533
33547 33563 33569 33577 33581 33587 33589 33599 33601 33613 33617 33619 33623
33629 33637 33641 33647 33679 33703 33713 33721 33739 33749 33751 33757 33767
33769 33773 33791 33797 33809 33811 33827 33829 33851 33857 33863 33871 33889
33893 33911 33923 33931 33937 33941 33961 33967 33997 34019 34031 34033 34039
34057 34061 34123 34127 34129 34141 34147 34157 34159 34171 34183 34211 34213
34217 34231 34253 34259 34261 34267 34273 34283 34297 34301 34303 34313 34319
34327 34337 34351 34361 34367 34369 34381 34403 34421 34429 34439 34457 34469
34471 34483 34487 34499 34501 34511 34513 34519 34537 34543 34549 34583 34589
34591 34603 34607 34613 34631 34649 34651 34667 34673 34679 34687 34693 34703
34721 34729 34739 34747 34757 34759 34763 34781 34807 34819 34841 34843 34847
34849 34871 34877 34883 34897 34913 34919 34939 34949 34961 34963 34981 35023
```

```
35027  35051  35053  35059  35069  35081  35083  35089  35099  35107  35111  35117  35129
35141  35149  35153  35159  35171  35201  35221  35227  35251  35257  35267  35279  35281
35291  35311  35317  35323  35327  35339  35353  35363  35381  35393  35401  35407  35419
35423  35437  35447  35449  35461  35491  35507  35509  35521  35527  35531  35533  35537
35543  35569  35573  35591  35593  35597  35603  35617  35671  35677  35729  35731  35747
35753  35759  35771  35797  35801  35803  35809  35831  35837  35839  35851  35863  35869
35879  35897  35899  35911  35923  35933  35951  35963  35969  35977  35983  35993  35999
36007  36011  36013  36017  36037  36061  36067  36073  36083  36097  36107  36109  36131
36137  36151  36161  36187  36191  36209  36217  36229  36241  36251  36263  36269  36277
36293  36299  36307  36313  36319  36341  36343  36353  36373  36383  36389  36433  36451
36457  36467  36469  36473  36479  36493  36497  36523  36527  36529  36541  36551  36559
36563  36571  36583  36587  36599  36607  36629  36637  36643  36653  36671  36677  36683
36691  36697  36709  36713  36721  36739  36749  36761  36767  36779  36781  36787  36791
36793  36809  36821  36833  36847  36857  36871  36877  36887  36899  36901  36913  36919
36923  36929  36931  36943  36947  36973  36979  36997  37003  37013  37019  37021  37039
37049  37057  37061  37087  37097  37117  37123  37139  37159  37171  37181  37189  37199
37201  37217  37223  37243  37253  37273  37277  37307  37309  37313  37321  37337  37339
37357  37361  37363  37369  37379  37397  37409  37423  37441  37447  37463  37483  37489
37493  37501  37507  37511  37517  37529  37537  37547  37549  37561  37567  37571  37573
37579  37589  37591  37607  37619  37633  37643  37649  37657  37663  37691  37693  37699
37717  37747  37781  37783  37799  37811  37813  37831  37847  37853  37861  37871  37879
37889  37897  37907  37951  37957  37963  37967  37987  37991  37993  37997  38011  38039
38047  38053  38069  38083  38113  38119  38149  38153  38167  38177  38183  38189  38197
38201  38219  38231  38237  38239  38261  38273  38281  38287  38299  38303  38317  38321
38327  38329  38333  38351  38371  38377  38393  38431  38447  38449  38453  38459  38461
38501  38543  38557  38561  38567  38569  38593  38603  38609  38611  38629  38639  38651
38653  38669  38671  38677  38693  38699  38707  38711  38713  38723  38729  38737  38747
38749  38767  38783  38791  38803  38821  38833  38839  38851  38861  38867  38873  38891
38903  38917  38921  38923  38933  38953  38959  38971  38977  38993  39019  39023  39041
39043  39047  39079  39089  39097  39103  39107  39113  39119  39133  39139  39157  39161
39163  39181  39191  39199  39209  39217  39227  39229  39233  39239  39241  39251  39293
39301  39313  39317  39323  39341  39343  39359  39367  39371  39373  39383  39397  39409
39419  39439  39443  39451  39461  39499  39503  39509  39511  39521  39541  39551  39563
39569  39581  39607  39619  39623  39631  39659  39667  39671  39679  39703  39709  39719
39727  39733  39749  39761  39769  39779  39791  39799  39821  39827  39829  39839  39841
39847  39857  39863  39869  39877  39883  39887  39901  39929  39937  39953  39971  39979
39983  39989  40009  40013  40031  40037  40039  40063  40087  40093  40099  40111  40123
40127  40129  40151  40153  40163  40169  40177  40189  40193  40213  40231  40237  40241
40253  40277  40283  40289  40343  40351  40357  40361  40387  40423  40427  40429  40433
40459  40471  40483  40487  40493  40499  40507  40519  40529  40531  40543  40559  40577
40583  40591  40597  40609  40627  40637  40639  40693  40697  40699  40709  40739  40751
40759  40763  40771  40787  40801  40813  40819  40823  40829  40841  40847  40849  40853
40867  40879  40883  40897  40903  40927  40933  40939  40949  40961  40973  40993  41011
41017  41023  41039  41047  41051  41057  41077  41081  41113  41117  41131  41141  41143
41149  41161  41177  41179  41183  41189  41201  41203  41213  41221  41227  41231  41233
41243  41257  41263  41269  41281  41299  41333  41341  41351  41357  41381  41387  41389
41399  41411  41413  41443  41453  41467  41479  41491  41507  41513  41519  41521  41539
41543  41549  41579  41593  41597  41603  41609  41611  41617  41621  41627  41641  41647
41651  41659  41669  41681  41687  41719  41729  41737  41759  41761  41771  41777  41801
41809  41813  41843  41849  41851  41863  41879  41887  41893  41897  41903  41911  41927
41941  41947  41953  41957  41959  41969  41981  41983  41999  42013  42017  42019  42023
42043  42061  42071  42073  42083  42089  42101  42131  42139  42157  42169  42179  42181
42187  42193  42197  42209  42221  42223  42227  42239  42257  42281  42283  42293  42299
42307  42323  42331  42337  42349  42359  42373  42379  42391  42397  42403  42407  42409
42433  42437  42443  42451  42457  42461  42463  42467  42473  42487  42491  42499  42509
42533  42557  42569  42571  42577  42589  42611  42641  42643  42649  42667  42677  42683
42689  42697  42701  42703  42709  42719  42727  42737  42743  42751  42767  42773  42787
42793  42797  42821  42829  42839  42841  42853  42859  42863  42899  42901  42923  42929
42937  42943  42953  42961  42967  42979  42989  43003  43013  43019  43037  43049  43051
43063  43067  43093  43103  43117  43133  43151  43159  43177  43189  43201  43207  43223
43237  43261  43271  43283  43291  43313  43319  43321  43331  43391  43397  43399  43403
43411  43427  43441  43451  43457  43481  43487  43499  43517  43541  43543  43573  43577
43579  43591  43597  43607  43609  43613  43627  43633  43649  43651  43661  43669  43691
43711  43717  43721  43753  43759  43777  43781  43783  43787  43789  43793  43801  43853
43867  43889  43891  43913  43933  43943  43951  43961  43963  43969  43973  43987  43991
43997  44017  44021  44027  44029  44041  44053  44059  44071  44087  44089  44101  44111
44119  44123  44129  44131  44159  44171  44179  44189  44201  44203  44207  44221  44249
44257  44263  44267  44269  44273  44279  44281  44293  44351  44357  44371  44381  44383
44389  44417  44449  44453  44483  44491  44497  44501  44507  44519  44531  44533  44537
44543  44549  44563  44579  44587  44617  44621  44623  44633  44641  44647  44651  44657
44683  44687  44699  44701  44711  44729  44741  44753  44771  44773  44777  44789  44797
44809  44819  44839  44843  44851  44867  44879  44887  44893  44909  44917  44927  44939
44953  44959  44963  44971  44983  44987  45007  45013  45053  45061  45077  45083  45119
45121  45127  45131  45137  45139  45161  45179  45181  45191  45197  45233  45247  45259
45263  45281  45289  45293  45307  45317  45319  45329  45337  45341  45343  45361  45377
45389  45403  45413  45427  45433  45439  45481  45491  45497  45503  45523  45533  45541
45553  45557  45569  45587  45589  45599  45613  45631  45641  45659  45667  45673  45677
45691  45697  45707  45737  45751  45757  45763  45767  45779  45817  45821  45823  45827
45833  45841  45853  45863  45869  45887  45893  45943  45949  45953  45959  45971  45979
45989  46021  46027  46049  46051  46061  46073  46091  46093  46099  46103  46133  46141
46147  46153  46171  46181  46183  46187  46199  46219  46229  46237  46261  46271  46273
46279  46301  46307  46309  46327  46337  46349  46351  46381  46399  46411  46439  46441
46447  46451  46457  46471  46477  46489  46499  46507  46511  46523  46549  46559  46567
46573  46589  46591  46601  46619  46633  46639  46643  46649  46663  46679  46681  46687
46691  46703  46723  46727  46747  46751  46757  46769  46771  46807  46811  46817  46819
46829  46831  46853  46861  46867  46877  46889  46901  46919  46933  46957  46993  46997
47017  47041  47051  47057  47059  47087  47093  47111  47119  47123  47129  47137  47143
47147  47149  47161  47189  47207  47221  47237  47251  47269  47279  47287  47293  47297
47303  47309  47317  47339  47351  47353  47363  47381  47387  47389  47407  47417  47419
```

```
47431  47441  47459  47491  47497  47501  47507  47513  47521  47527  47533  47543  47563
47569  47581  47591  47599  47609  47623  47629  47639  47653  47657  47659  47681  47699
47701  47711  47713  47717  47737  47741  47743  47777  47779  47791  47797  47807  47809
47819  47837  47843  47857  47869  47881  47903  47911  47917  47933  47939  47947  47951
47963  47969  47977  47981  48017  48023  48029  48049  48073  48079  48091  48109  48119
48121  48131  48157  48163  48187  48193  48197  48221  48239  48247  48259  48271
48281  48299  48311  48313  48337  48341  48353  48371  48383  48397  48407  48409  48413
48437  48449  48463  48473  48479  48481  48487  48491  48497  48523  48527  48533  48539
48541  48563  48571  48589  48593  48611  48619  48623  48647  48649  48661  48673  48677
48679  48731  48733  48751  48757  48761  48767  48779  48781  48787  48799  48809  48817
48821  48823  48847  48857  48859  48869  48871  48883  48889  48907  48947  48953  48973
48989  48991  49003  49009  49019  49031  49033  49037  49043  49057  49069  49081  49103
49109  49117  49121  49123  49139  49157  49169  49171  49177  49193  49199  49201  49207
49211  49223  49253  49261  49277  49279  49297  49307  49331  49333  49339  49363  49367
49369  49391  49393  49409  49411  49417  49429  49433  49451  49459  49463  49477  49481
49499  49523  49529  49531  49537  49547  49549  49559  49597  49603  49613  49627  49633
49639  49663  49667  49669  49681  49697  49711  49727  49739  49741  49747  49757  49783
49787  49789  49801  49807  49811  49823  49831  49843  49853  49871  49877  49891  49919
49921  49927  49937  49939  49943  49957  49991  49993  49999  50021  50023  50033  50047
50051  50053  50069  50077  50087  50093  50101  50111  50119  50123  50129  50131  50147
50153  50159  50177  50207  50221  50227  50231  50261  50263  50273  50287  50291  50311
50321  50329  50333  50341  50359  50363  50377  50383  50387  50411  50417  50423  50441
50459  50461  50497  50503  50513  50527  50539  50543  50549  50551  50581  50587  50591
50593  50599  50627  50647  50651  50671  50683  50707  50723  50741  50753  50767  50773
50777  50789  50821  50833  50839  50849  50857  50867  50873  50891  50893  50909  50923
50929  50951  50957  50969  50971  50989  50993  51001  51031  51043  51047  51059  51061
51071  51109  51131  51133  51137  51151  51157  51169  51193  51197  51199  51203  51217
51229  51239  51241  51257  51263  51283  51287  51307  51329  51341  51343  51347  51349
51361  51383  51407  51413  51419  51421  51427  51431  51437  51439  51449  51461  51473
51479  51481  51487  51503  51511  51517  51521  51539  51551  51563  51577  51581  51593
51599  51607  51613  51631  51637  51647  51659  51673  51679  51683  51691  51713  51719
51721  51749  51767  51769  51787  51797  51803  51817  51827  51829  51839  51853  51859
51869  51871  51893  51899  51907  51913  51929  51941  51949  51971  51973  51977  51991
52009  52021  52027  52051  52057  52067  52069  52081  52103  52121  52127  52147  52153
52163  52177  52181  52183  52189  52201  52223  52237  52249  52253  52259  52267  52289
52291  52301  52313  52321  52361  52363  52369  52379  52387  52391  52433  52453  52457
52489  52501  52511  52517  52529  52541  52543  52553  52561  52567  52571  52579  52583
52609  52627  52631  52639  52667  52673  52691  52697  52709  52711  52721  52727  52733
52747  52757  52769  52783  52807  52813  52817  52837  52859  52861  52879  52883  52889
52901  52903  52919  52937  52951  52957  52963  52967  52973  52981  52999  53003  53017
53047  53051  53069  53077  53087  53089  53093  53101  53113  53117  53129  53147  53149
53161  53171  53173  53189  53197  53201  53231  53233  53239  53267  53269  53279  53281
53299  53309  53323  53327  53353  53359  53377  53381  53401  53407  53411  53419  53437
53441  53453  53479  53503  53507  53527  53549  53551  53569  53591  53593  53597  53609
53611  53617  53623  53629  53633  53639  53653  53657  53681  53693  53699  53717  53719
53731  53759  53773  53777  53783  53791  53813  53819  53831  53849  53857  53861  53881
53887  53891  53897  53899  53917  53923  53927  53939  53951  53959  53987  53993  54001
54011  54013  54037  54049  54059  54083  54091  54101  54121  54133  54139  54151  54163
54167  54181  54193  54217  54251  54269  54277  54287  54293  54311  54319  54323  54331
54347  54361  54367  54371  54377  54401  54403  54409  54413  54419  54421  54437  54443
54449  54469  54493  54497  54499  54503  54517  54521  54539  54541  54547  54559  54563
54577  54581  54583  54601  54617  54623  54629  54631  54647  54667  54673  54679  54709
54713  54721  54727  54751  54767  54773  54779  54787  54799  54829  54833  54851  54869
54877  54881  54907  54917  54919  54941  54949  54959  54973  54979  54983  55001  55009
55021  55049  55051  55057  55061  55073  55079  55103  55109  55117  55127  55147  55163
55171  55201  55207  55213  55217  55219  55229  55243  55249  55259  55291  55313  55331
55333  55337  55339  55343  55351  55373  55381  55399  55411  55439  55441  55457  55469
55487  55501  55511  55529  55541  55547  55579  55589  55603  55609  55619  55621  55631
55633  55639  55661  55663  55667  55673  55681  55691  55697  55711  55717  55721  55733
55763  55787  55793  55799  55807  55813  55817  55819  55823  55829  55837  55843  55849
55871  55889  55897  55901  55903  55921  55927  55931  55933  55949  55967  55987  55997
56003  56009  56039  56041  56053  56081  56087  56093  56099  56101  56113  56123  56131
56149  56167  56171  56179  56197  56207  56209  56237  56239  56249  56263  56267  56269
56299  56311  56333  56359  56369  56377  56383  56393  56401  56417  56431  56437  56443
56453  56467  56473  56477  56489  56501  56503  56509  56519  56527  56531  56533
56543  56569  56591  56597  56599  56611  56629  56633  56659  56663  56671  56681  56687
56701  56711  56713  56731  56737  56747  56767  56773  56779  56783  56807  56809  56813
56821  56827  56843  56857  56873  56891  56893  56897  56909  56911  56921  56923  56929
56941  56951  56957  56963  56983  56989  56993  56999  57037  57041  57047  57059  57073
57077  57089  57097  57107  57119  57131  57139  57143  57149  57163  57173  57179  57191
57193  57203  57221  57223  57241  57251  57259  57269  57271  57283  57287  57301  57329
57331  57347  57349  57367  57373  57383  57389  57397  57413  57427  57457  57467  57487
57493  57503  57527  57529  57557  57559  57571  57587  57593  57601  57637  57641  57649
57653  57667  57679  57689  57697  57709  57713  57719  57727  57731  57737  57751  57773
57781  57787  57791  57793  57803  57809  57829  57839  57847  57853  57859  57881  57899
57901  57917  57923  57943  57947  57973  57977  57991  58013  58027  58031  58043  58049
58057  58061  58067  58073  58099  58109  58111  58129  58147  58151  58153  58169  58171
58189  58193  58199  58207  58211  58217  58229  58231  58237  58243  58271  58309  58313
58321  58337  58363  58367  58369  58379  58391  58393  58403  58411  58417  58427  58439
58441  58451  58453  58477  58481  58511  58537  58543  58549  58567  58573  58579  58601
58603  58613  58631  58657  58661  58679  58687  58693  58699  58711  58727  58733  58741
58757  58763  58771  58787  58789  58831  58889  58897  58901  58907  58909  58913  58921
58937  58943  58963  58967  58979  58991  58997  59009  59011  59021  59023  59029  59051
59053  59063  59069  59077  59083  59093  59107  59113  59119  59123  59141  59149  59159
59167  59183  59197  59207  59209  59219  59221  59233  59239  59243  59263  59273  59281
59333  59341  59351  59357  59359  59369  59377  59387  59393  59399  59407  59417  59419
59441  59443  59447  59453  59467  59471  59473  59497  59509  59513  59539  59557  59561
59567  59581  59611  59617  59621  59627  59629  59651  59659  59663  59669  59671  59693
59699  59707  59723  59729  59743  59747  59753  59771  59779  59791  59797  59809  59833
```

59863 59879 59887 59921 59929 59951 59957 59971 59981 59999 60013 60017 60029
60037 60041 60077 60083 60089 60091 60101 60103 60107 60127 60133 60139 60149
60161 60167 60169 60209 60217 60223 60251 60257 60259 60271 60289 60293 60317
60331 60337 60343 60353 60373 60383 60397 60413 60427 60443 60449 60457 60493
60497 60509 60521 60527 60539 60589 60601 60607 60611 60617 60623 60631 60637
60647 60649 60659 60661 60679 60689 60703 60719 60727 60733 60737 60757 60761
60763 60773 60779 60793 60811 60821 60859 60869 60887 60889 60899 60901 60913
60917 60919 60923 60937 60943 60953 60961 61001 61007 61027 61031 61043 61051
61057 61091 61099 61121 61129 61141 61151 61153 61169 61211 61223 61231 61253
61261 61283 61291 61297 61331 61333 61339 61343 61357 61363 61379 61381 61403
61409 61417 61441 61463 61469 61471 61483 61487 61493 61507 61511 61519 61543
61547 61553 61559 61561 61583 61603 61609 61613 61627 61631 61637 61643 61651
61657 61667 61673 61681 61687 61703 61717 61723 61729 61751 61757 61781 61813
61819 61837 61843 61861 61871 61879 61909 61927 61933 61949 61961 61967 61979
61981 61987 61991 62003 62011 62017 62039 62047 62053 62057 62071 62081 62099
62119 62129 62131 62137 62141 62143 62171 62189 62191 62201 62207 62213 62219
62233 62273 62297 62299 62303 62311 62323 62327 62347 62351 62383 62401 62417
62423 62459 62467 62473 62477 62483 62497 62501 62507 62533 62539 62549 62563
62581 62591 62597 62603 62617 62627 62633 62639 62653 62659 62683 62687 62701
62723 62731 62743 62753 62761 62773 62791 62801 62819 62827 62851 62861 62869
62873 62897 62903 62921 62927 62929 62939 62969 62971 62981 62983 62987 62989
63029 63031 63059 63067 63073 63079 63097 63103 63113 63127 63131 63149 63179
63197 63199 63211 63241 63247 63277 63281 63299 63311 63313 63317 63331 63337
63347 63353 63361 63367 63377 63389 63391 63397 63409 63419 63421 63439 63443
63463 63467 63473 63487 63493 63499 63521 63527 63533 63541 63559 63577 63587
63589 63599 63601 63607 63611 63617 63629 63647 63649 63659 63667 63671 63689
63691 63697 63703 63709 63719 63727 63737 63743 63761 63773 63781 63793 63799
63803 63809 63823 63839 63841 63853 63857 63863 63901 63907 63913 63929 63949
63977 63997 64007 64013 64019 64033 64037 64063 64067 64081 64091 64109 64123
64151 64153 64157 64171 64187 64189 64217 64223 64231 64237 64271 64279 64283
64301 64303 64319 64327 64333 64373 64381 64399 64403 64433 64439 64451 64453
64483 64489 64499 64513 64553 64567 64577 64579 64591 64601 64609 64613 64621
64627 64633 64661 64663 64667 64679 64693 64709 64717 64747 64763 64781 64783
64793 64811 64817 64849 64853 64871 64877 64879 64891 64901 64919 64921 64927
64937 64951 64969 64997 65003 65011 65027 65029 65033 65053 65063 65071 65089
65099 65101 65111 65119 65123 65129 65141 65147 65167 65171 65173 65179 65183
65203 65213 65239 65257 65267 65269 65287 65293 65309 65323 65327 65353 65357
65371 65381 65393 65407 65413 65419 65423 65437 65447 65449 65479 65497 65519
65521 65537 65539 65543 65551 65557 65563 65579 65581 65587 65599 65609 65617
65629 65633 65647 65651 65657 65677 65687 65699 65701 65707 65713 65717 65719
65729 65731 65761 65777 65789 65809 65827 65831 65837 65839 65843 65851 65867
65881 65899 65921 65927 65929 65951 65957 65963 65981 65983 65993 66029 66037
66041 66047 66067 66071 66083 66089 66103 66107 66109 66137 66161 66169 66173
66179 66191 66221 66239 66271 66293 66301 66337 66343 66347 66359 66361 66373
66377 66383 66403 66413 66431 66449 66457 66463 66467 66491 66499 66509 66523
66529 66533 66541 66553 66569 66571 66587 66593 66601 66617 66629 66643 66653
66683 66697 66701 66713 66721 66733 66739 66749 66751 66763 66791 66797 66809
66821 66841 66851 66853 66863 66877 66883 66889 66919 66923 66931 66943 66947
66949 66959 66973 66977 67003 67021 67033 67043 67049 67057 67061 67073 67079
67103 67121 67129 67139 67141 67153 67157 67169 67181 67187 67189 67211 67213
67217 67219 67231 67247 67261 67271 67273 67289 67307 67339 67343 67349 67369
67391 67399 67409 67411 67421 67427 67429 67433 67447 67453 67477 67481 67489
67493 67499 67511 67523 67531 67537 67547 67559 67567 67577 67579 67589 67601
67607 67619 67631 67651 67679 67699 67709 67723 67733 67741 67751 67757 67759
67763 67777 67783 67789 67801 67807 67819 67829 67843 67853 67867 67883 67891
67901 67927 67931 67933 67939 67943 67957 67961 67967 67979 67987 67993 68023
68041 68053 68059 68071 68087 68099 68111 68113 68141 68147 68161 68171 68207
68209 68213 68219 68227 68239 68261 68279 68281 68311 68329 68351 68371 68389
68399 68437 68443 68447 68449 68473 68477 68483 68489 68491 68501 68507 68521
68531 68539 68543 68567 68581 68597 68611 68633 68639 68659 68669 68683 68687
68699 68711 68713 68729 68737 68743 68749 68767 68771 68777 68791 68813 68819
68821 68863 68879 68881 68891 68897 68899 68903 68909 68917 68927 68947 68963
68993 69001 69011 69019 69029 69031 69061 69067 69073 69109 69119 69127 69143
69149 69151 69163 69191 69193 69197 69203 69221 69233 69239 69247 69257 69259
69263 69313 69317 69337 69341 69371 69379 69383 69389 69401 69403 69427 69431
69439 69457 69463 69467 69473 69481 69491 69493 69497 69499 69539 69557 69593
69623 69653 69661 69677 69691 69697 69709 69737 69739 69761 69763 69767 69779
69809 69821 69827 69829 69833 69847 69857 69859 69877 69899 69911 69929 69931
69941 69959 69991 69997 70001 70003 70009 70019 70039 70051 70061 70067 70079
70099 70111 70117 70121 70123 70139 70141 70157 70163 70177 70181 70183 70199
70201 70207 70223 70229 70237 70241 70249 70271 70289 70297 70309 70313 70321
70327 70351 70373 70379 70381 70393 70423 70429 70439 70451 70457 70459 70481
70487 70489 70501 70507 70529 70537 70549 70571 70573 70583 70589 70607 70619
70621 70627 70639 70657 70663 70667 70687 70709 70717 70729 70753 70769 70783
70793 70823 70841 70843 70849 70853 70867 70877 70879 70891 70901 70913 70919
70921 70937 70949 70951 70957 70969 70979 70981 70991 70997 70999 71011 71023
71039 71059 71069 71081 71089 71119 71129 71143 71147 71153 71161 71167 71171
71191 71209 71233 71237 71249 71257 71261 71263 71287 71293 71317 71327 71329
71333 71339 71341 71347 71353 71359 71363 71387 71389 71399 71411 71413 71419
71429 71437 71443 71453 71471 71473 71479 71483 71503 71527 71537 71549 71551
71563 71569 71593 71597 71633 71647 71663 71671 71693 71699 71707 71711 71713
71719 71741 71761 71777 71789 71807 71809 71821 71837 71843 71849 71861 71867
71879 71881 71887 71899 71909 71917 71933 71941 71947 71963 71971 71983 71987
71993 71999 72019 72031 72043 72047 72053 72073 72077 72089 72091 72101 72103
72109 72139 72161 72167 72169 72173 72211 72221 72223 72227 72229 72251 72253
72269 72271 72277 72287 72307 72313 72337 72341 72353 72367 72379 72383 72421
72431 72461 72467 72469 72481 72493 72497 72503 72533 72547 72551 72559 72577
72613 72617 72623 72643 72647 72649 72661 72671 72673 72679 72689 72701 72707
72719 72727 72733 72739 72763 72767 72797 72817 72823 72859 72869 72871 72883

```
72889  72893  72901  72907  72911  72923  72931  72937  72949  72953  72959  72973  72977
72997  73009  73013  73019  73037  73039  73043  73061  73063  73079  73091  73121  73127
73133  73141  73181  73189  73237  73243  73259  73277  73291  73303  73309  73327  73331
73351  73361  73363  73369  73379  73387  73417  73421  73433  73453  73459  73471  73477
73483  73517  73523  73529  73547  73553  73561  73571  73583  73589  73597  73607  73609
73613  73637  73643  73651  73673  73679  73681  73693  73699  73709  73721  73727  73751
73757  73771  73783  73819  73823  73847  73849  73859  73867  73877  73883  73897  73907
73939  73943  73951  73961  73973  73999  74017  74021  74027  74047  74051  74071  74077
74093  74099  74101  74131  74143  74149  74159  74161  74167  74177  74189  74197  74201
74203  74209  74219  74231  74257  74279  74287  74293  74297  74311  74317  74323  74353
74357  74363  74377  74381  74383  74411  74413  74419  74441  74449  74453  74471  74489
74507  74509  74521  74527  74531  74551  74561  74567  74573  74587  74597  74609  74611
74623  74653  74687  74699  74707  74713  74717  74719  74729  74731  74747  74759  74761
74771  74779  74797  74821  74827  74831  74843  74857  74861  74869  74873  74887  74891
74897  74903  74923  74929  74933  74941  74959  75011  75013  75017  75029  75037  75041
75079  75083  75109  75133  75149  75161  75167  75169  75181  75193  75209  75211  75217
75223  75227  75239  75253  75269  75277  75289  75307  75323  75329  75337  75347  75353
75367  75377  75389  75391  75401  75403  75407  75431  75437  75479  75503  75511  75521
75527  75533  75539  75541  75553  75557  75571  75577  75583  75611  75617  75619  75629
75641  75653  75659  75679  75683  75689  75703  75707  75709  75721  75731  75743  75767
75773  75781  75787  75793  75797  75821  75833  75853  75869  75883  75913  75931  75937
75941  75967  75979  75983  75989  75991  75997  76001  76003  76031  76039  76079  76081
76091  76099  76103  76123  76129  76147  76157  76159  76163  76207  76213  76231  76243
76249  76253  76259  76261  76283  76289  76303  76333  76343  76367  76369  76379  76387
76403  76421  76423  76441  76463  76471  76481  76487  76493  76507  76511  76519  76537
76541  76543  76561  76579  76597  76603  76607  76631  76649  76651  76667  76673  76679
76697  76717  76733  76753  76757  76771  76777  76781  76801  76819  76829  76831  76837
76847  76871  76873  76883  76907  76913  76919  76943  76949  76961  76963  76991  77003
77017  77023  77029  77041  77047  77069  77081  77093  77101  77137  77141  77153  77167
77171  77191  77201  77213  77237  77239  77243  77249  77261  77263  77267  77269  77279
77291  77317  77323  77339  77347  77351  77359  77369  77377  77383  77417  77419  77431
77447  77471  77477  77479  77489  77491  77509  77513  77521  77527  77543  77549  77551
77557  77563  77569  77573  77587  77591  77611  77617  77621  77641  77647  77659  77681
77687  77689  77699  77711  77713  77719  77723  77731  77743  77747  77761  77773  77783
77797  77801  77813  77839  77849  77863  77867  77893  77899  77929  77933  77951  77969
77977  77983  77999  78007  78017  78031  78041  78049  78059  78079  78101  78121  78137
78139  78157  78163  78167  78173  78179  78191  78193  78203  78229  78233  78241  78259
78277  78283  78301  78307  78311  78317  78341  78347  78367  78401  78427  78437  78439
78467  78479  78487  78497  78509  78511  78517  78539  78541  78553  78569  78571  78577
78583  78593  78607  78623  78643  78649  78653  78691  78697  78707  78713  78721  78737
78779  78781  78787  78791  78797  78803  78809  78823  78839  78853  78857  78877  78887
78889  78893  78901  78919  78929  78941  78977  78979  78989  79031  79039  79043  79063
79087  79103  79111  79133  79139  79147  79151  79153  79159  79181  79187  79193  79201
79229  79231  79241  79259  79273  79279  79283  79301  79309  79319  79333  79337  79349
79357  79367  79379  79393  79397  79399  79411  79423  79427  79433  79451  79481  79493
79531  79537  79549  79559  79561  79579  79589  79601  79609  79613  79621  79627  79631
79633  79657  79669  79687  79691  79693  79697  79699  79757  79769  79777  79801  79811
79813  79817  79823  79829  79841  79843  79847  79861  79867  79873  79889  79901  79903
79907  79939  79943  79967  79979  79987  79997  79999  80021  80039  80051  80071
80077  80107  80111  80141  80147  80149  80153  80167  80173  80177  80191  80207  80209
80221  80231  80233  80239  80251  80263  80273  80279  80287  80309  80317  80329  80341
80347  80363  80369  80387  80407  80429  80447  80449  80471  80473  80489  80491  80513
80527  80537  80557  80567  80599  80603  80611  80621  80627  80629  80651  80657  80669
80671  80677  80681  80683  80687  80701  80713  80737  80747  80749  80761  80777  80779
80783  80789  80803  80809  80819  80831  80833  80849  80863  80897  80909  80911  80917
80923  80929  80933  80953  80963  80989  81001  81013  81017  81019  81023  81031  81041
81043  81047  81049  81071  81077  81083  81097  81101  81119  81131  81157  81163  81173
81181  81197  81199  81203  81223  81233  81239  81281  81283  81293  81299  81307  81331
81343  81349  81353  81359  81371  81373  81401  81409  81421  81439  81457  81463  81509
81517  81527  81533  81547  81551  81553  81559  81563  81569  81611  81619  81629  81637
81647  81649  81667  81671  81689  81701  81703  81707  81727  81737  81749  81761
81769  81773  81799  81817  81839  81847  81853  81869  81883  81899  81901  81919  81929
81931  81937  81943  81953  81967  81971  81973  82003  82007  82009  82013  82021  82031
82037  82039  82051  82067  82073  82129  82139  82141  82153  82163  82171  82183  82189
82193  82207  82217  82219  82223  82231  82237  82241  82261  82267  82279  82301  82307
82339  82349  82351  82361  82373  82387  82393  82421  82457  82463  82469  82471  82483
82487  82493  82499  82507  82529  82531  82549  82559  82561  82567  82571  82591  82601
82609  82613  82619  82633  82651  82657  82699  82721  82723  82727  82729  82757  82759
82763  82781  82787  82793  82799  82811  82813  82837  82847  82883  82889  82891  82903
82913  82939  82963  82981  82997  83003  83009  83023  83047  83059  83063  83071  83077
83089  83093  83101  83117  83137  83177  83203  83207  83219  83221  83227  83231  83233
83243  83257  83267  83269  83273  83299  83311  83339  83341  83357  83383  83389  83399
83401  83407  83417  83423  83431  83437  83443  83449  83459  83471  83477  83497  83537
83557  83561  83563  83579  83591  83597  83609  83617  83621  83639  83641  83653  83663
83689  83701  83717  83719  83737  83761  83773  83777  83791  83813  83833  83843  83857
83869  83873  83891  83903  83911  83921  83933  83939  83969  83983  83987  84011  84017
84047  84053  84059  84061  84067  84089  84121  84127  84131  84137  84143  84163  84179
84181  84191  84199  84211  84223  84229  84239  84247  84263  84299  84307  84313
84317  84319  84347  84349  84377  84389  84391  84401  84407  84421  84431  84437  84443
84449  84457  84463  84467  84481  84499  84503  84509  84521  84523  84533  84551  84559
84589  84629  84631  84649  84653  84659  84673  84691  84697  84701  84713  84719  84731
84737  84751  84761  84787  84793  84809  84811  84827  84857  84859  84869  84871  84913
84919  84947  84961  84967  84977  84979  84991  85009  85021  85027  85037  85049  85061
85081  85087  85091  85093  85103  85109  85121  85133  85147  85159  85193  85199  85201
85213  85223  85229  85237  85243  85247  85259  85297  85303  85313  85331  85333  85361
85363  85369  85381  85411  85427  85429  85439  85447  85451  85453  85469  85487  85513
85517  85523  85531  85549  85571  85577  85597  85601  85607  85619  85621  85627  85639
85643  85661  85667  85669  85691  85703  85711  85717  85733  85751  85781  85793  85817
85819  85829  85831  85837  85843  85847  85853  85889  85903  85909  85931  85933  85991
```

```
85999  86011  86017  86027  86029  86069  86077  86083  86111  86113  86117  86131  86137
86143  86161  86171  86179  86183  86197  86201  86209  86239  86243  86249  86257  86263
86269  86287  86291  86293  86297  86311  86323  86341  86351  86353  86357  86369  86371
86381  86389  86399  86413  86423  86441  86453  86461  86467  86477  86491  86501  86509
86531  86533  86539  86561  86573  86579  86587  86599  86627  86629  86677  86689  86693
86711  86719  86729  86743  86753  86767  86771  86783  86813  86837  86843  86851  86857
86861  86869  86923  86927  86929  86939  86951  86959  86969  86981  86993  87011  87013
87037  87041  87049  87071  87083  87103  87107  87119  87121  87133  87149  87151  87179
87181  87187  87211  87221  87223  87251  87253  87257  87277  87281  87293  87299  87313
87317  87323  87337  87359  87383  87403  87407  87421  87427  87433  87443  87473  87481
87491  87509  87511  87517  87523  87539  87541  87547  87553  87557  87559  87583  87587
87589  87613  87623  87629  87631  87641  87643  87649  87671  87679  87683  87691  87697
87701  87719  87721  87739  87743  87751  87767  87793  87797  87803  87811  87833  87853
87869  87877  87881  87887  87911  87917  87931  87943  87959  87961  87973  87977  87991
88001  88003  88007  88019  88037  88069  88079  88093  88117  88129  88169  88177  88211
88223  88237  88241  88259  88261  88289  88301  88321  88327  88337  88339  88379  88397
88411  88423  88427  88463  88469  88471  88493  88499  88513  88523  88547  88589  88591
88607  88609  88643  88651  88657  88661  88663  88667  88681  88721  88729  88741  88747
88771  88789  88793  88799  88801  88807  88811  88813  88817  88819  88843  88853  88861
88867  88873  88883  88897  88903  88919  88937  88951  88969  88993  88997  89003  89009
89017  89021  89041  89051  89057  89069  89071  89083  89087  89101  89107  89113  89119
89123  89137  89153  89189  89203  89209  89213  89227  89231  89237  89261  89269  89273
89293  89303  89317  89329  89363  89371  89381  89387  89393  89399  89413  89417  89431
89443  89449  89459  89477  89491  89501  89513  89519  89521  89527  89533  89561  89563
89567  89591  89597  89599  89603  89611  89627  89633  89653  89657  89659  89669  89671
89681  89689  89753  89759  89767  89779  89783  89797  89809  89819  89821  89833  89839
89849  89867  89891  89897  89899  89909  89917  89923  89939  89959  89963  89977  89983
89989  90001  90007  90011  90017  90019  90023  90031  90053  90059  90067  90071  90073
90089  90107  90121  90127  90149  90163  90173  90187  90191  90197  90199  90203  90217
90227  90239  90247  90263  90271  90281  90289  90313  90353  90359  90371  90373  90379
90397  90401  90403  90407  90437  90439  90469  90473  90481  90499  90511  90523  90527
90529  90533  90547  90583  90599  90617  90619  90631  90641  90647  90659  90667  90679
90697  90703  90709  90731  90749  90787  90793  90803  90821  90823  90833  90841  90847
90863  90887  90901  90907  90911  90917  90931  90947  90971  90977  90989  90997  91009
91019  91033  91079  91081  91097  91099  91121  91127  91129  91139  91141  91151  91153
91159  91163  91183  91193  91199  91229  91237  91243  91249  91253  91283  91291  91297
91303  91309  91331  91367  91369  91373  91381  91387  91393  91397  91411  91423  91433
91453  91457  91459  91463  91493  91499  91513  91529  91541  91571  91573  91577  91583
91591  91621  91631  91639  91673  91691  91703  91711  91733  91753  91757  91771  91781
91801  91807  91811  91813  91823  91837  91841  91867  91873  91909  91921  91939  91943
91951  91957  91961  91969  91997  92003  92009  92033  92041  92051  92077  92083  92083
92107  92111  92119  92143  92153  92173  92177  92179  92189  92203  92219  92221  92227
92233  92237  92243  92251  92269  92297  92311  92317  92333  92347  92353  92357  92363
92369  92377  92381  92383  92387  92399  92401  92413  92419  92431  92459  92461  92467
92479  92489  92503  92507  92551  92557  92567  92569  92581  92593  92623  92627  92639
92641  92647  92657  92669  92671  92681  92683  92693  92699  92707  92717  92723  92737
92753  92761  92767  92779  92789  92791  92801  92809  92821  92831  92849  92857  92861
92863  92867  92893  92899  92921  92927  92941  92951  92957  92959  92987  92993  93001
93047  93053  93059  93077  93083  93089  93097  93103  93113  93131  93133  93139  93151
93169  93179  93187  93199  93229  93239  93241  93251  93253  93257  93263  93281  93283
93287  93307  93319  93323  93329  93337  93371  93377  93383  93407  93419  93427  93463
93479  93481  93487  93491  93493  93497  93503  93523  93529  93553  93557  93559  93563
93581  93601  93607  93629  93637  93683  93701  93703  93719  93739  93761  93763  93787
93809  93811  93827  93851  93871  93887  93889  93893  93901  93911  93913  93923  93937
93941  93949  93967  93971  93979  93983  93997  94007  94009  94033  94049  94057  94063
94079  94099  94109  94111  94117  94121  94151  94153  94169  94201  94207  94219  94229
94253  94261  94273  94291  94307  94309  94321  94327  94331  94343  94349  94351  94379
94397  94399  94421  94427  94433  94439  94447  94463  94477  94483  94513  94529
94531  94541  94543  94547  94559  94561  94573  94583  94597  94603  94613  94621  94649
94651  94687  94693  94709  94723  94727  94747  94771  94777  94781  94789  94793  94811
94819  94823  94837  94841  94847  94849  94873  94889  94903  94907  94933  94949  94951
94961  94993  94999  95003  95009  95021  95027  95063  95071  95083  95087  95089  95093
95101  95107  95111  95131  95143  95153  95177  95189  95191  95203  95213  95219  95231
95233  95239  95257  95261  95267  95273  95279  95287  95311  95317  95327  95339  95369
95383  95393  95401  95413  95419  95429  95441  95443  95461  95467  95471  95479  95483
95507  95527  95531  95539  95549  95561  95569  95581  95597  95603  95617  95621  95629
95633  95651  95701  95707  95713  95717  95723  95731  95737  95747  95773  95783  95789
95791  95801  95803  95813  95819  95857  95869  95873  95881  95891  95911  95917  95923
95929  95947  95957  95959  95971  95987  95989  96001  96013  96017  96043  96053  96059
96079  96097  96137  96149  96157  96167  96179  96181  96199  96211  96221  96223  96233
96259  96263  96269  96281  96289  96293  96323  96329  96331  96337  96353  96377  96401
96419  96431  96443  96451  96457  96461  96469  96479  96487  96493  96497  96517  96527
96553  96557  96581  96587  96589  96601  96643  96661  96667  96671  96697  96703  96731
96737  96739  96749  96757  96763  96769  96779  96787  96797  96799  96821  96823  96827
96847  96851  96857  96893  96907  96911  96931  96953  96959  96973  96979  96989  96997
97001  97003  97007  97021  97039  97073  97081  97103  97117  97127  97151  97157  97159
97169  97171  97177  97187  97213  97231  97241  97259  97283  97301  97303  97327  97367
97369  97373  97379  97381  97387  97397  97423  97429  97441  97453  97459  97463  97499
97501  97511  97523  97547  97549  97553  97561  97571  97577  97579  97583  97607  97609
97613  97649  97651  97673  97687  97711  97729  97771  97777  97787  97789  97813  97829
97841  97843  97847  97849  97859  97861  97871  97879  97883  97919  97927  97931  97943
97961  97967  97973  97987  98009  98011  98017  98041  98047  98057  98081  98101  98123
98129  98143  98179  98207  98213  98221  98227  98251  98257  98269  98297  98299  98317
98321  98323  98327  98347  98369  98377  98387  98389  98407  98411  98419  98429  98443
98453  98459  98467  98473  98479  98491  98507  98519  98533  98543  98561  98563  98573
98597  98621  98627  98639  98641  98663  98669  98689  98711  98713  98717  98729  98731
98737  98773  98779  98801  98807  98809  98837  98849  98867  98869  98873  98887  98893
98897  98899  98909  98911  98927  98929  98939  98947  98953  98963  98981  98993  98999
99013  99017  99023  99041  99053  99079  99083  99089  99103  99109  99119  99131  99133
```

```
99137   99139   99149   99173   99181   99191   99223   99233   99241   99251   99257   99259   99277
99289   99317   99347   99349   99367   99371   99377   99391   99397   99401   99409   99431   99439
99469   99487   99497   99523   99527   99529   99551   99559   99563   99571   99577   99581   99607
99611   99623   99643   99661   99667   99679   99689   99707   99709   99713   99719   99721   99733
99761   99767   99787   99793   99809   99817   99823   99829   99833   99839   99859   99871   99877
99881   99901   99907   99923   99929   99961   99971   99989   99991  100003  100019  100043  100049
100057  100069  100103  100109  100129  100151  100153  100169  100183  100189  100193
100207  100213  100237  100267  100271  100279  100291  100297  100313  100333  100343
100357  100361  100363  100379  100391  100393  100403  100411  100417  100447  100459
100469  100483  100493  100501  100511  100517  100519  100523  100537  100547  100549
100559  100591  100609  100613  100621  100649  100669  100673  100693  100699  100703
100733  100741  100747  100769  100787  100799  100801  100811  100823  100829  100847
100853  100907  100913  100927  100931  100937  100943  100957  100981  100987  100999
101009  101021  101027  101051  101063  101081  101089  101107  101111  101113  101117
101119  101141  101149  101159  101161  101173  101183  101197  101203  101207  101209
101221  101267  101273  101279  101281  101287  101293  101323  101333  101341  101347
101359  101363  101377  101383  101399  101411  101419  101429  101449  101467  101477
101483  101489  101501  101503  101513  101527  101531  101533  101537  101561  101573
101581  101599  101603  101611  101627  101641  101653  101663  101681  101693  101701
101719  101723  101737  101741  101747  101749  101771  101789  101797  101807  101833
101837  101839  101863  101869  101873  101879  101891  101917  101921  101929  101939
101957  101963  101977  101987  101999  102001  102013  102019  102023  102031  102043
102059  102061  102071  102077  102079  102101  102103  102107  102121  102139  102149
102161  102181  102191  102197  102199  102203  102217  102229  102233  102241  102251
102253  102259  102293  102299  102301  102317  102329  102337  102359  102367  102397
102407  102409  102433  102437  102451  102461  102481  102497  102499  102503  102523
102533  102539  102547  102551  102559  102563  102587  102593  102607  102611  102643
102647  102653  102667  102673  102677  102679  102701  102761  102763  102769  102793
102797  102811  102829  102841  102859  102871  102877  102881  102911  102913  102929
102931  102953  102967  102983  103001  103007  103043  103049  103067  103069  103079
103087  103091  103093  103099  103123  103141  103171  103177  103183  103217  103231
103237  103289  103291  103307  103319  103333  103349  103357  103387  103391  103393
103399  103409  103421  103423  103451  103457  103471  103483  103511  103529  103549
103553  103561  103567  103573  103577  103583  103591  103613  103619  103643  103651
103657  103669  103681  103687  103699  103703  103723  103769  103787  103801  103811
103813  103837  103841  103843  103867  103889  103903  103913  103919  103951  103963
103967  103969  103979  103981  103991  103993  103997  104003  104009  104021  104033
104047  104053  104059  104087  104089  104107  104113  104119  104123  104147  104149
104161  104173  104179  104183  104207  104231  104233  104239  104243  104281  104287
104297  104309  104311  104323  104327  104347  104369  104381  104383  104393  104399
104417  104459  104471  104473  104479  104491  104513  104527  104537  104543  104549
104551  104561  104579  104593  104597  104623  104639  104651  104659  104677  104681
104683  104693  104701  104707  104711  104717  104723  104729  104743  104759  104761
104773  104779  104789  104801  104803  104827  104831  104849  104851  104869  104879
104891  104911  104917  104933  104947  104953  104959  104971  104987  104999  105019
105023  105031  105037  105071  105097  105107  105137  105143  105167  105173  105199
105211  105227  105229  105239  105251  105253  105263  105269  105277  105319  105323
105331  105337  105341  105359  105361  105367  105373  105379  105389  105397  105401
105407  105437  105449  105467  105491  105499  105503  105509  105517  105527  105529
105533  105541  105557  105563  105601  105607  105613  105619  105649  105653  105667
105673  105683  105691  105701  105727  105733  105751  105761  105767  105769  105817
105829  105863  105871  105883  105899  105907  105913  105929  105943  105953  105967
105971  105977  105983  105997  106013  106019  106031  106033  106087  106103  106109
106121  106123  106129  106163  106181  106187  106189  106207  106213  106217  106219
106243  106261  106273  106277  106279  106291  106297  106303  106307  106319  106321
106349  106351  106357  106363  106367  106373  106391  106397  106411  106417  106427
106433  106441  106451  106453  106487  106501  106531  106537  106541  106543  106591
106619  106621  106627  106637  106649  106657  106661  106663  106669  106681  106693
106699  106703  106721  106727  106739  106747  106751  106753  106759  106781  106783
106787  106801  106823  106853  106859  106861  106867  106871  106877  106903  106907
106921  106937  106949  106957  106961  106963  106979  106993  107021  107033  107053
107057  107069  107071  107077  107089  107099  107101  107119  107123  107137  107171
107183  107197  107201  107209  107227  107243  107251  107269  107273  107279  107309
107323  107339  107347  107351  107357  107377  107441  107449  107453  107467  107473
107507  107509  107563  107581  107599  107603  107609  107621  107641  107647  107671
107687  107693  107699  107713  107717  107719  107741  107747  107761  107773  107777
107791  107827  107837  107839  107843  107857  107867  107873  107881  107897  107903
107923  107927  107941  107951  107971  107981  107999  108007  108011  108013  108023
108037  108041  108061  108079  108089  108107  108109  108127  108131  108139  108161
108179  108187  108191  108193  108203  108211  108217  108223  108233  108247  108263
108271  108287  108289  108293  108301  108343  108347  108359  108377  108379  108401
108413  108421  108439  108457  108461  108463  108497  108499  108503  108517  108529
108533  108541  108553  108557  108571  108587  108631  108637  108643  108649  108677
108707  108709  108727  108739  108751  108761  108769  108791  108793  108799  108803
108821  108827  108863  108869  108877  108881  108883  108887  108893  108907  108917
108923  108929  108943  108947  108949  108959  108961  108967  108971  108991  109001
109013  109037  109049  109063  109073  109097  109103  109111  109121  109133  109139
109141  109147  109159  109169  109171  109199  109201  109211  109229  109253  109267
109279  109297  109303  109313  109321  109331  109357  109363  109367  109379  109387
109391  109397  109423  109433  109441  109451  109453  109469  109471  109481  109507
109517  109519  109537  109541  109547  109567  109579  109583  109589  109597  109609
109619  109621  109639  109661  109663  109673  109717  109721  109741  109751  109789
109793  109807  109819  109829  109831  109841  109843  109847  109849  109859  109873
109883  109891  109897  109903  109913  109919  109937  109943  109961  109987  110017
110023  110039  110051  110059  110063  110069  110083  110119  110129  110161  110183
110221  110233  110237  110251  110261  110269  110273  110281  110291  110311  110321
110323  110339  110359  110419  110431  110437  110441  110459  110477  110479  110491
110501  110503  110527  110533  110543  110557  110563  110567  110569  110573  110581
110587  110597  110603  110609  110623  110629  110641  110647  110651  110681  110711
```

```
110729  110731  110749  110753  110771  110777  110807  110813  110819  110821  110849
110863  110881  110899  110909  110917  110921  110923  110927  110933  110939
110947  110951  110969  110977  110989  111029  111031  111043  111049  111053  111091
111103  111109  111119  111121  111127  111143  111149  111187  111191  111211  111217
111227  111229  111253  111263  111269  111271  111301  111317  111323  111337  111341
111347  111373  111409  111427  111431  111439  111443  111467  111487  111491  111493
111497  111509  111521  111533  111539  111577  111581  111593  111599  111611  111623
111637  111641  111653  111659  111667  111697  111721  111731  111733  111751  111767
111773  111779  111781  111791  111799  111821  111827  111829  111833  111847  111857
111863  111869  111871  111893  111913  111919  111949  111953  111959  111973  111977
111997  112019  112031  112061  112067  112069  112087  112097  112103  112111  112121
112129  112139  112153  112163  112181  112199  112207  112213  112223  112237  112241
112247  112249  112253  112261  112279  112289  112291  112297  112303  112327  112331
112337  112339  112349  112361  112363  112397  112403  112429  112459  112481  112501
112507  112543  112559  112571  112573  112577  112583  112589  112601  112603  112621
112643  112657  112663  112687  112691  112741  112757  112759  112771  112787  112799
112807  112831  112843  112859  112877  112901  112909  112913  112919  112921  112927
112939  112951  112967  112979  112997  113011  113017  113021  113023  113027  113039
113041  113051  113063  113081  113083  113089  113093  113111  113117  113123  113131
113143  113147  113149  113153  113159  113161  113167  113171  113173  113177  113189
113209  113213  113227  113233  113279  113287  113327  113329  113341  113357  113359
113363  113371  113381  113383  113417  113437  113453  113467  113489  113497  113501
113513  113537  113539  113557  113567  113591  113621  113623  113647  113657  113683
113717  113719  113723  113731  113749  113759  113761  113777  113779  113783  113797
113809  113819  113837  113843  113891  113899  113903  113909  113921  113933  113947
113957  113963  113969  113983  113989  114001  114013  114031  114041  114043  114067
114073  114077  114083  114089  114113  114143  114157  114161  114167  114193  114197
114199  114203  114217  114221  114229  114259  114269  114277  114281  114299  114311
114319  114329  114343  114371  114377  114407  114419  114451  114467  114473  114479
114487  114493  114547  114553  114571  114577  114593  114599  114601  114613  114617
114641  114643  114649  114659  114661  114671  114679  114689  114691  114713  114743
114749  114757  114761  114769  114773  114781  114797  114799  114809  114827  114833
114847  114859  114883  114889  114901  114913  114941  114967  114973  114997  115001
115013  115019  115021  115057  115061  115067  115079  115099  115117  115123  115127
115133  115151  115153  115163  115183  115201  115211  115223  115237  115249  115259
115279  115301  115303  115309  115319  115321  115327  115331  115337  115343  115361
115363  115399  115421  115429  115459  115469  115471  115499  115513  115523  115547
115553  115561  115571  115589  115597  115601  115603  115613  115631  115637  115657
115663  115679  115693  115727  115733  115741  115751  115757  115763  115769  115771
115777  115781  115783  115793  115807  115811  115823  115831  115837  115849  115853
115859  115861  115873  115877  115879  115883  115891  115901  115903  115931  115933
115963  115979  115981  115987  116009  116027  116041  116047  116089  116099  116101
116107  116113  116131  116141  116159  116167  116177  116189  116191  116201  116239
116243  116257  116269  116273  116279  116293  116329  116341  116351  116359  116371
116381  116387  116411  116423  116437  116443  116447  116461  116471  116483  116491
116507  116531  116533  116537  116539  116549  116579  116593  116639  116657  116663
116681  116687  116689  116707  116719  116731  116741  116747  116789  116791  116797
116803  116819  116827  116833  116849  116867  116881  116903  116911  116923  116927
116929  116933  116953  116959  116969  116981  116989  116993  117017  117023  117037
117041  117043  117053  117071  117101  117109  117119  117127  117133  117163  117167
117191  117193  117203  117209  117223  117239  117241  117251  117259  117269  117281
117307  117319  117329  117331  117353  117361  117371  117373  117389  117413  117427
117431  117437  117443  117497  117499  117503  117511  117517  117529  117539  117541
117563  117571  117577  117617  117619  117643  117659  117671  117673  117679  117701
117703  117709  117721  117727  117731  117751  117757  117763  117773  117779  117787
117797  117809  117811  117833  117839  117841  117851  117877  117881  117883  117889
117899  117911  117917  117937  117959  117973  117977  117979  117989  117991  118033
118037  118043  118051  118057  118061  118081  118093  118127  118147  118163  118169
118171  118189  118211  118213  118219  118247  118249  118253  118259  118273  118277
118297  118343  118361  118369  118373  118387  118399  118409  118411  118423  118429
118453  118457  118463  118471  118493  118529  118543  118549  118571  118583  118589
118603  118619  118621  118633  118661  118669  118673  118681  118687  118691  118709
118717  118739  118747  118751  118757  118787  118799  118801  118819  118831  118843
118861  118873  118891  118897  118901  118903  118907  118913  118927  118931  118967
118973  119027  119033  119039  119047  119057  119069  119083  119087  119089  119099
119101  119107  119129  119131  119159  119173  119179  119183  119191  119227  119233
119237  119243  119267  119291  119293  119297  119299  119311  119321  119359  119363
119389  119417  119419  119447  119489  119503  119513  119533  119549  119551
119557  119563  119569  119591  119611  119617  119627  119633  119653  119657  119669
119671  119677  119687  119689  119701  119723  119737  119747  119759  119771
119773  119783  119797  119809  119813  119827  119831  119839  119849  119851  119869
119881  119891  119921  119923  119929  119953  119963  119971  119981  119983  119993
120011  120017  120041  120047  120049  120067  120077  120079  120091  120097  120103
120121  120157  120163  120167  120181  120193  120199  120209  120223  120233  120247
120277  120283  120293  120299  120319  120331  120349  120371  120383  120391  120397
120401  120413  120427  120431  120473  120503  120511  120539  120551  120557  120563
120569  120577  120587  120607  120619  120623  120641  120647  120661  120671  120677
120689  120691  120709  120713  120721  120737  120739  120749  120763  120767  120779
120811  120817  120823  120829  120833  120847  120851  120863  120871  120877  120889
120899  120907  120917  120919  120929  120937  120941  120943  120947  120977  120997
121001  121007  121013  121019  121021  121039  121061  121063  121067  121081  121123
121139  121151  121157  121169  121171  121181  121189  121229  121259  121267  121271
121283  121291  121309  121313  121321  121327  121333  121343  121349  121351  121357
121367  121369  121379  121403  121421  121439  121441  121447  121453  121469  121487
121493  121501  121507  121523  121531  121547  121553  121559  121571  121577  121579
121591  121607  121609  121621  121631  121633  121637  121661  121687  121697  121711
121721  121727  121763  121787  121789  121843  121853  121867  121883  121889  121909
121921  121931  121937  121949  121951  121963  121967  121993  121997  122011  122021
122027  122029  122033  122039  122041  122051  122053  122069  122081  122099  122117
```

```
122131  122147  122149  122167  122173  122201  122203  122207  122209  122219  122231
122251  122263  122267  122273  122279  122299  122321  122323  122327  122347  122363
122387  122389  122393  122399  122401  122443  122449  122453  122471  122477  122489
122497  122501  122503  122509  122527  122533  122557  122561  122579  122597  122599
122609  122611  122651  122653  122663  122693  122701  122719  122741  122743  122753
122761  122777  122789  122819  122827  122833  122839  122849  122861  122867  122869
122887  122891  122921  122929  122939  122953  122957  122963  122971  123001  123007
123017  123031  123049  123059  123077  123083  123091  123113  123121  123127  123143
123169  123191  123203  123209  123217  123229  123239  123259  123269  123289  123307
123311  123323  123341  123373  123377  123379  123397  123401  123407  123419  123427
123433  123439  123449  123457  123479  123491  123493  123499  123503  123517  123527
123547  123551  123553  123581  123583  123593  123601  123619  123631  123637  123653
123661  123667  123677  123701  123707  123719  123727  123731  123733  123737  123757
123787  123791  123803  123817  123821  123829  123833  123853  123863  123887  123911
123923  123931  123941  123953  123973  123979  123983  123989  123997  124001  124021
124067  124087  124097  124121  124123  124133  124139  124147  124153  124171  124181
124183  124193  124199  124213  124231  124247  124249  124277  124291  124297  124301
124303  124309  124337  124339  124343  124349  124351  124363  124367  124427  124429
124433  124447  124459  124471  124477  124489  124493  124513  124529  124541  124543
124561  124567  124577  124601  124633  124643  124669  124673  124679  124693  124699
124703  124717  124721  124739  124753  124759  124769  124771  124777  124781  124783
124793  124799  124819  124823  124847  124853  124897  124907  124909  124919  124951
124979  124981  124987  124991  125003  125017  125029  125053  125063  125093  125101
125107  125113  125117  125119  125131  125141  125149  125183  125197  125201  125207
125219  125221  125231  125243  125261  125269  125287  125299  125303  125311  125329
125339  125353  125371  125383  125387  125399  125407  125423  125429  125441  125453
125471  125497  125507  125509  125527  125539  125551  125591  125597  125617  125621
125627  125639  125641  125651  125659  125669  125683  125687  125693  125707  125711
125717  125731  125737  125743  125753  125777  125789  125791  125803  125813  125821
125863  125887  125897  125899  125921  125927  125929  125933  125941  125959  125963
126001  126011  126013  126019  126023  126031  126037  126041  126047  126067  126079
126097  126107  126127  126131  126143  126151  126173  126199  126211  126223  126227
126229  126233  126241  126257  126271  126307  126311  126317  126323  126337  126341
126349  126359  126397  126421  126433  126443  126457  126461  126473  126481  126487
126491  126493  126499  126517  126541  126547  126551  126583  126601  126611  126613
126631  126641  126653  126683  126691  126703  126713  126719  126733  126739  126743
126751  126757  126761  126781  126823  126827  126839  126851  126857  126859  126913
126923  126943  126949  126961  126967  126989  127031  127033  127037  127051  127079
127081  127103  127123  127133  127139  127157  127163  127189  127207  127217  127219
127241  127247  127249  127261  127271  127277  127289  127291  127297  127301  127321
127331  127343  127363  127373  127399  127403  127423  127447  127453  127481  127487
127493  127507  127529  127541  127549  127579  127583  127591  127597  127601  127607
127609  127637  127643  127657  127663  127669  127679  127681  127691  127703
127709  127711  127717  127727  127733  127739  127747  127763  127781  127807  127817
127819  127837  127843  127849  127859  127867  127873  127877  127913  127921  127931
127951  127973  127979  127997  128021  128033  128047  128053  128099  128111  128113
128119  128147  128153  128159  128173  128189  128201  128203  128213  128221  128237
128239  128257  128273  128287  128291  128311  128321  128327  128339  128341  128347
128351  128377  128389  128393  128399  128411  128413  128431  128437  128449  128461
128467  128473  128477  128483  128489  128509  128519  128521  128549  128551  128563
128591  128599  128603  128621  128629  128657  128659  128663  128669  128677  128683
128693  128717  128747  128749  128761  128767  128813  128819  128831  128833  128837
128857  128861  128873  128879  128903  128923  128939  128941  128951  128959  128969
128971  128981  128983  128987  128993  129001  129011  129023  129037  129049  129061
129083  129089  129097  129113  129119  129121  129127  129169  129187  129193  129197
129209  129221  129223  129229  129263  129277  129281  129287  129289  129293  129313
129341  129347  129361  129379  129401  129403  129419  129439  129443  129449  129457
129461  129469  129491  129497  129499  129509  129517  129527  129529  129533  129539
129553  129581  129587  129589  129593  129607  129629  129631  129641  129643  129671
129707  129719  129733  129737  129749  129757  129763  129793  129803  129841
129853  129887  129893  129901  129917  129919  129937  129953  129959  129967  129971
130003  130021  130027  130043  130051  130057  130069  130073  130079  130087  130099
130121  130127  130147  130171  130183  130199  130201  130211  130223  130241  130253
130259  130261  130267  130279  130303  130307  130337  130343  130349  130363  130367
130379  130399  130409  130411  130423  130439  130447  130457  130469  130477
130483  130489  130513  130517  130523  130531  130547  130553  130579  130589  130619
130621  130631  130633  130639  130643  130649  130651  130657  130681  130687  130693
130699  130729  130769  130783  130787  130807  130811  130817  130829  130841  130843
130859  130873  130927  130957  130969  130973  130981  130987  131009  131011  131023
131041  131059  131063  131071  131101  131111  131113  131129  131143  131149  131171
131203  131213  131221  131231  131249  131251  131267  131293  131297  131303  131311
131317  131321  131357  131363  131371  131381  131413  131431  131437  131441  131447
131449  131477  131489  131497  131501  131507  131519  131543  131561  131581
131591  131611  131617  131627  131639  131641  131671  131687  131701  131707  131711
131713  131731  131743  131749  131759  131771  131777  131779  131783  131797  131837
131839  131849  131861  131891  131893  131899  131909  131927  131933  131939  131941
131947  131959  131969  132001  132019  132047  132049  132059  132071  132103  132109
132113  132137  132151  132157  132169  132173  132199  132229  132233  132241  132247
132257  132263  132283  132287  132299  132313  132329  132331  132347  132361  132367
132371  132383  132403  132409  132421  132437  132439  132469  132491  132499  132511
132523  132527  132529  132533  132541  132547  132589  132607  132611  132619  132623
132631  132637  132647  132661  132667  132679  132689  132697  132701  132707  132709
132721  132739  132749  132751  132757  132761  132763  132817  132833  132851  132857
132859  132863  132887  132893  132911  132929  132947  132949  132953  132961  132967
132971  132989  133013  133033  133039  133051  133069  133073  133087  133097  133103
133109  133117  133121  133153  133157  133169  133183  133187  133201  133213  133241
133253  133261  133271  133277  133279  133283  133303  133319  133321  133327  133337
133349  133351  133379  133387  133391  133403  133417  133439  133447  133451  133481
133493  133499  133519  133541  133543  133559  133571  133583  133597  133631  133633
```

```
133649  133657  133669  133673  133691  133697  133709  133711  133717  133723  133733
133769  133781  133801  133811  133813  133831  133843  133853  133873  133877  133919
133949  133963  133967  133979  133981  133993  133999  134033  134039  134047  134053
134059  134077  134081  134087  134089  134093  134129  134153  134161  134171  134177
134191  134207  134213  134219  134227  134243  134257  134263  134269  134287  134291
134293  134327  134333  134339  134341  134353  134359  134363  134369  134371  134399
134401  134417  134437  134443  134471  134489  134503  134507  134513  134581  134587
134591  134593  134597  134609  134639  134669  134677  134681  134683  134699  134707
134731  134741  134753  134777  134789  134807  134837  134839  134851  134857  134867
134873  134887  134909  134917  134921  134923  134947  134951  134989  134999  135007
135017  135019  135029  135043  135049  135059  135077  135089  135101  135119  135131
135151  135173  135181  135193  135197  135209  135211  135221  135241  135257  135271
135277  135281  135283  135301  135319  135329  135347  135349  135353  135367  135389
135391  135403  135409  135427  135431  135433  135449  135461  135463  135467  135469
135479  135497  135511  135533  135559  135571  135581  135589  135593  135599  135601
135607  135613  135617  135623  135637  135647  135649  135661  135671  135697  135701
135719  135721  135727  135731  135743  135757  135781  135787  135799  135829  135841
135851  135859  135887  135893  135899  135911  135913  135929  135937  135977  135979
136013  136027  136033  136043  136057  136067  136069  136093  136099  136111  136133
136139  136163  136177  136189  136193  136207  136217  136223  136237  136247  136261
136277  136297  136303  136309  136319  136327  136333  136337  136343  136351  136361
136373  136379  136393  136397  136399  136403  136417  136421  136429  136447  136453
136463  136471  136481  136483  136501  136511  136519  136523  136531  136537  136541
136547  136559  136573  136601  136603  136607  136621  136649  136651  136667  136691
136693  136709  136711  136727  136733  136739  136751  136753  136769  136777  136811
136813  136841  136849  136859  136861  136879  136883  136889  136897  136943  136949
136951  136963  136973  136979  136987  136991  136993  136999  137029  137077  137087
137089  137117  137119  137131  137143  137147  137153  137177  137183  137191  137197
137201  137209  137219  137239  137251  137273  137279  137303  137321  137339  137341
137353  137359  137363  137369  137383  137387  137393  137399  137413  137437  137443
137447  137453  137477  137483  137491  137507  137519  137537  137567  137573  137587
137593  137597  137623  137633  137639  137653  137659  137699  137707  137713  137723
137737  137743  137771  137777  137791  137803  137827  137831  137849  137867  137869
137873  137909  137911  137927  137933  137941  137947  137957  137983  137993  137999
138007  138041  138053  138059  138071  138077  138079  138101  138107  138113  138139
138143  138157  138163  138179  138181  138191  138197  138209  138239  138241  138247
138251  138283  138289  138311  138319  138323  138337  138349  138371  138373  138389
138401  138403  138407  138427  138433  138449  138451  138461  138469  138493  138497
138511  138517  138547  138559  138563  138569  138571  138577  138581  138587  138599
138617  138629  138637  138641  138647  138661  138679  138683  138727  138731  138739
138763  138793  138797  138799  138821  138829  138841  138863  138869  138883  138889
138893  138899  138917  138923  138937  138959  138967  138977  139021  139033  139067
139079  139091  139109  139121  139123  139133  139169  139177  139187  139199  139201
139241  139267  139273  139291  139297  139301  139303  139309  139313  139333  139339
139343  139361  139367  139369  139387  139393  139397  139409  139423  139429  139439
139457  139459  139483  139487  139493  139501  139511  139537  139547  139571  139589
139591  139597  139609  139619  139627  139661  139663  139681  139697  139703  139709
139721  139729  139739  139747  139753  139759  139787  139801  139813  139831  139837
139861  139871  139883  139891  139901  139907  139921  139939  139943  139967  139969
139981  139987  139991  139999  140009  140053  140057  140069  140071  140111  140123
140143  140159  140167  140171  140177  140191  140197  140207  140221  140227  140237
140249  140263  140269  140281  140297  140317  140321  140333  140339  140351  140363
140381  140401  140407  140411  140417  140419  140423  140443  140449  140453  140473
140477  140521  140527  140533  140549  140551  140557  140587  140593  140603  140611
140617  140627  140629  140659  140663  140677  140681  140683  140689  140717
140729  140731  140741  140759  140761  140773  140779  140797  140813  140827  140831
140837  140839  140863  140867  140869  140891  140893  140897  140909  140929  140939
140977  140983  140989  141023  141041  141061  141067  141073  141079  141101  141107
141121  141131  141157  141161  141179  141181  141199  141209  141221  141223  141233
141241  141257  141263  141269  141277  141283  141301  141307  141311  141319  141353
141359  141371  141397  141403  141413  141439  141443  141461  141481  141497  141499
141509  141511  141529  141539  141551  141587  141601  141613  141619  141623  141629
141637  141649  141653  141667  141671  141677  141679  141689  141697  141707  141709
141719  141731  141761  141767  141769  141773  141793  141803  141811  141829  141833
141851  141853  141863  141871  141907  141917  141931  141937  141941  141959  141961
141971  141991  142007  142019  142031  142039  142049  142057  142061  142067  142097
142099  142111  142123  142151  142157  142159  142169  142183  142189  142193  142211
142217  142223  142231  142237  142271  142297  142319  142327  142357  142369  142381
142391  142403  142421  142427  142433  142453  142469  142501  142529  142537  142543
142547  142553  142559  142567  142573  142589  142591  142601  142607  142609  142619
142657  142673  142697  142699  142711  142733  142757  142759  142771  142787  142789
142799  142811  142837  142841  142867  142871  142873  142897  142903  142907  142939
142949  142963  142969  142973  142979  142981  142993  143053  143063  143093  143107
143111  143113  143137  143141  143159  143177  143197  143239  143243  143249  143257
143261  143263  143281  143287  143291  143329  143333  143357  143387  143401  143413
143419  143443  143461  143467  143477  143483  143489  143501  143503  143509  143513
143519  143527  143537  143551  143567  143569  143573  143593  143609  143617  143629
143651  143653  143669  143677  143687  143699  143711  143719  143729  143743  143779
143791  143797  143807  143813  143821  143827  143831  143833  143873  143879  143881
143909  143947  143953  143971  143977  143981  143999  144013  144031  144037  144061
144071  144073  144103  144139  144161  144163  144167  144169  144173  144203  144223
144241  144247  144253  144259  144271  144289  144299  144307  144311  144323  144341
144349  144379  144383  144407  144409  144413  144427  144439  144451  144461  144479
144481  144497  144511  144539  144541  144563  144569  144577  144583  144589  144593
144611  144629  144659  144667  144671  144701  144709  144719  144731  144737  144751
144757  144763  144773  144779  144791  144817  144829  144839  144847  144883  144887
144889  144899  144917  144931  144941  144961  144967  144973  144983  145007  145009
145021  145031  145037  145043  145063  145069  145091  145109  145121  145133  145139
145177  145193  145207  145213  145219  145253  145259  145267  145283  145289  145303
```

```
145307  145349  145361  145381  145391  145399  145417  145423  145433  145441  145451
145459  145463  145471  145477  145487  145501  145511  145513  145517  145531  145543
145547  145549  145577  145589  145601  145603  145633  145637  145643  145661  145679
145681  145687  145703  145709  145721  145723  145753  145757  145759  145771  145777
145799  145807  145819  145823  145829  145861  145879  145897  145903  145931  145933
145949  145963  145967  145969  145987  145991  146009  146011  146021  146023  146033
146051  146057  146059  146063  146077  146093  146099  146117  146141  146161  146173
146191  146197  146203  146213  146221  146239  146249  146273  146291  146297  146299
146309  146317  146323  146347  146359  146369  146381  146383  146389  146407  146417
146423  146437  146449  146477  146513  146519  146521  146527  146539  146543  146563
146581  146603  146609  146617  146639  146647  146669  146677  146681  146683  146701
146719  146743  146749  146767  146777  146801  146807  146819  146833  146837  146843
146849  146857  146891  146893  146917  146921  146933  146941  146953  146977  146983
146987  146989  147011  147029  147031  147047  147073  147083  147089  147097  147107
147137  147139  147151  147163  147179  147197  147209  147211  147221  147227  147229
147253  147263  147283  147289  147293  147299  147311  147319  147331  147341  147347
147353  147377  147391  147397  147401  147409  147419  147449  147451  147457  147481
147487  147503  147517  147541  147547  147551  147557  147571  147583  147607  147613
147617  147629  147647  147661  147671  147673  147689  147703  147709  147727  147739
147743  147761  147769  147773  147779  147787  147793  147799  147811  147827  147853
147859  147863  147881  147919  147937  147949  147977  147997  148001  148021  148061
148063  148073  148079  148091  148123  148139  148147  148151  148153  148157  148171
148193  148199  148201  148207  148229  148243  148249  148279  148301  148303  148331
148339  148361  148367  148381  148387  148399  148403  148411  148429  148439  148457
148469  148471  148483  148501  148513  148517  148531  148537  148549  148573  148579
148609  148627  148633  148639  148663  148667  148669  148691  148693  148711  148721
148723  148727  148747  148763  148781  148783  148793  148817  148829  148853  148859
148861  148867  148873  148891  148913  148921  148927  148931  148933  148949  148957
148991  148997  148999  149011  149021  149027  149033  149053  149057  149059  149069
149077  149087  149099  149101  149111  149113  149119  149143  149153  149159  149161
149173  149183  149197  149213  149239  149249  149251  149257  149269  149287  149297
149309  149323  149333  149341  149351  149371  149377  149381  149393  149399  149411
149417  149419  149423  149441  149459  149489  149491  149497  149503  149519  149521
149531  149533  149543  149551  149561  149563  149579  149603  149623  149627  149629
149689  149711  149713  149717  149729  149731  149749  149759  149767  149771  149791
149803  149827  149837  149843  149861  149867  149873  149899  149909  149911
149921  149939  149953  149969  149971  149993  150001  150011  150041  150053  150061
150067  150077  150083  150089  150091  150097  150107  150131  150151  150169  150193
150197  150203  150209  150211  150217  150221  150223  150239  150247  150287  150299
150301  150323  150329  150343  150373  150377  150379  150383  150401  150407  150413
150427  150431  150439  150473  150497  150503  150517  150523  150533  150551  150559
150571  150583  150587  150589  150607  150611  150617  150649  150659  150697  150707
150721  150743  150767  150769  150779  150791  150797  150827  150833  150847  150869
150881  150883  150889  150893  150901  150907  150919  150929  150959  150961  150967
150979  150989  150991  151007  151009  151013  151027  151049  151051  151057  151091
151121  151141  151153  151157  151163  151169  151171  151189  151201  151213  151237
151241  151243  151247  151253  151273  151279  151289  151303  151337  151339  151343
151357  151379  151381  151391  151397  151423  151429  151433  151451  151471  151477
151483  151499  151507  151517  151523  151531  151537  151549  151553  151561  151573
151579  151597  151603  151607  151609  151631  151637  151643  151651  151667  151673
151681  151687  151693  151703  151717  151729  151733  151769  151771  151783  151787
151799  151813  151817  151841  151847  151849  151871  151883  151897  151901  151903
151909  151937  151939  151967  151969  152003  152017  152027  152029  152039  152041
152063  152077  152081  152083  152093  152111  152123  152147  152183  152189  152197
152203  152213  152219  152231  152239  152249  152267  152287  152293  152297  152311
152363  152377  152381  152389  152393  152407  152417  152419  152423  152429  152441
152443  152459  152461  152501  152519  152531  152533  152539  152563  152567  152597
152599  152617  152623  152629  152639  152641  152657  152671  152681  152717  152723
152729  152753  152767  152777  152783  152791  152809  152819  152821  152833  152837
152839  152843  152851  152857  152879  152897  152899  152909  152939  152941  152947
152953  152959  152981  152989  152993  153001  153059  153067  153071  153073  153077
153089  153107  153113  153133  153137  153151  153191  153247  153259  153269  153271
153277  153281  153287  153313  153319  153337  153343  153353  153359  153371  153379
153407  153409  153421  153427  153437  153443  153449  153457  153469  153487  153499
153509  153511  153521  153523  153529  153533  153557  153563  153589  153607  153611
153623  153641  153649  153689  153701  153719  153733  153739  153743  153749  153757
153763  153817  153841  153871  153877  153887  153889  153911  153913  153929  153941
153947  153949  153953  153991  153997  154001  154027  154043  154057  154061  154067
154073  154079  154081  154087  154097  154111  154127  154153  154157  154159  154181
154183  154211  154213  154229  154243  154247  154267  154277  154279  154291  154303
154313  154321  154333  154339  154351  154369  154373  154387  154409  154417  154423
154439  154459  154487  154493  154501  154523  154543  154571  154573  154579  154589
154591  154613  154619  154621  154643  154667  154669  154681  154691  154699  154723
154727  154733  154747  154753  154769  154787  154789  154799  154807  154823  154841
154849  154871  154873  154883  154897  154927  154943  154949  154963  154981
154991  155003  155009  155017  155027  155047  155069  155081  155083  155087  155119
155137  155153  155161  155167  155171  155191  155201  155203  155209  155219  155231
155251  155269  155291  155299  155303  155317  155327  155333  155371  155377  155381
155383  155387  155399  155413  155423  155443  155453  155461  155473  155501  155509
155521  155537  155539  155557  155569  155579  155581  155593  155599  155609  155621
155627  155653  155657  155663  155671  155689  155693  155699  155707  155717  155719
155723  155731  155741  155747  155773  155777  155783  155797  155801  155809  155821
155833  155849  155851  155861  155863  155887  155891  155893  155921  156007  156011
156019  156041  156059  156061  156071  156089  156109  156119  156127  156131  156139
156151  156157  156217  156227  156229  156241  156253  156257  156259  156269  156307
156319  156329  156347  156353  156361  156371  156419  156421  156437  156467  156487
156491  156493  156511  156521  156539  156577  156589  156593  156601  156619  156623
156631  156641  156659  156671  156677  156679  156683  156691  156703  156707  156719
156727  156733  156749  156781  156797  156799  156817  156823  156833  156841  156887
```

156899 156901 156913 156941 156943 156967 156971 156979 157007 157013 157019
157037 157049 157051 157057 157061 157081 157103 157109 157127 157133 157141
157163 157177 157181 157189 157207 157211 157217 157219 157229 157231 157243
157247 157253 157259 157271 157273 157277 157279 157291 157303 157307 157321
157327 157349 157351 157363 157393 157411 157427 157429 157433 157457 157477
157483 157489 157513 157519 157523 157543 157559 157561 157571 157579 157627
157637 157639 157649 157667 157669 157679 157721 157733 157739 157747 157769
157771 157793 157799 157813 157823 157831 157837 157841 157867 157877 157889
157897 157901 157907 157931 157933 157951 157991 157999 158003 158009 158017
158029 158047 158071 158077 158113 158129 158141 158143 158161 158189 158201
158209 158227 158231 158233 158243 158261 158269 158293 158303 158329 158341
158351 158357 158359 158363 158371 158393 158407 158419 158429 158443 158449
158489 158507 158519 158527 158537 158551 158563 158567 158573 158581 158591
158597 158611 158617 158621 158633 158647 158657 158663 158669 158731 158747
158749 158759 158761 158771 158777 158791 158803 158843 158849 158863 158867
158881 158909 158923 158927 158941 158959 158981 158993 159013 159017 159023
159059 159073 159079 159097 159113 159119 159157 159161 159167 159169 159179
159191 159193 159199 159209 159223 159227 159233 159287 159293 159311 159319
159337 159347 159349 159361 159389 159403 159407 159421 159431 159437 159457
159463 159469 159473 159491 159499 159503 159521 159539 159541 159553 159563
159569 159571 159589 159617 159623 159629 159631 159667 159671 159673 159683
159697 159701 159707 159721 159737 159739 159763 159769 159773 159779 159787
159791 159793 159799 159811 159833 159839 159853 159857 159869 159871 159899
159911 159931 159937 159977 159979 160001 160009 160019 160031 160033 160049
160073 160079 160081 160087 160091 160093 160117 160141 160159 160163 160169
160183 160201 160207 160217 160231 160243 160253 160309 160313 160319 160343
160357 160367 160373 160387 160397 160403 160409 160423 160441 160453 160481
160483 160499 160507 160541 160553 160579 160583 160591 160603 160619 160621
160627 160637 160639 160649 160651 160663 160669 160681 160687 160697 160709
160711 160723 160739 160751 160753 160757 160781 160789 160807 160813 160817
160829 160841 160861 160877 160879 160883 160903 160907 160933 160967 160969
160981 160997 161009 161017 161033 161039 161047 161053 161059 161071 161087
161093 161123 161137 161141 161149 161159 161167 161201 161221 161233 161237
161263 161267 161281 161303 161309 161323 161333 161339 161341 161363 161377
161387 161407 161411 161453 161459 161461 161471 161503 161507 161521 161527
161531 161543 161561 161563 161569 161573 161591 161599 161611 161627 161639
161641 161659 161683 161717 161729 161731 161741 161743 161753 161761 161771
161773 161779 161783 161807 161831 161839 161869 161873 161879 161881 161911
161921 161923 161947 161957 161969 161971 161977 161983 161999 162007 162011
162017 162053 162059 162079 162091 162109 162119 162143 162209 162221 162229
162251 162257 162263 162269 162277 162287 162289 162293 162343 162359 162389
162391 162413 162419 162439 162451 162457 162473 162493 162499 162517 162523
162527 162529 162553 162557 162563 162577 162593 162601 162611 162623 162629
162641 162649 162671 162677 162683 162691 162703 162709 162713 162727 162731
162739 162749 162751 162779 162787 162791 162821 162823 162829 162839 162847
162853 162859 162881 162889 162901 162907 162917 162937 162947 162971 162973
162989 162997 163003 163019 163021 163027 163061 163063 163109 163117 163127
163129 163147 163151 163169 163171 163181 163193 163199 163211 163223 163243
163249 163259 163307 163309 163321 163327 163337 163351 163363 163367 163393
163403 163409 163411 163417 163433 163469 163477 163481 163483 163487 163517
163543 163561 163567 163573 163601 163613 163621 163627 163633 163637 163643
163661 163673 163679 163697 163729 163733 163741 163753 163771 163781 163789
163811 163819 163841 163847 163853 163859 163861 163871 163883 163901 163909
163927 163973 163979 163981 163987 163991 163993 163997 164011 164023 164039
164051 164057 164071 164089 164093 164113 164117 164147 164149 164173 164183
164191 164201 164209 164231 164233 164239 164249 164251 164267 164279 164291
164299 164309 164321 164341 164357 164363 164371 164377 164387 164413 164419
164429 164431 164443 164447 164449 164471 164477 164503 164513 164531 164569
164581 164587 164599 164617 164621 164623 164627 164653 164663 164677 164683
164701 164707 164729 164743 164767 164771 164789 164809 164821 164831 164837
164839 164881 164893 164911 164953 164963 164987 164999 165001 165037 165041
165047 165049 165059 165079 165083 165089 165103 165133 165161 165173 165181
165203 165211 165229 165233 165247 165287 165293 165311 165313 165317 165331
165343 165349 165367 165379 165383 165391 165397 165437 165443 165449 165457
165463 165469 165479 165511 165523 165527 165533 165541 165551 165553 165559
165569 165587 165589 165601 165611 165617 165653 165667 165673 165701 165703
165707 165709 165713 165719 165721 165749 165779 165799 165811 165817 165829
165833 165857 165877 165887 165901 165931 165941 165947 165961 165983
166013 166021 166027 166031 166043 166063 166081 166099 166147 166151 166157
166169 166183 166189 166207 166219 166237 166247 166259 166273 166289 166297
166301 166303 166319 166349 166351 166357 166363 166393 166399 166403 166409
166417 166429 166457 166471 166487 166541 166561 166567 166571 166597 166601
166603 166609 166613 166619 166627 166631 166643 166657 166667 166669 166679
166693 166703 166723 166739 166741 166781 166783 166799 166807 166823 166841
166843 166847 166849 166853 166861 166867 166871 166909 166919 166931 166949
166967 166973 166979 166987 167009 167017 167021 167023 167033 167039 167047
167051 167071 167077 167081 167087 167099 167107 167113 167117 167119 167149
167159 167173 167177 167191 167197 167213 167221 167249 167261 167267 167269
167309 167311 167317 167329 167339 167341 167381 167393 167407 167413 167423
167429 167437 167441 167443 167449 167471 167483 167491 167521 167537 167543
167593 167597 167611 167621 167623 167627 167633 167641 167663 167677 167683
167711 167729 167747 167759 167771 167777 167779 167801 167809 167861 167863
167873 167879 167887 167891 167899 167911 167917 167953 167971 167987 168013
168023 168029 168037 168043 168067 168071 168083 168089 168109 168127 168143
168151 168193 168197 168211 168227 168247 168253 168263 168269 168277 168281
168293 168323 168331 168347 168353 168391 168409 168433 168449 168451 168457
168463 168481 168491 168499 168523 168527 168533 168541 168559 168599 168601
168617 168629 168631 168643 168673 168677 168697 168713 168719 168731 168737
168743 168761 168769 168781 168803 168851 168863 168869 168887 168893 168899

```
168901  168913  168937  168943  168977  168991  169003  169007  169009  169019  169049
169063  169067  169069  169079  169093  169097  169111  169129  169151  169159  169177
169181  169199  169217  169219  169241  169243  169249  169259  169283  169307  169313
169319  169321  169327  169339  169343  169361  169369  169373  169399  169409  169427
169457  169471  169483  169489  169493  169501  169523  169531  169553  169567  169583
169591  169607  169627  169633  169639  169649  169657  169661  169667  169681  169691
169693  169709  169733  169751  169753  169769  169777  169783  169789  169817  169823
169831  169837  169843  169859  169889  169891  169909  169913  169919  169933  169937
169943  169951  169957  169987  169991  170003  170021  170029  170047  170057  170063
170081  170099  170101  170111  170123  170141  170167  170179  170189  170197  170207
170213  170227  170231  170239  170243  170249  170263  170267  170279  170293  170299
170327  170341  170347  170351  170353  170363  170369  170371  170383  170389  170393
170413  170441  170447  170473  170483  170497  170503  170509  170537  170539  170551
170557  170579  170603  170609  170627  170633  170641  170647  170669  170689  170701
170707  170711  170741  170749  170759  170761  170767  170773  170777  170801  170809
170813  170827  170837  170843  170851  170857  170873  170881  170899  170909  170921
170927  170953  170957  170971  171007  171023  171029  171043  171047  171049  171053
171077  171079  171091  171103  171131  171161  171163  171167  171169  171179  171203
171233  171251  171253  171263  171271  171293  171299  171317  171329  171341  171383
171401  171403  171427  171439  171449  171467  171469  171473  171481  171491  171517
171529  171539  171541  171553  171559  171571  171583  171617  171629  171637  171641
171653  171659  171671  171673  171679  171697  171707  171713  171719  171733  171757
171761  171763  171793  171799  171803  171811  171823  171827  171851  171863  171869
171877  171881  171889  171917  171923  171929  171937  171947  172001  172009  172021
172027  172031  172049  172069  172079  172093  172097  172127  172147  172153  172157
172169  172171  172181  172199  172213  172217  172219  172223  172243  172259  172279
172283  172297  172307  172313  172321  172331  172343  172351  172357  172373  172399
172411  172421  172423  172427  172433  172439  172441  172489  172507  172517  172519
172541  172553  172561  172573  172583  172589  172597  172603  172607  172619  172633
172643  172649  172657  172663  172673  172681  172687  172709  172717  172721  172741
172751  172759  172787  172801  172807  172829  172849  172853  172859  172867  172871
172877  172883  172933  172969  172973  172981  172987  172993  172999  173021  173023
173039  173053  173059  173081  173087  173099  173137  173141  173149  173177  173183
173189  173191  173207  173209  173219  173249  173263  173267  173273  173291  173293
173297  173309  173347  173357  173359  173429  173431  173473  173483  173491  173497
173501  173531  173539  173543  173549  173561  173573  173599  173617  173629  173647
173651  173659  173669  173671  173683  173687  173699  173707  173713  173729  173741
173743  173773  173777  173779  173783  173807  173819  173827  173839  173851  173861
173867  173891  173897  173909  173917  173923  173933  173969  173977  173981  173993
174007  174017  174019  174047  174049  174061  174067  174071  174077  174079  174091
174101  174121  174137  174143  174149  174157  174169  174197  174221  174241  174257
174259  174263  174281  174289  174299  174311  174329  174331  174337  174347  174367
174389  174407  174413  174431  174443  174457  174467  174469  174481  174487  174491
174527  174533  174569  174571  174583  174599  174613  174617  174631  174637  174649
174653  174659  174673  174679  174703  174721  174737  174749  174761  174763  174767
174773  174799  174821  174829  174851  174859  174877  174893  174901  174907  174917
174929  174931  174943  174959  174989  174991  175003  175013  175039  175061  175067
175069  175079  175081  175103  175129  175141  175211  175229  175261  175267  175277
175291  175303  175309  175327  175333  175349  175361  175391  175393  175403  175411
175433  175447  175453  175463  175481  175493  175499  175519  175523  175543  175573
175601  175621  175631  175633  175649  175663  175673  175687  175691  175699  175709
175723  175727  175753  175757  175759  175781  175783  175811  175829  175837  175843
175853  175859  175873  175891  175897  175909  175919  175937  175939  175949  175961
175963  175979  175991  175993  176017  176021  176023  176041  176047  176051  176053
176063  176081  176087  176089  176123  176129  176153  176159  176161  176179  176191
176201  176207  176213  176221  176227  176237  176243  176261  176299  176303  176317
176321  176327  176329  176333  176347  176353  176357  176369  176383  176389  176401
176413  176417  176419  176431  176459  176461  176467  176489  176497  176503  176507
176509  176521  176531  176537  176549  176551  176557  176573  176591  176597  176599
176609  176611  176629  176641  176651  176677  176699  176711  176713  176741  176747
176753  176777  176779  176789  176791  176797  176807  176809  176819  176849  176857
176887  176899  176903  176921  176923  176927  176933  176951  176977  176983  176989
177007  177011  177013  177019  177043  177091  177101  177109  177113  177127  177131
177167  177173  177209  177211  177217  177223  177239  177257  177269  177283  177301
177319  177323  177337  177347  177379  177383  177409  177421  177427  177431  177433
177467  177473  177481  177487  177493  177511  177533  177539  177553  177589  177601
177623  177647  177677  177679  177691  177739  177743  177761  177763  177787  177791
177797  177811  177823  177839  177841  177883  177887  177889  177893  177907  177913
177917  177929  177943  177949  177953  177967  177979  178001  178021  178037  178039
178067  178069  178081  178093  178103  178117  178127  178141  178151  178169  178183
178187  178207  178223  178231  178247  178249  178259  178261  178289  178301  178307
178327  178333  178349  178351  178361  178393  178397  178403  178417  178439  178441
178447  178469  178481  178487  178489  178501  178513  178531  178537  178559  178561
178567  178571  178597  178601  178603  178609  178613  178621  178627  178639  178643
178681  178691  178693  178697  178753  178757  178781  178793  178807  178813  178813
178817  178819  178831  178853  178859  178873  178877  178889  178897  178903  178907
178909  178921  178931  178933  178939  178951  178973  178987  179021  179029  179033
179041  179051  179057  179083  179089  179099  179107  179111  179119  179143  179161
179167  179173  179203  179209  179213  179233  179243  179261  179269  179281  179287
179317  179321  179327  179351  179357  179369  179381  179383  179393  179407  179411
179429  179437  179441  179453  179461  179471  179479  179483  179497  179519  179527
179533  179549  179563  179573  179579  179581  179591  179593  179603  179623  179633
179651  179657  179659  179671  179687  179689  179693  179717  179719  179737  179743
179749  179779  179801  179807  179813  179819  179821  179827  179833  179849  179897
179899  179903  179909  179917  179923  179939  179947  179951  179957  179969  179981
179981  179989  179999  180001  180007  180023  180043  180053  180071  180073  180077
180097  180137  180161  180179  180181  180211  180221  180233  180239  180241  180247
180259  180263  180281  180287  180289  180307  180311  180317  180331  180337  180347
180361  180371  180379  180391  180413  180419  180437  180463  180473  180491  180497
```

```
180503 180511 180533 180539 180541 180547 180563 180569 180617 180623 180629
180647 180667 180679 180701 180731 180749 180751 180773 180779 180793 180797
180799 180811 180847 180871 180883 180907 180949 180959 181001 181003 181019
181031 181039 181061 181063 181081 181087 181123 181141 181157 181183 181199
181199 181201 181211 181213 181219 181243 181253 181273 181277 181283 181297
181301 181303 181361 181387 181397 181399 181409 181421 181439 181457 181459
181499 181501 181513 181523 181537 181549 181553 181603 181607 181609 181619
181639 181667 181669 181693 181711 181717 181721 181729 181739 181751 181757
181759 181763 181777 181787 181789 181813 181837 181871 181873 181889 181891
181903 181913 181919 181927 181931 181943 181957 181967 181981 181997 182009
182011 182027 182029 182041 182047 182057 182059 182089 182099 182101 182107
182111 182123 182129 182131 182141 182159 182167 182177 182179 182201 182209
182233 182239 182243 182261 182279 182297 182309 182333 182339 182341 182353
182387 182389 182417 182423 182431 182443 182453 182467 182471 182473 182489
182503 182509 182519 182537 182549 182561 182579 182587 182593 182599 182603
182617 182627 182641 182653 182657 182659 182681 182687 182701 182711
182713 182747 182773 182779 182789 182803 182813 182821 182839 182851 182857
182867 182887 182893 182899 182921 182927 182929 182933 182953 182957 182969
182981 182999 183023 183037 183041 183047 183059 183067 183089 183091 183119
183151 183167 183191 183203 183247 183259 183263 183283 183289 183299 183301
183307 183317 183319 183329 183343 183349 183361 183373 183377 183383 183389
183397 183437 183439 183451 183461 183473 183479 183487 183497 183499 183503
183509 183511 183523 183527 183569 183571 183577 183581 183587 183593 183611
183637 183661 183683 183691 183697 183707 183709 183713 183761 183763 183797
183809 183823 183829 183871 183877 183881 183907 183917 183919 183943 183949
183959 183971 183973 183979 184003 184007 184013 184031 184039 184043 184057
184073 184081 184087 184111 184117 184133 184153 184157 184181 184187 184189
184199 184211 184231 184241 184259 184271 184273 184279 184291 184309 184321
184333 184337 184351 184369 184409 184417 184441 184447 184463 184477 184487
184489 184511 184517 184523 184553 184559 184567 184571 184577 184607 184609
184627 184631 184633 184649 184651 184669 184687 184693 184703 184711 184721
184727 184733 184753 184777 184823 184829 184831 184837 184843 184859 184879
184901 184903 184913 184949 184957 184967 184969 184993 184997 184999 185021
185027 185051 185057 185063 185069 185071 185077 185089 185099 185123 185131
185137 185149 185153 185161 185167 185177 185183 185189 185221 185233 185243
185267 185291 185299 185303 185309 185323 185327 185359 185363 185369 185371
185401 185429 185441 185467 185477 185483 185491 185519 185527 185531 185533
185539 185543 185551 185557 185567 185569 185593 185599 185621 185641 185651
185677 185681 185683 185693 185699 185707 185711 185723 185737 185747 185749
185753 185767 185789 185797 185813 185819 185821 185831 185833 185849 185869
185873 185893 185897 185903 185917 185923 185947 185951 185957 185959 185971
185987 185993 186007 186013 186019 186023 186037 186041 186049 186071 186097
186103 186113 186119 186149 186161 186187 186191 186211
186227 186229 186239 186247 186253 186259 186271 186283 186299 186301 186311
186317 186343 186377 186379 186391 186397 186419 186437 186451 186469 186479
186481 186551 186569 186581 186583 186587 186601 186619 186629 186647 186649
186653 186671 186679 186689 186701 186707 186709 186727 186733 186743 186757
186761 186763 186773 186793 186799 186841 186859 186869 186871 186877 186883
186889 186917 186947 186959 187003 187009 187027 187043 187049 187067 187069
187073 187081 187091 187111 187123 187127 187129 187133 187139 187141 187163
187171 187177 187181 187189 187193 187211 187217 187219 187223 187237 187273
187277 187303 187337 187339 187349 187361 187367 187373 187379 187387 187393
187409 187417 187423 187433 187441 187463 187469 187471 187477 187507 187513
187531 187547 187559 187573 187597 187631 187633 187637 187639 187651 187661
187669 187687 187699 187711 187721 187751 187763 187787 187793 187823 187843
187861 187871 187877 187883 187897 187907 187909 187921 187927 187931 187951
187963 187973 187987 188011 188017 188021 188029 188107 188137 188143 188147
188159 188171 188179 188189 188197 188249 188261 188273 188281 188291 188299
188303 188311 188317 188323 188333 188351 188359 188369 188389 188401 188407
188417 188431 188437 188443 188459 188473 188483 188491 188519 188527 188533
188563 188579 188603 188609 188621 188633 188653 188677 188681 188687 188693
188701 188707 188711 188719 188729 188753 188767 188779 188791 188801 188827
188831 188833 188843 188857 188863 188869 188891 188911 188917 188927 188933
188939 188941 188953 188957 188983 188999 189011 189017 189019 189041 189043
189061 189067 189127 189139 189149 189151 189169 189187 189199 189223 189229
189239 189251 189253 189257 189271 189307 189311 189337 189347 189349 189353
189361 189377 189389 189391 189401 189407 189421 189433 189437 189439 189463
189467 189473 189479 189491 189493 189509 189517 189523 189529 189547 189559
189583 189593 189599 189613 189617 189619 189643 189653 189661 189671 189691
189697 189701 189713 189733 189743 189757 189767 189797 189799 189817 189823
189851 189853 189859 189877 189881 189887 189901 189913 189929 189947 189949
189961 189967 189977 189983 189989 189997 190027 190031 190051 190063 190093
190097 190121 190129 190147 190159 190181 190207 190243 190249 190261 190271
190283 190297 190301 190313 190321 190331 190339 190357 190367 190369 190387
190391 190403 190409 190471 190507 190523 190529 190537 190543 190573 190577
190579 190583 190591 190607 190613 190633 190639 190649 190657 190667 190669
190699 190709 190711 190717 190753 190759 190763 190769 190783 190787 190793
190807 190811 190823 190829 190837 190843 190871 190889 190891 190901 190909
190913 190921 190979 190997 191021 191027 191033 191039 191047 191057 191071
191089 191099 191119 191123 191137 191141 191143 191161 191173 191189 191227
191231 191237 191249 191251 191281 191297 191299 191339 191341 191353 191413
191441 191447 191449 191453 191459 191461 191467 191473 191491 191497 191507
191509 191519 191531 191533 191537 191551 191561 191563 191579 191599 191621
191627 191657 191669 191671 191677 191689 191693 191699 191707 191717 191747
191749 191773 191783 191791 191801 191803 191827 191831 191833 191837 191861
191899 191903 191911 191929 191953 191969 191977 191999 192007 192013 192029
192037 192043 192047 192053 192091 192097 192103 192113 192121 192133 192149
192161 192173 192187 192191 192193 192229 192233 192239 192251 192259 192263
192271 192307 192317 192319 192323 192341 192343 192347 192373 192377 192383
```

```
192391  192407  192431  192461  192463  192497  192499  192529  192539  192547  192553
192557  192571  192581  192583  192587  192601  192611  192613  192617  192629  192631
192637  192667  192677  192697  192737  192743  192749  192757  192767  192781  192791
192799  192811  192817  192833  192847  192853  192859  192877  192883  192887  192889
192917  192923  192931  192949  192961  192971  192977  192979  192991  193003  193009
193013  193031  193043  193051  193057  193073  193093  193133  193139  193147  193153
193163  193181  193183  193189  193201  193243  193247  193261  193283  193301  193327
193337  193357  193367  193373  193379  193381  193387  193393  193423  193433  193441
193447  193451  193463  193469  193493  193507  193513  193541  193549  193559  193573
193577  193597  193601  193603  193607  193619  193649  193663  193679  193703  193723
193727  193741  193751  193757  193763  193771  193789  193793  193799  193811  193813
193841  193847  193859  193861  193871  193873  193877  193883  193891  193937  193939
193943  193951  193957  193979  193993  194003  194017  194027  194057  194069  194071
194083  194087  194093  194101  194113  194119  194141  194149  194167  194179  194197
194203  194239  194263  194267  194269  194309  194323  194353  194371  194377  194413
194431  194443  194471  194479  194483  194507  194521  194527  194543  194569  194581
194591  194609  194647  194653  194659  194671  194681  194683  194687  194707  194713
194717  194723  194729  194749  194767  194771  194809  194813  194819  194827  194839
194861  194863  194867  194869  194891  194899  194911  194917  194933  194963  194977
194981  194989  195023  195029  195043  195047  195049  195053  195071  195077  195089
195103  195121  195127  195131  195137  195157  195161  195163  195193  195197  195203
195229  195241  195253  195259  195271  195277  195281  195311  195319  195329  195341
195343  195353  195359  195389  195401  195407  195413  195427  195443  195457  195469
195479  195493  195497  195511  195527  195539  195541  195581  195593  195599  195659
195677  195691  195697  195709  195731  195733  195737  195739  195743  195751  195761
195781  195787  195791  195809  195817  195863  195869  195883  195887  195893  195907
195913  195919  195929  195931  195967  195971  195973  195977  195991  195997  196003
196033  196039  196043  196051  196073  196081  196087  196111  196117  196139  196159
196169  196171  196177  196181  196187  196193  196201  196247  196271  196277  196279
196291  196303  196307  196331  196337  196379  196387  196429  196439  196453  196459
196477  196499  196501  196519  196523  196541  196543  196549  196561  196579  196583
196597  196613  196643  196657  196661  196663  196681  196687  196699  196709  196717
196727  196739  196751  196769  196771  196799  196817  196831  196837  196853  196871
196873  196879  196901  196907  196919  196927  196961  196991  196993  197003  197009
197023  197033  197059  197063  197077  197083  197089  197101  197117  197123  197137
197147  197159  197161  197203  197207  197221  197233  197243  197257  197261  197269
197273  197279  197293  197297  197299  197311  197339  197341  197347  197359  197369
197371  197381  197383  197389  197419  197423  197441  197453  197479  197507  197521
197539  197551  197567  197569  197573  197597  197599  197609  197621  197641  197647
197651  197677  197683  197689  197699  197711  197713  197741  197753  197759  197767
197773  197779  197803  197807  197831  197837  197887  197891  197893  197909  197921
197927  197933  197947  197957  197959  197963  197969  197971  198013  198017  198031
198043  198047  198073  198083  198091  198097  198109  198127  198139  198173  198179
198193  198197  198221  198223  198241  198251  198257  198259  198277  198281  198301
198313  198323  198337  198347  198349  198377  198391  198397  198409  198413  198427
198437  198439  198461  198463  198469  198479  198491  198503  198529  198533  198553
198571  198589  198593  198599  198613  198623  198637  198641  198647  198659  198673
198689  198701  198719  198733  198761  198769  198811  198817  198823  198827  198829
198833  198839  198841  198851  198859  198899  198901  198929  198937  198941  198943
198953  198959  198967  198971  198977  198997  199021  199033  199037  199039  199049
199081  199103  199109  199151  199153  199181  199193  199207  199211  199247  199261
199267  199289  199313  199321  199337  199343  199357  199373  199379  199399  199403
199411  199417  199429  199447  199453  199457  199483  199487  199489  199499  199501
199523  199559  199567  199583  199601  199603  199621  199637  199657  199669  199673
199679  199687  199697  199721  199729  199739  199741  199751  199753  199777  199783
199799  199807  199811  199813  199819  199831  199853  199873  199877  199889  199909
199921  199931  199933  199961  199967  199999  200003  200009  200017  200023  200029
200033  200041  200063  200087  200117  200131  200153  200159  200171  200177  200183
200191  200201  200227  200231  200237  200257  200273  200293  200297  200323  200329
200341  200351  200357  200363  200371  200381  200383  200401  200407  200437  200443
200461  200467  200483  200513  200569  200573  200579  200587  200591  200597  200609
200639  200657  200671  200689  200699  200713  200723  200731  200771  200779  200789
200797  200807  200843  200861  200867  200869  200881  200891  200899  200903  200909
200927  200929  200971  200983  200987  200989  201007  201011  201031  201037  201049
201073  201101  201107  201119  201121  201139  201151  201163  201167  201193  201203
201209  201211  201233  201247  201251  201281  201287  201307  201329  201337  201359
201389  201401  201403  201413  201437  201449  201451  201473  201491  201493  201497
201499  201511  201517  201547  201557  201577  201581  201589  201599  201611  201623
201629  201653  201661  201667  201673  201683  201701  201709  201731  201743  201757
201767  201769  201781  201787  201791  201797  201809  201821  201823  201827  201829
201833  201847  201881  201889  201893  201907  201911  201919  201923  201937  201947
201953  201961  201973  201979  201997  202001  202021  202031  202049  202061  202063
202067  202087  202099  202109  202121  202127  202129  202183  202187  202201  202219
202231  202243  202277  202289  202291  202309  202327  202339  202343  202357  202361
202381  202387  202393  202403  202409  202441  202471  202481  202493  202519  202529
202549  202567  202577  202591  202613  202621  202627  202637  202639  202661  202667
202679  202693  202717  202729  202733  202747  202751  202753  202757  202777  202799
202817  202823  202841  202859  202877  202879  202889  202907  202921  202931  202933
202949  202967  202973  202981  202987  202999  203011  203017  203023  203039  203051
203057  203117  203141  203173  203183  203207  203209  203213  203221  203227  203233
203249  203279  203293  203309  203311  203317  203321  203323  203339  203341  203351
203353  203363  203381  203383  203387  203393  203417  203419  203429  203431  203449
203459  203461  203531  203549  203563  203569  203579  203591  203617  203627  203641
203653  203657  203659  203663  203669  203713  203761  203767  203771  203773  203789
203807  203809  203821  203843  203857  203869  203873  203887  203909  203911  203921
203947  203953  203969  203971  203977  203989  203999  204007  204013  204019  204023
204047  204059  204067  204101  204107  204133  204137  204143  204151  204161  204163
204173  204233  204251  204299  204301  204311  204319  204329  204331  204353  204359
204361  204367  204371  204377  204397  204427  204431  204437  204439  204443  204461
```

```
204481  204487  204509  204511  204517  204521  204557  204563  204583  204587  204599
204601  204613  204623  204641  204667  204679  204707  204719  204733  204749  204751
204781  204791  204793  204797  204803  204821  204857  204859  204871  204887  204913
204917  204923  204931  204947  204973  204979  204983  205019  205031  205033  205043
205063  205069  205081  205097  205103  205111  205129  205133  205141  205151  205157
205171  205187  205201  205211  205213  205223  205237  205253  205267  205297  205307
205319  205327  205339  205357  205391  205397  205399  205417  205421  205423  205427
205433  205441  205453  205463  205477  205483  205487  205493  205507  205519  205529
205537  205549  205553  205559  205589  205603  205607  205619  205627  205633  205651
205657  205661  205663  205703  205721  205759  205763  205783  205817  205823  205837
205847  205879  205883  205913  205937  205949  205951  205957  205963  205967  205981
205991  205993  206009  206021  206027  206033  206039  206047  206051  206069  206077
206081  206083  206123  206153  206177  206179  206183  206191  206197  206203  206209
206221  206233  206237  206249  206251  206263  206273  206279  206281  206291  206299
206303  206341  206347  206351  206369  206383  206399  206407  206411  206413  206419
206447  206461  206467  206477  206483  206489  206501  206519  206527  206543  206551
206593  206597  206603  206623  206627  206639  206641  206651  206699  206749  206779
206783  206803  206807  206813  206819  206821  206827  206879  206887  206897  206909
206911  206917  206923  206933  206939  206951  206953  206993  207013  207017  207029
207037  207041  207061  207073  207079  207113  207121  207127  207139  207169  207187
207191  207197  207199  207227  207239  207241  207257  207269  207287  207293  207301
207307  207329  207331  207341  207343  207367  207371  207377  207401  207409  207433
207443  207457  207463  207469  207479  207481  207491  207497  207509  207511  207517
207523  207533  207541  207547  207551  207563  207569  207589  207593  207619  207629
207643  207653  207661  207671  207673  207679  207709  207719  207721  207743  207763
207769  207797  207799  207811  207821  207833  207847  207869  207877  207923  207931
207941  207947  207953  207967  207971  207973  207997  208001  208003  208009  208037
208049  208057  208067  208073  208099  208111  208121  208129  208139  208141  208147
208189  208207  208213  208217  208223  208231  208253  208261  208277  208279  208283
208291  208309  208319  208333  208337  208367  208379  208387  208391  208393  208409
208433  208441  208457  208459  208463  208469  208489  208493  208499  208501  208511
208513  208519  208529  208553  208577  208589  208591  208609  208627  208631  208657
208667  208673  208687  208697  208699  208721  208729  208739  208759  208787  208799
208807  208837  208843  208877  208889  208891  208907  208927  208931  208933  208961
208963  208991  208993  208997  209021  209029  209039  209063  209071  209089  209123
209147  209159  209173  209179  209189  209201  209203  209213  209221  209227  209233
209249  209257  209263  209267  209269  209299  209311  209317  209327  209333  209347
209353  209357  209359  209371  209381  209393  209401  209431  209441  209449  209459
209471  209477  209497  209519  209533  209543  209549  209563  209567  209569  209579
209581  209597  209621  209623  209639  209647  209659  209669  209687  209701  209707
209717  209719  209743  209767  209771  209789  209801  209809  209813  209819  209821
209837  209851  209857  209861  209887  209917  209927  209929  209939  209953  209959
209971  209977  209983  209987  210011  210019  210031  210037  210053  210071  210097
210101  210109  210113  210127  210131  210139  210143  210157  210169  210173  210187
210191  210193  210209  210229  210233  210241  210247  210257  210263  210277  210283
210299  210317  210319  210323  210347  210359  210361  210391  210401  210403  210407
210421  210437  210461  210467  210481  210487  210491  210499  210523  210527  210533
210557  210599  210601  210619  210631  210643  210659  210671  210709  210713  210719
210731  210739  210761  210773  210803  210809  210811  210823  210827  210839  210853
210857  210869  210901  210907  210911  210913  210923  210929  210943  210961  210967
211007  211039  211049  211051  211061  211063  211067  211073  211093  211097  211129
211151  211153  211177  211187  211193  211199  211213  211217  211219  211229  211231
211241  211247  211271  211283  211291  211297  211313  211319  211333  211339  211349
211369  211373  211403  211427  211433  211441  211457  211469  211493  211499  211501
211507  211543  211559  211571  211573  211583  211597  211619  211639  211643  211657
211661  211663  211681  211691  211693  211711  211723  211727  211741  211747  211777
211781  211789  211801  211811  211817  211859  211867  211873  211877  211879  211889
211891  211927  211931  211933  211943  211949  211969  211979  211997  212029  212039
212057  212081  212099  212117  212123  212131  212141  212161  212167  212183  212203
212207  212209  212227  212239  212243  212281  212293  212297  212353  212369  212383
212411  212419  212423  212437  212447  212453  212461  212467  212479  212501  212507
212557  212561  212573  212579  212587  212593  212627  212633  212651  212669  212671
212677  212683  212701  212777  212791  212801  212827  212837  212843  212851  212867
212869  212873  212881  212897  212903  212909  212917  212923  212969  212981  212987
212999  213019  213023  213029  213043  213067  213079  213091  213097  213119  213131
213133  213139  213149  213173  213181  213193  213203  213209  213217  213223  213229
213247  213253  213263  213281  213287  213289  213307  213319  213329  213337  213349
213359  213361  213383  213391  213397  213407  213449  213461  213467  213481  213491
213523  213533  213539  213553  213557  213589  213599  213611  213613  213623  213637
213641  213649  213659  213713  213721  213727  213737  213751  213791  213799  213821
213827  213833  213847  213859  213881  213887  213901  213919  213929  213943  213947
213949  213953  213973  213977  213989  214003  214007  214009  214021  214031  214033
214043  214051  214063  214069  214087  214091  214129  214133  214141  214147  214163
214177  214189  214211  214213  214219  214237  214243  214259  214283  214297  214309
214351  214363  214373  214381  214391  214399  214433  214439  214451  214457  214463
214469  214481  214483  214499  214507  214517  214519  214531  214541  214559  214561
214589  214603  214607  214631  214639  214651  214657  214663  214667  214673  214691
214723  214729  214733  214741  214759  214763  214771  214783  214787  214789  214807
214811  214817  214831  214849  214853  214867  214883  214891  214913  214939  214943
214967  214987  214993  215051  215063  215077  215087  215123  215141  215143  215153
215161  215179  215183  215191  215197  215239  215249  215261  215273  215279  215297
215309  215317  215329  215351  215353  215359  215381  215389  215393  215399  215417
215443  215447  215459  215461  215471  215483  215497  215503  215507  215521  215531
215563  215573  215587  215617  215653  215659  215681  215687  215689  215693  215723
215737  215753  215767  215771  215797  215801  215827  215833  215843  215851  215857
215863  215893  215899  215909  215921  215927  215939  215953  215959  215981  215983
216023  216037  216061  216071  216091  216103  216107  216113  216119  216127  216133
216149  216157  216173  216179  216211  216217  216233  216259  216263  216289  216317
216319  216329  216347  216371  216373  216379  216397  216401  216421  216431  216451
```

216481 216493 216509 216523 216551 216553 216569 216571 216577 216607 216617
216641 216647 216649 216653 216661 216679 216703 216719 216731 216743 216751
216757 216761 216779 216781 216787 216791 216803 216829 216841 216851 216859
216877 216899 216901 216911 216917 216919 216947 216967 216973 216991 217001
217003 217027 217033 217057 217069 217081 217111 217117 217121 217157 217163
217169 217199 217201 217207 217219 217223 217229 217241 217253 217271 217307
217309 217313 217319 217333 217337 217339 217351 217361 217363 217367 217369
217387 217397 217409 217411 217421 217429 217439 217457 217463 217489 217499
217517 217519 217559 217561 217573 217577 217579 217619 217643 217661 217667
217681 217687 217691 217697 217717 217727 217733 217739 217747 217771 217781
217793 217823 217829 217849 217859 217901 217907 217909 217933 217937 217969
217979 217981 218003 218021 218047 218069 218077 218081 218083 218087 218107
218111 218117 218131 218137 218143 218149 218171 218191 218213 218227 218233
218249 218279 218287 218357 218363 218371 218381 218389 218401 218417 218419
218423 218437 218447 218453 218459 218461 218479 218509 218513 218521 218527
218531 218549 218551 218579 218591 218599 218611 218623 218627 218629 218641
218651 218657 218677 218681 218711 218717 218719 218723 218737 218749 218761
218783 218797 218809 218819 218833 218839 218843 218849 218857 218873 218887
218923 218941 218947 218963 218969 218971 218987 218989 219001 219017
219019 219031 219041 219053 219059 219071 219083 219091 219097 219103 219119
219133 219143 219169 219187 219217 219223 219251 219277 219281 219293 219301
219311 219313 219353 219361 219371 219377 219389 219407 219409 219433 219437
219451 219463 219467 219491 219503 219517 219523 219529 219533 219547 219577
219587 219599 219607 219613 219619 219629 219647 219649 219677 219679 219683
219689 219707 219721 219727 219731 219749 219757 219761 219763 219767 219787
219797 219799 219809 219823 219829 219839 219847 219851 219871 219881 219889
219911 219917 219931 219937 219941 219943 219953 219959 219971 219977 219979
219983 220009 220013 220019 220021 220057 220063 220123 220141 220147 220151
220163 220169 220177 220189 220217 220243 220279 220291 220301 220307 220327
220333 220351 220357 220361 220369 220373 220391 220399 220403 220411 220421
220447 220469 220471 220511 220513 220529 220537 220543 220553 220559 220573
220579 220589 220613 220663 220667 220673 220681 220687 220699 220709 220721
220747 220757 220771 220783 220789 220793 220807 220811 220841 220859 220861
220873 220877 220879 220889 220897 220901 220903 220907 220919 220931 220933
220939 220973 221021 221047 221059 221069 221071 221077 221083 221087 221093
221101 221159 221171 221173 221197 221201 221203 221209 221219 221227 221233
221239 221251 221261 221281 221303 221311 221317 221327 221393 221399 221401
221411 221413 221447 221453 221461 221471 221477 221489 221497 221509 221537
221549 221567 221581 221587 221603 221621 221623 221653 221657 221659
221671 221677 221707 221713 221717 221719 221723 221729 221737 221747 221773
221797 221807 221813 221827 221831 221849 221873 221891 221909 221941 221951
221953 221957 221987 221989 221999 222007 222011 222023 222029 222041 222043
222059 222067 222073 222107 222109 222113 222127 222137 222149 222151 222161
222163 222193 222197 222199 222247 222269 222289 222293 222311 222317 222323
222329 222337 222347 222349 222361 222367 222379 222389 222403 222419 222437
222461 222493 222499 222511 222527 222533 222553 222557 222587 222601 222613
222619 222643 222647 222659 222679 222707 222713 222731 222773 222779 222787
222791 222793 222799 222823 222839 222841 222857 222863 222877 222883 222913
222919 222931 222941 222947 222953 222967 222977 222979 222991 223007 223009
223019 223037 223049 223051 223061 223063 223087 223099 223103 223129 223133
223151 223207 223211 223217 223219 223229 223241 223243 223247 223253 223259
223273 223277 223283 223291 223303 223313 223319 223331 223337 223339 223361
223367 223381 223403 223423 223429 223439 223441 223463 223469 223481 223493
223507 223529 223543 223547 223549 223577 223589 223621 223633 223637 223667
223679 223681 223697 223711 223747 223753 223757 223759 223781 223823 223829
223831 223837 223841 223843 223903 223919 223921 223939 223963 223969
223999 224011 224027 224033 224041 224047 224057 224069 224071 224101 224113
224129 224131 224149 224153 224171 224177 224197 224201 224209 224221 224243
224239 224251 224261 224267 224291 224299 224303 224309 224317 224327 224351
224359 224363 224401 224423 224429 224443 224449 224461 224467 224473 224491
224501 224513 224527 224563 224569 224579 224591 224603 224611 224617 224629
224633 224669 224677 224683 224699 224711 224717 224729 224737 224743 224759
224771 224797 224813 224831 224863 224869 224881 224891 224897 224909 224911
224921 224929 224947 224951 224969 224977 224993 225023 225037 225061 225067
225077 225079 225089 225109 225119 225133 225143 225149 225157 225161 225163
225167 225217 225221 225223 225227 225241 225257 225263 225287 225289 225299
225307 225341 225343 225347 225349 225353 225371 225373 225383 225427 225431
225457 225461 225479 225493 225499 225503 225509 225523 225527 225529 225569
225581 225583 225601 225611 225613 225619 225629 225637 225671 225683 225689
225697 225721 225733 225749 225751 225767 225769 225779 225781 225809 225821
225829 225839 225859 225871 225889 225919 225931 225941 225943 225949 225961
225977 225983 225989 226001 226007 226013 226027 226063 226087 226099 226103
226123 226129 226133 226141 226169 226183 226189 226199 226201 226217 226231
226241 226267 226283 226307 226313 226337 226357 226367 226379 226381 226397
226409 226427 226433 226451 226453 226463 226483 226487 226511 226531 226547
226549 226553 226571 226601 226609 226621 226631 226637 226643 226649 226657
226663 226669 226691 226697 226741 226753 226769 226777 226783 226789 226799
226813 226817 226819 226823 226843 226871 226901 226903 226907 226913 226937
226943 226991 227011 227027 227053 227081 227089 227093 227111 227113 227131
227147 227153 227159 227167 227177 227189 227191 227207 227219 227231 227233
227251 227257 227267 227281 227299 227303 227363 227371 227377 227387 227393
227399 227407 227419 227431 227453 227459 227467 227471 227473 227489 227497
227501 227519 227531 227533 227537 227561 227567 227569 227581 227593 227597
227603 227609 227611 227627 227629 227651 227653 227663 227671 227693 227699
227707 227719 227729 227743 227789 227797 227827 227849 227869 227873 227893
227947 227951 227977 227989 227993 228013 228023 228049 228061 228077 228097
228103 228113 228127 228131 228139 228181 228197 228199 228203 228211 228223
228233 228251 228257 228281 228299 228301 228307 228311 228331 228337 228341
228353 228359 228383 228409 228419 228421 228427 228443 228451 228457 228461

```
228469  228479  228509  228511  228517  228521  228523  228539  228559  228577  228581
228587  228593  228601  228611  228617  228619  228637  228647  228677  228707  228713
228731  228733  228737  228751  228757  228773  228793  228797  228799  228829  228841
228847  228853  228859  228869  228881  228883  228887  228901  228911  228913  228923
228929  228953  228959  228961  228983  228989  229003  229027  229037  229081  229093
229123  229127  229133  229139  229153  229157  229171  229181  229189  229199  229213
229217  229223  229237  229247  229249  229253  229261  229267  229283  229309  229321
229343  229351  229373  229393  229399  229403  229409  229423  229433  229459  229469
229487  229499  229507  229519  229529  229537  229547  229553  229561  229583  229589
229591  229601  229613  229627  229631  229637  229639  229681  229693  229699  229703
229711  229717  229727  229739  229751  229753  229759  229763  229769  229771  229777
229781  229799  229813  229819  229837  229841  229847  229849  229897  229903  229937
229939  229949  229961  229963  229979  229981  230003  230017  230047  230059  230063
230077  230081  230089  230101  230107  230117  230123  230137  230143  230149  230189
230203  230213  230221  230227  230233  230239  230257  230273  230281  230291  230303
230309  230311  230327  230339  230341  230353  230357  230369  230383  230387  230389
230393  230431  230449  230453  230467  230471  230479  230501  230507  230539  230551
230561  230563  230567  230597  230611  230647  230653  230663  230683  230693  230719
230729  230743  230761  230767  230771  230773  230779  230807  230819  230827  230833
230849  230861  230863  230873  230891  230929  230933  230939  230941  230959  230969
230977  230999  231001  231017  231019  231031  231041  231053  231067  231079  231107
231109  231131  231169  231197  231223  231241  231269  231271  231277  231289  231293
231299  231317  231323  231331  231347  231349  231359  231367  231379  231409  231419
231431  231433  231443  231461  231463  231479  231481  231493  231503  231529  231533
231547  231551  231559  231563  231571  231589  231599  231607  231611  231613  231631
231643  231661  231677  231701  231709  231719  231779  231799  231809  231821  231823
231827  231839  231841  231859  231871  231877  231893  231901  231919  231923  231943
231947  231961  231967  232003  232007  232013  232049  232051  232073  232079  232081
232091  232103  232109  232117  232129  232153  232171  232187  232189  232207  232217
232259  232303  232307  232333  232357  232363  232367  232381  232391  232409  232411
232417  232433  232439  232451  232457  232459  232487  232499  232513  232523  232549
232567  232571  232591  232597  232607  232621  232633  232643  232663  232669  232681
232699  232709  232711  232741  232751  232753  232777  232801  232811  232819  232823
232847  232853  232861  232871  232877  232891  232901  232907  232919  232937  232961
232963  232987  233021  233069  233071  233083  233113  233117  233141  233143  233159
233161  233173  233183  233201  233221  233231  233239  233251  233267  233279  233293
233297  233323  233327  233329  233341  233347  233353  233357  233371  233407  233417
233419  233423  233437  233477  233489  233509  233549  233551  233557  233591  233599
233609  233617  233621  233641  233663  233669  233683  233687  233689  233693  233713
233743  233747  233759  233777  233837  233851  233861  233879  233881  233911  233917
233921  233923  233939  233941  233969  233983  233993  234007  234029  234043  234067
234083  234089  234103  234121  234131  234139  234149  234161  234167  234181  234187
234193  234197  234199  234203  234211  234217  234239  234259  234271  234281  234287
234293  234317  234319  234323  234331  234341  234343  234361  234371  234431  234457
234461  234463  234467  234473  234499  234511  234527  234529  234539  234541  234547
234571  234587  234589  234599  234613  234629  234653  234659  234673  234683  234713
234721  234727  234733  234743  234749  234769  234781  234791  234799  234803  234809
234811  234833  234847  234851  234863  234869  234893  234907  234917  234931  234947
234959  234961  234967  234977  234979  234989  235003  235007  235009  235013  235043
235051  235057  235069  235091  235099  235111  235117  235159  235171  235177  235181
235199  235211  235231  235241  235243  235273  235289  235307  235309  235337  235349
235369  235397  235439  235441  235447  235483  235489  235493  235513  235519  235523
235537  235541  235553  235559  235577  235591  235601  235607  235621  235661  235663
235673  235679  235699  235723  235747  235751  235783  235787  235789  235793  235811
235813  235849  235871  235877  235889  235891  235901  235919  235927  235951  235967
235979  235997  236017  236021  236053  236063  236069  236077  236087  236107  236111
236129  236143  236153  236167  236207  236209  236219  236231  236261  236287  236293
236297  236323  236329  236333  236339  236377  236381  236387  236399  236407  236429
236449  236461  236471  236477  236479  236503  236507  236519  236527  236549  236563
236573  236609  236627  236641  236653  236659  236681  236699  236701  236707  236713
236723  236729  236737  236749  236771  236773  236779  236783  236807  236813  236867
236869  236879  236881  236891  236893  236897  236909  236917  236947  236981  236983
236993  237011  237019  237043  237053  237067  237071  237073  237089  237091  237137
237143  237151  237157  237161  237163  237173  237179  237203  237217  237233  237257
237271  237277  237283  237287  237301  237313  237319  237331  237343  237361  237373
237379  237401  237409  237467  237487  237509  237547  237563  237571  237581  237607
237619  237631  237673  237683  237689  237691  237701  237707  237733  237737  237749
237763  237767  237781  237791  237821  237851  237857  237859  237877  237883  237901
237911  237929  237959  237967  237971  237973  237977  237997  238001  238009  238019
238031  238037  238039  238079  238081  238093  238099  238103  238141  238151  238157
238159  238163  238171  238181  238201  238207  238213  238223  238229  238237
238247  238261  238267  238291  238307  238313  238321  238331  238339  238361  238363
238369  238373  238397  238417  238423  238439  238451  238463  238471  238477  238481
238499  238519  238529  238531  238547  238573  238591  238627  238639  238649  238657
238673  238681  238691  238703  238709  238723  238727  238729  238747  238759  238781
238789  238801  238829  238837  238841  238853  238859  238877  238879  238883  238897
238919  238921  238939  238943  238949  238967  238991  239017  239023  239027  239053
239069  239081  239087  239119  239137  239147  239167  239171  239179  239201  239231
239233  239237  239243  239251  239263  239273  239287  239297  239329  239333  239347
239357  239383  239387  239389  239401  239423  239429  239431  239441  239461  239489
239509  239521  239527  239531  239539  239543  239557  239567  239579  239587  239597
239611  239623  239633  239641  239671  239689  239699  239711  239713  239731  239737
239753  239779  239783  239803  239807  239831  239843  239849  239851  239857  239873
239879  239893  239929  239933  239947  239957  239963  239977  239999  240007  240011
240017  240041  240043  240047  240049  240059  240073  240089  240101  240109  240113
240131  240139  240151  240169  240173  240197  240203  240209  240257  240259  240263
240271  240283  240287  240319  240341  240347  240349  240353  240371  240379  240421
240433  240437  240473  240479  240491  240503  240509  240517  240551  240571  240587
240589  240599  240607  240623  240631  240641  240659  240677  240701  240707  240719
```

```
240727  240733  240739  240743  240763  240769  240797  240811  240829  240841  240853
240859  240869  240881  240883  240893  240899  240913  240943  240953  240959  240967
240997  241013  241027  241037  241049  241051  241061  241067  241069  241079  241093
241117  241127  241141  241169  241177  241183  241207  241229  241249  241253  241259
241261  241271  241291  241303  241313  241321  241327  241333  241337  241343  241361
241363  241391  241393  241421  241429  241441  241453  241463  241469  241489  241511
241513  241517  241537  241543  241559  241561  241567  241589  241597  241601  241603
241639  241643  241651  241663  241667  241679  241687  241691  241711  241727  241739
241771  241781  241783  241793  241807  241811  241817  241823  241847  241861  241867
241873  241877  241883  241903  241907  241919  241921  241931  241939  241951  241963
241973  241979  241981  241993  242009  242057  242059  242069  242083  242093  242101
242119  242129  242147  242161  242171  242173  242197  242201  242227  242243  242257
242261  242273  242279  242309  242329  242357  242371  242377  242393  242399  242413
242419  242441  242447  242449  242453  242467  242479  242483  242491  242509  242519
242521  242533  242551  242591  242603  242617  242621  242629  242633  242639  242647
242659  242677  242681  242689  242713  242729  242731  242747  242773  242779  242789
242797  242807  242813  242819  242863  242867  242873  242887  242911  242923  242927
242971  242989  242999  243011  243031  243073  243077  243091  243101  243109  243119
243121  243137  243149  243157  243161  243167  243197  243203  243209  243227  243233
243239  243259  243263  243301  243311  243343  243367  243391  243401  243403  243421
243431  243433  243437  243461  243469  243473  243479  243487  243517  243521  243527
243533  243539  243553  243577  243583  243587  243589  243613  243623  243631  243643
243647  243671  243673  243701  243703  243707  243709  243769  243781  243787  243799
243809  243829  243839  243851  243857  243863  243871  243889  243911  243917  243931
243953  243973  243989  244003  244009  244021  244033  244043  244087  244091  244109
244121  244129  244141  244147  244157  244159  244177  244199  244217  244219  244243
244247  244253  244261  244291  244297  244301  244303  244313  244333  244339  244351
244357  244367  244379  244381  244393  244399  244403  244411  244423  244429  244451
244457  244463  244471  244481  244493  244507  244529  244547  244553  244561  244567
244583  244589  244597  244603  244619  244633  244637  244639  244667  244669  244687
244691  244703  244711  244721  244733  244747  244753  244759  244781  244787  244813
244837  244841  244843  244859  244861  244873  244877  244889  244897  244901  244939
244943  244957  244997  245023  245029  245033  245039  245071  245083  245087  245107
245129  245131  245149  245171  245173  245177  245183  245209  245251  245257  245261
245269  245279  245291  245299  245317  245321  245339  245383  245389  245407  245411
245417  245419  245437  245471  245473  245477  245501  245513  245519  245521  245527
245533  245561  245563  245587  245591  245593  245621  245627  245629  245639  245653
245671  245681  245683  245711  245719  245723  245741  245747  245753  245759  245771
245783  245789  245821  245849  245851  245863  245881  245897  245899  245909  245911
245941  245963  245977  245981  245983  245989  246011  246017  246049  246073  246097
246119  246121  246131  246133  246151  246167  246173  246187  246193  246203  246209
246217  246223  246241  246247  246251  246271  246277  246289  246317  246319  246329
246343  246349  246361  246371  246391  246403  246439  246469  246473  246497  246509
246511  246523  246527  246539  246557  246569  246577  246599  246607  246611  246613
246637  246641  246643  246661  246683  246689  246707  246709  246713  246731  246739
246769  246773  246781  246787  246793  246803  246809  246811  246817  246833  246839
246889  246899  246907  246913  246919  246923  246929  246931  246937  246941  246947
246971  246979  247001  247007  247031  247067  247069  247073  247087  247099  247141
247183  247193  247201  247223  247229  247241  247249  247259  247279  247301  247309
247337  247339  247343  247363  247369  247381  247391  247393  247409  247421  247433
247439  247451  247463  247501  247519  247529  247531  247547  247553  247579  247591
247601  247603  247607  247609  247613  247633  247649  247651  247691  247693  247697
247711  247717  247729  247739  247759  247769  247771  247781  247799  247811  247813
247829  247847  247853  247873  247879  247889  247901  247913  247939  247943  247957
247991  247993  247997  247999  248021  248033  248041  248051  248057  248063  248071
248077  248089  248099  248117  248119  248137  248141  248161  248167  248177  248179
248189  248201  248203  248231  248243  248257  248267  248291  248293  248299  248309
248317  248323  248351  248357  248371  248389  248401  248407  248431  248441  248447
248461  248473  248477  248483  248509  248533  248537  248543  248569  248579  248587
248593  248597  248609  248621  248627  248639  248641  248657  248683  248701  248707
248719  248723  248737  248749  248753  248779  248783  248789  248797  248813  248821
248827  248839  248851  248861  248867  248869  248879  248887  248891  248893  248903
248909  248971  248981  248987  249017  249037  249059  249079  249089  249097  249103
249107  249127  249131  249133  249143  249181  249187  249199  249211  249217  249229
249233  249253  249257  249287  249311  249317  249329  249341  249367  249377  249383
249397  249419  249421  249427  249433  249437  249439  249449  249463  249497  249499
249503  249517  249521  249533  249539  249541  249563  249583  249589  249593  249607
249647  249659  249671  249677  249703  249721  249727  249737  249749  249763  249779
249797  249811  249827  249833  249853  249857  249859  249863  249871  249881  249911
249923  249943  249947  249967  249971  249973  249989  250007  250013  250027  250031
250037  250043  250049  250051  250057  250073  250091  250109  250123  250147  250153
250169  250199  250253  250259  250267  250279  250301  250307  250343  250361  250403
250409  250423  250433  250441  250451  250489  250499  250501  250543  250583  250619
250643  250673  250681  250687  250693  250703  250709  250721  250727  250739  250741
250751  250753  250777  250787  250793  250799  250807  250813  250829  250837  250841
250853  250867  250871  250889  250919  250949  250951  250963  250967  250969  250979
250993  251003  251033  251051  251057  251059  251063  251071  251081  251087  251099
251117  251143  251149  251159  251171  251177  251179  251191  251197  251201  251203
251219  251221  251231  251233  251257  251261  251263  251287  251291  251297  251323
251347  251353  251359  251387  251393  251417  251429  251431  251437  251443  251467
251473  251477  251483  251491  251501  251513  251519  251527  251533  251539  251543
251561  251567  251609  251611  251621  251623  251639  251653  251663  251677  251701
251707  251737  251761  251789  251791  251809  251831  251833  251843  251857  251861
251879  251887  251893  251897  251903  251917  251939  251941  251947  251969  251971
251983  252001  252013  252017  252029  252037  252079  252101  252139  252143  252151
252157  252163  252169  252173  252181  252193  252209  252223  252233  252253  252277
252283  252289  252293  252313  252319  252323  252341  252359  252383  252391  252401
252409  252419  252431  252443  252449  252457  252463  252481  252509  252533  252541
252559  252583  252589  252607  252611  252617  252641  252667  252691  252709  252713
```

```
252727  252731  252737  252761  252767  252779  252817  252823  252827  252829  252869
252877  252881  252887  252893  252899  252911  252913  252919  252937  252949  252971
252979  252983  253003  253013  253049  253063  253081  253103  253109  253133  253153
253157  253159  253229  253243  253247  253273  253307  253321  253343  253349  253361
253367  253369  253381  253387  253417  253423  253427  253433  253439  253447  253469
253481  253493  253501  253507  253531  253537  253543  253553  253567  253573  253601
253607  253609  253613  253633  253637  253639  253651  253661  253679  253681  253703
253717  253733  253741  253751  253763  253769  253777  253787  253789  253801  253811
253819  253823  253853  253867  253871  253879  253901  253907  253909  253919  253937
253949  253951  253969  253987  253993  253999  254003  254021  254027  254039  254041
254047  254053  254071  254083  254119  254141  254147  254161  254179  254197  254207
254209  254213  254249  254257  254279  254281  254291  254299  254329  254369  254377
254383  254389  254407  254413  254437  254447  254461  254489  254491  254519  254537
254557  254593  254623  254627  254647  254659  254663  254699  254713  254729  254731
254741  254747  254753  254773  254777  254783  254791  254803  254827  254831  254833
254857  254873  254879  254887  254899  254911  254927  254929  254941  254959
254963  254971  254977  254987  254993  255007  255019  255023  255043  255049  255053
255071  255077  255083  255097  255107  255121  255127  255133  255137  255149  255173
255179  255181  255191  255193  255197  255209  255217  255229  255247  255251  255253
255259  255313  255329  255349  255361  255371  255383  255413  255419  255443  255457
255467  255469  255473  255487  255499  255503  255511  255517  255523  255551  255571
255587  255589  255613  255617  255637  255641  255649  255653  255659  255667  255679
255709  255713  255733  255743  255757  255763  255767  255803  255839  255841  255847
255851  255859  255869  255877  255887  255907  255917  255919  255923  255947  255961
255971  255973  255977  255989  256019  256021  256031  256033  256049  256057  256079
256093  256117  256121  256129  256133  256147  256163  256169  256181  256187  256189
256199  256211  256219  256279  256301  256307  256313  256337  256349  256363  256369
256391  256393  256423  256441  256469  256471  256483  256489  256493  256499  256517
256541  256561  256567  256577  256579  256589  256603  256609  256639  256643  256651
256661  256687  256699  256721  256723  256757  256771  256799  256801  256813  256831
256873  256877  256889  256901  256903  256931  256939  256957  256967  256981  257003
257017  257053  257069  257077  257093  257099  257107  257123  257141  257161  257171
257177  257189  257219  257221  257239  257249  257263  257273  257281  257287  257293
257297  257311  257321  257339  257353  257363  257371  257381  257399  257401  257407
257437  257443  257447  257459  257473  257489  257497  257501  257503  257519  257539
257561  257591  257611  257627  257639  257657  257671  257687  257689  257707  257711
257713  257717  257731  257783  257791  257797  257837  257857  257861  257863  257867
257879  257879  257893  257903  257921  257947  257953  257981  257987  257989  257993
258019  258023  258031  258061  258067  258101  258107  258109  258113  258119  258127
258131  258143  258157  258161  258173  258197  258211  258233  258241  258253  258277
258283  258299  258317  258319  258329  258331  258337  258353  258373  258389  258403
258407  258413  258421  258437  258443  258449  258469  258487  258491  258499  258521
258527  258539  258551  258563  258569  258581  258607  258611  258613  258617  258623
258631  258637  258659  258673  258677  258691  258697  258703  258707  258721  258733
258737  258743  258763  258779  258787  258803  258809  258827  258847  258871  258887
258917  258919  258949  258959  258967  258971  258977  258983  258991  259001  259009
259019  259033  259099  259121  259123  259151  259157  259159  259163  259169  259177
259183  259201  259211  259213  259219  259229  259271  259277  259309  259321  259339
259379  259381  259387  259397  259411  259421  259429  259451  259453  259459  259499
259507  259517  259531  259537  259547  259577  259583  259603  259619  259621  259627
259631  259639  259643  259657  259667  259681  259691  259697  259717  259723  259733
259751  259771  259781  259783  259801  259813  259823  259829  259837  259841  259867
259907  259933  259937  259943  259949  259967  259991  259993  260003  260009  260011
260017  260023  260047  260081  260089  260111  260137  260171  260179  260189  260191
260201  260207  260209  260213  260231  260263  260269  260317  260329  260339  260363
260387  260399  260411  260413  260417  260419  260441  260453  260461  260467  260483
260489  260527  260539  260543  260549  260551  260569  260573  260581  260587  260609
260629  260647  260651  260671  260677  260713  260717  260723  260747  260753  260761
260773  260791  260807  260809  260849  260857  260861  260863  260879  260893
260921  260941  260951  260959  260969  260983  260987  260999  261011  261013  261017
261031  261043  261059  261061  261071  261077  261089  261101  261127  261167  261169
261223  261229  261241  261251  261271  261281  261301  261323  261329  261337  261347
261353  261379  261389  261407  261427  261431  261433  261439  261451  261463  261467
261509  261523  261529  261557  261563  261577  261581  261587  261593  261601  261619
261631  261637  261641  261643  261673  261697  261707  261713  261721  261739  261757
261761  261773  261787  261791  261799  261823  261847  261881  261887  261917  261959
261971  261973  261977  261983  262007  262027  262049  262051  262069  262079  262103
262109  262111  262121  262127  262133  262139  262147  262151  262153  262187  262193
262217  262231  262237  262253  262261  262271  262303  262313  262321  262331  262337
262349  262351  262369  262387  262391  262399  262411  262433  262459  262469  262489
262501  262511  262513  262519  262541  262543  262553  262567  262583  262597  262621
262627  262643  262649  262651  262657  262681  262693  262697  262709  262723  262733
262739  262741  262747  262781  262783  262807  262819  262853  262877  262883  262897
262901  262909  262937  262949  262957  262981  263009  263023  263047  263063  263071
263077  263083  263089  263101  263111  263119  263129  263167  263171  263183  263191
263201  263209  263213  263227  263239  263257  263267  263269  263273  263287  263293
263303  263323  263369  263383  263387  263399  263401  263411  263423  263429  263437
263443  263489  263491  263503  263513  263519  263521  263533  263537  263561  263567
263573  263591  263597  263609  263611  263621  263647  263651  263657  263677  263723
263737  263747  263759  263761  263803  263819  263821  263827  263843  263849  263863
263867  263869  263881  263899  263909  263911  263927  263933  263941  263951  263953
263957  263983  264007  264013  264029  264031  264053  264059  264071  264083  264091
264101  264113  264127  264133  264137  264139  264167  264169  264179  264211  264221
264263  264269  264283  264289  264301  264323  264331  264343  264349  264353  264359
264371  264391  264403  264437  264443  264463  264487  264527  264529  264553  264559
264577  264581  264599  264601  264619  264631  264637  264643  264659  264697  264731
264739  264743  264749  264757  264763  264769  264779  264787  264791  264793  264811
264827  264829  264839  264871  264881  264889  264893  264899  264919  264931  264949
264959  264961  264977  264991  264997  265003  265007  265021  265037  265079  265091
```

```
265093  265117  265123  265129  265141  265151  265157  265163  265169  265193  265207
265231  265241  265247  265249  265261  265271  265273  265277  265313  265333  265337
265339  265381  265399  265403  265417  265423  265427  265451  265459  265471  265483
265493  265511  265513  265541  265543  265547  265561  265567  265571  265579  265607
265613  265619  265621  265703  265709  265711  265717  265729  265739  265747  265757
265781  265787  265807  265813  265819  265831  265841  265847  265861  265871  265873
265883  265891  265921  265957  265961  265987  266003  266009  266023  266027  266029
266047  266051  266053  266059  266081  266083  266089  266093  266099  266111  266117
266129  266137  266153  266159  266177  266183  266221  266239  266261  266269  266281
266291  266293  266297  266333  266351  266353  266359  266369  266381  266401  266411
266417  266447  266449  266477  266479  266489  266491  266521  266549  266587  266599
266603  266633  266641  266647  266663  266671  266677  266681  266683  266687  266689
266701  266711  266719  266759  266767  266797  266801  266821  266837  266839  266863
266867  266891  266899  266909  266921  266927  266933  266947  266953  266957
266971  266977  266983  266993  266999  267017  267037  267049  267097  267131  267133
267139  267143  267167  267187  267193  267199  267203  267217  267227  267229  267233
267259  267271  267277  267299  267301  267307  267317  267341  267353  267373  267389
267391  267401  267403  267413  267419  267431  267433  267439  267451  267469  267479
267481  267493  267497  267511  267517  267521  267523  267541  267551  267557  267569
267581  267587  267593  267601  267611  267613  267629  267637  267643  267647  267649
267661  267667  267671  267679  267713  267719  267721  267727  267737  267739
267749  267763  267781  267791  267797  267803  267811  267829  267833  267857  267863
267877  267887  267893  267899  267901  267907  267913  267929  267941  267959  267961
268003  268013  268043  268049  268063  268069  268091  268123  268133  268153  268171
268189  268199  268207  268211  268237  268253  268267  268271  268283  268291  268297
268343  268403  268439  268459  268487  268493  268501  268507  268517  268519  268529
268531  268537  268547  268573  268607  268613  268637  268643  268661  268693  268721
268729  268733  268747  268757  268759  268771  268777  268781  268783  268789  268811
268813  268819  268823  268861  268883  268913  268843  268879  268909  268921  268913
268921  268927  268937  268969  268973  268979  268993  268997  268999  269023  269029
269039  269041  269057  269063  269069  269089  269117  269131  269141  269167  269177
269179  269183  269189  269201  269209  269219  269221  269231  269237  269251  269257
269281  269317  269327  269333  269341  269351  269377  269383  269387  269389  269393
269413  269419  269429  269431  269441  269461  269473  269513  269519  269527  269539
269543  269561  269573  269579  269597  269617  269623  269641  269651  269663  269683
269701  269713  269719  269723  269741  269749  269761  269779  269783  269791  269851
269879  269887  269891  269897  269923  269939  269947  269953  269981  269987  270001
270029  270031  270037  270059  270071  270073  270097  270121  270131  270133  270143
270157  270163  270167  270191  270209  270217  270223  270229  270239  270241  270269
270271  270287  270299  270307  270311  270323  270329  270337  270343  270371  270379
270407  270421  270437  270443  270451  270461  270463  270493  270509  270527  270539
270547  270551  270553  270563  270577  270583  270587  270593  270601  270619  270631
270653  270659  270667  270679  270689  270701  270709  270713  270737  270749  270761
270763  270791  270797  270799  270821  270833  270841  270859  270899  270913  270923
270931  270937  270953  270961  270967  270973  271003  271013  271021  271027  271043
271057  271067  271079  271097  271109  271127  271129  271163  271169  271177  271181
271211  271217  271231  271241  271253  271261  271273  271277  271279  271289  271333
271351  271357  271363  271367  271393  271409  271429  271451  271463  271471  271483
271489  271499  271501  271517  271549  271553  271571  271573  271597  271603  271619
271637  271639  271651  271657  271693  271703  271723  271729  271753  271769  271771
271787  271807  271811  271829  271841  271849  271853  271861  271867  271879  271897
271903  271919  271927  271939  271967  271969  271981  272003  272009  272011  272029
272039  272053  272059  272093  272131  272141  272171  272179  272183  272189  272191
272201  272203  272227  272231  272249  272257  272263  272267  272269  272287  272299
272317  272329  272333  272341  272347  272351  272353  272359  272369  272381  272383
272399  272407  272411  272417  272423  272449  272453  272477  272507  272533  272537
272539  272549  272563  272567  272581  272603  272621  272651  272659  272683  272693
272717  272719  272737  272759  272761  272771  272777  272807  272809  272813  272863
272879  272887  272903  272911  272917  272927  272933  272959  272971  272981  272983
272989  272999  273001  273029  273043  273047  273059  273061  273067  273073  273083
273107  273113  273127  273131  273149  273157  273181  273187  273193  273233  273253
273269  273271  273281  273283  273289  273311  273313  273323  273349  273359  273367
273433  273457  273473  273503  273517  273521  273527  273551  273569  273601  273613
273617  273629  273641  273643  273653  273697  273709  273719  273727  273739  273773
273787  273797  273803  273821  273827  273857  273881  273899  273901  273913  273919
273929  273941  273943  273967  273971  273979  273997  274007  274019  274033  274061
274069  274081  274093  274103  274117  274121  274123  274139  274147  274163  274171
274177  274187  274199  274201  274213  274223  274237  274243  274259  274271  274277
274283  274301  274333  274349  274357  274361  274403  274423  274441  274451  274453
274457  274471  274489  274517  274529  274579  274583  274591  274609  274627  274661
274667  274679  274693  274697  274709  274711  274723  274739  274751  274777  274783
274787  274811  274817  274829  274831  274837  274843  274847  274853  274861  274867
274871  274889  274909  274931  274943  274951  274957  274961  274973  274993  275003
275027  275039  275047  275053  275059  275083  275087  275129  275131  275147  275153
275159  275161  275167  275183  275201  275207  275227  275251  275263  275269  275299
275309  275321  275323  275339  275357  275371  275389  275393  275399  275419  275423
275447  275449  275453  275459  275461  275489  275491  275503  275521  275531  275543
275549  275557  275579  275581  275591  275593  275599  275623  275641  275651  275657
275669  275677  275699  275711  275719  275729  275741  275767  275773  275783  275813
275827  275837  275881  275897  275911  275917  275921  275923  275929  275939  275941
275963  275969  275981  275987  275999  276007  276011  276019  276037  276041  276043
276047  276049  276079  276083  276091  276113  276137  276151  276173  276181  276187
276191  276209  276229  276239  276247  276251  276257  276277  276293  276319  276323
276337  276343  276347  276359  276371  276373  276389  276401  276439  276443  276449
276461  276467  276487  276499  276503  276517  276527  276553  276557  276581  276587
276589  276593  276599  276623  276629  276637  276671  276673  276707  276721  276739
276763  276767  276779  276781  276817  276821  276823  276827  276833  276839  276847
276869  276883  276901  276907  276917  276919  276929  276949  276953  276961  276977
277003  277007  277021  277051  277063  277073  277087  277097  277099  277157  277163
```

```
277169  277177  277183  277213  277217  277223  277231  277247  277259  277261  277273
277279  277297  277301  277309  277331  277363  277373  277411  277421  277427  277429
277483  277493  277499  277513  277531  277547  277549  277567  277577  277579  277597
277601  277603  277637  277639  277643  277657  277663  277687  277691  277703  277741
277747  277751  277757  277787  277789  277793  277813  277829  277847  277859  277883
277889  277891  277897  277903  277919  277961  277993  277999  278017  278029  278041
278051  278063  278071  278087  278111  278119  278123  278143  278147  278149  278177
278191  278207  278209  278219  278227  278233  278237  278261  278269  278279  278321
278329  278347  278353  278363  278387  278393  278413  278437  278459  278479  278489
278491  278497  278501  278503  278543  278549  278557  278561  278563  278581  278591
278609  278611  278617  278623  278627  278639  278651  278671  278687  278689  278701
278717  278741  278743  278753  278767  278801  278807  278809  278813  278819  278827
278843  278849  278867  278879  278881  278891  278903  278909  278911  278917  278947
278981  279001  279007  279023  279029  279047  279073  279109  279119  279121  279127
279131  279137  279143  279173  279179  279187  279203  279211  279221  279269  279311
279317  279329  279337  279353  279397  279407  279413  279421  279431  279443  279451
279479  279481  279511  279523  279541  279551  279553  279557  279571  279577  279583
279593  279607  279613  279619  279637  279641  279649  279659  279679  279689  279707
279709  279731  279751  279761  279767  279779  279817  279823  279847  279857  279863
279883  279913  279919  279941  279949  279967  279977  279991  280001  280009  280013
280031  280037  280061  280069  280097  280099  280103  280121  280129  280139  280183
280187  280199  280207  280219  280223  280229  280243  280249  280253  280277  280297
280303  280321  280327  280337  280339  280351  280373  280409  280411  280451  280463
280487  280499  280507  280513  280537  280541  280549  280561  280583  280589
280591  280597  280603  280607  280613  280627  280639  280673  280681  280697  280699
280703  280717  280729  280751  280759  280769  280771  280811  280817  280837
280843  280859  280871  280879  280883  280897  280909  280913  280921  280927  280933
280939  280949  280957  280963  280967  280979  280997  281023  281033  281053  281063
281069  281081  281117  281131  281153  281159  281167  281189  281191  281207  281227
281233  281243  281249  281251  281273  281279  281291  281297  281317  281321  281327
281339  281353  281357  281363  281381  281419  281423  281429  281431  281509  281527
281531  281539  281549  281551  281557  281563  281579  281581  281609  281621  281623
281627  281641  281647  281651  281653  281663  281669  281683  281717  281719  281737
281747  281761  281767  281777  281783  281791  281797  281803  281807  281833  281837
281839  281849  281857  281867  281887  281893  281921  281923  281927  281933  281947
281959  281971  281989  281993  282001  282011  282019  282053  282059  282071  282089
282091  282097  282101  282103  282127  282143  282157  282167  282221  282229  282239
282241  282253  282281  282287  282299  282307  282311  282313  282349  282377  282383
282389  282391  282407  282409  282413  282427  282439  282461  282481  282487  282493
282559  282563  282571  282577  282589  282599  282617  282661  282671  282677  282679
282683  282691  282697  282703  282707  282713  282767  282769  282773  282797  282809
282827  282833  282847  282851  282869  282881  282889  282907  282911  282913  282917
282959  282973  282977  282991  283001  283007  283009  283027  283051  283079  283093
283097  283099  283111  283117  283121  283133  283139  283159  283163  283181  283183
283193  283207  283211  283267  283277  283289  283303  283369  283397  283403  283411
283447  283463  283487  283489  283501  283511  283519  283541  283553  283571  283573
283579  283583  283601  283607  283609  283631  283637  283639  283669  283687  283697
283721  283741  283763  283769  283771  283793  283799  283807  283813  283817  283831
283837  283859  283861  283873  283909  283937  283949  283957  283961  283979  284003
284023  284041  284051  284057  284059  284083  284093  284111  284117  284129  284131
284149  284153  284159  284161  284173  284191  284201  284227  284231  284233  284237
284243  284261  284267  284269  284293  284311  284341  284357  284369  284377  284387
284407  284413  284423  284429  284447  284467  284477  284483  284489  284507  284509
284521  284527  284539  284551  284561  284573  284587  284591  284593  284623  284633
284651  284657  284659  284681  284689  284701  284707  284723  284729  284731  284737
284741  284743  284747  284749  284759  284777  284783  284803  284807  284813  284819
284831  284833  284839  284857  284881  284897  284899  284917  284927  284957  284969
284989  285007  285023  285031  285049  285071  285079  285091  285101  285113  285119
285121  285139  285151  285161  285179  285191  285199  285221  285227  285251  285281
285283  285287  285289  285301  285317  285343  285377  285421  285433  285451  285457
285463  285469  285473  285497  285517  285521  285533  285539  285553  285557  285559
285569  285599  285611  285613  285629  285631  285641  285643  285661  285667  285673
285697  285707  285709  285721  285731  285749  285757  285763  285767  285773  285781
285823  285827  285839  285841  285871  285937  285949  285953  285977  285979  285983
285997  286001  286009  286019  286043  286049  286061  286063  286073  286103  286129
286163  286171  286199  286243  286249  286289  286301  286333  286367  286369  286381
286393  286397  286411  286421  286427  286453  286457  286459  286469  286477  286483
286487  286499  286513  286519  286541  286543  286547  286553  286589  286591
286609  286613  286619  286633  286651  286673  286687  286697  286703  286711  286721
286733  286751  286753  286763  286771  286777  286789  286801  286813  286831  286859
286873  286927  286973  286981  286987  286999  287003  287047  287057  287059  287087
287093  287099  287107  287117  287137  287141  287149  287159  287167  287173  287179
287191  287219  287233  287237  287239  287251  287257  287269  287279  287281  287291
287297  287321  287327  287333  287341  287347  287383  287387  287393  287437  287449
287491  287501  287503  287537  287549  287557  287579  287597  287611  287629  287669
287671  287681  287689  287701  287731  287747  287783  287789  287801  287809  287821
287849  287851  287857  287863  287867  287873  287887  287921  287933  287939  287977
288007  288023  288049  288053  288061  288077  288089  288109  288137  288179  288181
288191  288199  288203  288209  288227  288241  288247  288257  288283  288293  288307
288313  288317  288349  288359  288361  288383  288389  288403  288413  288427  288433
288461  288467  288481  288493  288499  288527  288529  288539  288551  288559  288571
288577  288583  288647  288649  288653  288661  288679  288683  288689  288697  288731
288733  288751  288767  288773  288803  288817  288823  288833  288851  288853
288877  288907  288913  288929  288931  288947  288973  288979  288989  288991  288997
289001  289019  289021  289031  289033  289039  289049  289063  289067  289099  289103
289109  289111  289127  289129  289139  289141  289151  289169  289171  289181  289189
289193  289213  289241  289243  289249  289253  289273  289283  289291  289297  289309
289319  289343  289349  289361  289369  289381  289397  289417  289423  289439  289453
289463  289469  289477  289489  289511  289543  289559  289573  289577  289589  289603
```

289607 289637 289643 289657 289669 289717 289721 289727 289733 289741 289759
289763 289771 289789 289837 289841 289843 289847 289853 289859 289871 289889
289897 289937 289951 289957 289967 289973 289987 289999 290011 290021 290023
290027 290033 290039 290041 290047 290057 290083 290107 290113 290119 290137
290141 290161 290183 290189 290201 290209 290219 290233 290243 290249 290317
290327 290347 290351 290359 290369 290383 290393 290399 290419 290429 290441
290443 290447 290471 290473 290489 290497 290509 290527 290531 290533 290539
290557 290593 290597 290611 290617 290621 290623 290627 290657 290659 290663
290669 290671 290677 290701 290707 290711 290737 290761 290767 290791 290803
290821 290827 290837 290839 290861 290869 290879 290897 290923 290959 290963
290971 290987 290993 290999 291007 291013 291037 291041 291043 291077 291089
291101 291103 291107 291113 291143 291167 291169 291173 291191 291199 291209
291217 291253 291257 291271 291287 291293 291299 291331 291337 291349 291359
291367 291371 291373 291377 291419 291437 291439 291443 291457 291481 291491
291503 291509 291521 291539 291547 291559 291563 291569 291619 291647 291649
291661 291677 291689 291691 291701 291721 291727 291743 291751 291779 291791
291817 291829 291833 291853 291857 291869 291887 291897 291899 291901 291923
291971 291979 291983 291997 292021 292027 292037 292057 292069 292079 292081
292091 292093 292133 292141 292147 292157 292181 292183 292223 292231 292241
292249 292267 292283 292301 292309 292319 292343 292351 292363 292367 292381
292393 292427 292441 292459 292469 292471 292477 292483 292489 292493 292517
292531 292541 292549 292561 292573 292577 292601 292627 292631 292661 292667
292673 292679 292693 292703 292709 292711 292717 292727 292753 292759 292777
292793 292801 292807 292819 292837 292841 292849 292867 292879 292909 292921
292933 292969 292973 292979 292993 293021 293071 293081 293087 293093 293099
293107 293123 293129 293147 293149 293173 293177 293179 293201 293207 293213
293221 293257 293261 293263 293269 293311 293329 293339 293351 293357 293399
293413 293431 293441 293453 293459 293467 293473 293483 293507 293543 293599
293603 293617 293621 293633 293639 293651 293659 293677 293681 293701 293717
293723 293729 293749 293767 293773 293791 293803 293827 293831 293861 293863
293893 293899 293941 293957 293983 293989 293999 294001 294013 294023 294029
294043 294053 294059 294067 294103 294127 294131 294149 294157 294167 294169
294179 294181 294199 294211 294223 294227 294241 294247 294251 294269 294277
294289 294293 294311 294313 294317 294319 294337 294341 294347 294353 294383
294391 294397 294403 294431 294439 294461 294467 294479 294499 294509 294523
294529 294551 294563 294629 294641 294647 294649 294659 294673 294703 294731
294751 294757 294761 294773 294781 294787 294793 294799 294803 294809 294821
294829 294859 294869 294887 294893 294911 294919 294923 294947 294949 294953
294979 294989 294991 294997 295007 295033 295037 295049 295073 295079
295081 295111 295123 295129 295153 295187 295199 295201 295219 295237 295247
295259 295271 295277 295283 295291 295313 295319 295333 295357 295363 295387
295411 295417 295429 295433 295439 295441 295459 295513 295517 295541 295553
295567 295571 295591 295601 295663 295693 295699 295703 295727 295751 295759
295769 295777 295787 295819 295831 295837 295843 295847 295853 295861 295871
295873 295877 295879 295901 295903 295909 295937 295943 295949 295951 295961
295973 295993 296011 296017 296027 296041 296047 296071 296083 296099 296117
296129 296137 296159 296183 296201 296213 296221 296237 296243 296249 296251
296269 296273 296279 296287 296299 296347 296353 296363 296369 296377 296437
296441 296473 296477 296479 296489 296503 296507 296509 296519 296551 296557
296561 296563 296579 296581 296587 296591 296627 296651 296663 296669 296683
296687 296693 296713 296719 296729 296731 296741 296749 296753 296767 296771
296773 296797 296801 296819 296827 296831 296833 296843 296909 296911 296921
296929 296941 296969 296971 296981 296983 296987 297019 297023 297049 297061
297067 297079 297083 297097 297113 297133 297151 297161 297169 297191 297233
297247 297251 297257 297263 297289 297317 297359 297371 297377 297391 297397
297403 297421 297439 297457 297467 297469 297481 297487 297503 297509 297523
297533 297581 297589 297601 297607 297613 297617 297623 297629 297641 297659
297683 297691 297707 297719 297727 297757 297779 297793 297797 297809 297811
297833 297841 297853 297881 297889 297893 297907 297911 297931 297953 297967
297971 297989 297991 298013 298021 298031 298043 298049 298063 298087 298093
298099 298153 298157 298159 298169 298171 298187 298201 298211 298213 298223
298237 298247 298261 298283 298303 298307 298327 298339 298343 298349 298369
298373 298399 298409 298411 298427 298451 298477 298483 298513 298559 298579
298583 298589 298601 298607 298621 298631 298651 298667 298679 298681 298687
298691 298693 298709 298723 298733 298757 298759 298777 298799 298801 298817
298819 298841 298847 298853 298861 298897 298937 298943 298993 298999 299011
299017 299027 299029 299053 299059 299063 299087 299099 299107 299113 299137
299147 299171 299179 299191 299197 299213 299239 299261 299281 299287 299311
299317 299329 299333 299357 299359 299363 299371 299389 299393 299401 299417
299419 299447 299471 299473 299477 299479 299501 299513 299521 299527 299539
299567 299569 299603 299617 299623 299653 299671 299681 299683 299699 299701
299711 299723 299731 299743 299749 299771 299777 299807 299843 299857 299861
299881 299891 299903 299909 299933 299941 299951 299969 299977 299993 299999
300007 300017 300023 300043 300073 300089 300109 300119 300137 300149 300151
300163 300187 300191 300193 300221 300229 300233 300239 300247 300277 300299
300317 300319 300323 300331 300343 300347 300367 300397 300413 300427
300431 300439 300463 300481 300491 300493 300497 300499 300511 300557 300569
300581 300583 300589 300593 300623 300631 300647 300649 300661 300667 300673
300683 300691 300719 300721 300733 300739 300743 300749 300757 300761 300779
300787 300799 300809 300821 300823 300851 300857 300869 300877 300889 300893
300929 300931 300953 300961 300967 300973 300977 300997 301013 301027 301039
301051 301057 301073 301079 301123 301127 301141 301153 301159 301177 301181
301183 301211 301219 301237 301241 301243 301247 301267 301303 301319 301331
301333 301349 301361 301363 301381 301403 301409 301423 301429 301447 301459
301463 301471 301487 301489 301493 301501 301531 301577 301579 301583 301591
301601 301619 301627 301643 301649 301657 301669 301673 301681 301703 301711
301747 301751 301753 301759 301789 301793 301813 301831 301841 301843 301867
301877 301897 301901 301907 301913 301927 301933 301943 301949 301979 301991
301993 301997 301999 302009 302053 302111 302123 302143 302167 302171 302173

302189 302191 302213 302221 302227 302261 302273 302279 302287 302297 302299
302317 302329 302399 302411 302417 302429 302443 302459 302483 302507 302513
302551 302563 302567 302573 302579 302581 302587 302593 302597 302609 302629
302647 302663 302681 302711 302723 302747 302759 302767 302779 302791 302801
302831 302833 302837 302843 302851 302857 302873 302891 302903 302909 302921
302927 302941 302959 302969 302971 302977 302983 302989 302999 303007 303011
303013 303019 303029 303049 303053 303073 303089 303091 303097 303119 303139
303143 303151 303157 303187 303217 303257 303271 303283 303287 303293 303299
303307 303313 303323 303337 303341 303361 303367 303371 303377 303379 303389
303409 303421 303431 303463 303469 303473 303491 303493 303497 303529 303539
303547 303551 303553 303571 303581 303587 303593 303613 303617 303619 303643
303647 303649 303679 303683 303689 303691 303703 303713 303727 303731 303749
303767 303781 303803 303817 303827 303839 303859 303871 303889 303907 303917
303931 303937 303959 303983 303997 304009 304013 304021 304033 304039 304049
304063 304067 304069 304081 304091 304099 304127 304151 304153 304163 304169
304193 304211 304217 304223 304253 304259 304279 304301 304303 304331 304349
304357 304363 304373 304391 304393 304411 304417 304429 304433 304439 304457
304459 304477 304481 304489 304501 304511 304517 304523 304537 304541 304553
304559 304561 304597 304609 304631 304643 304651 304663 304687 304709 304723
304729 304739 304751 304757 304763 304771 304781 304789 304807 304813 304831
304847 304849 304867 304879 304883 304897 304901 304903 304907 304933 304937
304943 304949 304961 304979 304981 305017 305021 305023 305029 305043 305047
305069 305093 305101 305111 305113 305119 305131 305143 305147 305209 305219
305221 305237 305243 305267 305281 305297 305329 305339 305351 305353 305363
305369 305377 305401 305407 305411 305413 305419 305423 305441 305449 305471
305477 305479 305483 305489 305497 305521 305533 305551 305563 305581 305593
305597 305603 305611 305621 305633 305639 305663 305717 305719 305741 305743
305749 305759 305761 305771 305783 305803 305821 305839 305849 305857 305861
305867 305873 305917 305927 305933 305947 305971 305999 306001 306023 306029
306041 306049 306083 306091 306121 306133 306139 306149 306157 306167 306169
306191 306193 306229 306247 306253 306263 306269 306301 306329 306331
306347 306349 306359 306367 306377 306389 306407 306419 306421 306431 306437
306457 306463 306473 306479 306491 306503 306511 306517 306529 306533 306541
306563 306577 306587 306589 306643 306653 306661 306689 306701 306703 306707
306727 306739 306749 306763 306781 306809 306821 306827 306829 306847 306853
306857 306871 306877 306883 306893 306899 306913 306919 306941 306947 306949
306953 306991 307009 307019 307031 307033 307067 307079 307091 307093 307103
307121 307129 307147 307163 307169 307171 307187 307189 307201 307243 307253
307259 307261 307267 307273 307277 307283 307289 307301 307337 307339 307361
307367 307381 307397 307399 307409 307423 307451 307471 307481 307511 307523
307529 307537 307543 307577 307583 307589 307609 307627 307631 307633 307639
307651 307669 307687 307691 307693 307711 307733 307759 307817 307823 307831
307843 307859 307871 307873 307891 307903 307919 307939 307969 308003 308017
308027 308041 308051 308081 308093 308101 308107 308117 308129 308137 308141
308149 308153 308213 308219 308249 308263 308291 308293 308303 308309 308311
308317 308323 308327 308333 308359 308383 308411 308423 308437 308447 308467
308489 308491 308501 308507 308509 308519 308521 308527 308537 308551 308569
308573 308587 308597 308621 308639 308641 308663 308681 308701 308713 308723
308761 308773 308801 308809 308813 308827 308849 308851 308857 308887 308899
308923 308927 308929 308933 308939 308951 308989 308999 309007 309011 309013
309019 309031 309037 309059 309079 309083 309091 309107 309109 309121 309131
309137 309157 309167 309173 309193 309223 309241 309251 309259 309269 309271
309277 309289 309293 309311 309313 309317 309359 309367 309371 309391 309403
309433 309437 309457 309461 309469 309479 309481 309493 309503 309521 309523
309539 309541 309559 309571 309577 309583 309599 309623 309629 309637 309667
309671 309677 309707 309713 309731 309737 309769 309779 309781 309797 309811
309823 309851 309853 309857 309877 309899 309929 309931 309937 309977 309989
310019 310021 310027 310043 310049 310081 310087 310091 310111 310117 310127
310129 310169 310181 310187 310223 310229 310231 310237 310243 310273 310283
310291 310313 310333 310357 310361 310363 310379 310397 310423 310433 310439
310447 310459 310463 310481 310489 310501 310507 310511 310547 310553 310559
310567 310571 310577 310591 310627 310643 310663 310693 310697 310711 310721
310727 310729 310733 310741 310747 310771 310781 310789 310801 310819 310823
310829 310831 310861 310867 310883 310889 310901 310927 310931 310949 310969
310987 310997 311009 311021 311027 311033 311041 311099 311111 311123 311137
311153 311173 311177 311183 311189 311197 311203 311237 311279 311291 311293
311299 311303 311323 311329 311341 311347 311359 311371 311393 311407 311419
311447 311453 311473 311533 311537 311539 311551 311557 311561 311567 311569
311603 311609 311653 311659 311677 311681 311683 311687 311711 311713 311737
311743 311747 311749 311791 311803 311807 311821 311827 311867 311869 311881
311897 311951 311957 311963 311981 312007 312023 312029 312031 312043 312047
312071 312073 312083 312089 312101 312107 312121 312161 312197 312199 312203
312209 312211 312217 312229 312233 312241 312251 312253 312269 312281 312283
312289 312311 312313 312331 312343 312349 312353 312371 312383 312397 312401
312407 312413 312427 312451 312469 312509 312517 312527 312551 312553 312563
312581 312583 312589 312601 312617 312619 312623 312643 312673 312677 312679
312701 312703 312709 312727 312737 312743 312757 312773 312779 312799 312839
312841 312857 312863 312887 312899 312929 312931 312937 312941 312943 312967
312971 312979 312989 313003 313009 313031 313037 313081 313087 313109 313127
313129 313133 313147 313151 313153 313163 313207 313211 313219 313241 313249
313267 313273 313289 313297 313301 313307 313321 313331 313333 313343 313351
313373 313381 313387 313399 313409 313471 313477 313507 313517 313543 313549
313553 313561 313567 313571 313583 313589 313597 313603 313613 313619 313637
313639 313661 313669 313679 313699 313711 313717 313721 313727 313739 313741
313763 313777 313783 313829 313849 313853 313879 313883 313889 313897 313909
313921 313931 313933 313949 313961 313969 313979 313981 313987 313991 313993
313997 314003 314021 314059 314063 314077 314107 314113 314117 314129 314137
314159 314161 314173 314189 314213 314219 314227 314233 314239 314243 314257
314261 314263 314267 314299 314329 314339 314351 314357 314359 314399 314401

```
314407  314423  314441  314453  314467  314491  314497  314513  314527  314543  314549
314569  314581  314591  314597  314599  314603  314623  314627  314641  314651  314693
314707  314711  314719  314723  314747  314761  314771  314777  314779  314807  314813
314827  314851  314879  314903  314917  314927  314933  314953  314957  314983  314989
315011  315013  315037  315047  315059  315067  315083  315097  315103  315109  315127
315179  315181  315193  315199  315223  315247  315251  315257  315269  315281  315313
315349  315361  315373  315377  315389  315407  315409  315421  315437  315449  315451
315461  315467  315481  315493  315517  315521  315527  315529  315547  315551  315559
315569  315589  315593  315599  315613  315617  315631  315641  315671  315677  315691
315697  315701  315703  315739  315743  315751  315779  315803  315811  315829  315851
315857  315881  315883  315893  315899  315907  315937  315949  315961  315967  315977
316003  316031  316033  316037  316051  316067  316073  316087  316097  316109  316133
316139  316153  316177  316189  316193  316201  316213  316219  316223  316241  316243
316259  316271  316291  316297  316301  316321  316339  316343  316363  316373  316391
316403  316423  316429  316439  316453  316469  316471  316493  316499  316501  316507
316531  316567  316571  316577  316583  316621  316633  316637  316649  316661  316663
316681  316691  316697  316699  316703  316717  316753  316759  316769  316777  316783
316793  316801  316817  316819  316847  316853  316859  316861  316879  316891  316903
316907  316919  316937  316951  316957  316961  316991  317003  317011  317021  317029
317047  317063  317071  317077  317087  317089  317123  317159  317171  317179  317189
317197  317209  317227  317257  317263  317267  317269  317279  317321  317323  317327
317333  317351  317353  317363  317371  317399  317411  317419  317431  317453  317453
317459  317483  317489  317491  317503  317539  317557  317563  317587  317591  317593
317599  317609  317617  317621  317651  317663  317671  317693  317701  317711  317717
317729  317731  317741  317743  317771  317773  317777  317783  317789  317797  317827
317831  317839  317857  317887  317903  317921  317923  317957  317959  317963  317969
317971  317983  317987  318001  318007  318023  318077  318103  318107  318127  318137
318161  318173  318179  318181  318191  318203  318209  318211  318229  318233  318247
318259  318271  318281  318287  318289  318299  318301  318313  318319  318323  318337
318347  318349  318377  318403  318407  318419  318431  318443  318457  318467  318473
318503  318523  318557  318559  318569  318581  318589  318601  318629  318641  318653
318671  318677  318679  318683  318691  318701  318713  318737  318743  318749  318751
318781  318793  318809  318811  318817  318823  318833  318841  318863  318881  318883
318889  318907  318911  318917  318919  318949  318979  319001  319027  319031  319037
319049  319057  319061  319069  319093  319097  319117  319127  319129  319133  319147
319159  319169  319183  319201  319211  319223  319237  319259  319279  319289  319313
319321  319327  319339  319343  319351  319357  319387  319391  319399  319411  319427
319433  319439  319441  319453  319469  319477  319483  319489  319499  319511  319519
319541  319547  319567  319577  319589  319591  319601  319607  319639  319673  319679
319681  319687  319691  319699  319727  319729  319733  319747  319757  319763  319811
319817  319819  319829  319831  319849  319883  319897  319901  319919  319927  319931
319937  319967  319973  319981  319993  320009  320011  320027  320039  320041  320053
320057  320063  320081  320083  320101  320107  320113  320119  320141  320143  320149
320153  320179  320209  320213  320219  320237  320239  320267  320269  320273  320291
320293  320303  320317  320329  320339  320377  320387  320389  320401  320417  320431
320449  320471  320477  320483  320513  320521  320533  320539  320561  320563  320591
320609  320611  320627  320647  320657  320659  320669  320687  320693  320699  320713
320741  320759  320767  320791  320821  320833  320839  320843  320851  320861  320867
320899  320911  320923  320927  320939  320941  320953  321007  321017  321031  321037
321047  321053  321073  321077  321091  321109  321143  321163  321169  321187  321193
321199  321203  321221  321227  321239  321247  321289  321301  321311  321313  321319
321323  321329  321331  321341  321359  321367  321371  321383  321397  321403  321413
321427  321443  321449  321467  321469  321509  321547  321553  321569  321571  321577
321593  321611  321617  321619  321631  321647  321661  321679  321707  321709  321721
321733  321743  321751  321757  321779  321799  321817  321821  321823  321829  321833
321847  321851  321889  321901  321911  321947  321949  321961  321983  321991  322001
322009  322013  322037  322039  322051  322057  322067  322073  322079  322093  322097
322109  322111  322139  322169  322171  322193  322213  322229  322237  322243  322247
322249  322261  322271  322319  322327  322339  322349  322351  322397  322403  322409
322417  322429  322433  322459  322463  322501  322513  322519  322523  322537  322549
322559  322571  322573  322583  322589  322591  322607  322613  322627  322631  322633
322649  322669  322709  322727  322747  322757  322769  322771  322781  322783  322807
322849  322859  322871  322877  322901  322919  322921  322939  322951  322963
322969  322997  322999  323003  323009  323027  323053  323077  323083  323087  323093
323101  323123  323131  323137  323149  323201  323207  323233  323243  323249  323251
323273  323333  323339  323341  323359  323369  323371  323377  323381  323383  323413
323419  323441  323443  323467  323471  323473  323507  323509  323537  323549  323567
323579  323581  323591  323597  323599  323623  323641  323647  323651  323659  323707
323711  323717  323759  323767  323789  323797  323801  323803  323819  323837  323879
323899  323903  323923  323927  323933  323951  323957  323987  324011  324031  324053
324067  324073  324089  324097  324101  324119  324131  324143  324151  324161
324179  324199  324209  324211  324217  324223  324239  324251  324293  324299  324301
324319  324329  324341  324361  324391  324397  324403  324419  324427  324431  324437
324439  324449  324451  324469  324473  324491  324497  324503  324517  324523  324529
324557  324587  324589  324593  324617  324619  324637  324641  324661  324673
324689  324697  324707  324733  324743  324757  324763  324773  324781  324791  324799
324809  324811  324839  324847  324869  324871  324889  324893  324901  324931  324941
324949  324953  324977  324979  324983  324991  324997  325001  325009  325019  325021
325027  325043  325051  325063  325079  325081  325093  325133  325153  325163  325181
325187  325189  325201  325217  325219  325229  325231  325249  325271  325301  325307
325309  325319  325333  325343  325349  325379  325411  325421  325439  325447  325453
325459  325463  325477  325487  325513  325517  325537  325541  325543  325571  325597
325607  325627  325631  325643  325667  325673  325681  325691  325693  325697  325709
325723  325729  325747  325751  325753  325769  325777  325781  325783  325807  325813
325849  325861  325877  325883  325889  325891  325901  325921  325939  325943  325951
325957  325987  325993  325999  326023  326057  326063  326083  326087  326099  326101
326113  326119  326141  326143  326147  326149  326153  326159  326171  326189  326203
326219  326251  326257  326309  326323  326351  326353  326369  326437  326441  326449
326467  326479  326497  326503  326537  326539  326549  326561  326563  326567  326581
```

326593	326597	326609	326611	326617	326633	326657	326659	326663	326681	326687
326693	326701	326707	326737	326741	326773	326779	326831	326863	326867	326869
326873	326881	326903	326923	326939	326941	326947	326951	326983	326993	326999
327007	327011	327017	327023	327059	327071	327079	327127	327133	327163	
327179	327193	327203	327209	327211	327247	327251	327263	327277	327289	327307
327311	327317	327319	327331	327337	327343	327347	327401	327407	327409	327419
327421	327433	327443	327463	327469	327473	327479	327491	327493	327499	327511
327517	327529	327553	327557	327559	327571	327581	327583	327599	327619	327629
327647	327661	327667	327673	327689	327707	327721	327737	327739	327757	327779
327797	327799	327809	327823	327827	327829	327839	327851	327853	327869	327871
327881	327889	327917	327923	327941	327953	327967	327979	327983	328007	328037
328043	328051	328061	328063	328067	328093	328103	328109	328121	328127	328129
328171	328177	328213	328243	328249	328271	328277	328283	328291	328303	328327
328331	328333	328343	328357	328373	328379	328381	328397	328411	328421	328429
328439	328481	328511	328513	328519	328543	328579	328589	328591	328619	328621
328633	328637	328639	328651	328667	328687	328709	328721	328723	328777	328781
328787	328789	328813	328829	328837	328847	328849	328883	328891	328897	328901
328919	328921	328931	328961	328981	329009	329027	329053	329059	329081	329083
329089	329101	329111	329123	329143	329167	329177	329191	329201	329207	329209
329233	329243	329257	329267	329269	329281	329293	329297	329299	329309	329317
329321	329333	329347	329387	329393	329401	329419	329431	329471	329473	329489
329503	329519	329533	329551	329557	329587	329591	329597	329603	329617	329627
329629	329639	329657	329663	329671	329677	329683	329687	329711	329717	329723
329729	329761	329773	329779	329789	329801	329803	329863	329867	329873	329891
329899	329941	329947	329951	329957	329969	329977	329993	329999	330017	330019
330037	330041	330047	330053	330061	330067	330097	330103	330131	330133	330139
330149	330167	330199	330203	330217	330227	330229	330233	330241	330247	330271
330287	330289	330311	330313	330329	330331	330347	330359	330383	330389	330409
330413	330427	330431	330433	330439	330469	330509	330557	330563	330569	330587
330607	330611	330623	330641	330643	330653	330661	330679	330683	330689	330697
330703	330719	330721	330731	330749	330767	330787	330791	330793	330821	330823
330839	330853	330857	330859	330877	330887	330899	330907	330917	330943	330983
330997	331013	331027	331031	331043	331063	331081	331099	331127	331141	331147
331153	331159	331171	331183	331207	331213	331217	331231	331241	331249	331259
331277	331283	331301	331307	331319	331333	331337	331339	331349	331367	331369
331399	331423	331447	331451	331489	331501	331511	331519	331523	331537	
331543	331547	331549	331553	331577	331579	331589	331603	331609	331613	331651
331663	331691	331693	331697	331711	331739	331753	331769	331777	331781	331801
331819	331841	331843	331871	331883	331889	331897	331907	331909	331921	331937
331943	331957	331967	331973	331997	331999	332009	332011	332039	332053	332069
332081	332099	332113	332117	332147	332159	332161	332179	332183	332191	332201
332203	332207	332219	332221	332251	332263	332273	332287	332303	332309	332317
332393	332399	332411	332417	332441	332447	332461	332467	332471	332473	332477
332489	332509	332513	332561	332567	332569	332573	332581	332611	332617	332623	332641
332687	332699	332711	332729	332743	332749	332767	332779	332791	332803	332837
332851	332873	332881	332887	332903	332921	332933	332947	332951	332987	332989
332993	333019	333023	333029	333031	333041	333049	333071	333097	333101	333103
333107	333131	333139	333161	333187	333197	333209	333227	333233	333253	333269
333271	333283	333287	333299	333323	333331	333337	333341	333349	333367	333383
333397	333419	333427	333433	333439	333449	333451	333457	333479	333491	333493
333497	333503	333517	333533	333563	333581	333589	333623	333631	333647	
333667	333673	333679	333691	333701	333713	333719	333721	333737	333757	333769
333779	333787	333791	333793	333803	333821	333857	333871	333911	333923	333929
333941	333959	333973	333989	333997	334021	334031	334043	334049	334057	334069
334093	334099	334127	334133	334157	334171	334177	334183	334189	334199	334231
334247	334261	334289	334297	334319	334331	334333	334349	334363	334379	334387
334393	334403	334421	334423	334427	334429	334447	334487	334493	334507	334511
334513	334541	334547	334549	334561	334603	334619	334637	334643	334651	334661
334667	334681	334693	334699	334717	334721	334727	334751	334753	334759	334771
334777	334783	334787	334793	334843	334861	334877	334889	334891	334897	334931
334963	334973	334987	334991	334993	335009	335021	335029	335033	335047	335051
335057	335077	335081	335089	335107	335113	335117	335123	335131	335149	335161
335171	335173	335207	335213	335221	335249	335261	335273	335281	335299	335323
335341	335347	335381	335383	335411	335417	335429	335449	335453	335459	335473
335477	335507	335519	335527	335539	335557	335567	335579	335591	335609	335633
335641	335653	335663	335669	335681	335689	335693	335719	335729	335743	335747
335771	335807	335809	335813	335821	335833	335843	335857	335879	335893	335897
335917	335941	335953	335957	335999	336029	336031	336041	336059	336079	336101
336103	336109	336113	336121	336143	336151	336157	336163	336181	336199	336211
336223	336227	336239	336247	336251	336253	336263	336307	336317	336353	
336361	336373	336397	336403	336419	336437	336463	336491	336499	336503	336521
336527	336529	336533	336551	336563	336571	336577	336587	336593	336599	336613
336631	336643	336649	336653	336667	336671	336683	336689	336703	336727	336757
336761	336767	336769	336773	336793	336799	336803	336823	336827	336829	336857
336863	336871	336887	336899	336901	336911	336929	336961	336977	336983	336989
336997	337013	337021	337031	337039	337049	337069	337081	337091	337097	
337153	337189	337201	337213	337217	337219	337223	337261	337277	337279	337283
337291	337301	337313	337327	337339	337343	337349	337361	337367	337369	337397
337411	337427	337453	337457	337487	337489	337511	337517	337529	337537	337541
337543	337583	337607	337609	337627	337633	337639	337651	337661	337669	337681
337691	337697	337721	337741	337751	337759	337781	337793	337817	337837	337853
337859	337861	337867	337871	337873	337891	337901	337903	337907	337919	337949
337957	337969	337973	337999	338017	338027	338033	338119	338137	338141	338153
338159	338161	338167	338171	338183	338197	338203	338207	338213	338231	338237
338251	338263	338267	338269	338279	338287	338293	338297	338309	338321	338323
338339	338341	338347	338369	338383	338389	338407	338411	338413	338423	338431
338441	338461	338473	338477	338497	338531	338543	338563	338567	338573	338579
338581	338609	338659	338669	338683	338687	338707	338717	338731	338747	338753
338761	338773	338777	338791	338803	338839	338851	338857	338867	338893	338909

```
338927  338959  338993  338999  339023  339049  339067  339071  339091  339103  339107
339121  339127  339137  339139  339151  339161  339173  339187  339211  339223  339239
339247  339257  339263  339289  339307  339323  339331  339341  339373  339389  339413
339433  339467  339491  339517  339527  339539  339557  339563  339589  339601  339613
339617  339631  339637  339649  339653  339659  339671  339673  339679  339707  339727
339749  339751  339761  339769  339799  339811  339817  339821  339827  339839  339841
339863  339887  339907  339943  339959  339991  340007  340027  340031  340037  340049
340057  340061  340063  340073  340079  340103  340111  340117  340121  340127  340129
340169  340183  340201  340211  340237  340261  340267  340283  340297  340321  340337
340339  340369  340381  340387  340393  340397  340409  340429  340447  340451  340453
340477  340481  340519  340541  340559  340573  340577  340579  340583  340591  340601
340619  340633  340643  340649  340657  340661  340687  340693  340709  340723  340757
340777  340787  340789  340793  340801  340811  340819  340849  340859  340877  340889
340897  340903  340909  340913  340919  340927  340931  340933  340937  340939  340957
340979  340999  341017  341027  341041  341057  341059  341063  341083  341087  341123
341141  341171  341179  341191  341203  341219  341227  341233  341269  341273  341281
341287  341293  341303  341311  341321  341323  341333  341339  341347  341357  341423
341443  341447  341459  341461  341477  341491  341501  341507  341521  341543  341557
341569  341587  341597  341603  341617  341623  341629  341641  341647  341659  341681
341687  341701  341729  341743  341749  341771  341773  341777  341813  341821  341827
341839  341851  341863  341879  341911  341927  341947  341951  341953  341963
341983  341993  342037  342047  342049  342059  342061  342071  342073  342077  342101
342107  342131  342143  342179  342187  342191  342197  342203  342211  342233  342239
342241  342257  342281  342283  342299  342319  342337  342341  342343  342347  342359
342371  342373  342379  342389  342413  342421  342449  342451  342467  342469  342481
342497  342521  342527  342547  342553  342569  342593  342599  342607  342647  342653
342659  342673  342679  342691  342697  342733  342757  342761  342791  342799  342803
342821  342833  342841  342847  342863  342869  342871  342889  342899  342929  342949
342971  342989  343019  343037  343051  343061  343073  343081  343087  343127  343141
343153  343163  343169  343177  343193  343199  343219  343237  343243  343253  343261
343267  343289  343303  343307  343309  343313  343327  343333  343337  343373  343379
343381  343391  343393  343411  343423  343433  343481  343489  343517  343529  343531
343543  343547  343559  343561  343579  343583  343589  343591  343601  343627  343631
343639  343649  343661  343667  343687  343709  343727  343769  343771  343787  343799
343801  343813  343817  343823  343829  343831  343891  343897  343901  343913  343933
343939  343943  343951  343963  343997  344017  344021  344039  344053  344083  344111
344117  344153  344161  344167  344171  344173  344177  344189  344207  344209  344213
344221  344231  344237  344243  344249  344251  344257  344263  344269  344273  344291
344293  344321  344327  344347  344353  344363  344371  344417  344423  344429  344453
344479  344483  344497  344543  344567  344587  344599  344611  344621  344629  344639
344653  344671  344681  344683  344693  344719  344749  344753  344759  344791  344797
344801  344807  344819  344821  344843  344857  344863  344873  344887  344893  344909
344917  344921  344941  344957  344959  344963  344969  344987  345001  345011  345017
345019  345041  345047  345067  345089  345109  345133  345139  345143  345181  345193
345221  345227  345229  345259  345263  345271  345307  345311  345329  345379  345413
345431  345461  345463  345473  345479  345487  345511  345517  345533  345547
345551  345571  345577  345581  345599  345601  345607  345637  345643  345647  345659
345673  345679  345689  345701  345707  345727  345731  345733  345739  345749  345757
345769  345773  345791  345803  345811  345817  345823  345853  345869  345881  345887
345889  345907  345923  345937  345953  345979  345997  346013  346039  346043  346051
346079  346091  346097  346111  346117  346133  346139  346141  346147  346169  346187
346201  346207  346217  346223  346259  346261  346277  346303  346309  346321  346331
346337  346349  346361  346369  346373  346391  346393  346399  346411  346417  346421
346429  346433  346439  346441  346447  346453  346469  346501  346529  346543  346547
346553  346559  346561  346589  346601  346607  346627  346639  346649  346651  346657
346667  346669  346699  346711  346721  346739  346751  346763  346793  346831  346849
346867  346873  346877  346891  346903  346933  346939  346943  346961  346963  347003
347033  347041  347051  347057  347059  347063  347069  347071  347099  347129  347131
347141  347143  347161  347167  347173  347177  347183  347197  347201  347209  347227
347239  347243  347251  347257  347287  347297  347299  347317  347329  347341  347359
347401  347411  347437  347443  347489  347509  347513  347519  347533  347539  347561
347563  347579  347587  347591  347609  347621  347629  347651  347671  347707  347717
347729  347731  347747  347759  347771  347773  347779  347801  347813  347821  347849
347873  347887  347891  347899  347929  347933  347951  347957  347959  347969  347981
347983  347989  348001  348011  348017  348031  348043  348053  348077
348083  348097  348149  348163  348181  348191  348209  348217  348221  348239  348241
348247  348253  348259  348269  348287  348307  348323  348353  348367  348389  348401
348407  348419  348421  348431  348433  348437  348443  348451  348457  348461  348463
348467  348527  348547  348553  348559  348563  348571  348583  348587  348617  348629
348637  348643  348661  348671  348709  348731  348739  348757  348763  348769  348779
348811  348827  348833  348839  348851  348883  348889  348911  348917  348919  348923
348937  348949  348989  348991  349007  349039  349043  349051  349079  349081  349093
349099  349109  349121  349133  349171  349177  349183  349187  349199  349207  349211
349241  349291  349303  349313  349331  349337  349343  349357  349369  349373  349379
349381  349387  349397  349399  349403  349409  349411  349423  349471  349477  349483
349493  349499  349507  349519  349529  349553  349567  349579  349589  349603  349637
349663  349667  349697  349709  349717  349729  349753  349759  349787  349793  349801
349813  349819  349829  349831  349837  349841  349849  349871  349903  349907  349913
349919  349927  349931  349933  349939  349949  349963  349967  349981  350003  350029
350033  350039  350087  350089  350093  350107  350111  350137  350159  350179  350191
350213  350219  350237  350249  350257  350281  350293  350347  350351  350377  350381
350411  350423  350429  350431  350437  350443  350447  350453  350459  350503  350521
350549  350561  350563  350587  350593  350617  350621  350629  350657  350663  350677
350699  350711  350719  350729  350731  350737  350741  350747  350767  350771  350783
350789  350803  350809  350843  350851  350869  350881  350887  350891  350909  350941
350947  350963  350971  350981  350983  350989  351011  351023  351031  351037  351041
351047  351053  351059  351061  351077  351079  351097  351121  351133  351151  351157
351179  351217  351223  351229  351257  351259  351269  351287  351289  351293  351301
351311  351341  351343  351347  351359  351361  351383  351391  351397  351401  351413
```

```
351427  351437  351457  351469  351479  351497  351503  351517  351529  351551  351563
351587  351599  351643  351653  351661  351667  351691  351707  351727  351731  351733
351749  351751  351763  351773  351779  351797  351803  351811  351829  351847  351851
351859  351863  351887  351913  351919  351929  351931  351959  351971  351991  352007
352021  352043  352049  352057  352069  352073  352081  352097  352109  352111  352123
352133  352181  352193  352201  352217  352229  352237  352249  352267  352271  352273
352301  352309  352327  352333  352349  352357  352361  352367  352369  352381  352399
352403  352409  352411  352421  352423  352441  352459  352463  352481  352483  352489
352493  352511  352523  352543  352549  352579  352589  352601  352607  352619  352633
352637  352661  352691  352711  352739  352741  352753  352757  352771  352813  352817
352819  352831  352837  352841  352853  352867  352883  352907  352909  352931  352939
352949  352951  352973  352991  353011  353021  353047  353053  353057  353069  353081
353099  353117  353123  353137  353147  353149  353161  353173  353179  353201  353203
353237  353263  353293  353317  353321  353329  353333  353341  353359  353389  353401
353411  353429  353443  353453  353459  353471  353473  353489  353501  353527  353531
353557  353567  353603  353611  353621  353627  353629  353641  353653  353657  353677
353681  353687  353699  353711  353737  353747  353767  353777  353783  353797  353807
353813  353819  353833  353867  353869  353879  353891  353897  353911  353917  353921
353939  353963  353983  354001  354007  354017  354023  354031  354037  354041  354043
354047  354073  354091  354097  354121  354139  354143  354149  354163  354169  354181
354209  354247  354251  354253  354257  354259  354271  354301  354307  354313  354317
354323  354329  354337  354353  354371  354373  354377  354383  354391  354401  354421
354439  354443  354451  354461  354463  354469  354479  354533  354539  354551  354553
354581  354587  354619  354643  354647  354661  354667  354677  354689  354701  354703
354727  354737  354743  354751  354763  354779  354791  354799  354829  354833  354839
354847  354869  354877  354881  354883  354911  354953  354961  354971  354973  354979
354983  354997  355007  355009  355027  355031  355037  355039  355049  355057  355063
355073  355087  355093  355099  355109  355111  355127  355139  355171  355193  355211
355261  355297  355307  355321  355331  355339  355343  355361  355363  355379  355417
355427  355441  355457  355463  355483  355499  355501  355507  355513  355517  355519
355529  355541  355549  355559  355571  355573  355591  355609  355633  355643  355651
355669  355679  355697  355717  355721  355723  355753  355763  355777  355783  355799
355811  355819  355841  355847  355853  355867  355891  355909  355913  355933  355937
355939  355951  355967  355969  356023  356039  356077  356093  356101  356113  356123
356129  356137  356141  356143  356171  356173  356197  356219  356243  356261  356263
356287  356299  356311  356327  356333  356351  356387  356399  356441  356443  356449
356453  356467  356479  356501  356509  356533  356549  356561  356563  356567  356579
356591  356621  356647  356663  356693  356701  356731  356737  356749  356761  356803
356819  356821  356869  356887  356893  356927  356929  356933  356947  356959  356969
356969  356977  356981  356989  356999  357031  357047  357073  357079  357083  357103
357109  357131  357139  357169  357179  357199  357211  357229  357239
357241  357263  357271  357281  357283  357293  357319  357347  357349  357353  357359
357377  357389  357421  357431  357437  357473  357503  357509  357517  357551  357559
357563  357569  357571  357583  357587  357593  357611  357613  357619  357649  357653
357659  357661  357667  357671  357677  357683  357689  357703  357727  357733  357737
357739  357767  357779  357781  357787  357793  357809  357817  357823  357829  357839
357859  357883  357913  357967  357977  357983  357989  357997  358031  358051  358069
358073  358079  358103  358109  358153  358157  358159  358181  358201  358213  358219
358223  358229  358243  358273  358277  358279  358289  358291  358297  358301  358313
358327  358331  358349  358373  358417  358427  358429  358441  358447  358459  358471
358483  358487  358543  358549  358551  358573  358591  358597  358601  358607
358613  358637  358667  358669  358681  358691  358697  358703  358711  358723  358727
358733  358747  358781  358783  358793  358811  358829  358847  358859  358861
358867  358877  358879  358901  358903  358907  358909  358931  358951  358973  358979
358987  358993  358999  359003  359017  359027  359041  359063  359069  359101  359111
359137  359143  359147  359153  359167  359171  359207  359209  359231  359243
359263  359267  359279  359291  359297  359299  359311  359323  359327  359353  359357
359389  359407  359417  359419  359441  359449  359477  359479  359483  359501
359509  359539  359549  359561  359563  359581  359587  359599  359621  359633  359641
359657  359663  359701  359713  359719  359731  359747  359753  359761  359767  359783
359837  359851  359869  359897  359911  359929  359981  359987  360007  360023  360037
360049  360053  360071  360089  360091  360163  360167  360169  360181  360187  360193
360197  360223  360229  360233  360257  360271  360277  360287  360289  360293  360307
360317  360323  360337  360391  360407  360421  360439  360457  360461  360497  360509
360511  360541  360551  360589  360593  360611  360637  360649  360653  360749  360769
360779  360781  360803  360817  360821  360823  360827  360851  360853  360863  360869
360901  360907  360947  360949  360953  360959  360973  360977  360979  360989  361001
361003  361013  361033  361069  361091  361093  361111  361159  361183  361211  361213
361217  361219  361223  361237  361241  361271  361279  361313  361321  361327  361337
361349  361351  361357  361363  361373  361409  361411  361421  361433  361441  361447
361451  361463  361469  361481  361499  361507  361511  361523  361531  361541  361549
361561  361577  361637  361643  361649  361651  361663  361679  361687  361723  361727
361747  361763  361769  361787  361789  361793  361799  361807  361843  361871  361873
361877  361901  361903  361909  361919  361927  361943  361961  361967  361973  361979
361993  362003  362027  362051  362053  362059  362069  362081  362093  362099  362107
362137  362143  362147  362161  362177  362191  362203  362213  362221  362233  362237
362281  362291  362293  362303  362309  362333  362339  362347  362353  362357  362363
362371  362377  362381  362393  362407  362419  362429  362431  362443  362449  362459
362473  362521  362561  362569  362581  362599  362629  362633  362657  362693  362707
362717  362723  362741  362743  362749  362753  362759  362801  362851  362863  362867
362897  362903  362911  362927  362941  362951  362953  362969  362977  362983  362987
363017  363019  363037  363043  363047  363059  363061  363067  363119  363149  363151
363157  363161  363173  363179  363199  363211  363217  363257  363269  363271  363277
363313  363317  363329  363343  363359  363361  363367  363371  363373  363379  363397
363401  363403  363431  363437  363439  363463  363481  363491  363497  363523  363529
363533  363541  363551  363557  363563  363569  363577  363581  363589  363611  363619
363659  363677  363683  363691  363719  363731  363751  363757  363761  363767  363773
363799  363809  363829  363833  363841  363871  363887  363889  363901  363911  363917
363941  363947  363949  363959  363967  363977  363989  364027  364031  364069  364073
```

364079 364103 364127 364129 364141 364171 364183 364187 364193 364213 364223
364241 364267 364271 364289 364291 364303 364313 364321 364333 364337 364349
364373 364379 364393 364411 364417 364423 364433 364447 364451 364459 364481
364499 364513 364523 364537 364541 364543 364571 364583 364601 364607 364621
364627 364643 364657 364669 364687 364691 364699 364717 364739 364747 364751
364753 364759 364801 364829 364853 364873 364879 364883 364891 364909 364919
364921 364937 364943 364961 364979 364993 364997 365003 365017 365021 365039
365063 365069 365089 365107 365119 365129 365137 365147 365159 365173 365179
365201 365213 365231 365249 365251 365257 365291 365293 365297 365303 365327
365333 365357 365369 365377 365411 365413 365419 365423 365441 365461 365467
365471 365473 365479 365489 365507 365509 365513 365527 365531 365537 365557
365567 365569 365587 365591 365611 365627 365639 365641 365669 365683 365689
365699 365747 365749 365759 365773 365779 365791 365797 365809 365837 365839
365851 365903 365929 365933 365941 365969 365983 366001 366013 366019 366029
366031 366053 366077 366097 366103 366127 366133 366139 366161 366167 366169
366173 366181 366193 366199 366211 366217 366221 366227 366239 366259 366269
366277 366287 366293 366307 366313 366329 366331 366343 366347 366383 366397
366409 366419 366433 366437 366439 366461 366463 366467 366479 366497 366511
366517 366521 366547 366593 366599 366607 366631 366677 366683 366697 366701
366703 366713 366721 366727 366733 366787 366791 366811 366829 366841 366851
366853 366859 366869 366881 366889 366901 366907 366917 366923 366941 366953
366967 366973 366983 366997 367001 367007 367019 367021 367027 367033 367049
367069 367097 367121 367123 367127 367139 367163 367181 367189 367201 367207
367219 367229 367231 367243 367259 367261 367273 367277 367307 367309 367313
367321 367357 367369 367391 367397 367427 367453 367457 367469 367501 367519
367531 367541 367547 367559 367561 367573 367597 367603 367613 367621 367637
367649 367651 367663 367673 367687 367699 367711 367721 367733 367739 367751
367771 367777 367781 367789 367819 367823 367831 367841 367849 367853 367867
367879 367883 367889 367909 367949 367957 368021 368029 368047 368059 368077
368083 368089 368099 368107 368111 368117 368129 368141 368149 368153 368171
368189 368197 368227 368231 368233 368243 368273 368279 368287 368293 368323
368327 368359 368363 368369 368399 368411 368443 368447 368453 368471 368491
368507 368513 368521 368531 368539 368551 368579 368593 368597 368609 368633
368647 368651 368653 368689 368717 368729 368737 368743 368773 368783 368789
368791 368801 368803 368833 368857 368873 368881 368899 368911 368939 368947
368957 369007 369013 369023 369029 369067 369071 369077 369079 369097 369119
369133 369137 369143 369169 369181 369191 369197 369211 369247 369253 369263
369269 369283 369293 369301 369319 369331 369353 369361 369407 369409 369419
369439 369449 369491 369539 369553 369557 369581 369637 369647 369659 369661
369673 369703 369709 369731 369739 369751 369791 369793 369821 369827 369829
369833 369841 369851 369877 369893 369913 369917 369947 369959 369961 369979
369983 369991 369997 370003 370009 370021 370033 370057 370061 370067 370081
370091 370103 370121 370133 370147 370159 370169 370193 370199 370207 370213
370217 370241 370247 370261 370373 370387 370399 370411 370421 370423 370427
370439 370441 370451 370463 370471 370477 370483 370493 370511 370529 370537
370547 370561 370571 370597 370603 370609 370613 370619 370631 370661 370663
370673 370679 370687 370693 370723 370759 370793 370801 370813 370837 370871
370873 370879 370883 370891 370897 370919 370949 371027 371029 371057 371069
371071 371083 371087 371099 371131 371141 371143 371153 371177 371179 371191
371213 371227 371233 371237 371249 371251 371257 371281 371291 371299 371303
371311 371321 371333 371339 371341 371353 371359 371383 371387 371389 371417
371447 371453 371471 371479 371491 371509 371513 371549 371561 371573 371587
371617 371627 371633 371663 371669 371699 371719 371737 371779 371797
371831 371837 371843 371851 371857 371869 371873 371897 371927 371929 371939
371941 371951 371957 371971 371981 371999 372013 372023 372037 372049 372059
372061 372067 372107 372121 372131 372137 372149 372167 372173 372179 372223
372241 372263 372269 372271 372277 372289 372293 372299 372311 372313 372353
372367 372371 372377 372397 372401 372409 372413 372443 372451 372461 372473
372481 372497 372511 372523 372539 372607 372611 372613 372629 372637 372653
372661 372667 372677 372689 372707 372709 372719 372733 372739 372751 372763
372769 372773 372797 372803 372809 372817 372829 372833 372839 372847 372859
372871 372877 372881 372901 372917 372941 372943 372971 372973 372979 373003
373007 373019 373049 373063 373073 373091 373127 373151 373157 373171 373181
373183 373187 373193 373199 373207 373211 373213 373229 373231 373273 373291
373297 373301 373327 373339 373343 373349 373357 373361 373363 373379 373393
373447 373453 373459 373463 373487 373489 373501 373517 373553 373561 373567
373613 373621 373631 373649 373657 373661 373669 373693 373717 373721 373753
373757 373777 373783 373823 373837 373859 373861 373903 373909 373937 373943
373951 373963 373969 373981 373987 373999 374009 374029 374039 374041 374047
374063 374069 374083 374089 374093 374111 374117 374123 374137 374149 374159
374173 374177 374189 374203 374219 374239 374287 374291 374293 374299 374317
374321 374333 374347 374351 374359 374389 374399 374441 374443 374447 374461
374483 374501 374531 374537 374557 374587 374603 374639 374641 374653 374669
374677 374681 374683 374687 374701 374713 374719 374729 374741 374753 374761
374771 374783 374789 374797 374807 374819 374837 374839 374849 374879 374887
374893 374903 374909 374929 374939 374953 374977 374981 374987 374989 374993
375017 375019 375029 375043 375049 375059 375083 375091 375097 375101 375103
375113 375119 375121 375127 375149 375157 375163 375169 375203 375209 375223
375227 375233 375247 375251 375253 375257 375259 375281 375283 375311 375341
375359 375367 375371 375373 375391 375407 375413 375443 375449 375451 375457
375467 375481 375509 375511 375523 375527 375533 375553 375559 375563 375569
375593 375607 375623 375631 375643 375647 375667 375673 375703 375707 375709
375743 375757 375761 375773 375779 375787 375799 375833 375841 375857 375899
375901 375923 375931 375967 375971 375979 375983 375997 376001 376003 376009
376021 376039 376049 376063 376081 376097 376099 376127 376133 376147 376153
376171 376183 376199 376231 376237 376241 376283 376291 376297 376307 376351
376373 376393 376399 376417 376463 376469 376471 376477 376483 376501 376511
376529 376531 376547 376573 376577 376583 376589 376603 376609 376627 376631
376633 376639 376657 376679 376687 376699 376709 376721 376729 376757 376759

```
376769  376787  376793  376801  376807  376811  376819  376823  376837  376841  376847
376853  376889  376891  376897  376921  376927  376931  376933  376949  376963  376969
377011  377021  377051  377059  377071  377099  377123  377129  377137  377147  377171
377173  377183  377197  377219  377231  377257  377263  377287  377291  377297  377327
377329  377339  377347  377353  377369  377371  377387  377393  377459  377471  377477
377491  377513  377521  377527  377537  377543  377557  377561  377563  377581  377593
377599  377617  377623  377633  377653  377681  377687  377711  377717  377737  377749
377761  377771  377779  377789  377801  377809  377827  377831  377843  377851  377873
377887  377911  377963  377981  377999  378011  378019  378023  378041  378071  378083
378089  378101  378127  378137  378149  378151  378163  378167  378179  378193  378223
378229  378239  378241  378253  378269  378277  378283  378289  378317  378353  378361
378379  378401  378407  378439  378449  378463  378467  378493  378503  378509  378523
378533  378551  378559  378569  378571  378583  378593  378601  378619  378629  378661
378667  378671  378683  378691  378713  378733  378739  378757  378761  378779  378793
378809  378817  378821  378823  378869  378883  378893  378901  378919  378929  378941
378949  378953  378967  378987  378989  379007  379009  379013  379033  379039  379073
379081  379087  379097  379103  379123  379133  379147  379157  379163  379177  379187
379189  379199  379207  379273  379277  379283  379289  379307  379319  379333  379343
379369  379387  379391  379397  379399  379417  379433  379439  379441  379451  379459
379499  379501  379513  379531  379541  379549  379571  379573  379579  379597  379607
379633  379649  379663  379667  379679  379681  379693  379699  379703  379721  379723
379727  379751  379777  379787  379811  379817  379837  379849  379853  379859  379877
379889  379903  379909  379913  379927  379931  379963  379979  379993  379997  379999
380041  380047  380059  380071  380117  380129  380131  380141  380147  380179  380189
380197  380201  380203  380207  380231  380251  380267  380269  380287  380291  380299
380309  380311  380327  380329  380333  380363  380377  380383  380401  380423  380441
380447  380453  380459  380461  380483  380503  380533  380557  380563  380591  380621
380623  380629  380641  380651  380657  380707  380713  380729  380753  380777  380797
380803  380819  380837  380839  380843  380867  380869  380879  380881  380909  380917
380929  380951  380957  380971  380977  380983  381001  381011  381019  381037  381047
381061  381071  381077  381097  381103  381167  381169  381181  381209  381221  381223
381233  381239  381253  381287  381289  381301  381319  381323  381343  381347  381371
381373  381377  381383  381389  381401  381413  381419  381439  381443  381461  381467
381481  381487  381509  381523  381527  381529  381533  381541  381559  381569  381607
381629  381631  381637  381659  381673  381697  381707  381713  381737  381739  381749
381757  381761  381791  381793  381817  381841  381853  381859  381911  381917  381937
381943  381949  381977  381989  381991  382001  382003  382021  382037  382061  382069
382073  382087  382103  382117  382163  382171  382189  382229  382231  382241  382253
382267  382271  382303  382331  382351  382357  382363  382373  382391  382427  382429
382457  382463  382493  382507  382511  382519  382541  382549  382553  382567  382579
382583  382589  382601  382621  382631  382643  382649  382661  382663  382693  382703
382709  382727  382729  382747  382751  382763  382769  382777  382801  382807  382813
382843  382847  382861  382867  382871  382873  382883  382919  382933  382939  382961
382979  382999  383011  383023  383029  383041  383051  383069  383077  383081  383083
383099  383101  383107  383113  383143  383147  383153  383171  383179  383219  383221
383261  383267  383281  383291  383297  383303  383321  383347  383371  383393  383399
383417  383419  383429  383459  383483  383489  383519  383521  383527  383533  383549
383557  383573  383587  383609  383611  383623  383627  383633  383651  383657  383659
383681  383683  383693  383723  383729  383753  383759  383767  383777  383791  383797
383807  383813  383821  383833  383837  383839  383869  383891  383909  383917  383923
383941  383951  383963  383969  383983  383987  384001  384017  384029  384049  384061
384067  384079  384089  384107  384113  384133  384143  384151  384157  384173  384187
384193  384203  384227  384247  384253  384257  384259  384269  384277  384287  384299
384301  384317  384331  384343  384359  384367  384383  384403  384407  384437  384469
384473  384479  384481  384487  384497  384509  384533  384547  384577  384581  384589
384599  384611  384619  384623  384641  384673  384691  384697  384701  384719  384733
384737  384751  384757  384773  384779  384817  384821  384827  384841  384847  384851
384889  384907  384913  384919  384941  384961  384973  385001  385013  385027  385039
385057  385069  385079  385081  385087  385109  385127  385129  385139  385141  385153
385159  385171  385193  385199  385223  385249  385261  385267  385279  385289  385291
385321  385327  385331  385351  385379  385391  385393  385397  385403  385417  385433
385471  385481  385493  385501  385519  385531  385537  385559  385571  385573  385579
385589  385591  385597  385607  385621  385631  385639  385657  385661  385663  385709
385739  385741  385771  385783  385793  385811  385817  385831  385837  385843  385859
385877  385897  385901  385907  385927  385939  385943  385957  385991  385999  386017
386039  386041  386047  386051  386083  386093  386117  386119  386129  386131  386143
386149  386153  386159  386161  386173  386219  386227  386233  386237  386249  386263
386279  386297  386299  386303  386329  386333  386339  386363  386369  386371  386381
386383  386401  386411  386413  386429  386431  386437  386471  386489  386501  386521
386557  386563  386569  386573  386587  386609  386611  386621  386629  386641  386647
386651  386677  386689  386693  386713  386719  386723  386731  386747  386777  386809
386839  386851  386857  386891  386921  386927  386963  386977  386987  386989  386993
387007  387017  387031  387047  387071  387077  387083  387089  387109  387137  387151
387161  387169  387173  387187  387197  387199  387203  387227  387253  387263  387269
387281  387307  387313  387329  387341  387371  387397  387403  387433  387437  387449
387463  387493  387503  387509  387529  387551  387577  387587  387613  387623  387631
387641  387659  387677  387679  387683  387707  387721  387727  387743  387749  387763
387781  387791  387799  387839  387853  387857  387911  387913  387917  387953  387967
387971  387973  387977  388009  388051  388057  388067  388081  388099  388109  388111
388117  388133  388159  388163  388169  388177  388181  388183  388187  388211  388217
388237  388253  388259  388273  388277  388301  388313  388319  388351  388363  388369
388373  388391  388403  388459  388471  388477  388481  388483  388489  388499  388519
388529  388541  388567  388573  388621  388651  388657  388673  388691  388693  388697
388699  388711  388727  388757  388777  388781  388789  388793  388813  388823  388837
388859  388879  388891  388897  388901  388903  388931  388933  388937  388961  388963
388991  389003  389023  389027  389029  389041  389047  389057  389083  389089  389099
389111  389117  389141  389149  389161  389167  389171  389173  389189  389219  389227
389231  389269  389273  389287  389297  389299  389303  389357  389369  389381  389399
389401  389437  389447  389461  389479  389483  389507  389513  389527  389531  389533
```

389539 389561 389563 389567 389569 389579 389591 389621 389629 389651 389659
389663 389687 389699 389713 389723 389743 389749 389761 389773 389783 389791
389797 389819 389839 389849 389867 389891 389897 389903 389911 389923 389927
389941 389947 389953 389957 389971 389981 389989 389999 390001 390043 390067
390077 390083 390097 390101 390107 390109 390113 390119 390151 390157 390161
390191 390193 390199 390209 390211 390223 390263 390281 390289 390307 390323
390343 390347 390353 390359 390367 390373 390389 390391 390407 390413 390419
390421 390433 390437 390449 390463 390479 390487 390491 390493 390499 390503
390527 390539 390553 390581 390647 390653 390671 390673 390703 390707 390721
390727 390737 390739 390743 390751 390763 390781 390791 390809 390821 390829
390851 390869 390877 390883 390889 390893 390953 390959 390961 390967 390989
390991 391009 391019 391021 391031 391049 391057 391063 391067 391073 391103
391117 391133 391151 391159 391163 391177 391199 391217 391219 391231 391247
391249 391273 391283 391291 391301 391331 391337 391351 391367 391373 391379
391387 391393 391397 391399 391403 391441 391451 391453 391487 391519 391537
391553 391579 391613 391619 391627 391631 391639 391661 391679 391691 391693
391711 391717 391733 391739 391751 391753 391757 391789 391801 391817 391823
391847 391861 391873 391879 391889 391891 391903 391907 391921 391939 391961
391967 391987 391999 392011 392033 392053 392069 392087 392099 392101
392111 392113 392131 392143 392149 392153 392159 392177 392201 392209 392213
392221 392233 392239 392251 392261 392263 392267 392269 392279 392281 392297
392299 392321 392333 392339 392347 392351 392363 392383 392389 392423 392437
392443 392467 392473 392477 392489 392503 392519 392531 392543 392549 392569
392593 392599 392611 392629 392647 392663 392669 392699 392723 392737 392741
392759 392761 392767 392803 392807 392809 392827 392831 392837 392849 392851
392857 392879 392893 392911 392923 392927 392929 392957 392963 392969 392981
392983 393007 393013 393017 393031 393059 393073 393077 393079 393083 393097
393103 393109 393121 393137 393143 393157 393161 393181 393187 393191 393203
393209 393241 393247 393257 393271 393287 393299 393301 393311 393331 393361
393373 393377 393383 393401 393403 393413 393451 393473 393479 393487 393517
393521 393539 393541 393551 393557 393571 393577 393581 393583 393587 393593
393611 393629 393637 393649 393667 393671 393677 393683 393697 393709 393713
393721 393727 393739 393749 393761 393779 393797 393847 393853 393857 393859
393863 393871 393901 393919 393929 393931 393947 393961 393977 393989 393997
394007 394019 394039 394049 394063 394073 394099 394123 394129 394153 394157
394169 394187 394201 394211 394223 394241 394249 394259 394271 394291 394319
394327 394357 394363 394367 394369 394393 394409 394411 394453 394481 394489
394501 394507 394523 394529 394549 394571 394577 394579 394601 394619 394631
394633 394637 394643 394673 394699 394717 394721 394727 394729 394733 394739
394747 394759 394787 394811 394813 394817 394819 394829 394837 394861 394879
394897 394943 394963 394967 394969 394981 394987 394993 395023 395027
395039 395047 395069 395089 395093 395107 395111 395113 395119 395137 395141
395147 395159 395173 395189 395191 395201 395231 395243 395251 395261 395273
395287 395293 395303 395309 395321 395323 395377 395383 395407 395429 395431
395443 395449 395453 395459 395491 395509 395513 395533 395537 395543 395581
395597 395611 395621 395627 395657 395671 395677 395687 395701 395719 395737
395741 395749 395767 395803 395849 395851 395873 395887 395891 395897 395909
395921 395953 395959 395971 396001 396029 396031 396041 396043 396061 396079
396091 396103 396107 396119 396157 396173 396181 396197 396199 396203 396217
396239 396247 396259 396269 396293 396299 396301 396311 396323 396349 396353
396373 396377 396379 396413 396427 396437 396443 396449 396479 396509 396523
396527 396533 396541 396547 396563 396577 396581 396601 396619 396623 396629
396631 396637 396647 396667 396679 396703 396709 396713 396719 396733 396833
396871 396881 396883 396887 396919 396931 396937 396943 396947 396953 396971
396983 396997 397013 397027 397037 397051 397057 397063 397073 397099
397127 397151 397153 397181 397183 397211 397217 397223 397237 397253 397259
397283 397289 397297 397301 397303 397337 397351 397357 397361 397373 397379
397427 397429 397433 397459 397469 397489 397493 397517 397519 397541 397543
397547 397549 397567 397589 397591 397597 397633 397643 397673 397687 397697
397721 397723 397729 397751 397753 397757 397759 397763 397799 397807 397811
397829 397849 397867 397897 397907 397921 397939 397951 397963 397973 397981
398011 398023 398029 398033 398039 398053 398059 398063 398077 398087 398113
398117 398119 398129 398143 398149 398171 398207 398213 398219 398227 398249
398261 398267 398273 398287 398303 398311 398323 398339 398341 398347 398353
398357 398369 398393 398407 398417 398423 398441 398459 398467 398471 398473
398477 398491 398509 398539 398543 398549 398557 398569 398581 398591 398609
398611 398621 398627 398669 398681 398683 398693 398711 398729 398731 398759
398771 398813 398819 398821 398833 398857 398887 398903 398917 398921
398933 398941 398969 398977 398989 399023 399031 399043 399059 399067 399071
399079 399097 399101 399107 399131 399137 399149 399151 399163 399173 399181
399197 399221 399227 399239 399241 399263 399271 399277 399281 399283 399353
399379 399389 399391 399401 399403 399409 399433 399439 399473 399481 399491
399493 399499 399523 399527 399541 399557 399571 399577 399583 399587 399601
399613 399617 399643 399647 399667 399677 399689 399691 399719 399727 399731
399739 399757 399761 399769 399781 399787 399793 399851 399853 399871 399887
399899 399911 399913 399937 399941 399953 399979 399983 399989 400009 400031
400033 400051 400067 400069 400087 400093 400109 400123 400151 400157 400187
400199 400207 400217 400237 400243 400247 400249 400261 400277 400291 400297
400307 400313 400321 400331 400339 400381 400391 400409 400417 400429 400441
400457 400471 400481 400523 400559 400579 400597 400601 400607 400619 400643
400651 400657 400679 400681 400703 400711 400721 400723 400739 400753 400759
400823 400837 400849 400853 400859 400871 400903 400927 400931 400943 400949
400963 400997 401017 401029 401039 401053 401057 401069 401077 401087 401101
401113 401119 401161 401173 401179 401201 401209 401231 401237 401243 401279
401287 401309 401311 401321 401329 401341 401347 401371 401381 401393 401407
401411 401417 401473 401477 401507 401519 401537 401539 401551 401567 401587
401593 401627 401629 401651 401669 401671 401689 401707 401711 401713 401771
401773 401809 401813 401827 401839 401861 401867 401887 401903 401909 401917
401939 401953 401957 401959 401981 401987 401993 402023 402029 402037 402043

```
402049 402053 402071 402089 402091 402107 402131 402133 402137 402139 402197
402221 402223 402239 402253 402263 402277 402299 402307 402313 402329 402331
402341 402343 402359 402361 402371 402379 402383 402403 402419 402443 402487
402503 402511 402517 402527 402529 402541 402551 402559 402581 402583 402587
402593 402601 402613 402631 402691 402697 402739 402751 402757 402761 402763
402767 402769 402797 402803 402817 402823 402847 402851 402859 402863 402869
402881 402923 402943 402947 402949 402991 403001 403003 403037 403043 403049
403057 403061 403063 403079 403097 403103 403133 403141 403159 403163 403181
403219 403241 403243 403253 403261 403267 403289 403301 403309 403327 403331
403339 403363 403369 403387 403391 403433 403439 403483 403499 403511 403537
403547 403553 403567 403577 403591 403603 403607 403621 403649 403661 403673
403679 403681 403687 403703 403717 403721 403729 403757 403783 403787 403817
403829 403831 403849 403861 403867 403877 403889 403901 403933 403951 403957
403969 403979 403981 403993 404009 404011 404017 404021 404029 404051 404081
404099 404113 404119 404123 404161 404167 404177 404189 404191 404197 404213
404221 404249 404251 404267 404269 404273 404291 404309 404321 404323 404357
404381 404387 404389 404399 404419 404423 404429 404431 404449 404461 404483
404489 404497 404507 404513 404527 404531 404533 404539 404557 404597 404671
404693 404699 404713 404773 404779 404783 404819 404827 404837 404843 404849
404851 404941 404951 404959 404969 404977 404981 404983 405001 405011 405029
405037 405047 405049 405071 405073 405089 405091 405143 405157 405179 405199
405211 405221 405227 405239 405241 405247 405253 405269 405277 405287 405299
405323 405341 405343 405347 405373 405401 405407 405413 405437 405439 405473
405479 405491 405497 405499 405521 405527 405529 405541 405553 405577 405599
405607 405611 405641 405659 405667 405677 405679 405683 405689 405701 405703
405709 405719 405731 405749 405763 405767 405781 405799 405817 405827 405839
405857 405863 405869 405871 405893 405901 405917 405947 405949 405959 405967
405989 405991 405997 406013 406027 406037 406067 406073 406093 406117 406123
406169 406171 406177 406183 406207 406247 406253 406267 406271 406309 406313
406327 406331 406339 406349 406361 406381 406397 406403 406423 406429 406481
406499 406501 406507 406513 406517 406531 406547 406559 406561 406573 406577
406579 406583 406591 406631 406633 406649 406661 406673 406697 406699 406717
406729 406739 406789 406807 406811 406817 406847 406859 406873 406883 406907
406951 406969 406981 406993 407023 407047 407059 407083 407119 407137 407149
407153 407177 407179 407191 407203 407207 407219 407221 407233 407249 407257
407263 407273 407287 407291 407299 407311 407317 407321 407347 407357 407359
407369 407377 407383 407401 407437 407471 407483 407489 407501 407503 407509
407521 407527 407567 407573 407579 407587 407599 407621 407633 407639 407651
407657 407669 407699 407707 407713 407717 407723 407741 407747 407783 407789
407791 407801 407807 407821 407833 407843 407857 407861 407879 407893 407899
407917 407923 407947 407959 407969 407971 407977 407993 408011 408019 408041
408049 408071 408077 408091 408127 408131 408137 408169 408173 408197 408203
408209 408211 408217 408223 408229 408241 408251 408263 408271 408283 408311
408337 408341 408347 408361 408379 408389 408403 408413 408427 408431 408433
408437 408461 408469 408479 408491 408497 408533 408539 408553 408563 408607
408623 408631 408637 408643 408659 408677 408689 408691 408701 408703 408713
408719 408743 408763 408769 408773 408787 408803 408809 408817 408841 408857
408869 408911 408913 408923 408943 408953 408959 408971 408979 408997 409007
409021 409027 409033 409043 409063 409069 409081 409099 409121 409153 409163
409177 409187 409217 409237 409259 409261 409267 409271 409289 409291 409327
409333 409337 409349 409351 409369 409379 409391 409397 409429 409433 409441
409463 409471 409477 409483 409499 409517 409523 409529 409543 409573 409579
409589 409597 409609 409639 409657 409691 409693 409709 409711 409723 409729
409733 409753 409769 409777 409781 409813 409817 409823 409831 409841 409861
409867 409879 409889 409891 409897 409901 409909 409933 409943 409951 409961
409967 409987 409993 409999 410009 410029 410063 410087 410093 410117 410119
410141 410143 410149 410171 410173 410203 410231 410233 410239 410243 410257
410279 410281 410299 410317 410323 410339 410341 410353 410359 410383 410387
410393 410401 410411 410413 410453 410461 410477 410489 410491 410497 410507
410513 410519 410551 410561 410587 410617 410621 410623 410629 410651 410659
410671 410687 410701 410717 410731 410741 410747 410749 410759 410783 410789
410801 410807 410819 410833 410857 410899 410903 410929 410953 410983 410999
411001 411007 411011 411013 411031 411041 411049 411067 411071 411083 411101
411113 411119 411127 411143 411157 411167 411193 411197 411211 411233 411241
411251 411253 411259 411287 411311 411337 411347 411361 411371 411379 411409
411421 411443 411449 411469 411473 411479 411491 411503 411527 411529 411557
411563 411569 411577 411583 411589 411611 411613 411617 411637 411641 411667
411679 411683 411703 411707 411709 411721 411727 411737 411739 411743 411751
411779 411799 411809 411821 411823 411833 411841 411883 411919 411923 411937
411941 411947 411967 411991 412001 412007 412019 412031 412033 412037 412039
412051 412067 412073 412081 412099 412109 412123 412127 412133 412147 412157
412171 412187 412189 412193 412201 412211 412213 412219 412249 412253 412273
412277 412289 412303 412333 412339 412343 412387 412397 412411 412457 412463
412481 412487 412493 412537 412561 412567 412571 412589 412591 412603 412609
412619 412627 412637 412639 412651 412663 412667 412717 412739 412771 412793
412807 412831 412849 412859 412891 412901 412903 412939 412943 412949 412967
412987 413009 413027 413033 413053 413069 413071 413081 413087 413089 413093
413111 413113 413129 413141 413143 413159 413167 413183 413197 413201 413207
413233 413243 413251 413263 413267 413293 413299 413353 413411 413417 413429
413443 413461 413477 413521 413527 413533 413537 413551 413557 413579 413587
413597 413629 413653 413681 413683 413689 413711 413713 413719 413737 413753
413759 413779 413783 413807 413827 413849 413863 413867 413869 413879 413887
413911 413923 413951 413981 414013 414017 414019 414031 414049 414053 414061
414077 414083 414097 414101 414107 414109 414131 414157 414179 414199 414203
414209 414217 414221 414241 414259 414269 414277 414283 414311 414313 414329
414331 414347 414361 414367 414383 414389 414397 414413 414431 414433 414451
414457 414461 414467 414487 414503 414521 414539 414553 414559 414571 414577
414607 414611 414629 414641 414643 414653 414677 414679 414683 414691 414697
414703 414707 414709 414721 414731 414737 414763 414767 414769 414773 414779
```

```
414793  414803  414809  414833  414857  414871  414889  414893  414899  414913  414923
414929  414949  414959  414971  414977  414991  415013  415031  415039  415061  415069
415073  415087  415097  415109  415111  415133  415141  415147  415153  415159  415171
415187  415189  415201  415213  415231  415253  415271  415273  415319  415343  415379
415381  415391  415409  415427  415447  415469  415477  415489  415507  415517  415523
415543  415553  415559  415567  415577  415603  415607  415609  415627  415631  415643
415661  415669  415673  415687  415691  415697  415717  415721  415729  415759
415783  415787  415799  415801  415819  415823  415861  415873  415879  415901  415931
415937  415949  415951  415957  415963  415969  415979  415993  415999  416011  416023
416071  416077  416089  416107  416147  416149  416153  416159  416167  416201  416219
416239  416243  416249  416257  416263  416281  416291  416333  416359  416387  416389
416393  416399  416401  416407  416413  416417  416419  416441  416443  416459  416473
416477  416491  416497  416501  416503  416513  416531  416543  416573  416579  416593
416621  416623  416629  416659  416677  416693  416719  416761  416797  416821  416833
416839  416849  416851  416873  416881  416887  416947  416957  416963  416989  417007
417017  417019  417023  417037  417089  417097  417113  417119  417127  417133  417161
417169  417173  417181  417187  417191  417203  417217  417227  417239  417251  417271
417283  417293  417311  417317  417331  417337  417371  417377  417379  417383  417419
417437  417451  417457  417479  417491  417493  417509  417511  417523  417541  417553
417559  417577  417581  417583  417617  417623  417631  417643  417649  417671  417691
417719  417721  417727  417731  417733  417737  417751  417763  417773  417793  417811
417821  417839  417863  417869  417881  417883  417899  417931  417941  417947  417953
417959  417961  417983  417997  418007  418009  418027  418031  418043  418051  418069
418073  418079  418087  418109  418129  418157  418169  418177  418181  418189  418199
418207  418219  418259  418273  418279  418289  418303  418321  418331  418337  418339
418343  418349  418351  418357  418373  418381  418391  418423  418427  418447  418459
418471  418493  418511  418553  418559  418597  418601  418603  418631  418633  418637
418657  418667  418699  418709  418721  418739  418751  418763  418771  418783  418787
418793  418799  418811  418813  418819  418837  418843  418849  418861  418867  418871
418883  418889  418909  418921  418927  418933  418939  418961  418981  418987  418993
418997  419041  419051  419053  419057  419059  419087  419141  419147  419161  419171
419183  419189  419191  419201  419231  419249  419261  419281  419291  419297  419303
419317  419329  419351  419383  419401  419417  419423  419429  419443  419449  419459
419467  419473  419477  419483  419491  419513  419527  419537  419557  419561  419563
419567  419579  419591  419597  419599  419603  419609  419623  419651  419687  419693
419701  419711  419743  419753  419777  419789  419791  419801  419803  419821  419827
419831  419873  419893  419921  419927  419929  419933  419953  419959  419999  420001
420029  420037  420041  420047  420073  420097  420103  420149  420163  420191  420193
420221  420241  420253  420263  420269  420271  420293  420307  420313  420317  420319
420323  420331  420341  420349  420353  420361  420367  420383  420397  420419  420421
420439  420457  420467  420479  420481  420499  420503  420521  420551  420557  420569
420571  420593  420599  420613  420671  420677  420683  420691  420731  420737  420743
420757  420769  420779  420781  420799  420803  420809  420811  420851  420853  420857
420859  420899  420919  420929  420941  420967  420977  420997  421009  421019  421033
421037  421049  421079  421081  421093  421103  421121  421123  421133  421147  421159
421163  421177  421181  421189  421207  421241  421273  421279  421303  421313  421331
421339  421349  421361  421381  421397  421409  421417  421423  421433  421453  421459
421469  421471  421483  421493  421501  421517  421559  421607  421609  421621  421633
421639  421643  421657  421661  421691  421697  421699  421703  421709  421711  421717
421727  421739  421741  421783  421801  421807  421831  421847  421891  421907  421913
421943  421973  421987  421997  422029  422041  422057  422063  422069  422077  422083
422087  422089  422099  422101  422111  422113  422129  422137  422141  422183  422203
422209  422231  422239  422243  422249  422267  422287  422291  422309  422311  422321
422339  422353  422363  422369  422377  422393  422407  422431  422453  422459  422479
422537  422549  422551  422557  422563  422567  422573  422581  422621  422627  422657
422689  422707  422717  422749  422753  422759  422761  422789  422797  422803
422827  422857  422861  422867  422869  422879  422881  422893  422897  422899  422911
422923  422927  422969  422987  423001  423013  423019  423043  423053  423061  423067
423083  423091  423097  423103  423109  423121  423127  423133  423173  423179  423191
423209  423221  423229  423233  423251  423257  423259  423277  423281  423287  423289
423299  423307  423323  423341  423347  423389  423403  423413  423427  423431  423439
423457  423461  423463  423469  423481  423497  423503  423509  423541  423547  423557
423559  423581  423601  423617  423649  423667  423697  423707  423713  423727
423749  423751  423763  423769  423779  423781  423791  423803  423823  423847  423853
423859  423869  423883  423887  423931  423949  423961  423977  423989  423991  424001
424003  424007  424019  424027  424037  424079  424091  424093  424103  424117  424121
424129  424139  424147  424157  424163  424169  424187  424199  424223  424231  424243
424247  424261  424267  424271  424273  424313  424331  424339  424343  424351  424397
424423  424429  424433  424451  424471  424481  424493  424519  424537  424547  424549
424559  424573  424577  424597  424601  424639  424661  424667  424679  424687  424693
424709  424727  424729  424757  424769  424771  424777  424811  424817  424819  424829
424841  424843  424849  424861  424867  424889  424891  424903  424909  424913  424939
424961  424967  424997  425003  425027  425039  425057  425059  425071  425083  425101
425107  425123  425147  425149  425189  425197  425207  425233  425237  425251  425273
425279  425281  425291  425297  425309  425317  425329  425333  425363  425377  425387
425393  425417  425419  425423  425441  425443  425471  425473  425489  425501  425519
425521  425533  425549  425563  425591  425603  425609  425641  425653  425681  425701
425773  425779  425783  425791  425801  425813  425819  425837  425839  425851  425857
425861  425869  425879  425899  425903  425911  425939  425959  425977  425987  425989
426007  426011  426061  426073  426077  426089  426091  426103  426131  426161  426163
426193  426197  426211  426229  426233  426253  426287  426301  426311  426319  426331
426353  426383  426389  426401  426407  426421  426427  426469  426487  426527  426541
426551  426553  426563  426583  426611  426631  426637  426641  426661  426691  426697
426707  426709  426731  426737  426739  426743  426757  426761  426763  426773  426779
426787  426799  426841  426859  426863  426871  426889  426893  426913  426917  426919
426931  426941  426971  426973  426997  427001  427013  427039  427043  427067  427069
427073  427079  427081  427103  427117  427151  427169  427181  427213  427237  427241
427243  427247  427249  427279  427283  427307  427309  427327  427333  427351  427369
427379  427381  427403  427417  427421  427423  427429  427433  427439  427447  427451
```

```
427457  427477  427513  427517  427523  427529  427541  427579  427591  427597  427619
427621  427681  427711  427717  427723  427727  427733  427751  427781  427787  427789
427813  427849  427859  427877  427879  427883  427913  427919  427939  427949  427951
427957  427967  427969  427991  427993  427997  428003  428023  428027  428033  428039
428041  428047  428083  428093  428137  428143  428147  428149  428161  428167  428173
428177  428221  428227  428231  428249  428251  428273  428297  428299  428303  428339
428353  428369  428401  428411  428429  428471  428473  428489  428503  428509  428531
428539  428551  428557  428563  428567  428569  428579  428629  428633  428639  428657
428663  428671  428677  428683  428693  428731  428741  428759  428777  428797  428801
428807  428809  428833  428843  428851  428863  428873  428899  428951  428957  428977
429007  429017  429043  429083  429101  429109  429119  429127  429137  429139  429161
429181  429197  429211  429217  429223  429227  429241  429259  429271  429277  429281
429283  429329  429347  429349  429361  429367  429389  429397  429409  429413  429427
429431  429449  429463  429467  429469  429487  429497  429503  429509  429511  429521
429529  429547  429551  429563  429581  429587  429589  429599  429631  429643  429659
429661  429673  429677  429679  429683  429701  429719  429727  429731  429733  429773
429791  429797  429817  429823  429827  429851  429853  429881  429887  429889  429899
429901  429907  429911  429917  429929  429931  429937  429943  429953  429971  429973
429991  430007  430009  430013  430019  430057  430061  430081  430091  430093  430121
430139  430147  430193  430259  430267  430277  430279  430289  430303  430319  430333
430343  430357  430393  430411  430427  430433  430453  430487  430499  430511  430513
430517  430543  430553  430571  430579  430589  430601  430603  430649  430663  430691
430697  430699  430709  430723  430739  430741  430747  430751  430753  430769  430783
430789  430799  430811  430819  430823  430841  430847  430861  430873  430879  430883
430891  430897  430907  430909  430921  430949  430957  430979  430981  430987  430999
431017  431021  431029  431047  431051  431063  431077  431083  431099  431107  431141
431147  431153  431173  431191  431203  431213  431219  431237  431251  431257  431267
431269  431287  431297  431311  431329  431339  431363  431369  431377  431381  431399
431423  431429  431441  431447  431449  431479  431513  431521  431533  431567  431581
431597  431603  431611  431617  431621  431657  431659  431663  431671  431693  431707
431729  431731  431759  431777  431797  431801  431803  431807  431831  431833  431857
431863  431867  431869  431881  431887  431891  431903  431911  431929  431933  431947
431983  431993  432001  432007  432023  432031  432037  432043  432053  432059  432067
432073  432097  432121  432137  432139  432143  432149  432161  432163  432167  432199
432203  432227  432241  432251  432277  432281  432287  432301  432317  432323  432337
432343  432349  432359  432373  432389  432391  432401  432413  432433  432437  432449
432457  432479  432491  432499  432503  432511  432527  432539  432557  432559  432569
432577  432587  432589  432613  432631  432637  432659  432661  432713  432721  432727
432737  432743  432749  432781  432793  432797  432799  432833  432847  432857  432869
432893  432907  432923  432931  432959  432961  432979  432983  432989  433003  433033
433049  433051  433061  433073  433079  433087  433093  433099  433117  433123  433141
433151  433187  433193  433201  433207  433229  433241  433249  433253  433259  433261
433271  433277  433291  433309  433319  433337  433351  433357  433361  433369  433373
433393  433399  433421  433429  433439  433453  433469  433471  433501  433507  433513
433549  433571  433577  433607  433627  433633  433639  433651  433661  433663  433673
433679  433681  433703  433723  433729  433747  433759  433777  433787  433789  433813
433817  433847  433859  433861  433877  433883  433889  433931  433943  433963  433967
433981  434009  434011  434029  434039  434081  434087  434107  434111  434113  434117
434141  434167  434179  434191  434201  434209  434221  434237  434243  434249  434261
434267  434293  434297  434303  434311  434323  434347  434353  434363  434377  434383
434387  434389  434407  434411  434431  434437  434459  434461  434471  434479  434501
434509  434521  434561  434563  434573  434593  434597  434611  434647  434659  434683
434689  434699  434717  434719  434743  434761  434783  434803  434807  434813  434821
434827  434831  434839  434849  434857  434867  434873  434881  434909  434921  434923
434927  434933  434939  434947  434957  434963  434977  434981  434989  435037  435041
435059  435103  435107  435109  435131  435139  435143  435151  435161  435179  435181
435187  435191  435221  435223  435247  435257  435263  435277  435283  435287  435307
435317  435343  435349  435359  435371  435397  435401  435403  435419  435427  435437
435439  435451  435481  435503  435529  435541  435553  435559  435563  435569  435571
435577  435583  435593  435619  435623  435637  435641  435647  435649  435653  435661
435679  435709  435731  435733  435739  435751  435763  435769  435779  435811  435839
435847  435857  435859  435881  435889  435893  435907  435913  435923  435947  435949
435973  435983  435997  436003  436013  436027  436061  436081  436087  436091  436097
436127  436147  436151  436157  436171  436181  436217  436231  436253  436273  436279
436283  436291  436307  436309  436313  436343  436357  436399  436417  436427  436439
436459  436463  436477  436481  436483  436507  436523  436529  436531  436547  436549
436571  436591  436607  436621  436627  436649  436651  436673  436687  436693  436717
436727  436729  436739  436741  436757  436801  436811  436819  436831  436841  436853
436871  436889  436913  436957  436963  436967  436973  436979  436993  436999  437011
437033  437071  437077  437083  437093  437111  437113  437137  437141  437149  437153
437159  437191  437201  437219  437237  437243  437263  437273  437279  437287  437293
437321  437351  437357  437363  437387  437389  437401  437413  437467  437471  437473
437497  437501  437509  437519  437527  437533  437539  437543  437557  437587  437629
437641  437651  437653  437677  437681  437687  437693  437719  437729  437743  437753
437771  437809  437819  437837  437849  437861  437867  437881  437909  437923  437947
437953  437959  437977  438001  438017  438029  438047  438049  438091  438131  438133
438143  438169  438203  438211  438223  438233  438241  438253  438259  438271  438281
438287  438301  438313  438329  438341  438377  438391  438401  438409  438419  438439
438443  438467  438479  438499  438517  438521  438523  438527  438533  438551  438569
438589  438601  438611  438623  438631  438637  438661  438667  438671  438701  438707
438721  438733  438761  438769  438793  438827  438829  438833  438847  438853  438869
438877  438887  438899  438913  438937  438941  438953  438961  438967  438979  438983
438989  439007  439009  439063  439081  439123  439133  439141  439157  439163  439171
439183  439199  439217  439253  439273  439279  439289  439303  439339  439349  439357
439367  439381  439409  439421  439427  439429  439441  439459  439463  439471  439493
439511  439519  439541  439559  439567  439573  439577  439583  439601  439613  439631
439639  439661  439667  439687  439693  439697  439709  439723  439729  439753  439759
439763  439771  439781  439787  439799  439811  439823  439849  439853  439861  439867
439883  439891  439903  439919  439949  439961  439969  439973  439981  439991  440009
```

```
440023 440039 440047 440087 440093 440101 440131 440159 440171 440177 440179
440183 440203 440207 440221 440227 440239 440261 440269 440281 440303 440311
440329 440333 440339 440347 440371 440383 440389 440393 440399 440431 440441
440443 440471 440497 440501 440507 440509 440527 440537 440543 440549 440551
440567 440569 440579 440581 440641 440651 440653 440669 440677 440681 440683
440711 440717 440723 440731 440753 440761 440773 440807 440809 440821 440831
440849 440863 440893 440903 440911 440939 440941 440953 440959 440983 440987
440989 441011 441029 441041 441043 441053 441073 441079 441101 441107 441109
441113 441121 441127 441157 441169 441179 441187 441191 441193 441229 441247
441251 441257 441263 441281 441307 441319 441349 441359 441361 441403 441421
441443 441449 441461 441479 441499 441517 441523 441527 441547 441557 441563
441569 441587 441607 441613 441619 441631 441647 441667 441697 441703 441713
441737 441751 441787 441797 441799 441811 441827 441829 441839 441841 441877
441887 441907 441913 441923 441937 441953 441971 442003 442007 442009 442019
442027 442031 442033 442061 442069 442097 442109 442121 442139 442147 442151
442157 442171 442177 442181 442193 442201 442207 442217 442229 442237 442243
442271 442283 442291 442319 442327 442333 442363 442367 442397 442399 442439
442447 442457 442469 442487 442489 442499 442501 442517 442531 442537 442571
442573 442577 442579 442589 442609 442619 442633 442691 442699 442703 442721
442733 442747 442753 442763 442769 442777 442781 442789 442807 442817 442823
442829 442831 442837 442843 442861 442879 442903 442919 442961 442963 442973
442979 442987 442991 442997 443011 443017 443039 443041 443057 443059 443063
443077 443089 443117 443123 443129 443147 443153 443159 443161 443167 443171
443189 443203 443221 443227 443231 443237 443243 443249 443263 443273 443281
443291 443293 443341 443347 443353 443363 443369 443389 443407 443413 443419
443423 443431 443437 443453 443467 443489 443501 443533 443543 443551 443561
443563 443567 443587 443591 443603 443609 443629 443659 443687 443689 443701
443711 443731 443749 443753 443759 443761 443771 443777 443791 443837 443851
443867 443869 443873 443879 443881 443893 443899 443909 443917 443939 443941
443953 443983 443987 443999 444001 444007 444029 444043 444047 444079 444089
444109 444113 444121 444127 444131 444151 444167 444173 444179 444181 444187
444209 444253 444271 444281 444287 444289 444293 444307 444341 444343 444347
444349 444401 444403 444421 444443 444449 444461 444463 444469 444473 444487
444517 444523 444527 444529 444539 444547 444553 444557 444569 444589 444607
444623 444637 444641 444649 444671 444677 444701 444713 444739 444767 444791
444793 444803 444811 444817 444833 444841 444859 444863 444869 444877 444883
444887 444893 444901 444929 444937 444953 444967 444971 444979 445001 445019
445021 445031 445033 445069 445087 445091 445097 445103 445141 445157 445169
445183 445187 445199 445229 445261 445271 445279 445283 445297 445307 445321
445339 445363 445427 445433 445447 445453 445463 445477 445499 445507 445537
445541 445567 445573 445583 445589 445597 445619 445631 445633 445649 445657
445691 445699 445703 445741 445747 445769 445771 445789 445799 445807 445829
445847 445853 445871 445877 445883 445891 445931 445937 445943 445967 445969
446003 446009 446041 446063 446081 446087 446111 446123 446129 446141 446179
446189 446191 446197 446221 446227 446231 446261 446263 446273 446279 446293
446309 446323 446333 446353 446363 446387 446389 446399 446401 446417 446441
446447 446461 446473 446477 446503 446533 446549 446561 446569 446597 446603
446609 446647 446657 446713 446717 446731 446753 446759 446767 446773 446819
446827 446839 446863 446881 446891 446893 446909 446911 446921 446933 446951
446969 446983 447001 447011 447019 447053 447067 447079 447101 447107 447119
447133 447137 447173 447179 447193 447197 447211 447217 447221 447233 447247
447257 447259 447263 447311 447319 447323 447331 447353 447401 447409 447427
447439 447443 447451 447463 447467 447481 447509 447521 447527 447541
447569 447571 447611 447617 447637 447641 447677 447683 447701 447703 447743
447749 447757 447779 447791 447793 447817 447823 447827 447829 447841 447859
447877 447883 447893 447901 447907 447943 447961 447983 447991 448003 448013
448027 448031 448057 448067 448073 448093 448111 448121 448139 448141 448157
448159 448169 448177 448187 448193 448199 448207 448241 448249 448303 448309
448313 448321 448351 448363 448367 448373 448379 448387 448397 448421 448451
448519 448531 448561 448597 448607 448627 448631 448633 448667 448687 448697
448703 448727 448733 448741 448769 448793 448801 448807 448813 448853
448859 448867 448871 448873 448879 448883 448907 448927 448939 448969 448993
448997 448999 449003 449011 449051 449077 449083 449093 449107 449117 449129
449131 449149 449153 449161 449171 449173 449201 449203 449209 449227 449243
449249 449261 449263 449269 449287 449299 449303 449311 449321 449333 449347
449353 449363 449381 449399 449411 449417 449419 449437 449441 449459 449473
449543 449549 449557 449563 449567 449569 449591 449609 449621 449629 449653
449663 449671 449677 449681 449689 449693 449699 449741 449759 449767 449773
449783 449797 449807 449821 449833 449851 449879 449921 449929 449941 449951
449959 449963 449971 449987 449989 450001 450011 450019 450029 450067 450071
450077 450083 450101 450103 450113 450127 450137 450161 450169 450193 450199
450209 450217 450223 450227 450239 450257 450259 450277 450287 450293 450299
450301 450311 450343 450349 450361 450367 450377 450383 450391 450403 450413
450421 450431 450451 450473 450479 450481 450487 450493 450503 450529 450533
450557 450563 450581 450587 450599 450601 450617 450641 450643 450649 450677
450691 450707 450719 450727 450761 450767 450787 450797 450799 450803 450809
450811 450817 450829 450839 450841 450847 450859 450881 450883 450887 450893
450899 450913 450917 450929 450943 450949 450971 450991 450997 451013 451039
451051 451057 451069 451093 451097 451103 451109 451159 451177 451181 451183
451201 451207 451249 451277 451279 451301 451303 451309 451313 451331 451337
451343 451361 451387 451397 451411 451439 451441 451481 451499 451519 451523
451541 451547 451553 451579 451601 451609 451621 451637 451657 451663 451667
451669 451679 451681 451691 451699 451709 451723 451747 451751 451771 451783
451793 451799 451823 451831 451837 451859 451873 451879 451897 451901 451903
451909 451921 451933 451937 451939 451961 451967 451987 452009 452017 452027
452033 452041 452077 452083 452087 452131 452159 452161 452171 452191 452201
452213 452227 452233 452239 452269 452279 452293 452297 452329 452363 452377
452393 452401 452443 452453 452497 452519 452521 452531 452533 452537 452539
452549 452579 452587 452597 452611 452629 452633 452671 452687 452689 452701
```

```
452731  452759  452773  452797  452807  452813  452821  452831  452857  452869  452873
452923  452953  452957  452983  452989  453023  453029  453053  453073  453107  453119
453133  453137  453143  453157  453161  453181  453197  453199  453209  453217  453227
453239  453247  453269  453289  453293  453301  453311  453317  453329  453347  453367
453371  453377  453379  453421  453451  453461  453527  453553  453559  453569  453571
453599  453601  453617  453631  453637  453641  453643  453659  453667  453671  453683
453703  453707  453709  453737  453757  453797  453799  453823  453833  453847  453851
453877  453889  453907  453913  453923  453931  453949  453961  453977  453983  453991
454009  454021  454031  454033  454039  454061  454063  454079  454109  454141  454151
454159  454183  454199  454211  454213  454219  454229  454231  454247  454253  454267
454297  454303  454313  454331  454351  454357  454361  454379  454387  454409  454417
454451  454453  454483  454501  454507  454513  454541  454543  454547  454577  454579
454603  454609  454627  454637  454673  454679  454709  454711  454721  454723  454759
454763  454777  454799  454823  454847  454849  454859  454889  454891  454907
454919  454921  454931  454943  454967  454969  454973  454991  455003  455011  455033
455047  455053  455093  455099  455123  455149  455159  455167  455171  455177  455201
455219  455227  455233  455237  455261  455263  455279  455291  455309  455317  455321
455333  455339  455341  455353  455381  455393  455401  455407  455419  455431  455437
455543  455461  455471  455473  455479  455489  455491  455513  455527  455531  455537
455557  455573  455579  455597  455599  455603  455627  455647  455659  455681  455683
455687  455701  455711  455717  455737  455761  455783  455789  455809  455827  455831
455849  455863  455881  455899  455921  455933  455941  455953  455969  455977  455989
455993  455999  456007  456013  456023  456037  456047  456061  456091  456107  456109
456119  456149  456151  456167  456193  456223  456233  456241  456283  456293  456329
456349  456353  456367  456377  456403  456409  456427  456439  456451  456457  456461
456499  456503  456517  456523  456529  456539  456553  456557  456559  456571  456581
456587  456607  456611  456613  456623  456641  456647  456649  456653  456679  456683
456697  456727  456737  456763  456767  456769  456791  456809  456811  456821  456871
456877  456881  456899  456901  456923  456949  456959  456979  456991  457001  457003
457013  457021  457043  457049  457057  457087  457091  457097  457099  457117  457139
457151  457153  457183  457189  457201  457213  457229  457241  457253  457267  457271
457277  457279  457307  457319  457333  457339  457363  457367  457381  457393  457397
457399  457403  457411  457421  457433  457459  457469  457507  457511  457517  457547
457553  457559  457571  457607  457609  457621  457643  457651  457661  457669  457673
457679  457687  457697  457711  457739  457757  457789  457799  457813  457817  457829
457837  457871  457889  457903  457913  457943  457979  457981  457987  457999  458027
458039  458047  458053  458057  458063  458069  458119  458123  458173  458179  458189
458191  458197  458207  458219  458239  458309  458317  458323  458327  458333  458357
458363  458377  458399  458401  458407  458449  458477  458483  458501  458531  458533
458543  458567  458569  458573  458593  458599  458611  458621  458629  458639  458651
458669  458683  458689  458701  458719  458729  458747  458789  458791  458797  458807
458819  458849  458863  458879  458891  458897  458917  458921  458929  458947  458957
458959  458963  458971  458977  458981  458987  458993  459007  459013  459023  459029
459031  459037  459047  459089  459091  459113  459127  459167  459169  459181  459209
459223  459229  459233  459257  459271  459293  459301  459313  459317  459337  459341
459343  459353  459373  459377  459383  459397  459427  459443  459463  459467  459487
459469  459479  459509  459521  459523  459593  459607  459611  459619  459623  459631
459647  459649  459671  459677  459691  459703  459749  459763  459791  459803  459817
459829  459841  459847  459883  459913  459923  459929  459937  459961  460013  460039
460051  460063  460073  460079  460081  460087  460091  460099  460111  460127  460147
460157  460171  460181  460189  460211  460217  460231  460247  460267  460289  460297
460301  460337  460349  460373  460379  460387  460393  460403  460409  460417  460451
460463  460477  460531  460543  460561  460571  460589  460609  460619  460627  460633
460637  460643  460657  460673  460697  460709  460711  460721  460771  460777  460787
460793  460813  460829  460841  460843  460871  460891  460903  460907  460913  460919
460937  460949  460951  460969  460973  460979  460981  460987  460991  461009  461011
461017  461051  461053  461059  461093  461101  461119  461143  461147  461171  461183
461191  461207  461233  461239  461257  461269  461273  461297  461299  461309  461317
461323  461327  461333  461359  461381  461393  461407  461411  461413  461437  461441
461443  461467  461479  461507  461521  461561  461569  461581  461599  461603  461609
461627  461639  461653  461677  461687  461689  461693  461707  461717  461801  461803
461819  461843  461861  461887  461891  461917  461921  461933  461957  461971  461977
461983  462001  462041  462067  462073  462079  462097  462103  462109  462113  462131
462149  462181  462191  462199  462221  462239  462263  462271  462307  462311  462331
462337  462361  462373  462377  462401  462409  462419  462421  462437  462443  462467
462481  462491  462493  462499  462529  462541  462547  462557  462569  462571  462577
462589  462607  462629  462641  462643  462653  462659  462667  462673  462677  462697
462713  462719  462727  462733  462739  462773  462827  462841  462851  462863  462871
462881  462887  462899  462901  462911  462937  462947  462953  462983  463003  463031
463033  463093  463103  463157  463181  463189  463207  463213  463219  463231  463237
463247  463249  463261  463283  463291  463297  463303  463313  463319  463321  463339
463343  463363  463387  463399  463433  463447  463451  463453  463457  463459  463483
463501  463511  463513  463523  463531  463537  463549  463579  463613  463627  463633
463643  463649  463663  463679  463693  463711  463717  463741  463747  463753  463763
463781  463787  463807  463823  463829  463831  463849  463861  463867  463873  463889
463891  463907  463919  463921  463949  463963  463973  463987  463993  464003  464011
464021  464033  464047  464069  464081  464089  464119  464129  464131  464137  464141
464143  464171  464173  464197  464201  464213  464237  464251  464257  464263  464279
464281  464291  464309  464311  464327  464351  464371  464381  464383  464413  464419
464437  464447  464459  464467  464479  464483  464521  464537  464539  464549  464557
464561  464587  464591  464603  464617  464621  464647  464663  464687  464699  464741
464747  464749  464753  464767  464773  464777  464801  464803  464809  464813
464819  464843  464857  464879  464897  464909  464917  464923  464927  464941
464951  464953  464963  464983  464993  464999  465007  465011  465013  465019  465041
465061  465067  465071  465079  465089  465107  465119  465133  465151  465161
465163  465167  465169  465173  465187  465209  465211  465259  465271  465277  465281
465293  465299  465317  465319  465331  465337  465373  465379  465383  465407  465419
465433  465463  465469  465523  465529  465539  465551  465581  465587  465611  465631
465643  465649  465659  465679  465701  465721  465739  465743  465761  465781  465797
```

465799 465809 465821 465833 465841 465887 465893 465901 465917 465929 465931
465947 465957 465989 466009 466019 466027 466033 466043 466061 466069 466073
466079 466087 466091 466121 466139 466153 466171 466181 466183 466201 466243
466247 466261 466267 466273 466283 466303 466321 466331 466339 466357 466369
466373 466409 466423 466441 466451 466483 466517 466537 466547 466553 466561
466567 466573 466579 466603 466619 466637 466649 466651 466673 466717 466723
466729 466733 466747 466751 466777 466787 466801 466819 466853 466859 466897
466909 466913 466919 466951 466957 466997 467003 467009 467017 467021 467063
467081 467083 467101 467119 467123 467141 467147 467171 467183 467197 467209
467213 467237 467239 467261 467293 467297 467317 467329 467333 467353 467371
467399 467417 467431 467437 467447 467471 467473 467477 467479 467491 467497
467503 467507 467527 467531 467543 467549 467557 467587 467591 467611 467617
467627 467629 467633 467641 467651 467657 467669 467671 467681 467689 467699
467713 467729 467737 467743 467749 467773 467783 467813 467827 467833 467867
467869 467879 467881 467893 467897 467899 467903 467927 467941 467953 467963
467977 468001 468011 468019 468029 468049 468059 468067 468071 468079 468107
468109 468113 468121 468131 468133 468137 468151 468157 468173 468187 468191 468199
468239 468241 468253 468271 468277 468289 468319 468323 468353 468359 468371
468389 468421 468439 468451 468463 468473 468491 468493 468499 468509 468527
468551 468557 468577 468581 468593 468599 468613 468619 468623 468641 468647
468653 468661 468667 468683 468691 468697 468703 468709 468719 468737 468739
468761 468773 468781 468803 468817 468821 468841 468851 468859 468869 468883
468887 468889 468893 468899 468913 468953 468967 468973 468983 469009 469031
469037 469069 469099 469121 469127 469141 469153 469169 469193 469207 469219
469229 469237 469241 469253 469267 469279 469283 469303 469321 469331 469351
469363 469367 469369 469379 469397 469411 469429 469439 469457 469487 469501
469529 469541 469543 469561 469583 469589 469613 469627 469631 469649 469657
469673 469687 469691 469717 469723 469747 469753 469757 469769 469787 469793
469801 469811 469823 469841 469849 469877 469879 469891 469907 469919 469939
469957 469969 469979 469993 470021 470039 470059 470077 470081 470083 470087
470089 470131 470149 470153 470161 470167 470179 470201 470207 470209 470213
470219 470227 470243 470251 470263 470279 470297 470299 470303 470317 470333
470347 470359 470389 470399 470411 470413 470417 470429 470443 470447 470453
470461 470471 470473 470489 470501 470513 470521 470531 470539 470551 470579
470593 470597 470599 470609 470621 470627 470647 470651 470653 470663 470669
470689 470711 470719 470731 470749 470779 470783 470791 470819 470831 470837
470863 470867 470881 470887 470891 470903 470927 470933 470941 470947 470957
470959 470993 470999 471007 471041 471061 471073 471089 471091 471101 471137
471139 471161 471173 471179 471187 471193 471209 471217 471241 471253 471259
471277 471281 471283 471299 471301 471313 471353 471389 471391 471403 471407
471439 471451 471467 471481 471487 471503 471509 471521 471533 471539 471553
471571 471589 471593 471607 471617 471619 471641 471649 471659 471671 471673
471677 471683 471697 471703 471719 471721 471749 471769 471781 471791 471803
471817 471841 471847 471859 471871 471893 471901 471907 471923 471929 471931
471943 471949 471959 471997 472019 472027 472051 472057 472063 472067 472103
472111 472123 472127 472133 472139 472151 472159 472163 472189 472193 472247
472249 472253 472261 472273 472289 472301 472309 472319 472331 472333 472349
472369 472391 472393 472399 472411 472421 472457 472469 472477 472523 472541
472543 472559 472561 472573 472597 472631 472639 472643 472669 472687 472691
472697 472709 472711 472721 472741 472751 472763 472793 472799 472817 472831
472837 472847 472859 472883 472907 472909 472921 472937 472963 472981 472993
473009 473021 473027 473089 473101 473117 473141 473147 473159 473167 473173
473191 473197 473201 473203 473219 473227 473257 473279 473287 473293 473311
473321 473327 473351 473353 473377 473381 473383 473411 473419 473441 473443
473453 473471 473477 473479 473497 473503 473507 473513 473519 473527 473531
473533 473549 473579 473597 473611 473617 473633 473647 473659 473719 473723
473729 473741 473743 473761 473789 473833 473839 473857 473861 473867 473887
473899 473911 473923 473929 473939 473951 473953 473971 473981 473987 473993
473999 474017 474029 474037 474043 474049 474059 474073 474077 474101 474119
474127 474137 474143 474151 474163 474169 474197 474211 474223 474241 474263
474307 474311 474319 474337 474343 474347 474359 474379 474389 474391
474413 474433 474437 474443 474479 474491 474497 474499 474503 474533 474541
474547 474557 474569 474571 474581 474583 474619 474629 474659 474667
474671 474707 474709 474737 474751 474757 474769 474779 474787 474809 474811
474839 474847 474857 474899 474907 474911 474917 474923 474931 474937 474941
474949 474959 474977 474983 475037 475051 475073 475081 475091 475093 475103
475109 475141 475147 475151 475159 475169 475207 475219 475229 475243 475271
475273 475283 475289 475297 475301 475327 475331 475333 475351 475367 475369
475379 475381 475403 475417 475421 475427 475429 475441 475457 475469 475483
475511 475523 475529 475559 475583 475597 475613 475619 475621 475637 475639
475649 475669 475679 475681 475691 475693 475697 475721 475729 475751 475753
475759 475763 475777 475789 475793 475807 475823 475831 475837 475841 475859
475879 475889 475897 475903 475907 475921 475927 475933 475957 475973
475991 475997 476009 476023 476027 476029 476039 476041 476059 476081 476087
476089 476101 476107 476111 476137 476143 476167 476183 476219 476233 476237
476243 476249 476279 476299 476317 476347 476351 476363 476369 476381 476401
476407 476419 476423 476429 476467 476477 476479 476507 476513 476519 476579
476587 476591 476599 476603 476611 476633 476639 476647 476659 476681 476683
476701 476713 476719 476737 476743 476753 476759 476783 476803 476831 476849
476851 476863 476869 476887 476891 476911 476921 476929 476977 476981 476989
477011 477013 477017 477019 477031 477047 477073 477077 477091 477131 477149
477163 477209 477221 477229 477259 477277 477293 477313 477317 477329 477341
477359 477361 477383 477409 477439 477461 477469 477497 477511 477517 477523
477539 477551 477553 477557 477571 477577 477593 477619 477623 477637 477671
477697 477721 477727 477731 477739 477751 477769 477791 477797 477809 477811
477821 477823 477839 477847 477857 477863 477881 477899 477913 477941 477947
477973 477977 477991 478001 478039 478063 478067 478069 478087 478099 478111
478129 478139 478157 478169 478171 478189 478199 478207 478213 478241 478243
478253 478259 478271 478273 478321 478339 478343 478351 478391 478399 478403

```
478411  478417  478421  478427  478433  478441  478451  478453  478459  478481  478483
478493  478523  478531  478571  478573  478579  478589  478603  478627  478631  478637
478651  478679  478697  478711  478727  478729  478739  478741  478747  478763  478769
478787  478801  478811  478813  478823  478831  478843  478853  478861  478871  478879
478897  478901  478913  478927  478931  478937  478943  478963  478967  478991  478999
479023  479027  479029  479041  479081  479131  479137  479147  479153  479189  479191
479201  479209  479221  479231  479239  479243  479263  479267  479287  479299  479309
479317  479327  479357  479371  479377  479387  479419  479429  479431  479441  479461
479473  479489  479497  479509  479513  479533  479543  479561  479569  479581  479593
479599  479623  479629  479639  479701  479749  479753  479761  479771  479777  479783
479797  479813  479821  479833  479839  479861  479879  479881  479891  479903  479909
479939  479951  479953  479957  479971  480013  480017  480019  480023  480043  480047
480049  480059  480061  480071  480091  480101  480107  480113  480133  480143  480157
480167  480169  480203  480209  480287  480299  480317  480329  480341  480343  480349
480367  480373  480379  480383  480391  480409  480419  480427  480449  480451  480461
480463  480499  480503  480509  480517  480521  480527  480533  480541  480553  480563
480569  480583  480587  480647  480661  480707  480713  480737  480749  480761
480773  480787  480803  480827  480839  480853  480881  480911  480919  480929  480937
480941  480959  480967  480989  480989  481001  481003  481009  481021  481043  481051
481067  481073  481087  481093  481097  481109  481123  481133  481141  481147  481153
481157  481177  481181  481199  481207  481211  481231  481249  481297  481301
481303  481307  481343  481363  481373  481379  481387  481409  481417  481433  481447
481469  481489  481501  481513  481531  481549  481571  481577  481589  481619  481633
481639  481651  481667  481673  481681  481693  481697  481699  481721  481751  481753
481769  481787  481801  481807  481813  481837  481843  481847  481849  481861  481867
481879  481883  481909  481939  481963  481997  482017  482021  482029  482033  482039
482051  482071  482093  482099  482101  482117  482123  482179  482189  482203  482213
482227  482231  482233  482243  482263  482281  482309  482323  482347  482351  482359
482371  482387  482393  482399  482401  482407  482413  482423  482437  482441  482483
482501  482507  482509  482513  482519  482527  482539  482569  482593  482597  482621
482627  482633  482641  482659  482663  482683  482687  482689  482707  482711  482717
482719  482731  482743  482753  482767  482773  482789  482803  482819  482827
482837  482861  482863  482873  482897  482899  482917  482941  482947  482957  482971
483017  483031  483061  483071  483097  483127  483139  483163  483167  483179  483209
483211  483221  483229  483233  483239  483247  483251  483281  483289  483317  483323
483337  483347  483367  483377  483389  483397  483407  483409  483433  483443  483467
483481  483491  483499  483503  483523  483541  483551  483557  483563  483577  483611
483619  483629  483643  483649  483671  483697  483709  483719  483727  483733  483751
483757  483761  483767  483773  483787  483809  483811  483827  483829  483839  483853
483863  483869  483883  483907  483929  483937  483953  483971  483991  484019  484027
484037  484061  484067  484079  484091  484111  484117  484123  484129  484151  484153
484171  484181  484193  484201  484207  484229  484243  484259  484283  484301  484303
484327  484339  484361  484369  484373  484397  484411  484417  484439  484447  484457
484459  484487  484489  484493  484531  484543  484577  484597  484607  484609  484613
484621  484639  484643  484691  484703  484727  484733  484751  484763  484769  484777
484787  484829  484853  484867  484927  484951  484987  484999  485021  485029  485041
485053  485059  485063  485081  485101  485113  485123  485131  485137  485161  485167
485201  485207  485209  485263  485303  485311  485347  485351  485363  485371  485383
485389  485411  485417  485423  485437  485447  485479  485497  485509  485519  485543
485567  485587  485593  485603  485609  485647  485657  485671  485689  485701  485717
485729  485731  485753  485777  485819  485827  485831  485833  485893  485899  485909
485923  485941  485959  485977  485993  486023  486037  486041  486043  486053  486061
486071  486091  486103  486119  486133  486139  486163  486179  486181  486193  486203
486221  486223  486247  486281  486293  486307  486313  486323  486329  486331  486341
486349  486377  486379  486389  486391  486397  486407  486433  486443  486449  486481
486491  486503  486509  486511  486527  486539  486559  486569  486583  486589  486601
486617  486637  486641  486643  486653  486667  486671  486677  486679  486683  486697
486713  486721  486757  486767  486769  486781  486797  486817  486821  486833  486839
486869  486907  486923  486929  486943  486947  486949  486971  486977  486991  487007
487013  487021  487049  487051  487057  487073  487079  487093  487099  487111  487133
487177  487183  487187  487211  487213  487219  487247  487261  487283  487303  487307
487313  487349  487363  487381  487387  487391  487397  487423  487427  487429  487447
487457  487463  487469  487471  487477  487481  487489  487507  487561  487601
487603  487607  487637  487649  487651  487657  487681  487691  487703  487709  487717
487727  487733  487741  487757  487769  487783  487789  487793  487811  487819  487829
487831  487843  487873  487889  487891  487897  487933  487943  487973  487979  487997
488003  488009  488011  488021  488051  488057  488069  488119  488143  488149  488153
488161  488171  488197  488203  488207  488209  488227  488231  488233  488239  488249
488261  488263  488287  488303  488309  488311  488317  488321  488329  488333  488339
488347  488353  488381  488399  488401  488407  488417  488419  488441  488447  488473
488503  488513  488539  488567  488573  488603  488611  488617  488627  488633  488639
488641  488651  488687  488689  488701  488711  488717  488723  488729  488743  488749
488759  488779  488791  488797  488821  488827  488833  488861  488879  488893  488897
488909  488921  488947  488959  488981  488993  489001  489011  489019  489043  489053
489061  489101  489109  489113  489127  489133  489157  489161  489191  489197
489217  489239  489241  489257  489263  489283  489299  489329  489337  489343  489361
489367  489389  489407  489409  489427  489431  489439  489449  489457  489479  489487
489493  489529  489539  489551  489553  489557  489571  489613  489631  489653  489659
489673  489677  489679  489689  489691  489733  489743  489761  489791  489793  489799
489803  489817  489823  489833  489851  489869  489887  489871  489899  489911
489913  489941  489943  489959  489961  489977  489989  490001  490003  490019  490031
490033  490057  490097  490103  490111  490117  490121  490151  490159  490169  490183
490201  490207  490223  490241  490247  490249  490267  490271  490277  490283  490309
490313  490339  490367  490393  490417  490421  490453  490459  490463  490481  490493
490499  490519  490537  490541  490543  490549  490559  490571  490573  490577  490579
490591  490619  490627  490631  490643  490661  490663  490697  490733  490741  490769
490771  490783  490829  490837  490849  490859  490877  490891  490913  490921  490927
490937  490949  490951  490957  490967  490969  490991  490993  491003  491039  491041
491059  491081  491083  491129  491137  491149  491159  491167  491171  491201  491213
```

```
491219  491251  491261  491273  491279  491297  491299  491327  491329  491333  491339
491341  491353  491357  491371  491377  491417  491423  491429  491461  491483  491489
491497  491501  491503  491527  491531  491537  491539  491581  491591  491593  491611
491627  491633  491639  491651  491653  491669  491677  491707  491719  491731  491737
491747  491773  491783  491789  491797  491819  491833  491837  491851  491857  491867
491873  491899  491923  491951  491969  491977  491983  492007  492013  492017  492029
492047  492053  492059  492061  492067  492077  492083  492103  492113  492227  492251
492253  492257  492281  492293  492299  492319  492377  492389  492397  492403  492409
492413  492431  492463  492467  492487  492491  492511  492523  492551  492563
492587  492601  492617  492619  492629  492631  492641  492647  492659  492671  492673
492707  492719  492721  492731  492757  492761  492763  492769  492781  492799  492839
492853  492871  492883  492893  492901  492911  492967  492979  493001  493013  493021
493027  493043  493049  493067  493093  493109  493111  493121  493123  493127  493133
493139  493147  493159  493169  493177  493193  493201  493211  493217  493219  493231
493243  493249  493277  493279  493291  493301  493313  493333  493351  493369  493393
493397  493399  493403  493433  493447  493457  493463  493481  493523  493531  493541
493567  493573  493579  493583  493607  493621  493627  493643  493657  493693  493709
493711  493721  493729  493733  493747  493777  493793  493807  493811  493813  493817
493853  493859  493873  493877  493897  493919  493931  493937  493939  493957  493973
493979  493993  494023  494029  494041  494051  494069  494077  494083  494093  494101
494107  494129  494141  494147  494167  494191  494213  494237  494251  494257  494267
494269  494281  494287  494317  494327  494341  494353  494359  494369  494381  494383
494387  494407  494413  494441  494443  494471  494497  494519  494521  494539  494561
494563  494567  494587  494591  494609  494617  494621  494639  494647  494651  494671
494677  494687  494693  494699  494713  494719  494723  494731  494737  494743  494749
494759  494761  494783  494789  494803  494843  494849  494873  494899  494903  494917
494927  494933  494939  494959  494987  495017  495037  495041  495043  495067  495071
495109  495113  495119  495133  495139  495149  495151  495161  495181  495199  495211
495221  495241  495269  495277  495289  495301  495307  495323  495337  495343  495347
495359  495361  495371  495377  495389  495401  495413  495421  495433  495437  495449
495457  495461  495491  495511  495527  495557  495559  495563  495569  495571  495587
495589  495611  495613  495617  495619  495629  495637  495647  495667  495679  495701
495707  495713  495749  495751  495757  495769  495773  495787  495791  495797  495799
495821  495827  495829  495851  495877  495893  495899  495923  495931  495947  495953
495959  495967  495973  495983  496007  496019  496039  496051  496063  496073  496079
496123  496127  496163  496187  496193  496211  496229  496231  496259  496283  496289
496291  496297  496303  496313  496333  496339  496343  496381  496399  496427  496439
496453  496459  496471  496477  496481  496487  496493  496499  496511  496549  496579
496583  496609  496631  496669  496681  496687  496703  496711  496733  496747  496763
496789  496813  496817  496841  496849  496871  496877  496889  496891  496897  496901
496913  496919  496949  496963  496997  496999  497011  497017  497041  497047  497051
497069  497093  497111  497113  497117  497137  497141  497153  497171  497177  497197
497239  497257  497261  497269  497279  497281  497291  497297  497303  497309  497323
497339  497351  497389  497411  497417  497423  497449  497461  497473  497479  497491
497501  497507  497509  497521  497537  497551  497557  497561  497579  497587  497597
497603  497633  497659  497663  497671  497677  497689  497701  497711  497719  497729
497737  497741  497771  497773  497801  497813  497831  497839  497851  497867  497869
497873  497899  497929  497957  497963  497969  497977  497989  497993  497999  498013
498053  498061  498073  498089  498101  498103  498119  498143  498163  498167  498181
498209  498227  498257  498259  498271  498301  498331  498343  498361  498367  498391
498397  498401  498403  498409  498439  498461  498481  498487  498497  498521
498523  498527  498551  498557  498577  498583  498599  498611  498613  498643  498647
498653  498679  498689  498691  498733  498739  498749  498761  498767  498779  498781
498787  498791  498803  498833  498857  498859  498881  498907  498923  498931  498937
498947  498961  498973  498977  498989  499021  499027  499033  499039  499063  499067
499099  499117  499127  499129  499133  499139  499141  499151  499157  499159  499181
499183  499189  499211  499229  499253  499267  499277  499283  499309  499321  499327
499349  499361  499363  499391  499397  499403  499423  499439  499459  499481  499483
499493  499507  499519  499523  499549  499559  499571  499591  499601  499607  499621
499633  499637  499649  499661  499663  499669  499673  499679  499687  499691  499693
499711  499717  499729  499739  499747  499781  499787  499801  499819  499853  499879
499883  499897  499903  499927  499943  499957  499969  499973  499979  500009  500029
500041  500057  500069  500083  500107  500111  500119  500153  500167  500173
500177  500179  500197  500209  500231  500233  500237  500239  500249  500257  500287
500299  500317  500321  500333  500341  500363  500369  500389  500393  500413  500417
500431  500443  500459  500471  500473  500483  500501  500509  500519  500527  500567
500579  500587  500603  500629  500671  500677  500693  500699  500713  500719  500723
500729  500741  500777  500791  500807  500809  500831  500839  500861  500873  500881
500887  500891  500909  500911  500921  500923  500933  500947  500953  500957  500977
501001  501013  501019  501029  501031  501037  501043  501077  501089  501103  501121
501131  501133  501139  501157  501173  501187  501191  501197  501203  501209  501217
501223  501229  501233  501257  501271  501287  501299  501317  501341  501343  501367
501383  501401  501409  501419  501427  501451  501463  501493  501503  501511  501563
501577  501593  501601  501617  501623  501637  501659  501691  501701  501703  501707
501719  501731  501769  501779  501803  501817  501821  501827  501829  501841  501863
501889  501911  501931  501947  501953  501967  501971  501997  502001  502013  502039
502043  502057  502063  502079  502081  502087  502093  502121  502133  502141  502171
502181  502217  502237  502247  502259  502261  502277  502301  502321  502339  502393
502409  502421  502429  502441  502451  502487  502499  502501  502507  502517  502543
502559  502553  502591  502597  502613  502631  502633  502643  502651  502669  502687
502699  502703  502717  502729  502769  502771  502781  502787  502807  502819  502829
502841  502847  502861  502883  502919  502921  502937  502961  502973  503003  503017
503039  503053  503077  503123  503131  503137  503147  503159  503197  503207  503213
503227  503231  503233  503249  503267  503287  503297  503303  503317  503339  503351
503359  503369  503381  503383  503389  503407  503423  503431  503441  503453
503483  503501  503543  503549  503551  503563  503593  503599  503609  503611  503621
503623  503647  503653  503663  503707  503717  503743  503753  503777  503779
503791  503803  503819  503821  503827  503851  503857  503869  503879  503911  503927
503929  503939  503947  503959  503963  503969  503983  503989  504001  504011  504017
```

```
504047  504061  504073  504103  504121  504139  504143  504149  504151  504157  504181
504187  504197  504209  504221  504247  504269  504289  504299  504307  504311  504323
504337  504349  504353  504359  504377  504379  504389  504403  504457  504461  504473
504479  504521  504523  504527  504547  504563  504593  504607  504617  504619
504631  504661  504667  504671  504677  504683  504727  504767  504787  504797  504799
504817  504821  504851  504853  504857  504871  504877  504893  504901  504929  504937
504943  504947  504953  504967  504983  504989  504991  505027  505031  505033  505049
505051  505061  505067  505073  505091  505097  505111  505117  505123  505129  505139
505157  505159  505181  505187  505201  505213  505231  505237  505277  505279  505283
505301  505313  505319  505321  505327  505339  505357  505367  505369  505399  505409
505411  505429  505447  505459  505469  505481  505493  505501  505511  505513  505523
505537  505559  505573  505601  505607  505613  505619  505633  505639  505643  505657
505663  505669  505691  505693  505709  505711  505727  505759  505763  505777  505781
505811  505819  505823  505867  505871  505877  505907  505919  505927  505949  505961
505969  505979  506047  506071  506083  506101  506113  506119  506131  506147  506171
506173  506183  506201  506213  506251  506263  506269  506281  506291  506327  506329
506333  506339  506347  506351  506357  506381  506393  506417  506423  506449  506459
506461  506479  506491  506501  506507  506531  506533  506537  506551  506563  506573
506591  506593  506599  506609  506629  506647  506663  506683  506687  506689  506699
506729  506731  506743  506773  506783  506791  506797  506809  506837  506843  506861
506873  506887  506893  506899  506903  506911  506929  506941  506963  506983  506993
506999  507029  507049  507071  507077  507079  507103  507109  507113  507119  507137
507139  507149  507151  507163  507193  507197  507217  507289  507301  507313  507317
507329  507347  507349  507359  507361  507371  507383  507401  507421  507431  507461
507491  507497  507499  507503  507523  507557  507571  507589  507593  507599  507607
507631  507641  507667  507673  507691  507697  507713  507719  507743  507757  507779
507781  507797  507803  507809  507821  507827  507839  507883  507901  507907  507917
507919  507937  507953  507961  507971  507979  508009  508019  508021  508033  508037
508073  508087  508097  508099  508103  508129  508159  508171  508213  508223
508229  508237  508243  508259  508271  508273  508297  508301  508327  508331  508349
508363  508367  508393  508433  508439  508451  508471  508477  508489  508499
508513  508517  508531  508549  508559  508567  508577  508579  508583  508619  508621
508637  508643  508661  508693  508709  508727  508771  508789  508799  508811  508817
508841  508847  508867  508901  508903  508909  508913  508919  508931  508943  508951
508957  508961  508969  508973  508987  509023  509027  509053  509063  509071  509087
509101  509123  509137  509147  509149  509203  509221  509227  509239  509263  509281
509287  509293  509297  509317  509329  509359  509363  509389  509393  509413  509417
509429  509441  509449  509477  509513  509521  509543  509549  509557  509563  509569
509573  509581  509591  509603  509623  509633  509647  509653  509659  509681  509687
509689  509693  509699  509723  509731  509737  509741  509767  509783  509797  509801
509837  509843  509863  509867  509879  509909  509911  509921  509939  509947
509959  509963  509989  510007  510031  510047  510049  510061  510067  510073  510077
510079  510089  510101  510121  510127  510137  510157  510179  510199  510203  510217
510227  510233  510241  510247  510253  510271  510287  510299  510311  510319  510331
510361  510379  510383  510401  510403  510449  510451  510457  510463  510481  510529
510551  510553  510569  510581  510583  510589  510611  510613  510617  510619  510677
510683  510691  510707  510709  510751  510767  510773  510793  510803  510817  510823
510827  510847  510889  510907  510919  510931  510941  510943  510989  511001  511013
511019  511033  511039  511057  511061  511087  511109  511111  511123  511151  511153
511163  511169  511171  511177  511193  511201  511211  511213  511223  511237  511243
511261  511279  511289  511297  511327  511333  511337  511351  511361  511387  511391
511409  511417  511439  511447  511453  511457  511463  511477  511487  511507  511519
511523  511541  511549  511559  511573  511579  511583  511591  511603  511627  511631
511633  511669  511691  511703  511711  511723  511757  511787  511793  511801  511811
511831  511843  511859  511867  511873  511891  511897  511909  511933  511939  511961
511963  511991  511997  512009  512011  512021  512047  512059  512093  512101  512137
512147  512167  512207  512249  512251  512269  512287  512311  512321  512333  512353
512389  512419  512429  512443  512467  512497  512503  512507  512521  512531  512537
512543  512569  512573  512579  512581  512591  512593  512597  512609  512621  512641
512657  512663  512671  512683  512711  512713  512717  512741  512747  512761  512767
512779  512797  512803  512819  512821  512843  512849  512891  512899  512903  512917
512921  512927  512929  512959  512977  512989  512999  513001  513013  513017  513031
513041  513047  513053  513059  513067  513083  513101  513103  513109  513131  513137
513157  513167  513169  513173  513203  513239  513257  513269  513277  513283  513307
513311  513313  513319  513341  513347  513353  513367  513371  513397  513407  513419
513427  513431  513439  513473  513479  513481  513509  513511  513529  513533  513593
513631  513641  513649  513673  513679  513683  513691  513697  513719  513727  513731
513739  513749  513761  513767  513769  513781  513839  513841  513871  513881
513899  513917  513923  513937  513943  513977  513991  514001  514009  514013  514021
514049  514051  514057  514061  514079  514081  514093  514103  514117  514123  514127
514147  514177  514187  514201  514219  514229  514243  514247  514249  514271  514277
514289  514309  514313  514333  514343  514357  514361  514379  514399  514417  514429
514453  514499  514513  514519  514523  514529  514531  514543  514561  514571
514621  514637  514639  514643  514649  514651  514669  514681  514711  514733  514739
514741  514747  514757  514767  514769  514783  514793  514819  514823  514831  514841
514847  514853  514859  514867  514873  514889  514903  514933  514939  514949  514967
515041  515087  515089  515111  515143  515149  515153  515173  515191  515227  515231
515233  515237  515279  515293  515311  515323  515333  515357  515369  515371  515377
515381  515401  515429  515477  515507  515519  515539  515563  515579  515587  515597
515611  515621  515639  515651  515653  515663  515677  515681  515687  515693  515701
515737  515741  515761  515771  515773  515777  515783  515803  515813  515839  515843
515857  515861  515873  515887  515917  515923  515929  515941  515951  515969  515993
516017  516023  516049  516053  516077  516091  516127  516151  516157  516161  516163
516169  516179  516193  516199  516209  516223  516227  516233  516247  516251  516253
516277  516283  516289  516319  516323  516349  516361  516371  516377  516391
516407  516421  516431  516433  516437  516449  516457  516469  516493  516499  516517
516521  516539  516541  516563  516587  516589  516599  516611  516617  516619  516623
516643  516653  516673  516679  516689  516701  516709  516713  516721  516727  516757
516793  516811  516821  516829  516839  516847  516871  516877  516883  516907  516911
```

```
516931  516947  516949  516959  516973  516977  516979  516991  517003  517043  517061
517067  517073  517079  517081  517087  517091  517129  517151  517169  517177  517183
517189  517207  517211  517217  517229  517241  517243  517249  517261  517267  517277
517289  517303  517337  517343  517367  517373  517381  517393  517399  517403  517411
517417  517457  517459  517469  517471  517481  517487  517499  517501  517507  517511
517513  517547  517549  517553  517571  517577  517589  517597  517603  517609  517613
517619  517637  517639  517711  517717  517721  517729  517733  517739  517747  517817
517823  517831  517861  517873  517877  517901  517919  517927  517931  517949  517967
517981  517991  517999  518017  518047  518057  518059  518083  518089  518101  518113
518123  518129  518131  518137  518153  518159  518171  518179  518191  518207  518209
518233  518237  518239  518249  518261  518291  518299  518311  518327  518341  518387
518389  518411  518417  518429  518431  518447  518467  518471  518473  518509  518521
518533  518543  518579  518587  518597  518611  518621  518657  518689  518699  518717
518729  518737  518741  518743  518747  518759  518761  518767  518779  518801  518803
518807  518809  518813  518831  518863  518867  518893  518911  518933  518953  518981
518983  518989  519011  519031  519037  519067  519083  519089  519091  519097  519107
519119  519121  519131  519157  519161  519193  519217  519227  519229  519247  519257
519269  519283  519287  519301  519307  519349  519353  519359  519371  519373  519383
519391  519413  519427  519433  519457  519487  519499  519509  519521  519523  519527
519539  519551  519553  519577  519581  519587  519611  519619  519643  519647  519667
519683  519691  519703  519713  519733  519737  519769  519787  519793  519797  519803
519817  519863  519881  519889  519907  519917  519919  519923  519931  519943  519947
519971  519989  519997  520019  520021  520031  520043  520063  520067  520073  520103
520111  520123  520129  520151  520193  520213  520241  520279  520291  520297  520307
520309  520313  520339  520349  520357  520361  520363  520369  520379  520381  520393
520409  520411  520423  520427  520433  520447  520451  520529  520547  520549  520567
520571  520589  520607  520609  520621  520631  520633  520649  520679  520691  520699
520703  520717  520721  520747  520759  520763  520787  520813  520837  520841  520853
520867  520889  520913  520921  520943  520957  520963  520967  520969  520981  521009
521021  521023  521039  521041  521047  521051  521063  521107  521119  521137  521153
521161  521167  521173  521177  521179  521201  521231  521243  521251  521267  521281
521299  521309  521317  521329  521357  521359  521363  521369  521377  521393  521399
521401  521429  521447  521471  521483  521491  521497  521503  521519  521527  521533
521537  521539  521551  521567  521581  521603  521641  521657  521659  521663  521669
521671  521693  521707  521723  521743  521749  521753  521767  521777  521789  521791
521809  521813  521819  521831  521861  521869  521889  521919  521923  521931  521947
521923  521929  521981  521993  521999  522017  522037  522047  522059  522061  522073
522079  522083  522113  522127  522157  522161  522167  522191  522199  522211  522227
522229  522233  522239  522251  522259  522281  522283  522289  522317  522323  522337
522371  522373  522383  522391  522409  522413  522439  522449  522469  522479  522497
522517  522521  522523  522551  522553  522559  522601  522623  522637  522659  522661
522673  522677  522679  522689  522703  522707  522719  522737  522749  522757  522761
522763  522787  522811  522827  522829  522839  522853  522857  522871  522881  522883
522887  522919  522943  522947  522959  522961  522989  523007  523021  523031  523049
523093  523097  523109  523129  523169  523177  523207  523213  523219  523261  523297
523333  523349  523351  523357  523387  523403  523417  523427  523433  523453  523459
523463  523487  523489  523493  523511  523519  523541  523543  523553  523571  523573
523577  523597  523603  523631  523637  523639  523657  523667  523669  523673  523681
523717  523729  523741  523759  523763  523771  523777  523793  523801  523829  523847
523867  523877  523903  523907  523927  523937  523949  523969  523987  523997  524047
524053  524057  524063  524071  524081  524087  524099  524113  524119  524123  524149
524171  524189  524197  524201  524203  524219  524221  524231  524243  524257  524261
524269  524287  524309  524341  524347  524351  524353  524369  524387  524389  524411
524413  524429  524453  524497  524507  524509  524519  524521  524591  524593  524599
524633  524669  524681  524683  524701  524707  524731  524743  524789  524801  524803
524827  524831  524857  524863  524869  524873  524893  524899  524921  524933  524939
524941  524947  524957  524959  524963  524969  524971  524981  524983  524999  525001
525013  525017  525029  525043  525101  525121  525127  525137  525143  525157  525167
525191  525193  525199  525209  525221  525241  525247  525253  525257  525299  525313
525353  525359  525361  525373  525377  525379  525391  525397  525409  525431  525433
525439  525457  525461  525467  525469  525493  525517  525529  525533  525541  525571
525583  525593  525599  525607  525641  525649  525671  525677  525697  525709  525713
525719  525727  525731  525739  525769  525773  525781  525809  525817  525839  525869
525871  525887  525893  525913  525923  525937  525947  525949  525953  525961  525979
525983  526027  526037  526049  526051  526063  526067  526069  526073  526087  526117
526121  526139  526157  526159  526189  526193  526199  526213  526223  526231  526249
526271  526283  526289  526291  526297  526307  526367  526373  526381  526387  526391
526397  526423  526429  526441  526453  526459  526483  526499  526501  526511  526531
526543  526571  526573  526583  526601  526619  526627  526633  526637  526649  526651
526657  526667  526679  526681  526703  526709  526717  526733  526739  526741  526759
526763  526777  526781  526829  526831  526837  526853  526859  526871  526909  526913
526931  526937  526943  526951  526957  526963  526993  526997  527053  527057  527063
527069  527071  527081  527099  527123  527129  527143  527159  527161  527173  527179
527203  527207  527209  527237  527251  527273  527281  527291  527327  527333  527347
527353  527377  527381  527393  527399  527407  527411  527419  527441  527447  527453
527489  527507  527533  527557  527563  527581  527591  527599  527603  527623  527627
527633  527671  527699  527701  527729  527741  527749  527753  527789  527803  527809
527819  527843  527851  527869  527881  527887  527909  527921  527929  527941  527981
527983  527987  527993  528001  528013  528041  528043  528053  528091  528097  528107
528127  528131  528137  528163  528167  528191  528197  528217  528223  528247  528263
528289  528299  528313  528317  528329  528373  528383  528391  528401  528403  528413
528419  528433  528469  528487  528491  528509  528511  528527  528559  528611  528623
528629  528631  528659  528667  528673  528679  528691  528707  528709  528719  528763
528779  528791  528799  528811  528821  528823  528833  528863  528877  528881  528883
528889  528911  528929  528947  528967  528973  528991  529003  529007  529027  529033
529037  529043  529049  529051  529097  529103  529117  529121  529127  529129  529153
529157  529181  529183  529213  529229  529237  529241  529259  529271  529273  529301
529307  529313  529327  529343  529349  529357  529381  529393  529411  529421  529423
529471  529489  529513  529517  529519  529531  529547  529577  529579  529603  529619
```

```
529637  529649  529657  529673  529681  529687  529691  529693  529709  529723  529741
529747  529751  529807  529811  529813  529819  529829  529847  529871  529927  529933
529939  529957  529961  529973  529979  529981  529987  529999  530017  530021  530027
530041  530051  530063  530087  530093  530129  530137  530143  530177  530183  530197
530203  530209  530227  530237  530249  530251  530261  530267  530279  530293  530297
530303  530329  530333  530339  530353  530359  530389  530393  530401  530429  530443
530447  530501  530507  530513  530527  530531  530533  530539  530549  530567  530597
530599  530603  530609  530641  530653  530659  530669  530693  530701  530711  530713
530731  530741  530743  530753  530767  530773  530797  530807  530833  530837  530843
530851  530857  530861  530869  530897  530911  530947  530969  530977  530983  530989
531017  531023  531043  531071  531079  531101  531103  531121  531133  531143  531163
531169  531173  531197  531203  531229  531239  531253  531263  531281  531287  531299
531331  531337  531343  531347  531353  531359  531383  531457  531481  531497  531521
531547  531551  531569  531571  531581  531589  531611  531613  531623  531631  531637
531667  531673  531689  531701  531731  531793  531799  531821  531823  531827  531833
531841  531847  531857  531863  531871  531877  531901  531911  531919  531977  531983
531989  531997  532001  532009  532027  532033  532061  532069  532093  532099  532141
532153  532159  532163  532183  532187  532193  532199  532241  532249  532261  532267
532277  532283  532307  532313  532327  532331  532333  532349  532373  532379  532391
532403  532417  532421  532439  532447  532451  532453  532489  532501  532523  532529
532531  532537  532547  532561  532601  532603  532607  532619  532621  532633  532639
532663  532669  532687  532691  532709  532733  532739  532751  532757  532771  532781
532783  532789  532801  532811  532823  532849  532853  532867  532907  532919  532949
532951  532981  532993  532999  533003  533009  533011  533033  533051  533053  533063
533077  533089  533111  533129  533149  533167  533177  533189  533191  533213  533219
533227  533237  533249  533257  533261  533263  533297  533303  533317  533321  533327
533353  533363  533371  533389  533399  533413  533447  533453  533459  533509  533543
533549  533573  533581  533593  533633  533641  533671  533693  533711  533713  533719
533723  533737  533747  533777  533801  533809  533821  533831  533837  533857  533879
533887  533893  533909  533921  533927  533959  533963  533969  533971  533989  533993
533999  534007  534013  534019  534029  534043  534047  534049  534059  534073  534077
534091  534101  534113  534137  534167  534173  534199  534203  534211  534229  534241
534253  534283  534301  534307  534311  534323  534329  534341  534367  534371  534403
534407  534431  534439  534473  534491  534511  534529  534553  534551  534577  534581
534601  534607  534617  534629  534631  534637  534647  534649  534659  534661  534671
534697  534707  534739  534749  534811  534827  534839  534841  534851  534857  534883
534889  534913  534923  534931  534943  534949  534971  535013  535019  535033  535037
535061  535099  535103  535123  535133  535151  535159  535169  535181  535193  535207
535219  535229  535237  535243  535273  535303  535319  535333  535349  535351  535361
535387  535391  535399  535481  535487  535489  535499  535511  535523  535529  535547
535571  535573  535589  535607  535609  535627  535637  535663  535669  535679
535697  535709  535727  535741  535751  535757  535771  535783  535793  535811  535849
535859  535861  535879  535919  535937  535939  535943  535957  535967  535973  535991
535999  536017  536023  536051  536057  536059  536069  536087  536099  536101  536111
536141  536147  536149  536189  536191  536203  536213  536219  536227  536233  536243
536267  536273  536279  536281  536287  536293  536311  536323  536353  536357  536377
536399  536407  536423  536441  536443  536447  536449  536453  536461  536467  536479
536491  536509  536513  536531  536533  536561  536563  536593  536609  536621  536633
536651  536671  536677  536687  536699  536717  536719  536729  536743  536749  536771
536773  536777  536779  536791  536801  536803  536839  536849  536857  536867  536869
536891  536909  536917  536929  536933  536947  536953  536971  536989  536999
537001  537007  537011  537023  537029  537037  537041  537067  537071  537079  537091
537127  537133  537143  537157  537169  537181  537191  537197  537221  537233  537241
537269  537281  537287  537307  537331  537343  537347  537373  537379  537401  537403
537413  537497  537527  537547  537569  537583  537587  537599  537611  537637  537661
537673  537679  537703  537709  537739  537743  537749  537769  537773  537781  537787
537793  537811  537841  537847  537853  537877  537883  537899  537913  537919  537941
537991  538001  538019  538049  538051  538073  538079  538093  538117  538121  538123
538127  538147  538151  538157  538159  538163  538199  538201  538247  538249  538259
538267  538283  538297  538301  538303  538309  538331  538333  538357  538367  538397
538399  538411  538423  538457  538471  538481  538487  538511  538513  538519  538523
538529  538553  538561  538567  538579  538589  538597  538621  538649  538651  538697
538711  538717  538721  538723  538739  538751  538763  538771  538777  538789  538799
538801  538817  538823  538829  538841  538871  538877  538921  538927  538931  538939
538943  538987  539003  539009  539039  539047  539089  539093  539101  539107  539111
539113  539129  539141  539153  539159  539167  539171  539207  539219  539233  539237
539261  539267  539269  539293  539303  539309  539311  539321  539323  539339  539347
539351  539389  539401  539447  539449  539479  539501  539503  539507  539509  539533
539573  539621  539629  539633  539639  539641  539653  539663  539677  539687  539711
539713  539729  539741  539743  539761  539783  539797  539837  539843  539849
539863  539881  539897  539899  539921  539947  539993  540041  540061  540079  540101
540119  540121  540139  540149  540157  540167  540173  540179  540181  540187  540203
540217  540233  540251  540269  540271  540283  540301  540307  540343  540347  540349
540367  540373  540377  540383  540389  540391  540433  540437  540461  540469  540509
540511  540517  540539  540541  540557  540559  540577  540587  540599  540611  540613
540619  540629  540677  540679  540689  540691  540697  540703  540713  540751  540769
540773  540779  540781  540803  540809  540823  540851  540863  540871  540877  540901
540907  540961  540989  541001  541007  541027  541049  541061  541087  541091  541129
541133  541141  541153  541181  541193  541201  541217  541231  541237  541249  541267
541271  541283  541301  541309  541339  541349  541361  541363  541369  541381  541391
541417  541439  541447  541469  541483  541507  541511  541523  541529  541531  541537
541543  541547  541549  541571  541577  541579  541589  541613  541631  541657  541661
541669  541693  541699  541711  541721  541727  541759  541763  541771  541777  541781
541799  541817  541831  541837  541859  541889  541901  541927  541951  541967  541987
541991  541993  541999  542021  542023  542027  542053  542063  542071  542081  542083
542093  542111  542117  542119  542123  542131  542141  542149  542153  542167  542183
542189  542197  542207  542219  542237  542251  542261  542263  542281  542293  542299
542323  542371  542401  542441  542447  542461  542467  542483  542489  542497  542519
542533  542537  542539  542551  542557  542567  542579  542587  542599  542603  542683
```

```
542687  542693  542713  542719  542723  542747  542761  542771  542783  542791  542797
542821  542831  542837  542873  542891  542911  542921  542923  542933  542939  542947
542951  542981  542987  542999  543017  543019  543029  543061  543097  543113  543131
543139  543143  543149  543157  543161  543163  543187  543203  543217  543223  543227
543233  543241  543253  543259  543281  543287  543289  543299  543307  543311  543313
543341  543349  543353  543359  543379  543383  543407  543427  543463  543497  543503
543509  543539  543551  543553  543593  543601  543607  543611  543617  543637  543659
543661  543671  543679  543689  543703  543707  543713  543769  543773  543787  543791
543793  543797  543811  543827  543841  543859  543867  543871  543877  543883
543887  543889  543901  543911  543929  543967  543971  543997  544001  544007  544009
544013  544021  544031  544097  544099  544109  544123  544129  544133  544139  544171
544177  544183  544199  544223  544259  544273  544277  544279  544367  544373  544399
544403  544429  544451  544471  544477  544487  544501  544513  544517  544543  544549
544601  544613  544627  544631  544651  544667  544699  544717  544721  544723  544727
544757  544759  544771  544781  544793  544807  544813  544837  544861  544877  544879
544883  544889  544897  544903  544919  544927  544937  544961  544963  544979  545023
545029  545033  545057  545063  545087  545089  545093  545117  545131  545141  545143
545161  545189  545203  545213  545231  545239  545257  545267  545291  545329  545371
545387  545429  545437  545443  545449  545473  545477  545483  545497  545521  545527
545533  545543  545549  545551  545579  545599  545609  545617  545621  545641  545647
545651  545663  545711  545723  545731  545747  545749  545759  545773  545789  545791
545827  545843  545863  545873  545893  545899  545911  545917  545929  545933  545939
545947  545959  546001  546017  546019  546031  546047  546053  546067  546071  546097
546101  546103  546109  546137  546149  546151  546173  546179  546197  546211  546233
546239  546241  546253  546263  546283  546289  546317  546323  546341  546349  546353
546361  546367  546373  546391  546461  546467  546479  546509  546523  546547  546569
546583  546587  546599  546613  546617  546619  546631  546643  546661  546671  546677
546683  546691  546709  546719  546731  546739  546781  546841  546859  546863  546869
546881  546893  546919  546937  546943  546947  546961  546967  546977  547007  547021
547037  547061  547087  547093  547097  547103  547121  547133  547139  547171  547223
547229  547237  547241  547249  547271  547273  547291  547301  547321  547357  547361
547363  547369  547373  547387  547397  547399  547411  547441  547453  547471  547483
547487  547493  547499  547501  547513  547529  547537  547559  547567  547577  547583
547601  547609  547619  547627  547639  547643  547661  547663  547681  547709  547727
547741  547747  547753  547763  547769  547787  547817  547819  547823  547831  547849
547853  547871  547889  547901  547909  547951  547957  547999  548003  548009  548059
548069  548083  548089  548099  548117  548123  548143  548153  548189  548201  548213
548221  548227  548239  548243  548263  548291  548309  548323  548347  548351  548363
548371  548393  548399  548407  548417  548443  548441  548453  548459  548461  548489
548501  548503  548519  548521  548533  548543  548557  548567  548579  548591  548623
548629  548657  548671  548687  548693  548707  548711  548719  548749  548753  548761
548771  548783  548791  548827  548831  548833  548837  548843  548851  548861  548869
548893  548897  548903  548909  548927  548953  548957  549001  549011  549013
549023  549037  549071  549089  549097  549121  549139  549149  549161
549163  549167  549169  549193  549203  549221  549229  549247  549257  549259  549281
549313  549319  549323  549331  549379  549391  549403  549421  549431  549443  549449
549481  549503  549509  549511  549517  549533  549547  549551  549553  549569  549587
549589  549607  549623  549641  549643  549649  549667  549683  549691  549701  549707
549719  549733  549737  549739  549749  549751  549767  549817  549833  549839
549863  549877  549883  549911  549937  549943  549949  549977  549979  550007  550009
550027  550049  550061  550063  550073  550111  550117  550127  550129  550139  550163
550169  550177  550181  550189  550211  550213  550241  550267  550279  550283  550289
550309  550337  550351  550369  550379  550427  550439  550441  550447  550457  550469
550471  550489  550513  550519  550531  550541  550553  550577  550607  550609  550621
550631  550637  550651  550657  550661  550663  550679  550691  550703  550717  550721
550757  550763  550769  550801  550811  550813  550831  550841  550843  550859
550861  550903  550909  550937  550939  550951  550961  550969  550973  550993  550997
551003  551017  551027  551039  551059  551063  551069  551093  551099  551107  551113
551129  551143  551179  551197  551207  551219  551231  551233  551269  551281  551297
551311  551321  551339  551347  551363  551381  551387  551407  551423  551443  551461
551483  551489  551503  551519  551539  551543  551549  551557  551569  551581  551587
551597  551651  551653  551659  551671  551689  551693  551713  551717  551723  551729
551731  551743  551753  551767  551773  551801  551809  551813  551849  551861
551909  551911  551917  551927  551933  551951  551959  551963  551981  552001  552011
552029  552031  552047  552053  552059  552089  552091  552103  552107  552113  552127
552173  552179  552193  552217  552239  552241  552259  552263  552271  552283  552301
552317  552341  552353  552379  552397  552401  552403  552469  552473  552481  552491
552493  552511  552523  552527  552553  552581  552583  552589  552611  552649  552659
552677  552703  552707  552709  552731  552749  552751  552757  552787  552791  552793
552809  552821  552833  552841  552847  552859  552883  552887  552899  552913  552917
552971  552983  552991  553013  553037  553043  553051  553057  553067  553073  553093
553097  553099  553103  553123  553139  553141  553153  553171  553181  553193  553207
553211  553229  553249  553253  553277  553279  553309  553351  553363  553369  553411
553417  553433  553439  553457  553463  553471  553481  553507  553513  553517
553529  553543  553549  553561  553573  553583  553589  553591  553601  553607  553627
553649  553667  553681  553687  553699  553703  553727  553733  553747  553757
553759  553769  553789  553811  553837  553849  553867  553873  553897  553901  553919
553921  553933  553961  553963  553981  553991  554003  554011  554017  554053  554077
554087  554089  554117  554123  554129  554137  554167  554171  554179  554189  554207
554209  554233  554237  554263  554269  554299  554303  554317  554347  554377
554383  554417  554419  554431  554447  554453  554467  554503  554527  554531  554569
554573  554597  554611  554627  554633  554639  554641  554663  554669  554677  554699
554707  554711  554731  554747  554753  554767  554779  554789  554791  554797
554803  554821  554833  554837  554839  554843  554849  554887  554891  554893  554899
554923  554947  554951  554959  554969  554977  555029  555041  555043  555053  555073
555077  555083  555091  555097  555109  555119  555143  555167  555209  555221  555251
555253  555257  555277  555287  555293  555301  555307  555337  555349  555361  555383
555391  555419  555421  555439  555461  555487  555491  555521  555523  555557  555589
555593  555637  555661  555671  555677  555683  555691  555697  555707  555739  555743
```

555761 555767 555823 555827 555829 555853 555857 555871 555931 555941 555953
555967 556007 556021 556027 556037 556043 556061 556067 556069 556093 556103
556123 556159 556177 556181 556211 556219 556229 556243 556253 556261 556267
556271 556273 556289 556289 556313 556321 556327 556331 556343 556351 556373
556399 556403 556441 556459 556477 556483 556487 556513 556519 556537 556559
556573 556579 556583 556601 556607 556609 556613 556627 556639 556651 556679
556687 556691 556693 556697 556709 556723 556727 556741 556753 556763 556769
556781 556789 556793 556799 556811 556817 556819 556823 556841 556849 556859
556867 556883 556891 556931 556939 556957 556967 556981 556987
556999 557017 557021 557027 557033 557041 557057 557059 557069 557087 557093
557153 557159 557197 557201 557261 557269 557273 557281 557303 557309 557321
557329 557339 557369 557371 557377 557423 557443 557449 557461 557483 557489
557519 557521 557533 557537 557551 557567 557573 557591 557611 557633 557639
557663 557671 557693 557717 557729 557731 557741 557743 557747 557759 557761
557779 557789 557801 557803 557831 557857 557861 557863 557891 557899 557903
557927 557981 557987 558007 558017 558029 558053 558067 558083 558091 558109
558113 558121 558139 558149 558167 558179 558197 558203 558209 558223 558241
558251 558253 558287 558289 558307 558319 558343 558401 558413 558421 558427
558431 558457 558469 558473 558479 558493 558497 558499 558521 558529 558533
558539 558541 558563 558583 558587 558599 558611 558629 558643 558661 558683
558703 558721 558731 558757 558769 558781 558787 558791 558793 558827 558829
558863 558869 558881 558883 558913 558931 558937 558947 558973 558979 558997
559001 559049 559051 559067 559081 559093 559099 559123 559133 559157 559177
559183 559201 559211 559213 559217 559219 559231 559243 559259 559277 559297
559313 559319 559343 559357 559367 559369 559397 559421 559451 559459 559469
559483 559501 559513 559523 559529 559541 559547 559549 559561 559571 559577
559583 559591 559597 559631 559633 559639 559649 559661 559673 559679 559687
559703 559709 559739 559747 559777 559781 559799 559807 559813 559831 559841
559849 559859 559877 559883 559901 559907 559913 559939 559957 559973 559991
560017 560023 560029 560039 560047 560081 560083 560089 560093 560107 560113
560117 560123 560137 560149 560159 560171 560173 560179 560191 560207 560213
560221 560227 560233 560237 560239 560243 560249 560281 560293 560297 560299
560311 560317 560341 560353 560393 560411 560437 560447 560459 560471 560477
560479 560489 560491 560501 560503 560531 560543 560551 560561 560597 560617
560621 560639 560641 560653 560669 560683 560689 560701 560719 560737 560753
560761 560767 560771 560783 560797 560803 560827 560837 560863 560869 560873
560887 560891 560893 560897 560929 560939 560941 560969 560977 561019 561047
561053 561059 561061 561079 561083 561091 561097 561101 561103 561109 561161
561173 561181 561191 561199 561229 561251 561277 561307 561313 561343 561347
561359 561367 561373 561377 561389 561409 561419 561439 561461 561521 561529
561551 561553 561559 561599 561607 561667 561703 561713 561733 561761 561767
561787 561797 561809 561829 561839 561907 561917 561923 561931 561943 561947
561961 561973 561983 561997 562007 562019 562021 562043 562091 562103 562129
562147 562169 562181 562193 562201 562231 562259 562271 562273 562283 562291
562297 562301 562307 562313 562333 562337 562349 562351 562357 562361 562399
562403 562409 562417 562421 562427 562439 562459 562477 562501 562517
562519 562537 562577 562579 562589 562591 562607 562613 562621 562631 562633
562651 562663 562669 562673 562691 562693 562699 562703 562711 562721 562739
562753 562759 562763 562781 562789 562813 562831 562841 562871 562897 562901
562909 562931 562943 562949 562963 562967 562973 562979 562987 562997 563009
563011 563021 563039 563041 563047 563051 563077 563081 563099 563113 563117
563119 563131 563149 563153 563183 563197 563219 563249 563263 563287 563327
563351 563357 563389 563401 563411 563413 563417 563419 563447 563449
563467 563489 563501 563503 563543 563551 563561 563587 563593 563599 563623
563657 563663 563723 563743 563747 563777 563809 563813 563821 563831 563837
563851 563869 563881 563887 563897 563929 563933 563947 563971 563987 563999
564013 564017 564041 564049 564059 564061 564089 564097 564103 564127 564133
564149 564163 564173 564191 564197 564227 564229 564233 564251 564257 564269
564271 564299 564301 564307 564313 564323 564353 564359 564367 564371 564373
564391 564401 564407 564409 564419 564437 564449 564457 564463 564467 564491
564497 564523 564533 564593 564607 564617 564643 564653 564661 564671 564679
564701 564703 564709 564713 564761 564779 564793 564797 564827 564871 564881
564899 564917 564919 564923 564943 564959 564973 564979 564983 564989 564997
565013 565039 565049 565057 565069 565109 565111 565127 565163 565171 565177
565183 565189 565207 565237 565241 565247 565259 565261 565273 565283 565289
565303 565319 565333 565337 565343 565361 565379 565381 565387 565391 565393
565427 565429 565441 565451 565463 565469 565483 565489 565507 565511 565517
565519 565549 565553 565559 565567 565571 565583 565589 565597 565603 565613
565637 565651 565661 565667 565723 565727 565769 565771 565787 565793 565813
565849 565867 565889 565891 565907 565909 565919 565921 565937 565973 565979
565997 566011 566023 566047 566057 566077 566089 566101 566107 566131 566149
566161 566173 566179 566183 566201 566213 566227 566231 566233 566273 566311
566323 566347 566387 566393 566413 566417 566429 566431 566437 566441 566443
566453 566521 566537 566539 566543 566549 566551 566557 566563 566567 566617
566623 566639 566653 566659 566677 566681 566683 566701 566707 566717 566719
566723 566737 566759 566767 566791 566821 566833 566851 566857 566879 566911
566939 566947 566963 566971 566977 566987 566999 567011 567013 567031 567053
567059 567067 567097 567101 567107 567121 567143 567179 567181 567203 567209
567257 567263 567277 567319 567323 567367 567377 567383 567389 567401 567407
567439 567449 567451 567467 567487 567493 567499 567527 567529 567533 567569
567601 567607 567631 567649 567653 567659 567661 567667 567673 567689 567719
567737 567751 567761 567767 567779 567793 567811 567829 567841 567857 567863
567871 567877 567881 567883 567899 567937 567943 567947 567961 567971 567979
567991 567997 568019 568027 568033 568049 568069 568091 568097 568109 568133
568151 568153 568163 568171 568177 568187 568189 568193 568201 568207 568231
568237 568241 568273 568279 568289 568303 568349 568363 568367 568387 568391
568433 568439 568441 568453 568471 568481 568493 568523 568541 568549 568577
568609 568619 568627 568643 568657 568669 568679 568691 568699 568709 568723
568751 568783 568787 568807 568823 568831 568853 568877 568891 568903 568907

```
568913  568921  568963  568979  568987  568991  568999  569003  569011  569021  569047
569053  569057  569071  569077  569081  569083  569111  569117  569137  569141  569159
569161  569189  569197  569201  569209  569213  569237  569243  569249  569251  569263
569267  569269  569321  569323  569369  569417  569419  569423  569431  569447  569461
569479  569497  569507  569533  569573  569579  569581  569599  569603  569609  569617
569623  569659  569663  569671  569683  569711  569713  569717  569729  569731  569747
569759  569771  569773  569797  569799  569809  569813  569819  569831  569839  569851
569861  569869  569887  569893  569897  569903  569927  569939  569957  569983  570001
570013  570029  570041  570043  570047  570049  570071  570077  570079  570083  570091
570107  570109  570113  570131  570139  570161  570173  570181  570191  570217  570221
570233  570253  570329  570359  570373  570379  570389  570391  570403  570407  570413
570419  570421  570461  570463  570467  570487  570491  570497  570499  570509  570511
570527  570529  570539  570547  570553  570569  570587  570601  570613  570637  570643
570649  570659  570667  570671  570677  570683  570697  570719  570733  570737  570743
570781  570821  570827  570839  570841  570851  570853  570859  570881  570887  570901
570919  570937  570949  570959  570961  570967  570991  571001  571019  571031  571037
571069  571093  571099  571111  571133  571147  571157  571163  571199  571201
571211  571223  571229  571231  571261  571267  571279  571303  571321  571331  571339
571369  571381  571397  571399  571409  571433  571453  571471  571477  571531  571541
571579  571583  571589  571601  571603  571633  571657  571673  571679  571699  571709
571717  571721  571741  571751  571759  571777  571783  571789  571799  571801  571811
571841  571847  571853  571861  571867  571871  571877  571883  571903  571933  571939
571969  571973  572023  572027  572041  572051  572053  572059  572063  572069  572087
572093  572107  572137  572161  572177  572179  572183  572207  572233  572239  572251
572269  572281  572303  572311  572321  572323  572329  572333  572357  572387  572399
572417  572419  572423  572437  572449  572461  572471  572479  572491  572497  572519
572521  572549  572567  572573  572581  572587  572597  572599  572609  572629  572633
572639  572651  572653  572657  572659  572683  572687  572699  572707  572711  572749
572777  572791  572801  572807  572813  572821  572827  572833  572843  572867  572879
572881  572903  572909  572927  572933  572939  572941  572963  572969  572993  573007
573031  573047  573101  573107  573109  573119  573143  573161  573163  573179  573197
573247  573253  573263  573277  573289  573299  573317  573329  573341  573343  573371
573379  573383  573409  573437  573451  573457  573473  573479  573481  573487  573493
573497  573509  573511  573523  573527  573557  573569  573571  573637  573647  573673
573679  573691  573719  573737  573739  573757  573761  573763  573787  573791  573809
573817  573829  573847  573853  573863  573871  573883  573887  573899  573901  573929
573941  573953  573967  573973  573977  574003  574031  574033  574051  574061  574081
574099  574109  574127  574157  574159  574163  574169  574181  574183  574201  574219
574261  574279  574283  574289  574297  574307  574309  574363  574367  574373  574393
574423  574429  574433  574439  574477  574489  574493  574501  574507  574529  574543
574547  574597  574619  574621  574627  574631  574643  574657  574667  574687  574699
574703  574711  574723  574727  574733  574741  574789  574799  574801  574813  574817
574859  574907  574913  574933  574939  574949  574963  574967  574969  575009  575027
575053  575063  575077  575087  575109  575123  575129  575131  575137  575153
575173  575177  575203  575213  575219  575231  575243  575249  575251  575257  575261
575303  575311  575359  575369  575371  575401  575417  575429  575531  575541  575473
575479  575489  575503  575513  575551  575557  575573  575579  575581  575591  575593
575611  575623  575647  575651  575669  575677  575689  575693  575699  575711  575717
575723  575747  575753  575777  575791  575821  575837  575849  575857  575863  575867
575893  575903  575921  575923  575941  575957  575959  575963  575987  576001  576013
576019  576029  576031  576049  576089  576101  576119  576131  576151  576161
576167  576179  576193  576203  576211  576217  576221  576223  576227  576287  576293
576299  576313  576319  576341  576377  576379  576391  576421  576467  576431  576439
576461  576469  576473  576493  576509  576523  576529  576533  576539  576551  576553
576577  576581  576613  576617  576637  576647  576649  576659  576671  576677  576683
576689  576701  576703  576721  576727  576731  576739  576743  576749  576757  576769
576787  576791  576881  576883  576889  576899  576943  576949  576967  576977  577007
577009  577033  577043  577063  577067  577069  577081  577097  577111  577123  577147
577151  577153  577169  577177  577193  577219  577249  577259  577271  577279  577307
577327  577331  577333  577349  577351  577363  577387  577397  577399  577427  577453
577457  577463  577471  577483  577513  577517  577523  577529  577531  577537  577547
577559  577573  577589  577601  577613  577627  577637  577639  577667  577721  577739
577751  577757  577781  577799  577807  577817  577831  577849  577867  577873  577879
577897  577901  577909  577919  577931  577937  577939  577957  577979  577981  578021
578029  578041  578047  578063  578077  578093  578117  578131  578167  578183  578191
578203  578209  578251  578267  578297  578299  578309  578311  578317  578327
578353  578363  578371  578399  578401  578407  578419  578441  578453  578467  578477
578483  578489  578497  578503  578533  578537  578563  578573  578581  578587
578597  578603  578609  578621  578647  578659  578687  578689  578693  578701  578759
578729  578741  578777  578779  578801  578803  578819  578827  578837  578839  578843
578857  578861  578881  578917  578923  578957  578959  578971  578999  579011  579017
579023  579053  579079  579083  579107  579113  579119  579133  579179  579197  579199
579239  579251  579259  579263  579277  579281  579283  579287  579311  579331  579353
579379  579407  579409  579427  579433  579451  579473  579497  579499  579503  579517
579521  579529  579533  579541  579563  579569  579571  579583  579587  579611
579613  579629  579637  579641  579643  579653  579673  579701  579707  579713  579721
579737  579757  579763  579773  579779  579809  579829  579851  579869  579877  579881
579883  579907  579917  579949  579967  579973  579983  580001  580031
580033  580079  580081  580093  580133  580163  580169  580183  580187  580201  580213
580219  580231  580259  580301  580303  580331  580339  580343  580357  580361
580373  580379  580381  580409  580417  580471  580477  580487  580513  580529  580549
580553  580561  580577  580607  580627  580631  580633  580639  580663  580673  580687
580691  580693  580711  580717  580733  580747  580757  580763  580787  580793
580807  580813  580837  580843  580859  580871  580889  580891  580901  580913  580919
580927  580939  580969  580981  580997  581029  581041  581047  581069  581089
581099  581101  581137  581143  581149  581171  581173  581177  581183  581197  581201
581227  581237  581239  581261  581263  581293  581303  581311  581323  581333  581341
581351  581353  581369  581377  581393  581407  581411  581429  581443  581447  581459
581473  581491  581521  581527  581549  581551  581557  581573  581597  581599  581617
```

```
581639  581657  581663  581683  581687  581699  581701  581729  581731  581743  581753
581767  581773  581797  581809  581821  581843  581857  581863  581869  581873  581891
581909  581921  581941  581947  581953  581981  581983  582011  582013  582017  582031
582037  582067  582083  582119  582137  582139  582157  582161  582167  582173  582181
582203  582209  582221  582223  582227  582247  582251  582299  582317  582319  582371
582391  582409  582419  582427  582433  582451  582457  582469  582499  582509  582511
582541  582551  582563  582587  582601  582623  582643  582649  582677  582689  582691
582719  582721  582727  582731  582737  582761  582763  582767  582773  582781  582793
582809  582821  582851  582853  582887  582899  582931  582937  582949  582961
582971  582973  582983  583007  583013  583019  583021  583031  583069  583087  583127
583139  583147  583153  583169  583171  583181  583189  583207  583213  583229  583237
583249  583267  583273  583279  583291  583301  583337  583339  583351  583367  583391
583397  583403  583409  583417  583421  583447  583459  583469  583481  583493  583501
583511  583519  583523  583537  583543  583577  583603  583613  583619  583621  583631
583651  583657  583669  583673  583697  583727  583733  583753  583769  583777  583783
583789  583801  583841  583853  583859  583861  583873  583879  583903  583909  583937
583969  583981  583991  583997  584011  584027  584033  584053  584057  584063  584081
584099  584141  584153  584167  584183  584203  584249  584261  584279  584281  584303
584347  584359  584377  584387  584393  584399  584411  584417  584429  584447
584471  584473  584509  584531  584557  584561  584587  584593  584599  584603  584609
584621  584627  584659  584663  584677  584693  584699  584707  584713  584719  584723
584737  584767  584777  584789  584791  584809  584843  584849  584863  584869  584873  584879
584897  584911  584917  584923  584951  584963  584971  584981  584993  584999  585019
585023  585031  585037  585041  585043  585049  585061  585071  585073  585077  585107
585113  585119  585131  585149  585163  585199  585217  585251  585269  585271  585283
585289  585313  585317  585337  585341  585367  585383  585391  585413  585437  585443
585461  585467  585493  585503  585517  585547  585551  585569  585577  585577  585587
585593  585601  585619  585643  585653  585671  585677  585691  585721  585727  585733
585737  585743  585749  585757  585779  585791  585799  585839  585841  585847  585853
585857  585863  585877  585881  585883  585889  585899  585911  585913  585917  585919
585953  585959  585989  586007  586037  586051  586057  586067  586073  586087  586111
586121  586123  586129  586139  586147  586153  586189  586213  586237  586273  586277
586291  586301  586309  586319  586349  586361  586363  586367  586387  586403  586429
586433  586457  586459  586463  586471  586493  586499  586501  586541  586543  586567
586571  586577  586589  586601  586603  586609  586627  586631  586633  586667  586679
586693  586711  586723  586741  586769  586787  586793  586801  586811  586813  586819
586837  586841  586849  586871  586897  586903  586909  586919  586921  586933  586939
586951  586961  586973  586979  586981  587017  587021  587033  587051  587053  587057
587063  587087  587101  587107  587117  587123  587131  587137  587143  587149  587173
587179  587189  587201  587219  587263  587267  587269  587281  587287  587297  587303
587341  587371  587381  587387  587413  587417  587429  587437  587441  587459  587467
587473  587497  587513  587519  587527  587533  587539  587549  587551  587563  587579
587599  587603  587617  587621  587623  587633  587659  587669  587677  587687  587693
587711  587731  587737  587747  587749  587753  587771  587773  587789  587813  587827
587833  587849  587863  587887  587891  587897  587927  587933  587947  587959  587969
587971  587987  587989  587999  588011  588019  588037  588043  588061  588073  588079
588083  588097  588113  588121  588131  588151  588167  588169  588173  588191  588199
588229  588239  588241  588257  588277  588293  588311  588337  588359  588361  588383
588389  588397  588403  588433  588437  588463  588481  588493  588503  588509  588517
588521  588529  588569  588571  588619  588631  588641  588647  588649  588667  588673
588683  588703  588733  588737  588743  588767  588773  588779  588811  588827  588839
588871  588877  588881  588893  588911  588937  588941  588947  588949  588953  588977
589021  589027  589049  589063  589069  589111  589123  589139  589159  589163  589181
589187  589189  589207  589213  589219  589231  589241  589243  589273  589289  589291
589297  589327  589331  589349  589357  589387  589409  589439  589451  589453  589471
589481  589493  589507  589529  589531  589579  589583  589591  589601  589607  589609
589639  589643  589681  589711  589717  589751  589753  589759  589763  589783  589793
589807  589811  589847  589859  589861  589873  589877  589903  589921  589933
589993  589997  590021  590027  590033  590041  590071  590077  590099  590119  590123
590129  590131  590137  590141  590153  590171  590201  590207  590243  590251  590263
590267  590269  590279  590309  590321  590323  590327  590357  590363  590377  590383
590389  590399  590407  590431  590437  590489  590537  590543  590567  590573  590593
590599  590609  590627  590641  590647  590657  590659  590669  590713  590717  590719
590741  590753  590771  590797  590809  590813  590819  590833  590839  590867  590899
590921  590923  590929  590959  590963  590983  590987  591023  591053  591061  591067
591079  591089  591091  591113  591127  591131  591137  591161  591163  591181  591193
591233  591259  591271  591287  591289  591301  591317  591319  591341  591377  591391
591403  591407  591421  591431  591443  591457  591469  591499  591509  591523  591553
591559  591581  591599  591601  591611  591623  591649  591653  591659  591673  591691
591739  591739  591743  591749  591751  591757  591779  591787  591841  591847
591863  591881  591887  591893  591901  591937  591959  591973  592019  592027  592049
592057  592061  592073  592087  592099  592121  592129  592133  592139  592157  592199
592217  592219  592223  592237  592261  592289  592303  592307  592309  592321  592337
592343  592351  592357  592367  592369  592387  592391  592393  592429  592451  592453
592463  592469  592489  592507  592517  592531  592547  592561  592577  592589
592597  592601  592609  592621  592639  592643  592649  592661  592663  592681  592693
592723  592727  592741  592747  592759  592763  592793  592843  592849  592853  592861
592873  592877  592897  592903  592919  592931  592939  592967  592973  592987  592993
593003  593029  593041  593051  593059  593071  593081  593083  593111  593119  593141
593143  593149  593171  593179  593183  593207  593209  593213  593227  593231  593233
593251  593261  593273  593291  593293  593297  593321  593323  593353  593381  593387
593399  593401  593407  593429  593447  593449  593473  593479  593491  593497  593501
593507  593513  593519  593531  593539  593573  593587  593597  593603  593627  593629
593633  593641  593647  593689  593903  593707  593711  593767  593777  593783  593839
593851  593863  593869  593899  593903  593933  593951  593969  593977  593987  593993
594023  594037  594047  594091  594103  594107  594119  594137  594151  594157  594161
594163  594179  594193  594203  594211  594227  594241  594271  594281  594283  594287
594299  594311  594313  594329  594359  594367  594379  594397  594401  594403  594421
594427  594449  594457  594467  594469  594499  594511  594521  594523  594533  594551
```

```
594563  594569  594571  594577  594617  594637  594641  594653  594667  594679  594697
594709  594721  594739  594749  594751  594781  594793  594811  594823  594827  594829
594857  594889  594899  594911  594917  594929  594931  594953  594959  594961  594977
594989  595003  595037  595039  595043  595057  595069  595073  595081  595087  595093
595097  595117  595123  595129  595139  595141  595157  595159  595181  595183  595201
595207  595229  595247  595253  595261  595267  595271  595277  595291  595303  595313
595319  595333  595339  595351  595363  595373  595379  595381  595411  595451  595453
595481  595513  595519  595523  595547  595549  595571  595577  595579  595613  595627
595687  595703  595709  595711  595717  595733  595741  595801  595807  595811  595843
595873  595877  595927  595939  595943  595949  595951  595957  595961  595963  595967
595981  596009  596021  596027  596047  596053  596059  596069  596081  596083  596093
596117  596119  596143  596147  596159  596179  596209  596227  596231  596243  596251
596257  596261  596273  596279  596291  596293  596317  596341  596363  596369  596399
596419  596423  596461  596489  596503  596507  596537  596569  596573  596579  596587
596593  596599  596611  596623  596633  596653  596663  596669  596671  596693  596707
596737  596741  596749  596767  596779  596789  596803  596821  596831  596839  596851
596857  596863  596869  596879  596899  596917  596927  596929  596933  596941  596963
596977  596983  596987  597031  597049  597053  597059  597073  597127  597131  597133
597137  597169  597209  597221  597239  597253  597263  597269  597271  597301  597307
597349  597353  597361  597367  597383  597391  597403  597407  597409  597419  597433
597437  597451  597473  597497  597521  597523  597539  597551  597559  597577  597581
597589  597593  597599  597613  597637  597643  597659  597671  597673  597677  597679
597689  597697  597757  597761  597767  597769  597781  597803  597823  597827  597833
597853  597859  597869  597889  597899  597901  597923  597929  597967  597997  598007
598049  598051  598057  598079  598093  598099  598123  598127  598141  598151  598159
598163  598187  598189  598193  598219  598229  598261  598303  598307  598333  598363
598369  598379  598387  598399  598421  598427  598439  598447  598457  598463  598487
598489  598501  598537  598541  598571  598613  598643  598649  598651  598657  598669
598681  598687  598691  598711  598721  598727  598759  598777  598783  598789  598799
598817  598841  598853  598867  598877  598883  598891  598903  598931  598933  598963
598967  598973  598981  598987  598999  599003  599009  599023  599069  599087
599117  599143  599147  599149  599153  599191  599213  599231  599243  599251  599273
599281  599303  599309  599321  599341  599353  599359  599371  599383  599387  599399
599407  599413  599419  599429  599477  599479  599491  599513  599519  599537  599551
599561  599591  599597  599603  599611  599623  599629  599657  599663  599681  599693
599699  599701  599713  599719  599741  599759  599779  599783  599803  599831  599843
599857  599869  599891  599899  599927  599933  599939  599941  599959  599983  599993
599999  600011  600043  600053  600071  600073  600091  600101  600109  600167  600169
600203  600217  600221  600233  600239  600241  600247  600269  600283  600289  600293
600307  600311  600317  600319  600337  600359  600361  600367  600371  600401  600403
600407  600421  600433  600451  600463  600469  600487  600517  600529  600557
600569  600577  600601  600623  600631  600641  600659  600673  600689  600697  600701
600703  600727  600751  600791  600823  600827  600833  600841  600857  600877  600881
600883  600889  600893  600931  600947  600949  600959  600961  600973  600979  600983
601021  601031  601037  601039  601043  601061  601067  601079  601093  601127  601147
601187  601189  601193  601201  601207  601219  601231  601241  601247  601259  601267
601283  601291  601297  601309  601313  601319  601333  601339  601357  601379  601397
601411  601423  601439  601451  601457  601487  601507  601541  601543  601589  601591
601607  601631  601651  601669  601681  601697  601717  601747  601751  601759  601763
601771  601801  601807  601813  601819  601823  601831  601849  601873  601883  601889
601897  601903  601943  601961  601969  601981  602029  602033  602039  602047
602057  602081  602083  602087  602093  602099  602111  602137  602141  602143  602153
602179  602197  602201  602221  602227  602233  602257  602267  602269  602279  602297
602309  602311  602317  602321  602333  602341  602351  602377  602383  602401  602411
602431  602453  602461  602477  602479  602489  602501  602513  602521  602543  602551
602593  602597  602603  602621  602627  602629  602647  602657  602687  602689  602711
602713  602717  602729  602743  602753  602759  602773  602779  602801  602821  602831
602839  602867  602873  602881  602891  602909  602929  602947  602951  602971  602977
602983  602999  603011  603013  603023  603047  603077  603091  603101  603103  603131
603133  603149  603173  603191  603203  603209  603217  603227  603257  603283  603311
603319  603349  603389  603391  603401  603431  603443  603457  603467  603487  603503
603521  603523  603529  603541  603553  603557  603563  603569  603607  603613  603623
603641  603667  603679  603689  603719  603731  603739  603749  603761  603769  603781
603791  603793  603817  603821  603833  603847  603851  603853  603859  603881  603893
603899  603901  603907  603913  603917  603919  603923  603931  603937  603947  603949
603989  604001  604007  604013  604031  604057  604063  604069  604073  604171  604189
604223  604237  604243  604249  604259  604277  604291  604309  604313  604319  604339
604343  604349  604361  604369  604379  604397  604411  604427  604433  604441  604477
604481  604517  604529  604547  604559  604579  604589  604603  604609  604613  604619
604649  604651  604661  604697  604699  604711  604727  604729  604733  604753  604759
604771  604787  604801  604811  604819  604849  604861  604867
604883  604907  604931  604939  604949  604957  604973  604997  605009  605021  605023
605039  605051  605069  605071  605113  605117  605123  605147  605167  605173  605177
605191  605221  605233  605237  605239  605249  605257  605261  605309  605323  605329
605333  605347  605369  605393  605401  605411  605413  605443  605471  605477  605497
605503  605509  605531  605533  605543  605551  605573  605593  605597  605599  605603
605609  605617  605629  605639  605641  605687  605707  605719  605779  605789  605809
605837  605843  605861  605873  605879  605887  605893  605909  605921  605933
605947  605953  605977  605987  605993  606017  606029  606031  606037  606041  606049
606059  606077  606079  606083  606091  606113  606121  606131  606173  606181  606223
606241  606247  606251  606299  606301  606311  606313  606323  606341  606379  606383
606413  606433  606443  606449  606493  606497  606503  606521  606527  606539  606559
606569  606581  606587  606589  606607  606643  606649  606653  606659  606673  606721
606731  606733  606737  606743  606757  606791  606811  606829  606833  606839  606847
606857  606863  606869  606913  606919  606943  606959  606967  606977  606991  606997
607001  607003  607007  607037  607043  607049  607063  607067  607081  607091  607093
607097  607109  607127  607129  607147  607151  607153  607157  607163  607181  607199
607213  607219  607249  607253  607261  607301  607303  607307  607309  607319  607331
607337  607339  607349  607357  607363  607417  607421  607423  607471  607493  607517
```

```
607531  607549  607573  607583  607619  607627  607667  607669  607681  607697  607703
607721  607723  607727  607741  607769  607813  607819  607823  607837  607843  607861
607883  607889  607909  607921  607931  607933  607939  607951  607961  607967  607991
607993  608011  608029  608033  608087  608089  608099  608117  608123  608129  608131
608147  608161  608177  608191  608207  608213  608269  608273  608297  608299  608303
608339  608347  608357  608359  608369  608371  608383  608389  608393  608401  608411
608423  608429  608431  608459  608471  608483  608497  608519  608521  608527  608581
608591  608593  608609  608611  608633  608653  608659  608669  608677  608693  608701
608737  608743  608749  608759  608767  608789  608819  608831  608843  608851  608857
608863  608873  608887  608897  608899  608903  608941  608947  608953  608977  608987
608989  608999  609043  609047  609067  609071  609079  609101  609107  609113  609143
609149  609163  609173  609179  609199  609209  609221  609227  609233  609241  609253
609269  609277  609283  609289  609307  609313  609337  609359  609361  609373  609379
609391  609397  609403  609407  609421  609437  609443  609461  609487  609503  609509
609517  609527  609533  609541  609571  609589  609593  609599  609601  609607  609613
609617  609619  609641  609673  609683  609701  609709  609743  609751  609757  609779
609781  609803  609809  609821  609859  609877  609887  609907  609911  609913  609923
609929  609979  609989  609991  609997  610031  610063  610081  610123  610157  610163
610187  610193  610199  610217  610219  610229  610243  610271  610279  610289  610301
610327  610331  610339  610391  610409  610417  610429  610439  610447  610457  610469
610501  610523  610541  610543  610553  610559  610567  610579  610583  610619  610633
610639  610651  610661  610667  610681  610699  610703  610721  610733  610739  610741
610763  610781  610783  610787  610801  610817  610823  610829  610837  610843  610847
610849  610867  610877  610879  610891  610913  610919  610921  610933  610957  610969
610993  611011  611027  611033  611057  611069  611071  611081  611101  611111  611113
611131  611137  611147  611159  611207  611213  611257  611263  611279  611293  611297
611323  611333  611389  611393  611411  611419  611441  611449  611453  611459  611467
611483  611497  611531  611543  611549  611551  611557  611561  611587  611603  611621
611641  611657  611671  611683  611707  611729  611753  611791  611801  611803  611827
611833  611837  611839  611873  611879  611887  611903  611921  611927  611939  611951
611957  611969  611977  611993  611999  612011  612023  612037  612041  612043
612049  612061  612067  612071  612083  612107  612109  612113  612133  612137  612149
612169  612173  612181  612193  612217  612223  612229  612259  612263  612301  612307
612317  612319  612331  612341  612349  612371  612373  612377  612383  612401  612407
612439  612481  612497  612511  612553  612583  612589  612611  612613  612637  612643
612649  612671  612679  612713  612719  612727  612737  612751  612763  612791  612797
612809  612811  612817  612823  612841  612847  612853  612869  612877  612889  612923
612929  612947  612967  612971  612977  613007  613009  613013  613049  613061  613097
613099  613141  613153  613163  613169  613177  613181  613189  613199  613213  613219
613229  613231  613243  613247  613253  613267  613279  613289  613297  613337  613357
613363  613367  613381  613421  613427  613439  613441  613447  613451  613463  613469
613471  613493  613499  613507  613523  613549  613559  613573  613577  613597  613607
613609  613633  613637  613651  613661  613667  613673  613699  613733  613741  613747
613759  613763  613787  613813  613817  613829  613841  613849  613861  613883  613889
613903  613957  613967  613969  613981  613993  613999  614041  614051  614063  614071
614093  614101  614113  614129  614143  614147  614153  614167  614177  614179  614183
614219  614267  614279  614291  614293  614297  614321  614333  614377  614387  614413
614417  614437  614447  614443  614503  614527  614531  614543  614561  614563  614569
614609  614611  614617  614623  614633  614639  614657  614669  614683  614687
614693  614701  614717  614729  614741  614743  614749  614753  614759  614773  614827
614843  614849  614851  614863  614881  614889  614909  614917  614927  614963  614981
614983  615019  615031  615047  615053  615067  615101  615103  615107  615137  615151
615161  615187  615229  615233  615253  615259  615269  615289  615299  615313  615337
615341  615343  615367  615379  615389  615401  615403  615413  615427  615431  615437
615449  615473  615479  615491  615493  615497  615509  615521  615539  615557  615577
615599  615607  615617  615623  615661  615677  615679  615709  615721  615731  615739
615743  615749  615751  615761  615767  615773  615793  615799  615821  615827  615829
615833  615869  615883  615887  615907  615919  615941  615949  615971  615997  616003
616027  616051  616069  616073  616079  616103  616111  616117  616129  616139  616141
616157  616169  616171  616181  616207  616211  616219  616223  616229  616243
616261  616277  616289  616307  616313  616321  616327  616361  616367  616387  616391
616393  616409  616411  616433  616439  616459  616463  616481  616489  616501  616507
616513  616519  616523  616529  616537  616547  616559  616589  616597  616603  616643
616669  616673  616703  616717  616723  616729  616741  616757  616769  616783  616787
616789  616793  616799  616829  616841  616843  616849  616871  616877  616897  616909
616933  616943  616951  616961  616991  616993  616999  617011  617027  617039  617051
617053  617059  617077  617087  617107  617119  617129  617131  617147  617153  617161
617189  617191  617231  617233  617237  617249  617257  617269  617273  617293  617311
617327  617333  617339  617341  617359  617363  617369  617387  617401  617411  617429
617447  617453  617467  617471  617473  617479  617509  617521  617531  617537  617579
617587  617647  617651  617657  617677  617681  617689  617693  617699  617707  617717
617719  617723  617731  617759  617761  617767  617777  617791  617801  617809  617819
617843  617857  617873  617879  617891  617917  617951  617959  617963  617971  617983
618029  618031  618041  618049  618053  618083  618119  618131  618161  618173  618199
618227  618229  618253  618257  618269  618271  618287  618301  618311  618313  618329
618337  618347  618349  618361  618377  618407  618413  618421  618437  618439  618463
618509  618521  618547  618559  618571  618577  618581  618587  618589  618593  618619
618637  618643  618671  618679  618703  618707  618719  618799  618823  618833  618841
618847  618857  618859  618869  618883  618913  618929  618941  618971  618979  618991
618997  619007  619009  619019  619027  619033  619057  619061  619067  619079  619111
619117  619139  619159  619169  619181  619187  619189  619207  619247  619253  619261
619273  619277  619279  619303  619309  619313  619331  619363  619373  619391  619397
619471  619477  619511  619537  619543  619561  619573  619583  619589  619603  619607
619613  619621  619657  619669  619681  619687  619693  619711  619739  619741  619753
619763  619771  619793  619807  619811  619813  619819  619831  619841  619849  619867
619897  619909  619921  619967  619979  619981  619987  619999  620003  620029  620033
620051  620099  620111  620117  620159  620161  620171  620183  620197  620201  620227
620233  620237  620239  620251  620261  620297  620303  620311  620317  620329  620351
620359  620363  620377  620383  620393  620401  620413  620429  620437  620441  620461
```

```
620467  620491  620507  620519  620531  620549  620561  620567  620569  620579  620603
620623  620639  620647  620657  620663  620671  620689  620693  620717  620731  620743
620759  620771  620773  620777  620813  620821  620827  620831  620849  620869  620887
620909  620911  620929  620933  620947  620957  620981  620999  621007  621013  621017
621029  621031  621043  621059  621083  621097  621113  621133  621139  621143  621217
621223  621227  621239  621241  621259  621289  621301  621317  621337  621343  621347
621353  621359  621371  621389  621419  621427  621431  621443  621451  621461  621473
621521  621527  621541  621583  621611  621617  621619  621629  621631  621641  621671
621679  621697  621701  621703  621721  621739  621749  621757  621769  621779  621799
621821  621833  621869  621871  621883  621893  621913  621923  621937  621941  621983
621997  622009  622019  622043  622049  622051  622067  622073  622091  622103  622109
622123  622129  622133  622151  622157  622159  622177  622187  622189  622241  622243
622247  622249  622277  622301  622313  622331  622333  622337  622351  622367  622397
622399  622423  622477  622481  622483  622493  622513  622519  622529  622547  622549
622561  622571  622577  622603  622607  622613  622619  622621  622637  622639  622663
622669  622709  622723  622729  622751  622777  622781  622793  622813  622849  622861
622889  622901  622927  622943  622957  622967  622987  622997  623003  623009
623017  623023  623041  623057  623059  623071  623107  623171  623209  623221  623261
623263  623269  623279  623281  623291  623299  623303  623321  623327  623341  623351
623353  623383  623387  623393  623401  623417  623423  623431  623437  623477  623521
623531  623537  623563  623591  623617  623621  623653  623641  623653  623669  623671
623677  623681  623683  623699  623717  623719  623723  623729  623743  623759  623767
623771  623803  623839  623851  623867  623869  623879  623881  623893  623923  623929
623933  623947  623957  623963  623977  623983  623989  624007  624031  624037  624047
624049  624067  624089  624097  624119  624133  624139  624149  624163  624191  624199
624203  624209  624229  624233  624241  624251  624259  624271  624277  624311  624313
624319  624329  624331  624347  624391  624401  624419  624443  624451  624467  624469
624479  624487  624497  624509  624517  624521  624539  624541  624577  624593  624599
624601  624607  624643  624649  624667  624683  624707  624709  624721  624727  624731
624737  624763  624769  624787  624791  624797  624803  624809  624829  624839  624847
624851  624859  624917  624961  624973  624977  624983  624999  625007  625033  625057
625063  625087  625103  625109  625111  625129  625133  625169  625171  625181  625187
625199  625213  625231  625237  625253  625267  625279  625283  625307  625319  625343
625351  625367  625369  625397  625409  625451  625477  625483  625489  625507  625517
625529  625543  625589  625591  625609  625621  625627  625631  625637  625643  625657
625661  625663  625697  625699  625763  625777  625789  625811  625819  625831  625837
625861  625871  625883  625909  625913  625927  625939  625943  625969  625979  625997
626009  626011  626033  626051  626063  626113  626117  626147  626159  626173  626177
626189  626191  626201  626207  626239  626251  626261  626317  626323  626333  626341
626347  626363  626377  626389  626393  626443  626477  626489  626519  626533  626539
626581  626597  626599  626611  626617  626621  626623  626627  626629  626663  626771
626683  626687  626693  626701  626711  626713  626723  626741  626749  626761  626771
626783  626797  626809  626833  626837  626861  626867  626879  626921  626929  626947
626953  626959  626963  626987  627017  627041  627059  627071  627073  627083  627089
627091  627101  627119  627131  627139  627163  627169  627191  627197  627217  627227
627251  627257  627269  627271  627293  627301  627329  627349  627353  627377  627379
627383  627391  627433  627449  627479  627481  627491  627511  627541  627547  627559
627593  627611  627617  627619  627637  627643  627659  627661  627667  627673  627709
627721  627733  627749  627773  627787  627791  627797  627799  627811  627841  627859
627901  627911  627919  627943  627947  627953  627961  627973  628013  628021  628037
628049  628057  628063  628093  628097  628127  628139  628171  628183  628189
628193  628207  628213  628217  628219  628231  628261  628267  628289  628301  628319
628357  628363  628373  628379  628391  628399  628423  628427  628441  628477  628487
628493  628499  628547  628561  628583  628591  628651  628673  628679  628681  628687
628699  628709  628721  628753  628757  628759  628781  628783  628787  628799  628801
628811  628819  628841  628861  628877  628909  628913  628921  628937  628939  628973
628993  628997  629003  629009  629011  629023  629029  629059  629081  629113  629137
629141  629171  629177  629203  629243  629249  629263  629303  629341  629483
629351  629371  629381  629383  629401  629411  629417  629429  629449  629467  629483
629491  629509  629513  629537  629567  629569  629591  629593  629609  629611  629617
629623  629653  629683  629687  629689  629701  629711  629723  629737  629743  629747
629767  629773  629779  629803  629807  629819  629843  629857  629861  629873  629891
629897  629899  629903  629921  629927  629939  629953  629963  629977  629987  629989
630017  630023  630029  630043  630067  630101  630107  630127  630151  630163  630167
630169  630181  630193  630197  630229  630247  630263  630281  630299  630307  630319
630349  630353  630391  630397  630401  630451  630467  630473  630481  630493  630523
630529  630559  630577  630583  630587  630589  630593  630607  630613  630659  630677
630689  630701  630709  630713  630719  630733  630737  630749  630803  630823  630827
630841  630863  630871  630893  630899  630901  630907  630911  630919  630941  630967
630997  631003  631013  631039  631061  631121  631133  631151  631153  631155  631157
631171  631181  631187  631223  631229  631247  631249  631259  631271  631273  631291
631307  631339  631357  631361  631387  631391  631399  631409  631429  631453  631457
631469  631471  631481  631487  631507  631513  631529  631531  631537  631543  631549
631559  631573  631577  631583  631597  631613  631619  631643  631667  631679  631681
631721  631727  631733  631739  631751  631753  631789  631817  631819  631843
631847  631853  631859  631861  631867  631889  631901  631903  631913  631927  631931
631937  631979  631987  631991  631993  632029  632041  632053  632081  632083  632087
632089  632101  632117  632123  632141  632147  632153  632189  632209  632221  632227
632231  632251  632257  632267  632273  632297  632299  632321  632323  632327  632329
632347  632351  632353  632363  632371  632381  632389  632393  632417  632459  632473
632483  632497  632501  632503  632521  632557  632561  632591  632609  632623  632627
632629  632647  632669  632677  632683  632699  632713  632717  632743  632747  632773
632777  632813  632839  632843  632851  632857  632887  632911  632921  632923  632939
632941  632971  632977  632987  632993  633001  633013  633037  633053  633067  633079
633091  633151  633161  633187  633197  633209  633221  633253  633257  633263
633271  633287  633307  633317  633337  633359  633377  633379  633383  633401  633407
633427  633449  633461  633463  633467  633469  633473  633487  633497  633559  633569
633571  633583  633599  633613  633623  633629  633649  633653  633667  633739  633751
633757  633767  633781  633791  633793  633797  633799  633803  633823  633833  633877
```

```
633883  633923  633931  633937  633943  633953  633961  633967  633991  634003  634013
634031  634061  634079  634091  634097  634103  634141  634157  634159  634169  634177
634181  634187  634199  634211  634223  634237  634241  634247  634261  634267  634273
634279  634301  634307  634313  634327  634331  634343  634367  634373  634397  634421
634441  634471  634483  634493  634499  634511  634519  634523  634531  634541  634567
634573  634577  634597  634603  634609  634643  634649  634651  634679  634681  634687
634703  634709  634717  634727  634741  634747  634757  634759  634793  634807  634817
634841  634853  634859  634861  634871  634891  634901  634903  634927  634937  634939
634943  634969  634979  635003  635021  635039  635051  635057  635087  635119  635147
635149  635197  635203  635207  635249  635251  635263  635267  635279  635287  635291
635293  635309  635317  635333  635339  635347  635351  635353  635359  635363  635387
635389  635413  635423  635431  635441  635449  635461  635471  635483  635507  635519
635527  635533  635563  635567  635599  635603  635617  635639  635653  635659  635689
635707  635711  635729  635731  635737  635801  635809  635813  635821  635837
635849  635867  635879  635891  635893  635909  635917  635923  635939  635959  635969
635977  635981  635983  635989  636017  636023  636043  636059  636061  636071  636073
636107  636109  636133  636137  636149  636193  636211  636217  636241  636247  636257
636263  636277  636283  636287  636301  636313  636319  636331  636343  636353  636359
636403  636407  636409  636421  636469  636473  636499  636533  636539  636541  636547
636553  636563  636569  636613  636619  636631  636653  636673  636697  636719  636721
636731  636739  636749  636761  636763  636773  636781  636809  636817  636821  636829
636851  636863  636877  636917  636919  636931  636947  636953  636967  636983  636997
637001  637003  637067  637073  637079  637097  637129  637139  637157  637163  637171
637199  637201  637229  637243  637271  637277  637283  637291  637297  637309  637319
637321  637327  637337  637339  637349  637369  637379  637409  637421  637423  637447
637459  637463  637471  637489  637499  637513  637519  637529  637531  637543  637573
637597  637601  637603  637607  637627  637657  637669  637691  637699  637709  637711
637717  637723  637727  637729  637751  637771  637781  637783  637787  637817  637829
637831  637841  637873  637883  637909  637933  637937  637939  638023  638047  638051
638059  638063  638081  638117  638123  638147  638159  638161  638171  638177  638179
638201  638233  638263  638269  638303  638317  638327  638347  638359  638371  638423
638431  638437  638453  638459  638467  638489  638501  638527  638567  638581  638587
638621  638629  638633  638663  638669  638689  638699  638717  638719  638767  638801
638819  638833  638857  638861  638893  638923  638933  638959  638971  638977  638993
638999  639007  639011  639043  639049  639053  639083  639091  639137  639143  639151
639157  639169  639181  639211  639253  639257  639259  639263  639269  639289
639307  639311  639329  639337  639361  639371  639391  639433  639439  639451  639487
639491  639493  639511  639517  639533  639547  639563  639571  639577  639589  639599
639601  639631  639647  639667  639671  639677  639679  639689  639697  639701  639703
639713  639719  639731  639739  639757  639833  639839  639851  639853  639857  639907
639911  639937  639941  639949  639959  639983  639997  640007  640009  640019  640027
640039  640043  640049  640061  640069  640099  640109  640121  640127  640139  640151
640153  640163  640193  640219  640223  640229  640231  640247  640249  640259  640261
640267  640279  640303  640307  640333  640363  640369  640411  640421  640457  640463
640477  640483  640499  640529  640531  640579  640583  640589  640613  640621  640631
640649  640663  640667  640669  640687  640691  640727  640733  640741  640771  640777
640793  640837  640847  640853  640859  640873  640891  640901  640907  640919  640933
640943  640949  640957  640963  640967  640973  640993  641051  641057  641077  641083
641089  641093  641101  641129  641131  641143  641167  641197  641203  641213  641227
641239  641261  641279  641287  641299  641317  641327  641371  641387  641411  641413
641419  641441  641447  641453  641467  641471  641479  641491  641513  641519  641521
641549  641551  641579  641581  641623  641633  641639  641681  641701  641713  641747
641749  641761  641789  641791  641803  641813  641819  641821  641827  641833  641843
641863  641867  641873  641881  641891  641897  641909  641923  641929  641959  641969
641981  642011  642013  642049  642071  642077  642079  642113  642121  642133  642149
642151  642157  642163  642197  642199  642211  642217  642223  642233  642241  642247
642253  642281  642359  642361  642373  642403  642407  642419  642427  642457  642487
642517  642527  642529  642533  642547  642557  642563  642581  642613  642623  642673
642683  642701  642737  642739  642769  642779  642791  642797  642799  642809  642833
642853  642869  642877  642881  642899  642907  642931  642937  642947  642953
642973  642977  642997  643009  643021  643031  643039  643043  643051  643061  643073
643081  643087  643099  643121  643129  643183  643187  643199  643213  643217  643231
643243  643273  643301  643303  643369  643373  643403  643421  643429  643439  643453
643463  643469  643493  643507  643523  643547  643553  643567  643583  643589
643619  643633  643639  643649  643651  643661  643681  643691  643693  643697  643703
643723  643729  643751  643781  643847  643849  643859  643873  643879  643883  643889
643919  643927  643949  643957  643961  643969  643991  644009  644029  644047  644051
644053  644057  644089  644101  644107  644117  644123  644129  644131  644141  644143
644153  644159  644173  644191  644197  644201  644227  644239  644257  644261  644291
644297  644327  644341  644353  644359  644363  644377  644381  644383  644401  644411
644431  644443  644447  644449  644507  644513  644519  644531  644549  644557
644563  644569  644593  644597  644599  644617  644629  644647  644653  644669  644671
644687  644701  644717  644729  644731  644747  644753  644767  644783  644789  644797
644801  644837  644843  644863  644867  644869  644881  644899  644909  644911
644923  644933  644951  644977  644999  645013  645019  645023  645037  645041
645049  645067  645077  645083  645091  645097  645131  645137  645169  645179  645187
645233  645257  645313  645329  645347  645353  645367  645383  645397  645409  645419
645431  645433  645453  645467  645481  645493  645497  645499  645503  645521  645527
645529  645571  645577  645581  645583  645599  645611  645629  645641  645647  645649
645661  645683  645691  645703  645713  645727  645737  645739  645751  645763  645787
645803  645833  645839  645851  645857  645877  645889  645893  645901  645907  645937
645941  645959  645979  646003  646013  646027  646039  646067  646073  646099  646103
646147  646157  646159  646169  646181  646183  646189  646193  646199  646237  646253
646259  646267  646271  646273  646291  646301  646307  646309  646339  646379  646397
646403  646411  646421  646423  646433  646463  646519  646523  646537  646543  646549
646571  646573  646577  646609  646619  646631  646637  646643  646669  646687  646721
646757  646771  646781  646823  646831  646837  646843  646859  646873  646879  646883
646889  646897  646909  646913  646927  646937  646957  646979  646981  646991  646993
647011  647033  647039  647047  647057  647069  647081  647099  647111  647113  647117
```

```
647131  647147  647161  647189  647201  647209  647219  647261  647263  647293  647303
647321  647327  647333  647341  647357  647363  647371  647399  647401  647417
647429  647441  647453  647477  647489  647503  647509  647527  647531  647551  647557
647579  647587  647593  647609  647617  647627  647641  647651  647659  647663  647809
647693  647719  647723  647741  647743  647747  647753  647771  647783  647789  647809
647821  647837  647839  647851  647861  647891  647893  647909  647917  647951  647953
647963  647987  648007  648019  648029  648041  648047  648059  648061  648073  648079
648097  648101  648107  648119  648133  648173  648181  648191  648199  648211  648217
648229  648239  648257  648259  648269  648283  648289  648293  648317  648331  648341
648343  648371  648377  648379  648391  648433  648437  648449  648481  648509
648563  648607  648617  648619  648629  648631  648649  648653  648671  648677  648689
648709  648719  648731  648763  648779  648803  648841  648859  648863  648881  648887
648889  648911  648917  648931  648937  648953  648961  648971  648997  649001  649007
649039  649063  649069  649073  649079  649087  649093  649123  649141  649147
649151  649157  649183  649217  649261  649273  649277  649279  649283  649291  649307
649321  649361  649379  649381  649403  649421  649423  649427  649457  649469  649471
649483  649487  649499  649501  649507  649511  649529  649531  649559  649567  649573
649577  649613  649619  649631  649633  649639  649643  649651  649657  649661  649697
649709  649717  649739  649751  649769  649771  649777  649783  649787  649793  649799
649801  649813  649829  649843  649849  649867  649871  649877  649879  649897  649907
649921  649937  649969  649981  649991  650011  650017  650059  650071  650081  650099
650107  650179  650183  650189  650213  650227  650261  650269  650281  650291  650317
650327  650329  650347  650359  650387  650401  650413  650449  650477  650479  650483
650519  650537  650543  650549  650563  650567  650581  650591  650599  650609  650623
650627  650669  650701  650759  650761  650779  650813  650821  650827  650833  650851
650861  650863  650869  650873  650911  650917  650927  650933  650953  650971  650987
651017  651019  651029  651043  651067  651071  651097  651103  651109  651127  651139
651143  651169  651179  651181  651191  651193  651221  651223  651239  651247  651251
651257  651271  651281  651289  651293  651323  651331  651347  651361  651397  651401
651437  651439  651461  651473  651481  651487  651503  651509  651517  651587  651617
651641  651647  651649  651667  651683  651689  651697  651727  651731  651733  651767
651769  651793  651803  651809  651811  651821  651839  651841  651853  651857  651863
651869  651877  651881  651901  651913  651943  651971  651997  652019  652033  652039
652063  652079  652081  652087  652117  652121  652153  652189  652207  652217  652229
652237  652241  652243  652261  652279  652283  652291  652319  652321  652331  652339
652343  652357  652361  652369  652373  652381  652411  652417  652429  652447  652451
652453  652493  652499  652507  652541  652543  652549  652559  652567  652573  652577
652591  652601  652607  652609  652621  652627  652651  652657  652667  652699  652723
652727  652733  652739  652741  652747  652753  652759  652787  652811  652831  652837
652849  652853  652871  652903  652909  652913  652921  652931  652933  652937  652943
652957  652969  652991  652997  652999  653033  653057  653083  653111  653113  653117
653143  653153  653197  653203  653207  653209  653243  653267  653273  653281  653311
653321  653339  653357  653363  653431  653461  653473  653491  653501  653503  653507
653519  653537  653539  653561  653563  653579  653593  653617  653621  653623  653641
653647  653651  653659  653687  653693  653707  653711  653713  653743  653761
653777  653789  653797  653801  653819  653831  653879  653881  653893  653899  653903
653927  653929  653941  653951  653963  653969  653977  653993  654001  654011  654019
654023  654029  654047  654053  654067  654089  654107  654127  654149  654161  654163
654169  654187  654191  654209  654221  654223  654229  654233  654257  654293
654301  654307  654323  654343  654349  654371  654397  654413  654421  654427  654439
654491  654499  654509  654527  654529  654539  654541  654553  654571  654587  654593
654601  654611  654613  654623  654629  654671  654679  654697  654701  654727  654739
654743  654749  654767  654779  654781  654799  654803  654817  654821  654827  654839
654853  654877  654889  654917  654923  654931  654943  654967  654991  655001  655003
655013  655021  655033  655037  655043  655069  655087  655103  655111  655121  655157
655181  655211  655219  655229  655243  655241  655261  655267  655273  655283
655289  655301  655331  655337  655351  655357  655373  655379  655387  655399  655439
655453  655471  655489  655507  655511  655517  655531  655541  655547  655559  655561
655579  655583  655597  655601  655637  655643  655649  655651  655657  655687  655693
655717  655723  655727  655757  655807  655847  655849  655859  655883  655901  655909
655913  655927  655943  655961  655987  656023  656039  656063  656077  656113  656119
656129  656141  656147  656153  656171  656221  656237  656263  656267  656273  656291
656297  656303  656311  656321  656323  656329  656333  656347  656371  656377  656389
656407  656423  656429  656459  656471  656479  656483  656519  656527  656561  656587
656597  656599  656603  656609  656651  656657  656671  656681  656683  656687  656701
656707  656737  656741  656749  656753  656771  656783  656791  656809  656819  656833
656839  656891  656917  656923  656939  656951  656959  656977  656989  656993  657017
657029  657047  657049  657061  657071  657079  657089  657091  657113  657121  657127
657131  657187  657193  657197  657233  657257  657269  657281  657289  657299  657311
657313  657323  657347  657361  657383  657403  657413  657431  657439  657451  657479
657473  657491  657493  657497  657499  657523  657529  657539  657557  657581  657583
657589  657607  657617  657649  657653  657659  657661  657703  657707  657719  657743
657779  657793  657809  657827  657841  657859  657893  657911  657929  657931  657947
657959  657973  657983  658001  658043  658051  658057  658069  658079  658111  658117
658123  658127  658139  658153  658159  658169  658187  658199  658211  658219  658247
658253  658261  658277  658279  658303  658309  658319  658321  658327  658349  658351
658367  658379  658391  658403  658417  658433  658447  658453  658477  658487  658507
658547  658549  658573  658579  658589  658591  658601  658607  658613  658633  658639
658643  658649  658663  658681  658703  658751  658753  658783  658807  658817  658831
658837  658841  658871  658873  658883  658897  658907  658913  658919  658943  658961
658963  658969  658979  658991  658997  659011  659023  659047  659059  659063  659069
659077  659101  659137  659159  659171  659173  659177  659189  659221  659231  659237
659251  659279  659299  659317  659327  659333  659351  659371  659419  659423  659437
659453  659467  659473  659497  659501  659513  659521  659531  659539  659563  659569
659591  659597  659609  659611  659621  659629  659653  659663  659677  659669  659671
659689  659693  659713  659723  659741  659759  659761  659783  659819  659831  659843
659849  659863  659873  659881  659899  659917  659941  659947  659951  659963  659983
659999  660001  660013  660029  660047  660053  660061  660067  660071  660073  660097
660103  660119  660131  660137  660157  660167  660181  660197  660199  660217  660227
```

```
660241  660251  660271  660277  660281  660299  660329  660337  660347  660349  660367
660377  660379  660391  660403  660409  660449  660493  660503  660509  660521  660529
660547  660557  660559  660563  660589  660593  660599  660601  660607  660617  660619
660643  660659  660661  660683  660719  660727  660731  660733  660757  660769  660787
660791  660799  660809  660811  660817  660833  660851  660853  660887  660893  660899
660901  660917  660923  660941  660949  660973  660983  661009  661019  661027  661049
661061  661091  661093  661097  661099  661103  661109  661117  661121  661139  661183
661187  661189  661201  661217  661231  661237  661253  661259  661267  661321  661327
661343  661361  661373  661393  661417  661421  661439  661459  661477  661481  661483
661513  661517  661541  661547  661553  661603  661607  661613  661621  661663  661673
661679  661697  661721  661741  661769  661777  661823  661849  661873  661877  661879
661883  661889  661897  661909  661931  661939  661949  661951  661961  661987  661993
662003  662021  662029  662047  662059  662063  662083  662107  662111  662141  662143
662149  662177  662203  662227  662231  662251  662261  662267  662281  662287  662309
662323  662327  662339  662351  662353  662357  662369  662401  662407  662443  662449
662477  662483  662491  662513  662527  662531  662537  662539  662551  662567  662591
662617  662639  662647  662657  662671  662681  662683  662689  662693  662713  662719  662743
662771  662773  662789  662797  662819  662833  662839  662843  662867  662897  662899
662917  662939  662941  662947  662951  662953  662957  662999  663001  663007  663031
663037  663049  663053  663071  663097  663127  663149  663161  663163  663167  663191
663203  663209  663239  663241  663263  663269  663281  663283  663301  663319  663331
663339  663359  663371  663407  663409  663437  663463  663517  663529  663539  663541
663547  663557  663563  663569  663571  663581  663583  663587  663589  663599  663601
663631  663653  663683  663703  663709  663713  663737  663763  663787  663797
663821  663823  663827  663853  663857  663869  663881  663893  663907  663937  663959
663961  663967  663973  663977  663979  663983  663991  663997  664009  664019  664043
664061  664067  664091  664099  664109  664117  664121  664123  664133  664141  664151
664177  664193  664199  664211  664243  664253  664271  664273  664289  664319  664331
664357  664369  664379  664381  664403  664421  664441  664447  664459  664471  664507
664511  664529  664537  664549  664561  664571  664579  664583  664589  664597  664603
664613  664619  664661  664663  664667  664669  664679  664687  664691
664693  664711  664739  664757  664771  664777  664789  664793  664799  664843  664847
664849  664879  664891  664933  664949  664967  664973  664997  665011  665017  665029
665039  665047  665051  665053  665069  665089  665099  665113  665117  665123  665131
665141  665153  665177  665179  665201  665207  665213  665221  665233  665239  665251
665267  665279  665293  665299  665303  665311  665351  665359  665369  665381  665387
665419  665429  665447  665479  665501  665503  665507  665527  665549  665557  665563
665569  665573  665591  665603  665617  665629  665633  665659  665677  665713  665719
665723  665743  665761  665773  665783  665789  665801  665803  665813  665843  665857
665897  665921  665923  665947  665953  665981  665983  665993  666013  666019  666023
666031  666041  666067  666079  666089  666091  666109  666119  666139  666143
666167  666173  666187  666191  666203  666229  666233  666269  666277  666301  666323
666353  666403  666427  666431  666433  666437  666439  666461  666467  666493  666511
666527  666529  666541  666557  666559  666599  666607  666637  666643  666647  666649
666667  666671  666683  666697  666707  666727  666733  666737  666749  666751  666769
666773  666811  666821  666823  666829  666857  666871  666881  666901  666929  666937
666959  666979  666983  666989  667013  667019  667021  667081  667091  667103  667123
667127  667129  667141  667171  667181  667211  667229  667241  667243  667273  667283
667309  667321  667333  667351  667361  667363  667367  667379  667417  667421  667423
667427  667441  667463  667477  667487  667501  667507  667519  667531  667547  667549
667553  667559  667561  667571  667631  667643  667649  667657  667673  667687  667691
667697  667699  667727  667741  667753  667769  667781  667801  667817  667819  667829
667837  667859  667861  667867  667883  667903  667921  667949  667963  667987  667991
667999  668009  668029  668033  668047  668051  668069  668089  668093  668111  668141
668153  668159  668179  668201  668203  668209  668221  668243  668273  668303  668347
668407  668417  668471  668509  668513  668527  668531  668533  668539  668543  668567
668579  668581  668599  668609  668611  668617  668623  668671  668677  668687  668699
668713  668719  668737  668741  668747  668761  668791  668803  668813  668821  668851
668867  668869  668873  668879  668903  668929  668939  668947  668959  668963  668989
668999  669023  669029  669049  669077  669089  669091  669107  669113  669121  669127
669133  669167  669173  669181  669241  669247  669271  669283  669287  669289  669301
669311  669329  669359  669371  669377  669379  669391  669401  669413  669419  669433
669437  669451  669463  669479  669481  669527  669551  669577  669601  669611  669637
669649  669659  669661  669667  669673  669677  669679  669689  669701  669707  669733
669763  669787  669791  669839  669847  669853  669857  669859  669863  669869  669887
669901  669913  669923  669931  669937  669943  669947  669971  669989  670001  670031
670037  670039  670049  670051  670097  670099  670129  670139  670147  670177  670193
670199  670211  670223  670231  670237  670249  670261  670279  670297  670303
670321  670333  670343  670349  670363  670379  670399  670409  670447  670457  670471
670487  670489  670493  670507  670511  670517  670541  670543  670559  670577  670583
670597  670613  670619  670627  670639  670669  670673  670693  670711  670717  670729
670739  670763  670777  670781  670811  670823  670849  670853  670867  670877  670897
670903  670919  670931  670951  670963  670987  670991  671003  671017  671029  671039
671059  671063  671081  671087  671093  671123  671131  671141  671159  671161  671189
671201  671219  671233  671249  671257  671261  671269  671287  671299  671303  671323
671339  671353  671357  671369  671383  671401  671411  671431  671443  671467  671471
671477  671501  671519  671533  671537  671557  671581  671591  671603  671609  671633
671647  671651  671701  671717  671729  671743  671753  671777  671779  671791
671831  671837  671851  671887  671893  671903  671911  671917  671921  671933  671939
671941  671947  671969  671971  671981  671999  672019  672029  672041  672043  672059
672073  672079  672097  672103  672107  672127  672131  672137  672143  672151  672157
672169  672181  672193  672209  672223  672227  672229  672251  672271  672283  672289
672293  672311  672317  672323  672341  672349  672377  672379  672409  672443  672473
672493  672499  672521  672557  672577  672587  672593  672629  672641  672643  672653
672667  672703  672733  672757  672767  672779  672781  672787  672799  672803  672811
672817  672823  672827  672863  672869  672871  672883  672901  672913  672937  672943
672949  672953  672967  672977  672983  673019  673039  673063  673069  673073  673091
673093  673109  673111  673117  673121  673129  673157  673193  673199  673201  673207
673223  673241  673247  673271  673273  673291  673297  673313  673327  673339  673349
```

```
673381  673391  673397  673399  673403  673411  673427  673429  673441  673447  673451
673457  673459  673469  673487  673499  673513  673529  673549  673553  673567  673573
673579  673609  673613  673619  673637  673639  673643  673649  673667  673669  673747
673769  673781  673787  673793  673801  673811  673817  673837  673879  673891  673921
673943  673951  673961  673979  673991  674017  674057  674059  674071  674083  674099
674117  674123  674131  674159  674161  674173  674183  674189  674227  674231  674239
674249  674263  674269  674273  674299  674321  674347  674357  674363  674371  674393
674419  674431  674449  674461  674483  674493  674501  674533  674537  674551  674563  674603
674647  674669  674677  674683  674693  674699  674701  674711  674717  674719  674731
674741  674749  674759  674761  674767  674771  674789  674813  674827  674831  674833
674837  674851  674857  674867  674879  674903  674929  674941  674953  674957  674977
674987  675029  675067  675071  675079  675083  675097  675109  675113  675131  675133
675151  675161  675163  675173  675179  675187  675197  675221  675239  675247  675251
675253  675263  675271  675299  675313  675319  675341  675347  675391  675407  675413
675419  675449  675457  675463  675481  675511  675539  675541  675551  675553  675559
675569  675581  675593  675601  675607  675611  675617  675629  675643  675713  675739
675743  675751  675781  675797  675817  675823  675827  675839  675841  675859  675863
675877  675881  675889  675923  675929  675931  675959  675973  675977  675979  676007
676009  676031  676037  676043  676051  676057  676061  676069  676099  676103  676111
676129  676147  676171  676211  676217  676219  676241  676253  676259  676279  676289
676297  676337  676339  676349  676363  676373  676387  676391  676409  676411  676421
676427  676463  676469  676493  676523  676573  676589  676597  676601  676649  676661
676679  676703  676717  676721  676727  676733  676747  676751  676763  676771  676807
676829  676859  676861  676883  676891  676903  676909  676919  676927  676931  676937
676943  676961  676967  676979  676981  676987  676993  677011  677021  677029  677041
677057  677077  677081  677107  677111  677113  677119  677147  677167  677177  677213
677227  677231  677233  677239  677309  677311  677321  677323  677333  677357  677371
677387  677423  677441  677447  677459  677461  677471  677473  677531  677533  677539
677543  677561  677563  677587  677627  677639  677647  677657  677663  677683  677687
677717  677737  677767  677779  677783  677791  677813  677827  677857  677891  677927
677947  677953  677959  677983  678023  678037  678047  678061  678077  678101  678103
678133  678157  678169  678179  678191  678199  678203  678211  678217  678221  678229
678253  678289  678299  678329  678341  678343  678367  678371  678383  678401  678407
678409  678413  678421  678437  678463  678473  678479  678481  678493  678499  678533
678541  678553  678563  678577  678581  678593  678599  678607  678611  678631  678637
678641  678647  678649  678653  678659  678719  678721  678731  678739  678749  678757
678761  678767  678773  678779  678809  678823  678829  678833  678859  678871
678883  678901  678907  678941  678943  678949  678959  678971  678989  679033  679037
679039  679051  679069  679087  679111  679123  679127  679153  679157  679169  679171
679183  679207  679219  679223  679229  679249  679277  679279  679297  679309  679319
679333  679361  679363  679369  679373  679381  679403  679409  679417  679423  679433
679451  679463  679487  679501  679517  679519  679531  679537  679561  679597  679603
679607  679633  679639  679669  679681  679691  679699  679709  679733  679741  679747
679751  679763  679781  679787  679807  679823  679829  679837  679843  679859  679867
679879  679883  679891  679897  679907  679909  679919  679933  679951  679957  679961
679969  679981  679993  679999  680003  680027  680039  680051  680057  680081  680083
680107  680123  680129  680159  680161  680177  680189  680203  680209  680213  680237
680249  680263  680291  680293  680297  680299  680321  680327  680341  680347  680353
680387  680399  680411  680417  680431  680441  680443  680453  680489
680503  680507  680509  680531  680539  680567  680569  680587  680597  680611  680623
680633  680651  680657  680707  680749  680759  680767  680783  680803  680809
680831  680857  680861  680873  680879  680881  680917  680929  680959  680971  680987
680989  680993  681001  681011  681019  681041  681047  681061  681067  681089
681091  681113  681127  681137  681151  681167  681179  681221  681229  681251  681253
681257  681259  681271  681293  681311  681337  681341  681361  681367  681371  681403
681407  681409  681419  681427  681449  681481  681487  681493  681499  681521
681523  681539  681557  681563  681589  681607  681613  681623  681631  681647  681673
681677  681689  681719  681727  681731  681763  681773  681781  681787  681809  681823
681833  681839  681853  681863  681899  681913  681931  681943  681949  681971  681977
681979  681983  681997  682001  682009  682037  682049  682063  682069  682079  682141
682147  682151  682153  682157  682207  682219  682229  682237  682247  682259  682277
682289  682291  682303  682307  682321  682327  682333  682337  682361  682373  682411
682417  682421  682427  682447  682463  682471  682483  682489  682511  682519
682531  682547  682597  682607  682637  682657  682673  682679  682697  682699  682723
682729  682733  682739  682751  682763  682777  682789  682811  682819  682901  682933
682943  682951  682963  683003  683021  683041  683047  683071  683083  683087  683119
683129  683143  683149  683159  683201  683231  683251  683257  683273  683299  683303
683323  683341  683351  683357  683377  683381  683401  683407  683437  683447
683453  683461  683471  683477  683479  683483  683489  683503  683513  683567  683591
683597  683603  683651  683653  683681  683687  683693  683699  683701  683713  683719
683731  683737  683747  683759  683777  683783  683789  683807  683819  683821  683831
683833  683843  683857  683861  683863  683873  683887  683899  683909  683911  683923
683933  683939  683957  684007  684017  684037  684053  684091  684109  684113
684119  684121  684127  684157  684163  684191  684217  684221  684239  684269  684287
684289  684293  684311  684329  684337  684347  684349  684373  684379  684407  684419
684427  684443  684443  684461  684469  684473  684493  684527  684547  684557  684559
684569  684581  684587  684599  684617  684637  684643  684647  684683  684713  684727
684731  684751  684757  684769  684769  684773  684791  684793  684799  684809  684829
684841  684857  684869  684889  684923  684949  684961  684973  684977  684989  685001
685019  685031  685039  685051  685057  685063  685073  685081  685093  685099  685103
685109  685121  685141  685169  685177  685199  685231  685247  685249  685271  685297
685301  685319  685337  685339  685361  685367  685369  685381  685393  685417  685427
685429  685453  685459  685489  685511  685519  685537  685541  685547
685591  685609  685613  685621  685631  685637  685649  685669  685679  685697  685717
685723  685733  685739  685747  685753  685759  685781  685793  685819  685849  685853
685907  685909  685963  685969  685973  685987  685991  686003  686009  686011  686027
686029  686039  686041  686051  686057  686087  686089  686099  686117  686131  686141
686143  686149  686173  686177  686197  686201  686209  686267  686269  686293  686317
686321  686333  686339  686353  686359  686363  686417  686423  686437  686449  686453
```

```
686473  686479  686503  686513  686519  686551  686563  686593  686611  686639  686669
686671  686687  686723  686729  686731  686737  686761  686773  686789  686797  686801
686837  686843  686863  686879  686891  686893  686897  686911  686947  686963  686969
686971  686977  686989  686993  687007  687013  687017  687019  687023  687031  687041
687163  687179  687223  687233  687277  687289  687299  687307  687311  687317  687331
687341  687343  687359  687383  687389  687397  687403  687413  687431  687433  687437
687443  687457  687461  687473  687481  687499  687517  687521  687523  687541  687551
687559  687581  687593  687623  687637  687641  687647  687679  687683  687691  687707
687721  687737  687749  687767  687773  687779  687787  687809  687823  687829  687839
687847  687893  687901  687917  687923  687931  687949  687961  687977  688003  688013
688027  688031  688063  688067  688073  688087  688097  688111  688133  688139  688141
688159  688187  688201  688217  688223  688249  688253  688277  688297  688309  688333
688339  688357  688379  688393  688397  688403  688411  688423  688433  688447  688451
688453  688477  688511  688531  688543  688561  688573  688591  688621  688627  688631
688757  688763  688771  688783  688799  688813  688861  688867  688871  688883  688907
688939  688951  688957  688969  688979  688999  689021  689033  689041  689063  689071
689077  689089  689093  689099  689107  689113  689131  689141  689167  689201  689219
689233  689237  689257  689261  689267  689279  689291  689309  689317  689321  689341
689357  689369  689383  689389  689393  689411  689431  689441  689459  689461  689467
689509  689551  689561  689581  689587  689597  689599  689603  689621  689629  689641
689693  689699  689713  689723  689761  689771  689779  689789  689797  689803  689807
689827  689831  689851  689867  689869  689873  689879  689891  689893  689903  689917
689921  689929  689951  689957  689959  689963  689981  689987  690037  690059  690073
690089  690103  690119  690127  690139  690143  690163  690187  690233  690259  690269
690271  690281  690293  690323  690341  690367  690397  690407  690419  690427
690433  690439  690449  690467  690491  690493  690509  690511  690533  690541  690553
690583  690589  690607  690611  690629  690641  690673  690689  690719  690721  690757
690787  690793  690817  690839  690841  690869  690871  690887  690889  690919  690929
690953  690997  691001  691037  691051  691063  691079  691109  691111  691121  691129
691147  691151  691153  691181  691183  691189  691193  691199  691231  691241  691267
691289  691297  691309  691333  691337  691343  691349  691363  691381  691399  691409
691433  691451  691463  691489  691499  691531  691553  691573  691583  691589  691591
691631  691637  691651  691661  691681  691687  691693  691697  691709  691721  691723
691727  691729  691739  691759  691763  691787  691799  691813  691829  691837  691841
691843  691871  691877  691891  691897  691903  691907  691919  691921  691931  691949
691973  691979  691991  691997  692009  692017  692051  692059  692063  692071  692089
692099  692117  692141  692147  692149  692161  692191  692221  692239  692249  692269
692273  692281  692287  692297  692299  692309  692327  692333  692347  692353  692371
692387  692399  692401  692407  692413  692423  692431  692441  692453  692459
692467  692513  692521  692537  692539  692543  692567  692581  692591  692621  692641
692647  692651  692663  692689  692707  692711  692717  692729  692743  692753  692761
692771  692779  692789  692821  692851  692863  692893  692917  692927  692929  692933
692957  692963  692969  692983  693019  693037  693041  693061  693079  693089  693097
693103  693127  693137  693149  693157  693167  693169  693179  693223  693257  693283
693317  693323  693337  693353  693359  693373  693397  693401  693403  693409  693421
693431  693467  693487  693493  693503  693523  693527  693529  693533  693569  693571
693601  693607  693619  693629  693659  693661  693677  693683  693689  693691  693697
693701  693727  693731  693733  693739  693743  693757  693779  693793  693799  693809
693827  693829  693851  693859  693871  693877  693881  693943  693961  693967  693989
694019  694033  694039  694061  694069  694079  694081  694087  694091  694123  694189
694193  694201  694207  694223  694259  694261  694271  694273  694277  694313  694319
694327  694333  694339  694349  694357  694361  694367  694373  694381  694387  694391
694409  694427  694457  694471  694481  694483  694487  694511  694513  694523  694541
694549  694559  694567  694571  694591  694597  694609  694619  694633  694649  694651
694717  694721  694747  694763  694781  694783  694789  694829  694831  694867  694871
694873  694901  694910  694919  694951  694957  694979  694987  694997  694999  695003
695017  695021  695047  695059  695069  695081  695087  695089  695099  695111  695117
695131  695141  695171  695207  695239  695243  695257  695263  695269  695281  695293
695297  695309  695323  695327  695329  695347  695369  695371  695377  695389  695407
695411  695441  695447  695467  695477  695491  695503  695509  695561  695567  695573
695581  695593  695599  695603  695621  695627  695641  695659  695663  695677  695687
695689  695701  695719  695743  695749  695771  695777  695791  695807  695809  695839
695843  695867  695873  695879  695881  695899  695917  695927  695939  695999  696019
696053  696061  696067  696077  696079  696083  696107  696109  696119  696149  696181
696239  696253  696257  696263  696271  696281  696313  696317  696323  696343  696349
696359  696361  696373  696379  696403  696413  696427  696433  696457  696481  696491
696497  696503  696517  696523  696533  696547  696569  696607  696611  696617  696623
696629  696653  696659  696679  696691  696719  696721  696737  696743  696757  696763
696793  696809  696811  696823  696827  696833  696851  696853  696887  696889  696893
696907  696929  696937  696961  696989  696991  697009  697013  697019  697033  697049
697063  697069  697079  697087  697093  697111  697121  697127  697133  697141  697157
697181  697201  697211  697217  697259  697261  697267  697271  697303  697327  697351
697373  697379  697381  697387  697397  697399  697409  697423  697441  697447  697453
697457  697481  697507  697511  697513  697519  697523  697553  697579  697583  697591
697601  697603  697637  697643  697673  697681  697687  697691  697693  697703  697727
697729  697733  697757  697759  697787  697813  697831  697877  697891  697897  697909
697913  697937  697951  697967  697973  697979  697993  697999  698017  698021  698039
698051  698053  698077  698083  698111  698171  698183  698239  698249  698251  698261
698273  698287  698293  698297  698311  698329  698339  698359  698371  698387
698393  698413  698417  698419  698437  698447  698471  698483  698491  698507  698521
698527  698531  698539  698543  698557  698561  698591  698641  698653  698669  698701
698713  698723  698729  698773  698779  698821  698827  698849  698891  698899  698903
698923  698939  698977  698983  699001  699007  699037  699053  699059  699073  699077
699089  699113  699119  699133  699151  699157  699169  699187  699191  699197  699211
699217  699221  699241  699253  699271  699287  699289  699299  699319  699323  699343
699367  699373  699379  699383  699401  699427  699437  699443  699449  699463  699469
699493  699511  699521  699527  699529  699539  699541  699557  699571  699581  699617
```

```
699631  699641  699649  699697  699709  699719  699733  699757  699761  699767  699791
699793  699817  699823  699863  699931  699943  699947  699953  699961  699967  700001
700027  700057  700067  700079  700081  700087  700099  700103  700109  700127  700129
700171  700199  700201  700211  700223  700229  700237  700241  700277  700279  700303
700307  700319  700331  700339  700361  700363  700367  700387  700391  700393  700423
700429  700433  700459  700471  700499  700523  700537  700561  700571  700573  700577
700591  700597  700627  700633  700639  700643  700673  700681  700703  700717  700751
700759  700781  700789  700801  700811  700831  700837  700849  700871  700877  700883
700897  700907  700919  700933  700937  700949  700963  700993  701009  701011  701023
701033  701047  701089  701117  701147  701159  701177  701179  701209  701219  701221
701227  701257  701279  701291  701299  701329  701341  701357  701359  701377  701383
701399  701401  701413  701417  701419  701443  701447  701453  701473  701479  701489
701497  701507  701509  701527  701531  701549  701579  701581  701593  701609  701611
701621  701627  701629  701653  701669  701671  701681  701699  701711  701719  701731
701741  701761  701783  701791  701819  701837  701863  701881  701903  701951  701957
701963  701969  702007  702011  702017  702067  702077  702101  702113  702127  702131
702137  702139  702173  702179  702193  702199  702203  702211  702239  702257  702269
702281  702283  702311  702313  702323  702329  702337  702341  702347  702349  702353
702379  702391  702407  702413  702431  702433  702439  702451  702469  702497  702503
702511  702517  702523  702529  702539  702551  702557  702587  702589  702599  702607
702613  702623  702671  702679  702683  702701  702707  702721  702731  702733  702743
702773  702787  702803  702809  702817  702827  702847  702851  702853  702869  702881
702887  702893  702913  702937  702983  702991  703013  703033  703039  703081  703117
703121  703123  703127  703139  703141  703169  703193  703211  703217  703223  703229
703231  703243  703249  703267  703277  703301  703309  703321  703327  703331  703349
703357  703379  703393  703411  703441  703447  703459  703463  703471  703489  703499
703531  703537  703559  703561  703631  703643  703657  703663  703673  703679  703691
703699  703709  703711  703721  703733  703753  703763  703789  703819  703837  703849
703861  703873  703883  703897  703903  703907  703943  703949  703957  703981  703991
704003  704009  704017  704023  704027  704029  704059  704069  704087  704101  704111
704117  704131  704141  704153  704161  704177  704183  704189  704213  704219  704233
704243  704251  704269  704279  704281  704287  704299  704303  704309  704321  704357
704393  704399  704419  704441  704447  704449  704453  704461  704477  704507  704521
704527  704549  704551  704563  704569  704579  704581  704593  704603  704611  704647
704657  704663  704681  704687  704713  704719  704731  704747  704761  704771  704777
704779  704783  704797  704801  704807  704819  704833  704839  704849  704857  704861
704863  704897  704899  704929  704933  704947  704983  704989  704993  704999  705011
705013  705017  705031  705043  705053  705073  705079  705097  705113  705119  705127
705137  705161  705163  705167  705169  705181  705191  705197  705209  705247  705259
705269  705277  705293  705307  705317  705389  705403  705409  705421  705427  705437
705461  705491  705493  705499  705521  705533  705559  705613  705631  705643  705689
705713  705737  705751  705763  705769  705779  705781  705787  705821  705827  705829
705833  705841  705863  705871  705883  705899  705919  705937  705949  705967  705973
705989  706001  706003  706019  706033  706039  706049  706051  706067  706069
706109  706117  706133  706141  706151  706157  706159  706183  706193  706201  706207
706213  706229  706253  706267  706283  706291  706297  706301  706309  706313  706337
706357  706369  706373  706403  706417  706427  706463  706481  706487  706499  706507
706523  706547  706561  706597  706603  706613  706621  706631  706633  706661  706669
706679  706703  706709  706729  706733  706747  706751  706753  706757  706763  706787
706793  706801  706829  706837  706841  706847  706883  706897  706907  706913  706919
706921  706943  706961  706973  706987  706999  707011  707027  707029  707053  707071
707099  707111  707117  707131  707143  707153  707159  707177  707191  707197  707219
707249  707261  707279  707293  707299  707321  707341  707359  707383  707407  707429
707431  707437  707459  707467  707501  707527  707543  707561  707563  707573  707627
707633  707647  707653  707669  707671  707677  707683  707689  707711  707717  707723
707747  707753  707767  707797  707801  707813  707827  707831  707849  707857
707869  707873  707887  707911  707923  707929  707933  707939  707951  707953  707957
707969  707981  707983  708007  708011  708017  708023  708031  708041  708047  708049
708053  708061  708091  708109  708119  708131  708137  708139  708161  708163  708179
708199  708221  708223  708229  708251  708269  708283  708287  708293  708311  708329
708343  708347  708353  708359  708361  708371  708403  708437  708457  708473  708479
708481  708493  708497  708517  708527  708559  708563  708569  708583  708593  708599
708601  708641  708647  708689  708703  708733  708751  708803  708823  708839
708857  708859  708893  708899  708907  708913  708923  708937  708943  708959  708979
708989  708991  708997  709043  709057  709097  709117  709123  709139  709141  709151
709153  709157  709201  709217  709231  709237  709253  709273  709279  709283
709307  709321  709337  709349  709351  709381  709409  709417  709421  709433  709447
709451  709453  709469  709519  709531  709537  709547  709561  709589  709603
709607  709609  709649  709651  709663  709673  709679  709691  709693  709703  709729
709739  709741  709769  709777  709789  709799  709817  709823  709831  709843  709847
709853  709861  709871  709879  709901  709909  709913  709921  709927  709957  709963
709967  709981  709991  710009  710023  710027  710051  710053  710081  710089  710119
710189  710207  710219  710221  710257  710261  710273  710293  710299  710321  710323
710327  710341  710351  710371  710377  710383  710389  710399  710441  710443  710449
710459  710473  710483  710491  710503  710513  710519  710527  710531  710557  710561
710573  710579  710599  710603  710609  710621  710623  710627  710641  710663  710683
710693  710713  710777  710779  710791  710813  710837  710839  710849  710851  710863
710867  710873  710887  710903  710909  710911  710917  710929  710933  710951  710959
710971  710977  710987  710989  711001  711017  711019  711023  711041  711049  711089
711097  711121  711131  711133  711143  711163  711173  711181  711187  711209  711223
711259  711287  711299  711307  711317  711329  711353  711371  711397  711409  711427
711437  711463  711479  711497  711499  711509  711517  711523  711539  711563  711577
711583  711589  711617  711629  711649  711653  711679  711691  711701  711707  711709
711713  711727  711731  711749  711751  711757  711793  711811  711817  711829  711839
711847  711859  711877  711889  711899  711913  711923  711929  711937  711947  711959
711967  711973  711983  712007  712021  712051  712067  712093  712109  712121  712133
712157  712169  712171  712183  712199  712219  712237  712279  712289  712301  712303
712319  712321  712331  712339  712357  712409  712417  712427  712429  712433  712447
712477  712483  712489  712493  712499  712507  712511  712531  712561  712571  712573
```

```
712601  712603  712631  712651  712669  712681  712687  712693  712697  712711  712717
712739  712787  712807  712819  712837  712841  712843  712847  712883  712889  712891
712909  712913  712927  712939  712951  712961  712967  712973  712981  713021  713039
713059  713077  713107  713117  713129  713147  713149  713159  713171  713177  713183
713189  713191  713227  713233  713239  713243  713261  713267  713281  713287  713309
713311  713329  713347  713351  713353  713357  713381  713389  713399  713407  713411
713417  713467  713477  713491  713497  713501  713509  713533  713563  713569  713597
713599  713611  713627  713653  713663  713681  713737  713743  713747  713753  713771
713807  713827  713831  713833  713861  713863  713873  713891  713903  713917  713927
713939  713941  713957  713981  713987  714029  714037  714061  714073  714107  714113
714139  714143  714151  714163  714169  714199  714223  714227  714247  714257  714283
714341  714349  714361  714377  714443  714463  714479  714481  714487  714503  714509
714517  714521  714529  714551  714557  714563  714569  714577  714601  714619  714673
714677  714691  714719  714739  714751  714773  714781  714787  714797  714809  714827
714839  714841  714851  714853  714869  714881  714887  714893  714907  714911  714919
714943  714947  714949  714971  714991  715019  715031  715049  715063  715069  715073
715087  715109  715123  715151  715153  715157  715159  715171  715189  715193  715223
715229  715237  715243  715249  715259  715289  715301  715303  715313  715339  715357
715361  715373  715397  715417  715423  715439  715441  715453  715457  715489  715499
715523  715537  715549  715567  715571  715577  715579  715613  715621  715639  715643
715651  715657  715679  715681  715699  715727  715739  715753  715777  715789  715801
715811  715817  715823  715843  715849  715867  715873  715877  715879  715889
715903  715909  715919  715927  715943  715961  715963  715969  715973  715991  715999
716003  716033  716063  716087  716117  716123  716137  716143  716161  716171  716173
716249  716257  716279  716291  716299  716321  716351  716383  716389  716399  716411
716413  716447  716449  716453  716459  716477  716479  716483  716491  716501  716531
716543  716549  716563  716581  716591  716621  716629  716633  716659  716663  716671
716687  716693  716707  716713  716731  716741  716743  716747  716783  716789  716809
716819  716827  716857  716861  716869  716897  716899  716917  716929  716951  716953
716959  716981  716987  717001  717011  717047  717089  717091  717103  717109  717113
717127  717133  717139  717149  717151  717161  717191  717229  717259  717271  717289
717293  717317  717323  717331  717341  717397  717413  717419  717427  717443  717449
717463  717491  717511  717527  717529  717533  717539  717551  717559  717583  717589
717593  717631  717653  717659  717667  717679  717683  717697  717719  717751  717797
717803  717811  717817  717841  717851  717883  717887  717917  717919  717923  717967
717979  717989  718007  718043  718049  718051  718087  718093  718121  718139  718163
718169  718171  718183  718187  718241  718259  718271  718303  718321  718331  718337
718343  718349  718357  718379  718381  718387  718391  718411  718423  718427  718433
718453  718457  718493  718511  718513  718541  718547  718559  718579  718603
718621  718633  718657  718661  718691  718703  718717  718723  718741  718747  718759
718801  718807  718813  718841  718847  718891  718897  718901  718919  718931  718937
718943  718973  718999  719009  719011  719027  719041  719057  719063  719071  719101
719119  719143  719149  719153  719167  719177  719179  719183  719189  719197  719203
719227  719237  719239  719267  719281  719297  719333  719351  719353  719377  719393
719413  719419  719441  719447  719483  719503  719533  719557  719567  719569  719573
719597  719599  719633  719639  719659  719671  719681  719683  719689  719699  719713
719717  719723  719731  719749  719753  719773  719779  719791  719801  719813  719821
719833  719863  719893  719903  719911  719941  719947  719951  719959  719981  719989
720007  720019  720023  720053  720059  720089  720091  720101  720127  720133  720151
720173  720179  720193  720197  720211  720221  720229  720241  720253  720257  720281
720283  720289  720299  720301  720311  720319  720359  720361  720367  720373  720397
720403  720407  720413  720439  720481  720491  720497  720527  720547  720569  720571
720607  720611  720617  720619  720653  720661  720677  720683  720697  720703  720743
720763  720767  720773  720779  720791  720793  720829  720847  720857  720869  720877
720887  720899  720901  720913  720931  720943  720947  720961  720971  720983  720991
720997  721003  721013  721037  721043  721051  721057  721079  721087  721109  721111
721117  721129  721139  721141  721159  721163  721169  721177  721181  721199  721207
721213  721219  721223  721229  721243  721261  721267  721283  721291  721307  721319
721321  721333  721337  721351  721363  721379  721381  721387  721397  721439  721451
721481  721499  721529  721547  721561  721571  721577  721597  721613  721619  721621
721631  721661  721663  721687  721697  721703  721709  721733  721739  721783  721793
721843  721849  721859  721883  721891  721909  721921  721951  721961  721979  721991
721997  722011  722023  722027  722047  722063  722069  722077  722093  722113  722123
722147  722149  722153  722159  722167  722173  722213  722237  722243  722257  722273
722287  722291  722299  722311  722317  722321  722333  722341  722353  722363  722369
722377  722389  722411  722417  722431  722449  722467  722479  722489  722509  722521
722537  722539  722563  722581  722599  722611  722633  722639  722663  722669  722713
722723  722737  722749  722783  722791  722797  722807  722819  722833  722849  722881
722899  722903  722921  722933  722963  722971  722977  722983  723029  723031  723043
723049  723053  723067  723071  723089  723101  723103  723109  723113  723119  723127
723133  723157  723161  723167  723169  723181  723193  723209  723221  723227  723257
723259  723263  723269  723271  723287  723293  723319  723337  723353  723361  723379
723391  723407  723409  723413  723421  723439  723451  723467  723473  723479  723491
723493  723529  723551  723553  723559  723563  723587  723589  723601  723607  723617
723623  723661  723721  723727  723739  723761  723791  723797  723799  723803  723823
723829  723839  723851  723857  723859  723893  723901  723907  723913  723917  723923
723949  723959  723967  723973  723977  723997  724001  724007  724021  724079  724093
724099  724111  724117  724121  724123  724153  724187  724211  724219  724259  724267
724277  724291  724303  724309  724313  724331  724393  724403  724433  724441  724447
724453  724459  724469  724481  724487  724499  724513  724517  724519  724531  724547
724553  724567  724573  724583  724597  724601  724609  724621  724627  724631  724639
724643  724651  724721  724723  724729  724733  724747  724751  724769  724777  724781
724783  724807  724813  724837  724847  724853  724879  724901  724903  724939  724949
724961  724967  724991  724993  725009  725041  725057  725071  725077  725099  725111
725113  725119  725147  725149  725159  725161  725189  725201  725209  725273  725293
725303  725317  725321  725323  725327  725341  725357  725359  725371  725381  725393
725399  725423  725437  725447  725449  725479  725507  725519  725531  725537  725579
725587  725597  725603  725639  725653  725663  725671  725687  725723  725731  725737
725749  725789  725801  725807  725827  725861  725863  725867  725891  725897  725909
```

```
725929  725939  725953  725981  725983  725993  725999  726007  726013  726023  726043
726071  726091  726097  726101  726107  726109  726137  726139  726149  726157  726163
726169  726181  726191  726221  726287  726289  726301  726307  726331  726337  726367
726371  726377  726379  726391  726413  726419  726431  726457  726463  726469  726487
726497  726521  726527  726533  726559  726589  726599  726601  726611  726619  726623
726629  726641  726647  726659  726679  726689  726697  726701  726707  726751  726779
726787  726797  726809  726811  726839  726841  726853  726893  726899  726911  726917
726923  726941  726953  726983  726989  726991  727003  727009  727019  727021  727049
727061  727063  727079  727121  727123  727157  727159  727169  727183  727189  727201
727211  727241  727247  727249  727261  727267  727271  727273  727289  727297  727313
727327  727343  727351  727369  727399  727409  727427  727451  727459  727471  727483
727487  727499  727501  727541  727561  727577  727589  727613  727621  727633  727667
727673  727691  727703  727711  727717  727729  727733  727747  727759  727763  727777
727781  727799  727807  727817  727823  727843  727847  727877  727879  727891  727933
727939  727949  727981  727997  728003  728017  728027  728047  728069  728087  728113
728129  728131  728173  728191  728207  728209  728261  728267  728269  728281  728293
728303  728317  728333  728369  728381  728383  728417  728423  728437  728471  728477
728489  728521  728527  728537  728551  728557  728561  728573  728579  728627  728639
728647  728659  728681  728687  728699  728701  728713  728723  728729  728731  728743
728747  728771  728809  728813  728831  728837  728839  728843  728851  728867  728869
728873  728881  728891  728899  728911  728921  728927  728929  728941  728947  728953
728969  728971  728993  729019  729023  729037  729041  729059  729073  729139  729143
729173  729187  729191  729199  729203  729217  729257  729269  729271  729293  729301
729329  729331  729359  729367  729371  729373  729389  729403  729413  729451  729457
729473  729493  729497  729503  729511  729527  729551  729557  729559  729569  729571
729577  729587  729601  729607  729613  729637  729643  729649  729661  729671  729679
729689  729713  729719  729737  729749  729761  729779  729787  729791  729821  729851
729871  729877  729907  729913  729919  729931  729941  729943  729947  729977  729979
729991  730003  730021  730033  730049  730069  730091  730111  730139  730157  730187
730199  730217  730237  730253  730277  730283  730297  730321  730339  730363  730397
730399  730421  730447  730451  730469  730487  730537  730553  730559  730567
730571  730573  730589  730591  730603  730619  730633  730637  730663  730669  730679
730727  730747  730753  730757  730777  730781  730783  730789  730799  730811  730819
730823  730837  730843  730853  730867  730879  730889  730901  730909  730913  730943
730969  730973  730993  730999  731033  731041  731047  731053  731057  731113  731117
731141  731173  731183  731189  731191  731201  731209  731219  731233  731243  731249
731251  731257  731261  731267  731287  731299  731327  731333  731359  731363  731369
731389  731413  731447  731483  731501  731503  731509  731531  731539  731567  731587
731593  731597  731603  731611  731623  731639  731651  731681  731683  731711  731713
731719  731729  731737  731741  731761  731767  731779  731803  731807  731821  731827
731831  731839  731851  731869  731881  731893  731909  731911  731921  731923  731933
731957  731981  731999  732023  732029  732041  732073  732077  732079  732097  732101
732133  732157  732169  732181  732187  732191  732197  732209  732211  732217  732229
732233  732239  732257  732271  732283  732287  732293  732299  732311  732323  732331
732373  732439  732449  732461  732467  732491  732493  732497  732509  732521  732533
732541  732601  732617  732631  732653  732673  732689  732703  732709  732713  732731
732749  732761  732769  732799  732817  732827  732829  732833  732841  732863  732877
732889  732911  732923  732943  732959  732967  732971  732997  733003  733009  733067
733097  733099  733111  733123  733127  733133  733141  733147  733157  733169  733177
733189  733237  733241  733273  733277  733283  733289  733301  733307  733321  733331
733333  733339  733351  733373  733387  733391  733393  733399  733409  733427  733433
733459  733477  733489  733511  733517  733519  733559  733561  733591  733619  733639
733651  733667  733697  733741  733751  733753  733757  733793  733807  733813  733823
733829  733841  733847  733849  733867  733871  733879  733883  733919  733921  733937
733939  733949  733963  733973  733981  733991  734003  734017  734021  734047  734057
734071  734131  734141  734143  734159  734171  734177  734189  734197  734203  734207
734221  734233  734263  734267  734273  734291  734303  734329  734347  734381  734389
734401  734411  734423  734429  734431  734443  734471  734473  734477  734479  734497
734537  734543  734549  734557  734567  734627  734647  734653  734659  734663  734687
734693  734707  734717  734729  734737  734743  734759  734771  734803  734807  734813
734819  734837  734849  734869  734879  734887  734897  734911  734933  734941  734953
734957  734959  734971  735001  735019  735043  735061  735067  735071  735073  735083
735107  735109  735113  735139  735143  735157  735169  735173  735181  735187  735193
735209  735211  735239  735247  735263  735271  735283  735307  735311  735331  735337
735341  735359  735367  735373  735389  735391  735419  735421  735431  735439  735443
735451  735461  735467  735473  735479  735491  735529  735533  735557  735571  735617
735649  735653  735659  735673  735689  735697  735719  735731  735733  735739  735751
735781  735809  735821  735829  735853  735871  735877  735883  735901  735919  735937
735949  735953  735979  735983  735997  736007  736013  736027  736037  736039  736051
736061  736063  736091  736093  736097  736111  736121  736147  736159  736181  736187
736243  736247  736249  736259  736273  736277  736279  736357  736361  736363  736367
736369  736381  736387  736399  736403  736409  736429  736433  736441  736447  736469
736471  736511  736577  736607  736639  736657  736679  736691  736699  736717  736721
736741  736787  736793  736817  736823  736843  736847  736867  736871  736889  736903
736921  736927  736951  736961  736973  736987  736993  737017  737039  737041
737047  737053  737059  737083  737089  737111  737119  737129  737131  737147  737159
737179  737183  737203  737207  737251  737263  737279  737281  737287  737291  737293
737309  737327  737339  737351  737353  737411  737413  737423  737431  737479  737483
737497  737501  737507  737509  737531  737533  737537  737563  737567  737573  737591
737593  737617  737629  737641  737657  737663  737683  737687  737717  737719  737729
737747  737753  737767  737773  737797  737801  737809  737819  737843  737857  737861
737873  737887  737897  737921  737927  737929  737969  737981  737999  738011  738029
738043  738053  738071  738083  738107  738109  738121  738151  738163  738173  738197
738211  738217  738223  738247  738263  738301  738313  738317  738319  738341  738349
738373  738379  738383  738391  738401  738403  738421  738443  738457  738469  738487
738499  738509  738523  738539  738547  738581  738583  738589  738623  738643  738677
738707  738713  738721  738743  738757  738781  738791  738797  738811  738827  738839
738847  738851  738863  738877  738889  738917  738919  738923  738937  738953  738961
738977  738989  739003  739021  739027  739031  739051  739061  739069  739087  739099
```

```
739103  739111  739117  739121  739153  739163  739171  739183  739187  739199  739201
739217  739241  739253  739273  739283  739301  739303  739307  739327  739331  739337
739351  739363  739369  739373  739379  739391  739393  739397  739399  739433  739439
739463  739469  739493  739507  739511  739513  739523  739549  739553  739579  739601
739603  739621  739631  739633  739637  739649  739693  739699  739723  739751  739759
739771  739777  739787  739799  739813  739829  739847  739853  739859  739861  739909
739931  739943  739951  739957  739967  739969  740011  740021  740023  740041  740053
740059  740087  740099  740123  740141  740143  740153  740161  740171  740189  740191
740227  740237  740279  740287  740303  740321  740323  740329  740351  740359  740371
740387  740423  740429  740461  740473  740477  740483  740513  740521  740527  740533
740549  740561  740581  740591  740599  740603  740651  740653  740659  740671  740681
740687  740693  740711  740713  740717  740737  740749  740801  740849  740891  740893
740897  740903  740923  740939  740951  740969  740989  741001  741007  741011  741031
741043  741053  741061  741071  741077  741079  741101  741119  741121  741127  741131
741137  741163  741187  741193  741227  741229  741233  741253  741283  741337  741341
741343  741347  741373  741401  741409  741413  741431  741457  741467  741469  741473
741479  741491  741493  741509  741541  741547  741563  741569  741593  741599  741641
741661  741667  741677  741679  741683  741691  741709  741721  741781  741787  741803
741809  741827  741833  741847  741857  741859  741877  741883  741913  741919  741929
741941  741967  741973  741991  742009  742031  742037  742057  742069  742073  742111
742117  742127  742151  742153  742193  742199  742201  742211  742213  742219  742229
742241  742243  742253  742277  742283  742289  742307  742327  742333  742351  742369
742381  742393  742409  742439  742457  742499  742507  742513  742519  742531  742537
742541  742549  742559  742579  742591  742607  742619  742657  742663  742673  742681
742697  742699  742711  742717  742723  742757  742759  742783  742789  742801  742817
742891  742897  742909  742913  742943  742949  742967  742981  742991  742993  742999
743027  743047  743059  743069  743089  743111  743123  743129  743131  743137  743143
743159  743161  743167  743173  743177  743179  743203  743209  743221  743251  743263
743269  743273  743279  743297  743321  743333  743339  743363  743377  743401  743423
743447  743507  743549  743551  743573  743579  743591  743609  743657  743669  743671
743689  743693  743711  743731  743747  743777  743779  743791  743803  743819  743833
743837  743849  743851  743881  743891  743917  743921  743923  743933  743947  743987
743989  744019  744043  744071  744077  744083  744113  744127  744137  744179  744187
744199  744203  744221  744239  744251  744253  744283  744301  744313  744353  744371
744377  744389  744391  744397  744407  744409  744431  744451  744493  744503  744511
744539  744547  744559  744599  744607  744637  744641  744649  744659  744661  744677
744701  744707  744721  744727  744739  744761  744767  744791  744811  744817  744823
744829  744833  744859  744893  744911  744917  744941  744949  744959  744977  745001
745013  745027  745033  745037  745051  745067  745103  745117  745133  745151  745181
745187  745189  745201  745231  745243  745247  745249  745273  745301  745307  745337
745343  745357  745369  745379  745391  745397  745471  745477  745511  745529  745531
745543  745567  745573  745601  745609  745621  745631  745649  745673  745697  745699
745709  745711  745727  745733  745741  745747  745751  745753  745757  745817  745837
745859  745873  745903  745931  745933  745939  745951  745973  745981  745993  745999
746017  746023  746033  746041  746047  746069  746099  746101  746107  746117  746129
746153  746167  746171  746177  746183  746191  746197  746203  746209  746227  746231
746233  746243  746267  746287  746303  746309  746329  746353  746363  746371  746411
746413  746429  746477  746479  746483  746497  746503  746507  746509  746531  746533
746561  746563  746597  746653  746659  746671  746677  746723  746737  746743  746747
746749  746773  746777  746791  746797  746807  746813  746839  746843  746869  746873
746881  746899  746903  746939  746951  746957  746969  746981  746989  747019  747037
747049  747053  747073  747107  747113  747139  747157  747161  747199  747203  747223
747239  747259  747277  747283  747287  747319  747323  747343  747361  747377  747391
747401  747407  747421  747427  747449  747451  747457  747463  747493  747497  747499
747521  747529  747547  747557  747563  747583  747587  747599  747611  747619  747647
747673  747679  747713  747731  747737  747743  747763  747781  747811  747827  747841
747833  747839  747841  747853  747863  747869  747871  747889  747917  747919  747941
747953  747977  747979  747991  748003  748019  748021  748039  748057  748091  748093
748133  748169  748183  748199  748207  748211  748217  748219  748249  748263  748273
748301  748331  748337  748339  748343  748361  748379  748387  748441  748453
748463  748471  748481  748487  748499  748513  748523  748541  748567  748589  748597
748603  748609  748613  748633  748637  748639  748669  748687  748691  748703  748711
748717  748723  748729  748763  748777  748789  748801  748807  748811  748819  748823
748829  748831  748849  748861  748871  748877  748883  748889  748921  748933  748963
748973  748981  748987  749011  749027  749051  749069  749081  749083  749093  749129
749137  749143  749149  749153  749167  749171  749183  749197  749209  749219  749237
749249  749257  749267  749279  749297  749299  749323  749339  749347  749351  749383
749393  749401  749423  749429  749431  749443  749449  749453  749461  749467  749471
749543  749557  749587  749641  749653  749659  749677  749701  749711  749729  749741
749747  749761  749771  749779  749803  749807  749809  749843  749851  749863  749891
749893  749899  749909  749923  749927  749939  749941  749971  749993  750019  750037
750059  750077  750083  750097  750119  750121  750131  750133  750137  750151  750157
750161  750163  750173  750179  750203  750209  750223  750229  750287  750311  750313
750353  750383  750401  750413  750419  750437  750457  750473  750487  750509  750517
750521  750553  750571  750599  750613  750641  750653  750661  750667  750679  750691
750707  750713  750719  750721  750749  750769  750787  750791  750797  750803  750809
750817  750829  750853  750857  750863  750917  750929  750943  750961  750977  750983
751001  751007  751021  751027  751057  751061  751087  751103  751123  751133  751139
751141  751147  751151  751181  751183  751189  751193  751199  751207  751217  751237
751259  751273  751277  751291  751297  751301  751307  751319  751321  751327  751343
751351  751357  751363  751367  751379  751411  751423  751447  751453  751463  751481
751523  751529  751549  751567  751579  751609  751613  751627  751631  751633  751637
751643  751661  751669  751691  751711  751717  751727  751739  751747  751753  751759
751763  751787  751799  751813  751823  751841  751853  751867  751871  751879  751901
751909  751913  751921  751943  751957  751969  751987  751997  752009  752023  752033
752053  752083  752093  752107  752111  752117  752137  752149  752177  752183  752189
752197  752201  752203  752207  752251  752263  752273  752281  752287  752291  752293
752299  752303  752351  752359  752383  752413  752431  752447  752449  752459  752483
752489  752503  752513  752519  752527  752569  752581  752593  752603  752627  752639
```

```
752651  752681  752683  752699  752701  752707  752747  752771  752789  752797  752803
752809  752819  752821  752831  752833  752861  752867  752881  752891  752903  752911
752929  752933  752977  752993  753001  753007  753019  753023  753031  753079  753091
753127  753133  753139  753143  753161  753187  753191  753197  753229  753257  753307
753329  753341  753353  753367  753373  753383  753409  753421  753427  753437  753439
753461  753463  753497  753499  753527  753547  753569  753583  753587  753589  753611
753617  753619  753631  753647  753659  753677  753679  753689  753691  753707  753719
753721  753737  753743  753751  753773  753793  753799  753803  753811  753821  753839
753847  753859  753931  753937  753941  753947  753959  753979  753983  754003  754027
754037  754043  754057  754067  754073  754081  754093  754099  754109  754111  754121
754123  754133  754153  754157  754181  754183  754207  754211  754217  754223  754241
754249  754267  754279  754283  754289  754297  754301  754333  754337  754343  754367
754373  754379  754381  754399  754417  754421  754427  754451  754463  754483  754489
754513  754531  754549  754573  754577  754583  754597  754627  754639  754651  754703
754709  754711  754717  754723  754739  754751  754771  754781  754811  754829  754861
754877  754891  754903  754907  754921  754931  754937  754939  754967  754969  754973
754979  754991  754993  754999  755009  755033  755057  755071  755077  755081  755087
755107  755137  755143  755147  755171  755173  755203  755213  755233  755239  755257
755267  755273  755309  755311  755317  755329  755333  755353  755357  755371  755387
755393  755399  755401  755413  755437  755441  755449  755473  755483  755509  755539
755551  755561  755567  755569  755593  755597  755617  755627  755663  755681  755707
755717  755719  755737  755759  755767  755771  755789  755791  755809  755813  755861
755863  755869  755879  755899  755903  755959  755969  755977  756011  756023  756043
756053  756097  756101  756127  756131  756139  756149  756167  756179  756191  756199
756227  756247  756251  756253  756271  756281  756289  756293  756319  756323  756331
756373  756403  756419  756421  756433  756443  756463  756467  756527  756533  756541
756563  756571  756593  756601  756607  756629  756641  756649  756667  756673  756683
756689  756703  756709  756719  756727  756739  756773  756799  756829  756839  756853
756869  756881  756887  756919  756923  756961  756967  756971  757019  757039  757063
757067  757109  757111  757151  757157  757171  757181  757201  757241  757243  757247
757259  757271  757291  757297  757307  757319  757327  757331  757343  757363  757381
757387  757403  757409  757417  757429  757433  757457  757481  757487  757507  757513
757517  757543  757553  757577  757579  757583  757607  757633  757651  757661  757693
757699  757709  757711  757727  757751  757753  757763  757793  757807  757811  757819
757829  757879  757903  757909  757927  757937  757943  757951  757993  757997  758003
758041  758053  758071  758081  758083  758099  758101  758111  758137  758141  758159
758179  758189  758201  758203  758227  758231  758237  758243  758267  758269  758273
758279  758299  758323  758339  758341  758357  758363  758383  758393  758411  758431
758441  758449  758453  758491  758501  758503  758519  758521  758551  758561  758573
758579  758599  758617  758629  758633  758671  758687  758699  758707  758711  758713
758729  758731  758741  758753  758767  758783  758789  758819  758827  758837
758851  758867  758887  758893  758899  758929  758941  758957  758963  758969  758971
758987  759001  759019  759029  759037  759047  759053  759089  759103  759113  759131
759119  759167  759173  759179  759181  759193  759223  759229  759263  759287  759293
759301  759313  759329  759359  759371  759377  759397  759401  759431  759433  759457
759463  759467  759491  759523  759547  759553  759557  759559  759569  759571
759581  759589  759599  759617  759623  759631  759637  759641  759653  759659  759673
759691  759697  759701  759709  759719  759727  759739  759751  759763  759797  759799
759821  759833  759881  759893  759911  759923  759929  759947  759953  759959  759961
759973  760007  760043  760063  760079  760093  760103  760117  760129  760141  760147
760151  760163  760169  760183  760187  760211  760229  760231  760237  760241  760261
760267  760273  760289  760297  760301  760321  760343  760367  760373  760411  760423
760433  760447  760453  760457  760477  760489  760499  760511  760519  760531  760537
760549  760553  760561  760567  760579  760607  760619  760621  760637  760649  760657
760693  760723  760729  760759  760769  760783  760807  760813  760841  760843  760847
760871  760891  760897  760913  760927  760933  760939  760951  760961  760993
760997  761003  761009  761023  761051  761069  761087  761113  761119  761129  761153
761161  761177  761179  761183  761203  761207  761213  761227  761249  761251  761261
761263  761291  761297  761347  761351  761357  761363  761377  761381  761389  761393
761399  761407  761417  761429  761437  761441  761443  761459  761471  761477  761483
761489  761521  761531  761533  761543  761561  761567  761591  761597  761603  761611
761623  761633  761669  761671  761681  761689  761711  761713  761731  761773  761777
761779  761807  761809  761833  761861  761863  761869  761879  761897  761927  761939
761963  761977  761983  761993  762001  762007  762017  762031  762037  762049  762053
762061  762101  762121  762187  762211  762227  762233  762239  762241  762253  762257
762277  762319  762329  762367  762371  762373  762379  762389  762397  762401  762407
762409  762479  762491  762529  762539  762547  762557  762563  762571  762577
762583  762599  762647  762653  762659  762667  762721  762737  762761  762779
762791  762809  762821  762823  762847  762871  762877  762893  762899  762901  762913
762917  762919  762959  762967  762973  762989  763001  763013  763027  763031  763039
763043  763067  763073  763093  763111  763123  763141  763157  763159  763183  763201
763223  763237  763261  763267  763271  763303  763307  763339  763349  763369  763381
763391  763403  763409  763417  763423  763429  763447  763457  763471  763541  763543
763513  763523  763549  763559  763573  763579  763583  763597  763601  763613  763619
763621  763627  763649  763663  763673  763699  763739  763751  763753  763757  763771
763787  763801  763811  763823  763843  763859  763879  763883  763897  763901  763907
763913  763921  763927  763937  763943  763957  763967  763999  764003  764011  764017
764021  764041  764051  764059  764081  764089  764111  764131  764143  764149
764171  764189  764209  764233  764249  764251  764261  764273  764293  764317  764321
764327  764339  764341  764369  764381  764399  764431  764447  764459  764471  764501
764521  764531  764551  764563  764587  764591  764593  764611  764623  764627  764629
764657  764683  764689  764717  764719  764723  764783  764789  764809  764837  764839
764849  764857  764887  764891  764893  764903  764947  764969  764971  764977
764989  764993  764999  765007  765031  765041  765043  765047  765059  765091  765097
765103  765109  765131  765137  765139  765143  765151  765169  765199  765203
765209  765211  765227  765229  765241  765251  765257  765283  765287  765293  765307
765313  765319  765329  765353  765379  765383  765389  765409  765437  765439  765461
765467  765487  765497  765503  765521  765533  765539  765577  765581  765587  765613
765619  765623  765649  765659  765673  765707  765727  765749  765763  765767  765773
```

```
765781  765823  765827  765847  765851  765857  765859  765881  765889  765893  765899
765907  765913  765931  765949  765953  765971  765973  765991  766021  766039  766049
766067  766079  766091  766097  766109  766111  766127  766163  766169  766177  766187
766211  766223  766229  766231  766237  766247  766261  766273  766277  766301  766313
766321  766333  766357  766361  766369  766373  766387  766393  766399  766421  766439
766453  766457  766471  766477  766487  766501  766511  766531  766541  766543  766553
766559  766583  766609  766637  766639  766651  766679  766687  766721  766739  766757
766763  766769  766793  766807  766811  766813  766817  766861  766867  766873  766877
766891  766901  766907  766937  766939  766957  766967  766999  767017  767029
767051  767071  767089  767093  767101  767111  767131  767147  767153  767161  767167
767203  767243  767279  767287  767293  767309  767317  767321  767323  767339  767357
767359  767381  767399  767423  767443  767471  767489  767509  767513  767521  767527
767537  767539  767549  767551  767587  767597  767603  767617  767623  767633  767647
767677  767681  767707  767729  767747  767749  767759  767761  767773  767783  767813
767827  767831  767843  767857  767863  767867  767869  767881  767909  767951  767957
768013  768029  768041  768049  768059  768073  768101  768107  768127  768133  768139
768161  768167  768169  768191  768193  768197  768199  768203  768221  768241  768259
768263  768301  768319  768323  768329  768343  768347  768353  768359  768371  768373
768377  768389  768401  768409  768419  768431  768437  768457  768461  768479  768491
768503  768541  768563  768571  768589  768613  768623  768629  768631  768641  768643
768653  768671  768727  768751  768767  768773  768787  768793  768799  768811  768841
768851  768853  768857  768869  768881  768923  768931  768941  768953  768979  768983
769003  769007  769019  769033  769039  769057  769073  769081  769091  769117  769123
769141  769151  769159  769169  769207  769231  769243  769247  769259  769261  769273
769289  769297  769309  769319  769339  769357  769387  769411  769421  769423  769429
769453  769459  769463  769469  769487  769541  769543  769547  769553  769577  769579
769589  769591  769597  769619  769627  769661  769663  769673  769687  769723  769729
769733  769739  769751  769781  769789  769799  769807  769837  769871  769903  769919
769927  769943  769961  769963  769973  769987  769997  769999  770027  770039  770041
770047  770053  770057  770059  770069  770101  770111  770113  770123  770129  770167
770177  770179  770183  770191  770207  770227  770233  770239  770261  770281  770291
770309  770311  770353  770359  770387  770401  770417  770437  770447  770449  770459
770503  770519  770527  770533  770537  770551  770557  770573  770579  770587  770591
770597  770611  770639  770641  770647  770657  770663  770669  770741  770761  770767
770771  770789  770801  770813  770837  770839  770843  770863  770867  770873  770881
770897  770909  770927  770929  770951  770971  770981  770993  771011  771013  771019
771031  771037  771047  771049  771073  771079  771091  771109  771143  771163  771179
771181  771209  771217  771227  771233  771269  771283  771289  771293  771299  771301
771349  771359  771389  771401  771403  771427  771431  771437  771439  771461  771473
771481  771499  771503  771509  771517  771527  771553  771569  771583  771587  771607
771619  771623  771629  771637  771643  771653  771679  771691  771697  771703  771739
771763  771769  771781  771809  771853  771863  771877  771887  771889  771899  771917
771937  771941  771961  771971  771973  771997  772001  772003  772019  772061  772073
772081  772091  772097  772127  772139  772147  772159  772169  772181  772207  772229
772231  772273  772279  772297  772313  772333  772339  772349  772367  772379  772381
772391  772393  772403  772439  772441  772451  772459  772477  772493  772517  772537
772567  772571  772573  772591  772619  772631  772649  772657  772661  772663  772669
772691  772697  772703  772721  772757  772771  772789  772843  772847  772853  772859
772867  772903  772907  772909  772913  772921  772949  772963  772987  772991  773021
773023  773027  773029  773039  773057  773063  773081  773083  773093  773117  773147
773153  773159  773207  773209  773231  773239  773249  773251  773273  773287  773299
773317  773341  773363  773371  773387  773393  773407  773417  773447  773453  773473
773491  773497  773501  773533  773537  773561  773567  773569  773579  773599  773603
773609  773611  773657  773659  773681  773683  773693  773713  773719  773723  773767
773777  773779  773803  773821  773831  773837  773849  773863  773867  773869  773879
773897  773909  773933  773939  773951  773953  773987  773989  773999  774001  774017
774023  774047  774071  774073  774083  774107  774119  774127  774131  774133  774143
774149  774161  774173  774181  774199  774217  774223  774229  774233  774239  774283
774289  774313  774317  774337  774343  774377  774427  774439  774463  774467  774491
774511  774523  774541  774551  774577  774583  774589  774593  774601  774629  774643
774661  774667  774671  774679  774691  774703  774733  774749  774757  774773  774779  774791
774797  774799  774803  774811  774821  774833  774853  774857  774863  774901  774919
774929  774931  774959  774997  775007  775037  775043  775057  775063  775079  775087
775091  775097  775121  775147  775153  775157  775163  775189  775193  775237  775241
775259  775261  775273  775309  775343  775349  775361  775363  775367  775393  775417
775441  775451  775477  775507  775513  775517  775531  775553  775573  775601  775603
775613  775627  775633  775639  775661  775669  775681  775711  775729  775739  775741
775757  775777  775787  775807  775811  775823  775861  775871  775889  775919  775933
775937  775939  775949  775963  775987  776003  776029  776047  776057  776059  776077
776099  776117  776119  776137  776143  776159  776173  776177  776179  776183  776201
776219  776221  776233  776249  776257  776267  776287  776317  776327  776357  776389
776401  776429  776449  776453  776467  776471  776483  776497  776507  776513  776521
776551  776557  776561  776563  776569  776599  776627  776651  776683  776693  776719
776729  776749  776753  776759  776801  776813  776819  776837  776851  776861  776869
776879  776887  776899  776921  776947  776969  776977  776983  776987  777001  777011
777013  777031  777041  777071  777097  777103  777109  777137  777143  777151  777167
777169  777173  777181  777187  777191  777199  777209  777221  777241  777247  777251
777269  777277  777313  777317  777349  777353  777373  777383  777389  777391  777419
777421  777431  777433  777437  777451  777463  777473  777479  777541  777551  777571
777583  777611  777617  777619  777641  777643  777661  777671  777677  777683  777731
777737  777743  777761  777769  777781  777787  777817  777839  777857  777859  777863
777871  777877  777901  777911  777919  777977  777979  777989  778013  778027  778049
778051  778061  778079  778081  778091  778097  778109  778111  778121  778123  778153
778163  778187  778201  778213  778223  778237  778241  778247  778301  778307  778313
778319  778333  778357  778361  778381  778391  778397  778403  778409  778417  778439
778469  778507  778511  778513  778523  778529  778537  778541  778553  778559  778567
778579  778597  778633  778643  778663  778667  778681  778693  778697  778699  778709
778717  778727  778733  778759  778763  778769  778777  778783  778793  778819  778831  778847
778871  778873  778879  778903  778907  778913  778927  778933  778951  778963  778979
```

```
778993  779003  779011  779021  779039  779063  779069  779081  779101  779111  779131
779137  779159  779173  779189  779221  779231  779239  779249  779267  779327  779329
779341  779347  779351  779353  779357  779377  779413  779477  779489  779507  779521
779531  779543  779561  779563  779573  779579  779591  779593  779599  779609  779617
779621  779657  779659  779663  779693  779699  779707  779731  779747  779749  779761
779767  779771  779791  779797  779827  779837  779869  779873  779879  779887  779899
779927  779939  779971  779981  779983  779993  780029  780037  780041  780047  780049
780061  780119  780127  780163  780173  780179  780191  780193  780211  780223  780233
780253  780257  780287  780323  780343  780347  780371  780379  780383  780389  780397
780401  780421  780433  780457  780469  780499  780523  780553  780583  780587  780601
780613  780631  780649  780667  780671  780679  780683  780697  780707  780719  780721
780733  780799  780803  780809  780817  780823  780833  780841  780851  780853  780869
780877  780887  780889  780917  780931  780953  780961  780971  780973  780991  781003
781007  781021  781043  781051  781063  781069  781087  781111  781117  781127  781129
781139  781163  781171  781199  781211  781217  781229  781243  781247  781271  781283
781301  781307  781309  781321  781327  781351  781357  781367  781369  781387  781397
781399  781409  781423  781433  781453  781481  781483  781493  781511  781513
781519  781523  781531  781559  781567  781589  781601  781607  781619  781631  781633
781661  781673  781681  781721  781733  781741  781771  781799  781801  781817  781819
781853  781861  781867  781883  781889  781897  781919  781951  781961  781967  781969
781973  781987  781997  781999  782003  782009  782011  782053  782057  782071  782083
782087  782107  782113  782123  782129  782137  782141  782147  782149  782183  782189
782191  782209  782219  782231  782251  782263  782267  782297  782311  782329  782339
782371  782381  782387  782389  782393  782429  782443  782461  782473  782489  782497
782501  782519  782539  782581  782611  782641  782659  782669  782671  782687  782689
782707  782711  782723  782777  782783  782791  782839  782849  782861  782891  782911
782921  782941  782963  782981  782983  782993  783007  783011  783019  783023  783043
783077  783089  783119  783121  783131  783137  783143  783149  783151  783191  783193
783197  783227  783247  783257  783259  783269  783283  783317  783323  783329  783337
783359  783361  783373  783379  783407  783413  783421  783473  783487  783527  783529
783533  783553  783557  783569  783571  783599  783613  783619  783641  783647  783661
783677  783689  783691  783701  783703  783707  783719  783721  783733  783737  783743
783749  783763  783767  783779  783781  783787  783791  783793  783799  783803  783829
783869  783877  783931  783953  784009  784019  784061  784081  784087  784097  784103
784109  784117  784129  784153  784171  784181  784183  784211  784213  784219  784229
784243  784249  784283  784307  784309  784313  784321  784327  784349  784351  784367
784373  784379  784387  784409  784411  784423  784447  784451  784457  784463  784471
784481  784489  784501  784513  784541  784543  784547  784561  784573  784577  784583
784603  784627  784649  784661  784687  784697  784717  784723  784747  784753  784789
784799  784831  784837  784841  784859  784867  784897  784913  784919  784939  784957
784961  784981  785003  785017  785033  785053  785093  785101  785107  785119  785123
785129  785143  785153  785159  785167  785203  785207  785219  785221  785227  785249
785269  785287  785293  785299  785303  785311  785321  785329  785333  785341  785347
785353  785357  785363  785377  785413  785423  785431  785459  785461  785483  785501
785503  785527  785537  785549  785569  785573  785579  785591  785597  785623  785627
785641  785651  785671  785693  785717  785731  785737  785753  785773  785777  785779
785801  785803  785809  785839  785857  785861  785879  785903  785921  785923  785947
785951  785963  786001  786013  786017  786031  786047  786053  786059  786061  786077
786109  786127  786151  786167  786173  786179  786197  786211  786223  786241  786251
786271  786307  786311  786319  786329  786337  786349  786371  786407  786419  786431
786443  786449  786469  786641  786547  786551  786553  786587  786589  786613  786629
786659  786661  786673  786691  786697  786701  786703  786707  786719  786739  786763
786803  786823  786829  786833  786859  786881  786887  786889  786901  786931  786937
786941  786949  786959  786971  786979  786983  787021  787043  787051  787057  787067
787069  787079  787091  787099  787123  787139  787153  787181  787187  787207  787217
787243  787261  787277  787289  787309  787331  787333  787337  787357  787361  787427
787429  787433  787439  787447  787469  787477  787483  787489  787513  787517  787519
787529  787537  787541  787547  787573  787601  787609  787621  787639  787649  787667
787697  787711  787747  787751  787757  787769  787771  787777  787783  787793  787807
787811  787817  787823  787837  787879  787883  787903  787907  787939  787973  787981
787993  787999  788003  788023  788027  788033  788041  788071  788077  788087  788089
788093  788107  788129  788153  788159  788167  788173  788189  788209  788213  788231
788261  788267  788287  788309  788317  788321  788351  788353  788357  788363  788369
788377  788383  788387  788393  788399  788413  788419  788429  788449  788467  788479
788497  788521  788527  788531  788537  788549  788561  788563  788569  788603  788621
788651  788659  788677  788687  788701  788719  788761  788779  788789  788813  788819
788849  788863  788867  788869  788873  788891  788897  788903  788927  788933  788941
788947  788959  788971  788993  788999  789001  789017  789029  789031  789067  789077
789091  789097  789101  789109  789121  789133  789137  789149  789169  789181  789221
789227  789251  789311  789323  789331  789343  789367  789377  789389  789391  789407
789419  789443  789473  789491  789493  789511  789527  789533  789557  789571  789577
789587  789589  789611  789623  789631  789653  789671  789673  789683  789689  789709
789713  789721  789731  789739  789749  789793  789823  789829  789847  789851  789857
789883  789941  789959  789961  789967  789977  789979  790003  790021  790033  790043
790051  790057  790063  790087  790093  790099  790121  790169  790171  790189  790199
790201  790219  790241  790261  790271  790277  790289  790291  790327  790331  790333
790351  790369  790379  790397  790403  790417  790421  790429  790451  790459  790481
790501  790513  790519  790523  790529  790547  790567  790583  790589  790607  790613
790633  790637  790649  790651  790693  790697  790703  790709  790733  790739  790747
790753  790781  790793  790817  790819  790831  790843  790861  790871  790879  790883
790897  790927  790957  790961  790967  790969  790991  790997  791003  791009  791017
791029  791047  791053  791081  791093  791099  791111  791117  791131  791159  791191
791201  791209  791227  791233  791251  791257  791261  791291  791309  791311  791317
791321  791347  791363  791377  791387  791411  791419  791431  791443  791447  791473
791489  791519  791543  791561  791563  791569  791573  791599  791627  791629  791657
791663  791677  791699  791773  791783  791789  791797  791801  791803  791827  791849
791851  791887  791891  791897  791899  791909  791927  791929  791933  791951  791969
791971  791993  792023  792031  792037  792041  792049  792061  792067  792073  792101
792107  792109  792119  792131  792151  792163  792179  792223  792227  792229  792241
```

792247	792257	792263	792277	792283	792293	792299	792301	792307	792317	792359
792371	792377	792383	792397	792413	792443	792461	792479	792481	792487	792521
792529	792551	792553	792559	792563	792581	792593	792601	792613	792629	792637
792641	792643	792647	792667	792679	792689	792691	792697	792703	792709	792713
792731	792751	792769	792793	792797	792821	792871	792881	792893	792907	792919
792929	792941	792959	792973	792983	792989	792991	793043	793069	793099	793103
793123	793129	793139	793159	793181	793187	793189	793207	793229	793253	793279
793297	793301	793327	793333	793337	793343	793379	793399	793439	793447	793453
793487	793493	793499	793511	793517	793519	793537	793547	793553	793561	793591
793601	793607	793621	793627	793633	793669	793673	793691	793699	793711	793717
793721	793733	793739	793757	793769	793777	793787	793789	793813	793841	793843
793853	793867	793889	793901	793927	793931	793939	793957	793967	793979	793981
793999	794009	794011	794023	794033	794039	794041	794063	794071	794077	794089
794111	794113	794119	794137	794141	794149	794153	794161	794173	794179	794191
794201	794203	794207	794221	794231	794239	794249	794327	794341	794363	794383
794389	794399	794407	794413	794449	794471	794473	794477	794483	794491	794509
794531	794537	794543	794551	794557	794569	794579	794587	794593	794641	794653
794657	794659	794669	794693	794711	794741	794743	794749	794779	794831	794879
794881	794887	794921	794923	794953	794957	794993	794999	795001	795007	795023
795071	795077	795079	795083	795097	795101	795103	795121	795127	795139	795149
795161	795187	795203	795211	795217	795233	795239	795251	795253	795299	795307
795323	795329	795337	795343	795349	795427	795449	795461	795467	795479	795493
795503	795517	795527	795533	795539	795551	795581	795589	795601	795643	795647
795649	795653	795659	795661	795667	795679	795703	795709	795713	795727	795737
795761	795763	795791	795793	795797	795799	795803	795827	795829	795871	795877
795913	795917	795931	795937	795941	795943	795947	795979	795983	795997	796001
796009	796063	796067	796091	796121	796139	796141	796151	796171	796177	796181
796189	796193	796217	796247	796259	796267	796291	796303	796307	796337	796339
796361	796363	796373	796379	796387	796391	796409	796447	796451	796459	796487
796493	796517	796531	796541	796553	796561	796567	796571	796583	796591	796619
796633	796657	796673	796687	796693	796699	796709	796711	796751	796759	796769
796777	796781	796799	796801	796813	796819	796847	796849	796853	796867	796871
796877	796889	796921	796931	796933	796937	796951	796967	796969	796981	797003
797009	797021	797029	797033	797039	797051	797053	797057	797063	797077	797119
797131	797143	797161	797171	797201	797207	797273	797281	797287	797309	797311
797333	797353	797359	797383	797389	797399	797417	797429	797473	797497	797507
797509	797539	797549	797551	797557	797561	797567	797569	797579	797581	797591
797593	797611	797627	797633	797647	797681	797689	797701	797711	797729	797743
797747	797767	797773	797813	797833	797851	797869	797887	797897	797911	797917
797933	797947	797957	797977	797987	798023	798043	798059	798067	798071	798079
798089	798097	798101	798121	798131	798139	798143	798151	798173	798179	798191
798197	798199	798221	798223	798227	798251	798257	798263	798271	798293	798319
798331	798341	798383	798397	798403	798409	798443	798451	798461	798481	798487
798503	798517	798521	798527	798533	798569	798599	798613	798641	798647	798649
798667	798691	798697	798701	798713	798727	798737	798751	798757	798773	798781
798799	798823	798871	798887	798911	798923	798929	798937	798943	798961	799003
799021	799031	799061	799063	799091	799093	799103	799147	799151	799171	799217
799219	799223	799259	799291	799301	799303	799307	799313	799333	799343	799361
799363	799369	799417	799427	799441	799453	799471	799481	799483	799489	799507
799523	799529	799543	799553	799573	799609	799613	799619	799621	799633	799637
799651	799657	799661	799679	799723	799727	799739	799741	799753	799759	799783
799801	799807	799817	799837	799853	799859	799873	799891	799921	799949	799961
799991	799993	799999	800011	800029	800053	800057	800077	800083	800099	
800113	800117	800119	800123	800131	800143	800159	800161	800209	800213	
800221	800231	800237	800243	800281	800287	800291	800311	800329	800333	800351
800357	800399	800407	800417	800419	800441	800447	800473	800477	800483	800497
800509	800519	800521	800533	800537	800539	800549	800557	800573	800587	800593
800599	800621	800623	800647	800651	800659	800663	800669	800677	800681	800693
800707	800711	800729	800731	800741	800743	800759	800773	800783	800801	800861
800873	800879	800897	800903	800909	800923	800953	800959	800971	800977	800993
800999	801001	801007	801011	801019	801037	801061	801077	801079	801103	801107
801127	801137	801179	801187	801197	801217	801247	801277	801289	801293	801301
801331	801337	801341	801349	801371	801379	801403	801407	801419	801421	801461
801469	801487	801503	801517	801539	801551	801557	801569	801571	801607	801611
801617	801631	801641	801677	801683	801701	801707	801709	801733	801761	801791
801809	801811	801817	801833	801841	801859	801883	801947	801959	801973	
801989	802007	802019	802027	802031	802037	802073	802103	802121	802127	802129
802141	802147	802159	802163	802177	802181	802183	802229	802231	802253	
802279	802283	802297	802331	802339	802357	802387	802421	802441	802453	802463
802471	802499	802511	802523	802531	802573	802583	802589	802597	802603	802609
802643	802649	802651	802661	802667	802709	802721	802729	802733	802751	802759
802777	802783	802787	802793	802799	802811	802829	802831	802873	802909	802913
802933	802951	802969	802999	803007	803027	803041	803053	803059	803069	803087
803093	803119	803141	803171	803189	803207	803227	803237	803251	803269	803273
803287	803311	803323	803333	803347	803359	803389	803393	803399	803417	803441
803443	803447	803449	803461	803479	803483	803497	803501	803513	803519	803549
803587	803591	803609	803611	803623	803629	803651	803659	803669	803687	803717
803729	803731	803737	803749	803813	803819	803849	803857	803867	803893	803897
803911	803921	803927	803939	803963	803977	803987	803989	804007	804017	804031
804043	804059	804073	804077	804091	804107	804113	804119	804127	804157	804161
804179	804191	804197	804203	804211	804239	804259	804281	804283	804313	804317
804329	804337	804341	804367	804371	804383	804409	804443	804449	804473	804493
804497	804511	804521	804523	804541	804553	804571	804577	804581	804589	804607
804611	804613	804619	804653	804689	804697	804703	804709	804743	804751	804757
804761	804769	804823	804829	804833	804847	804857	804859	804889	804893	
804901	804913	804919	804929	804941	804943	804983	804989	804997	805019	805027
805031	805033	805037	805061	805067	805073	805081	805097	805099	805109	805111
805121	805153	805159	805177	805181	805187	805219	805223	805241	805249	805267
805271	805279	805289	805297	805309	805313	805327	805331	805333	805339	805369

```
805381  805397  805403  805421  805451  805463  805471  805487  805499  805501  805507
805517  805523  805531  805537  805559  805573  805583  805589  805633  805639  805687
805703  805711  805723  805729  805741  805757  805789  805799  805807  805811  805843
805853  805859  805867  805873  805877  805891  805901  805913  805933  805967  805991
806009  806011  806017  806023  806027  806033  806041  806051  806059  806087  806107
806111  806129  806137  806153  806159  806177  806203  806213  806233  806257  806261
806263  806269  806291  806297  806317  806329  806363  806369  806371  806381  806383
806389  806447  806453  806467  806483  806503  806513  806521  806543  806549  806579
806581  806609  806639  806657  806671  806719  806737  806761  806783  806789  806791
806801  806807  806821  806857  806893  806903  806917  806929  806941  806947  806951
806977  806999  807011  807017  807071  807077  807083  807089  807097  807113  807119
807127  807151  807181  807187  807193  807197  807203  807217  807221  807241  807251
807259  807281  807299  807337  807371  807379  807383  807403  807407  807409  807419
807427  807463  807473  807479  807487  807491  807493  807509  807511  807523  807539
807559  807571  807607  807613  807629  807637  807647  807689  807707  807731  807733
807749  807757  807787  807797  807809  807817  807869  807871  807901  807907  807923
807931  807941  807943  807949  807973  807997  808019  808021  808039  808081  808097
808111  808147  808153  808169  808177  808187  808211  808217  808229  808237  808261
808267  808307  808309  808343  808349  808351  808361  808363  808369  808373  808391
808399  808417  808421  808439  808441  808459  808481  808517  808523  808553  808559
808579  808589  808597  808601  808603  808627  808637  808651  808679  808681  808693
808699  808721  808733  808739  808747  808751  808771  808777  808789  808793  808837
808853  808867  808919  808937  808957  808961  808981  808991  808993  809023  809041
809051  809063  809087  809093  809101  809141  809143  809147  809173  809177  809189
809201  809203  809213  809231  809239  809243  809261  809269  809273  809297  809309
809323  809339  809357  809359  809377  809383  809399  809401  809407  809423  809437
809443  809447  809453  809461  809491  809507  809521  809527  809563  809569  809579
809581  809587  809603  809629  809701  809707  809719  809729  809737  809741  809747
809749  809759  809771  809779  809797  809801  809803  809821  809827  809833  809839
809843  809869  809891  809903  809909  809917  809929  809981  809983  809993  810013
810023  810049  810053  810059  810071  810079  810091  810109  810137  810149  810151
810191  810193  810209  810223  810239  810253  810259  810269  810281  810307  810319
810343  810349  810353  810361  810367  810377  810379  810389  810391  810401  810409
810419  810427  810437  810443  810457  810473  810487  810493  810503  810517  810533
810539  810541  810547  810553  810571  810581  810583  810587  810643  810653  810659
810671  810697  810737  810757  810763  810769  810791  810809  810839  810853  810871
810881  810893  810907  810913  810923  810941  810949  810961  810967  810973  810989
811037  811039  811067  811081  811099  811123  811127  811147  811157  811163  811171
811183  811193  811199  811207  811231  811241  811253  811259  811273  811277  811289
811297  811337  811351  811379  811387  811411  811429  811441  811457  811469  811493
811501  811511  811519  811523  811553  811561  811583  811607  811619  811627  811637
811649  811651  811667  811691  811697  811703  811709  811729  811747  811753  811757
811763  811771  811777  811799  811819  811861  811871  811879  811897  811919  811931
811933  811957  811961  811981  811991  811997  812011  812033  812047  812051  812057
812081  812101  812129  812137  812167  812173  812179  812183  812191  812213  812221
812233  812249  812257  812267  812281  812297  812299  812309  812341  812347  812351
812353  812359  812363  812381  812387  812393  812401  812431  812443  812467  812473
812477  812491  812501  812503  812519  812527  812587  812597  812599  812627  812633
812639  812641  812671  812681  812689  812699  812701  812711  812717  812731  812759
812761  812807  812849  812857  812869  812921  812939  812963  812969  813013  813017
813023  813041  813049  813061  813083  813089  813091  813097  813107  813121  813133
813157  813167  813199  813203  813209  813217  813221  813227  813251  813269  813277
813283  813287  813299  813301  813311  813343  813361  813367  813377  813383  813401
813419  813427  813443  813493  813499  813503  813511  813529  813541  813559  813577
813583  813601  813613  813623  813647  813677  813697  813707  813721  813749  813767
813797  813811  813817  813833  813847  813863  813871  813893  813907  813931
813961  813971  813991  813997  814003  814007  814013  814019  814031  814043  814049
814061  814063  814067  814069  814081  814097  814127  814129  814139  814171  814183
814193  814199  814211  814213  814237  814241  814243  814279  814309  814327  814337
814367  814379  814381  814393  814399  814403  814423  814447  814469  814477  814493
814501  814531  814537  814543  814559  814577  814579  814601  814603  814609  814631
814633  814643  814687  814699  814717  814741  814747  814763  814771  814783  814789
814799  814823  814829  814841  814859  814873  814883  814889  814901  814903  814927
814937  814939  814943  814949  814991  815029  815033  815047  815053  815063  815123
815141  815149  815159  815173  815197  815209  815231  815251  815257  815261  815273
815279  815291  815317  815333  815341  815351  815389  815401  815411  815413  815417
815431  815453  815459  815471  815491  815501  815519  815527  815533  815539  815543
815569  815587  815599  815621  815623  815627  815663  815669  815671  815681
815687  815693  815713  815729  815809  815819  815821  815831  815851  815869  815891
815897  815923  815933  815939  815953  815963  815977  815999  816019  816037  816043
816047  816077  816091  816103  816113  816121  816131  816133  816157  816161  816163
816169  816191  816203  816209  816217  816223  816227  816239  816251  816271  816317
816329  816341  816353  816367  816377  816401  816427  816443  816451  816469  816499
816521  816539  816547  816559  816581  816587  816589  816593  816649  816653  816667
816689  816691  816703  816709  816743  816763  816769  816799  816811  816817  816821
816839  816841  816847  816857  816859  816869  816883  816887  816899  816911  816917
816919  816929  816941  816947  816961  816971  817013  817027  817039  817049  817051
817073  817081  817087  817093  817111  817123  817127  817147  817151  817153  817163
817169  817183  817211  817237  817273  817277  817279  817291  817303  817319  817321
817331  817337  817357  817379  817403  817409  817433  817457  817463  817483  817519
817529  817549  817561  817567  817603  817637  817651  817669  817679  817697  817709
817711  817721  817723  817727  817757  817769  817777  817783  817787  817793  817823
817837  817841  817867  817871  817877  817889  817891  817897  817907  817913  817919
817933  817951  817979  817987  818011  818017  818021  818093  818099  818101  818113
818123  818143  818171  818173  818189  818219  818231  818239  818249  818281  818287
818291  818303  818309  818327  818339  818341  818347  818353  818359  818371  818383
818393  818399  818413  818429  818453  818473  818509  818561  818569  818579  818581
818603  818621  818659  818683  818687  818689  818707  818717  818723  818813  818819
818821  818827  818837  818887  818897  818947  818959  818963  818969  818977  818999
```

```
819001  819017  819029  819031  819037  819061  819073  819083  819101  819131  819149
819157  819167  819173  819187  819229  819239  819241  819251  819253  819263  819271
819289  819307  819311  819317  819319  819367  819373  819389  819391  819407  819409
819419  819431  819437  819443  819449  819457  819463  819473  819487  819491  819493
819499  819503  819509  819523  819563  819583  819593  819607  819617  819619  819629
819647  819653  819659  819673  819691  819701  819719  819737  819739  819761  819769
819773  819781  819787  819799  819811  819823  819827  819829  819853  819889  819911
819913  819937  819943  819977  819989  819991  820037  820051  820067  820073  820093
820109  820117  820129  820133  820163  820177  820187  820201  820213  820223  820231
820241  820243  820247  820271  820273  820279  820319  820321  820331  820333  820343
820349  820361  820367  820399  820409  820411  820427  820429  820441  820459  820481
820489  820537  820541  820559  820577  820597  820609  820619  820627  820637  820643
820649  820657  820679  820681  820691  820711  820723  820733  820747  820753  820759
820763  820793  820837  820873  820891  820901  820907  820909  820921  820927
820957  820969  820991  820997  821003  821027  821039  821053  821057  821063  821069
821081  821089  821099  821101  821113  821131  821143  821147  821153  821167  821173
821207  821209  821263  821281  821291  821297  821311  821329  821333  821377  821383
821411  821441  821449  821459  821461  821467  821477  821479  821489  821497  821507
821519  821551  821573  821603  821641  821647  821651  821663  821677  821741  821747
821753  821759  821771  821801  821803  821809  821819  821827  821833  821851  821857
821861  821869  821879  821897  821911  821939  821941  821971  821993  821999  822007
822011  822013  822037  822049  822067  822079  822113  822131  822139  822161  822163
822167  822169  822191  822197  822221  822223  822229  822233  822253  822259  822277
822293  822299  822313  822317  822323  822329  822343  822347  822361  822379  822383
822389  822391  822407  822431  822433  822517  822539  822541  822551  822553  822557
822571  822581  822587  822589  822599  822607  822611  822631  822667  822671  822673
822683  822691  822697  822713  822721  822727  822739  822743  822761  822763  822781
822791  822793  822803  822821  822823  822839  822853  822881  822883  822889  822893
822901  822907  822949  822971  822973  822989  823001  823003  823013  823033  823051
823117  823127  823129  823153  823169  823177  823183  823201  823219  823231  823237
823241  823243  823261  823271  823283  823309  823337  823349  823351  823357  823373
823399  823421  823447  823451  823457  823481  823483  823489  823499  823519  823541
823547  823553  823573  823591  823601  823619  823621  823637  823643  823651  823663
823679  823703  823709  823717  823721  823723  823727  823739  823741  823747  823759
823777  823787  823789  823799  823819  823829  823831  823841  823843  823877  823903
823913  823961  823967  823969  823981  823993  823997  824017  824029  824039  824063
824069  824077  824081  824099  824123  824137  824147  824179  824183  824189  824191
824227  824231  824233  824269  824281  824287  824339  824393  824399  824401  824413
824419  824437  824443  824459  824477  824489  824497  824501  824513  824531  824539
824563  824591  824609  824641  824647  824651  824669  824671  824683  824699  824701
824723  824741  824747  824753  824773  824777  824779  824801  824821  824833  824843
824861  824893  824899  824911  824921  824933  824939  824947  824951  824977  824981
824983  825007  825017  825029  825047  825049  825059  825067  825073  825101
825107  825109  825131  825161  825191  825193  825199  825203  825229  825241  825247
825259  825277  825281  825283  825287  825301  825329  825337  825343  825347  825353
825361  825389  825397  825403  825413  825421  825439  825443  825467  825479  825491
825509  825527  825533  825547  825551  825553  825577  825593  825611  825613  825637
825647  825661  825679  825689  825697  825701  825709  825733  825739  825749  825763
825779  825791  825821  825827  825829  825857  825883  825889  825919  825947  825959
825961  825971  825983  825991  825997  826019  826037  826039  826051  826061  826069
826087  826093  826099  826129  826151  826153  826169  826171  826193  826201  826211
826271  826283  826289  826303  826313  826333  826339  826349  826351  826363  826379
826381  826391  826393  826403  826411  826453  826477  826493  826499  826541  826549
826559  826561  826571  826583  826603  826607  826613  826621  826663  826667  826669
826673  826681  826697  826699  826711  826717  826723  826729  826753  826759  826783
826799  826807  826831  826849  826867  826877  826879  826883  826907  826921  826927
826939  826957  826963  826967  826979  826997  827009  827023  827039  827041  827063
827087  827129  827131  827143  827147  827161  827213  827227  827231  827251  827269
827293  827303  827311  827327  827347  827369  827389  827417  827423  827429  827443
827447  827461  827473  827501  827521  827537  827539  827549  827581  827591  827599
827633  827639  827677  827681  827693  827699  827719  827737  827741  827767  827779
827791  827803  827809  827821  827833  827837  827843  827851  827857  827867  827873
827899  827903  827923  827927  827929  827941  827969  827987  827989  828007  828011
828013  828029  828043  828059  828067  828071  828101  828109  828119  828127  828131
828133  828169  828199  828209  828221  828239  828277  828349  828361  828371  828379
828383  828397  828407  828409  828431  828461  828517  828523  828547  828557  828577
828587  828601  828637  828643  828649  828673  828677  828691  828697  828701  828703
828721  828731  828743  828757  828787  828797  828809  828811  828823  828829  828833
828859  828871  828881  828889  828899  828901  828917  828923  828941  828953  828967
828977  829001  829013  829057  829063  829069  829093  829097  829111  829121  829123
829151  829159  829177  829187  829193  829211  829223  829229  829237  829249  829267
829273  829289  829319  829349  829399  829453  829457  829463  829469  829501  829511
829519  829537  829547  829561  829601  829613  829627  829637  829639  829643  829657
829687  829693  829709  829721  829723  829727  829729  829733  829757  829783  829811
829813  829819  829831  829841  829847  829849  829867  829877  829883  829949  829967
829979  829987  829993  830003  830017  830041  830051  830099  830111  830117  830131
830143  830153  830173  830177  830191  830233  830237  830257  830267  830279  830293
830309  830311  830327  830329  830339  830341  830353  830359  830363  830383  830387
830411  830413  830419  830441  830447  830449  830477  830483  830497  830503  830513
830549  830551  830561  830567  830579  830587  830591  830597  830617  830639  830657
830677  830693  830719  830729  830741  830743  830777  830789  830801  830827  830833
830839  830849  830861  830873  830887  830891  830899  830911  830923  830939  830957
830981  830989  831023  831031  831037  831043  831067  831071  831073  831091  831109
831139  831161  831163  831167  831191  831217  831221  831239  831253  831287  831301
831323  831329  831361  831367  831371  831373  831407  831409  831431  831433  831437
831443  831461  831503  831529  831539  831541  831547  831553  831559  831583  831587
831599  831617  831619  831631  831643  831647  831653  831659  831661  831679  831683
831697  831707  831709  831713  831731  831739  831751  831757  831769  831781  831799
831811  831821  831829  831847  831851  831863  831881  831889  831893  831899  831911
```

```
831913  831917  831967  831983  832003  832063  832079  832081  832103  832109  832121
832123  832129  832141  832151  832157  832159  832189  832211  832217  832253  832291
832297  832309  832327  832331  832339  832361  832367  832369  832373  832379  832399
832411  832421  832427  832451  832457  832477  832483  832487  832493  832499  832519
832583  832591  832597  832607  832613  832621  832627  832631  832633  832639  832673
832679  832681  832687  832693  832703  832709  832717  832721  832729  832747  832757
832763  832771  832787  832801  832837  832841  832861  832879  832883  832889  832913
832919  832927  832933  832943  832957  832963  832969  832973  832987  833009  833023
833033  833047  833057  833099  833101  833117  833171  833179  833191  833197  833237
833201  833219  833251  833269  833281  833293  833299  833309  833347  833353  833363
833377  833389  833429  833449  833453  833461  833467  833477  833479  833491  833509
833537  833557  833563  833593  833597  833617  833633  833659  833669  833689  833711
833713  833717  833719  833737  833747  833759  833783  833801  833821  833839  833843
833857  833873  833887  833893  833897  833923  833927  833933  833947  833977  833999
834007  834013  834023  834059  834107  834131  834133  834137  834143  834149  834151
834181  834199  834221  834257  834259  834269  834277  834283  834287  834299  834311
834341  834367  834433  834439  834469  834487  834497  834503  834511  834523  834527
834569  834571  834593  834599  834607  834611  834623  834629  834641  834643  834653
834671  834703  834709  834721  834761  834773  834781  834787  834809  834811
834829  834857  834859  834893  834913  834941  834947  834949  834959  834961  834983
834991  835001  835013  835019  835033  835039  835097  835099  835117  835123  835139
835151  835207  835213  835217  835249  835253  835271  835313  835319  835321  835327
835369  835379  835391  835399  835421  835427  835441  835451  835453  835459  835469
835549  835511  835531  835553  835559  835591  835603  835607  835609  835633  835643
835661  835663  835673  835687  835717  835721  835733  835739  835759  835789  835811
835817  835819  835823  835831  835841  835847  835859  835897  835909  835927  835931
835937  835951  835957  835973  835979  835987  835993  835997  836047  836063  836071
836107  836117  836131  836137  836149  836153  836159  836161  836183  836189  836191
836203  836219  836233  836239  836243  836267  836291  836299  836317  836327  836347
836351  836369  836377  836387  836413  836449  836471  836477  836491  836497  836501
836509  836567  836569  836573  836609  836611  836623  836657  836663  836677  836683
836699  836701  836707  836713  836729  836747  836749  836753  836761  836789  836807
836821  836833  836839  836861  836863  836873  836879  836881  836917  836921  836939
836951  836971  837017  837043  837047  837059  837071  837073  837077  837079  837107
837113  837139  837149  837157  837191  837203  837257  837271  837283  837293  837307
837313  837359  837367  837373  837377  837379  837409  837413  837439  837451  837461
837467  837497  837503  837509  837521  837533  837583  837601  837611  837619  837631
837659  837667  837673  837677  837679  837721  837731  837737  837773  837779  837797
837817  837833  837847  837853  837887  837923  837929  837931  837937  837943  837979
838003  838021  838037  838039  838043  838063  838069  838091  838093  838099  838133
838139  838141  838153  838157  838169  838171  838193  838207  838247  838249  838441
838351  838363  838367  838379  838391  838393  838399  838403  838421  838429  838441
838447  838459  838463  838471  838483  838517  838547  838553  838561  838571  838583
838589  838597  838601  838609  838613  838631  838633  838657  838667  838687  838693
838711  838751  838757  838769  838771  838777  838781  838807  838813  838837  838853
838889  838897  838909  838913  838919  838927  838931  838939  838949  838951  838963
838969  838991  838993  839009  839029  839051  839071  839087  839117  839131  839161
839203  839207  839221  839227  839261  839269  839303  839323  839327  839351  839353
839369  839381  839413  839429  839437  839441  839453  839459  839471  839473  839483
839491  839497  839519  839539  839551  839563  839599  839603  839609  839611  839617
839621  839633  839651  839653  839669  839693  839723  839731  839767  839771  839791
839801  839809  839831  839837  839873  839879  839887  839897  839899  839903  839911
839921  839957  839959  839963  839981  839999  840023  840053  840061  840067  840083
840109  840139  840149  840163  840179  840181  840187  840197  840223  840239
840241  840253  840269  840277  840289  840299  840319  840331  840341  840347  840353
840439  840451  840457  840467  840473  840479  840491  840523  840547  840557  840571
840589  840601  840611  840643  840661  840683  840703  840709  840713  840727  840733
840743  840757  840761  840767  840817  840821  840823  840839  840841  840859  840863
840907  840911  840923  840929  840941  840943  840967  840979  840989  840991  841003
841013  841019  841021  841063  841069  841079  841081  841091  841097  841103  841147
841157  841189  841193  841207  841213  841219  841223  841231  841237  841241  841259
841273  841277  841283  841297  841307  841327  841333  841349  841369  841391
841397  841411  841427  841447  841457  841459  841531  841549  841559  841573  841597
841601  841637  841651  841661  841663  841691  841697  841727  841741  841751  841793
841801  841849  841859  841873  841879  841889  841913  841921  841927  841931  841933
841979  841987  842003  842021  842041  842063  842071  842077  842081  842087
842089  842111  842113  842141  842147  842159  842161  842167  842173  842183  842203
842209  842249  842267  842279  842291  842293  842311  842321  842323  842339  842341
842351  842353  842371  842383  842393  842399  842407  842417  842419  842423  842447
842449  842473  842477  842483  842489  842497  842507  842519  842521  842531  842551
842581  842587  842599  842617  842623  842627  842657  842701  842729  842747  842759
842767  842771  842791  842801  842813  842819  842857  842869  842879  842887  842923
842939  842951  842957  842969  842981  842987  842993  843043  843067  843079
843091  843103  843113  843127  843131  843137  843173  843179  843181  843209  843211
843229  843253  843257  843289  843299  843301  843307  843331  843337  843361  843371
843377  843379  843383  843397  843443  843449  843457  843461  843473  843487  843497
843503  843527  843539  843553  843559  843587  843589  843607  843613  843629  843643
843649  843677  843679  843701  843737  843757  843763  843779  843781  843793  843797
843811  843823  843833  843841  843881  843883  843889  843901  843907  843911  844001
844013  844043  844061  844069  844087  844093  844111  844117  844121  844127  844139
844141  844153  844157  844183  844187  844199  844201  844243  844247  844253
844279  844289  844297  844309  844321  844351  844369  844421  844427  844429  844433
844439  844447  844453  844457  844463  844469  844489  844499  844507  844511
844513  844517  844523  844549  844553  844601  844603  844609  844619  844621  844631
844639  844643  844651  844709  844717  844733  844757  844763  844769  844777
844841  844847  844861  844867  844891  844897  844903  844913  844927  844957  844999
845003  845017  845021  845027  845041  845069  845083  845099  845111  845129  845137
845167  845179  845183  845197  845203  845209  845219  845231  845237  845261  845279
845287  845303  845309  845333  845347  845357  845363  845371  845381  845387  845431
```

845441 845447 845459 845489 845491 845531 845567 845599 845623 845653 845657
845659 845683 845717 845723 845729 845749 845753 845771 845777 845809 845833
845849 845863 845879 845881 845893 845909 845921 845927 845941 845951 845969
845981 845983 845987 845989 846037 846059 846061 846067 846113 846137 846149
846161 846179 846187 846217 846229 846233 846247 846259 846271 846323 846341
846343 846353 846359 846361 846383 846389 846397 846401 846403 846407 846421
846427 846437 846457 846487 846493 846499 846529 846563 846577 846589 846607
846661 846667 846673 846689 846721 846733 846739 846749 846751 846757 846779
846823 846841 846851 846869 846871 846877 846913 846917 846919 846931 846943
846949 846953 846961 846973 846977 846983 846997 847009 847031 847037 847043
847051 847069 847073 847079 847097 847103 847109 847129 847139 847151 847157
847163 847169 847193 847201 847213 847219 847237 847247 847271 847277 847279
847283 847309 847321 847339 847361 847367 847373 847393 847423 847453 847477
847493 847499 847507 847519 847531 847537 847543 847549 847577 847589 847601
847607 847621 847657 847663 847673 847681 847687 847697 847703 847727 847729
847741 847787 847789 847813 847817 847853 847871 847883 847901 847919 847933
847937 847949 847967 847969 847991 847993 847997 848017 848051 848087 848101
848119 848123 848131 848143 848149 848173 848201 848203 848213 848227 848251
848273 848297 848321 848359 848363 848383 848387 848399 848417 848423
848429 848443 848461 848467 848473 848489 848531 848537 848557 848567 848579
848591 848593 848599 848611 848629 848633 848647 848651 848671 848681 848699
848707 848713 848737 848747 848761 848779 848789 848791 848797 848803 848807
848839 848843 848849 848851 848857 848879 848893 848909 848921 848923 848927
848933 848941 848959 848983 848993 849019 849047 849049 849061 849083 849097
849103 849119 849127 849131 849143 849161 849179 849197 849203 849217 849221
849223 849241 849253 849271 849301 849311 849347 849349 849353 849383 849391
849419 849427 849461 849467 849481 849523 849533 849539 849571 849581 849587
849593 849599 849601 849649 849691 849701 849703 849721 849727 849731 849733
849743 849763 849767 849773 849829 849833 849839 849857 849863 849883 849917
849923 849931 849943 849967 849973 849991 849997 850009 850021 850027 850033
850039 850049 850061 850063 850081 850093 850121 850133 850139 850147 850177
850181 850189 850207 850211 850229 850243 850247 850253 850261 850271 850273
850301 850303 850331 850337 850349 850351 850373 850387 850393 850397 850403
850417 850427 850433 850439 850453 850457 850481 850529 850537 850567 850571
850613 850631 850637 850673 850679 850691 850711 850729 850753 850781 850807
850823 850849 850853 850879 850891 850897 850933 850943 850951 850973 850979
851009 851017 851033 851041 851051 851057 851087 851093 851113 851117 851131
851153 851159 851171 851177 851197 851203 851209 851231 851239 851251 851261
851267 851273 851293 851297 851303 851321 851327 851351 851359 851363 851381
851387 851393 851401 851413 851419 851423 851449 851471 851491 851507 851519
851537 851543 851569 851573 851597 851603 851623 851633 851639 851647 851659
851671 851677 851689 851723 851731 851749 851761 851797 851801 851803 851813
851821 851831 851839 851843 851863 851881 851891 851899 851953 851957 851971
852011 852013 852031 852037 852079 852101 852121 852139 852143 852149 852151
852167 852179 852191 852197 852199 852211 852233 852239 852253 852259 852263
852287 852289 852301 852323 852347 852367 852391 852409 852427 852437 852443
852463 852521 852557 852559 852563 852569 852581 852583 852589 852613 852617
852623 852641 852661 852671 852673 852689 852749 852751 852757 852763 852769
852793 852799 852809 852827 852829 852833 852847 852851 852857 852871 852881
852889 852893 852913 852937 852953 852959 852989 852997 853007 853031 853033
853049 853057 853079 853091 853103 853123 853133 853159 853187 853189 853211
853217 853241 853283 853289 853291 853319 853339 853357 853387 853403 853427
853429 853439 853477 853481 853493 853529 853543 853547 853571 853577 853597
853637 853663 853667 853669 853687 853693 853703 853717 853733 853739 853759
853763 853793 853799 853807 853813 853819 853823 853837 853843 853873 853889
853901 853903 853913 853933 853949 853969 853981 853999 854017 854033 854039
854041 854047 854053 854083 854089 854093 854099 854111 854123 854129 854141
854149 854159 854171 854213 854257 854263 854299 854303 854323 854327 854333
854351 854353 854363 854383 854387 854407 854417 854419 854423 854431 854443
854459 854461 854467 854479 854527 854533 854569 854587 854593 854599 854617
854621 854629 854647 854683 854713 854729 854747 854771 854801 854807 854849
854869 854881 854897 854899 854921 854923 854927 854929 854951 854957 854963
854993 854999 855031 855059 855061 855067 855079 855089 855119 855131 855143
855187 855191 855199 855203 855221 855229 855241 855269 855271 855277 855293
855307 855311 855317 855331 855359 855373 855377 855391 855397 855401 855419
855427 855431 855461 855467 855499 855511 855521 855527 855581 855601 855607
855619 855641 855667 855671 855683 855697 855709 855713 855719 855721 855727
855731 855733 855737 855739 855751 855757 855821 855851 855857 855863 855887
855889 855901 855919 855923 855937 855947 855983 855989 855997 856021 856043
856057 856061 856073 856081 856099 856111 856117 856133 856139 856147 856153
856169 856181 856187 856213 856237 856241 856249 856277 856279 856301 856309
856333 856343 856351 856369 856381 856391 856393 856411 856417 856421 856441
856459 856469 856483 856487 856507 856519 856529 856547 856549 856553 856567
856571 856627 856637 856649 856693 856697 856699 856703 856711 856717 856721
856733 856759 856787 856789 856811 856813 856831 856841 856849 856853 856861
856897 856901 856903 856909 856927 856939 856943 856949 856969 856993 857009
857011 857027 857029 857039 857047 857053 857069 857081 857083 857099 857107
857137 857167 857177 857201 857203 857221 857249 857267 857273 857281 857287
857309 857321 857333 857341 857347 857357 857369 857407 857411 857419 857431
857453 857459 857471 857513 857539 857551 857567 857569 857573 857579 857581
857629 857653 857663 857669 857671 857687 857707 857711 857713 857723 857737
857741 857743 857749 857809 857821 857827 857839 857851 857867 857873 857897
857903 857929 857951 857953 857957 857959 857963 857977 857981 858001 858029
858043 858073 858083 858101 858103 858113 858127 858149 858161 858167 858217
858223 858233 858239 858241 858251 858259 858269 858281 858293 858301 858307
858311 858317 858373 858397 858427 858433 858457 858463 858467 858479 858497
858503 858527 858563 858577 858589 858623 858631 858673 858691 858701 858707
858709 858713 858749 858757 858763 858769 858787 858817 858821 858833 858841
858859 858877 858883 858899 858911 858919 858931 858943 858953 858961 858989

```
858997  859003  859031  859037  859049  859051  859057  859081  859091  859093  859109
859121  859181  859189  859213  859223  859249  859259  859267  859273  859277  859279
859297  859321  859361  859363  859373  859381  859393  859423  859433  859447  859459
859477  859493  859513  859553  859559  859561  859567  859577  859601  859603  859609
859619  859633  859657  859667  859669  859679  859681  859697  859709  859751  859783
859787  859799  859801  859823  859841  859849  859853  859861  859891  859913  859919
859927  859933  859939  859973  859981  859987  860009  860011  860029  860051  860059
860063  860071  860077  860087  860089  860107  860113  860117  860143  860239  860257
860267  860291  860297  860309  860311  860317  860323  860333  860341  860351  860357
860369  860381  860383  860393  860399  860413  860417  860423  860441  860479  860501
860507  860513  860533  860543  860569  860579  860581  860593  860599  860609  860623
860641  860647  860663  860689  860701  860747  860753  860759  860779  860789  860791
860809  860813  860819  860843  860861  860887  860891  860911  860917  860921  860927
860929  860939  860941  860957  860969  860971  861001  861013  861019  861031  861037
861043  861053  861059  861079  861083  861089  861109  861121  861131  861139  861163
861167  861191  861199  861221  861239  861293  861299  861317  861347  861353  861361
861391  861433  861437  861439  861491  861493  861499  861541  861547  861551  861559
861563  861571  861589  861599  861613  861617  861647  861659  861691  861701  861703
861719  861733  861739  861743  861761  861797  861799  861803  861823  861829  861853
861857  861871  861877  861881  861899  861901  861907  861929  861937  861941  861947
861977  861979  861997  862009  862013  862031  862033  862061  862067  862097  862117
862123  862129  862139  862157  862159  862171  862177  862181  862187  862207  862219
862229  862231  862241  862249  862259  862261  862273  862283  862289  862297  862307
862319  862331  862343  862369  862387  862397  862399  862409  862417  862423  862441
862447  862471  862481  862483  862487  862493  862501  862541  862553  862559  862567
862571  862573  862583  862607  862627  862633  862649  862651  862669  862703  862727
862739  862769  862777  862783  862789  862811  862819  862861  862879  862907  862909
862913  862919  862921  862943  862957  862973  862987  862991  862997  863003  863017
863047  863081  863087  863119  863123  863131  863143  863153  863179  863197  863231
863251  863279  863287  863299  863309  863323  863363  863377  863393  863479  863491
863497  863509  863521  863537  863539  863561  863593  863609  863633  863641  863671
863689  863693  863711  863729  863743  863749  863767  863771  863783  863801  863803
863833  863843  863851  863867  863869  863879  863887  863897  863899  863909  863917
863921  863959  863983  864007  864011  864013  864029  864037  864047  864049  864053
864077  864079  864091  864103  864107  864119  864121  864131  864137  864151  864167
864169  864191  864203  864211  864221  864251  864257  864277  864289  864299  864301
864307  864319  864323  864341  864359  864361  864379  864407  864419  864427  864439
864449  864491  864503  864509  864511  864533  864541  864551  864581  864583  864587
864613  864623  864629  864631  864641  864673  864679  864691  864697  864733  864737
864757  864781  864793  864803  864811  864817  864883  864887  864901  864911  864917
864947  864953  864959  864967  864979  864989  865001  865003  865043  865049  865057
865061  865069  865087  865091  865103  865121  865153  865159  865177  865201  865211
865213  865217  865231  865247  865253  865259  865261  865301  865307  865313  865321
865327  865339  865343  865349  865363  865367  865379  865409  865457  865477  865481
865483  865493  865499  865511  865537  865577  865591  865597  865609  865619  865637
865639  865643  865661  865681  865687  865691  865721  865729  865741  865747  865751
865757  865769  865771  865783  865801  865807  865817  865819  865829  865847  865859
865867  865871  865877  865889  865933  865937  865957  865979  865993  866003  866009
866011  866029  866051  866053  866057  866081  866083  866087  866093  866101  866119
866123  866161  866183  866197  866213  866221  866231  866279  866293  866309  866311
866329  866353  866389  866399  866417  866431  866443  866461  866471  866477  866513
866519  866573  866581  866623  866629  866639  866641  866653  866683  866689  866693
866707  866713  866717  866737  866743  866759  866777  866783  866813  866843  866849
866851  866857  866869  866909  866917  866927  866933  866941  866953  866963  866969
867001  867007  867011  867023  867037  867059  867067  867079  867091  867121  867131
867143  867151  867161  867173  867203  867211  867227  867233  867253  867257  867259
867263  867271  867281  867301  867319  867337  867343  867371  867389  867397  867401
867409  867413  867431  867443  867457  867463  867467  867487  867509  867511  867541
867547  867553  867563  867571  867577  867589  867617  867619  867623  867631  867641
867653  867677  867679  867689  867701  867719  867733  867743  867773  867781  867793
867803  867817  867827  867829  867857  867871  867877  867913  867943  867947  867959
867991  868019  868033  868039  868051  868069  868073  868081  868103  868111  868121
868123  868151  868157  868171  868177  868199  868211  868229  868247  868267  868271
868277  868291  868313  868327  868331  868337  868349  868369  868379  868381  868397
868409  868423  868451  868453  868459  868487  868489  868493  868529  868531  868537
868559  868561  868577  868583  868603  868613  868639  868663  868669  868691  868697
868727  868739  868741  868771  868783  868787  868793  868799  868801  868817  868841
868849  868861  868873  868877  868883  868891  868909  868937  868939  868943  868951
868957  868993  868997  868999  869017  869021  869039  869053  869059  869069  869081
869119  869131  869137  869153  869173  869179  869203  869233  869249  869251  869257
869291  869293  869297  869299  869303  869317  869321  869339  869369  869371  869381
869399  869413  869419  869437  869443  869461  869467  869471  869489  869501  869521
869543  869551  869563  869579  869587  869597  869599  869657  869663  869669  869689
869707  869717  869747  869753  869773  869777  869779  869807  869809  869819  869849
869863  869879  869887  869891  869921  869923  869929  869951  869959  869983  869999
870007  870013  870031  870047  870049  870059  870083  870097  870109  870127  870131
870137  870151  870161  870169  870173  870197  870211  870223  870229  870239  870241
870253  870271  870283  870301  870323  870329  870341  870367  870391  870403  870407
870413  870431  870433  870437  870461  870479  870491  870497  870517  870533  870547
870557  870563  870589  870601  870613  870629  870641  870643  870679  870691  870703
870731  870739  870743  870773  870787  870809  870811  870823  870833  870847  870853
870871  870889  870901  870907  870911  870917  870929  870931  870953  870967  870977
870983  870997  871001  871021  871027  871037  871061  871073  871103  871147  871159
871177  871181  871229  871231  871249  871259  871271  871289  871303  871337  871349
871393  871439  871459  871463  871477  871513  871517  871531  871553  871571  871589
871597  871613  871621  871639  871643  871649  871657  871679  871681  871687  871727
871763  871771  871789  871817  871823  871837  871867  871883  871901  871919  871931
871957  871963  871973  871987  871993  872017  872023  872033  872041  872057  872071
872077  872089  872099  872107  872129  872141  872143  872149  872159  872161  872173
```

```
872177  872189  872203  872227  872231  872237  872243  872251  872257  872269  872281
872317  872323  872351  872353  872369  872381  872383  872387  872393  872411  872419
872429  872437  872441  872453  872471  872477  872479  872533  872549  872561  872563
872567  872587  872609  872611  872621  872623  872647  872657  872659  872671  872687
872731  872737  872747  872749  872761  872789  872791  872843  872863  872923  872947
872951  872953  872959  872999  873017  873043  873049  873073  873079  873083  873091
873109  873113  873121  873133  873139  873157  873209  873247  873251  873263  873293
873317  873319  873331  873343  873349  873359  873403  873407  873419  873421  873427
873437  873461  873463  873469  873497  873527  873529  873539  873541  873553  873569
873571  873617  873619  873641  873643  873659  873667  873671  873689  873707  873709
873721  873727  873739  873767  873773  873781  873787  873863  873877  873913  873959
873979  873989  873991  874001  874009  874037  874063  874087  874091  874099  874103
874109  874117  874121  874127  874151  874193  874213  874217  874229  874249  874267
874271  874277  874301  874303  874331  874337  874343  874351  874373  874387  874397
874403  874409  874427  874457  874459  874477  874487  874537  874543  874547  874567
874583  874597  874619  874637  874639  874651  874661  874673  874681  874693  874697
874711  874721  874723  874729  874739  874763  874771  874777  874799  874807  874813
874823  874831  874847  874859  874873  874879  874889  874891  874919  874957  874967
874987  875011  875027  875033  875089  875107  875117  875129  875141  875161  875163
875201  875209  875213  875233  875239  875243  875261  875263  875267  875269  875297
875299  875317  875323  875327  875333  875339  875341  875363  875377  875389  875393
875417  875419  875429  875443  875447  875477  875491  875501  875503  875509  875513
875521  875543  875579  875591  875593  875617  875621  875627  875629  875647  875659
875663  875681  875683  875689  875701  875711  875717  875731  875741  875759  875761
875773  875779  875783  875803  875821  875837  875851  875893  875923  875929  875933
875947  875969  875981  875983  876011  876013  876017  876019  876023  876041  876067
876077  876079  876097  876103  876107  876121  876131  876137  876149  876161  876181
876193  876199  876203  876229  876233  876257  876263  876287  876301  876307  876311
876329  876331  876341  876349  876371  876373  876441  876463  876469  876479  876481
876497  876523  876529  876569  876581  876593  876607  876611  876619  876643  876647
876653  876661  876677  876719  876721  876731  876749  876751  876761  876769  876787
876791  876797  876817  876823  876833  876851  876853  876871  876893  876913  876929
876947  876971  877003  877027  877043  877057  877073  877091  877109  877111  877117
877133  877169  877181  877187  877199  877213  877223  877237  877267  877291  877297
877301  877313  877321  877333  877343  877351  877361  877367  877379  877397  877399
877403  877411  877423  877463  877469  877531  877543  877567  877573  877577  877601
877609  877619  877621  877651  877661  877699  877739  877771  877783  877817  877823
877837  877843  877853  877867  877871  877873  877879  877883  877907  877909  877937
877939  877949  877997  878011  878021  878023  878039  878041  878077  878083  878089
878099  878107  878113  878131  878147  878153  878159  878167  878173  878183  878191
878201  878221  878239  878279  878287  878291  878299  878309  878359  878377
878387  878411  878413  878419  878443  878453  878467  878489  878513  878539  878551
878567  878573  878593  878597  878609  878621  878629  878641  878651  878659  878663
878677  878681  878699  878719  878737  878743  878749  878777  878783  878789  878797
878821  878831  878833  878837  878851  878863  878869  878873  878893  878929  878939
878953  878957  878987  878989  879001  879007  879023  879031  879061  879089  879097
879103  879113  879119  879133  879143  879167  879169  879181  879199  879227  879239
879247  879259  879269  879271  879283  879287  879299  879331  879341  879343  879353
879371  879391  879401  879413  879449  879457  879493  879523  879533  879539  879559
879679  879689  879691  879701  879707  879709  879713  879721  879743  879797  879799
879817  879821  879839  879859  879863  879881  879917  879919  879941  879953  879961
879973  879979  880001  880007  880021  880027  880043  880057  880067  880069
880091  880097  880109  880127  880133  880151  880153  880199  880211  880219  880223
880247  880249  880259  880283  880301  880303  880331  880337  880343  880349  880361
880367  880409  880421  880423  880427  880483  880487  880513  880519  880531  880541
880543  880553  880559  880571  880573  880589  880603  880661  880667  880673  880681
880687  880691  880703  880709  880723  880727  880729  880751  880793  880799  880801
880813  880819  880823  880853  880861  880871  880883  880903  880907  880909  880939
880949  880951  880961  880981  880993  881003  881009  881017  881029  881057  881071
881077  881099  881119  881141  881143  881147  881159  881171  881173  881191  881197
881207  881219  881233  881249  881269  881273  881311  881317  881327  881333  881351
881357  881369  881393  881407  881411  881417  881437  881449  881471  881473  881477
881479  881509  881527  881533  881537  881539  881591  881597  881611  881641  881663
881669  881681  881707  881711  881729  881743  881779  881813  881833  881849  881897
881899  881911  881917  881939  881953  881963  881983  881987  882017  882019  882029
882031  882047  882061  882067  882071  882083  882103  882139  882157  882169  882173
882179  882187  882199  882239  882241  882247  882251  882253  882263  882289  882313
882359  882367  882377  882389  882391  882433  882439  882449  882451  882461  882481
882491  882517  882529  882551  882571  882577  882587  882593  882599  882617  882631
882653  882659  882697  882701  882703  882719  882727  882733  882751  882773  882779
882823  882851  882863  882877  882881  882883  882907  882913  882923  882943  882953
882961  882967  882979  883013  883049  883061  883073  883087  883093  883109  883111
883117  883121  883163  883187  883193  883213  883217  883229  883231  883237  883241
883247  883249  883273  883279  883307  883327  883331  883339  883343  883357  883391
883397  883409  883411  883423  883429  883433  883451  883471  883483  883489  883517
883537  883549  883577  883579  883613  883621  883627  883639  883661  883667  883691
883697  883699  883703  883721  883733  883739  883763  883777  883781  883783  883807
883871  883877  883889  883921  883933  883963  883969  883973  883979  883991  884003
884011  884029  884057  884069  884077  884087  884111  884129  884131  884159  884167
884171  884183  884201  884227  884231  884243  884251  884267  884269  884287  884293
884309  884311  884321  884341  884353  884363  884369  884371  884417  884423  884437
884441  884453  884483  884489  884491  884497  884501  884537  884573  884579  884591
884593  884617  884651  884669  884693  884699  884717  884743  884789  884791  884803
884813  884827  884831  884857  884869  884899  884921  884951  884959  884977  884981
884987  884999  885023  885041  885061  885083  885091  885097  885103  885107  885127
885133  885161  885163  885169  885187  885217  885223  885233  885239  885251  885257
885263  885289  885301  885307  885331  885359  885371  885383  885389  885397  885403
885421  885427  885449  885473  885487  885497  885503  885509  885517  885529  885551
```

```
885553 885589 885607 885611 885623 885679 885713 885721 885727 885733 885737
885769 885791 885793 885803 885811 885821 885823 885839 885869 885881 885883
885889 885893 885919 885923 885931 885943 885947 885959 885961 885967 885971
885977 885991 886007 886013 886019 886021 886031 886043 886069 886097 886117
886129 886163 886177 886181 886183 886189 886199 886241 886243 886247 886271
886283 886307 886313 886337 886339 886349 886367 886381 886387 886421 886427
886429 886433 886453 886463 886469 886471 886493 886511 886517 886519 886537
886541 886547 886549 886583 886591 886607 886609 886619 886643 886651 886663
886667 886741 886747 886751 886759 886777 886793 886799 886807 886819 886859
886867 886891 886909 886913 886967 886969 886973 886979 886981 886987 886993
886999 887017 887057 887059 887069 887093 887101 887113 887141 887143 887153
887171 887177 887191 887203 887233 887261 887267 887269 887291 887311 887323
887333 887377 887387 887399 887401 887423 887441 887449 887459 887479 887483
887503 887533 887543 887567 887569 887573 887581 887599 887617 887629 887633
887641 887651 887657 887659 887669 887671 887681 887693 887701 887707 887717
887743 887749 887759 887819 887827 887837 887839 887849 887867 887903 887911
887923 887941 887947 887957 887987 887989 888001 888011 888047 888059 888061
888077 888091 888103 888109 888133 888143 888157 888161 888163 888179 888203
888211 888247 888257 888263 888271 888287 888313 888319 888323 888359 888361
888373 888389 888397 888409 888413 888427 888431 888443 888451 888457 888469
888479 888493 888499 888533 888541 888557 888623 888631 888637 888653 888659
888661 888683 888689 888691 888721 888737 888751 888761 888773 888779 888781
888793 888799 888809 888827 888857 888869 888871 888887 888917 888919 888931
888959 888961 888967 888983 888989 888997 889001 889027 889037 889039 889043
889051 889069 889081 889087 889123 889139 889171 889177 889211 889237 889247
889261 889271 889279 889289 889309 889313 889327 889337 889349 889351 889363
889367 889373 889391 889411 889429 889439 889453 889481 889489 889501 889519
889579 889589 889597 889631 889639 889657 889673 889687 889697 889699 889703
889727 889747 889769 889783 889829 889871 889873 889877 889879 889891 889901
889907 889909 889921 889937 889951 889957 889963 889969 889997 890003 890011 890027
890053 890063 890083 890107 890111 890117 890119 890129 890147 890159 890161
890177 890221 890231 890237 890287 890291 890303 890317 890333 890371 890377
890419 890429 890437 890441 890459 890467 890501 890531 890543 890551 890563
890597 890609 890653 890657 890671 890683 890707 890711 890717 890737 890761
890789 890797 890803 890809 890821 890833 890843 890861 890863 890867 890881
890887 890893 890927 890933 890941 890957 890963 890969 890993 890999 891001
891017 891047 891049 891061 891067 891091 891101 891103 891133 891151 891161
891173 891179 891223 891239 891251 891277 891287 891311 891323 891329 891349
891377 891379 891389 891391 891409 891421 891427 891439 891481 891487 891491
891493 891509 891521 891523 891551 891557 891559 891563 891571 891577 891587
891593 891601 891617 891629 891643 891647 891659 891661 891667 891679 891707
891743 891749 891763 891767 891797 891799 891809 891817 891823 891827 891829
891851 891859 891887 891889 891893 891899 891907 891913 891923 891967 891983
891991 891997 892019 892027 892049 892057 892079 892091 892093 892097 892103
892123 892141 892153 892159 892169 892189 892219 892237 892249 892253 892261
892267 892271 892291 892321 892351 892357 892387 892391 892421 892433 892439
892457 892471 892481 892513 892523 892531 892547 892553 892559 892579 892597
892603 892609 892627 892643 892657 892663 892667 892709 892733 892747 892757
892763 892777 892781 892783 892817 892841 892849 892861 892877 892901 892919
892933 892951 892973 892987 892999 893003 893023 893029 893033 893041 893051
893059 893093 893099 893107 893111 893117 893119 893131 893147 893149 893161
893183 893213 893219 893227 893237 893257 893261 893281 893317 893339 893341
893351 893359 893363 893381 893383 893407 893413 893419 893429 893441 893449
893479 893489 893509 893521 893549 893567 893591 893603 893609 893653 893657
893671 893681 893701 893719 893723 893743 893777 893797 893821 893839 893857
893863 893881 893897 893903 893917 893929 893933 893939 893959 893989 893999
894011 894037 894059 894067 894073 894097 894109 894119 894137 894139 894151
894161 894167 894181 894191 894193 894203 894209 894211 894221 894227 894233
894239 894247 894259 894277 894281 894287 894301 894329 894343 894371 894391
894403 894407 894409 894419 894427 894431 894449 894451 894503 894511 894521
894527 894541 894547 894559 894581 894589 894611 894613 894637 894643 894667
894689 894709 894713 894721 894731 894749 894763 894779 894791 894793 894811
894869 894871 894893 894917 894923 894947 894973 894997 895003 895007 895009
895039 895049 895051 895079 895087 895127 895133 895151 895157 895159 895171
895189 895211 895231 895241 895243 895247 895253 895277 895283 895291 895309
895313 895319 895333 895343 895351 895357 895361 895387 895393 895421 895423
895457 895463 895469 895471 895507 895529 895553 895571 895579 895591 895613
895627 895633 895649 895651 895667 895669 895673 895681 895691 895703 895709
895721 895729 895757 895771 895777 895787 895789 895799 895801 895813 895823
895841 895861 895879 895889 895901 895903 895913 895927 895933 895957 895987
896003 896009 896047 896069 896101 896107 896111 896113 896123 896143 896167
896191 896201 896263 896281 896293 896297 896299 896323 896327 896341 896347
896353 896369 896381 896417 896443 896447 896449 896453 896479 896491 896509
896521 896531 896537 896543 896549 896557 896561 896573 896587 896617 896633
896647 896669 896677 896681 896717 896719 896723 896771 896783 896803 896837
896867 896879 896897 896921 896927 896947 896953 896963 896983 897007 897011
897019 897049 897053 897059 897067 897077 897101 897103 897119 897133 897137
897157 897163 897191 897223 897229 897241 897251 897263 897269 897271 897301
897307 897317 897319 897329 897349 897359 897373 897401 897433 897443 897461
897469 897473 897497 897499 897517 897527 897553 897557 897563 897571
897577 897581 897593 897601 897607 897629 897647 897649 897671 897691 897703
897707 897709 897727 897751 897779 897781 897817 897829 897847 897877 897881
897887 897899 897907 897931 897947 897971 897983 898013 898019 898033 898063
898067 898069 898091 898097 898109 898129 898133 898147 898153 898171 898181
898189 898199 898211 898213 898223 898231 898241 898243 898253 898259 898279
898283 898291 898307 898319 898327 898361 898369 898409 898421 898423 898427
898439 898459 898477 898481 898483 898493 898519 898523 898543 898549 898553
898561 898607 898613 898621 898661 898663 898669 898673 898691 898717 898727
898753 898763 898769 898787 898813 898819 898823 898853 898867 898873 898889
```

```
898897  898921  898927  898951  898981  898987  899009  899051  899057  899069  899123
899149  899153  899159  899161  899177  899179  899183  899189  899209  899221  899233
899237  899263  899273  899291  899309  899321  899387  899401  899413  899429  899447
899467  899473  899477  899491  899519  899531  899537  899611  899617  899659  899671
899681  899687  899693  899711  899719  899749  899753  899761  899779  899791  899807
899831  899849  899851  899863  899881  899891  899893  899903  899917  899939  899971
899981  900001  900007  900019  900037  900061  900089  900091  900103  900121  900139
900143  900149  900157  900161  900169  900187  900217  900233  900241  900253  900259
900283  900287  900293  900307  900329  900331  900349  900397  900409  900443  900461
900481  900491  900511  900539  900551  900553  900563  900569  900577  900583  900587
900589  900593  900607  900623  900649  900659  900671  900673  900689  900701  900719
900737  900743  900759  900761  900763  900773  900797  900803  900817  900821  900863
900869  900917  900929  900931  900937  900959  900971  900973  900997  901007  901009
901013  901063  901067  901079  901093  901097  901111  901133  901141  901169  901171
901177  901183  901193  901207  901211  901213  901247  901249  901253  901273  901279
901309  901333  901339  901367  901399  901403  901423  901427  901429  901441  901447
901451  901457  901477  901489  901499  901501  901513  901517  901529  901547  901567
901591  901613  901643  901657  901679  901687  901709  901717  901739  901741  901751
901787  901811  901819  901841  901861  901891  901907  901909  901919  901931
901937  901963  901973  901993  901997  902009  902017  902029  902039  902047  902053
902087  902089  902119  902137  902141  902179  902191  902201  902227  902261  902263
902281  902299  902303  902311  902333  902347  902351  902357  902389  902401  902413
902437  902449  902471  902477  902483  902501  902507  902521  902563  902569  902579
902591  902597  902599  902611  902639  902653  902659  902669  902677  902687  902719
902723  902753  902761  902767  902771  902777  902789  902807  902821  902827  902849
902873  902903  902933  902953  902963  902971  902977  902981  902987  903017  903029
903037  903073  903079  903103  903109  903143  903151  903163  903179  903197  903211
903223  903251  903257  903269  903311  903323  903337  903347  903359  903367  903389
903391  903403  903407  903421  903443  903449  903457  903479  903493  903523  903527
903541  903547  903563  903569  903607  903613  903641  903649  903673  903677  903691
903701  903709  903751  903757  903761  903781  903803  903827  903841  903871  903883
903899  903913  903919  903949  903967  903979  904019  904027  904049  904067  904069
904073  904087  904093  904097  904103  904117  904121  904147  904157  904181  904193
904201  904207  904219  904261  904283  904289  904297  904303  904357  904361
904369  904399  904441  904459  904483  904489  904499  904511  904513  904517  904523
904531  904559  904573  904577  904601  904619  904627  904631  904637  904643  904661
904663  904667  904679  904681  904693  904697  904721  904727  904733  904759  904769
904879  904901  904903  904907  904919  904931  904933  904947  904997  905011
905053  905059  905071  905083  905087  905111  905123  905137  905143  905147  905161
905171  905189  905197  905207  905209  905213  905227  905249  905269  905291
905297  905299  905329  905339  905347  905381  905413  905449  905453  905461  905477
905491  905497  905507  905551  905581  905587  905599  905617  905621  905629  905647
905651  905659  905677  905683  905687  905693  905701  905713  905719  905759  905761
905767  905783  905803  905819  905833  905843  905897  905909  905917  905923  905951
905959  905963  906007  906011  906013  906023  906029  906043  906089  906107
906119  906121  906133  906179  906187  906197  906203  906211  906229  906233  906259
906263  906289  906293  906313  906317  906329  906331  906343  906349  906371  906377
906383  906391  906403  906421  906427  906431  906461  906473  906481  906487  906497
906517  906523  906539  906541  906557  906589  906601  906613  906617  906641  906649
906677  906699  906701  906707  906713  906727  906749  906751  906757  906767
906779  906793  906809  906817  906823  906839  906847  906869  906881  906901  906911
906923  906929  906943  906949  906973  907019  907021  907031  907063  907073
907099  907111  907133  907139  907141  907163  907169  907183  907199  907211  907213
907217  907223  907229  907237  907259  907267  907279  907297  907301  907321  907331
907363  907369  907391  907393  907397  907439  907447  907433  907447  907457
907469  907471  907481  907493  907507  907513  907549  907561  907567  907583  907589
907637  907651  907657  907663  907667  907691  907693  907703  907717  907723  907727
907733  907757  907759  907793  907807  907811  907813  907831  907843  907849  907871
907891  907909  907913  907927  907957  907967  907969  907997  907999  908003  908041
908053  908057  908071  908081  908101  908113  908129  908137  908153  908179  908183
908197  908213  908221  908233  908249  908287  908317  908321  908353  908359  908363
908377  908381  908417  908419  908441  908449  908489  908497  908641  908489  908503
908513  908521  908527  908533  908539  908543  908549  908573  908581  908591  908597
908603  908617  908623  908627  908653  908669  908671  908711  908723  908731  908741
908749  908759  908771  908797  908807  908813  908819  908821  908849  908851  908857
908861  908863  908879  908881  908893  908909  908911  908927  908953  908959  908993
909019  909023  909031  909037  909043  909047  909061  909071  909089  909091  909107
909113  909119  909133  909151  909173  909203  909217  909239  909241  909247  909253
909281  909287  909289  909299  909301  909317  909319  909329  909331  909341  909343
909371  909379  909383  909401  909409  909437  909451  909457  909463  909481  909521
909529  909539  909541  909547  909577  909599  909611  909613  909631  909637  909679
909683  909691  909697  909731  909737  909743  909761  909767  909773  909787  909791
909803  909809  909829  909833  909859  909863  909877  909889  909899  909901  909907
909911  909971  909973  909977  910003  910031  910051  910069  910093  910097
910099  910103  910109  910121  910127  910139  910141  910171  910177  910199  910201
910207  910213  910219  910229  910277  910279  910307  910361  910369  910421  910447
910453  910457  910467  910471  910519  910523  910561  910577  910583  910603  910619
910621  910627  910631  910643  910661  910691  910709  910711  910747  910751  910771
910781  910787  910799  910807  910817  910849  910853  910883  910909  910939  910957
910981  911003  911011  911023  911033  911039  911063  911077  911087  911089  911101
911111  911129  911147  911159  911161  911167  911171  911173  911179  911201  911219
911227  911231  911233  911249  911269  911291  911293  911303  911311  911321  911327
911341  911357  911359  911363  911371  911413  911419  911437  911453  911459  911503
911507  911527  911549  911593  911597  911621  911633  911657  911663  911671  911681
911683  911689  911707  911719  911723  911737  911749  911773  911777  911783  911819
911831  911837  911839  911851  911861  911873  911879  911893  911899  911903  911917
911947  911951  911957  911959  911969  912007  912031  912047  912049  912053  912061
912083  912089  912103  912167  912173  912187  912193  912211  912217  912227  912239
```

```
912251  912269  912287  912337  912343  912349  912367  912391  912397  912403  912409
912413  912449  912451  912463  912467  912469  912481  912487  912491  912497  912511
912521  912523  912533  912539  912559  912581  912631  912647  912649  912727  912763
912773  912797  912799  912809  912823  912829  912839  912851  912853  912859  912869
912871  912911  912929  912941  912953  912959  912971  912973  912979  912991  913013
913027  913037  913039  913063  913067  913103  913139  913151  913177  913183  913217
913247  913259  913279  913309  913321  913327  913331  913337  913373  913397  913417
913421  913433  913441  913447  913457  913483  913487  913513  913571  913573  913579
913589  913637  913639  913687  913709  913723  913739  913753  913771  913799  913811
913853  913873  913889  913907  913921  913933  913943  913981  913999  914021  914027
914041  914047  914117  914131  914161  914189  914191  914213  914219  914237  914239
914257  914269  914279  914293  914321  914327  914339  914351  914357  914359  914363
914369  914371  914429  914443  914449  914461  914467  914477  914491  914513  914519
914521  914533  914561  914569  914579  914581  914591  914597  914609  914611  914629
914647  914657  914701  914713  914723  914731  914737  914777  914783  914789  914791
914801  914813  914819  914827  914843  914857  914861  914867  914873  914887  914891
914897  914941  914951  914981  915007  915017  915029  915041  915049  915053
915067  915071  915113  915139  915143  915157  915181  915191  915197  915199  915203
915221  915223  915247  915251  915253  915259  915283  915301  915311  915353  915367
915379  915391  915437  915451  915479  915487  915527  915533  915539  915547  915557
915587  915589  915601  915611  915613  915623  915631  915641  915659  915683  915697
915703  915727  915731  915737  915757  915763  915769  915799  915839  915851  915869
915881  915911  915917  915919  915947  915949  915961  915973  915991  916031  916033
916049  916057  916061  916073  916099  916103  916109  916121  916127  916129  916141
916169  916177  916183  916187  916189  916213  916217  916219  916259  916261  916273
916291  916319  916337  916339  916361  916367  916387  916411  916417  916441  916451
916457  916463  916469  916471  916477  916501  916507  916511  916537  916561  916571
916583  916613  916621  916633  916649  916651  916679  916703  916733  916771  916781
916787  916831  916837  916841  916859  916871  916879  916907  916913  916931  916933
916939  916961  916973  916999  917003  917039  917041  917051  917053  917083  917089
917093  917101  917113  917117  917123  917141  917153  917159  917173  917179  917209
917219  917227  917237  917239  917243  917251  917281  917291  917317  917327  917333
917353  917363  917381  917407  917443  917459  917461  917471  917503  917513  917519
917549  917557  917573  917591  917593  917611  917617  917629  917633  917641  917659
917669  917687  917689  917713  917729  917737  917753  917759  917767  917771  917773
917783  917789  917803  917809  917827  917831  917837  917843  917849  917869  917887
917893  917923  917927  917951  917971  917993  918011  918019  918041  918067  918079
918089  918103  918109  918131  918139  918143  918149  918157  918161  918173  918193
918199  918209  918223  918257  918259  918263  918283  918301  918319  918329  918341
918347  918353  918361  918371  918389  918397  918431  918433  918439  918443  918469
918481  918497  918529  918539  918563  918581  918583  918587  918613  918641  918647
918653  918677  918679  918683  918733  918737  918751  918763  918767  918779  918787
918793  918823  918829  918839  918857  918877  918889  918899  918913  918943  918947
918949  918959  918971  918983  919013  919019  919021  919031  919033  919063  919067
919081  919109  919111  919129  919147  919153  919169  919183  919189  919223  919229
919231  919249  919253  919267  919301  919313  919319  919337  919349  919351  919381
919393  919409  919417  919421  919423  919427  919447  919511  919519  919531  919559
919571  919591  919613  919621  919631  919679  919691  919693  919703  919729  919757
919759  919769  919781  919799  919811  919817  919823  919859  919871  919883  919901
919903  919913  919927  919937  919939  919949  919951  919969  919979  920011  920021
920009  920053  920107  920123  920137  920149  920167  920197  920201  920203
920209  920219  920233  920263  920267  920273  920279  920281  920291  920323  920333
920357  920371  920377  920393  920399  920407  920411  920419  920441  920443  920467
920473  920477  920497  920509  920519  920539  920561  920609  920641  920651  920653
920677  920687  920701  920707  920729  920741  920743  920753  920761  920783  920789
920791  920807  920827  920833  920849  920863  920869  920891  920921  920947  920951
920957  920963  920971  920999  921001  921007  921013  921029  921031  921073  921079
921091  921121  921133  921143  921149  921157  921169  921191  921197  921199  921203
921223  921233  921241  921257  921259  921287  921293  921331  921353  921373  921379
921407  921409  921457  921463  921467  921491  921497  921499  921517  921523  921563
921581  921589  921601  921611  921629  921637  921643  921647  921667  921677  921703
921733  921737  921743  921749  921751  921761  921779  921791  921821  921839  921841
921871  921887  921889  921901  921911  921913  921919  921931  921959  921989  922021
922027  922037  922039  922043  922057  922067  922069  922073  922079  922081  922087
922099  922123  922169  922211  922217  922223  922237  922247  922261  922283  922289
922291  922303  922309  922321  922331  922333  922351  922357  922367  922391  922423
922451  922457  922463  922487  922489  922499  922511  922513  922517  922531  922549
922561  922601  922613  922619  922627  922631  922637  922639  922651  922667  922679
922681  922699  922717  922727  922739  922741  922781  922807  922813  922853  922861
922897  922907  922931  922973  922993  923017  923023  923029  923047  923051  923053
923107  923123  923129  923137  923141  923147  923171  923177  923179  923183  923201
923203  923227  923233  923239  923249  923309  923311  923333  923341  923347  923369
923371  923387  923399  923407  923411  923437  923441  923449  923453  923467  923471
923501  923509  923513  923539  923543  923551  923561  923567  923579  923581  923591
923599  923603  923617  923641  923653  923687  923693  923701  923711  923719  923743
923773  923789  923809  923833  923849  923851  923861  923869  923903  923917  923929
923939  923947  923953  923959  923963  923971  923977  923983  923987  924019  924023
924031  924037  924041  924043  924059  924073  924083  924097  924101  924109  924139
924151  924173  924191  924197  924241  924269  924281  924283  924299  924323  924337
924359  924361  924383  924397  924401  924403  924419  924421  924431  924437  924463
924493  924499  924503  924523  924527  924529  924551  924557  924601  924617  924641
924643  924659  924661  924683  924697  924709  924713  924719  924727  924731  924743
924751  924757  924769  924773  924779  924793  924809  924811  924827  924829  924841
924871  924877  924881  924907  924929  924961  924967  924997  925019  925027  925033
925039  925051  925063  925073  925079  925081  925087  925097  925103  925109  925117
925121  925147  925153  925159  925163  925181  925189  925193  925217  925237  925241
925271  925273  925279  925291  925307  925339  925349  925369  925373  925387  925391
925399  925409  925423  925447  925469  925487  925499  925501  925513  925523  925551
925559  925577  925579  925597  925607  925619  925621  925637  925649  925663  925669
```

```
925679  925697  925721  925733  925741  925783  925789  925823  925831  925843  925849
925891  925901  925913  925921  925937  925943  925949  925961  925979  925987  925997
926017  926027  926033  926077  926087  926089  926099  926111  926113  926129  926131
926153  926161  926171  926179  926183  926203  926227  926239  926251  926273  926293
926309  926327  926351  926353  926357  926377  926389  926399  926411  926423  926437
926461  926467  926489  926503  926507  926533  926537  926557  926561  926567  926581
926587  926617  926623  926633  926657  926659  926669  926671  926689  926701  926707
926741  926747  926767  926777  926797  926803  926819  926843  926851  926867  926879
926889  926903  926921  926957  926963  926971  926977  926983  927001  927007  927013
927049  927077  927083  927089  927097  927137  927149  927161  927167  927187  927191
927229  927233  927259  927287  927301  927313  927317  927323  927361  927373  927397
927403  927431  927439  927491  927497  927517  927529  927533  927541  927557  927569
927587  927629  927631  927643  927649  927653  927671  927677  927683  927709  927727
927743  927763  927769  927779  927791  927803  927821  927833  927841  927847  927853
927863  927869  927961  927967  927973  928001  928043  928051  928063  928079  928097
928099  928111  928139  928141  928153  928157  928159  928163  928177  928223  928231
928253  928267  928271  928273  928289  928307  928313  928331  928337  928361  928399
928409  928423  928427  928429  928453  928457  928463  928469  928471  928513  928547
928559  928561  928597  928607  928619  928621  928637  928643  928649  928661  928661
928679  928699  928703  928769  928771  928787  928793  928799  928813  928817  928819
928849  928859  928871  928883  928903  928913  928927  928933  928979  929003  929009
929011  929023  929029  929051  929057  929059  929063  929069  929077  929083  929087
929113  929129  929141  929153  929161  929171  929197  929207  929209  929239  929251
929261  929281  929293  929303  929311  929323  929333  929381  929389  929393  929399
929417  929419  929431  929459  929483  929497  929501  929507  929527  929549  929557
929561  929573  929581  929587  929609  929623  929627  929629  929639  929641  929647
929671  929693  929717  929737  929741  929743  929749  929777  929791  929807  929809
929813  929843  929861  929869  929881  929891  929897  929941  929953  929963  929977
929983  930001  930023  930043  930071  930073  930077  930089  930101  930113  930119
930157  930173  930179  930187  930191  930197  930199  930211  930229  930269  930277
930283  930287  930289  930301  930323  930337  930379  930389  930409  930437  930467
930469  930481  930491  930499  930509  930547  930551  930569  930571  930583  930593
930617  930619  930637  930653  930667  930689  930707  930719  930737  930749  930763
930773  930779  930817  930827  930841  930847  930859  930863  930889  930911  930931
930973  930977  930989  930991  931003  931013  931067  931087  931097  931123  931127
931153  931163  931169  931181  931193  931199  931213  931237  931241  931267
931289  931303  931309  931313  931319  931351  931363  931387  931417  931421  931487
931499  931517  931529  931537  931543  931571  931573  931577  931597  931621  931639
931657  931691  931709  931727  931729  931739  931747  931751  931757  931781  931783
931789  931811  931837  931849  931859  931873  931877  931883  931901  931907  931913
931921  931933  931943  931949  931967  931981  931991  931999  932003  932039  932051
932081  932101  932117  932119  932131  932149  932153  932177  932189  932203  932207
932219  932221  932227  932231  932257  932303  932317  932333  932341  932353
932357  932413  932417  932419  932431  932441  932447  932471  932473  932483  932497
932513  932521  932537  932549  932557  932563  932567  932579  932587  932593  932597
932609  932647  932651  932663  932687  932681  932683  932749  932761  932779  932783
932801  932803  932819  932839  932863  932879  932887  932917  932923  932927  932941
932947  932951  932963  932969  932983  932999  933001  933019  933047  933059  933061
933067  933073  933151  933157  933173  933199  933209  933217  933221  933241  933259
933263  933269  933293  933301  933313  933319  933329  933349  933389  933397  933403
933407  933421  933433  933463  933479  933487  933523  933551  933553  933563  933601
933607  933613  933643  933649  933671  933677  933703  933707  933739  933761  933781
933787  933797  933809  933811  933817  933839  933887  933851  933853  933883  933893
933923  933931  933943  933949  933953  933967  933973  933979  934001  934009  934033
934039  934049  934051  934057  934067  934069  934079  934111  934117  934121  934127
934151  934159  934187  934223  934229  934243  934253  934259  934277  934291  934301
934319  934343  934387  934393  934399  934403  934429  934441  934463  934469  934481
934487  934489  934499  934517  934523  934537  934543  934547  934561  934567  934579
934597  934603  934607  934613  934639  934669  934673  934693  934721  934723  934733
934753  934763  934771  934793  934799  934811  934831  934837  934853  934861  934883
934889  934891  934897  934907  934909  934919  934939  934943  934951  934961  934979
934981  935003  935021  935023  935059  935063  935071  935093  935107  935113  935147
935149  935167  935183  935189  935197  935201  935213  935243  935257  935261  935303
935339  935353  935359  935377  935381  935393  935399  935413  935423  935443  935447
935461  935489  935507  935513  935531  935537  935551  935557  935591  935599  935603
935621  935639  935651  935653  935677  935687  935689  935699  935707  935717  935719
935761  935771  935777  935791  935813  935819  935827  935839  935843  935861  935899
935903  935971  935999  936007  936029  936053  936097  936113  936119  936127  936151
936161  936179  936181  936197  936203  936223  936227  936233  936253  936259  936281
936283  936311  936319  936329  936361  936379  936391  936401  936407  936413  936437
936451  936469  936487  936493  936499  936511  936521  936527  936539  936557  936577
936587  936599  936619  936647  936659  936667  936673  936679  936697  936709  936713
936731  936737  936739  936769  936773  936779  936797  936811  936827  936869  936889
936907  936911  936917  936919  936937  936941  936953  936967  937003  937007  937009
937031  937033  937049  937067  937121  937127  937147  937151  937171  937187  937207
937229  937231  937241  937243  937253  937331  937337  937351  937373  937379  937421
937429  937459  937463  937477  937481  937501  937511  937537  937571  937577  937589
937591  937613  937627  937633  937637  937639  937661  937663  937667  937679  937681
937693  937709  937721  937747  937751  937777  937789  937801  937813  937819  937823
937841  937847  937877  937883  937891  937901  937903  937919  937927  937943  937949
937969  937991  938017  938023  938027  938033  938051  938053  938057  938059  938071
938083  938089  938099  938107  938117  938129  938183  938207  938219  938233  938243
938251  938257  938263  938279  938293  938309  938323  938347  938351  938353  938359
938369  938387  938393  938437  938447  938453  938459  938491  938507  938533  938537
938563  938569  938573  938591  938611  938617  938659  938677  938681  938713  938747
938761  938803  938807  938827  938831  938843  938857  938869  938879  938881  938921
938939  938947  938963  938963  938981  938983  938989  939007  939011  939019
939061  939089  939091  939109  939119  939121  939157  939167  939179  939181  939193
939203  939229  939247  939287  939293  939299  939317  939347  939349  939359  939361
```

```
939373  939377  939391  939413  939431  939439  939443  939451  939469  939487  939511
939551  939581  939599  939611  939613  939623  939649  939661  939677  939707  939713
939737  939739  939749  939767  939769  939773  939791  939793  939823  939839  939847
939853  939871  939881  939901  939923  939931  939971  939973  939989  939997  940001
940003  940019  940031  940067  940073  940087  940097  940127  940157  940169  940183
940189  940201  940223  940229  940241  940249  940259  940271  940279  940297  940301
940319  940327  940349  940351  940361  940369  940399  940403  940421  940469  940477
940483  940501  940523  940529  940531  940543  940547  940549  940553  940573  940607
940619  940649  940669  940691  940703  940721  940727  940733  940739  940759  940781
940787  940801  940813  940817  940829  940853  940871  940879  940889  940903
940913  940921  940931  940949  940957  940981  940993  941009  941011  941023  941027
941041  941093  941099  941117  941119  941123  941131  941153  941159  941167  941179
941201  941207  941209  941221  941249  941251  941263  941267  941299  941309  941323
941329  941351  941359  941383  941407  941429  941441  941449  941453  941461  941467
941471  941489  941491  941503  941509  941513  941519  941537  941557  941561  941573
941593  941599  941609  941617  941641  941653  941663  941669  941671  941683  941701
941723  941737  941741  941747  941753  941771  941791  941813  941839  941861  941879
941903  941911  941929  941933  941947  941971  941981  941989  941999  942013  942017
942037  942041  942047  942043  942049  942061  942079  942091  942101  942113  942143
942163  942167  942169  942187  942199  942217  942223  942247  942257  942269  942301
942311  942313  942317  942341  942367  942371  942401  942433  942437  942439  942449
942479  942509  942521  942527  942541  942569  942577  942583  942593  942607  942637
942653  942659  942661  942691  942709  942719  942727  942749  942763  942779  942787
942811  942827  942847  942853  942857  942859  942869  942883  942889  942901
942917  942943  942979  942983  943003  943009  943013  943031  943043  943057  943073
943079  943081  943091  943097  943127  943139  943153  943157  943183  943199  943213
943219  943231  943249  943273  943277  943289  943301  943303  943307  943321  943343
943357  943363  943367  943373  943387  943403  943409  943421  943429  943471  943477
943499  943511  943541  943543  943567  943571  943589  943601  943603  943637  943651
943693  943699  943729  943741  943751  943757  943763  943769  943777  943781  943783
943799  943801  943819  943837  943841  943843  943849  943859  943871  943903  943913
943931  943951  943967  944003  944017  944029  944039  944071  944077  944123  944137
944143  944147  944149  944161  944179  944191  944233  944239  944257  944261  944263
944297  944309  944329  944369  944387  944389  944393  944399  944417  944429  944431
944453  944467  944473  944491  944497  944519  944521  944527  944533  944543  944551
944561  944563  944579  944591  944609  944621  944651  944659  944677  944687  944689
944701  944711  944717  944729  944731  944773  944777  944803  944821  944833  944857
944873  944887  944893  944897  944899  944929  944953  944963  944969  944987  945031
945037  945059  945089  945103  945143  945151  945179  945209  945211  945227  945233
945289  945293  945331  945341  945349  945359  945367  945377  945389  945391  945397
945409  945431  945457  945463  945473  945479  945481  945521  945547  945577  945587
945589  945601  945629  945631  945647  945671  945673  945677  945701  945731  945733
945739  945767  945787  945799  945809  945811  945817  945823  945851  945881  945883
945887  945899  945907  945929  945937  945941  945943  945949  945961  945983  946003
946021  946031  946037  946079  946081  946091  946093  946109  946111  946123  946133
946163  946193  946201  946207  946223  946249  946273  946291  946307  946327  946331
946367  946369  946391  946397  946411  946417  946453  946459  946469  946487  946489
946507  946511  946513  946549  946573  946579  946607  946661  946663  946667  946669
946681  946697  946717  946727  946733  946741  946753  946769  946783  946801  946819
946823  946853  946859  946861  946873  946877  946901  946919  946931  946943  946949
946961  946969  946987  946991  946997  947027  947033  947039  947119  947129  947137
947171  947183  947197  947203  947239  947263  947299  947327  947341  947351  947357
947369  947377  947381  947383  947389  947407  947411  947413  947417  947423  947431
947443  947483  947501  947509  947539  947561  947579  947603  947621  947627  947641
947647  947651  947659  947707  947711  947719  947729  947741  947743  947747  947753
947773  947783  947803  947819  947833  947851  947857  947861  947873  947893  947911
947917  947927  947959  947963  947987  948007  948019  948029  948041  948049  948053
948061  948067  948089  948091  948133  948139  948149  948151  948169  948173  948187
948247  948253  948263  948287  948293  948317  948331  948349  948377  948391
948401  948403  948407  948427  948439  948443  948449  948457  948469  948487  948517
948533  948551  948557  948581  948593  948659  948667  948707  948713  948721
948749  948767  948797  948799  948839  948847  948853  948877  948887  948901  948907
948929  948943  948947  948971  948973  948989  949001  949019  949021  949033  949037
949043  949051  949111  949121  949129  949147  949153  949159  949171  949211  949213
949241  949243  949253  949261  949303  949307  949381  949387  949391  949409  949423
949427  949439  949441  949451  949453  949471  949477  949513  949517  949523  949567
949583  949589  949607  949609  949621  949631  949633  949643  949649  949651  949667
949673  949687  949691  949699  949733  949759  949771  949777  949789  949811  949849
949853  949889  949891  949903  949931  949937  949939  949951  949957  949961  949967
949973  949979  949987  949997  950009  950023  950029  950039  950041  950071  950083
950099  950111  950149  950161  950171  950179  950207  950221  950227  950231  950233
950239  950251  950269  950281  950329  950333  950347  950357  950363  950393  950401
950423  950447  950459  950461  950473  950479  950483  950497  950507  950519
950527  950531  950557  950569  950581  950611  950617  950633  950639  950647  950671  950681
950689  950693  950699  950717  950723  950737  950743  950753  950783  950807  950809
950813  950819  950837  950839  950867  950869  950879  950921  950927  950933  950947
950953  950959  950993  951001  951019  951023  951029  951047  951053  951059  951061
951079  951089  951091  951101  951107  951109  951131  951151  951161  951193  951221
951259  951277  951281  951283  951299  951331  951341  951343  951361  951367  951373
951389  951407  951413  951427  951437  951449  951469  951479  951491  951497  951553
951557  951571  951581  951583  951589  951623  951637  951641  951647  951649  951659
951689  951697  951749  951781  951787  951791  951803  951829  951851  951859  951887
951893  951911  951941  951959  951967  951997  952001  952009  952037  952057
952073  952087  952097  952111  952117  952123  952129  952141  952151  952163  952169
952183  952199  952207  952219  952229  952247  952253  952277  952283  952291  952297
952313  952349  952363  952379  952381  952397  952423  952429  952439  952481  952487
952507  952513  952541  952547  952559  952573  952583  952597  952619  952649  952657
952667  952669  952681  952687  952691  952709  952739  952741  952753  952771  952789
952811  952813  952823  952829  952843  952859  952873  952877  952883  952921  952927
```

952933 952937 952943 952957 952967 952979 952981 952997 953023 953039 953041
953053 953077 953081 953093 953111 953131 953149 953171 953179 953191 953221
953237 953243 953261 953273 953297 953321 953333 953341 953347 953399 953431
953437 953443 953473 953483 953497 953501 953503 953507 953521 953539 953543
953551 953567 953593 953621 953639 953647 953651 953671 953681 953699 953707
953731 953747 953773 953789 953791 953831 953851 953861 953873 953881 953917
953923 953929 953941 953969 953977 953983 953987 954001 954011 954043
954067 954097 954103 954131 954133 954139 954157 954167 954181 954203 954209
954221 954229 954253 954257 954259 954263 954269 954277 954287 954307 954319
954323 954367 954377 954379 954391 954409 954433 954451 954461 954469 954491
954497 954509 954517 954539 954571 954599 954619 954623 954641 954649 954671
954677 954697 954713 954719 954727 954743 954757 954763 954827 954829 954847
954851 954853 954857 954869 954871 954911 954917 954923 954929 954971 954973
954977 954979 954991 955037 955039 955051 955061 955063 955091 955093 955103
955127 955139 955147 955153 955183 955193 955211 955217 955223 955243 955261
955267 955271 955277 955307 955309 955313 955319 955333 955337 955363 955379
955391 955433 955441 955457 955469 955477 955481 955483 955501 955511
955541 955601 955607 955613 955649 955657 955693 955697 955709 955711 955727
955729 955769 955777 955781 955793 955807 955813 955819 955841 955853 955879
955883 955891 955901 955919 955937 955939 955951 955957 955963 955967 955987
955991 955993 956003 956051 956057 956083 956107 956113 956119 956143 956147
956177 956231 956237 956261 956269 956273 956281 956303 956311 956341 956353
956357 956377 956383 956387 956393 956399 956401 956429 956477 956503 956513
956521 956569 956587 956617 956633 956689 956699 956713 956723 956749 956759
956789 956801 956831 956843 956849 956861 956881 956903 956909 956929 956941
956951 956953 956987 956993 956999 957031 957037 957041 957043 957059 957071
957091 957097 957107 957109 957119 957133 957139 957161 957169 957181 957193
957211 957221 957241 957247 957263 957289 957317 957331 957337 957349 957361
957403 957409 957413 957419 957431 957433 957499 957529 957547 957553 957557
957563 957587 957599 957601 957611 957641 957643 957659 957701 957703 957709
957721 957731 957751 957769 957773 957811 957821 957823 957851 957871 957877
957889 957917 957937 957949 957953 957959 957977 957991 958007 958021 958039
958043 958049 958051 958057 958063 958121 958123 958141 958159 958163 958183
958193 958213 958259 958261 958289 958313 958319 958327 958333 958339 958343
958351 958357 958361 958367 958369 958381 958393 958423 958439 958459 958481
958487 958499 958501 958519 958523 958541 958543 958547 958549 958553 958577
958609 958627 958637 958667 958669 958673 958679 958687 958693 958729 958739
958747 958787 958807 958819 958829 958843 958849 958871 958877 958883 958897
958901 958921 958931 958933 958957 958963 958967 958973 959009 959083 959093
959237 959263 959267 959269 959279 959323 959333 959339 959351 959363 959369
959377 959383 959389 959449 959461 959467 959471 959473 959477 959479 959489
959533 959561 959579 959597 959603 959617 959627 959659 959677 959681 959689
959719 959723 959737 959759 959773 959779 959801 959809 959831 959863 959867
959869 959873 959879 959887 959911 959921 959927 959941 959947 959953 959969
960001 960019 960031 960049 960053 960059 960077 960119 960121 960131 960137
960139 960151 960173 960191 960199 960217 960229 960251 960259 960293 960299
960329 960331 960341 960353 960373 960383 960389 960419 960467 960493 960497
960499 960521 960523 960527 960569 960581 960587 960593 960601 960603 960643
960647 960649 960667 960677 960691 960703 960709 960737 960763 960793 960803
960809 960889 960833 960931 960937 960941 960961 960997 961009 961073 961091
960989 960991 961003 961021 961033 961063 961067 961069 961073 961087 961091
961099 961109 961117 961123 961133 961139 961147 961151 961157 961159
961183 961187 961189 961201 961241 961243 961273 961277 961283 961313 961319
961339 961393 961397 961399 961427 961447 961451 961453 961459 961487 961507
961511 961529 961531 961547 961549 961567 961601 961613 961619 961627 961633
961637 961643 961657 961661 961663 961679 961687 961691 961703 961729 961733
961747 961757 961769 961777 961783 961789 961811 961813 961817 961841
961847 961853 961861 961871 961879 961927 961937 961943 961957 961973 961981
961991 961993 962009 962011 962033 962041 962051 962063 962077 962099 962119
962131 962161 962177 962197 962233 962237 962243 962257 962267 962303 962309
962341 962363 962413 962417 962431 962441 962447 962459 962461 962471 962477
962497 962503 962509 962537 962561 962569 962587 962603 962609 962611
962623 962627 962653 962669 962671 962677 962681 962683 962737 962743 962747
962779 962783 962789 962791 962807 962837 962839 962861 962867 962869 962903
962909 962911 962921 962959 962963 962971 962993 963019 963031 963043 963047
963097 963103 963121 963143 963163 963173 963181 963187 963191 963211 963223
963227 963239 963241 963253 963283 963299 963301 963311 963323 963331 963341
963343 963349 963367 963379 963397 963419 963427 963461 963481 963491 963497
963499 963559 963581 963601 963619 963629 963643 963653 963659 963667 963689
963691 963701 963707 963709 963719 963731 963751 963761 963773 963779 963793
963799 963811 963817 963839 963841 963847 963863 963871 963877 963899 963901
963913 963943 963973 963979 964009 964021 964027 964039 964049 964081 964097
964133 964151 964153 964199 964207 964213 964217 964219 964253 964259 964261
964267 964283 964289 964297 964303 964309 964333 964339 964351 964357 964363
964373 964417 964423 964433 964463 964499 964501 964507 964517 964519 964531
964559 964571 964577 964583 964589 964609 964637 964661 964679 964693 964697
964703 964721 964753 964783 964787 964793 964823 964829 964861 964871 964873
964879 964883 964889 964897 964913 964927 964933 964939 964967 964969 964973
964981 965023 965047 965059 965087 965089 965101 965113 965117 965131 965147
965161 965171 965177 965179 965189 965191 965197 965201 965227 965233 965249
965267 965291 965303 965317 965329 965357 965369 965399 965401 965407 965411
965423 965429 965443 965453 965467 965483 965491 965507 965519 965533 965551
965567 965603 965611 965621 965623 965639 965647 965659 965677 965711 965749
965773 965777 965779 965801 965819 965843 965851 965857 965893 965927
965953 965963 965969 965983 965989 966011 966013 966029 966041 966109 966113
966139 966149 966157 966191 966197 966209 966211 966221 966227 966233 966241
966257 966271 966293 966307 966313 966319 966323 966337 966347 966353 966373
966377 966379 966389 966401 966409 966419 966431 966439 966463 966481 966491

966499 966509 966521 966527 966547 966557 966583 966613 966617 966619 966631
966653 966659 966661 966677 966727 966751 966781 966803 966817 966863 966869
966871 966883 966893 966907 966913 966919 966923 966937 966961 966971 966991
966997 967003 967019 967049 967061 967111 967129 967139 967171 967201 967229
967259 967261 967289 967297 967319 967321 967327 967333 967349 967361 967363
967391 967397 967427 967429 967441 967451 967459 967481 967493 967501 967507
967511 967529 967567 967583 967607 967627 967663 967667 967693 967699 967709
967721 967739 967751 967753 967763 967781 967787 967819 967823 967831 967843
967847 967859 967873 967877 967903 967919 967931 967937 967951 967961 967979
967999 968003 968017 968021 968027 968041 968063 968089 968101 968111 968113
968117 968137 968141 968147 968159 968173 968197 968213 968237 968239 968251
968263 968267 968273 968291 968299 968311 968321 968329 968333 968353 968377
968381 968389 968419 968423 968431 968437 968459 968467 968479 968501 968503
968519 968521 968537 968557 968567 968573 968593 968641 968647 968659 968663
968689 968699 968713 968729 968731 968761 968801 968809 968819 968827 968831
968857 968879 968897 968909 968911 968917 968939 968959 968963 968971 969011
969037 969041 969049 969071 969083 969097 969109 969113 969131 969139 969167
969179 969181 969233 969239 969253 969257 969259 969271 969301 969341 969343
969347 969359 969377 969403 969407 969421 969431 969443 969457 969461 969461
969467 969481 969497 969503 969509 969533 969559 969569 969593 969599 969637
969641 969667 969671 969677 969679 969713 969719 969721 969743 969757 969763
969767 969797 969809 969821 969851 969863 969869 969877 969889 969907
969911 969919 969923 969929 969977 969989 970027 970031 970043 970051 970061
970063 970069 970087 970091 970111 970133 970147 970201 970213 970217 970219
970231 970237 970247 970259 970261 970267 970279 970297 970303 970313 970351
970391 970421 970423 970433 970441 970447 970457 970469 970481 970493 970537
970549 970561 970573 970583 970603 970633 970643 970657 970667 970687 970699
970721 970747 970777 970787 970789 970793 970799 970813 970817 970829 970847
970859 970861 970867 970877 970883 970903 970909 970927 970939 970943 970961
970967 970969 970987 970997 970999 971021 971027 971029 971039 971051 971053
971063 971077 971093 971099 971111 971141 971143 971149 971153 971171 971177
971197 971207 971237 971251 971263 971273 971279 971281 971291 971309 971339
971353 971357 971371 971381 971387 971389 971401 971419 971429 971441 971473
971479 971483 971491 971501 971513 971521 971549 971561 971563 971569 971591
971639 971651 971653 971683 971693 971699 971713 971723 971753 971759 971767
971783 971821 971833 971851 971857 971863 971899 971903 971917 971921 971933
971939 971951 971959 971977 971981 971989 972001 972017 972029 972031 972047
972071 972079 972091 972113 972119 972121 972131 972133 972137 972161 972163
972197 972199 972221 972227 972229 972259 972263 972271 972277 972313 972319
972329 972337 972343 972347 972353 972373 972403 972407 972409 972427 972431
972443 972469 972473 972481 972493 972533 972557 972577 972581 972599 972611
972613 972623 972637 972649 972661 972679 972683 972701 972721 972787 972793
972799 972823 972827 972833 972847 972869 972887 972899 972901 972941 972943
972967 972971 972991 973001 973003 973031 973033 973051 973057 973067 973069
973073 973081 973099 973129 973151 973169 973177 973187 973213 973253 973277
973279 973283 973289 973321 973331 973333 973367 973373 973387 973397 973409
973411 973421 973439 973469 973487 973523 973529 973537 973547 973561 973591
973597 973631 973657 973669 973681 973693 973727 973757 973759 973781 973787
973789 973801 973813 973837 973853 973891 973897 973901 973919 973957
974003 974009 974033 974041 974053 974063 974089 974107 974123 974137 974143
974161 974167 974177 974179 974189 974213 974249 974261 974269
974273 974279 974293 974317 974329 974359 974383 974387 974401 974411 974417
974419 974431 974437 974443 974459 974473 974489 974497 974507 974513 974531
974537 974539 974551 974557 974563 974581 974591 974599 974651 974653 974657
974707 974711 974713 974737 974747 974749 974761 974773 974803 974819 974821
974837 974849 974861 974863 974867 974873 974879 974887 974891 974923 974927
974957 974959 974969 974971 974977 974983 974989 974999 975011 975017 975049
975053 975071 975083 975089 975133 975151 975157 975181 975187 975193 975199
975217 975257 975259 975263 975277 975281 975287 975313 975323 975343 975367
975379 975383 975389 975421 975427 975433 975439 975463 975493 975497 975509
975521 975523 975551 975553 975581 975599 975619 975629 975643 975649 975661
975671 975691 975701 975731 975739 975743 975797 975803 975811 975823 975827
975847 975857 975869 975883 975899 975901 975907 975941 975943 975967 975977
975991 976009 976013 976033 976039 976091 976093 976103 976109 976117 976127
976147 976177 976187 976193 976211 976231 976253 976271 976279 976301 976303
976307 976309 976351 976369 976403 976411 976439 976447 976453 976457 976471
976477 976483 976489 976501 976513 976537 976553 976559 976561 976571 976601
976607 976621 976637 976643 976669 976699 976709 976721 976727 976747 976777
976799 976817 976823 976849 976853 976883 976909 976919 976933 976951 976957
976991 977021 977023 977047 977057 977069 977087 977107 977147 977149 977167
977183 977191 977203 977209 977233 977239 977243 977257 977269 977299 977323
977351 977357 977359 977363 977369 977407 977411 977413 977437 977447 977507
977513 977521 977539 977567 977591 977593 977609 977611 977629 977671 977681
977693 977719 977723 977747 977761 977791 977803 977813 977819 977831 977849
977861 977881 977897 977923 977927 977971 978001 978007 978011 978017 978031
978037 978041 978049 978053 978067 978071 978073 978077 978079 978091 978113
978149 978151 978157 978179 978181 978203 978209 978217 978223 978233 978239
978269 978277 978283 978287 978323 978337 978343 978347 978349 978359 978389
978403 978413 978427 978449 978457 978463 978473 978479 978491 978511 978521
978541 978569 978599 978611 978617 978619 978643 978647 978683 978689 978697
978713 978727 978743 978749 978773 978797 978799 978821 978839 978851 978853
978863 978871 978883 978907 978917 978931 978947 978973 978997 979001 979009
979031 979037 979061 979063 979093 979103 979109 979117 979159 979163 979171
979177 979189 979201 979207 979211 979219 979229 979261 979273 979283 979291
979313 979327 979333 979337 979343 979361 979369 979373 979379 979403 979423
979439 979457 979471 979481 979519 979529 979541 979543 979549 979553 979567
979651 979691 979709 979717 979747 979757 979787 979807 979819 979831 979873
979883 979889 979907 979919 979921 979949 979969 979987 980027 980047 980069
980071 980081 980107 980117 980131 980137 980149 980159 980173 980179 980197

```
980219  980249  980261  980293  980299  980321  980327  980363  980377  980393  980401
980417  980423  980431  980449  980459  980471  980489  980491  980503  980549  980557
980579  980587  980591  980593  980599  980621  980641  980677  980687  980689  980711
980717  980719  980729  980731  980773  980801  980803  980827  980831  980851  980887
980893  980897  980899  980909  980911  980921  980957  980963  980999  981011  981017
981023  981037  981049  981061  981067  981073  981077  981091  981133  981137  981139
981151  981173  981187  981199  981209  981221  981241  981263  981271  981283  981287
981289  981301  981311  981319  981373  981377  981391  981397  981419  981437  981439
981443  981451  981467  981473  981481  981493  981517  981523  981527  981569  981577
981587  981599  981601  981623  981637  981653  981683  981691  981697  981703  981707
981713  981731  981769  981797  981809  981811  981817  981823  981887  981889  981913
981919  981941  981947  981949  981961  981979  981983  982021  982057  982061  982063
982067  982087  982097  982099  982103  982117  982133  982147  982151  982171  982183
982187  982211  982213  982217  982231  982271  982273  982301  982321  982337  982339
982343  982351  982363  982381  982393  982403  982453  982489  982493  982559  982571
982573  982577  982589  982603  982613  982621  982633  982643  982687  982693  982697
982703  982741  982759  982769  982777  982783  982789  982801  982819  982829  982841
982843  982847  982867  982871  982903  982909  982931  982939  982967  982973  982981
983063  983069  983083  983113  983119  983123  983131  983141  983149  983153  983173
983179  983189  983197  983209  983233  983239  983243  983261  983267  983299  983317
983327  983329  983347  983363  983371  983377  983407  983429  983431  983441  983443
983447  983449  983461  983491  983513  983519  983527  983531  983533  983557  983579
983581  983597  983617  983659  983699  983701  983737  983771  983777  983783  983789
983791  983803  983809  983813  983819  983849  983861  983863  983881  983911  983923
983929  983951  983987  983993  984007  984017  984037  984047  984059  984083  984091
984119  984121  984127  984149  984167  984199  984211  984241  984253  984299  984301
984307  984323  984329  984337  984341  984349  984353  984359  984367  984383  984391
984397  984407  984413  984421  984427  984437  984457  984461  984481  984491  984497
984539  984541  984563  984583  984587  984593  984611  984617  984667  984689  984701
984703  984707  984733  984749  984757  984761  984817  984847  984853  984859  984877
984881  984911  984913  984917  984923  984931  984947  984959  985003  985007  985013
985027  985057  985063  985079  985097  985109  985121  985129  985151  985177  985181
985213  985219  985253  985277  985279  985291  985301  985307  985331  985339  985351
985379  985399  985403  985417  985433  985447  985451  985463  985471  985483  985487
985493  985499  985519  985529  985531  985547  985571  985597  985601  985613  985631
985639  985657  985667  985679  985703  985709  985723  985729  985741  985759  985781
985783  985799  985807  985819  985867  985871  985877  985903  985921  985937  985951
985969  985973  985979  985981  985991  985993  985997  986023  986047  986053  986071
986101  986113  986131  986137  986143  986147  986149  986177  986189  986191  986197
986207  986213  986239  986257  986267  986281  986287  986333  986339  986351  986369
986411  986417  986429  986437  986471  986477  986497  986507  986509  986519  986533
986543  986563  986567  986569  986581  986593  986597  986599  986617  986633  986641
986659  986693  986707  986717  986719  986729  986737  986749  986759  986767  986779
986801  986813  986819  986837  986849  986851  986857  986903  986927  986929  986933
986941  986959  986963  986981  986983  986989  987013  987023  987029  987043  987053
987067  987079  987083  987089  987097  987101  987127  987143  987191  987193  987217
987199  987209  987211  987227  987251  987293  987299  987313  987353  987361  987383
987391  987433  987457  987463  987473  987491  987509  987523  987533  987541  987559
987587  987593  987599  987607  987631  987659  987697  987713  987739  987793  987799
987803  987809  987821  987851  987869  987911  987913  987929  987941  987971  987979
987983  987991  987997  988007  988021  988033  988051  988061  988067  988069  988093
988109  988111  988129  988147  988157  988199  988213  988217  988219  988231  988237
988243  988271  988279  988297  988313  988319  988321  988343  988357  988367  988409
988417  988439  988453  988459  988483  988489  988511  988541  988549  988559  988571
988577  988579  988583  988591  988607  988643  988649  988651  988661  988681  988693
988711  988727  988733  988759  988763  988783  988789  988829  988837  988849  988859
988861  988877  988901  988909  988937  988951  988963  988979  989011  989029  989059
989071  989081  989099  989119  989123  989171  989173  989231  989239  989249  989251
989279  989293  989309  989321  989323  989327  989341  989347  989353  989377  989381
989411  989419  989423  989441  989467  989477  989479  989507  989533  989557  989561
989579  989581  989623  989629  989641  989647  989663  989671  989687  989719  989743
989749  989753  989761  989777  989783  989797  989803  989827  989831  989837  989839
989869  989873  989887  989909  989917  989921  989929  989939  989951  989959  989971
989977  989981  989999  990001  990013  990023  990037  990043  990053  990137  990151
990163  990169  990179  990181  990211  990239  990259  990277  990281  990287  990289
990293  990307  990313  990323  990329  990331  990349  990359  990361  990371  990377
990383  990389  990397  990463  990469  990487  990497  990503  990511  990523  990529
990547  990559  990589  990593  990599  990631  990637  990643  990673  990707  990719
990733  990761  990767  990797  990799  990809  990841  990851  990881  990887  990889
990893  990917  990923  990953  990961  990967  990973  990989  991009  991027  991031
991037  991043  991057  991063  991069  991073  991079  991091  991127  991129  991147
991171  991181  991187  991201  991217  991223  991229  991261  991273  991313  991327
991343  991357  991381  991387  991409  991427  991429  991447  991453  991483  991493
991499  991511  991531  991541  991547  991567  991579  991603  991607  991619  991621
991633  991643  991651  991663  991693  991703  991717  991723  991733  991741  991751
991777  991811  991817  991867  991871  991873  991883  991889  991901  991909  991927
991931  991943  991951  991957  991961  991973  991979  991981  991987  991999  992011
992021  992023  992051  992087  992111  992113  992129  992141  992153  992179  992183
992219  992231  992249  992263  992267  992269  992281  992309  992317  992357  992359
992363  992371  992393  992417  992429  992437  992441  992449  992461  992513  992521
992539  992549  992561  992591  992603  992609  992623  992633  992659  992669  992701
992707  992723  992737  992777  992801  992809  992819  992843  992857  992861  992863
992867  992891  992903  992917  992923  992941  992947  992963  992983  993001  993011
993037  993049  993053  993079  993103  993107  993121  993137  993169  993197  993199
993203  993217  993233  993241  993247  993253  993269  993283  993287  993307  993319
993323  993341  993367  993397  993401  993407  993431  993437  993451  993467  993479
993481  993493  993527  993541  993557  993589  993611  993617  993647  993679  993683
993689  993703  993763  993779  993781  993793  993821  993823  993827  993841  993851
993869  993887  993893  993907  993913  993919  993943  993961  993977  993983  993997
```

```
994013  994027  994039  994051  994067  994069  994073  994087  994093  994141  994163
994181  994183  994193  994199  994229  994237  994241  994247  994249  994271  994297
994303  994307  994309  994319  994321  994337  994339  994363  994369  994391  994393
994417  994447  994453  994457  994471  994489  994501  994549  994559  994561  994571
994579  994583  994603  994621  994657  994663  994667  994691  994699  994709  994711
994717  994723  994751  994769  994793  994811  994813  994817  994831  994837  994853
994867  994871  994879  994901  994907  994913  994927  994933  994949  994963  994991
994997  995009  995023  995051  995053  995081  995117  995119  995147  995167  995173
995219  995227  995237  995243  995273  995303  995327  995339  995341  995347  995359
995363  995369  995377  995381  995387  995399  995431  995443  995447  995461  995471
995513  995531  995539  995549  995551  995567  995573  995587  995591  995593  995611
995623  995641  995651  995663  995669  995677  995699  995713  995719  995737  995747
995783  995791  995801  995833  995881  995887  995903  995909  995927  995941  995957
995959  995983  995987  995989  996001  996011  996019  996049  996067  996103  996109
996119  996143  996157  996161  996167  996169  996173  996187  996197  996209  996211
996253  996257  996263  996271  996293  996301  996311  996323  996329  996361  996367
996403  996407  996409  996431  996461  996487  996511  996529  996539  996551  996563
996571  996599  996601  996617  996629  996631  996637  996647  996649  996689  996703
996719  996763  996781  996803  996811  996841  996847  996857  996859  996871  996881
996883  996887  996899  996953  996967  996973  996979  997001  997013  997019  997021
997037  997043  997057  997069  997081  997091  997097  997099  997103  997109  997111
997121  997123  997141  997147  997151  997153  997163  997201  997207  997219  997247
997259  997267  997273  997279  997307  997309  997319  997327  997333  997343  997357
997369  997379  997391  997427  997433  997439  997453  997463  997511  997541  997547
997553  997573  997583  997589  997597  997609  997627  997637  997649  997651  997663
997681  997693  997699  997727  997739  997741  997751  997769  997783  997793  997807
997811  997813  997877  997879  997889  997891  997897  997933  997949  997961  997963
997973  997991  998009  998017  998027  998029  998069  998071  998077  998083  998111
998117  998147  998161  998167  998197  998201  998213  998219  998237  998243  998273
998281  998287  998311  998329  998353  998377  998381  998399  998411  998419  998423
998429  998443  998471  998497  998513  998527  998537  998539  998551  998561  998617
998623  998629  998633  998651  998653  998681  998687  998689  998717  998737  998743
998749  998759  998779  998813  998819  998831  998839  998843  998857  998861  998897
998909  998911  998917  998927  998941  998947  998951  998969  998983  998989  999007
999023  999029  999043  999049  999067  999083  999091  999101  999133  999149  999169
999181  999199  999217  999221  999233  999239  999269  999287  999307  999329  999331
999359  999371  999377  999389  999431  999433  999437  999451  999491  999499  999521
999529  999541  999553  999563  999599  999611  999613  999623  999631  999653  999667
999671  999683  999721  999727  999749  999763  999769  999773  999809  999853  999863
999883  999907  999917  999931  999953  999959  999961  999979  999983  1000003 1000033
1000037 1000039 1000081 1000099 1000117 1000121 1000133 1000151 1000159 1000171
1000183 1000193 1000199 1000211 1000213 1000231 1000249 1000253 1000273
1000289 1000291 1000303 1000313 1000333 1000357 1000367 1000381 1000393 1000397
1000403 1000409 1000423 1000427 1000429 1000453 1000457 1000507 1000537 1000541
1000547 1000577 1000579 1000589 1000609 1000619 1000621 1000639 1000651 1000667
1000669 1000679 1000691 1000697 1000721 1000723 1000763 1000777 1000793 1000829
1000847 1000849 1000859 1000861 1000889 1000907 1000919 1000921 1000931 1000969
1000973 1000981 1000999 1001003 1001017 1001023 1001027 1001041 1001069 1001081
1001087 1001089 1001093 1001107 1001123 1001153 1001159 1001173 1001177 1001191
1001197 1001219 1001237 1001267 1001279 1001291 1001303 1001311 1001321 1001323
1001327 1001347 1001353 1001369 1001381 1001387 1001389 1001401 1001411 1001431
1001447 1001459 1001467 1001491 1001501 1001527 1001531 1001549 1001551 1001563
1001569 1001587 1001593 1001621 1001629 1001639 1001659 1001669 1001683 1001687
1001713 1001723 1001743 1001797 1001801 1001807 1001809 1001821 1001831
1001839 1001911 1001933 1001941 1001947 1001953 1001977 1001981 1001983 1001989
1002017 1002049 1002061 1002073 1002077 1002083 1002091 1002101 1002109 1002121
1002143 1002149 1002151 1002173 1002191 1002227 1002241 1002247 1002257 1002259
1002263 1002289 1002299 1002341 1002343 1002347 1002349 1002359 1002361 1002377
1002403 1002427 1002433 1002451 1002457 1002467 1002481 1002487 1002493 1002503
1002511 1002517 1002523 1002527 1002553 1002569 1002577 1002583 1002619 1002623
1002647 1002653 1002679 1002709 1002713 1002719 1002721 1002739 1002751 1002767
1002769 1002773 1002787 1002797 1002809 1002817 1002821 1002851 1002853 1002857
1002863 1002871 1002887 1002893 1002899 1002913 1002917 1002929 1002931 1002973
1002979 1003001 1003003 1003019 1003039 1003049 1003087 1003091 1003097 1003103
1003109 1003111 1003133 1003141 1003193 1003199 1003201 1003241 1003259 1003273
1003279 1003291 1003307 1003337 1003349 1003351 1003361 1003363 1003367 1003369
1003381 1003397 1003411 1003417 1003433 1003463 1003469 1003507 1003517 1003543
1003549 1003589 1003601 1003609 1003619 1003621 1003627 1003631 1003679 1003693
1003711 1003729 1003733 1003741 1003747 1003753 1003757 1003763 1003771 1003787
1003817 1003819 1003841 1003879 1003889 1003897 1003907 1003909 1003913 1003931
1003943 1003957 1003963 1004027 1004033 1004053 1004057 1004063 1004077 1004089
1004117 1004119 1004137 1004141 1004161 1004167 1004209 1004221 1004233 1004273
1004279 1004287 1004293 1004303 1004317 1004323 1004363 1004371 1004401 1004429
1004441 1004449 1004453 1004461 1004477 1004483 1004501 1004527 1004537 1004551
1004561 1004567 1004599 1004651 1004657 1004659 1004669 1004671 1004677 1004687
1004723 1004737 1004743 1004747 1004749 1004761 1004779 1004797 1004873 1004903
1004911 1004917 1004963 1004977 1004981 1004987 1005007 1005013 1005019 1005029
1005041 1005049 1005071 1005073 1005079 1005101 1005107 1005131 1005133 1005143
1005161 1005187 1005203 1005209 1005217 1005223 1005229 1005239 1005241 1005269
1005287 1005293 1005313 1005317 1005331 1005349 1005359 1005371 1005373 1005391
1005409 1005413 1005427 1005437 1005439 1005457 1005467 1005481 1005493 1005503
1005527 1005541 1005551 1005553 1005581 1005593 1005617 1005619 1005637 1005643
1005647 1005661 1005677 1005679 1005701 1005709 1005751 1005761 1005821 1005827
1005833 1005883 1005911 1005913 1005931 1005937 1005959 1005971 1005989 1006003
1006007 1006021 1006037 1006063 1006087 1006091 1006123 1006133 1006147 1006151
1006153 1006163 1006169 1006171 1006177 1006189 1006193 1006217 1006219 1006231
1006237 1006241 1006249 1006253 1006267 1006279 1006301 1006303 1006307 1006309
1006331 1006333 1006337 1006339 1006351 1006361 1006367 1006391 1006393 1006433
1006441 1006463 1006469 1006471 1006493 1006507 1006513 1006531 1006543 1006547
```

```
1006559  1006583  1006589  1006609  1006613  1006633  1006637  1006651  1006711  1006721
1006739  1006751  1006769  1006781  1006783  1006799  1006847  1006853  1006861  1006877
1006879  1006883  1006891  1006897  1006933  1006937  1006949  1006969  1006979  1006987
1006991  1007021  1007023  1007047  1007059  1007081  1007089  1007099  1007117  1007119
1007129  1007137  1007161  1007173  1007179  1007203  1007231  1007243  1007249  1007297
1007299  1007309  1007317  1007339  1007353  1007359  1007381  1007387  1007401  1007417
1007429  1007441  1007459  1007467  1007483  1007497  1007519  1007527  1007549  1007557
1007597  1007599  1007609  1007647  1007651  1007681  1007683  1007693  1007701  1007711
1007719  1007723  1007729  1007731  1007749  1007753  1007759  1007767  1007771  1007789
1007801  1007807  1007813  1007819  1007827  1007857  1007861  1007873  1007887  1007891
1007921  1007933  1007939  1007957  1007959  1007971  1007977  1008001  1008013  1008017
1008031  1008037  1008041  1008043  1008101  1008131  1008157  1008181  1008187  1008193
1008199  1008209  1008223  1008229  1008233  1008239  1008247  1008257  1008263  1008317
1008323  1008331  1008347  1008353  1008373  1008379  1008401  1008407  1008409  1008419
1008421  1008433  1008437  1008451  1008467  1008493  1008499  1008503  1008517  1008541
1008547  1008563  1008571  1008587  1008589  1008607  1008611  1008613  1008617  1008659
1008701  1008719  1008743  1008773  1008779  1008781  1008793  1008809  1008811  1008829
1008851  1008853  1008857  1008859  1008863  1008871  1008901  1008911  1008913  1008923
1008937  1008947  1008979  1008983  1008989  1008991  1009007  1009037  1009049  1009061
1009097  1009121  1009139  1009153  1009157  1009159  1009163  1009189  1009193  1009199
1009201  1009207  1009237  1009243  1009247  1009259  1009289  1009291  1009301  1009303
1009319  1009321  1009343  1009357  1009361  1009369  1009373  1009387  1009399  1009417
1009433  1009439  1009457  1009483  1009487  1009499  1009501  1009507  1009531  1009537
1009559  1009573  1009601  1009609  1009621  1009627  1009631  1009643  1009649  1009651
1009669  1009727  1009741  1009747  1009781  1009787  1009807  1009819  1009837  1009843
1009859  1009873  1009901  1009909  1009927  1009937  1009951  1009963  1009991  1009993
1009997  1010003  1010033  1010069  1010081  1010083  1010129  1010131  1010143  1010167
1010179  1010201  1010203  1010237  1010263  1010291  1010297  1010329  1010353  1010357
1010381  1010407  1010411  1010419  1010423  1010431  1010461  1010467  1010473  1010491
1010501  1010509  1010519  1010549  1010567  1010579  1010617  1010623  1010627  1010671
1010683  1010687  1010717  1010719  1010747  1010749  1010753  1010759  1010767  1010771
1010783  1010791  1010797  1010809  1010833  1010843  1010861  1010881  1010897  1010899
1010903  1010917  1010929  1010957  1010981  1010983  1010993  1011001  1011013  1011029
1011037  1011067  1011071  1011077  1011079  1011091  1011107  1011137  1011139  1011163
1011167  1011191  1011217  1011221  1011229  1011233  1011239  1011271  1011277  1011281
1011289  1011331  1011343  1011349  1011359  1011371  1011377  1011391  1011397  1011407
1011431  1011443  1011509  1011539  1011553  1011559  1011583  1011587  1011589  1011599
1011601  1011631  1011641  1011649  1011667  1011671  1011677  1011697  1011719  1011733
1011737  1011749  1011763  1011779  1011797  1011799  1011817  1011827  1011889  1011893
1011917  1011937  1011943  1011947  1011961  1011973  1011979  1012007  1012009  1012031
1012043  1012049  1012079  1012087  1012093  1012097  1012103  1012133  1012147  1012159
1012171  1012183  1012189  1012201  1012213  1012217  1012229  1012241  1012259  1012261
1012267  1012279  1012289  1012307  1012321  1012369  1012373  1012379  1012397  1012399
1012411  1012421  1012423  1012433  1012439  1012447  1012457  1012463  1012481  1012489
1012507  1012513  1012519  1012523  1012547  1012549  1012559  1012573  1012591  1012597
1012601  1012619  1012631  1012633  1012637  1012657  1012663  1012679  1012691  1012699
1012703  1012717  1012721  1012733  1012751  1012763  1012769  1012771  1012789  1012811
1012829  1012831  1012861  1012903  1012919  1012931  1012967  1012981  1012993  1012997
1013003  1013009  1013029  1013041  1013053  1013063  1013143  1013153  1013197  1013203
1013227  1013237  1013239  1013249  1013263  1013267  1013279  1013291  1013321  1013329
1013377  1013399  1013401  1013429  1013431  1013471  1013477  1013501  1013503  1013527
1013531  1013533  1013563  1013569  1013581  1013603  1013609  1013627  1013629  1013641
1013671  1013681  1013687  1013699  1013711  1013713  1013717  1013729  1013741  1013767
1013773  1013791  1013813  1013819  1013827  1013833  1013839  1013843  1013851  1013879
1013891  1013893  1013899  1013921  1013923  1013933  1013993  1014007  1014029  1014037
1014061  1014089  1014113  1014121  1014127  1014131  1014137  1014149  1014157  1014161
1014173  1014193  1014197  1014199  1014229  1014257  1014259  1014263  1014287  1014301
1014317  1014319  1014331  1014337  1014341  1014359  1014361  1014371  1014389  1014397
1014451  1014457  1014469  1014487  1014493  1014521  1014539  1014547  1014557  1014571
1014593  1014617  1014631  1014641  1014649  1014677  1014697  1014719  1014721  1014731
1014743  1014763  1014779  1014787  1014817  1014821  1014833  1014863  1014869
1014877  1014887  1014889  1014907  1014941  1014953  1014973  1014989  1015009  1015039
1015043  1015051  1015057  1015061  1015067  1015073  1015081  1015093  1015097  1015123
1015127  1015139  1015159  1015163  1015171  1015199  1015207  1015277  1015309  1015349
1015361  1015363  1015367  1015369  1015403  1015409  1015423  1015433  1015451  1015453
1015459  1015463  1015471  1015481  1015499  1015501  1015507  1015517  1015523  1015541
1015549  1015559  1015561  1015571  1015601  1015603  1015627  1015661  1015691  1015697
1015709  1015723  1015727  1015739  1015747  1015753  1015769  1015813  1015823  1015829
1015843  1015853  1015871  1015877  1015891  1015897  1015907  1015913  1015919  1015967
1015981  1015991  1016009  1016011  1016023  1016027  1016033  1016051  1016053  1016069
1016083  1016089  1016111  1016123  1016137  1016143  1016153  1016159  1016173  1016201
1016203  1016221  1016227  1016231  1016237  1016263  1016303  1016339  1016341  1016357
1016359  1016371  1016399  1016401  1016419  1016423  1016441  1016453  1016489  1016497
1016527  1016567  1016569  1016573  1016581  1016597  1016599  1016611  1016621  1016641
1016663  1016681  1016689  1016731  1016737  1016749  1016773  1016777  1016783  1016789
1016839  1016843  1016849  1016879  1016881  1016891  1016909  1016921  1016927  1016929
1016941  1016947  1016959  1016971  1017007  1017011  1017031  1017041  1017043  1017061
1017077  1017097  1017119  1017131  1017139  1017157  1017173  1017179  1017193  1017199
1017209  1017227  1017277  1017293  1017299  1017301  1017307  1017311  1017319  1017323
1017329  1017347  1017353  1017361  1017371  1017377  1017383  1017391  1017437  1017439
1017449  1017473  1017479  1017481  1017539  1017551  1017553  1017559  1017607  1017613
1017617  1017623  1017647  1017649  1017673  1017683  1017703  1017713  1017719  1017721
1017749  1017781  1017787  1017799  1017827  1017847  1017851  1017857  1017859
1017881  1017889  1017923  1017953  1017959  1017997  1018007  1018019  1018021  1018057
1018091  1018109  1018123  1018177  1018201  1018207  1018217  1018223  1018247
1018253  1018271  1018291  1018301  1018309  1018313  1018337  1018357  1018411  1018421
1018429  1018439  1018447  1018471  1018477  1018489  1018513  1018543  1018559  1018583
1018613  1018621  1018643  1018649  1018651  1018669  1018673  1018679  1018697  1018709
1018711  1018729  1018733  1018763  1018769  1018777  1018789  1018807  1018811  1018813
```

```
1018817  1018859  1018873  1018879  1018889  1018903  1018907  1018931  1018937  1018949
1018957  1018967  1018981  1018987  1018993  1018999  1019023  1019033  1019059  1019069
1019071  1019077  1019093  1019119  1019129  1019173  1019177  1019197  1019209  1019237
1019251  1019257  1019261  1019267  1019273  1019281  1019297  1019329  1019339  1019351
1019353  1019357  1019377  1019399  1019411  1019413  1019423  1019443  1019449  1019453
1019467  1019471  1019479  1019503  1019509  1019531  1019533  1019537  1019549  1019563
1019567  1019639  1019647  1019657  1019663  1019687  1019693  1019699  1019701  1019713
1019717  1019723  1019729  1019731  1019741  1019747  1019771  1019783  1019801  1019819
1019827  1019839  1019849  1019857  1019861  1019873  1019899  1019903  1019927  1019971
1020001  1020007  1020011  1020013  1020023  1020037  1020043  1020049  1020059  1020077
1020079  1020101  1020109  1020113  1020137  1020143  1020157  1020163  1020223  1020233
1020247  1020259  1020269  1020293  1020301  1020329  1020337  1020353  1020361  1020379
1020389  1020401  1020407  1020413  1020419  1020431  1020451  1020457  1020491  1020517
1020529  1020541  1020557  1020583  1020589  1020599  1020619  1020631  1020667  1020683
1020689  1020707  1020709  1020743  1020751  1020757  1020779  1020797  1020821  1020823
1020827  1020839  1020841  1020847  1020853  1020881  1020893  1020907  1020913  1020931
1020959  1020961  1020967  1020973  1020977  1020979  1020989  1020991  1020997  1021001
1021019  1021043  1021067  1021073  1021081  1021087  1021091  1021093  1021123  1021127
1021129  1021157  1021159  1021183  1021199  1021217  1021243  1021253  1021259  1021261
1021271  1021283  1021289  1021291  1021297  1021301  1021303  1021327  1021331  1021333
1021367  1021369  1021373  1021381  1021387  1021403  1021417  1021429  1021441  1021457
1021463  1021483  1021487  1021541  1021561  1021567  1021577  1021621  1021627  1021651
1021661  1021663  1021673  1021697  1021711  1021747  1021753  1021759  1021777  1021793
1021799  1021807  1021831  1021837  1021849  1021861  1021879  1021889  1021907  1021919
1021961  1021963  1021973  1022011  1022017  1022033  1022053  1022059  1022071  1022083
1022113  1022123  1022129  1022137  1022141  1022167  1022179  1022183  1022191  1022201
1022209  1022237  1022243  1022249  1022251  1022291  1022303  1022341  1022377  1022381
1022383  1022387  1022389  1022429  1022443  1022449  1022467  1022491  1022501  1022503
1022507  1022509  1022513  1022519  1022531  1022573  1022591  1022611  1022629  1022633
1022639  1022653  1022677  1022683  1022689  1022701  1022719  1022729  1022761  1022773
1022797  1022821  1022837  1022843  1022849  1022869  1022881  1022891  1022899  1022911
1022929  1022933  1022963  1022977  1022981  1023019  1023037  1023041  1023047  1023067
1023079  1023083  1023101  1023107  1023133  1023163  1023167  1023173  1023199  1023203
1023221  1023227  1023229  1023257  1023259  1023263  1023277  1023289  1023299  1023301
1023311  1023313  1023317  1023329  1023353  1023361  1023367  1023389  1023391  1023409
1023413  1023419  1023461  1023467  1023487  1023499  1023521  1023541  1023551  1023557
1023571  1023577  1023601  1023643  1023653  1023697  1023719  1023721  1023731  1023733
1023751  1023769  1023821  1023833  1023839  1023851  1023857  1023871  1023941  1023943
1023947  1023949  1023973  1023977  1023991  1024021  1024031  1024061  1024073  1024087
1024091  1024099  1024103  1024151  1024159  1024171  1024183  1024189  1024207  1024249
1024277  1024307  1024313  1024319  1024321  1024327  1024337  1024339  1024357  1024379
1024391  1024399  1024411  1024421  1024427  1024433  1024447  1024481  1024511  1024523
1024547  1024559  1024577  1024579  1024589  1024591  1024609  1024633  1024663  1024669
1024693  1024697  1024703  1024711  1024721  1024729  1024757  1024783  1024799  1024823
1024843  1024853  1024871  1024883  1024901  1024909  1024921  1024931  1024939  1024943
1024951  1024957  1024963  1024987  1024997  1025009  1025021  1025029  1025039  1025047
1025081  1025093  1025099  1025111  1025113  1025119  1025137  1025147  1025149  1025153
1025161  1025197  1025203  1025209  1025231  1025239  1025257  1025261  1025267  1025273
1025279  1025281  1025303  1025327  1025333  1025347  1025351  1025383  1025393  1025407
1025413  1025417  1025419  1025443  1025459  1025477  1025483  1025503  1025509  1025513
1025537  1025543  1025551  1025561  1025579  1025611  1025621  1025623  1025641  1025653
1025569  1025669  1025693  1025707  1025741  1025747  1025749  1025767  1025789  1025803
1025807  1025819  1025839  1025873  1025887  1025891  1025897  1025909  1025911  1025917
1025939  1025957  1026029  1026031  1026037  1026041  1026043  1026061  1026073
1026101  1026119  1026127  1026139  1026143  1026167  1026197  1026199  1026217  1026227
1026229  1026251  1026253  1026257  1026293  1026299  1026313  1026331  1026359  1026371
1026383  1026391  1026401  1026407  1026413  1026427  1026439  1026449  1026457  1026479
1026481  1026521  1026541  1026563  1026577  1026581  1026583  1026587  1026593  1026661
1026667  1026673  1026677  1026679  1026709  1026733  1026757  1026761  1026791  1026799
1026811  1026829  1026833  1026847  1026853  1026859  1026887  1026899  1026911  1026913
1026917  1026941  1026943  1026947  1026979  1026989  1027001  1027003  1027027  1027031
1027051  1027067  1027097  1027127  1027129  1027139  1027153  1027163  1027181  1027189
1027199  1027207  1027211  1027223  1027241  1027261  1027277  1027289  1027319  1027321
1027331  1027357  1027391  1027409  1027417  1027421  1027427  1027459  1027471  1027483
1027487  1027489  1027493  1027519  1027547  1027549  1027567  1027591  1027597  1027613
1027643  1027679  1027687  1027693  1027703  1027717  1027727  1027739  1027751  1027753
1027757  1027759  1027777  1027783  1027787  1027799  1027841  1027853  1027883  1027891
1027931  1027969  1027987  1028003  1028011  1028017  1028023  1028029  1028047  1028051
1028063  1028081  1028089  1028099  1028101  1028107  1028113  1028117  1028129  1028141
1028149  1028189  1028191  1028201  1028207  1028213  1028221  1028231  1028243  1028263
1028273  1028303  1028309  1028317  1028327  1028329  1028333  1028389  1028393  1028411
1028437  1028471  1028473  1028479  1028509  1028557  1028561  1028569  1028579  1028581
1028597  1028617  1028647  1028663  1028669  1028681  1028683  1028737  1028747  1028749
1028761  1028773  1028777  1028803  1028809  1028837  1028843  1028873  1028893  1028903
1028939  1028941  1028953  1028957  1028969  1028981  1028989  1029001  1029013  1029023
1029037  1029103  1029109  1029113  1029139  1029151  1029157  1029167  1029179  1029191
1029199  1029209  1029247  1029251  1029263  1029277  1029289  1029307  1029323  1029331
1029337  1029341  1029349  1029359  1029361  1029383  1029403  1029407  1029409  1029433
1029467  1029473  1029481  1029487  1029499  1029517  1029521  1029527  1029533  1029547
1029563  1029569  1029577  1029583  1029593  1029601  1029617  1029643  1029647  1029653
1029689  1029697  1029731  1029751  1029757  1029767  1029803  1029823  1029827  1029839
1029841  1029859  1029881  1029883  1029907  1029929  1029937  1029943  1029953  1029967
1029983  1029989  1030019  1030021  1030031  1030033  1030043  1030049  1030051  1030061
1030067  1030069  1030091  1030111  1030121  1030153  1030157  1030181  1030201  1030213
1030219  1030241  1030247  1030291  1030297  1030307  1030349  1030357  1030361  1030369
1030411  1030417  1030429  1030439  1030441  1030451  1030493  1030511  1030529  1030537
1030543  1030571  1030583  1030619  1030637  1030639  1030643  1030681  1030703  1030723
1030739  1030741  1030751  1030759  1030763  1030787  1030793  1030801  1030811  1030817
1030823  1030831  1030847  1030867  1030873  1030889  1030919  1030933  1030949  1030951
```

```
1030957  1030987  1030993  1031003  1031047  1031053  1031057  1031081  1031117  1031119
1031137  1031141  1031161  1031189  1031231  1031267  1031279  1031281  1031291  1031299
1031309  1031323  1031347  1031357  1031399  1031411  1031413  1031423  1031431  1031447
1031461  1031477  1031479  1031483  1031489  1031507  1031521  1031531  1031533  1031549
1031561  1031593  1031609  1031623  1031629  1031633  1031669  1031677  1031707  1031717
1031729  1031731  1031741  1031753  1031759  1031761  1031809  1031813  1031831  1031837
1031869  1031911  1031923  1031981  1031999  1032007  1032047  1032049  1032067  1032071
1032107  1032131  1032151  1032191  1032193  1032211  1032221  1032233  1032259  1032287
1032299  1032307  1032319  1032329  1032341  1032347  1032349  1032373  1032377  1032391
1032397  1032407  1032419  1032433  1032457  1032463  1032467  1032491  1032497  1032509
1032511  1032527  1032541  1032571  1032583  1032601  1032607  1032613  1032617  1032643
1032649  1032679  1032683  1032697  1032701  1032709  1032721  1032727  1032739  1032751
1032763  1032793  1032799  1032803  1032833  1032839  1032841  1032847  1032851  1032853
1032881  1032887  1032901  1032943  1032949  1032959  1032961  1033001  1033007  1033027
1033033  1033037  1033057  1033061  1033063  1033069  1033079  1033099  1033127  1033139
1033171  1033181  1033189  1033223  1033271  1033273  1033289  1033297  1033303  1033309
1033313  1033339  1033343  1033343  1033449  1033463  1033383  1033387  1033393
1033421  1033423  1033427  1033441  1033451  1033457  1033463  1033469  1033489  1033493
1033499  1033507  1033517  1033537  1033541  1033559  1033567  1033601  1033603  1033631
1033661  1033663  1033667  1033679  1033687  1033693  1033741  1033751  1033759  1033777
1033783  1033789  1033793  1033801  1033807  1033829  1033841  1033843  1033867  1033927
1033951  1033987  1034003  1034009  1034027  1034029  1034069  1034071  1034101  1034119
1034123  1034147  1034167  1034171  1034177  1034183  1034197  1034207  1034219  1034221
1034233  1034237  1034239  1034249  1034251  1034281  1034309  1034317  1034323  1034339
1034353  1034357  1034359  1034381  1034387  1034419  1034443  1034461  1034477  1034479
1034489  1034491  1034503  1034513  1034549  1034567  1034581  1034591  1034597  1034599
1034617  1034639  1034651  1034653  1034659  1034707  1034729  1034731  1034767  1034771
1034783  1034791  1034809  1034827  1034833  1034837  1034849  1034857  1034861  1034863
1034867  1034879  1034903  1034941  1034951  1034953  1034959  1034983  1034989  1034993
1035007  1035019  1035043  1035061  1035077  1035107  1035131  1035163  1035187  1035191
1035197  1035211  1035241  1035247  1035257  1035263  1035277  1035301  1035313  1035323
1035341  1035343  1035361  1035379  1035383  1035403  1035409  1035413  1035427  1035449
1035451  1035467  1035469  1035473  1035479  1035499  1035527  1035533  1035547  1035563
1035571  1035581  1035599  1035607  1035613  1035631  1035637  1035641  1035649  1035659
1035707  1035733  1035743  1035761  1035763  1035781  1035791  1035829  1035869  1035893
1035917  1035949  1035953  1035959  1035973  1035977  1036001  1036003  1036027  1036039
1036067  1036069  1036073  1036093  1036109  1036117  1036121  1036129  1036153  1036163
1036183  1036213  1036223  1036229  1036247  1036249  1036253  1036261  1036267  1036271
1036291  1036297  1036307  1036319  1036327  1036331  1036339  1036349  1036351  1036363
1036367  1036369  1036391  1036411  1036459  1036471  1036493  1036499  1036513  1036531
1036537  1036561  1036579  1036613  1036619  1036631  1036649  1036661  1036667  1036669
1036681  1036729  1036747  1036751  1036757  1036759  1036769  1036787  1036793  1036799
1036829  1036831  1036853  1036873  1036877  1036883  1036913  1036921  1036943  1036951
1036957  1036979  1036991  1036993  1037001  1037053  1037059  1037081  1037087  1037089
1037123  1037129  1037137  1037143  1037213  1037233  1037249  1037261  1037273  1037293
1037297  1037303  1037317  1037327  1037329  1037339  1037347  1037401  1037411  1037437
1037441  1037447  1037471  1037479  1037489  1037497  1037503  1037537  1037557  1037563
1037567  1037593  1037611  1037627  1037653  1037657  1037677  1037681  1037683  1037741
1037747  1037753  1037759  1037767  1037791  1037801  1037819  1037831  1037857  1037873
1037879  1037893  1037903  1037917  1037929  1037941  1037957  1037963  1037983  1038001
1038017  1038019  1038029  1038041  1038043  1038047  1038073  1038077  1038119  1038127
1038143  1038157  1038187  1038199  1038203  1038209  1038211  1038227  1038251  1038253
1038259  1038263  1038269  1038307  1038311  1038319  1038329  1038337  1038383  1038391
1038409  1038421  1038449  1038463  1038487  1038497  1038503  1038523  1038529  1038539
1038563  1038589  1038599  1038601  1038617  1038619  1038623  1038629  1038637  1038643
1038671  1038689  1038691  1038707  1038721  1038727  1038731  1038757  1038797  1038803
1038811  1038823  1038827  1038833  1038881  1038913  1038937  1038941  1038953  1039001
1039007  1039021  1039033  1039037  1039039  1039043  1039067  1039069  1039081  1039109
1039111  1039127  1039139  1039153  1039169  1039187  1039229  1039249  1039279  1039289
1039307  1039321  1039327  1039343  1039349  1039351  1039387  1039421  1039427  1039429
1039463  1039469  1039477  1039481  1039513  1039517  1039537  1039543  1039553  1039603
1039607  1039631  1039651  1039657  1039667  1039681  1039733  1039763  1039769  1039789
1039799  1039817  1039823  1039837  1039889  1039891  1039901  1039921  1039931  1039943
1039949  1039979  1039999  1040021  1040029  1040051  1040057  1040059  1040069  1040071
1040089  1040093  1040101  1040113  1040119  1040141  1040153  1040159  1040161  1040167
1040183  1040189  1040191  1040203  1040219  1040227  1040311  1040327  1040339  1040353
1040371  1040381  1040387  1040407  1040411  1040419  1040447  1040449  1040483  1040489
1040503  1040521  1040531  1040563  1040571  1040581  1040597  1040629  1040651  1040657
1040659  1040671  1040717  1040731  1040747  1040749  1040771  1040777  1040779  1040783
1040797  1040803  1040807  1040813  1040821  1040827  1040833  1040857  1040861  1040873
1040881  1040891  1040899  1040929  1040939  1040947  1040951  1040959  1040981  1040989
1041041  1041077  1041083  1041091  1041109  1041119  1041121  1041127  1041137  1041149
1041151  1041163  1041167  1041169  1041203  1041221  1041223  1041239  1041241  1041253
1041269  1041281  1041283  1041289  1041307  1041311  1041317  1041329  1041343  1041349
1041373  1041421  1041427  1041449  1041451  1041461  1041497  1041511  1041517  1041529
1041553  1041559  1041563  1041571  1041577  1041583  1041617  1041619  1041643  1041653
1041671  1041673  1041701  1041731  1041737  1041757  1041779  1041787  1041793  1041823
1041829  1041841  1041853  1041857  1041863  1041869  1041889  1041893  1041907  1041919
1041949  1041961  1041983  1041991  1042001  1042021  1042039  1042043  1042081  1042087
1042091  1042099  1042103  1042109  1042121  1042123  1042133  1042141  1042183  1042187
1042193  1042211  1042241  1042243  1042259  1042267  1042271  1042273  1042309  1042331
1042333  1042357  1042369  1042373  1042381  1042399  1042427  1042439  1042451  1042469
1042487  1042519  1042529  1042571  1042583  1042597  1042607  1042609
1042619  1042631  1042633  1042681  1042687  1042693  1042703  1042709  1042733  1042759
1042781  1042799  1042819  1042829  1042837  1042861  1042897  1042901  1042903
1042931  1042949  1042961  1042997  1043011  1043023  1043047  1043083  1043089  1043111
1043113  1043117  1043131  1043167  1043173  1043177  1043183  1043191  1043201  1043209
1043213  1043221  1043279  1043291  1043293  1043299  1043311  1043323  1043351  1043369
1043377  1043401  1043453  1043467  1043479  1043489  1043501  1043513  1043521  1043531
```

```
1043543  1043557  1043587  1043591  1043593  1043597  1043599  1043617  1043639  1043657
1043663  1043683  1043701  1043723  1043743  1043747  1043753  1043759  1043761  1043767
1043773  1043831  1043837  1043839  1043843  1043849  1043857  1043869  1043873  1043897
1043899  1043921  1043923  1043929  1043951  1043969  1043981  1044019  1044023  1044041
1044053  1044079  1044091  1044097  1044133  1044139  1044149  1044161  1044167  1044179
1044181  1044187  1044193  1044209  1044217  1044227  1044247  1044257  1044271  1044283
1044287  1044289  1044299  1044343  1044347  1044353  1044367  1044371  1044383  1044391
1044397  1044409  1044437  1044443  1044451  1044457  1044479  1044509  1044517  1044529
1044559  1044569  1044583  1044587  1044613  1044619  1044629  1044653  1044689  1044697
1044727  1044733  1044737  1044739  1044749  1044751  1044761  1044767  1044779  1044781
1044809  1044811  1044833  1044839  1044847  1044851  1044859  1044877  1044889  1044893
1044931  1044941  1044971  1044997  1045003  1045013  1045021  1045027  1045043  1045061
1045063  1045081  1045111  1045117  1045123  1045129  1045151  1045153  1045157  1045183
1045193  1045199  1045223  1045229  1045237  1045241  1045273  1045277  1045307  1045309
1045321  1045349  1045367  1045391  1045393  1045397  1045409  1045411  1045423  1045427
1045469  1045487  1045493  1045507  1045523  1045529  1045543  1045547  1045549  1045559
1045571  1045573  1045607  1045621  1045633  1045643  1045651  1045663  1045679  1045691
1045727  1045729  1045739  1045763  1045799  1045801  1045819  1045829  1045841  1045859
1045903  1045907  1045963  1045981  1045997  1046009  1046047  1046051  1046053
1046069  1046077  1046081  1046113  1046119  1046179  1046183  1046189  1046191  1046203
1046207  1046237  1046239  1046257  1046263  1046329  1046347  1046351  1046369  1046371
1046389  1046393  1046399  1046413  1046441  1046449  1046459  1046497  1046519  1046527
1046557  1046579  1046587  1046597  1046599  1046627  1046641  1046657  1046659  1046677
1046681  1046687  1046701  1046711  1046779  1046791  1046797  1046807  1046827  1046833
1046849  1046863  1046867  1046897  1046917  1046933  1046951  1046959  1046977  1046993
1046999  1047031  1047041  1047043  1047061  1047077  1047089  1047097  1047107  1047119
1047127  1047131  1047133  1047139  1047157  1047173  1047197  1047199  1047229  1047239
1047247  1047271  1047281  1047283  1047289  1047307  1047311  1047313  1047317  1047323
1047341  1047367  1047373  1047379  1047391  1047419  1047467  1047469  1047479  1047491
1047499  1047511  1047533  1047539  1047551  1047559  1047587  1047589  1047647  1047649
1047653  1047667  1047671  1047689  1047691  1047701  1047703  1047713  1047721  1047737
1047751  1047763  1047773  1047779  1047821  1047833  1047841  1047859  1047881  1047883
1047887  1047923  1047929  1047941  1047961  1047971  1047979  1047989  1047997  1048007
1048009  1048013  1048027  1048043  1048049  1048051  1048063  1048123  1048127  1048129
1048139  1048189  1048193  1048213  1048217  1048219  1048261  1048273  1048291  1048309
1048343  1048357  1048361  1048367  1048387  1048391  1048433  1048447  1048507
1048517  1048549  1048559  1048571  1048573  1048583  1048589  1048601  1048609  1048613
1048627  1048633  1048661  1048681  1048703  1048709  1048717  1048721  1048759  1048783
1048793  1048799  1048807  1048829  1048837  1048847  1048867  1048877  1048889  1048891
1048897  1048909  1048919  1048963  1048991  1049011  1049023  1049039  1049051  1049057
1049063  1049077  1049089  1049093  1049101  1049117  1049129  1049131  1049137  1049141
1049143  1049171  1049173  1049177  1049183  1049201  1049219  1049227  1049239  1049263
1049281  1049297  1049333  1049339  1049387  1049413  1049429  1049437  1049459  1049471
1049473  1049479  1049483  1049497  1049509  1049519  1049527  1049533  1049537  1049549
1049569  1049599  1049603  1049611  1049623  1049639  1049663  1049677  1049681  1049683
1049687  1049707  1049717  1049747  1049773  1049791  1049809  1049821  1049827  1049833
1049837  1049843  1049849  1049857  1049861  1049863  1049891  1049897  1049899  1049941
1049953  1049963  1049977  1049999  1050011  1050013  1050031  1050041  1050053  1050079
1050083  1050139  1050151  1050167  1050169  1050191  1050197  1050229  1050233  1050239
1050241  1050253  1050281  1050307  1050317  1050323  1050331  1050337  1050349  1050367
1050383  1050421  1050431  1050437  1050449  1050451  1050457  1050473  1050503  1050509
1050523  1050563  1050593  1050611  1050631  1050713  1050727  1050733  1050737  1050739
1050743  1050769  1050773  1050781  1050811  1050817  1050851  1050853  1050887  1050899
1050901  1050913  1050949  1050961  1050977  1050997  1051003  1051007  1051009  1051019
1051027  1051051  1051069  1051079  1051081  1051139  1051147  1051151  1051153  1051157
1051177  1051181  1051247  1051277  1051283  1051291  1051301  1051313  1051319  1051333
1051373  1051397  1051409  1051417  1051423  1051459  1051469  1051471  1051481  1051499
1051507  1051543  1051549  1051553  1051559  1051571  1051591  1051601  1051607  1051619
1051621  1051639  1051643  1051649  1051663  1051697  1051709  1051717  1051747  1051759
1051763  1051781  1051789  1051811  1051819  1051829  1051847  1051849  1051879  1051889
1051903  1051913  1051927  1051949  1051957  1051961  1051979  1051987  1051991  1052027
1052039  1052041  1052063  1052083  1052099  1052111  1052119  1052137  1052141  1052179
1052197  1052203  1052221  1052231  1052237  1052269  1052279  1052281  1052287  1052299
1052309  1052321  1052327  1052329  1052333  1052413  1052417  1052431  1052437  1052459
1052473  1052479  1052489  1052531  1052533  1052537  1052551  1052561  1052563  1052567
1052573  1052609  1052629  1052663  1052693  1052707  1052719  1052731  1052743  1052747
1052767  1052797  1052801  1052803  1052813  1052819  1052851  1052873  1052881  1052893
1052897  1052899  1052939  1052971  1052981  1052993  1053007  1053029  1053061  1053067
1053071  1053079  1053083  1053089  1053097  1053103  1053179  1053181  1053191  1053197
1053253  1053257  1053259  1053263  1053271  1053293  1053301  1053319  1053347  1053361
1053383  1053401  1053407  1053421  1053449  1053461  1053467  1053487  1053491  1053497
1053509  1053511  1053529  1053539  1053551  1053557  1053571  1053581  1053583  1053589
1053593  1053617  1053691  1053697  1053707  1053713  1053727  1053737  1053739  1053749
1053757  1053769  1053809  1053817  1053821  1053827  1053863  1053953  1053959  1053967
1053971  1053989  1053991  1054001  1054007  1054013  1054033  1054043  1054049  1054061
1054073  1054091  1054133  1054169  1054171  1054181  1054189  1054199  1054201  1054213
1054219  1054243  1054247  1054259  1054267  1054301  1054303  1054309  1054321  1054327
1054331  1054337  1054363  1054369  1054373  1054381  1054393  1054423  1054429  1054439
1054441  1054457  1054477  1054483  1054517  1054523  1054531  1054549  1054577  1054583
1054597  1054607  1054609  1054621  1054639  1054649  1054667  1054673  1054679  1054717
1054721  1054723  1054733  1054769  1054813  1054819  1054831  1054843  1054853  1054903
1054909  1054927  1054931  1054951  1054957  1054993  1055017  1055039  1055057  1055063
1055077  1055083  1055113  1055137  1055141  1055143  1055167  1055189  1055191  1055231
1055233  1055251  1055261  1055267  1055269  1055303  1055321  1055347  1055359  1055363
1055371  1055387  1055399  1055407  1055413  1055423  1055429  1055437  1055441  1055489
1055501  1055503  1055531  1055543  1055567  1055591  1055597  1055603  1055609  1055611
1055671  1055689  1055713  1055731  1055737  1055741  1055771  1055783  1055801  1055809
1055827  1055839  1055851  1055863  1055867  1055881  1055893  1055897  1055911  1055917
1055933  1055939  1055947  1055959  1055969  1055981  1056007  1056019  1056047  1056049
```

```
1056053  1056061  1056071  1056073  1056089  1056109  1056113  1056149  1056161  1056169
1056173  1056179  1056203  1056217  1056241  1056247  1056269  1056271  1056281  1056287
1056311  1056317  1056323  1056347  1056353  1056361  1056371  1056373  1056379  1056401
1056443  1056463  1056469  1056479  1056481  1056493  1056509  1056521  1056541  1056563
1056569  1056577  1056589  1056599  1056613  1056617  1056623  1056641  1056659  1056667
1056707  1056719  1056721  1056739  1056773  1056779  1056793  1056823  1056829  1056833
1056863  1056871  1056893  1056911  1056917  1056929  1056949  1056959  1056971  1057003
1057013  1057019  1057033  1057037  1057051  1057087  1057093  1057117  1057129  1057157
1057163  1057181  1057183  1057219  1057223  1057237  1057249  1057271  1057279  1057291
1057307  1057361  1057367  1057387  1057391  1057393  1057411  1057421  1057477  1057487
1057489  1057493  1057531  1057541  1057561  1057577  1057579  1057603  1057607  1057613
1057631  1057633  1057643  1057657  1057663  1057681  1057699  1057703  1057739  1057741
1057753  1057781  1057807  1057831  1057853  1057879  1057883  1057897  1057907  1057919
1057951  1057957  1057963  1057981  1057993  1058009  1058011  1058021  1058027  1058041
1058059  1058077  1058093  1058107  1058117  1058143  1058147  1058149  1058153  1058171
1058179  1058203  1058221  1058227  1058249  1058257  1058263  1058287  1058303  1058329
1058339  1058341  1058353  1058377  1058381  1058383  1058389  1058419  1058423  1058443
1058461  1058479  1058489  1058503  1058507  1058543  1058549  1058567  1058591  1058593
1058597  1058627  1058639  1058653  1058657  1058663  1058671  1058677  1058683  1058693
1058711  1058723  1058731  1058747  1058749  1058753  1058767  1058773  1058779  1058791
1058803  1058807  1058809  1058821  1058839  1058861  1058891  1058921  1058951  1058983
1058999  1059001  1059007  1059017  1059029  1059059  1059061  1059067  1059073  1059077
1059103  1059119  1059131  1059137  1059161  1059169  1059181  1059197  1059209  1059217
1059221  1059251  1059257  1059259  1059263  1059271  1059293  1059299  1059313  1059323
1059343  1059349  1059413  1059419  1059433  1059437  1059439  1059467  1059479  1059503
1059511  1059517  1059547  1059557  1059571  1059599  1059613  1059637  1059647  1059671
1059683  1059697  1059701  1059703  1059713  1059733  1059743  1059749  1059757  1059769
1059787  1059823  1059833  1059847  1059857  1059871  1059889  1059893  1059923  1059931
1059937  1059941  1060009  1060019  1060021  1060039  1060043  1060051  1060061  1060091
1060097  1060123  1060133  1060151  1060177  1060187  1060201  1060207  1060223  1060229
1060237  1060249  1060253  1060271  1060303  1060313  1060321  1060343  1060349  1060351
1060357  1060361  1060373  1060379  1060391  1060393  1060403  1060421  1060427  1060441
1060453  1060463  1060469  1060481  1060487  1060513  1060519  1060529  1060567  1060571
1060573  1060589  1060597  1060621  1060673  1060687  1060721  1060723  1060739  1060747
1060769  1060777  1060781  1060861  1060867  1060883  1060937  1060949  1060963  1060981
1060991  1060993  1061033  1061057  1061069  1061087  1061101  1061107  1061117  1061129
1061141  1061143  1061149  1061171  1061189  1061227  1061251  1061261  1061273  1061279
1061287  1061297  1061311  1061317  1061323  1061353  1061363  1061377  1061393  1061407
1061413  1061441  1061453  1061483  1061509  1061513  1061527  1061561  1061569  1061573
1061591  1061597  1061609  1061617  1061623  1061629  1061647  1061651  1061677  1061689
1061699  1061707  1061717  1061729  1061733  1061759  1061771  1061773  1061779  1061783
1061807  1061831  1061849  1061867  1061869  1061881  1061897  1061903  1061909  1061911
1061917  1061959  1061969  1061993  1062001  1062013  1062031  1062073  1062107  1062121
1062169  1062197  1062203  1062251  1062253  1062263  1062293  1062311  1062343  1062349
1062361  1062367  1062379  1062407  1062409  1062427  1062443  1062469  1062497  1062511
1062521  1062547  1062557  1062563  1062599  1062601  1062643  1062671  1062673  1062683
1062697  1062701  1062707  1062731  1062779  1062781  1062793  1062797  1062827  1062847
1062869  1062871  1062877  1062881  1062907  1062911  1062913  1062931  1062947  1062949
1062977  1062979  1062989  1063001  1063009  1063019  1063033  1063039  1063043  1063067
1063079  1063087  1063109  1063123  1063151  1063157  1063159  1063177  1063189  1063193
1063201  1063213  1063219  1063241  1063243  1063273  1063303  1063319  1063351  1063379
1063397  1063399  1063409  1063427  1063441  1063453  1063457  1063463  1063471  1063477
1063483  1063501  1063523  1063529  1063541  1063547  1063553  1063561  1063597  1063609
1063613  1063619  1063627  1063637  1063649  1063661  1063693  1063709  1063721  1063729
1063739  1063747  1063757  1063771  1063781  1063813  1063823  1063831  1063837  1063847
1063849  1063871  1063873  1063891  1063897  1063903  1063913  1063919  1063921  1063927
1063961  1063963  1063967  1063969  1063973  1063987  1063999  1064017  1064029  1064059
1064069  1064087  1064117  1064131  1064153  1064159  1064177  1064179  1064191  1064197
1064201  1064243  1064257  1064263  1064269  1064281  1064311  1064317  1064321  1064333
1064339  1064341  1064359  1064377  1064383  1064407  1064411  1064431  1064467  1064471
1064473  1064477  1064507  1064519  1064521  1064533  1064549  1064587  1064593  1064629
1064653  1064669  1064671  1064681  1064689  1064699  1064731  1064737  1064743  1064753
1064771  1064783  1064801  1064813  1064867  1064873  1064891  1064927  1064933  1064939
1064941  1064951  1064953  1064957  1064977  1064989  1065011  1065013  1065017  1065019
1065037  1065041  1065047  1065059  1065073  1065089  1065091  1065109  1065131  1065133
1065137  1065173  1065209  1065217  1065263  1065269  1065277  1065283  1065307  1065313
1065319  1065331  1065343  1065347  1065391  1065409  1065433  1065469  1065479  1065503
1065511  1065523  1065527  1065529  1065557  1065569  1065593  1065601  1065629  1065643
1065667  1065677  1065683  1065689  1065697  1065709  1065733  1065763  1065773  1065787
1065791  1065809  1065817  1065821  1065829  1065839  1065847  1065851  1065887  1065893
1065899  1065901  1065937  1065941  1065949  1065973  1065979  1066001  1066031  1066049
1066063  1066067  1066111  1066133  1066139  1066141  1066157  1066159  1066217  1066231
1066253  1066253  1066267  1066279  1066283  1066297  1066313  1066319  1066327  1066333
1066339  1066343  1066367  1066379  1066399  1066409  1066411  1066423  1066433  1066447
1066511  1066517  1066523  1066531  1066553  1066561  1066567  1066577  1066619  1066621
1066643  1066651  1066669  1066687  1066693  1066721  1066729  1066753  1066757  1066777
1066789  1066811  1066817  1066847  1066859  1066867  1066883  1066889  1066909  1066913
1066931  1066973  1066979  1066981  1066987  1066999  1067009  1067023  1067029  1067047
1067057  1067063  1067069  1067083  1067137  1067147  1067159  1067167  1067179  1067203
1067207  1067221  1067229  1067263  1067293  1067327  1067329  1067347  1067351  1067359
1067371  1067383  1067387  1067411  1067441  1067459  1067467  1067471  1067489  1067491
1067497  1067509  1067537  1067551  1067557  1067567  1067569  1067593  1067597  1067611
1067621  1067639  1067653  1067669  1067687  1067701  1067707  1067711  1067741  1067747
1067749  1067761  1067767  1067777  1067789  1067797  1067831  1067837  1067849  1067851
1067879  1067893  1067903  1067909  1067921  1067939  1067951  1067969  1067999  1068019
1068037  1068061  1068083  1068101  1068103  1068107  1068113  1068131  1068149  1068191
1068203  1068217  1068233  1068241  1068247  1068251  1068253  1068257  1068259  1068271
1068307  1068311  1068323  1068329  1068343  1068367  1068371  1068377  1068383  1068407
1068409  1068437  1068439  1068461  1068469  1068481  1068491  1068497  1068499  1068517
```

```
1068559  1068577  1068589  1068611  1068619  1068629  1068631  1068677  1068701  1068703
1068707  1068709  1068713  1068719  1068721  1068751  1068757  1068761  1068779  1068803
1068811  1068817  1068857  1068871  1068877  1068887  1068889  1068901  1068913  1068917
1068941  1068989  1069001  1069007  1069031  1069039  1069043  1069051  1069087  1069099
1069127  1069129  1069141  1069171  1069183  1069193  1069199  1069207  1069217  1069219
1069223  1069267  1069273  1069291  1069303  1069307  1069349  1069363  1069379  1069421
1069427  1069429  1069441  1069459  1069489  1069463  1069499  1069501  1069507  1069517
1069543  1069547  1069553  1069561  1069571  1069573  1069577  1069583  1069591  1069597
1069603  1069609  1069631  1069639  1069667  1069687  1069693  1069697  1069727  1069741
1069751  1069777  1069807  1069811  1069819  1069823  1069853  1069867  1069919  1069921
1069927  1069931  1069933  1069949  1069951  1069973  1069979  1069987  1070009  1070011
1070021  1070033  1070039  1070063  1070081  1070087  1070093  1070131  1070149  1070171
1070189  1070197  1070203  1070207  1070221  1070231  1070233  1070243  1070249  1070257
1070287  1070291  1070309  1070317  1070323  1070339  1070341  1070347  1070357  1070369
1070389  1070411  1070417  1070423  1070429  1070431  1070453  1070471  1070491  1070497
1070501  1070513  1070527  1070533  1070543  1070557  1070561  1070567  1070569  1070579
1070621  1070659  1070681  1070683  1070689  1070753  1070761  1070777  1070789  1070803
1070827  1070843  1070851  1070869  1070873  1070899  1070921  1070933  1070939  1070947
1070981  1070987  1071023  1071047  1071053  1071061  1071067  1071121  1071131  1071139
1071149  1071151  1071157  1071181  1071193  1071197  1071223  1071227  1071229  1071233
1071373  1071377  1071379  1071401  1071407  1071419  1071439  1071443  1071451  1071457
1071479  1071487  1071529  1071533  1071541  1071563  1071569  1071571  1071589  1071601
1071641  1071643  1071659  1071661  1071671  1071683  1071703  1071739  1071743  1071761
1071773  1071787  1071803  1071817  1071821  1071841  1071857  1071871  1071899  1071907
1071911  1071919  1071937  1071943  1071977  1071979  1071991  1072009  1072039  1072103
1072129  1072133  1072147  1072157  1072163  1072187  1072199  1072213  1072219  1072229
1072231  1072301  1072327  1072339  1072363  1072367  1072373  1072381  1072387  1072397
1072429  1072433  1072439  1072447  1072457  1072459  1072471  1072517  1072537  1072543
1072613  1072627  1072633  1072637  1072657  1072711  1072733  1072763  1072793  1072801
1072811  1072823  1072829  1072831  1072837  1072843  1072849  1072859  1072867  1072901
1072919  1072931  1072943  1072937  1072943  1072957  1072961  1072969  1072991  1072997
1072999  1073053  1073069  1073077  1073089  1073099  1073113  1073117  1073131  1073141
1073143  1073147  1073153  1073183  1073201  1073209  1073213  1073221  1073239  1073243
1073263  1073279  1073297  1073311  1073321  1073351  1073353  1073381  1073383  1073393
1073399  1073411  1073441  1073447  1073461  1073491  1073507  1073509  1073521  1073537
1073563  1073573  1073587  1073593  1073599  1073603  1073627  1073647  1073651  1073687
1073711  1073713  1073717  1073729  1073773  1073789  1073791  1073803  1073819  1073837
1073857  1073869  1073879  1073881  1073909  1073911  1073921  1073939  1073953  1073983
1074001  1074023  1074041  1074061  1074067  1074071  1074079  1074083  1074107  1074109
1074113  1074121  1074133  1074167  1074223  1074251  1074253  1074259  1074277  1074287
1074289  1074299  1074329  1074343  1074361  1074371  1074377  1074379  1074389  1074427
1074433  1074461  1074473  1074481  1074509  1074511  1074523  1074533  1074559  1074581
1074607  1074617  1074641  1074643  1074649  1074673  1074683  1074691  1074701  1074707
1074709  1074713  1074719  1074751  1074761  1074763  1074833  1074839  1074847  1074851
1074887  1074883  1074889  1074901  1074907  1074917  1074919  1074923  1074929  1074949
1074971  1074973  1074977  1074989  1074991  1075007  1075013  1075021  1075027  1075069
1075073  1075079  1075091  1075093  1075103  1075133  1075141  1075147  1075159  1075163
1075169  1075171  1075177  1075187  1075201  1075231  1075237  1075241  1075259  1075279
1075289  1075303  1075337  1075339  1075351  1075357  1075391  1075397  1075409  1075429
1075441  1075537  1075453  1075463  1075469  1075489  1075493  1075499  1075507  1075519
1075531  1075537  1075561  1075577  1075601  1075619  1075621  1075643  1075649  1075651
1075663  1075667  1075673  1075681  1075691  1075693  1075699  1075703  1075727  1075729
1075757  1075759  1075769  1075771  1075787  1075807  1075843  1075853  1075859  1075897
1075909  1075957  1075973  1076003  1076011  1076017  1076029  1076039  1076051  1076057
1076063  1076069  1076077  1076107  1076111  1076113  1076123  1076129  1076137  1076143
1076167  1076171  1076191  1076203  1076213  1076237  1076263  1076279  1076281  1076303
1076323  1076329  1076353  1076359  1076381  1076399  1076401  1076417  1076429  1076443
1076447  1076461  1076473  1076477  1076501  1076503  1076507  1076513  1076519  1076557
1076563  1076587  1076611  1076617  1076639  1076651  1076657  1076671  1076707  1076717
1076731  1076753  1076767  1076771  1076773  1076813  1076821  1076827  1076843  1076861
1076869  1076879  1076893  1076903  1076917  1076921  1076953  1076981  1077017  1077023
1077047  1077059  1077079  1077101  1077127  1077143  1077161  1077179  1077191  1077203
1077221  1077227  1077233  1077289  1077299  1077301  1077311  1077337  1077347  1077353
1077371  1077397  1077413  1077421  1077449  1077457  1077469  1077499  1077533  1077539
1077541  1077563  1077599  1077607  1077641  1077673  1077677  1077691  1077697  1077707
1077719  1077721  1077733  1077743  1077751  1077761  1077763  1077793  1077799  1077821
1077823  1077827  1077833  1077859  1077863  1077893  1077911  1077913  1077917  1077949
1077971  1077977  1077997  1078001  1078009  1078019  1078027  1078031  1078043  1078081
1078109  1078111  1078127  1078151  1078153  1078159  1078163  1078169  1078183  1078199
1078219  1078241  1078247  1078331  1078333  1078367  1078369  1078373  1078387  1078393
1078403  1078409  1078411  1078417  1078471  1078489  1078507  1078537  1078559  1078589
1078643  1078657  1078673  1078681  1078691  1078699  1078711  1078717  1078733  1078739
1078757  1078787  1078789  1078807  1078813  1078817  1078841  1078849  1078853  1078873
1078879  1078919  1078927  1078937  1078943  1078951  1078967  1078981  1078993  1079009
1079011  1079021  1079033  1079053  1079059  1079069  1079077  1079081  1079087  1079093
1079101  1079107  1079123  1079147  1079153  1079173  1079189  1079213  1079227  1079233
1079251  1079269  1079297  1079311  1079317  1079329  1079339  1079357  1079359  1079363
1079369  1079383  1079399  1079417  1079431  1079453  1079461  1079471  1079473  1079503
1079509  1079527  1079531  1079539  1079569  1079593  1079609  1079621  1079629  1079633
1079647  1079651  1079669  1079671  1079681  1079711  1079717  1079753  1079777  1079779
1079783  1079797  1079809  1079821  1079831  1079849  1079861  1079867  1079879  1079887
1079917  1079927  1079947  1079963  1079969  1079977  1079983  1079987  1079999
1080007  1080029  1080043  1080049  1080059  1080073  1080077  1080083  1080089  1080091
1080097  1080119  1080137  1080143  1080173  1080199  1080217  1080223  1080229  1080251
1080259  1080263  1080269  1080271  1080281  1080301  1080307  1080311  1080329  1080341
1080347  1080353  1080383  1080413  1080419  1080433  1080439  1080449  1080451  1080463
1080479  1080481  1080491  1080523  1080539  1080553  1080557  1080559  1080589  1080613
1080647  1080649  1080661  1080679  1080683  1080713  1080749  1080757  1080763  1080767
```

```
1080773  1080787  1080791  1080797  1080803  1080811  1080817  1080823  1080841  1080847
1080851  1080857  1080899  1080901  1080907  1080913  1080923  1080941  1080943  1080971
1080973  1080983  1081027  1081037  1081051  1081061  1081079  1081097  1081099  1081121
1081123  1081127  1081133  1081139  1081153  1081163  1081219  1081229  1081231  1081237
1081243  1081247  1081277  1081279  1081291  1081303  1081307  1081331  1081337  1081351
1081361  1081369  1081403  1081417  1081429  1081441  1081477  1081501  1081513  1081541
1081583  1081631  1081637  1081657  1081679  1081681  1081687  1081699  1081709  1081711
1081721  1081723  1081733  1081741  1081757  1081763  1081771  1081777  1081781  1081789
1081793  1081813  1081823  1081853  1081859  1081891  1081901  1081907  1081919  1081937
1081939  1081979  1081981  1082017  1082023  1082027  1082047  1082083  1082089  1082093
1082099  1082129  1082141  1082143  1082149  1082153  1082161  1082171  1082177  1082189
1082197  1082209  1082231  1082233  1082243  1082273  1082317  1082321  1082351  1082369
1082377  1082381  1082383  1082387  1082399  1082429  1082443  1082447  1082467  1082491
1082527  1082531  1082533  1082573  1082579  1082581  1082593  1082597  1082603  1082621
1082629  1082647  1082659  1082681  1082699  1082707  1082717  1082723  1082729  1082743
1082761  1082777  1082801  1082881  1082891  1082911  1082969  1082971  1082989  1082993
1082999  1083007  1083031  1083037  1083059  1083073  1083077  1083079  1083083  1083107
1083113  1083119  1083151  1083167  1083191  1083193  1083211  1083241  1083253  1083283
1083287  1083289  1083301  1083307  1083311  1083317  1083319  1083337  1083349  1083367
1083371  1083377  1083391  1083409  1083431  1083443  1083449  1083451  1083463  1083473
1083497  1083517  1083541  1083559  1083571  1083583  1083601  1083611  1083613  1083659
1083689  1083707  1083713  1083721  1083743  1083749  1083757  1083793  1083809  1083827
1083833  1083839  1083847  1083851  1083871  1083881  1083899  1083911  1083913  1083923
1083941  1083947  1083949  1083983  1084001  1084019  1084043  1084051  1084067  1084079
1084087  1084093  1084103  1084133  1084147  1084157  1084177  1084217  1084219  1084247
1084253  1084267  1084297  1084301  1084309  1084313  1084333  1084357  1084367  1084373
1084403  1084423  1084429  1084451  1084459  1084469  1084471  1084477  1084483  1084493
1084543  1084547  1084553  1084579  1084609  1084613  1084621  1084627  1084637  1084649
1084661  1084669  1084673  1084697  1084711  1084723  1084747  1084757  1084771  1084777
1084793  1084799  1084817  1084823  1084829  1084859  1084871  1084891  1084927  1084939
1084949  1084969  1084981  1084987  1084997  1085003  1085011  1085017  1085023  1085047
1085053  1085101  1085111  1085113  1085131  1085137  1085141  1085143  1085153  1085159
1085179  1085197  1085221  1085269  1085309  1085317  1085327  1085351  1085353  1085369
1085389  1085407  1085419  1085429  1085431  1085443  1085459  1085473  1085509  1085521
1085551  1085587  1085611  1085627  1085633  1085657  1085663  1085677  1085681  1085687
1085719  1085737  1085753  1085767  1085771  1085779  1085801  1085809  1085813  1085827
1085857  1085863  1085867  1085873  1085881  1085891  1085911  1085933  1085957  1085971
1085989  1086031  1086047  1086073  1086089  1086091  1086101  1086103  1086119  1086133
1086139  1086149  1086161  1086179  1086191  1086199  1086199  1086203  1086247  1086251
1086257  1086259  1086263  1086277  1086299  1086301  1086307  1086331  1086343  1086347
1086353  1086361  1086373  1086389  1086391  1086413  1086439  1086443  1086461  1086469
1086493  1086509  1086511  1086523  1086529  1086557  1086559  1086587  1086607  1086611
1086619  1086637  1086641  1086647  1086677  1086689  1086703  1086731  1086749  1086763
1086769  1086791  1086809  1086817  1086859  1086863  1086881  1086893  1086901  1086913
1086919  1086923  1086931  1086937  1086989  1086991  1087001  1087019  1087027  1087061
1087091  1087109  1087117  1087129  1087147  1087159  1087231  1087241  1087249  1087259
1087271  1087291  1087301  1087309  1087349  1087357  1087379  1087381  1087391  1087409
1087423  1087433  1087451  1087453  1087459  1087483  1087487  1087517  1087519  1087543
1087553  1087561  1087589  1087591  1087621  1087631  1087657  1087663  1087673  1087679
1087687  1087717  1087729  1087741  1087747  1087753  1087781  1087787  1087789  1087799
1087811  1087817  1087829  1087841  1087843  1087861  1087873  1087897  1087903  1087907
1087937  1087963  1087967  1087973  1087981  1087987  1088023  1088027  1088039  1088053
1088063  1088071  1088081  1088089  1088093  1088123  1088159  1088161  1088209  1088233
1088237  1088239  1088251  1088267  1088273  1088293  1088309  1088371  1088387  1088389
1088393  1088407  1088413  1088419  1088431  1088443  1088447  1088449  1088467  1088471
1088489  1088519  1088533  1088537  1088543  1088569  1088579  1088603  1088611  1088617
1088621  1088623  1088639  1088641  1088657  1088669  1088671  1088687  1088693  1088707
1088723  1088749  1088753  1088761  1088777  1088783  1088807  1088827  1088831  1088839
1088851  1088903  1088917  1088933  1088953  1088957  1088959  1088977  1088987  1088993
1089017  1089029  1089047  1089091  1089103  1089107  1089113  1089133  1089161  1089191
1089197  1089217  1089223  1089227  1089239  1089259  1089299  1089313  1089359  1089383
1089397  1089401  1089421  1089427  1089457  1089461  1089463  1089469  1089481  1089497
1089503  1089509  1089523  1089551  1089563  1089611  1089629  1089653  1089661  1089677
1089679  1089703  1089709  1089713  1089757  1089793  1089799  1089841  1089863  1089877
1089919  1089941  1089943  1089961  1089967  1089997  1090003  1090013  1090021  1090027
1090031  1090097  1090099  1090127  1090129  1090151  1090153  1090169  1090181  1090189
1090211  1090213  1090217  1090241  1090249  1090267  1090273  1090303  1090333  1090373
1090381  1090387  1090403  1090409  1090421  1090423  1090457  1090459  1090469  1090471
1090483  1090493  1090519  1090553  1090577  1090589  1090597  1090613  1090627  1090681
1090697  1090709  1090711  1090717  1090721  1090757  1090759  1090769  1090783  1090799
1090807  1090819  1090841  1090849  1090877  1090879  1090883  1090889  1090891  1090897
1090909  1090919  1090927  1090937  1090939  1090949  1090963  1090967  1090979  1090997
1091003  1091017  1091021  1091023  1091033  1091047  1091053  1091059  1091063  1091071
1091119  1091137  1091147  1091149  1091159  1091161  1091173  1091177  1091191  1091219
1091221  1091239  1091243  1091257  1091261  1091263  1091267  1091269  1091273  1091287
1091329  1091339  1091359  1091369  1091371  1091381  1091393  1091399  1091401  1091411
1091413  1091443  1091459  1091471  1091477  1091509  1091521  1091527  1091549  1091551
1091561  1091581  1091591  1091609  1091617  1091627  1091633  1091639  1091659  1091663
1091681  1091687  1091711  1091729  1091731  1091737  1091749  1091777  1091807  1091809
1091837  1091843  1091869  1091887  1091907  1091917  1091919  1091957  1091983  1092019
1092023  1092041  1092043  1092059  1092061  1092067  1092089  1092103  1092107  1092127
1092137  1092151  1092163  1092173  1092181  1092191  1092209  1092229  1092241  1092251
1092257  1092269  1092307  1092331  1092337  1092349  1092353  1092361  1092371  1092373
1092379  1092389  1092391  1092397  1092419  1092433  1092451  1092461  1092463  1092473
1092479  1092493  1092541  1092583  1092593  1092601  1092629  1092643  1092659  1092667
1092677  1092713  1092731  1092733  1092757  1092779  1092803  1092821  1092827  1092829
1092851  1092853  1092863  1092887  1092893  1092901  1092907  1092911  1092919  1092929
1092961  1092977  1092989  1092991  1092997  1093007  1093033  1093061  1093063  1093067
1093069  1093087  1093109  1093111  1093129  1093133  1093159  1093163  1093177  1093199
```

```
1093201 1093223 1093237 1093243 1093249 1093273 1093283 1093289 1093297 1093307
1093327 1093331 1093357 1093363 1093381 1093399 1093403 1093409 1093427 1093441
1093487 1093493 1093517 1093529 1093531 1093537 1093541 1093553 1093571 1093577
1093591 1093633 1093637 1093639 1093657 1093663 1093667 1093679 1093681 1093699
1093717 1093723 1093733 1093739 1093747 1093751 1093753 1093777 1093789 1093823
1093837 1093843 1093847 1093871 1093889 1093901 1093907 1093927 1093943 1093951
1093957 1093969 1093991 1093997 1093999 1094011 1094029 1094047 1094057
1094059 1094081 1094089 1094099 1094101 1094123 1094129 1094131 1094143 1094147
1094161 1094183 1094209 1094237 1094263 1094293 1094299 1094321 1094333 1094339
1094371 1094377 1094407 1094411 1094417 1094437 1094441 1094449 1094453 1094461
1094473 1094491 1094519 1094531 1094539 1094543 1094549 1094551 1094557 1094567
1094573 1094603 1094629 1094633 1094657 1094669 1094671 1094683 1094689
1094693 1094701 1094711 1094747 1094759 1094773 1094791 1094801 1094803 1094809
1094831 1094833 1094843 1094881 1094887 1094897 1094911 1094921 1094923 1094939
1094957 1094963 1094969 1094983 1094999 1095023 1095043 1095047 1095049 1095067
1095071 1095091 1095119 1095161 1095169 1095173 1095209 1095221 1095223 1095229
1095239 1095247 1095251 1095257 1095287 1095313 1095319 1095343 1095349 1095401
1095403 1095427 1095433 1095439 1095443 1095449 1095461 1095481 1095487 1095491
1095503 1095529 1095541 1095551 1095557 1095569 1095581 1095583 1095613 1095631
1095671 1095691 1095713 1095719 1095727 1095733 1095739 1095751 1095779 1095781
1095791 1095793 1095811 1095821 1095833 1095839 1095841 1095847 1095851 1095859
1095907 1095931 1095947 1095959 1095961 1095979 1095989 1096031 1096057 1096061
1096079 1096097 1096099 1096127 1096133 1096141 1096159 1096163 1096189 1096201
1096219 1096267 1096289 1096307 1096327 1096349 1096351 1096363 1096373 1096379
1096393 1096399 1096423 1096427 1096451 1096477 1096481 1096489 1096493 1096499
1096507 1096541 1096549 1096553 1096559 1096561 1096583 1096609 1096621 1096631
1096639 1096673 1096691 1096703 1096727 1096741 1096763 1096787 1096793 1096807
1096817 1096829 1096831 1096853 1096859 1096861 1096871 1096883 1096919 1096951
1096957 1096967 1096969 1096981 1096999 1097009 1097017 1097029 1097039 1097051
1097069 1097081 1097101 1097111 1097113 1097141 1097143 1097147 1097179 1097189
1097203 1097209 1097221 1097237 1097267 1097293 1097297 1097321 1097323 1097351
1097359 1097377 1097381 1097413 1097419 1097423 1097441 1097443 1097461 1097483
1097501 1097513 1097533 1097539 1097543 1097549 1097557 1097599 1097627 1097633
1097651 1097653 1097659 1097669 1097699 1097711 1097717 1097729 1097743 1097783
1097791 1097797 1097819 1097849 1097851 1097861 1097869 1097879 1097891 1097893
1097897 1097903 1097909 1097923 1097933 1097947 1097983 1098017 1098023 1098037
1098073 1098077 1098101 1098109 1098121 1098133 1098151 1098187 1098191 1098193
1098203 1098211 1098221 1098233 1098269 1098287 1098301 1098311 1098313 1098341
1098379 1098397 1098401 1098439 1098443 1098461 1098463 1098469 1098479
1098481 1098509 1098511 1098533 1098541 1098593 1098613 1098623 1098631 1098649
1098667 1098673 1098689 1098707 1098709 1098731 1098737 1098787 1098791 1098803
1098821 1098833 1098847 1098953 1098967 1098973 1098989 1099031 1099051 1099057
1099079 1099081 1099097 1099103 1099117 1099121 1099139 1099171 1099177 1099181
1099199 1099223 1099247 1099249 1099261 1099279 1099289 1099309 1099313 1099327
1099337 1099363 1099369 1099391 1099393 1099409 1099411 1099421 1099433 1099459
1099463 1099487 1099489 1099493 1099499 1099507 1099513 1099519 1099523 1099541
1099547 1099559 1099573 1099589 1099619 1099621 1099627 1099633 1099649 1099669
1099687 1099711 1099717 1099723 1099727 1099729 1099741 1099757 1099771 1099783
1099793 1099799 1099807 1099817 1099823 1099841 1099843 1099859 1099867 1099927
1099933 1099957 1099961 1099997 1100009 1100023 1100027 1100039 1100041 1100051
1100063 1100089 1100093 1100101 1100123 1100131 1100147 1100149 1100161 1100167
1100171 1100179 1100213 1100219 1100243 1100249 1100261 1100273 1100279 1100303
1100311 1100321 1100353 1100357 1100377 1100381 1100387 1100419 1100441 1100443
1100447 1100467 1100471 1100483 1100503 1100509 1100513 1100543 1100557 1100569
1100581 1100591 1100611 1100641 1100653 1100681 1100683 1100747 1100773 1100777
1100783 1100797 1100807 1100831 1100833 1100837 1100839 1100851 1100857 1100887
1100893 1100899 1100909 1100921 1100933 1100947 1100977 1101071 1101091 1101097
1101103 1101109 1101127 1101143 1101169 1101179 1101193 1101211 1101229 1101253
1101283 1101299 1101307 1101319 1101323 1101341 1101349 1101371 1101377 1101389
1101403 1101407 1101409 1101421 1101431 1101433 1101439 1101467 1101473 1101509
1101511 1101517 1101521 1101533 1101559 1101571 1101577 1101587 1101593 1101613
1101619 1101641 1101649 1101671 1101673 1101689 1101691 1101697 1101733 1101743
1101761 1101763 1101771 1101781 1101803 1101811 1101839 1101851 1101871 1101883
1101901 1101917 1101929 1101931 1101937 1101941 1101959 1101967 1102001 1102007
1102021 1102027 1102063 1102069 1102111 1102117 1102147 1102151 1102159 1102163
1102169 1102181 1102187 1102201 1102237 1102243 1102249 1102253 1102259 1102271
1102279 1102301 1102307 1102313 1102333 1102337 1102393 1102397 1102411 1102427
1102429 1102441 1102447 1102457 1102463 1102481 1102483 1102523 1102537 1102547
1102553 1102567 1102571 1102583 1102663 1102669 1102679 1102681 1102691 1102693
1102709 1102721 1102727 1102729 1102733 1102747 1102757 1102813 1102823 1102831
1102847 1102853 1102861 1102879 1102883 1102891 1102901 1102903 1102921 1102939
1102951 1102963 1102967 1102979 1102991 1102999 1103009 1103017 1103029 1103041
1103059 1103087 1103101 1103107 1103111 1103119 1103129 1103143 1103171 1103183
1103191 1103203 1103213 1103237 1103257 1103279 1103281 1103293 1103309 1103339
1103341 1103353 1103371 1103437 1103449 1103461 1103467 1103483 1103489 1103497
1103519 1103533 1103549 1103561 1103579 1103581 1103587 1103591 1103603 1103611
1103617 1103621 1103629 1103633 1103639 1103699 1103723 1103737 1103749 1103779
1103797 1103803 1103849 1103857 1103863 1103873 1103899 1103903 1103911 1103923
1103933 1103981 1103987 1103989 1104017 1104041 1104079 1104097 1104101 1104107
1104113 1104119 1104137 1104139 1104157 1104179 1104193 1104203 1104209 1104217
1104221 1104241 1104247 1104289 1104293 1104307 1104319 1104331 1104343 1104353
1104373 1104377 1104379 1104403 1104409 1104427 1104431 1104449 1104479 1104491
1104511 1104517 1104533 1104557 1104559 1104589 1104599 1104613 1104619 1104659
1104661 1104671 1104683 1104703 1104707 1104731 1104737 1104739 1104743 1104749
1104751 1104767 1104769 1104781 1104787 1104791 1104797 1104811 1104821 1104823
1104833 1104853 1104877 1104889 1104899 1104913 1104919 1104937 1104941 1104947
1104959 1105009 1105019 1105033 1105061 1105063 1105067 1105109 1105141 1105157
1105163 1105171 1105177 1105193 1105201 1105207 1105213 1105217 1105231 1105261
1105267 1105271 1105309 1105327 1105333 1105337 1105339 1105343 1105387 1105397
```

```
1105427 1105441 1105457 1105463 1105501 1105513 1105519 1105537 1105547 1105549
1105571 1105579 1105583 1105589 1105603 1105607 1105609 1105613 1105619 1105627
1105639 1105649 1105651 1105661 1105669 1105691 1105693 1105711 1105757 1105759
1105787 1105807 1105813 1105823 1105847 1105861 1105873 1105879 1105883 1105891
1105913 1105919 1105943 1105961 1105963 1105997 1105999 1106029 1106069 1106087
1106099 1106101 1106129 1106137 1106159 1106167 1106177 1106179 1106197 1106201
1106213 1106219 1106233 1106243 1106249 1106257 1106267 1106279 1106293 1106311
1106317 1106363 1106381 1106401 1106407 1106419 1106423 1106429 1106447 1106449
1106471 1106477 1106489 1106491 1106509 1106527 1106531 1106543 1106563 1106569
1106593 1106621 1106627 1106629 1106653 1106671 1106687 1106689 1106741 1106747
1106761 1106767 1106771 1106779 1106789 1106801 1106821 1106827 1106837 1106839
1106851 1106881 1106891 1106909 1106923 1106927 1106939 1106953 1106957 1106977
1106993 1106999 1107019 1107031 1107047 1107049 1107053 1107083 1107101 1107107
1107109 1107157 1107167 1107173 1107199 1107203 1107217 1107269 1107317 1107319
1107341 1107347 1107383 1107389 1107401 1107409 1107419 1107433 1107439 1107467
1107479 1107487 1107497 1107503 1107511 1107523 1107527 1107553 1107569 1107571
1107581 1107583 1107593 1107619 1107677 1107679 1107721 1107727 1107751 1107763
1107773 1107781 1107787 1107791 1107793 1107797 1107803 1107811 1107823 1107851
1107853 1107881 1107887 1107913 1107917 1107923 1107929 1107937 1107989 1108001
1108007 1108021 1108049 1108057 1108069 1108073 1108091 1108103 1108123 1108127
1108147 1108169 1108171 1108181 1108201 1108207 1108223 1108229 1108241 1108253
1108259 1108267 1108313 1108321 1108337 1108357 1108361 1108363 1108369 1108397
1108423 1108427 1108447 1108453 1108463 1108469 1108477 1108487 1108489 1108501
1108507 1108537 1108543 1108559 1108561 1108567 1108571 1108573 1108579 1108603
1108609 1108619 1108633 1108663 1108691 1108693 1108697 1108703 1108711 1108717
1108727 1108729 1108733 1108739 1108747 1108753 1108759 1108771 1108781 1108801
1108817 1108819 1108823 1108867 1108903 1108907 1108909 1108957 1108967 1108993
1108997 1108999 1109021 1109033 1109057 1109113 1109117 1109123 1109159 1109161
1109167 1109189 1109197 1109219 1109231 1109243 1109249 1109257 1109281 1109287
1109291 1109309 1109327 1109347 1109351 1109363 1109387 1109393 1109399 1109401
1109411 1109431 1109473 1109477 1109489 1109491 1109509 1109513 1109531 1109533
1109561 1109579 1109609 1109611 1109629 1109639 1109653 1109663 1109723 1109737
1109749 1109761 1109783 1109789 1109791 1109813 1109821 1109839 1109851 1109861
1109869 1109881 1109887 1109891 1109897 1109903 1109909 1109921 1109951 1109987
1110007 1110013 1110019 1110023 1110041 1110061 1110077 1110089 1110103 1110127
1110133 1110167 1110181 1110223 1110229 1110247 1110269 1110271 1110289 1110301
1110311 1110313 1110331 1110349 1110353 1110367 1110397 1110401 1110413 1110427
1110433 1110449 1110467 1110479 1110517 1110521 1110523 1110533 1110539 1110541
1110547 1110583 1110587 1110589 1110611 1110617 1110643 1110667 1110679 1110709
1110713 1110719 1110727 1110743 1110773 1110779 1110803 1110817 1110821 1110839
1110859 1110881 1110887 1110913 1110917 1110919 1110929 1110931 1110943 1110953
1110959 1110971 1110973 1110979 1110983 1110997 1111007 1111013 1111021 1111031
1111043 1111049 1111057 1111067 1111081 1111087 1111091 1111151 1111157 1111169
1111181 1111183 1111189 1111211 1111213 1111219 1111247 1111259 1111283 1111289
1111301 1111333 1111339 1111351 1111361 1111379 1111393 1111399 1111423 1111427
1111433 1111447 1111457 1111489 1111493 1111499 1111531 1111543 1111547 1111553
1111559 1111573 1111577 1111637 1111639 1111651 1111661 1111667 1111673 1111687
1111703 1111711 1111723 1111727 1111741 1111757 1111771 1111787 1111793 1111801
1111841 1111853 1111867 1111897 1111921 1111933 1111949 1111963 1111967 1111991
1112003 1112011 1112017 1112047 1112057 1112077 1112081 1112087 1112093 1112107
1112113 1112129 1112131 1112141 1112143 1112147 1112159 1112171 1112197 1112201
1112239 1112269 1112273 1112291 1112323 1112333 1112339 1112341 1112351 1112359
1112369 1112381 1112383 1112389 1112413 1112467 1112471 1112477 1112483 1112509
1112513 1112519 1112543 1112549 1112561 1112567 1112569 1112581 1112591 1112597
1112611 1112623 1112651 1112653 1112663 1112677 1112689 1112707 1112723 1112729
1112731 1112737 1112747 1112777 1112779 1112789 1112821 1112827 1112831 1112833
1112857 1112897 1112899 1112911 1112921 1112941 1112953 1112959 1112971 1112977
1112983 1113011 1113019 1113029 1113043 1113059 1113083 1113089 1113103 1113137
1113149 1113157 1113173 1113181 1113187 1113193 1113197 1113199 1113221 1113239
1113253 1113257 1113317 1113319 1113337 1113349 1113373 1113379 1113401 1113403
1113421 1113451 1113461 1113481 1113491 1113509 1113521 1113527 1113557 1113569
1113587 1113599 1113617 1113643 1113667 1113701 1113703 1113713 1113719 1113751
1113773 1113781 1113787 1113793 1113797 1113809 1113859 1113863 1113877 1113883
1113887 1113899 1113941 1113949 1113953 1113961 1113971 1113991 1113997 1114019
1114031 1114037 1114039 1114049 1114063 1114111 1114117 1114159 1114193 1114207
1114213 1114241 1114249 1114261 1114271 1114273 1114283 1114297 1114301 1114303
1114349 1114361 1114381 1114397 1114423 1114427 1114447 1114471 1114489 1114493
1114501 1114507 1114523 1114541 1114549 1114567 1114573 1114577 1114591 1114601
1114613 1114651 1114657 1114661 1114681 1114693 1114697 1114709 1114721 1114723
1114733 1114753 1114759 1114801 1114807 1114811 1114829 1114837 1114849 1114859
1114873 1114891 1114907 1114909 1114931 1114937 1114943 1114969 1114973 1114987
1114999 1115011 1115027 1115029 1115057 1115071 1115089 1115099 1115113 1115117
1115131 1115189 1115207 1115227 1115237 1115239 1115267 1115269 1115273 1115297
1115299 1115321 1115327 1115329 1115351 1115363 1115381 1115399 1115407 1115417
1115419 1115447 1115449 1115453 1115467 1115497 1115501 1115519 1115531 1115533
1115539 1115551 1115561 1115567 1115573 1115579 1115581 1115599 1115627 1115633
1115641 1115657 1115683 1115701 1115711 1115713 1115731 1115743 1115759 1115767
1115771 1115773 1115789 1115831 1115839 1115843 1115857 1115879 1115899 1115911
1115923 1115929 1115941 1115987 1115993 1116001 1116053 1116077 1116091 1116107
1116133 1116163 1116173 1116187 1116209 1116223 1116229 1116257 1116277 1116281
1116289 1116301 1116317 1116319 1116329 1116337 1116347 1116371 1116419 1116431
1116439 1116449 1116461 1116469 1116473 1116491 1116499 1116523 1116541 1116547
1116569 1116571 1116593 1116601 1116631 1116637 1116641 1116653 1116659 1116677
1116701 1116743 1116749 1116751 1116809 1116821 1116851 1116853 1116859 1116887
1116889 1116893 1116911 1116937 1116977 1116989 1117009 1117013 1117021
1117027 1117031 1117033 1117057 1117069 1117073 1117079 1117099 1117111 1117117
1117153 1117169 1117177 1117199 1117243 1117247 1117253 1117267 1117273 1117279
1117301 1117307 1117309 1117321 1117349 1117367 1117379 1117433 1117439 1117451
1117463 1117471 1117477 1117481 1117483 1117489 1117513 1117549 1117553 1117579
```

1117591 1117601 1117603 1117607 1117609 1117657 1117661 1117673 1117679 1117681
1117709 1117729 1117741 1117757 1117759 1117763 1117769 1117793 1117799 1117811
1117813 1117817 1117819 1117861 1117867 1117877 1117889 1117901 1117913 1117931
1117933 1117939 1117943 1117967 1117973 1117993 1118003 1118009 1118011 1118021
1118023 1118027 1118041 1118063 1118081 1118101 1118113 1118123 1118137 1118147
1118149 1118189 1118197 1118203 1118219 1118261 1118267 1118291 1118303 1118309
1118317 1118339 1118363 1118371 1118393 1118419 1118437 1118441 1118479 1118483
1118497 1118519 1118527 1118563 1118567 1118569 1118599 1118629 1118653 1118659
1118713 1118717 1118723 1118737 1118749 1118773 1118779 1118783 1118797 1118807
1118809 1118827 1118837 1118851 1118857 1118861 1118863 1118867 1118869 1118893
1118911 1118921 1118941 1118947 1118951 1118969 1118987 1118993 1119029 1119037
1119047 1119049 1119077 1119091 1119109 1119121 1119169 1119179 1119221 1119227
1119241 1119269 1119281 1119299 1119319 1119323 1119343 1119359 1119389 1119397
1119403 1119449 1119473 1119523 1119527 1119529 1119557 1119577 1119589 1119607
1119611 1119623 1119649 1119653 1119659 1119673 1119691 1119697 1119707 1119733
1119737 1119779 1119793 1119799 1119809 1119817 1119821 1119823 1119857 1119863
1119871 1119907 1119913 1119947 1119949 1119959 1120001 1120019 1120051 1120073
1120081 1120087 1120109 1120121 1120153 1120157 1120159 1120187 1120211 1120219
1120237 1120271 1120277 1120289 1120291 1120303 1120313 1120319 1120321 1120337
1120349 1120363 1120369 1120391 1120423 1120429 1120459 1120481 1120499 1120501
1120507 1120513 1120517 1120519 1120529 1120541 1120543 1120547 1120549 1120573
1120577 1120591 1120607 1120627 1120633 1120649 1120661 1120663 1120667 1120673
1120687 1120711 1120723 1120727 1120739 1120741 1120747 1120771 1120781 1120783
1120787 1120799 1120807 1120811 1120831 1120837 1120849 1120871 1120883 1120901
1120907 1120913 1120919 1120939 1120957 1120961 1120969 1120993 1121011 1121017
1121023 1121027 1121033 1121047 1121051 1121083 1121093 1121101 1121143 1121147
1121179 1121189 1121191 1121203 1121221 1121231 1121249 1121257 1121261
1121293 1121297 1121317 1121333 1121347 1121357 1121369 1121377 1121383 1121387
1121389 1121423 1121431 1121443 1121447 1121453 1121509 1121539 1121543 1121557
1121599 1121621 1121629 1121651 1121671 1121689 1121693 1121699 1121707 1121723
1121737 1121819 1121831 1121833 1121837 1121839 1121867 1121899 1121933 1121941
1121947 1121987 1121993 1122001 1122029 1122041 1122053 1122071 1122089 1122091
1122103 1122113 1122131 1122133 1122137 1122139 1122157 1122179 1122181 1122227
1122241 1122259 1122263 1122269 1122281 1122283 1122287 1122367 1122371 1122389
1122397 1122419 1122427 1122431 1122437 1122449 1122467 1122481 1122491 1122529
1122533 1122551 1122571 1122587 1122599 1122623 1122643 1122647 1122659 1122679
1122683 1122701 1122721 1122739 1122749 1122757 1122761 1122811 1122841 1122857
1122887 1122899 1122923 1122937 1122941 1122983 1122997 1123051 1123079 1123081
1123093 1123127 1123151 1123181 1123189 1123211 1123217 1123219 1123231 1123247
1123267 1123279 1123303 1123307 1123319 1123327 1123349 1123351 1123361 1123379
1123391 1123399 1123403 1123427 1123429 1123439 1123477 1123483 1123487 1123501
1123511 1123517 1123531 1123541 1123553 1123561 1123567 1123589 1123597 1123601
1123621 1123631 1123637 1123651 1123667 1123669 1123691 1123693 1123699 1123709
1123729 1123739 1123741 1123747 1123777 1123807 1123841 1123867 1123873 1123879
1123883 1123897 1123901 1123909 1123919 1123931 1123943 1123951 1123961 1123973
1123979 1123999 1124027 1124041 1124051 1124063 1124087 1124107 1124113 1124119
1124131 1124141 1124147 1124197 1124203 1124209 1124219 1124239 1124251 1124267
1124269 1124293 1124297 1124303 1124317 1124341 1124353 1124369 1124377 1124423
1124429 1124437 1124441 1124443 1124449 1124509 1124531 1124551 1124561 1124581
1124593 1124597 1124603 1124639 1124647 1124653 1124659 1124681 1124687 1124699
1124719 1124741 1124749 1124759 1124789 1124797 1124803 1124807 1124813 1124831
1124833 1124867 1124869 1124951 1124957 1124969 1124983 1124987 1124993 1125001
1125013 1125017 1125029 1125053 1125097 1125109 1125121 1125127 1125139 1125143
1125151 1125167 1125169 1125193 1125203 1125209 1125217 1125221 1125253 1125259
1125283 1125317 1125323 1125329 1125343 1125359 1125361 1125379 1125391 1125401
1125407 1125419 1125431 1125433 1125469 1125473 1125479 1125499 1125529 1125539
1125557 1125559 1125569 1125571 1125581 1125599 1125629 1125647 1125653 1125679
1125701 1125713 1125739 1125763 1125767 1125793 1125797 1125811 1125823 1125833
1125857 1125871 1125899 1125907 1125911 1125913 1125923 1125931 1125941 1125953
1125973 1125991 1126031 1126033 1126043 1126067 1126093 1126159 1126189 1126201
1126211 1126219 1126247 1126253 1126259 1126283 1126313 1126319 1126343 1126351
1126357 1126361 1126381 1126387 1126397 1126399 1126421 1126439 1126441 1126457
1126483 1126489 1126501 1126513 1126519 1126523 1126537 1126553 1126561 1126577
1126579 1126597 1126627 1126649 1126661 1126663 1126667 1126669 1126693 1126703
1126711 1126751 1126759 1126771 1126781 1126787 1126823 1126831 1126837 1126843
1126847 1126859 1126861 1126889 1126897 1126963 1126973 1126991 1126999 1127011
1127029 1127033 1127039 1127051 1127081 1127101 1127111 1127123 1127149 1127153
1127171 1127177 1127183 1127197 1127209 1127221 1127227 1127239 1127249 1127263
1127281 1127297 1127303 1127309 1127311 1127323 1127333 1127351 1127359 1127369
1127381 1127383 1127393 1127407 1127411 1127441 1127447 1127453 1127461 1127507
1127513 1127527 1127531 1127537 1127557 1127561 1127573 1127587 1127603 1127617
1127629 1127641 1127657 1127663 1127683 1127701 1127741 1127767 1127773 1127801
1127803 1127809 1127813 1127837 1127849 1127857 1127881 1127891 1127911 1127947
1127957 1127969 1127981 1127983 1127993 1128031 1128037 1128089 1128091 1128107
1128109 1128143 1128151 1128161 1128181 1128209 1128223 1128227 1128233 1128247
1128251 1128287 1128289 1128293 1128299 1128301 1128313 1128349 1128371 1128373
1128383 1128397 1128427 1128433 1128451 1128497 1128499 1128503 1128509 1128521
1128527 1128539 1128553 1128557 1128577 1128583 1128599 1128601 1128623 1128629
1128637 1128641 1128643 1128661 1128667 1128691 1128697 1128703 1128713 1128719
1128727 1128731 1128737 1128761 1128763 1128769 1128773 1128779 1128787 1128811
1128821 1128823 1128889 1128899 1128901 1128917 1128931 1128937 1128943 1128947
1128949 1128977 1128979 1128997 1129013 1129019 1129033 1129043 1129103 1129109
1129111 1129127 1129133 1129153 1129159 1129169 1129187 1129211 1129213 1129217
1129229 1129253 1129283 1129307 1129313 1129333 1129343 1129367 1129391 1129399
1129409 1129433 1129439 1129441 1129459 1129477 1129489 1129501 1129507 1129511
1129519 1129523 1129559 1129561 1129571 1129577 1129603 1129619 1129643 1129663
1129679 1129693 1129699 1129717 1129729 1129741 1129747 1129757 1129763 1129787
1129789 1129819 1129831 1129841 1129847 1129853 1129859 1129861 1129889 1129897
1129951 1129957 1129963 1129991 1130011 1130023 1130039 1130047 1130053 1130057

```
1130081  1130099  1130117  1130123  1130131  1130191  1130237  1130251  1130257  1130267
1130273  1130281  1130287  1130293  1130309  1130317  1130321  1130351  1130359  1130369
1130407  1130413  1130417  1130429  1130431  1130447  1130471  1130497  1130501  1130527
1130561  1130579  1130581  1130587  1130621  1130627  1130629  1130639  1130641  1130651
1130677  1130693  1130699  1130711  1130719  1130737  1130741  1130777  1130783  1130803
1130807  1130809  1130813  1130819  1130827  1130863  1130929  1130939  1130947  1130951
1130957  1130963  1130981  1131023  1131047  1131049  1131077  1131079  1131083
1131103  1131113  1131121  1131131  1131133  1131139  1131157  1131181  1131191  1131217
1131223  1131239  1131253  1131259  1131269  1131271  1131307  1131323  1131329  1131331
1131341  1131343  1131353  1131379  1131397  1131413  1131419  1131421  1131437  1131451
1131463  1131467  1131479  1131491  1131509  1131523  1131547  1131553  1131569  1131617
1131629  1131643  1131653  1131671  1131677  1131701  1131721  1131727  1131737  1131749
1131751  1131763  1131769  1131787  1131799  1131821  1131827  1131829  1131839  1131857
1131863  1131869  1131881  1131883  1131913  1131917  1131919  1131937  1131943  1131959
1131961  1131973  1131997  1132003  1132009  1132063  1132067  1132091  1132123  1132139
1132141  1132177  1132199  1132223  1132249  1132259  1132291  1132301  1132309  1132321
1132333  1132393  1132403  1132409  1132423  1132429  1132447  1132463  1132471  1132477
1132487  1132499  1132507  1132511  1132519  1132529  1132541  1132561  1132567  1132583
1132597  1132601  1132603  1132627  1132633  1132639  1132643  1132661  1132667  1132673
1132679  1132697  1132721  1132739  1132753  1132783  1132787  1132793  1132811  1132823
1132861  1132877  1132883  1132909  1132919  1132927  1132933  1132949  1132969  1132979
1132987  1132991  1132993  1132997  1133009  1133017  1133039  1133047  1133053  1133071
1133131  1133147  1133149  1133159  1133173  1133177  1133183  1133189  1133191  1133219
1133227  1133239  1133257  1133261  1133263  1133287  1133303  1133317  1133333  1133357
1133359  1133381  1133387  1133459  1133467  1133477  1133479  1133501  1133507  1133513
1133519  1133533  1133537  1133551  1133579  1133591  1133621  1133623  1133633  1133641
1133651  1133653  1133659  1133677  1133681  1133683  1133689  1133731  1133737  1133789
1133809  1133819  1133827  1133837  1133843  1133851  1133857  1133861  1133893  1133897
1133903  1133911  1133933  1133947  1133959  1133963  1133971  1133989  1134031  1134037
1134043  1134047  1134059  1134071  1134079  1134113  1134137  1134143  1134149  1134151
1134163  1134169  1134179  1134187  1134193  1134239  1134241  1134247  1134271  1134283
1134299  1134311  1134313  1134389  1134391  1134403  1134421  1134437  1134443  1134449
1134467  1134479  1134481  1134487  1134503  1134517  1134541  1134557  1134559  1134583
1134587  1134607  1134611  1134619  1134649  1134667  1134673  1134691  1134697  1134703
1134709  1134719  1134769  1134781  1134787  1134811  1134821  1134841  1134863  1134871
1134877  1134883  1134907  1134923  1134929  1134961  1134967  1134977  1134989  1135007
1135009  1135019  1135021  1135061  1135063  1135081  1135087  1135091  1135093  1135103
1135111  1135129  1135133  1135159  1135171  1135187  1135201  1135217  1135229  1135237
1135241  1135247  1135261  1135279  1135283  1135291  1135327  1135333  1135339  1135363
1135367  1135403  1135411  1135427  1135429  1135439  1135451  1135469  1135483  1135513
1135531  1135597  1135613  1135619  1135663  1135643  1135657  1135663  1135699  1135703
1135711  1135721  1135733  1135751  1135777  1135819  1135831  1135837  1135847  1135853
1135859  1135861  1135873  1135879  1135891  1135903  1135913  1135919  1135921  1135951
1135963  1135969  1135979  1135999  1136041  1136053  1136063  1136077  1136081  1136087
1136089  1136111  1136117  1136123  1136129  1136147  1136153  1136183  1136203  1136221
1136227  1136231  1136237  1136287  1136299  1136309  1136327  1136329  1136339  1136357
1136363  1136383  1136389  1136393  1136411  1136417  1136449  1136459  1136461  1136477
1136483  1136557  1136567  1136579  1136587  1136593  1136609  1136617  1136623  1136627
1136633  1136647  1136651  1136659  1136669  1136699  1136717  1136719  1136741  1136749
1136767  1136809  1136813  1136819  1136831  1136833  1136843  1136869  1136897  1136917
1136921  1136939  1136951  1136959  1136981  1136983  1136999  1137001  1137007  1137029
1137067  1137091  1137109  1137137  1137139  1137161  1137163  1137167  1137179  1137203
1137209  1137229  1137233  1137247  1137263  1137271  1137289  1137313  1137329  1137337
1137341  1137403  1137407  1137427  1137439  1137457  1137481  1137503  1137527  1137529
1137547  1137551  1137553  1137569  1137611  1137613  1137629  1137659  1137667  1137673
1137677  1137707  1137733  1137743  1137749  1137767  1137781  1137803  1137809  1137811
1137817  1137859  1137863  1137869  1137881  1137883  1137887  1137889  1137911  1137919
1137937  1137953  1137959  1137973  1137977  1137991  1138019  1138057  1138061  1138091
1138097  1138117  1138127  1138141  1138147  1138171  1138183  1138213  1138237  1138273
1138363  1138367  1138369  1138391  1138393  1138409  1138411  1138427  1138429  1138433
1138441  1138451  1138457  1138483  1138519  1138547  1138559  1138567  1138589  1138591
1138637  1138639  1138649  1138667  1138673  1138679  1138681  1138703  1138717  1138729
1138733  1138741  1138751  1138757  1138771  1138777  1138793  1138829  1138831  1138849
1138853  1138867  1138883  1138901  1138919  1138957  1138961  1138967  1138979  1138987
1138997  1138999  1139003  1139011  1139041  1139059  1139081  1139087  1139123  1139141
1139143  1139147  1139191  1139197  1139227  1139239  1139249  1139263  1139269  1139273
1139287  1139291  1139293  1139309  1139321  1139329  1139353  1139387  1139393  1139407
1139423  1139461  1139471  1139473  1139483  1139491  1139503  1139519  1139521  1139531
1139539  1139549  1139557  1139573  1139587  1139623  1139669  1139681  1139683  1139687
1139713  1139717  1139741  1139771  1139773  1139779  1139807  1139819  1139843  1139849
1139851  1139861  1139863  1139869  1139909  1139911  1139917  1139921  1139951  1139959
1139989  1139993  1140091  1140101  1140103  1140121  1140127  1140131  1140137  1140143
1140157  1140163  1140197  1140203  1140253  1140259  1140253  1140257  1140281  1140289
1140311  1140319  1140341  1140353  1140371  1140379  1140383  1140389  1140413  1140421
1140431  1140449  1140449  1140463  1140487  1140493  1140533  1140539  1140563  1140569
1140571  1140577  1140611  1140619  1140637  1140677  1140691  1140697  1140709
1140721  1140749  1140787  1140803  1140847  1140851  1140859  1140863  1140871  1140901
1140911  1140913  1140929  1140949  1140959  1140967  1140973  1140983  1140991  1141009
1141013  1141027  1141031  1141033  1141039  1141061  1141067  1141081  1141087  1141093
1141097  1141103  1141109  1141123  1141139  1141171  1141219  1141223  1141229  1141241
1141243  1141253  1141267  1141271  1141277  1141279  1141289  1141291  1141303  1141319
1141321  1141351  1141373  1141379  1141381  1141391  1141417  1141423  1141447  1141453
1141477  1141507  1141523  1141529  1141531  1141541  1141571  1141573  1141597  1141631
1141633  1141649  1141661  1141667  1141717  1141739  1141757  1141769  1141801  1141813
1141837  1141849  1141853  1141867  1141871  1141901  1141909  1141949  1141963  1141967
1141969  1141999  1142003  1142017  1142021  1142039  1142041  1142059  1142069  1142083
1142129  1142131  1142159  1142161  1142171  1142191  1142201  1142233  1142237  1142243
1142263  1142269  1142279  1142287  1142311  1142321  1142333  1142353  1142357  1142359
1142363  1142389  1142423  1142431  1142473  1142483  1142503  1142507  1142509  1142539
```

1142549 1142569 1142573 1142593 1142599 1142633 1142651 1142677 1142693 1142707
1142737 1142759 1142773 1142777 1142783 1142789 1142809 1142821 1142833 1142837
1142851 1142863 1142881 1142891 1142909 1142917 1142923 1142929 1142941 1142959
1142969 1142971 1143013 1143019 1143047 1143049 1143053 1143061 1143067 1143071
1143073 1143089 1143091 1143101 1143113 1143143 1143161 1143167 1143193 1143217
1143223 1143227 1143239 1143257 1143269 1143281 1143283 1143299 1143341 1143347
1143371 1143391 1143407 1143433 1143469 1143473 1143481 1143487 1143529 1143551
1143563 1143577 1143587 1143589 1143601 1143619 1143643 1143647 1143661 1143679
1143697 1143719 1143749 1143763 1143799 1143803 1143809 1143817 1143829 1143851
1143887 1143893 1143943 1143949 1143953 1143959 1143977 1144001 1144007 1144019
1144037 1144061 1144081 1144103 1144139 1144141 1144147 1144153 1144163 1144183
1144193 1144211 1144223 1144243 1144249 1144261 1144271 1144277 1144279 1144291
1144301 1144327 1144333 1144343 1144349 1144357 1144379 1144393 1144399 1144417
1144439 1144441 1144453 1144477 1144483 1144499 1144511 1144519 1144523 1144529
1144537 1144573 1144589 1144603 1144607 1144621 1144643 1144657 1144667 1144681
1144691 1144721 1144723 1144727 1144739 1144757 1144783 1144823 1144837 1144867
1144877 1144879 1144889 1144901 1144903 1144907 1144919 1144931 1144939 1144951
1144973 1144981 1144993 1145003 1145021 1145057 1145059 1145077 1145093 1145099
1145107 1145129 1145141 1145143 1145173 1145189 1145191 1145203 1145213 1145227
1145269 1145281 1145293 1145299 1145303 1145311 1145323 1145327 1145329 1145359
1145369 1145371 1145381 1145387 1145393 1145411 1145429 1145461 1145479 1145497
1145509 1145533 1145537 1145539 1145593 1145611 1145621 1145623 1145659 1145689
1145693 1145713 1145723 1145741 1145743 1145747 1145773 1145789 1145797 1145801
1145803 1145831 1145843 1145849 1145873 1145897 1145899 1145971 1145983 1145999
1146037 1146043 1146049 1146071 1146083 1146091 1146097 1146133 1146143 1146179
1146217 1146221 1146263 1146281 1146307 1146323 1146329 1146331 1146347 1146367
1146391 1146407 1146413 1146419 1146421 1146461 1146487 1146491 1146511 1146521
1146533 1146539 1146559 1146569 1146581 1146661 1146671 1146679 1146697
1146703 1146709 1146763 1146727 1146731 1146769 1146773 1146779 1146781 1146787
1146791 1146793 1146797 1146799 1146809 1146823 1146829 1146833 1146841 1146857
1146869 1146877 1146881 1146911 1146917 1146931 1146947 1146953 1146967 1146989
1147009 1147021 1147039 1147043 1147051 1147067 1147073 1147099 1147103 1147117
1147127 1147141 1147169 1147183 1147187 1147189 1147193 1147213 1147229 1147231
1147243 1147247 1147249 1147253 1147271 1147273 1147291 1147301 1147331 1147339
1147351 1147379 1147387 1147409 1147417 1147423 1147427 1147441 1147451 1147453
1147459 1147463 1147499 1147507 1147511 1147561 1147567 1147571 1147579 1147583
1147591 1147613 1147621 1147637 1147639 1147669 1147697 1147709 1147711 1147717
1147739 1147759 1147793 1147819 1147841 1147843 1147889 1147897 1147903 1147921
1147931 1147969 1147981 1147987 1147997 1148039 1148049 1148087 1148047 1148089
1148099 1148111 1148167 1148171 1148177 1148219 1148249 1148261 1148263 1148291
1148293 1148297 1148311 1148327 1148339 1148359 1148377 1148387 1148437 1148453
1148489 1148501 1148507 1148513 1148527 1148549 1148561 1148593 1148599 1148621
1148629 1148647 1148663 1148677 1148681 1148687 1148701 1148713 1148729 1148731
1148737 1148747 1148753 1148761 1148773 1148837 1148839 1148857 1148867 1148899
1148921 1148933 1148941 1148957 1148963 1148971 1148977 1148981 1148989 1148999
1149007 1149017 1149037 1149053 1149059 1149061 1149131 1149151 1149157 1149163
1149167 1149191 1149193 1149209 1149221 1149227 1149229 1149233 1149259 1149283
1149307 1149341 1149349 1149361 1149373 1149403 1149409 1149413 1149427 1149457
1149469 1149487 1149493 1149503 1149509 1149521 1149527 1149539 1149559 1149569
1149581 1149587 1149593 1149601 1149607 1149619 1149637 1149641 1149661 1149679
1149689 1149737 1149749 1149769 1149779 1149809 1149817 1149857 1149859
1149881 1149887 1149901 1149913 1149917 1149919 1149943 1149971 1149979 1149983
1149989 1149991 1150027 1150031 1150057 1150063 1150073 1150081 1150103 1150117
1150139 1150141 1150151 1150159 1150183 1150187 1150199 1150211 1150213 1150217
1150229 1150243 1150249 1150301 1150309 1150349 1150351 1150363 1150397 1150403
1150411 1150417 1150421 1150423 1150447 1150499 1150511 1150519 1150531 1150557
1150547 1150561 1150579 1150603 1150609 1150631 1150649 1150651 1150657 1150661
1150673 1150687 1150703 1150717 1150729 1150733 1150739 1150741 1150757 1150763
1150769 1150777 1150783 1150823 1150837 1150847 1150861 1150867 1150871 1150873
1150879 1150909 1150921 1150927 1150939 1150949 1150957 1150973 1150987 1151021
1151041 1151047 1151057 1151063 1151069 1151083 1151089 1151113 1151141 1151147
1151159 1151167 1151177 1151179 1151203 1151209 1151221 1151233 1151237 1151243
1151251 1151287 1151303 1151317 1151327 1151333 1151363 1151369 1151383 1151389
1151399 1151401 1151413 1151417 1151431 1151441 1151443 1151471 1151473 1151483
1151519 1151537 1151569 1151581 1151593 1151599 1151603 1151611 1151629 1151639
1151651 1151653 1151659 1151661 1151687 1151701 1151713 1151729 1151737 1151747
1151753 1151779 1151807 1151861 1151873 1151879 1151881 1151911 1151933 1151963
1151987 1151993 1151999 1152023 1152029 1152037 1152071 1152077 1152079
1152091 1152113 1152119 1152121 1152149 1152157 1152161 1152163 1152181 1152187
1152227 1152233 1152287 1152313 1152317 1152337 1152343 1152367 1152383 1152391
1152397 1152419 1152421 1152493 1152509 1152517 1152523 1152527 1152589 1152623
1152629 1152631 1152637 1152643 1152649 1152653 1152667 1152677 1152707 1152733
1152751 1152757 1152761 1152763 1152773 1152791 1152799 1152841 1152857
1152881 1152887 1152913 1152917 1152937 1152941 1152979 1152989 1152997 1153001
1153007 1153021 1153027 1153049 1153057 1153063 1153073 1153099 1153109 1153123
1153147 1153153 1153157 1153171 1153177 1153183 1153199 1153211 1153219 1153223
1153237 1153241 1153247 1153249 1153261 1153267 1153277 1153309 1153337 1153343
1153349 1153367 1153393 1153421 1153429 1153441 1153457 1153459 1153463 1153483
1153487 1153511 1153517 1153531 1153553 1153573 1153577 1153589 1153597 1153609
1153613 1153639 1153643 1153681 1153687 1153721 1153729 1153751 1153753 1153759
1153769 1153777 1153799 1153811 1153849 1153853 1153871 1153891 1153921 1153967
1153973 1154017 1154029 1154033 1154039 1154047 1154051 1154119 1154123 1154129
1154159 1154173 1154177 1154183 1154207 1154221 1154227 1154233 1154239 1154243
1154267 1154291 1154297 1154299 1154311 1154323 1154327 1154339 1154353 1154359
1154369 1154401 1154411 1154431 1154449 1154467 1154473 1154509 1154513 1154537
1154539 1154551 1154561 1154563 1154567 1154579 1154581 1154603 1154633 1154639
1154651 1154653 1154707 1154723 1154737 1154753 1154771 1154789 1154819 1154821
1154849 1154863 1154887 1154893 1154897 1154911 1154927 1154947 1154969 1154971
1154987 1155001 1155017 1155019 1155053 1155061 1155071 1155097 1155101 1155107

```
1155127  1155149  1155151  1155169  1155179  1155211  1155223  1155233  1155239  1155247
1155263  1155293  1155311  1155317  1155373  1155397  1155379  1155403  1155419  1155431
1155437  1155449  1155457  1155461  1155499  1155527  1155529  1155569  1155577  1155601
1155607  1155611  1155613  1155617  1155619  1155629  1155631  1155653  1155659  1155689
1155697  1155701  1155703  1155709  1155733  1155821  1155823  1155829  1155841  1155851
1155859  1155863  1155899  1155901  1155907  1155919  1155923  1155929  1155937  1155943
1155953  1155961  1155967  1155971  1155977  1155997  1156009  1156013  1156019  1156031
1156033  1156037  1156039  1156073  1156079  1156087  1156097  1156109  1156121  1156151
1156157  1156171  1156217  1156229  1156231  1156249  1156261  1156271  1156291  1156297
1156303  1156307  1156327  1156333  1156343  1156367  1156369  1156387  1156403  1156423
1156427  1156429  1156451  1156453  1156457  1156483  1156501  1156523  1156537  1156541
1156553  1156567  1156591  1156613  1156627  1156633  1156637  1156643  1156681  1156699
1156709  1156711  1156721  1156741  1156747  1156751  1156769  1156783  1156801  1156807
1156819  1156823  1156847  1156849  1156873  1156907  1156927  1156949  1156963  1156997
1157011  1157017  1157033  1157053  1157059  1157063  1157069  1157077  1157099  1157111
1157131  1157159  1157171  1157179  1157183  1157201  1157203  1157209  1157213  1157227
1157237  1157243  1157251  1157257  1157263  1157279  1157293  1157327  1157333  1157339
1157341  1157357  1157363  1157369  1157381  1157393  1157413  1157437  1157449  1157489
1157491  1157503  1157531  1157539  1157557  1157579  1157591  1157609  1157621  1157627
1157641  1157669  1157671  1157699  1157701  1157711  1157713  1157729  1157747  1157749
1157759  1157771  1157773  1157791  1157831  1157833  1157837  1157839  1157851  1157869
1157873  1157899  1157929  1157953  1157969  1157977  1157987  1158007  1158011  1158037
1158071  1158077  1158089  1158121  1158133  1158139  1158161  1158187  1158197  1158203
1158217  1158247  1158251  1158263  1158271  1158293  1158301  1158307  1158317  1158323
1158341  1158361  1158383  1158389  1158401  1158407  1158419  1158427  1158457  1158461
1158467  1158473  1158481  1158491  1158523  1158529  1158539  1158541  1158551  1158569
1158587  1158593  1158607  1158611  1158613  1158617  1158629  1158643  1158653  1158673
1158679  1158683  1158713  1158719  1158743  1158757  1158761  1158769  1158799  1158821
1158823  1158827  1158841  1158847  1158863  1158881  1158887  1158923  1158953  1158961
1158977  1158991  1159001  1159007  1159027  1159031  1159049  1159063  1159073  1159079
1159087  1159091  1159127  1159139  1159153  1159187  1159189  1159199  1159201  1159229
1159231  1159241  1159243  1159259  1159271  1159283  1159303  1159337  1159339  1159381
1159393  1159397  1159421  1159423  1159429  1159447  1159463  1159489  1159517  1159523
1159531  1159541  1159577  1159583  1159597  1159601  1159633  1159649  1159661  1159663
1159709  1159721  1159777  1159787  1159789  1159811  1159813  1159843  1159853  1159861
1159877  1159889  1159901  1159909  1159919  1159967  1159973  1159981  1159993  1159997
1160009  1160039  1160041  1160057  1160077  1160111  1160129  1160141  1160147  1160161
1160167  1160179  1160207  1160213  1160219  1160221  1160227  1160251  1160279  1160287
1160297  1160303  1160309  1160317  1160351  1160359  1160363  1160371  1160407  1160413
1160429  1160443  1160447  1160449  1160459  1160473  1160479  1160491  1160503  1160513
1160519  1160543  1160567  1160569  1160581  1160597  1160611  1160639  1160659  1160681
1160689  1160713  1160717  1160749  1160771  1160807  1160813  1160837  1160839  1160867
1160893  1160903  1160911  1160927  1160941  1160953  1160977  1160983  1160987  1160989
1161001  1161007  1161011  1161031  1161037  1161047  1161059  1161077  1161091  1161101
1161107  1161113  1161137  1161143  1161163  1161169  1161203  1161217  1161227  1161233
1161239  1161241  1161263  1161269  1161289  1161313  1161317  1161331  1161343  1161371
1161397  1161401  1161403  1161437  1161439  1161443  1161449  1161463  1161481  1161487
1161493  1161497  1161499  1161509  1161521  1161529  1161547  1161551  1161553  1161581
1161599  1161617  1161619  1161637  1161647  1161659  1161683  1161691  1161703  1161749
1161757  1161761  1161767  1161781  1161791  1161829  1161833  1161841  1161851  1161857
1161871  1161877  1161883  1161893  1161929  1161931  1161947  1161949  1161991  1161997
1162009  1162037  1162043  1162061  1162067  1162079  1162081  1162093  1162099  1162129
1162193  1162219  1162223  1162229  1162243  1162253  1162261  1162277  1162279  1162297
1162303  1162321  1162339  1162361  1162367  1162373  1162417  1162423  1162453  1162463
1162471  1162481  1162493  1162501  1162507  1162529  1162537  1162541  1162543  1162547
1162559  1162571  1162573  1162583  1162589  1162597  1162619  1162621  1162631  1162649
1162663  1162669  1162687  1162691  1162709  1162727  1162729  1162741  1162751  1162753
1162771  1162789  1162793  1162807  1162853  1162859  1162867  1162877  1162879  1162897
1162901  1162907  1162927  1162937  1162943  1162951  1162957  1162961  1162969  1162981
1162991  1163003  1163011  1163017  1163033  1163039  1163069  1163077  1163081  1163083
1163093  1163111  1163119  1163131  1163137  1163143  1163147  1163159  1163167  1163177
1163189  1163207  1163221  1163231  1163233  1163251  1163257  1163263  1163273  1163311
1163329  1163333  1163339  1163353  1163417  1163423  1163431  1163441  1163467  1163473
1163479  1163483  1163507  1163521  1163543  1163551  1163557  1163581  1163587  1163609
1163611  1163627  1163629  1163641  1163651  1163653  1163663  1163671  1163689  1163699
1163711  1163713  1163717  1163719  1163737  1163753  1163759  1163783  1163791  1163821
1163831  1163843  1163849  1163873  1163879  1163891  1163923  1163947  1163969  1163971
1163977  1163989  1163993  1164001  1164029  1164043  1164067  1164071  1164077  1164091
1164101  1164173  1164179  1164181  1164193  1164199  1164203  1164217  1164221  1164253
1164287  1164323  1164343  1164367  1164409  1164413  1164419  1164431  1164433  1164439
1164461  1164479  1164497  1164503  1164511  1164521  1164533  1164557  1164571  1164587
1164589  1164593  1164599  1164607  1164617  1164623  1164629  1164641  1164659  1164671
1164689  1164731  1164749  1164791  1164799  1164803  1164811  1164817  1164829  1164841
1164853  1164859  1164869  1164899  1164937  1164941  1164953  1164967  1164979  1164991
1164997  1165001  1165037  1165049  1165051  1165057  1165069  1165079  1165081  1165103
1165121  1165127  1165139  1165147  1165183  1165187  1165189  1165193  1165201  1165207
1165211  1165217  1165223  1165273  1165279  1165301  1165303  1165349  1165357  1165361
1165363  1165369  1165397  1165399  1165421  1165447  1165453  1165471  1165511  1165529
1165531  1165579  1165583  1165643  1165667  1165691  1165711  1165721  1165727  1165729
1165739  1165751  1165777  1165789  1165799  1165819  1165823  1165831  1165837  1165849
1165861  1165873  1165889  1165903  1165909  1165919  1165921  1165933  1165937  1165943
1165949  1165951  1165991  1165993  1166021  1166027  1166041  1166057  1166083  1166089
1166093  1166101  1166107  1166131  1166141  1166147  1166153  1166213  1166219  1166227
1166237  1166287  1166311  1166323  1166329  1166359  1166383  1166393  1166401  1166411
1166413  1166441  1166453  1166479  1166483  1166497  1166507  1166527  1166531  1166533
1166549  1166563  1166567  1166569  1166579  1166597  1166603  1166609  1166617  1166639
1166663  1166677  1166687  1166713  1166723  1166729  1166741  1166773  1166779  1166801
1166807  1166827  1166833  1166839  1166849  1166857  1166861  1166903  1166927  1166929
1166947  1166953  1166969  1166987  1167011  1167013  1167053  1167059  1167077  1167083
```

```
1167139  1167143  1167157  1167167  1167193  1167209  1167211  1167217  1167233  1167241
1167251  1167277  1167289  1167293  1167307  1167317  1167329  1167347  1167349  1167359
1167391  1167409  1167421  1167443  1167449  1167469  1167473  1167539  1167547  1167559
1167571  1167581  1167587  1167599  1167613  1167623  1167637  1167653  1167659  1167667
1167689  1167697  1167701  1167703  1167707  1167709  1167731  1167763  1167773  1167791
1167799  1167811  1167821  1167823  1167833  1167839  1167841  1167847  1167853  1167869
1167889  1167899  1167913  1167919  1167937  1167953  1167973  1168001  1168007  1168031
1168039  1168043  1168093  1168133  1168151  1168169  1168183  1168187  1168231  1168241
1168243  1168247  1168249  1168261  1168301  1168319  1168327  1168337  1168339  1168351
1168357  1168361  1168397  1168399  1168403  1168411  1168451  1168463  1168477  1168487
1168493  1168501  1168523  1168537  1168553  1168619  1168621  1168627  1168637  1168639
1168693  1168711  1168841  1168751  1168757  1168763  1168771  1168789  1168799  1168819
1168829  1168831  1168841  1168847  1168859  1168877  1168879  1168897  1168919  1168927
1168931  1168933  1168957  1168969  1168987  1168997  1169009  1169011  1169017  1169023
1169027  1169029  1169059  1169081  1169131  1169137  1169149  1169171  1169177  1169183
1169191  1169249  1169257  1169261  1169269  1169281  1169293  1169323  1169327  1169341
1169347  1169353  1169363  1169381  1169383  1169401  1169411  1169419  1169419  1169449
1169453  1169473  1169477  1169491  1169513  1169521  1169563  1169587  1169591  1169593
1169603  1169627  1169633  1169647  1169669  1169677  1169683  1169713  1169713  1169741
1169747  1169759  1169761  1169767  1169789  1169801  1169809  1169827  1169873  1169879
1169899  1169929  1169933  1169939  1170007  1170011  1170019  1170023  1170031  1170049
1170061  1170067  1170089  1170107  1170109  1170119  1170131  1170133  1170137  1170139
1170167  1170173  1170193  1170203  1170209  1170233  1170251  1170271  1170277  1170311
1170317  1170329  1170349  1170361  1170373  1170397  1170437  1170443  1170451  1170461
1170487  1170497  1170511  1170517  1170523  1170541  1170553  1170563  1170581  1170583
1170593  1170599  1170607  1170641  1170649  1170661  1170667  1170679  1170683  1170707
1170709  1170713  1170721  1170727  1170751  1170779  1170781  1170787  1170803  1170811
1170821  1170833  1170853  1170857  1170863  1170899  1170941  1170947  1170971  1170979
1171031  1171033  1171057  1171057  1171061  1171069  1171073  1171109  1171111  1171117
1171123  1171133  1171189  1171201  1171207  1171231  1171241  1171243  1171253
1171259  1171267  1171301  1171319  1171343  1171393  1171399  1171421  1171427  1171447
1171451  1171463  1171477  1171517  1171523  1171529  1171549  1171553  1171561  1171579
1171591  1171601  1171619  1171633  1171637  1171661  1171669  1171699  1171721  1171747
1171771  1171783  1171789  1171801  1171811  1171813  1171823  1171837  1171847  1171867
1171921  1171927  1171931  1171957  1171967  1171969  1171979  1171981  1171991  1171999
1172009  1172021  1172023  1172027  1172029  1172047  1172063  1172069  1172081  1172107
1172111  1172147  1172179  1172207  1172233  1172257  1172261  1172273  1172279  1172317
1172329  1172351  1172377  1172393  1172401  1172407  1172411  1172417  1172429  1172443
1172447  1172461  1172467  1172491  1172497  1172503  1172531  1172533  1172537  1172539
1172543  1172573  1172579  1172657  1172659  1172663  1172671  1172681  1172683  1172687
1172713  1172749  1172777  1172783  1172797  1172803  1172807  1172819  1172833  1172867
1172893  1172903  1172921  1172929  1172933  1172939  1172953  1172957  1172959  1172981
1172993  1173001  1173013  1173043  1173059  1173101  1173121  1173127  1173157  1173163
1173173  1173181  1173191  1173199  1173223  1173239  1173259  1173281  1173283  1173301
1173343  1173349  1173373  1173397  1173401  1173407  1173433  1173439  1173463  1173481
1173511  1173521  1173539  1173541  1173551  1173553  1173581  1173583  1173587  1173589
1173593  1173617  1173631  1173709  1173743  1173749  1173779  1173787  1173803  1173811
1173827  1173829  1173841  1173853  1173881  1173883  1173917  1173937  1173941  1173947
1173959  1173961  1173979  1173983  1174021  1174027  1174031  1174049  1174073  1174079
1174091  1174093  1174099  1174141  1174163  1174171  1174193  1174211  1174213  1174231
1174237  1174247  1174259  1174267  1174273  1174301  1174307  1174319  1174331  1174337
1174339  1174361  1174387  1174399  1174423  1174441  1174451  1174463  1174469  1174477
1174487  1174489  1174499  1174507  1174519  1174531  1174549  1174571  1174583  1174601
1174603  1174619  1174627  1174669  1174673  1174681  1174687  1174709  1174721  1174727
1174739  1174759  1174763  1174769  1174781  1174783  1174793  1174801  1174829  1174847
1174889  1174883  1174919  1174897  1174913  1174919  1174949  1174951  1174969  1174973
1175003  1175021  1175029  1175039  1175071  1175077  1175099  1175107  1175123  1175143
1175149  1175173  1175191  1175219  1175243  1175249  1175257  1175267  1175297  1175351
1175353  1175371  1175387  1175389  1175407  1175411  1175413  1175417  1175437  1175467
1175479  1175483  1175497  1175509  1175521  1175561  1175569  1175579  1175591  1175617
1175623  1175627  1175651  1175659  1175677  1175683  1175687  1175711  1175717  1175723
1175729  1175743  1175767  1175789  1175791  1175803  1175807  1175813  1175819  1175821
1175833  1175849  1175857  1175887  1175899  1175927  1175939  1175953  1175959  1175963
1175969  1175981  1175989  1176023  1176029  1176031  1176041  1176061  1176083  1176089
1176113  1176121  1176127  1176137  1176163  1176173  1176187  1176191  1176221  1176223
1176239  1176277  1176293  1176323  1176353  1176361  1176367  1176377  1176391  1176397
1176403  1176407  1176421  1176433  1176449  1176463  1176509  1176521  1176529  1176533
1176557  1176583  1176589  1176599  1176601  1176607  1176631  1176641  1176647  1176671
1176673  1176701  1176709  1176713  1176737  1176767  1176779  1176787  1176793  1176797
1176811  1176827  1176869  1176871  1176881  1176899  1176911  1176937  1176943  1176947
1176949  1176983  1177009  1177019  1177027  1177037  1177067  1177073  1177087  1177093
1177103  1177129  1177147  1177153  1177157  1177159  1177171  1177181  1177201  1177207
1177219  1177223  1177237  1177243  1177247  1177277  1177291  1177331  1177387  1177399
1177427  1177433  1177447  1177453  1177459  1177481  1177489  1177499  1177507  1177513
1177529  1177541  1177543  1177549  1177571  1177609  1177613  1177619  1177621  1177637
1177651  1177667  1177681  1177697  1177711  1177717  1177723  1177733  1177739  1177741
1177751  1177763  1177769  1177801  1177843  1177859  1177873  1177877  1177901  1177919
1177921  1177933  1177949  1177987  1177997  1178003  1178017  1178033  1178039  1178041
1178059  1178069  1178087  1178101  1178113  1178123  1178131  1178141  1178159  1178161
1178167  1178173  1178189  1178197  1178201  1178207  1178213  1178227  1178231  1178237
1178239  1178263  1178269  1178273  1178297  1178347  1178363  1178369  1178371  1178377
1178393  1178417  1178447  1178461  1178479  1178483  1178521  1178533  1178537  1178549
1178557  1178591  1178609  1178621  1178623  1178633  1178641  1178659  1178669  1178689
1178699  1178701  1178707  1178711  1178717  1178719  1178743  1178753  1178767  1178803
1178809  1178833  1178843  1178851  1178887  1178897  1178909  1178921  1178927  1178939
1178953  1178959  1178963  1178971  1178977  1178981  1178993  1179011  1179019  1179047
1179109  1179127  1179149  1179151  1179173  1179179  1179193  1179203  1179223  1179251
1179253  1179259  1179263  1179281  1179287  1179289  1179293  1179317  1179319  1179323
1179329  1179331  1179337  1179379  1179383  1179389  1179403  1179413  1179419  1179421
```

```
1179427  1179467  1179491  1179499  1179527  1179547  1179551  1179553  1179569  1179571
1179583  1179589  1179599  1179637  1179641  1179649  1179677  1179733  1179751  1179757
1179779  1179793  1179797  1179839  1179847  1179853  1179859  1179863  1179869  1179883
1179901  1179907  1179929  1179947  1179961  1179973  1179977  1179979  1179989  1179991
1180009  1180013  1180019  1180027  1180031  1180043  1180057  1180073  1180087  1180093
1180099  1180111  1180117  1180121  1180133  1180141  1180159  1180171  1180219  1180237
1180241  1180243  1180247  1180253  1180279  1180303  1180313  1180351  1180369  1180373
1180381  1180391  1180397  1180409  1180423  1180427  1180447  1180477  1180493  1180507
1180519  1180537  1180547  1180549  1180577  1180591  1180631  1180637  1180643  1180657
1180661  1180691  1180693  1180709  1180721  1180723  1180727  1180733  1180757  1180771
1180799  1180807  1180811  1180819  1180847  1180849  1180853  1180859  1180873  1180877
1180891  1180897  1180901  1180903  1180913  1180931  1180937  1180951  1180957  1180961
1180979  1180987  1180997  1181017  1181023  1181039  1181051  1181053  1181057  1181093
1181099  1181137  1181149  1181153  1181171  1181183  1181197  1181203  1181209  1181237
1181263  1181267  1181269  1181281  1181293  1181309  1181311  1181321  1181329  1181407
1181413  1181437  1181443  1181461  1181471  1181473  1181501  1181507  1181519  1181527
1181549  1181561  1181563  1181573  1181581  1181611  1181617  1181633  1181647  1181681
1181699  1181701  1181723  1181729  1181731  1181759  1181767  1181771  1181773  1181777
1181839  1181879  1181881  1181893  1181897  1181911  1181923  1181927  1181963  1181969
1181981  1181987  1182007  1182019  1182023  1182031  1182043  1182073  1182121  1182133
1182143  1182157  1182211  1182253  1182277  1182281  1182283  1182287  1182289  1182331
1182341  1182343  1182347  1182353  1182383  1182397  1182403  1182413  1182421  1182431
1182437  1182439  1182449  1182451  1182463  1182479  1182487  1182491  1182509  1182521
1182539  1182547  1182581  1182593  1182611  1182659  1182677  1182679  1182689  1182691
1182697  1182703  1182737  1182739  1182757  1182763  1182767  1182781  1182787  1182791
1182817  1182847  1182869  1182889  1182893  1182901  1182917  1182919  1182947  1182953
1182967  1182989  1183003  1183027  1183031  1183033  1183057  1183079  1183093  1183101
1183121  1183123  1183141  1183151  1183157  1183159  1183163  1183181  1183199  1183201
1183213  1183241  1183261  1183267  1183271  1183277  1183279  1183333  1183337  1183339
1183349  1183381  1183393  1183397  1183409  1183411  1183423  1183447  1183451  1183471
1183477  1183531  1183537  1183541  1183561  1183571  1183579  1183597  1183607  1183613
1183687  1183697  1183709  1183723  1183729  1183733  1183739  1183753  1183759  1183769
1183771  1183781  1183799  1183811  1183813  1183837  1183843  1183877  1183913  1183933
1183939  1183943  1183951  1183961  1183969  1183981  1183993  1183997  1184003  1184011
1184047  1184059  1184069  1184077  1184081  1184083  1184093  1184119  1184123  1184129
1184143  1184149  1184171  1184173  1184207  1184219  1184243  1184269  1184291  1184299
1184303  1184317  1184329  1184347  1184357  1184363  1184369  1184377  1184399  1184411
1184413  1184423  1184429  1184453  1184459  1184461  1184471  1184473  1184483  1184489
1184507  1184527  1184537  1184539  1184551  1184551  1184587  1184609  1184653  1184663
1184671  1184683  1184731  1184741  1184749  1184759  1184767  1184791  1184797  1184837
1184839  1184867  1184881  1184893  1184903  1184923  1184927  1184933  1184947  1184957
1184959  1184987  1184993  1185013  1185017  1185071  1185077  1185089  1185103  1185109
1185113  1185127  1185131  1185179  1185181  1185241  1185281  1185287  1185299  1185307
1185313  1185319  1185329  1185337  1185343  1185361  1185367  1185377  1185383  1185389
1185403  1185439  1185463  1185469  1185493  1185497  1185511  1185523  1185551  1185559
1185577  1185589  1185601  1185617  1185623  1185637  1185643  1185647  1185659  1185661
1185671  1185677  1185683  1185689  1185697  1185703  1185707  1185721  1185749  1185787
1185791  1185797  1185817  1185823  1185827  1185851  1185859  1185871  1185883  1185889
1185893  1185907  1185929  1185931  1185953  1185979  1185997  1186001  1186033  1186049
1186051  1186057  1186063  1186067  1186079  1186099  1186111  1186117  1186121  1186127
1186147  1186169  1186181  1186217  1186231  1186249  1186259  1186291  1186321  1186337
1186349  1186351  1186373  1186397  1186403  1186411  1186439  1186441  1186489  1186517
1186519  1186541  1186573  1186589  1186597  1186621  1186631  1186657  1186673  1186693
1186697  1186699  1186739  1186741  1186751  1186769  1186789  1186793  1186811  1186813
1186837  1186841  1186847  1186879  1186931  1186937  1186963  1186973  1186981  1187003
1187009  1187023  1187047  1187051  1187089  1187107  1187111  1187117  1187141  1187159
1187167  1187189  1187201  1187227  1187233  1187239  1187261  1187279  1187287  1187309
1187311  1187317  1187321  1187339  1187341  1187353  1187357  1187363  1187369  1187383
1187387  1187411  1187413  1187419  1187429  1187453  1187471  1187479  1187489  1187507
1187509  1187539  1187551  1187561  1187567  1187587  1187623  1187629  1187639  1187657
1187687  1187689  1187699  1187701  1187707  1187717  1187723  1187741  1187749  1187761
1187801  1187803  1187819  1187821  1187833  1187839  1187863  1187867  1187873  1187887
1187897  1187911  1187931  1187939  1187941  1187947  1187981  1187993  1187999  1188001
1188007  1188017  1188029  1188037  1188041  1188049  1188059  1188071  1188073  1188149
1188151  1188167  1188169  1188179  1188197  1188223  1188227  1188233  1188247  1188259
1188263  1188269  1188277  1188287  1188289  1188293  1188307  1188353  1188359  1188361
1188377  1188389  1188409  1188413  1188457  1188491  1188511  1188527  1188529  1188553
1188557  1188559  1188581  1188587  1188601  1188613  1188619  1188637  1188653  1188661
1188667  1188679  1188689  1188721  1188727  1188731  1188763  1188769  1188787  1188839
1188841  1188851  1188857  1188889  1188917  1188931  1188937  1188947  1188973  1188977
1188991  1189003  1189007  1189021  1189033  1189057  1189061  1189063  1189093  1189109
1189121  1189127  1189151  1189159  1189163  1189171  1189189  1189193  1189213  1189219
1189231  1189277  1189277  1189301  1189313  1189327  1189333  1189339  1189361  1189387
1189403  1189417  1189453  1189469  1189471  1189481  1189483  1189553  1189567  1189577
1189579  1189603  1189607  1189613  1189621  1189627  1189631  1189633  1189637  1189649
1189651  1189673  1189703  1189709  1189717  1189751  1189757  1189759  1189763  1189789
1189801  1189807  1189823  1189831  1189843  1189871  1189879  1189891  1189897  1189901
1189907  1189919  1189933  1189967  1189999  1190011  1190023  1190029  1190041  1190047
1190069  1190071  1190081  1190143  1190149  1190159  1190177  1190201  1190237  1190249
1190261  1190263  1190279  1190291  1190311  1190347  1190359  1190381  1190417  1190429
1190447  1190467  1190473  1190477  1190489  1190491  1190507  1190509  1190513  1190533
1190573  1190587  1190591  1190611  1190633  1190639  1190647  1190671  1190699  1190701
1190719  1190723  1190737  1190743  1190753  1190773  1190789  1190807  1190809  1190821
1190831  1190837  1190851  1190873  1190897  1190899  1190911  1190923  1190929  1190947
1190951  1190953  1190983  1191011  1191013  1191019  1191031  1191061  1191077  1191079
1191089  1191097  1191103  1191107  1191109  1191119  1191131  1191149  1191163  1191187
1191191  1191199  1191209  1191221  1191247  1191277  1191283  1191293  1191301  1191313
1191341  1191347  1191353  1191373  1191409  1191431  1191439  1191457  1191481  1191499
1191529  1191539  1191551  1191559  1191565  1191571  1191577  1191601  1191611  1191613
```

```
1191637 1191643 1191667 1191679 1191691 1191703 1191719 1191727 1191731 1191739
1191761 1191767 1191769 1191781 1191793 1191809 1191821 1191833 1191847 1191899
1191923 1191937 1191941 1191947 1191973 1191979 1191991 1192013 1192027 1192039
1192069 1192073 1192097 1192099 1192109 1192127 1192141 1192151 1192153 1192171
1192181 1192183 1192187 1192199 1192201 1192207 1192211 1192241 1192253 1192259
1192267 1192271 1192327 1192337 1192339 1192349 1192357 1192369 1192391 1192409
1192417 1192423 1192427 1192453 1192469 1192483 1192517 1192549 1192559 1192561
1192571 1192579 1192589 1192603 1192651 1192673 1192679 1192699 1192717 1192721
1192753 1192781 1192811 1192817 1192823 1192831 1192837 1192847 1192853 1192879
1192883 1192889 1192903 1192903 1192927 1192937 1192951 1192967 1192969
1193011 1193021 1193041 1193047 1193057 1193081 1193107 1193119 1193123 1193131
1193149 1193161 1193173 1193183 1193209 1193233 1193237 1193239 1193243 1193261
1193267 1193299 1193303 1193329 1193351 1193363 1193369 1193399 1193429 1193431
1193443 1193459 1193473 1193483 1193497 1193501 1193503 1193513 1193537 1193557
1193567 1193573 1193603 1193609 1193617 1193653 1193663 1193683 1193693 1193701
1193707 1193711 1193729 1193737 1193741 1193743 1193761 1193767 1193771 1193783
1193821 1193833 1193837 1193839 1193849 1193867 1193869 1193887 1193909 1193911
1193939 1193947 1193963 1193971 1193989 1193993 1194019 1194023 1194031 1194041
1194047 1194059 1194103 1194157 1194161 1194163 1194203 1194209 1194211 1194241
1194251 1194253 1194269 1194293 1194311 1194329 1194341 1194343 1194373 1194379
1194383 1194407 1194421 1194439 1194443 1194449 1194463 1194493 1194517 1194521
1194541 1194547 1194553 1194581 1194593 1194601 1194631 1194659 1194667 1194671
1194679 1194707 1194727 1194731 1194733 1194751 1194757 1194763 1194769 1194797
1194799 1194803 1194821 1194847 1194857 1194877 1194883 1194889 1194901 1194907
1194917 1194923 1194959 1194961 1194971 1194979 1194997 1195021 1195031 1195037
1195039 1195067 1195091 1195121 1195123 1195127 1195141 1195153 1195169 1195171
1195189 1195193 1195217 1195223 1195231 1195237 1195247 1195277 1195291 1195361
1195387 1195421 1195429 1195459 1195463 1195477 1195483 1195489 1195501 1195543
1195547 1195549 1195561 1195567 1195573 1195589 1195669 1195673 1195679 1195681
1195693 1195703 1195709 1195721 1195723 1195741 1195751 1195759 1195771 1195801
1195807 1195811 1195837 1195849 1195891 1195897 1195907 1195919 1195927 1195937
1195979 1195991 1196003 1196029 1196033 1196059 1196077 1196087 1196089 1196119
1196123 1196141 1196177 1196191 1196201 1196219 1196227 1196231 1196267 1196269
1196281 1196287 1196309 1196323 1196329 1196347 1196357 1196359 1196399 1196401
1196413 1196431 1196471 1196473 1196491 1196501 1196509 1196513 1196519 1196521
1196537 1196539 1196593 1196597 1196603 1196609 1196653 1196663 1196683 1196707
1196717 1196719 1196729 1196731 1196773 1196809 1196813 1196837 1196843 1196857
1196861 1196863 1196869 1196873 1196891 1196911 1196927 1196939 1196959 1196999
1197011 1197013 1197017 1197029 1197037 1197041 1197059 1197067 1197073 1197103
1197107 1197113 1197121 1197167 1197181 1197187 1197193 1197197 1197199 1197211
1197221 1197239 1197257 1197263 1197269 1197277 1197281 1197289 1197307 1197337
1197347 1197349 1197353 1197359 1197367 1197389 1197407 1197409 1197433 1197451
1197467 1197473 1197479 1197509 1197527 1197571 1197577 1197601 1197617 1197619
1197631 1197649 1197697 1197709 1197733 1197743 1197751 1197767 1197799 1197821
1197827 1197829 1197881 1197901 1197907 1197923 1197929 1197941 1197947 1197953
1197971 1197997 1198013 1198033 1198037 1198049 1198051 1198063 1198069 1198073
1198081 1198103 1198123 1198133 1198151 1198157 1198187 1198189 1198201 1198217
1198229 1198247 1198259 1198261 1198289 1198291 1198297 1198303 1198321 1198343
1198363 1198397 1198399 1198403 1198411 1198427 1198433 1198447 1198451
1198469 1198481 1198511 1198513 1198523 1198537 1198583 1198607 1198609 1198621
1198643 1198651 1198661 1198669 1198679 1198699 1198727 1198751 1198783 1198811
1198819 1198849 1198853 1198861 1198867 1198877 1198903 1198927 1198949 1198973
1198979 1198991 1198997 1198999 1199003 1199047 1199069 1199083 1199087 1199089
1199117 1199123 1199131 1199137 1199167 1199183 1199189 1199203 1199257 1199309
1199329 1199351 1199357 1199369 1199371 1199377 1199389 1199417 1199423 1199437
1199441 1199447 1199459 1199461 1199467 1199477 1199491 1199507 1199509 1199521
1199551 1199557 1199573 1199587 1199591 1199593 1199617 1199621 1199623 1199629
1199659 1199663 1199677 1199683 1199689 1199699 1199711 1199719 1199767 1199777
1199789 1199801 1199813 1199819 1199833 1199839 1199851 1199857 1199879 1199893
1199899 1199909 1199923 1199929 1199953 1199969 1199993 1199999 1200007 1200061
1200077 1200083 1200109 1200139 1200161 1200167 1200179 1200187 1200191 1200233
1200253 1200307 1200313 1200323 1200341 1200349 1200359 1200361 1200371 1200373
1200377 1200383 1200389 1200403 1200443 1200449 1200461 1200467 1200491 1200499
1200509 1200527 1200581 1200583 1200607 1200611 1200637 1200643 1200673 1200679
1200691 1200697 1200701 1200739 1200751 1200779 1200799 1200809 1200811 1200833
1200859 1200869 1200883 1200887 1200889 1200917 1200929 1200937 1200943 1200949
1200959 1200989 1201001 1201003 1201019 1201021 1201027 1201043 1201049 1201061
1201073 1201087 1201097 1201103 1201111 1201117 1201141 1201153 1201163 1201171
1201183 1201201 1201217 1201229 1201241 1201247 1201261 1201283 1201307 1201309
1201327 1201337 1201381 1201439 1201469 1201481 1201483 1201489 1201493 1201513
1201523 1201531 1201553 1201559 1201567 1201583 1201601 1201633 1201637 1201643
1201687 1201691 1201699 1201703 1201709 1201729 1201787 1201793 1201813 1201829
1201841 1201843 1201853 1201873 1201909 1201919 1201933 1201961 1201969 1201999
1202009 1202017 1202023 1202027 1202029 1202041 1202057 1202063 1202077 1202081
1202099 1202107 1202129 1202147 1202153 1202183 1202191 1202219 1202221 1202231
1202239 1202251 1202261 1202269 1202293 1202303 1202317 1202321 1202329 1202347
1202363 1202387 1202423 1202429 1202437 1202447 1202471 1202473 1202477 1202483
1202497 1202501 1202507 1202549 1202561 1202569 1202603 1202609 1202627 1202629
1202633 1202689 1202741 1202743 1202771 1202779 1202783 1202791 1202807 1202813
1202819 1202827 1202837 1202843 1202849 1202857 1202863 1202867 1202881 1202939
1202959 1202963 1202977 1202987 1203019 1203067 1203077 1203101 1203121 1203127
1203149 1203151 1203161 1203179 1203193 1203211 1203217 1203221 1203229 1203233
1203263 1203283 1203287 1203329 1203331 1203343 1203359 1203361 1203421 1203437
1203443 1203457 1203463 1203467 1203487 1203493 1203509 1203533 1203557 1203571
1203581 1203607 1203611 1203619 1203641 1203661 1203667 1203689 1203691 1203731
1203733 1203739 1203757 1203773 1203779 1203791 1203793 1203799 1203809 1203817
1203827 1203841 1203863 1203887 1203893 1203899 1203901 1203913 1203919 1203929
1203931 1203941 1203949 1203953 1203959 1203971 1204003 1204019 1204037 1204097
1204103 1204117 1204139 1204141 1204153 1204169 1204171 1204183 1204207 1204219
```

```
1204243  1204271  1204279  1204289  1204309  1204337  1204363  1204369  1204397  1204409
1204421  1204447  1204451  1204453  1204471  1204477  1204493  1204507  1204519  1204529
1204561  1204583  1204597  1204607  1204613  1204633  1204649  1204669  1204681  1204699
1204711  1204729  1204741  1204781  1204783  1204787  1204813  1204823  1204859  1204871
1204873  1204883  1204891  1204937  1204967  1204969  1204981  1205027  1205047  1205081
1205089  1205093  1205101  1205117  1205119  1205123  1205159  1205173  1205179  1205219
1205231  1205251  1205257  1205287  1205293  1205339  1205377  1205383  1205411  1205437
1205447  1205459  1205467  1205471  1205473  1205489  1205513  1205527  1205537  1205539
1205549  1205557  1205563  1205609  1205627  1205629  1205639  1205647  1205653  1205663
1205669  1205681  1205693  1205707  1205713  1205717  1205731  1205749  1205753  1205767
1205773  1205779  1205819  1205843  1205891  1205899  1205903  1205921  1205947  1205951
1205969  1205977  1205999  1206013  1206017  1206043  1206053  1206059  1206061  1206071
1206113  1206131  1206151  1206157  1206169  1206173  1206181  1206187  1206199  1206209
1206223  1206229  1206259  1206263  1206277  1206307  1206319  1206323  1206341  1206347
1206353  1206377  1206383  1206391  1206407  1206433  1206449  1206461  1206467  1206479
1206497  1206529  1206539  1206553  1206563  1206577  1206581  1206587  1206619  1206637
1206679  1206683  1206691  1206701  1206703  1206713  1206721  1206731  1206743  1206749
1206761  1206767  1206769  1206773  1206781  1206791  1206809  1206827  1206841  1206869
1206941  1206973  1206979  1207001  1207027  1207033  1207039  1207043  1207079  1207093
1207097  1207111  1207117  1207121  1207123  1207133  1207147  1207159  1207211  1207223
1207237  1207249  1207259  1207267  1207291  1207307  1207309  1207313  1207319  1207331
1207343  1207351  1207363  1207379  1207387  1207403  1207417  1207429  1207439  1207441
1207447  1207489  1207501  1207511  1207519  1207529  1207537  1207597  1207603  1207627
1207649  1207681  1207699  1207721  1207727  1207751  1207757  1207769  1207841  1207883
1207903  1207909  1207919  1207933  1207957  1207961  1207979  1207981  1208017  1208021
1208023  1208027  1208033  1208057  1208069  1208089  1208113  1208117  1208131  1208149
1208159  1208177  1208189  1208209  1208219  1208237  1208239  1208243  1208269  1208279
1208297  1208299  1208303  1208341  1208371  1208387  1208399  1208407  1208413  1208423
1208447  1208461  1208507  1208521  1208561  1208569  1208573  1208591  1208651  1208657
1208663  1208677  1208681  1208689  1208707  1208731  1208741  1208777  1208789  1208791
1208797  1208813  1208821  1208833  1208843  1208849  1208863  1208873  1208927  1208939
1208941  1208957  1209007  1209017  1209029  1209053  1209073  1209079  1209083  1209107
1209113  1209121  1209139  1209151  1209163  1209181  1209191  1209199  1209209  1209223
1209233  1209239  1209251  1209269  1209277  1209281  1209287  1209311  1209337  1209347
1209353  1209367  1209379  1209427  1209437  1209457  1209463  1209469  1209487  1209491
1209517  1209539  1209557  1209563  1209577  1209583  1209587  1209617  1209629  1209631
1209647  1209671  1209697  1209707  1209709  1209739  1209757  1209763  1209773  1209779
1209781  1209809  1209811  1209821  1209841  1209853  1209877  1209883  1209889  1209931
1209947  1209959  1209973  1209979  1210003  1210019  1210037  1210039  1210049
1210051  1210067  1210093  1210103  1210123  1210127  1210151  1210163  1210169  1210177
1210193  1210207  1210211  1210229  1210241  1210259  1210289  1210351  1210369  1210379
1210387  1210393  1210397  1210399  1210403  1210409  1210411  1210427  1210439  1210441
1210459  1210477  1210483  1210499  1210523  1210541  1210549  1210597  1210609  1210613
1210631  1210637  1210639  1210711  1210717  1210747  1210753  1210777  1210787  1210793
1210799  1210801  1210817  1210819  1210831  1210843  1210871  1210873  1210877  1210879
1210883  1210897  1210903  1210921  1210933  1210939  1210949  1210967  1210987  1210999
1211027  1211039  1211051  1211057  1211059  1211081  1211083  1211087  1211141  1211167
1211179  1211183  1211191  1211207  1211227  1211261  1211279  1211281  1211303  1211311
1211333  1211339  1211381  1211389  1211393  1211407  1211411  1211423  1211443  1211447
1211489  1211501  1211503  1211531  1211537  1211543  1211549  1211563  1211593  1211597
1211599  1211603  1211621  1211629  1211647  1211663  1211657  1211669  1211669  1211677
1211689  1211701  1211719  1211723  1211731  1211737  1211741  1211761  1211767  1211779
1211789  1211797  1211807  1211813  1211827  1211843  1211857  1211863  1211897  1211911
1211921  1211923  1211933  1211983  1211999  1212011  1212017  1212023  1212047  1212053
1212061  1212103  1212119  1212121  1212149  1212173  1212187  1212191  1212199  1212221
1212227  1212241  1212251  1212259  1212283  1212293  1212301  1212319  1212331  1212347
1212361  1212373  1212397  1212401  1212427  1212433  1212437  1212439  1212443  1212473
1212479  1212487  1212517  1212521  1212551  1212559  1212611  1212613  1212641  1212649
1212671  1212677  1212683  1212697  1212703  1212709  1212719  1212737  1212769  1212773
1212781  1212787  1212793  1212811  1212817  1212839  1212847  1212851  1212853  1212857
1212877  1212889  1212907  1212917  1212919  1212923  1212931  1212943  1212973  1212989
1213007  1213019  1213021  1213027  1213033  1213049  1213057  1213063  1213081  1213087
1213097  1213109  1213129  1213133  1213141  1213151  1213153  1213183  1213189  1213213
1213241  1213253  1213259  1213271  1213301  1213327  1213339  1213357  1213367  1213379
1213427  1213439  1213451  1213469  1213481  1213483  1213517  1213529  1213547  1213561
1213577  1213577  1213591  1213601  1213607  1213627  1213631  1213633  1213643  1213651
1213657  1213661  1213673  1213721  1213741  1213747  1213757  1213759  1213763  1213781
1213801  1213829  1213837  1213841  1213873  1213879  1213897  1213907  1213909  1213913
1213921  1213931  1213939  1213943  1213951  1213981  1214011  1214023  1214039  1214047
1214077  1214093  1214113  1214117  1214131  1214137  1214141  1214159  1214167  1214183
1214189  1214197  1214219  1214221  1214237  1214261  1214273  1214281  1214299  1214333
1214357  1214371  1214393  1214401  1214407  1214413  1214417  1214431  1214441  1214453
1214459  1214471  1214483  1214489  1214519  1214533  1214567  1214573  1214579  1214593
1214617  1214623  1214639  1214641  1214657  1214659  1214663  1214669  1214671  1214683
1214687  1214711  1214729  1214737  1214743  1214749  1214767  1214819  1214827  1214849
1214867  1214891  1214909  1214923  1214933  1214947  1214957  1214959  1214963  1214971
1214977  1214981  1215017  1215029  1215047  1215079  1215083  1215103  1215121  1215133
1215157  1215161  1215167  1215173  1215197  1215209  1215229  1215239  1215271  1215283
1215299  1215301  1215311  1215329  1215349  1215359  1215367  1215391  1215397  1215407
1215421  1215433  1215437  1215439  1215451  1215457  1215463  1215497  1215499  1215509
1215521  1215553  1215569  1215583  1215587  1215623  1215629  1215631  1215637  1215647
1215649  1215673  1215679  1215703  1215719  1215743  1215769  1215779  1215787  1215827
1215839  1215847  1215853  1215859  1215881  1215899  1215917  1215919  1215923  1216009
1216013  1216021  1216043  1216067  1216069  1216087  1216091  1216109  1216123  1216147
1216151  1216177  1216213  1216249  1216273  1216277  1216337  1216339  1216349  1216351
1216373  1216379  1216387  1216393  1216417  1216421  1216433  1216441  1216451  1216459
1216489  1216507  1216529  1216543  1216547  1216559  1216561  1216577  1216583  1216591
1216601  1216603  1216619  1216681  1216693  1216711  1216717  1216729  1216751  1216759
1216763  1216777  1216793  1216799  1216807  1216823  1216841  1216847  1216849  1216867
```

```
1216871  1216879  1216903  1216913  1216937  1216939  1216951  1216961  1216973  1216987
1216997  1217009  1217017  1217023  1217033  1217053  1217057  1217063  1217071  1217077
1217089  1217093  1217107  1217113  1217119  1217131  1217141  1217143  1217147  1217171
1217179  1217191  1217207  1217213  1217219  1217233  1217261  1217269  1217297  1217299
1217303  1217309  1217317  1217329  1217351  1217393  1217399  1217407  1217417  1217423
1217443  1217467  1217471  1217473  1217477  1217483  1217509  1217521  1217533  1217537
1217561  1217617  1217647  1217651  1217663  1217669  1217677  1217683  1217687  1217719
1217731  1217753  1217759  1217771  1217809  1217813  1217831  1217833  1217861  1217893
1217899  1217903  1217917  1217921  1217927  1217933  1217941  1217947  1217963  1217977
1217989  1218017  1218043  1218089  1218121  1218131  1218157  1218167  1218179  1218197
1218199  1218209  1218211  1218221  1218247  1218251  1218257  1218263  1218277  1218281
1218307  1218313  1218367  1218383  1218391  1218401  1218421  1218433  1218449  1218457
1218463  1218467  1218473  1218487  1218533  1218557  1218559  1218571  1218583  1218601
1218617  1218631  1218649  1218653  1218683  1218691  1218709  1218717  1218731  1218739
1218761  1218773  1218787  1218797  1218821  1218829  1218853  1218859  1218901  1218911
1218913  1218923  1218941  1218949  1218953  1218989  1218991  1219003  1219061  1219081
1219091  1219109  1219111  1219123  1219129  1219147  1219177  1219213  1219237  1219241
1219271  1219279  1219297  1219301  1219303  1219307  1219313  1219343  1219349  1219357
1219399  1219411  1219433  1219453  1219457  1219469  1219481  1219487  1219489  1219501
1219507  1219549  1219577  1219607  1219613  1219619  1219639  1219643  1219649  1219651
1219657  1219663  1219679  1219703  1219717  1219721  1219727  1219739  1219747  1219753
1219763  1219783  1219787  1219789  1219793  1219807  1219811  1219831  1219837  1219843
1219847  1219849  1219859  1219861  1219871  1219877  1219879  1219891  1219909  1219913
1219919  1219931  1219949  1219951  1219957  1219971  1219981  1219993  1220027  1220029
1220041  1220071  1220077  1220099  1220147  1220171  1220203  1220239  1220249  1220251
1220257  1220309  1220327  1220333  1220347  1220353  1220363  1220369  1220393  1220411
1220423  1220437  1220483  1220491  1220497  1220507  1220591  1220599  1220623  1220657
1220663  1220669  1220689  1220699  1220711  1220717  1220729  1220743  1220761  1220773
1220797  1220813  1220827  1220861  1220869  1220833  1220839  1220883  1221019  1221029
1221049  1221061  1221079  1221083  1221089  1221097  1221113  1221119  1221131  1221163
1221167  1221193  1221197  1221221  1221223  1221239  1221247  1221251  1221289  1221299
1221373  1221379  1221383  1221391  1221421  1221427  1221443  1221449  1221457  1221463
1221469  1221499  1221503  1221523  1221527  1221533  1221541  1221551  1221557  1221559
1221589  1221593  1221601  1221631  1221641  1221653  1221659  1221667  1221707  1221749
1221751  1221761  1221767  1221791  1221793  1221811  1221821  1221823  1221853  1221863
1221907  1221917  1221937  1221959  1221971  1222003  1222019  1222027  1222037  1222049
1222057  1222063  1222097  1222129  1222157  1222159  1222171  1222187  1222219  1222229
1222231  1222241  1222253  1222259  1222267  1222271  1222279  1222307  1222373  1222393
1222409  1222411  1222433  1222471  1222483  1222493  1222499  1222513  1222523  1222537
1222561  1222567  1222583  1222597  1222601  1222603  1222633  1222643  1222651  1222667
1222679  1222681  1222693  1222717  1222723  1222729  1222751  1222757  1222769  1222777
1222789  1222801  1222811  1222829  1222831  1222847  1222853  1222889  1222909  1222913
1222931  1222943  1222957  1222967  1222993  1223003  1223021  1223029  1223039  1223051
1223059  1223077  1223083  1223093  1223119  1223149  1223161  1223177  1223179  1223197
1223203  1223207  1223231  1223237  1223263  1223279  1223281  1223309  1223311  1223323
1223329  1223351  1223357  1223381  1223419  1223437  1223447  1223449  1223459  1223471
1223489  1223491  1223527  1223533  1223549  1223561  1223569  1223587  1223591  1223603
1223633  1223683  1223687  1223689  1223693  1223723  1223731  1223749  1223753  1223767
1223773  1223777  1223857  1223863  1223867  1223879  1223897  1223921  1223939  1223941
1223953  1223977  1223987  1223993  1224029  1224031  1224053  1224059  1224077  1224079
1224089  1224109  1224121  1224131  1224133  1224149  1224163  1224169  1224193  1224203
1224217  1224229  1224233  1224239  1224257  1224259  1224269  1224271  1224281  1224287
1224299  1224329  1224337  1224347  1224389  1224403  1224413  1224437  1224439  1224473
1224479  1224481  1224529  1224533  1224577  1224599  1224637  1224673  1224677  1224701
1224703  1224709  1224751  1224763  1224767  1224809  1224823  1224851  1224859  1224869
1224863  1224869  1224887  1224889  1224893  1224913  1224919  1224943  1224953  1224967
1224973  1224983  1224991  1225009  1225019  1225061  1225067  1225073  1225079  1225087
1225093  1225097  1225109  1225111  1225117  1225123  1225127  1225129  1225147  1225153
1225157  1225183  1225219  1225223  1225261  1225283  1225297  1225303  1225319  1225327
1225331  1225361  1225373  1225381  1225397  1225453  1225459  1225493  1225501  1225507
1225517  1225529  1225541  1225559  1225571  1225577  1225579  1225589  1225591  1225603
1225621  1225643  1225657  1225663  1225687  1225691  1225703  1225723  1225727  1225729
1225759  1225769  1225787  1225817  1225849  1225871  1225883  1225891  1225897
1225907  1225909  1225919  1225927  1225933  1225949  1225963  1225981  1225997  1225999
1226011  1226041  1226053  1226063  1226077  1226083  1226087  1226101  1226111  1226117
1226179  1226189  1226191  1226209  1226213  1226237  1226257  1226263  1226293  1226297
1226299  1226311  1226321  1226339  1226341  1226347  1226353  1226377  1226387  1226417
1226461  1226471  1226479  1226483  1226501  1226503  1226531  1226539  1226549  1226557
1226581  1226593  1226609  1226611  1226623  1226629  1226651  1226663  1226677  1226681
1226683  1226699  1226707  1226711  1226713  1226741  1226767  1226779  1226783  1226789
1226801  1226803  1226807  1226821  1226831  1226851  1226857  1226861  1226867  1226891
1226899  1226959  1226977  1226983  1226993  1227047  1227053  1227101  1227103  1227131
1227133  1227143  1227151  1227157  1227167  1227173  1227241  1227271  1227277
1227299  1227301  1227319  1227323  1227329  1227337  1227353  1227379  1227407  1227431
1227437  1227463  1227469  1227491  1227497  1227539  1227547  1227559  1227563  1227619
1227637  1227649  1227659  1227683  1227701  1227703  1227713  1227719  1227769  1227797
1227829  1227833  1227841  1227847  1227871  1227881  1227887  1227911  1227917  1227929
1227943  1227949  1227973  1227977  1227979  1227983  1228001  1228009  1228013  1228021
1228091  1228099  1228109  1228133  1228147  1228153  1228159  1228163  1228181  1228187
1228193  1228219  1228243  1228247  1228273  1228277  1228291  1228303  1228309  1228327
1228333  1228351  1228373  1228391  1228393  1228397  1228399  1228429  1228441  1228457
1228469  1228489  1228501  1228519  1228537  1228541  1228543  1228547  1228567  1228571
1228583  1228589  1228603  1228613  1228631  1228651  1228657  1228679  1228691  1228693
1228741  1228763  1228783  1228789  1228837  1228841  1228849  1228859  1228883  1228889
1228891  1228907  1228919  1228937  1228943  1228949  1228951  1228961  1228963  1228987
1228993  1229021  1229023  1229071  1229077  1229093  1229113  1229131  1229141  1229149
1229159  1229197  1229201  1229203  1229209  1229213  1229227  1229237  1229257  1229269
1229273  1229279  1229297  1229309  1229311  1229317  1229329  1229351  1229353  1229359
```

```
1229369  1229377  1229381  1229401  1229443  1229447  1229453  1229461  1229483  1229489
1229519  1229521  1229531  1229561  1229563  1229581  1229597  1229617  1229633  1229647
1229663  1229689  1229707  1229719  1229731  1229743  1229773  1229783  1229807  1229827
1229869  1229873  1229897  1229903  1229911  1229939  1229941  1229957  1229981  1229993
1229999  1230013  1230023  1230029  1230067  1230071  1230107  1230127  1230167  1230169
1230181  1230199  1230223  1230227  1230233  1230241  1230263  1230301  1230311  1230329
1230331  1230337  1230343  1230347  1230349  1230367  1230371  1230373  1230377  1230379
1230391  1230401  1230433  1230461  1230469  1230479  1230491  1230521  1230529  1230539
1230547  1230571  1230587  1230599  1230629  1230631  1230637  1230667  1230689  1230727
1230739  1230743  1230751  1230769  1230791  1230829  1230863  1230869  1230871  1230881
1230907  1230913  1230941  1230949  1230967  1230997  1231001  1231003  1231039  1231049
1231051  1231063  1231073  1231091  1231093  1231099  1231127  1231129  1231141  1231171
1231177  1231193  1231199  1231201  1231207  1231229  1231231  1231247  1231261  1231267
1231277  1231283  1231301  1231303  1231309  1231313  1231319  1231337  1231339  1231357
1231379  1231381  1231387  1231411  1231421  1231423  1231453  1231457  1231459  1231469
1231481  1231487  1231511  1231513  1231547  1231553  1231577  1231579  1231589  1231597
1231613  1231631  1231663  1231669  1231687  1231691  1231697  1231709  1231721  1231733
1231753  1231757  1231771  1231781  1231787  1231799  1231807  1231817  1231829  1231831
1231843  1231859  1231873  1231877  1231883  1231889  1231943  1231961  1231981  1231987
1231999  1232003  1232069  1232071  1232083  1232089  1232171  1232183  1232201  1232213
1232221  1232227  1232243  1232269  1232291  1232299  1232327  1232339  1232351  1232353
1232377  1232389  1232393  1232401  1232411  1232417  1232431  1232437  1232453  1232461
1232477  1232527  1232531  1232537  1232563  1232573  1232603  1232611  1232617  1232657
1232659  1232683  1232689  1232713  1232719  1232771  1232797  1232801  1232809  1232831
1232843  1232849  1232851  1232879  1232893  1232909  1232941  1232947  1232977  1232981
1232983  1232999  1233019  1233047  1233073  1233079  1233097  1233101  1233107  1233121
1233143  1233179  1233181  1233187  1233209  1233241  1233251  1233259  1233263  1233301
1233313  1233319  1233361  1233371  1233373  1233377  1233409  1233431  1233433  1233437
1233439  1233473  1233493  1233497  1233509  1233523  1233527  1233539  1233563  1233569
1233577  1233587  1233593  1233599  1233607  1233611  1233619  1233641  1233647  1233653
1233709  1233721  1233751  1233761  1233763  1233779  1233781  1233851  1233887  1233899
1233907  1233923  1233929  1233949  1233983  1234001  1234003  1234039  1234049  1234063
1234067  1234099  1234109  1234117  1234133  1234147  1234187  1234231  1234237  1234241
1234243  1234253  1234271  1234309  1234333  1234349  1234351  1234367  1234379  1234391
1234393  1234417  1234439  1234463  1234511  1234517  1234531  1234537  1234543  1234547
1234577  1234603  1234613  1234627  1234657  1234687  1234703  1234721  1234747  1234757
1234759  1234769  1234777  1234787  1234789  1234799  1234813  1234819  1234837  1234841
1234843  1234853  1234873  1234889  1234901  1234951  1234967  1234969  1234991  1235021
1235027  1235041  1235063  1235083  1235093  1235099  1235131  1235137  1235141  1235159
1235159  1235167  1235177  1235183  1235191  1235239  1235243  1235249  1235251  1235263
1235281  1235287  1235303  1235309  1235321  1235327  1235363  1235369  1235383  1235389
1235417  1235419  1235431  1235447  1235449  1235459  1235473  1235477  1235497  1235501
1235503  1235539  1235569  1235573  1235593  1235651  1235653  1235659  1235669  1235701
1235711  1235761  1235789  1235791  1235803  1235807  1235821  1235831  1235833  1235867
1235879  1235887  1235891  1235909  1235929  1235933  1235947  1235977  1235981  1235987
1235999  1236017  1236073  1236077  1236161  1236163  1236173  1236203  1236211  1236229
1236233  1236239  1236259  1236307  1236317  1236329  1236337  1236383  1236397  1236419
1236439  1236449  1236467  1236479  1236481  1236491  1236517  1236527  1236533  1236541
1236553  1236583  1236611  1236623  1236629  1236643  1236659  1236661  1236667  1236701
1236709  1236713  1236727  1236737  1236743  1236751  1236757  1236761  1236769  1236787
1236791  1236797  1236803  1236811  1236827  1236857  1236883  1236901  1236953  1236959
1236979  1237001  1237013  1237031  1237037  1237043  1237051  1237057  1237063  1237079
1237091  1237121  1237129  1237139  1237151  1237163  1237177  1237199  1237207  1237211
1237213  1237217  1237231  1237253  1237273  1237279  1237283  1237297  1237309  1237349
1237363  1237373  1237387  1237393  1237403  1237417  1237433  1237441  1237471  1237487
1237493  1237499  1237501  1237513  1237519  1237529  1237531  1237543  1237547  1237567
1237571  1237589  1237619  1237627  1237661  1237721  1237727  1237739  1237757  1237763
1237783  1237813  1237823  1237829  1237843  1237849  1237853  1237867  1237877  1237897
1237919  1237931  1237939  1237949  1237961  1237963  1237967  1237973  1237993  1238023  1238033
1238051  1238063  1238071  1238087  1238089  1238101  1238119  1238129  1238137  1238177
1238179  1238189  1238197  1238201  1238219  1238267  1238269  1238273  1238291  1238317
1238327  1238333  1238371  1238381  1238383  1238407  1238411  1238423  1238429  1238431
1238437  1238449  1238459  1238491  1238509  1238521  1238533  1238537  1238551  1238557
1238599  1238621  1238647  1238659  1238681  1238683  1238687  1238693  1238717  1238719
1238747  1238749  1238759  1238761  1238767  1238771  1238789  1238801  1238821  1238827
1238833  1238843  1238863  1238893  1238903  1238911  1238921  1238947  1238989
1238999  1239001  1239013  1239023  1239041  1239067  1239089  1239103  1239109  1239127
1239151  1239179  1239191  1239197  1239223  1239229  1239239  1239247  1239269  1239281
1239311  1239319  1239323  1239341  1239347  1239353  1239361  1239367  1239377  1239379
1239397  1239421  1239443  1239449  1239457  1239461  1239481  1239499  1239509  1239517
1239523  1239529  1239533  1239551  1239569  1239583  1239593  1239599  1239607  1239619
1239643  1239661  1239671  1239697  1239727  1239737  1239739  1239751  1239761  1239773
1239803  1239817  1239839  1239877  1239899  1239911  1239913  1239919  1239923
1239943  1239961  1239971  1239983  1239989  1240007  1240009  1240013  1240021  1240027
1240039  1240081  1240087  1240097  1240117  1240139  1240153  1240159  1240181  1240193
1240199  1240207  1240219  1240231  1240241  1240247  1240271  1240273  1240307  1240319
1240333  1240361  1240363  1240387  1240391  1240399  1240423  1240483  1240507  1240511
1240517  1240523  1240543  1240553  1240559  1240607  1240621  1240637  1240667  1240669
1240691  1240699  1240703  1240709  1240717  1240739  1240741  1240751  1240763  1240769
1240777  1240793  1240807  1240817  1240831  1240861  1240901  1240931  1240957  1240973
1240979  1240991  1240999  1241003  1241027  1241033  1241039  1241059  1241077  1241081
1241087  1241159  1241161  1241173  1241197  1241203  1241243  1241249  1241257  1241263
1241267  1241269  1241291  1241321  1241341  1241347  1241351  1241369  1241377  1241381
1241389  1241407  1241413  1241417  1241423  1241437  1241447  1241467  1241477  1241483
1241489  1241491  1241507  1241509  1241549  1241551  1241557  1241573  1241579  1241587
1241627  1241651  1241659  1241677  1241699  1241741  1241743  1241761  1241771  1241789
1241813  1241819  1241827  1241869  1241879  1241893  1241921  1241923  1241927  1241939
1241941  1241951  1241957  1241963  1241971  1241987  1242001  1242029  1242061  1242067
1242089  1242097  1242103  1242107  1242119  1242121  1242151  1242167  1242169  1242181
```

```
1242191  1242193  1242217  1242221  1242233  1242251  1242271  1242289  1242317  1242347
1242359  1242361  1242379  1242403  1242407  1242413  1242419  1242421  1242457  1242487
1242503  1242517  1242569  1242601  1242611  1242617  1242623  1242629  1242641  1242643
1242739  1242757  1242763  1242767  1242781  1242803  1242811  1242817  1242823  1242827
1242841  1242859  1242869  1242889  1242893  1242929  1242931  1242937  1242947  1242959
1242977  1242979  1242991  1243003  1243013  1243093  1243097  1243111  1243129  1243133
1243141  1243147  1243157  1243169  1243181  1243211  1243271  1243273  1243309  1243337
1243343  1243349  1243367  1243369  1243373  1243387  1243391  1243393  1243421  1243427
1243439  1243471  1243477  1243481  1243483  1243511  1243523  1243537  1243547  1243559
1243577  1243579  1243609  1243631  1243639  1243643  1243663  1243673  1243691  1243709
1243717  1243741  1243747  1243783  1243789  1243793  1243807  1243811  1243819  1243841
1243843  1243859  1243877  1243883  1243889  1243927  1243933  1243939  1243943  1243951
1243961  1243967  1243969  1243997  1244003  1244021  1244027  1244029  1244039  1244041
1244053  1244057  1244059  1244083  1244099  1244141  1244143  1244149  1244153  1244167
1244183  1244197  1244203  1244233  1244249  1244261  1244263  1244279  1244293  1244333
1244357  1244359  1244363  1244381  1244393  1244401  1244423  1244429  1244437  1244447
1244449  1244471  1244479  1244483  1244501  1244521  1244531  1244533  1244543  1244567
1244591  1244603  1244609  1244611  1244627  1244629  1244647  1244687  1244699  1244713
1244729  1244741  1244753  1244759  1244777  1244797  1244813  1244819  1244821  1244833
1244839  1244857  1244863  1244879  1244909  1244911  1244923  1244953  1244987  1244989
1244993  1245001  1245017  1245019  1245037  1245067  1245091  1245103  1245113  1245121
1245137  1245149  1245169  1245187  1245191  1245217  1245227  1245281  1245331  1245353
1245379  1245397  1245401  1245421  1245449  1245451  1245479  1245509  1245527  1245529
1245551  1245557  1245589  1245613  1245617  1245619  1245623  1245653  1245683  1245689
1245691  1245701  1245707  1245719  1245721  1245763  1245767  1245779  1245781  1245791
1245799  1245817  1245833  1245847  1245863  1245877  1245883  1245917  1245929  1245943
1245953  1245961  1245971  1245973  1246013  1246033  1246057  1246061  1246073  1246081
1246093  1246099  1246103  1246181  1246187  1246199  1246207  1246213  1246241  1246243
1246247  1246249  1246261  1246283  1246303  1246307  1246313  1246319  1246327  1246331
1246339  1246351  1246361  1246363  1246367  1246369  1246373  1246379  1246387  1246397
1246429  1246433  1246451  1246459  1246471  1246477  1246481  1246489  1246499  1246501
1246513  1246517  1246529  1246537  1246543  1246561  1246573  1246579  1246589  1246591
1246601  1246631  1246639  1246667  1246673  1246697  1246703  1246711  1246733  1246747
1246757  1246781  1246823  1246829  1246841  1246867  1246879  1246891  1246907  1246919
1246943  1246961  1246963  1246997  1247009  1247017  1247033  1247053  1247063  1247089
1247101  1247107  1247117  1247119  1247167  1247177  1247189  1247209  1247231  1247243
1247263  1247269  1247291  1247297  1247303  1247317  1247321  1247327  1247329  1247371
1247383  1247401  1247417  1247419  1247429  1247447  1247453  1247459  1247479  1247501
1247509  1247527  1247549  1247557  1247563  1247569  1247581  1247591  1247599  1247611
1247621  1247627  1247641  1247651  1247663  1247693  1247699  1247737  1247759  1247761
1247777  1247797  1247801  1247803  1247837  1247861  1247867  1247879  1247887  1247881
1247893  1247923  1247947  1247951  1247959  1247969  1248001  1248007  1248011  1248017
1248019  1248031  1248041  1248059  1248061  1248083  1248101  1248103  1248113  1248119
1248151  1248193  1248199  1248209  1248211  1248217  1248229  1248239  1248241  1248253
1248271  1248323  1248329  1248337  1248341  1248347  1248349  1248353  1248383  1248391
1248407  1248413  1248427  1248449  1248451  1248469  1248493  1248503  1248529  1248539
1248551  1248553  1248563  1248571  1248589  1248593  1248631  1248641  1248671  1248673
1248691  1248697  1248703  1248721  1248757  1248781  1248799  1248809  1248829  1248833
1248847  1248857  1248859  1248869  1248881  1248893  1248917  1248941  1248953  1248977
1248979  1248991  1249013  1249019  1249033  1249037  1249043  1249049  1249057  1249063
1249091  1249099  1249111  1249121  1249133  1249139  1249141  1249151  1249159  1249163
1249187  1249201  1249217  1249243  1249247  1249273  1249301  1249319  1249321  1249333
1249343  1249361  1249363  1249373  1249397  1249411  1249427  1249433  1249477
1249481  1249487  1249499  1249509  1249511  1249519  1249531  1249559  1249603  1249621
1249627  1249631  1249643  1249657  1249669  1249681  1249691  1249693  1249727  1249733
1249739  1249741  1249747  1249757  1249799  1249811  1249817  1249819  1249837  1249841
1249847  1249849  1249861  1249873  1249901  1249921  1249939  1249943  1249999  1250003
1250009  1250021  1250023  1250057  1250069  1250083  1250087  1250099  1250107  1250141
1250147  1250149  1250173  1250177  1250189  1250201  1250207  1250237  1250243  1250273
1250281  1250297  1250309  1250351  1250357  1250407  1250413  1250437  1250443  1250449
1250461  1250467  1250471  1250479  1250497  1250507  1250519  1250521  1250527  1250551
1250593  1250609  1250611  1250629  1250647  1250653  1250677  1250701  1250737  1250749
1250761  1250771  1250779  1250783  1250801  1250813  1250831  1250839  1250867
1250917  1250923  1250929  1250939  1250969  1250971  1250981  1250983  1251011
1251037  1251043  1251053  1251071  1251083  1251097  1251101  1251109  1251121  1251157
1251161  1251179  1251227  1251247  1251259  1251281  1251287  1251301  1251317  1251323
1251329  1251409  1251427  1251431  1251433  1251461  1251463  1251527  1251529  1251533
1251571  1251577  1251581  1251583  1251641  1251661  1251667  1251671  1251697  1251703
1251707  1251713  1251721  1251743  1251787  1251791  1251797  1251827  1251841  1251851
1251857  1251869  1251871  1251881  1251907  1251911  1251919  1251923  1251937  1251947
1251953  1251961  1251983  1252021  1252037  1252049  1252057  1252063  1252073  1252079
1252103  1252109  1252123  1252129  1252151  1252159  1252177  1252187  1252193  1252201
1252211  1252217  1252231  1252247  1252259  1252267  1252283  1252331  1252343  1252357
1252399  1252403  1252411  1252421  1252429  1252439  1252451  1252457  1252469  1252483
1252507  1252523  1252579  1252609  1252631  1252643  1252661  1252681  1252711
1252717  1252721  1252729  1252739  1252751  1252777  1252799  1252817  1252819  1252843
1252873  1252877  1252897  1252903  1252913  1252921  1252943  1252957  1252963  1252987
1252991  1252997  1253011  1253023  1253027  1253047  1253059  1253071  1253089  1253093
1253099  1253111  1253137  1253167  1253171  1253249  1253251  1253261  1253279  1253323
1253327  1253333  1253347  1253377  1253381  1253401  1253437  1253453  1253471  1253479
1253513  1253519  1253521  1253557  1253587  1253591  1253599  1253621  1253627  1253683
1253689  1253701  1253717  1253723  1253729  1253737  1253741  1253761  1253783  1253803
1253831  1253839  1253869  1253851  1253887  1253909  1253911  1253947
1253953  1253963  1253969  1253999  1254013  1254017  1254023  1254031  1254037  1254049
1254053  1254059  1254061  1254079  1254091  1254109  1254119  1254131  1254137  1254151
1254157  1254161  1254179  1254193  1254203  1254217  1254241  1254251  1254257  1254269
1254293  1254301  1254317  1254329  1254367  1254371  1254373  1254377  1254427  1254433
1254467  1254469  1254479  1254497  1254503  1254523  1254527  1254529  1254541  1254553
1254557  1254577  1254593  1254607  1254613  1254619  1254623  1254637  1254647  1254653
```

```
1254661  1254667  1254683  1254689  1254731  1254733  1254739  1254751  1254761  1254767
1254791  1254793  1254823  1254833  1254839  1254863  1254899  1254907  1254941  1254959
1254971  1254983  1254997  1255013  1255021  1255039  1255049  1255063  1255069  1255081
1255103  1255109  1255117  1255123  1255129  1255139  1255147  1255153  1255157  1255169
1255181  1255183  1255187  1255201  1255211  1255237  1255249  1255253  1255259  1255269
1255301  1255307  1255313  1255321  1255333  1255337  1255357  1255361  1255367  1255391
1255393  1255421  1255427  1255451  1255453  1255477  1255519  1255549  1255559  1255567
1255591  1255601  1255609  1255619  1255633  1255651  1255663  1255679  1255687  1255693
1255721  1255747  1255757  1255759  1255799  1255801  1255811  1255829  1255831  1255847
1255861  1255907  1255913  1255927  1255931  1255939  1255949  1255963  1255967  1255993
1255997  1256009  1256023  1256029  1256041  1256063  1256107  1256149  1256161  1256197
1256201  1256209  1256231  1256243  1256267  1256279  1256303  1256323  1256347  1256369
1256383  1256389  1256393  1256407  1256429  1256449  1256477  1256531  1256533  1256543
1256573  1256579  1256587  1256597  1256611  1256617  1256621  1256659  1256681  1256687
1256693  1256707  1256711  1256729  1256737  1256747  1256753  1256777  1256797  1256809
1256813  1256819  1256821  1256837  1256863  1256867  1256873  1256887  1256891  1256897
1256903  1256911  1256917  1256923  1256939  1256953  1256989  1256993  1257013  1257017
1257029  1257041  1257043  1257049  1257071  1257073  1257077  1257079  1257089  1257103
1257119  1257131  1257163  1257169  1257209  1257229  1257233  1257239  1257241  1257247
1257251  1257253  1257281  1257293  1257307  1257313  1257317  1257323  1257331  1257359
1257397  1257409  1257437  1257457  1257461  1257463  1257491  1257493  1257499  1257517
1257521  1257547  1257559  1257563  1257569  1257587  1257589  1257611  1257647  1257653
1257689  1257691  1257713  1257719  1257721  1257749  1257787  1257827  1257829  1257853
1257869  1257889  1257897  1257911  1257931  1257953  1257959  1257961  1257973  1257989
1258001  1258013  1258027  1258039  1258079  1258087  1258097  1258099  1258109  1258133
1258139  1258141  1258151  1258163  1258171  1258177  1258181  1258183  1258207  1258211
1258217  1258219  1258241  1258267  1258291  1258297  1258303  1258319  1258337  1258343
1258349  1258373  1258403  1258409  1258417  1258421  1258423  1258429  1258441  1258451
1258459  1258469  1258471  1258483  1258487  1258511  1258531  1258559  1258589  1258597
1258601  1258627  1258637  1258639  1258643  1258657  1258661  1258667  1258681  1258709
1258711  1258717  1258723  1258753  1258777  1258787  1258793  1258807  1258811  1258819
1258837  1258847  1258871  1258877  1258889  1258903  1258927  1258931  1258937  1258967
1258973  1258993  1259017  1259029  1259033  1259039  1259047  1259051  1259053  1259057
1259077  1259081  1259087  1259099  1259107  1259113  1259123  1259129  1259143  1259171
1259179  1259191  1259213  1259231  1259243  1259249  1259287  1259299  1259317  1259329
1259371  1259389  1259393  1259429  1259449  1259477  1259509  1259527  1259537  1259539
1259543  1259551  1259563  1259569  1259593  1259603  1259627  1259639  1259653  1259659
1259663  1259669  1259677  1259689  1259701  1259737  1259743  1259749  1259759  1259767
1259777  1259803  1259821  1259851  1259873  1259899  1259903  1259927  1259939  1259953
1259977  1259983  1260011  1260019  1260031  1260047  1260059  1260067  1260113  1260121
1260131  1260143  1260157  1260163  1260167  1260169  1260191  1260223  1260269  1260277
1260283  1260293  1260317  1260319  1260323  1260341  1260359  1260361  1260383  1260401
1260419  1260437  1260439  1260461  1260473  1260481  1260487  1260509  1260541  1260547
1260551  1260569  1260577  1260583  1260599  1260629  1260641  1260643  1260661  1260673
1260691  1260713  1260719  1260731  1260733  1260751  1260757  1260767  1260769  1260797
1260799  1260827  1260829  1260841  1260851  1260877  1260881  1260887  1260893  1260899
1260901  1260911  1260971  1260979  1260989  1260991  1261033  1261069  1261079  1261081
1261109  1261121  1261133  1261157  1261171  1261177  1261199  1261217  1261223  1261259
1261261  1261279  1261289  1261301  1261313  1261321  1261327  1261333  1261357  1261363
1261373  1261387  1261411  1261427  1261459  1261487  1261489  1261523  1261531  1261549
1261567  1261571  1261627  1261639  1261643  1261649  1261697  1261699  1261717  1261721
1261739  1261747  1261759  1261763  1261769  1261789  1261801  1261823  1261829  1261831
1261837  1261861  1261889  1261891  1261901  1261913  1261933  1261943  1261963  1261969
1261973  1262011  1262017  1262057  1262071  1262081  1262083  1262087  1262099  1262101
1262119  1262143  1262147  1262203  1262207  1262221  1262231  1262237  1262269  1262281
1262291  1262293  1262299  1262311  1262321  1262363  1262377  1262411  1262419  1262441
1262453  1262461  1262479  1262483  1262491  1262509  1262519  1262543  1262557  1262563
1262581  1262587  1262617  1262621  1262623  1262629  1262653  1262669  1262671  1262693
1262711  1262713  1262717  1262731  1262741  1262753  1262771  1262783  1262819  1262839
1262851  1262869  1262881  1262887  1262893  1262897  1262903  1262917  1262927  1262929
1262939  1262941  1262957  1263007  1263047  1263071  1263077  1263079  1263103  1263107
1263109  1263113  1263121  1263133  1263173  1263179  1263181  1263187  1263191  1263193
1263209  1263239  1263247  1263259  1263263  1263299  1263307  1263319  1263323  1263331
1263337  1263341  1263347  1263373  1263377  1263391  1263403  1263461  1263463  1263473
1263487  1263499  1263503  1263511  1263539  1263541  1263547  1263569  1263583  1263599
1263607  1263629  1263631  1263659  1263667  1263677  1263697  1263701  1263751  1263761
1263767  1263793  1263799  1263803  1263817  1263853  1263863  1263887  1263917  1263929
1263931  1263943  1263947  1263949  1263953  1263961  1263973  1263979  1264009  1264027
1264033  1264037  1264049  1264061  1264063  1264129  1264177  1264189  1264199  1264213
1264231  1264259  1264261  1264267  1264271  1264301  1264303  1264331  1264337  1264363
1264387  1264411  1264447  1264451  1264499  1264537  1264541  1264559  1264561  1264573
1264577  1264597  1264607  1264643  1264649  1264651  1264657  1264663  1264667  1264687
1264699  1264733  1264741  1264763  1264787  1264801  1264807  1264819  1264829  1264853
1264859  1264867  1264873  1264877  1264883  1264889  1264897  1264903  1264909  1264933
1264969  1264979  1264981  1264987  1265029  1265041  1265051  1265053  1265063  1265081
1265083  1265087  1265093  1265101  1265111  1265113  1265119  1265129  1265167  1265177
1265179  1265197  1265233  1265249  1265273  1265279  1265281  1265311  1265321  1265333
1265347  1265353  1265377  1265387  1265393  1265431  1265443  1265449  1265461  1265471
1265477  1265479  1265503  1265519  1265521  1265527  1265549  1265557  1265573  1265581
1265597  1265603  1265611  1265617  1265623  1265639  1265653  1265657  1265681  1265729
1265741  1265777  1265779  1265801  1265813  1265827  1265843  1265857  1265861  1265863
1265867  1265899  1265903  1265909  1265911  1265921  1265923  1265941  1265959  1265969
1265977  1265981  1265987  1265993  1266019  1266047  1266057  1266059  1266063  1266077
1266079  1266091  1266101  1266107  1266113  1266149  1266157  1266163  1266191  1266197
1266229  1266241  1266247  1266259  1266263  1266269  1266271  1266277  1266281  1266301
1266323  1266337  1266341  1266359  1266371  1266373  1266379  1266389  1266409  1266413
1266431  1266451  1266469  1266487  1266491  1266493  1266511  1266523  1266527  1266539
1266557  1266563  1266583  1266589  1266593  1266611  1266631  1266677  1266719  1266731
1266743  1266751  1266757  1266761  1266763  1266767  1266779  1266781  1266799  1266841
```

```
1266847  1266851  1266869  1266883  1266893  1266899  1266913  1266919  1266929  1266931
1266943  1266949  1266953  1267009  1267043  1267051  1267067  1267103  1267109  1267117
1267121  1267127  1267151  1267157  1267159  1267183  1267193  1267199  1267223  1267237
1267291  1267297  1267303  1267307  1267349  1267381  1267403  1267411  1267429  1267447
1267451  1267459  1267463  1267481  1267501  1267517  1267529  1267531  1267549  1267577
1267579  1267589  1267613  1267633  1267649  1267663  1267681  1267709  1267711  1267723
1267727  1267757  1267771  1267787  1267789  1267823  1267831  1267837  1267859  1267873
1267883  1267891  1267897  1267907  1267933  1267939  1267943  1267951  1267957  1267961
1267999  1268011  1268017  1268039  1268051  1268053  1268077  1268093  1268119  1268143
1268147  1268167  1268173  1268177  1268207  1268213  1268221  1268233  1268261  1268279
1268287  1268291  1268299  1268327  1268341  1268357  1268359  1268369  1268413  1268419
1268429  1268447  1268453  1268461  1268467  1268479  1268537  1268549  1268563  1268567
1268593  1268599  1268621  1268623  1268627  1268633  1268669  1268681  1268713  1268731
1268741  1268747  1268753  1268759  1268777  1268783  1268789  1268791  1268797  1268803
1268807  1268843  1268849  1268867  1268881  1268899  1268921  1268929  1268947  1268963
1269001  1269007  1269013  1269017  1269041  1269043  1269049  1269061  1269077  1269091
1269113  1269119  1269131  1269167  1269173  1269179  1269187  1269193  1269197  1269221
1269223  1269239  1269241  1269253  1269263  1269283  1269287  1269299  1269311  1269337
1269343  1269377  1269379  1269383  1269391  1269413  1269427  1269461  1269467  1269493
1269497  1269529  1269547  1269559  1269563  1269571  1269589  1269601  1269641  1269643
1269683  1269691  1269703  1269731  1269733  1269743  1269757  1269797  1269847  1269859
1269869  1269871  1269901  1269907  1269911  1269923  1269929  1269937  1269953  1269971
1270001  1270013  1270033  1270051  1270063  1270067  1270079  1270097  1270103  1270111
1270123  1270141  1270147  1270151  1270183  1270193  1270201  1270231  1270237  1270249
1270271  1270279  1270301  1270309  1270319  1270327  1270333  1270337  1270343  1270361
1270391  1270417  1270421  1270429  1270433  1270441  1270471  1270483  1270499  1270513
1270531  1270537  1270541  1270547  1270559  1270561  1270567  1270571  1270573  1270579
1270609  1270627  1270639  1270649  1270651  1270657  1270667  1270669  1270679  1270747
1270757  1270771  1270817  1270823  1270849  1270859  1270861  1270879  1270897  1270901
1270909  1270933  1270943  1270961  1270981  1271027  1271029  1271033  1271047  1271051
1271059  1271069  1271087  1271089  1271111  1271117  1271129  1271147  1271161  1271167
1271173  1271183  1271197  1271201  1271203  1271213  1271227  1271239  1271251  1271293
1271299  1271317  1271321  1271339  1271351  1271353  1271359  1271383  1271393  1271399
1271401  1271419  1271429  1271449  1271471  1271483  1271503  1271507  1271513  1271521
1271531  1271551  1271561  1271597  1271603  1271609  1271657  1271659  1271671  1271687
1271701  1271717  1271731  1271747  1271749  1271791  1271797  1271807  1271813  1271827
1271833  1271839  1271843  1271849  1271903  1271927  1271929  1271939  1271953  1271971
1271987  1271999  1272001  1272043  1272049  1272067  1272071  1272079  1272091  1272109
1272113  1272133  1272151  1272157  1272163  1272169  1272191  1272203  1272211  1272223
1272233  1272247  1272253  1272269  1272281  1272283  1272287  1272289  1272329  1272343
1272347  1272361  1272367  1272377  1272379  1272409  1272421  1272443  1272451  1272461
1272539  1272547  1272559  1272577  1272589  1272617  1272629  1272631  1272641  1272647
1272653  1272673  1272679  1272749  1272811  1272827  1272833  1272847  1272851  1272857
1272863  1272881  1272883  1272893  1272899  1272913  1272917  1272919  1272937  1272941
1272961  1272983  1272989  1272991  1273001  1273021  1273033  1273037  1273039  1273087
1273099  1273109  1273117  1273121  1273127  1273157  1273159  1273199  1273213  1273231
1273241  1273267  1273289  1273291  1273301  1273309  1273313  1273331  1273333  1273343
1273367  1273381  1273403  1273409  1273411  1273417  1273421  1273423  1273457  1273463
1273471  1273483  1273499  1273507  1273541  1273543  1273549  1273561  1273567  1273609
1273637  1273639  1273663  1273673  1273681  1273687  1273693  1273721  1273729  1273733
1273739  1273757  1273771  1273781  1273787  1273823  1273843  1273879  1273889  1273891
1273903  1273907  1273919  1273933  1273939  1273957  1273981  1274011  1274017  1274041
1274051  1274071  1274087  1274089  1274111  1274113  1274129  1274137  1274149  1274183
1274209  1274227  1274249  1274267  1274291  1274293  1274297  1274309  1274323  1274333
1274353  1274363  1274381  1274389  1274401  1274411  1274423  1274437  1274461  1274509
1274549  1274557  1274561  1274599  1274617  1274621  1274629  1274633  1274671  1274701
1274719  1274723  1274737  1274759  1274771  1274773  1274803  1274851  1274857  1274873
1274879  1274899  1274921  1274929  1274939  1274941  1274989  1275011  1275019  1275041
1275067  1275107  1275121  1275133  1275173  1275179  1275193  1275199  1275203  1275227
1275269  1275277  1275283  1275293  1275319  1275341  1275349  1275359  1275361  1275401
1275431  1275457  1275467  1275499  1275503  1275523  1275539  1275541  1275553  1275559
1275563  1275569  1275583  1275601  1275611  1275643  1275661  1275667  1275683  1275691
1275707  1275709  1275719  1275737  1275749  1275751  1275779  1275803  1275811  1275823
1275829  1275839  1275847  1275851  1275863  1275877  1275889  1275893  1275899  1275931
1275947  1275973  1275977  1275979  1276001  1276007  1276013  1276027  1276031  1276039
1276049  1276057  1276069  1276103  1276117  1276123  1276129  1276133  1276147  1276157
1276169  1276183  1276193  1276213  1276237  1276243  1276271  1276279  1276307  1276313
1276351  1276357  1276361  1276397  1276409  1276433  1276441  1276481  1276491  1276501
1276511  1276529  1276543  1276571  1276579  1276589  1276603  1276619  1276621  1276631
1276657  1276667  1276679  1276687  1276711  1276721  1276733  1276739  1276747  1276763
1276771  1276777  1276817  1276829  1276861  1276867  1276871  1276889  1276897  1276903
1276927  1276949  1276967  1276969  1276973  1276987  1276999  1277011  1277021  1277039
1277041  1277063  1277069  1277071  1277083  1277093  1277099  1277113  1277137  1277147
1277197  1277207  1277209  1277233  1277249  1277257  1277267  1277299  1277321  1277323
1277357  1277359  1277369  1277387  1277429  1277449  1277461  1277477  1277483  1277491
1277501  1277543  1277557  1277569  1277593  1277597  1277621  1277629  1277651  1277657
1277677  1277699  1277723  1277729  1277741  1277743  1277753  1277761  1277791  1277803
1277813  1277819  1277833  1277849  1277863  1277867  1277879  1277897  1277909  1277911
1277957  1277971  1277993  1278007  1278029  1278031  1278047  1278097  1278107  1278113
1278131  1278139  1278163  1278181  1278191  1278197  1278203  1278209  1278217  1278227
1278253  1278287  1278289  1278323  1278337  1278341  1278371  1278373  1278379  1278391
1278397  1278401  1278419  1278437  1278439  1278463  1278467  1278479  1278481  1278493
1278527  1278551  1278583  1278601  1278611  1278617  1278619  1278623  1278631  1278637
1278659  1278671  1278701  1278709  1278713  1278721  1278733  1278769  1278779  1278787
1278799  1278803  1278811  1278817  1278839  1278857  1278881  1278899  1278911  1278983
1278997  1279001  1279013  1279021  1279027  1279039  1279043  1279081  1279087  1279093
1279111  1279123  1279133  1279141  1279163  1279171  1279177  1279181  1279183  1279189
1279193  1279211  1279249  1279253  1279303  1279307  1279309  1279319  1279321  1279337
1279357  1279361  1279417  1279427  1279457  1279459  1279483  1279493  1279507  1279511
```

```
1279519  1279541  1279547  1279549  1279561  1279583  1279601  1279609  1279627  1279643
1279657  1279661  1279667  1279673  1279679  1279687  1279693  1279703  1279727  1279753
1279757  1279787  1279801  1279807  1279813  1279819  1279823  1279843  1279847  1279853
1279871  1279877  1279907  1279919  1279921  1279931  1279937  1279961  1279969  1279997
1280023  1280101  1280107  1280113  1280119  1280129  1280131  1280141  1280159  1280161
1280173  1280179  1280183  1280221  1280231  1280267  1280281  1280291  1280297  1280309
1280317  1280333  1280371  1280399  1280401  1280407  1280417  1280431  1280453  1280473
1280519  1280537  1280549  1280561  1280567  1280597  1280603  1280623  1280633  1280651
1280659  1280677  1280693  1280707  1280737  1280743  1280759  1280761  1280767  1280789
1280791  1280803  1280821  1280833  1280837  1280857  1280863  1280869  1280887  1280921
1280947  1280969  1280987  1280989  1281029  1281041  1281043  1281047  1281083  1281089
1281097  1281101  1281131  1281149  1281157  1281167  1281187  1281193  1281211  1281221
1281229  1281253  1281257  1281263  1281281  1281283  1281317  1281331  1281349  1281367
1281383  1281389  1281407  1281431  1281433  1281439  1281451  1281457  1281463  1281503
1281521  1281523  1281541  1281547  1281551  1281563  1281587  1281649  1281653  1281667
1281673  1281677  1281691  1281697  1281703  1281727  1281739  1281751  1281773  1281779
1281781  1281799  1281803  1281809  1281821  1281823  1281827  1281853  1281871  1281883
1281899  1281937  1281941  1281961  1281971  1281979  1281983  1282007  1282009  1282031
1282033  1282051  1282069  1282079  1282081  1282093  1282109  1282117  1282121  1282133
1282153  1282163  1282187  1282201  1282213  1282231  1282241  1282261  1282277  1282279
1282289  1282297  1282343  1282349  1282363  1282381  1282387  1282399  1282417  1282423
1282427  1282451  1282469  1282471  1282493  1282499  1282507  1282511  1282513  1282517
1282529  1282543  1282571  1282577  1282597  1282607  1282613  1282627  1282637  1282639
1282649  1282657  1282661  1282681  1282693  1282703  1282717  1282739  1282751  1282763
1282781  1282783  1282807  1282817  1282867  1282877  1282903  1282907  1282909  1282913
1282933  1282943  1282951  1282961  1282969  1282993  1283011  1283017  1283021  1283027
1283063  1283069  1283083  1283099  1283111  1283119  1283129  1283137  1283159  1283167
1283171  1283173  1283179  1283207  1283237  1283297  1283323  1283333  1283339  1283353
1283383  1283389  1283417  1283437  1283441  1283473  1283479  1283509  1283521  1283537
1283539  1283543  1283549  1283563  1283573  1283591  1283603  1283677  1283683  1283701
1283707  1283717  1283719  1283731  1283753  1283759  1283767  1283771  1283797  1283831
1283839  1283873  1283879  1283881  1283897  1283903  1283939  1283941  1283957  1283969
1283981  1283983  1284007  1284037  1284043  1284047  1284053  1284083  1284131  1284169
1284187  1284209  1284211  1284223  1284263  1284271  1284287  1284293  1284301  1284313
1284317  1284329  1284341  1284373  1284379  1284383  1284421  1284427  1284433  1284443
1284467  1284473  1284487  1284541  1284543  1284551  1284565  1284583  1284599  1284583
1284601  1284617  1284623  1284631  1284641  1284659  1284691  1284709  1284713  1284737
1284739  1284763  1284769  1284791  1284793  1284823  1284841  1284847  1284851  1284863
1284889  1284901  1284917  1284931  1284937  1284967  1284971  1284977  1284991  1285021
1285049  1285051  1285057  1285061  1285069  1285099  1285111  1285117  1285129  1285139
1285147  1285159  1285169  1285181  1285199  1285213  1285223  1285231  1285237  1285247
1285259  1285267  1285279  1285283  1285289  1285301  1285351  1285381  1285393  1285397
1285411  1285429  1285441  1285451  1285469  1285481  1285507  1285511  1285513  1285517
1285519  1285547  1285549  1285553  1285607  1285619  1285633  1285649  1285679  1285699
1285703  1285717  1285741  1285747  1285759  1285763  1285777  1285789  1285793  1285799
1285811  1285813  1285841  1285847  1285853  1285859  1285871  1285877  1285891  1285903
1285913  1285937  1285943  1285969  1285981  1285993  1286011  1286017  1286039  1286071
1286081  1286093  1286099  1286107  1286109  1286147  1286149  1286177  1286189  1286191
1286209  1286227  1286239  1286261  1286267  1286269  1286273  1286287  1286303  1286323
1286359  1286371  1286381  1286387  1286399  1286419  1286447  1286489  1286491  1286503
1286513  1286521  1286533  1286557  1286561  1286569  1286581  1286591  1286617  1286629
1286633  1286641  1286647  1286653  1286657  1286669  1286683  1286693  1286707  1286711
1286773  1286777  1286783  1286797  1286807  1286819  1286821  1286833  1286837  1286839
1286843  1286881  1286939  1286941  1286953  1286959  1286969  1286981  1286983  1287007
1287047  1287059  1287061  1287067  1287071  1287101  1287109  1287131  1287133  1287157
1287163  1287173  1287179  1287197  1287199  1287217  1287233  1287239  1287289  1287323
1287329  1287343  1287347  1287353  1287361  1287371  1287373  1287401  1287431  1287457
1287467  1287469  1287479  1287487  1287491  1287499  1287511  1287541  1287551  1287553
1287569  1287589  1287593  1287607  1287613  1287623  1287661  1287683  1287691  1287697
1287707  1287731  1287739  1287743  1287749  1287751  1287757  1287761  1287787  1287799
1287817  1287821  1287829  1287841  1287857  1287883  1287887  1287899  1287917  1287947
1287961  1287967  1287973  1287983  1287989  1287997  1288003  1288009  1288013  1288033
1288037  1288043  1288051  1288057  1288061  1288099  1288103  1288109  1288117  1288163
1288169  1288171  1288187  1288193  1288201  1288213  1288247  1288249  1288291  1288307
1288337  1288349  1288361  1288363  1288367  1288393  1288421  1288423  1288429  1288439
1288487  1288513  1288519  1288531  1288541  1288543  1288559  1288571  1288597  1288603
1288607  1288613  1288643  1288649  1288657  1288691  1288697  1288699  1288709  1288711
1288733  1288769  1288783  1288799  1288817  1288823  1288829  1288831  1288843  1288849
1288853  1288871  1288873  1288877  1288891  1288919  1288921  1288933  1288939  1288951
1288967  1288981  1288993  1288997  1289003  1289009  1289027  1289039  1289053  1289077
1289083  1289111  1289129  1289149  1289153  1289159  1289179  1289213  1289231  1289237
1289261  1289273  1289287  1289303  1289329  1289333  1289341  1289363  1289371  1289381
1289401  1289411  1289423  1289429  1289447  1289459  1289513  1289531  1289537  1289551
1289557  1289567  1289593  1289597  1289599  1289621  1289623  1289627  1289653  1289657
1289687  1289711  1289713  1289731  1289747  1289749  1289753  1289779  1289789  1289801
1289803  1289831  1289839  1289851  1289867  1289881  1289921  1289927  1289933  1289963
1289969  1289971  1290013  1290019  1290031  1290049  1290077  1290083  1290109  1290131
1290143  1290151  1290161  1290167  1290169  1290173  1290199  1290203  1290209  1290257
1290259  1290287  1290293  1290299  1290319  1290329  1290371  1290379  1290427  1290431
1290433  1290439  1290463  1290467  1290469  1290491  1290503  1290533  1290539  1290551
1290563  1290571  1290581  1290593  1290607  1290629  1290631  1290637  1290643  1290647
1290659  1290673  1290683  1290719  1290791  1290811  1290823  1290847  1290853  1290857
1290869  1290901  1290907  1290923  1290937  1290983  1291001  1291007  1291009  1291019
1291021  1291063  1291079  1291111  1291117  1291139  1291153  1291159  1291163  1291177
1291193  1291211  1291217  1291219  1291223  1291229  1291249  1291271  1291313  1291321
1291327  1291343  1291349  1291357  1291369  1291379  1291387  1291391  1291421  1291447
1291453  1291471  1291481  1291483  1291489  1291501  1291523  1291547  1291567  1291579
1291603  1291637  1291669  1291673  1291691  1291783  1291793  1291799  1291817  1291819
1291831  1291861  1291877  1291883  1291907  1291909  1291931  1291957  1291963  1291967
```

```
1291991 1291999 1292009 1292023 1292029 1292063 1292069 1292089 1292099 1292113
1292131 1292141 1292143 1292149 1292167 1292177 1292219 1292237 1292249 1292251
1292257 1292261 1292281 1292293 1292309 1292329 1292339 1292353 1292371 1292383
1292387 1292419 1292429 1292441 1292477 1292491 1292503 1292509 1292539 1292549
1292563 1292567 1292579 1292587 1292593 1292597 1292609 1292633 1292639
1292653 1292657 1292659 1292693 1292701 1292713 1292717 1292729 1292737 1292783
1292789 1292801 1292813 1292831 1292843 1292857 1292887 1292927 1292947 1292953
1292957 1292971 1292983 1292989 1292999 1293001 1293011 1293031 1293077 1293119
1293133 1293137 1293157 1293169 1293179 1293199 1293203 1293233 1293239 1293247
1293251 1293277 1293283 1293287 1293307 1293317 1293319 1293323 1293329 1293361
1293367 1293373 1293401 1293419 1293421 1293433 1293473 1293491 1293493 1293499
1293529 1293533 1293541 1293553 1293559 1293583 1293587 1293613 1293619 1293647
1293659 1293701 1293739 1293757 1293763 1293791 1293797 1293821 1293829 1293839
1293841 1293857 1293869 1293899 1293917 1293923 1293931 1293947 1293949 1293961
1293967 1293977 1293979 1293983 1294019 1294021 1294031 1294037 1294039 1294061
1294081 1294087 1294103 1294121 1294123 1294129 1294169 1294177 1294199 1294201
1294231 1294253 1294273 1294277 1294301 1294303 1294309 1294339 1294351 1294361
1294367 1294369 1294393 1294399 1294453 1294459 1294471 1294477 1294483 1294561
1294571 1294583 1294597 1294609 1294621 1294627 1294633 1294639 1294649 1294661
1294691 1294721 1294723 1294729 1294753 1294757 1294759 1294817 1294823 1294841
1294849 1294939 1294957 1294967 1294973 1294987 1294999 1295003 1295027 1295033
1295051 1295057 1295069 1295071 1295081 1295089 1295113 1295131 1295137 1295159
1295183 1295191 1295201 1295207 1295219 1295221 1295243 1295263 1295279 1295293
1295297 1295299 1295309 1295317 1295321 1295323 1295339 1295347 1295369 1295377
1295387 1295389 1295447 1295473 1295491 1295501 1295513 1295533 1295543 1295549
1295551 1295561 1295563 1295603 1295611 1295617 1295639 1295647 1295653 1295681
1295711 1295717 1295737 1295741 1295747 1295761 1295783 1295803 1295809 1295813
1295839 1295849 1295867 1295869 1295873 1295881 1295947 1295953 1295989 1295993
1296007 1296011 1296019 1296023 1296037 1296041 1296059 1296077 1296089 1296101
1296109 1296137 1296143 1296167 1296181 1296187 1296209 1296227 1296277 1296283
1296287 1296293 1296319 1296331 1296341 1296343 1296371 1296391 1296409 1296413
1296419 1296467 1296473 1296481 1296499 1296511 1296521 1296523 1296551 1296557
1296563 1296571 1296583 1296587 1296593 1296601 1296613 1296623 1296629 1296649
1296679 1296689 1296703 1296721 1296727 1296749 1296781 1296787 1296803 1296817
1296829 1296833 1296839 1296877 1296899 1296907 1296929 1296949 1296973 1296983
1297001 1297003 1297013 1297019 1297027 1297057 1297061 1297063 1297091 1297103
1297123 1297129 1297139 1297147 1297157 1297169 1297171 1297193 1297201 1297211
1297217 1297229 1297243 1297249 1297271 1297273 1297279 1297297 1297313 1297333
1297337 1297349 1297367 1297369 1297393 1297397 1297399 1297403 1297411
1297421 1297447 1297451 1297459 1297477 1297487 1297501 1297507 1297519 1297523
1297537 1297561 1297573 1297601 1297607 1297619 1297631 1297633 1297649 1297651
1297657 1297669 1297687 1297693 1297727 1297739 1297771 1297781 1297799 1297841
1297847 1297853 1297873 1297927 1297963 1297973 1297979 1297993 1298027 1298039
1298047 1298053 1298057 1298111 1298113 1298117 1298119 1298131 1298149 1298161
1298173 1298191 1298197 1298221 1298261 1298279 1298291 1298309 1298317 1298329
1298333 1298351 1298357 1298371 1298387 1298467 1298489 1298491 1298537 1298551
1298573 1298581 1298611 1298617 1298641 1298651 1298653 1298699 1298719 1298723
1298747 1298771 1298779 1298789 1298797 1298809 1298819 1298831 1298849 1298863
1298887 1298909 1298911 1298923 1298951 1298963 1298981 1298989 1299007 1299013
1299019 1299029 1299041 1299059 1299061 1299079 1299097 1299101 1299143 1299169
1299173 1299187 1299209 1299211 1299223 1299227 1299257 1299269 1299283
1299289 1299299 1299317 1299323 1299341 1299343 1299349 1299359 1299367 1299377
1299379 1299437 1299439 1299449 1299451 1299457 1299491 1299499 1299533 1299541
1299553 1299583 1299601 1299631 1299637 1299647 1299653 1299673 1299689 1299709
1299721 1299743 1299763 1299791 1299811 1299817 1299821 1299827 1299833 1299841
1299853 1299869 1299877 1299887 1299899 1299917 1299919 1299941 1299953 1299979
1299989 1300021 1300027 1300031 1300051 1300073 1300097 1300111 1300127 1300129
1300133 1300139 1300141 1300147 1300153 1300181 1300199 1300199 1300237 1300253
1300283 1300289 1300297 1300307 1300309 1300319 1300333 1300339 1300367 1300391
1300421 1300423 1300433 1300451 1300457 1300463 1300471 1300477 1300487 1300501
1300511 1300553 1300571 1300573 1300583 1300597 1300609 1300613 1300633 1300639
1300669 1300681 1300709 1300711 1300727 1300751 1300769 1300771 1300781 1300813
1300829 1300837 1300841 1300843 1300907 1300921 1300927 1300931 1300963 1300967
1300979 1300997 1301011 1301017 1301021 1301023 1301033 1301057 1301077 1301081
1301099 1301119 1301123 1301147 1301149 1301171 1301173 1301219 1301221 1301233
1301239 1301243 1301249 1301257 1301273 1301281 1301297 1301323 1301347 1301353
1301387 1301389 1301393 1301413 1301423 1301437 1301453 1301459 1301467 1301471
1301497 1301507 1301527 1301533 1301539 1301543 1301551 1301561 1301581 1301591
1301603 1301617 1301621 1301669 1301693 1301701 1301711 1301719 1301761 1301779
1301821 1301827 1301849 1301851 1301857 1301863 1301879 1301887 1301893 1301909
1301921 1301929 1301939 1301941 1301957 1301959 1302017 1302019 1302029 1302043
1302061 1302079 1302107 1302121 1302137 1302151 1302163 1302173 1302179 1302181
1302199 1302209 1302221 1302227 1302233 1302239 1302253 1302269 1302277 1302281
1302293 1302313 1302331 1302347 1302349 1302373 1302377 1302383 1302391 1302397
1302443 1302461 1302461 1302491 1302493 1302563 1302587 1302607 1302617
1302647 1302667 1302673 1302683 1302689 1302701 1302737 1302739 1302757 1302787
1302803 1302827 1302839 1302841 1302869 1302901 1302911 1302919 1302929 1302937
1302953 1302991 1303009 1303013 1303031 1303037 1303051 1303061 1303069 1303077
1303091 1303097 1303109 1303117 1303121 1303129 1303139 1303151 1303163 1303171
1303189 1303199 1303213 1303219 1303223 1303241 1303243 1303261 1303279 1303283
1303297 1303307 1303321 1303327 1303331 1303363 1303409 1303411 1303417 1303427
1303439 1303453 1303469 1303481 1303493 1303499 1303507 1303517 1303537 1303541
1303553 1303567 1303591 1303597 1303613 1303633 1303693 1303703
1303703 1303711 1303739 1303741 1303751 1303787 1303789 1303793 1303807 1303823
1303831 1303853 1303867 1303871 1303873 1303879 1303903 1303919 1303931 1303933
1303961 1303963 1303979 1303987 1304003 1304029 1304033 1304071 1304081 1304089
1304111 1304113 1304129 1304131 1304137 1304167 1304183 1304207 1304209 1304221
1304227 1304231 1304239 1304243 1304249 1304267 1304273 1304299 1304309 1304321
1304357 1304371 1304389 1304411 1304419 1304477 1304503 1304519 1304531 1304539
```

```
1304543  1304551  1304581  1304591  1304599  1304603  1304609  1304627  1304659  1304669
1304687  1304707  1304713  1304741  1304753  1304783  1304803  1304833  1304837  1304867
1304867  1304887  1304893  1304923  1304929  1304957  1304969  1304981  1304983  1304987
1305011  1305013  1305047  1305061  1305097  1305121  1305137  1305149  1305151  1305163
1305169  1305229  1305233  1305247  1305251  1305253  1305287  1305289  1305301  1305307
1305371  1305373  1305383  1305391  1305401  1305427  1305431  1305449  1305511  1305517
1305527  1305533  1305559  1305571  1305581  1305587  1305589  1305593  1305599  1305607
1305637  1305643  1305653  1305659  1305679  1305691  1305701  1305709  1305713  1305739
1305743  1305749  1305757  1305803  1305823  1305869  1305881  1305893  1305907  1305919
1305947  1305959  1305961  1305971  1306001  1306007  1306027  1306033  1306051  1306069
1306087  1306099  1306103  1306121  1306133  1306139  1306157  1306159  1306169  1306181
1306213  1306223  1306237  1306241  1306243  1306259  1306267  1306273  1306289  1306313
1306339  1306343  1306351  1306367  1306373  1306381  1306387  1306391  1306411  1306429
1306439  1306447  1306451  1306477  1306483  1306489  1306499  1306517  1306519  1306541
1306589  1306597  1306601  1306633  1306661  1306663  1306667  1306691  1306693  1306717
1306733  1306751  1306757  1306759  1306777  1306817  1306819  1306829  1306831  1306849
1306853  1306883  1306889  1306891  1306901  1306913  1306933  1306961  1306973  1306979
1306997  1307051  1307057  1307063  1307069  1307077  1307081  1307083  1307087  1307093
1307101  1307107  1307123  1307153  1307161  1307181  1307197  1307209  1307221  1307261
1307281  1307303  1307309  1307311  1307347  1307353  1307393  1307417  1307431  1307437
1307441  1307461  1307473  1307479  1307483  1307497  1307507  1307519  1307539  1307557
1307591  1307627  1307633  1307641  1307651  1307671  1307689  1307693  1307701  1307729
1307731  1307741  1307753  1307767  1307771  1307809  1307821  1307833  1307863  1307893
1307909  1307923  1307927  1307951  1307981  1307993  1308011  1308019  1308029  1308037
1308049  1308077  1308091  1308121  1308137  1308157  1308173  1308191  1308193  1308221
1308247  1308287  1308299  1308301  1308313  1308323  1308331  1308343  1308353  1308367
1308383  1308403  1308413  1308421  1308457  1308467  1308491  1308497  1308499  1308521
1308523  1308529  1308547  1308551  1308557  1308563  1308581  1308583  1308589  1308599
1308607  1308611  1308613  1308647  1308649  1308691  1308707  1308709  1308719  1308731
1308737  1308757  1308773  1308803  1308829  1308841  1308863  1308869  1308883  1308887
1308899  1308911  1308917  1308919  1308943  1308977  1309013  1309039  1309057  1309067
1309073  1309079  1309093  1309103  1309117  1309123  1309127  1309129  1309163  1309177
1309181  1309207  1309211  1309219  1309237  1309249  1309283  1309291  1309313  1309333
1309337  1309339  1309343  1309351  1309369  1309397  1309411  1309421  1309463  1309501
1309513  1309531  1309549  1309559  1309571  1309589  1309591  1309601  1309631  1309639
1309661  1309673  1309691  1309699  1309709  1309717  1309723  1309739  1309747  1309753
1309757  1309769  1309793  1309801  1309807  1309811  1309817  1309829  1309831  1309849
1309877  1309883  1309907  1309921  1309927  1309939  1309949  1309961  1309963  1309999
1310033  1310039  1310041  1310053  1310063  1310077  1310083  1310087  1310093  1310117
1310119  1310123  1310137  1310143  1310147  1310171  1310189  1310209  1310233  1310251
1310261  1310269  1310279  1310293  1310311  1310327  1310329  1310359  1310363  1310369
1310371  1310381  1310383  1310389  1310399  1310417  1310431  1310467  1310473  1310489
1310509  1310527  1310537  1310549  1310579  1310591  1310599  1310611  1310627  1310629
1310633  1310657  1310669  1310681  1310693  1310719  1310723  1310741  1310759  1310779
1310789  1310797  1310801  1310807  1310809  1310851  1310891  1310899  1310923  1310927
1310963  1310987  1310993  1310999  1311001  1311029  1311031  1311043  1311047  1311053
1311067  1311097  1311103  1311109  1311127  1311131  1311143  1311173  1311181  1311217
1311223  1311229  1311239  1311241  1311251  1311259  1311263  1311287  1311301  1311307
1311311  1311341  1311353  1311367  1311377  1311383  1311403  1311407  1311419  1311433
1311449  1311473  1311481  1311493  1311503  1311509  1311523  1311547  1311553  1311559
1311577  1311599  1311617  1311619  1311623  1311643  1311689  1311691  1311701  1311721
1311733  1311749  1311767  1311769  1311773  1311797  1311799  1311829  1311847  1311853
1311857  1311899  1311901  1311917  1311923  1311967  1311971  1311991  1312001  1312019
1312027  1312079  1312093  1312133  1312139  1312153  1312169  1312177  1312183  1312187
1312189  1312211  1312229  1312237  1312277  1312301  1312303  1312319  1312331  1312343
1312351  1312373  1312379  1312391  1312393  1312397  1312411  1312459  1312471  1312513
1312517  1312523  1312543  1312547  1312559  1312561  1312567  1312579  1312583  1312601
1312603  1312637  1312657  1312667  1312669  1312673  1312681  1312733  1312739  1312769
1312777  1312789  1312813  1312823  1312841  1312847  1312853  1312867  1312873  1312877
1312889  1312891  1312907  1312921  1312931  1312937  1312951  1312963  1312967  1313041
1313057  1313069  1313083  1313087  1313141  1313153  1313161  1313171  1313219  1313237
1313239  1313293  1313297  1313311  1313317  1313329  1313339  1313357  1313359  1313363
1313371  1313383  1313423  1313443  1313447  1313449  1313453  1313463  1313467  1313569
1313579  1313597  1313621  1313623  1313629  1313633  1313651  1313657  1313677  1313699
1313701  1313723  1313731  1313747  1313761  1313771  1313797  1313813  1313827  1313839
1313843  1313857  1313863  1313881  1313891  1313899  1313911  1313929  1313953  1313957
1313959  1313987  1313999  1314011  1314017  1314023  1314043  1314101  1314109  1314113
1314127  1314133  1314143  1314149  1314161  1314163  1314169  1314179  1314191  1314199
1314217  1314233  1314239  1314259  1314283  1314301  1314317  1314359  1314361  1314371
1314377  1314409  1314433  1314437  1314451  1314463  1314479  1314497  1314503  1314517
1314527  1314539  1314563  1314569  1314571  1314587  1314601  1314611  1314613  1314671
1314673  1314701  1314767  1314769  1314779  1314809  1314821  1314823  1314851  1314853
1314871  1314883  1314893  1314917  1314941  1314953  1314997  1315003  1315007  1315019
1315037  1315049  1315073  1315081  1315087  1315151  1315159  1315177  1315183  1315187
1315211  1315213  1315229  1315231  1315243  1315253  1315283  1315289  1315291  1315297
1315309  1315367  1315373  1315397  1315399  1315441  1315451  1315453  1315463  1315481
1315487  1315493  1315507  1315519  1315537  1315543  1315549  1315553  1315591  1315597
1315603  1315607  1315621  1315627  1315637  1315651  1315661  1315673  1315697  1315711
1315723  1315729  1315747  1315771  1315781  1315801  1315823  1315837  1315849  1315861
1315871  1315889  1315891  1315901  1315907  1315927  1315931  1315943  1315949  1315961
1315967  1315969  1316009  1316017  1316033  1316039  1316041  1316071  1316099  1316143
1316177  1316209  1316213  1316239  1316251  1316257  1316261  1316279  1316299  1316303
1316311  1316321  1316323  1316347  1316363  1316389  1316401  1316407  1316417  1316431
1316437  1316479  1316507  1316509  1316519  1316527  1316533  1316537  1316591  1316593
1316603  1316621  1316639  1316647  1316657  1316669  1316671  1316677  1316699  1316717
1316729  1316741  1316743  1316761  1316767  1316779  1316801  1316813  1316831  1316869
1316873  1316881  1316899  1316921  1316923  1316951  1316963  1316971  1316983  1316989
1316999  1317013  1317031  1317059  1317067  1317079  1317083  1317091  1317119  1317131
1317157  1317161  1317191  1317193  1317223  1317227  1317229  1317247  1317257  1317259
```

```
1317271 1317299 1317301 1317307 1317317 1317319 1317359 1317361 1317377 1317397
1317401 1317409 1317413 1317419 1317427 1317443 1317451 1317461 1317487 1317493
1317521 1317523 1317541 1317553 1317571 1317583 1317587 1317599 1317629 1317671
1317677 1317683 1317691 1317697 1317703 1317713 1317727 1317751 1317761 1317763
1317773 1317787 1317793 1317817 1317839 1317853 1317881 1317887 1317917 1317929
1317941 1317947 1317961 1317971 1317989 1318003 1318013 1318019 1318033 1318039
1318063 1318067 1318073 1318099 1318103 1318139 1318147 1318157 1318169 1318183
1318193 1318211 1318241 1318249 1318259 1318267 1318279 1318283 1318301 1318313
1318349 1318379 1318409 1318411 1318441 1318451 1318459 1318463 1318477 1318487
1318489 1318517 1318549 1318553 1318579 1318609 1318633 1318661 1318663 1318697
1318699 1318703 1318711 1318721 1318727 1318729 1318739 1318753 1318781 1318783
1318789 1318829 1318831 1318841 1318859 1318861 1318879 1318883 1318897 1318901
1318903 1318913 1318927 1318931 1318937 1318943 1318963 1318973 1318987 1318991
1318997 1319023 1319033 1319053 1319057 1319077 1319083 1319107 1319137 1319147
1319167 1319191 1319207 1319209 1319261 1319273 1319281 1319293 1319321 1319323
1319333 1319371 1319377 1319389 1319399 1319401 1319407 1319411 1319419 1319429
1319443 1319459 1319477 1319509 1319543 1319561 1319567 1319609 1319623 1319651
1319687 1319707 1319711 1319719 1319723 1319729 1319737 1319741 1319743 1319777
1319779 1319803 1319821 1319839 1319861 1319869 1319883 1319909 1319911 1319917
1319933 1319951 1319963 1320019 1320023 1320031 1320037 1320061 1320091 1320107
1320113 1320119 1320127 1320149 1320157 1320161 1320173 1320181 1320191 1320199
1320211 1320247 1320251 1320287 1320301 1320307 1320331 1320337 1320343 1320353
1320377 1320379 1320391 1320409 1320413 1320421 1320427 1320433 1320437 1320533
1320541 1320607 1320617 1320623 1320667 1320721 1320727 1320731 1320749 1320751
1320773 1320791 1320799 1320811 1320859 1320871 1320881 1320887 1320889 1320901
1320911 1320923 1320929 1320931 1320947 1320961 1320973 1320983 1321007 1321031
1321063 1321079 1321093 1321109 1321139 1321141 1321157 1321163 1321169 1321171
1321193 1321213 1321219 1321247 1321249 1321259 1321267 1321273 1321283 1321289
1321301 1321303 1321319 1321349 1321351 1321357 1321363 1321379 1321391 1321399
1321409 1321417 1321421 1321429 1321447 1321451 1321457 1321459 1321477 1321483
1321487 1321513 1321517 1321549 1321571 1321577 1321589 1321601 1321627 1321633
1321637 1321651 1321657 1321669 1321679 1321681 1321693 1321711 1321729 1321753
1321757 1321759 1321763 1321769 1321813 1321823 1321841 1321847 1321867 1321891
1321897 1321919 1321921 1321939 1321951 1321961 1321981 1321991 1322003 1322011
1322021 1322033 1322089 1322117 1322129 1322137 1322143 1322147 1322149 1322159
1322161 1322171 1322173 1322177 1322179 1322203 1322219 1322221 1322227 1322257
1322261 1322281 1322287 1322303 1322317 1322323 1322327 1322329 1322333 1322341
1322357 1322359 1322369 1322389 1322423 1322437 1322443 1322449 1322467 1322471
1322483 1322501 1322507 1322521 1322527 1322543 1322557 1322579 1322591 1322593
1322597 1322599 1322611 1322621 1322641 1322669 1322681 1322689 1322693 1322731
1322743 1322747 1322749 1322767 1322813 1322831 1322843 1322851 1322857 1322869
1322873 1322887 1322897 1322903 1322917 1322921 1322927 1322939 1322941 1322953
1322963 1322977 1323001 1323017 1323041 1323043 1323053 1323073 1323079 1323107
1323109 1323131 1323137 1323139 1323143 1323149 1323169 1323187 1323197 1323199
1323221 1323233 1323247 1323253 1323281 1323307 1323319 1323323 1323337 1323349
1323367 1323373 1323389 1323409 1323431 1323437 1323457 1323461 1323479 1323499
1323503 1323529 1323533 1323541 1323551 1323571 1323577 1323593 1323599 1323611
1323629 1323649 1323659 1323689 1323691 1323727 1323733 1323737 1323743 1323779
1323797 1323799 1323851 1323869 1323871 1323877 1323883 1323899 1323919 1323923
1323941 1323967 1323997 1324007 1324033 1324039 1324051 1324061 1324069 1324093
1324097 1324117 1324123 1324151 1324159 1324171 1324187 1324199 1324201 1324217
1324223 1324261 1324313 1324327 1324361 1324369 1324381 1324387 1324391 1324403
1324429 1324441 1324451 1324457 1324481 1324511 1324513 1324567 1324571 1324573
1324577 1324579 1324591 1324607 1324613 1324619 1324621 1324627 1324649 1324651
1324663 1324667 1324679 1324681 1324717 1324721 1324733 1324753 1324783 1324819
1324831 1324837 1324849 1324867 1324871 1324907 1324913 1324949 1324951 1324967
1324969 1324979 1325011 1325017 1325021 1325047 1325063 1325083 1325089 1325111
1325119 1325123 1325143 1325173 1325179 1325183 1325197 1325227 1325251 1325263
1325267 1325273 1325287 1325293 1325309 1325333 1325351 1325399 1325417 1325419
1325431 1325449 1325483 1325491 1325501 1325509 1325521 1325543 1325557 1325567
1325579 1325581 1325611 1325627 1325633 1325657 1325659 1325663 1325669 1325693
1325707 1325761 1325771 1325773 1325791 1325803 1325861 1325867 1325873 1325903
1325911 1325923 1325939 1325941 1325959 1325977 1325993 1326001 1326037 1326041
1326047 1326049 1326053 1326071 1326089 1326097 1326109 1326133 1326137 1326151
1326161 1326167 1326197 1326239 1326251 1326253 1326271 1326277 1326287 1326301
1326307 1326313 1326319 1326343 1326349 1326359 1326389 1326419 1326421 1326427
1326443 1326449 1326461 1326463 1326467 1326491 1326499 1326503 1326511 1326529
1326551 1326587 1326607 1326613 1326623 1326631 1326641 1326649 1326653 1326659
1326673 1326683 1326691 1326701 1326727 1326739 1326757 1326781 1326791 1326797
1326817 1326821 1326823 1326839 1326859 1326869 1326881 1326887 1326889 1326917
1326929 1326943 1326967 1326971 1326989 1327001 1327009 1327013 1327019 1327043
1327063 1327091 1327099 1327111 1327133 1327147 1327159 1327181 1327199 1327201
1327217 1327231 1327237 1327267 1327289 1327297 1327303 1327349 1327351 1327363
1327369 1327373 1327379 1327387 1327409 1327427 1327481 1327489 1327517 1327561
1327577 1327603 1327619 1327631 1327673 1327679 1327709 1327759 1327769 1327783
1327789 1327793 1327801 1327831 1327841 1327849 1327871 1327877 1327889 1327901
1327903 1327933 1327973 1327987 1327999 1328003 1328017 1328051 1328077 1328087
1328099 1328101 1328111 1328143 1328161 1328167 1328179 1328183 1328203 1328207
1328213 1328219 1328231 1328237 1328269 1328279 1328297 1328311 1328317 1328323
1328351 1328357 1328387 1328407 1328417 1328447 1328449 1328473 1328477 1328479
1328491 1328497 1328501 1328507 1328521 1328531 1328539 1328563 1328573 1328603
1328611 1328617 1328647 1328653 1328671 1328683 1328699 1328711 1328729 1328731
1328741 1328749 1328777 1328783 1328797 1328807 1328827 1328843 1328861 1328863
1328891 1328893 1328897 1328909 1328911 1328923 1328927 1328953 1328969 1328981
1329011 1329061 1329067 1329073 1329091 1329103 1329109 1329127 1329131 1329143
1329161 1329197 1329217 1329233 1329241 1329269 1329277 1329283 1329287 1329313
1329337 1329353 1329359 1329371 1329379 1329397 1329407 1329437 1329439 1329457
1329479 1329499 1329509 1329529 1329533 1329541 1329569 1329593 1329599 1329619
1329623 1329631 1329637 1329661 1329673 1329701 1329703 1329707 1329709 1329719
```

```
1329721  1329733  1329761  1329763  1329767  1329787  1329799  1329847  1329863  1329871
1329899  1329907  1329941  1329949  1329953  1329971  1330001  1330003  1330009  1330031
1330061  1330073  1330093  1330103  1330111  1330129  1330157  1330177  1330207  1330211
1330213  1330223  1330229  1330237  1330249  1330253  1330309  1330313  1330321  1330337
1330393  1330397  1330411  1330423  1330453  1330487  1330493  1330499  1330501  1330519
1330529  1330541  1330547  1330559  1330577  1330583  1330601  1330603  1330621  1330633
1330649  1330691  1330699  1330727  1330733  1330751  1330783  1330787  1330789  1330831
1330843  1330859  1330867  1330873  1330909  1330933  1330943  1330957  1330961  1330963
1330997  1331023  1331039  1331041  1331051  1331059  1331063  1331093  1331107  1331119
1331123  1331153  1331207  1331227  1331243  1331249  1331251  1331261  1331269  1331279
1331293  1331299  1331327  1331329  1331333  1331339  1331347  1331377  1331381  1331383
1331399  1331411  1331431  1331437  1331443  1331471  1331489  1331497  1331513  1331521
1331527  1331549  1331567  1331573  1331579  1331587  1331591  1331597  1331599  1331611
1331633  1331641  1331647  1331657  1331663  1331683  1331699  1331711  1331719  1331749
1331761  1331773  1331779  1331783  1331789  1331801  1331821  1331851  1331857  1331921
1331923  1331929  1331951  1331959  1331969  1331987  1331989  1332017  1332047  1332059
1332077  1332119  1332127  1332151  1332167  1332169  1332181  1332187  1332193  1332217
1332251  1332277  1332281  1332283  1332313  1332319  1332329  1332343  1332361  1332371
1332379  1332389  1332421  1332427  1332431  1332433  1332439  1332449  1332467  1332479
1332491  1332503  1332509  1332517  1332547  1332553  1332557  1332571  1332587  1332589
1332631  1332649  1332671  1332673  1332691  1332701  1332713  1332719  1332733  1332739
1332757  1332763  1332767  1332769  1332797  1332803  1332823  1332833  1332841  1332847
1332853  1332893  1332913  1332917  1332941  1332949  1332959  1332973  1332979  1332997
1333019  1333027  1333091  1333117  1333121  1333133  1333139  1333141  1333151  1333153
1333169  1333181  1333193  1333219  1333231  1333253  1333261  1333271  1333273  1333289
1333291  1333313  1333331  1333357  1333393  1333411  1333417  1333457  1333483  1333489
1333511  1333537  1333543  1333547  1333567  1333571  1333583  1333597  1333601  1333613
1333621  1333649  1333663  1333669  1333679  1333687  1333691  1333697  1333721  1333723
1333733  1333741  1333751  1333777  1333799  1333807  1333831  1333833  1333841  1333867
1333883  1333889  1333901  1333909  1333919  1333949  1333963  1333967  1333991  1333993
1333999  1334057  1334071  1334077  1334093  1334101  1334107  1334111  1334117  1334119
1334129  1334141  1334233  1334239  1334273  1334287  1334297  1334327  1334329  1334339
1334341  1334353  1334357  1334363  1334369  1334371  1334393  1334401  1334407  1334413
1334423  1334441  1334453  1334461  1334477  1334491  1334501  1334507  1334537  1334549
1334561  1334563  1334569  1334603  1334629  1334633  1334651  1334681  1334717  1334719
1334737  1334743  1334747  1334771  1334797  1334813  1334819  1334833  1334881  1334903
1334933  1334947  1334969  1335007  1335023  1335043  1335053  1335067  1335079  1335137
1335157  1335167  1335199  1335209  1335211  1335233  1335239  1335241  1335259  1335277
1335287  1335289  1335319  1335331  1335343  1335349  1335361  1335371  1335379  1335391
1335407  1335409  1335413  1335431  1335457  1335461  1335497  1335527  1335533  1335557
1335563  1335611  1335617  1335619  1335637  1335641  1335647  1335661  1335667  1335683
1335689  1335743  1335749  1335751  1335781  1335791  1335797  1335847  1335853  1335869
1335889  1335899  1335907  1335941  1335949  1335953  1335977  1335989  1335991  1336003
1336009  1336019  1336021  1336031  1336037  1336039  1336057  1336091  1336103  1336121
1336133  1336141  1336151  1336169  1336171  1336177  1336187  1336189  1336201  1336211
1336229  1336241  1336253  1336261  1336267  1336271  1336273  1336333  1336337  1336339
1336343  1336393  1336399  1336417  1336429  1336453  1336457  1336463  1336469  1336481
1336487  1336493  1336499  1336519  1336529  1336547  1336561  1336567  1336579  1336589
1336597  1336603  1336613  1336619  1336637  1336649  1336663  1336729  1336747  1336781
1336793  1336799  1336801  1336817  1336861  1336873  1336877  1336883  1336891  1336901
1336919  1336927  1336939  1336943  1336957  1336961  1336963  1336967  1336997  1337003
1337023  1337027  1337057  1337071  1337093  1337153  1337159  1337173  1337209  1337227
1337261  1337263  1337267  1337269  1337293  1337299  1337317  1337327  1337333  1337351
1337359  1337363  1337377  1337383  1337389  1337411  1337419  1337431  1337441  1337447
1337459  1337489  1337507  1337527  1337551  1337563  1337591  1337593  1337603  1337617
1337621  1337627  1337629  1337647  1337663  1337671  1337689  1337701  1337723  1337729
1337731  1337753  1337779  1337783  1337801  1337803  1337813  1337851  1337873  1337891
1337899  1337909  1337911  1337969  1337971  1337977  1337981  1337983  1337989  1338013
1338041  1338049  1338101  1338107  1338109  1338167  1338217  1338229  1338241  1338247
1338269  1338277  1338299  1338319  1338331  1338343  1338349  1338361  1338367  1338371
1338377  1338391  1338397  1338413  1338443  1338451  1338457  1338473  1338479
1338481  1338499  1338517  1338521  1338539  1338551  1338559  1338581  1338587  1338637
1338641  1338647  1338653  1338661  1338671  1338679  1338703  1338731  1338737  1338749
1338751  1338781  1338787  1338791  1338793  1338803  1338809  1338811  1338823  1338851
1338863  1338871  1338877  1338881  1338907  1338923  1338941  1338979  1339001  1339003
1339027  1339031  1339057  1339061  1339069  1339087  1339097  1339109  1339111  1339127
1339147  1339153  1339157  1339187  1339199  1339207  1339211  1339223  1339229  1339259
1339297  1339333  1339337  1339339  1339343  1339357  1339381  1339391  1339399  1339409
1339411  1339427  1339433  1339463  1339487  1339523  1339529  1339567  1339571  1339577
1339601  1339607  1339619  1339627  1339631  1339643  1339661  1339669  1339673  1339687
1339691  1339693  1339711  1339729  1339759  1339777  1339781  1339813  1339817  1339843
1339853  1339859  1339873  1339901  1339903  1339907  1339909  1339931  1339951  1339969
1339993  1340011  1340021  1340023  1340039  1340041  1340047  1340069  1340071
1340083  1340107  1340113  1340153  1340159  1340179  1340221  1340237  1340243
1340281  1340291  1340321  1340323  1340327  1340329  1340333  1340357  1340359  1340363
1340369  1340387  1340401  1340407  1340411  1340419  1340441  1340447  1340459  1340477
1340489  1340491  1340497  1340527  1340557  1340561  1340587  1340617  1340627  1340639
1340653  1340681  1340687  1340701  1340707  1340723  1340743  1340747  1340753  1340879
1340761  1340767  1340777  1340789  1340797  1340803  1340827  1340837  1340861  1340879
1340891  1340897  1340903  1340929  1340947  1340959  1340981  1341007  1341017  1341019
1341023  1341071  1341073  1341089  1341097  1341101  1341103  1341121  1341143  1341167
1341173  1341187  1341203  1341209  1341217  1341257  1341259  1341293  1341313  1341323
1341359  1341371  1341409  1341433  1341447  1341449  1341467  1341469  1341481
1341491  1341493  1341523  1341539  1341547  1341551  1341553  1341559  1341577  1341581
1341617  1341619  1341661  1341689  1341701  1341707  1341713  1341733  1341737
1341757  1341779  1341787  1341839  1341841  1341863  1341869  1341871  1341881
1341883  1341911  1341919  1341931  1341947  1341983  1342001  1342007  1342049  1342051
1342063  1342067  1342069  1342079  1342087  1342093  1342109  1342111  1342139  1342153
1342163  1342177  1342181  1342199  1342213  1342219  1342223  1342241  1342247  1342259
```

```
1342261 1342267 1342277 1342279 1342283 1342291 1342333 1342339 1342343 1342361
1342379 1342403 1342409 1342423 1342433 1342469 1342493 1342499 1342501 1342519
1342531 1342547 1342567 1342571 1342573 1342591 1342633 1342651 1342657 1342661
1342667 1342669 1342697 1342699 1342723 1342727 1342739 1342741 1342751 1342753
1342799 1342801 1342829 1342849 1342871 1342877 1342883 1342897 1342907 1342909
1342963 1342969 1342973 1342987 1343003 1343009 1343029 1343033 1343047 1343057
1343059 1343071 1343081 1343113 1343161 1343183 1343197 1343203 1343219 1343233
1343257 1343263 1343299 1343311 1343317 1343327 1343333 1343341 1343351 1343369
1343383 1343387 1343389 1343413 1343423 1343431 1343467 1343477 1343479 1343491
1343501 1343519 1343549 1343567 1343569 1343579 1343593 1343597 1343627 1343651
1343653 1343669 1343677 1343681 1343689 1343717 1343723 1343743 1343747 1343759
1343767 1343789 1343791 1343801 1343863 1343873 1343887 1343893 1343899 1343911
1343917 1343941 1343957 1343963 1343971 1343983 1343987 1344011 1344017 1344029
1344043 1344053 1344073 1344113 1344127 1344151 1344157 1344163 1344169 1344181
1344199 1344227 1344271 1344283 1344311 1344319 1344337 1344347 1344359 1344389
1344401 1344403 1344407 1344457 1344461 1344463 1344487 1344491 1344503 1344509
1344569 1344583 1344589 1344593 1344599 1344601 1344641 1344647 1344667 1344669
1344671 1344709 1344727 1344743 1344767 1344779 1344781 1344793 1344797 1344799
1344823 1344829 1344847 1344859 1344869 1344889 1344899 1344901 1344907 1344943
1344947 1344949 1344979 1345009 1345013 1345027 1345033 1345037 1345051 1345079
1345117 1345129 1345139 1345153 1345177 1345207 1345229 1345231 1345241 1345243
1345271 1345273 1345277 1345297 1345301 1345303 1345343 1345349 1345361 1345423
1345441 1345451 1345453 1345457 1345471 1345481 1345507 1345537 1345541 1345549
1345559 1345577 1345583 1345621 1345627 1345633 1345649 1345651 1345667 1345691
1345693 1345699 1345711 1345733 1345759 1345777 1345781 1345783 1345787 1345811
1345859 1345879 1345889 1345913 1345921 1345931 1345933 1345935 1345957 1345973
1345987 1345997 1346003 1346021 1346039 1346063 1346083 1346117 1346119 1346123
1346129 1346143 1346159 1346161 1346173 1346183 1346243 1346249 1346273 1346309
1346311 1346333 1346351 1346361 1346363 1346369 1346377 1346417 1346419 1346437
1346447 1346461 1346479 1346483 1346491 1346533 1346537 1346539 1346567 1346591
1346593 1346603 1346623 1346629 1346641 1346661 1346669 1346693 1346711 1346729
1346743 1346747 1346753 1346773 1346827 1346831 1346843 1346861 1346881 1346899
1346909 1346951 1346953 1346957 1346971 1346977 1346987 1346993 1346999 1347001
1347013 1347019 1347053 1347077 1347091 1347103 1347113 1347127 1347149 1347191
1347209 1347211 1347221 1347223 1347263 1347277 1347287 1347289 1347293 1347329
1347337 1347341 1347377 1347389 1347391 1347397 1347413 1347427 1347433 1347457
1347469 1347473 1347481 1347487 1347527 1347553 1347557 1347569 1347587 1347611
1347617 1347623 1347637 1347667 1347679 1347707 1347713 1347733 1347739 1347757
1347763 1347767 1347769 1347781 1347791 1347817 1347877 1347881 1347893 1347901
1347919 1347937 1347953 1347967 1347971 1347989 1348001 1348013 1348027 1348033
1348051 1348063 1348073 1348111 1348129 1348133 1348157 1348177 1348211 1348223
1348231 1348247 1348271 1348309 1348313 1348331 1348357 1348363 1348379 1348381
1348387 1348393 1348409 1348427 1348441 1348443 1348489 1348493 1348507 1348511
1348517 1348537 1348541 1348547 1348549 1348553 1348561 1348573 1348577 1348583
1348597 1348619 1348621 1348637 1348673 1348727 1348733 1348747 1348757 1348769
1348793 1348843 1348847 1348849 1348871 1348873 1348889 1348891 1348901 1348913
1348931 1348937 1348939 1348951 1348957 1348961 1348987 1349003 1349017 1349053
1349059 1349063 1349077 1349087 1349119 1349129 1349143 1349147 1349149 1349177
1349189 1349207 1349219 1349233 1349251 1349281 1349287 1349317 1349339 1349357
1349363 1349371 1349393 1349401 1349407 1349423 1349471 1349473 1349531 1349533
1349651 1349669 1349671 1349683 1349687 1349701 1349707 1349713 1349737 1349753
1349773 1349807 1349809 1349827 1349867 1349891 1349897 1349903 1349917 1349927
1349947 1349971 1349977 1349993 1350001 1350011 1350023 1350029 1350047 1350049
1350053 1350059 1350061 1350073 1350101 1350119 1350127 1350133 1350187 1350203
1350229 1350247 1350257 1350277 1350287 1350313 1350317 1350319 1350331 1350341
1350367 1350373 1350379 1350383 1350403 1350449 1350457 1350469 1350487 1350509
1350473 1350487 1350509 1350511 1350521 1350533 1350541 1350551 1350553 1350563
1350599 1350607 1350623 1350641 1350647 1350659 1350697 1350703 1350709 1350731
1350743 1350749 1350751 1350761 1350773 1350779 1350799 1350809 1350823 1350847
1350851 1350857 1350883 1350889 1350893 1350911 1350959 1350961 1350977 1351019
1351027 1351037 1351039 1351061 1351069 1351079 1351087 1351093 1351099 1351111
1351117 1351121 1351123 1351127 1351151 1351169 1351171 1351183 1351199 1351213
1351241 1351243 1351247 1351249 1351253 1351267 1351283 1351289 1351291 1351309
1351327 1351373 1351387 1351397 1351403 1351417 1351421 1351423 1351439 1351459
1351523 1351529 1351541 1351543 1351547 1351589 1351621 1351639 1351663 1351667
1351697 1351703 1351711 1351747 1351751 1351781 1351783 1351799 1351813 1351829
1351837 1351841 1351843 1351853 1351897 1351901 1351913 1351919 1351921 1351949
1351957 1351967 1351979 1351981 1351991 1351997 1352069 1352093 1352107 1352111
1352119 1352123 1352149 1352167 1352171 1352191 1352201 1352203 1352207 1352209
1352227 1352257 1352269 1352279 1352291 1352293 1352311 1352317 1352347 1352359
1352369 1352371 1352383 1352389 1352419 1352441 1352443 1352447 1352459 1352489
1352521 1352543 1352557 1352597 1352599 1352627 1352641 1352657 1352669 1352749
1352753 1352761 1352773 1352777 1352779 1352783 1352803 1352807 1352839 1352849
1352861 1352863 1352873 1352881 1352893 1352903 1352917 1352921 1352957 1352963
1352969 1352977 1352987 1352993 1352999 1353007 1353019 1353029 1353043 1353059
1353089 1353091 1353101 1353133 1353137 1353173 1353179 1353197 1353221 1353223
1353239 1353241 1353257 1353259 1353269 1353277 1353281 1353293 1353301 1353311
1353329 1353371 1353377 1353383 1353397 1353433 1353449 1353463 1353479 1353487
1353551 1353581 1353593 1353607 1353613 1353629 1353641 1353679 1353689 1353701
1353707 1353713 1353733 1353743 1353763 1353767 1353791 1353809 1353827 1353839
1353857 1353881 1353887 1353893 1353901 1353917 1353949 1353967 1353973 1353977
1353983 1354007 1354009 1354013 1354019 1354021 1354037 1354043 1354051 1354057
1354063 1354069 1354081 1354127 1354153 1354159 1354181 1354193 1354207 1354229
1354231 1354247 1354267 1354289 1354291 1354303 1354307 1354321 1354333 1354337
1354343 1354349 1354361 1354391 1354393 1354411 1354487 1354489 1354501 1354507
1354523 1354547 1354571 1354583 1354589 1354601 1354603 1354637 1354649 1354651
1354663 1354687 1354711 1354741 1354757 1354811 1354813 1354819 1354823 1354841
1354853 1354877 1354889 1354901 1354931 1354937 1354939 1354943 1354949 1354957
1354981 1354987 1355021 1355047 1355063 1355071 1355089 1355113 1355119 1355129
```

```
1355131  1355153  1355191  1355219  1355243  1355261  1355267  1355269  1355279  1355281
1355293  1355297  1355303  1355309  1355311  1355323  1355329  1355353  1355357  1355363
1355371  1355399  1355401  1355423  1355429  1355443  1355447  1355449  1355483  1355503
1355507  1355513  1355533  1355573  1355579  1355591  1355609  1355623  1355647  1355657
1355659  1355677  1355681  1355693  1355713  1355741  1355743  1355749  1355759  1355771
1355777  1355803  1355807  1355819  1355831  1355843  1355857  1355863  1355867  1355881
1355891  1355917  1355923  1355933  1355941  1355947  1355957  1355983  1355987  1355989
1355999  1356007  1356037  1356053  1356059  1356067  1356077  1356079  1356083  1356101
1356109  1356133  1356143  1356151  1356167  1356169  1356181  1356197  1356221  1356227
1356247  1356253  1356259  1356269  1356319  1356331  1356337  1356371  1356389  1356401
1356409  1356427  1356431  1356451  1356461  1356463  1356473  1356491  1356497  1356499
1356503  1356539  1356547  1356571  1356577  1356599  1356611  1356623  1356629  1356643
1356647  1356659  1356671  1356689  1356697  1356709  1356713  1356721  1356727  1356737
1356743  1356757  1356763  1356811  1356829  1356857  1356869  1356871  1356877  1356899
1356907  1356911  1356913  1356919  1356947  1356973  1357001  1357003  1357009  1357021
1357039  1357043  1357061  1357063  1357079  1357091  1357129  1357163  1357183  1357193
1357201  1357333  1357337  1357351  1357361  1357423  1357427  1357429  1357453  1357463
1357507  1357513  1357537  1357547  1357549  1357561  1357571  1357589  1357619  1357651
1357661  1357669  1357673  1357679  1357703  1357717  1357729  1357753  1357771  1357781
1357787  1357801  1357817  1357823  1357843  1357871  1357883  1357901  1357907  1357919
1357927  1357969  1358009  1358029  1358033  1358039  1358047  1358057  1358059  1358083
1358087  1358111  1358143  1358153  1358167  1358171  1358179  1358183  1358197  1358209
1358213  1358221  1358251  1358257  1358263  1358281  1358297  1358299  1358303  1358309
1358323  1358333  1358353  1358359  1358363  1358369  1358377  1358387  1358393  1358411
1358417  1358437  1358459  1358471  1358477  1358479  1358491  1358507  1358509  1358537
1358561  1358611  1358629  1358647  1358689  1358701  1358713  1358717  1358729  1358741
1358743  1358779  1358783  1358801  1358803  1358807  1358809  1358813  1358821  1358831
1358837  1358857  1358881  1358887  1358891  1358927  1358933  1358939  1358953  1358957
1358977  1358983  1358993  1359023  1359053  1359077  1359091  1359097  1359161  1359173
1359179  1359181  1359209  1359223  1359233  1359247  1359271  1359283  1359307  1359311
1359313  1359329  1359349  1359361  1359367  1359373  1359377  1359401  1359427  1359467
1359487  1359493  1359499  1359509  1359521  1359529  1359563  1359571  1359581  1359619
1359641  1359647  1359661  1359679  1359689  1359719  1359727  1359731  1359733  1359739
1359769  1359803  1359817  1359823  1359853  1359857  1359859  1359871  1359901  1359913
1359937  1359947  1359959  1359971  1359977  1359979  1359991  1359997  1360027  1360049
1360067  1360069  1360081  1360087  1360097  1360103  1360141  1360159  1360171  1360189
1360193  1360201  1360207  1360213  1360223  1360237  1360241  1360253  1360259  1360277
1360279  1360283  1360309  1360313  1360319  1360327  1360349  1360367  1360409  1360417
1360423  1360439  1360441  1360451  1360507  1360511  1360517  1360529  1360531  1360537
1360589  1360591  1360607  1360613  1360631  1360637  1360673  1360687  1360699  1360729
1360747  1360753  1360759  1360763  1360769  1360781  1360783  1360787  1360789  1360811
1360819  1360829  1360847  1360861  1360873  1360889  1360903  1360921  1360943  1360967
1360973  1360981  1361011  1361021  1361023  1361029  1361047  1361051  1361053  1361069
1361081  1361089  1361099  1361123  1361131  1361137  1361149  1361153  1361183  1361197
1361273  1361279  1361287  1361291  1361299  1361317  1361357  1361363  1361383  1361387
1361389  1361401  1361417  1361431  1361441  1361453  1361471  1361491  1361541  1361547
1361533  1361573  1361587  1361593  1361599  1361603  1361609  1361629  1361677  1361699
1361707  1361713  1361741  1361743  1361777  1361791  1361803  1361809  1361813  1361827
1361831  1361839  1361849  1361879  1361911  1361929  1361953  1361957  1361959
1361963  1361999  1362017  1362019  1362041  1362059  1362071  1362089  1362103  1362131
1362161  1362181  1362203  1362209  1362211  1362223  1362247  1362271  1362287  1362293
1362299  1362301  1362337  1362341  1362343  1362349  1362353  1362367  1362371  1362401
1362407  1362409  1362421  1362437  1362443  1362457  1362461  1362463  1362479  1362511
1362521  1362523  1362551  1362607  1362619  1362629  1362631  1362637  1362643  1362653
1362689  1362701  1362707  1362709  1362719  1362731  1362761  1362763  1362787  1362833
1362863  1362869  1362883  1362919  1362929  1362931  1362937  1362967  1362973  1362989
1362997  1363027  1363031  1363051  1363069  1363081  1363093  1363099  1363121  1363133
1363139  1363151  1363157  1363171  1363183  1363189  1363207  1363217  1363223  1363259
1363267  1363273  1363277  1363301  1363309  1363321  1363331  1363333  1363361  1363367
1363381  1363393  1363403  1363409  1363429  1363433  1363447  1363469  1363477  1363489
1363511  1363513  1363541  1363547  1363559  1363577  1363603  1363627  1363631  1363673
1363679  1363717  1363727  1363751  1363753  1363771  1363781  1363787  1363793  1363807
1363811  1363837  1363847  1363867  1363883  1363891  1363897  1363909  1363913  1363933
1363937  1363949  1363963  1363979  1363993  1364009  1364017  1364039  1364047  1364059
1364071  1364101  1364137  1364141  1364161  1364177  1364179  1364183  1364191  1364201
1364203  1364213  1364221  1364239  1364243  1364263  1364287  1364299  1364303  1364309
1364323  1364327  1364329  1364339  1364351  1364359  1364381  1364399  1364401  1364417
1364423  1364431  1364453  1364477  1364483  1364491  1364533  1364569  1364581  1364609
1364617  1364621  1364633  1364663  1364677  1364717  1364719  1364731  1364747  1364761
1364771  1364773  1364791  1364809  1364821  1364861  1364897  1364911  1364917  1364953
1364963  1364969  1364971  1365011  1365019  1365029  1365037  1365043  1365047  1365071
1365079  1365097  1365103  1365107  1365109  1365127  1365137  1365139  1365149  1365163
1365167  1365181  1365193  1365197  1365223  1365239  1365251  1365269  1365281  1365289
1365307  1365311  1365313  1365347  1365361  1365367  1365373  1365383  1365431  1365449
1365461  1365467  1365499  1365503  1365547  1365557  1365563  1365571  1365577  1365583
1365659  1365667  1365703  1365709  1365719  1365731  1365733  1365761  1365767  1365799
1365811  1365821  1365869  1365877  1365907  1365911  1365913  1365919  1365977  1365979
1365983  1366009  1366019  1366021  1366031  1366087  1366093  1366109  1366117  1366121
1366159  1366163  1366187  1366213  1366241  1366279  1366289  1366291  1366297  1366303
1366327  1366333  1366349  1366367  1366397  1366427  1366433  1366459  1366471  1366481
1366483  1366493  1366507  1366517  1366523  1366529  1366531  1366543  1366549  1366577
1366597  1366601  1366609  1366627  1366639  1366643  1366649  1366657  1366661  1366663
1366667  1366693  1366709  1366721  1366747  1366753  1366763  1366769  1366793  1366801
1366829  1366831  1366837  1366843  1366861  1366877  1366889  1366903  1366907  1366921
1366943  1366963  1366967  1366979  1366991  1366997  1367017  1367027  1367057  1367059
1367077  1367087  1367101  1367117  1367137  1367141  1367153  1367159  1367161  1367167
1367203  1367231  1367257  1367279  1367291  1367299  1367323  1367339  1367341  1367383
1367393  1367417  1367423  1367447  1367459  1367461  1367479  1367501  1367507  1367519
1367521  1367533  1367539  1367543  1367551  1367573  1367579  1367581  1367593  1367617
```

1367647	1367687	1367711	1367713	1367749	1367761	1367777	1367783	1367789	1367819
1367827	1367831	1367851	1367857	1367869	1367881	1367887	1367893	1367903	1367921
1367929	1367953	1367963	1367987	1368013	1368053	1368071	1368077	1368079	1368083
1368119	1368121	1368127	1368161	1368163	1368167	1368173	1368181	1368187	1368203
1368229	1368233	1368251	1368253	1368259	1368271	1368281	1368287	1368319	1368329
1368331	1368337	1368343	1368349	1368373	1368377	1368397	1368401	1368439	1368443
1368461	1368463	1368467	1368469	1368473	1368481	1368491	1368509	1368527	1368529
1368547	1368599	1368617	1368643	1368659	1368673	1368683	1368727	1368737	1368739
1368761	1368791	1368793	1368797	1368803	1368811	1368827	1368839	1368841	1368847
1368869	1368907	1368911	1368943	1368967	1368971	1368979	1368989	1369009	1369013
1369019	1369021	1369033	1369051	1369057	1369097	1369099	1369103	1369133	1369139
1369153	1369169	1369201	1369217	1369219	1369223	1369229	1369243	1369297	1369309
1369309	1369321	1369337	1369339	1369369	1369373	1369391	1369393	1369411	1369427
1369429	1369451	1369457	1369483	1369499	1369517	1369531	1369541	1369559	1369561
1369597	1369607	1369619	1369651	1369667	1369723	1369727	1369733	1369747	1369759
1369763	1369783	1369787	1369789	1369793	1369801	1369813	1369831	1369853	1369861
1369871	1369883	1369897	1369943	1369949	1369981	1369991	1370027	1370051	1370053
1370059	1370063	1370069	1370077	1370093	1370099	1370101	1370111	1370113	1370143
1370177	1370189	1370197	1370219	1370227	1370263	1370269	1370287	1370297	1370311
1370321	1370323	1370329	1370359	1370377	1370389	1370407	1370431	1370449	1370459
1370461	1370471	1370483	1370491	1370503	1370519	1370521	1370531	1370533	1370537
1370587	1370597	1370599	1370617	1370623	1370657	1370669	1370683	1370687	1370701
1370723	1370741	1370749	1370773	1370779	1370819	1370821	1370833	1370839	1370857
1370861	1370881	1370899	1370909	1370921	1370933	1370953	1370977	1370981	1370987
1371001	1371017	1371031	1371047	1371061	1371079	1371089	1371103	1371107	1371113
1371119	1371121	1371137	1371151	1371157	1371177	1371187	1371193	1371217	1371229
1371259	1371263	1371301	1371343	1371353	1371389	1371397	1371431	1371449	1371493
1371499	1371511	1371541	1371551	1371563	1371569	1371581	1371583	1371589	1371593
1371599	1371607	1371619	1371641	1371647	1371653	1371661	1371683	1371703	1371731
1371749	1371763	1371767	1371779	1371803	1371817	1371821	1371841	1371863	1371893
1371899	1371911	1371913	1371947	1371949	1371989	1371991	1372027	1372043	1372051
1372051	1372079	1372081	1372097	1372103	1372109	1372127	1372139	1372171	1372183
1372187	1372207	1372211	1372243	1372253	1372271	1372303	1372307	1372331	1372363
1372369	1372373	1372379	1372391	1372403	1372411	1372417	1372421	1372451	1372471
1372493	1372531	1372537	1372543	1372549	1372559	1372583	1372607	1372621	1372627
1372633	1372661	1372667	1372673	1372727	1372739	1372747	1372757	1372759	1372771
1372799	1372829	1372843	1372849	1372867	1372879	1372913	1372933	1372951	1372957
1372961	1372963	1372979	1372981	1372991	1372999	1373027	1373041	1373051	1373059
1373081	1373087	1373129	1373137	1373147	1373153	1373159	1373161	1373167	1373173
1373189	1373191	1373201	1373219	1373227	1373233	1373321	1373341	1373347	1373357
1373363	1373369	1373371	1373381	1373417	1373419	1373431	1373441	1373473	1373483
1373497	1373501	1373521	1373531	1373539	1373543	1373557	1373563	1373591	1373611
1373627	1373639	1373677	1373683	1373689	1373717	1373761	1373777	1373789	1373803
1373819	1373839	1373843	1373849	1373851	1373861	1373873	1373881	1373887	1373891
1373959	1373989	1374007	1374019	1374029	1374041	1374053	1374067	1374073	1374077
1374083	1374101	1374133	1374157	1374173	1374187	1374209	1374211	1374239	1374257
1374271	1374277	1374299	1374301	1374311	1374313	1374341	1374367	1374377	1374379
1374407	1374413	1374431	1374437	1374473	1374481	1374499	1374511	1374533	1374539
1374547	1374551	1374557	1374559	1374589	1374601	1374613	1374617	1374619	1374673
1374677	1374683	1374691	1374697	1374713	1374719	1374721	1374731	1374743	1374749
1374761	1374787	1374827	1374833	1374847	1374851	1374869	1374887	1374929	1374937
1374941	1374953	1374983	1375007	1375013	1375019	1375021	1375037	1375039	1375043
1375051	1375063	1375091	1375103	1375109	1375111	1375117	1375133	1375141	1375159
1375189	1375211	1375219	1375223	1375237	1375243	1375261	1375303	1375307	1375313
1375337	1375357	1375373	1375379	1375411	1375417	1375421	1375433	1375457	1375481
1375513	1375531	1375547	1375567	1375571	1375597	1375601	1375609	1375637	1375639
1375669	1375679	1375681	1375709	1375723	1375727	1375729	1375739	1375747	1375757
1375769	1375783	1375799	1375807	1375813	1375817	1375819	1375823	1375853	1375877
1375879	1375901	1375921	1375937	1375949	1375951	1375981	1375987	1376003	1376009
1376017	1376033	1376071	1376077	1376093	1376131	1376147	1376153	1376161	1376171
1376173	1376191	1376197	1376203	1376213	1376231	1376237	1376257	1376317	1376321
1376339	1376359	1376377	1376383	1376393	1376407	1376423	1376429	1376443	1376447
1376449	1376461	1376467	1376471	1376491	1376497	1376503	1376509	1376513	1376533
1376539	1376567	1376591	1376603	1376621	1376623	1376653	1376693	1376699	1376701
1376719	1376723	1376729	1376737	1376747	1376773	1376777	1376789	1376819	1376827
1376839	1376897	1376899	1376923	1376929	1376939	1376957	1376971	1376981	1377023
1377031	1377037	1377041	1377043	1377071	1377107	1377121	1377127	1377133	1377137
1377151	1377157	1377169	1377179	1377191	1377223	1377269	1377281	1377293	1377317
1377347	1377349	1377353	1377359	1377371	1377377	1377403	1377407	1377421	1377427
1377427	1377451	1377457	1377469	1377479	1377487	1377491	1377499	1377517	1377533
1377553	1377577	1377589	1377601	1377637	1377643	1377653	1377659	1377667	1377679
1377713	1377737	1377749	1377751	1377757	1377773	1377781	1377787	1377791	1377793
1377811	1377821	1377829	1377847	1377851	1377853	1377881	1377911	1377913	1377923
1377931	1377967	1377973	1377977	1377983	1378001	1378007	1378009	1378019	1378031
1378033	1378057	1378061	1378067	1378073	1378081	1378099	1378103	1378129	1378141
1378147	1378151	1378163	1378187	1378189	1378199	1378217	1378219	1378231	1378249
1378253	1378271	1378277	1378301	1378319	1378337	1378339	1378373	1378387	1378397
1378427	1378439	1378441	1378499	1378501	1378511	1378519	1378529	1378541	1378561
1378567	1378579	1378589	1378591	1378603	1378613	1378639	1378669	1378673	1378679
1378691	1378697	1378703	1378721	1378733	1378759	1378763	1378777	1378799	1378801
1378807	1378813	1378823	1378831	1378841	1378843	1378847	1378859	1378903	1378907
1378943	1378957	1378961	1378969	1378997	1378999	1379003	1379017	1379029	1379047
1379069	1379071	1379089	1379099	1379107	1379111	1379129	1379137	1379141	1379167
1379173	1379201	1379207	1379237	1379239	1379251	1379263	1379291	1379321	1379353
1379359	1379369	1379383	1379387	1379423	1379447	1379449	1379461	1379467	1379473
1379489	1379491	1379503	1379509	1379513	1379519	1379549	1379579	1379603	1379621
1379629	1379633	1379639	1379641	1379657	1379659	1379663	1379681	1379699	1379753
1379797	1379801	1379803	1379809	1379813	1379821	1379857	1379867	1379869	1379879
1379887	1379897	1379923	1379929	1379947	1379953	1379957	1379969	1379981	1379993

```
1380007  1380013  1380031  1380047  1380053  1380083  1380149  1380157  1380163  1380199
1380221  1380227  1380233  1380241  1380251  1380259  1380271  1380277  1380283  1380289
1380307  1380317  1380319  1380329  1380341  1380377  1380389  1380397  1380419  1380427
1380439  1380443  1380469  1380499  1380517  1380551  1380557  1380563  1380571  1380607
1380611  1380619  1380623  1380629  1380637  1380653  1380671  1380677  1380679  1380707
1380721  1380727  1380763  1380779  1380781  1380793  1380811  1380817  1380853  1380881
1380887  1380889  1380913  1380931  1380947  1380949  1380959  1380971  1380983  1380997
1381027  1381033  1381043  1381057  1381069  1381103  1381109  1381111  1381141  1381147
1381153  1381187  1381207  1381213  1381217  1381229  1381231  1381271  1381273  1381277
1381279  1381291  1381297  1381307  1381313  1381327  1381337  1381349  1381381  1381397
1381409  1381411  1381421  1381427  1381439  1381441  1381451  1381459  1381483  1381487
1381489  1381493  1381507  1381517  1381519  1381529  1381537  1381553  1381559  1381609
1381613  1381621  1381637  1381643  1381649  1381693  1381697  1381727  1381739  1381747
1381759  1381769  1381819  1381837  1381859  1381871  1381883  1381901  1381907  1381921
1381967  1381969  1381973  1381979  1381993  1381997  1381999  1382021  1382023  1382039
1382057  1382089  1382099  1382107  1382113  1382123  1382159  1382167  1382177  1382179
1382189  1382191  1382201  1382207  1382221  1382237  1382243  1382279  1382291  1382309
1382327  1382393  1382419  1382449  1382477  1382501  1382503  1382519  1382527  1382533
1382543  1382551  1382567  1382597  1382609  1382621  1382629  1382651  1382663  1382671
1382677  1382681  1382753  1382767  1382779  1382819  1382827  1382861  1382891  1382893
1382939  1382957  1382959  1382977  1382987  1382989  1382999  1383037  1383043  1383047
1383077  1383089  1383113  1383121  1383139  1383169  1383191  1383199  1383203  1383209
1383287  1383301  1383323  1383331  1383359  1383367  1383377  1383379  1383391  1383401
1383433  1383449  1383451  1383479  1383493  1383497  1383509  1383517  1383521  1383553
1383583  1383589  1383593  1383607  1383653  1383659  1383667  1383691  1383731  1383737
1383743  1383757  1383761  1383769  1383797  1383799  1383803  1383829  1383853  1383857
1383881  1383901  1383913  1383917  1383923  1383937  1383947  1383959  1383961  1383983
1384013  1384027  1384043  1384067  1384069  1384079  1384087  1384091  1384099  1384109
1384121  1384139  1384171  1384189  1384193  1384219  1384231  1384237  1384241  1384247
1384249  1384303  1384309  1384337  1384343  1384349  1384351  1384387  1384391  1384403
1384433  1384477  1384499  1384501  1384507  1384561  1384601  1384613  1384619  1384631
1384661  1384673  1384679  1384697  1384699  1384711  1384717  1384727  1384741  1384781
1384787  1384813  1384829  1384843  1384847  1384849  1384861  1384879  1384909  1384913
1384919  1384921  1384937  1384951  1384961  1384963  1384979  1384993  1385003  1385009
1385017  1385023  1385039  1385051  1385057  1385071  1385077  1385093  1385099  1385101
1385113  1385117  1385147  1385149  1385171  1385179  1385183  1385191  1385203  1385213
1385273  1385287  1385291  1385299  1385303  1385327  1385333  1385341  1385369  1385383
1385387  1385389  1385393  1385399  1385401  1385411  1385429  1385437  1385441  1385459
1385471  1385477  1385479  1385507  1385521  1385561  1385563  1385569  1385603  1385609
1385621  1385647  1385693  1385743  1385749  1385753  1385767  1385777  1385779  1385801
1385809  1385827  1385833  1385837  1385843  1385861  1385863  1385869  1385873  1385887
1385893  1385899  1385921  1385929  1385947  1385953  1385963  1385977  1385987  1386013
1386037  1386043  1386053  1386079  1386083  1386089  1386097  1386139  1386149  1386167
1386179  1386181  1386193  1386199  1386211  1386223  1386239  1386263  1386271  1386283
1386293  1386311  1386313  1386317  1386337  1386361  1386377  1386379  1386383  1386419
1386443  1386457  1386479  1386491  1386499  1386551  1386557  1386569  1386587  1386607
1386611  1386617  1386631  1386643  1386659  1386667  1386691  1386703  1386731  1386733
1386757  1386767  1386773  1386779  1386787  1386811  1386821  1386823  1386839  1386857
1386863  1386881  1386883  1386901  1386929  1386947  1386949  1386953  1386977  1386991
1387007  1387021  1387037  1387039  1387069  1387109  1387117  1387121  1387123  1387129
1387147  1387151  1387163  1387189  1387207  1387213  1387231  1387259  1387261  1387271
1387289  1387313  1387327  1387349  1387357  1387363  1387367  1387403  1387417  1387427
1387433  1387499  1387501  1387517  1387531  1387571  1387579  1387583  1387597  1387601
1387649  1387667  1387669  1387681  1387691  1387717  1387721  1387733  1387781  1387783
1387801  1387807  1387819  1387823  1387847  1387849  1387871  1387877  1387879  1387913
1387921  1387927  1387943  1387961  1387987  1388003  1388011  1388021  1388029  1388041
1388053  1388059  1388063  1388069  1388077  1388081  1388113  1388117  1388141  1388161
1388171  1388183  1388227  1388243  1388269  1388279  1388287  1388293  1388297  1388323
1388327  1388353  1388357  1388363  1388369  1388381  1388393  1388411  1388419  1388449
1388461  1388467  1388473  1388477  1388479  1388483  1388587  1388593  1388603  1388623
1388627  1388633  1388641  1388659  1388669  1388687  1388693  1388701  1388719  1388743
1388773  1388789  1388791  1388797  1388819  1388837  1388873  1388887  1388927  1388941
1388953  1388963  1388969  1389001  1389007  1389083  1389097  1389107  1389133  1389139
1389149  1389163  1389169  1389173  1389191  1389209  1389211  1389217  1389221  1389229
1389233  1389251  1389259  1389277  1389281  1389301  1389319  1389329  1389347  1389371
1389383  1389403  1389431  1389433  1389439  1389469  1389473  1389481  1389491  1389511
1389533  1389539  1389547  1389551  1389559  1389569  1389587  1389589  1389623  1389629
1389643  1389667  1389673  1389691  1389697  1389727  1389749  1389769  1389797  1389809
1389811  1389833  1389841  1389851  1389853  1389877  1389887  1389893  1389911  1389917
1389919  1389941  1389961  1389989  1389991  1390003  1390019  1390027  1390043  1390069
1390087  1390111  1390117  1390121  1390157  1390159  1390177  1390199  1390219  1390241
1390247  1390253  1390283  1390297  1390309  1390331  1390339  1390343  1390357  1390369
1390387  1390391  1390399  1390409  1390421  1390457  1390469  1390471  1390483  1390489
1390507  1390517  1390541  1390547  1390573  1390601  1390607  1390619  1390621  1390633
1390639  1390643  1390681  1390693  1390699  1390703  1390709  1390729  1390733  1390757
1390759  1390771  1390783  1390789  1390801  1390813  1390841  1390847  1390859  1390891
1390901  1390903  1390913  1390919  1390931  1390937  1390967  1390969  1390979  1390993
1391011  1391023  1391029  1391041  1391051  1391057  1391081  1391083  1391087  1391113
1391119  1391129  1391183  1391189  1391207  1391233  1391239  1391261  1391267  1391281
1391287  1391317  1391323  1391353  1391363  1391381  1391393  1391407  1391413  1391419
1391441  1391447  1391461  1391479  1391483  1391519  1391521  1391549  1391557  1391561
1391563  1391567  1391573  1391587  1391597  1391627  1391629  1391641  1391647  1391651
1391663  1391669  1391701  1391713  1391729  1391779  1391849  1391861  1391893  1391899
1391917  1391927  1391933  1391941  1391969  1391981  1391989  1392007  1392089  1392101
1392133  1392143  1392163  1392197  1392221  1392229  1392233  1392253  1392269
1392271  1392277  1392311  1392323  1392353  1392361  1392367  1392373  1392379  1392407
1392431  1392449  1392451  1392463  1392473  1392481  1392497  1392527  1392539  1392541
1392553  1392557  1392607  1392619  1392631  1392649  1392679  1392697  1392701  1392707
1392731  1392733  1392763  1392773  1392779  1392803  1392817  1392829  1392847  1392851
```

```
1392877 1392883 1392889 1392901 1392943 1392953 1392959 1392977 1392983 1393003
1393019 1393027 1393039 1393043 1393069 1393079 1393097 1393103 1393121 1393123
1393141 1393159 1393181 1393187 1393193 1393219 1393229 1393241 1393253 1393261
1393283 1393297 1393313 1393331 1393333 1393361 1393367 1393373 1393387 1393397
1393417 1393451 1393453 1393459 1393489 1393493 1393523 1393559 1393577 1393581
1393589 1393607 1393619 1393627 1393633 1393649 1393657 1393661 1393663 1393681
1393687 1393693 1393697 1393723 1393739 1393751 1393771 1393781 1393807 1393817
1393837 1393871 1393883 1393891 1393913 1393919 1393921 1393927 1393933 1393937
1393939 1393957 1393963 1393967 1393969 1393979 1393981 1393991 1393999 1394009
1394021 1394023 1394027 1394047 1394083 1394089 1394131 1394137 1394141 1394149
1394167 1394177 1394209 1394251 1394269 1394273 1394293 1394297 1394299 1394321
1394359 1394383 1394389 1394401 1394413 1394417 1394423 1394431 1394441 1394453
1394479 1394489 1394501 1394509 1394539 1394557 1394573 1394579 1394599 1394633
1394669 1394671 1394681 1394699 1394707 1394711 1394713 1394737 1394747
1394753 1394777 1394821 1394831 1394849 1394857 1394891 1394893 1394909
1394917 1394933 1394941 1394977 1394983 1394989 1394993 1395001 1395029 1395047
1395059 1395067 1395073 1395077 1395083 1395109 1395127 1395137 1395167 1395179
1395181 1395187 1395209 1395263 1395283 1395293 1395301 1395319 1395323
1395337 1395347 1395361 1395413 1395419 1395439 1395463 1395467 1395469 1395481
1395487 1395491 1395523 1395533 1395551 1395553 1395571 1395577 1395593 1395613
1395623 1395629 1395643 1395659 1395661 1395671 1395673 1395679 1395697 1395739
1395743 1395749 1395773 1395781 1395791 1395809 1395817 1395829 1395839 1395859
1395869 1395871 1395883 1395907 1395923 1395943 1395983 1395991 1395997 1396001
1396007 1396013 1396027 1396033 1396037 1396049 1396051 1396061 1396069 1396093
1396099 1396103 1396127 1396141 1396183 1396189 1396207 1396211 1396217 1396223
1396237 1396247 1396259 1396273 1396301 1396303 1396327 1396331 1396387 1396393
1396411 1396427 1396429 1396433 1396453 1396469 1396487 1396513 1396517 1396523
1396529 1396531 1396541 1396547 1396559 1396561 1396579 1396607 1396613 1396627
1396657 1396663 1396667 1396673 1396679 1396687 1396691 1396697 1396711 1396723
1396751 1396753 1396757 1396789 1396817 1396819 1396841 1396847 1396849 1396867
1396877 1396903 1396909 1396939 1396949 1396967 1396979 1396991
1397021 1397023 1397029 1397041 1397057 1397059 1397063 1397069 1397087 1397101
1397107 1397117 1397119 1397131 1397153 1397159 1397161 1397167 1397177 1397189
1397219 1397233 1397251 1397257 1397261 1397263 1397287 1397303 1397311 1397329
1397339 1397359 1397437 1397441 1397443 1397447 1397477 1397483 1397491 1397497
1397509 1397521 1397531 1397551 1397563 1397569 1397579 1397581 1397603 1397609
1397633 1397657 1397681 1397717 1397719 1397729 1397743 1397761 1397783 1397833
1397839 1397857 1397861 1397873 1397881 1397909 1397933 1397939 1397951 1397953
1397959 1397983 1397989 1397999 1398011 1398017 1398031 1398037 1398043 1398049
1398053 1398079 1398083 1398091 1398107 1398113 1398121 1398127 1398139 1398151
1398161 1398197 1398209 1398211 1398217 1398227 1398247 1398251 1398259 1398263
1398281 1398283 1398307 1398323 1398329 1398347 1398349 1398367
1398401 1398407 1398413 1398421 1398427 1398451 1398473 1398493 1398497 1398511
1398521 1398541 1398557 1398559 1398569 1398577 1398581 1398599 1398611 1398619
1398623 1398659 1398667 1398701 1398707 1398721 1398731 1398737 1398763 1398769
1398773 1398779 1398803 1398841 1398871 1398881 1398911 1398967 1398973
1398977 1398979 1398997 1399003 1399009 1399019 1399033 1399037 1399039 1399063
1399109 1399121 1399129 1399133 1399183 1399187 1399193 1399199 1399201 1399213
1399231 1399261 1399271 1399273 1399283 1399301 1399319 1399351 1399357 1399361
1399367 1399373 1399381 1399393 1399399 1399403 1399417 1399427 1399439 1399441
1399469 1399471 1399481 1399493 1399499 1399507 1399513 1399529 1399537 1399541
1399547 1399549 1399553 1399577 1399579 1399583 1399589 1399603 1399609 1399621
1399633 1399639 1399663 1399679 1399687 1399691 1399709 1399721 1399733 1399751
1399777 1399789 1399793 1399813 1399817 1399819 1399837 1399843 1399847 1399861
1399883 1399913 1399919 1399943 1399963 1399999 1400017 1400023 1400029 1400039
1400051 1400081 1400093 1400107 1400131 1400141 1400143 1400159 1400173 1400197
1400249 1400251 1400261 1400287 1400297 1400299 1400303 1400327 1400353 1400369
1400383 1400387 1400411 1400417 1400423 1400449 1400453 1400479 1400489 1400507
1400527 1400543 1400557 1400587 1400599 1400627 1400653 1400669 1400687 1400689
1400701 1400731 1400747 1400753 1400801 1400803 1400807 1400809 1400861 1400863
1400873 1400879 1400881 1400887 1400899 1400909 1400923 1400939 1400941 1400947
1400989 1401007 1401017 1401031 1401053 1401067 1401083 1401119 1401131 1401139
1401151 1401167 1401187 1401199 1401203 1401217 1401233 1401247 1401263 1401287
1401317 1401319 1401349 1401371 1401377 1401401 1401403 1401409 1401437 1401443
1401461 1401481 1401487 1401511 1401529 1401559 1401571 1401601 1401607 1401613
1401623 1401629 1401641 1401679 1401683 1401703 1401713 1401721 1401737 1401739
1401761 1401767 1401791 1401793 1401809 1401811 1401817 1401821 1401823 1401857
1401931 1401943 1401971 1401977 1401979 1401989 1402003 1402019 1402031
1402061 1402081 1402087 1402123 1402127 1402129 1402147 1402153 1402157 1402169
1402201 1402231 1402249 1402267 1402277 1402283 1402301 1402309 1402361 1402363
1402367 1402369 1402391 1402397 1402399 1402417 1402421 1402439 1402459 1402477
1402493 1402501 1402519 1402529 1402543 1402547 1402567 1402571 1402589 1402603
1402673 1402693 1402699 1402721 1402727 1402763 1402771 1402799 1402801
1402811 1402829 1402847 1402859 1402871 1402873 1402883 1402901 1402937 1402943
1402957 1403009 1403021 1403057 1403071 1403081 1403113 1403137 1403147 1403159
1403167 1403189 1403239 1403249 1403251 1403257 1403261 1403287 1403309 1403323
1403327 1403351 1403357 1403371 1403377 1403383 1403393 1403399 1403407 1403411
1403417 1403429 1403443 1403453 1403459 1403461 1403489 1403491 1403531 1403533
1403557 1403569 1403579 1403603 1403609 1403617 1403627 1403641 1403651 1403653
1403657 1403681 1403683 1403693 1403747 1403789 1403791 1403807 1403813 1403819
1403827 1403833 1403849 1403869 1403879 1403887 1403893 1403903 1403921 1403923
1403933 1403939 1403951 1403953 1403957 1403971 1403981 1404059 1404061 1404071
1404107 1404131 1404133 1404163 1404181 1404191 1404211 1404229 1404257 1404283
1404287 1404289 1404323 1404367 1404371 1404391 1404397 1404419 1404427 1404437
1404439 1404467 1404479 1404497 1404503 1404527 1404539 1404547 1404569 1404577
1404581 1404583 1404617 1404643 1404649 1404653 1404671 1404709 1404721 1404737
1404743 1404749 1404763 1404791 1404797 1404811 1404833 1404859 1404869 1404881
1404883 1404899 1404911 1404919 1404937 1404959 1404961 1404973 1404979 1404989
1405007 1405009 1405039 1405087 1405097 1405099 1405109 1405127 1405133 1405141
```

```
1405147  1405153  1405163  1405171  1405181  1405207  1405211  1405241  1405247  1405249
1405267  1405289  1405309  1405319  1405333  1405343  1405351  1405361  1405363  1405367
1405387  1405403  1405421  1405451  1405477  1405493  1405511  1405513  1405529  1405531
1405561  1405583  1405597  1405631  1405637  1405643  1405669  1405681  1405693  1405699
1405709  1405721  1405751  1405759  1405769  1405787  1405801  1405813  1405823  1405841
1405879  1405919  1405927  1405939  1405979  1405997  1406011  1406033  1406039  1406051
1406071  1406077  1406081  1406089  1406101  1406159  1406161  1406173  1406213  1406221
1406231  1406267  1406281  1406311  1406351  1406357  1406387  1406389  1406417  1406429
1406441  1406443  1406453  1406459  1406479  1406497  1406521  1406533  1406539  1406543
1406549  1406557  1406591  1406593  1406609  1406617  1406633  1406651  1406677  1406683
1406689  1406701  1406707  1406771  1406773  1406789  1406803  1406807  1406827  1406837
1406849  1406857  1406861  1406879  1406897  1406927  1406939  1406947  1406953  1406959
1406983  1407011  1407017  1407019  1407023  1407037  1407041  1407047  1407053  1407061
1407101  1407113  1407143  1407151  1407181  1407187  1407193  1407223  1407229  1407247
1407251  1407253  1407257  1407271  1407281  1407293  1407317  1407319  1407323  1407337
1407361  1407383  1407389  1407391  1407397  1407409  1407449  1407467  1407473  1407487
1407491  1407499  1407503  1407533  1407547  1407551  1407557  1407559  1407569  1407587
1407599  1407607  1407611  1407613  1407619  1407629  1407647  1407661  1407667  1407671
1407709  1407727  1407751  1407793  1407811  1407823  1407827  1407829  1407841  1407851
1407869  1407877  1407883  1407893  1407937  1407971  1407997  1408007  1408009  1408021
1408027  1408031  1408067  1408079  1408087  1408111  1408123  1408151  1408177  1408181
1408201  1408217  1408219  1408241  1408279  1408289  1408301  1408339  1408349  1408367
1408373  1408397  1408409  1408411  1408417  1408453  1408493  1408499  1408523  1408529
1408567  1408573  1408577  1408597  1408601  1408613  1408619  1408621  1408633  1408651
1408661  1408663  1408669  1408697  1408699  1408703  1408709  1408741  1408763  1408769
1408787  1408789  1408817  1408829  1408843  1408859  1408867  1408871  1408873  1408879
1408889  1408961  1408963  1408987  1408991  1408993  1408999  1409017  1409027  1409033
1409041  1409053  1409063  1409069  1409101  1409117  1409159  1409171  1409203  1409207
1409209  1409227  1409231  1409237  1409251  1409263  1409299  1409311  1409327  1409329
1409341  1409357  1409381  1409393  1409399  1409407  1409459  1409467  1409489  1409491
1409503  1409519  1409531  1409533  1409537  1409543  1409549  1409579  1409581  1409587
1409633  1409651  1409659  1409677  1409713  1409717  1409731  1409741  1409753  1409773
1409783  1409789  1409791  1409797  1409803  1409833  1409843  1409851  1409869  1409879
1409899  1409917  1409957  1409977  1409999  1410007  1410023  1410037  1410043  1410049
1410053  1410077  1410103  1410109  1410139  1410163  1410169  1410179  1410187  1410197
1410203  1410217  1410223  1410239  1410247  1410257  1410289  1410293  1410301  1410307
1410319  1410361  1410373  1410377  1410397  1410401  1410413  1410421  1410449  1410457
1410463  1410467  1410499  1410509  1410527  1410553  1410571  1410587  1410599  1410623
1410653  1410679  1410683  1410697  1410707  1410709  1410727  1410733  1410743  1410757
1410767  1410781  1410803  1410809  1410811  1410823  1410833  1410859  1410887  1410907
1410923  1410931  1410943  1410947  1410961  1410971  1410973  1410977  1410979
1411013  1411021  1411037  1411043  1411049  1411061  1411099  1411117  1411127  1411141
1411159  1411171  1411181  1411183  1411199  1411219  1411243  1411247  1411271  1411283
1411297  1411307  1411313  1411331  1411369  1411387  1411411  1411427  1411429  1411433
1411471  1411481  1411499  1411519  1411541  1411559  1411573  1411583  1411603  1411607
1411609  1411621  1411663  1411669  1411667  1411679  1411703  1411721  1411727  1411759
1411769  1411777  1411783  1411789  1411793  1411829  1411831  1411847  1411873  1411889
1411897  1411903  1411931  1411937  1411961  1411979  1411987  1411997  1412009  1412011
1412017  1412041  1412051  1412053  1412057  1412087  1412093  1412107  1412141  1412153
1412171  1412183  1412189  1412197  1412219  1412221  1412227  1412231  1412239  1412273
1412287  1412297  1412317  1412321  1412339  1412347  1412351  1412357  1412363  1412381
1412393  1412399  1412413  1412419  1412429  1412447  1412461  1412471  1412473  1412483
1412497  1412527  1412539  1412563  1412597  1412603  1412617  1412629  1412633  1412641
1412647  1412651  1412659  1412681  1412689  1412693  1412711  1412713  1412753  1412759
1412767  1412777  1412779  1412791  1412797  1412813  1412833  1412837  1412849  1412857
1412861  1412863  1412893  1412903  1412911  1412947  1412969  1412981  1413001
1413007  1413017  1413029  1413031  1413043  1413077  1413079  1413089  1413103  1413107
1413131  1413133  1413161  1413169  1413171  1413179  1413211  1413221  1413233  1413253
1413271  1413283  1413301  1413341  1413361  1413371  1413413  1413427  1413439  1413443
1413449  1413479  1413481  1413487  1413509  1413521  1413523  1413527  1413541  1413551
1413571  1413593  1413623  1413641  1413643  1413661  1413663  1413673  1413679  1413689
1413691  1413749  1413751  1413773  1413781  1413793  1413827  1413829  1413851  1413859
1413889  1413931  1413949  1413959  1413991  1414001  1414027  1414031  1414061  1414067
1414073  1414081  1414097  1414123  1414129  1414181  1414207  1414211  1414241  1414261
1414267  1414291  1414297  1414307  1414319  1414321  1414331  1414373  1414381  1414393
1414397  1414409  1414423  1414453  1414463  1414481  1414507  1414513  1414549  1414573
1414577  1414597  1414613  1414619  1414627  1414631  1414663  1414681  1414697  1414703
1414709  1414733  1414741  1414801  1414837  1414843  1414913  1414921  1414943  1414957
1414979  1414993  1414999  1415023  1415039  1415059  1415069  1415077  1415081  1415083
1415093  1415137  1415143  1415179  1415191  1415207  1415221  1415231  1415237  1415263
1415273  1415303  1415317  1415321  1415339  1415341  1415357  1415377  1415387  1415411
1415419  1415441  1415459  1415467  1415473  1415497  1415507  1415567  1415569  1415591
1415611  1415629  1415639  1415647  1415651  1415681  1415707  1415741  1415753  1415773
1415779  1415783  1415803  1415831  1415833  1415837  1415851  1415861  1415899  1415929
1415933  1415957  1415971  1415977  1415989  1416007  1416011  1416029  1416031  1416043
1416047  1416053  1416061  1416067  1416071  1416073  1416097  1416109  1416113  1416137
1416143  1416161  1416167  1416187  1416197  1416199  1416209  1416211  1416223  1416277
1416293  1416299  1416329  1416341  1416433  1416449  1416461  1416473  1416479  1416487
1416497  1416511  1416551  1416577  1416587  1416601  1416617  1416629  1416631  1416641
1416671  1416691  1416703  1416713  1416739  1416749  1416757  1416769  1416799  1416869
1416809  1416829  1416851  1416859  1416871  1416913  1416931  1416937  1416941  1416949
1416953  1416977  1416997  1417019  1417033  1417051  1417057  1417067  1417093  1417123
1417159  1417183  1417189  1417217  1417219  1417223  1417253  1417261  1417271  1417277
1417301  1417303  1417309  1417313  1417319  1417331  1417337  1417349  1417363  1417369
1417393  1417399  1417417  1417439  1417453  1417459  1417463  1417469  1417487  1417489
1417499  1417523  1417541  1417543  1417561  1417573  1417583  1417597  1417631  1417639
1417649  1417679  1417693  1417699  1417727  1417747  1417751  1417769  1417771  1417777
1417807  1417831  1417841  1417873  1417883  1417891  1417901  1417907  1417931  1417967
1417979  1417991  1417993  1418009  1418023  1418047  1418051  1418059  1418063  1418077
```

1418093 1418101 1418107 1418117 1418119 1418147 1418159 1418161 1418167 1418201
1418213 1418233 1418239 1418243 1418251 1418257 1418267 1418297 1418299 1418353
1418363 1418399 1418423 1418447 1418449 1418453 1418491 1418513 1418551 1418561
1418567 1418569 1418579 1418581 1418611 1418621 1418687 1418689 1418693 1418741
1418759 1418771 1418783 1418797 1418831 1418849 1418867 1418869 1418873 1418881
1418917 1418951 1418953 1418959 1418983 1419001 1419023 1419029 1419037 1419059
1419073 1419079 1419083 1419097 1419137 1419157 1419161 1419163 1419179 1419199
1419233 1419239 1419247 1419251 1419263 1419269 1419293 1419311 1419317 1419337
1419349 1419359 1419371 1419373 1419377 1419389 1419403 1419427 1419469 1419487
1419493 1419497 1419511 1419527 1419533 1419557 1419563 1419589 1419611 1419617
1419641 1419643 1419673 1419679 1419683 1419689 1419697 1419701 1419713 1419739
1419749 1419763 1419791 1419799 1419809 1419827 1419829 1419833 1419839 1419877
1419883 1419911 1419919 1419947 1419961 1419967 1419973 1420009 1420031 1420037
1420039 1420057 1420063 1420073 1420091 1420093 1420099 1420109 1420121 1420123
1420151 1420169 1420201 1420207 1420253 1420259 1420261 1420277 1420283 1420291
1420301 1420303 1420357 1420369 1420373 1420399 1420403 1420429 1420483 1420493
1420501 1420511 1420519 1420561 1420577 1420583 1420603 1420607 1420613 1420621
1420631 1420633 1420651 1420667 1420697 1420717 1420721 1420729 1420753 1420777
1420789 1420807 1420817 1420819 1420831 1420841 1420847 1420879 1420883 1420891
1420901 1420919 1420921 1420931 1420933 1420949 1420967 1420981 1420999 1421011
1421027 1421039 1421041 1421083 1421093 1421099 1421113 1421141 1421153 1421159
1421191 1421213 1421221 1421227 1421243 1421249 1421267 1421291 1421293 1421309
1421317 1421339 1421351 1421389 1421401 1421417 1421437 1421449 1421461 1421471
1421479 1421489 1421501 1421521 1421527 1421543 1421549 1421569 1421603 1421611
1421621 1421627 1421639 1421647 1421663 1421669 1421677 1421689 1421711 1421731
1421737 1421741 1421747 1421759 1421773 1421779 1421801 1421813 1421857 1421867
1421909 1421911 1421933 1421963 1421969 1421977 1421989 1422007 1422011 1422013
1422023 1422061 1422089 1422097 1422103 1422107 1422119 1422133 1422163 1422191
1422199 1422209 1422221 1422227 1422229 1422241 1422257 1422277 1422281 1422293
1422367 1422409 1422419 1422433 1422437 1422439 1422461 1422469 1422493 1422521
1422523 1422541 1422563 1422583 1422593 1422599 1422601 1422603 1422637 1422661
1422671 1422677 1422691 1422709 1422721 1422727 1422749 1422763 1422797 1422821
1422833 1422857 1422877 1422899 1422907 1422923 1422937 1422961 1422973 1422977
1422979 1422991 1423003 1423039 1423061 1423067 1423073 1423091 1423111 1423127
1423129 1423159 1423181 1423183 1423187 1423193 1423231 1423237 1423243 1423259
1423273 1423277 1423283 1423297 1423307 1423319 1423321 1423327 1423333 1423339
1423361 1423369 1423379 1423381 1423391 1423399 1423403 1423417 1423439 1423441
1423451 1423453 1423463 1423469 1423481 1423483 1423507 1423511 1423547 1423553
1423579 1423589 1423603 1423607 1423627 1423637 1423663 1423691 1423703 1423711
1423717 1423753 1423757 1423759 1423781 1423789 1423819 1423843 1423853 1423897
1423901 1423909 1423921 1423931 1423943 1423949 1423957 1423967 1423969 1423979
1423991 1423997 1424021 1424023 1424041 1424077 1424119 1424123 1424149 1424177
1424191 1424231 1424237 1424257 1424261 1424263 1424317 1424323 1424341 1424347
1424351 1424359 1424369 1424399 1424407 1424417 1424431 1424441 1424443 1424471
1424477 1424483 1424497 1424503 1424513 1424519 1424531 1424539 1424557 1424561
1424569 1424573 1424581 1424603 1424669 1424681 1424699 1424701 1424707 1424723
1424737 1424743 1424749 1424767 1424771 1424779 1424789 1424803 1424809 1424831
1424837 1424849 1424851 1424869 1424881 1424903 1424911 1424933 1424939 1424947
1424959 1424963 1424989 1425007 1425029 1425049 1425071 1425077 1425079 1425091
1425097 1425113 1425121 1425139 1425169 1425187 1425199 1425217 1425227 1425251
1425253 1425271 1425293 1425299 1425301 1425311 1425337 1425343 1425367 1425371
1425427 1425439 1425451 1425469 1425481 1425491 1425497 1425503 1425511 1425521
1425527 1425539 1425547 1425583 1425601 1425607 1425629 1425649 1425653 1425661
1425667 1425707 1425733 1425757 1425769 1425791 1425797 1425811 1425821 1425863
1425877 1425881 1425883 1425889 1425899 1425911 1425913 1425917 1425929 1425953
1425967 1425973 1426003 1426043 1426057 1426063 1426067 1426081 1426097 1426109
1426111 1426123 1426127 1426129 1426141 1426151 1426153 1426157 1426163 1426169
1426171 1426199 1426211 1426213 1426223 1426231 1426237 1426247 1426277 1426289
1426291 1426301 1426303 1426331 1426343 1426361 1426367 1426379 1426393 1426427
1426429 1426457 1426471 1426489 1426499 1426511 1426519 1426541 1426543 1426553
1426559 1426567 1426583 1426613 1426619 1426627 1426643 1426669 1426673 1426693
1426699 1426703 1426717 1426723 1426741 1426751 1426753 1426781 1426801 1426807
1426811 1426847 1426877 1426883 1426889 1426891 1426907 1426913 1426927 1426933
1426939 1426949 1426951 1426969 1426981 1426987 1426991 1427017 1427021 1427039
1427047 1427089 1427093 1427117 1427141 1427143 1427191 1427221 1427227 1427233
1427281 1427291 1427297 1427323 1427329 1427341 1427347 1427359 1427383 1427389
1427399 1427401 1427407 1427411 1427431 1427453 1427479 1427483 1427501 1427509
1427513 1427521 1427539 1427551 1427561 1427563 1427567 1427599 1427617 1427627
1427653 1427663 1427681 1427687 1427707 1427737 1427747 1427749 1427753 1427773
1427809 1427821 1427843 1427851 1427879 1427887 1427893 1427897 1427911 1427917
1427927 1427957 1427963 1427969 1427999 1428013 1428029 1428041 1428079 1428109
1428113 1428127 1428137 1428143 1428151 1428157 1428169 1428179 1428197 1428199
1428209 1428233 1428247 1428253 1428257 1428281 1428359 1428389 1428409 1428419
1428431 1428473 1428491 1428521 1428529 1428541 1428571 1428587 1428593 1428601
1428631 1428637 1428649 1428671 1428673 1428677 1428689 1428703 1428709 1428751
1428767 1428769 1428787 1428793 1428811 1428839 1428851 1428853 1428863 1428887
1428893 1428899 1428923 1428929 1428937 1428949 1428953 1428979 1428991 1428997
1429027 1429061 1429063 1429067 1429081 1429093 1429097 1429117 1429133 1429163
1429187 1429201 1429231 1429247 1429249 1429261 1429279 1429283 1429303 1429319
1429349 1429367 1429369 1429387 1429397 1429399 1429403 1429409 1429423 1429451
1429469 1429481 1429507 1429523 1429529 1429531 1429543 1429553 1429567 1429573
1429583 1429591 1429601 1429609 1429619 1429633 1429651 1429661 1429669 1429697
1429721 1429733 1429741 1429759 1429763 1429777 1429783 1429801 1429811 1429817
1429829 1429837 1429843 1429849 1429859 1429861 1429867 1429871 1429889 1429907
1429913 1429927 1429943 1429951 1429959 1429969 1430027 1430063 1430089 1430119
1430131 1430167 1430179 1430183 1430197 1430201 1430237 1430239 1430243 1430279
1430281 1430287 1430291 1430293 1430321 1430357 1430381 1430413 1430419 1430441
1430461 1430479 1430503 1430521 1430543 1430587 1430593 1430603 1430617 1430641
1430647 1430659 1430677 1430683 1430687 1430707 1430711 1430713 1430717 1430729

```
1430749  1430783  1430789  1430797  1430801  1430813  1430851  1430857  1430861  1430879
1430881  1430887  1430903  1430921  1430939  1430953  1430959  1430969  1430971  1430987
1430993  1431007  1431013  1431029  1431047  1431071  1431097  1431107  1431113  1431119
1431127  1431139  1431149  1431161  1431173  1431191  1431193  1431203  1431211  1431217
1431223  1431253  1431257  1431263  1431277  1431307  1431317  1431323  1431337  1431347
1431361  1431373  1431377  1431379  1431389  1431413  1431421  1431439  1431449  1431461
1431467  1431491  1431503  1431511  1431523  1431539  1431557  1431569  1431571  1431581
1431601  1431607  1431613  1431637  1431649  1431659  1431713  1431721  1431733  1431737
1431751  1431763  1431769  1431779  1431799  1431809  1431827  1431841  1431847  1431851
1431869  1431907  1431917  1431919  1431923  1431929  1431959  1431967  1431977  1432001
1432019  1432021  1432031  1432073  1432091  1432103  1432111  1432129  1432139  1432147
1432177  1432181  1432217  1432243  1432271  1432273  1432297  1432303  1432313  1432351
1432357  1432363  1432411  1432423  1432427  1432439  1432441  1432447  1432451  1432469
1432481  1432489  1432493  1432511  1432517  1432531  1432547  1432549  1432559  1432577
1432583  1432589  1432591  1432621  1432637  1432649  1432667  1432679  1432681  1432699
1432703  1432723  1432729  1432741  1432757  1432799  1432801  1432807  1432813  1432841
1432859  1432891  1432897  1432903  1432927  1432931  1432943  1432957  1432979  1432987
1432997  1433011  1433017  1433021  1433041  1433053  1433057  1433059  1433071  1433101
1433119  1433123  1433129  1433137  1433149  1433177  1433203  1433207  1433213  1433239
1433251  1433273  1433293  1433309  1433329  1433351  1433353  1433357  1433363  1433371
1433413  1433437  1433473  1433477  1433489  1433503  1433513  1433519  1433527  1433539
1433573  1433581  1433587  1433591  1433603  1433623  1433629  1433633  1433669  1433681
1433689  1433699  1433711  1433717  1433723  1433737  1433741  1433743  1433767  1433777
1433801  1433813  1433819  1433821  1433833  1433849  1433891  1433903  1433909  1433941
1433947  1433953  1433989  1434011  1434019  1434023  1434031  1434067  1434077  1434089
1434107  1434109  1434131  1434133  1434143  1434149  1434161  1434187  1434203  1434217
1434229  1434241  1434247  1434259  1434281  1434283  1434289  1434337  1434353  1434359
1434373  1434383  1434397  1434421  1434431  1434439  1434451  1434457  1434469  1434473
1434491  1434493  1434497  1434539  1434541  1434553  1434571  1434593  1434599  1434607
1434617  1434623  1434637  1434661  1434677  1434679  1434691  1434707  1434731  1434737
1434743  1434757  1434779  1434791  1434793  1434803  1434827  1434841  1434847  1434857
1434883  1434887  1434911  1434913  1434929  1434941  1434943  1434991  1434997  1435001
1435009  1435037  1435061  1435069  1435079  1435097  1435103  1435111  1435117  1435121
1435129  1435139  1435141  1435151  1435163  1435171  1435183  1435201  1435219  1435229
1435237  1435243  1435249  1435261  1435271  1435277  1435289  1435307  1435339  1435363
1435373  1435403  1435409  1435417  1435457  1435459  1435547  1435493  1435501  1435519
1435523  1435537  1435543  1435559  1435561  1435571  1435573  1435589  1435597  1435607
1435613  1435627  1435631  1435657  1435663  1435669  1435739  1435741  1435751  1435783
1435787  1435793  1435801  1435829  1435831  1435853  1435901  1435909  1435919  1435921
1435937  1435997  1436003  1436021  1436023  1436027  1436063  1436069  1436087  1436089
1436093  1436101  1436111  1436131  1436141  1436159  1436173  1436203  1436207  1436221
1436231  1436249  1436251  1436257  1436263  1436269  1436291  1436297  1436311  1436333
1436339  1436363  1436387  1436411  1436417  1436429  1436431  1436437  1436441  1436443
1436467  1436471  1436507  1436527  1436531  1436537  1436563  1436593  1436623  1436627
1436639  1436651  1436693  1436711  1436731  1436737  1436749  1436767  1436779  1436797
1436801  1436803  1436849  1436867  1436899  1436909  1436923  1436929  1436933  1436957
1436999  1437011  1437013  1437019  1437031  1437041  1437047  1437049  1437053  1437097
1437101  1437133  1437187  1437193  1437199  1437203  1437223  1437229  1437239  1437251
1437257  1437263  1437283  1437287  1437301  1437313  1437323  1437329  1437341  1437347
1437349  1437379  1437389  1437391  1437409  1437421  1437427  1437451  1437461  1437467
1437481  1437493  1437511  1437517  1437551  1437557  1437581  1437607  1437613  1437629
1437641  1437647  1437659  1437691  1437697  1437713  1437719  1437739  1437743  1437757
1437773  1437797  1437817  1437833  1437841  1437847  1437851  1437853  1437869  1437883
1437899  1437913  1437949  1437959  1437967  1437991  1438001  1438009  1438033  1438057
1438061  1438067  1438069  1438093  1438097  1438103  1438109  1438117  1438123  1438159
1438163  1438169  1438181  1438207  1438211  1438223  1438231  1438237  1438253  1438267
1438271  1438279  1438291  1438303  1438379  1438399  1438417  1438447  1438457  1438477
1438483  1438501  1438517  1438537  1438583  1438609  1438643  1438663  1438667  1438681
1438687  1438709  1438721  1438729  1438747  1438751  1438753  1438763  1438771  1438793
1438817  1438831  1438837  1438847  1438849  1438867  1438883  1438891  1438901  1438907
1438919  1438933  1438937  1438961  1438963  1438973  1438979  1438981  1438991  1438993
1439017  1439023  1439027  1439047  1439071  1439077  1439089  1439107  1439111  1439129
1439147  1439161  1439171  1439177  1439209  1439223  1439239  1439261  1439267  1439279
1439287  1439293  1439309  1439323  1439329  1439359  1439369  1439371  1439377  1439381
1439393  1439401  1439413  1439429  1439437  1439443  1439447  1439513  1439521  1439527
1439549  1439561  1439579  1439651  1439663  1439681  1439693  1439699  1439701  1439717
1439719  1439729  1439743  1439749  1439759  1439773  1439791  1439803  1439827  1439833
1439881  1439891  1439903  1439909  1439927  1439947  1439969  1439989  1440011  1440017
1440037  1440079  1440107  1440119  1440203  1440209  1440211  1440233  1440239  1440247
1440253  1440269  1440289  1440293  1440301  1440317  1440349  1440379  1440391  1440403
1440419  1440437  1440443  1440449  1440469  1440473  1440479  1440493  1440499  1440511
1440533  1440553  1440557  1440577  1440581  1440583  1440587  1440589  1440611  1440619
1440623  1440641  1440679  1440689  1440707  1440727  1440731  1440737  1440763  1440779
1440779  1440799  1440811  1440823  1440847  1440851  1440853  1440877  1440883  1440889
1440913  1440949  1440953  1440961  1440983  1441001  1441007  1441009  1441031  1441049
1441051  1441057  1441061  1441081  1441117  1441127  1441133  1441151  1441189  1441199
1441201  1441217  1441241  1441259  1441289  1441301  1441309  1441313  1441327  1441331
1441339  1441343  1441351  1441361  1441367  1441373  1441381  1441411  1441423  1441439
1441459  1441463  1441471  1441523  1441529  1441543  1441553  1441567  1441579  1441589
1441591  1441603  1441633  1441637  1441669  1441673  1441679  1441681  1441697  1441703
1441721  1441723  1441729  1441751  1441757  1441771  1441807  1441837  1441849  1441871
1441877  1441879  1441883  1441931  1441933  1441949  1441963  1441981  1442003  1442009
1442017  1442053  1442057  1442069  1442071  1442087  1442143  1442159  1442173  1442191
1442209  1442227  1442251  1442267  1442279  1442299  1442317  1442321  1442327  1442333
1442341  1442351  1442377  1442393  1442411  1442429  1442437  1442453  1442459  1442509
1442513  1442527  1442531  1442549  1442579  1442591  1442599  1442611  1442621  1442627
1442633  1442641  1442653  1442657  1442669  1442717  1442723  1442731  1442743  1442783
1442797  1442827  1442849  1442863  1442869  1442873  1442887  1442899  1442911  1442921
1442923  1442939  1442941  1442971  1442983  1442989  1443007  1443053  1443059  1443067
```

```
1443073  1443083  1443103  1443119  1443131  1443139  1443151  1443157  1443161  1443193
1443203  1443223  1443257  1443271  1443293  1443307  1443311  1443331  1443341  1443353
1443383  1443389  1443397  1443401  1443427  1443437  1443439  1443461  1443469  1443473
1443509  1443517  1443523  1443529  1443551  1443557  1443571  1443581  1443587  1443613
1443647  1443653  1443679  1443683  1443697  1443709  1443713  1443719  1443727  1443781
1443787  1443797  1443803  1443817  1443839  1443857  1443859  1443899  1443913  1443941
1443961  1443971  1443977  1443989  1444007  1444043  1444063  1444067  1444081  1444087
1444103  1444109  1444111  1444181  1444187  1444213  1444217  1444237  1444249  1444271
1444273  1444279  1444291  1444309  1444411  1444441  1444447  1444459  1444463  1444477
1444481  1444483  1444489  1444493  1444501  1444523  1444529  1444543  1444567  1444571
1444613  1444633  1444649  1444657  1444661  1444679  1444687  1444697  1444747  1444753
1444759  1444763  1444771  1444777  1444787  1444789  1444801  1444811  1444819  1444823
1444873  1444897  1444901  1444903  1444909  1444913  1444943  1444957  1444967  1444973
1444979  1444981  1444999  1445033  1445039  1445047  1445053  1445057  1445071  1445077
1445107  1445117  1445137  1445149  1445161  1445173  1445177  1445179  1445207  1445237
1445239  1445261  1445287  1445303  1445317  1445329  1445333  1445341  1445351  1445371
1445401  1445407  1445413  1445417  1445419  1445429  1445443  1445453  1445467  1445497
1445503  1445513  1445519  1445533  1445557  1445567  1445569  1445581  1445593  1445599
1445657  1445669  1445671  1445687  1445699  1445707  1445713  1445723  1445749  1445753
1445771  1445797  1445827  1445831  1445863  1445879  1445887  1445921  1445929  1445953
1445959  1445963  1445971  1445981  1445989  1446001  1446007  1446019  1446023  1446041
1446043  1446059  1446073  1446077  1446083  1446089  1446091  1446097  1446113  1446131
1446167  1446169  1446187  1446191  1446197  1446227  1446233  1446239  1446251  1446257
1446281  1446301  1446311  1446323  1446353  1446359  1446383  1446397  1446409  1446427
1446437  1446449  1446457  1446469  1446509  1446551  1446559  1446587  1446611  1446617
1446619  1446629  1446637  1446659  1446673  1446689  1446701  1446703  1446713  1446719
1446761  1446779  1446791  1446803  1446829  1446833  1446871  1446881  1446889  1446899
1446901  1446917  1446919  1446923  1446941  1446971  1446997  1447001  1447003  1447007
1447009  1447031  1447037  1447063  1447067  1447073  1447099  1447123  1447139  1447151
1447153  1447169  1447189  1447213  1447217  1447219  1447223  1447231  1447241  1447247
1447273  1447279  1447283  1447291  1447309  1447331  1447333  1447343  1447349  1447351
1447373  1447379  1447387  1447399  1447409  1447427  1447429  1447441  1447471  1447487
1447507  1447529  1447543  1447549  1447559  1447561  1447571  1447583  1447609  1447627
1447631  1447639  1447661  1447711  1447717  1447727  1447759  1447777  1447799  1447807
1447811  1447813  1447843  1447861  1447867  1447877  1447889  1447891  1447913  1447949
1447951  1447961  1447969  1447973  1447981  1447987  1448003  1448021  1448039  1448053
1448059  1448063  1448081  1448087  1448171  1448177  1448189  1448191  1448203  1448207
1448219  1448221  1448303  1448309  1448357  1448371  1448387  1448401  1448411  1448423
1448431  1448443  1448449  1448459  1448477  1448497  1448533  1448569  1448593  1448611
1448659  1448663  1448683  1448687  1448717  1448737  1448743  1448761  1448767  1448771
1448779  1448789  1448801  1448803  1448819  1448827  1448833  1448849  1448857  1448873
1448879  1448903  1448929  1448947  1448983  1448989  1449001  1449013  1449017  1449061
1449067  1449089  1449113  1449121  1449127  1449163  1449167  1449169  1449191  1449193
1449209  1449211  1449271  1449289  1449293  1449307  1449311  1449319  1449337
1449361  1449367  1449379  1449389  1449431  1449439  1449443  1449479  1449509  1449517
1449521  1449523  1449551  1449557  1449563  1449577  1449583  1449587  1449589  1449599
1449601  1449611  1449619  1449647  1449649  1449661  1449671  1449673  1449683  1449691
1449733  1449779  1449817  1449823  1449827  1449829  1449841  1449863  1449869  1449893
1449907  1449911  1449937  1449941  1449949  1449953  1449967  1449977  1449979  1449983
1450019  1450021  1450051  1450063  1450069  1450073  1450103  1450109  1450139  1450147
1450157  1450177  1450199  1450201  1450231  1450237  1450243  1450249  1450271  1450277
1450283  1450297  1450307  1450331  1450333  1450367  1450391  1450399  1450429  1450439
1450447  1450453  1450469  1450481  1450487  1450489  1450499  1450507  1450513  1450531
1450543  1450571  1450573  1450577  1450613  1450619  1450637  1450639  1450651  1450697
1450699  1450711  1450727  1450739  1450741  1450747  1450753  1450759  1450819  1450847
1450849  1450853  1450861  1450871  1450873  1450877  1450903  1450907  1450913  1450919
1450927  1450931  1450963  1450979  1450991  1451003  1451039  1451041  1451053  1451057
1451059  1451081  1451083  1451119  1451123  1451143  1451147  1451161  1451179  1451209
1451213  1451237  1451243  1451249  1451257  1451267  1451291  1451321  1451339  1451347
1451371  1451383  1451393  1451423  1451509  1451521  1451531  1451539  1451557  1451561
1451573  1451603  1451609  1451623  1451633  1451641  1451663  1451677  1451713  1451717
1451719  1451729  1451741  1451743  1451759  1451767  1451797  1451831  1451833  1451837
1451839  1451867  1451893  1451899  1451909  1451911  1451929  1451959  1451969  1452047
1452079  1452083  1452109  1452127  1452131  1452149  1452169  1452181  1452193  1452203
1452211  1452221  1452223  1452229  1452247  1452263  1452271  1452277  1452281  1452299
1452301  1452317  1452323  1452329  1452377  1452383  1452413  1452419  1452421  1452433
1452439  1452449  1452457  1452461  1452487  1452491  1452511  1452527  1452533  1452541
1452553  1452557  1452559  1452613  1452631  1452637  1452653  1452709  1452713  1452727
1452743  1452751  1452767  1452779  1452791  1452809  1452827  1452833  1452839  1452851
1452853  1452859  1452863  1452907  1452923  1452947  1452961  1452977  1452991  1453003
1453009  1453019  1453033  1453037  1453043  1453057  1453061  1453091  1453093  1453129
1453141  1453169  1453171  1453181  1453201  1453223  1453241  1453267  1453307  1453321
1453337  1453339  1453343  1453369  1453391  1453399  1453411  1453427  1453429  1453453
1453457  1453469  1453477  1453489  1453493  1453499  1453513  1453537  1453547  1453549
1453553  1453597  1453603  1453607  1453609  1453643  1453651  1453657  1453681  1453703
1453723  1453729  1453759  1453783  1453817  1453831  1453847  1453871  1453877  1453883
1453889  1453897  1453909  1453913  1453919  1453927  1453939  1453943  1453957  1453961
1453997  1454003  1454021  1454029  1454041  1454053  1454059  1454071  1454081  1454099
1454119  1454143  1454149  1454177  1454191  1454207  1454209  1454239  1454249  1454261
1454273  1454339  1454347  1454351  1454371  1454377  1454381  1454399  1454417  1454419
1454441  1454443  1454459  1454461  1454477  1454513  1454521  1454533  1454539  1454549
1454567  1454569  1454573  1454587  1454591  1454597  1454599  1454633  1454657  1454683
1454689  1454699  1454701  1454711  1454731  1454743  1454759  1454767  1454779  1454801
1454807  1454821  1454839  1454851  1454863  1454891  1454897  1454899  1454927  1454939
1454941  1454953  1454969  1454977  1454983  1454987  1454989  1454993  1455007  1455011
1455019  1455023  1455029  1455031  1455037  1455043  1455053  1455067  1455079  1455089
1455119  1455121  1455127  1455143  1455151  1455193  1455197  1455199  1455203  1455211
1455227  1455241  1455253  1455257  1455263  1455301  1455317  1455323  1455329  1455341
1455359  1455361  1455367  1455373  1455379  1455383  1455403  1455409  1455431  1455437
```

```
1455439  1455491  1455499  1455527  1455563  1455569  1455599  1455607  1455613  1455653
1455661  1455673  1455677  1455683  1455697  1455703  1455721  1455757  1455767  1455781
1455809  1455821  1455827  1455833  1455841  1455847  1455859  1455871  1455893  1455901
1455907  1455911  1455929  1455941  1455947  1455953  1455959  1455973  1455983  1455991
1456001  1456019  1456057  1456087  1456099  1456121  1456123  1456127  1456157  1456159
1456171  1456187  1456219  1456229  1456241  1456243  1456267  1456289  1456313  1456321
1456333  1456381  1456391  1456393  1456417  1456439  1456451  1456501  1456517  1456519
1456529  1456537  1456541  1456547  1456561  1456603  1456627  1456633  1456643  1456657
1456667  1456687  1456691  1456703  1456709  1456717  1456739  1456759  1456789  1456799
1456823  1456837  1456867  1456877  1456891  1456919  1456921  1456927  1456937  1456943
1456963  1457011  1457021  1457033  1457039  1457051  1457059  1457069  1457077  1457083
1457111  1457143  1457147  1457149  1457161  1457177  1457201  1457207  1457213  1457219
1457251  1457273  1457293  1457321  1457333  1457353  1457363  1457371  1457381  1457389
1457411  1457419  1457429  1457437  1457459  1457479  1457483  1457497  1457501  1457503
1457513  1457551  1457633  1457639  1457647  1457653  1457663  1457683  1457741  1457749
1457783  1457791  1457803  1457821  1457849  1457857  1457861  1457867  1457873  1457879
1457887  1457891  1457921  1457933  1457941  1457957  1457959  1457969  1457983  1457999
1458011  1458019  1458031  1458049  1458053  1458071  1458097  1458101  1458113  1458151
1458157  1458167  1458179  1458199  1458203  1458229  1458253  1458263  1458267  1458283
1458293  1458319  1458337  1458343  1458349  1458371  1458397  1458403  1458409  1458427
1458433  1458461  1458463  1458469  1458473  1458487  1458521  1458533  1458547  1458593
1458599  1458601  1458607  1458619  1458623  1458629  1458631  1458641  1458659  1458697
1458671  1458683  1458707  1458907  1458911  1458971  1458973  1458997  1459027  1459061
1459069  1459091  1459099  1459109  1459111  1459123  1459141  1459153  1459163  1459177
1459207  1459217  1459253  1459259  1459261  1459277  1459301  1459319  1459351  1459369
1459411  1459421  1459427  1459429  1459439  1459453  1459457  1459481  1459517  1459531
1459537  1459543  1459583  1459589  1459597  1459609  1459631  1459651  1459663  1459681
1459691  1459709  1459727  1459771  1459793  1459811  1459823  1459849  1459853  1459873
1459891  1459901  1459907  1459921  1459933  1459937  1459949  1459951  1459957  1459963
1459993  1460003  1460021  1460027  1460029  1460033  1460059  1460071  1460077  1460087
1460089  1460099  1460101  1460111  1460117  1460143  1460153  1460161  1460167  1460171
1460177  1460189  1460213  1460233  1460267  1460269  1460281  1460311  1460341  1460369
1460377  1460383  1460423  1460429  1460447  1460467  1460479  1460483  1460491  1460497
1460507  1460567  1460593  1460603  1460609  1460617  1460629  1460633  1460651  1460653
1460671  1460681  1460687  1460729  1460731  1460737  1460741  1460743  1460747  1460773
1460821  1460857  1460863  1460867  1460887  1460903  1460911  1460923  1460941  1460951
1460957  1460971  1460981  1460989  1460993  1461001  1461073  1461077  1461079  1461091
1461101  1461127  1461139  1461151  1461169  1461179  1461181  1461191  1461209  1461211
1461283  1461287  1461289  1461293  1461301  1461311  1461329  1461349  1461353  1461359
1461367  1461391  1461401  1461403  1461407  1461409  1461411  1461419  1461437  1461451
1461479  1461497  1461511  1461517  1461553  1461563  1461583  1461587  1461599  1461601
1461623  1461637  1461643  1461641  1461659  1461661  1461667  1461671  1461683  1461697
1461701  1461703  1461709  1461731  1461749  1461763  1461769  1461781  1461791  1461797
1461809  1461821  1461851  1461853  1461877  1461883  1461913  1461923  1461931  1461953
1461973  1461979  1461989  1462001  1462009  1462033  1462037  1462039  1462049  1462057
1462061  1462063  1462099  1462127  1462157  1462163  1462169  1462171  1462189  1462193
1462199  1462213  1462229  1462247  1462249  1462313  1462319  1462327  1462337  1462339
1462367  1462381  1462397  1462399  1462403  1462421  1462423  1462427  1462457  1462463
1462477  1462507  1462519  1462523  1462567  1462589  1462603  1462607  1462613  1462619
1462621  1462627  1462631  1462651  1462679  1462691  1462693  1462711  1462717  1462723
1462739  1462751  1462759  1462763  1462801  1462807  1462819  1462861  1462871  1462873
1462883  1462891  1462897  1462927  1462933  1462939  1462957  1462973  1462999  1463009
1463027  1463047  1463089  1463113  1463117  1463123  1463149  1463153  1463177  1463179
1463183  1463197  1463201  1463219  1463221  1463233  1463243  1463257  1463261  1463263
1463303  1463327  1463339  1463359  1463369  1463447  1463453  1463469  1463471  1463489
1463503  1463507  1463509  1463521  1463537  1463557  1463563  1463569  1463587  1463597
1463599  1463611  1463617  1463621  1463641  1463647  1463719  1463767  1463773  1463797
1463821  1463837  1463857  1463863  1463873  1463879  1463897  1463899  1463911  1463933
1463941  1463947  1463953  1463971  1463981  1463983  1463999  1464011  1464031  1464049
1464079  1464101  1464103  1464131  1464137  1464143  1464149  1464163  1464173  1464179
1464241  1464251  1464257  1464259  1464263  1464269  1464271  1464277  1464283  1464289
1464293  1464299  1464343  1464371  1464373  1464383  1464391  1464401  1464403  1464409
1464467  1464481  1464493  1464503  1464559  1464563  1464569  1464583  1464611  1464641
1464649  1464689  1464713  1464721  1464731  1464733  1464751  1464769  1464773  1464787
1464809  1464811  1464817  1464823  1464829  1464863  1464899  1464901  1464917  1464929
1464949  1464959  1464961  1464977  1464997  1465007  1465019  1465021  1465027  1465049
1465067  1465073  1465081  1465097  1465127  1465129  1465133  1465141  1465171  1465181
1465187  1465193  1465229  1465231  1465249  1465253  1465259  1465273  1465279  1465301
1465313  1465351  1465361  1465367  1465391  1465393  1465421  1465423  1465427  1465433
1465439  1465441  1465469  1465481  1465487  1465493  1465523  1465547  1465549  1465559
1465561  1465567  1465571  1465577  1465591  1465637  1465643  1465661  1465663  1465669
1465691  1465693  1465703  1465727  1465729  1465771  1465777  1465801  1465819  1465823
1465837  1465843  1465847  1465853  1465861  1465889  1465901  1465931  1465943  1465957
1465963  1465987  1465991  1465993  1466009  1466053  1466057  1466069  1466107  1466111
1466117  1466123  1466137  1466147  1466167  1466177  1466183  1466191  1466203  1466243
1466251  1466261  1466279  1466291  1466293  1466299  1466303  1466317  1466323  1466329
1466371  1466383  1466389  1466407  1466417  1466449  1466459  1466461  1466473  1466519
1466533  1466551  1466557  1466567  1466599  1466603  1466639  1466653  1466657  1466659
1466667  1466701  1466711  1466713  1466719  1466741  1466747  1466753  1466767  1466771
1466783  1466797  1466821  1466833  1466869  1466873  1466887  1466893  1466897  1466911
1466929  1466953  1466957  1466999  1467001  1467007  1467017  1467043  1467061  1467091
1467097  1467107  1467121  1467131  1467143  1467149  1467157  1467173  1467187  1467209
1467211  1467217  1467223  1467229  1467241  1467281  1467283  1467299  1467307  1467317
1467329  1467337  1467341  1467353  1467359  1467391  1467397  1467413  1467419  1467437
1467443  1467493  1467497  1467511  1467527  1467533  1467539  1467553  1467581  1467589
1467611  1467629  1467673  1467691  1467703  1467749  1467751  1467773  1467779  1467787
1467821  1467839  1467859  1467863  1467869  1467889  1467901  1467913  1467919  1467937
1467953  1467971  1467989  1468079  1468109  1468163  1468189  1468193  1468211  1468213
```

```
1468219  1468261  1468267  1468277  1468387  1468391  1468399  1468403  1468427  1468447
1468457  1468459  1468499  1468499  1468507  1468513  1468517  1468543  1468547  1468553
1468559  1468561  1468591  1468603  1468631  1468633  1468637  1468639  1468651  1468657
1468667  1468673  1468717  1468723  1468729  1468739  1468741  1468759  1468781  1468799
1468801  1468807  1468877  1468889  1468897  1468913  1468921  1468927  1468933  1468939
1468949  1468963  1468967  1468969  1469047  1469057  1469081  1469087  1469129  1469131
1469141  1469147  1469161  1469179  1469189  1469197  1469201  1469231  1469239  1469249
1469257  1469287  1469291  1469311  1469323  1469341  1469357  1469359  1469383  1469393
1469407  1469437  1469467  1469477  1469509  1469511  1469521  1469527  1469543  1469543
1469557  1469561  1469569  1469581  1469591  1469597  1469621  1469623  1469627  1469641
1469659  1469687  1469693  1469717  1469729  1469731  1469747  1469753  1469761  1469773
1469777  1469801  1469833  1469843  1469851  1469857  1469879  1469887  1469893  1469921
1469933  1469947  1469957  1469969  1469977  1469983  1469987  1470023  1470043  1470059
1470067  1470071  1470149  1470151  1470173  1470187  1470193  1470199  1470233  1470241
1470251  1470281  1470289  1470307  1470319  1470323  1470373  1470377  1470401  1470407
1470419  1470431  1470437  1470451  1470461  1470487  1470493  1470523  1470529  1470559
1470571  1470577  1470611  1470613  1470641  1470659  1470683  1470709  1470727  1470757
1470797  1470817  1470829  1470839  1470841  1470869  1470871  1470913  1470941  1470947
1470949  1470977  1470983  1470991  1471007  1471021  1471031  1471033  1471069  1471069
1471079  1471091  1471117  1471123  1471133  1471177  1471181  1471213  1471219  1471271
1471277  1471279  1471289  1471297  1471307  1471313  1471321  1471339  1471343  1471361
1471397  1471403  1471409  1471411  1471423  1471427  1471433  1471441  1471481  1471487
1471499  1471501  1471511  1471513  1471529  1471543  1471553  1471567  1471573  1471579
1471583  1471619  1471621  1471633  1471649  1471661  1471667  1471669  1471681  1471693
1471697  1471703  1471709  1471751  1471763  1471807  1471817  1471819  1471829  1471853
1471867  1471879  1471891  1471903  1471907  1471909  1471913  1471919  1471937  1472017
1472021  1472033  1472041  1472077  1472083  1472111  1472117  1472137  1472143  1472153
1472167  1472173  1472197  1472203  1472209  1472239  1472249  1472257  1472279  1472293
1472297  1472333  1472371  1472389  1472399  1472411  1472423  1472423  1472441  1472447
1472453  1472461  1472467  1472491  1472501  1472507  1472539  1472543  1472551  1472561
1472573  1472579  1472587  1472599  1472623  1472657  1472663  1472677  1472687  1472689
1472701  1472719  1472743  1472767  1472777  1472789  1472791  1472813  1472831  1472837
1472857  1472869  1472893  1472909  1472927  1472929  1472951  1472953  1472959  1472963
1472971  1472981  1472987  1472993  1473011  1473019  1473023  1473041  1473047  1473049
1473061  1473077  1473083  1473091  1473097  1473103  1473149  1473187  1473191  1473193
1473221  1473239  1473247  1473257  1473301  1473319  1473331  1473341  1473343  1473379
1473383  1473389  1473391  1473419  1473421  1473443  1473467  1473473  1473487  1473503
1473529  1473533  1473551  1473553  1473557  1473569  1473601  1473607  1473613  1473631
1473649  1473671  1473677  1473737  1473743  1473749  1473763  1473767  1473793  1473803
1473841  1473847  1473853  1473869  1473919  1473937  1473949  1473959  1473961  1473971
1473973  1473977  1474003  1474021  1474027  1474037  1474049  1474069  1474079  1474097
1474103  1474127  1474129  1474141  1474159  1474171  1474177  1474181  1474199  1474211
1474217  1474241  1474243  1474247  1474259  1474261  1474271  1474283  1474307  1474313
1474321  1474349  1474357  1474397  1474411  1474433  1474439  1474441  1474489  1474519
1474523  1474549  1474559  1474579  1474589  1474591  1474633  1474637  1474643  1474663
1474703  1474717  1474721  1474727  1474751  1474757  1474769  1474787  1474793  1474843
1474849  1474859  1474861  1474873  1474877  1474901  1474961  1474981  1474999  1475003
1475017  1475021  1475051  1475087  1475113  1475129  1475137  1475147  1475203  1475213
1475219  1475233  1475237  1475239  1475251  1475261  1475281  1475291  1475297  1475323
1475339  1475351  1475363  1475371  1475387  1475399  1475401  1475431  1475443  1475489
1475503  1475527  1475561  1475563  1475567  1475587  1475609  1475647  1475687  1475701
1475729  1475731  1475737  1475743  1475759  1475777  1475797  1475813  1475827  1475833
1475843  1475861  1475869  1475899  1475911  1475917  1475927  1475953  1476001  1476011
1476023  1476031  1476043  1476047  1476067  1476073  1476089  1476109  1476149  1476151
1476169  1476173  1476179  1476191  1476193  1476199  1476203  1476217  1476227  1476253
1476259  1476283  1476311  1476323  1476329  1476359  1476379  1476401  1476403  1476407
1476413  1476457  1476463  1476469  1476473  1476511  1476523  1476529  1476539  1476551
1476581  1476641  1476647  1476649  1476659  1476677  1476689  1476691  1476701  1476703
1476719  1476743  1476751  1476791  1476793  1476799  1476803  1476817  1476823  1476857
1476859  1476869  1476877  1476887  1476911  1476913  1476919  1476949  1476953  1476961
1476967  1476973  1476983  1476989  1477001  1477027  1477031  1477039  1477043  1477051
1477061  1477067  1477081  1477087  1477097  1477103  1477109  1477111  1477127  1477139
1477159  1477169  1477177  1477207  1477219  1477291  1477309  1477319  1477321  1477331
1477337  1477339  1477361  1477363  1477369  1477381  1477393  1477397  1477403  1477409
1477457  1477477  1477499  1477501  1477507  1477513  1477519  1477547  1477559  1477577
1477583  1477607  1477613  1477621  1477631  1477639  1477643  1477661  1477699  1477703
1477711  1477747  1477757  1477769  1477771  1477787  1477789  1477807  1477823  1477831
1477843  1477871  1477879  1477901  1477907  1477913  1477937  1477951  1477961  1477979
1477999  1478017  1478021  1478027  1478033  1478047  1478051  1478063  1478069  1478083
1478089  1478119  1478123  1478129  1478161  1478179  1478189  1478203  1478207  1478209
1478231  1478237  1478251  1478263  1478273  1478287  1478293  1478353  1478357  1478369
1478381  1478387  1478413  1478423  1478429  1478437  1478443  1478459  1478467  1478471
1478513  1478549  1478563  1478591  1478593  1478611  1478627  1478639  1478663  1478683
1478689  1478699  1478707  1478723  1478759  1478767  1478777  1478809  1478837  1478839
1478843  1478857  1478863  1478863  1478887  1478909  1478921  1478929  1478933  1478947
1478957  1478963  1478987  1478999  1479007  1479011  1479013  1479031  1479047  1479059
1479073  1479083  1479089  1479109  1479113  1479133  1479139  1479151  1479161  1479173
1479193  1479197  1479209  1479211  1479217  1479229  1479251  1479253  1479263  1479271
1479277  1479281  1479287  1479301  1479341  1479343  1479409  1479437  1479449  1479451
1479469  1479479  1479481  1479487  1479497  1479539  1479547  1479553  1479557  1479559
1479571  1479581  1479589  1479617  1479671  1479679  1479713  1479721  1479727  1479733
1479757  1479761  1479763  1479773  1479781  1479791  1479809  1479817  1479823  1479839
1479851  1479857  1479859  1479883  1479887  1479911  1479913  1479913  1479941  1479941
1479991  1479997  1480001  1480013  1480019  1480021  1480067  1480079  1480093  1480099
1480153  1480163  1480181  1480201  1480229  1480243  1480261  1480273  1480277  1480291
1480301  1480313  1480319  1480321  1480331  1480379  1480393  1480397  1480417  1480429
1480433  1480459  1480483  1480517  1480519  1480541  1480543  1480553  1480561  1480571
1480573  1480597  1480601  1480621  1480627  1480631  1480643  1480663  1480669  1480673
1480679  1480691  1480709  1480733  1480741  1480757  1480771  1480781  1480783  1480793
```

1480811	1480837	1480861	1480883	1480891	1480903	1480907	1480909	1480931	1480933
1480937	1480991	1481003	1481021	1481027	1481033	1481041	1481047	1481071	1481099
1481113	1481143	1481153	1481167	1481173	1481189	1481197	1481219	1481231	1481239
1481257	1481281	1481309	1481321	1481339	1481353	1481357	1481377	1481387	1481413
1481477	1481483	1481489	1481497	1481503	1481527	1481537	1481539	1481551	1481573
1481603	1481611	1481663	1481671	1481693	1481717	1481719	1481731	1481743	1481747
1481749	1481759	1481773	1481783	1481797	1481801	1481819	1481849	1481881	1481891
1481897	1481899	1481911	1481917	1481927	1481947	1481951	1481971	1481989	1481993
1481999	1482007	1482011	1482023	1482029	1482049	1482053	1482059	1482101	1482121
1482127	1482137	1482163	1482181	1482193	1482199	1482211	1482233	1482263	1482289
1482293	1482301	1482307	1482319	1482337	1482343	1482359	1482407	1482413	1482421
1482431	1482443	1482449	1482457	1482461	1482469	1482487	1482491	1482499	1482541
1482577	1482581	1482583	1482599	1482617	1482631	1482647	1482659	1482661	1482671
1482707	1482737	1482739	1482743	1482763	1482773	1482797	1482809	1482821	1482827
1482851	1482853	1482863	1482869	1482883	1482889	1482907	1482919	1482937	1482959
1482967	1483003	1483019	1483021	1483039	1483043	1483049	1483061	1483073	1483087
1483091	1483103	1483123	1483151	1483169	1483171	1483177	1483187	1483193	1483231
1483241	1483249	1483253	1483259	1483277	1483283	1483289	1483309	1483327	1483331
1483333	1483343	1483357	1483393	1483397	1483411	1483423	1483429	1483439	1483451
1483453	1483507	1483519	1483529	1483549	1483561	1483597	1483621	1483627	1483631
1483633	1483637	1483681	1483693	1483697	1483711	1483717	1483721	1483733	1483739
1483759	1483763	1483787	1483793	1483813	1483819	1483861	1483883	1483903	1483907
1483927	1483967	1483969	1483987	1483991	1483997	1484009	1484023	1484039	1484047
1484051	1484057	1484081	1484111	1484137	1484141	1484143	1484177	1484183	1484201
1484207	1484209	1484221	1484227	1484233	1484237	1484243	1484257	1484281	1484291
1484303	1484347	1484359	1484369	1484377	1484387	1484393	1484407	1484419	1484437
1484449	1484453	1484459	1484467	1484473	1484479	1484501	1484507	1484531	1484537
1484563	1484573	1484579	1484591	1484629	1484633	1484657	1484663	1484671	1484677
1484701	1484723	1484737	1484741	1484803	1484827	1484837	1484849	1484911	1484927
1484929	1484947	1484969	1484999	1485013	1485017	1485019	1485023	1485031	1485037
1485047	1485049	1485067	1485101	1485109	1485139	1485191	1485193	1485199	1485221
1485227	1485233	1485251	1485259	1485269	1485277	1485347	1485353	1485373	1485383
1485397	1485413	1485433	1485461	1485469	1485479	1485487	1485503	1485541	1485557
1485559	1485563	1485571	1485581	1485599	1485619	1485683	1485703	1485713	1485719
1485721	1485733	1485739	1485751	1485761	1485763	1485787	1485793	1485821	1485853
1485871	1485877	1485889	1485917	1485937	1485947	1486003	1486019	1486057	1486081
1486087	1486091	1486097	1486103	1486117	1486139	1486141	1486153	1486181	1486183
1486189	1486223	1486241	1486249	1486267	1486271	1486297	1486301	1486321	1486333
1486339	1486343	1486349	1486363	1486367	1486379	1486399	1486403	1486409	1486411
1486451	1486493	1486501	1486517	1486523	1486541	1486561	1486571	1486577	1486591
1486603	1486607	1486609	1486637	1486649	1486687	1486691	1486699	1486711	1486733
1486747	1486757	1486777	1486781	1486787	1486799	1486813	1486829	1486841	1486843
1486847	1486867	1486873	1486907	1486909	1486943	1486951	1486957	1486963	1486987
1486999	1487009	1487027	1487051	1487053	1487071	1487081	1487093	1487099	1487113
1487117	1487131	1487159	1487173	1487179	1487191	1487197	1487201	1487219	1487231
1487251	1487273	1487303	1487351	1487359	1487383	1487389	1487399	1487401	1487417
1487429	1487441	1487459	1487461	1487471	1487489	1487509	1487527	1487539	1487543
1487557	1487569	1487579	1487581	1487593	1487599	1487623	1487641	1487711	1487713
1487743	1487749	1487753	1487777	1487779	1487797	1487809	1487819	1487821	1487867
1487873	1487887	1487917	1487933	1487951	1487953	1487963	1487977	1487987	1487989
1488007	1488017	1488043	1488073	1488119	1488121	1488127	1488131	1488133	1488139
1488143	1488167	1488173	1488181	1488199	1488209	1488211	1488233	1488239	1488241
1488301	1488337	1488343	1488371	1488379	1488419	1488419	1488427	1488433	1488451
1488467	1488481	1488493	1488499	1488533	1488559	1488563	1488577	1488581	1488607
1488623	1488653	1488661	1488667	1488671	1488701	1488727	1488737	1488749	1488761
1488763	1488787	1488791	1488793	1488797	1488803	1488811	1488847	1488857	1488869
1488871	1488901	1488931	1488943	1488953	1488959	1488967	1488989	1489003	1489009
1489021	1489031	1489039	1489051	1489057	1489067	1489069	1489093	1489097	1489099
1489109	1489129	1489153	1489157	1489171	1489177	1489199	1489207	1489223	1489231
1489249	1489253	1489259	1489261	1489283	1489291	1489297	1489303	1489309	1489321
1489351	1489393	1489399	1489403	1489409	1489441	1489451	1489463	1489507	1489511
1489513	1489529	1489531	1489541	1489561	1489577	1489589	1489597	1489613	1489627
1489633	1489637	1489661	1489667	1489669	1489673	1489717	1489721	1489723	1489729
1489751	1489753	1489757	1489769	1489781	1489783	1489799	1489819	1489841	1489867
1489889	1489903	1489909	1489937	1489951	1489973	1489979	1489989	1490011	1490029
1490039	1490051	1490059	1490081	1490089	1490117	1490119	1490129	1490161	1490171
1490179	1490183	1490207	1490213	1490233	1490243	1490257	1490267	1490273	1490287
1490297	1490299	1490317	1490327	1490329	1490347	1490351	1490353	1490369	1490371
1490381	1490429	1490443	1490459	1490477	1490479	1490507	1490527	1490557	1490591
1490603	1490609	1490627	1490633	1490639	1490641	1490647	1490663	1490669	1490677
1490701	1490711	1490717	1490729	1490737	1490743	1490773	1490789	1490807	1490813
1490833	1490843	1490869	1490893	1490899	1490921	1490933	1490941	1490953	1490959
1490963	1490969	1490999	1491001	1491013	1491031	1491041	1491079	1491097	1491103
1491109	1491157	1491179	1491199	1491227	1491233	1491239	1491241	1491247	1491271
1491299	1491377	1491401	1491403	1491407	1491419	1491421	1491437	1491439	1491449
1491491	1491493	1491509	1491517	1491521	1491547	1491571	1491577	1491583	1491587
1491601	1491629	1491641	1491643	1491649	1491653	1491661	1491667	1491683	1491701
1491719	1491727	1491739	1491761	1491769	1491773	1491797	1491821	1491839	1491851
1491859	1491863	1491911	1491913	1491929	1491943	1491947	1491953	1491961	1491967
1491977	1491979	1491989	1491991	1492009	1492019	1492063	1492069	1492087	1492097
1492103	1492111	1492133	1492147	1492159	1492163	1492177	1492181	1492187	1492189
1492201	1492213	1492219	1492223	1492261	1492273	1492289	1492303	1492307	1492313
1492331	1492343	1492357	1492411	1492417	1492453	1492457	1492459	1492499	1492501
1492511	1492529	1492541	1492567	1492571	1492577	1492597	1492607	1492627	1492637
1492643	1492649	1492657	1492661	1492703	1492709	1492733	1492747	1492783	1492789
1492793	1492801	1492807	1492819	1492823	1492859	1492871	1492873	1492879	1492901
1492919	1492943	1492951	1492969	1492993	1493027	1493057	1493071	1493099	1493101
1493159	1493171	1493189	1493197	1493207	1493213	1493221	1493249	1493257	1493273
1493279	1493281	1493291	1493293	1493299	1493311	1493329	1493333	1493339	1493369

```
1493377  1493383  1493389  1493423  1493441  1493447  1493449  1493461  1493473  1493483
1493489  1493491  1493537  1493539  1493563  1493567  1493573  1493581  1493599  1493617
1493621  1493623  1493633  1493641  1493651  1493659  1493663  1493677  1493683  1493693
1493717  1493719  1493729  1493731  1493741  1493743  1493749  1493759  1493771  1493783
1493813  1493839  1493867  1493879  1493903  1493927  1493929  1493963  1493971  1493981
1494019  1494029  1494037  1494047  1494049  1494061  1494067  1494071  1494089  1494133
1494137  1494151  1494161  1494187  1494191  1494197  1494247  1494253  1494257  1494263
1494289  1494299  1494313  1494343  1494347  1494349  1494359  1494371  1494373  1494377
1494391  1494401  1494403  1494421  1494461  1494463  1494473  1494481  1494509  1494511
1494539  1494557  1494583  1494599  1494607  1494613  1494617  1494641  1494643  1494659
1494671  1494677  1494679  1494697  1494707  1494709  1494719  1494739  1494743  1494781
1494799  1494803  1494811  1494853  1494859  1494869  1494881  1494887  1494907  1494937
1494943  1494947  1494973  1494989  1495003  1495009  1495019  1495063  1495073  1495093
1495097  1495157  1495159  1495163  1495177  1495181  1495231  1495261  1495267  1495279
1495283  1495297  1495301  1495321  1495343  1495349  1495363  1495369  1495379  1495381
1495387  1495421  1495447  1495451  1495463  1495469  1495477  1495489  1495511  1495517
1495553  1495561  1495567  1495597  1495601  1495631  1495633  1495687  1495691  1495717
1495723  1495727  1495751  1495771  1495777  1495783  1495817  1495829  1495831  1495853
1495859  1495861  1495867  1495877  1495919  1495939  1495961  1495973  1495979  1495987
1495993  1495999  1496009  1496039  1496059  1496069  1496071  1496083  1496111  1496129
1496141  1496149  1496167  1496171  1496189  1496203  1496227  1496237  1496251  1496267
1496273  1496291  1496309  1496321  1496353  1496359  1496387  1496393  1496399
1496423  1496431  1496437  1496471  1496477  1496479  1496489  1496491  1496507  1496519
1496533  1496543  1496549  1496563  1496567  1496569  1496581  1496597  1496639  1496641
1496647  1496657  1496669  1496707  1496717  1496723  1496741  1496749  1496753  1496767
1496779  1496783  1496791  1496797  1496827  1496837  1496917  1496927  1496939  1496941
1496987  1497019  1497031  1497043  1497049  1497053  1497061  1497103  1497107  1497121
1497127  1497149  1497151  1497161  1497187  1497193  1497211  1497227  1497229  1497233
1497253  1497263  1497271  1497281  1497283  1497289  1497313  1497317  1497337  1497341
1497347  1497359  1497407  1497421  1497439  1497493  1497511  1497521  1497533  1497541
1497557  1497571  1497577  1497593  1497619  1497653  1497659  1497667  1497673  1497701
1497707  1497719  1497721  1497731  1497757  1497787  1497799  1497803  1497809  1497841
1497851  1497857  1497863  1497869  1497877  1497911  1497949  1497961  1497983  1497997
1498009  1498017  1498027  1498073  1498097  1498121  1498129  1498139  1498141  1498153
1498213  1498223  1498229  1498279  1498303  1498309  1498319  1498327  1498333  1498349
1498361  1498379  1498391  1498403  1498411  1498417  1498429  1498433  1498439
1498457  1498481  1498489  1498513  1498529  1498531  1498543  1498561  1498577  1498583
1498619  1498621  1498649  1498661  1498667  1498687  1498697  1498729  1498741  1498751
1498789  1498799  1498801  1498811  1498813  1498823  1498829  1498843  1498921  1498927
1498951  1498961  1498969  1498993  1498997  1499011  1499041  1499053  1499059  1499123
1499149  1499153  1499161  1499167  1499189  1499207  1499219  1499221  1499227  1499231
1499237  1499243  1499257  1499273  1499287  1499291  1499321  1499353  1499357  1499359
1499369  1499389  1499413  1499419  1499429  1499447  1499467  1499471  1499497  1499521
1499549  1499551  1499567  1499569  1499579  1499593  1499609  1499611  1499627  1499681
1499683  1499699  1499713  1499759  1499767  1499779  1499831  1499843  1499857  1499881
1499921  1499933  1499959  1499963  1499977  1500007  1500019  1500031  1500043  1500047
1500061  1500071  1500073  1500101  1500113  1500127  1500133  1500139  1500143  1500151
1500157  1500181  1500229  1500241  1500269  1500277  1500283  1500293  1500337  1500341
1500347  1500349  1500353  1500371  1500379  1500397  1500407  1500409  1500413  1500419
1500463  1500467  1500469  1500479  1500491  1500503  1500511  1500517  1500523  1500529
1500533  1500593  1500613  1500619  1500643  1500647  1500649  1500691  1500701  1500703
1500713  1500731  1500739  1500761  1500767  1500769  1500781  1500787  1500797  1500799
1500817  1500823  1500827  1500833  1500839  1500847  1500853  1500857  1500859  1500871
1500893  1500899  1500929  1500931  1500937  1500973  1500991  1500997  1501009  1501021
1501037  1501043  1501081  1501139  1501169  1501177  1501193  1501207  1501217  1501223
1501229  1501261  1501303  1501307  1501333  1501343  1501351  1501363  1501369  1501411
1501427  1501429  1501441  1501447  1501471  1501481  1501483  1501499  1501501  1501523
1501529  1501541  1501561  1501573  1501583  1501597  1501607  1501613  1501639  1501663
1501667  1501673  1501679  1501681  1501699  1501723  1501777  1501781  1501783  1501807
1501811  1501837  1501847  1501849  1501859  1501873  1501889  1501897  1501901  1501909
1501921  1501937  1501943  1501949  1501957  1501961  1501999  1502021  1502023  1502041
1502047  1502057  1502063  1502093  1502099  1502101  1502141  1502143  1502161  1502183
1502191  1502201  1502203  1502209  1502219  1502227  1502233  1502269  1502297  1502309
1502323  1502327  1502329  1502381  1502407  1502419  1502437  1502467  1502471  1502503
1502551  1502563  1502569  1502581  1502591  1502621  1502629  1502639  1502651  1502687
1502689  1502717  1502719  1502723  1502741  1502747  1502759  1502771  1502801  1502819
1502827  1502861  1502863  1502869  1502887  1502909  1502923  1502929  1502933  1502939
1502947  1502959  1502971  1502989  1502993  1503017  1503031  1503037  1503043  1503049
1503053  1503059  1503091  1503113  1503127  1503137  1503149  1503163  1503169  1503181
1503233  1503241  1503247  1503253  1503263  1503269  1503287  1503311  1503317  1503319
1503329  1503353  1503367  1503371  1503373  1503377  1503401  1503419  1503431  1503461
1503473  1503479  1503499  1503503  1503517  1503521  1503529  1503583  1503611  1503613
1503637  1503647  1503653  1503659  1503661  1503683  1503713  1503721  1503731  1503739
1503751  1503767  1503781  1503787  1503811  1503823  1503829  1503847  1503863  1503881
1503883  1503899  1503913  1503919  1503937  1503941  1503959  1503961  1503967  1503989
1504033  1504037  1504057  1504067  1504073  1504093  1504103  1504117  1504121  1504147
1504157  1504171  1504187  1504231  1504247  1504267  1504271  1504289  1504297  1504319
1504339  1504379  1504409  1504411  1504417  1504421  1504429  1504463  1504469  1504471
1504487  1504493  1504501  1504513  1504519  1504537  1504543  1504571  1504579  1504583
1504589  1504609  1504627  1504631  1504651  1504661  1504663  1504669  1504673  1504681
1504691  1504693  1504697  1504717  1504733  1504739  1504747  1504757  1504777  1504793
1504801  1504813  1504841  1504831  1504843  1504847  1504859  1504861  1504879  1504903
1504907  1504949  1504961  1504967  1504969  1504981  1504991  1504999  1505003  1505011
1505033  1505083  1505087  1505089  1505093  1505099  1505107  1505111  1505117  1505131
1505137  1505167  1505173  1505177  1505183  1505191  1505201  1505209  1505227  1505243
1505261  1505279  1505291  1505293  1505311  1505323  1505341  1505353  1505369  1505381
1505407  1505411  1505417  1505431  1505437  1505449  1505467  1505499  1505489  1505507
1505519  1505521  1505563  1505587  1505591  1505599  1505611  1505657  1505659  1505681
1505683  1505687  1505711  1505723  1505729  1505737  1505743  1505747  1505753  1505761
```

```
1505773  1505797  1505813  1505831  1505837  1505849  1505851  1505873  1505893  1505899
1505929  1505953  1505983  1505993  1506007  1506023  1506031  1506059  1506077  1506079
1506091  1506103  1506121  1506137  1506157  1506163  1506179  1506191  1506199  1506203
1506223  1506229  1506257  1506269  1506287  1506317  1506341  1506359  1506371  1506389
1506391  1506413  1506433  1506443  1506457  1506473  1506487  1506493  1506497  1506499
1506509  1506511  1506551  1506553  1506559  1506563  1506587  1506607  1506611  1506613
1506619  1506623  1506641  1506649  1506653  1506689  1506697  1506721  1506731  1506733
1506749  1506779  1506781  1506797  1506803  1506809  1506823  1506839  1506851  1506877
1506887  1506889  1506907  1506917  1506929  1506943  1506959  1506977  1506979  1506997
1507007  1507019  1507039  1507057  1507069  1507073  1507091  1507097  1507111  1507123
1507139  1507141  1507153  1507171  1507183  1507211  1507229  1507291  1507301  1507321
1507369  1507379  1507421  1507423  1507427  1507439  1507453  1507469  1507481  1507483
1507487  1507501  1507531  1507559  1507591  1507603  1507607  1507609  1507613  1507637
1507651  1507657  1507687  1507697  1507699  1507729  1507763  1507769  1507771  1507789
1507813  1507837  1507841  1507853  1507867  1507879  1507889  1507907  1507921  1507993
1507997  1508033  1508047  1508051  1508063  1508077  1508081  1508093  1508113  1508131
1508141  1508147  1508173  1508197  1508207  1508219  1508249  1508251  1508263  1508279
1508281  1508293  1508303  1508321  1508323  1508383  1508389  1508401  1508407  1508413
1508417  1508449  1508459  1508471  1508473  1508489  1508509  1508519  1508531  1508561
1508579  1508587  1508621  1508623  1508627  1508629  1508651  1508659  1508671  1508687
1508693  1508707  1508711  1508719  1508723  1508729  1508743  1508753  1508779  1508789
1508797  1508803  1508813  1508833  1508851  1508867  1508873  1508879  1508893  1508909
1508911  1508921  1508929  1508933  1508939  1508951  1508953  1508959  1508977  1508981
1508993  1509019  1509031  1509059  1509061  1509071  1509077  1509099  1509127  1509133
1509143  1509163  1509187  1509197  1509203  1509229  1509269  1509289  1509307  1509331
1509353  1509367  1509371  1509377  1509407  1509427  1509437  1509439  1509457  1509463
1509491  1509509  1509517  1509523  1509533  1509551  1509553  1509581  1509587  1509589
1509623  1509631  1509643  1509659  1509701  1509727  1509733  1509737  1509749  1509757
1509779  1509841  1509857  1509863  1509887  1509899  1509913  1509919  1509929  1509941
1509947  1509953  1509961  1509967  1509971  1509997  1510013  1510021  1510039  1510043
1510049  1510057  1510087  1510109  1510121  1510141  1510147  1510163  1510189  1510199
1510207  1510213  1510217  1510219  1510259  1510273  1510279  1510307  1510309  1510319
1510321  1510337  1510339  1510343  1510357  1510361  1510363  1510373  1510391  1510393
1510417  1510423  1510427  1510429  1510469  1510477  1510489  1510493  1510507  1510511
1510541  1510573  1510583  1510591  1510601  1510643  1510651  1510669  1510679  1510681
1510687  1510693  1510703  1510741  1510753  1510757  1510759  1510763  1510777  1510781
1510799  1510819  1510843  1510853  1510867  1510877  1510889  1510897  1510913  1510921
1510933  1510961  1510963  1510967  1510991  1511017  1511021  1511047  1511053  1511099
1511101  1511119  1511129  1511143  1511179  1511201  1511207  1511227  1511231  1511233
1511239  1511243  1511269  1511273  1511287  1511291  1511303  1511327  1511329  1511371
1511387  1511423  1511429  1511441  1511443  1511449  1511459  1511527  1511533  1511539
1511563  1511569  1511597  1511599  1511617  1511633  1511647  1511651  1511663  1511669
1511687  1511689  1511723  1511737  1511743  1511747  1511779  1511791  1511801  1511819
1511821  1511863  1511891  1511897  1511911  1511921  1511927  1511933  1511941  1511947
1511953  1511971  1511977  1511999  1512019  1512023  1512029  1512041  1512083  1512097
1512109  1512113  1512127  1512169  1512197  1512209  1512221  1512223  1512233  1512241
1512253  1512281  1512283  1512289  1512293  1512299  1512307  1512311  1512323  1512331
1512361  1512383  1512421  1512431  1512479  1512481  1512493  1512517  1512527  1512547
1512551  1512557  1512559  1512569  1512607  1512619  1512629  1512661  1512683  1512689
1512691  1512703  1512713  1512751  1512767  1512773  1512787  1512809  1512817  1512827
1512829  1512857  1512877  1512923  1512941  1512947  1512961  1513013  1513019  1513021
1513033  1513037  1513049  1513067  1513069  1513073  1513091  1513093  1513111  1513117
1513121  1513123  1513139  1513151  1513159  1513163  1513199  1513207  1513219  1513229
1513271  1513273  1513277  1513319  1513321  1513361  1513367  1513381  1513387  1513397
1513399  1513417  1513427  1513429  1513441  1513453  1513487  1513489  1513511  1513517
1513529  1513531  1513537  1513543  1513553  1513573  1513583  1513591  1513601  1513609
1513619  1513621  1513651  1513657  1513661  1513667  1513669  1513693  1513717  1513727
1513739  1513741  1513751  1513777  1513807  1513819  1513859  1513871  1513891  1513909
1513913  1513921  1513927  1513937  1513949  1513957  1513973  1513991  1514027  1514033
1514039  1514059  1514063  1514099  1514101  1514131  1514147  1514153  1514179  1514197
1514209  1514213  1514241  1514273  1514291  1514321  1514323  1514327  1514329  1514363
1514399  1514407  1514413  1514423  1514437  1514441  1514453  1514459  1514489  1514497
1514507  1514537  1514549  1514551  1514561  1514563  1514587  1514593  1514599  1514603
1514633  1514647  1514651  1514657  1514659  1514671  1514701  1514713  1514719  1514731
1514741  1514749  1514783  1514791  1514797  1514801  1514831  1514837  1514867  1514879
1514897  1514911  1514917  1514959  1514963  1514981  1515011  1515029  1515049  1515053
1515089  1515109  1515119  1515149  1515169  1515197  1515229  1515251  1515259  1515271
1515281  1515313  1515317  1515347  1515359  1515377  1515391  1515413  1515419  1515461
1515469  1515487  1515509  1515541  1515571  1515583  1515599  1515617  1515623  1515643
1515671  1515691  1515697  1515713  1515719  1515721  1515727  1515733  1515739  1515749
1515757  1515791  1515809  1515817  1515821  1515823  1515841  1515847  1515881  1515919
1515923  1515929  1515947  1515961  1515971  1515973  1515979  1515989  1516007  1516019
1516037  1516039  1516049  1516061  1516087  1516093  1516103  1516127  1516129  1516153
1516157  1516187  1516189  1516199  1516217  1516231  1516243  1516259  1516261  1516279
1516289  1516331  1516337  1516343  1516357  1516363  1516369  1516391  1516393  1516397
1516421  1516433  1516441  1516483  1516499  1516513  1516531  1516547  1516583  1516589
1516591  1516607  1516609  1516633  1516639  1516651  1516657  1516661  1516663  1516681
1516687  1516693  1516709  1516733  1516759  1516763  1516771  1516817  1516819  1516829
1516843  1516847  1516871  1516883  1516897  1516909  1516951  1516967  1516987  1517023
1517027  1517039  1517051  1517053  1517059  1517099  1517101  1517107  1517141  1517143
1517161  1517179  1517189  1517209  1517213  1517227  1517239  1517261  1517273  1517279
1517297  1517311  1517317  1517339  1517363  1517377  1517387  1517393  1517401  1517413
1517423  1517441  1517449  1517507  1517519  1517521  1517531  1517557  1517561  1517567
1517569  1517591  1517603  1517611  1517627  1517639  1517647  1517651  1517653  1517671
1517687  1517689  1517699  1517707  1517713  1517719  1517753  1517783  1517807  1517819
1517837  1517843  1517849  1517869  1517881  1517917  1517921  1517927  1517933  1517939
1517941  1517983  1517993  1518001  1518007  1518061  1518067  1518071  1518089  1518091
1518103  1518109  1518133  1518137  1518149  1518191  1518199  1518203  1518239  1518263
1518277  1518281  1518311  1518313  1518329  1518337  1518343  1518359  1518379  1518383
```

1518427 1518449 1518463 1518467 1518481 1518497 1518521 1518533 1518551 1518553
1518563 1518571 1518577 1518581 1518589 1518623 1518677 1518679 1518691 1518707
1518709 1518731 1518733 1518743 1518749 1518773 1518779 1518799 1518809 1518827
1518863 1518871 1518883 1518893 1518901 1518931 1518947 1518949 1518971 1518973
1518977 1519039 1519051 1519097 1519099 1519121 1519123 1519129 1519153 1519159
1519163 1519169 1519201 1519213 1519237 1519253 1519261 1519267 1519277 1519283
1519291 1519313 1519333 1519363 1519391 1519417 1519421 1519423 1519433 1519439
1519447 1519451 1519499 1519517 1519519 1519523 1519547 1519549 1519561 1519591
1519597 1519607 1519619 1519631 1519657 1519667 1519673 1519691 1519703 1519709
1519711 1519729 1519733 1519751 1519759 1519769 1519789 1519807 1519831 1519871
1519883 1519891 1519901 1519907 1519913 1519939 1519951 1519967 1520003 1520009
1520011 1520069 1520083 1520107 1520131 1520143 1520153 1520159 1520173 1520203
1520213 1520221 1520227 1520251 1520287 1520291 1520329 1520339 1520341 1520347
1520357 1520359 1520381 1520401 1520417 1520423 1520443 1520447 1520473 1520483
1520501 1520503 1520509 1520527 1520537 1520539 1520543 1520549 1520579 1520587
1520611 1520621 1520639 1520653 1520681 1520683 1520689 1520693 1520707 1520711
1520719 1520723 1520747 1520759 1520777 1520801 1520821 1520851 1520879 1520887
1520903 1520923 1520947 1520971 1520983 1520989 1521011 1521017 1521029 1521031
1521043 1521049 1521067 1521089 1521103 1521119 1521133 1521193 1521199 1521209
1521217 1521227 1521229 1521241 1521269 1521281 1521293 1521301 1521323
1521337 1521361 1521371 1521391 1521397 1521479 1521491 1521497 1521547 1521563
1521571 1521589 1521593 1521599 1521613 1521621 1521623 1521629 1521643 1521649
1521671 1521673 1521677 1521731 1521739 1521757 1521763 1521769 1521781 1521791
1521803 1521809 1521853 1521859 1521869 1521893 1521901 1521913 1521937 1521973
1521983 1521991 1522009 1522019 1522021 1522049 1522051 1522057 1522063 1522067
1522097 1522111 1522127 1522153 1522159 1522187 1522201 1522249 1522253 1522321
1522343 1522357 1522361 1522363 1522369 1522387 1522399 1522427 1522447
1522457 1522459 1522463 1522483 1522487 1522511 1522517 1522541 1522553 1522579
1522589 1522601 1522607 1522643 1522663 1522681 1522691 1522693 1522711 1522727
1522733 1522769 1522771 1522789 1522799 1522811 1522837 1522841 1522897 1522933
1522951 1522973 1522981 1523003 1523009 1523063 1523069 1523077 1523087 1523089
1523099 1523101 1523107 1523117 1523131 1523141 1523153 1523161 1523177 1523219
1523233 1523261 1523281 1523293 1523297 1523311 1523323 1523329 1523339 1523351
1523369 1523377 1523381 1523393 1523407 1523419 1523429 1523441 1523443 1523453
1523491 1523503 1523507 1523521 1523527 1523531 1523539 1523551 1523563 1523567
1523569 1523581 1523603 1523609 1523617 1523633 1523651 1523653 1523663 1523671
1523701 1523707 1523737 1523749 1523783 1523789 1523801 1523807 1523813 1523849
1523861 1523891 1523917 1523939 1523941 1523953 1523969 1523981 1523983 1523987
1524007 1524013 1524023 1524059 1524067 1524073 1524077 1524079 1524097 1524109
1524113 1524119 1524137 1524139 1524143 1524179 1524181 1524217 1524223 1524241
1524247 1524253 1524277 1524287 1524293 1524319 1524337 1524349 1524359 1524361
1524377 1524379 1524401 1524403 1524409 1524431 1524433 1524449 1524469 1524473
1524493 1524517 1524529 1524533 1524547 1524569 1524571 1524587 1524613 1524629
1524631 1524637 1524641 1524683 1524689 1524697 1524701 1524703 1524707 1524763
1524767 1524773 1524799 1524811 1524827 1524829 1524839 1524841 1524847 1524851
1524871 1524931 1524953 1524989 1525021 1525031 1525033 1525039 1525049
1525057 1525063 1525067 1525093 1525099 1525109 1525123 1525133 1525157 1525163
1525171 1525207 1525217 1525219 1525229 1525243 1525261 1525267 1525273 1525297
1525333 1525343 1525351 1525357 1525367 1525409 1525421 1525423 1525471
1525477 1525493 1525501 1525507 1525561 1525571 1525607 1525609 1525633 1525637
1525639 1525669 1525673 1525697 1525703 1525709 1525717 1525723 1525729 1525747
1525763 1525781 1525787 1525819 1525831 1525837 1525859 1525873 1525877 1525921
1525933 1525957 1525961 1525963 1525967 1525969 1525987 1525999 1526053 1526069
1526071 1526087 1526089 1526093 1526117 1526123 1526149 1526167 1526179 1526191
1526227 1526263 1526267 1526269 1526279 1526297 1526321 1526339 1526341 1526351
1526363 1526377 1526381 1526387 1526401 1526411 1526423 1526431 1526449 1526467
1526521 1526537 1526557 1526561 1526587 1526597 1526611 1526621 1526633 1526639
1526641 1526653 1526659 1526687 1526741 1526747 1526807 1526813 1526831 1526867
1526873 1526909 1526929 1526933 1526977 1526999 1527017 1527023 1527041 1527047
1527061 1527079 1527083 1527107 1527109 1527121 1527133 1527137 1527143 1527157
1527173 1527179 1527197 1527203 1527247 1527271 1527287 1527289 1527299 1527311
1527313 1527347 1527349 1527371 1527389 1527443 1527457 1527497 1527521 1527523
1527529 1527541 1527551 1527553 1527563 1527577 1527583 1527599 1527607 1527613
1527629 1527677 1527679 1527689 1527703 1527709 1527727 1527731 1527737 1527761
1527769 1527791 1527793 1527803 1527811 1527839 1527857 1527859 1527887 1527893
1527899 1527901 1527931 1527941 1527949 1527971 1527973 1527979 1527983 1527997
1528001 1528013 1528019 1528061 1528073 1528103 1528127 1528139 1528141 1528157
1528171 1528187 1528199 1528223 1528229 1528237 1528243 1528253 1528259 1528291
1528313 1528321 1528333 1528399 1528409 1528421 1528427 1528441 1528447 1528459
1528463 1528469 1528529 1528537 1528543 1528577 1528601 1528609 1528613 1528621
1528627 1528633 1528643 1528661 1528669 1528687 1528697 1528717 1528733 1528771
1528781 1528789 1528799 1528811 1528823 1528831 1528853 1528859 1528871 1528897
1528937 1528939 1528973 1528993 1528999 1529009 1529027 1529029 1529041 1529053
1529069 1529071 1529081 1529089 1529093 1529119 1529149 1529153 1529189 1529191
1529233 1529243 1529249 1529263 1529267 1529273 1529279 1529309 1529327 1529357
1529369 1529377 1529383 1529387 1529389 1529393 1529401 1529413 1529419 1529449
1529459 1529471 1529501 1529503 1529513 1529531 1529533 1529537 1529573 1529581
1529599 1529603 1529611 1529621 1529629 1529659 1529683 1529701 1529741 1529761
1529777 1529791 1529797 1529807 1529831 1529849 1529851 1529863 1529867 1529893
1529903 1529909 1529917 1529933 1529947 1529963 1529971 1529977 1529989 1530019
1530037 1530067 1530073 1530077 1530091 1530097 1530103 1530107 1530131 1530143
1530149 1530157 1530173 1530197 1530227 1530229 1530233 1530281 1530293 1530311
1530313 1530329 1530343 1530349 1530409 1530457 1530511 1530517 1530521 1530523
1530539 1530541 1530553 1530559 1530569 1530589 1530601 1530611 1530623 1530631
1530647 1530667 1530691 1530703 1530709 1530713 1530721 1530779 1530791
1530803 1530827 1530829 1530839 1530847 1530853 1530863 1530869 1530871 1530911
1530913 1530937 1530943 1530953 1530967 1531021 1531027 1531031 1531051 1531081
1531091 1531093 1531111 1531129 1531147 1531157 1531181 1531199 1531217 1531253
1531279 1531297 1531303 1531331 1531333 1531337 1531357 1531367 1531373 1531379

```
1531447  1531469  1531477  1531487  1531499  1531549  1531561  1531567  1531591  1531619
1531627  1531631  1531633  1531657  1531661  1531669  1531681  1531697  1531709  1531721
1531729  1531769  1531793  1531807  1531811  1531813  1531843  1531847  1531861  1531897
1531909  1531987  1531991  1531997  1532009  1532017  1532021  1532029  1532033  1532039
1532077  1532081  1532093  1532107  1532117  1532123  1532131  1532143  1532161  1532173
1532183  1532231  1532243  1532249  1532257  1532287  1532291  1532303  1532327  1532351
1532353  1532359  1532371  1532413  1532449  1532471  1532507  1532543  1532551  1532579
1532581  1532593  1532603  1532611  1532627  1532633  1532639  1532647  1532659  1532681
1532693  1532701  1532719  1532723  1532731  1532767  1532779  1532803  1532827  1532833
1532849  1532887  1532899  1532903  1532917  1532929  1532933  1532957  1532963  1532983
1532987  1533029  1533041  1533083  1533101  1533107  1533109  1533127  1533137  1533139
1533163  1533197  1533199  1533211  1533221  1533239  1533283  1533293  1533307  1533313
1533331  1533347  1533379  1533397  1533401  1533407  1533431  1533437  1533439  1533443
1533457  1533461  1533463  1533481  1533487  1533503  1533517  1533527  1533533  1533557
1533583  1533593  1533599  1533619  1533629  1533643  1533659  1533673  1533683  1533691
1533713  1533731  1533743  1533793  1533797  1533799  1533809  1533817  1533841  1533871
1533877  1533881  1533899  1533901  1533907  1533937  1533947  1533953  1533971  1533977
1534019  1534021  1534051  1534061  1534067  1534069  1534073  1534081  1534103  1534121
1534133  1534139  1534147  1534151  1534153  1534171  1534189  1534207  1534213  1534217
1534219  1534223  1534289  1534321  1534327  1534331  1534349  1534373  1534397  1534411
1534451  1534453  1534457  1534483  1534499  1534513  1534517  1534549  1534579  1534591
1534601  1534609  1534633  1534657  1534661  1534667  1534727  1534739  1534751  1534783
1534787  1534789  1534823  1534837  1534843  1534853  1534861  1534873  1534889  1534901
1534921  1534931  1534957  1534961  1534963  1534969  1534979  1534993  1535011  1535041
1535069  1535071  1535077  1535101  1535111  1535119  1535123  1535137  1535153  1535179
1535243  1535249  1535269  1535279  1535291  1535293  1535299  1535311  1535323  1535341
1535351  1535353  1535363  1535377  1535381  1535393  1535441  1535453  1535459  1535467
1535473  1535477  1535489  1535497  1535507  1535531  1535539  1535543  1535563  1535581
1535587  1535603  1535609  1535621  1535629  1535663  1535669  1535671  1535689  1535717
1535719  1535741  1535747  1535761  1535767  1535773  1535777  1535791  1535803  1535813
1535837  1535843  1535857  1535861  1535867  1535879  1535909  1535923  1535929  1535939
1535959  1535969  1535971  1535987  1536011  1536013  1536023  1536037  1536047  1536049
1536077  1536083  1536097  1536107  1536121  1536133  1536149  1536167  1536173  1536187
1536191  1536211  1536221  1536251  1536257  1536263  1536281  1536287  1536343  1536349
1536373  1536389  1536401  1536439  1536467  1536487  1536497  1536527  1536533  1536539
1536547  1536553  1536581  1536583  1536589  1536593  1536599  1536611  1536617  1536631
1536641  1536643  1536649  1536659  1536673  1536677  1536679  1536683  1536719  1536737
1536781  1536793  1536809  1536811  1536823  1536839  1536881  1536889  1536893  1536907
1536959  1536961  1536989  1536991  1537001  1537007  1537013  1537027  1537031  1537037
1537051  1537061  1537099  1537141  1537147  1537153  1537163  1537169  1537177  1537183
1537199  1537223  1537241  1537247  1537279  1537301  1537337  1537357  1537369  1537373
1537391  1537397  1537399  1537411  1537421  1537427  1537439  1537441  1537457  1537469
1537489  1537513  1537517  1537559  1537561  1537607  1537621  1537639  1537643  1537661
1537681  1537691  1537709  1537721  1537729  1537751  1537771  1537799  1537801  1537807
1537813  1537819  1537847  1537853  1537867  1537883  1537889  1537897  1537933  1537937
1537961  1537967  1537983  1537997  1537999  1538011  1538023  1538027  1538029  1538039
1538057  1538059  1538077  1538081  1538083  1538087  1538093  1538101  1538111  1538167
1538179  1538191  1538203  1538213  1538227  1538233  1538261  1538267  1538281  1538293
1538311  1538321  1538353  1538389  1538393  1538399  1538413  1538419  1538429  1538441
1538461  1538473  1538491  1538501  1538503  1538507  1538519  1538531  1538569  1538573
1538587  1538597  1538599  1538609  1538611  1538617  1538627  1538629  1538633  1538657
1538701  1538731  1538743  1538773  1538777  1538807  1538837  1538839  1538851  1538879
1538893  1538909  1538917  1538939  1538951  1538963  1538983  1538989  1539011  1539029
1539049  1539053  1539073  1539103  1539127  1539149  1539193  1539199  1539211  1539217
1539227  1539253  1539257  1539259  1539281  1539301  1539313  1539331  1539347  1539359
1539389  1539397  1539403  1539449  1539451  1539463  1539467  1539479  1539521  1539547
1539557  1539563  1539569  1539583  1539613  1539619  1539641  1539649  1539653  1539661
1539679  1539691  1539719  1539721  1539731  1539737  1539763  1539773  1539793  1539799
1539821  1539847  1539859  1539869  1539883  1539887  1539913  1539917  1539943  1539961
1539971  1539973  1539983  1539991  1539997  1540003  1540009  1540027  1540031  1540039
1540073  1540079  1540109  1540139  1540141  1540151  1540153  1540157  1540169  1540171
1540177  1540193  1540207  1540211  1540223  1540229  1540243  1540249  1540289  1540309
1540321  1540337  1540367  1540403  1540423  1540447  1540453  1540477  1540481  1540499
1540541  1540543  1540559  1540573  1540603  1540619  1540621  1540631  1540639  1540661
1540673  1540681  1540687  1540697  1540699  1540709  1540711  1540751  1540753  1540783
1540787  1540789  1540807  1540813  1540823  1540831  1540841  1540849  1540859  1540867
1540871  1540873  1540879  1540901  1540927  1540949  1540961  1540963  1540967  1540969
1540997  1541003  1541009  1541051  1541063  1541117  1541119  1541143  1541171  1541191
1541209  1541251  1541273  1541279  1541291  1541297  1541303  1541317  1541333  1541341
1541347  1541357  1541359  1541363  1541377  1541381  1541389  1541429  1541431  1541453
1541471  1541497  1541503  1541513  1541539  1541581  1541591  1541597  1541629  1541651
1541663  1541671  1541681  1541689  1541693  1541699  1541707  1541731  1541773  1541779
1541783  1541791  1541797  1541809  1541819  1541821  1541863  1541867  1541873  1541891
1541921  1541923  1541933  1541941  1541957  1541963  1541987  1541999  1542007  1542029
1542031  1542041  1542043  1542071  1542077  1542089  1542091  1542119  1542131  1542137
1542179  1542187  1542193  1542217  1542221  1542239  1542251  1542259  1542283  1542347
1542349  1542361  1542377  1542383  1542421  1542433  1542451  1542473  1542479  1542487
1542503  1542509  1542511  1542517  1542521  1542523  1542533  1542551  1542571  1542581
1542589  1542599  1542661  1542689  1542691  1542703  1542727  1542811  1542823  1542841
1542851  1542889  1542899  1542911  1542917  1542941  1542973  1542991  1542997
1543007  1543013  1543019  1543033  1543037  1543051  1543063  1543067  1543081  1543099
1543103  1543111  1543127  1543133  1543169  1543181  1543187  1543207  1543229  1543259
1543271  1543279  1543291  1543309  1543319  1543337  1543357  1543391  1543393  1543417
1543429  1543441  1543463  1543489  1543501  1543511  1543513  1543537  1543543  1543559
1543589  1543631  1543637  1543639  1543649  1543687  1543709  1543733  1543741  1543777
1543793  1543811  1543813  1543819  1543823  1543859  1543879  1543891  1543909  1543951
1543961  1543979  1543981  1543999  1544003  1544021  1544027  1544033  1544051  1544063
1544071  1544077  1544083  1544113  1544119  1544129  1544131  1544159  1544167  1544171
1544177  1544201  1544209  1544219  1544227  1544311  1544317  1544341  1544357  1544363
```

```
1544383 1544407 1544423 1544437 1544441 1544449 1544479 1544483 1544489 1544503
1544507 1544509 1544527 1544533 1544537 1544563 1544573 1544623 1544633 1544651
1544659 1544663 1544693 1544729 1544789 1544831 1544849 1544863 1544869 1544891
1544903 1544923 1544929 1544941 1544957 1544987 1545001 1545007 1545017 1545029
1545041 1545043 1545059 1545067 1545073 1545097 1545101 1545107 1545121 1545127
1545139 1545143 1545169 1545179 1545217 1545233 1545239 1545241 1545253 1545259
1545277 1545287 1545311 1545329 1545343 1545353 1545361 1545367 1545371 1545389
1545391 1545421 1545431 1545433 1545449 1545461 1545473 1545493 1545499 1545503
1545529 1545539 1545547 1545553 1545563 1545569 1545581 1545587 1545617 1545619
1545641 1545647 1545653 1545667 1545701 1545703 1545743 1545751 1545769 1545773
1545779 1545799 1545809 1545811 1545839 1545847 1545857 1545871 1545911 1545913
1545917 1545949 1545959 1545983 1545989 1546003 1546033 1546057 1546073 1546081
1546093 1546117 1546121 1546141 1546147 1546157 1546189 1546199 1546211 1546217
1546219 1546229 1546231 1546241 1546247 1546261 1546271 1546273 1546291 1546297
1546301 1546327 1546351 1546357 1546361 1546379 1546387 1546393 1546399 1546403
1546423 1546453 1546463 1546469 1546477 1546499 1546537 1546547 1546549 1546627
1546639 1546663 1546669 1546679 1546687 1546697 1546709 1546729 1546757 1546759
1546781 1546799 1546823 1546837 1546861 1546873 1546879 1546901 1546903 1546907
1546927 1546939 1546967 1546969 1546981 1546991 1546997 1547009 1547023 1547027
1547069 1547093 1547101 1547129 1547131 1547173 1547177 1547191 1547197 1547201
1547207 1547213 1547239 1547251 1547257 1547261 1547267 1547339 1547347 1547383
1547389 1547407 1547419 1547423 1547431 1547437 1547449 1547453 1547471 1547477
1547479 1547501 1547519 1547521 1547537 1547543 1547563 1547573 1547591 1547593
1547597 1547603 1547641 1547657 1547659 1547671 1547677 1547713 1547717 1547719
1547723 1547771 1547773 1547779 1547803 1547807 1547827 1547837 1547839 1547849
1547857 1547879 1547881 1547893 1547921 1547927 1547929 1547939 1547941 1547947
1547989 1547993 1548031 1548059 1548067 1548073 1548083 1548097 1548103
1548121 1548137 1548143 1548149 1548161 1548179 1548181 1548187 1548221 1548247
1548251 1548277 1548307 1548311 1548317 1548331 1548347 1548359 1548389 1548401
1548409 1548427 1548433 1548461 1548481 1548493 1548497 1548517 1548527 1548539
1548541 1548553 1548577 1548587 1548593 1548619 1548623 1548641 1548647 1548653
1548719 1548721 1548733 1548739 1548761 1548763 1548769 1548779 1548787 1548793
1548847 1548871 1548881 1548893 1548901 1548913 1548917 1548923 1548929 1548941
1548947 1548949 1548961 1548983 1548991 1549003 1549013 1549033 1549049 1549061
1549081 1549087 1549099 1549129 1549139 1549157 1549169 1549183 1549199 1549213
1549271 1549277 1549283 1549319 1549321 1549351 1549367 1549369 1549391 1549403
1549409 1549417 1549439 1549447 1549459 1549463 1549477 1549481 1549489 1549501
1549511 1549519 1549529 1549531 1549547 1549549 1549553 1549573 1549577 1549609
1549619 1549631 1549657 1549699 1549733 1549739 1549741 1549787 1549817 1549831
1549837 1549843 1549853 1549883 1549897 1549921 1549931 1549937 1549943 1549957
1549987 1549997 1550027 1550033 1550051 1550053 1550069 1550083 1550099
1550119 1550141 1550147 1550161 1550167 1550173 1550203 1550207 1550209 1550221
1550231 1550233 1550243 1550257 1550287 1550299 1550309 1550321 1550327 1550359
1550363 1550371 1550377 1550387 1550401 1550431 1550441 1550443 1550449
1550467 1550477 1550503 1550509 1550513 1550539 1550551 1550567 1550597 1550603
1550611 1550617 1550629 1550663 1550669 1550683 1550701 1550737 1550741 1550753
1550771 1550777 1550779 1550789 1550819 1550827 1550831 1550851 1550873 1550897
1550947 1550963 1550971 1550993 1550999 1551001 1551013 1551019 1551037 1551041
1551049 1551083 1551089 1551107 1551113 1551133 1551157 1551163 1551167 1551191
1551197 1551203 1551229 1551241 1551269 1551289 1551343 1551371 1551383 1551449
1551463 1551467 1551479 1551497 1551499 1551551 1551577 1551593 1551601 1551617
1551619 1551623 1551647 1551659 1551661 1551677 1551691 1551701 1551707 1551731
1551733 1551757 1551763 1551773 1551791 1551793 1551853 1551859 1551871 1551883
1551887 1551889 1551899 1551911 1551917 1551919 1551929 1551943 1551959 1551961
1551967 1551997 1552007 1552037 1552079 1552087 1552121 1552123 1552147 1552169
1552207 1552217 1552223 1552227 1552241 1552277 1552289 1552307 1552333
1552337 1552351 1552367 1552373 1552379 1552381 1552393 1552403 1552417 1552451
1552469 1552501 1552513 1552517 1552531 1552541 1552543 1552553 1552561 1552567
1552571 1552583 1552589 1552597 1552613 1552619 1552643 1552651 1552657 1552669
1552693 1552709 1552723 1552757 1552781 1552807 1552819 1552843 1552861 1552867
1552871 1552879 1552909 1552913 1552919 1552949 1552963 1552981 1552987 1552997
1553009 1553011 1553017 1553023 1553053 1553063 1553081 1553089 1553093 1553099
1553107 1553119 1553129 1553147 1553159 1553173 1553177 1553191 1553249 1553281
1553287 1553291 1553309 1553311 1553329 1553333 1553339 1553347 1553369 1553381
1553389 1553401 1553407 1553413 1553417 1553423 1553429 1553437 1553467 1553471
1553479 1553507 1553509 1553527 1553537 1553543 1553557 1553561 1553567 1553597
1553653 1553701 1553707 1553711 1553723 1553729 1553737 1553743 1553753 1553771
1553803 1553807 1553809 1553821 1553869 1553873 1553887 1553897 1553927
1553947 1553971 1553983 1554019 1554043 1554073 1554083 1554101 1554103 1554107
1554151 1554169 1554173 1554193 1554221 1554227 1554233 1554239 1554277 1554281
1554283 1554299 1554307 1554347 1554349 1554359 1554367 1554379 1554383 1554391
1554401 1554419 1554439 1554451 1554461 1554521 1554529 1554559 1554569 1554583
1554589 1554611 1554613 1554653 1554659 1554697 1554733 1554737 1554739 1554757
1554779 1554781 1554797 1554811 1554821 1554841 1554853 1554863 1554877 1554881
1554899 1554913 1554977 1554989 1555013 1555027 1555033 1555039 1555051 1555061
1555079 1555091 1555111 1555117 1555123 1555129 1555133 1555153 1555157 1555159
1555163 1555187 1555189 1555193 1555199 1555223 1555231 1555243 1555247 1555249
1555259 1555261 1555291 1555319 1555327 1555343 1555349 1555409 1555423
1555429 1555469 1555471 1555481 1555507 1555523 1555529 1555553 1555571 1555573
1555579 1555607 1555633 1555637 1555639 1555643 1555657 1555661 1555669 1555679
1555691 1555693 1555699 1555711 1555717 1555727 1555733 1555751 1555759 1555781
1555787 1555793 1555817 1555819 1555831 1555837 1555847 1555861 1555901 1555907
1555913 1555919 1555943 1555951 1555963 1555969 1555997 1555999 1556003 1556011
1556017 1556039 1556059 1556069 1556083 1556117 1556147 1556173 1556179 1556189
1556201 1556251 1556263 1556267 1556297 1556323 1556327 1556339 1556351
1556363 1556369 1556371 1556393 1556413 1556431 1556441 1556449 1556453 1556473
1556491 1556501 1556509 1556519 1556551 1556561 1556563 1556567 1556573 1556587
1556591 1556609 1556623 1556641 1556657 1556669 1556671 1556717 1556719 1556747
1556759 1556761 1556767 1556771 1556773 1556791 1556837 1556839 1556869 1556873
```

```
1556881  1556897  1556909  1556927  1556963  1556977  1557001  1557007  1557019  1557029
1557041  1557043  1557053  1557067  1557079  1557089  1557091  1557103  1557109  1557113
1557119  1557131  1557137  1557151  1557211  1557239  1557247  1557287  1557289  1557301
1557313  1557337  1557341  1557343  1557359  1557371  1557377  1557389  1557397  1557403
1557407  1557419  1557427  1557433  1557443  1557469  1557481  1557499  1557509  1557547
1557551  1557559  1557593  1557607  1557613  1557623  1557637  1557641  1557649  1557653
1557667  1557707  1557709  1557733  1557763  1557769  1557797  1557823  1557833  1557839
1557869  1557883  1557889  1557947  1557949  1557973  1557991  1558009  1558061  1558079
1558087  1558099  1558103  1558129  1558177  1558189  1558201  1558213  1558217  1558223
1558243  1558267  1558279  1558283  1558289  1558303  1558307  1558309  1558313  1558321
1558327  1558343  1558351  1558357  1558387  1558397  1558409  1558423  1558439  1558483
1558511  1558517  1558523  1558541  1558559  1558561  1558573  1558597  1558619  1558631
1558637  1558643  1558651  1558673  1558681  1558691  1558709  1558717  1558727  1558729
1558759  1558769  1558771  1558787  1558789  1558807  1558811  1558813  1558819  1558829
1558831  1558841  1558867  1558873  1558877  1558891  1558901  1558913  1558919  1558933
1558937  1558939  1558967  1558979  1558981  1559017  1559057  1559059  1559093  1559113
1559119  1559123  1559153  1559161  1559171  1559177  1559183  1559203  1559209  1559213
1559227  1559267  1559281  1559297  1559303  1559329  1559333  1559347  1559351  1559357
1559399  1559407  1559431  1559443  1559447  1559449  1559477  1559497  1559499  1559483
1559491  1559521  1559527  1559531  1559549  1559573  1559581  1559603  1559609  1559611
1559617  1559647  1559651  1559669  1559683  1559689  1559713  1559731  1559749  1559759
1559773  1559777  1559797  1559807  1559821  1559839  1559849  1559851  1559879  1559891
1559893  1559933  1559963  1559969  1559983  1559989  1560007  1560011  1560023  1560037
1560047  1560049  1560059  1560077  1560121  1560127  1560131  1560133  1560149  1560187
1560193  1560203  1560211  1560217  1560227  1560239  1560241  1560257  1560263  1560271
1560289  1560371  1560391  1560407  1560409  1560421  1560441  1560457  1560473  1560511
1560523  1560529  1560539  1560547  1560569  1560589  1560593  1560653  1560659  1560673
1560677  1560683  1560707  1560709  1560733  1560739  1560743  1560749  1560781  1560799
1560817  1560847  1560859  1560877  1560883  1560893  1560901  1560913  1560953  1560967
1560973  1560997  1561003  1561013  1561019  1561037  1561039  1561069  1561111  1561117
1561121  1561123  1561139  1561151  1561159  1561163  1561169  1561187  1561193  1561213
1561243  1561247  1561267  1561279  1561303  1561337  1561349  1561367  1561393  1561421
1561423  1561429  1561453  1561457  1561463  1561499  1561519  1561529  1561537  1561541
1561559  1561577  1561579  1561589  1561597  1561601  1561607  1561633  1561639  1561657
1561673  1561697  1561711  1561727  1561741  1561753  1561757  1561759  1561801  1561817
1561823  1561829  1561883  1561891  1561919  1562051  1562053  1562063  1562081  1562087
1562089  1562101  1562107  1562111  1562129  1562131  1562159  1562173  1562191  1562207
1562219  1562243  1562263  1562269  1562279  1562287  1562291  1562293  1562347  1562357
1562359  1562371  1562377  1562381  1562411  1562417  1562423  1562447  1562471  1562513
1562527  1562531  1562543  1562567  1562591  1562593  1562611  1562647  1562653  1562707
1562713  1562719  1562753  1562833  1562863  1562887  1562897  1562933  1562947  1562971
1562983  1562993  1562999  1563017  1563019  1563041  1563047  1563061  1563077  1563083
1563091  1563097  1563101  1563109  1563119  1563131  1563137  1563143  1563157  1563161
1563209  1563217  1563227  1563229  1563239  1563253  1563257  1563259  1563271  1563277
1563281  1563283  1563293  1563319  1563329  1563389  1563407  1563409  1563413  1563421
1563427  1563431  1563433  1563469  1563461  1563467  1563469  1563481  1563487  1563503
1563511  1563533  1563539  1563571  1563577  1563599  1563619  1563623  1563629  1563631
1563649  1563689  1563703  1563707  1563739  1563743  1563773  1563791  1563811  1563817
1563829  1563851  1563893  1563901  1563911  1563937  1563943  1563959  1563967  1563971
1563973  1564001  1564007  1564037  1564049  1564063  1564067  1564081  1564091  1564097
1564103  1564111  1564117  1564139  1564151  1564159  1564183  1564237  1564243  1564307
1564309  1564313  1564337  1564349  1564361  1564363  1564369  1564373  1564379  1564393
1564399  1564411  1564417  1564421  1564427  1564457  1564487  1564499  1564501  1564543
1564553  1564559  1564571  1564573  1564597  1564603  1564643  1564657  1564679  1564699
1564721  1564729  1564741  1564747  1564751  1564777  1564781  1564807  1564831  1564837
1564853  1564861  1564877  1564907  1564909  1564921  1564933  1564949  1564991  1564993
1564999  1565009  1565017  1565023  1565027  1565033  1565041  1565051  1565059  1565099
1565117  1565129  1565141  1565149  1565153  1565167  1565171  1565177  1565183  1565189
1565191  1565203  1565209  1565233  1565251  1565261  1565269  1565281  1565287  1565293
1565323  1565341  1565351  1565381  1565383  1565413  1565437  1565441  1565471  1565489
1565491  1565519  1565521  1565539  1565549  1565561  1565563  1565569  1565579  1565591
1565609  1565611  1565651  1565659  1565671  1565693  1565737  1565741  1565743  1565747
1565789  1565791  1565807  1565813  1565821  1565827  1565833  1565867  1565869  1565873
1565891  1565897  1565911  1565917  1565929  1565933  1565947  1565969  1565987  1566031
1566043  1566049  1566079  1566083  1566101  1566107  1566121  1566137  1566143  1566163
1566179  1566197  1566199  1566209  1566211  1566217  1566239  1566251  1566263  1566281
1566283  1566289  1566307  1566343  1566349  1566353  1566359  1566371  1566401  1566403
1566427  1566449  1566451  1566479  1566517  1566529  1566559  1566571  1566577  1566583
1566613  1566637  1566659  1566673  1566731  1566739  1566743  1566749  1566751  1566767
1566769  1566779  1566793  1566811  1566821  1566823  1566827  1566847  1566857  1566881
1566883  1566889  1566893  1566923  1566937  1566953  1566997  1567001  1567003  1567031
1567037  1567039  1567057  1567067  1567079  1567087  1567103  1567109  1567117  1567127
1567133  1567141  1567147  1567169  1567171  1567219  1567249  1567259  1567261  1567271
1567297  1567301  1567303  1567327  1567333  1567339  1567343  1567361  1567373  1567409
1567411  1567429  1567469  1567477  1567483  1567487  1567493  1567499  1567513  1567541
1567549  1567567  1567589  1567603  1567607  1567627  1567637  1567661  1567667  1567679
1567721  1567727  1567729  1567759  1567771  1567789  1567829  1567837  1567847  1567901
1567903  1567931  1567951  1567987  1567999  1568033  1568041  1568053  1568087  1568107
1568123  1568129  1568141  1568143  1568153  1568159  1568173  1568179  1568207  1568213
1568221  1568243  1568251  1568257  1568263  1568293  1568309  1568341  1568351  1568353
1568377  1568389  1568419  1568423  1568449  1568453  1568459  1568503  1568509  1568519
1568521  1568533  1568543  1568561  1568563  1568579  1568599  1568629  1568657  1568687
1568729  1568741  1568767  1568771  1568867  1568873  1568891  1568909  1568921  1568923
1568927  1568933  1568951  1568969  1568971  1568977  1568993  1569011  1569013  1569023
1569047  1569053  1569061  1569101  1569121  1569131  1569149  1569157  1569163  1569171
1569181  1569187  1569203  1569209  1569241  1569257  1569259  1569263  1569289  1569301
1569307  1569311  1569317  1569319  1569329  1569331  1569349  1569367  1569391  1569397
1569401  1569413  1569431  1569443  1569473  1569479  1569487  1569517  1569541  1569551
1569553  1569599  1569611  1569619  1569637  1569643  1569649  1569677  1569703  1569731
```

```
1569749  1569781  1569787  1569793  1569803  1569811  1569817  1569833  1569839  1569859
1569889  1569901  1569923  1569937  1569961  1569977  1569983  1570007  1570043  1570061
1570067  1570073  1570081  1570087  1570091  1570097  1570099  1570117  1570123  1570189
1570193  1570199  1570229  1570237  1570241  1570267  1570271  1570291  1570319  1570339
1570343  1570351  1570357  1570381  1570399  1570421  1570427  1570433  1570447  1570451
1570453  1570487  1570493  1570501  1570519  1570531  1570577  1570603  1570607  1570619
1570631  1570633  1570637  1570649  1570663  1570697  1570729  1570753  1570759  1570763
1570769  1570771  1570781  1570837  1570841  1570847  1570859  1570871  1570873  1570879
1570883  1570889  1570897  1570903  1570913  1570927  1570931  1570937  1570951  1570957
1570963  1570967  1570981  1570991  1570999  1571023  1571027  1571029  1571093  1571113
1571137  1571149  1571183  1571189  1571201  1571209  1571221  1571233  1571237  1571239
1571267  1571287  1571309  1571329  1571363  1571377  1571387  1571393  1571411  1571417
1571419  1571461  1571467  1571477  1571513  1571551  1571569  1571579  1571587  1571611
1571621  1571629  1571657  1571663  1571681  1571683  1571707  1571711  1571719  1571729
1571741  1571743  1571747  1571749  1571761  1571777  1571783  1571789  1571807  1571827
1571833  1571839  1571849  1571873  1571881  1571893  1571897  1571923  1571929  1571953
1571957  1571959  1571989  1572017  1572023  1572029  1572047  1572083  1572091  1572097
1572101  1572113  1572149  1572163  1572187  1572191  1572203  1572217  1572239  1572247
1572251  1572253  1572271  1572281  1572283  1572287  1572323  1572331  1572341  1572353
1572359  1572367  1572377  1572379  1572401  1572407  1572419  1572427  1572433  1572443
1572509  1572511  1572521  1572539  1572547  1572559  1572569  1572577  1572587  1572589
1572607  1572617  1572629  1572643  1572647  1572677  1572679  1572689  1572713  1572731
1572749  1572751  1572773  1572799  1572803  1572821  1572841  1572853  1572869  1572871
1572887  1572911  1572919  1572929  1572997  1573009  1573021  1573037  1573051  1573057
1573079  1573081  1573087  1573109  1573111  1573133  1573139  1573141  1573151  1573153
1573183  1573193  1573207  1573217  1573237  1573283  1573301  1573303  1573339  1573357
1573379  1573387  1573391  1573399  1573477  1573483  1573487  1573501  1573541  1573543
1573547  1573549  1573553  1573577  1573603  1573613  1573643  1573651  1573667  1573669
1573679  1573699  1573709  1573717  1573723  1573727  1573753  1573771  1573799  1573811
1573813  1573823  1573829  1573837  1573879  1573907  1573909  1573921  1573927  1573931
1573933  1573937  1573939  1573961  1573969  1573973  1574003  1574009  1574011
1574029  1574039  1574057  1574059  1574071  1574107  1574123  1574129  1574137  1574159
1574161  1574173  1574197  1574201  1574219  1574231  1574249  1574269  1574311  1574317
1574333  1574341  1574357  1574369  1574371  1574393  1574401  1574411  1574431  1574437
1574467  1574479  1574491  1574501  1574527  1574543  1574563  1574569  1574579  1574597
1574611  1574623  1574627  1574647  1574653  1574719  1574681  1574717  1574737  1574747
1574773  1574791  1574827  1574843  1574849  1574857  1574869  1574873  1574917  1574939
1574953  1574957  1574981  1574987  1575011  1575029  1575031  1575071  1575083  1575113
1575131  1575137  1575139  1575143  1575151  1575187  1575199  1575209  1575227  1575239
1575253  1575263  1575269  1575281  1575283  1575289  1575307  1575331  1575337  1575341
1575397  1575401  1575421  1575433  1575437  1575443  1575463  1575467  1575473  1575479
1575481  1575517  1575521  1575547  1575551  1575557  1575583  1575697  1575709  1575731
1575641  1575643  1575647  1575653  1575659  1575667  1575683  1575697  1575709  1575731
1575733  1575757  1575767  1575811  1575817  1575829  1575869  1575887  1575913  1575919
1575961  1575989  1575991  1576007  1576013  1576021  1576033  1576037  1576039  1576049
1576073  1576093  1576097  1576103  1576111  1576117  1576139  1576177  1576229  1576241
1576243  1576247  1576277  1576283  1576321  1576339  1576343  1576357  1576363  1576391
1576403  1576417  1576483  1576493  1576499  1576501  1576507  1576511  1576517  1576537
1576543  1576559  1576571  1576579  1576583  1576613  1576649  1576651  1576661  1576669
1576693  1576703  1576717  1576721  1576723  1576747  1576763  1576769  1576777  1576781
1576793  1576837  1576843  1576849  1576871  1576879  1576889  1576891  1576907  1576921
1576931  1576951  1576957  1576973  1576997  1577021  1577027  1577071  1577099  1577101
1577117  1577119  1577137  1577143  1577153  1577163  1577189  1577201  1577203  1577221
1577231  1577267  1577291  1577293  1577297  1577299  1577309  1577321  1577341  1577353
1577357  1577377  1577383  1577431  1577449  1577453  1577479  1577489  1577503  1577507
1577509  1577531  1577533  1577539  1577561  1577567  1577573  1577579  1577591  1577599
1577623  1577657  1577659  1577663  1577671  1577689  1577699  1577701  1577711  1577729
1577759  1577767  1577801  1577813  1577843  1577879  1577897  1577903  1577909
1577941  1577959  1577963  1577987  1577999  1578001  1578011  1578019  1578023  1578029
1578043  1578047  1578061  1578077  1578091  1578133  1578169  1578193  1578217  1578221
1578257  1578277  1578281  1578289  1578293  1578299  1578323  1578347  1578361  1578389
1578397  1578407  1578439  1578469  1578509  1578517  1578553  1578581  1578607  1578611
1578631  1578641  1578701  1578713  1578719  1578727  1578749  1578769  1578779  1578793
1578803  1578809  1578821  1578823  1578833  1578839  1578851  1578853  1578859  1578877
1578883  1578911  1578931  1578961  1578979  1579001  1579009  1579013  1579027  1579031
1579037  1579043  1579051  1579057  1579091  1579099  1579103  1579139  1579141  1579163
1579169  1579183  1579187  1579217  1579219  1579231  1579297  1579313  1579321  1579339
1579343  1579363  1579367  1579381  1579397  1579399  1579421  1579429  1579439  1579469
1579511  1579517  1579541  1579553  1579561  1579579  1579583  1579597  1579609  1579619
1579621  1579631  1579637  1579669  1579691  1579693  1579703  1579723  1579727  1579733
1579751  1579769  1579783  1579807  1579813  1579819  1579867  1579873  1579883  1579889
1579901  1579909  1579931  1579933  1579951  1579969  1579979  1579993  1580003  1580023
1580027  1580041  1580053  1580057  1580081  1580087  1580107  1580119  1580141  1580171
1580177  1580203  1580213  1580251  1580273  1580279  1580309  1580339  1580351  1580357
1580387  1580393  1580417  1580419  1580429  1580431  1580437  1580441  1580459  1580461
1580479  1580483  1580489  1580503  1580521  1580533  1580561  1580567  1580573  1580581
1580617  1580627  1580633  1580647  1580651  1580653  1580671  1580687  1580699  1580707
1580713  1580717  1580737  1580753  1580759  1580771  1580773  1580797  1580801  1580849
1580851  1580861  1580897  1580911  1580921  1580923  1580959  1580977  1580987  1581007
1581031  1581037  1581053  1581061  1581077  1581079  1581091  1581111  1581113
1581131  1581157  1581163  1581169  1581191  1581193  1581211  1581257  1581271  1581287
1581299  1581311  1581317  1581367  1581379  1581413  1581421  1581431  1581439  1581443
1581469  1581473  1581479  1581487  1581499  1581533  1581539  1581553  1581573  1581577
1581581  1581607  1581611  1581623  1581637  1581649  1581653  1581673  1581707  1581709
1581719  1581721  1581727  1581743  1581751  1581757  1581829  1581857  1581859  1581869
1581889  1581911  1581919  1581929  1581949  1582001  1582019  1582033  1582043  1582069
1582079  1582081  1582109  1582117  1582127  1582151  1582159  1582169  1582171  1582177
1582247  1582267  1582283  1582297  1582319  1582337  1582351  1582363  1582381  1582387
1582391  1582393  1582409  1582429  1582447  1582459  1582463  1582489  1582517  1582531
```

```
1582541  1582549  1582573  1582577  1582579  1582583  1582589  1582597  1582621  1582673
1582697  1582703  1582709  1582729  1582753  1582759  1582799  1582811  1582813  1582877
1582901  1582927  1582937  1582949  1582957  1582961  1582963  1582967  1582981  1582991
1583003  1583027  1583033  1583039  1583047  1583053  1583089  1583093  1583107  1583117
1583149  1583161  1583167  1583171  1583177  1583191  1583203  1583233  1583249  1583273
1583287  1583291  1583293  1583299  1583311  1583321  1583339  1583347  1583353  1583357
1583359  1583369  1583447  1583459  1583471  1583497  1583509  1583521  1583531  1583539
1583591  1583599  1583629  1583651  1583653  1583657  1583671  1583689  1583731  1583741
1583749  1583753  1583761  1583767  1583773  1583801  1583807  1583809  1583833  1583837
1583843  1583851  1583861  1583863  1583867  1583887  1583899  1583909  1583917  1583927
1583929  1583999  1584001  1584017  1584031  1584047  1584059  1584083  1584101  1584103
1584113  1584127  1584137  1584139  1584151  1584157  1584169  1584203  1584227  1584257
1584259  1584269  1584283  1584307  1584311  1584343  1584367  1584371  1584389  1584403
1584409  1584413  1584431  1584433  1584437  1584439  1584469  1584481  1584487  1584491
1584509  1584547  1584551  1584571  1584577  1584607  1584613  1584623  1584629  1584641
1584643  1584697  1584701  1584703  1584721  1584731  1584743  1584767  1584797  1584811
1584827  1584829  1584881  1584889  1584899  1584901  1584929  1584931  1584941  1584943
1584949  1584959  1584967  1584971  1584983  1585007  1585009  1585013  1585021  1585027
1585033  1585093  1585127  1585147  1585201  1585219  1585249  1585253  1585261  1585279
1585289  1585291  1585313  1585319  1585373  1585387  1585393  1585399  1585411  1585427
1585447  1585457  1585469  1585477  1585481  1585483  1585489  1585499  1585513  1585523
1585537  1585541  1585547  1585559  1585583  1585589  1585603  1585631  1585637  1585657
1585663  1585669  1585673  1585679  1585687  1585697  1585699  1585723  1585747  1585763
1585769  1585799  1585819  1585889  1585897  1585901  1585937  1585963  1585967  1585973
1585993  1586023  1586027  1586041  1586077  1586089  1586093  1586099  1586111  1586113
1586147  1586161  1586191  1586197  1586201  1586209  1586251  1586257  1586309  1586311
1586327  1586339  1586371  1586381  1586393  1586401  1586419  1586437  1586467  1586513
1586527  1586531  1586537  1586539  1586551  1586567  1586581  1586587  1586617  1586621
1586623  1586647  1586663  1586699  1586707  1586719  1586723  1586737  1586771  1586773
1586777  1586789  1586791  1586813  1586821  1586857  1586867  1586869  1586881  1586887
1586891  1586911  1586939  1586951  1586953  1586971  1586989  1587007  1587011  1587067
1587077  1587101  1587109  1587121  1587167  1587197  1587221  1587251  1587283  1587301
1587323  1587343  1587349  1587361  1587389  1587407  1587413  1587449  1587473  1587491
1587499  1587503  1587527  1587533  1587557  1587563  1587569  1587577  1587581  1587587
1587611  1587617  1587629  1587637  1587653  1587673  1587679  1587683  1587701  1587709
1587737  1587739  1587743  1587787  1587799  1587809  1587829  1587841  1587847  1587869
1587871  1587877  1587899  1587917  1587923  1587959  1587961  1587973  1587977  1587991
1587997  1588019  1588031  1588043  1588049  1588051  1588063  1588073  1588087  1588091
1588117  1588121  1588133  1588141  1588159  1588163  1588183  1588187  1588189  1588193
1588211  1588231  1588253  1588273  1588289  1588297  1588303  1588309  1588333  1588387
1588393  1588399  1588423  1588439  1588451  1588507  1588511  1588513  1588523  1588567
1588577  1588597  1588603  1588661  1588663  1588673  1588681  1588687  1588711  1588729
1588733  1588747  1588751  1588753  1588757  1588759  1588777  1588793  1588801  1588813
1588819  1588841  1588859  1588861  1588877  1588879  1588883  1588889  1588901  1588903
1588907  1588921  1588931  1588933  1588949  1588963  1588987  1589017  1589053  1589059
1589069  1589083  1589089  1589123  1589129  1589183  1589207  1589209  1589219  1589239
1589249  1589251  1589257  1589281  1589297  1589299  1589303  1589317  1589327  1589333
1589359  1589363  1589377  1589387  1589389  1589411  1589431  1589443  1589453  1589459
1589473  1589501  1589503  1589513  1589537  1589561  1589563  1589569  1589573  1589591
1589633  1589641  1589647  1589657  1589663  1589669  1589671  1589677  1589683  1589689
1589701  1589713  1589719  1589747  1589771  1589803  1589813  1589827  1589831  1589837
1589849  1589851  1589881  1589893  1589899  1589911  1589923  1589933  1589941  1589969
1589981  1590019  1590037  1590047  1590049  1590073  1590077  1590079  1590101  1590107
1590119  1590131  1590133  1590137  1590161  1590203  1590221  1590229  1590233  1590241
1590247  1590263  1590271  1590293  1590311  1590317  1590343  1590373  1590377  1590383
1590397  1590403  1590437  1590461  1590467  1590481  1590487  1590493  1590521  1590539
1590541  1590551  1590553  1590559  1590643  1590653  1590671  1590683  1590713  1590727
1590731  1590739  1590791  1590793  1590803  1590829  1590857  1590893  1590907  1590913
1590917  1590931  1590937  1590949  1590961  1590991  1591001  1591021  1591033  1591097
1591099  1591103  1591127  1591141  1591159  1591189  1591207  1591211  1591229  1591237
1591241  1591253  1591267  1591273  1591277  1591313  1591339  1591351  1591363  1591367
1591391  1591397  1591417  1591441  1591463  1591483  1591487  1591507  1591511  1591547
1591553  1591567  1591589  1591621  1591631  1591637  1591663  1591697  1591721  1591729
1591753  1591783  1591787  1591813  1591841  1591859  1591871  1591873  1591883  1591901
1591913  1591921  1591927  1591949  1591969  1591973  1591981  1592027  1592047  1592051
1592069  1592081  1592099  1592111  1592113  1592117  1592159  1592167  1592183  1592197
1592207  1592243  1592251  1592263  1592273  1592281  1592321  1592323  1592329  1592341
1592387  1592401  1592411  1592429  1592431  1592471  1592489  1592533  1592557  1592573
1592579  1592581  1592609  1592621  1592623  1592639  1592653  1592659  1592663  1592671
1592683  1592693  1592699  1592729  1592737  1592753  1592761  1592777  1592779  1592797
1592807  1592821  1592831  1592861  1592863  1592867  1592869  1592879  1592881  1592923
1592939  1592947  1592953  1592963  1592993  1593029  1593037  1593043  1593047  1593061
1593071  1593133  1593149  1593167  1593181  1593191  1593197  1593199  1593217  1593227
1593239  1593247  1593269  1593271  1593281  1593299  1593323  1593329  1593341  1593349
1593377  1593379  1593401  1593409  1593421  1593433  1593467  1593481  1593491  1593497
1593499  1593523  1593539  1593541  1593583  1593589  1593593  1593607  1593619  1593643
1593653  1593659  1593703  1593743  1593749  1593773  1593797  1593799  1593821  1593827
1593833  1593841  1593847  1593857  1593859  1593887  1593899  1593931  1593947  1594027
1594031  1594037  1594049  1594057  1594063  1594093  1594097  1594111  1594123  1594127
1594129  1594133  1594141  1594169  1594183  1594207  1594211  1594223  1594249  1594253
1594259  1594261  1594267  1594273  1594279  1594283  1594289  1594297  1594301  1594331
1594339  1594387  1594403  1594421  1594433  1594451  1594459  1594471  1594477  1594517
1594529  1594553  1594559  1594597  1594631  1594633  1594639  1594643  1594657
1594661  1594669  1594693  1594709  1594721  1594729  1594763  1594771  1594783  1594793
1594807  1594819  1594837  1594849  1594861  1594867  1594871  1594883  1594897  1594903
1594909  1594921  1594927  1594933  1594937  1594951  1594961  1594987  1595003  1595047
1595051  1595053  1595057  1595063  1595071  1595081  1595101  1595117  1595149  1595173
1595189  1595197  1595201  1595213  1595219  1595239  1595267  1595273  1595287  1595309
1595311  1595317  1595323  1595327  1595339  1595357  1595369  1595381  1595389  1595393
```

```
1595401  1595417  1595431  1595437  1595453  1595483  1595507  1595513  1595527  1595557
1595567  1595593  1595611  1595623  1595647  1595653  1595669  1595701  1595719  1595723
1595729  1595731  1595743  1595749  1595767  1595771  1595801  1595813  1595819  1595827
1595831  1595833  1595857  1595861  1595863  1595887  1595903  1595927  1595929  1595953
1595983  1596013  1596029  1596043  1596047  1596059  1596061  1596071  1596107  1596121
1596139  1596163  1596169  1596211  1596229  1596233  1596251  1596277  1596299  1596311
1596313  1596319  1596341  1596347  1596349  1596367  1596373  1596377  1596379  1596383
1596389  1596433  1596451  1596467  1596493  1596503  1596509  1596527  1596541  1596563
1596629  1596631  1596641  1596649  1596659  1596667  1596689  1596701  1596713  1596737
1596739  1596743  1596767  1596781  1596787  1596839  1596851  1596863  1596869  1596871
1596941  1596961  1596989  1597033  1597039  1597067  1597069  1597081  1597091  1597103
1597109  1597111  1597129  1597139  1597147  1597153  1597157  1597171  1597181  1597187
1597229  1597243  1597259  1597289  1597331  1597357  1597361  1597369  1597381  1597391
1597397  1597411  1597417  1597423  1597433  1597441  1597447  1597451  1597457  1597469
1597489  1597499  1597513  1597553  1597567  1597597  1597601  1597619  1597621  1597657
1597663  1597679  1597693  1597699  1597703  1597721  1597723  1597747  1597753  1597759
1597763  1597777  1597781  1597793  1597801  1597819  1597823  1597829  1597861  1597873
1597877  1597913  1597927  1597931  1597943  1597951  1597961  1597969  1597991  1598011
1598021  1598039  1598053  1598089  1598099  1598111  1598131  1598137  1598167  1598171
1598183  1598197  1598209  1598213  1598227  1598237  1598239  1598257  1598263  1598273
1598279  1598309  1598327  1598341  1598371  1598381  1598447  1598449  1598501  1598503
1598507  1598521  1598539  1598543  1598551  1598557  1598563  1598573  1598581  1598587
1598617  1598633  1598651  1598669  1598677  1598689  1598699  1598711  1598743  1598767
1598789  1598791  1598801  1598813  1598819  1598827  1598843  1598873  1598897  1598899
1598911  1598923  1598941  1598951  1598953  1598963  1598999  1599023  1599047  1599053
1599067  1599083  1599109  1599119  1599131  1599137  1599151  1599181  1599203  1599229
1599253  1599271  1599293  1599307  1599319  1599331  1599347  1599361  1599373  1599407
1599413  1599421  1599427  1599449  1599461  1599463  1599469  1599509  1599511  1599523
1599529  1599539  1599571  1599581  1599583  1599601  1599607  1599613  1599617  1599691
1599707  1599709  1599803  1599809  1599823  1599827  1599839  1599841  1599863  1599869
1599877  1599883  1599889  1599919  1599931  1599937  1599977  1600033  1600037  1600051
1600061  1600069  1600097  1600099  1600121  1600141  1600153  1600177  1600187  1600201
1600211  1600217  1600219  1600223  1600241  1600243  1600253  1600259  1600267  1600273
1600279  1600283  1600321  1600337  1600343  1600349  1600367  1600373  1600387  1600393
1600421  1600433  1600451  1600483  1600519  1600531  1600537  1600603  1600607  1600631
1600633  1600637  1600649  1600663  1600691  1600699  1600721  1600727  1600733  1600741
1600787  1600793  1600811  1600813  1600861  1600877  1600889  1600891  1600897
1600901  1600909  1600913  1600919  1600957  1600967  1600969  1600981  1600993  1601023
1601051  1601059  1601071  1601107  1601111  1601123  1601137  1601147  1601161  1601203
1601207  1601209  1601219  1601227  1601231  1601239  1601261  1601267  1601269  1601273
1601287  1601309  1601317  1601359  1601371  1601381  1601389  1601399  1601423  1601441
1601443  1601447  1601459  1601473  1601477  1601489  1601503  1601507  1601521  1601527
1601533  1601543  1601563  1601569  1601573  1601591  1601599  1601609  1601617  1601623
1601627  1601629  1601647  1601663  1601669  1601671  1601687  1601711  1601729  1601731
1601741  1601749  1601773  1601777  1601779  1601783  1601797  1601813  1601843  1601849
1601857  1601861  1601867  1601869  1601953  1601969  1602011  1602059  1602067  1602071
1602077  1602079  1602091  1602101  1602103  1602113  1602119  1602121  1602143  1602151
1602169  1602187  1602193  1602241  1602269  1602281  1602283  1602311  1602317  1602323
1602347  1602353  1602361  1602379  1602383  1602389  1602397  1602401  1602407  1602427
1602451  1602463  1602473  1602487  1602493  1602509  1602527  1602529  1602551  1602553
1602589  1602599  1602611  1602637  1602661  1602677  1602691  1602697  1602703  1602719
1602721  1602737  1602749  1602751  1602761  1602817  1602823  1602827  1602829  1602833
1602851  1602857  1602863  1602869  1602883  1602899  1602901  1602907  1602919  1602929
1602941  1602943  1602949  1602959  1602961  1603009  1603013  1603027  1603039  1603051
1603057  1603067  1603073  1603079  1603081  1603093  1603111  1603139  1603159  1603183
1603193  1603237  1603241  1603249  1603267  1603279  1603291  1603297  1603319  1603331
1603333  1603337  1603339  1603361  1603363  1603397  1603403  1603411  1603417  1603421
1603453  1603471  1603489  1603493  1603501  1603517  1603519  1603529  1603531  1603541
1603573  1603597  1603601  1603631  1603649  1603663  1603669  1603673  1603681  1603697
1603699  1603709  1603711  1603747  1603769  1603793  1603799  1603801  1603807  1603817
1603837  1603843  1603853  1603867  1603891  1603897  1603907  1603909  1603919  1603949
1603957  1603963  1604003  1604017  1604021  1604051  1604059  1604081  1604087  1604093
1604101  1604111  1604123  1604129  1604131  1604143  1604147  1604149  1604167  1604177
1604179  1604191  1604231  1604237  1604243  1604263  1604279  1604293  1604297  1604299
1604311  1604329  1604333  1604347  1604359  1604381  1604399  1604413  1604419  1604437
1604441  1604461  1604479  1604497  1604501  1604509  1604513  1604521  1604539  1604543
1604557  1604567  1604573  1604593  1604597  1604609  1604611  1604621  1604651  1604711
1604719  1604731  1604737  1604747  1604753  1604809  1604821  1604833  1604857  1604923
1604929  1604951  1604957  1604983  1605001  1605013  1605017  1605029  1605031  1605041
1605047  1605053  1605083  1605103  1605127  1605151  1605169  1605173  1605187  1605199
1605209  1605217  1605257  1605269  1605277  1605287  1605299  1605313  1605323  1605341
1605349  1605389  1605413  1605419  1605421  1605427  1605431  1605433  1605509  1605511
1605533  1605547  1605551  1605553  1605559  1605563  1605587  1605619  1605629  1605631
1605677  1605691  1605697  1605719  1605739  1605743  1605757  1605761  1605767  1605811
1605829  1605839  1605853  1605859  1605869  1605881  1605887  1605889  1605907  1605913
1605931  1605941  1605971  1605979  1606009  1606081  1606097  1606117  1606123  1606139
1606151  1606153  1606201  1606237  1606247  1606249  1606259  1606261  1606273  1606277
1606289  1606291  1606309  1606321  1606331  1606349  1606379  1606387  1606399  1606403
1606427  1606433  1606439  1606457  1606463  1606487  1606499  1606529  1606537  1606541
1606543  1606547  1606559  1606567  1606603  1606639  1606643  1606663  1606669  1606681
1606723  1606733  1606739  1606741  1606751  1606753  1606763  1606771  1606777  1606783
1606793  1606817  1606837  1606841  1606853  1606859  1606879  1606889  1606897  1606901
1606909  1606921  1606951  1606967  1606981  1606991  1607003  1607029  1607051  1607057
1607063  1607069  1607083  1607087  1607107  1607113  1607131  1607141  1607143  1607149
1607173  1607183  1607201  1607233  1607237  1607261  1607273  1607293  1607321  1607327
1607357  1607371  1607377  1607399  1607407  1607449  1607471  1607477  1607479  1607491
1607509  1607513  1607519  1607527  1607563  1607579  1607591  1607597  1607603  1607611
1607621  1607659  1607663  1607681  1607699  1607701  1607713  1607747  1607773  1607791
1607807  1607821  1607831  1607833  1607839  1607849  1607857  1607863  1607867  1607873
```

```
1607923  1607929  1607941  1607981  1607987  1608007  1608017  1608023  1608037  1608041
1608083  1608107  1608109  1608127  1608133  1608197  1608209  1608227  1608239  1608241
1608259  1608283  1608323  1608337  1608349  1608359  1608371  1608379  1608401  1608433
1608437  1608443  1608449  1608461  1608463  1608473  1608479  1608487  1608493  1608511
1608527  1608569  1608571  1608577  1608583  1608599  1608611  1608617  1608637  1608653
1608661  1608667  1608671  1608697  1608703  1608707  1608713  1608743  1608751  1608769
1608773  1608821  1608823  1608863  1608883  1608911  1608913  1608941  1608979  1609009
1609021  1609037  1609043  1609061  1609063  1609079  1609087  1609099  1609109  1609141
1609147  1609163  1609177  1609193  1609199  1609211  1609219  1609247  1609249  1609261
1609301  1609367  1609381  1609403  1609417  1609423  1609457  1609477  1609493  1609501
1609507  1609511  1609519  1609523  1609549  1609561  1609567  1609571  1609583  1609589
1609627  1609631  1609667  1609669  1609693  1609693  1609717  1609739  1609757  1609763
1609771  1609789  1609801  1609807  1609843  1609871  1609873  1609879  1609897  1609901
1609903  1609913  1609969  1609991  1609997  1609999  1610009  1610017  1610027  1610057
1610083  1610093  1610101  1610107  1610123  1610131  1610149  1610153  1610177  1610179
1610183  1610227  1610237  1610239  1610251  1610293  1610309  1610311  1610333  1610347
1610353  1610369  1610377  1610387  1610417  1610423  1610429  1610431  1610443  1610467
1610471  1610473  1610501  1610513  1610519  1610527  1610533  1610537  1610551  1610561
1610569  1610579  1610591  1610627  1610639  1610657  1610659  1610681  1610701  1610753
1610761  1610771  1610773  1610779  1610783  1610789  1610797  1610809  1610813  1610837
1610867  1610887  1610893  1610899  1610923  1610927  1610933  1610941  1610957  1610963
1610969  1610981  1610993  1611031  1611053  1611059  1611079  1611089  1611097  1611131
1611139  1611151  1611157  1611161  1611187  1611199  1611217  1611223  1611227  1611241
1611251  1611289  1611293  1611299  1611307  1611319  1611331  1611343  1611353  1611361
1611367  1611391  1611397  1611419  1611433  1611439  1611451  1611469  1611479  1611499
1611517  1611529  1611553  1611563  1611593  1611601  1611607  1611613  1611667  1611677
1611689  1611691  1611697  1611707  1611737  1611749  1611761  1611763  1611773  1611781
1611809  1611851  1611853  1611877  1611881  1611899  1611901  1611917  1611947  1611949
1611971  1612007  1612019  1612033  1612063  1612069  1612073  1612111  1612123  1612133
1612141  1612157  1612181  1612183  1612189  1612211  1612213  1612223  1612249  1612267
1612271  1612307  1612309  1612319  1612327  1612333  1612361  1612363  1612393  1612427
1612439  1612451  1612463  1612477  1612493  1612517  1612537  1612561  1612601  1612609
1612619  1612621  1612649  1612669  1612679  1612693  1612697  1612703  1612727  1612733
1612747  1612759  1612763  1612771  1612781  1612823  1612859  1612903  1612913  1612927
1612931  1612937  1612957  1612991  1612997  1612999  1613033  1613041  1613057  1613069
1613093  1613099  1613123  1613141  1613149  1613153  1613173  1613179  1613201  1613279
1613321  1613323  1613329  1613363  1613371  1613393  1613399  1613407  1613411  1613413
1613441  1613471  1613483  1613497  1613503  1613509  1613539  1613543  1613587  1613593
1613597  1613609  1613621  1613639  1613641  1613653  1613669  1613671  1613683  1613707
1613713  1613741  1613761  1613771  1613809  1613813  1613831  1613867  1613873  1613921
1613947  1613951  1613959  1613981  1613987  1614001  1614007  1614017  1614023  1614037
1614073  1614083  1614149  1614157  1614187  1614191  1614229  1614233  1614241  1614247
1614251  1614257  1614281  1614289  1614307  1614311  1614317  1614329  1614331  1614359
1614367  1614377  1614383  1614391  1614397  1614409  1614413  1614443  1614461  1614463
1614467  1614479  1614491  1614493  1614533  1614553  1614559  1614583  1614589  1614593
1614619  1614629  1614631  1614637  1614647  1614649  1614659  1614661  1614671  1614707
1614719  1614721  1614733  1614757  1614787  1614793  1614803  1614817  1614859  1614863
1614871  1614911  1614913  1614917  1614929  1614947  1614961  1614973  1614989  1615001
1615021  1615027  1615043  1615049  1615067  1615073  1615079  1615121  1615139  1615151
1615157  1615177  1615181  1615183  1615199  1615223  1615231  1615253  1615279  1615307
1615331  1615333  1615337  1615351  1615363  1615403  1615421  1615433  1615447  1615477
1615483  1615487  1615499  1615501  1615511  1615529  1615541  1615591  1615613  1615631
1615633  1615637  1615643  1615651  1615657  1615661  1615673  1615699  1615709  1615717
1615723  1615739  1615763  1615777  1615781  1615837  1615841  1615843  1615847  1615849
1615853  1615871  1615891  1615919  1615921  1615949  1615963  1615981  1615987  1616009
1616029  1616033  1616039  1616047  1616057  1616063  1616077  1616099  1616113  1616119
1616161  1616171  1616183  1616201  1616221  1616227  1616231  1616269  1616281  1616291
1616297  1616347  1616359  1616401  1616429  1616437  1616443  1616453  1616473  1616491
1616497  1616519  1616533  1616543  1616551  1616569  1616597  1616603  1616609  1616611
1616617  1616621  1616623  1616627  1616633  1616639  1616651  1616669  1616677  1616687
1616689  1616711  1616723  1616749  1616801  1616803  1616807  1616809  1616821  1616827
1616833  1616851  1616861  1616891  1616897  1616899  1616939  1616947  1616963  1616983
1617019  1617029  1617037  1617043  1617047  1617079  1617103  1617137  1617139  1617149
1617211  1617247  1617251  1617269  1617277  1617283  1617289  1617311  1617347  1617349
1617373  1617391  1617433  1617437  1617439  1617443  1617463  1617493  1617503  1617509
1617523  1617541  1617547  1617557  1617563  1617569  1617589  1617619  1617647  1617661
1617689  1617691  1617697  1617727  1617739  1617743  1617757  1617767  1617769  1617773
1617779  1617809  1617817  1617827  1617871  1617883  1617893  1617923  1617929  1617943
1617949  1617971  1617977  1617989  1618003  1618007  1618033  1618039  1618049  1618051
1618079  1618081  1618087  1618091  1618093  1618129  1618139  1618153  1618181  1618187
1618189  1618207  1618217  1618223  1618241  1618261  1618271  1618277  1618291  1618307
1618319  1618327  1618333  1618367  1618369  1618373  1618387  1618399  1618411  1618433
1618453  1618457  1618459  1618471  1618481  1618489  1618501  1618517  1618531  1618537
1618549  1618559  1618601  1618613  1618619  1618627  1618637  1618663  1618679  1618681
1618703  1618739  1618741  1618769  1618777  1618807  1618817  1618823  1618829  1618831
1618849  1618853  1618891  1618909  1618931  1618937  1618943  1618957  1618963  1618973
1618979  1619021  1619053  1619069  1619071  1619087  1619113  1619119  1619153  1619159
1619171  1619179  1619207  1619209  1619227  1619239  1619243  1619249  1619257  1619281
1619287  1619311  1619327  1619329  1619339  1619341  1619353  1619381  1619383  1619417
1619419  1619473  1619507  1619531  1619549  1619551  1619557  1619561  1619593  1619599
1619603  1619633  1619647  1619663  1619669  1619671  1619677  1619687  1619689  1619699
1619713  1619741  1619747  1619753  1619759  1619773  1619791  1619831  1619837  1619857
1619861  1619887  1619899  1619903  1619909  1619929  1619941  1619957  1619983  1619987
1620001  1620013  1620019  1620041  1620071  1620103  1620107  1620121  1620133  1620161
1620209  1620217  1620233  1620239  1620247  1620251  1620257  1620271  1620319  1620329
1620331  1620337  1620347  1620371  1620379  1620391  1620403  1620413  1620431  1620439
1620449  1620461  1620467  1620469  1620497  1620517  1620523  1620539  1620547  1620551
1620569  1620571  1620589  1620611  1620613  1620617  1620629  1620631  1620667  1620677
1620679  1620733  1620739  1620743  1620769  1620803  1620811  1620823  1620841  1620881
```

```
1620887  1620893  1620917  1620923  1620929  1620961  1620973  1620977  1620989  1621019
1621031  1621033  1621043  1621049  1621079  1621093  1621097  1621127  1621133  1621141
1621153  1621163  1621177  1621219  1621231  1621237  1621241  1621259  1621283  1621309
1621349  1621351  1621357  1621363  1621369  1621381  1621391  1621397  1621421  1621423
1621439  1621457  1621469  1621471  1621481  1621489  1621519  1621537  1621541  1621559
1621583  1621597  1621619  1621621  1621637  1621639  1621643  1621657  1621667  1621679
1621699  1621717  1621721  1621723  1621727  1621729  1621751  1621769  1621771  1621777
1621819  1621843  1621849  1621861  1621871  1621877  1621909  1621931  1621933  1621979
1621993  1622009  1622039  1622041  1622053  1622059  1622063  1622077  1622081  1622141
1622143  1622149  1622189  1622207  1622209  1622233  1622263  1622273  1622287  1622297
1622311  1622333  1622359  1622377  1622407  1622419  1622431  1622437  1622449  1622471
1622473  1622479  1622483  1622549  1622557  1622573  1622587  1622591  1622597  1622609
1622617  1622639  1622641  1622659  1622669  1622671  1622681  1622693  1622707  1622711
1622729  1622743  1622749  1622773  1622779  1622791  1622813  1622827  1622833  1622839
1622849  1622861  1622867  1622879  1622917  1622947  1622953  1622977  1622981  1622987
1623023  1623029  1623047  1623053  1623059  1623071  1623077  1623091  1623107  1623137
1623157  1623161  1623163  1623169  1623173  1623197  1623203  1623229  1623233  1623263
1623269  1623283  1623287  1623289  1623299  1623319  1623361  1623367  1623403  1623421
1623431  1623437  1623451  1623463  1623467  1623473  1623487  1623533  1623539  1623553
1623599  1623631  1623647  1623667  1623679  1623701  1623707  1623733  1623763  1623767
1623781  1623793  1623799  1623827  1623829  1623833  1623847  1623859  1623863  1623883
1623901  1623907  1623917  1623929  1623931  1623943  1623977  1623989  1624001  1624019
1624037  1624057  1624069  1624081  1624111  1624141  1624151  1624159  1624169  1624171
1624193  1624199  1624201  1624213  1624223  1624241  1624277  1624297  1624309  1624321
1624327  1624331  1624349  1624351  1624361  1624373  1624387  1624417  1624423  1624429
1624453  1624471  1624487  1624501  1624507  1624523  1624529  1624573  1624589  1624591
1624603  1624607  1624627  1624661  1624663  1624681  1624687  1624691  1624699  1624717
1624729  1624757  1624807  1624811  1624813  1624829  1624849  1624913  1624933  1624943
1624963  1624967  1624969  1624991  1624993  1625017  1625021  1625027  1625059  1625123
1625147  1625153  1625167  1625171  1625177  1625179  1625201  1625207  1625223  1625227
1625257  1625263  1625287  1625297  1625303  1625311  1625321  1625329  1625339  1625347
1625359  1625383  1625417  1625419  1625453  1625461  1625471  1625483  1625497  1625501
1625513  1625539  1625543  1625551  1625573  1625581  1625587  1625629  1625647  1625677
1625699  1625707  1625717  1625719  1625747  1625749  1625759  1625791  1625803  1625807
1625809  1625821  1625831  1625837  1625839  1625843  1625851  1625861  1625867  1625879
1625903  1625909  1625927  1625933  1625951  1625969  1625977  1625989  1625993  1626013
1626017  1626047  1626071  1626073  1626083  1626089  1626091  1626109  1626127  1626133
1626137  1626143  1626173  1626181  1626193  1626197  1626211  1626227  1626239  1626259
1626263  1626269  1626277  1626281  1626283  1626301  1626311  1626319  1626329  1626337
1626371  1626377  1626379  1626431  1626433  1626437  1626451  1626461  1626467  1626479
1626481  1626487  1626503  1626533  1626589  1626613  1626617  1626619  1626637  1626649
1626673  1626701  1626707  1626739  1626749  1626763  1626769  1626773  1626791  1626803
1626817  1626829  1626881  1626887  1626893  1626901  1626923  1626943  1626949  1626953
1626959  1626971  1626989  1626993  1627007  1627013  1627033  1627051  1627057  1627061
1627063  1627069  1627079  1627099  1627111  1627117  1627123  1627127  1627133  1627147
1627169  1627177  1627193  1627201  1627237  1627247  1627253  1627267  1627309  1627333
1627337  1627357  1627361  1627403  1627429  1627441  1627459  1627481  1627487  1627489
1627501  1627513  1627523  1627537  1627553  1627573  1627579  1627583  1627601  1627603
1627607  1627609  1627627  1627643  1627649  1627651  1627669  1627693  1627723  1627727
1627729  1627739  1627763  1627771  1627781  1627783  1627793  1627807  1627819  1627831
1627837  1627849  1627853  1627859  1627861  1627867  1627877  1627883  1627919  1627943
1627979  1627981  1628051  1628057  1628059  1628063  1628071  1628093  1628117  1628131
1628149  1628153  1628161  1628171  1628173  1628177  1628183  1628191  1628197  1628203
1628227  1628261  1628279  1628293  1628299  1628309  1628317  1628323  1628329  1628353
1628359  1628369  1628381  1628383  1628387  1628401  1628441  1628467  1628477  1628489
1628491  1628507  1628551  1628567  1628579  1628587  1628591  1628593  1628603  1628621
1628633  1628689  1628701  1628729  1628747  1628773  1628779  1628801  1628839  1628857
1628867  1628873  1628887  1628909  1628917  1628933  1628947  1628983  1628987
1628989  1629007  1629011  1629013  1629031  1629071  1629077  1629083  1629091  1629101
1629107  1629109  1629119  1629137  1629149  1629163  1629169  1629197  1629203  1629209
1629211  1629233  1629253  1629259  1629281  1629293  1629317  1629319  1629337  1629359
1629361  1629367  1629377  1629409  1629427  1629431  1629449  1629451  1629457  1629469
1629479  1629541  1629547  1629557  1629559  1629581  1629583  1629587  1629599  1629601
1629623  1629643  1629647  1629663  1629673  1629689  1629721  1629731  1629767  1629809
1629851  1629853  1629869  1629893  1629899  1629919  1629923  1629937  1629977  1629997
1630019  1630021  1630049  1630051  1630091  1630093  1630117  1630127  1630129  1630133
1630141  1630159  1630169  1630193  1630199  1630243  1630247  1630253  1630261  1630273
1630303  1630357  1630361  1630367  1630379  1630381  1630393  1630399  1630403  1630411
1630423  1630427  1630429  1630441  1630451  1630457  1630459  1630463  1630471  1630483
1630501  1630543  1630547  1630549  1630597  1630621  1630633  1630663  1630669
1630721  1630751  1630771  1630777  1630781  1630801  1630813  1630829  1630841  1630843
1630859  1630891  1630897  1630913  1630919  1630927  1630933  1630943  1630987  1631023
1631027  1631029  1631051  1631053  1631057  1631059  1631101  1631117  1631143  1631153
1631159  1631171  1631177  1631191  1631209  1631243  1631257  1631261  1631263  1631297
1631299  1631309  1631341  1631351  1631363  1631369  1631407  1631447  1631471  1631489
1631491  1631503  1631519  1631521  1631537  1631543  1631557  1631573  1631579  1631611
1631629  1631633  1631639  1631647  1631657  1631659  1631683  1631723  1631731  1631741
1631761  1631771  1631783  1631797  1631821  1631837  1631843  1631869  1631879  1631897
1631899  1631911  1631921  1631939  1631951  1631957  1631969  1631989  1632013  1632019
1632041  1632047  1632079  1632101  1632109  1632121  1632133  1632139  1632143
1632167  1632173  1632179  1632193  1632199  1632209  1632227  1632259  1632307  1632311
1632313  1632317  1632341  1632359  1632383  1632427  1632431  1632437  1632457  1632467
1632469  1632473  1632479  1632481  1632487  1632509  1632523  1632557  1632569  1632571
1632599  1632611  1632619  1632623  1632637  1632647  1632649  1632679  1632691  1632703
1632749  1632751  1632767  1632769  1632779  1632781  1632797  1632809  1632817  1632821
1632853  1632871  1632881  1632887  1632893  1632899  1632913  1632919  1632941  1632949
1632979  1632997  1633007  1633033  1633039  1633043  1633057  1633067  1633081  1633103
1633117  1633123  1633127  1633129  1633133  1633157  1633169  1633171  1633187  1633201
1633211  1633223  1633231  1633237  1633243  1633249  1633267  1633277  1633319  1633321
```

```
1633337  1633339  1633361  1633363  1633369  1633403  1633409  1633447  1633459  1633531
1633549  1633553  1633559  1633561  1633573  1633589  1633603  1633609  1633627  1633633
1633679  1633691  1633693  1633703  1633711  1633729  1633741  1633747  1633757  1633777
1633787  1633789  1633811  1633817  1633823  1633837  1633843  1633847  1633873  1633903
1633913  1633939  1633949  1633967  1633987  1633991  1633993  1634011  1634027  1634047
1634051  1634053  1634069  1634071  1634089  1634099  1634107  1634117  1634141  1634153
1634167  1634177  1634183  1634201  1634203  1634231  1634233  1634239  1634257  1634267
1634279  1634291  1634293  1634309  1634317  1634333  1634341  1634371  1634393  1634407
1634417  1634441  1634443  1634447  1634453  1634461  1634471  1634489  1634497  1634531
1634557  1634569  1634579  1634593  1634597  1634603  1634609  1634657  1634681  1634683
1634687  1634693  1634719  1634753  1634761  1634767  1634791  1634797  1634803  1634819
1634833  1634837  1634849  1634869  1634879  1634881  1634911  1634923  1634929  1634939
1634947  1634951  1634953  1634959  1634987  1635013  1635031  1635037  1635041  1635061
1635079  1635091  1635119  1635133  1635143  1635163  1635169  1635173  1635181  1635187
1635199  1635217  1635229  1635241  1635287  1635299  1635307  1635313  1635317  1635329
1635341  1635353  1635371  1635373  1635377  1635401  1635479  1635497  1635499  1635503
1635509  1635541  1635547  1635551  1635559  1635563  1635583  1635607  1635611  1635619
1635631  1635637  1635649  1635661  1635703  1635713  1635721  1635727  1635761  1635773
1635811  1635817  1635827  1635863  1635889  1635899  1635913  1635937  1635943  1635947
1635971  1635973  1635983  1636001  1636007  1636009  1636039  1636043  1636049  1636067
1636069  1636079  1636091  1636111  1636121  1636139  1636157  1636181  1636189  1636213
1636231  1636237  1636249  1636277  1636291  1636303  1636331  1636333  1636339  1636343
1636363  1636367  1636373  1636379  1636391  1636423  1636457  1636463  1636469  1636501
1636513  1636529  1636541  1636543  1636549  1636553  1636561  1636571  1636577  1636609
1636627  1636637  1636651  1636667  1636669  1636697  1636699  1636711  1636721  1636729
1636741  1636751  1636757  1636759  1636781  1636787  1636819  1636823  1636849  1636867
1636871  1636883  1636891  1636909  1636919  1636927  1636931  1636937  1636951  1636961
1636969  1636997  1637029  1637087  1637093  1637147  1637161  1637177  1637183  1637197
1637221  1637239  1637243  1637261  1637299  1637357  1637371  1637381  1637407  1637429
1637437  1637459  1637479  1637497  1637501  1637521  1637539  1637549  1637551  1637563
1637599  1637611  1637617  1637633  1637639  1637641  1637677  1637683  1637687  1637693
1637707  1637711  1637719  1637723  1637737  1637759  1637773  1637777  1637813  1637851
1637863  1637887  1637927  1637963  1637983  1638011  1638019  1638023  1638031  1638053
1638059  1638061  1638067  1638089  1638097  1638107  1638121  1638127  1638139  1638149
1638167  1638191  1638209  1638211  1638251  1638269  1638311  1638331  1638347  1638349
1638353  1638431  1638463  1638473  1638487  1638547  1638551  1638563  1638569  1638583
1638599  1638641  1638649  1638653  1638673  1638677  1638683  1638701  1638719  1638733
1638743  1638797  1638799  1638809  1638821  1638869  1638899  1638907  1638913  1638929
1638943  1638947  1638977  1638983  1638991  1639019  1639061  1639067  1639081  1639087
1639091  1639097  1639147  1639151  1639153  1639159  1639193  1639199  1639201  1639217
1639223  1639229  1639241  1639243  1639271  1639307  1639349  1639357  1639367  1639381
1639387  1639409  1639427  1639459  1639471  1639481  1639493  1639511  1639513  1639577
1639579  1639597  1639607  1639609  1639613  1639663  1639699  1639711  1639717  1639723
1639733  1639751  1639763  1639789  1639793  1639811  1639817  1639823  1639829  1639849
1639853  1639861  1639879  1639889  1639901  1639907  1639919  1639927  1639949  1639987
1639991  1639999  1640017  1640021  1640033  1640053  1640057  1640059  1640071  1640077
1640083  1640131  1640147  1640167  1640183  1640189  1640201  1640207  1640231  1640263
1640267  1640273  1640281  1640299  1640311  1640323  1640333  1640393  1640399  1640423
1640447  1640461  1640467  1640497  1640503  1640519  1640531  1640539  1640549  1640557
1640599  1640609  1640621  1640623  1640633  1640641  1640657  1640663  1640677  1640689
1640701  1640729  1640741  1640753  1640761  1640773  1640803  1640809  1640819  1640843
1640851  1640869  1640879  1640887  1640927  1640929  1640939  1640941  1640953  1640971
1641007  1641043  1641053  1641077  1641089  1641091  1641103  1641131  1641137  1641161
1641217  1641229  1641253  1641281  1641301  1641323  1641329  1641359  1641361  1641373
1641377  1641379  1641389  1641403  1641407  1641457  1641473  1641509  1641539  1641559
1641583  1641587  1641589  1641593  1641613  1641617  1641623  1641631  1641637  1641641
1641659  1641709  1641713  1641721  1641737  1641751  1641797  1641799  1641811  1641817
1641821  1641833  1641841  1641863  1641881  1641889  1641907  1641917  1641929  1641931
1641953  1641971  1642021  1642031  1642033  1642049  1642051  1642057  1642079  1642093
1642117  1642141  1642153  1642187  1642211  1642231  1642243  1642247  1642259  1642273
1642279  1642283  1642297  1642309  1642313  1642327  1642339  1642363  1642373  1642397
1642423  1642441  1642447  1642451  1642463  1642481  1642483  1642513  1642517  1642519
1642549  1642559  1642567  1642579  1642601  1642631  1642633  1642649  1642657  1642661
1642679  1642699  1642709  1642717  1642723  1642741  1642769  1642777  1642787  1642801
1642807  1642811  1642813  1642831  1642847  1642853  1642859  1642903  1642909
1642919  1642939  1642943  1642951  1642997  1643003  1643021  1643027  1643039  1643069
1643077  1643099  1643123  1643129  1643137  1643141  1643171  1643179  1643197  1643219
1643221  1643231  1643233  1643251  1643269  1643273  1643293  1643311  1643347  1643351
1643357  1643363  1643387  1643423  1643431  1643461  1643491  1643497  1643501  1643513
1643539  1643581  1643591  1643597  1643599  1643617  1643623  1643639  1643641  1643659
1643669  1643683  1643687  1643693  1643701  1643717  1643729  1643743  1643773  1643779
1643791  1643797  1643801  1643809  1643819  1643821  1643827  1643839  1643843  1643857
1643867  1643869  1643881  1643891  1643959  1643963  1643979  1643987  1643989
1644001  1644031  1644061  1644067  1644073  1644079  1644103  1644143  1644163  1644173
1644193  1644197  1644199  1644217  1644221  1644229  1644233  1644283  1644287  1644299
1644311  1644341  1644347  1644361  1644367  1644371  1644373  1644413  1644421  1644437
1644439  1644451  1644491  1644493  1644497  1644547  1644571  1644593  1644607  1644611
1644623  1644637  1644641  1644653  1644667  1644673  1644689  1644691  1644703  1644719
1644751  1644757  1644781  1644791  1644817  1644823  1644871  1644883  1644893  1644899
1644901  1644931  1644943  1644949  1644989  1644991  1644997  1645003  1645009
1645019  1645087  1645093  1645099  1645123  1645129  1645151  1645157  1645169  1645183
1645187  1645211  1645249  1645253  1645291  1645327  1645337  1645349  1645363  1645367
1645409  1645417  1645421  1645429  1645433  1645439  1645459  1645477  1645481  1645487
1645499  1645529  1645537  1645543  1645559  1645561  1645601  1645603  1645607  1645613
1645643  1645661  1645667  1645669  1645681  1645721  1645727  1645729  1645733  1645747
1645757  1645769  1645771  1645801  1645829  1645843  1645849  1645867  1645873  1645879
1645901  1645907  1645909  1645927  1645933  1645937  1645939  1645961  1645967  1645979
1645999  1646017  1646023  1646033  1646101  1646107  1646111  1646143  1646147  1646149
1646153  1646171  1646173  1646189  1646209  1646219  1646221  1646237  1646261  1646287
```

```
1646291 1646299 1646303 1646311 1646321 1646347 1646357 1646371 1646377 1646383
1646387 1646413 1646423 1646443 1646461 1646473 1646479 1646497 1646509 1646527
1646543 1646563 1646581 1646609 1646629 1646633 1646641 1646647 1646669 1646677
1646689 1646717 1646719 1646737 1646741 1646747 1646783 1646797 1646819 1646839
1646849 1646861 1646893 1646899 1646903 1646921 1646923 1646933 1646947 1646951
1646959 1646971 1646989 1647001 1647013 1647031 1647047 1647059 1647067 1647083
1647097 1647101 1647119 1647127 1647137 1647161 1647179 1647193 1647227 1647241
1647251 1647253 1647299 1647307 1647311 1647323 1647353 1647361 1647377 1647379
1647383 1647389 1647407 1647439 1647469 1647473 1647497 1647523 1647551 1647553
1647563 1647599 1647601 1647617 1647649 1647673 1647677 1647689 1647707 1647719
1647727 1647761 1647769 1647781 1647797 1647847 1647853 1647857 1647859 1647871
1647887 1647911 1647917 1647931 1647937 1647941 1647949 1647953 1647959 1647977
1648001 1648021 1648039 1648057 1648063 1648067 1648069 1648081 1648181 1648187
1648217 1648223 1648237 1648253 1648259 1648261 1648277 1648289 1648291 1648349
1648379 1648391 1648417 1648429 1648441 1648453 1648481 1648483 1648499 1648513
1648523 1648529 1648531 1648553 1648567 1648579 1648583 1648589 1648601 1648613
1648687 1648723 1648739 1648753 1648771 1648781 1648789 1648793 1648811 1648817
1648837 1648879 1648909 1648919 1648943 1648951 1648963 1648987 1649003 1649023
1649059 1649099 1649101 1649111 1649129 1649147 1649149 1649161 1649171 1649173
1649213 1649237 1649243 1649251 1649267 1649287 1649299 1649303 1649309 1649311
1649327 1649341 1649359 1649363 1649369 1649377 1649381 1649393 1649411 1649419
1649429 1649443 1649449 1649489 1649507 1649521 1649533 1649539 1649567 1649587
1649591 1649597 1649611 1649621 1649639 1649647 1649651 1649657 1649671 1649677
1649689 1649693 1649707 1649737 1649743 1649759 1649771 1649773 1649783 1649797
1649801 1649803 1649807 1649819 1649831 1649861 1649863 1649887 1649917 1649927
1649959 1649981 1649987 1649993 1650001 1650023 1650031 1650041 1650059 1650079
1650089 1650091 1650097 1650101 1650107 1650109 1650133 1650137 1650157 1650167
1650179 1650191 1650199 1650221 1650263 1650281 1650287 1650293 1650301 1650317
1650349 1650353 1650361 1650371 1650379 1650401 1650413 1650427 1650437 1650463
1650487 1650491 1650521 1650529 1650553 1650557 1650563 1650569 1650577 1650589
1650601 1650611 1650613 1650617 1650623 1650637 1650647 1650659 1650667 1650673
1650703 1650743 1650757 1650763 1650769 1650793 1650823 1650877 1650881 1650889
1650907 1650911 1650923 1650931 1650937 1650949 1650959 1650983 1650991 1651007
1651019 1651033 1651073 1651093 1651151 1651163 1651171 1651183 1651201 1651207
1651211 1651213 1651219 1651229 1651259 1651267 1651283 1651291 1651297 1651313
1651343 1651361 1651369 1651379 1651387 1651409 1651411 1651457 1651471 1651477
1651493 1651511 1651513 1651541 1651547 1651553 1651571 1651589 1651591 1651597
1651609 1651621 1651667 1651681 1651691 1651693 1651723 1651747 1651757 1651781
1651787 1651801 1651829 1651843 1651847 1651861 1651877 1651891 1651921 1651943
1651961 1651981 1652011 1652033 1652039 1652047 1652051 1652081 1652089 1652129
1652137 1652141 1652171 1652237 1652243 1652263 1652267 1652279 1652291 1652317
1652347 1652351 1652353 1652359 1652363 1652369 1652377 1652407 1652419 1652459
1652479 1652489 1652491 1652503 1652509 1652513 1652543 1652569 1652591 1652597
1652611 1652617 1652627 1652671 1652687 1652701 1652719 1652731 1652737 1652741
1652747 1652771 1652773 1652789 1652801 1652821 1652831 1652837 1652839 1652843
1652863 1652869 1652873 1652879 1652881 1652891 1652893 1652899 1652903 1652909
1652921 1652923 1652929 1652933 1652947 1652993 1653007 1653011 1653023 1653031
1653059 1653061 1653083 1653101 1653103 1653107 1653109 1653149 1653167 1653181
1653191 1653193 1653227 1653251 1653259 1653287 1653293 1653313 1653317 1653329
1653331 1653341 1653343 1653347 1653383 1653389 1653409 1653427 1653433 1653439
1653451 1653469 1653473 1653497 1653499 1653503 1653511 1653517 1653521 1653541
1653557 1653583 1653599 1653611 1653623 1653643 1653671 1653679 1653689 1653697
1653721 1653731 1653739 1653749 1653763 1653767 1653791 1653853 1653901 1653917
1653919 1653923 1653929 1653959 1653973 1653989 1653997 1654013 1654019 1654021
1654027 1654031 1654033 1654039 1654043 1654057 1654111 1654123 1654127 1654153
1654157 1654171 1654193 1654199 1654201 1654217 1654223 1654231 1654241 1654267
1654271 1654291 1654313 1654319 1654337 1654343 1654351 1654357 1654361 1654369
1654397 1654403 1654427 1654441 1654519 1654531 1654547 1654561 1654567 1654573
1654579 1654649 1654651 1654663 1654673 1654693 1654703 1654717 1654721 1654727
1654733 1654739 1654787 1654789 1654799 1654817 1654841 1654853 1654859 1654871
1654879 1654889 1654897 1654903 1654921 1654931 1654963 1654979 1654981 1654987
1655021 1655023 1655029 1655039 1655051 1655077 1655089 1655099 1655123 1655131
1655141 1655153 1655167 1655177 1655189 1655197 1655201 1655207 1655209
1655231 1655237 1655249 1655257 1655263 1655279 1655281 1655309 1655317 1655321
1655323 1655327 1655377 1655383 1655393 1655413 1655449 1655461 1655471 1655483
1655497 1655509 1655531 1655551 1655557 1655569 1655573 1655587 1655593 1655597
1655623 1655627 1655653 1655659 1655663 1655671 1655677 1655683 1655707 1655807
1655809 1655821 1655827 1655873 1655893 1655897 1655909 1655921 1655939
1655947 1655959 1655963 1655981 1655999 1656007 1656013 1656019 1656043 1656047
1656049 1656073 1656079 1656101 1656107 1656119 1656121 1656131 1656163 1656167
1656169 1656199 1656203 1656209 1656223 1656227 1656229 1656247 1656251 1656257
1656283 1656301 1656311 1656313 1656323 1656367 1656383 1656427 1656491 1656517
1656521 1656533 1656541 1656559 1656563 1656583 1656587 1656593 1656607 1656617
1656631 1656647 1656649 1656659 1656673 1656679 1656689 1656719 1656761 1656773
1656791 1656793 1656827 1656829 1656839 1656841 1656847 1656869 1656877 1656883
1656887 1656899 1656901 1656911 1656917 1656931 1656937 1656947 1656953 1656979
1656997 1657001 1657013 1657021 1657037 1657039 1657049 1657067 1657087 1657093
1657099 1657121 1657129 1657153 1657157 1657169 1657181 1657199 1657207 1657213
1657231 1657247 1657277 1657283 1657303 1657339 1657399 1657421 1657429 1657441
1657457 1657459 1657463 1657519 1657561 1657571 1657573 1657583 1657603 1657609
1657627 1657631 1657639 1657651 1657661 1657673 1657697 1657699 1657729 1657741
1657783 1657793 1657801 1657811 1657861 1657867 1657871 1657889 1657897 1657927
1657937 1657939 1657949 1657963 1657987 1658009 1658023 1658029 1658039 1658051
1658053 1658089 1658101 1658119 1658147 1658161 1658201 1658203 1658213 1658233
1658263 1658273 1658291 1658309 1658311 1658353 1658359 1658383 1658387 1658393
1658411 1658413 1658417 1658429 1658441 1658443 1658471 1658479 1658483 1658497
1658509 1658513 1658533 1658561 1658611 1658617 1658623 1658627 1658669 1658711
1658749 1658753 1658759 1658801 1658807 1658827 1658837 1658849 1658857 1658869
1658873 1658893 1658927 1658941 1658957 1658963 1658971 1658977 1658989 1658999
```

```
1659011  1659029  1659041  1659067  1659083  1659101  1659103  1659107  1659109  1659131
1659169  1659181  1659187  1659211  1659223  1659233  1659239  1659263  1659269  1659277
1659299  1659323  1659347  1659349  1659373  1659401  1659407  1659431  1659443  1659451
1659457  1659491  1659527  1659533  1659547  1659551  1659569  1659571  1659587  1659613
1659629  1659643  1659649  1659653  1659661  1659667  1659673  1659683  1659719  1659731
1659737  1659787  1659797  1659809  1659811  1659817  1659851  1659877  1659881  1659883
1659893  1659913  1659919  1659971  1659997  1660007  1660037  1660039  1660063  1660069
1660073  1660097  1660103  1660111  1660121  1660133  1660177  1660189  1660199  1660207
1660229  1660231  1660247  1660259  1660261  1660283  1660289  1660297  1660357  1660367
1660387  1660409  1660411  1660423  1660433  1660457  1660469  1660471  1660489  1660493
1660499  1660507  1660517  1660553  1660559  1660573  1660601  1660609  1660661  1660663
1660667  1660691  1660697  1660699  1660709  1660721  1660723  1660727  1660739  1660741
1660751  1660783  1660793  1660837  1660843  1660871  1660873  1660889  1660921  1660943
1660957  1660963  1661003  1661021  1661029  1661059  1661063  1661069  1661111  1661117
1661123  1661137  1661141  1661159  1661161  1661173  1661237  1661243  1661249  1661251
1661273  1661281  1661293  1661311  1661327  1661333  1661347  1661353  1661431  1661437
1661441  1661447  1661479  1661489  1661503  1661519  1661549  1661557  1661567  1661587
1661599  1661623  1661629  1661641  1661659  1661663  1661669  1661677  1661713  1661731
1661741  1661789  1661813  1661827  1661831  1661833  1661839  1661851  1661857  1661861
1661887  1661893  1661899  1661917  1661939  1661953  1661969  1661977  1661983  1662007
1662013  1662029  1662041  1662083  1662103  1662119  1662121  1662149  1662161  1662163
1662191  1662211  1662217  1662223  1662229  1662257  1662281  1662293  1662307  1662319
1662341  1662347  1662361  1662377  1662383  1662389  1662403  1662439  1662449  1662457
1662467  1662487  1662491  1662503  1662517  1662527  1662547  1662553  1662559  1662571
1662581  1662589  1662593  1662611  1662629  1662631  1662637  1662641  1662643  1662653
1662667  1662697  1662701  1662707  1662733  1662737  1662751  1662757  1662761  1662779
1662781  1662803  1662833  1662839  1662841  1662851  1662863  1662883  1662893  1662901
1662929  1662943  1662953  1662959  1662961  1662977  1662979  1663009  1663027  1663031
1663073  1663091  1663099  1663117  1663133  1663147  1663157  1663169  1663183  1663217
1663219  1663223  1663267  1663273  1663289  1663301  1663303  1663309  1663327  1663349
1663351  1663373  1663379  1663381  1663391  1663397  1663457  1663463  1663477  1663481
1663513  1663517  1663523  1663537  1663547  1663549  1663579  1663589  1663609  1663619
1663681  1663687  1663693  1663703  1663709  1663721  1663747  1663763  1663771  1663777
1663789  1663793  1663813  1663861  1663867  1663873  1663877  1663891  1663913  1663919
1663951  1663967  1663973  1663997  1664009  1664017  1664021  1664053  1664063  1664071
1664083  1664101  1664123  1664227  1664251  1664261  1664279  1664287  1664291  1664353
1664387  1664407  1664417  1664431  1664437  1664447  1664459  1664461  1664501  1664543
1664549  1664557  1664561  1664563  1664569  1664627  1664633  1664651  1664653  1664681
1664701  1664711  1664713  1664717  1664797  1664801  1664807  1664821  1664833  1664849
1664857  1664863  1664867  1664869  1664893  1664903  1664909  1664941  1664959  1664987
1665007  1665023  1665029  1665043  1665061  1665067  1665071  1665073  1665091  1665107
1665109  1665121  1665137  1665143  1665149  1665161  1665173  1665197  1665211  1665221
1665233  1665247  1665263  1665271  1665277  1665311  1665317  1665343  1665421  1665427
1665451  1665457  1665467  1665479  1665493  1665523  1665527  1665529  1665553  1665563
1665569  1665571  1665577  1665581  1665583  1665611  1665619  1665623  1665647  1665649
1665659  1665679  1665689  1665701  1665709  1665757  1665761  1665767  1665823  1665827
1665841  1665869  1665877  1665889  1665899  1665907  1665919  1665929  1665931  1665941
1665943  1665967  1665973  1665997  1666003  1666019  1666037  1666039  1666043  1666061
1666081  1666111  1666127  1666139  1666151  1666177  1666201  1666211  1666213  1666237
1666261  1666271  1666279  1666297  1666303  1666307  1666309  1666321  1666339  1666351
1666361  1666387  1666393  1666397  1666403  1666409  1666447  1666461  1666469  1666471
1666477  1666481  1666487  1666499  1666507  1666519  1666523  1666531  1666541  1666559
1666589  1666597  1666607  1666619  1666627  1666657  1666711  1666727  1666729  1666733
1666757  1666771  1666781  1666783  1666789  1666793  1666807  1666811  1666823  1666843
1666853  1666871  1666897  1666909  1666913  1666919  1666933  1666939  1666943  1666991
1666999  1667033  1667047  1667051  1667053  1667077  1667131  1667143  1667147  1667179
1667189  1667209  1667213  1667227  1667233  1667243  1667249  1667251  1667279  1667287
1667291  1667311  1667321  1667329  1667353  1667357  1667359  1667363  1667389  1667401
1667417  1667423  1667441  1667443  1667447  1667461  1667473  1667489  1667507  1667509
1667537  1667543  1667551  1667579  1667597  1667599  1667609  1667623  1667629  1667639
1667641  1667647  1667651  1667663  1667689  1667693  1667711  1667723  1667741  1667747
1667749  1667773  1667777  1667779  1667789  1667791  1667821  1667833  1667837  1667843
1667851  1667863  1667867  1667873  1667881  1667899  1667917  1667933  1667947  1667951
1667957  1667959  1667969  1668001  1668011  1668019  1668031  1668053  1668061  1668083
1668089  1668113  1668119  1668131  1668133  1668137  1668197  1668211  1668229  1668241
1668253  1668299  1668301  1668307  1668313  1668319  1668323  1668347  1668361  1668379
1668427  1668437  1668449  1668467  1668473  1668479  1668481  1668503  1668509  1668517
1668521  1668539  1668551  1668553  1668587  1668593  1668617  1668619  1668629  1668647
1668649  1668679  1668683  1668721  1668727  1668739  1668743  1668757  1668773  1668791
1668803  1668833  1668847  1668869  1668883  1668889  1668911  1668913  1668929  1668943
1668971  1668983  1669027  1669049  1669061  1669091  1669097  1669099  1669103  1669121
1669127  1669141  1669147  1669163  1669177  1669193  1669201  1669219  1669223  1669231
1669237  1669243  1669249  1669253  1669259  1669289  1669301  1669309  1669313  1669323
1669331  1669351  1669357  1669361  1669391  1669399  1669427  1669433  1669441  1669463
1669463  1669469  1669471  1669489  1669513  1669537  1669541  1669543  1669571  1669579
1669589  1669597  1669627  1669637  1669649  1669651  1669687  1669697  1669727  1669741
1669747  1669751  1669763  1669781  1669783  1669793  1669799  1669813  1669817  1669861
1669873  1669879  1669883  1669897  1669931  1669933  1669937  1669951  1669963  1669979
1669999  1670003  1670017  1670057  1670059  1670089  1670093  1670129  1670161  1670171
1670183  1670213  1670269  1670281  1670287  1670303  1670327  1670341  1670353  1670359
1670399  1670407  1670411  1670413  1670419  1670447  1670477  1670489  1670491  1670503
1670519  1670527  1670531  1670533  1670551  1670561  1670563  1670567  1670569  1670579
1670597  1670623  1670629  1670633  1670639  1670653  1670657  1670669  1670687  1670717
1670723  1670741  1670761  1670783  1670813  1670819  1670827  1670831  1670833  1670857
1670863  1670887  1670891  1670899  1670923  1670953  1670959  1670971  1670983  1671041
1671053  1671073  1671077  1671097  1671101  1671121  1671133  1671139  1671161  1671191
1671199  1671209  1671211  1671223  1671227  1671277  1671289  1671311  1671337  1671343
1671347  1671349  1671359  1671379  1671421  1671431  1671437  1671443  1671451  1671463
1671493  1671497  1671511  1671517  1671521  1671577  1671581  1671599  1671619  1671629
```

```
1671641  1671643  1671671  1671679  1671689  1671707  1671713  1671727  1671731  1671739
1671757  1671781  1671907  1671941  1671947  1671961  1671977  1671983  1671997  1672003
1672009  1672037  1672051  1672063  1672079  1672081  1672087  1672091  1672117  1672129
1672199  1672219  1672243  1672271  1672301  1672331  1672337  1672339  1672379  1672381
1672393  1672421  1672423  1672441  1672453  1672457  1672469  1672471  1672487  1672499
1672501  1672507  1672519  1672523  1672529  1672549  1672553  1672603  1672607  1672609
1672631  1672637  1672639  1672651  1672663  1672747  1672751  1672753  1672771  1672787
1672799  1672849  1672861  1672873  1672889  1672897  1672901  1672921  1672927  1672939
1672949  1672961  1672963  1672967  1672999  1673011  1673017  1673027  1673053  1673069
1673071  1673081  1673099  1673107  1673131  1673137  1673167  1673171  1673179  1673183
1673207  1673209  1673237  1673249  1673279  1673281  1673297  1673317  1673339  1673377
1673381  1673389  1673393  1673401  1673407  1673437  1673447  1673453  1673461  1673489
1673509  1673513  1673519  1673527  1673543  1673563  1673569  1673591  1673627  1673629
1673663  1673669  1673681  1673713  1673719  1673723  1673731  1673741  1673747  1673753
1673759  1673797  1673807  1673809  1673813  1673827  1673831  1673839  1673849  1673857
1673897  1673923  1673927  1673933  1673941  1673951  1673953  1673981  1673983  1673993
1674011  1674047  1674053  1674067  1674073  1674107  1674133  1674151  1674157  1674161
1674163  1674181  1674203  1674209  1674259  1674269  1674271  1674289  1674301  1674319
1674329  1674353  1674357  1674391  1674433  1674437  1674457  1674461  1674473  1674503
1674523  1674539  1674557  1674559  1674577  1674581  1674587  1674593  1674599  1674601
1674613  1674623  1674637  1674643  1674649  1674667  1674683  1674703  1674733  1674737
1674763  1674767  1674769  1674787  1674797  1674817  1674821  1674847  1674887  1674889
1674901  1674913  1674917  1674919  1674931  1674941  1674947  1674949  1674971  1674989
1674991  1674997  1675001  1675007  1675013  1675039  1675049  1675057  1675073  1675087
1675109  1675111  1675117  1675133  1675139  1675181  1675183  1675199  1675213  1675217
1675259  1675273  1675279  1675283  1675291  1675307  1675321  1675327  1675339  1675351
1675361  1675369  1675379  1675393  1675411  1675441  1675447  1675459  1675463  1675507
1675561  1675567  1675577  1675579  1675589  1675607  1675613  1675627  1675631  1675637
1675679  1675697  1675703  1675717  1675721  1675733  1675747  1675759  1675763  1675769
1675771  1675787  1675789  1675799  1675801  1675831  1675847  1675859  1675867  1675873
1675931  1675937  1675943  1675951  1675963  1675967  1675981  1675991  1676023  1676027
1676029  1676041  1676053  1676069  1676071  1676083  1676111  1676167  1676173  1676221
1676243  1676261  1676267  1676281  1676303  1676321  1676333  1676347  1676383  1676393
1676413  1676417  1676431  1676453  1676471  1676473  1676497  1676501  1676533  1676551
1676561  1676569  1676593  1676599  1676611  1676621  1676627  1676629  1676641  1676651
1676663  1676687  1676711  1676713  1676749  1676767  1676771  1676783  1676813  1676827
1676833  1676837  1676869  1676879  1676887  1676891  1676893  1676911  1676923  1676947
1676963  1676971  1676981  1676993  1677001  1677019  1677031  1677037  1677047  1677083
1677089  1677113  1677121  1677133  1677163  1677167  1677191  1677197  1677199  1677209
1677217  1677251  1677253  1677281  1677283  1677287  1677323  1677329  1677337  1677343
1677349  1677353  1677359  1677443  1677451  1677457  1677461  1677463  1677499  1677521
1677523  1677527  1677539  1677569  1677583  1677589  1677593  1677631  1677667  1677673
1677703  1677707  1677721  1677727  1677733  1677743  1677773  1677779  1677787  1677791
1677811  1677847  1677857  1677877  1677887  1677899  1677941  1677961  1677971  1677997
1678009  1678013  1678021  1678031  1678037  1678067  1678069  1678073  1678091  1678093
1678111  1678129  1678151  1678153  1678181  1678199  1678207  1678217  1678219
1678231  1678249  1678267  1678277  1678301  1678319  1678321  1678331  1678337  1678349
1678361  1678363  1678367  1678381  1678399  1678409  1678421  1678423  1678429  1678459
1678463  1678507  1678531  1678543  1678553  1678571  1678577  1678601  1678603  1678613
1678627  1678639  1678657  1678673  1678679  1678687  1678693  1678697  1678711  1678717
1678739  1678751  1678753  1678757  1678759  1678769  1678771  1678777  1678837  1678843
1678847  1678861  1678871  1678877  1678879  1678883  1678889  1678891  1678921  1678951
1678961  1678979  1678993  1679009  1679017  1679033  1679057  1679059  1679077  1679099
1679101  1679113  1679123  1679131  1679143  1679159  1679189  1679203  1679213  1679233
1679261  1679267  1679273  1679281  1679287  1679291  1679323  1679329  1679333
1679351  1679371  1679383  1679417  1679443  1679459  1679471  1679473  1679501
1679521  1679533  1679539  1679599  1679603  1679609  1679627  1679633  1679641  1679653
1679659  1679669  1679681  1679683  1679687  1679693  1679701  1679723  1679773  1679779
1679801  1679807  1679831  1679833  1679849  1679857  1679863  1679903  1679917  1679939
1679959  1679963  1679981  1680013  1680023  1680071  1680079  1680089  1680101  1680103
1680121  1680131  1680149  1680167  1680179  1680181  1680191  1680247  1680253  1680269
1680271  1680277  1680313  1680317  1680319  1680323  1680359  1680361  1680373  1680377
1680401  1680407  1680421  1680431  1680439  1680457  1680461  1680491  1680509  1680527
1680529  1680551  1680557  1680583  1680589  1680593  1680617  1680643  1680647  1680659
1680689  1680697  1680703  1680709  1680743  1680761  1680779  1680787  1680793  1680803
1680821  1680839  1680859  1680881  1680893  1680901  1680907  1680919
1680929  1680961  1680967  1680979  1680983  1681003  1681007  1681027  1681033  1681061
1681073  1681091  1681103  1681129  1681151  1681157  1681187  1681193  1681201  1681219
1681241  1681247  1681259  1681261  1681271  1681279  1681289  1681307  1681321  1681349
1681363  1681397  1681403  1681411  1681423  1681469  1681501  1681513  1681517  1681541
1681571  1681573  1681591  1681597  1681619  1681621  1681639  1681649  1681651
1681661  1681679  1681703  1681711  1681717  1681721  1681723  1681787  1681807  1681817
1681837  1681853  1681873  1681877  1681889  1681891  1681903  1681907  1681931
1681957  1681973  1681991  1682017  1682047  1682069  1682081  1682101  1682111  1682119
1682123  1682143  1682159  1682179  1682207  1682237  1682249  1682251  1682257  1682281
1682287  1682293  1682311  1682333  1682363  1682383  1682389  1682399  1682407  1682413
1682423  1682449  1682477  1682479  1682489  1682509  1682521  1682531  1682537  1682539
1682543  1682557  1682567  1682573  1682581  1682627  1682663  1682669  1682671
1682693  1682701  1682713  1682717  1682753  1682801  1682809  1682827  1682831  1682833
1682843  1682867  1682893  1682911  1682939  1682951  1682987  1682999  1683007  1683013
1683029  1683037  1683041  1683043  1683049  1683053  1683067  1683089  1683103  1683113
1683169  1683223  1683233  1683239  1683251  1683259  1683271  1683293  1683299  1683313
1683317  1683359  1683383  1683397  1683403  1683433  1683467  1683469  1683491  1683497
1683503  1683523  1683553  1683581  1683589  1683601  1683631  1683637  1683667  1683673
1683679  1683691  1683719  1683733  1683749  1683767  1683779  1683817  1683839  1683841
1683887  1683949  1683971  1683977  1684019  1684031  1684063  1684079  1684091  1684097
1684099  1684127  1684169  1684171  1684187  1684223  1684229  1684231  1684237  1684247
1684259  1684283  1684289  1684297  1684301  1684303  1684307  1684327  1684337  1684373
1684379  1684387  1684399  1684409  1684427  1684477  1684481  1684489  1684511  1684531
```

```
1684537  1684549  1684561  1684577  1684591  1684607  1684609  1684667  1684679  1684691
1684693  1684703  1684733  1684741  1684763  1684769  1684787  1684789  1684801  1684829
1684843  1684861  1684867  1684873  1684877  1684883  1684919  1684937  1684951  1684973
1684979  1684993  1684999  1685011  1685039  1685051  1685071  1685077  1685087  1685093
1685107  1685111  1685113  1685119  1685153  1685171  1685179  1685207  1685209  1685221
1685231  1685267  1685269  1685273  1685297  1685317  1685323  1685381  1685399  1685407
1685419  1685423  1685429  1685441  1685443  1685447  1685449  1685459  1685473  1685477
1685479  1685483  1685503  1685521  1685527  1685543  1685549  1685573  1685581  1685591
1685599  1685617  1685627  1685681  1685701  1685707  1685711  1685713  1685731  1685759
1685767  1685773  1685777  1685779  1685809  1685819  1685821  1685833  1685837  1685861
1685863  1685869  1685881  1685897  1685911  1685917  1685933  1685951  1685953  1685963
1685977  1685989  1686017  1686029  1686049  1686067  1686071  1686109  1686119  1686133
1686137  1686143  1686149  1686169  1686173  1686197  1686203  1686229  1686239  1686257
1686259  1686271  1686287  1686319  1686329  1686341  1686343  1686353  1686367  1686389
1686403  1686409  1686439  1686449  1686473  1686479  1686491  1686511  1686527  1686547
1686551  1686563  1686569  1686583  1686593  1686631  1686637  1686647  1686661  1686667
1686673  1686677  1686683  1686697  1686701  1686703  1686743  1686749  1686779  1686823
1686827  1686851  1686857  1686871  1686907  1686913  1686931  1686943  1686967  1686973
1686983  1687009  1687033  1687039  1687057  1687061  1687087  1687111  1687117  1687129
1687139  1687151  1687157  1687171  1687177  1687183  1687187  1687193  1687247  1687289
1687297  1687319  1687327  1687331  1687339  1687373  1687381  1687393  1687421  1687451
1687453  1687489  1687507  1687531  1687549  1687559  1687571  1687583  1687591  1687603
1687613  1687627  1687633  1687643  1687649  1687661  1687667  1687669  1687729  1687739
1687757  1687759  1687781  1687783  1687799  1687801  1687823  1687831  1687837  1687843
1687849  1687853  1687859  1687909  1687937  1687949  1687963  1687969  1687991  1687999
1688041  1688047  1688069  1688077  1688101  1688123  1688143  1688147  1688153
1688161  1688173  1688179  1688189  1688201  1688213  1688231  1688237  1688243  1688261
1688263  1688279  1688299  1688311  1688317  1688327  1688329  1688341  1688363  1688369
1688371  1688387  1688411  1688413  1688443  1688471  1688497  1688509  1688543  1688573
1688579  1688623  1688629  1688651  1688657  1688669  1688677  1688681  1688741  1688759
1688773  1688789  1688803  1688809  1688837  1688857  1688861  1688887  1688893  1688903
1688909  1688917  1688923  1688927  1688969  1688971  1688977  1688987  1689031  1689049
1689053  1689067  1689071  1689109  1689113  1689167  1689197  1689199  1689211  1689217
1689253  1689263  1689277  1689287  1689319  1689343  1689353  1689367  1689377  1689379
1689397  1689431  1689437  1689451  1689497  1689503  1689521  1689533  1689551  1689553
1689601  1689607  1689617  1689641  1689659  1689661  1689703  1689707  1689713  1689719
1689739  1689757  1689763  1689767  1689773  1689781  1689829  1689847  1689869  1689881
1689893  1689907  1689911  1689913  1689923  1689929  1689931  1689967  1690009  1690019
1690043  1690057  1690067  1690079  1690081  1690097  1690099  1690103  1690121  1690153
1690187  1690189  1690193  1690211  1690217  1690219  1690229  1690231  1690253  1690267
1690277  1690303  1690309  1690319  1690349  1690357  1690387  1690393  1690421
1690427  1690433  1690441  1690483  1690519  1690529  1690537  1690547  1690571  1690573
1690597  1690603  1690609  1690621  1690651  1690669  1690673  1690681  1690687  1690691
1690693  1690727  1690739  1690757  1690781  1690783  1690811  1690831  1690847  1690849
1690853  1690883  1690901  1690933  1690967  1690993  1691003  1691023  1691033  1691051
1691069  1691087  1691093  1691099  1691111  1691113  1691119  1691141  1691161  1691189
1691219  1691227  1691231  1691237  1691243  1691257  1691269  1691273  1691293  1691297
1691303  1691321  1691359  1691369  1691387  1691401  1691411  1691413  1691419  1691423
1691429  1691441  1691461  1691479  1691507  1691519  1691527  1691531  1691533  1691561
1691567  1691593  1691611  1691621  1691633  1691647  1691659  1691681  1691689  1691693
1691737  1691747  1691759  1691771  1691803  1691821  1691827  1691839  1691843  1691849
1691861  1691863  1691867  1691869  1691897  1691917  1691927  1691933  1691939  1691983
1692013  1692023  1692043  1692049  1692059  1692071  1692091  1692107  1692137
1692139  1692149  1692161  1692167  1692181  1692191  1692199  1692203  1692217  1692221
1692233  1692239  1692241  1692247  1692253  1692283  1692293  1692337  1692377  1692407
1692413  1692421  1692433  1692461  1692473  1692479  1692499  1692511  1692541  1692563
1692583  1692589  1692629  1692637  1692641  1692667  1692679  1692683  1692697  1692709
1692721  1692727  1692737  1692749  1692763  1692791  1692827  1692829  1692839  1692857
1692863  1692871  1692883  1692907  1692917  1692947  1692949  1692959  1692967  1692983
1692989  1693001  1693031  1693051  1693067  1693073  1693091  1693093  1693103  1693129
1693169  1693171  1693187  1693201  1693249  1693267  1693271  1693273  1693277  1693303
1693309  1693327  1693331  1693333  1693343  1693357  1693361  1693411  1693427  1693429
1693441  1693493  1693501  1693511  1693529  1693537  1693541  1693553  1693577  1693579
1693583  1693607  1693613  1693621  1693631  1693633  1693639  1693649  1693661  1693663
1693667  1693691  1693711  1693729  1693753  1693763  1693777  1693807  1693817  1693841
1693859  1693883  1693889  1693891  1693921  1693943  1693957  1693987  1694023  1694027
1694029  1694051  1694081  1694083  1694089  1694123  1694129  1694141  1694159  1694167
1694171  1694177  1694191  1694197  1694207  1694213  1694221  1694227  1694233  1694239
1694263  1694281  1694291  1694309  1694311  1694327  1694351  1694353  1694359  1694369
1694377  1694393  1694423  1694443  1694447  1694449  1694467  1694503  1694507  1694513
1694521  1694533  1694551  1694573  1694599  1694603  1694621  1694647  1694681  1694689
1694701  1694717  1694723  1694729  1694761  1694767  1694779  1694809  1694821  1694831
1694837  1694851  1694879  1694897  1694909  1694921  1694929  1694941  1694977  1694989
1695041  1695061  1695073  1695091  1695107  1695131  1695139  1695143  1695157  1695163
1695191  1695209  1695233  1695259  1695283  1695289  1695293  1695319  1695329  1695341
1695347  1695349  1695401  1695403  1695413  1695433  1695437  1695439  1695457  1695467
1695481  1695493  1695509  1695511  1695527  1695553  1695559  1695581  1695593  1695611
1695623  1695641  1695643  1695653  1695671  1695691  1695697  1695709  1695737  1695751
1695761  1695763  1695779  1695781  1695797  1695809  1695817  1695823  1695839  1695847
1695853  1695871  1695887  1695889  1695913  1695929  1695961  1695989  1696001  1696021
1696027  1696033  1696069  1696081  1696099  1696109  1696127  1696153  1696157  1696169
1696193  1696199  1696207  1696213  1696231  1696237  1696241  1696249  1696259  1696283
1696291  1696313  1696327  1696333  1696363  1696369  1696391  1696417  1696421  1696423
1696439  1696451  1696459  1696463  1696493  1696501  1696511  1696517  1696523  1696543
1696547  1696571  1696579  1696589  1696601  1696609  1696649  1696657  1696661
1696693  1696697  1696711  1696729  1696801  1696811  1696859  1696861  1696879  1696883
1696943  1696951  1696969  1696973  1696979  1697027  1697039  1697041  1697053  1697057
1697063  1697071  1697077  1697083  1697107  1697149  1697159  1697173  1697191  1697197
1697231  1697243  1697257  1697261  1697287  1697291  1697299  1697309  1697317  1697321
```

```
1697347  1697351  1697357  1697383  1697389  1697401  1697407  1697411  1697413  1697419
1697453  1697459  1697461  1697471  1697477  1697491  1697503  1697519  1697523  1697551
1697581  1697587  1697621  1697623  1697627  1697651  1697677  1697701  1697719  1697723
1697737  1697741  1697743  1697753  1697767  1697771  1697797  1697803  1697827  1697833
1697869  1697873  1697881  1697887  1697903  1697953  1697957  1697959  1697987
1697989  1698001  1698007  1698013  1698023  1698029  1698043  1698061  1698071  1698077
1698089  1698101  1698119  1698121  1698127  1698131  1698133  1698139  1698167  1698217
1698227  1698233  1698241  1698247  1698253  1698259  1698271  1698289  1698311  1698313
1698349  1698377  1698379  1698409  1698413  1698427  1698449  1698461  1698469  1698497
1698509  1698511  1698539  1698553  1698569  1698607  1698611  1698643  1698647  1698679
1698689  1698701  1698709  1698713  1698727  1698751  1698773  1698797  1698799  1698821
1698833  1698857  1698859  1698869  1698871  1698877  1698881  1698883  1698913  1698943
1698947  1698953  1698967  1698971  1699001  1699007  1699039  1699043  1699063  1699067
1699069  1699073  1699091  1699109  1699111  1699129  1699153  1699157  1699177  1699193
1699213  1699219  1699223  1699237  1699249  1699279  1699289  1699297  1699301  1699307
1699319  1699331  1699333  1699349  1699361  1699381  1699391  1699393  1699421  1699427
1699457  1699469  1699471  1699499  1699501  1699517  1699543  1699547  1699571  1699597
1699619  1699627  1699639  1699651  1699667  1699679  1699681  1699703  1699717  1699727
1699739  1699741  1699751  1699783  1699793  1699799  1699801  1699829  1699831  1699837
1699853  1699871  1699877  1699879  1699897  1699921  1699933  1699937  1699939  1699969
1699993  1700021  1700047  1700053  1700059  1700077  1700087  1700099  1700107  1700129
1700141  1700143  1700161  1700173  1700189  1700197  1700219  1700233  1700267  1700269
1700287  1700297  1700327  1700339  1700341  1700353  1700359  1700371  1700383  1700423
1700431  1700437  1700441  1700471  1700477  1700513  1700533  1700549  1700563  1700591
1700593  1700603  1700609  1700617  1700627  1700651  1700659  1700669  1700683  1700687
1700719  1700723  1700729  1700749  1700759  1700761  1700767  1700771  1700801  1700807
1700813  1700819  1700849  1700851  1700917  1700921  1700981  1700983  1700987  1701017
1701019  1701023  1701041  1701043  1701047  1701059  1701061  1701079  1701101  1701121
1701137  1701151  1701179  1701181  1701199  1701233  1701239  1701263  1701269  1701277
1701289  1701299  1701307  1701313  1701361  1701367  1701389  1701391  1701397  1701433
1701437  1701439  1701449  1701461  1701487  1701493  1701503  1701509  1701521  1701523
1701527  1701533  1701571  1701577  1701589  1701607  1701613  1701617  1701629  1701641
1701643  1701647  1701653  1701709  1701719  1701727  1701731  1701743  1701757  1701761
1701767  1701803  1701809  1701827  1701829  1701841  1701851  1701857  1701859  1701871
1701877  1701881  1701899  1701901  1701911  1701913  1701967  1701971  1701979  1701991
1702009  1702013  1702061  1702079  1702087  1702093  1702109  1702121  1702133  1702169
1702171  1702177  1702189  1702219  1702237  1702243  1702249  1702291  1702313  1702319
1702321  1702339  1702369  1702373  1702409  1702417  1702423  1702429  1702507  1702511
1702523  1702543  1702549  1702553  1702573  1702577  1702627  1702637  1702639  1702643
1702661  1702663  1702697  1702709  1702711  1702717  1702721  1702739  1702741  1702747
1702751  1702781  1702783  1702801  1702807  1702817  1702819  1702823  1702849  1702867
1702879  1702891  1702901  1702903  1702927  1702931  1702933  1702949  1702963  1702969
1702991  1702993  1703041  1703063  1703071  1703089  1703113  1703123  1703159  1703183
1703203  1703227  1703231  1703237  1703267  1703269  1703287  1703291  1703297  1703323
1703381  1703399  1703413  1703437  1703447  1703453  1703461  1703467  1703479  1703501
1703557  1703563  1703573  1703593  1703599  1703627  1703651  1703683  1703687  1703693
1703707  1703717  1703719  1703731  1703773  1703783  1703809  1703833  1703843  1703851
1703857  1703899  1703903  1703941  1703957  1703963  1703983  1703993  1704023  1704041
1704067  1704077  1704103  1704119  1704121  1704137  1704149  1704161  1704169  1704181
1704187  1704203  1704211  1704217  1704229  1704251  1704271  1704289  1704299  1704343
1704371  1704377  1704397  1704407  1704421  1704431  1704449  1704463  1704487
1704499  1704511  1704517  1704529  1704551  1704559  1704587  1704589  1704601  1704611
1704613  1704671  1704673  1704683  1704689  1704713  1704727  1704751  1704757  1704763
1704793  1704799  1704803  1704809  1704841  1704847  1704877  1704887  1704893  1704919
1704929  1704931  1704943  1704953  1704961  1704971  1704979  1704991  1705001  1705009
1705021  1705051  1705097  1705103  1705111  1705127  1705129  1705139  1705141  1705153
1705157  1705181  1705189  1705199  1705211  1705241  1705247  1705267  1705271  1705273
1705303  1705309  1705331  1705339  1705369  1705387  1705393  1705397  1705399  1705409
1705433  1705447  1705463  1705481  1705493  1705549  1705579  1705591  1705597  1705601
1705637  1705667  1705679  1705721  1705747  1705757  1705799  1705807  1705813  1705817
1705819  1705829  1705843  1705849  1705859  1705861  1705871  1705883  1705889  1705897
1705903  1705931  1705943  1705973  1705997  1706009  1706057  1706063  1706077  1706087
1706113  1706129  1706141  1706153  1706167  1706179  1706191  1706213  1706227  1706233
1706249  1706251  1706281  1706291  1706293  1706311  1706317  1706323  1706363  1706381
1706387  1706399  1706417  1706437  1706449  1706459  1706473  1706483  1706489  1706491
1706501  1706527  1706533  1706539  1706567  1706569  1706591  1706603  1706629  1706633
1706641  1706651  1706657  1706659  1706687  1706689  1706701  1706741  1706743  1706777
1706791  1706797  1706801  1706821  1706843  1706849  1706857  1706863  1706867  1706869
1706897  1706927  1706951  1706977  1706981  1706989  1707067  1707071  1707073  1707107
1707113  1707119  1707127  1707137  1707161  1707163  1707179  1707197  1707253  1707257
1707301  1707331  1707341  1707347  1707353  1707367  1707371  1707379  1707389  1707403
1707413  1707421  1707437  1707443  1707457  1707467  1707499  1707509  1707521  1707523
1707529  1707533  1707539  1707551  1707577  1707581  1707611  1707617  1707631  1707647
1707649  1707707  1707709  1707733  1707737  1707757  1707767  1707779  1707787  1707791
1707833  1707851  1707863  1707869  1707887  1707889  1707899  1707907  1707913  1707919
1707931  1707941  1707943  1707947  1707977  1707983  1708009  1708033  1708037  1708039
1708051  1708067  1708079  1708087  1708103  1708159  1708163  1708169  1708181  1708207
1708219  1708229  1708283  1708307  1708321  1708339  1708351  1708363  1708373
1708387  1708391  1708397  1708409  1708411  1708439  1708453  1708457  1708493  1708507
1708513  1708523  1708529  1708541  1708543  1708571  1708573  1708579  1708607  1708621
1708639  1708649  1708657  1708669  1708703  1708717  1708741  1708769  1708781  1708783
1708799  1708807  1708829  1708853  1708859  1708871  1708909  1708939  1708943  1708951
1708961  1708963  1708979  1708981  1708997  1709009  1709017  1709033  1709047
1709077  1709087  1709093  1709131  1709137  1709143  1709161  1709189  1709203  1709209
1709233  1709243  1709251  1709261  1709263  1709269  1709287  1709317  1709321  1709327
1709339  1709341  1709353  1709359  1709377  1709387  1709443  1709453  1709473  1709479
1709483  1709489  1709497  1709501  1709507  1709509  1709527  1709593  1709599  1709611
1709633  1709663  1709671  1709689  1709693  1709699  1709711  1709713  1709749  1709767
1709783  1709789  1709837  1709861  1709863  1709909  1709923  1709933  1709941  1709951
```

```
1709959 1709963 1709969 1709971 1709989 1709993 1709999 1710011 1710017 1710061
1710077 1710083 1710091 1710097 1710131 1710139 1710161 1710167 1710179 1710193
1710197 1710199 1710221 1710229 1710253 1710263 1710287 1710299 1710307 1710311
1710337 1710341 1710343 1710347 1710383 1710389 1710403 1710407 1710409 1710413
1710419 1710431 1710439 1710493 1710517 1710529 1710539 1710593 1710601 1710607
1710613 1710617 1710619 1710629 1710647 1710661 1710677 1710689 1710691 1710697
1710701 1710757 1710767 1710781 1710791 1710799 1710833 1710851 1710853 1710857
1710869 1710871 1710881 1710923 1710937 1710953 1710959 1710997 1711019 1711043
1711049 1711051 1711069 1711081 1711091 1711093 1711097 1711103 1711117 1711123
1711153 1711163 1711181 1711189 1711207 1711277 1711279 1711289 1711291 1711327
1711351 1711379 1711397 1711399 1711427 1711447 1711459 1711471 1711481 1711487
1711511 1711517 1711519 1711547 1711553 1711561 1711573 1711613 1711621 1711639
1711643 1711651 1711669 1711673 1711687 1711753 1711763 1711793 1711799 1711811
1711813 1711817 1711819 1711859 1711889 1711891 1711901 1711909 1711921 1711937
1711949 1711961 1711967 1711973 1711979 1711981 1711993 1712017 1712047 1712057
1712077 1712129 1712141 1712149 1712153 1712171 1712173 1712177 1712197 1712203
1712213 1712219 1712231 1712237 1712267 1712287 1712311 1712329 1712339 1712353
1712369 1712371 1712383 1712387 1712401 1712407 1712411 1712437 1712467 1712497
1712509 1712519 1712531 1712549 1712551 1712567 1712569 1712617 1712621 1712629
1712639 1712707 1712743 1712747 1712759 1712761 1712771 1712791 1712807 1712813
1712839 1712861 1712881 1712891 1712899 1712917 1712927 1712929 1712933 1712951
1712969 1712981 1712987 1713007 1713043 1713071 1713083 1713121 1713133 1713167
1713181 1713221 1713223 1713227 1713251 1713281 1713289 1713317 1713319 1713329
1713343 1713353 1713373 1713389 1713403 1713449 1713457 1713469 1713493 1713497
1713511 1713521 1713541 1713557 1713559 1713599 1713601 1713637 1713641 1713671
1713683 1713689 1713709 1713713 1713737 1713749 1713763 1713769 1713779 1713791
1713797 1713809 1713823 1713847 1713853 1713863 1713883 1713913 1713919 1713931
1713941 1713977 1713979 1713989 1713997 1714003 1714049 1714057 1714067 1714091
1714117 1714133 1714147 1714151 1714157 1714159 1714171 1714177 1714183 1714187
1714189 1714211 1714241 1714253 1714261 1714289 1714327 1714369 1714387 1714403
1714409 1714411 1714417 1714421 1714423 1714439 1714441 1714457 1714477 1714483
1714499 1714507 1714519 1714529 1714547 1714577 1714591 1714621 1714631 1714633
1714639 1714651 1714663 1714667 1714723 1714729 1714747 1714751 1714759 1714777
1714787 1714789 1714793 1714813 1714819 1714831 1714837 1714849 1714859 1714861
1714871 1714891 1714901 1714919 1714931 1714939 1714957 1714963 1715033 1715039
1715047 1715059 1715099 1715107 1715117 1715123 1715143 1715167 1715177 1715213
1715237 1715243 1715269 1715293 1715309 1715341 1715353 1715369 1715387 1715393
1715407 1715411 1715429 1715449 1715459 1715471 1715473 1715479 1715489 1715507
1715513 1715533 1715537 1715561 1715569 1715599 1715603 1715617 1715621 1715627
1715683 1715711 1715713 1715717 1715723 1715729 1715737 1715741 1715761 1715767
1715771 1715783 1715789 1715797 1715807 1715821 1715849 1715851 1715867 1715873
1715887 1715899 1715911 1715927 1715971 1715983 1716037 1716041 1716047 1716049
1716059 1716079 1716089 1716103 1716107 1716109 1716139 1716149 1716163 1716181
1716203 1716217 1716241 1716263 1716271 1716277 1716287 1716311 1716313 1716317
1716343 1716359 1716361 1716367 1716389 1716391 1716397 1716401 1716413 1716419
1716427 1716443 1716457 1716469 1716489 1716499 1716529 1716521 1716529 1716551
1716557 1716577 1716599 1716613 1716619 1716623 1716647 1716653 1716661 1716667
1716683 1716691 1716703 1716733 1716751 1716761 1716767 1716787 1716791 1716797
1716853 1716889 1716893 1716901 1716917 1716931 1716937 1716941 1716943 1716971
1716991 1717007 1717043 1717063 1717081 1717099 1717117 1717129 1717139 1717151
1717169 1717181 1717217 1717229 1717237 1717241 1717283 1717297 1717321 1717337
1717343 1717349 1717361 1717363 1717379 1717393 1717399 1717439 1717447 1717451
1717477 1717489 1717501 1717517 1717553 1717567 1717591 1717603 1717609 1717621
1717627 1717631 1717637 1717669 1717673 1717687 1717739 1717747 1717787 1717817
1717829 1717853 1717861 1717913 1717951 1717957 1717973 1717981 1717993 1718011
1718027 1718033 1718039 1718053 1718069 1718083 1718107 1718131 1718137
1718141 1718153 1718159 1718177 1718191 1718203 1718219 1718251 1718267 1718281
1718287 1718291 1718293 1718333 1718357 1718369 1718371 1718383 1718389 1718393
1718401 1718407 1718429 1718441 1718447 1718449 1718459 1718467 1718471 1718473
1718477 1718489 1718503 1718551 1718557 1718567 1718573 1718593 1718599 1718653
1718663 1718669 1718693 1718699 1718701 1718707 1718711 1718713 1718719 1718723
1718747 1718749 1718771 1718789 1718791 1718807 1718861 1718863 1718867 1718869
1718879 1718881 1718891 1718923 1718929 1718933 1718947 1718971 1719001 1719049
1719059 1719143 1719187 1719197 1719203 1719209 1719217 1719233 1719239 1719241
1719271 1719293 1719299 1719301 1719317 1719337 1719343 1719359 1719409 1719413
1719433 1719451 1719469 1719491 1719493 1719517 1719541 1719547 1719551 1719583
1719607 1719611 1719623 1719629 1719643 1719647 1719659 1719667 1719701 1719719
1719721 1719743 1719749 1719763 1719799 1719829 1719841 1719853 1719857 1719859
1719863 1719869 1719877 1719901 1719919 1719923 1719931 1719943 1719947 1719967
1719983 1719989 1720003 1720031 1720039 1720049 1720057 1720063 1720109 1720123
1720133 1720151 1720157 1720163 1720171 1720177 1720181 1720183 1720189 1720211
1720217 1720219 1720223 1720231 1720273 1720289 1720291 1720297 1720307 1720321
1720339 1720361 1720363 1720379 1720399 1720421 1720427 1720429 1720457 1720471
1720513 1720517 1720549 1720591 1720597 1720603 1720613 1720619 1720633 1720639
1720643 1720669 1720679 1720703 1720709 1720711 1720769 1720777 1720781 1720787
1720799 1720843 1720847 1720867 1720897 1720909 1720931 1720933 1720937 1720949
1720951 1720973 1720991 1721003 1721009 1721011 1721023 1721081 1721123 1721143
1721147 1721149 1721183 1721197 1721201 1721227 1721243 1721257 1721261 1721273
1721299 1721323 1721327 1721339 1721347 1721371 1721383 1721407 1721417 1721441
1721449 1721453 1721477 1721497 1721501 1721507 1721509 1721513 1721521 1721543
1721557 1721567 1721569 1721579 1721593 1721633 1721639 1721651 1721659 1721683
1721689 1721693 1721717 1721719 1721729 1721749 1721767 1721773 1721779 1721807
1721809 1721827 1721831 1721857 1721887 1721891 1721893 1721899 1721903 1721911
1721921 1721927 1721983 1722013 1722029 1722031 1722037 1722053 1722067 1722073
1722089 1722113 1722131 1722137 1722163 1722173 1722181 1722187 1722191 1722199
1722209 1722211 1722241 1722251 1722283 1722307 1722319 1722323 1722359 1722373
1722377 1722419 1722431 1722443 1722449 1722463 1722481 1722529 1722551 1722557
1722563 1722587 1722599 1722601 1722607 1722619 1722647 1722649 1722653 1722667
1722713 1722719 1722731 1722737 1722739 1722751 1722793 1722821 1722829 1722839
```

```
1722857  1722869  1722883  1722893  1722923  1722937  1722983  1722989  1722991  1723003
1723027  1723031  1723037  1723063  1723109  1723147  1723177  1723193  1723219  1723223
1723231  1723247  1723277  1723291  1723303  1723327  1723333  1723339  1723361  1723577
1723417  1723451  1723453  1723481  1723487  1723489  1723523  1723541  1723573  1723577
1723583  1723609  1723619  1723621  1723627  1723637  1723639  1723651  1723669  1723721
1723723  1723727  1723747  1723751  1723769  1723801  1723807  1723811  1723823  1723837
1723853  1723861  1723903  1723957  1723961  1723973  1723991  1724027  1724029  1724033
1724059  1724083  1724113  1724131  1724147  1724153  1724183  1724201  1724209  1724221
1724227  1724263  1724273  1724299  1724309  1724321  1724329  1724339  1724347  1724351
1724357  1724363  1724389  1724399  1724407  1724413  1724417  1724423  1724441  1724447
1724449  1724453  1724473  1724483  1724507  1724509  1724537  1724551  1724557  1724579
1724581  1724587  1724617  1724627  1724641  1724663  1724669  1724677  1724683
1724689  1724699  1724713  1724741  1724743  1724761  1724783  1724791  1724813  1724819
1724843  1724857  1724861  1724887  1724893  1724923  1724927  1724929  1724969  1724971
1724981  1724999  1725011  1725013  1725071  1725077  1725079  1725083  1725089  1725091
1725121  1725127  1725133  1725151  1725173  1725179  1725197  1725221  1725223  1725233
1725247  1725259  1725287  1725301  1725307  1725343  1725359  1725379  1725389  1725419
1725463  1725469  1725481  1725497  1725499  1725509  1725527  1725539  1725541  1725557
1725583  1725593  1725613  1725641  1725671  1725683  1725691  1725707  1725743  1725767
1725781  1725811  1725821  1725833  1725859  1725869  1725907  1725923  1725929  1725931
1725937  1725947  1725953  1725961  1725967  1725991  1726003  1726009  1726031  1726033
1726037  1726079  1726091  1726103  1726139  1726147  1726159  1726171  1726189  1726199
1726201  1726211  1726217  1726237  1726253  1726259  1726267  1726273  1726289  1726303
1726313  1726327  1726339  1726343  1726349  1726363  1726379  1726409  1726411  1726429
1726433  1726441  1726447  1726453  1726471  1726477  1726481  1726489  1726513  1726561
1726577  1726577  1726591  1726597  1726601  1726603  1726609  1726643  1726651  1726661
1726667  1726691  1726693  1726729  1726757  1726759  1726787  1726811  1726841  1726859
1726883  1726897  1726903  1726913  1726919  1726927  1726931  1726937  1726939  1726943
1726951  1726957  1726969  1726993  1726997  1727021  1727023  1727029  1727051  1727057
1727069  1727071  1727101  1727113  1727129  1727137  1727161  1727179  1727189  1727191
1727221  1727261  1727263  1727273  1727287  1727291  1727293  1727317  1727321  1727329
1727339  1727377  1727381  1727393  1727417  1727437  1727441  1727483  1727491  1727503
1727513  1727521  1727527  1727533  1727563  1727569  1727573  1727587  1727597  1727623
1727639  1727653  1727669  1727683  1727701  1727711  1727717  1727743  1727749  1727771
1727773  1727777  1727779  1727797  1727813  1727819  1727827  1727839  1727851  1727881
1727903  1727911  1727921  1727939  1727941  1727951  1727969  1727987  1727989  1728017
1728019  1728043  1728061  1728071  1728091  1728119  1728121  1728149  1728163  1728177
1728193  1728229  1728247  1728253  1728257  1728269  1728317  1728319  1728323  1728329
1728341  1728361  1728403  1728409  1728439  1728451  1728457  1728481  1728511  1728527
1728539  1728541  1728547  1728581  1728583  1728593  1728659  1728689  1728691  1728697
1728733  1728737  1728739  1728761  1728767  1728773  1728809  1728821  1728823  1728827
1728871  1728889  1728907  1728911  1728949  1728953  1728959  1728967  1728971  1728977
1728983  1728997  1729001  1729033  1729037  1729043  1729051  1729103  1729109  1729127
1729129  1729141  1729153  1729157  1729187  1729193  1729207  1729229  1729237  1729249
1729253  1729261  1729279  1729283  1729307  1729309  1729327  1729333  1729363  1729369
1729373  1729379  1729391  1729433  1729447  1729459  1729477  1729481  1729493  1729499
1729517  1729523  1729543  1729591  1729621  1729633  1729681  1729687  1729697  1729709
1729711  1729723  1729727  1729747  1729757  1729759  1729771  1729789  1729799  1729813
1729823  1729829  1729841  1729843  1729877  1729891  1729901  1729909  1729921  1729927
1729943  1729957  1729961  1730041  1730063  1730081  1730087  1730089  1730101  1730119
1730147  1730149  1730153  1730167  1730171  1730177  1730207  1730213  1730237  1730263
1730299  1730303  1730317  1730353  1730357  1730371  1730429  1730431  1730437  1730441
1730461  1730471  1730473  1730507  1730551  1730567  1730579  1730581  1730591  1730623
1730657  1730671  1730683  1730693  1730713  1730717  1730723  1730741  1730779  1730789
1730791  1730797  1730809  1730831  1730849  1730851  1730863  1730867  1730873  1730887
1730891  1730899  1730917  1730921  1730929  1730941  1730959  1730983  1730999  1731007
1731013  1731053  1731073  1731083  1731091  1731113  1731167  1731179  1731181  1731199
1731209  1731221  1731227  1731251  1731253  1731287  1731311  1731313  1731349  1731361
1731377  1731383  1731397  1731407  1731421  1731437  1731449  1731479  1731491  1731493
1731497  1731511  1731539  1731551  1731559  1731571  1731589  1731593  1731617  1731643
1731659  1731701  1731703  1731721  1731731  1731733  1731767  1731823  1731853  1731857
1731871  1731887  1731893  1731913  1731929  1731931  1731937  1731941  1731949  1731953
1731971  1731979  1731991  1732037  1732039  1732043  1732051  1732057  1732109  1732117
1732139  1732193  1732219  1732231  1732253  1732261  1732267  1732271  1732273  1732277
1732301  1732307  1732319  1732321  1732327  1732331  1732333  1732343  1732361  1732369
1732387  1732397  1732399  1732421  1732447  1732457  1732463  1732469  1732483  1732499
1732501  1732519  1732529  1732531  1732579  1732597  1732609  1732631  1732649  1732669
1732681  1732697  1732723  1732727  1732763  1732777  1732799  1732811  1732817  1732831
1732847  1732859  1732867  1732873  1732879  1732883  1732891  1732901  1732903  1732909
1732921  1732941  1732957  1732979  1732987  1733003  1733021  1733033  1733041  1733057
1733063  1733077  1733087  1733101  1733113  1733129  1733141  1733143  1733159  1733177
1733183  1733197  1733213  1733227  1733231  1733267  1733273  1733279  1733297  1733309
1733321  1733321  1733327  1733353  1733363  1733383  1733393  1733399  1733449  1733519
1733527  1733539  1733549  1733569  1733581  1733623  1733639  1733647  1733651  1733653
1733663  1733663  1733701  1733713  1733723  1733729  1733741  1733777  1733791  1733801
1733827  1733843  1733869  1733873  1733899  1733903  1733909  1733911  1733917  1733929
1733981  1733989  1733999  1734011  1734023  1734037  1734041  1734043  1734049  1734067
1734091  1734097  1734101  1734121  1734133  1734143  1734151  1734167  1734179  1734193
1734197  1734203  1734247  1734277  1734281  1734311  1734349  1734353  1734367  1734371
1734373  1734401  1734427  1734431  1734463  1734497  1734503  1734511  1734533  1734547
1734559  1734583  1734589  1734599  1734611  1734641  1734647  1734673  1734709  1734713
1734721  1734727  1734737  1734739  1734763  1734767  1734769  1734787  1734793  1734797
1734827  1734841  1734869  1734883  1734899  1734907  1734917  1734937  1734973  1734989
1735001  1735009  1735033  1735043  1735049  1735067  1735103  1735109  1735117  1735121
1735159  1735183  1735199  1735211  1735259  1735271  1735277  1735291  1735301  1735313
1735333  1735339  1735361  1735369  1735397  1735399  1735421  1735423  1735463  1735469
1735477  1735499  1735507  1735519  1735529  1735541  1735549  1735553  1735579  1735627
1735651  1735661  1735673  1735681  1735687  1735703  1735733  1735739  1735753  1735771
1735807  1735813  1735823  1735829  1735831  1735843  1735847  1735849  1735871  1735883
```

```
1735889  1735913  1735919  1735931  1735933  1735961  1735967  1735997  1736029  1736051
1736071  1736099  1736101  1736131  1736149  1736153  1736173  1736177  1736179  1736191
1736197  1736213  1736219  1736221  1736233  1736237  1736257  1736269  1736281  1736303
1736347  1736369  1736387  1736389  1736393  1736417  1736419  1736437  1736453  1736459
1736461  1736519  1736531  1736557  1736563  1736599  1736617  1736621  1736639  1736653
1736671  1736677  1736681  1736687  1736689  1736701  1736711  1736729  1736759  1736767
1736789  1736797  1736821  1736827  1736831  1736849  1736851  1736879  1736881  1736921
1736927  1736939  1736951  1736963  1736971  1736981  1736989  1736993  1737007  1737017
1737031  1737041  1737049  1737053  1737059  1737079  1737089  1737101  1737103  1737161
1737199  1737221  1737257  1737269  1737311  1737317  1737331  1737371  1737391  1737401
1737403  1737413  1737427  1737431  1737433  1737479  1737497  1737517  1737521  1737523
1737529  1737551  1737559  1737563  1737599  1737611  1737613  1737623  1737647  1737653
1737661  1737667  1737677  1737679  1737691  1737733  1737739  1737761  1737773  1737793
1737809  1737821  1737863  1737871  1737887  1737899  1737959  1737979  1737991  1738003
1738019  1738021  1738039  1738043  1738049  1738067  1738117  1738127  1738129  1738141
1738153  1738157  1738169  1738171  1738183  1738207  1738211  1738273  1738283  1738307
1738313  1738327  1738343  1738357  1738379  1738381  1738391  1738411  1738417  1738421
1738423  1738427  1738433  1738459  1738487  1738493  1738543  1738549  1738567  1738571
1738589  1738591  1738603  1738609  1738613  1738621  1738651  1738657  1738661  1738669
1738691  1738699  1738703  1738727  1738733  1738739  1738783  1738799  1738813  1738819
1738831  1738837  1738843  1738873  1738901  1738903  1738909  1738921  1738931  1738943
1738951  1738967  1738969  1738973  1738987  1738991  1738993  1739009  1739021  1739039
1739041  1739057  1739063  1739147  1739167  1739173  1739189  1739197  1739201  1739207
1739209  1739233  1739239  1739251  1739291  1739303  1739347  1739351  1739357  1739359
1739377  1739383  1739399  1739401  1739411  1739417  1739443  1739447  1739453  1739461
1739473  1739477  1739483  1739533  1739539  1739557  1739561  1739579  1739581  1739587
1739599  1739603  1739609  1739641  1739653  1739657  1739669  1739677  1739687  1739693
1739719  1739723  1739741  1739747  1739767  1739791  1739807  1739821  1739827  1739833
1739839  1739867  1739869  1739879  1739891  1739897  1739911  1739921  1739951  1739957
1739977  1739981  1740041  1740047  1740049  1740097  1740113  1740119  1740121  1740143
1740169  1740173  1740181  1740187  1740197  1740199  1740209  1740223  1740241  1740251
1740257  1740259  1740283  1740289  1740293  1740301  1740317  1740337  1740353  1740359
1740367  1740373  1740379  1740421  1740437  1740439  1740451  1740461  1740481  1740499
1740503  1740521  1740523  1740527  1740581  1740589  1740611  1740623  1740631  1740649
1740689  1740691  1740701  1740703  1740721  1740731  1740763  1740779  1740787  1740793
1740811  1740821  1740829  1740853  1740857  1740877  1740881  1740911  1740917  1740931
1740943  1740971  1741007  1741013  1741037  1741049  1741063  1741079  1741099  1741111
1741127  1741151  1741153  1741163  1741171  1741213  1741231  1741241  1741249  1741273
1741291  1741319  1741321  1741339  1741351  1741373  1741379  1741381  1741387  1741409
1741427  1741447  1741451  1741459  1741469  1741477  1741511  1741517  1741529  1741541
1741547  1741553  1741603  1741609  1741613  1741651  1741657  1741683  1741693  1741697
1741699  1741723  1741741  1741757  1741781  1741793  1741807  1741811  1741841  1741877
1741879  1741891  1741897  1741903  1741913  1741969  1741979  1742017  1742021  1742033
1742051  1742063  1742077  1742101  1742161  1742171  1742173  1742179  1742197  1742249
1742261  1742297  1742303  1742309  1742339  1742359  1742369  1742383  1742387  1742393
1742401  1742413  1742423  1742443  1742453  1742467  1742473  1742497  1742501  1742513
1742527  1742537  1742539  1742563  1742579  1742591  1742593  1742617  1742647  1742659
1742669  1742677  1742681  1742701  1742707  1742711  1742723  1742731  1742753  1742771
1742773  1742791  1742809  1742843  1742861  1742893  1742899  1742903  1742941  1742947
1742969  1742971  1742989  1742999  1743013  1743017  1743023  1743031  1743047  1743059
1743067  1743113  1743127  1743143  1743149  1743179  1743221  1743229  1743233  1743241
1743271  1743283  1743317  1743341  1743353  1743359  1743397  1743419  1743433  1743437
1743457  1743461  1743463  1743473  1743487  1743491  1743517  1743523  1743527  1743529
1743557  1743569  1743589  1743593  1743601  1743613  1743629  1743631  1743641  1743659
1743661  1743671  1743701  1743713  1743727  1743737  1743739  1743761  1743793  1743803
1743811  1743823  1743827  1743829  1743851  1743869  1743871  1743881  1743919  1743923
1743941  1743971  1744007  1744009  1744027  1744049  1744063  1744087  1744097  1744103
1744111  1744139  1744151  1744187  1744213  1744231  1744243  1744247  1744261  1744273
1744279  1744289  1744307  1744313  1744331  1744357  1744361  1744363  1744367  1744397
1744423  1744429  1744433  1744441  1744469  1744493  1744507  1744517  1744531  1744543
1744549  1744559  1744579  1744583  1744597  1744609  1744621  1744643  1744657  1744663
1744679  1744697  1744709  1744723  1744733  1744753  1744777  1744793  1744801  1744817
1744819  1744889  1744871  1744877  1744891  1744947  1744991  1744993  1745011  1745039
1745057  1745077  1745087  1745111  1745113  1745137  1745141  1745143  1745147  1745153
1745173  1745197  1745213  1745231  1745239  1745257  1745281  1745297  1745311  1745333
1745351  1745353  1745371  1745389  1745431  1745437  1745453  1745459  1745461  1745467
1745479  1745489  1745501  1745519  1745537  1745561  1745581  1745593  1745599  1745621
1745629  1745647  1745669  1745687  1745693  1745699  1745707  1745717  1745729  1745741
1745749  1745753  1745761  1745773  1745789  1745803  1745813  1745831  1745839  1745851
1745879  1745897  1745911  1745921  1745923  1745957  1745967  1745969  1745971  1746007
1746023  1746029  1746037  1746109  1746127  1746139  1746161  1746169  1746179  1746181
1746193  1746203  1746209  1746211  1746259  1746263  1746281  1746287  1746299  1746301
1746307  1746317  1746331  1746337  1746343  1746383  1746389  1746397  1746401  1746419
1746421  1746439  1746443  1746449  1746463  1746497  1746517  1746533  1746539  1746541
1746557  1746581  1746587  1746599  1746601  1746607  1746629  1746667  1746669  1746673
1746677  1746683  1746697  1746707  1746713  1746737  1746743  1746751  1746761  1746763
1746779  1746821  1746847  1746859  1746883  1746893  1746907  1746911  1746923  1746929
1746947  1746949  1746967  1746973  1746991  1747001  1747003  1747007  1747013  1747027
1747033  1747043  1747061  1747063  1747079  1747087  1747099  1747117  1747121  1747153
1747169  1747171  1747181  1747201  1747217  1747231  1747237  1747247  1747271  1747289
1747301  1747303  1747307  1747313  1747327  1747331  1747363  1747367  1747387  1747429
1747433  1747441  1747483  1747489  1747513  1747519  1747531  1747541  1747573  1747579
1747591  1747607  1747619  1747633  1747643  1747661  1747669  1747721  1747723  1747727
1747729  1747763  1747783  1747799  1747847  1747877  1747891  1747903  1747939  1747951
1747969  1747979  1747987  1748003  1748009  1748027  1748029  1748033  1748041  1748051
1748053  1748083  1748107  1748113  1748119  1748129  1748137  1748143  1748167  1748177
1748179  1748189  1748237  1748239  1748261  1748267  1748269  1748291  1748333  1748339
1748353  1748377  1748401  1748407  1748417  1748441  1748459  1748471  1748473  1748477
1748479  1748489  1748491  1748503  1748519  1748563  1748587  1748599  1748611  1748623
```

```
1748639  1748647  1748653  1748699  1748707  1748711  1748723  1748737  1748743  1748749
1748777  1748783  1748787  1748833  1748843  1748849  1748863  1748881  1748891  1748899
1748911  1748933  1748941  1748951  1748959  1748963  1748993  1749001  1749023  1749029
1749031  1749047  1749049  1749067  1749071  1749073  1749089  1749091  1749107  1749119
1749133  1749149  1749151  1749157  1749179  1749191  1749211  1749217  1749221  1749229
1749233  1749239  1749247  1749257  1749259  1749263  1749269  1749271  1749277  1749281
1749287  1749313  1749329  1749337  1749359  1749373  1749383  1749389  1749413  1749431
1749439  1749443  1749457  1749467  1749469  1749491  1749493  1749497  1749499  1749509
1749529  1749533  1749569  1749581  1749611  1749617  1749641  1749647  1749673  1749697
1749701  1749703  1749731  1749749  1749779  1749833  1749851  1749859  1749877  1749887
1749899  1749911  1749941  1749949  1749959  1749961  1749967  1749991  1750009  1750013
1750037  1750061  1750069  1750081  1750103  1750123  1750127  1750129  1750141  1750153
1750159  1750169  1750181  1750183  1750193  1750253  1750267  1750271  1750283  1750289
1750297  1750319  1750351  1750361  1750379  1750381  1750391  1750409  1750423  1750447
1750453  1750459  1750493  1750499  1750501  1750513  1750519  1750523  1750531  1750549
1750579  1750583  1750591  1750597  1750607  1750621  1750631  1750657  1750669  1750673
1750681  1750687  1750699  1750733  1750747  1750751  1750769  1750807  1750811  1750871
1750873  1750901  1750909  1750913  1750919  1750927  1750937  1750979  1750981  1750999
1751011  1751023  1751033  1751039  1751041  1751047  1751053  1751063  1751083  1751093
1751117  1751131  1751143  1751149  1751177  1751207  1751213  1751231  1751273  1751291
1751293  1751311  1751327  1751333  1751353  1751377  1751411  1751413  1751419  1751437
1751443  1751467  1751507  1751551  1751557  1751567  1751569  1751573  1751579  1751587
1751599  1751623  1751627  1751639  1751647  1751653  1751671  1751683  1751689  1751693
1751699  1751707  1751719  1751741  1751753  1751767  1751773  1751791  1751801  1751821
1751837  1751851  1751879  1751891  1751923  1751929  1751941  1751947  1751993  1752001
1752007  1752011  1752013  1752029  1752031  1752077  1752097  1752119  1752131  1752137
1752181  1752187  1752193  1752197  1752211  1752221  1752227  1752229  1752239  1752253
1752263  1752269  1752271  1752307  1752319  1752323  1752341  1752353  1752371  1752397
1752403  1752407  1752419  1752437  1752449  1752467  1752481  1752497  1752521  1752529
1752539  1752563  1752599  1752601  1752607  1752613  1752629  1752631  1752643  1752659
1752679  1752691  1752701  1752703  1752719  1752721  1752749  1752757  1752781  1752799
1752811  1752823  1752827  1752831  1752841  1752851  1752857  1752871  1752889  1752901
1752913  1752917  1752923  1752937  1752941  1752943  1752953  1752977  1752979  1752983
1753007  1753013  1753039  1753049  1753051  1753069  1753093  1753109  1753139  1753151
1753177  1753181  1753229  1753243  1753249  1753289  1753291  1753309  1753343  1753373
1753379  1753403  1753417  1753439  1753441  1753469  1753481  1753513  1753517
1753519  1753537  1753547  1753553  1753559  1753561  1753579  1753597  1753603  1753607
1753613  1753637  1753649  1753651  1753673  1753691  1753733  1753747  1753753  1753769
1753777  1753789  1753799  1753831  1753849  1753853  1753867  1753877  1753883  1753889
1753897  1753901  1753903  1753931  1753943  1753951  1753963  1753967  1753979  1753981
1753991  1754033  1754063  1754113  1754143  1754147  1754153  1754171  1754173  1754189
1754209  1754231  1754237  1754273  1754287  1754293  1754303  1754309  1754323  1754359
1754377  1754381  1754387  1754407  1754411  1754419  1754437  1754447  1754453  1754461
1754491  1754497  1754527  1754531  1754549  1754561  1754567  1754579  1754581  1754591
1754609  1754617  1754629  1754639  1754653  1754659  1754681  1754699  1754713  1754729
1754743  1754749  1754801  1754803  1754849  1754861  1754867  1754891  1754899
1754911  1754939  1754953  1754957  1754971  1755023  1755037  1755041  1755043  1755059
1755101  1755113  1755133  1755161  1755179  1755181  1755197  1755209  1755241  1755253
1755263  1755287  1755319  1755331  1755343  1755359  1755371  1755401  1755421  1755443
1755451  1755487  1755491  1755493  1755503  1755511  1755517  1755527  1755553  1755563
1755569  1755571  1755583  1755587  1755599  1755629  1755643  1755653  1755697  1755701
1755707  1755713  1755727  1755739  1755749  1755757  1755769  1755773  1755799  1755821
1755823  1755827  1755829  1755839  1755851  1755877  1755883  1755893  1755911  1755937
1755953  1755959  1756009  1756021  1756063  1756093  1756109  1756127  1756141  1756171
1756177  1756187  1756199  1756207  1756213  1756229  1756231  1756259  1756267  1756273
1756319  1756331  1756333  1756357  1756361  1756369  1756393  1756397  1756409
1756463  1756471  1756483  1756499  1756511  1756519  1756523  1756541  1756549  1756567
1756591  1756597  1756613  1756633  1756639  1756663  1756687  1756691  1756697  1756709
1756747  1756787  1756789  1756793  1756817  1756819  1756823  1756837  1756877  1756883
1756903  1756913  1756919  1756921  1756927  1756939  1756943  1756957  1756969  1756991
1756999  1757033  1757057  1757071  1757083  1757087  1757089  1757143  1757153  1757191
1757201  1757221  1757233  1757237  1757257  1757267  1757309  1757311  1757323  1757339
1757347  1757351  1757383  1757387  1757401  1757411  1757417  1757447  1757449  1757467
1757479  1757491  1757521  1757527  1757531  1757549  1757597  1757617  1757653  1757663
1757677  1757687  1757699  1757741  1757771  1757779  1757801  1757809  1757813  1757827
1757849  1757863  1757869  1757881  1757887  1757897  1757911  1757923  1757927  1757939
1757963  1757971  1757983  1757989  1757993  1757999  1758007  1758019  1758073  1758101
1758131  1758139  1758149  1758161  1758179  1758187  1758193  1758209  1758221  1758233
1758247  1758257  1758269  1758283  1758287  1758301  1758307  1758311  1758329  1758347
1758359  1758371  1758389  1758391  1758397  1758401  1758403  1758433  1758437  1758439
1758443  1758503  1758527  1758539  1758541  1758553  1758623  1758629  1758641  1758689
1758709  1758719  1758727  1758737  1758739  1758761  1758781  1758793  1758797  1758839
1758851  1758857  1758863  1758877  1758899  1758923  1758929  1758947  1758959
1758983  1758989  1758997  1759003  1759049  1759097  1759103  1759129  1759133  1759159
1759171  1759181  1759213  1759223  1759231  1759249  1759271  1759283  1759291  1759333
1759337  1759349  1759361  1759363  1759379  1759397  1759399  1759427  1759453  1759463
1759469  1759481  1759489  1759493  1759507  1759543  1759553  1759561  1759573  1759579
1759607  1759627  1759643  1759649  1759651  1759663  1759669  1759673  1759711  1759717
1759729  1759763  1759787  1759847  1759867  1759909  1759921  1759939  1759943  1759969
1759987  1759991  1760021  1760047  1760069  1760071  1760081  1760113  1760117  1760131
1760159  1760173  1760203  1760221  1760233  1760261  1760267  1760279  1760281  1760287
1760309  1760327  1760359  1760371  1760389  1760419  1760431  1760449  1760467  1760477
1760491  1760527  1760533  1760557  1760567  1760569  1760593  1760599  1760609  1760641
1760657  1760659  1760669  1760699  1760701  1760723  1760743  1760747  1760753  1760767
1760777  1760779  1760783  1760797  1760813  1760849  1760873  1760881  1760897  1760917
1760921  1760923  1760947  1760953  1760959  1760981  1761029  1761049  1761059  1761077
1761101  1761103  1761107  1761127  1761139  1761161  1761169  1761173  1761187  1761289
1761299  1761301  1761307  1761337  1761367  1761371  1761379  1761407  1761413  1761437
1761449  1761467  1761493  1761503  1761517  1761527  1761553  1761583  1761601  1761611
```

```
1761629  1761671  1761677  1761689  1761691  1761703  1761733  1761751  1761757  1761763
1761787  1761797  1761817  1761821  1761827  1761833  1761847  1761853  1761857  1761883
1761901  1761911  1761919  1761941  1761943  1761959  1761973  1761989  1762031  1762039
1762049  1762073  1762087  1762129  1762141  1762157  1762177  1762207  1762213  1762217
1762247  1762259  1762261  1762279  1762297  1762309  1762333  1762361  1762391  1762399
1762427  1762429  1762451  1762457  1762471  1762477  1762499  1762511  1762517  1762531
1762561  1762571  1762583  1762589  1762601  1762603  1762609  1762619  1762627  1762637
1762661  1762681  1762693  1762711  1762721  1762751  1762771  1762777  1762793  1762843
1762853  1762897  1762903  1762907  1762909  1762919  1762921  1762931  1762933  1762963
1762987  1762993  1763011  1763057  1763081  1763089  1763093  1763131  1763137  1763147
1763149  1763159  1763173  1763191  1763207  1763231  1763243  1763263  1763269  1763273
1763297  1763303  1763323  1763381  1763401  1763407  1763413  1763417  1763423  1763429
1763431  1763453  1763459  1763477  1763491  1763513  1763539  1763543  1763549  1763551
1763579  1763603  1763611  1763623  1763627  1763639  1763651  1763677  1763701  1763717
1763719  1763747  1763759  1763803  1763813  1763821  1763843  1763849  1763851  1763857
1763873  1763887  1763897  1763911  1763921  1763929  1763953  1763959  1763963  1763969
1763977  1763981  1764001  1764013  1764029  1764047  1764053  1764067  1764071  1764089
1764097  1764101  1764127  1764151  1764173  1764187  1764193  1764199  1764221  1764223
1764227  1764249  1764251  1764253  1764263  1764281  1764289  1764293  1764299  1764313
1764319  1764349  1764377  1764391  1764407  1764431  1764437  1764449  1764457  1764461
1764463  1764479  1764487  1764541  1764557  1764559  1764577  1764589  1764611  1764619
1764661  1764667  1764671  1764683  1764691  1764727  1764731  1764733  1764743  1764767
1764779  1764809  1764811  1764817  1764823  1764839  1764871  1764877  1764881  1764887
1764899  1764901  1764949  1764977  1764979  1765013  1765033  1765051  1765061  1765063
1765079  1765087  1765121  1765123  1765129  1765139  1765147  1765163  1765187  1765207
1765277  1765289  1765301  1765343  1765349  1765363  1765369  1765403  1765417  1765429
1765469  1765507  1765513  1765541  1765553  1765559  1765567  1765573  1765579  1765597
1765609  1765619  1765627  1765639  1765657  1765661  1765679  1765697  1765703  1765741
1765759  1765769  1765787  1765789  1765817  1765823  1765831  1765843  1765861  1765873
1765877  1765891  1765901  1765913  1765949  1765957  1765969  1765979  1765987  1765997
1765999  1766021  1766041  1766057  1766087  1766089  1766099  1766117  1766123  1766137
1766153  1766159  1766161  1766173  1766179  1766201  1766209  1766227  1766231  1766243
1766251  1766279  1766291  1766309  1766327  1766333  1766353  1766357  1766363  1766399
1766441  1766447  1766459  1766461  1766507  1766509  1766533  1766537  1766539  1766573
1766579  1766581  1766587  1766603  1766617  1766627  1766629  1766663  1766689  1766701
1766707  1766717  1766719  1766729  1766747  1766749  1766761  1766773  1766801  1766803
1766879  1766881  1766899  1766903  1766911  1766939  1766971  1767001  1767011  1767023
1767037  1767041  1767043  1767053  1767071  1767079  1767089  1767091  1767121  1767131
1767137  1767149  1767187  1767203  1767211  1767229  1767239  1767281  1767307  1767313
1767317  1767329  1767331  1767373  1767383  1767397  1767401  1767407  1767419  1767421
1767427  1767449  1767461  1767487  1767499  1767503  1767509  1767517  1767523  1767539
1767553  1767559  1767569  1767593  1767611  1767617  1767641  1767679  1767683  1767691
1767697  1767707  1767737  1767739  1767751  1767763  1767767  1767781  1767809  1767833
1767863  1767877  1767889  1767907  1767911  1767917  1767919  1767923  1767937  1767943
1767947  1767959  1767973  1767979  1768001  1768003  1768037  1768057  1768069  1768127
1768141  1768157  1768181  1768199  1768229  1768241  1768243  1768253  1768271  1768281
1768303  1768313  1768321  1768339  1768343  1768367  1768373  1768379  1768381  1768399
1768411  1768421  1768423  1768433  1768439  1768441  1768471  1768477  1768499  1768517
1768523  1768537  1768541  1768553  1768583  1768589  1768597  1768607  1768609  1768619
1768639  1768651  1768661  1768667  1768673  1768709  1768721  1768727  1768747  1768757
1768759  1768771  1768787  1768801  1768831  1768849  1768853  1768873  1768903  1768927
1768937  1768951  1768967  1768973  1768993  1769017  1769023  1769041  1769069  1769093
1769099  1769101  1769111  1769113  1769129  1769153  1769161  1769167  1769171  1769189
1769197  1769227  1769239  1769281  1769291  1769293  1769297  1769323  1769329  1769333
1769357  1769371  1769399  1769401  1769423  1769431  1769441  1769473  1769501  1769507
1769531  1769539  1769543  1769563  1769591  1769623  1769627  1769633  1769639  1769687
1769701  1769737  1769741  1769749  1769771  1769777  1769791  1769813  1769839  1769851
1769863  1769881  1769891  1769893  1769897  1769909  1769917  1769927  1769947  1769981
1769987  1770001  1770029  1770053  1770061  1770071  1770077  1770089  1770113  1770127
1770143  1770151  1770163  1770167  1770169  1770187  1770199  1770217  1770221  1770233
1770239  1770259  1770271  1770277  1770313  1770331  1770337  1770409  1770427  1770437
1770449  1770463  1770481  1770491  1770493  1770497  1770511  1770521  1770539  1770547
1770551  1770557  1770583  1770589  1770617  1770679  1770683  1770707  1770719  1770739
1770757  1770763  1770773  1770787  1770799  1770817  1770829  1770841  1770851  1770859
1770871  1770883  1770887  1770893  1770911  1770919  1770949  1770961  1770973  1770983
1770991  1770997  1771027  1771031  1771039  1771051  1771057  1771087  1771093  1771097
1771103  1771139  1771151  1771157  1771169  1771177  1771183  1771193  1771201  1771223
1771261  1771271  1771283  1771327  1771337  1771361  1771373  1771387  1771397  1771411
1771421  1771423  1771453  1771457  1771459  1771463  1771481  1771489  1771493  1771507
1771531  1771543  1771559  1771607  1771613  1771633  1771657  1771673  1771687  1771717
1771741  1771747  1771751  1771787  1771793  1771799  1771849  1771877  1771879  1771937
1771963  1771981  1771993  1771999  1772003  1772011  1772033  1772047  1772077  1772087
1772101  1772107  1772119  1772167  1772201  1772209  1772213  1772227  1772237  1772249
1772273  1772291  1772293  1772297  1772317  1772327  1772333  1772341  1772359  1772387
1772399  1772401  1772423  1772461  1772467  1772473  1772483  1772497  1772501  1772531
1772557  1772569  1772579  1772581  1772591  1772593  1772597  1772609  1772623  1772629
1772647  1772677  1772711  1772713  1772723  1772737  1772747  1772759  1772767  1772783
1772801  1772809  1772851  1772867  1772883  1772887  1772893  1772923  1772959  1772971
1772987  1772989  1772993  1773007  1773017  1773029  1773041  1773059  1773067  1773071
1773131  1773143  1773157  1773173  1773179  1773181  1773203  1773227  1773229  1773241
1773259  1773271  1773281  1773283  1773307  1773319  1773337  1773349  1773361  1773371
1773377  1773397  1773407  1773413  1773419  1773439  1773469  1773487  1773511  1773523
1773571  1773581  1773587  1773589  1773601  1773613  1773637  1773641  1773643  1773649
1773671  1773677  1773679  1773683  1773689  1773703  1773713  1773719  1773721  1773749
1773767  1773781  1773791  1773799  1773803  1773823  1773841  1773847  1773853  1773869
1773881  1773883  1773887  1773907  1773911  1773917  1773923  1773949  1773971  1773977
1773979  1773997  1774007  1774009  1774021  1774027  1774043  1774061  1774067  1774117
1774121  1774139  1774159  1774169  1774177  1774183  1774207  1774217  1774247  1774259
1774271  1774301  1774303  1774313  1774321  1774327  1774337  1774349  1774363  1774369
```

```
1774373  1774403  1774433  1774447  1774453  1774463  1774489  1774499  1774517  1774523
1774529  1774541  1774547  1774559  1774583  1774601  1774609  1774621  1774637  1774639
1774649  1774667  1774691  1774697  1774699  1774723  1774741  1774757  1774769  1774777
1774813  1774819  1774823  1774859  1774879  1774901  1774909  1774921  1774937  1774939
1774951  1774957  1774991  1775009  1775017  1775041  1775063  1775069           1775171
1775173  1775183  1775201  1775203  1775219  1775231  1775243  1775261  1775269  1775273
1775281  1775309  1775317  1775329  1775353  1775359  1775387  1775399  1775419  1775441
1775471  1775483  1775489  1775491  1775503  1775533  1775537  1775549  1775551  1775563
1775573  1775591  1775597  1775611  1775629  1775647  1775663  1775671  1775687  1775689
1775717  1775729  1775731  1775737  1775743  1775747  1775777  1775783  1775819  1775831
1775843  1775867  1775869  1775881  1775887  1775903  1775909  1775927  1775933  1775953
1775981  1776011  1776013  1776023  1776031  1776053  1776067  1776091  1776097  1776113
1776119  1776133  1776149  1776169  1776193  1776197  1776209  1776223  1776227  1776239
1776241  1776251  1776263  1776277  1776289  1776301  1776311  1776317  1776319  1776323
1776389  1776403  1776419  1776421  1776433  1776457  1776461  1776469  1776493  1776499
1776539  1776581  1776587  1776617  1776623  1776637  1776659  1776673  1776683  1776701
1776739  1776751  1776757  1776767  1776779  1776787  1776791  1776793  1776821  1776833
1776839  1776847  1776881  1776913  1776923  1776941  1776953  1776961  1776967  1776989
1776997  1777007  1777031  1777043  1777057  1777067  1777079  1777081  1777093  1777103
1777109  1777121  1777133  1777169  1777213  1777219  1777247  1777267  1777289  1777313
1777339  1777351  1777379  1777403  1777411  1777423  1777427  1777441  1777453  1777459
1777481  1777483  1777487  1777513  1777541  1777543  1777547  1777553  1777609  1777661
1777687  1777691  1777703  1777717  1777733  1777751  1777753  1777771  1777781  1777799
1777807  1777823  1777859  1777861  1777871  1777879  1777891  1777907  1777927  1777931
1777933  1777939  1777957  1777973  1777981  1778003  1778009  1778011  1778027  1778033
1778041  1778059  1778069  1778071  1778099  1778111  1778137  1778141  1778159  1778171
1778177  1778197  1778209  1778213  1778219  1778221  1778239  1778243  1778261  1778263
1778279  1778299  1778303  1778317  1778321  1778323  1778341  1778347  1778393  1778411
1778417  1778423  1778443  1778453  1778459  1778461  1778471  1778473  1778477  1778531
1778537  1778549  1778551  1778561  1778593  1778597  1778611  1778633  1778639  1778663
1778677  1778683  1778719  1778729  1778731  1778743  1778747  1778753  1778759  1778801
1778807  1778813  1778851  1778857  1778869  1778879  1778899  1778921  1778927  1778929
1778963  1778971  1778977  1778983  1778993  1779007  1779013  1779017  1779053  1779097
1779109  1779131  1779133  1779137  1779149  1779161  1779163  1779191  1779223  1779227
1779241  1779247  1779269  1779287  1779289  1779299  1779301  1779311  1779329  1779341
1779347  1779361  1779403  1779409  1779443  1779451  1779457  1779461  1779497  1779511
1779529  1779541  1779571  1779601  1779607  1779619  1779623  1779647  1779649  1779677
1779683  1779689  1779691  1779703  1779709  1779761  1779779  1779821  1779823  1779829
1779857  1779871  1779881  1779889  1779893  1779913  1779931  1779941           1779961
1779983  1780001  1780003  1780007  1780013  1780021  1780027  1780061  1780067  1780069
1780081  1780099  1780127  1780133  1780147  1780151  1780169  1780171  1780187  1780201
1780231  1780253  1780271  1780277  1780283  1780301  1780307  1780309  1780321  1780333
1780349  1780351  1780367  1780379  1780381  1780399  1780411  1780439  1780447  1780459
1780469  1780481  1780483  1780487  1780489  1780517  1780523           1780549  1780573
1780577  1780579  1780601  1780607  1780613  1780619  1780627  1780633  1780643  1780663
1780703  1780711  1780717  1780771  1780777  1780787  1780799  1780817  1780829  1780837
1780873  1780879  1780901  1780939  1780943  1780957  1780967  1780969  1781009  1781027
1781029  1781047  1781053  1781057  1781063  1781089  1781099  1781113  1781119  1781173
1781231  1781233  1781239  1781287  1781293  1781309  1781317  1781321  1781341  1781357
1781359  1781363  1781369  1781393  1781399  1781407  1781449  1781453  1781467  1781503
1781509  1781519  1781531  1781537  1781543  1781551  1781561  1781567  1781569  1781581
1781609  1781621  1781641  1781653  1781669  1781677  1781693  1781699  1781707  1781743
1781771  1781777  1781779  1781783  1781803  1781827  1781831  1781837  1781851  1781863
1781873  1781881  1781893  1781903  1781921  1781939  1781981  1782043  1782061  1782071
1782083  1782103  1782113  1782139  1782167  1782169  1782173  1782197  1782199  1782203
1782211  1782239  1782241  1782269  1782271  1782281  1782289  1782301  1782329  1782373
1782377  1782379  1782413  1782461  1782463  1782493  1782497  1782499  1782503  1782509
1782511  1782527  1782533  1782551  1782553  1782559  1782563  1782577  1782589  1782607
1782611  1782619  1782629  1782647  1782667  1782679  1782689  1782709  1782743  1782769
1782791  1782797  1782811  1782817  1782829  1782839  1782863  1782883  1782887  1782901
1782917  1782929  1782931  1782947  1782959  1782961  1782971  1782997  1783009  1783037
1783043  1783051  1783069  1783073  1783087  1783099  1783129  1783139  1783163  1783189
1783193  1783211  1783219  1783237  1783241  1783261  1783273  1783277  1783319  1783333
1783361  1783373  1783387  1783391  1783409  1783423  1783427  1783429  1783447  1783469
1783477  1783493  1783499  1783501  1783517  1783519  1783531  1783543  1783553  1783571
1783601  1783609  1783643  1783667  1783669  1783693  1783699  1783711           1783723
1783729  1783751  1783781  1783783  1783799  1783801  1783813  1783829  1783841  1783843
1783867  1783879  1783883  1783889  1783897  1783907  1783921  1783933  1783937  1783981
1784021  1784023  1784053  1784137  1784171  1784173  1784191  1784203  1784213  1784227
1784231  1784239  1784243  1784257  1784273  1784281  1784287  1784291  1784297  1784327
1784333  1784353  1784389  1784401  1784429  1784441  1784459  1784527  1784533  1784551
1784557  1784561  1784567  1784579  1784581  1784599  1784603  1784611  1784617  1784633
1784641  1784647  1784683  1784689  1784707  1784719  1784723  1784737  1784743
1784753  1784767  1784773  1784789  1784807  1784833  1784873  1784891  1784903  1784911
1784929  1784941  1784963  1784989  1784997  1785001  1785019  1785023  1785029
1785041  1785071  1785079  1785097  1785101  1785103  1785109  1785143  1785149  1785151
1785209  1785227  1785241  1785253  1785257  1785293  1785313  1785319  1785331  1785337
1785347  1785367  1785401  1785419  1785431  1785439  1785457  1785473  1785481  1785491
1785503  1785541  1785557  1785587  1785593  1785599  1785613  1785643  1785647  1785683
1785689  1785691  1785701  1785709  1785713  1785727  1785761  1785769  1785779  1785793
1785803  1785811  1785821  1785851  1785853  1785857  1785869  1785913  1785947  1785961
1785977  1786021  1786039  1786079  1786087  1786093  1786097  1786117  1786121  1786129
1786159  1786193  1786201  1786217  1786223  1786223  1786229  1786261  1786271  1786277
1786283  1786327  1786331  1786333  1786339  1786357  1786363  1786381  1786391  1786439
1786441  1786451  1786463  1786483  1786489  1786489  1786501  1786511  1786541
1786553  1786583  1786591  1786597  1786613  1786621  1786637  1786639  1786667  1786679
1786691  1786699  1786711  1786721  1786727  1786753  1786769  1786781  1786787  1786831
1786843  1786861  1786867  1786909  1786913  1786937  1786943  1786949  1786963  1786973
1786979  1786997  1787011  1787021  1787029  1787033  1787039  1787041  1787087  1787089
```

```
1787101  1787129  1787143  1787161  1787167  1787173  1787179  1787189  1787237  1787249
1787251  1787267  1787281  1787293  1787309  1787323  1787333  1787339  1787341  1787347
1787351  1787369  1787377  1787393  1787407  1787417  1787437  1787447  1787453  1787459
1787479  1787509  1787519  1787521  1787557  1787561  1787573  1787587  1787603  1787633
1787651  1787659  1787663  1787683  1787699  1787701  1787707  1787717  1787719  1787741
1787783  1787827  1787831  1787837  1787861  1787869  1787893  1787899  1787911  1787923
1787953  1788011  1788013  1788023  1788037  1788041  1788067  1788097  1788103  1788139
1788151  1788187  1788191  1788211  1788217  1788221  1788229  1788239  1788253  1788257
1788263  1788271  1788313  1788331  1788341  1788361  1788373  1788377  1788433  1788439
1788443  1788473  1788487  1788497  1788509  1788511  1788529  1788539  1788547  1788551
1788571  1788601  1788613  1788623  1788629  1788637  1788649  1788653  1788659  1788667
1788673  1788727  1788739  1788763  1788767  1788769  1788827  1788847  1788863  1788881
1788901  1788911  1788931  1788937  1788949  1788973  1788991  1789001  1789003  1789027
1789033  1789037  1789091  1789093  1789153  1789159  1789163  1789169  1789181  1789201
1789217  1789219  1789223  1789247  1789261  1789309  1789343  1789349  1789367  1789373
1789391  1789399  1789427  1789433  1789451  1789457  1789481  1789483  1789493  1789499
1789517  1789519  1789559  1789583  1789597  1789603  1789621  1789649  1789681  1789687
1789693  1789721  1789751  1789769  1789783  1789787  1789829  1789849  1789867  1789891
1789897  1789919  1789927  1789951  1789973  1789979  1789987  1789993  1789999  1790029
1790051  1790053  1790059  1790071  1790077  1790081  1790111  1790137  1790149  1790203
1790209  1790213  1790221  1790231  1790233  1790263  1790279  1790291  1790293  1790303
1790309  1790311  1790323  1790339  1790353  1790357  1790359  1790363  1790401  1790417
1790419  1790443  1790479  1790483  1790501  1790507  1790521  1790531  1790539  1790557
1790561  1790587  1790599  1790603  1790611  1790623  1790641  1790647  1790651  1790669
1790671  1790683  1790707  1790713  1790743  1790749  1790753  1790759  1790771  1790783
1790791  1790809  1790819  1790857  1790863  1790869  1790879  1790897  1790917  1790939
1790951  1790969  1790989  1791017  1791019  1791037  1791043  1791047  1791077  1791089
1791091  1791113  1791121  1791161  1791169  1791173  1791191  1791193  1791203  1791221
1791247  1791269  1791277  1791289  1791319  1791323  1791329  1791343  1791371  1791403
1791407  1791421  1791431  1791451  1791457  1791463  1791473  1791487  1791497  1791523
1791541  1791551  1791553  1791563  1791599  1791617  1791623  1791637  1791679  1791683
1791689  1791697  1791701  1791709  1791731  1791733  1791737  1791739  1791773  1791787
1791791  1791793  1791847  1791857  1791863  1791883  1791899  1791901  1791941  1791943
1791961  1791967  1791973  1791989  1791991  1792013  1792027  1792031  1792033  1792039
1792051  1792073  1792093  1792103  1792117  1792121  1792129  1792139  1792159  1792163
1792177  1792201  1792207  1792237  1792247  1792249  1792267  1792277  1792279  1792309
1792313  1792319  1792331  1792337  1792339  1792379  1792381  1792387  1792409  1792423
1792433  1792477  1792489  1792493  1792501  1792507  1792523  1792543  1792547  1792559
1792579  1792591  1792601  1792603  1792621  1792663  1792673  1792691  1792709  1792711
1792753  1792757  1792759  1792771  1792787  1792789  1792793  1792849  1792891  1792913
1792927  1792933  1792957  1792979  1792981  1792991  1793017  1793023  1793047  1793059
1793081  1793101  1793107  1793117  1793119  1793123  1793137  1793147  1793153  1793161
1793171  1793173  1793179  1793203  1793219  1793227  1793237  1793251  1793263  1793303
1793321  1793329  1793357  1793359  1793369  1793383  1793387  1793399  1793417  1793419
1793459  1793479  1793497  1793503  1793507  1793569  1793579  1793591  1793599  1793611
1793633  1793639  1793647  1793663  1793669  1793699  1793717  1793719  1793731  1793761
1793767  1793773  1793819  1793833  1793843  1793863  1793887  1793921  1793927  1793929
1793941  1793947  1793963  1793971  1793983  1793989  1794007  1794017  1794029  1794041
1794049  1794053  1794083  1794127  1794137  1794179  1794181  1794203  1794217  1794223
1794229  1794239  1794257  1794269  1794271  1794277  1794293  1794301  1794313  1794323
1794343  1794349  1794361  1794371  1794427  1794433  1794439  1794517  1794521  1794523
1794539  1794547  1794557  1794587  1794589  1794599  1794619  1794623  1794647  1794649
1794659  1794671  1794677  1794679  1794697  1794703  1794719  1794731  1794733  1794757
1794761  1794763  1794769  1794773  1794787  1794811  1794817  1794823  1794829  1794841
1794893  1794913  1794929  1794941  1794967  1794973  1794983  1795007  1795009  1795033
1795039  1795043  1795049  1795061  1795067  1795091  1795109  1795133  1795141
1795151  1795153  1795181  1795201  1795223  1795229  1795247  1795271  1795273  1795279
1795307  1795327  1795331  1795333  1795337  1795363  1795369  1795411  1795439  1795483
1795487  1795511  1795517  1795529  1795531  1795537  1795543  1795559  1795561  1795571
1795583  1795601  1795603  1795621  1795627  1795639  1795649  1795663  1795669  1795687
1795697  1795699  1795733  1795763  1795769  1795777  1795793  1795811  1795813  1795837
1795847  1795853  1795867  1795877  1795889  1795891  1795921  1795951  1795957  1795961
1795967  1795979  1795987  1795991  1796009  1796021  1796059  1796071  1796099  1796107
1796111  1796129  1796131  1796143  1796147  1796167  1796177  1796183  1796189  1796191
1796219  1796227  1796269  1796281  1796309  1796321  1796341  1796351  1796363  1796413
1796437  1796477  1796479  1796489  1796503  1796519  1796527  1796567  1796573  1796581
1796591  1796617  1796657  1796671  1796677  1796693  1796699  1796759  1796761  1796777
1796779  1796801  1796803  1796819  1796833  1796843  1796863  1796897  1796911  1796941
1796947  1796953  1796959  1796983  1796987  1797011  1797017  1797031  1797049  1797067
1797097  1797109  1797161  1797167  1797181  1797193  1797203  1797209  1797227  1797239
1797241  1797277  1797281  1797293  1797307  1797319  1797331  1797337  1797371  1797373
1797377  1797379  1797407  1797413  1797437  1797463  1797469  1797503  1797539  1797541
1797547  1797581  1797589  1797617  1797637  1797641  1797667  1797673  1797751  1797769
1797773  1797779  1797781  1797821  1797823  1797827  1797833  1797839  1797847  1797857
1797877  1797893  1797911  1797947  1797953  1797967  1798001  1798003  1798009  1798021
1798033  1798037  1798051  1798057  1798081  1798109  1798123  1798127  1798129  1798133
1798151  1798157  1798171  1798177  1798183  1798187  1798189  1798201  1798207  1798211
1798241  1798253  1798271  1798273  1798289  1798309  1798327  1798333  1798351  1798367
1798387  1798409  1798421  1798427  1798429  1798441  1798451  1798457  1798469  1798487
1798519  1798523  1798529  1798543  1798571  1798591  1798603  1798613  1798619  1798631
1798633  1798637  1798639  1798649  1798679  1798697  1798703  1798717  1798721  1798723
1798729  1798739  1798747  1798759  1798763  1798781  1798801  1798813  1798817  1798861
1798871  1798891  1798897  1798913  1798919  1798921  1798931  1798943  1798963  1798967
1798987  1798997  1798999  1799003  1799009  1799011  1799041  1799071  1799081  1799089
1799099  1799107  1799117  1799123  1799137  1799141  1799153  1799173  1799177  1799179
1799219  1799227  1799233  1799251  1799261  1799269  1799279  1799309  1799311  1799381
1799393  1799407  1799417  1799423  1799453  1799477  1799503  1799521  1799527  1799533
1799549  1799563  1799573  1799579  1799591  1799599  1799617  1799621  1799627  1799639
1799701  1799713  1799731  1799741  1799753  1799761  1799783  1799797  1799801  1799803
```

```
1799839 1799843 1799849 1799867 1799881 1799887 1799923 1799929 1799951 1799969
1799983 1799999 1800017 1800037 1800047 1800067 1800083 1800091 1800103 1800119
1800121 1800137 1800157 1800167 1800179 1800191 1800199 1800209 1800221 1800257
1800259 1800277 1800301 1800311 1800313 1800341 1800343 1800361 1800377 1800389
1800397 1800401 1800413 1800431 1800451 1800473 1800493 1800499 1800529 1800541
1800551 1800553 1800563 1800577 1800593 1800599 1800613 1800619 1800637 1800641
1800677 1800707 1800709 1800713 1800719 1800727 1800731 1800767 1800787 1800803
1800809 1800811 1800823 1800829 1800833 1800853 1800859 1800863 1800889 1800907
1800913 1800937 1800949 1800959 1800961 1800973 1800979 1801003 1801013 1801021
1801039 1801073 1801091 1801109 1801117 1801187 1801207 1801213 1801223 1801229
1801237 1801259 1801273 1801297 1801309 1801339 1801357 1801361 1801363 1801403
1801411 1801433 1801453 1801469 1801477 1801489 1801517 1801529 1801531 1801549
1801577 1801589 1801601 1801619 1801669 1801673 1801691 1801717 1801727 1801733
1801747 1801759 1801769 1801771 1801777 1801781 1801817 1801819 1801823 1801853
1801867 1801871 1801873 1801897 1801901 1801907 1801913 1801927 1801931 1801967
1801997 1802029 1802039 1802057 1802077 1802081 1802083 1802107 1802113 1802117
1802137 1802149 1802189 1802197 1802219 1802221 1802259 1802261 1802267 1802279
1802287 1802293 1802327 1802347 1802363 1802393 1802407 1802419 1802491 1802503
1802519 1802531 1802551 1802597 1802599 1802609 1802621 1802641 1802651 1802653
1802657 1802659 1802683 1802687 1802693 1802699 1802707 1802711 1802719 1802737
1802753 1802791 1802797 1802803 1802821 1802837 1802839 1802897 1802909 1802923
1802989 1803001 1803023 1803029 1803031 1803059 1803077 1803079 1803089 1803097
1803101 1803103 1803127 1803149 1803163 1803167 1803169 1803203 1803209 1803211
1803227 1803251 1803253 1803289 1803293 1803299 1803317 1803323 1803337 1803349
1803353 1803371 1803379 1803383 1803419 1803421 1803449 1803457 1803469 1803493
1803497 1803509 1803511 1803517 1803523 1803533 1803541 1803551 1803553 1803563
1803569 1803577 1803583 1803629 1803647 1803667 1803671 1803677 1803689 1803691
1803701 1803743 1803761 1803799 1803811 1803817 1803863 1803881 1803889 1803947
1803973 1804007 1804037 1804063 1804073 1804079 1804093 1804129 1804133
1804139 1804199 1804207 1804213 1804219 1804249 1804267 1804273 1804303 1804307
1804321 1804349 1804381 1804391 1804399 1804403 1804411 1804433 1804447 1804459
1804463 1804469 1804489 1804493 1804501 1804507 1804513 1804529 1804547
1804549 1804559 1804577 1804609 1804613 1804619 1804631 1804643 1804657 1804687
1804709 1804711 1804763 1804793 1804799 1804801 1804813 1804819 1804841 1804871
1804919 1804921 1804927 1804937 1804939 1804951 1804961 1804963 1804973 1804991
1804993 1804997 1805003 1805039 1805053 1805059 1805081 1805087 1805093 1805117
1805123 1805137 1805143 1805147 1805203 1805227 1805231 1805239 1805261 1805263
1805299 1805303 1805327 1805357 1805359 1805369 1805371 1805381 1805393 1805413
1805473 1805483 1805491 1805497 1805501 1805521 1805537 1805549 1805561 1805579
1805581 1805591 1805593 1805597 1805603 1805633 1805641 1805651 1805653 1805663
1805701 1805707 1805729 1805747 1805761 1805767 1805773 1805789 1805819 1805821
1805827 1805833 1805857 1805863 1805873 1805879 1805887 1805897 1805911 1805941
1805963 1805989 1806001 1806011 1806017 1806023 1806031 1806041 1806059 1806061
1806097 1806107 1806113 1806137 1806143 1806151 1806191 1806193 1806209 1806221
1806223 1806227 1806241 1806247 1806251 1806263 1806269 1806281 1806313 1806331
1806341 1806347 1806353 1806361 1806373 1806379 1806383 1806407 1806421 1806461
1806479 1806487 1806491 1806499 1806503 1806509 1806527 1806533 1806551 1806557
1806569 1806589 1806617 1806631 1806643 1806683 1806689 1806697 1806703 1806713
1806733 1806769 1806781 1806797 1806803 1806839 1806841 1806859 1806863 1806869
1806877 1806887 1806899 1806901 1806941 1806943 1806953 1806971 1806977 1807027
1807037 1807061 1807063 1807067 1807093 1807097 1807121 1807129 1807153 1807171
1807177 1807187 1807189 1807199 1807213 1807231 1807237 1807243 1807249 1807277
1807297 1807301 1807313 1807327 1807357 1807361 1807387 1807391 1807397 1807439
1807469 1807483 1807493 1807499 1807511 1807513 1807537 1807543 1807549 1807571
1807577 1807607 1807609 1807633 1807643 1807691 1807693 1807697 1807711 1807723
1807733 1807759 1807769 1807781 1807801 1807811 1807829 1807837 1807853 1807867
1807891 1807903 1807909 1807913 1807921 1807943 1807957 1807963 1807969 1807987
1807997 1807999 1808003 1808017 1808029 1808033 1808039 1808041 1808071 1808077
1808083 1808099 1808117 1808119 1808161 1808167 1808207 1808243 1808269 1808281
1808293 1808297 1808309 1808327 1808377 1808399 1808431 1808453 1808459 1808479
1808491 1808493 1808497 1808501 1808507 1808539 1808543 1808557 1808561 1808567
1808581 1808617 1808627 1808669 1808683 1808687 1808699 1808707 1808713 1808761
1808767 1808773 1808801 1808803 1808813 1808831 1808843 1808863 1808869 1808887
1808923 1808951 1808959 1808969 1808977 1808981 1808993 1809029 1809079
1809083 1809091 1809097 1809113 1809121 1809133 1809149 1809163 1809167 1809169
1809193 1809211 1809217 1809227 1809229 1809233 1809271 1809277
1809287 1809299 1809319 1809323 1809331 1809349 1809373 1809383 1809391 1809403
1809419 1809421 1809449 1809469 1809481 1809487 1809491 1809517 1809523
1809527 1809529 1809539 1809551 1809553 1809557 1809581 1809583 1809601 1809631
1809671 1809673 1809683 1809751 1809757 1809763 1809767 1809793 1809799 1809823
1809833 1809851 1809853 1809859 1809869 1809881 1809887 1809901 1809911 1809937
1809949 1809953 1809967 1809971 1809979 1809991 1810001 1810013 1810033 1810043
1810057 1810063 1810069 1810087 1810097 1810129 1810153 1810199 1810213 1810217
1810219 1810241 1810243 1810247 1810253 1810271 1810283 1810309 1810337 1810357
1810363 1810397 1810409 1810421 1810423 1810439 1810451 1810469 1810477
1810481 1810507 1810511 1810531 1810553 1810561 1810573 1810577 1810579 1810597
1810603 1810607 1810609 1810649 1810667 1810693 1810709 1810723 1810733 1810747
1810751 1810771 1810799 1810819 1810867 1810877 1810889 1810931 1810937
1810967 1810969 1810973 1810979 1810981 1810999 1811041 1811053 1811059 1811071
1811081 1811083 1811107 1811119 1811141 1811167 1811179 1811209 1811219 1811287
1811291 1811297 1811321 1811323 1811347 1811353 1811357 1811371 1811377 1811387
1811389 1811413 1811431 1811443 1811473 1811489 1811507 1811519 1811527 1811533
1811539 1811561 1811567 1811569 1811603 1811617 1811647 1811651 1811657 1811681
1811683 1811723 1811731 1811737 1811743 1811759 1811767 1811791 1811819 1811827
1811837 1811851 1811867 1811893 1811899 1811903 1811923 1811939 1811959 1811983
1811987 1811993 1812037 1812053 1812059 1812061 1812073 1812089 1812091 1812103
1812121 1812131 1812137 1812157 1812199 1812227 1812233 1812263 1812269 1812271
1812301 1812311 1812341 1812347 1812359 1812361 1812379 1812383 1812401 1812403
1812409 1812431 1812439 1812443 1812449 1812457 1812509 1812511 1812527 1812541
```

1812553	1812563	1812571	1812589	1812611	1812623	1812661	1812673	1812677	1812683
1812689	1812721	1812749	1812763	1812773	1812793	1812817	1812821	1812823	1812827
1812851	1812869	1812871	1812907	1812917	1812947	1812949	1812959	1812983	1812989
1813001	1813003	1813039	1813073	1813081	1813121	1813139	1813157	1813177	1813211
1813219	1813223	1813277	1813291	1813313	1813319	1813321	1813327	1813337	1813351
1813367	1813369	1813387	1813391	1813421	1813429	1813447	1813459	1813477	1813499
1813517	1813523	1813547	1813561	1813579	1813583	1813597	1813613	1813627	1813639
1813667	1813673	1813681	1813699	1813729	1813739	1813741	1813751	1813789	1813793
1813813	1813817	1813829	1813843	1813853	1813897	1813901	1813913	1813937	1813939
1813943	1813961	1813969	1813991	1813993	1814003	1814011	1814023	1814039	1814047
1814051	1814069	1814083	1814107	1814117	1814119	1814129	1814143	1814161	1814167
1814179	1814233	1814237	1814261	1814279	1814311	1814339	1814347	1814357	1814363
1814377	1814381	1814383	1814413	1814429	1814431	1814453	1814459	1814467	1814473
1814507	1814509	1814531	1814543	1814569	1814573	1814581	1814599	1814609	1814611
1814639	1814641	1814651	1814653	1814669	1814693	1814713	1814719	1814737	1814749
1814753	1814759	1814777	1814803	1814807	1814809	1814819	1814821	1814843	1814851
1814909	1814921	1814927	1814929	1814951	1814993	1815001	1815007	1815017	1815043
1815053	1815061	1815083	1815101	1815103	1815131	1815179	1815199	1815217	1815221
1815223	1815251	1815259	1815269	1815271	1815287	1815301	1815323	1815337	1815343
1815347	1815349	1815353	1815361	1815377	1815383	1815389	1815397	1815403	1815427
1815449	1815461	1815467	1815491	1815497	1815509	1815523	1815533	1815547	1815557
1815559	1815587	1815599	1815629	1815631	1815637	1815647	1815673	1815691	1815703
1815707	1815731	1815733	1815739	1815799	1815809	1815817	1815823	1815839	1815841
1815859	1815871	1815881	1815883	1815889	1815907	1815911	1815917	1815941	1815943
1815959	1815977	1816007	1816027	1816051	1816063	1816069	1816091	1816099	1816117
1816121	1816141	1816147	1816159	1816187	1816189	1816193	1816207	1816211	1816237
1816247	1816253	1816261	1816271	1816279	1816301	1816337	1816387	1816403	1816411
1816421	1816429	1816439	1816453	1816489	1816511	1816523	1816543	1816553	1816559
1816567	1816583	1816613	1816627	1816643	1816651	1816679	1816699	1816729	1816769
1816777	1816783	1816813	1816831	1816849	1816853	1816861	1816901	1816933	1816949
1816957	1816963	1816979	1816987	1817009	1817041	1817063	1817077	1817083	1817087
1817093	1817099	1817131	1817149	1817159	1817177	1817197	1817213	1817261	1817267
1817269	1817273	1817279	1817281	1817303	1817311	1817327	1817341	1817383	1817393
1817399	1817411	1817447	1817449	1817471	1817507	1817513	1817533	1817539	1817549
1817581	1817603	1817611	1817663	1817677	1817687	1817689	1817701	1817707	1817737
1817779	1817789	1817791	1817801	1817821	1817843	1817859	1817863	1817873	1817891
1817909	1817947	1817969	1817987	1817999	1818013	1818017	1818023	1818049	1818067
1818077	1818079	1818107	1818109	1818151	1818161	1818163	1818199	1818209	1818221
1818233	1818241	1818247	1818293	1818307	1818317	1818331	1818347	1818353	1818373
1818379	1818407	1818409	1818413	1818419	1818431	1818437	1818451	1818457	1818469
1818499	1818521	1818527	1818529	1818533	1818539	1818559	1818569	1818577	1818611
1818617	1818631	1818647	1818667	1818689	1818703	1818721	1818727	1818743	1818769
1818781	1818787	1818799	1818833	1818871	1818919	1818923	1818931	1818937	1818977
1818979	1818989	1818991	1819007	1819043	1819057	1819061	1819063	1819067	1819109
1819123	1819151	1819157	1819183	1819189	1819217	1819261	1819271	1819273	1819283
1819333	1819339	1819343	1819361	1819381	1819387	1819393	1819397	1819409	1819423
1819471	1819481	1819487	1819513	1819523	1819541	1819577	1819583	1819591	1819603
1819637	1819651	1819667	1819679	1819693	1819709	1819711	1819723	1819729	1819739
1819747	1819751	1819757	1819759	1819781	1819819	1819841	1819843	1819847	1819849
1819871	1819879	1819891	1819913	1819931	1819933	1819957	1819999	1820009	1820023
1820033	1820051	1820057	1820087	1820089	1820111	1820123	1820129	1820153	1820171
1820201	1820213	1820237	1820249	1820261	1820267	1820279	1820281	1820293	1820303
1820311	1820339	1820341	1820347	1820353	1820387	1820389	1820407	1820419	1820431
1820449	1820461	1820471	1820501	1820509	1820521	1820527	1820549	1820551	1820557
1820573	1820579	1820597	1820617	1820629	1820633	1820641	1820647	1820669	1820671
1820677	1820699	1820701	1820711	1820737	1820743	1820747	1820759	1820773	1820783
1820809	1820813	1820821	1820837	1820843	1820857	1820869	1820891	1820899	1820927
1820947	1820957	1820969	1820977	1820983	1820999	1821013	1821019	1821037	1821067
1821101	1821107	1821121	1821137	1821139	1821151	1821167	1821181	1821191	1821233
1821257	1821263	1821289	1821311	1821319	1821331	1821353	1821371	1821373	1821377
1821401	1821409	1821427	1821433	1821481	1821487	1821497	1821509	1821541	1821551
1821553	1821571	1821583	1821613	1821641	1821649	1821679	1821691	1821707	1821709
1821713	1821731	1821733	1821749	1821763	1821779	1821791	1821821	1821847	1821857
1821871	1821877	1821893	1821913	1821923	1821943	1821959	1821997	1822003	1822013
1822019	1822021	1822027	1822063	1822091	1822109	1822123	1822147	1822169	1822181
1822187	1822189	1822207	1822217	1822229	1822241	1822259	1822277	1822307	1822319
1822321	1822367	1822391	1822393	1822411	1822427	1822439	1822441	1822463	1822477
1822481	1822487	1822493	1822501	1822517	1822529	1822547	1822559	1822571	1822577
1822633	1822637	1822649	1822661	1822663	1822669	1822673	1822693	1822703	1822781
1822787	1822811	1822823	1822837	1822867	1822871	1822903	1822907	1822939	1822943
1822963	1822967	1822981	1822999	1823009	1823011	1823021	1823023	1823047	1823051
1823053	1823057	1823077	1823093	1823099	1823117	1823119	1823123	1823149	1823153
1823179	1823189	1823191	1823197	1823207	1823219	1823231	1823257	1823281	1823287
1823291	1823293	1823303	1823357	1823377	1823383	1823401	1823407	1823413	1823429
1823431	1823443	1823447	1823483	1823489	1823531	1823533	1823537	1823543	1823567
1823579	1823581	1823599	1823603	1823609	1823617	1823621	1823659	1823663	1823669
1823671	1823681	1823683	1823687	1823713	1823719	1823729	1823737	1823771	1823779
1823797	1823813	1823827	1823837	1823849	1823863	1823903	1823911	1823953	1823957
1823963	1823993	1823999	1824001	1824007	1824037	1824041	1824047	1824073	1824077
1824113	1824139	1824143	1824167	1824169	1824227	1824239	1824259	1824269	1824271
1824281	1824289	1824307	1824331	1824341	1824349	1824353	1824367	1824371	1824373
1824379	1824391	1824397	1824401	1824409	1824421	1824451	1824461	1824463	1824467
1824479	1824481	1824499	1824523	1824539	1824577	1824583	1824601	1824607	1824611
1824649	1824673	1824677	1824679	1824689	1824701	1824707	1824721	1824727	1824731
1824743	1824749	1824761	1824773	1824827	1824829	1824839	1824841	1824847	1824857
1824859	1824871	1824881	1824887	1824917	1824919	1824943	1824947	1824959	1824971
1824973	1824989	1824997	1825003	1825039	1825079	1825081	1825129	1825139	1825141
1825157	1825163	1825169	1825177	1825183	1825193	1825207	1825217	1825261	1825277
1825297	1825309	1825319	1825331	1825333	1825337	1825357	1825379	1825381	1825391

```
1825403  1825429  1825451  1825457  1825459  1825489  1825493  1825513  1825517  1825531
1825553  1825591  1825597  1825601  1825627  1825631  1825661  1825667  1825673  1825679
1825687  1825693  1825699  1825711  1825723  1825739  1825757  1825781  1825787  1825819
1825829  1825861  1825867  1825871  1825883  1825891  1825897  1825933  1825937  1825963
1825969  1826003  1826023  1826047  1826051  1826059  1826063  1826093  1826107  1826113
1826119  1826129  1826137  1826141  1826161  1826171  1826173  1826183  1826189  1826197
1826207  1826239  1826257  1826281  1826291  1826311  1826323  1826329  1826371  1826389
1826399  1826411  1826417  1826423  1826443  1826459  1826477  1826491  1826501  1826519
1826521  1826537  1826543  1826549  1826557  1826563  1826567  1826609  1826611  1826639
1826651  1826659  1826687  1826689  1826711  1826723  1826743  1826753  1826761  1826771
1826777  1826807  1826819  1826849  1826863  1826873  1826879  1826887  1826893  1826897
1826899  1826917  1826933  1826947  1826969  1826977  1826987  1826999  1827017  1827071
1827101  1827103  1827107  1827127  1827139  1827151  1827179  1827181  1827193  1827197
1827209  1827227  1827229  1827253  1827257  1827269  1827271  1827277  1827283  1827307
1827311  1827337  1827341  1827361  1827367  1827379  1827389  1827421  1827431  1827479
1827487  1827509  1827533  1827563  1827583  1827589  1827593  1827613  1827647  1827659
1827673  1827697  1827703  1827731  1827733  1827737  1827751  1827757  1827767  1827773
1827779  1827799  1827803  1827809  1827817  1827829  1827863  1827869  1827901  1827929
1827937  1827949  1827953  1827983  1828003  1828019  1828051  1828069  1828093  1828117
1828121  1828153  1828193  1828217  1828223  1828243  1828249  1828259  1828271  1828273
1828279  1828283  1828291  1828301  1828303  1828319  1828331  1828361  1828373  1828381
1828397  1828399  1828423  1828433  1828439  1828451  1828471  1828481  1828487  1828499
1828501  1828507  1828517  1828531  1828543  1828549  1828583  1828591  1828601  1828609
1828627  1828633  1828637  1828649  1828663  1828667  1828669  1828681  1828691  1828703
1828709  1828727  1828759  1828763  1828781  1828789  1828793  1828829  1828831  1828847
1828867  1828901  1828903  1828933  1828973  1828993  1828999  1829011  1829017  1829027
1829041  1829057  1829089  1829119  1829137  1829141  1829143  1829171  1829197  1829203
1829209  1829221  1829227  1829249  1829257  1829281  1829293  1829299  1829309  1829389
1829417  1829441  1829447  1829449  1829473  1829479  1829483  1829497  1829501  1829519
1829533  1829537  1829549  1829551  1829563  1829579  1829587  1829609  1829617  1829621
1829623  1829629  1829647  1829671  1829683  1829699  1829701  1829717  1829743  1829747
1829753  1829759  1829771  1829777  1829797  1829801  1829803  1829827  1829831  1829843
1829873  1829879  1829911  1829923  1829959  1829963  1830011  1830013  1830029  1830047
1830053  1830071  1830077  1830079  1830083  1830089  1830113  1830119  1830163  1830181
1830211  1830223  1830253  1830263  1830287  1830307  1830319  1830331  1830337  1830341
1830343  1830347  1830349  1830379  1830391  1830401  1830419  1830421  1830431  1830443
1830469  1830481  1830511  1830523  1830533  1830539  1830557  1830559  1830571  1830583
1830589  1830599  1830613  1830617  1830623  1830629  1830637  1830659  1830677  1830701
1830733  1830739  1830749  1830757  1830817  1830833  1830839  1830863  1830887  1830889
1830901  1830911  1830923  1830931  1830943  1830967  1830971  1830977  1831001  1831003
1831009  1831021  1831021  1831033  1831051  1831079  1831103  1831111  1831127  1831129
1831133  1831153  1831169  1831171  1831187  1831211  1831243  1831253  1831267  1831273
1831289  1831307  1831331  1831339  1831343  1831369  1831373  1831381  1831399  1831411
1831441  1831447  1831451  1831469  1831477  1831481  1831483  1831493  1831507  1831517
1831523  1831589  1831591  1831601  1831633  1831667  1831673  1831679  1831681  1831693
1831703  1831723  1831741  1831747  1831751  1831783  1831787  1831799  1831807  1831811
1831831  1831849  1831853  1831861  1831867  1831877  1831909  1831913  1831933  1831939
1831967  1831969  1831979  1831987  1831993  1832011  1832029  1832057  1832063  1832071
1832093  1832099  1832119  1832123  1832137  1832143  1832147  1832177  1832179  1832183
1832197  1832213  1832219  1832221  1832239  1832251  1832261  1832279  1832291  1832293
1832309  1832329  1832333  1832353  1832371  1832377  1832381  1832393  1832407  1832419
1832459  1832461  1832471  1832477  1832497  1832513  1832543  1832561  1832629  1832641
1832653  1832657  1832669  1832681  1832693  1832707  1832711  1832719  1832819  1832833
1832839  1832851  1832861  1832863  1832881  1832927  1832933  1832947  1832969  1832977
1832983  1833001  1833019  1833023  1833067  1833079  1833089  1833113  1833121  1833131
1833137  1833157  1833163  1833173  1833179  1833257  1833259  1833269  1833317  1833319
1833341  1833343  1833347  1833383  1833389  1833401  1833427  1833431  1833437  1833439
1833451  1833457  1833473  1833487  1833509  1833521  1833523  1833527  1833529  1833551
1833571  1833613  1833631  1833647  1833653  1833673  1833677  1833679  1833697
1833701  1833731  1833737  1833749  1833751  1833761  1833763  1833781  1833787  1833803
1833809  1833817  1833851  1833863  1833883  1833911  1833919  1833947  1833961  1833983
1834031  1834033  1834037  1834039  1834067  1834069  1834099  1834109  1834111  1834117
1834139  1834141  1834153  1834159  1834193  1834199  1834207  1834229  1834237  1834243
1834253  1834303  1834307  1834309  1834321  1834333  1834373  1834397  1834403  1834421
1834429  1834433  1834439  1834447  1834451  1834477  1834501  1834513  1834523  1834597
1834601  1834603  1834607  1834619  1834631  1834639  1834643  1834663  1834667  1834669
1834717  1834727  1834741  1834747  1834751  1834753  1834757  1834783  1834799  1834813
1834831  1834879  1834883  1834901  1834907  1834909  1834919  1834967  1834969  1834981
1834991  1834993  1834999  1835003  1835017  1835027  1835051  1835081  1835083  1835087
1835117  1835129  1835131  1835161  1835177  1835189  1835227  1835257  1835263  1835291
1835297  1835299  1835321  1835329  1835333  1835359  1835363  1835399  1835401  1835411
1835413  1835453  1835461  1835467  1835501  1835527  1835557  1835569  1835573  1835591
1835593  1835633  1835651  1835657  1835689  1835737  1835741  1835753  1835767  1835797
1835809  1835819  1835839  1835861  1835863  1835879  1835909  1835921  1835923  1835941
1835947  1835957  1835969  1835993  1836011  1836031  1836041  1836047  1836053  1836059
1836061  1836073  1836091  1836151  1836157  1836239  1836259  1836271  1836277  1836287
1836299  1836301  1836319  1836379  1836383  1836413  1836427  1836433  1836437  1836449
1836461  1836467  1836473  1836479  1836511  1836517  1836539  1836553  1836563  1836581
1836623  1836641  1836647  1836689  1836691  1836727  1836733  1836761  1836763  1836797
1836811  1836827  1836839  1836853  1836911  1836929  1836931  1836937  1836943  1836949
1836959  1836971  1836973  1836979  1837007  1837009  1837027  1837061  1837067  1837097
1837103  1837117  1837123  1837127  1837151  1837159  1837181  1837189  1837223  1837249
1837271  1837273  1837289  1837313  1837349  1837361  1837379  1837387  1837391  1837393
1837397  1837399  1837427  1837453  1837477  1837481  1837489  1837529  1837541  1837573
1837601  1837607  1837621  1837639  1837657  1837663  1837681  1837687  1837709  1837727
1837729  1837733  1837739  1837741  1837763  1837789  1837831  1837837  1837867  1837873
1837879  1837903  1837919  1837931  1837937  1837943  1837961  1837967  1837973  1837981
1838033  1838047  1838051  1838063  1838069  1838087  1838101  1838131  1838141  1838143
1838167  1838173  1838191  1838203  1838209  1838233  1838237  1838257  1838297  1838299
```

```
1838327  1838341  1838371  1838377  1838401  1838407  1838423  1838429  1838453  1838461
1838519  1838521  1838527  1838531  1838549  1838569  1838587  1838591  1838621  1838659
1838671  1838693  1838717  1838719  1838741  1838743  1838747  1838761  1838773  1838791
1838807  1838813  1838819  1838843  1838869  1838909  1838911  1838923  1838933  1838957
1838983  1838987  1838989  1838999  1839001  1839059  1839073  1839091  1839121  1839127
1839133  1839169  1839203  1839221  1839283  1839293  1839317  1839329  1839347  1839353
1839359  1839361  1839373  1839377  1839401  1839413  1839427  1839433  1839449  1839457
1839463  1839469  1839473  1839479  1839491  1839493  1839511  1839559  1839589  1839601
1839611  1839631  1839647  1839653  1839659  1839667  1839671  1839697  1839727  1839737
1839743  1839763  1839767  1839769  1839787  1839809  1839833  1839853  1839857  1839907
1839911  1839913  1839919  1839923  1839947  1839949  1839953  1839967  1839983  1839991
1839997  1840019  1840031  1840043  1840049  1840051  1840057  1840073  1840087  1840109
1840117  1840123  1840171  1840183  1840219  1840231  1840259  1840261  1840297  1840313
1840327  1840331  1840337  1840351  1840393  1840429  1840441  1840453  1840457  1840459
1840469  1840493  1840519  1840537  1840541  1840561  1840577  1840591  1840603  1840633
1840649  1840651  1840669  1840673  1840679  1840697  1840703  1840711  1840723  1840733
1840747  1840771  1840781  1840789  1840829  1840843  1840847  1840871  1840877  1840921
1840939  1840957  1840961  1840973  1841003  1841011  1841039  1841057  1841069  1841071
1841087  1841089  1841107  1841111  1841113  1841141  1841153  1841171  1841201  1841221
1841237  1841249  1841251  1841261  1841267  1841291  1841293  1841299  1841317  1841327
1841339  1841377  1841383  1841387  1841401  1841429  1841443  1841447  1841473  1841479
1841513  1841519  1841531  1841557  1841579  1841599  1841603  1841621  1841639  1841641
1841657  1841659  1841681  1841699  1841701  1841711  1841713  1841759  1841779  1841783
1841821  1841837  1841849  1841857  1841869  1841891  1841911  1841923  1841929  1841941
1841947  1841951  1841969  1842011  1842023  1842041  1842067  1842073  1842079  1842083
1842097  1842101  1842131  1842133  1842151  1842161  1842173  1842187  1842199  1842229
1842233  1842251  1842263  1842287  1842289  1842293  1842311  1842317  1842329  1842349
1842377  1842391  1842413  1842419  1842431  1842469  1842473  1842479  1842481  1842493
1842497  1842509  1842523  1842527  1842539  1842551  1842557  1842569  1842583  1842587
1842611  1842619  1842641  1842661  1842667  1842703  1842719  1842727  1842767  1842769
1842779  1842781  1842793  1842803  1842809  1842811  1842829  1842847  1842853  1842877
1842887  1842889  1842899  1842901  1842913  1842931  1842941  1842949  1842961  1842977
1842989  1843003  1843027  1843033  1843063  1843067  1843087  1843091  1843099  1843111
1843117  1843129  1843139  1843141  1843147  1843159  1843169  1843183  1843189  1843201
1843207  1843213  1843217  1843241  1843253  1843273  1843277  1843313  1843321  1843349
1843357  1843421  1843423  1843433  1843447  1843487  1843489  1843493  1843511  1843537
1843547  1843549  1843561  1843571  1843579  1843591  1843607  1843619  1843631  1843643
1843649  1843687  1843697  1843753  1843757  1843771  1843783  1843789  1843801  1843823
1843843  1843859  1843867  1843889  1843901  1843909  1843943  1843949  1843967  1843981
1843993  1843997  1843999  1844021  1844027  1844033  1844039  1844077  1844093  1844099
1844111  1844119  1844123  1844131  1844153  1844179  1844189  1844201  1844207  1844243
1844257  1844263  1844287  1844291  1844299  1844317  1844329  1844333  1844341  1844357
1844369  1844377  1844383  1844411  1844417  1844441  1844473  1844477  1844497  1844503
1844519  1844527  1844537  1844567  1844569  1844581  1844617  1844641  1844659  1844677
1844681  1844683  1844707  1844723  1844737  1844741  1844747  1844749  1844813  1844819
1844827  1844837  1844863  1844867  1844889  1844917  1844923  1844939  1844963  1844971
1844977  1844981  1844987  1845017  1845023  1845029  1845047  1845049  1845073  1845119
1845133  1845139  1845143  1845149  1845157  1845161  1845167  1845187  1845199  1845209
1845211  1845229  1845271  1845289  1845293  1845307  1845317  1845331  1845353  1845373
1845379  1845419  1845421  1845427  1845457  1845463  1845491  1845499  1845509  1845521
1845539  1845541  1845551  1845559  1845563  1845577  1845581  1845583  1845601  1845611
1845637  1845713  1845719  1845721  1845731  1845751  1845757  1845769  1845791  1845827
1845829  1845881  1845901  1845913  1845919  1845931  1845941  1845959  1846001
1846037  1846057  1846063  1846067  1846073  1846079  1846093  1846099  1846121  1846129
1846139  1846153  1846157  1846171  1846177  1846181  1846219  1846223  1846231  1846241
1846253  1846261  1846283  1846289  1846297  1846321  1846331  1846333  1846357  1846367
1846373  1846379  1846393  1846399  1846441  1846457  1846469  1846487  1846511  1846529
1846547  1846549  1846561  1846567  1846571  1846609  1846613  1846619  1846631  1846643
1846657  1846673  1846703  1846711  1846729  1846751  1846769  1846777  1846811  1846837
1846843  1846847  1846861  1846879  1846903  1846909  1846913  1846921  1846939
1846951  1846963  1846967  1846993  1847023  1847051  1847071  1847093  1847117  1847129
1847143  1847149  1847179  1847221  1847233  1847239  1847243  1847267  1847273  1847281
1847297  1847303  1847309  1847327  1847333  1847341  1847347  1847353  1847357  1847359
1847369  1847381  1847393  1847401  1847413  1847423  1847431  1847471  1847473  1847477
1847513  1847537  1847539  1847563  1847591  1847603  1847609  1847623  1847627  1847641
1847647  1847653  1847687  1847689  1847701  1847737  1847767  1847777  1847779  1847789
1847803  1847809  1847827  1847831  1847861  1847863  1847869  1847887  1847897  1847903
1847929  1847933  1847969  1847971  1847983  1847999  1848013  1848023  1848029  1848031
1848043  1848103  1848107  1848151  1848167  1848169  1848193  1848221  1848227  1848233
1848241  1848247  1848277  1848281  1848289  1848311  1848323  1848331  1848337  1848347
1848367  1848397  1848439  1848443  1848449  1848467  1848503  1848551  1848569  1848577
1848589  1848593  1848599  1848607  1848617  1848641  1848667  1848673  1848677  1848697
1848713  1848751  1848787  1848787  1848811  1848823  1848827  1848841  1848859  1848863
1848877  1848907  1848919  1848923  1848929  1848943  1848949  1848983  1848997  1849013
1849021  1849037  1849049  1849051  1849063  1849079  1849087  1849091  1849097  1849103
1849109  1849147  1849151  1849171  1849189  1849201  1849207  1849217  1849229
1849231  1849241  1849259  1849271  1849273  1849279  1849283  1849291  1849319  1849333
1849349  1849357  1849381  1849391  1849399  1849423  1849453  1849457  1849459  1849457
1849483  1849487  1849493  1849511  1849513  1849577  1849579  1849609  1849643  1849663
1849681  1849691  1849699  1849711  1849721  1849723  1849733  1849751  1849759  1849811
1849829  1849831  1849843  1849847  1849849  1849853  1849877  1849909  1849919  1849921
1849973  1849979  1850021  1850029  1850033  1850041  1850053  1850089  1850119  1850129
1850131  1850141  1850159  1850179  1850227  1850243  1850257  1850267  1850269  1850279
1850293  1850309  1850341  1850347  1850357  1850369  1850413  1850423  1850441  1850447
1850489  1850491  1850503  1850509  1850521  1850561  1850573  1850587  1850593  1850609
1850633  1850687  1850689  1850701  1850749  1850759  1850767  1850789  1850803  1850831
1850837  1850839  1850843  1850887  1850939  1850941  1850951  1850969  1850987  1851019
1851023  1851029  1851043  1851071  1851077  1851089  1851097  1851119  1851127  1851133
1851139  1851163  1851173  1851203  1851217  1851253  1851259  1851271  1851287  1851299
```

```
1851301  1851313  1851319  1851329  1851337  1851349  1851359  1851371  1851373  1851391
1851401  1851403  1851407  1851433  1851457  1851463  1851469  1851491  1851503  1851511
1851539  1851541  1851547  1851557  1851559  1851571  1851581  1851587  1851611  1851637
1851643  1851649  1851667  1851671  1851677  1851701  1851719  1851727  1851749  1851757
1851761  1851763  1851769  1851779  1851781  1851803  1851809  1851821  1851841  1851851
1851859  1851869  1851877  1851901  1851907  1851917  1851919  1851931  1851953  1851973
1851991  1852003  1852009  1852013  1852049  1852051  1852057  1852073  1852079  1852087
1852091  1852111  1852153  1852159  1852163  1852171  1852181  1852189  1852211  1852217
1852241  1852243  1852247  1852261  1852271  1852273  1852283  1852289  1852307  1852327
1852363  1852373  1852393  1852427  1852429  1852447  1852451  1852457  1852469  1852493
1852511  1852523  1852559  1852579  1852597  1852601  1852621  1852637  1852649  1852663
1852679  1852681  1852699  1852703  1852727  1852771  1852789  1852793  1852817
1852819  1852843  1852859  1852909  1852951  1852957  1852969  1852973  1852987  1853011
1853053  1853063  1853081  1853083  1853107  1853161  1853167  1853177  1853183  1853191
1853207  1853209  1853231  1853239  1853263  1853281  1853309  1853321  1853329  1853333
1853339  1853377  1853381  1853387  1853399  1853443  1853447  1853461  1853471  1853479
1853483  1853497  1853503  1853513  1853549  1853557  1853563  1853581  1853587  1853591
1853611  1853617  1853627  1853641  1853647  1853669  1853671  1853701  1853711  1853713
1853723  1853743  1853749  1853771  1853779  1853789  1853801  1853807  1853809
1853857  1853861  1853879  1853927  1853939  1853947  1853977  1853987  1854011  1854019
1854029  1854067  1854089  1854101  1854109  1854113  1854119  1854131  1854157  1854163
1854179  1854187  1854211  1854227  1854233  1854247  1854257  1854269  1854271
1854277  1854299  1854313  1854317  1854331  1854337  1854341  1854353  1854373  1854379
1854383  1854407  1854409  1854439  1854487  1854491  1854497  1854527  1854529  1854563
1854599  1854607  1854613  1854617  1854623  1854653  1854659  1854661  1854673  1854679
1854689  1854701  1854703  1854709  1854731  1854739  1854763  1854769  1854781  1854791
1854793  1854833  1854851  1854859  1854863  1854883  1854889  1854893  1854899  1854907
1854911  1854917  1854943  1854971  1854991  1854997  1855001  1855013  1855031  1855033
1855039  1855093  1855097  1855099  1855109  1855123  1855153  1855169  1855171  1855187
1855207  1855211  1855219  1855229  1855237  1855247  1855253  1855267  1855279  1855303
1855307  1855313  1855327  1855349  1855361  1855393  1855411  1855421  1855423  1855457
1855463  1855501  1855517  1855519  1855523  1855531  1855541  1855549  1855577  1855589
1855591  1855603  1855613  1855621  1855627  1855649  1855687  1855697  1855723  1855729
1855741  1855747  1855757  1855759  1855769  1855807  1855811  1855813  1855817  1855823
1855849  1855853  1855891  1855921  1855927  1855933  1855949  1855951  1855961  1855969
1855981  1855993  1855999  1856003  1856017  1856021  1856027  1856033  1856039
1856059  1856069  1856083  1856089  1856119  1856137  1856147  1856149  1856159  1856191
1856201  1856207  1856221  1856227  1856233  1856237  1856269  1856287  1856293  1856297
1856303  1856333  1856339  1856347  1856363  1856411  1856419  1856441  1856443  1856507
1856513  1856581  1856599  1856639  1856651  1856713  1856719  1856747  1856753  1856759
1856773  1856801  1856819  1856821  1856837  1856843  1856857  1856861  1856891  1856903
1856909  1856917  1856941  1856947  1856963  1856969  1856971  1856983  1856989  1856999
1857001  1857049  1857091  1857101  1857109  1857113  1857139  1857151  1857157  1857161
1857169  1857197  1857203  1857209  1857217  1857257  1857281  1857283  1857287  1857293
1857313  1857343  1857347  1857353  1857371  1857377  1857391  1857407  1857439  1857461
1857473  1857481  1857509  1857517  1857521  1857533  1857547  1857553  1857577  1857589
1857593  1857599  1857617  1857671  1857673  1857677  1857679  1857689  1857701  1857707
1857719  1857731  1857761  1857767  1857773  1857797  1857803  1857829  1857859  1857887
1857893  1857899  1857929  1857931  1857941  1857949  1857959  1857967  1857971  1857979
1858007  1858033  1858057  1858061  1858081  1858091  1858093  1858133  1858139  1858163
1858169  1858183  1858187  1858189  1858201  1858211  1858217  1858249  1858261  1858267
1858279  1858303  1858309  1858313  1858319  1858343  1858369  1858403  1858421  1858433
1858469  1858529  1858531  1858537  1858541  1858553  1858573  1858579  1858583  1858603
1858613  1858631  1858643  1858651  1858663  1858669  1858691  1858693  1858711  1858721
1858733  1858739  1858741  1858757  1858807  1858819  1858823  1858849  1858861  1858867
1858873  1858889  1858919  1858921  1858931  1858937  1858957  1858973  1858999  1859009
1859023  1859041  1859057  1859071  1859083  1859087  1859111  1859119  1859141  1859167
1859173  1859177  1859197  1859201  1859203  1859233  1859243  1859269  1859279  1859281
1859311  1859323  1859327  1859329  1859353  1859369  1859387  1859441  1859453  1859467
1859471  1859479  1859489  1859491  1859497  1859513  1859519  1859521  1859531  1859537
1859551  1859563  1859569  1859603  1859609  1859617  1859629  1859633  1859639  1859651
1859653  1859677  1859687  1859699  1859771  1859779  1859813  1859827  1859831  1859843
1859863  1859881  1859899  1859911  1859917  1859927  1859933  1859983  1859999  1860007
1860013  1860017  1860037  1860059  1860071  1860083  1860097  1860109  1860127  1860139
1860143  1860163  1860179  1860181  1860193  1860197  1860251  1860253  1860277  1860281
1860289  1860301  1860337  1860343  1860359  1860373  1860377  1860407  1860421  1860427
1860431  1860449  1860479  1860503  1860517  1860533  1860559  1860569  1860571  1860581
1860583  1860629  1860641  1860643  1860647  1860659  1860679  1860707  1860709
1860721  1860731  1860737  1860743  1860757  1860763  1860799  1860821  1860829  1860847
1860851  1860853  1860857  1860869  1860877  1860893  1860923  1860941  1860967  1860977
1860979  1860983  1861001  1861009  1861019  1861021  1861033  1861039  1861061  1861081
1861103  1861121  1861141  1861151  1861157  1861187  1861219  1861253  1861261  1861267
1861303  1861309  1861331  1861337  1861339  1861351  1861397  1861403  1861417  1861469
1861471  1861493  1861501  1861511  1861543  1861547  1861567  1861579  1861583  1861589
1861591  1861621  1861631  1861637  1861649  1861661  1861663  1861697  1861709  1861711
1861747  1861751  1861757  1861759  1861787  1861807  1861817  1861831  1861859  1861861
1861879  1861889  1861897  1861913  1861921  1861927  1861961  1861973  1861991  1862009
1862017  1862023  1862081  1862087  1862101  1862111  1862123  1862141  1862153  1862213
1862219  1862221  1862227  1862233  1862243  1862249  1862251  1862279  1862297  1862317
1862341  1862359  1862381  1862383  1862407  1862411  1862417  1862429  1862447  1862477
1862489  1862501  1862519  1862521  1862561  1862587  1862591  1862593  1862611  1862621
1862633  1862647  1862659  1862669  1862683  1862687  1862711  1862737  1862761  1862797
1862837  1862851  1862869  1862891  1862909  1862923  1862933  1862947  1862953
1862957  1862981  1862983  1863011  1863041  1863049  1863053  1863067  1863073  1863077
1863089  1863091  1863101  1863107  1863151  1863157  1863181  1863223  1863229  1863241
1863247  1863263  1863269  1863271  1863307  1863313  1863331  1863347  1863361  1863371
1863377  1863401  1863403  1863413  1863451  1863457  1863461  1863473  1863479  1863481
1863493  1863497  1863509  1863517  1863527  1863541  1863559  1863581  1863583  1863593
1863601  1863607  1863613  1863637  1863647  1863649  1863671  1863677  1863683  1863707
```

```
1863721  1863731  1863769  1863779  1863787  1863811  1863839  1863853  1863857  1863871
1863877  1863889  1863893  1863899  1863913  1863923  1863929  1863941  1863971  1863997
1864001  1864003  1864039  1864043  1864069  1864087  1864111  1864117  1864151  1864153
1864189  1864217  1864241  1864253  1864259  1864267  1864297  1864307  1864361  1864363
1864391  1864399  1864417  1864427  1864453  1864463  1864469  1864483  1864507  1864517
1864529  1864547  1864549  1864553  1864559  1864567  1864571  1864589  1864591  1864601
1864649  1864657  1864661  1864691  1864693  1864703  1864711  1864739  1864769  1864783
1864789  1864801  1864823  1864847  1864853  1864859  1864861  1864871  1864873  1864879
1864897  1864901  1864921  1864939  1864979  1864987  1865011  1865023  1865027  1865057
1865063  1865069  1865081  1865107  1865119  1865137  1865141  1865147  1865159  1865161
1865179  1865203  1865221  1865233  1865243  1865261  1865263  1865267  1865299  1865321
1865327  1865329  1865333  1865341  1865371  1865389  1865399  1865411  1865417  1865419
1865431  1865443  1865447  1865453  1865467  1865471  1865489  1865491  1865509  1865527
1865533  1865537  1865543  1865551  1865561  1865569  1865573  1865579  1865587  1865603
1865609  1865659  1865671  1865681  1865687  1865693  1865711  1865719  1865729  1865791
1865821  1865827  1865837  1865839  1865849  1865863  1865881  1865887  1865893  1865911
1865917  1865939  1865957  1865959  1865987  1865999  1866001  1866019  1866031  1866037
1866043  1866049  1866083  1866091  1866101  1866113  1866127  1866131  1866143  1866191
1866203  1866211  1866223  1866233  1866239  1866247  1866251  1866269  1866281  1866283
1866301  1866307  1866331  1866341  1866343  1866349  1866367  1866373  1866409  1866437
1866439  1866451  1866457  1866461  1866467  1866499  1866517  1866521  1866547  1866551
1866569  1866577  1866593  1866637  1866649  1866659  1866677  1866679  1866721  1866737
1866751  1866757  1866779  1866827  1866833  1866847  1866857  1866859  1866863  1866869
1866871  1866901  1866941  1866961  1866967  1866971  1866973  1866989  1867001
1867003  1867009  1867013  1867039  1867051  1867069  1867079  1867109  1867123  1867147
1867157  1867183  1867193  1867211  1867213  1867219  1867231  1867237  1867241  1867249
1867253  1867259  1867303  1867319  1867321  1867337  1867343  1867351  1867367  1867373
1867421  1867423  1867429  1867469  1867477  1867553  1867573  1867597  1867601  1867609
1867631  1867651  1867693  1867709  1867711  1867717  1867727  1867729  1867751  1867753
1867769  1867771  1867783  1867787  1867799  1867813  1867819  1867823  1867847  1867849
1867867  1867883  1867897  1867907  1867913  1867927  1867949  1867951  1867969  1867973
1867979  1867993  1868017  1868033  1868039  1868051  1868057  1868059  1868063  1868107
1868149  1868159  1868173  1868179  1868183  1868189  1868201  1868231  1868239  1868257
1868261  1868287  1868291  1868309  1868333  1868371  1868381  1868387  1868407  1868423
1868443  1868459  1868483  1868501  1868513  1868519  1868527  1868533  1868549  1868561
1868567  1868569  1868591  1868599  1868617  1868627  1868639  1868641  1868663  1868677
1868687  1868693  1868701  1868717  1868719  1868723  1868747  1868749  1868753  1868777
1868807  1868813  1868837  1868843  1868851  1868863  1868879  1868917  1868947  1868983
1868987  1868989  1869029  1869041  1869053  1869071  1869073  1869097  1869113  1869139
1869169  1869173  1869181  1869191  1869193  1869199  1869209  1869221  1869227  1869251
1869271  1869293  1869299  1869319  1869341  1869379  1869383  1869389  1869403  1869407
1869419  1869433  1869443  1869449  1869487  1869521  1869529  1869547  1869551  1869563
1869577  1869617  1869631  1869649  1869691  1869709  1869719  1869731  1869737  1869757
1869761  1869793  1869823  1869839  1869853  1869859  1869871  1869929  1869949  1869953
1869971  1869991  1870019  1870021  1870049  1870067  1870079  1870097  1870103  1870111
1870117  1870129  1870139  1870147  1870159  1870163  1870207  1870213  1870223  1870229
1870247  1870249  1870259  1870279  1870307  1870327  1870343  1870361  1870369  1870373
1870381  1870399  1870403  1870411  1870433  1870441  1870469  1870499  1870507  1870511
1870541  1870577  1870591  1870597  1870601  1870619  1870639  1870643  1870651  1870667
1870669  1870709  1870711  1870717  1870723  1870733  1870777  1870783  1870787  1870793
1870807  1870829  1870853  1870859  1870861  1870879  1870907  1870919  1870927  1870933
1870951  1870961  1870991  1871017  1871021  1871029  1871039  1871057  1871081  1871083
1871099  1871113  1871137  1871147  1871153  1871171  1871183  1871213  1871249  1871263
1871279  1871293  1871321  1871327  1871339  1871351  1871383  1871413  1871417  1871437
1871447  1871449  1871459  1871461  1871473  1871477  1871491  1871503  1871509  1871531
1871543  1871549  1871561  1871591  1871603  1871621  1871627  1871629  1871641  1871651
1871669  1871677  1871693  1871699  1871711  1871713  1871743  1871777  1871783  1871789
1871813  1871827  1871839  1871843  1871851  1871879  1871917  1871923  1871927  1871929
1871951  1871957  1871981  1871983  1872001  1872007  1872043  1872049  1872097  1872109
1872113  1872137  1872149  1872173  1872217  1872229  1872239  1872253  1872259  1872271
1872281  1872287  1872289  1872301  1872313  1872319  1872323  1872337  1872389  1872419
1872421  1872427  1872461  1872463  1872473  1872491  1872503  1872529  1872547  1872553
1872557  1872569  1872581  1872587  1872589  1872623  1872631  1872667  1872671  1872691
1872713  1872721  1872727  1872743  1872751  1872763  1872769  1872799  1872817  1872841
1872847  1872859  1872889  1872911  1872919  1872929  1872943  1872953  1872971  1873013
1873019  1873021  1873031  1873049  1873057  1873093  1873099  1873111  1873133  1873141
1873147  1873159  1873163  1873171  1873181  1873211  1873217  1873219  1873231  1873271
1873283  1873297  1873307  1873321  1873337  1873357  1873367  1873373  1873409  1873411
1873433  1873441  1873471  1873499  1873507  1873513  1873517  1873523  1873541  1873549
1873567  1873583  1873589  1873607  1873633  1873637  1873657  1873679  1873681  1873687
1873699  1873721  1873727  1873769  1873771  1873783  1873831  1873849  1873867  1873877
1873889  1873967  1873969  1873979  1874003  1874021  1874039  1874051  1874083  1874099
1874101  1874107  1874111  1874143  1874153  1874177  1874189  1874207  1874209  1874261
1874263  1874303  1874311  1874317  1874351  1874377  1874387  1874399  1874417  1874441
1874443  1874449  1874461  1874491  1874503  1874513  1874527  1874549  1874599  1874603
1874611  1874623  1874627  1874629  1874633  1874657  1874659  1874669  1874699  1874723
1874729  1874759  1874767  1874791  1874797  1874819  1874833  1874837  1874839  1874857
1874869  1874881  1874893  1874903  1874921  1874923  1874941  1874953  1874959  1874987
1874993  1875007  1875011  1875037  1875043  1875059  1875061  1875067  1875073  1875077
1875103  1875109  1875131  1875143  1875149  1875161  1875163  1875173  1875179  1875191
1875229  1875233  1875239  1875241  1875277  1875311  1875317  1875331  1875337  1875361
1875371  1875373  1875403  1875427  1875431  1875439  1875449  1875451  1875479  1875481
1875487  1875499  1875521  1875529  1875541  1875553  1875557  1875569  1875583  1875611
1875619  1875677  1875683  1875707  1875743  1875751  1875773  1875793  1875803  1875821
1875833  1875859  1875869  1875877  1875883  1875901  1875931  1875943  1875947  1875959
1875971  1875977  1875983  1875989  1875997  1876009  1876019  1876057  1876073  1876081
1876093  1876109  1876123  1876129  1876157  1876163  1876169  1876181  1876183  1876187
1876211  1876223  1876241  1876247  1876249  1876261  1876267  1876289  1876291  1876309
1876327  1876331  1876333  1876339  1876367  1876373  1876379  1876403  1876417  1876451
```

```
1876453  1876481  1876499  1876507  1876513  1876517  1876519  1876541  1876549  1876559
1876597  1876607  1876627  1876631  1876643  1876667  1876669  1876697  1876703  1876711
1876717  1876733  1876741  1876747  1876781  1876807  1876829  1876841  1876859  1876949
1876951  1876999  1877003  1877009  1877011  1877017  1877023  1877033  1877041  1877059
1877069  1877077  1877087  1877107  1877111  1877137  1877147  1877159  1877171  1877177
1877179  1877189  1877209  1877221  1877231  1877233  1877243  1877261  1877279  1877297
1877299  1877303  1877347  1877353  1877357  1877363  1877389  1877399  1877401  1877443
1877459  1877461  1877471  1877479  1877483  1877501  1877503  1877521  1877573  1877609
1877621  1877669  1877671  1877683  1877693  1877717  1877723  1877741  1877753  1877761
1877773  1877797  1877801  1877819  1877833  1877839  1877857  1877873  1877891  1877917
1877933  1877951  1877959  1877977  1877983  1878013  1878043  1878047  1878049  1878053
1878059  1878061  1878089  1878091  1878119  1878139  1878181  1878187  1878193  1878199
1878209  1878221  1878223  1878229  1878257  1878263  1878277  1878281  1878287  1878293
1878299  1878319  1878323  1878353  1878367  1878389  1878403  1878419  1878421  1878431
1878439  1878451  1878463  1878491  1878493  1878553  1878557  1878559  1878563  1878577
1878581  1878593  1878623  1878629  1878641  1878659  1878677  1878683  1878689  1878697
1878733  1878757  1878769  1878781  1878791  1878803  1878827  1878839  1878841  1878869
1878883  1878887  1878889  1878911  1878913  1878931  1878949  1878977  1878979  1878991
1879049  1879067  1879069  1879079  1879099  1879103  1879109  1879121  1879151  1879187
1879211  1879243  1879253  1879279  1879291  1879301  1879351  1879357  1879363  1879379
1879387  1879391  1879421  1879429  1879439  1879453  1879459  1879463  1879477  1879511
1879517  1879523  1879543  1879567  1879589  1879597  1879601  1879607  1879621  1879643
1879663  1879723  1879729  1879781  1879789  1879807  1879811  1879817  1879847  1879849
1879873  1879897  1879901  1879909  1879921  1879931  1879937  1879939  1879949  1879961
1879967  1880017  1880023  1880027  1880093  1880111  1880117  1880129  1880159  1880167
1880189  1880201  1880209  1880233  1880257  1880267  1880287  1880309  1880321  1880323
1880327  1880339  1880341  1880357  1880363  1880369  1880381  1880401  1880413  1880441
1880467  1880497  1880509  1880513  1880521  1880537  1880551  1880561  1880573  1880581
1880597  1880603  1880633  1880647  1880653  1880657  1880663  1880689  1880701  1880707
1880729  1880741  1880789  1880803  1880807  1880819  1880831  1880833  1880839  1880843
1880849  1880869  1880881  1880887  1880899  1880903  1880909  1880929  1880933  1880939
1880941  1880947  1880951  1880959  1880971  1880993  1881031  1881037  1881041  1881071
1881079  1881083  1881109  1881119  1881127  1881151  1881157  1881161  1881163  1881181
1881197  1881199  1881211  1881221  1881223  1881241  1881263  1881277  1881289  1881307
1881311  1881329  1881343  1881349  1881389  1881391  1881401  1881403  1881419  1881431
1881461  1881463  1881479  1881493  1881499  1881511  1881521  1881533  1881559  1881587
1881601  1881617  1881619  1881631  1881641  1881697  1881749  1881751  1881757  1881767
1881769  1881787  1881799  1881811  1881821  1881823  1881851  1881853  1881863  1881881
1881889  1881899  1881907  1881937  1881949  1881961  1881983  1881989  1882009  1882031
1882037  1882039  1882051  1882063  1882073  1882081  1882099  1882117  1882141  1882147
1882163  1882169  1882171  1882183  1882207  1882221  1882229  1882247  1882253  1882259
1882271  1882313  1882319  1882327  1882367  1882369  1882403  1882409  1882417  1882421
1882429  1882453  1882457  1882459  1882469  1882471  1882519  1882541  1882561  1882579
1882589  1882607  1882667  1882681  1882703  1882717  1882721  1882747  1882781  1882787
1882823  1882861  1882877  1882891  1882921  1882939  1882963  1882997  1883003  1883017
1883023  1883027  1883047  1883051  1883053  1883083  1883113  1883129  1883153  1883177
1883183  1883191  1883197  1883201  1883207  1883213  1883227  1883237  1883257  1883267
1883279  1883293  1883317  1883341  1883351  1883359  1883363  1883369  1883377  1883381
1883389  1883393  1883407  1883429  1883459  1883471  1883477  1883491  1883501
1883503  1883513  1883533  1883551  1883573  1883599  1883611  1883621  1883627  1883639
1883647  1883659  1883669  1883671  1883689  1883699  1883731  1883737  1883743  1883759
1883773  1883857  1883879  1883881  1883939  1883941  1883969  1883971  1883989  1883993
1884007  1884011  1884013  1884053  1884061  1884083  1884109  1884119  1884121  1884133
1884193  1884199  1884209  1884221  1884227  1884247  1884293  1884313  1884341  1884343
1884347  1884353  1884359  1884409  1884427  1884437  1884451  1884461  1884469  1884479
1884481  1884503  1884517  1884523  1884527  1884529  1884539  1884563  1884577  1884587
1884593  1884599  1884601  1884607  1884611  1884677  1884679  1884713  1884721  1884731
1884791  1884793  1884799  1884803  1884809  1884821  1884829  1884833  1884853  1884927
1884881  1884887  1884889  1884901  1884907  1884917  1884923  1884947  1884973  1885007
1885021  1885033  1885043  1885069  1885151  1885153  1885159  1885171  1885183  1885201
1885207  1885243  1885253  1885259  1885267  1885277  1885291  1885307  1885309
1885321  1885339  1885349  1885363  1885381  1885391  1885393  1885423  1885439  1885459
1885469  1885489  1885501  1885519  1885523  1885529  1885553  1885561  1885567  1885573
1885577  1885601  1885603  1885607  1885613  1885619  1885627  1885633  1885649  1885673
1885703  1885711  1885717  1885729  1885733  1885753  1885757  1885789  1885801  1885811
1885847  1885859  1885867  1885879  1885907  1885909  1885913  1885943  1885979  1885981
1885991  1885993  1886011  1886021  1886029  1886047  1886051  1886081  1886107  1886113
1886119  1886153  1886173  1886179  1886197  1886231  1886233  1886237  1886243  1886267
1886279  1886293  1886317  1886327  1886329  1886347  1886351  1886389  1886411  1886413
1886447  1886449  1886459  1886471  1886503  1886509  1886513  1886527  1886543  1886557
1886561  1886569  1886611  1886623  1886657  1886659  1886663  1886671  1886693  1886699
1886701  1886723  1886743  1886749  1886777  1886783  1886809  1886821  1886849  1886867
1886869  1886887  1886901  1886903  1886917  1886923  1886957  1886981  1886993  1886999
1887013  1887019  1887029  1887049  1887071  1887079  1887091  1887103  1887113  1887131
1887133  1887143  1887161  1887167  1887169  1887181  1887199  1887209  1887211  1887217
1887229  1887247  1887253  1887283  1887307  1887341  1887359  1887409  1887419  1887421
1887433  1887437  1887443  1887451  1887463  1887499  1887511  1887521  1887539  1887563
1887569  1887577  1887607  1887617  1887619  1887637  1887643  1887659  1887667  1887671
1887713  1887719  1887727  1887737  1887749  1887757  1887773  1887797  1887803  1887811
1887857  1887877  1887883  1887917  1887923  1887941  1887947  1887967  1888031  1888063
1888069  1888079  1888097  1888121  1888123  1888129  1888151  1888157  1888169  1888171
1888189  1888193  1888199  1888213  1888217  1888223  1888247  1888253  1888267  1888279
1888283  1888301  1888307  1888333  1888349  1888351  1888361  1888399  1888409  1888421
1888441  1888457  1888463  1888483  1888487  1888559  1888561  1888571  1888597  1888609
1888633  1888651  1888673  1888723  1888727  1888753  1888759  1888763  1888769  1888793
1888807  1888837  1888841  1888849  1888879  1888887  1888907  1888919  1888927  1888933
1888963  1888979  1888981  1889009  1889011  1889029  1889039  1889051  1889053  1889077
1889081  1889087  1889099  1889101  1889117  1889131  1889143  1889177  1889191  1889201
1889213  1889219  1889221  1889267  1889273  1889287  1889309  1889311  1889317  1889347
```

```
1889351  1889359  1889369  1889383  1889387  1889389  1889399  1889401  1889411  1889423
1889429  1889441  1889453  1889471  1889477  1889483  1889491  1889497  1889501  1889509
1889521  1889527  1889539  1889551  1889561  1889579  1889603  1889617  1889621  1889647
1889651  1889653  1889677  1889689  1889707  1889717  1889743  1889747  1889753  1889761
1889801  1889803  1889819  1889831  1889957  1889981  1889999  1890019  1890023
1890029  1890037  1890041  1890079  1890089  1890103  1890107  1890113  1890121  1890149
1890167  1890173  1890193  1890211  1890221  1890227  1890241  1890257  1890269  1890277
1890283  1890289  1890299  1890313  1890319  1890331  1890337  1890373  1890379  1890389
1890397  1890401  1890403  1890467  1890479  1890487  1890509  1890521  1890523  1890527
1890529  1890541  1890547  1890571  1890593  1890599  1890601  1890611  1890617  1890631
1890799  1890809  1890827  1890851  1890869  1890877  1890901  1890913  1890923  1890953
1890997  1891007  1891027  1891039  1891049  1891069  1891073  1891103  1891111  1891133
1891147  1891163  1891171  1891187  1891189  1891213  1891223  1891243  1891249  1891273
1891277  1891283  1891291  1891297  1891303  1891319  1891333  1891361  1891367  1891381
1891387  1891391  1891429  1891433  1891447  1891457  1891489  1891499  1891501  1891529
1891537  1891541  1891567  1891599  1891601  1891619  1891627  1891639  1891657  1891661
1891663  1891667  1891679  1891711  1891739  1891753  1891789  1891807  1891829  1891843
1891859  1891861  1891889  1891907  1891909  1891927  1891933  1891949  1891951  1891969
1891987  1891991  1891997  1892017  1892021  1892029  1892057  1892089  1892113  1892119
1892123  1892161  1892167  1892171  1892183  1892197  1892203  1892239  1892249  1892257
1892299  1892309  1892311  1892329  1892353  1892357  1892383  1892399  1892413  1892431
1892441  1892461  1892477  1892489  1892497  1892503  1892507  1892531  1892537  1892551
1892563  1892591  1892599  1892617  1892621  1892629  1892633  1892651  1892663  1892669
1892677  1892687  1892699  1892701  1892713  1892719  1892749  1892753  1892771  1892773
1892777  1892783  1892827  1892833  1892843  1892857  1892861  1892867  1892879  1892887
1892893  1892911  1892921  1892927  1892977  1892999  1893029  1893049  1893071
1893083  1893131  1893163  1893173  1893181  1893187  1893191  1893193  1893197  1893209
1893211  1893223  1893277  1893289  1893299  1893317  1893329  1893347  1893349  1893361
1893371  1893373  1893377  1893391  1893403  1893413  1893427  1893431  1893457  1893467
1893469  1893473  1893481  1893517  1893527  1893533  1893539  1893581  1893587  1893589
1893599  1893607  1893643  1893701  1893707  1893713  1893719  1893733  1893737  1893757
1893779  1893781  1893799  1893809  1893823  1893877  1893887  1893911  1893917  1893929
1893937  1893949  1893967  1893971  1893973  1893979  1894001  1894003  1894033  1894037
1894043  1894049  1894051  1894063  1894099  1894103  1894117  1894121  1894127  1894163
1894171  1894181  1894213  1894229  1894247  1894253  1894267  1894277  1894283  1894307
1894337  1894339  1894369  1894381  1894393  1894397  1894411  1894439  1894481  1894489
1894577  1894583  1894601  1894603  1894609  1894631  1894639  1894643  1894663  1894687
1894691  1894727  1894729  1894741  1894757  1894787  1894793  1894811  1894817  1894853
1894859  1894873  1894883  1894913  1894931  1894933  1894969  1895009  1895011  1895017
1895027  1895051  1895057  1895071  1895081  1895093  1895099  1895119  1895129
1895141  1895167  1895189  1895191  1895207  1895219  1895233  1895239  1895249  1895261
1895263  1895273  1895287  1895317  1895321  1895351  1895357  1895359  1895479  1895489
1895501  1895507  1895513  1895521  1895533  1895539  1895563  1895567  1895581  1895587
1895599  1895603  1895609  1895623  1895627  1895633  1895657  1895693  1895711  1895713
1895749  1895753  1895767  1895779  1895797  1895809  1895833  1895851  1895869  1895893
1895903  1895909  1895939  1895981  1895989  1896001  1896017  1896019  1896023  1896031
1896043  1896047  1896071  1896077  1896091  1896101  1896109  1896133  1896149  1896151
1896157  1896161  1896173  1896199  1896203  1896211  1896221  1896227  1896229  1896241
1896247  1896259  1896263  1896269  1896313  1896317  1896331  1896341  1896353  1896407
1896413  1896421  1896431  1896443  1896451  1896463  1896473  1896527  1896529  1896547
1896563  1896577  1896581  1896593  1896607  1896617  1896647  1896659  1896667  1896677
1896683  1896689  1896721  1896737  1896761  1896767  1896781  1896823  1896847  1896871
1896883  1896887  1896889  1896893  1896899  1896901  1896959  1896989  1896991  1897001
1897009  1897037  1897057  1897069  1897073  1897079  1897087  1897097  1897099  1897121
1897127  1897139  1897141  1897163  1897171  1897177  1897199  1897219  1897229  1897237
1897243  1897277  1897279  1897327  1897361  1897367  1897403  1897409  1897429  1897459
1897481  1897517  1897529  1897537  1897561  1897573  1897583  1897589  1897601  1897627
1897639  1897667  1897669  1897681  1897691  1897703  1897711  1897717  1897729  1897733
1897741  1897751  1897787  1897793  1897801  1897807  1897823  1897843  1897871  1897939
1897943  1897949  1897957  1897969  1897979  1897991  1898009  1898011  1898023  1898027
1898047  1898051  1898053  1898069  1898077  1898087  1898107  1898123  1898131  1898153
1898179  1898201  1898209  1898227  1898243  1898249  1898257  1898279  1898297  1898317
1898353  1898363  1898371  1898383  1898389  1898417  1898419  1898431  1898447  1898467
1898483  1898521  1898527  1898539  1898549  1898557  1898563  1898569  1898573  1898591
1898593  1898609  1898621  1898629  1898641  1898681  1898693  1898711  1898737  1898749
1898759  1898761  1898773  1898783  1898801  1898807  1898861  1898863  1898867  1898873
1898881  1898887  1898893  1898921  1898959  1898977  1899011  1899017  1899047  1899049
1899059  1899077  1899083  1899089  1899101  1899109  1899119  1899137  1899167  1899187
1899193  1899197  1899199  1899253  1899263  1899281  1899301  1899307  1899311  1899323
1899341  1899343  1899347  1899371  1899377  1899419  1899421  1899437  1899473  1899481
1899497  1899503  1899509  1899511  1899523  1899589  1899637  1899641  1899647  1899659
1899661  1899673  1899683  1899701  1899709  1899721  1899757  1899769  1899797  1899809
1899827  1899847  1899901  1899907  1899917  1899923  1899929  1899949  1899983  1900009
1900037  1900043  1900049  1900079  1900111  1900121  1900147  1900153  1900159  1900169
1900177  1900181  1900189  1900201  1900219  1900231  1900253  1900267  1900273  1900291
1900303  1900313  1900337  1900363  1900369  1900373  1900397  1900429  1900433  1900441
1900463  1900487  1900489  1900499  1900501  1900511  1900529  1900531  1900537  1900541
1900543  1900553  1900571  1900597  1900603  1900607  1900609  1900621  1900667  1900673
1900687  1900709  1900711  1900721  1900733  1900757  1900763  1900777  1900813  1900831
1900861  1900867  1900879  1900891  1900903  1900907  1900937  1900991  1901021  1901027
1901033  1901087  1901089  1901117  1901131  1901147  1901177  1901191  1901201  1901209
1901219  1901231  1901267  1901299  1901303  1901353  1901357  1901359  1901363  1901369
1901371  1901377  1901407  1901413  1901429  1901437  1901461  1901489  1901507  1901519
1901531  1901551  1901563  1901567  1901597  1901639  1901651  1901681  1901699  1901717
1901719  1901749  1901759  1901771  1901777  1901803  1901831  1901833  1901839  1901857
1901891  1901897  1901899  1901917  1901923  1901947  1901951  1901969  1901981  1901987
1901993  1902007  1902029  1902037  1902049  1902053  1902097  1902107  1902119  1902127
1902143  1902157  1902193  1902203  1902209  1902217  1902221  1902239  1902269  1902287
```

```
1902289 1902293 1902301 1902311 1902319 1902343 1902347 1902367 1902379 1902389
1902391 1902403 1902421 1902427 1902431 1902437 1902457 1902463 1902469 1902497
1902517 1902539 1902569 1902611 1902613 1902617 1902619 1902643 1902653 1902671
1902737 1902743 1902757 1902763 1902779 1902829 1902833 1902839 1902847 1902863
1902877 1902881 1902883 1902899 1902917 1902931 1902961 1902973 1902977 1902991
1903003 1903007 1903061 1903063 1903073 1903081 1903091 1903103 1903117 1903123
1903147 1903159 1903199 1903207 1903229 1903247 1903271 1903277 1903289 1903301
1903313 1903339 1903373 1903379 1903381 1903387 1903409 1903441 1903459 1903463
1903471 1903483 1903487 1903501 1903511 1903513 1903529 1903579 1903597 1903619
1903639 1903651 1903661 1903669 1903673 1903703 1903709 1903747 1903757 1903787
1903789 1903801 1903807 1903817 1903859 1903861 1903873 1903877 1903897 1903907
1903921 1903931 1903961 1903969 1903973 1903981 1903987 1903991 1904011 1904027
1904029 1904041 1904069 1904087 1904093 1904099 1904117 1904129 1904143 1904167
1904171 1904179 1904191 1904233 1904249 1904263 1904267 1904281 1904293 1904297
1904311 1904407 1904429 1904447 1904467 1904471 1904473 1904477 1904479 1904489
1904509 1904519 1904521 1904531 1904533 1904537 1904543 1904549 1904587 1904597
1904621 1904647 1904681 1904687 1904701 1904719 1904729 1904741 1904753 1904761
1904803 1904809 1904827 1904831 1904849 1904869 1904879 1904891 1904897 1904939
1904941 1904951 1904963 1904971 1904977 1904999 1905017 1905023 1905031 1905041
1905049 1905053 1905077 1905109 1905121 1905131 1905157 1905161 1905179 1905181
1905199 1905247 1905257 1905269 1905283 1905317 1905331 1905347 1905359 1905361
1905367 1905383 1905391 1905433 1905437 1905443 1905473 1905493 1905499 1905517
1905577 1905583 1905593 1905599 1905613 1905653 1905661 1905667 1905671 1905679
1905689 1905691 1905697 1905703 1905713 1905727 1905733 1905737 1905767 1905773
1905779 1905781 1905791 1905797 1905821 1905863 1905899 1905923 1905979 1905983
1906007 1906013 1906043 1906063 1906087 1906109 1906117 1906123 1906133 1906139
1906153 1906183 1906187 1906211 1906237 1906241 1906243 1906259 1906271 1906297
1906321 1906337 1906343 1906361 1906379 1906381 1906391 1906393 1906417 1906439
1906453 1906477 1906481 1906511 1906523 1906537 1906543 1906559 1906579 1906589
1906603 1906607 1906613 1906621 1906627 1906637 1906643 1906673 1906691 1906693
1906699 1906711 1906727 1906733 1906739 1906747 1906757 1906811 1906829 1906831
1906843 1906867 1906871 1906889 1906909 1906963 1906969 1906987 1906997 1907023
1907029 1907041 1907053 1907063 1907071 1907107 1907123 1907141 1907153 1907189
1907203 1907209 1907231 1907233 1907249 1907291 1907303 1907309 1907317 1907329
1907333 1907357 1907369 1907371 1907377 1907431 1907441 1907447 1907449 1907453
1907471 1907473 1907483 1907501 1907527 1907561 1907567 1907573 1907593 1907599
1907611 1907617 1907623 1907627 1907639 1907669 1907687 1907693 1907701 1907713
1907729 1907743 1907747 1907749 1907761 1907767 1907783 1907797 1907803 1907819
1907837 1907849 1907861 1907863 1907903 1907909 1907911 1907933 1907963 1907981
1907987 1907989 1907993 1908013 1908031 1908041 1908043 1908047 1908061 1908077
1908083 1908089 1908091 1908121 1908133 1908157 1908167 1908169 1908173 1908197
1908209 1908217 1908221 1908223 1908239 1908251 1908259 1908289 1908299 1908311 1908317
1908323 1908343 1908367 1908373 1908407 1908421 1908433 1908443 1908449 1908451
1908499 1908521 1908523 1908527 1908581 1908601 1908611 1908617 1908631 1908659
1908661 1908667 1908679 1908703 1908707 1908713 1908737 1908749 1908757 1908761
1908769 1908779 1908787 1908817 1908857 1908869 1908881 1908883 1908923 1908943
1908967 1908971 1908979 1908989 1908997 1909003 1909021 1909027 1909043 1909051
1909079 1909081 1909087 1909091 1909109 1909111 1909121 1909129 1909147 1909153
1909183 1909199 1909213 1909217 1909223 1909231 1909241 1909267 1909279 1909283
1909307 1909309 1909319 1909333 1909343 1909363 1909373 1909381 1909399 1909409
1909421 1909429 1909441 1909451 1909463 1909477 1909487 1909489 1909513 1909561
1909573 1909603 1909619 1909637 1909651 1909669 1909703 1909717 1909741 1909757
1909769 1909777 1909783 1909799 1909801 1909807 1909811 1909837 1909841 1909907
1909909 1909927 1909949 1909951 1909987 1909991 1909997 1910009 1910023
1910047 1910059 1910063 1910071 1910087 1910101 1910107 1910119 1910123 1910131
1910147 1910159 1910177 1910179 1910257 1910261 1910263 1910267 1910269 1910287
1910297 1910323 1910333 1910339 1910369 1910399 1910401 1910413 1910417 1910423
1910429 1910471 1910509 1910527 1910537 1910551 1910567 1910593 1910611 1910651
1910663 1910669 1910677 1910683 1910687 1910693 1910719 1910729 1910737 1910759
1910767 1910813 1910827 1910837 1910869 1910873 1910891 1910899 1910903 1910911
1910917 1910927 1910941 1910971 1910977 1910989 1910999 1911011 1911017 1911029
1911031 1911037 1911043 1911053 1911061 1911073 1911079 1911083 1911101 1911103
1911109 1911121 1911149 1911163 1911167 1911199 1911209 1911211 1911227 1911251
1911253 1911263 1911269 1911281 1911289 1911311 1911317 1911319 1911347 1911373
1911401 1911433 1911439 1911451 1911467 1911493 1911517 1911523 1911529 1911583
1911589 1911607 1911617 1911619 1911641 1911653 1911661 1911671 1911673 1911697
1911713 1911733 1911757 1911787 1911839 1911841 1911851 1911857 1911881 1911887
1911893 1911911 1911919 1911929 1911937 1911961 1911977 1911991 1912019 1912061
1912063 1912067 1912069 1912087 1912093 1912121 1912129 1912133 1912139 1912147
1912159 1912193 1912213 1912241 1912259 1912277 1912283 1912301 1912307 1912357
1912373 1912387 1912423 1912429 1912451 1912453 1912457 1912459 1912481 1912487
1912489 1912499 1912507 1912513 1912529 1912531 1912541 1912543 1912553 1912577
1912583 1912601 1912613 1912621 1912633 1912639 1912643 1912661 1912679 1912681
1912693 1912709 1912727 1912733 1912739 1912741 1912763 1912829 1912831 1912843
1912847 1912873 1912879 1912903 1912913 1912919 1912921 1912943 1912949 1912951
1912969 1912991 1913003 1913017 1913039 1913047 1913063 1913081 1913087 1913089
1913099 1913123 1913147 1913161 1913201 1913213 1913221 1913251 1913269 1913273
1913287 1913291 1913293 1913297 1913341 1913377 1913389 1913407 1913419 1913437
1913441 1913447 1913467 1913473 1913477 1913489 1913497 1913501 1913533 1913539
1913551 1913581 1913609 1913627 1913641 1913651 1913683 1913687 1913701 1913719
1913749 1913773 1913789 1913803 1913819 1913827 1913831 1913833 1913861 1913867
1913893 1913903 1913917 1913939 1913941 1913957 1913959 1913963 1913969 1913983
1913993 1913999 1914001 1914007 1914023 1914043 1914053 1914061 1914067 1914097
1914103 1914127 1914131 1914139 1914163 1914179 1914197 1914239 1914247 1914259
1914323 1914361 1914371 1914379 1914389 1914427 1914433 1914439 1914443 1914457
1914469 1914481 1914487 1914499 1914503 1914509 1914511 1914527 1914541 1914569
1914581 1914587 1914593 1914613 1914623 1914637 1914641 1914673 1914691 1914707
1914709 1914719 1914739 1914743 1914751 1914767 1914769 1914791 1914811 1914817
1914821 1914853 1914883 1914889 1914923 1914947 1914949 1914959 1914961 1914967
```

1914971 1915007 1915019 1915031 1915051 1915057 1915099 1915103 1915117 1915153
1915163 1915183 1915201 1915213 1915223 1915229 1915241 1915253 1915259 1915267
1915289 1915307 1915313 1915321 1915337 1915343 1915399 1915411 1915423 1915427
1915439 1915451 1915469 1915471 1915477 1915481 1915483 1915489 1915499 1915517
1915531 1915567 1915591 1915609 1915619 1915633 1915649 1915663 1915687 1915691
1915703 1915721 1915729 1915733 1915741 1915757 1915759 1915763 1915777 1915799
1915811 1915813 1915817 1915841 1915843 1915853 1915891 1915909 1915919 1915931
1915933 1915937 1915939 1915957 1915961 1915981 1915993 1915997 1916021 1916023
1916027 1916051 1916069 1916099 1916129 1916147 1916179 1916183 1916231 1916249
1916251 1916269 1916279 1916281 1916287 1916293 1916309 1916311 1916333 1916339
1916351 1916353 1916363 1916371 1916413 1916419 1916423 1916443 1916471 1916531
1916539 1916543 1916573 1916591 1916599 1916611 1916617 1916633 1916641 1916647
1916653 1916687 1916689 1916729 1916731 1916737 1916741 1916749 1916753 1916773
1916779 1916809 1916833 1916839 1916857 1916867 1916881 1916909 1916917 1916921
1916939 1916951 1916953 1916977 1917001 1917017 1917023 1917029 1917049 1917059
1917077 1917079 1917089 1917101 1917121 1917137 1917173 1917187 1917191 1917197
1917203 1917239 1917259 1917281 1917287 1917301 1917313 1917317 1917329 1917337
1917341 1917343 1917353 1917367 1917373 1917397 1917407 1917427 1917431 1917463
1917467 1917479 1917493 1917511 1917521 1917523 1917527 1917541 1917557 1917563
1917569 1917571 1917581 1917623 1917631 1917653 1917659 1917667 1917697 1917703
1917731 1917733 1917737 1917739 1917743 1917749 1917767 1917793 1917847 1917859
1917871 1917887 1917893 1917899 1917931 1917943 1917959 1917961 1917967 1917977
1918003 1918013 1918019 1918027 1918067 1918079 1918087 1918097 1918121 1918129
1918151 1918157 1918181 1918193 1918219 1918237 1918243 1918247 1918283 1918303
1918307 1918313 1918327 1918351 1918363 1918391 1918417 1918429 1918439 1918451
1918463 1918471 1918489 1918507 1918517 1918519 1918523 1918529 1918537 1918549
1918571 1918607 1918643 1918649 1918661 1918667 1918687 1918733 1918747 1918769
1918771 1918799 1918811 1918817 1918837 1918849 1918859 1918879 1918897 1918919
1918921 1918933 1918967 1918979 1918991 1919009 1919039 1919041 1919053 1919063
1919119 1919123 1919149 1919161 1919231 1919273 1919279 1919287 1919293 1919297
1919299 1919311 1919341 1919347 1919363 1919369 1919377 1919383 1919387 1919429
1919431 1919441 1919459 1919461 1919471 1919479 1919503 1919509 1919549 1919581
1919591 1919633 1919647 1919669 1919677 1919689 1919693 1919711 1919719 1919761
1919767 1919773 1919783 1919789 1919833 1919843 1919851 1919881 1919891 1919917
1919927 1919947 1919959 1919987 1920001 1920011 1920013 1920043 1920049 1920089
1920101 1920143 1920161 1920173 1920187 1920199 1920203 1920211 1920221 1920223
1920227 1920239 1920257 1920271 1920283 1920299 1920343 1920361 1920377 1920379
1920383 1920397 1920403 1920407 1920427 1920433 1920437 1920469 1920487 1920497
1920521 1920533 1920551 1920571 1920587 1920593 1920599 1920601 1920613 1920617
1920631 1920637 1920671 1920679 1920683 1920701 1920713 1920731 1920739 1920761
1920769 1920797 1920803 1920811 1920817 1920839 1920851 1920859 1920883 1920889
1920901 1920911 1920913 1920917 1920923 1920959 1920991 1921013 1921021 1921027
1921037 1921063 1921069 1921079 1921097 1921103 1921123 1921133 1921159 1921169
1921177 1921181 1921211 1921229 1921247 1921253 1921267 1921273 1921277 1921307
1921319 1921327 1921363 1921393 1921417 1921427 1921457 1921477 1921481 1921483
1921499 1921529 1921531 1921537 1921553 1921559 1921573 1921631 1921657 1921681
1921687 1921691 1921693 1921709 1921723 1921729 1921739 1921747 1921763 1921769
1921771 1921781 1921789 1921813 1921819 1921823 1921841 1921847 1921849 1921873
1921879 1921883 1921889 1921919 1921921 1921937 1921967 1921981 1922027 1922047
1922077 1922111 1922119 1922147 1922153 1922209 1922213 1922233 1922269 1922273
1922329 1922339 1922351 1922353 1922383 1922387 1922407 1922423 1922429 1922447
1922461 1922471 1922491 1922507 1922519 1922533 1922551 1922561 1922563 1922567
1922579 1922603 1922611 1922621 1922663 1922677 1922689 1922693 1922719 1922749
1922771 1922773 1922783 1922803 1922807 1922813 1922821 1922863 1922867 1922873
1922891 1922909 1922923 1922951 1922957 1922983 1923013 1923017 1923029 1923037
1923049 1923059 1923073 1923079 1923083 1923107 1923109 1923127 1923133 1923137
1923139 1923151 1923157 1923167 1923169 1923197 1923203 1923221 1923253 1923263
1923277 1923281 1923289 1923293 1923307 1923323 1923349 1923353 1923377 1923401
1923403 1923409 1923419 1923437 1923443 1923463 1923469 1923479 1923491 1923521
1923547 1923611 1923613 1923653 1923659 1923671 1923683 1923689 1923707 1923709
1923749 1923751 1923763 1923781 1923787 1923791 1923793 1923797 1923811 1923833
1923841 1923853 1923869 1923871 1923877 1923893 1923917 1923979 1923983 1923989
1923991 1924003 1924031 1924033 1924067 1924079 1924081 1924093 1924129 1924141
1924147 1924199 1924217 1924231 1924243 1924261 1924283 1924289 1924291 1924297
1924303 1924327 1924331 1924343 1924393 1924397 1924409 1924457 1924459 1924463
1924487 1924501 1924513 1924523 1924537 1924547 1924561 1924579 1924601 1924619
1924627 1924631 1924649 1924651 1924661 1924669 1924679 1924693 1924721 1924751
1924753 1924781 1924799 1924829 1924849 1924861 1924889 1924903 1924921
1924957 1924963 1924969 1924973 1925017 1925039 1925041 1925047 1925057 1925059
1925071 1925081 1925087 1925117 1925129 1925149 1925171 1925177 1925179 1925191
1925219 1925227 1925243 1925257 1925293 1925299 1925311 1925321 1925323 1925333
1925359 1925381 1925383 1925387 1925389 1925393 1925431 1925459 1925461 1925489
1925501 1925507 1925509 1925531 1925533 1925557 1925563 1925579 1925603 1925611
1925621 1925639 1925653 1925681 1925711 1925717 1925719 1925747 1925753 1925773
1925779 1925801 1925827 1925837 1925863 1925881 1925887 1925893 1925957
1925881 1925899 1925909 1925929 1925933 1925971 1925993 1926007 1926019 1926031
1926037 1926047 1926053 1926077 1926079 1926097 1926149 1926157 1926161 1926167
1926187 1926191 1926217 1926241 1926259 1926263 1926269 1926283 1926289 1926293
1926299 1926329 1926341 1926343 1926359 1926361 1926367 1926377 1926403 1926413
1926427 1926437 1926439 1926461 1926469 1926473 1926481 1926487 1926493 1926521
1926523 1926541 1926569 1926571 1926601 1926611 1926623 1926637 1926647 1926649
1926653 1926667 1926697 1926703 1926707 1926721 1926739 1926767 1926773 1926791
1926803 1926811 1926833 1926851 1926863 1926893 1926901 1926907 1926913
1926919 1926931 1926937 1926949 1926973 1927007 1927019 1927031 1927033 1927067
1927073 1927087 1927097 1927109 1927111 1927129 1927139 1927157 1927187 1927223
1927241 1927249 1927259 1927271 1927279 1927297 1927313 1927319 1927327 1927333
1927337 1927349 1927351 1927357 1927361 1927397 1927399 1927411 1927421 1927433
1927459 1927481 1927483 1927501 1927507 1927537 1927547 1927553 1927559 1927567
1927571 1927573 1927577 1927591 1927603 1927619 1927631 1927633 1927669 1927687

1927691	1927693	1927703	1927729	1927741	1927753	1927781	1927789	1927813	1927823
1927853	1927867	1927879	1927897	1927901	1927903	1927909	1927957	1927963	1927967
1927969	1927979	1927993	1927997	1928011	1928023	1928029	1928041	1928071	1928093
1928099	1928141	1928161	1928167	1928183	1928203	1928207	1928219	1928237	1928257
1928261	1928287	1928317	1928321	1928323	1928351	1928359	1928369	1928371	1928383
1928387	1928401	1928411	1928419	1928447	1928449	1928467	1928473	1928489	1928501
1928513	1928539	1928543	1928561	1928567	1928569	1928621	1928623	1928629	1928653
1928659	1928677	1928687	1928741	1928743	1928753	1928767	1928791	1928807	1928809
1928813	1928821	1928831	1928869	1928873	1928899	1928947	1928951	1928957	1928959
1928963	1928989	1929043	1929047	1929049	1929061	1929071	1929073	1929113	1929119
1929121	1929149	1929157	1929163	1929197	1929199	1929227	1929229	1929251	1929271
1929287	1929289	1929307	1929311	1929329	1929331	1929349	1929407	1929413	1929451
1929467	1929481	1929497	1929503	1929509	1929523	1929527	1929541	1929553	1929559
1929563	1929569	1929581	1929589	1929601	1929607	1929611	1929617	1929637	1929647
1929649	1929671	1929691	1929731	1929749	1929751	1929779	1929793	1929803	1929821
1929827	1929839	1929841	1929847	1929869	1929871	1929877	1929899	1929913	1929923
1929929	1929943	1929947	1929971	1929973	1930021	1930043	1930057	1930073	1930079
1930081	1930087	1930099	1930133	1930139	1930147	1930177	1930199	1930219	1930237
1930249	1930259	1930261	1930289	1930297	1930301	1930307	1930309	1930349	1930351
1930373	1930391	1930417	1930427	1930429	1930433	1930447	1930451	1930477	1930483
1930493	1930517	1930519	1930541	1930543	1930553	1930573	1930583	1930603	1930627
1930633	1930667	1930679	1930693	1930729	1930757	1930763	1930783	1930793	1930801
1930811	1930823	1930879	1930883	1930927	1930931	1930937	1930939	1930961	1930963
1930969	1931009	1931011	1931053	1931093	1931101	1931113	1931123	1931143	1931159
1931177	1931203	1931213	1931227	1931239	1931261	1931273	1931291	1931297	1931299
1931309	1931317	1931323	1931329	1931339	1931341	1931357	1931381	1931383	1931399
1931411	1931453	1931473	1931477	1931497	1931513	1931519	1931533	1931537	1931539
1931549	1931569	1931593	1931623	1931627	1931647	1931651	1931663	1931669	1931681
1931717	1931723	1931729	1931751	1931759	1931771	1931773	1931789	1931801	1931819
1931821	1931833	1931843	1931851	1931887	1931921	1931927	1931933	1931957	1931983
1931987	1931989	1932001	1932011	1932017	1932037	1932059	1932061	1932071	1932089
1932107	1932109	1932113	1932121	1932131	1932181	1932193	1932197	1932209	1932223
1932247	1932263	1932277	1932283	1932317	1932331	1932341	1932353	1932361	1932367
1932379	1932397	1932401	1932421	1932431	1932439	1932467	1932487	1932493	1932503
1932523	1932533	1932563	1932599	1932631	1932641	1932677	1932703	1932719	1932731
1932739	1932761	1932797	1932803	1932823	1932829	1932841	1932859	1932869	
1932871	1932877	1932901	1932911	1932923	1932947	1932949	1932961	1933007	1933013
1933037	1933049	1933097	1933103	1933123	1933133	1933147	1933159	1933163	1933171
1933177	1933181	1933199	1933229	1933247	1933277	1933289	1933301	1933331	1933339
1933363	1933397	1933423	1933433	1933457	1933469	1933471	1933499	1933511	1933513
1933523	1933537	1933549	1933571	1933577	1933643	1933661	1933663	1933681	1933709
1933717	1933727	1933741	1933747	1933759	1933777	1933781	1933783	1933819	1933823
1933837	1933849	1933859	1933861	1933891	1933913	1933927	1933931	1933957	1933973
1933979	1933993	1934021	1934041	1934063	1934067	1934077	1934099	1934113	1934117
1934131	1934137	1934147	1934167	1934173	1934201	1934263	1934279	1934287	1934293
1934297	1934299	1934327	1934351	1934377	1934381	1934389	1934393	1934399	1934411
1934417	1934419	1934437	1934459	1934483	1934489	1934501	1934519	1934521	1934531
1934539	1934563	1934579	1934609	1934627	1934629	1934633	1934657	1934663	1934671
1934683	1934687	1934689	1934707	1934729	1934743	1934761	1934773	1934791	1934797
1934833	1934837	1934843	1934869	1934879	1934887	1934897	1934951	1934969	1934983
1934987	1934993	1935007	1935047	1935049	1935067	1935079	1935091	1935121	1935133
1935139	1935149	1935163	1935173	1935181	1935217	1935221	1935239	1935251	1935253
1935281	1935287	1935293	1935313	1935317	1935341	1935343	1935371	1935379	1935383
1935407	1935419	1935443	1935481	1935509	1935517	1935533	1935541	1935589	1935599
1935617	1935631	1935641	1935677	1935683	1935691	1935707	1935743	1935751	1935757
1935763	1935767	1935781	1935793	1935799	1935811	1935823	1935827	1935847	1935859
1935881	1935889	1935893	1935907	1935911	1935917	1935961	1935991	1936021	1936027
1936057	1936063	1936093	1936111	1936133	1936153	1936159	1936171	1936177	1936183
1936189	1936213	1936219	1936223	1936237	1936289	1936303	1936327	1936331	1936339
1936343	1936349	1936357	1936381	1936387	1936391	1936397	1936399	1936427	1936433
1936457	1936489	1936511	1936523	1936547	1936559	1936579	1936609	1936629	1936631
1936633	1936637	1936643	1936679	1936721	1936723	1936733	1936741	1936747	1936751
1936757	1936771	1936777	1936783	1936789	1936813	1936817	1936819	1936859	1936871
1936889	1936943	1936969	1936981	1936999	1937003	1937017	1937027	1937041	1937051
1937057	1937059	1937063	1937071	1937077	1937087	1937123	1937153	1937197	1937207
1937227	1937233	1937237	1937261	1937311	1937323	1937329	1937333	1937339	1937363
1937389	1937401	1937417	1937437	1937443	1937459	1937471	1937489	1937491	1937513
1937539	1937549	1937557	1937587	1937603	1937629	1937641	1937651	1937657	1937659
1937699	1937713	1937723	1937729	1937731	1937759	1937777	1937807	1937833	1937843
1937879	1937891	1937917	1937927	1937933	1937939	1937941	1937953	1937959	1937987
1937989	1937993	1938007	1938011	1938067	1938071	1938073	1938103	1938113	1938149
1938161	1938163	1938173	1938179	1938191	1938197	1938199	1938203	1938217	1938227
1938239	1938253	1938257	1938269	1938271	1938301	1938317	1938359	1938367	1938373
1938383	1938427	1938449	1938451	1938491	1938499	1938533	1938553	1938557	1938571
1938577	1938593	1938611	1938617	1938623	1938637	1938659	1938701	1938719	1938743
1938751	1938773	1938787	1938791	1938803	1938809	1938821	1938829	1938847	1938851
1938863	1938883	1938887	1938889	1938907	1938949	1938971	1938973	1938977	1938983
1938997	1939009	1939033	1939039	1939057	1939073	1939097	1939103	1939109	1939217
1939123	1939141	1939151	1939169	1939183	1939187	1939229	1939237	1939243	1939241
1939253	1939279	1939303	1939307	1939313	1939331	1939339	1939351	1939353	1939363
1939369	1939381	1939397	1939403	1939409	1939439	1939447	1939481	1939489	1939493
1939499	1939517	1939523	1939541	1939543	1939559	1939571	1939573	1939591	1939603
1939621	1939631	1939633	1939657	1939673	1939681	1939699	1939711	1939727	1939733
1939741	1939753	1939757	1939771	1939787	1939801	1939837	1939841	1939867	1939879
1939891	1939903	1939913	1939939	1939943	1939961	1939967	1939969	1939989	1939999
1940041	1940047	1940053	1940069	1940083	1940087	1940123	1940131	1940137	1940143
1940149	1940153	1940173	1940201	1940219	1940221	1940233	1940269	1940293	1940327
1940339	1940371	1940377	1940381	1940399	1940401	1940423	1940437	1940443	1940447
1940453	1940459	1940473	1940479	1940483	1940509	1940537	1940551	1940557	1940563

1940573 1940597 1940599 1940621 1940639 1940663 1940683 1940699 1940711 1940713
1940747 1940749 1940753 1940759 1940777 1940779 1940797 1940821 1940833 1940849
1940881 1940893 1940903 1940929 1940957 1940971 1940987 1941013 1941031 1941061
1941073 1941083 1941089 1941091 1941101 1941103 1941151 1941157 1941169 1941187
1941193 1941221 1941229 1941239 1941253 1941257 1941259 1941263 1941293 1941307
1941323 1941343 1941367 1941377 1941389 1941403 1941409 1941419 1941421 1941431
1941461 1941469 1941479 1941481 1941491 1941497 1941503 1941509 1941517 1941547
1941557 1941559 1941571 1941601 1941607 1941659 1941671 1941673 1941677 1941707
1941721 1941733 1941739 1941763 1941799 1941827 1941839 1941851 1941881 1941889
1941931 1941937 1941941 1941967 1941983 1942001 1942007 1942021 1942027 1942033
1942049 1942067 1942081 1942091 1942099 1942111 1942121 1942133 1942139 1942141
1942151 1942153 1942163 1942169 1942177 1942183 1942201 1942207 1942273 1942307
1942309 1942319 1942321 1942349 1942361 1942363 1942379 1942387 1942399 1942411
1942417 1942433 1942441 1942453 1942459 1942481 1942483 1942487 1942519 1942529
1942543 1942547 1942571 1942627 1942657 1942669 1942723 1942727 1942729 1942747
1942751 1942753 1942757 1942763 1942771 1942793 1942841 1942859 1942873 1942877
1942891 1942901 1942909 1942939 1942943 1942961 1942979 1943021 1943023 1943059
1943069 1943077 1943093 1943101 1943107 1943131 1943141 1943147 1943171 1943197
1943209 1943231 1943237 1943239 1943243 1943251 1943257 1943269 1943273 1943281
1943311 1943323 1943329 1943353 1943363 1943371 1943387 1943393 1943411 1943413
1943429 1943437 1943443 1943467 1943489 1943531 1943533 1943537 1943561
1943587 1943597 1943629 1943639 1943651 1943653 1943657 1943659 1943663 1943693
1943699 1943717 1943723 1943743 1943791 1943803 1943819 1943827 1943839 1943857
1943861 1943863 1943867 1943897 1943911 1943923 1943941 1943951 1943959 1943993
1944011 1944013 1944049 1944053 1944067 1944071 1944079 1944113 1944127 1944133
1944143 1944157 1944169 1944181 1944197 1944211 1944223 1944281 1944287 1944311
1944317 1944323 1944329 1944353 1944361 1944373 1944377 1944379 1944389 1944401
1944457 1944469 1944473 1944499 1944521 1944529 1944539 1944557 1944563 1944577
1944583 1944659 1944667 1944689 1944713 1944721 1944727 1944737 1944763 1944779
1944781 1944791 1944797 1944799 1944823 1944829 1944841 1944853 1944881 1944883
1944911 1944923 1944931 1944937 1944961 1944983 1944991 1944997 1945003 1945007
1945043 1945051 1945057 1945061 1945091 1945093 1945109 1945121 1945129 1945169
1945183 1945199 1945243 1945261 1945297 1945301 1945303 1945309 1945313 1945319
1945331 1945337 1945369 1945381 1945393 1945399 1945403 1945453 1945453 1945457
1945483 1945487 1945499 1945511 1945519 1945549 1945553 1945561 1945579 1945597
1945607 1945609 1945627 1945637 1945649 1945651 1945661 1945673 1945681 1945687
1945703 1945709 1945711 1945721 1945729 1945739 1945751 1945763 1945781 1945799
1945817 1945831 1945843 1945859 1945873 1945883 1945891 1945903 1945913 1945919
1945943 1945969 1945981 1945991 1946011 1946017 1946029 1946033 1946059 1946069
1946081 1946093 1946117 1946141 1946171 1946173 1946183 1946207 1946209 1946257
1946281 1946297 1946299 1946369 1946377 1946383 1946401 1946407 1946429 1946443
1946447 1946453 1946471 1946473 1946489 1946501 1946507 1946537 1946543 1946561
1946563 1946579 1946603 1946617 1946621 1946627 1946629 1946641 1946647 1946657
1946663 1946669 1946671 1946689 1946699 1946701 1946713 1946723 1946731 1946761
1946767 1946771 1946779 1946801 1946809 1946839 1946851 1946869 1946899 1946909
1946921 1946933 1946939 1946947 1946963 1946969 1946981 1946999 1947041 1947073
1947091 1947107 1947109 1947119 1947137 1947149 1947151 1947193 1947217 1947223
1947227 1947229 1947241 1947247 1947259 1947269 1947287 1947307 1947311 1947359
1947371 1947383 1947391 1947397 1947419 1947431 1947457 1947467 1947487 1947493
1947497 1947499 1947511 1947527 1947551 1947593 1947607 1947619 1947629 1947641
1947653 1947661 1947667 1947683 1947691 1947703 1947719 1947731 1947733 1947763
1947773 1947779 1947811 1947851 1947853 1947919 1947923 1947941 1947971 1947973
1947977 1947989 1947991 1947997 1948021 1948043 1948049 1948069 1948073
1948091 1948097 1948099 1948109 1948129 1948139 1948147 1948171 1948181 1948187
1948223 1948229 1948231 1948237 1948267 1948273 1948283 1948301 1948313 1948327
1948337 1948343 1948369 1948411 1948433 1948447 1948483 1948493 1948511 1948517
1948519 1948549 1948553 1948559 1948571 1948601 1948603 1948613 1948619 1948627
1948637 1948649 1948669 1948699 1948703 1948729 1948741 1948747 1948759 1948763
1948777 1948783 1948789 1948799 1948801 1948847 1948861 1948867 1948883 1948907
1948909 1948927 1948937 1948981 1948987 1948993 1949023 1949053 1949081 1949111
1949113 1949117 1949141 1949161 1949179 1949201 1949251 1949257 1949309 1949327
1949333 1949341 1949357 1949359 1949371 1949383 1949417 1949459 1949471 1949473
1949501 1949527 1949531 1949539 1949557 1949573 1949579 1949581 1949627 1949639
1949657 1949707 1949719 1949737 1949741 1949771 1949777 1949791 1949809 1949813
1949819 1949833 1949839 1949887 1949897 1949911 1949929 1949933 1949939
1949947 1949999 1950017 1950023 1950037 1950043 1950061 1950071 1950073 1950089
1950107 1950133 1950139 1950149 1950161 1950167 1950173 1950181 1950187 1950211
1950227 1950253 1950269 1950271 1950283 1950287 1950317 1950323 1950343 1950349
1950367 1950383 1950391 1950401 1950409 1950419 1950433 1950449 1950457 1950463
1950517 1950527 1950539 1950577 1950617 1950623 1950629 1950643 1950649 1950661
1950667 1950679 1950691 1950703 1950757 1950761 1950763 1950803 1950827 1950833
1950853 1950881 1950889 1950913 1950919 1950941 1950959 1950979 1950989 1951003
1951007 1951013 1951043 1951049 1951051 1951093 1951097 1951099 1951123 1951127
1951133 1951139 1951153 1951177 1951193 1951199 1951223 1951237 1951249 1951253
1951289 1951303 1951321 1951403 1951441 1951457 1951459 1951463 1951483
1951489 1951493 1951501 1951511 1951529 1951553 1951561 1951591 1951597 1951601
1951603 1951627 1951633 1951657 1951669 1951687 1951693 1951709 1951721 1951739
1951759 1951783 1951793 1951811 1951819 1951823 1951837 1951843 1951867 1951871
1951879 1951891 1951949 1951951 1951967 1951993 1951997 1952021 1952023 1952047
1952053 1952087 1952089 1952099 1952123 1952129 1952131 1952173 1952191 1952201
1952207 1952219 1952221 1952227 1952257 1952261 1952267 1952311 1952317 1952323
1952339 1952351 1952381 1952407 1952413 1952437 1952441 1952449 1952477 1952479
1952519 1952537 1952551 1952557 1952563 1952567 1952579 1952591 1952623 1952627
1952641 1952647 1952653 1952663 1952689 1952693 1952729 1952737 1952747 1952767
1952779 1952813 1952833 1952837 1952851 1952887 1952893 1952911 1952921 1952933
1952939 1952957 1952963 1952981 1952989 1953001 1953013 1953041 1953043 1953053
1953059 1953101 1953109 1953151 1953157 1953163 1953167 1953233 1953253 1953269
1953277 1953299 1953307 1953311 1953323 1953331 1953349 1953359 1953373 1953379
1953383 1953437 1953451 1953463 1953467 1953473 1953481 1953491 1953493 1953503

```
1953509  1953517  1953529  1953547  1953557  1953559  1953569  1953577  1953587  1953593
1953613  1953617  1953629  1953659  1953673  1953697  1953709  1953727  1953761  1953767
1953799  1953803  1953811  1953821  1953823  1953829  1953839  1953857  1953863  1953869
1953901  1953911  1953943  1953949  1953967  1953977  1953983  1954003  1954033  1954087
1954097  1954111  1954151  1954153  1954157  1954159  1954177  1954187  1954193  1954217
1954231  1954237  1954247  1954273  1954279  1954289  1954291  1954297  1954301  1954313
1954319  1954327  1954343  1954349  1954357  1954361  1954363  1954367  1954369  1954373
1954387  1954391  1954411  1954423  1954427  1954441  1954483  1954487  1954489  1954523
1954531  1954543  1954553  1954573  1954597  1954607  1954613  1954621  1954627  1954639
1954649  1954661  1954679  1954691  1954699  1954709  1954717  1954741  1954753  1954759
1954763  1954769  1954811  1954819  1954873  1954877  1954889  1954907  1954933  1954943
1954951  1954957  1954963  1954987  1954991  1955021  1955027  1955033  1955047  1955071
1955099  1955113  1955123  1955131  1955137  1955141  1955179  1955183  1955197  1955203
1955237  1955251  1955279  1955281  1955287  1955293  1955333  1955381  1955389  1955399
1955407  1955417  1955467  1955489  1955491  1955501  1955507  1955509  1955521  1955531
1955533  1955539  1955543  1955579  1955587  1955593  1955609  1955633  1955641  1955671
1955687  1955693  1955711  1955747  1955761  1955771  1955773  1955777  1955801  1955809
1955819  1955827  1955831  1955839  1955873  1955887  1955893  1955939  1955957  1955959
1955977  1955983  1956001  1956011  1956029  1956047  1956049  1956089  1956091  1956109
1956161  1956169  1956179  1956203  1956211  1956217  1956239  1956257  1956287  1956289
1956299  1956313  1956323  1956329  1956337  1956341  1956359  1956391  1956419  1956431
1956439  1956449  1956481  1956517  1956527  1956529  1956533  1956553  1956583  1956589
1956599  1956611  1956613  1956631  1956637  1956653  1956667  1956719  1956737  1956743
1956749  1956761  1956763  1956769  1956793  1956811  1956839  1956847  1956859  1956881
1956883  1956901  1956907  1956953  1956961  1956979  1956991  1957013  1957027  1957031
1957037  1957049  1957051  1957069  1957079  1957097  1957099  1957117  1957121  1957129
1957147  1957157  1957187  1957243  1957283  1957289  1957301  1957303  1957321  1957327
1957357  1957367  1957379  1957391  1957441  1957453  1957469  1957477  1957517  1957519
1957523  1957547  1957573  1957583  1957591  1957621  1957639  1957651  1957663  1957667
1957693  1957729  1957759  1957763  1957777  1957789  1957799  1957801  1957831  1957847
1957853  1957859  1957861  1957871  1957903  1957909  1957919  1957931  1957937  1957939
1957957  1957981  1957997  1957999  1958029  1958041  1958063  1958069  1958107  1958137
1958183  1958189  1958233  1958237  1958249  1958287  1958303  1958309  1958317  1958321
1958351  1958357  1958413  1958419  1958423  1958431  1958449  1958461  1958471  1958497
1958513  1958531  1958557  1958563  1958569  1958591  1958603  1958617  1958633  1958639
1958641  1958651  1958681  1958683  1958687  1958689  1958707  1958711  1958731  1958753
1958773  1958777  1958813  1958821  1958833  1958837  1958861  1958867  1958897  1958899
1958909  1958917  1958941  1958959  1958993  1959011  1959017  1959019  1959031  1959047
1959053  1959073  1959079  1959091  1959149  1959151  1959161  1959173  1959179  1959197
1959227  1959239  1959241  1959253  1959263  1959283  1959311  1959313  1959317  1959319
1959323  1959361  1959371  1959401  1959407  1959421  1959457  1959463  1959473  1959487
1959521  1959523  1959583  1959593  1959599  1959619  1959637  1959647  1959649  1959673
1959689  1959697  1959701  1959707  1959719  1959721  1959731  1959739  1959751  1959773
1959787  1959799  1959821  1959827  1959833  1959847  1959857  1959863  1959883  1959889
1959941  1959943  1959949  1959961  1959967  1959973  1960009  1960019  1960033  1960051
1960067  1960093  1960111  1960121  1960141  1960163  1960171  1960183  1960189  1960199
1960201  1960213  1960237  1960247  1960261  1960271  1960279  1960289  1960291  1960303
1960331  1960351  1960363  1960369  1960379  1960391  1960397  1960421  1960447  1960481
1960493  1960529  1960531  1960549  1960573  1960613  1960631  1960639  1960643  1960649
1960669  1960703  1960711  1960733  1960769  1960771  1960787  1960789  1960799  1960813
1960837  1960867  1960877  1960879  1960891  1960901  1960909  1960913  1960919  1960921
1960943  1960961  1960969  1960979  1960991  1960993  1961021  1961027  1961033  1961039
1961059  1961077  1961083  1961093  1961107  1961123  1961131  1961147  1961173  1961213
1961221  1961231  1961249  1961251  1961257  1961321  1961327  1961329  1961347  1961363
1961381  1961411  1961413  1961419  1961431  1961441  1961447  1961461  1961463  1961483
1961489  1961501  1961513  1961527  1961537  1961549  1961551  1961581  1961593  1961623
1961633  1961651  1961653  1961657  1961669  1961671  1961683  1961737  1961741  1961747
1961753  1961759  1961767  1961797  1961819  1961833  1961857  1961863  1961873  1961887
1961893  1961899  1961903  1961909  1961917  1961929  1961933  1961957  1961963  1961983
1961989  1962001  1962011  1962013  1962041  1962049  1962071  1962091  1962097  1962119
1962131  1962139  1962161  1962193  1962209  1962211  1962239  1962271  1962283  1962287
1962299  1962307  1962319  1962347  1962379  1962397  1962403  1962409  1962413  1962419
1962437  1962449  1962451  1962461  1962469  1962473  1962503  1962523  1962551  1962557
1962577  1962581  1962589  1962593  1962637  1962661  1962689  1962707  1962731  1962743
1962761  1962787  1962809  1962811  1962817  1962839  1962847  1962859  1962881  1962911
1962929  1962941  1962943  1962949  1962953  1962959  1962967  1962991  1962997  1963001
1963019  1963037  1963057  1963063  1963081  1963103  1963111  1963127  1963133  1963139
1963153  1963187  1963193  1963201  1963207  1963219  1963231  1963243  1963249  1963253
1963259  1963267  1963277  1963309  1963319  1963321  1963333  1963369  1963391  1963397
1963411  1963453  1963457  1963459  1963463  1963469  1963471  1963513  1963537  1963543
1963567  1963639  1963657  1963667  1963679  1963691  1963693  1963711  1963727  1963747
1963751  1963769  1963781  1963799  1963807  1963811  1963813  1963873  1963877  1963883
1963889  1963921  1963981  1963999  1964009  1964033  1964041  1964047  1964059  1964063
1964077  1964093  1964101  1964113  1964117  1964119  1964159  1964173  1964189
1964213  1964243  1964249  1964301  1964311  1964317  1964323  1964363  1964381  1964387
1964399  1964411  1964419  1964437  1964447  1964461  1964477  1964483  1964531  1964549
1964561  1964569  1964579  1964593  1964603  1964617  1964623  1964629  1964659  1964671
1964719  1964723  1964773  1964789  1964791  1964797  1964801  1964811  1964847  1964849
1964857  1964861  1964881  1964887  1964899  1964917  1964927  1964947  1964951  1964969
1964981  1964983  1965007  1965077  1965091  1965109  1965133  1965167  1965179  1965191
1965203  1965239  1965247  1965259  1965263  1965277  1965289  1965323  1965347  1965377
1965389  1965391  1965407  1965413  1965427  1965437  1965443  1965449  1965451  1965461
1965463  1965497  1965503  1965517  1965521  1965527  1965541  1965553  1965557  1965577
1965619  1965629  1965631  1965637  1965641  1965643  1965647  1965661  1965673  1965701
1965709  1965731  1965751  1965767  1965781  1965851  1965853  1965883  1965889  1965893
1965913  1965923  1965937  1965941  1965959  1965967  1965973  1965979  1965983  1966007
1966009  1966031  1966043  1966049  1966079  1966123  1966127  1966169  1966189  1966207
1966219  1966241  1966259  1966297  1966301  1966303  1966331  1966337  1966343  1966381
1966387  1966397  1966399  1966409  1966417  1966427  1966429  1966463  1966493  1966499
```

```
1966507  1966511  1966561  1966583  1966589  1966597  1966603  1966607  1966619  1966663
1966667  1966669  1966681  1966697  1966787  1966793  1966807  1966813  1966817  1966819
1966831  1966841  1966843  1966847  1966871  1966873  1966879  1966889  1966897  1966901
1966907  1966931  1966933  1966963  1966967  1966973  1966999  1967011  1967023  1967027
1967039  1967047  1967071  1967101  1967107  1967129  1967137  1967149  1967171  1967191
1967239  1967243  1967261  1967263  1967297  1967299  1967309  1967323  1967347  1967369
1967377  1967387  1967411  1967417  1967419  1967429  1967453  1967479  1967501  1967521
1967533  1967543  1967587  1967593  1967599  1967633  1967639  1967657  1967671  1967683
1967711  1967717  1967729  1967741  1967753  1967759  1967789  1967803  1967813  1967821
1967851  1967891  1967893  1967897  1967909  1967923  1967939  1967947  1968017  1968019
1968023  1968047  1968053  1968059  1968061  1968079  1968103  1968137  1968139  1968149
1968157  1968163  1968173  1968193  1968199  1968203  1968233  1968251  1968257  1968269
1968293  1968301  1968331  1968341  1968349  1968353  1968359  1968361  1968383  1968391
1968401  1968403  1968427  1968467  1968487  1968521  1968539  1968541  1968563  1968569
1968581  1968599  1968611  1968613  1968641  1968679  1968683  1968691  1968721  1968739
1968749  1968751  1968767  1968773  1968797  1968803  1968817  1968829  1968853  1968871
1968899  1968919  1968977  1968979  1968983  1968997  1969001  1969021  1969031  1969049
1969057  1969069  1969073  1969111  1969147  1969153  1969157  1969181  1969183  1969199
1969207  1969223  1969241  1969249  1969273  1969277  1969291  1969307  1969343  1969381
1969403  1969411  1969423  1969447  1969453  1969459  1969489  1969511  1969519  1969531
1969543  1969567  1969573  1969589  1969609  1969619  1969633  1969657  1969661  1969691
1969699  1969729  1969741  1969757  1969777  1969801  1969811  1969819  1969829  1969831
1969889  1969907  1969921  1969949  1969967  1969969  1969987  1969993  1969997  1970029
1970039  1970071  1970083  1970119  1970123  1970149  1970161  1970183  1970201  1970209
1970219  1970233  1970237  1970257  1970261  1970263  1970279  1970291  1970327  1970333
1970359  1970363  1970369  1970401  1970407  1970413  1970417  1970429  1970431  1970459
1970461  1970467  1970473  1970491  1970513  1970519  1970531  1970543  1970567  1970581
1970597  1970599  1970621  1970627  1970629  1970641  1970677  1970681  1970711  1970713
1970719  1970729  1970743  1970783  1970791  1970809  1970867  1970873  1970921  1970923
1970957  1970959  1970977  1970987  1970999  1971007  1971023  1971029  1971049  1971091
1971107  1971119  1971127  1971143  1971149  1971161  1971181  1971199  1971209  1971241
1971251  1971253  1971289  1971313  1971329  1971349  1971377  1971401  1971427  1971433
1971443  1971451  1971467  1971469  1971479  1971481  1971503  1971517  1971521  1971527
1971539  1971553  1971577  1971589  1971601  1971637  1971647  1971659  1971667  1971691
1971707  1971709  1971727  1971799  1971829  1971833  1971857  1971869  1971887  1971889
1971901  1971911  1971967  1972007  1972013  1972031  1972037  1972049  1972079  1972093
1972097  1972099  1972111  1972121  1972123  1972129  1972133  1972147  1972169  1972177
1972207  1972231  1972247  1972249  1972259  1972277  1972283  1972291  1972297  1972307
1972343  1972349  1972361  1972379  1972381  1972417  1972423  1972441  1972471  1972483
1972511  1972541  1972567  1972571  1972583  1972589  1972591  1972603  1972613  1972627
1972643  1972651  1972657  1972669  1972717  1972721  1972739  1972741  1972777  1972781
1972787  1972807  1972813  1972823  1972829  1972847  1972849  1972889  1972891  1972913
1972921  1972931  1972939  1972967  1972981  1972987  1973011  1973021  1973033  1973047
1973051  1973053  1973087  1973129  1973139  1973143  1973149  1973177  1973197  1973203
1973233  1973261  1973281  1973287  1973291  1973297  1973299  1973317  1973339  1973347
1973353  1973369  1973381  1973407  1973417  1973431  1973437  1973467  1973471  1973501
1973507  1973509  1973519  1973527  1973539  1973557  1973563  1973567  1973579  1973591
1973597  1973627  1973633  1973651  1973669  1973687  1973689  1973723  1973731  1973737
1973747  1973749  1973761  1973779  1973813  1973821  1973831  1973857  1973893  1973897
1973903  1973911  1973927  1973957  1973971  1973977  1973999  1974029  1974041  1974053
1974073  1974079  1974121  1974149  1974163  1974221  1974229  1974239  1974263  1974277
1974299  1974319  1974331  1974353  1974361  1974373  1974383  1974391  1974403  1974433
1974457  1974493  1974503  1974541  1974541  1974551  1974559  1974569  1974641  1974647
1974649  1974659  1974701  1974719  1974743  1974751  1974761  1974767  1974779  1974781
1974787  1974851  1974881  1974883  1974887  1974919  1974923  1974937  1974961  1974967
1974983  1974989  1975019  1975021  1975027  1975037  1975049  1975067  1975073  1975091
1975117  1975121  1975123  1975133  1975147  1975153  1975163  1975187  1975199  1975201
1975223  1975243  1975249  1975279  1975301  1975313  1975321  1975333  1975367  1975381
1975387  1975399  1975409  1975423  1975427  1975439  1975481  1975499  1975511  1975517
1975529  1975543  1975573  1975609  1975613  1975619  1975627  1975651  1975657  1975663
1975669  1975691  1975693  1975709  1975751  1975789  1975811  1975817  1975819  1975823
1975901  1975921  1975931  1975933  1975949  1975957  1975991  1975997  1976011  1976017
1976047  1976053  1976069  1976071  1976081  1976099  1976113  1976141  1976167  1976173
1976197  1976201  1976213  1976239  1976243  1976297  1976309  1976327  1976333  1976347
1976357  1976381  1976383  1976393  1976411  1976419  1976431  1976453  1976477  1976519
1976537  1976543  1976549  1976563  1976593  1976599  1976603  1976609  1976617  1976629
1976633  1976647  1976657  1976683  1976687  1976699  1976707  1976717  1976729  1976731
1976747  1976749  1976759  1976761  1976771  1976789  1976791  1976797  1976803  1976809
1976831  1976837  1976851  1976857  1976861  1976869  1976903  1976911  1976917  1976927
1976939  1976949  1976961  1976983  1976987  1976993  1977023  1977067  1977077  1977089
1977091  1977119  1977139  1977163  1977187  1977203  1977223  1977233  1977251  1977259
1977301  1977319  1977323  1977329  1977343  1977359  1977361  1977403  1977407  1977427
1977433  1977499  1977509  1977529  1977541  1977551  1977557  1977571  1977581  1977601
1977611  1977617  1977623  1977631  1977637  1977667  1977673  1977697  1977709  1977719
1977721  1977727  1977737  1977743  1977917  1977929  1977953  1977961  1977971  1977979
1977991  1978021  1978027  1978037  1978051  1978063  1978087  1978091  1978111  1978117
1978153  1978157  1978159  1978181  1978189  1978199  1978201  1978213  1978267  1978289
1978297  1978313  1978343  1978349  1978363  1978393  1978411  1978421  1978423  1978429
1978433  1978439  1978441  1978463  1978469  1978507  1978523  1978531  1978541  1978567
1978589  1978591  1978597  1978631  1978661  1978663  1978673  1978687  1978693  1978709
1978727  1978741  1978763  1978771  1978799  1978807  1978849  1978853  1978877  1978883
1978891  1978909  1978913  1978927  1978983  1978993  1978997  1979039  1979051  1979053
1979057  1979063  1979069  1979077  1979101  1979119  1979129  1979141  1979143  1979147
1979171  1979177  1979183  1979189  1979207  1979209  1979227  1979233  1979239  1979251
1979261  1979269  1979281  1979291  1979303  1979317  1979321  1979323  1979339  1979347
1979353  1979359  1979371  1979387  1979399  1979413  1979437  1979441  1979473  1979489
1979491  1979507  1979539  1979543  1979563  1979573  1979581  1979609  1979617  1979683
1979689  1979713  1979717  1979723  1979729  1979741  1979749  1979773  1979779  1979807
```

```
1979827  1979891  1979893  1979897  1979899  1979911  1979941  1979947  1979993  1980019
1980023  1980029  1980031  1980053  1980067  1980073  1980079  1980089  1980101  1980103
1980113  1980181  1980191  1980221  1980227  1980229  1980233  1980247  1980263  1980269
1980281  1980283  1980289  1980301  1980317  1980337  1980343  1980353  1980361  1980367
1980371  1980383  1980397  1980401  1980409  1980413  1980431  1980443  1980469  1980491
1980521  1980523  1980529  1980577  1980581  1980607  1980631  1980637  1980659  1980661
1980673  1980697  1980701  1980703  1980707  1980743  1980749  1980757  1980761  1980763
1980773  1980791  1980809  1980817  1980821  1980859  1980863  1980877  1980899  1980907
1980911  1980919  1980929  1980941  1980947  1980949  1980983  1980991  1981037  1981081
1981093  1981099  1981141  1981153  1981159  1981169  1981181  1981201  1981237  1981247
1981267  1981277  1981297  1981337  1981349  1981361  1981393  1981403  1981409  1981417
1981429  1981457  1981471  1981477  1981487  1981493  1981513  1981517  1981523  1981543
1981547  1981583  1981589  1981597  1981607  1981619  1981621  1981627  1981631  1981649
1981663  1981667  1981669  1981687  1981691  1981699  1981711  1981739  1981753  1981787
1981813  1981853  1981867  1981879  1981883  1981891  1981901  1981919  1981921  1981939
1981949  1981963  1981997  1982011  1982021  1982033  1982051  1982059  1982069  1982077
1982083  1982087  1982093  1982111  1982129  1982153  1982159  1982173  1982191  1982203
1982207  1982219  1982263  1982269  1982273  1982287  1982291  1982293  1982371  1982381
1982401  1982417  1982437  1982443  1982447  1982467  1982471  1982501  1982509  1982521
1982537  1982551  1982567  1982573  1982579  1982587  1982599  1982609  1982611  1982627
1982633  1982639  1982641  1982671  1982681  1982713  1982723  1982741  1982779  1982797
1982803  1982809  1982833  1982837  1982839  1982843  1982857  1982861  1982873  1982879
1982881  1982887  1982891  1982909  1982917  1982921  1982951  1982957  1982969  1982987
1982989  1982993  1983001  1983013  1983019  1983053  1983061  1983077  1983097  1983103
1983109  1983143  1983197  1983227  1983229  1983253  1983257  1983301  1983323  1983341
1983343  1983347  1983361  1983379  1983383  1983389  1983409  1983413  1983427  1983437
1983439  1983463  1983479  1983491  1983493  1983503  1983523  1983559  1983563  1983587
1983599  1983601  1983643  1983647  1983649  1983689  1983697  1983701  1983731  1983743
1983749  1983763  1983767  1983833  1983851  1983853  1983859  1983871  1983881  1983889
1983913  1983929  1983931  1983967  1983979  1983997  1984007  1984013  1984039  1984043
1984057  1984061  1984069  1984079  1984091  1984109  1984117  1984123  1984133  1984139
1984159  1984163  1984181  1984183  1984201  1984211  1984247  1984259  1984261  1984271
1984309  1984319  1984327  1984331  1984337  1984343  1984351  1984361  1984363  1984397
1984399  1984429  1984453  1984457  1984459  1984471  1984511  1984537  1984547  1984561
1984571  1984639  1984649  1984667  1984709  1984711  1984727  1984729  1984747  1984753
1984777  1984783  1984793  1984799  1984813  1984817  1984841  1984849  1984859  1984867
1984891  1984897  1984901  1984907  1984921  1984979  1984981  1984991  1985003  1985017
1985041  1985047  1985051  1985057  1985077  1985167  1985183  1985189  1985213  1985219
1985227  1985237  1985239  1985257  1985279  1985287  1985293  1985303  1985317  1985363
1985377  1985407  1985419  1985441  1985453  1985471  1985483  1985491  1985509  1985513
1985537  1985551  1985561  1985573  1985587  1985591  1985593  1985623  1985639  1985663
1985677  1985689  1985713  1985729  1985741  1985743  1985759  1985771  1985779  1985791
1985803  1985849  1985873  1985887  1985897  1985903  1985939  1985987  1985989  1986001
1986029  1986037  1986043  1986053  1986067  1986071  1986097  1986109  1986121  1986133
1986137  1986167  1986169  1986199  1986217  1986223  1986233  1986253  1986277  1986289
1986293  1986301  1986311  1986323  1986337  1986359  1986373  1986401  1986421  1986437
1986443  1986461  1986497  1986527  1986539  1986541  1986547  1986553  1986577  1986631
1986581  1986601  1986629  1986631  1986679  1986683  1986689  1986713  1986749  1986757
1986769  1986779  1986781  1986797  1986823  1986839  1986869  1986871  1986883  1986893
1986899  1986913  1986923  1986949  1986967  1986989  1986991  1986997  1987003  1987031
1987043  1987049  1987057  1987067  1987081  1987091  1987099  1987121  1987123  1987127
1987151  1987157  1987189  1987201  1987217  1987231  1987241  1987247  1987261  1987277
1987291  1987303  1987309  1987313  1987333  1987339  1987373  1987411  1987429  1987439
1987451  1987471  1987477  1987481  1987483  1987501  1987519  1987523  1987537  1987543
1987547  1987549  1987577  1987619  1987621  1987649  1987673  1987679  1987681  1987693
1987697  1987703  1987709  1987789  1987819  1987829  1987841  1987849  1987873  1987879
1987883  1987889  1987891  1987901  1987919  1987939  1987969  1987981  1987987  1987991
1988011  1988023  1988033  1988057  1988087  1988089  1988101  1988113  1988137  1988177
1988183  1988197  1988219  1988221  1988227  1988237  1988243  1988249  1988251  1988257
1988263  1988267  1988279  1988291  1988297  1988299  1988323  1988339  1988341  1988347
1988353  1988411  1988423  1988453  1988471  1988513  1988531  1988533  1988537  1988549
1988551  1988561  1988563  1988579  1988587  1988599  1988611  1988633  1988653  1988659
1988669  1988671  1988683  1988689  1988699  1988729  1988759  1988797  1988801  1988807
1988837  1988839  1988843  1988851  1988891  1988897  1988933  1988941  1988963  1988963
1988999  1989007  1989019  1989049  1989059  1989073  1989077  1989101  1989107  1989131
1989133  1989151  1989161  1989193  1989203  1989217  1989233  1989241  1989259  1989263
1989277  1989307  1989329  1989341  1989353  1989401  1989413  1989419  1989479  1989499
1989517  1989551  1989553  1989563  1989571  1989583  1989613  1989619  1989643  1989671
1989679  1989683  1989721  1989769  1989787  1989791  1989803  1989811  1989847  1989863
1989877  1989899  1989919  1989947  1989959  1989973  1989979  1989989  1990007  1990007
1990031  1990033  1990051  1990069  1990081  1990103  1990111  1990123  1990133  1990141
1990147  1990151  1990159  1990171  1990187  1990189  1990211  1990223  1990229  1990237
1990243  1990249  1990253  1990273  1990277  1990279  1990319  1990321  1990327  1990337
1990361  1990379  1990381  1990433  1990441  1990447  1990453  1990463  1990481  1990487
1990493  1990507  1990523  1990529  1990543  1990553  1990559  1990577  1990579  1990607
1990621  1990643  1990657  1990661  1990679  1990691  1990693  1990753  1990759  1990787
1990823  1990829  1990831  1990867  1990871  1990883  1990889  1990907  1990927  1990939
1990951  1990957  1990969  1990973  1990981  1990987  1991027  1991047  1991063  1991071
1991089  1991107  1991123  1991131  1991137  1991147  1991153  1991177  1991231  1991239
1991243  1991251  1991267  1991279  1991281  1991293  1991351  1991357  1991359  1991387
1991389  1991413  1991443  1991449  1991461  1991477  1991489  1991491  1991503  1991519
1991527  1991551  1991573  1991597  1991603  1991609  1991617  1991623  1991641  1991653
1991677  1991701  1991707  1991723  1991729  1991753  1991761  1991779  1991797  1991803
1991837  1991849  1991861  1991863  1991879  1991881  1991893  1991911  1991921  1991929
1991933  1991947  1991959  1991963  1991989  1991993  1991999  1992031  1992041  1992049
1992073  1992079  1992101  1992119  1992139  1992163  1992167  1992181  1992197  1992203
1992227  1992241  1992251  1992257  1992259  1992269  1992299  1992307  1992337  1992343
1992373  1992407  1992409  1992433  1992437  1992439  1992469  1992481  1992493  1992509
1992517  1992527  1992533  1992547  1992563  1992583  1992589  1992611  1992623  1992631
```

```
1992637  1992643  1992673  1992691  1992713  1992719  1992733  1992761  1992763  1992769
1992779  1992797  1992803  1992817  1992839  1992841  1992877  1992883  1992889  1992911
1992917  1992919  1992937  1992953  1992971  1992983  1993031  1993037  1993039  1993067
1993087  1993109  1993127  1993151  1993163  1993193  1993217  1993219  1993231  1993237
1993241  1993247  1993259  1993261  1993273  1993289  1993307  1993319  1993339  1993349
1993357  1993363  1993367  1993417  1993441  1993457  1993477  1993483  1993493  1993507
1993513  1993529  1993531  1993553  1993561  1993591  1993601  1993603  1993627  1993631
1993633  1993637  1993643  1993657  1993661  1993679  1993681  1993687  1993697  1993699
1993711  1993729  1993757  1993759  1993763  1993829  1993861  1993877  1993921  1993931
1993933  1993949  1993963  1993969  1993973  1993991  1993997  1994033  1994051  1994053
1994059  1994081  1994087  1994093  1994101  1994119  1994143  1994191  1994203  1994207
1994227  1994299  1994327  1994339  1994341  1994347  1994357  1994381  1994387  1994413
1994429  1994437  1994441  1994459  1994467  1994471  1994477  1994479  1994483  1994497
1994501  1994519  1994521  1994543  1994567  1994569  1994599  1994621  1994623  1994647
1994651  1994659  1994669  1994687  1994711  1994717  1994743  1994777  1994779  1994807
1994827  1994833  1994843  1994869  1994879  1994897  1994911  1994947  1994953  1994959
1994977  1994983  1994989  1995011  1995013  1995023  1995031  1995061  1995073  1995083
1995107  1995109  1995121  1995139  1995143  1995187  1995211  1995221  1995223  1995263
1995271  1995293  1995311  1995331  1995337  1995349  1995353  1995359  1995389  1995391
1995421  1995431  1995449  1995473  1995481  1995517  1995527  1995529  1995533  1995541
1995547  1995583  1995607  1995611  1995629  1995649  1995661  1995677  1995683  1995689
1995691  1995709  1995713  1995727  1995769  1995781  1995787  1995797  1995827  1995841
1995857  1995869  1995883  1995913  1995937  1995947  1995967  1995971  1995977  1995979
1995989  1995991  1996013  1996019  1996061  1996081  1996087  1996091  1996097  1996109
1996129  1996171  1996177  1996207  1996217  1996219  1996223  1996229  1996237  1996277
1996279  1996283  1996289  1996297  1996301  1996303  1996321  1996333  1996343  1996363
1996381  1996391  1996403  1996411  1996417  1996427  1996439  1996453  1996459  1996471
1996481  1996487  1996507  1996517  1996529  1996543  1996549  1996559  1996573  1996583
1996609  1996613  1996639  1996649  1996681  1996697  1996711  1996717  1996721  1996723
1996739  1996751  1996759  1996763  1996777  1996781  1996793  1996817  1996829  1996849
1996859  1996867  1996879  1996901  1996903  1996933  1996937  1996949  1996979  1997003
1997029  1997053  1997057  1997059  1997081  1997087  1997089  1997101  1997111  1997119
1997129  1997137  1997141  1997161  1997173  1997179  1997183  1997189  1997213  1997231
1997243  1997257  1997267  1997269  1997293  1997311  1997321  1997339  1997341  1997351
1997407  1997419  1997431  1997441  1997459  1997467  1997473  1997503  1997507  1997531
1997539  1997543  1997557  1997587  1997591  1997599  1997617  1997647  1997657  1997663
1997683  1997693  1997701  1997707  1997713  1997719  1997731  1997747  1997753  1997771
1997773  1997813  1997833  1997843  1997851  1997867  1997887  1997899  1997903  1997911
1997921  1997939  1997969  1997999  1998019  1998023  1998041  1998049  1998067  1998077
1998089  1998107  1998109  1998119  1998127  1998133  1998169  1998181  1998209  1998221
1998223  1998233  1998251  1998257  1998277  1998289  1998303  1998319  1998329  1998331
1998341  1998343  1998349  1998371  1998379  1998397  1998413  1998427  1998431  1998443
1998449  1998457  1998473  1998497  1998517  1998527  1998533  1998541  1998559  1998569
1998587  1998589  1998611  1998617  1998637  1998641  1998643  1998679  1998691  1998697
1998701  1998727  1998739  1998761  1998793  1998817  1998827  1998839  1998881  1998917
1998923  1998943  1998947  1998949  1998961  1998977  1998991  1999007  1999021  1999033
1999043  1999061  1999069  1999099  1999103  1999111  1999121  1999163  1999177  1999187
1999211  1999219  1999223  1999243  1999247  1999273  1999297  1999301  1999303  1999307
1999331  1999339  1999343  1999363  1999379  1999423  1999441  1999471  1999499  1999511
1999513  1999537  1999549  1999559  1999561  1999567  1999603  1999607  1999619  1999631
1999651  1999661  1999667  1999687  1999681  1999691  1999703  1999721  1999733  1999757
1999799  1999817  1999819  1999853  1999859  1999867  1999871  1999889  1999891  1999957
1999969  1999979  1999993  2000003  2000029  2000039  2000081  2000083  2000093  2000107
2000113  2000143  2000147  2000153  2000177  2000209  2000221  2000227  2000249  2000261
2000269  2000281  2000291  2000293  2000303  2000309  2000321  2000329  2000351  2000353
2000371  2000381  2000387  2000389  2000393  2000413  2000417  2000423  2000429  2000447
2000497  2000503  2000519  2000521  2000539  2000573  2000597  2000629  2000633  2000639
2000653  2000659  2000671  2000689  2000693  2000699  2000717  2000731  2000753  2000767
2000807  2000813  2000863  2000903  2000927  2000939  2000941  2000953  2000959  2000963
2000969  2000989  2001007  2001049  2001067  2001073  2001079  2001101  2001127  2001163
2001179  2001191  2001199  2001211  2001229  2001247  2001269  2001281  2001313  2001331
2001347  2001353  2001361  2001371  2001397  2001407  2001409  2001413  2001421  2001449
2001451  2001463  2001469  2001481  2001487  2001509  2001511  2001533  2001539  2001541
2001547  2001553  2001581  2001583  2001611  2001617  2001619  2001641  2001653  2001673
2001677  2001691  2001697  2001709  2001721  2001731  2001751  2001787  2001793  2001799
2001809  2001833  2001847  2001911  2001919  2001953  2001977  2001997  2002001  2002009
2002019  2002061  2002079  2002093  2002151  2002157  2002159  2002199  2002207  2002211
2002223  2002229  2002249  2002267  2002289  2002303  2002307  2002313  2002327  2002331
2002333  2002337  2002339  2002349  2002361  2002373  2002387  2002397  2002417  2002453
2002459  2002471  2002523  2002531  2002547  2002577  2002579  2002603  2002607  2002613
2002621  2002643  2002661  2002667  2002669  2002673  2002681  2002723  2002739  2002747
2002783  2002799  2002807  2002823  2002829  2002841  2002853  2002867  2002877  2002883
2002907  2002919  2002927  2002937  2002957  2002967  2002969  2002993  2002997  2003009
2003011  2003021  2003033  2003051  2003081  2003083  2003087  2003119  2003149  2003153
2003159  2003191  2003201  2003213  2003227  2003257  2003269  2003273  2003279  2003299
2003321  2003329  2003359  2003363  2003381  2003387  2003411  2003447  2003459  2003471
2003483  2003497  2003509  2003557  2003591  2003593  2003597  2003611  2003621  2003627
2003633  2003641  2003647  2003653  2003663  2003669  2003681  2003723  2003741  2003753
2003761  2003767  2003801  2003803  2003819  2003839  2003857  2003861  2003863  2003879
2003927  2003937  2003951  2003959  2003971  2003999  2004001  2004007  2004017  2004029
2004043  2004049  2004073  2004083  2004091  2004097  2004109  2004131  2004133  2004137
2004209  2004227  2004251  2004269  2004271  2004293  2004313  2004341  2004347  2004349
2004377  2004383  2004421  2004433  2004461  2004463  2004479  2004511  2004529  2004539
2004559  2004571  2004577  2004593  2004601  2004631  2004641  2004647  2004661  2004679
2004701  2004713  2004719  2004731  2004757  2004763  2004773  2004787  2004791  2004803
2004809  2004811  2004817  2004829  2004833  2004839  2004851  2004881  2004901  2004911
2004917  2004931  2004943  2004953  2004983  2004991  2005001  2005019  2005021  2005027
2005033  2005037  2005039  2005057  2005061  2005079  2005103  2005121  2005139  2005151
2005181  2005183  2005189  2005193  2005207  2005229  2005231  2005249  2005261  2005277
```

```
2005319  2005331  2005343  2005369  2005373  2005387  2005397  2005417  2005427  2005429
2005441  2005447  2005453  2005459  2005489  2005499  2005519  2005547  2005559  2005567
2005571  2005579  2005613  2005667  2005673  2005681  2005687  2005693  2005723  2005739
2005747  2005763  2005769  2005777  2005789  2005799  2005831  2005841  2005859  2005873
2005877  2005879  2005903  2005919  2005931  2005937  2005943  2005957  2005981  2006009
2006021  2006033  2006071  2006087  2006093  2006111  2006141  2006159  2006183  2006189
2006197  2006201  2006231  2006239  2006273  2006287  2006297  2006299  2006317  2006339
2006341  2006353  2006369  2006377  2006387  2006393  2006429  2006437  2006441  2006443
2006447  2006461  2006483  2006489  2006491  2006503  2006507  2006549  2006573  2006579
2006603  2006611  2006623  2006651  2006657  2006659  2006671  2006677  2006689  2006707
2006779  2006783  2006791  2006813  2006831  2006869  2006891  2006897  2006899  2006903
2006923  2006929  2006959  2007001  2007011  2007013  2007029  2007043  2007053  2007067
2007077  2007079  2007091  2007097  2007107  2007133  2007149  2007151  2007193  2007199
2007209  2007227  2007251  2007259  2007263  2007277  2007301  2007307  2007329  2007347
2007353  2007359  2007389  2007391  2007403  2007431  2007433  2007437  2007451  2007487
2007491  2007493  2007497  2007503  2007517  2007527  2007539  2007553  2007557  2007589
2007611  2007613  2007617  2007619  2007623  2007631  2007659  2007661  2007679  2007697
2007701  2007703  2007721  2007737  2007763  2007767  2007769  2007773  2007791  2007823
2007827  2007851  2007853  2007869  2007871  2007883  2007899  2007911  2007913  2007917
2007919  2007949  2007959  2007961  2007979  2008003  2008033  2008043  2008049  2008051
2008063  2008067  2008079  2008081  2008103  2008121  2008141  2008147  2008151  2008189
2008213  2008229  2008241  2008247  2008271  2008277  2008289  2008297  2008309
2008313  2008327  2008333  2008339  2008343  2008367  2008373  2008379  2008393  2008403
2008421  2008427  2008439  2008441  2008469  2008477  2008481  2008483  2008493  2008529
2008553  2008571  2008621  2008637  2008663  2008673  2008679  2008691  2008697  2008709
2008717  2008729  2008739  2008763  2008777  2008781  2008793  2008807  2008817  2008823
2008871  2008879  2008883  2008901  2008933  2008939  2008949  2008961  2008973  2009011
2009039  2009069  2009083  2009093  2009107  2009113  2009167  2009171  2009173  2009191
2009209  2009219  2009233  2009239  2009243  2009251  2009299  2009311  2009317  2009321
2009333  2009339  2009377  2009387  2009393  2009407  2009437  2009461  2009467  2009489
2009503  2009509  2009537  2009543  2009593  2009603  2009639  2009647  2009669  2009713
2009719  2009731  2009737  2009747  2009759  2009771  2009783  2009789  2009807  2009827
2009831  2009857  2009867  2009869  2009873  2009879  2009881  2009897  2009911  2009921
2009923  2009957  2009971  2009977  2009981  2009983  2009989  2009999  2010017  2010023
2010031  2010037  2010053  2010061  2010083  2010089  2010103  2010137  2010139  2010161
2010167  2010187  2010191  2010221  2010227  2010241  2010289  2010299  2010311  2010317
2010329  2010341  2010373  2010389  2010397  2010401  2010413  2010431  2010439  2010451
2010467  2010479  2010527  2010553  2010559  2010571  2010581  2010583  2010601  2010611
2010647  2010653  2010667  2010677  2010689  2010703  2010721  2010727  2010733  2010881
2010887  2010893  2010901  2010923  2010929  2010971  2010973  2010977  2011003  2011019
2011021  2011027  2011033  2011057  2011069  2011073  2011081  2011099  2011111  2011123
2011127  2011129  2011147  2011171  2011183  2011193  2011199  2011201  2011211  2011241
2011259  2011267  2011277  2011291  2011309  2011333  2011363  2011381  2011391  2011393
2011409  2011417  2011439  2011441  2011483  2011507  2011517  2011531  2011543  2011561
2011573  2011591  2011601  2011613  2011631  2011637  2011657  2011673  2011697  2011699
2011703  2011733  2011753  2011769  2011799  2011811  2011843  2011861  2011897  2011903
2011907  2011913  2011939  2011951  2011957  2011973  2011987  2012009  2012011  2012027
2012033  2012047  2012057  2012083  2012093  2012113  2012123  2012147  2012159  2012161
2012167  2012173  2012189  2012203  2012221  2012237  2012243  2012287  2012299  2012317
2012323  2012333  2012363  2012371  2012383  2012401  2012407  2012419  2012429  2012447
2012449  2012471  2012519  2012531  2012533  2012597  2012611  2012639  2012641  2012657
2012663  2012671  2012677  2012693  2012711  2012713  2012719  2012741  2012743  2012767
2012789  2012807  2012821  2012827  2012839  2012889  2012893  2012909  2012951
2012957  2012971  2013001  2013013  2013019  2013023  2013043  2013049  2013071  2013079
2013083  2013101  2013113  2013119  2013127  2013163  2013169  2013173  2013181  2013197
2013227  2013229  2013247  2013251  2013287  2013289  2013299  2013301  2013307
2013313  2013329  2013337  2013343  2013359  2013367  2013371  2013377  2013391  2013409
2013439  2013457  2013491  2013511  2013533  2013541  2013553  2013589  2013593  2013617
2013619  2013653  2013659  2013679  2013703  2013707  2013709  2013721  2013727  2013743
2013749  2013751  2013757  2013761  2013779  2013787  2013821  2013833  2013859  2013877
2013889  2013899  2013911  2013923  2013937  2013941  2013967  2013983  2013989  2014009
2014013  2014027  2014031  2014049  2014069  2014081  2014097  2014099  2014121  2014127
2014139  2014141  2014147  2014151  2014157  2014183  2014193  2014213  2014217  2014219
2014231  2014237  2014267  2014277  2014283  2014297  2014301  2014303  2014333  2014351
2014357  2014379  2014393  2014423  2014457  2014459  2014471  2014487  2014499  2014511
2014553  2014559  2014567  2014591  2014603  2014609  2014643  2014651  2014657
2014667  2014697  2014709  2014723  2014729  2014739  2014759  2014763  2014799  2014801
2014811  2014813  2014861  2014867  2014869  2014877  2014889  2014897  2014919
2014921  2014939  2014951  2014967  2014979  2014997  2015011  2015021  2015033  2015047
2015063  2015071  2015081  2015087  2015089  2015107  2015141  2015149  2015161  2015177
2015179  2015183  2015201  2015203  2015213  2015267  2015269  2015287  2015303  2015309
2015317  2015339  2015347  2015359  2015371  2015393  2015411  2015417  2015423  2015441
2015443  2015473  2015491  2015509  2015543  2015557  2015567  2015599  2015609
2015621  2015627  2015633  2015669  2015677  2015701  2015731  2015747  2015753  2015771
2015777  2015779  2015791  2015801  2015833  2015853  2015861  2015863  2015869
2015873  2015879  2015921  2015933  2015941  2015947  2015977  2015999  2016017  2016029
2016031  2016059  2016101  2016107  2016127  2016137  2016139  2016181  2016193  2016197
2016199  2016211  2016239  2016247  2016269  2016277  2016281  2016293  2016323  2016331
2016349  2016359  2016361  2016367  2016373  2016397  2016401  2016403  2016407  2016409
2016419  2016439  2016449  2016461  2016493  2016517  2016529  2016541  2016551  2016559
2016577  2016583  2016587  2016593  2016607  2016653  2016671  2016673  2016691  2016697
2016733  2016739  2016787  2016821  2016823  2016841  2016851  2016853  2016857  2016877
2016881  2016919  2016923  2016943  2016967  2016977  2016997  2017003  2017009  2017019
2017027  2017073  2017079  2017109  2017121  2017133  2017177  2017187  2017189  2017217
2017243  2017247  2017283  2017289  2017313  2017319  2017333  2017369  2017397  2017403
2017409  2017427  2017447  2017459  2017469  2017471  2017489  2017493  2017513  2017529
2017549  2017567  2017579  2017601  2017621  2017627  2017637  2017643  2017669  2017681
2017693  2017709  2017711  2017723  2017727  2017751  2017753  2017783  2017787  2017801
2017811  2017817  2017823  2017831  2017837  2017843  2017889  2017901  2017909  2017919
```

```
2017931  2017957  2017963  2017987  2017991  2018021  2018041  2018077  2018111  2018113
2018117  2018153  2018167  2018171  2018173  2018183  2018249  2018251  2018261  2018287
2018299  2018309  2018333  2018369  2018381  2018383  2018407  2018413  2018437  2018447
2018453  2018483  2018507  2018531  2018543  2018561  2018573  2018581  2018591  2018593
2018623  2018629  2018633  2018647  2018651  2018663  2018671  2018677  2018713  2018729
2018741  2018747  2018749  2018761  2018773  2018827  2018837  2018843  2018851  2018873
2018897  2018899  2018927  2018953  2018957  2018981  2018987  2018993  2019001  2019011
2019013  2019019  2019023  2019029  2019037  2019041  2019047  2019071  2019077  2019089
2019113  2019119  2019131  2019133  2019137  2019181  2019191  2019211  2019217  2019223
2019257  2019271  2019289  2019317  2019337  2019343  2019361  2019401  2019403  2019419
2019461  2019463  2019467  2019487  2019503  2019533  2019569  2019587  2019599  2019613
2019623  2019659  2019679  2019707  2019709  2019713  2019739  2019751  2019761  2019767
2019769  2019799  2019803  2019811  2019817  2019827  2019847  2019851  2019859  2019869
2019881  2019907  2019911  2019931  2019959  2019967  2019973  2019977  2020001  2020003
2020019  2020027  2020037  2020043  2020079  2020091  2020147  2020153  2020171  2020181
2020223  2020231  2020243  2020247  2020253  2020261  2020279  2020309  2020313  2020321
2020387  2020391  2020393  2020409  2020411  2020423  2020429  2020457  2020463  2020471
2020477  2020489  2020493  2020507  2020511  2020537  2020547  2020561  2020591  2020597
2020609  2020621  2020657  2020661  2020663  2020679  2020687  2020693  2020721  2020723
2020727  2020729  2020771  2020789  2020793  2020817  2020819  2020831  2020853  2020861
2020877  2020883  2020891  2020913  2020933  2020939  2020961  2020979  2020999  2021003
2021009  2021017  2021029  2021053  2021077  2021081  2021083  2021099  2021119  2021137
2021143  2021167  2021179  2021183  2021191  2021197  2021203  2021219  2021237  2021251
2021291  2021321  2021333  2021339  2021377  2021381  2021431  2021471  2021489  2021497
2021501  2021507  2021519  2021527  2021533  2021549  2021563  2021567  2021573  2021597
2021599  2021609  2021627  2021629  2021639  2021647  2021651  2021653  2021659  2021671
2021693  2021699  2021711  2021729  2021737  2021743  2021777  2021779  2021783  2021801
2021807  2021837  2021839  2021843  2021849  2021863  2021879  2021891  2021927  2021933
2021959  2022011  2022017  2022019  2022029  2022043  2022047  2022049  2022067  2022077
2022101  2022103  2022149  2022157  2022187  2022191  2022217  2022233  2022239  2022253
2022263  2022271  2022281  2022283  2022289  2022301  2022329  2022331  2022359  2022389
2022401  2022403  2022421  2022469  2022481  2022487  2022491  2022497  2022539  2022583
2022613  2022617  2022619  2022641  2022649  2022659  2022661  2022701  2022707  2022731
2022737  2022743  2022749  2022751  2022767  2022773  2022791  2022803  2022841  2022863
2022869  2022877  2022883  2022893  2022971  2022989  2022991  2023001  2023009  2023013
2023019  2023027  2023031  2023061  2023067  2023081  2023093  2023097  2023117  2023121
2023141  2023157  2023159  2023163  2023171  2023183  2023201  2023207  2023211  2023223
2023261  2023267  2023283  2023297  2023313  2023337  2023349  2023363  2023369  2023393
2023421  2023433  2023447  2023453  2023501  2023507  2023529  2023531  2023543  2023547
2023577  2023579  2023597  2023603  2023607  2023621  2023639  2023661  2023667  2023727
2023741  2023753  2023783  2023811  2023817  2023829  2023831  2023837  2023841  2023843
2023849  2023859  2023891  2023907  2023913  2023921  2023951  2023963  2023981  2023993
2024063  2024093  2024101  2024107  2024111  2024117  2024147  2024153  2024167  2024177
2024179  2024213  2024219  2024221  2024227  2024237  2024249  2024261  2024263  2024327
2024329  2024339  2024357  2024369  2024371  2024383  2024387  2024413  2024417  2024419
2024471  2024489  2024501  2024531  2024551  2024567  2024573  2024587  2024591  2024597
2024599  2024611  2024639  2024647  2024689  2024731  2024767  2024779  2024831  2024833
2024843  2024861  2024863  2024873  2024881  2024909  2024917  2024933  2024977  2025029
2025043  2025053  2025103  2025109  2025131  2025169  2025181  2025187  2025197  2025203
2025211  2025217  2025241  2025251  2025253  2025259  2025281  2025307  2025341  2025347
2025349  2025367  2025377  2025409  2025421  2025427  2025437  2025467  2025479  2025487
2025493  2025497  2025503  2025511  2025539  2025553  2025557  2025577  2025589  2025593
2025623  2025629  2025631  2025637  2025641  2025643  2025649  2025659  2025671  2025689
2025697  2025719  2025721  2025733  2025739  2025767  2025791  2025827  2025833  2025869
2025887  2025899  2025901  2025917  2025923  2025929  2025949  2025979  2026021  2026061
2026069  2026081  2026091  2026099  2026109  2026121  2026151  2026153  2026163  2026181
2026183  2026187  2026223  2026229  2026249  2026303  2026309  2026327  2026333  2026351
2026361  2026373  2026391  2026393  2026397  2026447  2026457  2026463  2026469  2026471
2026487  2026517  2026523  2026537  2026567  2026613  2026627  2026631  2026639  2026663
2026669  2026679  2026697  2026721  2026727  2026729  2026733  2026741  2026751  2026763
2026769  2026789  2026799  2026807  2026813  2026819  2026831  2026841  2026877  2026889
2026909  2026919  2026931  2026957  2026987  2027021  2027023  2027033  2027057  2027087
2027093  2027099  2027101  2027111  2027117  2027147  2027159  2027161  2027177  2027209
2027227  2027237  2027239  2027257  2027269  2027297  2027309  2027317  2027323  2027359
2027371  2027383  2027393  2027401  2027411  2027423  2027447  2027449  2027461  2027497
2027503  2027507  2027513  2027537  2027549  2027561  2027567  2027569  2027587  2027609
2027629  2027633  2027639  2027659  2027677  2027681  2027713  2027719  2027723  2027731
2027747  2027759  2027783  2027789  2027797  2027801  2027807  2027821  2027843  2027869
2027873  2027897  2027899  2027903  2027911  2027951  2027953  2027959  2028017  2028053
2028073  2028077  2028101  2028107  2028109  2028119  2028121  2028137  2028139  2028179
2028197  2028199  2028203  2028217  2028223  2028227  2028239  2028241  2028263  2028277
2028281  2028293  2028319  2028329  2028359  2028371  2028373  2028391  2028401  2028413
2028431  2028443  2028461  2028487  2028503  2028511  2028517  2028527  2028581
2028589  2028601  2028617  2028629  2028643  2028647  2028667  2028679  2028701  2028703
2028707  2028713  2028749  2028757  2028773  2028779  2028781  2028809  2028841  2028847
2028863  2028881  2028907  2028931  2028941  2028947  2028973  2029003  2029007  2029019
2029021  2029033  2029051  2029063  2029073  2029081  2029087  2029091  2029121  2029123
2029147  2029163  2029177  2029189  2029199  2029207  2029241  2029243  2029249  2029271
2029277  2029283  2029301  2029331  2029351  2029369  2029373  2029387  2029399  2029403
2029411  2029439  2029453  2029457  2029483  2029499  2029501  2029549  2029567
2029597  2029633  2029649  2029661  2029667  2029669  2029679  2029697  2029711  2029717
2029721  2029723  2029759  2029793  2029799  2029801  2029813  2029829  2029831  2029843
2029871  2029873  2029879  2029889  2029891  2029921  2029939  2029967  2029981  2029991
2029997  2030009  2030051  2030053  2030069  2030081  2030099  2030101  2030117  2030137
2030173  2030183  2030209  2030213  2030243  2030251  2030257  2030267  2030291  2030299
2030309  2030311  2030317  2030363  2030381  2030383  2030389  2030393  2030411  2030419
2030437  2030459  2030461  2030467  2030471  2030489  2030513  2030527  2030533  2030563
2030573  2030591  2030617  2030627  2030653  2030657  2030659  2030669  2030683  2030711
2030719  2030731  2030737  2030747  2030759  2030789  2030879  2030881  2030909  2030911
```

```
2030921  2030947  2030953  2030981  2030999  2031023  2031037  2031053  2031059  2031067
2031077  2031103  2031121  2031137  2031163  2031167  2031179  2031187  2031217  2031223
2031229  2031251  2031257  2031269  2031283  2031287  2031301  2031319  2031353  2031391
2031397  2031409  2031431  2031443  2031457  2031467  2031473  2031487  2031493  2031541
2031563  2031569  2031571  2031577  2031587  2031593  2031599  2031611  2031671  2031691
2031703  2031713  2031749  2031767  2031779  2031791  2031811  2031839  2031851  2031863
2031893  2031907  2031937  2031961  2031977  2031979  2031983  2032013  2032021  2032039
2032057  2032067  2032103  2032109  2032111  2032133  2032153  2032157  2032159  2032171
2032181  2032193  2032207  2032213  2032237  2032241  2032253  2032271  2032273  2032301
2032307  2032313  2032339  2032343  2032351  2032357  2032361  2032363  2032369  2032403
2032409  2032417  2032439  2032463  2032489  2032507  2032519  2032529  2032543  2032553
2032559  2032561  2032573  2032607  2032619  2032621  2032627  2032633  2032637  2032643
2032649  2032651  2032661  2032663  2032687  2032691  2032711  2032721  2032733  2032759
2032769  2032777  2032783  2032787  2032799  2032819  2032837  2032841  2032853  2032859
2032861  2032873  2032879  2032909  2032931  2032937  2032939  2032951  2032967  2032969
2032973  2032991  2032999  2033021  2033041  2033051  2033063  2033071  2033077  2033089
2033093  2033111  2033159  2033167  2033179  2033189  2033201  2033203  2033221  2033233
2033243  2033257  2033263  2033279  2033281  2033287  2033299  2033309  2033327  2033357
2033363  2033369  2033377  2033389  2033401  2033429  2033441  2033443  2033459  2033461
2033497  2033503  2033527  2033531  2033533  2033543  2033573  2033579  2033587  2033609
2033611  2033639  2033657  2033677  2033687  2033699  2033711  2033719  2033743  2033783
2033791  2033797  2033803  2033807  2033833  2033839  2033861  2033869  2033873  2033881
2033903  2033929  2033939  2033951  2033953  2033971  2033989  2034017  2034023  2034041
2034047  2034061  2034103  2034139  2034157  2034161  2034173  2034181  2034191  2034209
2034211  2034217  2034233  2034239  2034257  2034269  2034283  2034317  2034337  2034343
2034359  2034367  2034421  2034427  2034433  2034449  2034457  2034481  2034491  2034493
2034503  2034517  2034521  2034541  2034551  2034569  2034581  2034619  2034661  2034671
2034689  2034709  2034731  2034737  2034743  2034749  2034757  2034761  2034779  2034793
2034797  2034811  2034817  2034827  2034839  2034841  2034869  2034887  2034913  2034937
2034941  2034947  2034973  2034979  2034997  2035001  2035009  2035013  2035031  2035039
2035043  2035067  2035069  2035081  2035093  2035097  2035127  2035141  2035151  2035169
2035193  2035211  2035213  2035237  2035273  2035289  2035301  2035303  2035343  2035349
2035361  2035373  2035379  2035391  2035399  2035403  2035417  2035433  2035447  2035493
2035507  2035511  2035513  2035531  2035549  2035567  2035591  2035633  2035639  2035667
2035669  2035681  2035687  2035723  2035729  2035757  2035763  2035807  2035823  2035837
2035841  2035843  2035853  2035867  2035879  2035919  2035927  2035931  2035949  2035967
2035973  2036009  2036017  2036051  2036071  2036077  2036081  2036113  2036123  2036129
2036131  2036137  2036143  2036161  2036171  2036201  2036219  2036257  2036263  2036269
2036273  2036299  2036323  2036339  2036341  2036357  2036387  2036393  2036423  2036449
2036459  2036473  2036479  2036501  2036513  2036527  2036533  2036539  2036569  2036579
2036597  2036603  2036611  2036623  2036663  2036677  2036687  2036693  2036701  2036711
2036747  2036791  2036803  2036807  2036809  2036831  2036833  2036861  2036863  2036869
2036891  2036893  2036911  2036929  2036939  2036941  2036963  2036977  2036987  2037017
2037019  2037023  2037029  2037037  2037043  2037067  2037071  2037073  2037083  2037131
2037149  2037151  2037157  2037169  2037209  2037223  2037247  2037251  2037253  2037281
2037283  2037293  2037307  2037311  2037341  2037349  2037353  2037377  2037379  2037391
2037407  2037419  2037437  2037449  2037457  2037491  2037493  2037509  2037523  2037533
2037611  2037619  2037643  2037677  2037689  2037697  2037709  2037713  2037719  2037751
2037757  2037787  2037793  2037799  2037803  2037809  2037821  2037829  2037851  2037853
2037857  2037881  2037911  2037979  2038019  2038021  2038027  2038031  2038039  2038103
2038117  2038123  2038133  2038139  2038159  2038163  2038177  2038217  2038247  2038259
2038271  2038291  2038297  2038307  2038313  2038319  2038363  2038369  2038373  2038403
2038411  2038417  2038427  2038429  2038481  2038493  2038499  2038507  2038523  2038537
2038549  2038573  2038577  2038579  2038607  2038637  2038639  2038661  2038693  2038703
2038717  2038721  2038747  2038763  2038769  2038783  2038801  2038819  2038831  2038849
2038853  2038867  2038879  2038919  2038921  2038943  2038951  2038957  2038969  2038979
2039027  2039057  2039071  2039083  2039113  2039119  2039131  2039143  2039161  2039171
2039173  2039179  2039197  2039221  2039243  2039263  2039267  2039287  2039321  2039339
2039351  2039353  2039357  2039383  2039407  2039417  2039423  2039437  2039461  2039467
2039491  2039501  2039509  2039549  2039561  2039567  2039579  2039603  2039621  2039623
2039629  2039633  2039641  2039647  2039651  2039671  2039731  2039743  2039761  2039771
2039777  2039789  2039797  2039819  2039833  2039837  2039857  2039867  2039879  2039899
2039903  2039909  2039911  2039927  2039929  2039951  2039957  2039971  2039977  2039981
2039993  2040019  2040029  2040041  2040047  2040053  2040089  2040097  2040107  2040109
2040113  2040133  2040149  2040151  2040167  2040173  2040191  2040193  2040211  2040229
2040251  2040253  2040263  2040281  2040287  2040293  2040319  2040331  2040361  2040377
2040403  2040407  2040427  2040431  2040433  2040443  2040449  2040457  2040461  2040473
2040481  2040497  2040539  2040541  2040551  2040557  2040559  2040593  2040601  2040607
2040641  2040653  2040679  2040719  2040743  2040749  2040769  2040781  2040791  2040803
2040827  2040851  2040917  2040919  2040943  2040959  2040967  2040971  2040989  2041001
2041027  2041033  2041051  2041063  2041079  2041097  2041129  2041147  2041159  2041177
2041183  2041199  2041201  2041231  2041283  2041297  2041307  2041363  2041387  2041421
2041427  2041433  2041447  2041451  2041469  2041477  2041489  2041519  2041531  2041537
2041553  2041561  2041579  2041583  2041601  2041619  2041631  2041639  2041643  2041661
2041681  2041693  2041703  2041709  2041729  2041757  2041783  2041807  2041811  2041817
2041849  2041859  2041867  2041891  2041933  2041937  2041943  2041957  2041961  2041967
2041997  2042017  2042021  2042039  2042059  2042077  2042083  2042107  2042111  2042123
2042129  2042149  2042153  2042171  2042179  2042189  2042203  2042207  2042213  2042221
2042233  2042237  2042263  2042273  2042281  2042297  2042303  2042317  2042323  2042347
2042353  2042357  2042389  2042393  2042399  2042401  2042419  2042429  2042449  2042459
2042477  2042483  2042489  2042531  2042549  2042581  2042587  2042591  2042597  2042603
2042609  2042627  2042647  2042657  2042681  2042687  2042717  2042749  2042753  2042767
2042783  2042797  2042809  2042813  2042819  2042849  2042851  2042857  2042863  2042891
2042923  2042933  2042969  2042981  2042983  2043001  2043007  2043011  2043017  2043023
2043037  2043047  2043053  2043061  2043091  2043101  2043109  2043121  2043149  2043163
2043169  2043187  2043191  2043193  2043199  2043257  2043259  2043269  2043277  2043289
2043313  2043323  2043329  2043337  2043341  2043397  2043401  2043409  2043413  2043421
2043449  2043467  2043479  2043487  2043491  2043497  2043511  2043523  2043539  2043541
2043571  2043589  2043599  2043617  2043631  2043637  2043647  2043673  2043703  2043719
```

```
2043721 2043739 2043749 2043751 2043761 2043763 2043779 2043793 2043817 2043841
2043851 2043869 2043907 2043911 2043931 2043953 2043959 2043971 2043989 2043997
2044013 2044027 2044037 2044043 2044061 2044067 2044069 2044099 2044111 2044127
2044129 2044151 2044169 2044187 2044201 2044243 2044249 2044271 2044277 2044279
2044321 2044331 2044351 2044363 2044391 2044411 2044421 2044463 2044487 2044489
2044499 2044507 2044519 2044541 2044561 2044577 2044621 2044633 2044649 2044661
2044673 2044681 2044697 2044733 2044739 2044753 2044759 2044787 2044789 2044831
2044841 2044843 2044849 2044873 2044883 2044901 2044909 2044919 2044921 2044937
2044943 2044963 2044969 2044979 2045009 2045011 2045023 2045047 2045053 2045077
2045089 2045093 2045129 2045177 2045189 2045191 2045213 2045311 2045317 2045333
2045339 2045347 2045357 2045359 2045363 2045371 2045377 2045437 2045441 2045503
2045509 2045539 2045543 2045557 2045567 2045569 2045587 2045591 2045599 2045609
2045611 2045629 2045647 2045651 2045653 2045669 2045677 2045699 2045713 2045731
2045753 2045761 2045773 2045789 2045819 2045833 2045837 2045839 2045851 2045857
2045881 2045891 2045903 2045909 2045929 2045963 2045987 2045999 2046013 2046017
2046029 2046043 2046047 2046049 2046059 2046073 2046101 2046119 2046127 2046133
2046151 2046157 2046169 2046193 2046203 2046223 2046271 2046293 2046299 2046311
2046313 2046323 2046349 2046353 2046371 2046389 2046391 2046397 2046419 2046431
2046437 2046449 2046463 2046469 2046479 2046487 2046493 2046553 2046607 2046631
2046637 2046641 2046677 2046683 2046703 2046719 2046721 2046727 2046731 2046739
2046743 2046773 2046787 2046799 2046823 2046827 2046829 2046833 2046853 2046857
2046871 2046881 2046893 2046901 2046937 2046943 2046949 2046959 2046971 2046973
2046983 2047037 2047039 2047043 2047049 2047061 2047063 2047091 2047093 2047121
2047141 2047159 2047163 2047181 2047183 2047211 2047217 2047219 2047237 2047249
2047289 2047303 2047349 2047351 2047369 2047387 2047393 2047403 2047439 2047471
2047481 2047501 2047517 2047523 2047541 2047547 2047553 2047559 2047567 2047571
2047597 2047613 2047627 2047637 2047651 2047699 2047729 2047733 2047737 2047741
2047811 2047813 2047819 2047841 2047879 2047883 2047919 2047933 2047937 2047957
2047967 2047993 2048003 2048017 2048021 2048027 2048063 2048107 2048113 2048117
2048131 2048141 2048149 2048153 2048159 2048171 2048203 2048231 2048239 2048243
2048251 2048261 2048269 2048273 2048327 2048329 2048339 2048353 2048359 2048369
2048413 2048419 2048429 2048467 2048471 2048509 2048521 2048533 2048537 2048569
2048581 2048593 2048621 2048639 2048663 2048671 2048677 2048699 2048723 2048749
2048779 2048797 2048819 2048833 2048843 2048861 2048867 2048887 2048897 2048911
2048933 2048939 2048953 2048957 2048983 2049041 2049043 2049067 2049071 2049077
2049083 2049107 2049119 2049121 2049127 2049137 2049143 2049149 2049161 2049167
2049191 2049263 2049269 2049287 2049293 2049301 2049331 2049347 2049349 2049361
2049407 2049409 2049419 2049427 2049431 2049449 2049451 2049491 2049493 2049521
2049533 2049547 2049569 2049577 2049589 2049611 2049613 2049617 2049629 2049643
2049647 2049659 2049667 2049679 2049703 2049721 2049727 2049787 2049791 2049797
2049823 2049829 2049847 2049869 2049893 2049919 2049941 2049949 2049957 2049973
2049977 2049991 2050007 2050021 2050031 2050033 2050057 2050063 2050079 2050099
2050109 2050141 2050163 2050171 2050177 2050189 2050193 2050211 2050219 2050229
2050231 2050241 2050253 2050261 2050273 2050277 2050327 2050331 2050333 2050337
2050339 2050357 2050361 2050397 2050403 2050417 2050459 2050481 2050487 2050493
2050507 2050511 2050513 2050543 2050553 2050567 2050571 2050599 2050603 2050621
2050639 2050679 2050717 2050721 2050733 2050739 2050771 2050777 2050787 2050813
2050817 2050819 2050823 2050831 2050843 2050849 2050877 2050883 2050889 2050903
2050949 2050957 2050963 2050969 2050973 2050987 2051041 2051051 2051059 2051087
2051111 2051113 2051123 2051167 2051171 2051173 2051191 2051219 2051233 2051249
2051251 2051263 2051267 2051279 2051281 2051311 2051321 2051323 2051327 2051333
2051341 2051359 2051383 2051417 2051419 2051429 2051437 2051443 2051459 2051461
2051477 2051479 2051507 2051537 2051587 2051593 2051617 2051627 2051629 2051641
2051653 2051671 2051689 2051701 2051719 2051743 2051759 2051767 2051773 2051801
2051821 2051839 2051851 2051887 2051891 2051893 2051923 2051947 2051963 2051969
2051999 2052023 2052041 2052047 2052049 2052059 2052077 2052109 2052119 2052137
2052157 2052163 2052179 2052181 2052187 2052191 2052199 2052217 2052311 2052317
2052329 2052331 2052343 2052371 2052409 2052431 2052439 2052473 2052493 2052503
2052511 2052517 2052521 2052553 2052559 2052569 2052577 2052587 2052601 2052629
2052647 2052689 2052697 2052709 2052731 2052737 2052749 2052751 2052769 2052781
2052793 2052803 2052821 2052857 2052859 2052877 2052889 2052899 2052907 2052917
2052923 2052943 2052959 2052977 2052983 2052989 2053001 2053013 2053021 2053031
2053063 2053067 2053069 2053087 2053091 2053109 2053111 2053127 2053189 2053201
2053211 2053213 2053237 2053253 2053291 2053307 2053313 2053333 2053339 2053357
2053361 2053397 2053411 2053421 2053423 2053427 2053439 2053459 2053507 2053517
2053529 2053553 2053573 2053603 2053619 2053621 2053627 2053631 2053643 2053661
2053673 2053699 2053703 2053721 2053757 2053769 2053771 2053783 2053789 2053811
2053819 2053837 2053841 2053847 2053859 2053871 2053873 2053897 2053903 2053927
2053937 2053943 2053951 2053979 2054009 2054011 2054021 2054023 2054027 2054047
2054057 2054069 2054077 2054089 2054113 2054131 2054149 2054159 2054179 2054189
2054197 2054207 2054231 2054233 2054249 2054251 2054257 2054317 2054329 2054341
2054347 2054369 2054443 2054449 2054471 2054483 2054491 2054519 2054537 2054543
2054549 2054581 2054593 2054597 2054609 2054617 2054623 2054627 2054629 2054639
2054687 2054707 2054713 2054719 2054729 2054749 2054753 2054761 2054771 2054791
2054821 2054839 2054849 2054851 2054861 2054873 2054881 2054903 2054917 2054933
2054939 2054947 2054951 2054971 2054989 2054999 2055019 2055037 2055041 2055061
2055071 2055089 2055101 2055103 2055107 2055121 2055127 2055133 2055187 2055191
2055197 2055199 2055203 2055217 2055223 2055233 2055247 2055253 2055299 2055307
2055311 2055337 2055341 2055367 2055397 2055409 2055437 2055467 2055479 2055481
2055497 2055503 2055509 2055511 2055541 2055551 2055569 2055611 2055637 2055649
2055673 2055679 2055689 2055707 2055709 2055719 2055727 2055751 2055769 2055821
2055829 2055847 2055853 2055917 2055953 2055961 2056001 2056007 2056069 2056073
2056079 2056081 2056111 2056139 2056141 2056147 2056151 2056157 2056193 2056207
2056211 2056247 2056253 2056277 2056279 2056289 2056319 2056333 2056339 2056343
2056357 2056363 2056381 2056399 2056403 2056409 2056421 2056441 2056459 2056463
2056489 2056501 2056517 2056547 2056553 2056573 2056577 2056589 2056597 2056603
2056627 2056631 2056661 2056667 2056679 2056687 2056697 2056727 2056741 2056751
2056753 2056759 2056763 2056777 2056787 2056829 2056841 2056843 2056853 2056891
2056903 2056907 2056909 2056919 2056927 2056933 2056961 2056963 2056973 2056979
```

```
2056987  2056993  2057009  2057021  2057023  2057047  2057053  2057087  2057113  2057137
2057141  2057147  2057177  2057179  2057197  2057203  2057227  2057233  2057291  2057299
2057303  2057309  2057317  2057333  2057353  2057371  2057381  2057383  2057387  2057399
2057401  2057411  2057431  2057441  2057477  2057479  2057483  2057537  2057543  2057569
2057597  2057599  2057609  2057611  2057633  2057639  2057659  2057669  2057683  2057689
2057701  2057711  2057723  2057729  2057747  2057761  2057777  2057779  2057791  2057807
2057813  2057849  2057857  2057863  2057893  2057897  2057917  2057921  2057933  2057953
2057981  2057987  2057999  2058011  2058013  2058019  2058031  2058041  2058047  2058103
2058131  2058143  2058157  2058163  2058169  2058179  2058191  2058193  2058197  2058211
2058223  2058229  2058233  2058239  2058253  2058299  2058311  2058341  2058373  2058379
2058383  2058389  2058401  2058409  2058439  2058443  2058457  2058473  2058541  2058557
2058559  2058571  2058577  2058599  2058607  2058611  2058619  2058629  2058653  2058671
2058677  2058691  2058697  2058701  2058703  2058713  2058737  2058761  2058767  2058773
2058781  2058809  2058829  2058839  2058841  2058851  2058857  2058869  2058871
2058877  2058893  2058899  2058919  2058949  2058967  2059009  2059033  2059039  2059063
2059093  2059097  2059133  2059153  2059157  2059181  2059207  2059217  2059223  2059231
2059243  2059249  2059271  2059273  2059283  2059297  2059303  2059327  2059331  2059339
2059367  2059381  2059411  2059417  2059427  2059441  2059459  2059469  2059481  2059501
2059511  2059517  2059537  2059573  2059613  2059621  2059637  2059649  2059661  2059697
2059709  2059711  2059721  2059723  2059741  2059747  2059751  2059763  2059769  2059777
2059793  2059807  2059817  2059819  2059823  2059843  2059859  2059861  2059879  2059891
2059913  2059921  2059927  2059931  2059933  2059943  2059973  2059979  2060021  2060059
2060063  2060089  2060099  2060101  2060117  2060129  2060137  2060141  2060159  2060161
2060171  2060203  2060231  2060243  2060249  2060251  2060263  2060273  2060287  2060327
2060347  2060351  2060389  2060407  2060437  2060441  2060447  2060449  2060453  2060473
2060489  2060503  2060507  2060543  2060551  2060561  2060563  2060579  2060581  2060599
2060609  2060627  2060629  2060657  2060671  2060687  2060749  2060753  2060767  2060801
2060803  2060843  2060857  2060867  2060879  2060881  2060909  2060921  2060963  2060977
2061013  2061041  2061049  2061067  2061077  2061097  2061109  2061113  2061127  2061149
2061161  2061173  2061179  2061181  2061187  2061197  2061203  2061209  2061217  2061239
2061247  2061271  2061277  2061287  2061289  2061313  2061331  2061343  2061361  2061379
2061383  2061391  2061413  2061419  2061427  2061431  2061491  2061503  2061533  2061551
2061583  2061589  2061599  2061601  2061613  2061623  2061629  2061649  2061667  2061673
2061679  2061691  2061733  2061757  2061793  2061847  2061869  2061877  2061883  2061887
2061907  2061919  2061923  2061967  2061971  2062001  2062003  2062007  2062009  2062033
2062037  2062043  2062057  2062061  2062069  2062091  2062129  2062147  2062153
2062169  2062187  2062199  2062201  2062217  2062223  2062231  2062243  2062267  2062273
2062289  2062297  2062303  2062339  2062351  2062381  2062391  2062429  2062477  2062483
2062493  2062513  2062517  2062519  2062523  2062537  2062547  2062553  2062561  2062577
2062597  2062637  2062651  2062657  2062673  2062681  2062693  2062703  2062721  2062747
2062757  2062759  2062789  2062807  2062829  2062841  2062859  2062871  2062873  2062883
2062889  2062891  2062903  2062909  2062913  2062937  2062943  2062979  2062993  2062999
2063003  2063021  2063029  2063057  2063059  2063107  2063111  2063129  2063141  2063167
2063179  2063213  2063249  2063251  2063279  2063291  2063293  2063323  2063339  2063351
2063359  2063377  2063389  2063393  2063423  2063429  2063459  2063461  2063483  2063497
2063507  2063521  2063541  2063543  2063559  2063561  2063563  2063573  2063587
2063597  2063603  2063617  2063627  2063651  2063671  2063687  2063693  2063707  2063729
2063731  2063741  2063771  2063773  2063777  2063779  2063797  2063807  2063819  2063827
2063833  2063839  2063857  2063881  2063893  2063903  2063909  2063917  2063921
2063933  2063939  2063983  2063993  2064031  2064047  2064061  2064067  2064071  2064077
2064109  2064113  2064121  2064143  2064149  2064151  2064169  2064187  2064199  2064229
2064241  2064247  2064263  2064277  2064299  2064313  2064317  2064323  2064329  2064343
2064353  2064371  2064373  2064379  2064389  2064421  2064431  2064437  2064443  2064447
2064449  2064487  2064511  2064523  2064527  2064529  2064547  2064551  2064571  2064581
2064583  2064589  2064611  2064619  2064649  2064653  2064679  2064703  2064737  2064761
2064763  2064767  2064789  2064793  2064809  2064833  2064847  2064857  2064877  2064899
2064913  2064919  2064929  2064943  2064947  2064949  2064961  2064971  2064983  2065031
2065043  2065073  2065087  2065103  2065111  2065117  2065121  2065153  2065157  2065163
2065169  2065181  2065187  2065213  2065241  2065267  2065309  2065363  2065369  2065379
2065387  2065397  2065411  2065417  2065429  2065489  2065493  2065501  2065523  2065559
2065571  2065553  2065577  2065579  2065597  2065627  2065633  2065639  2065663  2065667
2065669  2065711  2065717  2065727  2065729  2065733  2065751  2065759  2065769  2065799
2065801  2065807  2065829  2065841  2065879  2065889  2065907  2065937  2065961  2065967
2065991  2065997  2066017  2066033  2066059  2066069  2066081  2066083  2066101  2066111
2066123  2066137  2066149  2066153  2066161  2066173  2066177  2066179  2066201  2066203
2066209  2066219  2066257  2066287  2066293  2066321  2066329  2066399  2066419
2066437  2066443  2066447  2066461  2066473  2066501  2066507  2066509  2066521  2066539
2066551  2066563  2066579  2066587  2066599  2066609  2066641  2066653  2066681
2066683  2066693  2066699  2066717  2066723  2066759  2066761  2066767  2066777  2066789
2066797  2066833  2066879  2066887  2066893  2066899  2066903  2066923  2066929  2066951
2066957  2066963  2066969  2066971  2066989  2066993  2067001  2067007  2067019  2067041
2067061  2067071  2067073  2067083  2067101  2067119  2067137  2067187  2067209  2067211
2067253  2067269  2067277  2067337  2067349  2067379  2067383  2067407  2067413  2067427
2067431  2067437  2067451  2067479  2067491  2067511  2067517  2067529  2067547  2067581
2067587  2067617  2067623  2067647  2067661  2067679  2067691  2067697  2067719  2067721
2067739  2067781  2067797  2067799  2067811  2067823  2067851  2067853  2067883  2067887
2067911  2067929  2067937  2067977  2067997  2068037  2068039  2068043  2068061  2068063
2068069  2068109  2068117  2068123  2068133  2068139  2068147  2068151  2068201  2068211
2068249  2068267  2068273  2068279  2068291  2068333  2068349  2068361  2068387  2068393
2068399  2068403  2068421  2068427  2068439  2068453  2068463  2068471  2068477  2068487
2068489  2068499  2068501  2068513  2068519  2068529  2068553  2068579  2068589  2068607
2068637  2068639  2068667  2068673  2068681  2068699  2068709  2068741  2068751  2068753
2068757  2068763  2068769  2068811  2068813  2068817  2068853  2068873  2068891  2068897
2068903  2068921  2068939  2068943  2068949  2068973  2068991  2068999  2069009  2069017
2069029  2069047  2069051  2069069  2069101  2069113  2069129  2069141  2069183  2069191
2069209  2069213  2069227  2069239  2069251  2069261  2069267  2069329  2069341  2069351
2069377  2069381  2069383  2069387  2069399  2069413  2069443  2069449  2069489  2069497
2069503  2069519  2069531  2069549  2069553  2069569  2069581  2069603  2069629  2069647
2069657  2069671  2069681  2069687  2069707  2069713  2069723  2069729  2069737  2069761
```

```
2069773 2069783 2069797 2069807 2069819 2069827 2069843 2069857 2069861 2069887
2069909 2069911 2069923 2069929 2069941 2069953 2069957 2069959 2069983 2069987
2069989 2069999 2070041 2070043 2070067 2070071 2070083 2070091 2070137 2070143
2070179 2070181 2070203 2070217 2070239 2070241 2070283 2070287 2070301 2070307
2070317 2070319 2070323 2070329 2070371 2070421 2070427 2070433 2070443 2070451
2070461 2070463 2070469 2070473 2070479 2070517 2070527 2070533 2070553 2070559
2070569 2070581 2070587 2070611 2070613 2070619 2070641 2070643 2070661 2070709
2070737 2070749 2070781 2070793 2070797 2070799 2070811 2070823 2070833 2070839
2070863 2070877 2070883 2070907 2070911 2070931 2070947 2070953 2070973 2070997
2071007 2071063 2071073 2071087 2071123 2071159 2071169 2071189 2071193 2071213
2071259 2071261 2071271 2071291 2071319 2071339 2071343 2071351 2071367 2071373
2071379 2071393 2071397 2071411 2071427 2071429 2071453 2071457 2071463 2071471
2071481 2071493 2071507 2071543 2071561 2071579 2071583 2071591 2071613 2071631
2071649 2071661 2071669 2071681 2071687 2071711 2071721 2071723 2071733 2071753
2071759 2071781 2071799 2071801 2071819 2071837 2071859 2071873 2071879 2071897
2071913 2071921 2071939 2071957 2071961 2071973 2071991 2071997 2071999 2072003
2072023 2072029 2072033 2072039 2072053 2072087 2072101 2072117 2072123 2072129
2072131 2072153 2072179 2072201 2072207 2072209 2072267 2072293 2072321 2072327
2072363 2072383 2072393 2072423 2072429 2072431 2072437 2072467 2072479 2072489
2072491 2072527 2072531 2072549 2072563 2072569 2072573 2072579 2072617 2072647
2072663 2072683 2072687 2072699 2072701 2072731 2072743 2072773 2072789 2072801
2072809 2072821 2072831 2072839 2072869 2072893 2072897 2072927 2072933 2072953
2072969 2072977 2073011 2073041 2073061 2073067 2073089 2073101 2073103 2073107
2073119 2073121 2073131 2073143 2073163 2073173 2073193 2073199 2073209 2073233
2073241 2073251 2073263 2073277 2073283 2073293 2073317 2073343 2073347 2073349
2073353 2073359 2073361 2073367 2073377 2073389 2073391 2073403 2073457 2073469
2073481 2073521 2073563 2073601 2073607 2073613 2073619 2073647 2073649 2073661
2073667 2073707 2073719 2073787 2073809 2073811 2073823 2073853 2073859 2073893
2073923 2073929 2073937 2073941 2073971 2073977 2073989 2073997 2074031 2074057
2074081 2074091 2074103 2074129 2074139 2074141 2074159 2074169 2074199 2074201
2074207 2074217 2074223 2074243 2074273 2074279 2074321 2074327 2074333 2074339
2074349 2074351 2074361 2074411 2074417 2074421 2074433 2074447 2074463 2074481
2074483 2074487 2074507 2074517 2074519 2074529 2074543 2074547 2074571 2074601
2074609 2074643 2074649 2074687 2074727 2074739 2074753 2074801 2074811 2074817
2074823 2074841 2074871 2074873 2074889 2074903 2074913 2074931 2074949 2074951
2074957 2074967 2074981 2074993 2075011 2075023 2075041 2075063 2075077 2075081
2075111 2075149 2075167 2075179 2075189 2075197 2075201 2075209 2075231 2075257
2075261 2075263 2075273 2075279 2075299 2075323 2075363 2075387 2075393 2075417
2075429 2075453 2075467 2075483 2075537 2075539 2075551 2075573 2075587 2075599
2075603 2075611 2075621 2075641 2075657 2075659 2075669 2075677 2075699 2075713
2075741 2075743 2075761 2075767 2075771 2075779 2075803 2075809 2075813 2075831
2075833 2075837 2075839 2075867 2075869 2075893 2075903 2075917 2075929 2075947
2075963 2075981 2075987 2075999 2076001 2076007 2076043 2076059 2076071 2076077
2076089 2076133 2076143 2076161 2076209 2076229 2076259 2076271 2076289 2076293
2076299 2076307 2076317 2076331 2076367 2076383 2076391 2076407 2076409 2076419
2076421 2076433 2076443 2076449 2076461 2076469 2076539 2076563 2076611 2076617
2076619 2076629 2076649 2076653 2076677 2076689 2076709 2076713 2076731 2076761
2076791 2076797 2076803 2076829 2076869 2076881 2076889 2076901 2076913 2076917
2076929 2076967 2076973 2077001 2077007 2077021 2077027 2077037 2077073 2077081
2077091 2077121 2077129 2077133 2077139 2077151 2077181 2077189 2077249 2077253
2077261 2077297 2077303 2077319 2077321 2077333 2077343 2077351 2077367 2077391
2077399 2077409 2077483 2077499 2077549 2077561 2077571 2077577 2077583 2077591
2077601 2077637 2077639 2077667 2077681 2077693 2077703 2077709 2077711 2077753
2077769 2077771 2077781 2077807 2077811 2077813 2077841 2077849 2077853 2077861
2077891 2077909 2077913 2077919 2077939 2077949 2077969 2077987 2077993 2077997
2078009 2078051 2078059 2078081 2078093 2078107 2078117 2078123 2078149 2078159
2078161 2078177 2078191 2078207 2078221 2078243 2078287 2078309 2078311 2078317
2078339 2078341 2078347 2078357 2078371 2078389 2078399 2078431 2078443 2078449
2078473 2078497 2078507 2078509 2078513 2078537 2078551 2078591 2078599 2078603
2078611 2078621 2078627 2078647 2078651 2078677 2078693 2078707 2078711 2078719
2078723 2078731 2078753 2078759 2078779 2078789 2078801 2078827 2078831 2078851
2078887 2078917 2078927 2078929 2078933 2078939 2078959 2078963 2078971 2078977
2079013 2079017 2079019 2079041 2079047 2079053 2079071 2079073 2079079 2079109
2079127 2079149 2079163 2079167 2079169 2079173 2079191 2079193 2079197 2079199
2079229 2079239 2079241 2079247 2079251 2079257 2079277 2079293 2079299 2079323
2079347 2079353 2079401 2079403 2079419 2079433 2079461 2079463 2079481 2079487
2079529 2079533 2079557 2079563 2079577 2079587 2079599 2079601 2079617 2079629
2079631 2079641 2079647 2079653 2079709 2079713 2079719 2079739 2079757 2079761
2079769 2079787 2079811 2079817 2079823 2079839 2079859 2079863 2079877 2079919
2079923 2079937 2079941 2079943 2079997 2080003 2080009 2080021 2080027 2080049
2080081 2080121 2080129 2080151 2080157 2080201 2080207 2080213 2080219 2080223
2080231 2080237 2080261 2080271 2080277 2080289 2080321 2080339 2080343 2080349
2080357 2080363 2080391 2080423 2080433 2080439 2080447 2080451 2080453 2080501
2080531 2080541 2080543 2080567 2080571 2080577 2080591 2080597 2080609 2080651
2080657 2080667 2080679 2080699 2080711 2080717 2080723 2080759 2080763 2080777
2080801 2080807 2080847 2080849 2080877 2080889 2080907 2080913 2080921 2080927
2080961 2080963 2080979 2081029 2081033 2081039 2081047 2081099 2081129 2081147
2081159 2081161 2081171 2081237 2081249 2081251 2081267 2081273 2081281 2081291
2081297 2081311 2081323 2081351 2081353 2081369 2081377 2081383 2081407 2081423
2081437 2081467 2081473 2081479 2081483 2081491 2081537 2081549 2081561 2081581
2081603 2081609 2081617 2081627 2081647 2081671 2081687 2081719 2081749 2081777
2081797 2081801 2081809 2081813 2081831 2081843 2081851 2081861 2081873 2081897
2081903 2081909 2081921 2081923 2081927 2081969 2082019 2082037 2082049 2082061
2082071 2082079 2082097 2082107 2082127 2082131 2082133 2082163 2082181 2082187
2082193 2082227 2082253 2082257 2082281 2082341 2082391 2082413 2082439 2082463
2082469 2082497 2082499 2082503 2082527 2082539 2082569 2082583 2082589 2082593
2082599 2082607 2082631 2082649 2082659 2082667 2082679 2082683 2082709 2082713
2082727 2082737 2082739 2082749 2082757 2082779 2082793 2082803 2082827 2082833
2082851 2082853 2082863 2082869 2082887 2082889 2082893 2082907 2082917 2082947
```

```
2082961 2082973 2082979 2083001 2083009 2083019 2083021 2083033 2083057 2083073
2083079 2083091 2083117 2083121 2083127 2083139 2083153 2083187 2083199 2083219
2083229 2083243 2083247 2083261 2083267 2083283 2083297 2083321 2083339 2083343
2083351 2083357 2083387 2083399 2083421 2083423 2083427 2083441 2083451 2083453
2083511 2083513 2083517 2083519 2083531 2083553 2083573 2083583 2083591 2083643
2083681 2083693 2083709 2083717 2083721 2083733 2083769 2083771 2083799 2083813
2083819 2083847 2083849 2083859 2083867 2083883 2083889 2083897 2083937 2083957
2083967 2083973 2083981 2084003 2084009 2084023 2084041 2084051 2084101 2084107
2084111 2084123 2084141 2084179 2084209 2084219 2084227 2084231 2084233 2084249
2084263 2084273 2084287 2084297 2084311 2084333 2084359 2084389 2084393 2084413
2084419 2084441 2084443 2084447 2084449 2084479 2084501 2084503 2084507 2084531
2084561 2084567 2084569 2084609 2084611 2084639 2084653 2084671 2084689 2084749
2084767 2084777 2084783 2084791 2084833 2084899 2084903 2084917 2084921 2084947
2084977 2084981 2084983 2084993 2085007 2085011 2085023 2085037 2085049
2085053 2085059 2085077 2085089 2085121 2085131 2085133 2085143 2085151 2085191
2085197 2085217 2085221 2085227 2085229 2085233 2085247 2085253 2085257 2085287
2085289 2085299 2085311 2085319 2085331 2085353 2085367 2085379 2085409 2085469
2085481 2085487 2085493 2085511 2085539 2085569 2085599 2085607 2085623 2085659
2085667 2085673 2085691 2085697 2085701 2085703 2085731 2085737 2085739 2085757
2085779 2085799 2085803 2085823 2085833 2085841 2085857 2085869 2085899 2085929
2085931 2085943 2085947 2085971 2085977 2085983 2085989 2086003 2086009 2086013
2086037 2086043 2086079 2086081 2086109 2086111 2086127 2086141 2086159 2086187
2086199 2086211 2086213 2086243 2086277 2086303 2086321 2086339 2086349 2086351
2086361 2086363 2086397 2086421 2086423 2086433 2086439 2086457 2086459 2086481
2086493 2086501 2086507 2086519 2086543 2086547 2086549 2086571 2086573 2086577
2086589 2086621 2086639 2086657 2086673 2086681 2086697 2086723 2086727 2086739
2086757 2086759 2086781 2086787 2086793 2086817 2086823 2086829 2086831 2086841
2086853 2086879 2086901 2086907 2086933 2086939 2086949 2086957 2086969 2087011
2087021 2087027 2087047 2087051 2087069 2087077 2087081 2087123 2087147 2087161
2087167 2087179 2087203 2087213 2087219 2087221 2087231 2087233 2087287 2087297
2087303 2087339 2087347 2087353 2087357 2087377 2087381 2087383 2087387 2087389
2087399 2087419 2087443 2087453 2087461 2087467 2087483 2087489 2087497 2087531
2087539 2087543 2087551 2087557 2087563 2087593 2087627 2087669 2087671 2087689
2087711 2087713 2087717 2087741 2087759 2087771 2087791 2087801 2087807 2087809
2087831 2087837 2087857 2087861 2087879 2087903 2087909 2087927 2087941 2087983
2087993 2087999 2088011 2088013 2088061 2088077 2088103 2088109 2088131 2088133
2088139 2088199 2088217 2088221 2088227 2088241 2088259 2088269 2088277 2088287
2088293 2088301 2088329 2088341 2088343 2088349 2088367 2088403 2088407 2088409
2088413 2088421 2088431 2088451 2088473 2088479 2088487 2088497 2088503
2088511 2088517 2088547 2088557 2088577 2088587 2088589 2088599 2088601 2088623
2088631 2088641 2088643 2088661 2088679 2088683 2088703 2088719 2088721 2088731
2088733 2088787 2088817 2088829 2088833 2088847 2088869 2088871 2088899 2088901
2088907 2088913 2088949 2088953 2088971 2088973 2088979 2089001 2089037 2089039
2089049 2089051 2089091 2089093 2089117 2089123 2089141 2089151 2089169 2089177
2089211 2089223 2089231 2089253 2089267 2089271 2089273 2089303 2089357 2089361
2089379 2089391 2089393 2089397 2089403 2089441 2089447 2089457 2089489 2089511
2089517 2089523 2089541 2089543 2089559 2089567 2089583 2089613 2089621 2089627
2089643 2089661 2089669 2089673 2089693 2089697 2089727 2089751 2089781 2089807
2089831 2089847 2089853 2089859 2089873 2089889 2089897 2089933 2089939 2089951
2089979 2090003 2090009 2090017 2090021 2090041 2090047 2090069 2090071 2090089
2090111 2090119 2090131 2090147 2090159 2090173 2090177 2090191 2090197 2090203
2090213 2090219 2090227 2090239 2090251 2090279 2090281 2090317 2090327 2090329
2090351 2090353 2090357 2090381 2090441 2090461 2090477 2090489 2090497 2090509
2090567 2090573 2090593 2090597 2090603 2090623 2090633 2090651 2090681 2090689
2090717 2090719 2090749 2090771 2090791 2090807 2090821 2090827 2090831 2090843
2090849 2090863 2090873 2090923 2090951 2090953 2091053 2091097 2091139 2091149
2091151 2091191 2091211 2091227 2091239 2091241 2091247 2091251 2091269 2091281
2091283 2091293 2091301 2091317 2091319 2091337 2091343 2091347 2091361 2091379
2091389 2091409 2091421 2091431 2091437 2091443 2091449 2091461 2091473 2091487
2091497 2091503 2091521 2091553 2091581 2091587 2091599 2091613 2091619 2091623
2091631 2091637 2091659 2091667 2091671 2091703 2091707 2091709 2091737 2091763
2091769 2091773 2091797 2091809 2091839 2091847 2091851 2091863 2091871 2091877
2091889 2091913 2091917 2091931 2091959 2091983 2091991 2091997 2092019 2092021
2092039 2092043 2092049 2092073 2092093 2092099 2092133 2092163 2092177 2092183
2092187 2092217 2092229 2092243 2092249 2092273 2092291 2092303 2092319 2092327
2092351 2092369 2092381 2092397 2092403 2092427 2092429 2092439 2092457 2092481
2092501 2092529 2092537 2092543 2092549 2092561 2092589 2092591 2092613 2092621
2092637 2092661 2092663 2092667 2092687 2092693 2092721 2092723 2092733 2092759
2092771 2092777 2092799 2092801 2092817 2092823 2092847 2092859 2092861
2092891 2092897 2092919 2092943 2092963 2092973 2092991 2092997 2092999 2093029
2093041 2093071 2093081 2093101 2093123 2093131 2093141 2093149 2093153 2093171
2093183 2093219 2093237 2093243 2093251 2093257 2093279 2093291 2093297 2093303
2093317 2093321 2093323 2093327 2093339 2093347 2093359 2093389 2093393 2093407
2093411 2093417 2093449 2093453 2093467 2093489 2093491 2093503 2093513 2093527
2093537 2093557 2093573 2093603 2093617 2093639 2093653 2093699 2093701 2093761
2093783 2093789 2093801 2093807 2093813 2093821 2093827 2093837 2093863 2093869
2093881 2093893 2093929 2093953 2093981 2094011 2094023 2094031 2094041 2094067
2094073 2094091 2094101 2094107 2094109 2094167 2094181 2094187 2094203 2094221
2094227 2094233 2094271 2094277 2094317 2094331 2094341 2094343 2094359 2094361
2094373 2094377 2094413 2094439 2094473 2094481 2094497 2094509 2094523 2094551
2094569 2094601 2094623 2094637 2094647 2094683 2094691 2094707 2094721 2094727
2094737 2094749 2094751 2094767 2094779 2094787 2094797 2094803 2094809 2094811
2094847 2094929 2094943 2094973 2094979 2095007 2095047 2095051 2095057 2095061
2095081 2095099 2095109 2095117 2095127 2095151 2095189 2095193 2095201 2095211
2095217 2095229 2095253 2095283 2095309 2095343 2095351 2095361 2095363
2095367 2095391 2095397 2095399 2095409 2095439 2095451 2095459 2095463 2095481
2095487 2095493 2095517 2095523 2095547 2095571 2095591 2095601 2095609 2095619
2095637 2095651 2095657 2095679 2095697 2095699 2095721 2095727 2095733 2095747
2095759 2095771 2095789 2095813 2095823 2095831 2095837 2095853 2095867 2095927
```

```
2095931  2095943  2095969  2095987  2095993  2095997  2096009  2096011  2096047  2096051
2096057  2096063  2096071  2096089  2096111  2096123  2096147  2096183  2096191  2096209
2096221  2096231  2096233  2096261  2096273  2096291  2096357  2096377  2096399  2096401
2096407  2096411  2096429  2096431  2096449  2096483  2096533  2096539  2096569  2096597
2096599  2096621  2096629  2096639  2096681  2096687  2096693  2096713  2096737  2096741
2096761  2096777  2096789  2096791  2096807  2096837  2096851  2096867  2096873  2096881
2096893  2096909  2096911  2096923  2096947  2096957  2096965  2096971  2096987  2096993
2097013  2097023  2097031  2097041  2097047  2097083  2097091  2097097  2097131  2097133
2097143  2097169  2097211  2097223  2097229  2097257  2097259  2097287  2097289  2097311
2097317  2097349  2097373  2097383  2097397  2097401  2097421  2097427  2097449  2097451
2097461  2097479  2097481  2097499  2097503  2097517  2097523  2097533  2097539  2097559
2097593  2097611  2097617  2097629  2097643  2097653  2097671  2097673  2097679  2097709
2097713  2097727  2097743  2097757  2097763  2097769  2097779  2097787  2097803  2097829
2097833  2097857  2097859  2097883  2097911  2097917  2097941  2097959  2097967  2097983
2097989  2098009  2098027  2098051  2098079  2098081  2098097  2098133  2098153  2098169
2098171  2098183  2098193  2098211  2098241  2098249  2098253  2098277  2098279  2098289
2098321  2098337  2098351  2098363  2098391  2098403  2098423  2098427  2098441  2098471
2098511  2098519  2098541  2098553  2098559  2098573  2098609  2098639  2098651  2098673
2098687  2098693  2098697  2098699  2098711  2098717  2098729  2098739  2098741  2098757
2098763  2098777  2098781  2098783  2098801  2098813  2098841  2098861  2098867  2098883
2098897  2098903  2098907  2098927  2098931  2098937  2098961  2098981  2099017  2099021
2099033  2099059  2099081  2099089  2099093  2099129  2099147  2099179  2099191  2099197
2099203  2099213  2099219  2099221  2099249  2099263  2099287  2099299  2099309  2099327
2099341  2099359  2099369  2099387  2099393  2099411  2099431  2099441  2099453  2099467
2099477  2099479  2099497  2099507  2099521  2099543  2099549  2099593  2099611  2099623
2099627  2099641  2099659  2099677  2099707  2099711  2099717  2099731  2099743  2099749
2099761  2099767  2099771  2099809  2099821  2099827  2099837  2099863  2099887  2099893
2099921  2099927  2099939  2099941  2099963  2100001  2100011  2100031  2100041  2100053
2100071  2100097  2100099  2100113  2100121  2100167  2100173  2100181  2100191  2100193
2100221  2100227  2100229  2100239  2100247  2100253  2100257  2100269  2100277  2100313
2100353  2100377  2100403  2100407  2100409  2100451  2100463  2100473  2100487  2100493
2100523  2100533  2100541  2100551  2100559  2100563  2100569  2100587  2100589  2100607
2100629  2100649  2100661  2100691  2100713  2100719  2100727  2100733  2100737  2100743
2100781  2100793  2100803  2100821  2100841  2100859  2100869  2100893  2100899  2100913
2100929  2100941  2100953  2100983  2100991  2100997  2101003  2101007  2101019  2101051
2101061  2101067  2101091  2101093  2101111  2101123  2101129  2101139  2101157  2101181
2101189  2101199  2101207  2101213  2101219  2101223  2101237  2101243  2101247  2101249
2101259  2101261  2101277  2101283  2101313  2101327  2101357  2101391  2101423  2101433
2101439  2101447  2101471  2101481  2101483  2101499  2101501  2101513  2101531  2101549
2101553  2101607  2101613  2101621  2101651  2101657  2101667  2101669  2101681  2101703
2101721  2101733  2101747  2101751  2101789  2101807  2101811  2101813  2101823  2101843
2101849  2101867  2101871  2101873  2101903  2101907  2101909  2101961  2102021  2102057
2102069  2102083  2102099  2102117  2102137  2102143  2102167  2102171  2102173  2102183
2102201  2102207  2102213  2102249  2102251  2102257  2102267  2102273  2102279  2102291
2102311  2102323  2102329  2102341  2102383  2102411  2102417  2102431  2102459  2102461
2102467  2102479  2102489  2102497  2102519  2102531  2102533  2102549  2102557  2102561
2102567  2102579  2102593  2102623  2102629  2102647  2102651  2102687  2102693  2102717
2102741  2102753  2102759  2102777  2102783  2102791  2102797  2102801  2102809  2102831
2102839  2102851  2102857  2102873  2102879  2102887  2102897  2102927  2102941  2102999
2103007  2103011  2103029  2103041  2103067  2103083  2103103  2103107  2103119  2103139
2103149  2103151  2103163  2103169  2103181  2103187  2103193  2103203  2103229  2103301
2103307  2103317  2103377  2103383  2103389  2103403  2103407  2103449  2103473  2103503
2103523  2103553  2103583  2103589  2103601  2103611  2103613  2103617  2103653  2103667
2103671  2103679  2103683  2103713  2103719  2103743  2103749  2103769  2103781  2103791
2103793  2103797  2103811  2103817  2103821  2103839  2103859  2103887  2103901  2103911
2103919  2103953  2103961  2103973  2103977  2103989  2104013  2104019  2104021  2104031
2104051  2104057  2104061  2104087  2104097  2104103  2104111  2104129  2104139  2104147
2104159  2104163  2104169  2104177  2104181  2104213  2104217  2104229  2104241  2104261
2104273  2104313  2104337  2104343  2104357  2104363  2104381  2104391  2104397  2104423
2104433  2104441  2104483  2104499  2104507  2104541  2104547  2104567  2104591  2104601
2104607  2104633  2104643  2104657  2104673  2104679  2104699  2104703  2104717  2104723
2104727  2104741  2104747  2104757  2104759  2104811  2104841  2104847  2104853  2104859
2104867  2104871  2104901  2104909  2104913  2104933  2104951  2104961  2104969  2104987
2105003  2105009  2105027  2105069  2105071  2105111  2105119  2105141  2105149  2105183
2105203  2105209  2105231  2105251  2105267  2105269  2105273  2105287  2105317  2105329
2105347  2105357  2105359  2105377  2105381  2105407  2105413  2105417  2105419  2105431
2105449  2105483  2105497  2105503  2105507  2105513  2105549  2105557  2105567  2105591
2105611  2105641  2105669  2105681  2105693  2105699  2105717  2105729  2105731  2105759
2105767  2105809  2105813  2105819  2105833  2105837  2105843  2105863  2105881  2105891
2105897  2105911  2105921  2105927  2105933  2105947  2105953  2105963  2105969  2105993
2106019  2106029  2106059  2106089  2106107  2106149  2106173  2106191  2106197  2106199
2106217  2106227  2106229  2106239  2106257  2106277  2106281  2106289  2106301  2106311
2106329  2106337  2106341  2106343  2106347  2106353  2106361  2106383  2106389  2106407
2106421  2106427  2106431  2106437  2106451  2106463  2106479  2106491  2106523  2106529
2106551  2106563  2106617  2106619  2106631  2106653  2106673  2106677  2106679  2106733
2106737  2106749  2106773  2106779  2106781  2106809  2106829  2106833  2106847  2106857
2106877  2106887  2106901  2106911  2106917  2106919  2106931  2106943  2106953  2106959
2106983  2106989  2106991  2107003  2107013  2107033  2107037  2107051  2107069  2107073
2107087  2107103  2107109  2107117  2107141  2107153  2107177  2107181  2107199  2107207
2107223  2107243  2107247  2107289  2107319  2107321  2107327  2107361  2107381  2107393
2107403  2107447  2107451  2107529  2107531  2107543  2107601  2107603  2107607  2107627
2107661  2107663  2107667  2107669  2107709  2107717  2107723  2107739  2107747  2107751
2107759  2107771  2107811  2107837  2107849  2107867  2107873  2107877  2107879  2107909
2107913  2107939  2107961  2107967  2107979  2107999  2108003  2108009  2108033  2108047
2108059  2108063  2108077  2108081  2108087  2108089  2108123  2108137  2108159  2108177
2108231  2108243  2108251  2108257  2108263  2108291  2108299  2108317  2108339  2108347
2108363  2108369  2108383  2108389  2108401  2108429  2108437  2108443  2108453  2108461
2108473  2108497  2108501  2108521  2108531  2108539  2108543  2108549  2108551  2108597
2108599  2108611  2108621  2108627  2108641  2108647  2108653  2108657  2108669  2108699
```

2108723 2108737 2108759 2108761 2108767 2108773 2108807 2108809 2108819 2108839
2108857 2108879 2108881 2108927 2108929 2108941 2108957 2108983 2108987 2108993
2109011 2109013 2109049 2109053 2109059 2109067 2109097 2109101 2109103 2109109
2109119 2109127 2109161 2109167 2109179 2109203 2109223 2109253 2109269 2109277
2109287 2109293 2109311 2109329 2109391 2109403 2109421 2109449 2109461 2109509
2109521 2109533 2109553 2109571 2109577 2109593 2109607 2109617 2109619 2109641
2109647 2109671 2109697 2109707 2109727 2109733 2109739 2109743 2109761 2109769
2109791 2109797 2109799 2109841 2109857 2109869 2109871 2109889 2109911 2109941
2109949 2109959 2109973 2109979 2110001 2110019 2110021 2110027 2110033 2110037
2110063 2110099 2110103 2110123 2110133 2110151 2110153 2110177 2110183 2110187
2110189 2110217 2110223 2110247 2110259 2110267 2110289 2110291 2110313 2110321
2110337 2110343 2110351 2110391 2110399 2110439 2110453 2110469 2110477 2110519
2110523 2110529 2110531 2110543 2110547 2110553 2110579 2110621 2110627 2110637
2110657 2110673 2110679 2110699 2110709 2110751 2110753 2110763 2110769 2110781
2110811 2110837 2110847 2110853 2110859 2110861 2110877 2110879 2110891 2110909
2110921 2110931 2110949 2110951 2110973 2110981 2111023 2111029 2111041 2111051
2111059 2111089 2111093 2111107 2111129 2111159 2111167 2111177 2111189 2111231
2111251 2111267 2111303 2111309 2111311 2111321 2111353 2111357 2111359 2111363
2111387 2111407 2111411 2111419 2111443 2111453 2111471 2111491 2111497 2111507
2111509 2111513 2111531 2111533 2111539 2111567 2111579 2111597 2111633 2111677
2111713 2111729 2111731 2111737 2111771 2111779 2111783 2111789 2111801 2111803
2111819 2111839 2111843 2111861 2111873 2111897 2111909 2111917 2111933 2111939
2111953 2111959 2111969 2111971 2112007 2112013 2112017 2112053 2112079 2112107
2112127 2112139 2112151 2112161 2112169 2112191 2112193 2112217 2112239 2112263
2112307 2112323 2112329 2112337 2112347 2112353 2112413 2112419 2112469 2112493
2112499 2112511 2112533 2112541 2112569 2112571 2112581 2112587 2112601 2112631
2112683 2112703 2112707 2112713 2112727 2112751 2112767 2112779 2112793 2112821
2112827 2112829 2112833 2112841 2112863 2112871 2112893 2112919 2112923 2112937
2112953 2112961 2112973 2112989 2112997 2113003 2113037 2113039 2113043 2113087
2113091 2113109 2113129 2113147 2113159 2113187 2113207 2113211 2113229 2113249
2113273 2113283 2113289 2113291 2113333 2113337 2113343 2113361 2113369 2113373
2113379 2113393 2113399 2113417 2113421 2113451 2113459 2113469 2113471 2113511
2113513 2113523 2113567 2113583 2113603 2113609 2113651 2113667 2113669 2113679
2113681 2113703 2113733 2113739 2113747 2113753 2113757 2113759 2113789 2113801
2113819 2113823 2113843 2113873 2113879 2113901 2113913 2113931 2113939 2113949
2113957 2113973 2113987 2114003 2114023 2114027 2114039 2114041 2114059 2114081
2114087 2114089 2114113 2114141 2114159 2114191 2114197 2114207 2114221 2114227
2114243 2114249 2114251 2114269 2114297 2114317 2114323 2114327 2114347 2114351
2114363 2114369 2114381 2114393 2114407 2114429 2114449 2114461 2114467 2114507
2114509 2114531 2114533 2114549 2114621 2114627 2114653 2114699 2114711 2114713
2114741 2114743 2114747 2114771 2114797 2114803 2114807 2114813 2114831 2114837
2114857 2114867 2114881 2114887 2114897 2114933 2114951 2114963 2114969 2114971
2114977 2115007 2115013 2115017 2115049 2115059 2115073 2115077 2115079 2115083
2115097 2115101 2115107 2115121 2115131 2115133 2115181 2115187 2115193 2115203
2115221 2115227 2115229 2115233 2115277 2115301 2115307 2115317 2115319 2115331
2115343 2115371 2115397 2115427 2115431 2115437 2115457 2115469 2115481 2115493
2115499 2115511 2115523 2115527 2115539 2115571 2115629 2115653 2115671 2115677
2115683 2115689 2115703 2115713 2115721 2115727 2115749 2115763 2115767 2115787
2115791 2115823 2115829 2115847 2115853 2115863 2115877 2115923 2115937 2115943
2115961 2115979 2115983 2116019 2116021 2116027 2116039 2116063 2116097 2116099
2116117 2116123 2116129 2116183 2116187 2116189 2116291 2116307 2116327 2116351
2116357 2116393 2116397 2116403 2116409 2116423 2116427 2116441 2116447 2116469
2116489 2116541 2116547 2116501 2116519 2116523 2116531 2116537 2116559 2116561
2116571 2116573 2116577 2116579 2116591 2116601 2116607 2116627 2116633 2116651
2116663 2116669 2116679 2116691 2116693 2116717 2116729 2116747 2116757 2116783
2116799 2116801 2116811 2116813 2116817 2116837 2116867 2116901 2116903 2116921
2116949 2116951 2116957 2116967 2116969 2116973 2116981 2116987 2116991 2116997
2117039 2117041 2117051 2117053 2117077 2117099 2117119 2117151 2117147 2117179
2117233 2117237 2117239 2117273 2117287 2117293 2117317 2117321 2117351 2117369
2117389 2117411 2117419 2117429 2117431 2117441 2117447 2117461 2117477 2117497
2117501 2117513 2117539 2117561 2117573 2117581 2117593 2117597 2117611 2117623
2117651 2117653 2117663 2117671 2117677 2117699 2117701 2117711 2117719 2117723
2117729 2117743 2117747 2117777 2117783 2117821 2117833 2117849 2117861 2117887
2117893 2117903 2117953 2117971 2117977 2118007 2118023 2118029 2118031 2118037
2118043 2118049 2118059 2118079 2118089 2118091 2118113 2118119 2118121 2118163
2118169 2118173 2118187 2118209 2118229 2118269 2118283 2118299 2118301 2118313
2118331 2118343 2118349 2118359 2118371 2118377 2118397 2118419 2118433 2118437
2118449 2118491 2118497 2118503 2118517 2118527 2118541 2118547 2118581 2118587
2118601 2118629 2118643 2118661 2118667 2118689 2118703 2118733 2118751 2118791
2118799 2118803 2118811 2118833 2118841 2118871 2118877 2118889 2118917 2118923
2118959 2118973 2119031 2119057 2119087 2119093 2119121 2119147 2119157 2119171
2119189 2119199 2119211 2119231 2119259 2119261 2119267 2119301 2119307 2119319
2119319 2119363 2119367 2119379 2119399 2119433 2119463 2119483 2119487 2119493
2119511 2119531 2119561 2119573 2119589 2119591 2119597 2119603 2119609 2119613
2119627 2119631 2119643 2119661 2119669 2119673 2119681 2119699 2119717 2119739
2119751 2119763 2119783 2119829 2119837 2119877 2119879 2119907 2119913 2119919
2119921 2119937 2119939 2119967 2119969 2120009 2120017 2120021 2120051 2120057
2120093 2120099 2120101 2120113 2120119 2120143 2120147 2120171 2120203 2120207
2120213 2120221 2120227 2120231 2120243 2120249 2120263 2120269 2120297 2120303
2120309 2120317 2120329 2120341 2120351 2120353 2120383 2120387 2120411 2120423
2120429 2120453 2120473 2120513 2120537 2120549 2120551 2120579 2120611 2120621
2120639 2120653 2120693 2120731 2120747 2120753 2120771 2120779 2120819 2120827
2120843 2120849 2120851 2120863 2120879 2120887 2120891 2120917 2120933 2120941
2120947 2120957 2120977 2120981 2121011 2121017 2121023 2121029 2121043 2121121
2121127 2121133 2121143 2121167 2121181 2121187 2121191 2121193 2121199 2121239
2121241 2121253 2121271 2121289 2121323 2121337 2121341 2121367 2121373 2121377
2121389 2121403 2121433 2121443 2121461 2121479 2121503 2121529 2121569 2121601
2121607 2121619 2121631 2121653 2121661 2121667 2121683 2121737 2121739 2121751
2121761 2121767 2121781 2121793 2121797 2121803 2121809 2121829

```
2121841  2121853  2121869  2121877  2121881  2121893  2121907  2121941  2121943  2121967
2121979  2121989  2122009  2122013  2122031  2122039  2122063  2122073  2122079  2122103
2122123  2122139  2122151  2122163  2122181  2122189  2122193  2122213  2122231  2122259
2122277  2122303  2122321  2122327  2122333  2122349  2122363  2122369  2122381  2122409
2122427  2122441  2122451  2122459  2122469  2122489  2122499  2122507  2122511  2122513
2122531  2122553  2122573  2122619  2122633  2122649  2122657  2122667  2122691  2122697
2122709  2122711  2122721  2122723  2122741  2122753  2122777  2122793  2122817  2122823
2122837  2122843  2122853  2122859  2122873  2122921  2122937  2122957  2122961  2122963
2122979  2123027  2123047  2123053  2123063  2123081  2123083  2123087  2123123  2123129
2123137  2123141  2123161  2123167  2123203  2123213  2123237  2123239  2123243  2123257
2123263  2123279  2123281  2123309  2123327  2123353  2123357  2123369  2123377  2123411
2123423  2123461  2123479  2123483  2123491  2123557  2123581  2123603  2123617  2123663
2123669  2123683  2123701  2123707  2123731  2123741  2123743  2123747  2123753  2123761
2123767  2123773  2123777  2123783  2123791  2123831  2123851  2123867  2123879  2123881
2123897  2123909  2123917  2123939  2123969  2123971  2123983  2123999  2124007  2124011
2124013  2124019  2124037  2124041  2124043  2124049  2124127  2124139  2124149  2124173
2124191  2124197  2124223  2124229  2124233  2124247  2124253  2124277  2124289  2124299
2124319  2124323  2124359  2124361  2124377  2124401  2124403  2124431  2124443  2124449
2124457  2124469  2124479  2124491  2124509  2124517  2124553  2124571  2124589  2124601
2124631  2124659  2124667  2124679  2124757  2124761  2124769  2124791  2124797  2124821
2124839  2124841  2124853  2124869  2124877  2124887  2124919  2124943  2124953  2124961
2124973  2125001  2125009  2125037  2125043  2125069  2125073  2125087  2125099  2125111
2125147  2125157  2125163  2125181  2125219  2125229  2125237  2125259  2125273  2125313
2125327  2125339  2125373  2125393  2125411  2125429  2125451  2125457  2125463  2125469
2125471  2125477  2125517  2125523  2125531  2125537  2125553  2125559  2125567  2125579
2125601  2125603  2125621  2125649  2125657  2125661  2125679  2125681  2125691  2125693
2125699  2125703  2125733  2125741  2125751  2125757  2125771  2125793  2125801  2125813
2125819  2125831  2125841  2125847  2125873  2125889  2125919  2125927  2125933  2125939
2125987  2125993  2126017  2126027  2126029  2126039  2126041  2126063  2126087  2126101
2126129  2126141  2126147  2126149  2126153  2126167  2126171  2126177  2126191  2126203
2126213  2126227  2126249  2126269  2126273  2126297  2126303  2126317  2126329  2126339
2126351  2126363  2126381  2126387  2126407  2126429  2126431  2126441  2126447  2126459
2126491  2126539  2126549  2126567  2126573  2126587  2126611  2126617  2126623  2126627
2126633  2126639  2126659  2126669  2126681  2126687  2126749  2126767  2126771  2126783
2126791  2126801  2126809  2126827  2126849  2126851  2126857  2126863  2126867  2126893
2126897  2126899  2126903  2126911  2126923  2126933  2126951  2126963  2127007  2127029
2127043  2127061  2127067  2127071  2127077  2127133  2127143  2127149  2127157  2127163
2127269  2127271  2127277  2127287  2127289  2127299  2127319  2127331  2127341  2127343
2127347  2127371  2127379  2127383  2127401  2127409  2127421  2127427  2127443  2127467
2127493  2127529  2127553  2127557  2127607  2127617  2127641  2127647  2127649  2127659
2127667  2127679  2127689  2127691  2127721  2127733  2127739  2127751  2127757  2127761
2127779  2127787  2127803  2127841  2127857  2127883  2127887  2127893  2127919  2127947
2127949  2127959  2127967  2127971  2127973  2127977  2127997  2128001  2128031  2128039
2128051  2128067  2128069  2128103  2128153  2128157  2128171  2128177  2128201  2128241
2128253  2128261  2128267  2128279  2128283  2128303  2128309  2128319  2128327  2128333
2128381  2128387  2128391  2128403  2128409  2128439  2128447  2128453  2128463  2128481
2128487  2128493  2128501  2128531  2128547  2128549  2128559  2128561  2128591  2128601
2128603  2128631  2128649  2128663  2128667  2128669  2128697  2128727  2128733  2128747
2128751  2128769  2128781  2128783  2128799  2128823  2128831  2128837  2128849  2128871
2128873  2128891  2128933  2128963  2128991  2128993  2129003  2129011  2129027  2129047
2129051  2129069  2129107  2129119  2129123  2129161  2129167  2129171  2129203  2129207
2129213  2129221  2129227  2129261  2129263  2129279  2129291  2129293  2129321  2129329
2129333  2129353  2129357  2129371  2129389  2129399  2129401  2129419  2129423  2129431
2129443  2129447  2129473  2129497  2129507  2129509  2129513  2129521  2129527  2129537
2129549  2129551  2129579  2129587  2129597  2129599  2129627  2129671  2129689  2129713
2129719  2129741  2129749  2129753  2129773  2129779  2129783  2129791  2129797  2129807
2129819  2129821  2129837  2129849  2129851  2129861  2129867  2129887  2129891  2129903
2129951  2129971  2129977  2129983  2130001  2130013  2130023  2130031  2130047  2130061  2130101
2130133  2130169  2130173  2130209  2130239  2130241  2130251  2130269  2130307  2130341
2130343  2130347  2130367  2130371  2130379  2130383  2130391  2130437  2130439  2130461
2130473  2130493  2130503  2130509  2130523  2130529  2130539  2130577  2130581  2130613
2130617  2130619  2130631  2130671  2130673  2130683  2130701  2130703  2130721  2130727
2130767  2130769  2130789  2130803  2130809  2130853  2130857  2130901  2130911  2130917
2130929  2130937  2130959  2130979  2131013  2131039  2131043  2131049  2131081  2131093
2131099  2131109  2131127  2131133  2131141  2131193  2131223  2131231  2131243  2131247
2131253  2131267  2131271  2131291  2131319  2131321  2131361  2131373  2131399  2131417
2131427  2131429  2131447  2131457  2131463  2131469  2131483  2131513  2131517  2131531
2131537  2131541  2131559  2131567  2131573  2131601  2131603  2131609  2131627  2131651
2131669  2131687  2131691  2131693  2131699  2131721  2131771  2131793  2131799  2131813
2131823  2131837  2131849  2131853  2131859  2131867  2131907  2131937  2131951  2131979
2131981  2131991  2132003  2132023  2132027  2132033  2132057  2132063  2132107  2132113
2132129  2132147  2132153  2132171  2132177  2132209  2132213  2132231  2132233  2132239
2132267  2132279  2132281  2132303  2132309  2132311  2132321  2132323  2132359  2132371
2132381  2132387  2132401  2132407  2132411  2132419  2132461  2132467  2132477  2132483
2132513  2132529  2132551  2132563  2132567  2132587  2132591  2132593  2132639  2132653
2132657  2132659  2132699  2132749  2132759  2132761  2132771  2132777  2132783  2132797
2132827  2132839  2132849  2132857  2132881  2132891  2132899  2132903  2132941  2132947
2132957  2132981  2132983  2132989  2132993  2133023  2133029  2133031  2133049  2133059
2133097  2133113  2133121  2133137  2133151  2133167  2133191  2133217  2133251  2133253
2133277  2133281  2133289  2133293  2133311  2133331  2133361  2133367  2133379  2133403
2133407  2133413  2133427  2133431  2133433  2133463  2133487  2133533  2133539  2133541
2133563  2133587  2133589  2133601  2133611  2133613  2133631  2133647  2133673  2133683
2133689  2133697  2133701  2133713  2133739  2133743  2133773  2133793  2133797  2133799
2133811  2133821  2133839  2133899  2133949  2133973  2133991  2133997  2134003  2134007
2134019  2134021  2134063  2134073  2134079  2134087  2134109  2134141  2134157  2134183
2134201  2134241  2134243  2134247  2134259  2134261  2134267  2134273  2134289  2134303
2134339  2134351  2134357  2134373  2134399  2134409  2134417  2134439  2134463  2134471
2134507  2134519  2134529  2134549  2134579  2134589  2134609  2134621  2134633  2134637
2134697  2134703  2134709  2134721  2134751  2134763  2134801  2134813  2134831  2134841
```

```
2134849  2134861  2134879  2134921  2134927  2134943  2134949  2134961  2134963  2134991
2135017  2135027  2135051  2135057  2135083  2135099  2135101  2135117  2135141  2135153
2135167  2135173  2135191  2135197  2135207  2135213  2135219  2135227  2135267  2135279
2135303  2135333  2135347  2135369  2135383  2135401  2135407  2135411  2135417  2135447
2135453  2135479  2135503  2135519  2135521  2135533  2135537  2135563  2135597  2135611
2135641  2135663  2135669  2135687  2135689  2135699  2135701  2135713  2135717  2135719
2135723  2135729  2135737  2135743  2135753  2135773  2135779  2135797  2135831  2135851
2135857  2135891  2135909  2135921  2135929  2135933  2135951  2135957  2135971  2136011
2136019  2136023  2136061  2136077  2136083  2136091  2136107  2136109  2136119  2136131
2136133  2136137  2136139  2136143  2136157  2136163  2136181  2136187  2136191  2136193
2136209  2136221  2136247  2136287  2136289  2136301  2136311  2136313  2136347  2136353
2136359  2136361  2136371  2136383  2136389  2136391  2136419  2136437  2136439  2136451
2136457  2136473  2136487  2136527  2136553  2136557  2136559  2136583  2136587  2136593
2136599  2136601  2136643  2136649  2136661  2136707  2136731  2136733  2136773  2136779
2136793  2136811  2136829  2136833  2136839  2136853  2136863  2136877  2136889
2136913  2136919  2136973  2136977  2136983  2136989  2136991  2136997  2137021  2137033
2137049  2137073  2137117  2137123  2137133  2137141  2137151  2137153  2137159  2137193
2137211  2137237  2137243  2137259  2137273  2137279  2137301  2137307  2137327
2137339  2137351  2137361  2137391  2137397  2137409  2137411  2137423  2137441  2137451
2137483  2137489  2137493  2137507  2137517  2137547  2137549  2137571  2137613  2137627
2137637  2137669  2137673  2137679  2137687  2137697  2137717  2137727  2137741  2137763
2137771  2137813  2137829  2137841  2137859  2137871  2137879  2137907  2137913  2137921
2137931  2137943  2137957  2137963  2137969  2137973  2137979  2137981  2137987  2137999
2138029  2138033  2138093  2138137  2138167  2138189  2138197  2138207  2138221  2138231
2138239  2138249  2138251  2138263  2138291  2138321  2138327  2138363  2138371  2138377
2138387  2138399  2138401  2138407  2138419  2138429  2138467  2138483  2138491  2138501
2138527  2138531  2138537  2138551  2138569  2138593  2138623  2138629  2138657
2138671  2138677  2138687  2138693  2138713  2138737  2138743  2138749  2138789  2138797
2138803  2138813  2138833  2138863  2138867  2138887  2138897  2138909  2138971
2138987  2138989  2138999  2139013  2139043  2139047  2139091  2139107  2139131  2139143
2139149  2139157  2139167  2139199  2139211  2139227  2139233  2139283  2139307  2139311
2139323  2139337  2139353  2139367  2139383  2139383  2139407  2139409  2139427  2139461
2139463  2139481  2139493  2139497  2139499  2139521  2139539  2139541  2139563  2139583
2139607  2139611  2139653  2139659  2139661  2139677  2139691  2139733  2139737  2139743
2139811  2139817  2139829  2139857  2139859  2139877  2139911  2139919  2139923
2139931  2139937  2139947  2139953  2139959  2139967  2139979  2140001  2140003  2140007
2140013  2140049  2140057  2140069  2140091  2140109  2140121  2140129  2140139  2140157
2140163  2140169  2140199  2140207  2140223  2140231  2140253  2140267  2140273  2140279
2140301  2140309  2140337  2140349  2140363  2140367  2140387  2140393  2140399  2140421
2140441  2140447  2140459  2140477  2140513  2140517  2140531  2140543  2140549  2140573
2140591  2140601  2140603  2140609  2140627  2140631  2140637  2140681  2140729  2140741
2140753  2140763  2140769  2140781  2140807  2140811  2140823  2140843  2140847  2140849
2140877  2140903  2140907  2140913  2140937  2140967  2140969  2140973  2140987  2140993
2141033  2141057  2141063  2141071  2141121  2141131  2141141  2141149  2141159
2141189  2141197  2141203  2141213  2141219  2141257  2141261  2141297  2141299  2141311
2141329  2141333  2141401  2141407  2141413  2141417  2141437  2141459  2141467  2141497
2141519  2141533  2141543  2141549  2141569  2141591  2141593  2141603  2141617  2141647
2141653  2141669  2141681  2141687  2141693  2141707  2141723  2141731  2141749  2141753
2141791  2141801  2141803  2141807  2141809  2141827  2141849  2141863  2141879  2141891
2141897  2141899  2141903  2141917  2141929  2141941  2141947  2141977  2141987  2142001
2142029  2142037  2142043  2142053  2142061  2142067  2142073  2142083  2142097  2142121
2142149  2142163  2142167  2142181  2142211  2142227  2142229  2142241  2142251
2142253  2142271  2142281  2142293  2142299  2142341  2142353  2142377  2142397  2142403
2142431  2142449  2142457  2142463  2142499  2142521  2142523  2142529  2142533  2142541
2142551  2142557  2142577  2142583  2142587  2142601  2142641  2142643  2142669  2142667
2142677  2142691  2142713  2142719  2142739  2142743  2142761  2142767  2142803  2142823
2142857  2142883  2142911  2142923  2142941  2142967  2142971  2143019  2143027  2143039
2143051  2143069  2143073  2143081  2143087  2143093  2143109  2143147  2143157  2143177
2143199  2143201  2143217  2143223  2143231  2143243  2143259  2143261  2143279  2143313
2143319  2143331  2143369  2143381  2143391  2143417  2143441  2143451  2143459  2143469
2143481  2143483  2143489  2143501  2143517  2143541  2143543  2143567  2143571
2143573  2143579  2143621  2143627  2143667  2143711  2143733  2143741  2143753  2143759
2143763  2143793  2143829  2143831  2143837  2143847  2143859  2143861  2143873  2143877
2143901  2143909  2143943  2143957  2143963  2143969  2143993  2144011  2144029  2144033
2144041  2144047  2144063  2144081  2144117  2144123  2144137  2144143  2144161  2144167
2144171  2144179  2144189  2144209  2144213  2144243  2144249  2144251  2144269
2144273  2144279  2144287  2144309  2144323  2144369  2144371  2144383  2144399  2144407
2144419  2144437  2144449  2144459  2144477  2144491  2144501  2144503
2144507  2144509  2144537  2144551  2144609  2144617  2144621  2144629  2144641  2144647
2144671  2144677  2144683  2144687  2144689  2144707  2144713  2144717  2144719  2144729
2144731  2144743  2144759  2144789  2144783  2144801  2144837  2144843  2144867
2144893  2144897  2144899  2144951  2144953  2144971  2144977  2144993  2144999  2145023
2145047  2145067  2145089  2145097  2145103  2145109  2145113  2145131  2145137
2145151  2145163  2145173  2145191  2145193  2145197  2145239  2145263  2145277  2145287
2145289  2145307  2145329  2145331  2145337  2145343  2145359  2145361  2145379  2145389
2145401  2145421  2145439  2145443  2145487  2145497  2145523  2145547
2145551  2145617  2145629  2145631  2145641  2145643  2145677  2145683  2145707  2145709
2145713  2145721  2145751  2145769  2145779  2145821  2145823  2145827  2145839  2145853
2145937  2145953  2145977  2145991  2146003  2146009  2146043  2146051  2146091  2146093
2146103  2146139  2146141  2146159  2146169  2146181  2146201  2146213  2146219  2146231
2146247  2146253  2146283  2146289  2146303  2146307  2146327  2146357  2146367  2146387
2146393  2146423  2146433  2146439  2146457  2146477  2146483  2146489  2146499  2146511
2146519  2146523  2146531  2146549  2146561  2146589  2146619  2146633  2146663  2146673
2146687  2146691  2146693  2146723  2146733  2146759  2146763  2146787  2146789  2146813
2146817  2146847  2146853  2146897  2146909  2146939  2146979  2146987  2146993  2147009
2147021  2147023  2147039  2147051  2147053  2147059  2147071  2147077  2147081  2147087
2147099  2147107  2147137  2147161  2147177  2147213  2147231  2147237  2147251  2147263
2147269  2147273  2147279  2147281  2147297  2147309  2147329  2147351  2147359  2147381
2147407  2147419  2147429  2147461  2147473  2147489  2147501  2147503  2147527  2147569
```

```
2147599 2147611 2147617 2147623 2147633 2147641 2147657 2147693 2147699 2147731
2147737 2147753 2147767 2147771 2147801 2147839 2147843 2147861 2147863 2147869
2147881 2147903 2147909 2147911 2147923 2147941 2147987 2147989 2148011 2148019
2148043 2148049 2148053 2148071 2148073 2148127 2148149 2148163 2148187 2148199
2148203 2148227 2148241 2148287 2148301 2148329 2148337 2148343 2148347 2148353
2148373 2148379 2148383 2148397 2148401 2148403 2148437 2148449 2148451 2148457
2148467 2148473 2148491 2148527 2148529 2148533 2148547 2148583 2148599 2148607
2148617 2148631 2148649 2148659 2148661 2148677 2148709 2148719 2148733 2148737
2148739 2148761 2148781 2148791 2148799 2148803 2148857 2148863 2148869 2148877
2148893 2148899 2148907 2148947 2148983 2148989 2149003 2149031 2149039 2149057
2149061 2149067 2149087 2149093 2149111 2149117 2149127 2149139 2149141 2149151
2149171 2149181 2149181 2149187 2149207 2149211 2149237 2149247 2149249 2149283
2149289 2149331 2149349 2149351 2149379 2149391 2149403 2149409 2149421 2149453
2149471 2149493 2149501 2149517 2149559 2149573 2149591 2149607 2149619 2149621
2149661 2149681 2149703 2149711 2149727 2149781 2149789 2149813 2149853
2149859 2149867 2149877 2149883 2149897 2149909 2149933 2149937 2149991 2149993
2150009 2150011 2150023 2150039 2150101 2150111 2150119 2150131 2150149 2150171
2150207 2150209 2150221 2150227 2150273 2150299 2150303 2150333 2150341 2150353
2150383 2150399 2150411 2150417 2150459 2150461 2150453 2150457 2150509 2150513
2150527 2150531 2150543 2150567 2150597 2150639 2150641 2150651 2150657 2150663
2150671 2150683 2150689 2150713 2150717 2150719 2150741 2150777 2150783 2150791
2150801 2150809 2150821 2150831 2150839 2150849 2150867 2150879 2150881 2150917
2150923 2150947 2150969 2150977 2151001 2151007 2151011 2151013 2151031 2151073
2151089 2151101 2151119 2151137 2151139 2151157 2151179 2151203 2151211 2151221
2151241 2151251 2151263 2151269 2151271 2151283 2151293 2151301 2151319 2151329
2151337 2151349 2151353 2151377 2151403 2151421 2151433 2151451 2151463 2151467
2151473 2151497 2151509 2151511 2151517 2151521 2151533 2151563 2151593 2151607
2151619 2151623 2151629 2151637 2151647 2151659 2151683 2151701 2151703 2151767
2151781 2151791 2151817 2151827 2151847 2151869 2151899 2151917 2151923 2151943
2151971 2151977 2151991 2152001 2152009 2152037 2152043 2152063 2152069 2152079
2152093 2152103 2152123 2152127 2152153 2152159 2152169 2152201 2152211 2152219
2152229 2152231 2152247 2152291 2152303 2152307 2152309 2152321 2152343 2152357
2152369 2152373 2152393 2152399 2152427 2152429 2152433 2152457 2152477 2152481
2152483 2152499 2152521 2152527 2152559 2152571 2152589 2152607 2152621 2152637
2152663 2152669 2152679 2152691 2152729 2152739 2152753 2152783 2152789 2152793
2152811 2152817 2152819 2152831 2152837 2152841 2152847 2152849 2152861 2152867
2152879 2152883 2152903 2152907 2152921 2152939 2152949 2152957 2152973 2153051
2153057 2153059 2153069 2153071 2153083 2153089 2153111 2153113 2153149 2153159
2153171 2153201 2153209 2153227 2153243 2153267 2153273 2153297 2153299 2153317
2153321 2153341 2153351 2153369 2153377 2153387 2153401 2153419 2153429 2153449
2153471 2153491 2153507 2153519 2153531 2153551 2153561 2153563 2153621 2153633
2153639 2153647 2153693 2153699 2153717 2153729 2153737 2153773 2153779 2153797
2153813 2153819 2153839 2153861 2153873 2153887 2153891 2153903 2153909 2153929
2153939 2153953 2153963 2153981 2153989 2153993 2154007 2154013 2154037 2154041
2154043 2154059 2154071 2154077 2154109 2154127 2154137 2154143 2154161 2154169
2154193 2154209 2154227 2154241 2154259 2154281 2154293 2154307 2154311 2154319
2154329 2154331 2154389 2154413 2154419 2154487 2154491 2154499 2154533 2154539
2154541 2154553 2154577 2154587 2154611 2154629 2154641 2154643 2154667 2154683
2154707 2154727 2154731 2154743 2154749 2154791 2154793 2154811 2154829 2154839
2154851 2154853 2154871 2154881 2154899 2154907 2154913 2154931 2154941 2154949
2154953 2154967 2154973 2154979 2155003 2155007 2155009 2155057 2155067 2155079
2155103 2155121 2155129 2155133 2155159 2155163 2155171 2155177 2155183 2155187
2155201 2155207 2155253 2155259 2155267 2155271 2155273 2155291 2155297 2155319
2155327 2155333 2155381 2155393 2155397 2155409 2155423 2155429 2155451 2155463
2155477 2155487 2155499 2155511 2155513 2155519 2155579 2155597 2155603 2155609
2155627 2155639 2155661 2155667 2155691 2155711 2155717 2155723 2155733
2155781 2155793 2155799 2155837 2155841 2155849 2155861 2155877 2155883 2155931
2155961 2155963 2155999 2156009 2156017 2156023 2156039 2156041 2156053 2156071
2156083 2156087 2156111 2156117 2156123 2156159 2156171 2156183 2156207 2156221
2156251 2156269 2156279 2156299 2156303 2156309 2156311 2156317 2156339 2156351
2156359 2156369 2156377 2156383 2156387 2156393 2156417 2156437 2156447 2156459
2156461 2156491 2156507 2156521 2156537 2156597 2156599 2156617 2156629 2156647
2156659 2156669 2156681 2156683 2156699 2156711 2156719 2156731 2156753 2156761
2156789 2156801 2156809 2156813 2156839 2156849 2156851 2156857 2156867 2156873
2156879 2156897 2156939 2156993 2157007 2157017 2157031 2157037 2157041 2157091
2157097 2157109 2157119 2157121 2157131 2157149 2157151 2157157 2157163 2157173
2157187 2157209 2157229 2157247 2157251 2157257 2157269 2157277 2157293 2157301
2157307 2157313 2157319 2157329 2157341 2157343 2157361 2157391 2157401 2157413
2157427 2157451 2157457 2157481 2157499 2157503 2157511 2157517 2157523 2157527
2157539 2157557 2157559 2157563 2157587 2157641 2157667 2157671 2157677 2157679
2157709 2157721 2157731 2157733 2157737 2157739 2157763 2157767 2157769 2157787
2157797 2157821 2157823 2157833 2157839 2157851 2157863 2157893 2157899 2157901
2157907 2157913 2157923 2157989 2158019 2158027 2158033 2158061 2158069 2158073
2158081 2158087 2158097 2158103 2158129 2158139 2158147 2158157 2158171 2158181
2158183 2158223 2158231 2158237 2158259 2158291 2158301 2158307 2158333 2158357
2158367 2158369 2158393 2158423 2158427 2158433 2158447 2158459 2158477 2158483
2158501 2158523 2158547 2158549 2158567 2158577 2158579 2158589 2158591 2158601
2158603 2158621 2158627 2158631 2158649 2158679 2158693 2158697 2158699 2158721
2158727 2158733 2158753 2158759 2158763 2158769 2158771 2158781 2158801 2158811
2158817 2158823 2158831 2158841 2158843 2158859 2158889 2158903 2158909 2158921
2158931 2158979 2158993 2158999 2159023 2159041 2159063 2159081 2159083 2159093
2159147 2159177 2159191 2159197 2159207 2159231 2159233 2159237 2159239 2159249
2159251 2159281 2159291 2159299 2159303 2159327 2159329 2159351 2159359 2159363
2159383 2159419 2159449 2159453 2159473 2159497 2159501 2159513 2159519 2159533
2159537 2159551 2159557 2159609 2159621 2159627 2159639 2159669 2159671 2159681
2159701 2159713 2159719 2159767 2159771 2159779 2159783 2159789 2159809 2159819
2159821 2159831 2159881 2159887 2159893 2159897 2159903 2159923 2159947 2159951
2159957 2159959 2160001 2160017 2160029 2160031 2160061 2160101 2160113 2160127
2160131 2160133 2160149 2160161 2160203 2160209 2160211 2160217 2160233 2160247
```

```
2160253  2160259  2160283  2160293  2160311  2160337  2160341  2160349  2160373  2160383
2160391  2160409  2160419  2160443  2160461  2160463  2160469  2160527  2160533  2160553
2160563  2160589  2160617  2160619  2160629  2160671  2160677  2160721  2160733  2160749
2160773  2160787  2160797  2160833  2160841  2160857  2160881  2160883  2160913  2160923
2160931  2160937  2160953  2160967  2160971  2160997  2161001  2161007  2161031  2161087
2161121  2161127  2161129  2161141  2161157  2161163  2161177  2161189  2161199  2161213
2161253  2161259  2161279  2161297  2161301  2161303  2161319  2161331  2161337  2161343
2161349  2161373  2161409  2161417  2161427  2161433  2161447  2161469  2161493  2161513
2161553  2161571  2161591  2161613  2161633  2161637  2161639  2161697  2161699  2161729
2161751  2161759  2161769  2161777  2161781  2161787  2161813  2161823  2161829  2161843
2161849  2161853  2161871  2161883  2161897  2161903  2161919  2161927  2161933  2161949
2161963  2161967  2161987  2162003  2162057  2162059  2162063  2162071  2162087  2162089
2162113  2162119  2162137  2162177  2162183  2162189  2162191  2162197  2162203  2162221
2162231  2162239  2162249  2162263  2162273  2162297  2162323  2162339  2162351  2162353
2162359  2162387  2162393  2162401  2162441  2162449  2162497  2162507  2162509  2162543
2162549  2162557  2162569  2162579  2162581  2162597  2162603  2162623  2162639  2162647
2162651  2162659  2162663  2162681  2162717  2162737  2162747  2162803  2162807  2162813
2162821  2162843  2162869  2162879  2162899  2162911  2162929  2162947  2162957  2162959
2162971  2162977  2163011  2163013  2163041  2163043  2163059  2163067  2163071  2163079
2163101  2163107  2163113  2163137  2163163  2163167  2163181  2163193  2163221  2163223
2163241  2163247  2163251  2163263  2163281  2163289  2163307  2163341  2163347  2163349
2163361  2163401  2163409  2163431  2163439  2163443  2163461  2163467  2163479  2163481
2163503  2163509  2163527  2163547  2163569  2163571  2163593  2163613  2163653  2163671
2163673  2163677  2163691  2163703  2163737  2163751  2163757  2163761  2163767  2163787
2163809  2163823  2163827  2163829  2163851  2163859  2163869  2163881  2163883  2163911
2163919  2163923  2163949  2163971  2163979  2163983  2164003  2164013  2164031  2164037
2164039  2164073  2164111  2164121  2164171  2164177  2164193  2164223  2164229  2164247
2164273  2164291  2164307  2164313  2164367  2164387  2164399  2164417  2164429  2164433
2164441  2164447  2164453  2164471  2164483  2164489  2164493  2164501  2164511  2164529
2164571  2164583  2164597  2164607  2164609  2164619  2164621  2164633  2164639  2164681
2164739  2164787  2164801  2164807  2164817  2164843  2164853  2164859  2164901  2164919
2164927  2164963  2164979  2164991  2165017  2165027  2165029  2165039  2165047  2165057
2165063  2165077  2165081  2165083  2165089  2165117  2165131  2165143  2165147  2165159
2165201  2165213  2165231  2165237  2165249  2165291  2165321  2165323  2165327  2165357
2165393  2165413  2165453  2165461  2165467  2165483  2165521  2165531  2165533  2165543
2165551  2165557  2165591  2165593  2165599  2165617  2165651  2165659  2165663  2165671
2165687  2165701  2165707  2165711  2165741  2165747  2165771  2165773  2165809  2165819
2165843  2165857  2165873  2165893  2165897  2165903  2165921  2165929  2165941  2165957
2165959  2165963  2165971  2166007  2166023  2166029  2166041  2166053  2166077  2166113
2166119  2166121  2166127  2166137  2166161  2166167  2166179  2166221  2166233  2166251
2166289  2166319  2166403  2166407  2166419  2166427  2166431  2166449  2166457  2166467
2166509  2166511  2166523  2166533  2166547  2166553  2166557  2166581  2166601
2166607  2166613  2166629  2166673  2166679  2166691  2166709  2166721  2166763  2166797
2166821  2166833  2166877  2166917  2166919  2166937  2166943  2166947  2166949  2166953
2166961  2166977  2167003  2167019  2167021  2167031  2167063  2167073  2167079  2167091
2167093  2167097  2167103  2167111  2167163  2167183  2167189  2167237  2167259  2167261
2167287  2167327  2167339  2167351  2167367  2167369  2167393  2167409  2167421  2167433
2167439  2167441  2167447  2167469  2167471  2167507  2167519  2167531  2167537  2167549
2167573  2167579  2167609  2167621  2167643  2167661  2167703  2167717  2167723  2167741
2167747  2167769  2167771  2167777  2167813  2167829  2167849  2167873  2167883  2167889
2167903  2167933  2167937  2167939  2167961  2167981  2167987  2167993  2167999  2168021
2168029  2168051  2168057  2168059  2168081  2168093  2168107  2168143  2168149  2168183
2168219  2168239  2168263  2168273  2168291  2168293  2168297  2168303  2168317  2168323
2168329  2168339  2168347  2168351  2168363  2168377  2168399  2168407  2168429  2168437
2168473  2168483  2168497  2168501  2168519  2168521  2168549  2168557  2168563  2168567
2168581  2168587  2168599  2168609  2168623  2168651  2168653  2168657  2168659  2168669
2168671  2168687  2168689  2168701  2168711  2168713  2168731  2168737  2168743  2168753
2168797  2168807  2168809  2168819  2168827  2168851  2168861  2168863  2168867  2168879
2168893  2168917  2168921  2168951  2168953  2168987  2168989  2169007  2169029  2169031
2169071  2169073  2169109  2169133  2169137  2169143  2169151  2169157  2169161  2169169
2169203  2169227  2169281  2169289  2169311  2169313  2169331  2169359  2169361  2169389
2169397  2169443  2169457  2169467  2169469  2169499  2169509  2169511  2169529  2169539
2169571  2169617  2169619  2169631  2169637  2169641  2169649  2169663  2169677  2169683
2169691  2169701  2169707  2169749  2169757  2169773  2169799  2169803  2169821  2169833
2169841  2169859  2169877  2169883  2169913  2169941  2169967  2169991  2169997  2170039
2170043  2170061  2170109  2170111  2170117  2170121  2170127  2170141  2170153  2170159
2170193  2170213  2170219  2170229  2170241  2170243  2170247  2170261  2170283  2170291
2170307  2170321  2170367  2170369  2170379  2170387  2170393  2170409  2170411  2170423
2170429  2170453  2170477  2170481  2170501  2170513  2170523  2170529  2170537  2170549
2170573  2170583  2170603  2170607  2170627  2170639  2170643  2170667  2170669  2170673
2170681  2170697  2170703  2170723  2170741  2170757  2170771  2170783  2170813  2170823
2170829  2170871  2170877  2170897  2170907  2170919  2170937  2170939  2170943  2171003
2171011  2171017  2171021  2171077  2171089  2171101  2171107  2171119  2171159  2171161
2171203  2171219  2171231  2171243  2171249  2171261  2171293  2171311  2171329  2171341
2171347  2171383  2171387  2171431  2171437  2171441  2171447  2171503  2171509  2171527
2171551  2171557  2171579  2171593  2171599  2171621  2171623  2171627  2171633  2171639
2171657  2171707  2171711  2171717  2171737  2171749  2171753  2171759  2171761  2171773
2171777  2171831  2171837  2171851  2171857  2171881  2171921  2171941  2171951  2171959
2171963  2171977  2171989  2171999  2172007  2172031  2172041  2172047  2172067  2172083
2172091  2172101  2172109  2172113  2172151  2172161  2172173  2172179  2172197  2172211
2172227  2172229  2172239  2172241  2172253  2172257  2172283  2172323  2172337  2172343
2172347  2172367  2172371  2172383  2172389  2172397  2172427  2172433  2172461  2172473
2172491  2172497  2172539  2172551  2172559  2172571  2172581  2172587  2172613
2172619  2172641  2172659  2172673  2172679  2172701  2172721  2172727  2172733  2172761
2172773  2172791  2172799  2172803  2172811  2172817  2172823  2172827  2172829  2172839
2172847  2172851  2172853  2172869  2172871  2172887  2172893  2172901  2172917  2172943
2172949  2172967  2172977  2172979  2172983  2172997  2173001  2173009  2173013  2173033
2173043  2173051  2173079  2173081  2173099  2173111  2173141  2173151  2173153  2173183
2173207  2173219  2173243  2173307  2173319  2173333  2173337  2173357  2173361  2173363
```

```
2173387  2173393  2173411  2173447  2173453  2173487  2173499  2173513  2173519  2173529
2173531  2173553  2173571  2173573  2173601  2173661  2173649  2173651  2173663  2173679
2173711  2173727  2173729  2173747  2173757  2173763  2173777  2173819  2173877  2173879
2173883  2173889  2173903  2173907  2173957  2173967  2173981  2173993  2174017  2174023
2174033  2174047  2174057  2174063  2174071  2174077  2174089  2174119  2174131  2174141
2174171  2174197  2174203  2174243  2174251  2174261  2174269  2174273  2174281  2174287
2174299  2174321  2174383  2174387  2174399  2174401  2174407  2174423  2174461  2174479
2174483  2174533  2174539  2174573  2174587  2174591  2174593  2174603  2174609  2174611
2174617  2174629  2174647  2174663  2174677  2174693  2174699  2174701  2174717  2174723
2174729  2174741  2174771  2174773  2174803  2174807  2174891  2174923  2174941  2174947
2174951  2174981  2174999  2175007  2175023  2175059  2175073  2175079  2175083  2175097
2175109  2175127  2175161  2175169  2175191  2175197  2175223  2175233  2175247  2175263
2175293  2175311  2175323  2175331  2175353  2175373  2175391  2175431  2175449  2175451
2175461  2175469  2175479  2175497  2175529  2175533  2175553  2175559  2175577  2175587
2175599  2175601  2175629  2175659  2175661  2175683  2175707  2175713  2175721  2175727
2175737  2175763  2175769  2175773  2175781  2175787  2175791  2175793  2175827  2175851
2175853  2175857  2175871  2175889  2175907  2175917  2175949  2175977  2175991  2175997
2176033  2176039  2176049  2176087  2176091  2176117  2176121  2176129  2176133  2176151
2176171  2176183  2176193  2176201  2176211  2176243  2176253  2176261  2176271  2176301
2176309  2176313  2176327  2176331  2176337  2176351  2176373  2176387  2176397  2176409
2176411  2176423  2176439  2176457  2176477  2176483  2176501  2176543  2176547  2176549
2176571  2176579  2176591  2176609  2176613  2176619  2176627  2176631  2176633  2176637
2176639  2176661  2176667  2176679  2176693  2176709  2176723  2176729  2176739  2176753
2176771  2176781  2176807  2176817  2176829  2176831  2176843  2176871  2176873  2176877
2176883  2176891  2176921  2176939  2176949  2176957  2176997  2177009  2177011  2177027
2177053  2177069  2177083  2177093  2177101  2177113  2177143  2177167  2177237  2177239
2177243  2177281  2177297  2177321  2177323  2177327  2177333  2177353  2177363  2177389
2177401  2177429  2177431  2177437  2177443  2177447  2177449  2177453  2177467  2177501
2177503  2177507  2177509  2177519  2177521  2177531  2177537  2177569  2177573  2177579
2177587  2177597  2177599  2177627  2177653  2177677  2177687  2177689  2177699  2177737
2177753  2177759  2177761  2177779  2177789  2177803  2177807  2177827  2177881  2177891
2177899  2177911  2177957  2177963  2177971  2177977  2177983  2177999  2178037  2178049
2178073  2178083  2178131  2178133  2178139  2178149  2178151  2178157  2178173  2178191
2178203  2178223  2178257  2178259  2178263  2178271  2178283  2178313  2178343  2178359
2178367  2178373  2178377  2178383  2178389  2178409  2178419  2178433  2178439  2178443
2178461  2178467  2178479  2178511  2178541  2178557  2178571  2178581  2178599  2178611
2178619  2178641  2178643  2178647  2178653  2178677  2178679  2178691  2178707  2178719
2178731  2178733  2178739  2178751  2178763  2178791  2178797  2178823  2178829  2178877
2178889  2178937  2178947  2178983  2178991  2179007  2179013  2179033  2179039  2179049
2179063  2179097  2179139  2179141  2179153  2179187  2179211  2179217  2179223  2179241
2179253  2179271  2179279  2179291  2179297  2179301  2179327  2179339  2179361  2179367
2179391  2179399  2179459  2179477  2179523  2179537  2179543  2179571  2179589  2179603
2179607  2179609  2179643  2179649  2179651  2179679  2179693  2179729  2179741  2179747
2179753  2179759  2179763  2179769  2179777  2179787  2179811  2179819  2179823  2179831
2179867  2179897  2179909  2179921  2179939  2179967  2179981  2179993  2179997  2180021
2180027  2180033  2180039  2180051  2180071  2180083  2180089  2180107  2180111  2180119
2180141  2180149  2180159  2180173  2180177  2180179  2180183  2180219  2180221  2180251
2180281  2180293  2180303  2180329  2180333  2180341  2180351  2180357  2180371  2180389
2180393  2180417  2180467  2180491  2180501  2180527  2180537  2180543  2180551  2180557
2180569  2180587  2180603  2180627  2180677  2180681  2180683  2180693  2180701  2180719
2180723  2180741  2180747  2180797  2180803  2180807  2180813  2180833  2180863  2180873
2180911  2180921  2180923  2180957  2180963  2180993  2180999  2181007  2181017  2181031
2181071  2181073  2181079  2181097  2181131  2181139  2181149  2181161  2181169  2181173
2181203  2181209  2181217  2181227  2181229  2181233  2181247  2181259  2181271  2181329
2181331  2181337  2181341  2181349  2181359  2181373  2181379  2181419  2181449  2181461
2181463  2181469  2181503  2181539  2181541  2181547  2181551  2181577  2181581  2181601
2181607  2181611  2181629  2181649  2181659  2181671  2181689  2181709  2181719  2181731
2181737  2181833  2181857  2181869  2181871  2181889  2181919  2181937  2181947  2181953
2181973  2182007  2182009  2182021  2182027  2182039  2182057  2182073  2182087  2182091
2182097  2182099  2182109  2182129  2182133  2182139  2182177  2182181  2182199  2182211
2182249  2182253  2182259  2182303  2182333  2182343  2182387  2182399  2182417  2182421
2182429  2182441  2182451  2182489  2182513  2182529  2182559  2182561  2182567  2182573
2182577  2182601  2182603  2182619  2182629  2182657  2182669  2182703  2182709  2182759
2182781  2182811  2182813  2182819  2182841  2182847  2182867  2182871  2182877  2182897
2182931  2182937  2182949  2182991  2182993  2182997  2183029  2183063  2183107  2183117
2183131  2183141  2183171  2183189  2183201  2183227  2183231  2183249  2183261  2183281
2183287  2183303  2183339  2183341  2183353  2183359  2183371  2183383  2183387  2183417
2183431  2183453  2183471  2183501  2183507  2183509  2183521  2183527  2183539  2183543
2183557  2183561  2183569  2183579  2183581  2183593  2183641  2183663  2183681  2183683
2183707  2183719  2183723  2183737  2183749  2183771  2183773  2183789  2183791  2183807
2183809  2183821  2183833  2183843  2183849  2183869  2183899  2183921  2183953  2183957
2183959  2183963  2183969  2184001  2184047  2184053  2184059  2184067  2184071  2184089
2184101  2184131  2184151  2184157  2184179  2184187  2184197  2184199  2184209  2184223
2184257  2184263  2184277  2184283  2184293  2184307  2184317  2184319  2184323  2184331
2184359  2184361  2184389  2184397  2184407  2184409  2184461  2184473  2184491  2184499
2184503  2184509  2184547  2184557  2184583  2184617  2184631  2184641  2184647  2184649
2184667  2184673  2184697  2184703  2184709  2184727  2184761  2184769  2184779  2184799
2184811  2184827  2184859  2184863  2184869  2184877  2184881  2184893  2184899  2184913
2184929  2184967  2184971  2184979  2184989  2184991  2184997  2185009  2185021  2185033
2185037  2185091  2185103  2185151  2185181  2185187  2185189  2185193  2185199  2185201
2185241  2185279  2185291  2185297  2185343  2185357  2185363  2185369  2185373  2185387
2185409  2185427  2185429  2185433  2185439  2185471  2185481  2185493  2185511  2185517
2185523  2185541  2185567  2185577  2185619  2185637  2185649  2185657  2185661  2185697
2185699  2185709  2185723  2185727  2185739  2185747  2185789  2185801  2185853  2185861
2185867  2185871  2185873  2185889  2185901  2185907  2185913  2185919  2185921  2185949
2185973  2185987  2185999  2186003  2186011  2186029  2186039  2186059  2186087  2186099
2186101  2186113  2186141  2186189  2186203  2186209  2186221  2186227  2186231  2186269
2186287  2186291  2186297  2186309  2186333  2186341  2186351  2186369  2186389  2186453
2186467  2186473  2186491  2186519  2186533  2186537  2186543  2186551  2186563  2186567
```

```
2186573  2186579  2186603  2186617  2186627  2186651  2186677  2186683  2186689  2186707
2186713  2186719  2186731  2186747  2186753  2186773  2186791  2186797  2186809  2186827
2186831  2186837  2186839  2186857  2186869  2186879  2186903  2186929  2186941  2186969
2186993  2187011  2187037  2187043  2187049  2187061  2187077  2187103  2187113  2187121
2187149  2187161  2187193  2187197  2187217  2187233  2187247  2187259  2187287  2187293
2187301  2187319  2187331  2187343  2187359  2187379  2187389  2187397  2187421  2187457
2187463  2187491  2187511  2187517  2187529  2187551  2187583  2187587  2187613  2187629
2187667  2187671  2187683  2187697  2187707  2187727  2187743  2187769  2187791  2187811
2187817  2187827  2187833  2187851  2187863  2187877  2187901  2187919  2187929  2187943
2187953  2187959  2187961  2187971  2187973  2187979  2188001  2188031  2188033  2188037
2188049  2188061  2188099  2188111  2188117  2188127  2188157  2188159  2188163  2188169
2188171  2188181  2188213  2188231  2188237  2188261  2188267  2188271  2188279  2188283
2188297  2188309  2188327  2188331  2188339  2188343  2188349  2188409  2188411  2188429
2188447  2188451  2188463  2188481  2188489  2188493  2188531  2188541  2188583  2188607
2188609  2188639  2188651  2188663  2188673  2188679  2188687  2188691  2188729  2188751
2188757  2188783  2188787  2188789  2188799  2188807  2188811  2188831  2188861  2188871
2188877  2188887  2188909  2188913  2188919  2188981  2188987  2188993  2189017  2189021
2189027  2189029  2189053  2189063  2189081  2189101  2189147  2189153  2189167  2189171
2189177  2189183  2189207  2189219  2189221  2189227  2189249  2189267  2189273  2189281
2189287  2189303  2189309  2189321  2189323  2189329  2189333  2189339  2189357  2189371
2189381  2189399  2189417  2189419  2189459  2189461  2189477  2189491  2189513  2189521
2189533  2189543  2189563  2189573  2189599  2189609  2189633  2189639  2189647  2189699
2189713  2189723  2189729  2189741  2189743  2189767  2189783  2189791  2189797  2189813
2189843  2189867  2189879  2189881  2189939  2189981  2189987  2189989  2190017  2190031
2190043  2190047  2190077  2190079  2190091  2190103  2190107  2190131  2190143  2190157
2190169  2190173  2190191  2190193  2190203  2190217  2190233  2190269  2190271  2190277
2190299  2190311  2190317  2190329  2190337  2190347  2190361  2190371  2190389  2190403
2190407  2190413  2190427  2190439  2190469  2190473  2190479  2190481  2190499  2190521
2190523  2190533  2190541  2190577  2190581  2190583  2190593  2190599  2190607  2190613
2190647  2190653  2190679  2190691  2190737  2190751  2190763  2190809  2190817  2190821
2190823  2190829  2190857  2190887  2190901  2190959  2190971  2190983  2190997  2191001
2191019  2191027  2191031  2191051  2191067  2191069  2191087  2191097  2191121  2191127
2191159  2191169  2191171  2191193  2191199  2191229  2191243  2191247  2191261  2191291
2191331  2191337  2191339  2191363  2191373  2191393  2191409  2191433  2191451  2191457
2191459  2191471  2191477  2191489  2191493  2191507  2191513  2191523  2191529  2191537
2191727  2191799  2191807  2191811  2191823  2191873  2191883  2191949  2191951  2191957
2191967  2191993  2192009  2192017  2192051  2192053  2192059  2192063  2192077  2192089
2192093  2192101  2192111  2192123  2192129  2192131  2192143  2192161  2192207  2192243
2192249  2192251  2192257  2192261  2192273  2192293  2192299  2192327  2192339  2192341
2192363  2192387  2192417  2192423  2192431  2192459  2192471  2192549  2192563  2192569
2192573  2192579  2192587  2192591  2192621  2192623  2192629  2192633  2192651  2192653
2192669  2192713  2192717  2192737  2192741  2192747  2192761  2192783  2192789  2192791
2192821  2192831  2192837  2192849  2192851  2192857  2192863  2192873  2192887  2192899
2192917  2192921  2192933  2192941  2192947  2192963  2193007  2193019  2193031  2193041
2193053  2193077  2193097  2193127  2193137  2193167  2193173  2193181  2193197  2193209
2193223  2193239  2193251  2193259  2193263  2193271  2193311  2193313  2193319  2193337
2193353  2193371  2193383  2193413  2193419  2193421  2193439  2193449  2193463  2193469
2193479  2193481  2193509  2193523  2193547  2193553  2193557  2193599  2193601  2193637
2193641  2193643  2193649  2193661  2193673  2193677  2193689  2193701  2193703  2193707
2193713  2193733  2193739  2193749  2193757  2193769  2193791  2193803  2193827  2193847
2193853  2193881  2193883  2193887  2193889  2193929  2193941  2193943  2193953  2193959
2193967  2193973  2193979  2194013  2194019  2194021  2194051  2194069  2194133  2194187
2194193  2194201  2194229  2194243  2194261  2194267  2194301  2194319  2194321  2194327
2194337  2194351  2194369  2194391  2194403  2194417  2194421  2194429  2194441  2194447
2194457  2194471  2194487  2194501  2194529  2194531  2194537  2194553  2194579  2194613
2194631  2194639  2194663  2194667  2194679  2194697  2194721  2194723  2194739  2194757
2194811  2194847  2194879  2194883  2194897  2194901  2194903  2194931  2194939  2194961
2194967  2194979  2194991  2194993  2195003  2195009  2195029  2195047  2195059  2195071
2195113  2195117  2195119  2195147  2195177  2195191  2195201  2195233  2195243  2195273
2195287  2195299  2195311  2195339  2195341  2195351  2195359  2195381  2195383  2195399
2195411  2195441  2195443  2195461  2195467  2195471  2195521  2195527  2195563  2195579
2195581  2195597  2195623  2195653  2195671  2195681  2195701  2195707  2195717  2195723
2195729  2195731  2195749  2195759  2195777  2195801  2195819  2195827  2195861  2195863
2195867  2195891  2195899  2195911  2195917  2195923  2195933  2195969  2195989  2196011
2196037  2196041  2196047  2196049  2196067  2196079  2196091  2196107  2196113  2196119
2196127  2196137  2196143  2196149  2196167  2196197  2196221  2196239  2196287  2196289
2196307  2196331  2196347  2196361  2196367  2196377  2196401  2196407  2196413  2196433
2196449  2196473  2196487  2196499  2196529  2196539  2196541  2196559  2196563  2196583
2196589  2196599  2196611  2196613  2196619  2196641  2196659  2196673  2196697  2196703
2196709  2196713  2196731  2196737  2196749  2196763  2196767  2196781  2196809  2196829
2196841  2196853  2196869  2196871  2196881  2196889  2196917  2196941  2196959  2196967
2196977  2196979  2197021  2197043  2197049  2197087  2197157  2197163  2197177  2197183
2197189  2197193  2197241  2197253  2197277  2197289  2197309  2197333  2197357  2197361
2197367  2197381  2197387  2197409  2197411  2197421  2197427  2197453  2197463  2197469
2197487  2197493  2197501  2197513  2197523  2197537  2197561  2197567  2197589  2197603
2197609  2197631  2197633  2197651  2197681  2197693  2197697  2197703  2197733  2197739
2197747  2197753  2197759  2197771  2197781  2197787  2197847  2197849  2197873  2197907
2197919  2197933  2197961  2197973  2198003  2198011  2198029  2198039  2198057  2198093
2198121  2198153  2198159  2198191  2198201  2198227  2198269  2198291  2198293  2198309
2198327  2198347  2198359  2198369  2198377  2198401  2198407  2198411  2198419  2198431
2198437  2198447  2198453  2198473  2198477  2198507  2198513  2198527  2198533  2198569
2198591  2198597  2198617  2198653  2198659  2198663  2198671  2198689  2198701  2198723
2198747  2198759  2198761  2198767  2198783  2198827  2198843  2198863  2198879  2198881
2198887  2198897  2198909  2198981  2199061  2199077  2199121  2199133  2199143  2199151
2199163  2199173  2199179  2199181  2199187  2199203  2199209  2199217  2199221  2199229
2199247  2199277  2199299  2199311  2199313  2199361  2199371  2199377  2199401  2199427
2199433  2199479  2199499  2199521  2199523  2199529  2199577  2199601  2199623  2199629
2199643  2199653  2199661  2199683  2199689  2199719  2199739  2199781  2199803  2199823
```

```
2199833  2199859  2199889  2199893  2199907  2199917  2199931  2199941  2199959  2199961
2199971  2199979  2200013  2200031  2200043  2200069  2200061  2200069  2200103  2200139
2200141  2200153  2200193  2200199  2200207  2200217  2200277  2200291  2200301  2200307
2200313  2200321  2200339  2200351  2200369  2200391  2200397  2200403  2200423  2200441
2200459  2200483  2200489  2200537  2200543  2200577  2200589  2200591  2200603  2200609
2200619  2200621  2200643  2200651  2200657  2200661  2200673  2200699  2200711  2200717
2200727  2200729  2200739  2200747  2200763  2200771  2200777  2200799  2200811  2200813
2200817  2200823  2200831  2200841  2200843  2200867  2200873  2200889  2200909  2200943
2200949  2200967  2200981  2200987  2200993  2200997  2201033  2201039  2201051  2201083
2201099  2201107  2201119  2201137  2201149  2201161  2201183  2201189  2201191  2201197
2201201  2201203  2201209  2201273  2201281  2201293  2201317  2201327  2201357  2201371
2201387  2201393  2201401  2201417  2201431  2201443  2201489  2201501  2201519  2201531
2201533  2201539  2201543  2201581  2201597  2201599  2201603  2201623  2201627  2201669
2201671  2201677  2201681  2201707  2201721  2201723  2201737  2201743  2201761  2201807
2201827  2201839  2201897  2201911  2201921  2201933  2201957  2201971  2201977  2201989
2202007  2202019  2202029  2202041  2202047  2202049  2202077  2202121  2202131  2202133
2202139  2202149  2202169  2202253  2202269  2202287  2202311  2202313  2202329  2202341
2202359  2202371  2202377  2202379  2202391  2202407  2202413  2202419  2202433  2202437
2202449  2202451  2202493  2202511  2202517  2202533  2202547  2202559  2202583  2202587
2202601  2202611  2202617  2202631  2202677  2202703  2202713  2202719  2202763  2202787
2202791  2202793  2202797  2202799  2202817  2202853  2202857  2202859  2202899  2202913
2202919  2202923  2202929  2202931  2202947  2202961  2202973  2202983  2202989  2202997
2203007  2203049  2203057  2203063  2203079  2203087  2203099  2203111  2203121  2203133
2203141  2203153  2203163  2203169  2203177  2203189  2203211  2203249  2203291  2203301
2203303  2203337  2203351  2203361  2203367  2203393  2203403  2203427  2203433  2203441
2203447  2203457  2203477  2203483  2203499  2203519  2203541  2203559  2203571  2203589
2203631  2203633  2203637  2203657  2203661  2203673  2203679  2203711  2203723  2203741
2203763  2203771  2203777  2203787  2203801  2203807  2203811  2203843  2203849  2203853
2203889  2203933  2203939  2203951  2203961  2203963  2203967  2203969  2203973  2203997
2204003  2204009  2204011  2204023  2204039  2204047  2204071  2204077  2204107  2204117
2204143  2204149  2204161  2204173  2204177  2204183  2204197  2204207  2204221  2204243
2204269  2204273  2204327  2204333  2204341  2204353  2204369  2204383  2204393  2204431
2204443  2204453  2204471  2204473  2204483  2204507  2204537  2204557  2204561  2204591
2204597  2204603  2204623  2204647  2204651  2204659  2204663  2204669  2204677  2204687
2204701  2204731  2204737  2204759  2204767  2204773  2204789  2204809  2204821  2204827
2204831  2204833  2204843  2204863  2204887  2204929  2204933  2204953  2204977  2205001
2205011  2205013  2205017  2205023  2205031  2205043  2205059  2205067  2205107  2205113
2205139  2205149  2205157  2205167  2205187  2205199  2205233  2205239  2205251  2205283
2205293  2205319  2205323  2205353  2205373  2205389  2205409  2205449  2205451  2205481
2205487  2205503  2205521  2205527  2205547  2205551  2205587  2205589  2205611  2205613
2205617  2205629  2205649  2205659  2205661  2205667  2205703  2205713  2205719  2205761
2205779  2205787  2205793  2205799  2205803  2205823  2205839  2205883  2205887  2205893
2205911  2205947  2205949  2205989  2206021  2206031  2206081  2206093  2206097  2206103
2206121  2206123  2206151  2206153  2206163  2206189  2206207  2206219  2206247  2206249
2206283  2206297  2206327  2206331  2206357  2206387  2206403  2206417  2206429  2206439
2206441  2206453  2206469  2206471  2206483  2206493  2206499  2206507  2206513  2206517
2206543  2206559  2206591  2206601  2206613  2206619  2206621  2206627  2206649  2206657
2206663  2206669  2206681  2206709  2206723  2206733  2206741  2206747  2206759  2206769
2206783  2206811  2206817  2206819  2206823  2206829  2206843  2206861  2206877  2206901
2206909  2206927  2206931  2206937  2206943  2206969  2206993  2206999  2207017  2207033
2207039  2207069  2207081  2207099  2207113  2207119  2207123  2207129  2207143  2207159
2207171  2207197  2207201  2207203  2207213  2207221  2207237  2207243  2207251  2207269
2207273  2207279  2207281  2207289  2207311  2207321  2207323  2207329  2207347  2207351
2207357  2207369  2207377  2207389  2207411  2207423  2207431  2207437  2207441  2207483
2207489  2207519  2207537  2207539  2207549  2207561  2207581  2207587  2207617  2207633
2207677  2207713  2207719  2207783  2207791  2207831  2207833  2207861  2207873  2207879
2207893  2207897  2207911  2207917  2207929  2207939  2207951  2207963  2207969  2207981
2207983  2207987  2207993  2208053  2208061  2208067  2208071  2208073  2208083  2208091
2208097  2208103  2208127  2208131  2208203  2208229  2208257  2208259  2208277  2208281
2208319  2208331  2208337  2208343  2208377  2208397  2208407  2208413  2208421  2208431
2208439  2208463  2208467  2208473  2208491  2208497  2208517  2208559  2208581  2208601
2208637  2208643  2208653  2208659  2208683  2208689  2208697  2208707  2208737  2208751
2208779  2208797  2208799  2208833  2208839  2208847  2208873  2208889  2208893  2208931
2208887  2208889  2208893  2208931  2208949  2208977  2208991  2209001  2209003  2209013
2209027  2209043  2209049  2209061  2209063  2209079  2209117  2209169  2209171  2209177
2209189  2209213  2209217  2209231  2209253  2209267  2209283  2209289  2209313  2209327
2209331  2209343  2209409  2209421  2209447  2209451  2209457  2209483  2209499  2209511
2209523  2209547  2209549  2209579  2209589  2209601  2209607  2209631  2209639  2209661
2209663  2209667  2209687  2209693  2209699  2209703  2209717  2209721  2209741  2209747
2209759  2209763  2209769  2209787  2209789  2209793  2209811  2209841  2209843  2209849
2209853  2209891  2209901  2209903  2209913  2209931  2209937  2209939  2209957  2209967
2209979  2209993  2209997  2210009  2210011  2210027  2210029  2210053  2210057  2210059
2210069  2210077  2210107  2210141  2210147  2210161  2210171  2210179  2210189  2210209
2210227  2210233  2210249  2210261  2210267  2210279  2210281  2210287  2210291  2210297
2210303  2210309  2210321  2210333  2210347  2210353  2210371  2210381  2210387  2210389
2210401  2210407  2210413  2210419  2210431  2210447  2210473  2210477  2210497
2210503  2210521  2210563  2210567  2210569  2210573  2210581  2210591  2210617  2210623
2210633  2210651  2210653  2210723  2210729  2210743  2210773  2210777  2210779  2210797
2210801  2210837  2210851  2210881  2210891  2210903  2210939  2210947  2210959  2210963
2210977  2210983  2210987  2210993  2211019  2211023  2211029  2211061  2211109  2211127
2211161  2211179  2211211  2211217  2211227  2211233  2211257  2211259  2211263  2211269
2211281  2211329  2211347  2211359  2211367  2211373  2211409  2211413  2211439  2211481
2211493  2211541  2211551  2211557  2211563  2211577  2211593  2211617  2211623  2211647
2211667  2211689  2211707  2211779  2211787  2211793  2211817  2211821  2211883  2211889
2211893  2211919  2211929  2211931  2211941  2211947  2211953  2211967  2211977  2211983
2211997  2212003  2212009  2212039  2212051  2212069  2212081  2212097  2212099  2212123
2212127  2212141  2212153  2212157  2212169  2212181  2212183  2212187  2212219  2212229
2212241  2212247  2212271  2212277  2212297  2212321  2212333  2212349  2212351  2212361
2212387  2212391  2212421  2212429  2212433  2212447  2212453  2212471  2212477  2212487
```

```
2212519  2212523  2212537  2212547  2212571  2212579  2212589  2212627  2212631  2212633
2212657  2212663  2212673  2212699  2212709  2212723  2212747  2212753  2212781  2212783
2212817  2212831  2212871  2212877  2212883  2212891  2212921  2212939  2212963  2212967
2212979  2213033  2213039  2213053  2213069  2213093  2213137  2213143  2213147  2213171
2213191  2213201  2213203  2213209  2213243  2213279  2213293  2213311  2213317  2213327
2213347  2213353  2213363  2213381  2213389  2213399  2213401  2213411  2213413  2213423
2213441  2213447  2213461  2213473  2213489  2213531  2213537  2213551  2213591  2213593
2213609  2213623  2213647  2213677  2213699  2213711  2213759  2213789  2213833  2213837
2213839  2213843  2213867  2213891  2213923  2213933  2213963  2213971  2213977  2213983
2214001  2214007  2214011  2214073  2214077  2214101  2214103  2214137  2214161  2214169
2214193  2214209  2214221  2214257  2214269  2214271  2214281  2214319  2214343  2214349
2214367  2214379  2214383  2214473  2214479  2214481  2214491  2214493  2214517  2214521
2214559  2214571  2214599  2214623  2214637  2214661  2214679  2214691  2214713  2214731
2214749  2214757  2214761  2214791  2214827  2214833  2214847  2214869  2214907  2214911
2214929  2214937  2214941  2214959  2214967  2214977  2214983  2214997  2215009  2215013
2215051  2215067  2215091  2215097  2215099  2215111  2215127  2215133  2215141  2215159
2215163  2215177  2215181  2215193  2215201  2215211  2215217  2215237  2215277  2215303
2215307  2215309  2215313  2215319  2215327  2215349  2215351  2215379  2215387  2215393
2215399  2215417  2215463  2215469  2215471  2215487  2215501  2215529  2215531  2215537
2215541  2215547  2215561  2215573  2215583  2215639  2215651  2215667  2215669  2215673
2215691  2215693  2215699  2215777  2215783  2215789  2215793  2215823  2215847  2215853
2215867  2215901  2215903  2215921  2215931  2215943  2215949  2215963  2215979  2215987
2215991  2215999  2216021  2216047  2216057  2216083  2216087  2216101  2216113  2216117
2216143  2216153  2216161  2216167  2216197  2216213  2216231  2216237  2216281  2216287
2216299  2216309  2216317  2216321  2216323  2216351  2216359  2216363  2216377  2216387
2216399  2216413  2216437  2216471  2216479  2216519  2216551  2216563  2216569  2216587
2216603  2216609  2216611  2216629  2216653  2216657  2216659  2216699  2216701  2216729
2216743  2216759  2216761  2216777  2216803  2216821  2216839  2216857  2216861  2216873
2216887  2216897  2216909  2216917  2216957  2216969  2216989  2216999  2217001
2217011  2217023  2217029  2217041  2217049  2217067  2217073  2217101  2217107  2217113
2217143  2217181  2217199  2217211  2217217  2217233  2217247  2217251  2217277  2217283
2217287  2217301  2217317  2217329  2217343  2217349  2217359  2217379  2217409  2217421
2217443  2217473  2217491  2217493  2217503  2217539  2217541  2217557  2217569  2217571
2217577  2217581  2217583  2217587  2217617  2217641  2217643  2217671  2217673  2217749
2217757  2217773  2217779  2217799  2217829  2217857  2217863  2217881  2217907  2217911
2217947  2217967  2217991  2218001  2218037  2218057  2218063  2218067  2218091  2218093
2218121  2218127  2218129  2218157  2218171  2218199  2218201  2218207  2218213  2218219
2218277  2218283  2218289  2218319  2218331  2218339  2218343  2218351  2218361  2218367
2218423  2218429  2218439  2218451  2218519  2218523  2218547  2218549  2218561
2218583  2218597  2218607  2218609  2218613  2218621  2218663  2218669  2218691  2218709
2218751  2218771  2218807  2218819  2218837  2218861  2218871  2218883  2218897  2218901
2218903  2218907  2218933  2218943  2218967  2218969  2218999  2219023  2219033  2219039
2219059  2219081  2219083  2219093  2219111  2219117  2219123  2219137  2219141  2219153
2219177  2219183  2219209  2219213  2219221  2219251  2219279  2219281  2219309  2219323
2219351  2219353  2219377  2219411  2219423  2219449  2219461  2219467  2219471  2219489
2219491  2219513  2219551  2219557  2219563  2219621  2219629  2219641
2219647  2219671  2219681  2219683  2219731  2219771  2219773  2219797  2219801  2219807
2219813  2219831  2219839  2219849  2219869  2219881  2219887  2219923  2219939  2219947
2219953  2219977  2219999  2220007  2220041  2220059  2220073  2220077  2220083  2220089
2220151  2220157  2220187  2220193  2220199  2220203  2220209  2220263  2220271  2220277
2220289  2220293  2220301  2220307  2220311  2220331  2220349  2220367  2220373  2220389
2220403  2220409  2220419  2220431  2220457  2220467  2220479  2220497  2220503  2220521
2220527  2220529  2220539  2220551  2220553  2220643  2220653  2220661  2220671  2220697
2220731  2220749  2220773  2220787  2220839  2220887  2220893  2220913  2220917  2220919
2220923  2220941  2220961  2220971  2220973  2220979  2221007  2221019  2221031  2221061
2221069  2221097  2221111  2221127  2221129  2221159  2221183  2221187  2221217  2221229
2221231  2221249  2221253  2221259  2221273  2221301  2221321  2221333  2221343  2221379
2221381  2221391  2221399  2221403  2221411  2221433  2221447  2221459  2221507  2221511
2221523  2221567  2221589  2221631  2221633  2221657  2221669  2221673  2221699  2221711
2221721  2221733  2221741  2221753  2221757  2221771  2221789  2221829  2221837  2221847
2221859  2221861  2221877  2221889  2221907  2221909  2221931  2221943  2221949  2221969
2221981  2221991  2221997  2222023  2222039  2222071  2222089  2222093  2222123  2222141
2222147  2222167  2222177  2222203  2222219  2222239  2222243  2222249  2222251  2222263
2222273  2222281  2222287  2222293  2222309  2222317  2222321  2222327  2222333  2222351
2222377  2222383  2222387  2222443  2222477  2222501  2222503  2222509  2222527  2222533
2222537  2222543  2222567  2222573  2222579  2222593  2222599  2222611  2222617  2222621
2222629  2222653  2222659  2222663  2222683  2222687  2222719  2222723  2222729  2222741
2222761  2222783  2222809  2222819  2222839  2222861  2222911  2222921  2222929  2222933
2222977  2223007  2223031  2223037  2223043  2223047  2223059  2223079  2223101  2223113
2223119  2223149  2223161  2223163  2223187  2223197  2223211  2223217  2223233  2223253
2223259  2223269  2223281  2223283  2223317  2223329  2223371  2223383  2223391  2223407
2223421  2223443  2223449  2223451  2223457  2223467  2223469  2223493  2223497  2223499
2223503  2223521  2223541  2223563  2223581  2223587  2223607  2223623  2223631  2223671
2223673  2223677  2223679  2223701  2223713  2223731  2223743  2223757  2223761  2223773
2223829  2223833  2223839  2223841  2223853  2223857  2223869  2223883  2223901  2223931
2223937  2223943  2223967  2223973  2223983  2224009  2224037  2224063  2224069  2224073
2224099  2224141  2224147  2224153  2224171  2224193  2224231  2224247  2224259  2224267
2224279  2224283  2224289  2224337  2224367  2224409  2224429  2224441  2224447  2224457
2224459  2224489  2224493  2224507  2224513  2224517  2224553  2224559  2224567  2224571
2224597  2224627  2224633  2224657  2224661  2224667  2224669  2224679  2224681  2224687
2224709  2224741  2224753  2224757  2224763  2224801  2224837  2224861  2224867  2224879
2224891  2224897  2224907  2224931  2224939  2224961  2224969  2224979  2224987  2224991
2225009  2225021  2225039  2225051  2225053  2225057  2225059  2225063  2225077  2225081
2225101  2225107  2225123  2225159  2225173  2225177  2225183  2225203  2225221  2225231
2225233  2225263  2225269  2225323  2225339  2225371  2225381  2225387  2225389  2225393
2225401  2225407  2225429  2225473  2225491  2225501  2225533  2225543  2225557  2225563
2225567  2225569  2225579  2225581  2225593  2225599  2225621  2225627  2225647  2225653
2225659  2225681  2225683  2225689  2225701  2225747  2225749  2225753  2225771  2225777
2225791  2225819  2225833  2225851  2225863  2225879  2225887  2225959  2225969  2225999
```

```
2226001 2226019 2226023 2226041 2226089 2226131 2226137 2226149 2226151 2226163
2226197 2226199 2226221 2226227 2226229 2226241 2226251 2226283 2226293 2226307
2226311 2226313 2226319 2226353 2226373 2226383 2226403 2226407 2226409 2226421
2226431 2226461 2226463 2226467 2226479 2226493 2226509 2226517 2226527 2226529
2226547 2226557 2226569 2226571 2226593 2226613 2226617 2226619 2226647 2226659
2226673 2226701 2226713 2226733 2226767 2226769 2226787 2226793 2226811 2226817
2226839 2226853 2226859 2226893 2226899 2226911 2226923 2226937 2226941 2226943
2226953 2226989 2227003 2227019 2227031 2227033 2227061 2227063 2227087 2227109
2227129 2227163 2227193 2227201 2227207 2227213 2227223 2227231 2227259 2227261
2227273 2227301 2227307 2227321 2227327 2227333 2227339 2227361 2227367 2227369
2227397 2227399 2227409 2227417 2227429 2227439 2227441 2227451 2227469 2227499
2227501 2227507 2227513 2227531 2227543 2227583 2227591 2227597 2227601 2227607
2227609 2227627 2227639 2227649 2227651 2227657 2227661 2227669 2227717 2227723
2227727 2227739 2227747 2227763 2227777 2227789 2227801 2227831 2227843 2227853
2227859 2227871 2227889 2227913 2227919 2227943 2227963 2228011 2228027 2228053
2228077 2228081 2228089 2228101 2228113 2228117 2228119 2228123 2228137 2228143
2228153 2228159 2228167 2228183 2228189 2228201 2228209 2228221 2228243 2228299
2228321 2228323 2228329 2228333 2228341 2228351 2228383 2228393 2228407 2228417
2228423 2228431 2228437 2228449 2228483 2228507 2228509 2228519 2228521 2228531
2228533 2228543 2228549 2228573 2228591 2228657 2228659 2228663 2228687 2228711
2228713 2228731 2228741 2228747 2228753 2228771 2228777 2228783 2228797 2228813
2228867 2228893 2228923 2228927 2228939 2228959 2228971 2228981 2228983 2228987
2229037 2229041 2229043 2229083 2229089 2229103 2229107 2229113 2229119 2229121
2229133 2229167 2229169 2229239 2229247 2229263 2229277 2229299 2229307 2229313
2229319 2229349 2229371 2229379 2229389 2229391 2229407 2229419 2229467 2229473
2229497 2229503 2229523 2229527 2229541 2229547 2229569 2229581 2229587 2229589
2229599 2229653 2229659 2229673 2229683 2229691 2229697 2229701 2229713 2229767
2229769 2229779 2229791 2229793 2229809 2229823 2229833 2229853 2229863 2229883
2229889 2229893 2229917 2229943 2229959 2229967 2229971 2229991 2230001 2230021
2230051 2230061 2230069 2230079 2230093 2230097 2230117 2230121 2230133 2230139
2230147 2230153 2230157 2230159 2230177 2230219 2230243 2230253 2230301 2230309
2230331 2230339 2230351 2230409 2230411 2230433 2230439 2230457 2230469 2230483
2230493 2230511 2230513 2230531 2230541 2230549 2230561 2230577 2230581 2230589
2230597 2230633 2230639 2230643 2230663 2230673 2230691 2230699 2230721 2230727
2230759 2230777 2230783 2230801 2230819 2230829 2230861 2230867 2230871 2230873
2230939 2230951 2230979 2231011 2231027 2231051 2231059 2231077 2231087 2231093
2231107 2231129 2231149 2231171 2231209 2231219 2231269 2231279 2231293 2231297
2231309 2231311 2231329 2231351 2231357 2231371 2231381 2231389 2231407 2231413
2231423 2231429 2231431 2231447 2231461 2231477 2231479 2231491 2231501 2231519
2231533 2231587 2231591 2231599 2231609 2231617 2231623 2231627 2231653 2231681
2231687 2231707 2231711 2231717 2231731 2231737 2231767 2231773 2231791 2231809
2231819 2231821 2231833 2231839 2231843 2231849 2231857 2231861 2231881 2231891
2231909 2231941 2232017 2232023 2232037 2232053 2232059 2232071 2232107 2232133
2232157 2232161 2232179 2232193 2232199 2232203 2232221 2232229 2232257 2232271
2232281 2232317 2232323 2232337 2232353 2232379 2232401 2232421 2232427 2232437
2232463 2232487 2232493 2232509 2232511 2232523 2232551 2232569 2232583 2232613
2232653 2232673 2232677 2232701 2232749 2232751 2232761 2232773 2232779 2232781
2232793 2232809 2232821 2232827 2232833 2232847 2232859 2232869 2232887 2232889
2232907 2232929 2232931 2232941 2232959 2232991 2233003 2233019 2233031 2233039
2233057 2233079 2233081 2233117 2233123 2233129 2233183 2233199 2233201 2233207
2233213 2233223 2233243 2233247 2233267 2233303 2233331 2233337 2233373 2233379
2233381 2233391 2233397 2233403 2233417 2233433 2233459 2233471 2233481 2233489
2233499 2233501 2233513 2233523 2233529 2233531 2233537 2233541 2233547 2233571
2233573 2233597 2233601 2233607 2233631 2233657 2233709 2233711 2233717 2233723
2233739 2233747 2233753 2233757 2233787 2233793 2233843 2233859 2233867 2233877
2233879 2233901 2233909 2233927 2233937 2233939 2233961 2233969 2233993
2233999 2234009 2234017 2234033 2234069 2234081 2234107 2234117 2234119 2234129
2234143 2234149 2234159 2234161 2234179 2234207 2234209 2234227 2234233 2234251
2234261 2234269 2234303 2234317 2234329 2234339 2234341 2234417 2234431 2234437
2234447 2234471 2234483 2234501 2234503 2234513 2234539 2234543 2234549 2234563
2234579 2234587 2234591 2234593 2234597 2234621 2234629 2234671 2234677 2234681
2234693 2234699 2234707 2234717 2234719 2234741 2234789 2234797 2234809 2234833
2234863 2234899 2234923 2234927 2234929 2234959 2234969 2234971 2234983 2234993
2235031 2235043 2235047 2235049 2235067 2235083 2235091 2235127 2235137 2235139
2235161 2235199 2235221 2235227 2235229 2235239 2235251 2235257 2235271 2235283
2235287 2235307 2235319 2235323 2235329 2235341 2235353 2235377 2235383 2235403
2235427 2235437 2235469 2235491 2235509 2235511 2235539 2235547 2235553 2235557
2235587 2235599 2235617 2235631 2235637 2235641 2235647 2235661 2235671 2235677
2235683 2235707 2235731 2235733 2235767 2235773 2235791 2235797 2235803 2235809
2235811 2235829 2235841 2235847 2235851 2235859 2235869 2235887 2235907 2235941
2235943 2235949 2235971 2235973 2235997 2236001 2236007 2236009 2236049 2236051
2236057 2236079 2236081 2236097 2236111 2236121 2236133 2236139 2236153 2236183
2236187 2236189 2236207 2236217 2236237 2236249 2236261 2236279 2236327 2236331
2236349 2236363 2236369 2236373 2236397 2236417 2236457 2236477 2236483 2236657
2236499 2236511 2236517 2236519 2236547 2236563 2236603 2236627 2236651 2236657
2236667 2236693 2236697 2236709 2236711 2236733 2236747 2236769 2236771 2236781
2236807 2236823 2236831 2236873 2236879 2236901 2236907 2236921 2236943 2236951
2236981 2236987 2236999 2237009 2237051 2237071 2237107 2237113 2237119 2237137
2237143 2237159 2237167 2237171 2237189 2237219 2237267 2237293 2237309 2237317
2237327 2237337 2237381 2237393 2237399 2237401 2237413 2237429 2237447 2237461
2237467 2237479 2237491 2237503 2237507 2237519 2237527 2237531 2237537 2237551
2237561 2237563 2237567 2237581 2237617 2237629 2237671 2237689 2237701 2237743
2237747 2237771 2237773 2237783 2237789 2237809 2237861 2237899 2237909 2237927
2237933 2237941 2237951 2237957 2238011 2238013 2238023 2238043 2238053 2238079
2238091 2238109 2238113 2238127 2238161 2238163 2238179 2238209 2238211 2238217
2238233 2238239 2238259 2238277 2238287 2238289 2238311 2238319 2238323 2238347
2238359 2238361 2238377 2238391 2238413 2238419 2238421 2238473 2238487 2238491
2238527 2238529 2238557 2238569 2238571 2238589 2238619 2238631 2238647 2238653
2238661 2238673 2238703 2238707 2238721 2238749 2238757 2238763 2238767 2238779
```

```
2238787 2238791 2238799 2238809 2238811 2238823 2238931 2238937 2238947 2238953
2238959 2238961 2238989 2238997 2239001 2239007 2239009 2239031 2239049 2239057
2239063 2239103 2239123 2239141 2239147 2239157 2239201 2239213 2239217 2239219
2239229 2239231 2239247 2239253 2239301 2239309 2239319 2239327 2239331 2239333
2239357 2239361 2239373 2239387 2239417 2239453 2239459 2239519 2239537 2239541
2239561 2239577 2239591 2239607 2239639 2239649 2239651 2239667 2239687 2239703
2239709 2239711 2239723 2239747 2239751 2239753 2239759 2239793 2239807 2239847
2239883 2239889 2239933 2239949 2239957 2239961 2239987 2239997 2240003 2240023
2240027 2240057 2240071 2240083 2240089 2240101 2240111 2240113 2240137 2240159
2240191 2240197 2240201 2240213 2240267 2240291 2240299 2240317 2240321 2240323
2240341 2240351 2240369 2240377 2240389 2240431 2240449 2240471 2240477 2240479
2240489 2240507 2240531 2240533 2240551 2240573 2240593 2240597 2240629 2240633
2240647 2240657 2240659 2240663 2240669 2240699 2240701 2240723 2240731 2240737
2240741 2240747 2240759 2240779 2240789 2240807 2240809 2240827 2240837 2240839
2240851 2240857 2240863 2240891 2240941 2240951 2240963 2240977 2241011 2241013
2241037 2241047 2241049 2241061 2241067 2241073 2241119 2241121 2241139 2241163
2241167 2241181 2241191 2241193 2241199 2241209 2241247 2241251 2241271 2241277
2241299 2241301 2241311 2241313 2241353 2241359 2241361 2241389 2241391 2241397
2241409 2241427 2241431 2241443 2241479 2241509 2241521 2241523 2241527 2241539
2241553 2241559 2241583 2241599 2241607 2241667 2241691 2241697 2241709 2241721
2241727 2241751 2241779 2241781 2241797 2241809 2241851 2241881 2241901 2241917
2241919 2241923 2241929 2241949 2241959 2241989 2242027 2242043 2242073 2242091
2242111 2242127 2242129 2242157 2242169 2242187 2242189 2242211 2242213 2242217
2242231 2242277 2242291 2242307 2242313 2242319 2242337 2242343 2242363 2242369
2242379 2242381 2242433 2242441 2242469 2242517 2242519 2242529 2242549 2242651
2242663 2242679 2242687 2242697 2242727 2242729 2242733 2242739 2242763 2242777
2242781 2242783 2242789 2242811 2242813 2242841 2242843 2242847 2242871 2242873
2242879 2242883 2242921 2242939 2242949 2242951 2242957 2242973 2242979 2242993
2243027 2243053 2243057 2243077 2243089 2243107 2243123 2243161 2243177 2243187
2243183 2243203 2243207 2243209 2243221 2243251 2243257 2243261 2243281 2243287
2243309 2243317 2243333 2243359 2243383 2243399 2243419 2243429 2243431
2243453 2243467 2243477 2243491 2243497 2243503 2243531 2243537 2243551 2243587
2243597 2243617 2243621 2243623 2243663 2243669 2243693 2243699 2243723 2243741
2243743 2243753 2243771 2243777 2243789 2243797 2243803 2243809 2243819 2243821
2243833 2243851 2243887 2243893 2243909 2243911 2243959 2243987 2244091 2244131
2244139 2244157 2244163 2244167 2244173 2244199 2244211 2244227 2244233 2244257
2244259 2244269 2244283 2244287 2244331 2244353 2244367 2244371 2244377 2244401
2244427 2244439 2244461 2244479 2244499 2244503 2244509 2244533 2244553 2244559
2244563 2244577 2244587 2244589 2244611 2244623 2244631 2244653 2244659 2244661
2244667 2244689 2244691 2244703 2244707 2244719 2244721 2244733 2244751 2244761
2244769 2244779 2244787 2244811 2244821 2244841 2244859 2244863 2244881 2244883
2244899 2244911 2244923 2244929 2244937 2244953 2244973 2245013 2245031 2245043
2245057 2245063 2245121 2245141 2245147 2245153 2245157 2245163 2245171 2245183
2245189 2245223 2245247 2245253 2245273 2245277 2245289 2245301 2245307 2245319
2245333 2245339 2245351 2245357 2245379 2245391 2245427 2245429 2245457 2245459
2245483 2245489 2245501 2245541 2245543 2245549 2245561 2245577 2245583 2245597
2245619 2245627 2245631 2245637 2245643 2245657 2245679 2245681 2245687 2245721
2245723 2245739 2245759 2245783 2245787 2245799 2245811 2245813 2245849 2245861
2245877 2245889 2245931 2245951 2245961 2245979 2245993 2246017 2246039 2246051
2246053 2246077 2246099 2246107 2246117 2246129 2246141 2246143 2246147 2246149
2246173 2246183 2246201 2246213 2246219 2246239 2246269 2246273 2246281 2246297
2246323 2246339 2246357 2246359 2246371 2246383 2246393 2246399 2246411 2246417
2246467 2246471 2246483 2246501 2246509 2246521 2246527 2246537 2246551 2246557
2246581 2246591 2246609 2246633 2246641 2246683 2246687 2246689 2246749 2246767
2246789 2246791 2246831 2246851 2246863 2246869 2246903 2246927 2246953 2246969
2246971 2246977 2246999 2247019 2247029 2247053 2247067 2247083 2247101 2247103
2247109 2247127 2247131 2247143 2247163 2247173 2247209 2247227 2247229 2247257
2247277 2247293 2247337 2247341 2247347 2247373 2247379 2247389 2247397 2247409
2247433 2247439 2247449 2247461 2247463 2247467 2247473 2247499 2247503 2247521
2247523 2247541 2247559 2247569 2247577 2247611 2247659 2247673 2247691 2247697
2247709 2247727 2247737 2247773 2247793 2247803 2247809 2247811 2247851
2247853 2247857 2247881 2247887 2247899 2247901 2247913 2247919 2247923 2247929
2247941 2247953 2247977 2247991 2248013 2248019 2248021 2248039 2248067 2248069
2248087 2248117 2248123 2248133 2248139 2248163 2248171 2248187 2248223 2248237
2248241 2248243 2248247 2248249 2248271 2248291 2248303 2248331 2248333 2248349
2248373 2248381 2248423 2248429 2248439 2248447 2248451 2248469 2248489 2248507
2248511 2248529 2248531 2248537 2248567 2248583 2248591 2248633 2248637 2248639
2248651 2248661 2248663 2248679 2248681 2248691 2248693 2248699 2248703 2248723
2248739 2248759 2248769 2248781 2248787 2248837 2248847 2248849 2248853 2248861
2248867 2248901 2248907 2248927 2248931 2248951 2248969 2248991 2248999 2249053
2249059 2249063 2249069 2249087 2249113 2249141 2249171 2249179 2249183 2249189
2249197 2249207 2249213 2249227 2249231 2249243 2249251 2249281 2249293 2249309
2249311 2249363 2249381 2249393 2249399 2249419 2249431 2249453 2249459 2249461
2249477 2249483 2249537 2249557 2249579 2249591 2249603 2249609 2249633 2249693
2249719 2249743 2249747 2249759 2249773 2249783 2249813 2249827 2249861 2249867
2249911 2249917 2249921 2249941 2249953 2249959 2249963 2249969 2249981 2249983
2249987 2250013 2250029 2250041 2250043 2250089 2250091 2250119 2250163 2250167
2250181 2250223 2250247 2250257 2250263 2250337 2250349 2250359 2250397 2250401
2250403 2250419 2250421 2250431 2250439 2250461 2250467 2250503 2250509 2250559
2250581 2250601 2250623 2250637 2250641 2250649 2250667 2250671 2250679 2250709
2250713 2250761 2250763 2250769 2250779 2250793 2250799 2250869 2250887 2250901
2250917 2250923 2250929 2250931 2250977 2250979 2251001 2251031 2251049 2251057
2251061 2251099 2251103 2251111 2251121 2251129 2251147 2251153 2251163 2251169
2251199 2251201 2251211 2251213 2251229 2251279 2251297 2251331 2251343 2251349
2251369 2251373 2251397 2251411 2251423 2251427 2251441 2251451 2251489 2251507
2251511 2251517 2251547 2251553 2251559 2251573 2251591 2251603 2251637 2251643
2251649 2251673 2251681 2251687 2251703 2251727 2251729 2251741 2251771 2251807
2251819 2251829 2251841 2251849 2251859 2251877 2251891 2251897 2251901 2251903
2251913 2251927 2251943 2251957 2251979 2251981 2251993 2252009 2252011 2252017
```

```
2252087 2252113 2252149 2252161 2252179 2252189 2252209 2252213 2252219 2252221
2252231 2252233 2252251 2252273 2252309 2252311 2252353 2252359 2252387 2252389
2252399 2252407 2252441 2252461 2252477 2252489 2252513 2252519 2252539 2252557
2252567 2252587 2252611 2252623 2252629 2252639 2252647 2252651 2252681 2252683
2252693 2252711 2252729 2252743 2252753 2252779 2252821 2252867 2252897 2252911
2252917 2252927 2252933 2252941 2252947 2252951 2252953 2252983 2253023 2253037
2253047 2253059 2253067 2253079 2253091 2253101 2253113 2253127 2253137 2253161
2253169 2253179 2253187 2253193 2253203 2253221 2253247 2253253 2253257 2253259
2253281 2253283 2253289 2253311 2253323 2253341 2253353 2253371 2253389 2253397
2253409 2253439 2253451 2253473 2253479 2253481 2253487 2253491 2253497 2253499
2253521 2253539 2253547 2253551 2253557 2253599 2253617 2253637 2253649 2253653
2253659 2253683 2253703 2253709 2253721 2253739 2253749 2253763 2253773 2253803
2253821 2253827 2253833 2253841 2253847 2253857 2253863 2253871 2253887 2253899
2253919 2253941 2253959 2253971 2253973 2253997 2254033 2254067 2254079 2254093
2254097 2254099 2254111 2254121 2254129 2254157 2254159 2254177 2254201 2254211
2254223 2254243 2254247 2254267 2254283 2254297 2254309 2254327 2254403 2254409
2254411 2254451 2254457 2254477 2254493 2254501 2254507 2254513 2254517 2254531
2254541 2254579 2254589 2254601 2254607 2254627 2254643 2254649 2254657 2254687
2254691 2254697 2254729 2254757 2254771 2254781 2254783 2254789 2254793 2254799
2254801 2254831 2254849 2254853 2254871 2254873 2254907 2254927 2254933 2254937
2254961 2254961 2254969 2255003 2255009 2255021 2255023 2255063 2255083 2255089
2255093 2255111 2255119 2255131 2255147 2255159 2255161 2255191 2255233 2255249
2255251 2255257 2255263 2255269 2255291 2255299 2255303 2255321 2255333 2255381
2255387 2255399 2255411 2255419 2255437 2255447 2255459 2255489 2255501 2255507
2255549 2255551 2255567 2255569 2255573 2255581 2255609 2255621 2255639 2255657
2255663 2255677 2255681 2255717 2255723 2255731 2255749 2255753 2255761 2255767
2255783 2255797 2255821 2255833 2255837 2255867 2255887 2255899 2255947 2255959
2255969 2255971 2255987 2255989 2255999 2256013 2256017 2256029 2256031 2256043
2256049 2256073 2256097 2256119 2256127 2256131 2256169 2256173 2256179 2256181
2256197 2256217 2256227 2256251 2256259 2256281 2256299 2256311 2256313 2256341
2256343 2256347 2256349 2256361 2256367 2256377 2256379 2256389 2256413 2256431
2256437 2256467 2256469 2256473 2256479 2256533 2256539 2256557 2256559 2256571
2256601 2256613 2256619 2256623 2256629 2256637 2256673 2256677 2256689 2256697
2256703 2256713 2256721 2256731 2256739 2256743 2256781 2256791 2256811 2256823
2256827 2256841 2256847 2256851 2256857 2256887 2256901 2256911 2256913 2256923
2256931 2256959 2256973 2257001 2257007 2257049 2257051 2257069 2257097 2257103
2257117 2257121 2257139 2257169 2257187 2257193 2257207 2257237 2257247 2257291
2257301 2257309 2257313 2257319 2257361 2257373 2257391 2257397 2257403 2257439
2257441 2257471 2257483 2257487 2257511 2257529 2257531 2257547 2257553 2257559
2257571 2257579 2257597 2257609 2257639 2257643 2257649 2257667 2257687 2257691
2257693 2257709 2257721 2257733 2257757 2257763 2257771 2257781 2257797 2257813
2257819 2257837 2257859 2257861 2257867 2257873 2257877 2257883 2257909 2257939
2257943 2257949 2257961 2257987 2258023 2258029 2258033 2258041 2258083 2258111
2258119 2258129 2258149 2258167 2258173 2258177 2258183 2258203 2258213 2258227
2258233 2258251 2258261 2258273 2258279 2258287 2258299 2258323 2258327 2258329
2258339 2258351 2258357 2258363 2258387 2258407 2258419 2258429 2258437 2258447
2258453 2258479 2258483 2258519 2258521 2258527 2258539 2258561 2258573 2258593
2258617 2258621 2258639 2258651 2258653 2258657 2258713 2258717 2258741 2258743
2258779 2258783 2258791 2258803 2258819 2258821 2258827 2258831 2258843 2258863
2258873 2258903 2258917 2258947 2258953 2258969 2258981 2258987 2259029 2259031
2259041 2259053 2259097 2259121 2259133 2259137 2259139 2259143 2259161 2259197
2259199 2259211 2259217 2259239 2259241 2259281 2259289 2259293 2259329 2259353
2259371 2259377 2259391 2259403 2259407 2259437 2259449 2259493 2259503 2259527
2259529 2259539 2259557 2259571 2259581 2259601 2259629 2259643 2259671 2259703
2259707 2259731 2259739 2259769 2259781 2259791 2259811 2259823 2259833 2259847
2259853 2259863 2259871 2259893 2259913 2259919 2259929 2259947 2259967 2260009
2260019 2260039 2260051 2260061 2260067 2260081 2260087 2260127 2260151 2260157
2260163 2260169 2260171 2260177 2260189 2260211 2260217 2260229 2260249 2260253
2260267 2260273 2260301 2260309 2260327 2260331 2260343 2260351 2260369 2260387
2260393 2260403 2260409 2260421 2260429 2260451 2260457 2260483 2260493 2260499
2260501 2260519 2260523 2260529 2260547 2260549 2260561 2260567 2260571 2260603
2260627 2260631 2260633 2260649 2260651 2260673 2260681 2260691 2260717 2260723
2260729 2260733 2260759 2260763 2260771 2260787 2260789 2260793 2260801 2260823
2260859 2260879 2260889 2260891 2260903 2260913 2260919 2260961 2260967 2261009
2261023 2261041 2261053 2261071 2261093 2261099 2261111 2261117 2261131 2261143
2261173 2261177 2261197 2261213 2261219 2261227 2261267 2261269 2261297 2261309
2261353 2261377 2261393 2261407 2261447 2261461 2261471 2261473 2261503 2261509
2261531 2261549 2261557 2261569 2261573 2261587 2261591 2261599 2261603 2261617
2261621 2261639 2261653 2261689 2261713 2261717 2261737 2261771 2261789 2261801
2261803 2261807 2261827 2261837 2261839 2261851 2261863 2261887 2261891 2261911
2261927 2261933 2261993 2262017 2262031 2262049 2262053 2262061 2262067 2262103
2262133 2262149 2262191 2262209 2262223 2262229 2262233 2262269 2262313 2262329
2262353 2262361 2262367 2262391 2262397 2262409 2262413 2262437 2262443 2262451
2262457 2262461 2262467 2262499 2262521 2262529 2262541 2262563 2262569 2262593
2262619 2262629 2262641 2262643 2262679 2262713 2262727 2262761 2262769 2262811
2262817 2262823 2262833 2262847 2262851 2262857 2262859 2262877 2262889 2262937
2262959 2262971 2262973 2262977 2262979 2263007 2263061 2263067 2263069 2263081
2263087 2263099 2263117 2263139 2263141 2263169 2263171 2263201 2263213 2263229
2263237 2263243 2263249 2263273 2263307 2263319 2263321 2263357 2263369 2263381
2263411 2263423 2263427 2263433 2263439 2263441 2263447 2263463 2263483 2263507
2263517 2263519 2263531 2263553 2263559 2263561 2263579 2263619 2263627 2263633
2263643 2263687 2263691 2263699 2263721 2263739 2263741 2263753 2263759 2263763
2263777 2263787 2263801 2263817 2263829 2263841 2263843 2263847 2263861 2263879
2263901 2263909 2263927 2263931 2263939 2263957 2263969 2264027 2264057 2264069
2264089 2264099 2264113 2264149 2264153 2264161 2264177 2264183 2264191
2264201 2264203 2264231 2264239 2264267 2264279 2264293 2264299 2264309 2264321
2264329 2264341 2264347 2264351 2264357 2264359 2264393 2264429 2264443 2264453
2264467 2264497 2264501 2264513 2264539 2264543 2264551 2264567 2264569 2264573
2264593 2264599 2264609 2264611 2264617 2264623 2264627 2264641 2264657 2264683
```

```
2264699 2264707 2264719 2264737 2264749 2264753 2264761 2264771 2264777 2264797
2264803 2264809 2264827 2264831 2264839 2264861 2264863 2264897 2264903 2264917
2264923 2264957 2264959 2265001 2265019 2265049 2265079 2265101 2265143 2265149
2265163 2265173 2265223 2265239 2265269 2265271 2265287 2265323 2265331 2265371
2265377 2265391 2265413 2265421 2265433 2265443 2265463 2265467 2265469 2265493
2265499 2265517 2265521 2265551 2265581 2265587 2265589 2265611 2265623 2265631
2265643 2265647 2265671 2265677 2265721 2265727 2265737 2265749 2265751 2265761
2265779 2265793 2265797 2265841 2265869 2265877 2265881 2265899 2265911 2265941
2265943 2265953 2265979 2266003 2266021 2266027 2266037 2266039 2266063 2266067
2266079 2266087 2266093 2266097 2266109 2266129 2266133 2266157 2266163 2266177
2266183 2266217 2266223 2266237 2266247 2266267 2266283 2266289 2266291 2266307
2266331 2266337 2266343 2266403 2266427 2266447 2266463 2266469 2266471 2266477
2266493 2266499 2266501 2266507 2266519 2266531 2266549 2266571 2266591 2266601
2266619 2266631 2266633 2266637 2266639 2266679 2266697 2266709 2266711 2266717
2266739 2266753 2266769 2266777 2266783 2266787 2266801 2266829 2266837 2266861
2266883 2266897 2266907 2266921 2266961 2266973 2266981 2266991 2266993 2267011
2267029 2267047 2267051 2267053 2267071 2267093 2267117 2267129 2267131 2267141
2267143 2267149 2267159 2267189 2267197 2267203 2267219 2267227 2267231 2267257
2267263 2267281 2267297 2267299 2267303 2267381 2267383 2267399 2267407 2267413
2267417 2267483 2267497 2267509 2267521 2267533 2267543 2267549 2267561 2267563
2267591 2267611 2267623 2267633 2267653 2267663 2267677 2267701 2267719 2267723
2267729 2267737 2267773 2267791 2267801 2267807 2267813 2267827 2267831 2267873
2267879 2267911 2267917 2267921 2267933 2267971 2267977 2267981 2267983 2268001
2268031 2268043 2268067 2268073 2268083 2268103 2268121 2268131 2268139 2268143
2268197 2268199 2268209 2268221 2268223 2268229 2268247 2268257 2268263 2268269
2268271 2268281 2268289 2268317 2268319 2268323 2268337 2268377 2268389 2268397
2268403 2268437 2268443 2268449 2268451 2268481 2268503 2268517 2268547 2268557
2268577 2268587 2268589 2268593 2268631 2268647 2268649 2268659 2268671 2268677
2268691 2268719 2268779 2268793 2268829 2268839 2268841 2268853 2268863 2268869
2268887 2268919 2268941 2268943 2268949 2268977 2268979 2268991 2268997 2269009
2269027 2269031 2269039 2269049 2269061 2269079 2269097 2269103 2269103 2269129
2269133 2269159 2269171 2269181 2269217 2269219 2269237 2269273 2269277 2269283
2269307 2269327 2269331 2269339 2269343 2269349 2269361 2269409 2269429 2269439
2269447 2269447 2269451 2269457 2269459 2269481 2269499 2269507 2269529 2269553
2269601 2269613 2269621 2269633 2269639 2269661 2269699 2269711 2269733 2269739
2269769 2269769 2269777 2269807 2269819 2269829 2269843 2269849 2269853 2269867
2269877 2269879 2269889 2269901 2269903 2269909 2269931 2269961 2269973 2269991
2270003 2270011 2270071 2270111 2270113 2270117 2270131 2270137 2270141 2270153
2270159 2270171 2270173 2270179 2270183 2270201 2270239 2270249 2270251 2270263
2270267 2270269 2270297 2270309 2270311 2270321 2270327 2270339 2270341 2270383
2270393 2270407 2270413 2270423 2270441 2270447 2270449 2270459 2270463 2270507
2270531 2270549 2270551 2270591 2270599 2270627 2270641 2270659 2270663 2270669
2270677 2270683 2270687 2270689 2270693 2270713 2270717 2270759 2270771 2270773
2270777 2270791 2270803 2270837 2270839 2270893 2270897 2270921 2270929 2270941
2270953 2270977 2270981 2270987 2271001 2271011 2271037 2271041 2271053 2271067
2271083 2271107 2271119 2271133 2271151 2271161 2271163 2271221 2271223 2271229
2271239 2271257 2271263 2271271 2271281 2271287 2271301 2271307 2271337 2271341
2271343 2271349 2271377 2271383 2271391 2271397 2271403 2271407 2271419 2271427
2271439 2271443 2271473 2271481 2271481 2271497 2271499 2271551 2271553 2271569
2271571 2271593 2271613 2271637 2271673 2271679 2271683 2271721 2271743 2271749
2271751 2271767 2271781 2271791 2271799 2271817 2271821 2271827 2271859 2271869
2271877 2271881 2271883 2271901 2271923 2271937 2271953 2271967 2271977 2271989
2272013 2272019 2272073 2272079 2272087 2272103 2272117 2272129 2272141 2272177
2272183 2272187 2272199 2272201 2272211 2272217 2272219 2272223 2272241 2272253
2272273 2272297 2272301 2272313 2272321 2272337 2272351 2272357 2272379 2272397
2272409 2272427 2272451 2272453 2272463 2272471 2272483 2272493 2272499 2272513
2272519 2272537 2272547 2272549 2272559 2272597 2272603 2272619 2272631 2272649
2272657 2272667 2272691 2272727 2272729 2272733 2272757 2272771 2272811 2272819
2272843 2272859 2272861 2272903 2272931 2272939 2272943 2272957 2272973 2272987
2272993 2272997 2273017 2273041 2273059 2273069 2273071 2273077 2273083 2273101
2273119 2273143 2273153 2273171 2273209 2273213 2273231 2273239 2273267 2273273
2273279 2273303 2273309 2273311 2273333 2273351 2273357 2273363 2273399 2273431
2273443 2273449 2273459 2273471 2273477 2273489 2273497 2273501 2273503 2273507
2273533 2273543 2273549 2273561 2273567 2273569 2273599 2273603 2273651 2273659
2273669 2273671 2273693 2273701 2273729 2273743 2273759 2273771 2273783 2273807
2273827 2273833 2273851 2273867 2273911 2273923 2273927 2273959 2273963 2273981
2273989 2273993 2274007 2274011 2274017 2274031 2274049 2274089 2274101 2274109
2274121 2274127 2274143 2274149 2274163 2274203 2274221 2274241 2274247 2274257
2274269 2274271 2274287 2274289 2274329 2274341 2274347 2274361 2274367 2274407
2274409 2274421 2274451 2274463 2274469 2274473 2274479 2274487 2274491 2274497
2274511 2274521 2274523 2274541 2274551 2274589 2274593 2274599 2274641 2274653
2274667 2274683 2274689 2274691 2274703 2274709 2274733 2274739 2274761 2274763
2274793 2274809 2274811 2274827 2274841 2274859 2274887 2274893 2274901 2274913
2274917 2274931 2274949 2274959 2274971 2274977 2275027 2275043 2275057 2275067
2275103 2275139 2275151 2275171 2275187 2275199 2275201 2275211 2275219 2275243
2275271 2275283 2275289 2275303 2275309 2275313 2275319 2275327 2275333 2275349
2275363 2275391 2275393 2275409 2275423 2275439 2275447 2275451 2275457 2275477
2275513 2275529 2275531 2275549 2275561 2275583 2275591 2275607 2275613 2275619
2275633 2275639 2275657 2275667 2275681 2275697 2275703 2275723 2275733 2275747
2275769 2275771 2275813 2275831 2275837 2275853 2275859 2275879 2275913
2275937 2275961 2275993 2276041 2276059 2276077 2276081 2276089 2276101 2276107
2276117 2276137 2276167 2276171 2276179 2276201 2276231 2276233 2276243 2276251
2276269 2276293 2276303 2276311 2276357 2276369 2276383 2276389 2276399 2276401
2276411 2276429 2276431 2276467 2276503 2276513 2276537 2276551 2276557 2276567
2276579 2276591 2276629 2276669 2276693 2276699 2276707 2276723 2276737 2276741
2276749 2276753 2276779 2276783 2276809 2276849 2276867 2276873 2276909 2276921
2276951 2276957 2276969 2276999 2277001 2277013 2277047 2277061 2277071 2277083
2277097 2277101 2277113 2277127 2277139 2277179 2277211 2277221 2277259 2277287
2277307 2277311 2277329 2277343 2277349 2277367 2277377 2277383 2277389 2277403
```

```
2277413  2277469  2277481  2277487  2277493  2277503  2277521  2277547  2277551  2277553
2277571  2277607  2277617  2277619  2277629  2277637  2277641  2277647  2277659  2277661
2277703  2277727  2277731  2277733  2277767  2277797  2277809  2277811  2277817  2277823
2277827  2277833  2277841  2277847  2277859  2277871  2277883  2277889  2277901  2277907
2277917  2277941  2278007  2278019  2278021  2278027  2278033  2278063  2278069  2278079
2278091  2278093  2278109  2278117  2278121  2278139  2278141  2278181  2278189  2278207
2278217  2278229  2278249  2278259  2278261  2278277  2278291  2278301  2278303  2278307
2278313  2278343  2278361  2278379  2278421  2278429  2278453  2278477  2278481  2278487
2278517  2278519  2278543  2278553  2278631  2278637  2278643  2278649  2278681  2278691
2278693  2278709  2278729  2278747  2278753  2278769  2278807  2278811  2278813  2278823
2278831  2278847  2278877  2278891  2278943  2278949  2278961  2278963  2278967  2278979
2278981  2279009  2279033  2279041  2279051  2279063  2279083  2279087  2279113  2279117
2279119  2279141  2279153  2279161  2279239  2279243  2279257  2279261  2279281  2279293
2279317  2279339  2279351  2279353  2279363  2279393  2279401  2279413  2279419  2279423
2279447  2279467  2279471  2279489  2279491  2279527  2279539  2279567  2279569  2279591
2279611  2279617  2279633  2279653  2279657  2279663  2279687  2279707  2279741  2279743
2279749  2279759  2279773  2279807  2279813  2279839  2279843  2279857  2279869  2279897
2279899  2279911  2279933  2279993  2280011  2280029  2280041  2280053  2280071  2280073
2280079  2280097  2280107  2280127  2280163  2280167  2280169  2280191  2280203  2280221
2280253  2280283  2280287  2280293  2280319  2280331  2280337  2280359  2280367  2280401
2280403  2280407  2280413  2280433  2280451  2280463  2280469  2280497  2280503  2280517
2280521  2280547  2280559  2280587  2280623  2280631  2280637  2280661  2280667  2280671
2280673  2280683  2280689  2280709  2280767  2280823  2280827  2280833  2280847  2280857
2280869  2280899  2280911  2280917  2280947  2280959  2280977  2280983  2280989  2281001
2281003  2281033  2281039  2281057  2281061  2281079  2281093  2281099  2281109  2281127
2281151  2281183  2281189  2281207  2281211  2281219  2281229  2281231  2281243  2281249
2281267  2281277  2281291  2281297  2281313  2281327  2281361  2281373  2281379  2281381
2281403  2281429  2281481  2281493  2281529  2281567  2281571  2281579  2281607  2281619
2281651  2281661  2281663  2281667  2281673  2281687  2281711  2281717  2281739  2281751
2281771  2281777  2281781  2281789  2281793  2281813  2281823  2281831  2281861  2281883
2281891  2281913  2281921  2281973  2281987  2282017  2282023  2282041  2282047  2282057
2282069  2282081  2282089  2282099  2282141  2282149  2282173  2282201  2282207  2282243
2282249  2282257  2282281  2282303  2282321  2282323  2282333  2282341  2282381  2282383
2282393  2282407  2282421  2282447  2282453  2282459  2282473  2282477  2282509  2282513
2282521  2282537  2282549  2282587  2282597  2282617  2282627  2282647  2282653  2282699
2282711  2282719  2282737  2282759  2282767  2282801  2282807  2282849  2282867  2282897
2282899  2282923  2282941  2282963  2282971  2282989  2283013  2283019  2283031  2283037
2283067  2283077  2283091  2283109  2283137  2283139  2283191  2283227  2283301  2283313
2283317  2283319  2283361  2283377  2283403  2283409  2283419  2283433  2283443  2283451
2283493  2283497  2283499  2283511  2283539  2283551  2283563  2283571  2283581  2283583
2283623  2283637  2283649  2283679  2283691  2283703  2283707  2283709  2283719  2283727
2283731  2283733  2283737  2283803  2283833  2283839  2283851  2283881  2283887  2283889
2283893  2283907  2283917  2283937  2283943  2283947  2283991  2283997  2284003  2284013
2284019  2284027  2284033  2284043  2284057  2284109  2284133  2284147  2284157  2284181
2284207  2284211  2284213  2284223  2284229  2284241  2284277  2284279  2284327  2284339
2284357  2284367  2284369  2284379  2284391  2284403  2284441  2284481  2284487  2284489
2284493  2284501  2284537  2284549  2284573  2284589  2284631  2284637  2284663  2284673
2284679  2284687  2284691  2284697  2284703  2284757  2284831  2284837  2284859  2284871
2284873  2284879  2284913  2284937  2284943  2284949  2284951  2284957  2284963  2285039
2285047  2285057  2285069  2285071  2285099  2285131  2285141  2285147  2285159  2285161
2285167  2285189  2285219  2285221  2285237  2285249  2285251  2285267  2285273  2285279
2285291  2285317  2285323  2285329  2285333  2285347  2285357  2285359  2285363  2285369
2285389  2285399  2285401  2285443  2285447  2285473  2285477  2285489  2285509  2285513
2285551  2285581  2285587  2285597  2285623  2285629  2285639  2285641  2285653  2285669
2285669  2285677  2285683  2285711  2285741  2285743  2285747  2285779  2285797  2285813
2285821  2285861  2285863  2285869  2285891  2285893  2285911  2285917  2285929  2285951
2285953  2285957  2285977  2285981  2286013  2286017  2286047  2286059  2286083  2286091
2286139  2286149  2286169  2286173  2286187  2286197  2286199  2286223  2286233  2286239
2286257  2286293  2286301  2286307  2286373  2286377  2286379  2286437  2286443  2286457
2286469  2286481  2286491  2286511  2286523  2286527  2286533  2286553  2286577  2286589
2286601  2286617  2286623  2286629  2286649  2286669  2286671  2286701  2286749  2286763
2286773  2286787  2286793  2286797  2286799  2286803  2286827  2286833  2286841  2286847
2286877  2286881  2286883  2286953  2286961  2286979  2286983  2286989  2287009  2287013
2287031  2287039  2287057  2287063  2287069  2287093  2287099  2287111  2287121  2287133
2287171  2287177  2287183  2287193  2287199  2287223  2287237  2287247  2287249  2287261
2287279  2287283  2287289  2287291  2287307  2287319  2287343  2287381  2287387  2287393
2287409  2287421  2287423  2287463  2287477  2287487  2287501  2287507  2287529  2287531
2287547  2287559  2287577  2287591  2287613  2287627  2287633  2287661  2287667  2287669
2287679  2287687  2287699  2287739  2287777  2287807  2287811  2287823  2287861  2287871
2287891  2287921  2287931  2287937  2287951  2287963  2287973  2287991  2287993  2288003
2288009  2288029  2288051  2288057  2288059  2288089  2288107  2288119  2288123  2288161
2288173  2288207  2288213  2288239  2288243  2288249  2288257  2288261  2288263  2288267
2288281  2288287  2288291  2288323  2288347  2288359  2288369  2288399  2288441  2288449
2288467  2288471  2288479  2288509  2288527  2288563  2288581  2288597  2288603  2288633
2288641  2288677  2288681  2288687  2288711  2288719  2288723  2288731  2288747  2288749
2288771  2288773  2288801  2288807  2288809  2288821  2288831  2288833  2288843  2288849
2288861  2288879  2288887  2288893  2288927  2288929  2288939  2288953  2289013  2289031
2289037  2289059  2289073  2289083  2289127  2289143  2289149  2289151  2289163  2289169
2289181  2289193  2289197  2289211  2289233  2289239  2289247  2289251  2289263  2289281
2289349  2289359  2289379  2289401  2289409  2289431  2289433  2289437  2289461  2289467
2289473  2289503  2289571  2289583  2289593  2289601  2289641  2289643  2289647  2289649
2289659  2289667  2289689  2289697  2289739  2289743  2289751  2289761  2289767  2289773
2289779  2289803  2289817  2289829  2289839  2289841  2289863  2289871  2289911  2289919
2289923  2289929  2289943  2289953  2289961  2289979  2290003  2290007  2290021  2290031
2290033  2290037  2290039  2290049  2290069  2290081  2290091  2290097  2290117  2290139
2290147  2290151  2290153  2290177  2290181  2290207  2290213  2290231  2290243  2290259
2290283  2290339  2290369  2290403  2290423  2290429  2290441  2290459  2290471  2290493
2290499  2290511  2290517  2290523  2290537  2290543  2290571  2290573  2290591  2290609
2290619  2290627  2290637  2290643  2290649  2290703  2290721  2290727  2290747  2290751
```

```
2290789  2290817  2290829  2290831  2290843  2290861  2290889  2290901  2290907  2290927
2290933  2290943  2290969  2290973  2290979  2290987  2290991  2290999  2291017  2291033
2291041  2291063  2291119  2291131  2291143  2291167  2291183  2291189  2291197  2291213
2291227  2291231  2291239  2291257  2291269  2291273  2291281  2291287  2291327  2291347
2291351  2291353  2291369  2291389  2291417  2291437  2291459  2291477  2291479  2291491
2291539  2291557  2291563  2291567  2291573  2291581  2291591  2291623  2291629  2291657
2291659  2291677  2291683  2291699  2291717  2291747  2291749  2291781  2291801  2291803
2291827  2291851  2291867  2291893  2291903  2291909  2291911  2291917  2291921  2291929
2291959  2291963  2291983  2291987  2291999  2292041  2292053  2292071  2292079
2292083  2292119  2292133  2292163  2292167  2292181  2292193  2292221  2292239  2292253
2292259  2292289  2292299  2292307  2292317  2292337  2292347  2292359  2292361  2292371
2292391  2292403  2292413  2292427  2292439  2292449  2292457  2292461  2292463  2292469
2292491  2292497  2292509  2292523  2292529  2292533  2292541  2292547  2292593  2292601
2292607  2292623  2292643  2292691  2292701  2292713  2292733  2292737  2292751  2292767
2292781  2292793  2292809  2292859  2292869  2292877  2292881  2292887  2292919  2292923
2292947  2292949  2292959  2292967  2293013  2293037  2293063  2293069  2293103  2293111
2293121  2293127  2293139  2293141  2293157  2293183  2293199  2293219  2293231  2293267
2293273  2293301  2293303  2293309  2293321  2293327  2293367  2293391  2293393  2293397
2293427  2293439  2293463  2293481  2293483  2293531  2293549  2293559  2293567
2293579  2293591  2293631  2293633  2293637  2293649  2293673  2293693  2293703  2293723
2293727  2293729  2293751  2293757  2293771  2293777  2293789  2293799  2293801  2293817
2293829  2293831  2293847  2293849  2293867  2293877  2293883  2293901  2293901  2293919
2293937  2293957  2293961  2293981  2294009  2294011  2294021  2294051  2294053  2294057
2294059  2294077  2294113  2294137  2294141  2294177  2294209  2294221  2294249  2294251
2294261  2294267  2294291  2294309  2294311  2294321  2294359  2294363  2294377  2294387
2294419  2294429  2294431  2294449  2294477  2294489  2294491  2294519  2294533  2294627
2294659  2294671  2294689  2294693  2294707  2294723  2294731  2294767  2294771  2294783
2294797  2294807  2294819  2294827  2294833  2294843  2294861  2294879  2294891  2294911
2294921  2294939  2294977  2294987  2294999  2295001  2295011  2295019  2295053  2295061
2295071  2295077  2295079  2295103  2295107  2295113  2295121  2295131  2295169  2295173
2295179  2295233  2295253  2295259  2295269  2295281  2295301  2295313  2295329  2295341
2295361  2295367  2295389  2295401  2295407  2295451  2295473  2295479  2295481  2295509
2295521  2295533  2295539  2295541  2295547  2295551  2295569  2295583  2295593  2295619
2295647  2295659  2295673  2295677  2295691  2295703  2295719  2295721  2295743  2295763
2295773  2295793  2295803  2295817  2295823  2295841  2295859  2295869  2295911  2295913
2295919  2295947  2295949  2295971  2295989  2296001  2296009  2296027  2296039  2296057
2296061  2296079  2296081  2296097  2296117  2296127  2296163  2296171  2296187  2296213
2296219  2296237  2296247  2296271  2296277  2296351  2296363  2296367  2296381  2296433
2296447  2296487  2296517  2296519  2296569  2296571  2296577  2296621  2296633  2296643
2296661  2296687  2296691  2296699  2296727  2296729  2296733  2296741  2296747  2296781
2296783  2296787  2296807  2296813  2296817  2296837  2296867  2296871  2296873  2296907
2296909  2296913  2296919  2296939  2296963  2296979  2296999  2297011  2297021  2297027
2297039  2297041  2297051  2297059  2297093  2297101  2297137  2297149  2297153  2297203
2297213  2297221  2297231  2297249  2297257  2297291  2297297  2297311  2297327  2297333
2297341  2297359  2297369  2297371  2297387  2297411  2297429  2297437  2297473  2297479
2297483  2297509  2297521  2297543  2297573  2297587  2297591  2297593  2297597  2297653
2297657  2297671  2297693  2297707  2297717  2297719  2297731  2297741  2297747  2297749
2297759  2297761  2297777  2297797  2297807  2297819  2297843  2297849  2297857  2297863
2297881  2297887  2297903  2297909  2297923  2297951  2297957  2297969  2297983  2297987
2298007  2298011  2298013  2298019  2298029  2298041  2298059  2298071  2298073  2298089
2298097  2298103  2298119  2298139  2298151  2298161  2298193  2298203  2298209
2298211  2298223  2298293  2298311  2298313  2298343  2298377  2298379  2298389  2298391
2298397  2298409  2298427  2298469  2298481  2298493  2298503  2298577  2298589  2298599
2298607  2298613  2298631  2298641  2298661  2298671  2298679  2298683  2298691  2298707
2298713  2298719  2298731  2298749  2298761  2298763  2298787  2298833  2298839  2298841
2298853  2298869  2298881  2298887  2298937  2298949  2298953  2298973  2298977
2298983  2299001  2299021  2299039  2299049  2299079  2299093  2299111  2299117  2299139
2299147  2299159  2299163  2299169  2299189  2299229  2299249  2299259  2299303  2299309
2299313  2299327  2299337  2299357  2299387  2299391  2299397  2299433  2299447  2299463
2299469  2299481  2299483  2299489  2299499  2299519  2299523  2299529  2299541  2299547
2299553  2299571  2299601  2299603  2299637  2299651  2299657  2299667  2299697  2299711
2299727  2299733  2299753  2299763  2299771  2299783  2299789  2299823  2299837  2299841
2299867  2299873  2299901  2299907  2299919  2299933  2299937  2299939  2299949  2299951
2299963  2300003  2300017  2300021  2300029  2300047  2300057  2300063  2300071  2300087
2300131  2300143  2300149  2300153  2300167  2300173  2300189  2300201  2300203  2300209
2300239  2300261  2300267  2300269  2300279  2300297  2300317  2300323  2300357
2300377  2300399  2300413  2300429  2300443  2300447  2300489  2300497  2300513  2300527
2300531  2300563  2300581  2300591  2300609  2300611  2300651  2300669  2300671  2300689
2300693  2300707  2300719  2300731  2300747  2300761  2300777  2300803  2300813  2300819
2300833  2300839  2300861  2300869  2300891  2300911  2300923  2300927  2300951  2300953
2300959  2300971  2300989  2300999  2301011  2301017  2301023  2301029  2301031  2301041
2301049  2301077  2301097  2301107  2301119  2301151  2301163  2301193  2301197  2301199
2301209  2301217  2301227  2301241  2301251  2301259  2301269  2301281  2301283  2301287
2301293  2301301  2301319  2301361  2301389  2301401  2301407  2301421  2301461  2301473
2301479  2301491  2301493  2301499  2301503  2301521  2301547  2301569  2301571  2301581
2301583  2301599  2301601  2301619  2301623  2301683  2301703  2301707  2301709  2301727
2301743  2301757  2301779  2301787  2301797  2301811  2301821  2301829  2301841  2301847
2301857  2301877  2301883  2301889  2301941  2301973  2301977  2301989  2301997
2302009  2302019  2302043  2302051  2302067  2302087  2302099  2302117  2302151  2302159
2302169  2302217  2302219  2302229  2302243  2302283  2302291  2302301  2302303
2302309  2302331  2302343  2302367  2302379  2302381  2302387  2302403  2302411  2302441
2302451  2302453  2302471  2302481  2302511  2302523  2302537  2302543  2302561  2302579
2302609  2302631  2302661  2302669  2302679  2302717  2302753  2302757  2302787
2302793  2302799  2302841  2302879  2302889  2302907  2302913  2302969  2302981  2302987
2302999  2303003  2303017  2303029  2303057  2303089  2303117  2303129  2303137  2303153
2303159  2303173  2303179  2303219  2303227  2303239  2303251  2303263  2303293  2303297
2303303  2303309  2303321  2303359  2303377  2303387  2303407  2303437  2303461  2303471
2303489  2303501  2303513  2303531  2303533  2303563  2303569  2303573  2303591  2303593
2303597  2303599  2303621  2303627  2303629  2303663  2303669  2303677  2303681  2303701
```

```
2303713  2303723  2303729  2303753  2303767  2303779  2303783  2303797  2303803  2303843
2303849  2303867  2303923  2303927  2303947  2303971  2303981  2303989  2303999  2304011
2304017  2304019  2304023  2304037  2304053  2304059  2304089  2304097  2304103  2304139
2304157  2304179  2304191  2304217  2304223  2304229  2304233  2304251  2304257  2304271
2304283  2304287  2304307  2304317  2304319  2304343  2304349  2304373  2304389  2304403
2304443  2304451  2304461  2304479  2304521  2304527  2304541  2304553  2304559  2304563
2304581  2304593  2304607  2304611  2304629  2304637  2304647  2304689  2304691  2304721
2304727  2304749  2304773  2304781  2304787  2304791  2304793  2304803  2304823  2304839
2304851  2304859  2304893  2304901  2304931  2304937  2304961  2304997  2305003  2305027
2305049  2305091  2305103  2305109  2305111  2305117  2305133  2305153  2305169  2305271
2305279  2305291  2305301  2305321  2305333  2305337  2305339  2305351  2305357  2305361
2305363  2305393  2305409  2305411  2305463  2305481  2305483  2305487  2305549  2305607
2305609  2305613  2305621  2305627  2305637  2305643  2305649  2305651  2305691  2305711
2305733  2305747  2305753  2305763  2305777  2305781  2305837  2305883  2305889  2305903
2305909  2305949  2305967  2305969  2305987  2306023  2306027  2306039  2306041  2306053
2306063  2306071  2306081  2306107  2306119  2306123  2306131  2306147  2306153  2306159
2306179  2306191  2306197  2306221  2306261  2306267  2306299  2306303  2306309  2306327
2306329  2306333  2306357  2306363  2306389  2306393  2306413  2306449  2306453
2306519  2306527  2306531  2306561  2306567  2306569  2306587  2306597  2306621  2306627
2306639  2306641  2306651  2306663  2306671  2306677  2306737  2306753  2306761  2306797
2306851  2306867  2306881  2306893  2306897  2306911  2306957  2306971  2306977  2306981
2307031  2307043  2307047  2307059  2307073  2307083  2307091  2307103  2307119  2307127
2307139  2307157  2307161  2307163  2307167  2307181  2307187  2307191  2307197  2307229
2307233  2307247  2307259  2307281  2307289  2307307  2307367  2307373  2307377  2307391
2307397  2307407  2307419  2307449  2307451  2307467  2307469  2307479  2307499  2307517
2307523  2307527  2307541  2307553  2307577  2307581  2307589  2307593  2307601  2307611
2307623  2307629  2307637  2307661  2307677  2307689  2307703  2307709  2307757  2307763
2307821  2307863  2307871  2307881  2307887  2307913  2307923  2307941  2307953  2307959
2307967  2307973  2307979  2307983  2307989  2308001  2308003  2308049  2308051  2308069
2308079  2308099  2308109  2308121  2308151  2308169  2308181  2308183  2308193  2308199
2308213  2308219  2308223  2308231  2308237  2308247  2308261  2308279  2308297  2308321
2308357  2308387  2308391  2308399  2308403  2308417  2308451  2308463  2308469  2308483
2308507  2308513  2308517  2308529  2308531  2308543  2308561  2308567  2308573  2308589
2308597  2308609  2308673  2308679  2308681  2308693  2308699  2308707  2308721  2308723
2308727  2308741  2308769  2308783  2308793  2308807  2308819  2308841  2308843  2308853
2308871  2308883  2308897  2308903  2308907  2308913  2308919  2308931  2308939  2308963
2308967  2309003  2309011  2309023  2309029  2309077  2309081  2309113  2309117  2309123
2309129  2309147  2309179  2309227  2309231  2309233  2309239  2309257  2309261  2309267
2309287  2309303  2309327  2309339  2309341  2309347  2309353  2309371  2309389
2309413  2309441  2309449  2309471  2309477  2309491  2309497  2309513  2309519  2309537
2309543  2309551  2309609  2309633  2309663  2309669  2309677  2309689  2309693  2309707
2309711  2309737  2309743  2309753  2309759  2309761  2309771  2309789  2309803  2309837
2309863  2309869  2309891  2309893  2309897  2309911  2309921  2309927  2309933  2309969
2309999  2310019  2310029  2310043  2310067  2310083  2310107  2310137  2310151  2310167
2310193  2310211  2310221  2310223  2310233  2310241  2310277  2310289  2310293  2310311
2310331  2310349  2310359  2310367  2310379  2310421  2310431  2310439  2310449  2310463
2310479  2310481  2310491  2310493  2310509  2310541  2310547  2310551  2310559  2310563
2310593  2310643  2310667  2310677  2310689  2310697  2310701  2310703  2310713  2310731
2310733  2310739  2310743  2310751  2310757  2310767  2310769  2310789  2310797  2310823
2310857  2310871  2310877  2310887  2310899  2310901  2310907  2310911  2310953  2310977
2310999  2311009  2311013  2311021  2311051  2311061  2311079  2311117  2311123  2311147
2311151  2311159  2311163  2311181  2311187  2311193  2311223  2311237  2311249  2311289
2311321  2311333  2311343  2311349  2311363  2311381  2311409  2311411  2311417  2311451
2311469  2311471  2311487  2311493  2311499  2311513  2311531  2311537  2311549  2311553
2311571  2311583  2311591  2311613  2311651  2311657  2311667  2311669  2311681  2311697
2311721  2311739  2311741  2311747  2311769  2311811  2311817  2311819  2311823  2311843
2311849  2311853  2311861  2311873  2311879  2311889  2311921  2311931  2311957  2311993
2312021  2312027  2312069  2312099  2312137  2312147  2312159  2312173  2312179  2312201
2312203  2312209  2312249  2312267  2312293  2312311  2312341  2312347  2312363  2312369
2312381  2312407  2312413  2312419  2312477  2312521  2312539  2312573  2312603  2312617
2312621  2312633  2312641  2312677  2312689  2312707  2312711  2312747  2312749
2312753  2312789  2312801  2312809  2312861  2312873  2312881  2312897  2312899  2312909
2312923  2312929  2312939  2312951  2312963  2312983  2312987  2313007  2313053  2313061
2313083  2313107  2313137  2313161  2313163  2313187  2313197  2313211  2313239  2313247
2313253  2313323  2313347  2313349  2313373  2313379  2313391  2313401  2313403  2313407
2313413  2313419  2313427  2313431  2313433  2313439  2313461  2313469  2313511  2313539
2313541  2313557  2313569  2313599  2313601  2313613  2313617  2313629  2313631  2313643
2313653  2313659  2313667  2313679  2313767  2313769  2313797  2313799  2313827  2313833
2313847  2313851  2313889  2313907  2313929  2313931  2313947  2313967  2313973  2313977
2314003  2314019  2314051  2314061  2314063  2314079  2314081  2314087  2314091  2314093
2314097  2314121  2314133  2314141  2314153  2314177  2314187  2314199  2314231  2314241
2314253  2314259  2314271  2314297  2314309  2314339  2314349  2314369  2314373  2314379
2314391  2314439  2314547  2314583  2314589  2314591  2314603  2314619  2314633  2314643
2314667  2314673  2314691  2314699  2314709  2314717  2314721  2314723  2314727  2314759
2314769  2314777  2314811  2314817  2314841  2314843  2314849  2314859  2314877  2314883
2314909  2314931  2314933  2314943  2314951  2314957  2314969  2314997  2314999  2315003
2315023  2315029  2315039  2315057  2315059  2315063  2315069  2315081  2315107  2315113
2315123  2315129  2315141  2315149  2315161  2315167  2315177  2315227  2315231  2315233
2315237  2315263  2315317  2315329  2315347  2315363  2315371  2315399  2315407  2315413
2315461  2315471  2315477  2315491  2315503  2315539  2315567  2315581  2315597  2315611
2315629  2315641  2315647  2315657  2315659  2315683  2315693  2315699  2315707  2315759
2315771  2315773  2315839  2315843  2315849  2315857  2315861  2315881  2315897  2315903
2315947  2315953  2315959  2315981  2315983  2315993  2316011  2316037  2316059  2316073
2316079  2316101  2316107  2316121  2316133  2316151  2316173  2316179  2316203  2316239
2316247  2316287  2316299  2316323  2316329  2316331  2316337  2316343  2316361  2316371
2316373  2316383  2316407  2316421  2316449  2316451  2316463  2316469  2316481  2316487
2316493  2316497  2316511  2316521  2316529  2316553  2316557  2316571  2316593  2316617
2316631  2316653  2316667  2316679  2316697  2316707  2316737  2316757  2316761  2316773
2316817  2316823  2316863  2316877  2316893  2316911  2316961  2316967  2316973  2317009
```

```
2317037  2317057  2317067  2317079  2317087  2317097  2317109  2317121  2317123  2317127
2317153  2317169  2317171  2317223  2317229  2317267  2317283  2317327  2317339  2317349
2317363  2317387  2317391  2317433  2317439  2317453  2317493  2317499  2317501  2317507
2317519  2317549  2317561  2317577  2317589  2317619  2317631  2317669  2317691  2317723
2317741  2317747  2317751  2317759  2317769  2317787  2317789  2317801  2317807  2317811
2317813  2317841  2317873  2317879  2317891  2317907  2317919  2317921  2317927  2317951
2317957  2317979  2318003  2318021  2318033  2318039  2318047  2318059  2318077  2318089
2318093  2318111  2318119  2318153  2318159  2318189  2318191  2318237  2318249  2318279
2318293  2318297  2318311  2318317  2318333  2318353  2318357  2318387  2318389  2318411
2318417  2318453  2318467  2318471  2318483  2318489  2318501  2318507  2318527  2318543
2318567  2318573  2318581  2318593  2318597  2318599  2318609  2318611  2318623  2318663
2318677  2318711  2318731  2318737  2318747  2318761  2318773  2318777  2318801  2318807
2318809  2318819  2318821  2318843  2318863  2318867  2318879  2318891  2318917  2318923
2318951  2318957  2318959  2319013  2319019  2319029  2319041  2319059  2319077  2319091
2319133  2319151  2319169  2319179  2319181  2319221  2319241  2319253  2319257  2319277
2319287  2319299  2319319  2319323  2319337  2319341  2319353  2319371  2319379  2319407
2319409  2319413  2319431  2319433  2319437  2319461  2319469  2319479  2319487  2319503
2319509  2319517  2319521  2319533  2319553  2319593  2319613  2319631  2319649  2319659
2319679  2319689  2319697  2319727  2319731  2319763  2319787  2319791  2319809  2319817
2319829  2319841  2319853  2319883  2319887  2319901  2319907  2319917  2319929  2319943
2319953  2319959  2319997  2320001  2320039  2320051  2320063  2320091  2320111  2320127
2320139  2320169  2320183  2320193  2320207  2320243  2320247  2320259  2320291  2320301
2320321  2320361  2320363  2320387  2320391  2320397  2320399  2320421  2320427  2320471
2320481  2320511  2320519  2320543  2320547  2320553  2320579  2320583  2320627  2320639
2320649  2320651  2320657  2320673  2320697  2320699  2320709  2320729  2320739  2320741
2320807  2320811  2320837  2320847  2320859  2320873  2320897  2320909  2320933  2320943
2320961  2320979  2320987  2320991  2321003  2321009  2321017  2321023  2321041  2321057
2321087  2321089  2321101  2321117  2321147  2321149  2321153  2321159  2321167  2321171
2321213  2321219  2321239  2321243  2321273  2321281  2321309  2321317  2321329  2321339
2321353  2321357  2321369  2321381  2321383  2321393  2321399  2321443  2321507  2321509
2321519  2321531  2321563  2321587  2321603  2321623  2321647  2321677  2321701  2321747
2321749  2321773  2321783  2321791  2321821  2321863  2321881  2321887  2321899  2321909
2321923  2321947  2321959  2321981  2321989  2321999  2322031  2322041  2322071  2322077
2322079  2322101  2322109  2322113  2322119  2322121  2322127  2322137  2322139  2322143
2322163  2322169  2322193  2322211  2322227  2322239  2322247  2322253  2322259  2322269
2322283  2322337  2322347  2322361  2322367  2322373  2322377  2322401  2322403  2322409
2322431  2322443  2322457  2322479  2322487  2322491  2322493  2322497  2322569  2322571
2322577  2322583  2322629  2322631  2322637  2322647  2322667  2322673  2322707  2322713
2322757  2322763  2322779  2322791  2322797  2322821  2322851  2322857  2322869
2322911  2322917  2322949  2322953  2322961  2322967  2322973  2323001  2323003  2323021
2323031  2323037  2323039  2323081  2323099  2323121  2323127  2323151  2323157  2323177
2323201  2323213  2323229  2323231  2323259  2323261  2323273  2323297  2323309  2323313
2323331  2323337  2323367  2323369  2323379  2323381  2323397  2323403  2323411  2323421
2323423  2323427  2323439  2323457  2323459  2323463  2323549  2323561  2323571  2323583
2323609  2323613  2323631  2323669  2323691  2323693  2323697  2323703  2323721  2323733
2323777  2323787  2323793  2323801  2323813  2323817  2323819  2323823  2323831  2323837
2323847  2323873  2323877  2323889  2323907  2323939  2323949  2323969  2323987  2323999
2324033  2324093  2324117  2324123  2324129  2324133  2324143  2324149  2324159  2324171
2324177  2324183  2324191  2324233  2324237  2324261  2324269  2324281  2324317  2324351
2324353  2324381  2324419  2324447  2324453  2324459  2324467  2324471  2324501  2324503
2324507  2324513  2324521  2324533  2324551  2324557  2324617  2324639  2324653  2324667
2324681  2324683  2324701  2324711  2324731  2324743  2324779  2324809  2324851  2324867
2324873  2324879  2324899  2324929  2324941  2324953  2324957  2324981  2324999  2325007
2325023  2325061  2325067  2325077  2325083  2325097  2325143  2325149  2325173  2325181
2325199  2325203  2325227  2325241  2325251  2325263  2325289  2325299  2325317  2325319
2325343  2325361  2325377  2325437  2325439  2325469  2325493  2325509  2325511  2325517
2325529  2325559  2325563  2325571  2325613  2325623  2325629  2325647  2325671  2325677
2325689  2325703  2325749  2325761  2325767  2325773  2325779  2325793  2325797  2325803
2325811  2325823  2325833  2325871  2325881  2325901  2325907  2325919  2325943  2326007
2326019  2326021  2326033  2326057  2326063  2326067  2326081  2326087  2326091  2326097
2326099  2326109  2326133  2326141  2326183  2326201  2326211  2326213  2326249  2326267
2326277  2326279  2326283  2326309  2326319  2326327  2326349  2326361  2326367  2326369
2326409  2326421  2326439  2326447  2326451  2326459  2326469  2326481  2326483  2326487
2326507  2326517  2326553  2326567  2326579  2326613  2326633  2326661  2326663  2326669
2326673  2326693  2326717  2326733  2326747  2326763  2326769  2326771  2326781  2326789
2326799  2326813  2326847  2326853  2326871  2326889  2326903  2326913  2326921  2326927
2326937  2326957  2326963  2326991  2326993  2327027  2327029  2327033  2327051  2327053
2327057  2327069  2327081  2327099  2327107  2327123  2327131  2327153  2327173  2327183
2327191  2327197  2327207  2327233  2327239  2327243  2327251  2327257  2327293  2327323
2327341  2327359  2327371  2327383  2327399  2327401  2327407  2327411  2327441  2327467
2327473  2327483  2327497  2327509  2327527  2327539  2327551  2327579  2327597  2327599
2327603  2327629  2327639  2327641  2327651  2327653  2327681  2327683  2327701  2327711
2327723  2327729  2327737  2327747  2327749  2327753  2327771  2327777  2327789  2327797
2327849  2327851  2327867  2327869  2327879  2327887  2327909  2327911  2327921  2327933
2327951  2327953  2327959  2327987  2328047  2328071  2328107  2328113
2328119  2328143  2328169  2328173  2328181  2328211  2328217  2328229  2328251  2328259
2328281  2328283  2328289  2328307  2328311  2328331  2328341  2328377  2328397  2328401
2328409  2328413  2328461  2328463  2328479  2328509  2328517  2328523  2328533  2328539
2328559  2328563  2328569  2328617  2328619  2328631  2328637  2328649  2328653  2328691
2328707  2328713  2328761  2328763  2328769  2328781  2328827  2328829  2328853  2328857
2328869  2328883  2328889  2328899  2328913  2328941  2328947  2328967  2328971  2328973
2329027  2329031  2329037  2329073  2329081  2329091  2329097  2329133  2329147  2329189
2329207  2329213  2329241  2329259  2329277  2329291  2329303  2329319  2329331
2329337  2329339  2329387  2329399  2329469  2329471  2329487  2329499  2329507  2329513
2329517  2329519  2329549  2329553  2329559  2329567  2329577  2329583  2329597  2329603
2329637  2329667  2329669  2329687  2329699  2329709  2329729  2329751  2329763  2329777
2329801  2329807  2329813  2329819  2329849  2329871  2329879  2329883  2329891  2329937
2329949  2329961  2329967  2329979  2329997  2330021  2330047  2330051  2330099  2330101
2330117  2330123  2330143  2330147  2330161  2330191  2330197  2330201  2330203  2330221
```

2330227 2330249 2330281 2330303 2330387 2330389 2330413 2330423 2330431 2330459
2330473 2330491 2330501 2330539 2330543 2330551 2330561 2330591 2330617 2330633
2330641 2330663 2330681 2330687 2330689 2330719 2330753 2330761 2330771 2330789
2330827 2330833 2330837 2330849 2330869 2330873 2330879 2330893 2330899 2330903
2330927 2330929 2330941 2330947 2330953 2330957 2330959 2331041 2331047 2331061
2331089 2331097 2331103 2331113 2331127 2331139 2331151 2331163 2331187 2331191
2331253 2331271 2331283 2331299 2331323 2331337 2331353 2331361 2331367 2331377
2331379 2331391 2331409 2331419 2331421 2331443 2331451 2331463 2331557 2331577
2331583 2331587 2331599 2331613 2331647 2331649 2331653 2331677 2331689 2331691
2331697 2331733 2331743 2331751 2331767 2331779 2331781 2331829 2331859 2331869
2331871 2331887 2331899 2331929 2331937 2331949 2331997 2332013 2332027 2332049
2332061 2332103 2332123 2332129 2332139 2332153 2332181 2332219 2332237 2332241
2332249 2332259 2332289 2332303 2332313 2332321 2332327 2332333 2332339 2332373
2332381 2332387 2332391 2332397 2332399 2332403 2332427 2332439 2332483 2332487
2332501 2332507 2332511 2332513 2332523 2332529 2332537 2332541 2332567 2332597
2332607 2332643 2332651 2332661 2332663 2332667 2332679 2332691 2332697 2332703
2332711 2332721 2332783 2332787 2332817 2332829 2332833 2332849 2332871 2332903
2332931 2332933 2332937 2332951 2332969 2332987 2332997 2333017 2333041 2333059
2333069 2333081 2333083 2333087 2333099 2333119 2333129 2333147 2333161 2333167
2333173 2333179 2333197 2333203 2333207 2333231 2333237 2333239 2333293 2333297
2333321 2333323 2333329 2333347 2333377 2333381 2333389 2333399 2333407 2333459
2333467 2333473 2333477 2333483 2333497 2333501 2333531 2333533 2333549 2333579
2333593 2333609 2333621 2333647 2333651 2333657 2333663 2333689 2333693 2333707
2333719 2333731 2333759 2333767 2333783 2333791 2333797 2333801 2333809 2333831
2333819 2333839 2333857 2333867 2333869 2333873 2333887 2333893 2333909 2333927
2333939 2333951 2333953 2333957 2333993 2333999 2334001 2334019 2334023 2334027
2334047 2334061 2334077 2334091 2334097 2334107 2334127 2334139 2334179 2334187
2334223 2334229 2334251 2334257 2334259 2334263 2334281 2334301 2334307 2334317
2334329 2334337 2334361 2334373 2334377 2334391 2334401 2334403 2334407 2334421
2334439 2334463 2334503 2334509 2334539 2334547 2334557 2334583 2334623 2334643
2334679 2334691 2334743 2334751 2334767 2334769 2334779 2334781 2334793 2334803
2334823 2334841 2334863 2334881 2334901 2334911 2334923 2334947 2334949 2334953
2334961 2334989 2335009 2335037 2335057 2335063 2335079 2335097 2335111 2335117
2335133 2335139 2335147 2335153 2335183 2335187 2335211 2335217 2335219 2335231
2335241 2335243 2335247 2335253 2335297 2335303 2335321 2335363 2335367 2335369
2335381 2335393 2335427 2335433 2335459 2335481 2335519 2335523 2335547 2335549
2335561 2335577 2335591 2335601 2335607 2335637 2335639 2335649 2335661 2335667
2335679 2335691 2335693 2335709 2335721 2335733 2335769 2335789 2335807 2335813
2335843 2335849 2335871 2335877 2335891 2335909 2335913 2335933 2335967 2335969
2335997 2336011 2336017 2336023 2336027 2336039 2336053 2336063 2336093 2336101
2336111 2336119 2336137 2336149 2336197 2336189 2336207 2336209 2336227 2336251
2336263 2336281 2336287 2336309 2336311 2336333 2336353 2336359 2336381 2336393
2336407 2336413 2336431 2336437 2336441 2336447 2336461 2336471 2336473 2336479
2336489 2336519 2336527 2336557 2336561 2336569 2336573 2336597 2336623 2336629
2336671 2336707 2336743 2336771 2336783 2336801 2336821 2336839 2336843 2336861
2336863 2336881 2336887 2336903 2336923 2336963 2336969 2336983 2336989 2336989
2336993 2337001 2337029 2337043 2337047 2337067 2337073 2337079 2337089 2337091
2337119 2337149 2337151 2337157 2337163 2337187 2337193 2337217 2337221 2337227
2337233 2337271 2337299 2337311 2337317 2337319 2337343 2337359 2337367 2337389
2337397 2337463 2337479 2337481 2337497 2337509 2337527 2337539 2337541 2337547
2337553 2337571 2337593 2337607 2337613 2337637 2337641 2337667 2337677 2337683
2337691 2337701 2337737 2337761 2337773 2337793 2337821 2337851 2337859 2337869
2337871 2337889 2337899 2337901 2337911 2337913 2337949 2337967 2337983 2338003
2338043 2338079 2338081 2338093 2338097 2338103 2338123 2338151 2338153 2338169
2338181 2338207 2338213 2338247 2338261 2338267 2338283 2338291 2338331 2338351
2338381 2338403 2338411 2338421 2338471 2338471 2338489 2338493 2338507 2338541
2338543 2338549 2338559 2338603 2338607 2338619 2338627 2338631 2338643 2338657
2338667 2338697 2338703 2338717 2338723 2338747 2338751 2338757 2338783 2338799
2338823 2338849 2338867 2338871 2338873 2338883 2338901 2338933 2338949 2338951
2338969 2338997 2339011 2339021 2339039 2339041 2339089 2339101 2339107 2339119
2339131 2339137 2339179 2339191 2339221 2339257 2339263 2339287 2339297 2339303
2339317 2339321 2339327 2339333 2339369 2339371 2339417 2339423 2339429 2339461
2339507 2339551 2339563 2339569 2339581 2339609 2339611 2339627 2339639 2339651
2339657 2339669 2339671 2339677 2339681 2339683 2339713 2339719 2339731 2339741
2339773 2339783 2339797 2339803 2339809 2339833 2339861 2339879 2339899 2339903
2339927 2339929 2339933 2339963 2339969 2339977 2340001 2340007 2340011 2340029
2340061 2340071 2340119 2340133 2340167 2340179 2340187 2340193 2340209 2340223
2340241 2340251 2340253 2340257 2340259 2340269 2340277 2340313 2340337 2340341
2340347 2340367 2340383 2340397 2340419 2340421 2340431 2340451 2340461 2340479
2340487 2340491 2340493 2340521 2340551 2340563 2340581 2340587 2340607 2340617
2340659 2340661 2340673 2340697 2340703 2340719 2340721 2340727 2340739 2340757
2340763 2340769 2340773 2340787 2340797 2340803 2340823 2340827 2340847 2340859
2340869 2340887 2340889 2340911 2340931 2340937 2340959 2340973 2340979 2340983
2341033 2341057 2341069 2341091 2341103 2341111 2341127 2341133 2341159 2341201
2341217 2341219 2341243 2341271 2341301 2341303 2341309 2341327 2341333 2341343
2341349 2341369 2341379 2341403 2341411 2341421 2341433 2341447 2341453 2341457
2341459 2341463 2341477 2341511 2341531 2341567 2341571 2341589 2341601 2341609
2341613 2341637 2341643 2341673 2341687 2341697 2341727 2341747 2341751 2341763
2341777 2341817 2341819 2341847 2341853 2341861 2341873 2341877 2341897 2341907
2341919 2341943 2341967 2341979 2341981 2341987 2341991 2341993 2341999 2342003
2342027 2342029 2342033 2342047 2342051 2342071 2342099 2342101 2342129 2342173
2342189 2342191 2342201 2342203 2342227 2342231 2342237 2342239 2342257 2342269
2342287 2342293 2342309 2342357 2342363 2342381 2342393 2342399 2342401 2342407
2342419 2342423 2342437 2342443 2342479 2342513 2342537 2342539 2342609 2342611
2342623 2342633 2342657 2342663 2342671 2342687 2342699 2342723 2342731 2342741
2342771 2342773 2342777 2342779 2342783 2342797 2342807 2342819 2342839 2342869
2342933 2342953 2342959 2342969 2342981 2342983 2342993 2343001 2343013 2343017
2343031 2343037 2343049 2343053 2343083 2343139 2343157 2343163 2343169 2343179
2343203 2343223 2343233 2343239 2343241 2343269 2343283 2343293 2343307 2343311

```
2343329  2343343  2343349  2343359  2343361  2343389  2343409  2343413  2343449  2343487
2343521  2343527  2343529  2343533  2343541  2343547  2343553  2343571  2343589  2343611
2343613  2343619  2343641  2343643  2343661  2343667  2343743  2343763  2343767  2343779
2343787  2343791  2343793  2343799  2343833  2343857  2343881  2343883  2343889  2343899
2343917  2343949  2343967  2343989  2343997  2344019  2344033  2344037  2344051  2344073
2344117  2344123  2344141  2344151  2344159  2344187  2344193  2344241  2344253  2344259
2344261  2344267  2344271  2344297  2344301  2344319  2344327  2344333  2344337  2344361
2344379  2344387  2344409  2344417  2344427  2344439  2344457  2344469  2344471  2344519
2344523  2344553  2344571  2344603  2344607  2344627  2344649  2344651  2344661  2344673
2344697  2344703  2344709  2344717  2344723  2344751  2344753  2344777  2344787
2344789  2344819  2344889  2344921  2344939  2344943  2344967  2344973  2344981  2344987
2345009  2345017  2345033  2345039  2345041  2345047  2345053  2345087  2345117  2345129
2345131  2345141  2345153  2345179  2345209  2345219  2345249  2345257  2345261  2345279
2345297  2345327  2345339  2345351  2345377  2345383  2345401  2345443  2345459  2345461
2345477  2345479  2345501  2345509  2345533  2345537  2345543  2345573  2345593  2345599
2345617  2345641  2345657  2345659  2345669  2345699  2345713  2345729  2345731  2345743
2345753  2345803  2345807  2345809  2345831  2345843  2345867  2345869  2345887  2345891
2345909  2345921  2345923  2345953  2345957  2345963  2345969  2345971  2345989  2346089
2346107  2346137  2346167  2346191  2346203  2346217  2346241  2346259  2346269  2346271
2346277  2346313  2346343  2346347  2346349  2346397  2346413  2346431  2346473  2346521
2346523  2346551  2346559  2346581  2346587  2346611  2346623  2346653  2346677  2346719
2346727  2346733  2346739  2346769  2346779  2346781  2346791  2346803  2346821  2346829
2346847  2346857  2346859  2346863  2346887  2346913  2346931  2346959  2346973  2346977
2346997  2347001  2347031  2347043  2347049  2347063  2347067  2347129  2347141  2347151
2347153  2347171  2347183  2347201  2347217  2347229  2347237  2347249  2347253  2347271
2347273  2347277  2347283  2347297  2347313  2347337  2347339  2347361  2347369  2347379
2347409  2347421  2347427  2347439  2347441  2347447  2347451  2347453  2347487  2347493
2347511  2347523  2347549  2347559  2347561  2347567  2347573  2347577  2347591  2347627
2347663  2347693  2347703  2347711  2347721  2347727  2347733  2347759  2347777  2347781
2347789  2347823  2347831  2347837  2347841  2347859  2347871  2347883  2347903  2347907
2347931  2347949  2347957  2347981  2347991  2347997  2347999  2348011  2348053  2348081
2348083  2348089  2348119  2348123  2348161  2348179  2348189  2348197  2348207  2348221
2348233  2348237  2348239  2348251  2348257  2348293  2348299  2348303  2348321  2348347
2348371  2348383  2348429  2348441  2348447  2348459  2348471  2348473  2348477  2348491
2348497  2348539  2348569  2348573  2348579  2348581  2348597  2348627  2348693  2348701
2348707  2348713  2348729  2348741  2348743  2348747  2348759  2348791  2348807  2348809
2348813  2348833  2348851  2348861  2348891  2348897  2348903  2348909  2348911  2348947
2348959  2348987  2348999  2349001  2349023  2349031  2349041  2349071  2349079  2349091
2349097  2349101  2349143  2349161  2349163  2349181  2349209  2349233  2349251  2349253
2349271  2349301  2349307  2349313  2349317  2349323  2349329  2349337  2349343  2349353
2349367  2349371  2349419  2349433  2349497  2349499  2349541  2349547  2349569  2349637
2349643  2349653  2349679  2349701  2349709  2349719  2349727  2349731  2349773  2349779
2349799  2349803  2349811  2349829  2349869  2349871  2349889  2349913  2349917  2349937
2349947  2349959  2349973  2350001  2350021  2350031  2350033  2350057  2350067  2350069
2350081  2350093  2350099  2350111  2350123  2350157  2350181  2350193  2350207  2350211
2350217  2350219  2350237  2350241  2350259  2350279  2350289  2350291  2350303  2350307
2350321  2350331  2350333  2350339  2350349  2350379  2350399  2350409  2350429  2350441
2350457  2350463  2350483  2350507  2350529  2350541  2350549  2350559  2350567  2350583
2350591  2350599  2350609  2350613  2350631  2350633  2350657  2350679  2350687  2350697
2350703  2350717  2350723  2350741  2350753  2350763  2350771  2350781  2350793  2350837
2350841  2350847  2350861  2350867  2350877  2350883  2350891  2350903  2350951  2350969
2350979  2350993  2351029  2351033  2351047  2351053  2351099  2351101  2351137  2351147
2351159  2351171  2351201  2351207  2351263  2351281  2351303  2351317  2351339
2351347  2351351  2351353  2351357  2351441  2351477  2351501  2351507  2351509  2351513
2351519  2351533  2351579  2351597  2351599  2351603  2351617  2351641  2351653  2351693
2351731  2351743  2351747  2351749  2351759  2351761  2351771  2351779  2351803  2351821
2351827  2351837  2351857  2351863  2351891  2351897  2351903  2351941  2351963  2351969
2351989  2352011  2352023  2352037  2352041  2352043  2352061  2352073  2352079  2352083
2352101  2352107  2352113  2352131  2352139  2352149  2352151  2352157  2352173  2352191
2352199  2352223  2352227  2352241  2352247  2352269  2352289  2352323  2352353  2352403
2352433  2352473  2352479  2352481  2352521  2352533  2352557  2352563  2352569  2352577
2352583  2352589  2352611  2352619  2352631  2352641  2352643  2352653  2352661  2352671
2352673  2352677  2352689  2352761  2352767  2352781  2352787  2352797  2352803  2352811
2352841  2352881  2352887  2352899  2352901  2352913  2352937  2352947  2352971  2352989
2353027  2353049  2353051  2353063  2353069  2353073  2353103  2353121  2353129  2353159
2353177  2353187  2353193  2353217  2353223  2353279  2353297  2353303  2353369  2353387
2353391  2353399  2353411  2353423  2353453  2353457  2353487  2353499  2353501  2353517
2353529  2353577  2353591  2353597  2353601  2353609  2353621  2353639  2353649  2353651
2353657  2353661  2353697  2353699  2353709  2353717  2353723  2353759  2353781  2353787
2353801  2353817  2353823  2353831  2353849  2353867  2353873  2353877  2353913  2353919
2353927  2353931  2353943  2353951  2353957  2353979  2353987  2353991  2353993  2354039
2354059  2354063  2354069  2354083  2354087  2354111  2354123  2354137  2354141  2354153
2354161  2354167  2354189  2354197  2354203  2354213  2354227  2354239  2354251  2354263
2354281  2354299  2354311  2354351  2354353  2354413  2354459  2354467  2354479  2354489
2354491  2354497  2354501  2354503  2354531  2354549  2354591  2354593  2354603  2354609
2354621  2354623  2354633  2354641  2354663  2354701  2354711  2354731  2354743  2354773
2354797  2354801  2354813  2354819  2354831  2354837  2354873  2354897  2354899  2354923
2354927  2354941  2354951  2354953  2354969  2355011  2355019  2355037  2355043  2355047
2355079  2355083  2355097  2355109  2355113  2355121  2355137  2355139  2355151  2355169
2355173  2355181  2355191  2355209  2355211  2355233  2355247  2355253  2355257  2355263
2355277  2355289  2355307  2355317  2355329  2355337  2355347  2355359  2355377  2355389
2355403  2355433  2355439  2355443  2355481  2355517  2355527  2355533  2355539  2355557
2355559  2355581  2355629  2355671  2355677  2355697  2355719  2355733  2355759  2355763
2355799  2355853  2355883  2355889  2355917  2355949  2355971  2355973  2356001  2356021
2356049  2356069  2356073  2356091  2356103  2356127  2356129  2356139  2356141  2356153
2356169  2356187  2356199  2356213  2356219  2356259  2356267  2356303  2356307  2356313
2356339  2356349  2356351  2356363  2356379  2356381  2356391  2356397  2356411  2356423
2356427  2356429  2356451  2356463  2356469  2356531  2356547  2356553  2356573  2356583
2356597  2356609  2356621  2356643  2356661  2356663  2356681  2356687  2356691  2356699
```

```
2356763  2356771  2356793  2356799  2356813  2356831  2356843  2356867  2356883  2356891
2356901  2356903  2356919  2356927  2356933  2356943  2356973  2356997  2357009  2357027
2357029  2357039  2357057  2357059  2357071  2357077  2357099  2357119  2357153  2357167
2357183  2357189  2357219  2357231  2357249  2357263  2357279  2357287  2357297  2357321
2357347  2357351  2357353  2357357  2357363  2357371  2357417  2357419  2357423  2357437
2357483  2357507  2357527  2357533  2357549  2357573  2357587  2357591  2357617  2357629
2357639  2357657  2357683  2357689  2357701  2357717  2357731  2357737  2357741  2357743
2357749  2357791  2357801  2357807  2357809  2357813  2357821  2357837  2357851  2357863
2357867  2357879  2357909  2357921  2357923  2357933  2357939  2357941  2357963  2357969
2357977  2358007  2358011  2358017  2358043  2358049  2358073  2358091  2358127  2358133
2358137  2358143  2358151  2358157  2358179  2358203  2358221  2358227  2358241  2358247
2358283  2358311  2358329  2358331  2358353  2358371  2358373  2358379  2358401  2358403
2358409  2358431  2358439  2358463  2358487  2358497  2358539  2358547  2358571  2358583
2358617  2358623  2358637  2358661  2358677  2358701  2358721  2358737  2358739  2358743
2358751  2358779  2358781  2358799  2358823  2358827  2358841  2358859  2358877  2358887
2358893  2358899  2358901  2358911  2358913  2358919  2358953  2358991  2359001  2359013
2359031  2359033  2359043  2359051  2359061  2359067  2359079  2359103  2359111  2359129
2359139  2359151  2359163  2359171  2359183  2359187  2359207  2359213  2359219  2359223
2359229  2359241  2359261  2359267  2359303  2359307  2359319  2359333  2359339  2359349
2359369  2359381  2359391  2359393  2359397  2359403  2359429  2359451  2359459  2359463
2359471  2359499  2359519  2359537  2359559  2359561  2359603  2359619  2359633  2359649
2359661  2359681  2359717  2359723  2359739  2359769  2359783  2359789  2359793  2359801
2359829  2359831  2359843  2359849  2359873  2359891  2359901  2359921  2359927  2359949
2359963  2359993  2359997  2360003  2360021  2360023  2360027  2360069  2360087  2360089
2360101  2360117  2360131  2360147  2360167  2360173  2360201  2360203  2360207  2360219
2360243  2360279  2360291  2360311  2360321  2360353  2360357  2360363  2360377  2360381
2360417  2360419  2360443  2360459  2360483  2360497  2360509  2360521  2360539  2360543
2360551  2360591  2360593  2360597  2360609  2360621  2360653  2360707  2360713  2360719
2360723  2360749  2360753  2360759  2360797  2360833  2360849  2360851  2360869  2360873
2360887  2360899  2360957  2360971  2360983  2360987  2360999  2361017  2361031  2361041
2361043  2361071  2361083  2361089  2361103  2361109  2361119  2361133  2361167  2361179
2361199  2361211  2361221  2361241  2361253  2361257  2361269  2361323  2361343  2361349
2361353  2361367  2361379  2361397  2361407  2361413  2361427  2361461  2361467  2361473
2361497  2361503  2361509  2361539  2361553  2361577  2361589  2361607  2361629  2361631
2361637  2361649  2361701  2361713  2361721  2361727  2361773  2361781  2361803  2361809
2361823  2361851  2361883  2361899  2361911  2361913  2361917  2361937  2361941  2361943
2361959  2361977  2361991  2362001  2362007  2362013  2362049  2362057  2362067  2362091
2362109  2362111  2362141  2362147  2362153  2362159  2362163  2362181  2362187  2362193
2362229  2362247  2362249  2362271  2362273  2362277  2362279  2362309  2362319  2362331
2362343  2362351  2362363  2362411  2362421  2362433  2362457  2362483  2362489  2362501
2362559  2362571  2362573  2362589  2362637  2362639  2362649  2362651  2362657  2362681
2362691  2362699  2362729  2362733  2362747  2362751  2362753  2362757  2362769  2362771
2362777  2362781  2362799  2362817  2362819  2362873  2362879  2362901  2362909  2362939
2362961  2362963  2362967  2362981  2363021  2363027  2363029  2363033  2363041  2363047
2363059  2363063  2363069  2363077  2363107  2363149  2363159  2363167  2363171  2363177
2363189  2363191  2363197  2363203  2363209  2363213  2363219  2363233  2363261  2363267
2363293  2363303  2363311  2363327  2363359  2363393  2363399  2363401  2363423  2363441
2363453  2363461  2363497  2363507  2363513  2363531  2363539  2363563  2363617  2363623
2363639  2363651  2363653  2363681  2363707  2363741  2363743  2363749  2363783  2363789
2363797  2363807  2363831  2363857  2363861  2363873  2363891  2363903  2363909  2363927
2363939  2363941  2363947  2363957  2363971  2363981  2363983  2364001  2364013  2364017
2364049  2364067  2364077  2364079  2364119  2364121  2364127  2364133  2364149  2364161
2364163  2364179  2364191  2364199  2364203  2364211  2364221  2364223  2364247  2364281
2364287  2364289  2364293  2364301  2364317  2364353  2364361  2364367  2364407  2364409
2364413  2364433  2364437  2364449  2364487  2364491  2364499  2364517  2364521  2364563
2364589  2364599  2364601  2364611  2364619  2364623  2364629  2364643  2364647  2364667
2364673  2364679  2364709  2364727  2364743  2364767  2364793  2364799  2364809  2364833
2364841  2364847  2364851  2364877  2364881  2364889  2364907  2364917  2364937  2364941
2364953  2364991  2365001  2365007  2365009  2365049  2365061  2365073  2365079  2365093
2365109  2365169  2365201  2365213  2365217  2365241  2365243  2365267  2365271  2365277
2365283  2365289  2365309  2365313  2365351  2365357  2365381  2365399  2365411  2365421
2365423  2365427  2365439  2365457  2365459  2365469  2365471  2365511  2365523  2365537
2365541  2365547  2365553  2365589  2365591  2365603  2365607  2365613  2365621  2365631
2365637  2365639  2365667  2365681  2365721  2365751  2365787  2365789  2365829  2365859
2365879  2365901  2365921  2365963  2365969  2365981  2365997  2365999  2366011  2366017
2366029  2366053  2366057  2366059  2366071  2366083  2366087  2366099  2366123  2366131
2366141  2366173  2366183  2366191  2366207  2366209  2366227  2366237  2366267  2366297
2366303  2366311  2366347  2366369  2366387  2366389  2366407  2366423  2366443  2366453
2366459  2366473  2366477  2366489  2366491  2366513  2366521  2366527  2366537  2366543
2366629  2366669  2366647  2366653  2366657  2366669  2366681  2366687  2366701  2366711
2366731  2366743  2366747  2366789  2366797  2366801  2366809  2366827  2366831  2366843
2366851  2366867  2366933  2366939  2366957  2366989  2366993  2367007  2367019  2367037
2367049  2367059  2367073  2367083  2367119  2367121  2367143  2367151  2367179  2367187
2367203  2367221  2367251  2367259  2367269  2367289  2367293  2367329  2367331  2367341
2367347  2367361  2367389  2367397  2367401  2367427  2367433  2367467  2367481  2367487
2367509  2367511  2367523  2367553  2367557  2367569  2367583  2367601  2367619  2367649
2367653  2367671  2367679  2367691  2367707  2367721  2367731  2367767  2367793  2367797
2367809  2367817  2367823  2367829  2367857  2367863  2367877  2367899  2367923  2367929
2367931  2367949  2367971  2367973  2367977  2367983  2368013  2368033  2368039  2368043
2368097  2368109  2368127  2368129  2368153  2368159  2368181  2368187  2368211  2368213
2368229  2368237  2368271  2368273  2368297  2368309  2368313  2368337  2368357  2368361
2368381  2368391  2368393  2368403  2368409  2368417  2368433  2368439  2368441  2368451
2368463  2368469  2368477  2368501  2368511  2368523  2368537  2368557  2368567  2368577
2368589  2368601  2368603  2368637  2368649  2368727  2368733  2368757  2368759  2368771
2368783  2368799  2368801  2368829  2368841  2368843  2368859  2368871  2368907  2368937
2368957  2368963  2368979  2368991  2368997  2369033  2369063  2369071  2369077  2369093
2369099  2369117  2369123  2369149  2369173  2369183  2369197  2369201  2369203  2369209
2369219  2369231  2369233  2369251  2369261  2369291  2369303  2369347  2369351  2369363
2369371  2369383  2369413  2369441  2369449  2369453  2369459  2369467  2369473  2369489
```

```
2369519  2369527  2369537  2369539  2369557  2369569  2369593  2369597  2369603  2369611
2369639  2369641  2369651  2369707  2369711  2369747  2369761  2369779  2369791  2369819
2369827  2369831  2369837  2369839  2369849  2369863  2369867  2369903  2369929  2369951
2369957  2369977  2369993  2369999  2370007  2370019  2370023  2370037  2370047  2370061
2370073  2370103  2370113  2370149  2370197  2370217  2370223  2370239  2370241  2370253
2370281  2370287  2370299  2370301  2370317  2370323  2370343  2370359  2370377  2370391
2370409  2370427  2370451  2370457  2370469  2370481  2370499  2370503  2370517  2370523
2370551  2370559  2370569  2370581  2370593  2370607  2370623  2370629  2370631  2370647
2370659  2370671  2370673  2370677  2370689  2370703  2370733  2370737  2370811  2370829
2370833  2370847  2370881  2370889  2370917  2370937  2370941  2370943  2370947  2370983
2371003  2371021  2371073  2371087  2371091  2371099  2371111  2371123  2371129  2371133
2371141  2371147  2371157  2371183  2371189  2371207  2371223  2371247  2371261  2371267
2371297  2371307  2371309  2371337  2371351  2371361  2371423  2371427  2371459  2371489
2371511  2371543  2371609  2371627  2371631  2371639  2371651  2371661  2371669  2371673
2371679  2371693  2371703  2371709  2371711  2371729  2371739  2371763  2371771  2371801
2371819  2371847  2371849  2371861  2371871  2371877  2371879  2371883  2371927  2371937
2371961  2371969  2371991  2372011  2372023  2372053  2372081  2372087  2372099  2372101
2372119  2372179  2372191  2372221  2372239  2372257  2372303  2372309  2372317  2372327
2372347  2372369  2372371  2372393  2372413  2372417  2372423  2372431  2372437  2372441
2372443  2372453  2372459  2372467  2372479  2372501  2372507  2372509  2372521  2372543
2372561  2372563  2372581  2372597  2372599  2372633  2372641  2372659  2372681  2372683
2372687  2372731  2372737  2372743  2372753  2372759  2372761  2372779  2372789  2372807
2372819  2372837  2372857  2372861  2372873  2372879  2372893  2372897  2372927  2372941
2372947  2372959  2372963  2372971  2372987  2372989  2372999  2373001  2373029  2373037
2373061  2373067  2373079  2373089  2373097  2373103  2373109  2373131  2373139  2373167
2373169  2373179  2373187  2373193  2373211  2373221  2373227  2373229  2373247  2373253
2373263  2373269  2373277  2373281  2373307  2373311  2373323  2373337  2373373  2373383
2373401  2373403  2373407  2373409  2373431  2373463  2373487  2373529  2373533  2373583
2373611  2373649  2373667  2373691  2373697  2373731  2373751  2373773  2373821  2373823
2373869  2373893  2373907  2373913  2373919  2373929  2373947  2373953  2373967  2373971
2373979  2373989  2374007  2374051  2374061  2374063  2374081  2374109  2374117  2374121
2374133  2374147  2374153  2374157  2374189  2374199  2374213  2374261  2374277  2374289
2374291  2374301  2374319  2374343  2374363  2374391  2374397  2374399  2374429  2374439
2374447  2374483  2374511  2374517  2374523  2374529  2374531  2374553  2374571  2374579
2374583  2374591  2374633  2374643  2374649  2374699  2374717  2374733  2374751  2374811
2374831  2374837  2374859  2374873  2374903  2374963  2374979  2374997  2375011  2375033
2375039  2375041  2375047  2375059  2375069  2375111  2375119  2375159  2375167  2375179
2375183  2375203  2375207  2375221  2375231  2375237  2375249  2375267  2375273  2375299
2375309  2375327  2375339  2375341  2375353  2375383  2375389  2375411  2375431  2375459
2375473  2375479  2375491  2375497  2375501  2375557  2375573  2375603  2375617  2375641
2375671  2375687  2375701  2375713  2375719  2375743  2375759  2375761  2375771  2375773
2375777  2375783  2375797  2375819  2375833  2375837  2375843  2375917  2375921  2375929
2375939  2375957  2375963  2375977  2375981  2375993  2376013  2376047  2376053  2376079
2376089  2376097  2376109  2376113  2376139  2376149  2376161  2376163  2376167  2376169
2376191  2376203  2376229  2376239  2376247  2376263  2376271  2376293  2376301  2376317
2376323  2376329  2376331  2376359  2376371  2376391  2376397  2376419  2376421  2376433
2376443  2376449  2376457  2376469  2376529  2376533  2376541  2376559  2376571  2376581
2376593  2376599  2376607  2376611  2376623  2376629  2376641  2376643  2376667  2376683
2376707  2376721  2376757  2376769  2376809  2376817  2376827  2376851  2376859
2376877  2376883  2376929  2376943  2376949  2376961  2376967  2376971  2376989  2377003
2377007  2377019  2377021  2377069  2377079  2377097  2377117  2377121  2377157  2377163
2377187  2377201  2377241  2377253  2377259  2377267  2377273  2377283  2377321  2377339
2377351  2377357  2377367  2377379  2377381  2377393  2377411  2377423  2377429  2377447
2377471  2377477  2377481  2377493  2377499  2377553  2377559  2377591  2377601  2377621
2377673  2377693  2377699  2377703  2377721  2377729  2377741  2377747  2377751  2377757
2377769  2377787  2377789  2377799  2377801  2377841  2377883  2377889  2377927  2377939
2377967  2377981  2377997  2378009  2378023  2378069  2378071  2378107  2378111  2378119
2378143  2378171  2378179  2378191  2378197  2378219  2378221  2378237  2378263  2378273
2378291  2378293  2378297  2378303  2378357  2378359  2378371  2378399  2378423  2378443
2378447  2378461  2378473  2378479  2378483  2378491  2378501  2378507  2378513  2378539
2378543  2378549  2378569  2378617  2378627  2378633  2378641  2378653  2378669  2378671
2378681  2378699  2378711  2378737  2378749  2378771  2378773  2378791  2378797  2378801
2378807  2378843  2378869  2378891  2378917  2378927  2378951  2378953  2378977  2378993
2379001  2379007  2379023  2379037  2379067  2379077  2379079  2379149  2379151  2379173
2379191  2379203  2379217  2379239  2379241  2379253  2379259  2379277  2379283  2379317
2379323  2379331  2379341  2379347  2379383  2379397  2379413  2379431  2379437  2379449
2379451  2379457  2379493  2379499  2379521  2379547  2379569  2379571  2379599  2379613
2379623  2379631  2379659  2379673  2379683  2379691  2379697  2379703  2379721  2379733
2379737  2379757  2379761  2379781  2379791  2379799  2379809  2379851  2379857  2379899
2379929  2379931  2379941  2379953  2379973  2379989  2380003  2380013  2380031  2380043
2380069  2380121  2380123  2380129  2380141  2380207  2380223  2380229  2380241
2380249  2380253  2380271  2380297  2380303  2380333  2380363  2380369  2380373  2380379
2380387  2380393  2380421  2380423  2380439  2380463  2380471  2380481  2380487
2380489  2380517  2380519  2380531  2380537  2380541  2380589  2380607  2380613  2380619
2380621  2380627  2380633  2380657  2380667  2380673  2380717  2380727  2380733  2380739
2380751  2380759  2380771  2380787  2380793  2380801  2380811  2380837  2380841  2380853
2380877  2380897  2380907  2380921  2380951  2380957  2380997  2381011  2381033  2381053
2381077  2381081  2381083  2381087  2381101  2381107  2381117  2381143  2381147
2381149  2381153  2381179  2381189  2381191  2381201  2381221  2381231  2381243  2381263
2381273  2381287  2381303  2381311  2381317  2381339  2381343  2381347  2381359
2381363  2381387  2381413  2381429  2381437  2381453  2381473  2381497  2381503  2381507
2381521  2381527  2381543  2381569  2381573  2381591  2381609  2381629  2381633  2381651
2381657  2381677  2381689  2381693  2381737  2381749  2381773  2381777  2381783  2381791
2381807  2381839  2381849  2381861  2381879  2381881  2381891  2381893  2381909  2381941
2381957  2381963  2381969  2381971  2381983  2381999  2382001  2382073  2382103  2382109
2382119  2382151  2382169  2382173  2382181  2382187  2382203  2382217  2382221  2382251
2382269  2382283  2382299  2382301  2382307  2382313  2382323  2382337  2382371  2382377
2382389  2382407  2382449  2382451  2382461  2382463  2382473  2382481  2382487  2382491
2382511  2382521  2382529  2382539  2382557  2382559  2382563  2382607  2382613  2382637
```

```
2382649  2382671  2382697  2382701  2382707  2382713  2382739  2382749  2382761  2382769
2382781  2382803  2382811  2382817  2382829  2382851  2382857  2382859  2382871  2382881
2382883  2382899  2382917  2382937  2382943  2382953  2382977  2382979  2383019  2383033
2383049  2383081  2383091  2383127  2383141  2383163  2383169  2383177  2383219  2383253
2383261  2383291  2383301  2383309  2383313  2383327  2383333  2383343  2383393  2383397
2383411  2383427  2383439  2383457  2383477  2383483  2383487  2383501  2383517  2383561
2383567  2383571  2383573  2383613  2383631  2383637  2383643  2383649  2383657  2383673
2383679  2383681  2383739  2383751  2383753  2383763  2383811  2383813  2383817  2383841
2383847  2383867  2383883  2383891  2383907  2383919  2383921  2383933  2383943  2383991
2383999  2384017  2384023  2384033  2384047  2384051  2384059  2384071  2384077  2384143
2384153  2384183  2384197  2384257  2384269  2384279  2384297  2384323  2384339  2384363
2384381  2384383  2384401  2384407  2384411  2384419  2384461  2384483  2384497  2384513
2384521  2384533  2384537  2384561  2384567  2384579  2384581  2384587  2384609  2384611
2384623  2384647  2384653  2384659  2384689  2384713  2384729  2384749  2384771  2384783
2384797  2384803  2384813  2384821  2384831  2384843  2384849  2384869  2384881  2384891
2384897  2384911  2384951  2384953  2384971  2385023  2385041  2385073  2385107  2385113
2385121  2385139  2385157  2385181  2385191  2385199  2385209  2385211  2385239  2385259
2385263  2385281  2385293  2385319  2385323  2385329  2385343  2385349  2385433  2385451
2385463  2385499  2385541  2385553  2385571  2385587  2385599  2385601  2385611  2385619
2385637  2385653  2385679  2385701  2385703  2385709  2385727  2385739  2385751  2385787
2385809  2385827  2385829  2385847  2385857  2385863  2385881  2385883  2385907  2385919
2385931  2385947  2385953  2385959  2385961  2385979  2385983  2385989  2385991  2386003
2386009  2386031  2386051  2386057  2386061  2386063  2386067  2386079  2386099  2386121
2386127  2386133  2386169  2386177  2386183  2386187  2386193  2386211  2386217  2386247
2386271  2386277  2386283  2386289  2386291  2386301  2386309  2386313  2386369  2386379
2386393  2386399  2386429  2386453  2386459  2386469  2386471  2386481  2386493  2386507
2386513  2386547  2386567  2386577  2386591  2386603  2386627  2386639  2386661  2386663
2386667  2386679  2386739  2386753  2386757  2386763  2386771  2386777  2386781  2386789
2386793  2386823  2386859  2386861  2386873  2386877  2386883  2386889  2386921  2386939
2386957  2386999  2387003  2387017  2387023  2387039  2387041  2387051  2387053  2387087
2387107  2387111  2387117  2387137  2387149  2387167  2387171  2387183  2387197  2387201
2387207  2387221  2387237  2387243  2387249  2387269  2387291  2387299  2387303  2387311
2387347  2387353  2387383  2387393  2387401  2387417  2387419  2387431  2387447  2387449
2387453  2387467  2387477  2387501  2387507  2387513  2387533  2387537  2387543  2387563
2387569  2387579  2387591  2387621  2387629  2387687  2387729  2387753  2387767  2387807
2387821  2387839  2387843  2387851  2387857  2387867  2387873  2387897  2387909  2387911
2387923  2387927  2387941  2387951  2387953  2387969  2387971  2388013  2388019  2388031
2388037  2388059  2388083  2388097  2388101  2388103  2388157  2388161  2388163  2388173
2388181  2388187  2388223  2388229  2388247  2388257  2388259  2388277  2388283  2388293
2388317  2388329  2388359  2388361  2388371  2388377  2388403  2388409  2388443  2388473
2388479  2388499  2388539  2388557  2388559  2388563  2388569  2388583  2388593  2388611
2388629  2388637  2388641  2388649  2388667  2388677  2388679  2388689  2388697  2388703
2388769  2388797  2388833  2388839  2388863  2388871  2388877  2388887  2388899  2388901
2388907  2388913  2388929  2388961  2388983  2389001  2389021  2389031  2389043  2389063
2389067  2389073  2389097  2389103  2389109  2389141  2389181  2389183  2389213  2389241
2389243  2389249  2389259  2389279  2389297  2389313  2389319  2389351  2389379  2389391
2389403  2389427  2389451  2389463  2389481  2389499  2389501  2389507  2389523  2389529
2389531  2389547  2389567  2389577  2389589  2389591  2389613  2389619  2389633  2389637
2389643  2389657  2389661  2389663  2389669  2389693  2389721  2389729  2389733  2389747
2389757  2389781  2389799  2389813  2389831  2389841  2389847  2389853  2389859  2389873
2389879  2389889  2389901  2389921  2389931  2389939  2389951  2389967  2389969  2389973
2389993  2390009  2390021  2390023  2390033  2390051  2390053  2390057  2390071  2390077
2390099  2390111  2390117  2390123  2390147  2390159  2390191  2390197  2390207  2390221
2390243  2390249  2390263  2390291  2390299  2390309  2390329  2390351  2390383  2390411
2390417  2390429  2390431  2390449  2390471  2390473  2390477  2390519  2390539  2390543
2390579  2390611  2390617  2390623  2390653  2390699  2390711  2390723  2390737  2390743
2390753  2390767  2390779  2390797  2390803  2390809  2390819  2390831  2390849  2390879
2390887  2390893  2390909  2390911  2390917  2390923  2390951  2390957  2390987  2391001
2391013  2391019  2391023  2391041  2391043  2391049  2391071  2391083  2391089  2391091
2391097  2391107  2391113  2391119  2391127  2391157  2391167  2391227  2391239  2391269
2391281  2391289  2391293  2391331  2391349  2391401  2391437  2391439  2391449  2391451
2391461  2391469  2391491  2391503  2391523  2391527  2391533  2391539  2391541  2391547
2391559  2391583  2391589  2391629  2391637  2391671  2391691  2391709  2391721  2391733
2391737  2391751  2391769  2391799  2391827  2391847  2391859  2391863  2391881  2391889
2391937  2391947  2391953  2391973  2391979  2391997  2392001  2392003  2392009  2392021
2392057  2392073  2392079  2392099  2392127  2392139  2392147  2392163  2392183
2392193  2392249  2392267  2392279  2392289  2392303  2392307  2392319  2392333  2392337
2392343  2392349  2392361  2392373  2392421  2392433  2392447  2392459  2392463  2392469
2392501  2392517  2392519  2392541  2392547  2392561  2392571  2392573  2392591  2392619
2392661  2392669  2392681  2392697  2392711  2392717  2392729  2392751  2392757  2392777
2392781  2392787  2392811  2392849  2392861  2392891  2392919  2392929  2392961  2392967
2392991  2392997  2393011  2393021  2393023  2393029  2393063  2393071  2393077  2393101
2393119  2393137  2393161  2393177  2393179  2393189  2393233  2393257  2393263  2393291
2393327  2393351  2393389  2393407  2393431  2393467  2393473  2393497  2393507  2393519
2393537  2393543  2393561  2393581  2393591  2393627  2393647  2393653  2393659  2393683
2393687  2393707  2393717  2393723  2393759  2393761  2393773  2393819  2393837  2393849
2393857  2393869  2393873  2393879  2393893  2393899  2393917  2393927  2393929  2393933
2393947  2393959  2393971  2393987  2394023  2394053  2394061  2394071  2394079
2394083  2394097  2394101  2394109  2394121  2394149  2394151  2394157  2394163  2394167
2394187  2394193  2394199  2394221  2394239  2394241  2394257  2394299  2394313  2394317
2394319  2394341  2394377  2394383  2394419  2394421  2394451  2394479  2394481  2394499
2394503  2394527  2394563  2394571  2394611  2394629  2394631  2394641  2394643  2394649
2394659  2394673  2394683  2394731  2394737  2394761  2394787  2394793  2394823  2394857
2394863  2394871  2394881  2394913  2394919  2394941  2394961  2395009  2395021  2395031
2395039  2395051  2395103  2395117  2395157  2395163  2395177  2395189  2395193  2395213
2395241  2395271  2395279  2395291  2395303  2395307  2395319  2395333  2395357  2395373
2395391  2395397  2395399  2395403  2395411  2395433  2395489  2395499  2395511  2395529
2395537  2395541  2395583  2395621  2395643  2395651  2395681  2395693  2395721  2395727
2395739  2395741  2395747  2395763  2395769  2395807  2395823  2395847  2395849  2395867
```

```
2395871  2395873  2395879  2395889  2395901  2395927  2395973  2396029  2396039  2396041
2396047  2396057  2396063  2396101  2396113  2396123  2396129  2396131  2396137  2396153
2396171  2396189  2396197  2396213  2396227  2396237  2396239  2396243  2396257  2396309
2396311  2396323  2396333  2396341  2396353  2396369  2396377  2396399  2396411  2396419
2396423  2396467  2396497  2396509  2396533  2396539  2396543  2396561  2396567  2396587
2396591  2396593  2396627  2396633  2396651  2396659  2396683  2396687  2396701  2396731
2396741  2396743  2396759  2396767  2396789  2396803  2396833  2396839  2396851  2396861
2396887  2396903  2396917  2396921  2396923  2396941  2396959  2396969  2396981  2396987
2397001  2397007  2397011  2397041  2397049  2397061  2397071  2397077  2397091  2397103
2397107  2397113  2397127  2397133  2397139  2397151  2397167  2397179  2397181  2397191
2397203  2397209  2397217  2397251  2397259  2397277  2397299  2397319  2397371  2397377
2397383  2397397  2397403  2397449  2397463  2397467  2397481  2397487  2397491  2397503
2397511  2397523  2397529  2397541  2397569  2397581  2397587  2397601  2397613  2397617
2397631  2397641  2397649  2397677  2397683  2397713  2397719  2397793  2397821  2397823
2397827  2397839  2397847  2397851  2397853  2397869  2397907  2397917  2397931  2397947
2397949  2397961  2397991  2398001  2398021  2398027  2398051  2398057  2398061  2398073
2398087  2398103  2398111  2398133  2398147  2398157  2398159  2398169  2398171  2398177
2398181  2398183  2398189  2398211  2398223  2398243  2398247  2398259  2398261  2398267
2398273  2398289  2398303  2398307  2398321  2398339  2398349  2398367  2398369  2398379
2398391  2398423  2398433  2398441  2398471  2398477  2398481  2398483  2398493  2398499
2398507  2398523  2398537  2398549  2398553  2398559  2398567  2398573  2398577  2398597
2398603  2398607  2398633  2398637  2398657  2398661  2398679  2398681  2398699  2398777
2398789  2398849  2398861  2398867  2398889  2398901  2398919  2398931  2398961  2398987
2399011  2399017  2399027  2399029  2399039  2399041  2399081  2399087  2399093  2399113
2399119  2399129  2399143  2399167  2399171  2399207  2399213  2399231  2399237  2399249
2399273  2399291  2399317  2399323  2399333  2399359  2399381  2399387  2399389  2399399
2399407  2399461  2399477  2399479  2399497  2399519  2399531  2399539  2399543  2399549
2399581  2399597  2399599  2399611  2399627  2399629  2399633  2399641  2399647  2399653
2399671  2399689  2399699  2399711  2399713  2399717  2399753  2399759  2399791  2399807
2399809  2399821  2399869  2399897  2399911  2399921  2399933  2399939  2399951  2399977
2399983  2399993  2400011  2400019  2400031  2400037  2400053  2400067  2400089  2400107
2400109  2400143  2400157  2400161  2400163  2400169  2400187  2400191  2400197  2400221
2400253  2400259  2400271  2400283  2400311  2400323  2400329  2400347  2400353  2400367
2400407  2400413  2400469  2400473  2400481  2400511  2400521  2400551  2400557  2400571
2400577  2400589  2400613  2400623  2400661  2400667  2400703  2400709  2400719  2400767
2400793  2400799  2400817  2400841  2400849  2400851  2400863  2400869  2400883  2400917
2400907  2400917  2400929  2400949  2400971  2400989  2401013  2401019  2401031  2401037
2401103  2401111  2401117  2401127  2401159  2401169  2401181  2401207  2401211  2401219
2401237  2401253  2401261  2401279  2401303  2401307  2401339  2401367  2401381  2401393
2401409  2401423  2401447  2401457  2401463  2401489  2401501  2401513  2401517  2401537
2401541  2401547  2401549  2401561  2401571  2401579  2401583  2401603  2401621  2401639
2401667  2401669  2401673  2401703  2401727  2401741  2401807  2401871  2401891  2401897
2401939  2401967  2401969  2401991  2402009  2402027  2402039  2402053  2402087  2402089
2402093  2402107  2402173  2402177  2402201  2402203  2402209  2402233  2402249  2402249
2402261  2402263  2402291  2402293  2402297  2402317  2402329  2402333  2402353  2402369
2402381  2402383  2402401  2402431  2402441  2402461  2402467  2402479  2402483  2402497
2402501  2402509  2402537  2402549  2402567  2402573  2402579  2402597  2402611  2402633
2402639  2402651  2402663  2402677  2402707  2402731  2402747  2402753  2402761  2402773
2402789  2402791  2402819  2402837  2402839  2402849  2402857  2402867  2402909  2402921
2402927  2402951  2402999  2403007  2403013  2403019  2403029  2403047  2403053  2403061
2403077  2403083  2403091  2403119  2403127  2403131  2403161  2403169  2403173  2403209
2403211  2403229  2403263  2403277  2403281  2403287  2403301  2403311  2403319  2403343
2403347  2403361  2403371  2403377  2403383  2403389  2403403  2403407  2403413  2403419
2403451  2403463  2403469  2403487  2403509  2403517  2403521  2403547  2403551  2403553
2403581  2403587  2403589  2403593  2403619  2403629  2403659  2403673  2403677  2403679
2403689  2403691  2403697  2403701  2403773  2403787  2403833  2403841  2403871  2403883
2403889  2403911  2403913  2403931  2403941  2403959  2403971  2403977  2404009  2404033
2404037  2404043  2404067  2404069  2404079  2404089  2404099  2404111  2404139  2404147
2404151  2404159  2404177  2404211  2404229  2404247  2404253  2404289  2404291  2404313
2404333  2404349  2404357  2404387  2404399  2404411  2404421  2404441  2404459  2404471
2404483  2404529  2404541  2404543  2404613  2404631  2404643  2404669  2404679  2404687
2404723  2404733  2404747  2404751  2404757  2404771  2404777  2404783  2404789  2404807
2404813  2404819  2404823  2404847  2404891  2404897  2404907  2404911  2404919  2404931
2404933  2404957  2404991  2404993  2405003  2405021  2405027  2405063  2405069  2405071
2405089  2405093  2405107  2405141  2405147  2405149  2405171  2405203  2405209  2405213
2405239  2405243  2405251  2405261  2405269  2405297  2405311  2405327  2405339  2405341
2405353  2405369  2405387  2405393  2405399  2405437  2405441  2405443  2405461  2405497
2405509  2405527  2405539  2405561  2405563  2405573  2405587  2405591  2405621  2405633
2405651  2405677  2405701  2405707  2405729  2405737  2405741  2405749  2405773  2405791
2405797  2405813  2405831  2405833  2405863  2405867  2405881  2405911  2405917  2405929
2405971  2405981  2405983  2405987  2406023  2406067  2406083  2406091  2406097  2406121
2406133  2406139  2406149  2406161  2406169  2406199  2406227  2406233  2406241  2406263
2406277  2406289  2406307  2406343  2406373  2406379  2406457  2406461  2406463  2406469
2406529  2406539  2406553  2406557  2406583  2406617  2406619  2406629  2406631  2406643
2406647  2406661  2406671  2406683  2406689  2406709  2406721  2406727  2406731  2406763
2406769  2406773  2406779  2406793  2406799  2406821  2406847  2406851  2406919  2406941
2406947  2406959  2406983  2406991  2406997  2407001  2407003  2407033  2407049  2407073
2407079  2407099  2407103  2407117  2407127  2407147  2407159  2407169  2407177  2407189
2407193  2407201  2407211  2407219  2407231  2407247  2407253  2407267  2407271  2407277
2407297  2407309  2407333  2407337  2407343  2407351  2407399  2407403  2407411  2407417
2407423  2407459  2407463  2407469  2407499  2407507  2407513  2407519  2407529  2407543
2407549  2407567  2407577  2407579  2407583  2407597  2407633  2407651  2407687  2407697
2407703  2407711  2407723  2407733  2407753  2407771  2407781  2407799  2407817  2407877
2407883  2407891  2407903  2407943  2407963  2408009  2408011  2408039  2408057  2408069
2408093  2408099  2408113  2408141  2408149  2408171  2408179  2408201  2408213  2408227
2408239  2408257  2408279  2408281  2408303  2408309  2408311  2408317  2408389  2408431
2408437  2408501  2408503  2408507  2408513  2408561  2408563  2408569  2408587  2408603
2408639  2408647  2408657  2408671  2408683  2408689  2408723  2408729  2408741  2408759
2408761  2408771  2408773  2408837  2408843  2408863  2408869  2408899  2408933  2408957
```

```
2408969 2408971 2408981 2408983 2408993 2408999 2409023 2409031 2409061 2409091
2409109 2409131 2409133 2409137 2409149 2409157 2409163 2409167 2409191 2409193
2409203 2409217 2409229 2409259 2409269 2409271 2409299 2409301 2409307 2409311
2409313 2409347 2409353 2409367 2409373 2409377 2409389 2409391 2409397 2409401
2409431 2409437 2409467 2409469 2409487 2409493 2409509 2409541 2409559 2409569
2409593 2409601 2409607 2409613 2409679 2409689 2409709 2409727 2409731 2409769
2409791 2409817 2409829 2409833 2409839 2409859 2409863 2409893 2409907 2409947
2409983 2409997 2410027 2410043 2410081 2410117 2410123 2410127 2410153 2410181
2410183 2410189 2410201 2410249 2410271 2410273 2410313 2410337 2410339 2410351
2410357 2410361 2410367 2410381 2410391 2410417 2410433 2410453 2410483 2410517
2410519 2410523 2410553 2410559 2410571 2410579 2410589 2410601 2410613 2410621
2410627 2410631 2410643 2410649 2410657 2410687 2410693 2410697 2410703 2410711
2410717 2410721 2410729 2410747 2410783 2410813 2410829 2410831 2410847 2410867
2410897 2410907 2410927 2410931 2410937 2410939 2410943 2410949 2410997 2410999
2411009 2411011 2411027 2411029 2411033 2411041 2411069 2411077 2411107 2411111
2411131 2411177 2411191 2411197 2411203 2411207 2411209 2411219 2411221 2411239
2411243 2411257 2411287 2411291 2411293 2411351 2411371 2411393 2411413 2411441
2411449 2411471 2411489 2411503 2411543 2411551 2411567 2411581 2411587 2411593
2411597 2411627 2411639 2411641 2411663 2411669 2411699 2411729 2411737 2411777
2411797 2411821 2411833 2411837 2411867 2411869 2411881 2411957 2411963 2411971
2412013 2412019 2412023 2412029 2412037 2412041 2412073 2412077 2412089 2412119
2412127 2412131 2412143 2412197 2412199 2412209 2412233 2412239 2412247 2412271
2412287 2412299 2412301 2412323 2412331 2412337 2412341 2412349 2412379 2412391
2412407 2412409 2412439 2412457 2412461 2412467 2412479 2412491 2412541 2412547
2412551 2412593 2412617 2412629 2412643 2412647 2412653 2412667 2412671 2412679
2412689 2412703 2412721 2412731 2412749 2412763 2412779 2412797 2412799 2412803
2412811 2412821 2412833 2412847 2412853 2412857 2412877 2412899 2412941 2412959
2412961 2413001 2413007 2413043 2413051 2413063 2413097 2413111 2413123 2413153
2413163 2413189 2413211 2413217 2413223 2413231 2413241 2413253 2413259 2413261
2413267 2413291 2413297 2413331 2413339 2413349 2413357 2413373 2413379 2413421
2413423 2413427 2413429 2413451 2413469 2413471 2413483 2413493 2413511 2413517
2413519 2413531 2413549 2413553 2413559 2413573 2413577 2413601 2413603 2413613
2413637 2413639 2413657 2413679 2413693 2413721 2413727 2413739 2413751 2413771
2413777 2413783 2413819 2413823 2413849 2413861 2413871 2413883 2413909 2413913
2413921 2413927 2413933 2413951 2413963 2413973 2413981 2413987 2413993 2414021
2414053 2414081 2414089 2414099 2414101 2414107 2414117 2414123 2414129 2414131
2414171 2414177 2414179 2414201 2414207 2414219 2414231 2414239 2414261 2414263
2414281 2414299 2414341 2414353 2414371 2414389 2414393 2414411 2414413 2414417
2414443 2414491 2414507 2414513 2414543 2414549 2414551 2414557 2414567 2414591
2414593 2414597 2414611 2414681 2414689 2414717 2414749 2414761 2414771 2414779
2414791 2414803 2414827 2414849 2414851 2414861 2414887 2414897 2414911 2414921
2414927 2414933 2414947 2414959 2414963 2414981 2414983 2414989 2414999 2415013
2415031 2415051 2415073 2415079 2415103 2415137 2415143 2415151 2415167 2415191
2415197 2415209 2415221 2415233 2415239 2415271 2415293 2415319 2415359 2415379
2415389 2415407 2415409 2415431 2415443 2415449 2415463 2415473 2415487 2415499
2415503 2415521 2415533 2415541 2415557 2415559 2415571 2415593 2415607 2415629
2415631 2415653 2415689 2415691 2415701 2415703 2415719 2415733 2415769 2415779
2415839 2415859 2415863 2415871 2415893 2415913 2415937 2415947 2415997 2416003
2416009 2416013 2416039 2416061 2416067 2416093 2416103 2416123 2416133 2416147
2416153 2416157 2416163 2416177 2416189 2416207 2416229 2416231 2416241 2416243
2416247 2416259 2416273 2416283 2416289 2416301 2416303 2416307 2416313 2416327
2416331 2416361 2416369 2416391 2416399 2416409 2416423 2416441 2416451 2416459
2416487 2416493 2416501 2416517 2416577 2416597 2416607 2416613 2416619 2416649
2416681 2416697 2416709 2416717 2416721 2416727 2416741 2416751 2416763 2416807
2416837 2416849 2416859 2416861 2416867 2416871 2416903 2416913 2416927 2416943
2416963 2416969 2417017 2417021 2417027 2417029 2417033 2417083 2417087 2417089
2417117 2417119 2417131 2417141 2417153 2417201 2417203 2417221 2417243 2417251
2417267 2417273 2417279 2417291 2417297 2417309 2417339 2417341 2417347 2417357
2417377 2417399 2417419 2417423 2417431 2417447 2417477 2417497 2417501 2417521
2417533 2417537 2417551 2417557 2417581 2417593 2417603 2417609 2417663 2417671
2417683 2417713 2417717 2417741 2417743 2417747 2417771 2417773 2417797 2417801
2417813 2417827 2417837 2417843 2417851 2417897 2417903 2417911 2417917 2417923
2417939 2417941 2417971 2417977 2417981 2417983 2417999 2418001
2418007 2418037 2418067 2418071 2418077 2418079 2418083 2418109 2418137 2418161
2418173 2418181 2418203 2418257 2418293 2418319 2418329 2418343 2418347 2418349
2418359 2418373 2418379 2418389 2418401 2418407 2418421 2418439 2418457 2418463
2418509 2418511 2418517 2418523 2418541 2418547 2418553 2418557 2418613 2418659
2418671 2418673 2418677 2418679 2418683 2418697 2418701 2418721 2418733 2418737
2418769 2418781 2418791 2418799 2418821 2418839 2418851 2418859 2418863 2418883
2418893 2418907 2418943 2418983 2418967 2419007 2419013 2419019 2419033 2419057
2419063 2419069 2419073 2419091 2419103 2419127 2419159 2419181 2419187 2419229
2419237 2419247 2419259 2419273 2419331 2419343 2419363 2419379 2419387 2419421
2419433 2419463 2419489 2419493 2419507 2419523 2419553 2419561 2419579 2419583
2419589 2419597 2419601 2419603 2419619 2419621 2419639 2419679 2419693 2419709
2419717 2419721 2419723 2419733 2419741 2419771 2419777 2419787 2419793 2419799
2419801 2419811 2419819 2419867 2419871 2419873 2419883 2419913 2419919 2419939
2419979 2419981 2419987 2419993 2420009 2420017 2420051 2420063 2420071 2420111
2420113 2420123 2420167 2420179 2420213 2420237 2420251 2420261 2420269 2420279
2420287 2420291 2420309 2420321 2420333 2420339 2420371 2420377 2420399 2420417
2420423 2420459 2420471 2420479 2420519 2420531 2420549 2420557 2420567 2420569
2420609 2420611 2420633 2420687 2420689 2420699 2420701 2420707 2420723 2420767
2420779 2420801 2420807 2420813 2420827 2420839 2420849 2420863 2420867 2420879
2420897 2420917 2420921 2420941 2420959 2420969 2420981 2420989 2420993 2421021
2421043 2421047 2421053 2421061 2421073 2421077 2421109 2421119 2421137 2421149
2421163 2421203 2421229 2421247 2421253 2421277 2421281 2421283 2421311 2421319
2421329 2421343 2421347 2421383 2421389 2421403 2421407 2421421 2421439 2421443
2421449 2421451 2421467 2421469 2421473 2421491 2421511 2421527 2421533 2421541
2421547 2421553 2421577 2421589 2421593 2421641 2421649 2421659 2421673 2421707
2421733 2421737 2421743 2421767 2421781 2421791 2421817 2421821 2421823 2421841
```

```
2421847  2421893  2421901  2421907  2421917  2421919  2421931  2421943  2421959  2421971
2421989  2421997  2422027  2422033  2422037  2422073  2422087  2422093  2422099  2422111
2422169  2422171  2422183  2422201  2422207  2422223  2422229  2422237  2422241  2422243
2422439  2422447  2422451  2422463  2422477  2422487  2422489  2422499  2422513  2422523
2422531  2422543  2422547  2422559  2422561  2422579  2422621  2422627  2422643  2422657
2422661  2422691  2422697  2422699  2422703  2422711  2422727  2422741  2422757  2422759
2422781  2422793  2422807  2422811  2422829  2422837  2422873  2422877  2422907  2422939
2422949  2422957  2422969  2422997  2422999  2423021  2423023  2423039  2423041  2423087
2423117  2423131  2423137  2423147  2423149  2423191  2423209  2423219  2423227  2423233
2423237  2423249  2423339  2423353  2423359  2423383  2423411  2423413  2423417  2423419
2423429  2423453  2423459  2423489  2423497  2423521  2423539  2423563  2423567  2423569
2423581  2423593  2423627  2423651  2423669  2423689  2423711  2423731  2423747  2423753
2423777  2423789  2423801  2423803  2423807  2423821  2423831  2423851  2423857  2423873
2423891  2423909  2423917  2423929  2423951  2423969  2423999  2424017  2424029  2424073
2424083  2424089  2424091  2424113  2424137  2424157  2424161  2424173  2424199  2424209
2424241  2424259  2424263  2424283  2424287  2424329  2424341  2424349  2424377  2424391
2424427  2424439  2424481  2424491  2424493  2424511  2424547  2424553  2424559  2424563
2424599  2424613  2424619  2424629  2424649  2424691  2424713  2424739  2424743  2424767
2424791  2424809  2424823  2424827  2424833  2424839  2424853  2424859  2424887  2424907
2424937  2424949  2424953  2424967  2424971  2424973  2424991  2424997  2425001  2425019
2425021  2425039  2425043  2425069  2425081  2425117  2425139  2425193  2425207  2425229
2425231  2425249  2425253  2425259  2425261  2425301  2425337  2425349  2425361  2425363
2425391  2425399  2425403  2425417  2425429  2425433  2425447  2425453  2425457  2425459
2425469  2425477  2425487  2425499  2425523  2425541  2425567  2425613  2425627  2425637
2425663  2425669  2425681  2425693  2425697  2425699  2425723  2425729  2425733  2425739
2425751  2425769  2425777  2425783  2425793  2425799  2425837  2425889  2425897  2425921
2425933  2425957  2425961  2425981  2425991  2426023  2426027  2426033  2426041  2426057
2426059  2426077  2426107  2426113  2426119  2426131  2426143  2426183  2426209  2426219
2426233  2426267  2426269  2426279  2426299  2426309  2426329  2426341  2426351  2426363
2426377  2426381  2426383  2426387  2426399  2426441  2426443  2426453  2426467  2426491
2426521  2426527  2426537  2426551  2426573  2426579  2426591  2426603  2426609  2426617
2426621  2426639  2426647  2426651  2426693  2426717  2426731  2426741  2426747  2426761
2426771  2426777  2426779  2426789  2426819  2426821  2426833  2426863  2426873  2426887
2426899  2426911  2426933  2426947  2426951  2426953  2426969  2426987  2427001  2427043
2427053  2427059  2427067  2427091  2427101  2427109  2427137  2427143  2427151  2427157
2427179  2427211  2427239  2427247  2427263  2427281  2427287  2427289  2427301  2427317
2427349  2427371  2427389  2427407  2427427  2427431  2427461  2427463  2427473  2427493
2427499  2427521  2427527  2427541  2427547  2427571  2427587  2427589  2427599  2427613
2427637  2427643  2427647  2427683  2427701  2427713  2427721  2427727  2427731  2427751
2427767  2427773  2427779  2427781  2427797  2427847  2427863  2427869  2427883  2427899
2427911  2427947  2427961  2427989  2428003  2428021  2428033  2428037  2428043  2428057
2428073  2428079  2428099  2428103  2428117  2428123  2428157  2428159  2428163  2428169
2428171  2428189  2428207  2428213  2428241  2428243  2428249  2428259  2428267  2428291
2428303  2428313  2428357  2428369  2428379  2428403  2428417  2428427  2428441  2428451
2428463  2428467  2428487  2428529  2428541  2428577  2428627  2428649  2428651  2428661
2428667  2428687  2428703  2428711  2428729  2428733  2428753  2428771  2428781  2428787
2428859  2428879  2428883  2428889  2428891  2428897  2428901  2428919  2428931  2428991
2428997  2428999  2429023  2429029  2429033  2429041  2429047  2429057  2429059  2429071
2429083  2429107  2429117  2429143  2429153  2429177  2429183  2429233  2429239  2429257
2429267  2429269  2429279  2429293  2429299  2429311  2429333  2429341  2429363  2429381
2429393  2429411  2429437  2429459  2429489  2429503  2429509  2429519  2429527  2429551
2429579  2429597  2429599  2429617  2429627  2429633  2429653  2429671  2429681  2429717
2429723  2429729  2429731  2429767  2429771  2429773  2429809  2429831  2429851  2429893
2429899  2429923  2429941  2429953  2429971  2429983  2430007  2430011  2430013  2430047
2430061  2430073  2430089  2430091  2430139  2430149  2430163  2430173  2430217  2430223
2430227  2430251  2430257  2430289  2430293  2430299  2430313  2430331  2430343  2430359
2430397  2430427  2430457  2430467  2430469  2430487  2430503  2430523  2430539  2430551
2430557  2430563  2430569  2430581  2430587  2430601  2430607  2430611  2430671  2430683
2430691  2430721  2430731  2430733  2430749  2430761  2430763  2430773  2430787  2430811
2430817  2430829  2430839  2430851  2430871  2430877  2430913  2430929  2430947  2430979
2430991  2430997  2431003  2431007  2431049  2431061  2431063  2431097  2431127  2431139
2431151  2431181  2431189  2431201  2431207  2431211  2431217  2431223  2431241  2431279
2431283  2431291  2431301  2431321  2431327  2431333  2431343  2431367  2431393  2431409
2431417  2431433  2431439  2431441  2431453  2431469  2431489  2431501  2431511  2431519
2431533  2431543  2431573  2431577  2431579  2431589  2431633  2431657  2431661  2431673
2431691  2431711  2431717  2431729  2431739  2431757  2431763  2431787  2431811  2431823
2431831  2431837  2431841  2431843  2431879  2431909  2431927  2431937  2431967  2431987
2431999  2432041  2432069  2432077  2432093  2432113  2432119  2432137  2432147  2432159
2432179  2432219  2432237  2432239  2432251  2432257  2432263  2432267  2432279  2432293
2432321  2432351  2432357  2432363  2432371  2432387  2432429  2432447  2432453  2432471
2432483  2432501  2432533  2432537  2432543  2432557  2432561  2432587  2432597  2432609
2432621  2432657  2432659  2432669  2432671  2432681  2432693  2432711  2432719  2432737
2432743  2432791  2432809  2432851  2432869  2432909  2432923  2432929  2432933  2432977
2432987  2432999  2433001  2433037  2433047  2433059  2433061  2433077  2433089  2433103
2433113  2433127  2433139  2433161  2433203  2433217  2433247  2433251  2433253  2433271
2433293  2433307  2433313  2433317  2433323  2433341  2433359  2433371  2433401  2433421
2433433  2433443  2433451  2433461  2433467  2433491  2433493  2433503  2433521  2433533
2433553  2433569  2433631  2433649  2433659  2433679  2433689  2433713  2433721  2433727
2433733  2433763  2433773  2433803  2433817  2433829  2433833  2433853  2433869  2433889
2433901  2433917  2433931  2433953  2433967  2433979  2434001  2434013  2434031  2434037
2434049  2434051  2434063  2434073  2434087  2434097  2434099  2434123  2434127  2434139
2434153  2434169  2434183  2434189  2434207  2434217  2434249  2434253  2434259  2434277
2434279  2434291  2434319  2434339  2434351  2434361  2434381  2434387  2434423  2434429
2434433  2434441  2434447  2434483  2434493  2434501  2434507  2434529  2434559  2434567
2434577  2434583  2434589  2434609  2434613  2434657  2434669  2434673  2434681  2434687
2434699  2434721  2434727  2434739  2434763  2434787  2434799  2434813  2434837  2434841
2434843  2434853  2434879  2434889  2434903  2434919  2434931  2434963  2434967  2434969
2434997  2435003  2435011  2435039  2435051  2435053  2435077  2435089  2435093  2435099
```

```
2435119 2435149 2435161 2435179 2435183 2435189 2435197 2435201 2435203 2435221
2435231 2435243 2435261 2435281 2435291 2435311 2435327 2435339 2435341 2435351
2435357 2435393 2435417 2435443 2435473 2435501 2435519 2435527 2435533 2435551
2435557 2435567 2435569 2435597 2435603 2435621 2435627 2435633 2435689 2435707
2435711 2435729 2435731 2435737 2435749 2435753 2435773 2435789 2435803 2435809
2435813 2435831 2435837 2435863 2435893 2435897 2435903 2435911 2435921 2435929
2435957 2435977 2436017 2436023 2436037 2436059 2436061 2436067 2436089 2436107
2436113 2436121 2436131 2436139 2436143 2436163 2436209 2436211 2436233 2436257
2436277 2436293 2436311 2436341 2436353 2436373 2436407 2436409 2436419 2436449
2436479 2436517 2436529 2436547 2436557 2436563 2436571 2436601 2436607 2436611
2436613 2436647 2436653 2436677 2436683 2436701 2436703 2436713 2436719 2436739
2436743 2436757 2436761 2436787 2436793 2436823 2436859 2436893 2436901 2436923
2436937 2436949 2436953 2436971 2436977 2436979 2437007 2437009 2437033 2437037
2437049 2437121 2437147 2437151 2437159 2437177 2437199 2437207 2437213 2437219
2437223 2437271 2437277 2437321 2437343 2437381 2437399 2437403 2437411 2437423
2437427 2437429 2437441 2437451 2437469 2437489 2437507 2437531 2437559 2437571
2437577 2437583 2437607 2437619 2437637 2437639 2437657 2437663 2437667 2437691
2437693 2437697 2437709 2437717 2437741 2437751 2437763 2437777 2437847 2437849
2437859 2437867 2437873 2437891 2437951 2437973 2437993 2437997 2437999 2438017
2438027 2438071 2438077 2438081 2438083 2438101 2438153 2438173 2438179 2438203
2438239 2438281 2438309 2438321 2438329 2438339 2438341 2438351 2438357 2438377
2438383 2438399 2438413 2438417 2438453 2438459 2438461 2438473 2438489 2438503
2438507 2438509 2438521 2438537 2438563 2438567 2438587 2438591 2438603 2438609
2438617 2438627 2438629 2438671 2438693 2438717 2438767 2438773 2438791 2438819
2438833 2438861 2438881 2438893 2438903 2438911 2438927 2438957 2438977 2439013
2439037 2439043 2439061 2439067 2439071 2439083 2439091 2439097 2439133 2439137
2439167 2439179 2439181 2439197 2439221 2439247 2439257 2439263 2439293 2439301
2439317 2439319 2439323 2439341 2439379 2439389 2439407 2439413 2439427 2439443
2439457 2439461 2439487 2439491 2439497 2439499 2439511 2439527 2439553 2439571
2439641 2439649 2439667 2439673 2439677 2439719 2439737 2439739 2439781 2439791
2439803 2439839 2439881 2439889 2439893 2439901 2439907 2439919 2439929 2439953
2439977 2439989 2439991 2440003 2440007 2440019 2440021 2440043 2440049 2440069
2440079 2440091 2440111 2440127 2440153 2440177 2440201 2440211 2440213 2440219
2440223 2440237 2440241 2440247 2440253 2440259 2440267 2440271 2440297 2440301
2440313 2440327 2440331 2440363 2440387 2440391 2440393 2440411 2440421 2440439
2440447 2440457 2440481 2440489 2440499 2440513 2440517 2440523 2440541 2440561
2440573 2440577 2440579 2440589 2440591 2440621 2440643 2440649 2440657 2440667
2440679 2440681 2440693 2440699 2440709 2440733 2440751 2440787 2440799 2440807
2440817 2440819 2440831 2440849 2440861 2440883 2440937 2440943 2440951 2440961
2440969 2440973 2440993 2441029 2441041 2441053 2441057 2441071 2441077 2441083
2441093 2441107 2441111 2441119 2441123 2441129 2441143 2441161 2441167 2441189
2441207 2441209 2441221 2441237 2441267 2441269 2441293 2441311 2441317 2441323
2441347 2441357 2441363 2441377 2441389 2441401 2441407 2441431 2441437 2441449
2441459 2441503 2441521 2441561 2441563 2441573 2441581 2441599 2441617 2441629
2441639 2441641 2441683 2441717 2441723 2441729 2441737 2441759 2441767 2441773
2441779 2441801 2441807 2441809 2441819 2441843 2441849 2441867 2441909 2441941
2441987 2442017 2442019 2442047 2442059 2442103 2442107 2442113 2442133 2442151
2442173 2442179 2442191 2442197 2442199 2442227 2442263 2442287 2442289 2442311
2442353 2442359 2442367 2442383 2442389 2442403 2442413 2442437 2442457 2442463
2442487 2442497 2442499 2442511 2442527 2442547 2442563 2442571 2442589 2442593
2442599 2442617 2442631 2442667 2442673 2442677 2442683 2442719 2442767 2442779
2442793 2442809 2442827 2442833 2442841 2442859 2442871 2442889 2442907 2442911
2442941 2442943 2442949 2442967 2442971 2442977 2443027 2443031 2443033 2443061
2443069 2443093 2443097 2443109 2443117 2443151 2443159 2443183 2443211 2443213
2443219 2443241 2443277 2443283 2443351 2443361 2443373 2443387 2443403 2443409
2443421 2443429 2443433 2443439 2443501 2443531 2443537 2443541 2443547 2443583
2443601 2443613 2443619 2443643 2443657 2443667 2443687 2443703 2443729 2443741
2443747 2443751 2443757 2443781 2443783 2443787 2443789 2443807 2443817 2443829
2443841 2443849 2443867 2443871 2443879 2443901 2443927 2443933 2443939 2443949
2443963 2443993 2443997 2443999 2444017 2444021 2444063 2444069 2444081 2444083
2444089 2444111 2444119 2444129 2444131 2444143 2444147 2444153 2444159 2444161
2444173 2444191 2444203 2444219 2444251 2444263 2444287 2444291 2444341 2444347
2444357 2444359 2444363 2444383 2444401 2444411 2444437 2444441 2444447 2444471
2444473 2444513 2444527 2444531 2444537 2444557 2444569 2444621 2444639 2444653
2444657 2444669 2444677 2444681 2444699 2444723 2444737 2444759 2444773 2444801
2444809 2444833 2444839 2444867 2444873 2444881 2444887 2444891 2444899 2444909
2444921 2444927 2444933 2444947 2444951 2444963 2444983 2445011 2445029 2445043
2445067 2445073 2445089 2445101 2445119 2445139 2445173 2445181 2445203 2445211
2445217 2445221 2445241 2445253 2445259 2445277 2445283 2445301 2445343 2445347
2445349 2445353 2445371 2445379 2445389 2445409 2445413 2445419 2445437 2445451
2445461 2445463 2445481 2445517 2445523 2445533 2445551 2445571 2445577 2445581
2445601 2445617 2445629 2445647 2445649 2445689 2445697 2445713 2445721 2445733
2445743 2445749 2445757 2445763 2445767 2445799 2445827 2445829 2445847 2445847
2445857 2445881 2445887 2445899 2445907 2445923 2445929 2445967 2445973 2445979
2445991 2446009 2446013 2446043 2446051 2446061 2446091 2446097 2446099 2446133
2446151 2446153 2446159 2446177 2446207 2446247 2446271 2446277 2446291 2446319
2446331 2446333 2446357 2446363 2446369 2446373 2446417 2446439 2446463 2446471
2446481 2446513 2446517 2446529 2446567 2446583 2446603 2446607 2446627 2446651
2446663 2446669 2446673 2446693 2446747 2446753 2446777 2446781 2446811 2446813
2446819 2446823 2446841 2446849 2446853 2446879 2446889 2446891 2446903 2446919
2446931 2446973 2446981 2447009 2447021 2447023 2447059 2447077 2447111 2447141
2447147 2447153 2447161 2447209 2447239 2447251 2447267 2447279 2447293 2447321
2447327 2447329 2447351 2447353 2447359 2447369 2447399 2447437 2447479 2447483
2447491 2447519 2447521 2447527 2447531 2447539 2447551 2447567 2447569 2447573
2447579 2447581 2447597 2447611 2447633 2447647 2447681 2447717 2447723 2447737
2447743 2447759 2447761 2447773 2447801 2447831 2447833 2447843 2447897 2447917
2447923 2447927 2447933 2447953 2447971 2447981 2448007 2448013 2448029 2448041
2448049 2448067 2448071 2448073 2448079 2448107 2448109 2448133 2448157 2448161
2448167 2448181 2448197 2448203 2448223 2448227 2448241 2448263 2448269 2448311
```

194

```
2448343  2448361  2448367  2448379  2448389  2448427  2448431  2448437  2448443  2448451
2448491  2448529  2448533  2448539  2448553  2448569  2448581  2448613  2448631  2448637
2448647  2448661  2448671  2448679  2448689  2448703  2448713  2448727  2448737  2448751
2448757  2448769  2448773  2448791  2448821  2448827  2448829  2448851  2448857  2448863
2448869  2448871  2448877  2448881  2448937  2448949  2448961  2448973  2448989
2449001  2449039  2449061  2449087  2449091  2449099  2449133  2449147  2449159  2449163
2449169  2449171  2449177  2449199  2449209  2449231  2449259  2449273  2449277  2449297
2449303  2449313  2449327  2449361  2449367  2449387  2449393  2449399  2449417  2449439
2449441  2449451  2449481  2449483  2449487  2449493  2449519  2449549  2449561  2449567
2449583  2449609  2449619  2449639  2449663  2449691  2449693  2449729  2449757  2449787
2449789  2449793  2449801  2449813  2449823  2449829  2449847  2449859  2449861  2449871
2449877  2449883  2449897  2449901  2449907  2449913  2449919  2449927  2449933  2449939
2449963  2449987  2449991  2449999  2450003  2450009  2450017  2450047  2450083  2450087
2450117  2450131  2450141  2450143  2450171  2450191  2450207  2450219  2450249  2450291
2450293  2450303  2450323  2450341  2450353  2450377  2450381  2450387  2450417  2450453
2450491  2450531  2450549  2450551  2450557  2450573  2450593  2450597  2450599  2450629
2450633  2450663  2450671  2450711  2450713  2450759  2450779  2450783  2450807  2450809
2450813  2450827  2450831  2450837  2450863  2450887  2450911  2450923  2450933  2450947
2450951  2450963  2450989  2450999  2451011  2451017  2451023  2451079  2451101  2451143
2451151  2451203  2451221  2451223  2451233  2451257  2451259  2451269  2451277  2451289
2451299  2451307  2451311  2451331  2451343  2451347  2451359  2451367  2451377  2451389
2451401  2451419  2451433  2451443  2451463  2451467  2451469  2451487  2451499  2451521
2451539  2451541  2451557  2451577  2451601  2451619  2451637  2451641  2451643  2451667
2451719  2451721  2451727  2451733  2451749  2451767  2451769  2451781  2451793  2451797
2451803  2451809  2451811  2451847  2451857  2451871  2451881  2451887  2451907  2451913
2451919  2451937  2451941  2451947  2451973  2451991  2452003  2452013  2452033  2452049
2452057  2452103  2452111  2452123  2452141  2452147  2452181  2452207  2452223  2452231
2452253  2452259  2452271  2452297  2452309  2452313  2452321  2452337  2452339  2452343
2452357  2452367  2452393  2452399  2452409  2452427  2452433  2452459  2452477  2452481
2452487  2452493  2452517  2452519  2452523  2452529  2452531  2452537  2452543  2452561
2452589  2452603  2452633  2452649  2452663  2452673  2452679  2452687  2452699  2452717
2452721  2452753  2452757  2452759  2452783  2452817  2452823  2452829  2452831  2452859
2452861  2452867  2452889  2452897  2452903  2452909  2452921  2452939  2452949  2452951
2452963  2453027  2453039  2453051  2453053  2453057  2453089  2453119  2453141  2453149
2453159  2453173  2453177  2453179  2453183  2453201  2453207  2453233  2453251  2453273
2453281  2453291  2453293  2453303  2453329  2453333  2453369  2453377  2453401  2453417
2453419  2453431  2453441  2453443  2453449  2453453  2453459  2453461  2453467  2453483
2453497  2453501  2453519  2453531  2453543  2453567  2453573  2453597  2453629  2453651
2453653  2453657  2453687  2453701  2453707  2453713  2453747  2453771  2453779  2453783
2453821  2453827  2453833  2453837  2453861  2453873  2453887  2453909  2453921  2453923
2453999  2454007  2454043  2454047  2454073  2454079  2454107  2454113  2454119
2454121  2454131  2454149  2454157  2454161  2454167  2454229  2454241  2454243  2454253
2454281  2454289  2454317  2454337  2454343  2454349  2454359  2454367  2454373  2454407
2454421  2454433  2454437  2454493  2454503  2454523  2454527  2454533  2454539  2454587
2454619  2454623  2454631  2454637  2454643  2454671  2454703  2454719  2454731  2454757
2454761  2454773  2454787  2454791  2454833  2454841  2454847  2454853  2454869  2454871
2454877  2454883  2454889  2454899  2454911  2454929  2454941  2454961  2455001  2455003
2455087  2455091  2455127  2455129  2455133  2455147  2455183  2455207  2455217  2455253
2455261  2455279  2455303  2455307  2455309  2455337  2455339  2455373  2455379  2455381
2455391  2455423  2455447  2455469  2455471  2455477  2455487  2455499  2455507  2455511
2455513  2455529  2455547  2455553  2455561  2455577  2455589  2455619  2455643  2455657
2455679  2455681  2455699  2455711  2455723  2455729  2455741  2455763  2455771  2455781
2455811  2455823  2455847  2455889  2455897  2455907  2455909  2455927  2455931  2455969
2455979  2455987  2456011  2456021  2456029  2456033  2456057  2456063  2456071  2456087
2456089  2456107  2456123  2456131  2456141  2456191  2456197  2456243  2456249  2456261
2456303  2456323  2456341  2456353  2456357  2456359  2456371  2456383  2456401  2456407
2456411  2456429  2456431  2456437  2456459  2456501  2456539  2456557  2456569  2456581
2456591  2456609  2456617  2456621  2456627  2456639  2456647  2456651  2456693  2456711
2456731  2456743  2456747  2456749  2456759  2456767  2456801  2456803  2456807  2456849
2456869  2456879  2456917  2456939  2456963  2456981  2456983  2456989  2456999  2457001
2457011  2457031  2457047  2457073  2457079  2457121  2457127  2457139  2457179  2457193
2457227  2457241  2457283  2457293  2457307  2457311  2457317  2457319  2457337  2457341
2457347  2457349  2457353  2457361  2457383  2457397  2457421  2457439  2457449  2457461
2457467  2457473  2457487  2457509  2457529  2457563  2457569  2457607  2457613  2457617
2457641  2457647  2457667  2457703  2457709  2457727  2457731  2457733  2457737  2457781
2457797  2457817  2457823  2457839  2457869  2457887  2457899  2457901  2457943  2457967
2457971  2457997  2458003  2458019  2458031  2458039  2458051  2458061  2458063  2458097
2458109  2458121  2458133  2458139  2458151  2458177  2458199  2458213  2458223
2458229  2458249  2458279  2458283  2458303  2458321  2458327  2458333  2458343  2458349
2458367  2458369  2458373  2458403  2458409  2458411  2458427  2458433  2458451  2458457
2458459  2458481  2458487  2458501  2458537  2458549  2458553  2458571  2458583  2458601
2458607  2458609  2458633  2458639  2458661  2458663  2458667  2458669  2458679  2458681
2458747  2458759  2458793  2458817  2458827  2458831  2458843  2458873  2458877  2458879
2458891  2458901  2458903  2458921  2458927  2458949  2458991  2459003  2459011  2459027
2459029  2459053  2459059  2459069  2459099  2459123  2459129  2459141  2459143  2459153
2459161  2459201  2459209  2459239  2459257  2459273  2459291  2459293  2459311  2459329
2459357  2459363  2459371  2459381  2459383  2459389  2459393  2459411  2459423  2459437
2459449  2459473  2459477  2459489  2459491  2459497  2459563  2459579  2459591  2459617
2459621  2459623  2459657  2459659  2459663  2459701  2459707  2459711  2459731  2459741
2459749  2459753  2459767  2459769  2459773  2459777  2459789  2459791  2459801  2459813
2459843  2459857  2459861  2459869  2459879  2459909  2459921  2459923  2459953  2459957
2459993  2460013  2460043  2460061  2460083  2460097  2460113  2460127  2460137  2460151
2460161  2460181  2460187  2460193  2460197  2460217  2460229  2460277  2460281  2460299
2460301  2460373  2460397  2460407  2460421  2460431  2460433  2460467  2460473  2460487
2460493  2460509  2460511  2460527  2460539  2460547  2460551  2460559  2460581  2460587
2460593  2460607  2460617  2460629  2460637  2460641  2460643  2460649  2460669  2460673
2460677  2460707  2460719  2460721  2460743  2460781  2460791  2460797  2460803  2460817
2460827  2460859  2460863  2460877  2460881  2460883  2460889  2460901  2460917  2460919
2460947  2460959  2460961  2460973  2460989  2461001  2461021  2461031  2461037  2461091
```

```
2461093 2461099 2461103 2461139 2461153 2461163 2461169 2461171 2461187 2461223
2461229 2461231 2461237 2461247 2461297 2461309 2461313 2461337 2461339 2461397
2461399 2461409 2461423 2461439 2461453 2461457 2461477 2461489 2461519 2461553
2461577 2461579 2461601 2461637 2461643 2461649 2461703 2461709 2461717 2461727
2461729 2461733 2461769 2461801 2461807 2461819 2461831 2461843 2461847 2461853
2461861 2461871 2461873 2461891 2461913 2461919 2461951 2461961 2461969 2461973
2461993 2461997 2462023 2462041 2462069 2462087 2462099 2462123 2462171 2462197
2462233 2462261 2462281 2462287 2462293 2462321 2462329 2462333 2462353 2462359
2462389 2462393 2462401 2462413 2462431 2462443 2462479 2462513 2462519 2462531
2462543 2462549 2462557 2462617 2462623 2462639 2462641 2462689 2462699 2462701
2462711 2462717 2462731 2462737 2462741 2462743 2462783 2462791 2462797 2462813
2462827 2462839 2462843 2462851 2462869 2462879 2462891 2462899 2462917 2462921
2462939 2462953 2463029 2463031 2463037 2463049 2463067 2463077 2463101 2463137
2463143 2463151 2463161 2463163 2463187 2463211 2463221 2463257 2463269 2463311
2463313 2463319 2463359 2463367 2463371 2463401 2463413 2463437 2463443 2463449
2463467 2463473 2463479 2463511 2463529 2463533 2463541 2463557 2463569 2463583
2463619 2463641 2463653 2463667 2463679 2463683 2463697 2463701 2463707 2463757
2463761 2463763 2463767 2463779 2463833 2463841 2463871 2463883 2463887 2463893
2463907 2463919 2463947 2463949 2463971 2463983 2463991 2464003 2464009 2464019
2464037 2464051 2464057 2464061 2464073 2464079 2464087 2464093 2464109 2464117
2464123 2464127 2464153 2464177 2464183 2464199 2464207 2464211 2464213 2464271
2464279 2464307 2464313 2464349 2464361 2464369 2464379 2464393 2464403 2464441
2464457 2464463 2464477 2464487 2464513 2464523 2464529 2464537 2464543 2464559
2464571 2464577 2464589 2464591 2464597 2464603 2464613 2464621 2464639 2464663
2464669 2464697 2464733 2464751 2464757 2464769 2464783 2464789 2464793 2464799
2464801 2464811 2464823 2464831 2464837 2464849 2464853 2464859 2464877 2464897
2464901 2464909 2464919 2464921 2464937 2464939 2464951 2464963 2464981 2465011
2465053 2465059 2465063 2465081 2465123 2465129 2465143 2465149 2465159 2465161
2465167 2465171 2465179 2465201 2465227 2465251 2465263 2465279 2465299 2465303
2465327 2465339 2465363 2465381 2465431 2465467 2465473 2465483 2465509 2465513
2465537 2465539 2465543 2465557 2465563 2465579 2465587 2465599 2465621 2465627
2465633 2465641 2465651 2465657 2465707 2465747 2465753 2465777 2465789 2465819
2465831 2465843 2465851 2465891 2465909 2465917 2465929 2465933 2465941 2465951
2465963 2465977 2465989 2465993 2466011 2466041 2466049 2466053 2466091 2466097
2466103 2466119 2466187 2466197 2466223 2466239 2466253 2466263 2466271 2466323
2466341 2466349 2466367 2466389 2466407 2466427 2466433 2466439 2466449 2466463
2466473 2466481 2466491 2466493 2466509 2466517 2466533 2466539 2466553 2466571
2466587 2466619 2466623 2466631 2466647 2466661 2466691 2466703 2466707 2466749
2466787 2466797 2466803 2466829 2466839 2466851 2466857 2466869 2466881 2466883
2466907 2466917 2466923 2466931 2466973 2466977 2467013 2467019 2467021 2467027
2467033 2467043 2467051 2467061 2467133 2467151 2467169 2467211 2467217 2467219
2467243 2467247 2467253 2467277 2467301 2467307 2467319 2467337 2467351 2467357
2467369 2467373 2467391 2467393 2467403 2467429 2467441 2467447 2467459 2467471
2467519 2467529 2467541 2467559 2467579 2467603 2467607 2467609 2467613 2467637
2467643 2467649 2467691 2467709 2467711 2467763 2467769 2467783 2467859 2467867
2467901 2467903 2467919 2467921 2467931 2467943 2467951 2467957 2467961 2467963
2467979 2467981 2468021 2468027 2468047 2468069 2468099 2468101 2468113 2468117
2468129 2468131 2468143 2468183 2468201 2468209 2468227 2468239 2468261 2468269
2468273 2468303 2468311 2468341 2468351 2468357 2468363 2468371 2468377 2468399
2468413 2468419 2468443 2468447 2468449 2468467 2468471 2468507 2468527 2468549
2468579 2468591 2468629 2468633 2468639 2468657 2468693 2468701 2468707 2468717
2468729 2468773 2468777 2468789 2468801 2468813 2468821 2468831 2468861 2468867
2468881 2468903 2468909 2468951 2468953 2468969 2468971 2469011 2469041 2469053
2469067 2469149 2469157 2469161 2469169 2469193 2469197 2469241 2469251 2469277
2469281 2469283 2469289 2469317 2469319 2469331 2469359 2469407 2469409 2469413
2469421 2469431 2469433 2469457 2469469 2469473 2469491 2469517 2469529 2469541
2469557 2469559 2469581 2469583 2469629 2469637 2469647 2469653 2469659 2469673
2469679 2469757 2469781 2469793 2469827 2469847 2469869 2469871 2469889 2469893
2469899 2469919 2469923 2469931 2469937 2469953 2469979 2469983 2469989 2470001
2470003 2470031 2470037 2470051 2470063 2470079 2470099 2470103 2470109 2470121
2470123 2470141 2470159 2470189 2470199 2470201 2470213 2470217 2470229 2470241
2470243 2470261 2470301 2470313 2470319 2470327 2470331 2470333 2470337 2470339
2470387 2470397 2470417 2470427 2470451 2470463 2470471 2470553 2470579 2470603
2470621 2470631 2470639 2470667 2470673 2470679 2470691 2470693 2470697 2470739
2470753 2470757 2470777 2470781 2470789 2470801 2470841 2470859 2470877 2470889
2470891 2470903 2470939 2470957 2470961 2470981 2470991 2471009 2471017 2471033
2471047 2471057 2471059 2471071 2471087 2471089 2471093 2471101 2471107 2471113
2471149 2471153 2471173 2471179 2471201 2471207 2471219 2471233 2471237 2471251
2471257 2471299 2471309 2471321 2471323 2471347 2471377 2471383 2471389 2471393
2471407 2471437 2471449 2471461 2471471 2471473 2471503 2471507 2471527 2471531
2471533 2471551 2471611 2471621 2471629 2471633 2471639 2471663 2471669 2471701
2471713 2471717 2471737 2471743 2471747 2471753 2471809 2471813 2471827 2471863
2471869 2471899 2471927 2471939 2471947 2471951 2471983 2471993 2472023 2472027
2472049 2472053 2472061 2472077 2472091 2472097 2472121 2472131 2472143 2472167
2472179 2472181 2472193 2472203 2472209 2472227 2472241 2472251 2472289 2472313
2472317 2472329 2472347 2472359 2472373 2472389 2472403 2472443 2472461 2472469
2472473 2472517 2472539 2472541 2472551 2472557 2472559 2472577 2472607 2472611
2472637 2472649 2472677 2472683 2472697 2472703 2472719 2472727 2472731 2472737
2472781 2472791 2472797 2472809 2472823 2472851 2472853 2472857 2472893 2472919
2472929 2472931 2472947 2472959 2472961 2472979 2473019 2473027 2473039 2473049
2473057 2473063 2473067 2473073 2473099 2473127 2473129 2473147 2473153 2473157
2473169 2473181 2473183 2473189 2473193 2473217 2473241 2473277 2473291 2473301
2473309 2473321 2473327 2473337 2473343 2473349 2473391 2473409 2473421 2473423
2473441 2473451 2473453 2473463 2473501 2473511 2473529 2473547 2473567 2473589
2473607 2473609 2473631 2473633 2473663 2473697 2473717 2473759 2473777 2473813
2473837 2473871 2473879 2473907 2473921 2473937 2473943 2473951 2473963 2473967
2473979 2473997 2474039 2474051 2474053 2474057 2474071 2474117 2474119 2474183
2474207 2474209 2474239 2474261 2474267 2474273 2474281 2474287 2474291 2474321
2474383 2474387 2474393 2474413 2474431 2474489 2474497 2474533 2474539 2474543
```

```
2474551 2474557 2474561 2474569 2474573 2474603 2474611 2474629 2474651 2474663
2474669 2474677 2474683 2474687 2474701 2474711 2474713 2474723 2474737 2474743
2474749 2474783 2474789 2474821 2474827 2474837 2474851 2474861 2474863 2474881
2474897 2474903 2474909 2474917 2474929 2474939 2474957 2474999 2475019 2475023
2475029 2475061 2475089 2475091 2475097 2475101 2475113 2475139 2475157 2475163
2475199 2475223 2475229 2475247 2475269 2475287 2475289 2475299 2475331 2475367
2475371 2475383 2475397 2475427 2475433 2475439 2475493 2475497 2475509
2475547 2475587 2475593 2475647 2475653 2475673 2475679 2475689 2475709 2475721
2475751 2475773 2475779 2475787 2475791 2475797 2475799 2475821 2475827 2475839
2475857 2475859 2475883 2475887 2475911 2475917 2475959 2475961 2475971 2475989
2476009 2476013 2476037 2476039 2476043 2476057 2476073 2476079 2476081 2476121
2476129 2476141 2476163 2476181 2476189 2476209 2476273 2476283 2476291 2476297
2476303 2476307 2476321 2476333 2476337 2476351 2476363 2476367 2476381 2476391
2476393 2476421 2476443 2476451 2476469 2476489 2476511 2476541 2476547 2476561
2476567 2476583 2476597 2476601 2476609 2476651 2476667 2476673 2476681 2476699
2476703 2476711 2476717 2476723 2476739 2476751 2476753 2476787 2476811 2476819
2476867 2476871 2476907 2476913 2476921 2476927 2476937 2476967 2476987 2477029
2477051 2477063 2477071 2477081 2477107 2477129 2477131 2477141 2477147 2477159
2477161 2477171 2477173 2477177 2477213 2477219 2477231 2477249 2477263 2477281
2477297 2477309 2477311 2477317 2477327 2477329 2477333 2477339 2477357 2477381
2477407 2477411 2477413 2477471 2477521 2477561 2477599 2477609 2477611 2477623
2477639 2477641 2477647 2477659 2477681 2477689 2477701 2477719 2477729 2477743
2477747 2477777 2477791 2477807 2477821 2477837 2477851 2477863 2477899 2477911
2477929 2477933 2477939 2477947 2477957 2477983 2477987 2478011 2478017 2478023
2478029 2478041 2478067 2478083 2478097 2478101 2478173 2478187 2478211 2478221
2478239 2478241 2478257 2478269 2478271 2478293 2478323 2478331 2478337 2478347
2478349 2478361 2478367 2478373 2478403 2478407 2478449 2478473 2478479 2478517
2478521 2478523 2478527 2478529 2478547 2478557 2478587 2478589 2478611 2478631
2478643 2478653 2478661 2478673 2478677 2478691 2478703 2478709 2478713 2478727
2478731 2478743 2478761 2478793 2478803 2478809 2478877 2478899 2478937 2478953
2478997 2479013 2479027 2479031 2479049 2479069 2479117 2479129 2479151
2479171 2479189 2479219 2479231 2479237 2479241 2479271 2479277 2479283 2479307
2479319 2479327 2479361 2479381 2479387 2479409 2479429 2479453 2479457 2479483
2479487 2479489 2479493 2479507 2479513 2479523 2479541 2479549 2479553 2479567
2479577 2479583 2479619 2479627 2479657 2479661 2479663 2479667 2479669 2479679
2479691 2479693 2479717 2479727 2479733 2479751 2479769 2479781 2479787 2479801
2479811 2479847 2479849 2479879 2479901 2479903 2479913 2479927 2479963 2479987
2479991 2480003 2480053 2480057 2480063 2480069 2480081 2480083 2480087 2480119
2480161 2480171 2480201 2480207 2480209 2480227 2480263 2480267 2480281
2480287 2480311 2480323 2480329 2480339 2480383 2480411 2480417 2480441 2480447
2480479 2480483 2480497 2480501 2480503 2480509 2480539 2480551 2480563 2480567
2480579 2480587 2480593 2480617 2480663 2480671 2480677 2480683 2480693 2480717
2480719 2480729 2480743 2480749 2480767 2480783 2480843 2480851 2480873 2480893
2480897 2480903 2480909 2480911 2480917 2480927 2480977 2481013 2481019
2481029 2481043 2481047 2481067 2481091 2481097 2481107 2481113 2481121 2481137
2481169 2481173 2481179 2481181 2481187 2481221 2481233 2481239 2481247
2481253 2481277 2481293 2481307 2481317 2481319 2481341 2481389 2481417 2481433
2481449 2481461 2481491 2481497 2481499 2481503 2481509 2481517 2481601 2481629
2481641 2481649 2481653 2481697 2481709 2481719 2481727 2481749 2481757 2481797
2481811 2481823 2481833 2481839 2481841 2481851 2481859 2481863 2481877 2481887
2481889 2481901 2481911 2481959 2481971 2481977 2481991 2481997 2482019 2482033
2482049 2482061 2482069 2482093 2482097 2482111 2482147 2482157 2482177 2482199
2482217 2482243 2482247 2482253 2482279 2482297 2482309 2482339 2482343 2482349
2482351 2482379 2482411 2482421 2482439 2482451 2482463 2482481 2482499 2482523
2482531 2482537 2482553 2482567 2482583 2482607 2482619 2482621 2482651 2482703
2482717 2482741 2482747 2482757 2482769 2482771 2482783 2482793 2482801 2482807
2482813 2482841 2482849 2482861 2482871 2482889 2482903 2482913 2482933 2482937
2482943 2482967 2482981 2482993 2482999 2483017 2483027 2483059 2483077
2483093 2483099 2483113 2483119 2483137 2483141 2483161 2483169 2483171 2483179
2483219 2483233 2483291 2483381 2483417 2483431 2483447 2483461 2483483 2483519
2483521 2483543 2483549 2483561 2483567 2483599 2483603 2483617 2483641 2483653
2483659 2483669 2483671 2483687 2483693 2483707 2483711 2483713 2483729 2483743
2483749 2483753 2483777 2483797 2483827 2483837 2483861 2483867 2483869 2483881
2483911 2483917 2483939 2483953 2484011 2484017 2484019 2484037 2484049 2484059
2484089 2484109 2484113 2484127 2484133 2484151 2484179 2484191 2484197
2484203 2484233 2484241 2484259 2484271 2484289 2484311 2484319 2484323 2484331
2484353 2484359 2484379 2484473 2484491 2484509 2484523 2484527 2484539 2484563
2484569 2484571 2484589 2484593 2484617 2484623 2484631 2484653 2484673 2484679
2484683 2484689 2484697 2484707 2484721 2484731 2484733 2484739 2484751 2484803
2484827 2484857 2484863 2484871 2484893 2484899 2484901 2484911 2484919 2484931
2484959 2484961 2484971 2484973 2485001 2485003 2485027 2485033 2485037 2485061
2485069 2485073 2485121 2485123 2485129 2485159 2485169 2485183 2485187 2485193
2485207 2485211 2485243 2485277 2485279 2485283 2485303 2485319 2485339 2485367
2485381 2485391 2485393 2485397 2485421 2485429 2485453 2485477 2485481 2485489
2485507 2485513 2485537 2485547 2485559 2485573 2485579 2485607 2485627 2485631
2485643 2485649 2485657 2485663 2485667 2485669 2485687 2485727 2485733 2485739
2485759 2485801 2485807 2485831 2485849 2485867 2485897 2485907 2485937 2485939
2485949 2485991 2485997 2485999 2486009 2486027 2486039 2486041 2486059 2486069
2486089 2486101 2486123 2486137 2486147 2486149 2486153 2486167 2486189 2486191
2486203 2486219 2486221 2486249 2486251 2486269 2486273 2486287 2486291 2486333
2486371 2486381 2486383 2486387 2486423 2486443 2486459 2486467 2486483 2486501
2486509 2486513 2486521 2486531 2486551 2486557 2486563 2486567 2486579 2486581
2486591 2486593 2486611 2486623 2486639 2486653 2486669 2486677 2486681 2486689
2486699 2486713 2486717 2486747 2486753 2486761 2486767 2486801 2486831 2486833
2486843 2486857 2486863 2486867 2486893 2486947 2486963 2486969 2486971 2486987
2486993 2487047 2487061 2487071 2487073 2487091 2487097 2487113 2487137 2487139
2487143 2487167 2487203 2487211 2487227 2487229 2487259 2487269 2487281 2487293
2487299 2487307 2487313 2487319 2487341 2487349 2487367 2487383 2487391 2487413
2487431 2487439 2487467 2487481 2487493 2487497 2487517 2487521 2487523 2487557
```

2487571 2487581 2487587 2487599 2487601 2487619 2487623 2487629 2487637 2487659
2487671 2487673 2487677 2487691 2487697 2487701 2487713 2487739 2487743 2487773
2487787 2487791 2487809 2487811 2487827 2487833 2487883 2487907 2487923 2487931
2487943 2487949 2487959 2487977 2487983 2488009 2488019 2488043 2488061 2488067
2488099 2488111 2488121 2488141 2488159 2488181 2488193 2488217 2488219 2488223
2488231 2488247 2488253 2488261 2488267 2488271 2488289 2488309 2488319 2488327
2488333 2488357 2488363 2488379 2488391 2488397 2488399 2488417 2488427 2488429
2488469 2488471 2488481 2488489 2488537 2488547 2488553 2488559 2488567 2488573
2488597 2488609 2488667 2488687 2488699 2488709 2488723 2488727 2488757 2488771
2488777 2488781 2488799 2488841 2488877 2488891 2488901 2488907 2488909 2488949
2488961 2488963 2488973 2489017 2489077 2489107 2489111 2489119 2489143 2489147
2489159 2489161 2489183 2489197 2489213 2489219 2489237 2489239 2489287 2489309
2489321 2489339 2489341 2489371 2489381 2489411 2489413 2489423 2489441 2489453
2489477 2489483 2489491 2489521 2489533 2489567 2489573 2489603 2489611 2489639
2489647 2489659 2489671 2489687 2489713 2489717 2489719 2489749 2489759 2489761
2489777 2489789 2489797 2489801 2489813 2489831 2489849 2489857 2489867 2489869
2489873 2489881 2489883 2489909 2489923 2489933 2489947 2489989 2490023 2490029
2490079 2490091 2490101 2490119 2490127 2490139 2490157 2490161 2490209 2490221
2490227 2490239 2490247 2490251 2490263 2490269 2490283 2490307 2490329 2490337
2490377 2490391 2490413 2490421 2490451 2490461 2490469 2490473 2490479 2490493
2490497 2490529 2490533 2490547 2490583 2490589 2490599 2490613 2490617 2490623
2490637 2490659 2490661 2490667 2490679 2490701 2490707 2490713 2490727 2490731
2490737 2490743 2490769 2490809 2490811 2490821 2490847 2490869 2490889 2490899
2490907 2490931 2490941 2490973 2490997 2491001 2491007 2491009 2491031 2491043
2491063 2491081 2491087 2491091 2491117 2491123 2491171 2491189 2491207 2491211
2491243 2491259 2491289 2491327 2491331 2491339 2491343 2491351 2491369 2491381
2491387 2491397 2491453 2491457 2491471 2491487 2491493 2491499 2491519 2491523
2491547 2491553 2491589 2491607 2491609 2491649 2491661 2491669 2491681 2491711
2491729 2491751 2491759 2491777 2491787 2491813 2491829 2491837 2491847 2491861
2491871 2491891 2491903 2491933 2491949 2491961 2491963 2491967 2492003 2492011
2492023 2492051 2492069 2492071 2492093 2492111 2492117 2492123 2492143 2492153
2492159 2492197 2492201 2492227 2492239 2492263 2492279 2492299 2492311 2492317
2492339 2492383 2492389 2492393 2492417 2492423 2492443 2492447 2492453 2492459
2492461 2492509 2492519 2492527 2492549 2492563 2492587 2492593 2492599 2492603
2492657 2492701 2492719 2492729 2492747 2492767 2492783 2492797 2492813 2492821
2492827 2492843 2492851 2492879 2492899 2492951 2492957 2493019 2493037 2493041
2493053 2493077 2493079 2493083 2493089 2493107 2493109 2493121 2493149 2493167
2493187 2493193 2493221 2493229 2493233 2493259 2493289 2493301 2493329 2493331
2493341 2493347 2493349 2493353 2493383 2493401 2493409 2493419 2493437 2493443
2493479 2493511 2493523 2493529 2493551 2493559 2493563 2493587 2493599 2493629
2493643 2493653 2493707 2493709 2493719 2493721 2493727 2493749 2493767 2493779
2493817 2493833 2493851 2493853 2493859 2493877 2493923 2493929 2493937 2493943
2493947 2493949 2493979 2493983 2493991 2494031 2494033 2494057 2494061 2494069
2494081 2494091 2494099 2494103 2494117 2494123 2494167 2494169 2494171 2494201
2494213 2494237 2494241 2494273 2494279 2494313 2494321 2494333 2494357 2494363
2494367 2494379 2494381 2494391 2494421 2494423 2494433 2494439 2494441 2494447
2494451 2494463 2494469 2494489 2494507 2494517 2494523 2494537 2494543 2494553
2494561 2494571 2494589 2494607 2494627 2494637 2494669 2494673 2494693 2494703
2494711 2494721 2494729 2494753 2494769 2494777 2494781 2494819 2494823 2494829
2494831 2494847 2494883 2494889 2494913 2494931 2494949 2494951 2494963 2494967
2494979 2494981 2494991 2494993 2495027 2495047 2495107 2495121 2495149 2495167
2495173 2495177 2495203 2495239 2495249 2495263 2495279 2495291 2495299 2495321
2495323 2495341 2495351 2495387 2495417 2495429 2495443 2495459 2495461 2495473
2495489 2495501 2495509 2495527 2495533 2495543 2495551 2495557 2495567 2495599
2495621 2495657 2495723 2495749 2495767 2495771 2495789 2495803 2495807 2495813
2495819 2495833 2495839 2495851 2495861 2495869 2495881 2495887 2495947 2495963
2495981 2495993 2496007 2496031 2496041 2496061 2496073 2496077 2496079 2496083
2496097 2496103 2496139 2496173 2496191 2496199 2496211 2496227 2496251 2496253
2496257 2496269 2496271 2496281 2496293 2496313 2496317 2496323 2496371 2496379
2496383 2496401 2496409 2496413 2496421 2496437 2496469 2496491 2496493 2496503
2496517 2496521 2496541 2496553 2496577 2496587 2496607 2496629 2496643 2496667
2496677 2496691 2496707 2496721 2496727 2496737 2496743 2496757 2496779 2496799
2496803 2496827 2496829 2496869 2496887 2496889 2496911 2496917 2496919 2496937
2496973 2496979 2497003 2497007 2497013 2497021 2497039 2497043 2497067 2497097
2497109 2497129 2497163 2497169 2497177 2497193 2497207 2497211 2497213 2497217
2497259 2497289 2497301 2497309 2497321 2497333 2497337 2497349 2497357 2497361
2497367 2497381 2497421 2497423 2497447 2497457 2497477 2497489 2497499 2497511
2497513 2497541 2497571 2497591 2497603 2497609 2497631 2497633 2497637 2497661
2497667 2497673 2497697 2497723 2497727 2497739 2497751 2497753 2497757 2497771
2497801 2497811 2497849 2497867 2497871 2497877 2497879 2497897 2497903 2497927
2497931 2497933 2497939 2497951 2497967 2497991 2498009 2498017 2498021 2498071
2498087 2498107 2498123 2498131 2498137 2498143 2498173 2498179 2498183 2498207
2498213 2498219 2498231 2498239 2498273 2498299 2498323 2498333 2498339 2498347
2498359 2498369 2498381 2498393 2498399 2498407 2498413 2498423 2498449 2498453
2498521 2498527 2498539 2498593 2498599 2498603 2498641 2498653 2498659 2498689
2498701 2498707 2498723 2498731 2498737 2498753 2498759 2498767 2498801 2498809
2498819 2498851 2498893 2498921 2498939 2498957 2498971 2498981 2498989 2499023
2499041 2499053 2499059 2499061 2499083 2499103 2499121 2499127 2499139 2499143
2499149 2499151 2499163 2499169 2499179 2499193 2499197 2499247 2499253 2499257
2499269 2499311 2499337 2499373 2499383 2499389 2499403 2499421 2499439 2499443
2499449 2499457 2499463 2499509 2499517 2499521 2499551 2499577 2499589 2499599
2499613 2499619 2499631 2499641 2499643 2499661 2499667 2499671 2499689 2499727
2499751 2499779 2499781 2499793 2499803 2499821 2499853 2499859 2499863 2499881
2499907 2499919 2499923 2499941 2499943 2499947 2499949 2499953 2499967 2499983
2499989 2499999 2500009 2500027 2500049 2500051 2500067 2500081 2500087 2500097
2500109 2500117 2500151 2500159 2500163 2500171 2500187 2500213 2500273 2500297
2500301 2500331 2500339 2500357 2500363 2500403 2500417 2500439 2500441 2500523
2500529 2500543 2500559 2500591 2500601 2500621 2500637 2500639 2500651 2500669
2500679 2500709 2500727 2500733 2500741 2500747 2500753 2500759 2500769 2500781

```
2500783  2500807  2500831  2500843  2500847  2500879  2500889  2500891  2500919  2500933
2500937  2500957  2500961  2500969  2500973  2500999  2501003  2501071  2501077  2501099
2501101  2501113  2501119  2501131  2501137  2501143  2501171  2501189  2501197  2501201
2501243  2501249  2501251  2501269  2501281  2501299  2501327  2501333  2501347  2501351
2501357  2501383  2501399  2501413  2501417  2501449  2501461  2501479  2501489  2501501
2501507  2501563  2501573  2501591  2501593  2501599  2501623  2501647  2501651  2501657
2501677  2501689  2501699  2501761  2501789  2501791  2501803  2501813  2501819  2501833
2501843  2501881  2501897  2501899  2501911  2501923  2501953  2501957  2501959  2501987
2501999  2502001  2502007  2502011  2502047  2502067  2502079  2502083  2502089  2502113
2502121  2502133  2502151  2502163  2502169  2502173  2502191  2502197  2502209  2502211
2502229  2502251  2502259  2502263  2502287  2502293  2502301  2502317  2502329  2502337
2502341  2502343  2502359  2502361  2502371  2502373  2502389  2502391  2502397  2502407
2502443  2502463  2502473  2502481  2502527  2502541  2502551  2502559  2502571  2502581
2502583  2502593  2502629  2502637  2502649  2502667  2502677  2502683  2502701  2502719
2502733  2502761  2502767  2502779  2502781  2502793  2502803  2502809  2502827  2502833
2502917  2502931  2502937  2502943  2502953  2502991  2503001  2503027  2503037  2503069
2503103  2503121  2503139  2503141  2503147  2503153  2503181  2503183  2503201  2503211
2503213  2503217  2503253  2503261  2503283  2503313  2503327  2503339  2503351  2503357
2503373  2503381  2503387  2503409  2503427  2503433  2503439  2503453  2503463  2503469
2503477  2503499  2503507  2503511  2503513  2503537  2503559  2503577  2503597  2503637
2503639  2503651  2503663  2503703  2503717  2503729  2503751  2503759  2503799  2503817
2503841  2503859  2503871  2503873  2503883  2503909  2503927  2503931  2503961  2503979
2503997  2503999  2504009  2504011  2504069  2504071  2504077  2504081  2504101  2504129
2504141  2504147  2504153  2504167  2504189  2504213  2504251  2504261  2504269  2504291
2504297  2504317  2504323  2504329  2504347  2504351  2504377  2504399  2504407  2504413
2504417  2504429  2504431  2504441  2504473  2504479  2504501  2504503  2504519  2504531
2504543  2504563  2504569  2504581  2504587  2504597  2504603  2504611  2504629  2504639
2504657  2504669  2504681  2504687  2504693  2504717  2504737  2504741  2504753  2504767
2504779  2504783  2504791  2504807  2504819  2504837  2504869  2504881  2504891  2504917
2504923  2504927  2504969  2504981  2504987  2505007  2505043  2505067  2505073  2505077
2505101  2505109  2505119  2505121  2505127  2505133  2505143  2505157  2505161  2505163
2505187  2505193  2505227  2505247  2505253  2505259  2505263  2505271  2505277  2505301
2505311  2505337  2505343  2505353  2505361  2505379  2505383  2505401  2505407  2505421
2505457  2505487  2505499  2505527  2505533  2505539  2505541  2505557  2505611  2505623
2505631  2505641  2505673  2505683  2505691  2505707  2505743  2505773  2505779  2505791
2505793  2505809  2505829  2505847  2505857  2505859  2505863  2505901  2505917  2505983
2505989  2505991  2506003  2506013  2506033  2506069  2506073  2506079  2506099  2506109
2506129  2506183  2506193  2506199  2506201  2506223  2506253  2506277  2506279  2506291
2506313  2506321  2506337  2506363  2506367  2506373  2506391  2506397  2506409  2506411
2506421  2506447  2506459  2506481  2506489  2506501  2506523  2506541  2506547  2506549
2506561  2506571  2506579  2506583  2506619  2506631  2506643  2506649  2506657  2506661
2506681  2506687  2506697  2506717  2506723  2506729  2506759  2506783  2506799  2506807
2506813  2506831  2506843  2506859  2506873  2506883  2506909  2506913  2506919  2506927
2506949  2506957  2506961  2506979  2506981  2506991  2506997  2507003  2507017  2507033
2507047  2507051  2507093  2507147  2507149  2507203  2507213  2507227  2507233  2507243
2507247  2507291  2507303  2507317  2507339  2507383  2507387  2507389  2507413  2507447
2507473  2507489  2507567  2507581  2507587  2507597  2507627  2507629  2507641  2507647
2507671  2507689  2507693  2507707  2507719  2507723  2507731  2507737  2507767  2507773
2507777  2507821  2507837  2507861  2507863  2507881  2507899  2507903  2507909  2507917
2507927  2507957  2507963  2508001  2508017  2508041  2508043  2508047  2508049  2508053
2508067  2508073  2508083  2508089  2508091  2508097  2508101  2508113  2508139  2508151
2508161  2508167  2508203  2508211  2508223  2508227  2508269  2508277  2508281  2508283
2508293  2508307  2508313  2508347  2508371  2508379  2508383  2508391  2508409  2508433
2508481  2508511  2508521  2508557  2508559  2508581  2508593  2508599  2508619  2508629
2508641  2508677  2508683  2508689  2508691  2508697  2508743  2508763  2508769  2508773
2508787  2508797  2508823  2508827  2508833  2508871  2508899  2508901  2508917  2508929
2508953  2508971  2509027  2509037  2509061  2509063  2509079  2509103  2509123  2509127
2509141  2509147  2509163  2509181  2509207  2509219  2509237  2509253  2509259  2509267
2509271  2509279  2509301  2509307  2509313  2509333  2509337  2509363  2509379  2509411
2509417  2509427  2509433  2509483  2509499  2509513  2509517  2509519  2509531  2509537
2509541  2509561  2509571  2509597  2509613  2509621  2509627  2509643  2509679  2509687
2509721  2509757  2509777  2509807  2509811  2509823  2509831  2509841  2509849  2509861
2509891  2509907  2509933  2509937  2509961  2509963  2509981  2509993  2510017  2510023
2510041  2510047  2510051  2510077  2510083  2510087  2510099  2510107  2510111  2510141
2510149  2510159  2510171  2510219  2510227  2510279  2510293  2510303  2510309  2510329
2510341  2510401  2510429  2510437  2510447  2510449  2510477  2510491  2510503  2510507
2510513  2510531  2510533  2510537  2510549  2510551  2510567  2510579  2510581  2510591
2510609  2510623  2510653  2510681  2510701  2510707  2510723  2510731  2510741  2510743
2510771  2510777  2510789  2510801  2510803  2510843  2510867  2510873  2510891  2510903
2510909  2510927  2510941  2510947  2510971  2511001  2511011  2511017  2511029  2511043
2511049  2511083  2511101  2511107  2511109  2511133  2511137  2511143  2511149  2511151
2511161  2511167  2511169  2511241  2511247  2511253  2511259  2511269  2511293  2511307
2511323  2511337  2511339  2511343  2511349  2511389  2511407  2511413  2511433  2511451
2511473  2511493  2511499  2511503  2511517  2511521  2511541  2511547  2511557  2511569
2511581  2511601  2511637  2511643  2511659  2511697  2511703  2511709  2511721  2511749
2511779  2511791  2511793  2511799  2511809  2511811  2511823  2511827  2511851  2511871
2511881  2511911  2511917  2511941  2511953  2511979  2511983  2511997  2512001  2512007
2512019  2512021  2512033  2512063  2512087  2512093  2512109  2512117  2512127  2512171
2512177  2512207  2512217  2512219  2512229  2512249  2512283  2512297  2512303  2512331
2512339  2512343  2512369  2512399  2512403  2512409  2512417  2512423  2512429  2512453
2512459  2512463  2512469  2512501  2512507  2512511  2512513  2512537  2512553  2512561
2512597  2512637  2512639  2512649  2512661  2512673  2512691  2512709  2512721  2512723
2512739  2512747  2512759  2512771  2512789  2512801  2512813  2512831  2512837  2512841
2512843  2512847  2512897  2512919  2512943  2512967  2512999  2513011  2513029  2513033
2513039  2513047  2513051  2513057  2513083  2513087  2513089  2513107  2513113  2513123
2513131  2513143  2513153  2513179  2513197  2513209  2513249  2513281  2513293  2513309
2513311  2513327  2513333  2513347  2513351  2513353  2513363  2513443  2513461  2513473
2513477  2513503  2513507  2513519  2513527  2513543  2513551  2513557  2513579  2513591
2513593  2513617  2513653  2513657  2513659  2513663  2513677  2513689  2513699  2513723
```

```
2513729  2513747  2513761  2513801  2513803  2513809  2513827  2513839  2513881  2513887
2513893  2513899  2513941  2514013  2514019  2514037  2514053  2514059  2514073  2514089
2514091  2514101  2514119  2514139  2514151  2514157  2514163  2514173  2514203  2514217
2514221  2514227  2514229  2514241  2514247  2514257  2514263  2514269  2514277  2514287
2514299  2514313  2514331  2514341  2514377  2514389  2514401  2514427  2514433  2514437
2514439  2514451  2514467  2514469  2514493  2514509  2514527  2514529  2514541  2514563
2514581  2514587  2514599  2514647  2514661  2514679  2514697  2514713  2514719  2514731
2514737  2514767  2514781  2514791  2514857  2514877  2514887  2514893  2514917  2514931
2514943  2514947  2514949  2514959  2514961  2514977  2514989  2514991  2515003  2515013
2515039  2515067  2515081  2515103  2515127  2515147  2515153  2515159  2515169  2515189
2515193  2515237  2515241  2515273  2515283  2515291  2515301  2515313  2515319  2515321
2515339  2515343  2515351  2515367  2515379  2515397  2515411  2515417  2515427  2515451
2515453  2515477  2515517  2515523  2515529  2515531  2515537  2515553  2515561  2515571
2515573  2515577  2515589  2515603  2515613  2515621  2515627  2515633  2515651  2515673
2515687  2515691  2515697  2515699  2515703  2515727  2515739  2515757  2515787  2515817
2515853  2515859  2515871  2515873  2515879  2515897  2515907  2515921  2515951  2515967
2516021  2516057  2516077  2516089  2516123  2516197  2516201  2516209  2516233  2516249
2516257  2516263  2516273  2516299  2516309  2516351  2516369  2516377  2516401  2516411
2516413  2516429  2516447  2516467  2516473  2516491  2516497  2516513  2516543  2516567
2516573  2516581  2516603  2516659  2516669  2516681  2516713  2516771  2516779  2516783
2516837  2516863  2516869  2516887  2516893  2516929  2516947  2516953  2516957  2516963
2516971  2516981  2516993  2517007  2517041  2517049  2517061  2517079  2517089  2517103
2517121  2517127  2517131  2517133  2517149  2517157  2517161  2517197  2517211  2517227
2517233  2517239  2517269  2517271  2517283  2517289  2517311  2517379  2517401  2517407
2517439  2517457  2517467  2517469  2517499  2517503  2517509  2517533  2517583  2517587
2517611  2517617  2517631  2517637  2517679  2517701  2517703  2517733  2517737
2517761  2517797  2517799  2517811  2517821  2517847  2517869  2517881  2517887  2517901
2517919  2517929  2517941  2517959  2518003  2518067  2518069  2518079  2518081  2518093
2518121  2518129  2518133  2518147  2518151  2518163  2518177  2518181  2518199  2518211
2518231  2518237  2518259  2518267  2518289  2518291  2518301  2518309  2518319  2518337
2518349  2518357  2518367  2518379  2518387  2518391  2518421  2518429  2518487  2518493
2518501  2518511  2518517  2518559  2518561  2518577  2518591  2518619  2518643  2518667
2518687  2518727  2518729  2518759  2518783  2518787  2518793  2518823  2518829  2518847
2518877  2518903  2518913  2518927  2518933  2518939  2518949  2518951  2518961  2518973
2518981  2518987  2519003  2519017  2519021  2519047  2519051  2519063  2519087  2519089
2519093  2519107  2519113  2519131  2519137  2519149  2519159  2519161  2519171  2519177
2519189  2519197  2519221  2519263  2519269  2519273  2519329  2519333  2519347  2519353
2519369  2519393  2519423  2519453  2519459  2519467  2519471  2519479  2519497  2519509
2519537  2519557  2519563  2519579  2519591  2519597  2519603  2519611  2519639  2519641
2519651  2519659  2519681  2519707  2519729  2519731  2519747  2519767  2519801  2519813
2519851  2519873  2519879  2519899  2519911  2519921  2519939  2519941  2519947  2519953
2519969  2519977  2519981  2520017  2520031  2520073  2520079  2520121  2520127  2520139
2520149  2520151  2520169  2520173  2520191  2520211  2520241  2520247  2520251  2520257
2520263  2520277  2520283  2520313  2520319  2520347  2520367  2520379  2520383  2520431
2520433  2520439  2520443  2520451  2520457  2520481  2520491  2520503  2520577  2520587
2520601  2520611  2520613  2520629  2520631  2520649  2520659  2520671  2520677  2520689
2520697  2520769  2520779  2520781  2520797  2520821  2520829  2520841  2520853  2520887
2520907  2520929  2520943  2520971  2520979  2520983  2521003  2521019  2521021  2521031
2521037  2521039  2521063  2521067  2521073  2521081  2521093  2521111  2521147  2521153
2521171  2521223  2521249  2521271  2521273  2521297  2521307  2521327  2521339  2521361
2521367  2521373  2521397  2521417  2521429  2521451  2521469  2521481  2521489  2521499
2521501  2521507  2521517  2521537  2521591  2521609  2521613  2521621  2521643  2521681
2521693  2521703  2521711  2521721  2521723  2521733  2521747  2521751  2521769  2521807
2521817  2521823  2521829  2521843  2521847  2521901  2521919  2521921  2521949  2521969
2521979  2522011  2522017  2522021  2522027  2522053  2522057  2522059  2522063  2522087
2522089  2522119  2522147  2522189  2522209  2522213  2522227  2522237  2522257  2522263
2522281  2522293  2522297  2522329  2522357  2522363  2522371  2522381  2522393  2522407
2522419  2522431  2522441  2522447  2522461  2522473  2522491  2522503  2522543  2522557
2522593  2522603  2522621  2522629  2522633  2522657  2522659  2522669  2522671  2522699
2522713  2522717  2522743  2522753  2522759  2522761  2522789  2522791  2522809  2522813
2522827  2522831  2522837  2522867  2522881  2522909  2522911  2522917  2522941  2522957
2522963  2522977  2522981  2522983  2522999  2523011  2523013  2523041  2523043  2523047
2523071  2523083  2523107  2523133  2523139  2523149  2523151  2523161  2523163  2523173
2523187  2523211  2523217  2523223  2523229  2523251  2523317  2523329  2523337  2523343
2523347  2523359  2523379  2523401  2523413  2523419  2523457  2523473  2523481  2523487
2523503  2523517  2523523  2523529  2523533  2523547  2523557  2523569  2523581  2523589
2523593  2523641  2523643  2523671  2523707  2523709  2523727  2523739  2523743  2523749
2523757  2523779  2523791  2523821  2523839  2523863  2523869  2523877  2523883  2523887
2523893  2523901  2523907  2523923  2523931  2523943  2523949  2523953  2523959  2523967
2523991  2524009  2524019  2524031  2524033  2524061  2524069  2524087  2524097  2524117
2524127  2524133  2524139  2524153  2524157  2524163  2524183  2524187  2524199  2524201
2524213  2524217  2524219  2524259  2524261  2524289  2524297  2524309  2524339  2524343
2524349  2524351  2524369  2524373  2524393  2524429  2524439  2524453  2524463  2524469
2524471  2524477  2524481  2524531  2524541  2524553  2524567  2524579  2524591  2524637
2524649  2524651  2524661  2524667  2524673  2524679  2524681  2524693  2524723  2524741
2524747  2524751  2524771  2524783  2524799  2524807  2524811  2524817  2524859  2524861
2524877  2524909  2524913  2524927  2524931  2524937  2524939  2524961  2524969  2524979
2524987  2525011  2525041  2525053  2525057  2525071  2525087  2525099  2525113  2525123
2525137  2525161  2525177  2525179  2525189  2525191  2525219  2525221  2525227  2525249
2525267  2525269  2525273  2525279  2525293  2525323  2525329  2525351  2525363  2525371
2525387  2525389  2525417  2525429  2525443  2525447  2525473  2525489  2525507  2525531
2525557  2525569  2525591  2525599  2525603  2525617  2525623  2525629  2525647  2525669
2525671  2525687  2525701  2525711  2525717  2525729  2525749  2525753  2525771  2525779
2525797  2525801  2525807  2525851  2525933  2525959  2525981  2525989  2526023  2526037
2526049  2526077  2526089  2526119  2526127  2526137  2526159  2526187  2526197  2526211
2526233  2526239  2526247  2526257  2526269  2526289  2526299  2526301  2526317  2526361
2526371  2526383  2526401  2526409  2526427  2526463  2526467  2526473  2526479  2526493
2526497  2526521  2526529  2526541  2526547  2526553  2526571  2526577  2526581  2526583
2526599  2526607  2526611  2526617  2526631  2526647  2526649  2526653  2526661  2526697
```

```
2526709  2526721  2526743  2526763  2526781  2526787  2526827  2526847  2526851  2526869
2526883  2526889  2526893  2526913  2526959  2526967  2526971  2526983  2526991  2527009
2527013  2527037  2527051  2527061  2527069  2527087  2527097  2527099  2527111  2527157
2527193  2527207  2527219  2527223  2527249  2527253  2527277  2527279  2527297  2527381
2527391  2527397  2527403  2527409  2527423  2527429  2527451  2527453  2527457  2527477
2527489  2527537  2527541  2527549  2527559  2527561  2527573  2527579  2527597  2527607
2527639  2527643  2527673  2527717  2527753  2527757  2527799  2527823  2527913  2527919
2527933  2527939  2527949  2527961  2527963  2527981  2527997  2528003  2528011  2528021
2528033  2528059  2528069  2528077  2528129  2528147  2528161  2528167  2528221  2528231
2528233  2528243  2528261  2528281  2528299  2528353  2528371  2528377  2528399  2528411
2528419  2528441  2528479  2528489  2528497  2528503  2528527  2528531  2528557  2528569
2528573  2528587  2528599  2528621  2528627  2528629  2528651  2528657  2528663  2528707
2528717  2528777  2528783  2528791  2528809  2528819  2528821  2528831  2528833  2528849
2528857  2528861  2528863  2528881  2528883  2528889  2528923  2528941  2528969  2528983
2528989  2528993  2529013  2529019  2529029  2529041  2529047  2529077  2529089  2529097
2529101  2529133  2529143  2529151  2529161  2529169  2529173  2529181  2529187  2529193
2529199  2529227  2529229  2529239  2529251  2529253  2529269  2529301  2529323  2529341
2529347  2529349  2529361  2529367  2529391  2529403  2529419  2529421  2529463  2529473
2529491  2529511  2529521  2529529  2529533  2529547  2529551  2529557  2529581  2529599
2529601  2529607  2529613  2529619  2529643  2529649  2529671  2529689  2529691  2529697
2529707  2529721  2529749  2529767  2529773  2529799  2529803  2529809  2529827  2529881
2529883  2529899  2529911  2529913  2529929  2529937  2529953  2529959  2529971  2529997
2530001  2530009  2530013  2530039  2530043  2530049  2530063  2530067  2530079  2530091
2530103  2530109  2530111  2530117  2530139  2530141  2530153  2530159  2530193  2530201
2530223  2530237  2530243  2530247  2530261  2530267  2530271  2530277  2530289  2530301
2530309  2530321  2530351  2530357  2530361  2530373  2530403  2530427  2530441  2530457
2530459  2530469  2530487  2530513  2530519  2530543  2530547  2530571  2530573  2530579
2530597  2530663  2530669  2530681  2530699  2530709  2530727  2530733  2530751  2530769
2530777  2530783  2530793  2530799  2530831  2530837  2530877  2530907  2530931  2530961
2530963  2530973  2530981  2530987  2530991  2530993  2530999  2531017  2531027  2531057
2531069  2531083  2531093  2531099  2531101  2531107  2531117  2531167  2531171  2531183
2531189  2531197  2531203  2531209  2531233  2531261  2531267  2531293  2531369  2531371
2531377  2531387  2531393  2531413  2531423  2531443  2531471  2531483  2531489  2531519
2531527  2531533  2531537  2531569  2531583  2531599  2531609  2531611  2531629  2531641
2531653  2531663  2531687  2531689  2531699  2531701  2531717  2531741  2531747  2531761
2531773  2531777  2531803  2531821  2531831  2531833  2531869  2531891  2531917  2531923
2531951  2531981  2531983  2531989  2531993  2532007  2532067  2532071  2532083  2532107
2532109  2532113  2532137  2532143  2532157  2532161  2532191  2532197  2532199  2532209
2532223  2532241  2532259  2532281  2532289  2532307  2532311  2532319  2532331  2532347
2532389  2532401  2532403  2532419  2532433  2532437  2532449  2532451  2532479  2532487
2532493  2532521  2532527  2532559  2532587  2532601  2532637  2532697  2532701  2532707
2532709  2532721  2532727  2532763  2532769  2532787  2532791  2532799  2532823  2532839
2532853  2532863  2532869  2532883  2532899  2532913  2532919  2532931  2532989  2532991
2533007  2533009  2533019  2533031  2533033  2533041  2533049  2533081  2533127  2533163
2533169  2533177  2533189  2533199  2533211  2533217  2533231  2533261  2533273  2533277
2533291  2533301  2533303  2533309  2533333  2533367  2533373  2533379  2533391  2533399
2533397  2533417  2533429  2533439  2533507  2533549  2533577  2533627  2533651  2533667
2533673  2533681  2533691  2533709  2533721  2533733  2533747  2533753  2533801  2533807
2533813  2533829  2533837  2533913  2533939  2533943  2533963  2533967  2534009  2534029
2534039  2534041  2534047  2534053  2534057  2534069  2534101  2534111  2534131  2534143
2534153  2534171  2534179  2534183  2534197  2534237  2534243  2534261  2534267  2534269
2534297  2534303  2534317  2534327  2534351  2534401  2534419  2534423  2534431  2534437
2534449  2534459  2534471  2534491  2534501  2534503  2534527  2534551  2534559  2534561
2534563  2534593  2534603  2534621  2534627  2534641  2534647  2534659  2534671  2534681
2534689  2534713  2534731  2534747  2534767  2534773  2534783  2534789  2534821  2534843
2534863  2534867  2534879  2534881  2534891  2534941  2534951  2534953  2534957  2534971
2534993  2535007  2535017  2535019  2535041  2535059  2535067  2535089  2535097  2535101
2535103  2535107  2535109  2535121  2535161  2535163  2535179  2535187  2535199  2535223
2535233  2535263  2535271  2535283  2535293  2535307  2535319  2535331  2535353  2535367
2535373  2535389  2535413  2535437  2535443  2535457  2535461  2535469  2535473  2535479
2535487  2535527  2535541  2535553  2535571  2535641  2535661  2535691  2535719  2535751
2535763  2535781  2535787  2535803  2535823  2535829  2535881  2535887  2535901  2535917
2535931  2535937  2535959  2535977  2535983  2536013  2536019  2536031  2536057  2536067
2536087  2536099  2536123  2536133  2536147  2536153  2536159  2536181  2536189  2536201
2536217  2536241  2536243  2536249  2536267  2536273  2536307  2536309  2536343  2536361
2536379  2536381  2536393  2536403  2536423  2536467  2536477  2536483  2536517  2536519
2536549  2536559  2536561  2536577  2536579  2536603  2536631  2536643  2536657  2536663
2536673  2536691  2536693  2536697  2536727  2536733  2536753  2536763  2536771  2536789
2536799  2536801  2536811  2536813  2536819  2536837  2536843  2536873  2536903  2536907
2536909  2536921  2536931  2536991  2536999  2537021  2537033  2537047  2537081  2537083
2537111  2537113  2537141  2537147  2537159  2537191  2537219  2537237  2537287  2537303
2537323  2537329  2537341  2537347  2537363  2537419  2537459  2537461  2537467  2537501
2537503  2537527  2537537  2537543  2537551  2537563  2537593  2537621  2537627  2537653
2537663  2537669  2537677  2537681  2537701  2537729  2537741  2537749  2537779  2537789
2537803  2537837  2537851  2537869  2537881  2537911  2537917  2537923  2537959  2537987
2537999  2538017  2538031  2538059  2538061  2538079  2538091  2538097  2538101  2538103
2538113  2538127  2538131  2538139  2538157  2538169  2538203  2538241  2538281  2538293
2538299  2538301  2538307  2538313  2538317  2538323  2538331  2538337  2538353  2538359
2538377  2538397  2538401  2538407  2538421  2538427  2538443  2538449  2538451  2538467
2538493  2538499  2538509  2538511  2538521  2538527  2538577  2538589  2538607  2538617
2538619  2538623  2538659  2538667  2538673  2538691  2538703  2538707  2538709  2538713
2538733  2538749  2538751  2538769  2538773  2538779  2538787  2538791  2538803  2538817
2538821  2538827  2538871  2538883  2538917  2538953  2538959  2538971
2538983  2539049  2539063  2539067  2539073  2539087  2539093  2539123  2539151  2539157
2539181  2539189  2539213  2539231  2539261  2539267  2539297  2539309  2539319  2539321
2539337  2539343  2539349  2539351  2539357  2539379  2539387  2539393  2539399  2539423
2539429  2539441  2539463  2539469  2539513  2539519  2539529  2539531  2539543  2539567
2539571  2539573  2539577  2539583  2539627  2539631  2539633  2539639  2539651  2539657
2539661  2539699  2539753  2539777  2539829  2539841  2539871  2539951  2539961  2539963
```

```
2539981 2539997 2540011 2540033 2540071 2540093 2540099 2540113 2540141 2540173
2540177 2540179 2540183 2540201 2540203 2540231 2540249 2540261 2540269 2540323
2540339 2540341 2540389 2540393 2540407 2540413 2540423 2540431 2540441 2540443
2540479 2540513 2540519 2540533 2540537 2540539 2540563 2540567 2540581 2540591
2540597 2540609 2540617 2540627 2540641 2540663 2540677 2540689 2540693
2540723 2540743 2540749 2540761 2540771 2540789 2540821 2540831 2540849 2540869
2540887 2540903 2540933 2540957 2540963 2540969 2540981 2540983 2541001 2541023
2541029 2541043 2541047 2541053 2541061 2541089 2541127 2541131 2541151 2541157
2541169 2541173 2541229 2541233 2541251 2541281 2541289 2541323 2541391 2541401
2541433 2541439 2541457 2541479 2541499 2541503 2541527 2541529 2541533 2541541
2541547 2541559 2541563 2541593 2541599 2541613 2541677 2541683 2541689 2541697
2541701 2541733 2541739 2541743 2541757 2541769 2541811 2541817 2541829
2541841 2541853 2541883 2541899 2541911 2541919 2541923 2541941 2541943 2541947
2541949 2541961 2541967 2541997 2542009 2542021 2542037 2542049 2542051 2542087
2542091 2542097 2542103 2542109 2542139 2542147 2542151 2542187 2542193 2542201
2542223 2542229 2542237 2542327 2542363 2542391 2542399 2542417 2542429 2542453
2542471 2542481 2542483 2542511 2542513 2542531 2542549 2542567 2542577 2542591
2542597 2542607 2542609 2542619 2542621 2542649 2542669 2542681 2542699 2542703
2542733 2542739 2542759 2542817 2542823 2542829 2542849 2542853 2542879 2542913
2542919 2542933 2542951 2542957 2542987 2542999 2543027 2543033 2543059 2543111
2543113 2543117 2543129 2543141 2543143 2543153 2543159 2543171 2543201 2543221
2543237 2543239 2543249 2543257 2543279 2543287 2543309 2543323 2543327 2543341
2543351 2543371 2543381 2543389 2543399 2543413 2543423 2543441 2543459 2543461
2543479 2543507 2543509 2543537 2543551 2543573 2543609 2543617 2543621 2543623
2543633 2543641 2543647 2543657 2543699 2543707 2543719 2543729 2543747 2543753
2543771 2543797 2543809 2543813 2543833 2543843 2543873 2543899 2543917 2543921
2543939 2543963 2543971 2544011 2544029 2544041 2544049 2544079 2544121 2544131
2544133 2544137 2544161 2544163 2544167 2544181 2544209 2544211 2544221 2544229
2544239 2544247 2544253 2544281 2544287 2544293 2544299 2544301 2544307 2544313
2544331 2544343 2544349 2544359 2544361 2544383 2544391 2544403 2544457 2544463
2544469 2544481 2544497 2544517 2544523 2544539 2544571 2544617 2544623 2544629
2544631 2544637 2544643 2544691 2544733 2544739 2544757 2544761 2544767 2544769
2544791 2544793 2544797 2544809 2544811 2544833 2544851 2544887 2544907 2544923
2544929 2544931 2544943 2544959 2544967 2544977 2545001 2545013 2545021 2545057
2545073 2545079 2545093 2545117 2545141 2545159 2545163 2545171 2545177 2545187
2545211 2545237 2545241 2545253 2545261 2545271 2545307 2545313 2545327 2545343
2545357 2545363 2545369 2545429 2545447 2545451 2545453 2545481 2545493 2545513
2545519 2545523 2545553 2545561 2545573 2545603 2545619 2545633 2545651 2545657
2545679 2545681 2545687 2545691 2545703 2545727 2545757 2545759 2545769 2545771
2545783 2545811 2545817 2545843 2545853 2545861 2545883 2545889 2545891 2545919
2545927 2545967 2545973 2545993 2546009 2546017 2546029 2546051 2546083 2546101
2546119 2546129 2546143 2546149 2546161 2546177 2546179 2546183 2546207 2546213
2546227 2546231 2546233 2546237 2546239 2546267 2546281 2546293 2546317 2546321
2546329 2546339 2546351 2546363 2546393 2546429 2546443 2546497 2546521 2546539
2546543 2546561 2546563 2546569 2546581 2546611 2546657 2546659 2546669 2546671
2546683 2546701 2546729 2546749 2546759 2546773 2546777 2546837 2546839 2546849
2546891 2546899 2546903 2546909 2546911 2546941 2546959 2546987 2547029 2547031
2547037 2547073 2547107 2547113 2547131 2547137 2547151 2547173 2547199 2547203
2547211 2547247 2547253 2547257 2547271 2547313 2547323 2547341 2547361 2547397
2547431 2547451 2547469 2547473 2547491 2547529 2547583 2547599 2547607
2547613 2547619 2547631 2547647 2547659 2547667 2547683 2547689 2547719 2547757
2547761 2547791 2547817 2547821 2547833 2547847 2547887 2547893 2547913 2547929
2547949 2547959 2547967 2547971 2547973 2547989 2547997 2548003 2548019 2548061
2548069 2548097 2548103 2548111 2548127 2548141 2548157 2548163 2548171 2548177
2548219 2548229 2548243 2548277 2548279 2548289 2548291 2548297 2548319 2548327
2548333 2548361 2548367 2548379 2548391 2548409 2548421 2548459 2548477 2548493
2548499 2548501 2548517 2548531 2548537 2548543 2548547 2548571 2548573 2548577
2548583 2548591 2548621 2548627 2548631 2548639 2548643 2548673 2548697 2548703
2548751 2548753 2548757 2548769 2548771 2548783 2548813 2548817 2548849 2548853
2548877 2548879 2548891 2548901 2548927 2548933 2548939 2548957 2548961 2548969
2548979 2549003 2549009 2549039 2549051 2549069 2549077 2549081 2549089 2549101
2549111 2549119 2549123 2549143 2549171 2549177 2549191 2549203 2549207 2549219
2549237 2549279 2549291 2549293 2549299 2549311 2549317 2549357 2549359 2549369
2549381 2549383 2549387 2549423 2549429 2549431 2549447 2549453 2549461 2549479
2549531 2549557 2549563 2549579 2549587 2549597 2549611 2549621 2549623 2549647
2549669 2549683 2549699 2549713 2549731 2549737 2549753 2549759 2549773 2549783
2549801 2549821 2549863 2549867 2549873 2549879 2549887 2549893 2549903 2549927
2549951 2549993 2550001 2550013 2550019 2550059 2550073 2550083 2550089 2550101
2550133 2550139 2550167 2550179 2550181 2550203 2550209 2550253 2550269 2550281
2550319 2550329 2550337 2550343 2550367 2550403 2550407 2550437 2550467 2550469
2550479 2550497 2550551 2550563 2550577 2550601 2550607 2550619 2550641 2550659
2550683 2550689 2550703 2550721 2550727 2550739 2550763 2550767 2550791 2550853
2550857 2550859 2550871 2550887 2550937 2550941 2550949 2550967 2550971 2550973
2550991 2551009 2551013 2551027 2551033 2551057 2551063 2551069 2551079 2551097
2551099 2551103 2551123 2551127 2551169 2551177 2551223 2551247 2551249 2551273
2551279 2551313 2551349 2551357 2551369 2551397 2551403 2551421 2551429 2551433
2551441 2551457 2551469 2551481 2551499 2551501 2551511 2551531 2551543 2551559
2551603 2551607 2551639 2551651 2551657 2551687 2551697 2551709 2551723 2551729
2551733 2551793 2551817 2551823 2551831 2551841 2551859 2551867 2551877 2551883
2551903 2551933 2551943 2551957 2551961 2551979 2551981 2551987 2551999 2552009
2552021 2552027 2552041 2552047 2552059 2552107 2552111 2552113 2552117 2552119
2552171 2552183 2552191 2552197 2552201 2552219 2552233 2552239 2552279 2552293
2552317 2552357 2552359 2552369 2552383 2552387 2552393 2552413 2552449 2552461
2552477 2552483 2552503 2552507 2552513 2552527 2552531 2552581 2552587 2552597
2552603 2552611 2552621 2552623 2552647 2552651 2552653 2552657 2552659
2552677 2552687 2552713 2552717 2552729 2552761 2552773 2552777 2552779 2552807
2552833 2552843 2552857 2552861 2552887 2552917 2552939 2552951 2552959 2552969
2552983 2552987 2553017 2553041 2553053 2553071 2553101 2553113 2553119 2553139
2553149 2553151 2553157 2553203 2553209 2553217 2553223 2553227 2553233 2553241
```

```
2553251 2553283 2553289 2553293 2553301 2553337 2553347 2553371 2553389 2553403
2553409 2553427 2553431 2553433 2553457 2553491 2553497 2553503 2553511 2553527
2553539 2553541 2553547 2553559 2553599 2553601 2553611 2553631 2553637 2553647
2553659 2553671 2553701 2553739 2553751 2553781 2553797 2553823 2553829 2553853
2553857 2553869 2553871 2553907 2553917 2553937 2553949 2553959 2554003 2554007
2554021 2554039 2554043 2554049 2554067 2554087 2554093 2554099 2554103 2554109
2554129 2554133 2554141 2554171 2554187 2554231 2554247 2554249 2554261 2554271
2554273 2554283 2554289 2554313 2554319 2554333 2554337 2554339 2554397 2554399
2554421 2554439 2554451 2554457 2554459 2554469 2554481 2554529
2554543 2554549 2554553 2554561 2554583 2554589 2554621 2554637 2554649 2554663
2554711 2554729 2554733 2554753 2554757 2554763 2554787 2554789 2554801 2554807
2554819 2554829 2554831 2554843 2554891 2554897 2554907 2554921 2554963 2554969
2554973 2554991 2555009 2555011 2555027 2555041 2555057 2555081 2555089 2555099
2555123 2555129 2555131 2555141 2555159 2555167 2555171 2555173 2555191 2555197
2555213 2555221 2555227 2555233 2555251 2555261 2555263 2555281 2555303 2555309
2555317 2555347 2555353 2555363 2555429 2555453 2555459 2555477 2555521 2555543
2555549 2555551 2555561 2555569 2555591 2555617 2555629 2555639 2555647
2555669 2555687 2555699 2555711 2555731 2555753 2555767 2555779 2555809 2555837
2555863 2555873 2555881 2555883 2555893 2555911 2555921 2555951 2555957 2555989
2556011 2556019 2556023 2556041 2556061 2556067 2556079 2556091 2556101 2556107
2556121 2556133 2556139 2556143 2556149 2556161 2556163 2556179 2556187 2556193
2556217 2556233 2556259 2556277 2556331 2556373 2556397 2556403 2556419 2556451
2556457 2556461 2556467 2556487 2556493 2556503 2556509 2556523 2556559 2556569
2556577 2556607 2556641 2556661 2556683 2556689 2556713 2556739 2556761 2556791
2556793 2556803 2556821 2556839 2556857 2556871 2556877 2556907 2556913 2556943
2556977 2556991 2556997 2557007 2557013 2557063 2557067 2557099 2557111 2557127
2557169 2557171 2557199 2557201 2557213 2557231 2557241 2557273 2557277 2557279
2557297 2557333 2557337 2557351 2557367 2557369 2557397 2557417 2557433 2557441
2557447 2557453 2557501 2557507 2557517 2557519 2557553 2557561 2557567 2557601
2557603 2557613 2557631 2557649 2557663 2557673 2557691 2557697 2557729 2557741
2557757 2557777 2557813 2557817 2557823 2557843 2557861 2557877 2557889
2557897 2557901 2557909 2557931 2557937 2557957 2557963 2557967 2557999 2558009
2558011 2558021 2558029 2558047 2558077 2558081 2558093 2558131 2558137 2558173
2558189 2558197 2558219 2558239 2558243 2558249 2558251 2558287
2558317 2558321 2558323 2558333 2558341 2558377 2558411 2558419 2558429 2558471
2558473 2558489 2558503 2558509 2558527 2558531 2558533 2558599 2558609
2558639 2558671 2558683 2558701 2558719 2558729 2558737 2558747 2558753 2558779
2558783 2558791 2558813 2558837 2558849 2558861 2558879 2558909 2558917 2558929
2558953 2559013 2559041 2559043 2559077 2559079 2559083 2559101
2559121 2559131 2559149 2559173 2559181 2559191 2559223 2559229 2559247 2559251
2559269 2559283 2559287 2559289 2559313 2559341 2559379 2559383 2559397 2559409
2559421 2559437 2559439 2559449 2559457 2559461 2559481 2559493 2559497 2559517
2559523 2559541 2559553 2559581 2559587 2559593 2559607 2559611 2559617 2559619
2559631 2559677 2559691 2559703 2559721 2559727 2559731 2559751 2559769 2559773
2559787 2559797 2559811 2559827 2559829 2559839 2559857 2559863 2559901 2559913
2559937 2559959 2559989 2560021 2560031 2560039 2560049 2560057 2560087
2560093 2560099 2560123 2560127 2560141 2560147 2560157 2560169 2560171 2560211
2560213 2560219 2560243 2560247 2560273 2560279 2560297 2560303 2560339 2560343
2560351 2560357 2560361 2560367 2560373 2560379 2560399 2560417 2560427 2560433
2560457 2560471 2560487 2560499 2560517 2560543 2560549 2560583 2560601 2560603
2560637 2560639 2560651 2560661 2560669 2560687 2560721 2560739 2560741 2560759
2560783 2560793 2560823 2560837 2560847 2560849 2560871 2560891 2560927 2560937
2560939 2560967 2560973 2560979 2560993 2560997 2561017 2561021 2561023 2561051
2561063 2561071 2561089 2561093 2561099 2561129 2561137 2561159 2561179 2561191
2561201 2561227 2561231 2561233 2561239 2561261 2561263 2561267 2561269 2561291
2561323 2561327 2561341 2561387 2561389 2561409 2561411 2561423 2561431 2561469
2561513 2561521 2561527 2561549 2561551 2561593 2561627 2561633 2561651 2561653
2561659 2561681 2561683 2561723 2561729 2561731 2561737 2561747 2561749 2561753
2561759 2561761 2561771 2561807 2561813 2561821 2561833 2561857 2561863 2561873
2561899 2561921 2561927 2561929 2561953 2561959 2561963 2561969 2561981 2561987
2562011 2562023 2562029 2562031 2562097 2562143 2562163 2562167 2562191 2562199
2562233 2562239 2562251 2562253 2562277 2562289 2562317 2562323 2562337 2562347
2562349 2562383 2562389 2562403 2562421 2562431 2562433 2562451 2562463 2562467
2562503 2562517 2562533 2562551 2562557 2562559 2562589 2562601 2562611 2562613
2562619 2562629 2562641 2562661 2562667 2562689 2562691 2562713 2562719 2562737
2562751 2562803 2562809 2562827 2562841 2562881 2562907 2562941 2562943 2562947
2562977 2562979 2562983 2563003 2563007 2563009 2563013 2563063 2563079 2563087
2563109 2563117 2563139 2563147 2563151 2563153 2563181 2563193 2563199 2563207
2563217 2563229 2563237 2563261 2563291 2563303 2563307 2563331 2563343 2563357
2563367 2563369 2563381 2563387 2563409 2563417 2563433 2563441 2563453 2563489
2563493 2563507 2563523 2563543 2563553 2563601 2563633 2563643 2563657 2563661
2563667 2563679 2563711 2563723 2563733 2563747 2563751 2563763 2563777 2563811
2563819 2563837 2563849 2563859 2563867 2563897 2563901 2563907 2563909 2563921
2563927 2563933 2563937 2563943 2563969 2563997 2564011 2564027 2564039 2564053
2564057 2564071 2564077 2564101 2564117 2564123 2564143 2564147 2564171 2564203
2564207 2564249 2564251 2564279 2564321 2564323 2564327 2564329 2564333 2564347
2564363 2564369 2564381 2564407 2564423 2564447 2564459 2564489 2564519 2564521
2564539 2564561 2564567 2564579 2564593 2564609 2564621 2564633 2564651 2564657
2564663 2564669 2564701 2564711 2564719 2564741 2564747 2564759 2564813 2564819
2564831 2564843 2564887 2564899 2564917 2564921 2564957 2564999 2565007 2565023
2565047 2565049 2565053 2565061 2565067 2565089 2565103 2565109 2565139 2565149
2565151 2565161 2565191 2565203 2565221 2565239 2565257 2565263 2565289 2565319
2565337 2565349 2565377 2565383 2565389 2565391 2565403 2565449 2565461 2565463
2565559 2565569 2565593 2565611 2565643 2565649 2565671 2565679 2565701 2565709
2565713 2565757 2565769 2565791 2565799 2565809 2565847 2565863 2565881 2565907
2565917 2565947 2565989 2566001 2566013 2566019 2566021 2566027 2566049 2566051
2566063 2566073 2566093 2566097 2566127 2566129 2566139 2566141 2566163 2566171
2566177 2566183 2566189 2566199 2566219 2566229 2566237 2566241 2566253 2566259
2566261 2566279 2566307 2566327 2566339 2566351 2566367 2566411 2566423 2566427
```

```
2566433 2566469 2566481 2566489 2566513 2566517 2566519 2566549 2566561 2566567
2566589 2566591 2566601 2566633 2566637 2566651 2566661 2566667 2566673 2566679
2566687 2566699 2566709 2566747 2566757 2566771 2566783 2566787 2566807 2566829
2566859 2566867 2566897 2566909 2566931 2566939 2566981 2566997 2567009 2567029
2567041 2567083 2567111 2567113 2567129 2567177 2567179 2567197 2567219 2567233
2567269 2567287 2567303 2567311 2567321 2567333 2567339 2567347 2567351 2567353
2567363 2567371 2567377 2567387 2567417 2567423 2567437 2567443 2567447 2567449
2567471 2567491 2567519 2567531 2567533 2567557 2567569 2567581 2567599 2567611
2567623 2567627 2567633 2567639 2567647 2567671 2567683 2567693 2567701 2567729
2567749 2567753 2567759 2567767 2567779 2567783 2567801 2567809 2567819 2567821
2567827 2567849 2567879 2567891 2567923 2567933 2567941 2567963 2567977 2567987
2568001 2568011 2568023 2568029 2568031 2568061 2568079 2568091 2568101 2568111
2568121 2568131 2568169 2568187 2568191 2568197 2568233 2568239 2568253 2568259
2568263 2568271 2568299 2568323 2568331 2568341 2568373 2568389 2568403 2568407
2568413 2568427 2568431 2568457 2568469 2568473 2568481 2568497 2568499 2568509
2568523 2568541 2568557 2568563 2568569 2568619 2568623 2568641 2568653 2568659
2568673 2568689 2568697 2568701 2568703 2568719 2568739 2568757 2568793 2568817
2568823 2568827 2568833 2568869 2568871 2568901 2568911 2568913 2568931 2568941
2568953 2568983 2568997 2569003 2569013 2569027 2569079 2569093 2569103 2569109
2569117 2569157 2569181 2569201 2569213 2569253 2569267 2569279 2569297 2569309
2569321 2569327 2569331 2569361 2569393 2569421 2569423 2569439 2569451 2569459
2569477 2569481 2569513 2569529 2569543 2569549 2569571 2569577 2569607 2569649
2569667 2569681 2569691 2569717 2569739 2569741 2569751 2569753 2569759 2569789
2569799 2569817 2569823 2569841 2569891 2569927 2569937 2569939 2569943 2569961
2569969 2569979 2570011 2570017 2570047 2570069 2570083 2570119 2570137 2570177
2570189 2570201 2570203 2570207 2570219 2570221 2570233 2570251 2570311 2570317
2570327 2570333 2570363 2570369 2570371 2570387 2570389 2570401 2570419 2570429
2570431 2570437 2570441 2570459 2570467 2570471 2570507 2570509 2570537 2570539
2570563 2570573 2570591 2570599 2570609 2570611 2570627 2570639 2570651 2570657
2570663 2570671 2570677 2570683 2570693 2570699 2570713 2570717 2570749 2570761
2570773 2570783 2570801 2570809 2570831 2570849 2570851 2570891 2570903 2570921
2570933 2570941 2570951 2570957 2570969 2570989 2571001 2571007 2571011 2571017
2571031 2571059 2571067 2571071 2571073 2571113 2571119 2571139 2571181 2571197
2571203 2571209 2571269 2571277 2571281 2571287 2571307 2571313 2571329 2571337
2571409 2571421 2571427 2571449 2571451 2571461 2571473 2571497 2571509 2571551
2571553 2571557 2571563 2571581 2571599 2571619 2571649 2571671 2571697 2571703
2571713 2571721 2571731 2571733 2571757 2571773 2571809 2571823 2571827 2571851
2571871 2571893 2571911 2571937 2571949 2571953 2571979 2572001 2572019 2572027
2572033 2572043 2572057 2572079 2572081 2572091 2572093 2572099 2572103 2572109
2572121 2572123 2572127 2572133 2572139 2572153 2572183 2572211 2572231 2572237
2572243 2572261 2572267 2572279 2572289 2572307 2572327 2572363 2572373 2572379
2572393 2572397 2572399 2572417 2572421 2572433 2572469 2572483 2572487 2572489
2572513 2572517 2572519 2572523 2572529 2572589 2572607 2572613 2572621 2572649
2572651 2572663 2572667 2572679 2572681 2572693 2572697 2572699 2572741 2572747
2572769 2572777 2572781 2572789 2572799 2572811 2572859 2572877 2572937 2572939
2572949 2572981 2572993 2573003 2573023 2573047 2573057 2573059 2573063 2573071
2573099 2573101 2573107 2573143 2573149 2573161 2573209 2573231 2573237 2573251
2573261 2573287 2573293 2573339 2573353 2573357 2573359 2573383 2573393 2573413
2573423 2573437 2573449 2573453 2573471 2573479 2573491 2573509 2573533 2573551
2573561 2573591 2573617 2573621 2573633 2573653 2573657 2573689 2573707 2573717
2573729 2573737 2573777 2573803 2573807 2573827 2573833 2573869 2573881 2573887
2573891 2573927 2573947 2573957 2573983 2574007 2574029 2574031 2574037 2574043
2574059 2574071 2574113 2574149 2574151 2574167 2574179 2574181 2574193 2574203
2574211 2574217 2574223 2574233 2574239 2574251 2574289 2574311 2574317 2574323
2574337 2574353 2574391 2574401 2574409 2574433 2574437 2574449 2574461 2574469
2574487 2574493 2574499 2574511 2574521 2574529 2574541 2574553 2574563 2574569
2574587 2574589 2574601 2574617 2574623 2574653 2574661 2574683 2574703 2574721
2574727 2574731 2574751 2574757 2574763 2574799 2574811 2574839 2574851 2574853
2574889 2574917 2574947 2574959 2574967 2574977 2574983 2575019 2575021 2575043
2575049 2575061 2575063 2575073 2575081 2575091 2575093 2575117 2575123 2575129
2575147 2575187 2575193 2575219 2575231 2575247 2575277 2575283 2575289 2575297
2575301 2575319 2575327 2575337 2575351 2575361 2575369 2575373 2575411 2575421
2575439 2575453 2575457 2575487 2575493 2575499 2575523 2575537 2575543 2575549
2575589 2575627 2575633 2575663 2575673 2575679 2575717 2575723 2575733 2575753
2575757 2575777 2575787 2575799 2575801 2575817 2575819 2575831 2575843 2575861
2575871 2575877 2575879 2575897 2575901 2575919 2575921 2575933 2575939 2575943
2575967 2576003 2576033 2576047 2576053 2576081 2576089 2576107 2576113 2576137
2576159 2576183 2576209 2576219 2576221 2576227 2576251 2576257 2576261 2576263
2576279 2576293 2576297 2576323 2576341 2576363 2576369 2576393 2576407 2576411
2576423 2576459 2576467 2576473 2576477 2576507 2576517 2576549 2576551 2576557
2576573 2576591 2576593 2576597 2576599 2576617 2576633 2576641 2576653 2576663
2576669 2576683 2576699 2576719 2576729 2576731 2576767 2576771 2576773 2576779
2576789 2576797 2576801 2576831 2576857 2576863 2576883 2576909 2576929 2576933
2576953 2576983 2576993 2577007 2577011 2577031 2577037 2577041 2577049 2577073
2577077 2577079 2577083 2577097 2577101 2577167 2577187 2577203 2577221 2577241
2577283 2577287 2577299 2577307 2577313 2577329 2577343 2577347 2577389 2577397
2577401 2577409 2577413 2577427 2577431 2577437 2577439 2577473 2577479 2577493
2577511 2577539 2577563 2577569 2577571 2577581 2577593 2577599 2577611 2577623
2577637 2577661 2577667 2577671 2577683 2577697 2577733 2577739 2577763 2577767
2577791 2577821 2577833 2577851 2577857 2577871 2577877 2577881 2577889 2577899
2577907 2577917 2577919 2577923 2577941 2577943 2577947 2577989 2578003 2578019
2578027 2578031 2578057 2578061 2578087 2578099 2578109 2578111 2578117 2578133
2578153 2578157 2578201 2578207 2578217 2578249 2578253 2578259 2578267 2578273
2578297 2578343 2578349 2578351 2578391 2578393 2578403 2578417 2578423 2578451
2578453 2578463 2578469 2578489 2578517 2578519 2578529 2578559 2578573 2578757
2578591 2578603 2578621 2578643 2578657 2578717 2578721 2578729 2578733 2578757
2578759 2578787 2578799 2578801 2578817 2578819 2578837 2578847 2578861 2578879
2578907 2578931 2578943 2578963 2578969 2578973 2578987 2578991 2578993 2579009
2579051 2579063 2579081 2579111 2579119 2579167 2579177 2579179 2579191 2579201
```

```
2579209  2579221  2579249  2579273  2579287  2579323  2579329  2579333  2579341  2579363
2579377  2579387  2579389  2579399  2579411  2579419  2579443  2579453  2579477  2579513
2579537  2579581  2579593  2579617  2579623  2579627  2579651  2579663  2579659  2579683
2579693  2579711  2579719  2579729  2579737  2579741  2579777  2579803  2579807  2579809
2579813  2579821  2579827  2579891  2579911  2579921  2579939  2579963  2579977  2579989
2579999  2580031  2580049  2580079  2580119  2580131  2580167  2580169  2580173  2580187
2580197  2580203  2580241  2580251  2580287  2580289  2580313  2580323  2580337  2580341
2580401  2580407  2580419  2580421  2580443  2580463  2580467  2580469  2580493  2580497
2580509  2580511  2580521  2580527  2580541  2580547  2580563  2580587  2580607  2580619
2580631  2580647  2580649  2580653  2580659  2580661  2580667  2580671  2580673  2580689
2580691  2580701  2580703  2580707  2580737  2580749  2580757  2580791  2580803  2580811
2580839  2580841  2580847  2580857  2580859  2580887  2580901  2580917  2580931  2580937
2580953  2580959  2580973  2580997  2581003  2581013  2581027  2581031  2581049  2581069
2581079  2581081  2581097  2581121  2581123  2581133  2581141  2581147  2581171  2581177
2581181  2581211  2581213  2581219  2581223  2581253  2581273  2581279  2581289  2581349
2581357  2581367  2581373  2581391  2581393  2581409  2581417  2581429  2581441  2581457
2581477  2581487  2581507  2581531  2581541  2581559  2581561  2581573  2581583  2581597
2581613  2581633  2581639  2581643  2581651  2581669  2581673  2581687  2581697  2581699
2581721  2581741  2581769  2581771  2581829  2581837  2581847  2581861  2581877  2581907
2581913  2581919  2581921  2581927  2581933  2581939  2581951  2581961  2581963  2581973
2581991  2582009  2582029  2582033  2582053  2582059  2582071  2582077  2582087  2582089
2582093  2582143  2582149  2582159  2582161  2582171  2582197  2582201  2582219  2582243
2582257  2582311  2582323  2582329  2582353  2582357  2582369  2582383  2582399  2582401
2582407  2582441  2582443  2582491  2582501  2582543  2582551  2582581  2582609  2582611
2582627  2582663  2582677  2582681  2582687  2582707  2582719  2582729  2582731  2582737
2582753  2582761  2582771  2582773  2582779  2582837  2582863  2582897  2582903  2582911
2582939  2582947  2582953  2582971  2582981  2582999  2583011  2583017  2583019  2583029
2583083  2583089  2583101  2583103  2583109  2583127  2583131  2583143  2583169  2583173
2583179  2583181  2583187  2583211  2583223  2583239  2583241  2583253  2583257  2583283
2583299  2583331  2583341  2583353  2583359  2583389  2583391  2583419  2583431  2583437
2583457  2583461  2583463  2583467  2583491  2583499  2583517  2583527  2583547  2583557
2583577  2583589  2583611  2583629  2583631  2583661  2583667  2583671  2583703  2583709
2583719  2583727  2583733  2583739  2583743  2583767  2583769  2583781  2583793  2583811
2583837  2583839  2583857  2583859  2583863  2583877  2583887  2583907  2583947  2583979
2584007  2584009  2584031  2584033  2584037  2584061  2584079  2584081  2584091  2584097
2584141  2584147  2584159  2584207  2584213  2584229  2584249  2584261  2584279  2584291
2584301  2584319  2584331  2584367  2584369  2584381  2584403  2584411  2584433  2584457
2584469  2584481  2584511  2584523  2584529  2584559  2584573  2584583  2584591  2584597
2584607  2584619  2584661  2584679  2584693  2584739  2584787  2584789  2584807  2584819
2584843  2584847  2584853  2584871  2584877  2584889  2584891  2584909  2584913  2584937
2584949  2584981  2585111  2585113  2585123  2585129  2585137  2585161  2585179  2585237
2585057  2585081  2585111  2585113  2585123  2585129  2585137  2585161  2585179  2585237
2585243  2585251  2585267  2585279  2585293  2585333  2585347  2585351  2585353  2585357
2585381  2585389  2585399  2585413  2585417  2585447  2585459  2585467  2585477  2585491
2585507  2585509  2585521  2585549  2585579  2585603  2585623  2585641  2585647  2585659
2585707  2585743  2585777  2585783  2585797  2585813  2585827  2585833  2585837  2585839
2585899  2585909  2585929  2585941  2585951  2585953  2585963  2585969  2585971  2585981
2585983  2586011  2586037  2586047  2586061  2586127  2586137  2586139  2586161  2586167
2586169  2586173  2586187  2586209  2586253  2586271  2586277  2586289  2586293  2586301
2586313  2586341  2586343  2586359  2586377  2586379  2586391  2586421  2586443  2586497
2586503  2586517  2586541  2586569  2586581  2586589  2586593  2586599  2586611  2586629
2586631  2586643  2586659  2586667  2586673  2586709  2586719  2586721  2586767  2586769
2586797  2586799  2586809  2586861  2586821  2586823  2586841  2586847  2586853  2586911
2586917  2586931  2586943  2586953  2586959  2586967  2586979  2586989  2587001  2587007
2587019  2587031  2587049  2587069  2587073  2587093  2587099  2587103  2587121  2587127
2587129  2587139  2587147  2587157  2587159  2587163  2587183  2587187  2587217  2587253
2587271  2587279  2587289  2587337  2587357  2587399  2587411  2587421  2587423  2587441
2587499  2587531  2587537  2587547  2587549  2587567  2587589  2587609  2587639  2587649
2587693  2587709  2587727  2587747  2587751  2587759  2587771  2587789  2587801  2587829
2587841  2587847  2587861  2587877  2587889  2587903  2587909  2587913  2587939  2587943
2587957  2587967  2587969  2587979  2587993  2587997  2588051  2588059  2588071  2588077
2588087  2588093  2588101  2588107  2588129  2588141  2588177  2588203  2588219  2588227
2588231  2588249  2588263  2588269  2588281  2588293  2588297  2588303  2588309  2588323
2588347  2588353  2588357  2588359  2588363  2588401  2588419  2588441  2588461  2588473
2588477  2588501  2588513  2588527  2588543  2588567  2588591  2588611  2588629  2588669
2588671  2588681  2588689  2588701  2588711  2588723  2588753  2588767  2588771  2588809
2588819  2588821  2588827  2588869  2588893  2588897  2588899  2588923  2588969  2588983
2589007  2589011  2589029  2589047  2589053  2589071  2589101  2589107  2589113  2589121
2589127  2589131  2589143  2589161  2589193  2589199  2589203  2589217  2589227  2589229
2589233  2589239  2589247  2589269  2589281  2589289  2589313  2589319  2589341  2589343
2589347  2589359  2589397  2589407  2589427  2589443  2589469  2589473  2589479  2589487
2589533  2589551  2589553  2589557  2589563  2589577  2589599  2589607  2589611  2589619
2589623  2589641  2589649  2589659  2589677  2589679  2589701  2589703  2589737  2589749
2589779  2589791  2589793  2589799  2589809  2589817  2589859  2589883  2589887  2589893
2589913  2589931  2589971  2589991  2590013  2590031  2590033  2590039  2590051  2590079
2590087  2590097  2590117  2590127  2590129  2590139  2590157  2590169  2590177  2590183
2590223  2590249  2590271  2590279  2590349  2590361  2590369  2590373  2590381  2590387
2590397  2590411  2590417  2590429  2590433  2590439  2590457  2590463  2590493  2590501
2590507  2590537  2590547  2590583  2590589  2590597  2590633  2590649  2590691  2590717
2590723  2590729  2590769  2590771  2590811  2590829  2590837  2590841  2590873  2590877
2590883  2590891  2590909  2590921  2590937  2590943  2590979  2590997  2591023  2591027
2591041  2591053  2591059  2591093  2591119  2591131  2591143  2591153  2591167  2591189
2591191  2591213  2591233  2591243  2591261  2591263  2591269  2591273  2591333  2591363
2591389  2591401  2591419  2591441  2591447  2591453  2591461  2591471  2591513  2591521
2591539  2591551  2591579  2591587  2591609  2591623  2591669  2591681  2591683  2591711
2591717  2591731  2591737  2591747  2591749  2591767  2591773  2591777  2591779  2591783
2591791  2591807  2591819  2591821  2591839  2591843  2591851  2591857  2591891  2591899
2591917  2591921  2591969  2591971  2591987  2592043  2592053  2592067  2592089  2592103
2592119  2592133  2592167  2592193  2592199  2592209  2592221  2592229  2592241  2592253
```

```
2592259  2592263  2592269  2592277  2592287  2592311  2592329  2592361  2592383  2592409
2592413  2592419  2592467  2592487  2592521  2592523  2592539  2592547  2592581  2592587
2592589  2592593  2592631  2592647  2592649  2592673  2592677  2592691  2592697  2592719
2592731  2592761  2592763  2592769  2592773  2592781  2592791  2592829  2592847  2592851
2592853  2592869  2592899  2592901  2592913  2592929  2592983  2593039  2593051  2593067
2593079  2593091  2593099  2593117  2593121  2593141  2593147  2593159  2593183  2593211
2593223  2593247  2593249  2593259  2593271  2593277  2593301  2593309  2593337  2593361
2593363  2593379  2593391  2593397  2593399  2593403  2593421  2593439  2593453  2593477
2593511  2593517  2593529  2593543  2593561  2593607  2593609  2593621  2593627  2593651
2593681  2593691  2593693  2593697  2593729  2593751  2593753  2593757  2593769  2593777
2593793  2593841  2593853  2593859  2593891  2593897  2593907  2593919  2593933  2593939
2593957  2593961  2593991  2593993  2594003  2594017  2594023  2594027  2594057  2594063
2594077  2594093  2594099  2594131  2594143  2594153  2594161  2594167  2594209  2594213
2594219  2594227  2594237  2594243  2594257  2594303  2594321  2594327  2594351  2594381
2594399  2594413  2594437  2594443  2594453  2594479  2594503  2594531  2594533  2594539
2594549  2594567  2594569  2594573  2594609  2594611  2594671  2594677  2594681  2594689
2594701  2594707  2594719  2594723  2594741  2594747  2594759  2594777  2594789  2594803
2594807  2594821  2594831  2594861  2594869  2594873  2594881  2594909  2594923  2594939
2594947  2594951  2594953  2594957  2594959  2594971  2594981  2594983  2594987  2594989
2595017  2595023  2595029  2595031  2595037  2595049  2595059  2595079  2595097  2595107
2595139  2595149  2595157  2595167  2595193  2595247  2595277  2595283  2595287  2595311
2595319  2595323  2595331  2595337  2595349  2595353  2595377  2595401  2595421  2595433
2595451  2595473  2595479  2595487  2595491  2595517  2595521  2595559  2595563  2595583
2595589  2595601  2595613  2595629  2595631  2595641  2595643  2595653  2595667  2595683
2595731  2595737  2595743  2595773  2595787  2595793  2595821  2595851  2595871  2595893
2595899  2595919  2595937  2595947  2595961  2595979  2596001  2596021  2596057  2596063
2596067  2596091  2596123  2596127  2596129  2596133  2596147  2596151  2596163  2596213
2596229  2596241  2596247  2596277  2596303  2596333  2596339  2596351  2596361  2596367
2596379  2596387  2596439  2596441  2596459  2596481  2596487  2596499  2596501  2596513
2596553  2596577  2596579  2596589  2596603  2596613  2596619  2596621  2596637  2596639
2596661  2596663  2596667  2596669  2596679  2596681  2596687  2596717  2596729  2596739
2596793  2596799  2596819  2596837  2596849  2596871  2596873  2596883  2596889  2596897
2596927  2596933  2596943  2596949  2596969  2596973  2596991  2597011  2597029  2597041
2597047  2597057  2597059  2597081  2597083  2597093  2597099  2597113  2597117  2597191
2597207  2597233  2597237  2597263  2597279  2597297  2597299  2597303  2597323  2597333
2597339  2597347  2597359  2597377  2597401  2597407  2597453  2597461  2597467  2597489
2597503  2597513  2597519  2597533  2597537  2597591  2597603  2597611  2597627  2597629
2597641  2597663  2597669  2597681  2597687  2597701  2597713  2597723  2597729  2597743
2597761  2597773  2597777  2597809  2597857  2597867  2597869  2597897  2597899  2597909
2597911  2597939  2597953  2597963  2597971  2597977  2597981  2598091  2598109  2598119
2598121  2598133  2598137  2598151  2598157  2598163  2598179  2598181  2598191  2598199
2598217  2598247  2598259  2598283  2598311  2598317  2598341  2598347  2598367  2598397
2598403  2598439  2598443  2598503  2598509  2598511  2598521  2598523  2598553  2598571
2598583  2598593  2598599  2598601  2598631  2598653  2598689  2598691  2598697  2598707
2598721  2598731  2598733  2598737  2598751  2598767  2598779  2598811  2598829  2598847
2598857  2598859  2598889  2598899  2598913  2598919  2598929  2598941  2598971  2598983
2598989  2599013  2599039  2599043  2599073  2599087  2599099  2599109  2599111  2599117
2599141  2599153  2599187  2599189  2599193  2599199  2599217  2599231  2599237  2599243
2599273  2599297  2599321  2599327  2599349  2599397  2599403  2599427  2599451  2599489
2599501  2599507  2599543  2599549  2599559  2599573  2599577  2599591  2599609  2599613
2599627  2599631  2599633  2599661  2599669  2599673  2599679  2599699  2599721  2599739
2599741  2599747  2599777  2599783  2599787  2599813  2599819  2599829  2599843  2599847
2599859  2599867  2599871  2599889  2599907  2599931  2599937  2599981  2599991  2599999
2600011  2600033  2600051  2600057  2600089  2600113  2600119  2600137  2600161  2600177
2600209  2600231  2600239  2600251  2600267  2600287  2600291  2600309  2600317  2600327
2600329  2600341  2600347  2600383  2600387  2600393  2600407  2600417  2600453  2600461
2600467  2600483  2600489  2600503  2600509  2600519  2600531  2600561  2600567  2600569
2600581  2600593  2600599  2600603  2600627  2600681  2600687  2600707  2600761  2600783
2600803  2600809  2600821  2600837  2600867  2600887  2600903  2600911  2600947  2600951
2600957  2600963  2600977  2601023  2601029  2601041  2601083  2601089  2601091  2601127
2601143  2601149  2601167  2601197  2601239  2601253  2601259  2601281  2601299  2601301
2601311  2601331  2601337  2601349  2601367  2601377  2601383  2601413  2601437  2601439
2601451  2601463  2601479  2601481  2601509  2601517  2601523  2601539  2601563  2601569
2601583  2601601  2601607  2601617  2601661  2601671  2601679  2601713  2601757  2601761
2601763  2601773  2601787  2601817  2601821  2601827  2601839  2601847  2601853  2601857
2601869  2601899  2601913  2601931  2601943  2601979  2601997  2602007  2602009  2602043
2602057  2602073  2602081  2602087  2602097  2602111  2602121  2602163  2602169  2602177
2602189  2602217  2602261  2602267  2602273  2602279  2602283  2602291  2602307  2602319
2602331  2602333  2602337  2602349  2602351  2602367  2602399  2602417  2602429  2602441
2602447  2602451  2602463  2602477  2602507  2602511  2602541  2602571  2602573  2602597
2602603  2602637  2602673  2602679  2602681  2602693  2602697  2602711  2602723  2602741
2602771  2602781  2602783  2602793  2602849  2602877  2602879  2602889  2602909  2602927
2602937  2602939  2602973  2602993  2603039  2603047  2603059  2603063  2603077  2603087
2603093  2603099  2603141  2603143  2603219  2603231  2603233  2603239  2603269  2603281
2603291  2603299  2603311  2603333  2603353  2603369  2603371  2603399  2603401  2603409
2603441  2603443  2603467  2603479  2603483  2603509  2603537  2603543  2603561  2603563
2603569  2603581  2603617  2603621  2603639  2603647  2603677  2603681  2603701  2603719
2603723  2603743  2603759  2603789  2603791  2603819  2603831  2603849  2603851  2603857
2603879  2603897  2603911  2603921  2603927  2603929  2603933  2603981  2604011  2604013
2604053  2604061  2604071  2604079  2604101  2604127  2604139  2604163  2604167  2604187
2604191  2604211  2604227  2604253  2604257  2604263  2604269  2604289  2604293  2604299
2604307  2604347  2604377  2604391  2604401  2604431  2604439  2604499  2604509  2604521
2604523  2604529  2604557  2604559  2604583  2604593  2604601  2604611  2604617  2604647
2604661  2604671  2604677  2604683  2604703  2604731  2604733  2604737  2604739  2604743
2604769  2604779  2604799  2604803  2604821  2604829  2604839  2604857  2604869  2604887
2604907  2604913  2604949  2604977  2604997  2605007  2605013  2605019  2605021  2605039
2605073  2605081  2605087  2605091  2605103  2605139  2605159  2605171  2605177  2605189
2605201  2605231  2605237  2605243  2605259  2605289  2605303  2605313  2605319  2605349
2605363  2605373  2605387  2605391  2605409  2605411  2605433  2605439  2605481  2605483
```

```
2605501 2605523 2605529 2605531 2605543 2605579 2605609 2605613 2605627 2605637
2605661 2605663 2605741 2605747 2605751 2605753 2605763 2605769 2605781 2605787
2605819 2605847 2605849 2605871 2605909 2605927 2605931 2605943 2605973 2605979
2605987 2605991 2606011 2606017 2606039 2606041 2606053 2606069 2606129 2606161
2606171 2606179 2606183 2606189 2606221 2606231 2606251 2606267 2606269 2606281
2606297 2606311 2606353 2606377 2606393 2606407 2606431 2606437 2606459 2606473
2606489 2606497 2606503 2606509 2606519 2606551 2606579 2606587 2606603 2606633
2606651 2606677 2606683 2606693 2606717 2606731 2606741 2606753 2606767 2606771
2606783 2606803 2606809 2606833 2606873 2606881 2606887 2606917 2606927 2606939
2606941 2606951 2606963 2606969 2606999 2607029 2607041 2607061 2607083 2607097
2607107 2607109 2607139 2607167 2607169 2607173 2607179 2607181 2607217 2607271
2607277 2607289 2607301 2607337 2607347 2607359 2607373 2607377 2607383 2607403
2607413 2607431 2607461 2607469 2607481 2607491 2607509 2607523 2607529 2607551
2607557 2607571 2607581 2607587 2607589 2607599 2607601 2607637 2607659 2607673
2607677 2607721 2607733 2607743 2607791 2607793 2607799 2607823 2607827 2607853
2607863 2607929 2607973 2607989 2607991 2608007 2608013 2608033 2608037 2608049
2608091 2608097 2608103 2608117 2608121 2608127 2608129 2608139 2608147 2608159
2608169 2608181 2608211 2608219 2608237 2608253 2608283 2608303 2608313 2608349
2608351 2608367 2608381 2608387 2608393 2608409 2608439 2608447 2608471
2608483 2608513 2608517 2608519 2608549 2608559 2608561 2608577 2608583 2608589
2608601 2608631 2608649 2608663 2608693 2608699 2608703 2608721 2608733 2608741
2608751 2608763 2608777 2608813 2608847 2608861 2608873 2608883 2608889 2608897
2608919 2608933 2608943 2608951 2608993 2609021 2609027 2609029 2609059 2609069
2609071 2609081 2609083 2609107 2609147 2609171 2609207 2609209 2609219 2609231
2609237 2609249 2609261 2609263 2609267 2609287 2609297 2609309 2609311 2609329
2609339 2609353 2609357 2609371 2609377 2609401 2609407 2609413 2609417 2609423
2609443 2609471 2609489 2609491 2609501 2609513 2609521 2609533 2609539 2609587
2609597 2609599 2609639 2609657 2609671 2609683 2609693 2609699 2609701 2609731
2609753 2609767 2609777 2609791 2609809 2609813 2609839 2609899 2609903 2609947
2609953 2609963 2609989 2610059 2610077 2610089 2610121 2610131 2610133 2610137
2610161 2610191 2610193 2610199 2610211 2610221 2610227 2610233 2610241 2610259
2610263 2610287 2610317 2610341 2610343 2610359 2610379 2610383 2610449 2610451
2610463 2610473 2610497 2610499 2610529 2610533 2610539 2610577 2610583 2610589
2610607 2610611 2610613 2610623 2610649 2610653 2610677 2610679 2610701 2610719
2610721 2610737 2610761 2610781 2610787 2610791 2610821 2610823 2610827 2610859
2610889 2610901 2610919 2610929 2610943 2610953 2610967 2610973 2610977 2610989
2611001 2611009 2611027 2611039 2611043 2611051 2611061 2611087 2611093 2611111
2611117 2611123 2611139 2611157 2611159 2611199 2611207 2611211 2611229 2611237
2611277 2611291 2611321 2611361 2611369 2611391 2611403 2611439 2611457 2611481
2611487 2611507 2611513 2611529 2611541 2611559 2611573 2611579 2611597 2611603
2611613 2611621 2611663 2611669 2611643 2611663 2611667 2611669 2611699 2611703
2611723 2611729 2611733 2611751 2611799 2611801 2611813 2611841 2611849 2611859
2611879 2611901 2611907 2611909 2611937 2611951 2611963 2611979 2611981 2611991
2611997 2612003 2612017 2612021 2612039 2612083 2612123 2612131 2612143 2612167
2612171 2612201 2612209 2612243 2612249 2612251 2612257 2612287 2612297 2612321
2612327 2612333 2612341 2612347 2612353 2612369 2612377 2612383 2612399 2612411
2612413 2612419 2612429 2612431 2612437 2612471 2612483 2612497 2612503 2612507
2612521 2612537 2612539 2612549 2612647 2612651 2612677 2612699 2612707 2612719
2612749 2612759 2612789 2612791 2612821 2612843 2612851 2612867 2612873 2612879
2612881 2612893 2612921 2612927 2612947 2612957 2612969 2612983 2612989 2612999
2613011 2613029 2613041 2613043 2613073 2613079 2613109 2613113 2613133 2613139
2613151 2613167 2613187 2613197 2613211 2613227 2613313 2613313 2613323 2613343
2613349 2613353 2613361 2613371 2613389 2613397 2613413 2613487 2613503 2613521
2613539 2613547 2613601 2613607 2613613 2613647 2613649 2613671 2613673 2613679
2613701 2613707 2613713 2613719 2613727 2613731 2613739 2613757 2613761 2613763
2613769 2613817 2613829 2613833 2613839 2613847 2613883 2613901 2613931 2613931
2613953 2613977 2613979 2613983 2613991 2613997 2614043 2614061 2614063 2614067
2614069 2614081 2614103 2614121 2614123 2614133 2614159 2614163 2614169 2614177
2614181 2614193 2614211 2614219 2614223 2614237 2614279 2614301 2614303 2614307
2614327 2614333 2614351 2614361 2614363 2614369 2614373 2614393 2614397 2614427
2614441 2614453 2614459 2614463 2614471 2614487 2614499 2614511 2614517 2614519
2614559 2614567 2614607 2614613 2614621 2614627 2614631 2614681 2614687 2614691
2614699 2614729 2614739 2614747 2614763 2614771 2614793 2614813 2614817 2614819
2614823 2614841 2614849 2614853 2614883 2614987 2614993 2614999 2615047 2615051
2615069 2615083 2615089 2615101 2615111 2615113 2615117 2615147 2615177 2615183
2615189 2615209 2615219 2615227 2615233 2615243 2615257 2615279 2615281 2615287
2615299 2615309 2615317 2615329 2615341 2615351 2615357 2615359 2615383 2615441
2615447 2615449 2615497 2615519 2615527 2615531 2615533 2615551 2615581 2615581
2615593 2615617 2615623 2615651 2615653 2615669 2615681 2615699 2615707 2615719
2615731 2615737 2615761 2615779 2615783 2615791 2615797 2615803 2615827 2615833
2615839 2615857 2615861 2615869 2615897 2615903 2615917 2615929 2615953 2615957
2615959 2615969 2615971 2615981 2615983 2615989 2615999 2616007 2616017 2616023
2616041 2616071 2616139 2616143 2616179 2616191 2616193 2616199 2616209 2616217
2616221 2616241 2616269 2616277 2616287 2616331 2616347 2616353 2616359 2616371
2616379 2616407 2616437 2616461 2616469 2616491 2616533 2616553 2616577 2616599
2616613 2616637 2616643 2616659 2616667 2616671 2616673 2616683 2616701 2616703
2616707 2616721 2616739 2616749 2616767 2616773 2616781 2616787 2616791 2616797
2616821 2616829 2616839 2616869 2616877 2616881 2616883 2616941 2616947 2616947
2616959 2617001 2617037 2617061 2617067 2617081 2617091 2617093 2617103 2617129
2617141 2617169 2617171 2617183 2617187 2617189 2617207 2617211 2617243 2617247
2617253 2617259 2617261 2617267 2617271 2617301 2617313 2617319 2617379 2617393
2617397 2617403 2617409 2617411 2617427 2617429 2617457 2617471 2617499 2617513
2617519 2617523 2617553 2617567 2617577 2617583 2617591 2617603 2617613 2617621
2617631 2617633 2617651 2617673 2617691 2617697 2617717 2617721 2617777 2617793
2617799 2617807 2617817 2617837 2617873 2617883 2617907 2617951 2617961 2617993
2617997 2618003 2618023 2618027 2618039 2618047 2618053 2618081 2618089 2618093
2618101 2618107 2618111 2618117 2618173 2618179 2618191 2618197 2618237 2618249
2618261 2618263 2618279 2618281 2618339 2618347 2618387 2618411 2618423 2618449
2618461 2618467 2618501 2618521 2618531 2618533 2618537 2618543 2618579 2618587
```

```
2618593  2618617  2618633  2618653  2618659  2618717  2618741  2618747  2618761  2618767
2618773  2618779  2618797  2618807  2618813  2618831  2618839  2618843  2618873  2618879
2618881  2618893  2618909  2618923  2618927  2618933  2618953  2618983  2619007  2619011
2619013  2619049  2619053  2619059  2619103  2619163  2619179  2619209  2619223  2619229
2619257  2619277  2619289  2619293  2619299  2619301  2619329  2619347  2619361  2619373
2619389  2619391  2619413  2619433  2619443  2619457  2619481  2619521  2619557  2619559
2619611  2619641  2619647  2619653  2619667  2619671  2619691  2619761  2619787  2619809
2619817  2619821  2619833  2619847  2619857  2619871  2619913  2619917  2619919  2619931
2619937  2619961  2619973  2619997  2620003  2620019  2620021  2620031  2620039  2620073
2620087  2620097  2620099  2620129  2620139  2620141  2620147  2620153  2620171  2620181
2620199  2620207  2620223  2620231  2620253  2620259  2620273  2620279  2620283  2620301
2620307  2620313  2620339  2620369  2620379  2620403  2620417  2620421  2620439  2620441
2620477  2620483  2620493  2620507  2620511  2620529  2620531  2620573  2620577  2620589
2620591  2620619  2620633  2620637  2620661  2620663  2620741  2620811  2620819  2620829
2620847  2620883  2620897  2620901  2620909  2620913  2620921  2620927  2620939  2620951
2620967  2620999  2621023  2621027  2621033  2621053  2621063  2621119  2621131  2621137
2621147  2621159  2621167  2621197  2621207  2621219  2621229  2621257  2621263  2621279
2621303  2621309  2621347  2621351  2621369  2621371  2621387  2621431  2621447  2621459
2621467  2621477  2621501  2621527  2621551  2621569  2621573  2621579  2621603  2621611
2621617  2621669  2621693  2621699  2621737  2621761  2621767  2621779  2621789  2621797
2621807  2621819  2621837  2621849  2621863  2621881  2621897  2621903  2621917  2621921
2621923  2621929  2621933  2621947  2621951  2621987  2622013  2622017  2622031  2622049
2622091  2622119  2622121  2622143  2622157  2622167  2622173  2622203  2622211  2622229
2622241  2622283  2622287  2622293  2622307  2622311  2622337  2622341  2622343  2622349
2622353  2622377  2622397  2622407  2622413  2622419  2622427  2622439  2622443  2622461
2622469  2622479  2622511  2622517  2622533  2622559  2622577  2622583  2622593  2622601
2622611  2622619  2622623  2622637  2622679  2622691  2622707  2622733  2622749  2622757
2622761  2622773  2622799  2622821  2622827  2622857  2622863  2622889  2622911  2622923
2622937  2622959  2623039  2623051  2623073  2623087  2623091  2623099  2623111  2623123
2623133  2623141  2623147  2623157  2623163  2623169  2623193  2623207  2623217  2623223
2623241  2623249  2623259  2623267  2623279  2623289  2623331  2623333  2623339  2623343
2623351  2623367  2623373  2623391  2623409  2623421  2623429  2623441  2623451  2623459
2623477  2623487  2623529  2623531  2623567  2623571  2623573  2623583  2623589  2623591
2623597  2623639  2623651  2623667  2623711  2623721  2623723  2623757  2623759  2623769
2623783  2623801  2623807  2623847  2623861  2623867  2623883  2623897  2623913  2623937
2623939  2623969  2623979  2623991  2623993  2623997  2624023  2624029  2624051  2624053
2624059  2624087  2624099  2624107  2624113  2624173  2624177  2624179  2624183  2624191
2624203  2624233  2624257  2624263  2624267  2624269  2624291  2624309  2624311  2624317
2624327  2624353  2624357  2624371  2624381  2624387  2624411  2624431  2624437  2624467
2624483  2624513  2624539  2624549  2624561  2624563  2624581  2624593  2624623  2624627
2624639  2624653  2624659  2624663  2624693  2624701  2624711  2624753  2624759  2624767
2624771  2624777  2624803  2624807  2624813  2624837  2624857  2624899  2624911  2624927
2624939  2624957  2624959  2624971  2624977  2624981  2624989  2625001  2625011  2625017
2625023  2625061  2625067  2625071  2625079  2625137  2625149  2625163  2625169  2625223
2625229  2625241  2625247  2625253  2625263  2625277  2625307  2625313  2625317  2625333
2625349  2625397  2625433  2625449  2625481  2625487  2625503  2625521  2625523  2625533
2625541  2625551  2625563  2625569  2625577  2625587  2625613  2625617  2625619  2625641
2625643  2625653  2625671  2625691  2625761  2625809  2625811  2625817  2625829  2625839
2625851  2625859  2625869  2625901  2625907  2625911  2625929  2625947  2625949  2625977
2626003  2626021  2626027  2626049  2626051  2626061  2626069  2626073  2626079  2626087
2626121  2626171  2626181  2626229  2626249  2626259  2626277  2626291  2626307  2626319
2626363  2626367  2626399  2626433  2626447  2626451  2626457  2626471  2626493  2626499
2626511  2626543  2626567  2626571  2626597  2626607  2626633  2626639  2626643  2626649
2626691  2626699  2626703  2626727  2626751  2626753  2626763  2626777  2626781  2626801
2626817  2626837  2626861  2626873  2626879  2626901  2626903  2626927  2626931  2626933
2626937  2626969  2626973  2627021  2627041  2627047  2627059  2627069  2627083  2627113
2627117  2627123  2627143  2627167  2627173  2627179  2627189  2627201  2627203  2627237
2627243  2627267  2627291  2627297  2627357  2627381  2627393  2627399  2627413  2627419
2627423  2627431  2627473  2627477  2627479  2627483  2627507  2627509  2627519  2627557
2627561  2627563  2627593  2627617  2627627  2627657  2627671  2627689  2627693  2627699
2627701  2627711  2627759  2627767  2627771  2627789  2627791  2627837  2627857  2627869
2627879  2627897  2627921  2627929  2627953  2627959  2627971  2627981  2627983  2627987
2627993  2628053  2628077  2628083  2628089  2628103  2628107  2628113  2628127  2628133
2628139  2628163  2628167  2628169  2628191  2628229  2628277  2628331  2628341  2628347
2628359  2628383  2628401  2628407  2628481  2628487  2628499  2628533  2628539  2628541
2628553  2628559  2628581  2628599  2628607  2628617  2628649  2628667  2628679  2628683
2628697  2628709  2628713  2628737  2628749  2628779  2628781  2628809  2628811  2628817
2628823  2628827  2628833  2628839  2628889  2628911  2628919  2628953  2628979  2629001
2629009  2629021  2629031  2629051  2629057  2629073  2629091  2629093  2629103  2629117
2629127  2629129  2629139  2629177  2629213  2629223  2629243  2629247  2629261  2629267
2629307  2629309  2629351  2629369  2629381  2629409  2629421  2629423  2629433  2629447
2629457  2629469  2629481  2629483  2629499  2629507  2629511  2629519  2629537  2629541
2629547  2629589  2629591  2629621  2629639  2629643  2629651  2629661  2629669  2629687
2629703  2629721  2629723  2629729  2629763  2629777  2629787  2629789  2629811  2629829
2629841  2629853  2629859  2629867  2629873  2629877  2629897  2629901  2629903  2629909
2629927  2629931  2629933  2629943  2629969  2629973  2630041  2630077  2630093  2630099
2630107  2630129  2630143  2630153  2630171  2630179  2630197  2630207  2630237  2630239
2630281  2630317  2630321  2630323  2630333  2630339  2630351  2630357  2630363  2630371
2630377  2630389  2630399  2630423  2630429  2630431  2630447  2630471  2630477  2630483
2630489  2630491  2630501  2630521  2630539  2630557  2630583  2630591  2630599  2630609
2630623  2630627  2630681  2630689  2630707  2630713  2630729  2630741  2630743  2630773
2630791  2630819  2630833  2630839  2630843  2630857  2630861  2630863  2630879  2630891
2630917  2630923  2630951  2630959  2630989  2631007  2631019  2631029  2631037  2631043
2631049  2631053  2631067  2631071  2631077  2631091  2631103  2631133  2631137  2631143
2631149  2631179  2631203  2631217  2631221  2631241  2631247  2631259  2631263  2631269
2631271  2631281  2631283  2631323  2631337  2631347  2631401  2631427  2631437  2631449
2631457  2631467  2631469  2631487  2631493  2631509  2631511  2631523  2631527  2631529
2631533  2631539  2631553  2631581  2631631  2631647  2631649  2631653  2631661  2631679
2631689  2631691  2631701  2631731  2631743  2631767  2631793  2631817  2631833  2631851
```

```
2631887  2631917  2631919  2631929  2631947  2631949  2631971  2631973  2631983  2631989
2632001  2632009  2632021  2632031  2632037  2632057  2632061  2632067  2632079  2632099
2632111  2632121  2632129  2632151  2632153  2632163  2632169  2632177  2632187  2632213
2632219  2632247  2632249  2632271  2632277  2632309  2632313  2632319  2632339  2632361
2632369  2632379  2632387  2632391  2632397  2632411  2632429  2632447  2632463  2632471
2632477  2632493  2632499  2632523  2632537  2632543  2632549  2632573  2632579  2632601
2632627  2632633  2632657  2632673  2632687  2632691  2632717  2632723  2632727  2632759
2632781  2632789  2632793  2632801  2632829  2632831  2632859  2632867  2632873  2632901
2632907  2632919  2632937  2632967  2632999  2633023  2633041  2633053  2633083
2633101  2633107  2633123  2633129  2633131  2633161  2633173  2633203  2633207  2633219
2633221  2633227  2633261  2633263  2633273  2633291  2633297  2633303  2633311  2633321
2633333  2633353  2633359  2633387  2633399  2633417  2633429  2633437  2633441  2633443
2633447  2633459  2633467  2633473  2633483  2633489  2633497  2633509  2633531  2633537
2633539  2633557  2633563  2633581  2633593  2633597  2633629  2633639  2633641  2633651
2633663  2633677  2633681  2633689  2633711  2633713  2633737  2633749  2633783  2633789
2633831  2633843  2633857  2633863  2633899  2633909  2633923  2633947  2633987  2634001
2634011  2634013  2634083  2634109  2634119  2634131  2634139  2634161  2634193  2634199
2634227  2634241  2634251  2634263  2634301  2634319  2634341  2634353  2634377  2634403
2634419  2634427  2634433  2634449  2634461  2634479  2634487  2634493  2634509  2634517
2634523  2634539  2634551  2634557  2634607  2634613  2634623  2634629  2634631  2634649
2634689  2634691  2634707  2634713  2634727  2634743  2634761  2634769  2634781  2634791
2634823  2634829  2634833  2634839  2634859  2634881  2634883  2634893  2634923  2634941
2634943  2634953  2634967  2634991  2635007  2635019  2635033  2635037  2635057  2635063
2635079  2635097  2635099  2635109  2635121  2635141  2635163  2635189  2635229  2635247
2635253  2635267  2635313  2635331  2635349  2635387  2635411  2635429  2635447  2635481
2635483  2635487  2635489  2635543  2635553  2635583  2635597  2635613  2635643  2635673
2635691  2635693  2635709  2635727  2635747  2635757  2635783  2635793  2635819  2635861
2635877  2635879  2635883  2635891  2635907  2635909  2635933  2635939  2635949  2635967
2635973  2635979  2635987  2636009  2636021  2636027  2636033  2636059  2636063  2636077
2636087  2636107  2636119  2636143  2636149  2636171  2636197  2636203  2636233  2636243
2636251  2636261  2636279  2636311  2636317  2636323  2636339  2636353  2636357  2636369
2636401  2636407  2636437  2636449  2636453  2636471  2636483  2636503  2636507  2636527
2636539  2636549  2636567  2636597  2636609  2636617  2636633  2636663  2636671  2636677
2636701  2636713  2636719  2636759  2636773  2636779  2636791  2636797  2636813  2636831
2636857  2636863  2636873  2636897  2636917  2636929  2636939  2636957  2636971  2636983
2637001  2637013  2637017  2637043  2637083  2637119  2637133  2637163  2637169  2637191
2637197  2637199  2637209  2637221  2637251  2637253  2637259  2637269  2637281  2637287
2637301  2637331  2637343  2637353  2637361  2637373  2637379  2637419  2637451  2637469
2637493  2637497  2637529  2637539  2637541  2637553  2637581  2637587  2637611  2637631
2637647  2637659  2637667  2637671  2637673  2637683  2637689  2637707  2637743  2637763
2637769  2637773  2637779  2637787  2637797  2637799  2637911  2637919  2637931  2637937
2637953  2637959  2637961  2637983  2637997  2638003  2638039  2638057  2638061  2638073
2638087  2638177  2638187  2638199  2638201  2638231  2638243  2638253  2638267  2638271
2638297  2638301  2638319  2638327  2638331  2638357  2638367  2638369  2638381  2638403
2638411  2638469  2638477  2638501  2638529  2638543  2638561  2638567  2638579  2638589
2638607  2638613  2638631  2638633  2638651  2638667  2638673  2638687  2638693  2638697
2638717  2638747  2638771  2638787  2638793  2638841  2638843  2638849  2638873  2638879
2638887  2638901  2638907  2638931  2638949  2638973  2639041  2639069  2639071
2639083  2639093  2639107  2639111  2639149  2639171  2639177  2639179  2639183  2639201
2639207  2639213  2639239  2639251  2639291  2639303  2639323  2639333  2639339  2639353
2639383  2639393  2639401  2639407  2639419  2639431  2639447  2639477  2639489  2639491
2639501  2639509  2639513  2639521  2639561  2639569  2639587  2639597  2639633  2639639
2639669  2639699  2639701  2639711  2639723  2639759  2639761  2639773  2639789  2639801
2639809  2639827  2639863  2639869  2639873  2639881  2639887  2639891  2639911  2639921
2639927  2639939  2639941  2639953  2639969  2639971  2639999  2640013  2640017  2640023
2640041  2640059  2640067  2640137  2640139  2640161  2640167  2640181  2640217  2640227
2640251  2640271  2640289  2640299  2640317  2640343  2640347  2640349  2640361  2640367
2640371  2640383  2640397  2640409  2640497  2640503  2640509  2640511  2640527  2640551
2640571  2640577  2640581  2640643  2640683  2640689  2640707  2640709  2640713  2640721
2640739  2640749  2640761  2640767  2640779  2640821  2640823  2640853  2640857  2640863
2640871  2640881  2640889  2640893  2640901  2640907  2640917  2640919  2640941  2640947
2640959  2640973  2640997  2641013  2641027  2641031  2641039  2641061  2641063  2641099
2641109  2641123  2641127  2641151  2641153  2641187  2641193  2641217  2641237  2641277
2641279  2641283  2641313  2641337  2641351  2641357  2641363  2641367  2641369  2641391
2641411  2641421  2641423  2641433  2641451  2641459  2641469  2641487  2641493  2641501
2641517  2641519  2641531  2641543  2641547  2641549  2641553  2641559  2641567  2641571
2641577  2641631  2641633  2641637  2641649  2641657  2641663  2641669  2641687  2641739
2641747  2641759  2641777  2641799  2641801  2641811  2641829  2641831  2641841  2641879
2641889  2641901  2641907  2641909  2641921  2641927  2641939  2641949  2641993  2642039
2642041  2642063  2642077  2642111  2642117  2642137  2642141  2642147  2642149  2642173
2642179  2642201  2642203  2642231  2642239  2642257  2642287  2642291  2642323  2642329
2642333  2642351  2642357  2642359  2642369  2642383  2642389  2642449  2642473  2642483
2642513  2642537  2642543  2642561  2642569  2642579  2642603  2642609  2642621  2642639
2642693  2642699  2642707  2642713  2642771  2642777  2642789  2642791  2642797  2642821
2642839  2642863  2642869  2642879  2642891  2642897  2642929  2642933  2642971  2642987
2642993  2643013  2643019  2643037  2643059  2643061  2643073  2643079  2643097  2643107
2643119  2643131  2643133  2643161  2643181  2643209  2643227  2643239  2643241  2643247
2643283  2643307  2643331  2643341  2643343  2643349  2643353  2643383  2643397  2643427
2643439  2643457  2643461  2643479  2643491  2643497  2643523  2643547  2643559  2643569
2643581  2643583  2643593  2643607  2643629  2643637  2643659  2643661  2643671  2643673
2643677  2643691  2643709  2643713  2643733  2643737  2643743  2643757  2643779  2643791
2643821  2643833  2643853  2643871  2643889  2643899  2643913  2643917  2643943  2643947
2643959  2643989  2644003  2644007  2644039  2644049  2644063  2644067  2644073  2644091
2644093  2644121  2644127  2644139  2644141  2644151  2644153  2644157  2644171  2644177
2644181  2644183  2644219  2644247  2644261  2644277  2644339  2644357  2644381  2644387
2644399  2644403  2644409  2644429  2644451  2644489  2644507  2644513  2644531  2644547
2644561  2644573  2644613  2644619  2644627  2644637  2644667  2644669  2644687  2644709
2644727  2644729  2644751  2644769  2644799  2644823  2644847  2644849  2644853  2644879
2644883  2644891  2644903  2644907  2644913  2644919  2644921  2644927  2644981  2645011
```

```
2645051 2645057 2645063 2645087 2645099 2645101 2645129 2645131 2645141 2645171
2645189 2645191 2645213 2645219 2645221 2645233 2645239 2645257 2645263 2645267
2645297 2645311 2645329 2645341 2645359 2645371 2645393 2645399 2645413 2645417
2645429 2645431 2645453 2645477 2645479 2645507 2645519 2645521 2645527 2645543
2645549 2645551 2645561 2645567 2645569 2645581 2645597 2645603 2645639 2645647
2645651 2645663 2645681 2645701 2645711 2645717 2645723 2645743 2645749 2645777
2645779 2645809 2645827 2645831 2645843 2645849 2645861 2645879 2645887 2645891
2645893 2645899 2645911 2645917 2645927 2645933 2645941 2645971 2645977 2645987
2646001 2646011 2646013 2646019 2646023 2646029 2646041 2646071 2646079 2646089
2646107 2646109 2646113 2646167 2646179 2646211 2646227 2646233 2646247 2646269
2646353 2646361 2646409 2646443 2646463 2646473 2646493 2646517 2646533 2646551
2646571 2646583 2646599 2646613 2646619 2646641 2646649 2646653 2646659 2646671
2646733 2646769 2646773 2646793 2646797 2646803 2646841 2646881 2646887 2646893
2646901 2646923 2646937 2646983 2646989 2646991 2647003 2647009 2647013
2647027 2647031 2647039 2647049 2647063 2647067 2647079 2647081 2647097 2647111
2647133 2647157 2647159 2647163 2647187 2647193 2647243 2647259 2647279 2647303
2647319 2647321 2647331 2647343 2647349 2647361 2647363 2647367 2647373 2647391
2647397 2647429 2647459 2647471 2647481 2647499 2647531 2647537 2647549 2647559
2647571 2647573 2647577 2647607 2647627 2647643 2647649 2647681 2647693 2647709
2647717 2647751 2647759 2647763 2647769 2647781 2647793 2647807 2647817 2647847
2647873 2647889 2647891 2647919 2647943 2647951 2647969 2647987 2647993 2647999
2648021 2648029 2648033 2648047 2648057 2648081 2648083 2648099 2648101 2648123
2648131 2648137 2648161 2648167 2648183 2648189 2648207 2648213 2648227 2648249
2648263 2648267 2648273 2648287 2648291 2648323 2648351 2648363
2648369 2648377 2648383 2648419 2648449 2648479 2648501 2648507 2648509 2648531
2648533 2648537 2648557 2648563 2648567 2648593 2648623 2648629 2648669 2648687
2648693 2648699 2648707 2648713 2648717 2648731 2648761 2648801 2648813 2648827
2648861 2648879 2648897 2648903 2648909 2648911 2648917 2648953 2648959 2648963
2649001 2649011 2649067 2649077 2649083 2649091 2649109 2649137 2649139 2649173
2649193 2649197 2649203 2649217 2649233 2649281 2649293 2649299 2649307 2649319
2649323 2649329 2649371 2649391 2649397 2649403 2649421 2649431 2649473 2649481
2649487 2649497 2649499 2649503 2649529 2649541 2649547 2649551 2649553 2649557
2649587 2649593 2649611 2649613 2649677 2649679 2649709 2649727 2649733 2649769
2649781 2649799 2649811 2649821 2649851 2649863 2649869 2649877 2649887 2649893
2649923 2649929 2649931 2649967 2649979 2649989 2650007 2650009 2650013 2650027
2650033 2650057 2650061 2650073 2650091 2650093 2650127 2650157 2650163 2650169
2650183 2650211 2650229 2650231 2650237 2650247 2650259 2650301 2650321 2650337
2650357 2650369 2650379 2650381 2650387 2650399 2650409 2650429 2650433 2650463
2650493 2650517 2650537 2650541 2650559 2650567 2650573 2650577 2650579 2650597
2650603 2650619 2650621 2650639 2650663 2650667 2650699 2650751 2650757 2650783
2650787 2650789 2650799 2650807 2650829 2650853 2650873 2650897 2650931 2650933
2650943 2650961 2650969 2650981 2650987 2651017 2651039 2651041 2651053 2651059
2651063 2651083 2651111 2651119 2651137 2651189 2651191 2651197 2651237 2651239
2651273 2651281 2651291 2651293 2651329 2651333 2651339 2651359 2651377 2651387
2651413 2651419 2651437 2651443 2651447 2651471 2651483 2651489 2651491 2651497
2651501 2651503 2651513 2651549 2651569 2651581 2651603 2651611 2651617 2651629
2651639 2651651 2651669 2651683 2651687 2651699 2651707 2651713 2651717 2651729
2651741 2651743 2651777 2651783 2651791 2651807 2651819 2651821 2651837 2651861
2651893 2651899 2651911 2651947 2651953 2651959 2651989 2652007 2652011 2652029
2652031 2652037 2652043 2652047 2652101 2652103 2652113 2652131 2652149 2652151
2652157 2652161 2652179 2652203 2652217 2652223 2652269 2652301 2652313 2652367
2652371 2652373 2652379 2652389 2652401 2652407 2652409 2652421 2652437 2652439
2652443 2652473 2652479 2652487 2652511 2652553 2652557 2652569 2652599 2652607
2652623 2652667 2652677 2652709 2652719 2652737 2652743 2652757 2652779 2652791
2652827 2652841 2652847 2652883 2652911 2652941 2652943 2652953 2652961 2652983
2652997 2653019 2653033 2653051 2653067 2653081 2653097 2653109 2653111 2653121
2653187 2653193 2653219 2653237 2653249 2653271 2653319 2653327 2653333 2653337
2653351 2653363 2653421 2653429 2653433 2653459 2653481 2653489 2653499 2653517
2653537 2653543 2653549 2653571 2653583 2653591 2653601 2653613 2653619 2653621
2653633 2653681 2653687 2653697 2653699 2653723 2653727 2653733 2653741 2653753
2653789 2653801 2653811 2653813 2653841 2653867 2653873 2653883 2653897 2653907
2653913 2653951 2653957 2653967 2653969 2653979 2653991 2653999 2654011 2654021
2654027 2654059 2654083 2654107 2654111 2654117 2654123 2654143 2654149 2654161
2654209 2654213 2654221 2654237 2654263 2654273 2654291 2654297 2654303 2654317
2654359 2654371 2654383 2654387 2654389 2654401 2654447 2654467 2654489 2654497
2654501 2654503 2654507 2654539 2654543 2654557 2654581 2654593 2654609 2654621
2654647 2654651 2654653 2654671 2654677 2654693 2654711 2654719 2654753 2654759
2654767 2654779 2654783 2654801 2654803 2654831 2654833 2654849 2654857 2654863
2654881 2654893 2654909 2654917 2654957 2654963 2654989 2654999 2655017 2655047
2655049 2655053 2655061 2655071 2655113 2655127 2655139 2655151 2655167 2655173
2655199 2655209 2655217 2655221 2655241 2655251 2655259 2655313 2655343 2655347
2655361 2655371 2655397 2655403 2655407 2655409 2655431 2655437 2655439 2655449
2655461 2655463 2655469 2655479 2655481 2655517 2655559 2655563 2655571 2655577
2655607 2655623 2655643 2655661 2655691 2655701 2655727 2655761 2655773 2655781
2655797 2655799 2655803 2655817 2655827 2655831 2655841 2655853 2655883 2655899
2655911 2655929 2655937 2655941 2655943 2655949 2655973 2655977 2656009 2656013
2656033 2656051 2656057 2656079 2656091 2656099 2656117 2656141 2656163 2656169
2656183 2656189 2656207 2656211 2656229 2656243 2656261 2656271 2656273 2656289
2656309 2656319 2656321 2656337 2656351 2656361 2656363 2656373 2656387 2656391
2656417 2656427 2656441 2656453 2656457 2656477 2656499 2656501 2656529 2656547
2656553 2656601 2656627 2656639 2656649 2656663 2656673 2656681 2656699 2656721
2656727 2656729 2656757 2656783 2656807 2656813 2656831 2656847 2656853 2656861
2656867 2656877 2656883 2656889 2656909 2656919 2656921 2656949 2656961 2656987
2656991 2656993 2657003 2657023 2657027 2657047 2657059 2657069 2657071 2657077
2657101 2657111 2657119 2657129 2657143 2657159 2657173 2657189 2657191 2657197
2657201 2657203 2657231 2657243 2657257 2657279 2657293 2657309 2657327 2657329
2657339 2657341 2657353 2657371 2657381 2657393 2657399 2657401 2657407 2657429
2657461 2657477 2657483 2657513 2657527 2657533 2657561 2657563 2657569 2657573
2657591 2657609 2657617 2657651 2657657 2657671 2657687 2657731 2657741 2657761
```

```
2657771 2657779 2657801 2657843 2657861 2657867 2657887 2657911 2657939 2657947
2657951 2657999 2658013 2658023 2658049 2658059 2658067 2658077 2658079 2658101
2658107 2658193 2658199 2658203 2658209 2658221 2658247 2658251 2658259 2658263
2658287 2658289 2658301 2658323 2658349 2658353 2658361 2658373 2658377 2658379
2658391 2658437 2658449 2658451 2658457 2658463 2658497 2658503 2658521 2658553
2658559 2658569 2658577 2658583 2658611 2658637 2658641 2658659 2658661 2658671
2658683 2658701 2658703 2658707 2658751 2658757 2658769 2658779 2658787 2658793
2658797 2658827 2658833 2658847 2658863 2658871 2658881 2658883 2658889 2658899
2658913 2658941 2658947 2658977 2658979 2658983 2658989 2659001 2659037 2659043
2659067 2659073 2659081 2659091 2659127 2659133 2659159 2659177 2659187
2659201 2659243 2659247 2659277 2659289 2659309 2659331 2659337 2659339 2659343
2659367 2659379 2659399 2659439 2659441 2659451 2659453 2659469 2659471 2659483
2659493 2659511 2659519 2659537 2659549 2659567 2659571 2659607 2659621 2659627
2659637 2659663 2659673 2659687 2659691 2659717 2659751 2659763 2659771 2659801
2659841 2659849 2659859 2659861 2659879 2659883 2659903 2659931 2659949 2659963
2659999 2660003 2660011 2660029 2660069 2660071 2660087 2660089 2660107 2660117
2660131 2660137 2660173 2660179 2660183 2660219 2660237 2660291 2660303 2660311
2660351 2660353 2660377 2660401 2660417 2660429 2660447 2660461 2660467 2660473
2660509 2660521 2660527 2660533 2660557 2660569 2660573 2660579 2660587 2660591
2660597 2660611 2660621 2660639 2660657 2660659 2660719 2660737 2660743 2660753
2660767 2660773 2660783 2660803 2660809 2660831 2660839 2660849 2660863 2660869
2660873 2660887 2660899 2660963 2660989 2661013 2661067 2661079 2661089 2661097
2661103 2661107 2661119 2661137 2661157 2661161 2661181 2661199 2661221 2661233
2661251 2661271 2661283 2661317 2661331 2661341 2661371 2661391 2661397 2661403
2661409 2661413 2661419 2661427 2661457 2661473 2661481 2661487 2661493 2661497
2661517 2661541 2661553 2661557 2661569 2661611 2661641 2661643 2661647 2661661
2661689 2661731 2661733 2661739 2661779 2661781 2661797 2661821 2661833 2661853
2661863 2661871 2661899 2661917 2661929 2661931 2661937 2661943 2661947 2661949
2661959 2661961 2661991 2662027 2662067 2662069 2662097 2662103 2662117 2662123
2662129 2662133 2662141 2662157 2662159 2662193 2662201 2662207 2662211 2662271
2662291 2662307 2662339 2662381 2662399 2662453 2662469 2662489 2662477 2662487
2662501 2662507 2662511 2662547 2662567 2662601 2662607 2662651 2662657 2662661
2662669 2662697 2662721 2662753 2662757 2662763 2662769 2662771 2662783 2662787
2662811 2662813 2662841 2662883 2662901 2662903 2662921 2662929 2662943 2662949
2662951 2662981 2663027 2663029 2663039 2663051 2663057 2663069 2663081 2663107
2663137 2663153 2663159 2663189 2663209 2663231 2663251 2663267 2663279 2663293
2663299 2663347 2663351 2663357 2663359 2663393 2663429 2663431 2663459 2663461
2663467 2663491 2663497 2663501 2663513 2663527 2663533 2663539 2663567 2663569
2663579 2663581 2663603 2663627 2663651 2663669 2663677 2663687 2663693 2663701
2663711 2663761 2663779 2663783 2663803 2663813 2663827 2663831 2663867 2663887
2663897 2663953 2663977 2663993 2664001 2664017 2664029 2664041 2664061 2664043
2664049 2664059 2664061 2664071 2664073 2664083 2664089 2664097 2664127 2664149
2664163 2664169 2664173 2664187 2664191 2664197 2664203 2664227 2664229 2664241
2664247 2664253 2664271 2664293 2664307 2664329 2664341 2664353 2664367 2664379
2664397 2664401 2664439 2664443 2664449 2664451 2664479 2664511 2664517 2664521
2664533 2664539 2664547 2664551 2664553 2664577 2664589 2664593 2664601 2664643
2664647 2664661 2664689 2664691 2664707 2664709 2664721 2664763 2664793 2664811
2664817 2664829 2664847 2664859 2664889 2664899 2664901 2664911 2664923 2664929
2664943 2664953 2664967 2664989 2665001 2665007 2665009 2665021 2665027
2665031 2665037 2665043 2665051 2665057 2665063 2665081 2665093 2665109 2665121
2665139 2665153 2665177 2665181 2665189 2665199 2665231 2665237 2665241 2665249
2665253 2665261 2665291 2665319 2665321 2665343 2665357 2665363 2665367 2665373
2665387 2665391 2665409 2665427 2665433 2665459 2665469 2665483 2665499 2665501
2665513 2665547 2665589 2665601 2665627 2665667 2665669 2665687 2665717 2665727
2665763 2665771 2665781 2665799 2665801 2665811 2665823 2665841 2665843 2665849
2665867 2665879 2665891 2665913 2665931 2665939 2665967 2665973 2666001 2666021
2666029 2666039 2666051 2666071 2666087 2666089 2666101 2666117 2666141 2666177
2666197 2666201 2666221 2666227 2666267 2666273 2666281 2666291 2666303 2666309
2666381 2666383 2666393 2666423 2666429 2666453 2666491 2666507 2666513 2666519
2666537 2666539 2666561 2666581 2666591 2666633 2666641 2666647 2666659 2666663
2666693 2666699 2666717 2666743 2666747 2666759 2666779 2666789 2666809 2666819
2666861 2666863 2666887 2666891 2666929 2666947 2666953 2666969 2666987 2667019
2667047 2667053 2667059 2667061 2667097 2667131 2667167 2667187 2667191
2667193 2667199 2667211 2667221 2667227 2667263 2667289 2667307 2667311 2667319
2667341 2667349 2667359 2667361 2667383 2667433 2667439 2667451 2667461 2667463
2667481 2667499 2667503 2667569 2667571 2667601 2667611 2667631 2667641 2667647
2667659 2667667 2667689 2667727 2667757 2667761 2667779 2667799 2667851 2667859
2667871 2667881 2667883 2667887 2667919 2667937 2667941 2667947 2667949 2667979
2667983 2667989 2668027 2668051 2668063 2668091 2668093 2668097 2668103 2668123
2668129 2668163 2668177 2668199 2668213 2668217 2668219 2668229 2668231 2668241
2668243 2668247 2668249 2668271 2668277 2668297 2668301 2668307 2668313 2668333
2668343 2668357 2668363 2668399 2668411 2668427 2668433 2668453 2668459 2668469
2668559 2668571 2668577 2668583 2668591 2668619 2668637 2668663
2668669 2668693 2668727 2668733 2668769 2668781 2668793 2668829 2668837 2668849
2668877 2668879 2668883 2668903 2668907 2668909 2668931 2668963 2668993 2669003
2669011 2669047 2669057 2669077 2669111 2669123 2669137 2669167 2669201 2669203
2669209 2669231 2669237 2669243 2669257 2669263 2669267 2669269 2669281 2669321
2669327 2669339 2669341 2669351 2669369 2669389 2669393 2669417 2669419 2669423
2669431 2669437 2669461 2669477 2669497 2669507 2669509 2669521 2669549 2669581
2669591 2669603 2669659 2669669 2669687 2669699 2669717 2669729 2669753 2669767
2669789 2669801 2669803 2669837 2669857 2669873 2669881 2669897 2669903 2669951
2669959 2669977 2669987 2670011 2670029 2670049 2670053 2670067 2670079 2670113
2670131 2670167 2670181 2670191 2670197 2670223 2670301 2670331 2670337 2670341
2670373 2670439 2670443 2670449 2670457 2670463 2670467 2670491 2670533 2670539
2670571 2670589 2670611 2670637 2670643 2670653 2670667 2670673 2670707 2670709
2670719 2670721 2670739 2670749 2670761 2670769 2670791 2670793 2670797 2670809
2670817 2670881 2670923 2670931 2670973 2671021 2671033 2671037 2671043 2671063
2671073 2671087 2671093 2671121 2671133 2671139 2671169 2671171 2671181 2671183
2671187 2671199 2671211 2671231 2671241 2671271 2671297 2671309 2671327 2671337
```

```
2671351  2671367  2671369  2671391  2671447  2671489  2671507  2671523  2671541  2671561
2671573  2671577  2671583  2671589  2671597  2671607  2671619  2671631  2671649  2671651
2671661  2671663  2671667  2671679  2671681  2671693  2671729  2671751  2671777  2671787
2671793  2671813  2671819  2671829  2671843  2671849  2671883  2671901  2671909  2671919
2671927  2671931  2671939  2671961  2671969  2671987  2672003  2672023  2672039  2672053
2672057  2672083  2672099  2672113  2672123  2672143  2672171  2672183  2672203  2672233
2672237  2672249  2672273  2672303  2672309  2672317  2672323  2672357  2672363  2672377
2672381  2672387  2672389  2672401  2672413  2672431  2672443  2672477  2672497  2672507
2672533  2672557  2672567  2672573  2672599  2672617  2672629  2672633  2672639  2672671
2672687  2672701  2672731  2672767  2672779  2672783  2672797  2672821  2672833  2672867
2672881  2672903  2672921  2672947  2672987  2673019  2673059  2673061  2673067  2673089
2673103  2673107  2673119  2673127  2673137  2673149  2673173  2673193  2673197  2673211
2673217  2673227  2673257  2673259  2673263  2673271  2673277  2673283  2673289  2673311
2673329  2673331  2673343  2673397  2673431  2673449  2673457  2673469  2673491  2673499
2673511  2673521  2673523  2673527  2673529  2673557  2673577  2673599  2673617  2673631
2673637  2673653  2673673  2673677  2673683  2673701  2673707  2673721  2673739  2673751
2673761  2673763  2673767  2673787  2673797  2673871  2673883  2673857  2673859  2673871
2673883  2673899  2673929  2673941  2673977  2673989  2673991  2674013  2674031  2674039
2674043  2674069  2674093  2674121  2674123  2674169  2674201  2674207  2674223  2674241
2674247  2674267  2674271  2674291  2674297  2674303  2674313  2674319  2674333  2674337
2674349  2674363  2674367  2674369  2674381  2674393  2674403  2674429  2674453  2674487
2674513  2674517  2674523  2674531  2674537  2674541  2674543  2674547  2674549  2674561
2674577  2674579  2674621  2674631  2674673  2674691  2674733  2674829  2674843  2674849
2674853  2674871  2674879  2674913  2674921  2674927  2674937  2674943  2674957  2674961
2674979  2674981  2675003  2675009  2675011  2675017  2675027  2675039  2675053  2675077
2675081  2675087  2675089  2675093  2675111  2675117  2675129  2675131  2675147  2675149
2675161  2675191  2675201  2675203  2675213  2675227  2675249  2675261  2675293  2675297
2675303  2675317  2675327  2675329  2675347  2675369  2675419  2675423  2675441  2675461
2675467  2675471  2675479  2675483  2675527  2675531  2675557  2675587  2675609  2675633
2675653  2675657  2675683  2675693  2675731  2675737  2675741  2675753  2675759  2675773
2675807  2675821  2675831  2675833  2675839  2675857  2675863  2675867  2675879  2675909
2675921  2675923  2675927  2675957  2675983  2675989  2675993  2676001  2676031  2676049
2676053  2676067  2676077  2676127  2676139  2676143  2676151  2676161  2676187  2676217
2676221  2676239  2676241  2676269  2676301  2676307  2676313  2676329  2676337  2676343
2676347  2676353  2676367  2676371  2676383  2676403  2676407  2676409  2676419  2676433
2676451  2676467  2676491  2676493  2676523  2676529  2676539  2676547  2676563  2676577
2676581  2676589  2676593  2676637  2676643  2676673  2676679  2676683  2676689  2676719
2676721  2676727  2676731  2676743  2676761  2676811  2676823  2676827  2676847  2676887
2676893  2676907  2676911  2676917  2676923  2676953  2676959  2676969  2676997  2677069
2677093  2677097  2677099  2677121  2677127  2677133  2677151  2677153  2677159  2677183
2677187  2677201  2677217  2677267  2677273  2677277  2677289  2677291  2677319  2677343
2677349  2677369  2677373  2677393  2677447  2677471  2677513  2677523  2677531  2677559
2677573  2677583  2677589  2677607  2677627  2677639  2677643  2677673  2677681  2677693
2677709  2677733  2677747  2677757  2677769  2677783  2677793  2677817  2677819  2677837
2677847  2677861  2677901  2677903  2677937  2677963  2677967  2677973  2678009  2678017
2678041  2678047  2678101  2678111  2678119  2678131  2678141  2678147  2678149  2678153
2678167  2678173  2678177  2678209  2678219  2678227  2678251  2678311  2678321  2678323
2678329  2678359  2678363  2678381  2678383  2678387  2678399  2678437  2678441  2678447
2678471  2678497  2678519  2678531  2678539  2678551  2678567  2678587  2678591  2678623
2678629  2678651  2678681  2678699  2678719  2678729  2678737  2678743  2678747  2678749
2678789  2678807  2678831  2678839  2678887  2678897  2678903  2678909  2678941  2678983
2678993  2679031  2679037  2679041  2679073  2679077  2679091  2679101  2679119  2679139
2679143  2679163  2679191  2679199  2679211  2679233  2679239  2679241  2679253  2679269
2679277  2679283  2679289  2679301  2679307  2679331  2679337  2679349  2679371  2679379
2679389  2679401  2679403  2679407  2679427  2679433  2679449  2679461  2679463  2679491
2679493  2679497  2679509  2679511  2679533  2679541  2679553  2679559  2679587  2679613
2679617  2679619  2679641  2679643  2679647  2679653  2679667  2679673  2679697  2679709
2679731  2679737  2679749  2679763  2679773  2679811  2679841  2679847  2679869  2679871
2679877  2679899  2679949  2679953  2679959  2679967  2679973  2679979  2680003  2680009
2680031  2680039  2680079  2680087  2680091  2680103  2680109  2680123  2680127  2680133
2680141  2680231  2680261  2680267  2680277  2680283  2680297  2680313  2680357  2680367
2680393  2680399  2680409  2680421  2680427  2680451  2680471  2680481  2680493  2680519
2680541  2680553  2680567  2680571  2680583  2680597  2680607  2680609  2680619  2680661
2680661  2680681  2680693  2680697  2680709  2680721  2680753  2680763  2680771  2680801
2680807  2680813  2680819  2680823  2680831  2680837  2680877  2680879  2680891  2680897
2680907  2680943  2680969  2680987  2680999  2681009  2681017  2681021  2681027  2681033
2681039  2681059  2681069  2681117  2681141  2681167  2681183  2681191  2681197  2681201
2681207  2681213  2681249  2681267  2681293  2681297  2681321  2681347  2681381  2681387
2681389  2681417  2681423  2681443  2681447  2681453  2681467  2681473  2681477  2681507
2681521  2681533  2681557  2681561  2681573  2681579  2681611  2681617  2681663  2681681
2681683  2681713  2681719  2681729  2681803  2681807  2681827  2681843  2681849  2681857
2681863  2681873  2681879  2681881  2681893  2681897  2681927  2681929  2681951  2681969
2681989  2681993  2682011  2682013  2682037  2682041  2682061  2682067  2682079  2682101
2682103  2682131  2682143  2682161  2682217  2682221  2682227  2682247  2682269  2682271
2682299  2682301  2682307  2682313  2682319  2682331  2682347  2682359  2682373  2682377
2682391  2682397  2682457  2682497  2682503  2682509  2682517  2682527  2682539  2682541
2682551  2682569  2682577  2682623  2682649  2682653  2682679  2682689  2682731  2682739
2682751  2682767  2682773  2682793  2682803  2682829  2682853  2682859  2682887  2682937
2682947  2682949  2682961  2682983  2683003  2683007  2683013  2683049  2683061  2683063
2683073  2683097  2683099  2683103  2683133  2683139  2683147  2683151  2683159  2683169
2683181  2683201  2683211  2683217  2683223  2683259  2683319  2683321  2683339  2683361
2683363  2683381  2683397  2683423  2683463  2683477  2683489  2683511  2683517  2683519
2683529  2683537  2683543  2683561  2683567  2683589  2683591  2683609  2683613  2683621
2683649  2683657  2683661  2683669  2683679  2683697  2683717  2683727  2683753  2683757
2683771  2683777  2683781  2683783  2683787  2683789  2683799  2683823  2683829  2683861
2683897  2683903  2683981  2683987  2683999  2684021  2684023  2684041  2684053  2684057
2684063  2684069  2684081  2684083  2684093  2684141  2684161  2684177  2684179  2684203
2684207  2684219  2684233  2684237  2684257  2684273  2684287  2684293  2684299  2684333
2684347  2684371  2684389  2684401  2684431  2684449  2684467  2684471  2684477  2684509
```

2684527 2684531 2684551 2684587 2684599 2684611 2684641 2684651 2684659 2684663
2684701 2684707 2684711 2684743 2684749 2684753 2684771 2684777 2684807 2684809
2684819 2684837 2684881 2684893 2684897 2684917 2684923 2684933 2684939 2684953
2684959 2684971 2684977 2684989 2684999 2685017 2685019 2685029 2685073 2685077
2685083 2685097 2685101 2685113 2685121 2685169 2685173 2685187 2685191 2685211
2685217 2685229 2685239 2685247 2685257 2685259 2685301 2685311 2685323 2685343
2685373 2685383 2685401 2685407 2685409 2685461 2685467 2685481 2685509 2685511
2685521 2685523 2685539 2685547 2685577 2685581 2685583 2685587 2685601 2685607
2685629 2685649 2685653 2685667 2685673 2685689 2685703 2685731 2685757 2685803
2685817 2685827 2685877 2685883 2685887 2685901 2685911 2685913 2685929 2685937
2685959 2685961 2685967 2685971 2685989 2686007 2686037 2686039 2686043 2686063
2686111 2686133 2686141 2686207 2686213 2686217 2686219 2686223 2686259 2686267
2686273 2686283 2686291 2686303 2686309 2686319 2686337 2686373 2686381 2686393
2686451 2686457 2686471 2686477 2686483 2686487 2686513 2686547 2686559 2686573
2686577 2686591 2686603 2686631 2686667 2686669 2686693 2686709 2686751 2686759
2686777 2686781 2686787 2686811 2686813 2686819 2686861 2686867 2686883 2686889
2686897 2686907 2686913 2686921 2686949 2686973 2686979 2686993 2687023 2687029
2687033 2687039 2687059 2687063 2687081 2687093 2687117 2687123 2687129 2687141
2687143 2687149 2687161 2687183 2687213 2687219 2687221 2687231 2687239 2687249
2687257 2687261 2687281 2687323 2687329 2687353 2687357 2687383 2687393 2687423
2687467 2687473 2687491 2687497 2687521 2687537 2687549 2687551 2687557 2687567
2687593 2687603 2687609 2687611 2687621 2687639 2687647 2687653 2687677 2687723
2687747 2687761 2687767 2687771 2687777 2687779 2687809 2687813 2687821 2687827
2687851 2687857 2687869 2687879 2687891 2687897 2687899 2687953 2687957 2687969
2687983 2687999 2688017 2688019 2688053 2688073 2688137 2688143 2688167 2688173
2688181 2688187 2688221 2688223 2688233 2688239 2688299 2688313 2688337 2688349
2688373 2688377 2688391 2688419 2688421 2688451 2688467 2688473 2688479 2688487
2688523 2688527 2688529 2688547 2688559 2688563 2688611 2688617 2688629 2688659
2688667 2688701 2688731 2688733 2688757 2688761 2688767 2688781 2688787 2688797
2688799 2688811 2688817 2688859 2688863 2688869 2688877 2688883 2688889 2688913
2688929 2688943 2688947 2688949 2688977 2688989 2688997 2689007 2689019 2689031
2689073 2689079 2689103 2689109 2689121 2689129 2689151 2689163 2689171 2689187
2689189 2689223 2689243 2689249 2689259 2689261 2689277 2689289 2689303 2689333
2689339 2689361 2689369 2689381 2689391 2689403 2689411 2689439 2689457 2689473
2689483 2689487 2689499 2689501 2689523 2689537 2689543 2689549 2689571 2689573
2689601 2689613 2689619 2689637 2689649 2689651 2689657 2689667 2689679 2689691
2689699 2689711 2689717 2689727 2689747 2689783 2689807 2689861 2689867 2689877
2689889 2689891 2689903 2689931 2689943 2689957 2689979 2689991 2689997 2690003
2690027 2690041 2690043 2690053 2690059 2690071 2690081 2690089 2690099
2690111 2690137 2690141 2690147 2690167 2690173 2690179 2690197 2690201 2690239
2690249 2690263 2690293 2690299 2690321 2690329 2690351 2690353 2690357 2690371
2690377 2690383 2690411 2690431 2690473 2690491 2690497 2690507 2690531 2690557
2690579 2690581 2690587 2690593 2690599 2690621 2690629 2690657 2690659 2690663
2690671 2690689 2690711 2690717 2690719 2690767 2690773 2690783 2690803 2690827
2690851 2690887 2690911 2690923 2690957 2690959 2690993 2691001 2691011 2691019
2691031 2691041 2691043 2691053 2691061 2691067 2691097 2691119 2691127 2691131
2691149 2691163 2691187 2691191 2691193 2691197 2691209 2691223 2691233 2691239
2691251 2691277 2691317 2691329 2691373 2691401 2691421 2691427 2691431 2691433
2691439 2691443 2691463 2691467 2691517 2691523 2691551 2691571 2691581 2691587
2691589 2691599 2691617 2691631 2691641 2691659 2691677 2691701 2691719 2691721
2691739 2691743 2691781 2691803 2691811 2691827 2691839 2691841 2691853 2691883
2691907 2691911 2691917 2691959 2691979 2692003 2692043 2692051 2692061 2692087
2692093 2692117 2692121 2692139 2692147 2692159 2692169 2692199 2692213 2692223
2692237 2692247 2692259 2692289 2692297 2692303 2692337 2692343 2692363 2692367
2692411 2692427 2692439 2692463 2692493 2692507 2692513 2692519 2692537 2692549
2692553 2692561 2692577 2692609 2692619 2692631 2692637 2692639 2692643 2692667
2692709 2692727 2692733 2692741 2692747 2692759 2692763 2692777 2692787 2692799
2692801 2692843 2692849 2692861 2692871 2692931 2692933 2692951 2692961 2692973
2692981 2692999 2693023 2693039 2693057 2693059 2693071 2693107 2693111 2693113
2693149 2693153 2693177 2693183 2693203 2693213 2693227 2693237 2693239 2693261
2693263 2693279 2693287 2693309 2693321 2693351 2693353 2693357 2693359 2693363
2693371 2693377 2693381 2693389 2693393 2693441 2693443 2693447 2693449 2693501
2693503 2693521 2693533 2693563 2693609 2693623 2693651 2693653 2693671 2693707
2693729 2693731 2693749 2693767 2693777 2693791 2693813 2693833 2693849 2693851
2693857 2693891 2693893 2693903 2693917 2693923 2693927 2693969 2693989 2694001
2694017 2694023 2694031 2694037 2694047 2694049 2694053 2694061 2694089 2694103
2694121 2694157 2694161 2694169 2694173 2694191 2694199 2694203 2694217 2694221
2694239 2694253 2694281 2694287 2694299 2694301 2694323 2694343 2694359 2694383
2694389 2694401 2694407 2694413 2694421 2694457 2694481 2694493 2694499
2694511 2694533 2694541 2694569 2694577 2694607 2694623 2694631 2694641 2694647
2694661 2694667 2694677 2694689 2694691 2694719 2694733 2694739 2694743 2694787
2694803 2694829 2694833 2694847 2694851 2694863 2694869 2694871 2694877 2694893
2694899 2694907 2694911 2694973 2694977 2695003 2695031 2695037 2695051 2695073
2695127 2695139 2695141 2695151 2695177 2695181 2695183 2695211 2695229 2695237
2695249 2695267 2695279 2695291 2695313 2695331 2695337 2695351 2695391 2695409
2695411 2695447 2695453 2695457 2695471 2695493 2695499 2695507 2695523 2695573
2695597 2695601 2695607 2695619 2695643 2695661 2695697 2695699 2695703 2695711
2695733 2695751 2695787 2695789 2695793 2695813 2695831 2695837 2695867 2695871
2695883 2695909 2695933 2695943 2695949 2695961 2695981 2695997 2695999 2696003
2696009 2696011 2696021 2696051 2696053 2696063 2696069 2696087 2696093 2696107
2696117 2696131 2696137 2696167 2696171 2696189 2696203 2696209 2696257 2696273
2696279 2696299 2696303 2696311 2696329 2696363 2696377 2696399 2696413 2696429
2696459 2696469 2696471 2696483 2696501 2696513 2696527 2696543 2696569 2696581
2696593 2696609 2696621 2696633 2696641 2696647 2696653 2696663 2696669 2696677
2696699 2696717 2696731 2696831 2696851 2696861 2696873 2696909 2696921
2696923 2696927 2696929 2696959 2696977 2696989 2697007 2697043 2697053 2697059
2697061 2697073 2697109 2697113 2697133 2697137 2697151 2697173 2697179 2697193
2697199 2697209 2697229 2697239 2697241 2697269 2697281 2697301 2697307 2697379
2697389 2697397 2697413 2697419 2697437 2697439 2697451 2697479 2697491 2697511

```
2697517  2697529  2697533  2697547  2697553  2697571  2697581  2697587  2697599  2697637
2697661  2697689  2697697  2697701  2697719  2697727  2697733  2697743  2697757  2697763
2697767  2697769  2697797  2697803  2697809  2697823  2697853  2697869  2697887  2697911
2697913  2697931  2697953  2697971  2697973  2697977  2697983  2697991  2697997  2698001
2698009  2698021  2698027  2698049  2698063  2698079  2698097  2698099  2698103  2698109
2698159  2698181  2698183  2698187  2698193  2698211  2698217  2698229  2698231  2698253
2698261  2698273  2698277  2698279  2698303  2698321  2698331  2698357  2698387  2698441
2698453  2698463  2698471  2698481  2698499  2698517  2698541  2698571  2698573  2698583
2698607  2698609  2698649  2698651  2698667  2698679  2698681  2698687  2698691  2698697
2698721  2698727  2698739  2698753  2698771  2698777  2698789  2698799  2698807  2698819
2698841  2698847  2698853  2698867  2698921  2698933  2698951  2698967  2698979  2699009
2699017  2699051  2699087  2699093  2699101  2699111  2699129  2699143  2699149  2699171
2699183  2699269  2699287  2699297  2699299  2699327  2699339  2699341  2699357  2699369
2699371  2699377  2699383  2699393  2699419  2699423  2699429  2699453  2699461  2699471
2699479  2699507  2699513  2699531  2699561  2699569  2699591  2699597  2699611  2699621
2699623  2699647  2699657  2699659  2699687  2699689  2699701  2699713  2699743  2699747
2699761  2699773  2699777  2699803  2699839  2699867  2699869  2699887  2699903  2699911
2699951  2699971  2699981  2699989  2699999  2700023  2700037  2700067  2700079  2700083
2700091  2700101  2700107  2700119  2700121  2700143  2700151  2700163  2700169  2700179
2700199  2700209  2700211  2700227  2700233  2700241  2700281  2700319  2700323  2700329
2700367  2700377  2700389  2700391  2700419  2700427  2700431  2700449  2700463  2700469
2700487  2700493  2700497  2700517  2700521  2700541  2700559  2700563  2700583  2700601
2700611  2700613  2700617  2700623  2700647  2700707  2700713  2700727  2700743  2700767
2700779  2700809  2700811  2700823  2700829  2700833  2700839  2700847  2700851  2700853
2700881  2700899  2700917  2700967  2700979  2700989  2701007  2701009  2701091  2701099
2701103  2701109  2701117  2701151  2701177  2701183  2701201  2701207  2701261  2701267
2701271  2701277  2701297  2701301  2701319  2701331  2701339  2701343  2701393  2701403
2701409  2701411  2701423  2701427  2701459  2701471  2701483  2701493  2701529  2701571
2701577  2701579  2701583  2701597  2701627  2701631  2701637  2701661  2701663  2701679
2701687  2701693  2701709  2701723  2701739  2701789  2701847  2701849  2701871  2701877
2701883  2701903  2701913  2701927  2701931  2701957  2701967  2701969  2701987  2702003
2702033  2702041  2702057  2702059  2702069  2702081  2702083  2702093  2702107  2702113
2702143  2702153  2702159  2702173  2702197  2702209  2702213  2702233  2702243  2702257
2702261  2702309  2702317  2702321  2702327  2702347  2702393  2702449  2702467  2702471
2702489  2702509  2702551  2702603  2702639  2702647  2702653  2702657  2702671  2702681
2702701  2702719  2702723  2702737  2702741  2702747  2702759  2702773  2702789  2702803
2702809  2702837  2702839  2702857  2702879  2702893  2702897  2702929  2702951  2702977
2702993  2703011  2703013  2703031  2703047  2703049  2703067  2703101  2703137  2703139
2703163  2703191  2703193  2703199  2703251  2703269  2703271  2703313  2703331  2703341
2703347  2703373  2703401  2703403  2703413  2703419  2703427  2703433  2703461  2703473
2703497  2703551  2703577  2703587  2703593  2703599  2703601  2703607  2703611  2703619
2703637  2703653  2703667  2703671  2703677  2703683  2703707  2703733  2703739  2703761
2703763  2703781  2703787  2703809  2703829  2703859  2703887  2703889  2703907  2703917
2703929  2703941  2703973  2703979  2703983  2704019  2704021  2704027  2704043  2704049
2704067  2704103  2704109  2704111  2704127  2704129  2704157  2704189  2704193  2704199
2704217  2704253  2704277  2704283  2704291  2704297  2704301  2704349  2704357  2704381
2704391  2704393  2704417  2704421  2704447  2704451  2704469  2704519  2704529  2704543
2704549  2704553  2704567  2704579  2704591  2704607  2704661  2704693  2704697  2704703
2704711  2704733  2704739  2704747  2704753  2704769  2704771  2704789  2704813  2704817
2704831  2704837  2704841  2704847  2704873  2704901  2704903  2704907  2704909  2704927
2704931  2704937  2704939  2704943  2704957  2704963  2704969  2704979  2704981  2704987
2704993  2704997  2705009  2705041  2705047  2705051  2705063  2705069  2705071  2705077
2705081  2705093  2705111  2705113  2705133  2705141  2705147  2705189  2705203  2705243
2705249  2705251  2705257  2705291  2705299  2705317  2705321  2705341  2705359  2705377
2705383  2705413  2705419  2705441  2705447  2705471  2705509  2705519  2705531  2705537
2705539  2705561  2705569  2705617  2705623  2705627  2705629  2705641  2705663  2705687
2705693  2705741  2705761  2705779  2705819  2705821  2705827  2705831  2705849  2705851
2705863  2705869  2705909  2705933  2705939  2705951  2705957  2705971  2705977  2705981
2705993  2706017  2706029  2706047  2706059  2706061  2706073  2706079  2706089  2706097
2706101  2706107  2706139  2706149  2706163  2706167  2706169  2706173  2706211  2706241
2706257  2706283  2706293  2706313  2706317  2706323  2706337  2706343  2706391  2706413
2706419  2706427  2706437  2706443  2706481  2706503  2706527  2706559  2706563  2706577
2706593  2706601  2706629  2706637  2706653  2706667  2706673  2706677  2706679  2706701
2706719  2706727  2706731  2706787  2706793  2706799  2706817  2706841  2706857  2706923
2706929  2706953  2706959  2706967  2706971  2706973  2706989  2707007  2707037  2707039
2707049  2707057  2707073  2707079  2707087  2707091  2707099  2707109  2707127  2707129
2707163  2707183  2707213  2707223  2707273  2707283  2707297  2707319  2707321  2707339
2707343  2707349  2707357  2707373  2707379  2707387  2707391  2707417  2707423  2707457
2707459  2707477  2707489  2707499  2707501  2707511  2707541  2707559  2707589  2707591
2707603  2707609  2707619  2707651  2707657  2707693  2707733  2707711  2707739  2707741
2707751  2707769  2707781  2707799  2707801  2707841  2707843  2707847  2707853  2707867
2707897  2707909  2707921  2707931  2707961  2707967  2707979  2707987  2708053  2708071
2708077  2708099  2708149  2708171  2708177  2708201  2708213  2708221  2708243  2708249
2708257  2708261  2708263  2708267  2708291  2708297  2708309  2708311  2708327  2708333
2708347  2708351  2708371  2708401  2708417  2708429  2708443  2708467  2708477  2708483
2708509  2708521  2708533  2708543  2708551  2708557  2708581  2708597  2708603  2708611
2708623  2708633  2708647  2708653  2708663  2708669  2708681  2708683  2708689  2708701
2708711  2708737  2708753  2708767  2708801  2708809  2708813  2708819  2708821  2708833
2708837  2708843  2708851  2708869  2708879  2708891  2708903  2708941  2708983  2708999
2709019  2709023  2709061  2709073  2709079  2709097  2709107  2709167  2709169  2709173
2709197  2709199  2709233  2709253  2709257  2709263  2709269  2709271  2709283  2709293
2709313  2709319  2709323  2709359  2709361  2709391  2709397  2709467  2709479  2709481
2709491  2709517  2709569  2709583  2709589  2709593  2709599  2709601  2709611  2709643
2709659  2709667  2709671  2709677  2709709  2709713  2709727  2709737  2709739  2709767
2709787  2709791  2709793  2709797  2709821  2709841  2709859  2709871  2709877
2709887  2709899  2709907  2709923  2710003  2710007  2710009  2710013  2710039  2710063
2710087  2710093  2710111  2710117  2710151  2710177  2710187  2710189  2710193  2710207
2710241  2710249  2710273  2710289  2710303  2710313  2710321  2710339  2710363  2710373
2710381  2710397  2710399  2710403  2710439  2710441  2710447  2710451  2710453  2710457
```

```
2710517  2710541  2710553  2710571  2710621  2710649  2710663  2710679  2710681  2710693
2710699  2710723  2710759  2710777  2710781  2710823  2710831  2710847  2710861  2710867
2710889  2710907  2710909  2710921  2710927  2710931  2710933  2710937  2710943  2710957
2710963  2710969  2710997  2711017  2711039  2711047  2711057  2711077  2711081  2711087
2711099  2711119  2711153  2711197  2711213  2711231  2711237  2711287  2711327
2711329  2711333  2711339  2711341  2711351  2711363  2711377  2711399  2711411  2711417
2711431  2711437  2711459  2711461  2711497  2711503  2711521  2711549  2711567  2711573
2711591  2711629  2711647  2711669  2711707  2711717  2711729  2711743  2711747  2711771
2711777  2711783  2711803  2711827  2711837  2711867  2711873  2711899  2711921  2711939
2711941  2711977  2711981  2712001  2712007  2712011  2712019  2712037  2712043  2712049
2712067  2712077  2712089  2712119  2712131  2712133  2712161  2712173  2712179  2712181
2712223  2712233  2712239  2712251  2712253  2712257  2712287  2712293  2712317  2712329
2712337  2712371  2712373  2712377  2712379  2712389  2712419  2712427  2712431  2712443
2712449  2712481  2712491  2712517  2712529  2712533  2712539  2712547  2712553  2712559
2712583  2712587  2712613  2712637  2712641  2712653  2712659  2712667  2712691  2712709
2712713  2712719  2712733  2712767  2712769  2712811  2712823  2712851  2712859  2712883
2712893  2712923  2712947  2712971  2712973  2712989  2713003  2713019  2713033
2713043  2713049  2713069  2713079  2713111  2713127  2713133  2713157  2713177  2713189
2713223  2713237  2713253  2713259  2713267  2713273  2713283  2713289  2713297  2713301
2713309  2713313  2713349  2713369  2713391  2713411  2713423  2713427  2713453  2713457
2713493  2713499  2713507  2713531  2713541  2713553  2713577  2713589  2713603  2713619
2713649  2713651  2713657  2713673  2713679  2713703  2713717  2713721  2713783  2713811
2713813  2713817  2713853  2713871  2713873  2713883  2713933  2713937  2713939  2713943
2713961  2713967  2713973  2713981  2713993  2714009  2714011  2714021  2714027  2714029
2714039  2714057  2714071  2714083  2714087  2714099  2714111  2714141  2714167  2714171
2714221  2714227  2714249  2714263  2714273  2714279  2714281  2714287  2714293  2714303
2714311  2714353  2714377  2714389  2714419  2714443  2714449  2714507  2714513  2714539
2714557  2714563  2714567  2714573  2714597  2714609  2714617  2714627  2714629  2714641
2714659  2714707  2714711  2714729  2714731  2714737  2714743  2714749  2714753  2714783
2714791  2714807  2714813  2714837  2714843  2714867  2714903  2714909  2714941  2714947
2714953  2714963  2714983  2715007  2715071  2715079  2715101  2715109  2715113  2715161
2715169  2715191  2715211  2715217  2715221  2715247  2715263  2715269  2715281  2715283
2715287  2715289  2715313  2715329  2715337  2715353  2715367  2715371  2715409  2715413
2715421  2715437  2715439  2715457  2715469  2715481  2715487  2715491  2715497  2715521
2715523  2715533  2715547  2715551  2715571  2715599  2715607  2715617  2715619  2715623
2715637  2715649  2715653  2715683  2715701  2715737  2715749  2715787  2715793  2715809
2715847  2715851  2715857  2715859  2715893  2715899  2715913  2715929  2715931  2715949
2715959  2715961  2715983  2715997  2716027  2716061  2716067  2716079  2716117  2716157
2716159  2716163  2716187  2716201  2716223  2716237  2716249  2716253  2716261  2716279
2716289  2716309  2716319  2716327  2716333  2716349  2716393  2716397  2716423  2716451
2716453  2716457  2716463  2716471  2716501  2716523  2716541  2716543  2716579  2716591
2716603  2716613  2716661  2716669  2716687  2716699  2716709  2716711  2716729  2716733
2716739  2716751  2716759  2716771  2716781  2716789  2716811  2716823  2716843  2716849
2716883  2716907  2716913  2716927  2716951  2716969  2716979  2716993  2716997  2716999
2717027  2717063  2717069  2717087  2717089  2717107  2717129  2717131  2717137  2717147
2717149  2717159  2717173  2717177  2717189  2717201  2717219  2717227  2717233  2717249
2717251  2717287  2717291  2717293  2717321  2717327  2717339  2717359  2717369  2717401
2717411  2717413  2717423  2717441  2717447  2717461  2717497  2717507  2717527  2717549
2717563  2717567  2717573  2717581  2717593  2717609  2717623  2717629  2717639  2717651
2717663  2717683  2717711  2717713  2717731  2717753  2717783  2717791  2717821  2717831
2717833  2717839  2717873  2717881  2717889  2717903  2717921  2717929  2717993  2718017
2718041  2718059  2718061  2718097  2718101  2718103  2718109  2718127  2718137  2718139
2718143  2718169  2718179  2718187  2718193  2718203  2718223  2718227  2718229  2718241
2718251  2718263  2718269  2718277  2718281  2718293  2718299  2718319  2718329  2718337
2718367  2718371  2718383  2718389  2718409  2718413  2718437  2718449  2718461  2718493
2718497  2718509  2718523  2718533  2718553  2718557  2718559  2718571  2718601  2718613
2718629  2718647  2718671  2718673  2718679  2718713  2718719  2718743  2718773  2718799
2718811  2718817  2718823  2718829  2718839  2718841  2718851  2718857  2718869  2718883
2718887  2718889  2718901  2718907  2718931  2718941  2718949  2718959  2718967  2718971
2718973  2718983  2719001  2719009  2719027  2719043  2719081  2719111  2719117  2719121
2719139  2719141  2719153  2719169  2719187  2719207  2719219  2719231
2719273  2719291  2719307  2719331  2719349  2719357  2719391  2719393  2719403  2719411
2719421  2719427  2719433  2719447  2719459  2719471  2719477  2719481  2719501  2719511
2719517  2719523  2719529  2719531  2719553  2719559  2719567  2719583  2719601  2719631
2719637  2719663  2719667  2719669  2719699  2719709  2719741  2719747  2719753  2719781
2719789  2719811  2719933  2719943  2719987  2719991  2720009
2720071  2720089  2720101  2720117  2720147  2720149  2720183  2720189  2720191  2720197
2720239  2720243  2720251  2720269  2720273  2720297  2720299  2720303  2720321  2720329
2720359  2720381  2720383  2720387  2720411  2720441  2720447  2720503  2720513  2720551
2720563  2720579  2720593  2720603  2720609  2720623  2720671  2720677  2720687  2720713
2720717  2720723  2720737  2720747  2720789  2720797  2720807  2720821  2720843  2720849
2720881  2720891  2720897  2720899  2720917  2720953  2720981  2720987  2720999  2721007
2721013  2721023  2721043  2721053  2721067  2721109  2721113  2721119  2721127  2721133
2721137  2721143  2721163  2721167  2721193  2721197  2721223  2721227  2721253  2721259
2721307  2721317  2721319  2721371  2721401  2721413  2721419  2721421  2721431  2721437
2721443  2721449  2721451  2721517  2721533  2721553  2721557  2721577  2721619  2721671
2721701  2721721  2721727  2721767  2721773  2721793  2721799  2721811  2721821  2721827
2721841  2721863  2721869  2721871  2721877  2721889  2721913  2721947  2722001  2722007
2722021  2722033  2722043  2722061  2722063  2722067  2722087  2722117  2722147  2722163
2722189  2722207  2722219  2722231  2722241  2722249  2722273  2722309  2722337  2722351
2722361  2722369  2722387  2722399  2722417  2722427  2722439  2722457  2722469  2722471
2722477  2722507  2722541  2722547  2722553  2722561  2722591  2722619  2722639  2722661
2722691  2722729  2722751  2722789  2722799  2722801  2722831  2722843  2722861  2722877
2722879  2722883  2722891  2722913  2722919  2722931  2722939  2722943  2722949  2722957
2722963  2722969  2722987  2722999  2723003  2723033  2723041  2723047  2723057  2723069
2723107  2723113  2723143  2723153  2723159  2723167  2723183  2723197  2723207  2723221
2723239  2723243  2723249  2723293  2723317  2723323  2723333  2723339  2723341  2723351
2723353  2723363  2723387  2723393  2723401  2723431  2723437  2723447  2723473  2723503
2723521  2723543  2723549  2723551  2723561  2723563  2723569  2723579  2723599  2723627
```

```
2723641  2723687  2723701  2723717  2723719  2723731  2723737  2723759  2723761  2723771
2723779  2723789  2723797  2723813  2723827  2723837  2723839  2723863  2723879  2723881
2723887  2723909  2723911  2723923  2723933  2723947  2723951  2723969  2723989  2724013
2724031  2724047  2724053  2724061  2724067  2724079  2724109  2724119  2724121  2724151
2724181  2724193  2724209  2724217  2724223  2724229  2724251  2724257  2724263  2724269
2724283  2724299  2724329  2724367  2724377  2724383  2724389  2724401  2724427  2724479
2724481  2724499  2724503  2724529  2724551  2724563  2724583  2724587  2724599  2724629
2724653  2724661  2724697  2724703  2724719  2724721  2724727  2724739  2724749  2724773
2724779  2724803  2724829  2724859  2724877  2724929  2724937  2724949  2724959  2724979
2724989  2725001  2725003  2725027  2725057  2725127  2725153  2725157  2725181  2725187
2725199  2725231  2725237  2725259  2725267  2725271  2725279  2725337  2725343  2725357
2725361  2725367  2725369  2725433  2725439  2725451  2725453  2725501  2725517  2725519
2725529  2725537  2725543  2725553  2725561  2725571  2725621  2725643  2725649  2725669
2725691  2725693  2725699  2725711  2725769  2725781  2725783  2725817  2725819  2725823
2725829  2725837  2725841  2725847  2725871  2725897  2725927  2725939  2725963  2725997
2726023  2726033  2726051  2726057  2726081  2726089  2726093  2726107  2726149  2726153
2726179  2726183  2726201  2726209  2726221  2726231  2726237  2726249  2726263  2726281
2726287  2726299  2726303  2726327  2726363  2726387  2726389  2726401  2726407  2726411
2726441  2726453  2726461  2726473  2726483  2726491  2726509  2726561  2726569  2726617
2726657  2726683  2726687  2726701  2726723  2726741  2726743  2726771  2726809  2726819
2726821  2726831  2726837  2726839  2726873  2726879  2726887  2726891  2726917  2726923
2726939  2726959  2726981  2726989  2727007  2727037  2727059  2727077  2727083  2727097
2727107  2727113  2727119  2727121  2727143  2727149  2727173  2727187  2727199  2727209
2727223  2727229  2727253  2727299  2727301  2727311  2727313  2727331  2727359  2727367
2727379  2727383  2727401  2727407  2727419  2727427  2727437  2727449  2727451  2727521
2727559  2727563  2727577  2727623  2727661  2727679  2727713  2727727  2727733  2727763
2727779  2727793  2727797  2727817  2727821  2727839  2727841  2727847  2727913  2727919
2727941  2727953  2727971  2727979  2727997  2728013  2728027  2728043  2728051  2728067
2728073  2728079  2728097  2728129  2728163  2728169  2728171  2728199  2728207  2728241
2728247  2728259  2728261  2728277  2728289  2728301  2728321  2728331  2728351  2728357
2728373  2728409  2728447  2728471  2728499  2728507  2728519  2728541  2728543  2728547
2728549  2728553  2728567  2728577  2728603  2728631  2728643  2728657  2728669  2728703
2728711  2728741  2728751  2728753  2728763  2728769  2728771  2728777  2728801  2728807
2728819  2728841  2728853  2728877  2728883  2728889  2728907  2728931  2728933  2728939
2728967  2728981  2728997  2729003  2729017  2729029  2729059  2729071  2729087  2729093
2729099  2729101  2729107  2729113  2729117  2729119  2729137  2729143  2729159  2729173
2729183  2729189  2729227  2729239  2729261  2729303  2729317  2729327  2729347  2729351
2729359  2729381  2729383  2729413  2729417  2729423  2729429  2729437  2729443  2729459
2729473  2729491  2729497  2729501  2729533  2729539  2729549  2729557  2729563  2729569
2729591  2729593  2729633  2729651  2729653  2729681  2729717  2729723  2729729  2729747
2729777  2729803  2729813  2729819  2729827  2729833  2729861  2729869  2729887  2729917
2729921  2729957  2729959  2729983  2730001  2730011  2730017  2730041  2730071  2730109
2730121  2730157  2730173  2730179  2730181  2730191  2730197  2730229  2730239  2730241
2730257  2730271  2730347  2730383  2730397  2730439  2730463  2730487  2730493  2730517
2730521  2730529  2730569  2730571  2730577  2730587  2730593  2730599  2730601  2730643
2730649  2730671  2730677  2730683  2730691  2730703  2730709  2730713  2730743  2730751
2730769  2730781  2730797  2730803  2730811  2730817  2730823  2730869  2730899  2730907
2730911  2730919  2730929  2730947  2730953  2730967  2730979  2730983  2730989  2730991
2731013  2731049  2731061  2731063  2731087  2731103  2731111  2731129  2731147  2731159
2731163  2731177  2731187  2731189  2731199  2731207  2731241  2731243  2731277  2731279
2731291  2731327  2731331  2731349  2731357  2731367  2731381  2731427  2731429  2731493
2731501  2731511  2731517  2731541  2731559  2731571  2731579  2731591  2731607  2731609
2731621  2731637  2731667  2731669  2731681  2731691  2731693  2731697  2731699  2731709
2731721  2731739  2731753  2731783  2731787  2731819  2731823  2731831  2731837  2731847
2731853  2731889  2731901  2731903  2731907  2731909  2731921  2731933  2731961  2731979
2731987  2731997  2732017  2732021  2732027  2732047  2732069  2732099  2732137  2732161
2732173  2732179  2732183  2732201  2732207  2732209  2732221  2732237  2732243  2732269
2732273  2732297  2732311  2732329  2732341  2732357  2732381  2732383  2732407  2732437
2732441  2732449  2732473  2732489  2732491  2732497  2732501  2732503  2732507  2732519
2732537  2732539  2732549  2732579  2732581  2732593  2732603  2732629  2732651  2732671
2732701  2732749  2732753  2732759  2732761  2732797  2732813  2732819  2732831  2732843
2732893  2732897  2732911  2732921  2732953  2732963  2732987  2732993  2733001  2733007
2733011  2733041  2733043  2733061  2733077  2733091  2733103  2733119  2733127  2733173
2733179  2733187  2733197  2733233  2733253  2733257  2733259  2733271  2733329  2733331
2733361  2733371  2733373  2733391  2733403  2733427  2733431  2733461  2733463  2733469
2733499  2733539  2733541  2733547  2733551  2733559  2733589  2733607  2733613  2733799
2733817  2733823  2733827  2733887  2733893  2733899  2733901  2733931  2733947  2733971
2733979  2734007  2734009  2734019  2734027  2734097  2734099  2734117  2734129  2734133
2734141  2734153  2734159  2734177  2734181  2734187  2734201  2734211  2734219  2734243
2734253  2734279  2734283  2734289  2734307  2734321  2734339  2734343  2734387  2734393
2734397  2734409  2734421  2734441  2734451  2734477  2734481  2734513  2734549  2734553
2734561  2734579  2734589  2734607  2734609  2734619  2734643  2734663  2734673  2734717
2734733  2734763  2734793  2734801  2734817  2734819  2734867  2734891  2734967  2734969
2734981  2735009  2735017  2735021  2735023  2735081  2735087  2735093  2735119  2735129
2735143  2735153  2735167  2735177  2735189  2735191  2735197  2735207  2735231  2735263
2735267  2735269  2735279  2735281  2735287  2735323  2735329  2735339  2735357  2735377
2735387  2735437  2735441  2735443  2735477  2735501  2735507  2735519  2735527  2735581
2735587  2735609  2735611  2735641  2735671  2735683  2735699  2735713  2735717  2735723
2735737  2735747  2735767  2735797  2735809  2735839  2735857  2735869  2735881  2735899
2735921  2735923  2735951  2735959  2735977  2735983  2736043  2736049  2736061  2736067
2736077  2736089  2736131  2736137  2736143  2736157  2736169  2736193  2736203  2736211
2736221  2736229  2736233  2736257  2736263  2736313  2736317  2736329  2736359  2736367
2736397  2736403  2736413  2736431  2736451  2736491  2736497  2736499  2736511  2736523
2736533  2736571  2736581  2736583  2736623  2736637  2736673  2736689  2736691  2736707
2736733  2736737  2736757  2736787  2736863  2736869  2736889  2736911  2736917  2736941
2736947  2736961  2736967  2736997  2737003  2737013  2737027  2737043  2737057  2737061
2737067  2737073  2737081  2737093  2737103  2737109  2737127  2737129  2737157  2737169
2737171  2737183  2737211  2737213  2737219  2737247  2737309  2737313  2737321  2737333
```

```
2737351  2737363  2737367  2737409  2737411  2737433  2737439  2737477  2737487  2737489
2737523  2737543  2737583  2737597  2737607  2737639  2737649  2737661  2737673  2737699
2737717  2737723  2737727  2737747  2737751  2737759  2737793  2737817  2737841  2737849
2737871  2737873  2737937  2737949  2737961  2737979  2737981  2737991  2737997  2738017
2738027  2738039  2738051  2738059  2738063  2738077  2738117  2738119  2738123  2738129
2738149  2738167  2738179  2738191  2738201  2738227  2738231  2738243  2738251  2738269
2738273  2738279  2738287  2738291  2738317  2738321  2738327  2738341  2738347  2738353
2738371  2738381  2738387  2738389  2738423  2738453  2738459  2738467  2738503  2738507
2738573  2738573  2738579  2738599  2738621  2738623  2738639  2738647  2738651  2738653
2738657  2738707  2738719  2738753  2738761  2738773  2738779  2738783  2738803  2738809
2738821  2738861  2738899  2738933  2738941  2738947  2739013  2739017  2739031  2739043
2739049  2739053  2739071  2739089  2739103  2739119  2739127  2739133  2739151  2739181
2739203  2739223  2739239  2739241  2739259  2739271  2739281  2739283  2739293  2739299
2739313  2739337  2739353  2739371  2739379  2739383  2739389  2739403  2739409  2739419
2739421  2739433  2739437  2739479  2739523  2739557  2739559  2739577  2739587  2739613
2739619  2739631  2739637  2739643  2739647  2739673  2739683  2739701  2739707  2739713
2739719  2739721  2739731  2739733  2739757  2739761  2739769  2739773  2739787  2739809
2739817  2739853  2739859  2739871  2739881  2739899  2739931  2739973  2739977  2739983
2739991  2740027  2740037  2740039  2740051  2740057  2740061  2740069  2740093  2740139
2740141  2740169  2740187  2740189  2740207  2740211  2740217  2740219  2740223  2740249
2740267  2740291  2740301  2740319  2740333  2740337  2740343  2740357  2740379  2740393
2740403  2740421  2740453  2740459  2740469  2740477  2740483  2740489  2740511  2740513
2740537  2740559  2740567  2740583  2740597  2740601  2740603  2740607  2740631  2740643
2740649  2740667  2740721  2740733  2740739  2740763  2740799  2740811  2740817  2740831
2740853  2740867  2740889  2740919  2740937  2740943  2740957  2740987  2740999  2741003
2741009  2741021  2741033  2741047  2741059  2741083  2741093  2741119  2741143  2741147
2741159  2741183  2741201  2741227  2741231  2741251  2741257  2741261  2741269  2741273
2741281  2741287  2741303  2741309  2741351  2741353  2741357  2741363  2741411  2741449
2741483  2741489  2741509  2741513  2741521  2741533  2741561  2741579  2741581  2741593
2741597  2741603  2741617  2741621  2741633  2741653  2741657  2741659  2741693  2741729
2741731  2741741  2741759  2741773  2741779  2741797  2741801  2741813  2741821  2741867
2741873  2741887  2741891  2741903  2741927  2741929  2741939  2741941  2741971  2741989
2741993  2742007  2742013  2742017  2742029  2742031  2742041  2742073  2742119  2742127
2742129  2742161  2742163  2742197  2742199  2742209  2742217  2742227  2742241  2742247
2742263  2742277  2742283  2742293  2742317  2742323  2742343  2742347  2742361  2742371
2742407  2742409  2742427  2742461  2742463  2742469  2742473  2742503  2742521  2742529
2742533  2742541  2742547  2742563  2742587  2742629  2742637  2742647  2742653  2742667
2742671  2742673  2742679  2742689  2742703  2742721  2742737  2742739  2742749  2742757
2742769  2742781  2742793  2742799  2742809  2742811  2742853  2742863  2742871  2742881
2742889  2742893  2742917  2742919  2742931  2742937  2742953  2742977  2742979  2742983
2742989  2742991  2743007  2743019  2743031  2743043  2743057  2743079  2743093  2743129
2743133  2743177  2743183  2743207  2743219  2743229  2743243  2743259  2743289  2743297
2743381  2743387  2743397  2743423  2743457  2743483  2743493  2743501  2743523  2743541
2743547  2743549  2743561  2743567  2743571  2743577  2743589  2743621  2743627  2743669
2743673  2743691  2743703  2743709  2743711  2743723  2743747  2743751  2743759  2743789
2743823  2743849  2743859  2743861  2743901  2743931  2743933  2743943  2743967  2743991
2744003  2744017  2744029  2744039  2744051  2744081  2744083  2744087  2744099  2744111
2744117  2744129  2744197  2744223  2744237  2744243  2744257  2744263  2744279  2744297
2744309  2744317  2744323  2744347  2744351  2744359  2744411  2744419  2744447  2744449
2744453  2744459  2744491  2744501  2744509  2744513  2744519  2744543  2744551  2744557
2744563  2744579  2744587  2744591  2744593  2744611  2744617  2744629  2744639  2744689
2744699  2744713  2744719  2744723  2744743  2744747  2744761  2744773  2744779  2744783
2744867  2744881  2744891  2744921  2744933  2744953  2744969  2745011  2745031  2745047
2745049  2745091  2745103  2745107  2745121  2745131  2745151  2745157  2745161  2745179
2745209  2745229  2745251  2745263  2745269  2745277  2745283  2745287  2745307  2745361
2745373  2745377  2745379  2745397  2745419  2745433  2745451  2745467  2745473  2745497
2745503  2745521  2745529  2745541  2745569  2745571  2745581  2745607  2745637  2745643
2745661  2745697  2745719  2745731  2745737  2745761  2745767  2745781  2745797  2745829
2745833  2745839  2745859  2745863  2745907  2745913  2745929  2745931  2745971  2745979
2745989  2746021  2746031  2746033  2746063  2746091  2746111  2746123  2746147  2746151
2746169  2746181  2746189  2746199  2746201  2746207  2746217  2746229  2746283  2746297
2746309  2746319  2746327  2746339  2746379  2746409  2746417  2746421  2746423  2746433
2746459  2746463  2746481  2746483  2746511  2746529  2746543  2746577  2746603  2746607
2746609  2746643  2746651  2746661  2746663  2746669  2746699  2746717  2746739  2746753
2746781  2746787  2746789  2746801  2746813  2746819  2746829  2746847  2746873  2746889
2746901  2746921  2746949  2746957  2746973  2746999  2747021  2747023  2747033  2747071
2747089  2747093  2747111  2747117  2747119  2747131  2747161  2747177  2747179  2747207
2747229  2747231  2747237  2747243  2747249  2747263  2747273  2747279  2747293  2747309
2747321  2747323  2747347  2747351  2747357  2747359  2747363  2747389  2747401  2747429
2747441  2747447  2747449  2747473  2747483  2747491  2747497  2747527  2747531  2747533
2747551  2747567  2747579  2747597  2747611  2747617  2747621  2747627  2747639  2747671
2747683  2747687  2747707  2747711  2747713  2747749  2747753  2747791  2747803  2747819
2747831  2747851  2747869  2747873  2747903  2747909  2747923  2747947  2747959  2747963
2747977  2748013  2748019  2748037  2748041  2748059  2748061  2748077  2748089  2748113
2748131  2748133  2748149  2748157  2748167  2748191  2748227  2748241  2748253  2748257
2748281  2748283  2748287  2748313  2748371  2748391  2748401  2748413  2748433  2748439
2748443  2748457  2748467  2748469  2748497  2748503  2748547  2748563  2748583  2748589
2748593  2748601  2748617  2748643  2748659  2748703  2748719  2748727  2748731  2748769
2748803  2748817  2748827  2748829  2748833  2748857  2748859  2748919  2748923  2748931
2748953  2748971  2748973  2749007  2749027  2749061  2749067  2749069  2749081  2749093
2749127  2749133  2749147  2749157  2749183  2749193  2749207  2749231  2749237  2749247
2749277  2749283  2749289  2749301  2749303  2749309  2749339  2749343  2749361  2749363
2749387  2749391  2749441  2749447  2749499  2749511  2749531  2749543  2749567  2749573
2749589  2749609  2749639  2749667  2749679  2749687  2749709  2749711  2749717  2749723
2749763  2749777  2749787  2749823  2749847  2749849  2749853  2749891  2749907  2749913
2749919  2749921  2749991  2750021  2750029  2750053  2750071  2750123  2750131  2750159
2750161  2750177  2750197  2750201  2750207  2750213  2750219  2750249  2750261  2750263
2750287  2750291  2750303  2750339  2750347  2750353  2750357  2750369  2750387  2750399
2750401  2750431  2750437  2750453  2750471  2750479  2750491  2750509  2750513  2750557
```

```
2750569  2750597  2750603  2750623  2750641  2750653  2750663  2750677  2750707  2750729
2750743  2750749  2750771  2750773  2750779  2750789  2750791  2750809  2750827  2750831
2750851  2750857  2750861  2750893  2750899  2750903  2750933  2750939  2750959  2750963
2750981  2750983  2750989  2750999  2751041  2751083  2751101  2751103  2751109  2751113
2751137  2751163  2751187  2751193  2751241  2751247  2751251  2751253  2751293  2751299
2751313  2751319  2751323  2751337  2751349  2751361  2751379  2751383  2751391  2751403
2751407  2751449  2751457  2751461  2751479  2751481  2751493  2751509  2751517  2751557
2751571  2751577  2751587  2751611  2751647  2751667  2751677  2751689  2751703  2751733
2751761  2751779  2751787  2751799  2751809  2751811  2751817  2751821  2751823  2751829
2751857  2751863  2751869  2751883  2751887  2751899  2751907  2751953  2751967  2751989
2751997  2752003  2752021  2752033  2752049  2752051  2752069  2752081  2752103  2752109
2752117  2752121  2752151  2752153  2752177  2752199  2752201  2752219  2752223  2752229
2752231  2752247  2752261  2752271  2752307  2752313  2752331  2752349  2752357  2752391
2752403  2752417  2752423  2752447  2752481  2752493  2752499  2752513  2752517  2752523
2752531  2752543  2752591  2752601  2752609  2752613  2752619  2752637  2752639  2752667
2752669  2752679  2752697  2752721  2752723  2752733  2752787  2752811  2752823  2752843
2752877  2752879  2752889  2752901  2752909  2752921  2752933  2752951  2752961  2752987
2752993  2753029  2753033  2753039  2753063  2753111  2753129  2753131  2753137  2753143
2753147  2753189  2753197  2753221  2753237  2753263  2753279  2753287  2753291  2753323
2753351  2753363  2753369  2753407  2753411  2753417  2753441  2753453  2753459  2753467
2753477  2753497  2753501  2753533  2753549  2753551  2753567  2753573  2753581  2753587
2753599  2753693  2753719  2753743  2753759  2753783  2753791  2753809  2753819  2753831
2753851  2753867  2753887  2753897  2753903  2753909  2753921  2753939  2753941  2753957
2753977  2753999  2754001  2754041  2754047  2754049  2754053  2754067  2754083  2754091
2754109  2754113  2754127  2754137  2754151  2754197  2754203  2754239  2754263  2754281
2754299  2754329  2754361  2754379  2754397  2754403  2754407  2754419  2754431  2754467
2754473  2754481  2754491  2754497  2754523  2754541  2754547  2754551  2754599  2754599
2754617  2754649  2754673  2754683  2754701  2754707  2754721  2754743  2754751  2754803
2754847  2754859  2754883  2754889  2754893  2754907  2754911  2754923  2754937  2754949
2754991  2755021  2755031  2755033  2755043  2755073  2755097  2755111  2755117  2755121
2755127  2755141  2755153  2755157  2755163  2755177  2755199  2755201  2755211  2755213
2755219  2755223  2755231  2755237  2755243  2755267  2755289  2755301  2755303  2755307
2755369  2755387  2755393  2755409  2755421  2755429  2755447  2755463  2755471  2755499
2755541  2755549  2755567  2755601  2755619  2755633  2755637  2755661  2755663  2755669
2755721  2755747  2755759  2755769  2755789  2755793  2755801  2755813  2755829  2755859
2755861  2755877  2755881  2755943  2755967  2755981  2755997  2756009  2756011  2756059
2756069  2756071  2756077  2756099  2756101  2756107  2756111  2756119  2756123  2756129
2756147  2756153  2756161  2756191  2756207  2756219  2756249  2756267  2756269  2756279
2756309  2756339  2756357  2756381  2756401  2756417  2756423  2756437  2756441  2756459
2756483  2756491  2756497  2756519  2756521  2756549  2756557  2756561  2756563  2756569
2756587  2756599  2756603  2756609  2756627  2756629  2756639  2756669  2756671  2756681
2756683  2756693  2756707  2756713  2756723  2756731  2756749  2756753  2756777  2756783
2756791  2756797  2756801  2756821  2756869  2756903  2756909  2756933  2756939  2756959
2756977  2756989  2756993  2757019  2757037  2757049  2757061  2757091  2757119  2757121
2757133  2757151  2757163  2757169  2757187  2757191  2757193  2757211  2757221  2757229
2757257  2757259  2757311  2757317  2757319  2757323  2757329  2757347  2757361  2757367
2757371  2757379  2757397  2757437  2757457  2757463  2757529  2757533  2757541  2757563
2757577  2757593  2757607  2757611  2757617  2757649  2757659  2757661  2757691  2757709
2757731  2757743  2757761  2757767  2757773  2757817  2757829  2757851  2757863  2757877
2757883  2757889  2757901  2757917  2758003  2758033  2758037  2758051  2758061  2758069
2758079  2758087  2758099  2758109  2758117  2758121  2758141  2758157  2758169  2758181
2758213  2758241  2758243  2758247  2758253  2758291  2758297  2758307  2758319  2758331
2758337  2758361  2758373  2758397  2758409  2758429  2758447  2758463  2758489  2758499
2758507  2758517  2758519  2758529  2758531  2758537  2758541  2758543  2758589  2758631
2758633  2758661  2758711  2758771  2758787  2758793  2758801  2758807  2758817  2758823
2758829  2758841  2758843  2758871  2758891  2758897  2758901  2758937  2758949  2758957
2758963  2758999  2759023  2759027  2759039  2759059  2759063  2759069  2759087  2759111
2759137  2759153  2759167  2759171  2759173  2759189  2759203  2759227  2759231  2759249
2759257  2759269  2759291  2759293  2759297  2759299  2759303  2759311  2759357  2759369
2759387  2759411  2759413  2759431  2759441  2759443  2759453  2759459  2759461  2759467
2759479  2759483  2759507  2759513  2759521  2759531  2759539  2759599  2759621  2759677
2759683  2759689  2759711  2759717  2759723  2759761  2759789  2759803  2759819  2759821
2759849  2759857  2759873  2759879  2759881  2759891  2759909  2759917  2759929  2759947
2759951  2759957  2759963  2759971  2760013  2760019  2760031  2760049  2760053  2760061
2760077  2760097  2760101  2760113  2760143  2760151  2760179  2760193  2760221  2760223
2760259  2760269  2760283  2760287  2760313  2760319  2760323  2760337  2760361  2760371
2760379  2760403  2760421  2760449  2760463  2760469  2760473  2760487  2760509  2760521
2760559  2760577  2760587  2760617  2760629  2760631  2760649  2760671  2760673  2760683
2760697  2760701  2760721  2760739  2760743  2760761  2760763  2760773  2760781  2760811
2760839  2760847  2760881  2760883  2760889  2760913  2760931  2760937  2760949  2760959
2760983  2760991  2761007  2761009  2761013  2761027  2761039  2761091  2761093  2761097
2761111  2761147  2761151  2761153  2761163  2761169  2761181  2761183  2761189  2761193
2761207  2761217  2761223  2761229  2761267  2761277  2761279  2761301  2761303  2761307
2761333  2761379  2761393  2761397  2761411  2761439  2761453  2761471  2761477  2761481
2761489  2761501  2761529  2761543  2761547  2761553  2761559  2761567  2761571  2761597
2761609  2761621  2761657  2761711  2761721  2761723  2761727  2761729  2761741  2761747
2761751  2761789  2761793  2761819  2761831  2761841  2761853  2761877  2761901  2761903
2761907  2761943  2761961  2761981  2761987  2761999  2762003  2762009  2762027  2762029
2762033  2762063  2762083  2762117  2762119  2762147  2762159  2762167  2762171  2762173
2762183  2762189  2762197  2762213  2762233  2762251  2762261  2762267  2762273  2762281
2762297  2762329  2762339  2762351  2762371  2762401  2762407  2762411  2762423  2762437
2762443  2762447  2762479  2762491  2762497  2762527  2762533  2762537  2762549  2762561
2762567  2762587  2762593  2762647  2762651  2762671  2762699  2762713  2762741  2762759
2762761  2762777  2762779  2762803  2762807  2762819  2762833  2762839  2762849  2762861
2762869  2762909  2762927  2762933  2762939  2762941  2762951  2762953  2762957  2763001
2763011  2763053  2763071  2763097  2763109  2763119  2763127  2763133  2763169  2763179
2763203  2763209  2763221  2763251  2763263  2763287  2763301  2763311  2763317  2763331
2763347  2763353  2763373  2763377  2763407  2763413  2763421  2763443  2763457  2763463
2763487  2763491  2763511  2763529  2763559  2763577  2763583  2763587  2763589  2763599
```

```
2763601  2763617  2763623  2763643  2763659  2763661  2763667  2763679  2763751  2763757
2763763  2763773  2763779  2763781  2763793  2763811  2763823  2763829  2763833  2763881
2763883  2763931  2763947  2763967  2763977  2763989  2764001  2764007  2764033  2764039
2764049  2764057  2764087  2764121  2764123  2764127  2764129  2764133  2764147  2764171
2764187  2764199  2764207  2764213  2764247  2764271  2764277  2764283  2764313  2764331
2764361  2764369  2764373  2764423  2764441  2764453  2764469  2764499  2764537  2764543
2764561  2764579  2764609  2764637  2764649  2764651  2764667  2764679  2764687  2764711
2764739  2764757  2764787  2764789  2764819  2764837  2764841  2764847  2764871  2764873
2764891  2764901  2764903  2764907  2764913  2764933  2764939  2764967  2765039  2765053
2765093  2765099  2765117  2765123  2765131  2765143  2765173  2765177  2765183  2765197
2765207  2765209  2765219  2765227  2765233  2765239  2765251  2765281  2765297  2765299
2765303  2765309  2765333  2765351  2765363  2765369  2765383  2765387  2765419  2765429
2765437  2765453  2765461  2765471  2765473  2765513  2765519  2765531  2765551  2765579
2765591  2765597  2765611  2765641  2765671  2765677  2765689  2765731  2765753  2765767
2765771  2765779  2765783  2765797  2765813  2765821  2765831  2765837  2765839  2765857
2765863  2765879  2765891  2765921  2765927  2765929  2765941  2765953  2765969  2765977
2766007  2766013  2766059  2766109  2766119  2766131  2766151  2766163  2766193  2766199
2766217  2766227  2766251  2766259  2766263  2766277  2766287  2766293  2766301  2766317
2766329  2766331  2766341  2766349  2766367  2766389  2766431  2766487  2766493  2766521
2766539  2766551  2766581  2766583  2766593  2766611  2766623  2766637  2766649  2766661
2766667  2766671  2766677  2766679  2766691  2766713  2766727  2766737  2766763  2766769
2766779  2766787  2766791  2766793  2766821  2766859  2766887  2766893  2766901  2766917
2766931  2766943  2766979  2766983  2766997  2767001  2767013  2767019  2767043  2767067
2767069  2767081  2767087  2767111  2767117  2767129  2767139  2767147  2767157  2767189
2767201  2767223  2767229  2767231  2767241  2767249  2767279  2767319  2767321  2767327
2767333  2767343  2767361  2767363  2767393  2767397  2767409  2767411  2767417  2767423
2767477  2767511  2767517  2767529  2767543  2767553  2767561  2767571  2767573  2767579
2767603  2767627  2767643  2767657  2767663  2767669  2767693  2767697  2767717  2767729
2767747  2767759  2767763  2767771  2767799  2767823  2767829  2767871  2767883  2767913
2767927  2767937  2767949  2767993  2768011  2768041  2768057  2768069  2768071  2768123
2768177  2768179  2768191  2768201  2768203  2768209  2768231  2768237  2768251
2768261  2768267  2768287  2768291  2768317  2768323  2768329  2768341  2768351  2768371
2768401  2768407  2768413  2768417  2768419  2768429  2768431  2768449  2768453  2768461
2768483  2768489  2768497  2768539  2768551  2768567  2768573  2768587  2768609  2768611
2768627  2768639  2768651  2768657  2768663  2768677  2768681  2768683  2768767  2768783
2768789  2768791  2768803  2768819  2768863  2768873  2768893  2768897  2768903  2768923
2768933  2768939  2768957  2768959  2768989  2769001  2769031  2769037  2769049  2769061
2769073  2769077  2769083  2769097  2769101  2769121  2769133  2769139  2769149  2769163
2769167  2769241  2769257  2769259  2769281  2769289  2769301  2769313  2769337
2769343  2769359  2769391  2769433  2769439  2769443  2769451  2769457  2769467  2769479
2769493  2769511  2769523  2769527  2769541  2769551  2769553  2769563  2769577  2769593
2769601  2769617  2769619  2769631  2769647  2769677  2769719  2769751  2769787  2769791
2769841  2769887  2769889  2769911  2769917  2769937  2769941  2769967  2769983  2770043
2770087  2770091  2770093  2770121  2770169  2770171  2770199  2770211  2770217  2770231
2770237  2770241  2770259  2770267  2770309  2770319  2770367  2770381  2770387  2770393
2770429  2770459  2770489  2770499  2770513  2770549  2770553  2770571  2770577  2770583
2770589  2770591  2770613  2770627  2770639  2770667  2770673  2770693  2770723  2770753
2770769  2770771  2770783  2770793  2770799  2770829  2770841  2770843  2770849  2770883
2770891  2770907  2770913  2770927  2770939  2770973  2770987  2770991  2770993  2771003
2771011  2771023  2771033  2771039  2771057  2771081  2771113  2771117  2771123  2771141
2771143  2771147  2771159  2771173  2771177  2771191  2771203  2771213  2771223  2771233
2771239  2771257  2771273  2771281  2771297  2771309  2771333  2771341  2771381  2771383
2771389  2771401  2771437  2771467  2771471  2771491  2771497  2771513  2771519  2771533
2771537  2771563  2771579  2771597  2771603  2771609  2771611  2771623  2771669  2771687
2771693  2771711  2771719  2771729  2771759  2771767  2771773  2771789  2771801  2771809
2771819  2771831  2771837  2771843  2771861  2771863  2771893  2771933  2771947  2771957
2771959  2771963  2771971  2771999  2772017  2772019  2772041  2772047  2772061  2772067
2772079  2772089  2772097  2772101  2772127  2772131  2772137  2772179  2772191  2772193
2772199  2772227  2772239  2772247  2772257  2772281  2772293  2772311  2772317  2772331
2772383  2772391  2772409  2772421  2772433  2772437  2772457  2772481  2772529  2772533
2772569  2772571  2772593  2772607  2772629  2772631  2772643  2772647  2772697  2772703
2772709  2772713  2772761  2772767  2772827  2772829  2772839  2772881  2772883  2772901
2772923  2772967  2772971  2772977  2772997  2773003  2773007  2773019  2773021  2773033
2773037  2773049  2773061  2773073  2773079  2773081  2773093  2773097  2773123  2773153
2773171  2773201  2773207  2773213  2773219  2773223  2773231  2773237  2773249  2773273
2773289  2773301  2773307  2773313  2773319  2773321  2773339  2773349  2773387  2773391
2773403  2773439  2773447  2773471  2773523  2773549  2773579  2773583  2773591  2773597
2773613  2773621  2773627  2773633  2773637  2773651  2773657  2773679  2773681  2773697
2773699  2773721  2773747  2773759  2773789  2773817  2773819  2773843  2773871  2773891
2773919  2773921  2773931  2773949  2773997  2773999  2774011  2774027  2774039  2774047
2774063  2774071  2774089  2774117  2774129  2774137  2774141  2774143  2774173  2774203
2774207  2774251  2774257  2774267  2774273  2774279  2774287  2774293  2774309  2774311
2774327  2774339  2774353  2774381  2774389  2774393  2774411  2774419  2774477  2774479
2774483  2774501  2774503  2774539  2774543  2774557  2774561  2774567  2774581  2774599
2774623  2774669  2774677  2774683  2774687  2774699  2774713  2774719  2774729  2774731
2774767  2774771  2774777  2774801  2774819  2774843  2774851  2774867  2774869  2774873
2774897  2774909  2774917  2774929  2774953  2774957  2774971  2775001  2775011  2775041
2775043  2775067  2775103  2775107  2775119  2775137  2775161  2775163  2775173  2775181
2775187  2775193  2775221  2775247  2775257  2775277  2775281  2775293  2775299  2775313
2775323  2775347  2775359  2775389  2775391  2775431  2775449  2775457  2775469  2775499
2775517  2775527  2775551  2775559  2775569  2775583  2775593  2775599  2775611  2775613
2775637  2775649  2775667  2775673  2775697  2775701  2775713  2775719  2775733  2775737
2775739  2775761  2775787  2775841  2775859  2775863  2775889  2775907  2775911  2775931
2775943  2775959  2775989  2775991  2776001  2776003  2776013  2776027  2776051  2776061
2776063  2776091  2776129  2776133  2776157  2776181  2776183  2776217  2776259  2776289
2776303  2776309  2776343  2776351  2776357  2776421  2776427  2776439  2776471  2776493
2776519  2776541  2776589  2776621  2776649  2776651  2776667  2776673  2776687  2776699
2776727  2776733  2776747  2776751  2776769  2776783  2776789  2776799  2776801  2776817
2776841  2776843  2776849  2776867  2776871  2776883  2776909  2776927  2776957  2776973
```

```
2776979 2776981 2776987 2776999 2777003 2777009 2777029 2777039 2777057 2777107
2777111 2777113 2777141 2777143 2777149 2777161 2777213 2777219 2777231 2777233
2777251 2777261 2777267 2777293 2777303 2777309 2777311 2777317 2777329 2777339
2777353 2777387 2777407 2777441 2777447 2777473 2777483 2777491 2777501 2777521
2777527 2777531 2777539 2777557 2777573 2777581 2777597 2777603 2777609 2777623
2777633 2777651 2777657 2777669 2777689 2777699 2777717 2777729 2777741 2777767
2777771 2777813 2777821 2777833 2777837 2777839 2777903 2777909 2777921 2777959
2777969 2777977 2777981 2777993 2778011 2778019 2778023 2778049 2778067 2778073
2778079 2778091 2778107 2778109 2778121 2778131 2778143 2778151 2778173 2778197
2778203 2778227 2778233 2778241 2778257 2778263 2778277 2778299 2778323 2778329
2778341 2778343 2778353 2778383 2778401 2778421 2778439 2778467 2778481 2778521
2778527 2778533 2778539 2778547 2778583 2778619 2778647 2778649 2778673 2778689
2778697 2778739 2778779 2778793 2778799 2778823 2778827 2778829 2778833 2778851
2778863 2778877 2778901 2778907 2778911 2778913 2778917 2778967 2778989 2779001
2779013 2779031 2779061 2779069 2779097 2779129 2779151 2779163 2779171 2779193
2779201 2779229 2779237 2779247 2779253 2779261 2779277 2779289 2779303 2779327
2779351 2779363 2779411 2779417 2779423 2779463 2779487 2779489 2779493 2779501
2779507 2779537 2779541 2779561 2779571 2779597 2779603 2779613 2779631 2779633
2779657 2779663 2779669 2779703 2779717 2779727 2779741 2779747 2779769 2779771
2779781 2779783 2779787 2779793 2779807 2779811 2779859 2779873 2779877 2779939
2779943 2779949 2779961 2779981 2779991 2780039 2780047 2780053 2780077 2780083
2780101 2780119 2780123 2780131 2780149 2780153 2780161 2780177 2780179 2780203
2780207 2780209 2780233 2780243 2780273 2780303 2780329 2780339 2780353 2780357
2780369 2780399 2780413 2780419 2780443 2780467 2780501 2780507 2780521 2780527
2780597 2780599 2780621 2780623 2780641 2780647 2780671 2780683 2780693 2780719
2780753 2780761 2780773 2780777 2780779 2780797 2780801 2780831 2780837 2780873
2780887 2780891 2780909 2780923 2780933 2780951 2780971 2780993 2781001 2781007
2781017 2781019 2781029 2781059 2781061 2781067 2781073 2781089 2781109 2781133
2781139 2781143 2781193 2781199 2781203 2781209 2781211 2781221 2781271
2781293 2781301 2781307 2781313 2781329 2781343 2781347 2781349 2781377 2781379
2781397 2781433 2781451 2781463 2781469 2781487 2781491 2781497 2781503 2781521
2781577 2781589 2781617 2781629 2781637 2781677 2781683 2781703 2781707 2781731
2781743 2781749 2781797 2781803 2781817 2781853 2781887 2781901 2781913 2781929
2781937 2781949 2781959 2781983 2781991 2782001 2782009 2782019 2782049 2782061
2782063 2782069 2782081 2782097 2782099 2782111 2782123 2782127 2782139 2782147
2782159 2782163 2782183 2782187 2782193 2782201 2782211 2782217 2782279 2782291
2782319 2782331 2782337 2782349 2782361 2782391 2782397 2782411 2782421 2782469
2782489 2782501 2782523 2782567 2782597 2782601 2782613 2782631 2782643 2782649
2782667 2782691 2782693 2782709 2782723 2782727 2782757 2782771 2782783 2782789
2782841 2782847 2782859 2782861 2782877 2782903 2782921 2782937 2782939 2782973
2782981 2782991 2782993 2782999 2783009 2783017 2783021 2783041 2783047 2783107
2783111 2783117 2783153 2783167 2783173 2783191 2783213 2783219 2783227 2783243
2783267 2783281 2783311 2783317 2783321 2783323 2783353 2783371 2783377 2783411
2783419 2783423 2783447 2783477 2783497 2783503 2783513 2783527 2783537 2783549
2783579 2783581 2783593 2783603 2783611 2783647 2783657 2783659 2783663 2783687
2783689 2783717 2783731 2783741 2783749 2783771 2783773 2783779 2783789 2783821
2783849 2783873 2783887 2783909 2783923 2783927 2783933 2783939 2783947 2783959
2783999 2784007 2784043 2784049 2784053 2784059 2784071 2784083 2784091 2784097
2784109 2784113 2784137 2784149 2784157 2784167 2784169 2784181 2784217 2784227
2784239 2784253 2784259 2784263 2784281 2784283 2784307 2784329 2784337 2784347
2784349 2784359 2784367 2784371 2784373 2784443 2784491 2784493 2784517
2784533 2784539 2784547 2784553 2784557 2784563 2784569 2784571 2784581 2784599
2784619 2784629 2784643 2784647 2784653 2784689 2784701 2784707 2784713 2784757
2784791 2784827 2784853 2784857 2784871 2784883 2784911 2784913 2784917 2784937
2784941 2784949 2784961 2784973 2784979 2784997 2785019 2785021 2785031 2785033
2785037 2785043 2785051 2785087 2785091 2785099 2785129 2785157 2785177 2785187
2785201 2785207 2785219 2785241 2785261 2785273 2785301 2785313 2785333 2785339
2785351 2785357 2785379 2785423 2785439 2785451 2785463 2785469 2785483 2785487
2785511 2785513 2785577 2785579 2785589 2785591 2785597 2785613 2785631 2785633
2785639 2785649 2785667 2785697 2785703 2785709 2785721 2785751 2785759 2785763
2785781 2785813 2785843 2785847 2785859 2785873 2785879 2785891 2785901 2785903
2785907 2785961 2785963 2785973 2785987 2785997 2786009 2786041 2786081 2786083
2786089 2786129 2786153 2786177 2786183 2786209 2786213 2786219 2786221 2786257
2786281 2786321 2786327 2786339 2786347 2786353 2786363 2786383 2786389 2786411
2786417 2786423 2786429 2786431 2786437 2786461 2786471 2786477 2786479 2786491
2786503 2786523 2786527 2786551 2786561 2786569 2786573 2786579 2786587 2786617
2786633 2786659 2786669 2786681 2786699 2786741 2786743 2786753 2786779 2786783
2786789 2786809 2786843 2786867 2786909 2786923 2786947 2786957 2786969 2786981
2787013 2787017 2787019 2787023 2787049 2787061 2787073 2787097 2787107 2787119
2787121 2787143 2787149 2787157 2787181 2787227 2787229 2787233 2787251 2787259
2787271 2787283 2787293 2787299 2787307 2787329 2787331 2787349 2787361 2787373
2787377 2787383 2787403 2787409 2787419 2787443 2787461 2787479 2787481 2787497
2787503 2787511 2787527 2787529 2787553 2787557 2787559 2787571 2787583 2787593
2787601 2787619 2787649 2787689 2787703 2787727 2787739 2787749 2787751 2787767
2787769 2787781 2787859 2787907 2787919 2787931 2787947 2787971 2787977 2788007
2788021 2788033 2788057 2788069 2788081 2788091 2788133 2788199 2788213 2788217
2788273 2788297 2788301 2788309 2788327 2788333 2788337 2788343 2788349 2788367
2788393 2788403 2788417 2788427 2788433 2788439 2788447 2788453 2788469 2788483
2788523 2788529 2788531 2788549 2788567 2788603 2788619 2788627 2788633 2788661
2788693 2788699 2788769 2788781 2788783 2788813 2788817 2788823 2788829 2788831
2788889 2788927 2788939 2788979 2788987 2788997 2789011 2789057 2789063 2789069
2789077 2789081 2789089 2789099 2789117 2789119 2789123 2789161 2789167 2789177
2789197 2789203 2789239 2789251 2789263 2789273 2789299 2789323 2789327 2789329
2789341 2789351 2789387 2789399 2789407 2789441 2789459 2789477 2789483 2789489
2789491 2789503 2789551 2789573 2789587 2789593 2789609 2789617 2789621 2789627
2789629 2789669 2789701 2789707 2789729 2789747 2789767 2789777 2789791 2789821
2789849 2789861 2789881 2789893 2789929 2789939 2789951 2789993 2790001 2790019
2790041 2790077 2790089 2790101 2790103 2790113 2790143 2790149 2790157 2790181
2790187 2790191 2790197 2790209 2790223 2790233 2790251 2790253 2790257 2790259
```

```
2790289  2790299  2790311  2790331  2790391  2790401  2790407  2790421  2790449  2790451
2790461  2790479  2790481  2790497  2790547  2790563  2790569  2790629  2790643  2790647
2790649  2790653  2790673  2790679  2790707  2790721  2790769  2790779  2790841  2790857
2790859  2790871  2790883  2790901  2790923  2790943  2790971  2790979  2791007  2791031
2791037  2791039  2791051  2791057  2791069  2791091  2791093  2791097  2791109  2791121
2791123  2791141  2791181  2791183  2791193  2791199  2791237  2791241  2791253  2791267
2791297  2791331  2791339  2791357  2791363  2791367  2791379  2791387  2791409  2791419
2791463  2791469  2791483  2791493  2791501  2791513  2791531  2791541  2791549  2791559
2791561  2791577  2791583  2791589  2791597  2791631  2791637  2791639  2791661  2791673
2791681  2791697  2791699  2791709  2791721  2791751  2791777  2791783  2791799  2791807
2791837  2791843  2791849  2791897  2791907  2791913  2791937  2791949  2791963  2791967
2791969  2791973  2791979  2791981  2791991  2792011  2792051  2792057  2792087  2792089
2792099  2792123  2792137  2792143  2792147  2792159  2792161  2792171  2792173  2792189
2792191  2792213  2792219  2792249  2792261  2792281  2792299  2792303  2792311  2792333
2792341  2792351  2792357  2792389  2792399  2792401  2792423  2792429  2792431  2792459
2792473  2792477  2792483  2792509  2792513  2792521  2792557  2792561  2792617  2792659
2792663  2792687  2792711  2792717  2792737  2792747  2792749  2792767  2792771  2792773
2792809  2792827  2792831  2792833  2792843  2792861  2792863  2792891  2792897  2792939
2792957  2792987  2792989  2793013  2793017  2793023  2793041  2793067  2793071  2793073
2793101  2793103  2793107  2793121  2793149  2793157  2793173  2793179  2793181  2793191
2793223  2793227  2793233  2793239  2793269  2793277  2793319  2793337  2793341  2793347
2793359  2793377  2793383  2793391  2793407  2793433  2793451  2793467  2793481  2793499
2793509  2793523  2793563  2793569  2793587  2793607  2793643  2793647  2793673  2793691
2793701  2793731  2793733  2793737  2793793  2793809  2793811  2793823  2793853  2793859
2793883  2793887  2793911  2793941  2793943  2793949  2793991  2794003  2794019  2794031
2794079  2794093  2794111  2794117  2794147  2794163  2794189  2794193  2794199  2794217
2794219  2794223  2794229  2794241  2794243  2794249  2794261  2794271  2794283  2794289
2794301  2794303  2794313  2794321  2794331  2794343  2794357  2794397  2794399  2794403
2794427  2794439  2794453  2794457  2794487  2794507  2794529  2794537  2794541  2794543
2794549  2794553  2794567  2794607  2794639  2794657  2794703  2794711  2794717  2794723
2794739  2794747  2794763  2794769  2794787  2794789  2794807  2794811  2794879  2794907
2794921  2794931  2794963  2794993  2794997  2795003  2795027  2795047  2795059  2795063
2795069  2795077  2795083  2795101  2795119  2795159  2795189  2795201  2795209  2795227
2795237  2795267  2795269  2795279  2795291  2795297  2795311  2795321  2795323  2795381
2795383  2795393  2795399  2795411  2795417  2795423  2795431  2795437  2795453  2795459
2795467  2795477  2795491  2795501  2795521  2795537  2795543  2795557  2795561  2795563
2795567  2795593  2795621  2795647  2795669  2795677  2795693  2795713  2795753  2795777
2795791  2795809  2795873  2795879  2795887  2795899  2795911  2795917  2795927  2795963
2795971  2795981  2795993  2795999  2796011  2796019  2796037  2796043  2796083  2796091
2796103  2796139  2796163  2796181  2796203  2796221  2796223  2796229  2796259  2796329
2796337  2796341  2796361  2796373  2796397  2796403  2796427  2796433  2796467  2796503
2796509  2796523  2796527  2796529  2796559  2796583  2796587  2796611  2796617  2796623
2796649  2796701  2796707  2796709  2796737  2796751  2796767  2796779  2796797  2796803
2796839  2796877  2796887  2796901  2796919  2796929  2796943  2796949  2796967
2796977  2797019  2797031  2797043  2797057  2797063  2797073  2797117  2797121  2797133
2797159  2797169  2797211  2797213  2797217  2797229  2797241  2797247  2797259  2797273
2797303  2797309  2797337  2797339  2797357  2797363  2797373  2797381  2797387  2797391
2797411  2797439  2797441  2797447  2797453  2797463  2797477  2797481  2797489  2797493
2797507  2797517  2797523  2797549  2797567  2797589  2797637  2797667  2797679  2797699
2797723  2797727  2797733  2797757  2797783  2797793  2797813  2797819  2797841  2797849
2797867  2797889  2797901  2797913  2797919  2797939  2797961  2797999  2798011  2798023
2798069  2798083  2798087  2798093  2798099  2798113  2798119  2798129  2798137  2798141
2798143  2798161  2798167  2798171  2798177  2798207  2798233  2798261  2798269  2798281
2798293  2798303  2798317  2798321  2798329  2798351  2798359  2798363  2798381  2798437
2798449  2798459  2798461  2798503  2798513  2798519  2798527  2798539  2798597  2798599
2798603  2798611  2798623  2798639  2798641  2798647  2798651  2798669  2798687  2798707
2798713  2798729  2798737  2798743  2798759  2798767  2798777  2798821  2798837  2798849
2798867  2798869  2798899  2798903  2798921  2798923  2798927  2798933  2798941  2798951
2798963  2798969  2798981  2798989  2799001  2799037  2799053  2799073  2799091  2799103
2799113  2799119  2799131  2799133  2799143  2799149  2799151  2799157  2799163  2799187
2799191  2799211  2799217  2799221  2799233  2799239  2799253  2799259  2799281  2799299
2799361  2799371  2799397  2799409  2799413  2799431  2799443  2799449  2799451  2799463
2799469  2799493  2799497  2799499  2799529  2799539  2799551  2799557  2799581  2799607
2799637  2799647  2799661  2799733  2799749  2799751  2799757  2799779  2799787  2799791
2799793  2799803  2799809  2799817  2799829  2799833  2799847  2799857  2799871  2799877
2799893  2799899  2799911  2799913  2799919  2799941  2799947  2799959  2799967  2799977
2799989  2799991  2800001  2800003  2800033  2800051  2800069  2800073  2800079  2800103
2800141  2800159  2800241  2800247  2800267  2800283  2800309
2800321  2800331  2800333  2800339  2800373  2800379  2800397  2800403  2800439  2800451
2800469  2800481  2800489  2800507  2800513  2800519  2800531  2800541  2800561  2800583
2800601  2800607  2800621  2800627  2800639  2800643  2800663  2800703  2800709  2800729
2800769  2800781  2800783  2800799  2800823  2800843  2800859  2800873  2800877  2800883
2800921  2800927  2800949  2800951  2800957  2800969  2800979  2800987  2800991  2801003
2801017  2801041  2801047  2801087  2801111  2801119  2801137  2801179  2801219  2801221
2801237  2801251  2801257  2801273  2801287  2801299  2801317  2801339  2801347  2801353
2801363  2801369  2801401  2801431  2801441  2801443  2801459  2801473  2801479  2801483
2801509  2801543  2801573  2801587  2801593  2801597  2801599  2801611  2801621  2801641
2801681  2801693  2801707  2801713  2801737  2801741  2801767  2801783  2801789  2801801
2801803  2801819  2801833  2801857  2801863  2801891  2801917  2801921  2801927  2801941
2801971  2801977  2802011  2802013  2802017  2802029  2802053  2802077  2802083  2802089
2802091  2802097  2802109  2802131  2802143  2802169  2802179  2802193  2802199  2802211
2802257  2802277  2802301  2802311  2802313  2802337  2802341  2802347  2802377  2802383
2802403  2802407  2802451  2802479  2802487  2802497  2802511  2802551  2802557  2802581
2802593  2802599  2802601  2802623  2802641  2802643  2802659  2802673  2802707  2802743
2802749  2802797  2802847  2802857  2802869  2802871  2802881  2802893  2802901
2802907  2802911  2802923  2802929  2802931  2802949  2802959  2802967  2802973  2802979
2802983  2802991  2802997  2803001  2803019  2803037  2803057  2803061  2803067  2803069
2803081  2803091  2803103  2803109  2803121  2803123  2803139  2803183  2803187  2803193
2803201  2803253  2803259  2803291  2803303  2803327  2803331  2803337  2803357  2803369
```

```
2803399 2803403 2803421 2803433 2803441 2803477 2803511 2803519 2803543 2803561
2803571 2803573 2803579 2803607 2803637 2803639 2803649 2803651 2803663 2803667
2803673 2803679 2803687 2803693 2803699 2803727 2803741 2803751 2803771 2803777
2803781 2803783 2803799 2803813 2803817 2803819 2803837 2803847 2803873 2803877
2803891 2803903 2803909 2803937 2803939 2803967 2803991 2804023 2804027 2804029
2804041 2804051 2804057 2804059 2804069 2804083 2804111 2804117 2804129 2804141
2804143 2804147 2804171 2804189 2804203 2804209 2804227 2804237 2804239 2804251
2804257 2804273 2804293 2804299 2804309 2804311 2804323 2804327 2804377 2804383
2804407 2804411 2804437 2804449 2804471 2804497 2804509 2804519 2804521 2804531
2804567 2804569 2804573 2804591 2804617 2804639 2804693 2804699 2804717 2804729
2804731 2804749 2804759 2804807 2804831 2804833 2804839 2804843 2804861 2804887
2804891 2804899 2804917 2804927 2804939 2804941 2804953 2804959 2804993 2805001
2805031 2805041 2805043 2805071 2805091 2805107 2805113 2805137 2805157 2805161
2805163 2805167 2805169 2805181 2805193 2805203 2805227 2805233 2805247 2805251
2805259 2805263 2805311 2805353 2805367 2805371 2805389 2805403 2805443 2805457
2805461 2805487 2805497 2805511 2805529 2805533 2805577 2805587 2805601 2805619
2805631 2805637 2805643 2805653 2805659 2805683 2805689 2805703 2805709 2805713
2805757 2805763 2805773 2805791 2805809 2805827 2805851 2805899 2805911 2805923
2805949 2805967 2805973 2805989 2806007 2806021 2806031 2806049 2806073 2806087
2806093 2806109 2806121 2806123 2806157 2806169 2806187 2806201 2806211 2806231
2806247 2806249 2806261 2806267 2806277 2806283 2806291 2806333 2806351 2806361
2806367 2806369 2806373 2806379 2806381 2806387 2806439 2806457 2806459 2806469
2806493 2806499 2806519 2806537 2806543 2806589 2806597 2806603 2806607 2806613
2806619 2806651 2806663 2806673 2806679 2806691 2806693 2806711 2806757 2806781
2806787 2806789 2806801 2806829 2806847 2806849 2806861 2806907 2806913 2806919
2806961 2806963 2806987 2807009 2807017 2807027 2807071 2807087 2807089 2807111
2807131 2807141 2807177 2807179 2807191 2807197 2807209 2807213 2807239 2807303
2807323 2807353 2807369 2807381 2807407 2807443 2807473 2807477 2807479 2807521
2807527 2807531 2807537 2807549 2807551 2807561 2807591 2807593 2807603 2807657
2807659 2807663 2807689 2807729 2807741 2807767 2807789 2807821 2807851 2807879
2807881 2807899 2807927 2807929 2807933 2807947 2807969 2807971 2807977 2808007
2808017 2808023 2808031 2808059 2808061 2808079 2808083 2808101 2808107 2808119
2808149 2808161 2808187 2808193 2808229 2808241 2808251 2808269 2808293 2808301
2808307 2808313 2808319 2808329 2808347 2808353 2808359 2808361 2808397 2808413
2808419 2808427 2808433 2808437 2808469 2808479 2808497 2808499 2808511 2808517
2808521 2808527 2808551 2808571 2808583 2808593 2808601 2808607 2808647 2808661
2808667 2808677 2808683 2808697 2808703 2808719 2808721 2808733 2808739 2808761
2808763 2808779 2808797 2808809 2808811 2808833 2808847 2808863 2808877 2808881
2808901 2808917 2808919 2808959 2808977 2808983 2808997 2809007 2809019 2809069
2809073 2809087 2809091 2809099 2809117 2809141 2809181 2809187 2809211 2809223
2809241 2809249 2809253 2809271 2809273 2809277 2809291 2809297 2809307 2809309
2809327 2809343 2809349 2809351 2809363 2809409 2809423 2809439 2809451 2809453
2809483 2809487 2809489 2809493 2809507 2809523 2809529 2809537 2809553 2809559
2809567 2809603 2809619 2809627 2809637 2809643 2809649 2809661 2809673 2809679
2809687 2809691 2809699 2809711 2809717 2809727 2809759 2809769 2809783 2809787
2809813 2809823 2809831 2809837 2809847 2809883 2809889 2809903 2809909 2809931
2809973 2809987 2810009 2810011 2810021 2810029 2810051 2810069 2810077 2810089
2810107 2810147 2810153 2810161 2810167 2810173 2810191 2810201 2810207 2810221
2810231 2810237 2810257 2810279 2810299 2810317 2810323 2810329 2810333 2810341
2810359 2810369 2810371 2810399 2810407 2810411 2810413 2810471 2810501 2810503
2810513 2810539 2810579 2810581 2810597 2810617 2810641 2810653 2810657 2810663
2810671 2810683 2810693 2810699 2810707 2810711 2810713 2810737 2810747 2810827
2810833 2810849 2810861 2810881 2810893 2810897 2810909 2810911 2810921 2810957
2810959 2810981 2810989 2811013 2811041 2811073 2811079 2811089 2811091 2811097
2811113 2811131 2811161 2811163 2811169 2811181 2811187 2811191 2811197 2811203
2811209 2811227 2811229 2811241 2811257 2811269 2811283 2811287 2811299 2811301
2811311 2811317 2811331 2811337 2811343 2811349 2811353 2811379 2811397 2811407
2811427 2811439 2811503 2811509 2811517 2811533 2811539 2811559 2811569 2811583
2811617 2811619 2811623 2811629 2811631 2811649 2811659 2811661 2811691 2811707
2811709 2811719 2811761 2811803 2811833 2811841 2811863 2811871 2811877 2811883
2811931 2811947 2811959 2811973 2811983 2811989 2812001 2812013 2812031 2812063
2812099 2812129 2812153 2812169 2812181 2812189 2812193 2812207 2812211 2812219
2812223 2812237 2812241 2812261 2812267 2812291 2812297 2812301 2812307 2812319
2812331 2812343 2812357 2812379 2812393 2812421 2812423 2812441 2812451 2812493
2812499 2812519 2812541 2812549 2812553 2812571 2812577 2812583 2812597 2812609
2812619 2812631 2812639 2812643 2812651 2812679 2812687 2812697 2812717 2812729
2812751 2812753 2812801 2812811 2812813 2812819 2812829 2812853 2812867 2812883
2812897 2812907 2812919 2812937 2812961 2812967 2812993 2813011 2813039 2813047
2813053 2813071 2813077 2813099 2813117 2813123 2813131 2813141 2813149 2813171
2813183 2813191 2813207 2813227 2813249 2813257 2813267 2813287 2813299 2813309
2813323 2813329 2813333 2813339 2813341 2813353 2813401 2813411 2813413 2813423
2813441 2813453 2813477 2813479 2813497 2813507 2813509 2813513 2813519 2813549
2813563 2813579 2813581 2813593 2813627 2813633 2813641 2813647 2813663 2813669
2813677 2813683 2813693 2813711 2813719 2813731 2813737 2813807 2813809 2813819
2813821 2813827 2813849 2813851 2813879 2813897 2813903 2813917 2813927 2813947
2813969 2813977 2813983 2813989 2814001 2814013 2814017 2814041 2814083 2814089
2814103 2814127 2814139 2814143 2814151 2814167 2814169 2814173 2814179 2814233
2814277 2814311 2814319 2814341 2814347 2814389 2814403 2814419 2814431 2814433
2814439 2814481 2814499 2814509 2814541 2814551 2814557 2814563 2814569 2814587
2814599 2814607 2814629 2814683 2814697 2814709 2814719 2814727 2814733 2814739
2814743 2814751 2814761 2814787 2814811 2814817 2814821 2814829 2814839 2814841
2814857 2814863 2814881 2814899 2814913 2814941 2814991 2815003 2815009 2815049
2815061 2815069 2815073 2815091 2815103 2815123 2815129 2815157 2815171 2815187
2815207 2815237 2815247 2815259 2815271 2815289 2815301 2815313 2815331 2815343
2815369 2815399 2815403 2815411 2815427 2815447 2815457 2815469 2815493 2815507
2815517 2815529 2815559 2815573 2815607 2815613 2815627 2815633 2815649 2815669
2815691 2815733 2815739 2815741 2815759 2815763 2815793 2815807 2815843 2815853
2815861 2815877 2815879 2815903 2815927 2815937 2815963 2815973 2815979 2815993
2815997 2816017 2816029 2816053 2816057 2816059 2816083 2816087 2816089 2816131
```

2816141 2816147 2816171 2816173 2816197 2816213 2816221 2816239 2816243 2816251
2816263 2816269 2816291 2816293 2816311 2816353 2816377 2816399 2816453 2816459
2816501 2816507 2816519 2816531 2816533 2816537 2816549 2816563 2816573 2816581
2816623 2816633 2816647 2816651 2816657 2816701 2816707 2816711 2816717 2816767
2816777 2816809 2816819 2816831 2816839 2816861 2816873 2816899 2816909 2816927
2816941 2816953 2816963 2816969 2816981 2817007 2817011 2817029 2817043 2817077
2817079 2817083 2817091 2817127 2817137 2817161 2817167 2817169 2817173 2817181
2817197 2817211 2817229 2817239 2817251 2817253 2817259 2817271 2817299 2817307
2817337 2817341 2817361 2817371 2817383 2817389 2817441 2817443 2817447 2817449
2817467 2817469 2817481 2817487 2817499 2817511 2817517 2817539 2817547 2817557
2817583 2817593 2817599 2817613 2817623 2817629 2817649 2817667 2817671 2817673
2817677 2817701 2817709 2817713 2817721 2817743 2817769 2817779 2817797 2817817
2817821 2817847 2817877 2817887 2817907 2817917 2817929 2817943 2817967 2817973
2818027 2818033 2818043 2818103 2818111 2818147 2818157 2818159 2818163 2818171
2818181 2818219 2818223 2818229 2818237 2818267 2818271 2818279 2818297 2818337
2818357 2818369 2818391 2818393 2818399 2818411 2818421 2818429 2818451 2818469
2818471 2818499 2818507 2818513 2818523 2818531 2818537 2818547 2818553 2818561
2818577 2818609 2818619 2818639 2818643 2818649 2818657 2818661 2818667 2818687
2818733 2818789 2818817 2818831 2818841 2818853 2818877 2818883 2818909
2818939 2818967 2818987 2818997 2818999 2819009 2819021 2819023 2819039 2819051
2819053 2819099 2819101 2819137 2819143 2819147 2819149 2819153 2819189 2819203
2819221 2819231 2819269 2819281 2819287 2819303 2819309 2819329 2819347 2819371
2819387 2819393 2819407 2819413 2819423 2819449 2819471 2819473 2819477 2819489
2819491 2819497 2819519 2819521 2819549 2819587 2819599 2819627 2819629 2819633
2819647 2819651 2819681 2819683 2819701 2819711 2819717 2819723 2819741 2819743
2819749 2819753 2819767 2819779 2819783 2819797 2819801 2819827 2819867 2819899
2819903 2819911 2819933 2819951 2819959 2819981 2819987 2820001 2820017 2820019
2820031 2820043 2820071 2820089 2820109 2820119 2820127 2820131 2820179 2820193
2820197 2820211 2820229 2820239 2820263 2820271 2820313 2820319 2820331 2820343
2820347 2820359 2820361 2820373 2820383 2820401 2820403 2820407 2820479 2820481
2820491 2820509 2820527 2820541 2820553 2820557 2820563 2820619 2820641 2820667
2820673 2820679 2820689 2820703 2820707 2820709 2820733 2820737 2820749 2820751
2820773 2820781 2820787 2820791 2820803 2820809 2820817 2820821 2820833 2820863
2820869 2820877 2820887 2820889 2820899 2820913 2820919 2820941 2820943 2820947
2820971 2820977 2821001 2821009 2821057 2821073 2821079 2821097 2821103 2821109
2821141 2821151 2821153 2821163 2821183 2821229 2821267 2821277 2821289 2821319
2821331 2821369 2821393 2821411 2821421 2821451 2821459 2821463 2821471 2821477
2821493 2821501 2821513 2821517 2821537 2821543 2821549 2821573 2821591 2821601
2821607 2821627 2821649 2821661 2821669 2821717 2821733 2821759 2821769 2821771
2821807 2821811 2821817 2821829 2821831 2821849 2821859 2821867 2821877 2821909
2821913 2821919 2821933 2821957 2821969 2821979 2821981 2821991 2821997 2821999
2822003 2822009 2822011 2822033 2822069 2822093 2822129 2822137 2822143 2822159
2822189 2822191 2822201 2822207 2822213 2822233 2822263 2822269 2822297 2822299
2822311 2822371 2822377 2822381 2822387 2822411 2822423 2822429 2822441 2822447
2822461 2822473 2822503 2822513 2822539 2822543 2822557 2822569 2822579 2822587
2822593 2822609 2822623 2822641 2822669 2822681 2822689 2822707 2822711 2822713
2822717 2822719 2822723 2822741 2822761 2822791 2822819 2822851 2822857 2822879
2822881 2822893 2822899 2822903 2822909 2822917 2822923 2822929 2822933 2822959
2822971 2822987 2823047 2823053 2823059 2823101 2823109 2823113 2823133 2823143
2823167 2823193 2823203 2823217 2823221 2823269 2823277 2823283 2823287 2823311
2823329 2823361 2823371 2823389 2823407 2823437 2823439 2823451 2823463 2823467
2823473 2823487 2823493 2823497 2823517 2823521 2823523 2823529 2823559 2823589
2823607 2823617 2823631 2823637 2823661 2823671 2823673 2823679 2823721 2823731
2823749 2823763 2823773 2823791 2823809 2823811 2823823 2823829 2823833 2823839
2823857 2823869 2823889 2823911 2823923 2823943 2823971 2823973 2824021 2824043
2824067 2824079 2824097 2824109 2824123 2824127 2824139 2824163 2824177 2824181
2824187 2824189 2824201 2824207 2824259 2824291 2824303 2824307 2824313 2824319
2824337 2824351 2824361 2824373 2824387 2824399 2824411 2824417 2824421 2824429
2824433 2824439 2824447 2824463 2824477 2824553 2824579 2824583 2824603 2824609
2824621 2824631 2824637 2824643 2824649 2824651 2824681 2824697 2824709 2824721
2824781 2824793 2824799 2824807 2824819 2824853 2824853 2824879 2824889 2824903
2824909 2824933 2824967 2824973 2824993 2825003 2825033 2825047 2825051 2825063
2825083 2825099 2825101 2825117 2825131 2825149 2825153 2825191 2825227 2825239
2825261 2825287 2825293 2825299 2825353 2825363 2825387 2825411 2825413 2825419
2825423 2825429 2825447 2825461 2825467 2825477 2825479 2825489 2825491 2825497
2825503 2825521 2825551 2825561 2825567 2825639 2825651 2825657 2825671 2825701
2825741 2825749 2825759 2825773 2825777 2825783 2825819 2825821 2825827 2825833
2825857 2825861 2825863 2825869 2825891 2825939 2825951 2825957 2825959 2825981
2825983 2826037 2826059 2826071 2826073 2826091 2826101 2826107 2826113 2826121
2826143 2826149 2826151 2826167 2826173 2826179 2826181 2826281 2826293 2826323
2826337 2826361 2826367 2826371 2826379 2826413 2826431 2826443 2826457 2826463
2826491 2826521 2826553 2826559 2826563 2826613 2826623 2826643 2826661 2826667
2826671 2826683 2826713 2826727 2826737 2826739 2826757 2826773 2826793 2826821
2826829 2826847 2826851 2826853 2826883 2826899 2826917 2826919 2826979 2826997
2827031 2827043 2827051 2827061 2827073 2827087 2827109 2827159 2827211 2827213
2827241 2827267 2827277 2827327 2827337 2827369 2827381 2827387 2827393 2827397
2827403 2827421 2827427 2827439 2827469 2827481 2827493 2827499 2827507 2827519
2827547 2827549 2827553 2827571 2827621 2827631 2827633 2827639 2827667 2827673
2827679 2827681 2827687 2827753 2827793 2827813 2827823 2827901 2827907 2827927
2827931 2827939 2827961 2827969 2827973 2827987 2828053 2828083 2828107 2828113
2828123 2828129 2828141 2828173 2828179 2828183 2828191 2828197 2828209 2828219
2828237 2828257 2828281 2828291 2828297 2828299 2828311 2828327 2828339 2828351
2828363 2828383 2828389 2828429 2828431 2828453 2828461 2828491 2828521 2828563
2828593 2828597 2828599 2828611 2828627 2828629 2828633 2828641 2828717 2828731
2828741 2828743 2828767 2828779 2828797 2828809 2828857 2828867 2828869 2828879
2828887 2828893 2828897 2828923 2828939 2828951 2828971 2828989 2828993 2828999
2829007 2829041 2829049 2829061 2829083 2829097 2829103 2829107 2829121 2829133
2829139 2829143 2829173 2829217 2829223 2829247 2829251 2829257 2829263 2829289
2829301 2829311 2829317 2829329 2829341 2829349 2829367 2829373 2829383 2829397

```
2829403  2829413  2829439  2829467  2829473  2829479  2829487  2829493  2829503  2829509
2829527  2829539  2829557  2829569  2829571  2829583  2829641  2829653  2829661  2829677
2829679  2829683  2829691  2829703  2829707  2829709  2829737  2829751  2829767  2829793
2829809  2829821  2829839  2829863  2829877  2829881  2829887  2829889  2829899  2829913
2829923  2829949  2829961  2829977  2830027  2830033  2830039  2830049  2830067  2830073
2830097  2830099  2830123  2830129  2830133  2830141  2830151  2830153  2830181  2830187
2830229  2830237  2830249  2830277  2830291  2830301  2830349  2830351  2830361  2830367
2830379  2830391  2830397  2830433  2830439  2830469  2830489  2830501  2830507  2830511
2830523  2830547  2830559  2830567  2830573  2830577  2830591  2830609  2830613  2830627
2830631  2830637  2830651  2830657  2830741  2830781  2830787  2830801  2830813  2830837
2830843  2830853  2830859  2830871  2830873  2830897  2830913  2830921  2830937  2830939
2830963  2830967  2830969  2830973  2830979  2831011  2831039  2831051  2831069  2831089
2831141  2831167  2831177  2831189  2831221  2831237  2831263  2831273  2831293  2831317
2831321  2831329  2831341  2831347  2831359  2831377  2831393  2831407  2831417  2831429
2831449  2831459  2831467  2831471  2831489  2831497  2831533  2831539  2831557  2831561
2831603  2831617  2831623  2831641  2831651  2831657  2831659  2831663  2831669  2831671
2831677  2831687  2831687  2831701  2831729  2831749  2831753  2831767  2831789  2831791
2831839  2831849  2831861  2831863  2831903  2831909  2831947  2831951  2831953  2831971
2831999  2832001  2832019  2832031  2832041  2832073  2832077  2832097  2832103  2832113
2832127  2832131  2832133  2832143  2832163  2832187  2832211  2832223  2832257  2832259
2832283  2832287  2832329  2832331  2832359  2832371  2832383  2832391  2832419  2832433
2832443  2832449  2832457  2832491  2832503  2832509  2832527  2832553  2832569  2832589
2832593  2832601  2832617  2832623  2832629  2832631  2832637  2832667  2832679  2832701
2832719  2832743  2832787  2832793  2832799  2832803  2832847  2832853  2832857  2832871
2832877  2832889  2832917  2832941  2832953  2832967  2832983  2833001  2833007  2833013
2833021  2833027  2833031  2833043  2833049  2833063  2833069  2833073  2833081  2833093
2833099  2833111  2833123  2833133  2833139  2833157  2833189  2833199  2833211  2833231
2833241  2833247  2833279  2833283  2833291  2833309  2833319  2833321  2833331  2833333
2833343  2833381  2833403  2833409  2833421  2833447  2833463  2833471  2833477  2833483
2833487  2833507  2833517  2833529  2833541  2833549  2833553  2833559  2833573  2833591
2833601  2833609  2833613  2833627  2833637  2833643  2833667  2833687  2833709  2833723
2833729  2833739  2833759  2833763  2833769  2833777  2833799  2833801  2833811  2833813
2833837  2833843  2833889  2833903  2833921  2833937  2833969  2833973  2833993  2833997
2834011  2834017  2834047  2834057  2834063  2834077  2834093  2834101  2834123  2834131
2834159  2834171  2834179  2834191  2834197  2834203  2834213  2834233  2834261  2834263
2834269  2834309  2834317  2834329  2834339  2834347  2834369  2834399  2834411  2834413
2834417  2834443  2834449  2834467  2834473  2834479  2834483  2834501  2834509  2834521
2834527  2834539  2834551  2834567  2834581  2834639  2834647  2834651  2834653  2834659
2834677  2834683  2834693  2834701  2834707  2834717  2834719  2834729  2834737  2834747
2834749  2834753  2834759  2834789  2834807  2834813  2834833  2834849  2834873  2834893
2834921  2834939  2834983  2834989  2835037  2835061  2835071  2835089  2835103  2835113
2835121  2835137  2835139  2835149  2835163  2835169  2835211  2835221  2835223  2835241
2835253  2835269  2835271  2835289  2835293  2835307  2835319  2835323  2835331  2835367
2835383  2835397  2835401  2835409  2835419  2835433  2835439  2835479  2835491  2835499
2835517  2835523  2835563  2835587  2835589  2835593  2835653  2835661  2835667  2835671
2835673  2835689  2835691  2835697  2835733  2835737  2835751  2835779  2835793  2835841
2835851  2835857  2835869  2835887  2835901  2835913  2835941  2835967  2835971  2836003
2836007  2836033  2836069  2836079  2836081  2836103  2836109  2836117  2836129  2836139
2836201  2836241  2836243  2836259  2836261  2836271  2836279  2836303  2836313  2836321
2836343  2836357  2836367  2836369  2836381  2836387  2836391  2836397  2836423  2836447
2836481  2836487  2836489  2836499  2836553  2836597  2836601  2836607  2836609  2836619
2836621  2836627  2836633  2836651  2836699  2836703  2836711  2836721  2836727  2836733
2836741  2836747  2836759  2836763  2836777  2836781  2836789  2836793  2836817  2836849
2836861  2836879  2836919  2836937  2836949  2836961  2836963  2836973  2836991  2836993
2837017  2837033  2837039  2837047  2837057  2837059  2837063  2837069  2837071  2837083
2837101  2837111  2837141  2837167  2837173  2837179  2837201  2837209  2837221  2837227
2837239  2837243  2837279  2837281  2837287  2837297  2837309  2837339  2837353  2837357
2837363  2837371  2837377  2837381  2837441  2837459  2837473  2837477  2837491  2837501
2837503  2837519  2837551  2837557  2837581  2837599  2837609  2837617  2837629  2837633
2837677  2837693  2837711  2837713  2837741  2837773  2837777  2837801  2837803  2837839
2837843  2837851  2837867  2837873  2837881  2837909  2837927  2837951  2837953  2837977
2837981  2837983  2837987  2838007  2838013  2838023  2838037  2838047  2838067  2838071
2838079  2838091  2838103  2838109  2838119  2838137  2838139  2838149  2838151  2838169
2838191  2838211  2838217  2838247  2838271  2838281  2838287  2838289  2838293  2838359
2838373  2838397  2838401  2838421  2838443  2838449  2838457  2838461  2838463  2838481
2838487  2838547  2838557  2838569  2838587  2838593  2838601  2838611  2838617  2838629
2838631  2838697  2838713  2838721  2838727  2838743  2838749  2838767  2838769  2838827
2838841  2838851  2838853  2838859  2838863  2838889  2838907  2838911  2838917  2838919
2838931  2838937  2839007  2839019  2839049  2839063  2839069  2839087  2839099  2839117
2839141  2839159  2839171  2839183  2839201  2839217  2839271  2839283  2839301  2839307
2839313  2839337  2839349  2839363  2839381  2839399  2839409  2839429  2839433  2839451
2839457  2839469  2839471  2839483  2839519  2839541  2839547  2839549  2839553  2839567
2839589  2839601  2839621  2839657  2839691  2839699  2839717  2839757  2839769  2839789
2839801  2839819  2839831  2839841  2839843  2839853  2839871  2839913  2839927  2839931
2839933  2839937  2839939  2839943  2839951  2839957  2839961  2839981  2840023  2840027
2840039  2840041  2840059  2840077  2840087  2840093  2840113  2840119  2840161  2840171
2840179  2840183  2840191  2840203  2840209  2840237  2840239  2840249  2840261  2840263
2840267  2840269  2840273  2840281  2840303  2840353  2840359  2840393  2840417  2840419
2840447  2840449  2840459  2840483  2840507  2840549  2840627  2840647  2840653  2840657
2840681  2840687  2840689  2840699  2840723  2840731  2840741  2840759  2840771  2840777
2840779  2840801  2840857  2840911  2840917  2840939  2840951  2840987  2841011  2841019
2841031  2841067  2841071  2841073  2841079  2841109  2841131  2841133  2841151  2841161
2841187  2841199  2841211  2841223  2841287  2841301  2841313  2841337  2841347  2841353
2841361  2841373  2841401  2841407  2841413  2841427  2841437  2841439  2841451  2841457
2841463  2841467  2841473  2841493  2841497  2841511  2841523  2841529  2841541  2841547
2841557  2841589  2841593  2841653  2841679  2841691  2841733  2841749  2841757  2841763
2841767  2841781  2841793  2841799  2841803  2841821  2841823  2841847  2841851  2841869
2841893  2841911  2841931  2841961  2841967  2841973  2841989  2842031  2842033  2842061
2842069  2842097  2842127  2842139  2842157  2842159  2842181  2842187  2842193  2842199
```

```
2842211  2842219  2842223  2842237  2842253  2842283  2842291  2842309  2842331  2842351
2842361  2842373  2842397  2842403  2842439  2842459  2842487  2842517  2842529  2842531
2842537  2842559  2842573  2842579  2842583  2842589  2842591  2842597  2842603  2842643
2842649  2842663  2842681  2842691  2842711  2842717  2842727  2842729  2842733  2842739
2842751  2842753  2842787  2842789  2842811  2842813  2842843  2842849  2842871  2842873
2842891  2842897  2842901  2842937  2842943  2842949  2842963  2842991  2843003  2843017
2843021  2843023  2843039  2843051  2843059  2843081  2843089  2843101  2843107  2843111
2843119  2843143  2843147  2843153  2843177  2843207  2843213  2843219  2843221  2843249
2843257  2843261  2843263  2843273  2843287  2843317  2843327  2843333  2843341  2843353
2843377  2843389  2843411  2843429  2843501  2843507  2843527  2843531  2843549  2843557
2843567  2843587  2843611  2843627  2843671  2843677  2843683  2843689  2843693  2843699
2843717  2843747  2843767  2843791  2843803  2843809  2843831  2843833  2843837  2843851
2843873  2843887  2843899  2843903  2843941  2843969  2843987  2843993  2843999  2844013
2844031  2844043  2844067  2844071  2844103  2844109  2844119  2844133  2844197  2844199
2844221  2844223  2844229  2844239  2844251  2844263  2844269  2844271  2844277  2844311
2844313  2844329  2844337  2844353  2844367  2844379  2844397  2844421  2844427  2844437
2844469  2844481  2844557  2844587  2844601  2844607  2844629  2844641  2844649  2844677
2844691  2844701  2844713  2844731  2844739  2844761  2844767  2844833  2844911  2844917
2844937  2844943  2844953  2844971  2844973  2844983  2845019  2845033  2845043  2845051
2845061  2845091  2845097  2845099  2845109  2845127  2845133  2845147  2845151  2845177
2845201  2845207  2845279  2845303  2845309  2845319  2845357  2845361  2845363  2845369
2845373  2845387  2845391  2845417  2845433  2845457  2845463  2845481  2845499  2845519
2845529  2845547  2845553  2845561  2845571  2845603  2845631  2845637  2845639  2845667
2845673  2845693  2845699  2845723  2845727  2845739  2845811  2845823  2845837  2845841
2845853  2845873  2845891  2845903  2845907  2845949  2845963  2845967  2845979  2845981
2846009  2846027  2846033  2846057  2846071  2846083  2846111  2846113  2846119  2846161
2846167  2846183  2846189  2846243  2846287  2846323  2846329  2846339  2846351  2846359
2846377  2846387  2846399  2846401  2846413  2846479  2846491  2846527  2846533  2846537
2846539  2846551  2846593  2846609  2846617  2846621  2846647  2846677  2846693  2846717
2846719  2846731  2846737  2846741  2846749  2846759  2846771  2846773  2846777  2846783
2846791  2846797  2846801  2846813  2846821  2846861  2846863  2846867  2846869  2846873
2846929  2846951  2846953  2846957  2846969  2846981  2846989  2847011  2847043  2847059
2847067  2847079  2847083  2847127  2847139  2847167  2847179  2847181  2847197  2847203
2847209  2847217  2847227  2847253  2847259  2847269  2847277  2847287  2847289  2847293
2847301  2847323  2847337  2847343  2847349  2847379  2847389  2847413  2847431  2847457
2847479  2847497  2847499  2847521  2847527  2847529  2847563  2847583  2847599  2847601
2847623  2847643  2847661  2847671  2847679  2847697  2847707  2847727  2847731  2847749
2847763  2847769  2847787  2847797  2847799  2847833  2847839  2847863  2847893  2847917
2847931  2847937  2847961  2847973  2847991  2848009  2848031  2848033  2848037  2848051
2848057  2848091  2848117  2848121  2848123  2848127  2848133  2848141  2848171  2848193
2848199  2848201  2848207  2848213  2848243  2848283  2848319  2848327  2848337  2848361
2848369  2848381  2848399  2848411  2848421  2848453  2848459  2848471  2848493  2848501
2848507  2848511  2848513  2848541  2848561  2848567  2848577  2848589  2848597  2848603
2848607  2848609  2848627  2848631  2848633  2848663  2848669  2848687  2848691  2848693
2848709  2848723  2848739  2848753  2848771  2848777  2848787  2848789  2848799  2848823
2848829  2848831  2848837  2848847  2848871  2848887  2848913  2848919  2848921  2848927
2848939  2848949  2848957  2848973  2848981  2849009  2849053  2849057  2849087  2849123
2849129  2849153  2849173  2849177  2849201  2849207  2849233  2849291  2849299  2849317
2849321  2849339  2849351  2849389  2849419  2849423  2849461  2849477  2849479  2849481
2849507  2849519  2849537  2849593  2849617  2849633  2849647  2849663  2849669  2849681
2849683  2849687  2849689  2849699  2849713  2849741  2849771  2849773  2849779  2849783
2849797  2849807  2849809  2849813  2849831  2849839  2849843  2849849  2849857  2849887
2849893  2849927  2849929  2849933  2849941  2849947  2849969  2849989  2849983  2850013
2850037  2850041  2850059  2850061  2850079  2850097  2850157  2850161  2850173  2850179
2850187  2850191  2850193  2850223  2850251  2850257  2850259  2850299  2850301  2850311
2850313  2850317  2850329  2850343  2850371  2850377  2850383  2850389  2850401  2850433
2850451  2850461  2850479  2850487  2850493  2850511  2850541  2850563  2850571  2850583
2850619  2850623  2850647  2850697  2850719  2850727  2850737  2850761  2850763  2850767
2850773  2850797  2850811  2850823  2850829  2850851  2850871  2850899  2850929  2850941
2850949  2850959  2850971  2850979  2850989  2850997  2851001  2851049  2851061  2851081
2851091  2851097  2851111  2851141  2851151  2851153  2851169  2851171  2851187  2851231
2851249  2851253  2851267  2851313  2851327  2851337  2851351  2851361  2851391  2851397
2851399  2851403  2851421  2851423  2851441  2851451  2851469  2851481  2851513  2851523
2851543  2851561  2851571  2851601  2851603  2851613  2851621  2851633  2851643  2851661
2851727  2851741  2851777  2851787  2851789  2851799  2851813  2851817  2851829  2851841
2851847  2851853  2851861  2851867  2851873  2851879  2851909  2851921  2851939  2851943
2851949  2851951  2851973  2851991  2852027  2852041  2852051  2852053  2852077  2852081
2852099  2852117  2852149  2852159  2852167  2852189  2852191  2852197  2852249  2852281
2852303  2852309  2852327  2852351  2852371  2852387  2852389  2852401  2852429  2852449
2852467  2852471  2852501  2852503  2852519  2852569  2852581  2852587  2852599  2852609
2852669  2852671  2852677  2852699  2852711  2852743  2852747  2852771  2852779  2852797
2852807  2852809  2852813  2852819  2852833  2852849  2852873  2852879  2852887  2852893
2852917  2852939  2852963  2852977  2852981  2852987  2852999  2853001  2853013  2853017
2853047  2853079  2853083  2853101  2853113  2853121  2853131  2853157  2853167  2853187
2853197  2853217  2853233  2853241  2853247  2853269  2853307  2853337  2853371  2853373
2853391  2853413  2853427  2853443  2853451  2853481  2853493  2853503  2853509  2853533
2853547  2853577  2853601  2853611  2853647  2853659  2853661  2853673  2853677  2853689
2853701  2853707  2853709  2853737  2853751  2853757  2853761  2853779  2853787  2853791
2853811  2853833  2853853  2853869  2853871  2853881  2853883  2853911  2853913  2853923
2853937  2853973  2853979  2853989  2854003  2854021  2854037  2854043  2854063  2854067
2854073  2854091  2854099  2854127  2854157  2854171  2854207  2854223  2854253  2854259
2854261  2854273  2854289  2854301  2854303  2854309  2854321  2854331  2854337  2854343
2854363  2854367  2854381  2854391  2854399  2854403  2854433  2854447  2854459  2854463
2854517  2854547  2854549  2854561  2854567  2854571  2854591  2854603  2854609  2854627
2854637  2854651  2854703  2854717  2854723  2854729  2854751  2854763  2854781  2854799
2854837  2854843  2854889  2854903  2854919  2854927  2854933  2854939  2854993  2855003
2855009  2855023  2855029  2855033  2855051  2855063  2855077  2855089  2855093  2855101
2855107  2855113  2855119  2855129  2855141  2855159  2855161  2855183  2855189  2855207
2855213  2855221  2855231  2855233  2855239  2855257  2855261  2855267  2855273  2855309
```

```
2855323  2855353  2855357  2855383  2855393  2855399  2855429  2855431  2855443  2855459
2855467  2855483  2855497  2855513  2855557  2855581  2855591  2855599  2855603  2855617
2855653  2855683  2855701  2855707  2855729  2855731  2855747  2855761  2855791  2855807
2855819  2855843  2855851  2855857  2855869  2855873  2855893  2855899  2855911  2855927
2855953  2855989  2856001  2856037  2856059  2856079  2856083  2856097  2856107  2856121
2856149  2856167  2856173  2856197  2856229  2856241  2856253  2856283  2856349  2856353
2856377  2856379  2856397  2856409  2856419  2856421  2856431  2856449  2856461  2856473
2856509  2856521  2856547  2856551  2856559  2856599  2856617  2856653  2856673  2856677
2856683  2856773  2856779  2856803  2856809  2856823  2856857  2856863  2856871  2856883
2856923  2856961  2856967  2856977  2857009  2857013  2857039  2857061  2857067  2857073
2857079  2857093  2857097  2857123  2857159  2857181  2857187  2857199  2857219  2857223
2857237  2857247  2857259  2857297  2857303  2857319  2857321  2857333  2857339  2857357
2857369  2857381  2857397  2857403  2857417  2857427  2857433  2857453  2857469  2857471
2857493  2857501  2857507  2857511  2857531  2857541  2857559  2857567  2857571  2857579
2857609  2857633  2857637  2857639  2857643  2857661  2857663  2857693  2857697  2857709
2857711  2857721  2857753  2857759  2857763  2857801  2857831  2857849  2857861  2857867
2857889  2857891  2857903  2857913  2857931  2857937  2857949  2857951  2857973  2857993
2858029  2858041  2858059  2858071  2858101  2858123  2858129  2858161  2858173  2858179
2858183  2858209  2858221  2858243  2858249  2858263  2858309  2858333  2858347  2858357
2858369  2858381  2858393  2858423  2858441  2858447  2858459  2858467  2858483  2858489
2858503  2858519  2858543  2858573  2858579  2858599  2858621  2858623  2858627  2858633
2858641  2858651  2858699  2858701  2858711  2858741  2858747  2858749  2858777  2858803
2858819  2858827  2858833  2858893  2858903  2858927  2858929  2858951  2858959  2858981
2859001  2859019  2859029  2859047  2859049  2859067  2859071  2859097  2859121  2859133
2859137  2859163  2859173  2859187  2859211  2859229  2859251  2859271  2859287  2859289
2859301  2859331  2859341  2859343  2859377  2859391  2859407  2859413  2859427  2859469
2859473  2859491  2859499  2859503  2859551  2859559  2859607  2859617  2859631  2859641
2859673  2859677  2859697  2859707  2859713  2859733  2859743  2859749  2859763  2859793
2859799  2859803  2859847  2859849  2859919  2859919  2859929  2859943  2859949  2859971
2859977  2859979  2859991  2860007  2860019  2860021  2860043  2860057  2860061  2860087
2860103  2860129  2860133  2860141  2860157  2860177  2860181  2860223  2860237  2860259
2860271  2860289  2860307  2860309  2860327  2860331  2860337  2860409  2860411  2860457
2860477  2860483  2860493  2860499  2860523  2860553  2860567  2860577  2860601  2860609
2860631  2860633  2860639  2860643  2860657  2860673  2860679  2860681  2860687  2860691
2860721  2860723  2860751  2860757  2860769  2860771  2860787  2860789  2860799  2860801
2860807  2860817  2860829  2860841  2860853  2860883  2860903  2860931  2860973  2860999
2861009  2861041  2861051  2861059  2861063  2861081  2861107  2861113  2861119  2861129
2861137  2861147  2861161  2861189  2861197  2861203  2861213  2861231  2861233  2861239
2861249  2861251  2861279  2861291  2861297  2861303  2861317  2861347  2861363  2861377
2861387  2861399  2861447  2861461  2861471  2861479  2861483  2861497  2861531  2861539
2861549  2861557  2861561  2861569  2861587  2861603  2861623  2861657  2861659  2861669
2861671  2861699  2861711  2861737  2861741  2861743  2861767  2861777  2861801  2861809
2861849  2861851  2861861  2861869  2861887  2861909  2861917  2861921  2861927  2861941
2861977  2862011  2862017  2862043  2862047  2862049  2862077  2862109  2862113  2862127
2862131  2862163  2862187  2862203  2862221  2862227  2862259  2862289  2862311  2862313
2862337  2862359  2862361  2862367  2862397  2862401  2862413  2862437  2862463  2862469
2862487  2862491  2862493  2862499  2862523  2862529  2862539  2862551  2862569  2862577
2862589  2862593  2862599  2862611  2862617  2862623  2862641  2862683  2862701  2862703
2862731  2862733  2862751  2862803  2862829  2862859  2862883  2862887  2862917  2862929
2862931  2862941  2862947  2862973  2862991  2862997  2863009  2863019  2863031  2863037
2863057  2863061  2863079  2863117  2863121  2863127  2863139  2863169  2863181  2863207
2863229  2863277  2863283  2863291  2863303  2863309  2863313  2863331  2863351  2863363
2863369  2863387  2863391  2863403  2863423  2863453  2863457  2863493  2863517  2863519
2863559  2863573  2863577  2863589  2863591  2863603  2863607  2863649  2863697  2863703
2863733  2863739  2863741  2863771  2863787  2863793  2863823  2863841  2863849  2863853
2863859  2863867  2863877  2863879  2863907  2863909  2863921  2863943  2863951  2863955
2863967  2863969  2863979  2864021  2864023  2864027  2864033  2864051  2864077  2864083
2864087  2864089  2864093  2864129  2864149  2864153  2864159  2864201  2864203  2864209
2864221  2864237  2864249  2864261  2864291  2864293  2864299  2864339  2864341  2864357
2864363  2864371  2864401  2864419  2864423  2864441  2864453  2864467  2864473  2864479
2864527  2864539  2864557  2864569  2864599  2864623  2864633  2864647  2864657  2864671
2864677  2864681  2864683  2864689  2864713  2864717  2864723  2864737  2864749  2864761
2864831  2864833  2864843  2864867  2864879  2864887  2864909  2864963  2864969  2864977
2865001  2865007  2865043  2865059  2865091  2865097  2865131  2865157  2865173  2865193
2865199  2865209  2865211  2865241  2865259  2865277  2865307  2865311  2865319  2865329
2865337  2865383  2865397  2865413  2865427  2865431  2865433  2865439  2865463  2865479
2865481  2865487  2865491  2865493  2865497  2865509  2865521  2865529  2865557  2865559
2865581  2865587  2865589  2865601  2865607  2865617  2865623  2865641  2865659  2865661
2865679  2865683  2865691  2865697  2865701  2865727  2865739  2865743  2865749  2865787
2865803  2865817  2865839  2865871  2865881  2865899  2865901  2865913  2865917  2865923
2865931  2865949  2865953  2865971  2865977  2866001  2866033  2866049  2866051  2866069
2866109  2866117  2866121  2866139  2866147  2866151  2866159  2866163  2866189  2866211
2866223  2866247  2866261  2866267  2866271  2866277  2866289  2866309  2866333  2866343
2866363  2866403  2866417  2866429  2866439  2866441  2866453  2866463  2866469  2866499
2866519  2866529  2866537  2866543  2866553  2866579  2866583  2866603  2866607  2866609
2866613  2866627  2866657  2866667  2866691  2866709  2866711  2866741  2866753  2866781
2866793  2866807  2866811  2866819  2866837  2866841  2866847  2866867  2866873  2866883
2866901  2866907  2866921  2866937  2866943  2866951  2866961  2867003  2867009  2867017
2867021  2867023  2867071  2867077  2867083  2867099  2867107  2867213  2867219  2867231
2867239  2867243  2867269  2867281  2867287  2867297  2867299  2867303  2867321  2867327
2867351  2867357  2867377  2867383  2867429  2867437  2867467  2867471  2867497  2867503
2867507  2867519  2867561  2867569  2867573  2867597  2867629  2867633  2867677  2867699
2867719  2867737  2867741  2867743  2867771  2867783  2867797  2867809  2867819  2867831
2867857  2867861  2867867  2867869  2867873  2867911  2867923  2867929  2867933  2867941
2867947  2867957  2867959  2868001  2868007  2868011  2868017  2868023  2868029  2868043
2868067  2868083  2868109  2868113  2868119  2868137  2868139  2868149  2868161  2868163
2868181  2868191  2868211  2868251  2868263  2868289  2868293  2868323  2868331  2868343
2868367  2868407  2868409  2868421  2868443  2868451  2868473  2868479  2868493  2868497
2868511  2868527  2868539  2868557  2868571  2868577  2868617  2868673  2868689  2868707
```

```
2868713  2868773  2868779  2868787  2868793  2868799  2868809  2868823  2868851  2868857
2868871  2868919  2868947  2868949  2868959  2868961  2868977  2869001  2869033  2869051
2869063  2869079  2869103  2869117  2869123  2869127  2869159  2869187  2869199  2869213
2869219  2869241  2869249  2869253  2869259  2869301  2869321  2869327  2869351  2869369
2869403  2869429  2869441  2869459  2869499  2869541  2869547  2869553  2869567  2869613
2869621  2869649  2869663  2869693  2869721  2869729  2869747  2869751  2869759  2869771
2869781  2869793  2869799  2869807  2869813  2869837  2869859  2869873  2869879  2869883
2869901  2869943  2869967  2869973  2869981  2869987  2870017  2870027  2870039  2870047
2870051  2870081  2870089  2870099  2870107  2870113  2870171  2870183  2870227  2870237
2870249  2870269  2870279  2870323  2870353  2870393  2870401  2870407  2870411  2870429
2870437  2870443  2870447  2870453  2870471  2870473  2870513  2870519  2870531  2870537
2870557  2870573  2870581  2870591  2870597  2870611  2870617  2870627  2870641  2870657
2870663  2870669  2870683  2870689  2870701  2870711  2870717  2870753  2870761  2870789
2870801  2870821  2870831  2870839  2870863  2870893  2870899  2870911  2870953  2870969
2870983  2870993  2871013  2871019  2871031  2871049  2871061  2871091  2871101  2871119
2871133  2871137  2871139  2871173  2871191  2871199  2871221  2871227  2871233  2871257
2871287  2871289  2871293  2871347  2871359  2871361  2871367  2871391  2871409  2871433
2871439  2871457  2871467  2871469  2871503  2871509  2871563  2871587  2871611  2871613
2871629  2871643  2871689  2871719  2871721  2871731  2871749  2871761  2871767  2871797
2871811  2871833  2871853  2871857  2871877  2871881  2871901  2871917  2871919  2871937
2871959  2871961  2871991  2872003  2872007  2872019  2872027  2872043  2872069
2872081  2872109  2872139  2872141  2872151  2872153  2872183  2872187  2872237  2872277
2872283  2872291  2872301  2872313  2872327  2872333  2872351  2872369  2872379  2872391
2872393  2872409  2872417  2872423  2872427  2872433  2872451  2872453  2872459  2872481
2872523  2872531  2872543  2872559  2872577  2872579  2872601  2872607  2872621  2872669
2872691  2872693  2872697  2872703  2872721  2872729  2872741  2872757  2872763  2872771
2872783  2872789  2872811  2872817  2872823  2872853  2872889  2872897  2872921  2872937
2872967  2872973  2872981  2872997  2873023  2873029  2873033  2873041  2873053  2873069
2873081  2873099  2873107  2873113  2873141  2873149  2873177  2873203  2873209
2873231  2873249  2873261  2873267  2873279  2873281  2873287  2873293  2873333  2873341
2873347  2873363  2873371  2873393  2873401  2873417  2873447  2873459  2873461  2873471
2873473  2873489  2873491  2873509  2873513  2873537  2873539  2873557  2873573  2873587
2873621  2873623  2873641  2873657  2873659  2873671  2873677  2873701  2873707  2873711
2873723  2873729  2873743  2873749  2873777  2873789  2873797  2873809  2873837  2873839
2873851  2873863  2873879  2873887  2873891  2873911  2873933  2873939  2873947  2873953
2873989  2873999  2874007  2874023  2874029  2874089  2874107  2874119  2874121  2874169
2874181  2874211  2874217  2874251  2874253  2874269  2874281  2874299  2874307  2874317
2874331  2874337  2874353  2874409  2874437  2874449  2874457  2874463  2874467  2874481
2874499  2874511  2874523  2874559  2874569  2874589  2874617  2874629  2874647  2874673
2874691  2874709  2874721  2874727  2874733  2874737  2874743  2874749  2874791  2874811
2874829  2874841  2874877  2874881  2874901  2874917  2874929  2874941  2874979  2875001
2875007  2875013  2875021  2875027  2875049  2875051  2875063  2875079  2875097  2875111
2875127  2875133  2875151  2875163  2875183  2875199  2875211  2875267  2875331  2875333
2875337  2875339  2875349  2875361  2875373  2875387  2875393  2875417  2875421  2875423
2875427  2875447  2875469  2875489  2875519  2875541  2875549  2875577  2875619  2875627
2875633  2875643  2875673  2875681  2875709  2875739  2875753  2875757  2875811  2875813
2875823  2875861  2875871  2875903  2875913  2875921  2875927  2875933  2875937  2875987
2875991  2876021  2876051  2876057  2876117  2876119  2876131  2876143  2876161  2876171
2876207  2876221  2876233  2876261  2876287  2876297  2876299  2876303  2876329  2876339
2876347  2876369  2876387  2876389  2876411  2876443  2876453  2876473  2876479  2876483
2876507  2876509  2876513  2876527  2876537  2876551  2876557  2876567  2876579  2876591
2876593  2876603  2876609  2876611  2876647  2876669  2876717  2876737  2876759  2876761
2876773  2876777  2876801  2876803  2876813  2876827  2876833  2876869  2876879  2876881
2876903  2876911  2876921  2876933  2876941  2876953  2876959  2876971  2876981  2876983
2877013  2877019  2877031  2877053  2877109  2877143  2877167  2877179  2877191  2877197
2877221  2877223  2877239  2877247  2877263  2877271  2877283  2877307  2877313
2877331  2877349  2877359  2877367  2877373  2877397  2877401  2877419  2877443  2877463
2877473  2877487  2877533  2877547  2877557  2877571  2877593  2877617  2877619  2877631
2877649  2877659  2877661  2877673  2877703  2877713  2877773  2877779  2877803  2877817
2877833  2877841  2877863  2877871  2877877  2877881  2877883  2877887  2877899  2877907
2877929  2877937  2877943  2877983  2878003  2878021  2878027  2878037  2878039  2878067
2878093  2878123  2878147  2878153  2878181  2878229  2878231  2878247  2878297  2878303
2878313  2878331  2878333  2878361  2878373  2878391  2878397  2878409  2878429  2878439
2878451  2878537  2878543  2878573  2878591  2878597  2878613  2878639  2878679  2878693
2878697  2878699  2878717  2878723  2878727  2878741  2878751  2878769  2878783  2878793
2878819  2878847  2878849  2878853  2878867  2878873  2878879  2878903  2878919  2878921
2878957  2878961  2878973  2878999  2879003  2879027  2879039  2879053  2879083  2879087
2879099  2879101  2879111  2879131  2879147  2879161  2879179  2879183  2879189  2879197
2879213  2879243  2879257  2879291  2879293  2879297  2879299  2879351  2879363  2879399
2879411  2879423  2879447  2879467  2879479  2879491  2879501  2879509  2879521
2879533  2879551  2879563  2879609  2879641  2879651  2879687  2879693  2879699  2879713
2879719  2879741  2879759  2879771  2879791  2879801  2879803  2879819  2879837  2879843
2879857  2879873  2879879  2879893  2879909  2879911  2879927  2879971  2879999  2880029
2880041  2880049  2880067  2880071  2880109  2880121  2880131  2880149  2880167  2880169
2880173  2880181  2880187  2880197  2880223  2880239  2880271  2880281  2880299  2880329
2880331  2880341  2880347  2880379  2880389  2880407  2880421  2880433  2880443  2880461
2880467  2880469  2880473  2880499  2880503  2880509  2880511  2880529  2880569  2880607
2880629  2880641  2880649  2880659  2880671  2880707  2880719  2880733  2880739
2880763  2880767  2880797  2880809  2880811  2880817  2880827  2880851  2880859  2880863
2880869  2880877  2880881  2880883  2880887  2880907  2880949  2880991  2881009
2881031  2881057  2881061  2881097  2881117  2881127  2881139  2881159  2881163  2881169
2881181  2881183  2881243  2881253  2881261  2881267  2881271  2881273  2881289  2881303
2881327  2881337  2881343  2881349  2881379  2881391  2881397  2881399  2881409  2881427
2881433  2881441  2881447  2881453  2881471  2881499  2881513  2881531  2881547  2881561
2881573  2881589  2881591  2881621  2881639  2881649  2881667  2881699  2881709  2881717
2881727  2881733  2881783  2881799  2881859  2881861  2881867  2881873  2881883  2881889
2881897  2881937  2881943  2881951  2882021  2882023  2882029  2882057  2882059  2882071
2882081  2882083  2882093  2882111  2882123  2882141  2882149  2882179  2882183  2882203
2882207  2882213  2882221  2882227  2882239  2882251  2882261  2882267  2882279  2882303
```

```
2882309 2882323 2882351 2882359 2882371 2882377 2882389 2882413 2882441 2882447
2882449 2882461 2882479 2882483 2882489 2882491 2882497 2882501 2882527 2882533
2882543 2882599 2882603 2882609 2882647 2882653 2882657 2882717 2882729 2882731
2882753 2882767 2882771 2882777 2882801 2882807 2882837 2882857 2882863 2882897
2882923 2882953 2882963 2882993 2883007 2883011 2883017 2883019 2883059 2883061
2883071 2883091 2883109 2883113 2883143 2883157 2883163 2883173 2883187 2883191
2883197 2883229 2883233 2883259 2883289 2883313 2883317 2883323 2883367 2883371
2883379 2883431 2883437 2883443 2883457 2883467 2883469 2883473 2883509 2883541
2883547 2883553 2883563 2883577 2883593 2883599 2883631 2883641 2883667 2883697
2883733 2883767 2883773 2883781 2883799 2883823 2883827 2883851 2883893
2883911 2883913 2883929 2883973 2883983 2883989 2883997 2884051 2884069 2884073
2884081 2884087 2884093 2884109 2884117 2884129 2884151 2884153 2884163 2884171
2884183 2884201 2884229 2884243 2884267 2884279 2884289 2884319 2884327 2884337
2884351 2884367 2884379 2884381 2884403 2884411 2884433 2884439 2884471 2884481
2884493 2884513 2884537 2884547 2884559 2884571 2884573 2884589 2884603 2884621
2884627 2884633 2884639 2884649 2884657 2884663 2884681 2884691 2884699 2884709
2884711 2884723 2884733 2884753 2884759 2884769 2884787 2884793 2884799 2884807
2884811 2884823 2884897 2884901 2884919 2884933 2884939 2884957 2884961 2884963
2884967 2884991 2884993 2885021 2885039 2885063 2885089 2885101 2885107 2885111
2885119 2885173 2885177 2885191 2885203 2885209 2885219 2885237 2885243 2885249
2885251 2885261 2885269 2885273 2885279 2885287 2885299 2885341 2885353 2885417
2885423 2885431 2885453 2885497 2885527 2885551 2885569 2885579 2885581 2885591
2885599 2885611 2885627 2885639 2885669 2885677 2885689 2885693 2885713 2885719
2885783 2885789 2885803 2885807 2885837 2885863 2885887 2885893 2885917 2885923
2885933 2885947 2885951 2885977 2885983 2886011 2886019 2886029 2886049 2886053
2886067 2886077 2886083 2886089 2886127 2886139 2886161 2886187 2886197 2886199
2886217 2886227 2886229 2886239 2886251 2886253 2886263 2886281 2886287 2886319
2886353 2886361 2886371 2886383 2886409 2886419 2886451 2886463 2886467 2886487
2886509 2886511 2886517 2886529 2886553 2886557 2886563 2886571 2886593 2886607
2886619 2886643 2886649 2886659 2886673 2886679 2886683 2886743 2886757 2886761
2886773 2886791 2886809 2886833 2886839 2886859 2886899 2886901 2886907 2886911
2886941 2886971 2886973 2886997 2887007 2887009 2887019 2887021 2887033 2887039
2887043 2887051 2887067 2887081 2887117 2887133 2887139 2887141 2887151 2887201
2887207 2887217 2887237 2887279 2887289 2887307 2887319 2887333 2887337 2887349
2887363 2887439 2887441 2887459 2887463 2887481 2887513 2887523 2887537 2887541
2887567 2887583 2887607 2887631 2887649 2887657 2887663 2887669 2887693 2887697
2887699 2887711 2887721 2887741 2887747 2887763 2887771 2887777 2887789 2887793
2887799 2887817 2887847 2887861 2887879 2887883 2887921 2887933 2887939 2887979
2887987 2887993 2888021 2888027 2888029 2888059 2888069 2888071 2888077 2888089
2888117 2888141 2888143 2888189 2888191 2888201 2888213 2888231 2888233 2888243
2888269 2888273 2888287 2888299 2888311 2888321 2888339 2888357 2888381 2888383
2888387 2888441 2888443 2888449 2888467 2888489 2888497 2888507 2888527 2888531
2888539 2888569 2888591 2888597 2888617 2888621 2888629 2888647 2888651 2888653
2888671 2888693 2888723 2888747 2888749 2888773 2888789 2888807 2888843 2888863
2888887 2888891 2888909 2888917 2888953 2888971 2889001 2889011 2889013 2889023
2889049 2889079 2889091 2889113 2889119 2889149 2889151 2889163 2889179 2889181
2889209 2889217 2889221 2889233 2889247 2889251 2889277 2889287 2889317 2889319
2889331 2889343 2889347 2889353 2889361 2889373 2889389 2889427 2889437 2889443
2889449 2889457 2889461 2889493 2889499 2889503 2889511 2889529 2889547 2889569
2889571 2889587 2889599 2889617 2889637 2889641 2889683 2889703 2889707 2889739
2889769 2889781 2889787 2889797 2889823 2889829 2889833 2889839 2889849 2889853
2889863 2889869 2889877 2889883 2889923 2889947 2889979 2890001 2890003 2890031
2890061 2890079 2890081 2890087 2890091 2890093 2890103 2890117 2890127 2890141
2890183 2890189 2890207 2890211 2890231 2890259 2890267 2890271 2890301 2890319
2890369 2890379 2890397 2890399 2890411 2890421 2890423 2890429 2890439 2890441
2890457 2890463 2890483 2890487 2890499 2890507 2890513 2890523 2890529 2890577
2890583 2890597 2890619 2890627 2890637 2890649 2890669 2890687 2890703 2890711
2890739 2890753 2890759 2890763 2890813 2890861 2890871 2890883 2890889 2890897
2890913 2890919 2890949 2890957 2890961 2890997 2890999 2891011 2891023 2891041
2891051 2891081 2891087 2891093 2891101 2891129 2891137 2891171 2891201 2891219
2891233 2891237 2891243 2891257 2891263 2891281 2891293 2891303 2891323 2891341
2891359 2891381 2891389 2891407 2891417 2891419 2891429 2891431 2891453 2891459
2891489 2891501 2891509 2891527 2891543 2891569 2891573 2891597 2891599 2891639
2891657 2891671 2891687 2891701 2891729 2891737 2891741 2891761 2891789 2891821
2891831 2891891 2891893 2891899 2891927 2891929 2891963 2891981 2892013 2892027
2892049 2892053 2892073 2892077 2892079 2892107 2892119 2892133 2892143 2892151
2892191 2892217 2892221 2892251 2892259 2892271 2892277 2892283 2892287 2892289
2892299 2892311 2892341 2892359 2892367 2892371 2892403 2892419 2892473 2892511
2892563 2892569 2892577 2892583 2892619 2892629 2892649 2892667 2892671 2892683
2892689 2892749 2892763 2892781 2892787 2892797 2892811 2892817 2892823 2892847
2892853 2892881 2892887 2892893 2892931 2892937 2892949 2892971 2892973 2892977
2892983 2893003 2893019 2893031 2893057 2893081 2893091 2893097 2893103 2893117
2893129 2893157 2893159 2893201 2893207 2893211 2893229 2893237 2893249 2893279
2893283 2893307 2893309 2893313 2893327 2893351 2893357 2893369 2893379 2893391
2893393 2893399 2893409 2893421 2893439 2893477 2893481 2893483 2893487 2893489
2893507 2893523 2893531 2893543 2893547 2893589 2893619 2893637 2893651 2893661
2893679 2893703 2893717 2893721 2893727 2893741 2893753 2893763 2893777 2893811
2893831 2893843 2893867 2893879 2893897 2893937 2893951 2893967 2893987
2893993 2894041 2894053 2894069 2894071 2894123 2894153 2894161 2894167 2894179
2894209 2894219 2894239 2894263 2894273 2894279 2894299 2894303 2894321 2894329
2894341 2894351 2894387 2894407 2894413 2894417 2894431 2894447 2894449
2894453 2894483 2894509 2894513 2894533 2894537 2894543 2894557 2894561 2894579
2894587 2894603 2894627 2894629 2894653 2894657 2894659 2894677 2894719 2894737
2894747 2894753 2894767 2894813 2894831 2894833 2894839 2894861 2894863 2894893
2894909 2894911 2894929 2894939 2894959 2894971 2894989 2894993 2895001 2895023
2895029 2895031 2895037 2895047 2895073 2895077 2895089 2895091 2895103 2895119
2895127 2895169 2895187 2895203 2895229 2895241 2895281 2895293 2895301 2895323
2895329 2895349 2895359 2895371 2895377 2895407 2895419 2895421 2895439 2895449
2895463 2895479 2895511 2895521 2895523 2895533 2895589 2895637 2895643 2895647
```

```
2895743  2895757  2895773  2895791  2895799  2895821  2895833  2895857  2895859  2895869
2895881  2895887  2895901  2895913  2895917  2895929  2895943  2895979  2896013  2896031
2896039  2896057  2896063  2896067  2896073  2896087  2896099  2896109  2896111  2896121
2896123  2896139  2896147  2896207  2896213  2896241  2896247  2896253  2896261  2896277
2896297  2896319  2896339  2896349  2896357  2896373  2896393  2896403  2896427  2896447
2896483  2896501  2896507  2896519  2896559  2896561  2896571  2896573  2896601  2896627
2896631  2896637  2896649  2896661  2896663  2896667  2896687  2896703  2896717  2896739
2896741  2896763  2896769  2896787  2896793  2896799  2896813  2896837  2896847  2896849
2896853  2896877  2896903  2896913  2896931  2896963  2896967  2896969  2896973  2896979
2897003  2897023  2897047  2897051  2897053  2897087  2897093  2897107  2897113  2897119
2897131  2897171  2897173  2897179  2897197  2897227  2897249  2897263  2897269  2897273
2897299  2897311  2897341  2897357  2897369  2897371  2897381  2897393  2897417  2897423
2897437  2897449  2897491  2897501  2897527  2897533  2897579  2897611  2897621  2897627
2897689  2897707  2897711  2897717  2897731  2897753  2897789  2897801  2897819  2897827
2897833  2897887  2897893  2897897  2897933  2897959  2897963  2897971  2897981  2897989
2898017  2898029  2898031  2898047  2898053  2898061  2898079  2898083  2898101  2898121
2898131  2898151  2898169  2898187  2898191  2898197  2898227  2898229  2898239  2898359
2898367  2898383  2898409  2898421  2898451  2898479  2898481  2898499  2898503  2898527
2898551  2898557  2898559  2898569  2898601  2898607  2898613  2898661  2898671  2898677
2898683  2898733  2898739  2898743  2898761  2898793  2898803  2898809  2898821  2898827
2898853  2898871  2898881  2898883  2898901  2898919  2898923  2898937  2898947  2898949
2898977  2898979  2898983  2898991  2899009  2899019  2899021  2899031  2899037  2899051
2899067  2899079  2899087  2899109  2899121  2899133  2899139  2899181  2899187  2899199
2899261  2899271  2899277  2899279  2899313  2899321  2899327  2899339  2899349  2899363
2899373  2899417  2899433  2899459  2899483  2899489  2899499  2899511  2899517  2899529
2899549  2899559  2899573  2899583  2899597  2899601  2899613  2899627  2899649  2899651
2899657  2899661  2899691  2899697  2899703  2899717  2899747  2899751  2899753  2899763
2899777  2899781  2899783  2899823  2899829  2899847  2899859  2899861  2899867  2899873
2899903  2899907  2899927  2899927  2899931  2899943  2899991  2899997  2899997  2900017
2900039  2900057  2900059  2900063  2900069  2900077  2900083  2900099  2900113  2900119
2900129  2900147  2900159  2900167  2900189  2900207  2900237  2900281  2900297  2900309
2900311  2900333  2900341  2900347  2900351  2900357  2900383  2900389  2900399  2900411
2900413  2900419  2900437  2900441  2900477  2900503  2900533  2900581  2900587  2900603
2900621  2900629  2900633  2900641  2900647  2900669  2900683  2900719  2900731  2900747
2900753  2900771  2900797  2900803  2900809  2900813  2900819  2900827  2900831  2900839
2900851  2900857  2900869  2900893  2900903  2900923  2900929  2900951  2900989  2901001
2901029  2901043  2901047  2901071  2901077  2901097  2901109  2901121  2901127  2901161
2901181  2901187  2901191  2901193  2901209  2901211  2901229  2901293  2901313  2901317
2901323  2901337  2901341  2901359  2901361  2901391  2901397  2901401  2901403  2901419
2901463  2901469  2901487  2901491  2901499  2901527  2901553  2901559  2901571  2901583
2901591  2901593  2901601  2901607  2901613  2901643  2901649  2901707  2901719  2901721
2901739  2901757  2901761  2901779  2901791  2901793  2901839  2901853  2901893  2901901
2901911  2901919  2901931  2901989  2902049  2902057  2902063  2902091  2902099  2902111
2902147  2902153  2902157  2902171  2902183  2902187  2902213  2902217  2902219  2902259
2902271  2902279  2902303  2902309  2902321  2902327  2902351  2902357  2902369  2902397
2902411  2902423  2902429  2902433  2902447  2902453  2902477  2902483  2902489  2902511
2902517  2902519  2902591  2902607  2902609  2902637  2902657  2902661  2902663  2902717
2902723  2902729  2902771  2902777  2902787  2902789  2902793  2902811  2902819  2902831
2902873  2902883  2902897  2902927  2902931  2902943  2902951  2902957  2902981  2902993
2903003  2903023  2903027  2903041  2903063  2903071  2903077  2903081  2903099  2903101
2903111  2903123  2903179  2903183  2903191  2903203  2903207  2903227  2903249  2903273
2903291  2903323  2903363  2903387  2903389  2903399  2903419  2903437  2903443  2903477
2903479  2903503  2903507  2903513  2903561  2903569  2903581  2903587  2903603  2903623
2903627  2903633  2903639  2903657  2903669  2903671  2903689  2903699  2903717  2903731
2903737  2903749  2903767  2903777  2903837  2903893  2903897  2903899  2903909  2903933
2903937  2903947  2903959  2903969  2904001  2904041  2904061  2904067  2904073  2904103
2904107  2904133  2904137  2904163  2904179  2904193  2904197  2904203  2904211  2904217
2904221  2904227  2904247  2904257  2904259  2904269  2904281  2904287  2904299  2904311
2904313  2904323  2904329  2904353  2904403  2904409  2904413  2904427  2904469  2904487
2904491  2904529  2904533  2904541  2904547  2904571  2904599  2904613  2904619  2904623
2904641  2904653  2904661  2904667  2904673  2904689  2904709  2904719  2904749  2904757
2904763  2904767  2904791  2904821  2904827  2904829  2904851  2904857  2904883  2904887
2904893  2904947  2904949  2904989  2905027  2905031  2905043  2905057  2905069  2905073
2905087  2905093  2905099  2905109  2905139  2905151  2905163  2905171  2905183  2905193
2905213  2905223  2905237  2905241  2905267  2905303  2905313  2905319  2905339  2905363
2905367  2905393  2905403  2905411  2905417  2905421  2905433  2905439  2905447  2905451
2905459  2905471  2905477  2905489  2905549  2905559  2905571  2905577  2905601  2905603
2905607  2905621  2905627  2905631  2905669  2905687  2905733  2905739  2905753  2905769
2905783  2905787  2905789  2905807  2905823  2905853  2905867  2905891  2905901  2905919
2905921  2905949  2905961  2905999  2906009  2906011  2906053  2906077  2906081  2906089
2906129  2906131  2906143  2906147  2906153  2906159  2906161  2906179  2906207  2906213
2906231  2906261  2906263  2906279  2906291  2906333  2906347  2906357  2906363  2906381
2906401  2906419  2906443  2906459  2906471  2906483  2906509  2906513  2906521  2906537
2906539  2906549  2906567  2906569  2906581  2906593  2906597  2906623  2906627  2906633
2906663  2906681  2906707  2906719  2906723  2906741  2906747  2906801  2906803  2906807
2906851  2906857  2906861  2906863  2906879  2906887  2906951  2906987  2906999  2907011
2907013  2907029  2907043  2907049  2907059  2907061  2907067  2907089  2907097  2907109
2907137  2907143  2907181  2907193  2907217  2907227  2907239  2907257  2907263  2907271
2907287  2907293  2907301  2907313  2907319  2907329  2907347  2907367  2907383  2907389
2907419  2907427  2907451  2907469  2907481  2907491  2907529  2907533  2907547  2907563
2907577  2907601  2907623  2907631  2907647  2907649  2907677  2907691  2907713  2907721
2907727  2907763  2907767  2907803  2907823  2907851  2907857  2907869  2907871  2907881
2907887  2907889  2907899  2907907  2907923  2907929  2907943  2907953  2907967  2907977
2907979  2907997  2908013  2908021  2908027  2908039  2908043  2908049  2908063  2908123
2908151  2908177  2908183  2908261  2908267  2908271  2908277  2908291  2908307  2908319
2908333  2908361  2908363  2908369  2908379  2908397  2908421  2908429  2908441  2908471
2908483  2908487  2908519  2908531  2908567  2908573  2908579  2908583  2908597  2908601
2908621  2908627  2908651  2908667  2908669  2908673  2908679  2908687  2908721  2908723
2908747  2908753  2908757  2908771  2908781  2908793  2908811  2908817  2908837  2908847
```

```
2908861  2908889  2908891  2908931  2908937  2908951  2908963  2908979  2908981  2908999
2909003  2909041  2909047  2909059  2909087  2909107  2909119  2909129  2909141  2909149
2909161  2909167  2909177  2909183  2909191  2909219  2909239  2909243  2909267  2909279
2909281  2909311  2909323  2909353  2909359  2909369  2909377  2909383  2909393  2909407
2909419  2909429  2909447  2909453  2909461  2909513  2909519  2909521  2909551  2909563
2909573  2909581  2909587  2909591  2909597  2909611  2909617  2909623  2909633  2909659
2909663  2909671  2909689  2909701  2909741  2909747  2909749  2909789  2909813  2909827
2909833  2909849  2909867  2909909  2909923  2909957  2909971  2909981  2909989  2909993
2910007  2910031  2910041  2910049  2910073  2910091  2910101  2910107  2910133  2910137
2910143  2910151  2910169  2910199  2910203  2910209  2910217  2910227  2910233  2910241
2910251  2910253  2910301  2910307  2910319  2910329  2910419  2910433  2910449  2910461
2910463  2910487  2910499  2910511  2910553  2910539  2910577  2910599  2910613  2910617
2910637  2910641  2910671  2910697  2910709  2910731  2910749  2910751  2910769  2910779
2910797  2910823  2910829  2910833  2910841  2910863  2910889  2910907  2910911  2910917
2910979  2910997  2911003  2911043  2911061  2911079  2911081  2911091  2911093  2911141
2911159  2911163  2911169  2911177  2911187  2911189  2911193  2911211  2911243  2911247
2911291  2911297  2911309  2911327  2911353  2911357  2911361  2911367  2911373  2911379
2911393  2911399  2911421  2911423  2911429  2911453  2911477  2911481  2911483  2911507
2911523  2911523  2911537  2911543  2911549  2911561  2911583  2911621  2911651  2911663
2911679  2911721  2911757  2911759  2911771  2911819  2911829  2911837  2911847  2911859
2911871  2911877  2911901  2911903  2911927  2911933  2911969  2911973  2912009  2912023
2912033  2912051  2912059  2912069  2912081  2912131  2912141  2912197  2912213  2912227
2912243  2912257  2912269  2912291  2912293  2912303  2912309  2912333  2912341  2912359
2912369  2912401  2912407  2912411  2912431  2912447  2912473  2912477  2912479  2912501
2912521  2912527  2912551  2912561  2912573  2912579  2912617  2912621  2912641  2912659
2912683  2912699  2912717  2912753  2912759  2912761  2912779  2912783  2912803  2912839
2912849  2912851  2912887  2912891  2912893  2912929  2912951  2912953  2912957  2912969
2912971  2912989  2913011  2913037  2913041  2913067  2913083  2913139  2913151  2913167
2913179  2913187  2913191  2913193  2913223  2913233  2913241  2913247  2913257  2913259
2913263  2913271  2913319  2913329  2913331  2913347  2913353  2913359  2913367  2913371
2913377  2913401  2913413  2913431  2913451  2913457  2913487  2913497  2913509  2913523
2913529  2913541  2913553  2913563  2913587  2913607  2913619  2913641  2913697  2913719
2913727  2913733  2913739  2913751  2913773  2913791  2913797  2913803  2913811  2913863
2913871  2913913  2913929  2913943  2913961  2913979  2913997  2914001  2914013  2914019
2914027  2914033  2914081  2914097  2914103  2914111  2914129  2914133  2914139  2914147
2914151  2914159  2914183  2914189  2914193  2914199  2914211  2914229  2914237  2914267
2914283  2914309  2914313  2914319  2914363  2914369  2914393  2914421  2914441  2914447
2914477  2914481  2914487  2914489  2914501  2914507  2914511  2914553  2914577  2914579
2914607  2914673  2914687  2914693  2914697  2914739  2914741  2914801  2914831  2914843
2914861  2914867  2914883  2914909  2914913  2914921  2914931  2914937  2914957  2914979
2914991  2915027  2915039  2915069  2915071  2915093  2915111  2915123  2915137  2915149
2915161  2915173  2915191  2915201  2915219  2915243  2915257  2915261  2915281  2915293
2915299  2915309  2915317  2915321  2915323  2915327  2915351  2915369  2915413  2915431
2915441  2915453  2915461  2915467  2915491  2915501  2915509  2915527  2915533  2915537
2915543  2915557  2915587  2915597  2915599  2915611  2915623  2915663  2915677  2915681
2915699  2915713  2915719  2915753  2915791  2915807  2915831  2915837  2915849  2915893
2915897  2915903  2915923  2915951  2915977  2915981  2915989  2915999  2916013  2916019
2916031  2916059  2916073  2916103  2916107  2916119  2916143  2916149  2916161  2916167
2916169  2916181  2916203  2916241  2916257  2916271  2916281  2916283  2916293  2916307
2916313  2916317  2916323  2916337  2916343  2916373  2916383  2916391  2916409  2916439
2916457  2916479  2916493  2916497  2916509  2916521  2916523  2916527  2916539  2916553
2916581  2916583  2916587  2916611  2916629  2916649  2916677  2916691  2916701  2916737
2916757  2916763  2916769  2916787  2916799  2916811  2916827  2916841  2916919  2916931
2916941  2916943  2916971  2917001  2917003  2917037  2917049  2917073  2917091  2917097
2917099  2917129  2917147  2917157  2917171  2917181  2917199  2917219  2917223  2917237
2917253  2917259  2917261  2917289  2917303  2917307  2917309  2917333  2917357  2917361
2917403  2917423  2917427  2917433  2917457  2917463  2917477  2917483  2917493  2917511
2917513  2917517  2917529  2917543  2917635  2917667  2917633  2917637  2917639  2917643
2917667  2917723  2917753  2917769  2917771  2917781  2917799  2917801  2917823  2917841
2917853  2917861  2917877  2917891  2917909  2917913  2917927  2917939  2917949  2917969
2917973  2918059  2918107  2918117  2918119  2918129  2918131  2918137  2918141  2918173
2918177  2918207  2918213  2918231  2918239  2918249  2918261  2918273  2918291  2918297
2918303  2918323  2918327  2918329  2918351  2918359  2918369  2918387  2918389  2918393
2918411  2918413  2918417  2918431  2918437  2918471  2918477  2918479  2918491  2918501
2918517  2918519  2918521  2918537  2918561  2918563  2918567  2918586  2918581  2918593
2918603  2918621  2918689  2918717  2918719  2918731  2918737  2918767  2918777  2918779
2918803  2918807  2918809  2918857  2918873  2918887  2918891  2918897  2918899  2918921
2918939  2918959  2918963  2918977  2919011  2919013  2919017  2919031  2919047  2919061
2919071  2919079  2919083  2919097  2919107  2919109  2919113  2919127  2919149  2919157
2919191  2919209  2919211  2919221  2919251  2919269  2919299  2919317  2919341  2919353
2919361  2919377  2919383  2919419  2919443  2919451  2919463  2919473  2919479  2919481
2919491  2919503  2919509  2919541  2919557  2919577  2919589  2919599  2919613  2919619
2919629  2919647  2919667  2919671  2919677  2919701  2919703  2919727  2919757  2919769
2919779  2919803  2919811  2919821  2919841  2919853  2919899  2919907  2919913  2919941
2919949  2919967  2919989  2920013  2920019  2920031  2920037  2920051  2920069  2920079
2920109  2920117  2920123  2920139  2920163  2920171  2920187  2920193  2920201  2920207
2920237  2920249  2920273  2920279  2920289  2920303  2920321  2920327  2920339  2920343
2920349  2920361  2920363  2920367  2920381  2920391  2920397  2920399  2920403  2920409
2920427  2920453  2920457  2920469  2920487  2920501  2920507  2920513  2920523  2920531
2920543  2920571  2920579  2920591  2920633  2920637  2920649  2920691  2920693  2920739
2920751  2920783  2920811  2920829  2920831  2920837  2920871  2920877  2920901  2920903
2920943  2920969  2920979  2920987  2921027  2921029  2921047  2921053  2921057  2921063
2921089  2921111  2921129  2921131  2921137  2921147  2921173  2921179  2921189  2921197
2921203  2921213  2921221  2921227  2921239  2921249  2921273  2921293  2921327  2921329
2921339  2921371  2921417  2921423  2921507  2921509  2921531  2921539  2921561  2921563
2921591  2921593  2921599  2921617  2921623  2921629  2921647  2921689  2921729  2921753
2921761  2921767  2921771  2921777  2921819  2921861  2921869  2921873  2921879  2921881
2921899  2921903  2921911  2921921  2921923  2921929  2921951  2921957  2921981  2921987
2922041  2922043  2922047  2922061  2922077  2922097  2922103  2922107  2922121  2922133
```

```
2922167  2922191  2922203  2922209  2922221  2922229  2922247  2922259  2922287  2922307
2922313  2922331  2922343  2922349  2922373  2922383  2922391  2922407  2922433
2922443  2922457  2922461  2922497  2922509  2922527  2922529  2922539  2922547  2922551
2922553  2922559  2922583  2922613  2922631  2922641  2922663  2922659  2922677  2922697
2922709  2922721  2922737  2922739  2922743  2922749  2922757  2922761  2922769  2922779
2922797  2922809  2922811  2922833  2922841  2922853  2922859  2922893  2922911  2922961
2922967  2922973  2922989  2922991  2923007  2923033  2923043  2923049  2923051  2923069
2923087  2923091  2923103  2923121  2923127  2923147  2923153  2923157  2923163  2923199
2923211  2923213  2923247  2923253  2923279  2923313  2923351  2923367  2923379  2923387
2923409  2923421  2923433  2923457  2923463  2923469  2923471  2923477  2923493  2923499
2923513  2923523  2923559  2923589  2923597  2923619  2923633  2923651  2923727  2923741
2923747  2923763  2923787  2923787  2923799  2923807  2923831  2923859  2923897  2923901
2923903  2923927  2923933  2923961  2923969  2924021  2924023  2924029  2924069  2924087
2924111  2924167  2924177  2924183  2924189  2924191  2924209  2924213  2924227
2924231  2924237  2924263  2924267  2924269  2924281  2924287  2924303  2924321  2924329
2924351  2924353  2924371  2924393  2924399  2924413  2924431  2924437  2924477  2924491
2924497  2924503  2924513  2924521  2924533  2924557  2924567  2924569  2924573  2924587
2924609  2924627  2924641  2924711  2924717  2924723  2924729  2924777  2924791  2924827
2924839  2924851  2924861  2924869  2924893  2924897  2924921  2924923  2924927  2924939
2924953  2924963  2924983  2925001  2925023  2925029  2925049  2925053  2925077  2925079
2925089  2925103  2925113  2925119  2925127  2925137  2925149  2925151  2925157  2925179
2925193  2925199  2925203  2925211  2925281  2925313  2925353  2925359  2925367  2925383
2925389  2925401  2925407  2925427  2925437  2925443  2925463  2925467  2925469  2925511
2925521  2925523  2925539  2925551  2925583  2925613  2925619  2925631  2925641  2925679
2925691  2925707  2925721  2925731  2925733  2925739  2925773  2925779  2925799  2925809
2925817  2925821  2925827  2925841  2925847  2925851  2925859  2925889  2925893  2925917
2925919  2925931  2925941  2925973  2925977  2926003  2926031  2926039  2926051  2926067
2926069  2926103  2926111  2926117  2926139  2926141  2926151  2926163  2926169  2926177
2926181  2926201  2926271  2926277  2926283  2926291  2926309  2926321  2926327  2926337
2926349  2926379  2926387  2926403  2926411  2926421  2926453  2926481  2926487  2926507
2926519  2926559  2926571  2926579  2926591  2926603  2926633  2926657  2926661  2926673
2926687  2926699  2926717  2926733  2926739  2926751  2926757  2926769  2926783  2926787
2926793  2926799  2926801  2926823  2926843  2926897  2926909  2926919  2926939  2926961
2926981  2927011  2927021  2927027  2927047  2927087  2927101  2927123  2927129  2927131
2927143  2927147  2927149  2927189  2927191  2927219  2927257  2927261  2927263  2927293
2927303  2927339  2927341  2927389  2927459  2927473  2927531  2927537  2927581  2927591
2927593  2927597  2927599  2927611  2927651  2927663  2927669  2927681  2927707  2927711
2927713  2927737  2927747  2927777  2927779  2927789  2927797  2927801  2927803  2927807
2927809  2927861  2927863  2927867  2927891  2927917  2927947  2927971  2927983  2928007
2928017  2928019  2928049  2928059  2928083  2928089  2928113  2928119  2928137  2928151
2928181  2928203  2928209  2928227  2928251  2928259  2928271  2928281  2928283
2928287  2928307  2928311  2928319  2928361  2928377  2928397  2928421  2928461  2928463
2928479  2928481  2928491  2928509  2928517  2928529  2928547  2928553  2928559  2928571
2928583  2928647  2928677  2928691  2928713  2928719  2928779  2928769  2928791  2928817
2928823  2928829  2928839  2928851  2928881  2928929  2928931  2928943  2928953  2928967
2928997  2929007  2929009  2929033  2929051  2929061  2929067  2929093  2929099  2929103
2929111  2929133  2929177  2929183  2929187  2929189  2929207  2929231  2929237  2929243
2929259  2929301  2929331  2929337  2929343  2929351  2929357  2929373  2929391  2929393
2929411  2929427  2929453  2929483  2929501  2929513  2929517  2929519  2929523  2929529
2929571  2929601  2929603  2929607  2929621  2929637  2929639  2929643  2929657  2929669
2929687  2929699  2929711  2929723  2929741  2929747  2929753  2929757  2929789  2929793
2929807  2929813  2929859  2929867  2929879  2929921  2929937  2929939  2929943  2929951
2929961  2929963  2929973  2929991  2930003  2930021  2930033  2930071  2930093  2930113
2930119  2930153  2930159  2930167  2930173  2930197  2930201  2930219  2930231  2930243
2930261  2930267  2930281  2930287  2930299  2930303  2930329  2930357  2930359  2930371
2930381  2930401  2930413  2930419  2930449  2930489  2930491  2930507  2930509
2930519  2930527  2930533  2930539  2930561  2930563  2930593  2930633  2930651  2930657
2930689  2930699  2930713  2930723  2930737  2930743  2930747  2930761  2930773  2930777
2930789  2930791  2930819  2930831  2930839  2930843  2930849  2930861  2930869  2930887
2930897  2930911  2930947  2930969  2930999  2931041  2931043  2931053  2931067  2931079
2931083  2931101  2931113  2931127  2931151  2931161  2931167  2931193  2931197  2931209
2931211  2931217  2931221  2931223  2931241  2931289  2931307  2931319  2931413  2931421
2931427  2931433  2931443  2931457  2931493  2931503  2931527  2931561  2931569  2931583
2931587  2931619  2931629  2931637  2931647  2931653  2931671  2931683  2931707  2931713
2931739  2931751  2931779  2931793  2931823  2931827  2931829  2931847  2931883  2931889
2931931  2931941  2931961  2931983  2931997  2932003  2932021  2932031  2932037  2932043
2932067  2932091  2932117  2932147  2932151  2932169  2932183  2932231  2932271  2932273
2932297  2932301  2932309  2932343  2932351  2932357  2932367  2932373  2932379  2932387
2932399  2932409  2932411  2932429  2932439  2932459  2932481  2932487  2932493  2932499
2932511  2932537  2932541  2932547  2932561  2932577  2932591  2932597  2932609  2932651
2932679  2932681  2932691  2932703  2932711  2932739  2932757  2932777  2932781  2932793
2932807  2932829  2932837  2932841  2932843  2932871  2932883  2932889  2932903  2932913
2932931  2932933  2932957  2932961  2932981  2932997  2932999  2933009  2933023  2933071
2933083  2933093  2933113  2933143  2933171  2933219  2933233  2933257  2933267  2933279
2933291  2933297  2933311  2933339  2933347  2933383  2933393  2933423  2933453  2933479
2933501  2933531  2933549  2933563  2933597  2933629  2933633  2933641  2933647  2933659
2933677  2933681  2933683  2933687  2933713  2933717  2933731  2933743  2933753  2933759
2933773  2933789  2933803  2933807  2933849  2933867  2933869  2933893  2933917  2933927
2933947  2933963  2933971  2933993  2934059  2934067  2934073  2934077  2934079  2934091
2934097  2934103  2934109  2934143  2934167  2934189  2934223  2934229  2934233  2934263
2934289  2934293  2934301  2934311  2934313  2934343  2934361  2934401  2934409  2934461
2934467  2934473  2934479  2934499  2934509  2934511  2934517  2934559  2934563  2934571
2934577  2934583  2934587  2934623  2934629  2934643  2934647  2934661  2934671  2934697
2934703  2934733  2934749  2934751  2934773  2934787  2934809  2934839  2934847  2934859
2934871  2934881  2934901  2934913  2934917  2934923  2934937  2934941  2934973  2934983
2934989  2935013  2935019  2935027  2935039  2935057  2935091  2935109  2935133  2935147
2935157  2935171  2935183  2935189  2935213  2935217  2935241  2935243  2935249  2935267
2935279  2935301  2935327  2935357  2935379  2935391  2935399  2935411  2935417  2935423
2935433  2935447  2935453  2935459  2935463  2935507  2935531  2935547  2935553  2935571
```

```
2935589  2935601  2935609  2935613  2935619  2935687  2935703  2935717  2935727  2935729
2935733  2935741  2935753  2935763  2935769  2935799  2935811  2935813  2935817  2935831
2935837  2935871  2935879  2935897  2935903  2935909  2935939  2935957  2935981  2935993
2936023  2936039  2936069  2936071  2936077  2936099  2936107  2936117  2936159  2936161
2936177  2936179  2936183  2936191  2936207  2936233  2936237  2936239  2936251  2936267
2936273  2936293  2936309  2936327  2936369  2936383  2936389  2936407  2936411  2936429
2936441  2936443  2936447  2936459  2936473  2936491  2936503  2936519  2936533  2936539
2936551  2936567  2936573  2936587  2936603  2936611  2936639  2936657  2936683  2936693
2936711  2936719  2936729  2936737  2936741  2936753  2936767  2936803  2936807  2936821
2936831  2936833  2936837  2936851  2936867  2936873  2936929  2936933  2936957  2936959
2936977  2936981  2936987  2936993  2937013  2937019  2937037  2937047  2937049  2937059
2937083  2937113  2937119  2937127  2937167  2937173  2937203  2937217  2937239  2937241
2937269  2937271  2937283  2937329  2937371  2937377  2937391  2937397  2937401  2937409
2937421  2937427  2937437  2937443  2937461  2937463  2937469  2937499  2937509  2937511
2937521  2937523  2937553  2937559  2937563  2937581  2937589  2937601  2937611  2937643
2937667  2937673  2937677  2937679  2937709  2937731  2937733  2937743  2937751  2937757
2937769  2937791  2937793  2937817  2937827  2937831  2937881  2937929  2937947  2937959
2937967  2937971  2937983  2938003  2938009  2938021  2938037  2938057  2938069  2938073
2938079  2938081  2938097  2938123  2938163  2938189  2938213  2938219  2938223
2938237  2938241  2938261  2938277  2938279  2938291  2938301  2938307  2938333  2938337
2938343  2938357  2938361  2938379  2938381  2938391  2938409  2938423  2938451  2938489
2938493  2938517  2938543  2938547  2938561  2938571  2938589  2938591  2938601  2938609
2938627  2938667  2938669  2938679  2938697  2938703  2938709  2938717  2938729  2938753
2938763  2938777  2938783  2938801  2938813  2938843  2938853  2938861  2938927  2938931
2938951  2938973  2938981  2938987  2938993  2939023  2939039  2939059  2939071  2939081
2939087  2939107  2939117  2939119  2939137  2939143  2939149  2939159  2939171  2939173
2939177  2939191  2939207  2939213  2939219  2939227  2939231  2939257  2939263  2939267
2939269  2939273  2939291  2939297  2939347  2939371  2939393  2939399  2939401  2939449
2939473  2939479  2939533  2939543  2939563  2939567  2939589  2939591  2939593  2939597
2939633  2939639  2939641  2939663  2939683  2939689  2939693  2939707  2939747  2939749
2939753  2939767  2939821  2939869  2939873  2939879  2939891  2939899  2939917  2939921
2939957  2939971  2939977  2939999  2940011  2940013  2940043  2940053  2940059  2940061
2940073  2940083  2940089  2940097  2940101  2940127  2940163  2940169  2940173  2940187
2940229  2940239  2940247  2940263  2940271  2940277  2940313  2940317  2940391  2940401
2940407  2940409  2940419  2940437  2940449  2940517  2940521  2940523  2940551  2940559
2940577  2940593  2940601  2940631  2940667  2940671  2940673  2940689  2940709  2940731
2940733  2940761  2940781  2940787  2940793  2940799  2940853  2940857  2940863  2940887
2940893  2940907  2940911  2940937  2940947  2940989  2941007  2941031  2941039  2941049
2941073  2941087  2941123  2941139  2941201  2941207  2941223  2941231  2941247
2941283  2941291  2941297  2941313  2941319  2941339  2941349  2941363  2941387  2941397
2941403  2941451  2941453  2941483  2941487  2941531  2941541  2941567  2941571  2941573
2941579  2941607  2941613  2941649  2941651  2941669  2941691  2941699  2941703  2941711
2941733  2941753  2941781  2941811  2941819  2941831  2941837  2941843  2941849  2941859
2941877  2941889  2941891  2941921  2941927  2941943  2941951  2941957  2942011  2942033
2942041  2942063  2942089  2942099  2942113  2942141  2942161  2942221  2942227  2942243
2942249  2942257  2942263  2942273  2942281  2942287  2942293  2942323  2942327  2942383
2942399  2942431  2942441  2942449  2942461  2942477  2942503  2942519  2942521  2942531
2942539  2942561  2942609  2942627  2942629  2942657  2942669  2942677  2942699  2942713
2942729  2942741  2942749  2942759  2942761  2942767  2942783  2942809  2942843  2942881
2942909  2942959  2942977  2942981  2943001  2943079  2943089  2943113  2943121  2943133
2943137  2943167  2943173  2943191  2943217  2943223  2943229  2943247  2943257
2943289  2943301  2943323  2943341  2943359  2943361  2943371  2943373  2943389  2943403
2943427  2943467  2943473  2943503  2943527  2943539  2943541  2943559  2943571  2943599
2943607  2943631  2943641  2943643  2943649  2943653  2943671  2943691  2943697  2943713
2943739  2943749  2943767  2943769  2943781  2943797  2943821  2943827  2943833  2943859
2943869  2943887  2943911  2943929  2943937  2943947  2943949  2943961  2943971  2944003
2944021  2944027  2944057  2944061  2944063  2944099  2944103  2944129  2944133  2944147
2944153  2944189  2944211  2944219  2944229  2944231  2944243  2944289  2944301
2944303  2944307  2944321  2944343  2944363  2944379  2944397  2944427  2944429  2944433
2944439  2944463  2944471  2944493  2944499  2944507  2944517  2944523  2944537  2944547
2944561  2944577  2944589  2944619  2944637  2944657  2944673  2944679  2944681  2944693
2944699  2944703  2944709  2944727  2944751  2944763  2944789  2944807  2944813  2944817
2944819  2944831  2944841  2944847  2944861  2944891  2944913  2944919  2944933  2944937
2944967  2944999  2945021  2945069  2945101  2945123  2945147  2945149  2945167  2945177
2945179  2945191  2945203  2945207  2945227  2945249  2945287  2945291  2945303  2945309
2945321  2945333  2945351  2945359  2945377  2945381  2945401  2945407  2945417  2945429
2945441  2945447  2945461  2945473  2945479  2945483  2945489  2945497  2945519  2945531
2945609  2945611  2945639  2945647  2945659  2945669  2945707  2945711  2945731  2945749
2945773  2945807  2945851  2945857  2945869  2945933  2945939  2945941  2945951  2945959
2945983  2945993  2946011  2946029  2946037  2946043  2946067  2946089  2946091  2946107
2946127  2946131  2946133  2946143  2946149  2946157  2946169  2946187  2946211  2946221
2946227  2946241  2946247  2946257  2946259  2946263  2946299  2946319  2946331  2946337
2946341  2946343  2946367  2946373  2946407  2946409  2946431  2946439  2946443  2946451
2946467  2946469  2946479  2946511  2946533  2946563  2946589  2946611  2946623  2946649
2946659  2946667  2946679  2946683  2946743  2946761  2946799  2946803  2946809  2946821
2946841  2946859  2946863  2946871  2946883  2946901  2946907  2946913  2946929  2946941
2946943  2946961  2946973  2947027  2947097  2947099  2947111  2947117  2947123  2947127
2947157  2947159  2947169  2947199  2947207  2947211  2947213  2947249  2947271  2947283
2947291  2947331  2947333  2947339  2947363  2947403  2947429  2947447  2947471  2947487
2947499  2947517  2947523  2947537  2947541  2947547  2947559  2947561  2947583  2947601
2947621  2947649  2947661  2947669  2947673  2947691  2947709  2947723  2947729  2947741
2947781  2947801  2947823  2947843  2947853  2947877  2947891  2947897  2947939  2947949
2947999  2948009  2948039  2948041  2948063  2948087  2948119  2948159  2948161  2948167
2948177  2948189  2948203  2948207  2948213  2948219  2948233  2948261  2948273  2948279
2948299  2948311  2948321  2948333  2948353  2948369  2948389  2948399  2948411  2948423
2948437  2948447  2948453  2948479  2948483  2948489  2948513  2948521  2948527  2948537
2948551  2948563  2948573  2948579  2948587  2948611  2948677  2948681  2948683  2948711
2948713  2948723  2948747  2948779  2948783  2948797  2948839  2948851  2948861  2948873
2948887  2948903  2948909  2948917  2948929  2948951  2948963  2948969  2948977  2948987
```

```
2949013 2949029 2949043 2949049 2949059 2949077 2949101 2949103 2949113 2949119
2949137 2949151 2949169 2949173 2949179 2949209 2949217 2949223 2949227 2949229
2949251 2949257 2949259 2949263 2949277 2949281 2949283 2949319 2949337 2949343
2949361 2949377 2949403 2949409 2949421 2949461 2949467 2949487 2949491 2949493
2949509 2949511 2949521 2949523 2949539 2949577 2949593 2949629 2949637 2949643
2949647 2949679 2949701 2949703 2949707 2949733 2949763 2949797 2949799 2949803
2949839 2949841 2949887 2949889 2949899 2949901 2949913 2949917 2949923
2949931 2949949 2949953 2950001 2950009 2950019 2950037 2950063 2950093 2950127
2950133 2950147 2950151 2950153 2950159 2950183 2950193 2950223 2950247 2950253
2950267 2950271 2950291 2950307 2950361 2950393 2950399 2950403 2950421 2950427
2950447 2950459 2950477 2950499 2950511 2950517 2950559 2950561 2950579 2950583
2950589 2950609 2950637 2950657 2950667 2950687 2950697 2950709 2950711 2950751
2950771 2950793 2950799 2950807 2950813 2950817 2950819 2950853 2950867 2950873
2950889 2950891 2950903 2950931 2950939 2950943 2950949 2950951 2950963
2950991 2950999 2951021 2951027 2951029 2951033 2951041 2951051 2951059 2951063
2951071 2951077 2951087 2951089 2951159 2951161 2951189 2951209 2951233 2951237
2951269 2951279 2951297 2951309 2951323 2951341 2951371 2951413 2951423
2951449 2951471 2951483 2951491 2951497 2951503 2951513 2951537 2951539 2951569
2951573 2951579 2951617 2951621 2951629 2951639 2951653 2951657 2951687 2951699
2951717 2951719 2951723 2951731 2951743 2951747 2951771 2951777 2951779 2951801
2951803 2951813 2951827 2951831 2951833 2951849 2951857 2951867 2951873 2951887
2951891 2951933 2951957 2951977 2951987 2952007 2952017 2952029 2952097 2952127
2952133 2952143 2952149 2952167 2952191 2952197 2952199 2952241 2952263 2952269
2952281 2952283 2952293 2952307 2952311 2952317 2952319 2952329 2952359 2952361
2952371 2952377 2952379 2952401 2952413 2952421 2952427 2952431 2952437 2952479
2952511 2952527 2952553 2952557 2952569 2952601 2952613 2952617 2952629 2952647
2952659 2952661 2952667 2952689 2952721 2952737 2952739 2952749 2952769 2952787
2952791 2952793 2952797 2952799 2952839 2952863 2952881 2952893 2952913 2952953
2952959 2952977 2952991 2952997 2953003 2953021 2953063 2953079 2953117 2953123
2953129 2953141 2953163 2953183 2953199 2953201 2953207 2953219 2953231 2953243
2953261 2953297 2953373 2953399 2953411 2953421 2953429 2953439 2953459 2953469
2953487 2953501 2953523 2953571 2953589 2953603 2953609 2953619 2953661
2953667 2953697 2953703 2953777 2953793 2953807 2953817 2953823 2953831 2953837
2953843 2953859 2953861 2953879 2953883 2953893 2953931 2953957 2953961
2953967 2953981 2953991 2954023 2954033 2954041 2954059 2954069 2954089 2954093
2954113 2954129 2954137 2954179 2954183 2954213 2954233 2954249 2954293 2954299
2954323 2954333 2954353 2954387 2954389 2954411 2954423 2954437
2954449 2954453 2954459 2954461 2954489 2954503 2954507 2954509 2954513 2954531
2954537 2954563 2954569 2954587 2954599 2954621 2954639 2954681 2954687 2954691
2954689 2954737 2954771 2954773 2954797 2954801 2954851 2954863 2954891
2954893 2954927 2954933 2954947 2954977 2954989 2955011 2955037 2955041
2955047 2955053 2955097 2955101 2955103 2955107 2955119 2955131 2955167 2955181
2955191 2955209 2955217 2955223 2955257 2955269 2955283 2955287 2955307 2955319
2955371 2955373 2955397 2955427 2955443 2955457 2955479 2955481 2955497
2955521 2955527 2955529 2955539 2955541 2955559 2955581 2955599 2955607 2955613
2955629 2955653 2955683 2955721 2955727 2955737 2955749 2955751 2955761 2955781
2955803 2955817 2955829 2955833 2955847 2955851 2955853 2955859 2955889 2955907
2955917 2955919 2955923 2955929 2955947 2955961 2956003 2956007 2956013 2956021
2956033 2956061 2956097 2956099 2956111 2956123 2956133 2956157 2956171 2956183
2956199 2956201 2956237 2956297 2956301 2956307 2956357 2956363 2956399 2956403
2956477 2956483 2956493 2956523 2956531 2956553 2956561 2956621 2956631
2956649 2956651 2956693 2956703 2956727 2956729 2956741 2956747 2956763 2956769
2956783 2956813 2956819 2956831 2956841 2956889 2956907 2956931 2956939 2956969
2956973 2956979 2956991 2956999 2957023 2957051 2957057 2957107 2957111 2957161
2957177 2957189 2957191 2957197 2957231 2957237 2957243 2957261 2957267 2957321
2957327 2957329 2957377 2957387 2957389 2957399 2957401 2957413 2957417 2957429
2957441 2957443 2957459 2957477 2957489 2957531 2957579 2957621 2957641 2957651
2957657 2957659 2957683 2957687 2957753 2957761 2957767 2957783 2957791 2957807
2957809 2957819 2957827 2957831 2957833 2957861 2957873 2957879 2957897 2957917
2957947 2957963 2958019 2958023 2958031 2958041 2958049 2958061 2958077 2958079
2958101 2958139 2958149 2958169 2958173 2958223 2958233 2958239 2958247 2958253
2958257 2958259 2958269 2958311 2958331 2958341 2958353 2958359 2958379 2958383
2958413 2958419 2958427 2958463 2958479 2958503 2958511 2958521 2958539
2958563 2958569 2958577 2958583 2958607 2958647 2958677 2958707 2958713 2958721
2958727 2958749 2958773 2958793 2958803 2958811 2958821 2958827 2958829 2958859
2958877 2958887 2958911 2958913 2958941 2958947 2958953 2958961 2958971
2959031 2959051 2959069 2959081 2959091 2959097 2959127 2959133 2959141 2959183
2959213 2959219 2959259 2959267 2959273 2959277 2959283 2959301 2959321 2959391
2959393 2959403 2959409 2959417 2959441 2959447 2959469 2959487 2959501 2959507
2959549 2959559 2959589 2959597 2959609 2959613 2959631 2959633 2959643 2959651
2959661 2959669 2959673 2959681 2959699 2959703 2959739 2959753 2959757 2959771
2959783 2959793 2959823 2959837 2959841 2959843 2959861 2959867 2959937 2959949
2959951 2959961 2959969 2959981 2960003 2960011 2960017 2960033 2960039
2960047 2960071 2960101 2960137 2960161 2960173 2960189 2960197
2960213 2960231 2960267 2960273 2960281 2960297 2960303 2960317 2960327 2960341
2960351 2960357 2960381 2960387 2960393 2960413 2960417 2960423 2960437 2960449
2960453 2960459 2960467 2960471 2960479 2960509 2960543 2960557 2960563 2960597
2960603 2960609 2960621 2960623 2960641 2960647 2960653 2960681 2960687 2960689
2960701 2960719 2960729 2960747 2960753 2960759 2960773 2960791 2960801 2960809
2960819 2960821 2960861 2960869 2960891 2960917 2960927 2960957 2960987
2960989 2961019 2961037 2961053 2961067 2961083 2961113 2961121 2961137 2961139
2961149 2961187 2961209 2961229 2961239 2961253 2961271 2961289 2961311 2961331
2961377 2961433 2961437 2961463 2961479 2961499 2961521 2961527 2961531 2961533
2961557 2961577 2961583 2961589 2961593 2961599 2961613 2961619 2961659 2961667
2961671 2961677 2961691 2961713 2961727 2961737 2961739 2961743 2961769 2961781
2961787 2961809 2961821 2961823 2961839 2961851 2961863 2961877 2961899 2961901
2961923 2961949 2961953 2961979 2961983 2961989 2961991 2961997 2962007 2962013
2962033 2962039 2962067 2962073 2962093 2962103 2962111 2962133 2962151 2962159
2962163 2962207 2962231 2962237 2962241 2962247 2962249 2962261 2962273 2962277
```

```
2962307 2962319 2962327 2962361 2962367 2962381 2962397 2962409 2962411 2962417
2962429 2962441 2962451 2962459 2962481 2962483 2962489 2962493 2962501 2962517
2962549 2962591 2962621 2962637 2962681 2962693 2962697 2962703 2962711 2962717
2962733 2962741 2962787 2962793 2962801 2962819 2962823 2962853 2962871 2962873
2962891 2962903 2962907 2962931 2962933 2962943 2962961 2962963 2962979 2962991
2963027 2963041 2963047 2963101 2963131 2963137 2963161 2963167 2963179 2963189
2963201 2963203 2963231 2963243 2963267 2963269 2963273 2963281 2963299 2963333
2963339 2963347 2963353 2963371 2963377 2963381 2963399 2963407 2963417 2963437
2963453 2963459 2963473 2963479 2963497 2963501 2963509 2963533 2963549 2963551
2963567 2963599 2963617 2963621 2963647 2963657 2963669 2963671 2963683 2963687
2963717 2963743 2963777 2963809 2963833 2963837 2963869 2963881 2963903 2963911
2963923 2963951 2963953 2963957 2963971 2963977 2963999 2964011 2964041 2964067
2964077 2964089 2964097 2964121 2964151 2964161 2964163 2964191 2964211 2964229
2964233 2964253 2964257 2964277 2964289 2964301 2964319 2964331 2964347 2964349
2964359 2964371 2964383 2964397 2964413 2964427 2964433 2964461 2964491 2964497
2964509 2964523 2964527 2964547 2964553 2964557 2964571 2964581 2964601 2964617
2964667 2964671 2964697 2964719 2964727 2964737 2964739 2964743 2964811 2964821
2964823 2964827 2964839 2964853 2964859 2964869 2964881 2964883 2964943 2964947
2964967 2964971 2965003 2965019 2965033 2965037 2965043 2965073 2965087 2965093
2965097 2965099 2965111 2965117 2965139 2965141 2965147 2965153 2965177 2965189
2965199 2965211 2965223 2965247 2965253 2965289 2965307 2965331 2965351 2965357
2965363 2965373 2965379 2965381 2965397 2965411 2965421 2965471 2965477 2965481
2965483 2965499 2965519 2965537 2965541 2965549 2965561 2965579 2965591 2965601
2965603 2965609 2965631 2965681 2965687 2965693 2965717 2965733 2965757 2965763
2965777 2965783 2965793 2965799 2965811 2965819 2965847 2965849 2965861 2965867
2965877 2965891 2965901 2965903 2965909 2965951 2965961 2965979 2965993 2966009
2966017 2966059 2966069 2966081 2966083 2966099 2966113 2966129 2966141 2966153
2966189 2966219 2966221 2966231 2966267 2966321 2966329 2966351 2966389 2966407
2966419 2966479 2966507 2966519 2966531 2966533 2966539 2966551 2966597 2966599
2966617 2966627 2966633 2966651 2966657 2966659 2966681 2966713 2966723 2966737
2966741 2966749 2966759 2966767 2966773 2966783 2966791 2966807 2966809 2966819
2966837 2966861 2966863 2966879 2966881 2966893 2966897 2966911 2966921 2966923
2966963 2966981 2966987 2967011 2967031 2967049 2967073 2967091 2967109 2967119
2967131 2967187 2967199 2967203 2967221 2967241 2967247 2967259 2967269 2967271
2967277 2967317 2967323 2967329 2967331 2967337 2967343 2967347 2967353 2967359
2967361 2967373 2967379 2967383 2967389 2967397 2967403 2967407 2967409 2967421
2967427 2967443 2967491 2967509 2967551 2967583 2967607 2967637 2967647 2967649
2967689 2967691 2967697 2967709 2967737 2967749 2967751 2967779 2967787 2967799
2967803 2967823 2967827 2967847 2967901 2967919 2967947 2967953 2967967 2967977
2967983 2968001 2968019 2968027 2968037 2968039 2968057 2968099 2968111 2968139
2968169 2968181 2968193 2968201 2968213 2968223 2968241 2968243 2968261 2968271
2968279 2968283 2968291 2968307 2968309 2968337 2968367 2968373 2968391 2968409
2968447 2968451 2968463 2968457 2968463 2968487 2968513 2968517 2968519 2968531
2968549 2968573 2968601 2968627 2968631 2968639 2968673 2968681 2968697 2968709
2968711 2968717 2968733 2968747 2968753 2968781 2968783 2968787 2968813 2968831
2968841 2968859 2968871 2968881 2968901 2968907 2968913 2968937 2968961 2968967
2969003 2969009 2969011 2969017 2969023 2969039 2969041 2969059 2969063 2969089
2969137 2969147 2969167 2969171 2969173 2969177 2969189 2969207 2969233 2969249
2969251 2969257 2969303 2969311 2969333 2969359 2969363 2969389 2969423 2969437
2969467 2969471 2969479 2969489 2969497 2969503 2969569 2969573 2969591 2969597
2969609 2969627 2969651 2969669 2969683 2969693 2969699 2969723 2969741 2969767
2969773 2969777 2969779 2969797 2969807 2969809 2969821 2969867 2969879 2969899
2969923 2969929 2969939 2969933 2969959 2969963 2969971 2969981 2969987 2970031
2970047 2970049 2970091 2970109 2970127 2970133 2970157 2970161 2970167 2970179
2970181 2970193 2970217 2970229 2970239 2970263 2970269 2970277 2970281 2970287
2970293 2970299 2970301 2970313 2970329 2970343 2970347 2970371 2970413 2970421
2970433 2970437 2970439 2970467 2970469 2970503 2970509 2970521 2970523 2970533
2970551 2970559 2970599 2970601 2970629 2970659 2970661 2970677 2970679 2970689
2970701 2970719 2970769 2970787 2970791 2970797 2970833 2970857 2970893 2970907
2970923 2970941 2970943 2970959 2970967 2970977 2970991 2971019 2971043 2971051
2971081 2971093 2971099 2971103 2971121 2971123 2971159 2971169 2971183
2971193 2971223 2971247 2971259 2971261 2971271 2971273 2971307 2971321 2971333
2971337 2971349 2971357 2971363 2971399 2971459 2971469 2971471 2971489 2971499
2971511 2971537 2971541 2971547 2971559 2971597 2971603 2971607 2971663 2971693
2971699 2971741 2971747 2971751 2971841 2971849 2971873 2971879 2971883
2971897 2971909 2971963 2971973 2971987 2971993 2972027 2972029 2972033 2972041
2972069 2972071 2972107 2972119 2972141 2972149 2972159 2972171 2972183 2972197
2972219 2972251 2972257 2972269 2972279 2972287 2972309 2972323 2972351 2972363
2972369 2972383 2972419 2972429 2972447 2972449 2972483 2972491 2972503 2972507
2972527 2972537 2972549 2972551 2972573 2972639 2972663 2972687 2972693 2972701
2972729 2972731 2972741 2972747 2972771 2972777 2972789 2972791 2972803 2972821
2972831 2972843 2972863 2972881 2972887 2972897 2972899 2972903 2972939 2972947
2972969 2972971 2972981 2973017 2973023 2973029 2973031 2973043 2973053 2973059
2973073 2973077 2973083 2973097 2973119 2973121 2973151 2973161 2973163 2973199
2973221 2973239 2973251 2973263 2973277 2973331 2973337 2973343 2973359 2973379
2973391 2973403 2973413 2973433 2973437 2973449 2973461 2973479 2973491 2973497
2973511 2973517 2973539 2973547 2973559 2973563 2973577 2973583 2973611 2973617
2973667 2973673 2973701 2973703 2973721 2973767 2973787 2973809 2973833 2973857
2973871 2973881 2973889 2973913 2973917 2973931 2973941 2973953 2973961 2974001
2974003 2974033 2974057 2974079 2974091 2974121 2974123 2974129 2974141 2974159
2974187 2974193 2974219 2974289 2974297 2974351 2974369 2974379 2974397 2974409
2974417 2974423 2974441 2974451 2974459 2974463 2974511 2974513 2974529 2974547
2974553 2974561 2974577 2974589 2974607 2974619 2974627 2974633 2974639
2974649 2974651 2974661 2974669 2974691 2974723 2974747 2974757 2974759 2974781
2974789 2974799 2974817 2974819 2974859 2974861 2974883 2974891 2974927 2974931
2974967 2974973 2974987 2974991 2974997 2974999 2975009 2975029 2975047 2975057
2975099 2975111 2975117 2975123 2975129 2975131 2975149 2975171 2975173 2975183
2975209 2975227 2975237 2975243 2975251 2975263 2975279 2975293 2975317 2975321
2975339 2975341 2975351 2975353 2975363 2975383 2975389 2975393 2975417 2975443
```

```
2975449 2975477 2975491 2975501 2975507 2975513 2975521 2975543 2975569 2975593
2975639 2975653 2975677 2975683 2975689 2975741 2975747 2975759 2975771 2975779
2975801 2975807 2975813 2975839 2975849 2975857 2975879 2975881 2975887 2975909
2975911 2975957 2975963 2975983 2976011 2976023 2976053 2976089 2976091 2976097
2976101 2976133 2976151 2976187 2976199 2976203 2976209 2976221 2976229 2976247
2976257 2976263 2976277 2976289 2976319 2976329 2976349 2976359 2976397 2976401
2976409 2976433 2976437 2976481 2976509 2976529 2976541 2976551 2976553 2976569
2976583 2976601 2976619 2976643 2976653 2976661 2976667 2976671 2976689 2976691
2976697 2976707 2976709 2976719 2976731 2976733 2976767 2976781 2976793 2976797
2976829 2976881 2976889 2976893 2976923 2976929 2976931 2976971 2976973 2976991
2977001 2977003 2977021 2977033 2977043 2977049 2977067 2977069 2977087 2977099
2977151 2977153 2977171 2977213 2977231 2977253 2977259 2977283 2977313 2977361
2977367 2977369 2977391 2977399 2977409 2977417 2977441 2977493 2977523 2977529
2977531 2977537 2977549 2977571 2977573 2977619 2977651 2977657 2977679 2977693
2977697 2977717 2977721 2977727 2977729 2977739 2977753 2977763 2977781 2977801
2977817 2977831 2977841 2977861 2977883 2977901 2977903 2977913 2977921 2977937
2977939 2977951 2977963 2977979 2977991 2978011 2978033 2978047 2978071 2978089
2978113 2978119 2978147 2978161 2978177 2978189 2978197 2978219 2978233 2978251
2978267 2978273 2978299 2978303 2978317 2978321 2978323 2978357 2978377 2978399
2978401 2978407 2978411 2978413 2978419 2978429 2978453 2978483 2978489 2978491
2978501 2978533 2978539 2978543 2978551 2978593 2978627 2978629 2978681 2978683
2978699 2978711 2978713 2978737 2978749 2978771 2978783 2978797 2978819 2978869
2978917 2978923 2978933 2978959 2978977 2978999 2979013 2979017 2979023 2979043
2979047 2979049 2979059 2979073 2979091 2979107 2979133 2979139 2979149 2979173
2979191 2979227 2979239 2979253 2979271 2979281 2979299 2979307 2979311 2979313
2979329 2979337 2979343 2979359 2979367 2979391 2979407 2979419 2979421 2979439
2979463 2979469 2979479 2979491 2979497 2979541 2979551 2979563 2979569 2979583
2979611 2979619 2979623 2979649 2979653 2979661 2979671 2979679 2979701 2979731
2979737 2979749 2979761 2979773 2979797 2979811 2979833 2979841 2979863 2979877
2979901 2979917 2979919 2979931 2979967 2979971 2979989 2979997 2980001 2980007
2980027 2980037 2980039 2980051 2980063 2980067 2980121 2980139 2980141 2980157
2980163 2980177 2980181 2980183 2980189 2980193 2980217 2980231 2980261 2980291
2980297 2980319 2980333 2980337 2980357 2980391 2980403 2980421 2980427 2980441
2980463 2980469 2980477 2980487 2980489 2980493 2980513 2980531 2980541 2980543
2980553 2980573 2980583 2980669 2980673 2980687 2980697 2980711 2980721 2980723
2980759 2980771 2980787 2980799 2980801 2980811 2980819 2980829 2980843 2980847
2980849 2980871 2980883 2980903 2980909 2980921 2980931 2980949 2980951 2980969
2980973 2980981 2980993 2981021 2981023 2981029 2981039 2981057 2981059 2981063
2981087 2981089 2981123 2981149 2981159 2981179 2981183 2981189 2981221 2981243
2981263 2981311 2981323 2981333 2981339 2981357 2981369 2981371 2981383 2981387
2981401 2981417 2981421 2981431 2981447 2981449 2981453 2981471 2981483 2981501
2981509 2981527 2981533 2981543 2981551 2981569 2981581 2981597 2981653 2981669
2981677 2981707 2981711 2981753 2981761 2981773 2981777 2981779 2981819 2981827
2981837 2981857 2981873 2981887 2981897 2981899 2981903 2981911 2981933 2981947
2981959 2981963 2981981 2981999 2982011 2982017 2982059 2982061 2982097 2982121
2982137 2982139 2982141 2982149 2982173 2982181 2982193 2982223 2982233 2982247
2982277 2982281 2982283 2982289 2982377 2982379 2982431 2982443 2982451 2982457
2982461 2982491 2982517 2982521 2982527 2982557 2982559 2982569 2982583 2982587
2982589 2982593 2982611 2982643 2982647 2982649 2982659 2982671 2982673 2982689
2982691 2982697 2982751 2982757 2982779 2982799 2982809 2982817 2982821 2982823
2982827 2982841 2982869 2982883 2982887 2982899 2982919 2982929 2982971 2982979
2982997 2983021 2983049 2983067 2983069 2983073 2983081 2983091 2983111 2983117
2983139 2983147 2983151 2983153 2983161 2983181 2983213 2983219 2983243 2983271
2983289 2983301 2983319 2983333 2983363 2983367 2983373 2983397 2983403 2983411
2983417 2983441 2983451 2983457 2983459 2983489 2983493 2983499 2983511 2983523
2983543 2983553 2983557 2983559 2983573 2983597 2983621 2983639 2983661 2983679
2983681 2983697 2983709 2983759 2983763 2983769 2983777 2983793 2983801 2983819
2983831 2983837 2983873 2983889 2983927 2983943 2983949 2983957 2983961 2983987
2984039 2984057 2984063 2984101 2984117 2984131 2984141 2984143 2984183 2984203
2984207 2984209 2984221 2984237 2984239 2984263 2984269 2984281 2984287 2984291
2984297 2984327 2984351 2984357 2984363 2984389 2984407 2984417 2984441 2984447
2984461 2984479 2984521 2984533 2984561 2984563 2984567 2984581 2984591 2984599
2984603 2984609 2984621 2984623 2984649 2984671 2984689 2984701 2984713 2984717
2984731 2984743 2984749 2984771 2984777 2984803 2984831 2984833 2984867 2984873
2984887 2984897 2984903 2984909 2984921 2984951 2984953 2984977 2985001 2985007
2985011 2985029 2985061 2985067 2985077 2985079 2985107 2985113 2985127 2985133
2985163 2985179 2985187 2985209 2985211 2985221 2985247 2985253 2985259 2985263
2985287 2985293 2985317 2985329 2985373 2985379 2985391 2985397 2985431 2985443
2985457 2985467 2985491 2985503 2985511 2985529 2985539 2985547 2985551 2985553
2985571 2985583 2985601 2985611 2985613 2985617 2985629 2985667 2985673 2985677
2985691 2985701 2985713 2985733 2985739 2985751 2985781 2985809 2985817 2985847
2985881 2985893 2985901 2985943 2985947 2985949 2985953 2985971 2985973 2985979
2985991 2986003 2986031 2986037 2986063 2986103 2986111 2986129 2986163 2986171
2986177 2986183 2986201 2986223 2986229 2986241 2986253 2986259 2986301 2986309
2986349 2986351 2986367 2986387 2986397 2986409 2986411 2986421 2986429 2986433
2986453 2986483 2986493 2986513 2986519 2986531 2986541 2986547 2986559 2986561
2986567 2986579 2986583 2986601 2986609 2986637 2986657 2986661 2986663 2986673
2986699 2986721 2986723 2986729 2986741 2986769 2986777 2986787 2986799 2986801
2986811 2986817 2986829 2986859 2986871 2986889 2986937 2986939 2986957 2986967
2986979 2986993 2986999 2987021 2987057 2987071 2987099 2987113 2987141 2987143
2987147 2987207 2987209 2987251 2987279 2987287 2987297 2987371 2987407 2987429
2987437 2987441 2987443 2987449 2987459 2987473 2987477 2987483 2987489 2987497
2987519 2987521 2987533 2987561 2987573 2987591 2987623 2987651 2987659 2987707
2987729 2987737 2987753 2987771 2987773 2987791 2987821 2987827 2987839 2987843
2987849 2987857 2987863 2987911 2987923 2987947 2987969 2987983 2987989 2988019
2988023 2988049 2988053 2988061 2988067 2988071 2988077 2988079 2988101 2988143
2988151 2988169 2988191 2988233 2988253 2988257 2988259 2988281 2988289 2988331
2988341 2988343 2988347 2988373 2988389 2988407 2988439 2988443 2988497 2988499
2988509 2988521 2988523 2988533 2988539 2988571 2988607 2988611 2988619 2988631
```

```
2988637  2988647  2988659  2988673  2988677  2988701  2988703  2988707  2988721  2988731
2988761  2988767  2988779  2988841  2988847  2988863  2988877  2988899  2988901  2988907
2988911  2988949  2988961  2989003  2989009  2989031  2989033  2989037  2989039  2989043
2989069  2989073  2989087  2989097  2989139  2989141  2989169  2989177  2989201  2989211
2989219  2989223  2989271  2989279  2989309  2989319  2989321  2989367  2989373  2989391
2989409  2989417  2989429  2989447  2989451  2989487  2989513  2989531  2989537  2989541
2989573  2989579  2989619  2989621  2989633  2989673  2989691  2989757  2989759  2989769
2989771  2989799  2989823  2989849  2989879  2989927  2989937  2989963  2989997  2990017
2990021  2990027  2990033  2990041  2990051  2990059  2990063  2990083  2990123  2990131
2990137  2990189  2990191  2990213  2990227  2990231  2990237  2990279  2990333  2990347
2990359  2990369  2990371  2990381  2990401  2990423  2990441  2990443  2990447  2990459
2990497  2990501  2990513  2990527  2990531  2990551  2990557  2990587  2990609  2990629
2990639  2990677  2990707  2990717  2990719  2990749  2990753  2990761  2990773  2990777
2990783  2990791  2990797  2990831  2990833  2990837  2990839  2990879  2990881  2990893
2990899  2990917  2990927  2990941  2990957  2990983  2990987  2990993  2991041  2991047
2991049  2991067  2991077  2991083  2991091  2991103  2991139  2991143  2991187  2991193
2991199  2991203  2991217  2991229  2991239  2991253  2991277  2991293  2991299  2991353
2991361  2991367  2991377  2991397  2991421  2991431  2991433  2991451  2991463  2991481
2991497  2991511  2991517  2991523  2991551  2991559  2991589  2991601  2991619  2991629
2991631  2991649  2991661  2991671  2991673  2991701  2991707  2991719  2991731  2991733
2991743  2991757  2991761  2991773  2991803  2991853  2991871  2991883  2991887  2991889
2991899  2991907  2991917  2991929  2991971  2992007  2992013  2992037  2992039  2992043
2992049  2992081  2992097  2992109  2992117  2992123  2992141  2992147  2992169  2992183
2992201  2992207  2992219  2992229  2992237  2992243  2992259  2992261  2992267  2992273
2992279  2992321  2992331  2992333  2992361  2992373  2992387  2992393  2992403  2992417
2992453  2992513  2992543  2992559  2992567  2992573  2992589  2992607  2992609  2992621
2992651  2992667  2992679  2992687  2992711  2992723  2992729  2992733  2992739  2992763
2992777  2992789  2992793  2992817  2992837  2992841  2992849  2992853  2992859  2992879
2992903  2992907  2992909  2992919  2992939  2992949  2992973  2992987  2992999  2993027
2993033  2993047  2993057  2993083  2993093  2993099  2993131  2993149  2993153  2993167
2993171  2993213  2993227  2993269  2993297  2993299  2993303  2993311  2993327  2993339
2993357  2993363  2993371  2993399  2993407  2993423  2993437  2993443  2993447  2993491
2993521  2993527  2993563  2993567  2993579  2993591  2993597  2993603  2993609  2993629
2993647  2993651  2993663  2993681  2993687  2993721  2993723  2993791  2993797  2993801
2993813  2993827  2993831  2993839  2993867  2993869  2993891  2993897  2993899  2993909
2993923  2993927  2993951  2993957  2993959  2993981  2993983  2993993  2994031  2994037
2994067  2994083  2994097  2994113  2994119  2994127  2994137  2994149  2994169  2994223
2994281  2994311  2994317  2994319  2994361  2994367  2994377  2994389  2994403  2994413
2994421  2994437  2994443  2994449  2994463  2994469  2994493  2994503  2994527  2994539
2994547  2994581  2994587  2994611  2994637  2994643  2994661  2994671  2994697  2994701
2994713  2994727  2994731  2994757  2994767  2994777  2994809  2994829  2994847  2994857
2994863  2994869  2994877  2994881  2994923  2994947  2994949  2994961  2994973  2994983
2994997  2995001  2995051  2995067  2995081  2995093  2995099  2995121  2995133  2995151
2995159  2995163  2995171  2995193  2995199  2995249  2995271  2995301  2995303  2995309
2995319  2995351  2995367  2995379  2995397  2995411  2995427  2995459  2995463  2995469
2995477  2995481  2995493  2995511  2995513  2995529  2995551  2995571  2995579  2995609
2995627  2995633  2995661  2995667  2995669  2995687  2995691  2995693  2995697  2995709
2995753  2995763  2995781  2995789  2995799  2995801  2995807  2995823  2995831  2995873
2995879  2995891  2995973  2995981  2995997  2995999  2996011  2996017  2996023  2996027
2996033  2996041  2996047  2996087  2996089  2996099  2996113  2996117  2996153  2996171
2996179  2996183  2996207  2996219  2996237  2996263  2996291  2996299  2996317  2996333
2996339  2996341  2996347  2996377  2996387  2996393  2996419  2996443  2996449  2996453
2996479  2996489  2996507  2996527  2996531  2996537  2996557  2996561  2996563  2996603
2996611  2996629  2996633  2996663  2996671  2996681  2996683  2996717  2996729  2996761
2996783  2996789  2996803  2996809  2996827  2996857  2996891  2996893  2996899  2996909
2996933  2997011  2997017  2997019  2997031  2997067  2997077  2997089  2997091  2997101
2997109  2997131  2997133  2997157  2997209  2997221  2997227  2997233  2997263  2997271
2997277  2997283  2997301  2997311  2997329  2997341  2997361  2997373  2997409  2997413
2997419  2997439  2997443  2997451  2997461  2997473  2997499  2997503  2997509  2997523
2997529  2997557  2997563  2997583  2997587  2997619  2997623  2997637  2997641  2997653
2997667  2997689  2997719  2997721  2997727  2997737  2997767  2997769  2997773  2997779
2997811  2997821  2997823  2997829  2997847  2997853  2997857  2997859  2997871  2997887
2997893  2997901  2997913  2997919  2997947  2997949  2997959  2997977  2997997  2998007
2998013  2998019  2998031  2998063  2998081  2998097  2998109  2998111  2998133  2998139
2998141  2998153  2998159  2998169  2998187  2998199  2998201  2998213  2998217  2998231
2998241  2998243  2998253  2998279  2998291  2998301  2998313  2998319  2998337  2998357
2998363  2998381  2998393  2998399  2998403  2998417  2998421  2998423  2998483  2998531
2998573  2998573  2998601  2998631  2998649  2998651  2998657  2998663  2998679  2998693
2998729  2998747  2998753  2998759  2998771  2998811  2998823  2998829  2998837  2998841
2998859  2998867  2998883  2998921  2998927  2998937  2998939  2998981  2998991  2998997
2998999  2999041  2999047  2999063  2999069  2999071  2999099  2999107  2999119  2999141
2999167  2999173  2999189  2999231  2999233  2999251  2999261  2999263  2999287  2999299
2999303  2999333  2999357  2999387  2999419  2999441  2999447  2999449  2999459  2999461
2999483  2999509  2999539  2999543  2999569  2999597  2999603  2999609  2999611  2999617
2999639  2999651  2999661  2999677  2999693  2999707  2999767  2999783  2999807  2999813
2999819  2999827  2999831  2999833  2999851  2999863  2999873  2999879  2999897  2999903
2999911  2999921  2999933  2999951  2999957  2999999  3000017  3000029  3000047  3000061
3000073  3000077  3000089  3000103  3000131  3000133  3000161  3000181  3000199  3000223
3000229  3000251  3000289  3000299  3000301  3000317  3000331  3000343  3000359  3000377
3000379  3000409  3000463  3000469  3000479  3000523  3000539  3000541  3000553  3000607
3000611  3000617  3000637  3000643  3000671  3000677  3000709  3000733  3000743  3000757
3000761  3000779  3000791  3000797  3000821  3000847  3000859  3000869  3000887  3000919
3000929  3000931  3000947  3000953  3000961  3000967  3000979  3000983  3001001  3001003
3001021  3001049  3001057  3001067  3001073  3001081  3001087  3001121  3001127  3001133
3001147  3001151  3001171  3001213  3001217  3001223  3001237  3001253  3001267  3001283
3001291  3001303  3001321  3001351  3001387  3001421  3001423  3001429  3001441  3001459
3001463  3001489  3001499  3001501  3001543  3001547  3001553  3001577  3001591  3001597
3001613  3001631  3001633  3001643  3001657  3001681  3001697  3001711  3001721  3001727
3001759  3001769  3001777  3001811  3001837  3001853  3001879  3001883  3001907  3001909
```

```
3001919  3001927  3001931  3001939  3001963  3001991  3002003  3002039  3002089  3002101
3002107  3002113  3002117  3002123  3002147  3002161  3002173  3002177  3002189  3002191
3002221  3002231  3002239  3002243  3002269  3002273  3002281  3002327  3002369  3002393
3002401  3002411  3002413  3002429  3002431  3002449  3002453  3002459  3002473  3002491
3002507  3002509  3002521  3002533  3002537  3002599  3002611  3002617  3002621  3002639
3002641  3002653  3002663  3002669  3002677  3002683  3002723  3002729  3002737  3002743
3002773  3002789  3002801  3002807  3002833  3002843  3002849  3002861  3002891  3002899
3002911  3002917  3002933  3002953  3002977  3002981  3003017  3003029  3003043  3003053
3003061  3003071  3003073  3003079  3003113  3003131  3003149  3003157  3003167  3003173
3003181  3003191  3003223  3003227  3003233  3003241  3003251  3003257  3003281  3003307
3003323  3003331  3003337  3003353  3003359  3003367  3003379  3003389  3003391  3003397
3003419  3003431  3003433  3003449  3003461  3003487  3003491  3003499  3003527  3003529
3003551  3003557  3003569  3003571  3003607  3003641  3003643  3003647  3003673  3003703
3003709  3003719  3003739  3003743  3003757  3003761  3003773  3003779  3003787  3003821
3003827  3003859  3003863  3003887  3003899  3003941  3003943  3003967  3003971  3003977
3003997  3004013  3004037  3004049  3004051  3004061  3004063  3004091  3004097  3004123
3004153  3004159  3004181  3004217  3004229  3004231  3004271  3004277  3004279
3004301  3004307  3004319  3004321  3004327  3004343  3004349  3004361  3004369  3004387
3004409  3004423  3004493  3004499  3004523  3004531  3004537  3004543  3004549
3004553  3004583  3004591  3004633  3004637  3004643  3004669  3004681  3004723  3004741
3004759  3004787  3004829  3004847  3004867  3004877  3004901  3004909  3004913  3004919
3004943  3004957  3004961  3004979  3004987  3004993  3005011  3005027  3005033  3005063
3005071  3005083  3005087  3005117  3005129  3005131  3005147  3005161  3005179  3005207
3005213  3005221  3005237  3005267  3005269  3005279  3005281  3005291  3005293  3005297
3005329  3005339  3005377  3005381  3005383  3005393  3005417  3005449  3005459  3005489
3005491  3005503  3005507  3005521  3005551  3005573  3005579  3005581  3005599  3005609
3005623  3005627  3005633  3005671  3005677  3005693  3005701  3005711  3005731  3005747
3005749  3005771  3005773  3005809  3005831  3005839  3005851  3005881  3005909  3005911
3005929  3005941  3005953  3005969  3005983  3005987  3005999  3006013  3006037  3006119
3006121  3006151  3006193  3006233  3006239  3006247  3006277  3006299  3006301  3006317
3006323  3006347  3006371  3006383  3006391  3006397  3006413  3006439  3006457  3006461
3006469  3006511  3006529  3006533  3006551  3006599  3006623  3006631  3006649  3006667
3006677  3006701  3006713  3006719  3006733  3006737  3006761  3006763  3006781  3006791
3006793  3006821  3006823  3006827  3006847  3006851  3006881  3006901  3006917  3006937
3006967  3006973  3006989  3007001  3007003  3007009  3007019  3007049  3007057  3007091
3007129  3007139  3007141  3007153  3007159  3007177  3007183  3007189  3007219  3007223
3007229  3007241  3007247  3007253  3007261  3007297  3007313  3007321  3007327  3007349
3007369  3007373  3007393  3007409  3007421  3007423  3007447  3007469  3007481  3007493
3007507  3007531  3007541  3007547  3007573  3007583  3007603  3007607  3007621  3007633
3007639  3007661  3007709  3007717  3007723  3007747  3007777  3007783  3007789
3007811  3007813  3007843  3007847  3007853  3007889  3007897  3007919  3007937  3007957
3007969  3007973  3007981  3007987  3008011  3008017  3008021  3008029  3008041  3008053
3008077  3008087  3008107  3008113  3008119  3008149  3008179  3008189  3008191  3008197
3008207  3008219  3008221  3008267  3008273  3008281  3008311  3008339  3008347  3008353
3008363  3008389  3008393  3008417  3008419  3008429  3008437  3008449  3008477  3008513
3008521  3008543  3008563  3008567  3008569  3008617  3008623  3008633  3008641  3008659
3008683  3008693  3008713  3008723  3008741  3008743  3008773  3008801  3008807  3008809
3008827  3008849  3008857  3008861  3008879  3008911  3008921  3008923  3008981  3009023
3009043  3009089  3009091  3009101  3009103  3009131  3009137  3009151  3009157  3009203
3009233  3009241  3009271  3009311  3009317  3009319  3009329  3009337  3009341  3009361
3009371  3009373  3009379  3009397  3009401  3009407  3009421  3009431  3009437  3009443
3009451  3009473  3009491  3009541  3009553  3009563  3009577  3009593  3009607  3009631
3009637  3009659  3009683  3009689  3009701  3009703  3009709  3009719  3009749  3009751
3009779  3009781  3009827  3009857  3009859  3009887  3009899  3009907  3009931  3009953
3009959  3009967  3009971  3009973  3009977  3009991  3010001  3010013  3010019  3010039
3010067  3010093  3010123  3010153  3010157  3010177  3010181  3010199  3010213  3010219
3010229  3010291  3010297  3010313  3010339  3010349  3010363  3010367  3010391  3010457
3010459  3010463  3010477  3010481  3010489  3010499  3010517  3010523  3010529  3010537
3010541  3010543  3010583  3010591  3010597  3010621  3010633  3010639  3010643  3010669
3010673  3010681  3010691  3010697  3010699  3010703  3010729  3010757  3010807  3010811
3010831  3010841  3010871  3010901  3010939  3010951  3010957  3010967  3010979  3010991
3011003  3011009  3011011  3011017  3011027  3011051  3011053  3011077  3011083  3011093
3011117  3011119  3011131  3011147  3011167  3011179  3011189  3011191  3011209  3011213
3011219  3011221  3011231  3011237  3011251  3011257  3011263  3011279  3011287  3011293
3011299  3011311  3011341  3011369  3011377  3011383  3011399  3011429  3011441  3011453
3011483  3011507  3011527  3011531  3011543  3011549  3011581  3011587  3011599  3011627
3011629  3011641  3011647  3011653  3011663  3011707  3011711  3011741  3011759  3011791
3011797  3011803  3011809  3011843  3011857  3011881  3011887  3011909  3011917  3011923
3011927  3011951  3011959  3011963  3011971  3011989  3012001  3012007  3012017  3012019
3012041  3012049  3012067  3012071  3012073  3012101  3012109  3012131  3012137  3012161
3012181  3012187  3012209  3012211  3012221  3012223  3012227  3012271  3012283
3012323  3012337  3012343  3012353  3012367  3012377  3012389  3012409  3012413  3012419
3012421  3012437  3012439  3012461  3012473  3012479  3012497  3012509  3012511  3012523
3012533  3012539  3012551  3012571  3012589  3012593  3012619  3012629  3012641  3012649
3012683  3012719  3012727  3012769  3012809  3012827  3012871  3012883  3012899  3012901
3012907  3012913  3012937  3012941  3012949  3012979  3012991  3013007  3013019  3013037
3013051  3013067  3013081  3013091  3013099  3013147  3013151  3013159  3013177  3013193
3013211  3013237  3013259  3013271  3013277  3013289  3013313  3013319  3013321  3013331
3013337  3013349  3013357  3013379  3013427  3013433  3013447  3013463  3013489  3013501
3013519  3013531  3013549  3013559  3013567  3013579  3013601  3013619  3013643  3013663
3013669  3013691  3013697  3013721  3013733  3013753  3013783  3013817  3013841  3013847
3013853  3013859  3013873  3013889  3013919  3013957  3013963  3013973  3013987  3013991
3014003  3014009  3014041  3014047  3014051  3014059  3014093  3014107  3014119  3014147
3014153  3014159  3014189  3014191  3014201  3014203  3014227  3014237  3014239  3014261
3014281  3014299  3014303  3014333  3014371  3014377  3014383  3014387  3014393  3014399
3014461  3014497  3014513  3014537  3014549  3014551  3014563  3014567  3014573  3014581
3014611  3014617  3014621  3014629  3014639  3014647  3014653  3014659  3014699  3014701
3014741  3014743  3014747  3014777  3014779  3014789  3014801  3014813  3014819  3014839
3014881  3014887  3014903  3014911  3014923  3014929  3014941  3014981  3014983  3014989
```

```
3015007 3015037 3015059 3015071 3015109 3015113 3015121 3015127 3015161 3015163
3015197 3015209 3015211 3015247 3015269 3015283 3015293 3015301 3015343 3015349
3015373 3015403 3015407 3015421 3015437 3015487 3015497 3015503 3015517 3015521
3015527 3015539 3015577 3015589 3015601 3015619 3015637 3015643 3015671 3015689
3015697 3015721 3015757 3015763 3015769 3015787 3015791 3015799 3015809 3015811
3015839 3015841 3015847 3015863 3015877 3015893 3015899 3015911 3015937 3015997
3016007 3016019 3016031 3016033 3016043 3016049 3016051 3016061 3016067 3016093
3016099 3016103 3016133 3016147 3016171 3016199 3016201 3016219 3016229 3016241
3016249 3016291 3016301 3016337 3016367 3016379 3016399 3016417 3016483 3016523
3016529 3016543 3016547 3016549 3016583 3016589 3016613 3016621 3016627 3016639
3016679 3016691 3016693 3016697 3016709 3016747 3016753 3016757 3016759 3016777
3016781 3016817 3016823 3016859 3016879 3016901 3016907 3016921 3016927 3016963
3016997 3017023 3017033 3017051 3017081 3017087 3017093 3017099 3017129 3017159
3017167 3017171 3017191 3017207 3017233 3017249 3017251 3017263 3017281 3017291
3017297 3017303 3017317 3017321 3017327 3017341 3017351 3017359 3017369 3017411
3017419 3017423 3017459 3017471 3017489 3017491 3017519 3017527 3017543 3017557
3017569 3017579 3017587 3017593 3017603 3017617 3017627 3017671 3017681 3017689
3017701 3017717 3017719 3017741 3017743 3017753 3017759 3017771 3017801 3017809
3017821 3017837 3017849 3017851 3017869 3017879 3017921 3017929 3017939 3017957
3017983 3017999 3018013 3018019 3018023 3018031 3018047 3018091 3018121 3018137
3018161 3018173 3018181 3018187 3018217 3018227 3018229 3018241 3018277 3018289
3018307 3018311 3018317 3018329 3018347 3018413 3018427 3018437 3018467 3018479
3018487 3018493 3018517 3018527 3018529 3018539 3018559 3018583 3018593 3018601
3018607 3018629 3018637 3018649 3018661 3018667 3018679 3018683 3018703
3018709 3018733 3018803 3018881 3018919 3018947 3018949 3018989 3019019 3019031
3019057 3019063 3019067 3019091 3019109 3019111 3019127 3019151 3019153 3019169
3019201 3019213 3019229 3019241 3019243 3019253 3019259 3019273 3019283 3019333
3019337 3019339 3019349 3019351 3019361 3019381 3019391 3019397 3019411 3019453
3019469 3019481 3019501 3019507 3019529 3019571 3019573 3019579 3019603 3019619
3019633 3019657 3019661 3019663 3019697 3019711 3019717 3019721 3019729 3019763
3019769 3019777 3019787 3019801 3019811 3019837 3019853 3019867 3019873 3019883
3019921 3019949 3019957 3019967 3019981 3020021 3020023 3020027 3020077 3020117
3020119 3020123 3020161 3020167 3020177 3020189 3020201 3020219 3020231 3020233
3020239 3020261 3020279 3020309 3020317 3020323 3020327 3020333 3020351 3020357
3020359 3020371 3020389 3020399 3020401 3020431 3020443 3020471 3020491 3020497
3020513 3020527 3020533 3020539 3020551 3020557 3020579 3020581 3020587 3020599
3020617 3020651 3020653 3020657 3020683 3020687 3020701 3020761 3020767 3020779
3020783 3020789 3020803 3020807 3020819 3020827 3020833 3020851 3020869 3020873
3020891 3020893 3020911 3020923 3020929 3020957 3020971 3020989 3020993 3020999
3021001 3021059 3021061 3021077 3021079 3021089 3021091 3021101 3021107 3021131
3021157 3021163 3021169 3021173 3021241 3021313 3021367 3021373 3021377 3021407
3021419 3021439 3021463 3021467 3021479 3021493 3021497 3021503 3021509 3021523
3021527 3021541 3021553 3021569 3021581 3021587 3021611 3021619 3021643 3021649
3021691 3021701 3021719 3021727 3021737 3021751 3021761 3021769 3021773 3021797
3021833 3021839 3021847 3021853 3021871 3021881 3021883 3021913 3021919 3021923
3021929 3021943 3021979 3021983 3021989 3022027 3022031 3022043 3022067 3022079
3022081 3022087 3022091 3022163 3022171 3022181 3022189 3022207 3022211 3022237
3022249 3022259 3022267 3022289 3022297 3022307 3022309 3022339 3022343 3022363
3022373 3022391 3022403 3022441 3022457 3022471 3022477 3022507 3022517 3022543
3022601 3022661 3022667 3022681 3022687 3022693 3022697 3022751 3022759 3022769
3022801 3022813 3022819 3022823 3022837 3022849 3022853 3022863 3022861 3022871
3022883 3022907 3022909 3022933 3022949 3022963 3023017 3023039 3023057 3023077
3023081 3023113 3023123 3023129 3023177 3023183 3023191 3023197 3023257 3023303
3023309 3023329 3023341 3023347 3023351 3023353 3023357 3023401 3023417 3023429
3023437 3023443 3023477 3023479 3023497 3023507 3023513 3023519 3023543 3023549
3023561 3023563 3023599 3023617 3023621 3023623 3023633 3023653 3023659 3023681
3023687 3023689 3023701 3023723 3023729 3023747 3023749 3023759 3023821 3023843
3023849 3023851 3023867 3023887 3023903 3023921 3023941 3023947 3023959 3023963
3023981 3023989 3024013 3024023 3024071 3024083 3024101 3024137 3024157 3024167
3024187 3024191 3024193 3024209 3024221 3024227 3024311 3024337 3024341 3024349
3024377 3024407 3024409 3024433 3024443 3024449 3024451 3024457 3024481 3024493
3024499 3024533 3024547 3024583 3024599 3024607 3024617 3024643 3024649 3024653
3024677 3024683 3024689 3024709 3024733 3024737 3024739 3024767 3024797 3024803
3024809 3024817 3024821 3024829 3024839 3024841 3024863 3024877 3024881 3024899
3024907 3024941 3024943 3024947 3024943 3024979 3024991 3025003 3025027
3025037 3025049 3025069 3025079 3025109 3025111 3025129 3025153 3025159 3025163
3025177 3025207 3025219 3025241 3025261 3025271 3025277 3025291 3025301 3025307
3025327 3025331 3025357 3025361 3025369 3025387 3025409 3025423 3025459 3025471
3025487 3025499 3025511 3025559 3025567 3025571 3025577 3025619 3025651 3025667
3025669 3025679 3025681 3025691 3025699 3025703 3025709 3025739 3025741 3025747
3025793 3025819 3025837 3025849 3025871 3025909 3025927 3025961 3025963 3025973
3025987 3025999 3026021 3026053 3026057 3026059 3026071 3026077 3026081 3026113
3026123 3026129 3026131 3026143 3026147 3026159 3026173 3026183 3026197 3026203
3026213 3026227 3026249 3026279 3026293 3026299 3026321 3026329 3026351 3026369
3026371 3026389 3026417 3026423 3026431 3026473 3026477 3026483 3026503 3026509
3026521 3026531 3026539 3026549 3026581 3026587 3026609 3026633 3026669 3026677
3026687 3026707 3026717 3026767 3026773 3026783 3026789 3026827 3026831 3026839
3026843 3026851 3026857 3026873 3026879 3026893 3026897 3026911 3026921
3026929 3026951 3026953 3026957 3026971 3026977 3026987 3026999 3027001 3027041
3027047 3027077 3027083 3027121 3027131 3027133 3027161 3027163 3027169 3027179
3027187 3027221 3027263 3027287 3027293 3027301 3027319 3027337 3027347 3027361
3027371 3027379 3027389 3027389 3027391 3027407 3027419 3027439 3027457 3027461
3027469 3027473 3027487 3027503 3027509 3027523 3027527 3027533 3027539 3027617
3027623 3027637 3027643 3027659 3027719 3027733 3027737 3027749 3027763 3027769
3027793 3027799 3027811 3027823 3027889 3027901 3027907 3027917 3027971
3028001 3028007 3028021 3028027 3028031 3028033 3028063 3028073 3028099 3028121
3028141 3028147 3028153 3028171 3028187 3028213 3028217 3028229 3028241 3028247
3028271 3028313 3028321 3028331 3028343 3028349 3028357 3028379 3028423 3028427
3028453 3028457 3028469 3028471 3028489 3028507 3028511 3028517 3028523 3028537
```

```
3028541 3028559 3028577 3028583 3028591 3028603 3028609 3028621 3028639 3028643
3028651 3028667 3028681 3028691 3028699 3028721 3028747 3028763 3028769 3028799
3028807 3028811 3028813 3028819 3028841 3028867 3028871 3028891 3028903 3028913
3028943 3028969 3028973 3028997 3029017 3029023 3029051 3029071 3029083 3029087
3029099 3029101 3029141 3029167 3029171 3029177 3029183 3029239 3029249 3029263
3029287 3029309 3029329 3029339 3029359 3029381 3029401 3029419 3029447 3029459
3029483 3029501 3029561 3029563 3029581 3029603 3029623 3029633 3029647 3029711
3029713 3029731 3029753 3029771 3029779 3029801 3029837 3029843 3029857 3029861
3029863 3029867 3029947 3029953 3029959 3029963 3029969 3029981 3030017 3030019
3030031 3030037 3030047 3030107 3030113 3030119 3030127 3030143 3030149 3030151
3030163 3030179 3030191 3030193 3030197 3030217 3030221 3030229 3030241 3030259
3030277 3030283 3030289 3030317 3030331 3030353 3030359 3030371 3030373 3030383
3030389 3030407 3030409 3030431 3030463 3030473 3030479 3030497 3030509 3030523
3030551 3030553 3030581 3030619 3030623 3030661 3030667 3030673 3030689 3030691
3030719 3030739 3030749 3030767 3030791 3030799 3030803 3030817 3030821 3030829
3030847 3030857 3030869 3030893 3030931 3030949 3030953 3030971 3030997 3031001
3031019 3031031 3031043 3031069 3031079 3031121 3031129 3031141 3031157
3031163 3031169 3031177 3031183 3031201 3031247 3031267 3031271 3031291 3031319
3031333 3031337 3031351 3031381 3031387 3031403 3031421 3031463 3031481 3031489
3031519 3031529 3031531 3031537 3031571 3031577 3031579 3031603 3031619 3031657
3031667 3031681 3031687 3031711 3031727 3031753 3031757 3031793 3031799 3031807
3031813 3031823 3031841 3031843 3031867 3031901 3031927 3031937 3031949 3031957
3031969 3031981 3031999 3032033 3032041 3032047 3032063 3032083 3032087 3032089
3032093 3032119 3032143 3032149 3032177 3032179 3032207 3032209 3032213 3032233
3032243 3032279 3032287 3032321 3032333 3032357 3032363 3032369 3032377 3032383
3032399 3032417 3032429 3032431 3032441 3032453 3032459 3032467 3032531 3032537
3032543 3032551 3032567 3032569 3032591 3032593 3032599 3032611 3032641 3032651
3032669 3032677 3032693 3032717 3032759 3032767 3032773 3032789 3032801 3032831
3032839 3032867 3032879 3032917 3032921 3032933 3032963 3032969 3032971 3032983
3032993 3032999 3033007 3033011 3033053 3033059 3033061 3033067 3033073 3033097
3033101 3033161 3033167 3033169 3033181 3033187 3033229 3033253 3033269 3033281
3033301 3033307 3033323 3033341 3033353 3033383 3033389 3033403 3033409 3033413
3033419 3033431 3033449 3033473 3033509 3033517 3033529 3033533 3033551 3033571
3033587 3033643 3033647 3033671 3033689 3033697 3033703 3033707 3033727
3033731 3033739 3033757 3033761 3033763 3033781 3033791 3033847 3033851 3033859
3033881 3033883 3033911 3033913 3033917 3033931 3033941 3033971 3033983 3034013
3034019 3034027 3034033 3034049 3034069 3034093 3034117 3034127 3034133 3034151
3034159 3034169 3034189 3034217 3034219 3034253 3034261 3034289 3034301 3034307
3034331 3034349 3034351 3034379 3034403 3034439 3034441 3034453 3034457 3034463
3034487 3034489 3034501 3034511 3034513 3034523 3034529 3034543 3034561 3034573
3034579 3034607 3034613 3034657 3034667 3034679 3034693 3034709 3034711 3034739
3034751 3034769 3034771 3034793 3034819 3034831 3034853 3034859 3034883 3034903
3034907 3034909 3034921 3034951 3034973 3034979 3034987 3035009 3035017 3035029
3035047 3035051 3035059 3035063 3035083 3035099 3035113 3035143 3035183 3035191
3035203 3035239 3035273 3035341 3035371 3035381 3035387 3035407 3035419 3035437
3035441 3035453 3035467 3035477 3035479 3035507 3035531 3035561 3035579 3035581
3035587 3035647 3035653 3035677 3035693 3035713 3035717 3035723 3035731 3035743
3035761 3035771 3035779 3035789 3035803 3035819 3035821 3035833 3035863 3035869
3035873 3035939 3035947 3035957 3035969 3035983 3035993 3036001 3036037 3036043
3036053 3036073 3036119 3036127 3036151 3036167 3036193 3036221 3036269 3036281
3036283 3036287 3036301 3036343 3036349 3036367 3036379 3036401 3036427 3036431
3036433 3036461 3036463 3036491 3036497 3036499 3036511 3036521 3036533 3036547
3036569 3036571 3036577 3036589 3036601 3036613 3036643 3036661 3036731 3036739
3036757 3036797 3036799 3036809 3036823 3036833 3036857 3036871 3036881 3036899
3036919 3036937 3036949 3036959 3036983 3037009 3037031 3037049 3037057 3037079
3037087 3037109 3037123 3037147 3037159 3037183 3037189 3037193 3037201 3037213
3037217 3037231 3037247 3037259 3037267 3037273 3037277 3037297 3037319 3037343
3037369 3037393 3037399 3037417 3037421 3037423 3037429 3037453 3037501 3037513
3037519 3037523 3037561 3037583 3037591 3037607 3037613 3037631 3037637 3037669
3037673 3037681 3037687 3037691 3037703 3037709 3037711 3037763 3037765 3037769
3037789 3037799 3037807 3037819 3037823 3037829 3037843 3037871 3037873 3037889
3037901 3037919 3037921 3037927 3037933 3037963 3037973 3037999 3038003 3038017
3038023 3038027 3038039 3038071 3038089 3038111 3038129 3038131 3038143 3038153
3038171 3038177 3038179 3038183 3038197 3038201 3038207 3038209 3038213 3038219
3038239 3038263 3038267 3038281 3038293 3038311 3038317 3038351 3038353 3038363
3038389 3038429 3038459 3038467 3038501 3038513 3038561 3038579 3038627 3038639
3038647 3038653 3038657 3038687 3038701 3038731 3038741 3038747 3038753 3038779
3038813 3038839 3038847 3038851 3038873 3038887 3038891 3038923 3038927 3038933
3038947 3038951 3038963 3038969 3038999 3039011 3039017 3039037 3039041 3039061
3039077 3039089 3039103 3039109 3039131 3039139 3039163 3039173 3039181 3039193
3039263 3039269 3039293 3039299 3039307 3039313 3039319 3039329 3039341 3039343
3039347 3039353 3039389 3039419 3039467 3039469 3039493 3039499 3039523 3039529
3039551 3039559 3039623 3039649 3039667 3039671 3039721 3039727 3039737
3039761 3039811 3039823 3039833 3039847 3039851 3039859 3039917 3039919 3039929
3039937 3039941 3039947 3039989 3039997 3040003 3040021 3040043 3040049 3040061
3040087 3040091 3040111 3040153 3040187 3040189 3040217 3040223 3040241 3040243
3040249 3040267 3040277 3040283 3040307 3040313 3040321 3040333 3040343 3040351
3040357 3040369 3040381 3040391 3040409 3040469 3040481 3040483 3040489 3040517
3040547 3040553 3040561 3040579 3040591 3040613 3040633 3040649 3040657 3040691
3040693 3040699 3040711 3040727 3040729 3040733 3040753 3040757 3040777 3040781
3040787 3040811 3040819 3040823 3040861 3040867 3040889 3040907 3040913 3040927
3040949 3040963 3040967 3040979 3040987 3040997 3041029 3041039 3041053 3041057
3041111 3041117 3041161 3041173 3041177 3041189 3041191 3041231 3041251
3041279 3041303 3041309 3041321 3041327 3041333 3041341 3041371 3041377 3041383
3041393 3041407 3041411 3041429 3041443 3041471 3041473 3041531 3041551 3041553
3041557 3041581 3041587 3041603 3041611 3041651 3041663 3041669 3041671 3041683
3041707 3041713 3041741 3041771 3041789 3041791 3041803 3041809 3041821 3041833
3041849 3041851 3041879 3041893 3041917 3041921 3041923 3041933 3041939 3041947
3041953 3041959 3041971 3041977 3041989 3042007 3042023 3042037 3042059 3042079
```

```
3042107 3042157 3042161 3042163 3042173 3042181 3042191 3042203 3042209 3042227
3042229 3042257 3042283 3042307 3042317 3042329 3042349 3042353 3042367 3042397
3042401 3042407 3042437 3042449 3042461 3042467 3042469 3042491 3042493 3042553
3042577 3042581 3042607 3042629 3042653 3042661 3042667 3042701 3042703 3042707
3042719 3042731 3042749 3042757 3042761 3042763 3042803 3042829 3042833 3042839
3042857 3042899 3042901 3042911 3042913 3042937 3042943 3042947 3042959 3042971
3042997 3043009 3043013 3043037 3043049 3043063 3043069 3043081 3043093 3043111
3043121 3043123 3043129 3043133 3043141 3043169 3043193 3043217 3043219 3043223
3043237 3043247 3043267 3043277 3043283 3043303 3043309 3043321 3043331 3043333
3043349 3043367 3043379 3043387 3043393 3043421 3043423 3043427 3043441 3043451
3043457 3043483 3043489 3043507 3043529 3043541 3043543 3043559 3043577 3043597
3043603 3043619 3043627 3043643 3043681 3043687 3043721 3043723 3043739 3043741
3043769 3043783 3043787 3043793 3043823 3043849 3043871 3043883 3043891 3043903
3043907 3043913 3043939 3043951 3043973 3043993 3044017 3044021 3044023 3044029
3044033 3044051 3044057 3044081 3044087 3044089 3044113 3044137 3044147 3044177
3044179 3044183 3044201 3044213 3044221 3044269 3044287 3044299 3044347 3044359
3044369 3044381 3044401 3044407 3044449 3044473 3044491 3044497 3044521 3044527
3044549 3044567 3044597 3044609 3044633 3044641 3044651 3044653 3044663 3044711
3044729 3044737 3044749 3044753 3044759 3044773 3044777 3044791 3044803 3044827
3044831 3044837 3044843 3044857 3044863 3044879 3044891 3044893 3044929 3044983
3045017 3045019 3045041 3045043 3045047 3045067 3045101 3045103 3045109 3045127
3045139 3045157 3045169 3045173 3045179 3045191 3045209 3045241 3045253 3045257
3045281 3045283 3045293 3045311 3045323 3045379 3045421 3045437 3045443 3045451
3045461 3045503 3045563 3045583 3045589 3045593 3045599 3045611 3045613
3045631 3045661 3045671 3045677 3045697 3045701 3045727 3045739 3045743 3045761
3045773 3045793 3045797 3045811 3045853 3045863 3045869 3045883 3045893 3045901
3045919 3045937 3045949 3045953 3045979 3045989 3046031 3046033 3046039 3046067
3046079 3046081 3046103 3046133 3046139 3046159 3046201 3046231 3046237 3046273
3046297 3046301 3046331 3046333 3046343 3046391 3046407 3046447 3046453 3046471
3046487 3046489 3046501 3046513 3046529 3046531 3046541 3046577 3046579 3046591
3046597 3046601 3046607 3046609 3046627 3046639 3046651 3046657 3046661 3046663
3046709 3046717 3046721 3046733 3046753 3046763 3046789 3046829 3046831 3046837
3046871 3046903 3046909 3046921 3046933 3046949 3046969 3046991 3046993 3047027
3047047 3047053 3047071 3047089 3047101 3047123 3047141 3047153 3047167
3047183 3047189 3047197 3047203 3047221 3047237 3047251 3047257 3047273 3047299
3047309 3047311 3047323 3047327 3047333 3047351 3047389 3047399 3047411 3047413
3047417 3047419 3047423 3047441 3047479 3047483 3047507 3047509 3047537 3047549
3047557 3047563 3047567 3047587 3047591 3047593 3047599 3047609 3047617 3047623
3047647 3047651 3047669 3047683 3047689 3047699 3047713 3047729 3047731 3047767
3047773 3047789 3047791 3047819 3047861 3047909 3047911 3047921 3047953 3047963
3047971 3048011 3048041 3048043 3048047 3048053 3048077 3048107 3048139 3048163
3048173 3048197 3048211 3048217 3048247 3048257 3048271 3048289 3048301 3048329
3048337 3048343 3048359 3048413 3048497 3048499 3048503 3048511 3048523 3048533
3048557 3048587 3048599 3048601 3048611 3048623 3048629 3048631 3048653 3048663
3048671 3048679 3048691 3048709 3048713 3048737 3048761 3048767 3048769 3048781
3048823 3048827 3048833 3048863 3048869 3048883 3048901 3048917 3048971 3048977
3048989 3049003 3049009 3049019 3049027 3049073 3049091 3049099 3049127 3049153
3049157 3049181 3049183 3049199 3049201 3049261 3049289 3049301 3049309 3049331
3049349 3049351 3049369 3049381 3049391 3049421 3049427 3049441 3049447 3049463
3049469 3049507 3049523 3049537 3049589 3049591 3049597 3049609 3049643 3049649
3049661 3049667 3049699 3049723 3049729 3049741 3049751 3049759 3049789
3049801 3049807 3049841 3049859 3049883 3049889 3049903 3049909 3049927 3049931
3049951 3049957 3049967 3049993 3049999 3050009 3050023 3050047 3050057 3050069
3050071 3050083 3050093 3050101 3050107 3050129 3050141 3050153 3050197
3050213 3050221 3050227 3050233 3050239 3050251 3050261 3050263 3050303 3050321
3050363 3050371 3050381 3050389 3050401 3050419 3050447 3050459 3050473 3050479
3050483 3050533 3050543 3050561 3050573 3050581 3050587 3050591 3050603 3050681
3050683 3050693 3050737 3050759 3050777 3050779 3050783 3050791 3050797 3050809
3050813 3050821 3050833 3050867 3050899 3050917 3050947 3050951 3050953 3050959
3050969 3050977 3051011 3051017 3051029 3051043 3051047 3051071 3051079 3051089
3051091 3051101 3051133 3051149 3051161 3051173 3051227 3051233 3051241 3051253
3051259 3051317 3051337 3051397 3051431 3051439 3051463 3051481 3051487 3051491
3051493 3051511 3051553 3051557 3051563 3051593 3051599 3051611 3051613 3051623
3051637 3051677 3051689 3051703 3051707 3051743 3051749 3051751 3051767 3051773
3051779 3051821 3051833 3051863 3051869 3051877 3051889 3051901 3051929 3051943
3051947 3051953 3051977 3052003 3052033 3052037 3052069 3052073 3052079 3052099
3052117 3052139 3052157 3052177 3052187 3052193 3052211 3052213 3052249 3052253
3052267 3052271 3052297 3052351 3052363 3052373 3052381 3052397 3052403 3052417
3052421 3052447 3052451 3052471 3052499 3052513 3052519 3052529 3052541 3052549
3052561 3052589 3052591 3052607 3052619 3052631 3052633 3052649 3052661 3052669
3052691 3052717 3052727 3052729 3052733 3052739 3052757 3052769 3052781 3052783
3052793 3052873 3052879 3052891 3052897 3052919 3052937 3052943 3052949 3052961
3052963 3052969 3052991 3052993 3053009 3053021 3053041 3053051 3053059 3053101
3053117 3053119 3053131 3053143 3053161 3053173 3053177 3053189 3053201 3053209
3053231 3053249 3053263 3053279 3053291 3053293 3053317 3053329 3053333 3053339
3053341 3053359 3053363 3053389 3053399 3053423 3053431 3053441 3053443 3053467
3053483 3053507 3053521 3053537 3053551 3053563 3053569 3053579 3053629 3053669
3053689 3053707 3053719 3053747 3053749 3053753 3053759 3053767 3053777 3053783
3053789 3053801 3053821 3053833 3053849 3053861 3053873 3053881 3053891 3053909
3053933 3053951 3053959 3053971 3053987 3053993 3054001 3054011 3054043 3054047
3054059 3054097 3054109 3054113 3054119 3054167 3054179 3054187 3054197 3054199
3054211 3054217 3054221 3054229 3054241 3054283 3054299 3054319 3054323 3054353
3054409 3054413 3054437 3054589 3054449 3054517 3054521 3054533 3054551 3054553
3054559 3054563 3054587 3054589 3054613 3054629 3054637 3054643 3054673 3054691
3054707 3054709 3054769 3054809 3054811 3054827 3054829 3054841 3054847
3054871 3054899 3054913 3054923 3054937 3054949 3054967 3054971 3055043 3055049
3055057 3055093 3055097 3055153 3055163 3055177 3055187 3055211 3055229 3055231
3055249 3055259 3055277 3055309 3055319 3055321 3055331 3055357 3055363 3055369
3055373 3055399 3055417 3055439 3055441 3055457 3055471 3055477 3055487 3055489
```

```
3055501  3055513  3055519  3055567  3055583  3055589  3055601  3055603  3055621  3055649
3055651  3055687  3055693  3055721  3055727  3055739  3055753  3055777  3055807  3055831
3055847  3055873  3055901  3055909  3055919  3055931  3055951  3055961  3055963  3055973
3056041  3056047  3056051  3056057  3056069  3056077  3056083  3056111  3056129  3056149
3056173  3056201  3056213  3056219  3056227  3056231  3056233  3056239  3056327  3056329  3056341
3056353  3056357  3056371  3056381  3056387  3056393  3056399  3056407  3056411  3056419
3056423  3056429  3056453  3056467  3056489  3056491  3056497  3056519  3056531  3056561
3056579  3056593  3056597  3056611  3056639  3056653  3056657  3056671  3056689  3056699
3056717  3056759  3056789  3056791  3056797  3056813  3056843  3056857  3056863  3056887
3056897  3056939  3056951  3056959  3056969  3056971  3056981  3056983  3056993  3057007
3057011  3057013  3057023  3057037  3057053  3057077  3057079  3057113  3057163  3057227
3057253  3057281  3057287  3057289  3057293  3057317  3057319  3057323  3057361  3057377
3057403  3057427  3057451  3057469  3057479  3057487  3057521  3057533  3057539  3057541
3057547  3057577  3057581  3057611  3057617  3057619  3057631  3057641  3057647  3057661
3057701  3057707  3057709  3057713  3057721  3057763  3057767  3057797  3057811  3057823
3057833  3057839  3057851  3057877  3057881  3057883  3057913  3057931  3057949  3057959
3057983  3057997  3058001  3058007  3058037  3058051  3058127  3058157  3058163  3058171
3058193  3058199  3058201  3058219  3058229  3058267  3058303  3058331  3058339  3058343
3058361  3058387  3058397  3058399  3058403  3058421  3058441  3058491  3058493  3058499
3058511  3058519  3058529  3058537  3058567  3058579  3058597  3058603  3058607  3058613
3058631  3058637  3058661  3058667  3058669  3058681  3058687  3058697  3058703  3058711
3058729  3058763  3058787  3058817  3058837  3058843  3058849  3058859  3058871  3058873
3058877  3058879  3058883  3058889  3058897  3058903  3058907  3058921  3058927  3058933
3058999  3059003  3059009  3059011  3059029  3059033  3059047  3059053  3059059  3059063
3059087  3059113  3059129  3059137  3059141  3059143  3059179  3059219  3059233  3059257
3059261  3059267  3059281  3059291  3059293  3059339  3059341  3059377  3059383  3059387
3059389  3059393  3059401  3059423  3059431  3059447  3059449  3059453  3059467  3059491
3059501  3059509  3059519  3059527  3059549  3059561  3059569  3059597  3059611  3059633
3059659  3059723  3059753  3059803  3059827  3059843  3059857  3059873  3059891  3059911
3059921  3059951  3059963  3060047  3060053  3060067  3060077  3060089  3060097  3060107
3060137  3060139  3060143  3060149  3060151  3060163  3060179  3060191  3060203  3060209
3060241  3060247  3060257  3060259  3060287  3060301  3060329  3060361  3060373  3060383
3060397  3060419  3060427  3060433  3060451  3060461  3060467  3060481  3060487  3060503
3060511  3060517  3060557  3060559  3060569  3060571  3060581  3060583  3060601  3060623
3060637  3060649  3060667  3060683  3060703  3060749  3060763  3060769  3060793  3060809
3060821  3060823  3060839  3060853  3060857  3060859  3060913  3060917  3060923  3060929
3060931  3060947  3060983  3060989  3060997  3061021  3061027  3061049  3061067  3061087
3061099  3061103  3061111  3061117  3061129  3061133  3061141  3061159  3061181  3061187
3061229  3061237  3061243  3061249  3061259  3061271  3061291  3061301  3061313  3061321
3061363  3061367  3061379  3061381  3061391  3061403  3061427  3061433  3061441  3061459
3061481  3061489  3061517  3061523  3061537  3061543  3061561  3061571  3061579  3061609
3061631  3061637  3061661  3061673  3061703  3061739  3061759  3061763  3061781  3061811
3061823  3061837  3061841  3061847  3061859  3061873  3061897  3061913  3061931  3061937
3061939  3061943  3061951  3061973  3061991  3061997  3062011  3062039  3062047  3062051
3062053  3062063  3062077  3062089  3062093  3062107  3062113  3062117  3062123  3062141
3062161  3062177  3062201  3062203  3062207  3062209  3062237  3062239  3062263  3062291
3062317  3062327  3062341  3062359  3062377  3062399  3062407  3062461  3062467  3062483
3062497  3062509  3062531  3062539  3062551  3062557  3062561  3062621  3062641  3062651
3062663  3062671  3062677  3062681  3062693  3062723  3062747  3062779  3062803  3062821
3062833  3062837  3062863  3062879  3062881  3062921  3062929  3062957  3062963  3062989
3062999  3063013  3063023  3063041  3063059  3063083  3063097  3063121  3063133  3063139
3063149  3063157  3063167  3063169  3063187  3063197  3063217  3063253  3063257  3063287
3063289  3063371  3063373  3063377  3063391  3063407  3063409  3063419  3063433  3063443
3063461  3063491  3063493  3063497  3063499  3063539  3063569  3063581  3063583  3063607
3063629  3063653  3063673  3063677  3063701  3063703  3063713  3063727  3063733  3063739
3063803  3063817  3063829  3063839  3063869  3063913  3063917  3063919  3063923  3063967
3063989  3064013  3064027  3064079  3064109  3064121  3064123  3064141  3064151  3064157
3064177  3064207  3064241  3064247  3064291  3064297  3064307  3064337  3064351  3064361
3064363  3064367  3064417  3064421  3064427  3064429  3064433  3064469  3064493  3064531
3064561  3064571  3064577  3064591  3064601  3064603  3064631  3064651  3064657  3064661
3064679  3064687  3064693  3064723  3064741  3064751  3064861  3064883  3064903
3064907  3064933  3064949  3064967  3064979  3064987  3064993  3065053  3065059  3065077
3065081  3065131  3065143  3065147  3065159  3065221  3065243  3065261  3065263  3065291
3065299  3065333  3065347  3065353  3065369  3065393  3065401  3065411  3065431  3065449
3065453  3065459  3065477  3065483  3065507  3065519  3065521  3065533  3065539  3065549
3065563  3065591  3065603  3065609  3065617  3065633  3065639  3065641  3065651  3065663
3065681  3065717  3065723  3065737  3065743  3065747  3065749  3065773  3065779  3065789
3065803  3065813  3065833  3065837  3065849  3065861  3065863  3065893  3065917  3065929
3065947  3065971  3065981  3065983  3065989  3065999  3066017  3066067  3066071  3066097
3066109  3066127  3066157  3066169  3066187  3066211  3066223  3066229  3066247  3066251
3066253  3066263  3066293  3066311  3066319  3066347  3066377  3066397  3066451  3066493
3066499  3066517  3066529  3066533  3066541  3066559  3066563  3066571  3066587  3066589
3066599  3066611  3066617  3066641  3066649  3066659  3066691  3066709  3066731  3066743
3066769  3066773  3066787  3066793  3066821  3066823  3066827  3066829  3066853  3066857
3066863  3066881  3066883  3066901  3066911  3066971  3066989  3066991  3066997  3067003
3067007  3067013  3067039  3067049  3067063  3067081  3067111  3067121  3067139  3067153
3067199  3067219  3067223  3067231  3067261  3067279  3067297  3067331  3067367  3067373
3067381  3067391  3067397  3067403  3067409  3067423  3067433  3067439  3067453  3067457
3067459  3067483  3067501  3067511  3067513  3067517  3067553  3067573  3067601  3067621
3067637  3067639  3067657  3067699  3067703  3067709  3067733  3067739  3067747  3067777
3067783  3067789  3067793  3067817  3067829  3067849  3067859  3067861  3067877  3067879
3067891  3067903  3067927  3067931  3067951  3067961  3067969  3067979  3068027  3068029
3068047  3068069  3068081  3068083  3068089  3068099  3068111  3068119  3068137  3068141
3068159  3068161  3068173  3068189  3068201  3068203  3068227  3068231  3068237  3068293
3068297  3068311  3068333  3068353  3068393  3068419  3068423  3068431  3068477  3068489
3068491  3068497  3068503  3068509  3068539  3068561  3068567  3068579  3068581  3068599
3068621  3068627  3068641  3068649  3068659  3068711  3068713  3068747  3068749  3068777
3068827  3068831  3068839  3068851  3068869  3068873  3068887  3068903  3068909  3068911
3068921  3068927  3068929  3068939  3068941  3068951  3068957  3069007  3069019  3069029
```

```
3069037 3069047 3069083 3069103 3069107 3069119 3069133 3069161 3069167 3069169
3069173 3069181 3069223 3069233 3069263 3069271 3069277 3069323 3069329 3069347
3069359 3069361 3069379 3069397 3069413 3069421 3069427 3069433 3069439 3069449
3069467 3069481 3069497 3069499 3069529 3069533 3069541 3069551 3069569 3069587
3069607 3069611 3069623 3069637 3069643 3069653 3069667 3069683 3069743 3069757
3069769 3069791 3069797 3069817 3069823 3069841 3069863 3069883 3069889 3069893
3069917 3069923 3069929 3069931 3069949 3069959 3069967 3070003 3070009 3070021
3070031 3070037 3070043 3070049 3070057 3070061 3070073 3070079 3070091 3070117
3070127 3070129 3070139 3070169 3070187 3070213 3070273 3070289 3070321 3070337
3070349 3070351 3070357 3070373 3070391 3070393 3070399 3070427 3070429 3070447
3070451 3070469 3070471 3070481 3070499 3070513 3070541 3070547 3070553 3070559
3070567 3070601 3070619 3070621 3070637 3070657 3070663 3070681 3070699 3070709
3070783 3070787 3070789 3070807 3070817 3070831 3070853 3070861 3070867 3070871
3070877 3070883 3070901 3070939 3070943 3070961 3070973 3070993 3070997 3071011
3071021 3071041 3071053 3071069 3071087 3071093 3071113 3071137 3071143 3071153
3071161 3071177 3071197 3071207 3071219 3071231 3071239 3071251 3071261 3071267
3071279 3071281 3071287 3071317 3071323 3071353 3071359 3071377 3071381 3071429
3071437 3071473 3071501 3071503 3071507 3071513 3071539 3071567 3071569 3071587
3071603 3071617 3071623 3071633 3071641 3071647 3071659 3071661 3071671 3071693
3071701 3071707 3071723 3071741 3071753 3071797 3071801 3071813 3071833 3071837
3071839 3071869 3071879 3071881 3071897 3071909 3071911 3071923 3071927 3071969
3071983 3071987 3071993 3072001 3072029 3072067 3072101 3072107 3072119 3072127
3072137 3072161 3072163 3072169 3072197 3072211 3072227 3072229 3072233 3072239
3072263 3072269 3072283 3072301 3072353 3072373 3072403 3072413 3072431 3072439
3072449 3072451 3072457 3072467 3072469 3072473 3072481 3072523 3072533 3072539
3072541 3072557 3072607 3072611 3072613 3072659 3072677 3072679 3072683 3072701
3072703 3072709 3072749 3072791 3072829 3072841 3072847 3072857 3072859 3072871
3072911 3072929 3072941 3072943 3072947 3072959 3072977 3072983 3073013 3073027
3073033 3073051 3073067 3073069 3073087 3073121 3073141 3073153 3073171 3073181
3073201 3073207 3073229 3073249 3073271 3073289 3073313 3073349 3073351 3073393
3073451 3073453 3073493 3073517 3073529 3073537 3073541 3073547 3073559 3073621
3073633 3073657 3073667 3073669 3073673 3073699 3073703 3073709 3073711 3073727
3073747 3073757 3073771 3073783 3073799 3073813 3073817 3073831 3073853 3073879
3073883 3073891 3073901 3073919 3073921 3073933 3073937 3073943 3073951 3073963
3073979 3073981 3073999 3074009 3074011 3074021 3074023 3074033 3074039 3074041
3074047 3074051 3074063 3074081 3074089 3074101 3074107 3074131 3074153 3074167
3074171 3074173 3074179 3074189 3074213 3074233 3074243 3074251 3074273 3074287
3074299 3074329 3074347 3074353 3074369 3074381 3074389 3074413 3074419 3074459
3074471 3074473 3074497 3074507 3074509 3074521 3074537 3074557 3074567 3074581
3074587 3074593 3074597 3074623 3074627 3074633 3074641 3074651 3074657 3074677
3074681 3074699 3074707 3074711 3074719 3074723 3074741 3074777 3074779 3074791
3074821 3074837 3074849 3074867 3074873 3074879 3074923 3074927 3074969 3074987
3074989 3074993 3075013 3075019 3075029 3075043 3075047 3075049 3075053 3075089
3075091 3075109 3075119 3075151 3075161 3075167 3075173 3075179 3075203 3075209
3075221 3075227 3075251 3075253 3075263 3075299 3075301 3075311 3075313 3075323
3075341 3075343 3075377 3075379 3075383 3075389 3075407 3075409 3075433 3075459
3075467 3075481 3075497 3075547 3075557 3075577 3075581 3075593 3075601 3075607
3075617 3075619 3075671 3075679 3075703 3075713 3075797 3075817 3075829 3075857
3075869 3075881 3075899 3075901 3075911 3075949 3075953 3075959 3075971 3075979
3076013 3076019 3076039 3076049 3076057 3076093 3076097 3076109 3076111 3076127
3076141 3076153 3076163 3076193 3076211 3076219 3076231 3076237 3076243 3076259
3076261 3076289 3076313 3076327 3076331 3076363 3076369 3076373 3076387 3076391
3076393 3076397 3076399 3076417 3076421 3076427 3076429 3076433 3076483 3076511
3076529 3076543 3076559 3076589 3076621 3076631 3076649 3076679 3076691 3076699
3076709 3076721 3076741 3076751 3076753 3076757 3076783 3076789 3076807 3076811
3076817 3076823 3076859 3076861 3076867 3076891 3076897 3076903 3076921 3076933
3076939 3076973 3076991 3077033 3077047 3077057 3077071 3077093 3077111 3077143
3077149 3077159 3077171 3077203 3077251 3077257 3077273 3077279 3077281 3077293
3077299 3077303 3077311 3077317 3077341 3077351 3077359 3077383 3077407 3077413
3077429 3077443 3077453 3077479 3077483 3077489 3077491 3077507 3077533 3077539
3077573 3077579 3077593 3077597 3077609 3077611 3077621 3077647 3077681 3077687
3077689 3077693 3077717 3077759 3077783 3077801 3077803 3077813 3077819 3077827
3077839 3077849 3077861 3077881 3077903 3077927 3077939 3077947 3077951 3077953
3078001 3078043 3078059 3078073 3078109 3078137 3078149 3078151 3078161 3078169
3078193 3078199 3078203 3078211 3078217 3078223 3078227 3078259 3078329 3078367
3078371 3078373 3078391 3078401 3078409 3078419 3078431 3078451 3078457 3078463
3078469 3078503 3078521 3078541 3078563 3078571 3078577 3078587 3078601 3078623
3078637 3078643 3078653 3078661 3078667 3078689 3078721 3078731 3078737 3078743
3078767 3078769 3078781 3078791 3078799 3078821 3078833 3078839 3078857 3078871
3078883 3078899 3078919 3078947 3078953 3078967 3078973 3078983 3078997 3079003
3079009 3079031 3079039 3079049 3079081 3079093 3079129 3079157 3079163 3079189
3079207 3079229 3079259 3079277 3079283 3079289 3079291 3079303 3079319 3079331
3079339 3079357 3079379 3079381 3079411 3079429 3079441 3079451 3079507 3079513
3079523 3079537 3079543 3079553 3079579 3079603 3079613 3079619 3079627 3079649
3079697 3079711 3079717 3079721 3079751 3079753 3079759 3079763 3079799 3079801
3079831 3079837 3079841 3079849 3079871 3079891 3079903 3079927 3079931 3079933
3079939 3079987 3080017 3080029 3080039 3080093 3080107 3080113 3080117 3080123
3080141 3080149 3080153 3080159 3080167 3080237 3080243 3080251 3080263 3080269
3080291 3080303 3080347 3080353 3080359 3080369 3080387 3080393 3080401 3080419
3080431 3080443 3080461 3080479 3080503 3080507 3080513 3080531 3080543 3080549
3080569 3080573 3080633 3080647 3080653 3080669 3080677 3080713 3080729 3080743
3080747 3080771 3080783 3080789 3080797 3080807 3080809 3080813 3080839 3080843
3080849 3080867 3080881 3080887 3080893 3080933 3080939 3080941 3080947 3080951
3080963 3080969 3080971 3080981 3081007 3081017 3081031 3081037 3081053 3081061
3081073 3081081 3081107 3081119 3081127 3081139 3081151 3081161 3081181 3081203
3081217 3081223 3081259 3081271 3081311 3081313 3081319 3081343 3081347 3081349
3081361 3081373 3081389 3081391 3081413 3081433 3081443 3081467 3081479 3081497
3081499 3081503 3081523 3081577 3081581 3081583 3081599 3081643 3081677 3081691
3081697 3081703 3081713 3081719 3081721 3081731 3081737 3081751 3081761 3081763
```

```
3081779  3081797  3081809  3081817  3081823  3081833  3081851  3081877  3081901  3081907
3081919  3081937  3081943  3081959  3082021  3082031  3082073  3082087  3082103  3082127
3082129  3082139  3082169  3082171  3082187  3082231  3082241  3082259  3082267  3082271
3082309  3082327  3082333  3082367  3082393  3082397  3082441  3082451  3082463
3082477  3082489  3082511  3082517  3082523  3082543  3082567  3082577  3082591  3082601
3082649  3082657  3082663  3082669  3082697  3082699  3082711  3082721  3082727  3082741
3082747  3082771  3082801  3082841  3082843  3082873  3082889  3082901  3082907  3082909
3082939  3082949  3082993  3082999  3083021  3083023  3083029  3083039  3083071  3083083
3083089  3083131  3083141  3083147  3083161  3083177  3083189  3083191  3083203  3083209
3083221  3083231  3083233  3083237  3083279  3083293  3083303  3083329  3083359  3083369
3083371  3083383  3083387  3083389  3083417  3083467  3083473  3083503  3083513  3083519
3083537  3083581  3083621  3083627  3083653  3083683  3083693  3083701  3083711  3083713
3083737  3083741  3083767  3083779  3083803  3083813  3083827  3083837  3083869  3083879
3083881  3083891  3083929  3083957  3083959  3083963  3083981  3084013  3084019  3084041
3084049  3084073  3084079  3084083  3084101  3084127  3084149  3084163  3084173  3084203
3084217  3084223  3084227  3084247  3084287  3084317  3084329  3084331  3084371  3084377
3084391  3084413  3084427  3084437  3084443  3084451  3084467  3084481  3084491  3084493
3084509  3084511  3084569  3084581  3084583  3084607  3084611  3084617  3084619  3084629
3084637  3084647  3084649  3084673  3084689  3084721  3084733  3084743  3084749  3084797
3084833  3084839  3084847  3084857  3084869  3084877  3084883  3084889  3084901  3084911
3084929  3084931  3084937  3084941  3084943  3084947  3084979  3084989  3085001  3085009
3085037  3085039  3085057  3085063  3085067  3085073  3085123  3085129  3085139  3085189
3085231  3085237  3085259  3085273  3085297  3085307  3085309  3085321  3085331  3085333
3085349  3085351  3085367  3085403  3085421  3085451  3085457  3085471  3085477  3085487
3085493  3085499  3085531  3085547  3085553  3085561  3085567  3085591  3085601  3085603
3085609  3085613  3085631  3085633  3085639  3085673  3085711  3085717  3085727  3085739
3085741  3085751  3085769  3085787  3085793  3085813  3085843  3085903  3085921  3085931
3085949  3085963  3085969  3086003  3086009  3086011  3086021  3086033  3086047  3086063
3086077  3086089  3086099  3086101  3086107  3086131  3086141  3086159  3086177  3086179
3086183  3086191  3086219  3086261  3086269  3086287  3086309  3086311  3086353  3086359
3086371  3086389  3086407  3086423  3086437  3086471  3086507  3086527  3086533  3086549
3086563  3086579  3086599  3086617  3086621  3086627  3086641  3086653  3086693  3086711
3086717  3086729  3086737  3086749  3086779  3086791  3086801  3086813  3086861  3086903
3086933  3086957  3086959  3086971  3086977  3086981  3086983  3086999  3087023  3087031
3087053  3087059  3087061  3087089  3087103  3087107  3087109  3087113  3087167  3087173
3087181  3087199  3087209  3087211  3087223  3087229  3087233  3087239  3087281
3087283  3087307  3087323  3087349  3087373  3087407  3087419  3087431  3087437  3087439
3087449  3087457  3087463  3087467  3087473  3087479  3087509  3087521  3087533  3087547
3087583  3087599  3087619  3087649  3087653  3087661  3087673  3087703  3087731
3087737  3087739  3087743  3087757  3087767  3087769  3087793  3087811  3087839  3087841
3087857  3087859  3087869  3087871  3087893  3087901  3087907  3087923  3087943  3087961
3087971  3087977  3087979  3087989  3087991  3088009  3088021  3088039  3088061  3088073
3088081  3088087  3088091  3088093  3088121  3088139  3088147  3088159  3088171  3088199
3088201  3088213  3088219  3088289  3088291  3088307  3088321  3088333  3088343  3088357
3088367  3088381  3088387  3088399  3088439  3088447  3088451  3088453  3088457  3088483
3088487  3088493  3088517  3088537  3088559  3088573  3088607  3088609  3088619  3088627
3088639  3088643  3088667  3088669  3088691  3088711  3088717  3088721  3088741  3088753
3088783  3088801  3088823  3088837  3088843  3088847  3088859  3088861  3088873
3088879  3088913  3088931  3088949  3088957  3088961  3088973  3089027  3089029  3089059
3089069  3089083  3089117  3089123  3089131  3089143  3089147  3089171  3089173  3089183
3089221  3089231  3089233  3089239  3089269  3089293  3089311  3089321  3089323  3089327
3089329  3089369  3089371  3089377  3089407  3089431  3089441  3089447  3089459  3089477
3089479  3089483  3089497  3089501  3089519  3089531  3089539  3089549  3089557  3089561
3089587  3089591  3089621  3089627  3089629  3089631  3089641  3089657  3089663  3089687
3089693  3089701  3089717  3089729  3089731  3089753  3089789  3089791  3089803  3089857
3089881  3089887  3089889  3089899  3089923  3089941  3089959  3089993  3090011  3090013
3090019  3090067  3090071  3090079  3090089  3090097  3090127  3090161  3090181  3090187
3090193  3090221  3090223  3090229  3090233  3090247  3090253  3090287  3090289  3090301
3090313  3090319  3090337  3090371  3090383  3090389  3090397  3090431  3090449  3090463
3090469  3090473  3090491  3090497  3090511  3090523  3090551  3090587  3090599  3090613
3090641  3090653  3090679  3090697  3090713  3090727  3090743  3090757  3090761  3090779
3090781  3090817  3090827  3090839  3090851  3090853  3090877  3090887  3090959  3090961
3090973  3091001  3091007  3091009  3091019  3091021  3091027  3091037  3091057  3091087
3091111  3091117  3091147  3091159  3091171  3091181  3091201  3091213  3091217  3091219
3091259  3091261  3091267  3091273  3091279  3091321  3091327  3091367  3091373  3091379
3091381  3091391  3091393  3091397  3091409  3091421  3091427  3091457  3091463  3091481
3091483  3091489  3091493  3091511  3091549  3091559  3091573  3091577  3091579  3091589
3091607  3091633  3091639  3091643  3091703  3091721  3091727  3091733  3091741  3091747
3091763  3091799  3091811  3091819  3091853  3091873  3091883  3091897  3091901
3091903  3091919  3091961  3091973  3091987  3091997  3092017  3092021  3092039
3092057  3092071  3092077  3092093  3092101  3092107  3092119  3092137  3092171  3092203
3092209  3092213  3092237  3092279  3092291  3092321  3092347  3092359  3092363  3092371
3092387  3092389  3092393  3092413  3092491  3092503  3092513  3092539
3092549  3092561  3092563  3092567  3092569  3092581  3092587  3092597  3092629  3092669
3092681  3092699  3092701  3092711  3092717  3092723  3092729  3092731  3092767  3092783
3092797  3092813  3092851  3092857  3092891  3092893  3092909  3092951  3092959  3092977
3092981  3092983  3092989  3092993  3093011  3093043  3093047  3093059  3093061  3093071
3093113  3093121  3093133  3093137  3093151  3093173  3093197  3093199  3093203  3093217
3093221  3093241  3093253  3093271  3093281  3093283  3093317  3093319  3093353  3093359
3093361  3093383  3093407  3093421  3093479  3093481  3093487  3093511  3093527  3093539
3093581  3093589  3093611  3093613  3093617  3093641  3093647  3093689  3093703  3093709
3093733  3093743  3093763  3093767  3093803  3093817  3093823  3093841  3093851  3093863
3093889  3093889  3093899  3093913  3093931  3093937  3093943  3093947  3093971
3093973  3093989  3094027  3094033  3094037  3094043  3094061  3094067  3094073  3094099
3094111  3094123  3094129  3094163  3094181  3094241  3094243  3094277  3094291  3094297
3094303  3094309  3094331  3094361  3094411  3094417  3094423  3094439  3094453  3094457
3094463  3094471  3094501  3094523  3094541  3094573  3094607  3094633  3094661  3094669
3094687  3094709  3094711  3094747  3094757  3094769  3094783  3094787  3094789  3094801
3094807  3094813  3094849  3094859  3094873  3094877  3094907  3094913  3094951  3094991
```

```
3095063  3095069  3095077  3095101  3095107  3095111  3095123  3095149  3095203  3095221
3095227  3095231  3095237  3095243  3095263  3095291  3095311  3095321  3095327  3095329
3095341  3095353  3095357  3095369  3095429  3095437  3095453  3095471  3095483  3095497
3095503  3095507  3095539  3095551  3095557  3095563  3095579  3095597  3095611  3095621
3095627  3095641  3095647  3095681  3095707  3095713  3095723  3095747  3095759  3095761
3095791  3095797  3095801  3095809  3095821  3095839  3095849  3095863  3095867  3095893
3095899  3095903  3095941  3095959  3095969  3095971  3095977  3095999  3096017  3096047
3096059  3096061  3096073  3096083  3096103  3096109  3096151  3096157  3096161  3096167
3096169  3096173  3096179  3096199  3096209  3096217  3096229  3096251  3096253  3096257
3096277  3096287  3096319  3096323  3096349  3096377  3096389  3096391  3096403  3096409
3096413  3096427  3096433  3096437  3096439  3096461  3096463  3096479  3096491  3096529
3096547  3096551  3096553  3096571  3096589  3096617  3096619  3096623  3096629  3096637
3096659  3096661  3096679  3096701  3096719  3096727  3096739  3096757  3096811  3096827
3096889  3096911  3096913  3096917  3096959  3096967  3096983  3097001  3097021  3097027
3097033  3097049  3097051  3097079  3097097  3097103  3097121  3097123  3097141  3097151
3097169  3097177  3097183  3097187  3097207  3097223  3097261  3097271  3097273  3097279
3097291  3097309  3097319  3097327  3097363  3097439  3097469  3097481  3097483  3097487
3097499  3097531  3097537  3097541  3097547  3097631  3097639  3097649  3097687  3097711
3097727  3097739  3097769  3097777  3097781  3097789  3097793  3097813  3097841  3097873
3097883  3097891  3097907  3097909  3097921  3097951  3097979  3097993  3097999  3098033
3098057  3098059  3098071  3098089  3098101  3098119  3098153  3098191  3098209  3098213
3098237  3098239  3098243  3098297  3098299  3098317  3098321  3098341  3098371  3098383
3098393  3098423  3098429  3098443  3098453  3098479  3098489  3098497  3098507  3098509
3098519  3098521  3098531  3098561  3098597  3098633  3098647  3098677  3098681  3098687
3098699  3098707  3098717  3098723  3098731  3098741  3098747  3098749  3098759  3098783
3098789  3098801  3098807  3098819  3098833  3098839  3098863  3098867  3098869  3098873
3098899  3098939  3098941  3098959  3098999  3099011  3099029  3099059  3099073  3099127
3099169  3099179  3099193  3099199  3099203  3099209  3099233  3099241  3099269  3099293
3099307  3099323  3099331  3099347  3099359  3099367  3099391  3099403  3099409  3099419
3099431  3099443  3099449  3099461  3099463  3099497  3099511  3099517  3099529  3099539
3099541  3099557  3099563  3099571  3099581  3099587  3099617  3099623  3099667  3099709
3099713  3099727  3099731  3099757  3099809  3099893  3099911  3099937  3099953  3099961
3099977  3099997  3100007  3100043  3100057  3100061  3100067  3100079  3100087  3100099
3100127  3100151  3100169  3100177  3100199  3100219  3100231  3100259  3100271  3100277
3100289  3100301  3100309  3100313  3100327  3100351  3100367  3100373  3100421  3100463
3100501  3100519  3100549  3100597  3100621  3100633  3100649  3100661  3100663  3100697
3100703  3100733  3100739  3100807  3100843  3100847  3100861  3100873  3100913  3100927
3100939  3100949  3100957  3100991  3101029  3101039  3101041  3101051  3101069  3101141
3101143  3101149  3101171  3101177  3101183  3101207  3101233  3101239  3101249  3101257
3101279  3101291  3101299  3101309  3101311  3101321  3101339  3101353  3101359  3101369
3101387  3101393  3101419  3101437  3101459  3101471  3101473  3101477  3101479  3101491
3101509  3101537  3101557  3101591  3101597  3101611  3101629  3101653  3101663  3101669
3101677  3101699  3101729  3101741  3101743  3101759  3101771  3101779  3101827  3101831
3101851  3101863  3101867  3101881  3101897  3101947  3101951  3101957  3101971  3101999
3102017  3102023  3102059  3102067  3102097  3102103  3102107  3102131  3102173  3102179
3102181  3102193  3102199  3102223  3102227  3102233  3102259  3102269  3102271  3102289
3102293  3102299  3102311  3102317  3102331  3102343  3102353  3102367  3102371  3102373
3102383  3102389  3102419  3102431  3102433  3102439  3102469  3102481  3102497  3102499
3102503  3102509  3102523  3102557  3102571  3102581  3102587  3102601  3102613  3102637
3102661  3102667  3102707  3102713  3102727  3102731  3102733  3102763  3102767  3102773
3102787  3102793  3102809  3102811  3102817  3102829  3102851  3102859  3102877  3102889
3102889  3102901  3102917  3102919  3102929  3102941  3102949  3102961  3102977  3102989
3103013  3103019  3103021  3103033  3103043  3103049  3103057  3103063  3103073  3103109
3103147  3103151  3103159  3103171  3103189  3103207  3103211  3103237  3103241  3103271
3103273  3103277  3103279  3103283  3103297  3103313  3103333  3103381  3103391  3103393
3103409  3103411  3103417  3103421  3103423  3103483  3103501  3103531  3103543  3103547
3103549  3103553  3103579  3103589  3103601  3103649  3103679  3103687  3103691  3103693
3103729  3103757  3103769  3103789  3103799  3103801  3103811  3103817  3103829  3103847
3103861  3103871  3103879  3103939  3103943  3103949  3103981  3104063  3104071  3104083
3104089  3104093  3104099  3104113  3104137  3104159  3104173  3104197  3104219  3104221
3104237  3104243  3104249  3104267  3104293  3104327  3104329  3104347  3104357  3104377
3104393  3104407  3104417  3104459  3104461  3104477  3104483  3104501  3104503  3104509
3104513  3104531  3104533  3104551  3104573  3104597  3104603  3104611  3104623  3104627
3104641  3104669  3104671  3104677  3104683  3104723  3104737  3104741  3104749  3104753
3104767  3104789  3104797  3104813  3104843  3104851  3104869  3104879  3104889  3104891
3104903  3104939  3104951  3104957  3104963  3105007  3105041  3105071  3105079  3105097
3105103  3105107  3105119  3105131  3105143  3105163  3105173  3105181  3105199  3105211
3105251  3105257  3105259  3105269  3105283  3105293  3105307  3105317  3105329  3105343
3105371  3105413  3105419  3105433  3105439  3105451  3105467  3105481  3105491  3105497
3105499  3105527  3105533  3105539  3105551  3105559  3105629  3105631  3105637  3105643
3105659  3105689  3105691  3105703  3105719  3105749  3105763  3105769  3105787  3105799
3105803  3105811  3105821  3105841  3105857  3105863  3105877  3105887  3105913  3105923
3105941  3105961  3105967  3105979  3106003  3106007  3106013  3106021  3106027  3106049
3106057  3106067  3106069  3106073  3106079  3106091  3106111  3106133  3106151  3106153
3106157  3106163  3106193  3106199  3106237  3106273  3106297  3106307  3106319  3106339
3106349  3106351  3106361  3106381  3106387  3106421  3106423  3106429  3106459  3106469
3106487  3106577  3106601  3106637  3106639  3106643  3106651  3106657  3106667  3106673
3106703  3106729  3106751  3106757  3106769  3106777  3106781  3106783  3106787  3106837
3106847  3106849  3106867  3106877  3106891  3106897  3106919  3106921  3106969  3106981
3106993  3107009  3107011  3107033  3107053  3107077  3107081  3107101  3107113  3107119
3107131  3107171  3107177  3107183  3107249  3107303  3107327  3107329  3107333  3107339
3107359  3107381  3107383  3107411  3107417  3107441  3107449  3107453  3107473  3107483
3107491  3107497  3107509  3107561  3107569  3107581  3107591  3107597  3107609  3107633
3107639  3107647  3107701  3107711  3107729  3107743  3107747  3107749  3107789  3107803
3107809  3107813  3107827  3107831  3107861  3107871  3107873  3107881  3107891  3107893
3107899  3107903  3107927  3107933  3107947  3107971  3107981  3107983  3107993  3108019
3108023  3108031  3108041  3108043  3108047  3108067  3108103  3108109  3108139  3108163
3108173  3108199  3108221  3108227  3108239  3108253  3108257  3108269  3108283  3108293
3108317  3108319  3108337  3108349  3108359  3108361  3108367  3108373  3108379  3108383
```

```
3108409  3108431  3108449  3108461  3108487  3108491  3108493  3108509  3108529  3108541
3108551  3108557  3108577  3108583  3108607  3108613  3108689  3108691  3108697  3108701
3108719  3108727  3108731  3108737  3108751  3108779  3108793  3108797  3108817  3108823
3108827  3108839  3108863  3108869  3108893  3108901  3108949  3108961  3108967  3108991
3109031  3109069  3109081  3109091  3109111  3109121  3109157  3109159  3109187  3109193
3109199  3109213  3109247  3109259  3109273  3109279  3109297  3109307  3109319  3109333
3109343  3109349  3109367  3109387  3109391  3109397  3109411  3109427  3109441  3109451
3109471  3109501  3109511  3109523  3109541  3109549  3109553  3109607  3109619  3109621
3109633  3109637  3109649  3109651  3109681  3109693  3109697  3109709  3109747  3109751
3109781  3109783  3109789  3109801  3109811  3109817  3109819  3109823  3109829  3109837
3109859  3109867  3109913  3109921  3109937  3109969  3109979  3109999  3110011  3110027
3110033  3110057  3110059  3110069  3110101  3110143  3110153  3110179  3110213  3110227
3110231  3110249  3110251  3110273  3110287  3110293  3110299  3110321  3110339  3110353
3110369  3110377  3110381  3110399  3110417  3110423  3110431  3110477  3110489  3110519
3110531  3110537  3110561  3110563  3110567  3110579  3110593  3110617  3110621  3110647
3110651  3110669  3110671  3110683  3110689  3110707  3110717  3110741  3110753  3110759
3110761  3110771  3110791  3110797  3110803  3110837  3110843  3110867  3110879  3110903
3110929  3110953  3110963  3110981  3110993  3110999  3111001  3111013  3111023  3111029
3111037  3111083  3111103  3111107  3111131  3111137  3111151  3111161  3111169  3111197
3111217  3111223  3111271  3111281  3111287  3111299  3111301  3111313  3111319  3111331
3111337  3111341  3111343  3111349  3111397  3111403  3111419  3111431  3111457  3111481
3111487  3111491  3111539  3111569  3111593  3111599  3111607  3111631  3111653  3111659
3111673  3111677  3111679  3111721  3111727  3111743  3111769  3111803  3111809  3111817
3111821  3111827  3111847  3111853  3111863  3111931  3111973  3112007  3112069  3112091
3112093  3112099  3112103  3112111  3112117  3112127  3112129  3112141  3112147  3112237
3112247  3112253  3112259  3112267  3112271  3112279  3112283  3112301  3112303  3112313
3112321  3112327  3112331  3112357  3112381  3112391  3112399  3112423  3112441  3112463
3112471  3112489  3112507  3112519  3112609  3112621  3112639  3112661  3112667  3112687
3112693  3112709  3112721  3112729  3112757  3112771  3112783  3112787  3112801  3112807
3112829  3112859  3112873  3112909  3112913  3112919  3112933  3112943  3112973  3112987
3113009  3113039  3113053  3113059  3113083  3113087  3113101  3113111  3113129  3113147
3113177  3113189  3113197  3113213  3113221  3113239  3113249  3113267  3113269  3113281
3113317  3113333  3113339  3113387  3113389  3113393  3113399  3113401  3113437  3113443
3113447  3113449  3113459  3113471  3113483  3113497  3113521  3113531  3113569  3113573
3113611  3113633  3113639  3113641  3113647  3113683  3113687  3113707  3113723  3113767
3113787  3113801  3113819  3113821  3113833  3113837  3113861  3113863  3113881  3113893
3113897  3113899  3113917  3113921  3113923  3113927  3113939  3113963  3113969  3113977
3113983  3113987  3114019  3114029  3114047  3114091  3114109  3114143  3114161  3114169
3114191  3114203  3114211  3114277  3114283  3114289  3114299  3114301  3114313  3114317
3114329  3114343  3114359  3114367  3114389  3114403  3114431  3114437  3114473  3114479
3114487  3114493  3114497  3114509  3114521  3114523  3114541  3114563  3114577  3114589
3114593  3114607  3114611  3114673  3114679  3114701  3114719  3114731  3114743  3114781
3114809  3114817  3114833  3114847  3114857  3114869  3114871  3114889  3114899  3114931
3114949  3114953  3114967  3114971  3114989  3114997  3115003  3115009  3115027  3115033
3115061  3115103  3115109  3115117  3115153  3115157  3115169  3115171  3115187  3115193
3115201  3115237  3115241  3115249  3115253  3115261  3115271  3115279  3115291  3115319
3115361  3115379  3115381  3115397  3115417  3115423  3115429  3115439  3115451  3115457
3115477  3115481  3115493  3115529  3115537  3115559  3115561  3115577  3115579  3115591
3115597  3115621  3115627  3115633  3115643  3115657  3115667  3115727  3115729  3115751
3115769  3115781  3115799  3115813  3115831  3115873  3115883  3115897  3115907  3115919
3115927  3115933  3115991  3115999  3116011  3116033  3116039  3116051
3116077  3116093  3116111  3116129  3116131  3116149  3116159  3116173  3116189  3116207
3116227  3116233  3116257  3116263  3116273  3116299  3116303  3116317  3116327  3116341
3116353  3116381  3116417  3116447  3116459  3116497  3116501  3116507  3116521  3116537
3116549  3116563  3116573  3116587  3116591  3116609  3116611  3116623  3116651  3116657
3116669  3116671  3116689  3116693  3116699  3116719  3116747  3116749  3116761  3116767
3116777  3116783  3116807  3116809  3116819  3116837  3116849  3116851  3116857  3116863
3116873  3116947  3116951  3116959  3116977  3117011  3117013  3117031  3117043
3117053  3117071  3117097  3117109  3117119  3117151  3117187  3117203  3117209  3117211
3117217  3117221  3117223  3117241  3117251  3117269  3117281  3117293  3117299  3117421
3117431  3117437  3117451  3117461  3117467  3117479  3117481  3117487  3117493  3117497
3117503  3117523  3117553  3117559  3117571  3117589  3117593  3117601  3117623  3117637
3117661  3117679  3117683  3117713  3117721  3117739  3117781  3117787  3117791  3117797
3117799  3117809  3117827  3117833  3117847  3117853  3117889  3117899  3117901  3117911
3117923  3117941  3117943  3117967  3117991  3117997  3118007  3118013  3118067  3118069
3118081  3118099  3118139  3118151  3118153  3118169  3118183  3118201  3118207  3118211
3118229  3118237  3118243  3118253  3118267  3118289  3118307  3118319  3118333  3118343
3118387  3118411  3118417  3118433  3118439  3118459  3118469  3118481  3118499
3118513  3118519  3118523  3118537  3118541  3118553  3118561  3118567  3118579  3118597
3118601  3118607  3118637  3118651  3118657  3118663  3118669  3118673  3118691  3118697
3118699  3118721  3118723  3118727  3118733  3118741  3118757  3118763  3118789  3118807
3118847  3118849  3118853  3118859  3118861  3118867  3118883  3118889  3118897  3118901
3118909  3118931  3118933  3118937  3118949  3118987  3119009  3119023  3119069  3119087
3119089  3119107  3119111  3119117  3119131  3119161  3119167  3119197  3119201  3119219
3119257  3119267  3119293  3119309  3119317  3119341  3119377  3119383  3119387  3119407
3119411  3119429  3119447  3119491  3119497  3119533  3119537  3119563  3119569  3119573
3119647  3119659  3119663  3119681  3119707  3119713  3119737  3119749  3119759  3119761
3119771  3119783  3119787  3119807  3119821  3119843  3119861  3119869  3119899  3119903
3119923  3119929  3119957  3119981  3119999  3120011  3120017  3120067  3120071  3120077
3120079  3120083  3120127  3120137  3120217  3120233  3120253  3120277  3120281
3120287  3120311  3120317  3120319  3120323  3120331  3120373  3120407  3120413  3120437
3120443  3120457  3120461  3120463  3120473  3120493  3120497  3120499  3120527  3120529
3120539  3120547  3120563  3120589  3120599  3120613  3120619  3120629  3120643  3120647
3120653  3120671  3120697  3120703  3120713  3120727  3120757  3120763  3120791  3120827
3120833  3120841  3120859  3120881  3120889  3120907  3120919  3120937  3120973
3120977  3120989  3120991  3121007  3121033  3121037  3121039  3121051  3121057  3121087
3121091  3121109  3121121  3121163  3121177  3121189  3121193  3121199  3121201  3121219
3121229  3121249  3121253  3121259  3121267  3121273  3121291  3121303  3121333  3121361
3121367  3121379  3121409  3121423  3121427  3121429  3121441  3121457  3121487  3121493
```

```
3121519  3121543  3121561  3121571  3121603  3121609  3121619  3121627  3121633  3121663
3121667  3121691  3121711  3121717  3121739  3121747  3121771  3121817  3121831  3121837
3121841  3121873  3121891  3121901  3121913  3121927  3121933  3121961  3121973  3121981
3122003  3122017  3122059  3122107  3122113  3122117  3122143  3122149  3122173  3122179
3122183  3122201  3122219  3122233  3122261  3122279  3122281  3122299  3122309  3122321
3122341  3122347  3122381  3122419  3122447  3122453  3122461  3122473  3122489  3122491
3122513  3122533  3122551  3122563  3122569  3122579  3122597  3122627  3122657  3122671
3122711  3122719  3122729  3122731  3122737  3122761  3122771  3122797  3122809  3122827
3122851  3122863  3122869  3122879  3122881  3122893  3122927  3122939  3122947  3122953
3122957  3122969  3122983  3122989  3122993  3123007  3123023  3123037  3123061  3123073
3123089  3123091  3123137  3123143  3123149  3123151  3123167  3123173  3123181  3123187
3123203  3123209  3123217  3123221  3123227  3123233  3123287  3123317  3123349  3123403
3123413  3123431  3123481  3123493  3123499  3123509  3123511  3123521  3123541  3123553
3123557  3123583  3123587  3123599  3123611  3123623  3123629  3123641  3123643  3123671
3123683  3123689  3123709  3123713  3123721  3123727  3123751  3123773  3123779  3123781
3123797  3123803  3123823  3123833  3123853  3123859  3123863  3123881  3123893  3123931
3123959  3123973  3123977  3123983  3123997  3124001  3124013  3124019  3124027  3124057
3124061  3124063  3124103  3124117  3124123  3124127  3124129  3124171  3124193  3124217
3124279  3124291  3124301  3124307  3124313  3124321  3124361  3124367  3124393  3124399
3124409  3124421  3124427  3124441  3124469  3124519  3124543  3124567  3124571  3124577
3124579  3124609  3124631  3124633  3124657  3124673  3124691  3124717  3124727  3124729
3124741  3124747  3124801  3124811  3124829  3124843  3124861  3124871  3124883  3124903
3124943  3124963  3124967  3124997  3124999  3125009  3125021  3125027  3125029  3125051
3125099  3125113  3125117  3125147  3125153  3125159  3125173  3125179  3125183  3125189
3125191  3125209  3125219  3125257  3125261  3125293  3125299  3125323  3125341  3125351
3125387  3125449  3125459  3125461  3125497  3125503  3125527  3125537  3125561  3125587
3125593  3125611  3125651  3125659  3125669  3125711  3125719  3125729  3125737  3125753
3125767  3125777  3125779  3125789  3125803  3125809  3125819  3125821  3125831  3125833
3125839  3125867  3125873  3125893  3125921  3125957  3125959  3125989  3126001  3126007
3126023  3126031  3126061  3126077  3126083  3126103  3126121  3126131  3126139  3126163
3126173  3126187  3126191  3126199  3126223  3126239  3126269  3126293  3126307  3126313
3126323  3126353  3126377  3126379  3126397  3126427  3126437  3126449  3126451  3126457
3126491  3126509  3126511  3126533  3126547  3126553  3126559  3126653  3126661  3126667
3126679  3126713  3126727  3126731  3126733  3126737  3126743  3126749  3126779  3126791
3126797  3126803  3126821  3126847  3126857  3126869  3126881  3126901  3126961  3126973
3126979  3127009  3127013  3127021  3127037  3127079  3127081  3127087  3127097  3127109
3127123  3127127  3127139  3127141  3127147  3127181  3127213  3127219  3127237  3127253
3127259  3127279  3127291  3127297  3127301  3127339  3127387  3127403  3127417  3127429
3127441  3127451  3127459  3127469  3127483  3127499  3127513  3127529  3127543  3127561
3127567  3127577  3127601  3127613  3127633  3127637  3127669  3127673  3127681  3127687
3127693  3127699  3127703  3127753  3127757  3127759  3127771  3127781  3127783  3127819
3127823  3127829  3127841  3127843  3127877  3127879  3127889  3127903  3127907  3127909
3127919  3127921  3127937  3127979  3127981  3127987  3127997  3128009  3128011  3128033
3128039  3128053  3128057  3128101  3128107  3128129  3128131  3128159  3128171  3128173
3128197  3128227  3128233  3128249  3128291  3128311  3128329  3128339  3128381  3128393
3128399  3128401  3128443  3128453  3128501  3128533  3128579  3128581  3128599  3128611
3128623  3128633  3128641  3128647  3128651  3128659  3128687  3128689  3128693  3128701
3128729  3128747  3128761  3128767  3128779  3128789  3128791  3128803  3128813  3128819
3128821  3128843  3128849  3128869  3128887  3128891  3128893  3128921  3128927  3128933
3128941  3128987  3129011  3129019  3129023  3129031  3129043  3129059  3129073  3129089
3129103  3129121  3129169  3129193  3129199  3129209  3129221  3129223  3129253  3129257
3129263  3129271  3129289  3129323  3129383  3129391  3129421  3129431  3129439  3129443
3129461  3129463  3129487  3129517  3129521  3129523  3129557  3129559  3129601  3129611
3129613  3129617  3129619  3129629  3129641  3129677  3129687  3129691  3129701  3129733
3129757  3129769  3129781  3129787  3129799  3129803  3129811  3129821  3129827  3129839
3129859  3129911  3129913  3129923  3129937  3129947  3129953  3129961
3129991  3130007  3130019  3130027  3130031  3130037  3130087  3130097  3130111  3130129
3130147  3130187  3130199  3130207  3130229  3130241  3130243  3130249  3130279  3130291
3130297  3130327  3130331  3130333  3130367  3130373  3130399  3130403  3130409  3130417
3130427  3130429  3130451  3130453  3130483  3130487  3130493  3130513  3130537  3130541
3130549  3130559  3130571  3130577  3130583  3130619  3130627  3130663  3130667  3130679
3130693  3130711  3130733  3130739  3130759  3130789  3130817  3130819  3130823  3130871
3130901  3130913  3130943  3130949  3130957  3130961  3130979  3130987  3130993  3130997
3131017  3131021  3131027  3131041  3131053  3131057  3131087  3131099  3131113  3131123
3131137  3131153  3131173  3131203  3131209  3131221  3131231  3131237  3131239  3131251
3131263  3131267  3131299  3131309  3131311  3131321  3131327  3131329  3131339  3131351
3131353  3131357  3131369  3131377  3131419  3131431  3131437  3131441  3131467  3131477
3131483  3131489  3131497  3131501  3131503  3131537  3131549  3131551  3131593  3131603
3131629  3131641  3131669  3131671  3131699  3131701  3131743  3131747  3131761  3131771
3131833  3131851  3131857  3131861  3131879  3131911  3131917  3131951  3131977  3131981
3131983  3132007  3132037  3132083  3132119  3132121  3132139  3132149  3132179  3132187
3132257  3132263  3132281  3132287  3132299  3132323  3132329  3132331  3132343  3132379
3132407  3132413  3132431  3132443  3132461  3132469  3132499  3132517  3132529  3132541
3132553  3132559  3132599  3132601  3132629  3132631  3132637  3132653  3132659  3132677
3132707  3132737  3132749  3132751  3132763  3132781  3132793  3132799  3132803  3132823
3132839  3132847  3132859  3132881  3132887  3132907  3132917  3132923  3132971  3132977
3132979  3133019  3133027  3133033  3133057  3133111  3133153  3133171  3133177  3133181
3133183  3133211  3133213  3133237  3133243  3133259  3133279  3133283  3133289  3133297
3133303  3133331  3133337  3133357  3133381  3133397  3133399  3133411  3133433  3133439
3133441  3133447  3133463  3133469  3133513  3133531  3133541  3133547  3133583  3133591
3133597  3133607  3133609  3133633  3133639  3133643  3133673  3133699  3133721  3133733
3133751  3133777  3133783  3133787  3133799  3133811  3133843  3133847  3133853  3133861
3133873  3133891  3133901  3133909  3133919  3133927  3133931  3133939  3133961  3133987
3134017  3134023  3134029  3134039  3134041  3134057  3134063  3134071  3134093  3134113
3134123  3134143  3134147  3134203  3134207  3134213  3134231  3134249  3134251  3134267
3134303  3134309  3134321  3134347  3134353  3134357  3134387  3134389  3134413  3134419
3134431  3134447  3134459  3134479  3134497  3134519  3134543  3134557  3134561  3134591
3134597  3134623  3134633  3134671  3134683  3134707  3134713  3134723  3134771  3134773
3134797  3134801  3134821  3134837  3134843  3134881  3134891  3134893  3134903  3134909
```

```
3134917  3134921  3134927  3134941  3135017  3135023  3135029  3135031  3135037  3135043
3135049  3135059  3135071  3135073  3135079  3135113  3135127  3135151  3135163  3135211
3135221  3135227  3135283  3135287  3135299  3135313  3135317  3135329  3135373  3135389
3135397  3135401  3135403  3135409  3135413  3135443  3135449  3135469  3135487  3135523
3135527  3135529  3135547  3135553  3135571  3135593  3135607  3135617  3135623  3135641
3135661  3135677  3135707  3135709  3135731  3135739  3135767  3135773  3135809  3135833
3135841  3135859  3135877  3135883  3135943  3135953  3135959  3135961  3135983  3136019
3136037  3136079  3136087  3136097  3136099  3136103  3136123  3136127  3136129  3136163
3136201  3136207  3136223  3136229  3136249  3136253  3136261  3136267  3136307  3136319
3136327  3136333  3136339  3136351  3136361  3136373  3136403  3136409  3136417  3136423
3136429  3136433  3136447  3136457  3136477  3136513  3136531  3136543  3136561  3136571
3136589  3136597  3136603  3136607  3136631  3136633  3136643  3136649  3136657  3136667
3136759  3136769  3136781  3136799  3136817  3136841  3136849  3136867  3136877  3136907
3136909  3136933  3136943  3136949  3136961  3137003  3137051  3137059  3137063  3137081
3137083  3137087  3137093  3137117  3137137  3137143  3137159  3137171  3137179  3137201
3137209  3137243  3137257  3137263  3137311  3137357  3137371  3137389  3137399  3137447
3137461  3137471  3137507  3137509  3137513  3137521  3137531  3137551  3137567  3137569
3137573  3137593  3137609  3137611  3137623  3137627  3137663  3137669  3137681  3137699
3137723  3137731  3137747  3137749  3137777  3137803  3137837  3137857  3137863  3137879
3137881  3137899  3137903  3137923  3137941  3137977  3137993  3137999  3138029  3138041
3138067  3138071  3138073  3138103  3138127  3138131  3138137  3138167  3138193  3138209
3138221  3138283  3138299  3138329  3138337  3138361  3138371  3138383  3138391  3138397
3138403  3138449  3138469  3138491  3138493  3138503  3138521  3138529  3138539  3138547
3138559  3138563  3138571  3138581  3138589  3138593  3138601  3138637  3138647  3138661
3138671  3138691  3138767  3138769  3138791  3138799  3138803  3138809  3138847  3138851
3138853  3138869  3138881  3138883  3138899  3138911  3138913  3138917  3138929  3138943
3138953  3138991  3138997  3139007  3139021  3139049  3139061  3139069  3139111  3139141
3139187  3139189  3139193  3139207  3139231  3139259  3139261  3139267  3139291  3139303
3139307  3139321  3139327  3139333  3139363  3139369  3139379  3139391  3139393  3139399
3139403  3139417  3139421  3139447  3139471  3139483  3139489  3139517  3139519  3139537
3139547  3139571  3139573  3139583  3139597  3139601  3139607  3139621  3139639  3139651
3139663  3139673  3139681  3139699  3139723  3139727  3139733  3139757  3139771  3139789
3139811  3139813  3139837  3139841  3139847  3139861  3139867  3139889  3139901  3139907
3139909  3139919  3139943  3139967  3139979  3139991  3139993  3140041  3140057  3140069
3140099  3140107  3140113  3140131  3140147  3140183  3140209  3140233  3140237  3140243
3140251  3140273  3140297  3140299  3140309  3140317  3140321  3140353  3140363  3140369
3140407  3140413  3140437  3140441  3140447  3140507  3140513  3140517  3140593  3140623
3140639  3140653  3140659  3140693  3140701  3140711  3140713  3140717  3140741  3140749
3140777  3140783  3140791  3140807  3140821  3140843  3140861  3140873  3140881  3140911
3140933  3140959  3140981  3140993  3141001  3141007  3141011  3141043  3141049  3141059
3141067  3141097  3141139  3141143  3141163  3141167  3141197  3141211  3141217  3141221
3141223  3141233  3141239  3141241  3141247  3141269  3141283  3141319  3141329  3141331
3141343  3141361  3141371  3141373  3141389  3141419  3141431  3141443  3141473  3141487
3141491  3141493  3141497  3141503  3141553  3141557  3141569  3141601  3141641  3141643
3141647  3141659  3141667  3141673  3141689  3141713  3141763  3141769  3141811  3141829
3141833  3141863  3141877  3141883  3141889  3141911  3141913  3141937  3141959  3142019
3142021  3142043  3142079  3142123  3142157  3142177  3142187  3142193  3142219  3142231
3142259  3142267  3142273  3142301  3142303  3142309  3142313  3142319  3142333  3142343
3142351  3142357  3142379  3142387  3142393  3142441  3142453  3142457  3142459  3142481
3142487  3142493  3142499  3142507  3142511  3142519  3142547  3142589  3142591  3142613
3142627  3142639  3142649  3142661  3142681  3142693  3142709  3142717  3142721  3142729
3142747  3142751  3142757  3142793  3142813  3142819  3142829  3142831  3142837  3142849
3142859  3142861  3142877  3142879  3142901  3142907  3142939  3142949  3142963  3142969
3142981  3142987  3143003  3143027  3143029  3143033  3143051  3143053  3143057  3143069
3143071  3143087  3143117  3143131  3143137  3143141  3143149  3143159  3143167  3143197
3143209  3143243  3143263  3143299  3143323  3143353  3143389  3143401  3143411  3143447
3143467  3143471  3143477  3143533  3143537  3143549  3143551  3143561  3143563  3143587
3143641  3143671  3143711  3143713  3143719  3143729  3143731  3143761  3143771  3143807
3143813  3143851  3143857  3143863  3143897  3143953  3143969  3143993  3144007  3144019
3144023  3144059  3144067  3144079  3144083  3144091  3144137  3144143  3144157  3144161
3144173  3144179  3144181  3144191  3144217  3144221  3144257  3144259  3144263  3144283
3144293  3144301  3144313  3144343  3144359  3144373  3144389  3144403  3144419  3144431
3144457  3144467  3144469  3144509  3144527  3144529  3144539  3144551  3144571  3144587
3144599  3144607  3144613  3144619  3144689  3144697  3144707  3144727  3144737  3144749
3144751  3144761  3144773  3144793  3144811  3144823  3144829  3144853  3144871  3144883
3144893  3144907  3144923  3144931  3144941  3144959  3144961  3144971  3144989  3145019
3145027  3145049  3145057  3145091  3145097  3145117  3145123  3145133  3145141  3145147
3145157  3145169  3145183  3145189  3145201  3145211  3145223  3145243  3145253  3145283
3145297  3145327  3145339  3145361  3145367  3145399  3145447  3145453  3145463  3145487
3145489  3145511  3145529  3145547  3145553  3145559  3145573  3145577  3145589  3145607
3145609  3145627  3145633  3145661  3145669  3145673  3145679  3145711  3145721  3145759
3145741  3145771  3145781  3145801  3145817  3145819  3145823  3145841  3145873  3145897
3145903  3145913  3145927  3145943  3145981  3145997  3146021  3146023  3146029  3146041
3146069  3146089  3146107  3146131  3146137  3146141  3146149  3146161  3146183  3146203
3146219  3146237  3146243  3146261  3146263  3146279  3146303  3146327  3146359  3146371
3146393  3146399  3146431  3146459  3146461  3146467  3146483  3146497  3146501  3146567
3146573  3146579  3146591  3146599  3146611  3146623  3146629  3146651  3146657  3146659
3146687  3146701  3146707  3146719  3146729  3146743  3146749  3146771  3146809  3146827
3146831  3146833  3146839  3146861  3146863  3146867  3146879  3146909  3146911  3146953
3146987  3146997  3147007  3147017  3147049  3147061  3147077  3147083  3147097  3147121
3147143  3147149  3147161  3147169  3147181  3147197  3147203  3147211  3147223  3147229
3147233  3147239  3147241  3147253  3147259  3147269  3147311  3147323  3147349  3147421
3147427  3147433  3147451  3147467  3147497  3147503  3147563  3147581  3147587  3147589
3147623  3147629  3147649  3147653  3147659  3147679  3147707  3147719  3147721  3147751
3147763  3147773  3147779  3147797  3147843  3147883  3147887  3147889  3147899  3147929
3147953  3147959  3147961  3147967  3147971  3147973  3147983  3148001  3148003  3148031
3148039  3148051  3148097  3148099  3148109  3148121  3148139  3148151  3148157  3148163
3148193  3148231  3148259  3148279  3148283  3148291  3148297  3148303  3148307  3148333
3148337  3148339  3148351  3148361  3148399  3148421  3148459  3148463  3148469  3148477
```

```
3148487  3148499  3148511  3148517  3148543  3148567  3148573  3148583  3148597  3148601
3148603  3148609  3148619  3148627  3148633  3148657  3148667  3148679  3148681  3148687
3148693  3148697  3148741  3148751  3148793  3148801  3148807  3148829  3148867  3148883
3148887  3148913  3148919  3148931  3148939  3148969  3148973  3148987  3148991  3148993
3149009  3149051  3149057  3149059  3149071  3149077  3149123  3149129  3149143  3149173
3149203  3149221  3149249  3149261  3149273  3149309  3149339  3149353  3149357  3149359
3149381  3149387  3149441  3149447  3149467  3149531  3149533  3149537  3149543  3149561
3149563  3149591  3149599  3149609  3149639  3149647  3149659  3149677  3149681  3149683
3149747  3149749  3149753  3149761  3149771  3149791  3149803  3149807  3149813  3149821
3149831  3149837  3149849  3149851  3149897  3149899  3149903  3149911  3149917  3149929
3149959  3149963  3149969  3149983  3149999  3150001  3150031  3150047  3150053  3150097
3150107  3150113  3150131  3150167  3150193  3150197  3150211  3150229  3150233  3150247
3150263  3150271  3150281  3150293  3150311  3150319  3150331  3150337  3150347  3150349
3150377  3150391  3150397  3150421  3150443  3150449  3150451  3150509  3150529  3150547
3150557  3150569  3150571  3150577  3150601  3150611  3150617  3150619  3150643  3150649
3150677  3150683  3150709  3150733  3150761  3150769  3150773  3150781  3150787
3150799  3150817  3150841  3150857  3150869  3150877  3150887  3150893  3150907  3150913
3150919  3150923  3150947  3151007  3151033  3151067  3151097  3151117  3151129  3151133
3151139  3151153  3151157  3151163  3151217  3151229  3151241  3151259  3151319  3151333
3151361  3151373  3151381  3151387  3151399  3151403  3151417  3151439  3151469  3151481
3151487  3151493  3151501  3151507  3151523  3151543  3151559  3151567  3151573  3151583
3151601  3151607  3151609  3151637  3151639  3151649  3151657  3151669  3151699  3151703
3151717  3151741  3151763  3151769  3151781  3151787  3151789  3151829  3151831  3151843
3151847  3151849  3151859  3151861  3151871  3151877  3151879  3151901  3151913  3151927
3151979  3151999  3152003  3152033  3152041  3152047  3152057  3152059  3152077  3152087
3152099  3152101  3152117  3152147  3152153  3152159  3152161  3152167  3152189  3152207
3152221  3152239  3152249  3152251  3152263  3152273  3152321  3152333  3152339  3152341
3152377  3152399  3152441  3152447  3152453  3152467  3152489  3152509  3152519  3152533
3152557  3152573  3152593  3152603  3152609  3152621  3152623  3152627  3152641  3152657
3152671  3152683  3152693  3152707  3152719  3152749  3152753  3152759  3152761  3152767
3152801  3152827  3152833  3152857  3152861  3152867  3152873  3152911  3152927  3152957
3152959  3152977  3152983  3152987  3153011  3153037  3153053  3153071  3153077  3153121
3153131  3153149  3153169  3153173  3153191  3153203  3153209  3153217  3153223  3153281
3153299  3153317  3153331  3153343  3153361  3153377  3153383  3153391  3153401  3153407
3153421  3153439  3153463  3153467  3153481  3153497  3153499  3153529  3153533  3153569
3153571  3153581  3153583  3153587  3153589  3153593  3153629  3153637  3153641  3153643
3153649  3153671  3153707  3153713  3153719  3153739  3153743  3153763  3153767  3153793
3153797  3153809  3153827  3153853  3153863  3153881  3153901  3153907  3153911  3153919
3153923  3153929  3153947  3153949  3153961  3153989  3154001  3154003  3154009  3154031
3154037  3154043  3154079  3154091  3154097  3154103  3154141  3154147  3154153  3154187
3154201  3154211  3154223  3154237  3154241  3154259  3154267  3154271  3154297  3154303
3154321  3154337  3154339  3154357  3154363  3154373  3154379  3154387  3154397  3154409
3154421  3154443  3154449  3154483  3154439  3154441  3154471  3154477  3154489  3154511
3154531  3154573  3154597  3154607  3154631  3154637  3154669  3154693  3154717  3154729
3154757  3154759  3154763  3154769  3154799  3154831  3154849  3154871  3154889  3154903
3154967  3154999  3155003  3155017  3155021  3155029  3155041  3155051  3155057  3155069
3155077  3155137  3155147  3155153  3155203  3155213  3155221  3155239  3155263  3155267
3155281  3155303  3155329  3155333  3155359  3155363  3155371  3155377  3155381  3155389
3155407  3155417  3155429  3155437  3155473  3155513  3155549  3155563  3155573  3155597
3155599  3155609  3155617  3155629  3155651  3155687  3155689  3155699  3155723  3155731
3155741  3155771  3155773  3155777  3155783  3155791  3155819  3155827  3155837  3155857
3155839  3155923  3155939  3155959  3155963  3155987  3155993  3156001  3156019  3156031
3156059  3156061  3156073  3156091  3156103  3156107  3156113  3156121  3156151
3156161  3156187  3156193  3156199  3156227  3156239  3156259  3156277  3156289  3156311
3156317  3156319  3156341  3156347  3156371  3156383  3156397  3156401  3156409  3156427
3156431  3156443  3156449  3156457  3156463  3156469  3156481  3156493  3156511  3156529
3156533  3156541  3156557  3156583  3156599  3156613  3156619  3156649  3156653  3156667
3156683  3156697  3156701  3156709  3156719  3156743  3156763  3156779  3156787  3156809
3156817  3156841  3156871  3156887  3156929  3156941  3156949  3156971  3156977  3156991
3156997  3157001  3157013  3157057  3157061  3157067  3157081  3157109  3157111  3157117
3157127  3157139  3157151  3157163  3157171  3157181  3157199  3157207  3157213  3157229
3157243  3157277  3157283  3157303  3157309  3157313  3157337  3157339  3157367  3157373
3157379  3157391  3157397  3157411  3157417  3157441  3157487  3157501  3157517  3157531
3157541  3157547  3157571  3157573  3157577  3157579  3157589  3157603  3157613  3157639
3157657  3157669  3157703  3157711  3157751  3157777  3157783  3157807  3157811  3157829
3157837  3157853  3157859  3157873  3157879  3157919  3157927  3157949  3157961  3157981
3157991  3157993  3158033  3158041  3158069  3158081  3158087  3158119  3158131  3158143
3158159  3158161  3158203  3158213  3158227  3158257  3158287  3158299  3158339  3158359
3158377  3158381  3158401  3158443  3158473  3158489  3158509  3158513  3158531  3158537
3158557  3158569  3158591  3158609  3158623  3158653  3158671  3158713  3158717  3158759
3158761  3158791  3158819  3158839  3158851  3158873  3158879  3158887  3158891  3158933
3158951  3158963  3158971  3158989  3159001  3159017  3159029  3159031  3159041  3159043
3159061  3159067  3159089  3159133  3159151  3159157  3159181  3159197  3159203  3159209
3159223  3159227  3159239  3159271  3159307  3159313  3159323  3159353  3159361  3159371
3159397  3159413  3159421  3159437  3159439  3159451  3159461  3159469  3159517  3159553
3159557  3159577  3159619  3159623  3159641  3159647  3159649  3159677  3159691  3159697
3159707  3159721  3159733  3159743  3159749  3159781  3159791  3159797  3159803  3159823
3159853  3159859  3159881  3159883  3159889  3159907  3159917  3159929  3159931  3159953
3159973  3159991  3160007  3160009  3160021  3160033  3160037  3160051  3160063  3160103
3160111  3160117  3160121  3160127  3160151  3160153  3160169  3160187  3160193  3160211
3160219  3160247  3160291  3160303  3160307  3160309  3160331  3160363  3160369  3160379
3160393  3160397  3160411  3160427  3160519  3160541  3160559  3160561  3160583  3160601
3160607  3160613  3160621  3160643  3160687  3160699  3160709  3160741  3160747
3160753  3160757  3160769  3160777  3160811  3160841  3160877  3160879  3160909  3160919
3160931  3160933  3160943  3160951  3160957  3160979  3161003  3161009  3161017  3161023
3161057  3161071  3161089  3161107  3161129  3161131  3161149  3161159  3161183  3161209
3161227  3161237  3161273  3161293  3161297  3161299  3161309  3161321  3161329  3161339
3161341  3161351  3161407  3161437  3161449  3161453  3161461  3161479  3161491  3161497
3161519  3161567  3161579  3161593  3161611  3161617  3161629  3161647  3161651  3161681
```

```
3161689  3161693  3161707  3161749  3161773  3161777  3161801  3161819  3161857  3161867
3161887  3161891  3161897  3161953  3161993  3162001  3162011  3162041  3162059  3162067
3162101  3162143  3162149  3162157  3162167  3162253  3162277  3162283  3162317  3162319
3162331  3162347  3162359  3162373  3162413  3162443  3162463  3162473  3162487  3162499
3162503  3162517  3162529  3162539  3162557  3162587  3162611  3162619  3162623  3162637
3162641  3162647  3162659  3162671  3162673  3162703  3162727  3162739  3162743  3162749
3162763  3162767  3162773  3162787  3162811  3162829  3162839  3162847  3162857  3162877
3162883  3162889  3162893  3162941  3162947  3162977  3162989  3163051  3163067  3163087
3163099  3163103  3163133  3163141  3163157  3163159  3163169  3163201  3163231  3163243
3163247  3163249  3163261  3163283  3163297  3163331  3163357  3163361  3163373  3163387
3163409  3163417  3163423  3163427  3163451  3163453  3163469  3163471  3163483  3163487
3163493  3163499  3163529  3163541  3163543  3163549  3163561  3163571  3163577  3163579
3163583  3163591  3163597  3163603  3163609  3163619  3163631  3163637  3163663  3163681
3163687  3163703  3163723  3163733  3163739  3163753  3163763  3163793  3163799  3163801
3163837  3163841  3163879  3163913  3163933  3163957  3163961  3163967  3163969  3163991
3164003  3164053  3164059  3164071  3164081  3164101  3164123  3164137  3164141  3164143
3164167  3164173  3164177  3164191  3164197  3164221  3164233  3164243  3164251  3164269
3164303  3164323  3164333  3164353  3164377  3164401  3164407  3164419  3164429  3164443
3164519  3164521  3164531  3164541  3164543  3164549  3164569  3164591  3164627  3164647
3164653  3164663  3164677  3164687  3164699  3164719  3164723  3164747  3164761  3164779
3164783  3164801  3164803  3164807  3164813  3164827  3164851  3164867  3164893  3164911
3164921  3164923  3164927  3164939  3164951  3164957  3164969  3164981  3164983  3164989
3165011  3165023  3165049  3165059  3165067  3165073  3165079  3165083  3165133  3165139
3165143  3165163  3165181  3165203  3165209  3165223  3165259  3165269  3165271  3165287
3165289  3165299  3165301  3165307  3165311  3165341  3165367  3165373  3165377  3165389
3165397  3165427  3165439  3165479  3165511  3165517  3165521  3165523  3165541  3165557
3165563  3165577  3165581  3165583  3165599  3165601  3165607  3165619  3165649  3165653
3165661  3165667  3165671  3165707  3165709  3165713  3165739  3165769  3165781  3165797
3165829  3165847  3165853  3165857  3165859  3165889  3165907  3165917  3165919  3165941
3165947  3165971  3165991  3166001  3166013  3166039  3166043  3166049  3166067  3166099
3166129  3166151  3166159  3166169  3166171  3166181  3166183  3166187  3166193  3166211
3166213  3166223  3166231  3166253  3166259  3166271  3166277  3166279  3166283  3166297
3166313  3166321  3166333  3166351  3166357  3166363  3166393  3166409  3166411  3166439
3166441  3166447  3166453  3166463  3166469  3166517  3166519  3166523  3166543  3166547
3166549  3166561  3166577  3166613  3166627  3166637  3166643  3166651  3166661  3166679
3166727  3166729  3166733  3166741  3166747  3166753  3166769  3166781  3166817  3166831
3166859  3166871  3166883  3166897  3166903  3166921  3166949  3166951  3166973  3166979
3166987  3166997  3167009  3167033  3167041  3167081  3167107  3167113  3167137  3167141
3167149  3167191  3167201  3167207  3167231  3167233  3167249  3167257  3167267  3167273
3167279  3167317  3167327  3167401  3167407  3167413  3167429  3167443  3167453  3167473
3167497  3167501  3167513  3167519  3167551  3167557  3167561  3167569  3167573  3167581
3167587  3167597  3167617  3167621  3167653  3167657  3167687  3167707  3167741  3167771
3167809  3167833  3167837  3167839  3167849  3167869  3167881  3167897  3167909  3167917
3167929  3167953  3167963  3167987  3167993  3167999  3168007  3168017  3168019  3168023
3168031  3168037  3168097  3168119  3168167  3168203  3168247  3168257  3168259  3168271
3168289  3168313  3168323  3168331  3168343  3168349  3168353  3168367  3168371  3168449
3168461  3168467  3168493  3168509  3168533  3168563  3168617  3168619  3168629  3168653
3168679  3168689  3168701  3168709  3168719  3168721  3168757  3168821  3168827  3168829
3168833  3168863  3168911  3168937  3168941  3168959  3168961  3168973  3168983  3168989
3169007  3169027  3169039  3169043  3169051  3169063  3169093  3169097  3169109  3169121
3169169  3169211  3169217  3169237  3169241  3169261  3169273  3169277  3169289  3169291
3169297  3169307  3169319  3169321  3169337  3169343  3169349  3169357  3169417  3169427
3169433  3169451  3169459  3169477  3169483  3169489  3169501  3169519  3169541  3169547
3169549  3169567  3169583  3169603  3169643  3169681  3169693  3169697  3169721  3169723
3169739  3169741  3169757  3169759  3169783  3169811  3169813  3169819  3169847  3169849
3169867  3169889  3169909  3169919  3169921  3169931  3169949  3169951  3169963  3169981
3170039  3170051  3170053  3170059  3170099  3170107  3170119  3170137  3170149  3170179
3170183  3170201  3170213  3170227  3170249  3170263  3170267  3170281  3170287  3170311
3170327  3170333  3170341  3170357  3170369  3170371  3170383  3170393  3170399  3170413
3170417  3170423  3170437  3170459  3170467  3170521  3170533  3170543  3170579  3170603
3170617  3170621  3170659  3170669  3170681  3170689  3170723  3170737  3170743  3170747
3170753  3170759  3170767  3170807  3170851  3170861  3170879  3170887  3170903  3170911
3170927  3170941  3170953  3170957  3170969  3170983  3171013  3171017  3171029  3171031
3171041  3171053  3171059  3171067  3171071  3171089  3171101  3171107  3171131  3171143
3171187  3171199  3171209  3171251  3171253  3171257  3171277  3171281  3171313  3171323
3171349  3171359  3171383  3171403  3171407  3171409  3171431  3171433  3171439  3171449
3171479  3171481  3171521  3171547  3171559  3171577  3171583  3171593  3171599  3171601
3171611  3171653  3171661  3171667  3171671  3171683  3171697  3171709  3171731  3171733
3171737  3171739  3171743  3171761  3171787  3171793  3171799  3171811  3171823  3171853
3171859  3171863  3171871  3171881  3171883  3171913  3171941  3171943  3171947  3171967
3171977  3171989  3172003  3172007  3172019  3172021  3172027  3172051  3172063  3172073
3172093  3172097  3172123  3172133  3172159  3172163  3172189  3172193  3172201  3172207
3172237  3172243  3172271  3172277  3172289  3172303  3172313  3172327  3172349  3172357
3172363  3172391  3172399  3172423  3172439  3172441  3172451  3172471  3172501  3172529
3172531  3172541  3172553  3172567  3172573  3172577  3172627  3172649  3172667  3172681
3172691  3172699  3172711  3172717  3172721  3172723  3172733  3172747  3172751  3172801
3172811  3172817  3172823  3172831  3172837  3172847  3172879  3172889  3172901  3172907
3172909  3172913  3172921  3172933  3172937  3172957  3172973  3172987  3172991  3172997
3173021  3173029  3173039  3173069  3173081  3173089  3173119  3173189  3173207  3173243
3173249  3173257  3173263  3173273  3173293  3173309  3173311  3173329  3173341  3173353
3173369  3173371  3173381  3173389  3173413  3173419  3173477  3173479  3173497  3173503
3173519  3173537  3173539  3173561  3173579  3173617  3173623  3173633  3173641  3173657
3173669  3173683  3173689  3173699  3173703  3173773  3173777  3173791  3173801
3173803  3173813  3173887  3173899  3173903  3173923  3173927  3173953  3173987  3174001
3174029  3174037  3174043  3174049  3174071  3174091  3174103  3174109  3174163
3174167  3174181  3174187  3174191  3174221  3174247  3174251  3174263  3174287  3174293
3174313  3174317  3174319  3174337  3174361  3174371  3174373  3174401  3174419  3174439
3174467  3174487  3174497  3174499  3174511  3174517  3174533  3174547  3174553  3174571
3174593  3174599  3174607  3174641  3174643  3174649  3174707  3174737  3174739  3174781
```

```
3174793 3174799 3174811 3174817 3174823 3174827 3174841 3174863 3174887 3174889
3174893 3174901 3174911 3174947 3174953 3174959 3174973 3174979 3175001 3175009
3175013 3175021 3175027 3175031 3175037 3175057 3175079 3175093 3175097 3175099
3175121 3175157 3175169 3175259 3175313 3175343 3175351 3175363 3175373 3175391
3175399 3175433 3175441 3175463 3175517 3175531 3175553 3175559 3175561 3175567
3175577 3175591 3175597 3175607 3175619 3175643 3175661 3175687 3175691 3175751
3175763 3175769 3175789 3175801 3175811 3175847 3175853 3175859 3175871 3175891
3175897 3175927 3175943 3175951 3175961 3175967 3175973 3175987 3176003 3176009
3176027 3176053 3176057 3176077 3176099 3176101 3176111 3176113 3176137 3176149
3176171 3176177 3176197 3176203 3176221 3176273 3176293 3176333 3176351 3176377
3176387 3176389 3176419 3176423 3176441 3176443 3176447 3176471 3176479 3176483
3176491 3176513 3176519 3176533 3176597 3176609 3176617 3176627 3176681 3176699
3176717 3176729 3176749 3176759 3176779 3176801 3176809 3176813 3176821 3176837
3176839 3176843 3176851 3176861 3176867 3176869 3176879 3176891 3176897 3176951
3176981 3176989 3176993 3177007 3177017 3177061 3177067 3177077 3177089 3177101
3177107 3177121 3177137 3177149 3177169 3177193 3177203 3177217 3177253 3177257
3177259 3177271 3177281 3177299 3177311 3177329 3177331 3177337 3177343 3177373
3177379 3177397 3177457 3177497 3177511 3177533 3177547 3177553 3177583 3177607
3177613 3177619 3177631 3177637 3177641 3177649 3177659 3177661 3177683 3177689
3177701 3177709 3177737 3177739 3177809 3177847 3177851 3177857 3177901 3177913
3177919 3177943 3177947 3177949 3177953 3177961 3177971 3178003 3178013 3178037
3178051 3178057 3178061 3178079 3178103 3178127 3178141 3178157 3178159 3178169
3178193 3178199 3178207 3178211 3178223 3178237 3178267 3178289 3178297 3178321
3178327 3178363 3178367 3178379 3178381 3178387 3178397 3178403 3178421 3178423
3178433 3178451 3178459 3178489 3178499 3178543 3178583 3178589 3178601 3178619
3178631 3178667 3178691 3178717 3178729 3178733 3178739 3178753 3178759 3178783
3178789 3178793 3178823 3178837 3178841 3178843 3178849 3178873 3178891 3178897
3178907 3178913 3178919 3178927 3178933 3178943 3178961 3178963 3178997 3178999
3179027 3179063 3179087 3179107 3179117 3179147 3179173 3179201 3179227 3179237
3179243 3179257 3179269 3179279 3179287 3179303 3179339 3179387 3179389 3179399
3179413 3179419 3179437 3179461 3179467 3179483 3179489 3179551 3179557 3179587
3179611 3179621 3179651 3179653 3179689 3179717 3179741 3179749 3179789 3179797
3179801 3179831 3179843 3179851 3179863 3179873 3179921 3179941 3179971 3179977
3179983 3179993 3179999 3180007 3180013 3180017 3180029 3180031 3180101 3180103
3180131 3180143 3180167 3180193 3180209 3180223 3180251 3180257 3180271 3180283
3180313 3180319 3180337 3180407 3180413 3180427 3180431 3180451 3180473 3180481
3180491 3180503 3180521 3180523 3180553 3180559 3180563 3180577 3180589 3180599
3180613 3180641 3180677 3180679 3180701 3180707 3180719 3180721 3180757 3180761
3180767 3180769 3180773 3180781 3180787 3180797 3180799 3180803 3180823 3180841
3180869 3180893 3180899 3180907 3180911 3180917 3180929 3180937 3180971 3180979
3180997 3181021 3181033 3181043 3181049 3181051 3181069 3181081 3181109 3181111
3181163 3181169 3181181 3181207 3181229 3181237 3181249 3181253 3181259 3181301
3181327 3181331 3181349 3181351 3181357 3181369 3181391 3181411 3181421 3181447
3181471 3181481 3181489 3181501 3181543 3181573 3181579 3181603 3181609 3181627
3181637 3181657 3181663 3181679 3181681 3181691 3181709 3181727 3181733 3181753
3181757 3181777 3181781 3181813 3181823 3181831 3181837 3181847 3181861 3181877
3181879 3181901 3181921 3181931 3181951 3181973 3181999 3182021 3182029 3182033
3182059 3182071 3182087 3182093 3182107 3182131 3182147 3182159 3182167 3182189
3182191 3182197 3182203 3182219 3182237 3182261 3182293 3182317 3182321 3182341
3182351 3182359 3182369 3182371 3182393 3182411 3182423 3182437 3182467 3182471
3182477 3182479 3182483 3182503 3182507 3182521 3182527 3182537 3182549 3182561
3182573 3182591 3182603 3182609 3182623 3182653 3182657 3182659 3182687 3182713
3182719 3182741 3182743 3182759 3182761 3182771 3182807 3182819 3182827 3182833
3182843 3182849 3182857 3182869 3182911 3182917 3182923 3182939 3182941 3182951
3182957 3183023 3183043 3183067 3183071 3183079 3183083 3183091 3183101 3183107
3183119 3183137 3183139 3183151 3183179 3183197 3183211 3183259 3183277 3183287
3183289 3183293 3183307 3183319 3183331 3183337 3183343 3183347 3183353 3183377
3183391 3183409 3183461 3183491 3183503 3183511 3183541 3183559 3183577 3183589
3183599 3183601 3183611 3183613 3183617 3183623 3183643 3183647 3183671 3183673
3183679 3183689 3183703 3183721 3183727 3183737 3183751 3183757 3183767 3183769
3183799 3183809 3183839 3183857 3183863 3183871 3183877 3183883 3183893 3183899
3183911 3183923 3183941 3183953 3183967 3183977 3183989 3183991 3184003 3184007
3184009 3184057 3184063 3184079 3184091 3184099 3184121 3184123 3184133 3184147
3184157 3184163 3184169 3184177 3184241 3184243 3184273 3184277 3184283 3184303
3184319 3184367 3184393 3184397 3184409 3184469 3184471 3184481 3184483 3184501
3184513 3184529 3184541 3184549 3184561 3184613 3184619 3184633 3184637 3184639
3184651 3184697 3184733 3184747 3184789 3184807 3184859 3184901 3184903 3184919
3184927 3184943 3184963 3184967 3184969 3184999 3185009 3185011 3185023
3185029 3185051 3185081 3185087 3185093 3185101 3185107 3185111 3185123 3185177
3185197 3185207 3185227 3185243 3185251 3185257 3185261 3185263 3185267 3185279
3185317 3185321 3185327 3185363 3185417 3185423 3185437 3185453 3185461 3185473
3185489 3185503 3185513 3185531 3185543 3185551 3185561 3185599 3185627 3185629
3185639 3185669 3185713 3185717 3185723 3185729 3185759 3185773 3185797 3185803
3185821 3185837 3185849 3185857 3185867 3185869 3185873 3185881 3185887 3185899
3185909 3185921 3185929 3185947 3185957 3185981 3186013 3186023 3186037 3186041
3186047 3186061 3186103 3186119 3186133 3186137 3186163 3186187 3186203 3186217
3186223 3186229 3186241 3186263 3186269 3186277 3186283 3186347 3186349 3186367
3186371 3186373 3186389 3186401 3186427 3186437 3186439 3186451 3186461 3186473
3186481 3186517 3186559 3186569 3186571 3186593 3186611 3186637 3186671 3186679
3186683 3186691 3186697 3186709 3186739 3186749 3186761 3186763 3186769 3186791
3186793 3186809 3186877 3186881 3186899 3186901 3186907 3186913 3186917 3186919
3186941 3186959 3186979 3186983 3187021 3187027 3187033 3187039 3187043 3187061
3187073 3187091 3187111 3187127 3187147 3187153 3187159 3187169 3187201 3187213
3187241 3187243 3187267 3187273 3187277 3187309 3187321 3187343 3187397 3187411
3187427 3187441 3187469 3187489 3187507 3187523 3187531 3187537 3187553 3187567
3187601 3187603 3187607 3187609 3187621 3187631 3187643 3187663 3187669 3187703
3187733 3187739 3187753 3187757 3187789 3187787 3187813 3187819 3187831 3187841
3187859 3187879 3187901 3187903 3187907 3187913 3187931 3187939 3187967 3187969
3187973 3187979 3188033 3188077 3188083 3188089 3188093 3188123 3188131 3188161
```

```
3188177 3188221 3188239 3188249 3188261 3188291 3188303 3188323 3188369 3188377
3188387 3188399 3188411 3188413 3188417 3188429 3188431 3188459 3188461 3188473
3188483 3188491 3188501 3188509 3188543 3188551 3188557 3188569 3188573 3188587
3188609 3188617 3188641 3188657 3188659 3188687 3188699 3188701 3188711 3188723
3188761 3188767 3188791 3188797 3188807 3188819 3188821 3188831 3188833 3188879
3188893 3188917 3188929 3188947 3188951 3188953 3188963 3188981 3188987 3188989
3189007 3189029 3189037 3189059 3189061 3189083 3189089 3189119 3189139 3189161
3189167 3189191 3189227 3189229 3189239 3189253 3189259 3189269 3189281 3189287
3189293 3189299 3189301 3189313 3189317 3189331 3189343 3189371 3189377 3189379
3189383 3189409 3189413 3189419 3189427 3189451 3189463 3189491 3189499 3189503
3189517 3189539 3189541 3189547 3189551 3189553 3189581 3189583 3189619 3189647
3189653 3189673 3189679 3189689 3189713 3189731 3189737 3189743 3189779 3189793
3189799 3189811 3189821 3189827 3189833 3189839 3189871 3189889 3189899 3189943
3189961 3189973 3189983 3189997 3190001 3190049 3190051 3190069 3190079 3190091
3190093 3190111 3190129 3190139 3190147 3190151 3190153 3190163 3190181 3190183
3190207 3190211 3190217 3190247 3190249 3190267 3190283 3190289 3190301 3190349
3190393 3190403 3190417 3190457 3190459 3190463 3190519 3190553 3190559 3190567
3190571 3190589 3190591 3190597 3190601 3190637 3190673 3190687 3190697 3190699
3190751 3190753 3190787 3190789 3190819 3190829 3190853 3190871 3190909 3190919
3190949 3190961 3190969 3190979 3190981 3191003 3191017 3191021 3191039 3191059
3191099 3191113 3191117 3191137 3191161 3191179 3191191 3191197 3191207 3191219
3191261 3191263 3191281 3191299 3191303 3191323 3191327 3191329 3191333 3191351
3191381 3191389 3191407 3191413 3191423 3191429 3191437 3191443 3191453 3191471
3191477 3191497 3191527 3191533 3191557 3191561 3191569 3191593 3191603 3191609
3191611 3191621 3191623 3191627 3191681 3191693 3191707 3191719 3191737 3191743
3191759 3191777 3191803 3191821 3191831 3191849 3191861 3191893 3191897 3191899
3191921 3191927 3191987 3191999 3192017 3192037 3192041 3192043 3192047 3192061
3192083 3192113 3192121 3192139 3192143 3192149 3192151 3192157 3192169 3192181
3192187 3192221 3192227 3192251 3192253 3192271 3192289 3192347 3192353 3192389
3192391 3192419 3192433 3192439 3192451 3192457 3192463 3192487 3192491 3192499
3192503 3192521 3192529 3192571 3192577 3192599 3192611 3192613 3192647 3192649
3192661 3192677 3192713 3192727 3192731 3192733 3192737 3192769 3192781 3192803
3192809 3192829 3192877 3192881 3192887 3192901 3192919 3192953 3192961 3192967
3192977 3192983 3192997 3193013 3193027 3193033 3193049 3193081 3193087 3193097
3193129 3193147 3193171 3193187 3193189 3193213 3193237 3193241 3193243 3193249
3193261 3193271 3193283 3193313 3193319 3193327 3193339 3193361 3193363 3193381
3193397 3193423 3193429 3193439 3193447 3193453 3193457 3193469 3193471 3193483
3193511 3193513 3193543 3193549 3193559 3193601 3193627 3193633 3193639 3193643
3193667 3193679 3193703 3193709 3193717 3193747 3193759 3193763 3193769 3193789
3193831 3193871 3193873 3193889 3193901 3193903 3193913 3193921 3193937 3193991
3194017 3194041 3194047 3194053 3194069 3194101 3194111 3194119 3194123 3194129
3194131 3194153 3194159 3194161 3194179 3194183 3194189 3194227 3194273 3194291
3194293 3194353 3194357 3194371 3194377 3194381 3194383 3194393 3194417 3194441
3194459 3194461 3194483 3194497 3194507 3194531 3194533 3194537 3194549 3194551
3194557 3194561 3194563 3194567 3194573 3194593 3194629 3194647 3194651 3194683
3194687 3194743 3194777 3194783 3194797 3194801 3194803 3194813 3194837 3194843
3194879 3194881 3194897 3194923 3194927 3194941 3194951 3194981 3195001 3195019
3195037 3195047 3195079 3195103 3195109 3195121 3195131 3195149 3195151 3195161
3195169 3195217 3195223 3195233 3195259 3195271 3195299 3195319 3195323 3195331
3195347 3195377 3195383 3195397 3195403 3195407 3195427 3195433 3195457 3195461
3195487 3195547 3195557 3195571 3195589 3195593 3195601 3195611 3195623 3195637
3195641 3195649 3195679 3195683 3195691 3195707 3195739 3195761 3195763 3195791
3195809 3195817 3195823 3195839 3195869 3195877 3195893 3195911 3195947 3195961
3195977 3196001 3196021 3196031 3196033 3196087 3196093 3196099 3196111 3196129
3196133 3196157 3196163 3196169 3196183 3196189 3196201 3196211 3196223 3196229
3196231 3196243 3196253 3196283 3196301 3196307 3196321 3196343 3196373 3196381
3196397 3196421 3196429 3196433 3196447 3196469 3196477 3196481 3196489 3196499
3196507 3196511 3196559 3196573 3196607 3196631 3196639 3196649 3196651 3196681
3196691 3196703 3196709 3196723 3196741 3196759 3196783 3196789 3196819 3196847
3196849 3196859 3196871 3196877 3196889 3196903 3196909 3196913 3196927 3196933
3196939 3196951 3196957 3196979 3196981 3197009 3197011 3197027 3197063 3197101
3197107 3197137 3197141 3197143 3197167 3197171 3197177 3197203 3197219 3197231
3197239 3197251 3197273 3197287 3197321 3197323 3197353 3197399 3197401 3197407
3197419 3197449 3197461 3197497 3197501 3197533 3197563 3197573 3197587 3197591
3197599 3197611 3197633 3197641 3197647 3197657 3197659 3197669 3197687 3197693
3197707 3197723 3197767 3197771 3197783 3197797 3197809 3197813 3197837 3197839
3197849 3197863 3197879 3197881 3197891 3197893 3197899 3197903 3197923 3197939
3197983 3198007 3198011 3198031 3198067 3198083 3198109 3198113 3198119 3198131
3198133 3198161 3198163 3198191 3198197 3198199 3198257 3198269 3198277 3198281
3198313 3198319 3198341 3198347 3198353 3198359 3198389 3198407 3198409 3198421
3198427 3198463 3198511 3198523 3198553 3198557 3198581 3198599 3198607 3198617
3198619 3198649 3198653 3198659 3198661 3198667 3198683 3198719 3198721 3198731
3198733 3198739 3198743 3198751 3198799 3198803 3198827 3198829 3198841 3198883
3198887 3198893 3198913 3198919 3198929 3198931 3198953 3198959 3198967 3198977
3198991 3198997 3199011 3199033 3199037 3199051 3199061 3199069 3199099 3199117
3199121 3199127 3199129 3199153 3199171 3199177 3199187 3199223 3199249 3199253
3199291 3199297 3199303 3199307 3199319 3199321 3199327 3199333 3199379 3199387
3199411 3199433 3199453 3199459 3199463 3199489 3199523 3199549 3199561 3199571
3199577 3199589 3199591 3199597 3199601 3199613 3199631 3199643 3199661 3199709
3199741 3199751 3199753 3199787 3199811 3199813 3199837 3199849 3199883 3199883
3199891 3199943 3199951 3199957 3199969 3199979 3199991 3199993 3199997 3200003
3200027 3200033 3200039 3200051 3200069 3200081 3200111 3200117 3200123 3200129
3200137 3200149 3200159 3200177 3200191 3200201 3200203 3200207 3200209 3200213
3200251 3200257 3200279 3200287 3200291 3200297 3200311 3200317 3200333 3200339
3200357 3200359 3200363 3200383 3200401 3200413 3200423 3200429 3200443 3200453
3200459 3200479 3200507 3200543 3200551 3200557 3200579 3200581 3200597 3200599
3200621 3200629 3200663 3200671 3200677 3200689 3200737 3200767 3200773 3200779
3200789 3200801 3200807 3200837 3200839 3200861 3200881 3200891 3200909 3200917
3200929 3200941 3200971 3200983 3200999 3201007 3201043 3201047 3201067 3201103
```

```
3201109  3201113  3201131  3201161  3201167  3201173  3201179  3201181  3201197  3201199
3201229  3201251  3201257  3201259  3201271  3201293  3201299  3201349  3201361  3201371
3201379  3201391  3201409  3201421  3201427  3201431  3201437  3201469  3201487  3201521
3201529  3201551  3201581  3201589  3201617  3201619  3201641  3201643  3201689  3201697
3201713  3201719  3201727  3201743  3201749  3201767  3201799  3201817  3201833
3201839  3201851  3201857  3201893  3201901  3201911  3201917  3201923  3201929  3201931
3201941  3201971  3201973  3201983  3202019  3202027  3202039  3202049  3202079  3202097
3202099  3202117  3202123  3202139  3202153  3202163  3202169  3202181  3202183  3202187
3202201  3202217  3202229  3202231  3202237  3202247  3202249  3202259  3202271  3202301
3202319  3202321  3202327  3202333  3202337  3202349  3202351  3202363  3202369  3202379
3202391  3202411  3202429  3202453  3202471  3202481  3202483  3202501  3202513  3202519
3202523  3202531  3202541  3202603  3202607  3202663  3202669  3202679  3202687  3202691
3202709  3202723  3202733  3202741  3202753  3202763  3202777  3202799  3202841  3202873
3202883  3202891  3202921  3202937  3202939  3202943  3202967  3202993  3203009  3203017
3203041  3203047  3203059  3203063  3203071  3203093  3203099  3203107  3203111  3203117
3203129  3203147  3203149  3203177  3203243  3203251  3203257  3203273  3203281  3203309
3203339  3203341  3203353  3203359  3203407  3203411  3203413  3203443  3203461  3203467
3203477  3203483  3203503  3203507  3203527  3203539  3203549  3203569  3203573  3203579
3203581  3203593  3203621  3203639  3203653  3203657  3203677  3203689  3203729  3203731
3203737  3203741  3203743  3203747  3203771  3203773  3203777  3203789  3203807  3203857
3203861  3203869  3203909  3203917  3203927  3203929  3203933  3203957  3203999  3204011
3204013  3204029  3204073  3204101  3204127  3204137  3204139  3204203  3204209  3204247
3204251  3204259  3204263  3204281  3204283  3204307  3204373  3204389  3204401  3204419
3204451  3204463  3204469  3204473  3204493  3204503  3204511  3204557  3204569  3204581
3204611  3204631  3204647  3204667  3204679  3204689  3204697  3204701  3204739  3204767
3204769  3204779  3204781  3204791  3204809  3204827  3204853  3204871  3204893  3204899
3204907  3204911  3204913  3204917  3204937  3204953  3204961  3204973  3204983  3204991
3205003  3205009  3205039  3205049  3205063  3205087  3205141  3205217  3205219  3205253
3205261  3205289  3205291  3205297  3205331  3205337  3205351  3205361  3205373  3205393
3205403  3205417  3205427  3205429  3205453  3205459  3205507  3205519  3205523  3205589
3205597  3205603  3205627  3205637  3205651  3205681  3205687  3205703  3205751  3205759
3205777  3205789  3205793  3205837  3205849  3205859  3205871  3205879  3205897  3205903
3205907  3205919  3205949  3205957  3205973  3205981  3205997  3205999  3206009  3206029
3206083  3206101  3206143  3206167  3206171  3206179  3206197  3206213  3206219  3206227
3206239  3206243  3206249  3206257  3206261  3206267  3206297  3206303  3206311  3206321
3206339  3206347  3206363  3206377  3206393  3206417  3206429  3206471  3206477  3206509
3206519  3206537  3206543  3206551  3206561  3206563  3206579  3206597  3206633  3206653
3206677  3206701  3206711  3206713  3206717  3206741  3206747  3206767  3206773  3206783
3206789  3206809  3206813  3206837  3206843  3206873  3206881  3206887  3206891  3206893
3206899  3206909  3206911  3206921  3206933  3206939  3206941  3206971  3206993  3207007
3207013  3207019  3207031  3207041  3207047  3207077  3207079  3207091  3207119  3207121
3207133  3207137  3207151  3207157  3207161  3207173  3207187  3207199  3207221  3207227
3207251  3207263  3207277  3207289  3207301  3207329  3207331  3207341  3207361  3207367
3207377  3207397  3207431  3207433  3207437  3207439  3207443  3207461  3207473  3207517
3207527  3207551  3207571  3207583  3207587  3207623  3207629  3207643  3207689  3207691
3207697  3207707  3207727  3207733  3207739  3207749  3207767  3207769  3207779  3207791
3207803  3207817  3207847  3207899  3207901  3207913  3207923  3207943  3207949
3207961  3207983  3207989  3207991  3208001  3208013  3208021  3208039  3208043  3208091
3208103  3208123  3208151  3208193  3208211  3208213  3208253  3208319  3208327  3208333
3208343  3208351  3208367  3208379  3208399  3208421  3208451  3208453  3208459  3208463
3208481  3208483  3208489  3208493  3208501  3208507  3208547  3208553  3208573  3208607
3208613  3208657  3208679  3208687  3208691  3208693  3208721  3208727  3208729  3208769
3208771  3208781  3208787  3208811  3208813  3208817  3208819  3208837  3208847  3208859
3208867  3208873  3208883  3208889  3208913  3208921  3208927  3208939  3208957  3208969
3208979  3208999  3209009  3209033  3209057  3209077  3209083  3209117  3209131  3209147
3209161  3209177  3209183  3209201  3209221  3209231  3209257  3209263  3209267  3209279
3209281  3209293  3209317  3209321  3209329  3209333  3209341  3209363  3209387  3209407
3209419  3209431  3209441  3209449  3209459  3209509  3209513  3209543  3209561  3209579
3209593  3209597  3209611  3209621  3209623  3209641  3209653  3209681  3209683  3209699
3209741  3209761  3209797  3209809  3209813  3209837  3209867  3209887  3209891  3209929
3209933  3209939  3209951  3209953  3209971  3210001  3210017  3210023  3210043  3210049
3210061  3210073  3210089  3210091  3210101  3210113  3210121  3210167  3210199  3210203
3210209  3210211  3210223  3210227  3210239  3210253  3210257  3210277  3210287  3210289
3210293  3210301  3210307  3210313  3210349  3210353  3210359  3210371  3210413  3210419
3210457  3210463  3210469  3210479  3210511  3210517  3210521  3210533  3210551  3210553
3210583  3210589  3210607  3210629  3210631  3210643  3210653  3210661  3210667  3210673
3210703  3210709  3210719  3210743  3210803  3210817  3210821  3210827  3210847  3210859
3210863  3210871  3210877  3210881  3210917  3210929  3210947  3210953  3210959  3211001
3211003  3211009  3211027  3211037  3211049  3211069  3211123  3211127  3211129  3211151
3211163  3211189  3211207  3211213  3211279  3211289  3211291  3211301  3211303  3211309
3211319  3211331  3211357  3211363  3211367  3211393  3211409  3211427  3211433  3211441
3211451  3211457  3211459  3211469  3211499  3211501  3211517  3211529  3211531  3211583
3211601  3211603  3211613  3211639  3211667  3211669  3211673  3211717  3211723  3211739
3211751  3211753  3211757  3211763  3211771  3211777  3211811  3211829  3211841  3211843
3211867  3211883  3211889  3211891  3211909  3211919  3211937  3211939  3211979  3211987
3212009  3212021  3212023  3212029  3212039  3212071  3212087  3212089  3212093  3212101
3212117  3212119  3212123  3212147  3212173  3212191  3212213  3212233  3212257  3212263
3212267  3212317  3212323  3212329  3212347  3212353  3212381  3212389  3212413
3212431  3212453  3212471  3212483  3212509  3212519  3212527  3212551  3212581  3212593
3212597  3212603  3212611  3212639  3212647  3212689  3212723  3212743  3212753  3212777
3212791  3212819  3212849  3212857  3212861  3212863  3212927  3212947  3212953  3212959
3212971  3212977  3212981  3213011  3213029  3213059  3213073  3213083  3213101  3213127
3213131  3213137  3213139  3213149  3213151  3213163  3213233  3213239  3213269  3213277
3213281  3213283  3213349  3213373  3213377  3213383  3213401  3213421  3213439  3213473
3213479  3213499  3213559  3213589  3213599  3213601  3213619  3213631  3213689  3213737
3213757  3213773  3213779  3213803  3213811  3213827  3213829  3213839  3213851  3213853
3213877  3213883  3213893  3213937  3213961  3213979  3214007  3214019  3214027  3214039
3214051  3214061  3214073  3214087  3214091  3214103  3214109  3214129  3214147  3214171
3214187  3214199  3214201  3214213  3214223  3214229  3214231  3214247  3214271  3214279
```

```
3214313  3214327  3214333  3214349  3214369  3214373  3214381  3214399  3214417  3214423
3214427  3214433  3214451  3214481  3214487  3214489  3214493  3214499  3214529  3214531
3214537  3214543  3214559  3214567  3214571  3214573  3214613  3214619  3214633  3214657
3214663  3214681  3214691  3214693  3214703  3214711  3214759  3214763  3214777  3214787
3214811  3214831  3214837  3214867  3214877  3214879  3214891  3214901  3214903  3214909
3214949  3214997  3215011  3215021  3215039  3215071  3215081  3215083  3215099  3215111
3215117  3215119  3215131  3215137  3215141  3215183  3215197  3215207  3215213  3215231
3215257  3215273  3215281  3215291  3215297  3215299  3215309  3215339  3215341  3215347
3215369  3215383  3215417  3215447  3215467  3215473  3215479  3215539  3215543  3215587
3215591  3215593  3215603  3215623  3215629  3215651  3215687  3215711  3215713  3215741
3215743  3215747  3215749  3215759  3215761  3215777  3215783  3215789  3215809  3215819
3215833  3215879  3215893  3215899  3215903  3215911  3215923  3215939  3215963  3215977
3215983  3216007  3216023  3216029  3216041  3216047  3216049  3216053  3216061  3216079
3216089  3216091  3216107  3216119  3216121  3216127  3216131  3216137  3216139  3216197
3216209  3216211  3216221  3216233  3216259  3216277  3216287  3216289  3216331  3216337
3216341  3216359  3216403  3216407  3216413  3216431  3216449  3216457  3216487  3216497
3216509  3216511  3216523  3216559  3216569  3216571  3216583  3216589  3216601  3216611
3216613  3216637  3216649  3216659  3216667  3216671  3216677  3216683  3216691  3216751
3216779  3216781  3216799  3216827  3216853  3216881  3216887  3216911  3216931  3216937
3216949  3216977  3216979  3216991  3217001  3217003  3217007  3217021  3217043  3217069
3217073  3217091  3217121  3217133  3217141  3217157  3217177  3217189  3217219  3217241
3217243  3217297  3217307  3217321  3217337  3217343  3217351  3217363  3217367  3217381
3217391  3217399  3217421  3217429  3217453  3217477  3217481  3217519  3217537  3217547
3217549  3217553  3217559  3217619  3217633  3217663  3217673  3217681  3217693  3217699
3217727  3217741  3217757  3217763  3217771  3217787  3217793  3217807  3217813  3217817
3217829  3217843  3217847  3217849  3217873  3217891  3217931  3217937  3217939  3217969
3217979  3217997  3218003  3218009  3218027  3218041  3218057  3218063  3218069  3218081
3218093  3218119  3218123  3218143  3218153  3218161  3218167  3218191  3218207  3218209
3218221  3218227  3218233  3218261  3218279  3218311  3218317  3218323  3218357  3218399
3218417  3218431  3218437  3218447  3218471  3218473  3218477  3218483  3218503  3218533
3218569  3218587  3218609  3218629  3218639  3218641  3218653  3218659  3218669  3218693
3218707  3218711  3218713  3218717  3218737  3218749  3218767  3218773  3218777  3218791
3218807  3218819  3218837  3218843  3218861  3218893  3218911  3218939  3218953  3218987
3218993  3219019  3219067  3219107  3219121  3219127  3219131  3219157  3219179  3219193
3219199  3219221  3219233  3219247  3219253  3219269  3219289  3219299  3219301  3219311
3219331  3219343  3219371  3219389  3219401  3219421  3219431  3219449  3219457  3219473
3219479  3219497  3219499  3219529  3219553  3219583  3219589  3219631  3219659  3219707
3219757  3219761  3219767  3219781  3219787  3219847  3219857  3219859  3219863  3219889
3219893  3219901  3219917  3219929  3219947  3219959  3219967  3219973  3219989  3220003
3220027  3220033  3220037  3220051  3220081  3220093  3220097  3220117  3220127  3220153
3220169  3220193  3220201  3220211  3220219  3220267  3220271  3220289  3220297
3220307  3220309  3220319  3220351  3220381  3220409  3220411  3220423  3220433  3220447
3220453  3220471  3220499  3220513  3220523  3220543  3220549  3220561  3220577  3220579
3220597  3220601  3220603  3220619  3220627  3220639  3220661  3220663  3220669  3220681
3220699  3220703  3220727  3220771  3220793  3220799  3220801  3220817  3220831  3220849
3220859  3220873  3220879  3220883  3220901  3220907  3220951  3220963  3220967  3221017
3221033  3221063  3221069  3221093  3221107  3221111  3221123  3221129  3221137  3221167
3221189  3221237  3221243  3221261  3221269  3221297  3221299  3221321  3221327  3221353
3221359  3221371  3221401  3221419  3221423  3221429  3221437  3221441  3221443  3221453
3221473  3221497  3221501  3221503  3221509  3221513  3221539  3221549  3221557  3221567
3221573  3221591  3221599  3221629  3221641  3221677  3221707  3221717  3221719  3221731
3221747  3221753  3221761  3221783  3221791  3221807  3221809  3221819  3221899  3221917
3221941  3221951  3221957  3221971  3221983  3222007  3222031  3222041  3222053  3222059
3222083  3222101  3222113  3222137  3222151  3222169  3222187  3222199  3222209  3222211
3222217  3222221  3222223  3222239  3222251  3222253  3222269  3222281  3222287  3222301
3222337  3222379  3222389  3222397  3222409  3222413  3222467  3222487  3222493  3222547
3222551  3222581  3222613  3222617  3222629  3222643  3222677  3222679  3222689  3222697
3222727  3222763  3222773  3222781  3222787  3222797  3222823  3222833  3222841  3222847
3222859  3222871  3222881  3222883  3222899  3222917  3222929  3222937  3222953  3222971
3222991  3223007  3223009  3223043  3223049  3223061  3223063  3223069  3223079  3223109
3223127  3223153  3223159  3223189  3223201  3223211  3223223  3223247  3223261  3223273
3223291  3223309  3223333  3223343  3223357  3223373  3223391  3223399  3223439  3223459
3223463  3223481  3223499  3223501  3223529  3223531  3223537  3223541  3223547  3223567
3223603  3223621  3223631  3223663  3223687  3223709  3223729  3223739  3223741  3223751
3223757  3223769  3223771  3223793  3223799  3223811  3223813  3223817  3223837  3223849
3223853  3223859  3223867  3223873  3223903  3223919  3223943  3223963  3223967  3223991
3224009  3224027  3224047  3224051  3224057  3224077  3224099  3224113  3224119  3224131
3224159  3224161  3224171  3224189  3224197  3224233  3224239  3224251  3224261  3224267
3224293  3224297  3224317  3224321  3224401  3224413  3224447  3224449  3224453  3224461
3224489  3224491  3224497  3224509  3224533  3224557  3224561  3224563  3224567  3224569
3224593  3224647  3224677  3224687  3224707  3224719  3224723  3224731  3224743  3224783
3224789  3224791  3224797  3224801  3224833  3224857  3224861  3224863  3224867  3224869
3224909  3224929  3224971  3224981  3224987  3225011  3225029  3225071  3225073  3225091
3225097  3225127  3225137  3225139  3225143  3225149  3225151  3225161  3225163  3225181
3225191  3225197  3225203  3225227  3225247  3225259  3225283  3225289  3225319  3225323
3225329  3225349  3225371  3225373  3225377  3225389  3225407  3225413  3225433  3225437
3225479  3225487  3225493  3225499  3225503  3225517  3225539  3225647  3225653  3225667
3225671  3225679  3225737  3225749  3225769  3225779  3225787  3225791  3225793  3225821
3225823  3225841  3225847  3225853  3225883  3225889  3225899  3225907  3225947  3225949
3225973  3226001  3226021  3226031  3226079  3226099  3226129  3226133
3226147  3226151  3226159  3226183  3226189  3226207  3226217  3226231  3226241  3226271
3226309  3226313  3226319  3226343  3226357  3226393  3226397  3226403  3226411  3226423
3226441  3226469  3226471  3226477  3226493  3226501  3226529  3226537  3226541  3226543
3226547  3226571  3226579  3226603  3226621  3226631  3226649  3226669  3226679  3226711
3226777  3226781  3226787  3226793  3226829  3226837  3226841  3226843  3226871  3226891
3226901  3226907  3226933  3226939  3226967  3226981  3226997  3226999  3227009  3227027
3227039  3227041  3227129  3227137  3227141  3227143  3227171  3227201  3227207  3227219
3227221  3227239  3227243  3227249  3227261  3227267  3227269  3227293  3227353
3227363  3227369  3227417  3227423  3227431  3227459  3227507  3227509  3227513  3227519
```

```
3227551  3227579  3227597  3227611  3227617  3227639  3227641  3227669  3227681  3227683
3227717  3227723  3227743  3227747  3227761  3227767  3227771  3227789  3227801  3227803
3227821  3227827  3227837  3227839  3227849  3227867  3227879  3227893  3227897  3227899
3227911  3227921  3227933  3227947  3227951  3227957  3227963  3227989  3228023  3228037
3228041  3228047  3228097  3228103  3228107  3228109  3228143  3228149  3228151  3228161
3228163  3228179  3228187  3228191  3228209  3228221  3228223  3228227  3228241  3228259
3228293  3228341  3228343  3228359  3228373  3228403  3228413  3228427  3228437  3228439
3228443  3228457  3228469  3228517  3228527  3228559  3228581  3228593  3228661  3228683
3228703  3228713  3228733  3228737  3228739  3228751  3228769  3228779  3228781  3228811
3228829  3228847  3228857  3228871  3228877  3228887  3228899  3228937  3228943  3228959
3228961  3228977  3228983  3229001  3229003  3229021  3229049  3229067  3229081  3229091
3229097  3229103  3229111  3229117  3229123  3229139  3229141  3229169  3229181  3229189
3229207  3229231  3229241  3229243  3229267  3229271  3229309  3229319  3229321  3229327
3229349  3229351  3229357  3229379  3229381  3229393  3229399  3229403  3229409  3229433
3229463  3229481  3229517  3229531  3229537  3229547  3229559  3229573  3229579  3229621
3229627  3229631  3229649  3229663  3229691  3229703  3229741  3229769  3229781  3229783
3229819  3229823  3229843  3229901  3229909  3229927  3229937  3229951  3229957  3229973
3229987  3230023  3230039  3230047  3230053  3230093  3230099  3230113  3230131  3230141
3230167  3230173  3230179  3230207  3230237  3230243  3230257  3230273  3230299  3230321
3230341  3230347  3230363  3230369  3230371  3230387  3230393  3230401  3230411  3230441
3230449  3230477  3230483  3230489  3230501  3230519  3230531  3230537  3230543  3230567
3230573  3230587  3230593  3230599  3230659  3230671  3230681  3230683  3230707  3230723
3230737  3230749  3230791  3230797  3230809  3230813  3230831  3230849  3230873  3230881
3230957  3230963  3230993  3230999  3231001  3231023  3231029  3231049  3231097  3231101
3231103  3231113  3231119  3231127  3231131  3231143  3231187  3231191  3231211  3231227
3231233  3231259  3231269  3231287  3231301  3231313  3231329  3231331  3231367  3231379
3231401  3231413  3231421  3231427  3231433  3231443  3231451  3231511  3231517  3231521
3231541  3231559  3231563  3231583  3231589  3231593  3231619  3231643  3231667  3231671
3231689  3231703  3231727  3231737  3231757  3231773  3231779  3231791  3231803  3231817
3231821  3231829  3231863  3231869  3231871  3231883  3231931  3231947  3231953  3231971
3231973  3231979  3232003  3232027  3232039  3232043  3232063  3232067  3232081  3232093
3232129  3232157  3232189  3232199  3232231  3232247  3232249  3232279  3232291  3232297
3232301  3232319  3232321  3232373  3232379  3232381  3232387  3232393  3232423  3232429
3232447  3232449  3232469  3232477  3232501  3232507  3232511  3232517  3232529  3232547
3232553  3232589  3232597  3232631  3232637  3232643  3232651  3232657  3232661  3232693
3232699  3232729  3232739  3232741  3232751  3232753  3232769  3232777  3232799  3232813
3232819  3232829  3232837  3232847  3232871  3232883  3232927  3232937  3232961  3232963
3232981  3232987  3232991  3232997  3233011  3233029  3233033  3233047  3233051  3233071
3233081  3233093  3233119  3233149  3233201  3233221  3233227  3233241  3233257  3233261
3233291  3233303  3233311  3233323  3233327  3233333  3233339  3233357  3233359  3233369
3233381  3233387  3233407  3233437  3233441  3233443  3233453  3233491  3233509  3233521
3233533  3233561  3233563  3233599  3233609  3233617  3233623  3233651  3233653  3233663
3233683  3233687  3233719  3233753  3233767  3233771  3233773  3233779  3233803  3233809
3233851  3233863  3233873  3233887  3233897  3233903  3233917  3233939  3233941  3233953
3233959  3233969  3233977  3233983  3233999  3234017  3234031  3234041  3234061  3234079
3234103  3234107  3234163  3234193  3234197  3234221  3234227  3234239  3234241  3234251
3234277  3234299  3234307  3234311  3234317  3234337  3234373  3234377  3234379  3234383
3234463  3234481  3234533  3234551  3234599  3234601  3234611  3234619  3234629  3234653
3234667  3234677  3234683  3234691  3234701  3234713  3234719  3234733  3234767  3234773
3234779  3234787  3234797  3234809  3234821  3234823  3234839  3234857  3234871  3234877
3234887  3234893  3234901  3234919  3234923  3234943  3235007  3235027  3235033  3235039
3235069  3235087  3235093  3235109  3235121  3235123  3235159  3235171  3235181  3235189
3235207  3235217  3235223  3235231  3235247  3235261  3235283  3235289  3235319  3235361
3235367  3235369  3235381  3235403  3235409  3235411  3235451  3235459  3235471  3235483
3235487  3235489  3235493  3235499  3235543  3235553  3235577  3235591  3235601  3235607
3235633  3235649  3235661  3235667  3235691  3235693  3235697  3235711  3235717  3235723
3235741  3235747  3235751  3235753  3235769  3235777  3235789  3235807  3235819  3235829
3235889  3235891  3235901  3235903  3235963  3235979  3235987  3235993  3236041  3236047
3236053  3236063  3236071  3236083  3236117  3236147  3236153  3236173  3236201  3236203
3236221  3236231  3236237  3236243  3236249  3236263  3236267  3236269  3236287  3236291
3236297  3236323  3236329  3236333  3236347  3236357  3236377  3236407  3236411  3236413
3236423  3236437  3236447  3236449  3236459  3236483  3236489  3236503  3236507  3236509
3236531  3236539  3236543  3236557  3236587  3236591  3236621  3236633  3236641  3236683
3236689  3236693  3236699  3236711  3236713  3236729  3236743  3236759  3236773  3236789
3236791  3236861  3236873  3236881  3236903  3236923  3236929  3236957  3236963  3236969
3236977  3236983  3236993  3237023  3237029  3237037  3237053  3237061  3237077  3237079
3237097  3237107  3237109  3237127  3237139  3237161  3237193  3237211  3237217  3237233
3237257  3237263  3237287  3237317  3237329  3237347  3237371  3237379  3237383  3237397
3237413  3237419  3237431  3237433  3237461  3237469  3237491  3237523  3237527  3237539
3237551  3237557  3237583  3237593  3237601  3237607  3237617  3237631  3237643  3237653
3237659  3237677  3237679  3237683  3237709  3237719  3237761  3237781  3237799  3237827
3237851  3237859  3237869  3237889  3237901  3237947  3237967  3237977  3237991  3238019
3238021  3238031  3238033  3238049  3238051  3238093  3238099  3238117  3238121  3238127
3238133  3238153  3238163  3238171  3238181  3238187  3238199  3238219  3238223  3238231
3238237  3238243  3238267  3238273  3238309  3238337  3238349  3238357  3238393  3238397
3238399  3238409  3238421  3238453  3238463  3238471  3238481  3238489  3238507  3238511
3238513  3238537  3238541  3238553  3238567  3238583  3238589  3238591  3238597  3238643
3238649  3238661  3238667  3238679  3238681  3238727  3238751  3238769  3238771  3238801
3238811  3238819  3238831  3238843  3238853  3238861  3238867  3238901  3238913  3238931
3238951  3238957  3238979  3238999  3239003  3239011  3239023  3239051  3239053  3239059
3239077  3239081  3239107  3239141  3239143  3239183  3239191  3239219  3239261  3239267
3239279  3239293  3239303  3239309  3239311  3239347  3239351  3239377  3239393  3239417
3239419  3239429  3239449  3239459  3239473  3239479  3239507  3239539  3239549  3239563
3239591  3239603  3239617  3239627  3239629  3239641  3239647  3239669  3239681  3239693
3239699  3239713  3239723  3239729  3239737  3239759  3239773  3239783  3239791  3239833
3239857  3239927  3239947  3239953  3239963  3239969  3239983  3239989  3240019  3240031
3240037  3240043  3240073  3240101  3240113  3240119  3240131  3240143  3240161  3240163
3240169  3240191  3240197  3240247  3240253  3240269  3240283  3240299  3240311  3240329
3240359  3240371  3240389  3240407  3240409  3240449  3240451  3240467  3240491  3240499
```

```
3240527  3240529  3240551  3240553  3240577  3240581  3240607  3240617  3240619  3240649
3240667  3240683  3240701  3240703  3240707  3240733  3240737  3240739  3240751  3240767
3240841  3240851  3240877  3240911  3240917  3240943  3240947  3240959  3240961  3240967
3240971  3240983  3241093  3241097  3241103  3241123  3241129  3241151  3241159  3241201
3241213  3241219  3241253  3241289  3241309  3241349  3241369  3241379  3241387  3241397
3241409  3241423  3241429  3241451  3241471  3241477  3241487  3241489  3241507  3241523
3241531  3241547  3241549  3241569  3241573  3241627  3241633  3241657  3241669  3241673
3241699  3241739  3241753  3241757  3241759  3241783  3241801  3241807  3241811  3241817
3241853  3241859  3241867  3241877  3241879  3241921  3241933  3241937  3241943  3241961
3241963  3241969  3241981  3242009  3242017  3242023  3242033  3242039  3242047  3242093
3242111  3242137  3242147  3242159  3242191  3242203  3242209  3242221  3242237  3242251
3242263  3242279  3242311  3242339  3242341  3242353  3242363  3242377  3242399  3242417
3242429  3242431  3242479  3242497  3242509  3242531  3242549  3242557  3242573  3242579
3242623  3242627  3242633  3242647  3242677  3242683  3242689  3242741  3242753  3242773
3242777  3242779  3242803  3242831  3242843  3242851  3242881  3242891  3242909  3242923
3242929  3242947  3242959  3242969  3242999  3243007  3243043  3243049  3243061  3243101
3243109  3243113  3243131  3243133  3243143  3243169  3243173  3243181  3243193  3243197
3243221  3243239  3243271  3243293  3243323  3243337  3243341  3243343  3243347  3243349
3243353  3243377  3243397  3243469  3243473  3243497  3243511  3243521  3243523  3243587
3243589  3243613  3243629  3243637  3243649  3243677  3243683  3243697  3243727  3243733
3243739  3243763  3243769  3243781  3243811  3243833  3243839  3243841  3243859  3243881
3243883  3243917  3243931  3243937  3243941  3243967  3243973  3243979  3243983  3244001
3244009  3244013  3244039  3244051  3244067  3244097  3244099  3244147  3244151  3244159
3244187  3244211  3244223  3244237  3244247  3244253  3244261  3244273  3244277  3244291
3244301  3244313  3244327  3244333  3244337  3244361  3244369  3244379  3244391  3244441
3244447  3244463  3244481  3244489  3244499  3244519  3244543  3244559  3244589  3244613
3244621  3244627  3244667  3244691  3244693  3244697  3244711  3244721  3244729  3244741
3244751  3244753  3244837  3244859  3244867  3244889  3244907  3244919  3244921  3244931
3244939  3244951  3244957  3244963  3244981  3245003  3245009  3245023  3245041  3245057
3245063  3245087  3245101  3245107  3245131  3245153  3245171  3245189  3245201  3245213
3245237  3245239  3245251  3245267  3245287  3245299  3245321  3245327  3245357  3245387
3245401  3245423  3245441  3245467  3245471  3245479  3245503  3245537  3245551  3245569
3245573  3245579  3245581  3245587  3245591  3245611  3245659  3245687  3245689  3245701
3245707  3245729  3245747  3245761  3245771  3245779  3245791  3245797  3245833  3245843
3245849  3245857  3245897  3245927  3245939  3245947  3245951  3245959  3245971  3245987
3245989  3246007  3246073  3246077  3246079  3246101  3246107  3246109  3246119  3246127
3246137  3246143  3246157  3246179  3246193  3246203  3246223  3246253  3246259  3246277
3246281  3246301  3246307  3246317  3246319  3246323  3246329  3246367  3246401  3246403
3246407  3246449  3246461  3246469  3246479  3246499  3246527  3246547  3246557  3246559
3246563  3246577  3246583  3246589  3246601  3246613  3246641  3246653  3246671  3246673
3246679  3246689  3246707  3246709  3246721  3246743  3246751  3246767  3246769  3246799
3246857  3246883  3246889  3246899  3246907  3246923  3246931  3246937  3246941  3246977
3246989  3247003  3247007  3247039  3247073  3247087  3247093  3247109  3247121  3247133
3247147  3247171  3247177  3247199  3247207  3247243  3247249  3247253  3247267  3247291
3247297  3247313  3247331  3247337  3247339  3247351  3247367  3247399  3247417  3247421
3247427  3247429  3247451  3247471  3247477  3247483  3247511  3247513  3247523  3247547
3247567  3247571  3247589  3247603  3247609  3247619  3247627  3247631  3247639  3247667
3247679  3247687  3247703  3247759  3247763  3247781  3247789  3247813  3247817  3247819
3247831  3247837  3247847  3247889  3247903  3247921  3247931  3247943  3247961  3247973
3247987  3248017  3248023  3248027  3248033  3248041  3248053  3248081  3248111  3248131
3248137  3248159  3248171  3248197  3248209  3248213  3248237  3248251  3248257  3248269
3248293  3248303  3248327  3248351  3248369  3248387  3248393  3248417  3248431
3248437  3248461  3248467  3248473  3248503  3248549  3248561  3248603  3248617  3248621
3248653  3248657  3248689  3248699  3248701  3248731  3248743  3248759  3248761  3248771
3248797  3248803  3248807  3248827  3248837  3248849  3248879  3248891  3248909  3248939
3248947  3248977  3249013  3249053  3249061  3249083  3249097  3249107  3249109  3249137
3249143  3249149  3249151  3249163  3249179  3249199  3249217  3249221  3249241  3249263
3249277  3249289  3249293  3249313  3249331  3249343  3249391  3249401  3249419  3249443
3249461  3249469  3249481  3249497  3249517  3249527  3249557  3249563  3249581  3249583
3249593  3249613  3249629  3249641  3249643  3249667  3249679  3249707  3249709  3249713
3249733  3249749  3249793  3249809  3249833  3249847  3249859  3249863  3249871  3249889
3249901  3249913  3249919  3249971  3249977  3249991  3249997  3250021  3250063  3250067
3250073  3250081  3250099  3250109  3250123  3250127  3250129  3250147  3250157  3250193
3250207  3250211  3250223  3250229  3250243  3250253  3250259  3250283  3250301  3250333
3250343  3250393  3250421  3250427  3250433  3250441  3250459  3250469  3250477  3250493
3250507  3250549  3250573  3250589  3250591  3250609  3250619  3250627  3250631  3250633
3250651  3250657  3250669  3250673  3250679  3250693  3250711  3250721  3250727  3250747
3250759  3250769  3250789  3250799  3250801  3250811  3250817  3250831  3250837  3250853
3250901  3250913  3250979  3250991  3250993  3250997  3251009  3251023  3251047  3251057
3251069  3251093  3251099  3251111  3251137  3251159  3251173  3251191  3251197  3251207
3251221  3251231  3251241  3251251  3251279  3251317  3251333  3251357  3251363  3251377
3251389  3251399  3251407  3251411  3251447  3251453  3251467  3251473  3251503  3251513
3251519  3251557  3251563  3251593  3251609  3251653  3251659  3251663  3251681  3251693
3251701  3251707  3251723  3251747  3251749  3251761  3251767  3251779  3251783  3251791
3251803  3251839  3251851  3251861  3251863  3251873  3251887  3251891  3251909  3251917
3251923  3251929  3251999  3252017  3252043  3252061  3252091  3252121  3252163
3252169  3252191  3252203  3252209  3252217  3252281  3252283  3252289  3252299  3252307
3252311  3252329  3252349  3252367  3252371  3252377  3252397  3252409  3252413  3252419
3252421  3252443  3252449  3252463  3252467  3252481  3252523  3252527  3252533  3252547
3252577  3252583  3252607  3252617  3252619  3252631  3252643  3252677  3252679  3252713
3252731  3252761  3252773  3252779  3252787  3252827  3252833  3252839  3252859  3252863
3252869  3252871  3252877  3252941  3252943  3252961  3252979  3253013  3253021  3253027
3253043  3253057  3253073  3253091  3253093  3253111  3253123  3253127  3253139  3253147
3253153  3253177  3253219  3253223  3253231  3253241  3253253  3253297  3253301  3253321
3253333  3253343  3253361  3253417  3253463  3253469  3253489  3253493  3253499
3253519  3253529  3253531  3253553  3253559  3253561  3253571  3253631  3253697  3253709
3253711  3253739  3253753  3253777  3253781  3253799  3253813  3253823  3253841  3253871
3253889  3253933  3253937  3253949  3253961  3253963  3253967  3253981  3254023  3254033
3254051  3254057  3254071  3254077  3254081  3254117  3254131  3254137  3254159  3254183
```

```
3254203  3254213  3254219  3254221  3254227  3254231  3254249  3254269  3254281  3254291
3254299  3254323  3254333  3254341  3254353  3254371  3254389  3254393  3254423  3254437
3254441  3254443  3254501  3254509  3254519  3254521  3254527  3254549  3254579  3254591
3254623  3254653  3254683  3254689  3254729  3254731  3254737  3254749  3254759  3254761
3254773  3254789  3254791  3254807  3254809  3254813  3254821  3254843  3254863  3254869
3254893  3254897  3254921  3254929  3254959  3255059  3255071  3255127  3255139  3255157
3255179  3255181  3255193  3255199  3255209  3255227  3255233  3255247  3255269  3255281
3255283  3255293  3255299  3255311  3255319  3255367  3255377  3255379  3255389  3255431
3255433  3255437  3255451  3255467  3255491  3255493  3255529  3255547  3255557  3255559
3255583  3255587  3255601  3255613  3255641  3255649  3255661  3255671  3255683  3255691
3255701  3255739  3255751  3255761  3255767  3255773  3255779  3255781  3255787  3255793
3255803  3255817  3255853  3255871  3255877  3255881  3255893  3255913  3255929  3255943
3255953  3255971  3255979  3255983  3255991  3256021  3256031  3256039  3256051  3256067
3256069  3256081  3256093  3256171  3256181  3256217  3256229  3256247  3256249  3256289
3256303  3256313  3256327  3256361  3256369  3256397  3256399  3256411  3256417  3256423
3256427  3256441  3256453  3256471  3256483  3256499  3256523  3256531  3256549  3256553
3256567  3256573  3256579  3256601  3256621  3256637  3256681  3256697  3256711  3256717
3256723  3256727  3256739  3256789  3256793  3256807  3256817  3256831  3256861  3256871
3256879  3256889  3256927  3256931  3256943  3256951  3256987  3256997  3257011  3257017
3257027  3257063  3257069  3257083  3257101  3257117  3257119  3257129  3257153  3257161
3257167  3257171  3257173  3257179  3257203  3257231  3257239  3257257  3257269  3257291
3257297  3257299  3257347  3257363  3257377  3257381  3257383  3257399  3257413  3257447
3257453  3257497  3257503  3257509  3257519  3257521  3257533  3257549  3257603  3257609
3257623  3257641  3257663  3257671  3257689  3257699  3257707  3257713  3257717  3257719
3257731  3257747  3257753  3257777  3257783  3257791  3257801  3257851  3257861  3257869
3257879  3257923  3257941  3257959  3258001  3258029  3258037  3258041  3258049  3258053
3258077  3258089  3258091  3258097  3258103  3258107  3258113  3258137  3258149  3258161
3258163  3258173  3258217  3258223  3258247  3258293  3258301  3258323  3258349  3258371
3258383  3258389  3258391  3258413  3258421  3258427  3258449  3258461  3258467  3258487
3258491  3258499  3258523  3258529  3258539  3258547  3258551  3258569  3258587  3258601
3258623  3258631  3258649  3258659  3258667  3258691  3258707  3258719  3258727  3258737
3258743  3258763  3258769  3258797  3258863  3258869  3258877  3258889  3258911  3258919
3258929  3258943  3258953  3258977  3258979  3258989  3259001  3259037  3259073  3259097
3259111  3259117  3259177  3259181  3259183  3259199  3259211  3259237  3259253  3259283
3259301  3259369  3259379  3259387  3259429  3259439  3259453  3259457  3259463  3259471
3259481  3259489  3259517  3259519  3259547  3259559  3259561  3259567  3259579  3259601
3259603  3259609  3259639  3259643  3259649  3259661  3259667  3259679  3259703  3259717
3259723  3259727  3259771  3259783  3259793  3259799  3259807  3259829  3259843  3259853
3259891  3259909  3259931  3259933  3259957  3259973  3259979  3259987  3259999  3260003
3260017  3260021  3260027  3260029  3260041  3260051  3260063  3260071  3260087  3260099
3260111  3260113  3260119  3260123  3260129  3260137  3260143  3260149  3260167  3260203
3260207  3260219  3260237  3260261  3260263  3260291  3260293  3260297  3260317  3260321
3260339  3260347  3260371  3260407  3260417  3260423  3260431  3260449  3260473  3260497
3260501  3260513  3260519  3260539  3260563  3260573  3260591  3260597  3260599  3260623
3260629  3260639  3260657  3260659  3260669  3260683  3260701  3260711  3260717  3260729
3260749  3260791  3260809  3260827  3260833  3260839  3260857  3260863  3260867  3260869
3260879  3260891  3260897  3260899  3260903  3260911  3260947  3260969  3260977  3260993
3261007  3261023  3261029  3261113  3261119  3261131  3261133  3261151  3261157  3261173
3261191  3261197  3261211  3261221  3261241  3261257  3261259  3261281  3261299  3261317
3261337  3261353  3261371  3261373  3261397  3261403  3261413  3261437  3261451  3261473
3261481  3261491  3261497  3261523  3261539  3261547  3261551  3261553  3261583  3261617
3261619  3261631  3261641  3261667  3261683  3261703  3261721  3261733  3261737  3261743
3261799  3261803  3261827  3261829  3261857  3261877  3261889  3261899  3261911
3261931  3261961  3261967  3262003  3262009  3262019  3262033  3262081  3262139  3262153
3262157  3262177  3262183  3262187  3262201  3262241  3262277  3262289  3262307  3262313
3262321  3262331  3262339  3262361  3262373  3262387  3262393  3262397  3262403  3262421
3262429  3262439  3262451  3262477  3262499  3262507  3262531  3262559  3262579  3262591
3262601  3262613  3262629  3262673  3262681  3262687  3262717  3262723  3262741  3262769
3262799  3262807  3262823  3262837  3262859  3262879  3262891  3262907  3262913  3262921
3262933  3262949  3262957  3262981  3263009  3263017  3263047  3263053  3263059  3263077
3263081  3263083  3263107  3263119  3263123  3263131  3263137  3263147  3263189  3263191
3263207  3263213  3263219  3263233  3263237  3263243  3263287  3263291  3263297  3263333
3263353  3263389  3263413  3263417  3263431  3263441  3263443  3263453  3263461  3263471
3263483  3263489  3263501  3263509  3263551  3263597  3263599  3263627  3263629  3263639
3263647  3263671  3263693  3263713  3263791  3263797  3263803  3263831  3263833  3263837
3263849  3263851  3263879  3263893  3263917  3263933  3263947  3263957  3263971  3263977
3263989  3263993  3264007  3264011  3264047  3264059  3264071  3264073  3264077  3264101
3264109  3264139  3264161  3264179  3264193  3264199  3264203  3264227  3264241  3264263
3264271  3264301  3264311  3264319  3264343  3264383  3264397  3264403  3264419  3264427
3264449  3264491  3264531  3264533  3264539  3264553  3264571  3264581  3264589  3264593
3264601  3264607  3264631  3264649  3264691  3264719  3264721  3264743  3264749  3264773
3264809  3264817  3264823  3264829  3264839  3264851  3264857  3264887  3264893  3264929
3264931  3264973  3264983  3265007  3265019  3265021  3265049  3265051  3265061  3265063
3265069  3265079  3265099  3265109  3265123  3265127  3265133  3265151  3265153  3265159
3265181  3265183  3265187  3265201  3265247  3265331  3265337  3265349  3265357  3265369
3265373  3265393  3265399  3265403  3265433  3265439  3265441  3265459  3265477  3265541
3265543  3265567  3265573  3265579  3265589  3265597  3265601  3265621  3265627  3265631
3265637  3265643  3265667  3265673  3265679  3265681  3265693  3265711  3265723  3265727
3265733  3265741  3265771  3265799  3265817  3265831  3265837  3265859  3265861  3265877
3265883  3265901  3265903  3265907  3265949  3265957  3265973  3265981  3265987  3265991
3265993  3266041  3266047  3266089  3266113  3266117  3266141  3266143  3266147  3266167
3266177  3266189  3266209  3266243  3266251  3266257  3266269  3266279  3266287  3266293
3266297  3266327  3266339  3266369  3266371  3266381  3266383  3266387  3266399  3266401
3266407  3266447  3266477  3266479  3266503  3266513  3266519  3266521  3266551  3266561
3266573  3266573  3266579  3266587  3266591  3266597  3266611  3266671  3266677  3266681
3266743  3266773  3266779  3266801  3266827  3266831  3266843  3266849  3266881  3266899
3266909  3266927  3266933  3266957  3266999  3267001  3267023  3267029  3267037  3267041
3267067  3267071  3267073  3267109  3267113  3267133  3267139  3267149  3267151  3267157
3267161  3267193  3267197  3267217  3267223  3267233  3267289  3267317  3267337  3267347
```

```
3267353  3267367  3267371  3267377  3267409  3267419  3267427  3267443  3267463  3267497
3267499  3267529  3267547  3267557  3267569  3267571  3267611  3267623  3267631  3267643
3267647  3267697  3267703  3267713  3267727  3267731  3267743  3267763  3267773  3267787
3267799  3267809  3267839  3267841  3267883  3267899  3267907  3267931  3267937  3267941
3267947  3267967  3267973  3268009  3268021  3268037  3268049  3268061  3268079  3268103
3268121  3268127  3268141  3268157  3268159  3268163  3268183  3268207  3268211  3268219
3268229  3268241  3268253  3268297  3268303  3268337  3268339  3268373  3268379  3268381
3268417  3268439  3268451  3268453  3268477  3268481  3268483  3268487  3268493  3268519
3268523  3268537  3268549  3268571  3268591  3268621  3268649  3268651  3268667  3268687
3268693  3268711  3268723  3268739  3268753  3268781  3268787  3268799  3268813  3268819
3268823  3268831  3268847  3268849  3268861  3268871  3268891  3268901  3268907  3268927
3268943  3268961  3268963  3269009  3269011  3269029  3269039  3269047  3269069  3269081
3269111  3269143  3269153  3269177  3269207  3269213  3269239  3269267  3269303  3269327
3269339  3269351  3269363  3269369  3269377  3269393  3269401  3269407  3269437  3269443
3269447  3269449  3269503  3269509  3269531  3269537  3269561  3269639  3269641  3269659
3269681  3269683  3269687  3269699  3269701  3269711  3269713  3269719  3269723  3269753
3269789  3269803  3269807  3269809  3269821  3269863  3269897  3269921  3269923  3269927
3269963  3269969  3269977  3269983  3269989  3269993  3270031  3270049  3270061  3270073
3270083  3270101  3270121  3270139  3270143  3270187  3270191  3270199  3270217  3270227
3270229  3270247  3270251  3270257  3270277  3270287  3270313  3270343  3270373  3270383
3270419  3270427  3270431  3270433  3270457  3270461  3270497  3270499  3270517  3270523
3270569  3270571  3270581  3270583  3270599  3270607  3270629  3270643  3270653  3270667
3270671  3270691  3270697  3270719  3270727  3270733  3270737  3270769  3270797  3270803
3270821  3270829  3270833  3270863  3270889  3270893  3270913  3270923  3270929  3270959
3270961  3270973  3270979  3271031  3271033  3271039  3271043  3271049  3271069  3271109
3271117  3271127  3271157  3271159  3271189  3271217  3271223  3271253  3271271  3271277
3271321  3271357  3271381  3271391  3271441  3271447  3271459  3271481  3271487  3271493
3271501  3271507  3271517  3271537  3271547  3271561  3271571  3271601  3271657  3271661
3271669  3271673  3271679  3271687  3271691  3271703  3271711  3271733  3271753  3271813
3271817  3271823  3271843  3271861  3271883  3271889  3271903  3271927  3271967  3271981
3271991  3271993  3272011  3272023  3272029  3272033  3272039  3272051  3272053  3272069
3272077  3272083  3272089  3272119  3272147  3272173  3272197  3272201  3272207  3272221
3272231  3272239  3272303  3272309  3272323  3272327  3272359  3272369  3272377  3272383
3272387  3272419  3272431  3272443  3272459  3272473  3272491  3272527  3272531  3272543
3272567  3272587  3272609  3272629  3272651  3272669  3272677  3272681  3272707  3272713
3272723  3272729  3272741  3272747  3272779  3272783  3272791  3272813  3272837  3272839
3272849  3272861  3272869  3272873  3272879  3272881  3272897  3272903  3272963  3272999
3273001  3273013  3273019  3273043  3273059  3273079  3273089  3273091  3273119  3273139
3273157  3273169  3273181  3273191  3273209  3273211  3273217  3273233  3273239  3273269
3273287  3273307  3273323  3273329  3273343  3273349  3273371  3273397  3273407  3273421
3273449  3273467  3273493  3273527  3273533  3273581  3273593  3273601  3273617  3273661
3273671  3273703  3273737  3273761  3273763  3273773  3273791  3273799  3273811  3273827
3273857  3273869  3273899  3273901  3273937  3273961  3273967  3273983  3273989  3274001
3274009  3274031  3274039  3274049  3274057  3274069  3274079  3274097  3274111  3274121
3274151  3274153  3274157  3274169  3274171  3274177  3274199  3274207  3274231  3274237
3274247  3274253  3274261  3274273  3274277  3274279  3274283  3274291  3274331  3274333
3274343  3274363  3274367  3274379  3274391  3274409  3274451  3274457  3274459  3274511
3274529  3274543  3274553  3274589  3274619  3274633  3274637  3274643  3274657  3274681
3274697  3274699  3274721  3274729  3274753  3274757  3274771  3274801  3274811  3274813
3274823  3274841  3274847  3274867  3274879  3274891  3274903  3274961  3274963  3274987
3275003  3275021  3275053  3275081  3275085  3275093  3275113  3275117  3275137
3275143  3275173  3275179  3275189  3275191  3275197  3275213  3275219  3275221  3275249
3275309  3275317  3275357  3275359  3275369  3275381  3275401  3275411  3275413  3275417
3275471  3275473  3275479  3275483  3275497  3275501  3275507  3275513  3275537  3275551
3275567  3275599  3275603  3275609  3275627  3275633  3275651  3275663  3275669  3275687
3275689  3275693  3275703  3275719  3275731  3275737  3275743  3275749  3275803  3275819
3275843  3275851  3275873  3275891  3275897  3275903  3275911  3275929  3275933  3275939
3275953  3275957  3275963  3275969  3275991  3275989  3276029  3276061  3276067  3276071
3276073  3276083  3276103  3276107  3276109  3276131  3276139  3276149  3276157  3276181
3276199  3276241  3276253  3276263  3276271  3276277  3276283  3276293  3276319  3276331
3276337  3276347  3276349  3276397  3276401  3276409  3276457  3276479  3276487  3276491
3276503  3276509  3276517  3276521  3276523  3276527  3276551  3276587  3276599  3276601
3276617  3276641  3276653  3276667  3276671  3276677  3276719  3276773  3276781  3276799
3276803  3276809  3276817  3276827  3276847  3276853  3276881  3276883  3276941  3276961
3276967  3276983  3276989  3276997  3277003  3277009  3277019  3277031  3277033  3277049
3277051  3277067  3277081  3277091  3277093  3277097  3277111  3277117  3277121  3277123
3277133  3277181  3277217  3277279  3277283  3277297  3277301  3277321  3277327  3277343
3277363  3277387  3277397  3277399  3277403  3277409  3277411  3277427  3277457  3277471
3277501  3277507  3277513  3277531  3277541  3277543  3277559  3277579  3277597  3277601
3277607  3277613  3277621  3277643  3277649  3277657  3277687  3277691  3277693  3277697
3277699  3277721  3277763  3277777  3277801  3277811  3277817  3277829  3277843  3277853
3277903  3277913  3277943  3277949  3277951  3277961  3277969  3277987  3277993  3278021
3278039  3278047  3278053  3278057  3278063  3278071  3278081  3278083  3278087  3278101
3278113  3278117  3278129  3278147  3278173  3278179  3278207  3278221  3278227  3278239
3278257  3278267  3278269  3278291  3278299  3278321  3278329  3278333  3278339  3278347
3278369  3278371  3278381  3278389  3278413  3278423  3278437  3278461  3278477  3278519
3278521  3278531  3278551  3278557  3278573  3278599  3278609  3278629  3278651  3278669
3278683  3278699  3278701  3278741  3278753  3278761  3278771  3278783  3278789  3278791
3278797  3278809  3278819  3278831  3278833  3278837  3278867  3278917  3278927  3278939
3278969  3278981  3278983  3278989  3278999  3279007  3279037  3279127  3279131
3279173  3279187  3279193  3279197  3279209  3279251  3279257  3279281  3279293  3279329
3279337  3279361  3279377  3279391  3279401  3279431  3279439  3279491  3279499  3279503
3279511  3279517  3279541  3279559  3279607  3279641  3279673  3279677  3279709  3279737
3279743  3279763  3279767  3279781  3279803  3279811  3279833  3279841  3279949  3279953
3279973  3279977  3279983  3280009  3280033  3280037  3280061  3280073  3280111  3280127
3280139  3280157  3280181  3280187  3280213  3280229  3280231  3280279  3280289  3280297
3280307  3280313  3280339  3280357  3280363  3280367  3280373  3280391  3280423  3280441
3280463  3280469  3280471  3280477  3280481  3280489  3280493  3280499  3280517  3280523
3280549  3280561  3280579  3280583  3280591  3280603  3280621  3280639  3280649  3280657
```

```
3280661  3280663  3280681  3280687  3280691  3280703  3280747  3280757  3280759  3280793
3280801  3280811  3280867  3280877  3280889  3280897  3280903  3280957  3280961  3280967
3280969  3281011  3281021  3281039  3281041  3281059  3281063  3281077  3281081  3281087
3281093  3281101  3281137  3281141  3281149  3281171  3281183  3281207  3281209  3281233
3281269  3281273  3281293  3281297  3281303  3281351  3281359  3281363  3281393  3281401
3281417  3281431  3281441  3281449  3281461  3281483  3281497  3281503  3281507  3281513
3281533  3281543  3281557  3281563  3281573  3281627  3281657  3281687  3281689  3281693
3281701  3281723  3281767  3281777  3281783  3281791  3281821  3281827  3281849  3281857
3281909  3281911  3281933  3281981  3281987  3282029  3282047  3282067  3282089  3282101
3282121  3282127  3282143  3282161  3282163  3282203  3282211  3282281  3282283  3282289
3282341  3282379  3282407  3282427  3282437  3282443  3282451  3282457  3282463  3282469
3282473  3282493  3282509  3282511  3282523  3282533  3282551  3282563  3282571  3282599
3282641  3282667  3282673  3282689  3282691  3282703  3282709  3282731  3282739  3282743
3282757  3282761  3282779  3282791  3282811  3282833  3282841  3282847  3282857  3282889
3282893  3282901  3282907  3282913  3282977  3283001  3283009  3283019  3283031  3283037
3283051  3283069  3283079  3283087  3283097  3283103  3283127  3283129  3283139  3283141
3283151  3283153  3283199  3283213  3283271  3283283  3283289
3283307  3283327  3283337  3283339  3283349  3283361  3283381  3283393  3283421  3283429
3283433  3283451  3283463  3283471  3283483  3283507  3283517  3283529  3283531  3283541
3283543  3283571  3283573  3283589  3283619  3283627  3283633  3283663  3283681  3283711
3283717  3283727  3283747  3283769  3283783  3283807  3283817  3283823  3283829  3283831
3283837  3283853  3283879  3283897  3283901  3283909  3283913  3283921  3283927  3283939
3283967  3283981  3283991  3283993  3283997  3284003  3284023  3284033  3284041  3284063
3284069  3284137  3284143  3284161  3284173  3284191  3284201  3284243  3284257  3284263
3284269  3284293  3284311  3284339  3284341  3284363  3284371  3284441  3284443  3284447
3284461  3284467  3284483  3284507  3284521  3284537  3284539  3284599  3284639  3284647
3284657  3284669  3284681  3284693  3284713  3284719  3284737  3284747  3284753  3284761
3284767  3284779  3284807  3284833  3284839  3284843  3284851  3284857  3284867  3284873
3284909  3284921  3284923  3284947  3284959  3284989  3284999  3285019  3285041  3285083
3285089  3285103  3285127  3285167  3285169  3285173  3285181  3285197  3285203  3285229
3285239  3285259  3285263  3285283  3285299  3285319  3285353  3285367  3285377  3285407
3285419  3285421  3285427  3285431  3285433  3285449  3285467  3285509  3285517  3285559
3285571  3285577  3285593  3285647  3285677  3285679  3285683  3285697  3285703  3285713
3285719  3285739  3285749  3285823  3285827  3285839  3285851  3285857  3285889  3285901
3285923  3285929  3285943  3285959  3285979  3285983  3285991  3286013  3286021  3286043
3286057  3286067  3286091  3286097  3286111  3286121  3286133  3286139  3286141  3286177
3286181  3286207  3286247  3286249  3286267  3286277  3286301  3286307  3286319  3286331
3286369  3286391  3286399  3286427  3286429  3286441  3286453  3286471  3286501  3286511
3286513  3286529  3286531  3286553  3286561  3286567  3286571  3286573  3286579  3286603
3286607  3286643  3286649  3286667  3286669  3286687  3286691  3286693  3286697  3286721
3286739  3286771  3286781  3286799  3286807  3286823  3286841  3286849  3286873  3286891
3286909  3286937  3286939  3286951  3286957  3286991  3286993  3287003  3287017  3287027
3287029  3287033  3287047  3287051  3287059  3287071  3287077  3287083  3287099  3287101
3287143  3287149  3287177  3287189  3287261  3287267  3287293  3287309  3287311  3287327
3287329  3287359  3287429  3287441  3287447  3287461  3287467  3287483  3287491  3287497
3287507  3287521  3287533  3287563  3287567  3287573  3287587  3287593  3287617  3287629
3287639  3287653  3287677  3287699  3287719  3287747  3287761  3287771  3287773  3287777
3287803  3287807  3287813  3287819  3287821  3287833  3287861  3287871  3287887  3287897
3287899  3287917  3287941  3287957  3287959  3287989  3288023  3288029  3288037  3288053
3288091  3288097  3288113  3288143  3288151  3288163  3288169  3288179  3288193  3288209
3288269  3288317  3288319  3288343  3288347  3288353  3288359  3288367  3288371  3288403
3288419  3288433  3288437  3288451  3288457  3288473  3288479  3288499  3288503  3288529
3288541  3288547  3288559  3288587  3288611  3288613  3288619  3288631  3288673  3288707
3288713  3288721  3288737  3288751  3288757  3288763  3288781  3288787  3288797  3288811
3288823  3288827  3288833  3288841  3288847  3288889  3288899  3288911  3288917  3288947
3288949  3288953  3288983  3288997  3289001  3289019  3289037  3289043  3289067  3289087
3289123  3289141  3289159  3289163  3289171  3289229  3289241  3289243  3289259  3289277
3289283  3289291  3289327  3289331  3289361  3289369  3289387  3289393  3289397  3289423
3289439  3289459  3289463  3289493  3289513  3289519  3289523  3289549  3289567  3289571
3289579  3289591  3289597  3289613  3289631  3289651  3289661  3289691  3289697  3289709
3289711  3289723  3289739  3289753  3289757  3289777  3289787  3289817  3289843  3289849
3289861  3289877  3289879  3289889  3289931  3289933  3289961  3289967  3289969  3289981
3289987  3289997  3290009  3290029  3290039  3290041  3290051  3290057  3290083  3290087
3290093  3290107  3290117  3290149  3290153  3290159  3290167  3290171  3290179  3290201
3290207  3290213  3290237  3290239  3290257  3290263  3290267  3290281  3290321  3290323
3290341  3290347  3290377  3290389  3290411  3290431  3290453  3290459  3290473  3290509
3290519  3290533  3290549  3290561  3290579  3290593  3290641  3290647  3290653  3290657
3290663  3290671  3290689  3290699  3290711  3290723  3290737  3290773  3290789
3290797  3290801  3290803  3290821  3290827  3290831  3290849  3290873  3290879  3290887
3290927  3290977  3290983  3291017  3291031  3291073  3291083  3291109  3291137
3291143  3291163  3291179  3291221  3291227  3291259  3291271  3291283  3291293  3291311
3291317  3291331  3291341  3291359  3291361  3291367  3291371  3291373  3291383  3291391
3291401  3291437  3291457  3291481  3291493  3291511  3291539  3291569  3291581  3291583
3291593  3291647  3291653  3291661  3291667  3291679  3291683  3291689  3291707  3291709
3291721  3291733  3291749  3291751  3291763  3291787  3291791  3291793  3291817
3291823  3291839  3291881  3291901  3291907  3291917  3291919  3291923  3291929  3291943
3291947  3291949  3291979  3291991  3292019  3292027  3292031  3292039  3292043  3292049
3292063  3292087  3292103  3292129  3292147  3292183  3292213  3292217  3292229  3292241
3292249  3292279  3292309  3292327  3292337  3292343  3292349  3292351  3292369  3292391
3292403  3292421  3292433  3292439  3292451  3292463  3292489  3292501  3292507  3292511
3292537  3292561  3292579  3292589  3292609  3292633  3292637  3292673  3292687  3292691
3292697  3292717  3292753  3292759  3292769  3292787  3292801  3292813  3292843  3292873
3292907  3292931  3292969  3292973  3292981  3293009  3293021  3293029  3293033  3293047
3293057  3293113  3293123  3293167  3293177  3293183  3293197  3293221  3293231  3293233
3293239  3293281  3293287  3293299  3293309  3293351  3293363  3293387  3293399  3293419
3293429  3293447  3293449  3293453  3293497  3293503  3293527  3293551  3293561  3293603
3293621  3293639  3293651  3293681  3293683  3293701  3293737  3293749  3293789  3293813
3293819  3293839  3293861  3293863  3293867  3293879  3293881  3293893  3293923  3293957
3293959  3293977  3293987  3293989  3293993  3294007  3294013  3294041  3294077  3294079
```

```
3294097  3294103  3294127  3294143  3294169  3294173  3294191  3294233  3294251  3294259
3294281  3294287  3294293  3294299  3294301  3294337  3294349  3294373  3294397  3294407
3294437  3294449  3294461  3294479  3294491  3294493  3294503  3294509  3294523  3294527
3294541  3294553  3294593  3294631  3294659  3294667  3294677  3294679  3294689  3294701
3294749  3294751  3294763  3294769  3294791  3294817  3294827  3294829  3294833  3294857
3294871  3294881  3294899  3294901  3294913  3294917  3294919  3294931  3294953  3294979
3294983  3294989  3295007  3295013  3295027  3295069  3295111  3295121  3295199  3295213
3295223  3295249  3295267  3295277  3295291  3295307  3295309  3295321  3295333  3295337
3295339  3295343  3295351  3295361  3295363  3295367  3295441  3295447  3295451  3295471
3295483  3295489  3295507  3295541  3295543  3295547  3295549  3295559  3295561  3295583
3295597  3295657  3295661  3295673  3295679  3295709  3295711  3295723  3295729  3295741
3295751  3295753  3295757  3295771  3295783  3295793  3295811  3295843  3295883  3295913
3295939  3295967  3295991  3296003  3296021  3296039  3296047  3296077  3296081  3296089
3296093  3296119  3296129  3296143  3296149  3296207  3296213  3296221  3296231  3296233
3296263  3296281  3296287  3296311  3296339  3296347  3296369  3296387  3296393  3296399
3296417  3296437  3296473  3296477  3296479  3296497  3296537  3296551  3296561  3296569
3296581  3296593  3296597  3296599  3296603  3296661  3296647  3296651  3296669  3296693
3296701  3296707  3296723  3296729  3296731  3296771  3296773  3296779  3296789  3296791
3296801  3296831  3296837  3296849  3296863  3296897  3296903  3296983  3296999  3297011
3297017  3297029  3297037  3297043  3297059  3297061  3297071  3297083  3297101  3297103
3297109  3297113  3297143  3297149  3297163  3297187  3297193  3297199  3297209  3297251
3297263  3297293  3297299  3297313  3297319  3297323  3297331  3297353  3297367  3297383
3297397  3297421  3297433  3297449  3297457  3297461  3297467  3297479  3297493  3297499
3297509  3297517  3297521  3297527  3297557  3297571  3297587  3297601  3297611  3297617
3297647  3297683  3297691  3297731  3297733  3297739  3297743  3297769  3297781  3297787
3297803  3297823  3297841  3297857  3297859  3297869  3297871  3297883  3297907  3297911
3297919  3297937  3297937  3297989  3298003  3298007  3298019  3298033  3298049  3298091
3298103  3298111  3298117  3298129  3298151  3298181  3298189  3298193  3298201  3298247
3298259  3298261  3298279  3298297  3298313  3298367  3298387  3298403  3298411  3298423
3298441  3298481  3298483  3298511  3298517  3298523  3298543  3298577  3298579  3298597
3298613  3298619  3298621  3298627  3298639  3298643  3298657  3298681  3298699  3298717
3298739  3298769  3298807  3298811  3298817  3298843  3298847  3298849  3298853  3298861
3298871  3298877  3298891  3298907  3298909  3298921  3298979  3299017  3299033  3299057
3299059  3299081  3299117  3299123  3299129  3299137  3299161  3299183  3299201  3299213
3299239  3299251  3299267  3299269  3299273  3299279  3299291  3299297  3299323  3299357
3299363  3299383  3299389  3299417  3299459  3299477  3299489  3299503  3299509  3299537
3299563  3299579  3299617  3299633  3299641  3299651  3299677  3299687  3299689  3299761
3299789  3299797  3299827  3299837  3299851  3299869  3299927  3299941  3299957  3299969
3300001  3300007  3300019  3300029  3300041  3300061  3300071  3300097  3300103  3300127
3300133  3300139  3300149  3300169  3300179  3300181  3300191  3300203  3300211  3300217
3300223  3300263  3300301  3300313  3300331  3300337  3300343  3300359  3300389  3300413
3300419  3300443  3300449  3300491  3300503  3300529  3300559  3300571  3300593  3300613
3300679  3300683  3300691  3300697  3300721  3300749  3300757  3300767  3300779  3300811
3300821  3300823  3300853  3300859  3300863  3300883  3300887  3300917  3300923  3300943
3300949  3300953  3300959  3300961  3300967  3300971  3300989  3301019  3301027  3301037
3301073  3301091  3301093  3301147  3301163  3301169  3301187  3301217  3301229  3301237
3301267  3301303  3301321  3301343  3301357  3301369  3301379  3301391  3301409  3301427
3301471  3301477  3301481  3301499  3301511  3301513  3301541  3301561  3301579  3301591
3301601  3301603  3301631  3301637  3301663  3301681  3301709  3301733  3301751  3301759
3301777  3301787  3301789  3301799  3301807  3301819  3301861  3301901  3301919  3301931
3301943  3301957  3301981  3301999  3302003  3302011  3302069  3302071  3302081  3302083
3302107  3302119  3302129  3302137  3302149  3302153  3302161  3302177  3302183  3302291
3302191  3302197  3302203  3302207  3302209  3302237  3302251  3302261  3302269  3302291
3302303  3302329  3302339  3302353  3302359  3302389  3302393  3302413  3302449  3302459
3302473  3302477  3302503  3302527  3302531  3302557  3302567  3302569  3302603  3302617
3302681  3302683  3302693  3302711  3302749  3302797  3302807  3302813  3302821  3302843
3302851  3302857  3302861  3302891  3302917  3302921  3302927  3302939  3302987  3302993
3303011  3303023  3303059  3303109  3303127  3303137  3303149  3303161  3303163  3303173
3303193  3303199  3303229  3303259  3303263  3303269  3303271  3303281  3303319  3303337
3303341  3303343  3303347  3303353  3303371  3303373  3303379  3303383  3303401  3303403
3303409  3303439  3303449  3303499  3303523  3303533  3303539  3303551  3303557  3303557
3303571  3303607  3303617  3303623  3303637  3303667  3303673  3303679  3303683  3303691
3303731  3303737  3303737  3303749  3303799  3303809  3303827  3303829  3303857  3303871
3303889  3303893  3303953  3303961  3303977  3304003  3304033  3304061  3304079  3304087
3304097  3304099  3304123  3304129  3304151  3304153  3304181  3304219  3304237  3304243
3304261  3304277  3304297  3304291  3304297  3304319  3304331  3304349  3304361  3304363
3304369  3304397  3304403  3304451  3304487  3304489  3304493  3304513  3304529  3304541
3304589  3304597  3304601  3304607  3304627  3304643  3304649  3304657  3304661  3304669
3304673  3304687  3304751  3304757  3304759  3304787  3304813  3304823  3304843  3304849
3304883  3304943  3304871  3304883  3304891  3304897  3304901  3304913  3304933  3304943
3304949  3304957  3304963  3304981  3304991  3305009  3305011  3305017  3305033  3305039
3305047  3305063  3305111  3305117  3305119  3305147  3305149  3305171  3305179  3305201
3305209  3305227  3305233  3305249  3305257  3305273  3305279  3305287  3305299  3305303
3305317  3305329  3305377  3305381  3305389  3305417  3305447  3305459  3305473  3305479
3305483  3305501  3305503  3305509  3305527  3305557  3305581  3305587  3305591  3305611
3305657  3305671  3305693  3305699  3305717  3305719  3305749  3305759  3305761  3305777
3305779  3305821  3305833  3305851  3305873  3305879  3305891  3305917  3305923  3305927
3305941  3305959  3305963  3305983  3305989  3305999  3306001  3306011  3306013  3306049
3306059  3306091  3306131  3306137  3306151  3306157  3306169  3306179  3306217  3306223
3306253  3306269  3306271  3306287  3306293  3306341  3306343  3306349  3306371  3306387
3306379  3306397  3306427  3306451  3306461  3306467  3306469  3306473  3306481  3306487
3306509  3306521  3306529  3306533  3306539  3306547  3306557  3306559  3306587  3306593
3306599  3306601  3306607  3306623  3306629  3306631  3306643  3306647  3306659  3306679
3306701  3306707  3306713  3306731  3306763  3306791  3306799  3306811  3306839  3306847
3306853  3306859  3306869  3306883  3306907  3306911  3306913  3306943  3306971  3306977
3306991  3307033  3307067  3307099  3307141  3307153  3307201  3307211  3307219  3307223
3307229  3307267  3307277  3307279  3307289  3307307  3307327  3307351  3307361  3307373
3307379  3307399  3307417  3307439  3307457  3307459  3307487  3307489  3307523  3307529
3307559  3307567  3307573  3307609  3307613  3307621  3307627  3307631  3307643  3307663
```

```
3307679  3307693  3307721  3307727  3307739  3307747  3307753  3307781  3307789  3307807
3307831  3307853  3307859  3307873  3307891  3307903  3307939  3307973  3308027  3308057
3308077  3308083  3308087  3308089  3308093  3308153  3308161  3308203  3308209  3308237
3308243  3308267  3308273  3308303  3308309  3308321  3308323  3308341  3308359  3308369
3308381  3308399  3308423  3308447  3308449  3308467  3308483  3308497  3308507  3308509
3308519  3308521  3308531  3308533  3308551  3308563  3308567  3308587  3308593  3308609
3308611  3308621  3308623  3308633  3308653  3308663  3308677  3308713  3308719  3308749
3308759  3308777  3308783  3308791  3308801  3308819  3308867  3308881  3308887  3308891
3308917  3308921  3308923  3308927  3308939  3308951  3308953  3308957  3308983  3308989
3308993  3309001  3309011  3309013  3309037  3309041  3309071  3309077  3309083  3309091
3309107  3309121  3309139  3309143  3309149  3309167  3309179  3309193  3309209  3309221
3309227  3309247  3309253  3309269  3309301  3309307  3309347  3309353  3309359  3309367
3309377  3309379  3309413  3309437  3309461  3309463  3309469  3309473  3309491  3309499
3309511  3309517  3309541  3309563  3309571  3309583  3309623  3309637  3309659  3309661
3309673  3309689  3309701  3309703  3309721  3309739  3309749  3309751  3309763  3309809
3309821  3309827  3309829  3309833  3309847  3309851  3309869  3309919  3309923  3309961
3309979  3309991  3309997  3310049  3310061  3310063  3310079  3310117  3310127  3310129
3310133  3310141  3310169  3310171  3310187  3310193  3310201  3310207  3310253  3310261
3310267  3310271  3310283  3310297  3310301  3310357  3310387  3310399  3310423  3310429
3310451  3310453  3310457  3310469  3310507  3310547  3310577  3310589  3310609  3310639
3310663  3310667  3310691  3310717  3310721  3310739  3310753  3310757  3310771  3310777
3310789  3310793  3310799  3310819  3310829  3310837  3310849  3310859  3310861  3310877
3310891  3310927  3310933  3310987  3310999  3311027  3311029  3311041  3311051  3311059
3311081  3311089  3311101  3311117  3311123  3311131  3311137  3311173  3311177  3311179
3311183  3311213  3311219  3311233  3311251  3311299  3311303  3311309  3311317  3311359
3311411  3311411  3311419  3311431  3311437  3311467  3311501  3311509  3311519  3311521
3311527  3311531  3311579  3311587  3311591  3311593  3311603  3311621  3311639  3311641
3311647  3311657  3311669  3311683  3311717  3311723  3311741  3311797  3311807  3311809
3311813  3311827  3311831  3311837  3311849  3311851  3311881  3311897  3311899  3311911
3311921  3311927  3311929  3311933  3311941  3311951  3311969  3311983  3311999  3312013
3312019  3312031  3312041  3312053  3312077  3312091  3312097  3312107  3312109  3312139
3312151  3312163  3312167  3312173  3312181  3312187  3312191  3312193  3312209  3312217
3312227  3312307  3312347  3312367  3312383  3312389  3312451  3312457  3312503  3312511
3312527  3312539  3312563  3312571  3312577  3312581  3312587  3312599  3312601  3312623
3312653  3312679  3312689  3312697  3312719  3312731  3312733  3312737  3312761  3312767
3312781  3312811  3312817  3312823  3312853  3312863  3312881  3312887  3312893  3312899
3312919  3312929  3312941  3313003  3313043  3313067  3313099  3313109  3313117  3313139
3313153  3313159  3313183  3313199  3313213  3313223  3313237  3313241  3313253  3313259
3313267  3313291  3313319  3313327  3313361  3313363  3313369  3313399  3313411  3313417
3313421  3313433  3313439  3313477  3313481  3313483  3313489  3313561  3313571  3313573
3313577  3313591  3313601  3313631  3313637  3313649  3313663  3313669  3313697  3313699
3313727  3313741  3313747  3313763  3313769  3313777  3313787  3313823  3313837  3313841
3313867  3313873  3313879  3313883  3313901  3313903  3313913  3313939  3313943  3313949
3313957  3313969  3313987  3314009  3314027  3314029  3314039  3314119  3314137  3314141
3314147  3314159  3314173  3314203  3314219  3314237  3314239  3314243  3314257  3314261
3314281  3314309  3314329  3314347  3314383  3314387  3314401  3314407  3314411  3314413
3314429  3314447  3314459  3314471  3314477  3314501  3314503  3314513  3314527  3314537
3314579  3314593  3314639  3314651  3314657  3314669  3314681  3314687  3314699  3314713
3314747  3314767  3314791  3314819  3314837  3314879  3314893  3314917  3314929  3314933
3314939  3314951  3314953  3314963  3314977  3314981  3315001  3315007  3315031  3315041
3315049  3315071  3315073  3315079  3315107  3315121  3315127  3315131  3315133  3315137
3315173  3315209  3315211  3315223  3315271  3315281  3315283  3315287  3315317  3315337
3315353  3315353  3315371  3315373  3315379  3315401  3315407  3315409  3315421  3315439
3315457  3315461  3315469  3315491  3315509  3315511  3315523  3315577  3315581  3315593
3315619  3315643  3315649  3315661  3315679  3315701  3315721  3315727  3315737  3315757
3315761  3315769  3315779  3315817  3315827  3315857  3315863  3315877  3315883  3315929
3315943  3315971  3315989  3316007  3316057  3316067  3316069  3316073  3316087  3316129
3316147  3316151  3316153  3316169  3316189  3316199  3316223  3316253  3316259  3316267
3316277  3316283  3316297  3316321  3316337  3316361  3316363  3316399  3316403  3316427
3316441  3316451  3316457  3316459  3316471  3316483  3316487  3316517  3316519  3316529
3316541  3316549  3316553  3316559  3316571  3316589  3316601  3316603  3316627  3316637
3316639  3316661  3316667  3316673  3316681  3316699  3316711  3316723  3316799  3316813
3316823  3316843  3316847  3316867  3316879  3316897  3316903  3316919  3316927  3316949
3316961  3316967  3316981  3316987  3316993  3317009  3317011  3317021  3317033  3317117
3317123  3317147  3317177  3317179  3317183  3317189  3317201  3317203  3317231  3317233
3317239  3317243  3317257  3317263  3317273  3317291  3317299  3317357  3317417  3317423
3317441  3317449  3317507  3317521  3317537  3317551  3317557  3317563  3317569  3317581
3317591  3317599  3317603  3317663  3317669  3317683  3317701  3317707  3317711  3317719
3317779  3317807  3317813  3317849  3317857  3317869  3317879  3317887  3317891  3317903
3317933  3317947  3318001  3318011  3318013  3318031  3318063  3318067  3318083  3318097
3318109  3318137  3318143  3318149  3318157  3318167  3318173  3318193  3318221  3318223
3318229  3318239  3318241  3318251  3318283  3318299  3318307  3318319  3318323  3318373
3318377  3318389  3318409  3318421  3318431  3318433  3318449  3318479  3318503  3318533
3318547  3318569  3318571  3318599  3318613  3318629  3318631  3318671  3318683  3318703
3318709  3318719  3318769  3318793  3318803  3318817  3318841  3318853  3318857  3318911
3318919  3318929  3318943  3318947  3318983  3318989  3319003  3319009  3319031  3319039
3319051  3319067  3319081  3319103  3319109  3319117  3319123  3319133  3319157  3319171
3319177  3319207  3319219  3319229  3319249  3319289  3319313  3319333  3319361  3319363
3319391  3319411  3319417  3319439  3319447  3319489  3319493  3319499  3319513  3319531
3319541  3319553  3319577  3319579  3319583  3319597  3319609  3319619  3319621  3319627
3319633  3319637  3319639  3319703  3319727  3319733  3319741  3319763  3319781  3319807
3319819  3319829  3319831  3319837  3319861  3319919  3319931  3319937  3319951  3319957
3319963  3319969  3319997  3320029  3320059  3320071  3320081  3320089  3320099  3320101
3320129  3320137  3320143  3320189  3320197  3320201  3320237  3320263  3320281  3320299
3320309  3320311  3320341  3320351  3320357  3320363  3320371  3320377  3320381  3320431
3320477  3320509  3320519  3320521  3320539  3320543  3320557  3320561  3320567  3320591
3320623  3320651  3320663  3320683  3320699  3320749  3320753  3320767  3320771  3320773
3320777  3320791  3320803  3320827  3320833  3320869  3320873  3320881  3320887  3320909
3320939  3320969  3320971  3321037  3321049  3321053  3321077  3321089  3321107  3321113
```

```
3321119 3321151 3321163 3321179 3321203 3321217 3321229 3321233 3321251 3321259
3321271 3321289 3321293 3321301 3321317 3321319 3321323 3321401 3321403 3321419
3321421 3321467 3321469 3321491 3321497 3321503 3321517 3321529 3321541 3321551
3321553 3321559 3321583 3321589 3321607 3321611 3321623 3321629 3321653 3321667
3321677 3321679 3321709 3321733 3321737 3321739 3321757 3321761 3321763 3321781
3321841 3321859 3321887 3321889 3321911 3321917 3321937 3321947 3321949 3321973
3321977 3322001 3322003 3322009 3322013 3322027 3322043 3322049 3322069 3322073
3322091 3322117 3322129 3322133 3322139 3322141 3322147 3322159 3322171 3322181
3322213 3322217 3322219 3322237 3322261 3322273 3322279 3322337 3322343 3322351
3322357 3322367 3322369 3322379 3322393 3322399 3322421 3322433 3322439 3322441
3322507 3322513 3322519 3322523 3322537 3322547 3322577 3322607 3322621 3322639
3322643 3322679 3322687 3322699 3322721 3322723 3322727 3322747 3322757 3322771
3322783 3322793 3322807 3322831 3322843 3322861 3322867 3322873 3322877 3322889
3322897 3322901 3322903 3322919 3322931 3322961 3322981 3322987 3323003 3323027
3323029 3323051 3323059 3323069 3323093 3323113 3323129 3323137 3323141 3323183
3323189 3323191 3323207 3323213 3323239 3323249 3323311 3323399 3323447 3323473
3323497 3323543 3323549 3323557 3323561 3323563 3323597 3323611 3323623 3323633
3323641 3323659 3323681 3323693 3323711 3323729 3323731 3323783 3323797 3323833
3323843 3323861 3323867 3323869 3323921 3323923 3323933 3323939 3323941 3323977
3323989 3324017 3324019 3324047 3324049 3324053 3324077 3324089 3324091 3324103
3324109 3324127 3324133 3324137 3324143 3324151 3324179 3324187 3324193 3324199
3324203 3324227 3324247 3324257 3324283 3324301 3324311 3324323 3324329 3324341
3324353 3324359 3324361 3324371 3324389 3324407 3324421 3324437 3324457 3324467
3324491 3324499 3324509 3324521 3324523 3324527 3324551 3324569 3324577 3324593
3324599 3324611 3324613 3324619 3324623 3324641 3324661 3324679 3324689 3324697
3324701 3324703 3324721 3324751 3324757 3324779 3324793 3324817 3324847 3324863
3324913 3324929 3324941 3324947 3324961 3324983 3324989 3324991 3325027 3325033
3325039 3325043 3325051 3325067 3325093 3325097 3325099 3325121 3325123 3325159
3325177 3325187 3325211 3325219 3325237 3325243 3325249 3325253 3325261 3325279
3325291 3325303 3325313 3325321 3325327 3325331 3325349 3325351 3325373 3325381
3325393 3325403 3325429 3325433 3325447 3325457 3325519 3325541 3325549 3325573
3325631 3325643 3325657 3325681 3325687 3325709 3325717 3325733 3325739 3325747
3325759 3325769 3325787 3325789 3325793 3325801 3325811 3325831 3325849 3325859
3325867 3325877 3325901 3325913 3325937 3325943 3325957 3325963 3325991 3325997
3326009 3326023 3326047 3326051 3326069 3326107 3326111 3326117 3326119 3326123
3326129 3326153 3326171 3326173 3326177 3326201 3326209 3326249 3326287 3326291
3326299 3326327 3326347 3326363 3326377 3326383 3326399 3326413 3326417 3326423
3326431 3326443 3326471 3326489 3326507 3326549 3326567 3326569 3326573 3326581
3326599 3326621 3326623 3326627 3326629 3326663 3326669 3326671 3326711 3326717
3326753 3326761 3326773 3326783 3326821 3326831 3326857 3326861 3326887 3326891
3326899 3326933 3326971 3326977 3327011 3327031 3327043 3327061 3327089
3327091 3327101 3327167 3327169 3327177 3327179 3327193 3327227 3327229 3327239
3327251 3327253 3327281 3327283 3327329 3327347 3327349 3327353 3327361 3327371
3327377 3327397 3327403 3327407 3327409 3327419 3327441 3327497 3327517 3327523
3327551 3327607 3327629 3327637 3327673 3327677 3327697 3327707 3327713 3327749
3327761 3327763 3327773 3327787 3327787 3327803 3327811 3327813 3327839
3327859 3327871 3327901 3327911 3327931 3327941 3327949 3327967 3327991 3328007
3328019 3328037 3328043 3328049 3328063 3328111 3328121 3328133 3328139 3328153
3328163 3328177 3328201 3328207 3328219 3328219 3328223 3328231 3328271 3328291
3328319 3328327 3328373 3328387 3328393 3328411 3328427 3328433 3328441 3328459
3328463 3328469 3328487 3328499 3328513 3328519 3328531 3328541 3328561 3328573
3328597 3328601 3328621 3328679 3328697 3328723 3328729 3328739 3328747 3328763
3328777 3328783 3328789 3328799 3328807 3328837 3328849 3328879 3328883 3328891
3328901 3328903 3328907 3328909 3328961 3328967 3328979 3328987 3328993 3329003
3329023 3329033 3329041 3329083 3329087 3329101 3329129 3329141 3329147 3329173
3329177 3329201 3329231 3329233 3329251 3329257 3329267 3329281 3329303 3329309
3329327 3329341 3329353 3329363 3329377 3329387 3329423 3329437 3329449 3329453
3329477 3329483 3329507 3329531 3329539 3329551 3329561 3329567 3329581 3329587
3329609 3329611 3329629 3329633 3329653 3329657 3329659 3329707 3329713 3329717
3329723 3329737 3329743 3329747 3329759 3329761 3329789 3329801 3329819 3329839
3329861 3329873 3329881 3329899 3329923 3329933 3329939 3329981 3329993 3329999
3330013 3330053 3330083 3330121 3330133 3330139 3330167 3330169 3330179 3330211
3330227 3330247 3330251 3330281 3330287 3330289 3330293 3330311 3330323 3330391
3330401 3330409 3330421 3330427 3330461 3330473 3330493 3330497 3330511 3330527
3330557 3330577 3330583 3330611 3330617 3330641 3330659 3330667 3330697 3330721
3330731 3330739 3330763 3330783 3330787 3330809 3330863 3330869 3330899 3330907
3330913 3330923 3330941 3330949 3330959 3330961 3330967 3330973 3330979 3330983
3331001 3331033 3331037 3331051 3331079 3331087 3331091 3331093 3331109 3331133
3331151 3331157 3331169 3331171 3331177 3331187 3331189 3331217 3331247 3331267
3331301 3331309 3331319 3331331 3331333 3331357 3331381 3331399 3331409 3331423
3331451 3331453 3331457 3331463 3331487 3331499 3331519 3331561 3331577 3331621
3331639 3331649 3331651 3331661 3331673 3331733 3331747 3331753 3331763 3331799
3331829 3331831 3331837 3331891 3331921 3331931 3331943 3331951 3331957 3331963
3331981 3331997 3332039 3332041 3332053 3332059 3332083 3332089 3332093 3332107
3332137 3332149 3332167 3332191 3332207 3332213 3332233 3332267 3332279 3332281
3332291 3332297 3332321 3332339 3332341 3332363 3332383 3332387 3332389 3332393
3332411 3332431 3332437 3332471 3332489 3332501 3332503 3332507 3332551 3332579
3332591 3332611 3332617 3332687 3332713 3332737 3332741 3332743 3332761 3332807
3332827 3332831 3332843 3332863 3332869 3332897 3332921 3332929 3332933 3332957
3332963 3332983 3333007 3333019 3333047 3333053 3333061 3333067 3333097 3333103
3333119 3333131 3333133 3333163 3333199 3333203 3333217 3333221 3333233 3333251
3333257 3333263 3333277 3333283 3333301 3333307 3333311 3333313 3333331 3333373
3333383 3333391 3333397 3333401 3333419 3333431 3333433 3333439 3333459 3333469
3333481 3333497 3333509 3333511 3333527 3333593 3333601 3333611 3333619 3333641
3333653 3333679 3333697 3333703 3333727 3333739 3333749 3333761 3333767 3333773
3333787 3333809 3333823 3333893 3333901 3333907 3333917 3333923 3333931
3333943 3333961 3333971 3333977 3334049 3334087 3334099 3334109 3334117 3334127
3334141 3334147 3334153 3334171 3334189 3334223 3334237 3334271 3334273 3334297
3334301 3334307 3334337 3334339 3334351 3334361 3334393 3334399 3334411 3334451
```

```
3334493 3334531 3334543 3334549 3334559 3334561 3334579 3334613 3334651 3334663
3334673 3334679 3334711 3334733 3334753 3334787 3334789 3334801 3334811 3334813
3334829 3334841 3334843 3334879 3334889 3334901 3334939 3334943 3334963 3334967
3334973 3334987 3334999 3335021 3335047 3335071 3335081 3335099 3335113 3335119
3335141 3335149 3335159 3335173 3335201 3335221 3335239 3335249 3335251 3335257
3335263 3335273 3335303 3335351 3335359 3335369 3335389 3335413 3335471 3335489
3335503 3335531 3335533 3335537 3335561 3335567 3335573 3335581 3335593 3335597
3335599 3335611 3335623 3335627 3335669 3335671 3335677 3335701 3335707 3335737
3335743 3335747 3335749 3335753 3335771 3335777 3335789 3335803 3335807 3335819
3335821 3335833 3335867 3335903 3335923 3335947 3335951 3335953 3335971 3335999
3336017 3336071 3336089 3336101 3336103 3336161 3336167 3336181 3336209 3336227
3336239 3336269 3336271 3336283 3336299 3336317 3336323 3336341 3336379 3336383
3336409 3336451 3336461 3336467 3336469 3336481 3336491 3336511 3336523 3336547
3336563 3336569 3336583 3336601 3336617 3336629 3336643 3336649 3336659 3336661
3336677 3336689 3336713 3336727 3336731 3336779 3336797 3336803 3336829 3336833
3336887 3336899 3336917 3336923 3336937 3336941 3336967 3336979 3337007 3337013
3337021 3337043 3337051 3337063 3337073 3337109 3337111 3337121 3337123 3337129
3337133 3337171 3337177 3337189 3337199 3337211 3337237 3337261 3337283 3337307
3337309 3337319 3337333 3337339 3337351 3337361 3337379 3337381 3337391 3337393
3337403 3337409 3337421 3337427 3337447 3337469 3337489 3337501 3337561 3337577
3337583 3337591 3337601 3337603 3337619 3337637 3337643 3337669 3337709 3337721
3337723 3337757 3337759 3337777 3337823 3337837 3337847 3337861 3337879 3337883
3337889 3337891 3337903 3337909 3337927 3337931 3337937 3337951 3337969 3337973
3337979 3337991 3338003 3338017 3338033 3338039 3338051 3338057 3338089 3338117
3338119 3338131 3338143 3338147 3338189 3338201 3338213 3338249 3338263 3338329
3338339 3338351 3338369 3338371 3338407 3338429 3338431 3338437 3338441 3338501
3338513 3338527 3338537 3338549 3338557 3338581 3338593 3338597 3338603 3338609
3338617 3338627 3338639 3338651 3338689 3338701 3338717 3338719 3338747 3338759
3338767 3338773 3338791 3338807 3338849 3338861 3338873 3338879 3338893 3338897
3338899 3338903 3338921 3338939 3338963 3338971 3338977 3338981 3338989 3339019
3339029 3339043 3339047 3339067 3339113 3339121 3339131 3339137 3339143 3339151
3339169 3339179 3339221 3339229 3339247 3339257 3339283 3339313 3339317 3339319
3339331 3339353 3339367 3339373 3339403 3339407 3339431 3339449 3339451 3339467
3339493 3339499 3339503 3339521 3339527 3339529 3339563 3339571 3339587 3339601
3339607 3339617 3339629 3339643 3339647 3339653 3339659 3339673 3339709 3339751
3339797 3339857 3339859 3339863 3339881 3339887 3339893 3339913 3339937 3339943
3339949 3339967 3339977 3339979 3339989 3340009 3340021 3340039 3340061 3340079
3340091 3340093 3340097 3340123 3340153 3340159 3340163 3340189 3340193 3340201
3340217 3340223 3340291 3340297 3340301 3340303 3340327 3340331 3340339 3340349
3340367 3340387 3340391 3340411 3340417 3340427 3340429 3340453 3340459 3340487
3340499 3340507 3340511 3340531 3340549 3340577 3340609 3340633 3340657 3340669
3340679 3340691 3340697 3340703 3340709 3340723 3340747 3340769 3340811 3340817
3340837 3340847 3340849 3340853 3340859 3340871 3340873 3340877 3340879 3340907
3340913 3340919 3340927 3340933 3340949 3340951 3340961 3340969 3340979 3341021
3341029 3341033 3341053 3341059 3341069 3341077 3341083 3341099 3341101 3341113
3341161 3341167 3341171 3341191 3341203 3341227 3341237 3341251 3341267 3341269
3341281 3341291 3341309 3341311 3341323 3341341 3341363 3341369 3341389 3341399
3341411 3341413 3341419 3341449 3341483 3341489 3341501 3341531 3341539 3341557
3341561 3341579 3341599 3341603 3341609 3341617 3341627 3341669 3341677 3341689
3341719 3341731 3341743 3341753 3341761 3341773 3341783 3341801 3341813 3341827
3341839 3341857 3341879 3341881 3341903 3341953 3341959 3341971 3341993 3342023
3342037 3342067 3342071 3342077 3342091 3342103 3342113 3342133 3342137 3342139
3342151 3342167 3342179 3342193 3342223 3342239 3342257 3342263 3342277 3342293
3342299 3342301 3342307 3342323 3342331 3342341 3342371 3342379 3342413 3342419
3342439 3342457 3342473 3342481 3342487 3342491 3342503 3342509 3342529 3342539
3342541 3342553 3342571 3342583 3342587 3342589 3342601 3342611 3342623 3342629
3342667 3342671 3342673 3342679 3342683 3342709 3342719 3342721 3342733 3342737
3342793 3342809 3342821 3342847 3342877 3342883 3342887 3342901 3342943 3342959
3342961 3342973 3342979 3343013 3343037 3343051 3343097 3343111 3343127 3343129
3343141 3343147 3343217 3343229 3343243 3343247 3343261 3343273 3343279 3343289
3343309 3343337 3343343 3343369 3343387 3343391 3343397 3343409 3343421 3343433
3343447 3343453 3343469 3343481 3343499 3343511 3343531 3343547 3343553 3343559
3343607 3343631 3343649 3343651 3343661 3343663 3343693 3343699 3343733 3343741
3343751 3343757 3343771 3343777 3343789 3343817 3343831 3343853 3343861 3343871
3343889 3343891 3343897 3343957 3344021 3344027 3344041 3344113 3344119 3344147
3344161 3344213 3344227 3344261 3344267 3344273 3344279 3344287 3344303 3344317
3344321 3344333 3344339 3344351 3344371 3344377 3344387 3344389 3344401 3344417
3344423 3344431 3344441 3344449 3344489 3344491 3344501 3344503 3344507 3344519
3344521 3344527 3344543 3344557 3344587 3344611 3344617 3344629 3344633 3344647
3344681 3344701 3344711 3344717 3344723 3344749 3344791 3344819 3344827 3344833
3344897 3344899 3344909 3344921 3344941 3344951 3344977 3344987 3345029 3345047
3345071 3345091 3345119 3345127 3345137 3345161 3345169 3345187 3345191 3345193
3345217 3345229 3345233 3345247 3345253 3345259 3345263 3345317 3345323 3345361
3345383 3345401 3345409 3345431 3345439 3345451 3345457 3345467 3345479 3345491
3345493 3345509 3345523 3345541 3345581 3345593 3345607 3345611 3345659 3345679
3345703 3345709 3345721 3345739 3345757 3345763 3345781 3345829 3345841 3345849
3345857 3345877 3345893 3345907 3345917 3345929 3345931 3345941 3345961 3345967
3345989 3346003 3346019 3346039 3346061 3346099 3346111 3346139 3346151 3346157
3346199 3346219 3346237 3346241 3346253 3346267 3346279 3346307 3346309 3346327
3346333 3346351 3346363 3346383 3346403 3346417 3346457 3346463 3346471 3346493
3346507 3346517 3346531 3346537 3346547 3346549 3346559 3346589 3346591 3346601
3346621 3346633 3346649 3346663 3346669 3346709 3346711 3346723 3346751 3346757
3346781 3346801 3346817 3346843 3346849 3346867 3346877 3346883 3346901 3346913
3346921 3346927 3346951 3346961 3346963 3346979 3346999 3347033 3347053 3347081
3347087 3347161 3347171 3347231 3347243 3347251 3347257 3347261 3347263 3347273
3347291 3347297 3347299 3347303 3347327 3347329 3347341 3347369 3347413 3347417
3347423 3347431 3347441 3347447 3347459 3347471 3347503 3347543 3347549 3347551
3347573 3347599 3347633 3347647 3347651 3347653 3347671 3347677 3347683 3347689
3347699 3347713 3347749 3347753 3347767 3347779 3347831 3347833 3347843 3347867
```

```
3347873  3347879  3347887  3347891  3347893  3347909  3347921  3347947  3347959  3347983
3347987  3347989  3348001  3348011  3348013  3348017  3348029  3348043  3348053  3348061
3348067  3348083  3348097  3348113  3348119  3348131  3348157  3348223  3348227  3348239
3348263  3348283  3348287  3348307  3348349  3348353  3348361  3348377  3348391  3348407
3348413  3348419  3348461  3348479  3348481  3348493  3348497  3348533  3348551  3348557
3348563  3348571  3348577  3348581  3348599  3348613  3348623  3348641  3348647  3348661
3348673  3348707  3348733  3348767  3348773  3348809  3348811  3348817  3348827  3348841
3348853  3348887  3348893  3348913  3348929  3348937  3348953  3348973  3348977  3348991
3349001  3349013  3349033  3349037  3349039  3349057  3349061  3349069  3349097  3349103
3349109  3349121  3349127  3349139  3349163  3349183  3349201  3349211  3349217
3349231  3349259  3349273  3349279  3349309  3349321  3349343  3349349  3349393  3349403
3349417  3349427  3349429  3349439  3349447  3349469  3349501  3349517  3349543  3349579
3349597  3349601  3349603  3349613  3349637  3349639  3349649  3349667  3349673  3349691
3349699  3349727  3349733  3349763  3349769  3349771  3349777  3349783  3349793  3349807
3349817  3349847  3349859  3349861  3349873  3349903  3349919  3349921  3349939  3349999
3350021  3350027  3350029  3350107  3350131  3350143  3350147  3350159  3350161  3350209
3350219  3350261  3350273  3350279  3350297  3350299  3350329  3350339  3350351  3350353
3350371  3350381  3350383  3350393  3350407  3350423  3350429  3350453  3350467  3350471
3350519  3350527  3350531  3350549  3350559  3350569  3350579  3350597  3350621  3350629
3350651  3350653  3350657  3350681  3350687  3350719  3350723  3350729  3350741  3350777
3350779  3350803  3350827  3350833  3350839  3350843  3350857  3350881  3350909  3350911
3350923  3350929  3350951  3350953  3350969  3350981  3350983  3350993  3350999  3351001
3351013  3351071  3351083  3351097  3351107  3351109  3351113  3351121  3351191  3351197
3351209  3351223  3351233  3351251  3351263  3351287  3351289  3351301  3351319
3351331  3351343  3351367  3351371  3351389  3351419  3351421  3351427  3351449  3351451
3351511  3351521  3351527  3351553  3351589  3351599  3351611  3351631  3351637
3351643  3351653  3351671  3351679  3351683  3351743  3351749  3351763  3351779  3351797
3351823  3351841  3351851  3351869  3351877  3351883  3351947  3351949  3352003  3352031
3352033  3352067  3352073  3352093  3352099  3352147  3352169  3352177  3352183
3352187  3352199  3352249  3352267  3352277  3352289  3352339  3352343  3352361  3352373
3352381  3352387  3352397  3352403  3352469  3352471  3352477  3352483  3352511  3352537
3352571  3352627  3352633  3352639  3352669  3352703  3352709  3352711  3352729  3352763
3352787  3352807  3352831  3352837  3352841  3352879  3352889  3352901  3352919  3352957
3352967  3352969  3352981  3353003  3353023  3353041  3353047  3353057  3353069  3353081
3353087  3353089  3353093  3353111  3353113  3353153  3353171  3353191  3353197
3353209  3353213  3353219  3353221  3353227  3353237  3353243  3353249  3353281
3353293  3353297  3353303  3353321  3353323  3353333  3353341  3353351  3353359  3353381
3353393  3353411  3353429  3353447  3353461  3353477  3353491  3353533  3353579  3353587
3353599  3353617  3353621  3353627  3353663  3353683  3353687  3353711  3353729  3353767
3353773  3353789  3353803  3353807  3353813  3353851  3353869  3353881  3353891  3353927
3354007  3354017  3354031  3354037  3354059  3354073  3354079  3354097  3354111  3354121
3354133  3354149  3354157  3354173  3354187  3354191  3354233  3354269  3354283  3354289
3354313  3354331  3354341  3354349  3354359  3354367  3354371  3354391  3354397  3354409
3354427  3354433  3354443  3354467  3354493  3354503  3354509  3354511  3354521  3354539
3354553  3354581  3354587  3354599  3354613  3354641  3354647  3354649  3354667  3354671
3354683  3354707  3354721  3354733  3354737  3354739  3354761  3354781  3354787
3354823  3354853  3354881  3354929  3354971  3354973  3354983  3354991  3355013  3355021
3355031  3355057  3355063  3355067  3355073  3355081  3355087  3355127  3355141  3355151
3355181  3355193  3355207  3355241  3355243  3355259  3355291  3355337  3355349
3355357  3355369  3355403  3355411  3355423  3355439  3355453  3355459  3355487  3355489
3355519  3355529  3355543  3355553  3355577  3355601  3355603  3355621  3355633  3355643
3355661  3355663  3355669  3355699  3355711  3355717  3355733  3355739  3355747  3355757
3355771  3355811  3355813  3355819  3355831  3355853  3355867  3355871  3355873  3355901
3355949  3355991  3355993  3355997  3356039  3356047  3356051  3356053  3356057  3356081
3356117  3356147  3356149  3356161  3356173  3356203  3356209  3356237  3356239  3356263
3356267  3356273  3356303  3356323  3356341  3356347  3356357  3356387  3356389  3356393
3356417  3356447  3356449  3356471  3356513  3356539  3356557  3356567  3356581  3356593
3356641  3356651  3356657  3356699  3356707  3356723  3356741  3356761  3356777  3356783
3356791  3356797  3356833  3356887  3356893  3356921  3356929  3356933  3356971  3356981
3356987  3356993  3356999  3357001  3357019  3357037  3357043  3357061  3357071  3357113
3357161  3357181  3357199  3357209  3357217  3357223  3357239  3357247  3357251
3357253  3357259  3357293  3357307  3357323  3357337  3357349  3357353  3357407  3357413
3357439  3357443  3357451  3357457  3357469  3357479  3357493  3357511  3357521  3357559
3357577  3357593  3357667  3357677  3357689  3357691  3357719  3357751  3357769  3357779
3357797  3357799  3357801  3357811  3357817  3357829  3357833  3357843  3357847  3357863
3357877  3357899  3357901  3357929  3357943  3357979  3358001  3358031  3358037  3358039
3358057  3358063  3358067  3358099  3358123  3358141  3358151  3358169  3358213  3358217
3358249  3358267  3358293  3358309  3358321  3358337  3358349  3358357  3358373  3358423
3358441  3358463  3358471  3358501  3358507  3358543  3358547  3358549  3358559  3358567
3358591  3358651  3358661  3358669  3358681  3358687  3358703  3358723  3358753  3358787
3358799  3358841  3358847  3358853  3358889  3358903  3358913  3358937  3358963  3358967
3358973  3358987  3358997  3359011  3359021  3359033  3359039  3359063  3359071  3359101
3359107  3359113  3359221  3359243  3359261  3359281  3359287  3359309  3359327  3359337
3359347  3359351  3359359  3359381  3359383  3359393  3359413  3359423  3359431  3359437
3359443  3359459  3359471  3359497  3359509  3359527  3359567  3359569  3359597  3359639
3359641  3359669  3359683  3359689  3359729  3359743  3359747  3359773  3359779  3359803
3359809  3359821  3359843  3359857  3359861  3359869  3359899  3359921  3359927  3359953
3359959  3359987  3359989  3360011  3360013  3360023  3360031  3360037  3360043  3360053
3360061  3360083  3360103  3360113  3360127  3360157  3360163  3360167  3360173  3360197
3360209  3360211  3360223  3360239  3360289  3360301  3360337  3360341  3360347  3360391
3360403  3360419  3360439  3360443  3360449  3360457  3360503  3360523  3360529  3360557
3360563  3360569  3360583  3360601  3360613  3360629  3360649  3360659  3360661  3360667
3360683  3360689  3360703  3360719  3360727  3360757  3360767  3360769  3360779
3360793  3360809  3360823  3360827  3360857  3360859  3360869  3360937  3360941  3360943
3360947  3360983  3360997  3361031  3361037  3361049  3361063  3361073  3361091  3361093
3361097  3361123  3361133  3361153  3361177  3361229  3361247  3361249  3361273  3361297
3361301  3361327  3361331  3361333  3361357  3361363  3361367  3361373  3361387  3361429
3361433  3361447  3361459  3361469  3361471  3361483  3361489  3361493  3361507  3361511
3361513  3361517  3361601  3361607  3361621  3361627  3361639  3361661  3361667  3361679
```

```
3361739 3361741 3361747 3361751 3361753 3361759 3361781 3361793 3361807 3361811
3361819 3361823 3361829 3361847 3361889 3361901 3361907 3361913 3361951 3361973
3361991 3362017 3362059 3362077 3362111 3362113 3362119 3362129 3362143 3362159
3362207 3362237 3362251 3362263 3362273 3362279 3362327 3362329 3362363 3362371
3362383 3362399 3362417 3362431 3362441 3362461 3362473 3362497 3362519 3362537
3362581 3362591 3362603 3362627 3362633 3362657 3362683 3362693 3362701 3362713
3362717 3362731 3362741 3362809 3362831 3362857 3362917 3362929 3362959 3362971
3362999 3363007 3363011 3363023 3363029 3363049 3363071 3363089 3363091 3363103
3363119 3363131 3363167 3363169 3363181 3363193 3363197 3363203 3363211 3363233
3363257 3363277 3363317 3363343 3363389 3363419 3363421 3363427 3363431 3363443
3363457 3363463 3363473 3363491 3363499 3363527 3363541 3363571 3363587 3363617
3363629 3363641 3363643 3363653 3363667 3363673 3363677 3363691 3363713 3363721
3363733 3363749 3363757 3363769 3363791 3363793 3363803 3363809 3363823 3363839
3363853 3363859 3363883 3363887 3363901 3363937 3363959 3363961 3363979 3364037
3364043 3364061 3364093 3364117 3364133 3364139 3364171 3364199 3364219 3364223
3364237 3364241 3364243 3364253 3364259 3364267 3364297 3364301 3364303 3364313
3364343 3364369 3364379 3364393 3364397 3364409 3364421 3364423 3364429 3364433
3364441 3364451 3364457 3364469 3364489 3364507 3364511 3364513 3364541 3364547
3364553 3364561 3364573 3364579 3364591 3364607 3364633 3364637 3364649 3364651
3364661 3364679 3364681 3364687 3364717 3364723 3364727 3364741 3364763 3364787
3364799 3364813 3364853 3364873 3364897 3364913 3364931 3364937 3364951 3364961
3364973 3364979 3364987 3365003 3365009 3365029 3365041 3365057 3365077 3365093
3365101 3365111 3365161 3365171 3365177 3365191 3365207 3365213 3365233 3365237
3365249 3365251 3365281 3365287 3365311 3365317 3365339 3365377 3365381 3365387
3365389 3365393 3365399 3365423 3365437 3365441 3365443 3365449 3365491 3365533
3365539 3365543 3365563 3365569 3365581 3365587 3365591 3365597 3365599 3365617
3365629 3365633 3365647 3365651 3365671 3365683 3365693 3365699 3365707 3365723
3365741 3365743 3365749 3365759 3365771 3365777 3365801 3365807 3365809 3365819
3365833 3365839 3365849 3365851 3365863 3365867 3365893 3365903 3365909 3365917
3365963 3365969 3365987 3366007 3366019 3366023 3366031 3366037 3366043 3366049
3366053 3366067 3366079 3366089 3366107 3366109 3366131 3366133 3366179 3366193
3366203 3366217 3366239 3366271 3366283 3366299 3366317 3366329 3366347 3366359
3366361 3366367 3366409 3366413 3366437 3366449 3366463 3366497 3366509 3366511
3366557 3366577 3366589 3366611 3366619 3366647 3366659 3366673 3366677 3366679
3366689 3366703 3366707 3366709 3366739 3366767 3366821 3366823 3366827 3366829
3366841 3366859 3366877 3366889 3366911 3366917 3366973 3366977 3366983 3366989
3366991 3367027 3367057 3367069 3367079 3367087 3367097 3367109 3367121 3367129
3367141 3367157 3367159 3367163 3367171 3367181 3367193 3367211 3367213 3367253
3367283 3367291 3367319 3367327 3367339 3367363 3367367 3367369 3367381 3367387
3367421 3367423 3367433 3367447 3367457 3367477 3367517 3367531 3367571 3367577
3367583 3367589 3367603 3367613 3367669 3367681 3367687 3367697 3367711 3367723
3367733 3367757 3367759 3367783 3367787 3367789 3367801 3367811 3367813 3367823
3367829 3367841 3367843 3367901 3367907 3367909 3367919 3367927 3367943 3367951
3367957 3367963 3367981 3368003 3368009 3368011 3368017 3368021 3368041 3368059
3368077 3368081 3368093 3368107 3368117 3368171 3368201 3368207 3368213 3368231
3368257 3368269 3368297 3368303 3368317 3368333 3368353 3368381 3368401 3368411
3368413 3368423 3368461 3368489 3368507 3368509 3368513 3368531 3368543 3368551
3368569 3368581 3368593 3368609 3368623 3368633 3368641 3368657 3368707 3368747
3368753 3368773 3368777 3368779 3368789 3368791 3368803 3368809 3368837 3368851
3368857 3368881 3368899 3368903 3368923 3368951 3368957 3368993 3369001 3369019
3369029 3369031 3369059 3369073 3369083 3369089 3369097 3369131 3369143 3369161
3369167 3369181 3369187 3369193 3369199 3369203 3369209 3369227 3369283 3369287
3369319 3369329 3369341 3369347 3369367 3369371 3369389 3369391 3369397 3369409
3369419 3369433 3369463 3369469 3369473 3369491 3369493 3369511 3369529 3369533
3369563 3369577 3369599 3369617 3369623 3369637 3369643 3369647 3369649 3369659
3369679 3369697 3369703 3369727 3369739 3369761 3369767 3369787 3369797 3369803
3369809 3369811 3369827 3369841 3369869 3369929 3369931 3369941 3369943 3369959
3369991 3370001 3370009 3370013 3370043 3370051 3370069 3370093 3370109 3370117
3370127 3370141 3370151 3370153 3370181 3370183 3370243 3370249 3370253 3370261
3370273 3370291 3370309 3370313 3370327 3370331 3370357 3370361 3370363 3370387
3370421 3370457 3370481 3370501 3370517 3370531 3370541 3370567 3370571 3370597
3370621 3370637 3370639 3370649 3370667 3370669 3370687 3370691 3370711 3370739
3370751 3370769 3370781 3370789 3370817 3370819 3370823 3370831 3370841 3370849
3370877 3370883 3370907 3370919 3370933 3370937 3370943 3370951 3370957 3370963
3370967 3370973 3370987 3370993 3371059 3371063 3371089 3371101 3371111 3371119
3371149 3371153 3371183 3371191 3371209 3371233 3371237 3371257 3371297 3371299
3371311 3371339 3371351 3371353 3371371 3371393 3371399 3371413 3371419 3371441
3371443 3371447 3371449 3371461 3371497 3371509 3371513 3371519 3371527 3371539
3371561 3371579 3371617 3371633 3371647 3371659 3371663 3371671 3371747 3371779
3371783 3371803 3371813 3371821 3371833 3371843 3371867 3371887 3371947 3371969
3371989 3371993 3371999 3372013 3372023 3372037 3372059 3372067 3372073 3372077
3372079 3372119 3372151 3372157 3372163 3372167 3372169 3372179 3372197 3372199
3372221 3372227 3372233 3372247 3372251 3372269 3372331 3372349 3372353 3372371
3372379 3372407 3372419 3372427 3372437 3372451 3372461 3372503 3372541 3372547
3372581 3372601 3372623 3372641 3372643 3372653 3372689 3372703 3372727 3372731
3372737 3372757 3372763 3372773 3372779 3372781 3372797 3372799 3372821 3372839
3372841 3372907 3372911 3372917 3372923 3372977 3372979 3372983 3373001 3373043
3373059 3373067 3373091 3373103 3373109 3373121 3373129 3373151 3373159 3373169
3373171 3373177 3373213 3373217 3373219 3373229 3373243 3373267 3373283 3373289
3373303 3373319 3373343 3373411 3373427 3373453 3373471 3373481 3373499 3373511
3373543 3373547 3373553 3373589 3373627 3373631 3373681 3373687 3373693 3373717
3373729 3373753 3373763 3373781 3373787 3373789 3373813 3373829 3373859 3373861
3373879 3373891 3373907 3373921 3373961 3373969 3374017 3374023 3374029
3374047 3374057 3374069 3374089 3374099 3374113 3374159 3374183 3374197 3374201
3374233 3374251 3374281 3374291 3374297 3374311 3374317 3374333 3374359 3374377
3374389 3374407 3374431 3374467 3374471 3374473 3374477 3374479 3374489 3374507
3374509 3374513 3374521 3374543 3374549 3374557 3374599 3374603 3374611 3374617
3374621 3374671 3374677 3374681 3374689 3374719 3374729 3374731 3374743 3374747
3374783 3374797 3374803 3374821 3374827 3374849 3374867 3374869 3374879 3374893
```

```
3374909  3374911  3374923  3374927  3374957  3374963  3374983  3375007  3375017  3375019
3375037  3375077  3375083  3375109  3375121  3375137  3375139  3375149  3375167  3375173
3375209  3375221  3375233  3375247  3375257  3375287  3375289  3375329  3375347  3375349
3375389  3375391  3375409  3375419  3375431  3375439  3375451  3375467  3375479  3375481
3375503  3375509  3375511  3375523  3375539  3375559  3375577  3375583  3375599  3375601
3375611  3375613  3375667  3375703  3375719  3375721  3375731  3375737  3375751  3375767
3375781  3375793  3375811  3375821  3375829  3375833  3375857  3375881  3375959  3375961
3376003  3376007  3376049  3376067  3376097  3376099  3376111  3376123  3376133  3376141
3376159  3376181  3376187  3376229  3376249  3376253  3376271  3376273  3376291  3376297
3376301  3376313  3376333  3376343  3376363  3376369  3376379  3376397  3376409  3376453
3376459  3376463  3376487  3376501  3376507  3376519  3376537  3376559  3376567  3376579
3376589  3376603  3376609  3376619  3376627  3376643  3376669  3376687  3376739  3376753
3376759  3376771  3376781  3376783  3376811  3376817  3376819  3376823  3376843  3376853
3376859  3376937  3376939  3376943  3376949  3376969  3376979  3376981  3376987  3376991
3376993  3377009  3377029  3377051  3377069  3377081  3377083  3377089  3377093  3377111
3377119  3377141  3377161  3377167  3377173  3377189  3377191  3377201  3377207  3377221
3377229  3377243  3377261  3377281  3377287  3377299  3377303  3377317  3377321  3377347
3377359  3377371  3377377  3377393  3377401  3377431  3377447  3377449  3377483  3377503
3377513  3377557  3377567  3377579  3377587  3377593  3377597  3377599  3377603  3377609
3377629  3377651  3377653  3377657  3377701  3377723  3377741  3377807  3377813  3377821
3377837  3377861  3377863  3377873  3377879  3377887  3377893  3377903  3377911  3377923
3377947  3377963  3377981  3377993  3377999  3378013  3378041  3378043  3378047  3378049
3378059  3378071  3378083  3378103  3378107  3378127  3378131  3378149  3378157  3378187
3378191  3378197  3378203  3378229  3378253  3378259  3378289  3378293  3378301  3378307
3378317  3378329  3378337  3378343  3378373  3378377  3378383  3378391  3378439  3378449
3378451  3378457  3378481  3378497  3378499  3378509  3378527  3378533  3378559  3378589
3378611  3378619  3378629  3378643  3378647  3378649  3378667  3378671  3378691  3378701
3378719  3378731  3378757  3378763  3378787  3378799  3378839  3378857  3378889  3378901
3378913  3378919  3378923  3378929  3378931  3378967  3378987  3379001  3379003  3379021
3379027  3379037  3379043  3379049  3379087  3379127  3379139  3379147  3379177  3379223
3379231  3379249  3379273  3379289  3379297  3379301  3379331  3379351  3379357  3379361
3379373  3379391  3379393  3379417  3379427  3379429  3379463  3379477  3379487  3379501
3379513  3379517  3379559  3379603  3379613  3379619  3379633  3379639  3379667  3379687
3379709  3379721  3379729  3379741  3379751  3379793  3379799  3379801  3379819  3379829
3379847  3379877  3379879  3379897  3379903  3379939  3379963  3379997  3380017  3380033
3380089  3380123  3380129  3380137  3380141  3380189  3380197  3380203  3380207  3380213
3380227  3380243  3380249  3380281  3380317  3380387  3380401  3380407  3380441  3380449
3380453  3380459  3380473  3380483  3380497  3380527  3380539  3380549  3380551  3380561
3380567  3380599  3380623  3380627  3380633  3380659  3380669  3380683  3380687  3380723
3380731  3380743  3380761  3380771  3380777  3380779  3380809  3380813  3380833  3380837
3380857  3380863  3380869  3380873  3380893  3380929  3380933  3380941  3380947  3380957
3380969  3380981  3380987  3380999  3381017  3381019  3381089  3381101  3381127  3381143
3381149  3381151  3381163  3381173  3381179  3381187  3381193  3381211  3381223  3381239
3381251  3381269  3381271  3381281  3381331  3381359  3381361  3381401  3381409  3381431
3381451  3381463  3381473  3381479  3381481  3381493  3381523  3381527  3381551  3381569
3381613  3381641  3381647  3381673  3381683  3381701  3381709  3381727  3381743  3381757
3381767  3381769  3381773  3381787  3381823  3381839  3381841  3381881  3381913  3381919
3381923  3381971  3382003  3382013  3382039  3382063  3382103  3382109  3382117  3382123
3382129  3382147  3382153  3382157  3382177  3382189  3382199  3382217  3382229  3382231
3382237  3382243  3382259  3382271  3382277  3382279  3382297  3382307  3382319  3382321
3382331  3382339  3382349  3382367  3382373  3382381  3382387  3382409  3382427  3382433
3382451  3382453  3382493  3382501  3382517  3382537  3382549  3382571  3382607  3382649
3382657  3382663  3382693  3382697  3382733  3382759  3382777  3382781  3382783  3382807
3382849  3382861  3382867  3382889  3382943  3382957  3382961  3382987  3382991  3382993
3383041  3383059  3383077  3383087  3383099  3383101  3383113  3383117  3383131  3383137
3383161  3383173  3383179  3383203  3383207  3383209  3383239  3383249  3383267  3383269
3383291  3383293  3383297  3383321  3383327  3383339  3383377  3383381  3383383  3383411
3383423  3383431  3383441  3383449  3383453  3383503  3383509  3383519  3383531  3383537
3383543  3383551  3383563  3383581  3383593  3383603  3383617  3383621  3383669  3383683
3383693  3383741  3383747  3383753  3383773  3383777  3383791  3383801  3383819  3383837
3383879  3383893  3383899  3383903  3383917  3383927  3383951  3383959  3383999  3384049
3384119  3384127  3384133  3384149  3384179  3384187  3384191  3384203  3384217  3384221
3384247  3384257  3384259  3384287  3384313  3384319  3384331  3384361  3384379  3384383
3384389  3384431  3384461  3384467  3384481  3384523  3384529  3384551  3384553  3384569
3384583  3384587  3384593  3384599  3384607  3384617  3384629  3384637  3384691  3384697
3384697  3384709  3384713  3384727  3384737  3384743  3384767  3384769
3384779  3384781  3384803  3384809  3384811  3384817  3384839  3384847  3384863  3384877
3384883  3384943  3384959  3384961  3384969  3384973  3384991  3384997  3385013
3385033  3385049  3385079  3385087  3385099  3385103  3385111  3385127  3385139  3385147
3385153  3385157  3385181  3385201  3385223  3385253  3385267  3385273  3385279  3385297
3385303  3385313  3385331  3385339  3385357  3385399  3385409  3385423  3385441  3385453
3385469  3385511  3385517  3385559  3385573  3385579  3385583  3385589  3385609  3385633
3385637  3385661  3385699  3385709  3385717  3385741  3385747  3385757  3385763  3385793
3385817  3385829  3385841  3385843  3385847  3385859  3385883  3385891  3385897  3385931
3385937  3385961  3385969  3385973  3385997  3386017  3386023  3386027  3386029  3386041
3386057  3386063  3386081  3386087  3386093  3386153  3386167  3386191  3386197  3386249
3386261  3386263  3386297  3386311  3386321  3386353  3386363  3386371  3386387  3386393
3386399  3386407  3386419  3386431  3386473  3386507  3386527  3386557  3386563  3386567
3386569  3386597  3386599  3386609  3386611  3386633  3386639  3386653  3386671  3386683
3386711  3386729  3386737  3386741  3386749  3386759  3386767  3386797  3386813  3386839
3386849  3386857  3386861  3386863  3386891  3386897  3386899  3386909  3386923  3386941
3386947  3386951  3386983  3386987  3386989  3386993  3387001  3387011  3387019  3387061
3387077  3387079  3387089  3387103  3387107  3387119  3387157  3387161  3387169  3387173
3387203  3387253  3387271  3387281  3387289  3387311  3387317  3387323  3387331  3387341
3387357  3387407  3387413  3387421  3387443  3387451  3387457  3387469  3387471  3387473
3387487  3387493  3387499  3387511  3387523  3387533  3387541  3387551  3387557  3387563
3387581  3387613  3387653  3387673  3387677  3387679  3387689  3387691  3387697  3387701
3387731  3387733  3387749  3387799  3387803  3387817  3387821  3387823  3387827  3387863
3387869  3387887  3387893  3387899  3387911  3387931  3387949  3387961  3387971  3387991
```

```
3387997  3388019  3388037  3388043  3388057  3388067  3388069  3388081  3388087  3388093
3388097  3388109  3388169  3388171  3388181  3388211  3388223  3388241  3388243  3388261
3388279  3388351  3388361  3388379  3388387  3388397  3388433  3388439  3388459  3388471
3388477  3388481  3388493  3388499  3388523  3388573  3388589  3388643  3388657  3388663
3388673  3388687  3388717  3388727  3388753  3388769  3388789  3388799  3388813  3388817
3388829  3388837  3388849  3388877  3388907  3388921  3388939  3388949  3388961  3388963
3388993  3388997  3388999  3389003  3389017  3389053  3389063  3389077  3389081  3389093
3389107  3389117  3389147  3389161  3389219  3389233  3389251  3389279  3389299  3389333
3389339  3389359  3389369  3389371  3389381  3389401  3389411  3389413  3389417  3389423
3389437  3389453  3389461  3389479  3389489  3389513  3389521  3389527  3389531  3389537
3389539  3389557  3389591  3389621  3389629  3389651  3389663  3389689  3389693  3389699
3389713  3389719  3389747  3389767  3389773  3389797  3389801  3389857  3389861  3389879
3389891  3389927  3389929  3389941  3389951  3389959  3389989  3390017  3390019  3390029
3390031  3390041  3390043  3390061  3390073  3390083  3390091  3390097  3390109  3390119
3390139  3390143  3390161  3390169  3390209  3390217  3390221  3390229  3390239  3390271
3390287  3390307  3390323  3390329  3390371  3390389  3390391  3390427  3390437  3390461
3390479  3390523  3390529  3390547  3390551  3390571  3390581  3390587  3390589  3390619
3390641  3390649  3390661  3390689  3390691  3390697  3390703  3390707  3390719  3390731
3390743  3390749  3390763  3390787  3390809  3390839  3390847  3390869  3390899  3390901
3390931  3390953  3390971  3390977  3390979  3390983  3390991  3391021  3391033  3391039
3391049  3391061  3391067  3391081  3391103  3391117  3391123  3391127  3391133  3391163
3391181  3391187  3391229  3391237  3391301  3391303  3391321  3391331  3391343  3391351
3391363  3391387  3391393  3391433  3391441  3391471  3391477  3391489  3391499  3391537
3391543  3391547  3391559  3391601  3391613  3391627  3391631  3391639  3391651  3391657
3391667  3391669  3391673  3391693  3391697  3391769  3391771  3391813  3391819  3391831
3391859  3391877  3391887  3391897  3391903  3391907  3391909  3391933  3391939  3391957
3391963  3391967  3391987  3391991  3392021  3392041  3392047  3392069  3392071  3392083
3392093  3392111  3392161  3392171  3392173  3392209  3392219  3392239  3392243  3392261
3392269  3392281  3392327  3392341  3392443  3392479  3392491  3392509  3392533  3392539
3392549  3392561  3392563  3392617  3392633  3392651  3392663  3392693  3392723  3392729
3392737  3392771  3392777  3392801  3392803  3392827  3392833  3392867  3392869  3392899
3392933  3392941  3392951  3392953  3392959  3392993  3392999  3393017  3393023  3393053
3393067  3393073  3393107  3393109  3393127  3393151  3393163  3393197  3393199  3393211
3393223  3393227  3393239  3393311  3393317  3393323  3393329  3393331  3393343  3393359
3393361  3393367  3393371  3393373  3393409  3393413  3393427  3393433  3393437  3393449
3393451  3393461  3393463  3393469  3393499  3393547  3393553  3393563  3393583  3393619
3393623  3393629  3393653  3393671  3393683  3393703  3393707  3393713  3393721  3393757
3393779  3393781  3393791  3393809  3393833  3393839  3393851  3393853  3393881  3393883
3393893  3393959  3393967  3393997  3394031  3394037  3394043  3394049  3394051  3394057
3394063  3394091  3394099  3394109  3394123  3394129  3394163  3394177  3394201  3394207
3394219  3394229  3394231  3394277  3394301  3394333  3394337  3394351  3394367  3394379
3394381  3394403  3394411  3394429  3394453  3394459  3394471  3394477  3394487  3394553
3394561  3394579  3394591  3394607  3394613  3394619  3394627  3394637  3394661  3394663
3394681  3394687  3394691  3394693  3394733  3394739  3394757  3394771  3394799  3394813
3394819  3394843  3394847  3394871  3394873  3394879  3394891  3394907  3394921  3394927
3394973  3394981  3394987  3394999  3395003  3395039  3395047  3395057  3395069  3395071
3395081  3395101  3395107  3395123  3395131  3395141  3395143  3395159  3395173  3395177
3395207  3395209  3395219  3395221  3395269  3395279  3395299  3395309  3395347  3395363
3395369  3395417  3395423  3395437  3395477  3395479  3395489  3395501  3395503  3395521
3395531  3395569  3395573  3395603  3395629  3395633  3395641  3395653  3395659  3395663
3395669  3395671  3395681  3395701  3395713  3395719  3395723  3395747  3395759  3395773
3395803  3395831  3395867  3395893  3395911  3395921  3395939  3395941  3395947  3395963
3395969  3395983  3395999  3396009  3396023  3396037  3396047  3396049  3396059  3396067
3396091  3396121  3396139  3396149  3396181  3396191  3396199  3396223  3396227  3396229
3396233  3396241  3396257  3396259  3396313  3396319  3396347  3396353  3396373  3396377
3396389  3396397  3396401  3396403  3396439  3396457  3396461  3396469  3396473  3396487
3396493  3396511  3396517  3396551  3396581  3396587  3396593  3396619  3396661  3396671
3396677  3396691  3396703  3396707  3396713  3396721  3396739  3396751  3396761  3396781
3396793  3396803  3396829  3396917  3396931  3396937  3396971  3396979  3396983  3396997
3397001  3397003  3397013  3397027  3397033  3397039  3397057  3397063  3397091  3397103
3397117  3397133  3397139  3397153  3397157  3397159  3397187  3397193  3397211  3397213
3397243  3397253  3397267  3397291  3397309  3397313  3397327  3397343  3397351  3397363
3397391  3397393  3397403  3397411  3397423  3397469  3397481  3397483  3397487  3397519
3397531  3397549  3397567  3397579  3397591  3397601  3397607  3397609  3397621  3397627
3397649  3397663  3397679  3397703  3397717  3397729  3397759  3397763  3397769  3397781
3397783  3397811  3397829  3397831  3397837  3397853  3397861  3397871  3397873  3397897
3397907  3397939  3397967  3397973  3397991  3397993  3398029  3398033  3398047  3398051
3398063  3398099  3398107  3398111  3398123  3398141  3398149  3398153  3398177  3398179
3398209  3398221  3398261  3398267  3398309  3398327  3398357  3398363  3398389  3398399
3398401  3398407  3398431  3398443  3398467  3398471  3398477  3398489  3398491  3398497
3398543  3398573  3398581  3398599  3398621  3398627  3398639  3398651  3398669  3398671
3398683  3398719  3398723  3398741  3398753  3398761  3398851  3398869  3398873  3398939
3398957  3398959  3398971  3398987  3399001  3399007  3399017  3399041  3399059  3399063
3399083  3399089  3399127  3399131  3399169  3399173  3399241  3399259  3399281  3399287
3399289  3399299  3399307  3399311  3399313  3399329  3399343  3399349  3399359  3399373
3399397  3399427  3399443  3399457  3399503  3399509  3399563  3399569  3399577  3399589
3399593  3399631  3399637  3399659  3399661  3399667  3399673  3399707  3399731  3399751
3399769  3399799  3399811  3399821  3399827  3399859  3399887  3399899  3399901  3399911
3399919  3399937  3399941  3399943  3399959  3399961  3399971  3399973  3399997  3400043
3400063  3400073  3400087  3400091  3400093  3400097  3400123  3400127  3400157  3400193
3400207  3400211  3400213  3400217  3400219  3400223  3400231  3400247  3400273  3400291
3400301  3400303  3400333  3400361  3400379  3400393  3400399  3400409  3400457  3400469
3400471  3400517  3400531  3400541  3400547  3400577  3400589  3400597  3400603  3400609
3400613  3400637  3400673  3400681  3400693  3400703  3400717  3400739  3400823  3400841
3400843  3400847  3400877  3400883  3400897  3400907  3400909  3400919  3400931  3400949
3400963  3400993  3401009  3401011  3401017  3401039  3401051  3401053  3401081  3401087
3401089  3401107  3401117  3401119  3401129  3401131  3401147  3401159  3401183  3401197
3401213  3401221  3401273  3401297  3401311  3401317  3401327  3401329  3401347  3401357
3401383  3401393  3401417  3401443  3401449  3401467  3401471  3401501  3401509  3401549
```

3401557	3401561	3401569	3401591	3401597	3401603	3401611	3401621	3401659	3401663
3401689	3401707	3401711	3401731	3401737	3401753	3401759	3401767	3401771	3401777
3401807	3401809	3401831	3401833	3401843	3401869	3401899	3401917	3401927	3401929
3401933	3401941	3401947	3401963	3402013	3402037	3402053	3402071	3402079	3402097
3402109	3402127	3402131	3402143	3402149	3402151	3402169	3402173	3402211	3402233
3402239	3402241	3402263	3402271	3402277	3402307	3402313	3402319	3402323	3402331
3402341	3402359	3402379	3402383	3402389	3402403	3402407	3402437	3402439	3402473
3402517	3402521	3402523	3402527	3402563	3402593	3402613	3402647	3402649	3402671
3402673	3402697	3402709	3402727	3402731	3402733	3402739	3402743	3402787
3402793	3402799	3402803	3402821	3402823	3402851	3402899	3402911	3402913	3402923
3402929	3402953	3402967	3402979	3402989	3402991	3403003	3403013	3403019	3403021
3403031	3403039	3403067	3403073	3403079	3403117	3403133	3403139	3403151	3403157
3403159	3403171	3403177	3403181	3403193	3403199	3403201	3403229	3403259	3403291
3403313	3403339	3403381	3403391	3403403	3403409	3403423	3403427	3403441	3403453
3403457	3403487	3403523	3403529	3403531	3403549	3403559	3403571	3403573	3403577
3403591	3403601	3403613	3403619	3403639	3403661	3403663	3403681	3403703	3403711
3403783	3403783	3403787	3403843	3403849	3403853	3403871	3403877	3403879	3403891
3403901	3403903	3403919	3403921	3403937	3403951	3403957	3403969	3403973	3403997
3403999	3404033	3404041	3404057	3404081	3404083	3404087	3404099	3404113	3404119
3404143	3404147	3404153	3404171	3404183	3404197	3404201	3404213	3404221	3404239
3404251	3404273	3404279	3404309	3404311	3404321	3404329	3404341	3404377	3404381
3404383	3404393	3404399	3404431	3404441	3404447	3404449	3404473	3404491	3404497
3404503	3404507	3404509	3404519	3404537	3404549	3404551	3404563	3404567	3404579
3404651	3404657	3404669	3404671	3404683	3404689	3404719	3404729	3404741	3404747
3404777	3404801	3404827	3404839	3404867	3404881	3404887	3404893	3404911	3404923
3404969	3404983	3405019	3405023	3405037	3405079	3405109	3405113	3405121	3405131
3405163	3405167	3405179	3405191	3405217	3405247	3405263	3405277	3405289	3405293
3405301	3405359	3405371	3405397	3405431	3405463	3405473	3405509	3405527	3405529
3405547	3405601	3405613	3405637	3405641	3405653	3405671	3405697	3405709	3405713
3405737	3405749	3405757	3405781	3405791	3405793	3405803	3405823	3405829	3405839
3405841	3405889	3405907	3405907	3405929	3405931	3405937	3405943	3405947	3405953
3405973	3405979	3406003	3406009	3406027	3406033	3406049	3406061	3406087	3406099
3406147	3406153	3406163	3406181	3406189	3406217	3406219	3406223	3406259	3406279
3406303	3406309	3406343	3406387	3406393	3406421	3406433	3406463	3406489	3406493
3406523	3406531	3406541	3406547	3406673	3406591	3406619	3406631	3406661	3406679
3406687	3406703	3406709	3406723	3406727	3406729	3406747	3406759	3406763	3406801
3406811	3406841	3406853	3406873	3406877	3406913	3406937	3406939	3406943	3406957
3406961	3406969	3406973	3406979	3406981	3407003	3407039	3407051	3407081	3407083
3407087	3407093	3407101	3407111	3407119	3407143	3407147	3407149	3407161	3407177
3407203	3407207	3407221	3407267	3407273	3407279	3407281	3407311	3407323	3407329
3407333	3407347	3407351	3407353	3407357	3407389	3407401	3407431	3407447	3407483
3407501	3407527	3407533	3407557	3407597	3407609	3407647	3407659	3407681	3407683
3407693	3407743	3407753	3407771	3407773	3407777	3407813	3407851	3407857	3407881
3407893	3407893	3407909	3407941	3407947	3407977	3407983	3408001	3408023	3408037
3408073	3408079	3408121	3408127	3408133	3408161	3408191	3408203	3408241
3408247	3408259	3408263	3408281	3408287	3408313	3408319	3408323	3408331	3408337
3408343	3408389	3408407	3408409	3408413	3408421	3408437	3408473	3408479	3408511
3408527	3408533	3408541	3408547	3408563	3408569	3408583	3408593	3408599	3408641
3408659	3408661	3408679	3408707	3408719	3408731	3408737	3408749	3408767	3408787
3408793	3408799	3408803	3408827	3408829	3408869	3408877	3408887	3408917	3408919
3408943	3408947	3408949	3408953	3408973	3408983	3408989	3409019	3409031	3409033
3409057	3409073	3409093	3409099	3409111	3409117	3409121	3409139	3409141	3409171
3409177	3409187	3409199	3409201	3409213	3409223	3409247	3409249	3409261	3409271
3409277	3409279	3409283	3409297	3409309	3409321	3409337	3409339	3409361	3409369
3409387	3409409	3409459	3409463	3409477	3409481	3409499	3409507	3409529	3409573
3409577	3409579	3409583	3409591	3409603	3409621	3409643	3409663	3409687	3409699
3409711	3409729	3409739	3409751	3409753	3409781	3409789	3409801	3409807	3409811
3409853	3409891	3409927	3409937	3409981	3410009	3410051	3410053	3410089
3410111	3410131	3410137	3410153	3410161	3410167	3410171	3410189	3410202	3410207
3410237	3410243	3410249	3410261	3410269	3410311	3410317	3410347	3410369	3410383
3410389	3410399	3410419	3410431	3410437	3410441	3410447	3410471	3410479	3410507
3410513	3410543	3410567	3410581	3410587	3410597	3410599	3410611	3410629	3410677
3410681	3410683	3410689	3410699	3410711	3410723	3410753	3410767	3410773	3410783
3410791	3410791	3410801	3410807	3410819	3410821	3410851	3410857	3410881	3410909
3410917	3410929	3410933	3410941	3410963	3410971	3410989	3411007	3411011	3411017
3411043	3411047	3411049	3411091	3411097	3411137	3411143	3411151	3411157	3411173
3411193	3411197	3411211	3411223	3411229	3411259	3411263	3411269	3411277	3411283
3411293	3411311	3411313	3411329	3411349	3411361	3411367	3411377	3411389	3411391
3411433	3411461	3411493	3411503	3411517	3411523	3411533	3411539	3411559	3411571
3411593	3411599	3411641	3411649	3411671	3411673	3411689	3411701	3411703	3411719
3411721	3411739	3411743	3411757	3411761	3411787	3411803	3411823	3411839	3411851
3411853	3411857	3411893	3411901	3411907	3411923	3411929	3411943	3411949	3411971
3411997	3412009	3412021	3412049	3412063	3412067	3412069	3412091	3412099	3412117
3412127	3412133	3412141	3412151	3412159	3412163	3412181	3412187	3412207	3412271
3412273	3412301	3412309	3412313	3412327	3412333	3412361	3412373	3412391	3412403
3412411	3412421	3412439	3412469	3412477	3412481	3412483	3412489	3412499	3412537
3412559	3412561	3412567	3412583	3412613	3412637	3412649	3412657	3412663	3412679
3412687	3412727	3412729	3412741	3412753	3412777	3412793	3412813	3412817	3412831
3412841	3412859	3412861	3412907	3412909	3412921	3412931	3412949	3412957	3412987
3413017	3413021	3413051	3413063	3413077	3413083	3413087	3413099	3413101	3413119
3413129	3413153	3413167	3413191	3413197	3413227	3413233	3413251	3413257	3413273
3413279	3413299	3413309	3413321	3413357	3413363	3413381	3413401	3413411	3413429
3413437	3413489	3413507	3413513	3413519	3413539	3413741	3413573	3413587	3413611
3413623	3413639	3413671	3413693	3413723	3413737	3413741	3413759	3413779	3413789
3413791	3413801	3413807	3413819	3413831	3413849	3413857	3413877	3413911	3413929
3413933	3413941	3413983	3414001	3414011	3414013	3414017	3414023	3414031	3414041
3414043	3414077	3414079	3414107	3414121	3414163	3414179	3414181	3414197	3414209
3414211	3414217	3414223	3414227	3414233	3414239	3414241	3414259	3414269	3414287
3414289	3414293	3414311	3414337	3414343	3414349	3414377	3414379	3414391	3414401

```
3414403 3414413 3414421 3414427 3414457 3414473 3414487 3414527 3414533 3414577
3414581 3414583 3414589 3414629 3414647 3414679 3414689 3414701 3414707 3414713
3414727 3414751 3414757 3414769 3414809 3414857 3414863 3414877 3414883 3414893
3414913 3414937 3414941 3414947 3414997 3415021 3415033 3415037 3415051 3415099
3415123 3415183 3415187 3415219 3415241 3415261 3415277 3415303 3415309 3415319
3415327 3415337 3415343 3415381 3415393 3415397 3415403 3415409 3415427 3415429
3415439 3415441 3415463 3415471 3415481 3415511 3415567 3415579 3415609 3415627
3415679 3415681 3415697 3415717 3415747 3415757 3415777 3415781 3415813 3415831
3415847 3415871 3415883 3415897 3415901 3415931 3415943 3415949 3415957 3415961
3415967 3415987 3415999 3416011 3416033 3416051 3416053 3416057 3416059
3416069 3416071 3416111 3416141 3416191 3416207 3416227 3416239 3416267 3416279
3416297 3416311 3416323 3416353 3416359 3416381 3416389 3416401 3416423 3416429
3416431 3416453 3416459 3416467 3416503 3416509 3416521 3416533 3416551 3416557
3416563 3416579 3416639 3416641 3416663 3416683 3416701 3416717 3416731 3416741
3416747 3416753 3416761 3416767 3416773 3416783 3416797 3416837 3416887 3416891
3416893 3416929 3416939 3416951 3416953 3416971 3416993 3416999 3417013 3417023
3417047 3417077 3417079 3417083 3417091 3417097 3417101 3417121 3417143 3417151
3417163 3417173 3417199 3417251 3417263 3417299 3417307 3417311 3417313 3417341
3417343 3417353 3417361 3417371 3417377 3417383 3417413 3417439 3417467 3417487
3417503 3417521 3417523 3417539 3417541 3417551 3417553 3417559 3417569 3417607
3417649 3417671 3417677 3417703 3417707 3417721 3417749 3417751 3417763 3417767
3417779 3417797 3417809 3417829 3417839 3417847 3417859 3417863 3417881 3417889
3417893 3417899 3417907 3417923 3417937 3417943 3417977 3418001 3418021 3418033
3418049 3418061 3418067 3418069 3418073 3418087 3418109 3418111 3418117 3418133
3418141 3418159 3418193 3418213 3418229 3418231 3418243 3418249 3418267 3418279
3418291 3418301 3418313 3418321 3418351 3418381 3418397 3418399 3418403 3418439
3418469 3418511 3418601 3418603 3418627 3418633 3418661 3418669 3418693
3418699 3418729 3418739 3418747 3418759 3418769 3418771 3418783 3418787 3418799
3418829 3418843 3418859 3418861 3418889 3418901 3418913 3418931 3418937 3418939
3418957 3418963 3418981 3418997 3419027 3419029 3419033 3419051 3419063 3419131
3419149 3419167 3419179 3419191 3419197 3419201 3419239 3419243 3419257 3419279
3419287 3419293 3419309 3419321 3419333 3419407 3419413 3419443 3419453 3419461
3419467 3419483 3419491 3419509 3419519 3419531 3419543 3419569 3419587 3419609
3419623 3419663 3419681 3419701 3419707 3419711 3419777 3419803 3419809 3419813
3419821 3419837 3419863 3419869 3419887 3419891 3419917 3419921 3419953 3419957
3419959 3419963 3420023 3420047 3420059 3420061 3420071 3420083 3420089 3420101
3420107 3420121 3420127 3420139 3420161 3420187 3420191 3420203 3420211 3420227
3420239 3420251 3420253 3420257 3420271 3420293 3420299 3420337 3420341 3420367
3420371 3420401 3420409 3420421 3420427 3420433 3420457 3420481 3420493 3420497
3420499 3420517 3420523 3420533 3420563 3420569 3420577 3420581 3420601 3420617
3420631 3420647 3420649 3420653 3420667 3420691 3420701 3420713 3420727 3420749
3420751 3420763 3420773 3420787 3420793 3420799 3420821 3420827 3420829 3420839
3420871 3420877 3420913 3420919 3420959 3420973 3421003 3421013 3421021 3421039
3421049 3421069 3421079 3421109 3421131 3421151 3421157 3421169 3421193
3421219 3421237 3421241 3421321 3421331 3421373 3421393 3421399 3421417 3421423
3421433 3421447 3421499 3421513 3421531 3421567 3421591 3421597 3421603 3421631
3421633 3421637 3421657 3421661 3421667 3421669 3421679 3421699 3421711 3421751
3421793 3421799 3421801 3421807 3421813 3421853 3421861 3421867 3421877 3421903
3421907 3421921 3421927 3421937 3421939 3421993 3422011 3422017 3422047 3422053
3422057 3422077 3422099 3422119 3422131 3422137 3422141 3422143 3422171 3422179
3422189 3422191 3422197 3422207 3422227 3422231 3422233 3422249 3422267 3422291
3422297 3422303 3422323 3422383 3422387 3422401 3422407 3422411 3422429 3422437
3422453 3422483 3422501 3422509 3422519 3422521 3422539 3422543 3422563 3422567
3422569 3422599 3422621 3422623 3422633 3422647 3422651 3422669 3422687 3422693
3422707 3422723 3422737 3422747 3422753 3422773 3422801 3422807 3422813 3422917
3422987 3422989 3423011 3423023 3423047 3423053 3423139 3423143 3423157 3423179
3423181 3423191 3423223 3423229 3423263 3423271 3423289 3423311 3423313 3423317
3423347 3423349 3423367 3423379 3423383 3423403 3423419 3423457 3423461 3423463
3423467 3423473 3423487 3423517 3423523 3423529 3423557 3423559 3423569 3423571
3423587 3423599 3423611 3423631 3423643 3423659 3423661 3423677 3423683 3423697
3423713 3423727 3423751 3423811 3423821 3423839 3423859 3423863 3423877 3423881
3423899 3423913 3423929 3423949 3423967 3423983 3424019 3424037 3424049 3424061
3424063 3424067 3424073 3424093 3424103 3424111 3424121 3424151 3424159 3424163
3424177 3424181 3424207 3424231 3424241 3424243 3424249 3424261 3424271 3424283
3424297 3424307 3424363 3424381 3424397 3424409 3424411 3424417 3424423 3424433
3424457 3424459 3424469 3424481 3424507 3424549 3424559 3424567 3424573 3424613
3424621 3424643 3424651 3424657 3424661 3424679 3424699 3424703 3424711 3424727
3424739 3424747 3424753 3424763 3424777 3424781 3424783 3424789 3424801 3424819
3424879 3424901 3424903 3424909 3424933 3424951 3424957 3424961 3424991 3425021
3425027 3425029 3425033 3425047 3425069 3425077 3425083 3425101 3425117 3425129
3425131 3425141 3425189 3425197 3425207 3425243 3425249 3425267 3425273 3425281
3425291 3425293 3425297 3425341 3425351 3425371 3425399 3425419 3425431 3425441
3425447 3425467 3425473 3425479 3425489 3425507 3425579 3425581 3425603 3425621
3425627 3425629 3425641 3425651 3425663 3425693 3425729 3425731 3425753 3425759
3425791 3425797 3425803 3425809 3425831 3425843 3425869 3425879 3425893 3425921
3425927 3425951 3425977 3425987 3425999 3426029 3426037 3426041 3426053 3426077
3426091 3426113 3426119 3426121 3426127 3426131 3426139 3426161 3426167 3426169
3426217 3426221 3426229 3426277 3426317 3426343 3426359 3426361 3426373 3426377
3426383 3426391 3426407 3426413 3426419 3426433 3426443 3426463 3426473 3426487
3426491 3426497 3426509 3426529 3426557 3426559 3426569 3426583 3426601 3426623
3426637 3426641 3426649 3426653 3426667 3426671 3426677 3426691 3426697 3426721
3426733 3426737 3426757 3426763 3426769 3426811 3426823 3426827 3426853 3426887
3426937 3426949 3426967 3426989 3426991 3427009 3427027 3427063 3427079 3427093
3427111 3427121 3427129 3427141 3427147 3427157 3427169 3427181 3427187 3427211
3427223 3427243 3427271 3427279 3427289 3427309 3427327 3427331 3427339 3427343
3427363 3427367 3427379 3427393 3427397 3427399 3427409 3427439 3427441 3427469
3427507 3427511 3427513 3427537 3427547 3427561 3427579 3427583 3427607 3427673
3427687 3427691 3427703 3427709 3427747 3427751 3427769 3427777 3427783 3427789
3427793 3427799 3427811 3427813 3427819 3427843 3427849 3427859 3427871 3427891
```

```
3427903 3427913 3427933 3427967 3427973 3427981 3428021 3428023 3428027 3428057
3428059 3428071 3428083 3428099 3428137 3428141 3428143 3428209 3428231 3428239
3428251 3428263 3428267 3428279 3428281 3428287 3428329 3428353 3428371 3428389
3428413 3428419 3428423 3428437 3428471 3428473 3428479 3428489 3428497 3428501
3428563 3428567 3428573 3428597 3428599 3428609 3428617 3428651 3428657 3428671
3428681 3428717 3428743 3428783 3428801 3428807 3428819 3428833 3428839 3428851
3428861 3428869 3428891 3428897 3428899 3428921 3428923 3428947 3428977 3428981
3429007 3429017 3429067 3429077 3429079 3429089 3429091 3429109 3429113 3429131
3429149 3429157 3429191 3429193 3429203 3429287 3429299 3429301 3429331 3429341
3429347 3429353 3429373 3429389 3429403 3429409 3429431 3429451 3429473 3429479
3429487 3429509 3429523 3429581 3429583 3429589 3429593 3429617 3429619 3429653
3429659 3429667 3429689 3429697 3429703 3429721 3429749 3429757 3429761
3429763 3429779 3429781 3429791 3429799 3429821 3429857 3429883 3429893 3429901
3429961 3429977 3429983 3429989 3430027 3430043 3430079 3430087 3430093 3430117
3430123 3430171 3430249 3430253 3430261 3430291 3430303 3430331 3430337 3430351
3430363 3430369 3430373 3430387 3430391 3430403 3430423 3430433 3430451 3430463
3430487 3430499 3430513 3430517 3430523 3430541 3430547 3430573 3430597 3430619
3430631 3430633 3430643 3430663 3430711 3430717 3430727 3430771 3430783 3430813
3430829 3430831 3430873 3430877 3430879 3430883 3430897 3430901 3430907 3430913
3430939 3430949 3430951 3430967 3431009 3431011 3431017 3431053 3431063 3431069
3431089 3431119 3431123 3431143 3431147 3431171 3431179 3431201 3431203 3431213
3431221 3431237 3431243 3431261 3431287 3431317 3431327 3431333 3431353 3431377
3431401 3431411 3431431 3431437 3431447 3431453 3431459 3431473 3431479 3431489
3431491 3431503 3431507 3431509 3431521 3431537 3431551 3431567 3431587 3431621
3431629 3431641 3431689 3431693 3431699 3431719 3431749 3431759 3431767 3431783
3431789 3431797 3431819 3431821 3431843 3431851 3431867 3431881 3431891 3431903
3431933 3431941 3431983 3431993 3431999 3432001 3432007 3432019 3432031 3432061
3432067 3432071 3432073 3432097 3432101 3432109 3432127 3432137 3432161 3432173
3432203 3432223 3432229 3432251 3432257 3432263 3432271 3432277 3432323 3432329
3432347 3432361 3432367 3432383 3432421 3432431 3432433 3432437 3432503 3432509
3432511 3432523 3432529 3432547 3432553 3432557 3432571 3432577 3432613 3432619
3432677 3432697 3432703 3432707 3432713 3432721 3432743 3432761 3432763 3432799
3432841 3432851 3432853 3432857 3432899 3432907 3432931 3432941 3432953 3432959
3432967 3432983 3433007 3433009 3433037 3433039 3433043 3433051 3433061 3433069
3433097 3433123 3433127 3433139 3433153 3433169 3433189 3433207 3433211 3433229
3433231 3433237 3433253 3433273 3433301 3433307 3433321 3433327 3433333
3433349 3433351 3433369 3433373 3433411 3433447 3433453 3433457 3433459 3433477
3433481 3433487 3433511 3433517 3433537 3433543 3433553 3433561 3433567 3433583
3433597 3433613 3433649 3433657 3433669 3433673 3433691 3433723 3433753 3433769
3433783 3433789 3433819 3433823 3433849 3433879 3433883 3433909 3433943 3433967
3433973 3433979 3434047 3434059 3434069 3434083 3434089 3434099 3434111 3434129
3434131 3434141 3434147 3434161 3434173 3434177 3434203 3434227 3434237 3434251
3434257 3434279 3434287 3434293 3434309 3434311 3434317 3434351 3434359 3434363
3434369 3434381 3434399 3434407 3434411 3434413 3434419 3434437 3434443 3434467
3434471 3434489 3434581 3434603 3434609 3434633 3434657 3434671 3434677 3434681
3434701 3434721 3434729 3434749 3434759 3434771 3434779 3434791 3434813 3434819
3434887 3434891 3434903 3434927 3434929 3434933 3435007 3435011 3435059 3435101
3435109 3435151 3435163 3435167 3435169 3435197 3435221 3435233 3435239 3435247
3435251 3435281 3435283 3435293 3435323 3435331 3435347 3435361 3435373 3435379
3435391 3435403 3435457 3435461 3435463 3435469 3435491 3435499 3435503 3435521
3435541 3435557 3435563 3435577 3435593 3435613 3435623 3435661 3435673
3435689 3435697 3435701 3435727 3435739 3435767 3435769 3435779 3435793 3435799
3435821 3435847 3435851 3435863 3435881 3435889 3435907 3435911
3435959 3435967 3435997 3436003 3436019 3436021 3436033 3436049 3436067 3436127
3436129 3436151 3436157 3436163 3436171 3436189 3436211 3436231 3436241 3436243
3436247 3436249 3436253 3436267 3436273 3436283 3436291 3436309 3436327 3436331
3436339 3436357 3436373 3436399 3436403 3436409 3436417 3436423 3436439 3436451
3436481 3436483 3436487 3436501 3436507 3436513 3436541 3436547 3436561 3436571
3436577 3436583 3436607 3436627 3436639 3436649 3436651 3436681 3436709 3436711
3436717 3436723 3436757 3436793 3436813 3436817 3436831 3436841 3436843 3436847
3436871 3436883 3436889 3436903 3436921 3436933 3436949 3436957 3436981 3436987
3437017 3437023 3437029 3437069 3437101 3437107 3437117 3437123 3437141 3437149
3437171 3437173 3437177 3437191 3437197 3437221 3437227 3437243 3437257
3437261 3437297 3437299 3437321 3437339 3437353 3437359 3437363 3437381 3437387
3437393 3437407 3437429 3437431 3437443 3437459 3437477 3437501 3437521 3437543
3437561 3437591 3437597 3437617 3437639 3437641 3437647 3437653 3437657 3437659
3437669 3437699 3437701 3437711 3437713 3437717 3437719 3437743 3437761 3437801
3437813 3437847 3437849 3437857 3437897 3437901 3437911 3437921 3437923 3437953
3437957 3437963 3438007 3438013 3438023 3438041 3438047 3438049 3438067 3438073
3438091 3438103 3438133 3438139 3438157 3438161 3438173 3438203 3438209 3438217
3438223 3438263 3438277 3438283 3438313 3438349 3438353 3438367 3438377
3438389 3438397 3438419 3438439 3438451 3438469 3438511 3438517 3438527 3438529
3438571 3438583 3438593 3438637 3438647 3438673 3438681 3438683 3438689
3438691 3438713 3438731 3438749 3438751 3438761 3438763 3438767 3438781 3438797
3438803 3438821 3438883 3438889 3438931 3438979 3439001 3439003 3439013
3439063 3439091 3439099 3439123 3439129 3439147 3439153 3439193 3439199 3439201
3439207 3439217 3439229 3439237 3439283 3439291 3439297 3439307 3439309 3439333
3439339 3439343 3439397 3439399 3439411 3439417 3439427 3439457 3439459 3439477
3439529 3439537 3439547 3439549 3439561 3439567 3439573 3439577 3439591 3439609
3439621 3439633 3439637 3439643 3439649 3439651 3439663 3439669 3439679 3439691
3439693 3439697 3439741 3439781 3439801 3439823 3439829 3439841 3439861 3439867
3439873 3439889 3439901 3439907 3439913 3439921 3439937 3439987 3439999 3440011
3440029 3440051 3440053 3440077 3440099 3440119 3440123 3440131 3440137
3440153 3440167 3440189 3440209 3440237 3440243 3440263 3440291 3440293 3440309
3440323 3440347 3440369 3440377 3440399 3440413 3440419 3440429 3440491 3440513
3440527 3440533 3440537 3440543 3440551 3440561 3440573 3440581 3440603 3440609
3440621 3440627 3440663 3440683 3440719 3440771 3440807 3440819 3440839 3440849
3440861 3440863 3440867 3440893 3440897 3440929 3440933 3440947 3440951 3440971
3440993 3441017 3441019 3441041 3441043 3441047 3441059 3441077 3441091 3441101
```

```
3441103 3441121 3441133 3441149 3441167 3441173 3441181 3441197 3441203 3441211
3441233 3441241 3441257 3441287 3441311 3441313 3441367 3441371 3441377 3441379
3441391 3441409 3441433 3441443 3441469 3441491 3441509 3441511 3441521 3441533
3441587 3441611 3441617 3441623 3441631 3441649 3441653 3441673 3441689 3441707
3441709 3441727 3441773 3441797 3441799 3441811 3441817 3441821 3441829 3441847
3441859 3441887 3441901 3441913 3441929 3441931 3441937 3441941 3441943 3441947
3441953 3441959 3441967 3441989 3442027 3442031 3442051 3442063 3442091 3442121
3442123 3442133 3442141 3442163 3442171 3442183 3442189 3442217 3442223 3442273
3442277 3442301 3442331 3442337 3442339 3442343 3442357 3442379 3442409 3442423
3442427 3442441 3442469 3442471 3442487 3442489 3442493 3442499 3442567 3442597
3442631 3442633 3442639 3442651 3442679 3442693 3442697 3442717 3442727 3442759
3442763 3442799 3442807 3442841 3442849 3442867 3442871 3442877 3442883 3442889
3442903 3442913 3442921 3442949 3442963 3442979 3442987 3442991 3443017 3443021
3443051 3443059 3443071 3443087 3443101 3443113 3443117 3443131 3443137 3443159
3443171 3443177 3443179 3443207 3443227 3443233 3443239 3443243 3443317 3443327
3443329 3443339 3443347 3443369 3443411 3443413 3443437 3443441 3443443 3443501
3443509 3443513 3443519 3443521 3443533 3443563 3443567 3443591 3443603 3443621
3443623 3443641 3443659 3443669 3443681 3443683 3443719 3443723 3443729 3443743
3443749 3443773 3443777 3443819 3443851 3443861 3443863 3443893 3443897 3443903
3443917 3443927 3443933 3443963 3443969 3443977 3443983 3443987 3443989 3444017
3444029 3444031 3444037 3444053 3444059 3444061 3444079 3444083 3444097 3444101
3444107 3444143 3444167 3444169 3444173 3444197 3444209 3444247 3444253 3444289
3444299 3444307 3444313 3444323 3444341 3444349 3444391 3444401 3444407 3444431
3444443 3444481 3444481 3444499 3444517 3444521 3444527 3444541 3444563 3444569
3444577 3444587 3444607 3444619 3444631 3444647 3444653 3444667 3444673 3444713
3444739 3444743 3444767 3444781 3444787 3444799 3444803 3444809 3444817 3444821
3444827 3444851 3444877 3444893 3444899 3444901 3444911 3444913 3444919 3444929
3444941 3444967 3444971 3444989 3445003 3445019 3445021 3445027 3445093 3445109
3445121 3445153 3445157 3445199 3445201 3445217 3445231 3445249 3445259 3445283
3445297 3445301 3445303 3445357 3445361 3445369 3445391 3445397 3445399 3445411
3445451 3445459 3445471 3445487 3445493 3445499 3445501 3445511 3445513 3445529
3445549 3445567 3445597 3445601 3445613 3445627 3445639 3445643 3445649 3445667
3445691 3445703 3445723 3445753 3445759 3445769 3445787 3445789 3445801 3445807
3445811 3445823 3445853 3445873 3445907 3445909 3445913 3445919 3445931 3445933
3445943 3445963 3445999 3446029 3446033 3446039 3446081 3446101 3446117 3446137
3446171 3446197 3446203 3446231 3446269 3446299 3446323 3446327 3446341 3446351
3446371 3446381 3446383 3446437 3446441 3446453 3446459 3446473 3446477 3446491
3446503 3446551 3446567 3446609 3446659 3446669 3446671 3446687 3446693 3446717
3446719 3446731 3446743 3446753 3446761 3446789 3446819 3446843 3446853 3446857
3446873 3446887 3446917 3446939 3446951 3446959 3447011 3447013 3447019 3447043
3447071 3447077 3447091 3447131 3447139 3447203 3447221 3447233 3447247 3447251
3447281 3447289 3447313 3447319 3447329 3447347 3447349 3447373 3447377 3447407
3447419 3447443 3447463 3447469 3447503 3447511 3447523 3447533 3447551 3447553
3447557 3447581 3447599 3447601 3447629 3447641 3447643 3447673 3447679 3447709
3447713 3447733 3447739 3447749 3447757 3447767 3447791 3447799 3447817 3447827
3447853 3447863 3447883 3447893 3447931 3447943 3447947 3447959 3447971 3447989
3448001 3448007 3448033 3448043 3448079 3448097 3448103 3448111 3448117 3448121
3448157 3448163 3448171 3448189 3448243 3448259 3448267 3448273 3448283 3448309
3448327 3448351 3448369 3448381 3448397 3448439 3448453 3448463 3448507 3448517
3448537 3448553 3448561 3448573 3448579 3448583 3448607 3448631 3448639 3448649
3448663 3448667 3448673 3448681 3448693 3448703 3448721 3448751 3448759 3448771
3448777 3448787 3448799 3448801 3448817 3448829 3448831 3448853 3448859 3448867
3448871 3448877 3448889 3448891 3448897 3448933 3448957 3448981 3448993 3448997
3449003 3449053 3449063 3449077 3449107 3449111 3449119 3449137 3449143 3449179
3449191 3449209 3449233 3449239 3449261 3449291 3449297 3449309 3449353 3449363
3449389 3449423 3449429 3449437 3449441 3449443 3449449 3449461 3449477 3449483
3449491 3449497 3449513 3449519 3449531 3449539 3449549 3449557 3449561 3449591
3449597 3449599 3449603 3449653 3449669 3449683 3449689 3449707 3449713 3449723
3449731 3449737 3449767 3449783 3449791 3449801 3449807 3449821 3449879 3449891
3449903 3449909 3449939 3449947 3449951 3449969 3449981 3449983 3449989 3450011
3450017 3450047 3450049 3450079 3450107 3450109 3450127 3450121 3450127 3450131
3450137 3450149 3450151 3450157 3450169 3450179 3450197 3450203 3450211 3450233
3450241 3450259 3450281 3450283 3450289 3450301 3450311 3450313 3450319 3450329
3450347 3450367 3450383 3450401 3450407 3450427 3450431 3450467 3450487 3450521
3450523 3450539 3450569 3450589 3450607 3450611 3450631 3450649 3450659 3450673
3450679 3450719 3450737 3450743 3450749 3450751 3450763 3450767 3450773 3450781
3450791 3450817 3450829 3450841 3450869 3450871 3450899 3450911 3450917 3450947
3450959 3450977 3450991 3451003 3451009 3451031 3451043 3451061 3451073 3451079
3451099 3451111 3451157 3451159 3451171 3451181 3451193 3451207 3451211 3451229
3451241 3451297 3451321 3451363 3451373 3451379 3451387 3451411 3451417 3451423
3451439 3451453 3451477 3451517 3451537 3451549 3451573 3451577 3451579 3451603
3451607 3451621 3451627 3451631 3451649 3451661 3451681 3451699 3451759 3451769
3451781 3451793 3451829 3451859 3451871 3451873 3451897 3451933 3451937 3451961
3451963 3451967 3451991 3451993 3452017 3452039 3452069 3452081 3452087 3452107
3452143 3452179 3452203 3452227 3452237 3452249 3452257 3452279 3452287 3452297
3452329 3452333 3452353 3452381 3452387 3452413 3452431 3452441 3452453 3452459
3452497 3452543 3452549 3452557 3452567 3452609 3452627 3452671 3452689 3452723
3452747 3452753 3452759 3452773 3452789 3452797 3452809 3452821 3452831 3452861
3452893 3452903 3452923 3452929 3452957 3452959 3452971 3452987 3452993 3453017
3453019 3453031 3453053 3453071 3453077 3453083 3453097 3453101 3453127 3453133
3453139 3453179 3453181 3453199 3453217 3453251 3453277 3453283 3453301 3453313
3453337 3453341 3453343 3453361 3453367 3453371 3453379 3453403 3453409 3453451
3453479 3453551 3453559 3453563 3453587 3453619 3453623 3453629 3453641 3453647
3453673 3453677 3453689 3453707 3453719 3453721 3453731 3453739 3453743 3453757
3453767 3453769 3453773 3453809 3453811 3453829 3453833 3453929 3453943 3453949
3453971 3453973 3453997 3454013 3454021 3454027 3454081 3454091 3454093 3454097
3454109 3454123 3454153 3454159 3454183 3454189 3454193 3454201 3454223 3454249
3454261 3454279 3454303 3454307 3454313 3454327 3454331 3454343 3454387 3454397
3454403 3454421 3454457 3454469 3454481 3454483 3454489 3454501 3454511 3454541
```

```
3454573  3454597  3454603  3454631  3454643  3454651  3454667  3454673  3454679  3454681
3454687  3454697  3454739  3454753  3454769  3454771  3454793  3454813  3454817  3454819
3454837  3454861  3454873  3454877  3454883  3454889  3454897  3454901  3454909  3454933
3454937  3454943  3454967  3454987  3454993  3455009  3455033  3455051  3455057  3455059
3455077  3455087  3455113  3455141  3455143  3455159  3455189  3455203  3455209  3455213
3455219  3455227  3455251  3455269  3455281  3455293  3455303  3455317  3455323  3455339
3455363  3455371  3455383  3455407  3455443  3455447  3455479  3455483  3455489  3455509
3455519  3455527  3455531  3455533  3455561  3455563  3455567  3455591  3455593  3455597
3455629  3455633  3455719  3455723  3455729  3455741  3455761  3455791  3455801  3455821
3455827  3455857  3455861  3455873  3455887  3455897  3455909  3455923  3455939  3455941
3455951  3455999  3456001  3456023  3456029  3456031  3456053  3456071  3456073  3456091
3456107  3456109  3456127  3456139  3456169  3456197  3456217  3456227  3456241  3456269
3456301  3456317  3456319  3456337  3456361  3456377  3456379  3456403  3456413  3456419
3456433  3456451  3456473  3456511  3456517  3456533  3456547  3456553  3456569  3456571
3456611  3456617  3456637  3456653  3456667  3456703  3456721  3456737  3456743  3456749
3456767  3456781  3456793  3456821  3456847  3456863  3456881  3456889  3456911  3456941
3456953  3456977  3456979  3457007  3457019  3457037  3457049  3457081  3457087  3457093
3457109  3457117  3457121  3457123  3457141  3457163  3457187  3457189  3457193  3457217
3457229  3457241  3457253  3457261  3457271  3457301  3457303  3457309  3457319  3457327
3457339  3457343  3457357  3457361  3457381  3457397  3457403  3457417  3457427  3457453
3457463  3457471  3457481  3457513  3457537  3457549  3457591  3457609  3457631  3457633
3457651  3457703  3457721  3457723  3457763  3457777  3457787  3457789  3457801  3457819
3457841  3457849  3457859  3457871  3457897  3457921  3457967  3457969  3457973  3457991
3457997  3457999  3458053  3458087  3458093  3458099  3458111  3458149  3458173  3458177
3458179  3458201  3458207  3458219  3458233  3458237  3458249  3458251  3458261  3458281
3458297  3458311  3458317  3458333  3458359  3458363  3458381  3458393  3458407  3458417
3458423  3458471  3458489  3458499  3458501  3458503  3458519  3458537  3458557  3458563
3458573  3458597  3458603  3458617  3458641  3458657  3458659  3458677  3458687  3458731
3458747  3458771  3458783  3458821  3458827  3458849  3458863  3458869  3458879  3458891
3458909  3458911  3458921  3458927  3458929  3458933  3458977  3458999  3459017  3459037
3459077  3459089  3459097  3459101  3459103  3459107  3459119  3459179  3459187  3459199
3459227  3459233  3459263  3459271  3459283  3459299  3459301  3459319  3459329  3459343
3459373  3459403  3459409  3459413  3459419  3459433  3459437  3459473  3459487  3459541
3459559  3459563  3459587  3459601  3459641  3459649  3459669  3459713  3459719  3459749
3459751  3459763  3459779  3459791  3459829  3459847  3459851  3459853  3459887  3459899
3459917  3459923  3459971  3459977  3459997  3460049  3460063  3460069  3460091  3460099
3460117  3460133  3460139  3460141  3460157  3460181  3460201  3460207  3460213  3460217
3460243  3460271  3460307  3460319  3460357  3460363  3460381  3460393  3460397  3460403
3460411  3460421  3460427  3460433  3460447  3460453  3460463  3460517  3460531  3460543
3460553  3460559  3460577  3460579  3460601  3460609  3460619  3460643  3460661  3460663
3460693  3460733  3460739  3460771  3460781  3460783  3460799  3460813  3460819
3460867  3460883  3460921  3460927  3460973  3460981  3460987  3460993  3460997  3461009
3461011  3461053  3461083  3461089  3461099  3461123  3461137  3461141  3461147  3461167
3461197  3461203  3461231  3461233  3461257  3461273  3461279  3461281  3461291  3461309
3461317  3461329  3461347  3461351  3461357  3461369  3461383  3461389  3461399  3461417
3461453  3461459  3461509  3461537  3461551  3461561  3461581  3461593  3461599  3461603
3461617  3461641  3461651  3461663  3461687  3461699  3461713  3461719  3461723  3461729
3461749  3461767  3461791  3461797  3461803  3461807  3461827  3461839  3461849  3461867
3461921  3461923  3461951  3461993  3462023  3462037  3462079  3462089  3462103
3462113  3462131  3462133  3462181  3462187  3462229  3462233  3462241  3462247  3462269
3462287  3462289  3462293  3462301  3462307  3462311  3462323  3462337  3462343  3462353
3462377  3462379  3462391  3462419  3462439  3462449  3462451  3462469  3462517  3462523
3462587  3462593  3462619  3462623  3462687  3462707  3462743  3462751  3462777  3462779
3462791  3462829  3462839  3462847  3462853  3462863  3462881  3462889  3462911  3462937
3462947  3462961  3462971  3462973  3462989  3463001  3463027  3463037  3463043  3463049
3463051  3463067  3463069  3463081  3463099  3463139  3463157  3463171  3463181  3463183
3463199  3463217  3463231  3463249  3463259  3463277  3463303  3463307  3463319  3463333
3463357  3463367  3463381  3463387  3463399  3463439  3463489  3463511  3463513
3463517  3463531  3463541  3463573  3463583  3463591  3463601  3463609  3463619  3463627
3463657  3463667  3463679  3463687  3463727  3463729  3463751  3463769  3463783  3463807
3463819  3463843  3463849  3463861  3463879  3463907  3463919  3463927  3463939  3463981
3464003  3464047  3464057  3464093  3464117  3464119  3464173  3464183  3464207  3464221
3464233  3464249  3464291  3464299  3464309  3464333  3464341  3464353  3464359  3464371
3464389  3464407  3464411  3464423  3464429  3464431  3464437  3464453  3464471  3464473
3464491  3464497  3464509  3464537  3464561  3464567  3464579  3464581  3464599  3464621
3464627  3464633  3464647  3464683  3464699  3464737  3464779  3464801  3464803  3464807
3464827  3464843  3464849  3464863  3464873  3464911  3464917  3464921  3464959  3464969
3464971  3464977  3465029  3465031  3465047  3465053  3465067  3465071  3465079  3465089
3465101  3465103  3465107  3465139  3465151  3465179  3465199  3465233  3465257  3465269
3465271  3465281  3465283  3465317  3465347  3465367  3465373  3465377  3465379  3465389
3465421  3465463  3465481  3465487  3465491  3465503  3465533  3465559  3465577  3465599
3465611  3465629  3465659  3465667  3465673  3465677  3465691  3465697  3465727  3465731
3465743  3465793  3465797  3465799  3465811  3465817  3465851  3465857  3465859  3465863
3465871  3465881  3465899  3465911  3465937  3465941  3465947  3465949  3465953  3465971
3465989  3465991  3466003  3466009  3466013  3466019  3466033  3466069  3466103  3466117
3466139  3466157  3466171  3466193  3466201  3466223  3466231  3466241  3466247  3466277
3466313  3466319  3466321  3466343  3466349  3466363  3466367  3466369  3466409  3466423
3466429  3466469  3466471  3466499  3466543  3466549  3466559  3466597  3466601  3466613
3466621  3466627  3466633  3466643  3466651  3466667  3466669  3466679  3466681  3466709
3466711  3466733  3466739  3466741  3466751  3466763  3466769  3466787  3466811  3466829
3466849  3466867  3466871  3466891  3466901  3466909  3466913  3466933  3466943  3467039
3467053  3467117  3467119  3467131  3467161  3467171  3467203  3467213  3467221  3467239
3467251  3467263  3467279  3467289  3467297  3467309  3467323  3467341  3467353  3467357
3467377  3467383  3467437  3467449  3467467  3467479  3467483  3467521  3467531  3467533
3467537  3467539  3467543  3467579  3467593  3467621  3467623  3467647  3467669  3467689
3467693  3467713  3467729  3467731  3467743  3467759  3467773  3467797  3467803  3467809
3467819  3467831  3467833  3467839  3467869  3467909  3467921  3467923  3467929  3467941
3467951  3467953  3467999  3468007  3468019  3468029  3468061  3468071  3468077  3468097
3468107  3468109  3468133  3468163  3468167  3468169  3468209  3468233  3468253  3468259
```

```
3468263 3468281 3468293 3468301 3468307 3468329 3468341 3468349 3468359 3468379
3468401 3468407 3468427 3468461 3468463 3468481 3468499 3468511 3468533 3468541
3468547 3468557 3468581 3468587 3468593 3468599 3468611 3468613 3468631 3468637
3468649 3468667 3468677 3468679 3468701 3468709 3468721 3468727 3468733 3468739
3468743 3468779 3468781 3468821 3468851 3468859 3468863 3468877 3468889 3468911
3468919 3468943 3468961 3468991 3469013 3469019 3469031 3469049 3469061 3469069
3469073 3469079 3469093 3469097 3469099 3469163 3469177 3469181 3469201 3469217
3469223 3469237 3469247 3469313 3469321 3469337 3469363 3469373 3469387 3469393
3469421 3469441 3469447 3469463 3469469 3469519 3469523 3469537 3469549 3469559
3469567 3469577 3469591 3469607 3469633 3469639 3469663 3469679 3469691 3469693
3469703 3469709 3469721 3469727 3469747 3469771 3469777 3469783 3469793 3469859
3469867 3469877 3469901 3469919 3469931 3469933 3469943 3469957 3469969 3470003
3470009 3470011 3470017 3470029 3470039 3470063 3470081 3470083 3470087 3470099
3470101 3470113 3470153 3470161 3470167 3470183 3470191 3470209 3470213 3470221
3470237 3470239 3470249 3470251 3470287 3470297 3470353 3470417 3470443 3470477
3470491 3470501 3470581 3470587 3470611 3470617 3470627 3470629 3470647 3470653
3470671 3470683 3470689 3470699 3470713 3470741 3470743 3470821 3470827 3470837
3470851 3470867 3470881 3470891 3470897 3470927 3470947 3470963 3470983 3470993
3471011 3471031 3471059 3471103 3471121 3471133 3471191 3471227 3471233 3471241
3471263 3471283 3471301 3471311 3471317 3471331 3471343 3471359 3471371 3471379
3471389 3471397 3471407 3471421 3471431 3471439 3471463 3471487 3471493 3471521
3471527 3471533 3471539 3471563 3471569 3471577 3471607 3471613 3471617 3471647
3471817 3471833 3471841 3471847 3471857 3471883 3471899 3471901 3471917 3471929
3471931 3471947 3471959 3471989 3471997 3472013 3472033 3472061 3472067 3472153
3472169 3472171 3472177 3472211 3472213 3472223 3472237 3472247 3472277 3472289
3472291 3472319 3472321 3472349 3472363 3472367 3472387 3472411 3472423 3472433
3472451 3472453 3472457 3472463 3472493 3472499 3472523 3472531 3472549 3472583
3472591 3472597 3472619 3472627 3472633 3472639 3472643 3472657 3472673 3472717
3472739 3472751 3472757 3472769 3472771 3472787 3472817 3472831 3472853 3472867
3472871 3472883 3472897 3472933 3472943 3472949 3472951 3472957 3472967 3472993
3472993 3472999 3473009 3473017 3473021 3473027 3473033 3473039 3473053 3473101
3473111 3473131 3473149 3473177 3473191 3473221 3473237 3473251 3473269 3473273
3473291 3473297 3473317 3473329 3473341 3473357 3473363 3473383 3473399 3473419
3473443 3473501 3473521 3473527 3473537 3473549 3473557 3473609 3473611 3473623
3473641 3473647 3473653 3473663 3473677 3473681 3473683 3473689 3473699 3473711
3473719 3473731 3473737 3473741 3473747 3473753 3473773 3473777 3473791 3473801
3473809 3473843 3473849 3473887 3473917 3473923 3473947 3473957 3473983 3473993
3473999 3474047 3474049 3474059 3474067 3474071 3474073 3474083 3474099 3474109
3474161 3474167 3474179 3474197 3474209 3474223 3474241 3474257 3474259 3474277
3474281 3474301 3474313 3474323 3474329 3474347 3474353 3474371 3474411 3474433
3474437 3474439 3474467 3474469 3474479 3474503 3474509 3474517 3474533 3474539
3474547 3474551 3474577 3474599 3474607 3474619 3474623 3474631 3474641 3474643
3474659 3474677 3474683 3474719 3474721 3474763 3474773 3474797 3474833 3474841
3474859 3474871 3474893 3474899 3474901 3474931 3474949 3475013 3475027 3475049
3475057 3475061 3475079 3475141 3475163 3475177 3475181 3475187 3475207 3475229
3475243 3475249 3475261 3475267 3475343 3475349 3475363 3475391 3475393 3475403
3475421 3475427 3475453 3475469 3475477 3475477 3475489 3475543 3475559 3475579
3475601 3475639 3475673 3475699 3475711 3475721 3475739 3475753 3475757 3475781
3475799 3475807 3475811 3475847 3475861 3475873 3475877 3475883 3475889 3475897
3475903 3475909 3475931 3475949 3475951 3475959 3476017 3476023 3476029 3476063
3476087 3476093 3476129 3476131 3476141 3476149 3476159 3476173 3476203 3476257
3476293 3476299 3476303 3476311 3476321 3476327 3476351 3476357 3476377 3476387
3476413 3476419 3476423 3476453 3476471 3476477 3476489 3476503 3476569 3476579
3476581 3476587 3476651 3476689 3476713 3476719 3476741 3476761 3476783 3476821
3476827 3476843 3476861 3476873 3476881 3476903 3476911 3476947 3476951 3476983
3476987 3476999 3477011 3477037 3477041 3477043 3477091 3477101 3477113 3477121
3477137 3477139 3477157 3477161 3477193 3477203 3477213 3477259 3477263 3477269
3477289 3477293 3477317 3477337 3477359 3477373 3477377 3477407 3477421 3477431
3477443 3477449 3477493 3477499 3477517 3477527 3477541 3477557 3477559 3477569
3477583 3477583 3477587 3477613 3477619 3477631 3477653 3477679 3477697 3477713
3477737 3477751 3477757 3477763 3477781 3477811 3477827 3477829 3477833 3477839
3477841 3477857 3477869 3477917 3477959 3477967 3477973 3477977 3478009 3478039
3478051 3478061 3478073 3478087 3478099 3478103 3478127 3478147 3478151 3478157
3478199 3478201 3478229 3478243 3478247 3478261 3478271 3478283 3478303 3478309
3478327 3478357 3478367 3478381 3478411 3478459 3478459 3478469 3478471 3478477
3478487 3478493 3478513 3478561 3478597 3478621 3478627 3478661 3478663 3478667
3478679 3478687 3478697 3478721 3478747 3478751 3478759 3478763 3478771 3478781
3478801 3478807 3478831 3478847 3478859 3478873 3478883 3478901 3478903 3478907
3478939 3478949 3478991 3478997 3479017 3479027 3479039 3479051 3479057 3479083
3479089 3479129 3479143 3479153 3479183 3479207 3479209 3479249 3479303 3479321
3479323 3479341 3479351 3479353 3479381 3479393 3479423 3479429 3479453 3479459
3479461 3479479 3479513 3479537 3479557 3479563 3479569 3479573 3479627 3479653
3479659 3479669 3479677 3479687 3479699 3479731 3479737 3479741 3479743 3479767
3479771 3479783 3479789 3479807 3479837 3479873 3479881 3479891 3479893 3479897
3479899 3479909 3479921 3479933 3479977 3479999 3480007 3480011 3480013 3480017
3480031 3480049 3480067 3480073 3480101 3480131 3480133 3480151 3480161 3480163
3480221 3480229 3480251 3480271 3480283 3480289 3480293 3480299 3480329 3480341
3480353 3480403 3480409 3480413 3480419 3480431 3480437 3480443 3480487 3480509
3480511 3480517 3480569 3480611 3480619 3480623 3480641 3480643 3480647 3480671
3480677 3480683 3480691 3480703 3480727 3480749 3480761 3480769 3480791 3480809
3480821 3480833 3480839 3480853 3480863 3480871 3480877 3480913 3480929 3480947
3480973 3480989 3480991 3481001 3481007 3481019 3481043 3481069 3481099 3481109
3481111 3481117 3481139 3481147 3481157 3481169 3481171 3481193 3481213 3481217
3481229 3481241 3481259 3481267 3481273 3481301 3481319 3481321 3481327 3481339
3481391 3481397 3481399 3481403 3481463 3481469 3481477 3481483 3481493 3481519
3481529 3481553 3481559 3481561 3481567 3481573 3481633 3481637 3481657 3481691
3481721 3481741 3481747 3481759 3481781 3481799 3481801 3481813 3481823 3481847
3481859 3481879 3481927 3481937 3481967 3481969 3481979 3481999 3482021 3482023
```

```
3482029  3482041  3482051  3482071  3482077  3482147  3482159  3482179  3482189  3482197
3482201  3482207  3482231  3482249  3482251  3482257  3482273  3482287  3482293  3482333
3482341  3482351  3482389  3482393  3482411  3482443  3482461  3482519  3482539  3482543
3482561  3482573  3482579  3482599  3482623  3482627  3482669  3482693  3482707  3482723
3482737  3482741  3482761  3482767  3482779  3482851  3482887  3482939  3482953  3482971
3482981  3482989  3482993  3483013  3483017  3483019  3483041  3483059  3483083  3483089
3483091  3483133  3483167  3483199  3483209  3483223  3483239  3483241  3483247  3483257
3483287  3483299  3483323  3483329  3483343  3483383  3483409  3483413  3483433  3483437
3483443  3483449  3483463  3483481  3483497  3483523  3483539  3483541  3483547  3483553
3483577  3483581  3483607  3483611  3483617  3483619  3483643  3483659  3483709  3483713
3483719  3483761  3483763  3483797  3483803  3483839  3483841  3483847  3483853  3483863
3483869  3483881  3483901  3483913  3483917  3483919  3483937  3483943  3483947  3483959
3484001  3484007  3484021  3484037  3484043  3484051  3484073  3484079  3484081  3484093
3484097  3484111  3484123  3484141  3484153  3484171  3484177  3484189  3484211  3484213
3484219  3484231  3484237  3484249  3484267  3484279  3484297  3484319  3484331  3484361
3484373  3484421  3484427  3484433  3484441  3484447  3484489  3484501  3484513  3484529
3484561  3484567  3484571  3484573  3484577  3484583  3484597  3484639  3484667  3484687
3484709  3484729  3484759  3484783  3484829  3484837  3484841  3484861  3484883  3484889
3484903  3484909  3484931  3484967  3484979  3484997  3485011  3485017  3485047  3485059
3485077  3485129  3485137  3485159  3485161  3485171  3485179  3485197  3485203  3485219
3485233  3485257  3485269  3485291  3485297  3485327  3485353  3485359  3485381  3485393
3485411  3485441  3485477  3485483  3485513  3485549  3485563  3485593  3485599  3485617
3485633  3485639  3485641  3485681  3485687  3485701  3485737  3485743  3485753  3485789
3485803  3485819  3485831  3485837  3485843  3485851  3485869  3485891  3485899  3485921
3485939  3485947  3485957  3485983  3486013  3486017  3486019  3486059  3486079  3486097
3486113  3486121  3486127  3486143  3486149  3486151  3486169  3486187  3486199  3486209
3486221  3486227  3486233  3486257  3486269  3486283  3486289  3486299  3486331  3486337
3486341  3486347  3486361  3486391  3486403  3486463  3486491  3486521  3486523  3486529
3486551  3486559  3486563  3486589  3486611  3486617  3486619  3486629  3486631  3486643
3486647  3486677  3486689  3486713  3486727  3486737  3486767  3486781  3486803  3486829
3486839  3486863  3486871  3486877  3486907  3486919  3486941  3486953  3486971  3486979
3486997  3487021  3487031  3487037  3487049  3487063  3487069  3487073  3487111  3487123
3487129  3487147  3487151  3487157  3487181  3487189  3487199  3487201  3487207  3487219
3487229  3487273  3487277  3487291  3487301  3487303  3487321  3487331  3487333  3487339
3487369  3487373  3487381  3487387  3487391  3487403  3487427  3487439  3487489  3487529
3487597  3487607  3487637  3487639  3487661  3487691  3487699  3487709  3487751  3487753
3487769  3487787  3487793  3487807  3487817  3487831  3487843  3487871  3487921  3487931
3487933  3487961  3487987  3487997  3488003  3488029  3488057  3488059  3488063  3488071
3488099  3488119  3488141  3488143  3488161  3488167  3488171  3488201  3488209  3488227
3488231  3488263  3488273  3488291  3488297  3488311  3488333  3488339  3488351  3488369
3488371  3488383  3488393  3488437  3488449  3488453  3488473  3488501  3488543  3488591
3488599  3488603  3488627  3488629  3488657  3488659  3488677  3488687  3488701  3488707
3488741  3488753  3488777  3488783  3488809  3488839  3488851  3488879  3488887  3488897
3488921  3488929  3488939  3488959  3488971  3488987  3488999  3489001  3489007  3489023
3489037  3489041  3489047  3489049  3489053  3489061  3489089  3489091  3489127  3489173
3489197  3489203  3489209  3489257  3489263  3489269  3489287  3489347  3489349  3489371
3489373  3489389  3489397  3489413  3489457  3489463  3489481  3489487  3489503  3489517
3489523  3489529  3489533  3489571  3489587  3489589  3489593  3489613  3489617  3489649
3489683  3489691  3489699  3489707  3489713  3489757  3489781  3489793  3489817  3489821
3489823  3489841  3489847  3489869  3489881  3489883  3489907  3489917  3489919  3489931
3489973  3489979  3490021  3490031  3490033  3490051  3490127  3490139  3490153  3490159
3490171  3490177  3490183  3490187  3490199  3490217  3490229  3490271  3490303  3490307
3490337  3490363  3490367  3490379  3490387  3490393  3490427  3490441  3490451  3490463
3490483  3490493  3490517  3490577  3490589  3490607  3490609  3490639  3490649  3490651
3490673  3490681  3490703  3490709  3490727  3490769  3490771  3490777  3490789  3490793
3490809  3490811  3490841  3490843  3490861  3490863  3490865  3490867  3490883  3490891
3490937  3490939  3490957  3490961  3490973  3491011  3491017  3491021  3491029  3491051
3491053  3491071  3491077  3491083  3491087  3491093  3491099  3491119  3491123  3491129
3491143  3491149  3491179  3491183  3491197  3491227  3491233  3491237  3491249  3491261
3491287  3491291  3491311  3491317  3491333  3491347  3491359  3491363  3491401  3491413
3491419  3491429  3491441  3491447  3491461  3491473  3491479  3491491  3491533  3491549
3491569  3491581  3491599  3491617  3491627  3491639  3491651  3491669  3491689  3491707
3491723  3491743  3491767  3491773  3491777  3491821  3491827  3491841  3491843  3491857
3491867  3491881  3491897  3491899  3491923  3491927  3491947  3491951  3491963  3491981
3492001  3492007  3492017  3492019  3492031  3492043  3492061  3492077  3492091  3492103
3492109  3492131  3492161  3492173  3492187  3492193  3492233  3492283  3492287  3492299
3492301  3492317  3492323  3492337  3492341  3492397  3492407  3492413  3492431  3492439
3492457  3492487  3492493  3492529  3492547  3492551  3492563  3492569  3492571  3492583
3492607  3492611  3492631  3492641  3492661  3492691  3492707  3492719  3492733  3492737
3492743  3492773  3492787  3492791  3492793  3492823  3492829  3492869  3492877  3492893
3492917  3492953  3492959  3492961  3492967  3492971  3492989  3492991  3493001  3493003
3493013  3493027  3493031  3493051  3493057  3493073  3493081  3493099  3493103  3493121
3493151  3493163  3493183  3493219  3493223  3493229  3493291  3493307  3493319  3493327
3493333  3493337  3493349  3493351  3493361  3493367  3493379  3493403  3493411  3493417
3493423  3493433  3493471  3493507  3493513  3493519  3493537  3493541  3493547  3493571
3493573  3493583  3493591  3493597  3493661  3493667  3493703  3493727  3493747  3493753
3493759  3493781  3493783  3493811  3493817  3493829  3493859  3493883  3493909  3493927
3493937  3493939  3493951  3493957  3493961  3494009  3494011  3494017  3494033  3494053
3494063  3494077  3494083  3494089  3494093  3494107  3494149  3494159  3494173  3494177
3494191  3494209  3494221  3494269  3494273  3494279  3494303  3494339  3494357  3494363
3494369  3494377  3494399  3494417  3494441  3494443  3494453  3494467  3494483  3494489
3494501  3494509  3494521  3494527  3494531  3494563  3494573  3494609  3494627  3494641
3494657  3494669  3494681  3494693  3494719  3494749  3494753  3494789  3494801  3494807
3494831  3494837  3494839  3494849  3494851  3494857  3494861  3494863  3494891  3494899
3494923  3494947  3494949  3494969  3494987  3494989  3494999  3495001  3495017  3495043
3495049  3495071  3495073  3495077  3495097  3495137  3495139  3495161  3495179  3495181
3495229  3495253  3495269  3495277  3495293  3495299  3495301  3495397  3495409  3495413
3495439  3495451  3495469  3495497  3495539  3495551  3495553  3495571  3495577  3495581
3495607  3495617  3495623  3495643  3495647  3495673  3495683  3495697  3495707  3495731
```

```
3495733 3495743 3495749 3495773 3495781 3495799 3495823 3495847 3495851 3495883
3495889 3495911 3495917 3495941 3495953 3495959 3495983 3496007 3496021 3496061
3496063 3496081 3496091 3496099 3496109 3496117 3496123 3496147 3496151 3496177
3496217 3496219 3496223 3496249 3496291 3496307 3496309 3496313 3496343 3496349
3496351 3496387 3496403 3496421 3496433 3496453 3496457 3496469 3496477 3496487
3496489 3496499 3496511 3496561 3496579 3496607 3496609 3496613 3496657 3496673
3496693 3496697 3496709 3496711 3496723 3496729 3496751 3496771 3496789 3496799
3496807 3496811 3496841 3496853 3496859 3496877 3496901 3496937 3496939 3496949
3496957 3496973 3496979 3496991 3497003 3497029 3497051 3497063 3497071 3497093
3497113 3497119 3497161 3497201 3497209 3497213 3497227 3497231 3497243 3497267
3497279 3497281 3497293 3497297 3497303 3497321 3497323 3497369 3497381 3497419
3497437 3497443 3497447 3497471 3497479 3497519 3497521 3497591 3497609 3497617
3497623 3497671 3497713 3497717 3497743 3497759 3497779 3497827 3497849 3497861
3497867 3497873 3497891 3497899 3497911 3497929 3497959 3497987 3497993 3497999
3498013 3498023 3498031 3498037 3498043 3498049 3498083 3498101 3498113 3498119
3498191 3498193 3498211 3498247 3498251 3498259 3498263 3498283 3498293 3498301
3498307 3498343 3498349 3498359 3498373 3498377 3498403 3498409 3498419 3498457
3498479 3498487 3498493 3498503 3498557 3498559 3498577 3498581 3498587 3498613
3498623 3498643 3498661 3498667 3498701 3498709 3498739 3498743 3498749 3498767
3498773 3498797 3498799 3498811 3498823 3498827 3498841 3498851 3498853 3498863
3498871 3498893 3498919 3498947 3498949 3498959 3498973 3498997 3499019 3499043
3499049 3499087 3499091 3499099 3499129 3499163 3499183 3499189 3499193 3499217
3499247 3499253 3499259 3499261 3499267 3499277 3499313 3499319 3499333 3499337
3499339 3499351 3499361 3499367 3499369 3499409 3499411 3499417 3499429 3499453
3499481 3499499 3499511 3499513 3499523 3499541 3499567 3499577 3499583 3499589
3499597 3499607 3499609 3499619 3499651 3499673 3499679 3499681 3499697 3499709
3499711 3499721 3499757 3499759 3499763 3499787 3499799 3499823 3499829 3499831
3499843 3499871 3499877 3499889 3499897 3499913 3499921 3499967 3499973 3499999
3500017 3500023 3500033 3500041 3500059 3500111 3500149 3500177 3500183 3500197
3500201 3500207 3500227 3500251 3500261 3500269 3500297 3500323 3500327 3500353
3500381 3500383 3500407 3500429 3500443 3500447 3500461 3500473 3500477 3500509
3500537 3500557 3500573 3500593 3500671 3500687 3500689 3500699 3500711 3500747
3500771 3500773 3500779 3500789 3500803 3500831 3500863 3500869 3500873 3500891
3500897 3500941 3500953 3500957 3500969 3500999 3501041 3501089 3501097 3501101
3501107 3501137 3501139 3501163 3501193 3501209 3501229 3501247 3501259 3501283
3501287 3501293 3501331 3501341 3501343 3501391 3501413 3501427 3501437 3501467
3501469 3501479 3501493 3501503 3501587 3501593 3501601 3501607 3501611 3501613
3501623 3501629 3501637 3501647 3501679 3501689 3501703 3501713 3501731 3501733
3501739 3501749 3501787 3501787 3501809 3501811 3501821 3501863 3501887 3501907
3501917 3501919 3501961 3501989 3501997 3502001 3502007 3502021 3502043 3502073
3502091 3502117 3502123 3502129 3502151 3502159 3502183 3502189 3502207 3502231
3502237 3502241 3502253 3502259 3502273 3502277 3502283 3502297 3502313 3502319
3502333 3502337 3502363 3502409 3502427 3502439 3502489 3502511 3502519 3502529
3502549 3502553 3502567 3502571 3502607 3502619 3502621 3502627 3502633 3502657
3502673 3502687 3502699 3502711 3502727 3502729 3502777 3502789 3502813 3502847
3502853 3502871 3502879 3502943 3502949 3502963 3502979 3502987 3503009 3503021
3503029 3503039 3503053 3503057 3503063 3503083 3503089 3503099 3503111 3503117
3503119 3503147 3503161 3503189 3503191 3503221 3503237 3503249 3503261 3503263
3503267 3503273 3503281 3503293 3503299 3503303 3503321 3503323 3503329 3503371
3503389 3503393 3503399 3503407 3503431 3503449 3503453 3503473 3503477 3503483
3503503 3503509 3503531 3503557 3503561 3503569 3503579 3503603 3503609 3503623
3503627 3503629 3503639 3503677 3503699 3503701 3503711 3503719 3503761 3503783
3503807 3503813 3503821 3503831 3503839 3503849 3503869 3503881 3503891 3503893
3503909 3503911 3503917 3503933 3503939 3503947 3503953 3503959 3503963 3503971
3503977 3504001 3504013 3504031 3504043 3504047 3504079 3504089 3504101 3504103
3504107 3504131 3504133 3504139 3504169 3504173 3504217 3504223 3504239 3504251
3504253 3504287 3504289 3504313 3504317 3504373 3504377 3504407 3504419 3504427
3504437 3504439 3504443 3504451 3504467 3504491 3504497 3504499 3504517 3504523
3504551 3504577 3504593 3504619 3504637 3504647 3504667 3504673 3504689 3504691
3504701 3504719 3504727 3504757 3504769 3504779 3504793 3504811 3504821 3504857
3504869 3504889 3504923 3504949 3504961 3504979 3504997 3505031 3505067 3505079
3505091 3505097 3505109 3505123 3505127 3505129 3505133 3505169 3505171 3505181
3505189 3505207 3505219 3505237 3505267 3505273 3505277 3505297 3505301 3505319
3505321 3505351 3505363 3505391 3505409 3505421 3505457 3505471 3505477 3505493
3505501 3505517 3505529 3505531 3505543 3505547 3505559 3505571 3505577 3505583
3505597 3505613 3505627 3505631 3505651 3505673 3505681 3505699 3505727 3505751
3505753 3505763 3505771 3505793 3505807 3505813 3505819 3505829 3505847 3505849
3505889 3505921 3505933 3505949 3505963 3505969 3505973 3505979 3505981 3505991
3506023 3506039 3506047 3506077 3506101 3506123 3506137 3506141 3506147 3506149
3506159 3506171 3506179 3506201 3506207 3506213 3506249 3506287 3506291 3506297
3506323 3506329 3506339 3506351 3506381 3506383 3506387 3506401 3506407 3506423
3506479 3506483 3506519 3506549 3506567 3506663 3506669 3506687 3506719 3506753
3506801 3506809 3506819 3506863 3506869 3506873 3506891 3506929 3506933 3506939
3506969 3506983 3506989 3507029 3507041 3507043 3507059 3507079 3507089 3507113
3507143 3507157 3507197 3507199 3507211 3507227 3507233 3507241 3507269 3507299
3507313 3507323 3507367 3507379 3507391 3507397 3507403 3507421 3507443 3507451
3507461 3507473 3507479 3507481 3507527 3507529 3507541 3507551 3507587 3507589
3507601 3507643 3507649 3507667 3507671 3507677 3507697 3507707 3507709 3507713
3507719 3507731 3507737 3507739 3507809 3507817 3507821 3507827 3507839 3507841
3507877 3507883 3507887 3507901 3507941 3507949 3507953 3507971 3507991 3508003
3508009 3508031 3508061 3508067 3508073 3508079 3508111 3508139 3508147 3508163
3508189 3508201 3508231 3508243 3508277 3508279 3508313 3508319 3508339 3508357
3508361 3508367 3508381 3508387 3508399 3508429 3508447 3508471 3508481 3508487
3508501 3508523 3508529 3508541 3508591 3508619 3508621 3508649 3508651 3508667
3508669 3508679 3508689 3508697 3508699 3508709 3508717 3508721 3508733 3508741
3508753 3508823 3508829 3508831 3508849 3508853 3508867 3508889 3508909 3508951
3508957 3508997 3509017 3509027 3509039 3509057 3509059 3509063 3509069 3509071
3509081 3509113 3509153 3509221 3509251 3509257 3509263 3509267 3509287 3509291
3509299 3509321 3509347 3509353 3509371 3509381 3509383 3509411 3509419 3509437
```

3509449	3509453	3509461	3509491	3509503	3509521	3509533	3509543	3509549	3509567
3509579	3509587	3509591	3509659	3509663	3509677	3509687	3509689	3509711	3509717
3509719	3509729	3509741	3509749	3509761	3509773	3509791	3509801	3509827	3509843
3509861	3509873	3509881	3509903	3509911	3509917	3509941	3509951	3509981	3509983
3509999	3510029	3510097	3510103	3510107	3510121	3510151	3510163	3510179	3510187
3510203	3510233	3510239	3510271	3510277	3510317	3510359	3510371	3510373	3510401
3510413	3510431	3510443	3510469	3510487	3510491	3510499	3510503	3510509	3510511
3510539	3510547	3510553	3510557	3510569	3510581	3510587	3510601	3510607	3510613
3510623	3510629	3510641	3510673	3510679	3510701	3510709	3510713	3510751	3510779
3510791	3510803	3510809	3510811	3510833	3510851	3510871	3510883	3510889	3510911
3510919	3510937	3511007	3511033	3511037	3511043	3511051	3511069	3511073	3511087
3511103	3511121	3511127	3511133	3511171	3511187	3511201	3511213	3511223	3511237
3511241	3511243	3511247	3511271	3511273	3511283	3511297	3511301	3511307	3511327
3511331	3511369	3511393	3511397	3511421	3511427	3511429	3511439	3511441	3511457
3511477	3511489	3511493	3511507	3511513	3511517	3511531	3511553	3511567	3511577
3511601	3511603	3511667	3511679	3511687	3511693	3511733	3511759	3511763	3511769
3511771	3511777	3511799	3511817	3511819	3511841	3511861	3511891	3511913	3511951
3511961	3511967	3511969	3511973	3511993	3511999	3512011	3512051	3512053	3512057
3512059	3512087	3512103	3512129	3512141	3512143	3512147	3512167	3512189	3512209
3512213	3512227	3512231	3512233	3512237	3512239	3512279	3512291	3512293	3512297
3512303	3512309	3512317	3512323	3512351	3512389	3512401	3512413	3512417	3512459
3512471	3512479	3512501	3512513	3512519	3512533	3512573	3512603	3512611	3512623
3512633	3512647	3512651	3512653	3512657	3512671	3512689	3512699	3512737	3512749
3512771	3512779	3512783	3512797	3512819	3512837	3512849	3512851	3512869	
3512909	3512911	3512923	3512963	3512969	3512981	3512983	3512987	3512989	3513007
3513017	3513019	3513023	3513047	3513071	3513073	3513077	3513079	3513121	3513127
3513149	3513163	3513193	3513221	3513239	3513253	3513277	3513299	3513313	3513329
3513359	3513371	3513403	3513421	3513427	3513431	3513439	3513443	3513449	3513451
3513463	3513467	3513469	3513481	3513491	3513511	3513527	3513541	3513581	3513583
3513589	3513593	3513599	3513607	3513617	3513623	3513637	3513649	3513667	3513677
3513701	3513703	3513721	3513737	3513739	3513761	3513787	3513799	3513821	3513859
3513877	3513893	3513907	3513931	3513941	3513967	3513977	3513997	3514013	3514073
3514079	3514103	3514109	3514123	3514127	3514163	3514177	3514207	3514211	3514241
3514243	3514267	3514279	3514289	3514321	3514361	3514363	3514367	3514381	3514387
3514391	3514403	3514409	3514417	3514451	3514493	3514499	3514517	3514531	3514543
3514547	3514549	3514559	3514583	3514649	3514657	3514663	3514673	3514697	3514717
3514729	3514739	3514747	3514757	3514783	3514793	3514799	3514813	3514817	3514859
3514871	3514879	3514891	3514897	3514909	3514913	3514919	3514933	3514939	3514957
3514993	3515011	3515027	3515041	3515047	3515051	3515063	3515087	3515089	
3515101	3515131	3515147	3515153	3515167	3515173	3515179	3515189	3515203	3515219
3515257	3515269	3515321	3515329	3515339	3515353	3515363	3515371	3515381	3515383
3515417	3515419	3515441	3515443	3515453	3515483	3515489	3515509	3515537	3515539
3515587	3515593	3515597	3515599	3515623	3515639	3515657	3515669	3515671	3515689
3515693	3515713	3515717	3515731	3515761	3515783	3515801	3515807	3515819	3515833
3515839	3515867	3515891	3515903	3515917	3515933	3515977	3516001	3516011	3516031
3516049	3516061	3516077	3516089	3516103	3516109	3516137	3516143	3516157	3516187
3516199	3516209	3516269	3516277	3516281	3516307	3516313	3516319	3516353	3516367
3516397	3516399	3516407	3516413	3516421	3516427	3516437	3516509	3516521	3516533
3516551	3516553	3516593	3516599	3516641	3516659	3516661	3516697	3516713	3516727
3516731	3516749	3516787	3516803	3516809	3516811	3516817	3516823	3516827	3516871
3516889	3516893	3516923	3516937	3516971	3516973	3517009	3517037	3517093	3517097
3517121	3517139	3517153	3517169	3517177	3517193	3517237	3517247	3517253	3517273
3517279	3517289	3517301	3517303	3517313	3517333	3517343	3517361	3517387	3517399
3517417	3517421	3517427	3517429	3517441	3517463	3517471	3517483	3517531	3517541
3517543	3517561	3517573	3517583	3517607	3517637	3517693	3517733	3517747	3517751
3517753	3517783	3517799	3517867	3517879	3517883	3517889	3517897	3517901	3517909
3517937	3517939	3517957	3517967	3517991	3517999	3518017	3518033	3518041	3518063
3518069	3518083	3518101	3518113	3518117	3518143	3518147	3518161	3518173	3518183
3518209	3518227	3518231	3518239	3518243	3518261	3518311	3518321	3518323	3518327
3518329	3518353	3518357	3518387	3518447	3518461	3518479	3518491	3518513	3518521
3518549	3518551	3518553	3518597	3518623	3518633	3518651	3518653	3518659	3518687
3518693	3518699	3518719	3518741	3518759	3518771	3518777	3518783	3518807	3518833
3518849	3518863	3518873	3518887	3518893	3518911	3518923	3518939	3518953	3518981
3518987	3519013	3519049	3519067	3519083	3519091	3519097	3519127	3519137	3519157
3519167	3519169	3519209	3519211	3519227	3519239	3519247	3519251	3519259	3519281
3519287	3519301	3519311	3519331	3519343	3519349	3519361	3519377	3519379	3519413
3519419	3519433	3519457	3519473	3519479	3519487	3519497	3519511	3519521	3519533
3519553	3519559	3519569	3519589	3519599	3519601	3519623	3519631	3519641	
3519661	3519707	3519739	3519743	3519757	3519767	3519787	3519793	3519797	3519811
3519821	3519823	3519829	3519853	3519863	3519869	3519871	3519899	3519911	3519913
3519917	3519949	3519953	3519983	3520007	3520009	3520021	3520043	3520051	3520079
3520091	3520093	3520141	3520147	3520151	3520157	3520163	3520183	3520201	3520211
3520229	3520243	3520261	3520303	3520333	3520351	3520399	3520427	3520457	3520481
3520483	3520487	3520499	3520507	3520511	3520519	3520537	3520549	3520579	3520597
3520603	3520607	3520663	3520667	3520669	3520691	3520697	3520729	3520733	
3520739	3520787	3520789	3520799	3520801	3520813	3520837	3520841	3520873	3520879
3520889	3520897	3520901	3520903	3520927	3520939	3520973	3520987	3520991	3520999
3521029	3521033	3521053	3521059	3521071	3521083	3521101	3521113	3521117	3521131
3521143	3521153	3521173	3521183	3521191	3521201	3521237	3521239	3521249	3521257
3521281	3521291	3521293	3521299	3521303	3521341	3521377	3521389	3521417	3521437
3521473	3521489	3521513	3521519	3521527	3521537	3521543	3521561	3521627	3521633
3521653	3521659	3521677	3521689	3521699	3521723	3521729	3521747	3521753	3521767
3521803	3521831	3521857	3521867	3521909	3521923	3521927	3521929	3521933	3521951
3521953	3521977	3522007	3522019	3522053	3522061	3522073	3522083	3522109	3522131
3522139	3522161	3522191	3522199	3522203	3522209	3522217	3522263	3522301	
3522307	3522317	3522319	3522329	3522331	3522341	3522347	3522367	3522403	3522413
3522439	3522479	3522487	3522503	3522521	3522529	3522551	3522559	3522569	3522583
3522637	3522641	3522643	3522647	3522653	3522667	3522671	3522737	3522763	3522767
3522773	3522787	3522797	3522817	3522823	3522863	3522877	3522889	3522901	3522913

```
3522917 3522971 3522973 3522977 3522991 3523019 3523027 3523031 3523043 3523081
3523087 3523109 3523111 3523141 3523147 3523153 3523159 3523187 3523231 3523279
3523307 3523309 3523313 3523327 3523337 3523339 3523343 3523357 3523363 3523381
3523391 3523397 3523447 3523447 3523469 3523477 3523483 3523501 3523519 3523561
3523579 3523589 3523603 3523613 3523627 3523649 3523651 3523691 3523711 3523763
3523771 3523781 3523799 3523823 3523829 3523841 3523901 3523903 3523921 3523957
3523963 3523969 3523997 3524029 3524033 3524041 3524047 3524071 3524077 3524093
3524099 3524113 3524119 3524159 3524161 3524197 3524207 3524231 3524233 3524239
3524243 3524249 3524273 3524281 3524299 3524309 3524317 3524347 3524363 3524371
3524383 3524387 3524393 3524407 3524413 3524431 3524441 3524453 3524459 3524467
3524471 3524503 3524531 3524537 3524561 3524567 3524569 3524603 3524611 3524617
3524621 3524699 3524701 3524711 3524713 3524737 3524767 3524777 3524779 3524789
3524821 3524827 3524867 3524891 3524903 3524923 3524929 3524947 3524959 3524971
3524981 3524993 3524999 3525017 3525029 3525029 3525031 3525043 3525061 3525133
3525143 3525157 3525161 3525167 3525199 3525209 3525229 3525293 3525299 3525311
3525359 3525367 3525377 3525391 3525419 3525433 3525437 3525451 3525461 3525479
3525491 3525497 3525499 3525521 3525539 3525541 3525551 3525553 3525563 3525581
3525593 3525623 3525637 3525671 3525673 3525679 3525727 3525761 3525779 3525803
3525829 3525833 3525859 3525869 3525883 3525889 3525931 3525937 3525941 3525943
3525961 3525979 3526027 3526049 3526057 3526079 3526087 3526097 3526099 3526111
3526147 3526151 3526163 3526169 3526177 3526181 3526183 3526207 3526217 3526223
3526231 3526247 3526273 3526279 3526283 3526307 3526319 3526331 3526333 3526373
3526379 3526427 3526441 3526469 3526483 3526511 3526513 3526541 3526573 3526583
3526619 3526637 3526657 3526693 3526709 3526711 3526741 3526771 3526781 3526793
3526867 3526909 3526931 3526933 3526937 3526949 3526987 3526993 3526997 3527023
3527033 3527057 3527059 3527071 3527077 3527089 3527101 3527129 3527137 3527213
3527219 3527233 3527239 3527243 3527261 3527263 3527267 3527281 3527291 3527311
3527327 3527371 3527383 3527399 3527411 3527443 3527453 3527471 3527477 3527479
3527497 3527501 3527507 3527519 3527527 3527549 3527581 3527611 3527621 3527639
3527659 3527663 3527723 3527731 3527743 3527759 3527761 3527767 3527779 3527791
3527803 3527819 3527827 3527833 3527851 3527869 3527889 3527917 3527941 3527957
3527963 3527969 3527981 3527983 3528001 3528011 3528029 3528037 3528043 3528047
3528067 3528089 3528101 3528103 3528113 3528127 3528137 3528143 3528191 3528211
3528229 3528241 3528251 3528253 3528257 3528271 3528277 3528289 3528293 3528311
3528313 3528323 3528331 3528341 3528347 3528359 3528373 3528379 3528397 3528403
3528409 3528463 3528479 3528521 3528533 3528541 3528559 3528563 3528587 3528589
3528593 3528607 3528631 3528641 3528647 3528649 3528659 3528743 3528751 3528773
3528779 3528781 3528799 3528803 3528827 3528853 3528857 3528859 3528871 3528887
3528907 3528961 3528989 3528991 3528997 3529037 3529063 3529067 3529069 3529087
3529109 3529129 3529147 3529153 3529159 3529177 3529187 3529199 3529219 3529241
3529247 3529249 3529259 3529283 3529291 3529301 3529303 3529367 3529369 3529417
3529423 3529433 3529441 3529451 3529499 3529543 3529553 3529583 3529601 3529607
3529621 3529633 3529637 3529657 3529703 3529759 3529783 3529789 3529807 3529817
3529843 3529861 3529873 3529919 3529921 3529937 3529943 3529949 3529951 3529961
3529963 3529973 3529979 3529997 3530011 3530027 3530039 3530041 3530069 3530071
3530081 3530089 3530099 3530113 3530159 3530179 3530209 3530221 3530227 3530231
3530243 3530287 3530299 3530323 3530341 3530347 3530369 3530381 3530389 3530393
3530399 3530413 3530453 3530467 3530507 3530519 3530537 3530539 3530563 3530587
3530591 3530603 3530609 3530623 3530629 3530647 3530669 3530671 3530677 3530689
3530693 3530717 3530729 3530731 3530803 3530809 3530819 3530851 3530867 3530887
3530909 3530921 3530939 3530957 3530967 3530969 3530977 3530987 3530999 3531001
3531007 3531013 3531037 3531041 3531049 3531071 3531079 3531089 3531097 3531109
3531113 3531119 3531129 3531161 3531173 3531181 3531193 3531197 3531211 3531223
3531247 3531271 3531277 3531287 3531293 3531299 3531313 3531323 3531329 3531331
3531343 3531347 3531361 3531377 3531383 3531389 3531403 3531413 3531433 3531467
3531481 3531487 3531497 3531499 3531509 3531523 3531559 3531569 3531571 3531599
3531601 3531623 3531659 3531677 3531683 3531691 3531713 3531727 3531757 3531779
3531791 3531797 3531809 3531833 3531841 3531887 3531907 3531911 3531911 3531989
3531991 3532007 3532019 3532021 3532033 3532049 3532091 3532103 3532121 3532147
3532183 3532187 3532213 3532219 3532237 3532241 3532247 3532253 3532261 3532289
3532297 3532301 3532313 3532367 3532381 3532387 3532393 3532429 3532439 3532453
3532457 3532469 3532483 3532511 3532517 3532523 3532531 3532541 3532553 3532559
3532561 3532597 3532603 3532619 3532621 3532631 3532637 3532663 3532673 3532679
3532681 3532687 3532691 3532703 3532717 3532721 3532733 3532741 3532757 3532769
3532811 3532813 3532817 3532829 3532877 3532891 3532897 3532913 3532931 3532933
3532967 3532973 3532999 3533021 3533063 3533077 3533087 3533113 3533119 3533129
3533141 3533147 3533197 3533203 3533207 3533239 3533293 3533317 3533357 3533359
3533363 3533371 3533377 3533381 3533401 3533423 3533441 3533443 3533471 3533477
3533479 3533483 3533489 3533531 3533533 3533539 3533549 3533557 3533561 3533573
3533581 3533609 3533627 3533633 3533653 3533657 3533683 3533693 3533701 3533707
3533723 3533729 3533731 3533767 3533779 3533813 3533819 3533839 3533851 3533861
3533863 3533879 3533897 3533899 3533903 3533921 3533939 3533953 3533963 3533993
3534017 3534043 3534053 3534061 3534067 3534121 3534151 3534173 3534187 3534197
3534211 3534257 3534263 3534269 3534281 3534287 3534313 3534337 3534343 3534347
3534359 3534371 3534373 3534379 3534397 3534407 3534413 3534431 3534449 3534467
3534469 3534473 3534493 3534497 3534529 3534533 3534547 3534611 3534613 3534659
3534667 3534673 3534683 3534701 3534731 3534743 3534757 3534763 3534787 3534799
3534803 3534809 3534821 3534829 3534841 3534863 3534881 3534907 3534913 3534919
3534967 3534989 3535001 3535003 3535009 3535027 3535033 3535043 3535057 3535067
3535069 3535087 3535097 3535117 3535127 3535139 3535141 3535163 3535177 3535193
3535237 3535241 3535243 3535247 3535253 3535277 3535283 3535289 3535291 3535319
3535321 3535327 3535369 3535373 3535379 3535391 3535397 3535403 3535421 3535423
3535447 3535451 3535459 3535489 3535513 3535517 3535529 3535547 3535561 3535573
3535579 3535603 3535607 3535613 3535627 3535639 3535663 3535673 3535687 3535699
3535733 3535739 3535751 3535769 3535771 3535781 3535793 3535817 3535841 3535849
3535853 3535867 3535877 3535879 3535907 3535913 3535927 3535943 3535969 3535981
3535989 3536009 3536041 3536081 3536101 3536123 3536129 3536131 3536161 3536167
3536171 3536177 3536189 3536207 3536219 3536249 3536257 3536303 3536341 3536369
3536371 3536389 3536437 3536441 3536443 3536453 3536471 3536479 3536501 3536513
```

```
3536539  3536551  3536563  3536567  3536627  3536633  3536647  3536653  3536657  3536669
3536681  3536693  3536699  3536737  3536749  3536789  3536791  3536801  3536807  3536809
3536837  3536843  3536851  3536881  3536899  3536903  3536933  3536957  3536959  3536977
3536987  3536999  3537019  3537031  3537047  3537073  3537103  3537113  3537119  3537151
3537161  3537169  3537179  3537181  3537187  3537197  3537199  3537269  3537271  3537277
3537293  3537307  3537337  3537407  3537421  3537427  3537431  3537467  3537487  3537491
3537517  3537551  3537559  3537563  3537571  3537601  3537631  3537641  3537647  3537659
3537673  3537701  3537713  3537719  3537731  3537733  3537749  3537763  3537769  3537773
3537811  3537823  3537827  3537841  3537847  3537851  3537869  3537871  3537899  3537907
3537943  3537949  3537953  3537959  3537973  3537979  3537983  3537991  3538027  3538033
3538039  3538103  3538127  3538133  3538147  3538151  3538187  3538189  3538201  3538211
3538217  3538219  3538231  3538267  3538307  3538357  3538361  3538387  3538391  3538399
3538411  3538453  3538477  3538517  3538519  3538531  3538547  3538559  3538589  3538627
3538649  3538673  3538687  3538697  3538699  3538747  3538753  3538763  3538781  3538813
3538831  3538859  3538889  3538891  3538901  3538919  3538933  3538949  3538973  3538979
3538999  3539021  3539027  3539051  3539059  3539083  3539089  3539099  3539117  3539119
3539143  3539167  3539257  3539267  3539269  3539297  3539299  3539311  3539317  3539321
3539329  3539359  3539387  3539399  3539413  3539443  3539449  3539461  3539483  3539507
3539509  3539521  3539533  3539561  3539573  3539579  3539593  3539597  3539603  3539609
3539623  3539639  3539651  3539659  3539663  3539687  3539693  3539699  3539713  3539743
3539761  3539777  3539779  3539809  3539819  3539831  3539839  3539849  3539857  3539863
3539869  3539897  3539917  3539929  3539957  3539959  3539971  3540041  3540067  3540071
3540077  3540101  3540109  3540127  3540133  3540139  3540149  3540157  3540161  3540167
3540203  3540223  3540247  3540259  3540263  3540269  3540283  3540311  3540323  3540371
3540373  3540377  3540401  3540421  3540443  3540451  3540457  3540461  3540487  3540499
3540503  3540521  3540529  3540533  3540553  3540583  3540587  3540599  3540611  3540619
3540661  3540671  3540673  3540679  3540683  3540703  3540721  3540763  3540773  3540787
3540793  3540829  3540893  3540917  3540931  3540991  3541019  3541033  3541051  3541063
3541073  3541079  3541091  3541127  3541133  3541147  3541177  3541189  3541193  3541199
3541229  3541249  3541259  3541271  3541273  3541289  3541297  3541319  3541327  3541337
3541339  3541397  3541411  3541441  3541453  3541459  3541481  3541493  3541511  3541537
3541541  3541547  3541579  3541589  3541607  3541613  3541631  3541633  3541651  3541663
3541667  3541669  3541679  3541691  3541709  3541723  3541739  3541753  3541757  3541777
3541787  3541789  3541801  3541817  3541823  3541871  3541877  3541883  3541907  3541919
3541921  3541939  3541957  3541987  3541991  3541997  3542009  3542051  3542053  3542059
3542081  3542083  3542093  3542101  3542117  3542141  3542159  3542167  3542233  3542243
3542251  3542267  3542293  3542323  3542327  3542333  3542353  3542369  3542377  3542387
3542423  3542447  3542489  3542503  3542507  3542519  3542543  3542549  3542551  3542557
3542593  3542603  3542653  3542677  3542687  3542701  3542717  3542723  3542729  3542743
3542753  3542761  3542767  3542771  3542779  3542809  3542831  3542837  3542839  3542849
3542863  3542923  3542927  3542939  3542951  3542963  3542969  3542977  3542983  3542993
3543011  3543037  3543041  3543047  3543049  3543053  3543073  3543079  3543143  3543151
3543193  3543203  3543221  3543227  3543257  3543289  3543299  3543301  3543349  3543359
3543373  3543389  3543391  3543409  3543433  3543451  3543467  3543469  3543487  3543499
3543503  3543511  3543523  3543569  3543571  3543577  3543581  3543583  3543611  3543613
3543643  3543649  3543677  3543721  3543731  3543737  3543763  3543781  3543787  3543791
3543797  3543811  3543821  3543857  3543877  3543893  3543901  3543913  3543919  3543923
3543949  3543959  3543979  3543983  3543997  3544027  3544043  3544063  3544067  3544111
3544117  3544133  3544141  3544147  3544157  3544159  3544169  3544171  3544187  3544201
3544213  3544217  3544237  3544297  3544309  3544319  3544339  3544357  3544427  3544433
3544459  3544453  3544531  3544537  3544549  3544559  3544577  3544579  3544583  3544633
3544643  3544657  3544669  3544703  3544727  3544733  3544741  3544753  3544759  3544763
3544777  3544837  3544841  3544849  3544861  3544867  3544883  3544889  3544907  3544927
3544939  3544969  3544973  3544987  3545021  3545029  3545041  3545051  3545053  3545057
3545063  3545071  3545083  3545111  3545119  3545123  3545131  3545161  3545167  3545177
3545183  3545189  3545203  3545207  3545209  3545219  3545237  3545239  3545249  3545261
3545263  3545273  3545281  3545287  3545291  3545293  3545317  3545327  3545357  3545359
3545383  3545387  3545407  3545411  3545429  3545461  3545467  3545483  3545489  3545497
3545567  3545617  3545623  3545629  3545693  3545699  3545701  3545719  3545767  3545771
3545779  3545783  3545791  3545797  3545819  3545833  3545851  3545881  3545897  3545903
3545929  3545947  3545957  3545963  3545999  3546001  3546007  3546017  3546019  3546031
3546041  3546061  3546089  3546119  3546133  3546139  3546143  3546161  3546173  3546181
3546199  3546233  3546239  3546241  3546247  3546259  3546269  3546271  3546281  3546287
3546299  3546311  3546371  3546373  3546397  3546409  3546427  3546437  3546449  3546451
3546467  3546469  3546469  3546509  3546539  3546551  3546583  3546589  3546593  3546607
3546619  3546637  3546643  3546661  3546677  3546689  3546691  3546713  3546721  3546737
3546743  3546757  3546799  3546833  3546847  3546859  3546871  3546877  3546883  3546889
3546901  3546921  3546953  3546971  3546979  3547001  3547007  3547013  3547031  3547039
3547069  3547073  3547097  3547099  3547109  3547111  3547151  3547163  3547177  3547189
3547207  3547213  3547223  3547249  3547253  3547259  3547283  3547307  3547321  3547331
3547363  3547393  3547399  3547403  3547417  3547421  3547429  3547459  3547469  3547499
3547507  3547517  3547519  3547529  3547553  3547567  3547571  3547591  3547613  3547619
3547631  3547633  3547639  3547661  3547667  3547669  3547721  3547723  3547741  3547751
3547757  3547759  3547763  3547769  3547777  3547823  3547829  3547837  3547867  3547871
3547879  3547909  3547913  3547931  3547933  3547939  3547961  3547963  3547991  3547993
3548009  3548023  3548033  3548071  3548081  3548089  3548101  3548107  3548147  3548159
3548161  3548173  3548177  3548183  3548197  3548213  3548219  3548221  3548261  3548267
3548299  3548327  3548329  3548339  3548381  3548401  3548407  3548409  3548471  3548473
3548483  3548491  3548513  3548549  3548557  3548569  3548579  3548581  3548593  3548621
3548627  3548639  3548681  3548683  3548689  3548719  3548723  3548731  3548737  3548783
3548803  3548807  3548851  3548863  3548879  3548891  3548899  3548957  3548977  3548983
3548989  3549011  3549019  3549037  3549047  3549059  3549079  3549089  3549101  3549113
3549131  3549137  3549157  3549173  3549179  3549193  3549197  3549253  3549307  3549317
3549319  3549323  3549331  3549341  3549347  3549401  3549419  3549421  3549437  3549457
3549467  3549461  3549473  3549509  3549517  3549547  3549619  3549631  3549641  3549647
3549649  3549673  3549677  3549683  3549691  3549697  3549701  3549731  3549737  3549757
3549811  3549823  3549839  3549851  3549877  3549881  3549901  3549911  3549913  3549947
3549967  3549983  3550007  3550009  3550069  3550091  3550109  3550111  3550163  3550177
3550189  3550201  3550219  3550249  3550259  3550271  3550277  3550279  3550289  3550301
```

```
3550319 3550357 3550363 3550373 3550387 3550411 3550439 3550447 3550471 3550489
3550517 3550537 3550541 3550567 3550571 3550609 3550619 3550633 3550643 3550649
3550667 3550681 3550691 3550693 3550697 3550699 3550711 3550721 3550727 3550733
3550741 3550751 3550759 3550783 3550787 3550817 3550831 3550837 3550843 3550861
3550873 3550889 3550931 3550949 3550979 3550999 3551003 3551027 3551029 3551057
3551077 3551089 3551099 3551101 3551123 3551161 3551173 3551209 3551213 3551221
3551227 3551239 3551243 3551257 3551291 3551323 3551363 3551389 3551411 3551441
3551447 3551467 3551473 3551489 3551501 3551503 3551507 3551549 3551551 3551563
3551573 3551599 3551621 3551627 3551629 3551641 3551663 3551677 3551687 3551699
3551719 3551747 3551753 3551767 3551771 3551777 3551797 3551813 3551839 3551851
3551881 3551893 3551903 3551909 3551921 3551927 3551939 3551941 3551957 3551981
3551987 3552001 3552013 3552023 3552041 3552047 3552053 3552071 3552083 3552103
3552137 3552149 3552163 3552173 3552179 3552203 3552217 3552233 3552247 3552251
3552277 3552299 3552301 3552313 3552347 3552391 3552397 3552421 3552427 3552433
3552463 3552491 3552503 3552509 3552517 3552533 3552559 3552583 3552611 3552641
3552667 3552671 3552673 3552697 3552707 3552713 3552751 3552781 3552793 3552797
3552811 3552839 3552841 3552853 3552859 3552869 3552883 3552893 3552907 3552917
3552929 3552931 3552947 3552953 3552959 3552977 3553001 3553007 3553009 3553021
3553037 3553049 3553061 3553087 3553097 3553111 3553139 3553141 3553163 3553217
3553223 3553229 3553241 3553243 3553267 3553271 3553273 3553307 3553309 3553321
3553327 3553351 3553409 3553411 3553423 3553427 3553441 3553447 3553453 3553463
3553469 3553471 3553507 3553531 3553541 3553553 3553559 3553579 3553601 3553673
3553699 3553721 3553723 3553729 3553751 3553777 3553783 3553787 3553793 3553819
3553843 3553853 3553877 3553903 3553943 3553967 3553981 3553997 3554011 3554039
3554051 3554059 3554069 3554081 3554099 3554107 3554137 3554141 3554147 3554171
3554179 3554203 3554227 3554231 3554237 3554263 3554267 3554333 3554359 3554363
3554399 3554401 3554407 3554431 3554437 3554449 3554461 3554477 3554519 3554527
3554557 3554561 3554569 3554587 3554591 3554597 3554611 3554651 3554669 3554671
3554687 3554689 3554711 3554713 3554723 3554731 3554773 3554777 3554779 3554797
3554813 3554821 3554827 3554851 3554891 3554893 3554909 3554933 3554959 3554963
3554981 3554983 3555001 3555007 3555011 3555017 3555029 3555031 3555037 3555043
3555053 3555059 3555067 3555073 3555089 3555103 3555107 3555113 3555121 3555131
3555137 3555143 3555157 3555161 3555169 3555191 3555217 3555229 3555239 3555241
3555247 3555257 3555269 3555311 3555353 3555361 3555379 3555403 3555427 3555443
3555449 3555463 3555469 3555509 3555521 3555551 3555557 3555571 3555599 3555613
3555647 3555649 3555667 3555697 3555701 3555743 3555749 3555763 3555767 3555779
3555781 3555787 3555829 3555833 3555857 3555859 3555883 3555901 3555913 3555943
3555947 3555949 3555953 3555967 3555977 3556001 3556019 3556031 3556061 3556073
3556087 3556093 3556121 3556123 3556129 3556139 3556151 3556169 3556199 3556219
3556243 3556253 3556261 3556271 3556277 3556297 3556307 3556309 3556321 3556331
3556337 3556367 3556369 3556379 3556387 3556391 3556393 3556447 3556457 3556469
3556493 3556499 3556507 3556517 3556523 3556543 3556547 3556571 3556583 3556601
3556607 3556649 3556669 3556681 3556687 3556691 3556703 3556711 3556717 3556733
3556739 3556747 3556753 3556769 3556783 3556793 3556801 3556811 3556843 3556853
3556877 3556897 3556939 3556951 3556967 3556979 3556981 3556991 3556999 3557017
3557023 3557039 3557041 3557083 3557117 3557129 3557153 3557167 3557189 3557207
3557243 3557251 3557263 3557269 3557273 3557293 3557299 3557303 3557327 3557339
3557377 3557381 3557431 3557441 3557473 3557483 3557497 3557501 3557507 3557527
3557531 3557551 3557557 3557563 3557599 3557621 3557639 3557647 3557681 3557683
3557689 3557699 3557713 3557737 3557761 3557773 3557779 3557783 3557797 3557803
3557821 3557831 3557833 3557843 3557867 3557903 3557933 3557951 3557977 3557987
3557999 3558001 3558007 3558011 3558019 3558029 3558043 3558059 3558067 3558089
3558109 3558133 3558163 3558167 3558193 3558221 3558223 3558241 3558259 3558281
3558283 3558299 3558337 3558343 3558361 3558371 3558403 3558407 3558409 3558421
3558433 3558439 3558461 3558463 3558469 3558479 3558481 3558517 3558553 3558587
3558589 3558613 3558649 3558671 3558683 3558689 3558691 3558739 3558749 3558761
3558803 3558811 3558829 3558853 3558869 3558881 3558883 3558901 3558911 3558913
3558917 3558931 3558941 3558943 3558953 3558979 3558983 3558991 3559009 3559013
3559019 3559037 3559063 3559091 3559093 3559097 3559111 3559117 3559151 3559183
3559201 3559207 3559217 3559229 3559247 3559249 3559253 3559267 3559279 3559313
3559337 3559343 3559349 3559351 3559379 3559393 3559399 3559417 3559421 3559433
3559447 3559453 3559459 3559463 3559469 3559481 3559487 3559519 3559537 3559559
3559561 3559571 3559597 3559603 3559607 3559627 3559649 3559679 3559697 3559709
3559711 3559729 3559741 3559747 3559753 3559771 3559789 3559793 3559799 3559861
3559867 3559903 3559909 3559931 3559949 3559951 3559961 3559967 3559979 3559999
3560003 3560023 3560027 3560033 3560047 3560059 3560077 3560107 3560111 3560113
3560129 3560159 3560173 3560197 3560209 3560213 3560261 3560269 3560299 3560311
3560329 3560339 3560363 3560371 3560393 3560411 3560419 3560461 3560471 3560477
3560503 3560507 3560519 3560521 3560527 3560537 3560539 3560549 3560569 3560587
3560597 3560611 3560647 3560659 3560671 3560681 3560741 3560747 3560759 3560779
3560789 3560797 3560819 3560831 3560833 3560897 3560903 3560927 3560969 3560989
3560987 3560993 3561023 3561053 3561059 3561071 3561073 3561091 3561097 3561127
3561133 3561149 3561167 3561181 3561193 3561197 3561203 3561209 3561221 3561247
3561253 3561263 3561293 3561317 3561359 3561367 3561377 3561391 3561407 3561413
3561433 3561443 3561479 3561499 3561511 3561521 3561529 3561539 3561541 3561581
3561611 3561631 3561641 3561643 3561659 3561661 3561671 3561673 3561689 3561703
3561749 3561773 3561799 3561827 3561841 3561847 3561853 3561881 3561893 3561907
3561931 3561947 3561977 3561997 3562019 3562043 3562051 3562057 3562067 3562093
3562103 3562109 3562193 3562199 3562211 3562219 3562259 3562267 3562301 3562343
3562369 3562373 3562381 3562387 3562393 3562399 3562409 3562417 3562423 3562439
3562451 3562453 3562463 3562499 3562511 3562513 3562529 3562541 3562547 3562561
3562577 3562579 3562627 3562651 3562661 3562681 3562711 3562717 3562729 3562733
3562751 3562753 3562771 3562781 3562789 3562813 3562831 3562847 3562849 3562901
3562903 3562913 3562919 3562927 3562931 3562939 3562943 3562957 3562961 3562967
3562991 3562997 3563009 3563033 3563039 3563041 3563059 3563063 3563093 3563099
3563111 3563141 3563159 3563167 3563191 3563221 3563237 3563249 3563291 3563297
3563299 3563303 3563309 3563311 3563323 3563341 3563377 3563383 3563389 3563401
3563407 3563467 3563473 3563477 3563479 3563501 3563503 3563513 3563519 3563531
3563563 3563569 3563653 3563657 3563671 3563699 3563701 3563717 3563719 3563731
```

```
3563741  3563753  3563767  3563779  3563783  3563789  3563801  3563831  3563837  3563851
3563867  3563881  3563893  3563909  3563929  3563953  3563957  3563971  3563983  3563993
3564017  3564019  3564049  3564059  3564061  3564073  3564097  3564137  3564139  3564157
3564181  3564193  3564221  3564257  3564259  3564283  3564293  3564299  3564307  3564317
3564331  3564383  3564389  3564397  3564437  3564443  3564461  3564479  3564487  3564493
3564497  3564503  3564529  3564551  3564553  3564557  3564569  3564619  3564623  3564629
3564643  3564661  3564677  3564683  3564689  3564703  3564707  3564719  3564733  3564739
3564749  3564751  3564787  3564791  3564817  3564823  3564857  3564859  3564863  3564871
3564893  3564923  3564929  3564937  3564961  3564971  3564983  3565013  3565021
3565039  3565043  3565049  3565097  3565117  3565127  3565129  3565147  3565153  3565169
3565171  3565181  3565183  3565187  3565213  3565241  3565249  3565273  3565277  3565297
3565307  3565321  3565333  3565337  3565339  3565351  3565381  3565399  3565409  3565411
3565423  3565447  3565451  3565459  3565487  3565531  3565537  3565543  3565553  3565567
3565571  3565577  3565591  3565613  3565619  3565669  3565687  3565693  3565697  3565721
3565739  3565741  3565747  3565777  3565789  3565799  3565813  3565819  3565829  3565841
3565867  3565871  3565879  3565889  3565907  3565909  3565921  3565931  3565979  3566027
3566029  3566047  3566063  3566099  3566131  3566149  3566177  3566183  3566191  3566197
3566231  3566239  3566249  3566263  3566263  3566267  3566273  3566293  3566309  3566327
3566341  3566351  3566363  3566369  3566383  3566429  3566441  3566443  3566461  3566473
3566513  3566527  3566539  3566551  3566573  3566579  3566599  3566659  3566669  3566687
3566701  3566711  3566723  3566729  3566743  3566749  3566789  3566791  3566809  3566819
3566831  3566839  3566861  3566867  3566869  3566897  3566917  3566939  3566951  3566977
3566989  3567007  3567019  3567089  3567101  3567103  3567107  3567119  3567121  3567149
3567163  3567191  3567211  3567217  3567227  3567233  3567247  3567251  3567257  3567283
3567293  3567299  3567301  3567337  3567353  3567359  3567367  3567371  3567373  3567379
3567397  3567401  3567407  3567419  3567439  3567457  3567469  3567517  3567539  3567541
3567547  3567559  3567587  3567593  3567601  3567631  3567643  3567659  3567661  3567673
3567703  3567709  3567721  3567727  3567761  3567769  3567791  3567793  3567797  3567803
3567833  3567847  3567853  3567859  3567869  3567881  3567901  3567913  3567917  3567919
3567923  3567937  3567959  3567961  3567973  3567983  3567989  3568003  3568029  3568043
3568051  3568057  3568063  3568091  3568093  3568109  3568127  3568133  3568141  3568153
3568157  3568163  3568207  3568211  3568217  3568231  3568237  3568241  3568259  3568307
3568337  3568361  3568399  3568403  3568417  3568423  3568451  3568457  3568463  3568483
3568489  3568501  3568529  3568549  3568567  3568577  3568597  3568603  3568651  3568679
3568693  3568709  3568717  3568729  3568753  3568781  3568783  3568787  3568801  3568837
3568853  3568883  3568891  3568907  3568949  3568951  3568973  3568991  3568993
3569003  3569021  3569051  3569063  3569077  3569089  3569107  3569113  3569143  3569161
3569191  3569221  3569231  3569257  3569263  3569287  3569297  3569311  3569317  3569329
3569333  3569369  3569399  3569411  3569429  3569431  3569437  3569453  3569459
3569477  3569483  3569491  3569513  3569519  3569521  3569539  3569551  3569563  3569591
3569597  3569611  3569633  3569647  3569651  3569653  3569707  3569717  3569719  3569759
3569771  3569789  3569831  3569833  3569849  3569857  3569869  3569873  3569887  3569893
3569897  3569927  3569939  3569941  3569947  3569953  3569957  3569963  3569971  3569977
3570001  3570011  3570013  3570067  3570071  3570107  3570113  3570121  3570131  3570139
3570169  3570179  3570181  3570191  3570199  3570223  3570227  3570263  3570311  3570317
3570319  3570341  3570349  3570361  3570373  3570383  3570401  3570407  3570409  3570431
3570433  3570439  3570481  3570491  3570517  3570551  3570569  3570571  3570583  3570599
3570601  3570607  3570643  3570647  3570659  3570703  3570713  3570719  3570733  3570737
3570761  3570767  3570779  3570781  3570811  3570817  3570821  3570823  3570839  3570869
3570877  3570881  3570887  3570923  3570943  3570953  3570971  3570989  3570991  3571039
3571067  3571091  3571097  3571103  3571111  3571133  3571151  3571153  3571157  3571163
3571181  3571199  3571237  3571247  3571261  3571283  3571289  3571291  3571307  3571313
3571333  3571369  3571397  3571423  3571427  3571429  3571433  3571439  3571441  3571457
3571459  3571471  3571501  3571507  3571517  3571531  3571543  3571549  3571559  3571583
3571609  3571619  3571627  3571651  3571661  3571681  3571699  3571741  3571747  3571759
3571787  3571793  3571849  3571871  3571873  3571883  3571889  3571927  3571933  3571973
3571987  3571991  3571993  3571999  3572003  3572027  3572029  3572059  3572069  3572077
3572113  3572119  3572137  3572167  3572183  3572189  3572203  3572243  3572267
3572279  3572287  3572321  3572339  3572351  3572357  3572377  3572389  3572407  3572411
3572417  3572419  3572447  3572449  3572467  3572473  3572477  3572519  3572531  3572561
3572599  3572599  3572663  3572687  3572689  3572707  3572729  3572731  3572819  3572857
3572867  3572879  3572897  3572903  3572917  3572923  3572939  3572963  3572983  3572993
3573001  3573013  3573041  3573049  3573107  3573137  3573139  3573149  3573181  3573187
3573203  3573209  3573221  3573223  3573239  3573253  3573259  3573263  3573331  3573337
3573341  3573373  3573391  3573403  3573413  3573431  3573461  3573469  3573473  3573491
3573499  3573503  3573509  3573511  3573517  3573523  3573527  3573529  3573599  3573607
3573613  3573623  3573629  3573637  3573673  3573679  3573697  3573709  3573727  3573733
3573749  3573751  3573761  3573769  3573799  3573803  3573821  3573827  3573839  3573877
3573887  3573917  3573937  3573953  3573971  3573979  3574013  3574037  3574049  3574061
3574079  3574091  3574111  3574127  3574141  3574157  3574169  3574187  3574189  3574201
3574231  3574247  3574253  3574297  3574309  3574313  3574343  3574357  3574379  3574381
3574391  3574411  3574423  3574429  3574457  3574463  3574523  3574531  3574541  3574577
3574583  3574589  3574609  3574619  3574621  3574631  3574639  3574649  3574657  3574663
3574687  3574721  3574757  3574759  3574771  3574789  3574799  3574817  3574819  3574847
3574849  3574853  3574861  3574897  3574927  3574933  3574937  3574943  3574997
3575003  3575017  3575057  3575071  3575087  3575093  3575101  3575113  3575119  3575147
3575153  3575183  3575251  3575263  3575269  3575291  3575317  3575333  3575339  3575357
3575371  3575413  3575437  3575441  3575449  3575471  3575483  3575503  3575519  3575521
3575531  3575549  3575573  3575581  3575597  3575599  3575609  3575617  3575639  3575647
3575653  3575657  3575687  3575701  3575707  3575717  3575783  3575821  3575839  3575843
3575849  3575861  3575863  3575867  3575893  3575909  3575911  3575917  3575921  3575927
3575941  3575959  3575981  3575983  3575987  3575993  3576029  3576031  3576037  3576043
3576073  3576091  3576121  3576119  3576127  3576151  3576161  3576163  3576179  3576187
3576217  3576227  3576233  3576257  3576269  3576283  3576289  3576299  3576311  3576319
3576323  3576329  3576359  3576361  3576373  3576401  3576407  3576413  3576421  3576437
3576451  3576467  3576473  3576479  3576509  3576557  3576571  3576577  3576583  3576593
3576607  3576637  3576649  3576673  3576691  3576721  3576733  3576761  3576779  3576791
3576803  3576809  3576829  3576847  3576863  3576907  3576913  3576941  3576943  3576961
3576967  3576971  3576977  3577019  3577027  3577031  3577037  3577061  3577081  3577099
```

```
3577109  3577141  3577151  3577153  3577159  3577169  3577181  3577247  3577253  3577261
3577267  3577289  3577297  3577313  3577333  3577337  3577349  3577391  3577393  3577417
3577459  3577487  3577501  3577507  3577513  3577517  3577543  3577571  3577573  3577577
3577597  3577631  3577649  3577661  3577663  3577669  3577699  3577703  3577727  3577771
3577793  3577799  3577829  3577859  3577877  3577891  3577897  3577907  3577913  3577921
3577957  3577961  3577963  3577967  3577997  3578017  3578021  3578033  3578053  3578059
3578089  3578093  3578101  3578119  3578129  3578131  3578149  3578167  3578191  3578203
3578209  3578221  3578227  3578231  3578243  3578249  3578257  3578261  3578273  3578293
3578353  3578359  3578383  3578437  3578453  3578461  3578467  3578473  3578539  3578543
3578567  3578569  3578573  3578581  3578591  3578599  3578633  3578651  3578657  3578681
3578683  3578693  3578717  3578723  3578737  3578741  3578759  3578791  3578801  3578807
3578819  3578837  3578843  3578863  3578873  3578879  3578893  3578903  3578917  3578947
3578951  3578969  3578989  3579071  3579077  3579083  3579089  3579119  3579127  3579133
3579139  3579157  3579161  3579179  3579187  3579211  3579221  3579271  3579281  3579287
3579347  3579349  3579371  3579377  3579403  3579481  3579487  3579493  3579497  3579509
3579523  3579529  3579533  3579547  3579551  3579613  3579623  3579629  3579647  3579649
3579679  3579683  3579691  3579703  3579761  3579767  3579769  3579799  3579803  3579817
3579827  3579841  3579857  3579859  3579869  3579871  3579893  3579931  3579949  3579959
3580001  3580067  3580069  3580099  3580103  3580123  3580127  3580133  3580141  3580153
3580163  3580169  3580207  3580211  3580229  3580259  3580261  3580271  3580289  3580301
3580331  3580333  3580337  3580351  3580363  3580373  3580393  3580397  3580403  3580411
3580429  3580441  3580457  3580463  3580487  3580513  3580519  3580553  3580579  3580583
3580597  3580609  3580613  3580649  3580657  3580669  3580673  3580679  3580691  3580697
3580747  3580761  3580763  3580771  3580793  3580807  3580813  3580831  3580849  3580859
3580861  3580901  3580909  3580919  3580943  3580957  3580963  3581003  3581021  3581029
3581041  3581047  3581087  3581099  3581107  3581113  3581117  3581129  3581131  3581153
3581167  3581189  3581191  3581219  3581251  3581257  3581269  3581293  3581321  3581363
3581377  3581381  3581393  3581419  3581429  3581467  3581497  3581503  3581507  3581521
3581549  3581551  3581579  3581593  3581597  3581609  3581621  3581639  3581651  3581663
3581681  3581689  3581693  3581701  3581717  3581723  3581731  3581741  3581749  3581777
3581779  3581791  3581803  3581821  3581827  3581839  3581843  3581867  3581869  3581873
3581881  3581911  3581923  3581927  3581953  3581971  3581999  3582001  3582017  3582077
3582079  3582083  3582091  3582101  3582107  3582119  3582149  3582179  3582191  3582193
3582233  3582239  3582259  3582269  3582277  3582281  3582343  3582353  3582361  3582389
3582401  3582419  3582433  3582437  3582463  3582493  3582499  3582521  3582547  3582559
3582611  3582613  3582617  3582629  3582637  3582643  3582653  3582661  3582671  3582707
3582727  3582737  3582739  3582743  3582749  3582757  3582769  3582781  3582791  3582793
3582809  3582823  3582829  3582833  3582877  3582883  3582899  3582923  3582967  3582973
3582977  3582989  3583007  3583033  3583057  3583067  3583081  3583091  3583103  3583123
3583127  3583133  3583159  3583169  3583187  3583189  3583199  3583207  3583213  3583219
3583231  3583241  3583271  3583273  3583289  3583297  3583309  3583313  3583357  3583403
3583409  3583417  3583529  3583543  3583579  3583597  3583603  3583633  3583639  3583661
3583667  3583669  3583673  3583681  3583711  3583717  3583721  3583739  3583757  3583771
3583777  3583781  3583793  3583819  3583829  3583841  3583843  3583847  3583861  3583871
3583903  3583919  3583927  3583939  3583949  3583963  3583967  3583997  3583999  3584011
3584017  3584033  3584047  3584051  3584069  3584089  3584099  3584101  3584107  3584111
3584123  3584129  3584137  3584143  3584149  3584171  3584183  3584201  3584221  3584237
3584249  3584303  3584311  3584323  3584327  3584333  3584341  3584353  3584359  3584363
3584377  3584381  3584417  3584419  3584423  3584459  3584461  3584479  3584509  3584563
3584593  3584599  3584611  3584617  3584641  3584681  3584689  3584723  3584729  3584741
3584743  3584759  3584767  3584771  3584797  3584813  3584851  3584869  3584873  3584921
3584923  3584927  3584929  3584947  3584981  3584983  3585013  3585073  3585097  3585133
3585137  3585139  3585143  3585149  3585161  3585173  3585209  3585221  3585229  3585233
3585247  3585251  3585259  3585271  3585289  3585293  3585311  3585331  3585347  3585349
3585353  3585359  3585389  3585391  3585403  3585443  3585451  3585457  3585467  3585481
3585497  3585557  3585581  3585611  3585629  3585667  3585671  3585679  3585689  3585697
3585709  3585733  3585749  3585767  3585779  3585787  3585809  3585817  3585823  3585859
3585913  3585917  3585931  3585941  3585949  3585959  3585971  3585977  3586001  3586019
3586021  3586057  3586073  3586081  3586087  3586097  3586109  3586123  3586159  3586171
3586189  3586199  3586217  3586223  3586237  3586259  3586267  3586277  3586279  3586283
3586301  3586327  3586333  3586379  3586391  3586397  3586399  3586411  3586441  3586469
3586481  3586487  3586493  3586511  3586529  3586537  3586543  3586547  3586549  3586553
3586559  3586571  3586619  3586631  3586637  3586651  3586657  3586717  3586727  3586729
3586741  3586753  3586757  3586771  3586777  3586783  3586811  3586819  3586823  3586829
3586853  3586859  3586867  3586871  3586879  3586883  3586889  3586897  3586901  3586903
3586907  3586909  3586927  3586943  3586951  3586997  3587009  3587021  3587099  3587117
3587123  3587137  3587161  3587167  3587179  3587183  3587197  3587201  3587203  3587237
3587249  3587251  3587263  3587267  3587279  3587303  3587317  3587321  3587347  3587359
3587393  3587399  3587407  3587429  3587431  3587443  3587449  3587453  3587461  3587477
3587497  3587513  3587531  3587569  3587579  3587581  3587587  3587611  3587641  3587657
3587659  3587669  3587671  3587687  3587693  3587699  3587707  3587711  3587719  3587741
3587761  3587777  3587797  3587803  3587809  3587813  3587819  3587821  3587861  3587873
3587879  3587891  3587923  3587929  3587939  3587957  3587989  3588019  3588029  3588041
3588061  3588073  3588077  3588097  3588103  3588113  3588133  3588163  3588181  3588209
3588217  3588239  3588251  3588289  3588337  3588341  3588349  3588379  3588383
3588401  3588407  3588421  3588427  3588451  3588457  3588469  3588493  3588499  3588503
3588509  3588517  3588527  3588589  3588601  3588617  3588619  3588647  3588677  3588679
3588707  3588763  3588769  3588773  3588787  3588791  3588797  3588803  3588811  3588841
3588859  3588869  3588877  3588881  3588883  3588913  3588917  3588919  3588931  3588941
3588947  3588961  3588971  3588973  3589031  3589073  3589133  3589139  3589141  3589151
3589153  3589163  3589189  3589247  3589279  3589283  3589297  3589361  3589367  3589373
3589381  3589441  3589451  3589457  3589471  3589477  3589489  3589493  3589513  3589549
3589571  3589589  3589603  3589609  3589661  3589693  3589699  3589709  3589717  3589721
3589739  3589741  3589753  3589757  3589763  3589783  3589801  3589819  3589847  3589853
3589871  3589881  3589903  3589913  3589933  3589973  3589991  3590011  3590021  3590023
3590029  3590039  3590051  3590057  3590063  3590087  3590089  3590099  3590101  3590117
3590137  3590143  3590149  3590161  3590173  3590201  3590207  3590219  3590239  3590243
3590263  3590291  3590299  3590303  3590309  3590311  3590339  3590347  3590381  3590387
3590407  3590413  3590429  3590437  3590441  3590467  3590473  3590501  3590537  3590539
```

3590549 3590551 3590567 3590593 3590603 3590623 3590627 3590641 3590647 3590669
3590687 3590707 3590759 3590767 3590773 3590777 3590779 3590831 3590833 3590837
3590849 3590863 3590879 3590897 3590911 3590929 3590933 3590953 3590957 3590963
3590971 3591017 3591023 3591047 3591073 3591079 3591083 3591101 3591139 3591143
3591163 3591167 3591169 3591173 3591187 3591191 3591193 3591281 3591283 3591299
3591311 3591337 3591359 3591383 3591397 3591449 3591451 3591481 3591487 3591499
3591503 3591509 3591517 3591529 3591547 3591569 3591571 3591587 3591613 3591631
3591649 3591667 3591671 3591719 3591733 3591761 3591767 3591769 3591781 3591793
3591839 3591851 3591869 3591871 3591949 3591953 3591967 3591977 3591989 3592009
3592019 3592037 3592067 3592081 3592109 3592213 3592217 3592223 3592231 3592243
3592261 3592289 3592291 3592319 3592327 3592397 3592399 3592411 3592427 3592447
3592483 3592493 3592517 3592553 3592571 3592579 3592583 3592591 3592597 3592613
3592619 3592637 3592639 3592643 3592649 3592651 3592657 3592679 3592747 3592751
3592759 3592777 3592801 3592819 3592829 3592847 3592859 3592861 3592867 3592879
3592889 3592891 3592903 3592907 3592913 3592921 3592969 3592973 3592997 3593003
3593017 3593021 3593039 3593047 3593053 3593063 3593077 3593087 3593089 3593101
3593113 3593201 3593203 3593211 3593321 3593323 3593333 3593351 3593353 3593371
3593377 3593399 3593407 3593417 3593423 3593441 3593483 3593501 3593503 3593507
3593509 3593519 3593531 3593539 3593549 3593563 3593581 3593587 3593617 3593627
3593633 3593659 3593663 3593669 3593687 3593701 3593713 3593747 3593791 3593797
3593803 3593827 3593833 3593873 3593881 3593903 3593917 3593927 3593929 3593939
3593959 3593969 3593977 3593981 3594001 3594011 3594037 3594053 3594061 3594067
3594083 3594113 3594121 3594131 3594161 3594167 3594169 3594197 3594223 3594251
3594277 3594299 3594307 3594317 3594319 3594323 3594343 3594377 3594389
3594403 3594427 3594431 3594433 3594449 3594467 3594473 3594523 3594541 3594551
3594557 3594559 3594583 3594589 3594623 3594631 3594641 3594649 3594653 3594673
3594683 3594697 3594707 3594713 3594719 3594727 3594733 3594761 3594763 3594793
3594797 3594821 3594827 3594863 3594881 3594887 3594901 3594907 3594911 3594931
3594953 3594959 3594961 3594967 3595001 3595027 3595051 3595057 3595063 3595069
3595079 3595087 3595091 3595099 3595103 3595117 3595121 3595127 3595129 3595133
3595139 3595181 3595201 3595213 3595231 3595247 3595271 3595289 3595301 3595303
3595309 3595363 3595367 3595387 3595393 3595399 3595409 3595441 3595451 3595463
3595481 3595489 3595589 3595591 3595601 3595607 3595609 3595621 3595633 3595639
3595649 3595663 3595667 3595673 3595733 3595777 3595793
3595811 3595847 3595859 3595861 3595877 3595897 3595909 3595939 3595951 3595967
3595973 3596003 3596009 3596023 3596059 3596063 3596083 3596107 3596123 3596137
3596143 3596147 3596161 3596167 3596171 3596183 3596189 3596191 3596213 3596239
3596251 3596267 3596287 3596297 3596309 3596323 3596353 3596357 3596371 3596381
3596383 3596407 3596419 3596429 3596431 3596447 3596449 3596521 3596531 3596543
3596557 3596573 3596587 3596599 3596611 3596617 3596641 3596653 3596687 3596689
3596693 3596701 3596731 3596737 3596759 3596771 3596773 3596777 3596819 3596849
3596851 3596869 3596893 3596897 3596927 3596933 3596959 3596981 3597001 3597017
3597037 3597043 3597049 3597059 3597067 3597071 3597091 3597127 3597133 3597151
3597161 3597173 3597179 3597193 3597197 3597199 3597203 3597211 3597227 3597241
3597257 3597259 3597263 3597277 3597281 3597311 3597329 3597343 3597359 3597379
3597383 3597389 3597397 3597401 3597409 3597413 3597437 3597449 3597487 3597491
3597493 3597511 3597527 3597533 3597541 3597551 3597553 3597563 3597569 3597571
3597589 3597611 3597613 3597617 3597673 3597677 3597703 3597749 3597751 3597773
3597793 3597809 3597817 3597883 3597887 3597901 3597907 3597911 3597929 3597941
3597947 3597949 3597977 3597983 3597989 3598009 3598013 3598019 3598027 3598039
3598061 3598081 3598093 3598109 3598141 3598157 3598221 3598229 3598241 3598253
3598261 3598279 3598307 3598313 3598319 3598337 3598363 3598379 3598381 3598393
3598403 3598411 3598421 3598423 3598453 3598459 3598477 3598487 3598501 3598519
3598549 3598589 3598591 3598601 3598607 3598613 3598643 3598667 3598691 3598703
3598709 3598723 3598729 3598739 3598757 3598789 3598801 3598811 3598831 3598841
3598843 3598867 3598883 3598891 3598921 3598927 3598943 3598949 3598957 3598967
3598981 3599009 3599023 3599033 3599041 3599047 3599083 3599093 3599107 3599111
3599117 3599137 3599147 3599149 3599171 3599179 3599191 3599207 3599231 3599243
3599251 3599263 3599269 3599279 3599327 3599357 3599369 3599371 3599383 3599423
3599429 3599437 3599447 3599459 3599467 3599473 3599483 3599501 3599527 3599581
3599621 3599639 3599641 3599649 3599653 3599663 3599719 3599737 3599773
3599779 3599821 3599833 3599837 3599839 3599851 3599879 3599881 3599887 3599899
3599927 3599929 3599933 3599941 3599963 3599969 3600001 3600011 3600013 3600017
3600041 3600053 3600097 3600119 3600133 3600173 3600187 3600193 3600203 3600217
3600221 3600269 3600283 3600301 3600307 3600319 3600361 3600383 3600407 3600409
3600419 3600431 3600451 3600461 3600463 3600469 3600473 3600479 3600491 3600511
3600521 3600523 3600533 3600539 3600547 3600559 3600563 3600587 3600601 3600607
3600613 3600629 3600659 3600679 3600683 3600689 3600697 3600721 3600731 3600739
3600749 3600757 3600761 3600763 3600791 3600799 3600809 3600841 3600847 3600853
3600881 3600887 3600911 3600913 3600917 3600941 3600983 3600997 3601001
3601007 3601009 3601019 3601027 3601043 3601061 3601063 3601079 3601111 3601123
3601139 3601141 3601151 3601193 3601211 3601219 3601237 3601243 3601253 3601267
3601291 3601313 3601327 3601337 3601361 3601363 3601369 3601421 3601427 3601447
3601457 3601463 3601489 3601517 3601523 3601529 3601541 3601553 3601567 3601571
3601579 3601589 3601607 3601627 3601669 3601681 3601693 3601709 3601711
3601729 3601753 3601781 3601783 3601837 3601877 3601879 3601883 3601889 3601903
3601931 3601937 3601957 3601967 3601991 3601993 3602021 3602041 3602047 3602057
3602059 3602083 3602087 3602089 3602149 3602167 3602171 3602173 3602197 3602201
3602243 3602257 3602279 3602297 3602299 3602309 3602353 3602359 3602371 3602377
3602393 3602437 3602441 3602461 3602471 3602491 3602527 3602537 3602549 3602561
3602581 3602587 3602591 3602593 3602617 3602633 3602659 3602681 3602693 3602707
3602713 3602719 3602737 3602747 3602749 3602773 3602783 3602803 3602821 3602831
3602869 3602891 3602897 3602899 3602903 3602921 3602923 3602941 3602959 3602971
3602983 3602999 3603007 3603049 3603053 3603073 3603077 3603079 3603101 3603107
3603151 3603169 3603227 3603251 3603253 3603277 3603287 3603289 3603317 3603323
3603329 3603361 3603373 3603389 3603401 3603419 3603421 3603437 3603451 3603469
3603491 3603527 3603539 3603547 3603563 3603577 3603583 3603619 3603623 3603659
3603667 3603703 3603713 3603727 3603731 3603737 3603797 3603799 3603829 3603833
3603857 3603869 3603871 3603883 3603923 3603931 3603953 3603961 3603989 3603991

```
3604019  3604021  3604037  3604039  3604043  3604057  3604067  3604087  3604099  3604121
3604127  3604141  3604147  3604151  3604157  3604163  3604177  3604189  3604199  3604213
3604241  3604247  3604273  3604283  3604297  3604301  3604309  3604313  3604327  3604373
3604417  3604421  3604427  3604451  3604481  3604507  3604511  3604529  3604541  3604543
3604553  3604567  3604591  3604603  3604609  3604619  3604621  3604631  3604681  3604693
3604703  3604709  3604717  3604747  3604753  3604763  3604771  3604781  3604789  3604793
3604807  3604817  3604829  3604871  3604879  3604891  3604907  3604933  3604943  3604963
3604967  3604981  3604999  3605027  3605033  3605051  3605057  3605059  3605081  3605087
3605093  3605099  3605111  3605141  3605143  3605153  3605159  3605197  3605201  3605221
3605233  3605257  3605263  3605279  3605281  3605291  3605293  3605299  3605311  3605341
3605351  3605369  3605387  3605419  3605443  3605473  3605477  3605489  3605531  3605561
3605621  3605629  3605633  3605647  3605653  3605669  3605669  3605671  3605705  3605711
3605741  3605743  3605747  3605759  3605783  3605803  3605809  3605813  3605821  3605837
3605843  3605857  3605867  3605869  3605879  3605881  3605891  3605897  3605923  3605929
3605939  3605957  3605969  3605999  3606011  3606017  3606041  3606059  3606061  3606089
3606103  3606151  3606157  3606187  3606209  3606223  3606233  3606277  3606283  3606287
3606289  3606293  3606301  3606341  3606347  3606359  3606389  3606413  3606437  3606443
3606461  3606467  3606487  3606497  3606511  3606529  3606541  3606553  3606563  3606569
3606583  3606593  3606613  3606661  3606679  3606689  3606697  3606719  3606721  3606727
3606731  3606763  3606767  3606769  3606773  3606781  3606829  3606833  3606851  3606859
3606887  3606899  3606901  3606917  3606947  3606949  3606959  3606961  3606973  3606983
3606989  3606997  3607001  3607031  3607063  3607069  3607091  3607099  3607103  3607117
3607133  3607147  3607151  3607157  3607183  3607187  3607199  3607211  3607217  3607229
3607231  3607237  3607249  3607277  3607301  3607309  3607327  3607361  3607381  3607393
3607411  3607421  3607423  3607433  3607447  3607453  3607459  3607489  3607493  3607507
3607517  3607523  3607531  3607543  3607547  3607561  3607567  3607589  3607603  3607607
3607627  3607633  3607649  3607691  3607697  3607727  3607729  3607741  3607771  3607787
3607801  3607817  3607819  3607831  3607837  3607841  3607867  3607897  3607921  3607931
3607939  3607949  3607957  3607963  3607969  3607979  3607991  3607999  3608003  3608009
3608051  3608053  3608057  3608071  3608117  3608153  3608161  3608179  3608191  3608207
3608219  3608221  3608239  3608249  3608251  3608257  3608273  3608279  3608293  3608303
3608377  3608389  3608393  3608417  3608477  3608489  3608491  3608503  3608513  3608531
3608543  3608551  3608569  3608621  3608639  3608653  3608669  3608681  3608701  3608713
3608729  3608747  3608767  3608771  3608783  3608791  3608797  3608807  3608837  3608849
3608851  3608863  3608867  3608873  3608887  3608897  3608903  3608909  3608921  3608939
3608951  3608977  3609007  3609013  3609029  3609041  3609059  3609061  3609071  3609077
3609101  3609103  3609161  3609163  3609191  3609209  3609211  3609241  3609251  3609257
3609283  3609289  3609301  3609329  3609337  3609349  3609379  3609383  3609391  3609407
3609409  3609433  3609439  3609451  3609479  3609481  3609491  3609493  3609497  3609499
3609503  3609509  3609523  3609533  3609581  3609583  3609611  3609623  3609629  3609637
3609649  3609673  3609703  3609719  3609721  3609731  3609737  3609743  3609769  3609773
3609787  3609799  3609803  3609817  3609821  3609847  3609863  3609871  3609877  3609887
3609889  3609911  3609953  3609959  3609973  3609997  3609997  3610003  3610021
3610037  3610051  3610081  3610097  3610109  3610111  3610129  3610153  3610157  3610169
3610177  3610183  3610199  3610219  3610283  3610301  3610303  3610319  3610331  3610339
3610351  3610357  3610363  3610367  3610381  3610391  3610393  3610403  3610427  3610469
3610499  3610519  3610531  3610543  3610547  3610549  3610553  3610577  3610591  3610597  3610619
3610657  3610669  3610679  3610693  3610699  3610709  3610721  3610723  3610729  3610759
3610771  3610781  3610807  3610811  3610861  3610883  3610891  3610897  3610921  3610933
3610949  3610951  3610961  3610979  3611059  3611063  3611071  3611093  3611119  3611129
3611147  3611171  3611177  3611189  3611203  3611243  3611281  3611287  3611291  3611297
3611303  3611317  3611323  3611329  3611347  3611351  3611369  3611381  3611389  3611393
3611401  3611411  3611417  3611423  3611431  3611453  3611477  3611479  3611513  3611521
3611549  3611551  3611561  3611563  3611603  3611623  3611669  3611677  3611711  3611719
3611761  3611771  3611789  3611827  3611831  3611833  3611849  3611869  3611873  3611891
3611893  3611941  3611947  3611981  3611987  3612019  3612023  3612029  3612047  3612053
3612061  3612083  3612097  3612121  3612137  3612149  3612179  3612181  3612187  3612197
3612209  3612221  3612227  3612233  3612239  3612241  3612247  3612263  3612277  3612281
3612283  3612289  3612293  3612307  3612317  3612319  3612331  3612341  3612391  3612407
3612419  3612431  3612437  3612457  3612487  3612491  3612493  3612503  3612509  3612529
3612547  3612577  3612607  3612613  3612659  3612667  3612671  3612673  3612677  3612683
3612689  3612703  3612737  3612743  3612761  3612773  3612779  3612781  3612787  3612799
3612809  3612811  3612821  3612853  3612883  3612893  3612899  3612919  3612923  3612929
3612943  3612967  3612979  3612991  3613003  3613009  3613033  3613039  3613079  3613121
3613123  3613151  3613157  3613171  3613187  3613189  3613193  3613199  3613201  3613217
3613237  3613271  3613301  3613307  3613321  3613327  3613331  3613349  3613361  3613387
3613397  3613417  3613433  3613447  3613481  3613513  3613517  3613523  3613543  3613559
3613601  3613607  3613609  3613619  3613637  3613663  3613681  3613693  3613703
3613717  3613721  3613723  3613733  3613739  3613747  3613759  3613787  3613789  3613807
3613811  3613837  3613847  3613867  3613871  3613889  3613931  3613957  3613963
3613991  3613993  3613999  3614003  3614033  3614041  3614057  3614087  3614099  3614101
3614111  3614129  3614137  3614147  3614153  3614173  3614179  3614203  3614207  3614209
3614227  3614239  3614249  3614263  3614267  3614269  3614291  3614309  3614323  3614339
3614363  3614407  3614411  3614431  3614447  3614459  3614461  3614477  3614497  3614509
3614561  3614581  3614587  3614603  3614609  3614669  3614671  3614687  3614707  3614711
3614719  3614747  3614773  3614777  3614783  3614791  3614813  3614833  3614839  3614843
3614867  3614873  3614893  3614903  3614909  3614917  3614927  3614939  3614951  3614953
3614957  3614969  3614981  3614987  3614993  3615037  3615089  3615097  3615103  3615133
3615167  3615173  3615211  3615217  3615221  3615229  3615259  3615299  3615319  3615329
3615331  3615341  3615389  3615413  3615419  3615431  3615433  3615449  3615457
3615467  3615473  3615523  3615559  3615571  3615581  3615583  3615587  3615641  3615649
3615671  3615701  3615709  3615721  3615727  3615737  3615739  3615743  3615769  3615791
3615793  3615811  3615839  3615847  3615863  3615893  3615919  3615929  3615943  3615949
3615961  3615967  3615977  3616001  3616007  3616009  3616013  3616027  3616033  3616049
3616069  3616073  3616079  3616111  3616117  3616127  3616147  3616183  3616229  3616231
3616259  3616297  3616303  3616351  3616357  3616369  3616373  3616381  3616397  3616399
3616409  3616421  3616423  3616447  3616453  3616463  3616477  3616489  3616519  3616531
3616537  3616549  3616573  3616583  3616621  3616633  3616637  3616649  3616661  3616673
3616703  3616721  3616741  3616747  3616757  3616813  3616829  3616831  3616841  3616843
```

```
3616853  3616883  3616889  3616901  3616913  3616933  3616939  3616969  3616993  3616997
3616999  3617027  3617059  3617063  3617069  3617071  3617093  3617099  3617101  3617137
3617147  3617149  3617153  3617177  3617179  3617221  3617267  3617269  3617281  3617291
3617293  3617309  3617321  3617323  3617329  3617347  3617351  3617363  3617401  3617407
3617441  3617443  3617473  3617477  3617479  3617491  3617501  3617503  3617533  3617557
3617561  3617569  3617587  3617597  3617599  3617609  3617611  3617623  3617629  3617639
3617641  3617659  3617683  3617687  3617689  3617701  3617711  3617723  3617737  3617767
3617773  3617797  3617813  3617843  3617857  3617879  3617899  3617903  3617927  3617951
3617983  3617987  3617989  3617993  3618007  3618029  3618047  3618049  3618071  3618077
3618101  3618137  3618143  3618157  3618163  3618187  3618191  3618211  3618217  3618233
3618239  3618247  3618259  3618269  3618281  3618283  3618311  3618317  3618323  3618343
3618347  3618397  3618403  3618409  3618421  3618443  3618457  3618463  3618479  3618497
3618499  3618509  3618523  3618547  3618553  3618583  3618631  3618653  3618679  3618697
3618709  3618743  3618757  3618761  3618793  3618803  3618809  3618827  3618833  3618851
3618869  3618907  3618913  3618919  3618929  3618959  3618961  3618991  3619013  3619019
3619037  3619039  3619093  3619103  3619117  3619123  3619151  3619159  3619183  3619199
3619207  3619243  3619261  3619289  3619307  3619327  3619339  3619393  3619397  3619411
3619433  3619459  3619463  3619471  3619477  3619501  3619507  3619531  3619549  3619571
3619573  3619597  3619607  3619613  3619619  3619639  3619643  3619663  3619669  3619687
3619711  3619723  3619769  3619771  3619787  3619807  3619813  3619817  3619843  3619873
3619877  3619883  3619907  3619909  3619921  3619961  3619981  3619991  3620011  3620021
3620033  3620053  3620069  3620083  3620093  3620119  3620129  3620153  3620159  3620161
3620207  3620209  3620231  3620249  3620257  3620291  3620293  3620311  3620327  3620329
3620369  3620387  3620401  3620437  3620443  3620467  3620489  3620497  3620501  3620537
3620567  3620597  3620599  3620623  3620627  3620641  3620657  3620671  3620681  3620689
3620693  3620713  3620723  3620741  3620753  3620767  3620789  3620791  3620803  3620819
3620839  3620843  3620879  3620909  3620917  3620921  3620923  3620933  3620941  3620957
3620977  3620989  3620993  3620999  3621011  3621031  3621043  3621049  3621067  3621083
3621103  3621113  3621127  3621139  3621157  3621181  3621199  3621217  3621223  3621239
3621251  3621253  3621257  3621263  3621269  3621271  3621287  3621313  3621329  3621341
3621347  3621353  3621379  3621403  3621461  3621463  3621469  3621473  3621481
3621517  3621521  3621529  3621559  3621577  3621581  3621587  3621593  3621613  3621617
3621623  3621643  3621661  3621691  3621701  3621713  3621721  3621727  3621733  3621767
3621797  3621803  3621851  3621857  3621881  3621887  3621889  3621907  3621911  3621929
3621931  3621941  3621973  3621977  3621983  3622001  3622007  3622039  3622043  3622051
3622061  3622079  3622081  3622097  3622111  3622121  3622123  3622159  3622169  3622183
3622193  3622219  3622231  3622253  3622259  3622261  3622273  3622279  3622313  3622321
3622327  3622351  3622357  3622373  3622379  3622393  3622427  3622429  3622433  3622439
3622453  3622459  3622469  3622481  3622499  3622501  3622511  3622517  3622529  3622537
3622573  3622579  3622583  3622589  3622601  3622609  3622631  3622643  3622679  3622687
3622727  3622729  3622733  3622739  3622741  3622747  3622763  3622783  3622787  3622811
3622813  3622831  3622837  3622847  3622859  3622873  3622889  3622897  3622903  3622909
3622919  3622951  3622963  3622967  3622979  3622987  3622991  3623017  3623069  3623071
3623099  3623107  3623117  3623143  3623171  3623197  3623203  3623237  3623251  3623267
3623273  3623287  3623353  3623359  3623369  3623377  3623381  3623393  3623401  3623413
3623423  3623441  3623449  3623483  3623491  3623507  3623519  3623537  3623569  3623597
3623639  3623657  3623671  3623681  3623689  3623701  3623707  3623713  3623723  3623729
3623731  3623773  3623783  3623803  3623821  3623861  3623881  3623887  3623897  3623899
3623909  3623929  3623933  3623947  3623951  3623953  3623969  3623987  3623999  3624001
3624011  3624013  3624059  3624073  3624091  3624107  3624109  3624139  3624143  3624157
3624161  3624167  3624191  3624221  3624223  3624233  3624239  3624287  3624289  3624293
3624301  3624319  3624323  3624331  3624353  3624367  3624371  3624373  3624407  3624431
3624443  3624449  3624457  3624461  3624463  3624469  3624473  3624493  3624503  3624521
3624529  3624539  3624541  3624563  3624581  3624601  3624629  3624637  3624653  3624667
3624671  3624679  3624683  3624697  3624721  3624727  3624773  3624787  3624811  3624821
3624833  3624847  3624911  3624917  3624919  3624931  3624937  3624949  3624977  3624983
3625003  3625031  3625033  3625043  3625049  3625051  3625079  3625081  3625093  3625103
3625121  3625133  3625151  3625177  3625211  3625213  3625229  3625243  3625277  3625309
3625339  3625351  3625361  3625367  3625387  3625397  3625411  3625423  3625429  3625477
3625487  3625511  3625577  3625579  3625591  3625603  3625619  3625661  3625669  3625669
3625679  3625681  3625693  3625711  3625733  3625759  3625781  3625793  3625807  3625813
3625829  3625849  3625859  3625873  3625883  3625939  3625943  3625961  3625969  3625987
3625991  3625997  3626009  3626011  3626033  3626053  3626059  3626087  3626099  3626113
3626141  3626149  3626153  3626159  3626171  3626173  3626201  3626221  3626239  3626257
3626269  3626279  3626281  3626291  3626297  3626299  3626309  3626339  3626351  3626383
3626401  3626417  3626429  3626431  3626437  3626443  3626449  3626453  3626471  3626501
3626521  3626531  3626533  3626561  3626563  3626569  3626611  3626639  3626641  3626657
3626669  3626677  3626683  3626717  3626723  3626741  3626743  3626759  3626771  3626773
3626803  3626807  3626813  3626837  3626873  3626881  3626897  3626941  3626947  3626951
3626971  3626981  3626989  3627023  3627053  3627067  3627079  3627083  3627097  3627101
3627109  3627139  3627167  3627181  3627199  3627203  3627223  3627251  3627257  3627263
3627269  3627277  3627287  3627289  3627317  3627329  3627331  3627359  3627367  3627383
3627391  3627401  3627427  3627431  3627469  3627523  3627587  3627641  3627649
3627653  3627661  3627671  3627677  3627683  3627707  3627737  3627769  3627787  3627791
3627823  3627829  3627839  3627857  3627863  3627889  3627893  3627901  3627931  3627937
3627941  3627947  3627971  3627973  3627979  3627989  3628007  3628033  3628057  3628061
3628063  3628067  3628073  3628111  3628127  3628129  3628133  3628153  3628169  3628187
3628193  3628199  3628201  3628243  3628249  3628267  3628279  3628291  3628309
3628321  3628337  3628351  3628357  3628363  3628397  3628399  3628403  3628421  3628439
3628453  3628481  3628483  3628561  3628571  3628591  3628621  3628631  3628657  3628663
3628679  3628697  3628711  3628747  3628759  3628763  3628777  3628783  3628789  3628811
3628819  3628841  3628847  3628853  3628883  3628887  3628907  3628931  3628949  3628967
3628969  3628987  3628991  3629027  3629029  3629039  3629051  3629053  3629063  3629081
3629099  3629107  3629111  3629117  3629123  3629141  3629159  3629161  3629167  3629173
3629179  3629183  3629203  3629207  3629257  3629261  3629287  3629291  3629299  3629303
3629357  3629359  3629363  3629389  3629393  3629401  3629407  3629413  3629459  3629471
3629477  3629497  3629519  3629537  3629543  3629557  3629567  3629581  3629597  3629609
3629623  3629629  3629657  3629671  3629719  3629729  3629749  3629777  3629783  3629803
3629831  3629863  3629867  3629869  3629887  3629897  3629909  3629921  3629933  3629939
```

```
3629947 3629953 3629987 3629999 3630019 3630037 3630047 3630097 3630101 3630149
3630157 3630161 3630167 3630169 3630199 3630203 3630223 3630227 3630229 3630241
3630247 3630257 3630259 3630269 3630271 3630281 3630323 3630331 3630359 3630371
3630377 3630391 3630397 3630433 3630437 3630461 3630521 3630547 3630559 3630593
3630611 3630629 3630631 3630643 3630667 3630701 3630709 3630733 3630743 3630749
3630769 3630779 3630793 3630817 3630821 3630827 3630833 3630841 3630857 3630859
3630883 3630901 3630917 3630923 3630929 3630943 3630953 3630959 3630961 3630967
3630971 3630973 3630983 3630997 3631007 3631009 3631027 3631031 3631039 3631073
3631139 3631141 3631163 3631169 3631169 3631211 3631213 3631219 3631237 3631249
3631321 3631339 3631343 3631349 3631379 3631423 3631427 3631457 3631469 3631487
3631501 3631517 3631519 3631541 3631543 3631561 3631597 3631609 3631633 3631637
3631703 3631729 3631741 3631751 3631753 3631759 3631763 3631781 3631783 3631787
3631799 3631801 3631807 3631811 3631813 3631841 3631871 3631877 3631889 3631919
3631921 3631937 3631951 3631963 3631973 3632009 3632011 3632023 3632029 3632051
3632087 3632141 3632171 3632191 3632201 3632243 3632267 3632269 3632273 3632297
3632303 3632309 3632323 3632333 3632351 3632353 3632371 3632381 3632383 3632389
3632399 3632411 3632423 3632429 3632443 3632449 3632479 3632491 3632507 3632513
3632521 3632537 3632557 3632579 3632599 3632609 3632621 3632633 3632653 3632663
3632701 3632719 3632729 3632737 3632753 3632767 3632773 3632777 3632789 3632803
3632813 3632821 3632831 3632833 3632879 3632903 3632929 3632939 3632953 3632957
3632963 3632987 3632989 3633001 3633013 3633017 3633029 3633037 3633041 3633059
3633073 3633083 3633101 3633109 3633127 3633139 3633151 3633167 3633181 3633187
3633191 3633193 3633229 3633233 3633263 3633269 3633299 3633317 3633337 3633347
3633349 3633353 3633361 3633367 3633373 3633391 3633401 3633403 3633431 3633449
3633499 3633551 3633559 3633569 3633571 3633577 3633583 3633647 3633653 3633661
3633673 3633683 3633689 3633697 3633703 3633713 3633719 3633741 3633773 3633797
3633803 3633821 3633853 3633857 3633859 3633863 3633893 3633901 3633907 3633919
3633923 3633941 3633983 3633991 3634009 3634021 3634027 3634031 3634061 3634097
3634123 3634129 3634171 3634201 3634219 3634249 3634261 3634271 3634289 3634291
3634297 3634303 3634307 3634313 3634343 3634373 3634417 3634439 3634457 3634507
3634511 3634513 3634531 3634559 3634571 3634591 3634601 3634607 3634619 3634627
3634637 3634639 3634663 3634669 3634679 3634693 3634699 3634717 3634723 3634727
3634777 3634789 3634801 3634811 3634859 3634861 3634877 3634901 3634907 3634913
3634927 3634949 3634993 3634999 3635001 3635057 3635069 3635077 3635087
3635113 3635147 3635171 3635189 3635197 3635201 3635207 3635209 3635221 3635227
3635239 3635243 3635257 3635273 3635299 3635321 3635353 3635369 3635371 3635377
3635393 3635407 3635431 3635447 3635453 3635459 3635551 3635563 3635579 3635581
3635617 3635623 3635647 3635651 3635689 3635699 3635717 3635719 3635729 3635743
3635761 3635767 3635789 3635791 3635803 3635809 3635831 3635857 3635877 3635881
3635923 3635969 3635971 3635987 3635999 3636013 3636019 3636043 3636053 3636071
3636077 3636097 3636103 3636119 3636169 3636211 3636221 3636233 3636247 3636257
3636263 3636289 3636301 3636329 3636341 3636359 3636361 3636371 3636389 3636401
3636403 3636427 3636439 3636443 3636463 3636469 3636481 3636491 3636499 3636511
3636527 3636539 3636541 3636547 3636551 3636569 3636593 3636617 3636631 3636667
3636683 3636709 3636757 3636769 3636779 3636781 3636791 3636797 3636799 3636839
3636877 3636901 3636911 3636943 3636947 3636983 3636991 3637043 3637057 3637061
3637087 3637097 3637103 3637121 3637129 3637141 3637157 3637159 3637169 3637171
3637187 3637217 3637223 3637273 3637279 3637287 3637301 3637331 3637333 3637343
3637367 3637391 3637393 3637411 3637453 3637481 3637523 3637547 3637573 3637577
3637589 3637591 3637603 3637619 3637637 3637681 3637691 3637693 3637709 3637723
3637771 3637793 3637801 3637811 3637813 3637849 3637859 3637883 3637891 3637897
3637901 3637903 3637913 3637927 3637937 3637939 3637957 3637967 3637981 3638003
3638009 3638023 3638027 3638039 3638057 3638059 3638077 3638087 3638113 3638147
3638149 3638171 3638183 3638203 3638207 3638213 3638227 3638233 3638237 3638249
3638251 3638267 3638279 3638287 3638293 3638303 3638333 3638351 3638407 3638413
3638417 3638419 3638473 3638477 3638489 3638491 3638497 3638507 3638513 3638523
3638549 3638573 3638639 3638641 3638651 3638653 3638699 3638753 3638759 3638771
3638773 3638777 3638809 3638827 3638851 3638879 3638903 3638909 3638917 3638923
3638941 3638951 3638953 3638959 3638993 3639017 3639019 3639029 3639043 3639067
3639079 3639107 3639109 3639143 3639151 3639157 3639161 3639193 3639197 3639211
3639217 3639277 3639281 3639287 3639289 3639319 3639323 3639347 3639379 3639397
3639403 3639407 3639409 3639421 3639473 3639481 3639487 3639499 3639509 3639521
3639523 3639527 3639541 3639551 3639569 3639577 3639593 3639631 3639637 3639661
3639667 3639689 3639719 3639733 3639739 3639743 3639763 3639781 3639817 3639827
3639829 3639841 3639847 3639851 3639869 3639913 3639919 3639929 3639941 3639959
3639967 3639971 3639973 3639983 3639991 3639997 3640019 3640027 3640031 3640037
3640061 3640073 3640081 3640121 3640151 3640163 3640181 3640207 3640223 3640243
3640249 3640289 3640309 3640327 3640331 3640333 3640369 3640379 3640391 3640409
3640447 3640451 3640471 3640487 3640493 3640519 3640523 3640537 3640543 3640561
3640577 3640589 3640591 3640597 3640603 3640643 3640649 3640661 3640669 3640711
3640717 3640753 3640781 3640789 3640801 3640807 3640817 3640823 3640829 3640843
3640849 3640859 3640867 3640891 3640909 3640933 3640937 3640991 3640993 3640999
3641041 3641051 3641069 3641081 3641083 3641119 3641123 3641147 3641149 3641159
3641171 3641191 3641201 3641219 3641221 3641233 3641237 3641243 3641263 3641311
3641357 3641371 3641381 3641387 3641389 3641399 3641401 3641423 3641431 3641437
3641441 3641461 3641467 3641489 3641507 3641509 3641537 3641549 3641551 3641563
3641569 3641591 3641593 3641609 3641611 3641623 3641629 3641633 3641641 3641647
3641653 3641747 3641731 3641753 3641767 3641773 3641777 3641783 3641801 3641819
3641819 3641831 3641851 3641857 3641861 3641867 3641881 3641887 3641917 3641923
3641933 3641951 3641987 3641999 3642019 3642031 3642049 3642061 3642101 3642157
3642203 3642209 3642227 3642239 3642241 3642251 3642269 3642299 3642307 3642323
3642337 3642341 3642343 3642347 3642377 3642427 3642449 3642451 3642467 3642479
3642491 3642547 3642559 3642571 3642577 3642581 3642629 3642631 3642631 3642733
3642649 3642673 3642677 3642679 3642697 3642701 3642707 3642721 3642731 3642733
3642737 3642761 3642791 3642803 3642823 3642839 3642881 3642911 3642931 3642941
3642959 3642971 3643001 3643033 3643043 3643063 3643099 3643127 3643139 3643141
3643147 3643181 3643201 3643217 3643267 3643271 3643291 3643303 3643331 3643351
3643363 3643369 3643403 3643411 3643429 3643447 3643463 3643477 3643481 3643483
3643511 3643513 3643517 3643529 3643537 3643561 3643579 3643603 3643609 3643613
```

```
3643621  3643631  3643639  3643657  3643669  3643681  3643699  3643721  3643733  3643747
3643751  3643799  3643807  3643811  3643819  3643841  3643853  3643859  3643873  3643883
3643891  3643897  3643901  3643919  3643921  3643951  3643961  3643963  3643973  3644021
3644023  3644057  3644059  3644071  3644117  3644129  3644149  3644153  3644159  3644183
3644213  3644231  3644237  3644279  3644297  3644309  3644317  3644321  3644339  3644351
3644357  3644411  3644423  3644437  3644479  3644483  3644497  3644503  3644513  3644569
3644575  3644587  3644593  3644617  3644621  3644629  3644653  3644657  3644659  3644669
3644731  3644743  3644747  3644761  3644791  3644801  3644831  3644873  3644899  3644947
3644951  3644957  3644959  3644983  3644999  3645007  3645013  3645049  3645053  3645071
3645077  3645101  3645107  3645119  3645121  3645133  3645137  3645143  3645149  3645151
3645193  3645227  3645251  3645253  3645263  3645289  3645307  3645347  3645349  3645371
3645373  3645377  3645391  3645407  3645409  3645419  3645449  3645469  3645527  3645533
3645539  3645557  3645559  3645563  3645571  3645581  3645589  3645611  3645623  3645643
3645659  3645683  3645703  3645709  3645713  3645727  3645731  3645737  3645749  3645767
3645773  3645781  3645791  3645809  3645823  3645877  3645893  3645899  3645913  3645949
3645953  3645959  3645977  3645979  3645997  3646001  3646009  3646021  3646033  3646037
3646039  3646057  3646067  3646079  3646103  3646117  3646129  3646183  3646187  3646219
3646229  3646231  3646261  3646289  3646319  3646337  3646339  3646343  3646361  3646369
3646393  3646399  3646411  3646421  3646427  3646441  3646463  3646471  3646481  3646493
3646507  3646523  3646541  3646553  3646567  3646583  3646603  3646633  3646637  3646661
3646681  3646693  3646711  3646717  3646723  3646729  3646739  3646751  3646759  3646781
3646793  3646817  3646829  3646859  3646883  3646889  3646913  3646919  3646927  3646931
3646957  3646961  3646963  3646997  3647003  3647023  3647029  3647071  3647093  3647101
3647167  3647173  3647177  3647207  3647233  3647257  3647261  3647263  3647291  3647327
3647339  3647353  3647377  3647381  3647383  3647393  3647419  3647431  3647459  3647461
3647489  3647531  3647551  3647573  3647597  3647599  3647627  3647629  3647641
3647671  3647687  3647689  3647711  3647713  3647723  3647747  3647759  3647773
3647779  3647797  3647803  3647807  3647827  3647851  3647873  3647921  3647927  3647947
3647953  3647971  3647989  3648031  3648037  3648041  3648067  3648079  3648101  3648107
3648131  3648137  3648167  3648179  3648241  3648263  3648269  3648277  3648289  3648301
3648331  3648343  3648391  3648409  3648413  3648419  3648427  3648439  3648451  3648479
3648487  3648493  3648511  3648521  3648527  3648539  3648553  3648581  3648587  3648643
3648647  3648649  3648653  3648661  3648683  3648691  3648707  3648739  3648767  3648769
3648781  3648797  3648833  3648847  3648857  3648899  3648913  3648919  3648923
3648941  3648943  3648947  3648989  3649001  3649003  3649027  3649049  3649057  3649097
3649133  3649147  3649153  3649181  3649193  3649201  3649207  3649229  3649241  3649253
3649259  3649297  3649301  3649307  3649313  3649337  3649357  3649363  3649397  3649403
3649411  3649417  3649469  3649487  3649511  3649517  3649531  3649549  3649559  3649567
3649579  3649601  3649609  3649637  3649669  3649693  3649699  3649741  3649753
3649771  3649777  3649831  3649871  3649889  3649903  3649907  3649913  3649931  3649949
3649967  3649993  3649999  3650051  3650063  3650069  3650081  3650111  3650113
3650117  3650137  3650159  3650167  3650173  3650183  3650197  3650203  3650221  3650233
3650237  3650249  3650263  3650327  3650329  3650333  3650341  3650357  3650369  3650419
3650429  3650431  3650441  3650447  3650483  3650497  3650501  3650503  3650509  3650533
3650561  3650567  3650573  3650579  3650593  3650609  3650617  3650651  3650663  3650677
3650683  3650687  3650701  3650707  3650729  3650741  3650761  3650783  3650791  3650797
3650809  3650833  3650837  3650849  3650851  3650863  3650887  3650929  3650939  3650953
3650957  3650989  3651019  3651023  3651083  3651119  3651127  3651133  3651157  3651169
3651191  3651217  3651239  3651269  3651281  3651293  3651341  3651407  3651409  3651443
3651449  3651463  3651467  3651491  3651497  3651539  3651547  3651559  3651607  3651611
3651619  3651623  3651653  3651671  3651673  3651731  3651757  3651761  3651763  3651793
3651797  3651811  3651839  3651847  3651919  3651929  3651943  3651959  3651979  3651983
3651997  3652007  3652031  3652049  3652063  3652067  3652081  3652097  3652151  3652153
3652163  3652171  3652189  3652211  3652219  3652223  3652279  3652303  3652333  3652357
3652361  3652367  3652373  3652387  3652391  3652421  3652447  3652459  3652477  3652487
3652507  3652531  3652543  3652547  3652553  3652559  3652573  3652589  3652591  3652609
3652613  3652633  3652643  3652661  3652669  3652679  3652697  3652703  3652757  3652763
3652771  3652777  3652783  3652819  3652829  3652843  3652871  3652889  3652897  3652903
3652931  3652933  3652937  3652939  3652949  3652967  3652969  3652991  3653029  3653051
3653053  3653057  3653077  3653081  3653129  3653137  3653161  3653171  3653173  3653189
3653191  3653201  3653203  3653213  3653219  3653227  3653267  3653291  3653303  3653329
3653359  3653369  3653383  3653393  3653401  3653423  3653467  3653471  3653483  3653501
3653509  3653557  3653577  3653599  3653603  3653647  3653651  3653659  3653669  3653687
3653701  3653737  3653761  3653777  3653779  3653791  3653809  3653821  3653831  3653851
3653863  3653911  3653959  3653977  3653981  3653989  3653999  3654017  3654037  3654067
3654089  3654143  3654149  3654151  3654173  3654179  3654181  3654193  3654197  3654199
3654227  3654317  3654323  3654331  3654349  3654353  3654361  3654367  3654383  3654389
3654397  3654419  3654437  3654451  3654457  3654463  3654481  3654487
3654503  3654529  3654557  3654569  3654577  3654587  3654641  3654647  3654671  3654689
3654709  3654713  3654719  3654743  3654757  3654787  3654793  3654809  3654829
3654851  3654853  3654857  3654883  3654913  3654919  3654923  3654929  3654947  3654961
3654997  3655007  3655019  3655021  3655079  3655081  3655103  3655111  3655121  3655133
3655139  3655159  3655199  3655217  3655219  3655231  3655243  3655259  3655261  3655271
3655279  3655307  3655339  3655343  3655349  3655361  3655369  3655373  3655397  3655411
3655447  3655451  3655469  3655481  3655499  3655501  3655513  3655541  3655579
3655609  3655627  3655633  3655649  3655651  3655661  3655667  3655681  3655693  3655703
3655709  3655723  3655727  3655739  3655741  3655747  3655753  3655759  3655763  3655783
3655789  3655793  3655807  3655831  3655837  3655849  3655877  3655879  3655891  3655907
3655921  3655937  3655957  3655987  3656017  3656033  3656039  3656069  3656087  3656089
3656101  3656111  3656129  3656137  3656141  3656179  3656183  3656231  3656239  3656249
3656251  3656267  3656269  3656273  3656281  3656321  3656327  3656329  3656353  3656363
3656369  3656371  3656383  3656413  3656437  3656441  3656447  3656453  3656467  3656483
3656509  3656537  3656539  3656551  3656573  3656581  3656599  3656617  3656621
3656633  3656641  3656651  3656657  3656663  3656669  3656689  3656699  3656707  3656753
3656773  3656777  3656801  3656827  3656833  3656837  3656843  3656857  3656867  3656887
3656903  3656909  3656923  3656953  3656981  3656993  3657013  3657029  3657037  3657041
3657079  3657083  3657089  3657097  3657119  3657131  3657151  3657167  3657169  3657179
3657187  3657217  3657223  3657239  3657259  3657271  3657289  3657293  3657307  3657317
3657319  3657331  3657337  3657341  3657343  3657347  3657361  3657383  3657419  3657439
```

```
3657449  3657457  3657497  3657517  3657523  3657527  3657539  3657547  3657571  3657607
3657613  3657617  3657631  3657637  3657649  3657653  3657677  3657679  3657691  3657749
3657751  3657761  3657769  3657791  3657793  3657803  3657827  3657847  3657859  3657877
3657887  3657911  3657919  3657949  3657959  3657961  3657977  3658001  3658019  3658021
3658049  3658073  3658087  3658091  3658097  3658117  3658129  3658141  3658157  3658159
3658181  3658189  3658199  3658201  3658211  3658283  3658297  3658309  3658327  3658331
3658337  3658351  3658381  3658387  3658399  3658409  3658423  3658427  3658429  3658459
3658463  3658477  3658493  3658513  3658547  3658607  3658631  3658637  3658639  3658661
3658667  3658673  3658693  3658703  3658709  3658729  3658747  3658751  3658769  3658801
3658807  3658813  3658829  3658847  3658867  3658871  3658873  3658877  3658891  3658943
3658981  3659009  3659011  3659069  3659083  3659099  3659111  3659113  3659141  3659143
3659177  3659179  3659203  3659213  3659237  3659261  3659273  3659303  3659309  3659311
3659317  3659321  3659347  3659351  3659353  3659363  3659371  3659393  3659399  3659401
3659441  3659443  3659449  3659477  3659479  3659497  3659501  3659527  3659531  3659543
3659567  3659587  3659611  3659627  3659629  3659651  3659657  3659659  3659683  3659717
3659779  3659791  3659797  3659801  3659813  3659819  3659849  3659861  3659917  3659923
3659933  3659941  3659959  3659993  3660011  3660017  3660023  3660037  3660053  3660071
3660073  3660109  3660131  3660187  3660191  3660211  3660221  3660259  3660269  3660281
3660317  3660323  3660343  3660347  3660353  3660359  3660367  3660379  3660401  3660403
3660413  3660443  3660463  3660469  3660487  3660493  3660497  3660523  3660541  3660563
3660571  3660581  3660607  3660617  3660619  3660637  3660647  3660653  3660667  3660677
3660707  3660721  3660733  3660739  3660799  3660823  3660827  3660847  3660871  3660889
3660893  3660911  3660913  3660919  3660949  3660953  3660961  3661019  3661043  3661093
3661111  3661123  3661139  3661157  3661181  3661211  3661247  3661249  3661271  3661277
3661289  3661291  3661303  3661327  3661367  3661369  3661381  3661391  3661417  3661421
3661429  3661447  3661457  3661499  3661501  3661507  3661517  3661529  3661543  3661561
3661573  3661583  3661591  3661597  3661601  3661633  3661643  3661649  3661673  3661703
3661733  3661739  3661759  3661771  3661781  3661831  3661841  3661871  3661907  3661909
3661913  3661943  3661949  3661951  3661963  3661979  3662011  3662039  3662051  3662053
3662069  3662077  3662081  3662093  3662101  3662107  3662111  3662119  3662137  3662167
3662177  3662201  3662213  3662227  3662249  3662311  3662363  3662389  3662401  3662411
3662419  3662437  3662441  3662453  3662467  3662471  3662473  3662521  3662537  3662539
3662551  3662579  3662587  3662591  3662597  3662609  3662621  3662639  3662641  3662651
3662657  3662683  3662699  3662713  3662719  3662723  3662731  3662753  3662759  3662761
3662767  3662797  3662809  3662831  3662833  3662849  3662861  3662881  3662887  3662909
3662917  3662927  3662933  3662941  3662951  3662977  3662983  3662987  3662999  3663001
3663017  3663031  3663043  3663059  3663071  3663073  3663083  3663089  3663097  3663113
3663137  3663157  3663161  3663197  3663199  3663203  3663217  3663241  3663263  3663271
3663277  3663293  3663311  3663323  3663337  3663343  3663377  3663383  3663419  3663421
3663427  3663433  3663437  3663461  3663469  3663497  3663503  3663533  3663547  3663559
3663563  3663581  3663587  3663617  3663661  3663683  3663691  3663707
3663743  3663749  3663757  3663763  3663767  3663811  3663833  3663887  3663893  3663899
3663911  3663917  3663929  3663949  3663971  3664013  3664033  3664039  3664043  3664067
3664069  3664081  3664091  3664103  3664117  3664139  3664183  3664189  3664247  3664249
3664259  3664273  3664279  3664301  3664303  3664307  3664319  3664327  3664343  3664351
3664361  3664399  3664421  3664439  3664447  3664483  3664487  3664499  3664519
3664547  3664561  3664631  3664649  3664651  3664657  3664679  3664681  3664683  3664693
3664709  3664711  3664721  3664723  3664747  3664763  3664781  3664783  3664799  3664811
3664823  3664831  3664841  3664861  3664873  3664879  3664883  3664901  3664937  3664943
3664957  3664963  3665017  3665023  3665029  3665033  3665041  3665087  3665089  3665117
3665131  3665141  3665147  3665153  3665159  3665171  3665177  3665203  3665227  3665237
3665239  3665261  3665267  3665279  3665293  3665297  3665317  3665327  3665329  3665357
3665371  3665377  3665393  3665399  3665401  3665407  3665413  3665419  3665437  3665443
3665477  3665491  3665507  3665509  3665527  3665539  3665573  3665581  3665587  3665609
3665633  3665653  3665657  3665731  3665747  3665759  3665777  3665791  3665797  3665807
3665813  3665819  3665839  3665869  3665881  3665899  3665903  3665911  3665939  3665941
3665989  3666001  3666007  3666011  3666023  3666037  3666041  3666049  3666073  3666077
3666119  3666121  3666127  3666149  3666163  3666173  3666197  3666233  3666241
3666251  3666253  3666263  3666281  3666301  3666317  3666323  3666331  3666347  3666371
3666409  3666413  3666419  3666427  3666461  3666473  3666499  3666521  3666529  3666539
3666581  3666583  3666599  3666613  3666629  3666647  3666659  3666661  3666703  3666727
3666743  3666757  3666787  3666797  3666809  3666823  3666827  3666833  3666841  3666853
3666877  3666881  3666907  3666919  3666947  3666961  3666979  3666991  3667003  3667031
3667043  3667061  3667063  3667073  3667091  3667093  3667117  3667127  3667129  3667141
3667159  3667201  3667219  3667231  3667243  3667249  3667273  3667289  3667303  3667333
3667343  3667357  3667387  3667429  3667453  3667471  3667483  3667501  3667537  3667541
3667553  3667561  3667567  3667577  3667591  3667621  3667637  3667669  3667673  3667679
3667723  3667733  3667751  3667753  3667823  3667843  3667849  3667871  3667887  3667889
3667907  3667913  3667919  3667967  3667973  3667981  3667987  3667997  3667999  3668009
3668033  3668051  3668057  3668059  3668081  3668087  3668099  3668117  3668129  3668179
3668213  3668221  3668227  3668233  3668251  3668257  3668263  3668279  3668299  3668359
3668369  3668377  3668381  3668383  3668389  3668407  3668419  3668461  3668503  3668507
3668531  3668543  3668563  3668579  3668593  3668603  3668611  3668629  3668647  3668671
3668699  3668701  3668741  3668747  3668759  3668801  3668807  3668837  3668851  3668857
3668879  3668887  3668893  3668897  3668909  3668911  3668921  3668927  3668939
3668941  3668953  3668969  3668971  3668981  3668989  3668999  3669007  3669011  3669013
3669023  3669047  3669073  3669077  3669091  3669097  3669101  3669119  3669163  3669173
3669187  3669217  3669221  3669227  3669241  3669251  3669257  3669277  3669287  3669307
3669311  3669343  3669353  3669359  3669371  3669373  3669383  3669427  3669469  3669473
3669487  3669499  3669511  3669521  3669553  3669557  3669583  3669587  3669599
3669613  3669643  3669647  3669649  3669691  3669709  3669727  3669751  3669761  3669763
3669767  3669799  3669803  3669829  3669833  3669839  3669847  3669851  3669881  3669883
3669893  3669899  3669931  3669937  3669959  3669961  3670001  3670013  3670027  3670039
3670049  3670063  3670081  3670109  3670123  3670151  3670169  3670171  3670231  3670237
3670243  3670253  3670259  3670291  3670301  3670319  3670321  3670333  3670349  3670393
3670397  3670417  3670423  3670463  3670481  3670483  3670517  3670549  3670561  3670571
3670603  3670633  3670637  3670649  3670651  3670661  3670669  3670673  3670687  3670697
3670717  3670721  3670739  3670757  3670763  3670769  3670783  3670789  3670813  3670837
3670871  3670873  3670879  3670883  3670903  3670949  3670957  3670967  3670969  3670973
```

```
3670981 3670987 3670991 3670999 3671021 3671027 3671069 3671071 3671077 3671089
3671117 3671119 3671147 3671149 3671179 3671183 3671203 3671219 3671221 3671231
3671267 3671273 3671281 3671309 3671321 3671333 3671341 3671347 3671401 3671411
3671419 3671431 3671441 3671449 3671453 3671461 3671471 3671477 3671497 3671501
3671527 3671531 3671543 3671561 3671567 3671573 3671587 3671599 3671627 3671663
3671669 3671761 3671797 3671831 3671839 3671849 3671851 3671861 3671869 3671891
3671897 3671901 3671923 3671929 3671939 3671971 3671989 3672007 3672013 3672023
3672029 3672037 3672041 3672047 3672059 3672089 3672107 3672113 3672127 3672143
3672181 3672197 3672199 3672209 3672217 3672223 3672233 3672257 3672281 3672283
3672293 3672307 3672311 3672343 3672349 3672359 3672367 3672373 3672379 3672413
3672419 3672421 3672437 3672451 3672457 3672463 3672499 3672511 3672521 3672541
3672547 3672563 3672577 3672593 3672611 3672619 3672623 3672659 3672661 3672677
3672689 3672727 3672733 3672737 3672751 3672761 3672769 3672791 3672793 3672803
3672811 3672827 3672829 3672853 3672857 3672881 3672887 3672899 3672917 3672919
3672923 3672959 3672961 3672971 3672997 3673009 3673013 3673039 3673069 3673073
3673091 3673093 3673127 3673133 3673147 3673151 3673181 3673183 3673193 3673199
3673211 3673217 3673223 3673253 3673273 3673277 3673279 3673337 3673349 3673357
3673367 3673387 3673393 3673429 3673457 3673463 3673489 3673493 3673507 3673519
3673529 3673597 3673599 3673601 3673609 3673613 3673639 3673651 3673687 3673837
3673697 3673699 3673727 3673741 3673763 3673771 3673777 3673781 3673793 3673837
3673861 3673867 3673919 3673937 3673939 3673949 3673961 3673979 3673987 3673993
3674003 3674029 3674071 3674081 3674101 3674129 3674149 3674173 3674197 3674207
3674219 3674233 3674249 3674269 3674287 3674291 3674299 3674303 3674317 3674323
3674339 3674351 3674357 3674417 3674441 3674443 3674453 3674459 3674521 3674537
3674557 3674591 3674597 3674599 3674603 3674609 3674617 3674623 3674639 3674653
3674663 3674689 3674711 3674719 3674753 3674761 3674767 3674773 3674777 3674813
3674819 3674837 3674849 3674857 3674863 3674897 3674911 3674921 3674927 3674929
3674947 3674969 3674971 3674989 3675011 3675041 3675053 3675059 3675079 3675107
3675131 3675149 3675181 3675187 3675197 3675211 3675229 3675241 3675271 3675277
3675283 3675313 3675337 3675359 3675361 3675401 3675403 3675439 3675443 3675449
3675461 3675473 3675479 3675481 3675499 3675509 3675563 3675583 3675593 3675601
3675613 3675629 3675631 3675647 3675649 3675667 3675671 3675697 3675703 3675713
3675719 3675733 3675739 3675743 3675767 3675781 3675803 3675809 3675817 3675829
3675853 3675857 3675869 3675899 3675901 3675907 3675923 3675943 3675977 3675983
3675989 3676033 3676037 3676039 3676051 3676087 3676091 3676093 3676103 3676109
3676111 3676129 3676147 3676151 3676157 3676163 3676181 3676187 3676193 3676201
3676213 3676219 3676237 3676273 3676279 3676289 3676303 3676307 3676313 3676327
3676339 3676373 3676399 3676433 3676441 3676459 3676489 3676493 3676513 3676529
3676549 3676553 3676567 3676571 3676577 3676583 3676597 3676609 3676637 3676639
3676643 3676667 3676721 3676723 3676733 3676741 3676753 3676781 3676789 3676793
3676819 3676831 3676847 3676853 3676859 3676867 3676889 3676891 3676903 3676909
3676927 3676931 3676957 3676963 3676993 3676999 3677017 3677029 3677041 3677071
3677077 3677081 3677101 3677111 3677119 3677123 3677129 3677137 3677147 3677207
3677209 3677227 3677239 3677257 3677273 3677281 3677291 3677329 3677339 3677341
3677347 3677353 3677357 3677363 3677369 3677381 3677383 3677441 3677459 3677473
3677477 3677533 3677537 3677549 3677567 3677573 3677579 3677585 3677591 3677599
3677633 3677657 3677671 3677683 3677699 3677701 3677717 3677731 3677743 3677753
3677779 3677783 3677803 3677819 3677827 3677851 3677857 3677881 3677887 3677897
3677909 3677917 3677923 3677929 3677951 3677957 3677977 3677981 3678007 3678011
3678023 3678043 3678053 3678061 3678067 3678071 3678083 3678089 3678097 3678107
3678109 3678113 3678121 3678131 3678149 3678163 3678179 3678211 3678217 3678221
3678223 3678247 3678287 3678289 3678293 3678299 3678317 3678347 3678377 3678391
3678407 3678431 3678461 3678481 3678497 3678517 3678527 3678529 3678539 3678541
3678557 3678583 3678589 3678599 3678601 3678617 3678659 3678671 3678683 3678713
3678743 3678751 3678791 3678797 3678803 3678811 3678821 3678823 3678833 3678839
3678841 3678847 3678869 3678877 3678881 3678893 3678923 3678929 3678931
3678937 3678943 3678949 3678967 3678973 3678977 3678979 3679003 3679009 3679031
3679033 3679051 3679061 3679079 3679087 3679121 3679129 3679139 3679147 3679153
3679163 3679183 3679189 3679211 3679213 3679219 3679229 3679231 3679237 3679261
3679271 3679279 3679289 3679309 3679339 3679363 3679373 3679387 3679427 3679451
3679453 3679457 3679499 3679519 3679541 3679567 3679579 3679591 3679601 3679603
3679649 3679661 3679679 3679681 3679691 3679693 3679729 3679751 3679757 3679759
3679789 3679799 3679807 3679813 3679817 3679843 3679847 3679861 3679867 3679887
3679891 3679913 3679919 3679933 3679967 3679969 3679993 3679999 3680011 3680029
3680059 3680081 3680101 3680111 3680113 3680123 3680153 3680203 3680213
3680249 3680263 3680269 3680291 3680321 3680363 3680371 3680399 3680401 3680407
3680431 3680459 3680461 3680489 3680491 3680503 3680507 3680519 3680527 3680533
3680539 3680549 3680563 3680627 3680647 3680657 3680659 3680669 3680685
3680741 3680753 3680791 3680837 3680863 3680867 3680869 3680881 3680893 3680917
3680947 3680953 3680987 3681001 3681017 3681023 3681031 3681037 3681043
3681049 3681059 3681113 3681131 3681149 3681151 3681191 3681199 3681217 3681239
3681253 3681277 3681283 3681287 3681319 3681341 3681371 3681373 3681407 3681413
3681451 3681481 3681487 3681499 3681511 3681523 3681553 3681569
3681577 3681593 3681599 3681619 3681683 3681697 3681709 3681719 3681731 3681749
3681761 3681767 3681781 3681791 3681813 3681823 3681827 3681889
3681917 3681947 3681949 3681967 3682031 3682037 3682057 3682061 3682079 3682103
3682109 3682117 3682123 3682171 3682177 3682187 3682199 3682201 3682213 3682223
3682229 3682243 3682321 3682337 3682361 3682363 3682429
3682439 3682451 3682457 3682501 3682513 3682519 3682531 3682537 3682543 3682571
3682597 3682607 3682639 3682643 3682667 3682687 3682703 3682709 3682727
3682733 3682759 3682781 3682787 3682801 3682813 3682817 3682823 3682837 3682843
3682853 3682867 3682891 3682933 3682961 3683011 3683021
3683027 3683077 3683081 3683089 3683107 3683111 3683117 3683143 3683149 3683159
3683171 3683179 3683189 3683201 3683209 3683213 3683227 3683233 3683257 3683263
3683279 3683287 3683293 3683297 3683333 3683353 3683357 3683401 3683411 3683413
3683431 3683453 3683479 3683503 3683527 3683569 3683597 3683599 3683627 3683651
3683671 3683677 3683717 3683723 3683731 3683741 3683803 3683819 3683821 3683833
3683837 3683839 3683879 3683909 3683921 3683941 3683959 3683969 3683971 3683993
3684011 3684013 3684029 3684041 3684047 3684059 3684061 3684101 3684103 3684151
```

```
3684169  3684173  3684179  3684181  3684193  3684203  3684211  3684221  3684229  3684253
3684293  3684299  3684311  3684337  3684353  3684371  3684389  3684391  3684407  3684419
3684451  3684463  3684467  3684487  3684509  3684517  3684523  3684539  3684553  3684559
3684587  3684589  3684601  3684607  3684641  3684643  3684647  3684671  3684677  3684679
3684683  3684697  3684701  3684721  3684749  3684757  3684763  3684781  3684809  3684833
3684859  3684871  3684881  3684913  3684929  3684953  3684959  3684977  3685007  3685009
3685021  3685027  3685049  3685051  3685111  3685133  3685147  3685151  3685153  3685169
3685211  3685219  3685247  3685273  3685289  3685301  3685303  3685309  3685327  3685337
3685369  3685387  3685403  3685417  3685427  3685441  3685453  3685463  3685471  3685477
3685483  3685489  3685501  3685511  3685519  3685541  3685571  3685597  3685631  3685657
3685663  3685687  3685691  3685699  3685729  3685739  3685741  3685751  3685763  3685783
3685811  3685837  3685849  3685861  3685879  3685883  3685939  3685949  3685951  3685963  3685973
3685999  3686009  3686027  3686029  3686063  3686071  3686083  3686087  3686099  3686101
3686119  3686131  3686153  3686159  3686167  3686183  3686237  3686239  3686251  3686299
3686321  3686327  3686329  3686339  3686341  3686357  3686369  3686383  3686387  3686401
3686411  3686447  3686477  3686479  3686483  3686503  3686531  3686537  3686549  3686561
3686587  3686591  3686609  3686621  3686623  3686629  3686651  3686663  3686677  3686701
3686713  3686723  3686729  3686731  3686743  3686747  3686797  3686801  3686833  3686849
3686867  3686927  3686929  3686941  3686951  3686953  3686957  3686971  3686993  3686997
3686989  3686999  3687029  3687037  3687041  3687043  3687049  3687071  3687097  3687119
3687127  3687133  3687139  3687163  3687169  3687209  3687227  3687239  3687241  3687247
3687251  3687287  3687301  3687319  3687373  3687391  3687401  3687403  3687407  3687413
3687421  3687427  3687433  3687443  3687451  3687461  3687469  3687557  3687583  3687631
3687683  3687703  3687707  3687713  3687731  3687737  3687743  3687757  3687763  3687769
3687787  3687823  3687833  3687839  3687847  3687857  3687869  3687911  3687923  3687941
3687967  3687973  3687979  3687989  3688001  3688021  3688057  3688063  3688081  3688093
3688117  3688127  3688129  3688141  3688151  3688171  3688189  3688193  3688199  3688219
3688241  3688247  3688277  3688301  3688309  3688313  3688331  3688343  3688357  3688361
3688367  3688369  3688393  3688453  3688463  3688469  3688501  3688511  3688519  3688537
3688543  3688549  3688561  3688571  3688591  3688613  3688627  3688631  3688637  3688649
3688661  3688667  3688681  3688691  3688693  3688697  3688703  3688709  3688757  3688759
3688777  3688781  3688787  3688801  3688837  3688849  3688859  3688871  3688877  3688897
3688903  3688933  3688939  3688963  3688967  3688981  3688991  3689009  3689069  3689113
3689117  3689129  3689137  3689141  3689143  3689149  3689183  3689207  3689209  3689237
3689263  3689281  3689291  3689297  3689299  3689311  3689327  3689377  3689417  3689423
3689461  3689473  3689479  3689501  3689503  3689507  3689513  3689519  3689551  3689573
3689579  3689597  3689611  3689617  3689633  3689669  3689689  3689711  3689717  3689723
3689753  3689761  3689771  3689773  3689779  3689797  3689809  3689843  3689863  3689869
3689887  3689911  3689927  3689947  3689963  3689993  3690013  3690031  3690053  3690067
3690079  3690091  3690101  3690107  3690119  3690149  3690151  3690187  3690191  3690227
3690233  3690251  3690257  3690259  3690301  3690307  3690329  3690341  3690347  3690361
3690371  3690397  3690437  3690473  3690497  3690499  3690517  3690521  3690523  3690527
3690529  3690539  3690551  3690553  3690571  3690587  3690607  3690611  3690613  3690619
3690623  3690629  3690671  3690677  3690689  3690691  3690703  3690721  3690727  3690737
3690763  3690773  3690781  3690803  3690821  3690823  3690839  3690851  3690857  3690871
3690881  3690889  3690899  3690923  3690941  3690961  3690977  3690983  3691003  3691007
3691013  3691019  3691021  3691027  3691031  3691043  3691087  3691147  3691151  3691153
3691183  3691199  3691213  3691223  3691253  3691273  3691277  3691283  3691307  3691309
3691313  3691327  3691343  3691349  3691351  3691357  3691367  3691403  3691447  3691451
3691459  3691469  3691489  3691531  3691547  3691549  3691553  3691559  3691561  3691577
3691603  3691619  3691621  3691627  3691657  3691673  3691687  3691691  3691693  3691717
3691747  3691783  3691789  3691801  3691811  3691813  3691819  3691841  3691843  3691847
3691859  3691913  3691921  3691949  3691951  3691957  3692021  3692041  3692053  3692057
3692063  3692081  3692107  3692123  3692159  3692177  3692197  3692201  3692207  3692209
3692231  3692239  3692243  3692261  3692263  3692291  3692321  3692323  3692329  3692333
3692347  3692357  3692363  3692401  3692407  3692411  3692431  3692449  3692467  3692471
3692477  3692527  3692531  3692543  3692551  3692567  3692573  3692617  3692641  3692651
3692659  3692671  3692681  3692683  3692701  3692737  3692761  3692771  3692803  3692807
3692827  3692849  3692873  3692929  3692951  3692971  3692977  3693037  3693043  3693077
3693089  3693113  3693161  3693167  3693169  3693187  3693191  3693197  3693203  3693211
3693253  3693257  3693259  3693299  3693311  3693323  3693331  3693337  3693343  3693359
3693373  3693397  3693413  3693427  3693449  3693463  3693479  3693493  3693499  3693511
3693563  3693601  3693617  3693637  3693653  3693659  3693661  3693689  3693691  3693707
3693719  3693721  3693737  3693761  3693763  3693769  3693773  3693779  3693787  3693791
3693839  3693841  3693853  3693863  3693881  3693883  3693953  3693959  3693973  3693983
3693997  3694013  3694027  3694039  3694057  3694063  3694091  3694109  3694111  3694121
3694127  3694129  3694133  3694139  3694147  3694181  3694183  3694193  3694199  3694217
3694241  3694267  3694279  3694297  3694319  3694351  3694357  3694373  3694393  3694409
3694429  3694433  3694451  3694459  3694463  3694477  3694499  3694501  3694511  3694547
3694553  3694567  3694573  3694583  3694597  3694601  3694609  3694619  3694631  3694637
3694643  3694667  3694679  3694693  3694699  3694711  3694723  3694727  3694741  3694787
3694799  3694807  3694813  3694829  3694841  3694843  3694877  3694891  3694897  3694913
3694937  3694981  3694997  3695009  3695011  3695039  3695057  3695059  3695071  3695089
3695099  3695113  3695123  3695141  3695143  3695149  3695173  3695183  3695189  3695201
3695233  3695257  3695261  3695297  3695303  3695317  3695333  3695353  3695357  3695381
3695389  3695399  3695401  3695407  3695411  3695437  3695467  3695491  3695501  3695507
3695509  3695513  3695521  3695539  3695551  3695559  3695581  3695599  3695611  3695659
3695669  3695677  3695683  3695687  3695693  3695711  3695717  3695729  3695737  3695753
3695761  3695773  3695803  3695821  3695833  3695869  3695911  3695933  3695947  3695957
3695969  3695971  3695977  3695981  3695983  3696001  3696019  3696053  3696059  3696067
3696071  3696097  3696103  3696107  3696113  3696131  3696139  3696163  3696179  3696181
3696193  3696197  3696227  3696233  3696247  3696257  3696269  3696271  3696281  3696283
3696313  3696349  3696359  3696377  3696383  3696391  3696401  3696403  3696419  3696421
3696449  3696461  3696479  3696481  3696487  3696493  3696523  3696551  3696557  3696577
3696593  3696619  3696643  3696703  3696713  3696727  3696731  3696733  3696761  3696779
3696787  3696799  3696821  3696827  3696851  3696853  3696863  3696877  3696883  3696893
3696907  3696911  3696923  3696929  3696941  3696947  3696977  3696989  3696991  3697009
3697013  3697019  3697033  3697037  3697049  3697051  3697061  3697073  3697081  3697103
3697139  3697147  3697159  3697163  3697207  3697223  3697241  3697249  3697289  3697321
```

```
3697361  3697363  3697403  3697409  3697423  3697427  3697429  3697433  3697451  3697487
3697511  3697531  3697559  3697579  3697583  3697591  3697633  3697657  3697691  3697709
3697717  3697741  3697777  3697781  3697783  3697787  3697843  3697847  3697849  3697853
3697867  3697907  3697909  3697919  3697921  3697927  3697933  3697949  3697997  3698029
3698053  3698063  3698081  3698087  3698099  3698111  3698117  3698119  3698131  3698137
3698143  3698153  3698183  3698203  3698209  3698213  3698237  3698243  3698251  3698257
3698273  3698311  3698327  3698351  3698363  3698371  3698389  3698417  3698419  3698441
3698447  3698489  3698507  3698509  3698531  3698551  3698581  3698623  3698647  3698657
3698663  3698683  3698671  3698683  3698693  3698713  3698719  3698753  3698767  3698771
3698789  3698797  3698801  3698819  3698831  3698839  3698861  3698873  3698887  3698909
3698917  3698941  3698953  3698957  3698963  3698969  3698999  3699011  3699023  3699049
3699079  3699089  3699103  3699121  3699127  3699131  3699139  3699169  3699181  3699187
3699191  3699193  3699197  3699203  3699209  3699233  3699239  3699253  3699257  3699263
3699277  3699287  3699299  3699301  3699329  3699331  3699337  3699373  3699379  3699401
3699407  3699413  3699427  3699431  3699439  3699457  3699497  3699499  3699517  3699533
3699581  3699599  3699601  3699607  3699613  3699629  3699671  3699679  3699691  3699697
3699701  3699719  3699721  3699743  3699767  3699769  3699781  3699797  3699841  3699847
3699853  3699869  3699893  3699901  3699919  3699947  3699961  3700001  3700009  3700013
3700031  3700043  3700049  3700051  3700087  3700091  3700093  3700097  3700133  3700141
3700153  3700157  3700159  3700187  3700241  3700261  3700267  3700283  3700289  3700349
3700363  3700369  3700387  3700391  3700393  3700397  3700409  3700423  3700457  3700483
3700511  3700517  3700523  3700547  3700549  3700601  3700607  3700691  3700699  3700717
3700727  3700751  3700757  3700771  3700789  3700793  3700817  3700819  3700843  3700847
3700867  3700871  3700889  3700891  3700901  3700903  3700909  3700919  3700927  3700933
3700969  3700979  3700987  3700993  3701021  3701063  3701069  3701077  3701101  3701119
3701123  3701141  3701179  3701207  3701213  3701227  3701249  3701251  3701263  3701267
3701273  3701287  3701293  3701303  3701317  3701323  3701339  3701351  3701353  3701363
3701377  3701381  3701417  3701429  3701437  3701471  3701479  3701507  3701513  3701527
3701539  3701543  3701557  3701587  3701623  3701627  3701629  3701639  3701641  3701653
3701701  3701707  3701723  3701729  3701743  3701759  3701773  3701779  3701783  3701791
3701807  3701809  3701839  3701881  3701917  3701939  3701959  3701963  3701969  3701977
3701983  3702007  3702031  3702037  3702043  3702047  3702059  3702071  3702079  3702089
3702091  3702119  3702161  3702163  3702187  3702197  3702211  3702229  3702233  3702263
3702269  3702271  3702289  3702301  3702313  3702323  3702329  3702337  3702371  3702389
3702409  3702443  3702449  3702463  3702467  3702497  3702499  3702509  3702529  3702533
3702551  3702571  3702577  3702581  3702593  3702607  3702623  3702649  3702679  3702689
3702697  3702757  3702791  3702817  3702823  3702841  3702869  3702887  3702893  3702901
3702911  3702913  3702943  3702947  3702971  3702983  3703001  3703013  3703019  3703027
3703033  3703061  3703067  3703087  3703109  3703111  3703121  3703151  3703171  3703187
3703199  3703223  3703237  3703241  3703267  3703277  3703279  3703313  3703319  3703327
3703333  3703351  3703369  3703373  3703393  3703417  3703429  3703439  3703451  3703457
3703463  3703471  3703487  3703507  3703549  3703597  3703631  3703639  3703643  3703649
3703673  3703691  3703703  3703723  3703747  3703753  3703769  3703781  3703823  3703831
3703853  3703871  3703877  3703883  3703901  3703907  3703919  3703927  3703939  3703949
3703957  3703969  3703979  3704003  3704009  3704017  3704053  3704059  3704087  3704111
3704119  3704123  3704137  3704143  3704153  3704161  3704167  3704171  3704179  3704201
3704203  3704213  3704237  3704243  3704251  3704279  3704291  3704293  3704303  3704341
3704353  3704369  3704381  3704387  3704417  3704443  3704461  3704507  3704513  3704537
3704543  3704573  3704581  3704599  3704611  3704621  3704629  3704651  3704653  3704671
3704689  3704693  3704707  3704731  3704737  3704741  3704747  3704749  3704761  3704819
3704821  3704843  3704849  3704873  3704879  3704887  3704941  3704947  3704951  3704959
3705017  3705029  3705041  3705059  3705067  3705077  3705083  3705101  3705113  3705137
3705161  3705187  3705193  3705197  3705199  3705227  3705241  3705257  3705271  3705281
3705287  3705311  3705329  3705343  3705347  3705367  3705379  3705391  3705409  3705421
3705431  3705451  3705463  3705467  3705469  3705491  3705503  3705509  3705511  3705521
3705593  3705617  3705619  3705623  3705629  3705659  3705679  3705719  3705739  3705749
3705763  3705769  3705773  3705799  3705827  3705839  3705841  3705851  3705853  3705887
3705899  3705901  3705917  3705929  3705941  3705959  3706009  3706039  3706067  3706069
3706093  3706097  3706099  3706111  3706123  3706133  3706139  3706141  3706163  3706181
3706189  3706193  3706201  3706247  3706259  3706301  3706303  3706309  3706369  3706379
3706393  3706399  3706433  3706447  3706487  3706489  3706499  3706529  3706609  3706621
3706627  3706631  3706649  3706669  3706679  3706723  3706733  3706741  3706753  3706777
3706811  3706819  3706837  3706861  3706883  3706889  3706891  3706897  3706921  3706931
3706961  3707021  3707051  3707063  3707069  3707087  3707101  3707107  3707111  3707113
3707149  3707161  3707167  3707189  3707203  3707213  3707237  3707239  3707287  3707293
3707317  3707339  3707351  3707359  3707369  3707381  3707399  3707401  3707419  3707449
3707453  3707461  3707471  3707477  3707491  3707497  3707533  3707537  3707573  3707593
3707611  3707617  3707629  3707633  3707653  3707663  3707677  3707681  3707699  3707701
3707719  3707741  3707749  3707771  3707773  3707777  3707789  3707791  3707797  3707813
3707839  3707849  3707857  3707861  3707863  3707867  3707923  3707927  3707947  3707953
3707987  3708017  3708031  3708041  3708043  3708049  3708073  3708077  3708101  3708119
3708121  3708137  3708139  3708151  3708157  3708161  3708169  3708203  3708223  3708241
3708269  3708283  3708293  3708301  3708307  3708319  3708323  3708349  3708371  3708421
3708443  3708469  3708487  3708493  3708503  3708511  3708521  3708539  3708559  3708571
3708577  3708581  3708587  3708611  3708613  3708623  3708637  3708641  3708643  3708673
3708697  3708709  3708751  3708791  3708797  3708841  3708847  3708853  3708863  3708869
3708877  3708883  3708889  3708893  3708899  3708923  3708931  3708949  3708959  3708961
3708967  3708977  3708997  3709007  3709019  3709031  3709033  3709039  3709061  3709073
3709081  3709091  3709103  3709109  3709117  3709157  3709163  3709249  3709259  3709291
3709301  3709319  3709327  3709331  3709333  3709337  3709357  3709397  3709403  3709421
3709423  3709441  3709457  3709487  3709499  3709501  3709513  3709561  3709577  3709631
3709633  3709661  3709681  3709687  3709691  3709703  3709711  3709733  3709747  3709759
3709771  3709813  3709817  3709819  3709829  3709843  3709873  3709907  3709913  3709939
3709943  3709949  3710009  3710089  3710123  3710137  3710167  3710171  3710209  3710243
3710253  3710279  3710281  3710293  3710299  3710303  3710387  3710407  3710411  3710417
3710419  3710431  3710461  3710467  3710501  3710507  3710543  3710549  3710561  3710593
3710611  3710617  3710621  3710627  3710647  3710651  3710683  3710699  3710701  3710711
3710713  3710723  3710741  3710761  3710783  3710801  3710821  3710827  3710831  3710851
3710873  3710881  3710891  3710893  3710921  3710963  3711017  3711047  3711053  3711077
```

```
3711091  3711107  3711109  3711121  3711131  3711139  3711157  3711199  3711203  3711209
3711221  3711229  3711233  3711263  3711269  3711271  3711299  3711307  3711311  3711313
3711319  3711329  3711343  3711353  3711371  3711377  3711401  3711419  3711451  3711473
3711481  3711493  3711497  3711527  3711529  3711541  3711557  3711563  3711577  3711611
3711613  3711647  3711679  3711683  3711691  3711709  3711713  3711727  3711737  3711751
3711761  3711769  3711779  3711781  3711787  3711793  3711817  3711833  3711857  3711863
3711881  3711893  3711907  3711941  3711943  3711959  3711989  3712019  3712021  3712043
3712063  3712073  3712081  3712091  3712097  3712117  3712127  3712139  3712141  3712169
3712187  3712199  3712207  3712231  3712249  3712253  3712259  3712271  3712283  3712297
3712301  3712309  3712327  3712333  3712349  3712363  3712369  3712381  3712393  3712417
3712421  3712441  3712459  3712463  3712487  3712517  3712523  3712531  3712547  3712549
3712559  3712567  3712571  3712573  3712589  3712601  3712627  3712669  3712679  3712697
3712699  3712711  3712717  3712721  3712739  3712747  3712757  3712769  3712801  3712823
3712831  3712843  3712871  3712873  3712889  3712897  3712909  3712927  3712949  3712979
3712981  3713027  3713041  3713053  3713057  3713069  3713071  3713077  3713081  3713147
3713153  3713159  3713161  3713219  3713239  3713251  3713261  3713263  3713267  3713279
3713287  3713299  3713309  3713317  3713323  3713387  3713399  3713407  3713441  3713443
3713447  3713449  3713453  3713461  3713473  3713477  3713483  3713491  3713533  3713561
3713573  3713581  3713587  3713617  3713621  3713623  3713627  3713639  3713681  3713737
3713747  3713753  3713767  3713771  3713789  3713807  3713849  3713851  3713887  3713891
3713909  3713917  3713921  3713923  3713929  3713993  3713999  3714013  3714019  3714031
3714037  3714043  3714049  3714089  3714091  3714103  3714121  3714131  3714133  3714157
3714163  3714181  3714239  3714241  3714259  3714307  3714311  3714323  3714331  3714341
3714397  3714399  3714409  3714419  3714433  3714437  3714439  3714461  3714479  3714493
3714521  3714527  3714553  3714563  3714587  3714589  3714617  3714629  3714631  3714643
3714647  3714673  3714691  3714701  3714703  3714713  3714731  3714743  3714769  3714773
3714779  3714797  3714803  3714811  3714827  3714859  3714863  3714883  3714889  3714913
3714943  3714967  3714973  3714979  3714989  3715031  3715037  3715069  3715079  3715087
3715093  3715109  3715111  3715169  3715183  3715193  3715211  3715253  3715307  3715343
3715363  3715373  3715399  3715409  3715417  3715421  3715423  3715433  3715457  3715471
3715477  3715493  3715511  3715513  3715541  3715559  3715561  3715589  3715601  3715631
3715637  3715667  3715669  3715687  3715703  3715709  3715717  3715727  3715729  3715739
3715757  3715781  3715783  3715787  3715793  3715807  3715813  3715823  3715837  3715841
3715853  3715889  3715909  3715913  3715951  3715957  3715981  3715991  3716029
3716057  3716071  3716107  3716123  3716131  3716143  3716161  3716171  3716173  3716177
3716197  3716221  3716227  3716257  3716269  3716291  3716299  3716309  3716333  3716341
3716359  3716369  3716371  3716393  3716429  3716459  3716467  3716483  3716543  3716567
3716569  3716597  3716599  3716617  3716623  3716627  3716633  3716641  3716653  3716663
3716677  3716681  3716701  3716707  3716719  3716747  3716753  3716759  3716771  3716819
3716821  3716827  3716831  3716833  3716857  3716879  3716887  3716903  3716917  3716969
3716971  3716981  3717011  3717023  3717031  3717041  3717047  3717061  3717071  3717083
3717107  3717113  3717127  3717139  3717149  3717173  3717209  3717223  3717239  3717247
3717257  3717269  3717281  3717299  3717313  3717317  3717319  3717323  3717341  3717359
3717377  3717391  3717397  3717409  3717431  3717437  3717449  3717451  3717457  3717499
3717533  3717547  3717557  3717563  3717583  3717589  3717599  3717601  3717607  3717641
3717647  3717667  3717683  3717689  3717731  3717739  3717751  3717761  3717803  3717809
3717811  3717821  3717853  3717859  3717869  3717893  3717899  3717919  3717937  3717941
3717947  3717953  3717971  3717979  3718021  3718027  3718037  3718051  3718067  3718069
3718097  3718103  3718139  3718147  3718159  3718181  3718207  3718229  3718259  3718277
3718279  3718303  3718307  3718327  3718349  3718361  3718373  3718381  3718397  3718411
3718417  3718423  3718439  3718457  3718459  3718489  3718501  3718513  3718549  3718553
3718573  3718607  3718613  3718619  3718633  3718643  3718651  3718657  3718669  3718681
3718739  3718751  3718763  3718777  3718783  3718789  3718807  3718831  3718837  3718849
3718861  3718867  3718877  3718879  3718901  3718919  3718951  3718963  3718993  3718997
3719011  3719017  3719029  3719057  3719059  3719087  3719119  3719153  3719159  3719161
3719167  3719179  3719197  3719201  3719207  3719239  3719267  3719273  3719291  3719299
3719321  3719323  3719329  3719333  3719341  3719347  3719377  3719389  3719393  3719431
3719461  3719467  3719519  3719531  3719559  3719563  3719567  3719579  3719597  3719623
3719633  3719657  3719663  3719669  3719693  3719701  3719707  3719711  3719713  3719717
3719747  3719759  3719777  3719789  3719791  3719797  3719803  3719827  3719831  3719851
3719857  3719867  3719879  3719897  3719899  3719921  3719939  3719959  3719981  3719983
3719987  3719993  3719999  3720011  3720023  3720037  3720103  3720113  3720121  3720137
3720151  3720163  3720169  3720179  3720209  3720247  3720251  3720253  3720293  3720337
3720349  3720359  3720361  3720373  3720383  3720391  3720397  3720401  3720407  3720413
3720421  3720427  3720469  3720487  3720491  3720511  3720551  3720553  3720571  3720581
3720583  3720617  3720623  3720649  3720667  3720677  3720697  3720701  3720707  3720767
3720781  3720797  3720811  3720839  3720851  3720853  3720859  3720869  3720877  3720887
3720889  3720907  3720911  3720923  3720929  3720947  3720989  3721027  3721033  3721049
3721051  3721063  3721087  3721097  3721099  3721117  3721129  3721141  3721153  3721163
3721171  3721199  3721213  3721217  3721229  3721259  3721273  3721279  3721297  3721301
3721303  3721327  3721337  3721339  3721363  3721379  3721391  3721409  3721411  3721439
3721451  3721463  3721477  3721489  3721537  3721559  3721583  3721603  3721621  3721631
3721673  3721717  3721721  3721727  3721741  3721771  3721787  3721799  3721807  3721811
3721813  3721847  3721849  3721859  3721873  3721877  3721901  3721919  3721931  3721933
3721943  3721957  3721973  3721981  3722009  3722011  3722027  3722029  3722039  3722053
3722083  3722087  3722101  3722129  3722143  3722149  3722171  3722177  3722183  3722189
3722207  3722219  3722221  3722231  3722249  3722273  3722291  3722293  3722339  3722351
3722357  3722393  3722411  3722419  3722437  3722443  3722479  3722491  3722519  3722549
3722567  3722591  3722599  3722611  3722617  3722623  3722629  3722683  3722687  3722699
3722713  3722767  3722771  3722801  3722809  3722819  3722827  3722833  3722843  3722861
3722867  3722893  3722899  3722911  3722921  3722947  3722951  3723001  3723019  3723023
3723029  3723047  3723053  3723059  3723061  3723067  3723089  3723121  3723149  3723211
3723227  3723233  3723271  3723277  3723283  3723287  3723299  3723319  3723329  3723337
3723359  3723383  3723389  3723407  3723427  3723439  3723443  3723451  3723469  3723521
3723529  3723547  3723581  3723589  3723593  3723607  3723617  3723637  3723641  3723647
3723649  3723679  3723719  3723721  3723739  3723749  3723773  3723779  3723781  3723787
3723809  3723847  3723869  3723871  3723893  3723913  3723931  3723947  3723959  3724001
3724031  3724033  3724043  3724051  3724067  3724069  3724073  3724079  3724099  3724103
3724109  3724117  3724129  3724157  3724159  3724169  3724181  3724211  3724213  3724223
```

```
3724243  3724249  3724261  3724277  3724289  3724291  3724307  3724313  3724319  3724333
3724339  3724379  3724393  3724403  3724423  3724429  3724439  3724471  3724489  3724507
3724519  3724537  3724541  3724543  3724559  3724573  3724579  3724603  3724621  3724631
3724657  3724661  3724663  3724667  3724709  3724711  3724733  3724757  3724807  3724813
3724823  3724837  3724849  3724859  3724879  3724883  3724907  3724913  3724927  3724933
3724937  3724939  3724943  3724967  3724979  3724993  3724997  3725017  3725027  3725041
3725069  3725077  3725101  3725107  3725119  3725147  3725153  3725179  3725203  3725207
3725213  3725221  3725231  3725233  3725251  3725257  3725279  3725303  3725347  3725357
3725389  3725411  3725413  3725443  3725459  3725461  3725473  3725489  3725503  3725507
3725521  3725551  3725569  3725573  3725591  3725597  3725651  3725663  3725677  3725681
3725693  3725699  3725707  3725713  3725731  3725753  3725759  3725783  3725809  3725849
3725857  3725879  3725893  3725899  3725923  3725929  3725933  3725951  3725959  3725963
3725971  3725987  3726001  3726013  3726029  3726083  3726089  3726097  3726103  3726127
3726131  3726137  3726143  3726157  3726187  3726197  3726211  3726221  3726241  3726259
3726277  3726311  3726313  3726319  3726323  3726329  3726347  3726353  3726361  3726397
3726403  3726407  3726409  3726419  3726421  3726439  3726461  3726467  3726469  3726491
3726511  3726523  3726533  3726539  3726559  3726571  3726581  3726599  3726623  3726629
3726631  3726647  3726661  3726683  3726691  3726721  3726731  3726733  3726739  3726743
3726763  3726769  3726773  3726787  3726797  3726803  3726809  3726817  3726823  3726839
3726841  3726847  3726871  3726881  3726889  3726911  3726923  3726929  3726953  3726977
3726979  3726991  3727019  3727027  3727033  3727049  3727057  3727067  3727091  3727103
3727123  3727153  3727159  3727169  3727177  3727189  3727193  3727243  3727259  3727279
3727291  3727303  3727309  3727313  3727387  3727397  3727441  3727459  3727463  3727483
3727487  3727489  3727501  3727513  3727579  3727609  3727621  3727663  3727681  3727687
3727693  3727699  3727721  3727723  3727727  3727729  3727741  3727751  3727753  3727769
3727793  3727837  3727847  3727849  3727853  3727859  3727873  3727877  3727903  3727937
3727939  3727949  3727951  3727961  3727991  3728017  3728041  3728051  3728063  3728069
3728099  3728113  3728141  3728149  3728173  3728177  3728189  3728203  3728243  3728251
3728267  3728273  3728297  3728297  3728303  3728311  3728317  3728357  3728359  3728363
3728371  3728377  3728393  3728407  3728411  3728429  3728441  3728447  3728471  3728479
3728489  3728509  3728513  3728533  3728537  3728561  3728591  3728597  3728611  3728633
3728671  3728687  3728713  3728717  3728719  3728743  3728759  3728779  3728789  3728821
3728861  3728863  3728867  3728873  3728891  3728911  3728939  3728947  3728957  3728969
3728983  3728987  3729007  3729017  3729031  3729041  3729043  3729049  3729053  3729067
3729071  3729097  3729109  3729157  3729161  3729169  3729179  3729181  3729191  3729199
3729203  3729227  3729233  3729241  3729259  3729293  3729311  3729317  3729329  3729337
3729373  3729379  3729389  3729391  3729413  3729419  3729437  3729457  3729461  3729463
3729493  3729499  3729503  3729521  3729533  3729541  3729547  3729569  3729571  3729581
3729587  3729589  3729629  3729659  3729667  3729673  3729697  3729709  3729721  3729727
3729731  3729751  3729767  3729793  3729797  3729799  3729809  3729853  3729877  3729883
3729899  3729911  3729931  3729959  3729961  3729977  3729983  3729989  3729991  3729997
3730003  3730019  3730033  3730063  3730093  3730141  3730147  3730159  3730171  3730187
3730189  3730201  3730219  3730231  3730247  3730267  3730271  3730277  3730283  3730297
3730303  3730319  3730339  3730367  3730381  3730387  3730423  3730427  3730453  3730457
3730471  3730483  3730499  3730537  3730541  3730547  3730561  3730579  3730583  3730607
3730619  3730651  3730669  3730681  3730693  3730697  3730703  3730721  3730729  3730733
3730739  3730759  3730777  3730781  3730787  3730799  3730801  3730817  3730823  3730841
3730847  3730849  3730861  3730889  3730901  3730919  3730949  3730967  3730997  3731003
3731009  3731017  3731069  3731071  3731081  3731089  3731093  3731107  3731137  3731141
3731173  3731207  3731209  3731213  3731237  3731251  3731257  3731303  3731311  3731333
3731341  3731393  3731417  3731443  3731447  3731461  3731473  3731477  3731489  3731491
3731509  3731513  3731521  3731527  3731531  3731549  3731557  3731579  3731591  3731593
3731603  3731621  3731627  3731683  3731701  3731711  3731713  3731731  3731737  3731747
3731759  3731801  3731803  3731821  3731843  3731851  3731863  3731867  3731869  3731887
3731909  3731933  3731947  3731953  3731963  3731969  3731983  3731989  3732007  3732019
3732031  3732071  3732077  3732083  3732103  3732109  3732139  3732143  3732161  3732167
3732173  3732191  3732203  3732217  3732221  3732241  3732259  3732293  3732343  3732347
3732359  3732373  3732383  3732389  3732397  3732409  3732423  3732437  3732439  3732461
3732467  3732479  3732499  3732511  3732551  3732577  3732581  3732587  3732629  3732649
3732653  3732661  3732691  3732697  3732719  3732727  3732761  3732769  3732779  3732791
3732853  3732857  3732887  3732899  3732907  3732917  3732919  3732931  3732961  3732973
3732977  3732983  3732997  3733003  3733021  3733027  3733031  3733049  3733057  3733099
3733111  3733133  3733157  3733159  3733193  3733207  3733211  3733229  3733231  3733259
3733271  3733273  3733297  3733313  3733321  3733333  3733363  3733381  3733397  3733399
3733417  3733447  3733453  3733459  3733463  3733507  3733511  3733517  3733531  3733537
3733549  3733607  3733621  3733637  3733649  3733669  3733687  3733703  3733729  3733739
3733757  3733771  3733787  3733789  3733799  3733801  3733831  3733879  3733883  3733913
3733963  3733967  3733969  3733973  3733987  3734039  3734053  3734057  3734083  3734113
3734117  3734123  3734141  3734149  3734153  3734179  3734183  3734191  3734219  3734261
3734293  3734323  3734329  3734371  3734383  3734399  3734411  3734413  3734429  3734443
3734453  3734473  3734491  3734501  3734519  3734531  3734557  3734569  3734587  3734609
3734617  3734657  3734681  3734693  3734699  3734711  3734719  3734737  3734741  3734749
3734767  3734779  3734831  3734833  3734837  3734839  3734867  3734893  3734903  3734909
3734953  3734957  3734987  3734999  3735007  3735013  3735047  3735073  3735101  3735119
3735139  3735161  3735163  3735167  3735169  3735181  3735209  3735217  3735227  3735253
3735247  3735253  3735271  3735293  3735299  3735301  3735323  3735341  3735353  3735371
3735377  3735379  3735401  3735439  3735443  3735449  3735481  3735497  3735517  3735527
3735547  3735547  3735553  3735569  3735583  3735587  3735601  3735617  3735619  3735643
3735653  3735661  3735671  3735679  3735709  3735713  3735731  3735737  3735763  3735773
3735793  3735817  3735829  3735833  3735847  3735857  3735859  3735883  3735887  3735889
3735911  3735923  3735929  3735931  3735943  3735967  3736003  3736037  3736049  3736063
3736069  3736081  3736087  3736111  3736133  3736153  3736163  3736169  3736199  3736211
3736231  3736231  3736241  3736247  3736253  3736259  3736261  3736289  3736283  3736301
3736307  3736349  3736351  3736367  3736391  3736393  3736409  3736423  3736429  3736471
3736477  3736501  3736507  3736541  3736543  3736567  3736573  3736589  3736591  3736609
3736613  3736619  3736639  3736669  3736717  3736723  3736739  3736763  3736769  3736783
3736793  3736807  3736813  3736823  3736841  3736849  3736861  3736867  3736877  3736927
3736933  3736951  3736981  3736987  3737003  3737009  3737029  3737039  3737047  3737057
3737077  3737117  3737131  3737137  3737141  3737147  3737159  3737177  3737179  3737183
```

3737197	3737203	3737231	3737233	3737269	3737291	3737311	3737323	3737347	3737351
3737353	3737359	3737387	3737417	3737423	3737449	3737521	3737543	3737557	3737563
3737579	3737593	3737597	3737599	3737609	3737611	3737621	3737633	3737647	3737659
3737663	3737677	3737687	3737711	3737731	3737743	3737749	3737791	3737821	3737837
3737843	3737857	3737869	3737873	3737879	3737893	3737933	3737939	3737941	3737953
3737959	3737969	3737989	3738001	3738017	3738023	3738047	3738101	3738103	3738107
3738157	3738169	3738173	3738191	3738209	3738211	3738223	3738227	3738233	3738247
3738253	3738277	3738281	3738289	3738311	3738323	3738353	3738391	3738401	3738409
3738431	3738437	3738451	3738457	3738479	3738481	3738529	3738539	3738547	3738551
3738563	3738583	3738587	3738607	3738617	3738659	3738661	3738701	3738733	3738743
3738769	3738781	3738829	3738853	3738859	3738869	3738881	3738907	3738923	3738937
3738947	3738967	3738971	3739009	3739019	3739039	3739051	3739061	3739063	3739079
3739103	3739111	3739123	3739129	3739139	3739163	3739187	3739193	3739199	3739247
3739249	3739259	3739291	3739301	3739319	3739339	3739349	3739381	3739387	3739391
3739397	3739403	3739427	3739429	3739433	3739441	3739459	3739469	3739481	3739493
3739511	3739531	3739573	3739577	3739591	3739613	3739661	3739663	3739669	3739699
3739759	3739763	3739793	3739819	3739831	3739843	3739859	3739867	3739877	3739889
3739891	3739909	3739921	3739943	3739987	3739991	3739993	3739999	3740021	3740039
3740059	3740081	3740083	3740089	3740161	3740171	3740173	3740179	3740189	3740197
3740201	3740251	3740267	3740281	3740287	3740291	3740309	3740311	3740339	3740371
3740393	3740419	3740447	3740453	3740461	3740483	3740497	3740501	3740519	3740537
3740557	3740567	3740573	3740579	3740591	3740609	3740669	3740689	3740707	3740747
3740767	3740773	3740783	3740809	3740837	3740843	3740851	3740873	3740879	3740897
3740903	3740909	3740911	3740923	3740981	3740993	3741011	3741047	3741053	3741077
3741097	3741103	3741113	3741121	3741151	3741161	3741163	3741167	3741169	3741197
3741211	3741223	3741239	3741253	3741259	3741299	3741307	3741337	3741349	3741379
3741383	3741401	3741407	3741431	3741443	3741449	3741457	3741497	3741523	3741533
3741541	3741583	3741587	3741589	3741593	3741599	3741611	3741653	3741671	3741707
3741713	3741737	3741733	3741737	3741739	3741743	3741757	3741767	3741799	3741809
3741821	3741823	3741833	3741863	3741877	3741919	3741929	3741943	3741961	3741971
3741977	3741997	3742009	3742033	3742043	3742049	3742051	3742061	3742087	3742099
3742117	3742121	3742127	3742133	3742139	3742201	3742223	3742229	3742231	3742237
3742241	3742243	3742267	3742273	3742279	3742283	3742301	3742331	3742337	3742367
3742369	3742379	3742391	3742451	3742457	3742477	3742493	3742523	3742561	3742573
3742577	3742579	3742621	3742631	3742633	3742649	3742667	3742681	3742693	3742699
3742709	3742727	3742729	3742741	3742789	3742793	3742841	3742861	3742877	3742891
3742919	3742933	3742961	3742987	3742993	3743011	3743017	3743023	3743039	3743041
3743053	3743081	3743083	3743133	3743141	3743149	3743153	3743183	3743203	3743237
3743239	3743249	3743263	3743269	3743297	3743303	3743309	3743317	3743321	3743371
3743381	3743393	3743419	3743447	3743449	3743459	3743461	3743473	3743477	3743479
3743483	3743489	3743497	3743527	3743533	3743539	3743543	3743557	3743599	3743647
3743651	3743657	3743671	3743681	3743683	3743699	3743711	3743717	3743737	3743749
3743797	3743837	3743843	3743851	3743863	3743897	3743903	3743959	3743981	3743983
3743989	3744001	3744017	3744019	3744023	3744031	3744049	3744071	3744089	3744109
3744113	3744133	3744163	3744179	3744187	3744217	3744227	3744253	3744263	3744287
3744313	3744329	3744353	3744361	3744371	3744383	3744401	3744409	3744431	3744449
3744467	3744493	3744523	3744527	3744541	3744551	3744613	3744619	3744623	3744647
3744661	3744667	3744673	3744677	3744701	3744731	3744737	3744757	3744761	3744781
3744787	3744809	3744823	3744863	3744869	3744941	3744943	3744953	3744967	3744971
3744991	3744997	3745019	3745051	3745069	3745087	3745111	3745127	3745129	3745163
3745187	3745193	3745199	3745201	3745211	3745229	3745241	3745243	3745249	3745253
3745303	3745331	3745361	3745393	3745397	3745439	3745453	3745459	3745471	3745487
3745493	3745499	3745507	3745519	3745529	3745531	3745537	3745543	3745589	3745591
3745597	3745607	3745613	3745631	3745649	3745663	3745691	3745697	3745723	3745739
3745771	3745783	3745789	3745811	3745813	3745829	3745867	3745877	3745879	3745891
3745897	3745913	3745939	3745957	3745961	3745997	3745999	3746027	3746051	3746053
3746077	3746081	3746089	3746107	3746111	3746143	3746147	3746153	3746167	3746179
3746201	3746209	3746219	3746227	3746233	3746269	3746299	3746317	3746329	3746333
3746339	3746359	3746377	3746383	3746387	3746399	3746453	3746471	3746473	3746497
3746503	3746507	3746513	3746521	3746527	3746549	3746551	3746557	3746563	3746581
3746593	3746641	3746651	3746663	3746671	3746689	3746693	3746711	3746737	3746747
3746767	3746773	3746779	3746789	3746791	3746801	3746837	3746839	3746843	3746909
3746921	3746923	3746927	3746969	3746983	3747019	3747043	3747053	3747067	3747071
3747077	3747083	3747097	3747131	3747181	3747197	3747223	3747241	3747299	3747307
3747319	3747329	3747343	3747347	3747349	3747371	3747379	3747383	3747391	3747431
3747479	3747521	3747539	3747547	3747581	3747587	3747589	3747607	3747629	3747637
3747649	3747671	3747691	3747703	3747707	3747713	3747719	3747721	3747727	3747749
3747761	3747787	3747811	3747823	3747833	3747847	3747899	3747917	3747929	3747949
3747979	3748021	3748027	3748033	3748037	3748049	3748051	3748079	3748099	3748123
3748127	3748133	3748139	3748141	3748153	3748169	3748189	3748193	3748207	3748219
3748229	3748231	3748243	3748289	3748307	3748309	3748351	3748357	3748361	3748387
3748397	3748399	3748417	3748441	3748463	3748469	3748487	3748499	3748519	3748523
3748541	3748543	3748553	3748559	3748561	3748571	3748573	3748597	3748603	3748607
3748651	3748663	3748669	3748699	3748709	3748711	3748733	3748739	3748741	3748751
3748763	3748781	3748813	3748819	3748831	3748841	3748847	3748867	3748879	3748883
3748889	3748897	3748903	3748907	3748933	3748939	3748957	3748963	3748967	3748973
3748981	3748991	3749021	3749029	3749071	3749077	3749087	3749093	3749101	3749111
3749117	3749153	3749183	3749189	3749191	3749219	3749257	3749267	3749281	3749293
3749309	3749311	3749329	3749363	3749371	3749377	3749393	3749399	3749407	3749443
3749477	3749497	3749527	3749531	3749533	3749549	3749561	3749563	3749587	3749597
3749597	3749611	3749623	3749633	3749653	3749657	3749677	3749687	3749699	3749761
3749771	3749773	3749807	3749833	3749849	3749861	3749869	3749873	3749881	3749891
3749939	3749947	3749951	3749957	3749959	3749969	3749971	3750001	3750017	3750031
3750037	3750041	3750067	3750079	3750113	3750119	3750151	3750157	3750167	3750169
3750199	3750203	3750211	3750221	3750223	3750233	3750247	3750269	3750293	3750301
3750317	3750323	3750337	3750347	3750361	3750379	3750389	3750407	3750419	3750443
3750451	3750493	3750499	3750511	3750517	3750529	3750533	3750547	3750559	3750563
3750577	3750611	3750613	3750623	3750631	3750697	3750701	3750731	3750737	3750739
3750751	3750767	3750781	3750787	3750797	3750827	3750833	3750839	3750869	3750883

```
3750917  3750919  3750937  3750953  3750977  3750979  3750997  3751003  3751009  3751021
3751057  3751081  3751091  3751103  3751133  3751141  3751177  3751183  3751207  3751219
3751229  3751243  3751259  3751273  3751283  3751289  3751291  3751301  3751309  3751343
3751357  3751367  3751381  3751387  3751409  3751421  3751457  3751463  3751477  3751481
3751511  3751519  3751523  3751547  3751549  3751567  3751571  3751591  3751597  3751603
3751609  3751613  3751637  3751639  3751663  3751673  3751703  3751717  3751723  3751729
3751733  3751739  3751753  3751777  3751801  3751807  3751819  3751823  3751831  3751843
3751859  3751861  3751871  3751901  3751907  3751919  3752009  3752017  3752039  3752069
3752081  3752093  3752117  3752131  3752141  3752149  3752153  3752159  3752183  3752191
3752219  3752237  3752239  3752249  3752261  3752299  3752303  3752317  3752321  3752327
3752351  3752369  3752387  3752389  3752401  3752407  3752431  3752447  3752467  3752477
3752531  3752533  3752549  3752561  3752569  3752587  3752591  3752641  3752647  3752663
3752669  3752677  3752681  3752719  3752729  3752731  3752741  3752759  3752773  3752779
3752783  3752789  3752807  3752831  3752839  3752849  3752851  3752909  3752921  3752923
3752929  3752939  3752981  3752993  3752999  3753007  3753023  3753031  3753067  3753109
3753133  3753137  3753143  3753157  3753179  3753193  3753199  3753223  3753229  3753251
3753257  3753287  3753289  3753307  3753329  3753331  3753349  3753353  3753359  3753361
3753367  3753371  3753377  3753419  3753433  3753437  3753457  3753487  3753493  3753523
3753551  3753553  3753559  3753569  3753593  3753611  3753643  3753647  3753653  3753661
3753671  3753679  3753683  3753691  3753707  3753721  3753751  3753767  3753773  3753781
3753791  3753793  3753823  3753829  3753833  3753839  3753859  3753877  3753913  3753917
3753929  3753947  3753949  3753961  3753979  3753989  3754019  3754033  3754087
3754099  3754103  3754117  3754133  3754139  3754141  3754147  3754151  3754169  3754183
3754187  3754241  3754243  3754259  3754277  3754291  3754301  3754307  3754319  3754321
3754349  3754357  3754363  3754391  3754393  3754397  3754403  3754423  3754469  3754507
3754511  3754519  3754567  3754577  3754607  3754669  3754687  3754691  3754697  3754711
3754721  3754741  3754757  3754763  3754769  3754771  3754787  3754789  3754811  3754823
3754843  3754867  3754873  3754897  3754921  3754963  3754973  3754979  3754981  3755023
3755041  3755051  3755053  3755057  3755069  3755077  3755083  3755117  3755137  3755153
3755183  3755189  3755197  3755203  3755237  3755243  3755267  3755273  3755287  3755299
3755333  3755359  3755383  3755387  3755429  3755431  3755443  3755447  3755449  3755459
3755489  3755513  3755539  3755561  3755617  3755621  3755627  3755651  3755669  3755671
3755677  3755701  3755707  3755729  3755747  3755753  3755779  3755783  3755797  3755803
3755809  3755821  3755837  3755849  3755879  3755891  3755909  3755959  3756001  3756019
3756023  3756029  3756037  3756041  3756059  3756073  3756079  3756097  3756119  3756139
3756143  3756149  3756157  3756161  3756173  3756209  3756211  3756223  3756227  3756229
3756241  3756251  3756253  3756257  3756271  3756289  3756299  3756317  3756323  3756367
3756373  3756377  3756391  3756413  3756421  3756443  3756451  3756479  3756491  3756503
3756517  3756527  3756551  3756559  3756581  3756607  3756617  3756619  3756629  3756637
3756667  3756671  3756691  3756703  3756733  3756763  3756773  3756791  3756793  3756803
3756817  3756821  3756827  3756833  3756839  3756887  3756917  3756923  3756937  3756941
3756947  3756989  3757007  3757009  3757043  3757063  3757067  3757069  3757081  3757087
3757093  3757097  3757109  3757111  3757147  3757151  3757157  3757163  3757177  3757189
3757207  3757261  3757267  3757279  3757283  3757331  3757361  3757367  3757393  3757399
3757423  3757433  3757447  3757451  3757463  3757471  3757511  3757513  3757571  3757577
3757583  3757601  3757619  3757643  3757657  3757673  3757703  3757709  3757711  3757723
3757729  3757777  3757781  3757807  3757811  3757823  3757837  3757861  3757879  3757891
3757909  3757927  3757933  3757939  3757961  3757981  3758017  3758021  3758023
3758077  3758087  3758089  3758093  3758107  3758137  3758141  3758159  3758189  3758221
3758233  3758263  3758273  3758281  3758297  3758299  3758317  3758341  3758351  3758353
3758369  3758383  3758387  3758413  3758431  3758467  3758473  3758483  3758507  3758509
3758537  3758539  3758569  3758597  3758609  3758611  3758621  3758627  3758639  3758659
3758663  3758693  3758701  3758723  3758747  3758761  3758767  3758791  3758809  3758851
3758857  3758861  3758879  3758891  3758927  3758929  3758933  3758939  3758947  3758969
3758971  3758999  3759001  3759011  3759031  3759037  3759047  3759053  3759101  3759127
3759137  3759149  3759199  3759209  3759211  3759221  3759251  3759253  3759257  3759263
3759289  3759323  3759341  3759367  3759377  3759407  3759433  3759439  3759451  3759461
3759479  3759487  3759517  3759527  3759563  3759593  3759611  3759617  3759647  3759667
3759677  3759683  3759713  3759727  3759751  3759757  3759761  3759779  3759781  3759793
3759797  3759799  3759851  3759863  3759869  3759881  3759883  3759901  3759907  3759919
3759949  3759961  3759989  3759991  3760007  3760027  3760033  3760037  3760039  3760067
3760073  3760079  3760103  3760117  3760121  3760123  3760147  3760171  3760193  3760243
3760249  3760261  3760279  3760283  3760319  3760327  3760333  3760357  3760363  3760381
3760411  3760433  3760441  3760447  3760453  3760487  3760489  3760507  3760511  3760529
3760531  3760541  3760561  3760577  3760591  3760639  3760693  3760759  3760763  3760769
3760789  3760811  3760819  3760831  3760843  3760871  3760903  3760919  3760921  3760973
3760997  3761003  3761027  3761047  3761059  3761071  3761117  3761119  3761123  3761159
3761171  3761189  3761203  3761227  3761231  3761239  3761279  3761293  3761333  3761359
3761393  3761413  3761419  3761423  3761441  3761473  3761501  3761507  3761557  3761591
3761599  3761629  3761647  3761669  3761701  3761707  3761711  3761713  3761729  3761731
3761741  3761749  3761773  3761789  3761801  3761831  3761837  3761843  3761861  3761893
3761897  3761929  3761959  3761963  3761971  3761977  3761999  3762001  3762007  3762047
3762061  3762091  3762097  3762103  3762131  3762137  3762139  3762163  3762169  3762173
3762181  3762211  3762259  3762263  3762277  3762299  3762329  3762331  3762349  3762359
3762379  3762383  3762403  3762433  3762449  3762461  3762469  3762487  3762587  3762599
3762601  3762613  3762623  3762631  3762667  3762673  3762683  3762701  3762709  3762719
3762739  3762767  3762799  3762821  3762833  3762839  3762877  3762881  3762911  3762917
3762949  3762977  3762991  3763003  3763027  3763031  3763033  3763043  3763057
3763063  3763093  3763141  3763153  3763169  3763211  3763217  3763229  3763241  3763247
3763259  3763271  3763313  3763321  3763327  3763339  3763343  3763363  3763399  3763423
3763427  3763429  3763453  3763471  3763483  3763523  3763531  3763537  3763561  3763567
3763589  3763601  3763609  3763621  3763653  3763657  3763663  3763667  3763673  3763699
3763709  3763717  3763733  3763757  3763763  3763769  3763777  3763811  3763813  3763819
3763829  3763831  3763861  3763867  3763871  3763873  3763897  3763931  3763933  3763937
3763979  3763999  3764003  3764009  3764041  3764053  3764093  3764107  3764119  3764149
3764197  3764209  3764213  3764227  3764239  3764273  3764291  3764303  3764311  3764323
3764329  3764339  3764357  3764363  3764383  3764393  3764399  3764401  3764437
3764441  3764443  3764447  3764459  3764471  3764477  3764503  3764543  3764569  3764591
3764597  3764647  3764659  3764669  3764687  3764711  3764759  3764767  3764771  3764773
```

3764791 3764807 3764843 3764863 3764879 3764899 3764911 3764923 3764933 3764947
3764953 3764993 3765011 3765019 3765023 3765049 3765079 3765089 3765101 3765107
3765127 3765149 3765161 3765197 3765227 3765233 3765239 3765241 3765247 3765253
3765257 3765263 3765271 3765299 3765319 3765329 3765341 3765367 3765373 3765383
3765397 3765409 3765427 3765431 3765457 3765493 3765497 3765511 3765521 3765523
3765529 3765533 3765547 3765569 3765571 3765581 3765589 3765599 3765607 3765611
3765613 3765661 3765673 3765689 3765701 3765709 3765757 3765761 3765779
3765799 3765829 3765833 3765871 3765889 3765893 3765917 3765919 3765941 3765967
3765977 3766013 3766031 3766057 3766073 3766093 3766099 3766109 3766111 3766117
3766121 3766141 3766153 3766207 3766223 3766229 3766249 3766253 3766261 3766297
3766303 3766307 3766331 3766349 3766387 3766397 3766409 3766417 3766421 3766453
3766459 3766471 3766487 3766499 3766513 3766517 3766519 3766523 3766559 3766573
3766577 3766591 3766601 3766613 3766663 3766691 3766699 3766703 3766709 3766739
3766751 3766753 3766759 3766783 3766787 3766817 3766853 3766891 3766907 3766913
3766937 3766943 3766969 3766993 3766999 3767011 3767017 3767021 3767041 3767053
3767063 3767069 3767077 3767083 3767087 3767117 3767119 3767123 3767131 3767161
3767173 3767207 3767219 3767221 3767227 3767237 3767249 3767261 3767297 3767321
3767333 3767341 3767389 3767411 3767437 3767441 3767447 3767471 3767483 3767497
3767501 3767509 3767521 3767527 3767539 3767549 3767551 3767573 3767587 3767597
3767609 3767623 3767627 3767633 3767657 3767671 3767683 3767689 3767707 3767723
3767741 3767779 3767783 3767801 3767807 3767809 3767831 3767851 3767861 3767867
3767887 3767891 3767893 3767921 3767923 3767971 3767977 3767983 3767987 3768053
3768059 3768077 3768097 3768109 3768119 3768139 3768181 3768199 3768227 3768241
3768253 3768257 3768277 3768287 3768299 3768301 3768307 3768311 3768341 3768367
3768377 3768409 3768431 3768473 3768493 3768497 3768503 3768529 3768533 3768539
3768551 3768553 3768559 3768581 3768587 3768589 3768607 3768617 3768643 3768673
3768697 3768703 3768719 3768727 3768731 3768769 3768799 3768823 3768827 3768839
3768841 3768847 3768899 3768901 3768911 3768913 3768929 3768937 3768967 3768971
3768983 3768991 3769027 3769067 3769069 3769081 3769091 3769109 3769187 3769193
3769229 3769231 3769237 3769243 3769247 3769273 3769303 3769313 3769331 3769349
3769351 3769361 3769379 3769387 3769397 3769399 3769411 3769433 3769439 3769453
3769471 3769489 3769511 3769531 3769553 3769559 3769573 3769583 3769589 3769607
3769609 3769613 3769637 3769651 3769669 3769673 3769679 3769709 3769751 3769763
3769781 3769783 3769807 3769811 3769813 3769841 3769873 3769877 3769891 3769897
3769901 3769949 3769973 3769979 3769981 3769993 3770009 3770033 3770047 3770051
3770057 3770059 3770071 3770083 3770089 3770093 3770101 3770119 3770153 3770161
3770167 3770219 3770233 3770257 3770269 3770279 3770281 3770287 3770297 3770317
3770323 3770357 3770381 3770443 3770449 3770467 3770479 3770489 3770491 3770497
3770527 3770537 3770539 3770567 3770659 3770677 3770687 3770699 3770717 3770761
3770779 3770807 3770813 3770831 3770839 3770861 3770863 3770869 3770891 3770903
3770909 3770917 3770941 3770947 3770953 3770969 3770989 3770999 3771007 3771013
3771017 3771029 3771043 3771049 3771067 3771071 3771091 3771133 3771137 3771169
3771179 3771191 3771193 3771211 3771277 3771281 3771289 3771323 3771343 3771347
3771377 3771407 3771431 3771451 3771461 3771499 3771503 3771529 3771577 3771583
3771589 3771617 3771623 3771641 3771661 3771667 3771673 3771679 3771689 3771707
3771737 3771749 3771751 3771767 3771821 3771847 3771853 3771871 3771881 3771907
3771913 3771923 3771949 3771953 3771967 3771973 3771979 3771991 3772007 3772009
3772019 3772031 3772099 3772103 3772121 3772141 3772151 3772177 3772183 3772189
3772193 3772217 3772229 3772243 3772259 3772271 3772303 3772319 3772331 3772337
3772339 3772343 3772387 3772397 3772459 3772493 3772537 3772541 3772547 3772577
3772579 3772603 3772619 3772627 3772633 3772679 3772687 3772693 3772709 3772711
3772721 3772733 3772739 3772753 3772757 3772763 3772771 3772801 3772883 3772889
3772907 3772913 3772919 3772981 3772999 3773023 3773027 3773047 3773051 3773053
3773071 3773087 3773111 3773129 3773131 3773137 3773171 3773177 3773179 3773197
3773213 3773221 3773243 3773249 3773257 3773279 3773281 3773291 3773317 3773321
3773327 3773359 3773369 3773377 3773387 3773401 3773411 3773417 3773431 3773447
3773453 3773467 3773477 3773491 3773501 3773503 3773513 3773527 3773543 3773563
3773573 3773597 3773617 3773621 3773629 3773639 3773657 3773701 3773713 3773743
3773747 3773773 3773797 3773821 3773831 3773839 3773849 3773851 3773873 3773879
3773893 3773897 3773911 3773921 3773941 3773947 3773993 3773999 3774013 3774019
3774061 3774079 3774101 3774107 3774109 3774143 3774161 3774163 3774181 3774191
3774193 3774203 3774227 3774233 3774257 3774271 3774283 3774307 3774347 3774359
3774361 3774373 3774379 3774409 3774413 3774427 3774439 3774443 3774451 3774457
3774469 3774473 3774479 3774499 3774509 3774517 3774569 3774571 3774577 3774581
3774587 3774593 3774601 3774623 3774649 3774671 3774677 3774689 3774707 3774709
3774739 3774763 3774767 3774769 3774773 3774781 3774809 3774811 3774817 3774871
3774889 3774893 3774907 3774919 3774929 3774943 3774973 3774983 3774989 3775007
3775019 3775039 3775043 3775061 3775063 3775081 3775097 3775103 3775127 3775169
3775171 3775193 3775199 3775201 3775297 3775313 3775333 3775339 3775361 3775363
3775367 3775391 3775393 3775399 3775417 3775439 3775441 3775501 3775507 3775543
3775549 3775553 3775559 3775571 3775573 3775579 3775589 3775601 3775619 3775621
3775637 3775643 3775663 3775679 3775697 3775729 3775757 3775763 3775777 3775781
3775789 3775799 3775801 3775817 3775859 3775861 3775883 3775889 3775897 3775909
3775913 3775939 3775943 3775973 3775987 3775999 3776009 3776011 3776029 3776039
3776077 3776081 3776093 3776153 3776161 3776167 3776173 3776189 3776237 3776239
3776249 3776263 3776273 3776291 3776317 3776369 3776411 3776429 3776441 3776471
3776483 3776489 3776503 3776527 3776543 3776557 3776569 3776581 3776587 3776593
3776603 3776609 3776639 3776651 3776653 3776659 3776671 3776677 3776681 3776683
3776713 3776719 3776743 3776783 3776789 3776809 3776831 3776837 3776863 3776867
3776869 3776881 3776893 3776933 3776957 3776999 3777013 3777031 3777051 3777073
3777089 3777091 3777101 3777119 3777131 3777139 3777157 3777161 3777173 3777187
3777197 3777209 3777211 3777217 3777223 3777229 3777233 3777253 3777283 3777307
3777311 3777317 3777329 3777331 3777341 3777377 3777379 3777391 3777401 3777419
3777439 3777463 3777467 3777479 3777481 3777491 3777503 3777509 3777517 3777539
3777551 3777559 3777569 3777581 3777601 3777607 3777611 3777623 3777667 3777671
3777721 3777749 3777769 3777779 3777793 3777799 3777817 3777853 3777857 3777871
3777883 3777887 3777889 3777899 3777901 3777923 3777931 3777953 3777967 3777971
3777973 3777989 3777997 3778007 3778039 3778043 3778051 3778067 3778079 3778081
3778087 3778111 3778121 3778127 3778163 3778213 3778217 3778237 3778241 3778253

```
3778297  3778319  3778343  3778391  3778399  3778421  3778427  3778429  3778447  3778451
3778457  3778459  3778469  3778499  3778517  3778531  3778571  3778583  3778589  3778591
3778603  3778627  3778637  3778651  3778661  3778667  3778679  3778681  3778717  3778727
3778759  3778769  3778771  3778793  3778823  3778837  3778861  3778897  3778909  3778939
3778949  3778963  3778987  3778997  3779003  3779021  3779033  3779053  3779057  3779071
3779101  3779131  3779159  3779161  3779183  3779201  3779203  3779213  3779231  3779249
3779261  3779263  3779267  3779273  3779297  3779299  3779311  3779327  3779329  3779333
3779341  3779353  3779359  3779371  3779387  3779417  3779437  3779441  3779443  3779453
3779459  3779467  3779473  3779509  3779527  3779533  3779539  3779579  3779623  3779639
3779653  3779663  3779669  3779687  3779707  3779753  3779759  3779761  3779771  3779779
3779813  3779819  3779821  3779849  3779851  3779857  3779863  3779873  3779891  3779921
3779929  3780017  3780037  3780041  3780043  3780053  3780059  3780061  3780067  3780079
3780083  3780113  3780143  3780149  3780151  3780169  3780181  3780191  3780193  3780199
3780247  3780251  3780281  3780313  3780319  3780367  3780377  3780389  3780391  3780397
3780407  3780433  3780473  3780479  3780499  3780503  3780509  3780521  3780541  3780559
3780583  3780589  3780599  3780607  3780611  3780619  3780653  3780709  3780731  3780737
3780739  3780757  3780781  3780787  3780793  3780797  3780811  3780823  3780839  3780857
3780863  3780869  3780871  3780893  3780929  3780937  3780941  3780949  3780961  3780971
3780989  3781007  3781079  3781087  3781117  3781121  3781147  3781153  3781187  3781189
3781213  3781229  3781237  3781243  3781249  3781277  3781301  3781303  3781313  3781367
3781387  3781403  3781423  3781433  3781447  3781457  3781489  3781501  3781507  3781517
3781543  3781559  3781567  3781579  3781639  3781643  3781649  3781663  3781669  3781691
3781711  3781727  3781747  3781759  3781777  3781781  3781801  3781819  3781829  3781849
3781853  3781873  3781883  3781901  3781903  3781909  3781951  3781961  3781993  3782011
3782021  3782039  3782059  3782063  3782069  3782081  3782087  3782111  3782117  3782123
3782153  3782161  3782167  3782171  3782179  3782201  3782213  3782243  3782249  3782257
3782293  3782297  3782309  3782333  3782353  3782369  3782371  3782377  3782407  3782413
3782417  3782437  3782447  3782453  3782459  3782461  3782477  3782479  3782491  3782503
3782507  3782509  3782521  3782531  3782533  3782543  3782561  3782567  3782573  3782579
3782591  3782617  3782629  3782657  3782677  3782683  3782689  3782699  3782773  3782803
3782813  3782819  3782869  3782893  3782897  3782921  3782927  3782929  3782939  3782953
3783001  3783007  3783041  3783047  3783049  3783053  3783083  3783089  3783113  3783119
3783181  3783211  3783251  3783313  3783317  3783343  3783391  3783407  3783419  3783421
3783433  3783449  3783463  3783467  3783473  3783487  3783491  3783497  3783539  3783541
3783551  3783589  3783629  3783631  3783649  3783671  3783677  3783697  3783709  3783713
3783727  3783733  3783737  3783739  3783793  3783821  3783827  3783839  3783851  3783853
3783859  3783889  3783893  3783919  3783929  3783943  3783961  3783971  3783977  3783991
3784003  3784009  3784019  3784037  3784051  3784057  3784063  3784073  3784103  3784127
3784133  3784141  3784159  3784163  3784169  3784189  3784199  3784223  3784241  3784267
3784271  3784273  3784309  3784321  3784331  3784343  3784357  3784367  3784373  3784381
3784399  3784411  3784427  3784433  3784441  3784447  3784457  3784463  3784469  3784493
3784499  3784507  3784519  3784531  3784541  3784577  3784603  3784631  3784633  3784639
3784643  3784657  3784667  3784691  3784723  3784733  3784741  3784747  3784757  3784777
3784787  3784793  3784813  3784849  3784861  3784873  3784901  3784919  3784927  3784943
3784967  3784973  3784987  3785011  3785021  3785029  3785053  3785071  3785083  3785143
3785149  3785153  3785183  3785191  3785209  3785213  3785227  3785261  3785263  3785273
3785279  3785281  3785291  3785293  3785303  3785323  3785347  3785357  3785371  3785393
3785401  3785417  3785449  3785459  3785471  3785479  3785491  3785527  3785531  3785539
3785549  3785569  3785623  3785629  3785641  3785651  3785669  3785681  3785687  3785753
3785779  3785797  3785801  3785809  3785819  3785851  3785857  3785861  3785891  3785893
3785911  3785923  3785927  3785939  3785953  3785963  3785987  3785993  3786011  3786047
3786049  3786059  3786067  3786071  3786077  3786091  3786109  3786119  3786127  3786131
3786151  3786157  3786169  3786197  3786199  3786203  3786229  3786241  3786253  3786259
3786271  3786281  3786287  3786311  3786319  3786337  3786347  3786353  3786397  3786401
3786403  3786413  3786449  3786463  3786481  3786493  3786509  3786511  3786521  3786533
3786539  3786553  3786569  3786571  3786577  3786581  3786593  3786613  3786641  3786647
3786659  3786661  3786667  3786677  3786689  3786703  3786749  3786751  3786779  3786781
3786803  3786821  3786829  3786847  3786857  3786859  3786899  3786919  3786953  3786989
3787031  3787057  3787067  3787097  3787109  3787117  3787123  3787153  3787163  3787183
3787193  3787219  3787229  3787237  3787247  3787261  3787279  3787291  3787297  3787319
3787321  3787349  3787351  3787361  3787367  3787369  3787391  3787417  3787471  3787493
3787501  3787507  3787513  3787519  3787523  3787529  3787547  3787561  3787591  3787627
3787649  3787657  3787687  3787691  3787723  3787733  3787757  3787759  3787769  3787777
3787781  3787793  3787799  3787811  3787843  3787853  3787877  3787919  3787933  3787937
3787943  3787957  3787967  3787969  3787981  3787997  3788003  3788017  3788033  3788041
3788047  3788051  3788111  3788117  3788159  3788209  3788219  3788221  3788227  3788243
3788249  3788251  3788273  3788303  3788311  3788321  3788329  3788333  3788383  3788401
3788417  3788419  3788423  3788431  3788453  3788459  3788483  3788497  3788503  3788509
3788563  3788573  3788597  3788621  3788633  3788639  3788663  3788669  3788683  3788711
3788713  3788737  3788747  3788779  3788833  3788839  3788843  3788861  3788903  3788929
3788963  3788969  3788989  3789013  3789029  3789067  3789073  3789103  3789109  3789119
3789127  3789131  3789139  3789143  3789173  3789193  3789197  3789221  3789239  3789241
3789257  3789277  3789287  3789293  3789323  3789329  3789337  3789361  3789367  3789371
3789377  3789389  3789413  3789427  3789451  3789463  3789481  3789497  3789523  3789529
3789571  3789581  3789593  3789601  3789613  3789701  3789703  3789709  3789713  3789739
3789743  3789757  3789761  3789769  3789787  3789809  3789811  3789817  3789839  3789853
3789857  3789859  3789883  3789889  3789893  3789899  3789931  3789937  3789953  3789971
3790001  3790057  3790067  3790069  3790103  3790121  3790187  3790229  3790247  3790273
3790279  3790289  3790309  3790333  3790349  3790373  3790393  3790433  3790441  3790447
3790453  3790459  3790471  3790483  3790487  3790513  3790517  3790531  3790537  3790543
3790547  3790559  3790571  3790583  3790621  3790651  3790667  3790697  3790729  3790739
3790747  3790753  3790757  3790763  3790769  3790771  3790781  3790783  3790789  3790807
3790889  3790921  3790933  3790939  3790951  3790961  3790981  3790991  3790993  3790999
3791027  3791033  3791059  3791063  3791069  3791087  3791093  3791101  3791107  3791167
3791173  3791189  3791197  3791209  3791213  3791219  3791231  3791233  3791243  3791261
3791273  3791303  3791309  3791321  3791339  3791341  3791371  3791377  3791383  3791387
3791423  3791429  3791449  3791453  3791459  3791479  3791483  3791497  3791509  3791549
3791551  3791563  3791569  3791647  3791651  3791657  3791677  3791681  3791687  3791701
3791717  3791719  3791741  3791789  3791791  3791807  3791831  3791861  3791863  3791873
```

```
3791899  3791903  3791911  3791927  3791933  3791959  3791981  3792017  3792029  3792043
3792073  3792091  3792109  3792119  3792121  3792149  3792161  3792169  3792179  3792193
3792209  3792221  3792223  3792227  3792233  3792251  3792253  3792259  3792281  3792293
3792307  3792317  3792331  3792367  3792391  3792421  3792427  3792443  3792487  3792491
3792499  3792511  3792527  3792577  3792589  3792599  3792629  3792637  3792641  3792661
3792671  3792673  3792709  3792721  3792727  3792731  3792739  3792743  3792773  3792779
3792781  3792791  3792793  3792809  3792821  3792827  3792857  3792863  3792871  3792883
3792889  3792917  3792949  3792959  3792967  3792973  3792977  3792979  3792983  3793001
3793003  3793019  3793021  3793039  3793061  3793079  3793081  3793087  3793117  3793121
3793133  3793177  3793199  3793211  3793241  3793259  3793289  3793313  3793333  3793357
3793373  3793381  3793423  3793429  3793457  3793463  3793469  3793481  3793487  3793507
3793549  3793561  3793571  3793583  3793613  3793619  3793627  3793633  3793649  3793723
3793733  3793747  3793753  3793763  3793789  3793807  3793813  3793819  3793837  3793849
3793903  3793921  3793927  3793931  3793949  3793973  3794003  3794039  3794047  3794051
3794071  3794081  3794083  3794101  3794107  3794117  3794123  3794137  3794171  3794207
3794227  3794257  3794269  3794279  3794299  3794309  3794317  3794339  3794341  3794347
3794353  3794359  3794377  3794419  3794423  3794459  3794503  3794507  3794521  3794537
3794599  3794647  3794711  3794719  3794729  3794743  3794753  3794767  3794771  3794773
3794789  3794809  3794863  3794867  3794891  3794897  3794909  3794929  3794941  3794951
3794953  3794963  3794971  3794981  3794983  3795007  3795013  3795031  3795059  3795061
3795067  3795073  3795091  3795149  3795151  3795157  3795221  3795251  3795263  3795283
3795287  3795289  3795347  3795367  3795373  3795377  3795401  3795419  3795427  3795439
3795443  3795457  3795469  3795499  3795503  3795511  3795521  3795523  3795541  3795551
3795553  3795563  3795569  3795581  3795587  3795593  3795619  3795637  3795643  3795661
3795677  3795691  3795697  3795703  3795749  3795773  3795797  3795853  3795887  3795899
3795907  3795917  3795923  3795931  3795937  3795959  3795977  3795983  3796003  3796027
3796031  3796057  3796061  3796063  3796087  3796097  3796099  3796109  3796183  3796193
3796201  3796211  3796217  3796223  3796241  3796277  3796279  3796283  3796301  3796307
3796339  3796343  3796349  3796363  3796367  3796399  3796439  3796453  3796457  3796459
3796469  3796487  3796493  3796501  3796531  3796537  3796543  3796567  3796577  3796589
3796603  3796609  3796619  3796621  3796669  3796673  3796693  3796697  3796711  3796733
3796739  3796753  3796777  3796783  3796799  3796811  3796813  3796843  3796847  3796861
3796873  3796879  3796907  3796921  3796927  3796939  3796951  3796963  3796997  3797023
3797041  3797071  3797077  3797081  3797089  3797111  3797113  3797117  3797141  3797161
3797179  3797191  3797203  3797219  3797249  3797251  3797281  3797327  3797357  3797371
3797377  3797383  3797389  3797419  3797429  3797441  3797447  3797489  3797491  3797501
3797509  3797527  3797539  3797551  3797557  3797567  3797597  3797603  3797611  3797623
3797641  3797657  3797659  3797671  3797683  3797687  3797693  3797699  3797711  3797723
3797743  3797797  3797809  3797819  3797837  3797863  3797867  3797873  3797879  3797909
3797917  3797933  3797951  3797957  3797993  3798001  3798017  3798019  3798031  3798037
3798049  3798071  3798073  3798077  3798079  3798097  3798107  3798121  3798131  3798149
3798169  3798173  3798181  3798187  3798239  3798251  3798283  3798299  3798317  3798343
3798349  3798367  3798371  3798373  3798397  3798407  3798413  3798419  3798437  3798451
3798469  3798489  3798491  3798517  3798523  3798533  3798539  3798547  3798569  3798581
3798583  3798589  3798593  3798629  3798631  3798637  3798643  3798649  3798659  3798671
3798677  3798733  3798737  3798767  3798779  3798793  3798829  3798853  3798857  3798859
3798877  3798889  3798919  3798923  3798931  3798941  3798943  3798953  3798961  3798983
3799013  3799027  3799039  3799043  3799051  3799063  3799067  3799079  3799097  3799099
3799111  3799121  3799127  3799129  3799153  3799157  3799171  3799193  3799217  3799219
3799223  3799241  3799247  3799273  3799291  3799333  3799337  3799349  3799379  3799403
3799409  3799427  3799447  3799469  3799489  3799513  3799547  3799559  3799571  3799589
3799597  3799603  3799643  3799661  3799681  3799699  3799703  3799709  3799717  3799727
3799759  3799769  3799787  3799799  3799801  3799811  3799813  3799819  3799837  3799877
3799883  3799897  3799919  3799927  3799931  3799951  3799973  3800021  3800051  3800053
3800059  3800063  3800081  3800107  3800113  3800119  3800149  3800177  3800183  3800201
3800213  3800219  3800227  3800257  3800263  3800273  3800281  3800287  3800309  3800311
3800347  3800369  3800371  3800387  3800393  3800429  3800443  3800449  3800473  3800477
3800491  3800501  3800521  3800549  3800579  3800581  3800591  3800593  3800609  3800611
3800623  3800633  3800647  3800669  3800689  3800723  3800737  3800761  3800777  3800801
3800807  3800857  3800861  3800887  3800917  3800947  3800963  3800999  3801011  3801029
3801041  3801043  3801053  3801067  3801073  3801097  3801117  3801143  3801163  3801169
3801173  3801179  3801211  3801221  3801223  3801229  3801241  3801247  3801253  3801257
3801263  3801283  3801299  3801331  3801341  3801359  3801361  3801367  3801373  3801377
3801403  3801419  3801431  3801439  3801443  3801449  3801461  3801487  3801493  3801503
3801533  3801541  3801571  3801583  3801599  3801617  3801619  3801631  3801661  3801667
3801671  3801709  3801731  3801757  3801769  3801779  3801793  3801797  3801799  3801823
3801827  3801839  3801857  3801869  3801883  3801899  3801937  3801949  3801953  3801977
3801983  3802003  3802027  3802037  3802081  3802093  3802129  3802133  3802151  3802171
3802187  3802193  3802207  3802213  3802229  3802241  3802283  3802319  3802321  3802333
3802343  3802363  3802369  3802391  3802417  3802471  3802481  3802483  3802493  3802511
3802523  3802529  3802531  3802541  3802583  3802607  3802621  3802649  3802651  3802663
3802681  3802693  3802699  3802753  3802759  3802763  3802769  3802783  3802787  3802837
3802861  3802867  3802871  3802913  3802919  3802949  3802957  3802961  3802969  3802979
3802993  3802999  3803017  3803029  3803047  3803077  3803113  3803117  3803131  3803141
3803153  3803161  3803171  3803197  3803203  3803209  3803231  3803253  3803311  3803329
3803339  3803347  3803351  3803369  3803377  3803419  3803453  3803473  3803491  3803497
3803507  3803509  3803543  3803551  3803557  3803561  3803581  3803587  3803599  3803603
3803609  3803617  3803623  3803627  3803647  3803659  3803677  3803689  3803707  3803709
3803783  3803797  3803827  3803831  3803861  3803867  3803879  3803887  3803911  3803923
3803941  3803951  3803977  3803983  3803989  3804011  3804029  3804043  3804063  3804067
3804071  3804083  3804089  3804091  3804113  3804121  3804137  3804149  3804169  3804179
3804187  3804197  3804211  3804217  3804221  3804233  3804259  3804263  3804271  3804301
3804319  3804331  3804337  3804341  3804373  3804397  3804409  3804411  3804421  3804433
3804457  3804473  3804491  3804517  3804527  3804533  3804547  3804551  3804553  3804587
3804589  3804601  3804613  3804623  3804629  3804643  3804653  3804659  3804667  3804701
3804707  3804709  3804721  3804737  3804739  3804743  3804751  3804763  3804767  3804797
3804799  3804811  3804859  3804869  3804881  3804893  3804907  3804917  3804919  3804929
3804937  3804943  3804947  3804949  3804953  3804989  3805001  3805037  3805057  3805063
3805069  3805091  3805099  3805121  3805133  3805159  3805171  3805183  3805211  3805223
```

```
3805231 3805237 3805253 3805259 3805273 3805279 3805289 3805309 3805313 3805357
3805367 3805369 3805379 3805391 3805393 3805463 3805469 3805471 3805489 3805499
3805531 3805537 3805547 3805573 3805621 3805639 3805663 3805673 3805679 3805687
3805717 3805721 3805733 3805811 3805817 3805819 3805829 3805831 3805849 3805853
3805861 3805889 3805897 3805903 3805927 3805933 3805951 3805979 3805987 3805999
3806003 3806009 3806021 3806027 3806029 3806051 3806083 3806093 3806111 3806119
3806123 3806167 3806177 3806189 3806191 3806197 3806207 3806233 3806281 3806287
3806291 3806303 3806321 3806333 3806347 3806423 3806437 3806447 3806501 3806507
3806527 3806549 3806557 3806567 3806587 3806591 3806599 3806609 3806617 3806639
3806641 3806653 3806659 3806683 3806687 3806689 3806701 3806711 3806741 3806749
3806767 3806837 3806839 3806843 3806849 3806851 3806867 3806903 3806909 3806911
3806923 3806927 3806981 3806983 3807053 3807059 3807061 3807101 3807109 3807113 3807119
3807173 3807187 3807217 3807227 3807229 3807257 3807281 3807289 3807313 3807317
3807341 3807359 3807379 3807413 3807421 3807431 3807449 3807457 3807491 3807499
3807511 3807523 3807527 3807533 3807539 3807553 3807577 3807589 3807593 3807647
3807649 3807689 3807691 3807701 3807709 3807731 3807737 3807743 3807751 3807757
3807827 3807833 3807851 3807861 3807871 3807877 3807883 3807889 3807901 3807907
3807911 3807931 3807941 3807959 3808001 3808031 3808033 3808061 3808073 3808109
3808127 3808139 3808141 3808157 3808159 3808163 3808177 3808223 3808229 3808241
3808243 3808253 3808261 3808267 3808283 3808307 3808327 3808333 3808397 3808403
3808411 3808429 3808477 3808487 3808513 3808549 3808559 3808579 3808591 3808667
3808709 3808711 3808757 3808757 3808789 3808793 3808801 3808813 3808829 3808841
3808843 3808853 3808907 3808913 3808963 3808967 3808979 3808993 3808999 3809051
3809077 3809081 3809089 3809107 3809123 3809131 3809137 3809149 3809153 3809159
3809161 3809167 3809171 3809189 3809251 3809257 3809279 3809297 3809321 3809339
3809341 3809369 3809381 3809383 3809387 3809423 3809431 3809461 3809471 3809489
3809503 3809523 3809539 3809543 3809549 3809551 3809567 3809591 3809593 3809599
3809623 3809639 3809653 3809677 3809681 3809699 3809711 3809719 3809723 3809731
3809737 3809749 3809753 3809777 3809791 3809803 3809809 3809831 3809837 3809849
3809857 3809891 3809903 3809909 3809917 3809941 3809947 3809957 3809959 3809963
3809977 3809983 3809987 3810017 3810031 3810047 3810071 3810077 3810083 3810097
3810119 3810133 3810137 3810143 3810151 3810167 3810173 3810181 3810199 3810211
3810221 3810229 3810251 3810269 3810277 3810293 3810299 3810319 3810343 3810349
3810353 3810379 3810383 3810403 3810409 3810413 3810419 3810421 3810461 3810463
3810481 3810493 3810497 3810503 3810509 3810511 3810517 3810523 3810529 3810553
3810557 3810559 3810563 3810577 3810589 3810623 3810637 3810643 3810661 3810679
3810701 3810707 3810721 3810727 3810733 3810739 3810743 3810757 3810761 3810767
3810769 3810797 3810809 3810817 3810823 3810841 3810899 3810931 3810979 3811007
3811013 3811057 3811063 3811081 3811099 3811117 3811121 3811127 3811139 3811141
3811147 3811163 3811189 3811193 3811201 3811207 3811217 3811253 3811273 3811279
3811289 3811303 3811321 3811331 3811369 3811373 3811387 3811411 3811427 3811433
3811453 3811469 3811487 3811501 3811523 3811529 3811541 3811547 3811579 3811589
3811627 3811631 3811657 3811669 3811681 3811711 3811733 3811741 3811763 3811771
3811783 3811817 3811877 3811889 3811891 3811909 3811921 3811939 3811949 3811967
3811979 3812023 3812033 3812059 3812071 3812077 3812111 3812119 3812129 3812153
3812177 3812183 3812189 3812191 3812201 3812209 3812213 3812219 3812257 3812261
3812269 3812309 3812357 3812363 3812371 3812381 3812383 3812387 3812399 3812441
3812453 3812477 3812513 3812527 3812531 3812533 3812569 3812581 3812587 3812603
3812617 3812623 3812647 3812651 3812657 3812663 3812689 3812693 3812701 3812707
3812719 3812729 3812737 3812741 3812759 3812773 3812791 3812797 3812801 3812807
3812819 3812839 3812923 3812929 3812941 3812951 3812983 3812987 3812989
3813001 3813013 3813023 3813067 3813097 3813113 3813143 3813149 3813169 3813211
3813221 3813223 3813233 3813289 3813307 3813311 3813317 3813323 3813349 3813353
3813379 3813391 3813401 3813419 3813421 3813427 3813461 3813463 3813493 3813499
3813503 3813517 3813521 3813559 3813571 3813577 3813581 3813599 3813611 3813617
3813619 3813631 3813643 3813647 3813673 3813679 3813751 3813757 3813769 3813773
3813811 3813847 3813869 3813871 3813893 3813913 3813941 3813949 3813959 3813983
3814009 3814033 3814043 3814061 3814081 3814087 3814091 3814093 3814121 3814123
3814127 3814183 3814207 3814211 3814253 3814267 3814301 3814309 3814313 3814319
3814337 3814339 3814351 3814361 3814373 3814381 3814387 3814397 3814403 3814417
3814423 3814427 3814429 3814439 3814483 3814493 3814501 3814529 3814543 3814553
3814561 3814583 3814607 3814609 3814621 3814627 3814633 3814637 3814639 3814667
3814691 3814693 3814697 3814703 3814709 3814717 3814721 3814729 3814739 3814751
3814753 3814771 3814777 3814787 3814793 3814799 3814813 3814841 3814903 3814931
3814957 3814961 3814963 3814973 3814981 3814997 3815041 3815051 3815057 3815069
3815081 3815083 3815087 3815101 3815111 3815159 3815167 3815179 3815197 3815209
3815221 3815243 3815249 3815267 3815281 3815291 3815303 3815321 3815351 3815363
3815377 3815381 3815389 3815407 3815423 3815431 3815453 3815459 3815467 3815473
3815503 3815509 3815521 3815527 3815533 3815549 3815557 3815563 3815569 3815579
3815597 3815627 3815639 3815641 3815653 3815681 3815683 3815687 3815711 3815719
3815737 3815761 3815767 3815771 3815797 3815807 3815809 3815813 3815843 3815869
3815879 3815891 3815893 3815909 3815923 3815927 3815957 3815963 3816011 3816013
3816019 3816031 3816061 3816067 3816073 3816089 3816103 3816117 3816133 3816149
3816167 3816173 3816187 3816191 3816203 3816233 3816277 3816287 3816299 3816311
3816317 3816383 3816389 3816391 3816407 3816431 3816437 3816467 3816469 3816497
3816499 3816539 3816557 3816559 3816563 3816581 3816599 3816601 3816623 3816629
3816641 3816647 3816667 3816677 3816679 3816691 3816697 3816713 3816733 3816737
3816763 3816767 3816793 3816803 3816811 3816847 3816863 3816877 3816881 3816907
3816913 3816941 3816973 3816979 3817039 3817063 3817111 3817117 3817127 3817133
3817147 3817159 3817189 3817193 3817199 3817201 3817211 3817213 3817217 3817223
3817249 3817259 3817273 3817277 3817279 3817291 3817301 3817313 3817339 3817343
3817349 3817351 3817369 3817381 3817391 3817393 3817397 3817447 3817501 3817511
3817541 3817543 3817557 3817559 3817573 3817579 3817607 3817621 3817657 3817679
3817687 3817691 3817717 3817721 3817739 3817753 3817757 3817777 3817783 3817789
3817811 3817813 3817817 3817819 3817829 3817853 3817859 3817903 3817907 3817939
3817963 3817967 3817969 3817981 3817987 3817999 3818021 3818027 3818029 3818033
3818039 3818063 3818071 3818077 3818093 3818123 3818131 3818137 3818179 3818201
3818209 3818219 3818231 3818237 3818261 3818267 3818291 3818293 3818317 3818329
3818333 3818341 3818351 3818359 3818369 3818389 3818393 3818407 3818431 3818447
```

```
3818461  3818473  3818501  3818513  3818527  3818533  3818537  3818543  3818561  3818587
3818603  3818641  3818651  3818661  3818687  3818707  3818719  3818729  3818741  3818767
3818803  3818831  3818839  3818869  3818879  3818887  3818909  3818917  3818929  3818951
3818953  3818963  3818977  3819007  3819031  3819037  3819041  3819059  3819073  3819077
3819083  3819089  3819139  3819143  3819187  3819197  3819199  3819223  3819227  3819229
3819259  3819269  3819301  3819313  3819331  3819337  3819341  3819353  3819367  3819371
3819379  3819421  3819461  3819463  3819481  3819511  3819521  3819523  3819527  3819559
3819583  3819617  3819631  3819661  3819671  3819691  3819707  3819709  3819731  3819757
3819773  3819797  3819811  3819821  3819833  3819853  3819857  3819877  3819899  3819901
3819923  3819943  3819979  3819983  3819997  3820009  3820031  3820043  3820051  3820057
3820067  3820097  3820109  3820111  3820127  3820129  3820133  3820153  3820171  3820177
3820181  3820237  3820253  3820259  3820279  3820303  3820319  3820321  3820343  3820351
3820357  3820363  3820379  3820391  3820423  3820429  3820441  3820447  3820457  3820477
3820499  3820511  3820513  3820517  3820543  3820549  3820567  3820571  3820589  3820591
3820603  3820627  3820651  3820673  3820709  3820711  3820727  3820759  3820763  3820769
3820787  3820799  3820811  3820813  3820841  3820847  3820849  3820853  3820867  3820871
3820889  3820903  3820933  3820963  3820987  3820997  3821003  3821009  3821057  3821099
3821117  3821119  3821123  3821131  3821137  3821171  3821173  3821177  3821183  3821203
3821221  3821241  3821231  3821239  3821263  3821267  3821269  3821273  3821311  3821327
3821329  3821347  3821351  3821387  3821399  3821407  3821423  3821437  3821483  3821491
3821497  3821513  3821563  3821579  3821581  3821627  3821633  3821639  3821647  3821669
3821681  3821687  3821689  3821723  3821729  3821731  3821737  3821771  3821789  3821791
3821801  3821803  3821809  3821813  3821819  3821827  3821837  3821863  3821893  3821903
3821911  3821929  3821947  3821953  3821963  3821971  3821981  3822017  3822029  3822031
3822037  3822041  3822047  3822053  3822073  3822103  3822107  3822109  3822139  3822157
3822167  3822191  3822223  3822241  3822251  3822255  3822271  3822277  3822281  3822289
3822311  3822317  3822349  3822367  3822383  3822397  3822407  3822409  3822419  3822421
3822473  3822491  3822493  3822509  3822523  3822527  3822529  3822541  3822583  3822587
3822589  3822593  3822601  3822613  3822619  3822631  3822669  3822665  3822661  3822683
3822701  3822727  3822737  3822757  3822769  3822779  3822811  3822821  3822823  3822851
3822869  3822883  3822913  3822919  3822941  3822947  3822967  3823007  3823031  3823067
3823069  3823091  3823097  3823103  3823117  3823139  3823151  3823159  3823163  3823177
3823187  3823201  3823207  3823213  3823219  3823223  3823241  3823243  3823271  3823277
3823289  3823301  3823307  3823319  3823349  3823399  3823411  3823429  3823433  3823439
3823441  3823459  3823511  3823513  3823553  3823559  3823577  3823597  3823609  3823627
3823649  3823661  3823697  3823711  3823717  3823723  3823733  3823739  3823747  3823753
3823777  3823789  3823801  3823811  3823867  3823871  3823877  3823879  3823889  3823901
3823927  3823931  3823933  3823951  3823973  3823991  3824017  3824053  3824057  3824069
3824083  3824089  3824113  3824123  3824137  3824147  3824173  3824189  3824207  3824231
3824243  3824267  3824281  3824297  3824323  3824333  3824347  3824413  3824441  3824461
3824479  3824491  3824497  3824503  3824519  3824537  3824551  3824573  3824591  3824599
3824617  3824641  3824651  3824663  3824669  3824671  3824683  3824713  3824729  3824741
3824753  3824759  3824771  3824827  3824837  3824861  3824867  3824869  3824879  3824921
3824927  3824933  3824993  3824999  3825011  3825043  3825049  3825053  3825079  3825083
3825089  3825091  3825103  3825109  3825167  3825179  3825181  3825191  3825193  3825209
3825223  3825229  3825257  3825271  3825281  3825293  3825299  3825301  3825313  3825329
3825343  3825347  3825359  3825373  3825379  3825397  3825401  3825413  3825421  3825427
3825439  3825457  3825463  3825473  3825509  3825511  3825529  3825533  3825557  3825559
3825599  3825623  3825637  3825643  3825649  3825671  3825677  3825683  3825691  3825713
3825721  3825739  3825743  3825781  3825793  3825817  3825823  3825827  3825851  3825853
3825869  3825893  3825907  3825919  3825923  3825931  3825947  3825949  3825953  3825979
3826001  3826007  3826019  3826157  3826177  3826187  3826219  3826259  3826279  3826283
3826297  3826313  3826337  3826367  3826373  3826393  3826399  3826409  3826439  3826453
3826481  3826499  3826517  3826541  3826573  3826583  3826597  3826601  3826621  3826631
3826639  3826661  3826673  3826703  3826721  3826723  3826729  3826741  3826769  3826777
3826843  3826859  3826861  3826877  3826897  3826931  3826943  3826951  3826967  3827003
3827029  3827053  3827059  3827071  3827093  3827143  3827149  3827191  3827207  3827209
3827221  3827231  3827249  3827273  3827293  3827297  3827339  3827347  3827357  3827381
3827393  3827401  3827419  3827429  3827437  3827441  3827479  3827489  3827519  3827561
3827563  3827573  3827581  3827599  3827611  3827617  3827627  3827639  3827647  3827651
3827657  3827671  3827693  3827701  3827723  3827741  3827749  3827767  3827783  3827809
3827833  3827843  3827869  3827881  3827893  3827897  3827899  3827927  3827939  3827947
3827953  3827977  3827981  3828007  3828023  3828037  3828049  3828053  3828059  3828061
3828067  3828073  3828079  3828091  3828109  3828113  3828119  3828133  3828151  3828169
3828217  3828229  3828239  3828259  3828263  3828269  3828287  3828311  3828343  3828359
3828361  3828371  3828379  3828389  3828397  3828401  3828413  3828431  3828437  3828449
3828463  3828467  3828497  3828499  3828509  3828521  3828523  3828571  3828589  3828599
3828611  3828637  3828659  3828661  3828673  3828683  3828701  3828719  3828733  3828743
3828749  3828751  3828821  3828857  3828887  3828901  3828917  3828919  3828931  3828941
3828947  3828953  3828973  3829079  3829081  3829087  3829103  3829121  3829123  3829129
3829139  3829141  3829157  3829169  3829171  3829181  3829183  3829219  3829223  3829229
3829237  3829253  3829271  3829283  3829289  3829291  3829307  3829321  3829333  3829351
3829373  3829379  3829381  3829391  3829429  3829433  3829447  3829459  3829487  3829489
3829493  3829499  3829531  3829559  3829597  3829601  3829603  3829613  3829633  3829649
3829667  3829673  3829681  3829691  3829729  3829733  3829751  3829757  3829781  3829783
3829801  3829807  3829817  3829823  3829829  3829831  3829843  3829853  3829873  3829883
3829897  3829901  3829919  3829927  3829949  3829961  3829979  3829993  3829997  3830003
3830017  3830023  3830027  3830033  3830051  3830087  3830093  3830111  3830119  3830131
3830137  3830147  3830149  3830159  3830161  3830207  3830231  3830243  3830263  3830269
3830273  3830303  3830317  3830327  3830347  3830357  3830371  3830401  3830411  3830413
3830429  3830441  3830459  3830461  3830509  3830513  3830527  3830531  3830537  3830539
3830543  3830549  3830557  3830579  3830597  3830599  3830611  3830623  3830669  3830689
3830707  3830713  3830731  3830737  3830759  3830773  3830791  3830803  3830819
3830843  3830863  3830867  3830881  3830891  3830909  3830927  3830963  3830969  3830977
3831007  3831019  3831043  3831067  3831097  3831101  3831119  3831131  3831167  3831169
3831181  3831199  3831221  3831253  3831287  3831301  3831319  3831329  3831339  3831413
3831427  3831431  3831439  3831449  3831467  3831473  3831493  3831517  3831523  3831557
3831571  3831577  3831587  3831599  3831623  3831643  3831649  3831661  3831689  3831691
3831719  3831721  3831727  3831733  3831743  3831767  3831781  3831811  3831827  3831871
```

```
3831889  3831907  3831911  3831913  3831917  3831923  3831929  3831937  3832001  3832009
3832019  3832061  3832067  3832079  3832097  3832111  3832121  3832133  3832159  3832163
3832177  3832183  3832207  3832219  3832223  3832247  3832249  3832253  3832267  3832273
3832291  3832303  3832307  3832337  3832343  3832351  3832397  3832399  3832403  3832417
3832481  3832487  3832489  3832501  3832511  3832579  3832597  3832603  3832613  3832627
3832637  3832643  3832657  3832663  3832679  3832687  3832723  3832729  3832757  3832783
3832811  3832831  3832853  3832877  3832879  3832903  3832919  3832921  3832931  3832937
3832949  3832957  3832993  3832999  3833009  3833033  3833047  3833059  3833069  3833087
3833099  3833101  3833107  3833129  3833153  3833183  3833197  3833201  3833209  3833233
3833239  3833257  3833261  3833281  3833293  3833327  3833329  3833339  3833359  3833369
3833371  3833411  3833413  3833419  3833441  3833443  3833513  3833527  3833567  3833569
3833591  3833629  3833647  3833651  3833699  3833701  3833707  3833719  3833723  3833729
3833737  3833747  3833777  3833833  3833867  3833873  3833881  3833897  3833899  3833909
3833927  3833971  3833989  3834013  3834023  3834043  3834053  3834059  3834079  3834091
3834109  3834121  3834139  3834157  3834161  3834167  3834191  3834221  3834223  3834227
3834251  3834253  3834283  3834287  3834301  3834377  3834407  3834431  3834433  3834437
3834451  3834473  3834499  3834529  3834533  3834539  3834541  3834547  3834553  3834557
3834577  3834601  3834613  3834619  3834631  3834647  3834653  3834703  3834797  3834829
3834833  3834841  3834851  3834893  3834899  3834907  3834913  3834937  3834953  3834959
3834967  3834983  3834991  3835001  3835021  3835031  3835049  3835057  3835061  3835067
3835079  3835109  3835123  3835157  3835187  3835199  3835231  3835241  3835243  3835259
3835261  3835267  3835291  3835301  3835303  3835313  3835331  3835339  3835343  3835361
3835367  3835373  3835379  3835399  3835439  3835441  3835483  3835487  3835501  3835519
3835547  3835567  3835577  3835597  3835603  3835607  3835613  3835621  3835631  3835651
3835669  3835681  3835691  3835697  3835747  3835751  3835757  3835759  3835763  3835771
3835831  3835861  3835873  3835883  3835903  3835907  3835913  3835921  3835927
3835939  3835957  3835969  3835973  3835991  3836047  3836069  3836113  3836143  3836153
3836171  3836179  3836213  3836227  3836243  3836257  3836263  3836267  3836279  3836291
3836293  3836317  3836321  3836341  3836359  3836363  3836383  3836387  3836389  3836401
3836431  3836449  3836471  3836489  3836501  3836513  3836519  3836587  3836603  3836629
3836639  3836663  3836669  3836681  3836683  3836731  3836741  3836743  3836771  3836801
3836809  3836827  3836831  3836843  3836851  3836867  3836869  3836887  3836891  3836893
3836927  3836941  3836957  3836977  3836983  3837013  3837017  3837049  3837079  3837101
3837103  3837131  3837133  3837137  3837139  3837143  3837151  3837167  3837179  3837187
3837199  3837209  3837217  3837241  3837247  3837263  3837287  3837289  3837311  3837319
3837329  3837331  3837347  3837349  3837371  3837377  3837401  3837403  3837437  3837439
3837451  3837467  3837469  3837497  3837499  3837511  3837553  3837557  3837569  3837577
3837629  3837643  3837653  3837661  3837689  3837703  3837721  3837727  3837737  3837739
3837749  3837787  3837851  3837853  3837857  3837859  3837863  3837871  3837877  3837901
3837917  3837923  3837949  3837979  3837989  3837991  3837997  3838001  3838013  3838027
3838097  3838099  3838103  3838111  3838117  3838123  3838129  3838139  3838157  3838183
3838187  3838201  3838213  3838231  3838253  3838259  3838283  3838333  3838381  3838391
3838397  3838409  3838423  3838433  3838441  3838477  3838507  3838519  3838529  3838561
3838591  3838609  3838613  3838619  3838621  3838657  3838661  3838711  3838729  3838771
3838777  3838801  3838811  3838831  3838841  3838853  3838859  3838867  3838883  3838897
3838903  3838921  3838937  3838973  3838979  3838981  3838991  3838993  3839023
3839027  3839029  3839039  3839047  3839051  3839113  3839131  3839153  3839177  3839201
3839203  3839221  3839233  3839237  3839239  3839261  3839293  3839299  3839309  3839317
3839327  3839347  3839351  3839359  3839369  3839417  3839419  3839449  3839471  3839503
3839509  3839519  3839533  3839573  3839579  3839587  3839593  3839611  3839621  3839623
3839639  3839651  3839677  3839681  3839683  3839701  3839707  3839711  3839713  3839747
3839777  3839783  3839809  3839813  3839833  3839839  3839851  3839911  3839923  3839929
3839951  3839959  3839987  3839999  3840007  3840017  3840037  3840043  3840059
3840061  3840077  3840091  3840107  3840127  3840139  3840157  3840163  3840169  3840173
3840191  3840203  3840211  3840227  3840253  3840257  3840259  3840271  3840289  3840301
3840307  3840313  3840349  3840359  3840391  3840401  3840409  3840449  3840469
3840479  3840481  3840503  3840523  3840533  3840541  3840547  3840601  3840647  3840649
3840667  3840671  3840703  3840713  3840719  3840721  3840737  3840761  3840787
3840791  3840821  3840829  3840853  3840911  3840913  3840923  3840953  3840961  3840971
3841009  3841027  3841039  3841049  3841063  3841073  3841087  3841091  3841111  3841121
3841127  3841129  3841139  3841141  3841153  3841181  3841199  3841219  3841223  3841237
3841247  3841259  3841261  3841267  3841283  3841291  3841301  3841307  3841309  3841339
3841351  3841361  3841367  3841373  3841381  3841393  3841399  3841403  3841429  3841433
3841457  3841469  3841499  3841517  3841531  3841559  3841561  3841567  3841573  3841603
3841619  3841627  3841631  3841657  3841679  3841681  3841693  3841709  3841729  3841751
3841753  3841757  3841763  3841777  3841787  3841807  3841829  3841843  3841867  3841883
3841889  3841907  3841909  3841913  3841919  3841927  3841961  3841973  3841991  3841993
3841999  3842011  3842029  3842077  3842089  3842101  3842143  3842147  3842149  3842171
3842183  3842197  3842213  3842227  3842231  3842269  3842281  3842287  3842299  3842303
3842317  3842327  3842353  3842369  3842381  3842401  3842411  3842431  3842483  3842507
3842519  3842539  3842549  3842551  3842557  3842569  3842599  3842603  3842627  3842669
3842677  3842687  3842689  3842711  3842717  3842737  3842749  3842759  3842777  3842779
3842801  3842803  3842809  3842831  3842843  3842851  3842873  3842887  3842899  3842903
3842929  3842941  3842947  3842957  3842963  3842981  3842989  3842999  3843023  3843029
3843031  3843041  3843067  3843097  3843107  3843121  3843127  3843131  3843137  3843179
3843181  3843197  3843199  3843221  3843223  3843247  3843251  3843253  3843311  3843313
3843317  3843347  3843361  3843379  3843407  3843419  3843451  3843467  3843533  3843551
3843557  3843571  3843581  3843611  3843617  3843629  3843661  3843677  3843701  3843713
3843731  3843733  3843739  3843743  3843773  3843781  3843823  3843841  3843859  3843881
3843883  3843919  3843923  3843937  3843971  3843943  3843979
3844021  3844067  3844069  3844079  3844097  3844109  3844111  3844117  3844121  3844133
3844187  3844199  3844229  3844241  3844273  3844277  3844301  3844303  3844307  3844313
3844333  3844339  3844363  3844391  3844409  3844433  3844439  3844469  3844537  3844541
3844549  3844571  3844583  3844591  3844613  3844619  3844627  3844637  3844649  3844663
3844667  3844697  3844717  3844747  3844751  3844777  3844801  3844807  3844823  3844829
3844843  3844847  3844861  3844877  3844901  3844909  3844921  3844927  3844943  3844949
3844957  3844963  3844987  3844999  3845027  3845029  3845033  3845041  3845057  3845113
3845119  3845123  3845143  3845159  3845173  3845183  3845221  3845251  3845263  3845273
3845279  3845287  3845291  3845293  3845297  3845311  3845321  3845327  3845329  3845341
```

```
3845351  3845357  3845363  3845381  3845389  3845407  3845441  3845449  3845459  3845461
3845477  3845489  3845497  3845537  3845539  3845549  3845557  3845563  3845579  3845593
3845651  3845663  3845693  3845701  3845717  3845741  3845747  3845753  3845837  3845861
3845873  3845887  3845903  3845909  3845921  3845929  3845939  3845977  3845981  3845983
3845987  3845993  3846013  3846019  3846023  3846103  3846109  3846127  3846133  3846149
3846163  3846191  3846197  3846203  3846209  3846217  3846223  3846229  3846239  3846247
3846257  3846259  3846277  3846281  3846287  3846289  3846331  3846347  3846371  3846373
3846389  3846397  3846413  3846421  3846439  3846461  3846463  3846467  3846481  3846487
3846499  3846509  3846523  3846529  3846541  3846571  3846583  3846613  3846617  3846629
3846643  3846649  3846653  3846659  3846673  3846691  3846701  3846707  3846751  3846761
3846767  3846769  3846833  3846841  3846863  3846877  3846917  3846929  3846943  3846961
3846991  3847013  3847021  3847037  3847061  3847079  3847093  3847127  3847147  3847157
3847159  3847201  3847237  3847241  3847243  3847271  3847273  3847303  3847309  3847351
3847357  3847397  3847409  3847421  3847433  3847439  3847451  3847469  3847471  3847477
3847489  3847499  3847549  3847553  3847577  3847583  3847589  3847603  3847619  3847621
3847637  3847639  3847651  3847663  3847673  3847687  3847711  3847717  3847783  3847799
3847817  3847829  3847849  3847859  3847867  3847871  3847873  3847897  3847927  3847931
3847939  3848017  3848021  3848029  3848057  3848059  3848083  3848099  3848101  3848161
3848167  3848177  3848191  3848197  3848209  3848231  3848233  3848237  3848249  3848261
3848263  3848269  3848287  3848293  3848303  3848347  3848357  3848359  3848381  3848417
3848419  3848437  3848447  3848473  3848491  3848497  3848513  3848527  3848531  3848539
3848563  3848569  3848573  3848591  3848597  3848599  3848609  3848623  3848639  3848651
3848653  3848657  3848671  3848687  3848699  3848707  3848717  3848753  3848791  3848809
3848813  3848821  3848827  3848833  3848837  3848861  3848869  3848881  3848891  3848903
3848921  3848939  3848941  3848947  3848951  3848969  3849017  3849023  3849029  3849031
3849061  3849091  3849107  3849113  3849127  3849133  3849137  3849143  3849149  3849151
3849187  3849193  3849233  3849269  3849281  3849299  3849319  3849341  3849359  3849379
3849383  3849389  3849397  3849401  3849409  3849421  3849437  3849467  3849479  3849491
3849499  3849511  3849523  3849529  3849541  3849569  3849581  3849583  3849617  3849653
3849679  3849683  3849707  3849737  3849743  3849757  3849767  3849787  3849793  3849821
3849823  3849827  3849829  3849841  3849847  3849863  3849869  3849929  3849943  3849949
3849977  3849997  3850003  3850009  3850013  3850043  3850061  3850073  3850081  3850129
3850151  3850153  3850159  3850199  3850219  3850237  3850241  3850247  3850267  3850271
3850277  3850303  3850339  3850373  3850387  3850391  3850393  3850403  3850421  3850459
3850463  3850477  3850481  3850489  3850507  3850547  3850571  3850589  3850621  3850633
3850657  3850661  3850699  3850703  3850723  3850811  3850813  3850829  3850831  3850837
3850841  3850883  3850909  3850921  3850937  3850949  3850963  3850967  3850981  3851009
3851011  3851017  3851041  3851047  3851059  3851063  3851077  3851083  3851087  3851101
3851147  3851149  3851173  3851179  3851213  3851279  3851291  3851303  3851317  3851359
3851363  3851369  3851371  3851377  3851387  3851389  3851399  3851413  3851423  3851429
3851431  3851443  3851459  3851587  3851593  3851597  3851599  3851611  3851641  3851651
3851677  3851689  3851713  3851747  3851759  3851761  3851767  3851779  3851789  3851797
3851801  3851807  3851819  3851839  3851857  3851863  3851873  3851899  3851909  3851923
3851977  3851989  3851993  3852001  3852011  3852019  3852049  3852059  3852067  3852077
3852083  3852103  3852127  3852131  3852133  3852139  3852143  3852151  3852209  3852221
3852253  3852257  3852263  3852271  3852301  3852313  3852323  3852337  3852341  3852347
3852361  3852367  3852379  3852391  3852419  3852427  3852451  3852487  3852493  3852503
3852539  3852547  3852553  3852559  3852581  3852601  3852631  3852643  3852677  3852683
3852689  3852691  3852697  3852703  3852713  3852733  3852767  3852781  3852787  3852809
3852881  3852889  3852907  3852913  3852917  3852923  3852949  3852973  3852997  3853007
3853009  3853037  3853039  3853049  3853081  3853093  3853097  3853111  3853141  3853151
3853163  3853183  3853193  3853211  3853247  3853249  3853261  3853279  3853301  3853313
3853321  3853379  3853403  3853411  3853417  3853427  3853429  3853469  3853501  3853511
3853529  3853537  3853547  3853559  3853567  3853583  3853589  3853609  3853613  3853621
3853643  3853663  3853669  3853687  3853693  3853697  3853709  3853711  3853727  3853741
3853753  3853757  3853763  3853793  3853813  3853847  3853857  3853873  3853909  3853933
3853937  3853943  3853991  3854003  3854023  3854027  3854029  3854063  3854077  3854083
3854089  3854099  3854111  3854113  3854117  3854119  3854143  3854153  3854159  3854167
3854171  3854197  3854203  3854231  3854237  3854243  3854251  3854273  3854281  3854297
3854311  3854341  3854387  3854429  3854449  3854453  3854467  3854471  3854483  3854497
3854537  3854551  3854573  3854579  3854581  3854621  3854629  3854671  3854677  3854681
3854693  3854717  3854723  3854729  3854737  3854749  3854761  3854783  3854797  3854827
3854843  3854849  3854899  3854923  3854927  3854933  3854947  3854957  3854969  3854989
3855013  3855023  3855029  3855041  3855083  3855091  3855127  3855133  3855143  3855149
3855151  3855161  3855169  3855179  3855197  3855211  3855221  3855223  3855239  3855287
3855323  3855331  3855359  3855361  3855367  3855409  3855419  3855431  3855469  3855479
3855493  3855497  3855503  3855539  3855541  3855547  3855557  3855571  3855581  3855623
3855647  3855667  3855703  3855757  3855769  3855779  3855781  3855793  3855799  3855829
3855851  3855857  3855913  3855919  3855937  3855949  3855953  3855961  3855967  3855977
3855983  3855989  3855989  3856001  3856007  3856033  3856037  3856067  3856109  3856123
3856129  3856133  3856141  3856147  3856187  3856199  3856213  3856231  3856243  3856253
3856261  3856267  3856273  3856289  3856357  3856361  3856367  3856379  3856381  3856393
3856403  3856409  3856451  3856469  3856477  3856499  3856511  3856513  3856519  3856537
3856549  3856561  3856579  3856591  3856597  3856607  3856613  3856631  3856661  3856667
3856703  3856717  3856729  3856733  3856751  3856763  3856777  3856793  3856813  3856823
3856837  3856861  3856873  3856877  3856891  3856903  3856907  3856921  3856949  3856967
3856973  3856987  3856997  3856999  3857003  3857023  3857027  3857039  3857053  3857081
3857107  3857137  3857141  3857153  3857167  3857179  3857207  3857233  3857263  3857267
3857297  3857309  3857311  3857327  3857339  3857341  3857369  3857383  3857417  3857429
3857443  3857449  3857459  3857467  3857489  3857519  3857531  3857533  3857543  3857549
3857561  3857569  3857611  3857621  3857641  3857663  3857681  3857683  3857717  3857719
3857723  3857743  3857747  3857761  3857773  3857801  3857803  3857809  3857939  3857953
3857869  3857873  3857891  3857911  3857921  3857941  3857983  3857989  3857993  3858011
3858017  3858037  3858053  3858079  3858091  3858103  3858143  3858157  3858163  3858191
3858193  3858199  3858233  3858251  3858259  3858287  3858289  3858299  3858307  3858317
3858367  3858401  3858403  3858427  3858431  3858461  3858487  3858493  3858497  3858499
3858509  3858511  3858523  3858529  3858581  3858583  3858593  3858607  3858629  3858667
3858671  3858719  3858721  3858727  3858737  3858749  3858761  3858763  3858781  3858791
3858793  3858817  3858839  3858851  3858859  3858889  3858901  3858923  3858929  3858931
```

```
3858941  3858947  3858971  3858991  3858997  3859003  3859007  3859019  3859027  3859039
3859049  3859067  3859073  3859081  3859099  3859127  3859139  3859151  3859157  3859171
3859181  3859183  3859189  3859201  3859213  3859231  3859243  3859253  3859259  3859277
3859279  3859309  3859313  3859319  3859321  3859327  3859333  3859381  3859393  3859399
3859411  3859439  3859447  3859477  3859481  3859483  3859501  3859511  3859517  3859529
3859567  3859573  3859621  3859649  3859673  3859693  3859759  3859769  3859771  3859783
3859787  3859789  3859819  3859829  3859847  3859879  3859927  3859931  3859939  3859963
3859979  3859993  3860009  3860023  3860029  3860033  3860039  3860041  3860083  3860093
3860107  3860117  3860123  3860137  3860147  3860163  3860183  3860189  3860209  3860221  3860231
3860237  3860267  3860281  3860291  3860293  3860299  3860303  3860317  3860333  3860347
3860357  3860359  3860369  3860383  3860387  3860431  3860471  3860489  3860501  3860537
3860557  3860561  3860587  3860611  3860639  3860641  3860657  3860663  3860687  3860723
3860729  3860737  3860777  3860807  3860821  3860827  3860863  3860867  3860869  3860893
3860903  3860917  3860939  3860947  3860953  3860959  3860993  3861007  3861017  3861041
3861059  3861073  3861083  3861113  3861119  3861167  3861173  3861203  3861211  3861223
3861233  3861241  3861251  3861259  3861269  3861289  3861293  3861317  3861337  3861343
3861349  3861383  3861413  3861419  3861433  3861439  3861441  3861461  3861463  3861521
3861547  3861551  3861563  3861581  3861587  3861589  3861593  3861607  3861659  3861709
3861713  3861719  3861721  3861743  3861751  3861811  3861817  3861821  3861841  3861857
3861863  3861877  3861881  3861889  3861899  3861911  3861929  3861961  3861967  3861983
3861989  3862003  3862007  3862013  3862039  3862049  3862051  3862063  3862087  3862099
3862109  3862121  3862141  3862147  3862151  3862153  3862169  3862181  3862189  3862193
3862219  3862237  3862253  3862267  3862277  3862279  3862289  3862291  3862343  3862361
3862363  3862373  3862403  3862409  3862421  3862427  3862433  3862447  3862477  3862489
3862493  3862531  3862549  3862559  3862577  3862589  3862591  3862609  3862673  3862699
3862709  3862711  3862717  3862739  3862741  3862769  3862783  3862787  3862811  3862841
3862847  3862849  3862853  3862861  3862891  3862921  3862933  3862939  3862987  3862993
3862997  3863009  3863017  3863107  3863173  3863183  3863201  3863203  3863239  3863243
3863257  3863269  3863273  3863291  3863297  3863303  3863309  3863311  3863317  3863339
3863347  3863393  3863399  3863407  3863411  3863417  3863423  3863443  3863473  3863477
3863501  3863513  3863521  3863533  3863569  3863581  3863591  3863603  3863611
3863677  3863681  3863683  3863687  3863737  3863759  3863771  3863773  3863789  3863803
3863831  3863833  3863837  3863843  3863857  3863861  3863863  3863887  3863903  3863911
3863971  3863987  3864019  3864037  3864059  3864089  3864097  3864101  3864131  3864137
3864139  3864187  3864191  3864193  3864197  3864233  3864247  3864269  3864307  3864313
3864319  3864331  3864347  3864349  3864403  3864407  3864409  3864433  3864449  3864451
3864461  3864463  3864473  3864479  3864499  3864521  3864541  3864551  3864557  3864583
3864587  3864599  3864607  3864629  3864643  3864671  3864673  3864683  3864691  3864697
3864703  3864709  3864719  3864767  3864787  3864793  3864803  3864813  3864811  3864821
3864827  3864829  3864841  3864871  3864901  3864929  3864941  3864953  3864977  3864979
3865007  3865009  3865013  3865019  3865063  3865079  3865093  3865117  3865123  3865133
3865153  3865157  3865187  3865229  3865231  3865243  3865247  3865283  3865289  3865321
3865331  3865333  3865349  3865361  3865363  3865429  3865447  3865457  3865469  3865481
3865513  3865517  3865523  3865529  3865553  3865567  3865577  3865591  3865601  3865637
3865663  3865691  3865733  3865747  3865769  3865777  3865801  3865819  3865847  3865853
3865859  3865867  3865879  3865889  3865907  3865911  3865933  3865943  3865951  3865957
3865963  3865969  3865991  3865993  3866011  3866033  3866039  3866081  3866099  3866117
3866141  3866143  3866147  3866171  3866183  3866201  3866237  3866243  3866263  3866281
3866287  3866333  3866393  3866399  3866419  3866437  3866441  3866453  3866479  3866543
3866581  3866609  3866617  3866623  3866627  3866647  3866651  3866713  3866717  3866719
3866741  3866749  3866767  3866797  3866811  3866809  3866839  3866857  3866867  3866869
3866879  3866881  3866903  3866911  3866917  3866923  3866927  3866957  3866963  3866969
3866977  3866983  3867001  3867011  3867047  3867077  3867091  3867107  3867131  3867133
3867137  3867163  3867169  3867181  3867191  3867209  3867221  3867223  3867229  3867233
3867239  3867257  3867263  3867271  3867323  3867337  3867349  3867359  3867361  3867371
3867393  3867401  3867421  3867433  3867443  3867481  3867491  3867503  3867533  3867541
3867557  3867587  3867599  3867601  3867623  3867629  3867649  3867679  3867683  3867691
3867707  3867713  3867733  3867739  3867757  3867763  3867767  3867789  3867779  3867797
3867803  3867847  3867859  3867881  3867889  3867911  3867923  3867931  3867937  3867947
3867961  3868003  3868013  3868019  3868021  3868031  3868043  3868057  3868079  3868093
3868097  3868121  3868133  3868141  3868159  3868169  3868177  3868187  3868201  3868213
3868219  3868243  3868247  3868253  3868259  3868261  3868279  3868283  3868297  3868321
3868331  3868357  3868399  3868427  3868441  3868463  3868477  3868481  3868483  3868493
3868517  3868541  3868549  3868567  3868591  3868619  3868649  3868679  3868699  3868717
3868721  3868729  3868751  3868763  3868789  3868793  3868811  3868817  3868847  3868849
3868897  3868901  3868933  3868937  3868957  3868961  3868973  3868981  3868987  3868999
3869009  3869023  3869029  3869051  3869057  3869069  3869101  3869111  3869113  3869123
3869153  3869167  3869183  3869191  3869197  3869213  3869231  3869263  3869297  3869311
3869321  3869329  3869351  3869399  3869417  3869461  3869473  3869501  3869561  3869573
3869581  3869603  3869611  3869623  3869627  3869629  3869639  3869641  3869647  3869653
3869683  3869687  3869729  3869741  3869743  3869753  3869759  3869791  3869797  3869807
3869849  3869857  3869861  3869881  3869917  3869959  3869989  3869993  3870001  3870011
3870037  3870047  3870059  3870073  3870077  3870149  3870157  3870173  3870179  3870193
3870197  3870199  3870211  3870227  3870239  3870247  3870259  3870283  3870299  3870337
3870401  3870413  3870437  3870439  3870457  3870467  3870469  3870479  3870499  3870527
3870551  3870557  3870563  3870599  3870613  3870617  3870619  3870631  3870649  3870653
3870667  3870689  3870697  3870703  3870709  3870719  3870721  3870751  3870767  3870773
3870793  3870803  3870821  3870827  3870847  3870863  3870869  3870899  3870913  3870929
3870941  3870947  3870953  3870959  3870983  3871009  3871013  3871039  3871073  3871081
3871103  3871111  3871129  3871139  3871151  3871159  3871171  3871177  3871201  3871211
3871271  3871303  3871319  3871321  3871331  3871339  3871363  3871381  3871391  3871397
3871423  3871433  3871447  3871481  3871499  3871501  3871523  3871537  3871547  3871579
3871583  3871601  3871603  3871607  3871619  3871657  3871661  3871663  3871669  3871691
3871759  3871781  3871783  3871787  3871811  3871817  3871823  3871831  3871841  3871871
3871883  3871909  3871919  3871921  3871961  3871969  3872017  3872023  3872041  3872047
3872059  3872101  3872129  3872153  3872201  3872203  3872207  3872221  3872237  3872249
3872273  3872287  3872291  3872293  3872299  3872317  3872329  3872359  3872381  3872387
3872389  3872417  3872423  3872459  3872503  3872507  3872521  3872527  3872543  3872567
3872587  3872591  3872647  3872669  3872677  3872681  3872731  3872761  3872767  3872773
```

```
3872777  3872797  3872807  3872833  3872839  3872851  3872873  3872887  3872893  3872899
3872917  3872929  3872933  3872959  3872963  3872969  3872971  3872977  3873007  3873011
3873041  3873061  3873071  3873091  3873101  3873151  3873157  3873179  3873193  3873209
3873239  3873257  3873281  3873299  3873313  3873323  3873329  3873343  3873349  3873367
3873371  3873379  3873383  3873391  3873413  3873427  3873431  3873437  3873461  3873479
3873487  3873491  3873497  3873509  3873517  3873577  3873629  3873631  3873647  3873659
3873677  3873679  3873691  3873697  3873707  3873713  3873719  3873731  3873743  3873761
3873769  3873781  3873799  3873809  3873811  3873817  3873829  3873833  3873839  3873847
3873871  3873883  3873901  3873911  3873931  3873941  3873983  3873997  3874009  3874027
3874067  3874093  3874099  3874103  3874109  3874111  3874133  3874151  3874153  3874193
3874201  3874219  3874229  3874231  3874237  3874243  3874279  3874319  3874333  3874337
3874361  3874369  3874379  3874391  3874393  3874417  3874433  3874439  3874441  3874469
3874501  3874513  3874531  3874547  3874561  3874571  3874573  3874579  3874583  3874639
3874669  3874679  3874693  3874697  3874711  3874723  3874733  3874747  3874753  3874763
3874799  3874807  3874823  3874831  3874837  3874853  3874867  3874877  3874889  3874891
3874919  3874933  3874939  3874957  3874979  3874987  3875041  3875051  3875057  3875087
3875089  3875101  3875141  3875143  3875159  3875161  3875173  3875177  3875239  3875243
3875273  3875281  3875309  3875317  3875321  3875323  3875329  3875359  3875363  3875369
3875381  3875383  3875387  3875401  3875407  3875429  3875447  3875453  3875467  3875537
3875539  3875549  3875551  3875567  3875591  3875603  3875617  3875623  3875629  3875653
3875671  3875681  3875693  3875699  3875741  3875743  3875747  3875797  3875803  3875827
3875869  3875873  3875909  3875917  3875929  3875933  3875939  3875947  3875951  3875957
3875987  3876007  3876011  3876031  3876073  3876079  3876091  3876101  3876107  3876109
3876143  3876161  3876179  3876203  3876253  3876269  3876287  3876301  3876307  3876311
3876317  3876319  3876329  3876347  3876371  3876403  3876413  3876449  3876469  3876491
3876497  3876539  3876557  3876569  3876577  3876583  3876599  3876617  3876619  3876641
3876659  3876661  3876679  3876707  3876709  3876739  3876773  3876781  3876787  3876793
3876827  3876869  3876881  3876907  3876913  3876937  3876941  3876947  3876959  3876973
3876979  3876991  3876997  3877033  3877043  3877057  3877061  3877063  3877073  3877079
3877123  3877151  3877189  3877219  3877243  3877259  3877283  3877331  3877337  3877339
3877361  3877373  3877397  3877403  3877417  3877441  3877451  3877477  3877481  3877483
3877487  3877507  3877543  3877571  3877589  3877597  3877603  3877609  3877613  3877631
3877633  3877663  3877667  3877669  3877673  3877681  3877703  3877733  3877763  3877771
3877781  3877789  3877799  3877801  3877813  3877817  3877837  3877849  3877871  3877877
3877879  3877889  3877891  3877897  3877901  3877927  3877943  3877987  3877999  3878003
3878051  3878093  3878101  3878107  3878113  3878137  3878143  3878177  3878183  3878207
3878209  3878219  3878221  3878263  3878267  3878269  3878279  3878291  3878297  3878323
3878359  3878389  3878401  3878423  3878447  3878449  3878491  3878519  3878521  3878543
3878549  3878561  3878597  3878617  3878621  3878629  3878647  3878653  3878657  3878681
3878687  3878701  3878713  3878741  3878753  3878759  3878761  3878767  3878773  3878783
3878843  3878887  3878889  3878893  3878899  3878921  3878923  3878947  3878991  3878993
3879023  3879047  3879049  3879067  3879101  3879119  3879121  3879143  3879149  3879151
3879163  3879167  3879181  3879193  3879199  3879221  3879257  3879259  3879263  3879269
3879277  3879283  3879307  3879311  3879319  3879329  3879347  3879353  3879361  3879397
3879437  3879509  3879517  3879527  3879529  3879541  3879569  3879581  3879593  3879607
3879641  3879671  3879679  3879691  3879697  3879719  3879721  3879727  3879737  3879739
3879749  3879751  3879773  3879793  3879797  3879817  3879829  3879839  3879851  3879853
3879913  3879917  3879919  3879923  3879943  3879959  3879979  3879983  3879989  3880003
3880007  3880033  3880043  3880049  3880057  3880061  3880067  3880069  3880091  3880099
3880127  3880139  3880147  3880157  3880159  3880181  3880189  3880193  3880207  3880223
3880241  3880249  3880259  3880337  3880343  3880361  3880381  3880411  3880421  3880441
3880447  3880451  3880453  3880507  3880517  3880543  3880553  3880561  3880567  3880589
3880601  3880603  3880627  3880631  3880633  3880661  3880663  3880729  3880733  3880757
3880763  3880771  3880781  3880801  3880817  3880847  3880853  3880861  3880871  3880889
3880897  3880901  3880907  3880927  3880949  3880999  3881021  3881027  3881029  3881057
3881063  3881071  3881071  3881077  3881093  3881113  3881131  3881147  3881161  3881173
3881177  3881203  3881209  3881221  3881239  3881249  3881291  3881299  3881303  3881323
3881333  3881341  3881351  3881359  3881363  3881387  3881393  3881401  3881413  3881419
3881431  3881441  3881443  3881461  3881467  3881509  3881543  3881573  3881587  3881597
3881609  3881611  3881659  3881671  3881699  3881711  3881723  3881741  3881743  3881803
3881807  3881837  3881863  3881867  3881873  3881883  3881887  3881951  3881953  3881959
3881987  3881989  3882007  3882019  3882029  3882031  3882071  3882079  3882089  3882107
3882121  3882133  3882149  3882157  3882163  3882191  3882227  3882233  3882311  3882313
3882343  3882353  3882367  3882383  3882397  3882401  3882407  3882421  3882451  3882481
3882523  3882539  3882547  3882553  3882559  3882563  3882569  3882587  3882601  3882643
3882661  3882669  3882679  3882691  3882713  3882717  3882721  3882731  3882737  3882763
3882773  3882787  3882799  3882841  3882871  3882877  3882881  3882887  3882889  3882899
3882911  3882913  3882937  3882941  3882947  3882959  3883001  3883027  3883031  3883037
3883051  3883063  3883073  3883079  3883109  3883111  3883127  3883133  3883169  3883171
3883177  3883183  3883189  3883207  3883211  3883213  3883219  3883223  3883247  3883249
3883273  3883283  3883291  3883301  3883307  3883309  3883333  3883379  3883393  3883417
3883423  3883427  3883433  3883441  3883489  3883493  3883499  3883501  3883519  3883541
3883547  3883549  3883559  3883571  3883591  3883597  3883601  3883637  3883639  3883669
3883679  3883699  3883703  3883727  3883811  3883823  3883829  3883843  3883903  3883921
3883933  3883937  3883951  3883963  3883967  3883969  3884011  3884047  3884051  3884063
3884071  3884081  3884093  3884099  3884117  3884123  3884131  3884141  3884159  3884161
3884183  3884203  3884213  3884239  3884261  3884267  3884291  3884311  3884333  3884389
3884399  3884407  3884411  3884429  3884431  3884473  3884497  3884533  3884547  3884591
3884609  3884659  3884689  3884693  3884707  3884717  3884729  3884731  3884747  3884767
3884807  3884819  3884831  3884833  3884843  3884849  3884899  3884917  3884929  3884947
3884989  3885001  3885017  3885019  3885031  3885041  3885047  3885071  3885073  3885103
3885107  3885109  3885121  3885127  3885149  3885181  3885187  3885221  3885223  3885241
3885247  3885251  3885281  3885293  3885319  3885331  3885337  3885347  3885361  3885373
3885379  3885403  3885421  3885433  3885461  3885487  3885499  3885521  3885533  3885569
3885577  3885599  3885619  3885641  3885647  3885653  3885667  3885687  3885691  3885697
3885719  3885727  3885733  3885737  3885743  3885751  3885767  3885779  3885787  3885803
3885821  3885841  3885859  3885941  3885961  3885967  3885983  3885989  3885991  3885997
3886027  3886031  3886037  3886049  3886061  3886063  3886079  3886093  3886109  3886117
3886121  3886151  3886159  3886171  3886187  3886193  3886199  3886229  3886231  3886237
```

```
3886273  3886283  3886291  3886303  3886307  3886321  3886339  3886343  3886357  3886361
3886391  3886397  3886403  3886417  3886423  3886429  3886433  3886453  3886457  3886459
3886481  3886537  3886559  3886573  3886577  3886601  3886637  3886643  3886651  3886661
3886679  3886699  3886709  3886717  3886723  3886733  3886741  3886769  3886777  3886787
3886789  3886801  3886819  3886823  3886837  3886843  3886867  3886867  3886889  3886919
3886937  3886951  3886991  3887003  3887011  3887017  3887021  3887047  3887053  3887057
3887083  3887111  3887129  3887167  3887171  3887173  3887197  3887227  3887239  3887281
3887291  3887293  3887297  3887311  3887357  3887383  3887393  3887399  3887449  3887453
3887461  3887467  3887473  3887489  3887491  3887503  3887519  3887531  3887549  3887551
3887557  3887561  3887563  3887567  3887573  3887581  3887623  3887641  3887657  3887659
3887671  3887683  3887707  3887731  3887749  3887753  3887771  3887777  3887783  3887789
3887831  3887839  3887843  3887861  3887867  3887881  3887893  3887899  3887903  3887911
3887959  3887963  3887971  3887993  3887999  3888007  3888013  3888023  3888029  3888047
3888067  3888083  3888091  3888107  3888149  3888151  3888163  3888193  3888253  3888271
3888281  3888337  3888341  3888347  3888383  3888389  3888397  3888413  3888421  3888431
3888463  3888503  3888509  3888517  3888527  3888539  3888551  3888553  3888571  3888593
3888607  3888611  3888629  3888653  3888683  3888713  3888719  3888721  3888761  3888763
3888823  3888847  3888851  3888887  3888889  3888893  3888917  3888923  3888931  3888967
3888999  3889007  3889009  3889013  3889027  3889031  3889037  3889063  3889079  3889157
3889159  3889163  3889169  3889183  3889187  3889189  3889199  3889201  3889217  3889241
3889253  3889261  3889279  3889289  3889313  3889331  3889337  3889349  3889351  3889373
3889387  3889397  3889399  3889411  3889423  3889427  3889441  3889453  3889489  3889493
3889519  3889537  3889591  3889607  3889621  3889631  3889649  3889657  3889667  3889679
3889727  3889729  3889733  3889759  3889763  3889777  3889801  3889807  3889817  3889843
3889859  3889867  3889891  3889901  3889913  3889933  3889937  3889939  3889969  3889993
3890011  3890021  3890027  3890053  3890057  3890063  3890071  3890083  3890111  3890113
3890119  3890129  3890141  3890171  3890179  3890189  3890191  3890219  3890239  3890261
3890267  3890309  3890311  3890317  3890323  3890329  3890333  3890347  3890351  3890353
3890357  3890377  3890387  3890417  3890423  3890443  3890431  3890503  3890507  3890521
3890527  3890543  3890561  3890563  3890581  3890591  3890609  3890633  3890639  3890651
3890699  3890693  3890701  3890713  3890737  3890741  3890743  3890753  3890759  3890771
3890819  3890833  3890849  3890851  3890863  3890879  3890927  3890951  3890963  3890969
3890981  3891037  3891049  3891053  3891061  3891077  3891103  3891131  3891137  3891157
3891161  3891197  3891203  3891229  3891241  3891247  3891259  3891263  3891287  3891323
3891331  3891343  3891353  3891359  3891379  3891383  3891389  3891403  3891431  3891449
3891451  3891467  3891469  3891493  3891527  3891541  3891551  3891571  3891593  3891659
3891673  3891677  3891683  3891689  3891707  3891721  3891733  3891743  3891749  3891757
3891763  3891773  3891779  3891781  3891803  3891821  3891841  3891847  3891851  3891857
3891863  3891869  3891871  3891883  3891893  3891907  3891913  3891917  3891971  3891977
3892001  3892027  3892039  3892051  3892069  3892087  3892103  3892111  3892123  3892151
3892153  3892181  3892183  3892193  3892199  3892219  3892247  3892249  3892261  3892271
3892279  3892309  3892331  3892333  3892367  3892379  3892387  3892393  3892411  3892457
3892459  3892463  3892477  3892481  3892519  3892571  3892573  3892601  3892607  3892619
3892621  3892627  3892631  3892649  3892657  3892691  3892741  3892751  3892753  3892789
3892799  3892817  3892829  3892831  3892841  3892849  3892877  3892897  3892907  3892913
3892921  3892939  3892943  3892951  3892961  3892969  3892979  3893023  3893027  3893053
3893059  3893063  3893069  3893089  3893093  3893101  3893107  3893111  3893137  3893159
3893167  3893171  3893173  3893179  3893191  3893207  3893209  3893213  3893243  3893249
3893257  3893269  3893273  3893287  3893291  3893299  3893317  3893353  3893359  3893363
3893369  3893381  3893387  3893419  3893431  3893471  3893479  3893489  3893497  3893531
3893543  3893557  3893563  3893567  3893579  3893597  3893609  3893633  3893657  3893671
3893683  3893707  3893719  3893741  3893749  3893753  3893759  3893819  3893849  3893861
3893863  3893881  3893903  3893909  3893909  3893927  3893933  3893937  3893959  3893971
3893977  3893983  3894001  3894013  3894019  3894029  3894041  3894043  3894047  3894049
3894053  3894083  3894101  3894103  3894113  3894119  3894131  3894133  3894151  3894157
3894167  3894169  3894193  3894197  3894203  3894211  3894217  3894223  3894227
3894229  3894239  3894269  3894307  3894329  3894347  3894349  3894353  3894391  3894409
3894419  3894431  3894433  3894469  3894481  3894511  3894523  3894529  3894557  3894571
3894587  3894589  3894593  3894619  3894637  3894673  3894689  3894691  3894697  3894703
3894707  3894733  3894763  3894833  3894857  3894859  3894881  3894883  3894893  3894899
3894923  3894949  3894973  3894977  3894991  3895037  3895039  3895043  3895049  3895051
3895079  3895097  3895117  3895127  3895139  3895153  3895169  3895183  3895231  3895289
3895291  3895337  3895343  3895351  3895379  3895387  3895391  3895403  3895421  3895427
3895433  3895453  3895459  3895481  3895511  3895531  3895543  3895561  3895571  3895583
3895597  3895603  3895667  3895673  3895679  3895681  3895691  3895709  3895721  3895729
3895733  3895747  3895777  3895781  3895789  3895799  3895813  3895847  3895867  3895883
3895891  3895909  3895921  3895949  3895963  3895967  3895981  3895999  3896003  3896017
3896023  3896029  3896041  3896059  3896089  3896099  3896129
3896141  3896161  3896171  3896203  3896219  3896231  3896239  3896257  3896287  3896303
3896317  3896323  3896329  3896339  3896341  3896351  3896357  3896363  3896369  3896371
3896381  3896413  3896443  3896447  3896449  3896461  3896467  3896489  3896491  3896513
3896561  3896569  3896573  3896597  3896609  3896657  3896677  3896699  3896707  3896743
3896777  3896801  3896807  3896819  3896831  3896861  3896863  3896903  3896923  3896929
3896941  3896947  3896969  3896987  3896993  3896999  3897001  3897013  3897059  3897073
3897079  3897083  3897121  3897139  3897151  3897161  3897181  3897191  3897203  3897209
3897217  3897241  3897259  3897263  3897269  3897331  3897347  3897353  3897359  3897389
3897401  3897407  3897409  3897449  3897463  3897497  3897499  3897521  3897559  3897581
3897587  3897611  3897631  3897637  3897653  3897659  3897671  3897683  3897703  3897721
3897727  3897739  3897749  3897797  3897799  3897823  3897827  3897841  3897853  3897871
3897877  3897889  3897899  3897937  3897941  3897967  3897973  3898001  3898003  3898007
3898019  3898031  3898043  3898057  3898073  3898081  3898091  3898123  3898163  3898177
3898183  3898207  3898243  3898291  3898303  3898319  3898351  3898361  3898369  3898373
3898379  3898393  3898409  3898417  3898421  3898451  3898459  3898463  3898483  3898487
3898507  3898511  3898513  3898537  3898541  3898547  3898549  3898561  3898589  3898597
3898619  3898633  3898637  3898639  3898651  3898717  3898747  3898751  3898757  3898771
3898841  3898871  3898879  3898887  3898907  3898913  3898919  3898927  3898943  3898957
3898981  3898991  3899011  3899033  3899053  3899057  3899101  3899117  3899131  3899143
3899153  3899173  3899177  3899191  3899201  3899209  3899219  3899227  3899243  3899279
3899297  3899299  3899309  3899321  3899327  3899339  3899347  3899353  3899381  3899383
```

```
3899407  3899411  3899429  3899453  3899471  3899507  3899513  3899527  3899549  3899569
3899573  3899603  3899611  3899639  3899653  3899657  3899699  3899737  3899747  3899761
3899767  3899771  3899773  3899801  3899809  3899813  3899827  3899839  3899843  3899867
3899881  3899887  3899927  3899941  3899947  3899957  3899963  3899977  3899981  3899983
3899989  3900067  3900097  3900121  3900131  3900167  3900199  3900223  3900227  3900233
3900269  3900277  3900287  3900307  3900311  3900329  3900331  3900341  3900343  3900349
3900359  3900367  3900397  3900433  3900439  3900469  3900473  3900499  3900509  3900517
3900563  3900569  3900581  3900583  3900623  3900649  3900679  3900691  3900697  3900707
3900733  3900737  3900749  3900779  3900817  3900829  3900839  3900847  3900857  3900881
3900887  3900893  3900907  3900929  3900931  3900937  3900943  3900989  3901013  3901019
3901031  3901033  3901043  3901069  3901087  3901103  3901111  3901127  3901147  3901153
3901187  3901199  3901201  3901217  3901223  3901229  3901259  3901301  3901333  3901351
3901363  3901367  3901369  3901397  3901411  3901427  3901439  3901453  3901463  3901481
3901487  3901511  3901523  3901531  3901543  3901553  3901561  3901571  3901589  3901609
3901649  3901657  3901661  3901673  3901679  3901693  3901717  3901727  3901741  3901757
3901787  3901801  3901819  3901829  3901837  3901841  3901853  3901867  3901871  3901901
3901907  3901943  3901951  3901957  3901967  3901981  3901991  3902009  3902033  3902039
3902053  3902071  3902137  3902141  3902149  3902167  3902209  3902219  3902237  3902243
3902263  3902291  3902317  3902347  3902351  3902369  3902377  3902399  3902417  3902419
3902441  3902453  3902461  3902471  3902473  3902477  3902489  3902491  3902531  3902557
3902573  3902579  3902609  3902641  3902651  3902677  3902687  3902713  3902747  3902779
3902783  3902803  3902813  3902819  3902827  3902839  3902851  3902861  3902879  3902881
3902887  3902929  3903001  3903007  3903017  3903071  3903073  3903101  3903127  3903131
3903143  3903187  3903191  3903203  3903223  3903233  3903247  3903269  3903271  3903281
3903293  3903299  3903331  3903337  3903373  3903401  3903413  3903433  3903437  3903443
3903457  3903461  3903479  3903481  3903511  3903533  3903539  3903547  3903563  3903577
3903589  3903593  3903619  3903623  3903631  3903637  3903643  3903649  3903667  3903671
3903673  3903689  3903703  3903749  3903769  3903787  3903839  3903857  3903871  3903877
3903883  3903899  3903901  3903917  3903929  3903937  3903947  3903953  3903971  3904001
3904003  3904031  3904039  3904051  3904057  3904081  3904111  3904123  3904127  3904141
3904189  3904217  3904249  3904261  3904283  3904289  3904309  3904321  3904333  3904349
3904379  3904387  3904409  3904447  3904469  3904477  3904487  3904493  3904501  3904517
3904547  3904591  3904597  3904603  3904631  3904639  3904643  3904651  3904657  3904673
3904699  3904727  3904741  3904753  3904757  3904763  3904801  3904829  3904877  3904887
3904903  3904907  3904909  3904913  3904919  3904921  3904931  3904933  3904973  3904981
3904997  3905003  3905023  3905059  3905107  3905113  3905119  3905149  3905173  3905177
3905191  3905197  3905201  3905219  3905221  3905263  3905273  3905299  3905323  3905327
3905329  3905351  3905357  3905383  3905413  3905417  3905441  3905443  3905449  3905467
3905471  3905477  3905491  3905501  3905513  3905527  3905533  3905543  3905599  3905641
3905651  3905663  3905669  3905677  3905687  3905711  3905717  3905753  3905777  3905789
3905809  3905833  3905857  3905859  3905861  3905879  3905911  3905933  3905963  3905987
3905999  3906017  3906043  3906059  3906061  3906101  3906103  3906109  3906137  3906151
3906169  3906173  3906187  3906247  3906263  3906269  3906283  3906293  3906307  3906319
3906323  3906361  3906367  3906373  3906401  3906407  3906431  3906433  3906437  3906461
3906473  3906479  3906493  3906541  3906547  3906557  3906559  3906563  3906599  3906601
3906607  3906611  3906613  3906641  3906653  3906659  3906667  3906691  3906701  3906701
3906709  3906731  3906733  3906751  3906769  3906779  3906797  3906809  3906811  3906827
3906839  3906853  3906857  3906883  3906907  3906911  3906919  3906949  3906953  3906967
3907003  3907009  3907019  3907021  3907031  3907037  3907049  3907051  3907061  3907067
3907069  3907081  3907091  3907097  3907121  3907133  3907153  3907159  3907187  3907193
3907207  3907219  3907231  3907249  3907283  3907291  3907303  3907313  3907313  3907327
3907339  3907349  3907361  3907363  3907403  3907417  3907441  3907481  3907487  3907499
3907523  3907529  3907537  3907571  3907583  3907601  3907613  3907619  3907621  3907649
3907661  3907667  3907693  3907699  3907727  3907733  3907777  3907781  3907789  3907793
3907801  3907811  3907817  3907831  3907847  3907873  3907913  3907919  3907927  3907933
3907949  3907951  3907957  3907963  3907979  3907987  3907991  3908017  3908027  3908033
3908059  3908071  3908081  3908083  3908089  3908119  3908131  3908153  3908159  3908173
3908207  3908213  3908237  3908239  3908287  3908291  3908309  3908329  3908339  3908363
3908369  3908371  3908381  3908393  3908423  3908441  3908467  3908477  3908491  3908497
3908501  3908503  3908537  3908539  3908543  3908549  3908561  3908563  3908581  3908587
3908609  3908617  3908629  3908659  3908687  3908693  3908701  3908711  3908731  3908741
3908753  3908761  3908767  3908771  3908831  3908837  3908857  3908867  3908869  3908887
3908893  3908911  3908921  3909019  3909023  3909043  3909049  3909083  3909091  3909107
3909127  3909179  3909209  3909211  3909221  3909233  3909247  3909251  3909253  3909263
3909271  3909277  3909289  3909293  3909329  3909341  3909343  3909359  3909361  3909397
3909401  3909427  3909463  3909467  3909469  3909481  3909491  3909509  3909523  3909527
3909533  3909547  3909559  3909589  3909593  3909613  3909617  3909641  3909667  3909671
3909691  3909707  3909709  3909733  3909739  3909749  3909761  3909767  3909769  3909797
3909799  3909803  3909817  3909853  3909889  3909907  3909911  3909923  3909943  3909959
3909967  3910003  3910007  3910003  3910009  3910019  3910031  3910043  3910057  3910063
3910079  3910087  3910091  3910097  3910111  3910121  3910133  3910141  3910147  3910169
3910171  3910177  3910201  3910229  3910237  3910241  3910243  3910261  3910267  3910297
3910301  3910337  3910339  3910349  3910351  3910363  3910367  3910381  3910397  3910411
3910427  3910429  3910441  3910451  3910469  3910477  3910507  3910513  3910519  3910531
3910553  3910559  3910573  3910597  3910631  3910651  3910661  3910691  3910693  3910717
3910727  3910733  3910747  3910763  3910787  3910843  3910849  3910861  3910909  3910913
3910919  3910967  3910981  3910993  3910997  3910999  3911009  3911021  3911057  3911059
3911069  3911077  3911087  3911099  3911111  3911123  3911129  3911153  3911179  3911191
3911203  3911221  3911227  3911249  3911251  3911261  3911263  3911273  3911279  3911291
3911339  3911351  3911417  3911423  3911429  3911431  3911459  3911497  3911507  3911519
3911521  3911539  3911543  3911563  3911573  3911617  3911623  3911627  3911647  3911653
3911681  3911689  3911693  3911711  3911741  3911749  3911767  3911773  3911779  3911783
3911807  3911821  3911849  3911861  3911879  3911881  3911911  3911923  3911927  3911939
3911977  3912017  3912031  3912037  3912061  3912109  3912121  3912131  3912199  3912211
3912221  3912229  3912239  3912247  3912263  3912319  3912367  3912379  3912401
3912413  3912439  3912443  3912451  3912457  3912463  3912481  3912487  3912497  3912509
3912521  3912547  3912551  3912569  3912607  3912611  3912647  3912673  3912679  3912719
3912721  3912749  3912757  3912763  3912781  3912809  3912817  3912823  3912827  3912833
3912859  3912877  3912893  3912899  3912901  3912919  3912943  3912947  3912959  3912973
```

```
3912983  3913027  3913033  3913051  3913061  3913067  3913093  3913103  3913109  3913121
3913127  3913139  3913159  3913171  3913181  3913193  3913199  3913237  3913249  3913277
3913309  3913319  3913331  3913369  3913391  3913397  3913421  3913489  3913499  3913501
3913513  3913531  3913541  3913543  3913561  3913583  3913589  3913627  3913633  3913667
3913669  3913673  3913687  3913697  3913717  3913727  3913747  3913771  3913787  3913807
3913837  3913907  3913963  3913969  3913991  3913993  3914003  3914011  3914069  3914077
3914083  3914087  3914089  3914107  3914111  3914129  3914143  3914179  3914189  3914201
3914203  3914221  3914249  3914257  3914263  3914269  3914279  3914291  3914293  3914303
3914321  3914329  3914353  3914357  3914359  3914377  3914387  3914413  3914419  3914429
3914441  3914453  3914459  3914461  3914467  3914503  3914509  3914549  3914569  3914579
3914593  3914597  3914621  3914663  3914671  3914689  3914699  3914723  3914747  3914749
3914783  3914819  3914837  3914851  3914857  3914863  3914873  3914887  3914891  3914901
3914903  3914921  3914923  3914941  3914957  3914983  3914987  3915013  3915031  3915047
3915061  3915073  3915077  3915101  3915127  3915139  3915143  3915157  3915167  3915169
3915187  3915239  3915251  3915257  3915259  3915277  3915293  3915341  3915343  3915361
3915371  3915397  3915403  3915419  3915421  3915427  3915433  3915469  3915473  3915479
3915487  3915503  3915511  3915521  3915533  3915553  3915557  3915601  3915629  3915631
3915683  3915689  3915697  3915707  3915713  3915719  3915731  3915739  3915761  3915781
3915803  3915809  3915817  3915823  3915839  3915853  3915887  3915893  3915907  3915913
3915937  3915941  3915953  3915959  3915971  3915979  3915997  3916019  3916021  3916027
3916037  3916039  3916057  3916067  3916079  3916091  3916097  3916153  3916169  3916177
3916183  3916193  3916229  3916271  3916301  3916303  3916309  3916313  3916321  3916327
3916343  3916373  3916387  3916391  3916403  3916411  3916433  3916439  3916453  3916459
3916481  3916499  3916529  3916543  3916609  3916621  3916631  3916637  3916639  3916641
3916643  3916663  3916667  3916673  3916691  3916721  3916733  3916751  3916799  3916811
3916813  3916819  3916849  3916883  3916889  3916901  3916903  3916921  3916981  3917009
3917033  3917041  3917047  3917063  3917087  3917093  3917101  3917113  3917119  3917131
3917149  3917161  3917167  3917183  3917189  3917201  3917203  3917209  3917261  3917267
3917281  3917297  3917323  3917411  3917413  3917453  3917461  3917467  3917471  3917479
3917483  3917489  3917491  3917527  3917549  3917561  3917587  3917609  3917623  3917681
3917699  3917717  3917729  3917731  3917737  3917759  3917761  3917791  3917801  3917827
3917833  3917863  3917909  3917923  3917989  3918011  3918029  3918037  3918043  3918053
3918067  3918071  3918127  3918137  3918139  3918149  3918151  3918157  3918179  3918193
3918197  3918209  3918251  3918259  3918269  3918281  3918283  3918293  3918301  3918311
3918323  3918353  3918359  3918377  3918379  3918391  3918401  3918413  3918443  3918491
3918511  3918529  3918539  3918553  3918557  3918569  3918571  3918583  3918587  3918589
3918613  3918641  3918667  3918689  3918697  3918743  3918751  3918757  3918793  3918797
3918829  3918851  3918853  3918869  3918881  3918899  3918913  3918919  3918923  3918949
3918983  3919007  3919021  3919033  3919037  3919049  3919057  3919079  3919081  3919087
3919099  3919109  3919133  3919169  3919171  3919183  3919199  3919211  3919213  3919217
3919229  3919241  3919243  3919247  3919249  3919259  3919261  3919297  3919309  3919313
3919319  3919327  3919369  3919381  3919387  3919393  3919397  3919411  3919417  3919441
3919457  3919463  3919481  3919501  3919519  3919523  3919541  3919543  3919549  3919577
3919583  3919603  3919607  3919613  3919621  3919627  3919667  3919679  3919687  3919711
3919717  3919763  3919771  3919777  3919781  3919787  3919789  3919807  3919813  3919823
3919859  3919873  3919889  3919907  3919943  3919951  3919961  3919973  3919999  3919999
3920003  3920011  3920029  3920057  3920069  3920071  3920087  3920089  3920131  3920141
3920153  3920177  3920179  3920197  3920201  3920209  3920227  3920233  3920239  3920243
3920263  3920269  3920299  3920303  3920311  3920359  3920377  3920383  3920401  3920417
3920429  3920431  3920453  3920459  3920467  3920471  3920509  3920513  3920551  3920561
3920629  3920677  3920681  3920687  3920689  3920729  3920737  3920743  3920747  3920759
3920797  3920843  3920857  3920867  3920899  3920909  3920923  3920929  3920933  3920941
3920947  3920957  3920977  3920981  3920989  3921023  3921037  3921059  3921079  3921089
3921121  3921139  3921143  3921161  3921173  3921179  3921193  3921209  3921217  3921219
3921227  3921287  3921289  3921301  3921343  3921347  3921367  3921377  3921383  3921413
3921451  3921497  3921499  3921503  3921521  3921529  3921551  3921559  3921601  3921637
3921649  3921677  3921683  3921689  3921719  3921721  3921761  3921769  3921791  3921817
3921823  3921851  3921859  3921877  3921881  3921883  3921913  3921919  3921941  3921949
3921959  3921971  3921991  3921997  3922003  3922007  3922013  3922031  3922033  3922063
3922067  3922081  3922099  3922109  3922123  3922153  3922157  3922169  3922187  3922207
3922231  3922249  3922267  3922273  3922277  3922309  3922313  3922327  3922349  3922357
3922367  3922403  3922409  3922423  3922433  3922439  3922459  3922463  3922487  3922507
3922523  3922543  3922553  3922559  3922561  3922577  3922579  3922601  3922613  3922619
3922621  3922637  3922651  3922657  3922691  3922717  3922729  3922741  3922747  3922753
3922769  3922781  3922819  3922843  3922871  3922907  3922909  3922931  3922939  3922967
3922973  3922979  3922981  3922993  3923009  3923011  3923047  3923071  3923077  3923083
3923089  3923099  3923159  3923173  3923189  3923203  3923233  3923261  3923263  3923279
3923287  3923303  3923321  3923347  3923357  3923399  3923407  3923427  3923429  3923431
3923429  3923471  3923477  3923483  3923527  3923539  3923567  3923599  3923609  3923611
3923627  3923629  3923641  3923653  3923669  3923681  3923687  3923723  3923737  3923761
3923771  3923779  3923789  3923791  3923827  3923837  3923839  3923863  3923867  3923893
3923897  3923911  3923917  3923963  3923971  3923977  3923981  3923993  3924017  3924023
3924047  3924071  3924079  3924083  3924097  3924101  3924103  3924113  3924119  3924119
3924121  3924139  3924163  3924181  3924187  3924199  3924209  3924211  3924227  3924247
3924253  3924281  3924287  3924289  3924293  3924307  3924311  3924337  3924341  3924343
3924353  3924409  3924413  3924443  3924449  3924451  3924457  3924461  3924497  3924499
3924517  3924527  3924533  3924539  3924581  3924593  3924611  3924617  3924649  3924677
3924689  3924719  3924721  3924731  3924757  3924761  3924781  3924787  3924797  3924803
3924827  3924839  3924847  3924853  3924863  3924871  3924883  3924901  3924929  3924931
3924953  3924959  3924961  3925013  3925027  3925037  3925043  3925069  3925087  3925091
3925109  3925123  3925133  3925151  3925171  3925177  3925193  3925213  3925223  3925253
3925261  3925277  3925279  3925297  3925301  3925307  3925309  3925357  3925373  3925379
3925391  3925403  3925409  3925459  3925483  3925489  3925541  3925549  3925553  3925583
3925591  3925613  3925631  3925637  3925667  3925693  3925699  3925717  3925729  3925739
3925741  3925751  3925783  3925787  3925807  3925829  3925841  3925843  3925877  3925897
3925903  3925927  3925949  3925967  3925969  3925973  3925981  3925993  3926017  3926023
3926047  3926089  3926093  3926101  3926113  3926129  3926137  3926147  3926171  3926203
3926213  3926227  3926231  3926233  3926249  3926291  3926297  3926311  3926323  3926341
3926347  3926357  3926423  3926431  3926441  3926467  3926471  3926479  3926497  3926501
```

```
3926539  3926543  3926561  3926569  3926603  3926621  3926623  3926633  3926639  3926641
3926651  3926707  3926719  3926729  3926731  3926737  3926759  3926771  3926789  3926827
3926849  3926869  3926891  3926893  3926903  3926911  3926917  3926933  3926941  3926957
3926959  3926963  3927013  3927019  3927037  3927047  3927059  3927067  3927073  3927083
3927097  3927107  3927109  3927113  3927127  3927137  3927139  3927197  3927199  3927251
3927257  3927269  3927271  3927293  3927299  3927307  3927337  3927347  3927361  3927373
3927377  3927409  3927419  3927437  3927449  3927463  3927467  3927479  3927523  3927529
3927551  3927559  3927563  3927593  3927601  3927611  3927647  3927667  3927691  3927701
3927709  3927713  3927727  3927739  3927751  3927761  3927769  3927823  3927827  3927829
3927839  3927877  3927887  3927893  3927907  3927919  3927929  3927941  3927943  3927961
3927967  3927971  3927997  3928013  3928019  3928027  3928039  3928049  3928069  3928091
3928097  3928109  3928123  3928151  3928157  3928159  3928163  3928189  3928229  3928247
3928259  3928261  3928273  3928283  3928303  3928313  3928319  3928361  3928367  3928373
3928381  3928391  3928399  3928417  3928429  3928447  3928451  3928453  3928487  3928493
3928553  3928577  3928619  3928621  3928637  3928651  3928663  3928667  3928669  3928681
3928703  3928709  3928721  3928733  3928739  3928753  3928783  3928807  3928811  3928817
3928823  3928831  3928843  3928849  3928913  3928931  3928937  3928941  3928961  3928979
3928997  3929011  3929017  3929027  3929047  3929053  3929063  3929099  3929117  3929129
3929131  3929161  3929173  3929183  3929201  3929209  3929213  3929221  3929249  3929267
3929269  3929291  3929309  3929311  3929323  3929327  3929351  3929357  3929369  3929407
3929417  3929449  3929461  3929477  3929479  3929501  3929503  3929509  3929521  3929531
3929537  3929543  3929551  3929557  3929581  3929593  3929609  3929621  3929633  3929657
3929671  3929683  3929687  3929699  3929707  3929719  3929729  3929741  3929747  3929749
3929753  3929773  3929797  3929831  3929833  3929843  3929857  3929879  3929917  3929923
3929927  3929951  3929957  3929969  3929977  3930001  3930023  3930037  3930061  3930139
3930191  3930197  3930209  3930221  3930229  3930257  3930259  3930271  3930293  3930307
3930317  3930319  3930323  3930331  3930337  3930361  3930371  3930373  3930389  3930391
3930439  3930461  3930463  3930467  3930481  3930491  3930497  3930517  3930527  3930529
3930541  3930559  3930569  3930571  3930581  3930593  3930601  3930607  3930611  3930613
3930637  3930653  3930671  3930683  3930709  3930721  3930727  3930737  3930743  3930761
3930763  3930767  3930799  3930811  3930827  3930841  3930869  3930887  3930919  3930923
3930973  3930989  3931001  3931027  3931049  3931051  3931087  3931093  3931159  3931177
3931231  3931241  3931247  3931259  3931261  3931273  3931283  3931307  3931331  3931349
3931357  3931363  3931373  3931379  3931387  3931393  3931399  3931411  3931457  3931463
3931469  3931481  3931517  3931519  3931523  3931541  3931547  3931553  3931567  3931589
3931639  3931649  3931661  3931667  3931669  3931693  3931721  3931729  3931747  3931757
3931783  3931787  3931799  3931801  3931813  3931817  3931831  3931847  3931861  3931891
3931927  3931933  3931943  3931969  3931997  3932003  3932021  3932039  3932053  3932059
3932063  3932077  3932099  3932119  3932129  3932147  3932153  3932167  3932179  3932207
3932209  3932237  3932239  3932281  3932303  3932309  3932347  3932377  3932387  3932399
3932413  3932447  3932473  3932483  3932503  3932521  3932543  3932573  3932581  3932633
3932641  3932647  3932657  3932659  3932681  3932689  3932707  3932713  3932717  3932723
3932741  3932743  3932749  3932771  3932779  3932783  3932801  3932813  3932827  3932861
3932869  3932897  3932917  3932921  3932927  3932941  3932947  3932953  3932959  3932963
3932969  3932993  3933011  3933037  3933053  3933071  3933073  3933091  3933109  3933119
3933131  3933143  3933151  3933197  3933199  3933203  3933221  3933227  3933233  3933257
3933269  3933277  3933301  3933337  3933343  3933367  3933379  3933431  3933439  3933469
3933481  3933491  3933493  3933509  3933539  3933547  3933557  3933569  3933577  3933583
3933593  3933599  3933731  3933733  3933767  3933773  3933781  3933791  3933823  3933841
3933857  3933859  3933871  3933887  3933901  3933907  3933929  3933959  3933961  3933971
3933973  3933977  3933997  3934001  3934009  3934013  3934033  3934067  3934087  3934093
3934103  3934109  3934153  3934187  3934201  3934207  3934261  3934267  3934289  3934309
3934339  3934351  3934363  3934367  3934369  3934373  3934421  3934433  3934451  3934453
3934471  3934477  3934493  3934499  3934507  3934519  3934523  3934537  3934583  3934589
3934603  3934621  3934631  3934639  3934669  3934717  3934727  3934739  3934741  3934751
3934783  3934813  3934823  3934849  3934867  3934873  3934877  3934901  3934943  3934963
3934967  3934979  3934991  3934993  3935003  3935011  3935023  3935027  3935089  3935101
3935117  3935119  3935153  3935161  3935179  3935203  3935207  3935219  3935257  3935273
3935287  3935291  3935297  3935311  3935333  3935363  3935383  3935389  3935411  3935417
3935423  3935443  3935453  3935471  3935479  3935497  3935501  3935509  3935521  3935539
3935563  3935573  3935573  3935587  3935609  3935627  3935629  3935651  3935683  3935699  3935719
3935753  3935759  3935761  3935779  3935797  3935809  3935819  3935821  3935837  3935839
3935861  3935879  3935887  3935917  3935947  3935951  3935989  3935999  3936001  3936007
3936011  3936019  3936043  3936103  3936113  3936131  3936137  3936139  3936161  3936167
3936181  3936187  3936217  3936223  3936227  3936239  3936241  3936271  3936293  3936301
3936307  3936313  3936329  3936353  3936437  3936463  3936487  3936509  3936523  3936577
3936587  3936589  3936593  3936599  3936623  3936631  3936641  3936643  3936683  3936727
3936731  3936733  3936769  3936791  3936799  3936811  3936827  3936853  3936859  3936869
3936883  3936899  3936913  3936917  3936923  3936929  3936967  3936973  3936997  3937019
3937039  3937051  3937057  3937061  3937067  3937079  3937097  3937099  3937103  3937111
3937139  3937147  3937159  3937169  3937177  3937181  3937187  3937201  3937229  3937249
3937253  3937261  3937267  3937273  3937289  3937291  3937303  3937321  3937337  3937357
3937363  3937393  3937397  3937399  3937411  3937469  3937477  3937481  3937487  3937499
3937501  3937513  3937537  3937559  3937561  3937567  3937573  3937607  3937621  3937631
3937643  3937673  3937679  3937691  3937697  3937709  3937721  3937751  3937753  3937757
3937771  3937777  3937781  3937783  3937789  3937819  3937831  3937849  3937861  3937877
3937903  3937919  3937943  3937949  3937951  3937981  3937993  3938029  3938057  3938063
3938087  3938089  3938107  3938117  3938119  3938141  3938153  3938167  3938197  3938251
3938257  3938273  3938281  3938303  3938321  3938329  3938351  3938357  3938371  3938381
3938383  3938393  3938437  3938447  3938449  3938471  3938489  3938513  3938521
3938527  3938531  3938549  3938593  3938603  3938609  3938629  3938633  3938639  3938653
3938657  3938699  3938707  3938717  3938723  3938731  3938743  3938771  3938783  3938789
3938791  3938821  3938827  3938839  3938897  3938903  3938923  3938927  3938939  3938941
3938971  3938981  3938999  3939031  3939043  3939059  3939071  3939149  3939181  3939191
3939203  3939209  3939227  3939241  3939259  3939269  3939277  3939337  3939349  3939361
3939367  3939373  3939379  3939421  3939433  3939443  3939457  3939469  3939473  3939497
3939499  3939521  3939539  3939541  3939569  3939589  3939619  3939641  3939671  3939673
3939713  3939721  3939743  3939769  3939773  3939779  3939781  3939787  3939791  3939811
3939829  3939839  3939841  3939851  3939899  3939907  3939917  3939919  3939931  3939953
```

```
3939959  3939989  3939997  3940009  3940021  3940033  3940063  3940091  3940099  3940117
3940121  3940127  3940147  3940159  3940171  3940177  3940207  3940213  3940217  3940231
3940247  3940249  3940253  3940267  3940271  3940273  3940289  3940301  3940303  3940309
3940319  3940351  3940367  3940369  3940373  3940381  3940397  3940411  3940427  3940439
3940451  3940457  3940483  3940487  3940499  3940507  3940513  3940523  3940553  3940561
3940577  3940579  3940589  3940597  3940609  3940631  3940637  3940663  3940667  3940679
3940691  3940693  3940697  3940721  3940747  3940763  3940777  3940793  3940799  3940801
3940823  3940837  3940841  3940891  3940931  3940933  3940939  3940943  3940967  3940969
3940987  3941011  3941017  3941029  3941039  3941053  3941057  3941081  3941083  3941099
3941107  3941111  3941117  3941137  3941159  3941183  3941209  3941233  3941243  3941293
3941299  3941317  3941359  3941363  3941369  3941381  3941411  3941437  3941447  3941449
3941471  3941473  3941507  3941537  3941551  3941611  3941629  3941633  3941653  3941669
3941687  3941689  3941711  3941719  3941741  3941801  3941803  3941831  3941837  3941887
3941891  3941923  3941933  3941957  3941963  3941969  3942007  3942023  3942041  3942047
3942061  3942067  3942089  3942097  3942121  3942137  3942209  3942217  3942227  3942241
3942259  3942287  3942293  3942307  3942311  3942331  3942349  3942353  3942359  3942373
3942377  3942383  3942397  3942401  3942403  3942409  3942413  3942467  3942469  3942479
3942493  3942503  3942509  3942527  3942551  3942553  3942569  3942571  3942577  3942581
3942619  3942643  3942647  3942661  3942667  3942721  3942727  3942739  3942751  3942767
3942769  3942773  3942781  3942839  3942871  3942889  3942907  3942919  3942923  3942931
3942941  3942947  3942977  3942989  3943007  3943019  3943021  3943061  3943087  3943091
3943103  3943109  3943111  3943117  3943123  3943129  3943139  3943153  3943171  3943187
3943193  3943207  3943211  3943243  3943249  3943259  3943267  3943283  3943301  3943307
3943319  3943367  3943397  3943399  3943403  3943409  3943427  3943451  3943481  3943517
3943523  3943529  3943531  3943543  3943547  3943559  3943591  3943613  3943627  3943631
3943633  3943637  3943651  3943661  3943663  3943673  3943691  3943703  3943717  3943721
3943757  3943763  3943769  3943777  3943799  3943829  3943843  3943853  3943859  3943871
3943873  3943883  3943921  3943931  3943937  3943939  3943957  3943967  3943993  3943999
3944009  3944011  3944033  3944041  3944103  3944131  3944141  3944173  3944183  3944189
3944219  3944231  3944249  3944251  3944257  3944309  3944329  3944351  3944359  3944371
3944389  3944399  3944407  3944411  3944449  3944461  3944463  3944481  3944511  3944523
3944497  3944503  3944509  3944513  3944537  3944539  3944557  3944581  3944593  3944597
3944599  3944617  3944621  3944627  3944669  3944671  3944683  3944711  3944729  3944767
3944789  3944791  3944807  3944813  3944821  3944827  3944839  3944861  3944869  3944873
3944881  3944909  3944911  3944921  3944933  3944953  3944987  3944999  3945013  3945017
3945031  3945047  3945059  3945077  3945079  3945101  3945107  3945119  3945127  3945157
3945163  3945203  3945233  3945287  3945299  3945301  3945313  3945323  3945329  3945341
3945349  3945353  3945367  3945391  3945413  3945427  3945449  3945457  3945467  3945527
3945607  3945631  3945647  3945659  3945661  3945671  3945677  3945701  3945703  3945727
3945731  3945757  3945761  3945803  3945841  3945883  3945913  3945917  3945919  3945923
3945959  3945973  3945983  3946027  3946037  3946051  3946059  3946123  3946139  3946141
3946157  3946177  3946183  3946211  3946213  3946219  3946223  3946231  3946237  3946247
3946249  3946259  3946289  3946297  3946337  3946339  3946379  3946381  3946387  3946391
3946399  3946403  3946421  3946427  3946429  3946447  3946463  3946469  3946477  3946483
3946489  3946493  3946507  3946511  3946541  3946549  3946571  3946589  3946597  3946643
3946673  3946681  3946721  3946727  3946729  3946739  3946741  3946757  3946759  3946763
3946793  3946799  3946801  3946829  3946837  3946843  3946853  3946879  3946913  3946933
3946937  3946939  3946951  3946991  3946993  3947017  3947023  3947051  3947059
3947071  3947087  3947089  3947101  3947113  3947131  3947143  3947147  3947173  3947189
3947227  3947233  3947297  3947299  3947309  3947311  3947327  3947351  3947353  3947369
3947407  3947413  3947431  3947453  3947473  3947479  3947491  3947501  3947507
3947533  3947549  3947557  3947561  3947569  3947579  3947591  3947597  3947623  3947627
3947659  3947663  3947693  3947747  3947759  3947771  3947807  3947809
3947831  3947833  3947843  3947851  3947861  3947891  3947897  3947899  3947903  3947921
3947939  3947941  3947963  3947971  3947987  3948071  3948073  3948101  3948121  3948137
3948151  3948161  3948163  3948171  3948179  3948187  3948223  3948229  3948247  3948251
3948271  3948277  3948281  3948283  3948289  3948293  3948311  3948317  3948353  3948361
3948383  3948431  3948439  3948463  3948467  3948469  3948487  3948493  3948521  3948533
3948541  3948547  3948551  3948569  3948577  3948583  3948589  3948613  3948619  3948653
3948667  3948673  3948683  3948689  3948697  3948701  3948719  3948731  3948781  3948803
3948809  3948817  3948821  3948839  3948853  3948859  3948881  3948883  3948887  3948907
3948911  3948953  3949003  3949007  3949013  3949027  3949037  3949039  3949051  3949061
3949069  3949073  3949083  3949087  3949097  3949109  3949111  3949147  3949157  3949177
3949193  3949199  3949213  3949217  3949241  3949247  3949271  3949273  3949291  3949301
3949313  3949333  3949339  3949349  3949357  3949367  3949391  3949409  3949411  3949433
3949441  3949453  3949459  3949469  3949487  3949501  3949529  3949531  3949541  3949579
3949609  3949619  3949643  3949651  3949657  3949669  3949703  3949711  3949723  3949733
3949799  3949819  3949849  3949867  3949871  3949877  3949889  3949903  3949919  3949961
3949969  3950029  3950033  3950039  3950041  3950099  3950101  3950117  3950123  3950129
3950147  3950159  3950161  3950173  3950179  3950181  3950189  3950197  3950201  3950203
3950207  3950213  3950257  3950263  3950267  3950291  3950321  3950327  3950339  3950363
3950383  3950389  3950393  3950399  3950417  3950449  3950459  3950497  3950501  3950509
3950533  3950563  3950599  3950603  3950627  3950629  3950657  3950659  3950693  3950701
3950731  3950753  3950759  3950767  3950777  3950809  3950813  3950827  3950887  3950893
3950899  3950911  3950927  3950929  3950939  3950941  3950951  3951001  3951023  3951071
3951083  3951109  3951113  3951121  3951127  3951131  3951133  3951139  3951151  3951161
3951169  3951173  3951179  3951187  3951197  3951209  3951247  3951251  3951253  3951263
3951283  3951301  3951307  3951319  3951323  3951361  3951373  3951379  3951391  3951401
3951413  3951419  3951421  3951427  3951443  3951461  3951481  3951503  3951509  3951517
3951551  3951553  3951559  3951571  3951587  3951601  3951707  3951719  3951737  3951749
3951767  3951781  3951793  3951797  3951811  3951841  3951863  3951869  3951881  3951887
3951907  3951917  3951947  3951967  3951977  3951989  3952009  3952027  3952037  3952043
3952079  3952099  3952103  3952111  3952121  3952127  3952163  3952181  3952189  3952199
3952217  3952219  3952243  3952301  3952307  3952309  3952321  3952327  3952331  3952337
3952387  3952391  3952393  3952423  3952453  3952463  3952477  3952489  3952493  3952511
3952519  3952537  3952549  3952561  3952567  3952583  3952601  3952633  3952649  3952651
3952691  3952733  3952759  3952763  3952771  3952813  3952873  3952909  3952919
3952937  3952967  3952981  3952997  3953009  3953011  3953017  3953051  3953071  3953093
3953107  3953143  3953149  3953161  3953189  3953233  3953249  3953267  3953269  3953281
```

```
3953293  3953303  3953317  3953353  3953393  3953437  3953473  3953479  3953489  3953491
3953497  3953513  3953519  3953527  3953581  3953591  3953597  3953617  3953627  3953629
3953669  3953689  3953699  3953701  3953717  3953749  3953759  3953779  3953791  3953797
3953801  3953813  3953819  3953827  3953839  3953849  3953863  3953867  3953879  3953909
3953921  3953923  3953927  3953993  3954001  3954007  3954017  3954053  3954077  3954101
3954127  3954131  3954199  3954211  3954221  3954233  3954241  3954253  3954257  3954259
3954281  3954283  3954317  3954331  3954361  3954371  3954373  3954397  3954437  3954443
3954473  3954481  3954493  3954499  3954529  3954547  3954563  3954571  3954583  3954611
3954617  3954623  3954637  3954649  3954683  3954697  3954707  3954719  3954749  3954751
3954767  3954799  3954803  3954823  3954833  3954851  3954859  3954871  3954877  3954889
3954959  3954961  3954971  3954997  3955001  3955009  3955013  3955027  3955043  3955069
3955079  3955087  3955109  3955117  3955121  3955123  3955139  3955141  3955151  3955153
3955157  3955163  3955177  3955187  3955243  3955267  3955277  3955279  3955291  3955307
3955309  3955313  3955319  3955331  3955387  3955403  3955417  3955421  3955429  3955433
3955447  3955459  3955493  3955499  3955529  3955561  3955579  3955597  3955603  3955621
3955643  3955649  3955657  3955663  3955673  3955691  3955703  3955709  3955717  3955723
3955727  3955733  3955753  3955759  3955771  3955799  3955813  3955823  3955859  3955877
3955909  3955927  3955949  3955969  3955979  3955993  3955999  3956027  3956041  3956059
3956081  3956101  3956119  3956143  3956153  3956159  3956171  3956179  3956203  3956219
3956221  3956233  3956261  3956263  3956269  3956279  3956287  3956297  3956311  3956327
3956347  3956353  3956401  3956419  3956429  3956453  3956471  3956501  3956509  3956543
3956549  3956569  3956581  3956587  3956639  3956647  3956651  3956663  3956671  3956677
3956681  3956737  3956741  3956749  3956779  3956783  3956803  3956831  3956833  3956857
3956863  3956867  3956881  3956917  3956941  3956957  3956983  3956999  3957007  3957013
3957017  3957047  3957049  3957053  3957059  3957077  3957091  3957097  3957103  3957133
3957143  3957167  3957169  3957171  3957223  3957227  3957229  3957251  3957269  3957271
3957287  3957299  3957313  3957337  3957341  3957383  3957389  3957397  3957431  3957433
3957439  3957451  3957479  3957487  3957493  3957509  3957521  3957571  3957637  3957647
3957671  3957673  3957683  3957691  3957703  3957713  3957743  3957749  3957761  3957769
3957773  3957781  3957799  3957829  3957839  3957847  3957857  3957859  3957883  3957907
3957929  3957937  3957953  3957959  3957973  3957983  3958013  3958033  3958039  3958063
3958069  3958091  3958103  3958109  3958147  3958153  3958169  3958177  3958183  3958211
3958217  3958219  3958243  3958259  3958261  3958313  3958337  3958343  3958349  3958363
3958373  3958391  3958397  3958439  3958457  3958459  3958477  3958499  3958523  3958531
3958543  3958583  3958589  3958601  3958621  3958627  3958657  3958687  3958697  3958727
3958733  3958751  3958753  3958777  3958789  3958811  3958813  3958817  3958831  3958847
3958879  3958883  3958891  3958931  3958937  3958949  3958957  3959003  3959027  3959029
3959063  3959089  3959093  3959119  3959129  3959141  3959143  3959159  3959171  3959177
3959191  3959203  3959209  3959237  3959257  3959261  3959269  3959279  3959287  3959297
3959299  3959303  3959323  3959339  3959357  3959359  3959363  3959387  3959393  3959441
3959477  3959491  3959507  3959531  3959539  3959551  3959587  3959591  3959651  3959663
3959663  3959677  3959687  3959701  3959707  3959719  3959729  3959801  3959803  3959807
3959819  3959833  3959843  3959849  3959869  3959873  3959899  3959911  3959947  3959953
3959957  3959959  3959981  3959983  3960007  3960029  3960049  3960053  3960083  3960101
3960137  3960161  3960193  3960217  3960223  3960251  3960263  3960283  3960289  3960317
3960329  3960367  3960373  3960377  3960401  3960403  3960419  3960421  3960427  3960431
3960433  3960457  3960497  3960499  3960521  3960557  3960581  3960587  3960599  3960613
3960631  3960667  3960673  3960689  3960701  3960707  3960727  3960731  3960751  3960757
3960769  3960799  3960811  3960829  3960833  3960841  3960857  3960871  3960883  3960889
3960893  3960937  3960941  3960959  3960967  3960977  3960997  3961007  3961021  3961039
3961049  3961057  3961061  3961147  3961159  3961171  3961193  3961213  3961229  3961231
3961259  3961261  3961271  3961283  3961327  3961333  3961337  3961339  3961343  3961393
3961411  3961417  3961427  3961439  3961453  3961457  3961469  3961501  3961513  3961517
3961541  3961579  3961597  3961609  3961619  3961631  3961649  3961651  3961669  3961691
3961721  3961723  3961753  3961759  3961781  3961813  3961817  3961847  3961877  3961883
3961897  3961907  3961933  3961949  3961969  3961961  3961963  3961973  3961979  3961981
3961987  3962029  3962039  3962047  3962081  3962093  3962107  3962113  3962137  3962143
3962201  3962213  3962227  3962243  3962251  3962299  3962303  3962311  3962323  3962339
3962351  3962359  3962437  3962443  3962461  3962467  3962471  3962489  3962521  3962549
3962557  3962587  3962591  3962593  3962599  3962603  3962611  3962627  3962641  3962653
3962671  3962689  3962707  3962713  3962729  3962731  3962747  3962759  3962789  3962807
3962813  3962839  3962843  3962851  3962857  3962887  3962897  3962909  3962927  3962939
3962941  3962977  3963013  3963017  3963031  3963041  3963119  3963121  3963161  3963209
3963221  3963241  3963263  3963269  3963277  3963283  3963293  3963299  3963301  3963317
3963359  3963361  3963373  3963391  3963409  3963467  3963469  3963473  3963493  3963497
3963503  3963523  3963529  3963539  3963559  3963569  3963577  3963581  3963587  3963607
3963623  3963637  3963643  3963649  3963683  3963709  3963721  3963763  3963803  3963809
3963829  3963833  3963853  3963857  3963887  3963899  3963931  3963951  3963959  3963977
3963979  3963991  3964007  3964013  3964021  3964031  3964061  3964087  3964091  3964117
3964123  3964133  3964177  3964181  3964193  3964201  3964229  3964237  3964273  3964277
3964283  3964297  3964307  3964319  3964333  3964357  3964381  3964393  3964397  3964399
3964421  3964423  3964463  3964481  3964489  3964507  3964511  3964517  3964523  3964531
3964549  3964589  3964603  3964607  3964613  3964627  3964633  3964651  3964663  3964679
3964693  3964699  3964733  3964759  3964777  3964783  3964789  3964801  3964811  3964819
3964837  3964841  3964843  3964847  3964867  3964871  3964889  3964891  3964897  3964903
3964907  3964913  3964937  3964943  3964949  3964951  3964963  3964973  3965021  3965023
3965033  3965041  3965123  3965147  3965153  3965161  3965197  3965219  3965231  3965309
3965317  3965341  3965347  3965359  3965371  3965383  3965393  3965419  3965441  3965443
3965447  3965461  3965483  3965537  3965569  3965581  3965587  3965617  3965629  3965639
3965653  3965659  3965681  3965701  3965707  3965723  3965783  3965789  3965827  3965833
3965839  3965849  3965869  3965881  3965887  3965903  3965911  3965939  3965963  3966007
3966029  3966059  3966089  3966091  3966113  3966119  3966121  3966139  3966161  3966173
3966197  3966211  3966223  3966229  3966239  3966247  3966271  3966293  3966323  3966329
3966331  3966349  3966407  3966409  3966433  3966439  3966503  3966517  3966539  3966541
3966563  3966581  3966583  3966607  3966617  3966623  3966631  3966689  3966691  3966701
3966719  3966727  3966761  3966773  3966779  3966799  3966803  3966817  3966857  3966863
3966871  3966883  3966887  3966889  3966913  3966923  3966929  3966961  3967027  3967043
3967049  3967057  3967081  3967087  3967111  3967121  3967123  3967127  3967133  3967141
3967147  3967157  3967189  3967193  3967207  3967231  3967237  3967241  3967253  3967259
```

```
3967277 3967289 3967297 3967321 3967343 3967351 3967357 3967363 3967373 3967417
3967429 3967441 3967451 3967487 3967489 3967493 3967499 3967507 3967517 3967541
3967553 3967571 3967609 3967619 3967627 3967651 3967669 3967679 3967687 3967699
3967727 3967741 3967793 3967801 3967811 3967819 3967829 3967837 3967841 3967871
3967877 3967913 3967961 3967963 3967973 3967993 3968009 3968011 3968023 3968047
3968053 3968071 3968077 3968113 3968137 3968149 3968177 3968183 3968201 3968203
3968219 3968227 3968231 3968291 3968297 3968299 3968303 3968323 3968329 3968339
3968357 3968381 3968387 3968411 3968417 3968453 3968483 3968491 3968501 3968507
3968521 3968533 3968537 3968543 3968551 3968567 3968597 3968603 3968617 3968647
3968669 3968717 3968729 3968743 3968761 3968801 3968807 3968813 3968819 3968827
3968863 3968869 3968873 3968893 3968897 3968917 3968941 3968947 3968957 3968981
3968983 3969001 3969019 3969037 3969059 3969061 3969067 3969071 3969137 3969151
3969167 3969181 3969191 3969193 3969221 3969241 3969247 3969253 3969263 3969269
3969289 3969307 3969349 3969367 3969377 3969389 3969391 3969419 3969421 3969437
3969443 3969451 3969467 3969481 3969487 3969503 3969527 3969529 3969557 3969569
3969571 3969583 3969601 3969611 3969629 3969649 3969659 3969673 3969677 3969703
3969709 3969733 3969737 3969751 3969769 3969773 3969787 3969793 3969809 3969811
3969821 3969827 3969853 3969863 3969871 3969899 3969923 3969937 3969943 3969971
3969983 3969997 3970009 3970033 3970039 3970049 3970073 3970097 3970103 3970111
3970121 3970133 3970151 3970157 3970159 3970181 3970199 3970223 3970247 3970261
3970271 3970273 3970277 3970289 3970313 3970321 3970331 3970339 3970349 3970357
3970363 3970409 3970423 3970441 3970453 3970459 3970489 3970493 3970529 3970531
3970567 3970579 3970583 3970591 3970633 3970643 3970649 3970657 3970679 3970691
3970711 3970723 3970739 3970751 3970763 3970781 3970787 3970793 3970801 3970819
3970823 3970831 3970849 3970859 3970903 3970949 3970991 3970997 3971027 3971041
3971053 3971063 3971087 3971117 3971119 3971129 3971141 3971147 3971153 3971167
3971207 3971213 3971239 3971257 3971263 3971267 3971281 3971287 3971299 3971309
3971311 3971333 3971377 3971393 3971411 3971413 3971423 3971431 3971459 3971477
3971483 3971501 3971531 3971533 3971537 3971549 3971581 3971587 3971599 3971621
3971651 3971677 3971687 3971713 3971719 3971731 3971743 3971749 3971791 3971797
3971809 3971833 3971843 3971861 3971879 3971881 3971887 3971899 3971911 3971917
3971963 3971977 3971983 3971993 3972011 3972019 3972029 3972037 3972071 3972091
3972103 3972107 3972113 3972119 3972139 3972151 3972167 3972173 3972181 3972187
3972193 3972223 3972233 3972251 3972263 3972301 3972329 3972341 3972343 3972359
3972377 3972413 3972427 3972439 3972467 3972499 3972517 3972523 3972533 3972541
3972569 3972593 3972601 3972643 3972649 3972671 3972697 3972737 3972751 3972757
3972791 3972809 3972811 3972817 3972833 3972841 3972851 3972877 3972901 3972911
3972923 3972931 3972937 3972953 3972959 3972973 3972979 3973007 3973009 3973027
3973031 3973061 3973063 3973093 3973111 3973117 3973129 3973133 3973139 3973153
3973163 3973183 3973213 3973219 3973241 3973247 3973253 3973259 3973279 3973283
3973289 3973297 3973303 3973309 3973331 3973339 3973381 3973391 3973421 3973429
3973439 3973447 3973469 3973481 3973483 3973499 3973511 3973517 3973531 3973553
3973561 3973577 3973579 3973633 3973639 3973649 3973661 3973691 3973727 3973729
3973741 3973747 3973751 3973757 3973787 3973807 3973811 3973829 3973847 3973861
3973877 3973919 3973927 3973933 3973943 3973973 3973997 3974023 3974027 3974041
3974053 3974057 3974071 3974077 3974093 3974129 3974143 3974167 3974177 3974191
3974213 3974219 3974221 3974227 3974237 3974261 3974279 3974291 3974309 3974351
3974353 3974357 3974359 3974371 3974387 3974389 3974393 3974419 3974437 3974441
3974459 3974483 3974491 3974497 3974501 3974527 3974539 3974563 3974567 3974609
3974611 3974623 3974657 3974681 3974683 3974687 3974689 3974701 3974713 3974717
3974723 3974741 3974749 3974759 3974779 3974783 3974797 3974801 3974833 3974849
3974881 3974897 3974911 3974917 3974921 3974939 3974951 3974959 3974969 3974981
3974987 3975011 3975017 3975031 3975089 3975091 3975107 3975109 3975151 3975163
3975173 3975193 3975197 3975217 3975239 3975247 3975253 3975269 3975271 3975277
3975281 3975289 3975341 3975353 3975379 3975383 3975437 3975449 3975463 3975473
3975487 3975493 3975509 3975511 3975529 3975547 3975577 3975593 3975599 3975649
3975659 3975661 3975667 3975677 3975701 3975703 3975707 3975709 3975721 3975749
3975779 3975791 3975827 3975857 3975863 3975887 3975911 3975947 3975971 3976001
3976003 3976009 3976019 3976031 3976043 3976061 3976087 3976097 3976099 3976121
3976129 3976169 3976177 3976183 3976199 3976207 3976223 3976229 3976241 3976261
3976267 3976289 3976319 3976327 3976331 3976337 3976361 3976367 3976381 3976387
3976391 3976397 3976403 3976409 3976417 3976439 3976459 3976477 3976481 3976507
3976519 3976523 3976547 3976573 3976579 3976601 3976607 3976619 3976633 3976663
3976667 3976669 3976703 3976733 3976783 3976801 3976807 3976829 3976831 3976849
3976853 3976859 3976867 3976873 3976879 3976913 3976927 3976943 3976949 3976969
3976979 3976981 3976991 3977003 3977011 3977059 3977063 3977069 3977081 3977087
3977101 3977107 3977117 3977153 3977159 3977161 3977177 3977203 3977209 3977219
3977221 3977273 3977293 3977317 3977339 3977341 3977353 3977377 3977381 3977387
3977401 3977411 3977419 3977429 3977431 3977447 3977453 3977461 3977471 3977483
3977489 3977497 3977503 3977509 3977527 3977549 3977569 3977573 3977587 3977599
3977621 3977639 3977647 3977653 3977663 3977681 3977693 3977717 3977719 3977731
3977741 3977761 3977777 3977791 3977797 3977807 3977819 3977849 3977851 3977863
3977867 3977891 3977893 3977903 3977921 3977927 3977929 3977933 3977947 3977977
3977999 3978031 3978043 3978053 3978071 3978101 3978109 3978113 3978167 3978179
3978181 3978197 3978217 3978229 3978253 3978257 3978263 3978269 3978283 3978301
3978329 3978349 3978421 3978431 3978433 3978451 3978473 3978479 3978497 3978511
3978523 3978553 3978587 3978593 3978641 3978643 3978659 3978671 3978673 3978683
3978707 3978727 3978739 3978743 3978749 3978761 3978773 3978781 3978803 3978811
3978817 3978823 3978841 3978859 3978883 3978893 3978899 3978917 3978967 3978971
3978979 3979013 3979021 3979039 3979043 3979117 3979127 3979133 3979141 3979147
3979159 3979163 3979181 3979193 3979201 3979211 3979219 3979229 3979237 3979247
3979259 3979267 3979289 3979357 3979361 3979363 3979427 3979433 3979463 3979499
3979511 3979517 3979523 3979543 3979553 3979561 3979567 3979583 3979603 3979627
3979637 3979639 3979643 3979663 3979669 3979691 3979711 3979739 3979771 3979837
3979843 3979861 3979883 3979889 3979891 3979901 3979957 3979967 3979981 3979999
3980003 3980017 3980027 3980051 3980069 3980071 3980087 3980089 3980113 3980117
3980143 3980147 3980161 3980191 3980203 3980231 3980281 3980287 3980299 3980303
3980323 3980341 3980359 3980377 3980387 3980399 3980401 3980407 3980419 3980429
3980461 3980479 3980491 3980503 3980513 3980521 3980527 3980531 3980549 3980551
```

```
3980579  3980591  3980593  3980611  3980621  3980629  3980653  3980657  3980663  3980687
3980689  3980693  3980729  3980749  3980761  3980801  3980819  3980827  3980831  3980843  3980857
3980887  3980891  3980957  3980971  3980987  3981017  3981037  3981067  3981071  3981097
3981101  3981119  3981137  3981157  3981161  3981167  3981169  3981181  3981191  3981193
3981209  3981217  3981227  3981253  3981301  3981331  3981343  3981389  3981391  3981401
3981403  3981407  3981421  3981449  3981463  3981473  3981479  3981491  3981503  3981517
3981539  3981541  3981563  3981569  3981581  3981589  3981617  3981619  3981629  3981641
3981643  3981647  3981683  3981707  3981709  3981739  3981749  3981763  3981767  3981821
3981823  3981827  3981833  3981839  3981847  3981863  3981869  3981871  3981881  3981883
3981889  3981899  3981911  3981917  3981937  3981953  3981959  3981973  3982031  3982037
3982057  3982067  3982073  3982079  3982117  3982123  3982129  3982157  3982171  3982183
3982201  3982247  3982249  3982259  3982271  3982283  3982333  3982351  3982373  3982379
3982393  3982397  3982399  3982411  3982417  3982481  3982493  3982499  3982513  3982549
3982567  3982591  3982597  3982631  3982679  3982687  3982691  3982697  3982721  3982739
3982747  3982763  3982801  3982813  3982819  3982877  3982883  3982903  3982931  3982967
3982987  3982991  3982999  3983009  3983011  3983033  3983039  3983041  3983059  3983069
3983093  3983123  3983129  3983131  3983153  3983197  3983201  3983227  3983249  3983261
3983263  3983279  3983299  3983303  3983333  3983341  3983377  3983381  3983387  3983401
3983431  3983443  3983453  3983459  3983461  3983467  3983471  3983479  3983509  3983543
3983587  3983633  3983641  3983657  3983663  3983689  3983699  3983719  3983747  3983773
3983789  3983809  3983839  3983869  3983873  3983893  3983897  3983909  3983911  3983927
3983951  3983963  3983981  3983983  3983989  3983999  3984031  3984047  3984061  3984073
3984109  3984131  3984133  3984139  3984161  3984173  3984181  3984191  3984199  3984217
3984229  3984259  3984269  3984283  3984287  3984293  3984301  3984317  3984347  3984389
3984391  3984403  3984439  3984457  3984467  3984473  3984479  3984499  3984517  3984521
3984587  3984599  3984611  3984649  3984653  3984677  3984679  3984731  3984751  3984769
3984781  3984791  3984793  3984809  3984823  3984859  3984917  3984941  3984943  3984949
3984971  3984983  3985013  3985027  3985031  3985039  3985057  3985063  3985067  3985073
3985087  3985099  3985103  3985181  3985207  3985211  3985213  3985217  3985237  3985243
3985249  3985277  3985297  3985337  3985349  3985351  3985363  3985393  3985403  3985409
3985433  3985451  3985469  3985511  3985519  3985523  3985537  3985543  3985549  3985567
3985589  3985591  3985609  3985621  3985637  3985661  3985669  3985697  3985711  3985717
3985721  3985777  3985829  3985843  3985853  3985859  3985867  3985879  3985889  3985903
3985951  3985999  3986009  3986033  3986051  3986063  3986111  3986113  3986159  3986161
3986173  3986189  3986201  3986207  3986209  3986231  3986237  3986243  3986263  3986273
3986287  3986293  3986303  3986309  3986329  3986351  3986357  3986377  3986393  3986413
3986431  3986441  3986459  3986467  3986473  3986497  3986503  3986513  3986519  3986531
3986537  3986539  3986581  3986597  3986611  3986617  3986623  3986641  3986651  3986663
3986669  3986677  3986699  3986711  3986729  3986737  3986747  3986761  3986767  3986771
3986783  3986803  3986809  3986813  3986839  3986897  3986921  3986923  3986929  3986951
3986953  3986971  3986977  3986987  3986989  3986999  3987001  3987013  3987019  3987023
3987029  3987037  3987077  3987079  3987107  3987121  3987149  3987167  3987173  3987199
3987227  3987229  3987259  3987271  3987287  3987301  3987311  3987317  3987323  3987353
3987407  3987409  3987421  3987427  3987449  3987481  3987517  3987521  3987523  3987551
3987559  3987589  3987593  3987629  3987649  3987677  3987727  3987733  3987757  3987769
3987791  3987799  3987811  3987821  3987833  3987839  3987847  3987859  3987883  3987887
3987913  3987931  3987937  3987943  3988003  3988007  3988021  3988027  3988069  3988073
3988087  3988093  3988097  3988129  3988147  3988151  3988213  3988247  3988249  3988273
3988277  3988289  3988291  3988297  3988301  3988321  3988331  3988343  3988351  3988381
3988403  3988427  3988433  3988441  3988451  3988471  3988477  3988487  3988513  3988519
3988531  3988541  3988583  3988601  3988619  3988627  3988643  3988661  3988667  3988679
3988681  3988687  3988703  3988717  3988753  3988759  3988763  3988771  3988781  3988783
3988823  3988889  3988903  3988961  3988969  3988991  3989003  3989009
3989021  3989023  3989039  3989057  3989093  3989119  3989123  3989137  3989147  3989159
3989171  3989191  3989233  3989243  3989261  3989267  3989287  3989311  3989317  3989329
3989333  3989351  3989371  3989383  3989387  3989389  3989393  3989413  3989429  3989431
3989437  3989467  3989471  3989477  3989519  3989533  3989569  3989593  3989641  3989651
3989653  3989663  3989683  3989701  3989723  3989729  3989759  3989761  3989801  3989807
3989809  3989831  3989837  3989857  3989863  3989891  3989897  3989903  3989929  3989941
3989957  3989963  3989983  3989989  3990001  3990011  3990029  3990031  3990037  3990047
3990061  3990073  3990083  3990097  3990113  3990127  3990157  3990169  3990179  3990187
3990241  3990251  3990269  3990281  3990307  3990331  3990353  3990373  3990379  3990383
3990419  3990449  3990451  3990463  3990473  3990509  3990521  3990593  3990601
3990607  3990617  3990619  3990641  3990689  3990731  3990737  3990761  3990773  3990827
3990841  3990851  3990859  3990863  3990901  3990907  3990913  3990919  3990929
3990967  3990977  3990979  3990997  3991019  3991021  3991037  3991051  3991087  3991093
3991103  3991111  3991139  3991181  3991189  3991199  3991223  3991237  3991261  3991279
3991289  3991297  3991313  3991321  3991333  3991369  3991399  3991441  3991451
3991469  3991511  3991517  3991543  3991571  3991573  3991579  3991601  3991607  3991609
3991613  3991619  3991639  3991649  3991667  3991679  3991681  3991693  3991703  3991711
3991717  3991723  3991727  3991747  3991751  3991807  3991817  3991829  3991831  3991853
3991877  3991891  3991943  3991961  3991973  3991993  3991997  3992011  3992029  3992057
3992069  3992081  3992083  3992089  3992099  3992123  3992141  3992143  3992159  3992171
3992201  3992203  3992207  3992213  3992221  3992231  3992243  3992251  3992257  3992279
3992291  3992309  3992323  3992327  3992341  3992347  3992357  3992371  3992377
3992381  3992393  3992407  3992419  3992441  3992447  3992453  3992477  3992479  3992503
3992519  3992531  3992533  3992563  3992567  3992587  3992609  3992623  3992627  3992683
3992687  3992689  3992699  3992701  3992713  3992719  3992741  3992761  3992771  3992797
3992837  3992843  3992873  3992887  3992899  3992903  3992917  3992927  3992939  3992951
3992959  3992987  3993019  3993029  3993037  3993043  3993049  3993071  3993083  3993089
3993091  3993103  3993107  3993127  3993161  3993193  3993217  3993221  3993229  3993233
3993239  3993247  3993251  3993257  3993259  3993263  3993313  3993323  3993343  3993377
3993397  3993427  3993443  3993469  3993481  3993511  3993527  3993547  3993559  3993569
3993571  3993581  3993593  3993601  3993617  3993631  3993653  3993659  3993683  3993701
3993713  3993721  3993733  3993739  3993751  3993779  3993791  3993839  3993889
3993889  3993893  3993901  3993907  3993911  3993943  3993949  3993953  3993959  3993991
3994007  3994021  3994069  3994079  3994103  3994121  3994147  3994171  3994183  3994189
3994213  3994223  3994229  3994253  3994267  3994271  3994279  3994357  3994369  3994391
3994411  3994421  3994429  3994453  3994481  3994493  3994499  3994513  3994537  3994553
```

```
3994559  3994561  3994591  3994597  3994619  3994621  3994681  3994687  3994699  3994717
3994723  3994729  3994733  3994747  3994759  3994763  3994777  3994787  3994789  3994799
3994817  3994841  3994843  3994849  3994891  3994897  3994909  3994931  3994933  3994937
3994961  3994993  3995021  3995023  3995029  3995083  3995093  3995113  3995129  3995161
3995183  3995191  3995207  3995219  3995231  3995269  3995279  3995281  3995347  3995351
3995413  3995429  3995437  3995441  3995443  3995447  3995449  3995461  3995471  3995489
3995503  3995507  3995531  3995543  3995557  3995571  3995587  3995609  3995623  3995627
3995633  3995639  3995647  3995653  3995659  3995671  3995687  3995699  3995713  3995729
3995743  3995749  3995753  3995777  3995779  3995797  3995837  3995843  3995851  3995891
3995897  3995903  3995921  3995923  3995933  3995941  3995977  3995989  3996007  3996017
3996059  3996067  3996073  3996077  3996079  3996107  3996131  3996149  3996151  3996193
3996199  3996211  3996221  3996277  3996281  3996283  3996323  3996337  3996341  3996347
3996353  3996361  3996379  3996397  3996413  3996431  3996439  3996467  3996511  3996521
3996523  3996527  3996529  3996541  3996569  3996583  3996589  3996647  3996653  3996743
3996763  3996791  3996793  3996827  3996857  3996869  3996911  3996919  3996931  3996959
3996961  3996977  3997001  3997003  3997039  3997043  3997051  3997061  3997069  3997111
3997117  3997129  3997141  3997181  3997211  3997241  3997267  3997271  3997297  3997307
3997319  3997339  3997349  3997361  3997381  3997403  3997453  3997457  3997463  3997471
3997493  3997507  3997547  3997549  3997559  3997577  3997583  3997597  3997603  3997639
3997649  3997673  3997723  3997751  3997759  3997769  3997801  3997811  3997849  3997859
3997871  3997891  3997909  3997919  3997921  3997927  3997933  3997963  3997967
3997979  3997993  3997997  3998003  3998041  3998069  3998089  3998107  3998119  3998131
3998171  3998173  3998177  3998191  3998209  3998219  3998221  3998233  3998249  3998261
3998263  3998273  3998299  3998333  3998339  3998353  3998369  3998377  3998399  3998413
3998419  3998459  3998461  3998497  3998521  3998537  3998539  3998551  3998557  3998567
3998581  3998591  3998609  3998623  3998629  3998639  3998641  3998653  3998669  3998671
3998677  3998693  3998707  3998717  3998719  3998737  3998741  3998749  3998773  3998779
3998789  3998801  3998809  3998821  3998831  3998837  3998881  3998899  3998959  3998971
3998983  3998993  3998999  3999001  3999053  3999067  3999109  3999113  3999143  3999161
3999209  3999211  3999239  3999251  3999283  3999311  3999313  3999323  3999337  3999379
3999383  3999389  3999421  3999439  3999449  3999461  3999467  3999487  3999491  3999497
3999511  3999517  3999529  3999547  3999563  3999577  3999581  3999599  3999623  3999629
3999637  3999647  3999659  3999661  3999683  3999703  3999707  3999719  3999727  3999733
3999739  3999763  3999773  3999781  3999791  3999803  3999851  3999859  3999871  3999893
3999901  3999917  3999923  3999929  3999949  3999971  4000037  4000039  4000043  4000063
4000067  4000079  4000081  4000093  4000133  4000153  4000159  4000169  4000189  4000237
4000261  4000267  4000273  4000277  4000291  4000301  4000303  4000309  4000343  4000357
4000361  4000379  4000439  4000489  4000511  4000523  4000541  4000543  4000553  4000561
4000567  4000573  4000589  4000631  4000649  4000651  4000669  4000673  4000679  4000691
4000693  4000709  4000723  4000741  4000747  4000751  4000813  4000823  4000853  4000861
4000879  4000883  4000889  4000897  4000901  4000907  4000937  4000939  4000949  4000951
4000957  4000979  4000987  4000993  4001003  4001009  4001017  4001027  4001029  4001059
4001071  4001089  4001111  4001117  4001119  4001141  4001147  4001167  4001177  4001183
4001197  4001213  4001219  4001227  4001237  4001243  4001269  4001303  4001339  4001357
4001369  4001383  4001399  4001407  4001411  4001453  4001461  4001467  4001483  4001509
4001521  4001527  4001531  4001549  4001551  4001561  4001567  4001593  4001597  4001603
4001611  4001617  4001629  4001639  4001689  4001713  4001719  4001741  4001743  4001771
4001779  4001791  4001807  4001827  4001831  4001849  4001863  4001867  4001873  4001891
4001939  4001947  4001999  4002001  4002013  4002017  4002041  4002043  4002049  4002067
4002077  4002101  4002109  4002113  4002127  4002137  4002143  4002169  4002197  4002209
4002221  4002223  4002239  4002247  4002263  4002269  4002281  4002301  4002307  4002329
4002337  4002353  4002389  4002403  4002431  4002457  4002499  4002527  4002547  4002553
4002563  4002571  4002577  4002611  4002631  4002641  4002643  4002671  4002679  4002709
4002721  4002727  4002743  4002773  4002797  4002811  4002821  4002829  4002833  4002839
4002847  4002857  4002877  4002893  4002907  4002917  4002923  4002949  4002959  4002961
4002979  4002983  4002991  4002997  4003001  4003019  4003033  4003039  4003057  4003079
4003099  4003121  4003133  4003147  4003151  4003187  4003201  4003213  4003231  4003253
4003271  4003273  4003291  4003297  4003333  4003361  4003387  4003397  4003423  4003427
4003453  4003459  4003501  4003513  4003523  4003529  4003577  4003579  4003663  4003667
4003669  4003697  4003709  4003717  4003729  4003757  4003763  4003781  4003793  4003819
4003841  4003847  4003861  4003871  4003873  4003877  4003913  4003939  4003949  4003963
4003973  4003981  4003999  4004009  4004023  4004057  4004069  4004081  4004087  4004089
4004137  4004141  4004179  4004191  4004207  4004213  4004219  4004227  4004237  4004249
4004267  4004279  4004281  4004293  4004339  4004359  4004387  4004393  4004417  4004449
4004453  4004489  4004509  4004513  4004527  4004579  4004591  4004597  4004617  4004629
4004653  4004659  4004669  4004677  4004681  4004683  4004699  4004713  4004717  4004731
4004753  4004773  4004779  4004789  4004807  4004821  4004837  4004851  4004867  4004873
4004881  4004887  4004909  4004933  4004939  4004951  4004989  4005019  4005049  4005091
4005119  4005121  4005137  4005173  4005203  4005223  4005229  4005233  4005241  4005271
4005301  4005307  4005317  4005341  4005343  4005347  4005367  4005373  4005377  4005433
4005457  4005467  4005499  4005527  4005539  4005553  4005613  4005619  4005643  4005649
4005653  4005691  4005733  4005767  4005769  4005791  4005817  4005821  4005839  4005847
4005889  4005893  4005901  4005921  4005959  4005971  4005977  4005981  4005983  4006001
4006007  4006019  4006039  4006063  4006091  4006097  4006103  4006109  4006129  4006133
4006141  4006153  4006183  4006201  4006229  4006231  4006241  4006243  4006253  4006259
4006273  4006307  4006309  4006319  4006333  4006337  4006349  4006351  4006361  4006363
4006381  4006403  4006411  4006417  4006423  4006451  4006463  4006477  4006481  4006489
4006517  4006523  4006529  4006537  4006547  4006567  4006571  4006589  4006591  4006603
4006621  4006633  4006637  4006649  4006661  4006687  4006699  4006721  4006729  4006741
4006763  4006789  4006811  4006823  4006837  4006859  4006861  4006879  4006913  4006927
4006931  4006939  4006957  4006963  4006969  4006979  4006993  4007021  4007023  4007033
4007039  4007071  4007077  4007099  4007123  4007131  4007141  4007147  4007149  4007183
4007207  4007209  4007219  4007239  4007251  4007261  4007279  4007281  4007321  4007351
4007363  4007369  4007407  4007411  4007413  4007429  4007431  4007441  4007447  4007459
4007477  4007483  4007497  4007513  4007519  4007527  4007551  4007561  4007569  4007573
4007593  4007599  4007611  4007623  4007629  4007657  4007659  4007671  4007677  4007687
4007723  4007741  4007747  4007777  4007789  4007797  4007813  4007827  4007837  4007851
4007863  4007881  4007893  4007921  4007933  4007953  4007963  4007981  4007989  4008001
4008013  4008023  4008029  4008077  4008089  4008091  4008097  4008131  4008133  4008143
```

```
4008149 4008157 4008161 4008181 4008203 4008217 4008227 4008239 4008253 4008271
4008287 4008289 4008307 4008313 4008317 4008349 4008377 4008391 4008397 4008421
4008427 4008437 4008439 4008461 4008523 4008551 4008559 4008577 4008581 4008619
4008629 4008643 4008661 4008671 4008673 4008679 4008689 4008701 4008709 4008713
4008727 4008749 4008769 4008779 4008793 4008799 4008841 4008853 4008869 4008881
4008883 4008887 4008919 4008947 4008967 4008971 4008997 4009001 4009003 4009007
4009037 4009039 4009051 4009091 4009097 4009139 4009141 4009151 4009193 4009207
4009219 4009237 4009249 4009307 4009319 4009321 4009333 4009339 4009373 4009381
4009391 4009409 4009417 4009451 4009477 4009483 4009507 4009529 4009531 4009545
4009547 4009549 4009619 4009631 4009639 4009667 4009669 4009679 4009721 4009729
4009769 4009777 4009781 4009787 4009799 4009823 4009849 4009861 4009891 4009897
4009919 4009919 4009921 4009933 4009939 4009991 4010021 4010029 4010047 4010063
4010081 4010089 4010101 4010117 4010131 4010141 4010143 4010161 4010173 4010177
4010179 4010189 4010189 4010203 4010221 4010231 4010261 4010267 4010269 4010297
4010299 4010339 4010353 4010371 4010399 4010423 4010431 4010443 4010471 4010491
4010507 4010509 4010519 4010527 4010537 4010543 4010549 4010551 4010561 4010569
4010581 4010597 4010599 4010603 4010621 4010627 4010639 4010641 4010647 4010663
4010701 4010707 4010731 4010771 4010777 4010789 4010801 4010803 4010807 4010819
4010833 4010839 4010857 4010893 4010921 4010927 4010939 4010953 4010977 4011011
4011017 4011037 4011043 4011053 4011061 4011103 4011113 4011127 4011157 4011181
4011197 4011209 4011221 4011239 4011247 4011257 4011263 4011283 4011289 4011313
4011331 4011347 4011349 4011353 4011373 4011377 4011409 4011443 4011467 4011479
4011487 4011523 4011529 4011533 4011551 4011559 4011583 4011647 4011649 4011653
4011671 4011673 4011701 4011703 4011719 4011731 4011737 4011767 4011769 4011781
4011797 4011811 4011817 4011827 4011859 4011863 4011871 4011883 4011899 4011911
4011923 4011929 4011977 4011979 4011991 4012013 4012033 4012037 4012067 4012069
4012079 4012081 4012103 4012109 4012111 4012133 4012147 4012157 4012163 4012171
4012193 4012199 4012207 4012213 4012241 4012247 4012271 4012273 4012297 4012321
4012339 4012367 4012369 4012381 4012441 4012451 4012457 4012483 4012487 4012499
4012507 4012537 4012549 4012573 4012601 4012621 4012627 4012633 4012639 4012669
4012681 4012703 4012709 4012721 4012747 4012769 4012783 4012829 4012837 4012841
4012861 4012871 4012873 4012927 4012949 4012993 4012997 4012999 4013021 4013027
4013059 4013089 4013111 4013153 4013159 4013179 4013183 4013197 4013209 4013227
4013267 4013287 4013297 4013323 4013329 4013363 4013369 4013407 4013419 4013423
4013441 4013461 4013473 4013497 4013507 4013519 4013521 4013543 4013557 4013561
4013563 4013567 4013573 4013591 4013621 4013623 4013641 4013651 4013671 4013699
4013729 4013761 4013783 4013827 4013837 4013851 4013857 4013881 4013897 4013909
4013917 4013929 4013939 4013951 4013953 4013981 4013987 4013993 4014001 4014011
4014047 4014053 4014071 4014113 4014133 4014137 4014139 4014161 4014163 4014173
4014191 4014203 4014211 4014217 4014229 4014239 4014251 4014271 4014277 4014281
4014289 4014293 4014313 4014331 4014347 4014391 4014401 4014403 4014421 4014449
4014457 4014467 4014473 4014497 4014503 4014559 4014587 4014607 4014617 4014623
4014653 4014667 4014671 4014683 4014691 4014709 4014713 4014721 4014739 4014743
4014749 4014763 4014767 4014809 4014817 4014821 4014827 4014863 4014877 4014887
4014889 4014893 4014929 4014931 4014937 4014971 4014973 4014977 4015013 4015031
4015049 4015051 4015117 4015139 4015147 4015159 4015169 4015177 4015183
4015189 4015199 4015201 4015237 4015259 4015267 4015273 4015279 4015283 4015303
4015307 4015309 4015313 4015331 4015339 4015367 4015373 4015379 4015381 4015411
4015421 4015463 4015471 4015483 4015489 4015493 4015513 4015537 4015549 4015559
4015567 4015577 4015579 4015619 4015637 4015643 4015673 4015679 4015729 4015741
4015787 4015793 4015799 4015801 4015811 4015819 4015829 4015841 4015873 4015877
4015883 4015931 4015933 4015937 4015939 4015981 4015987 4015993 4016003 4016021
4016027 4016039 4016041 4016059 4016093 4016101 4016113 4016119 4016141 4016149
4016153 4016161 4016167 4016171 4016203 4016213 4016219 4016231 4016261 4016269
4016317 4016321 4016339 4016347 4016351 4016357 4016371 4016377 4016381 4016407
4016443 4016473 4016477 4016503 4016549 4016561 4016563 4016567 4016569 4016611
4016671 4016689 4016713 4016731 4016741 4016773 4016791 4016797 4016801 4016827
4016833 4016839 4016843 4016849 4016861 4016863 4016869 4016917 4016959 4016963
4016983 4017001 4017007 4017023 4017031 4017067 4017089 4017107 4017121 4017131
4017173 4017179 4017191 4017199 4017217 4017257 4017269 4017271 4017311 4017313
4017353 4017359 4017367 4017397 4017407 4017427 4017437 4017439 4017443 4017463
4017499 4017509 4017511 4017523 4017527 4017539 4017547 4017551 4017553 4017557
4017581 4017589 4017599 4017623 4017647 4017649 4017653 4017659 4017667 4017691
4017697 4017707 4017731 4017737 4017773 4017803 4017821 4017823 4017833 4017857
4017869 4017883 4017919 4017931 4017977 4017989 4017991 4017997 4018039 4018043
4018061 4018081 4018087 4018093 4018097 4018099 4018109 4018151 4018159 4018181
4018207 4018243 4018247 4018249 4018277 4018297 4018309 4018321 4018337 4018349
4018361 4018363 4018373 4018379 4018397 4018403 4018423 4018433 4018457 4018463
4018471 4018489 4018507 4018523 4018541 4018543 4018589 4018627 4018631 4018643
4018649 4018699 4018711 4018717 4018739 4018753 4018757 4018769 4018799 4018837
4018843 4018853 4018867 4018873 4018877 4018879 4018897 4018901 4018921 4018979
4018981 4019003 4019009 4019047 4019063 4019069 4019077 4019083 4019101 4019117
4019131 4019153 4019159 4019173 4019177 4019207 4019219 4019221 4019231 4019251
4019311 4019341 4019359 4019363 4019377 4019383 4019387 4019401 4019413 4019419
4019437 4019447 4019461 4019479 4019501 4019513 4019527 4019557 4019567 4019579
4019591 4019623 4019627 4019647 4019657 4019663 4019689 4019693 4019707 4019713
4019731 4019753 4019767 4019789 4019797 4019809 4019831 4019833 4019843 4019861
4019867 4019879 4019909 4019993 4020011 4020017 4020031 4020119 4020139 4020151
4020157 4020167 4020197 4020217 4020221 4020223 4020227 4020257 4020277 4020281
4020283 4020287 4020293 4020307 4020323 4020349 4020353 4020361 4020407 4020409
4020431 4020433 4020461 4020463 4020493 4020503 4020529 4020563 4020587 4020593
4020617 4020623 4020631 4020637 4020641 4020671 4020691 4020701 4020713 4020719
4020727 4020733 4020749 4020773 4020781 4020833 4020847 4020869 4020889 4020923
4020949 4020977 4021001 4021009 4021013 4021019 4021033 4021051 4021079 4021081
4021091 4021097 4021099 4021151 4021153 4021177 4021183 4021187 4021189 4021201
4021211 4021229 4021243 4021247 4021249 4021261 4021301 4021309 4021349 4021357
4021379 4021387 4021397 4021399 4021417 4021427 4021439 4021447 4021471
4021477 4021513 4021519 4021529 4021531 4021543 4021561 4021579 4021601 4021607
4021613 4021627 4021651 4021657 4021663 4021727 4021733 4021739 4021751 4021769
```

```
4021777  4021867  4021873  4021879  4021889  4021891  4021903  4021907  4021933  4021949
4021961  4021967  4021973  4022003  4022017  4022021  4022027  4022041  4022063  4022069
4022071  4022087  4022099  4022101  4022107  4022111  4022113  4022143  4022147  4022153
4022173  4022189  4022191  4022197  4022201  4022203  4022257  4022287  4022297  4022303
4022323  4022339  4022341  4022371  4022383  4022407  4022419  4022437  4022441  4022449
4022477  4022483  4022507  4022549  4022563  4022567  4022569  4022581  4022587  4022593
4022611  4022657  4022663  4022671  4022701  4022717  4022719  4022741  4022749  4022773
4022783  4022803  4022807  4022827  4022831  4022849  4022857  4022867  4022869  4022873
4022891  4022903  4022911  4022929  4022933  4022959  4022981  4023001  4023017
4023023  4023031  4023049  4023053  4023109  4023113  4023127  4023161  4023163  4023167
4023179  4023181  4023191  4023221  4023223  4023241  4023263  4023277  4023281  4023287
4023293  4023311  4023317  4023319  4023323  4023337  4023347  4023353  4023359  4023401
4023469  4023473  4023479  4023493  4023511  4023533  4023563  4023599  4023619  4023629
4023631  4023653  4023659  4023661  4023671  4023673  4023703  4023727  4023731  4023737
4023749  4023751  4023791  4023809  4023821  4023829  4023841  4023853  4023871  4023881
4023889  4023907  4023913  4023937  4023947  4023973  4023997  4024001  4024003  4024021
4024037  4024039  4024049  4024051  4024061  4024063  4024073  4024091  4024123  4024129
4024133  4024147  4024183  4024211  4024259  4024277  4024289  4024303  4024309
4024337  4024357  4024367  4024369  4024399  4024411  4024429  4024487  4024507  4024511
4024541  4024549  4024571  4024577  4024583  4024589  4024667  4024673  4024679  4024687
4024693  4024697  4024703  4024711  4024717  4024723  4024729  4024739  4024759  4024781
4024807  4024817  4024819  4024849  4024861  4024879  4024957  4024961  4024973  4024989
4025003  4025027  4025029  4025041  4025051  4025053  4025057  4025081  4025083  4025089
4025111  4025167  4025179  4025227  4025239  4025249  4025269  4025279  4025303  4025317
4025327  4025347  4025353  4025369  4025377  4025387  4025389  4025407  4025429  4025431
4025453  4025491  4025501  4025507  4025521  4025543  4025551  4025599  4025627
4025633  4025653  4025657  4025683  4025689  4025699  4025717  4025743  4025779  4025783
4025797  4025807  4025837  4025839  4025849  4025863  4025873  4025881  4025893  4025899
4025909  4025911  4025921  4025927  4025941  4025981  4025993  4025999  4026017  4026031
4026053  4026073  4026079  4026083  4026103  4026107  4026109  4026131  4026137  4026149
4026181  4026199  4026199  4026221  4026223  4026227  4026257  4026259  4026277  4026283
4026287  4026301  4026313  4026329  4026343  4026353  4026359  4026371  4026383  4026397
4026401  4026409  4026437  4026469  4026493  4026509  4026511  4026521  4026523  4026527
4026571  4026593  4026611  4026619  4026643  4026647  4026653  4026667  4026677  4026703
4026713  4026719  4026721  4026751  4026791  4026799  4026823  4026829  4026857  4026889
4026937  4026949  4026961  4026967  4026973  4026989  4027021  4027033  4027057  4027073
4027097  4027103  4027123  4027129  4027141  4027151  4027171  4027187  4027189  4027193
4027211  4027213  4027217  4027229  4027237  4027273  4027279  4027291  4027367  4027379
4027381  4027391  4027393  4027421  4027451  4027459  4027481  4027493  4027501  4027511
4027519  4027547  4027559  4027579  4027627  4027631  4027643  4027669  4027687  4027693
4027697  4027703  4027711  4027733  4027739  4027747  4027763  4027787  4027789  4027811
4027817  4027819  4027823  4027831  4027843  4027879  4027883  4027889  4027909  4027913
4027927  4027957  4027993  4028009  4028069  4028077  4028093  4028137  4028173  4028177
4028179  4028191  4028221  4028231  4028251  4028261  4028267  4028273  4028279  4028281
4028287  4028293  4028309  4028333  4028341  4028347  4028363  4028389  4028413  4028429
4028441  4028471  4028491  4028533  4028539  4028561  4028573  4028599  4028603  4028621
4028641  4028663  4028681  4028683  4028693  4028707  4028723  4028743  4028747  4028771
4028807  4028833  4028839  4028851  4028863  4028891  4028917  4028923  4028929  4028939
4028953  4028963  4028987  4028993  4029001  4029013  4029031  4029049  4029097  4029107
4029127  4029131  4029161  4029199  4029203  4029217  4029227  4029239  4029253  4029271
4029323  4029341  4029359  4029367  4029371  4029373  4029379  4029383  4029397  4029409
4029413  4029433  4029437  4029457  4029461  4029479  4029497  4029517  4029541  4029563
4029587  4029589  4029593  4029611  4029617  4029631  4029661  4029667  4029677  4029679
4029703  4029709  4029757  4029763  4029787  4029791  4029793  4029797  4029803  4029829
4029841  4029847  4029863  4029871  4029911  4029913  4029923  4029937  4029943  4029959
4029973  4029979  4030007  4030051  4030063  4030069  4030121  4030123  4030127  4030133
4030141  4030153  4030157  4030189  4030193  4030199  4030219  4030277  4030319  4030321
4030339  4030357  4030363  4030379  4030387  4030393  4030399  4030409  4030417  4030421
4030441  4030463  4030469  4030483  4030487  4030511  4030529  4030541  4030553  4030561
4030567  4030571  4030573  4030577  4030591  4030613  4030633  4030657  4030687  4030693
4030709  4030757  4030759  4030781  4030783  4030831  4030847  4030849  4030867  4030877
4030889  4030903  4030909  4030919  4030927  4030933  4030937  4030963  4030973  4030979
4030981  4030993  4031041  4031081  4031089  4031101  4031117  4031119  4031129  4031177
4031179  4031201  4031219  4031221  4031231  4031239  4031267  4031273  4031281  4031297
4031303  4031327  4031337  4031351  4031353  4031369  4031389  4031399  4031441  4031453
4031471  4031473  4031491  4031497  4031537  4031539  4031543  4031561  4031563  4031579
4031597  4031627  4031633  4031639  4031641  4031681  4031711  4031719  4031759  4031761
4031771  4031803  4031821  4031827  4031837  4031843  4031849  4031861  4031879  4031887
4031893  4031897  4031903  4031947  4031977  4031987  4032029  4032031  4032059  4032071
4032097  4032101  4032113  4032151  4032157  4032163  4032167  4032173  4032191  4032211
4032221  4032257  4032269  4032299  4032307  4032317  4032341  4032361  4032401  4032403
4032407  4032409  4032433  4032437  4032443  4032463  4032491  4032493  4032517  4032533
4032557  4032571  4032599  4032601  4032629  4032641  4032671  4032683  4032703  4032727
4032733  4032767  4032773  4032779  4032781  4032793  4032811  4032839  4032851  4032863
4032877  4032881  4032901  4032907  4032911  4032913  4032923  4032947  4032949  4032953
4032967  4032971  4032979  4032989  4032991  4033009  4033019  4033039  4033079  4033087
4033091  4033147  4033153  4033157  4033201  4033207  4033229  4033231  4033241  4033243
4033261  4033283  4033307  4033313  4033321  4033331  4033343  4033409  4033411  4033423
4033451  4033483  4033489  4033499  4033511  4033537  4033559  4033571  4033577  4033591
4033597  4033609  4033613  4033619  4033633  4033649  4033651  4033663  4033721  4033727
4033741  4033753  4033759  4033781  4033817  4033829  4033831  4033849  4033853  4033891
4033903  4033921  4033927  4033933  4033943  4033957  4033961  4033979  4034011  4034021
4034027  4034029  4034047  4034059  4034071  4034077  4034089  4034101  4034141  4034143
4034167  4034183  4034189  4034203  4034207  4034209  4034249  4034273  4034297  4034311
4034333  4034341  4034383  4034399  4034411  4034449  4034467  4034477  4034489
4034497  4034501  4034507  4034543  4034549  4034573  4034579  4034599  4034623  4034629
4034633  4034651  4034659  4034689  4034699  4034747  4034759  4034761  4034773  4034777
4034791  4034803  4034827  4034869  4034873  4034881  4034893  4034911  4034923  4034957
4034969  4034971  4034977  4034999  4035007  4035013  4035019  4035023  4035029  4035041
```

```
4035043  4035047  4035079  4035107  4035113  4035121  4035131  4035139  4035149  4035191
4035203  4035217  4035223  4035259  4035271  4035293  4035299  4035313  4035323  4035337
4035359  4035397  4035401  4035403  4035431  4035433  4035439  4035457  4035469  4035481
4035497  4035517  4035523  4035533  4035539  4035547  4035599  4035601  4035607  4035617
4035623  4035637  4035641  4035653  4035677  4035697  4035737  4035739  4035743  4035751
4035761  4035763  4035781  4035799  4035803  4035827  4035839  4035841  4035869  4035887
4035893  4035907  4035929  4035947  4035973  4035989  4036001  4036007  4036009  4036033
4036049  4036051  4036057  4036069  4036091  4036093  4036099  4036103  4036117  4036139
4036141  4036159  4036171  4036177  4036181  4036183  4036199  4036213  4036217  4036229
4036273  4036283  4036289  4036297  4036301  4036349  4036363  4036387  4036391  4036393
4036397  4036433  4036451  4036457  4036489  4036517  4036519  4036537  4036547  4036567
4036577  4036601  4036621  4036649  4036657  4036687  4036691  4036693  4036709  4036717
4036723  4036733  4036757  4036763  4036777  4036801  4036841  4036861  4036889  4036909
4036927  4036931  4036933  4036943  4036961  4036993  4036997  4036999  4037017  4037023
4037039  4037069  4037083  4037149  4037153  4037171  4037179  4037183  4037197  4037221
4037233  4037263  4037281  4037303  4037309  4037321  4037333  4037359  4037389  4037401
4037413  4037417  4037419  4037437  4037447  4037461  4037479  4037507  4037521  4037531
4037543  4037563  4037573  4037587  4037591  4037599  4037609  4037617  4037681  4037707
4037729  4037731  4037741  4037749  4037767  4037771  4037777  4037779  4037797  4037807
4037809  4037821  4037827  4037851  4037863  4037881  4037923  4037933  4037939  4037947
4037951  4037953  4037963  4037981  4037987  4038007  4038011  4038043  4038053  4038071
4038079  4038113  4038121  4038161  4038169  4038187  4038191  4038211  4038239  4038247
4038253  4038257  4038269  4038289  4038301  4038311  4038319  4038323  4038379  4038403
4038421  4038443  4038463  4038481  4038487  4038489  4038491  4038493  4038521
4038533  4038539  4038563  4038581  4038607  4038611  4038613  4038631  4038637  4038641
4038647  4038667  4038677  4038679  4038701  4038703  4038709  4038719  4038721  4038737
4038739  4038761  4038763  4038767  4038781  4038791  4038799  4038803  4038817  4038829
4038833  4038857  4038893  4038899  4038907  4038949  4038953  4038967  4038973  4038989
4038997  4039019  4039037  4039043  4039051  4039067  4039069  4039073  4039093  4039097
4039111  4039117  4039127  4039157  4039169  4039181  4039219  4039247  4039249  4039271
4039307  4039333  4039367  4039391  4039397  4039429  4039433  4039447  4039471  4039487
4039537  4039543  4039547  4039561  4039583  4039589  4039597  4039639  4039661  4039663
4039667  4039669  4039681  4039709  4039733  4039741  4039753  4039769  4039781  4039793
4039801  4039831  4039843  4039873  4039901  4039949  4039957  4039967  4039991  4040009
4040011  4040021  4040041  4040053  4040059  4040083  4040093  4040119  4040123  4040129
4040159  4040161  4040173  4040207  4040219  4040227  4040233  4040279  4040287  4040291
4040299  4040317  4040327  4040353  4040359  4040371  4040383  4040389  4040401  4040411
4040419  4040429  4040431  4040459  4040461  4040467  4040473  4040501  4040507  4040513
4040527  4040549  4040563  4040573  4040593  4040627  4040629  4040653  4040669  4040677
4040683  4040717  4040719  4040723  4040737  4040741  4040779  4040783  4040789  4040797
4040833  4040873  4040887  4040891  4040903  4040921  4040941  4040963  4040989  4041007
4041043  4041047  4041049  4041073  4041101  4041109  4041119  4041127  4041133  4041137
4041139  4041151  4041157  4041173  4041199  4041203  4041209  4041211  4041217  4041229
4041241  4041287  4041299  4041343  4041347  4041361  4041371  4041379  4041383  4041407
4041413  4041419  4041431  4041437  4041467  4041503  4041511  4041517  4041539  4041553
4041571  4041581  4041589  4041593  4041599  4041601  4041619  4041683  4041689  4041691
4041731  4041761  4041773  4041781  4041787  4041803  4041827  4041847  4041881  4041883
4041887  4041899  4041907  4041929  4041931  4041941  4041943  4041949  4041977  4041979
4042001  4042019  4042033  4042037  4042057  4042063  4042069  4042081  4042091  4042097
4042111  4042153  4042163  4042211  4042217  4042249  4042253  4042271  4042303  4042309
4042327  4042331  4042333  4042343  4042391  4042393  4042417  4042427  4042429  4042433
4042463  4042471  4042501  4042523  4042543  4042547  4042561  4042601  4042603  4042607
4042609  4042613  4042627  4042631  4042639  4042673  4042693  4042697  4042721  4042729
4042757  4042769  4042777  4042789  4042807  4042823  4042849  4042859  4042873  4042891
4042901  4042933  4042939  4042943  4042967  4042979  4042993  4043023  4043047  4043071
4043087  4043111  4043119  4043129  4043159  4043167  4043173  4043177  4043189  4043191
4043233  4043243  4043287  4043293  4043321  4043341  4043353  4043357  4043387  4043401
4043407  4043411  4043437  4043443  4043449  4043483  4043489  4043491  4043503  4043509
4043513  4043519  4043527  4043539  4043549  4043587  4043597  4043621  4043623  4043657
4043681  4043687  4043701  4043717  4043719  4043723  4043729  4043747  4043749  4043759
4043761  4043771  4043777  4043813  4043821  4043869  4043887  4043891  4043899  4043917
4043957  4043959  4043983  4043999  4044013  4044023  4044031  4044041  4044049  4044077
4044179  4044221  4044223  4044241  4044263  4044269  4044289  4044319  4044323  4044329
4044331  4044347  4044371  4044379  4044401  4044407  4044413  4044421  4044431  4044437
4044449  4044463  4044479  4044497  4044499  4044503  4044517  4044529  4044533  4044541
4044553  4044559  4044571  4044583  4044617  4044629  4044631  4044641  4044643  4044661
4044683  4044697  4044713  4044731  4044743  4044749  4044751  4044763  4044767  4044769
4044779  4044797  4044811  4044841  4044847  4044851  4044869  4044881  4044883  4044889
4044893  4044917  4044959  4044977  4044983  4045009  4045049  4045051  4045091  4045103
4045117  4045121  4045127  4045141  4045147  4045163  4045213  4045219  4045229  4045253
4045267  4045273  4045277  4045289  4045291  4045313  4045333  4045357  4045361  4045369
4045381  4045387  4045399  4045417  4045421  4045501  4045523  4045549  4045567  4045577
4045583  4045597  4045603  4045633  4045663  4045681  4045687  4045693  4045697  4045721
4045763  4045771  4045781  4045787  4045817  4045829  4045831  4045837  4045843  4045849
4045883  4045891  4045927  4045933  4045961  4045963  4045969  4045973  4045997  4046011
4046033  4046057  4046059  4046083  4046087  4046099  4046101  4046111  4046117  4046123
4046129  4046131  4046173  4046177  4046233  4046239  4046269  4046291  4046293  4046299
4046303  4046309  4046311  4046327  4046351  4046353  4046377  4046381  4046387  4046389
4046401  4046423  4046437  4046443  4046447  4046453  4046467  4046473  4046477  4046479
4046489  4046507  4046513  4046521  4046543  4046587  4046591  4046653  4046657  4046671
4046683  4046699  4046701  4046711  4046719  4046723  4046737  4046759  4046761  4046797
4046803  4046807  4046821  4046849  4046851  4046857  4046879  4046881  4046897  4046899
4046927  4046941  4046953  4046963  4046993  4047013  4047041  4047049  4047053
4047067  4047077  4047079  4047089  4047101  4047157  4047257  4047271  4047283  4047299
4047301  4047317  4047331  4047347  4047349  4047359  4047367  4047371  4047383  4047409
4047413  4047419  4047431  4047469  4047473  4047487  4047509  4047529  4047539  4047569
4047583  4047587  4047599  4047601  4047607  4047619  4047623  4047629  4047647  4047697
4047709  4047721  4047737  4047739  4047763  4047767  4047787  4047803  4047811  4047821
4047829  4047847  4047929  4047961  4047973  4047983  4047991  4047997  4048001  4048013
```

```
4048043  4048061  4048103  4048111  4048123  4048129  4048171  4048189  4048199  4048211
4048223  4048229  4048241  4048243  4048249  4048267  4048271  4048277  4048283  4048307
4048309  4048339  4048393  4048417  4048433  4048441  4048453  4048459  4048477  4048481
4048519  4048523  4048531  4048537  4048549  4048553  4048573  4048589  4048613  4048619
4048637  4048643  4048673  4048679  4048687  4048697  4048711  4048727  4048739  4048741
4048747  4048769  4048783  4048813  4048819  4048831  4048853  4048859  4048861  4048867
4048871  4048901  4048921  4048927  4048939  4048969  4048973  4048991  4049029  4049039
4049047  4049051  4049057  4049063  4049069  4049093  4049107  4049131  4049153  4049167
4049203  4049207  4049231  4049273  4049291  4049293  4049327  4049329  4049351  4049369
4049387  4049389  4049399  4049401  4049429  4049431  4049443  4049467  4049471  4049483
4049497  4049533  4049537  4049543  4049569  4049579  4049593  4049609  4049707  4049711
4049743  4049753  4049759  4049789  4049803  4049813  4049827  4049833  4049873
4049887  4049891  4049897  4049921  4049923  4049953  4049959  4049977  4049987  4049989
4050019  4050023  4050031  4050049  4050071  4050077  4050089  4050121  4050133  4050149
4050161  4050187  4050191  4050197  4050209  4050223  4050229  4050253  4050281  4050283
4050289  4050311  4050329  4050341  4050359  4050377  4050433  4050451  4050457  4050469
4050481  4050493  4050499  4050503  4050521  4050523  4050547  4050581  4050587  4050589
4050611  4050617  4050647  4050671  4050701  4050703  4050719  4050721  4050727  4050731
4050733  4050751  4050769  4050779  4050793  4050803  4050821  4050833  4050847  4050853
4050859  4050869  4050899  4050931  4050941  4050979  4050983  4050997  4051001  4051007
4051051  4051057  4051063  4051067  4051081  4051121  4051133  4051139  4051181  4051261
4051273  4051277  4051279  4051309  4051337  4051339  4051343  4051361  4051363  4051367
4051379  4051403  4051429  4051469  4051477  4051499  4051511  4051513  4051517  4051529
4051583  4051591  4051601  4051603  4051613  4051631  4051633  4051667  4051709  4051717
4051727  4051741  4051753  4051781  4051813  4051819  4051829  4051837  4051843  4051867
4051877  4051891  4051939  4051951  4051987  4051991  4052021  4052029  4052051  4052053
4052057  4052063  4052077  4052089  4052099  4052101  4052107  4052173  4052201  4052207
4052231  4052249  4052261  4052299  4052311  4052333  4052359  4052371  4052383  4052401
4052407  4052429  4052441  4052471  4052473  4052479  4052497  4052501  4052507  4052509
4052513  4052527  4052549  4052551  4052561  4052611  4052627  4052683  4052687  4052701
4052717  4052743  4052767  4052773  4052777  4052791  4052801  4052803  4052813  4052821
4052849  4052911  4052921  4052927  4052929  4052933  4052941  4052957  4052959  4052969
4052977  4052989  4052999  4053001  4053019  4053041  4053059  4053067  4053079  4053103
4053107  4053113  4053121  4053131  4053163  4053173  4053187  4053229  4053311
4053317  4053323  4053331  4053349  4053367  4053373  4053397  4053407  4053437  4053443
4053449  4053457  4053473  4053503  4053523  4053527  4053541  4053551  4053557  4053559
4053571  4053587  4053607  4053611  4053613  4053641  4053659  4053671  4053689  4053691
4053697  4053719  4053737  4053743  4053761  4053779  4053781  4053787  4053799  4053851
4053869  4053919  4053923  4053941  4053947  4053953  4053961  4053971  4053983  4053989
4053991  4054009  4054019  4054031  4054033  4054069  4054091  4054093  4054111  4054117
4054139  4054147  4054151  4054159  4054207  4054231  4054247  4054261  4054283  4054291
4054321  4054331  4054387  4054411  4054451  4054481  4054489  4054499  4054537  4054559
4054591  4054607  4054621  4054627  4054667  4054669  4054681  4054709  4054711  4054723
4054727  4054741  4054753  4054759  4054763  4054807  4054811  4054837  4054873  4054879
4054889  4054913  4054933  4054949  4054957  4054987  4054997  4055021  4055033  4055053
4055057  4055071  4055087  4055137  4055143  4055147  4055159  4055167  4055179  4055221
4055257  4055267  4055281  4055321  4055329  4055347  4055353  4055357  4055371  4055377
4055393  4055399  4055423  4055431  4055461  4055477  4055497  4055539  4055543  4055549
4055551  4055561  4055573  4055581  4055593  4055599  4055627  4055633  4055647  4055651
4055657  4055669  4055671  4055687  4055747  4055767  4055773  4055791  4055801  4055833
4055839  4055851  4055893  4055897  4055899  4055917  4055923  4055927  4055957  4055963
4055983  4055993  4056023  4056067  4056077  4056079  4056109  4056121  4056131  4056137
4056161  4056179  4056193  4056209  4056229  4056287  4056359  4056379  4056383  4056389
4056407  4056419  4056431  4056457  4056467  4056473  4056509  4056517  4056527  4056529
4056539  4056553  4056583  4056589  4056601  4056623  4056641  4056697  4056719  4056721
4056733  4056737  4056739  4056743  4056751  4056769  4056803  4056847  4056851
4056853  4056859  4056883  4056893  4056919  4056967  4056971  4056977  4056979  4056989
4057019  4057021  4057043  4057061  4057091  4057111  4057117  4057139  4057147
4057159  4057199  4057211  4057213  4057217  4057231  4057247  4057297  4057321  4057331
4057343  4057349  4057357  4057379  4057381  4057397  4057409  4057423  4057451  4057511
4057513  4057553  4057561  4057567  4057589  4057597  4057601  4057631  4057633  4057639
4057649  4057657  4057661  4057663  4057667  4057673  4057681  4057687  4057693  4057699
4057723  4057727  4057759  4057769  4057783  4057789  4057799  4057823  4057829  4057841
4057847  4057853  4057861  4057871  4057873  4057897  4057909  4057927  4057939  4057967
4057969  4058011  4058017  4058029  4058059  4058063  4058071  4058081  4058083  4058099
4058101  4058107  4058111  4058113  4058137  4058141  4058149  4058167  4058209  4058227
4058237  4058251  4058261  4058273  4058279  4058317  4058321  4058333  4058339  4058357
4058363  4058371  4058387  4058389  4058399  4058401  4058423  4058429  4058443  4058449
4058471  4058473  4058477  4058479  4058501  4058519  4058543  4058569  4058599  4058629
4058633  4058683  4058693  4058701  4058731  4058749  4058777  4058797  4058809  4058819
4058839  4058849  4058863  4058869  4058887  4058891  4058903  4058907  4058917  4058933
4058947  4058953  4058963  4058969  4058981  4059037  4059049  4059059  4059067  4059079
4059113  4059119  4059131  4059149  4059161  4059169  4059191  4059193  4059197  4059199
4059203  4059221  4059227  4059229  4059271  4059313  4059317  4059337  4059347  4059361
4059371  4059389  4059397  4059403  4059439  4059443  4059499  4059509  4059511  4059527
4059563  4059571  4059581  4059593  4059599  4059619  4059637  4059647  4059659  4059683
4059761  4059763  4059817  4059823  4059827  4059833  4059871  4059877  4059883  4059919
4059949  4059953  4060009  4060019  4060037  4060061  4060073  4060109  4060117
4060123  4060139  4060151  4060159  4060181  4060207  4060211  4060219  4060237  4060249
4060253  4060289  4060291  4060313  4060337  4060339  4060369  4060379  4060387  4060391
4060403  4060409  4060423  4060481  4060487  4060531  4060579  4060583  4060591  4060601
4060613  4060631  4060633  4060643  4060663  4060691  4060717  4060729  4060741  4060747
4060751  4060759  4060769  4060789  4060799  4060801  4060853  4060867  4060871  4060873
4060879  4060883  4060891  4060897  4060933  4060951  4060967  4060999  4061017  4061021
4061023  4061027  4061033  4061047  4061051  4061059  4061077  4061081  4061137  4061143
4061149  4061177  4061191  4061203  4061207  4061227  4061237  4061243  4061251  4061261
4061263  4061329  4061347  4061353  4061377  4061381  4061401  4061429  4061461  4061467
4061483  4061489  4061543  4061557  4061567  4061569  4061579  4061581  4061609  4061621
4061633  4061641  4061663  4061669  4061671  4061677  4061699  4061767  4061791  4061803
```

```
4061809  4061833  4061843  4061857  4061873  4061887  4061903  4061921  4061923  4061927
4061951  4061957  4061969  4061977  4061983  4061987  4061999  4062013  4062077  4062083
4062089  4062127  4062131  4062139  4062151  4062161  4062197  4062203  4062221  4062241
4062251  4062281  4062287  4062301  4062307  4062319  4062347  4062361  4062413  4062419
4062431  4062451  4062491  4062493  4062521  4062533  4062547  4062551  4062557  4062571
4062577  4062587  4062589  4062607  4062613  4062623  4062631  4062659  4062671  4062673
4062701  4062749  4062781  4062787  4062791  4062797  4062809  4062811  4062823  4062841
4062853  4062869  4062889  4062893  4062911  4062923  4062931  4062959  4062967  4062991
4063013  4063021  4063061  4063063  4063067  4063091  4063097  4063123  4063127  4063133
4063159  4063177  4063181  4063183  4063211  4063217  4063237  4063273  4063307  4063309
4063327  4063337  4063363  4063369  4063373  4063403  4063417  4063421  4063429  4063441
4063447  4063471  4063487  4063513  4063517  4063537  4063547  4063559  4063583  4063589
4063601  4063603  4063627  4063643  4063693  4063699  4063711  4063721  4063723  4063733
4063757  4063781  4063793  4063841  4063859  4063877  4063889  4063897  4063909  4063919
4063931  4063951  4063957  4063963  4063991  4064023  4064033  4064051  4064083  4064107
4064113  4064141  4064143  4064149  4064161  4064167  4064171  4064183  4064189  4064197
4064209  4064213  4064227  4064237  4064247  4064299  4064311  4064323  4064327  4064329
4064351  4064383  4064393  4064407  4064447  4064477  4064509  4064519  4064529  4064531
4064539  4064549  4064579  4064597  4064603  4064633  4064639  4064649  4064659  4064663
4064681  4064693  4064707  4064741  4064831  4064839  4064849  4064861  4064873
4064881  4064899  4064909  4064933  4064971  4065001  4065007  4065013  4065029  4065059
4065073  4065097  4065119  4065137  4065157  4065161  4065179  4065197  4065199  4065203
4065209  4065211  4065241  4065283  4065287  4065289  4065293  4065317  4065331  4065361
4065377  4065379  4065403  4065409  4065427  4065461  4065463  4065469  4065473  4065491
4065517  4065527  4065541  4065569  4065571  4065583  4065587  4065599  4065613  4065637
4065653  4065661  4065667  4065697  4065701  4065727  4065731  4065751  4065757  4065767
4065773  4065781  4065821  4065823  4065857  4065877  4065913  4065937  4065947  4065953
4065973  4065979  4065983  4065989  4066021  4066031  4066033  4066039  4066063  4066067
4066121  4066129  4066141  4066151  4066187  4066219  4066229  4066259  4066261  4066267
4066273  4066289  4066313  4066327  4066333  4066357  4066369  4066379  4066441  4066453
4066507  4066523  4066537  4066567  4066577  4066591  4066597  4066609  4066613  4066619
4066661  4066669  4066679  4066691  4066709  4066721  4066729  4066747  4066759  4066789
4066801  4066807  4066823  4066847  4066861  4066871  4066877  4066879  4066891  4066901
4066943  4066949  4066981  4066987  4066991  4067009  4067027  4067039  4067071  4067081
4067087  4067099  4067123  4067137  4067143  4067149  4067171  4067179  4067201  4067207
4067213  4067227  4067237  4067243  4067257  4067263  4067291  4067303  4067309  4067321
4067363  4067381  4067407  4067411  4067423  4067467  4067477  4067489  4067509  4067513
4067543  4067561  4067579  4067587  4067593  4067597  4067599  4067611  4067617  4067621
4067629  4067639  4067647  4067677  4067699  4067717  4067731  4067737  4067741  4067753
4067797  4067813  4067827  4067831  4067837  4067857  4067863  4067893  4067939  4067951
4067963  4067971  4067981  4067983  4068011  4068017  4068023  4068041  4068047  4068073
4068107  4068131  4068137  4068139  4068203  4068241  4068257  4068269  4068271
4068283  4068301  4068313  4068319  4068329  4068331  4068343  4068349  4068353  4068373
4068419  4068433  4068443  4068469  4068473  4068479  4068487  4068503  4068511  4068529
4068541  4068563  4068569  4068587  4068607  4068611  4068619  4068653  4068667  4068683
4068697  4068707  4068731  4068733  4068739  4068749  4068751  4068811  4068823  4068833
4068839  4068847  4068851  4068871  4068877  4068887  4068893  4068913  4068923  4068943
4068949  4068959  4068973  4068979  4069003  4069027  4069033  4069049  4069063
4069073  4069099  4069139  4069157  4069159  4069187  4069199  4069201  4069217  4069237
4069267  4069271  4069279  4069301  4069327  4069333  4069343  4069349  4069381  4069397
4069421  4069433  4069451  4069487  4069489  4069501  4069523  4069529  4069543  4069567
4069603  4069609  4069627  4069651  4069661  4069679  4069687  4069693  4069699  4069717
4069721  4069727  4069729  4069753  4069757  4069771  4069787  4069819  4069831  4069837
4069847  4069861  4069889  4069913  4069937  4069991  4070051  4070069  4070093  4070113
4070117  4070119  4070137  4070167  4070197  4070201  4070203  4070219  4070221  4070243
4070267  4070303  4070309  4070321  4070323  4070329  4070371  4070377  4070383  4070399
4070431  4070447  4070459  4070483  4070489  4070519  4070533  4070537  4070543
4070557  4070567  4070621  4070653  4070669  4070683  4070687  4070711  4070723  4070741
4070749  4070761  4070789  4070797  4070813  4070819  4070821  4070831  4070861  4070867
4070873  4070879  4070903  4070909  4070923  4070947  4070953  4070971  4070981  4071017
4071019  4071031  4071037  4071043  4071047  4071061  4071071  4071077  4071097  4071157
4071181  4071217  4071227  4071241  4071257  4071271  4071289  4071307  4071317  4071329
4071337  4071359  4071371  4071373  4071383  4071401  4071421  4071427  4071431  4071439
4071451  4071467  4071479  4071497  4071511  4071527  4071533  4071539  4071553  4071559
4071569  4071589  4071593  4071601  4071647  4071659  4071679  4071701  4071703  4071733
4071761  4071763  4071793  4071827  4071829  4071869  4071877  4071917  4071931  4071941
4071953  4071967  4071983  4072007  4072009  4072039  4072049  4072073  4072091  4072097
4072139  4072147  4072171  4072207  4072223  4072249  4072259  4072291  4072293  4072297
4072301  4072309  4072337  4072399  4072417  4072427  4072433  4072447  4072457  4072459
4072463  4072477  4072483  4072507  4072513  4072531  4072559  4072577  4072583  4072593
4072609  4072613  4072619  4072637  4072661  4072667  4072697  4072699  4072709  4072721
4072751  4072753  4072793  4072801  4072807  4072813  4072819  4072837  4072841  4072853
4072867  4072883  4072903  4072919  4072927  4072931  4072949  4072951  4072961  4072967
4072987  4073009  4073023  4073029  4073033  4073039  4073053  4073077  4073101  4073107
4073123  4073129  4073143  4073159  4073171  4073177  4073191  4073197  4073203  4073233
4073243  4073249  4073257  4073287  4073291  4073339  4073351  4073359  4073371  4073411
4073413  4073423  4073437  4073449  4073453  4073491  4073497  4073501  4073513  4073521
4073551  4073561  4073567  4073569  4073593  4073609  4073621  4073627  4073677  4073683
4073687  4073689  4073701  4073711  4073731  4073747  4073749  4073791  4073807  4073821
4073831  4073837  4073851  4073873  4073879  4073887  4073893  4073899  4073917  4073929
4073933  4073939  4073941  4073957  4073963  4073983  4074011  4074023  4074041  4074043
4074053  4074061  4074071  4074073  4074089  4074137  4074143  4074149  4074167  4074173
4074209  4074241  4074247  4074253  4074263  4074277  4074281  4074313  4074319  4074347
4074353  4074377  4074409  4074419  4074437  4074439  4074443  4074449  4074451  4074461
4074463  4074487  4074523  4074527  4074533  4074557  4074559  4074589  4074593  4074601
4074613  4074647  4074649  4074677  4074689  4074701  4074709  4074731  4074743  4074757
4074767  4074769  4074793  4074817  4074823  4074839  4074869  4074871  4074901  4074929
4074943  4074977  4074991  4075003  4075021  4075039  4075073  4075091  4075103  4075111
4075129  4075133  4075147  4075171  4075193  4075199  4075207  4075213  4075219  4075231
```

4075241	4075243	4075271	4075289	4075297	4075319	4075327	4075369	4075391	4075397
4075429	4075433	4075447	4075459	4075469	4075493	4075499	4075507	4075537	4075559
4075567	4075579	4075609	4075627	4075637	4075657	4075679	4075693	4075717	4075723
4075741	4075759	4075771	4075817	4075831	4075871	4075879	4075889	4075891	4075909
4075913	4075919	4075931	4075963	4075987	4075993	4076003	4076021	4076027	4076063
4076069	4076077	4076087	4076113	4076123	4076143	4076167	4076183	4076197	4076201
4076207	4076227	4076257	4076287	4076291	4076299	4076333	4076339	4076351	4076363
4076377	4076381	4076383	4076411	4076417	4076419	4076441	4076459	4076473	4076477
4076483	4076489	4076537	4076557	4076563	4076587	4076591	4076599	4076627	4076629
4076641	4076647	4076713	4076729	4076741	4076759	4076777	4076783	4076803	4076833
4076837	4076857	4076861	4076867	4076869	4076879	4076881	4076951	4076981	4076987
4077011	4077013	4077037	4077041	4077061	4077079	4077097	4077103	4077121	4077137
4077149	4077167	4077169	4077211	4077221	4077223	4077239	4077247	4077253	4077259
4077299	4077319	4077323	4077341	4077347	4077349	4077361	4077373	4077397	4077407
4077413	4077421	4077439	4077443	4077473	4077481	4077497	4077499	4077527	4077529
4077547	4077551	4077559	4077583	4077607	4077611	4077617	4077629	4077631	4077643
4077649	4077653	4077677	4077701	4077751	4077757	4077763	4077779	4077781	4077817
4077823	4077847	4077859	4077863	4077869	4077883	4077917	4077919	4077929	4077947
4077949	4077967	4077971	4078003	4078013	4078031	4078043	4078073	4078099	4078117
4078133	4078159	4078187	4078201	4078211	4078213	4078219	4078231	4078253	4078259
4078273	4078301	4078339	4078343	4078363	4078367	4078387	4078397	4078409	4078411
4078439	4078441	4078457	4078469	4078489	4078511	4078513	4078523	4078561	4078573
4078579	4078601	4078609	4078619	4078631	4078637	4078649	4078651	4078663	4078667
4078687	4078693	4078699	4078709	4078717	4078741	4078747	4078757	4078771	4078777
4078783	4078799	4078807	4078817	4078819	4078829	4078831	4078871	4078883	4078891
4078897	4078951	4078969	4078993	4078999	4079003	4079029	4079041	4079059	4079071
4079081	4079123	4079143	4079159	4079191	4079203	4079219	4079221	4079237	4079261
4079267	4079297	4079347	4079353	4079359	4079381	4079399	4079419	4079423	4079431
4079477	4079479	4079483	4079489	4079519	4079527	4079531	4079557	4079573	4079617
4079629	4079641	4079651	4079653	4079669	4079683	4079687	4079689	4079701	4079707
4079729	4079753	4079759	4079767	4079771	4079783	4079819	4079821	4079837	4079857
4079861	4079891	4079893	4079963	4079987	4079989	4080001	4080007	4080029	4080047
4080049	4080071	4080077	4080103	4080121	4080133	4080137	4080143	4080149	4080151
4080161	4080163	4080191	4080199	4080217	4080239	4080253	4080259	4080281	4080287
4080301	4080331	4080341	4080347	4080359	4080403	4080409	4080413	4080431	4080449
4080451	4080457	4080463	4080469	4080509	4080511	4080533	4080539	4080541	4080547
4080589	4080613	4080647	4080679	4080691	4080707	4080719	4080737	4080749	4080751
4080761	4080787	4080803	4080827	4080847	4080859	4080889	4080907	4080911	4080931
4080941	4080943	4080993	4080997	4081013	4081039	4081073	4081079	4081099	4081111
4081153	4081157	4081163	4081177	4081183	4081201	4081213	4081229	4081261	4081271
4081283	4081303	4081307	4081331	4081351	4081361	4081381	4081387	4081393	
4081397	4081421	4081423	4081453	4081459	4081463	4081481	4081487	4081501	4081541
4081543	4081549	4081579	4081601	4081607	4081613	4081657	4081661	4081669	4081703
4081711	4081733	4081747	4081771	4081793	4081799	4081811	4081813	4081849	4081867
4081871	4081897	4081933	4081949	4081963	4081969	4081991	4081999	4082021	4082027
4082041	4082053	4082101	4082107	4082123	4082147	4082171	4082237	4082249	4082251
4082257	4082311	4082327	4082333	4082347	4082357	4082389	4082401	4082413	4082423
4082447	4082479	4082489	4082513	4082527	4082531	4082539	4082563	4082579	4082599
4082609	4082629	4082651	4082681	4082693	4082711	4082719	4082747	4082759	4082761
4082783	4082789	4082797	4082809	4082831	4082849	4082857	4082879	4082909	4082921
4082933	4082971	4082989	4082993	4083059	4083071	4083073	4083083	4083089	4083097
4083137	4083143	4083161	4083199	4083203	4083223	4083239	4083241	4083251	4083253
4083269	4083307	4083341	4083361	4083371	4083377	4083379	4083419	4083421	4083427
4083437	4083463	4083479	4083487	4083509	4083511	4083533	4083539	4083551	4083557
4083571	4083619	4083631	4083637	4083659	4083671	4083691	4083697	4083701	4083721
4083731	4083749	4083763	4083769	4083787	4083817	4083829	4083853	4083881	4083883
4083899	4083901	4083907	4083913	4083931	4083953	4083979	4083997	4084001	4084019
4084027	4084037	4084049	4084057	4084061	4084079	4084081	4084109	4084139	4084141
4084147	4084163	4084169	4084177	4084207	4084211	4084217	4084229	4084231	4084247
4084261	4084279	4084303	4084307	4084313	4084349	4084391	4084397	4084427	4084439
4084517	4084519	4084567	4084571	4084589	4084603	4084609	4084631	4084637	4084643
4084651	4084667	4084687	4084693	4084697	4084721	4084739	4084741	4084757	4084771
4084799	4084807	4084823	4084889	4084891	4084907	4084909	4084931	4084937	4084991
4084999	4085033	4085041	4085047	4085051	4085069	4085089	4085111	4085113	4085119
4085167	4085173	4085183	4085239	4085243	4085261	4085267	4085309	4085311	4085339
4085357	4085359	4085369	4085371	4085377	4085383	4085401	4085407	4085413	4085447
4085453	4085489	4085507	4085519	4085531	4085537	4085539	4085561	4085563	4085567
4085579	4085603	4085623	4085629	4085633	4085639	4085657	4085659	4085669	4085677
4085687	4085693	4085699	4085747	4085749	4085761	4085771	4085777	4085791	4085803
4085819	4085827	4085849	4085857	4085891	4085923	4085941	4085951	4085953	4085957
4085981	4085987	4085993	4086011	4086023	4086031	4086041	4086053	4086059	4086073
4086091	4086097	4086109	4086119	4086143	4086149	4086151	4086167	4086179	4086217
4086241	4086253	4086287	4086289	4086293	4086337	4086343	4086363	4086373	4086377
4086403	4086413	4086421	4086427	4086431	4086449	4086457	4086473	4086481	4086491
4086493	4086499	4086521	4086527	4086559	4086569	4086611	4086631		
4086673	4086679	4086683	4086713	4086721	4086743	4086751	4086773	4086781	4086809
4086811	4086821	4086829	4086833	4086853	4086877	4086889	4086911	4086913	4086923
4086949	4086967	4086997	4087001	4087007	4087019	4087037	4087093	4087141	4087151
4087163	4087177	4087189	4087199	4087207	4087211	4087229	4087253	4087267	
4087271	4087273	4087277	4087297	4087301	4087333	4087351	4087357	4087373	4087379
4087397	4087403	4087423	4087439	4087453	4087477	4087487	4087513	4087597	
4087607	4087613	4087619	4087621	4087627	4087631	4087639	4087661	4087663	4087673
4087711	4087729	4087739	4087747	4087751	4087757	4087771	4087801	4087807	4087829
4087843	4087847	4087873	4087883	4087891	4087901	4087913	4087931	4087949	4087957
4087969	4087991	4088009	4088011	4088017	4088027	4088039	4088087	4088111	
4088137	4088141	4088153	4088179	4088191	4088197	4088209	4088213	4088221	4088237
4088239	4088267	4088299	4088309	4088317	4088321	4088323	4088339	4088351	4088353
4088377	4088387	4088417	4088423	4088431	4088443	4088467	4088471	4088521	4088527
4088533	4088543	4088563	4088587	4088593	4088599	4088633	4088639	4088659	4088713

```
4088723 4088731 4088761 4088767 4088771 4088801 4088813 4088839 4088849 4088863
4088867 4088873 4088879 4088893 4088899 4088911 4088923 4088941 4088947 4088957
4088977 4089011 4089017 4089037 4089073 4089079 4089083 4089089 4089097 4089133
4089139 4089143 4089149 4089157 4089167 4089191 4089209 4089221 4089227 4089259
4089263 4089269 4089271 4089287 4089289 4089307 4089311 4089341 4089347 4089413
4089431 4089439 4089473 4089509 4089521 4089559 4089563 4089581 4089599 4089619
4089643 4089677 4089697 4089713 4089719 4089763 4089779 4089823 4089829 4089847
4089853 4089871 4089887 4089889 4089907 4089937 4089947 4089949 4089973 4090001
4090003 4090019 4090033 4090049 4090061 4090069 4090103 4090127 4090129 4090133
4090139 4090147 4090153 4090193 4090223 4090237 4090241 4090243 4090253 4090259
4090267 4090279 4090309 4090349 4090379 4090397 4090403 4090423 4090433 4090441
4090451 4090507 4090511 4090519 4090531 4090553 4090561 4090577 4090579 4090589
4090637 4090649 4090651 4090663 4090673 4090679 4090703 4090733 4090747 4090753
4090763 4090777 4090787 4090789 4090799 4090813 4090837 4090841 4090859 4090861
4090901 4090903 4090907 4090913 4090921 4090937 4090967 4090969 4090973 4090991
4090997 4091011 4091047 4091069 4091071 4091081 4091083 4091161 4091177 4091239
4091249 4091257 4091273 4091279 4091281 4091293 4091299 4091317 4091323 4091357
4091369 4091371 4091383 4091393 4091459 4091471 4091537 4091561 4091569 4091587
4091599 4091603 4091609 4091621 4091627 4091657 4091663 4091671 4091693 4091729
4091741 4091749 4091753 4091767 4091771 4091777 4091797 4091809 4091831 4091833
4091863 4091873 4091909 4091911 4091921 4091933 4091947 4091957 4091959 4091993
4092007 4092013 4092029 4092041 4092043 4092059 4092061 4092071 4092073 4092079
4092083 4092113 4092133 4092157 4092167 4092173 4092197 4092233 4092247 4092259
4092269 4092271 4092287 4092317 4092323 4092343 4092349 4092377 4092379 4092383
4092401 4092433 4092443 4092469 4092479 4092503 4092523 4092547 4092559 4092587
4092593 4092629 4092637 4092659 4092667 4092677 4092679 4092691 4092701 4092703
4092707 4092709 4092727 4092749 4092757 4092761 4092763 4092769 4092791 4092811
4092839 4092859 4092871 4092883 4092887 4092931 4092941 4092943 4092947 4092983
4092997 4093013 4093027 4093043 4093081 4093087 4093129 4093163 4093169 4093171
4093181 4093217 4093223 4093237 4093247 4093249 4093253 4093259 4093279 4093289
4093301 4093307 4093313 4093339 4093343 4093351 4093367 4093391 4093403 4093409
4093451 4093469 4093483 4093487 4093489 4093501 4093511 4093541 4093567 4093571
4093589 4093601 4093603 4093627 4093637 4093679 4093709 4093751 4093777 4093781
4093801 4093807 4093811 4093813 4093823 4093847 4093849 4093853 4093861 4093871
4093883 4093897 4093907 4093919 4093933 4093937 4093961 4093979 4093993 4094003
4094009 4094011 4094021 4094047 4094113 4094117 4094131 4094171 4094173 4094177
4094183 4094203 4094221 4094231 4094239 4094243 4094257 4094269 4094281 4094287
4094317 4094323 4094359 4094369 4094393 4094407 4094411 4094413 4094429 4094479
4094513 4094521 4094533 4094537 4094543 4094549 4094561 4094579 4094591 4094599
4094609 4094617 4094627 4094663 4094677 4094681 4094683 4094693 4094719 4094731
4094743 4094767 4094791 4094809 4094813 4094819 4094837 4094879 4094903 4094911
4094917 4094921 4094927 4094953 4094999 4095001 4095017 4095023 4095037 4095043
4095053 4095059 4095071 4095097 4095103 4095109 4095139 4095163 4095187 4095199
4095229 4095263 4095269 4095319 4095331 4095337 4095359 4095391 4095397 4095401
4095451 4095461 4095473 4095491 4095517 4095523 4095529 4095547 4095577 4095593
4095599 4095607 4095617 4095629 4095647 4095649 4095661 4095667 4095671 4095673
4095677 4095683 4095703 4095709 4095713 4095719 4095727 4095731 4095737 4095779
4095797 4095799 4095823 4095829 4095857 4095881 4095899 4095901 4095953 4095979
4095991 4096013 4096021 4096033 4096049 4096073 4096109 4096117 4096129 4096151
4096171 4096189 4096199 4096219 4096241 4096259 4096271 4096273 4096283 4096297
4096319 4096327 4096331 4096349 4096357 4096397 4096399 4096427 4096441 4096451
4096471 4096489 4096493 4096513 4096517 4096523 4096531 4096537 4096579 4096583
4096607 4096621 4096633 4096657 4096663 4096667 4096693 4096717 4096721 4096727
4096753 4096769 4096789 4096793 4096819 4096823 4096831 4096853 4096871 4096877
4096879 4096891 4096927 4096931 4096933 4096957 4096969 4096999 4097021 4097057
4097063 4097069 4097077 4097081 4097099 4097101 4097111 4097113 4097143 4097167
4097173 4097189 4097209 4097213 4097227 4097231 4097257 4097263 4097279 4097281
4097299 4097321 4097333 4097347 4097371 4097383 4097389 4097393 4097441 4097447
4097453 4097503 4097537 4097551 4097567 4097573 4097579 4097603 4097617 4097633
4097647 4097683 4097693 4097699 4097707 4097741 4097767 4097773 4097777 4097783
4097813 4097837 4097843 4097869 4097879 4097917 4097923 4097953 4097957 4097981
4097987 4098011 4098043 4098079 4098089 4098097 4098103 4098113 4098121 4098131
4098161 4098179 4098187 4098217 4098229 4098233 4098247 4098271 4098299 4098313
4098337 4098349 4098359 4098371 4098389 4098403 4098427 4098449 4098461 4098463
4098467 4098469 4098481 4098491 4098499 4098503 4098511 4098533 4098551 4098557
4098559 4098569 4098571 4098583 4098587 4098607 4098613 4098637 4098641 4098659
4098673 4098691 4098697 4098701 4098709 4098713 4098719 4098763 4098767 4098779
4098791 4098793 4098797 4098817 4098821 4098839 4098847 4098863 4098869 4098911
4098923 4098937 4098949 4098953 4098959 4098973 4099001 4099009 4099027 4099033
4099049 4099087 4099093 4099133 4099141 4099171 4099187 4099189 4099213 4099229
4099247 4099259 4099273 4099283 4099289 4099309 4099321 4099331 4099339 4099357
4099367 4099369 4099441 4099463 4099477 4099493 4099517 4099523 4099531 4099541
4099561 4099591 4099597 4099621 4099661 4099679 4099699 4099717 4099721 4099723
4099729 4099789 4099807 4099811 4099853 4099861 4099867 4099883 4099889 4099897
4099903 4099943 4099961 4099981 4100023 4100051 4100069 4100099 4100137
4100167 4100171 4100177 4100207 4100221 4100227 4100231 4100249 4100251 4100263
4100269 4100293 4100311 4100381 4100399 4100407 4100413 4100419 4100423 4100443
4100479 4100489 4100521 4100527 4100531 4100539 4100543 4100549 4100573 4100581
4100597 4100611 4100627 4100641 4100651 4100659 4100729 4100731 4100737 4100741
4100743 4100749 4100777 4100807 4100809 4100813 4100819 4100849 4100879 4100887
4100909 4100911 4100939 4100951 4100963 4100983 4101011 4101023 4101037 4101049
4101059 4101073 4101101 4101103 4101133 4101179 4101187 4101197 4101241 4101247
4101259 4101263 4101277 4101287 4101289 4101313 4101319 4101329 4101347 4101367
4101371 4101373 4101379 4101389 4101401 4101431 4101467 4101481 4101491 4101527
4101529 4101533 4101541 4101571 4101593 4101623 4101653 4101679 4101689 4101733
4101761 4101767 4101791 4101793 4101817 4101841 4101863 4101869 4101907 4101919
4101949 4101961 4101971 4101983 4101989 4101991 4102037 4102039 4102069 4102097
4102121 4102123 4102129 4102141 4102169 4102171 4102193 4102223 4102229 4102237
4102247 4102249 4102283 4102289 4102291 4102327 4102331 4102333 4102339 4102363
```

```
4102379 4102393 4102409 4102453 4102471 4102493 4102517 4102529 4102541 4102561
4102573 4102577 4102591 4102603 4102649 4102663 4102667 4102687 4102697 4102699
4102711 4102723 4102733 4102753 4102793 4102807 4102823 4102843 4102853 4102867
4102883 4102907 4102909 4102927 4102937 4102957 4102961 4102963 4102979 4102991
4102997 4102999 4103009 4103083 4103119 4103149 4103153 4103159 4103173 4103179
4103213 4103219 4103227 4103233 4103237 4103249 4103261 4103279 4103291 4103293
4103299 4103329 4103347 4103353 4103371 4103381 4103383 4103389 4103401 4103431
4103441 4103467 4103503 4103521 4103543 4103581 4103597 4103611 4103621 4103631
4103651 4103657 4103689 4103699 4103713 4103719 4103767 4103797 4103807
4103809 4103831 4103833 4103839 4103861 4103881 4103887 4103893 4103903 4103923
4103941 4103999 4104007 4104011 4104031 4104041 4104043 4104053 4104083 4104091
4104103 4104127 4104131 4104169 4104187 4104193 4104203 4104239 4104251 4104271
4104277 4104313 4104319 4104343 4104371 4104391 4104403 4104421 4104427 4104449
4104461 4104467 4104473 4104481 4104491 4104509 4104517 4104523 4104553 4104563
4104577 4104587 4104593 4104601 4104619 4104643 4104647 4104673 4104677 4104697
4104707 4104713 4104721 4104733 4104757 4104791 4104799 4104811 4104827 4104851
4104853 4104857 4104869 4104883 4104887 4104907 4104913 4104929 4104937 4104967
4104977 4105001 4105019 4105033 4105069 4105091 4105093 4105103 4105111 4105161
4105169 4105181 4105183 4105193 4105217 4105219 4105229 4105243 4105249 4105259
4105307 4105319 4105333 4105337 4105351 4105363 4105373 4105391 4105399 4105457
4105459 4105469 4105487 4105499 4105531 4105553 4105567 4105571 4105573 4105579
4105583 4105601 4105613 4105627 4105637 4105639 4105657 4105663 4105667 4105677
4105679 4105681 4105711 4105763 4105793 4105811 4105817 4105831 4105847 4105861
4105879 4105901 4105903 4105931 4105939 4105943 4105949 4105979 4105999 4106009
4106017 4106041 4106057 4106059 4106077 4106083 4106087 4106111 4106117 4106119
4106131 4106153 4106161 4106189 4106227 4106237 4106239 4106243 4106251 4106269
4106279 4106287 4106293 4106303 4106317 4106321 4106327 4106381 4106383 4106393
4106407 4106411 4106419 4106423 4106441 4106447 4106471 4106491 4106513 4106521
4106551 4106563 4106567 4106573 4106579 4106587 4106617 4106621 4106651 4106653
4106659 4106677 4106681 4106699 4106701 4106723 4106743 4106749 4106771 4106779
4106783 4106789 4106803 4106807 4106819 4106821 4106827 4106863 4106867 4106891
4106897 4106939 4106953 4106957 4106959 4106969 4106987 4107007 4107069 4107101
4107127 4107143 4107151 4107157 4107163 4107247 4107263 4107281 4107329 4107347
4107349 4107371 4107373 4107391 4107413 4107419 4107427 4107431 4107449 4107461
4107479 4107487 4107497 4107511 4107517 4107527 4107529 4107533 4107541 4107577
4107581 4107583 4107613 4107641 4107643 4107683 4107689 4107707 4107721 4107737
4107739 4107751 4107769 4107787 4107791 4107793 4107799 4107809 4107811 4107827
4107839 4107877 4107881 4107893 4107907 4107911 4107947 4107953 4107979 4107991
4107997 4108021 4108063 4108087 4108121 4108141 4108163 4108183 4108193 4108217
4108243 4108249 4108253 4108259 4108261 4108297 4108309 4108331 4108387 4108393
4108397 4108439 4108451 4108453 4108457 4108463 4108469 4108471 4108477 4108483
4108499 4108529 4108549 4108571 4108589 4108609 4108627 4108661 4108667 4108669
4108673 4108681 4108717 4108757 4108763 4108801 4108837 4108843 4108873 4108889
4108903 4108913 4108919 4108969 4108987 4108991 4108999 4109003
4109011 4109023 4109029 4109051 4109059 4109071 4109089 4109093 4109101 4109107
4109113 4109117 4109129 4109137 4109141 4109153 4109167 4109197 4109201 4109227
4109233 4109251 4109279 4109293 4109297 4109309 4109317 4109321 4109323 4109327
4109383 4109401 4109407 4109411 4109419 4109423 4109429 4109431 4109447 4109459
4109477 4109489 4109507 4109519 4109531 4109537 4109543 4109557 4109591 4109621
4109629 4109641 4109653 4109669 4109671 4109683 4109689 4109723 4109737 4109761
4109771 4109783 4109839 4109843 4109857 4109873 4109879 4109891 4109899 4109921
4109927 4109929 4109933 4109951 4109953 4109957 4109969 4110017 4110047 4110049
4110059 4110079 4110089 4110121 4110131 4110143 4110151 4110157 4110163 4110167
4110179 4110217 4110233 4110247 4110269 4110283 4110313 4110317 4110319 4110331
4110341 4110343 4110347 4110349 4110361 4110401 4110419 4110433 4110437 4110439
4110443 4110451 4110467 4110473 4110493 4110527 4110541 4110553 4110571 4110611
4110637 4110661 4110677 4110679 4110709 4110713 4110727 4110751 4110781 4110793
4110797 4110803 4110853 4110877 4110901 4110917 4110961 4110979
4110989 4111007 4111021 4111027 4111067 4111091 4111097 4111123 4111139 4111147
4111169 4111171 4111183 4111199 4111207 4111213 4111241 4111249 4111253 4111259
4111271 4111291 4111333 4111337 4111361 4111363 4111379 4111409 4111423 4111427
4111447 4111463 4111487 4111489 4111519 4111529 4111553 4111573 4111577 4111621
4111633 4111643 4111663 4111693 4111717 4111721 4111727 4111753 4111763 4111787
4111801 4111813 4111817 4111819 4111829 4111837 4111853 4111859 4111867 4111901
4111951 4111967 4111969 4111973 4111993 4112021 4112023 4112027 4112051 4112063
4112083 4112089 4112093 4112099 4112137 4112149 4112161 4112191 4112197 4112209
4112231 4112233 4112237 4112261 4112263 4112281 4112293 4112299 4112321 4112333
4112347 4112357 4112363 4112371 4112399 4112413 4112431 4112447 4112467 4112497
4112539 4112551 4112557 4112573 4112579 4112597 4112609 4112621 4112627 4112629
4112701 4112707 4112711 4112723 4112753 4112761 4112777 4112807 4112813 4112851
4112881 4112887 4112891 4112903 4112917 4112939 4112971 4112981 4112989 4113029
4113059 4113061 4113073 4113077 4113097 4113103 4113119 4113121 4113127 4113143
4113181 4113191 4113203 4113209 4113211 4113233 4113259 4113311 4113341 4113349
4113353 4113379 4113419 4113437 4113449 4113469 4113517 4113521 4113533 4113547
4113553 4113569 4113589 4113601 4113631 4113647 4113661 4113667 4113691 4113713
4113719 4113721 4113743 4113749 4113761 4113763 4113773 4113787 4113827 4113833
4113839 4113877 4113883 4113887 4113929 4113931 4113943 4113947 4113959 4113997
4114003 4114009 4114021 4114057 4114069 4114073 4114087 4114133 4114139 4114151
4114157 4114163 4114183 4114189 4114193 4114199 4114211 4114223 4114249 4114277
4114307 4114321 4114349 4114373 4114421 4114463 4114477 4114489 4114501 4114519
4114571 4114577 4114589 4114597 4114603 4114613 4114651 4114667 4114687 4114699
4114703 4114717 4114741 4114753 4114771 4114777 4114783 4114787 4114819 4114823
4114843 4114871 4114879 4114931 4114951 4114997 4115009 4115017 4115021
4115051 4115053 4115087 4115099 4115101 4115117 4115119 4115123 4115131 4115141
4115147 4115149 4115201 4115213 4115239 4115249 4115257 4115263 4115269 4115297
4115299 4115311 4115317 4115333 4115351 4115369 4115393 4115407 4115417 4115429
4115437 4115443 4115453 4115471 4115509 4115537 4115543 4115549 4115563 4115569
4115599 4115603 4115633 4115641 4115681 4115701 4115707 4115753 4115773 4115779
4115789 4115791 4115801 4115803 4115833 4115849 4115863 4115869 4115879 4115893
```

```
4115897  4115933  4115939  4115953  4115957  4115971  4115981  4115987  4116019  4116029
4116041  4116043  4116059  4116061  4116071  4116107  4116127  4116143  4116157  4116163
4116169  4116181  4116187  4116209  4116221  4116223  4116257  4116271  4116311  4116313
4116317  4116323  4116337  4116353  4116373  4116377  4116391  4116449  4116443  4116449
4116467  4116473  4116479  4116491  4116527  4116529  4116557  4116569  4116571  4116577
4116587  4116617  4116641  4116643  4116649  4116661  4116667  4116727  4116743  4116751
4116757  4116779  4116781  4116817  4116823  4116857  4116887  4116899  4116911  4116919
4116923  4116967  4116989  4116991  4116997  4117007  4117021  4117031  4117033  4117037
4117081  4117109  4117123  4117133  4117151  4117171  4117181  4117189  4117193  4117231
4117237  4117259  4117271  4117277  4117279  4117283  4117291  4117297  4117307  4117313
4117339  4117409  4117427  4117441  4117453  4117457  4117489  4117501  4117511  4117523
4117541  4117549  4117567  4117571  4117577  4117601  4117609  4117613  4117657  4117691
4117697  4117709  4117727  4117777  4117781  4117783  4117793  4117829  4117831  4117843
4117847  4117873  4117877  4117903  4117909  4117957  4117969  4117979  4117987  4117991
4118057  4118069  4118077  4118111  4118123  4118143  4118161  4118167  4118197  4118201
4118227  4118243  4118251  4118273  4118287  4118321  4118333  4118339  4118417  4118419
4118467  4118479  4118499  4118501  4118519  4118531  4118579  4118591  4118599  4118603
4118627  4118693  4118707  4118711  4118749  4118759  4118761  4118773  4118797  4118809
4118833  4118861  4118893  4118897  4118971  4118977  4118993  4119007  4119043  4119053
4119061  4119077  4119079  4119091  4119097  4119103  4119109  4119113  4119119  4119133
4119149  4119163  4119169  4119191  4119211  4119217  4119233  4119239  4119259  4119263
4119281  4119289  4119307  4119329  4119331  4119343  4119347  4119359  4119377  4119383
4119397  4119419  4119509  4119527  4119541  4119551  4119569  4119589  4119601  4119623
4119667  4119677  4119697  4119719  4119761  4119767  4119779  4119781  4119809  4119833
4119847  4119851  4119853  4119859  4119883  4119887  4119889  4119893  4119919  4119923
4119937  4119949  4119961  4119977  4119991  4120003  4120021  4120033  4120079  4120097
4120111  4120133  4120141  4120159  4120163  4120177  4120183  4120187  4120189  4120211
4120219  4120223  4120229  4120231  4120253  4120279  4120301  4120313  4120331  4120393
4120411  4120423  4120429  4120471  4120483  4120517  4120547  4120553  4120559  4120573
4120577  4120583  4120603  4120607  4120609  4120621  4120651  4120661  4120673  4120679
4120709  4120723  4120729  4120741  4120747  4120793  4120807  4120829  4120847  4120849
4120873  4120889  4120903  4120931  4120937  4120939  4120957  4120981  4120993  4120999
4121003  4121009  4121011  4121017  4121063  4121087  4121107  4121111  4121113  4121137
4121141  4121147  4121149  4121153  4121167  4121177  4121203  4121213  4121231  4121261
4121269  4121291  4121297  4121311  4121321  4121387  4121401  4121413  4121431  4121441
4121459  4121471  4121503  4121527  4121539  4121549  4121561  4121573  4121591  4121603
4121609  4121629  4121641  4121647  4121657  4121687  4121693  4121699  4121707  4121717
4121737  4121743  4121749  4121753  4121779  4121783  4121797  4121809  4121827  4121839
4121849  4121861  4121867  4121869  4121881  4121891  4121893  4121903  4121927  4121933
4121941  4121959  4121987  4122043  4122067  4122073  4122077  4122103  4122119  4122121
4122179  4122217  4122218  4122227  4122247  4122277  4122289  4122301  4122317  4122329
4122343  4122401  4122413  4122421  4122479  4122493  4122557  4122571  4122583  4122607
4122623  4122631  4122641  4122647  4122661  4122667  4122689  4122691  4122697  4122709
4122731  4122749  4122751  4122779  4122827  4122851  4122863  4122893  4122913  4122941
4122953  4122971  4122973  4122997  4123037  4123039  4123043  4123069  4123079  4123087
4123099  4123111  4123121  4123127  4123153  4123181  4123199  4123201  4123211  4123253
4123261  4123283  4123297  4123303  4123319  4123321  4123337  4123349  4123369  4123387
4123421  4123439  4123447  4123477  4123489  4123507  4123529  4123531  4123541  4123547
4123583  4123591  4123621  4123633  4123643  4123667  4123681  4123727  4123747  4123753
4123759  4123781  4123787  4123793  4123799  4123813  4123841  4123849  4123871  4123891
4123897  4123901  4123907  4123913  4123927  4123943  4123949  4123957  4123963  4123967
4123997  4124009  4124069  4124093  4124123  4124137  4124167  4124179  4124189  4124191
4124207  4124213  4124221  4124227  4124243  4124257  4124287  4124299  4124303  4124317
4124321  4124427  4124347  4124357  4124369  4124377  4124381  4124411  4124437  4124443
4124459  4124473  4124479  4124503  4124507  4124509  4124563  4124569  4124597  4124599
4124609  4124611  4124621  4124623  4124633  4124639  4124647  4124651  4124677  4124687
4124707  4124711  4124717  4124737  4124753  4124777  4124801  4124803  4124819  4124821
4124837  4124899  4124909  4124917  4124921  4124929  4124951  4124959  4124971  4124993
4125013  4125053  4125083  4125089  4125097  4125113  4125127  4125131  4125137  4125151
4125181  4125229  4125259  4125281  4125287  4125307  4125311  4125343  4125347  4125353
4125371  4125383  4125403  4125419  4125421  4125427  4125431  4125439  4125479  4125493
4125497  4125521  4125551  4125553  4125559  4125571  4125581  4125587  4125593  4125601
4125619  4125623  4125629  4125631  4125637  4125647  4125673  4125677  4125691  4125703
4125727  4125767  4125769  4125787  4125827  4125829  4125839  4125851  4125853  4125899
4125941  4125967  4125971  4125973  4125991  4126009  4126043  4126049  4126051  4126063
4126081  4126093  4126099  4126139  4126141  4126159  4126201  4126247  4126261  4126267
4126289  4126301  4126313  4126327  4126333  4126337  4126349  4126373  4126391  4126399
4126417  4126429  4126433  4126457  4126481  4126483  4126501  4126513  4126523  4126531
4126537  4126543  4126561  4126567  4126571  4126579  4126607  4126621  4126651  4126657
4126693  4126697  4126757  4126769  4126777  4126783  4126789  4126799  4126807  4126817
4126823  4126861  4126891  4126897  4126907  4126921  4126939  4126963  4126979  4126987
4127003  4127021  4127027  4127029  4127033  4127069  4127083  4127111  4127131  4127147
4127153  4127171  4127173  4127177  4127191  4127231  4127257  4127273  4127287  4127293
4127297  4127303  4127359  4127363  4127377  4127381  4127393  4127407  4127467  4127471
4127477  4127479  4127489  4127521  4127533  4127537  4127573  4127597  4127611  4127621
4127633  4127647  4127653  4127659  4127707  4127713  4127723  4127737  4127749  4127771
4127791  4127797  4127801  4127843  4127861  4127863  4127891  4127897  4127899  4127933
4127951  4127983  4127989  4127993  4127999  4128013  4128023  4128031  4128041  4128049
4128079  4128097  4128101  4128107  4128119  4128133  4128139  4128181  4128193  4128199
4128217  4128233  4128251  4128253  4128281  4128283  4128287  4128307  4128323  4128359
4128361  4128367  4128379  4128391  4128401  4128409  4128427  4128451  4128493  4128511
4128517  4128521  4128533  4128539  4128547  4128557  4128581  4128589  4128599  4128601
4128613  4128617  4128623  4128689  4128697  4128713  4128747  4128749  4128763  4128767
4128781  4128821  4128827  4128829  4128857  4128869  4128877  4128883  4128899  4128911
4128913  4128931  4128959  4128967  4129003  4129007  4129031  4129033  4129039  4129057
4129063  4129087  4129109  4129129  4129141  4129157  4129171  4129187  4129189  4129199
4129241  4129243  4129309  4129313  4129319  4129331  4129343  4129361  4129369  4129381
4129393  4129397  4129409  4129439  4129493  4129501  4129507  4129519  4129523  4129529
4129553  4129597  4129613  4129633  4129637  4129649  4129651  4129661  4129667  4129721
```

```
4129729  4129751  4129753  4129771  4129777  4129787  4129799  4129817  4129841  4129871
4129907  4129921  4129927  4129933  4129943  4129981  4129987  4130003  4130023  4130033
4130039  4130111  4130123  4130129  4130143  4130149  4130153  4130171  4130207  4130213
4130221  4130227  4130233  4130251  4130261  4130281  4130293  4130297  4130309  4130323
4130327  4130333  4130339  4130359  4130369  4130389  4130437  4130459  4130461  4130479
4130519  4130527  4130563  4130573  4130591  4130603  4130641  4130647  4130671  4130681
4130683  4130699  4130713  4130723  4130729  4130741  4130803  4130807  4130837  4130839
4130849  4130887  4130897  4130899  4130911  4130927  4130933  4130947  4130957  4130977
4131031  4131047  4131059  4131073  4131077  4131089  4131097  4131107  4131109  4131223
4131229  4131241  4131293  4131301  4131307  4131313  4131317  4131331  4131353  4131367
4131371  4131373  4131409  4131443  4131451  4131473  4131487  4131539  4131577  4131583
4131599  4131613  4131623  4131637  4131641  4131643  4131653  4131661  4131667  4131707
4131709  4131719  4131763  4131767  4131781  4131791  4131839  4131851  4131859  4131877
4131889  4131917  4131923  4131961  4131971  4131977  4131979  4131983  4132001  4132031
4132033  4132043  4132061  4132067  4132069  4132087  4132097  4132151  4132153  4132159
4132211  4132229  4132231  4132259  4132273  4132277  4132279  4132313  4132339  4132351
4132361  4132363  4132369  4132379  4132391  4132409  4132421  4132439  4132477  4132489
4132507  4132511  4132553  4132559  4132577  4132591  4132607  4132619  4132621  4132637
4132643  4132673  4132679  4132693  4132769  4132783  4132829  4132831  4132867  4132873
4132883  4132897  4132901  4132903  4132913  4132927  4132943  4132949  4132963  4132967
4132969  4132979  4132987  4133047  4133069  4133113  4133119  4133131  4133147  4133149
4133179  4133183  4133189  4133209  4133219  4133237  4133263  4133273  4133293  4133369
4133377  4133383  4133401  4133411  4133413  4133419  4133449  4133453  4133473  4133513
4133527  4133551  4133557  4133561  4133581  4133587  4133593  4133609  4133611  4133617
4133639  4133641  4133663  4133693  4133713  4133741  4133749  4133761  4133777  4133807
4133821  4133837  4133869  4133893  4133911  4133923  4133933  4133939  4133957  4133971
4134023  4134049  4134059  4134061  4134107  4134133  4134161  4134187  4134203  4134217
4134257  4134283  4134287  4134289  4134293  4134311  4134323  4134329  4134337  4134341
4134391  4134409  4134413  4134421  4134433  4134437  4134463  4134467  4134469  4134497
4134499  4134509  4134539  4134541  4134547  4134551  4134569  4134589  4134619  4134629
4134649  4134659  4134667  4134671  4134677  4134679  4134701  4134703  4134707  4134719
4134737  4134743  4134769  4134803  4134817  4134829  4134847  4134857  4134869  4134877
4134881  4134883  4134887  4134931  4134937  4134971  4135003  4135037  4135049  4135057
4135069  4135093  4135123  4135127  4135151  4135169  4135211  4135237  4135249  4135273
4135279  4135283  4135297  4135303  4135343  4135349  4135357  4135363  4135381  4135427
4135457  4135463  4135499  4135507  4135519  4135529  4135531  4135541  4135567  4135591
4135591  4135609  4135613  4135627  4135717  4135721  4135763  4135771  4135829  4135847
4135853  4135889  4135907  4135909  4135921  4135933  4135987  4135991  4135993  4135997
4136003  4136023  4136029  4136057  4136059  4136123  4136137  4136147  4136149  4136161
4136179  4136189  4136191  4136221  4136239  4136261  4136269  4136303  4136309  4136311
4136317  4136333  4136339  4136347  4136351  4136359  4136381  4136383  4136411  4136437
4136459  4136467  4136477  4136497  4136521  4136537  4136551  4136567  4136579  4136581
4136599  4136617  4136633  4136641  4136651  4136653  4136663  4136669  4136681  4136689
4136701  4136707  4136719  4136723  4136747  4136749  4136753  4136761  4136767  4136773
4136819  4136833  4136861  4136863  4136887  4136917  4136939  4136963  4136971  4136999
4137013  4137031  4137037  4137047  4137059  4137083  4137097  4137101  4137113  4137121
4137149  4137157  4137173  4137179  4137181  4137223  4137271  4137277  4137299  4137311
4137323  4137337  4137347  4137359  4137389  4137437  4137449  4137473  4137491  4137509
4137527  4137541  4137559  4137563  4137571  4137587  4137593  4137607  4137619  4137629
4137643  4137659  4137671  4137697  4137701  4137709  4137733  4137737  4137751  4137773
4137781  4137823  4137829  4137857  4137863  4137871  4137883  4137893  4137901  4137929
4137949  4137961  4137971  4137977  4137979  4137997  4138033  4138051  4138073  4138111
4138129  4138139  4138153  4138217  4138223  4138241  4138243  4138247  4138249  4138261
4138279  4138289  4138291  4138307  4138331  4138349  4138369  4138373  4138391  4138451
4138483  4138489  4138507  4138513  4138529  4138543  4138567  4138577  4138579  4138583
4138591  4138601  4138609  4138627  4138649  4138681  4138691  4138703  4138711  4138727
4138741  4138747  4138753  4138777  4138807  4138817  4138819  4138829  4138843  4138847
4138853  4138861  4138877  4138933  4138943  4138951  4138957  4138963  4138969  4138987
4138993  4138997  4138999  4139029  4139063  4139101  4139111  4139119  4139129  4139147
4139159  4139171  4139189  4139203  4139209  4139221  4139249  4139273  4139297  4139299
4139323  4139329  4139339  4139341  4139351  4139383  4139389  4139417  4139419  4139423
4139477  4139491  4139497  4139501  4139503  4139533  4139537  4139539  4139557  4139573
4139579  4139581  4139591  4139593  4139599  4139627  4139659  4139677  4139699  4139741
4139749  4139753  4139761  4139767  4139801  4139803  4139809  4139827  4139831  4139873
4139881  4139899  4139909  4139917  4139921  4139923  4139951  4139983  4139999  4140001
4140029  4140047  4140053  4140077  4140079  4140107  4140109  4140113  4140121  4140133
4140173  4140211  4140217  4140259  4140281  4140307  4140361  4140373  4140377  4140379
4140397  4140419  4140421  4140439  4140457  4140477  4140481  4140511  4140557  4140569
4140589  4140607  4140611  4140623  4140629  4140637  4140641  4140683  4140691  4140709
4140733  4140749  4140757  4140761  4140767  4140769  4140811  4140817  4140821  4140827
4140839  4140847  4140853  4140869  4140883  4140893  4140923  4140931  4140937  4140947
4140967  4140973  4141001  4141009  4141057  4141061  4141063  4141079  4141091  4141117
4141121  4141133  4141147  4141169  4141177  4141187  4141211  4141213  4141223  4141243
4141273  4141279  4141283  4141289  4141301  4141307  4141309  4141331  4141339  4141349
4141381  4141391  4141399  4141409  4141439  4141441  4141457  4141469  4141481  4141483
4141493  4141513  4141517  4141549  4141559  4141573  4141589  4141603  4141663  4141681
4141691  4141699  4141703  4141721  4141723  4141747  4141759  4141763  4141769  4141799
4141807  4141811  4141831  4141843  4141847  4141849  4141853  4141871  4141877  4141903
4141919  4141937  4141957  4141967  4142011  4142023  4142027  4142029  4142053  4142059
4142087  4142119  4142129  4142161  4142167  4142179  4142227  4142267  4142287  4142293
4142297  4142309  4142311  4142363  4142371  4142387  4142393  4142401  4142417  4142423
4142429  4142473  4142497  4142519  4142521  4142569  4142573  4142591  4142609  4142629
4142641  4142651  4142657  4142659  4142669  4142689  4142701  4142707  4142753  4142767
4142791  4142797  4142813  4142857  4142863  4142891  4142899  4142903  4142939  4142947
4142989  4142993  4143011  4143023  4143037  4143043  4143047  4143049  4143067  4143071
4143077  4143101  4143109  4143163  4143187  4143193  4143221  4143229  4143233  4143241
4143253  4143281  4143287  4143299  4143301  4143329  4143331  4143341  4143353  4143383
4143389  4143397  4143401  4143409  4143413  4143421  4143449  4143467  4143479  4143493
4143497  4143499  4143509  4143521  4143551  4143569  4143571  4143599  4143613  4143617
```

```
4143637  4143641  4143647  4143673  4143683  4143697  4143707  4143709  4143719  4143731
4143757  4143779  4143803  4143827  4143833  4143847  4143851  4143857  4143859  4143863
4143877  4143901  4143947  4143959  4143961  4143967  4143973  4144001  4144031  4144043
4144051  4144061  4144067  4144069  4144079  4144081  4144087  4144099  4144121  4144159
4144177  4144181  4144201  4144237  4144241  4144247  4144249  4144253  4144267  4144271
4144291  4144307  4144331  4144363  4144367  4144369  4144373  4144409  4144423  4144457
4144471  4144487  4144537  4144541  4144579  4144589  4144631  4144633  4144663  4144667
4144681  4144711  4144729  4144739  4144741  4144757  4144781  4144783  4144801  4144817
4144849  4144871  4144873  4144879  4144913  4144919  4144961  4144963  4144967  4144969
4144981  4145003  4145017  4145023  4145027  4145033  4145047  4145069  4145111  4145117
4145171  4145177  4145189  4145191  4145201  4145213  4145257  4145261  4145291  4145293
4145299  4145333  4145341  4145371  4145389  4145419  4145423  4145459  4145473  4145503
4145509  4145527  4145539  4145549  4145567  4145611  4145639  4145641  4145653  4145677
4145689  4145693  4145699  4145707  4145711  4145717  4145731  4145737  4145777  4145783
4145803  4145809  4145837  4145839  4145849  4145851  4145861  4145863  4145873  4145891
4145951  4145959  4145969  4145983  4145993  4146001  4146013  4146053  4146067  4146073
4146119  4146133  4146139  4146173  4146179  4146193  4146203  4146211  4146221  4146227
4146253  4146277  4146323  4146341  4146347  4146367  4146377  4146379  4146383  4146397
4146403  4146407  4146409  4146451  4146497  4146517  4146539  4146547  4146559  4146577
4146587  4146661  4146671  4146679  4146743  4146767  4146803  4146811  4146833  4146859
4146881  4146907  4146917  4146929  4146973  4146977  4146979  4147001  4147007
4147009  4147019  4147021  4147037  4147043  4147079  4147081  4147093  4147103  4147147
4147151  4147159  4147163  4147229  4147237  4147249  4147267  4147289  4147309  4147313
4147321  4147331  4147357  4147361  4147373  4147379  4147391  4147399  4147411  4147417
4147457  4147483  4147499  4147511  4147531  4147537  4147547  4147553  4147571  4147597
4147639  4147657  4147673  4147679  4147687  4147697  4147709  4147721  4147729  4147739
4147747  4147753  4147771  4147789  4147799  4147837  4147867  4147873  4147879  4147883
4147921  4147943  4147961  4147963  4147973  4147987  4147991  4148003  4148009  4148029
4148041  4148057  4148059  4148071  4148077  4148083  4148087  4148101  4148129  4148143
4148147  4148159  4148161  4148219  4148227  4148233  4148239  4148269  4148279  4148293
4148321  4148341  4148351  4148381  4148393  4148401  4148407  4148413  4148437  4148461
4148453  4148461  4148483  4148489  4148567  4148581  4148591  4148603  4148609  4148611
4148621  4148633  4148647  4148657  4148659  4148687  4148689  4148719  4148741  4148759
4148791  4148797  4148813  4148819  4148849  4148857  4148861  4148863  4148873  4148887
4148891  4148899  4148909  4148917  4148923  4148927  4148933  4148953  4148957  4148971
4148983  4148987  4149007  4149023  4149029  4149053  4149107  4149121  4149137  4149151
4149161  4149179  4149191  4149227  4149259  4149263  4149283  4149287  4149337  4149347
4149359  4149367  4149373  4149389  4149401  4149413  4149427  4149433  4149437  4149451
4149469  4149517  4149533  4149553  4149557  4149559  4149589  4149599  4149601
4149617  4149623  4149641  4149643  4149653  4149659  4149679  4149703  4149707  4149713
4149721  4149731  4149749  4149763  4149793  4149811  4149833  4149839  4149881  4149889
4149907  4149911  4149919  4149931  4149941  4149947  4149967  4149983  4149991  4149997
4150007  4150019  4150069  4150033  4150039  4150043  4150049  4150073  4150093  4150109
4150127  4150129  4150169  4150171  4150177  4150213  4150243  4150247  4150259  4150283
4150297  4150301  4150309  4150313  4150319  4150331  4150343  4150351  4150357  4150369
4150381  4150411  4150439  4150441  4150453  4150457  4150459  4150463  4150507  4150513
4150519  4150529  4150547  4150577  4150613  4150633  4150667  4150673  4150681  4150691
4150723  4150733  4150753  4150763  4150781  4150793  4150813  4150819  4150823  4150847
4150849  4150859  4150889  4150901  4150903  4150933  4150943  4150967  4150969  4150981
4151011  4151023  4151027  4151029  4151039  4151053  4151057  4151099  4151113  4151129
4151131  4151153  4151159  4151167  4151197  4151207  4151219  4151239  4151261  4151267
4151269  4151297  4151317  4151341  4151347  4151351  4151359  4151377  4151423  4151461
4151467  4151471  4151473  4151479  4151501  4151531  4151533  4151549  4151629  4151639
4151647  4151663  4151677  4151681  4151683  4151699  4151711  4151713  4151717  4151801
4151803  4151809  4151813  4151821  4151879  4151887  4151911  4151929  4151941  4151963
4151969  4151971  4151977  4151989  4152019  4152061  4152067  4152077  4152079  4152091
4152101  4152107  4152119  4152139  4152143  4152157  4152217  4152229  4152257  4152271
4152283  4152289  4152299  4152311  4152329  4152341  4152353  4152371  4152373  4152377
4152389  4152409  4152433  4152503  4152509  4152517  4152523  4152527  4152529  4152541
4152557  4152587  4152601  4152653  4152677  4152679  4152721  4152737  4152761  4152763
4152787  4152803  4152809  4152823  4152839  4152847  4152859  4152877  4152893  4152901
4152919  4152923  4152937  4152943  4152959  4152971  4152989  4152997  4153021  4153067
4153081  4153099  4153111  4153159  4153169  4153183  4153199  4153207  4153217  4153223
4153231  4153273  4153277  4153283  4153291  4153301  4153309  4153333  4153367  4153393
4153399  4153417  4153421  4153433  4153447  4153453  4153463  4153469  4153477  4153483
4153489  4153493  4153507  4153517  4153519  4153529  4153543  4153561  4153579  4153607
4153613  4153649  4153687  4153697  4153711  4153717  4153753  4153759  4153771  4153817
4153819  4153829  4153841  4153867  4153871  4153909  4153927  4153943  4153973  4153979
4153987  4153991  4153999  4154009  4154041  4154077  4154083  4154089  4154107  4154149
4154173  4154177  4154197  4154203  4154207  4154209  4154263  4154287  4154303  4154309
4154333  4154347  4154363  4154383  4154389  4154417  4154419  4154461  4154473  4154497
4154509  4154519  4154543  4154561  4154581  4154593  4154621  4154629  4154639  4154641
4154669  4154677  4154687  4154699  4154719  4154729  4154741  4154779  4154791  4154797
4154809  4154819  4154831  4154833  4154861  4154867  4154869  4154879  4154903  4154911
4154923  4154929  4154933  4154947  4154951  4154959  4154999  4155007  4155013  4155017
4155029  4155037  4155049  4155061  4155077  4155079  4155103  4155113  4155119  4155121
4155161  4155169  4155187  4155197  4155247  4155251  4155257  4155269  4155301  4155331
4155337  4155343  4155367  4155401  4155409  4155413  4155419  4155427  4155467  4155469
4155511  4155517  4155521  4155523  4155533  4155539  4155551  4155583  4155589  4155607
4155611  4155629  4155631  4155647  4155653  4155659  4155673  4155703  4155721  4155731
4155733  4155743  4155751  4155761  4155763  4155779  4155791  4155793  4155797  4155839
4155841  4155857  4155863  4155887  4155911  4155913  4155917  4155919  4155923  4155929
4155989  4155997  4156001  4156037  4156039  4156043  4156063  4156073  4156081  4156091
4156093  4156151  4156157  4156181  4156183  4156199  4156213  4156219  4156249  4156277
4156291  4156297  4156301  4156331  4156333  4156349  4156379  4156409  4156417  4156433
4156441  4156447  4156507  4156519  4156531  4156549  4156561  4156571  4156589  4156591
4156627  4156639  4156643  4156651  4156673  4156709  4156739  4156751  4156769  4156777
4156783  4156787  4156793  4156799  4156807  4156819  4156829  4156847  4156871  4156903
4156907  4156909  4156921  4156937  4156969  4156981  4157011  4157053  4157077  4157093
```

```
4157099  4157119  4157123  4157141  4157147  4157159  4157171  4157173  4157177  4157189
4157191  4157201  4157227  4157239  4157269  4157287  4157303  4157311  4157339  4157347
4157399  4157429  4157437  4157449  4157459  4157471  4157473  4157477  4157501  4157509
4157513  4157563  4157591  4157603  4157611  4157617  4157623  4157663  4157669  4157677
4157693  4157717  4157723  4157729  4157731  4157749  4157753  4157771  4157773  4157807
4157833  4157837  4157863  4157869  4157887  4157891  4157893  4157897  4157899  4157927
4157929  4157947  4157981  4158001  4158019  4158031  4158041  4158053  4158067  4158073
4158083  4158103  4158109  4158139  4158151  4158157  4158163  4158173  4158181  4158197
4158211  4158233  4158289  4158307  4158313  4158337  4158367  4158391  4158403  4158409
4158443  4158449  4158457  4158461  4158491  4158499  4158521  4158527  4158529  4158547
4158551  4158559  4158569  4158611  4158613  4158617  4158631  4158641  4158673  4158697
4158731  4158779  4158789  4158823  4158827  4158857  4158887  4158893  4158899  4158907
4158941  4158943  4158953  4158961  4158971  4158989  4159007  4159013  4159027  4159049
4159091  4159097  4159147  4159153  4159187  4159193  4159217  4159219  4159223  4159229
4159231  4159241  4159247  4159273  4159277  4159279  4159289  4159291  4159303  4159319
4159333  4159349  4159361  4159367  4159403  4159447  4159451  4159459  4159471  4159501
4159511  4159517  4159523  4159531  4159541  4159553  4159583  4159601  4159621  4159627
4159637  4159663  4159667  4159669  4159681  4159693  4159699  4159717  4159723  4159741
4159769  4159787  4159801  4159829  4159843  4159889  4159907  4159937  4159943  4159987
4159979  4159997  4160003  4160011  4160027  4160041  4160047  4160063  4160077  4160099
4160113  4160119  4160141  4160159  4160173  4160179  4160227  4160237  4160269  4160281
4160323  4160327  4160329  4160333  4160347  4160353  4160357  4160363  4160371  4160381
4160389  4160399  4160407  4160413  4160423  4160437  4160459  4160467  4160473  4160491
4160509  4160521  4160531  4160549  4160561  4160567  4160579  4160591  4160593  4160603
4160609  4160617  4160641  4160669  4160711  4160713  4160719  4160729  4160797  4160843
4160849  4160881  4160899  4160929  4160941  4160951  4160969  4160987  4161011  4161013
4161013  4161023  4161061  4161077  4161103  4161109  4161119  4161149  4161151  4161163
4161173  4161187  4161191  4161193  4161197  4161221  4161233  4161251  4161257  4161263
4161271  4161299  4161307  4161331  4161341  4161343  4161349  4161389  4161407  4161419
4161433  4161439  4161457  4161461  4161463  4161499  4161527  4161539  4161557  4161559
4161581  4161593  4161607  4161611  4161629  4161631  4161637  4161653  4161667  4161671
4161673  4161679  4161691  4161697  4161701  4161713  4161721  4161727  4161737  4161757
4161763  4161767  4161769  4161791  4161793  4161809  4161811  4161823  4161851  4161853
4161881  4161943  4161953  4161959  4161977  4162003  4162009  4162021  4162027  4162049
4162063  4162069  4162087  4162097  4162117  4162133  4162157  4162177  4162183  4162187
4162189  4162211  4162217  4162219  4162231  4162243  4162247  4162253  4162261  4162309
4162313  4162321  4162337  4162343  4162351  4162363  4162373  4162381  4162421  4162423
4162439  4162447  4162469  4162481  4162493  4162507  4162511  4162519  4162547  4162549
4162583  4162591  4162657  4162661  4162667  4162681  4162687  4162693  4162703  4162709
4162721  4162727  4162733  4162751  4162757  4162783  4162811  4162859  4162861  4162867
4162877  4162889  4162901  4162913  4162937  4162967  4162973  4162979  4162993  4162999
4162999  4163009  4163039  4163041  4163051  4163077  4163123  4163149  4163171  4163177
4163219  4163231  4163233  4163251  4163267  4163281  4163287  4163297  4163329  4163333
4163347  4163353  4163359  4163371  4163381  4163387  4163399  4163417  4163429  4163459
4163461  4163479  4163491  4163503  4163539  4163563  4163597  4163611  4163629  4163651
4163659  4163669  4163671  4163681  4163693  4163699  4163707  4163723  4163741  4163743
4163749  4163767  4163773  4163801  4163813  4163821  4163833  4163843  4163857  4163879
4163881  4163893  4163903  4163911  4163933  4163941  4163953  4163983  4163987  4164007
4164019  4164047  4164049  4164053  4164071  4164101  4164107  4164131  4164179  4164191
4164217  4164233  4164241  4164253  4164271  4164289  4164299  4164317  4164319  4164343
4164367  4164379  4164427  4164437  4164451  4164463  4164467  4164481  4164497  4164499
4164521  4164527  4164539  4164551  4164569  4164583  4164607  4164613  4164631  4164637
4164673  4164697  4164709  4164737  4164749  4164767  4164773  4164791  4164799  4164803
4164827  4164829  4164859  4164877  4164887  4164907  4164913  4164917  4164947  4164967
4164977  4164989  4165037  4165039  4165043  4165061  4165079  4165097  4165099  4165103
4165157  4165163  4165169  4165177  4165181  4165193  4165229  4165243  4165267  4165283
4165297  4165303  4165319  4165327  4165331  4165333  4165339  4165361  4165379  4165393
4165397  4165411  4165451  4165463  4165489  4165517  4165523  4165547  4165549  4165553
4165583  4165597  4165607  4165613  4165619  4165621  4165627  4165631  4165633  4165643
4165661  4165699  4165709  4165729  4165741  4165757  4165781  4165787  4165849  4165927
4165933  4165943  4165949  4165951  4165957  4165961  4165963  4165979  4165991  4165999
4166011  4166017  4166023  4166027  4166047  4166069  4166081  4166087  4166093  4166101
4166119  4166137  4166143  4166147  4166153  4166159  4166177  4166191  4166203  4166221
4166231  4166233  4166251  4166257  4166287  4166293  4166299  4166303  4166317  4166321
4166333  4166341  4166363  4166389  4166411  4166419  4166441  4166447  4166501  4166507
4166509  4166527  4166551  4166557  4166563  4166593  4166599  4166629  4166641  4166647
4166651  4166671  4166689  4166693  4166731  4166737  4166809  4166831  4166837  4166843
4166863  4166867  4166873  4166893  4166899  4167017  4167043  4167049  4167073  4167077
4167109  4167127  4167133  4167143  4167157  4167187  4167197  4167223  4167239  4167257
4167263  4167269  4167287  4167307  4167311  4167341  4167367  4167377  4167379  4167389
4167391  4167407  4167413  4167419  4167433  4167437  4167451  4167473  4167481  4167491
4167509  4167521  4167523  4167551  4167587  4167607  4167641  4167649  4167659  4167661
4167673  4167697  4167719  4167721  4167731  4167763  4167767  4167797  4167809  4167827
4167829  4167841  4167847  4167881  4167893  4167923  4167931  4167949  4167953  4167979
4168001  4168057  4168063  4168091  4168097  4168117  4168121  4168123  4168127  4168133
4168159  4168181  4168207  4168223  4168253  4168259  4168273  4168279  4168301  4168303
4168319  4168327  4168331  4168337  4168369  4168379  4168387  4168403  4168421  4168433
4168447  4168459  4168469  4168501  4168517  4168523  4168529  4168537  4168559  4168561
4168579  4168583  4168627  4168649  4168651  4168667  4168691  4168709  4168741  4168831
4168861  4168883  4168889  4168891  4168933  4168939  4168943  4168951  4168981  4168987
4169057  4169083  4169093  4169101  4169119  4169129  4169147  4169161  4169171  4169177
4169203  4169213  4169251  4169257  4169273  4169281  4169293  4169299  4169327  4169329
4169387  4169393  4169401  4169423  4169441  4169443  4169453  4169497  4169507  4169513
4169521  4169527  4169549  4169551  4169579  4169597  4169603  4169609  4169621  4169623
4169651  4169653  4169657  4169663  4169689  4169693  4169713  4169719  4169723  4169729
4169731  4169747  4169771  4169783  4169807  4169821  4169827  4169849  4169909  4169929
4169941  4169951  4169953  4170007  4170017  4170031  4170041  4170053  4170071  4170079
4170091  4170109  4170119  4170121  4170191  4170193  4170209  4170211  4170227  4170247
4170251  4170277  4170289  4170301  4170343  4170347  4170349  4170359  4170371  4170377
```

```
4170379  4170407  4170427  4170431  4170433  4170473  4170493  4170497  4170499  4170541
4170547  4170583  4170599  4170601  4170641  4170679  4170703  4170707  4170721  4170731
4170737  4170739  4170743  4170757  4170773  4170781  4170839  4170851  4170863  4170877
4170911  4170913  4170953  4170977  4170979  4170989  4171003  4171009  4171021  4171031
4171087  4171091  4171093  4171117  4171151  4171177  4171183  4171187  4171201  4171207
4171213  4171229  4171231  4171243  4171261  4171283  4171289  4171313  4171319  4171327
4171337  4171357  4171361  4171411  4171421  4171423  4171429  4171451  4171459  4171481
4171483  4171499  4171523  4171543  4171547  4171591  4171619  4171633  4171667  4171691
4171721  4171751  4171759  4171771  4171777  4171781  4171793  4171799  4171801  4171813
4171819  4171837  4171841  4171879  4171883  4171907  4171931  4171933  4171943  4171967
4171991  4172029  4172041  4172057  4172059  4172071  4172087  4172099  4172101  4172111
4172117  4172141  4172159  4172167  4172171  4172183  4172239  4172243  4172257  4172279
4172309  4172323  4172341  4172353  4172359  4172369  4172417  4172431  4172471  4172479
4172489  4172513  4172521  4172537  4172551  4172561  4172573  4172579  4172621  4172627
4172639  4172653  4172681  4172699  4172711  4172717  4172719  4172731  4172737  4172747
4172759  4172783  4172789  4172807  4172851  4172863  4172869  4172873  4172881  4172887
4172929  4172953  4172957  4172981  4173023  4173031  4173047  4173049  4173073  4173077
4173079  4173089  4173139  4173149  4173151  4173161  4173181  4173209  4173223  4173241
4173269  4173277  4173287  4173311  4173319  4173329  4173343  4173353  4173359  4173371
4173383  4173409  4173413  4173467  4173469  4173473  4173479  4173487  4173493  4173523
4173539  4173569  4173571  4173577  4173607  4173613  4173641  4173683  4173703  4173727
4173733  4173739  4173751  4173761  4173769  4173773  4173779  4173811  4173817  4173847
4173853  4173887  4173907  4173919  4173943  4173947  4173973  4173989  4174013  4174021
4174039  4174043  4174069  4174097  4174103  4174111  4174133  4174141  4174151  4174171
4174193  4174207  4174237  4174249  4174259  4174271  4174273  4174277  4174283  4174297
4174327  4174343  4174349  4174351  4174369  4174393  4174409  4174411  4174421  4174453
4174501  4174507  4174517  4174529  4174531  4174549  4174561  4174567  4174601  4174603
4174607  4174609  4174631  4174649  4174669  4174691  4174711  4174717  4174727  4174733
4174759  4174769  4174771  4174777  4174789  4174823  4174847  4174853  4174861  4174873
4174879  4174949  4174967  4174981  4174991  4174993  4174997  4175053  4175063  4175077
4175123  4175131  4175141  4175177  4175189  4175201  4175203  4175209  4175243  4175261
4175263  4175273  4175279  4175291  4175299  4175309  4175321  4175341  4175377  4175411
4175417  4175453  4175467  4175471  4175473  4175477  4175491  4175503  4175513  4175519
4175531  4175539  4175551  4175579  4175597  4175653  4175657  4175663  4175671  4175683
4175737  4175747  4175777  4175779  4175789  4175803  4175827  4175837  4175867  4175869
4175879  4175881  4175933  4175939  4175957  4175981  4175989  4176001  4176013
4176037  4176049  4176061  4176071  4176077  4176097  4176113  4176127  4176157  4176163
4176167  4176187  4176191  4176217  4176229  4176233  4176239  4176253  4176259  4176269
4176281  4176283  4176287  4176307  4176313  4176331  4176379  4176391  4176397  4176421
4176443  4176457  4176517  4176521  4176539  4176541  4176563  4176569  4176587  4176617
4176647  4176677  4176691  4176701  4176709  4176721  4176727  4176737  4176743  4176761
4176769  4176773  4176779  4176791  4176803  4176817  4176833  4176863  4176871  4176919
4176929  4176947  4176973  4177051  4177079  4177081  4177123  4177127  4177139  4177153
4177163  4177183  4177193  4177211  4177231  4177309  4177333  4177339  4177351  4177357
4177373  4177379  4177391  4177403  4177409  4177423  4177447  4177451  4177469  4177477
4177483  4177487  4177519  4177543  4177553  4177573  4177609  4177673  4177687  4177703
4177709  4177729  4177741  4177753  4177759  4177763  4177787  4177793  4177799  4177807
4177843  4177847  4177867  4177897  4177907  4177909  4177913  4177931  4177939  4177969
4177993  4177997  4178021  4178033  4178047  4178051  4178063  4178071  4178093  4178101
4178113  4178129  4178131  4178171  4178177  4178191  4178197  4178219  4178221  4178261
4178287  4178327  4178329  4178333  4178357  4178359  4178393  4178399  4178411  4178417
4178431  4178443  4178453  4178483  4178491  4178497  4178501  4178509  4178513  4178519
4178527  4178543  4178569  4178579  4178591  4178599  4178609  4178633  4178641  4178677
4178701  4178711  4178717  4178729  4178737  4178749  4178767  4178771  4178773  4178777
4178789  4178791  4178809  4178827  4178849  4178851  4178861  4178873  4178887  4178897
4178903  4178959  4178963  4178969  4178971  4178983  4179001  4179013  4179023  4179037
4179053  4179067  4179073  4179101  4179139  4179143  4179151  4179163  4179247  4179251
4179257  4179269  4179289  4179311  4179317  4179319  4179341  4179347  4179359  4179361
4179367  4179377  4179379  4179391  4179403  4179419  4179437  4179457  4179463  4179473
4179493  4179517  4179521  4179533  4179541  4179551  4179577  4179587  4179607  4179641
4179647  4179649  4179667  4179673  4179691  4179701  4179709  4179713  4179727  4179731
4179743  4179803  4179839  4179863  4179881  4179893  4179899  4179913  4179919  4179941
4179949  4179953  4179971  4179979  4180051  4180067  4180069  4180081  4180093  4180097
4180153  4180157  4180201  4180217  4180219  4180229  4180243  4180271  4180277  4180301
4180303  4180313  4180333  4180343  4180367  4180369  4180373  4180387  4180441  4180447
4180469  4180471  4180489  4180499  4180507  4180541  4180607  4180609  4180613  4180621
4180633  4180663  4180679  4180723  4180739  4180747  4180763  4180769  4180777  4180789
4180801  4180819  4180823  4180831  4180837  4180909  4180921  4180927  4180949
4180961  4180987  4181041  4181059  4181069  4181071  4181077  4181081  4181087  4181129
4181137  4181141  4181171  4181173  4181183  4181209  4181213  4181251  4181257  4181263
4181267  4181279  4181293  4181321  4181323  4181347  4181351  4181357  4181383  4181393
4181413  4181417  4181431  4181447  4181459  4181461  4181479  4181483  4181503  4181509
4181521  4181531  4181533  4181557  4181603  4181633  4181657  4181669  4181693
4181717  4181741  4181747  4181759  4181761  4181773  4181797  4181819  4181839  4181857
4181867  4181873  4181897  4181899  4181909  4181917  4181927  4181941  4181953  4181981
4181987  4182011  4182019  4182037  4182043  4182047  4182049  4182077  4182083  4182089
4182103  4182127  4182131  4182133  4182151  4182163  4182169  4182173  4182193  4182203
4182209  4182239  4182253  4182257  4182263  4182271  4182301  4182307  4182313  4182317
4182329  4182331  4182361  4182379  4182403  4182407  4182419  4182421  4182433  4182461
4182463  4182487  4182547  4182553  4182557  4182561  4182571  4182589  4182593  4182599
4182611  4182631  4182667  4182691  4182701  4182721  4182749  4182751  4182769  4182791
4182809  4182821  4182839  4182853  4182863  4182881  4182883  4182947  4182949  4182979
4182991  4183001  4183007  4183009  4183013  4183019  4183027  4183031  4183043  4183057
4183061  4183063  4183087  4183099  4183103  4183111  4183121  4183133  4183177  4183199
4183229  4183243  4183259  4183273  4183297  4183301  4183303  4183327  4183349  4183351
4183369  4183381  4183393  4183397  4183429  4183457  4183499  4183537  4183559  4183567
4183583  4183639  4183643  4183651  4183687  4183691  4183693  4183727  4183733  4183741
4183759  4183783  4183787  4183789  4183813  4183831  4183841  4183847  4183889  4183891
4183897  4183903  4183909  4183913  4183931  4183937  4183951  4183957  4183961  4183967
```

```
4183973  4184017  4184027  4184087  4184099  4184107  4184111  4184119  4184143  4184153
4184179  4184197  4184203  4184233  4184239  4184251  4184263  4184273  4184281  4184303
4184309  4184311  4184347  4184353  4184357  4184359  4184377  4184399  4184407  4184423
4184429  4184437  4184443  4184507  4184549  4184561  4184563  4184569  4184573  4184591
4184599  4184603  4184629  4184633  4184641  4184647  4184657  4184681  4184707  4184711
4184743  4184759  4184767  4184773  4184797  4184809  4184813  4184821  4184849  4184857
4184861  4184881  4184893  4184897  4184899  4184909  4184977  4184989  4185007  4185029
4185037  4185067  4185101  4185121  4185131  4185133  4185143  4185173  4185191  4185197
4185211  4185229  4185253  4185257  4185277  4185343  4185347  4185353  4185359  4185361
4185373  4185409  4185413  4185431  4185437  4185439  4185449  4185469  4185473  4185479
4185481  4185497  4185509  4185523  4185547  4185583  4185593  4185613  4185617  4185619
4185641  4185661  4185673  4185683  4185697  4185703  4185739  4185751  4185763  4185767
4185787  4185799  4185803  4185821  4185823  4185829  4185851  4185869  4185901  4185911
4185913  4185917  4185919  4185941  4185943  4185949  4185953  4185967  4185971  4185989
4185997  4186009  4186019  4186031  4186033  4186043  4186073  4186079  4186087  4186103
4186123  4186129  4186151  4186153  4186181  4186183  4186201  4186211  4186219  4186241
4186283  4186307  4186313  4186319  4186339  4186393  4186397  4186409  4186421
4186433  4186459  4186487  4186489  4186493  4186531  4186547  4186571  4186579  4186591
4186639  4186673  4186681  4186691  4186703  4186717  4186723  4186747  4186771  4186801
4186823  4186837  4186843  4186849  4186877  4186907  4186927  4186937  4186951  4186997
4186999  4187009  4187021  4187023  4187047  4187059  4187069  4187093  4187111  4187123
4187129  4187137  4187147  4187177  4187189  4187213  4187233  4187251  4187257  4187269
4187291  4187303  4187329  4187333  4187363  4187369  4187399  4187411  4187413  4187419
4187437  4187459  4187471  4187479  4187483  4187489  4187501  4187503  4187507  4187531
4187537  4187563  4187569  4187591  4187597  4187611  4187647  4187663  4187669  4187707
4187719  4187731  4187737  4187741  4187753  4187773  4187779  4187789  4187801  4187819
4187839  4187851  4187891  4187927  4187929  4187941  4187951  4187957  4187971  4187983
4187987  4188011  4188017  4188043  4188053  4188059  4188089  4188101  4188127  4188133
4188161  4188187  4188203  4188221  4188257  4188259  4188269  4188271  4188281  4188299
4188313  4188337  4188347  4188367  4188403  4188407  4188413  4188419  4188427  4188433
4188449  4188451  4188467  4188473  4188479  4188491  4188497  4188533  4188551  4188559
4188577  4188617  4188619  4188631  4188649  4188671  4188677  4188697  4188703  4188713
4188719  4188727  4188739  4188763  4188791  4188799  4188803  4188827  4188853  4188857
4188893  4188901  4188917  4188973  4188997  4189001  4189019  4189027
4189039  4189057  4189069  4189091  4189099  4189117  4189121  4189147  4189153  4189181
4189183  4189187  4189217  4189219  4189223  4189261  4189267  4189271  4189277  4189307
4189313  4189337  4189351  4189363  4189373  4189403  4189417  4189453  4189459  4189477
4189483  4189489  4189499  4189513  4189517  4189553  4189561  4189567  4189583  4189609
4189631  4189651  4189661  4189673  4189693  4189697  4189699  4189723  4189727  4189729
4189733  4189741  4189763  4189791  4189793  4189807  4189819  4189847  4189849  4189879
4189883  4189897  4189903  4189951  4189957  4189961  4189987  4190009  4190023  4190027
4190033  4190057  4190059  4190063  4190083  4190093  4190101  4190107  4190119  4190149
4190161  4190167  4190171  4190183  4190189  4190231  4190237  4190257  4190261  4190269
4190293  4190299  4190309  4190321  4190359  4190369  4190371  4190383  4190399  4190411
4190429  4190447  4190453  4190467  4190477  4190489  4190503  4190513  4190533  4190573
4190617  4190629  4190663  4190677  4190689  4190699  4190701  4190707  4190717  4190729
4190759  4190777  4190803  4190833  4190861  4190863  4190867  4190903  4190933  4190957
4190969  4190981  4190987  4190999  4191013  4191017  4191041  4191043  4191049  4191067
4191071  4191073  4191091  4191097  4191119  4191137  4191151  4191157  4191179  4191181
4191193  4191217  4191227  4191233  4191259  4191311  4191329  4191337  4191349  4191353
4191373  4191391  4191403  4191427  4191443  4191461  4191463  4191487  4191493  4191521
4191527  4191529  4191563  4191581  4191599  4191613  4191623  4191641  4191659  4191679
4191701  4191709  4191739  4191757  4191763  4191787  4191793  4191797  4191829  4191857
4191893  4191907  4191919  4191931  4191947  4191949  4191953  4191973  4191983  4191991
4192007  4192021  4192033  4192039  4192051  4192073  4192087  4192091  4192093  4192121
4192129  4192157  4192163  4192169  4192189  4192219  4192229  4192231  4192261  4192267
4192271  4192273  4192277  4192283  4192289  4192301  4192339  4192343  4192351  4192361
4192381  4192399  4192403  4192411  4192427  4192429  4192477  4192493  4192499  4192511
4192519  4192547  4192553  4192561  4192567  4192571  4192603  4192607  4192613  4192627
4192637  4192667  4192697  4192709  4192753  4192757  4192759  4192789  4192841  4192861
4192871  4192873  4192923  4192943  4192963  4192987  4192997  4193039  4193041  4193051
4193087  4193089  4193113  4193131  4193141  4193149  4193171  4193191  4193209  4193221
4193239  4193249  4193261  4193263  4193269  4193279  4193297  4193303  4193309  4193327
4193353  4193359  4193369  4193377  4193381  4193389  4193393  4193411  4193417  4193443
4193447  4193459  4193507  4193513  4193531  4193549  4193551  4193569  4193573  4193633
4193663  4193701  4193743  4193753  4193759  4193789  4193801  4193803  4193807  4193869
4193909  4193929  4193939  4193957  4193963  4193971  4193977  4194007  4194011  4194023
4194101  4194107  4194131  4194137  4194143  4194167  4194173  4194181  4194187  4194191
4194199  4194217  4194247  4194271  4194277  4194287  4194301  4194319  4194329  4194353
4194371  4194389  4194397  4194403  4194409  4194419  4194433  4194439  4194451  4194493
4194511  4194523  4194527  4194559  4194581  4194583  4194599  4194601  4194637
4194643  4194661  4194677  4194679  4194713  4194719  4194739  4194761  4194769  4194781
4194793  4194823  4194847  4194851  4194857  4194871  4194887  4194907  4194917
4194919  4194961  4194973  4194989  4195001  4195019  4195021  4195027  4195033  4195057
4195063  4195117  4195127  4195129  4195157  4195183  4195189  4195201  4195211  4195229
4195231  4195249  4195253  4195259  4195271  4195273  4195283  4195291  4195297  4195307
4195309  4195327  4195349  4195357  4195421  4195441  4195463  4195483  4195487  4195493
4195501  4195531  4195547  4195559  4195573  4195579  4195589  4195619  4195621  4195649
4195657  4195679  4195703  4195747  4195759  4195771  4195777  4195801  4195823  4195847
4195859  4195861  4195871  4195879  4195883  4195921  4195937  4195949  4195951  4195969
4195973  4195999  4196011  4196057  4196077  4196081  4196089  4196099  4196119  4196147
4196149  4196167  4196177  4196183  4196233  4196237  4196239  4196249  4196267  4196299
4196303  4196333  4196341  4196347  4196363  4196369  4196371  4196389  4196393  4196407
4196417  4196459  4196497  4196509  4196513  4196527  4196567  4196573  4196581  4196629
4196641  4196657  4196659  4196683  4196713  4196737  4196747  4196779  4196789  4196791
4196809  4196821  4196837  4196839  4196849  4196867  4196869  4196893  4196897  4196903
4196917  4196923  4196939  4196953  4196981  4196987  4196993  4196999  4197007  4197019
4197031  4197091  4197097  4197103  4197107  4197133  4197139  4197143  4197161  4197163
4197197  4197203  4197239  4197251  4197253  4197299  4197311  4197313  4197337  4197343
```

```
4197367  4197407  4197409  4197443  4197463  4197467  4197469  4197511  4197527  4197533
4197541  4197553  4197577  4197587  4197601  4197629  4197631  4197647  4197667  4197671
4197737  4197749  4197757  4197763  4197769  4197797  4197821  4197829  4197833  4197839
4197857  4197871  4197877  4197883  4197887  4197913  4197923  4197967  4198003  4198013
4198037  4198039  4198049  4198079  4198093  4198097  4198111  4198141  4198211  4198247
4198261  4198307  4198309  4198319  4198321  4198331  4198333  4198339  4198343  4198349
4198357  4198379  4198409  4198429  4198433  4198457  4198471  4198511  4198517  4198529
4198543  4198549  4198553  4198567  4198577  4198583  4198631  4198637  4198669  4198703
4198709  4198729  4198757  4198759  4198763  4198781  4198793  4198807  4198837  4198877
4198879  4198889  4198891  4198921  4198927  4198937  4198963  4198973  4199003  4199009
4199021  4199023  4199029  4199071  4199077  4199131  4199141  4199149  4199177  4199183
4199189  4199201  4199213  4199231  4199257  4199269  4199281  4199297  4199303  4199311
4199341  4199347  4199383  4199387  4199411  4199441  4199473  4199483  4199491  4199543
4199557  4199563  4199567  4199599  4199603  4199609  4199633  4199647  4199653  4199659
4199669  4199707  4199711  4199747  4199749  4199771  4199791  4199801  4199803  4199813
4199827  4199837  4199851  4199861  4199887  4199891  4199903  4199927  4199929  4199957
4199963  4199971  4199977  4199999  4200013  4200019  4200023  4200043  4200047  4200073
4200103  4200109  4200113  4200127  4200137  4200143  4200149  4200167  4200187  4200199
4200211  4200223  4200227  4200233  4200239  4200247  4200257  4200263  4200299  4200307
4200319  4200341  4200397  4200401  4200403  4200419  4200433  4200439  4200451  4200481
4200487  4200523  4200527  4200529  4200583  4200587  4200601  4200607  4200611  4200617
4200629  4200661  4200671  4200689  4200701  4200709  4200731  4200733  4200739  4200761
4200769  4200797  4200803  4200809  4200821  4200827  4200863  4200877  4200883  4200923
4200941  4200947  4200949  4200953  4200991  4201003  4201007  4201013  4201051  4201063
4201069  4201073  4201079  4201103  4201123  4201177  4201181  4201199  4201207  4201217
4201243  4201247  4201271  4201279  4201289  4201291  4201303  4201319  4201321  4201343
4201357  4201367  4201391  4201409  4201429  4201447  4201459  4201493  4201501  4201513
4201529  4201531  4201537  4201577  4201579  4201583  4201621  4201633  4201649  4201699
4201711  4201727  4201739  4201751  4201763  4201789  4201811  4201817  4201837  4201843
4201849  4201853  4201861  4201889  4201891  4201933  4201937  4201961  4201963  4201969
4202017  4202027  4202047  4202057  4202063  4202069  4202083  4202113  4202117  4202141
4202147  4202153  4202161  4202167  4202171  4202183  4202203  4202227  4202257  4202269
4202273  4202279  4202293  4202311  4202321  4202327  4202339  4202369  4202371  4202381
4202389  4202413  4202447  4202449  4202461  4202467  4202479  4202483  4202489  4202501
4202521  4202567  4202579  4202633  4202641  4202657  4202663  4202677  4202687  4202729
4202761  4202771  4202773  4202789  4202797  4202827  4202851  4202897  4202899  4202903
4202911  4202923  4202929  4202959  4202963  4202969  4202981  4202993  4203013  4203019
4203041  4203049  4203053  4203071  4203109  4203113  4203119  4203127  4203139  4203169
4203187  4203191  4203193  4203209  4203217  4203229  4203239  4203247  4203263  4203307
4203349  4203371  4203373  4203391  4203421  4203431  4203473  4203491  4203509  4203517
4203523  4203527  4203581  4203583  4203587  4203593  4203599  4203601  4203611  4203613
4203643  4203649  4203677  4203707  4203757  4203767  4203791  4203799  4203841  4203847
4203863  4203887  4203889  4203893  4203911  4203919  4203929  4203931  4203961  4203967
4203973  4204001  4204007  4204027  4204037  4204061  4204063  4204069  4204091  4204097
4204121  4204133  4204139  4204141  4204157  4204169  4204223  4204237  4204243  4204279
4204283  4204307  4204309  4204337  4204363  4204367  4204379  4204429  4204439  4204441
4204471  4204477  4204481  4204489  4204493  4204511  4204523  4204537  4204553  4204579
4204601  4204609  4204633  4204639  4204657  4204663  4204679  4204687  4204703  4204709
4204723  4204741  4204751  4204799  4204807  4204819  4204859  4204903  4204943
4204961  4204973  4204997  4204999  4205009  4205011  4205017  4205027  4205039  4205041
4205053  4205059  4205063  4205077  4205081  4205093  4205129  4205143  4205147  4205153
4205177  4205183  4205189  4205191  4205219  4205233  4205269  4205281  4205303  4205317
4205321  4205323  4205347  4205353  4205363  4205371  4205381  4205393  4205437  4205459
4205473  4205507  4205533  4205549  4205569  4205581  4205587  4205599  4205611  4205623
4205651  4205659  4205671  4205687  4205689  4205699  4205713  4205717  4205731  4205737
4205743  4205777  4205779  4205797  4205809  4205813  4205819  4205833  4205837  4205857
4205869  4205879  4205891  4205909  4205911  4205917  4205923  4205947  4205951  4205977
4205989  4206019  4206023  4206029  4206053  4206061  4206091  4206101  4206107  4206109
4206119  4206127  4206151  4206179  4206203  4206221  4206227  4206233  4206281  4206283
4206299  4206317  4206329  4206331  4206337  4206373  4206379  4206383  4206409  4206413
4206427  4206431  4206439  4206443  4206469  4206473  4206481  4206487  4206511  4206529
4206533  4206551  4206569  4206577  4206583  4206593  4206611  4206613  4206659  4206673
4206691  4206703  4206721  4206737  4206739  4206749  4206757  4206767  4206773  4206779
4206781  4206791  4206817  4206823  4206857  4206883  4206893  4206899  4206901  4206929
4206931  4206947  4206967  4206971  4207003  4207031  4207039  4207043  4207061  4207079
4207097  4207139  4207141  4207201  4207213  4207219  4207237  4207243  4207253  4207261
4207267  4207277  4207283  4207309  4207319  4207331  4207337  4207339  4207373  4207397
4207433  4207453  4207471  4207477  4207481  4207571  4207583  4207591  4207613  4207627
4207631  4207633  4207657  4207663  4207691  4207717  4207729  4207733  4207771  4207799
4207807  4207837  4207843  4207867  4207877  4207883  4207901  4207913  4207933  4207943
4207961  4207969  4207981  4207991  4208053  4208059  4208077  4208081  4208107  4208123
4208131  4208143  4208159  4208173  4208179  4208189  4208209  4208221  4208227  4208249
4208257  4208261  4208273  4208297  4208311  4208339  4208341  4208357  4208371  4208387
4208419  4208429  4208437  4208441  4208447  4208473  4208483  4208489  4208507  4208549
4208579  4208593  4208621  4208623  4208627  4208629  4208641  4208657  4208689  4208717
4208731  4208753  4208759  4208761  4208779  4208801  4208821  4208849  4208863  4208879
4208887  4208891  4208903  4208923  4208933  4208947  4208959  4208983  4208999  4209011
4209017  4209097  4209103  4209109  4209113  4209131  4209151  4209167  4209169  4209181
4209187  4209209  4209221  4209223  4209229  4209259  4209269  4209281  4209311  4209349
4209371  4209383  4209389  4209407  4209451  4209463  4209481  4209493  4209497  4209503
4209533  4209539  4209559  4209563  4209587  4209613  4209617  4209629  4209643  4209679
4209683  4209719  4209739  4209763  4209767  4209787  4209797  4209809  4209817  4209833
4209853  4209859  4209869  4209871  4209883  4209889  4209899  4209911  4209913  4209929
4209937  4209977  4209979  4209991  4210013  4210021  4210043  4210049  4210061  4210069
4210093  4210103  4210109  4210121  4210139  4210187  4210207  4210211  4210247  4210253
4210277  4210279  4210291  4210303  4210309  4210321  4210337  4210361  4210391  4210397
4210399  4210411  4210429  4210433  4210447  4210469  4210487  4210499  4210519  4210523
4210553  4210559  4210573  4210579  4210601  4210607  4210627  4210631  4210639  4210643
4210649  4210667  4210693  4210709  4210721  4210763  4210783  4210793  4210807  4210813
```

```
4210819  4210831  4210841  4210853  4210879  4210919  4210931  4210963  4210967  4210981
4211021  4211023  4211029  4211063  4211083  4211099  4211101  4211107  4211111  4211113
4211117  4211131  4211143  4211147  4211149  4211159  4211161  4211167  4211173  4211203
4211219  4211267  4211279  4211281  4211299  4211321  4211371  4211387  4211399  4211401
4211423  4211491  4211497  4211513  4211533  4211551  4211579  4211591  4211593  4211609
4211633  4211639  4211653  4211657  4211659  4211671  4211681  4211693  4211707  4211723
4211729  4211743  4211759  4211761  4211797  4211819  4211861  4211887  4211891  4211899
4211917  4211927  4211929  4211981  4211983  4211993  4212023  4212029  4212071  4212097
4212101  4212113  4212119  4212121  4212127  4212137  4212139  4212161  4212179  4212181
4212199  4212203  4212211  4212227  4212239  4212251  4212283  4212287  4212317  4212331
4212343  4212353  4212361  4212367  4212371  4212401  4212421  4212431  4212437  4212443
4212449  4212457  4212479  4212521  4212529  4212557  4212577  4212587  4212589  4212601
4212629  4212641  4212647  4212653  4212679  4212701  4212707  4212713  4212727  4212731
4212739  4212763  4212773  4212797  4212799  4212827  4212847  4212863  4212881  4212883
4212907  4212919  4212941  4212973  4212977  4212983  4213019  4213031  4213043  4213063
4213073  4213081  4213103  4213133  4213141  4213147  4213151  4213159  4213189  4213199
4213217  4213277  4213309  4213333  4213337  4213357  4213369  4213379  4213397  4213411
4213423  4213457  4213463  4213471  4213483  4213519  4213543  4213567  4213589  4213591
4213609  4213639  4213673  4213679  4213681  4213717  4213747  4213753  4213757  4213771
4213793  4213813  4213817  4213837  4213843  4213889  4213897  4213901  4213907  4213949
4213969  4213999  4214003  4214009  4214051  4214053  4214057  4214069  4214087  4214117
4214131  4214173  4214183  4214191  4214201  4214207  4214209  4214213  4214227
4214237  4214269  4214279  4214281  4214291  4214293  4214323  4214377  4214381  4214383
4214393  4214407  4214437  4214479  4214503  4214519  4214549  4214569  4214591  4214603
4214611  4214627  4214641  4214647  4214653  4214659  4214669  4214671  4214687  4214699
4214701  4214711  4214741  4214753  4214761  4214779  4214807  4214851  4214867  4214879
4214891  4214893  4214909  4214933  4214939  4214953  4214971  4214981  4215011  4215023
4215041  4215047  4215059  4215073  4215083  4215089  4215091  4215103  4215157  4215191
4215193  4215217  4215221  4215227  4215229  4215241  4215259  4215301  4215317  4215319
4215347  4215389  4215401  4215403  4215413  4215427  4215443  4215451  4215457  4215493
4215503  4215517  4215539  4215551  4215553  4215577  4215599  4215613  4215619  4215641
4215683  4215689  4215697  4215719  4215749  4215751  4215773  4215781  4215787  4215803
4215811  4215821  4215829  4215833  4215839  4215859  4215863  4215889  4215899  4215919
4215941  4215971  4215979  4216001  4216007  4216027  4216057  4216063  4216067  4216073
4216117  4216127  4216129  4216133  4216171  4216189  4216211  4216231  4216237  4216241
4216283  4216297  4216327  4216343  4216351  4216363  4216367  4216393  4216411  4216439
4216441  4216469  4216501  4216507  4216517  4216523  4216573  4216579  4216591  4216603
4216607  4216633  4216657  4216661  4216669  4216691  4216721  4216741  4216753  4216787
4216801  4216811  4216819  4216847  4216871  4216897  4216931  4216937  4216939
4216943  4216951  4216957  4216963  4216999  4217011  4217029  4217039  4217041  4217063
4217077  4217111  4217117  4217131  4217141  4217159  4217167  4217203  4217231  4217233
4217237  4217281  4217287  4217321  4217341  4217359  4217363  4217387  4217393  4217401
4217413  4217417  4217431  4217453  4217459  4217461  4217489  4217501  4217503  4217531
4217539  4217561  4217597  4217611  4217617  4217623  4217669  4217693  4217699  4217701
4217713  4217729  4217737  4217749  4217761  4217771  4217779  4217783  4217813  4217831
4217839  4217849  4217881  4217883  4217903  4217909  4217911  4217923  4217929
4217959  4217971  4217987  4218001  4218007  4218031  4218061  4218103  4218107  4218113
4218157  4218163  4218167  4218169  4218173  4218199  4218241  4218251  4218271  4218281
4218283  4218287  4218289  4218293  4218299  4218317  4218349  4218353  4218359  4218371
4218377  4218413  4218439  4218463  4218469  4218497  4218509  4218517  4218541  4218547
4218563  4218569  4218581  4218583  4218623  4218631  4218667  4218671  4218701  4218707
4218713  4218733  4218751  4218763  4218791  4218793  4218803  4218829  4218847  4218857
4218869  4218899  4218901  4218917  4218947  4218961  4218967  4218971  4218979  4218989
4218997  4219001  4219013  4219027  4219079  4219093  4219099  4219133  4219151  4219183
4219211  4219217  4219219  4219231  4219261  4219283  4219301  4219333  4219357  4219361
4219363  4219427  4219429  4219447  4219487  4219507  4219513  4219549  4219571  4219573
4219583  4219609  4219651  4219673  4219681  4219687  4219693  4219697  4219711  4219753
4219769  4219771  4219781  4219799  4219823  4219847  4219849  4219871  4219909  4219933
4219939  4219949  4219951  4219967  4219979  4219981  4219987  4219991  4220039  4220053
4220059  4220077  4220081  4220137  4220141  4220143  4220173  4220189  4220207  4220239
4220243  4220269  4220287  4220297  4220323  4220327  4220347  4220351  4220353  4220357
4220387  4220393  4220423  4220441  4220449  4220473  4220483  4220497  4220509  4220519
4220521  4220533  4220537  4220543  4220551  4220563  4220597  4220599  4220609  4220617
4220639  4220653  4220659  4220687  4220693  4220719  4220729  4220731  4220767  4220771
4220789  4220791  4220803  4220809  4220813  4220819  4220851  4220857  4220861  4220873
4220911  4220917  4220927  4220939  4220941  4220961  4220963  4220969  4220971  4220977
4220987  4221011  4221031  4221047  4221109  4221169  4221179  4221193  4221197  4221209
4221223  4221227  4221229  4221247  4221263  4221271  4221281  4221299  4221307  4221311
4221313  4221323  4221337  4221361  4221379  4221407  4221409  4221419  4221421  4221433
4221449  4221467  4221473  4221479  4221499  4221521  4221523  4221531  4221551  4221563
4221571  4221577  4221583  4221619  4221631  4221641  4221643  4221649  4221653  4221671
4221677  4221683  4221691  4221703  4221713  4221751  4221761  4221769  4221779  4221787
4221799  4221827  4221833  4221851  4221883  4221911  4221913  4221923  4221941  4221953
4221977  4221989  4222003  4222007  4222013  4222037  4222051  4222061  4222063  4222067
4222091  4222093  4222117  4222177  4222219  4222243  4222277  4222289  4222297  4222319
4222343  4222367  4222373  4222381  4222391  4222397  4222399  4222483  4222489  4222513
4222529  4222553  4222577  4222591  4222597  4222601  4222619  4222627  4222637  4222649
4222657  4222667  4222679  4222703  4222711  4222717  4222721  4222723  4222739  4222747
4222759  4222763  4222781  4222793  4222811  4222837  4222843  4222849  4222859  4222871
4222909  4222927  4222937  4222963  4222973  4223003  4223027  4223039  4223053  4223057
4223071  4223083  4223117  4223171  4223179  4223189  4223207  4223231  4223239  4223243
4223251  4223257  4223267  4223311  4223333  4223353  4223363  4223371  4223381  4223383
4223393  4223407  4223413  4223431  4223441  4223459  4223501  4223507  4223509  4223519
4223521  4223537  4223539  4223543  4223551  4223563  4223617  4223627  4223629  4223663
4223669  4223677  4223689  4223699  4223717  4223741  4223753  4223759  4223767  4223773
4223777  4223783  4223801  4223831  4223839  4223873  4223897  4223903  4223911  4223959
4223963  4223977  4223981  4223983  4223993  4224037  4224049  4224097  4224127  4224131
4224139  4224161  4224167  4224197  4224229  4224247  4224281  4224317  4224331  4224361
4224371  4224373  4224377  4224379  4224383  4224391  4224397  4224427  4224439  4224443
```

```
4224457  4224461  4224469  4224491  4224503  4224511  4224529  4224541  4224557  4224559
4224589  4224601  4224607  4224611  4224613  4224629  4224637  4224667  4224673  4224679
4224719  4224733  4224739  4224743  4224761  4224769  4224791  4224809  4224811  4224827
4224839  4224851  4224889  4224901  4224911  4224917  4224947  4224967  4224977  4224991
4225003  4225007  4225019  4225037  4225069  4225073  4225079  4225099  4225103  4225121
4225147  4225171  4225189  4225211  4225219  4225229  4225237  4225283  4225297  4225301
4225303  4225339  4225357  4225373  4225381  4225411  4225427  4225439  4225451  4225457
4225477  4225483  4225499  4225513  4225519  4225523  4225541  4225547  4225549  4225589
4225597  4225607  4225609  4225633  4225649  4225651  4225679  4225691  4225709  4225729
4225769  4225783  4225787  4225799  4225811  4225841  4225853  4225873  4225901  4225931
4225933  4225937  4225943  4225957  4225973  4225981  4226009  4226063  4226077  4226093
4226107  4226153  4226161  4226171  4226203  4226207  4226213  4226219  4226221  4226231
4226249  4226279  4226281  4226291  4226297  4226309  4226333  4226351  4226359  4226371
4226377  4226389  4226401  4226413  4226423  4226429  4226459  4226471  4226477  4226479
4226501  4226527  4226533  4226543  4226611  4226617  4226623  4226647  4226657  4226671
4226681  4226689  4226707  4226711  4226713  4226767  4226791  4226809  4226839  4226867
4226891  4226903  4226933  4226939  4226993  4227023  4227031  4227037  4227043  4227049
4227061  4227077  4227089  4227103  4227109  4227137  4227149  4227161  4227187  4227229
4227247  4227257  4227277  4227281  4227283  4227299  4227313  4227317  4227323  4227337
4227341  4227371  4227383  4227389  4227397  4227401  4227413  4227427  4227451  4227491
4227511  4227521  4227523  4227529  4227571  4227599  4227637  4227659  4227661  4227667
4227689  4227701  4227719  4227739  4227761  4227787  4227793  4227809  4227827  4227859
4227869  4227877  4227887  4227893  4227931  4227959  4227967  4227973  4227983  4227989
4227991  4228031  4228039  4228079  4228097  4228099  4228109  4228111  4228141  4228157
4228177  4228199  4228243  4228247  4228267  4228271  4228309  4228313  4228349  4228351
4228361  4228363  4228373  4228381  4228387  4228391  4228423  4228429  4228457  4228487
4228489  4228501  4228513  4228531  4228537  4228559  4228561  4228591  4228603  4228613
4228649  4228669  4228673  4228723  4228727  4228739  4228759  4228771  4228787  4228789
4228793  4228813  4228837  4228843  4228853  4228859  4228879  4228883  4228891  4228897
4228901  4228907  4228951  4228979  4228993  4229003  4229021  4229023  4229047  4229059
4229081  4229089  4229101  4229117  4229119  4229129  4229143  4229167  4229207  4229213
4229231  4229249  4229279  4229287  4229317  4229339  4229383  4229387  4229411  4229417
4229429  4229441  4229443  4229461  4229473  4229479  4229503  4229521  4229543  4229573
4229579  4229587  4229623  4229633  4229639  4229657  4229689  4229699  4229707  4229711
4229713  4229717  4229741  4229747  4229749  4229759  4229767  4229783  4229809  4229833
4229843  4229851  4229873  4229881  4229891  4229921  4229933  4229941  4229947  4229971
4229993  4230007  4230071  4230101  4230113  4230119  4230133  4230139  4230169  4230197
4230199  4230203  4230209  4230221  4230223  4230227  4230283  4230311  4230337  4230377
4230379  4230389  4230397  4230403  4230419  4230451  4230463  4230481  4230487  4230493
4230571  4230623  4230631  4230649  4230659  4230661  4230683  4230719  4230731  4230757
4230763  4230791  4230797  4230803  4230817  4230847  4230851  4230857  4230859  4230871
4230883  4230917  4230923  4230929  4230953  4230959  4230997  4231027  4231033  4231039
4231049  4231063  4231069  4231099  4231109  4231111  4231121  4231177  4231189  4231207
4231211  4231219  4231229  4231247  4231261  4231267  4231277  4231291  4231309  4231313
4231321  4231369  4231373  4231391  4231393  4231399  4231417  4231427  4231429  4231459
4231463  4231483  4231537  4231541  4231553  4231559  4231561  4231567  4231603  4231607
4231627  4231637  4231663  4231687  4231697  4231723  4231741  4231751  4231763  4231769
4231771  4231781  4231783  4231789  4231811  4231817  4231823  4231831  4231837  4231843
4231853  4231859  4231873  4231901  4231919  4231943  4231967  4231991  4231993  4232009
4232051  4232101  4232113  4232131  4232147  4232159  4232183  4232191  4232197  4232233
4232237  4232257  4232279  4232287  4232309  4232351  4232353  4232357  4232407  4232413
4232443  4232453  4232477  4232509  4232519  4232537  4232539  4232549  4232581  4232593
4232597  4232603  4232623  4232629  4232651  4232653  4232659  4232693  4232707  4232731
4232737  4232743  4232747  4232777  4232819  4232821  4232827  4232849  4232863  4232873
4232887  4232903  4232909  4232933  4232999  4233001  4233007  4233013  4233023  4233041
4233071  4233077  4233079  4233109  4233113  4233121  4233139  4233161  4233167  4233169
4233179  4233199  4233247  4233259  4233263  4233287  4233301  4233331  4233347  4233349
4233367  4233389  4233401  4233419  4233421  4233433  4233457  4233473  4233499  4233521
4233533  4233539  4233547  4233553  4233563  4233569  4233571  4233589  4233601  4233611
4233613  4233631  4233653  4233661  4233667  4233673  4233707  4233709  4233743  4233767
4233769  4233773  4233787  4233793  4233811  4233839  4233851  4233857  4233869  4233871
4233877  4233907  4233919  4233937  4233959  4233961  4233967  4233973  4233989  4234007
4234019  4234033  4234039  4234049  4234057  4234063  4234067  4234091  4234099  4234103
4234141  4234157  4234177  4234187  4234189  4234201  4234211  4234213  4234229  4234247
4234249  4234271  4234273  4234291  4234301  4234337  4234361  4234367  4234379  4234381
4234387  4234393  4234409  4234421  4234423  4234427  4234429  4234453  4234459  4234463
4234469  4234481  4234487  4234501  4234537  4234651  4234673  4234679  4234697  4234721
4234723  4234733  4234771  4234781  4234787  4234793  4234801  4234823  4234861  4234873
4234877  4234907  4234927  4234933  4234939  4234943  4234963  4234973  4234987  4234991
4235017  4235041  4235083  4235129  4235141  4235149  4235201  4235237  4235263  4235281
4235293  4235299  4235321  4235327  4235351  4235377  4235383  4235401  4235411  4235419
4235443  4235453  4235467  4235471  4235503  4235521  4235531  4235549  4235557  4235563
4235591  4235603  4235633  4235639  4235659  4235663  4235683  4235713  4235717  4235719
4235731  4235741  4235761  4235767  4235773  4235783  4235837  4235851  4235863  4235867
4235897  4235899  4235923  4235939  4235947  4235951  4235953  4235963  4235977  4235999
4236049  4236061  4236097  4236101  4236103  4236109  4236121  4236137  4236139  4236149
4236187  4236191  4236203  4236269  4236283  4236307  4236313  4236319  4236329  4236341
4236359  4236361  4236371  4236431  4236433  4236437  4236461  4236527  4236541  4236619
4236643  4236679  4236703  4236707  4236719  4236737  4236773  4236779  4236797  4236803
4236811  4236821  4236887  4236889  4236917  4236937  4236941  4236971  4236983  4236989
4236997  4237031  4237033  4237043  4237069  4237087  4237117  4237127  4237151  4237153
4237183  4237229  4237237  4237241  4237271  4237279  4237283  4237319  4237333  4237397
4237417  4237423  4237427  4237433  4237459  4237463  4237469  4237477  4237501  4237507
4237529  4237531  4237537  4237559  4237601  4237603  4237619  4237621  4237631  4237643
4237663  4237679  4237687  4237697  4237699  4237733  4237747  4237757  4237759  4237763
4237769  4237781  4237787  4237813  4237829  4237841  4237843  4237861  4237867  4237873
4237889  4237921  4237927  4237939  4237963  4237967  4237993  4237999  4238011  4238033
4238053  4238057  4238071  4238077  4238093  4238107  4238119  4238149  4238153  4238167
4238177  4238189  4238231  4238237  4238257  4238261  4238281  4238303  4238309  4238393
```

```
4238407  4238431  4238459  4238513  4238519  4238543  4238551  4238567  4238573  4238579
4238617  4238651  4238657  4238687  4238699  4238719  4238747  4238753  4238761  4238783
4238791  4238807  4238813  4238833  4238837  4238851  4238873  4238911  4238929  4238953
4238963  4238989  4238999  4239013  4239041  4239043  4239047  4239069  4239101  4239121
4239149  4239161  4239163  4239167  4239173  4239187  4239211  4239229  4239247  4239251
4239269  4239271  4239289  4239293  4239331  4239371  4239373  4239379  4239397  4239401
4239419  4239449  4239457  4239463  4239469  4239479  4239491  4239493  4239509  4239533
4239577  4239593  4239601  4239607  4239611  4239649  4239667  4239673  4239701  4239721
4239731  4239733  4239737  4239739  4239743  4239761  4239803  4239811  4239821  4239847
4239853  4239857  4239877  4239881  4239923  4239931  4239971  4239979  4239997  4240007
4240037  4240043  4240063  4240069  4240079  4240091  4240109  4240111  4240127  4240139
4240147  4240151  4240169  4240183  4240207  4240217  4240219  4240267  4240277  4240279
4240289  4240319  4240381  4240399  4240417  4240421  4240433  4240447  4240451  4240469
4240493  4240499  4240501  4240513  4240519  4240541  4240547  4240559  4240567  4240597
4240603  4240619  4240627  4240661  4240673  4240679  4240693  4240697  4240711  4240721
4240729  4240741  4240783  4240787  4240801  4240807  4240811  4240823  4240843
4240853  4240909  4240913  4240927  4240963  4240967  4240969  4240981  4240991
4241021  4241023  4241057  4241059  4241063  4241071  4241077  4241089  4241093  4241099
4241101  4241119  4241129  4241173  4241183  4241189  4241191  4241201  4241207  4241239
4241261  4241291  4241297  4241317  4241329  4241339  4241353  4241357  4241371  4241399
4241411  4241429  4241443  4241459  4241507  4241509  4241521  4241539  4241581  4241593
4241597  4241599  4241603  4241621  4241623  4241639  4241641  4241647  4241659  4241663
4241689  4241711  4241723  4241759  4241771  4241773  4241779  4241813  4241827  4241833
4241843  4241851  4241873  4241893  4241903  4241929  4241977  4241987  4241989  4242019
4242023  4242031  4242059  4242109  4242127  4242131  4242137  4242167  4242169  4242191
4242209  4242211  4242223  4242233  4242239  4242247  4242253  4242269  4242283
4242289  4242307  4242317  4242349  4242353  4242391  4242397  4242409  4242421  4242437
4242449  4242451  4242461  4242473  4242517  4242523  4242547  4242551  4242569  4242593
4242617  4242619  4242659  4242661  4242677  4242709  4242713  4242751  4242761  4242781
4242829  4242839  4242841  4242851  4242859  4242869  4242883  4242893  4242907  4242913
4242919  4242929  4242963  4242983  4242989  4242991  4243003  4243009  4243039
4243051  4243067  4243069  4243087  4243091  4243093  4243117  4243121  4243139  4243147
4243181  4243189  4243199  4243219  4243237  4243243  4243279  4243297  4243307  4243321
4243357  4243361  4243391  4243397  4243409  4243411  4243427  4243429  4243433  4243439
4243453  4243469  4243487  4243511  4243529  4243543  4243549  4243571  4243573  4243597
4243607  4243619  4243633  4243639  4243649  4243667  4243699  4243711  4243721  4243747
4243781  4243793  4243819  4243859  4243861  4243879  4243903  4243927  4243933  4243949
4243957  4243961  4243969  4243979  4243991  4243997  4244003  4244017  4244021  4244027
4244059  4244069  4244083  4244099  4244129  4244137  4244153  4244161  4244183  4244221
4244299  4244311  4244329  4244333  4244341  4244347  4244363  4244377  4244389  4244417
4244423  4244431  4244437  4244447  4244473  4244477  4244479  4244491  4244497  4244503
4244507  4244521  4244533  4244549  4244567  4244579  4244609  4244621  4244629  4244633
4244641  4244663  4244693  4244707  4244729  4244743  4244753  4244767  4244777  4244791
4244819  4244827  4244833  4244837  4244881  4244893  4244909  4244927  4244963  4244969
4244971  4244983  4244987  4245013  4245029  4245077  4245079  4245091  4245103  4245119
4245149  4245167  4245193  4245203  4245209  4245217  4245239  4245259  4245289  4245301
4245313  4245331  4245337  4245361  4245407  4245413  4245443  4245469  4245473  4245487
4245499  4245511  4245517  4245551  4245581  4245599  4245601  4245611  4245613  4245617
4245623  4245643  4245679  4245743  4245779  4245793  4245799  4245811  4245821  4245827
4245833  4245847  4245851  4245881  4245907  4245929  4245947  4245973  4246003  4246019
4246043  4246049  4246051  4246057  4246061  4246087  4246111  4246127  4246129  4246147
4246159  4246181  4246199  4246213  4246217  4246241  4246273  4246301  4246303  4246327
4246331  4246357  4246381  4246387  4246391  4246397  4246409  4246433  4246469  4246507
4246511  4246523  4246547  4246553  4246577  4246603  4246609  4246679  4246681  4246691
4246717  4246727  4246741  4246751  4246763  4246769  4246771  4246799  4246807  4246817
4246819  4246831  4246843  4246877  4246883  4246919  4246939  4246987  4246993  4247011
4247017  4247039  4247053  4247057  4247069  4247071  4247081  4247101  4247107  4247129
4247147  4247167  4247209  4247227  4247251  4247273  4247281  4247333  4247363  4247371
4247377  4247381  4247389  4247407  4247417  4247429  4247443  4247447  4247449  4247459
4247461  4247471  4247513  4247539  4247549  4247561  4247567  4247597  4247609  4247611
4247623  4247629  4247687  4247689  4247693  4247707  4247729  4247741  4247743  4247753
4247759  4247767  4247777  4247809  4247819  4247821  4247827  4247863  4247917  4247923
4247981  4247983  4248017  4248019  4248037  4248043  4248061  4248071  4248073  4248091
4248103  4248121  4248131  4248151  4248173  4248187  4248193  4248227  4248253
4248259  4248281  4248287  4248319  4248323  4248331  4248337  4248347  4248371  4248389
4248397  4248401  4248421  4248449  4248463  4248479  4248481  4248539  4248551  4248553
4248557  4248611  4248617  4248631  4248661  4248667  4248683  4248689  4248709  4248719
4248731  4248733  4248737  4248743  4248749  4248757  4248779  4248791  4248809  4248817
4248823  4248869  4248883  4248901  4248911  4248917  4248919  4248931  4248947  4248967
4248971  4248977  4248983  4248991  4249067  4249087  4249097  4249123  4249151  4249159
4249163  4249211  4249237  4249241  4249249  4249253  4249261  4249277  4249307  4249309
4249313  4249327  4249361  4249391  4249409  4249417  4249423  4249429  4249433  4249447
4249451  4249459  4249463  4249477  4249481  4249501  4249513  4249523  4249537  4249543
4249571  4249577  4249579  4249613  4249621  4249627  4249633  4249669  4249703  4249717
4249723  4249741  4249753  4249757  4249769  4249789  4249793  4249799  4249807  4249823
4249831  4249853  4249867  4249873  4249897  4249913  4249943  4249951  4249957  4249961
4249967  4249969  4249981  4250021  4250023  4250027  4250039  4250041  4250047  4250063
4250083  4250107  4250111  4250149  4250159  4250169  4250171  4250177  4250179  4250189
4250209  4250219  4250231  4250251  4250261  4250287  4250291  4250293  4250299  4250303
4250321  4250329  4250333  4250353  4250359  4250369  4250387  4250431  4250447  4250453
4250479  4250483  4250489  4250531  4250567  4250569  4250573  4250591  4250599  4250611
4250621  4250639  4250657  4250711  4250723  4250747  4250749  4250767  4250777  4250809
4250843  4250861  4250879  4250887  4250899  4250903  4250923  4250933  4250941  4250951
4250957  4250959  4250963  4250977  4250993  4251019  4251031  4251043  4251053  4251073
4251131  4251157  4251161  4251199  4251223  4251239  4251253  4251259  4251277  4251283
4251293  4251311  4251323  4251329  4251347  4251349  4251353  4251361  4251397  4251407
4251419  4251449  4251451  4251461  4251463  4251491  4251493  4251523  4251553  4251563
4251589  4251601  4251617  4251623  4251629  4251631  4251647  4251691  4251697  4251703
4251721  4251727  4251733  4251749  4251769  4251773  4251799  4251809  4251817  4251829
```

```
4251847  4251857  4251869  4251889  4251917  4251931  4251967  4251971  4252019  4252037
4252051  4252063  4252081  4252093  4252097  4252103  4252109  4252111  4252117  4252121
4252123  4252147  4252163  4252169  4252187  4252207  4252211  4252229  4252253  4252271
4252277  4252279  4252319  4252327  4252337  4252351  4252393  4252421  4252433  4252439
4252459  4252463  4252471  4252477  4252481  4252489  4252511  4252519  4252541  4252553
4252559  4252583  4252679  4252681  4252709  4252711  4252727  4252739  4252747  4252753
4252757  4252777  4252793  4252799  4252813  4252819  4252823  4252841  4252847  4252867
4252877  4252883  4252901  4252933  4252939  4252951  4252961  4252987  4252991  4252993
4253023  4253027  4253047  4253057  4253083  4253089  4253099  4253101  4253129  4253147
4253153  4253167  4253201  4253203  4253209  4253233  4253237  4253257  4253267  4253273
4253309  4253311  4253317  4253329  4253341  4253351  4253371  4253387  4253393  4253419
4253423  4253429  4253437  4253443  4253449  4253461  4253467  4253477  4253489  4253531
4253537  4253563  4253567  4253573  4253593  4253609  4253617  4253651  4253653  4253671
4253693  4253699  4253707  4253719  4253731  4253737  4253741  4253759  4253803  4253813
4253831  4253839  4253849  4253863  4253867  4253869  4253917  4253941  4253969  4254007
4254013  4254049  4254053  4254083  4254091  4254101  4254109  4254113  4254127  4254139
4254163  4254179  4254181  4254191  4254193  4254197  4254203  4254227  4254247  4254251
4254253  4254259  4254269  4254277  4254311  4254319  4254353  4254361  4254389  4254449
4254451  4254473  4254491  4254527  4254541  4254553  4254557  4254559  4254571  4254583
4254587  4254599  4254623  4254629  4254637  4254643  4254647  4254671  4254683  4254707
4254739  4254763  4254779  4254797  4254799  4254821  4254853  4254869  4254883  4254911
4254949  4254961  4254983  4255039  4255057  4255061  4255067  4255073  4255079  4255081
4255087  4255093  4255109  4255133  4255157  4255169  4255187  4255193  4255213  4255249
4255301  4255313  4255351  4255369  4255387  4255399  4255403  4255429  4255439  4255461
4255477  4255501  4255519  4255523  4255541  4255549  4255553  4255561  4255577  4255579
4255583  4255591  4255597  4255609  4255619  4255637  4255673  4255679  4255697  4255739
4255747  4255751  4255781  4255789  4255807  4255817  4255859  4255877  4255879  4255913
4255921  4255931  4255939  4255949  4255963  4255987  4255997  4256003  4256009  4256029
4256051  4256089  4256101  4256117  4256141  4256159  4256167  4256191  4256227  4256233
4256249  4256257  4256261  4256267  4256281  4256293  4256297  4256327  4256347  4256381
4256383  4256389  4256407  4256429  4256431  4256459  4256467  4256471  4256491  4256501
4256507  4256509  4256537  4256561  4256563  4256573  4256617  4256639  4256653  4256669
4256671  4256701  4256717  4256723  4256729  4256737  4256761  4256797  4256803  4256807
4256831  4256839  4256897  4256921  4256927  4256929  4256933  4256963  4256977  4256981
4257017  4257023  4257037  4257041  4257053  4257061  4257067  4257101  4257131  4257133
4257161  4257163  4257193  4257203  4257217  4257221  4257223  4257241  4257269  4257271
4257283  4257289  4257313  4257353  4257359  4257371  4257391  4257413  4257467  4257469
4257503  4257521  4257523  4257527  4257529  4257541  4257551  4257557  4257569  4257587
4257593  4257611  4257613  4257641  4257647  4257677  4257679  4257697  4257733  4257749
4257763  4257787  4257821  4257833  4257889  4257899  4257931  4257937  4257949  4257959
4257961  4257977  4257991  4258019  4258031  4258043  4258057  4258061  4258069  4258081
4258087  4258091  4258103  4258117  4258127  4258139  4258171  4258181  4258193  4258217
4258237  4258249  4258259  4258307  4258339  4258357  4258361  4258363  4258369  4258379
4258393  4258403  4258409  4258411  4258459  4258469  4258477  4258531  4258537  4258567
4258571  4258607  4258609  4258643  4258649  4258673  4258693  4258697  4258699  4258729
4258733  4258753  4258757  4258769  4258777  4258781  4258801  4258819  4258829  4258879
4258883  4258889  4258897  4258909  4258937  4258949  4258951  4258967  4258973  4258987
4259053  4259063  4259113  4259119  4259131  4259141  4259147  4259149  4259159  4259191
4259207  4259221  4259237  4259243  4259251  4259263  4259267  4259291  4259303  4259323
4259327  4259351  4259357  4259371  4259383  4259389  4259399  4259419  4259459  4259461
4259483  4259501  4259527  4259533  4259543  4259579  4259597  4259599  4259621  4259627
4259641  4259653  4259677  4259681  4259683  4259687  4259701  4259711  4259713  4259719
4259729  4259753  4259791  4259797  4259833  4259837  4259863  4259887  4259891  4259903
4259909  4259923  4259951  4260001  4260007  4260019  4260041  4260043  4260049  4260073
4260077  4260097  4260107  4260121  4260131  4260133  4260167  4260173  4260209  4260229
4260247  4260257  4260259  4260271  4260283  4260293  4260317  4260323  4260343  4260367
4260371  4260383  4260401  4260413  4260437  4260457  4260461  4260467  4260479  4260481
4260517  4260521  4260527  4260551  4260601  4260623  4260629  4260643  4260647  4260649
4260677  4260689  4260703  4260713  4260719  4260721  4260743  4260749  4260757  4260793
4260799  4260821  4260833  4260859  4260877  4260899  4260901  4260917  4260967  4261009
4261013  4261021  4261027  4261051  4261079  4261087  4261093  4261109  4261129  4261139
4261151  4261177  4261183  4261189  4261193  4261199  4261211  4261219  4261223  4261249
4261261  4261273  4261319  4261321  4261331  4261333  4261351  4261357  4261363  4261381
4261391  4261421  4261423  4261483  4261519  4261541  4261547  4261553  4261583  4261589
4261597  4261613  4261627  4261651  4261661  4261709  4261711  4261723  4261727  4261759
4261793  4261837  4261841  4261843  4261853  4261867  4261903  4261931  4261949  4261963
4261979  4261981  4261987  4261997  4262003  4262029  4262033  4262047  4262051  4262077
4262119  4262143  4262147  4262153  4262161  4262171  4262173  4262177  4262179  4262183
4262191  4262197  4262233  4262239  4262249  4262261  4262267  4262281  4262303  4262311
4262329  4262351  4262353  4262387  4262389  4262399  4262417  4262431  4262459  4262491
4262509  4262513  4262549  4262551  4262561  4262581  4262611  4262617  4262639  4262653
4262677  4262683  4262693  4262701  4262743  4262749  4262777  4262803  4262813  4262831
4262849  4262851  4262873  4262887  4262889  4262933  4262941  4262969  4262983
4263001  4263013  4263037  4263047  4263059  4263079  4263113  4263121  4263131  4263137
4263157  4263169  4263187  4263197  4263199  4263223  4263227  4263253  4263283  4263289
4263299  4263313  4263331  4263341  4263359  4263361  4263397  4263403  4263421  4263431
4263433  4263449  4263491  4263509  4263527  4263529  4263541  4263557  4263559  4263569
4263587  4263593  4263607  4263641  4263659  4263683  4263689  4263703  4263731
4263739  4263761  4263773  4263781  4263803  4263811  4263823  4263827  4263859  4263863
4263869  4263881  4263911  4263913  4263929  4263937  4263977  4263979  4264021
4264027  4264033  4264049  4264063  4264067  4264069  4264109  4264157  4264171  4264187
4264193  4264201  4264207  4264219  4264237  4264259  4264261  4264289  4264307
4264313  4264319  4264333  4264339  4264373  4264409  4264471  4264487  4264511  4264517
4264543  4264549  4264553  4264567  4264597  4264609  4264619  4264621  4264627  4264633
4264651  4264661  4264669  4264681  4264691  4264709  4264781  4264811  4264817  4264823
4264829  4264831  4264837  4264847  4264849  4264859  4264877  4264889  4264901  4264919
4264951  4264957  4264961  4264979  4264991  4264999  4265003  4265017  4265021  4265029
4265047  4265057  4265077  4265081  4265083  4265087  4265089  4265099  4265119  4265123
4265137  4265141  4265159  4265161  4265179  4265207  4265227  4265231  4265263  4265267
```

```
4265273 4265293 4265311 4265357 4265363 4265369 4265377 4265399 4265413 4265431
4265441 4265473 4265477 4265489 4265537 4265561 4265567 4265593 4265617 4265629
4265663 4265683 4265687 4265699 4265711 4265713 4265717 4265719 4265731 4265783
4265797 4265801 4265831 4265837 4265843 4265881 4265887 4265897 4265903 4265939
4265969 4265977 4265999 4266029 4266061 4266149 4266169 4266179 4266181
4266217 4266221 4266253 4266257 4266263 4266271 4266287 4266289 4266307 4266329
4266343 4266347 4266377 4266391 4266397 4266443 4266481 4266487 4266497 4266511
4266517 4266527 4266529 4266547 4266551 4266557 4266593 4266599 4266601 4266611
4266617 4266629 4266637 4266667 4266673 4266679 4266709 4266717 4266721 4266733
4266797 4266817 4266827 4266833 4266841 4266853 4266859 4266893 4266907 4266943
4266961 4266967 4266991 4267007 4267033 4267079 4267091 4267111 4267117 4267141
4267169 4267183 4267199 4267201 4267261 4267301 4267303 4267337 4267339 4267349
4267369 4267399 4267409 4267421 4267427 4267441 4267447 4267451 4267463 4267517
4267531 4267537 4267541 4267573 4267579 4267603 4267619 4267631 4267651 4267657
4267661 4267667 4267693 4267721 4267729 4267759 4267763 4267787 4267819 4267831
4267841 4267847 4267859 4267889 4267891 4267927 4267937 4267973 4267981 4268009
4268021 4268029 4268039 4268063 4268107 4268149 4268153 4268167 4268171 4268177
4268183 4268189 4268197 4268213 4268219 4268233 4268261 4268267 4268269 4268279
4268287 4268311 4268321 4268323 4268333 4268339 4268401 4268413 4268437 4268471
4268477 4268491 4268507 4268531 4268533 4268543 4268557 4268569 4268573 4268599
4268603 4268609 4268611 4268617 4268623 4268647 4268651 4268689 4268699 4268729
4268743 4268791 4268809 4268813 4268843 4268857 4268861 4268867 4268881 4268893
4268899 4268909 4268933 4268951 4268981 4268993 4269019 4269029 4269037 4269047
4269049 4269071 4269077 4269101 4269127 4269137 4269149 4269157 4269179 4269211
4269217 4269263 4269277 4269313 4269347 4269379 4269383 4269403 4269439 4269469
4269491 4269497 4269511 4269523 4269539 4269563 4269571 4269589 4269593 4269607
4269619 4269631 4269637 4269647 4269667 4269677 4269679 4269691 4269721 4269767
4269779 4269787 4269803 4269821 4269823 4269833 4269841 4269877 4269883 4269887
4269899 4269901 4269913 4269919 4269949 4269961 4269973 4270031 4270039 4270069
4270073 4270081 4270087 4270093 4270099 4270103 4270139 4270169 4270177 4270181
4270199 4270223 4270229 4270261 4270283 4270289 4270297 4270303 4270319 4270327
4270363 4270391 4270397 4270411 4270447 4270463 4270471 4270499 4270501 4270507
4270517 4270523 4270531 4270537 4270543 4270559 4270589 4270603 4270633 4270639
4270667 4270697 4270699 4270703 4270727 4270741 4270751 4270789 4270807 4270811
4270817 4270829 4270837 4270841 4270853 4270879 4270891 4270907 4270909 4270921
4270943 4270949 4270957 4270969 4270997 4271009 4271017 4271027 4271039 4271041
4271081 4271117 4271129 4271153 4271161 4271167 4271171 4271173 4271177 4271203
4271213 4271221 4271227 4271237 4271251 4271269 4271279 4271297 4271299 4271321
4271327 4271347 4271357 4271363 4271387 4271389 4271401 4271413 4271417 4271441
4271453 4271461 4271467 4271479 4271489 4271557 4271563 4271567 4271569 4271581
4271587 4271591 4271611 4271621 4271623 4271627 4271711 4271717 4271731 4271737
4271753 4271759 4271791 4271801 4271803 4271809 4271833 4271843 4271851 4271873
4271881 4271923 4271929 4271963 4272001 4272029 4272031 4272053 4272091 4272113
4272119 4272139 4272157 4272161 4272167 4272173 4272187 4272211 4272221 4272223
4272239 4272263 4272269 4272311 4272341 4272343 4272349 4272377 4272409 4272413
4272419 4272449 4272461 4272469 4272481 4272497 4272529 4272533 4272553 4272563
4272571 4272589 4272601 4272613 4272659 4272683 4272707 4272727 4272731
4272743 4272767 4272769 4272799 4272803 4272809 4272811 4272833 4272841 4272859
4272881 4272883 4272901 4272907 4272941 4272943 4272949 4272959 4272971 4272973
4273033 4273037 4273051 4273057 4273067 4273079 4273091 4273097 4273117 4273123
4273151 4273153 4273163 4273183 4273187 4273207 4273249 4273253 4273261 4273289
4273301 4273343 4273361 4273387 4273391 4273393 4273397 4273417 4273427 4273439
4273459 4273481 4273519 4273523 4273543 4273559 4273597 4273601 4273609
4273627 4273631 4273667 4273669 4273679 4273693 4273739 4273741 4273769 4273793
4273807 4273823 4273831 4273849 4273853 4273873 4273889 4273891 4273903 4273909
4273937 4273949 4273957 4273961 4273967 4274003 4274009 4274027 4274029 4274041
4274051 4274057 4274059 4274093 4274099 4274147 4274161 4274173 4274177 4274189
4274201 4274213 4274233 4274239 4274261 4274273 4274287 4274299 4274317 4274377
4274381 4274393 4274401 4274407 4274419 4274423 4274437 4274443 4274447 4274461
4274467 4274471 4274489 4274521 4274549 4274551 4274579 4274591 4274593 4274597
4274651 4274671 4274689 4274707 4274713 4274731 4274737 4274747 4274761 4274773
4274789 4274797 4274813 4274827 4274833 4274843 4274857 4274863 4274873 4274891
4274899 4274911 4274917 4274951 4274957 4274969 4274983 4274989 4274999 4275013
4275023 4275031 4275043 4275049 4275053 4275059 4275083 4275119 4275127 4275149
4275157 4275181 4275233 4275251 4275253 4275259 4275287 4275289 4275301 4275319
4275329 4275343 4275353 4275371 4275377 4275389 4275419 4275451 4275473 4275497
4275503 4275511 4275541 4275547 4275571 4275611 4275617 4275641 4275643 4275679
4275707 4275727 4275751 4275781 4275787 4275793 4275797 4275809 4275811 4275841
4275851 4275871 4275883 4275937 4275941 4275967 4275983 4275989 4275991 4276001
4276031 4276043 4276067 4276073 4276099 4276157 4276211 4276213 4276241 4276247
4276289 4276303 4276313 4276339 4276373 4276381 4276421 4276429 4276451 4276499
4276511 4276513 4276529 4276541 4276549 4276553 4276567 4276579 4276583 4276607
4276621 4276627 4276637 4276661 4276693 4276721 4276739 4276763 4276777 4276787
4276799 4276807 4276819 4276829 4276843 4276861 4276871 4276879 4276903 4276927
4276931 4276933 4276963 4276967 4276973 4276999 4277017 4277023 4277029 4277059
4277093 4277099 4277113 4277159 4277171 4277179 4277197 4277201 4277209 4277219
4277227 4277257 4277263 4277267 4277279 4277293 4277303 4277327 4277341 4277359
4277419 4277437 4277443 4277453 4277477 4277479 4277501 4277519 4277521 4277531
4277561 4277579 4277593 4277621 4277633 4277639 4277671 4277699 4277719 4277723
4277743 4277753 4277759 4277843 4277847 4277851 4277857 4277887 4277889
4277951 4277953 4277957 4277971 4277989 4278013 4278037 4278041 4278047 4278049
4278073 4278077 4278089 4278091 4278103 4278121 4278133 4278139 4278143 4278179
4278211 4278223 4278229 4278233 4278257 4278289 4278343 4278349 4278353 4278361
4278367 4278377 4278383 4278413 4278431 4278433 4278451 4278467 4278481 4278487
4278499 4278511 4278523 4278539 4278557 4278577 4278607 4278613 4278619 4278641
4278649 4278661 4278671 4278691 4278697 4278709 4278731 4278737 4278751 4278761
4278773 4278829 4278839 4278847 4278881 4278883 4278931 4278941 4278947 4278983
4278959 4278991 4279007 4279027 4279039 4279043 4279057 4279063 4279069 4279091
4279111 4279117 4279141 4279157 4279159 4279201 4279213 4279217 4279229 4279267
```

```
4279283 4279337 4279343 4279369 4279391 4279409 4279411 4279417 4279421 4279433
4279439 4279453 4279459 4279481 4279487 4279507 4279523 4279537 4279553 4279567
4279589 4279601 4279603 4279619 4279637 4279651 4279657 4279669 4279687 4279741
4279757 4279763 4279777 4279789 4279813 4279819 4279831 4279837 4279841 4279843
4279853 4279871 4279879 4279889 4279897 4279939 4279963 4279967 4279969 4279973
4279981 4279991 4279999 4280009 4280011 4280021 4280033 4280041 4280051 4280053
4280071 4280083 4280117 4280131 4280137 4280147 4280153 4280173 4280179 4280183
4280191 4280203 4280249 4280257 4280267 4280329 4280347 4280351 4280363 4280383
4280389 4280399 4280407 4280417 4280459 4280467 4280477 4280483 4280503 4280527
4280531 4280533 4280537 4280561 4280581 4280593 4280611 4280623 4280629 4280657
4280659 4280741 4280747 4280767 4280827 4280873 4280879 4280897 4280917 4280929
4280959 4280971 4280999 4281019 4281047 4281049 4281083 4281091 4281103 4281107
4281133 4281157 4281169 4281191 4281203 4281227 4281253 4281259 4281271 4281283
4281293 4281301 4281311 4281313 4281323 4281337 4281341 4281349 4281353 4281359
4281373 4281383 4281413 4281439 4281443 4281449 4281463 4281469 4281481 4281493
4281533 4281539 4281581 4281583 4281587 4281601 4281619 4281643 4281649 4281679
4281691 4281709 4281731 4281733 4281757 4281779 4281787 4281791 4281799 4281803
4281833 4281839 4281853 4281857 4281863 4281869 4281889 4281911 4281913 4281931
4281941 4281967 4281971 4281989 4282001 4282007 4282009 4282013 4282021 4282027
4282051 4282063 4282093 4282129 4282133 4282141 4282151 4282177 4282183 4282193
4282219 4282231 4282237 4282273 4282303 4282319 4282331 4282337 4282357 4282367
4282373 4282379 4282403 4282423 4282441 4282457 4282469 4282471 4282513 4282519
4282549 4282571 4282601 4282609 4282631 4282651 4282661 4282673 4282693 4282699
4282711 4282723 4282727 4282753 4282763 4282777 4282799 4282801 4282823 4282829
4282849 4282879 4282897 4282903 4282907 4282909 4282921 4282939 4282951 4282973
4282979 4283017 4283029 4283047 4283057 4283087 4283131 4283137 4283171 4283173
4283183 4283197 4283203 4283261 4283297 4283299 4283333 4283351 4283353 4283369
4283399 4283401 4283413 4283429 4283441 4283479 4283519 4283537 4283581 4283593
4283623 4283633 4283647 4283651 4283663 4283687 4283689 4283693 4283701 4283707
4283723 4283729 4283737 4283743 4283753 4283767 4283777 4283801 4283821 4283843
4283849 4283861 4283869 4283963 4283989 4284011 4284013 4284019 4284023 4284037
4284041 4284061 4284103 4284113 4284121 4284157 4284209 4284223 4284227 4284229
4284251 4284263 4284277 4284283 4284299 4284307 4284311 4284317 4284331 4284349
4284383 4284389 4284419 4284421 4284437 4284439 4284461 4284503 4284523 4284551
4284559 4284569 4284593 4284607 4284613 4284641 4284659 4284667 4284677 4284713
4284737 4284743 4284809 4284811 4284817 4284827 4284857 4284871 4284887 4284893
4284919 4284941 4284967 4284971 4284977 4284979 4284989 4285009 4285019 4285049
4285087 4285123 4285129 4285147 4285157 4285159 4285163 4285187 4285201 4285217
4285219 4285247 4285249 4285313 4285321 4285327 4285331 4285339 4285349 4285357
4285367 4285381 4285399 4285427 4285447 4285453 4285481 4285499 4285511 4285517
4285543 4285559 4285563 4285573 4285577 4285579 4285597 4285609 4285627 4285643
4285651 4285661 4285663 4285667 4285669 4285679 4285693 4285753 4285763 4285769
4285777 4285783 4285793 4285807 4285817 4285847 4285859 4285861 4285901 4285907
4285913 4285949 4285961 4285993 4286011 4286033 4286047 4286053 4286059 4286081
4286089 4286131 4286147 4286167 4286179 4286209 4286213 4286221 4286237 4286239
4286251 4286279 4286281 4286309 4286311 4286323 4286351 4286357 4286393 4286417
4286423 4286453 4286467 4286473 4286489 4286537 4286543 4286649 4286663 4286673
4286699 4286617 4286629 4286657 4286663 4286677 4286687 4286699 4286719 4286731
4286747 4286749 4286753 4286801 4286803 4286827 4286833 4286851 4286903 4286923
4286929 4286957 4286969 4286981 4286987 4287037 4287047 4287067 4287089 4287097
4287121 4287137 4287181 4287187 4287197 4287209 4287211 4287221 4287233 4287253
4287271 4287287 4287289 4287299 4287313 4287319 4287337 4287341 4287359 4287373
4287379 4287403 4287419 4287427 4287431 4287457 4287463 4287467 4287473 4287511
4287539 4287557 4287583 4287593 4287599 4287601 4287607 4287611 4287617 4287623
4287643 4287667 4287677 4287719 4287721 4287727 4287743 4287769 4287781 4287793
4287809 4287823 4287841 4287847 4287851 4287887 4287919 4287923 4287937 4287949
4287971 4287973 4287979 4287989 4287991 4288021 4288043 4288049 4288073 4288087
4288103 4288111 4288121 4288127 4288133 4288147 4288159 4288171 4288183 4288223
4288217 4288223 4288253 4288307 4288309 4288321 4288391 4288397 4288439 4288441
4288457 4288481 4288489 4288517 4288541 4288577 4288579 4288589 4288619 4288621
4288637 4288661 4288729 4288733 4288747 4288759 4288789 4288793 4288799 4288801
4288867 4288873 4288883 4288901 4288909 4288937 4288939 4288951 4288957 4288979
4288993 4289011 4289053 4289057 4289099 4289101 4289107 4289111 4289113 4289119
4289137 4289149 4289213 4289239 4289249 4289251 4289279 4289291 4289317 4289347
4289353 4289371 4289381 4289387 4289471 4289473 4289479 4289489 4289507 4289513
4289531 4289539 4289599 4289603 4289609 4289617 4289629 4289633 4289639 4289647
4289653 4289657 4289683 4289693 4289717 4289741 4289771 4289783 4289821 4289827
4289833 4289837 4289849 4289861 4289869 4289893 4289911 4289917 4289921 4289927
4289939 4289959 4289963 4289969 4289977 4290017 4290023 4290037 4290043 4290047
4290071 4290079 4290089 4290107 4290109 4290133 4290151 4290161 4290163 4290179
4290193 4290217 4290233 4290269 4290277 4290287 4290311 4290331 4290337 4290359
4290373 4290413 4290427 4290437 4290449 4290467 4290469 4290487 4290491 4290499
4290529 4290541 4290547 4290553 4290641 4290661 4290667 4290683 4290697 4290701
4290757 4290761 4290763 4290799 4290823 4290833 4290887 4290889 4290899 4290911
4290931 4290943 4290947 4290961 4290971 4290973 4290991 4290997 4291031 4291033
4291057 4291061 4291073 4291097 4291103 4291109 4291117 4291121 4291141 4291163
4291171 4291181 4291193 4291211 4291213 4291219 4291249 4291267 4291291 4291307
4291319 4291337 4291369 4291381 4291387 4291403 4291409 4291447 4291471 4291493
4291537 4291559 4291583 4291589 4291603 4291607 4291619 4291621 4291631 4291649
4291673 4291697 4291709 4291717 4291747 4291751 4291759 4291813 4291829 4291841
4291843 4291867 4291933 4291943 4291949 4291979 4292009 4292011 4292017 4292023
4292027 4292033 4292047 4292051 4292059 4292063 4292069 4292083 4292089 4292107
4292117 4292129 4292137 4292159 4292161 4292173 4292209 4292213 4292251 4292257
4292269 4292273 4292287 4292293 4292317 4292339 4292341 4292357 4292363 4292383
4292411 4292419 4292437 4292441 4292443 4292471 4292479 4292501 4292503 4292507
4292521 4292543 4292549 4292567 4292569 4292573 4292579 4292581 4292591 4292593
4292597 4292611 4292627 4292681 4292683 4292707 4292711 4292719 4292723 4292749
4292759 4292767 4292773 4292809 4292867 4292887 4292903 4292921
4292923 4292941 4292963 4292989 4293007 4293011 4293013 4293041 4293059 4293071
```

```
4293083  4293089  4293101  4293109  4293127  4293167  4293173  4293187  4293199  4293227
4293239  4293269  4293313  4293319  4293323  4293343  4293347  4293353  4293361  4293389
4293437  4293451  4293461  4293463  4293473  4293481  4293547  4293551  4293559  4293577
4293581  4293599  4293613  4293623  4293629  4293631  4293637  4293649  4293683  4293701
4293713  4293721  4293727  4293749  4293763  4293767  4293781  4293799  4293811  4293833
4293853  4293869  4293923  4293929  4293931  4293941  4294039  4294051  4294067  4294099
4294153  4294163  4294189  4294207  4294223  4294229  4294237  4294259  4294313
4294321  4294327  4294351  4294357  4294363  4294369  4294373  4294393  4294417  4294439
4294441  4294457  4294469  4294471  4294529  4294541  4294547  4294559  4294567  4294607
4294637  4294649  4294657  4294681  4294687  4294691  4294699  4294723  4294729  4294751
4294753  4294769  4294783  4294799  4294811  4294831  4294837  4294847  4294867  4294877
4294879  4294891  4294903  4294919  4294921  4294933  4294943  4294953  4294967  4294973
4294991  4295021  4295029  4295041  4295059  4295077  4295113  4295129  4295131  4295149
4295153  4295177  4295183  4295209  4295231  4295261  4295281  4295321  4295323  4295351
4295371  4295383  4295413  4295443  4295449  4295461  4295477  4295479  4295507  4295519
4295527  4295531  4295537  4295563  4295569  4295573  4295587  4295593  4295609  4295617
4295623  4295651  4295671  4295689  4295699  4295717  4295719  4295723  4295761  4295789
4295791  4295801  4295861  4295897  4295899  4295903  4295911  4295923  4295927  4295953
4295969  4295971  4295981  4295999  4296013  4296023  4296043  4296067  4296077  4296079
4296091  4296137  4296167  4296217  4296221  4296277  4296289  4296319  4296323  4296343
4296353  4296361  4296389  4296401  4296419  4296433  4296443  4296449  4296463  4296473
4296491  4296497  4296499  4296511  4296533  4296559  4296571  4296577  4296581  4296613
4296647  4296667  4296673  4296701  4296703  4296709  4296739  4296749  4296751  4296757
4296781  4296797  4296821  4296823  4296829  4296833  4296839  4296857  4296863  4296893
4296899  4296913  4296917  4296973  4296977  4296979  4296989  4296997  4297001  4297019
4297031  4297037  4297043  4297061  4297063  4297091  4297093  4297199  4297201  4297207
4297259  4297261  4297289  4297301  4297303  4297327  4297361  4297369  4297387  4297409
4297429  4297451  4297453  4297457  4297519  4297523  4297529  4297537  4297541  4297571
4297603  4297609  4297613  4297621  4297627  4297637  4297649  4297663  4297669  4297673
4297681  4297697  4297703  4297759  4297763  4297793  4297817  4297841  4297847  4297861
4297897  4297901  4297927  4297939  4297961  4297963  4297981  4298011  4298023  4298027
4298039  4298051  4298069  4298081  4298089  4298113  4298131  4298137  4298143  4298149
4298183  4298191  4298213  4298219  4298233  4298279  4298299  4298339  4298341  4298377
4298381  4298383  4298387  4298417  4298419  4298423  4298431  4298443  4298453  4298461
4298471  4298477  4298507  4298509  4298513  4298533  4298543  4298551  4298557  4298561
4298587  4298629  4298663  4298669  4298683  4298687  4298713  4298729  4298759
4298779  4298783  4298797  4298803  4298821  4298843  4298849  4298857  4298867  4298869
4298881  4298887  4298927  4298929  4298933  4298941  4298947  4298951  4298963  4298971
4298981  4299007  4299013  4299041  4299089  4299101  4299107  4299133  4299157  4299179
4299203  4299209  4299241  4299247  4299277  4299299  4299319  4299329  4299391  4299397
4299403  4299433  4299439  4299443  4299467  4299473  4299497  4299499  4299509  4299517
4299539  4299553  4299557  4299563  4299587  4299599  4299637  4299653  4299667  4299683
4299697  4299703  4299709  4299721  4299727  4299739  4299751  4299761  4299767  4299769
4299791  4299803  4299809  4299811  4299821  4299853  4299859  4299863  4299887  4299899
4299901  4299937  4299959  4299961  4300003  4300007  4300013  4300063  4300067  4300069
4300081  4300111  4300141  4300151  4300157  4300181  4300183  4300187  4300189  4300217
4300229  4300237  4300253  4300259  4300267  4300273  4300279  4300291  4300297  4300319
4300343  4300349  4300363  4300369  4300393  4300397  4300423  4300427  4300447  4300459
4300463  4300477  4300487  4300489  4300493  4300519  4300553  4300573  4300577  4300591
4300627  4300633  4300657  4300669  4300691  4300693  4300717  4300753  4300759  4300789
4300801  4300823  4300837  4300853  4300867  4300871  4300913  4300921  4300937  4300939
4300943  4300951  4300957  4300963  4300993  4300999  4301009  4301021  4301039  4301047
4301053  4301057  4301113  4301117  4301137  4301147  4301149  4301189  4301197  4301217
4301243  4301257  4301261  4301263  4301273  4301279  4301303  4301327  4301347  4301359
4301369  4301371  4301399  4301411  4301417  4301449  4301461  4301477  4301497  4301501
4301519  4301551  4301569  4301587  4301593  4301603  4301611  4301623  4301669  4301699
4301701  4301707  4301723  4301747  4301789  4301837  4301861  4301881  4301917  4301929
4301959  4301971  4301981  4301987  4302013  4302017  4302019  4302041  4302043  4302049
4302061  4302073  4302083  4302097  4302131  4302143  4302157  4302161  4302167  4302187
4302191  4302197  4302203  4302229  4302247  4302251  4302257  4302293  4302299  4302301
4302307  4302317  4302359  4302367  4302371  4302373  4302409  4302439  4302461  4302481
4302491  4302503  4302509  4302517  4302523  4302533  4302553  4302563  4302601  4302631
4302661  4302703  4302733  4302737  4302743  4302761  4302763  4302773  4302799  4302829
4302833  4302847  4302869  4302871  4302889  4302901  4302917  4302919  4302931  4302937
4302959  4302973  4302979  4302983  4303007  4303021  4303027  4303043  4303067  4303069
4303081  4303087  4303099  4303109  4303111  4303121  4303127  4303133  4303133  4303157
4303163  4303171  4303181  4303199  4303207  4303217  4303241  4303259  4303267  4303279
4303289  4303303  4303309  4303337  4303357  4303361  4303369  4303391  4303393  4303399
4303447  4303457  4303459  4303463  4303471  4303487  4303493  4303501  4303511  4303529
4303543  4303561  4303573  4303577  4303591  4303603  4303609  4303613  4303631  4303639
4303643  4303657  4303661  4303667  4303679  4303681  4303723  4303727  4303753  4303763
4303769  4303777  4303787  4303813  4303853  4303867  4303889  4303891  4303927  4303963
4303969  4303973  4304011  4304017  4304027  4304023  4304033  4304039  4304081
4304101  4304107  4304137  4304141  4304143  4304159  4304161  4304191  4304207  4304219
4304231  4304249  4304291  4304309  4304323  4304327  4304347  4304353  4304359  4304369
4304371  4304389  4304407  4304423  4304437  4304497  4304527  4304533  4304539  4304561
4304579  4304603  4304609  4304623  4304627  4304633  4304669  4304693  4304719  4304761
4304779  4304803  4304821  4304847  4304851  4304869  4304879  4304891  4304897  4304899
4304903  4304917  4304929  4304941  4304981  4304999  4305011  4305017  4305073  4305083
4305101  4305109  4305121  4305143  4305157  4305167  4305179  4305211  4305221  4305241
4305269  4305271  4305281  4305307  4305337  4305361  4305383  4305401  4305409  4305443
4305449  4305473  4305479  4305491  4305523  4305527  4305569  4305583  4305593  4305611
4305619  4305629  4305661  4305673  4305689  4305701  4305703  4305739  4305751  4305767
4305781  4305793  4305817  4305823  4305863  4305881  4305893  4305901  4305953  4305967
4306019  4306031  4306033  4306061  4306109  4306139  4306147  4306193  4306199
4306229  4306231  4306261  4306273  4306277  4306279  4306283  4306301  4306333  4306349
4306373  4306381  4306399  4306433  4306439  4306441  4306447  4306453  4306459  4306501
4306507  4306537  4306553  4306571  4306583  4306591  4306609  4306633  4306639  4306651
4306663  4306691  4306717  4306723  4306733  4306747  4306777  4306793  4306801  4306811
```

```
4306817  4306829  4306847  4306849  4306853  4306867  4306889  4306891  4306921  4306937
4306969  4306979  4306987  4306999  4307021  4307041  4307057  4307077  4307081  4307087
4307089  4307099  4307111  4307113  4307117  4307131  4307153  4307161  4307183  4307201
4307203  4307213  4307227  4307231  4307249  4307263  4307287  4307291  4307297  4307299
4307309  4307323  4307327  4307351  4307377  4307383  4307423  4307437  4307453  4307461
4307467  4307473  4307483  4307489  4307491  4307507  4307519  4307533  4307539  4307557
4307561  4307581  4307587  4307591  4307603  4307629  4307669  4307691  4307697  4307701
4307711  4307717  4307731  4307741  4307761  4307827  4307833  4307857  4307887  4307909
4307939  4307957  4307959  4307971  4308001  4308013  4308023  4308043  4308047  4308063
4308071  4308077  4308097  4308103  4308133  4308173  4308179  4308217  4308251  4308257
4308263  4308277  4308319  4308329  4308331  4308341  4308371  4308377  4308379  4308397
4308413  4308419  4308431  4308439  4308461  4308467  4308481  4308509  4308517  4308527
4308541  4308553  4308571  4308589  4308637  4308653  4308671  4308673  4308677  4308691
4308697  4308713  4308727  4308737  4308749  4308781  4308793  4308817  4308823  4308827
4308841  4308853  4308881  4308883  4308893  4308923  4308937  4308943  4308949  4308961
4308989  4309001  4309003  4309013  4309033  4309043  4309049  4309069  4309079  4309121
4309153  4309169  4309187  4309199  4309243  4309259  4309267  4309273
4309297  4309309  4309339  4309343  4309363  4309369  4309391  4309399  4309411  4309423
4309433  4309451  4309453  4309457  4309471  4309489  4309499  4309519  4309531  4309541
4309549  4309553  4309559  4309577  4309583  4309621  4309673  4309693  4309709  4309729
4309733  4309741  4309757  4309787  4309817  4309819  4309831  4309841  4309861  4309867
4309873  4309897  4309927  4309937  4309939  4309957  4310021  4310057  4310063  4310069
4310071  4310081  4310083  4310099  4310171  4310179  4310203  4310219  4310227  4310237
4310261  4310263  4310279  4310347  4310351  4310353  4310387  4310393  4310429  4310441
4310461  4310491  4310497  4310533  4310561  4310563  4310569  4310573  4310609  4310629
4310633  4310651  4310659  4310671  4310681  4310689  4310693  4310711  4310731  4310737
4310743  4310753  4310783  4310791  4310819  4310827  4310851  4310897  4310927  4310947
4310963  4310989  4311001  4311007  4311011  4311019  4311031  4311037  4311101  4311107
4311113  4311121  4311127  4311133  4311163  4311173  4311193  4311211  4311221  4311247
4311257  4311283  4311299  4311301  4311311  4311317  4311323  4311331  4311337  4311361
4311367  4311371  4311379  4311403  4311407  4311409  4311413  4311447  4311473  4311487
4311529  4311533  4311539  4311547  4311551  4311563  4311569  4311577  4311607  4311611
4311631  4311667  4311673  4311677  4311701  4311743  4311751  4311757  4311781  4311809
4311823  4311871  4311877  4311887  4311893  4311913  4311947  4311959  4311977  4312003
4312013  4312019  4312051  4312073  4312079  4312103  4312111  4312117  4312123  4312141
4312153  4312157  4312171  4312177  4312181  4312223  4312229  4312261  4312267  4312279
4312283  4312291  4312309  4312331  4312333  4312337  4312351  4312361  4312381  4312393
4312403  4312417  4312433  4312447  4312463  4312471  4312481  4312489  4312493  4312499
4312501  4312519  4312537  4312541  4312547  4312549  4312559  4312571  4312631  4312643
4312657  4312691  4312697  4312699  4312703  4312727  4312729  4312733  4312739  4312741
4312783  4312787  4312807  4312811  4312823  4312837  4312853  4312859  4312873  4312879
4312907  4312939  4312961  4312969  4313027  4313033  4313041  4313081  4313093  4313107
4313119  4313129  4313131  4313147  4313149  4313161  4313173  4313191  4313219  4313251
4313269  4313273  4313293  4313297  4313303  4313311  4313317  4313327  4313329  4313333
4313339  4313341  4313381  4313383  4313389  4313417  4313429  4313467  4313471  4313483
4313501  4313503  4313509  4313531  4313539  4313579  4313591  4313599  4313611  4313629
4313641  4313653  4313669  4313671  4313677  4313689  4313693  4313713  4313731  4313783
4313791  4313797  4313807  4313819  4313831  4313843  4313849  4313851  4313861  4313873
4313891  4313899  4313917  4313921  4313927  4313977  4313983  4313999  4314017  4314029
4314043  4314059  4314119  4314169  4314181  4314187  4314217  4314241  4314281  4314287
4314293  4314313  4314337  4314341  4314383  4314391  4314403  4314419  4314433  4314451
4314467  4314509  4314529  4314551  4314559  4314581  4314587  4314643  4314671  4314683
4314689  4314701  4314703  4314721  4314769  4314781  4314803  4314833  4314839  4314857
4314887  4314899  4314911  4314913  4314943  4314949  4314953  4315013  4315027  4315039
4315057  4315061  4315063  4315067  4315097  4315111  4315123  4315141  4315151  4315159
4315183  4315187  4315219  4315243  4315277  4315279  4315301  4315303  4315349  4315361
4315369  4315379  4315387  4315397  4315411  4315439  4315453  4315463  4315469  4315477
4315541  4315529  4315543  4315573  4315579  4315589  4315601  4315607  4315709  4315723
4315733  4315741  4315757  4315763  4315769  4315777  4315799  4315819  4315823  4315837
4315847  4315873  4315891  4315897  4315901  4315903  4315919  4315921  4315931  4315981
4315991  4315999  4316003  4316017  4316023  4316047  4316051  4316071  4316107  4316129
4316141  4316153  4316159  4316171  4316197  4316201  4316219  4316231  4316239  4316251
4316293  4316311  4316321  4316327  4316329  4316359  4316371  4316399  4316407  4316423
4316443  4316461  4316483  4316489  4316497  4316503  4316519  4316539  4316561  4316567
4316569  4316573  4316593  4316647  4316651  4316659  4316681  4316693  4316707  4316717
4316749  4316771  4316773  4316777  4316779  4316789  4316803  4316821  4316867  4316881
4316887  4316891  4316941  4316951  4316959  4316981  4316989  4316999  4317017  4317023
4317037  4317041  4317059  4317073  4317083  4317097  4317107  4317121  4317127  4317139
4317151  4317191  4317193  4317211  4317239  4317251  4317253  4317263  4317283  4317289
4317311  4317319  4317323  4317347  4317361  4317377  4317403  4317407  4317409  4317421
4317437  4317449  4317457  4317461  4317487  4317497  4317517  4317529  4317553  4317569
4317571  4317601  4317611  4317623  4317631  4317637  4317661  4317667  4317683  4317689
4317697  4317701  4317727  4317737  4317739  4317791  4317799  4317811  4317821  4317823
4317827  4317853  4317869  4317889  4317893  4317899  4317913  4317917  4317919  4317923
4317961  4317967  4317979  4317991  4318049  4318057  4318063  4318081  4318087  4318091
4318099  4318109  4318121  4318123  4318133  4318157  4318163  4318183  4318201  4318211
4318213  4318231  4318247  4318267  4318271  4318277  4318283  4318337  4318399  4318403
4318409  4318429  4318441  4318451  4318463  4318469  4318487  4318507  4318511  4318513
4318541  4318543  4318553  4318577  4318597  4318621  4318637  4318649  4318661  4318667
4318669  4318723  4318729  4318759  4318767  4318777  4318781  4318789  4318793  4318801
4318813  4318823  4318829  4318837  4318849  4318879  4318891  4318933  4318949  4318987
4318991  4318997  4319017  4319027  4319041  4319069  4319089  4319093  4319111  4319131
4319141  4319149  4319153  4319177  4319209  4319233  4319243  4319257  4319297  4319299
4319303  4319311  4319339  4319351  4319353  4319363  4319369  4319383  4319401  4319407
4319431  4319453  4319461  4319477  4319489  4319501  4319503  4319519  4319527  4319531
4319551  4319563  4319591  4319597  4319599  4319603  4319621  4319671  4319677  4319681
4319687  4319729  4319743  4319761  4319767  4319771  4319773  4319827  4319831  4319849
4319863  4319873  4319879  4319891  4319893  4319933  4319941  4319947  4319951  4319963
4319969  4319993  4320059  4320061  4320079  4320097  4320109  4320119  4320187  4320223
```

```
4320241 4320247 4320257 4320269 4320299 4320311 4320313 4320319 4320341 4320347
4320373 4320383 4320419 4320443 4320461 4320469 4320473 4320479 4320487 4320493
4320509 4320517 4320521 4320529 4320559 4320571 4320583 4320593 4320607 4320637
4320643 4320689 4320697 4320707 4320709 4320713 4320721 4320761 4320787 4320793
4320817 4320821 4320829 4320853 4320857 4320863 4320893 4320917 4320919 4320929
4320959 4321003 4321019 4321049 4321061 4321067 4321081 4321091 4321103 4321123
4321121 4321139 4321157 4321169 4321181 4321231 4321237 4321241 4321243
4321259 4321327 4321357 4321363 4321393 4321397 4321411 4321439 4321481 4321483
4321501 4321507 4321529 4321601 4321613 4321627 4321633 4321643 4321657 4321663
4321703 4321717 4321729 4321747 4321753 4321781 4321787 4321799 4321813 4321817
4321829 4321831 4321871 4321883 4321897 4321901 4321931 4321981 4321997 4322009
4322027 4322047 4322069 4322077 4322089 4322117 4322119 4322173 4322209 4322221
4322243 4322287 4322293 4322323 4322347 4322359 4322387 4322389 4322401 4322419
4322429 4322441 4322453 4322467 4322473 4322491 4322503 4322509 4322533 4322569
4322581 4322587 4322603 4322651 4322663 4322683 4322687 4322701 4322713 4322741
4322749 4322779 4322783 4322803 4322809 4322863 4322881 4322891 4322897 4322909
4322951 4322963 4323023 4323037 4323047 4323061 4323071 4323073 4323101
4323161 4323197 4323199 4323217 4323239 4323247 4323251 4323257 4323283 4323289
4323307 4323311 4323313 4323323 4323329 4323331 4323337 4323359 4323377 4323401
4323419 4323427 4323439 4323467 4323479 4323499 4323503 4323541 4323551 4323569
4323589 4323611 4323629 4323643 4323647 4323653 4323679 4323689 4323691 4323707
4323713 4323721 4323731 4323743 4323751 4323757 4323769 4323791 4323817 4323841
4323877 4323883 4323919 4323923 4323941 4323947 4323959 4323961 4323997 4324003
4324007 4324027 4324037 4324057 4324063 4324081 4324093 4324109 4324127 4324157
4324211 4324231 4324259 4324261 4324279 4324289 4324297 4324303 4324321 4324337
4324339 4324363 4324367 4324373 4324399 4324417 4324433 4324471 4324501 4324519
4324547 4324559 4324561 4324583 4324601 4324627 4324631 4324637 4324643
4324669 4324699 4324711 4324751 4324753 4324781 4324787 4324807 4324843
4324861 4324907 4324909 4324927 4324979 4324997 4325033 4325039 4325059
4325071 4325099 4325117 4325119 4325137 4325143 4325149 4325159 4325161 4325201
4325203 4325207 4325257 4325267 4325273 4325281 4325303 4325317 4325333 4325339
4325341 4325351 4325359 4325389 4325393 4325401 4325417 4325423 4325441 4325443
4325473 4325491 4325509 4325513 4325537 4325539 4325543 4325549 4325557 4325569
4325579 4325593 4325617 4325621 4325627 4325639 4325641 4325657 4325687 4325731
4325743 4325759 4325767 4325773 4325779 4325791 4325813 4325851 4325861 4325873
4325879 4325887 4325891 4325921 4325933 4325953 4325963 4325969 4325987 4326011
4326029 4326031 4326067 4326071 4326073 4326079 4326083 4326121 4326131 4326137
4326149 4326163 4326169 4326173 4326229 4326233 4326239 4326247 4326253 4326263
4326269 4326271 4326349 4326367 4326383 4326401 4326403 4326407 4326409 4326437
4326451 4326457 4326473 4326493 4326499 4326503 4326533 4326559 4326571 4326583
4326587 4326589 4326611 4326629 4326631 4326643 4326649 4326667 4326671 4326677
4326683 4326697 4326709 4326719 4326727 4326757 4326769 4326797 4326821 4326827
4326841 4326859 4326863 4326877 4326893 4326901 4326911 4326937 4326947 4326979
4326991 4326997 4327007 4327019 4327031 4327033 4327049 4327051 4327087 4327093
4327097 4327111 4327123 4327153 4327159 4327171 4327189 4327199 4327201 4327217
4327229 4327241 4327247 4327277 4327283 4327313 4327327 4327331 4327357 4327361
4327363 4327369 4327373 4327387 4327423 4327439 4327441 4327451 4327481 4327489
4327493 4327501 4327511 4327549 4327553 4327577 4327579 4327607 4327621 4327633
4327643 4327669 4327711 4327721 4327723 4327727 4327759 4327777 4327789 4327793
4327823 4327859 4327861 4327867 4327909 4327913 4327937 4327943 4327963 4328017
4328021 4328053 4328057 4328059 4328069 4328087 4328099 4328111 4328123 4328147
4328167 4328179 4328213 4328219 4328249 4328273 4328293 4328309 4328327 4328339
4328341 4328407 4328413 4328419 4328459 4328461 4328497 4328521 4328537 4328539
4328543 4328551 4328567 4328573 4328579 4328581 4328603 4328609 4328617 4328629
4328641 4328671 4328677 4328711 4328719 4328749 4328773 4328777 4328783 4328813
4328833 4328837 4328843 4328851 4328861 4328867 4328873 4328887 4328889 4328893
4328921 4328923 4328927 4328953 4328957 4328969 4328981 4328983 4328993 4329011
4329023 4329041 4329043 4329053 4329079 4329089 4329097 4329107 4329137 4329139
4329151 4329167 4329173 4329179 4329191 4329209 4329211 4329229 4329239 4329253
4329257 4329263 4329277 4329293 4329301 4329307 4329331 4329379 4329383 4329389
4329421 4329449 4329469 4329487 4329503 4329539 4329547 4329551 4329581 4329601
4329631 4329649 4329653 4329659 4329667 4329697 4329709 4329733 4329737 4329757
4329763 4329797 4329821 4329847 4329881 4329887 4329907 4329941 4329947 4329953
4329973 4329977 4329979 4330013 4330021 4330037 4330097 4330099 4330103 4330127
4330163 4330169 4330181 4330199 4330201 4330231 4330241 4330253 4330301 4330303
4330321 4330331 4330343 4330349 4330351 4330357 4330373 4330409 4330453 4330457
4330481 4330489 4330493 4330507 4330511 4330523 4330559 4330567 4330583 4330589
4330603 4330621 4330631 4330637 4330649 4330661 4330663 4330667 4330687 4330717
4330757 4330763 4330783 4330819 4330847 4330853 4330867 4330913 4330927 4330943
4330973 4330987 4331009 4331021 4331027 4331051 4331057 4331059 4331083 4331087
4331099 4331123 4331137 4331161 4331167 4331207 4331219 4331251 4331267 4331269
4331273 4331287 4331293 4331323 4331339 4331357 4331359 4331377 4331381 4331389
4331417 4331441 4331471 4331489 4331513 4331543 4331557 4331573 4331581 4331583
4331611 4331641 4331647 4331653 4331683 4331711 4331713 4331731 4331741 4331749
4331779 4331801 4331809 4331827 4331837 4331851 4331857 4331861 4331869 4331911
4331917 4331939 4331941 4331947 4331953 4331963 4331969 4331983 4331989 4332001
4332011 4332043 4332047 4332067 4332079 4332089 4332091 4332143 4332149 4332151
4332179 4332187 4332191 4332199 4332203 4332217 4332239 4332241 4332259
4332277 4332299 4332313 4332371 4332389 4332407 4332409 4332443 4332469 4332479
4332499 4332509 4332521 4332527 4332539 4332577 4332583 4332599 4332607 4332611
4332613 4332617 4332619 4332631 4332649 4332659 4332673 4332677 4332707 4332709
4332719 4332721 4332733 4332743 4332761 4332767 4332791 4332793 4332821 4332833
4332851 4332857 4332867 4332877 4332907 4332929 4332947 4332949 4332953
4332961 4332967 4332971 4332973 4332997 4333009 4333027 4333057 4333081 4333097
4333099 4333103 4333129 4333187 4333193 4333213 4333237 4333243 4333253 4333279
4333327 4333337 4333339 4333363 4333391 4333423 4333457 4333471 4333481 4333507
4333517 4333523 4333529 4333531 4333543 4333547 4333597 4333601 4333613 4333633
4333649 4333661 4333697 4333709 4333711 4333733 4333739 4333751 4333753 4333829
4333837 4333853 4333877 4333891 4333909 4333933 4333939 4333943 4333991 4333999
```

```
4334003  4334023  4334027  4334039  4334041  4334087  4334089  4334107  4334119  4334123
4334171  4334191  4334221  4334257  4334263  4334273  4334279  4334321  4334339  4334347
4334353  4334359  4334381  4334399  4334401  4334417  4334441  4334453  4334459  4334467
4334483  4334497  4334563  4334569  4334579  4334581  4334593  4334597  4334653  4334657
4334663  4334713  4334719  4334731  4334749  4334753  4334767  4334777  4334791  4334797
4334801  4334839  4334893  4334899  4334903  4334917  4334933  4334969  4334977  4334989
4334999  4335041  4335043  4335049  4335073  4335103  4335137  4335151  4335157  4335203
4335229  4335259  4335263  4335269  4335281  4335301  4335307  4335313  4335329  4335337
4335341  4335367  4335377  4335403  4335407  4335427  4335433  4335437  4335467  4335469
4335479  4335481  4335491  4335511  4335557  4335571  4335577  4335581  4335589  4335593
4335607  4335619  4335631  4335649  4335677  4335679  4335739  4335763  4335767  4335787
4335823  4335841  4335853  4335883  4335887  4335949  4335959  4335967  4335979  4336019
4336027  4336061  4336091  4336093  4336097  4336099  4336103  4336117  4336133  4336147
4336151  4336153  4336159  4336219  4336223  4336229  4336247  4336253  4336279  4336303
4336327  4336331  4336333  4336337  4336357  4336379  4336393  4336439  4336463  4336471
4336481  4336483  4336487  4336523  4336531  4336537  4336567  4336571  4336583  4336589
4336597  4336613  4336639  4336663  4336687  4336691  4336697  4336699  4336723  4336727
4336729  4336741  4336753  4336757  4336763  4336777  4336781  4336793  4336799  4336837
4336847  4336859  4336861  4336867  4336873  4336889  4336901  4336907  4336909  4336919
4336951  4336957  4336963  4336973  4336987  4337027  4337033  4337051  4337063  4337071
4337077  4337083  4337101  4337107  4337119  4337129  4337131  4337143  4337147  4337167
4337171  4337183  4337209  4337213  4337231  4337233  4337257  4337273  4337287  4337297
4337321  4337341  4337351  4337353  4337371  4337381  4337383  4337393  4337401  4337423
4337429  4337447  4337449  4337471  4337479  4337483  4337519  4337521  4337537  4337561
4337569  4337581  4337591  4337609  4337623  4337633  4337651  4337689  4337693  4337701
4337713  4337717  4337741  4337779  4337783  4337819  4337821  4337863  4337881  4337899
4337911  4337951  4337953  4337987  4337999  4338011  4338013  4338041  4338049  4338073
4338083  4338121  4338133  4338151  4338167  4338199  4338203  4338221  4338223  4338239
4338277  4338293  4338319  4338331  4338343  4338353  4338391  4338401  4338407
4338427  4338431  4338437  4338449  4338457  4338491  4338511  4338533  4338539  4338547
4338563  4338569  4338577  4338613  4338623  4338629  4338643  4338647  4338671  4338703
4338709  4338721  4338769  4338787  4338799  4338811  4338823  4338847  4338871  4338883
4338913  4338923  4338937  4338949  4338959  4338979  4339021  4339031  4339043  4339073
4339091  4339103  4339123  4339129  4339133  4339141  4339147  4339169  4339177  4339181
4339189  4339207  4339217  4339243  4339253  4339271  4339289  4339297  4339303  4339333
4339337  4339343  4339363  4339421  4339451  4339457  4339459  4339469  4339477  4339487
4339499  4339501  4339513  4339519  4339529  4339537  4339541  4339547  4339561  4339567
4339609  4339613  4339639  4339649  4339669  4339681  4339697  4339703  4339747  4339757
4339781  4339787  4339793  4339817  4339823  4339843  4339849  4339859  4339877  4339883
4339889  4339897  4339901  4339919  4339927  4339931  4339943  4339957  4339963  4340003
4340009  4340171  4340207  4340233  4340239  4340251  4340257  4340267  4340269  4340299
4340351  4340363  4340381  4340407  4340411  4340429  4340431  4340447  4340449  4340471
4340477  4340503  4340521  4340533  4340573  4340587  4340589  4340621  4340639  4340641
4340659  4340663  4340719  4340731  4340737  4340747  4340761  4340773  4340783  4340789
4340827  4340839  4340849  4340881  4340887  4340891  4340909  4340927  4340939  4340969
4340977  4340989  4340993  4341013  4341017  4341019  4341037  4341049  4341053  4341067
4341079  4341083  4341107  4341157  4341163  4341167  4341181  4341193  4341199  4341211
4341223  4341229  4341251  4341257  4341263  4341269  4341277  4341299  4341371  4341373
4341377  4341419  4341427  4341433  4341439  4341451  4341461  4341487  4341497  4341517
4341527  4341563  4341569  4341577  4341593  4341599  4341607  4341637  4341653  4341661
4341679  4341697  4341763  4341769  4341787  4341791  4341803  4341853  4341877  4341881
4341893  4341923  4341947  4341971  4341973  4341983  4341991  4342007  4342013  4342067
4342081  4342087  4342099  4342103  4342111  4342133  4342153  4342207  4342213  4342229
4342231  4342267  4342271  4342277  4342301  4342309  4342319  4342321  4342333  4342339
4342363  4342367  4342397  4342409  4342411  4342417  4342427  4342429  4342453  4342487
4342517  4342523  4342549  4342567  4342571  4342589  4342619  4342627  4342631  4342649
4342687  4342717  4342757  4342771  4342811  4342829  4342841  4342859  4342861  4342879
4342889  4342901  4342907  4342913  4342927  4342937  4342967  4342969  4342991  4342993
4343029  4343057  4343071  4343099  4343117  4343123  4343147  4343179  4343189  4343203
4343219  4343221  4343249  4343257  4343291  4343293  4343299  4343309  4343321  4343327
4343329  4343357  4343363  4343377  4343401  4343429  4343459  4343489  4343491  4343497
4343519  4343539  4343561  4343569  4343579  4343587  4343617  4343621  4343639  4343641
4343659  4343671  4343681  4343699  4343701  4343747  4343771  4343791  4343821  4343831
4343839  4343869  4343873  4343887  4343893  4343897  4343917  4343921  4343923  4343957
4343981  4344007  4344019  4344023  4344029  4344031  4344037  4344077  4344083  4344101
4344107  4344121  4344139  4344143  4344149  4344169  4344173  4344187  4344227  4344239
4344253  4344269  4344271  4344283  4344323  4344337  4344349  4344377  4344383  4344391
4344397  4344427  4344443  4344451  4344467  4344479  4344499  4344517  4344523  4344551
4344601  4344607  4344649  4344653  4344667  4344679  4344689  4344721  4344733  4344773
4344779  4344803  4344827  4344829  4344833  4344841  4344853  4344871  4344881  4344889
4344931  4344959  4344961  4344997  4345031  4345039  4345043  4345049  4345063  4345073
4345087  4345093  4345097  4345111  4345127  4345147  4345153  4345199  4345207  4345223
4345249  4345277  4345283  4345307  4345337  4345343  4345349  4345351  4345361  4345373
4345381  4345403  4345423  4345427  4345463  4345469  4345477  4345493  4345511  4345529
4345541  4345543  4345567  4345571  4345577  4345609  4345633  4345639  4345651  4345669
4345703  4345723  4345729  4345739  4345741  4345751  4345769  4345787  4345793  4345799
4345801  4345811  4345819  4345837  4345849  4345903  4345997  4346009  4346029  4346049
4346063  4346077  4346081  4346087  4346119  4346141  4346161  4346183  4346197  4346207
4346219  4346249  4346269  4346247  4346261  4346267  4346281  4346323  4346327
4346341  4346393  4346399  4346401  4346429  4346431  4346437  4346453  4346467  4346521
4346557  4346561  4346581  4346623  4346647  4346651  4346663  4346717  4346729  4346731
4346761  4346767  4346773  4346803  4346807  4346809  4346819  4346821  4346831  4346857
4346863  4346891  4346899  4346911  4346929  4346933  4346941  4346981  4346989  4347001
4347011  4347041  4347059  4347073  4347097  4347103  4347149  4347151  4347169
4347191  4347197  4347227  4347229  4347263  4347269  4347281  4347307  4347311  4347313
4347319  4347331  4347341  4347349  4347367  4347377  4347379  4347403  4347407  4347467
4347479  4347481  4347491  4347521  4347557  4347559  4347569  4347583  4347589  4347613
4347617  4347619  4347647  4347659  4347689  4347701  4347703  4347737  4347757  4347799
```

```
4347803 4347817 4347821 4347823 4347839 4347841 4347857 4347877 4347899 4347911
4347919 4347929 4347947 4347977 4347983 4347991 4347997 4348007 4348027 4348037
4348063 4348109 4348133 4348139 4348171 4348177 4348181 4348189 4348193 4348213
4348217 4348229 4348247 4348259 4348261 4348271 4348301 4348307 4348313 4348343
4348369 4348411 4348417 4348433 4348441 4348459 4348471 4348489 4348493 4348523
4348529 4348543 4348559 4348571 4348577 4348601 4348621 4348667 4348681 4348691
4348699 4348709 4348717 4348727 4348759 4348781 4348783 4348789 4348793
4348819 4348823 4348843 4348859 4348901 4348907 4348913 4348919 4348933 4348937
4348973 4348979 4348987 4348997 4349011 4349027 4349053 4349071 4349089 4349113
4349131 4349141 4349153 4349167 4349179 4349183 4349201 4349227 4349237 4349251
4349273 4349281 4349287 4349291 4349299 4349311 4349353 4349357 4349377 4349417
4349419 4349453 4349473 4349479 4349489 4349533 4349549 4349581 4349591 4349617
4349621 4349663 4349669 4349677 4349687 4349693 4349699 4349701 4349711 4349729
4349743 4349753 4349759 4349777 4349801 4349833 4349843 4349861 4349881 4349899
4349903 4349927 4349959 4349987 4350023 4350043 4350067 4350077 4350091 4350103
4350119 4350121 4350133 4350139 4350163 4350167 4350173 4350209 4350217 4350251
4350263 4350271 4350277 4350287 4350329 4350331 4350341 4350347 4350389 4350391
4350397 4350403 4350421 4350433 4350443 4350499 4350503 4350523 4350527 4350539
4350553 4350557 4350569 4350629 4350631 4350659 4350679 4350699 4350681 4350701
4350707 4350713 4350733 4350761 4350769 4350803 4350817 4350821 4350833 4350877
4350883 4350889 4350901 4350911 4350917 4350919 4350937 4350967 4350971 4350977
4350991 4351001 4351021 4351027 4351049 4351063 4351091 4351103 4351159 4351177
4351187 4351199 4351219 4351231 4351271 4351273 4351279 4351283 4351297 4351327
4351331 4351339 4351349 4351357 4351397 4351409 4351411 4351423 4351429 4351433
4351483 4351489 4351493 4351499 4351511 4351547 4351561 4351573 4351579 4351601
4351619 4351621 4351631 4351637 4351649 4351651 4351693 4351709 4351723 4351747
4351757 4351759 4351793 4351819 4351849 4351859 4351891 4351933 4351967 4351979
4351981 4352003 4352009 4352039 4352063 4352069 4352077 4352081 4352111 4352113
4352123 4352143 4352147 4352171 4352177 4352203 4352209 4352227 4352239 4352251
4352269 4352279 4352377 4352389 4352399 4352419 4352423 4352441 4352443 4352461
4352473 4352477 4352483 4352563 4352567 4352573 4352587 4352597 4352599 4352611
4352641 4352651 4352687 4352707 4352713 4352747 4352753 4352779 4352801 4352807
4352827 4352839 4352849 4352851 4352857 4352863 4352893 4352903 4352921 4352941
4352947 4352951 4352963 4352977 4352983 4353001 4353007 4353023 4353047 4353053
4353091 4353121 4353127 4353131 4353149 4353157 4353163 4353169 4353203 4353219
4353221 4353247 4353253 4353259 4353289 4353301 4353311 4353313 4353317 4353319
4353329 4353331 4353347 4353353 4353373 4353397 4353407 4353409 4353431 4353443
4353467 4353493 4353497 4353499 4353511 4353521 4353529 4353539 4353553 4353577
4353607 4353623 4353653 4353659 4353673 4353677 4353691 4353709 4353719 4353731
4353737 4353743 4353757 4353761 4353773 4353781 4353803 4353821 4353823 4353847
4353851 4353859 4353883 4353889 4353917 4353949 4353959 4353961 4353967 4353971
4354001 4354027 4354067 4354079 4354093 4354099 4354111 4354117 4354121 4354171
4354177 4354183 4354201 4354213 4354253 4354277 4354279 4354289 4354297 4354307
4354333 4354349 4354367 4354369 4354373 4354381 4354391 4354423 4354433 4354457
4354463 4354513 4354517 4354529 4354547 4354549 4354561 4354573 4354577 4354627
4354631 4354633 4354661 4354673 4354687 4354697 4354711 4354741 4354747 4354759
4354807 4354811 4354813 4354837 4354853 4354913 4354921 4354939 4354951 4354963
4354969 4355053 4355059 4355129 4355137 4355167 4355173 4355177 4355207 4355209
4355227 4355231 4355243 4355269 4355279 4355291 4355311 4355317 4355327 4355333
4355347 4355363 4355369 4355371 4355401 4355411 4355437 4355453 4355459 4355467
4355489 4355497 4355501 4355509 4355551 4355567 4355573 4355581 4355623 4355639
4355647 4355657 4355669 4355683 4355707 4355753 4355759 4355777 4355789 4355797
4355801 4355831 4355833 4355873 4355909 4355933 4355941 4355951 4355957 4355969
4355971 4355977 4355987 4355999 4356013 4356041 4356043 4356049 4356083 4356091
4356103 4356109 4356133 4356167 4356169 4356181 4356211 4356217 4356221 4356239
4356257 4356277 4356289 4356307 4356311 4356353 4356371 4356389 4356397
4356419 4356427 4356431 4356449 4356479 4356487 4356493 4356503 4356511 4356533
4356553 4356563 4356661 4356679 4356689 4356691 4356697 4356721 4356727 4356733
4356739 4356749 4356761 4356763 4356767 4356791 4356823 4356829 4356841 4356881
4356883 4356887 4356893 4356899 4356923 4356967 4356977 4356983 4356991 4356997
4357027 4357033 4357063 4357081 4357127 4357139 4357159
4357201 4357217 4357247 4357259 4357271 4357277 4357307 4357349 4357369 4357387
4357429 4357433 4357447 4357459 4357471 4357481 4357499 4357513 4357519 4357523
4357537 4357541 4357543 4357567 4357571 4357579 4357597 4357609 4357637 4357651
4357673 4357679 4357693 4357721 4357733 4357739 4357757 4357777 4357781 4357807
4357811 4357853 4357861 4357867 4357889 4357891 4357907 4357943 4357961 4357993
4358009 4358021 4358059 4358111 4358129 4358141 4358143 4358161 4358191 4358203
4358209 4358257 4358261 4358279 4358281 4358287 4358311 4358327 4358329 4358359
4358369 4358371 4358377 4358407 4358411 4358441 4358447 4358449 4358461 4358503
4358521 4358527 4358531 4358539 4358593 4358603 4358617 4358621 4358659 4358687
4358701 4358719 4358741 4358747 4358759 4358777 4358779 4358789 4358797 4358803
4358807 4358813 4358821 4358843 4358863 4358873 4358881 4358899 4358909 4358927
4358951 4358957 4358969 4358989 4359001 4359031 4359101 4359107 4359133 4359139
4359163 4359169 4359209 4359233 4359239 4359241 4359247 4359253 4359281 4359301
4359307 4359317 4359319 4359343 4359347 4359349 4359353 4359373 4359389 4359401
4359403 4359503 4359517 4359527 4359533 4359539 4359557 4359583 4359587 4359629
4359631 4359643 4359647 4359661 4359671 4359679 4359697 4359713 4359739 4359749
4359781 4359787 4359787 4359829 4359841 4359847 4359863 4359937 4359941
4359959 4359961 4359983 4359991 4360001 4360003 4360009 4360019 4360033 4360051
4360061 4360067 4360079 4360091 4360123 4360127 4360141 4360163 4360171 4360189
4360193 4360207 4360229 4360231 4360241 4360267 4360273 4360303 4360333 4360373
4360393 4360397 4360399 4360417 4360423 4360439 4360457 4360459 4360529 4360541
4360567 4360577 4360579 4360583 4360589 4360627 4360649 4360651 4360663 4360669
4360679 4360703 4360717 4360751 4360757 4360781 4360793 4360813 4360819 4360843
4360849 4360907 4360919 4360927 4360949 4360973 4361003 4361011 4361039
4361041 4361087 4361101 4361113 4361131 4361171 4361179 4361183 4361207 4361209
4361219 4361233 4361243 4361249 4361251 4361257 4361261 4361263 4361311 4361323
4361341 4361347 4361363 4361381 4361419 4361429 4361437 4361471 4361473 4361477
4361479 4361501 4361509 4361519 4361551 4361563 4361569 4361579 4361593 4361611
```

```
4361653  4361663  4361689  4361699  4361711  4361719  4361723  4361729  4361737  4361761
4361779  4361783  4361807  4361813  4361821  4361837  4361897  4361909  4361941  4361957
4361971  4361983  4362011  4362037  4362053  4362073  4362079  4362091  4362101  4362107
4362109  4362119  4362121  4362133  4362167  4362179  4362181  4362199  4362223  4362233
4362269  4362299  4362313  4362329  4362331  4362349  4362361  4362367  4362389  4362403
4362427  4362451  4362461  4362469  4362481  4362487  4362503  4362511  4362521  4362551
4362569  4362581  4362583  4362593  4362601  4362607  4362613  4362619  4362623  4362629
4362641  4362649  4362653  4362671  4362689  4362719  4362739  4362749  4362751  4362763
4362773  4362797  4362801  4362821  4362833  4362857  4362859  4362877  4362889  4362901
4362923  4362947  4362949  4362961  4362983  4362997  4363049  4363069  4363111  4363127
4363129  4363159  4363189  4363193  4363199  4363201  4363207  4363213  4363223  4363231
4363243  4363259  4363267  4363277  4363279  4363291  4363297  4363309  4363319  4363321
4363327  4363357  4363361  4363363  4363397  4363409  4363421  4363439  4363451  4363453
4363459  4363477  4363487  4363493  4363523  4363531  4363561  4363571  4363607  4363613
4363631  4363633  4363637  4363651  4363663  4363693  4363703  4363771  4363783  4363789
4363819  4363829  4363837  4363889  4363897  4363927  4363943  4363969  4363973  4363979
4363981  4364011  4364021  4364023  4364029  4364047  4364069  4364077  4364093  4364111
4364147  4364161  4364177  4364201  4364203  4364231  4364233  4364237  4364249  4364267
4364303  4364329  4364351  4364383  4364401  4364429  4364431  4364441  4364501  4364519
4364533  4364539  4364551  4364567  4364593  4364621  4364653  4364663  4364677  4364681
4364693  4364713  4364719  4364741  4364747  4364771  4364777  4364783  4364791  4364797
4364809  4364837  4364861  4364873  4364891  4364909  4364911  4364933  4364947  4364951
4364959  4364989  4364999  4365007  4365013  4365019  4365029  4365061  4365083  4365089
4365103  4365113  4365121  4365139  4365143  4365157  4365191  4365197  4365199  4365211
4365247  4365271  4365281  4365287  4365289  4365301  4365337  4365359  4365367  4365397
4365401  4365409  4365419  4365433  4365443  4365509  4365511  4365521  4365527  4365533
4365541  4365553  4365589  4365623  4365677  4365703  4365727  4365731  4365737  4365749
4365773  4365793  4365811  4365827  4365859  4365869  4365871  4365887  4365899  4365913
4365931  4365961  4365997  4366007  4366027  4366031  4366039  4366051  4366079  4366097
4366121  4366123  4366163  4366171  4366183  4366217  4366231  4366237  4366267  4366277
4366283  4366289  4366303  4366309  4366337  4366363  4366367  4366379  4366393  4366403
4366421  4366469  4366471  4366477  4366493  4366499  4366513  4366519  4366577  4366627
4366633  4366639  4366643  4366667  4366669  4366673  4366697  4366699  4366709  4366717
4366721  4366727  4366729  4366741  4366771  4366781  4366783  4366793  4366811  4366819
4366823  4366837  4366847  4366853  4366861  4366871  4366889  4366897  4366919  4366927
4366931  4366961  4366969  4366981  4367029  4367047  4367057  4367059  4367087  4367101
4367107  4367137  4367159  4367177  4367179  4367189  4367203  4367213  4367219  4367243
4367257  4367267  4367299  4367329  4367353  4367383  4367393  4367411  4367413  4367431
4367477  4367483  4367491  4367501  4367507  4367527  4367533  4367557  4367567  4367581
4367609  4367617  4367647  4367681  4367749  4367761  4367801  4367819  4367821  4367833
4367837  4367843  4367863  4367873  4367879  4367897  4367941  4367959  4367969  4367981
4368011  4368029  4368053  4368059  4368071  4368079  4368083  4368107  4368113  4368121
4368131  4368139  4368151  4368163  4368173  4368187  4368193  4368197  4368239  4368251
4368253  4368277  4368281  4368293  4368307  4368311  4368319  4368323  4368341  4368349
4368359  4368379  4368389  4368391  4368407  4368409  4368431  4368449  4368451  4368487
4368491  4368503  4368521  4368523  4368527  4368569  4368571  4368583  4368593  4368599
4368629  4368641  4368649  4368659  4368667  4368691  4368709  4368713  4368731  4368739
4368751  4368761  4368787  4368809  4368811  4368817  4368823  4368863  4368899  4368907
4368911  4368943  4368953  4368967  4368971  4368989  4369033  4369039  4369069
4369061  4369097  4369117  4369133  4369139  4369147  4369163  4369199  4369201  4369213
4369229  4369249  4369279  4369283  4369291  4369303  4369349  4369381  4369397  4369399
4369423  4369427  4369429  4369439  4369447  4369451  4369457  4369489  4369499  4369501
4369511  4369513  4369529  4369537  4369579  4369591  4369649  4369661  4369669  4369679
4369693  4369699  4369711  4369721  4369741  4369759  4369763  4369777  4369801  4369891
4369907  4369921  4369933  4369949  4369957  4369973  4369991  4370017  4370027  4370063
4370081  4370083  4370087  4370089  4370111  4370123  4370129  4370143  4370147  4370159
4370203  4370237  4370273  4370279  4370281  4370297  4370339  4370357  4370383  4370407
4370447  4370449  4370453  4370459  4370461  4370497  4370507  4370521  4370533  4370537
4370549  4370579  4370591  4370609  4370633  4370651  4370657  4370687  4370693  4370719
4370731  4370747  4370749  4370753  4370761  4370767  4370777  4370789  4370803  4370809
4370813  4370867  4370903  4370911  4370929  4370939  4370941  4370957  4370987  4371019
4371041  4371043  4371049  4371053  4371061  4371067  4371089  4371097  4371119  4371131
4371137  4371139  4371151  4371161  4371163  4371203  4371209  4371221  4371223  4371229
4371239  4371247  4371253  4371277  4371293  4371347  4371371  4371377  4371383  4371391
4371407  4371421  4371457  4371473  4371481  4371491  4371503  4371529  4371551  4371569
4371581  4371593  4371613  4371617  4371641  4371649  4371659  4371673  4371677  4371701
4371743  4371761  4371791  4371803  4371847  4371869  4371877  4371911  4371937  4371943
4371949  4371973  4371977  4371989  4372003  4372007  4372013  4372019  4372037  4372051
4372061  4372063  4372073  4372087  4372091  4372133  4372141  4372153  4372157  4372163
4372177  4372183  4372201  4372211  4372237  4372241  4372259  4372267  4372273  4372279
4372289  4372307  4372321  4372339  4372343  4372351  4372367  4372373  4372397  4372399
4372409  4372411  4372421  4372429  4372441  4372477  4372493  4372499  4372513  4372517
4372531  4372559  4372567  4372573  4372597  4372631  4372637  4372639  4372651  4372657
4372673  4372699  4372721  4372727  4372733  4372747  4372759  4372763  4372777  4372813
4372817  4372847  4372873  4372877  4372883  4372897  4372909  4372913  4372931  4372933
4372957  4372969  4372981  4373003  4373009  4373011  4373027  4373041  4373053  4373069
4373081  4373087  4373099  4373107  4373119  4373123  4373129  4373137  4373147  4373153
4373167  4373179  4373191  4373207  4373219  4373221  4373227  4373231  4373251  4373261
4373269  4373293  4373297  4373309  4373311  4373321  4373323  4373333  4373351  4373389
4373399  4373417  4373419  4373431  4373441  4373453  4373459  4373489  4373513  4373531
4373533  4373557  4373561  4373569  4373581  4373587  4373617  4373623  4373647  4373651
4373653  4373683  4373687  4373701  4373713  4373717  4373731  4373767  4373771  4373791
4373801  4373833  4373861  4373869  4373899  4373911  4373927  4373931  4373951  4373969
4373977  4373987  4373989  4374001  4374031  4374059  4374077  4374079  4374113  4374119
4374133  4374137  4374173  4374179  4374187  4374203  4374217  4374247  4374257  4374269
4374277  4374289  4374299  4374311  4374323  4374341  4374353  4374361  4374373  4374401
4374421  4374451  4374463  4374499  4374511  4374521  4374527  4374551  4374553  4374571
4374583  4374637  4374641  4374647  4374653  4374677  4374683  4374701  4374739  4374743
4374749  4374767  4374787  4374793  4374803  4374809  4374829  4374833  4374857  4374869
```

```
4374893 4374907 4374913 4374919 4374947 4374961 4374977 4375039 4375043 4375051
4375093 4375127 4375141 4375153 4375157 4375169 4375177 4375193 4375249 4375253
4375321 4375331 4375363 4375367 4375387 4375403 4375411 4375429 4375439 4375447
4375457 4375471 4375487 4375493 4375519 4375523 4375537 4375577 4375603 4375621
4375633 4375639 4375649 4375667 4375669 4375673 4375683 4375689 4375691 4375697 4375717
4375729 4375739 4375759 4375771 4375811 4375831 4375849 4375883 4375907 4375913
4375937 4375949 4375951 4375963 4375967 4375993 4375997 4376011 4376059 4376063
4376083 4376117 4376143 4376147 4376159 4376167 4376173 4376189 4376221 4376231
4376237 4376243 4376261 4376287 4376321 4376347 4376353 4376357 4376401 4376413
4376447 4376461 4376467 4376483 4376501 4376513 4376527 4376539 4376551 4376557
4376587 4376597 4376629 4376663 4376681 4376683 4376717 4376719 4376731 4376741
4376747 4376759 4376789 4376833 4376843 4376849 4376851 4376857 4376863 4376881
4376887 4376917 4376929 4376947 4376951 4376959 4376963 4376993 4377001 4377017
4377019 4377029 4377053 4377067 4377089 4377091 4377101 4377167 4377179 4377181
4377193 4377203 4377227 4377229 4377257 4377341 4377343 4377379 4377407 4377409
4377413 4377427 4377473 4377487 4377493 4377497 4377509 4377511 4377539 4377547
4377557 4377559 4377587 4377589 4377599 4377601 4377629 4377649 4377661 4377671
4377673 4377677 4377679 4377697 4377739 4377749 4377757 4377799 4377833 4377839
4377871 4377881 4377887 4377899 4377929 4377953 4377973 4377983 4378007 4378009
4378013 4378019 4378057 4378069 4378079 4378093 4378123 4378133 4378139 4378141
4378181 4378201 4378207 4378219 4378229 4378237 4378243 4378271 4378273 4378279
4378301 4378307 4378327 4378351 4378373 4378399 4378403 4378447 4378453 4378463
4378477 4378481 4378511 4378523 4378541 4378553 4378559 4378609 4378631 4378697
4378727 4378753 4378757 4378771 4378789 4378811 4378813 4378817 4378837 4378887
4378909 4378939 4378951 4378963 4378981 4379003 4379009 4379017 4379021 4379027
4379033 4379071 4379083 4379099 4379107 4379143 4379159 4379161 4379171 4379173
4379227 4379233 4379239 4379257 4379267 4379273 4379279 4379281 4379303 4379311
4379327 4379359 4379369 4379371 4379381 4379399 4379437 4379447 4379449 4379467
4379477 4379483 4379491 4379509 4379521 4379533 4379539 4379561 4379567 4379569
4379581 4379597 4379603 4379611 4379623 4379677 4379689 4379707 4379717 4379719
4379731 4379737 4379741 4379759 4379797 4379803 4379819 4379833 4379873 4379887
4379911 4379917 4379923 4379931 4379933 4379939 4379971 4379987 4380001 4380017
4380031 4380037 4380043 4380049 4380059 4380091 4380107 4380113 4380119 4380121
4380133 4380151 4380157 4380163 4380179 4380193 4380197 4380199 4380209
4380221 4380223 4380239 4380251 4380263 4380283 4380287 4380289 4380293 4380323
4380361 4380391 4380401 4380403 4380421 4380433 4380437 4380449 4380461 4380463
4380499 4380547 4380553 4380559 4380589 4380599 4380637 4380647 4380683 4380707
4380709 4380737 4380751 4380757 4380767 4380793 4380839 4380841 4380851 4380853
4380881 4380919 4380931 4380979 4380983 4380991 4381007 4381009 4381031 4381043
4381049 4381051 4381067 4381073 4381093 4381127 4381147 4381151 4381159 4381177
4381183 4381187 4381249 4381253 4381271 4381297 4381303 4381319 4381357 4381361
4381367 4381379 4381409 4381411 4381423 4381441 4381453 4381459 4381469 4381493
4381499 4381501 4381513 4381537 4381541 4381549 4381561 4381591 4381607 4381667
4381681 4381693 4381703 4381709 4381739 4381747 4381771 4381777 4381787 4381807
4381823 4381847 4381859 4381877 4381879 4381921 4381931 4381939 4381961 4381963
4381967 4381973 4381999 4382003 4382023 4382041 4382047 4382069 4382071
4382083 4382089 4382101 4382143 4382149 4382153 4382159 4382177 4382197 4382201
4382207 4382227 4382251 4382267 4382281 4382291 4382297 4382299 4382303 4382309
4382359 4382381 4382383 4382387 4382419 4382429 4382437 4382453 4382459 4382467
4382471 4382503 4382507 4382519 4382527 4382533 4382561 4382591 4382593 4382611
4382629 4382647 4382657 4382663 4382699 4382713 4382723 4382731 4382737 4382747
4382773 4382779 4382783 4382801 4382813 4382843 4382849 4382869 4382879 4382881
4382887 4382893 4382921 4382927 4382929 4382951 4382953 4383017 4383017 4383061
4383101 4383107 4383109 4383149 4383163 4383191 4383199 4383209 4383227 4383241
4383257 4383293 4383311 4383343 4383349 4383367 4383389 4383397 4383403 4383413
4383439 4383443 4383449 4383451 4383461 4383481 4383497 4383503 4383529 4383539
4383551 4383571 4383581 4383601 4383607 4383619 4383629 4383667 4383677 4383689
4383697 4383713 4383719 4383733 4383751 4383763 4383767 4383779 4383791 4383817
4383833 4383839 4383853 4383857 4383919 4383923 4383931 4383937 4383949
4383991 4384013 4384021 4384043 4384057 4384063 4384067 4384087 4384091 4384097
4384103 4384129 4384141 4384153 4384157 4384183 4384187 4384189 4384243 4384271
4384273 4384277 4384291 4384313 4384333 4384337 4384343 4384357 4384379 4384433
4384447 4384451 4384469 4384483 4384493 4384507 4384517 4384529 4384543 4384553
4384561 4384577 4384591 4384603 4384621 4384631 4384673 4384711 4384727 4384769
4384777 4384781 4384799 4384823 4384837 4384841 4384847 4384867 4384871 4384873
4384879 4384901 4384931 4384937 4384943 4384951 4384957 4384979 4384987 4384993
4385009 4385021 4385027 4385041 4385047 4385063 4385071 4385093 4385123 4385131
4385137 4385141 4385149 4385159 4385209 4385243 4385263 4385267 4385281 4385287
4385317 4385323 4385327 4385347 4385357 4385389 4385393 4385399 4385461 4385489
4385501 4385509 4385519 4385531 4385533 4385569 4385603 4385611 4385627 4385629
4385639 4385669 4385681 4385683 4385687 4385701 4385743 4385783 4385791 4385807
4385819 4385837 4385863 4385879 4385897 4385923 4385947 4385963 4385971 4385981
4385987 4386023 4386029 4386061 4386071 4386073 4386089 4386101 4386133 4386149
4386191 4386197 4386211 4386229 4386233 4386241 4386247 4386257 4386259 4386271
4386293 4386331 4386341 4386379 4386383 4386419 4386443 4386457 4386517 4386521
4386523 4386533 4386541 4386553 4386601 4386611 4386617 4386623 4386637 4386647
4386649 4386653 4386671 4386673 4386689 4386719 4386763 4386769 4386787 4386793
4386803 4386821 4386847 4386869 4386871 4386881 4386883 4386883 4386913 4386919
4386947 4386971 4386973 4387013 4387021 4387039 4387049 4387067 4387069 4387073
4387087 4387099 4387133 4387147 4387153 4387169 4387171 4387177 4387183 4387193
4387211 4387217 4387223 4387231 4387249 4387267 4387283 4387289 4387291 4387301
4387351 4387363 4387367 4387379 4387391 4387429 4387441 4387477 4387483 4387501
4387517 4387529 4387543 4387553 4387567 4387609 4387619 4387633 4387661 4387673
4387681 4387693 4387703 4387741 4387753 4387769 4387777 4387783 4387807 4387829
4387847 4387867 4387891 4387907 4387919 4387931 4387937 4387939 4387969 4387979
4387987 4387991 4387997 4388017 4388039 4388063 4388071 4388099 4388113 4388117
4388171 4388173 4388179 4388191 4388201 4388207 4388257 4388269 4388291 4388333
4388359 4388381 4388387 4388393 4388407 4388413 4388429 4388443 4388473 4388477
4388507 4388519 4388539 4388557 4388609 4388611 4388617 4388641 4388651 4388689
```

```
4388711  4388731  4388743  4388749  4388779  4388803  4388821  4388827  4388843  4388861
4388869  4388897  4388911  4388971  4388987  4389017  4389023  4389029  4389031  4389041
4389071  4389083  4389131  4389137  4389169  4389191  4389193  4389221  4389223  4389227
4389233  4389241  4389257  4389263  4389269  4389293  4389299  4389313  4389367  4389379
4389401  4389403  4389439  4389443  4389449  4389457  4389467  4389479  4389491  4389503
4389509  4389521  4389523  4389533  4389547  4389557  4389559  4389571  4389577  4389601
4389607  4389611  4389647  4389653  4389667  4389673  4389677  4389691  4389727  4389731
4389769  4389799  4389809  4389821  4389823  4389839  4389841  4389851  4389857  4389871
4389881  4389883  4389899  4389901  4389919  4389947  4389971  4389977  4389989  4389997
4390021  4390039  4390051  4390069  4390073  4390091  4390093  4390117  4390151  4390181
4390207  4390219  4390229  4390237  4390247  4390279  4390283  4390289  4390291  4390307
4390327  4390357  4390381  4390409  4390417  4390433  4390453  4390469  4390481  4390483
4390489  4390523  4390541  4390553  4390559  4390613  4390619  4390621  4390651  4390657
4390663  4390667  4390697  4390703  4390717  4390733  4390739  4390751  4390759  4390781
4390801  4390817  4390823  4390829  4390849  4390873  4390889  4390909  4390921  4390937
4391003  4391011  4391017  4391027  4391039  4391041  4391063  4391081  4391087  4391089
4391099  4391131  4391161  4391221  4391227  4391249  4391263  4391323  4391339  4391341
4391353  4391363  4391369  4391371  4391393  4391399  4391411  4391417  4391437  4391449
4391483  4391503  4391521  4391549  4391579  4391587  4391591  4391609  4391617  4391651
4391659  4391671  4391683  4391687  4391707  4391711  4391713  4391741  4391767  4391771
4391773  4391791  4391813  4391819  4391839  4391843  4391851  4391857  4391867  4391887
4391897  4391903  4391909  4391911  4391921  4391923  4391929  4391941  4391953  4391957
4391969  4391993  4391999  4392007  4392013  4392077  4392107  4392109  4392119  4392133
4392151  4392169  4392181  4392203  4392209  4392217  4392221  4392259  4392263  4392281
4392313  4392317  4392331  4392343  4392383  4392397  4392403  4392433  4392461  4392463
4392473  4392483  4392497  4392499  4392503  4392523  4392541  4392547  4392559
4392571  4392589  4392593  4392611  4392653  4392679  4392683  4392691  4392719  4392737
4392757  4392763  4392769  4392779  4392797  4392811  4392853  4392881  4392887  4392911
4392929  4392937  4393001  4393003  4393019  4393031  4393061  4393063  4393079  4393093
4393097  4393127  4393139  4393153  4393163  4393177  4393201  4393217  4393219  4393229
4393243  4393247  4393271  4393283  4393309  4393321  4393369  4393387  4393397  4393423
4393447  4393451  4393481  4393489  4393507  4393511  4393517  4393523  4393549  4393559
4393583  4393591  4393637  4393643  4393687  4393699  4393717  4393729  4393751  4393799
4393811  4393813  4393817  4393849  4393853  4393903  4393919  4393933  4393937  4393967
4393969  4393979  4393981  4393999  4394021  4394023  4394029  4394063  4394099  4394107
4394113  4394123  4394183  4394189  4394191  4394209  4394227  4394237  4394249  4394267
4394287  4394293  4394297  4394303  4394309  4394321  4394323  4394353  4394371  4394413
4394419  4394431  4394437  4394441  4394447  4394461  4394473  4394561  4394563  4394603
4394609  4394617  4394627  4394639  4394651  4394717  4394737  4394743  4394783
4394791  4394801  4394827  4394837  4394843  4394879  4394881  4394893  4394899  4394903
4394911  4394917  4394927  4394983  4395029  4395031  4395049  4395067  4395103  4395109
4395143  4395151  4395161  4395173  4395179  4395199  4395221  4395227  4395229  4395271
4395283  4395301  4395317  4395329  4395353  4395379  4395389  4395409  4395421  4395427
4395437  4395439  4395463  4395493  4395497  4395511  4395527  4395541  4395551  4395557
4395613  4395619  4395623  4395641  4395653  4395659  4395689  4395697  4395701  4395709
4395719  4395739  4395751  4395779  4395793  4395817  4395827  4395857  4395869  4395887
4395917  4395949  4395953  4395959  4395983  4395997  4396001  4396003  4396027  4396033
4396037  4396057  4396069  4396097  4396099  4396111  4396121  4396123  4396127  4396181
4396199  4396207  4396211  4396219  4396237  4396283  4396291  4396321  4396361  4396367
4396369  4396393  4396397  4396409  4396411  4396417  4396423  4396439  4396459  4396463
4396481  4396493  4396517  4396529  4396531  4396537  4396549  4396559  4396573  4396577
4396583  4396589  4396597  4396627  4396633  4396643  4396669  4396681  4396687  4396729
4396751  4396781  4396783  4396787  4396789  4396801  4396811  4396813  4396831  4396849
4396853  4396871  4396877  4396907  4396919  4396937  4396939  4396981  4396993  4397023
4397047  4397053  4397069  4397077  4397083  4397087  4397131  4397147  4397149  4397167
4397171  4397177  4397201  4397207  4397233  4397249  4397279  4397287  4397311  4397353
4397363  4397383  4397389  4397399  4397431  4397453  4397467  4397483  4397501  4397521
4397557  4397581  4397587  4397599  4397651  4397663  4397677  4397681  4397717  4397737
4397777  4397779  4397803  4397831  4397863  4397867  4397893  4397909  4397923  4397933
4397941  4397957  4397959  4397969  4397983  4397999  4398007  4398011  4398013  4398047
4398049  4398061  4398071  4398089  4398091  4398101  4398131  4398133  4398143  4398151
4398181  4398197  4398211  4398217  4398239  4398241  4398263  4398287  4398293  4398319
4398337  4398347  4398353  4398371  4398397  4398421  4398431  4398463  4398467  4398487
4398503  4398553  4398571  4398577  4398623  4398637  4398677  4398679  4398689  4398697
4398703  4398707  4398731  4398743  4398769  4398787  4398811  4398817  4398829  4398839
4398851  4398859  4398887  4398941  4398949  4398959  4398991  4398997  4399001  4399007
4399061  4399063  4399067  4399079  4399103  4399123  4399133  4399147  4399163  4399169
4399193  4399223  4399227  4399289  4399301  4399309  4399313  4399327  4399331  4399333
4399361  4399363  4399397  4399399  4399457  4399471  4399511  4399513  4399517  4399531
4399541  4399543  4399553  4399573  4399609  4399627  4399639  4399663  4399667  4399673
4399679  4399699  4399709  4399711  4399721  4399723  4399729  4399763  4399771  4399789
4399817  4399819  4399847  4399853  4399873  4399883  4399903  4399907  4399931  4399933
4399939  4399943  4399961  4400011  4400021  4400023  4400027  4400041  4400081  4400093
4400101  4400111  4400129  4400131  4400167  4400183  4400189  4400197  4400203  4400213
4400261  4400269  4400293  4400309  4400311  4400317  4400329  4400351  4400353  4400369
4400377  4400387  4400393  4400401  4400413  4400443  4400477  4400483  4400497  4400503
4400507  4400527  4400549  4400551  4400587  4400621  4400623  4400629  4400639  4400687
4400701  4400717  4400719  4400731  4400771  4400777  4400801  4400813  4400819  4400821
4400839  4400861  4400887  4400917  4400923  4400927  4400959  4400969  4400989  4400993
4401043  4401071  4401083  4401107  4401121  4401143  4401191  4401193  4401203  4401209
4401233  4401251  4401259  4401269  4401281  4401289  4401329  4401337  4401343  4401347
4401373  4401403  4401413  4401421  4401427  4401433  4401443  4401451  4401457  4401493
4401497  4401517  4401563  4401581  4401601  4401641  4401653  4401673  4401697  4401701
4401737  4401743  4401767  4401791  4401799  4401811  4401829  4401841  4401847  4401857
4401869  4401883  4401889  4401899  4401931  4401941  4401949  4401979  4401983
4402003  4402007  4402009  4402019  4402033  4402037  4402043  4402063  4402081  4402157
4402159  4402189  4402193  4402199  4402219  4402241  4402247  4402249  4402253  4402259
4402271  4402273  4402283  4402291  4402327  4402351  4402373  4402379  4402381  4402393
4402399  4402421  4402423  4402429  4402441  4402451  4402459  4402481  4402493  4402501
```

```
4402511  4402513  4402543  4402549  4402561  4402597  4402613  4402627  4402633  4402663
4402669  4402679  4402689  4402721  4402747  4402787  4402789  4402799  4402807  4402817
4402823  4402831  4402841  4402859  4402861  4402873  4402877  4402891  4402897  4402903
4402933  4402987  4402991  4402997  4402999  4403033  4403053  4403057  4403059  4403089
4403093  4403129  4403149  4403159  4403167  4403171  4403183  4403213  4403219  4403227
4403237  4403251  4403257  4403279  4403291  4403299  4403309  4403341  4403393  4403411
4403429  4403431  4403461  4403473  4403489  4403533  4403537  4403543  4403569  4403617
4403627  4403639  4403647  4403653  4403657  4403669  4403677  4403683  4403689  4403699
4403713  4403719  4403747  4403753  4403783  4403803  4403821  4403837  4403849  4403857
4403881  4403909  4403923  4403939  4403951  4403963  4403981  4403983  4403989  4404019
4404047  4404079  4404107  4404121  4404133  4404137  4404149  4404151  4404157  4404161
4404167  4404193  4404251  4404271  4404287  4404299  4404319  4404341  4404347  4404391
4404397  4404419  4404427  4404437  4404451  4404457  4404469  4404503  4404551  4404553
4404557  4404559  4404583  4404593  4404623  4404641  4404643  4404677  4404679  4404689
4404691  4404703  4404709  4404731  4404733  4404737  4404773  4404797  4404809  4404811
4404817  4404833  4404847  4404857  4404859  4404863  4404889  4404899  4404929  4404931
4404943  4404971  4404973  4404977  4405003  4405021  4405031  4405043  4405067  4405073
4405097  4405111  4405127  4405133  4405147  4405151  4405153  4405157  4405189  4405199
4405217  4405231  4405243  4405253  4405267  4405309  4405333  4405343  4405367  4405381
4405403  4405417  4405421  4405433  4405439  4405447  4405459  4405493  4405501  4405517
4405523  4405543  4405547  4405559  4405571  4405579  4405591  4405633  4405637  4405679
4405691  4405693  4405697  4405699  4405717  4405741  4405747  4405759  4405789  4405829
4405831  4405867  4405871  4405879  4405913  4405927  4405979  4405991  4406021  4406023
4406069  4406089  4406093  4406099  4406141  4406159  4406177  4406197  4406201  4406251
4406267  4406287  4406291  4406323  4406329  4406341  4406351  4406357  4406359  4406401
4406411  4406429  4406431  4406449  4406453  4406459  4406477  4406491  4406503  4406509
4406531  4406527  4406531  4406539  4406551  4406573  4406599  4406627  4406653  4406659
4406671  4406707  4406713  4406741  4406747  4406749  4406797  4406813  4406819  4406821
4406827  4406837  4406881  4406891  4406903  4406911  4406939  4406947  4406949  4406953
4406957  4406999  4407017  4407023  4407071  4407089  4407103  4407119  4407127  4407163
4407203  4407211  4407257  4407269  4407287  4407289  4407307  4407313  4407317
4407323  4407343  4407349  4407367  4407397  4407401  4407409  4407413  4407429  4407439
4407463  4407479  4407493  4407497  4407509  4407523  4407577  4407581  4407589  4407593
4407653  4407671  4407691  4407719  4407731  4407761  4407763  4407779  4407817  4407827
4407839  4407857  4407883  4407917  4407929  4407937  4407961  4407967  4408007  4408031
4408073  4408093  4408097  4408099  4408109  4408123  4408139  4408141  4408147
4408153  4408163  4408199  4408267  4408277  4408289  4408301  4408307  4408309  4408331
4408333  4408337  4408343  4408363  4408427  4408429  4408451  4408483  4408499  4408501
4408517  4408561  4408577  4408583  4408597  4408601  4408619  4408637  4408639  4408643
4408681  4408687  4408693  4408697  4408739  4408757  4408759  4408769  4408777  4408787
4408813  4408837  4408849  4408861  4408867  4408889  4408891  4408903  4408909  4408951
4408961  4408973  4408991  4408993  4408997  4409003  4409033  4409063  4409081  4409087
4409101  4409107  4409113  4409143  4409183  4409221  4409257  4409269  4409281  4409287
4409291  4409297  4409299  4409303  4409333  4409371  4409381  4409389  4409393  4409411
4409437  4409453  4409459  4409473  4409513  4409519  4409527  4409551  4409557  4409569
4409609  4409611  4409633  4409651  4409677  4409687  4409723  4409737  4409747  4409753
4409773  4409777  4409803  4409807  4409809  4409849  4409887  4409891  4409897  4409903
4409917  4409921  4409927  4409939  4409941  4409981  4410019  4410041  4410047  4410061
4410079  4410097  4410103  4410113  4410121  4410127  4410137  4410139  4410143
4410163  4410173  4410187  4410193  4410199  4410221  4410229  4410253  4410283  4410317
4410323  4410347  4410353  4410359  4410379  4410389  4410397  4410403  4410431  4410443
4410473  4410479  4410481  4410499  4410517  4410547  4410551  4410589  4410611  4410613
4410619  4410631  4410643  4410683  4410691  4410719  4410737  4410743  4410761  4410767
4410787  4410799  4410827  4410829  4410839  4410841  4410859  4410877  4410893
4410911  4410919  4410937  4410947  4410949  4410953  4410961  4410977  4411013  4411019
4411049  4411061  4411063  4411073  4411083  4411087  4411117  4411129  4411133  4411139
4411153  4411189  4411217  4411247  4411261  4411333  4411343  4411357  4411369  4411391
4411397  4411403  4411409  4411417  4411427  4411447  4411453  4411477  4411493  4411501
4411507  4411523  4411531  4411541  4411549  4411571  4411573  4411577  4411601  4411637
4411643  4411661  4411663  4411669  4411679  4411697  4411711  4411739  4411747  4411801
4411817  4411829  4411831  4411867  4411873  4411877  4411963  4412033
4412041  4412053  4412059  4412063  4412077  4412081  4412087  4412099  4412141  4412183
4412189  4412201  4412227  4412249  4412257  4412269  4412279  4412281  4412293  4412327
4412347  4412377  4412381  4412383  4412393  4412399  4412411  4412413  4412423  4412449
4412453  4412459  4412467  4412477  4412497  4412533  4412539  4412563  4412567  4412581
4412587  4412593  4412659  4412663  4412671  4412713  4412719  4412729  4412743  4412747
4412753  4412773  4412797  4412813  4412839  4412857  4412867  4412893  4412897  4412917
4412927  4412977  4412981  4413007  4413011  4413019  4413029  4413037  4413041
4413043  4413049  4413053  4413061  4413077  4413091  4413119  4413121  4413131  4413137
4413139  4413161  4413163  4413169  4413173  4413179  4413197  4413203  4413229  4413239
4413247  4413271  4413287  4413293  4413313  4413317  4413329  4413337  4413341  4413349
4413371  4413373  4413379  4413419  4413443  4413457  4413467  4413503  4413509  4413511
4413547  4413553  4413571  4413581  4413583  4413587  4413589  4413593  4413611  4413623
4413637  4413671  4413683  4413697  4413701  4413707  4413751  4413763  4413781  4413793
4413797  4413823  4413841  4413853  4413869  4413883  4413889  4413917  4413919  4413923
4413943  4413949  4413971  4413973  4413991  4414001  4414013  4414037  4414049  4414073
4414087  4414093  4414097  4414127  4414129  4414147  4414153  4414159  4414171  4414199
4414217  4414219  4414247  4414253  4414259  4414261  4414279  4414297  4414301  4414303
4414309  4414313  4414343  4414349  4414357  4414379  4414411  4414427  4414447  4414451
4414457  4414463  4414519  4414537  4414591  4414601  4414607  4414621  4414633  4414637
4414649  4414673  4414703  4414723  4414727  4414759  4414763  4414769  4414777  4414789
4414807  4414843  4414867  4414909  4414913  4414937  4414957  4414961  4414999  4415009
4415041  4415069  4415123  4415143  4415153  4415161  4415171  4415183  4415207  4415219
4415269  4415273  4415297  4415303  4415329  4415357  4415371  4415387  4415399  4415401
4415407  4415431  4415441  4415443  4415447  4415459  4415473  4415497  4415503
4415513  4415527  4415531  4415533  4415549  4415573  4415591  4415633  4415639  4415641
4415669  4415681  4415687  4415707  4415717  4415753  4415777  4415779  4415813  4415819
4415881  4415893  4415899  4415909  4415933  4415941  4415951  4415953  4415963  4415969
4415993  4416007  4416011  4416017  4416029  4416047  4416053  4416067  4416079  4416089
```

```
4416101 4416131 4416133 4416157 4416163 4416187 4416193 4416221 4416241 4416257
4416259 4416263 4416287 4416301 4416319 4416329 4416343 4416359 4416371 4416409
4416421 4416443 4416473 4416499 4416521 4416523 4416527 4416541 4416547 4416551
4416553 4416589 4416611 4416623 4416641 4416661 4416673 4416677 4416689 4416691
4416703 4416733 4416751 4416757 4416773 4416793 4416823 4416829 4416857 4416869
4416871 4416877 4416913 4416931 4416947 4416953 4416977 4417009 4417027 4417031
4417043 4417051 4417087 4417099 4417111 4417121 4417141 4417151 4417163 4417169
4417199 4417207 4417211 4417213 4417223 4417241 4417247 4417267 4417279 4417307
4417313 4417321 4417333 4417351 4417363 4417379 4417397 4417409 4417411 4417421
4417429 4417453 4417471 4417487 4417489 4417493 4417499 4417513 4417537 4417591
4417597 4417607 4417613 4417663 4417669 4417703 4417723 4417727 4417729 4417753
4417757 4417769 4417783 4417793 4417799 4417811 4417813 4417883 4417927 4417957
4417967 4417969 4417981 4417993 4418009 4418017 4418023 4418041 4418069 4418077
4418081 4418083 4418107 4418111 4418123 4418131 4418143 4418149 4418159 4418171
4418189 4418191 4418209 4418221 4418243 4418261 4418269 4418273 4418303 4418311
4418321 4418341 4418357 4418389 4418417 4418437 4418459 4418467 4418483 4418489
4418497 4418537 4418539 4418563 4418567 4418581 4418587 4418627 4418633 4418669
4418677 4418683 4418719 4418731 4418741 4418747 4418749 4418789 4418797 4418801
4418807 4418819 4418831 4418839 4418881 4418903 4418917 4418941 4418951 4418977
4418983 4418989 4419011 4419017 4419071 4419073 4419083 4419089 4419097 4419101
4419109 4419113 4419131 4419137 4419157 4419161 4419179 4419199 4419211 4419263
4419271 4419293 4419307 4419323 4419341 4419353 4419367 4419377 4419379 4419383
4419407 4419409 4419451 4419461 4419469 4419479 4419487 4419509 4419517 4419529
4419553 4419557 4419559 4419563 4419581 4419587 4419589 4419593 4419599 4419601
4419661 4419671 4419673 4419683 4419691 4419713 4419731 4419743 4419773 4419791
4419797 4419823 4419851 4419853 4419869 4419889 4419901 4419907 4419911 4419937
4419941 4419953 4419967 4419973 4419991 4420001 4420019 4420037 4420043 4420049
4420067 4420069 4420081 4420127 4420139 4420159 4420183 4420189 4420219 4420231
4420249 4420309 4420319 4420337 4420373 4420379 4420417 4420421 4420453 4420463
4420469 4420513 4420517 4420519 4420523 4420543 4420547 4420553 4420567 4420573
4420583 4420589 4420601 4420607 4420613 4420627 4420639 4420667 4420687 4420699
4420721 4420729 4420733 4420739 4420747 4420751 4420753 4420769 4420777 4420813
4420831 4420837 4420849 4420859 4420891 4420903 4420987 4420993 4421023 4421029
4421033 4421041 4421063 4421113 4421117 4421141 4421143 4421147 4421159 4421177
4421201 4421203 4421213 4421227 4421237 4421257 4421297 4421299 4421321 4421323
4421353 4421371 4421407 4421413 4421423 4421447 4421449 4421461 4421491 4421507
4421533 4421539 4421567 4421579 4421587 4421597 4421603 4421617 4421621 4421633
4421653 4421671 4421689 4421693 4421719 4421723 4421731 4421741 4421743 4421749
4421771 4421779 4421783 4421789 4421797 4421801 4421831 4421839 4421849 4421861
4421863 4421869 4421897 4421899 4421903 4421909 4421929 4421941 4421947 4421953
4421987 4421989 4421999 4422017 4422037 4422043 4422071 4422101 4422127 4422139
4422151 4422169 4422191 4422211 4422221 4422241 4422247 4422263 4422287 4422289
4422311 4422331 4422343 4422347 4422359 4422361 4422391 4422401 4422403 4422409
4422419 4422427 4422443 4422461 4422493 4422503 4422527 4422557 4422571 4422577
4422589 4422599 4422617 4422619 4422623 4422643 4422667 4422673 4422749 4422757
4422773 4422787 4422791 4422799 4422809 4422811 4422823 4422827 4422829 4422853
4422857 4422881 4422919 4422931 4422959 4422961 4422967 4422989 4423019 4423021
4423031 4423037 4423057 4423063 4423117 4423127 4423157 4423163 4423169 4423183
4423189 4423201 4423207 4423231 4423249 4423253 4423259 4423261 4423271 4423277
4423301 4423339 4423351 4423357 4423361 4423379 4423381 4423403 4423411 4423423
4423427 4423481 4423493 4423511 4423543 4423579 4423583 4423603 4423619 4423649
4423667 4423673 4423681 4423691 4423697 4423703 4423717 4423721 4423729 4423733
4423807 4423823 4423829 4423841 4423849 4423871 4423877 4423897 4423907 4423919
4423931 4423933 4423973 4423987 4423999 4424009 4424039 4424059 4424083 4424087
4424111 4424113 4424117 4424137 4424143 4424171 4424179 4424191 4424209 4424213
4424239 4424249 4424261 4424291 4424293 4424297 4424317 4424323 4424333 4424341
4424347 4424353 4424363 4424383 4424389 4424411 4424429 4424447 4424467 4424489
4424491 4424503 4424527 4424531 4424561 4424569 4424621 4424639 4424653 4424659
4424669 4424677 4424687 4424699 4424729 4424759 4424767 4424773 4424789 4424801
4424803 4424831 4424851 4424857 4424863 4424873 4424887 4424921 4424923 4424939
4424951 4424957 4424969 4424977 4425011 4425017 4425019 4425053 4425079 4425107
4425133 4425143 4425181 4425221 4425227 4425229 4425241 4425251 4425257 4425293
4425299 4425307 4425329 4425349 4425353 4425373 4425391 4425397 4425401 4425403
4425409 4425427 4425433 4425437 4425497 4425503 4425521 4425539 4425541 4425571
4425587 4425599 4425623 4425647 4425671 4425677 4425679 4425691 4425697 4425709
4425713 4425721 4425737 4425739 4425749 4425779 4425781 4425787 4425791 4425833
4425851 4425853 4425877 4425887 4425907 4425919 4425923 4425929 4425931 4425979
4425983 4425989 4425997 4426007 4426021 4426049 4426057 4426091 4426109 4426117
4426129 4426139 4426151 4426157 4426159 4426181 4426193 4426223 4426231 4426249
4426277 4426283 4426309 4426313 4426337 4426349 4426361 4426363 4426369 4426379
4426417 4426423 4426441 4426451 4426481 4426493 4426517 4426529 4426561 4426571
4426573 4426577 4426627 4426651 4426663 4426673 4426699 4426739 4426777 4426781
4426813 4426843 4426847 4426853 4426859 4426861 4426901 4426907
4426913 4426927 4426957 4426967 4426993 4426999 4427009 4427029 4427039 4427041
4427047 4427051 4427069 4427077 4427083 4427107 4427113 4427117 4427119 4427131
4427147 4427149 4427167 4427173 4427251 4427261 4427263 4427273 4427279 4427281
4427287 4427299 4427329 4427341 4427369 4427393 4427417 4427443 4427491 4427503
4427509 4427519 4427543 4427587 4427597 4427609 4427611 4427617 4427623 4427629
4427639 4427641 4427659 4427681 4427711 4427719 4427723 4427737 4427747 4427771
4427777 4427789 4427807 4427831 4427849 4427851 4427879 4427881 4427887 4427891
4427921 4427933 4427957 4427971 4428001 4428013 4428023 4428031 4428037 4428043
4428059 4428079 4428091 4428103 4428113 4428139 4428161 4428163 4428169 4428181
4428191 4428223 4428227 4428233 4428239 4428247 4428259 4428289 4428301 4428317
4428323 4428331 4428337 4428353 4428379 4428383 4428421 4428427 4428433 4428439
4428467 4428497 4428499 4428509 4428511 4428553 4428559 4428587 4428601
4428607 4428643 4428689 4428701 4428703 4428709 4428713 4428737 4428751 4428773
4428817 4428821 4428843 4428847 4428859 4428869 4428883 4428899
4428911 4428913 4428917 4428947 4428961 4428971 4429031 4429037 4429039 4429049
4429057 4429069 4429079 4429093 4429171 4429211 4429213 4429237 4429253 4429259
```

```
4429273 4429277 4429289 4429291 4429297 4429331 4429343 4429349 4429351 4429357
4429391 4429417 4429457 4429429 4429457 4429469 4429463 4429471 4429483 4429493
4429499 4429511 4429531 4429549 4429553 4429561 4429583 4429589 4429591 4429597
4429631 4429643 4429657 4429669 4429723 4429739 4429753 4429757 4429769 4429771
4429783 4429787 4429801 4429811 4429813 4429819 4429829 4429853 4429861 4429871
4429883 4429933 4429937 4429963 4429969 4429981 4429987 4429991 4430017 4430033
4430039 4430051 4430093 4430113 4430137 4430143 4430147 4430159 4430171 4430201
4430213 4430219 4430221 4430227 4430263 4430273 4430299 4430311 4430351 4430411
4430431 4430441 4430473 4430479 4430483 4430507 4430561 4430563 4430593 4430597
4430599 4430603 4430609 4430611 4430653 4430663 4430689 4430711 4430719 4430729
4430731 4430749 4430753 4430771 4430773 4430779 4430801 4430807 4430809 4430837
4430851 4430869 4430887 4430891 4430941 4430947 4430963 4430969 4431001
4431017 4431023 4431029 4431059 4431079 4431103 4431127 4431131 4431143 4431149
4431151 4431187 4431227 4431241 4431257 4431269 4431283 4431289 4431293 4431307
4431311 4431367 4431443 4431457 4431463 4431487 4431491 4431499 4431523 4431533
4431551 4431563 4431569 4431587 4431641 4431643 4431653 4431659 4431671 4431673
4431683 4431697 4431703 4431719 4431727 4431733 4431743 4431787 4431793 4431799
4431803 4431811 4431827 4431829 4431839 4431841 4431851 4431857 4431871 4431899
4431901 4431923 4431943 4431949 4431961 4431963 4431991 4432007 4432009 4432069
4432081 4432091 4432093 4432097 4432151 4432177 4432201 4432217 4432229 4432243
4432247 4432249 4432271 4432279 4432343 4432357 4432367 4432381 4432391 4432457
4432471 4432513 4432517 4432531 4432541 4432559 4432591 4432607 4432613 4432619
4432627 4432657 4432661 4432667 4432669 4432693 4432723 4432739 4432751 4432759
4432763 4432793 4432807 4432817 4432819 4432829 4432837 4432843 4432861 4432873
4432889 4432943 4432949 4432963 4432979 4433021 4433029 4433047 4433057 4433059
4433063 4433069 4433119 4433129 4433131 4433147 4433167 4433173 4433203 4433237
4433249 4433263 4433267 4433269 4433281 4433287 4433309 4433333 4433339 4433381
4433393 4433399 4433423 4433449 4433459 4433467 4433477 4433489 4433497 4433519
4433533 4433567 4433573 4433581 4433587 4433603 4433621 4433623 4433629 4433633
4433647 4433657 4433701 4433729 4433771 4433809 4433827 4433833 4433843 4433881
4433887 4433893 4433903 4433911 4433929 4433941 4433953 4433959 4433971 4433977
4433981 4433999 4434019 4434041 4434061 4434077 4434083 4434097 4434107 4434119
4434149 4434173 4434179 4434181 4434197 4434251 4434257 4434259 4434281 4434299
4434307 4434329 4434337 4434341 4434343 4434371 4434383 4434421 4434427 4434431
4434449 4434473 4434491 4434503 4434511 4434527 4434539 4434541 4434571 4434629
4434631 4434673 4434691 4434697 4434721 4434737 4434769 4434799 4434811 4434817
4434839 4434851 4434863 4434877 4434889 4434901 4434907 4434949 4434973 4434979
4435001 4435031 4435069 4435087 4435091 4435097 4435103 4435111 4435117 4435121
4435129 4435133 4435169 4435177 4435183 4435237 4435241 4435243 4435253 4435259
4435279 4435313 4435357 4435367 4435369 4435373 4435381 4435397 4435423 4435429
4435433 4435439 4435447 4435451 4435469 4435477 4435513 4435549 4435559 4435567
4435577 4435609 4435631 4435643 4435661 4435663 4435709 4435723 4435733 4435741
4435763 4435777 4435787 4435801 4435817 4435889 4435891 4435897 4435903 4435919
4435933 4435939 4435943 4435961 4435969 4435993 4436011 4436017 4436023 4436039
4436051 4436059 4436071 4436093 4436111 4436119 4436123 4436143 4436183 4436207
4436209 4436219 4436227 4436231 4436249 4436251 4436273 4436287 4436297 4436321
4436339 4436351 4436359 4436363 4436389 4436407 4436413 4436431 4436459 4436461
4436477 4436483 4436501 4436521 4436527 4436567 4436581 4436587 4436603 4436639
4436647 4436657 4436669 4436687 4436693 4436699 4436701 4436737 4436749 4436759
4436771 4436801 4436821 4436827 4436863 4436879 4436891 4436893 4436903 4436909
4436923 4436933 4436947 4436959 4436987 4436989 4437007 4437011 4437053 4437067
4437113 4437131 4437161 4437163 4437179 4437197 4437211 4437217 4437227 4437259
4437283 4437311 4437313 4437337 4437341 4437347 4437359 4437361 4437379 4437383
4437403 4437409 4437421 4437427 4437439 4437443 4437457 4437463 4437473 4437479
4437487 4437491 4437497 4437523 4437529 4437539 4437547 4437593 4437613 4437617
4437673 4437677 4437701 4437703 4437709 4437721 4437733 4437737 4437749 4437751
4437757 4437767 4437779 4437857 4437863 4437869 4437877 4437883 4437911 4437913
4437941 4437943 4437959 4437967 4437973 4437977 4437989 4438009 4438019 4438033
4438043 4438051 4438067 4438079 4438087 4438097 4438111 4438117 4438123 4438151
4438169 4438171 4438183 4438199 4438201 4438211 4438219 4438223 4438237 4438271
4438279 4438283 4438303 4438321 4438339 4438349 4438361 4438391 4438397 4438451
4438463 4438481 4438501 4438507 4438529 4438541 4438559 4438573 4438583 4438597
4438601 4438613 4438639 4438667 4438691 4438699 4438703 4438739 4438741 4438771
4438789 4438813 4438823 4438829 4438831 4438843 4438867 4438871 4438891 4438901
4438919 4438939 4438961 4438981 4438991 4438997 4438999 4439003 4439033
4439047 4439063 4439077 4439081 4439087 4439119 4439129 4439137 4439143 4439167
4439209 4439213 4439257 4439269 4439273 4439287 4439317 4439341 4439377 4439381
4439389 4439401 4439411 4439419 4439423 4439443 4439447 4439453 4439459 4439473
4439503 4439507 4439509 4439531 4439543 4439569 4439627 4439653 4439663 4439671
4439693 4439717 4439719 4439723 4439777 4439797 4439801 4439807 4439821 4439833
4439837 4439857 4439861 4439867 4439887 4439899 4439909 4439917 4439921 4439923
4439947 4439951 4439971 4439993 4440001 4440011 4440017 4440019 4440031 4440041
4440049 4440067 4440071 4440089 4440131 4440133 4440169 4440187 4440193 4440197
4440199 4440209 4440221 4440239 4440253 4440257 4440323 4440343 4440367 4440379
4440389 4440413 4440421 4440427 4440437 4440439 4440461 4440479 4440487 4440497
4440503 4440521 4440523 4440529 4440571 4440613 4440619 4440637 4440641 4440659
4440673 4440677 4440691 4440707 4440721 4440727 4440731 4440763 4440767 4440773
4440797 4440803 4440823 4440841 4440847 4440881 4440899 4440901 4440913 4440929
4440937 4440959 4440991 4441007 4441009 4441033 4441037 4441043 4441103 4441109
4441111 4441133 4441159 4441163 4441187 4441207 4441211 4441219 4441237 4441271
4441279 4441289 4441303 4441309 4441313 4441351 4441357 4441361 4441387 4441397
4441399 4441417 4441433 4441439 4441441 4441457 4441477 4441483 4441493 4441499
4441523 4441529 4441531 4441543 4441561 4441589 4441597 4441601 4441621 4441627
4441643 4441663 4441667 4441673 4441693 4441721 4441729 4441733 4441747 4441751
4441757 4441769 4441793 4441823 4441841 4441861 4441867 4441883 4441903 4441909
4441919 4441939 4441949 4441963 4441979 4441999 4442003 4442027 4442041 4442047
4442069 4442071 4442093 4442099 4442101 4442117 4442131 4442159 4442161 4442171
4442189 4442209 4442213 4442231 4442233 4442261 4442267 4442279 4442303 4442311
4442327 4442357 4442363 4442387 4442401 4442413 4442429 4442437 4442441 4442443
```

```
4442453  4442483  4442489  4442507  4442521  4442527  4442531  4442549  4442551  4442573
4442609  4442623  4442639  4442663  4442681  4442689  4442743  4442777  4442807  4442819
4442839  4442843  4442861  4442869  4442897  4442909  4442917  4442927  4442929  4442939
4442953  4442987  4442989  4442993  4443037  4443041  4443079  4443083  4443097  4443107
4443121  4443139  4443143  4443157  4443181  4443191  4443203  4443221  4443227  4443247
4443253  4443259  4443289  4443311  4443331  4443353  4443371  4443379  4443391  4443401
4443403  4443419  4443421  4443431  4443433  4443463  4443487  4443493  4443497  4443529
4443533  4443541  4443553  4443557  4443559  4443563  4443581  4443599  4443601  4443619
4443631  4443653  4443689  4443707  4443713  4443743  4443767  4443781  4443793  4443797
4443809  4443827  4443841  4443863  4443877  4443889  4443893  4443937  4443941  4443973
4443983  4444001  4444049  4444087  4444091  4444109  4444127  4444147  4444159  4444169
4444171  4444201  4444207  4444213  4444217  4444229  4444241  4444261  4444289  4444291
4444331  4444339  4444357  4444369  4444381  4444397  4444409  4444469  4444471  4444483
4444487  4444507  4444519  4444549  4444591  4444607  4444621  4444639  4444663  4444669
4444697  4444703  4444711  4444717  4444729  4444747  4444753  4444771  4444787  4444789
4444793  4444799  4444807  4444823  4444829  4444861  4444877  4444907  4444943  4444949
4444967  4444991  4444997  4445017  4445027  4445029  4445047  4445083  4445087  4445099
4445113  4445153  4445159  4445167  4445197  4445201  4445227  4445257  4445267  4445281
4445303  4445317  4445321  4445333  4445387  4445393  4445429  4445437  4445443  4445447
4445453  4445459  4445477  4445479  4445491  4445501  4445503  4445521  4445527  4445531
4445543  4445557  4445561  4445569  4445593  4445603  4445621  4445629  4445633  4445657
4445659  4445663  4445681  4445711  4445719  4445723  4445737  4445767  4445797  4445821
4445839  4445849  4445851  4445869  4445879  4445921  4445933  4445939  4445941  4445953
4445983  4446007  4446037  4446047  4446067  4446073  4446097  4446103  4446119  4446131
4446137  4446161  4446191  4446203  4446217  4446241  4446259  4446269  4446293  4446317
4446319  4446331  4446347  4446353  4446359  4446371  4446373  4446389  4446413  4446419
4446427  4446433  4446451  4446457  4446461  4446467  4446499  4446509  4446553  4446581
4446583  4446593  4446601  4446641  4446643  4446661  4446667  4446677  4446679  4446683
4446721  4446731  4446763  4446769  4446787  4446821  4446823  4446829  4446853  4446863
4446887  4446899  4446971  4446977  4446997  4447019  4447031  4447033  4447049  4447061
4447099  4447109  4447111  4447151  4447153  4447169  4447171  4447181  4447199  4447207
4447249  4447253  4447297  4447301  4447321  4447423  4447427  4447433  4447439  4447453
4447459  4447483  4447493  4447507  4447529  4447537  4447543  4447549  4447559  4447589
4447607  4447609  4447627  4447637  4447649  4447679  4447687  4447697  4447739  4447747
4447753  4447757  4447769  4447783  4447801  4447811  4447819  4447823  4447841  4447847
4447853  4447871  4447879  4447889  4447903  4447907  4447909  4447913  4447943  4447987
4447997  4448009  4448011  4448021  4448023  4448027  4448077  4448089  4448099  4448111
4448113  4448117  4448149  4448167  4448179  4448183  4448207  4448231  4448239  4448267
4448273  4448287  4448291  4448317  4448321  4448333  4448347  4448357  4448359  4448371
4448383  4448419  4448443  4448447  4448501  4448533  4448537  4448539  4448557  4448573
4448579  4448657  4448671  4448677  4448699  4448701  4448723  4448769  4448797  4448813
4448833  4448837  4448863  4448881  4448921  4448929  4448933  4448947  4448957  4448989
4449017  4449023  4449037  4449077  4449079  4449083  4449103  4449113  4449119  4449127
4449163  4449227  4449233  4449239  4449259  4449283  4449299  4449301  4449307  4449317
4449323  4449329  4449331  4449343  4449371  4449391  4449397  4449407  4449409  4449413
4449421  4449433  4449449  4449457  4449469  4449479  4449481  4449491  4449493  4449503
4449521  4449527  4449539  4449541  4449551  4449559  4449589  4449593  4449617  4449619
4449637  4449659  4449661  4449691  4449701  4449749  4449751  4449763  4449773  4449793
4449799  4449811  4449817  4449821  4449829  4449859  4449871  4449877  4449883  4449899
4449901  4449919  4449923  4449947  4449983  4449997  4450003  4450013  4450031  4450051
4450057  4450097  4450111  4450129  4450139  4450151  4450163  4450169  4450177  4450213
4450261  4450273  4450283  4450291  4450297  4450301  4450319  4450331  4450333  4450337
4450349  4450373  4450399  4450409  4450441  4450489  4450507  4450517  4450519
4450553  4450561  4450573  4450603  4450613  4450627  4450637  4450657  4450669  4450679
4450681  4450687  4450697  4450703  4450711  4450729  4450739  4450751  4450757  4450811
4450829  4450847  4450861  4450871  4450909  4450913  4450931  4450933  4450951  4450961
4450967  4450981  4451017  4451023  4451053  4451071  4451081  4451087  4451119  4451129
4451141  4451179  4451191  4451219  4451257  4451261  4451269  4451273  4451281  4451291
4451309  4451341  4451357  4451387  4451389  4451393  4451401  4451407  4451423  4451429
4451437  4451441  4451449  4451459  4451479  4451483  4451527  4451533  4451537  4451543
4451563  4451591  4451593  4451599  4451611  4451617  4451633  4451639  4451653  4451677
4451701  4451723  4451743  4451767  4451779  4451791  4451813  4451827  4451849  4451891
4451893  4451921  4451929  4451939  4451957  4451983  4451999  4452001  4452013  4452017
4452043  4452073  4452131  4452139  4452143  4452157  4452187  4452191  4452209  4452211
4452229  4452233  4452241  4452251  4452277  4452293  4452307  4452337  4452347  4452353
4452379  4452391  4452407  4452431  4452433  4452443  4452449  4452473  4452491  4452509
4452523  4452533  4452571  4452599  4452647  4452649  4452653  4452673  4452683  4452719
4452727  4452737  4452739  4452743  4452751  4452761  4452769  4452797  4452803  4452829
4452841  4452857  4452881  4452893  4452919  4452941  4452947  4452953  4453013  4453063
4453069  4453081  4453093  4453121  4453129  4453139  4453147  4453159  4453171
4453177  4453187  4453213  4453223  4453231  4453259  4453271  4453291  4453321  4453331
4453349  4453387  4453399  4453403  4453409  4453417  4453433  4453441  4453451  4453457
4453481  4453483  4453487  4453489  4453499  4453517  4453567  4453573  4453583  4453591
4453613  4453621  4453637  4453663  4453681  4453693  4453703  4453717  4453747  4453751
4453769  4453777  4453787  4453807  4453817  4453837  4453853  4453859  4453877  4453903
4453909  4453913  4453919  4453931  4453937  4453951  4453957  4453963  4453991  4453997
4454003  4454027  4454041  4454059  4454071  4454077  4454083  4454101  4454141  4454147
4454179  4454207  4454209  4454213  4454239  4454269  4454273  4454291  4454293  4454299
4454321  4454339  4454353  4454369  4454377  4454381  4454383  4454399  4454407  4454423
4454447  4454449  4454473  4454477  4454501  4454521  4454537  4454543  4454551  4454563
4454579  4454599  4454621  4454657  4454687  4454699  4454711  4454741  4454767  4454771
4454783  4454789  4454819  4454839  4454861  4454869  4454881  4454887  4454903  4454921
4454927  4454963  4454977  4454993  4455001  4455007  4455023  4455029  4455043  4455203
4455079  4455091  4455097  4455107  4455119  4455151  4455161  4455167  4455181  4455203
4455221  4455223  4455229  4455239  4455259  4455301  4455323  4455331  4455361  4455371
4455383  4455391  4455397  4455403  4455461  4455467  4455469  4455487  4455497  4455509
4455527  4455533  4455559  4455569  4455611  4455631  4455637  4455641  4455667  4455691
4455707  4455727  4455743  4455749  4455761  4455779  4455793  4455797  4455833
4455851  4455863  4455877  4455881  4455901  4455911  4455949  4455953  4455959  4455967
```

```
4455973  4455977  4455991  4456007  4456063  4456079  4456121  4456147  4456183  4456189
4456213  4456223  4456297  4456301  4456327  4456339  4456349  4456357  4456367  4456369
4456373  4456421  4456427  4456429  4456433  4456451  4456453  4456511  4456513  4456541
4456547  4456553  4456559  4456561  4456579  4456589  4456609  4456619  4456631  4456643
4456651  4456663  4456679  4456693  4456709  4456769  4456783  4456787  4456789  4456799
4456819  4456831  4456847  4456861  4456867  4456877  4456889  4456891  4456897  4456931
4456937  4456939  4456951  4456957  4456961  4456973  4456997  4457093  4457099  4457113
4457129  4457143  4457171  4457197  4457203  4457221  4457249  4457263  4457269  4457287
4457293  4457303  4457311  4457317  4457347  4457357  4457359  4457371  4457389  4457399
4457407  4457413  4457429  4457437  4457447  4457449  4457461  4457471  4457473  4457477
4457489  4457491  4457507  4457539  4457543  4457549  4457597  4457603  4457611  4457623
4457639  4457657  4457663  4457693  4457729  4457753  4457759  4457771  4457801  4457813
4457839  4457857  4457867  4457881  4457897  4457911  4457923  4457933  4457953  4457977
4457983  4457987  4458001  4458043  4458071  4458073  4458101  4458109  4458127  4458133
4458151  4458163  4458169  4458187  4458193  4458253  4458263  4458269  4458281  4458287
4458313  4458317  4458319  4458359  4458361  4458367  4458371  4458379  4458409  4458457
4458491  4458491  4458497  4458499  4458529  4458533  4458557  4458563  4458569  4458599
4458617  4458647  4458653  4458659  4458661  4458667  4458697  4458737  4458739  4458793
4458809  4458821  4458827  4458829  4458841  4458877  4458887  4458889  4458893  4458899
4458911  4458919  4458929  4458931  4458959  4458967  4458983  4458991  4459001  4459003
4459027  4459073  4459099  4459141  4459157  4459159  4459163  4459177  4459193  4459199
4459211  4459237  4459241  4459267  4459303  4459333  4459339  4459361  4459363  4459369
4459373  4459379  4459409  4459451  4459531  4459531  4459541  4459549  4459561  4459577
4459589  4459597  4459601  4459603  4459619  4459639  4459657  4459667  4459669  4459687
4459709  4459711  4459717  4459727  4459733  4459739  4459747  4459757  4459759  4459781
4459799  4459811  4459817  4459841  4459849  4459901  4459921  4459951  4459981
4459993  4460009  4460023  4460039  4460077  4460083  4460107  4460111  4460119  4460147
4460153  4460161  4460167  4460173  4460177  4460191  4460207  4460219  4460237  4460243
4460251  4460279  4460297  4460303  4460327  4460353  4460359  4460369  4460377  4460399
4460411  4460429  4460437  4460447  4460453  4460471  4460479  4460483  4460537  4460549
4460557  4460581  4460587  4460593  4460623  4460633  4460641  4460653  4460657  4460699
4460711  4460713  4460741  4460761  4460767  4460773  4460779  4460803  4460837  4460879
4460891  4460899  4460903  4460909  4460917  4460921  4460941  4460959  4460971  4460977
4460999  4461007  4461019  4461031  4461047  4461059  4461073  4461091  4461109  4461161
4461203  4461211  4461221  4461227  4461253  4461277  4461283  4461307  4461313  4461319
4461341  4461377  4461419  4461421  4461433  4461439  4461449  4461451  4461461  4461491
4461493  4461539  4461547  4461553  4461577  4461617  4461623  4461641  4461643  4461649
4461671  4461673  4461689  4461703  4461707  4461727  4461733  4461749  4461763  4461767
4461773  4461791  4461797  4461811  4461817  4461823  4461869  4461881  4461887  4461889
4461893  4461901  4461913  4461929  4461943  4461971  4462009  4462013  4462021  4462033
4462037  4462049  4462091  4462099  4462121  4462141  4462151  4462181  4462187  4462223
4462231  4462243  4462261  4462277  4462307  4462309  4462319  4462331  4462343  4462349
4462361  4462363  4462373  4462379  4462387  4462429  4462457  4462463  4462489  4462519
4462531  4462537  4462567  4462571  4462589  4462609  4462637  4462643  4462651  4462657
4462673  4462691  4462693  4462751  4462753  4462763  4462771  4462793  4462811  4462813
4462817  4462831  4462837  4462867  4462877  4462879  4462883  4462889  4462919  4462921
4462949  4462951  4462957  4462963  4463003  4463009  4463023  4463033  4463057  4463059
4463111  4463113  4463141  4463143  4463153  4463177  4463189  4463191  4463203
4463209  4463213  4463243  4463257  4463317  4463321  4463341  4463351  4463363  4463369
4463377  4463399  4463413  4463453  4463467  4463489  4463497  4463513  4463521  4463539
4463549  4463551  4463567  4463603  4463611  4463647  4463663  4463671  4463729  4463747
4463761  4463773  4463779  4463813  4463827  4463831  4463857  4463887  4463903  4463929
4463947  4463971  4464007  4464011  4464017  4464049  4464071  4464073  4464079  4464091
4464101  4464133  4464157  4464179  4464181  4464227  4464233  4464253  4464269  4464331
4464337  4464359  4464371  4464377  4464379  4464401  4464413  4464443  4464451  4464469
4464491  4464497  4464511  4464533  4464547  4464569  4464571  4464587  4464623  4464641
4464643  4464661  4464673  4464689  4464721  4464731  4464739  4464751  4464763  4464767
4464781  4464793  4464799  4464821  4464839  4464841  4464853  4464857  4464877  4464881
4464893  4464917  4464937  4464949  4464959  4464983  4465009  4465031  4465037  4465051
4465063  4465073  4465093  4465099  4465103  4465117  4465127  4465157  4465177  4465199
4465207  4465211  4465231  4465259  4465273  4465277  4465291  4465301  4465319  4465327
4465343  4465367  4465369  4465379  4465387  4465411  4465429  4465453  4465459  4465471
4465499  4465501  4465537  4465553  4465561  4465603  4465607  4465609  4465619  4465631
4465639  4465661  4465667  4465691  4465693  4465697  4465723  4465733  4465763  4465787
4465801  4465807  4465819  4465831  4465837  4465861  4465907  4465919  4465957  4465963
4465973  4466009  4466017  4466027  4466039  4466041  4466051  4466069  4466093  4466129
4466131  4466141  4466149  4466167  4466191  4466219  4466221  4466227  4466239  4466243
4466249  4466251  4466299  4466303  4466323  4466327  4466339  4466401  4466411  4466419
4466443  4466447  4466459  4466471  4466491  4466503  4466507  4466513  4466521  4466569
4466591  4466593  4466617  4466621  4466639  4466641  4466719  4466723  4466741  4466747
4466771  4466773  4466779  4466789  4466837  4466857  4466863  4466867  4466873  4466879
4466911  4466923  4466939  4466941  4466951  4466963  4466981  4466983  4466989  4466993
4467011  4467013  4467017  4467019  4467041  4467049  4467053  4467059  4467077  4467119
4467137  4467139  4467181  4467187  4467191  4467217  4467241  4467257  4467263  4467271
4467293  4467301  4467329  4467347  4467367  4467377  4467383  4467389  4467403  4467439
4467443  4467461  4467469  4467499  4467509  4467511  4467521  4467553  4467559  4467563
4467569  4467577  4467601  4467611  4467613  4467643  4467649  4467677  4467709  4467767
4467779  4467781  4467791  4467803  4467809  4467833  4467839  4467851  4467857  4467863
4467887  4467901  4467919  4467929  4467949  4467971  4467979  4467997  4468007  4468033
4468039  4468043  4468069  4468091  4468099  4468103  4468109  4468153  4468159  4468171
4468183  4468199  4468273  4468301  4468307  4468313  4468327  4468333  4468339  4468351
4468367  4468369  4468393  4468421  4468441  4468447  4468469  4468487  4468493  4468537
4468547  4468559  4468567  4468573  4468577  4468579  4468609  4468613  4468621  4468643
4468649  4468661  4468663  4468687  4468721  4468727  4468729  4468741  4468747  4468757
4468777  4468787  4468817  4468843  4468847  4468859  4468873  4468883  4468887  4468889
4468903  4468927  4468939  4468979  4469027  4469051  4469063  4469083  4469099  4469111
4469131  4469141  4469167  4469189  4469197  4469203  4469207  4469233  4469243  4469261
4469293  4469299  4469303  4469321  4469323  4469329  4469347  4469357  4469359  4469401
4469411  4469417  4469431  4469447  4469461  4469483  4469501  4469519  4469561  4469581
```

4469587 4469599 4469609 4469627 4469629 4469651 4469671 4469677 4469681 4469719
4469723 4469737 4469743 4469749 4469753 4469767 4469813 4469821 4469831 4469833
4469837 4469849 4469869 4469879 4469911 4469923 4469939 4469951 4469977 4469987
4469989 4470013 4470043 4470047 4470049 4470061 4470077 4470083 4470121 4470143
4470163 4470209 4470223 4470233 4470239 4470241 4470247 4470251 4470281 4470287
4470289 4470329 4470331 4470383 4470397 4470407 4470413 4470419 4470421 4470443
4470449 4470461 4470467 4470469 4470539 4470569 4470577 4470589 4470623 4470649
4470659 4470679 4470707 4470731 4470743 4470761 4470769 4470773 4470793 4470803
4470811 4470857 4470859 4470863 4470877 4470911 4470919 4470923 4470929 4470931
4470937 4470943 4470953 4470971 4470989 4470997 4471001 4471003 4471007 4471013
4471067 4471069 4471073 4471081 4471121 4471123 4471141 4471171 4471189 4471193
4471211 4471217 4471237 4471267 4471279 4471303 4471319 4471349 4471381 4471387
4471393 4471421 4471427 4471477 4471529 4471547 4471549 4471559 4471567 4471609
4471619 4471633 4471661 4471681 4471693 4471711 4471717 4471739 4471741 4471751
4471757 4471801 4471811 4471837 4471847 4471853 4471879 4471889 4471891 4471921
4471927 4471933 4471939 4471949 4471979 4471997 4472021 4472081 4472089 4472101
4472107 4472113 4472131 4472137 4472147 4472159 4472197 4472203 4472213 4472233
4472261 4472263 4472267 4472287 4472297 4472311 4472323 4472341 4472357 4472359
4472371 4472399 4472431 4472437 4472443 4472477 4472497 4472509 4472527 4472539
4472551 4472563 4472591 4472593 4472609 4472627 4472651 4472687 4472693 4472701
4472747 4472749 4472753 4472759 4472777 4472779 4472789 4472801 4472807 4472821
4472827 4472851 4472857 4472869 4472911 4472917 4472927 4472933 4472957 4473011
4473013 4473019 4473089 4473097 4473101 4473103 4473107 4473127 4473143 4473149
4473169 4473173 4473181 4473211 4473241 4473277 4473281 4473283 4473289 4473299
4473347 4473361 4473373 4473377 4473383 4473409 4473421 4473449 4473457 4473463
4473473 4473479 4473503 4473541 4473583 4473587 4473611 4473613 4473619 4473631
4473647 4473653 4473671 4473697 4473701 4473713 4473727 4473731 4473751 4473757
4473761 4473767 4473769 4473773 4473779 4473809 4473811 4473853 4473863 4473869
4473877 4473881 4473901 4473971 4474027 4474031 4474037 4474039 4474073 4474079
4474081 4474087 4474103 4474109 4474133 4474153 4474157 4474159 4474163 4474181
4474201 4474219 4474241 4474243 4474303 4474307 4474331 4474361 4474369 4474399
4474409 4474427 4474433 4474441 4474469 4474471 4474493 4474511 4474517 4474523
4474543 4474573 4474601 4474609 4474643 4474649 4474661 4474693 4474697 4474703
4474711 4474721 4474733 4474739 4474741 4474763 4474783 4474801 4474807 4474837
4474849 4474867 4474879 4474907 4474919 4474931 4474933 4474963 4474969 4474999
4475017 4475033 4475047 4475057 4475069 4475071 4475083 4475117 4475123 4475137
4475147 4475153 4475171 4475173 4475189 4475197 4475239 4475243 4475257 4475291
4475323 4475329 4475333 4475351 4475357 4475389 4475407 4475413 4475417 4475423
4475447 4475459 4475461 4475467 4475473 4475503 4475551 4475567 4475579 4475617
4475623 4475633 4475663 4475671 4475689 4475701 4475707 4475711 4475717 4475719
4475747 4475803 4475813 4475837 4475839 4475843 4475851 4475881 4475893 4475957
4475959 4475969 4475983 4475987 4475993 4476013 4476019 4476023 4476041 4476047
4476067 4476079 4476089 4476091 4476133 4476137 4476167 4476181 4476187 4476193
4476247 4476281 4476289 4476301 4476313 4476317 4476319 4476331 4476341 4476379
4476383 4476397 4476403 4476427 4476463 4476473 4476481 4476487 4476497 4476509
4476517 4476547 4476553 4476569 4476581 4476583 4476599 4476613 4476631 4476653
4476671 4476677 4476691 4476707 4476713 4476757 4476767 4476779 4476781 4476793
4476809 4476811 4476821 4476827 4476833 4476847 4476863 4476883 4476893 4476907
4476911 4476917 4476929 4476931 4476949 4476959 4476961 4476971 4476977 4477013
4477043 4477061 4477073 4477091 4477133 4477139 4477153 4477181 4477199 4477261
4477271 4477279 4477283 4477313 4477337 4477349 4477351 4477367 4477373 4477379
4477381 4477391 4477411 4477427 4477439 4477441 4477453 4477457 4477463 4477471
4477489 4477519 4477523 4477537 4477541 4477553 4477567 4477573 4477619 4477661
4477667 4477691 4477717 4477721 4477727 4477729 4477741 4477751 4477769 4477789
4477813 4477819 4477841 4477849 4477871 4477873 4477883 4477903 4477931 4477937
4477951 4477961 4477969 4478009 4478011 4478017 4478059 4478069 4478081 4478083
4478087 4478137 4478153 4478161 4478189 4478197 4478203 4478231 4478233 4478237
4478249 4478251 4478269 4478317 4478323 4478339 4478351 4478359 4478381 4478387
4478413 4478417 4478423 4478527 4478533 4478549 4478561 4478563 4478567 4478641
4478647 4478653 4478657 4478671 4478687 4478693 4478707 4478741 4478777 4478779
4478783 4478801 4478807 4478809 4478821 4478827 4478833 4478843 4478857 4478861
4478863 4478869 4478879 4478891 4478899 4478917 4478983 4478987 4478989 4478993
4479001 4479023 4479029 4479031 4479049 4479071 4479073 4479121 4479133 4479149
4479157 4479179 4479187 4479197 4479199 4479203 4479239 4479247 4479259 4479263
4479287 4479317 4479323 4479361 4479389 4479443 4479463 4479473 4479481 4479487
4479491 4479493 4479509 4479581 4479661 4479667 4479691 4479707 4479731 4479743
4479749 4479793 4479799 4479803 4479809 4479829 4479851 4479863 4479883 4479889
4479907 4479911 4479919 4479941 4479967 4479973 4479989 4480001 4480013 4480031
4480033 4480039 4480043 4480081 4480093 4480097 4480141 4480153 4480183 4480187
4480199 4480211 4480241 4480243 4480247 4480253 4480261 4480271 4480277 4480291
4480303 4480319 4480339 4480351 4480361 4480363 4480379 4480403 4480429 4480453
4480481 4480507 4480513 4480517 4480547 4480559 4480573 4480583 4480591 4480613
4480621 4480627 4480631 4480649 4480661 4480681 4480691 4480757 4480769 4480783
4480787 4480793 4480799 4480807 4480831 4480841 4480867 4480871 4480897 4480909
4480951 4480961 4480981 4481003 4481041 4481069 4481077 4481083 4481101
4481123 4481129 4481137 4481153 4481171 4481173 4481179 4481189 4481201 4481233
4481249 4481261 4481263 4481273 4481287 4481291 4481293 4481299 4481311 4481327
4481333 4481339 4481363 4481369 4481383 4481401 4481431 4481441 4481443 4481459
4481461 4481479 4481501 4481537 4481567 4481569 4481579 4481593 4481597 4481599
4481611 4481621 4481629 4481677 4481683 4481707 4481713 4481717 4481723 4481767
4481791 4481797 4481801 4481819 4481837 4481843 4481857 4481881 4481899 4481927
4481989 4482001 4482007 4482031 4482047 4482059 4482091 4482101 4482131 4482167
4482173 4482209 4482227 4482239 4482253 4482281 4482287 4482299 4482311 4482319
4482323 4482329 4482349 4482389 4482391 4482409 4482431 4482451 4482469 4482479
4482497 4482547 4482553 4482589 4482593 4482601 4482619 4482623 4482637
4482641 4482649 4482659 4482701 4482703 4482721 4482739 4482743 4482749 4482767
4482787 4482799 4482809 4482847 4482871 4482887 4482901 4482911 4482931 4482937
4482943 4482971 4482977 4482983 4483009 4483021 4483027 4483033 4483043 4483057
4483067 4483093 4483097 4483103 4483123 4483147 4483159 4483163 4483181 4483201

```
4483207  4483231  4483247  4483249  4483273  4483277  4483307  4483319  4483337  4483363
4483387  4483397  4483399  4483403  4483421  4483433  4483447  4483483  4483489  4483517
4483519  4483537  4483541  4483543  4483571  4483607  4483649  4483651  4483657  4483663
4483681  4483709  4483741  4483751  4483769  4483789  4483793  4483807  4483811  4483813
4483837  4483849  4483859  4483877  4483889  4483891  4483901  4483907  4483939  4483957
4483991  4484021  4484023  4484027  4484033  4484041  4484069  4484089  4484099  4484111
4484113  4484131  4484143  4484167  4484189  4484191  4484197  4484201  4484203  4484219
4484231  4484239  4484251  4484267  4484273  4484321  4484327  4484329  4484339  4484371
4484387  4484419  4484423  4484449  4484483  4484503  4484509  4484521  4484561  4484567
4484569  4484591  4484611  4484633  4484653  4484657  4484663  4484671  4484687  4484729
4484731  4484737  4484743  4484749  4484759  4484761  4484773  4484789  4484791  4484803
4484813  4484819  4484827  4484833  4484849  4484861  4484869  4484873  4484891  4484897
4484899  4484911  4484917  4484927  4484933  4484941  4484947  4484959  4484971  4484981
4484983  4484993  4485001  4485043  4485073  4485097  4485109  4485139  4485149  4485157
4485167  4485179  4485191  4485209  4485211  4485223  4485301  4485317  4485319  4485323
4485329  4485353  4485367  4485379  4485389  4485409  4485413  4485451  4485469  4485479
4485487  4485497  4485527  4485557  4485581  4485587  4485589  4485599  4485601  4485617
4485619  4485623  4485629  4485643  4485661  4485683  4485707  4485721  4485737  4485743
4485763  4485781  4485797  4485799  4485809  4485823  4485827  4485839  4485853  4485869
4485883  4485907  4485931  4485937  4485941  4485953  4485967  4485983  4485997  4486003
4486019  4486037  4486051  4486073  4486087  4486093  4486099  4486129  4486151  4486169
4486171  4486177  4486187  4486193  4486199  4486217  4486231  4486247  4486259  4486297
4486303  4486309  4486327  4486333  4486373  4486379  4486381  4486411  4486421  4486429
4486457  4486459  4486463  4486477  4486483  4486499  4486511  4486519  4486543  4486553
4486567  4486571  4486591  4486607  4486621  4486631  4486637  4486639  4486649  4486673
4486681  4486711  4486721  4486751  4486777  4486787  4486813  4486819  4486829  4486841
4486843  4486849  4486877  4486883  4486919  4486939  4486943  4486957  4486961  4486973
4487003  4487011  4487029  4487039  4487051  4487053  4487089  4487107  4487111  4487159
4487177  4487183  4487207  4487213  4487233  4487239  4487243  4487297  4487299  4487311
4487321  4487339  4487341  4487359  4487381  4487387  4487393  4487407  4487411  4487411
4487423  4487449  4487479  4487503  4487519  4487521  4487537  4487543  4487557  4487579
4487597  4487621  4487627  4487671  4487683  4487699  4487719  4487723  4487729  4487741
4487761  4487789  4487797  4487801  4487803  4487807  4487809  4487843  4487849  4487869
4487887  4487891  4487939  4487969  4488007  4488023  4488037  4488049  4488061  4488073
4488079  4488083  4488089  4488091  4488101  4488103  4488157  4488163  4488167  4488179
4488193  4488203  4488217  4488233  4488271  4488277  4488283  4488299  4488331  4488343
4488349  4488353  4488371  4488373  4488401  4488409  4488439  4488457  4488469  4488479
4488487  4488499  4488509  4488553  4488559  4488569  4488571  4488593  4488599  4488607
4488613  4488643  4488667  4488683  4488689  4488713  4488719  4488739  4488751  4488761
4488763  4488773  4488791  4488797  4488817  4488839  4488853  4488907  4488937  4488943
4488949  4488961  4488973  4488983  4489007  4489013  4489021  4489027  4489031  4489033
4489057  4489061  4489081  4489103  4489109  4489129  4489159  4489169  4489189  4489193
4489237  4489267  4489273  4489279  4489291  4489297  4489307  4489319  4489351  4489357
4489367  4489409  4489421  4489423  4489477  4489481  4489483  4489493  4489517  4489549
4489559  4489571  4489579  4489591  4489609  4489619  4489621  4489651  4489663  4489687
4489697  4489703  4489721  4489739  4489741  4489747  4489799  4489813  4489843
4489847  4489861  4489883  4489897  4489937  4489943  4489967  4489973  4489981  4489999
4490029  4490053  4490063  4490081  4490113  4490119  4490131  4490141  4490147  4490179
4490183  4490201  4490207  4490231  4490237  4490243  4490249  4490263  4490293  4490309
4490347  4490371  4490377  4490399  4490401  4490419  4490459  4490471  4490477  4490503
4490509  4490581  4490587  4490599  4490617  4490623  4490639  4490657  4490659  4490663
4490687  4490699  4490701  4490729  4490747  4490749  4490767  4490777  4490779  4490831
4490861  4490879  4490921  4490933  4490947  4490953  4490977  4490987  4490989
4490999  4491007  4491013  4491031  4491037  4491079  4491089  4491107  4491121  4491133
4491161  4491169  4491173  4491191  4491203  4491217  4491241  4491301  4491313  4491323
4491329  4491337  4491341  4491359  4491401  4491407  4491413  4491419  4491439  4491469
4491481  4491503  4491533  4491551  4491569  4491623  4491631  4491653  4491659  4491667
4491671  4491677  4491679  4491701  4491709  4491719  4491749  4491761  4491769  4491787
4491793  4491811  4491827  4491829  4491833  4491841  4491871  4491887  4491899  4491913
4491937  4491941  4491943  4491953  4491989  4491997  4492003  4492009  4492021  4492049
4492051  4492069  4492087  4492123  4492157  4492171  4492193  4492211  4492231  4492237
4492249  4492259  4492273  4492277  4492289  4492297  4492309  4492321  4492343  4492349
4492357  4492373  4492387  4492391  4492399  4492409  4492421  4492441  4492451  4492457
4492459  4492469  4492487  4492507  4492513  4492529  4492549  4492591  4492603  4492627
4492633  4492643  4492679  4492681  4492687  4492693  4492699  4492717  4492723  4492727
4492753  4492793  4492837  4492853  4492877  4492919  4492927  4492997  4493003  4493009
4493023  4493029  4493033  4493051  4493053  4493081  4493129  4493147  4493179  4493197
4493201  4493207  4493213  4493239  4493261  4493273  4493297  4493309  4493353  4493383
4493399  4493407  4493413  4493417  4493459  4493473  4493483  4493501  4493507  4493509
4493513  4493527  4493551  4493561  4493563  4493569  4493597  4493647  4493651  4493659
4493663  4493689  4493701  4493707  4493759  4493773  4493777  4493779  4493789  4493813
4493821  4493837  4493843  4493849  4493851  4493857  4493873  4493921  4493939  4494019
4494067  4494071  4494079  4494097  4494121  4494143  4494151  4494157  4494167  4494169
4494181  4494209  4494211  4494221  4494227  4494247  4494251  4494257  4494263  4494271
4494299  4494311  4494313  4494331  4494359  4494377  4494383  4494401  4494463  4494467
4494481  4494487  4494491  4494509  4494517  4494521  4494527  4494551  4494571  4494577
4494587  4494593  4494619  4494629  4494641  4494643  4494653  4494671  4494701  4494703
4494719  4494727  4494731  4494733  4494757  4494761  4494769  4494781  4494793  4494839
4494857  4494859  4494881  4494901  4494923  4494929  4494937  4494947  4494961  4494977
4494989  4494991  4495009  4495013  4495037  4495061  4495063  4495069  4495079  4495103
4495109  4495111  4495133  4495171  4495193  4495219  4495237  4495289  4495297  4495303
4495313  4495331  4495339  4495357  4495397  4495411  4495417  4495453  4495471  4495481
4495523  4495541  4495553  4495573  4495577  4495591  4495627  4495637  4495643  4495663
4495679  4495681  4495697  4495717  4495721  4495727  4495739  4495747  4495763  4495781
4495801  4495817  4495867  4495873  4495891  4495919  4495931  4495961  4495979  4495991
4495993  4496039  4496057  4496059  4496069  4496071  4496083  4496099  4496111  4496113
4496153  4496159  4496171  4496197  4496207  4496227  4496243  4496257  4496263  4496267
4496269  4496273  4496287  4496291  4496299  4496309  4496311  4496329  4496341  4496353
4496377  4496389  4496411  4496441  4496473  4496491  4496497  4496507  4496509  4496533
```

```
4496539  4496543  4496549  4496563  4496579  4496599  4496627  4496633  4496641  4496651
4496669  4496683  4496717  4496731  4496741  4496761  4496771  4496777  4496797  4496801
4496813  4496831  4496861  4496879  4496881  4496909  4496923  4496929  4496941  4496963
4497011  4497047  4497049  4497071  4497079  4497089  4497109  4497149  4497151  4497161
4497169  4497173  4497179  4497191  4497217  4497221  4497223  4497247  4497271  4497293
4497329  4497343  4497359  4497373  4497377  4497403  4497431  4497439  4497473  4497491
4497529  4497533  4497539  4497541  4497583  4497589  4497601  4497611  4497641  4497653
4497679  4497721  4497743  4497751  4497761  4497769  4497781  4497791  4497799  4497803
4497817  4497839  4497841  4497919  4497923  4497931  4497937  4497943  4497953  4497973
4497989  4497991  4498001  4498009  4498027  4498049  4498061  4498073  4498093  4498099
4498111  4498129  4498141  4498177  4498189  4498199  4498211  4498223  4498283  4498297
4498303  4498331  4498343  4498357  4498367  4498369  4498381  4498391  4498411  4498427
4498453  4498463  4498469  4498493  4498513  4498553  4498589  4498597  4498603  4498609
4498619  4498633  4498651  4498661  4498667  4498679  4498709  4498717  4498729  4498759
4498787  4498817  4498831  4498841  4498847  4498853  4498859  4498873  4498883  4498891
4498903  4498919  4498939  4498951  4498979  4498987  4499003  4499009  4499021  4499059
4499069  4499081  4499087  4499107  4499111  4499119  4499167  4499171  4499189  4499207
4499221  4499239  4499269  4499273  4499317  4499323  4499351  4499359  4499377  4499389
4499401  4499423  4499431  4499449  4499503  4499507  4499527  4499531  4499567  4499581
4499587  4499591  4499597  4499617  4499623  4499659  4499683  4499689  4499717  4499723
4499731  4499741  4499779  4499783  4499801  4499809  4499819  4499837  4499839  4499851
4499863  4499879  4499889  4499923  4499933  4499947  4499953  4499969  4500007  4500029
4500043  4500047  4500049  4500061  4500103  4500127  4500137  4500143  4500161  4500163
4500211  4500217  4500229  4500233  4500259  4500263  4500269  4500271  4500281  4500289
4500299  4500317  4500319  4500329  4500361  4500371  4500383  4500401  4500407  4500409
4500439  4500461  4500491  4500493  4500541  4500547  4500553  4500557  4500577  4500581
4500589  4500599  4500623  4500637  4500649  4500653  4500667  4500689  4500721  4500731
4500737  4500751  4500757  4500779  4500787  4500799  4500851  4500871  4500877  4500883
4500901  4500907  4500913  4500917  4500943  4500989  4501001  4501009  4501027  4501037
4501069  4501093  4501097  4501099  4501109  4501153  4501171  4501199  4501201  4501213
4501219  4501223  4501229  4501241  4501279  4501303  4501319  4501333  4501381  4501391
4501397  4501403  4501411  4501421  4501429  4501451  4501459  4501477  4501489  4501493
4501507  4501547  4501573  4501577  4501619  4501621  4501649  4501667  4501669  4501711
4501723  4501733  4501781  4501817  4501829  4501831  4501843  4501853  4501891  4501919
4501921  4501927  4501933  4501949  4501963  4501969  4501999  4502009  4502011  4502021
4502051  4502053  4502063  4502101  4502117  4502137  4502149  4502159  4502167  4502171
4502189  4502203  4502207  4502213  4502237  4502257  4502261  4502269  4502287  4502293
4502317  4502321  4502327  4502341  4502359  4502363  4502371  4502389  4502413  4502423
4502431  4502437  4502441  4502461  4502489  4502513  4502539  4502543  4502551  4502581
4502591  4502609  4502611  4502621  4502623  4502651  4502653  4502699  4502717  4502747
4502759  4502783  4502809  4502857  4502873  4502879  4502887  4502893  4502903  4502941
4502957  4502983  4503001  4503007  4503013  4503041  4503047  4503049  4503061  4503067
4503077  4503119  4503127  4503139  4503143  4503157  4503173  4503179  4503197  4503199
4503217  4503241  4503253  4503259  4503313  4503337  4503341  4503353  4503371  4503391
4503397  4503403  4503407  4503409  4503413  4503427  4503431  4503467  4503479  4503491
4503503  4503517  4503533  4503557  4503559  4503571  4503593  4503599  4503637  4503641
4503643  4503659  4503661  4503679  4503683  4503689  4503731  4503761  4503769  4503797
4503799  4503803  4503833  4503839  4503901  4503913  4503923  4503937  4503953  4503977
4503991  4504009  4504013  4504039  4504043  4504061  4504063  4504069  4504079  4504091
4504103  4504109  4504111  4504127  4504147  4504153  4504163  4504187  4504189  4504211
4504223  4504243  4504249  4504259  4504261  4504267  4504321  4504333  4504351  4504363
4504369  4504391  4504397  4504399  4504403  4504411  4504429  4504441  4504447  4504457
4504537  4504559  4504561  4504571  4504597  4504601  4504603  4504607  4504627  4504651
4504663  4504673  4504681  4504699  4504727  4504733  4504741  4504751  4504769  4504781
4504853  4504873  4504883  4504891  4504897  4504901  4504921  4504931  4504933  4504939
4504961  4504967  4504979  4504993  4505003  4505029  4505041  4505057  4505069
4505107  4505113  4505131  4505141  4505167  4505177  4505183  4505191  4505201  4505209
4505213  4505227  4505233  4505257  4505287  4505311  4505317  4505329  4505351  4505377
4505381  4505393  4505419  4505437  4505491  4505503  4505533  4505537  4505551  4505569
4505581  4505591  4505593  4505597  4505617  4505621  4505623  4505647  4505651  4505671
4505681  4505687  4505693  4505707  4505713  4505719  4505729  4505737  4505741  4505773
4505783  4505789  4505791  4505797  4505801  4505807  4505849  4505863  4505899  4505929
4505947  4505993  4506001  4506017  4506043  4506053  4506109  4506121  4506127  4506133
4506149  4506167  4506181  4506197  4506199  4506221  4506233  4506247  4506251  4506259
4506283  4506289  4506301  4506311  4506331  4506349  4506373  4506389  4506419  4506427
4506451  4506457  4506473  4506493  4506499  4506503  4506511  4506517  4506521  4506539
4506569  4506577  4506587  4506589  4506611  4506617  4506647  4506653  4506659  4506703
4506707  4506709  4506731  4506739  4506757  4506763  4506767  4506769  4506841  4506869
4506893  4506907  4506913  4506917  4506937  4506973  4506991  4507003  4507021  4507033
4507043  4507051  4507073  4507079  4507099  4507133  4507147  4507189  4507201  4507211
4507247  4507249  4507277  4507289  4507297  4507309  4507319  4507331  4507337  4507339
4507361  4507381  4507387  4507421  4507429  4507453  4507463  4507469  4507483  4507487
4507507  4507519  4507537  4507603  4507619  4507637  4507639  4507651  4507667  4507691
4507729  4507751  4507753  4507759  4507787  4507799  4507837  4507849  4507859  4507879
4507891  4507927  4507949  4507957  4507967  4507981  4507999  4508011  4508027  4508029
4508039  4508041  4508047  4508071  4508081  4508087  4508089  4508093  4508107  4508123
4508129  4508197  4508201  4508209  4508227  4508239  4508243  4508267  4508291  4508297
4508303  4508321  4508333  4508431  4508461  4508501  4508509  4508513  4508521
4508549  4508597  4508599  4508611  4508617  4508633  4508641  4508653  4508687  4508701
4508711  4508737  4508771  4508773  4508789  4508797  4508821  4508831  4508879  4508887
4508923  4508939  4508953  4508971  4508983  4509013  4509017  4509019  4509047  4509049
4509053  4509073  4509077  4509101  4509107  4509119  4509143  4509149  4509161  4509163
4509179  4509191  4509209  4509223  4509257  4509259  4509269  4509277  4509287  4509317
4509341  4509343  4509361  4509371  4509377  4509409  4509419  4509451  4509457  4509469
4509493  4509499  4509503  4509551  4509559  4509599  4509613  4509619  4509623  4509647
4509667  4509727  4509731  4509737  4509749  4509763  4509779  4509793  4509851  4509853
4509881  4509887  4509889  4509899  4509907  4509919  4509931  4509941  4509961  4509983
4509997  4510021  4510039  4510057  4510067  4510091  4510147  4510153  4510229  4510241
4510243  4510273  4510291  4510301  4510307  4510327  4510333  4510343  4510349  4510351
```

```
4510367  4510381  4510393  4510397  4510421  4510427  4510439  4510477  4510481  4510483
4510487  4510489  4510501  4510577  4510579  4510601  4510651  4510669  4510687  4510703
4510711  4510739  4510757  4510789  4510813  4510819  4510853  4510859  4510867  4510871
4510873  4510879  4510897  4510907  4510927  4510937  4510939  4510949  4510973  4510991
4510993  4511021  4511029  4511041  4511051  4511053  4511057  4511083  4511093  4511099
4511123  4511141  4511149  4511161  4511191  4511209  4511219  4511231  4511249  4511251
4511261  4511263  4511281  4511291  4511293  4511323  4511329  4511333  4511359  4511363
4511369  4511383  4511387  4511449  4511467  4511489  4511491  4511527  4511537  4511543
4511581  4511587  4511597  4511609  4511651  4511627  4511629  4511653  4511699  4511711
4511737  4511747  4511753  4511777  4511779  4511809  4511827  4511867  4511893  4511909
4511917  4511939  4511951  4511971  4511989  4512007  4512037  4512043  4512059  4512061
4512073  4512077  4512097  4512103  4512107  4512127  4512133  4512161  4512199  4512217
4512223  4512229  4512241  4512283  4512317  4512331  4512341  4512397  4512407  4512427
4512449  4512451  4512479  4512499  4512503  4512527  4512551  4512553  4512587  4512589
4512617  4512619  4512653  4512707  4512713  4512727  4512737  4512743  4512749  4512751
4512797  4512811  4512839  4512847  4512857  4512863  4512869  4512877  4512901  4512929
4512931  4512941  4512943  4512947  4512961  4512971  4513021  4513031  4513039  4513043
4513057  4513063  4513097  4513099  4513111  4513123  4513181  4513189  4513213  4513247
4513253  4513273  4513277  4513283  4513309  4513331  4513351  4513373  4513391
4513417  4513433  4513447  4513459  4513463  4513471  4513477  4513499  4513513  4513549
4513577  4513609  4513627  4513637  4513643  4513661  4513669  4513679  4513699  4513709
4513711  4513757  4513759  4513771  4513777  4513781  4513783  4513793  4513801  4513807
4513829  4513837  4513897  4513921  4513931  4513933  4513973  4513979  4513987  4513997
4514023  4514033  4514051  4514071  4514087  4514113  4514131  4514137  4514173  4514207
4514219  4514239  4514249  4514273  4514281  4514291  4514309  4514317  4514327  4514339
4514351  4514357  4514359  4514369  4514423  4514429  4514431  4514443  4514449  4514473
4514479  4514483  4514501  4514507  4514513  4514519  4514557  4514567  4514569  4514591
4514597  4514603  4514641  4514669  4514681  4514687  4514701  4514711  4514729  4514743
4514751  4514759  4514791  4514813  4514821  4514833  4514863  4514869  4514893  4514899
4514903  4514927  4514947  4514953  4514959  4514971  4514987  4515001  4515011  4515023
4515041  4515053  4515067  4515083  4515089  4515101  4515113  4515139  4515151  4515167
4515169  4515191  4515209  4515227  4515241  4515299  4515311  4515317  4515323  4515341
4515347  4515349  4515359  4515361  4515419  4515457  4515461  4515479  4515487  4515493
4515541  4515551  4515601  4515607  4515629  4515631  4515689  4515691  4515697  4515737
4515767  4515779  4515799  4515809  4515821  4515839  4515857  4515871  4515881  4515893
4515913  4515923  4515937  4515941  4515943  4515997  4516003  4516021  4516051
4516069  4516081  4516093  4516103  4516117  4516123  4516133  4516139  4516151  4516157
4516159  4516163  4516177  4516189  4516201  4516207  4516217  4516219  4516229  4516231
4516283  4516307  4516313  4516327  4516367  4516387  4516399  4516411  4516427  4516429
4516439  4516453  4516469  4516481  4516507  4516517  4516529  4516541  4516571  4516573
4516597  4516621  4516643  4516649  4516651  4516691  4516693  4516711  4516727  4516739
4516741  4516751  4516769  4516783  4516789  4516817  4516823  4516829  4516873  4516879
4516907  4516913  4516929  4516931  4516937  4516969  4516973  4516987  4516991  4517033
4517081  4517089  4517113  4517119  4517143  4517147  4517153  4517173  4517179  4517213
4517237  4517267  4517281  4517321  4517323  4517327  4517347  4517353  4517363  4517399
4517411  4517419  4517431  4517437  4517473  4517509  4517521  4517543  4517587  4517603
4517651  4517657  4517671  4517693  4517701  4517713  4517719  4517731  4517753  4517759
4517761  4517783  4517787  4517791  4517809  4517813  4517833  4517837  4517857  4517873
4517893  4517911  4517921  4517923  4517927  4517951  4517957  4517977  4517987  4517993
4517999  4518023  4518037  4518049  4518061  4518083  4518109  4518121  4518133  4518169
4518187  4518191  4518211  4518221  4518233  4518259  4518307  4518313  4518337
4518347  4518389  4518391  4518401  4518421  4518427  4518431  4518443  4518463  4518469
4518491  4518499  4518517  4518539  4518541  4518569  4518571  4518581  4518601  4518623
4518641  4518643  4518667  4518691  4518737  4518739  4518743  4518749  4518779  4518793
4518803  4518823  4518859  4518863  4518881  4518883  4518887  4518893  4518907  4518929
4518947  4518953  4518959  4518967  4518989  4519007  4519019  4519049  4519057  4519103
4519117  4519121  4519139  4519189  4519231  4519241  4519259  4519261  4519271  4519289
4519301  4519337  4519349  4519367  4519381  4519391  4519393  4519421  4519423
4519441  4519453  4519457  4519483  4519499  4519517  4519519  4519547  4519561  4519583
4519591  4519597  4519607  4519639  4519643  4519657  4519667  4519699  4519709  4519721
4519727  4519733  4519747  4519811  4519817  4519819  4519829  4519843  4519871  4519877
4519901  4519913  4519919  4519939  4519973  4519979  4519981  4519993  4519997  4520003
4520023  4520051  4520059  4520063  4520069  4520099  4520101  4520123  4520129
4520137  4520149  4520171  4520177  4520183  4520227  4520237  4520239  4520261  4520267
4520273  4520279  4520281  4520293  4520303  4520371  4520381  4520393  4520407  4520431
4520449  4520497  4520519  4520531  4520533  4520539  4520543  4520563  4520573  4520587
4520599  4520603  4520609  4520611  4520629  4520647  4520687  4520693  4520713  4520729
4520737  4520743  4520753  4520767  4520797  4520807  4520843  4520849  4520869  4520887
4520909  4520911  4520983  4521001  4521037  4521047  4521053  4521061  4521079  4521103
4521113  4521151  4521161  4521173  4521217  4521241  4521289  4521301  4521311  4521313
4521331  4521343  4521359  4521367  4521379  4521383  4521389  4521403  4521421  4521427
4521509  4521523  4521527  4521533  4521551  4521553  4521557  4521599  4521607  4521611
4521617  4521623  4521631  4521637  4521653  4521679  4521689  4521707  4521721  4521739
4521743  4521761  4521773  4521793  4521799  4521817  4521821  4521827  4521833  4521841
4521863  4521889  4521893  4521899  4521929  4521971  4521973  4521977  4522027  4522033
4522069  4522079  4522097  4522123  4522127  4522129  4522157  4522169  4522201  4522211
4522213  4522223  4522229  4522241  4522253  4522261  4522303  4522319  4522327  4522333
4522337  4522339  4522351  4522367  4522369  4522379  4522403  4522411  4522447  4522457
4522471  4522499  4522501  4522517  4522523  4522549  4522577  4522591  4522613  4522619
4522623  4522657  4522681  4522709  4522729  4522777  4522787  4522831  4522841  4522849
4522853  4522883  4522933  4522937  4522949  4522957  4522961  4522963  4523011  4523023
4523027  4523053  4523059  4523063  4523081  4523093  4523107  4523137  4523147  4523149
4523171  4523191  4523201  4523221  4523231  4523263  4523269  4523279  4523291  4523293
4523297  4523357  4523369  4523381  4523383  4523399  4523423  4523443  4523447  4523521
4523531  4523543  4523549  4523567  4523569  4523579  4523593  4523599  4523621  4523633
4523647  4523669  4523671  4523677  4523693  4523713  4523719  4523747  4523791  4523807
4523833  4523837  4523851  4523917  4523941  4523951  4523963  4523969  4523993
4523999  4524007  4524011  4524017  4524019  4524043  4524053  4524059  4524083  4524097
4524139  4524199  4524209  4524229  4524253  4524277  4524283  4524287  4524313  4524341
```

```
4524343  4524349  4524367  4524427  4524449  4524479  4524521  4524523  4524529  4524539
4524547  4524563  4524571  4524607  4524623  4524631  4524647  4524649  4524661  4524673
4524677  4524691  4524697  4524701  4524713  4524731  4524733  4524787  4524803  4524823
4524827  4524829  4524851  4524857  4524889  4524913  4524931  4524959  4524991  4525007
4525013  4525033  4525057  4525067  4525091  4525109  4525117  4525121  4525139  4525151
4525177  4525187  4525201  4525217  4525219  4525223  4525229  4525231  4525253  4525259
4525289  4525291  4525303  4525307  4525309  4525321  4525333  4525337  4525373  4525393
4525397  4525399  4525427  4525463  4525501  4525517  4525523  4525531  4525541  4525567
4525579  4525589  4525601  4525603  4525607  4525627  4525663  4525693  4525747  4525751
4525799  4525811  4525823  4525837  4525841  4525847  4525849  4525861  4525883  4525889
4525891  4525901  4525909  4525981  4525987  4525991  4525999  4526003  4526033  4526057
4526083  4526089  4526107  4526111  4526143  4526167  4526177  4526189  4526209  4526213
4526227  4526243  4526251  4526287  4526297  4526299  4526329  4526339  4526363  4526371
4526393  4526411  4526413  4526419  4526447  4526449  4526461  4526479  4526507  4526521
4526531  4526549  4526551  4526591  4526593  4526597  4526603  4526609  4526611  4526623
4526633  4526659  4526663  4526681  4526689  4526701  4526707  4526723  4526729  4526771
4526789  4526801  4526827  4526831  4526833  4526843  4526857  4526861  4526867  4526881
4526887  4526897  4526909  4526917  4526927  4526939  4526941  4526971  4526983  4527007
4527043  4527053  4527071  4527079  4527109  4527137  4527139  4527157  4527197  4527217
4527223  4527233  4527239  4527269  4527293  4527307  4527311  4527331  4527337  4527361
4527371  4527373  4527379  4527403  4527421  4527437  4527469  4527473  4527487  4527493
4527517  4527521  4527541  4527547  4527553  4527563  4527623  4527637  4527641  4527673
4527689  4527701  4527709  4527739  4527769  4527781  4527791  4527811  4527821  4527823
4527851  4527869  4527877  4527883  4527907  4527911  4527923  4527937  4527979  4528009
4528019  4528021  4528087  4528093  4528109  4528141  4528151  4528157  4528169  4528177
4528193  4528207  4528211  4528219  4528229  4528241  4528243  4528247  4528253  4528257
4528301  4528313  4528331  4528357  4528361  4528367  4528369  4528399  4528417  4528421
4528429  4528487  4528507  4528519  4528523  4528529  4528543  4528547  4528549  4528567
4528583  4528607  4528609  4528627  4528653  4528661  4528679  4528703  4528709  4528721
4528751  4528753  4528757  4528787  4528813  4528829  4528831  4528891  4528913  4528921
4528949  4528957  4528961  4529003  4529023  4529029  4529047  4529071  4529081  4529099
4529101  4529117  4529141  4529159  4529167  4529177  4529179  4529197  4529243  4529251
4529257  4529263  4529269  4529279  4529297  4529309  4529323  4529333  4529341  4529347
4529359  4529363  4529377  4529381  4529383  4529387  4529389  4529407  4529411  4529419
4529449  4529453  4529461  4529471  4529509  4529521  4529533  4529549  4529561  4529563
4529611  4529641  4529653  4529683  4529687  4529699  4529711  4529717  4529731  4529747
4529773  4529779  4529783  4529839  4529851  4529867  4529893  4529897  4529911  4529929
4529957  4529969  4529977  4529983  4529989  4530017  4530023  4530067  4530091  4530107
4530121  4530157  4530173  4530181  4530193  4530199  4530203  4530257  4530263  4530271
4530277  4530301  4530319  4530343  4530353  4530359  4530401  4530431  4530443  4530451
4530469  4530481  4530497  4530499  4530503  4530511  4530527  4530529  4530577  4530587
4530593  4530601  4530629  4530637  4530649  4530667  4530671  4530679  4530703  4530707
4530709  4530719  4530731  4530737  4530739  4530751  4530763  4530791  4530817  4530821
4530829  4530833  4530853  4530871  4530893  4530907  4530913  4530937  4530943  4530997
4531003  4531049  4531081  4531091  4531097  4531117  4531123  4531127  4531157  4531171
4531199  4531217  4531217  4531243  4531249  4531271  4531283  4531313  4531321  4531327
4531339  4531357  4531379  4531399  4531403  4531409  4531441  4531451  4531463  4531517
4531543  4531547  4531559  4531561  4531573  4531603  4531609  4531619  4531643  4531651
4531663  4531729  4531739  4531763  4531777  4531781  4531783  4531789  4531799  4531811
4531829  4531837  4531841  4531847  4531867  4531903  4531931  4531939  4531949  4531951
4531973  4531987  4531991  4531999  4532009  4532023  4532041  4532053  4532063  4532113
4532123  4532137  4532153  4532191  4532197  4532201  4532221  4532233  4532237  4532267
4532291  4532327  4532369  4532377  4532399  4532419  4532441  4532447  4532453  4532471
4532513  4532527  4532531  4532581  4532599  4532609  4532629  4532639  4532653  4532657
4532663  4532669  4532677  4532683  4532699  4532707  4532743  4532767  4532791  4532807
4532813  4532819  4532831  4532893  4532917  4532923  4532951  4532953  4532959  4532977
4533007  4533031  4533041  4533049  4533059  4533073  4533079  4533091  4533097  4533107
4533121  4533131  4533149  4533163  4533173  4533181  4533187  4533209  4533239  4533241
4533253  4533259  4533281  4533283  4533293  4533299  4533301  4533313  4533317  4533349
4533371  4533379  4533391  4533439  4533443  4533449  4533497  4533511  4533521  4533523
4533527  4533547  4533569  4533583  4533593  4533601  4533631  4533643  4533649  4533671
4533677  4533701  4533733  4533743  4533769  4533797  4533803  4533827  4533833  4533853
4533929  4533931  4533941  4533953  4533959  4533961  4533979  4534007  4534009  4534021
4534031  4534037  4534039  4534081  4534099  4534109  4534111  4534129  4534139  4534147
4534177  4534181  4534183  4534199  4534247  4534253  4534267  4534279  4534297  4534357
4534367  4534391  4534403  4534417  4534421  4534423  4534447  4534471  4534487  4534489
4534501  4534549  4534567  4534571  4534589  4534603  4534619  4534633  4534637  4534667
4534669  4534709  4534721  4534729  4534741  4534753  4534763  4534771  4534807  4534843
4534853  4534861  4534867  4534883  4534891  4534919  4534927  4534949  4534951  4534961
4534973  4534993  4535017  4535087  4535099  4535123  4535143  4535147  4535159  4535161
4535189  4535197  4535213  4535221  4535227  4535239  4535249  4535273  4535291  4535299
4535303  4535329  4535341  4535371  4535383  4535437  4535441  4535449  4535467  4535483
4535491  4535501  4535519  4535521  4535537  4535539  4535561  4535591  4535593  4535603
4535611  4535639  4535647  4535653  4535689  4535717  4535819  4535831  4535849  4535863
4535873  4535879  4535881  4535893  4535911  4535917  4535929  4535959  4535963  4535969
4535983  4535989  4536019  4536023  4536029  4536047  4536061  4536067  4536071  4536073
4536109  4536121  4536131  4536139  4536149  4536157  4536167  4536173  4536179  4536283
4536317  4536341  4536361  4536373  4536377  4536401  4536407  4536431  4536437  4536449
4536463  4536491  4536517  4536523  4536529  4536547  4536551  4536559  4536563  4536583
4536599  4536601  4536619  4536643  4536647  4536667  4536677  4536703  4536761  4536767
4536781  4536793  4536797  4536803  4536809  4536811  4536827  4536859  4536869  4536871
4536893  4536913  4536929  4536941  4536947  4536967  4536989  4537007  4537033  4537061
4537069  4537081  4537087  4537111  4537123  4537139  4537151  4537157  4537163  4537189
4537201  4537213  4537229  4537243  4537259  4537261  4537297  4537301  4537319  4537373
4537387  4537391  4537433  4537493  4537499  4537517  4537529  4537531  4537541  4537571
4537579  4537591  4537597  4537613  4537619  4537633  4537669  4537699  4537711  4537723
4537727  4537733  4537769  4537777  4537781  4537783  4537787  4537817  4537853  4537909
4537927  4537937  4537961  4537987  4537993  4538033  4538041  4538063  4538069  4538081
4538089  4538101  4538113  4538129  4538137  4538143  4538147  4538159  4538173  4538197
```

```
4538227  4538243  4538251  4538257  4538267  4538323  4538329  4538333  4538407  4538441
4538447  4538477  4538491  4538497  4538503  4538509  4538519  4538537  4538543  4538557
4538561  4538563  4538581  4538603  4538621  4538627  4538641  4538657  4538669  4538671
4538687  4538707  4538717  4538731  4538747  4538749  4538759  4538771  4538791  4538851
4538887  4538899  4538917  4538923  4538939  4538953  4538957  4538969  4538977  4538999
4539011  4539013  4539083  4539091  4539121  4539131  4539133  4539149  4539163  4539169
4539173  4539191  4539203  4539217  4539247  4539251  4539263  4539277  4539329  4539331
4539343  4539371  4539373  4539377  4539383  4539413  4539427  4539433  4539481  4539511
4539517  4539541  4539551  4539569  4539571  4539581  4539593  4539607  4539617  4539649
4539653  4539659  4539673  4539679  4539701  4539737  4539739  4539749  4539751  4539761
4539767  4539779  4539791  4539817  4539823  4539827  4539859  4539877  4539883  4539907
4539911  4539923  4539929  4539949  4539973  4539989  4540007  4540009  4540013  4540027
4540049  4540061  4540079  4540091  4540093  4540097  4540099  4540103  4540111  4540127
4540147  4540171  4540181  4540187  4540189  4540201  4540219  4540231  4540303  4540313
4540337  4540357  4540363  4540369  4540397  4540423  4540427  4540429  4540439  4540469
4540493  4540507  4540517  4540531  4540541  4540573  4540579  4540589  4540607  4540609
4540619  4540633  4540651  4540661  4540687  4540727  4540741  4540763  4540769  4540771
4540777  4540807  4540883  4540889  4540903  4540909  4540919  4540927  4540969  4540979
4540993  4540997  4541003  4541011  4541021  4541029  4541039  4541041  4541063  4541071
4541083  4541087  4541099  4541107  4541113  4541123  4541129  4541137  4541149  4541153
4541183  4541191  4541203  4541219  4541233  4541237  4541287  4541291  4541309  4541321
4541333  4541347  4541351  4541387  4541477  4541479  4541497  4541501  4541503  4541519
4541521  4541561  4541573  4541591  4541597  4541599  4541609  4541629  4541671  4541681
4541699  4541701  4541707  4541711  4541723  4541743  4541783  4541813  4541819  4541821
4541827  4541851  4541891  4541897  4541909  4541917  4541963  4541981  4541989  4542001
4542011  4542019  4542029  4542049  4542053  4542059  4542061  4542107  4542113  4542119
4542143  4542149  4542173  4542191  4542203  4542211  4542253  4542277  4542283  4542301
4542323  4542331  4542361  4542371  4542389  4542407  4542437  4542449  4542457  4542467
4542479  4542491  4542511  4542521  4542529  4542547  4542581  4542583  4542611  4542631
4542697  4542719  4542739  4542743  4542751  4542761  4542779  4542781  4542787  4542803
4542809  4542817  4542851  4542877  4542883  4542887  4542911  4542913  4542929  4542947
4542953  4542977  4542991  4543003  4543013  4543031  4543039  4543043  4543051  4543117
4543127  4543129  4543139  4543207  4543237  4543241  4543243  4543247  4543249  4543277
4543291  4543303  4543313  4543321  4543339  4543367  4543373  4543379  4543381  4543387
4543393  4543417  4543421  4543477  4543481  4543507  4543519  4543523  4543543  4543549
4543559  4543571  4543597  4543619  4543657  4543667  4543703  4543723  4543729  4543751
4543753  4543757  4543769  4543801  4543813  4543817  4543823  4543837  4543871  4543897
4543901  4543921  4543927  4543937  4543943  4543961  4543963  4543991  4543993  4544009
4544063  4544093  4544119  4544123  4544129  4544143  4544147  4544149  4544171  4544201
4544203  4544207  4544209  4544233  4544261  4544279  4544291  4544297  4544311  4544339
4544359  4544411  4544413  4544417  4544431  4544437  4544443  4544453  4544461  4544473
4544479  4544489  4544509  4544513  4544539  4544549  4544557  4544567  4544587  4544597
4544621  4544623  4544641  4544663  4544681  4544689  4544699  4544717  4544719  4544753
4544773  4544779  4544833  4544849  4544873  4544887  4544921  4544951  4544959  4545011
4545017  4545031  4545059  4545067  4545071  4545077  4545089  4545097  4545109  4545113
4545133  4545139  4545157  4545169  4545173  4545179  4545181  4545193  4545197  4545209
4545223  4545241  4545259  4545269  4545337  4545361  4545371  4545377  4545379  4545397
4545403  4545433  4545449  4545451  4545461  4545469  4545473  4545479  4545509  4545521
4545551  4545557  4545571  4545577  4545587  4545599  4545601  4545641  4545643  4545683
4545689  4545691  4545701  4545703  4545713  4545719  4545727  4545733  4545767  4545799
4545833  4545839  4545859  4545869  4545889  4545899  4545901  4545911  4545913  4545929
4545943  4545967  4545977  4545979  4546001  4546007  4546027  4546037  4546043  4546049
4546051  4546081  4546133  4546141  4546163  4546193  4546207  4546211  4546229  4546231
4546247  4546253  4546271  4546277  4546291  4546307  4546309  4546319  4546331  4546349
4546351  4546397  4546403  4546411  4546427  4546447  4546471  4546489  4546511  4546517
4546563  4546573  4546579  4546589  4546603  4546609  4546631  4546637  4546651
4546669  4546679  4546697  4546699  4546721  4546753  4546771  4546783  4546793  4546807
4546811  4546813  4546831  4546849  4546889  4546891  4546903  4546931  4546937  4546943
4546963  4546979  4546991  4546999  4547051  4547057  4547083  4547087  4547093  4547117
4547129  4547149  4547159  4547183  4547197  4547209  4547219  4547227  4547237  4547239
4547267  4547281  4547303  4547311  4547329  4547339  4547341  4547363  4547369  4547377
4547383  4547401  4547419  4547437  4547443  4547447  4547467  4547503  4547507  4547513
4547531  4547539  4547549  4547561  4547567  4547581  4547657  4547689  4547701  4547713
4547729  4547737  4547749  4547773  4547791  4547831  4547833  4547839  4547887  4547899
4547909  4547923  4547947  4547953  4547957  4548001  4548013  4548023  4548029  4548053
4548079  4548083  4548091  4548101  4548107  4548121  4548127  4548179  4548191  4548199
4548209  4548217  4548241  4548259  4548287  4548293  4548307  4548311  4548329  4548347
4548359  4548403  4548421  4548443  4548449  4548533  4548539  4548541  4548553  4548559
4548611  4548631  4548637  4548647  4548653  4548667  4548671  4548683  4548727  4548751
4548769  4548781  4548787  4548793  4548799  4548833  4548857  4548883  4548893  4548919
4548931  4548967  4548983  4549003  4549021  4549079  4549087  4549117  4549121  4549123
4549133  4549159  4549169  4549199  4549211  4549213  4549229  4549241  4549249  4549253
4549283  4549291  4549297  4549301  4549309  4549351  4549393  4549439  4549453  4549471
4549477  4549487  4549507  4549511  4549537  4549547  4549583  4549627  4549639  4549651
4549669  4549687  4549691  4549697  4549709  4549711  4549733  4549739  4549757  4549763
4549789  4549799  4549801  4549841  4549849  4549859  4549861  4549933  4549939  4549943
4549957  4549967  4549973  4549991  4550003  4550009  4550011  4550027  4550059  4550069
4550093  4550111  4550137  4550167  4550179  4550197  4550201  4550207  4550213  4550229
4550239  4550243  4550261  4550263  4550267  4550281  4550317  4550323  4550333  4550341
4550369  4550383  4550387  4550401  4550411  4550431  4550449  4550453  4550477
4550489  4550501  4550563  4550569  4550591  4550617  4550627  4550639  4550657  4550677
4550683  4550701  4550731  4550737  4550771  4550773  4550779  4550789  4550813  4550839
4550851  4550857  4550867  4550873  4550879  4550921  4550927  4550933  4550971  4550977
4550983  4550993  4551023  4551049  4551061  4551073  4551091  4551097  4551101  4551103
4551119  4551137  4551169  4551181  4551191  4551199  4551227  4551233  4551293  4551307
4551311  4551341  4551343  4551353  4551361  4551397  4551413  4551419  4551439  4551473
4551479  4551487  4551497  4551509  4551517  4551523  4551559  4551571  4551601  4551619
4551641  4551649  4551661  4551671  4551691  4551709  4551737  4551763  4551793  4551817
4551821  4551829  4551839  4551847  4551853  4551863  4551871  4551917  4551923  4551929
```

```
4551973  4551983  4552019  4552021  4552033  4552049  4552057  4552069  4552087  4552123
4552139  4552151  4552187  4552193  4552201  4552211  4552213  4552231  4552237  4552259
4552283  4552297  4552309  4552313  4552337  4552349  4552351  4552357  4552363  4552393
4552403  4552409  4552417  4552421  4552423  4552433  4552441  4552451  4552469  4552487
4552519  4552531  4552543  4552547  4552573  4552589  4552601  4552607  4552619  4552627
4552637  4552649  4552661  4552673  4552687  4552697  4552699  4552727  4552741  4552759
4552771  4552789  4552811  4552831  4552861  4552879  4552897  4552901  4552903  4552907
4552931  4552943  4552949  4552967  4552997  4553033  4553069  4553099  4553111  4553113
4553123  4553137  4553147  4553191  4553209  4553221  4553231  4553233  4553239  4553243
4553251  4553267  4553279  4553281  4553303  4553317  4553327  4553371  4553401  4553411
4553413  4553431  4553441  4553447  4553453  4553459  4553473  4553489  4553491  4553503
4553509  4553531  4553537  4553543  4553573  4553579  4553587  4553601  4553623  4553641
4553651  4553663  4553669  4553677  4553687  4553699  4553713  4553719  4553723  4553729
4553737  4553741  4553771  4553819  4553821  4553827  4553831  4553851  4553873  4553891
4553897  4553903  4553917  4553921  4553929  4553933  4553951  4553963  4553981  4553999
4554007  4554029  4554031  4554059  4554083  4554097  4554119  4554133  4554139  4554149
4554163  4554169  4554203  4554211  4554217  4554227  4554307  4554313  4554323  4554331
4554337  4554353  4554359  4554401  4554409  4554461  4554467  4554469  4554481  4554491
4554493  4554499  4554523  4554527  4554541  4554553  4554559  4554569  4554577  4554611
4554617  4554619  4554631  4554637  4554643  4554647  4554673  4554677  4554707  4554733
4554743  4554749  4554751  4554761  4554773  4554779  4554821  4554841  4554871  4554877
4554881  4554899  4554937  4554941  4554967  4554971  4554983  4555021  4555027  4555037
4555043  4555049  4555051  4555073  4555087  4555091  4555121  4555139  4555151  4555153
4555163  4555183  4555207  4555211  4555237  4555241  4555247  4555249  4555253  4555261
4555283  4555301  4555319  4555321  4555339  4555367  4555373  4555391  4555409  4555417
4555427  4555429  4555433  4555489  4555493  4555501  4555511  4555513  4555517  4555547
4555559  4555561  4555583  4555597  4555601  4555613  4555619  4555631  4555637  4555673
4555709  4555717  4555723  4555741  4555753  4555783  4555829  4555843  4555867  4555883
4555891  4555897  4555913  4555937  4555997  4556021  4556023  4556033  4556077  4556089
4556099  4556131  4556137  4556147  4556159  4556173  4556179  4556183  4556203  4556213
4556239  4556249  4556263  4556267  4556269  4556327  4556329  4556347  4556351  4556389
4556399  4556401  4556407  4556417  4556423  4556437  4556467  4556471  4556477  4556491
4556501  4556521  4556557  4556579  4556621  4556623  4556627  4556653  4556681  4556689
4556693  4556701  4556707  4556719  4556729  4556759  4556767  4556771  4556777  4556779
4556813  4556831  4556861  4556873  4556891  4556897  4556911  4556917  4556933  4556939
4556947  4556953  4556989  4556999  4557041  4557043  4557053  4557079  4557103  4557143
4557193  4557199  4557209  4557211  4557229  4557233  4557257  4557271  4557307  4557323
4557349  4557353  4557361  4557373  4557391  4557409  4557433  4557439  4557461  4557467
4557499  4557521  4557529  4557533  4557557  4557559  4557571  4557577  4557599  4557607
4557673  4557677  4557689  4557719  4557743  4557757  4557767  4557781  4557793  4557803
4557821  4557823  4557837  4557857  4557881  4557893  4557937  4557941  4557977  4557983
4557997  4558003  4558009  4558019  4558049  4558069  4558079  4558087  4558097  4558109
4558139  4558153  4558207  4558217  4558243  4558247  4558273  4558291  4558319  4558349
4558369  4558427  4558429  4558441  4558451  4558487  4558501  4558513  4558523  4558529
4558549  4558553  4558571  4558607  4558627  4558633  4558639  4558649  4558657  4558661
4558693  4558717  4558721  4558739  4558769  4558781  4558793  4558811  4558819  4558823
4558843  4558861  4558867  4558889  4558909  4558921  4558927  4558943  4558963  4558973
4558999  4559021  4559041  4559053  4559063  4559081  4559101  4559147  4559153  4559167
4559189  4559227  4559231  4559237  4559279  4559287  4559299  4559311  4559353  4559369
4559371  4559389  4559393  4559441  4559447  4559453  4559459  4559483  4559491  4559509
4559521  4559531  4559539  4559557  4559561  4559593  4559609  4559623  4559629  4559647
4559657  4559669  4559683  4559693  4559729  4559741  4559767  4559777  4559803  4559809
4559813  4559827  4559831  4559837  4559857  4559861  4559869  4559879  4559887  4559903
4559963  4559969  4559983  4560001  4560013  4560041  4560053  4560071  4560079  4560109
4560121  4560151  4560181  4560211  4560217  4560223  4560263  4560277  4560293  4560331
4560373  4560427  4560467  4560469  4560473  4560487  4560497  4560527  4560533  4560541
4560547  4560557  4560571  4560581  4560587  4560599  4560631  4560637  4560643  4560667
4560691  4560707  4560713  4560719  4560727  4560733  4560761  4560769  4560791  4560797
4560841  4560847  4560851  4560869  4560883  4560901  4560929  4560961  4560971  4560973
4560977  4561001  4561003  4561009  4561043  4561057  4561069  4561079  4561093  4561097
4561129  4561157  4561163  4561177  4561181  4561211  4561213  4561217  4561237  4561241
4561267  4561283  4561301  4561307  4561327  4561331  4561343  4561351  4561363  4561367
4561369  4561379  4561393  4561399  4561409  4561421  4561477  4561489  4561507  4561523
4561547  4561553  4561589  4561591  4561603  4561607  4561621  4561631  4561633  4561637
4561639  4561651  4561663  4561723  4561727  4561747  4561769  4561789  4561801  4561807
4561849  4561853  4561859  4561877  4561883  4561891  4561897  4561901  4561937  4561943
4561979  4561993  4562003  4562017  4562021  4562039  4562083  4562087  4562099  4562113
4562141  4562143  4562153  4562161  4562189  4562197  4562209  4562213  4562219  4562227
4562269  4562279  4562287  4562291  4562317  4562321  4562333  4562347  4562351  4562353
4562381  4562401  4562419  4562497  4562501  4562513  4562539  4562553  4562557  4562561
4562563  4562567  4562627  4562639  4562653  4562659  4562669  4562683  4562689  4562693
4562707  4562711  4562731  4562741  4562743  4562771  4562791  4562813  4562821  4562837
4562843  4562867  4562869  4562903  4562921  4562923  4562941  4562917  4562923  4562933
4562939  4562963  4562981  4563007  4563017  4563023  4563029  4563037  4563043  4563049
4563061  4563071  4563073  4563077  4563101  4563103  4563109  4563113  4563127  4563133
4563137  4563149  4563151  4563197  4563217  4563239  4563253  4563263  4563271  4563301
4563311  4563319  4563323  4563331  4563337  4563347  4563367  4563373  4563409  4563413
4563421  4563457  4563467  4563487  4563521  4563523  4563529  4563551  4563557  4563577
4563583  4563619  4563623  4563641  4563649  4563659  4563661  4563679  4563697  4563703
4563733  4563737  4563749  4563761  4563763  4563773  4563799  4563829  4563847  4563863
4563869  4563877  4563893  4563901  4563907  4563919  4563929  4563931  4563983  4564013
4564039  4564057  4564073  4564103  4564111  4564117  4564121  4564151  4564193  4564207
4564247  4564271  4564303  4564319  4564331  4564333  4564337  4564363  4564367  4564369
4564387  4564393  4564411  4564421  4564423  4564457  4564459  4564477  4564487  4564523
4564531  4564537  4564559  4564589  4564591  4564597  4564601  4564607  4564613  4564627
4564631  4564633  4564663  4564667  4564669  4564697  4564711  4564753  4564757  4564759
4564793  4564799  4564829  4564831  4564841  4564853  4564867  4564871  4564873  4564877
4564907  4564927  4564933  4564939  4564961  4564991  4565003  4565039  4565047  4565051
4565053  4565069  4565101  4565107  4565131  4565137  4565159  4565167  4565189  4565191
```

```
4565203  4565257  4565273  4565287  4565291  4565311  4565357  4565359  4565381  4565399
4565411  4565413  4565543  4565471  4565497  4565501  4565543  4565549  4565551  4565563
4565599  4565609  4565621  4565623  4565629  4565633  4565641  4565653  4565663  4565669
4565677  4565723  4565749  4565761  4565831  4565839  4565851  4565861  4565863  4565903
4565917  4565921  4565927  4565929  4565933  4565971  4565987  4565999  4566007  4566019
4566043  4566049  4566053  4566071  4566091  4566103  4566113  4566131  4566143  4566151
4566161  4566169  4566179  4566181  4566203  4566209  4566229  4566241  4566257  4566271
4566301  4566329  4566343  4566361  4566377  4566383  4566409  4566431  4566433  4566451
4566467  4566481  4566491  4566553  4566563  4566589  4566607  4566623  4566629  4566643
4566647  4566671  4566689  4566713  4566721  4566739  4566767  4566781  4566797  4566803
4566823  4566841  4566847  4566853  4566869  4566871  4566883  4566907  4566923  4566929
4566937  4566941  4566977  4566979  4566997  4567039  4567061  4567103  4567109  4567117
4567151  4567153  4567177  4567183  4567187  4567193  4567207  4567219  4567231  4567247
4567259  4567267  4567273  4567289  4567313  4567327  4567333  4567349  4567357  4567369
4567379  4567393  4567397  4567399  4567411  4567421  4567481  4567483  4567489  4567513
4567531  4567553  4567559  4567567  4567579  4567583  4567597  4567621  4567627  4567637
4567649  4567669  4567861  4567691  4567751  4567763  4567793  4567813  4567817  4567831
4567841  4567861  4567867  4567873  4567891  4567907  4567919  4567931  4567963  4567967
4567973  4567987  4568009  4568023  4568029  4568033  4568059  4568077  4568089  4568093
4568111  4568119  4568141  4568143  4568149  4568159  4568183  4568197  4568209  4568219
4568231  4568243  4568269  4568273  4568297  4568309  4568323  4568327  4568339  4568371
4568381  4568383  4568387  4568419  4568437  4568453  4568471  4568479  4568497  4568519
4568521  4568527  4568537  4568567  4568581  4568591  4568609  4568623  4568633  4568639
4568647  4568657  4568677  4568693  4568713  4568719  4568731  4568737  4568741  4568761
4568777  4568803  4568819  4568821  4568827  4568831  4568833  4568891  4568899  4568909
4568923  4568933  4568947  4568951  4568957  4568969  4568981  4568989  4569001  4569013
4569023  4569029  4569043  4569049  4569127  4569133  4569151  4569161  4569179  4569193
4569197  4569217  4569259  4569317  4569319  4569337  4569353  4569377  4569391  4569401
4569419  4569421  4569437  4569469  4569497  4569529  4569533  4569541  4569547  4569553
4569563  4569569  4569577  4569589  4569613  4569619  4569641  4569659  4569667  4569683
4569701  4569703  4569769  4569779  4569781  4569791  4569797  4569811  4569839
4569853  4569931  4569941  4569959  4569973  4569977  4570001  4570037  4570067  4570079
4570087  4570099  4570133  4570171  4570177  4570201  4570207  4570211  4570217  4570219
4570249  4570253  4570259  4570283  4570301  4570367  4570403  4570409  4570411  4570441
4570453  4570463  4570477  4570481  4570519  4570541  4570549  4570567  4570571  4570589
4570591  4570607  4570613  4570627  4570633  4570663  4570679  4570691  4570693  4570723
4570729  4570747  4570751  4570757  4570759  4570763  4570781  4570801  4570831  4570837
4570843  4570847  4570877  4570883  4570889  4570897  4570901  4570903  4570927  4570949
4570987  4571023  4571033  4571053  4571057  4571071  4571081  4571101  4571107  4571207
4571219  4571233  4571251  4571263  4571297  4571309  4571323  4571341  4571363
4571407  4571417  4571423  4571443  4571447  4571467  4571471  4571491  4571519  4571561
4571573  4571579  4571597  4571603  4571629  4571681  4571731  4571741  4571747  4571783
4571947  4571953  4571971  4571999  4572017  4572023  4572037  4572049  4572059  4572077
4572107  4572109  4572119  4572131  4572157  4572163  4572181  4572199  4572229  4572247
4572251  4572259  4572263  4572277  4572299  4572307  4572317  4572353  4572383  4572391
4572427  4572433  4572437  4572487  4572509  4572511  4572523  4572527  4572551  4572569
4572611  4572619  4572629  4572641  4572671  4572679  4572707  4572709  4572721  4572727
4572751  4572761  4572767  4572803  4572809  4572811  4572823  4572829  4572833  4572899
4572907  4572917  4572979  4572989  4572991  4573001  4573033  4573069  4573081  4573103
4573111  4573117  4573123  4573133  4573141  4573157  4573169  4573171  4573183  4573201
4573207  4573273  4573279  4573321  4573333  4573363  4573367  4573409  4573421  4573441
4573451  4573483  4573489  4573519  4573537  4573553  4573571  4573589  4573627  4573631
4573633  4573637  4573649  4573687  4573691  4573693  4573703  4573717  4573727  4573733
4573747  4573753  4573763  4573769  4573783  4573787  4573801  4573819  4573831  4573843
4573861  4573871  4573913  4573883  4573897  4573931  4573937  4573949  4573961  4573981
4573991  4573997  4573999  4574027  4574029  4574069  4574077  4574111  4574123  4574147
4574149  4574153  4574161  4574177  4574183  4574233  4574237  4574239  4574261  4574269
4574287  4574299  4574327  4574393  4574407  4574417  4574419  4574429  4574441  4574443
4574461  4574467  4574477  4574533  4574543  4574587  4574597  4574599  4574659  4574671
4574707  4574719  4574741  4574749  4574753  4574761  4574767  4574771  4574777  4574783
4574789  4574797  4574803  4574807  4574849  4574863  4574873  4574879  4574881  4574891
4574897  4574917  4574923  4574963  4574971  4574981  4574987  4575001  4575017  4575047
4575049  4575059  4575079  4575083  4575089  4575107  4575133  4575139  4575163  4575167
4575173  4575187  4575203  4575211  4575217  4575239  4575269  4575271  4575281  4575283
4575287  4575289  4575323  4575341  4575377  4575379  4575469  4575481  4575503  4575517
4575521  4575539  4575547  4575553  4575563  4575581  4575583  4575589  4575619  4575647
4575653  4575661  4575691  4575731  4575733  4575749  4575773  4575797  4575799  4575803
4575821  4575833  4575841  4575847  4575853  4575869  4575871  4575877  4575911  4575913
4575947  4575971  4575973  4575983  4576001  4576027  4576031  4576063  4576067  4576087
4576097  4576109  4576141  4576153  4576157  4576177  4576193  4576259  4576261  4576277
4576279  4576303  4576307  4576309  4576331  4576381  4576409  4576421  4576423  4576427
4576433  4576441  4576457  4576459  4576477  4576487  4576501  4576541  4576591  4576597
4576601  4576631  4576639  4576651  4576661  4576667  4576669  4576673  4576679  4576681
4576687  4576697  4576717  4576721  4576727  4576729  4576753  4576763  4576771  4576799
4576841  4576849  4576879  4576889  4576903  4576939  4576951  4576973  4576981  4576991
4576993  4576997  4577039  4577051  4577059  4577071  4577077  4577093  4577101  4577107
4577123  4577129  4577141  4577147  4577149  4577179  4577191  4577213  4577231  4577249
4577297  4577311  4577317  4577323  4577329  4577371  4577383  4577411  4577413  4577431
4577467  4577467  4577473  4577477  4577509  4577513  4577543  4577549  4577561  4577569
4577627  4577647  4577653  4577669  4577693  4577701  4577711  4577717  4577719  4577723
4577731  4577761  4577779  4577789  4577821  4577827  4577849  4577861  4577887  4577927
4577929  4577933  4577953  4577957  4577959  4577977  4578017  4578023  4578029  4578037
4578053  4578059  4578097  4578103  4578113  4578139  4578163  4578179  4578187  4578199
4578227  4578241  4578257  4578263  4578271  4578281  4578289  4578307  4578313  4578361
4578377  4578383  4578391  4578407  4578437  4578439  4578443  4578451  4578463  4578467
4578481  4578493  4578499  4578503  4578517  4578547  4578569  4578571  4578589  4578611
4578619  4578631  4578643  4578653  4578667  4578701  4578703  4578709  4578727  4578733
4578751  4578767  4578811  4578823  4578841  4578857  4578869  4578883  4578901  4578907
```

```
4578913  4578923  4578929  4578947  4578949  4578953  4578971  4578989  4578991  4579007
4579021  4579033  4579039  4579063  4579067  4579073  4579111  4579117  4579151  4579153
4579181  4579213  4579259  4579283  4579301  4579319  4579327  4579339  4579343  4579349
4579381  4579387  4579397  4579423  4579427  4579433  4579439  4579447  4579451  4579459
4579501  4579529  4579541  4579559  4579567  4579609  4579621  4579637  4579657  4579667
4579669  4579693  4579711  4579721  4579733  4579753  4579759  4579769  4579787  4579807
4579831  4579837  4579849  4579859  4579871  4579873  4579877  4579879  4579901  4579903
4579933  4579937  4579951  4579961  4579963  4579979  4580011  4580027  4580039  4580041
4580077  4580117  4580131  4580141  4580143  4580201  4580209  4580227  4580269  4580287
4580299  4580339  4580351  4580357  4580363  4580369  4580377  4580399  4580413  4580417
4580441  4580449  4580453  4580503  4580533  4580549  4580557  4580593  4580603  4580617
4580621  4580627  4580629  4580651  4580663  4580669  4580683  4580689  4580699  4580731
4580743  4580773  4580783  4580791  4580809  4580831  4580879  4580893  4580897  4580903
4580909  4580911  4580923  4580941  4580959  4580981  4580999  4581011  4581037  4581067
4581077  4581079  4581107  4581113  4581119  4581121  4581139  4581151  4581191  4581193
4581221  4581233  4581251  4581277  4581281  4581287  4581293  4581307  4581329  4581331
4581383  4581389  4581403  4581427  4581431  4581433  4581469  4581481  4581497  4581523
4581529  4581547  4581569  4581581  4581589  4581611  4581613  4581617  4581637  4581659
4581671  4581697  4581703  4581713  4581719  4581727  4581781  4581803  4581817  4581833
4581839  4581859  4581911  4581919  4581931  4581937  4581943  4581947  4581977  4582049
4582051  4582057  4582073  4582091  4582103  4582139  4582147  4582153  4582159
4582177  4582199  4582213  4582217  4582223  4582229  4582241  4582271  4582273  4582289
4582297  4582307  4582309  4582321  4582337  4582349  4582351  4582387  4582393  4582421
4582423  4582441  4582463  4582481  4582483  4582499  4582517  4582531  4582559  4582577
4582601  4582621  4582631  4582717  4582723  4582759  4582763  4582769  4582777  4582789
4582807  4582817  4582847  4582849  4582859  4582861  4582871  4582889  4582891  4582901
4582909  4582913  4582927  4582967  4582973  4582997  4583039  4583041  4583057  4583063
4583083  4583087  4583093  4583099  4583119  4583147  4583197  4583213  4583219  4583221
4583239  4583261  4583273  4583309  4583317  4583321  4583323  4583329  4583333  4583339
4583377  4583419  4583429  4583437  4583459  4583471  4583473  4583507  4583521  4583531
4583543  4583549  4583561  4583563  4583569  4583573  4583627  4583633  4583639  4583669
4583681  4583699  4583701  4583713  4583717  4583741  4583749  4583771  4583779  4583783
4583801  4583833  4583849  4583851  4583857  4583861  4583867  4583869  4583899  4583903
4583911  4583933  4583941  4583951  4583963  4583977  4583989  4584031  4584037  4584043
4584077  4584103  4584113  4584119  4584121  4584143  4584161  4584179  4584193  4584227
4584247  4584277  4584287  4584299  4584323  4584331  4584343  4584347  4584361  4584367
4584379  4584389  4584401  4584403  4584409  4584413  4584445  4584469  4584487  4584493
4584499  4584527  4584533  4584551  4584589  4584599  4584647  4584653  4584677  4584689
4584691  4584721  4584731  4584733  4584773  4584779  4584787  4584791  4584793  4584799
4584817  4584823  4584829  4584841  4584847  4584851  4584859  4584863  4584887  4584901
4584913  4584959  4584971  4584997  4585007  4585033  4585039  4585043  4585051  4585069
4585123  4585127  4585129  4585183  4585249  4585261  4585283  4585297  4585307  4585313
4585331  4585333  4585351  4585363  4585379  4585387  4585411  4585423  4585429  4585433
4585439  4585453  4585459  4585463  4585523  4585531  4585541  4585561  4585573  4585577
4585583  4585619  4585621  4585687  4585697  4585723  4585729  4585751  4585769  4585771
4585793  4585811  4585829  4585831  4585877  4585883  4585909  4585927  4585939  4585943
4585967  4585969  4585979  4585991  4586003  4586017  4586051  4586059  4586069  4586077
4586111  4586123  4586149  4586173  4586189  4586191  4586203  4586207  4586227  4586287
4586291  4586293  4586297  4586303  4586327  4586333  4586339  4586347  4586377  4586411
4586443  4586459  4586479  4586531  4586551  4586563  4586587  4586597  4586633  4586653
4586689  4586707  4586717  4586723  4586731  4586737  4586741  4586759  4586797  4586831
4586833  4586849  4586851  4586863  4586891  4586893  4586903  4586917  4586921  4586947
4586951  4586963  4586969  4586987  4587007  4587013  4587019  4587029  4587041  4587043
4587049  4587061  4587067  4587103  4587119  4587131  4587137  4587157  4587169  4587173
4587179  4587181  4587199  4587211  4587221  4587241  4587269  4587301  4587313  4587337
4587343  4587347  4587361  4587389  4587391  4587403  4587431  4587437  4587463  4587469
4587487  4587491  4587497  4587503  4587533  4587559  4587563  4587571  4587589  4587599
4587619  4587643  4587647  4587673  4587677  4587679  4587703  4587731  4587743  4587757
4587761  4587763  4587769  4587851  4587853  4587881  4587883  4587893  4587901  4587953
4587967  4587997  4588007  4588019  4588021  4588099  4588117  4588121  4588141  4588153
4588159  4588193  4588211  4588219  4588223  4588231  4588271  4588277  4588289  4588319
4588321  4588357  4588373  4588387  4588411  4588417  4588421  4588427  4588429  4588457
4588459  4588471  4588483  4588499  4588559  4588609  4588621  4588663  4588667
4588669  4588681  4588693  4588697  4588711  4588769  4588781  4588789  4588811  4588813
4588819  4588879  4588889  4588897  4588923  4588931  4588933  4588949  4588957  4588967
4588979  4589017  4589027  4589069  4589071  4589083  4589093  4589119  4589131  4589141
4589159  4589161  4589173  4589177  4589183  4589219  4589237  4589239  4589243  4589281
4589293  4589297  4589309  4589329  4589359  4589407  4589413  4589419  4589423  4589441
4589467  4589477  4589479  4589483  4589491  4589521  4589549  4589561  4589587  4589593
4589623  4589633  4589639  4589657  4589671  4589681  4589693  4589707  4589731  4589737
4589759  4589771  4589791  4589797  4589803  4589807  4589831  4589833  4589843  4589861
4589869  4589873  4589933  4589951  4589971  4589999  4590007  4590011  4590013  4590029
4590031  4590043  4590071  4590101  4590107  4590181  4590199  4590203  4590217  4590227
4590239  4590241  4590251  4590253  4590281  4590283  4590307  4590337  4590347  4590367
4590373  4590389  4590403  4590427  4590437  4590457  4590461  4590491  4590499  4590503
4590517  4590557  4590559  4590563  4590583  4590617  4590643  4590661  4590667
4590673  4590679  4590683  4590689  4590713  4590739  4590743  4590767  4590793  4590797
4590829  4590841  4590857  4590871  4590877  4590889  4590899  4590917  4590919  4590941
4590959  4590973  4590977  4591001  4591009  4591033  4591051  4591061  4591063  4591079
4591091  4591117  4591121  4591127  4591133  4591159  4591163  4591183  4591187  4591201
4591211  4591267  4591271  4591273  4591297  4591313  4591319  4591333  4591361  4591373
4591381  4591387  4591393  4591399  4591403  4591451  4591453  4591459  4591463  4591487
4591493  4591507  4591511  4591519  4591523  4591567  4591579  4591591  4591607  4591619
4591621  4591633  4591661  4591667  4591687  4591709  4591721  4591723  4591729  4591739
4591747  4591757  4591771  4591781  4591801  4591817  4591823  4591837  4591861  4591873
4591891  4591903  4591913  4591933  4591949  4591991  4591997  4592009  4592017  4592039
4592051  4592059  4592069  4592089  4592117  4592131  4592149  4592153  4592171  4592183
4592201  4592219  4592233  4592257  4592303  4592317  4592321  4592327  4592339  4592347
4592359  4592389  4592429  4592453  4592519  4592521  4592531  4592543  4592563  4592569
```

```
4592579  4592587  4592591  4592593  4592597  4592611  4592641  4592647  4592657  4592671
4592683  4592711  4592713  4592717  4592723  4592741  4592789  4592803  4592827  4592843
4592857  4592869  4592881  4592899  4592911  4592947  4592953  4592957  4592963  4592969
4592983  4592989  4592993  4592999  4593007  4593011  4593037  4593059  4593067  4593089
4593097  4593133  4593157  4593161  4593181  4593187  4593191  4593221  4593227  4593229
4593283  4593293  4593299  4593313  4593317  4593331  4593367  4593371  4593377  4593401
4593409  4593427  4593431  4593437  4593461  4593481  4593499  4593527  4593529  4593539
4593541  4593569  4593601  4593607  4593619  4593623  4593637  4593643  4593679  4593683
4593703  4593707  4593709  4593737  4593761  4593769  4593847  4593851  4593857  4593863
4593907  4593923  4593931  4593937  4593943  4593959  4593973  4594001  4594013  4594019
4594027  4594033  4594049  4594099  4594127  4594129  4594141  4594147  4594159  4594171
4594189  4594207  4594223  4594229  4594277  4594279  4594283  4594307  4594309  4594357
4594379  4594397  4594399  4594433  4594439  4594451  4594453  4594463  4594483  4594489
4594493  4594511  4594519  4594529  4594537  4594543  4594553  4594559  4594567  4594589
4594609  4594619  4594621  4594633  4594649  4594657  4594661  4594663  4594691  4594721
4594739  4594753  4594763  4594769  4594781  4594783  4594801  4594817  4594819  4594823
4594859  4594883  4594889  4594897  4594921  4594939  4594949  4594957  4594963  4594969
4594973  4594991  4594999  4595027  4595033  4595039  4595051  4595077  4595089  4595179
4595189  4595207  4595221  4595243  4595257  4595263  4595299  4595303  4595341  4595387
4595407  4595411  4595413  4595441  4595443  4595477  4595489  4595527  4595531  4595537
4595579  4595581  4595599  4595603  4595609  4595621  4595671  4595677  4595713  4595737
4595809  4595821  4595827  4595849  4595863  4595867  4595869  4595879  4595887  4595893
4595897  4595947  4595951  4595953  4595993  4596013  4596017  4596019  4596037  4596047
4596073  4596077  4596079  4596089  4596099  4596101  4596121  4596131  4596139  4596143
4596149  4596161  4596173  4596187  4596191  4596197  4596199  4596211  4596217  4596247
4596283  4596287  4596289  4596301  4596311  4596323  4596329  4596331  4596337  4596349
4596353  4596359  4596373  4596377  4596379  4596407  4596419  4596491  4596497  4596503
4596517  4596521  4596569  4596577  4596589  4596607  4596617  4596653  4596661  4596671
4596677  4596697  4596707  4596721  4596731  4596833  4596847  4596853  4596859  4596901
4596967  4596971  4596979  4596983  4596997  4597003  4597007  4597013  4597027  4597039
4597063  4597081  4597091  4597111  4597121  4597141  4597163  4597169  4597189  4597193
4597231  4597237  4597253  4597277  4597279  4597291  4597301  4597303  4597337  4597357
4597363  4597367  4597381  4597391  4597421  4597423  4597427  4597459  4597471  4597499
4597511  4597519  4597543  4597577  4597589  4597597  4597609  4597669  4597673  4597679
4597709  4597717  4597727  4597739  4597751  4597771  4597787  4597793  4597807  4597819
4597841  4597847  4597849  4597881  4597903  4597919  4597927  4597933  4597949  4597961
4597993  4598063  4598071  4598081  4598107  4598123  4598141  4598147  4598149  4598159
4598161  4598179  4598189  4598201  4598203  4598207  4598213  4598221  4598233  4598239
4598257  4598281  4598299  4598303  4598323  4598329  4598351  4598359  4598371  4598389
4598423  4598453  4598491  4598533  4598557  4598563  4598567  4598569  4598579  4598591
4598593  4598603  4598623  4598647  4598677  4598701  4598731  4598743  4598747  4598771
4598801  4598821  4598831  4598837  4598843  4598887  4598899  4598911  4598917  4598921
4598933  4598939  4598941  4598963  4598977  4598983  4598999  4599019  4599059  4599071
4599131  4599169  4599173  4599209  4599223  4599229  4599233  4599251  4599269  4599271
4599277  4599281  4599289  4599293  4599307  4599319  4599337  4599341  4599407  4599437
4599493  4599509  4599527  4599533  4599557  4599587  4599613  4599619  4599659  4599677
4599709  4599731  4599737  4599739  4599757  4599761  4599773  4599797  4599799  4599841
4599857  4599863  4599883  4599887  4599929  4599941  4599953  4599961  4599971  4599983
4599989  4600003  4600007  4600021  4600027  4600051  4600061  4600073  4600087  4600093
4600103  4600129  4600151  4600157  4600163  4600177  4600181  4600187  4600199  4600231
4600259  4600279  4600291  4600301  4600331  4600333  4600339  4600361  4600363  4600367
4600373  4600397  4600399  4600411  4600423  4600429  4600439  4600447  4600471  4600481
4600507  4600513  4600531  4600553  4600573  4600607  4600627  4600633  4600637  4600639
4600657  4600669  4600697  4600711  4600721  4600751  4600753  4600801  4600811  4600847
4600861  4600889  4600901  4600933  4600949  4600963  4600991  4600993  4601011  4601029
4601099  4601119  4601121  4601131  4601137  4601141  4601147  4601153  4601167  4601171
4601189  4601239  4601243  4601251  4601273  4601293  4601323  4601341  4601507  4601537
4601417  4601447  4601453  4601479  4601483  4601497  4601501  4601507  4601537  4601549
4601551  4601561  4601593  4601599  4601617  4601621  4601677  4601687  4601697  4601719
4601741  4601759  4601789  4601809  4601833  4601843  4601879  4601887  4601897  4601921
4601929  4601939  4601957  4601959  4601969  4601977  4602011  4602041  4602071  4602077
4602083  4602107  4602109  4602113  4602131  4602137  4602173  4602179  4602181  4602187
4602211  4602217  4602233  4602239  4602251  4602281  4602289  4602293  4602317  4602331
4602341  4602343  4602347  4602371  4602383  4602397  4602407  4602439  4602443  4602463
4602487  4602509  4602517  4602557  4602571  4602581  4602583  4602589  4602593  4602629
4602659  4602673  4602713  4602721  4602727  4602749  4602779  4602781  4602791  4602797
4602799  4602803  4602811  4602821  4602827  4602839  4602841  4602847  4602853  4602863
4602889  4602893  4602977  4602989  4603007  4603031  4603043  4603051  4603087  4603091
4603099  4603117  4603139  4603147  4603153  4603171  4603189  4603211  4603229  4603241
4603253  4603259  4603273  4603297  4603309  4603327  4603331  4603351  4603393  4603399
4603411  4603441  4603483  4603513  4603517  4603559  4603573  4603589  4603601  4603607
4603619  4603631  4603639  4603661  4603667  4603691  4603699  4603723  4603741  4603747
4603751  4603759  4603763  4603769  4603777  4603783  4603789  4603811  4603813  4603817
4603831  4603843  4603861  4603867  4603897  4603901  4603913  4603919  4603981  4603983
4603989  4604063  4604101  4604111  4604123  4604129  4604143  4604147  4604189  4604191
4604221  4604233  4604267  4604291  4604293  4604309  4604321  4604323  4604333  4604351
4604363  4604377  4604387  4604389  4604447  4604491  4604497  4604507  4604521  4604547
4604549  4604573  4604597  4604599  4604609  4604617  4604641  4604651  4604657  4604659
4604681  4604689  4604701  4604711  4604713  4604723  4604741  4604753  4604759  4604791
4604797  4604801  4604837  4604849  4604851  4604859  4604903  4604911  4604921  4604927
4604933  4604953  4604969  4604993  4605001  4605017  4605023  4605031  4605061  4605067
4605071  4605077  4605101  4605121  4605137  4605179  4605197  4605199  4605217  4605241
4605247  4605299  4605301  4605311  4605323  4605331  4605361  4605383  4605397  4605409
4605437  4605443  4605449  4605473  4605479  4605493  4605509  4605511  4605527  4605539
4605547  4605551  4605553  4605569  4605607  4605613  4605617  4605641  4605659  4605673
4605703  4605709  4605719  4605721  4605737  4605743  4605787  4605791  4605869  4605893
4605901  4605917  4605947  4605959  4605967  4605973  4605977  4606001  4606033  4606039
4606051  4606079  4606109  4606127  4606153  4606169  4606181  4606193  4606213  4606229
4606237  4606249  4606313  4606319  4606363  4606367
```

```
4606369  4606397  4606403  4606429  4606477  4606487  4606489  4606499  4606501  4606513
4606529  4606549  4606559  4606561  4606571  4606577  4606579  4606597  4606607  4606619
4606639  4606649  4606663  4606669  4606673  4606691  4606697  4606699  4606703  4606709
4606733  4606741  4606751  4606769  4606783  4606807  4606829  4606837  4606871  4606933
4606937  4606939  4606963  4606967  4606991  4606997  4607011  4607021  4607023  4607033
4607059  4607077  4607093  4607167  4607171  4607191  4607219  4607227  4607233  4607243
4607257  4607279  4607297  4607299  4607303  4607311  4607327  4607333  4607347  4607353
4607377  4607387  4607411  4607417  4607423  4607431  4607461  4607467  4607483  4607531
4607543  4607563  4607569  4607589  4607591  4607593  4607599  4607609  4607611  4607627
4607641  4607651  4607653  4607677  4607683  4607689  4607693  4607699  4607719  4607749
4607777  4607789  4607803  4607807  4607819  4607857  4607881  4607887  4607893  4607903
4607909  4607917  4607929  4607947  4607951  4607957  4607963  4607987  4608007  4608049
4608053  4608083  4608101  4608133  4608143  4608151  4608199  4608217  4608223  4608251
4608259  4608281  4608283  4608287  4608293  4608301  4608311  4608319  4608337  4608347
4608379  4608389  4608391  4608407  4608413  4608433  4608437  4608463  4608473  4608493
4608517  4608521  4608551  4608557  4608577  4608587  4608589  4608599  4608601  4608607
4608613  4608619  4608631  4608661  4608689  4608691  4608701  4608707  4608727  4608743
4608787  4608797  4608833  4608841  4608859  4608881  4608889  4608899  4608911  4608917
4608943  4608949  4608953  4608959  4608971  4608983  4609009  4609013  4609027  4609037
4609063  4609067  4609079  4609081  4609093  4609109  4609123  4609133  4609169  4609207
4609217  4609237  4609247  4609259  4609271  4609273  4609277  4609301  4609303  4609307
4609309  4609313  4609321  4609327  4609333  4609351  4609369  4609393  4609411  4609427
4609433  4609441  4609447  4609481  4609489  4609511  4609513  4609519  4609523  4609531
4609543  4609547  4609597  4609621  4609651  4609663  4609673  4609681  4609687  4609691
4609699  4609721  4609727  4609733  4609747  4609751  4609763  4609783  4609849  4609897
4609909  4609921  4609949  4610003  4610017  4610029  4610033  4610057  4610063  4610087
4610093  4610107  4610147  4610149  4610153  4610173  4610239  4610267  4610269  4610303
4610317  4610321  4610341  4610357  4610363  4610377  4610381  4610387  4610393  4610399
4610443  4610447  4610453  4610479  4610509  4610531  4610569  4610579  4610581  4610609
4610611  4610633  4610651  4610659  4610687  4610693  4610699  4610707  4610719  4610729
4610731  4610743  4610759  4610773  4610777  4610779  4610783  4610789  4610813  4610821
4610831  4610839  4610843  4610849  4610867  4610869  4610897  4610911  4610917  4610923
4610959  4610987  4610999  4611011  4611041  4611059  4611067  4611071  4611077  4611083
4611119  4611127  4611133  4611137  4611143  4611149  4611163  4611181  4611193  4611209
4611221  4611227  4611241  4611251  4611287  4611289  4611307  4611323  4611329  4611353
4611359  4611391  4611407  4611419  4611443  4611457  4611461  4611469  4611479  4611487
4611511  4611553  4611571  4611601  4611613  4611631  4611637  4611647  4611683  4611697
4611731  4611749  4611767  4611779  4611787  4611809  4611821  4611829  4611833  4611847
4611911  4611923  4611931  4611953  4611973  4611989  4611991  4612001  4612009  4612019
4612037  4612043  4612081  4612103  4612123  4612129  4612133  4612147  4612163  4612177
4612183  4612187  4612219  4612227  4612229  4612241  4612261  4612277  4612297  4612301
4612303  4612313  4612319  4612339  4612343  4612369  4612381  4612409  4612427  4612451
4612477  4612483  4612493  4612511  4612523  4612529  4612549  4612571  4612579  4612609
4612613  4612631  4612633  4612639  4612669  4612693  4612697  4612709  4612717  4612723
4612789  4612793  4612807  4612813  4612819  4612843  4612847  4612849  4612859  4612871
4612873  4612913  4612919  4612921  4612931  4612957  4612963  4612969  4612987  4613023
4613027  4613051  4613053  4613071  4613099  4613101  4613113  4613209  4613237  4613243
4613251  4613261  4613263  4613293  4613299  4613303  4613311  4613333  4613347  4613359
4613423  4613437  4613449  4613459  4613461  4613467  4613471  4613489  4613507  4613533
4613551  4613563  4613569  4613573  4613591  4613603  4613617  4613627  4613629  4613657
4613669  4613683  4613701  4613711  4613717  4613729  4613743  4613747  4613753  4613767
4613773  4613803  4613881  4613891  4613893  4613911  4613957  4613969  4613971  4613981
4613993  4614031  4614047  4614061  4614067  4614109  4614119  4614139  4614151  4614163
4614173  4614179  4614187  4614209  4614217  4614221  4614271  4614341  4614347  4614349
4614353  4614391  4614419  4614431  4614433  4614439  4614479  4614487  4614499  4614521
4614523  4614553  4614563  4614583  4614593  4614603  4614607  4614613  4614619  4614637
4614641  4614671  4614689  4614713  4614719  4614749  4614809  4614821  4614829  4614839
4614887  4614901  4614913  4614923  4614937  4614947  4614959  4614971  4614983  4614989
4614991  4614997  4615003  4615057  4615069  4615073  4615099  4615123  4615139  4615141
4615153  4615183  4615201  4615223  4615229  4615241  4615253  4615267  4615283  4615291
4615297  4615333  4615337  4615349  4615363  4615367  4615409  4615439  4615453  4615469
4615477  4615489  4615519  4615529  4615531  4615549  4615601  4615603  4615607  4615609
4615627  4615661  4615673  4615679  4615709  4615753  4615783  4615817  4615829  4615867
4615927  4615967  4615969  4615973  4615979  4615991  4615999  4616033  4616039  4616063
4616071  4616089  4616111  4616113  4616119  4616147  4616153  4616167  4616177  4616189
4616237  4616251  4616257  4616267  4616291  4616317  4616321  4616347  4616363  4616369
4616371  4616393  4616413  4616431  4616461  4616473  4616497  4616509  4616531  4616567
4616569  4616587  4616603  4616611  4616617  4616627  4616657  4616687  4616693  4616719
4616743  4616747  4616761  4616779  4616783  4616789  4616797  4616803  4616819  4616827
4616849  4616863  4616879  4616881  4616893  4616929  4616933  4616939  4616957  4616959
4616977  4616993  4617001  4617073  4617077  4617083  4617097  4617101  4617113  4617143
4617161  4617187  4617191  4617199  4617203  4617257  4617259  4617269  4617271  4617287
4617299  4617317  4617331  4617337  4617359  4617391  4617401  4617427  4617433  4617431
4617463  4617479  4617493  4617497  4617511  4617521  4617533  4617541  4617559  4617577
4617581  4617601  4617607  4617617  4617643  4617649  4617653  4617671  4617709  4617713
4617737  4617749  4617773  4617793  4617803  4617839  4617857  4617869  4617887  4617901
4617919  4617941  4617947  4617959  4617967  4617979  4618001  4618027  4618063  4618069
4618091  4618093  4618129  4618139  4618153  4618171  4618177  4618181  4618183  4618213
4618217  4618219  4618231  4618241  4618247  4618253  4618259  4618291  4618307  4618309
4618319  4618333  4618351  4618357  4618381  4618391  4618399  4618403  4618409  4618429
4618433  4618447  4618459  4618483  4618489  4618499  4618507  4618513  4618529  4618541
4618567  4618583  4618589  4618619  4618639  4618687  4618693  4618703  4618709  4618711
4618717  4618723  4618727  4618741  4618753  4618771  4618777  4618787  4618807  4618807
4618813  4618841  4618847  4618853  4618871  4618879  4618921  4618949  4618961  4618967
4618979  4618987  4618993  4619009  4619023  4619029  4619039  4619063  4619077  4619081
4619089  4619099  4619107  4619123  4619137  4619141  4619143  4619177  4619179  4619203
4619213  4619227  4619233  4619249  4619269  4619281  4619309  4619333  4619353  4619357
4619399  4619441  4619443  4619471  4619491  4619501  4619507  4619509  4619519
4619521  4619539  4619557  4619569  4619579  4619609  4619621  4619623  4619627  4619647
```

```
4619669  4619701  4619743  4619749  4619773  4619789  4619807  4619809  4619821  4619827
4619833  4619843  4619873  4619893  4619897  4619929  4619947  4619969  4619981  4620001
4620037  4620061  4620067  4620101  4620103  4620127  4620137  4620139  4620149  4620151
4620179  4620191  4620223  4620229  4620269  4620281  4620283  4620289  4620299  4620359
4620377  4620391  4620397  4620403  4620409  4620419  4620431  4620437  4620443  4620463
4620491  4620503  4620529  4620547  4620557  4620559  4620563  4620569  4620571  4620589
4620601  4620611  4620673  4620697  4620709  4620731  4620757  4620761  4620779  4620793
4620797  4620799  4620809  4620817  4620839  4620841  4620853  4620871  4620877  4620881
4620901  4620919  4620929  4620943  4620961  4620977  4621007  4621021  4621031  4621037
4621049  4621073  4621129  4621153  4621157  4621159  4621163  4621171  4621187  4621207
4621217  4621219  4621231  4621259  4621261  4621277  4621283  4621289  4621307  4621327
4621343  4621381  4621439  4621447  4621453  4621481  4621483  4621499  4621517  4621531
4621537  4621571  4621577  4621583  4621619  4621621  4621649  4621679  4621691  4621711
4621723  4621777  4621823  4621847  4621853  4621867  4621891  4621913  4621931  4621949
4621951  4621957  4621961  4621963  4621979  4621999  4622017  4622047  4622081  4622083
4622143  4622161  4622209  4622213  4622257  4622273  4622311  4622323  4622329  4622357
4622389  4622399  4622411  4622417  4622437  4622461  4622477  4622479  4622489  4622509
4622533  4622539  4622557  4622561  4622573  4622593  4622599  4622603  4622617  4622647
4622671  4622677  4622693  4622699  4622707  4622711  4622741  4622753  4622767  4622771
4622789  4622831  4622857  4622867  4622869  4622879  4622897  4622899  4622903  4622911
4622939  4622941  4622951  4622971  4622983  4623019  4623029  4623043  4623053  4623097
4623107  4623127  4623131  4623139  4623191  4623197  4623211  4623217  4623239  4623257
4623259  4623271  4623287  4623301  4623329  4623331  4623341  4623347  4623379  4623401
4623413  4623427  4623431  4623457  4623467  4623491  4623497  4623503  4623523  4623527
4623539  4623547  4623551  4623559  4623569  4623581  4623589  4623599  4623607  4623623
4623629  4623649  4623659  4623683  4623691  4623709  4623761  4623769  4623781  4623793
4623797  4623809  4623811  4623823  4623863  4623869  4623877  4623911  4623953  4623967
4624003  4624019  4624027  4624031  4624033  4624057  4624069  4624093  4624099  4624111
4624129  4624133  4624157  4624171  4624211  4624229  4624231  4624237  4624241  4624261
4624313  4624339  4624343  4624381  4624387  4624393  4624439  4624441  4624453  4624457
4624481  4624489  4624507  4624517  4624523  4624531  4624537  4624547  4624553  4624573
4624577  4624579  4624583  4624591  4624603  4624637  4624639  4624643  4624649  4624661
4624681  4624691  4624699  4624703  4624721  4624723  4624747  4624757  4624777  4624783
4624787  4624801  4624813  4624819  4624831  4624849  4624853  4624871  4624877  4624883
4624903  4624913  4624931  4624933  4624957  4624967  4624987  4624993  4625021  4625029
4625059  4625119  4625141  4625167  4625183  4625191  4625219  4625221  4625233  4625237
4625249  4625263  4625267  4625273  4625279  4625287  4625311  4625321  4625329  4625339
4625389  4625393  4625431  4625441  4625443  4625449  4625459  4625519  4625549  4625557
4625567  4625609  4625611  4625617  4625641  4625651  4625657  4625701  4625707  4625713
4625723  4625729  4625767  4625771  4625773  4625779  4625801  4625807  4625843  4625849
4625867  4625879  4625891  4625903  4625909  4625917  4625927  4625939  4626001  4626007
4626019  4626031  4626043  4626053  4626113  4626121  4626133  4626137  4626157  4626169
4626191  4626203  4626217  4626233  4626239  4626247  4626269  4626277  4626299  4626313
4626331  4626361  4626373  4626379  4626383  4626389  4626407  4626421  4626437  4626439
4626449  4626463  4626467  4626469  4626497  4626511  4626547  4626577  4626617  4626619
4626623  4626637  4626659  4626647  4626653  4626659  4626679  4626691  4626707  4626733
4626751  4626761  4626779  4626799  4626827  4626829  4626833  4626851  4626859  4626871
4626877  4626889  4626913  4626917  4626977  4627003  4627031  4627039  4627061  4627067
4627121  4627169  4627177  4627201  4627223  4627229  4627243  4627253  4627289  4627303
4627307  4627361  4627367  4627373  4627387  4627409  4627421  4627423  4627459  4627487
4627523  4627529  4627549  4627591  4627603  4627631  4627633  4627639  4627663  4627673
4627681  4627691  4627699  4627717  4627747  4627751  4627759  4627787  4627817  4627823
4627841  4627871  4627873  4627877  4627879  4627913  4627937  4627943  4628003  4628017
4628033  4628051  4628069  4628093  4628101  4628111  4628177  4628201  4628209  4628227
4628257  4628279  4628287  4628291  4628297  4628311  4628317  4628321  4628341  4628363
4628389  4628399  4628401  4628411  4628417  4628431  4628447  4628453  4628461  4628479
4628483  4628489  4628501  4628551  4628567  4628581  4628599  4628621  4628627  4628629
4628651  4628669  4628677  4628699  4628731  4628747  4628749  4628753  4628759  4628783
4628797  4628803  4628807  4628849  4628851  4628867  4628891  4628917  4628929  4628969
4628977  4628999  4629007  4629017  4629041  4629043  4629047  4629059  4629089  4629091
4629101  4629127  4629139  4629161  4629167  4629169  4629173  4629197  4629239  4629283
4629311  4629347  4629349  4629353  4629377  4629379  4629397  4629419  4629421  4629431
4629439  4629451  4629461  4629467  4629481  4629487  4629511  4629517  4629523  4629529
4629539  4629563  4629577  4629607  4629613  4629617  4629623  4629629  4629631  4629659
4629707  4629719  4629721  4629727  4629731  4629743  4629769  4629803  4629809  4629817
4629827  4629841  4629871  4629887  4629893  4629913  4629917  4629929  4629931  4629959
4629971  4629979  4629983  4629991  4630009  4630013  4630019  4630051  4630063  4630079
4630081  4630097  4630099  4630121  4630139  4630177  4630181  4630187  4630201  4630207
4630231  4630237  4630247  4630271  4630277  4630309  4630313  4630331  4630349  4630363
4630387  4630397  4630399  4630401  4630447  4630453  4630469  4630519  4630529  4630553
4630583  4630589  4630597  4630601  4630603  4630607  4630643  4630651  4630657  4630669
4630673  4630697  4630709  4630721  4630723  4630753  4630757  4630763  4630789  4630831
4630837  4630849  4630859  4630861  4630867  4630891  4630897  4630903  4630907  4630921
4630931  4630933  4630949  4630961  4630979  4630999  4631017  4631093  4631111  4631131
4631141  4631147  4631171  4631203  4631233  4631237  4631251  4631279  4631287  4631311
4631351  4631353  4631359  4631371  4631399  4631413  4631453  4631467  4631477  4631479
4631489  4631513  4631527  4631537  4631551  4631567  4631569  4631593  4631597  4631629
4631639  4631651  4631663  4631681  4631689  4631699  4631719  4631743  4631747  4631749
4631761  4631797  4631813  4631821  4631843  4631863  4631867  4631881  4631899  4631903
4631989  4631999  4632011  4632053  4632073  4632077  4632091  4632097  4632151  4632161
4632167  4632169  4632191  4632197  4632233  4632239  4632241  4632247  4632281  4632301
4632307  4632317  4632337  4632343  4632349  4632377  4632403  4632443  4632457  4632473
4632487  4632497  4632527  4632577  4632611  4632613  4632629  4632647  4632673  4632689
4632697  4632701  4632703  4632709  4632757  4632781  4632787  4632809  4632829  4632841
4632851  4632853  4632869  4632871  4632893  4632907  4632911  4632937  4632973  4632989
4632997  4633001  4633003  4633019  4633021  4633037  4633039  4633067  4633141  4633157
4633159  4633183  4633193  4633199  4633201  4633217  4633219  4633259  4633261  4633267
4633273  4633289  4633303  4633319  4633331  4633361  4633381  4633403  4633411  4633423
4633439  4633457  4633463  4633471  4633483  4633487  4633501  4633507  4633513  4633543
```

4633553 4633579 4633583 4633609 4633627 4633633 4633679 4633687 4633693 4633709
4633747 4633753 4633757 4633763 4633793 4633813 4633819 4633841 4633847 4633873
4633883 4633897 4633901 4633913 4633931 4633961 4633969 4633999 4634009 4634011
4634023 4634027 4634029 4634051 4634057 4634089 4634093 4634111 4634117 4634173
4634177 4634191 4634197 4634207 4634209 4634249 4634263 4634281 4634291 4634297
4634317 4634321 4634327 4634351 4634359 4634363 4634389 4634393 4634401 4634419
4634429 4634447 4634459 4634473 4634501 4634503 4634521 4634527 4634561 4634633
4634639 4634687 4634699 4634701 4634713 4634723 4634737 4634743 4634767 4634783
4634801 4634821 4634827 4634837 4634869 4634881 4634899 4634923 4634933 4634947
4634957 4634977 4635011 4635017 4635023 4635047 4635061 4635073 4635079 4635083
4635097 4635131 4635143 4635149 4635161 4635181 4635223 4635263 4635269 4635277
4635287 4635289 4635311 4635313 4635317 4635341 4635343 4635353 4635359 4635361
4635383 4635391 4635403 4635437 4635439 4635457 4635473 4635503 4635517 4635541
4635551 4635559 4635569 4635613 4635623 4635629 4635637 4635649 4635703 4635707
4635731 4635733 4635773 4635779 4635793 4635809 4635821 4635847 4635859 4635863
4635871 4635877 4635887 4635893 4635899 4635907 4635913 4635937 4635941 4635971
4635973 4635977 4635979 4635991 4636003 4636013 4636031 4636039 4636111 4636123
4636129 4636141 4636147 4636169 4636207 4636231 4636237 4636243 4636249 4636319
4636327 4636337 4636343 4636351 4636369 4636381 4636441 4636447 4636451 4636633
4636477 4636519 4636531 4636543 4636553 4636559 4636579 4636591 4636603 4636609
4636613 4636651 4636657 4636661 4636663 4636669 4636679 4636693 4636711 4636717
4636721 4636739 4636769 4636771 4636799 4636829 4636837 4636847 4636871 4636883
4636909 4636913 4636921 4636943 4636963 4636967 4636993 4636999 4637027 4637041
4637069 4637093 4637111 4637117 4637119 4637123 4637131 4637189 4637201 4637231
4637233 4637239 4637251 4637261 4637263 4637287 4637323 4637333 4637351 4637359
4637363 4637371 4637389 4637411 4637417 4637429 4637449 4637453 4637461 4637483
4637489 4637497 4637519 4637561 4637573 4637579 4637603 4637627 4637639 4637657
4637669 4637683 4637687 4637707 4637713 4637723 4637749 4637771 4637783 4637803
4637827 4637837 4637873 4637903 4637939 4637947 4637951 4637981 4638001
4638017 4638037 4638041 4638077 4638089 4638103 4638113 4638119 4638133 4638143
4638149 4638181 4638187 4638191 4638197 4638199 4638211 4638239 4638241 4638247
4638287 4638301 4638307 4638323 4638329 4638353 4638377 4638397 4638407 4638419
4638449 4638457 4638461 4638509 4638511 4638523 4638541 4638547 4638551 4638553
4638583 4638587 4638589 4638607 4638629 4638631 4638659 4638677 4638691 4638721
4638737 4638743 4638761 4638791 4638827 4638833 4638857 4638859 4638899 4638911
4638937 4638961 4638967 4638971 4638979 4639003 4639049 4639051 4639067 4639073
4639081 4639099 4639121 4639127 4639133 4639139 4639189 4639237 4639259 4639267
4639277 4639289 4639291 4639309 4639321 4639331 4639343 4639361 4639373 4639379
4639381 4639387 4639423 4639447 4639457 4639483 4639489 4639493 4639499 4639513
4639529 4639543 4639561 4639597 4639631 4639633 4639643 4639651 4639693 4639697
4639703 4639709 4639717 4639741 4639751 4639757 4639771 4639787 4639799 4639823
4639849 4639853 4639867 4639871 4639879 4639883 4639891 4639903 4639909 4639927
4639931 4639963 4639967 4639969 4639993 4640003 4640017 4640057 4640081 4640113
4640117 4640131 4640137 4640143 4640147 4640159 4640171 4640177 4640179 4640183
4640197 4640213 4640221 4640231 4640249 4640267 4640287 4640329 4640369 4640387
4640393 4640399 4640401 4640417 4640423 4640437 4640443 4640477 4640479 4640491
4640497 4640501 4640543 4640557 4640567 4640591 4640593 4640599 4640717 4640719
4640723 4640737 4640747 4640759 4640761 4640777 4640789 4640791 4640803 4640821
4640833 4640837 4640843 4640863 4640869 4640929 4640953 4640969 4640971 4640981
4640989 4641001 4641011 4641019 4641029 4641037 4641047 4641059 4641061 4641067
4641089 4641107 4641121 4641139 4641151 4641179 4641191 4641209 4641211 4641223
4641229 4641251 4641271 4641281 4641293 4641347 4641361 4641379 4641389 4641397
4641401 4641437 4641451 4641467 4641473 4641503 4641509 4641557 4641563 4641583
4641587 4641631 4641641 4641647 4641667 4641683 4641709 4641713 4641739 4641773
4641781 4641787 4641811 4641829 4641841 4641853 4641863 4641877 4641887 4641907
4641913 4641919 4641991 4642009 4642013 4642069 4642081 4642087 4642091 4642093
4642123 4642163 4642171 4642181 4642199 4642223 4642259 4642271 4642361 4642373
4642381 4642387 4642397 4642399 4642423 4642457 4642459 4642483 4642489 4642493
4642499 4642531 4642537 4642541 4642549 4642601 4642607 4642609 4642621 4642643
4642657 4642661 4642679 4642721 4642733 4642741 4642787 4642789 4642811 4642817
4642823 4642843 4642867 4642877 4642889 4642907 4642927 4642949 4642951 4642969
4642997 4642999 4643003 4643039 4643047 4643063 4643069 4643077 4643113 4643117
4643143 4643153 4643189 4643203 4643213 4643231 4643237 4643251 4643257 4643279
4643297 4643299 4643321 4643323 4643333 4643339 4643357 4643371 4643407 4643413
4643417 4643437 4643453 4643461 4643473 4643491 4643497 4643563 4643579 4643591
4643593 4643621 4643623 4643629 4643633 4643641 4643659 4643663 4643671 4643687
4643689 4643711 4643719 4643729 4643761 4643789 4643801 4643843 4643867 4643909
4643911 4643921 4643939 4643959 4643963 4643983 4643987 4643993 4644001 4644011
4644053 4644061 4644097 4644131 4644139 4644149 4644161 4644209 4644221 4644251
4644257 4644259 4644319 4644329 4644347 4644361 4644371 4644377 4644401 4644403
4644433 4644463 4644481 4644509 4644511 4644527 4644533 4644581 4644583 4644589
4644593 4644617 4644623 4644631 4644667 4644671 4644677 4644691 4644697 4644707
4644719 4644737 4644769 4644799 4644811 4644833 4644843 4644851 4644871 4644881
4644883 4644907 4644953 4644971 4645007 4645019 4645027 4645037 4645061 4645073
4645099 4645111 4645117 4645141 4645153 4645163 4645169 4645171 4645181 4645187
4645231 4645237 4645243 4645271 4645283 4645309 4645343 4645349 4645363 4645409
4645411 4645429 4645441 4645477 4645489 4645499 4645507 4645523 4645541 4645547
4645549 4645559 4645561 4645583 4645631 4645637 4645639 4645649 4645651 4645681
4645687 4645721 4645733 4645783 4645799 4645801 4645813 4645841 4645843 4645867
4645873 4645891 4645909 4645919 4645933 4645951 4645961 4645967 4645987 4645999
4646017 4646071 4646099 4646111 4646113 4646123 4646129 4646137 4646141 4646143
4646149 4646153 4646167 4646171 4646179 4646197 4646209 4646233 4646263 4646273
4646281 4646297 4646329 4646339 4646347 4646357 4646359 4646363 4646371 4646381
4646401 4646413 4646417 4646429 4646459 4646479 4646501 4646513 4646519 4646527
4646533 4646557 4646567 4646573 4646597 4646599 4646617 4646633 4646647 4646659
4646671 4646693 4646711 4646731 4646743 4646753 4646777 4646783 4646791 4646801
4646809 4646849 4646857 4646891 4646911 4646923 4646927 4646951 4646959
4646977 4647007 4647029 4647037 4647061 4647073 4647079 4647091 4647101 4647113
4647119 4647121 4647133 4647157 4647193 4647197 4647211 4647259 4647263 4647271

```
4647277  4647281  4647283  4647287  4647289  4647301  4647317  4647319  4647323  4647329
4647347  4647353  4647361  4647373  4647413  4647431  4647437  4647439  4647469  4647479
4647493  4647497  4647499  4647509  4647521  4647523  4647527  4647547  4647559  4647563
4647581  4647583  4647611  4647631  4647653  4647661  4647667  4647701  4647707  4647707
4647733  4647763  4647779  4647791  4647793  4647809  4647823  4647871  4647887  4647889
4647893  4647943  4647947  4647959  4648003  4648009  4648031  4648037  4648067  4648069
4648099  4648151  4648169  4648181  4648183  4648201  4648213  4648219  4648229  4648243
4648283  4648289  4648307  4648313  4648321  4648333  4648349  4648351  4648373  4648387
4648403  4648409  4648417  4648447  4648459  4648477  4648487  4648489  4648513  4648519
4648561  4648591  4648603  4648619  4648639  4648663  4648681  4648739  4648753  4648757
4648799  4648801  4648807  4648811  4648843  4648849  4648879  4648907  4648937  4648957
4648979  4648991  4649017  4649027  4649033  4649069  4649083  4649119  4649123
4649137  4649147  4649149  4649153  4649171  4649179  4649189  4649191  4649201  4649207
4649209  4649219  4649231  4649261  4649269  4649291  4649303  4649311  4649339  4649341
4649353  4649371  4649399  4649401  4649413  4649417  4649431  4649459  4649467  4649497
4649503  4649507  4649521  4649527  4649537  4649539  4649549  4649573  4649581  4649587
4649591  4649609  4649621  4649629  4649651  4649677  4649681  4649683  4649693  4649741
4649747  4649759  4649779  4649797  4649803  4649809  4649819  4649863  4649873  4649893
4649903  4649923  4649929  4649941  4649963  4649967  4650001  4650007  4650011  4650029
4650053  4650077  4650101  4650109  4650131  4650137  4650169  4650187  4650199  4650253
4650259  4650281  4650311  4650323  4650337  4650389  4650391  4650427  4650461  4650463
4650467  4650479  4650487  4650491  4650511  4650521  4650551  4650559  4650587  4650601
4650617  4650637  4650647  4650661  4650677  4650689  4650691  4650719  4650727  4650749
4650781  4650797  4650827  4650847  4650851  4650857  4650869  4650871  4650883  4650887
4650901  4650907  4650931  4650983  4651001  4651007  4651019  4651021  4651027  4651033
4651043  4651061  4651063  4651091  4651093  4651099  4651133  4651169  4651177  4651187
4651201  4651249  4651259  4651289  4651291  4651301  4651303  4651321  4651331
4651343  4651349  4651369  4651373  4651391  4651399  4651429  4651453  4651459  4651463
4651469  4651483  4651499  4651511  4651547  4651553  4651579  4651597  4651601  4651607
4651639  4651663  4651709  4651711  4651721  4651729  4651733  4651739  4651741  4651769
4651771  4651781  4651807  4651811  4651813  4651831  4651837  4651841  4651859  4651873
4651909  4651939  4651963  4651967  4651981  4651987  4652027  4652029  4652099  4652117
4652129  4652149  4652173  4652189  4652239  4652251  4652273  4652293  4652303  4652309
4652317  4652353  4652507  4652513  4652521  4652533  4652551  4652567  4652579  4652581
4652603  4652617  4652623  4652677  4652689  4652699  4652711  4652723  4652737  4652741
4652747  4652749  4652771  4652783  4652807  4652827  4652833  4652839  4652881  4652887
4652909  4652911  4652927  4652933  4652939  4652941  4652957  4652971  4652981  4653017
4653031  4653041  4653059  4653071  4653113  4653139  4653151  4653169  4653191  4653197
4653211  4653221  4653247  4653277  4653281  4653287  4653293  4653301  4653307  4653343
4653349  4653353  4653401  4653403  4653413  4653421  4653433  4653443  4653449  4653457
4653491  4653497  4653511  4653533  4653547  4653577  4653587  4653647  4653667  4653673
4653697  4653703  4653707  4653713  4653739  4653757  4653763  4653793  4653827  4653829
4653853  4653883  4653893  4653907  4653911  4653919  4653923  4653941  4653953  4653977
4653989  4654009  4654043  4654049  4654051  4654063  4654099  4654103  4654109  4654129
4654147  4654163  4654187  4654201  4654207  4654213  4654217  4654229  4654231  4654241
4654271  4654291  4654319  4654327  4654337  4654339  4654343  4654381  4654387  4654399
4654417  4654421  4654439  4654453  4654459  4654469  4654477  4654493  4654541  4654543
4654567  4654577  4654591  4654597  4654603  4654609  4654631  4654649  4654669  4654697
4654709  4654721  4654729  4654733  4654747  4654781  4654799  4654801  4654807  4654813
4654817  4654843  4654907  4654919  4654963  4655009  4655029  4655033  4655047  4655069
4655071  4655111  4655113  4655129  4655143  4655171  4655201  4655213  4655251  4655279
4655317  4655333  4655369  4655381  4655383  4655389  4655411  4655419  4655461  4655471
4655473  4655503  4655507  4655531  4655533  4655537  4655561  4655579  4655587  4655593
4655597  4655617  4655657  4655659  4655663  4655687  4655723  4655737  4655743  4655753
4655767  4655789  4655801  4655809  4655831  4655851  4655869  4655873  4655881  4655887
4655899  4655923  4655927  4655929  4655933  4655957  4655971  4656053  4656061  4656077
4656089  4656139  4656151  4656163  4656167  4656173  4656187  4656193  4656203  4656227
4656229  4656241  4656263  4656331  4656343  4656367  4656397  4656409  4656467  4656469
4656481  4656503  4656517  4656551  4656563  4656581  4656607  4656629  4656643
4656661  4656703  4656757  4656763  4656779  4656797  4656809  4656823  4656853  4656869
4656877  4656887  4656893  4656937  4656947  4656973  4656979  4656983  4656989  4657001
4657007  4657019  4657021  4657039  4657049  4657061  4657117  4657123  4657141  4657151
4657171  4657187  4657189  4657193  4657199  4657229  4657241  4657267  4657291  4657297
4657321  4657343  4657349  4657361  4657363  4657381  4657397  4657417  4657423  4657427
4657441  4657453  4657493  4657537  4657547  4657553  4657561  4657567  4657571  4657577
4657579  4657607  4657613  4657621  4657687  4657691  4657703  4657727  4657729  4657739
4657769  4657771  4657787  4657789  4657811  4657823  4657853  4657879  4657883  4657901
4657909  4657921  4657927  4657931  4657957  4657963  4657981  4657987  4657997  4657999
4658047  4658053  4658099  4658107  4658141  4658149  4658161  4658177  4658197  4658207
4658237  4658279  4658281  4658321  4658327  4658341  4658359  4658383  4658389  4658399
4658419  4658431  4658447  4658483  4658497  4658503  4658513  4658539  4658553  4658567
4658569  4658579  4658597  4658603  4658611  4658617  4658623  4658653  4658659  4658671
4658677  4658701  4658713  4658723  4658729  4658767  4658777  4658779  4658791
4658809  4658831  4658837  4658869  4658893  4658911  4658917  4658923  4658939  4658947
4658957  4658963  4658989  4659013  4659023  4659043  4659049  4659059  4659073  4659131
4659181  4659197  4659203  4659209  4659211  4659223  4659229  4659257  4659287  4659293
4659307  4659311  4659323  4659367  4659443  4659449  4659451  4659469  4659481  4659491
4659493  4659497  4659511  4659569  4659587  4659619  4659623  4659637  4659647  4659673
4659679  4659689  4659719  4659727  4659763  4659793  4659797  4659803  4659833  4659841
4659847  4659857  4659871  4659881  4659887  4659901  4659907  4659913  4659919  4659929
4659947  4659979  4660001  4660009  4660043  4660067  4660079  4660087  4660093  4660127
4660133  4660147  4660151  4660153  4660157  4660169  4660177  4660189  4660219  4660223
4660259  4660267  4660277  4660291  4660303  4660309  4660321  4660349  4660361  4660423
4660427  4660433  4660457  4660471  4660489  4660493  4660501  4660507  4660517  4660541
4660543  4660547  4660549  4660573  4660577  4660589  4660597  4660627  4660637  4660687
4660693  4660709  4660717  4660723  4660729  4660741  4660759  4660769  4660781  4660783
4660801  4660807  4660867  4660871  4660889  4660909  4660919  4660933  4660951  4660961
4660969  4660993  4661011  4661017  4661029  4661039  4661053  4661057  4661089  4661093
4661113  4661117  4661119  4661161  4661183  4661207  4661231  4661233  4661263  4661291
```

```
4661299  4661303  4661309  4661317  4661323  4661333  4661347  4661351  4661353  4661359
4661399  4661429  4661443  4661477  4661491  4661497  4661513  4661537  4661539  4661543
4661551  4661557  4661567  4661581  4661609  4661639  4661651  4661693  4661717  4661719
4661729  4661743  4661747  4661773  4661777  4661807  4661819  4661849  4661851  4661863
4661887  4661911  4661941  4661959  4661983  4661989  4662019  4662023  4662067  4662083
4662101  4662109  4662113  4662137  4662149  4662167  4662179  4662181  4662197  4662209
4662221  4662223  4662227  4662241  4662263  4662269  4662271  4662293  4662299  4662319
4662331  4662337  4662341  4662347  4662349  4662373  4662377  4662389  4662401  4662419
4662433  4662451  4662457  4662461  4662487  4662503  4662527  4662529  4662547  4662557
4662571  4662587  4662601  4662611  4662631  4662653  4662661  4662667  4662673  4662689
4662773  4662821  4662863  4662871  4662893  4662899  4662919  4662967  4662979  4663003
4663007  4663013  4663019  4663039  4663063  4663079  4663111  4663121  4663159  4663163
4663177  4663201  4663223  4663231  4663249  4663259  4663277  4663279  4663283  4663289
4663297  4663327  4663331  4663339  4663349  4663363  4663367  4663427  4663429  4663433
4663441  4663447  4663499  4663501  4663507  4663513  4663541  4663543  4663553  4663573
4663579  4663583  4663597  4663601  4663613  4663621  4663643  4663649  4663657  4663691
4663697  4663699  4663717  4663727  4663741  4663781  4663787  4663793  4663801  4663807
4663817  4663847  4663859  4663913  4663921  4663927  4663931  4663969  4663973  4663979
4663991  4664003  4664017  4664057  4664059  4664083  4664087  4664089  4664111  4664113
4664117  4664129  4664131  4664141  4664173  4664197  4664213  4664221  4664227  4664249
4664263  4664279  4664287  4664311  4664321  4664323  4664357  4664381  4664393  4664399
4664419  4664431  4664441  4664449  4664453  4664459  4664467  4664497  4664507  4664521
4664531  4664533  4664567  4664573  4664581  4664591  4664593  4664603  4664641  4664657
4664659  4664669  4664687  4664707  4664711  4664789  4664801  4664809  4664813  4664819
4664839  4664867  4664909  4664917  4664921  4664927  4664951  4664971  4664977  4664993
4665019  4665047  4665049  4665109  4665119  4665139  4665149  4665161  4665163  4665169
4665209  4665247  4665263  4665281  4665299  4665301  4665313  4665319  4665329  4665373
4665377  4665379  4665413  4665449  4665461  4665467  4665473  4665487  4665499  4665509
4665533  4665539  4665547  4665553  4665563  4665573  4665719  4665721  4665733  4665751
4665761  4665767  4665799  4665833  4665847  4665851  4665863  4665877  4665889  4665893
4665901  4665911  4665917  4665919  4665931  4665937  4665967  4665971  4665979  4666021
4666031  4666037  4666069  4666117  4666121  4666127  4666139  4666141  4666159  4666183
4666219  4666223  4666243  4666247  4666253  4666261  4666273  4666283  4666289  4666297
4666327  4666373  4666393  4666397  4666421  4666423  4666433  4666463  4666477  4666499
4666549  4666553  4666559  4666589  4666633  4666637  4666639  4666643  4666663  4666667
4666679  4666681  4666691  4666693  4666741  4666777  4666801  4666807  4666813  4666819
4666867  4666873  4666877  4666889  4666903  4666931  4666943  4666967  4666973  4666979
4666997  4667017  4667023  4667041  4667051  4667063  4667101  4667107  4667111  4667161
4667189  4667209  4667251  4667261  4667269  4667303  4667309  4667323  4667363  4667371
4667381  4667387  4667389  4667393  4667417  4667423  4667437  4667449  4667471  4667473
4667477  4667527  4667539  4667567  4667569  4667573  4667581  4667591  4667599  4667603
4667609  4667623  4667629  4667647  4667653  4667669  4667681  4667687  4667699  4667731
4667743  4667771  4667777  4667791  4667797  4667807  4667813  4667821  4667851  4667881
4667893  4667921  4667933  4667947  4667963  4667969  4667981  4667983  4667989  4668023
4668049  4668061  4668071  4668107  4668109  4668113  4668121  4668133  4668163  4668199
4668211  4668221  4668229  4668233  4668247  4668283  4668299  4668331  4668337  4668371
4668373  4668397  4668407  4668409  4668413  4668427  4668431  4668439  4668451  4668457
4668473  4668479  4668481  4668487  4668491  4668511  4668527  4668529  4668539  4668541
4668551  4668571  4668577  4668581  4668583  4668589  4668637  4668641  4668679  4668683
4668691  4668721  4668733  4668749  4668767  4668773  4668779  4668787  4668791  4668799
4668803  4668827  4668877  4668883  4668907  4668943  4668949  4668973  4668989  4668953
4668973  4668991  4668997  4669009  4669013  4669019  4669037  4669051  4669061  4669109
4669111  4669139  4669157  4669177  4669187  4669199  4669211  4669229  4669243  4669277
4669279  4669283  4669303  4669321  4669333  4669351  4669369  4669381  4669387  4669393
4669411  4669429  4669447  4669463  4669471  4669477  4669481  4669501  4669507  4669517
4669519  4669523  4669537  4669549  4669559  4669583  4669589  4669627  4669681  4669697
4669703  4669729  4669751  4669799  4669811  4669813  4669817  4669823  4669831  4669853
4669879  4669891  4669913  4669961  4669963  4670009  4670033  4670041
4670051  4670059  4670089  4670093  4670111  4670129  4670179  4670191  4670203  4670207
4670213  4670227  4670293  4670297  4670317  4670353  4670377  4670387  4670411  4670423
4670431  4670441  4670459  4670507  4670509  4670513  4670527  4670573  4670591  4670609
4670639  4670641  4670651  4670663  4670671  4670681  4670683  4670707  4670737  4670749
4670753  4670773  4670779  4670791  4670797  4670807  4670819  4670849  4670851  4670857
4670867  4670873  4670879  4670891  4670893  4670923  4670929  4670957  4670959  4670969
4670989  4670999  4671011  4671013  4671031  4671071  4671077  4671097  4671101  4671109
4671113  4671137  4671151  4671167  4671193  4671203  4671223  4671257  4671259  4671269
4671281  4671301  4671341  4671347  4671353  4671383  4671389  4671427  4671439  4671449
4671463  4671467  4671471  4671493  4671503  4671517  4671529  4671539  4671547  4671571
4671613  4671647  4671671  4671677  4671683  4671703  4671707  4671713  4671749  4671757
4671761  4671763  4671781  4671799  4671803  4671809  4671817  4671833  4671839  4671857
4671859  4671869  4671893  4671899  4671913  4671937  4671973  4671983  4672001  4672009
4672021  4672037  4672039  4672049  4672097  4672099  4672117  4672121  4672141  4672147
4672177  4672181  4672189  4672201  4672231  4672253  4672273  4672301  4672303  4672307
4672333  4672357  4672373  4672441  4672453  4672463  4672469  4672487  4672523
4672529  4672531  4672553  4672561  4672573  4672579  4672597  4672607  4672621  4672627
4672631  4672649  4672667  4672669  4672687  4672699  4672709  4672747  4672751  4672757
4672769  4672813  4672823  4672873  4672883  4672891  4672907  4672919  4672937  4672951
4672963  4673003  4673023  4673029  4673051  4673077  4673099  4673131  4673143  4673159
4673171  4673173  4673189  4673191  4673237  4673261  4673287  4673309  4673323  4673327
4673329  4673353  4673399  4673401  4673407  4673413  4673429  4673441  4673443  4673447
4673477  4673483  4673489  4673491  4673497  4673503  4673509  4673519  4673527  4673551
4673569  4673609  4673621  4673631  4673651  4673659  4673681  4673693  4673701  4673707
4673723  4673731  4673737  4673741  4673783  4673789  4673833  4673863
4673909  4673917  4673923  4673927  4673939  4673957  4673983  4673989  4674023  4674049
4674067  4674071  4674077  4674091  4674101  4674113  4674127  4674151  4674161  4674169
4674181  4674199  4674217  4674223  4674233  4674239  4674251  4674253  4674289  4674347
4674349  4674353  4674367  4674377  4674391  4674403  4674407  4674421  4674433  4674443
4674463  4674503  4674517  4674529  4674557  4674563  4674581  4674587  4674647  4674661
4674671  4674673  4674739  4674767  4674793  4674797  4674821  4674833  4674841  4674863
```

```
4674883  4674889  4674899  4674907  4674919  4674941  4674947  4674959  4674961  4674973
4674991  4675037  4675063  4675091  4675093  4675103  4675117  4675123  4675129  4675133
4675147  4675157  4675163  4675169  4675171  4675199  4675207  4675217  4675241  4675243
4675247  4675249  4675267  4675277  4675291  4675309  4675313  4675343  4675361  4675369
4675373  4675379  4675397  4675403  4675423  4675439  4675453  4675477  4675481  4675487
4675507  4675511  4675523  4675547  4675571  4675591  4675597  4675603  4675609  4675613
4675631  4675633  4675667  4675669  4675679  4675703  4675709  4675717  4675733  4675751
4675753  4675771  4675787  4675813  4675817  4675841  4675849  4675859  4675861  4675883
4675889  4675921  4675933  4675939  4675943  4675961  4675963  4676011  4676029  4676041
4676051  4676057  4676059  4676081  4676093  4676101  4676117  4676141  4676159  4676179
4676201  4676213  4676219  4676227  4676233  4676237  4676239  4676249  4676297  4676311
4676317  4676323  4676333  4676339  4676351  4676369  4676387  4676407  4676417  4676437
4676447  4676449  4676461  4676473  4676491  4676537  4676587  4676593  4676657  4676669
4676671  4676713  4676729  4676741  4676759  4676761  4676767  4676779  4676783  4676803
4676807  4676827  4676839  4676849  4676851  4676941  4676951  4676953  4676963  4677011
4677019  4677031  4677083  4677089  4677121  4677137  4677139  4677161  4677191  4677199
4677241  4677247  4677263  4677269  4677289  4677301  4677313  4677319  4677331  4677341
4677359  4677383  4677389  4677391  4677427  4677433  4677443  4677451  4677457  4677467
4677473  4677479  4677481  4677493  4677509  4677521  4677523  4677529  4677587  4677599
4677619  4677623  4677653  4677677  4677679  4677691  4677709  4677713  4677779  4677817
4677821  4677847  4677853  4677859  4677877  4677889  4677899  4677917  4677919  4677923
4677943  4677973  4677989  4677991  4678031  4678033  4678049  4678057  4678061  4678073
4678103  4678109  4678133  4678181  4678183  4678187  4678211  4678217  4678231  4678249
4678259  4678283  4678319  4678321  4678327  4678337  4678343  4678381  4678397  4678477
4678481  4678501  4678537  4678547  4678549  4678561  4678567  4678631  4678649  4678651
4678679  4678703  4678721  4678727  4678741  4678753  4678771  4678777  4678781  4678791
4678783  4678801  4678823  4678837  4678901  4678907  4678937  4678939  4678943  4678951
4678957  4678963  4678967  4678979  4679009  4679011  4679023  4679039  4679041  4679069
4679083  4679089  4679099  4679107  4679117  4679119  4679137  4679141  4679153  4679159
4679161  4679167  4679177  4679197  4679201  4679203  4679221  4679287  4679293  4679321
4679333  4679359  4679383  4679387  4679401  4679413  4679417  4679429  4679447  4679447
4679449  4679459  4679473  4679483  4679489  4679533  4679537  4679551  4679579  4679581
4679621  4679627  4679629  4679639  4679651  4679659  4679677  4679683  4679687  4679693
4679707  4679711  4679747  4679761  4679767  4679771  4679803  4679809  4679813  4679839
4679849  4679867  4679869  4679891  4679897  4679903  4679911  4679921  4679923  4679929
4679951  4679963  4679999  4680001  4680007  4680041  4680043  4680049  4680079  4680131
4680149  4680161  4680173  4680199  4680211  4680301  4680311  4680317  4680323  4680353
4680371  4680373  4680383  4680407  4680409  4680413  4680443  4680451  4680497  4680503
4680527  4680539  4680551  4680563  4680583  4680587  4680607  4680623  4680653  4680667
4680673  4680677  4680701  4680719  4680727  4680733  4680743  4680749  4680757  4680769
4680779  4680789  4680791  4680811  4680827  4680853  4680857  4680881  4680887  4680889
4680901  4680913  4680941  4680953  4680961  4680971  4680997  4681003  4681007  4681009
4681037  4681043  4681063  4681081  4681097  4681147  4681169  4681199  4681211  4681241
4681253  4681289  4681291  4681297  4681301  4681309  4681321  4681337  4681343  4681349
4681361  4681379  4681399  4681423  4681433  4681459  4681463  4681471  4681507  4681513
4681519  4681559  4681559  4681561  4681597  4681603  4681609  4681631  4681637  4681639
4681661  4681693  4681697  4681727  4681739  4681751  4681753  4681757  4681763  4681793
4681801  4681829  4681841  4681843  4681871  4681889  4681891  4681909  4681921  4681939
4681951  4681973  4681981  4681991  4681993  4681997  4682003  4682009  4682011  4682033
4682039  4682053  4682059  4682081  4682101  4682129  4682143  4682149  4682173  4682203
4682207  4682219  4682231  4682233  4682243  4682257  4682261  4682267  4682273  4682297
4682309  4682347  4682351  4682357  4682371  4682401  4682411  4682423  4682443  4682449
4682479  4682479  4682507  4682527  4682537  4682551  4682597  4682647  4682677  4682687
4682689  4682851  4682861  4682863  4682903  4682917  4682927  4682929  4682933  4682957
4682959  4682989  4682999  4683011  4683017  4683037  4683047  4683073  4683079  4683083
4683097  4683103  4683121  4683131  4683149  4683157  4683167  4683179  4683187  4683193
4683197  4683209  4683227  4683229  4683247  4683271  4683277  4683293  4683317  4683323
4683337  4683377  4683383  4683391  4683463  4683473  4683487  4683491  4683493  4683499
4683521  4683527  4683563  4683577  4683589  4683599  4683611  4683631  4683643  4683661
4683667  4683713  4683733  4683739  4683751  4683779  4683797  4683817  4683827  4683829
4683841  4683851  4683853  4683859  4683871  4683901  4683907  4683919  4683923  4683953
4683967  4683977  4683983  4683997  4684003  4684039  4684049  4684073  4684079  4684091
4684093  4684103  4684117  4684123  4684151  4684177  4684181  4684201  4684213  4684223
4684243  4684259  4684297  4684301  4684313  4684319  4684357  4684391  4684447  4684451
4684483  4684489  4684501  4684523  4684529  4684553  4684579  4684597  4684601  4684613
4684633  4684661  4684699  4684703  4684733  4684759  4684763  4684789  4684817  4684859
4684879  4684879  4684891  4684907  4684909  4684949  4684951  4684957  4684969  4684973
4684987  4684991  4684993  4685033  4685059  4685063  4685071  4685119  4685129  4685137
4685141  4685167  4685179  4685189  4685201  4685223  4685227  4685221  4685231  4685257
4685299  4685321  4685333  4685341  4685389  4685393  4685407  4685413  4685431  4685437
4685441  4685449  4685459  4685467  4685479  4685497  4685509  4685531  4685539  4685561
4685567  4685579  4685623  4685633  4685641  4685657  4685663  4685669  4685687  4685689
4685699  4685701  4685713  4685719  4685729  4685731  4685749  4685773  4685777  4685789
4685809  4685827  4685833  4685833  4685843  4685869  4685873  4685887  4685893  4685903
4685911  4685917  4685921  4685927  4685953  4685963  4685969  4685971  4685987  4686007
4686029  4686037  4686079  4686083  4686113  4686119  4686131  4686133  4686137  4686163
4686247  4686257  4686277  4686281  4686287  4686289  4686307  4686317  4686343  4686347
4686349  4686377  4686379  4686389  4686431  4686443  4686463  4686467  4686481  4686491
4686499  4686523  4686529  4686533  4686541  4686553  4686557  4686571  4686589  4686593
4686599  4686601  4686623  4686637  4686653  4686677  4686697  4686701  4686709  4686811
4686817  4686821  4686839  4686881  4686911  4686919  4686931  4686937  4686947  4686959
4686961  4686967  4686973  4686989  4687003  4687013  4687021  4687027  4687031  4687037
4687051  4687063  4687069  4687073  4687097  4687099  4687103  4687139  4687141  4687153
4687159  4687171  4687187  4687211  4687213  4687217  4687229  4687247  4687273  4687283
4687303  4687313  4687321  4687337  4687351  4687367  4687369  4687399  4687409  4687421
4687439  4687447  4687453  4687483  4687499  4687517  4687519  4687601  4687637  4687643
4687651  4687663  4687673  4687679  4687681  4687693  4687721  4687723  4687741  4687747
4687751  4687769  4687783  4687799  4687829  4687849  4687853  4687871  4687873  4687901
```

4687919	4687931	4687933	4687961	4687967	4687979	4687993	4687999	4688017	4688069
4688071	4688083	4688087	4688137	4688143	4688147	4688149	4688153	4688171	4688179
4688183	4688207	4688219	4688239	4688249	4688261	4688267	4688273	4688287	4688323
4688329	4688339	4688351	4688353	4688357	4688371	4688377	4688393	4688407	4688441
4688449	4688503	4688543	4688557	4688561	4688569	4688581	4688641	4688653	4688669
4688683	4688693	4688699	4688707	4688741	4688743	4688759	4688771	4688773	4688777
4688813	4688867	4688897	4688903	4688909	4688921	4688927	4688933	4688951	4688977
4688993	4689017	4689031	4689043	4689089	4689109	4689133	4689149	4689151	4689163
4689169	4689173	4689187	4689197	4689239	4689247	4689259	4689283	4689287	4689299
4689341	4689353	4689359	4689389	4689403	4689413	4689427	4689437	4689439	4689449
4689473	4689481	4689547	4689551	4689557	4689577	4689589	4689611	4689661	4689667
4689689	4689697	4689719	4689731	4689743	4689757	4689779	4689781	4689803	4689809
4689829	4689847	4689859	4689869	4689871	4689901	4689911	4689947	4689973	4689991
4690001	4690027	4690069	4690099	4690109	4690111	4690117	4690121	4690123	4690219
4690261	4690303	4690307	4690313	4690333	4690349	4690363	4690369	4690381	4690409
4690417	4690451	4690463	4690471	4690481	4690493	4690519	4690531	4690537	4690571
4690591	4690619	4690633	4690639	4690661	4690667	4690709	4690711	4690727	4690747
4690753	4690789	4690799	4690801	4690811	4690817	4690831	4690843	4690859	4690867
4690877	4690879	4690921	4690937	4690943	4690949	4690957	4690981	4690991	4690993
4691009	4691039	4691047	4691087	4691107	4691123	4691143	4691153	4691173	4691177
4691191	4691207	4691213	4691227	4691237	4691293	4691321	4691329	4691353	4691363
4691369	4691381	4691383	4691413	4691431	4691437	4691443	4691459	4691501	4691513
4691521	4691539	4691567	4691569	4691623	4691627	4691699	4691717	4691749	4691759
4691767	4691777	4691789	4691801	4691807	4691821	4691831	4691837	4691849	4691851
4691867	4691887	4691899	4691903	4691909	4691927	4691957	4691969	4691989	4692001
4692011	4692041	4692047	4692043	4692053	4692071	4692089	4692091	4692109	4692137
4692139	4692173	4692227	4692241	4692251	4692257	4692277	4692283	4692313	4692349
4692361	4692383	4692397	4692407	4692427	4692431	4692463	4692469	4692473	4692497
4692503	4692509	4692539	4692553	4692557	4692593	4692617	4692631	4692637	4692641
4692671	4692689	4692733	4692757	4692769	4692773	4692797	4692817	4692823	4692839
4692841	4692847	4692869	4692889	4692917	4692923	4692931	4692949	4692953	4692959
4692967	4692979	4693001	4693021	4693027	4693033	4693067	4693079	4693093	4693103
4693123	4693141	4693177	4693187	4693189	4693193	4693217	4693223	4693261	4693267
4693277	4693291	4693303	4693327	4693363	4693387	4693421	4693447	4693439	4693457
4693463	4693471	4693477	4693499	4693501	4693517	4693529	4693553	4693573	4693609
4693631	4693643	4693661	4693669	4693673	4693687	4693691	4693693	4693697	4693699
4693727	4693747	4693753	4693763	4693811	4693823	4693831	4693849	4693859	4693879
4693883	4693901	4693903	4693933	4693939	4693987	4693993	4693999	4694003	4694017
4694029	4694033	4694069	4694071	4694077	4694111	4694141	4694147	4694161	4694167
4694171	4694233	4694243	4694269	4694293	4694309	4694341	4694381	4694401	4694413
4694419	4694441	4694467	4694479	4694513	4694519	4694527	4694531	4694551	4694603
4694617	4694629	4694659	4694663	4694681	4694693	4694699	4694713	4694749	4694759
4694773	4694777	4694779	4694791	4694797	4694801	4694803	4694821	4694827	4694831
4694861	4694863	4694887	4694903	4694917	4694923	4694927	4694933	4694939	4694969
4694983	4694993	4694999	4695001	4695011	4695023	4695029	4695073	4695079	4695107
4695113	4695121	4695137	4695143	4695149	4695157	4695169	4695181	4695191	4695199
4695203	4695221	4695233	4695239	4695259	4695269	4695277	4695311	4695329	4695331
4695343	4695359	4695371	4695377	4695391	4695407	4695465	4695487	4695491	4695499
4695517	4695533	4695547	4695563	4695569	4695589	4695623	4695631	4695653	4695659
4695661	4695701	4695731	4695737	4695763	4695797	4695799	4695809	4695811	4695833
4695851	4695857	4695863	4695877	4695881	4695913	4695917	4695919	4695931	4695937
4695947	4695953	4695989	4695991	4696001	4696007	4696019	4696031	4696039	4696047
4696093	4696121	4696127	4696129	4696147	4696177	4696183	4696187	4696213	4696217
4696229	4696247	4696259	4696261	4696271	4696273	4696291	4696297	4696303	4696319
4696327	4696339	4696343	4696357	4696361	4696379	4696387	4696409	4696429	4696453
4696457	4696487	4696507	4696513	4696529	4696537	4696567	4696583	4696597	4696613
4696631	4696639	4696651	4696687	4696691	4696711	4696723	4696733	4696739	4696763
4696789	4696799	4696801	4696823	4696829	4696831	4696843	4696859	4696871	4696873
4696877	4696883	4696897	4696943	4696957	4696961	4696973	4696987	4696999	4697003
4697023	4697057	4697059	4697081	4697093	4697107	4697141	4697177	4697179	4697197
4697201	4697239	4697249	4697257	4697269	4697279	4697291	4697293	4697299	4697317
4697327	4697347	4697369	4697377	4697383	4697387	4697393	4697417	4697447	4697453
4697467	4697479	4697519	4697527	4697531	4697533	4697569	4697587	4697599	4697629
4697633	4697659	4697663	4697689	4697711	4697723	4697741	4697743	4697747	4697753
4697789	4697801	4697809	4697827	4697843	4697851	4697873	4697881	4697897	4697909
4697923	4697929	4697947	4697951	4697963	4697977	4697981	4697983	4698007	4698013
4698047	4698059	4698091	4698097	4698101	4698121	4698151	4698157	4698173	4698179
4698181	4698193	4698251	4698259	4698269	4698271	4698293	4698299	4698311	4698349
4698359	4698361	4698383	4698431	4698433	4698437	4698457	4698461	4698479	4698497
4698521	4698527	4698541	4698553	4698557	4698563	4698569	4698581	4698599	4698607
4698611	4698671	4698677	4698679	4698697	4698721	4698737	4698761	4698767	4698773
4698779	4698857	4698893	4698917	4698943	4698961	4698977	4698983	4698989	4699003
4699043	4699081	4699087	4699091	4699103	4699109	4699129	4699141	4699147	4699151
4699159	4699183	4699187	4699217	4699231	4699267	4699283	4699339	4699367	4699369
4699391	4699393	4699399	4699417	4699423	4699459	4699477	4699493	4699549	4699571
4699579	4699619	4699621	4699637	4699657	4699679	4699691	4699697	4699727	4699733
4699757	4699801	4699831	4699853	4699861	4699873	4699931	4699949	4699951	4699963
4699967	4699969	4699991	4699997	4700023	4700039	4700053	4700057	4700063	
4700071	4700077	4700089	4700099	4700107	4700123	4700131	4700161	4700167	4700183
4700191	4700197	4700203	4700219	4700231	4700243	4700249	4700261	4700299	4700317
4700323	4700327	4700341	4700351	4700359	4700383	4700401	4700417	4700419	4700473
4700491	4700497	4700537	4700557	4700567	4700573	4700593	4700603	4700621	4700627
4700629	4700659	4700669	4700677	4700693	4700699	4700723	4700741	4700743	4700753
4700767	4700777	4700783	4700791	4700797	4700807	4700821	4700827	4700833	4700837
4700851	4700863	4700867	4700879	4700939	4700951	4700953	4700957	4700963	4700989
4701001	4701007	4701013	4701017	4701029	4701031	4701049	4701071	4701107	4701121
4701143	4701157	4701167	4701199	4701239	4701253	4701293	4701311	4701317	4701329
4701337	4701343	4701349	4701353	4701371	4701373	4701377	4701383	4701391	4701421
4701443	4701467	4701523	4701539	4701547	4701563	4701583	4701589	4701601	4701611

```
4701617  4701643  4701661  4701709  4701731  4701733  4701737  4701743  4701751  4701761
4701787  4701791  4701803  4701811  4701841  4701869  4701871  4701883  4701889  4701899
4701919  4701929  4701937  4701943  4701971  4702037  4702069  4702079  4702099  4702109
4702133  4702141  4702153  4702163  4702169  4702207  4702211  4702237  4702267  4702277
4702279  4702283  4702289  4702309  4702333  4702337  4702349  4702361  4702381  4702393
4702403  4702409  4702417  4702427  4702433  4702469  4702471  4702499  4702501  4702513
4702549  4702571  4702573  4702583  4702597  4702601  4702613  4702619  4702627  4702681
4702699  4702723  4702729  4702771  4702777  4702783  4702807  4702853  4702871  4702889
4702909  4702921  4702929  4702939  4703003  4703021  4703047  4703053  4703057  4703059
4703071  4703077  4703081  4703099  4703123  4703129  4703131  4703141  4703143  4703147
4703159  4703189  4703207  4703219  4703261  4703263  4703287  4703291  4703311  4703323
4703341  4703353  4703371  4703389  4703411  4703417  4703429  4703437  4703443  4703453
4703471  4703497  4703519  4703521  4703533  4703557  4703579  4703593  4703639  4703663
4703681  4703683  4703711  4703717  4703731  4703767  4703779  4703789  4703791  4703819
4703837  4703843  4703857  4703863  4703879  4703911  4703927  4703929  4703939  4703957
4703969  4703981  4703987  4704013  4704023  4704031  4704097  4704101  4704107  4704127
4704149  4704151  4704179  4704181  4704187  4704199  4704211  4704233  4704239  4704241
4704251  4704253  4704263  4704283  4704307  4704353  4704367  4704373  4704383
4704391  4704407  4704421  4704433  4704437  4704449  4704481  4704487  4704499  4704509
4704517  4704551  4704577  4704589  4704593  4704599  4704613  4704617  4704619  4704643
4704659  4704697  4704737  4704751  4704769  4704773  4704779  4704781  4704787  4704793
4704797  4704823  4704827  4704829  4704851  4704853  4704859  4704871  4704893  4704919
4704929  4705007  4705013  4705049  4705093  4705097  4705109  4705117  4705139  4705153
4705157  4705159  4705177  4705199  4705219  4705237  4705247  4705249  4705291  4705297
4705301  4705303  4705313  4705381  4705387  4705391  4705403  4705417  4705423  4705429
4705439  4705451  4705471  4705537  4705541  4705543  4705553  4705573  4705577  4705579
4705607  4705609  4705637  4705669  4705681  4705693  4705709  4705747  4705751  4705759
4705783  4705807  4705829  4705837  4705849  4705853  4705891  4705903  4705931  4705949
4705997  4706011  4706027  4706047  4706057  4706077  4706081  4706083  4706101  4706117
4706153  4706189  4706197  4706201  4706213  4706279  4706287  4706291  4706309  4706311
4706321  4706341  4706353  4706369  4706407  4706411  4706413  4706417  4706419  4706473
4706483  4706491  4706503  4706521  4706531  4706539  4706557  4706567  4706579  4706591
4706599  4706633  4706657  4706711  4706717  4706749  4706783  4706809  4706827  4706831
4706839  4706857  4706883  4706917  4706939  4706941  4706953  4706959  4706987  4706993
4707007  4707023  4707083  4707107  4707127  4707149  4707161  4707173  4707211  4707221
4707239  4707249  4707269  4707281  4707323  4707343  4707347  4707349  4707359  4707361
4707377  4707389  4707413  4707427  4707449  4707491  4707499  4707517  4707533  4707539
4707569  4707581  4707613  4707641  4707643  4707667  4707671  4707713  4707719  4707721
4707733  4707737  4707757  4707779  4707799  4707803  4707809  4707817  4707841  4707851
4707853  4707863  4707869  4707881  4707883  4707887  4707931  4707949  4707971  4707973
4707977  4707979  4708013  4708021  4708049  4708073  4708079  4708087  4708097  4708117
4708127  4708129  4708147  4708159  4708177  4708183  4708211  4708267  4708289  4708309
4708313  4708339  4708349  4708351  4708357  4708381  4708387  4708393  4708397  4708421
4708423  4708433  4708441  4708463  4708493  4708511  4708513  4708531  4708547  4708567
4708579  4708589  4708603  4708607  4708619  4708631  4708681  4708687  4708699  4708703
4708709  4708729  4708747  4708757  4708763  4708787  4708793  4708811  4708841  4708853
4708861  4708867  4708871  4708877  4708889  4708919  4708939  4708969  4708999  4709009
4709021  4709041  4709069  4709087  4709099  4709113  4709129  4709143  4709147  4709149
4709161  4709183  4709191  4709197  4709213  4709239  4709251  4709267  4709291  4709293
4709333  4709347  4709351  4709371  4709377  4709387  4709399  4709401  4709417  4709423
4709429  4709461  4709479  4709483  4709491  4709519  4709591  4709597  4709599  4709603
4709609  4709651  4709657  4709659  4709681  4709689  4709699  4709717  4709723  4709753
4709759  4709797  4709807  4709813  4709821  4709827  4709839  4709849  4709851  4709857
4709879  4709909  4709941  4709959  4709981  4709987  4710053  4710103  4710107  4710113
4710127  4710133  4710161  4710187  4710221  4710227  4710229  4710253  4710259  4710281
4710283  4710289  4710313  4710317  4710319  4710323  4710341  4710371  4710373  4710379
4710397  4710413  4710427  4710443  4710457  4710463  4710473  4710491  4710493  4710523
4710577  4710583  4710599  4710623  4710647  4710669  4710677  4710697  4710701  4710749
4710767  4710773  4710787  4710809  4710821  4710829  4710833  4710869  4710899  4710907
4710919  4710949  4710961  4710967  4710983  4711001  4711013  4711033  4711051  4711073
4711087  4711093  4711097  4711099  4711121  4711129  4711141  4711169  4711171  4711181
4711211  4711229  4711241  4711277  4711303  4711331  4711337  4711361  4711367  4711379
4711399  4711409  4711417  4711423  4711439  4711451  4711453  4711471  4711501  4711517
4711537  4711547  4711559  4711561  4711583  4711591  4711621  4711627  4711657  4711699
4711739  4711741  4711781  4711789  4711793  4711801  4711807  4711831  4711853  4711871
4711879  4711919  4711921  4711933  4711937  4711963  4711979  4711997  4712003  4712011
4712021  4712039  4712051  4712053  4712063  4712083  4712087  4712117  4712119  4712137
4712203  4712207  4712221  4712231  4712237  4712243  4712249  4712251  4712261  4712287
4712291  4712299  4712317  4712321  4712329  4712371  4712377  4712381  4712443  4712453
4712467  4712473  4712479  4712489  4712501  4712503  4712531  4712537  4712557  4712563
4712567  4712599  4712629  4712633  4712641  4712681  4712683  4712711  4712717  4712731
4712749  4712759  4712783  4712789  4712797  4712821  4712863  4712933  4712941  4712947
4712957  4712959  4712977  4713001  4713011  4713013  4713017  4713031  4713047  4713053
4713067  4713089  4713103  4713127  4713139  4713151  4713161  4713169  4713179  4713227
4713239  4713251  4713257  4713259  4713277  4713281  4713299  4713323  4713329  4713337
4713347  4713389  4713427  4713433  4713439  4713461  4713479  4713481  4713493  4713547
4713557  4713559  4713563  4713587  4713593  4713649  4713659  4713697  4713701  4713721
4713727  4713739  4713769  4713791  4713853  4713857  4713869  4713871  4713883  4713887
4713889  4713899  4713901  4713941  4713967  4713971  4713977  4713983  4713991  4714067
4714079  4714097  4714163  4714181  4714183  4714189  4714217  4714249  4714273  4714279
4714301  4714309  4714331  4714351  4714361  4714363  4714393  4714397  4714417  4714427
4714439  4714441  4714447  4714459  4714469  4714481  4714487  4714499  4714519  4714537
4714547  4714561  4714601  4714607  4714637  4714639  4714643  4714657  4714669  4714687
4714691  4714757  4714771  4714777  4714789  4714811  4714819  4714823  4714837  4714841
4714847  4714861  4714869  4714881  4714901  4714903  4714909  4714921  4714939  4714951
4714961  4714973  4714979  4714987  4714999  4715027  4715033  4715047  4715077  4715089
4715099  4715107  4715111  4715141  4715149  4715159  4715167  4715177  4715189  4715201
4715203  4715209  4715219  4715233  4715257  4715261  4715279  4715281  4715311  4715329
4715407  4715411  4715413  4715419  4715453  4715467  4715497  4715507  4715519  4715521
```

4715531	4715549	4715551	4715561	4715563	4715573	4715587	4715609	4715611	4715653
4715657	4715699	4715707	4715717	4715723	4715729	4715771	4715801	4715863	4715899
4715911	4715947	4715959	4715969	4716001	4716007	4716013	4716017	4716031	4716053
4716083	4716091	4716097	4716109	4716133	4716137	4716139	4716149	4716163	4716167
4716193	4716203	4716209	4716211	4716223	4716253	4716263	4716269	4716287	4716289
4716301	4716307	4716319	4716323	4716329	4716343	4716347	4716367	4716373	4716391
4716407	4716443	4716469	4716487	4716511	4716521	4716527	4716529	4716553	4716559
4716563	4716571	4716583	4716661	4716671	4716689	4716707	4716709	4716737	4716739
4716793	4716809	4716823	4716827	4716839	4716847	4716851	4716857	4716869	4716889
4716913	4716919	4716931	4716941	4716949	4716953	4716961	4716983	4717021	4717039
4717067	4717079	4717087	4717099	4717103	4717117	4717121	4717123	4717133	
4717151	4717157	4717183	4717199	4717213	4717217	4717247	4717253	4717259	4717283
4717289	4717303	4717319	4717351	4717367	4717373	4717387	4717393	4717397	4717409
4717421	4717429	4717451	4717469	4717511	4717513	4717519	4717543	4717547	4717561
4717571	4717577	4717589	4717597	4717607	4717613	4717631	4717639	4717649	4717651
4717667	4717717	4717729	4717733	4717751	4717753	4717777	4717793	4717819	4717837
4717841	4717861	4717873	4717877	4717897	4717913	4717919	4717927	4717961	4717963
4717997	4718009	4718029	4718033	4718071	4718083	4718093	4718111	4718149	4718183
4718191	4718201	4718221	4718249	4718257	4718269	4718279	4718281	4718317	4718353
4718353	4718369	4718419	4718429	4718437	4718443	4718449	4718477	4718491	4718507
4718509	4718521	4718531	4718557	4718563	4718569	4718579	4718617	4718621	4718627
4718653	4718663	4718671	4718683	4718689	4718699	4718711	4718713	4718723	4718737
4718771	4718773	4718837	4718849	4718867	4718881	4718891	4718927	4718947	4718951
4718963	4718971	4718981	4718983	4718999	4719007	4719031	4719041	4719053	4719061
4719073	4719079	4719097	4719107	4719109	4719119	4719133	4719167	4719181	4719191
4719229	4719241	4719259	4719269	4719271	4719287	4719289	4719307	4719311	4719329
4719331	4719343	4719361	4719401	4719443	4719457	4719479	4719493	4719541	4719571
4719593	4719607	4719641	4719643	4719647	4719661	4719667	4719677	4719679	4719691
4719707	4719713	4719731	4719751	4719763	4719791	4719811	4719821	4719839	4719857
4719889	4719893	4719901	4719907	4719917	4719943	4719973	4719977	4719989	4720003
4720019	4720039	4720049	4720057	4720087	4720097	4720099	4720141	4720147	4720159
4720187	4720193	4720211	4720223	4720229	4720231	4720259	4720273	4720283	4720291
4720297	4720307	4720321	4720327	4720333	4720343	4720361	4720367	4720369	4720381
4720393	4720403	4720427	4720433	4720477	4720481	4720501	4720517	4720553	4720559
4720561	4720601	4720603	4720613	4720621	4720627	4720637	4720663	4720693	4720697
4720741	4720777	4720787	4720811	4720817	4720843	4720853	4720871	4720879	4720889
4720901	4720907	4720909	4720913	4720921	4720931	4720943	4720981	4721011	4721047
4721077	4721107	4721137	4721149	4721153	4721173	4721179	4721201	4721221	4721243
4721261	4721263	4721303	4721323	4721333	4721341	4721351	4721369	4721377	4721383
4721407	4721411	4721419	4721441	4721449	4721467	4721477	4721491	4721513	4721527
4721531	4721569	4721581	4721609	4721617	4721627	4721653	4721657	4721659	4721663
4721677	4721687	4721719	4721723	4721729	4721737	4721741	4721749	4721753	4721779
4721791	4721813	4721819	4721839	4721879	4721887	4721891	4721897	4721911	4721933
4721957	4721963	4721999	4722001	4722031	4722049	4722077	4722079	4722083	4722097
4722101	4722103	4722121	4722163	4722169	4722173	4722187	4722197	4722229	4722233
4722239	4722269	4722271	4722283	4722293	4722299	4722313	4722343	4722371	4722373
4722397	4722407	4722409	4722433	4722449	4722463	4722479	4722491	4722493	4722499
4722533	4722539	4722547	4722551	4722587	4722631	4722661	4722703	4722709	4722713
4722721	4722761	4722769	4722799	4722829	4722841	4722847	4722863	4722869	4722871
4722899	4722919	4722931	4722941	4722947	4722953	4722959	4722961	4722967	4722979
4723021	4723049	4723051	4723057	4723091	4723097	4723139	4723183	4723193	4723207
4723219	4723223	4723237	4723247	4723283	4723321	4723337	4723351	4723361	4723373
4723391	4723409	4723423	4723427	4723451	4723463	4723517	4723561	4723573	4723591
4723601	4723633	4723661	4723699	4723721	4723727	4723759	4723777	4723783	4723813
4723847	4723861	4723877	4723879	4723921	4723933	4723949	4723981	4723987	4724047
4724051	4724053	4724063	4724077	4724087	4724089	4724099	4724101	4724117	4724173
4724201	4724207	4724219	4724221	4724227	4724231	4724233	4724243	4724309	4724327
4724329	4724339	4724353	4724381	4724383	4724429	4724441	4724479	4724491	4724497
4724509	4724513	4724519	4724537	4724557	4724561	4724569	4724611	4724627	4724647
4724653	4724659	4724663	4724669	4724677	4724689	4724693	4724723	4724747	4724771
4724801	4724807	4724809	4724813	4724831	4724851	4724873	4724879	4724887	4724891
4724903	4724917	4724947	4724953	4724981	4724987	4725001	4725029	4725059	4725067
4725089	4725101	4725131	4725137	4725139	4725151	4725169	4725179	4725191	4725197
4725199	4725221	4725223	4725241	4725247	4725257	4725271	4725283	4725293	4725311
4725317	4725323	4725341	4725353	4725389	4725389	4725397	4725401	4725431	4725437
4725451	4725467	4725493	4725499	4725503	4725527	4725551	4725569	4725587	4725601
4725607	4725613	4725629	4725631	4725641	4725647	4725659	4725667	4725673	4725683
4725691	4725713	4725727	4725739	4725757	4725781	4725821	4725827	4725839	4725863
4725883	4725887	4725893	4725911	4725923	4725943	4725953	4725967	4725997	4726009
4726013	4726021	4726031	4726037	4726067	4726069	4726081	4726123	4726133	4726151
4726157	4726181	4726199	4726213	4726237	4726243	4726261	4726277	4726279	4726301
4726303	4726369	4726387	4726409	4726427	4726441	4726457	4726471	4726481	4726483
4726499	4726537	4726543	4726583	4726591	4726597	4726607	4726619	4726669	4726679
4726721	4726723	4726741	4726747	4726759	4726769	4726793	4726817	4726819	4726831
4726859	4726919	4726921	4726927	4726957	4726963	4726993	4726999	4726999	4727069
4727081	4727089	4727147	4727171	4727183	4727189	4727197	4727201	4727209	4727227
4727237	4727243	4727249	4727279	4727287	4727293	4727297	4727299	4727311	4727329
4727339	4727347	4727353	4727381	4727399	4727417	4727449	4727461	4727473	4727477
4727483	4727497	4727501	4727519	4727533	4727537	4727557	4727563	4727573	4727579
4727617	4727623	4727633	4727641	4727647	4727687	4727689	4727707	4727711	4727731
4727743	4727747	4727761	4727771	4727791	4727797	4727809	4727813	4727837	4727851
4727867	4727869	4727881	4727939	4727953	4727969	4727977	4727981	4727993	4727999
4728001	4728011	4728013	4728019	4728037	4728043	4728047	4728109	4728121	4728127
4728149	4728173	4728181	4728203	4728211	4728221	4728233	4728239	4728253	4728287
4728301	4728313	4728343	4728349	4728379	4728401	4728403	4728413	4728433	4728487
4728497	4728527	4728539	4728551	4728553	4728557	4728599	4728611	4728613	4728617
4728631	4728649	4728677	4728697	4728733	4728743	4728749	4728761	4728767	4728797
4728799	4728883	4728887	4728917	4728931	4728947	4728973	4728989	4729033	4729037
4729069	4729133	4729139	4729189	4729199	4729211	4729217	4729223	4729261	4729297

4729321	4729327	4729331	4729337	4729339	4729343	4729367	4729369	4729393	4729397
4729427	4729433	4729447	4729457	4729477	4729481	4729531	4729547	4729567	4729573
4729579	4729583	4729591	4729603	4729609	4729631	4729649	4729663	4729687	4729691
4729693	4729759	4729777	4729793	4729799	4729811	4729819	4729831	4729843	4729849
4729867	4729873	4729877	4729891	4729897	4729903	4729913	4729919	4729937	4729943
4729979	4729981	4730003	4730009	4730023	4730027	4730039	4730041	4730057	4730059
4730071	4730081	4730101	4730153	4730171	4730177	4730179	4730213	4730227	4730229
4730251	4730269	4730287	4730291	4730311	4730317	4730347	4730353	4730357	4730359
4730381	4730389	4730417	4730431	4730447	4730461	4730477	4730483	4730533	4730603
4730647	4730653	4730689	4730699	4730701	4730707	4730711	4730717	4730723	4730729
4730771	4730779	4730807	4730809	4730813	4730819	4730821	4730837	4730839	4730851
4730861	4730863	4730897	4730909	4730923	4730933	4730951	4730953	4730959	4730963
4730969	4730987	4730993	4731011	4731037	4731043	4731053	4731059	4731061	4731091
4731101	4731109	4731119	4731163	4731173	4731191	4731211	4731239	4731241	4731271
4731281	4731289	4731299	4731319	4731341	4731367	4731371	4731373	4731383	4731403
4731409	4731431	4731439	4731451	4731479	4731481	4731487	4731527	4731539	4731541
4731557	4731577	4731599	4731613	4731637	4731669	4731679	4731689	4731691	4731697
4731707	4731719	4731733	4731751	4731821	4731833	4731847	4731889	4731907	4731929
4731941	4731943	4731971	4731973	4731983	4731989	4732003	4732019	4732027	4732031
4732033	4732037	4732061	4732067	4732073	4732081	4732087	4732093	4732109	4732139
4732157	4732163	4732177	4732183	4732187	4732199	4732229	4732237	4732241	4732271
4732297	4732303	4732309	4732313	4732333	4732361	4732369	4732373	4732417	4732433
4732447	4732459	4732471	4732489	4732499	4732513	4732543	4732547	4732561	4732583
4732591	4732601	4732603	4732619	4732621	4732639	4732643	4732649	4732657	4732661
4732667	4732669	4732703	4732711	4732751	4732757	4732769	4732837	4732841	4732867
4732877	4732891	4732901	4732927	4732979	4732991	4732993	4733011	4733017	4733023
4733063	4733083	4733093	4733117	4733129	4733167	4733189	4733203	4733207	4733221
4733233	4733237	4733243	4733251	4733257	4733263	4733269	4733273	4733279	4733291
4733317	4733329	4733341	4733347	4733353	4733369	4733371	4733381	4733387	4733389
4733401	4733411	4733419	4733437	4733441	4733461	4733471	4733473	4733479	4733501
4733507	4733513	4733537	4733549	4733563	4733587	4733591	4733611	4733623	4733627
4733639	4733647	4733681	4733689	4733719	4733723	4733753	4733767	4733789	4733797
4733809	4733843	4733851	4733857	4733863	4733867	4733881	4733893	4733903	4733941
4733951	4733959	4733969	4733987	4734017	4734029	4734031	4734043	4734061	4734073
4734091	4734139	4734151	4734167	4734193	4734203	4734217	4734253	4734259	4734299
4734319	4734329	4734349	4734383	4734397	4734407	4734427	4734461	4734463	4734469
4734487	4734503	4734523	4734529	4734547	4734559	4734563	4734571	4734581	4734589
4734593	4734623	4734647	4734671	4734673	4734677	4734679	4734701	4734703	4734727
4734767	4734787	4734787	4734797	4734797	4734799	4734811	4734817	4734833	4734839
4734841	4734871	4734893	4734911	4734929	4734937	4734949	4734979	4734991	4734997
4735037	4735043	4735063	4735103	4735121	4735127	4735147	4735151	4735153	4735169
4735177	4735189	4735193	4735201	4735229	4735253	4735267	4735271	4735273	4735301
4735319	4735331	4735349	4735361	4735363	4735387	4735417	4735433	4735441	4735453
4735481	4735513	4735531	4735559	4735561	4735573	4735589	4735609	4735651	4735669
4735681	4735697	4735699	4735711	4735727	4735733	4735751	4735793	4735799	4735817
4735823	4735849	4735859	4735867	4735879	4735909	4735919	4735931	4735933	4735937
4735967	4735987	4735993	4736023	4736041	4736051	4736057	4736071	4736093	4736099
4736131	4736153	4736177	4736189	4736231	4736243	4736257	4736261	4736269	4736299
4736311	4736323	4736341	4736351	4736357	4736359	4736383	4736401	4736429	4736437
4736441	4736447	4736649	4736477	4736497	4736507	4736513	4736531	4736573	4736581
4736647	4736653	4736701	4736713	4736717	4736723	4736729	4736731	4736737	4736749
4736759	4736779	4736789	4736791	4736803	4736807	4736819	4736839	4736843	4736861
4736881	4736887	4736891	4736903	4736911	4736929	4736939	4736957	4736983	4736993
4737037	4737053	4737071	4737097	4737107	4737113	4737119	4737127	4737133	4737143
4737151	4737163	4737217	4737223	4737233	4737253	4737277	4737283	4737301	4737307
4737311	4737319	4737329	4737347	4737349	4737367	4737371	4737377	4737409	4737413
4737433	4737437	4737449	4737461	4737487	4737493	4737497	4737521	4737529	4737533
4737539	4737541	4737547	4737569	4737581	4737599	4737619	4737661	4737671	4737721
4737727	4737731	4737743	4737749	4737763	4737767	4737769	4737779	4737787	4737797
4737827	4737847	4737851	4737899	4737907	4737911	4737923	4737949	4737959	4737979
4738003	4738007	4738023	4738031	4738057	4738061	4738073	4738079	4738099	4738141
4738157	4738169	4738177	4738193	4738241	4738249	4738259	4738273	4738289	4738303
4738351	4738361	4738367	4738369	4738379	4738403	4738421	4738423	4738439	4738451
4738463	4738457	4738463	4738477	4738523	4738537	4738549	4738561	4738577	4738583
4738589	4738603	4738607	4738609	4738651	4738777	4738781	4738793	4738807	4738817
4738831	4738837	4738841	4738881	4738873	4738883	4738891	4738933	4738949	4738957
4738969	4738991	4739017	4739023	4739027	4739041	4739047	4739089	4739099	4739117
4739143	4739153	4739171	4739183	4739213	4739221	4739237	4739239	4739257	4739279
4739291	4739297	4739327	4739363	4739377	4739381	4739407	4739443	4739473	4739479
4739489	4739491	4739519	4739521	4739563	4739573	4739599	4739599	4739659	4739687
4739689	4739699	4739717	4739729	4739743	4739803	4739831	4739837	4739857	4739879
4739893	4739899	4739929	4739947	4739989	4740023	4740037	4740053	4740077	4740089
4740097	4740103	4740143	4740149	4740157	4740167	4740193	4740199	4740217	4740223
4740227	4740247	4740257	4740259	4740271	4740287	4740289	4740299	4740319	4740349
4740353	4740361	4740383	4740389	4740397	4740409	4740413	4740419	4740469	4740499
4740509	4740511	4740521	4740523	4740559	4740583	4740623	4740641	4740643	4740647
4740649	4740653	4740667	4740679	4740683	4740713	4740721	4740727	4740731	4740779
4740787	4740803	4740817	4740887	4740893	4740907	4740961	4740971	4740979	4741003
4741019	4741039	4741049	4741057	4741067	4741073	4741081	4741097	4741111	4741129
4741133	4741169	4741207	4741207	4741229	4741237	4741259	4741267	4741271	4741301
4741307	4741333	4741339	4741361	4741397	4741403	4741441	4741447	4741459	4741463
4741483	4741511	4741547	4741553	4741559	4741577	4741579	4741601	4741603	4741613
4741673	4741673	4741717	4741717	4741727	4741733	4741741	4741747	4741753	4741769
4741787	4741801	4741813	4741829	4741837	4741859	4741879	4741897	4741901	4741931
4741951	4741969	4741973	4741991	4742011	4742021	4742027	4742029	4742047	4742057
4742063	4742081	4742107	4742113	4742119	4742131	4742137	4742141	4742147	4742173
4742189	4742197	4742207	4742219	4742239	4742251	4742261	4742273	4742279	4742317
4742321	4742329	4742351	4742357	4742359	4742377	4742383	4742407	4742417	4742431
4742443	4742447	4742467	4742471	4742483	4742489	4742519	4742557	4742603	4742611

```
4742641  4742651  4742671  4742681  4742687  4742693  4742701  4742707  4742713  4742719
4742753  4742809  4742821  4742827  4742831  4742861  4742873  4742887  4742891  4742897
4742909  4742939  4742953  4742957  4742971  4742977  4742981  4743001  4743007  4743019
4743041  4743049  4743073  4743091  4743107  4743113  4743133  4743139  4743149  4743161
4743191  4743197  4743199  4743223  4743241  4743247  4743257  4743281  4743283  4743307
4743311  4743317  4743329  4743337  4743383  4743461  4743469  4743503  4743509  4743587
4743593  4743601  4743623  4743637  4743671  4743677  4743691  4743701  4743703  4743707
4743709  4743719  4743737  4743743  4743769  4743779  4743797  4743821  4743839  4743841
4743847  4743857  4743859  4743883  4743887  4743923  4743941  4743953  4743971  4743983
4743989  4744001  4744021  4744027  4744057  4744063  4744093  4744097  4744099  4744109
4744111  4744127  4744163  4744171  4744183  4744199  4744211  4744213  4744219  4744237
4744247  4744261  4744277  4744297  4744301  4744307  4744331  4744349  4744373  4744379
4744387  4744391  4744393  4744409  4744423  4744459  4744469  4744511  4744543  4744573
4744589  4744591  4744609  4744639  4744657  4744669  4744703  4744711  4744741  4744787
4744793  4744811  4744837  4744849  4744897  4744907  4744913  4744937  4744963  4744997
4745021  4745029  4745047  4745051  4745063  4745071  4745087  4745089  4745099  4745123
4745131  4745137  4745149  4745177  4745189  4745197  4745243  4745267  4745281  4745303
4745317  4745339  4745369  4745401  4745413  4745423  4745441  4745467  4745491  4745513
4745537  4745539  4745551  4745561  4745579  4745591  4745593  4745597  4745603  4745623
4745641  4745651  4745681  4745683  4745701  4745707  4745729  4745743  4745749  4745761
4745773  4745813  4745833  4745837  4745849  4745869  4745881  4745903  4745911  4745921
4745929  4745957  4745963  4745987  4746011  4746017  4746031  4746041  4746047  4746059
4746061  4746089  4746139  4746149  4746151  4746163  4746173  4746191  4746229  4746233
4746239  4746251  4746253  4746263  4746271  4746289  4746299  4746311  4746341  4746359
4746377  4746407  4746419  4746431  4746437  4746457  4746473  4746493  4746499  4746551
4746559  4746569  4746571  4746589  4746607  4746617  4746647  4746649  4746659  4746667
4746673  4746683  4746701  4746737  4746739  4746743  4746769  4746773  4746787  4746799
4746803  4746817  4746821  4746823  4746877  4746881  4746919  4746983  4746997  4747009
4747033  4747073  4747079  4747091  4747121  4747129  4747139  4747159  4747181  4747217
4747229  4747231  4747241  4747279  4747291  4747297  4747313  4747331  4747339  4747343
4747357  4747381  4747427  4747441  4747451  4747481  4747487  4747489  4747493  4747531
4747537  4747559  4747577  4747583  4747597  4747601  4747609  4747651  4747657  4747661
4747667  4747669  4747679  4747703  4747727  4747741  4747747  4747751  4747753  4747819
4747829  4747871  4747889  4747903  4747927  4747933  4747937  4747943  4747949  4747957
4747961  4747969  4747973  4747997  4747999  4748011  4748033  4748039  4748047  4748063
4748071  4748077  4748113  4748123  4748131  4748153  4748171  4748201  4748207  4748209
4748221  4748231  4748279  4748299  4748351  4748371  4748377  4748399  4748407  4748411
4748413  4748437  4748449  4748467  4748477  4748479  4748483  4748503  4748509  4748519
4748521  4748531  4748563  4748581  4748587  4748591  4748621  4748629  4748633  4748647
4748683  4748699  4748707  4748713  4748719  4748749  4748753  4748771  4748813  4748819
4748867  4748887  4748903  4748929  4748941  4748957  4748999  4749013  4749029  4749037
4749047  4749053  4749083  4749091  4749097  4749131  4749139  4749179  4749191  4749193
4749203  4749223  4749229  4749253  4749257  4749263  4749271  4749289  4749299  4749377
4749391  4749421  4749427  4749463  4749467  4749497  4749499  4749527  4749529  4749551
4749557  4749571  4749581  4749593  4749607  4749629  4749631  4749637  4749659  4749671
4749691  4749709  4749751  4749757  4749761  4749763  4749779  4749781  4749793  4749803
4749827  4749839  4749853  4749883  4749907  4749911  4749967  4749989  4749991  4750001
4750003  4750013  4750063  4750069  4750073  4750087  4750091  4750103  4750117  4750127
4750129  4750159  4750169  4750189  4750199  4750217  4750241  4750279  4750297  4750303
4750307  4750313  4750363  4750373  4750379  4750387  4750391  4750411  4750423  4750439
4750457  4750477  4750517  4750561  4750579  4750609  4750631  4750639  4750643  4750651
4750661  4750679  4750699  4750717  4750723  4750729  4750771  4750787  4750789  4750813
4750829  4750831  4750841  4750849  4750853  4750861  4750873  4750877  4750889  4750919
4750891  4750919  4750927  4750951  4750987  4750997  4751011  4751017  4751051  4751053
4751057  4751077  4751101  4751111  4751137  4751161  4751167  4751209  4751213  4751221
4751231  4751237  4751261  4751267  4751269  4751293  4751303  4751333  4751359  4751393
4751441  4751459  4751477  4751479  4751489  4751491  4751519  4751557  4751567  4751599
4751611  4751627  4751641  4751657  4751701  4751713  4751723  4751741  4751743  4751749
4751753  4751779  4751783  4751807  4751809  4751849  4751893  4751909  4751917  4751951
4752001  4752017  4752019  4752031  4752043  4752047  4752067  4752089  4752091  4752113
4752131  4752133  4752157  4752161  4752173  4752179  4752193  4752199  4752221  4752229
4752247  4752257  4752263  4752277  4752289  4752301  4752313  4752323  4752347  4752359
4752361  4752379  4752409  4752411  4752443  4752481  4752521  4752551  4752569  4752577
4752581  4752599  4752623  4752677  4752691  4752731  4752733  4752739  4752767  4752773
4752791  4752817  4752821  4752823  4752841  4752851  4752871  4752887  4752899  4752901
4752929  4752931  4752949  4752977  4753003  4753009  4753033  4753037  4753051  4753061
4753087  4753109  4753121  4753123  4753127  4753159  4753169  4753201  4753207  4753213
4753219  4753267  4753277  4753289  4753313  4753393  4753403  4753423  4753449  4753459
4753537  4753543  4753549  4753561  4753577  4753589  4753601  4753613  4753643  4753657
4753681  4753711  4753739  4753741  4753753  4753787  4753789  4753813  4753823  4753831
4753841  4753849  4753877  4753891  4753901  4753919  4753921  4753927  4753937  4753961
4753963  4753981  4753993  4753997  4754011  4754017  4754021  4754027  4754039  4754051
4754053  4754063  4754083  4754107  4754111  4754131  4754147  4754159  4754159  4754177
4754227  4754273  4754287  4754303  4754317  4754329  4754333  4754357  4754359  4754371
4754413  4754429  4754437  4754443  4754447  4754459  4754479  4754507  4754513  4754531
4754549  4754551  4754591  4754597  4754599  4754609  4754621  4754623  4754627  4754653
4754663  4754669  4754677  4754681  4754741  4754779  4754791  4754837  4754851  4754861
4754863  4754903  4754909  4754929  4754933  4754947  4754957  4754963  4754977  4754993
4754999  4755013  4755017  4755031  4755061  4755067  4755077  4755103  4755119  4755137
4755143  4755151  4755173  4755193  4755197  4755209  4755211  4755229  4755239  4755253
4755269  4755281  4755299  4755323  4755337  4755347  4755349  4755371  4755389  4755397
4755403  4755419  4755433  4755437  4755451  4755463  4755469  4755479  4755481  4755497
4755511  4755521  4755523  4755533  4755539  4755557  4755559  4755571  4755581  4755589
4755599  4755629  4755649  4755677  4755689  4755691  4755701  4755703  4755761  4755781
4755791  4755811  4755827  4755853  4755857  4755899  4755911  4755923  4755941  4755967
4755979  4756013  4756019  4756021  4756027  4756033  4756067  4756079  4756093  4756121
4756133  4756159  4756181  4756183  4756253  4756307  4756333  4756337  4756343  4756357
4756373  4756417  4756421  4756429  4756439  4756459  4756483  4756489  4756513  4756523
4756537  4756553  4756579  4756603  4756613  4756621  4756627  4756637  4756649  4756657
```

```
4756663  4756679  4756693  4756709  4756711  4756723  4756747  4756751  4756769  4756771
4756793  4756811  4756819  4756847  4756853  4756867  4756877  4756891  4756901  4756931
4756937  4757009  4757033  4757041  4757057  4757101  4757117  4757119  4757147  4757153
4757173  4757177  4757183  4757189  4757209  4757231  4757267  4757273  4757281  4757309
4757323  4757339  4757341  4757351  4757359  4757383  4757393  4757411  4757419  4757447
4757449  4757453  4757461  4757471  4757491  4757507  4757521  4757531  4757549  4757551
4757561  4757567  4757591  4757593  4757609  4757647  4757659  4757677  4757707  4757713
4757723  4757743  4757749  4757759  4757777  4757783  4757861  4757869  4757881  4757887
4757899  4757957  4757971  4757983  4758007  4758023  4758031  4758041  4758043  4758049
4758071  4758073  4758077  4758101  4758107  4758121  4758157  4758167  4758179  4758197
4758209  4758223  4758239  4758269  4758277  4758301  4758323  4758343  4758367  4758373
4758389  4758437  4758443  4758449  4758503  4758511  4758517  4758553  4758557  4758571
4758587  4758617  4758619  4758629  4758643  4758653  4758659  4758661  4758673  4758679
4758701  4758707  4758713  4758727  4758731  4758737  4758749  4758751  4758757  4758791
4758799  4758811  4758821  4758823  4758833  4758847  4758857  4758863  4758893  4758913
4758931  4758937  4758959  4758961  4758973  4758991  4759003  4759009  4759021  4759081
4759093  4759109  4759123  4759127  4759129  4759163  4759169  4759171  4759189  4759193
4759217  4759231  4759301  4759309  4759327  4759331  4759351  4759357  4759373  4759387
4759397  4759411  4759427  4759429  4759457  4759463  4759477  4759493  4759533  4759543
4759553  4759561  4759571  4759577  4759583  4759591  4759607  4759621  4759637  4759639
4759661  4759663  4759679  4759697  4759721  4759723  4759739  4759751  4759753  4759787
4759793  4759817  4759837  4759841  4759871  4759901  4759903  4759907  4759913  4759927
4759933  4760003  4760009  4760023  4760027  4760039  4760047  4760069  4760071  4760099
4760101  4760117  4760123  4760137  4760167  4760177  4760183  4760201  4760209  4760213
4760219  4760227  4760233  4760237  4760243  4760251  4760269  4760281  4760291  4760311
4760347  4760363  4760369  4760419  4760429  4760443  4760449  4760467  4760543  4760579
4760597  4760603  4760617  4760627  4760647  4760653  4760687  4760689  4760713  4760719
4760759  4760761  4760779  4760783  4760801  4760807  4760809  4760851  4760881  4760891
4760893  4760927  4760929  4760939  4760941  4760981  4760999  4761007  4761013  4761019
4761041  4761059  4761061  4761079  4761083  4761101  4761109  4761121  4761137  4761143
4761151  4761203  4761209  4761217  4761223  4761247  4761269  4761283  4761301  4761311
4761313  4761319  4761329  4761349  4761373  4761397  4761403  4761413  4761431  4761469
4761487  4761499  4761509  4761511  4761517  4761521  4761527  4761551  4761553  4761557
4761563  4761583  4761619  4761629  4761643  4761661  4761677  4761689  4761697  4761703
4761727  4761733  4761763  4761769  4761773  4761791  4761803  4761811  4761857  4761917
4761923  4761947  4761973  4761979  4762013  4762031  4762039  4762073  4762099
4762111  4762117  4762133  4762151  4762187  4762211  4762213  4762231  4762237  4762253
4762259  4762267  4762271  4762309  4762321  4762327  4762333  4762337  4762361  4762367
4762399  4762441  4762451  4762469  4762477  4762489  4762493  4762501  4762507  4762523
4762583  4762799  4762801  4762811  4762841  4762843  4762859  4762867  4762889  4762913
4762943  4762949  4762957  4762969  4762997  4762999  4763021  4763041  4763071  4763081
4763089  4763107  4763117  4763123  4763131  4763137  4763149  4763159  4763197  4763201
4763203  4763207  4763233  4763237  4763249  4763267  4763273  4763299  4763321  4763327
4763329  4763333  4763351  4763359  4763387  4763393  4763399  4763401  4763443  4763449
4763459  4763477  4763527  4763531  4763557  4763581  4763609  4763641  4763653  4763659
4763663  4763683  4763701  4763753  4763789  4763797  4763809  4763833  4763839  4763849
4763879  4763923  4763929  4763933  4763939  4763959  4763971  4763981  4764037  4764043
4764103  4764121  4764143  4764181  4764187  4764203  4764211  4764217  4764229  4764239
4764257  4764293  4764311  4764317  4764337  4764341  4764371  4764373  4764391  4764401
4764407  4764413  4764433  4764469  4764481  4764493  4764509  4764511  4764517  4764521
4764547  4764559  4764563  4764577  4764581  4764583  4764619  4764629  4764631  4764667
4764673  4764689  4764691  4764707  4764713  4764751  4764757  4764769  4764779  4764791
4764821  4764853  4764857  4764869  4764901  4764911  4764923  4764937  4764967  4764983
4764989  4765003  4765021  4765027  4765039  4765051  4765063  4765069  4765073  4765087
4765093  4765099  4765109  4765121  4765127  4765129  4765133  4765141  4765157  4765171
4765183  4765199  4765207  4765213  4765223  4765249  4765331  4765339  4765361  4765379
4765391  4765399  4765417  4765427  4765451  4765463  4765469  4765487  4765499  4765511
4765529  4765543  4765573  4765583  4765597  4765603  4765609  4765613  4765619  4765633
4765667  4765687  4765693  4765697  4765699  4765721  4765727  4765741  4765757  4765759
4765769  4765771  4765781  4765793  4765801  4765829  4765837  4765841  4765867  4765879
4765883  4765897  4765907  4765927  4765931  4765939  4765973  4765987  4765997  4766009
4766029  4766057  4766059  4766071  4766087  4766107  4766117  4766123  4766147  4766189
4766213  4766261  4766263  4766287  4766297  4766299  4766309  4766329  4766351  4766369
4766371  4766381  4766383  4766387  4766431  4766459  4766491  4766501  4766533
4766539  4766557  4766561  4766563  4766611  4766621  4766627  4766633  4766651  4766689
4766711  4766717  4766719  4766753  4766761  4766791  4766803  4766807  4766837  4766843
4766863  4766887  4766899  4766903  4766917  4766941  4766977  4766981  4766999  4767013
4767017  4767019  4767053  4767067  4767079  4767083  4767121  4767143  4767151  4767167
4767173  4767179  4767181  4767197  4767229  4767239  4767241  4767253  4767277  4767299
4767311  4767331  4767337  4767341  4767353  4767379  4767383  4767391  4767409  4767419
4767421  4767431  4767449  4767457  4767473  4767479  4767481  4767493  4767527  4767533
4767569  4767589  4767611  4767617  4767643  4767649  4767661  4767673  4767751  4767761
4767773  4767779  4767781  4767799  4767817  4767823  4767853  4767899  4767947  4767949
4767953  4768003  4768019  4768021  4768033  4768051  4768063  4768067  4768073  4768087
4768091  4768097  4768129  4768133  4768139  4768163  4768171  4768193  4768207  4768219
4768223  4768237  4768243  4768271  4768273  4768307  4768331  4768339  4768349  4768369
4768391  4768397  4768403  4768417  4768427  4768459  4768471  4768481  4768493  4768501
4768507  4768529  4768541  4768549  4768583  4768607  4768609  4768627  4768633  4768661
4768681  4768689  4768693  4768703  4768727  4768747  4768763  4768769  4768783
4768801  4768817  4768831  4768849  4768861  4768873  4768879  4768889  4768901  4768909
4768913  4768921  4768927  4768937  4768961  4768969  4768987  4769011  4769047  4769053
4769059  4769081  4769111  4769113  4769117  4769153  4769159  4769201  4769207  4769213
4769227  4769239  4769269  4769273  4769279  4769291  4769339  4769351  4769357  4769377
4769447  4769449  4769459  4769473  4769519  4769521  4769539  4769549  4769573  4769581
4769593  4769623  4769647  4769657  4769669  4769693  4769711  4769719  4769759  4769767
4769771  4769789  4769803  4769873  4769877  4769881  4769887  4769903  4769909  4769917
4769923  4769957  4769959  4769971  4769977  4769987  4770011  4770019  4770023  4770037
4770043  4770061  4770067  4770071  4770079  4770097  4770109  4770127  4770163  4770173
```

```
4770191 4770221 4770253 4770263 4770281 4770287 4770313 4770317 4770323 4770329
4770343 4770347 4770379 4770397 4770401 4770427 4770433 4770439 4770443 4770449
4770487 4770509 4770511 4770517 4770527 4770541 4770551 4770569 4770581 4770593
4770599 4770611 4770629 4770631 4770643 4770671 4770677 4770713 4770737 4770763
4770793 4770827 4770839 4770841 4770851 4770911 4770929 4770967 4770971 4770977
4771001 4771021 4771037 4771049 4771069 4771093 4771121 4771159 4771163 4771171
4771177 4771181 4771229 4771243 4771267 4771279 4771289 4771297 4771307 4771321
4771331 4771381 4771391 4771397 4771411 4771433 4771439 4771447 4771463 4771493
4771519 4771541 4771549 4771567 4771579 4771589 4771619 4771633 4771687 4771699
4771709 4771763 4771777 4771813 4771817 4771829 4771841 4771843 4771873 4771889
4771891 4771903 4771909 4771939 4771967 4771973 4771993 4771997 4771999 4772057
4772069 4772071 4772077 4772107 4772111 4772137 4772143 4772147 4772177 4772179
4772191 4772227 4772237 4772281 4772309 4772323 4772353 4772381 4772387 4772399
4772413 4772437 4772459 4772479 4772483 4772489 4772503 4772507 4772513 4772531
4772557 4772561 4772623 4772653 4772659 4772671 4772683 4772717 4772731 4772759
4772771 4772797 4772821 4772837 4772839 4772861 4772863 4772909 4772939 4772951
4772953 4772993 4773019 4773049 4773053 4773059 4773061 4773089 4773133 4773143
4773157 4773169 4773173 4773191 4773203 4773227 4773229 4773239 4773257 4773269
4773283 4773289 4773331 4773359 4773383 4773403 4773409 4773449 4773451 4773479
4773497 4773499 4773523 4773529 4773533 4773553 4773557 4773599 4773607 4773611
4773641 4773701 4773707 4773709 4773737 4773739 4773757 4773767 4773773 4773779
4773793 4773809 4773823 4773829 4773833 4773841 4773859 4773863 4773877 4773887
4773913 4773929 4773941 4773953 4773961 4773983 4774001 4774051 4774069 4774123
4774129 4774151 4774171 4774177 4774181 4774199 4774201 4774249 4774261 4774267
4774283 4774321 4774349 4774351 4774361 4774379 4774387 4774391 4774411 4774417
4774423 4774439 4774459 4774469 4774477 4774489 4774499 4774513 4774519 4774543
4774559 4774571 4774579 4774597 4774613 4774619 4774663 4774667 4774673 4774687
4774699 4774709 4774723 4774727 4774733 4774747 4774751 4774753 4774769 4774793
4774801 4774817 4774829 4774831 4774843 4774859 4774867 4774873 4774877 4774883
4774921 4774949 4774951 4774967 4774969 4774993 4774999 4775027 4775039 4775051
4775063 4775077 4775087 4775093 4775119 4775123 4775131 4775143 4775159 4775167
4775171 4775201 4775207 4775219 4775231 4775233 4775293 4775297 4775299 4775321
4775339 4775357 4775359 4775369 4775371 4775377 4775383 4775413 4775417 4775423
4775431 4775437 4775447 4775461 4775477 4775489 4775497 4775503 4775539 4775543
4775549 4775569 4775591 4775621 4775647 4775653 4775681 4775689 4775711 4775713
4775723 4775741 4775747 4775791 4775809 4775819 4775839 4775843 4775851 4775863
4775887 4775909 4775917 4775921 4775933 4775941 4775951 4775959 4775977 4775993
4776001 4776017 4776029 4776073 4776113 4776127 4776137 4776143 4776151 4776173
4776209 4776217 4776221 4776223 4776251 4776287 4776313 4776323 4776347 4776403
4776451 4776461 4776481 4776487 4776491 4776517 4776521 4776523 4776529 4776539
4776599 4776601 4776637 4776641 4776647 4776671 4776679 4776683 4776689 4776691
4776713 4776721 4776749 4776767 4776769 4776803 4776833 4776839 4776841 4776853
4776857 4776887 4776907 4776929 4776931 4776953 4776977 4776979 4777001 4777009
4777027 4777043 4777057 4777061 4777063 4777081 4777099 4777103 4777139 4777163
4777183 4777207 4777211 4777217 4777219 4777237 4777247 4777249 4777273 4777277
4777351 4777363 4777433 4777453 4777463 4777469 4777471 4777481 4777499 4777501
4777517 4777523 4777559 4777567 4777573 4777621 4777679 4777681 4777711 4777723
4777727 4777733 4777739 4777769 4777781 4777789 4777793 4777807 4777811 4777819
4777823 4777831 4777891 4777907 4777909 4777933 4777939 4777943 4777961 4777967
4778009 4778021 4778027 4778029 4778041 4778051 4778077 4778107 4778113 4778119
4778129 4778153 4778167 4778171 4778183 4778197 4778231 4778237 4778303 4778311
4778339 4778341 4778357 4778381 4778383 4778387 4778399 4778407 4778413 4778429
4778437 4778441 4778453 4778459 4778483 4778489 4778491 4778539 4778567 4778569
4778593 4778603 4778611 4778659 4778663 4778693 4778701 4778713 4778723 4778729
4778731 4778759 4778777 4778783 4778791 4778803 4778827 4778831 4778833 4778843
4778863 4778869 4778927 4778933 4778953 4778981 4778993 4779029 4779037 4779067
4779079 4779107 4779119 4779143 4779157 4779163 4779191 4779199 4779209 4779221
4779251 4779277 4779337 4779343 4779347 4779349 4779353 4779371 4779427 4779433
4779443 4779449 4779491 4779497 4779503 4779517 4779521 4779547 4779553 4779557
4779563 4779589 4779631 4779661 4779701 4779743 4779757 4779769 4779779 4779799
4779829 4779851 4779871 4779877 4779889 4779913 4779949 4779953 4779959 4779961
4779979 4779989 4779991 4779997 4780007 4780033 4780037 4780051 4780079 4780081
4780093 4780117 4780133 4780151 4780177 4780183 4780187 4780199 4780201 4780241
4780261 4780283 4780291 4780337 4780361 4780379 4780397 4780403 4780409 4780411
4780427 4780429 4780453 4780459 4780463 4780471 4780483 4780487 4780499 4780507
4780513 4780543 4780549 4780561 4780597 4780637 4780639 4780649 4780663 4780667
4780669 4780673 4780681 4780687 4780693 4780703 4780729 4780739 4780751 4780771
4780777 4780781 4780819 4780823 4780861 4780871 4780877 4780891 4780903 4780931
4780933 4780939 4780943 4780949 4780957 4780967 4780973 4781009 4781011 4781017
4781039 4781047 4781057 4781089 4781111 4781129 4781137 4781167 4781173 4781191
4781197 4781237 4781243 4781323 4781333 4781341 4781351 4781383 4781389 4781411
4781417 4781429 4781431 4781443 4781449 4781489 4781507 4781519 4781527 4781531
4781551 4781561 4781587 4781611 4781629 4781653 4781659 4781663 4781669 4781671
4781731 4781737 4781747 4781759 4781761 4781767 4781783 4781807 4781831 4781837
4781867 4781873 4781911 4781923 4781929 4781941 4781951 4781963 4781971 4781983
4781989 4781993 4782023 4782061 4782077 4782097 4782101 4782103 4782119 4782121
4782131 4782133 4782143 4782161 4782179 4782191 4782223 4782227 4782241 4782251
4782263 4782269 4782301 4782311 4782317 4782329 4782341 4782359 4782383 4782397
4782409 4782431 4782443 4782469 4782473 4782487 4782493 4782497 4782511 4782523
4782529 4782539 4782571 4782577 4782607 4782637 4782641 4782647 4782671 4782677
4782683 4782697 4782707 4782719 4782749 4782769 4782787 4782803 4782821 4782823
4782829 4782839 4782853 4782871 4782881 4782893 4782907 4782913 4782961 4782971
4782977 4782991 4782997 4783039 4783043 4783061 4783067 4783099 4783109
4783147 4783151 4783157 4783169 4783187 4783223 4783279 4783283 4783291 4783321
4783327 4783343 4783349 4783369 4783391 4783399 4783411 4783433 4783439 4783447
4783451 4783469 4783487 4783489 4783501 4783523 4783531 4783553 4783567 4783577
4783589 4783631 4783643 4783651 4783673 4783687 4783699 4783717 4783721 4783729
4783739 4783741 4783769 4783781 4783793 4783819 4783837 4783853 4783859
4783861 4783873 4783973 4783979 4783993 4783997 4784009 4784057 4784071 4784093
```

```
4784107  4784141  4784149  4784183  4784237  4784239  4784243  4784267  4784279  4784281
4784287  4784303  4784317  4784321  4784341  4784401  4784411  4784419  4784431  4784443
4784467  4784501  4784503  4784543  4784597  4784617  4784627  4784629  4784641  4784669
4784677  4784683  4784693  4784699  4784747  4784753  4784777  4784807  4784809
4784821  4784833  4784839  4784863  4784869  4784887  4784909  4784921  4784947  4784953
4784957  4784963  4785031  4785043  4785059  4785091  4785101  4785113  4785119  4785161
4785181  4785197  4785227  4785239  4785251  4785271  4785281  4785289  4785293  4785307
4785323  4785331  4785343  4785367  4785371  4785373  4785379  4785383  4785401  4785419
4785421  4785463  4785467  4785499  4785503  4785509  4785523  4785527  4785553  4785559
4785581  4785593  4785601  4785607  4785611  4785623  4785629  4785647  4785669  4785673
4785707  4785733  4785761  4785769  4785773  4785787  4785791  4785793  4785799  4785827
4785881  4785901  4785931  4785941  4785947  4785961  4786007  4786013  4786037  4786049
4786051  4786079  4786091  4786097  4786109  4786141  4786147  4786193  4786213  4786219
4786241  4786253  4786259  4786261  4786267  4786291  4786297  4786303  4786321  4786343
4786393  4786399  4786403  4786409  4786429  4786447  4786451  4786471  4786477  4786541
4786543  4786559  4786577  4786583  4786603  4786619  4786633  4786657  4786667  4786669
4786697  4786703  4786739  4786751  4786753  4786763  4786777  4786799  4786807  4786861
4786811  4786819  4786823  4786861  4786883  4786897  4786913  4786937  4786939  4786961
4786963  4786973  4786983  4786987  4787039  4787053  4787063  4787077  4787089  4787093
4787099  4787161  4787173  4787177  4787179  4787213  4787231  4787239  4787249  4787257
4787261  4787273  4787281  4787311  4787329  4787339  4787347  4787371  4787441  4787477
4787483  4787507  4787513  4787527  4787533  4787537  4787551  4787567  4787569  4787593
4787597  4787599  4787603  4787621  4787633  4787641  4787647  4787669  4787683  4787701
4787719  4787729  4787737  4787747  4787767  4787779  4787789  4787803  4787831
4787833  4787869  4787873  4787879  4787903  4787941  4787957  4787963  4787969  4787971
4788011  4788023  4788037  4788061  4788079  4788083  4788097  4788109  4788127  4788131
4788197  4788221  4788233  4788241  4788257  4788283  4788307  4788331  4788337  4788379
4788389  4788397  4788401  4788403  4788419  4788457  4788461  4788463  4788473  4788481
4788491  4788493  4788517  4788533  4788541  4788559  4788569  4788583  4788593  4788613
4788631  4788647  4788653  4788661  4788673  4788731  4788733  4788739  4788757  4788767
4788769  4788803  4788811  4788821  4788863  4788871  4788881  4788887  4788897  4788907
4788929  4788937  4788941  4788961  4788989  4789003  4789013  4789033  4789061  4789069
4789073  4789091  4789123  4789139  4789177  4789193  4789199  4789201  4789219  4789231
4789237  4789241  4789247  4789249  4789277  4789303  4789339  4789363  4789373  4789381
4789399  4789409  4789453  4789471  4789487  4789513  4789517  4789541  4789549  4789559
4789567  4789573  4789583  4789591  4789601  4789619  4789621  4789633  4789637  4789639
4789651  4789667  4789721  4789739  4789747  4789777  4789783  4789789  4789793  4789823
4789831  4789853  4789877  4789949  4789951  4789963  4789969  4789973  4789987  4789991
4789999  4790011  4790029  4790047  4790053  4790063  4790111  4790117  4790143  4790167
4790237  4790239  4790273  4790293  4790297  4790309  4790321  4790339  4790351  4790363
4790369  4790377  4790389  4790393  4790419  4790437  4790459  4790473  4790483  4790503
4790521  4790537  4790551  4790557  4790573  4790579  4790593  4790609  4790627  4790671
4790699  4790707  4790743  4790749  4790761  4790827  4790857  4790893  4790897  4790911
4790963  4790971  4790987  4790999  4791011  4791013  4791023  4791043  4791049  4791067
4791077  4791089  4791109  4791181  4791187  4791197  4791221  4791223  4791239  4791247
4791257  4791277  4791299  4791307  4791343  4791373  4791377  4791379  4791403  4791407
4791431  4791443  4791481  4791491  4791497  4791503  4791511  4791517
4791557  4791559  4791623  4791643  4791649  4791653  4791737  4791767  4791769  4791771
4791799  4791811  4791817  4791847  4791851  4791859  4791863  4791881  4791883  4791901
4791911  4791923  4791929  4791937  4791947  4791953  4791959  4791961  4791973  4792001
4792013  4792019  4792031  4792057  4792063  4792069  4792097  4792127  4792133  4792141
4792153  4792159  4792169  4792201  4792241  4792247  4792297  4792301  4792331  4792339
4792369  4792387  4792391  4792409  4792439  4792451  4792457  4792471  4792481  4792519
4792547  4792553  4792603  4792607  4792609  4792633  4792639  4792643  4792661  4792663
4792703  4792727  4792729  4792751  4792783  4792787  4792789  4792811  4792829  4792841
4792849  4792867  4792871  4792873  4792889  4792913  4792927  4792933  4792951  4792967
4792987  4792999  4793011  4793027  4793029  4793051  4793059  4793069  4793077  4793123
4793147  4793167  4793183  4793203  4793209  4793221  4793227  4793231  4793233  4793237
4793317  4793363  4793413  4793417  4793429  4793431  4793471  4793489  4793501  4793513
4793519  4793531  4793533  4793543  4793557  4793587  4793599  4793603  4793627  4793639
4793651  4793653  4793669  4793687  4793713  4793741  4793749  4793753  4793771  4793851
4793853  4793861  4793863  4793879  4793897  4793923  4793951  4793963  4793969  4793981
4794001  4794037  4794043  4794059  4794067  4794071  4794073  4794103  4794149  4794151
4794161  4794191  4794197  4794203  4794211  4794217  4794239  4794241  4794247  4794259
4794263  4794269  4794281  4794299  4794301  4794331  4794337  4794343  4794347  4794353
4794379  4794407  4794437  4794443  4794463  4794473  4794481  4794523  4794533  4794551
4794577  4794607  4794619  4794637  4794641  4794653  4794679  4794683  4794709  4794733
4794743  4794749  4794761  4794767  4794781  4794791  4794809  4794817  4794841  4794877
4794899  4794913  4794931  4794949  4794953  4794961  4794983  4794997  4795013  4795039
4795051  4795067  4795081  4795093  4795097  4795103  4795129  4795157  4795171  4795183
4795187  4795199  4795223  4795243  4795249  4795253  4795261  4795313  4795331
4795333  4795337  4795367  4795369  4795433  4795451  4795481  4795501  4795507  4795519
4795529  4795561  4795603  4795613  4795627  4795631  4795663  4795667  4795699  4795709
4795711  4795723  4795727  4795741  4795757  4795781  4795787  4795789  4795801  4795807
4795831  4795841  4795867  4795871  4795883  4795897  4795909  4795913  4795919  4795939
4795951  4795963  4795969  4795993  4795997  4796017  4796039  4796047  4796053  4796081
4796083  4796087  4796089  4796111  4796119  4796131  4796149  4796153  4796179  4796191
4796203  4796237  4796249  4796257  4796279  4796291  4796317  4796357  4796371  4796381
4796383  4796387  4796399  4796411  4796423  4796437  4796461  4796479  4796483  4796501
4796509  4796543  4796573  4796593  4796609  4796621  4796633  4796639  4796647  4796651
4796657  4796677  4796699  4796707  4796711  4796749  4796761  4796767  4796783  4796789
4796807  4796837  4796843  4796851  4796879  4796893  4796899  4796921  4796923  4796929
4796983  4796987  4796993  4797007  4797017  4797031  4797059  4797061  4797071  4797073
4797167  4797173  4797193  4797211  4797227  4797229  4797241  4797251  4797259  4797263
4797269  4797277  4797281  4797301  4797311  4797313  4797361  4797371  4797389  4797407
4797413  4797439  4797469  4797497  4797503  4797511  4797517  4797521  4797539  4797563
4797571  4797577  4797581  4797599  4797607  4797629  4797631  4797643  4797647  4797659
4797677  4797701  4797707  4797721  4797733  4797739  4797769  4797781  4797809  4797851
4797857  4797883  4797913  4797941  4797953  4797959  4797971  4797973  4798009  4798019
```

```
4798033  4798039  4798061  4798081  4798091  4798121  4798163  4798181  4798193  4798219
4798229  4798243  4798259  4798307  4798309  4798331  4798333  4798337  4798349  4798357
4798361  4798373  4798379  4798439  4798477  4798481  4798483  4798489  4798511  4798523
4798531  4798537  4798571  4798609  4798627  4798639  4798649  4798657  4798669  4798679
4798693  4798711  4798721  4798727  4798733  4798751  4798793  4798817  4798823  4798837
4798861  4798867  4798877  4798889  4798901  4798907  4798919  4798921  4798933  4798967
4798987  4798993  4798999  4799021  4799023  4799027  4799059  4799071  4799087  4799099
4799129  4799131  4799189  4799213  4799227  4799231  4799243  4799251  4799261  4799279
4799281  4799299  4799303  4799317  4799323  4799339  4799351  4799369  4799383  4799393
4799401  4799407  4799429  4799437  4799453  4799467  4799477  4799507  4799551  4799563
4799573  4799623  4799651  4799659  4799689  4799693  4799713  4799719  4799731  4799771
4799777  4799783  4799791  4799833  4799843  4799849  4799857  4799863  4799867  4799897
4799909  4799923  4799941  4799953  4799957  4799981  4799983  4799987  4799999  4800007
4800023  4800043  4800049  4800053  4800067  4800073  4800083  4800091  4800101  4800113
4800149  4800163  4800193  4800199  4800209  4800221  4800241  4800253  4800281  4800287
4800317  4800347  4800361  4800373  4800401  4800421  4800427  4800431  4800437  4800451
4800487  4800541  4800547  4800557  4800599  4800619  4800623  4800641  4800659  4800661
4800667  4800683  4800703  4800707  4800709  4800737  4800773  4800779  4800781  4800799
4800811  4800827  4800841  4800853  4800857  4800881  4800893  4800911  4800931  4800937
4800941  4800947  4800973  4800989  4801033  4801039  4801051  4801057  4801061  4801099
4801109  4801117  4801133  4801151  4801163  4801169  4801171  4801177  4801183  4801189
4801201  4801207  4801213  4801253  4801267  4801289  4801309  4801339  4801351  4801369
4801393  4801409  4801441  4801451  4801499  4801507  4801513  4801519  4801553  4801561
4801579  4801603  4801607  4801609  4801613  4801627  4801631  4801673  4801679  4801691
4801697  4801711  4801717  4801723  4801729  4801781  4801789  4801793  4801829  4801847
4801861  4801873  4801903  4801921  4801933  4801949  4801969  4801999  4802011  4802047
4802051  4802059  4802071  4802087  4802089  4802093  4802099  4802107  4802123  4802129
4802137  4802153  4802191  4802209  4802219  4802243  4802249  4802257  4802293  4802299
4802321  4802323  4802327  4802333  4802339  4802353  4802393  4802411  4802443  4802461
4802491  4802513  4802519  4802521  4802527  4802531  4802533  4802537  4802543  4802557
4802569  4802599  4802621  4802641  4802657  4802683  4802689  4802723  4802729  4802731
4802741  4802771  4802779  4802783  4802803  4802813  4802843  4802851  4802873  4802879
4802881  4802899  4802911  4802921  4802927  4802939  4802947  4802989  4803031  4803037
4803049  4803053  4803059  4803091  4803103  4803119  4803137  4803151  4803157  4803167
4803173  4803179  4803187  4803193  4803209  4803217  4803223  4803247  4803277  4803283
4803301  4803307  4803317  4803319  4803341  4803347  4803361  4803373  4803391  4803397
4803413  4803427  4803439  4803467  4803479  4803493  4803497  4803509  4803511  4803529
4803563  4803569  4803581  4803583  4803593  4803607  4803641  4803649  4803653  4803677
4803679  4803709  4803719  4803737  4803749  4803767  4803769  4803781  4803787  4803799
4803857  4803871  4803881  4803899  4803907  4803913  4803919  4803923  4803947  4803949
4803959  4803961  4803971  4803983  4803989  4803991  4804021  4804027  4804049  4804061
4804087  4804091  4804109  4804133  4804157  4804159  4804187  4804201  4804213  4804231
4804249  4804253  4804271  4804273  4804277  4804297  4804307  4804333  4804337  4804351
4804361  4804363  4804399  4804409  4804417  4804427  4804439  4804463  4804529  4804567
4804571  4804573  4804577  4804589  4804607  4804619  4804627  4804643  4804661  4804697
4804699  4804703  4804711  4804717  4804733  4804741  4804753  4804759  4804781  4804799
4804823  4804837  4804841  4804867  4804883  4804889  4804937  4804939  4804957  4804979
4804991  4804993  4804997  4805011  4805041  4805063  4805069  4805111  4805149  4805161
4805179  4805189  4805191  4805231  4805249  4805257  4805267  4805287  4805291  4805303
4805357  4805393  4805401  4805419  4805429  4805431  4805443  4805453  4805467  4805513
4805531  4805533  4805539  4805557  4805579  4805587  4805599  4805621  4805629  4805639
4805653  4805657  4805659  4805683  4805693  4805699  4805707  4805711  4805719  4805737
4805743  4805753  4805761  4805791  4805821  4805831  4805861  4805903  4805929  4805939
4805953  4805959  4806001  4806013  4806029  4806071  4806077  4806127  4806161  4806167
4806181  4806187  4806211  4806233  4806283  4806299  4806301  4806313  4806323  4806341
4806367  4806377  4806383  4806391  4806401  4806407  4806409  4806413  4806419  4806421
4806433  4806437  4806443  4806463  4806469  4806493  4806499  4806509  4806523  4806541
4806551  4806577  4806587  4806589  4806649  4806661  4806667  4806673  4806689  4806709
4806713  4806719  4806731  4806743  4806751  4806773  4806803  4806821  4806827  4806853
4806863  4806871  4806877  4806883  4806887  4806899  4806911  4806917  4806947  4806959
4806961  4806973  4807001  4807021  4807027  4807031  4807063  4807079  4807081  4807087
4807091  4807093  4807097  4807109  4807129  4807147  4807169  4807181  4807199  4807217
4807219  4807241  4807303  4807337  4807343  4807393  4807409  4807423  4807427  4807433
4807441  4807459  4807463  4807469  4807477  4807487  4807493  4807501  4807519  4807531
4807559  4807631  4807639  4807643  4807679  4807681  4807687  4807717  4807757  4807793
4807807  4807813  4807819  4807841  4807849  4807877  4807909  4807921  4807951  4807961
4807967  4807973  4808003  4808009  4808017  4808021  4808033  4808051  4808071  4808077
4808101  4808123  4808129  4808137  4808207  4808227  4808231  4808233  4808239  4808249
4808257  4808267  4808269  4808299  4808327  4808329  4808339  4808351  4808359  4808369
4808383  4808393  4808417  4808469  4808491  4808497  4808507  4808513  4808527  4808533
4808543  4808579  4808593  4808599  4808611  4808621  4808623  4808641  4808659  4808701
4808707  4808717  4808719  4808737  4808747  4808777  4808803  4808821  4808827  4808857
4808873  4808911  4808929  4808933  4808939  4808959  4808963  4808987  4809017  4809023
4809037  4809097  4809107  4809121  4809137  4809143  4809187  4809197  4809209  4809251
4809253  4809257  4809263  4809271  4809281  4809289  4809307  4809319  4809347  4809349
4809359  4809377  4809383  4809401  4809443  4809457  4809473  4809479  4809509  4809547
4809559  4809577  4809583  4809643  4809653  4809661  4809671  4809677  4809683  4809689
4809703  4809719  4809773  4809731  4809787  4809797  4809809  4809811  4809887  4809899
4809901  4809941  4809943  4809947  4809949  4809977  4810019  4810063  4810081  4810087
4810103  4810129  4810147  4810153  4810159  4810163  4810171  4810187  4810193  4810199
4810217  4810229  4810261  4810307  4810313  4810343  4810349  4810397  4810411  4810441
4810457  4810469  4810483  4810493  4810499  4810501  4810511  4810513  4810517  4810579
4810583  4810649  4810661  4810691  4810697  4810721  4810727  4810733  4810739  4810753
4810787  4810789  4810807  4810823  4810837  4810843  4810849  4810853  4810867  4810877
4810879  4810891  4810901  4810903  4810907  4810913  4810943  4810961  4810973  4810987
4811057  4811087  4811089  4811101  4811111  4811137  4811159  4811167  4811171  4811189
4811197  4811239  4811263  4811267  4811269  4811281  4811299  4811311  4811321  4811329
4811363  4811371  4811381  4811383  4811407  4811413  4811441  4811447  4811449  4811453
4811461  4811483  4811507  4811533  4811537  4811549  4811551  4811567  4811581  4811647
```

```
4811659  4811687  4811701  4811713  4811717  4811777  4811783  4811791  4811797  4811809
4811819  4811831  4811839  4811843  4811861  4811869  4811909  4811927  4811953  4811993
4812011  4812043  4812053  4812061  4812077  4812079  4812089  4812097  4812113  4812121
4812131  4812133  4812151  4812169  4812179  4812191  4812193  4812209  4812239  4812251
4812271  4812281  4812287  4812299  4812307  4812329  4812337  4812349  4812371  4812373
4812383  4812413  4812419  4812421  4812427  4812433  4812481  4812487  4812499  4812503
4812523  4812527  4812569  4812583  4812607  4812611  4812631  4812641  4812653  4812707
4812713  4812721  4812733  4812739  4812761  4812767  4812779  4812791  4812799  4812827
4812851  4812859  4812883  4812889  4812931  4812937  4812943  4812991  4813027  4813051
4813063  4813069  4813073  4813093  4813103  4813139  4813177  4813183  4813189  4813201
4813229  4813243  4813283  4813297  4813307  4813309  4813313  4813321  4813337  4813349
4813373  4813399  4813421  4813423  4813433  4813439  4813451  4813469  4813477  4813483
4813511  4813531  4813537  4813541  4813561  4813573  4813577  4813579  4813583  4813591
4813597  4813607  4813621  4813639  4813643  4813651  4813667  4813673  4813691  4813717
4813723  4813741  4813747  4813759  4813793  4813799  4813801  4813817  4813829  4813841
4813843  4813849  4813909  4813943  4813951  4813957  4813961  4813991  4813997  4814039
4814053  4814093  4814123  4814129  4814137  4814143  4814167  4814171  4814191  4814209
4814219  4814221  4814231  4814233  4814263  4814273  4814287  4814321  4814357  4814363
4814399  4814413  4814449  4814461  4814471  4814473  4814489  4814503  4814533  4814597
4814599  4814603  4814617  4814629  4814647  4814651  4814683  4814707  4814713  4814717
4814743  4814759  4814779  4814789  4814801  4814833  4814837  4814863  4814867  4814881
4814903  4814911  4814947  4814959  4814963  4814987  4815023  4815047  4815053  4815059
4815067  4815071  4815101  4815121  4815127  4815179  4815193  4815221  4815229  4815253
4815259  4815281  4815289  4815311  4815329  4815337  4815359  4815367  4815389  4815397
4815443  4815451  4815457  4815463  4815467  4815469  4815529  4815553  4815581  4815583
4815589  4815593  4815599  4815617  4815619  4815623  4815631  4815647  4815673  4815677
4815689  4815697  4815731  4815773  4815787  4815791  4815799  4815817  4815821  4815823
4815847  4815857  4815887  4815917  4815931  4815973  4815989  4815997  4816003  4816033
4816037  4816051  4816061  4816069  4816073  4816079  4816087  4816103  4816109  4816121
4816153  4816157  4816169  4816183  4816187  4816193  4816213  4816243  4816249  4816267
4816277  4816283  4816297  4816303  4816309  4816337  4816351  4816363  4816373  4816417
4816421  4816433  4816459  4816463  4816517  4816531  4816541  4816561  4816597  4816619
4816649  4816657  4816663  4816673  4816681  4816717  4816727  4816751  4816787  4816789
4816837  4816841  4816843  4816849  4816859  4816883  4816897  4816901  4816907  4816909
4816921  4816949  4816957  4816963  4816969  4817003  4817009  4817017  4817027  4817039
4817041  4817047  4817053  4817083  4817093  4817101  4817107  4817119  4817123  4817129
4817149  4817177  4817179  4817209  4817221  4817257  4817261  4817269  4817339  4817357
4817381  4817387  4817399  4817411  4817441  4817467  4817471  4817479  4817497  4817513
4817537  4817539  4817543  4817551  4817573  4817581  4817627  4817629  4817633  4817639
4817651  4817653  4817663  4817669  4817689  4817707  4817713  4817717  4817731  4817737
4817761  4817779  4817789  4817797  4817809  4817819  4817821  4817867  4817873  4817899
4817921  4817929  4817933  4817941  4817947  4817959  4817977  4818013  4818043  4818053
4818061  4818091  4818119  4818133  4818137  4818161  4818167  4818169  4818181
4818199  4818211  4818221  4818239  4818241  4818269  4818271  4818277  4818287  4818301
4818347  4818349  4818383  4818409  4818413  4818421  4818461  4818467  4818469  4818481
4818491  4818503  4818509  4818521  4818551  4818559  4818577  4818587  4818617  4818629
4818637  4818677  4818679  4818691  4818719  4818721  4818743  4818757  4818767  4818773
4818791  4818797  4818829  4818887  4818889  4818893  4818899  4818907  4818923  4818941
4818953  4819021  4819033  4819039  4819049  4819069  4819081  4819091  4819093  4819123
4819127  4819147  4819151  4819153  4819159  4819163  4819169  4819189  4819201  4819223
4819271  4819273  4819327  4819357  4819369  4819379  4819411  4819413  4819423
4819447  4819469  4819471  4819499  4819501  4819513  4819519  4819531  4819537  4819543
4819579  4819603  4819609  4819631  4819637  4819643  4819667  4819669  4819697  4819729
4819733  4819739  4819751  4819783  4819799  4819807  4819813  4819817  4819831  4819847
4819853  4819861  4819889  4819909  4819937  4819943  4819961  4819963  4819967  4819981
4819987  4820009  4820021  4820033  4820051  4820069  4820093  4820107  4820113  4820131
4820149  4820161  4820173  4820183  4820201  4820203  4820219  4820227  4820237  4820239
4820251  4820269  4820327  4820341  4820369  4820383  4820419  4820423  4820437
4820441  4820443  4820447  4820479  4820483  4820489  4820533  4820579  4820587  4820617
4820633  4820653  4820663  4820681  4820689  4820719  4820747  4820759  4820791  4820807
4820833  4820857  4820899  4820909  4820923  4820929  4820939  4820951  4820983
4820987  4821017  4821029  4821043  4821049  4821059  4821073  4821077  4821083  4821097
4821101  4821109  4821127  4821143  4821161  4821191  4821199  4821209  4821239  4821241
4821247  4821263  4821281  4821293  4821317  4821331  4821373  4821389  4821407  4821451
4821473  4821489  4821503  4821517  4821529  4821541  4821563  4821613  4821617  4821629
4821631  4821637  4821643  4821653  4821667  4821671  4821689  4821721  4821731  4821737
4821749  4821767  4821769  4821779  4821793  4821797  4821799  4821821  4821847  4821853
4821889  4821899  4821907  4821911  4821913  4821931  4821937  4821997  4822001  4822003
4822007  4822031  4822039  4822061  4822073  4822079  4822117  4822121  4822123  4822141
4822159  4822163  4822187  4822189  4822193  4822199  4822201  4822211  4822229  4822231
4822273  4822277  4822291  4822309  4822313  4822319  4822331  4822343  4822351  4822361
4822369  4822393  4822421  4822423  4822427  4822451  4822481  4822513  4822541  4822553
4822567  4822589  4822591  4822621  4822627  4822633  4822661  4822667  4822669  4822687
4822703  4822711  4822723  4822759  4822771  4822777  4822799  4822819  4822859  4822879
4822889  4822907  4822919  4822921  4822931  4822943  4822963  4822967  4822973  4822991
4822997  4823003  4823023  4823033  4823059  4823081  4823083  4823099  4823111  4823149
4823167  4823171  4823173  4823201  4823219  4823227  4823233  4823297  4823303  4823339
4823347  4823369  4823381  4823389  4823407  4823417  4823437  4823447  4823459  4823471
4823479  4823521  4823557  4823573  4823591  4823627  4823639  4823641  4823677  4823681
4823719  4823723  4823729  4823743  4823761  4823779  4823803  4823807  4823809  4823821
4823837  4823839  4823843  4823849  4823851  4823887  4823909  4823911  4823957  4823981
4823983  4823999  4824011  4824031  4824037  4824047  4824091  4824103  4824109  4824133
4824151  4824161  4824163  4824167  4824187  4824191  4824203  4824223  4824247  4824257
4824263  4824283  4824317  4824329  4824331  4824359  4824373  4824383  4824401  4824403
4824419  4824427  4824433  4824439  4824473  4824479  4824493  4824517  4824529  4824559
4824563  4824569  4824581  4824619  4824629  4824647  4824649  4824653  4824671  4824697
4824739  4824751  4824773  4824791  4824847  4824863  4824881  4824893  4824907  4824929
4824943  4824959  4824971  4824977  4824997  4825001  4825013  4825019  4825021  4825027
4825091  4825109  4825129  4825169  4825187  4825189  4825199  4825201  4825211  4825217
```

4825267 4825307 4825333 4825343 4825351 4825361 4825369 4825427 4825441 4825453
4825517 4825523 4825529 4825549 4825559 4825621 4825627 4825633 4825643 4825673
4825693 4825759 4825763 4825789 4825813 4825817 4825831 4825853 4825871 4825879
4825889 4825897 4825901 4825903 4825921 4825937 4825939 4825963 4825967 4825969
4825979 4825991 4825993 4826027 4826033 4826051 4826053 4826071 4826119 4826153
4826161 4826179 4826197 4826207 4826231 4826273 4826279 4826281 4826291 4826293
4826309 4826357 4826369 4826401 4826407 4826431 4826447 4826473 4826491 4826501
4826531 4826537 4826543 4826587 4826597 4826611 4826641 4826693 4826713 4826719
4826729 4826753 4826771 4826777 4826797 4826813 4826831 4826863 4826867 4826897
4826903 4826911 4826923 4826933 4826951 4826953 4827029 4827037 4827059 4827071
4827073 4827107 4827139 4827157 4827169 4827191 4827211 4827233 4827239 4827241
4827257 4827259 4827287 4827307 4827313 4827359 4827373 4827377 4827391 4827409
4827419 4827421 4827437 4827443 4827457 4827461 4827491 4827499 4827521 4827523
4827533 4827547 4827553 4827569 4827583 4827587 4827617 4827619 4827623 4827673
4827671 4827703 4827707 4827721 4827737 4827751 4827763 4827773 4827799 4827817
4827821 4827827 4827829 4827853 4827859 4827863 4827869 4827877 4827899 4827913
4827943 4827959 4827973 4827989 4828009 4828049 4828067 4828069 4828073 4828079
4828099 4828111 4828121 4828129 4828133 4828139 4828163 4828171 4828177 4828207
4828217 4828237 4828249 4828253 4828303 4828349 4828363 4828379 4828381 4828393
4828399 4828403 4828409 4828429 4828433 4828457 4828469 4828477 4828519 4828531
4828543 4828553 4828567 4828573 4828583 4828613 4828631 4828661 4828669 4828723
4828727 4828729 4828739 4828751 4828763 4828787 4828801 4828807 4828843 4828847
4828871 4828927 4828937 4828961 4828979 4828987 4828991 4828997 4829009 4829047
4829081 4829089 4829093 4829101 4829107 4829117 4829137 4829141 4829147 4829161
4829171 4829177 4829183 4829197 4829219 4829257 4829263 4829269 4829317 4829323
4829329 4829347 4829359 4829369 4829371 4829389 4829423 4829437 4829441 4829443
4829449 4829453 4829467 4829497 4829501 4829509 4829543 4829549 4829551 4829557
4829593 4829603 4829651 4829653 4829663 4829711 4829723 4829729 4829749 4829761
4829771 4829777 4829779 4829789 4829809 4829843 4829911 4829947 4829953 4829969
4829983 4829999 4830011 4830043 4830053 4830071 4830073 4830103 4830107 4830113
4830127 4830149 4830151 4830167 4830197 4830223 4830229 4830247 4830263 4830277
4830281 4830289 4830307 4830349 4830359 4830361 4830373 4830377 4830383 4830401
4830409 4830421 4830439 4830481 4830487 4830547 4830569 4830571 4830593 4830599
4830607 4830611 4830619 4830649 4830659 4830677 4830689 4830719 4830751 4830797
4830799 4830817 4830827 4830841 4830853 4830857 4830869 4830871 4830877 4830899
4830913 4830923 4830937 4830967 4831019 4831037 4831039 4831051 4831069 4831091
4831121 4831147 4831159 4831163 4831193 4831237 4831243 4831273 4831283 4831289
4831291 4831297 4831363 4831367 4831373 4831391 4831441 4831457 4831493 4831507
4831531 4831549 4831559 4831577 4831591 4831601 4831613 4831637 4831657 4831669
4831693 4831699 4831703 4831709 4831733 4831751 4831759 4831787 4831789 4831807
4831823 4831829 4831831 4831837 4831843 4831889 4831901 4831903 4831907 4831933
4831949 4831963 4831987 4831991 4831999 4832017 4832021 4832027 4832033 4832053
4832059 4832071 4832081 4832123 4832147 4832167 4832171 4832173 4832203 4832207
4832209 4832221 4832239 4832257 4832263 4832273 4832281 4832287 4832293 4832309
4832329 4832339 4832353 4832363 4832411 4832413 4832417 4832419 4832423 4832467
4832483 4832489 4832521 4832537 4832543 4832549 4832551 4832557 4832561 4832563
4832567 4832579 4832591 4832609 4832651 4832677 4832689 4832693 4832701 4832719
4832741 4832747 4832759 4832761 4832767 4832797 4832801 4832809 4832833 4832837
4832851 4832857 4832887 4832909 4832929 4832939 4832941 4832953 4832987 4832999
4833019 4833029 4833047 4833067 4833109 4833131 4833133 4833137 4833139 4833149
4833161 4833167 4833181 4833187 4833193 4833209 4833211 4833233 4833247 4833271
4833307 4833371 4833379 4833383 4833397 4833443 4833463 4833487 4833523 4833533
4833553 4833571 4833583 4833617 4833623 4833641 4833649 4833683 4833721 4833727
4833739 4833743 4833761 4833767 4833779 4833821 4833853 4833863 4833869 4833877
4833883 4833901 4833911 4833937 4833943 4833947 4833953 4833977 4833989 4833991
4834021 4834073 4834079 4834111 4834121 4834127 4834129 4834147 4834201 4834211
4834217 4834223 4834229 4834231 4834241 4834267 4834321 4834327 4834331 4834363
4834381 4834397 4834399 4834411 4834441 4834451 4834469 4834471 4834489 4834499
4834513 4834523 4834537 4834549 4834553 4834573 4834589 4834601 4834631 4834639
4834649 4834663 4834673 4834699 4834699 4834723 4834727 4834733 4834747 4834777
4834801 4834813 4834829 4834847 4834849 4834861 4834871 4834883 4834889 4834891
4834897 4834961 4834979 4834981 4834993 4834997 4835003 4835011 4835023 4835027
4835057 4835071 4835081 4835099 4835111 4835113 4835143 4835147 4835153 4835161
4835179 4835203 4835213 4835231 4835249 4835251 4835261 4835263 4835269 4835273
4835279 4835297 4835321 4835333 4835357 4835381 4835387 4835461 4835471 4835477
4835483 4835503 4835513 4835521 4835527 4835533 4835539 4835549 4835563 4835569
4835573 4835617 4835629 4835639 4835647 4835683 4835693 4835707 4835711 4835713
4835717 4835723 4835731 4835749 4835767 4835771 4835791 4835797 4835801 4835807
4835821 4835833 4835839 4835843 4835849 4835851 4835867 4835891 4835893 4835903
4835917 4835921 4835923 4835927 4835933 4835947 4835951 4835977 4835983 4835989
4836037 4836059 4836067 4836101 4836107 4836113 4836119 4836121 4836131 4836133
4836149 4836151 4836157 4836173 4836193 4836229 4836239 4836257 4836259 4836269
4836277 4836281 4836283 4836353 4836367 4836383 4836413 4836451 4836457 4836467
4836497 4836521 4836523 4836539 4836553 4836563 4836569 4836577 4836587 4836593
4836607 4836613 4836631 4836641 4836679 4836701 4836703 4836737 4836743 4836749
4836757 4836763 4836779 4836781 4836787 4836809 4836827 4836829 4836859 4836919
4836929 4836943 4836947 4836967 4836971 4836977 4836989 4837003 4837009 4837033
4837051 4837073 4837087 4837141 4837169 4837187 4837201 4837213 4837219 4837223
4837237 4837241 4837247 4837277 4837297 4837307 4837309 4837331 4837369 4837373
4837379 4837411 4837423 4837433 4837439 4837447 4837451 4837453 4837463 4837471
4837477 4837493 4837499 4837501 4837513 4837517 4837531 4837541 4837559 4837561
4837579 4837589 4837603 4837633 4837649 4837661 4837669 4837687 4837697 4837709
4837717 4837733 4837739 4837759 4837769 4837771 4837793 4837817 4837831 4837841
4837853 4837871 4837873 4837879 4837883 4837919 4837927 4837933 4837939 4837967
4837969 4837991 4837997 4838017 4838021 4838023 4838033 4838063 4838087 4838089
4838101 4838107 4838111 4838117 4838131 4838143 4838159 4838167 4838189 4838209
4838213 4838261 4838279 4838297 4838333 4838341 4838347 4838363 4838377 4838399
4838443 4838461 4838467 4838473 4838497 4838501 4838507 4838543 4838551 4838569
4838593 4838599 4838609 4838611 4838633 4838653 4838681 4838683 4838689 4838699

```
4838707 4838719 4838753 4838789 4838797 4838819 4838831 4838839 4838843 4838851
4838857 4838881 4838887 4838891 4838893 4838903 4838917 4838923 4838927 4838963
4838989 4839001 4839013 4839047 4839049 4839071 4839077 4839103 4839113 4839127
4839137 4839151 4839157 4839179 4839187 4839227 4839229 4839253 4839257 4839283
4839311 4839347 4839403 4839409 4839421 4839437 4839469 4839487 4839529 4839539
4839581 4839587 4839613 4839631 4839649 4839671 4839673 4839691 4839719 4839721
4839727 4839761 4839767 4839797 4839803 4839811 4839817 4839833 4839847 4839871
4839881 4839893 4839899 4839911 4839929 4839941 4839949 4839953 4839977 4839997
4840027 4840049 4840103 4840127 4840133 4840139 4840151 4840159 4840169 4840177
4840211 4840217 4840219 4840243 4840249 4840259 4840261 4840267 4840313 4840333
4840349 4840357 4840379 4840387 4840399 4840417 4840439 4840441 4840447 4840457
4840489 4840499 4840541 4840559 4840571 4840579 4840601 4840637 4840657
4840663 4840679 4840711 4840723 4840727 4840729 4840751 4840753 4840757 4840789
4840793 4840813 4840819 4840841 4840921 4840931 4840933 4840939 4840943 4840949
4840963 4840981 4841003 4841051 4841071 4841087 4841101 4841119 4841149 4841153
4841183 4841197 4841203 4841261 4841279 4841297 4841303 4841323 4841341 4841351
4841359 4841377 4841381 4841383 4841393 4841399 4841401 4841407 4841461 4841467
4841483 4841491 4841519 4841527 4841531 4841533 4841563 4841581 4841587 4841593
4841609 4841633 4841647 4841657 4841687 4841693 4841699 4841729 4841737 4841741
4841743 4841777 4841779 4841801 4841819 4841849 4841887 4841897 4841899 4841909
4841933 4841951 4841981 4842007 4842031 4842067 4842073 4842077 4842083 4842091
4842109 4842113 4842139 4842179 4842181 4842197 4842203 4842221 4842247 4842251
4842287 4842289 4842317 4842329 4842347 4842349 4842361 4842367 4842371 4842403
4842407 4842427 4842493 4842521 4842533 4842577 4842583 4842589 4842599 4842611
4842631 4842641 4842653 4842679 4842683 4842689 4842707 4842709 4842731 4842737
4842743 4842749 4842767 4842781 4842787 4842821 4842847 4842863 4842869 4842883
4842911 4842917 4842923 4842941 4842953 4842983 4843001 4843009 4843019 4843057
4843061 4843093 4843103 4843117 4843127 4843129 4843151 4843171 4843183 4843211
4843213 4843231 4843243 4843247 4843259 4843277 4843297 4843343 4843357 4843367
4843381 4843403 4843417 4843427 4843429 4843441 4843451 4843457 4843507 4843541
4843561 4843571 4843603 4843621 4843637 4843669 4843681 4843687 4843693
4843697 4843747 4843757 4843789 4843819 4843831 4843873 4843877 4843913 4843933
4843939 4843973 4843981 4843991 4844017 4844023 4844039 4844051 4844057 4844087
4844093 4844101 4844123 4844137 4844141 4844143 4844171 4844179 4844227 4844233
4844239 4844267 4844293 4844311 4844317 4844321 4844327 4844347 4844377 4844381
4844383 4844387 4844437 4844419 4844443 4844459 4844491 4844501 4844527 4844531
4844561 4844573 4844599 4844603 4844617 4844629 4844633 4844641 4844647 4844659
4844669 4844717 4844729 4844747 4844761 4844797 4844809 4844831 4844839 4844843
4844887 4844899 4844909 4844911 4844921 4844933 4844947 4844951 4844977 4844989
4845013 4845023 4845031 4845037 4845041 4845073 4845077 4845079 4845143 4845151
4845173 4845199 4845241 4845251 4845259 4845263 4845271 4845293 4845299 4845353
4845359 4845367 4845389 4845397 4845443 4845461 4845473 4845481 4845487 4845499
4845539 4845569 4845583 4845593 4845601 4845613 4845647 4845661 4845671 4845683
4845689 4845707 4845719 4845721 4845727 4845761 4845767 4845793 4845811 4845823
4845851 4845859 4845877 4845881 4845899 4845917 4845943 4845989 4845991 4846019
4846021 4846027 4846033 4846063 4846069 4846073 4846087 4846091 4846109 4846111
4846117 4846129 4846147 4846157 4846181 4846183 4846187 4846211 4846213 4846271
4846279 4846321 4846333 4846339 4846357 4846367 4846379 4846409 4846421 4846427
4846441 4846469 4846477 4846481 4846529 4846553 4846561 4846603
4846627 4846631 4846679 4846693 4846697 4846727 4846739 4846753 4846759 4846771
4846789 4846801 4846811 4846817 4846823 4846837 4846873 4846879 4846883 4846901
4846927 4846937 4846939 4846987 4847021 4847039 4847041 4847053 4847081 4847083
4847093 4847107 4847137 4847149 4847153 4847177 4847189 4847231 4847237 4847239
4847257 4847267 4847279 4847291 4847309 4847317 4847341 4847371 4847387 4847443
4847449 4847461 4847467 4847473 4847477 4847497 4847537 4847543 4847551 4847561
4847569 4847573 4847593 4847597 4847621 4847639 4847653 4847657 4847659 4847671
4847681 4847683 4847699 4847719 4847729 4847743 4847747 4847753 4847807 4847819
4847827 4847833 4847861 4847867 4847891 4847893 4847897 4847923 4847933 4847939
4847957 4847981 4847987 4847989 4848001 4848007 4848023 4848029 4848037 4848071
4848079 4848083 4848091 4848119 4848139 4848163 4848167 4848169 4848199 4848223
4848227 4848229 4848241 4848251 4848253 4848269 4848289 4848299 4848323 4848359
4848391 4848407 4848413 4848421 4848427 4848499 4848509 4848523 4848527 4848533
4848541 4848559 4848563 4848577 4848583 4848601 4848643 4848653 4848673 4848709
4848719 4848721 4848731 4848763 4848773 4848787 4848839 4848847 4848869 4848871
4848881 4848889 4848901 4848911 4848913 4848929 4848937 4848953 4848959 4848979
4848997 4849001 4849007 4849027 4849043 4849049 4849057 4849079 4849081 4849121
4849147 4849157 4849189 4849211 4849213 4849219 4849223 4849249 4849261 4849277
4849279 4849283 4849291 4849307 4849337 4849349 4849367 4849379 4849381 4849399
4849417 4849459 4849477 4849487 4849517 4849529 4849531 4849543 4849567 4849577
4849589 4849591 4849597 4849613 4849631 4849639 4849651 4849687 4849697 4849703
4849721 4849723 4849727 4849753 4849759 4849787 4849813 4849843 4849861 4849907
4849909 4849951 4849967 4849973 4850009 4850011 4850017 4850023 4850051 4850059
4850077 4850101 4850107 4850123 4850137 4850159 4850161 4850179 4850191 4850207
4850231 4850239 4850243 4850273 4850297 4850303 4850317 4850327 4850347 4850353
4850369 4850371 4850383 4850387 4850393 4850399 4850413 4850459 4850467 4850471
4850501 4850513 4850519 4850533 4850543 4850557 4850563 4850581 4850597 4850617
4850621 4850623 4850633 4850641 4850647 4850653 4850689 4850707 4850711 4850749
4850753 4850761 4850819 4850843 4850887 4850891 4850939 4850941 4850957 4850969
4850987 4851013 4851017 4851029 4851053 4851071 4851073 4851083 4851109 4851113
4851127 4851139 4851151 4851163 4851169 4851173 4851179 4851191 4851193 4851211
4851227 4851233 4851241 4851277 4851299 4851317 4851331 4851337 4851347 4851377
4851383 4851397 4851463 4851491 4851493 4851529 4851541 4851547 4851557 4851565
4851563 4851569 4851577 4851617 4851619 4851659 4851661 4851683 4851697 4851703
4851709 4851719 4851731 4851761 4851793 4851797 4851809 4851829 4851839 4851877
4851883 4851893 4851901 4851907 4851923 4851929 4851941 4851947 4851949 4851953
4851989 4852007 4852039 4852051 4852061 4852079 4852093 4852117 4852171 4852181
4852189 4852223 4852247 4852261 4852271 4852273 4852279 4852283 4852301
4852303 4852313 4852321 4852339 4852349 4852363 4852381 4852387 4852409 4852411
4852423 4852427 4852447 4852451 4852453 4852457 4852459 4852469 4852481 4852487
```

```
4852493  4852537  4852567  4852577  4852591  4852607  4852621  4852643  4852663  4852669
4852681  4852693  4852697  4852699  4852711  4852741  4852753  4852787  4852807  4852811
4852817  4852843  4852849  4852873  4852879  4852901  4852909  4852919  4852963  4852979
4852997  4853039  4853053  4853059  4853077  4853083  4853087  4853089  4853111  4853117
4853171  4853183  4853203  4853243  4853249  4853273  4853287  4853297  4853309  4853323
4853333  4853351  4853383  4853389  4853393  4853423  4853441  4853461  4853467  4853473
4853477  4853479  4853503  4853507  4853509  4853533  4853573  4853599  4853609  4853617
4853657  4853659  4853671  4853677  4853699  4853729  4853731  4853791  4853803  4853819
4853837  4853909  4853917  4853921  4853957  4853983  4853999  4854001  4854037  4854053
4854077  4854079  4854121  4854137  4854151  4854167  4854169  4854181  4854193  4854203
4854211  4854229  4854233  4854247  4854251  4854257  4854263  4854307  4854337  4854361
4854371  4854373  4854379  4854389  4854391  4854407  4854413  4854431  4854433  4854439
4854457  4854497  4854539  4854547  4854581  4854589  4854599  4854607  4854617  4854623
4854637  4854653  4854667  4854691  4854701  4854727  4854737  4854739  4854761  4854763
4854779  4854781  4854793  4854797  4854799  4854821  4854827  4854833  4854841  4854847
4854893  4854917  4854923  4854931  4854961  4854989  4855007  4855027  4855031  4855033
4855049  4855057  4855063  4855069  4855073  4855079  4855099  4855129  4855133  4855153
4855163  4855211  4855219  4855223  4855237  4855273  4855297  4855327  4855363  4855391
4855471  4855483  4855511  4855519  4855531  4855537  4855541  4855549  4855559  4855567
4855579  4855597  4855601  4855651  4855667  4855679  4855681  4855699  4855703  4855717
4855787  4855801  4855813  4855817  4855831  4855867  4855891  4855901  4855919  4855951
4855957  4855973  4855987  4856003  4856011  4856023  4856029  4856053  4856063  4856083
4856143  4856147  4856161  4856177  4856183  4856207  4856219  4856233  4856261  4856263
4856273  4856279  4856297  4856303  4856309  4856321  4856323  4856351  4856359  4856369
4856399  4856417  4856447  4856461  4856479  4856503  4856531  4856561  4856567  4856569
4856597  4856603  4856639  4856653  4856669  4856701  4856707  4856711  4856741  4856771
4856777  4856779  4856783  4856791  4856809  4856827  4856843  4856869  4856899  4856903
4856921  4856923  4856947  4856963  4856981  4857023  4857037  4857059  4857067  4857089
4857091  4857113  4857131  4857143  4857161  4857169  4857187  4857199  4857211  4857221
4857227  4857233  4857253  4857269  4857271  4857277  4857287  4857289  4857329  4857337
4857341  4857343  4857371  4857373  4857389  4857449  4857451  4857481  4857487  4857499
4857511  4857527  4857533  4857547  4857551  4857569  4857637  4857649  4857659  4857679
4857683  4857691  4857707  4857719  4857739  4857751  4857781  4857791  4857799  4857829
4857893  4857943  4857949  4857953  4857959  4857973  4857997  4858019  4858031  4858043
4858057  4858067  4858079  4858081  4858093  4858111  4858159  4858163  4858171  4858177
4858193  4858207  4858229  4858247  4858253  4858279  4858291  4858297  4858307  4858309
4858327  4858331  4858349  4858361  4858393  4858411  4858417  4858423  4858453  4858463
4858487  4858493  4858499  4858517  4858519  4858523  4858559  4858561  4858577  4858603
4858627  4858643  4858657  4858673  4858703  4858717  4858739  4858751  4858781  4858783
4858793  4858811  4858817  4858823  4858831  4858837  4858859  4858879  4858891  4858897
4858901  4858933  4858943  4858949  4858961  4858963  4858967  4858981  4859017  4859081
4859083  4859087  4859123  4859137  4859167  4859171  4859177  4859201  4859207  4859209
4859227  4859237  4859243  4859249  4859273  4859287  4859317  4859341  4859353  4859357
4859359  4859419  4859429  4859431  4859441  4859461  4859479  4859507  4859513  4859521
4859531  4859539  4859549  4859551  4859557  4859563  4859581  4859593  4859597  4859627
4859629  4859651  4859713  4859717  4859741  4859747  4859749  4859759  4859819  4859821
4859837  4859861  4859863  4859891  4859947  4859957  4859971  4859993  4859999  4860013
4860041  4860043  4860049  4860059  4860077  4860083  4860091  4860101  4860103  4860133
4860137  4860151  4860157  4860179  4860203  4860217  4860227  4860241  4860269  4860277
4860281  4860293  4860299  4860301  4860307  4860311  4860329  4860341  4860343  4860347
4860389  4860391  4860407  4860421  4860431  4860443  4860449  4860451  4860461  4860463
4860481  4860511  4860517  4860533  4860547  4860553  4860601  4860607  4860617  4860629
4860631  4860643  4860689  4860701  4860721  4860749  4860761  4860773  4860799  4860803
4860809  4860829  4860847  4860853  4860859  4860871  4860883  4860901  4860931  4860937
4860953  4860959  4860971  4860991  4861013  4861033  4861049  4861057  4861063  4861111
4861121  4861139  4861217  4861237  4861243  4861261  4861267  4861271  4861277  4861301
4861313  4861361  4861399  4861403  4861421  4861427  4861429  4861471  4861501  4861529
4861547  4861553  4861561  4861567  4861573  4861601  4861603  4861607  4861621  4861631
4861667  4861673  4861679  4861691  4861697  4861729  4861733  4861751  4861771  4861781
4861799  4861807  4861811  4861859  4861867  4861877  4861889  4861907  4861921  4861939
4861943  4861951  4861957  4861979  4861991  4861999  4862003  4862027  4862041  4862047
4862063  4862087  4862089  4862101  4862107  4862141  4862161  4862171  4862173  4862219
4862243  4862251  4862261  4862279  4862303  4862339  4862353  4862383  4862399  4862411
4862413  4862437  4862441  4862471  4862489  4862509  4862519  4862531  4862549  4862579
4862581  4862593  4862609  4862621  4862699  4862717  4862743  4862747  4862771  4862777
4862791  4862797  4862813  4862831  4862843  4862863  4862911  4862941  4862983  4862989
4863007  4863011  4863013  4863017  4863029  4863059  4863073  4863077  4863083  4863091
4863101  4863103  4863109  4863179  4863217  4863223  4863233  4863239  4863263  4863269
4863277  4863283  4863293  4863301  4863323  4863337  4863349  4863371  4863401  4863403
4863437  4863457  4863461  4863467  4863473  4863491  4863493  4863553  4863569  4863577
4863589  4863611  4863623  4863629  4863631  4863641  4863653  4863671  4863673  4863679
4863709  4863721  4863737  4863767  4863769  4863779  4863797  4863799  4863809  4863821
4863823  4863827  4863839  4863841  4863847  4863877  4863913  4863919  4863923  4863941
4863959  4863961  4863979  4864003  4864009  4864021  4864033  4864039  4864043  4864051
4864061  4864073  4864081  4864087  4864121  4864141  4864151  4864169  4864177  4864187
4864207  4864217  4864229  4864231  4864243  4864253  4864271  4864273  4864283  4864297
4864309  4864313  4864319  4864369  4864417  4864429  4864451  4864493  4864511  4864529
4864553  4864573  4864577  4864601  4864603  4864619  4864667  4864681  4864709  4864729
4864759  4864777  4864781  4864787  4864789  4864801  4864813  4864823  4864831  4864843
4864859  4864889  4864901  4864903  4864907  4864919  4864927  4864949  4864967  4864987
4865023  4865033  4865051  4865059  4865087  4865089  4865123  4865129  4865131  4865137
4865141  4865143  4865207  4865219  4865221  4865227  4865257  4865261  4865263  4865303
4865327  4865353  4865431  4865447  4865459  4865467  4865477  4865479  4865507  4865521
4865551  4865557  4865561  4865569  4865573  4865603  4865629  4865647  4865657  4865659
4865683  4865699  4865711  4865717  4865737  4865743  4865747  4865753  4865761  4865799
4865803  4865821  4865827  4865849  4865891  4865899  4865929  4865933  4865947  4865951
4865953  4865963  4865969  4865989  4865999  4866007  4866011  4866013  4866019  4866023
4866047  4866049  4866061  4866073  4866091  4866139  4866149  4866151  4866187  4866193
4866209  4866221  4866227  4866241  4866263  4866283  4866307  4866313  4866341  4866343
```

```
4866359  4866371  4866383  4866391  4866401  4866443  4866469  4866481  4866503  4866517
4866541  4866551  4866557  4866559  4866569  4866581  4866583  4866599  4866601  4866623
4866629  4866643  4866649  4866677  4866683  4866703  4866707  4866727  4866737  4866749
4866761  4866773  4866791  4866821  4866847  4866857  4866859  4866863  4866877  4866893
4866899  4866919  4866923  4866929  4866941  4866949  4866973  4866977  4866989  4866997
4867003  4867013  4867019  4867033  4867063  4867067  4867073  4867103  4867123  4867133
4867139  4867147  4867171  4867207  4867223  4867229  4867243  4867259  4867297  4867301
4867307  4867309  4867319  4867327  4867333  4867337  4867339  4867399  4867409  4867411
4867417  4867433  4867451  4867453  4867457  4867469  4867481  4867487  4867501  4867543  4867607
4867619  4867631  4867637  4867653  4867657  4867691  4867693  4867711  4867717  4867753  4867771
4867777  4867799  4867801  4867813  4867817  4867823  4867843  4867871  4867873  4867879
4867903  4867909  4867921  4867939  4867949  4867957  4867963  4867999  4868011  4868029
4868041  4868107  4868113  4868131  4868141  4868167  4868173  4868177  4868189  4868207
4868221  4868231  4868233  4868243  4868251  4868293  4868309  4868323  4868329  4868359
4868363  4868371  4868377  4868407  4868419  4868431  4868447  4868453  4868467  4868483
4868509  4868543  4868557  4868561  4868573  4868587  4868597  4868599  4868609  4868623
4868651  4868653  4868657  4868669  4868671  4868687  4868711  4868729  4868741  4868771
4868779  4868789  4868797  4868813  4868819  4868827  4868833  4868861  4868869  4868909
4868911  4868947  4868977  4868993  4869017  4869043  4869047  4869049  4869061
4869083  4869097  4869103  4869121  4869131  4869139  4869143  4869167  4869181  4869209  4869223
4869229  4869239  4869257  4869281  4869289  4869317  4869349  4869407  4869433  4869461
4869479  4869499  4869503  4869517  4869521  4869523  4869539  4869547  4869551  4869559
4869563  4869617  4869637  4869649  4869669  4869679  4869703  4869713  4869727  4869731
4869743  4869749  4869751  4869763  4869773  4869791  4869817  4869841  4869853  4869863
4869877  4869889  4869911  4869913  4869929  4869959  4869979  4869989  4870001  4870009
4870013  4870027  4870039  4870067  4870081  4870087  4870133  4870139  4870157  4870171
4870183  4870207  4870219  4870241  4870247  4870253  4870259  4870291  4870337  4870361
4870367  4870373  4870409  4870417  4870427  4870433  4870471  4870477  4870493  4870499
4870511  4870531  4870559  4870583  4870589  4870597  4870609  4870651  4870681  4870693
4870709  4870729  4870763  4870771  4870777  4870799  4870819  4870837  4870843  4870861
4870867  4870907  4870909  4870933  4870949  4870969  4870979  4870991  4871017  4871029
4871057  4871063  4871077  4871081  4871089  4871093  4871107  4871137  4871143  4871149
4871173  4871183  4871203  4871213  4871227  4871233  4871261  4871267  4871281  4871291
4871297  4871303  4871311  4871323  4871329  4871351  4871359  4871393  4871407  4871413
4871431  4871441  4871443  4871459  4871473  4871479  4871491  4871527  4871567  4871569
4871609  4871617  4871641  4871663  4871687  4871701  4871717  4871723  4871747  4871773
4871819  4871821  4871831  4871833  4871849  4871861  4871863  4871869  4871873  4871897
4871903  4871921  4871927  4871939  4871941  4871953  4871957  4871959  4871963  4871969
4871981  4871983  4872001  4872041  4872059  4872083  4872097  4872103  4872107  4872121
4872157  4872163  4872169  4872187  4872223  4872229  4872269  4872277  4872281  4872289
4872293  4872311  4872313  4872323  4872331  4872337  4872391  4872403  4872431  4872451
4872467  4872473  4872479  4872503  4872509  4872521  4872529  4872533  4872541  4872547
4872577  4872583  4872587  4872589  4872599  4872613  4872617  4872629  4872643  4872649
4872691  4872719  4872733  4872739  4872743  4872781  4872793  4872817  4872853  4872871
4872877  4872919  4872929  4872961  4873019  4873027  4873031  4873039  4873049  4873051
4873091  4873103  4873129  4873133  4873151  4873157  4873163  4873181  4873199
4873207  4873243  4873259  4873279  4873283  4873303  4873321  4873327  4873333  4873391
4873397  4873399  4873411  4873433  4873483  4873507  4873559  4873573  4873579  4873591
4873601  4873607  4873613  4873619  4873621  4873639  4873643  4873657  4873669  4873697
4873703  4873753  4873763  4873777  4873783  4873801  4873811  4873819  4873831  4873859
4873871  4873903  4873907  4873993  4873997  4874007  4874017  4874021  4874027  4874033
4874069  4874081  4874113  4874119  4874123  4874131  4874141  4874173  4874197  4874201
4874213  4874231  4874249  4874267  4874273  4874293  4874297  4874339  4874377  4874381
4874399  4874411  4874447  4874453  4874473  4874489  4874501  4874503  4874543  4874561
4874567  4874579  4874587  4874603  4874633  4874651  4874663  4874669  4874687  4874717
4874741  4874747  4874791  4874803  4874851  4874879  4874911  4874939  4874959
4874977  4874983  4874999  4875037  4875049  4875061  4875067  4875071  4875097  4875109
4875119  4875127  4875133  4875137  4875151  4875163  4875179  4875193  4875197
4875203  4875217  4875223  4875251  4875253  4875257  4875259  4875271  4875281  4875289
4875293  4875319  4875323  4875329  4875341  4875359  4875397  4875407  4875439  4875487
4875491  4875529  4875551  4875581  4875613  4875623  4875653  4875667  4875677  4875707
4875713  4875721  4875751  4875763  4875779  4875797  4875803  4875809  4875817  4875833
4875847  4875851  4875859  4875881  4875887  4875901  4875907  4875943  4875979  4876009
4876019  4876049  4876051  4876057  4876073  4876111  4876129  4876133  4876189  4876211
4876219  4876231  4876271  4876301  4876307  4876337  4876357  4876367  4876397  4876423
4876427  4876429  4876441  4876447  4876451  4876453  4876511  4876513  4876607  4876609
4876631  4876639  4876643  4876657  4876681  4876687  4876691  4876693  4876709  4876717
4876721  4876733  4876747  4876757  4876783  4876799  4876829  4876849  4876867  4876873
4876877  4876903  4876913  4876957  4876961  4876969  4876973  4876979  4876981  4877003
4877009  4877021  4877027  4877029  4877051  4877069  4877071  4877077  4877083  4877087
4877099  4877141  4877161  4877179  4877183  4877207  4877209  4877221  4877227  4877251
4877263  4877267  4877287  4877293  4877297  4877321  4877339  4877347  4877387  4877393
4877429  4877441  4877459  4877489  4877497  4877501  4877503  4877507  4877513  4877527
4877557  4877563  4877573  4877581  4877617  4877651  4877659  4877669  4877701  4877711
4877723  4877731  4877773  4877783  4877843  4877849  4877857  4877867  4877869  4877891
4877897  4877911  4877941  4877959  4877981  4878007  4878011  4878019  4878073  4878089
4878091  4878103  4878113  4878121  4878149  4878151  4878163  4878187  4878217  4878233
4878239  4878241  4878341  4878281  4878283  4878299  4878301  4878319  4878361  4878373
4878397  4878431  4878443  4878463  4878469  4878499  4878509  4878527  4878529  4878551
4878581  4878589  4878593  4878617  4878661  4878667  4878673  4878683  4878697  4878701
4878721  4878767  4878791  4878793  4878799  4878817  4878821  4878827  4878851  4878869
4878871  4878889  4878893  4878919  4878941  4878943  4878977  4879009  4879033  4879057
4879087  4879097  4879103  4879109  4879111  4879147  4879157  4879159  4879177  4879201
4879223  4879261  4879267  4879291  4879313  4879319  4879331  4879349  4879363  4879397
4879421  4879429  4879471  4879481  4879489  4879499  4879507  4879513  4879517  4879531
4879541  4879547  4879549  4879571  4879583  4879591  4879607  4879631  4879639  4879643
4879669  4879687  4879709  4879711  4879729  4879733  4879739  4879747  4879753  4879807
4879813  4879829  4879837  4879871  4879879  4879909  4879913  4879921  4879937  4879951
4879957  4879961  4879993  4879997  4880011  4880021  4880059  4880069  4880087  4880089
```

```
4880101 4880111 4880119 4880129 4880147 4880153 4880159 4880177 4880179 4880191
4880201 4880203 4880221 4880231 4880251 4880261 4880279 4880287 4880311 4880329
4880333 4880387 4880401 4880413 4880417 4880419 4880431 4880437 4880441 4880443
4880453 4880461 4880489 4880507 4880521 4880537 4880573 4880593 4880639 4880713
4880723 4880741 4880747 4880779 4880789 4880791 4880797 4880803 4880839 4880867
4880879 4880917 4880923 4880933 4880947 4880951 4880957 4880959 4880963 4880969
4880971 4880977 4880987 4881001 4881007 4881029 4881049 4881053 4881061 4881089
4881101 4881103 4881109 4881113 4881127 4881131 4881133 4881139 4881169 4881187
4881199 4881203 4881211 4881223 4881277 4881293 4881301 4881307 4881341 4881343
4881379 4881407 4881413 4881421 4881427 4881433 4881469 4881473 4881491 4881511
4881517 4881559 4881563 4881581 4881587 4881623 4881629 4881631 4881641 4881649
4881659 4881677 4881683 4881691 4881707 4881731 4881733 4881757 4881763 4881791
4881809 4881823 4881827 4881853 4881859 4881869 4881871 4881881 4881901 4881931
4881949 4881953 4881959 4881967 4881979 4881983 4882019 4882027 4882057 4882061
4882093 4882099 4882103 4882109 4882127 4882133 4882147 4882153 4882211 4882217
4882271 4882277 4882289 4882327 4882333 4882339 4882351 4882363 4882369 4882387
4882393 4882399 4882421 4882429 4882433 4882453 4882489 4882499 4882523 4882529
4882541 4882547 4882571 4882597 4882609 4882651 4882667 4882673 4882681 4882687
4882697 4882699 4882711 4882721 4882727 4882733 4882771 4882777 4882789 4882811
4882819 4882847 4882861 4882907 4882919 4882939 4882957 4882963 4882979 4882987
4882993 4883003 4883033 4883071 4883083 4883101 4883119 4883129 4883147 4883183
4883191 4883231 4883237 4883239 4883269 4883279 4883293 4883303 4883311 4883321
4883327 4883357 4883363 4883393 4883401 4883413 4883423 4883453 4883503 4883507
4883509 4883537 4883569 4883591 4883597 4883609 4883611 4883623 4883651 4883663
4883677 4883699 4883719 4883729 4883759 4883789 4883839 4883863 4883881 4883887
4883899 4883903 4883917 4883929 4883941 4883953 4883971 4883987 4883989 4883993
4883999 4884001 4884029 4884031 4884041 4884059 4884097 4884101 4884127 4884137
4884149 4884169 4884179 4884223 4884227 4884247 4884263 4884277 4884281 4884307
4884323 4884337 4884343 4884361 4884377 4884401 4884419 4884421 4884431 4884437
4884449 4884469 4884479 4884493 4884497 4884511 4884521 4884553 4884563 4884589
4884601 4884611 4884613 4884619 4884631 4884643 4884683 4884707 4884721 4884727
4884739 4884749 4884773 4884779 4884791 4884793 4884811 4884821 4884827 4884833
4884857 4884883 4884889 4884907 4884911 4884923 4884937 4884977 4884983 4884989
4885007 4885019 4885031 4885043 4885051 4885081 4885091 4885099 4885117 4885129
4885201 4885219 4885247 4885249 4885277 4885289 4885301 4885319 4885333 4885339
4885351 4885357 4885367 4885373 4885411 4885423 4885469 4885481 4885483 4885493
4885501 4885523 4885537 4885541 4885547 4885549 4885553 4885567 4885571 4885577
4885583 4885607 4885609 4885619 4885627 4885633 4885669 4885687 4885691 4885753
4885801 4885807 4885823 4885843 4885861 4885883 4885889 4885897 4885901 4885943
4885957 4885973 4885981 4885999 4886027 4886029 4886041 4886053 4886069 4886081
4886083 4886087 4886111 4886117 4886129 4886131 4886137 4886159 4886177 4886197
4886201 4886207 4886213 4886227 4886237 4886263 4886269 4886303 4886317 4886333
4886347 4886393 4886411 4886443 4886461 4886473 4886489 4886491 4886501 4886513
4886537 4886551 4886573 4886593 4886597 4886617 4886639 4886641 4886647 4886663
4886669 4886677 4886689 4886699 4886729 4886737 4886767 4886789 4886807 4886863
4886867 4886881 4886891 4886897 4886929 4886929 4886941 4886951 4886963 4886969
4886977 4886983 4886989 4887023 4887031 4887037 4887049 4887053 4887073 4887139
4887149 4887163 4887173 4887187 4887193 4887209 4887227 4887269 4887287 4887299
4887301 4887317 4887331 4887343 4887353 4887371 4887391 4887397 4887401 4887409
4887437 4887481 4887529 4887559 4887563 4887581 4887587 4887593 4887599 4887601
4887611 4887629 4887637 4887643 4887667 4887683 4887697 4887703 4887709 4887763
4887781 4887793 4887829 4887833 4887847 4887871 4887893 4887899 4887901 4887907
4887913 4887917 4887919 4887929 4887941 4887943 4887947 4887977 4887989 4888043
4888063 4888067 4888069 4888087 4888109 4888123 4888127 4888139 4888157 4888199
4888217 4888223 4888241 4888249 4888271 4888309 4888313 4888319 4888321 4888337
4888343 4888363 4888379 4888391 4888399 4888409 4888427 4888447 4888487 4888511
4888519 4888523 4888531 4888547 4888549 4888577 4888579 4888589 4888619 4888621
4888633 4888649 4888651 4888661 4888679 4888687 4888691 4888693 4888711 4888739
4888753 4888813 4888831 4888837 4888841 4888861 4888867 4888889 4888901 4888913
4888931 4888943 4888951 4888957 4888969 4888973 4888981 4888997 4888999 4889033
4889063 4889077 4889083 4889113 4889147 4889173 4889207 4889219 4889233 4889237
4889239 4889243 4889249 4889257 4889263 4889267 4889279 4889293 4889299 4889347
4889359 4889369 4889377 4889383 4889399 4889407 4889411 4889419 4889431 4889453
4889461 4889471 4889477 4889483 4889491 4889497 4889509 4889539 4889543 4889561
4889567 4889609 4889611 4889641 4889671 4889711 4889741 4889747 4889771 4889789
4889803 4889813 4889851 4889879 4889891 4889921 4889923 4889933 4889953 4889977
4889981 4889987 4889993 4890001 4890013 4890019 4890023 4890037 4890043 4890047
4890091 4890103 4890113 4890133 4890139 4890143 4890161 4890199 4890211 4890217
4890227 4890229 4890247 4890251 4890269 4890289 4890293 4890307 4890311 4890323
4890331 4890341 4890367 4890371 4890383 4890419 4890481 4890493 4890497 4890499
4890511 4890517 4890533 4890539 4890541 4890547 4890563 4890593 4890617 4890629
4890631 4890637 4890659 4890661 4890667 4890671 4890701 4890703 4890709 4890731
4890751 4890761 4890779 4890791 4890793 4890803 4890827 4890833 4890851 4890857
4890859 4890869 4890871 4890887 4890889 4890911 4890913 4890943 4890971 4890983
4891001 4891027 4891039 4891043 4891057 4891063 4891079 4891091 4891093 4891099
4891129 4891153 4891171 4891193 4891213 4891217 4891241 4891247 4891253 4891283
4891297 4891307 4891331 4891333 4891339 4891349 4891361 4891399 4891429 4891457
4891463 4891477 4891483 4891489 4891499 4891501 4891507 4891519 4891547 4891559
4891567 4891591 4891639 4891643 4891661 4891681 4891703 4891717 4891727 4891729
4891763 4891781 4891787 4891831 4891841 4891853 4891879 4891889 4891897 4891933
4891961 4891969 4891973 4891979 4891993 4892003 4892009 4892011 4892021 4892047
4892051 4892071 4892057 4892087 4892099 4892149 4892159 4892189 4892197 4892201
4892207 4892257 4892287 4892297 4892309 4892323 4892351 4892359 4892369 4892401
4892429 4892449 4892471 4892479 4892501 4892507 4892527 4892543 4892579 4892581
4892609 4892639 4892647 4892687 4892689 4892717 4892729 4892731 4892737 4892773
4892791 4892819 4892827 4892837 4892857 4892873 4892887 4892891 4892893 4892897
4892941 4892977 4892983 4892999 4893001 4893019 4893037 4893041 4893067 4893073
4893079 4893101 4893103 4893113 4893137 4893151 4893157 4893167 4893169 4893179
4893191 4893193 4893197 4893209 4893247 4893253 4893277 4893281 4893293 4893299
```

```
4893307 4893313 4893341 4893367 4893377 4893389 4893397 4893419 4893451 4893461
4893463 4893491 4893517 4893521 4893523 4893527 4893541 4893563 4893571 4893589
4893599 4893617 4893619 4893631 4893643 4893667 4893673 4893683 4893689 4893703
4893709 4893727 4893737 4893743 4893751 4893761 4893809 4893827 4893829 4893851
4893853 4893857 4893869 4893899 4893907 4893913 4893923 4893937 4893947 4893949
4893961 4893983 4894031 4894037 4894049 4894081 4894093 4894103 4894111 4894117
4894121 4894151 4894171 4894189 4894231 4894259 4894271 4894277 4894289 4894297
4894319 4894321 4894349 4894361 4894367 4894387 4894403 4894441 4894451 4894457
4894489 4894493 4894499 4894511 4894517 4894529 4894543 4894571 4894573 4894577
4894583 4894597 4894601 4894633 4894639 4894651 4894697 4894711 4894753 4894777
4894781 4894843 4894847 4894849 4894853 4894871 4894889 4894933 4894943 4894957
4894969 4894973 4894979 4894987 4894999 4895017 4895029 4895039 4895041 4895057
4895069 4895071 4895119 4895131 4895153 4895173 4895197 4895207 4895213 4895243
4895263 4895279 4895291 4895309 4895323 4895327 4895329 4895347 4895351 4895377
4895399 4895419 4895459 4895477 4895479 4895491 4895497 4895503 4895533 4895533
4895537 4895549 4895587 4895591 4895603 4895621 4895629 4895641 4895651 4895659
4895701 4895713 4895731 4895743 4895753 4895767 4895771 4895777 4895783 4895789
4895797 4895819 4895827 4895843 4895857 4895887 4895893 4895897 4895909 4895959
4895963 4895993 4896011 4896013 4896019 4896049 4896061 4896077 4896083 4896103
4896113 4896127 4896137 4896149 4896161 4896169 4896181 4896191 4896209 4896211
4896239 4896277 4896313 4896317 4896337 4896349 4896361 4896377 4896383 4896421
4896431 4896439 4896443 4896449 4896469 4896487 4896491 4896497 4896503 4896503
4896523 4896533 4896557 4896559 4896569 4896571 4896583 4896613 4896637 4896643
4896659 4896701 4896709 4896713 4896719 4896721 4896733 4896757 4896761 4896781
4896803 4896809 4896811 4896821 4896863 4896887 4896923 4896943 4896949 4896971
4896979 4897001 4897007 4897021 4897031 4897051 4897103 4897153 4897157 4897171
4897181 4897199 4897213 4897219 4897237 4897267 4897273 4897279 4897297 4897331
4897337 4897363 4897379 4897381 4897391 4897397 4897423 4897439 4897441 4897463
4897469 4897471 4897483 4897489 4897523 4897553 4897559 4897561 4897567 4897577
4897583 4897601 4897603 4897631 4897639 4897681 4897693 4897703 4897709 4897741
4897757 4897769 4897771 4897777 4897787 4897811 4897831 4897847 4897859 4897861
4897891 4897903 4897909 4897927 4897931 4897933 4897951 4897973 4897993 4898017
4898021 4898027 4898039 4898051 4898053 4898059 4898083 4898099 4898119 4898123
4898183 4898203 4898213 4898233 4898249 4898269 4898273 4898291 4898297 4898317
4898323 4898339 4898381 4898389 4898417 4898429 4898441 4898449 4898459 4898461
4898473 4898479 4898497 4898507 4898549 4898573 4898587 4898623 4898627 4898629
4898633 4898653 4898657 4898687 4898723 4898741 4898753 4898797 4898809 4898809
4898813 4898819 4898821 4898833 4898851 4898863 4898917 4898923 4898939 4898981
4899001 4899019 4899029 4899031 4899053 4899061 4899067 4899073 4899079 4899091
4899101 4899113 4899121 4899143 4899149 4899151 4899157 4899197 4899199 4899203
4899211 4899217 4899229 4899263 4899277 4899311 4899317 4899329 4899331 4899353
4899371 4899379 4899403 4899431 4899439 4899443 4899467 4899481 4899493 4899523
4899527 4899547 4899551 4899563 4899569 4899571 4899593 4899599 4899619 4899641
4899647 4899673 4899677 4899683 4899733 4899737 4899803 4899809 4899821 4899823
4899841 4899847 4899857 4899863 4899871 4899883 4899887 4899907 4899931 4899941
4899971 4899997 4900001 4900003 4900031 4900037 4900057 4900067 4900087 4900099
4900109 4900111 4900117 4900121 4900123 4900153 4900177 4900183 4900187 4900193
4900211 4900241 4900277 4900289 4900297 4900307 4900319 4900321 4900331 4900339
4900351 4900367 4900381 4900393 4900397 4900421 4900439 4900451 4900453 4900457
4900459 4900477 4900501 4900513 4900517 4900523 4900529 4900543 4900547 4900559
4900589 4900591 4900601 4900603 4900619 4900631 4900639 4900657 4900663 4900669
4900673 4900741 4900747 4900757 4900783 4900789 4900793 4900799 4900877 4900927
4900939 4900943 4900957 4900979 4900997 4900999 4901009 4901021 4901023 4901023
4901051 4901053 4901063 4901077 4901089 4901101 4901111 4901129 4901153 4901159
4901177 4901179 4901191 4901209 4901213 4901243 4901249 4901257 4901291 4901327
4901329 4901333 4901339 4901357 4901359 4901371 4901381 4901401 4901417 4901419
4901431 4901437 4901443 4901453 4901471 4901473 4901513 4901521 4901537 4901539
4901549 4901579 4901581 4901623 4901647 4901657 4901681 4901683 4901693 4901707
4901711 4901717 4901719 4901749 4901773 4901801 4901803 4901807 4901849 4901851
4901857 4901879 4901887 4901903 4901909 4901947 4901969 4901971 4901989 4902049
4902077 4902097 4902101 4902127 4902173 4902193 4902199 4902211 4902217 4902253
4902257 4902259 4902263 4902269 4902299 4902349 4902353 4902367 4902379 4902383
4902431 4902451 4902467 4902497 4902529 4902533 4902539 4902563 4902571 4902577
4902587 4902593 4902643 4902649 4902691 4902701 4902713 4902721 4902757 4902767
4902773 4902787 4902791 4902797 4902803 4902811 4902823 4902829 4902839 4902853
4902857 4902869 4902901 4902913 4902917 4902923 4902941 4902949 4902967 4902971
4903043 4903049 4903051 4903069 4903079 4903081 4903111 4903187 4903193 4903201
4903207 4903219 4903237 4903243 4903289 4903319 4903357 4903373 4903397 4903399
4903403 4903411 4903417 4903421 4903433 4903453 4903513 4903519 4903553 4903571
4903579 4903589 4903637 4903663 4903681 4903693 4903733 4903741 4903753 4903753
4903777 4903783 4903819 4903823 4903841 4903867 4903879 4903901 4903907 4903909
4903949 4903961 4903963 4903979 4903981 4903999 4904023 4904047 4904057 4904077
4904089 4904099 4904101 4904111 4904113 4904197 4904201 4904203 4904227 4904233
4904269 4904303 4904311 4904321 4904327 4904351 4904353 4904357 4904363 4904369
4904401 4904407 4904437 4904441 4904443 4904477 4904491 4904531 4904561 4904563
4904569 4904573 4904587 4904593 4904597 4904629 4904657 4904659 4904663 4904699
4904759 4904777 4904803 4904807 4904813 4904821 4904843 4904849 4904893 4904899
4904923 4904927 4904969 4904971 4904989 4905001 4905007 4905029 4905067 4905079
4905101 4905143 4905149 4905157 4905179 4905181 4905209 4905221 4905227 4905253
4905259 4905269 4905283 4905289 4905301 4905317 4905337 4905353 4905377 4905389
4905391 4905421 4905427 4905431 4905473 4905479 4905487 4905491 4905493 4905529
4905541 4905547 4905577 4905587 4905617 4905619 4905623 4905653 4905661 4905701
4905713 4905721 4905731 4905799 4905829 4905869 4905899 4905917 4905931 4905931
4905949 4905973 4905977 4905983 4905991 4906003 4906007 4906021 4906039 4906063
4906067 4906079 4906087 4906103 4906127 4906147 4906159 4906177 4906193 4906193
4906207 4906229 4906241 4906243 4906247 4906259 4906261 4906267 4906273 4906301
4906309 4906327 4906331 4906333 4906361 4906373 4906393 4906399 4906439 4906469
4906483 4906493 4906507 4906513 4906543 4906547 4906589 4906609 4906619 4906621
4906631 4906633 4906637 4906651 4906661 4906663 4906673 4906691 4906709 4906717
```

```
4906723  4906763  4906787  4906801  4906819  4906823  4906849  4906861  4906873  4906907
4906919  4906933  4906943  4906949  4906963  4906969  4906973  4906991  4907009  4907011
4907029  4907039  4907041  4907081  4907087  4907093  4907099  4907107  4907113  4907131
4907143  4907159  4907173  4907183  4907191  4907219  4907223  4907233  4907239  4907261
4907297  4907333  4907359  4907369  4907381  4907417  4907423  4907431  4907437  4907447
4907459  4907473  4907501  4907519  4907531  4907537  4907563  4907587  4907593  4907603
4907627  4907647  4907657  4907677  4907687  4907711  4907729  4907743  4907753  4907761
4907789  4907801  4907807  4907813  4907821  4907831  4907857  4907867  4907869  4907897
4907923  4907923  4907933  4907941  4907957  4907971  4908011  4908031  4908037  4908041
4908049  4908067  4908073  4908077  4908089  4908091  4908097  4908107  4908109  4908133
4908139  4908143  4908179  4908181  4908187  4908193  4908217  4908247  4908311  4908317
4908329  4908331  4908347  4908373  4908377  4908389  4908391  4908413  4908433  4908437
4908451  4908467  4908469  4908481  4908503  4908521  4908551  4908559  4908577  4908581
4908583  4908647  4908653  4908661  4908667  4908691  4908697  4908713  4908719
4908737  4908749  4908769  4908773  4908793  4908803  4908811  4908817  4908829  4908857
4908863  4908907  4908941  4908947  4908949  4908961  4908979  4908991  4908997  4909007
4909013  4909027  4909057  4909109  4909117  4909147  4909169  4909183  4909193
4909199  4909241  4909249  4909259  4909279  4909283  4909301  4909319  4909321  4909343
4909349  4909357  4909361  4909393  4909403  4909409  4909427  4909441  4909451  4909477
4909483  4909523  4909537  4909577  4909601  4909609  4909637  4909643  4909679  4909717
4909739  4909747  4909763  4909781  4909823  4909837  4909841  4909843  4909859  4909871
4909939  4909969  4909981  4910027  4910033  4910047  4910069  4910071  4910089  4910099
4910107  4910117  4910131  4910141  4910173  4910177  4910179  4910203  4910207  4910221
4910239  4910287  4910327  4910329  4910351  4910357  4910359  4910371  4910377  4910407
4910413  4910429  4910441  4910449  4910461  4910509  4910537  4910539  4910567  4910579
4910597  4910621  4910639  4910651  4910663  4910669  4910681  4910687  4910699  4910749
4910767  4910813  4910833  4910837  4910887  4910897  4910921  4910953  4910957  4910959
4910981  4911017  4911019  4911031  4911043  4911061  4911083  4911089  4911097  4911107
4911119  4911131  4911149  4911157  4911161  4911163  4911169  4911191  4911197  4911199
4911229  4911233  4911241  4911251  4911311  4911371  4911373  4911383  4911391  4911409
4911427  4911433  4911451  4911463  4911497  4911499  4911523  4911539  4911551  4911593
4911601  4911607  4911617  4911619  4911629  4911653  4911661  4911707  4911721  4911727
4911737  4911743  4911749  4911757  4911763  4911769  4911773  4911791  4911799  4911839
4911853  4911859  4911871  4911883  4911887  4911901  4911931  4911941  4911943  4911961
4912007  4912027  4912057  4912067  4912069  4912073  4912079  4912091  4912151  4912207
4912213  4912247  4912249  4912253  4912267  4912283  4912301  4912309  4912343  4912351
4912357  4912361  4912367  4912403  4912421  4912423  4912433  4912441  4912447  4912459
4912471  4912489  4912493  4912511  4912529  4912543  4912553  4912559  4912591  4912613
4912627  4912667  4912669  4912673  4912693  4912709  4912717  4912727  4912751  4912763
4912771  4912781  4912807  4912837  4912841  4912891  4912903  4912937  4912939  4912951
4912967  4912981  4912991  4913009  4913011  4913021  4913063  4913081  4913101  4913113
4913131  4913143  4913189  4913197  4913257  4913261  4913263  4913269  4913273  4913281
4913287  4913303  4913339  4913369  4913387  4913401  4913443  4913449  4913473  4913477
4913479  4913497  4913537  4913539  4913543  4913569  4913581  4913591  4913599  4913603
4913617  4913621  4913627  4913639  4913677  4913681  4913693  4913707  4913747  4913767
4913773  4913791  4913801  4913813  4913861  4913873  4913917  4913921  4913929  4913939
4913947  4913959  4913971  4913999  4914029  4914059  4914101  4914109  4914127  4914131
4914167  4914187  4914197  4914209  4914211  4914223  4914227  4914263  4914271  4914277
4914281  4914289  4914307  4914373  4914379  4914389  4914391  4914397  4914431  4914443
4914457  4914473  4914487  4914499  4914509  4914527  4914529  4914541  4914551  4914563
4914577  4914583  4914589  4914607  4914619  4914653  4914661  4914667  4914671  4914677
4914719  4914731  4914737  4914739  4914769  4914781  4914797  4914799  4914809  4914817
4914829  4914841  4914869  4914881  4914883  4914907  4914911  4914913  4914937  4914941
4914947  4914961  4914991  4914997  4915013  4915037  4915049  4915051  4915067  4915093
4915109  4915111  4915133  4915139  4915147  4915151  4915153  4915171  4915217  4915219
4915223  4915241  4915249  4915271  4915277  4915279  4915303  4915331  4915369  4915403
4915409  4915411  4915447  4915451  4915489  4915501  4915511  4915523  4915549  4915571
4915597  4915607  4915609  4915621  4915633  4915637  4915663  4915711  4915727  4915751
4915753  4915759  4915769  4915817  4915831  4915837  4915843  4915847  4915853  4915879
4915891  4915961  4915987  4916027  4916033  4916053  4916063  4916069  4916081  4916083
4916099  4916123  4916137  4916143  4916161  4916183  4916189  4916201  4916203  4916221
4916237  4916239  4916257  4916279  4916287  4916309  4916311  4916323  4916347  4916357
4916369  4916371  4916381  4916413  4916419  4916423  4916441  4916447  4916453  4916467
4916489  4916557  4916581  4916591  4916603  4916629  4916633  4916669  4916683  4916707
4916719  4916741  4916759  4916771  4916773  4916777  4916789  4916803  4916809  4916827
4916831  4916867  4916869  4916887  4916909  4916939  4916957  4916993  4917019  4917023
4917049  4917071  4917079  4917103  4917109  4917113  4917139  4917151  4917173  4917203
4917217  4917277  4917329  4917359  4917361  4917391  4917401  4917413  4917431  4917457
4917461  4917467  4917481  4917503  4917511  4917527  4917533  4917551  4917557  4917571
4917593  4917631  4917659  4917721  4917761  4917763  4917779  4917793  4917797  4917799
4917823  4917839  4917853  4917859  4917863  4917901  4917943  4917967  4917973  4917989
4918007  4918009  4918019  4918027  4918061  4918079  4918091  4918097  4918129  4918171
4918183  4918187  4918259  4918261  4918267  4918271  4918273  4918283  4918301  4918337
4918357  4918387  4918391  4918399  4918411  4918427  4918439  4918451  4918477  4918493
4918513  4918517  4918519  4918541  4918547  4918567  4918577  4918601  4918609  4918631
4918633  4918637  4918649  4918673  4918681  4918687  4918699  4918703  4918709  4918717
4918721  4918733  4918747  4918759  4918769  4918783  4918787  4918789  4918799  4918807
4918841  4918861  4918871  4918887  4918883  4918943  4918961  4918981  4918993  4918997
4918999  4919011  4919017  4919021  4919023  4919029  4919063  4919077  4919107  4919143
4919147  4919153  4919179  4919191  4919197  4919209  4919219  4919231  4919249  4919267
4919269  4919323  4919333  4919339  4919351  4919353  4919363  4919381  4919393  4919413
4919417  4919431  4919441  4919449  4919471  4919491  4919507  4919527  4919561  4919569
4919573  4919581  4919591  4919623  4919639  4919657  4919671  4919699  4919701  4919729
4919737  4919767  4919773  4919777  4919791  4919813  4919839  4919867  4919891  4919899
4919903  4919911  4919921  4919939  4919977  4919983  4919989  4920023  4920059  4920061
4920067  4920073  4920109  4920163  4920193  4920197  4920203  4920217  4920233  4920239
4920241  4920247  4920257  4920263  4920269  4920271  4920299  4920329  4920347  4920359
4920389  4920397  4920403  4920407  4920437  4920439  4920457  4920473  4920493  4920499
4920511  4920527  4920529  4920569  4920577  4920581  4920583  4920589  4920613  4920623
```

```
4920631  4920647  4920649  4920683  4920703  4920709  4920719  4920737  4920743  4920757
4920761  4920763  4920787  4920793  4920833  4920841  4920887  4920901  4920911  4920961
4920967  4920983  4920991  4921009  4921027  4921043  4921051  4921061  4921067  4921073
4921079  4921093  4921099  4921117  4921121  4921127  4921129  4921139  4921151  4921159
4921181  4921187  4921199  4921201  4921243  4921253  4921261  4921283  4921289  4921291
4921309  4921337  4921339  4921349  4921369  4921373  4921391  4921403  4921409  4921429
4921447  4921453  4921487  4921493  4921523  4921537  4921549  4921577  4921583  4921597
4921601  4921607  4921613  4921643  4921667  4921673  4921711  4921717  4921757  4921787
4921769  4921771  4921781  4921783  4921811  4921841  4921849  4921853  4921871  4921883
4921913  4921919  4921921  4921949  4922011  4922039  4922051  4922053  4922089  4922101
4922117  4922123  4922143  4922179  4922191  4922201  4922213  4922227  4922233  4922237
4922243  4922251  4922287  4922293  4922303  4922327  4922329  4922341  4922353  4922377
4922383  4922389  4922399  4922417  4922441  4922447  4922461  4922497  4922509  4922527
4922531  4922543  4922563  4922573  4922579  4922581  4922623  4922627  4922629  4922633
4922641  4922669  4922677  4922681  4922711  4922717  4922719  4922773  4922803  4922807
4922867  4922873  4922891  4922903  4922917  4922923  4922933  4922971  4922987  4923001
4923007  4923029  4923031  4923067  4923073  4923101  4923119  4923143  4923151  4923167
4923179  4923187  4923209  4923221  4923229  4923253  4923277  4923283  4923287  4923293
4923307  4923341  4923391  4923397  4923409  4923427  4923433  4923439  4923461  4923463
4923467  4923473  4923481  4923487  4923509  4923539  4923563  4923571  4923577  4923593
4923599  4923601  4923613  4923619  4923671  4923689  4923691  4923697  4923703  4923719
4923739  4923757  4923769  4923791  4923811  4923839  4923883  4923889  4923899  4923901
4923913  4923929  4923937  4923943  4923953  4923967  4923979  4924013  4924019  4924027
4924043  4924061  4924079  4924147  4924163  4924181  4924189  4924207  4924243  4924267
4924289  4924291  4924303  4924313  4924321  4924333  4924357  4924391  4924397  4924411
4924471  4924473  4924481  4924487  4924499  4924501  4924523  4924531  4924537
4924541  4924547  4924559  4924571  4924573  4924597  4924607  4924609  4924627  4924643
4924649  4924651  4924657  4924669  4924687  4924697  4924721  4924727  4924763  4924771
4924787  4924823  4924837  4924841  4924847  4924903  4924943  4924973  4924979  4924987
4924991  4924999  4925017  4925023  4925029  4925071  4925077  4925093  4925101  4925119
4925153  4925159  4925183  4925209  4925213  4925233  4925251  4925267  4925281  4925293
4925299  4925309  4925321  4925339  4925353  4925363  4925399  4925411  4925419  4925443
4925471  4925489  4925509  4925513  4925533  4925537  4925539  4925549  4925573  4925581
4925603  4925633  4925651  4925663  4925663  4925677  4925707  4925719  4925747  4925759
4925761  4925797  4925803  4925831  4925861  4925867  4925881  4925923  4925941  4925957
4925983  4925989  4926007  4926011  4926013  4926041  4926049  4926059  4926079  4926091
4926101  4926157  4926161  4926167  4926169  4926199  4926221  4926227  4926247  4926269
4926283  4926287  4926331  4926367  4926371  4926401  4926407  4926409  4926419  4926451
4926469  4926499  4926511  4926527  4926539  4926541  4926547  4926563  4926569  4926589
4926629  4926637  4926641  4926653  4926659  4926671  4926673  4926689  4926703  4926709
4926731  4926743  4926749  4926751  4926767  4926791  4926793  4926851  4926863  4926907
4926937  4926941  4926949  4926953  4926967  4926973  4926997  4927007  4927009  4927049
4927063  4927067  4927073  4927079  4927081  4927103  4927121  4927141  4927147  4927157
4927163  4927177  4927189  4927193  4927199  4927201  4927207  4927231  4927249  4927259
4927261  4927271  4927283  4927291  4927319  4927337  4927387  4927409  4927423  4927453
4927459  4927493  4927511  4927513  4927523  4927529  4927537  4927541  4927547  4927567
4927577  4927607  4927639  4927661  4927673  4927679  4927687  4927711  4927721  4927763
4927733  4927751  4927781  4927787  4927789  4927791  4927801  4927823  4927861  4927873
4927921  4927927  4927931  4927933  4928029  4928069  4928071  4928081  4928117  4928123
4928149  4928153  4928177  4928179  4928207  4928213  4928219  4928221  4928237  4928267
4928281  4928293  4928299  4928321  4928369  4928377  4928381  4928383  4928389  4928461
4928471  4928477  4928479  4928491  4928501  4928503  4928513  4928519  4928533  4928537
4928549  4928563  4928591  4928603  4928611  4928639  4928663  4928681  4928687  4928713
4928717  4928719  4928723  4928747  4928761  4928773  4928779  4928797  4928837  4928857
4928863  4928867  4928873  4928879  4928899  4928933  4928941  4928951  4928953  4928971
4928977  4928993  4929013  4929049  4929073  4929083  4929091  4929109  4929157  4929161
4929163  4929187  4929191  4929193  4929203  4929209  4929229  4929233  4929259  4929263
4929277  4929343  4929379  4929361  4929373  4929377  4929401  4929427  4929433  4929451
4929467  4929469  4929511  4929523  4929539  4929559  4929599  4929641  4929647  4929703
4929707  4929719  4929731  4929737  4929773  4929781  4929791  4929809  4929817  4929823
4929833  4929857  4929871  4929887  4929893  4929919  4929937  4929943  4929989  4929997
4930001  4930019  4930021  4930033  4930039  4930043  4930049  4930097  4930103  4930109
4930129  4930151  4930157  4930171  4930181  4930193  4930199  4930207  4930231  4930243
4930273  4930279  4930297  4930309  4930313  4930339  4930363  4930379  4930381  4930403
4930417  4930421  4930433  4930439  4930451  4930483  4930489  4930531  4930543  4930547
4930553  4930567  4930589  4930613  4930631  4930637  4930649  4930693  4930699  4930703
4930711  4930721  4930729  4930741  4930759  4930771  4930777  4930789  4930811  4930819
4930831  4930837  4930843  4930847  4930873  4930889  4930927  4930939  4930951  4930963
4930973  4930997  4931011  4931023  4931063  4931119  4931141  4931149  4931153  4931159
4931183  4931191  4931209  4931219  4931221  4931231  4931237  4931261  4931299  4931327
4931389  4931441  4931461  4931467  4931473  4931477  4931489  4931497  4931539  4931543
4931557  4931561  4931587  4931593  4931599  4931623  4931639  4931651  4931657  4931671
4931687  4931699  4931749  4931753  4931761  4931769  4931783  4931813  4931833  4931837
4931879  4931881  4931893  4931897  4931903  4931909  4931917  4931939  4931947  4931957
4931999  4932017  4932043  4932047  4932073  4932079  4932089  4932101  4932107  4932119
4932121  4932139  4932163  4932167  4932173  4932181  4932199  4932209  4932241  4932247
4932251  4932269  4932271  4932287  4932293  4932311  4932313  4932331  4932371  4932383
4932409  4932427  4932437  4932439  4932449  4932461  4932463  4932467  4932489  4932493
4932497  4932541  4932559  4932611  4932619  4932623  4932637  4932671  4932673  4932677
4932691  4932713  4932727  4932731  4932743  4932757  4932769  4932779  4932797  4932817
4932821  4932827  4932853  4932859  4932881  4932883  4932901  4932947  4932953  4933007
4933031  4933039  4933069  4933087  4933127  4933147  4933153  4933157  4933171  4933177
4933207  4933223  4933259  4933283  4933289  4933297  4933301  4933303  4933307  4933333
4933351  4933361  4933363  4933367  4933373  4933381  4933387  4933421  4933427  4933457
4933493  4933493  4933499  4933501  4933529  4933531  4933549  4933573  4933583  4933589
4933601  4933631  4933633  4933697  4933727  4933751  4933759  4933783  4933793  4933801
4933811  4933829  4933843  4933849  4933871  4933889  4933897  4933909  4933967  4933969
4933979  4934023  4934047  4934057  4934087  4934093  4934113  4934117  4934119  4934123
4934161  4934183  4934197  4934203  4934219  4934221  4934231  4934257  4934269  4934291
```

```
4934297 4934311 4934317 4934327 4934341 4934383 4934387 4934399 4934401 4934407
4934441 4934453 4934467 4934477 4934491 4934507 4934513 4934521 4934533 4934537
4934543 4934561 4934569 4934591 4934621 4934647 4934651 4934659 4934663 4934689
4934747 4934773 4934779 4934791 4934807 4934837 4934849 4934863 4934869 4934889
4934929 4934939 4934971 4934977 4935011 4935013 4935043 4935053 4935061 4935089
4935101 4935103 4935121 4935127 4935131 4935149 4935157 4935167 4935187 4935197
4935199 4935221 4935223 4935241 4935247 4935257 4935283 4935299 4935313 4935323
4935331 4935341 4935361 4935377 4935379 4935391 4935407 4935419 4935431 4935443
4935461 4935487 4935499 4935503 4935521 4935523 4935529 4935533 4935563 4935569
4935607 4935613 4935617 4935641 4935647 4935653 4935691 4935719 4935739 4935743
4935757 4935779 4935787 4935793 4935809 4935811 4935817 4935859 4935871 4935919
4935929 4935941 4935947 4935977 4935979 4935989 4936033 4936073 4936079 4936097
4936111 4936121 4936123 4936153 4936163 4936189 4936193 4936201 4936213 4936241
4936249 4936279 4936291 4936297 4936301 4936319 4936339 4936343 4936381 4936391
4936411 4936423 4936433 4936439 4936453 4936469 4936483 4936499 4936507 4936531
4936537 4936541 4936549 4936567 4936601 4936619 4936649 4936667 4936693 4936703
4936717 4936721 4936727 4936753 4936793 4936819 4936823 4936831 4936837 4936847
4936859 4936861 4936879 4936891 4936909 4936951 4936961 4936963 4936993 4937027
4937033 4937041 4937113 4937129 4937147 4937161 4937167 4937171 4937173 4937197
4937201 4937237 4937239 4937267 4937281 4937287 4937291 4937323 4937329 4937347
4937363 4937371 4937381 4937399 4937417 4937423 4937441 4937461 4937467 4937483
4937509 4937551 4937563 4937573 4937641 4937657 4937659 4937677 4937683 4937719
4937731 4937791 4937797 4937813 4937839 4937843 4937869 4937873 4937879 4937899
4937903 4937921 4937941 4937953 4937963 4937971 4937993 4938029 4938047 4938049
4938071 4938097 4938103 4938113 4938127 4938137 4938139 4938151 4938161 4938181
4938187 4938191 4938203 4938209 4938217 4938229 4938239 4938247 4938259 4938277
4938281 4938287 4938289 4938293 4938301 4938317 4938319 4938341 4938361 4938379
4938383 4938389 4938397 4938403 4938407 4938413 4938443 4938467 4938473 4938509
4938529 4938539 4938559 4938583 4938587 4938589 4938599 4938601 4938617 4938623
4938643 4938673 4938683 4938701 4938707 4938733 4938761 4938779 4938833 4938853
4938881 4938887 4938907 4938929 4938931 4938943 4938979 4939003 4939021 4939037
4939049 4939073 4939079 4939091 4939111 4939127 4939139 4939141 4939169 4939171
4939211 4939213 4939223 4939237 4939243 4939271 4939279 4939289 4939313 4939331
4939339 4939349 4939357 4939369 4939387 4939391 4939423 4939427 4939433 4939439
4939471 4939511 4939523 4939567 4939573 4939577 4939609 4939621 4939631 4939637
4939661 4939667 4939679 4939681 4939717 4939729 4939751 4939763 4939769 4939783
4939787 4939789 4939807 4939813 4939817 4939853 4939859 4939861 4939901 4939903
4939933 4939939 4939973 4939993 4939997 4940017 4940051 4940071 4940137 4940153
4940161 4940197 4940219 4940231 4940233 4940263 4940279 4940289 4940281 4940291
4940293 4940303 4940321 4940333 4940339 4940359 4940363 4940371 4940381 4940389
4940407 4940413 4940417 4940431 4940443 4940447 4940461 4940503 4940519 4940521
4940531 4940539 4940587 4940609 4940629 4940641 4940651 4940669 4940671 4940711
4940717 4940729 4940731 4940753 4940759 4940797 4940809 4940813 4940827 4940867
4940879 4940891 4940899 4940909 4940911 4940959 4940977 4940983 4941043 4941047
4941071 4941127 4941149 4941161 4941163 4941187 4941193 4941217 4941221 4941227
4941229 4941241 4941247 4941253 4941257 4941263 4941269 4941283 4941289 4941319
4941323 4941337 4941347 4941353 4941359 4941383 4941413 4941421 4941449 4941487
4941511 4941551 4941557 4941569 4941593 4941613 4941623 4941637 4941641 4941649
4941659 4941661 4941709 4941731 4941749 4941751 4941763 4941787 4941817 4941821
4941847 4941857 4941863 4941901 4941907 4941913 4941929 4941931 4941943 4941961
4941967 4941971 4941979 4941983 4942013 4942039 4942057 4942061 4942073 4942111
4942123 4942177 4942183 4942193 4942199 4942211 4942213 4942241 4942271 4942283
4942313 4942339 4942351 4942373 4942397 4942411 4942501 4942513 4942519 4942541
4942573 4942579 4942601 4942627 4942633 4942687 4942697 4942703 4942709 4942711
4942739 4942747 4942753 4942771 4942781 4942799 4942811 4942877 4942879 4942901
4942909 4942913 4942951 4942969 4942991 4942993 4942997 4942999 4943009 4943011
4943017 4943027 4943051 4943053 4943063 4943069 4943077 4943087 4943093 4943101
4943111 4943119 4943143 4943153 4943177 4943189 4943201 4943207 4943219 4943227
4943261 4943269 4943273 4943299 4943317 4943333 4943339 4943347 4943357 4943377
4943383 4943387 4943417 4943429 4943431 4943441 4943467 4943473 4943479 4943483
4943489 4943503 4943509 4943531 4943567 4943573 4943641 4943657 4943693 4943699
4943707 4943711 4943713 4943723 4943737 4943747 4943749 4943767 4943777 4943797
4943831 4943837 4943843 4943921 4943927 4943939 4943963 4944019 4944029 4944053
4944073 4944077 4944083 4944101 4944113 4944119 4944139 4944143 4944157 4944169
4944197 4944209 4944223 4944257 4944281 4944299 4944307 4944311 4944319 4944337
4944341 4944343 4944361 4944367 4944371 4944383 4944391 4944397 4944409 4944421
4944437 4944451 4944463 4944473 4944479 4944481 4944487 4944497 4944521 4944523
4944539 4944547 4944557 4944571 4944581 4944607 4944623 4944631 4944659 4944661
4944679 4944683 4944691 4944697 4944707 4944713 4944733 4944743 4944781 4944787
4944803 4944817 4944827 4944833 4944849 4944869 4944883 4944899 4944911 4944923
4944949 4944983 4944991 4945001 4945007 4945009 4945019 4945033 4945081 4945091
4945103 4945121 4945123 4945141 4945153 4945159 4945183 4945231 4945243 4945261
4945267 4945273 4945277 4945279 4945307 4945327 4945333 4945373 4945393 4945397
4945411 4945469 4945477 4945511 4945513 4945519 4945537 4945541 4945553 4945579
4945597 4945601 4945609 4945613 4945639 4945651 4945663 4945673 4945687 4945693
4945711 4945723 4945727 4945741 4945777 4945783 4945807 4945813 4945849 4945859
4945867 4945879 4945937 4945939 4945961 4945973 4945981 4945987 4946003 4946009
4946017 4946027 4946033 4946041 4946047 4946057 4946083 4946087 4946089 4946101
4946107 4946113 4946129 4946131 4946171 4946189 4946191 4946203 4946209 4946231
4946237 4946257 4946299 4946323 4946341 4946351 4946387 4946393 4946399 4946401
4946411 4946413 4946467 4946471 4946497 4946509 4946519 4946533 4946557 4946581
4946603 4946647 4946653 4946657 4946663 4946671 4946681 4946687 4946713 4946723
4946729 4946731 4946741 4946747 4946759 4946761 4946789 4946803 4946809 4946827
4946833 4946857 4946873 4946899 4946923 4946927 4946939 4946947 4946951 4946989
4947013 4947029 4947043 4947083 4947109 4947121 4947143 4947167 4947181 4947191
4947199 4947203 4947251 4947263 4947269 4947287 4947301 4947311 4947329 4947331
4947337 4947367 4947373 4947377 4947403 4947413 4947431 4947463 4947499 4947517
4947521 4947557 4947559 4947571 4947573 4947589 4947601 4947613 4947617 4947641
4947653 4947659 4947727 4947743 4947763 4947779 4947789 4947797 4947821 4947841
```

4947853	4947857	4947863	4947871	4947949	4947959	4947979	4947991	4948039	4948057
4948079	4948087	4948093	4948109	4948117	4948201	4948213	4948219	4948231	4948247
4948267	4948283	4948291	4948337	4948351	4948367	4948369	4948387	4948393	4948409
4948423	4948441	4948457	4948459	4948501	4948523	4948529	4948571	4948579	4948613
4948621	4948631	4948633	4948637	4948661	4948673	4948679	4948681	4948693	4948729
4948733	4948739	4948777	4948807	4948829	4948831	4948849	4948859	4948883	4948891
4948897	4948901	4948939	4948961	4948963	4948969	4949003	4949027	4949029	4949033
4949051	4949059	4949081	4949093	4949107	4949141	4949143	4949167	4949179	4949213
4949221	4949239	4949249	4949267	4949279	4949293	4949297	4949341	4949353	4949359
4949369	4949389	4949407	4949419	4949423	4949437	4949447	4949449	4949471	4949489
4949501	4949521	4949551	4949579	4949591	4949557	4949599	4949603	4949611	4949621
4949627	4949641	4949663	4949667	4949683	4949689	4949699	4949717	4949719	4949741
4949743	4949753	4949779	4949797	4949827	4949837	4949843	4949881	4949891	4949921
4949939	4949951	4949963	4949977	4949983	4950067	4950103	4950107	4950109	4950131
4950133	4950137	4950139	4950151	4950157	4950199	4950259	4950287	4950307	4950311
4950331	4950343	4950353	4950373	4950389	4950397	4950401	4950403	4950409	4950419
4950427	4950433	4950467	4950479	4950487	4950493	4950499	4950509	4950511	4950521
4950527	4950541	4950559	4950581	4950593	4950599	4950611	4950613	4950623	4950629
4950661	4950683	4950707	4950707	4950713	4950733	4950739	4950779	4950797	4950817
4950833	4950853	4950857	4950871	4950923	4950931	4950937	4950941	4950971	4950991
4951013	4951019	4951021	4951057	4951073	4951091	4951109	4951127	4951151	4951157
4951183	4951189	4951213	4951217	4951231	4951253	4951259	4951277	4951333	4951357
4951361	4951379	4951393	4951399	4951409	4951421	4951439	4951459	4951511	4951549
4951561	4951567	4951589	4951613	4951621	4951627	4951633	4951637	4951643	4951649
4951657	4951679	4951691	4951703	4951729	4951733	4951741	4951757	4951783	4951787
4951789	4951813	4951819	4951823	4951829	4951861	4951867	4951883	4951897	4951901
4951907	4951943	4951963	4951987	4951997	4952023	4952071	4952081	4952089	4952093
4952113	4952119	4952147	4952149	4952173	4952177	4952183	4952201	4952203	4952209
4952231	4952239	4952257	4952261	4952279	4952317	4952323	4952327	4952351	4952357
4952371	4952377	4952399	4952443	4952447	4952449	4952461	4952477	4952489	4952501
4952503	4952543	4952551	4952569	4952587	4952609	4952619	4952663	4952669	4952671
4952681	4952683	4952699	4952713	4952743	4952767	4952771	4952807	4952809	4952819
4952833	4952837	4952861	4952887	4952891	4952897	4952921	4952929	4952947	4952953
4952957	4952971	4952989	4952993	4953023	4953043	4953049	4953059	4953061	4953077
4953083	4953089	4953101	4953121	4953133	4953199	4953209	4953233	4953259	4953271
4953293	4953313	4953317	4953331	4953353	4953391	4953413	4953439	4953451	4953479
4953491	4953493	4953527	4953541	4953551	4953569	4953587	4953593	4953601	4953607
4953617	4953629	4953631	4953667	4953673	4953677	4953679	4953701	4953709	4953713
4953719	4953761	4953787	4953791	4953797	4953811	4953827	4953833	4953869	4953877
4953899	4953911	4953917	4953929	4953931	4953943	4953961	4953973	4953979	4953997
4954013	4954031	4954049	4954051	4954063	4954067	4954087	4954091	4954109	4954121
4954127	4954139	4954199	4954211	4954219	4954241	4954247	4954249	4954253	4954267
4954277	4954303	4954321	4954333	4954351	4954409	4954423	4954457	4954471	4954487
4954507	4954511	4954549	4954553	4954561	4954577	4954597	4954601	4954613	4954619
4954627	4954639	4954661	4954669	4954721	4954751	4954771	4954777	4954793	4954799
4954841	4954843	4954883	4954903	4954909	4954919	4954921	4954927	4954931	4954951
4954967	4954979	4954981	4954987	4955011	4955033	4955039	4955059	4955081	4955087
4955089	4955099	4955101	4955107	4955123	4955131	4955147	4955179	4955221	4955263
4955297	4955311	4955323	4955329	4955339	4955359	4955393	4955399	4955407	4955417
4955581	4955593	4955597	4955611	4955627	4955641	4955647	4955693	4955719	4955737
4955747	4955761	4955771	4955773	4955791	4955801	4955803	4955809	4955831	4955851
4955869	4955887	4955893	4955911	4955917	4955933	4955947	4955953	4955963	4955981
4955987	4955989	4955999	4956011	4956023	4956073	4956097	4956139	4956151	4956157
4956173	4956181	4956221	4956227	4956233	4956241	4956251	4956253	4956269	4956313
4956337	4956349	4956353	4956379	4956383	4956389	4956437	4956443	4956451	4956461
4956467	4956487	4956491	4956509	4956521	4956529	4956533	4956541	4956547	4956563
4956577	4956599	4956607	4956617	4956629	4956643	4956691	4956703	4956733	4956781
4956793	4956803	4956811	4956817	4956821	4956823	4956827	4956829	4956857	4956871
4956893	4956899	4956901	4956943	4956947	4956977	4957019	4957021	4957031	4957039
4957049	4957063	4957087	4957091	4957093	4957097	4957103	4957109	4957123	4957153
4957159	4957177	4957207	4957219	4957229	4957243	4957247	4957261	4957283	4957301
4957307	4957321	4957327	4957333	4957349	4957361	4957363	4957373	4957391	4957399
4957411	4957441	4957457	4957471	4957483	4957529	4957549	4957553	4957559	4957583
4957609	4957633	4957639	4957663	4957691	4957703	4957709	4957721	4957723	4957739
4957747	4957751	4957769	4957769	4957781	4957789	4957801	4957817	4957819	4957837
4957847	4957871	4957873	4957891	4957913	4957919	4957921	4957937	4957969	4957987
4958011	4958017	4958021	4958131	4958189	4958209	4958227	4958231	4958251	4958257
4958299	4958311	4958321	4958323	4958329	4958347	4958351	4958377	4958381	4958383
4958399	4958413	4958423	4958467	4958491	4958497	4958539	4958549	4958561	4958567
4958579	4958587	4958617	4958633	4958647	4958651	4958659	4958693	4958719	4958761
4958771	4958801	4958819	4958843	4958861	4958879	4958893	4958903	4958911	4958957
4958983	4959013	4959037	4959041	4959043	4959047	4959049	4959079	4959083	4959113
4959151	4959161	4959181	4959197	4959277	4959289	4959313	4959341	4959371	4959379
4959389	4959397	4959413	4959419	4959431	4959463	4959469	4959497	4959503	4959511
4959523	4959527	4959533	4959569	4959583	4959587	4959593	4959637	4959641	4959653
4959673	4959679	4959701	4959719	4959751	4959761	4959833	4959853	4959883	4959919
4959923	4959947	4959949	4959959	4959991	4960001	4960013	4960027	4960037	4960049
4960097	4960117	4960127	4960129	4960133	4960147	4960169	4960181	4960187	4960201
4960213	4960223	4960231	4960259	4960283	4960297	4960301	4960309	4960313	4960327
4960339	4960343	4960367	4960391	4960393	4960451	4960453	4960457	4960471	4960477
4960499	4960507	4960511	4960519	4960531	4960561	4960567	4960591	4960601	4960603
4960607	4960639	4960673	4960687	4960693	4960717	4960727	4960741	4960751	4960757
4960763	4960807	4960811	4960829	4960831	4960859	4960883	4960903	4960909	4960913
4960927	4960931	4960933	4960937	4960951	4960973	4960979	4960981	4960987	4961017
4961027	4961053	4961057	4961063	4961083	4961087	4961107	4961113	4961119	4961129
4961141	4961183	4961207	4961213	4961237	4961249	4961311	4961317	4961321	4961323
4961329	4961339	4961351	4961371	4961377	4961389	4961443	4961449	4961459	4961471
4961477	4961479	4961497	4961503	4961507	4961513	4961521	4961531	4961543	4961549

```
4961563  4961587  4961599  4961609  4961633  4961659  4961669  4961689  4961699  4961707
4961713  4961741  4961777  4961783  4961791  4961797  4961809  4961821  4961833  4961851
4961863  4961897  4961903  4961917  4961921  4961927  4961939  4961941  4961947  4961963
4961969  4962037  4962047  4962049  4962053  4962073  4962091  4962109  4962131  4962137
4962143  4962151  4962163  4962187  4962193  4962239  4962257  4962259  4962301  4962311
4962323  4962341  4962343  4962359  4962361  4962367  4962389  4962407  4962409  4962421
4962427  4962469  4962491  4962493  4962527  4962539  4962557  4962569  4962571  4962577
4962583  4962611  4962619  4962631  4962637  4962647  4962649  4962677  4962703  4962707
4962709  4962719  4962721  4962731  4962751  4962787  4962791  4962803  4962833  4962863
4962869  4962877  4962911  4962949  4962953  4962967  4962977  4962983  4962989  4963001
4963003  4963019  4963027  4963037  4963043  4963061  4963067  4963093  4963109  4963121
4963157  4963163  4963171  4963181  4963183  4963207  4963213  4963243  4963253  4963267
4963279  4963307  4963327  4963349  4963363  4963369  4963391  4963403  4963411  4963417
4963421  4963429  4963451  4963463  4963471  4963481  4963487  4963499  4963523  4963547
4963559  4963571  4963573  4963589  4963597  4963603  4963613  4963633  4963639  4963663
4963667  4963687  4963697  4963723  4963771  4963787  4963801  4963853  4963859  4963891
4963897  4963909  4963943  4963961  4963967  4964009  4964041  4964053  4964059  4964087
4964101  4964129  4964171  4964173  4964189  4964209  4964227  4964243  4964261  4964273
4964279  4964293  4964317  4964341  4964369  4964381  4964383  4964387  4964411  4964413
4964417  4964447  4964461  4964467  4964471  4964473  4964483  4964489  4964503  4964543
4964569  4964579  4964591  4964599  4964621  4964627  4964639  4964647  4964699  4964741
4964753  4964761  4964777  4964779  4964789  4964797  4964801  4964819  4964821  4964831
4964837  4964863  4964873  4964879  4964891  4964893  4964899  4964903  4964951  4964957
4965001  4965007  4965013  4965019  4965029  4965047  4965049  4965083  4965089  4965091
4965131  4965151  4965157  4965161  4965179  4965187  4965193  4965197  4965203  4965209
4965227  4965269  4965271  4965283  4965287  4965299  4965307  4965347  4965349  4965353
4965361  4965371  4965379  4965383  4965391  4965397  4965413  4965419  4965421  4965449
4965451  4965481  4965509  4965523  4965557  4965563  4965589  4965599  4965601  4965607
4965613  4965629  4965637  4965649  4965661  4965671  4965689  4965731  4965739  4965743
4965761  4965767  4965773  4965781  4965787  4965791  4965799  4965803  4965833  4965841
4965847  4965869  4965893  4965899  4965911  4965923  4965943  4965959  4965967  4965979
4965991  4966001  4966007  4966033  4966051  4966061  4966099  4966123  4966127  4966147
4966151  4966189  4966243  4966267  4966301  4966343  4966373  4966393  4966411  4966421
4966441  4966483  4966501  4966513  4966519  4966523  4966529  4966531  4966553  4966571
4966579  4966613  4966639  4966649  4966667  4966673  4966697  4966711  4966723  4966783
4966799  4966807  4966811  4966813  4966817  4966831  4966837  4966849  4966853  4966889
4966891  4966901  4966903  4966909  4966937  4966939  4966963  4966979  4967023  4967041
4967051  4967069  4967087  4967093  4967143  4967147  4967153  4967167  4967177
4967197  4967201  4967203  4967219  4967233  4967243  4967257  4967267  4967279  4967293
4967297  4967309  4967311  4967321  4967329  4967353  4967377  4967401  4967407  4967411
4967419  4967423  4967449  4967453  4967461  4967491  4967513  4967537  4967549  4967579
4967617  4967629  4967647  4967653  4967659  4967681  4967687  4967737  4967761  4967773
4967777  4967783  4967801  4967803  4967813  4967821  4967827  4967857  4967861  4967867
4967881  4967899  4967909  4967917  4967923  4967933  4967969  4967971  4967981  4967993
4968017  4968037  4968059  4968109  4968121  4968127  4968133  4968149  4968151  4968157
4968169  4968179  4968203  4968209  4968239  4968241  4968283  4968287  4968289  4968317
4968319  4968343  4968347  4968371  4968373  4968407  4968409  4968427  4968473  4968479
4968487  4968499  4968517  4968559  4968563  4968577  4968583  4968589  4968611  4968637
4968643  4968647  4968661  4968679  4968683  4968707  4968721  4968727  4968731  4968739
4968757  4968763  4968797  4968809  4968827  4968829  4968857  4968869  4968871  4968881
4968883  4968907  4968917  4968967  4968979  4968991  4969031  4969057  4969061  4969067
4969087  4969091  4969093  4969141  4969163  4969177  4969193  4969199  4969231  4969267
4969271  4969277  4969291  4969297  4969309  4969313  4969319  4969339  4969351  4969369
4969373  4969399  4969417  4969427  4969463  4969477  4969483  4969567  4969571  4969589
4969603  4969619  4969631  4969649  4969681  4969691  4969693  4969709  4969751  4969777
4969793  4969799  4969801  4969807  4969813  4969823  4969837  4969841  4969843  4969847
4969873  4969879  4969883  4969901  4969931  4969961  4969973  4969997  4970029  4970057
4970083  4970089  4970131  4970177  4970209  4970221  4970227  4970233  4970237  4970249
4970263  4970279  4970309  4970333  4970347  4970353  4970401  4970417  4970429  4970453
4970479  4970489  4970503  4970519  4970551  4970557  4970569  4970587  4970591  4970611
4970657  4970659  4970683  4970689  4970699  4970701  4970729  4970743  4970773  4970827
4970831  4970857  4970863  4970873  4970887  4970891  4970897  4970909  4970941  4970947
4970969  4970981  4970993  4971007  4971017  4971019  4971023  4971037  4971047  4971053
4971133  4971137  4971139  4971171  4971173  4971181  4971193  4971203  4971223  4971229
4971257  4971269  4971271  4971287  4971301  4971313  4971341  4971397  4971409  4971419
4971433  4971437  4971443  4971493  4971529  4971553  4971583  4971587  4971643  4971671
4971677  4971679  4971691  4971709  4971721  4971737  4971739  4971751  4971763  4971773
4971781  4971797  4971823  4971833  4971839  4971851  4971859  4971881  4971893  4971907
4971931  4971943  4971959  4971971  4971991  4972001  4972013  4972031  4972061  4972063
4972067  4972069  4972081  4972127  4972147  4972151  4972153  4972159  4972189  4972199
4972207  4972223  4972229  4972267  4972283  4972291  4972309  4972321  4972327  4972333
4972337  4972349  4972351  4972379  4972399  4972411  4972417  4972423  4972469  4972481
4972501  4972507  4972523  4972529  4972549  4972559  4972567  4972571  4972573  4972589
4972607  4972609  4972621  4972633  4972651  4972663  4972691  4972727  4972729  4972739
4972771  4972783  4972829  4972841  4972843  4972861  4972867  4972909  4972917  4972921
4972951  4972969  4972987  4972999  4973009  4973011  4973021  4973029  4973047  4973057
4973069  4973071  4973077  4973107  4973119  4973131  4973141  4973167  4973179  4973233
4973249  4973263  4973279  4973303  4973317  4973327  4973329  4973347  4973357  4973363
4973369  4973377  4973387  4973393  4973411  4973483  4973539  4973557  4973567  4973581
4973597  4973623  4973627  4973663  4973711  4973719  4973743  4973747  4973753  4973791
4973807  4973821  4973827  4973861  4973867  4973887  4973897  4973929  4973959  4973989
4974007  4974019  4974023  4974041  4974071  4974083  4974097  4974127  4974131  4974133
4974139  4974157  4974163  4974199  4974227  4974239  4974241  4974287  4974311  4974313
4974329  4974337  4974377  4974397  4974401  4974413  4974427  4974443  4974449  4974479
4974491  4974493  4974501  4974503  4974511  4974517  4974521  4974559  4974577  4974581
4974583  4974587  4974649  4974691  4974707  4974711  4974721  4974743  4974773  4974779
4974793  4974811  4974883  4974887  4974889  4974901  4974913  4974919  4974929
4974943  4974953  4975001  4975013  4975021  4975027  4975031  4975039  4975043  4975049
4975073  4975079  4975081  4975109  4975111  4975121  4975127  4975129  4975141  4975151
```

```
4975177  4975193  4975213  4975241  4975247  4975253  4975297  4975301  4975319  4975331
4975349  4975351  4975387  4975403  4975409  4975417  4975457  4975459  4975463  4975493
4975507  4975513  4975517  4975519  4975549  4975547  4975571  4975589  4975631  4975639
4975643  4975651  4975661  4975669  4975673  4975757  4975759  4975769  4975787  4975793
4975807  4975813  4975819  4975823  4975829  4975837  4975847  4975877  4975879  4975897
4975909  4975913  4975921  4975931  4975963  4975969  4975979  4975991  4976017  4976029
4976039  4976057  4976063  4976107  4976113  4976137  4976143  4976149  4976161  4976171
4976173  4976183  4976203  4976263  4976269  4976281  4976299  4976317  4976333  4976341
4976351  4976369  4976381  4976383  4976401  4976437  4976443  4976449  4976453  4976459
4976467  4976497  4976509  4976549  4976551  4976557  4976567  4976581  4976593  4976623
4976639  4976663  4976683  4976687  4976701  4976707  4976711  4976723  4976731  4976747
4976761  4976773  4976789  4976813  4976837  4976843  4976849  4976861  4976897  4976899
4976911  4976927  4976941  4976953  4976963  4976987  4976999  4977017  4977023  4977041
4977053  4977059  4977061  4977097  4977103  4977109  4977127  4977139  4977157  4977163
4977169  4977197  4977211  4977227  4977233  4977239  4977251  4977263  4977317  4977331
4977337  4977341  4977367  4977403  4977409  4977419  4977421  4977431  4977433  4977437
4977439  4977443  4977461  4977491  4977493  4977517  4977521  4977527  4977529  4977541
4977547  4977559  4977569  4977571  4977611  4977649  4977659  4977667  4977671  4977673
4977689  4977691  4977697  4977733  4977743  4977751  4977757  4977767  4977781  4977799
4977823  4977853  4977871  4977877  4977893  4977901  4977953  4977971  4977977  4977979
4978003  4978009  4978031  4978031  4978069  4978079  4978081  4978109  4978121  4978147
4978151  4978157  4978159  4978163  4978187  4978199  4978213  4978217  4978219  4978241
4978277  4978279  4978283  4978291  4978349  4978367  4978397  4978403  4978417  4978427
4978429  4978447  4978451  4978453  4978471  4978483  4978487  4978543  4978553  4978559
4978577  4978579  4978607  4978651  4978657  4978681  4978697  4978709  4978723  4978751
4978763  4978783  4978801  4978829  4978847  4978867  4978879  4978889  4978901  4978903
4978907  4978937  4978957  4978973  4978993  4979021  4979027  4979033  4979047  4979057
4979059  4979071  4979101  4979131  4979137  4979141  4979153  4979171  4979173  4979209
4979263  4979267  4979281  4979287  4979309  4979333  4979347  4979353  4979363
4979371  4979393  4979411  4979413  4979467  4979473  4979479  4979489  4979519  4979531
4979537  4979551  4979563  4979581  4979587  4979591  4979599  4979609  4979617  4979627
4979633  4979647  4979651  4979669  4979671  4979683  4979687  4979693  4979713  4979717
4979743  4979749  4979761  4979789  4979801  4979831  4979837  4979839  4979879  4979893
4979903  4979911  4979921  4979939  4979969  4979977  4979981  4979993  4979999  4980047
4980067  4980097  4980103  4980113  4980127  4980161  4980169  4980179  4980187  4980191
4980193  4980211  4980229  4980253  4980281  4980289  4980301  4980323  4980331  4980347
4980383  4980401  4980419  4980421  4980427  4980499  4980551  4980583  4980587
4980601  4980611  4980617  4980629  4980631  4980671  4980683  4980691  4980727  4980749
4980763  4980797  4980809  4980817  4980827  4980863  4980883  4980889  4980893  4980901
4980929  4980947  4980959  4980961  4980971  4981019  4981027  4981057  4981091  4981103
4981157  4981217  4981231  4981237  4981259  4981261  4981303  4981309  4981313  4981337
4981349  4981351  4981367  4981373  4981387  4981393  4981423  4981441  4981451  4981469
4981481  4981513  4981519  4981531  4981549  4981579  4981589  4981601  4981609
4981631  4981633  4981637  4981673  4981699  4981709  4981727  4981729  4981747  4981751
4981759  4981763  4981771  4981789  4981807  4981811  4981861  4981877  4981903  4981913
4981927  4981967  4981979  4981993  4982011  4982039  4982051  4982059  4982077  4982093
4982101  4982119  4982129  4982147  4982179  4982183  4982189  4982203  4982209  4982221
4982231  4982233  4982249  4982269  4982273  4982291  4982311  4982317  4982333  4982339
4982357  4982359  4982381  4982401  4982429  4982437  4982441  4982449  4982501  4982507
4982533  4982563  4982569  4982587  4982603  4982629  4982641  4982657  4982707  4982729
4982741  4982773  4982777  4982833  4982837  4982869  4982887  4982897  4982899  4982903
4982933  4982941  4982977  4982981  4983001  4983031  4983047  4983079  4983107  4983127
4983131  4983137  4983163  4983169  4983179  4983191  4983211  4983217  4983229  4983233
4983283  4983287  4983299  4983323  4983359  4983361  4983379  4983383  4983401  4983421
4983437  4983439  4983443  4983463  4983469  4983481  4983497  4983521  4983523  4983547
4983581  4983599  4983613  4983623  4983631  4983647  4983669  4983689  4983691  4983697
4983701  4983707  4983721  4983731  4983751  4983767  4983773  4983787  4983791  4983793
4983809  4983821  4983857  4983859  4983877  4983887  4983917  4983931  4983949  4983959
4983971  4983973  4983977  4983983  4984013  4984019  4984033  4984037  4984039  4984073
4984117  4984139  4984153  4984163  4984171  4984181  4984207  4984241  4984253  4984277
4984283  4984313  4984321  4984333  4984337  4984339  4984351  4984361  4984373  4984391
4984423  4984429  4984439  4984481  4984487  4984489  4984523  4984531  4984541  4984547
4984561  4984571  4984579  4984589  4984591  4984633  4984667  4984673  4984687  4984699
4984709  4984711  4984717  4984729  4984741  4984753  4984799  4984817  4984829  4984841
4984849  4984853  4984871  4984871  4984919  4984919  4984933  4984937
4984939  4984949  4984999  4985003  4985027  4985041  4985051  4985059  4985069  4985081
4985083  4985107  4985159  4985161  4985177  4985209  4985213  4985249  4985251  4985257
4985261  4985263  4985287  4985317  4985359  4985371  4985381  4985399  4985423  4985443
4985473  4985483  4985489  4985507  4985521  4985527  4985557  4985569  4985597  4985599
4985609  4985623  4985627  4985647  4985663  4985693  4985711  4985731  4985741  4985749
4985753  4985789  4985797  4985801  4985803  4985819  4985821  4985831  4985837  4985839
4985863  4985881  4985909  4985951  4985971  4985989  4985993  4986001  4986011  4986013
4986019  4986029  4986041  4986061  4986077  4986097  4986103  4986109  4986131  4986139
4986143  4986167  4986169  4986181  4986197  4986199  4986203  4986209  4986211  4986221
4986229  4986251  4986269  4986283  4986299  4986313  4986323  4986337  4986349  4986353
4986361  4986367  4986383  4986407  4986413  4986419  4986427  4986431  4986439  4986481
4986511  4986517  4986523  4986529  4986547  4986551  4986613  4986647  4986649  4986677
4986679  4986697  4986701  4986713  4986719  4986767  4986769  4986799  4986809  4986847
4986853  4986887  4986893  4986901  4986913  4986923  4986931  4986941  4986959  4986977
4986979  4986983  4987007  4987009  4987019  4987027  4987057  4987079  4987091
4987109  4987127  4987207  4987223  4987231  4987259  4987271  4987303  4987319  4987321
4987327  4987331  4987351  4987393  4987397  4987399  4987403  4987427  4987429  4987439
4987453  4987457  4987501  4987523  4987531  4987561  4987567  4987589  4987597  4987607
4987627  4987639  4987657  4987663  4987667  4987669  4987673  4987693  4987721  4987729
4987769  4987771  4987793  4987813  4987819  4987847  4987867  4987877  4987891
4987901  4987903  4987907  4987921  4987943  4987951  4987967  4987973  4987979  4987999
4988003  4988023  4988057  4988077  4988099  4988111  4988119  4988131  4988141  4988143
4988173  4988177  4988189  4988197  4988209  4988219  4988227  4988231  4988299  4988311
4988323  4988339  4988353  4988363  4988369  4988381  4988407  4988411  4988437  4988449
```

```
4988453  4988513  4988527  4988537  4988563  4988569  4988579  4988591  4988651  4988653
4988657  4988663  4988681  4988689  4988699  4988713  4988719  4988741  4988749  4988759
4988761  4988831  4988833  4988843  4988891  4988917  4988927  4988947  4988959  4988983
4988987  4988993  4989029  4989053  4989067  4989079  4989107  4989113  4989119  4989121
4989133  4989139  4989151  4989157  4989169  4989181  4989199  4989203  4989209  4989221
4989277  4989287  4989293  4989301  4989337  4989349  4989353  4989359  4989371  4989377
4989409  4989427  4989431  4989437  4989443  4989451  4989461  4989463  4989469  4989499
4989503  4989511  4989541  4989581  4989599  4989613  4989637  4989641  4989697  4989701
4989707  4989713  4989757  4989767  4989773  4989779  4989797  4989811  4989821  4989841
4989847  4989851  4989863  4989917  4989937  4989947  4989949  4989953  4989973  4989979
4989991  4989997  4990019  4990031  4990049  4990067  4990091  4990121  4990133  4990157
4990177  4990187  4990189  4990199  4990201  4990213  4990229  4990243  4990259  4990261
4990267  4990273  4990277  4990303  4990313  4990327  4990339  4990343  4990357  4990393
4990409  4990421  4990429  4990439  4990441  4990463  4990477  4990493  4990501  4990529
4990543  4990547  4990567  4990577  4990589  4990591  4990603  4990613  4990631  4990637
4990649  4990679  4990693  4990717  4990723  4990753  4990759  4990771  4990781  4990823
4990831  4990849  4990891  4990919  4990927  4990933  4990949  4990961  4990981  4991009
4991011  4991029  4991033  4991101  4991123  4991131  4991137  4991143  4991153  4991159
4991171  4991201  4991237  4991249  4991257  4991267  4991291  4991293  4991297  4991303
4991317  4991333  4991339  4991347  4991359  4991383  4991401  4991407  4991417  4991419
4991423  4991429  4991431  4991449  4991453  4991461  4991473  4991479  4991491  4991507
4991543  4991551  4991561  4991563  4991573  4991587  4991617  4991647  4991653  4991663
4991671  4991677  4991681  4991687  4991719  4991771  4991801  4991803  4991839  4991843
4991849  4991867  4991879  4991881  4991893  4991923  4991933  4991951  4991953  4991963
4991977  4991983  4992007  4992019  4992061  4992073  4992083  4992107  4992109  4992133
4992137  4992149  4992157  4992181  4992187  4992233  4992241  4992259  4992287  4992341
4992347  4992349  4992353  4992359  4992389  4992401  4992409  4992413  4992419  4992439
4992461  4992487  4992499  4992511  4992517  4992539  4992551  4992569  4992583  4992593
4992619  4992623  4992629  4992661  4992671  4992677  4992683  4992703  4992707  4992709
4992731  4992737  4992769  4992787  4992809  4992821  4992833  4992913  4992919  4992929
4992937  4992943  4992947  4992961  4992973  4992997  4993003  4993007  4993049  4993057
4993061  4993097  4993123  4993129  4993147  4993151  4993159  4993199  4993207  4993213
4993237  4993271  4993283  4993321  4993343  4993379  4993397  4993403  4993411  4993433
4993441  4993451  4993453  4993459  4993517  4993537  4993559  4993579  4993591  4993603
4993613  4993619  4993621  4993627  4993661  4993673  4993679  4993687  4993693  4993741
4993757  4993777  4993811  4993817  4993823  4993837  4993843  4993847  4993867  4993871
4993873  4993897  4993907  4993909  4993913  4993931  4993943  4993949  4993951  4993987
4993993  4993999  4994051  4994081  4994089  4994117  4994123  4994153  4994179  4994203
4994219  4994221  4994233  4994237  4994257  4994263  4994273  4994309  4994329  4994357
4994369  4994387  4994393  4994401  4994411  4994417  4994419  4994461  4994471  4994477
4994501  4994513  4994543  4994557  4994569  4994599  4994603  4994621  4994659  4994669
4994723  4994729  4994761  4994789  4994791  4994807  4994819  4994851  4994897  4994903
4994909  4994981  4994987  4994993  4995007  4995017  4995031  4995041  4995049  4995073
4995079  4995083  4995097  4995101  4995139  4995169  4995187  4995203  4995227  4995241
4995253  4995281  4995283  4995299  4995311  4995323  4995349  4995373  4995377  4995379
4995383  4995421  4995427  4995449  4995457  4995479  4995493  4995503  4995517  4995527
4995539  4995541  4995547  4995553  4995581  4995607  4995643  4995647  4995649  4995667
4995673  4995691  4995701  4995709  4995713  4995719  4995779  4995827  4995863  4995871
4995877  4995883  4995889  4995911  4995919  4995923  4995931  4995941  4995953  4995983
4995997  4996003  4996049  4996051  4996081  4996087  4996097  4996099  4996111  4996141
4996169  4996223  4996247  4996273  4996289  4996291  4996309  4996319  4996333  4996477
4996349  4996361  4996367  4996399  4996421  4996423  4996441  4996457  4996463  4996477
4996493  4996501  4996507  4996531  4996553  4996559  4996573  4996609  4996619  4996627
4996637  4996679  4996687  4996697  4996703  4996709  4996723  4996757  4996841  4996879
4996883  4996891  4996913  4996919  4996933  4996949  4996967  4996991  4997011  4997017
4997029  4997033  4997063  4997093  4997101  4997119  4997173  4997191  4997219  4997227
4997243  4997273  4997281  4997287  4997297  4997327  4997339  4997353  4997381  4997383
4997387  4997389  4997393  4997401  4997471  4997491  4997521  4997533  4997539  4997549
4997563  4997567  4997569  4997579  4997593  4997611  4997621  4997659  4997683  4997687
4997689  4997717  4997747  4997753  4997801  4997813  4997837  4997887  4997891  4997899
4997917  4997921  4997929  4997981  4997989  4998001  4998013  4998031  4998073  4998089
4998101  4998109  4998113  4998131  4998137  4998181  4998211  4998229  4998233  4998241
4998319  4998341  4998359  4998361  4998373  4998407  4998419  4998437  4998439  4998467
4998479  4998541  4998547  4998557  4998559  4998563  4998569  4998571  4998583  4998599
4998601  4998611  4998619  4998641  4998647  4998667  4998671  4998673  4998683  4998689
4998713  4998733  4998739  4998743  4998757  4998769  4998787  4998823  4998839  4998853
4998859  4998869  4998887  4998911  4998913  4998941  4998943  4998947  4998971  4998979
4998989  4998997  4999021  4999031  4999081  4999087  4999097  4999103  4999117  4999121
4999151  4999177  4999187  4999201  4999217  4999231  4999237  4999243  4999273  4999297
4999301  4999307  4999321  4999327  4999363  4999387  4999391  4999409  4999427  4999439
4999447  4999453  4999457  4999469  4999493  4999507  4999523  4999529  4999537  4999559
4999591  4999597  4999613  4999627  4999633  4999637  4999639  4999651  4999661  4999667
4999681  4999693  4999703  4999727  4999733  4999759  4999769  4999781  4999783  4999801
4999823  4999849  4999867  4999871  4999879  4999889  4999913  4999933  4999949  4999957
4999961  4999963  4999999  5000011  5000077  5000081  5000087  5000101  5000111  5000113
5000153  5000161  5000167  5000197  5000201  5000213  5000251  5000257  5000263  5000299
5000311  5000321  5000339  5000381  5000389  5000399  5000423  5000473  5000491  5000503
5000519  5000539  5000543  5000549  5000551  5000563  5000581  5000623  5000627  5000651
5000657  5000687  5000689  5000701  5000713  5000741  5000747  5000759  5000761  5000777
5000783  5000791  5000797  5000851  5000861  5000881  5000903  5000917  5000923  5000927
5000929  5000939  5000977  5000981  5000987  5000993  5001001  5001019  5001023  5001049
5001053  5001067  5001071  5001083  5001089  5001119  5001121  5001127  5001163  5001167
5001173  5001193  5001197  5001203  5001233  5001251  5001277  5001289  5001299  5001301
5001307  5001319  5001343  5001361  5001379  5001391  5001397  5001407  5001413  5001421
5001431  5001433  5001443  5001461  5001481  5001487  5001523  5001539  5001547  5001559
5001593  5001629  5001643  5001653  5001671  5001679  5001691  5001701  5001707  5001739
5001743  5001749  5001761  5001767  5001779  5001809  5001907  5001911  5001923  5001967
5001979  5002001  5002003  5002051  5002057  5002093  5002103  5002133  5002157  5002189
5002211  5002219  5002223  5002229  5002237  5002241  5002259  5002273  5002313  5002321
```

```
5002331 5002373 5002379 5002391 5002457 5002463 5002489 5002499 5002507 5002519
5002537 5002541 5002553 5002561 5002579 5002583 5002637 5002639 5002649 5002651
5002691 5002721 5002729 5002741 5002747 5002771 5002801 5002817 5002841 5002843
5002847 5002859 5002883 5002889 5002901 5002903 5002927 5002939 5002979 5003003
5003039 5003071 5003077 5003081 5003101 5003111 5003113 5003123 5003143 5003191
5003203 5003227 5003231 5003239 5003249 5003261 5003263 5003267 5003303 5003309
5003329 5003371 5003387 5003407 5003429 5003459 5003477 5003483 5003503 5003507
5003513 5003519 5003539 5003543 5003549 5003591 5003597 5003633 5003653 5003657
5003659 5003671 5003699 5003701 5003711 5003717 5003737 5003743 5003749 5003759
5003771 5003773 5003809 5003813 5003819 5003827 5003837 5003839 5003881 5003893
5003909 5003923 5003951 5003959 5003963 5003969 5003981 5003983 5003993 5004007
5004017 5004019 5004031 5004053 5004059 5004067 5004071 5004073 5004089 5004119
5004121 5004127 5004143 5004149 5004157 5004193 5004217 5004221 5004227 5004281
5004323 5004359 5004367 5004401 5004403 5004437 5004451 5004457 5004491 5004539
5004553 5004569 5004599 5004611 5004653 5004677 5004679 5004697 5004707 5004721
5004739 5004751 5004757 5004767 5004799 5004803 5004821 5004827 5004841 5004859
5004871 5004877 5004893 5004929 5004931 5004941 5004971 5004977 5004991 5005001
5005031 5005057 5005067 5005087 5005127 5005129 5005141 5005159 5005177 5005199
5005201 5005213 5005219 5005223 5005261 5005289 5005307 5005309 5005337 5005339
5005367 5005381 5005411 5005423 5005433 5005439 5005489 5005523 5005549 5005613
5005621 5005639 5005643 5005669 5005687 5005703 5005709 5005757 5005783 5005799
5005817 5005823 5005859 5005867 5005877 5005883 5005907 5005909 5005921 5005933
5005961 5005969 5005981 5005991 5006003 5006011 5006021 5006047 5006069 5006077
5006081 5006083 5006119 5006123 5006129 5006147 5006149 5006153 5006171 5006179
5006191 5006207 5006231 5006233 5006237 5006269 5006273 5006297 5006317 5006369
5006377 5006383 5006399 5006401 5006411 5006429 5006431 5006437 5006459 5006489
5006497 5006501 5006503 5006509 5006513 5006527 5006537 5006543 5006579 5006587
5006591 5006597 5006609 5006611 5006621 5006623 5006657 5006669 5006693 5006711
5006719 5006737 5006741 5006753 5006761 5006767 5006773 5006831 5006859 5006867
5006909 5006923 5006929 5006971 5006983 5007001 5007007 5007011 5007017 5007047
5007059 5007071 5007109 5007113 5007137 5007157 5007179 5007181 5007187 5007191
5007193 5007209 5007251 5007253 5007263 5007283 5007313 5007319 5007323 5007341
5007347 5007377 5007383 5007391 5007397 5007413 5007421 5007433 5007439 5007449
5007463 5007467 5007481 5007529 5007533 5007539 5007553 5007577 5007589 5007593
5007601 5007619 5007623 5007637 5007643 5007661 5007671 5007679 5007689 5007703
5007719 5007733 5007791 5007791 5007797 5007817 5007841 5007851 5007853 5007881
5007907 5007929 5007943 5007949 5007967 5007983 5008007 5008009 5008021 5008057
5008063 5008079 5008099 5008103 5008111 5008121 5008123 5008139 5008147
5008151 5008187 5008193 5008219 5008231 5008259 5008277 5008279 5008291 5008369
5008379 5008417 5008429 5008433 5008481 5008483 5008513 5008517 5008529 5008537
5008559 5008567 5008573 5008607 5008651 5008681 5008691 5008699 5008709
5008711 5008721 5008739 5008741 5008807 5008811 5008819 5008841 5008859 5008867
5008873 5008901 5008921 5009003 5009021 5009051 5009057 5009063 5009077
5009087 5009089 5009099 5009107 5009117 5009129 5009149 5009167 5009233 5009269
5009281 5009287 5009317 5009327 5009341 5009359 5009413 5009443 5009449 5009453
5009491 5009497 5009519 5009527 5009539 5009599 5009543 5009559 5009579 5009581
5009591 5009593 5009603 5009617 5009621 5009623 5009651 5009659 5009677 5009707
5009719 5009723 5009729 5009737 5009761 5009783 5009803 5009821 5009839 5009857
5009881 5009891 5009897 5009909 5009947 5009957 5009959 5009969 5009971 5009987
5009989 5009993 5010013 5010017 5010041 5010043 5010073 5010079 5010107 5010119
5010163 5010169 5010217 5010233 5010263 5010283 5010287 5010289 5010293 5010329
5010337 5010349 5010353 5010361 5010367 5010373 5010407 5010409 5010419 5010431
5010449 5010451 5010463 5010491 5010493 5010497 5010517 5010539 5010557 5010559
5010583 5010589 5010613 5010637 5010667 5010671 5010679 5010689 5010701 5010727
5010751 5010763 5010769 5010781 5010787 5010791 5010827 5010877 5010883 5010893
5010931 5010949 5010953 5010977 5011001 5011007 5011031 5011041 5011051 5011063
5011099 5011121 5011129 5011133 5011147 5011151 5011189 5011199 5011213 5011249
5011271 5011271 5011273 5011301 5011313 5011319 5011327 5011337 5011339 5011343
5011351 5011361 5011381 5011387 5011439 5011451 5011507 5011529 5011537 5011543
5011561 5011579 5011609 5011619 5011621 5011639 5011661 5011729 5011759 5011771
5011781 5011807 5011817 5011829 5011843 5011847 5011849 5011859 5011879 5011901
5011927 5011931 5011967 5011969 5011973 5012003 5012011 5012023 5012027 5012039
5012047 5012053 5012101 5012113 5012129 5012141 5012153 5012159 5012167 5012177
5012239 5012243 5012251 5012261 5012299 5012303 5012323 5012347 5012377 5012383
5012407 5012411 5012417 5012429 5012473 5012489 5012507 5012519 5012521 5012531
5012533 5012543 5012549 5012573 5012587 5012591 5012627 5012633 5012647 5012653
5012659 5012663 5012719 5012729 5012741 5012743 5012767 5012803 5012831 5012849
5012857 5012867 5012881 5012923 5012927 5012929 5012939 5012957 5012971 5012981
5012993 5012999 5013023 5013037 5013083 5013089 5013101 5013119 5013133 5013137
5013139 5013179 5013191 5013199 5013209 5013221 5013247 5013257 5013269 5013277
5013293 5013301 5013311 5013331 5013341 5013343 5013347 5013377 5013383 5013427
5013451 5013457 5013479 5013527 5013551 5013581 5013629 5013647 5013649 5013667
5013683 5013719 5013737 5013751 5013769 5013779 5013787 5013797 5013817 5013829
5013851 5013857 5013871 5013917 5013919 5013961 5013979 5013991 5014003 5014019
5014049 5014049 5014057 5014073 5014103 5014111 5014117 5014123 5014169 5014181
5014183 5014189 5014193 5014199 5014237 5014249 5014267 5014291 5014301 5014357
5014363 5014379 5014381 5014403 5014409 5014417 5014421 5014433 5014441 5014447
5014463 5014501 5014547 5014553 5014561 5014577 5014579 5014663 5014673 5014687
5014693 5014699 5014717 5014739 5014747 5014771 5014783 5014799 5014819 5014829
5014831 5014873 5014903 5014921 5014927 5014931 5014939 5014951 5014973 5014979
5014979 5015033 5015039 5015063 5015077 5015083 5015089 5015099 5015117 5015123
5015137 5015141 5015167 5015189 5015201 5015207 5015209 5015233 5015249 5015251
5015261 5015267 5015287 5015291 5015293 5015299 5015317 5015321 5015371 5015383
5015389 5015399 5015429 5015431 5015453 5015467 5015471 5015501 5015503 5015509
5015519 5015519 5015557 5015581 5015599 5015617 5015623 5015637 5015657 5015669
5015711 5015713 5015719 5015723 5015729 5015737 5015741 5015743 5015749 5015783
5015797 5015807 5015809 5015827 5015873 5015897 5015911 5015917 5015921 5015953
5015971 5015977 5015987 5016013 5016023 5016029 5016031 5016059 5016061 5016063
5016097 5016113 5016149 5016163 5016181 5016197 5016229 5016269 5016281 5016283
```

5016287 5016299 5016301 5016311 5016313 5016317 5016331 5016353 5016379 5016413
5016433 5016439 5016443 5016467 5016469 5016499 5016521 5016533 5016541 5016559
5016563 5016601 5016607 5016611 5016631 5016643 5016653 5016659 5016667 5016679
5016689 5016707 5016721 5016727 5016731 5016757 5016773 5016787 5016799 5016811
5016839 5016857 5016859 5016863 5016901 5016923 5016929 5016953 5016959 5016961
5016983 5017003 5017021 5017031 5017037 5017043 5017049 5017069 5017079 5017093
5017097 5017099 5017127 5017141 5017231 5017241 5017253 5017279 5017321 5017343
5017361 5017399 5017417 5017423 5017447 5017451 5017471 5017477 5017487 5017489
5017511 5017513 5017559 5017583 5017589 5017603 5017613 5017633 5017637 5017679
5017687 5017699 5017709 5017721 5017739 5017769 5017811 5017819 5017871 5017879
5017889 5017913 5017927 5017951 5017981 5017993 5017997 5018003 5018017 5018023
5018047 5018081 5018119 5018129 5018137 5018141 5018149 5018161 5018177 5018197
5018201 5018203 5018207 5018219 5018269 5018297 5018309 5018323 5018327 5018333
5018341 5018357 5018369 5018371 5018381 5018399 5018437 5018467 5018491 5018513
5018521 5018539 5018543 5018551 5018567 5018591 5018593 5018597 5018609 5018617
5018627 5018639 5018647 5018693 5018701 5018731 5018737 5018749 5018753 5018789
5018803 5018813 5018821 5018833 5018837 5018843 5018861 5018863 5018879 5018887
5018891 5018911 5018929 5018947 5018957 5018971 5018987 5018999 5019017 5019023
5019031 5019041 5019043 5019067 5019103 5019139 5019163 5019169 5019181 5019187
5019193 5019227 5019251 5019253 5019257 5019277 5019281 5019299 5019319 5019331
5019353 5019361 5019373 5019389 5019431 5019463 5019473 5019481 5019491 5019529
5019541 5019557 5019563 5019569 5019587 5019593 5019601 5019617 5019631 5019649
5019659 5019701 5019713 5019719 5019767 5019787 5019793 5019797 5019803 5019821
5019869 5019877 5019899 5019919 5019943 5019961 5019967 5019977 5019979 5019983
5019997 5020007 5020019 5020021 5020031 5020033 5020061 5020063 5020069 5020079
5020087 5020097 5020111 5020129 5020139 5020159 5020177 5020189 5020201 5020217
5020229 5020231 5020247 5020259 5020261 5020291 5020307 5020331 5020343 5020349
5020373 5020381 5020387 5020391 5020403 5020441 5020447 5020453 5020469 5020471
5020489 5020507 5020513 5020517 5020537 5020553 5020577 5020583 5020591 5020619
5020621 5020643 5020651 5020657 5020669 5020711 5020781 5020783 5020787 5020793
5020861 5020871 5020891 5020903 5020909 5020943 5020949 5020957 5020987 5020993
5020999 5021033 5021087 5021117 5021119 5021143 5021173 5021183 5021197 5021201
5021207 5021209 5021213 5021221 5021227 5021231 5021243 5021257 5021279 5021299
5021327 5021329 5021347 5021351 5021363 5021369 5021407 5021447 5021479 5021503
5021507 5021509 5021519 5021531 5021537 5021543 5021551 5021561 5021573 5021587
5021609 5021633 5021641 5021657 5021663 5021683 5021693 5021701 5021729 5021771
5021773 5021777 5021789 5021791 5021801 5021827 5021837 5021869 5021879 5021881
5021893 5021917 5021923 5021977 5021983 5021999 5022019 5022029 5022041 5022067
5022079 5022097 5022167 5022169 5022187 5022207 5022221 5022233 5022301 5022317
5022319 5022323 5022331 5022389 5022421 5022449 5022461 5022503 5022509 5022547
5022571 5022607 5022613 5022617 5022637 5022643 5022649 5022653 5022659 5022673
5022683 5022691 5022733 5022739 5022779 5022791 5022811 5022817 5022833 5022881
5022883 5022889 5022917 5022943 5022971 5022991 5023013 5023019 5023069 5023079
5023091 5023097 5023099 5023111 5023121 5023127 5023133 5023141 5023153 5023159
5023169 5023199 5023229 5023253 5023259 5023261 5023267 5023297 5023301 5023307
5023309 5023331 5023363 5023387 5023399 5023429 5023471 5023481 5023489 5023493
5023507 5023511 5023537 5023547 5023553 5023559 5023567 5023589 5023609 5023631
5023639 5023651 5023663 5023679 5023693 5023703 5023709 5023717 5023751 5023769
5023831 5023849 5023859 5023871 5023901 5023903 5023951 5023957 5023969 5023973
5023979 5023987 5024009 5024011 5024023 5024039 5024053 5024057 5024059 5024081
5024083 5024101 5024111 5024141 5024147 5024161 5024171 5024177 5024183 5024203
5024207 5024219 5024233 5024251 5024269 5024273 5024287 5024293 5024311 5024323
5024329 5024359 5024363 5024389 5024407 5024473 5024477 5024483 5024491 5024519
5024527 5024533 5024549 5024567 5024581 5024587 5024623 5024633 5024641 5024647
5024659 5024671 5024687 5024693 5024717 5024731 5024777 5024779 5024783 5024807
5024819 5024849 5024857 5024861 5024867 5024869 5024881 5024893 5024897 5024951
5024959 5024963 5024969 5024977 5025037 5025049 5025071 5025073 5025077 5025079
5025107 5025113 5025133 5025143 5025151 5025157 5025173 5025181 5025199 5025203
5025211 5025221 5025239 5025257 5025277 5025299 5025311 5025313 5025337 5025373
5025389 5025403 5025409 5025437 5025467 5025479 5025487 5025509 5025521 5025529
5025533 5025541 5025547 5025589 5025617 5025637 5025649 5025653 5025677 5025697
5025701 5025703 5025719 5025721 5025731 5025749 5025781 5025791 5025817 5025847
5025857 5025859 5025869 5025883 5025907 5025929 5025941 5025947 5025953 5025959
5025967 5025971 5025989 5025997 5026001 5026003 5026027 5026031 5026037 5026057
5026069 5026093 5026103 5026129 5026157 5026159 5026171 5026183 5026187 5026207
5026211 5026223 5026243 5026253 5026261 5026289 5026349 5026369 5026381 5026391
5026403 5026421 5026423 5026429 5026447 5026451 5026457 5026493 5026501 5026519
5026523 5026531 5026559 5026597 5026613 5026633 5026649 5026661 5026687 5026711
5026717 5026733 5026739 5026751 5026759 5026771 5026789 5026793 5026807 5026817
5026823 5026837 5026841 5026843 5026873 5026877 5026907 5026909 5026937 5026961
5026981 5026993 5027003 5027017 5027021 5027023 5027059 5027069 5027081 5027101
5027107 5027117 5027119 5027123 5027131 5027137 5027147 5027149 5027159 5027171
5027203 5027221 5027233 5027251 5027263 5027287 5027293 5027299 5027329 5027339
5027357 5027383 5027443 5027467 5027471 5027509 5027537 5027557 5027569 5027579
5027591 5027621 5027629 5027651 5027653 5027657 5027663 5027669 5027677 5027713
5027741 5027773 5027783 5027791 5027807 5027821 5027833 5027851 5027873 5027887
5027909 5027917 5027923 5027929 5027941 5027959 5027963 5027969 5027977 5027987
5027993 5028011 5028017 5028059 5028071 5028091 5028097 5028109 5028131 5028181
5028197 5028241 5028259 5028299 5028301 5028307 5028319 5028323 5028343 5028347
5028367 5028389 5028391 5028409 5028431 5028437 5028449 5028461 5028473 5028509
5028523 5028533 5028539 5028547 5028557 5028581 5028593 5028599 5028607 5028623
5028631 5028641 5028649 5028703 5028733 5028739 5028757 5028761 5028791 5028811
5028817 5028827 5028841 5028847 5028857 5028869 5028911 5028917 5028931 5028943
5028949 5028997 5029007 5029009 5029027 5029033 5029067 5029081 5029103 5029109
5029121 5029139 5029163 5029169 5029187 5029201 5029207 5029217 5029247 5029253
5029259 5029261 5029273 5029289 5029303 5029307 5029309 5029333 5029351 5029361
5029393 5029397 5029403 5029411 5029417 5029457 5029459 5029463 5029469 5029477
5029487 5029513 5029523 5029529 5029537 5029547 5029561 5029567 5029579 5029589
5029601 5029643 5029649 5029679 5029697 5029727 5029729 5029751 5029763 5029811

5029819 5029823 5029831 5029837 5029907 5029933 5029951 5029957 5029991 5030027
5030033 5030063 5030087 5030099 5030101 5030107 5030111 5030131 5030143 5030173
5030197 5030203 5030219 5030227 5030239 5030251 5030257 5030273 5030287 5030299
5030303 5030309 5030327 5030329 5030341 5030359 5030371 5030411 5030423 5030449
5030449 5030461 5030471 5030477 5030479 5030489 5030567 5030581 5030591 5030593
5030621 5030639 5030653 5030671 5030681 5030689 5030693 5030719 5030723 5030747
5030761 5030771 5030791 5030797 5030807 5030821 5030917 5030923 5030939 5030969
5030981 5031011 5031017 5031023 5031041 5031071 5031101 5031121 5031127 5031139
5031157 5031161 5031193 5031199 5031217 5031251 5031253 5031281 5031287 5031329
5031353 5031361 5031373 5031401 5031407 5031419 5031427 5031443 5031451 5031469
5031493 5031497 5031547 5031553 5031563 5031569 5031583 5031601 5031623 5031659
5031673 5031683 5031701 5031721 5031727 5031737 5031749 5031769 5031781 5031791
5031799 5031809 5031811 5031821 5031823 5031833 5031857 5031863 5031899 5031907
5031911 5031919 5031931 5031959 5031967 5031991 5031997 5032019 5032031 5032033
5032039 5032043 5032057 5032061 5032067 5032081 5032087 5032099 5032127 5032129
5032133 5032151 5032189 5032201 5032219 5032249 5032253 5032319 5032361 5032367
5032383 5032387 5032411 5032427 5032453 5032471 5032487 5032501 5032507 5032513
5032519 5032529 5032543 5032579 5032583 5032603 5032613 5032649 5032661 5032667
5032669 5032691 5032711 5032717 5032723 5032771 5032823 5032843 5032847 5032887
5032919 5032939 5032957 5032961 5032987 5032997 5033023 5033047 5033053 5033057
5033059 5033069 5033087 5033099 5033111 5033117 5033143 5033167 5033177 5033179
5033219 5033227 5033291 5033299 5033317 5033321 5033339 5033341 5033351 5033383
5033393 5033401 5033407 5033417 5033437 5033449 5033453 5033459 5033473 5033477
5033503 5033531 5033543 5033549 5033593 5033599 5033629 5033641 5033647 5033663
5033669 5033671 5033681 5033723 5033731 5033737 5033741 5033759 5033761 5033771
5033789 5033807 5033837 5033839 5033843 5033863 5033869 5033893 5033909 5033923
5033927 5033933 5033957 5033969 5033981 5033999 5034061 5034077 5034089 5034097
5034131 5034149 5034181 5034191 5034209 5034229 5034233 5034247 5034283 5034301
5034317 5034343 5034347 5034353 5034361 5034377 5034389 5034413 5034427 5034451
5034467 5034503 5034509 5034521 5034541 5034559 5034571 5034583 5034587 5034607
5034683 5034691 5034707 5034709 5034721 5034751 5034761 5034763 5034767 5034773
5034787 5034797 5034811 5034817 5034847 5034851 5034871 5034881 5034889 5034901
5034917 5034919 5034929 5034937 5034959 5034961 5034971 5034973 5035003 5035021
5035027 5035031 5035033 5035039 5035049 5035073 5035103 5035109 5035139 5035181
5035189 5035207 5035243 5035253 5035267 5035273 5035307 5035309 5035319
5035339 5035351 5035369 5035379 5035403 5035423 5035443 5035447 5035453 5035463
5035469 5035483 5035493 5035507 5035529 5035543 5035549 5035571 5035573 5035577
5035631 5035633 5035637 5035651 5035673 5035711 5035717 5035729 5035739 5035747
5035777 5035819 5035841 5035843 5035853 5035897 5035903 5035913 5035933 5035951
5035957 5035973 5035999 5036039 5036041 5036047 5036069 5036077 5036081 5036147
5036173 5036183 5036201 5036209 5036231 5036237 5036261 5036263 5036281 5036293
5036309 5036347 5036351 5036371 5036389 5036393 5036413 5036453 5036503 5036509
5036513 5036519 5036533 5036543 5036569 5036617 5036621 5036623 5036627 5036639
5036651 5036657 5036671 5036683 5036711 5036723 5036741 5036753 5036783 5036789
5036821 5036851 5036869 5036873 5036893 5036897 5036939 5036959 5036987 5036989
5037001 5037017 5037029 5037091 5037101 5037157 5037167 5037181 5037191 5037199
5037211 5037229 5037233 5037247 5037269 5037281 5037293 5037317 5037341 5037349
5037359 5037371 5037377 5037419 5037433 5037449 5037463 5037467 5037497 5037509
5037517 5037523 5037569 5037581 5037607 5037611 5037631 5037647 5037673 5037689
5037691 5037701 5037707 5037731 5037733 5037737 5037743 5037749 5037757 5037761
5037817 5037823 5037827 5037853 5037859 5037883 5037887 5037911 5037913 5037917
5037919 5037953 5037961 5037997 5038003 5038013 5038037 5038043 5038057 5038063
5038073 5038079 5038091 5038109 5038123 5038133 5038147 5038153 5038157 5038169
5038207 5038237 5038289 5038321 5038343 5038351 5038381 5038421 5038427 5038433
5038441 5038457 5038499 5038507 5038529 5038559 5038567 5038571 5038573 5038577
5038597 5038609 5038637 5038643 5038673 5038739 5038753 5038757 5038769 5038793
5038801 5038807 5038811 5038841 5038849 5038853 5038861 5038867 5038871 5038883
5038923 5038927 5038931 5038939 5038963 5038967 5038973 5038981 5039017
5039051 5039059 5039071 5039077 5039087 5039101 5039107 5039113 5039119 5039129
5039147 5039159 5039171 5039183 5039189 5039197 5039207 5039219 5039227 5039239
5039273 5039291 5039297 5039303 5039311 5039347 5039357 5039371 5039383 5039407
5039459 5039467 5039477 5039501 5039519 5039521 5039537 5039547 5039557 5039561
5039569 5039581 5039621 5039623 5039641 5039653 5039681 5039711 5039719 5039743
5039747 5039767 5039773 5039779 5039789 5039813 5039821 5039831 5039849 5039863
5039891 5039911 5039933 5039953 5039971 5039977 5039999 5040031 5040037 5040043
5040047 5040053 5040067 5040071 5040127 5040131 5040163 5040179 5040181 5040221
5040241 5040257 5040317 5040359 5040379 5040389 5040391 5040397 5040401 5040407
5040433 5040439 5040443 5040467 5040481 5040493 5040523 5040527 5040533 5040571
5040583 5040593 5040599 5040601 5040647 5040649 5040661 5040667 5040683 5040689
5040697 5040713 5040727 5040731 5040767 5040773 5040779 5040781 5040793 5040803
5040829 5040851 5040853 5040899 5040913 5040943 5040949 5040953 5040961 5041007
5041009 5041067 5041081 5041087 5041103 5041109 5041111 5041121 5041133 5041151
5041181 5041199 5041207 5041219 5041241 5041243 5041259 5041261 5041271 5041291
5041303 5041321 5041343 5041369 5041409 5041411 5041417 5041433 5041451 5041457
5041489 5041493 5041501 5041513 5041523 5041529 5041559 5041567
5041573 5041601 5041627 5041633 5041637 5041649 5041661 5041667 5041681 5041691
5041693 5041697 5041703 5041709 5041723 5041759 5041801 5041823 5041847 5041849
5041889 5041901 5041903 5041913 5041919 5041921 5041931 5041937 5041999 5042029
5042033 5042039 5042053 5042099 5042111 5042131 5042171 5042179 5042189 5042203
5042273 5042287 5042299 5042309 5042311 5042327 5042341 5042357 5042363 5042371
5042381 5042383 5042393 5042407 5042413 5042419 5042423 5042437 5042459 5042483
5042507 5042539 5042551 5042563 5042573 5042599 5042603 5042617 5042629 5042641
5042647 5042707 5042711 5042717 5042729 5042747 5042753 5042773 5042797 5042827
5042837 5042857 5042861 5042867 5042881 5042887 5042893 5042903 5042927 5042929
5042953 5042963 5042969 5042971 5042977 5043001 5043011 5043019 5043079 5043121
5043149 5043161 5043167 5043193 5043209 5043217 5043223 5043239 5043251 5043253
5043263 5043277 5043293 5043299 5043301 5043307 5043317 5043319 5043323 5043331
5043347 5043349 5043413 5043431 5043443 5043449 5043457 5043461 5043491 5043517
5043527 5043547 5043553 5043587 5043613 5043629 5043641 5043653 5043667 5043673

```
5043691 5043707 5043761 5043809 5043811 5043817 5043821 5043833 5043847 5043869
5043881 5043919 5043947 5043953 5043959 5043967 5043971 5044003 5044007 5044009
5044021 5044027 5044031 5044049 5044069 5044073 5044093 5044129 5044133 5044141
5044147 5044187 5044211 5044261 5044267 5044297 5044307 5044343 5044357 5044379
5044397 5044409 5044423 5044439 5044453 5044489 5044499 5044511 5044513 5044531
5044541 5044547 5044561 5044577 5044583 5044591 5044607 5044619 5044643 5044649
5044667 5044673 5044769 5044783 5044789 5044807 5044817 5044829 5044859 5044877
5044891 5044901 5044939 5044951 5044967 5044969 5044979 5044997 5044999 5045003
5045011 5045023 5045057 5045059 5045063 5045071 5045077 5045081 5045083 5045087
5045113 5045137 5045191 5045251 5045263 5045269 5045273 5045291 5045297 5045347
5045407 5045423 5045437 5045459 5045461 5045471 5045477 5045479 5045483 5045531
5045539 5045543 5045567 5045581 5045609 5045611 5045669 5045683 5045693 5045701
5045707 5045741 5045743 5045771 5045791 5045827 5045861 5045879 5045881 5045893
5045897 5045903 5045933 5045939 5045941 5045951 5045959 5045977 5045987 5046011
5046031 5046047 5046049 5046053 5046071 5046079 5046089 5046101 5046113 5046133
5046163 5046187 5046199 5046233 5046247 5046253 5046259 5046277 5046281 5046313
5046341 5046359 5046367 5046383 5046401 5046409 5046449 5046491 5046511 5046529
5046539 5046553 5046557 5046577 5046589 5046611 5046623 5046653 5046659 5046697
5046703 5046721 5046733 5046737 5046787 5046817 5046831 5046859 5046883 5046883
5046901 5046949 5046961 5046967 5046971 5046973 5046983 5046991 5046997 5047033
5047057 5047067 5047087 5047093 5047111 5047117 5047121 5047123 5047127 5047129
5047139 5047151 5047157 5047171 5047187 5047193 5047213 5047261 5047267 5047271
5047277 5047291 5047303 5047333 5047379 5047397 5047403 5047411 5047417 5047423
5047447 5047499 5047501 5047517 5047519 5047531 5047543 5047571 5047573 5047607
5047631 5047639 5047643 5047661 5047663 5047697 5047703 5047709 5047717 5047733
5047739 5047747 5047789 5047807 5047817 5047831 5047837 5047843 5047849 5047883
5047891 5047897 5047907 5047921 5047937 5047951 5047993 5048003 5048011 5048047
5048077 5048083 5048093 5048101 5048119 5048137 5048149 5048221 5048231 5048237
5048261 5048279 5048297 5048353 5048359 5048369 5048387 5048399 5048401 5048413
5048423 5048441 5048467 5048489 5048513 5048557 5048573 5048579 5048591 5048627
5048647 5048663 5048669 5048671 5048713 5048717 5048723 5048731 5048741 5048749
5048767 5048773 5048777 5048783 5048801 5048809 5048821 5048839 5048843 5048867
5048903 5048917 5048921 5048933 5048951 5048977 5048999 5049007 5049047 5049049
5049061 5049067 5049071 5049097 5049169 5049173 5049203 5049211 5049217 5049241
5049263 5049283 5049287 5049313 5049329 5049347 5049349 5049371 5049377 5049403
5049431 5049463 5049481 5049487 5049503 5049511 5049521 5049523 5049557 5049571
5049607 5049613 5049623 5049659 5049677 5049689 5049713 5049721 5049739 5049749
5049761 5049773 5049823 5049827 5049841 5049853 5049881 5049883 5049887 5049907
5049911 5049959 5049977 5049983 5049997 5050013 5050021 5050033 5050039 5050051
5050063 5050091 5050099 5050109 5050121 5050141 5050151 5050163 5050187 5050189
5050217 5050249 5050261 5050267 5050273 5050277 5050289 5050327 5050349 5050361
5050369 5050403 5050417 5050433 5050453 5050471 5050477 5050511 5050517 5050543
5050559 5050567 5050571 5050583 5050597 5050601 5050607 5050609 5050631 5050657
5050679 5050681 5050687 5050691 5050697 5050699 5050709 5050711 5050723 5050763
5050781 5050783 5050817 5050841 5050849 5050891 5050897 5050919 5050937 5050939
5050963 5050993 5050999 5051009 5051029 5051041 5051069 5051087 5051107 5051113
5051117 5051141 5051143 5051147 5051209 5051219 5051243 5051251 5051257 5051269
5051281 5051287 5051303 5051309 5051341 5051369 5051383 5051393 5051401 5051407
5051411 5051413 5051443 5051447 5051503 5051509 5051531 5051581 5051603 5051609
5051611 5051617 5051621 5051633 5051653 5051681 5051687 5051689 5051693 5051707
5051723 5051741 5051747 5051749 5051797 5051803 5051807 5051821 5051843 5051861
5051903 5051911 5051939 5051947 5051951 5051953 5051957 5051987 5051989 5051999
5052037 5052037 5052049 5052059 5052071 5052079 5052097 5052109 5052167 5052169
5052181 5052197 5052209 5052217 5052227 5052241 5052283 5052301 5052317 5052337
5052353 5052361 5052373 5052391 5052401 5052407 5052469 5052491 5052497 5052503
5052521 5052527 5052529 5052533 5052557 5052559 5052563 5052577 5052589 5052599
5052623 5052637 5052643 5052653 5052673 5052679 5052713 5052737 5052743 5052763
5052767 5052769 5052781 5052787 5052821 5052823 5052833 5052851 5052863 5052869
5052889 5052911 5052947 5052997 5053039 5053051 5053117 5053121 5053151 5053159
5053187 5053189 5053193 5053211 5053219 5053229 5053249 5053271 5053273 5053277
5053303 5053309 5053313 5053351 5053357 5053379 5053381 5053387 5053397 5053417
5053421 5053429 5053441 5053459 5053469 5053493 5053501 5053507 5053523 5053541
5053547 5053549 5053553 5053561 5053577 5053579 5053591 5053597 5053613 5053637
5053649 5053663 5053681 5053691 5053693 5053723 5053739 5053751 5053771 5053781
5053817 5053843 5053883 5053889 5053891 5053897 5053903 5053927 5053933 5053949
5053967 5053973 5054017 5054047 5054053 5054059 5054069 5054087 5054099 5054113
5054129 5054131 5054143 5054167 5054173 5054197 5054213 5054233 5054243 5054249
5054251 5054261 5054267 5054281 5054293 5054299 5054303 5054317 5054327 5054339
5054351 5054363 5054369 5054383 5054417 5054431 5054443 5054449 5054453 5054479
5054507 5054531 5054537 5054639 5054669 5054677 5054713 5054719 5054737
5054743 5054771 5054773 5054789 5054801 5054807 5054809 5054813 5054821 5054839
5054843 5054851 5054857 5054867 5054869 5054921 5054939 5054957 5054983 5054989
5054999 5055023 5055047 5055053 5055059 5055067 5055107 5055109 5055133 5055151
5055157 5055173 5055181 5055191 5055203 5055221 5055223 5055241 5055247 5055277
5055283 5055287 5055293 5055319 5055359 5055361 5055383 5055389 5055397 5055403
5055431 5055439 5055473 5055487 5055493 5055503 5055509 5055521 5055551 5055559
5055563 5055571 5055581 5055593 5055601 5055623 5055629 5055641 5055667 5055671
5055679 5055707 5055709 5055781 5055793 5055803 5055859 5055877 5055901 5055913
5055917 5055923 5055937 5055943 5055949 5055977 5055979 5055991 5056027 5056031
5056039 5056043 5056049 5056057 5056133 5056151 5056153 5056169 5056171 5056187
5056201 5056211 5056217 5056231 5056267 5056273 5056279 5056283 5056291 5056321
5056339 5056349 5056369 5056397 5056417 5056427 5056433 5056439 5056453 5056459
5056487 5056501 5056517 5056529 5056543 5056559 5056561 5056567 5056577 5056591
5056607 5056621 5056651 5056657 5056663 5056669 5056673 5056697 5056699 5056721
5056729 5056739 5056763 5056771 5056777 5056781 5056811 5056819 5056823 5056829
5056859 5056861 5056867 5056873 5056913 5056921 5056951 5056957 5056979 5057009
5057023 5057029 5057047 5057051 5057053 5057071 5057077 5057099 5057111 5057113
5057119 5057137 5057147 5057149 5057159 5057161 5057167 5057191 5057203 5057219
5057243 5057251 5057291 5057293 5057323 5057329 5057369 5057387 5057407 5057413
```

```
5057453  5057461  5057467  5057471  5057497  5057509  5057519  5057527  5057561  5057573
5057579  5057587  5057593  5057597  5057621  5057639  5057651  5057669  5057671  5057707
5057711  5057747  5057797  5057831  5057837  5057839  5057851  5057869  5057879  5057911
5057917  5057947  5057963  5057981  5057989  5058013  5058023  5058037  5058073  5058083
5058089  5058101  5058107  5058113  5058127  5058139  5058143  5058169  5058173  5058191
5058203  5058217  5058257  5058271  5058289  5058311  5058323  5058329  5058341  5058359
5058397  5058409  5058419  5058421  5058437  5058461  5058467  5058491  5058497  5058509
5058511  5058517  5058523  5058527  5058569  5058577  5058583  5058589  5058593  5058619
5058623  5058629  5058631  5058637  5058653  5058659  5058667  5058709  5058721  5058733
5058737  5058743  5058749  5058761  5058793  5058803  5058829  5058857  5058881  5058887
5058917  5058929  5058947  5058961  5059001  5059007  5059063  5059091  5059097  5059133
5059139  5059151  5059163  5059181  5059189  5059199  5059207  5059211  5059213  5059259
5059261  5059283  5059289  5059291  5059303  5059321  5059363  5059367  5059403  5059451
5059459  5059499  5059507  5059511  5059519  5059573  5059619  5059627  5059633  5059651
5059657  5059661  5059679  5059697  5059711  5059721  5059729  5059741  5059759  5059771
5059783  5059799  5059837  5059847  5059877  5059903  5059919  5059927  5059937  5059961
5059979  5059987  5059993  5060021  5060039  5060047  5060051  5060053  5060063  5060071
5060087  5060113  5060119  5060129  5060131  5060149  5060171  5060173  5060177  5060221
5060233  5060243  5060257  5060269  5060317  5060329  5060333  5060357  5060381
5060401  5060431  5060449  5060459  5060467  5060477  5060521  5060551  5060591  5060597
5060603  5060609  5060617  5060623  5060639  5060663  5060677  5060681  5060687  5060701
5060717  5060723  5060767  5060771  5060777  5060791  5060801  5060813  5060827  5060833
5060837  5060857  5060863  5060873  5060899  5060921  5060953  5060959  5060981  5060983
5061013  5061031  5061047  5061061  5061073  5061103  5061107  5061137  5061139  5061181
5061187  5061253  5061263  5061281  5061299  5061323  5061347  5061349  5061367  5061379
5061389  5061443  5061473  5061493  5061499  5061517  5061527  5061533  5061599
5061607  5061613  5061629  5061643  5061673  5061677  5061731  5061743  5061757  5061761
5061799  5061821  5061827  5061829  5061857  5061883  5061887  5061907  5061911  5061919
5061943  5061949  5061989  5062033  5062049  5062091  5062097  5062103  5062133  5062157
5062163  5062171  5062177  5062181  5062199  5062201  5062217  5062219  5062237  5062247
5062249  5062279  5062283  5062289  5062297  5062301  5062307  5062313  5062349  5062357
5062367  5062381  5062397  5062403  5062411  5062429  5062457  5062459  5062469  5062483
5062489  5062529  5062543  5062567  5062591  5062597  5062609  5062619  5062621  5062633
5062637  5062649  5062661  5062663  5062669  5062693  5062697  5062711  5062727  5062741
5062819  5062847  5062853  5062859  5062861  5062867  5062891  5062901  5062903  5062909
5062913  5062927  5062963  5062973  5062997  5062999  5063021  5063027  5063033  5063039
5063087  5063089  5063099  5063111  5063119  5063129  5063141  5063147  5063167  5063173
5063209  5063237  5063239  5063251  5063287  5063309  5063327  5063369  5063389  5063431
5063437  5063449  5063453  5063479  5063489  5063503  5063533  5063563  5063587  5063593
5063621  5063629  5063647  5063677  5063699  5063713  5063717  5063743  5063753  5063759
5063761  5063797  5063801  5063803  5063843  5063867  5063879  5063939  5063957  5063959
5063999  5064019  5064023  5064043  5064047  5064053  5064077  5064091  5064119  5064121
5064131  5064139  5064149  5064151  5064167  5064173  5064193  5064223  5064251  5064259
5064263  5064277  5064287  5064307  5064331  5064337  5064341  5064343  5064373  5064401
5064421  5064461  5064503  5064509  5064511  5064517  5064533  5064539  5064551  5064557
5064559  5064571  5064581  5064599  5064601  5064629  5064677  5064679  5064701  5064713
5064727  5064739  5064779  5064781  5064791  5064809  5064817  5064823  5064833  5064859
5064877  5064881  5064883  5064889  5064907  5064919  5064949  5064971  5064979  5064989
5065003  5065019  5065033  5065057  5065061  5065063  5065103  5065139  5065199  5065217
5065253  5065259  5065283  5065289  5065297  5065351  5065373  5065391  5065393  5065409
5065421  5065429  5065433  5065471  5065481  5065531  5065537  5065547  5065561  5065583
5065601  5065603  5065607  5065651  5065661  5065663  5065693  5065699  5065703  5065729
5065747  5065751  5065759  5065769  5065777  5065783  5065789  5065817  5065831  5065843
5065861  5065871  5065883  5065889  5065897  5065909  5065939  5065961  5065979  5065987
5065997  5066011  5066021  5066029  5066041  5066069  5066081  5066099  5066107  5066137
5066141  5066161  5066183  5066207  5066219  5066221  5066239  5066251  5066267  5066287
5066291  5066297  5066309  5066311  5066333  5066351  5066353  5066363  5066381  5066401
5066431  5066441  5066449  5066461  5066471  5066491  5066497  5066513  5066519  5066533
5066563  5066573  5066587  5066603  5066623  5066639  5066653  5066683  5066713  5066717
5066723  5066729  5066753  5066771  5066791  5066797  5066801  5066813  5066837  5066839
5066869  5066881  5066921  5066927  5066933  5066951  5066987  5066993  5067047  5067079
5067089  5067109  5067119  5067121  5067133  5067151  5067197  5067217  5067247  5067253
5067263  5067287  5067299  5067317  5067329  5067371  5067389  5067401  5067407
5067443  5067449  5067463  5067467  5067481  5067511  5067527  5067533  5067551  5067553
5067583  5067589  5067599  5067607  5067617  5067619  5067637  5067653  5067707  5067709
5067739  5067757  5067761  5067763  5067781  5067793  5067809  5067817  5067823  5067827
5067847  5067857  5067859  5067871  5067883  5067899  5067901  5067943  5067961  5067967
5067977  5067991  5068031  5068043  5068067  5068093  5068103  5068111  5068151
5068169  5068177  5068201  5068213  5068249  5068253  5068267  5068279  5068289  5068291
5068313  5068319  5068333  5068361  5068411  5068423  5068439  5068447  5068451  5068489
5068493  5068501  5068507  5068517  5068523  5068529  5068537  5068559  5068571  5068597
5068627  5068633  5068691  5068709  5068747  5068757  5068781  5068787  5068793  5068807
5068829  5068849  5068879  5068891  5068909  5068927  5068933  5068937  5068957
5068961  5068967  5068979  5068981  5069003  5069011  5069017  5069023  5069033  5069063
5069081  5069083  5069093  5069107  5069159  5069189  5069201  5069203  5069231  5069243
5069297  5069299  5069321  5069327  5069353  5069357  5069359  5069369  5069413  5069423
5069431  5069437  5069473  5069483  5069497  5069507  5069513  5069539  5069543  5069549
5069551  5069563  5069567  5069573  5069579  5069627  5069633  5069639  5069661  5069663
5069671  5069681  5069759  5069761  5069783  5069797  5069803  5069807  5069819  5069849
5069861  5069863  5069873  5069879  5069881  5069887  5069891  5069921  5069947  5069959
5069963  5069989  5070007  5070049  5070061  5070071  5070089  5070113  5070133  5070151
5070167  5070179  5070187  5070193  5070209  5070217  5070223  5070227  5070239  5070251
5070253  5070257  5070269  5070277  5070293  5070311  5070341  5070343  5070379  5070413
5070421  5070433  5070449  5070469  5070479  5070497  5070509  5070521  5070523  5070529
5070547  5070551  5070599  5070601  5070613  5070631  5070643  5070647  5070661  5070671
5070673  5070683  5070691  5070697  5070707  5070721  5070727  5070733  5070809  5070817
5070823  5070827  5070829  5070841  5070847  5070853  5070883  5070899  5070937  5070959
5070973  5071009  5071013  5071019  5071057  5071061  5071067  5071097  5071103  5071111
5071127  5071133  5071139  5071147  5071169  5071177  5071181  5071189  5071193  5071211
```

```
5071229  5071267  5071273  5071277  5071301  5071343  5071351  5071361  5071369  5071373
5071379  5071453  5071471  5071481  5071483  5071501  5071511  5071519  5071543  5071567
5071579  5071589  5071597  5071609  5071639  5071657  5071667  5071669  5071673  5071679
5071687  5071697  5071709  5071747  5071751  5071771  5071777  5071783  5071789  5071793
5071813  5071837  5071873  5071883  5071889  5071901  5071903  5071909  5071919  5071921
5071931  5071943  5071949  5071951  5071973  5072057  5072063  5072117  5072141  5072143
5072161  5072173  5072191  5072201  5072261  5072269  5072299  5072329  5072359  5072363
5072371  5072393  5072399  5072429  5072497  5072519  5072531  5072537  5072539  5072603
5072621  5072653  5072659  5072671  5072687  5072689  5072693  5072707  5072729
5072731  5072741  5072773  5072777  5072779  5072797  5072801  5072803  5072813  5072831
5072863  5072869  5072891  5072897  5072939  5072983  5072993  5073017  5073031  5073067
5073077  5073139  5073149  5073161  5073169  5073221  5073241  5073287  5073311  5073337
5073353  5073371  5073373  5073377  5073379  5073389  5073401  5073421  5073443  5073451
5073457  5073493  5073511  5073517  5073539  5073539  5073557  5073559  5073583  5073631
5073643  5073647  5073659  5073661  5073683  5073689  5073721  5073737  5073749  5073763
5073767  5073781  5073787  5073821  5073839  5073851  5073857  5073877  5073889  5073923
5073949  5073967  5073989  5073997  5074001  5074009  5074033  5074051  5074063  5074067
5074079  5074081  5074087  5074093  5074103  5074123  5074127  5074133  5074141  5074151
5074183  5074187  5074189  5074207  5074213  5074229  5074231  5074247  5074259  5074271
5074337  5074351  5074357  5074369  5074373  5074393  5074417  5074423  5074429  5074451
5074453  5074457  5074469  5074481  5074567  5074571  5074603  5074627  5074633  5074639
5074673  5074709  5074733  5074747  5074753  5074777  5074787  5074801  5074807  5074819
5074831  5074841  5074847  5074859  5074871  5074873  5074877  5074879  5074897  5074907
5074933  5074961  5074967  5074981  5074987  5074991  5074997  5074999  5075011  5075023
5075051  5075069  5075099  5075101  5075113  5075123  5075143  5075153  5075159  5075167
5075171  5075173  5075177  5075207  5075221  5075233  5075237  5075251  5075263  5075269
5075309  5075359  5075381  5075407  5075423  5075437  5075453  5075459  5075491  5075501
5075509  5075519  5075561  5075573  5075579  5075597  5075611  5075633  5075659  5075669
5075683  5075687  5075689  5075747  5075767  5075779  5075797  5075821  5075827  5075867
5075879  5075881  5075891  5075897  5075927  5075929  5075933  5075951  5075989  5075999
5076017  5076037  5076041  5076053  5076083  5076089  5076091  5076109  5076133  5076139
5076151  5076161  5076179  5076199  5076209  5076221  5076223  5076229  5076241  5076283
5076349  5076377  5076391  5076397  5076403  5076413  5076427  5076431  5076433  5076443
5076473  5076503  5076509  5076527  5076541  5076551  5076559  5076569  5076581  5076587
5076593  5076601  5076607  5076613  5076637  5076671  5076677  5076679  5076683  5076691
5076703  5076719  5076763  5076787  5076793  5076803  5076821  5076833  5076853  5076899
5076913  5076941  5076947  5076949  5076959  5076979  5076983  5076991  5077013  5077021
5077057  5077063  5077097  5077099  5077129  5077151  5077157  5077201  5077207  5077217
5077229  5077243  5077249  5077277  5077279  5077283  5077297  5077321  5077367  5077379
5077393  5077417  5077421  5077447  5077451  5077477  5077489  5077493  5077507  5077517
5077519  5077529  5077561  5077607  5077609  5077619  5077627  5077643  5077673  5077711
5077753  5077757  5077759  5077777  5077783  5077789  5077811  5077817  5077819  5077829
5077847  5077873  5077889  5077901  5077907  5077931  5077951  5077967  5077993  5078011
5078039  5078057  5078077  5078081  5078083  5078119  5078123  5078167  5078191  5078207
5078237  5078243  5078261  5078273  5078279  5078309  5078321  5078329  5078347  5078351
5078363  5078369  5078387  5078401  5078431  5078443  5078449  5078459  5078501  5078503
5078519  5078531  5078539  5078551  5078573  5078581  5078599  5078609  5078617  5078651
5078659  5078663  5078729  5078737  5078743  5078747  5078753  5078771  5078783  5078789
5078797  5078807  5078809  5078813  5078839  5078849  5078851  5078861  5078863  5078873
5078891  5078893  5078911  5078933  5078939  5078951  5078959  5078977  5078993  5079037
5079047  5079049  5079059  5079079  5079083  5079097  5079103  5079143  5079157  5079163
5079169  5079197  5079223  5079227  5079233  5079241  5079247  5079253  5079259  5079299
5079307  5079341  5079359  5079377  5079401  5079407  5079419  5079433  5079493  5079499
5079511  5079533  5079539  5079577  5079587  5079589  5079623  5079661  5079667  5079673
5079703  5079709  5079731  5079743  5079749  5079751  5079773  5079817  5079827  5079829
5079839  5079869  5079871  5079883  5079911  5079913  5079917  5079947  5079961  5079967
5080003  5080013  5080021  5080037  5080043  5080051  5080067  5080069  5080073  5080081
5080091  5080109  5080123  5080129  5080139  5080151  5080169  5080177  5080193  5080213
5080219  5080223  5080237  5080241  5080259  5080267  5080279  5080301  5080333  5080357
5080403  5080451  5080463  5080483  5080529  5080541  5080553  5080561  5080567  5080571
5080577  5080583  5080591  5080627  5080639  5080643  5080651  5080661  5080687  5080703
5080709  5080711  5080717  5080721  5080741  5080793  5080799  5080813  5080849  5080853
5080879  5080883  5080937  5080939  5080963  5080967  5080997  5081017  5081023
5081033  5081047  5081051  5081077  5081081  5081101  5081149  5081159  5081161  5081191
5081231  5081287  5081291  5081339  5081369  5081381  5081387  5081393  5081407  5081437
5081441  5081477  5081491  5081519  5081561  5081563  5081567  5081579  5081591  5081599
5081627  5081647  5081669  5081677  5081707  5081717  5081719  5081731  5081743  5081761
5081767  5081773  5081777  5081789  5081801  5081803  5081807  5081819  5081821  5081837
5081893  5081897  5081899  5081903  5081939  5081941  5081953  5081959  5081981  5081983
5082001  5082013  5082029  5082037  5082043  5082053  5082059  5082067  5082071  5082079
5082089  5082097  5082131  5082137  5082169  5082191  5082193  5082199  5082211  5082227
5082271  5082277  5082281  5082293  5082313  5082317  5082323  5082331  5082353  5082359
5082373  5082377  5082409  5082433  5082463  5082491  5082521  5082529  5082551  5082577
5082587  5082589  5082593  5082601  5082613  5082617  5082619  5082629  5082631  5082641
5082691  5082697  5082713  5082731  5082739  5082751  5082761  5082767  5082773  5082787
5082809  5082817  5082827  5082887  5082907  5082911  5082919  5082929  5082967  5082991
5083019  5083021  5083031  5083049  5083061  5083087  5083121  5083123  5083151  5083157
5083213  5083217  5083219  5083231  5083237  5083297  5083301  5083307  5083321  5083339
5083343  5083363  5083367  5083399  5083423  5083451  5083453  5083471  5083487  5083489
5083511  5083513  5083517  5083523  5083579  5083619  5083643  5083649  5083657
5083669  5083681  5083691  5083693  5083699  5083709  5083711  5083723  5083733  5083753
5083823  5083879  5083889  5083909  5083913  5083927  5083931  5083957  5083973  5083993
5084017  5084033  5084069  5084099  5084111  5084113  5084117  5084129  5084141  5084147
5084171  5084179  5084197  5084213  5084221  5084243  5084249  5084263  5084269  5084333
5084371  5084383  5084393  5084399  5084407  5084423  5084437  5084447  5084461  5084473
5084477  5084489  5084501  5084509  5084531  5084537  5084543  5084549  5084551  5084557
5084567  5084593  5084617  5084627  5084641  5084671  5084689  5084693  5084711  5084731
5084743  5084749  5084753  5084803  5084809  5084813  5084843  5084851  5084867  5084869
5084897  5084903  5084917  5084927  5084929  5084939  5084957  5084969  5084987  5084999
```

```
5085011 5085013 5085019 5085049 5085079 5085083 5085089 5085131 5085133 5085149
5085167 5085187 5085239 5085251 5085263 5085299 5085313 5085319 5085337 5085343
5085347 5085349 5085359 5085361 5085383 5085401 5085413 5085427 5085433 5085439
5085449 5085463 5085473 5085491 5085497 5085523 5085547 5085571 5085583 5085589
5085607 5085611 5085629 5085637 5085649 5085677 5085679 5085683 5085709 5085713
5085719 5085779 5085797 5085803 5085809 5085841 5085853 5085869 5085881 5085887
5085889 5085893 5085929 5085947 5085973 5085989 5086007 5086021 5086033 5086051
5086063 5086079 5086087 5086093 5086117 5086121 5086141 5086153 5086163 5086177
5086189 5086219 5086229 5086271 5086297 5086303 5086309 5086313 5086321 5086327
5086351 5086379 5086409 5086423 5086429 5086441 5086447 5086483 5086493 5086507
5086517 5086531 5086541 5086561 5086579 5086589 5086591 5086597 5086603 5086619
5086633 5086681 5086691 5086709 5086717 5086751 5086769 5086793 5086799 5086811
5086817 5086847 5086849 5086891 5086897 5086909 5086931 5086967 5086997 5087011
5087021 5087051 5087053 5087057 5087087 5087107 5087111 5087119 5087129 5087141
5087143 5087149 5087161 5087179 5087183 5087191 5087197 5087213 5087219 5087227
5087237 5087263 5087279 5087281 5087293 5087309 5087323 5087351 5087353 5087399
5087413 5087419 5087431 5087447 5087449 5087473 5087501 5087527 5087543 5087549
5087569 5087581 5087587 5087591 5087603 5087633 5087639 5087653 5087657 5087681
5087699 5087701 5087707 5087711 5087713 5087741 5087749 5087767 5087773 5087783
5087791 5087809 5087821 5087851 5087861 5087869 5087893 5087897 5087921 5087923
5087933 5087939 5087959 5087969 5088007 5088023 5088089 5088113 5088119 5088121
5088157 5088169 5088179 5088199 5088217 5088227 5088241 5088263 5088269 5088283
5088301 5088331 5088341 5088353 5088379 5088383 5088401 5088407 5088439 5088443
5088467 5088511 5088521 5088529 5088539 5088541 5088569 5088613 5088617 5088631
5088649 5088653 5088679 5088701 5088709 5088731 5088739 5088761 5088793 5088821
5088823 5088871 5088877 5088887 5088907 5088913 5088937 5088947 5088971
5088973 5088989 5089013 5089031 5089057 5089061 5089079 5089081 5089121 5089129
5089151 5089159 5089199 5089213 5089223 5089229 5089237 5089243 5089261 5089277
5089339 5089361 5089373 5089391 5089411 5089423 5089429 5089439 5089451 5089459
5089499 5089501 5089519 5089541 5089547 5089559 5089561 5089571 5089573 5089597
5089607 5089619 5089631 5089697 5089709 5089729 5089741 5089751 5089769 5089793
5089807 5089811 5089829 5089837 5089849 5089873 5089879 5089897 5089913 5089927
5089933 5089939 5089943 5089957 5089963 5090003 5090009 5090017 5090077 5090087
5090093 5090117 5090131 5090149 5090171 5090209 5090219 5090227 5090237 5090243
5090249 5090251 5090257 5090303 5090317 5090339 5090369 5090377 5090381 5090387
5090401 5090419 5090447 5090467 5090481 5090483 5090489 5090507 5090539 5090543
5090549 5090551 5090557 5090563 5090587 5090609 5090621 5090623 5090669 5090671
5090693 5090699 5090713 5090737 5090741 5090749 5090753 5090773 5090777 5090779
5090807 5090819 5090831 5090849 5090857 5090881 5090903 5090923 5090927 5090951
5090963 5090977 5091001 5091013 5091019 5091061 5091091 5091101 5091113 5091173
5091199 5091227 5091241 5091253 5091271 5091301 5091323 5091341 5091343
5091367 5091371 5091377 5091379 5091407 5091413 5091451 5091467 5091473 5091491
5091509 5091521 5091529 5091547 5091553 5091589 5091613 5091637 5091643 5091649
5091659 5091661 5091689 5091703 5091707 5091743 5091761 5091767 5091769 5091797
5091803 5091817 5091833 5091841 5091847 5091881 5091883 5091887 5091899 5091923
5091929 5091937 5091953 5091973 5091991 5092007 5092069 5092099 5092111
5092127 5092141 5092147 5092169 5092181 5092183 5092193 5092229 5092271 5092291
5092289 5092303 5092327 5092337 5092343 5092357 5092369 5092379 5092387 5092391
5092393 5092397 5092411 5092441 5092481 5092489 5092501 5092517 5092519 5092523
5092541 5092561 5092567 5092579 5092613 5092657 5092693 5092709 5092721 5092727
5092757 5092771 5092783 5092793 5092799 5092811 5092819 5092831 5092849 5092853
5092861 5092883 5092889 5092891 5092909 5092921 5092933 5092937 5092943 5092949
5092961 5092973 5092987 5092993 5093003 5093017 5093027 5093029 5093059
5093063 5093069 5093089 5093107 5093111 5093167 5093173 5093191 5093201 5093213
5093227 5093233 5093279 5093303 5093321 5093323 5093339 5093351 5093359 5093423
5093447 5093467 5093503 5093507 5093509 5093519 5093527 5093537 5093549
5093573 5093609 5093623 5093657 5093663 5093677 5093681 5093689 5093713 5093731
5093747 5093749 5093771 5093773 5093789 5093791 5093801 5093819 5093839
5093857 5093887 5093899 5093917 5093923 5093929 5093939 5093941 5093947 5093983
5093993 5094007 5094029 5094043 5094049 5094083 5094091 5094113 5094121 5094151
5094181 5094191 5094233 5094241 5094259 5094263 5094269 5094281 5094301 5094311
5094329 5094359 5094361 5094371 5094403 5094409 5094433 5094437 5094487 5094533
5094539 5094553 5094559 5094601 5094629 5094647 5094653 5094667 5094673 5094703
5094773 5094779 5094787 5094797 5094821 5094829 5094833 5094839 5094841 5094853
5094871 5094899 5094919 5094931 5094949 5094951 5094961
5095009 5095037 5095073 5095081 5095091 5095117 5095127 5095133 5095151 5095157
5095163 5095169 5095171 5095183 5095187 5095201 5095219 5095229 5095231 5095243
5095267 5095273 5095319 5095333 5095361 5095379 5095399 5095403 5095429 5095471
5095483 5095523 5095537 5095547 5095549 5095567 5095633 5095637 5095639 5095663
5095669 5095681 5095697 5095709 5095711 5095721 5095723 5095729 5095733 5095837
5095841 5095847 5095877 5095919 5095921 5095927 5095939 5095957 5095991 5096011
5096023 5096029 5096093 5096111 5096137 5096153 5096159 5096171 5096173 5096207
5096213 5096239 5096243 5096251 5096279 5096281 5096291 5096323 5096327 5096347
5096381 5096387 5096393 5096411 5096437 5096461 5096467 5096471 5096473 5096519
5096563 5096569 5096573 5096621 5096627 5096647 5096653 5096657 5096683 5096687
5096701 5096711 5096717 5096737 5096759 5096771 5096783 5096789 5096797 5096809
5096813 5096827 5096849 5096857 5096863 5096867 5096873 5096879 5096887 5096893
5096911 5096929 5096939 5096969 5096983 5096999 5097013 5097017 5097023 5097031
5097041 5097049 5097089 5097097 5097109 5097137 5097139 5097143 5097151 5097163
5097179 5097193 5097199 5097223 5097237 5097241 5097251 5097259
5097289 5097353 5097401 5097403 5097409 5097419 5097431 5097457 5097461 5097473
5097511 5097523 5097539 5097551 5097553 5097563 5097577 5097581 5097583 5097613
5097619 5097629 5097647 5097683 5097751 5097767 5097787 5097793 5097797 5097803
5097811 5097839 5097847 5097863 5097887 5097893 5097901 5097923 5097931 5097941
5097979 5097991 5098007 5098031 5098033 5098069 5098081 5098087 5098091
5098117 5098129 5098133 5098139 5098141 5098153 5098169 5098189 5098201 5098207
5098211 5098237 5098241 5098253 5098259 5098279 5098307 5098337 5098369
5098399 5098421 5098427 5098463 5098469 5098501 5098523 5098529 5098531 5098549
5098559 5098567 5098573 5098627 5098649 5098661 5098679 5098697 5098733 5098741
```

```
5098747  5098763  5098771  5098789  5098799  5098813  5098823  5098853  5098903  5098909
5098927  5098943  5098967  5098969  5098979  5098981  5098987  5098993  5099009  5099021
5099023  5099033  5099053  5099057  5099063  5099071  5099089  5099093  5099113  5099131
5099141  5099153  5099191  5099197  5099219  5099233  5099243  5099251  5099257  5099267
5099309  5099317  5099329  5099333  5099357  5099383  5099411  5099443  5099459  5099519
5099527  5099533  5099557  5099569  5099587  5099597  5099617  5099623  5099669  5099683
5099701  5099729  5099741  5099749  5099753  5099777  5099797  5099807  5099827  5099849
5099851  5099873  5099879  5099893  5099933  5099959  5099977  5099981  5099987  5099989
5099993  5100071  5100077  5100079  5100083  5100097  5100127  5100157  5100167  5100169
5100211  5100229  5100239  5100253  5100257  5100269  5100287  5100311  5100331  5100343
5100353  5100367  5100371  5100397  5100409  5100467  5100479  5100521  5100541  5100587
5100593  5100611  5100619  5100631  5100649  5100653  5100659  5100661  5100671  5100673
5100691  5100713  5100737  5100749  5100751  5100757  5100763  5100791  5100811  5100817
5100827  5100829  5100841  5100859  5100877  5100889  5100899  5100913  5100929  5100941
5100943  5100959  5100971  5100973  5100989  5101007  5101043  5101049  5101067  5101093
5101099  5101127  5101141  5101157  5101171  5101181  5101189  5101211  5101223  5101231
5101237  5101249  5101259  5101273  5101289  5101297  5101307  5101351  5101357  5101363
5101373  5101379  5101381  5101387  5101399  5101403  5101417  5101441  5101451  5101471
5101493  5101501  5101511  5101517  5101529  5101531  5101541  5101549  5101559  5101567
5101573  5101609  5101627  5101631  5101643  5101661  5101669  5101673  5101687  5101697
5101711  5101739  5101757  5101771  5101781  5101783  5101787  5101807  5101841  5101879
5101913  5101961  5101969  5101997  5102059  5102087  5102107  5102129  5102137  5102177
5102219  5102239  5102243  5102249  5102269  5102303  5102309  5102323  5102333  5102353
5102359  5102369  5102371  5102381  5102407  5102429  5102437  5102443  5102453  5102473
5102501  5102543  5102561  5102563  5102593  5102599  5102611  5102623  5102639  5102651
5102663  5102683  5102717  5102719  5102731  5102759  5102761  5102777  5102789  5102821
5102827  5102831  5102861  5102863  5102953  5103029  5103031  5103037  5103047  5103061
5103067  5103071  5103083  5103097  5103103  5103121  5103139  5103143  5103149  5103157
5103169  5103173  5103209  5103221  5103223  5103233  5103239  5103257  5103269  5103277
5103289  5103331  5103337  5103377  5103379  5103389  5103403  5103407  5103431  5103433
5103467  5103473  5103481  5103487  5103509  5103517  5103523  5103577  5103601  5103607
5103611  5103613  5103619  5103653  5103671  5103691  5103701  5103727  5103733  5103751
5103773  5103779  5103781  5103811  5103829  5103863  5103877  5103881  5103887  5103929
5103937  5103947  5103949  5103983  5103991  5103997  5104009  5104013  5104051  5104067
5104081  5104109  5104117  5104123  5104129  5104147  5104163  5104189  5104193  5104201
5104207  5104249  5104259  5104289  5104291  5104303  5104313  5104327  5104339  5104343
5104349  5104357  5104373  5104387  5104391  5104397  5104399  5104423  5104433  5104447
5104453  5104457  5104469  5104513  5104523  5104537  5104571  5104601  5104613  5104633
5104661  5104669  5104679  5104691  5104699  5104741  5104747  5104753  5104769  5104837
5104849  5104859  5104867  5104877  5104909  5104921  5104933  5104937  5104943  5104949
5104961  5104973  5104991  5104993  5105021  5105047  5105063  5105101  5105123  5105141
5105143  5105161  5105171  5105179  5105183  5105203  5105231  5105237  5105267  5105299
5105327  5105341  5105377  5105381  5105393  5105407  5105431  5105473  5105497  5105531
5105561  5105587  5105629  5105641  5105671  5105707  5105753  5105759  5105791  5105809
5105833  5105843  5105857  5105879  5105897  5105921  5105923  5105951  5105957  5105981
5105993  5105999  5106011  5106029  5106047  5106053  5106083  5106089  5106091  5106097
5106109  5106113  5106133  5106139  5106149  5106151  5106163  5106173  5106203  5106217
5106229  5106247  5106251  5106287  5106317  5106319  5106347  5106373  5106397  5106419
5106433  5106469  5106473  5106487  5106527  5106547  5106557  5106559  5106571  5106589
5106601  5106617  5106631  5106641  5106643  5106653  5106679  5106701  5106707  5106719
5106757  5106781  5106793  5106821  5106823  5106841  5106869  5106901  5106947  5106961
5106967  5106979  5107009  5107013  5107019  5107043  5107061  5107079  5107111  5107117
5107129  5107139  5107163  5107177  5107189  5107199  5107213  5107231  5107237  5107241
5107253  5107303  5107307  5107309  5107313  5107331  5107337  5107351  5107373  5107379
5107381  5107391  5107423  5107433  5107439  5107457  5107481  5107483  5107499  5107507
5107511  5107549  5107601  5107607  5107643  5107649  5107651  5107691  5107693  5107699
5107703  5107709  5107717  5107721  5107747  5107757  5107759  5107787  5107793  5107801
5107829  5107831  5107891  5107897  5107919  5107933  5107937  5107951  5107967  5107997
5108003  5108009  5108011  5108021  5108023  5108027  5108039  5108053  5108057  5108107
5108113  5108119  5108137  5108153  5108189  5108197  5108203  5108209  5108221  5108227
5108239  5108251  5108267  5108269  5108291  5108293  5108297  5108317  5108351  5108353
5108387  5108393  5108399  5108413  5108423  5108429  5108447  5108497  5108533  5108539
5108557  5108561  5108569  5108573  5108581  5108591  5108639  5108647  5108657  5108669
5108713  5108717  5108731  5108749  5108767  5108771  5108773  5108813  5108821  5108827
5108879  5108887  5108941  5108963  5108977  5108989  5109019  5109023  5109029  5109037
5109047  5109067  5109107  5109113  5109121  5109149  5109161  5109173  5109179  5109193
5109199  5109211  5109239  5109241  5109259  5109283  5109311  5109317  5109329  5109331
5109371  5109383  5109407  5109409  5109413  5109431  5109439  5109463  5109469  5109479
5109491  5109497  5109509  5109529  5109541  5109547  5109551  5109553  5109557  5109569
5109583  5109617  5109631  5109661  5109683  5109697  5109719  5109721  5109739  5109751
5109773  5109791  5109821  5109847  5109857  5109859  5109883  5109899  5109919  5109961
5109967  5109971  5109989  5110019  5110037  5110043  5110093  5110097  5110103  5110123
5110129  5110141  5110159  5110211  5110223  5110229  5110241  5110243  5110267  5110283
5110289  5110307  5110327  5110331  5110337  5110361  5110379  5110423  5110433  5110459
5110471  5110481  5110493  5110513  5110517  5110529  5110541  5110549  5110561  5110579
5110597  5110603  5110619  5110627  5110643  5110661  5110709  5110711  5110717  5110723
5110739  5110741  5110751  5110759  5110769  5110783  5110801  5110811  5110813  5110817
5110823  5110871  5110883  5110907  5110909  5110913  5110933  5110937  5110957  5110979
5110997  5111011  5111017  5111039  5111089  5111123  5111131  5111137  5111149  5111153
5111159  5111177  5111179  5111189  5111201  5111231  5111233  5111261  5111287  5111299
5111303  5111317  5111341  5111377  5111401  5111413  5111419  5111423  5111459  5111461
5111467  5111471  5111521  5111527  5111563  5111567  5111599  5111641  5111647  5111651
5111693  5111699  5111707  5111719  5111723  5111749  5111753  5111759  5111761  5111791
5111833  5111837  5111879  5111891  5111923  5111927  5111933  5111941  5111963  5111999
5112001  5112017  5112047  5112059  5112067  5112073  5112089  5112097  5112101  5112103
5112109  5112113  5112119  5112127  5112137  5112181  5112193  5112271  5112277  5112293
5112299  5112307  5112329  5112361  5112379  5112383  5112389  5112403  5112421  5112451
5112467  5112469  5112473  5112479  5112487  5112491  5112511  5112517  5112533  5112553
5112581  5112587  5112629  5112649  5112661  5112673  5112683  5112713  5112727  5112749
```

```
5112769  5112791  5112803  5112827  5112841  5112851  5112859  5112871  5112889  5112901
5112917  5112929  5112949  5112973  5112979  5112997  5113007  5113021  5113037  5113051
5113063  5113093  5113099  5113103  5113111  5113123  5113127  5113133  5113169  5113187
5113189  5113201  5113211  5113217  5113219  5113231  5113247  5113267  5113279  5113307
5113319  5113321  5113331  5113343  5113351  5113369  5113391  5113399  5113403  5113417
5113441  5113477  5113487  5113513  5113519  5113573  5113579  5113597  5113601  5113607
5113609  5113631  5113639  5113649  5113681  5113687  5113709  5113721  5113747  5113769
5113777  5113781  5113783  5113789  5113819  5113837  5113859  5113877  5113891  5113931
5113939  5113963  5113967  5113993  5114003  5114047  5114051  5114077  5114089  5114099
5114111  5114143  5114149  5114159  5114167  5114191  5114233  5114269  5114273  5114293
5114309  5114321  5114323  5114327  5114339  5114357  5114359  5114387  5114393  5114413
5114419  5114437  5114443  5114449  5114471  5114479  5114489  5114491  5114503  5114507
5114509  5114513  5114581  5114609  5114623  5114639  5114647  5114653  5114663  5114687
5114689  5114699  5114731  5114737  5114749  5114771  5114779  5114801  5114803  5114821
5114827  5114831  5114833  5114881  5114899  5114929  5114939  5114957  5114959  5114983
5114999  5115023  5115067  5115073  5115133  5115137  5115167  5115193  5115203  5115211
5115233  5115239  5115247  5115251  5115259  5115301  5115343  5115353  5115367  5115371
5115379  5115413  5115421  5115431  5115449  5115469  5115491  5115493  5115497  5115511
5115553  5115559  5115569  5115577  5115599  5115601  5115619  5115647  5115653  5115659
5115661  5115673  5115679  5115703  5115709  5115727  5115743  5115749  5115779  5115787
5115797  5115823  5115833  5115841  5115853  5115863  5115881  5115911  5115917  5115923
5115937  5115947  5116039  5116043  5116049  5116057  5116061  5116123  5116127  5116141
5116169  5116171  5116193  5116211  5116229  5116291  5116297  5116361  5116367  5116381
5116393  5116411  5116417  5116427  5116429  5116469  5116477  5116483  5116493  5116537
5116543  5116571  5116577  5116583  5116597  5116607  5116621  5116627  5116667  5116669
5116679  5116687  5116691  5116717  5116727  5116739  5116763  5116823  5116831  5116849
5116861  5116873  5116889  5116897  5116901  5116907  5116921  5116927  5116967  5116973
5116981  5116987  5117003  5117027  5117039  5117053  5117069  5117071  5117083  5117089
5117111  5117113  5117117  5117131  5117141  5117149  5117173  5117197  5117207  5117269
5117297  5117317  5117341  5117347  5117363  5117377  5117389  5117401  5117419  5117471
5117491  5117503  5117509  5117533  5117551  5117557  5117587  5117597  5117599  5117603
5117611  5117621  5117633  5117653  5117687  5117701  5117713  5117737  5117741  5117747
5117773  5117779  5117797  5117807  5117809  5117813  5117851  5117869  5117899  5117923
5117927  5117941  5117947  5117953  5117977  5117993  5117999  5118013  5118017  5118023
5118031  5118059  5118067  5118079  5118089  5118101  5118107  5118143  5118149  5118187
5118199  5118203  5118209  5118251  5118283  5118287  5118293  5118307  5118341  5118349
5118359  5118367  5118371  5118389  5118403  5118409  5118431  5118433  5118439  5118517
5118557  5118569  5118577  5118583  5118613  5118637  5118653  5118661  5118667  5118697
5118709  5118713  5118767  5118779  5118789  5118829  5118871  5118881  5118889  5118901
5118907  5118917  5118929  5118931  5118943  5118947  5118959  5119007  5119019  5119027
5119043  5119063  5119067  5119069  5119097  5119117  5119129  5119139  5119157  5119199
5119207  5119229  5119267  5119273  5119277  5119297  5119307  5119319  5119321  5119327
5119333  5119337  5119343  5119351  5119423  5119427  5119447  5119459  5119463  5119469
5119507  5119529  5119549  5119571  5119603  5119633  5119637  5119643  5119649  5119661
5119679  5119687  5119693  5119717  5119733  5119769  5119783  5119811  5119813  5119819
5119841  5119847  5119859  5119861  5119871  5119879  5119897  5119901  5119909  5119931
5119963  5119969  5119973  5119997  5120029  5120033  5120047  5120051  5120113  5120117
5120119  5120123  5120131  5120183  5120189  5120201  5120221  5120231  5120249  5120251
5120257  5120263  5120267  5120273  5120287  5120299  5120333  5120351  5120359  5120371
5120399  5120411  5120413  5120419  5120441  5120459  5120461  5120477  5120491  5120503
5120537  5120539  5120567  5120573  5120597  5120629  5120657  5120677  5120681  5120707
5120719  5120729  5120737  5120809  5120813  5120831  5120833  5120839  5120879  5120887
5120891  5120939  5120957  5120959  5120963  5121007  5121031  5121037  5121041  5121071
5121113  5121119  5121143  5121161  5121173  5121191  5121209  5121211  5121223  5121227
5121247  5121251  5121271  5121287  5121289  5121323  5121329  5121331  5121353  5121359
5121367  5121379  5121383  5121419  5121421  5121439  5121463  5121481  5121511  5121521
5121527  5121533  5121551  5121553  5121559  5121581  5121593  5121631  5121643  5121653
5121667  5121673  5121689  5121691  5121703  5121713  5121737  5121749  5121751  5121763
5121791  5121793  5121797  5121821  5121833  5121839  5121841  5121871  5121877  5121889
5121901  5121911  5121917  5121923  5121929  5121931  5121937  5121943  5121953  5121959
5121971  5121979  5121989  5122069  5122081  5122111  5122121  5122127  5122141  5122147
5122163  5122181  5122189  5122193  5122211  5122213  5122259  5122277  5122297  5122301
5122303  5122331  5122339  5122361  5122363  5122367  5122379  5122387  5122393  5122421
5122427  5122433  5122463  5122477  5122489  5122517  5122529  5122541  5122631  5122639
5122643  5122651  5122669  5122679  5122681  5122697  5122699  5122717  5122727  5122739
5122757  5122759  5122771  5122783  5122787  5122807  5122847  5122849  5122853  5122867
5122877  5122883  5122889  5122903  5122907  5122919  5122939  5122961  5122969  5122973
5122981  5122987  5123003  5123011  5123051  5123077  5123099  5123119  5123143  5123177
5123189  5123191  5123197  5123201  5123203  5123219  5123221  5123231  5123257  5123263
5123269  5123281  5123299  5123303  5123311  5123317  5123357  5123399  5123429  5123441
5123449  5123453  5123467  5123471  5123479  5123491  5123509  5123527  5123537  5123551
5123603  5123621  5123623  5123627  5123639  5123683  5123693  5123707  5123719  5123743
5123747  5123753  5123761  5123771  5123779  5123791  5123821  5123849  5123869  5123873
5123879  5123887  5123891  5123927  5123933  5123947  5123969  5123983  5124001  5124011
5124013  5124017  5124023  5124037  5124043  5124047  5124059  5124107  5124121  5124127
5124131  5124143  5124151  5124169  5124173  5124179  5124187  5124247  5124253  5124263
5124289  5124299  5124307  5124349  5124373  5124397  5124401  5124407  5124409  5124419
5124443  5124451  5124479  5124491  5124499  5124521  5124523  5124529  5124541  5124569
5124571  5124583  5124593  5124617  5124643  5124649  5124659  5124683  5124761  5124781
5124797  5124811  5124817  5124829  5124839  5124869  5124943  5124961  5124991  5124997
5125009  5125019  5125027  5125039  5125049  5125051  5125061  5125073  5125093  5125139
5125151  5125157  5125163  5125171  5125187  5125201  5125223  5125247  5125273  5125319
5125321  5125327  5125363  5125391  5125399  5125411  5125427  5125429  5125453  5125487
5125493  5125511  5125513  5125529  5125531  5125541  5125543  5125553  5125559  5125583
5125597  5125609  5125639  5125651  5125661  5125669  5125693  5125699  5125709  5125723
5125733  5125753  5125759  5125781  5125787  5125807  5125811  5125843  5125871  5125907
5125919  5125921  5125927  5125931  5125933  5125949  5125951  5125963  5125999  5126003
5126021  5126057  5126059  5126063  5126081  5126083  5126089  5126113  5126117  5126123
5126131  5126141  5126153  5126167  5126179  5126183  5126221  5126267  5126269  5126291
```

```
5126323  5126339  5126347  5126351  5126357  5126369  5126393  5126411  5126419  5126437
5126449  5126479  5126483  5126491  5126497  5126543  5126549  5126551  5126557  5126567
5126579  5126581  5126587  5126603  5126617  5126629  5126647  5126651  5126657  5126669
5126689  5126701  5126711  5126747  5126753  5126767  5126777  5126783  5126791  5126813
5126819  5126833  5126851  5126897  5126899  5126909  5126917  5126929  5126959  5126963
5126971  5126977  5126983  5126987  5127007  5127011  5127037  5127043  5127071  5127103
5127107  5127139  5127181  5127197  5127203  5127247  5127257  5127289  5127299  5127313
5127341  5127347  5127427  5127433  5127481  5127487  5127503  5127527  5127533  5127541
5127553  5127569  5127611  5127613  5127641  5127673  5127709  5127737  5127743  5127763
5127767  5127769  5127779  5127797  5127839  5127869  5127877  5127901  5127917  5127943
5127949  5127961  5127971  5127973  5127977  5128007  5128021  5128027  5128037  5128063
5128153  5128213  5128219  5128229  5128231  5128261  5128283  5128297  5128303  5128307
5128327  5128337  5128349  5128351  5128363  5128369  5128391  5128393  5128399  5128421
5128427  5128433  5128463  5128489  5128493  5128507  5128521  5128523  5128549  5128553
5128573  5128583  5128603  5128633  5128637  5128639  5128657  5128661  5128667  5128691
5128723  5128751  5128771  5128789  5128817  5128847  5128859  5128861  5128867  5128873
5128889  5128891  5128897  5128901  5128921  5128943  5128967  5128973  5128987  5128993
5129011  5129021  5129039  5129041  5129057  5129077  5129081  5129099  5129101  5129129
5129147  5129153  5129171  5129177  5129197  5129227  5129249  5129261  5129279  5129303
5129309  5129321  5129329  5129339  5129351  5129357  5129363  5129381  5129389  5129407
5129419  5129459  5129479  5129489  5129557  5129581  5129617  5129647  5129659  5129671
5129681  5129731  5129737  5129749  5129779  5129807  5129809  5129819  5129827  5129833
5129837  5129863  5129893  5129933  5129947  5129953  5129959  5129983  5129987  5130001
5130017  5130067  5130079  5130089  5130101  5130113  5130119  5130143  5130157  5130163
5130179  5130253  5130259  5130263  5130269  5130271  5130299  5130331  5130343  5130397
5130409  5130421  5130443  5130467  5130487  5130493  5130509  5130511  5130529  5130547
5130553  5130557  5130571  5130577  5130607  5130623  5130641  5130647  5130683  5130689
5130701  5130707  5130721  5130731  5130733  5130743  5130773  5130791  5130809  5130823
5130847  5130857  5130869  5130913  5130919  5130947  5130949  5130959  5130989  5130997
5131013  5131019  5131039  5131043  5131067  5131069  5131079  5131081  5131111  5131141
5131157  5131163  5131177  5131183  5131199  5131201  5131207  5131211  5131219  5131223
5131237  5131249  5131253  5131267  5131283  5131307  5131333  5131339  5131351  5131363
5131367  5131417  5131421  5131439  5131447  5131457  5131459  5131481  5131517  5131541
5131543  5131571  5131627  5131631  5131649  5131657  5131673  5131697  5131757  5131759
5131781  5131787  5131799  5131801  5131813  5131823  5131849  5131853  5131871  5131877
5131891  5131897  5131961  5131963  5131969  5131981  5131993  5132009  5132051  5132053
5132069  5132087  5132111  5132117  5132123  5132131  5132137  5132161  5132167  5132177
5132189  5132191  5132201  5132207  5132209  5132213  5132219  5132221  5132227  5132273
5132279  5132287  5132311  5132321  5132327  5132341  5132359  5132417  5132429  5132443
5132459  5132461  5132497  5132513  5132531  5132537  5132539  5132549  5132563  5132581
5132591  5132597  5132599  5132629  5132653  5132671  5132689  5132741  5132747  5132753
5132767  5132773  5132821  5132833  5132837  5132839  5132843  5132851  5132857  5132873
5132893  5132903  5132909  5132923  5132927  5132947  5132957  5132989  5132993  5132999
5133001  5133013  5133017  5133043  5133049  5133053  5133091  5133101  5133109  5133113
5133119  5133127  5133157  5133179  5133187  5133239  5133263  5133277  5133299  5133307
5133311  5133313  5133353  5133361  5133379  5133389  5133391  5133397  5133407  5133437
5133451  5133461  5133463  5133503  5133509  5133511  5133517  5133523  5133529  5133559
5133571  5133581  5133593  5133613  5133617  5133619  5133637  5133659  5133671  5133673
5133697  5133701  5133719  5133749  5133757  5133773  5133809  5133839  5133851  5133859
5133883  5133907  5133911  5133913  5133917  5133923  5133937  5133977  5134013  5134039
5134043  5134067  5134069  5134079  5134091  5134097  5134099  5134109  5134117
5134147  5134159  5134169  5134183  5134193  5134201  5134219  5134249  5134253  5134273
5134279  5134301  5134303  5134331  5134333  5134361  5134369  5134373  5134417  5134429
5134457  5134477  5134487  5134511  5134517  5134567  5134573  5134643  5134667  5134669
5134687  5134691  5134699  5134709  5134721  5134729  5134733  5134751  5134757  5134771
5134781  5134783  5134793  5134841  5134847  5134853  5134861  5134903  5134907  5134939
5134949  5134951  5134979  5134981  5134993  5135023  5135027  5135029  5135063  5135093
5135113  5135129  5135131  5135147  5135153  5135161  5135167  5135177  5135191  5135197
5135201  5135219  5135231  5135257  5135281  5135297  5135321  5135323  5135327  5135357
5135363  5135381  5135387  5135401  5135413  5135423  5135437  5135441  5135443  5135503
5135521  5135527  5135531  5135539  5135569  5135573  5135579  5135591  5135597  5135609
5135621  5135653  5135657  5135659  5135671  5135687  5135707  5135723  5135731  5135743
5135747  5135759  5135761  5135789  5135807  5135839  5135873  5135899  5135917  5135953
5135959  5135983  5136011  5136013  5136031  5136037  5136041  5136067  5136073  5136083
5136121  5136143  5136163  5136199  5136229  5136269  5136281  5136311  5136323  5136331
5136347  5136361  5136367  5136371  5136401  5136427  5136437  5136449  5136463  5136473
5136491  5136493  5136511  5136529  5136553  5136559  5136577  5136581  5136611  5136623
5136629  5136661  5136667  5136701  5136709  5136721  5136727  5136743  5136757  5136773
5136809  5136811  5136841  5136847  5136853  5136863  5136881  5136893  5136947  5136977
5137001  5137019  5137037  5137021  5137037  5137039  5137051  5137057  5137123  5137127
5137141  5137183  5137193  5137199  5137207  5137219  5137243  5137267  5137273  5137283
5137309  5137357  5137361  5137367  5137373  5137381  5137387  5137393  5137399  5137403
5137453  5137459  5137469  5137477  5137499  5137507  5137513  5137529  5137547  5137651
5137663  5137673  5137681  5137721  5137739  5137747  5137777  5137787  5137789  5137793
5137801  5137829  5137831  5137849  5137861  5137871  5137903  5137919  5137921  5137939
5137943  5137963  5137973  5137987  5138009  5138041  5138053  5138069  5138071  5138083
5138093  5138099  5138101  5138117  5138137  5138149  5138167  5138171  5138179  5138183
5138207  5138257  5138279  5138291  5138311  5138317  5138321  5138333  5138347  5138359
5138363  5138377  5138383  5138387  5138443  5138477  5138479  5138491  5138503  5138513
5138519  5138533  5138537  5138561  5138603  5138611  5138633  5138657  5138663  5138677
5138687  5138717  5138719  5138747  5138753  5138789  5138803  5138807  5138831  5138849
5138857  5138863  5138869  5138891  5138923  5138929  5138941  5138953  5138957  5138977
5139019  5139047  5139073  5139089  5139109  5139131  5139137  5139161  5139179  5139203
5139221  5139223  5139257  5139259  5139271  5139301  5139319  5139341  5139347  5139349
5139359  5139371  5139377  5139393  5139401  5139431  5139437  5139451  5139461  5139479
5139493  5139509  5139517  5139527  5139539  5139551  5139581  5139601  5139611  5139613
5139623  5139643  5139647  5139653  5139679  5139683  5139691  5139697  5139713  5139721
5139731  5139737  5139751  5139767  5139791  5139793  5139811  5139821  5139859  5139863
5139877  5139881  5139907  5139913  5139917  5139923  5139949  5139973  5139983  5140007
```

5140027 5140049 5140067 5140073 5140087 5140117 5140123 5140133 5140147 5140153
5140181 5140183 5140189 5140207 5140217 5140237 5140253 5140259 5140271 5140277
5140283 5140297 5140357 5140361 5140367 5140381 5140397 5140403 5140411 5140459
5140463 5140481 5140489 5140501 5140517 5140543 5140547 5140561 5140573 5140589
5140591 5140633 5140643 5140657 5140673 5140687 5140691 5140727 5140741 5140747
5140763 5140769 5140777 5140781 5140829 5140853 5140871 5140873 5140901 5140909
5140913 5140921 5140939 5140957 5140969 5140973 5140979 5140991 5140997
5140999 5141011 5141023 5141027 5141051 5141063 5141093 5141099 5141117 5141137
5141177 5141179 5141219 5141237 5141249 5141251 5141273 5141309 5141321 5141347
5141363 5141369 5141393 5141401 5141407 5141431 5141449 5141453 5141491 5141501
5141519 5141527 5141537 5141573 5141579 5141603 5141621 5141663 5141677 5141681
5141693 5141699 5141743 5141771 5141789 5141813 5141819 5141831 5141833 5141867
5141869 5141921 5141947 5141953 5141959 5141963 5141971 5141977 5141987 5141993
5141999 5142013 5142017 5142043 5142061 5142083 5142089 5142091 5142101 5142107
5142119 5142121 5142131 5142173 5142197 5142199 5142227 5142229 5142257 5142259
5142289 5142323 5142329 5142337 5142349 5142353 5142383 5142419 5142421 5142461
5142469 5142493 5142503 5142523 5142539 5142587 5142623 5142637 5142647
5142661 5142677 5142679 5142689 5142713 5142733 5142751 5142779 5142793 5142799
5142811 5142817 5142829 5142847 5142877 5142899 5142911 5142913 5142919
5142937 5142953 5142967 5142989 5143013 5143031 5143051 5143087 5143097 5143109
5143133 5143147 5143153 5143183 5143189 5143217 5143249 5143253 5143267 5143277
5143291 5143301 5143321 5143339 5143343 5143349 5143363 5143381 5143403 5143423
5143429 5143447 5143451 5143483 5143487 5143493 5143499 5143543 5143583 5143591
5143603 5143609 5143637 5143667 5143669 5143687 5143693 5143709 5143711 5143729
5143751 5143753 5143757 5143771 5143781 5143783 5143793 5143807 5143837 5143847
5143849 5143871 5143891 5143903 5143907 5143913 5143921 5143967 5143987 5144011
5144023 5144053 5144077 5144093 5144119 5144137 5144141 5144143 5144177 5144189
5144263 5144273 5144287 5144303 5144309 5144317 5144323 5144351 5144371 5144411
5144413 5144437 5144441 5144471 5144483 5144519 5144521 5144533 5144537 5144539
5144549 5144561 5144567 5144569 5144597 5144599 5144603 5144621 5144647 5144653
5144669 5144677 5144681 5144701 5144707 5144719 5144743 5144749 5144753 5144759
5144809 5144827 5144831 5144837 5144849 5144851 5144879 5144899 5144903 5144911
5144917 5144929 5144933 5144941 5144947 5144957 5144959 5144963 5144981 5144983
5144989 5145011 5145017 5145037 5145053 5145059 5145061 5145071 5145083 5145139
5145149 5145197 5145211 5145233 5145263 5145269 5145311 5145313 5145317 5145323
5145347 5145389 5145403 5145433 5145463 5145493 5145521 5145529 5145589 5145593
5145601 5145619 5145631 5145643 5145661 5145671 5145677 5145689 5145703 5145719
5145727 5145733 5145743 5145757 5145761 5145769 5145773 5145779 5145809 5145817
5145821 5145841 5145851 5145871 5145887 5145901 5145937 5145949 5145967 5145971
5145977 5145991 5146003 5146061 5146091 5146103 5146109 5146147 5146153 5146159
5146177 5146199 5146213 5146237 5146243 5146261 5146269 5146303 5146307 5146343
5146381 5146391 5146409 5146417 5146451 5146469 5146481 5146483 5146487 5146489
5146513 5146517 5146523 5146567 5146579 5146591 5146619 5146621 5146633 5146637
5146639 5146649 5146667 5146681 5146711 5146721 5146727 5146741 5146751 5146763
5146769 5146783 5146789 5146793 5146819 5146831 5146847 5146879 5146901 5146919
5146927 5146943 5146951 5146957 5147041 5147047 5147059 5147069 5147159 5147161
5147167 5147179 5147213 5147249 5147251 5147267 5147273 5147279 5147281 5147291
5147293 5147323 5147339 5147353 5147357 5147369 5147371 5147379 5147399 5147431
5147479 5147497 5147507 5147531 5147539 5147563 5147603 5147609 5147621 5147627
5147629 5147633 5147647 5147657 5147687 5147707 5147711 5147749 5147789 5147797
5147827 5147839 5147867 5147881 5147893 5147897 5147939 5147951 5147959
5147963 5147981 5148007 5148041 5148047 5148119 5148131 5148151 5148173 5148181
5148191 5148197 5148203 5148233 5148257 5148271 5148277 5148287 5148289 5148293
5148301 5148313 5148337 5148359 5148371 5148379 5148463 5148497 5148499 5148503
5148523 5148541 5148547 5148551 5148553 5148557 5148581 5148589 5148623 5148659
5148701 5148713 5148719 5148721 5148761 5148779 5148799 5148817 5148823
5148853 5148859 5148893 5148937 5148959 5148967 5148971 5148973 5149009 5149013
5149021 5149049 5149061 5149063 5149093 5149097 5149099 5149103 5149139 5149159
5149187 5149189 5149219 5149223 5149229 5149259 5149267 5149289 5149301 5149303
5149307 5149337 5149349 5149393 5149409 5149411 5149421 5149423 5149429 5149471
5149483 5149517 5149519 5149531 5149537 5149567 5149577 5149583 5149597 5149601
5149619 5149621 5149643 5149667 5149673 5149679 5149699 5149709 5149717 5149721
5149747 5149763 5149783 5149801 5149829 5149841 5149847 5149853 5149867 5149889
5149913 5149927 5149943 5149951 5149961 5149973 5149979 5149987 5150027 5150059
5150079 5150107 5150129 5150143 5150147 5150149 5150161 5150177 5150191 5150203
5150207 5150209 5150219 5150221 5150237 5150251 5150267 5150279 5150333 5150347
5150351 5150377 5150389 5150407 5150419 5150423 5150441 5150443 5150477 5150489
5150513 5150549 5150567 5150581 5150599 5150617 5150633 5150671 5150693 5150701
5150713 5150723 5150737 5150741 5150773 5150819 5150833 5150839 5150851 5150869
5150909 5150917 5150939 5150941 5150947 5150969 5150987 5151001 5151007
5151019 5151031 5151043 5151049 5151061 5151131 5151137 5151151 5151163 5151169
5151191 5151193 5151197 5151203 5151217 5151227 5151253 5151257 5151269 5151277
5151319 5151343 5151347 5151359 5151361 5151371 5151373 5151407 5151431
5151437 5151457 5151463 5151469 5151481 5151491 5151521 5151533 5151539 5151541
5151551 5151571 5151581 5151583 5151589 5151599 5151607 5151617 5151637 5151659
5151661 5151677 5151737 5151739 5151779 5151781 5151791 5151823 5151841 5151847
5151851 5151871 5151889 5151899 5151919 5151929 5151947 5151953 5151967 5151989
5151997 5152001 5152027 5152031 5152039 5152051 5152087 5152109 5152127 5152151
5152153 5152177 5152181 5152237 5152247 5152261 5152297 5152319 5152327 5152331
5152333 5152351 5152379 5152387 5152397 5152403 5152421 5152423 5152447 5152453
5152457 5152463 5152471 5152481 5152493 5152507 5152519 5152531 5152549 5152571
5152579 5152613 5152639 5152643 5152669 5152681 5152699 5152711 5152739 5152747
5152753 5152783 5152801 5152811 5152813 5152837 5152841 5152843 5152859 5152877
5152909 5152937 5152949 5152957 5152993 5153017 5153021 5153041 5153063 5153089
5153111 5153117 5153129 5153149 5153153 5153179 5153191 5153201 5153207 5153209
5153257 5153299 5153321 5153327 5153353 5153359 5153381 5153383 5153437 5153443
5153459 5153483 5153509 5153521 5153531 5153537 5153539 5153543 5153549 5153569
5153623 5153639 5153641 5153647 5153651 5153663 5153689 5153699 5153711 5153747
5153749 5153777 5153779 5153831 5153833 5153849 5153867 5153887 5153891 5153899

```
5153903 5153917 5153923 5153927 5153957 5153963 5153971 5153983 5154007 5154013
5154049 5154089 5154101 5154133 5154143 5154157 5154167 5154173 5154209 5154221
5154229 5154239 5154271 5154287 5154293 5154307 5154313 5154343 5154353 5154361
5154371 5154379 5154389 5154419 5154421 5154427 5154469 5154473 5154493 5154497
5154509 5154533 5154551 5154557 5154559 5154563 5154577 5154593 5154619 5154629
5154641 5154673 5154701 5154703 5154707 5154713 5154733 5154739 5154761 5154763
5154767 5154769 5154811 5154817 5154823 5154827 5154839 5154857 5154869 5154887
5154901 5154907 5154911 5154917 5154923 5154973 5154979 5154983 5154997 5155001
5155027 5155037 5155043 5155067 5155103 5155109 5155133 5155159 5155193 5155219
5155229 5155237 5155261 5155277 5155279 5155307 5155309 5155351 5155387 5155433
5155439 5155481 5155483 5155489 5155499 5155511 5155547 5155561 5155567 5155603
5155639 5155643 5155673 5155679 5155697 5155699 5155727 5155729 5155753 5155769
5155789 5155817 5155849 5155861 5155907 5155957 5155961 5155993 5156017 5156023
5156033 5156051 5156059 5156089 5156101 5156111 5156141 5156153 5156159 5156161
5156183 5156189 5156213 5156227 5156231 5156237 5156243 5156267 5156273 5156279
5156297 5156299 5156309 5156339 5156363 5156383 5156399 5156413 5156419
5156441 5156449 5156471 5156477 5156479 5156497 5156527 5156533 5156537 5156539
5156549 5156551 5156561 5156563 5156573 5156587 5156609 5156663 5156719 5156731
5156737 5156743 5156747 5156773 5156779 5156783 5156803 5156813 5156839 5156849
5156891 5156897 5156911 5156917 5156929 5156941 5156951 5156969 5156971 5156993
5157007 5157017 5157029 5157049 5157073 5157101 5157133 5157143 5157179 5157197
5157203 5157241 5157247 5157277 5157281 5157287 5157323 5157329 5157403 5157407
5157419 5157421 5157457 5157479 5157487 5157491 5157499 5157517 5157533 5157547
5157557 5157571 5157577 5157599 5157617 5157619 5157623 5157629 5157661 5157709
5157731 5157739 5157743 5157787 5157791 5157793 5157821 5157829 5157847 5157857
5157877 5157883 5157917 5157941 5157947 5157967 5157983 5157991 5158001 5158007
5158019 5158031 5158033 5158037 5158039 5158057 5158061 5158067 5158073 5158081
5158103 5158117 5158189 5158199 5158211 5158261 5158267 5158271 5158273 5158277
5158289 5158303 5158313 5158339 5158357 5158379 5158381 5158393 5158411 5158423
5158427 5158441 5158451 5158453 5158457 5158469 5158477 5158487 5158499 5158501
5158511 5158537 5158537 5158591 5158597 5158603 5158663 5158669 5158711 5158721
5158733 5158759 5158763 5158793 5158801 5158817 5158841 5158843 5158847 5158883
5158903 5158913 5158921 5158987 5158991 5158999 5159023 5159039 5159047 5159053
5159057 5159059 5159081 5159093 5159111 5159117 5159149 5159159 5159171 5159207
5159213 5159227 5159239 5159249 5159251 5159257 5159261 5159281 5159321 5159351
5159377 5159389 5159443 5159447 5159461 5159489 5159509 5159513 5159533 5159549
5159573 5159611 5159617 5159633 5159639 5159657 5159663 5159669 5159677 5159681
5159683 5159701 5159711 5159717 5159723 5159729 5159731 5159741 5159743 5159779
5159813 5159827 5159839 5159879 5159881 5159893 5159897 5159899 5159911 5159927
5159969 5159977 5160007 5160011 5160037 5160041 5160047 5160049 5160079 5160101
5160143 5160149 5160157 5160161 5160179 5160187 5160217 5160223 5160283 5160293
5160307 5160313 5160319 5160329 5160361 5160373 5160377 5160409 5160413 5160439
5160461 5160479 5160499 5160509 5160511 5160523 5160527 5160563 5160569 5160581
5160583 5160587 5160593 5160607 5160613 5160643 5160677 5160679 5160719 5160721
5160733 5160737 5160767 5160773 5160781 5160791 5160803 5160821 5160829 5160839
5160851 5160887 5160893 5160917 5160923 5160941 5160959 5160971 5160983 5160997
5161003 5161031 5161063 5161073 5161099 5161111 5161129 5161133 5161139 5161181
5161187 5161229 5161231 5161243 5161249 5161253 5161267 5161291 5161309 5161327
5161337 5161339 5161349 5161357 5161363 5161381 5161411 5161417 5161423 5161427
5161439 5161451 5161517 5161529 5161549 5161553 5161561 5161567 5161571 5161579
5161609 5161619 5161631 5161643 5161669 5161691 5161697 5161699 5161703 5161789
5161799 5161811 5161813 5161831 5161837 5161843 5161847 5161873 5161879 5161909
5161921 5161927 5161943 5161967 5161993 5161997 5162011 5162063 5162071 5162077
5162081 5162083 5162093 5162099 5162123 5162141 5162159 5162177 5162219 5162221
5162231 5162233 5162291 5162299 5162303 5162323 5162329 5162371 5162383 5162387
5162389 5162393 5162447 5162459 5162467 5162473 5162477 5162483 5162489 5162497
5162501 5162513 5162561 5162569 5162587 5162593 5162617 5162627 5162653 5162671
5162681 5162711 5162719 5162743 5162749 5162753 5162767 5162789 5162789 5162803
5162827 5162831 5162837 5162863 5162891 5162893 5162909 5162923 5162933 5162947
5162981 5162987 5163001 5163023 5163061 5163077 5163097 5163113 5163127 5163163
5163167 5163199 5163229 5163233 5163241 5163283 5163289 5163317 5163343 5163349
5163371 5163377 5163409 5163437 5163443 5163451 5163469 5163481 5163491 5163511
5163517 5163527 5163547 5163583 5163593 5163607 5163629 5163659 5163671 5163727
5163751 5163773 5163787 5163791 5163793 5163797 5163817 5163859 5163871 5163883
5163911 5163919 5163923 5163939 5163959 5163997 5164007 5164009 5164013 5164021
5164069 5164079 5164087 5164091 5164097 5164123 5164129 5164139 5164147 5164157
5164169 5164189 5164193 5164207 5164217 5164241 5164253 5164261 5164273 5164283
5164303 5164331 5164361 5164363 5164381 5164387 5164417 5164441 5164451 5164463
5164517 5164519 5164541 5164543 5164547 5164567 5164589 5164591 5164597 5164603
5164609 5164619 5164657 5164669 5164699 5164703 5164717 5164723 5164739 5164741
5164769 5164771 5164787 5164799 5164807 5164849 5164853 5164897 5164921 5164961
5164993 5165021 5165051 5165063 5165077 5165107 5165113 5165119 5165123 5165137
5165191 5165201 5165227 5165243 5165267 5165269 5165299 5165309 5165323 5165333
5165387 5165389 5165411 5165417 5165423 5165429 5165431 5165453 5165483 5165497
5165513 5165519 5165527 5165543 5165551 5165557 5165579 5165581 5165591 5165597
5165621 5165647 5165653 5165659 5165687 5165689 5165707 5165711 5165717 5165729
5165749 5165753 5165771 5165791 5165801 5165803 5165813 5165821 5165833 5165887
5165899 5165939 5165947 5165969 5165983 5165987 5165999 5166001 5166013 5166017
5166019 5166023 5166037 5166061 5166071 5166101 5166103 5166107 5166121 5166131
5166143 5166179 5166209 5166211 5166221 5166223 5166253 5166257 5166269 5166289
5166311 5166323 5166331 5166353 5166373 5166383 5166389 5166391 5166401 5166443
5166449 5166481 5166527 5166541 5166563 5166619 5166631 5166647 5166649 5166653
5166661 5166671 5166673 5166701 5166703 5166737 5166787 5166817 5166829 5166869
5166871 5166877 5166893 5166919 5166961 5166971 5166983 5167003 5167021 5167051
5167061 5167067 5167079 5167081 5167103 5167109 5167121 5167139 5167163 5167187
5167199 5167207 5167213 5167223 5167231 5167247 5167291 5167301 5167333 5167339
5167343 5167367 5167399 5167403 5167427 5167441 5167471 5167489 5167501 5167511
5167523 5167529 5167549 5167559 5167577 5167583 5167619 5167621 5167637 5167649
5167651 5167661 5167667 5167691 5167693 5167703 5167733 5167739 5167741 5167769
```

```
5167781  5167787  5167807  5167817  5167823  5167837  5167853  5167861  5167879  5167891
5167907  5167913  5167919  5167933  5167937  5167957  5167973  5167991  5168021  5168047
5168071  5168087  5168089  5168113  5168117  5168129  5168147  5168201  5168237  5168239
5168249  5168263  5168269  5168287  5168291  5168309  5168311  5168329  5168333  5168369
5168377  5168381  5168389  5168393  5168407  5168411  5168431  5168441  5168477  5168479
5168539  5168573  5168621  5168623  5168677  5168687  5168707  5168711  5168717  5168743
5168749  5168753  5168777  5168791  5168803  5168837  5168851  5168857  5168861  5168869
5168879  5168887  5168897  5168921  5168923  5168927  5168929  5168939  5168941  5168953
5168963  5168981  5169019  5169023  5169053  5169061  5169091  5169103  5169113  5169137
5169149  5169187  5169191  5169211  5169247  5169253  5169299  5169301  5169317  5169347
5169361  5169379  5169383  5169397  5169401  5169419  5169427  5169431  5169433  5169443
5169449  5169469  5169481  5169487  5169497  5169509  5169551  5169559  5169583  5169599
5169601  5169607  5169613  5169617  5169623  5169631  5169643  5169667  5169679  5169713
5169721  5169727  5169763  5169781  5169793  5169799  5169817  5169823  5169833  5169841
5169893  5169907  5169943  5169947  5169949  5169961  5169971  5170001  5170013  5170027
5170031  5170049  5170063  5170073  5170129  5170163  5170181  5170183  5170201  5170213
5170237  5170241  5170247  5170271  5170279  5170283  5170289  5170303  5170307  5170339
5170351  5170357  5170369  5170393  5170411  5170427  5170463  5170483  5170513  5170539
5170551  5170553  5170559  5170577  5170579  5170609  5170619  5170637  5170643  5170657
5170667  5170673  5170687  5170691  5170709  5170727  5170741  5170751  5170777  5170813
5170829  5170853  5170871  5170889  5170927  5170933  5170967  5170999  5171011  5171029
5171039  5171041  5171057  5171063  5171071  5171087  5171093  5171119  5171123  5171129
5171161  5171171  5171183  5171189  5171191  5171197  5171209  5171237  5171239  5171279
5171293  5171311  5171317  5171323  5171329  5171333  5171347  5171357  5171359  5171381
5171407  5171429  5171437  5171449  5171459  5171461  5171473  5171521  5171531  5171533
5171549  5171557  5171561  5171597  5171609  5171623  5171627  5171633  5171659  5171681
5171693  5171729  5171753  5171779  5171783  5171801  5171807  5171809  5171839  5171843
5171891  5171909  5171917  5171923  5171951  5171953  5171963  5171981  5171983  5171989
5171993  5172001  5172017  5172019  5172043  5172049  5172053  5172061  5172073  5172077
5172107  5172127  5172149  5172151  5172163  5172187  5172197  5172221  5172227  5172239
5172253  5172259  5172283  5172287  5172289  5172317  5172337  5172347  5172361  5172371
5172379  5172383  5172407  5172449  5172451  5172457  5172463  5172473  5172481  5172521
5172523  5172547  5172551  5172553  5172569  5172571  5172647  5172653  5172659  5172697
5172703  5172733  5172749  5172751  5172767  5172787  5172793  5172803  5172821  5172823
5172829  5172851  5172889  5172899  5172901  5172919  5172941  5172949  5172977  5173013
5173019  5173039  5173057  5173067  5173079  5173097  5173193  5173211  5173213  5173237
5173241  5173247  5173261  5173283  5173309  5173313  5173319  5173331  5173379  5173387
5173409  5173439  5173477  5173499  5173537  5173541  5173543  5173561  5173579  5173589
5173591  5173603  5173607  5173613  5173657  5173703  5173711  5173723  5173741  5173759
5173787  5173799  5173813  5173829  5173843  5173849  5173859  5173867  5173877  5173879
5173891  5173897  5173907  5173947  5173939  5173943  5173951  5173957  5173963  5173979
5173981  5173991  5174003  5174017  5174033  5174047  5174063  5174119  5174177  5174189
5174219  5174237  5174243  5174261  5174291  5174293  5174347  5174363  5174387  5174399
5174401  5174419  5174423  5174431  5174461  5174467  5174473  5174483  5174501  5174503
5174509  5174527  5174531  5174537  5174567  5174573  5174581  5174591  5174633  5174639
5174657  5174671  5174677  5174699  5174723  5174759  5174773  5174777  5174791  5174803
5174809  5174833  5174843  5174849  5174863  5174881  5174887  5174891  5174903  5174927
5174929  5174933  5174941  5174947  5174957  5174959  5174989  5174999  5175019  5175031
5175041  5175059  5175097  5175101  5175103  5175187  5175193  5175199  5175229  5175251
5175271  5175283  5175323  5175329  5175337  5175343  5175347  5175383  5175407  5175409
5175433  5175461  5175473  5175491  5175493  5175509  5175517  5175551  5175557
5175563  5175571  5175587  5175637  5175661  5175673  5175691  5175719  5175721  5175727
5175757  5175763  5175767  5175811  5175839  5175857  5175869  5175887  5175899  5175913
5175917  5175931  5175991  5176009  5176027  5176051  5176069  5176079  5176091  5176097
5176141  5176169  5176183  5176187  5176217  5176229  5176243  5176253  5176273  5176289
5176307  5176309  5176319  5176321  5176343  5176387  5176429  5176433  5176459  5176477
5176489  5176511  5176543  5176547  5176571  5176573  5176579  5176583  5176603  5176631
5176637  5176663  5176667  5176693  5176709  5176711  5176723  5176729  5176739  5176747
5176757  5176763  5176799  5176807  5176811  5176841  5176849  5176861  5176879  5176903
5176933  5176943  5176961  5176973  5177033  5177059  5177069  5177099  5177113
5177119  5177147  5177149  5177203  5177209  5177239  5177261  5177273  5177281  5177287
5177327  5177339  5177351  5177363  5177387  5177413  5177441  5177449  5177453  5177467
5177477  5177479  5177489  5177509  5177551  5177591  5177593  5177597  5177617  5177621
5177647  5177657  5177659  5177687  5177701  5177719  5177723  5177761  5177771  5177791
5177797  5177801  5177803  5177807  5177813  5177869  5177881  5177903  5177923
5177947  5177969  5177971  5177983  5177989  5178001  5178007  5178029  5178031  5178049
5178053  5178067  5178073  5178077  5178083  5178091  5178133  5178137  5178139  5178143
5178161  5178163  5178181  5178191  5178193  5178301  5178311  5178337  5178379  5178389
5178391  5178403  5178419  5178487  5178499  5178517  5178521  5178541  5178553  5178571
5178599  5178623  5178629  5178647  5178653  5178661  5178689  5178709  5178731  5178739
5178743  5178781  5178787  5178809  5178827  5178857  5178869  5178871  5178889  5178893
5178919  5178923  5178941  5178947  5178949  5178967  5178973  5178983  5178989  5178991
5179019  5179021  5179061  5179073  5179061  5179063  5179093  5179099  5179103  5179123
5179127  5179133  5179151  5179159  5179199  5179219  5179231  5179241  5179249  5179289
5179303  5179337  5179351  5179367  5179403  5179411  5179481  5179507  5179513  5179523
5179547  5179567  5179579  5179589  5179591  5179597  5179613  5179619  5179627  5179633
5179639  5179699  5179709  5179739  5179831  5179841  5179843  5179859  5179891  5179903
5179907  5179919  5179931  5179939  5179943  5179961  5179969  5179997  5180003  5180017
5180029  5180041  5180047  5180051  5180057  5180099  5180101  5180117  5180137  5180143
5180159  5180171  5180213  5180233  5180237  5180241  5180281  5180297  5180321  5180323
5180341  5180347  5180353  5180419  5180437  5180447  5180449  5180459  5180467  5180471
5180477  5180489  5180501  5180537  5180569  5180573  5180579  5180587  5180599  5180603
5180621  5180653  5180677  5180687  5180713  5180717  5180743  5180759  5180761  5180771
5180807  5180809  5180827  5180839  5180887  5180897  5180921  5180927  5180933  5180953
5180963  5180969  5180983  5180993  5181013  5181017  5181019  5181023  5181067  5181079
5181101  5181103  5181133  5181151  5181173  5181191  5181217  5181223  5181251  5181269
5181283  5181287  5181299  5181301  5181307  5181321  5181347  5181349  5181353  5181383
5181391  5181431  5181469  5181497  5181499  5181511  5181529  5181541  5181551  5181559
5181563  5181569  5181581  5181587  5181599  5181611  5181637  5181641  5181653  5181667
```

5181677 5181679 5181697 5181721 5181733 5181769 5181779 5181811 5181817 5181829
5181859 5181881 5181893 5181899 5181901 5181907 5181919 5181941 5181947 5181971
5181977 5181983 5181989 5181997 5182027 5182057 5182063 5182091 5182103 5182139
5182141 5182157 5182171 5182189 5182201 5182207 5182217 5182253 5182313 5182319
5182339 5182349 5182367 5182379 5182417 5182427 5182447 5182451 5182453 5182469
5182477 5182531 5182537 5182543 5182571 5182601 5182609 5182631 5182663 5182669
5182691 5182699 5182717 5182721 5182757 5182777 5182799 5182811 5182813 5182819
5182829 5182867 5182871 5182897 5182913 5182939 5182949 5182951 5182963 5182979
5182993 5183033 5183047 5183051 5183077 5183089 5183131 5183137 5183153 5183159
5183183 5183201 5183221 5183279 5183281 5183291 5183309 5183323 5183329 5183357
5183363 5183369 5183383 5183393 5183411 5183459 5183461 5183471 5183473 5183483
5183527 5183531 5183537 5183557 5183567 5183569 5183587 5183609 5183611 5183641
5183683 5183687 5183699 5183701 5183707 5183729 5183747 5183749 5183813 5183819
5183821 5183831 5183839 5183863 5183869 5183879 5183881 5183891 5183897 5183909
5183933 5183939 5183957 5183977 5183987 5184001 5184007 5184029 5184061 5184073
5184103 5184121 5184139 5184143 5184187 5184191 5184197 5184199 5184227 5184233
5184247 5184283 5184287 5184293 5184307 5184317 5184323 5184343 5184373 5184391
5184401 5184419 5184427 5184433 5184457 5184479 5184493 5184497 5184539 5184563
5184577 5184581 5184593 5184607 5184623 5184631 5184689 5184703 5184721 5184727
5184733 5184757 5184763 5184769 5184787 5184791 5184793 5184797 5184799 5184833
5184841 5184857 5184859 5184863 5184871 5184877 5184889 5184911 5184919 5184931
5184943 5184947 5184953 5184961 5185001 5185003 5185009 5185027 5185057 5185067
5185121 5185127 5185129 5185139 5185199 5185211 5185223 5185253 5185261 5185267
5185307 5185321 5185337 5185351 5185379 5185381 5185399 5185417 5185421 5185429
5185447 5185483 5185487 5185507 5185529 5185559 5185567 5185589 5185619 5185633
5185669 5185681 5185699 5185703 5185709 5185729 5185753 5185781 5185801
5185811 5185813 5185823 5185837 5185849 5185853 5185877 5185889 5185913 5185919
5185927 5185931 5185937 5185949 5185979 5185981 5185987 5185991 5186009 5186033
5186039 5186059 5186081 5186087 5186123 5186141 5186149 5186161 5186177 5186191
5186197 5186219 5186261 5186263 5186267 5186287 5186303 5186317 5186333 5186341
5186351 5186353 5186371 5186381 5186383 5186387 5186407 5186463 5186501 5186417
5186483 5186491 5186501 5186509 5186521 5186543 5186551 5186557 5186603 5186627
5186651 5186659 5186663 5186681 5186689 5186729 5186759 5186761 5186773 5186777
5186803 5186821 5186833 5186837 5186849 5186851 5186861 5186879 5186899 5186927
5186933 5186941 5186947 5186953 5186963 5187011 5187089 5187109 5187113 5187131
5187139 5187151 5187173 5187181 5187233 5187239 5187271 5187277 5187283 5187293
5187313 5187353 5187359 5187367 5187383 5187401 5187449 5187487 5187503 5187517
5187527 5187529 5187547 5187577 5187593 5187617 5187629 5187667 5187671 5187683
5187691 5187697 5187739 5187761 5187769 5187797 5187803 5187827 5187841 5187859
5187863 5187869 5187883 5187887 5187901 5187911 5187913 5187937 5187961 5187971
5187977 5187979 5187991 5188019 5188021 5188061 5188069 5188091 5188121 5188141
5188163 5188171 5188193 5188207 5188219 5188229 5188231 5188241 5188243 5188259
5188277 5188289 5188297 5188301 5188319 5188333 5188343 5188411 5188429 5188441
5188457 5188459 5188481 5188489 5188507 5188531 5188543 5188549 5188571 5188619
5188633 5188643 5188649 5188661 5188669 5188679 5188697 5188717 5188739 5188763
5188793 5188801 5188817 5188819 5188829 5188849 5188877 5188887 5188889 5188901
5188933 5188943 5188951 5188969 5188979 5189027 5189039 5189047 5189069 5189081
5189113 5189117 5189141 5189153 5189159 5189161 5189167 5189201 5189207 5189251
5189263 5189269 5189291 5189293 5189309 5189311 5189333 5189339 5189357 5189363
5189377 5189399 5189441 5189473 5189479 5189491 5189507 5189519 5189531 5189533
5189537 5189543 5189551 5189557 5189563 5189567 5189621 5189623 5189629 5189633
5189659 5189669 5189677 5189687 5189711 5189759 5189761 5189783 5189797 5189809
5189839 5189851 5189893 5189917 5189923 5189929 5189939 5189957 5189993 5190001
5190007 5190011 5190023 5190037 5190041 5190047 5190061 5190071 5190077 5190091
5190103 5190127 5190139 5190167 5190169 5190181 5190191 5190197 5190247 5190259
5190277 5190281 5190293 5190301 5190319 5190331 5190347 5190377 5190403 5190413
5190421 5190431 5190443 5190467 5190511 5190583 5190587 5190599 5190607 5190611
5190637 5190649 5190701 5190707 5190719 5190721 5190769 5190791 5190817 5190839
5190851 5190859 5190863 5190869 5190877 5190929 5190947 5190953 5190973 5191013
5191019 5191027 5191033 5191049 5191057 5191091 5191099 5191129 5191139 5191141
5191177 5191181 5191187 5191213 5191231 5191243 5191247 5191253 5191259 5191267
5191271 5191279 5191289 5191301 5191331 5191337 5191339 5191349 5191363 5191367
5191369 5191391 5191393 5191397 5191411 5191421 5191429 5191441 5191447 5191451
5191453 5191457 5191481 5191489 5191513 5191597 5191603 5191651 5191673 5191699
5191709 5191723 5191727 5191741 5191751 5191793 5191799 5191819 5191831 5191843
5191853 5191861 5191873 5191883 5191909 5191931 5191963 5191981 5191999 5192009
5192023 5192029 5192041 5192051 5192071 5192081 5192087 5192113 5192129 5192153
5192167 5192179 5192183 5192219 5192233 5192267 5192269 5192287 5192311 5192323
5192351 5192353 5192359 5192371 5192387 5192393 5192399 5192441 5192449 5192477
5192483 5192519 5192521 5192587 5192597 5192639 5192647 5192657 5192659 5192669
5192699 5192743 5192783 5192797 5192801 5192813 5192819 5192821 5192879 5192893
5192899 5192927 5192959 5192977 5192989 5193037 5193043 5193047 5193049 5193053
5193091 5193107 5193127 5193137 5193163 5193169 5193187 5193191 5193197 5193203
5193217 5193229 5193257 5193271 5193277 5193281 5193299 5193301 5193317 5193329
5193341 5193361 5193401 5193421 5193427 5193443 5193451 5193493 5193499 5193509
5193527 5193553 5193557 5193563 5193571 5193613 5193623 5193637 5193649 5193667
5193677 5193679 5193691 5193703 5193719 5193733 5193737 5193739 5193743 5193751
5193763 5193767 5193781 5193817 5193847 5193869 5193889 5193901 5193931 5193977
5193983 5193989 5193997 5194001 5194009 5194037 5194069 5194073 5194093 5194109
5194117 5194193 5194199 5194207 5194213 5194229 5194237 5194261 5194279 5194283
5194303 5194337 5194349 5194351 5194361 5194369 5194379 5194381 5194403 5194411
5194417 5194421 5194433 5194439 5194457 5194459 5194489 5194493 5194499 5194507
5194549 5194559 5194561 5194601 5194603 5194639 5194649 5194661 5194669 5194691
5194697 5194703 5194727 5194729 5194751 5194781 5194789 5194793 5194807 5194811
5194817 5194879 5194883 5194907 5194913 5194921 5194927 5194933 5194939 5194951
5194963 5194967 5194991 5194993 5194997 5195027 5195063 5195077 5195083 5195123
5195129 5195153 5195161 5195173 5195213 5195221 5195249 5195269 5195317 5195327
5195357 5195369 5195413 5195419 5195441 5195459 5195467 5195471 5195497 5195501
5195543 5195549 5195573 5195579 5195587 5195609 5195639 5195653 5195657 5195737

```
5195741  5195747  5195777  5195789  5195791  5195809  5195831  5195837  5195849  5195857
5195887  5195891  5195899  5195903  5195923  5195963  5195969  5195977  5195977  5195989
5196001  5196007  5196011  5196013  5196029  5196043  5196047  5196073  5196097  5196119
5196131  5196151  5196157  5196167  5196181  5196187  5196197  5196199  5196209  5196211
5196221  5196223  5196227  5196259  5196281  5196287  5196293  5196311  5196337  5196341
5196343  5196361  5196371  5196379  5196397  5196427  5196431  5196439  5196449  5196467
5196473  5196479  5196511  5196511  5196517  5196523  5196553  5196563  5196601  5196619
5196629  5196641  5196647  5196701  5196707  5196731  5196733  5196749  5196767  5196769
5196803  5196817  5196839  5196859  5196881  5196913  5196923  5196949  5196953  5196973
5196979  5197063  5197067  5197081  5197091  5197099  5197111  5197117  5197147  5197151
5197169  5197183  5197187  5197193  5197217  5197249  5197253  5197259  5197289  5197303
5197319  5197327  5197337  5197343  5197363  5197397  5197403  5197417  5197421  5197459
5197463  5197477  5197481  5197513  5197519  5197537  5197573  5197601  5197603  5197607
5197637  5197639  5197663  5197691  5197721  5197727  5197769  5197771  5197781  5197783
5197789  5197823  5197831  5197847  5197853  5197877  5197879  5197889  5197897  5197909
5197943  5197957  5197967  5198003  5198027  5198029  5198033  5198057  5198119  5198143
5198147  5198159  5198189  5198197  5198201  5198203  5198213  5198251  5198261  5198269
5198273  5198287  5198309  5198317  5198321  5198357  5198363  5198371  5198377  5198387
5198423  5198429  5198441  5198443  5198449  5198467  5198471  5198497  5198503  5198507
5198509  5198519  5198551  5198563  5198573  5198581  5198591  5198629  5198639  5198653
5198663  5198671  5198681  5198689  5198693  5198729  5198737  5198747  5198749  5198789
5198797  5198803  5198807  5198813  5198819  5198827  5198839  5198849  5198861  5198867
5198873  5198881  5198887  5198927  5198939  5198959  5198983  5199011  5199043  5199049
5199079  5199083  5199109  5199119  5199137  5199157  5199163  5199167  5199197  5199221
5199239  5199241  5199269  5199301  5199307  5199319  5199329  5199391  5199427  5199437
5199461  5199463  5199473  5199479  5199503  5199529  5199533  5199539  5199547  5199553
5199577  5199583  5199589  5199629  5199631  5199641  5199643  5199697  5199703  5199707
5199713  5199731  5199757  5199769  5199781  5199793  5199797  5199809  5199811  5199829
5199853  5199877  5199911  5199917  5199959  5199973  5199993  5200007  5200021  5200049
5200051  5200061  5200081  5200099  5200103  5200123  5200133  5200141  5200159  5200163
5200171  5200177  5200211  5200229  5200297  5200331  5200337  5200379  5200397  5200421
5200423  5200427  5200439  5200441  5200451  5200477  5200493  5200511  5200561  5200567
5200579  5200627  5200631  5200651  5200667  5200669  5200681  5200687  5200703  5200711
5200729  5200751  5200753  5200781  5200787  5200801  5200843  5200847  5200859  5200883
5200903  5200913  5200919  5200933  5200957  5200969  5200981  5200991  5200999  5201023
5201033  5201039  5201057  5201069  5201081  5201083  5201089  5201101  5201107  5201111
5201113  5201129  5201159  5201171  5201173  5201213  5201267  5201291  5201293  5201297
5201299  5201309  5201311  5201327  5201341  5201359  5201387  5201393  5201401  5201437
5201467  5201477  5201509  5201513  5201533  5201563  5201569  5201593  5201621  5201627
5201633  5201639  5201641  5201659  5201663  5201671  5201681  5201683  5201689  5201699
5201717  5201723  5201731  5201741  5201767  5201773  5201827  5201837  5201849  5201851
5201857  5201863  5201873  5201909  5201923  5201939  5201951  5201969  5201981  5201993
5202023  5202073  5202077  5202091  5202103  5202133  5202137  5202151  5202157  5202167
5202247  5202251  5202259  5202271  5202293  5202299  5202331  5202341  5202343  5202359
5202361  5202377  5202413  5202433  5202437  5202469  5202473  5202479  5202481  5202487
5202497  5202499  5202503  5202511  5202521  5202541  5202553  5202559  5202569  5202619
5202641  5202643  5202647  5202653  5202671  5202709  5202727  5202733  5202737  5202739
5202749  5202767  5202773  5202779  5202781  5202787  5202793  5202811  5202863  5202877
5202887  5202893  5202907  5202913  5202917  5202971  5202973  5203001  5203039  5203057
5203061  5203069  5203097  5203111  5203141  5203147  5203157  5203171  5203181  5203183
5203201  5203213  5203243  5203249  5203271  5203279  5203337  5203339  5203349  5203357
5203369  5203379  5203391  5203399  5203409  5203423  5203439  5203453  5203477  5203529
5203531  5203577  5203579  5203591  5203603  5203607  5203609  5203619  5203631  5203637
5203669  5203687  5203697  5203703  5203711  5203721  5203729  5203733  5203771  5203787
5203813  5203831  5203837  5203841  5203867  5203871  5203873  5203883  5203889  5203897
5203901  5203907  5203909  5203927  5203937  5203943  5203949  5203969  5203997  5204009
5204011  5204027  5204039  5204041  5204047  5204077  5204083  5204107  5204113  5204117
5204131  5204167  5204179  5204191  5204197  5204207  5204209  5204231  5204239  5204257
5204267  5204321  5204323  5204327  5204377  5204387  5204411  5204413  5204443  5204467
5204471  5204473  5204477  5204489  5204491  5204501  5204503  5204519  5204527  5204557
5204603  5204611  5204629  5204687  5204701  5204713  5204741  5204743  5204747  5204779
5204789  5204791  5204813  5204821  5204867  5204887  5204897  5204911  5204933  5204951
5204957  5204959  5204977  5204981  5204999  5205001  5205019  5205037  5205047  5205071
5205089  5205103  5205113  5205127  5205139  5205149  5205169  5205173  5205227  5205251
5205253  5205269  5205283  5205307  5205329  5205341  5205367  5205371  5205377  5205407
5205433  5205437  5205461  5205463  5205467  5205469  5205479  5205481  5205491  5205523
5205527  5205539  5205583  5205593  5205617  5205619  5205653  5205667  5205671  5205701
5205719  5205721  5205727  5205749  5205763  5205769  5205773  5205787  5205793  5205817
5205839  5205853  5205883  5205887  5205901  5205913  5205917  5205931  5205953  5205971
5205979  5205989  5205997  5206007  5206013  5206037  5206081  5206121  5206127  5206147
5206151  5206153  5206163  5206169  5206177  5206193  5206207  5206213  5206231  5206241
5206259  5206261  5206273  5206291  5206297  5206309  5206319  5206321  5206339  5206343
5206363  5206367  5206373  5206379  5206387  5206391  5206393  5206417  5206423  5206427
5206447  5206459  5206477  5206489  5206511  5206541  5206567  5206571  5206609  5206633
5206639  5206657  5206661  5206679  5206681  5206687  5206711  5206739  5206783  5206787
5206793  5206819  5206823  5206829  5206837  5206841  5206849  5206867  5206889  5206891
5206897  5206937  5206939  5206963  5206967  5206991  5206997  5207003  5207009  5207011
5207023  5207071  5207089  5207113  5207129  5207149  5207161  5207179  5207183  5207201
5207203  5207207  5207221  5207239  5207243  5207249  5207261  5207291  5207329  5207339
5207341  5207347  5207383  5207413  5207467  5207471  5207513  5207519  5207549  5207557
5207563  5207567  5207569  5207599  5207611  5207633  5207677  5207681  5207707  5207711
5207723  5207731  5207737  5207743  5207749  5207771  5207777  5207801  5207803  5207827
5207879  5207897  5207921  5207941  5207947  5207953  5207963  5207971  5207981  5208041
5208043  5208059  5208079  5208131  5208149  5208169  5208173  5208179  5208193  5208209
5208227  5208253  5208263  5208277  5208293  5208367  5208383  5208389  5208407  5208421
5208433  5208457  5208473  5208479  5208481  5208521  5208523  5208529  5208551  5208559
5208569  5208583  5208617  5208659  5208673  5208683  5208689  5208701  5208727  5208739
5208751  5208779  5208799  5208809  5208821  5208829  5208859  5208871  5208881  5208887
5208911  5208913  5208923  5208937  5208941  5208967  5208979  5208989  5209013  5209027
```

```
5209031 5209069 5209093 5209111 5209117 5209129 5209177 5209279 5209283 5209291
5209297 5209301 5209307 5209313 5209319 5209381 5209387 5209397 5209403 5209409
5209411 5209441 5209453 5209471 5209481 5209507 5209513 5209517 5209537 5209541
5209543 5209559 5209573 5209577 5209601 5209619 5209627 5209657 5209669 5209679
5209709 5209717 5209727 5209777 5209783 5209817 5209823 5209849 5209861 5209889
5209901 5209913 5209943 5209951 5209957 5209999 5210003 5210017 5210027 5210033
5210039 5210057 5210063 5210087 5210099 5210119 5210131 5210141 5210189 5210197
5210203 5210207 5210209 5210243 5210269 5210273 5210281 5210297 5210311 5210323
5210329 5210339 5210363 5210369 5210393 5210399 5210411 5210423 5210473 5210479
5210497 5210507 5210519 5210531 5210537 5210539 5210563 5210591 5210609 5210629
5210651 5210669 5210677 5210729 5210753 5210767 5210771 5210773 5210827 5210837
5210839 5210851 5210867 5210911 5210929 5210941 5210951 5210957 5210999 5211023
5211071 5211083 5211091 5211109 5211209 5211211 5211229 5211233 5211247 5211257
5211259 5211277 5211289 5211307 5211347 5211359 5211373 5211383 5211389 5211391
5211421 5211431 5211443 5211449 5211457 5211467 5211473 5211497 5211509 5211523
5211539 5211541 5211581 5211587 5211589 5211607 5211623 5211631 5211637 5211641
5211659 5211667 5211671 5211683 5211721 5211727 5211743 5211749 5211761 5211781
5211803 5211827 5211839 5211841 5211853 5211881 5211919 5211949 5211959 5212003
5212019 5212027 5212033 5212037 5212057 5212069 5212087 5212091 5212093 5212111
5212133 5212139 5212157 5212171 5212201 5212219 5212231 5212241 5212303 5212313
5212343 5212357 5212367 5212381 5212393 5212409 5212447 5212451 5212457 5212469
5212477 5212507 5212541 5212549 5212561 5212573 5212579 5212583 5212637 5212673
5212703 5212717 5212729 5212733 5212759 5212769 5212777 5212787 5212793 5212799
5212807 5212811 5212813 5212841 5212843 5212853 5212861 5212873 5212901 5212937
5212939 5212943 5212979 5212993 5213023 5213057 5213059 5213077 5213081 5213083
5213093 5213113 5213119 5213129 5213137 5213141 5213161 5213171 5213179 5213183
5213207 5213209 5213213 5213231 5213233 5213251 5213267 5213269 5213279 5213291
5213297 5213309 5213311 5213321 5213323 5213333 5213347 5213357 5213371 5213389
5213399 5213413 5213419 5213423 5213431 5213491 5213501 5213539 5213561 5213563
5213567 5213597 5213603 5213627 5213629 5213639 5213671 5213693 5213717 5213737
5213773 5213777 5213821 5213827 5213833 5213839 5213861 5213867 5213891 5213899
5213909 5213927 5213941 5213947 5213959 5213993 5214017 5214043 5214049 5214059
5214061 5214071 5214103 5214119 5214161 5214179 5214191 5214197 5214199 5214211
5214221 5214259 5214269 5214271 5214277 5214283 5214289 5214301 5214323 5214329
5214331 5214337 5214367 5214383 5214413 5214437 5214439 5214467 5214487 5214497
5214499 5214527 5214571 5214593 5214613 5214637 5214669 5214679 5214691 5214701
5214719 5214761 5214763 5214779 5214793 5214821 5214823 5214857 5214883 5214889
5214899 5214917 5214919 5214929 5214941 5214947 5214953 5214959 5214961 5214991
5215003 5215013 5215033 5215051 5215057 5215061 5215081 5215097 5215121 5215127
5215151 5215183 5215201 5215207 5215211 5215229 5215247 5215267 5215271 5215279
5215297 5215303 5215313 5215321 5215333 5215349 5215361 5215363 5215369 5215381
5215387 5215393 5215403 5215417 5215421 5215429 5215433 5215451 5215459 5215477
5215499 5215517 5215537 5215547 5215559 5215579 5215597 5215619 5215643 5215649
5215663 5215669 5215673 5215699 5215703 5215729 5215739 5215751 5215789 5215799
5215801 5215811 5215841 5215849 5215867 5215891 5215901 5215907 5215913 5215921
5215939 5215961 5215997 5215999 5216021 5216039 5216053 5216083 5216111 5216119
5216129 5216137 5216173 5216191 5216209 5216213 5216219 5216221 5216227 5216231
5216243 5216251 5216269 5216273 5216303 5216311 5216327 5216333 5216353 5216381
5216411 5216443 5216461 5216473 5216509 5216521 5216567 5216573 5216581 5216591
5216599 5216623 5216663 5216681 5216683 5216689 5216693 5216747 5216749 5216753
5216759 5216767 5216777 5216797 5216803 5216833 5216873 5216917 5216921 5216933
5216941 5216947 5216971 5216993 5217007 5217019 5217029 5217031 5217049 5217059
5217101 5217133 5217139 5217143 5217169 5217203 5217221 5217253 5217257 5217263
5217271 5217299 5217341 5217349 5217353 5217367 5217379 5217403 5217413 5217431
5217439 5217449 5217461 5217469 5217493 5217523 5217557 5217587 5217601 5217607
5217631 5217649 5217661 5217673 5217689 5217697 5217731 5217733 5217743 5217887
5217763 5217781 5217787 5217809 5217841 5217847 5217859 5217869 5217881 5217887
5217907 5217911 5217917 5217923 5217931 5217937 5217949 5217991 5218021 5218051
5218061 5218067 5218091 5218121 5218139 5218151 5218181 5218189 5218207 5218211
5218229 5218243 5218247 5218271 5218277 5218307 5218313 5218319 5218321 5218349
5218361 5218391 5218397 5218417 5218441 5218471 5218481 5218487 5218511 5218519
5218529 5218531 5218537 5218547 5218553 5218567 5218573 5218589 5218601 5218607
5218613 5218627 5218639 5218651 5218657 5218667 5218669 5218681 5218721 5218729
5218793 5218817 5218823 5218853 5218879 5218883 5218919 5218933 5218937 5218951
5218987 5218991 5219003 5219009 5219047 5219057 5219063 5219077 5219083 5219089
5219111 5219117 5219143 5219219 5219261 5219267 5219273 5219287 5219309 5219327
5219339 5219351 5219363 5219371 5219381 5219393 5219441 5219443 5219447 5219453
5219477 5219503 5219531 5219537 5219549 5219569 5219603 5219611 5219639 5219651
5219653 5219657 5219717 5219723 5219729 5219743 5219759 5219771 5219777 5219783
5219791 5219801 5219803 5219807 5219857 5219881 5219887 5219891 5219917 5219927
5219911 5219933 5219941 5219947 5219959 5220001 5220013 5220031 5220043 5220049
5220053 5220073 5220077 5220091 5220097 5220101 5220107 5220113 5220151 5220167
5220199 5220211 5220217 5220223 5220227 5220233 5220239 5220247 5220251 5220277
5220283 5220323 5220331 5220353 5220359 5220361 5220389 5220403 5220409 5220427
5220463 5220469 5220491 5220511 5220521 5220529 5220533 5220539 5220541 5220569
5220599 5220601 5220613 5220641 5220647 5220661 5220689 5220731 5220749 5220767
5220797 5220799 5220823 5220847 5220869 5220883 5220889 5220907 5220911 5220923
5220961 5220973 5220983 5220997 5221001 5221003 5221009 5221021 5221039 5221049
5221079 5221093 5221123 5221129 5221133 5221157 5221169 5221171 5221181 5221199
5221211 5221217 5221231 5221283 5221289 5221301 5221303 5221319 5221327 5221331
5221343 5221369 5221373 5221387 5221399 5221451 5221457 5221459 5221501 5221543
5221549 5221577 5221583 5221591 5221597 5221603 5221631 5221639 5221649 5221651
5221673 5221691 5221693 5221709 5221717 5221721 5221729 5221757 5221781 5221787
5221793 5221817 5221819 5221829 5221849 5221889 5221891 5221927 5221933 5221939
5221949 5221969 5221973 5221987 5222011 5222023 5222051 5222057 5222071 5222083
5222099 5222141 5222153 5222159 5222171 5222183 5222197 5222237 5222251 5222297
5222309 5222323 5222333 5222339 5222341 5222363 5222401 5222411 5222423 5222429
5222447 5222501 5222507 5222509 5222533 5222573 5222579 5222597 5222627 5222629
5222641 5222653 5222671 5222699 5222713 5222719 5222729 5222731 5222753 5222761
```

```
5222797 5222801 5222807 5222837 5222843 5222869 5222873 5222879 5222887 5222923
5222933 5222963 5222977 5222981 5222993 5223007 5223017 5223037 5223067 5223079
5223083 5223109 5223121 5223181 5223187 5223191 5223227 5223263 5223287 5223293
5223299 5223343 5223349 5223367 5223371 5223377 5223397 5223409 5223431 5223457
5223467 5223473 5223503 5223557 5223571 5223577 5223583 5223601 5223611 5223629
5223643 5223649 5223671 5223679 5223703 5223707 5223731 5223763 5223773 5223781
5223793 5223853 5223859 5223863 5223871 5223901 5223929 5223961 5223971
5223983 5223997 5224001 5224073 5224111 5224127 5224133 5224169 5224171 5224187
5224201 5224217 5224229 5224231 5224237 5224277 5224279 5224291 5224309 5224319
5224327 5224333 5224339 5224361 5224367 5224421 5224433 5224441 5224447 5224451
5224481 5224501 5224529 5224547 5224561 5224573 5224577 5224579 5224591 5224603
5224607 5224613 5224619 5224631 5224643 5224649 5224663 5224691 5224693 5224699
5224717 5224721 5224757 5224759 5224783 5224789 5224811 5224837 5224847 5224853
5224873 5224883 5224889 5224897 5224903 5224913 5224931 5224937 5224939 5224963
5224969 5224987 5224991 5224997 5225027 5225039 5225041 5225047 5225083 5225107
5225123 5225141 5225147 5225153 5225159 5225167 5225173 5225179 5225183 5225201
5225219 5225237 5225243 5225261 5225287 5225309 5225333 5225369 5225371 5225377
5225383 5225401 5225419 5225461 5225471 5225501 5225503 5225509 5225527 5225533
5225537 5225567 5225587 5225593 5225599 5225609 5225629 5225653 5225677 5225683
5225699 5225707 5225719 5225723 5225729 5225743 5225777 5225791 5225797 5225821
5225839 5225867 5225887 5225921 5225971 5225993 5225999 5226017 5226019 5226029
5226049 5226077 5226079 5226101 5226107 5226113 5226127 5226163 5226203 5226211
5226227 5226251 5226257 5226271 5226281 5226283 5226301 5226307 5226317 5226343
5226367 5226371 5226391 5226421 5226433 5226437 5226439 5226461 5226479 5226491
5226511 5226517 5226547 5226553 5226587 5226619 5226643 5226647 5226671 5226707
5226733 5226763 5226791 5226797 5226799 5226811 5226829 5226833 5226839 5226841
5226847 5226853 5226857 5226883 5226887 5226899 5226901 5226929 5226943 5226959
5226983 5226997 5227009 5227021 5227063 5227067 5227073 5227081 5227093 5227111
5227121 5227153 5227171 5227219 5227241 5227253 5227283 5227291 5227297 5227301
5227303 5227331 5227333 5227349 5227361 5227363 5227379 5227393 5227433 5227441
5227487 5227501 5227507 5227513 5227529 5227591 5227613 5227631 5227643 5227657
5227661 5227681 5227697 5227709 5227723 5227727 5227741 5227753 5227757 5227759
5227769 5227777 5227829 5227853 5227889 5227909 5227919 5227961 5227979 5227987
5227991 5227997 5228017 5228029 5228071 5228081 5228089 5228101 5228123 5228131
5228143 5228147 5228159 5228161 5228189 5228213 5228219 5228239 5228263 5228273
5228297 5228309 5228317 5228329 5228339 5228347 5228351 5228389 5228393 5228417
5228423 5228437 5228441 5228449 5228453 5228473 5228501 5228513 5228527 5228533
5228539 5228543 5228593 5228611 5228617 5228633 5228651 5228683 5228687 5228723
5228731 5228749 5228761 5228777 5228779 5228789 5228813 5228827 5228833 5228837
5228851 5228869 5228893 5228921 5228941 5228953 5228959 5228963 5228969 5229011
5229023 5229031 5229043 5229053 5229061 5229071 5229109 5229113 5229143 5229151
5229157 5229223 5229233 5229253 5229269 5229293 5229299 5229317 5229331 5229337
5229377 5229391 5229401 5229403 5229407 5229409 5229431 5229437 5229439 5229443
5229461 5229463 5229481 5229491 5229517 5229547 5229569 5229577 5229589 5229593
5229611 5229613 5229649 5229661 5229683 5229689 5229709 5229739 5229767 5229781
5229787 5229797 5229799 5229803 5229817 5229823 5229857 5229871 5229899 5229911
5229923 5229943 5229967 5229971 5229989 5230003 5230007 5230013 5230021 5230091
5230097 5230109 5230129 5230157 5230163 5230171 5230189 5230193 5230213 5230217
5230229 5230259 5230261 5230279 5230297 5230321 5230327 5230349 5230363 5230367
5230387 5230397 5230399 5230403 5230417 5230427 5230429 5230439 5230447 5230457
5230471 5230513 5230553 5230573 5230597 5230601 5230609 5230613 5230627 5230633
5230651 5230663 5230691 5230703 5230717 5230733 5230741 5230751 5230789 5230829
5230831 5230837 5230843 5230873 5230877 5230881 5230921 5230937 5230957 5230963
5230969 5230997 5231011 5231021 5231027 5231029 5231041 5231059 5231069 5231077
5231089 5231101 5231111 5231119 5231129 5231131 5231141 5231173 5231197 5231203
5231207 5231263 5231287 5231297 5231309 5231311 5231329 5231341 5231371 5231389
5231411 5231417 5231431 5231453 5231483 5231491 5231503 5231521 5231531 5231533
5231537 5231579 5231581 5231599 5231623 5231647 5231657 5231663 5231671 5231701
5231713 5231717 5231753 5231773 5231797 5231827 5231843 5231857 5231881 5231917
5231923 5231929 5231951 5231957 5231981 5231987 5232023 5232041 5232047 5232067
5232077 5232079 5232089 5232113 5232119 5232121 5232127 5232131 5232173 5232187
5232223 5232229 5232251 5232257 5232287 5232299 5232317 5232323 5232329 5232341
5232401 5232419 5232443 5232449 5232457 5232497 5232511 5232547 5232553 5232569
5232571 5232607 5232613 5232659 5232671 5232677 5232679 5232683 5232697 5232701
5232727 5232737 5232741 5232761 5232793 5232803 5232823 5232841 5232863 5232869
5232959 5232973 5232977 5232979 5233003 5233043 5233051 5233069 5233073 5233087
5233091 5233133 5233139 5233147 5233153 5233157 5233171 5233177 5233183 5233219
5233223 5233231 5233271 5233301 5233307 5233313 5233321 5233343 5233353 5233367
5233381 5233387 5233409 5233411 5233439 5233447 5233469 5233499 5233511 5233523
5233549 5233559 5233567 5233573 5233619 5233621 5233639 5233649 5233667 5233681
5233693 5233703 5233727 5233741 5233751 5233763 5233771 5233777 5233783 5233793
5233817 5233847 5233849 5233867 5233871 5233883 5233889 5233919 5233927 5233951
5233957 5233961 5233979 5233981 5233991 5234017 5234029 5234039 5234081 5234111
5234143 5234149 5234153 5234167 5234189 5234213 5234219 5234233 5234237 5234263
5234267 5234269 5234287 5234321 5234389 5234399 5234401 5234417 5234431 5234447
5234473 5234477 5234483 5234491 5234513 5234543 5234549 5234569 5234573 5234591
5234597 5234599 5234609 5234627 5234641 5234653 5234659 5234681 5234683 5234687
5234689 5234693 5234743 5234767 5234771 5234787 5234809 5234821 5234843 5234849
5234857 5234909 5234917 5234923 5234927 5234987 5234989 5235017 5235029 5235037
5235073 5235077 5235079 5235091 5235137 5235143 5235149 5235151 5235193 5235199
5235229 5235233 5235253 5235259 5235281 5235299 5235319 5235323 5235353 5235359
5235361 5235367 5235383 5235401 5235437 5235441 5235509 5235523 5235539 5235553
5235563 5235599 5235613 5235619 5235641 5235647 5235649 5235661 5235667 5235673
5235679 5235721 5235731 5235733 5235749 5235751 5235757 5235761 5235803 5235827
5235851 5235871 5235913 5235917 5235943 5235947 5236013 5236027 5236031
5236043 5236061 5236087 5236093 5236097 5236109 5236123 5236139 5236141 5236159
5236163 5236183 5236193 5236213 5236237 5236247 5236261 5236271 5236279 5236291
5236313 5236331 5236333 5236367 5236369 5236373 5236379 5236393 5236409 5236447
5236481 5236487 5236541 5236579 5236597 5236601 5236607 5236631 5236633 5236661
```

```
5236691  5236717  5236727  5236741  5236753  5236811  5236823  5236843  5236853  5236879
5236897  5236909  5236919  5236937  5236949  5236961  5236967  5236981  5236991  5236999
5237009  5237039  5237041  5237059  5237129  5237131  5237137  5237143  5237191  5237209
5237227  5237237  5237251  5237263  5237269  5237273  5237279  5237291  5237303  5237311
5237327  5237333  5237347  5237389  5237417  5237423  5237467  5237473  5237501  5237503
5237509  5237527  5237563  5237567  5237569  5237579  5237593  5237623  5237641  5237651
5237671  5237681  5237689  5237693  5237707  5237723  5237731  5237747  5237753  5237761
5237789  5237809  5237833  5237839  5237849  5237851  5237867  5237899  5237909  5237923
5237929  5237933  5237941  5237983  5237987  5238007  5238011  5238019  5238029  5238031
5238041  5238049  5238059  5238061  5238071  5238083  5238113  5238137  5238139  5238143
5238151  5238161  5238179  5238187  5238199  5238203  5238209  5238221  5238229  5238251
5238257  5238293  5238301  5238307  5238313  5238323  5238353  5238367  5238371  5238377
5238383  5238403  5238419  5238421  5238437  5238439  5238449  5238461  5238487  5238523
5238577  5238581  5238671  5238677  5238689  5238713  5238731  5238773  5238791  5238799
5238809  5238811  5238817  5238829  5238847  5238853  5238869  5238899  5238911  5238913
5238923  5238929  5238943  5238953  5238967  5238973  5238977  5238979  5239007  5239033
5239051  5239061  5239063  5239081  5239097  5239139  5239153  5239159  5239177  5239181
5239183  5239187  5239189  5239207  5239211  5239271  5239277  5239319  5239337  5239357
5239369  5239373  5239391  5239393  5239397  5239411  5239427  5239433  5239447  5239463
5239477  5239483  5239499  5239501  5239511  5239523  5239529  5239543  5239547  5239567
5239571  5239583  5239603  5239627  5239631  5239657  5239669  5239673  5239753  5239777
5239783  5239789  5239811  5239813  5239879  5239891  5239901  5239907  5239909  5239931
5239943  5239987  5240017  5240033  5240069  5240089  5240093  5240099  5240101  5240107
5240117  5240141  5240177  5240197  5240201  5240227  5240239  5240243  5240299  5240303
5240309  5240317  5240351  5240357  5240377  5240381  5240383  5240399  5240413  5240423
5240441  5240461  5240483  5240501  5240507  5240509  5240533  5240549  5240551  5240591
5240593  5240603  5240617  5240621  5240639  5240647  5240663  5240681  5240707  5240731
5240737  5240747  5240761  5240771  5240773  5240779  5240783  5240819  5240821  5240831
5240839  5240843  5240857  5240863  5240867  5240881  5240887  5240897  5240899  5240929
5240951  5240957  5240959  5240993  5241037  5241043  5241101  5241107  5241113  5241143
5241157  5241167  5241239  5241241  5241251  5241277  5241281  5241289  5241293  5241311
5241319  5241331  5241349  5241403  5241407  5241409  5241419  5241421  5241427  5241437
5241463  5241469  5241479  5241497  5241517  5241521  5241529  5241557  5241569  5241583
5241601  5241617  5241667  5241673  5241689  5241707  5241751  5241787  5241793  5241839
5241857  5241877  5241881  5241889  5241893  5241931  5241937  5241959  5241961  5241983
5241989  5242021  5242067  5242079  5242117  5242141  5242163  5242169  5242199  5242201
5242213  5242217  5242231  5242241  5242249  5242291  5242313  5242319  5242357  5242381
5242399  5242411  5242421  5242439  5242451  5242469  5242483  5242487  5242513  5242561
5242571  5242577  5242583  5242609  5242619  5242661  5242667  5242669  5242673  5242693
5242697  5242703  5242729  5242763  5242771  5242777  5242801  5242807  5242819  5242837
5242843  5242847  5242861  5242877  5242883  5242891  5242903  5242907  5242921
5242927  5242931  5242949  5242961  5242967  5242969  5242981  5243003  5243023  5243059
5243071  5243081  5243083  5243093  5243099  5243101  5243143  5243167  5243177  5243201
5243207  5243239  5243243  5243263  5243267  5243269  5243281  5243317  5243323  5243339
5243341  5243363  5243369  5243387  5243393  5243417  5243419  5243423  5243443  5243453
5243477  5243479  5243489  5243501  5243503  5243509  5243521  5243527  5243543  5243551
5243569  5243573  5243587  5243591  5243593  5243597  5243611  5243629  5243647  5243669
5243683  5243687  5243699  5243717  5243729  5243737  5243759  5243761  5243801  5243813
5243827  5243831  5243869  5243879  5243891  5243897  5243911  5243923  5243947  5243971
5243993  5244011  5244013  5244017  5244037  5244049  5244059  5244067  5244073  5244077
5244103  5244139  5244167  5244179  5244203  5244251  5244259  5244263  5244277  5244293
5244311  5244319  5244341  5244367  5244373  5244383  5244427  5244431  5244439  5244457
5244467  5244469  5244493  5244511  5244527  5244553  5244583  5244587  5244601  5244637
5244641  5244643  5244647  5244661  5244671  5244691  5244709  5244727  5244739  5244751
5244763  5244791  5244803  5244809  5244869  5244881  5244901  5244913  5244917  5244919
5244937  5244947  5245003  5245013  5245021  5245049  5245067  5245073  5245091  5245099
5245103  5245111  5245133  5245139  5245151  5245193  5245211  5245223  5245241  5245243
5245271  5245283  5245297  5245301  5245309  5245313  5245321  5245391  5245397  5245411
5245421  5245423  5245439  5245459  5245483  5245489  5245511  5245523  5245543  5245553
5245609  5245619  5245651  5245667  5245711  5245733  5245759  5245763  5245783  5245813
5245831  5245861  5245873  5245883  5245901  5245907  5245921  5245931  5245937  5245943
5245963  5245967  5245969  5245973  5245997  5246009  5246011  5246023  5246027  5246029
5246053  5246057  5246069  5246083  5246089  5246107  5246113  5246173  5246179  5246191
5246203  5246249  5246257  5246287  5246309  5246321  5246333  5246363  5246389  5246393
5246399  5246407  5246411  5246429  5246431  5246441  5246447  5246453  5246459  5246491
5246503  5246509  5246519  5246539  5246561  5246567  5246573  5246581  5246609  5246611
5246617  5246621  5246623  5246663  5246677  5246707  5246713  5246723  5246743  5246771
5246777  5246779  5246809  5246823  5246851  5246867  5246873  5246883  5246909  5246911
5246953  5246957  5246977  5246981  5246993  5247001  5247019  5247031  5247041  5247043
5247071  5247083  5247107  5247131  5247157  5247163  5247191  5247199  5247217
5247223  5247227  5247233  5247241  5247257  5247269  5247299  5247311  5247323  5247349
5247353  5247379  5247391  5247421  5247433  5247443  5247449  5247461  5247469  5247479
5247491  5247499  5247533  5247581  5247589  5247653  5247659  5247661  5247701  5247709
5247757  5247761  5247787  5247791  5247793  5247871  5247881  5247889  5247899  5247911
5247919  5247937  5247941  5247947  5247961  5247967  5247997  5248003  5248037  5248057
5248069  5248073  5248079  5248081  5248091  5248093  5248097  5248099  5248127  5248129
5248141  5248151  5248153  5248157  5248169  5248181  5248183  5248231  5248247  5248259
5248261  5248273  5248283  5248289  5248297  5248303  5248343  5248363  5248381  5248421
5248423  5248429  5248433  5248447  5248469  5248471  5248493  5248499  5248513  5248519
5248543  5248547  5248553  5248559  5248567  5248583  5248589  5248601  5248603
5248637  5248687  5248723  5248741  5248759  5248787  5248811  5248829  5248843  5248877
5248879  5248891  5248907  5248927  5248933  5248953  5248973  5248987  5249009  5249011
5249017  5249033  5249051  5249063  5249077  5249081  5249093  5249143  5249147  5249159
5249161  5249183  5249191  5249207  5249219  5249239  5249269  5249287  5249297  5249303
5249333  5249341  5249371  5249381  5249389  5249399  5249401  5249411  5249441  5249447
5249423  5249437  5249441  5249473  5249479  5249507  5249513  5249537  5249539  5249557
5249579  5249581  5249591  5249611  5249627  5249639  5249653  5249659  5249663  5249683
5249687  5249693  5249701  5249707  5249729  5249731  5249771  5249791  5249801  5249813
5249831  5249851  5249857  5249861  5249869  5249873  5249887  5249897  5249903  5249921
```

```
5249929  5249939  5249983  5249987  5249989  5250029  5250043  5250071  5250079  5250107
5250109  5250121  5250143  5250149  5250151  5250181  5250211  5250227  5250277  5250281
5250299  5250317  5250341  5250353  5250359  5250361  5250367  5250373  5250391  5250407
5250409  5250437  5250449  5250451  5250461  5250491  5250493  5250503  5250523  5250527
5250529  5250533  5250541  5250571  5250617  5250643  5250649  5250659  5250673  5250677
5250683  5250689  5250691  5250701  5250703  5250709  5250727  5250731  5250743  5250757
5250761  5250779  5250787  5250803  5250809  5250851  5250871  5250899  5250913  5250919
5250953  5250961  5250967  5251007  5251009  5251019  5251027  5251039  5251097  5251123
5251139  5251189  5251193  5251217  5251229  5251237  5251241  5251247  5251261  5251271
5251273  5251331  5251333  5251361  5251409  5251417  5251423  5251457  5251459  5251469
5251481  5251507  5251513  5251529  5251537  5251541  5251549  5251573  5251591  5251601
5251607  5251627  5251663  5251711  5251769  5251781  5251783  5251787  5251789  5251819
5251859  5251877  5251879  5251903  5251919  5251933  5251949  5251951  5252011  5252017
5252021  5252029  5252033  5252041  5252047  5252057  5252069  5252081  5252087  5252089
5252111  5252123  5252129  5252147  5252153  5252179  5252209  5252231  5252249  5252263
5252287  5252311  5252327  5252329  5252333  5252347  5252363  5252369  5252381  5252389
5252411  5252413  5252419  5252447  5252449  5252461  5252477  5252491  5252497  5252501
5252537  5252543  5252549  5252563  5252581  5252587  5252591  5252603  5252617  5252623
5252627  5252641  5252657  5252669  5252693  5252701  5252713  5252719  5252729  5252743
5252747  5252761  5252773  5252783  5252791  5252803  5252831  5252839  5252887  5252917
5252921  5252939  5252957  5252963  5252977  5252999  5253013  5253019  5253023
5253029  5253041  5253071  5253091  5253097  5253109  5253121  5253151  5253161  5253169
5253173  5253203  5253217  5253277  5253317  5253343  5253349  5253359  5253383  5253397
5253431  5253433  5253449  5253463  5253467  5253487  5253509  5253511  5253529  5253587
5253607  5253623  5253631  5253643  5253649  5253679  5253713  5253719  5253739  5253751
5253761  5253763  5253767  5253769  5253773  5253791  5253803  5253827  5253837  5253847
5253881  5253893  5253907  5253961  5253967  5254001  5254019  5254031  5254033  5254063
5254069  5254079  5254091  5254141  5254153  5254157  5254163  5254169  5254201  5254229
5254231  5254247  5254253  5254297  5254313  5254349  5254351  5254397  5254421  5254427
5254429  5254439  5254453  5254463  5254489  5254493  5254499  5254537  5254559  5254567
5254591  5254607  5254619  5254637  5254651  5254661  5254673  5254687  5254693  5254699
5254709  5254721  5254757  5254763  5254789  5254793  5254801  5254817  5254831  5254859
5254861  5254889  5254891  5254927  5254937  5254943  5255009  5255021  5255053  5255059
5255069  5255083  5255099  5255101  5255113  5255123  5255137  5255141  5255149  5255161
5255167  5255179  5255203  5255209  5255219  5255233  5255251  5255281  5255297  5255303
5255357  5255359  5255407  5255423  5255429  5255449  5255479  5255507  5255527  5255531
5255561  5255573  5255603  5255617  5255623  5255629  5255651  5255659  5255671  5255683
5255687  5255693  5255711  5255713  5255741  5255771  5255777  5255797  5255801  5255819
5255843  5255863  5255867  5255879  5255903  5255911  5255953  5255959  5255993  5256001
5256037  5256049  5256061  5256071  5256131  5256137  5256197  5256233  5256239  5256253
5256263  5256269  5256271  5256283  5256287  5256299  5256311  5256313  5256319  5256341
5256347  5256353  5256359  5256367  5256371  5256379  5256389  5256401  5256413  5256463
5256467  5256469  5256509  5256547  5256589  5256599  5256613  5256643  5256649
5256653  5256661  5256679  5256683  5256697  5256737  5256751  5256773  5256781  5256817
5256821  5256829  5256847  5256851  5256883  5256929  5256931  5256941  5256943  5256967
5256989  5257003  5257009  5257013  5257037  5257059  5257103  5257111  5257117  5257121
5257157  5257159  5257169  5257171  5257201  5257253  5257261  5257277  5257331  5257349
5257361  5257379  5257391  5257393  5257451  5257453  5257463  5257489  5257493  5257517
5257519  5257531  5257541  5257559  5257583  5257591  5257597  5257619  5257627  5257711
5257723  5257727  5257741  5257771  5257781  5257783  5257789  5257793  5257807  5257829
5257877  5257883  5257907  5257933  5257943  5257949  5257951  5257957  5257991  5257999
5258023  5258027  5258059  5258063  5258081  5258089  5258167  5258171  5258173  5258179
5258221  5258233  5258249  5258293  5258303  5258317  5258327  5258333  5258369  5258371
5258377  5258381  5258399  5258413  5258419  5258431  5258443  5258447  5258489  5258503
5258531  5258549  5258557  5258567  5258569  5258579  5258633  5258639  5258647  5258677
5258683  5258707  5258723  5258731  5258741  5258761  5258777  5258779  5258791  5258807
5258821  5258863  5258867  5258873  5258917  5258959  5258977  5258987  5258999  5259011
5259047  5259053  5259071  5259073  5259091  5259127  5259151  5259161  5259167
5259169  5259173  5259209  5259223  5259227  5259229  5259251  5259263  5259269  5259301
5259311  5259313  5259323  5259329  5259337  5259361  5259379  5259389  5259391  5259407
5259413  5259421  5259427  5259473  5259487  5259503  5259517  5259533  5259547  5259563
5259581  5259593  5259601  5259619  5259623  5259641  5259671  5259689  5259721  5259731
5259733  5259743  5259763  5259823  5259833  5259857  5259887  5259913  5259923  5259929
5259967  5259973  5259977  5259983  5259997  5260001  5260007  5260009  5260051  5260081
5260117  5260127  5260133  5260159  5260163  5260183  5260201  5260217  5260219  5260243
5260247  5260267  5260279  5260289  5260337  5260349  5260357  5260363  5260369  5260379
5260391  5260417  5260433  5260439  5260459  5260469  5260481  5260487  5260501  5260529
5260559  5260561  5260573  5260589  5260597  5260613  5260627  5260643  5260649  5260657
5260679  5260681  5260691  5260693  5260699  5260711  5260747  5260763  5260799  5260807
5260811  5260819  5260873  5260883  5260889  5260897  5260901  5260903  5260909  5260943
5260949  5260999  5261021  5261023  5261027  5261033  5261051  5261063  5261071  5261077
5261099  5261101  5261111  5261117  5261129  5261147  5261153  5261173  5261203  5261251
5261261  5261317  5261323  5261341  5261351  5261359  5261387  5261419  5261429  5261471
5261497  5261519  5261527  5261563  5261569  5261573  5261587  5261611  5261617  5261623
5261629  5261647  5261671  5261693  5261699  5261701  5261717  5261719  5261741  5261743
5261747  5261749  5261761  5261771  5261777  5261783  5261801  5261813  5261821  5261827
5261833  5261869  5261887  5261923  5261933  5261941  5261957  5261971  5261989  5262001
5262013  5262017  5262041  5262053  5262077  5262091  5262097  5262109  5262121  5262133
5262143  5262149  5262181  5262203  5262209  5262217  5262223  5262263  5262277  5262289
5262319  5262329  5262349  5262359  5262371  5262379  5262437  5262443  5262451  5262457
5262463  5262511  5262533  5262539  5262553  5262557  5262559  5262583  5262599  5262611
5262617  5262619  5262661  5262667  5262683  5262689  5262701  5262703  5262721  5262737
5262757  5262767  5262793  5262799  5262811  5262821  5262823  5262827  5262841  5262853
5262857  5262863  5262869  5262871  5262923  5262931  5262997  5263003  5263031  5263033
5263061  5263109  5263169  5263177  5263189  5263229  5263241  5263253  5263259  5263267
5263309  5263327  5263333  5263337  5263393  5263417  5263429  5263439  5263441  5263451
5263463  5263477  5263493  5263499  5263541  5263547  5263561  5263571  5263579  5263597
5263607  5263613  5263631  5263637  5263639  5263649  5263667  5263669  5263673  5263697
5263729  5263733  5263747  5263771  5263787  5263789  5263793  5263813  5263861  5263883
```

```
5263891  5263901  5263913  5263919  5263933  5263939  5263961  5263963  5263991  5263997
5264003  5264009  5264029  5264041  5264057  5264059  5264071  5264081  5264087  5264089
5264099  5264107  5264111  5264137  5264143  5264173  5264177  5264179  5264191  5264213
5264251  5264267  5264269  5264279  5264291  5264299  5264333  5264351  5264353  5264377
5264381  5264383  5264417  5264429  5264443  5264449  5264473  5264477  5264489  5264521
5264537  5264549  5264593  5264603  5264621  5264627  5264641  5264647  5264657  5264663
5264671  5264683  5264711  5264741  5264771  5264789  5264801  5264813  5264821  5264837
5264839  5264867  5264873  5264887  5264891  5264899  5264911  5264923  5264929  5264969
5264977  5265023  5265059  5265067  5265077  5265079  5265103  5265107  5265119  5265131
5265167  5265187  5265193  5265203  5265209  5265241  5265263  5265277  5265287  5265311
5265313  5265331  5265347  5265353  5265371  5265373  5265383  5265401  5265419  5265439
5265473  5265487  5265499  5265517  5265539  5265571  5265583  5265593  5265607  5265649
5265653  5265683  5265697  5265707  5265721  5265727  5265761  5265763  5265773  5265787
5265829  5265847  5265851  5265853  5265859  5265881  5265889  5265901  5265909  5265943
5265961  5265973  5265979  5266013  5266031  5266043  5266067  5266109  5266123  5266127
5266153  5266159  5266169  5266181  5266189  5266193  5266199  5266201  5266207  5266237
5266271  5266273  5266291  5266297  5266301  5266307  5266319  5266337  5266351  5266361
5266381  5266423  5266441  5266453  5266463  5266483  5266507  5266519  5266531  5266537
5266577  5266589  5266619  5266631  5266669  5266673  5266711  5266727  5266739  5266741
5266757  5266799  5266823  5266831  5266841  5266873  5266883  5266897  5266903  5266907
5266909  5266927  5266967  5266969  5266979  5266997  5267039  5267077  5267083  5267089
5267099  5267137  5267153  5267159  5267173  5267177  5267191  5267201  5267221  5267257
5267279  5267291  5267309  5267323  5267341  5267359  5267363  5267369  5267377  5267401
5267413  5267417  5267441  5267443  5267447  5267459  5267491  5267497  5267519  5267527
5267539  5267567  5267573  5267593  5267599  5267609  5267611  5267623  5267657  5267659
5267663  5267669  5267701  5267707  5267711  5267719  5267747  5267767  5267771  5267783
5267789  5267797  5267809  5267837  5267849  5267863  5267869  5267881  5267891  5267953
5268001  5268007  5268013  5268017  5268031  5268077  5268083  5268091  5268101  5268119
5268121  5268163  5268203  5268209  5268217  5268229  5268257  5268269  5268281  5268293
5268299  5268397  5268407  5268409  5268437  5268451  5268457  5268493  5268499  5268539
5268547  5268551  5268577  5268583  5268607  5268619  5268647  5268671  5268673  5268701
5268709  5268713  5268721  5268727  5268737  5268743  5268761  5268773  5268779  5268803
5268811  5268899  5268937  5268953  5268959  5268971  5268973  5268979  5269003  5269007
5269009  5269013  5269021  5269027  5269037  5269049  5269059  5269079  5269109  5269111
5269129  5269151  5269181  5269193  5269211  5269219  5269247  5269259  5269283  5269307
5269339  5269343  5269363  5269373  5269399  5269409  5269447  5269463  5269469  5269473
5269471  5269487  5269489  5269493  5269501  5269513  5269543  5269559  5269567  5269573
5269603  5269613  5269633  5269639  5269673  5269679  5269681  5269709  5269717  5269723
5269727  5269739  5269757  5269769  5269787  5269801  5269811  5269819  5269841  5269861
5269867  5269879  5269933  5269993  5270003  5270009  5270029  5270039  5270081  5270101
5270113  5270129  5270131  5270143  5270149  5270171  5270173  5270183  5270203  5270219
5270231  5270233  5270273  5270303  5270311  5270347  5270359  5270383  5270387  5270389
5270393  5270399  5270413  5270423  5270443  5270449  5270453  5270497  5270501  5270521
5270537  5270549  5270557  5270563  5270567  5270579  5270597  5270599  5270609  5270623
5270633  5270641  5270653  5270677  5270701  5270719  5270723  5270729  5270737  5270747
5270767  5270773  5270789  5270807  5270821  5270843  5270849  5270851  5270861  5270869
5270873  5270921  5270929  5270939  5270971  5270977  5270981  5270987  5271041  5271053
5271059  5271061  5271067  5271109  5271121  5271143  5271157  5271169  5271179  5271199
5271223  5271281  5271283  5271289  5271293  5271307  5271313  5271319  5271323  5271361
5271373  5271397  5271401  5271419  5271443  5271451  5271463  5271481  5271491  5271509
5271517  5271521  5271529  5271551  5271557  5271599  5271613  5271619  5271651  5271653
5271667  5271677  5271701  5271703  5271719  5271727  5271731  5271733  5271743  5271781
5271787  5271793  5271811  5271817  5271839  5271869  5271883  5271901  5271913  5271919
5271923  5271941  5271961  5271967  5271977  5272009  5272013  5272021  5272031  5272039
5272051  5272061  5272079  5272081  5272097  5272103  5272121  5272123  5272147  5272153
5272207  5272219  5272237  5272249  5272259  5272283  5272307  5272321  5272327  5272339
5272369  5272411  5272429  5272433  5272441  5272447  5272453  5272459  5272471  5272483
5272489  5272513  5272517  5272541  5272583  5272591  5272613  5272621  5272637  5272643
5272649  5272651  5272667  5272739  5272753  5272763  5272781  5272783  5272793  5272801
5272807  5272837  5272843  5272859  5272871  5272877  5272909  5272921  5272951  5272963
5272979  5272987  5272991  5272999  5273011  5273053  5273063  5273087  5273117  5273123
5273137  5273173  5273189  5273197  5273201  5273209  5273221  5273227  5273231  5273251
5273263  5273287  5273309  5273327  5273347  5273363  5273381  5273399  5273407  5273419
5273449  5273453  5273459  5273483  5273491  5273531  5273537  5273581  5273603  5273617
5273629  5273651  5273657  5273663  5273669  5273677  5273683  5273711  5273717  5273731
5273743  5273753  5273759  5273767  5273777  5273783  5273819  5273837  5273839  5273857
5273861  5273921  5273941  5273959  5273971  5273981  5274007  5274023  5274037  5274041
5274047  5274067  5274109  5274127  5274133  5274151  5274161  5274163  5274167  5274169
5274197  5274211  5274221  5274257  5274287  5274289  5274299  5274319  5274329  5274331
5274341  5274359  5274391  5274397  5274427  5274441  5274443  5274449  5274463  5274551
5274553  5274559  5274583  5274587  5274589  5274601  5274611  5274617  5274623  5274629
5274631  5274649  5274653  5274667  5274671  5274673  5274677  5274679  5274701  5274707
5274713  5274739  5274817  5274827  5274833  5274841  5274859  5274869  5274877  5274881
5274917  5274923  5274949  5274967  5275007  5275021  5275051  5275057  5275063  5275079
5275099  5275121  5275133  5275159  5275163  5275243  5275247  5275271  5275279  5275307
5275313  5275373  5275381  5275399  5275409  5275411  5275427  5275451  5275481  5275499
5275537  5275547  5275553  5275561  5275573  5275577  5275583  5275639  5275657  5275663
5275679  5275681  5275723  5275727  5275747  5275751  5275759  5275771  5275793  5275799
5275807  5275811  5275813  5275841  5275889  5275903  5275909  5275987  5275997  5276017
5276021  5276027  5276077  5276093  5276101  5276111  5276113  5276119  5276149  5276153
5276189  5276191  5276197  5276207  5276233  5276261  5276263  5276279  5276303  5276329
5276333  5276339  5276351  5276371  5276377  5276387  5276399  5276419  5276423  5276431
5276437  5276441  5276449  5276483  5276497  5276501  5276503  5276519  5276539  5276563
5276599  5276617  5276629  5276653  5276657  5276671  5276701  5276707  5276731  5276743
5276767  5276771  5276779  5276807  5276809  5276819  5276827  5276833  5276843  5276861
5276863  5276911  5276923  5276939  5276969  5276983  5277001  5277007  5277029  5277031
5277059  5277061  5277109  5277119  5277131  5277163  5277169  5277179  5277187  5277197
5277211  5277221  5277227  5277247  5277253  5277257  5277269  5277313  5277329  5277331
5277341  5277343  5277379  5277403  5277407  5277427  5277469  5277473  5277487  5277499
```

```
5277509  5277527  5277539  5277551  5277589  5277607  5277641  5277661  5277707  5277709
5277749  5277751  5277761  5277773  5277799  5277847  5277851  5277901  5277917  5277919
5277929  5277941  5277947  5277983  5278001  5278033  5278037  5278043  5278051  5278073
5278093  5278099  5278127  5278139  5278151  5278171  5278223  5278237  5278249  5278253
5278271  5278289  5278291  5278297  5278303  5278321  5278331  5278337  5278349  5278373
5278393  5278397  5278421  5278423  5278439  5278451  5278459  5278499  5278519  5278529
5278541  5278547  5278571  5278573  5278577  5278579  5278591  5278601  5278607  5278621
5278657  5278681  5278697  5278699  5278727  5278733  5278739  5278769  5278771  5278787
5278813  5278829  5278831  5278843  5278877  5278913  5278927  5278939  5278943  5278951
5278961  5278969  5278991  5279003  5279011  5279033  5279039  5279041  5279051  5279089
5279107  5279117  5279149  5279161  5279177  5279179  5279191  5279203  5279221  5279233
5279237  5279243  5279257  5279279  5279291  5279297  5279303  5279311  5279341  5279353
5279357  5279377  5279387  5279423  5279429  5279437  5279453  5279501  5279509  5279513
5279531  5279539  5279543  5279609  5279621  5279623  5279629  5279671  5279683  5279689
5279731  5279737  5279767  5279783  5279831  5279837  5279867  5279873  5279881  5279887
5279899  5279909  5279941  5279947  5279959  5279993  5279999  5280007  5280031  5280049
5280071  5280073  5280083  5280091  5280101  5280109  5280139  5280161  5280169  5280173
5280229  5280239  5280257  5280259  5280263  5280277  5280329  5280361  5280367  5280371
5280383  5280397  5280427  5280433  5280447  5280449  5280463  5280481  5280487
5280491  5280493  5280503  5280521  5280553  5280589  5280617  5280619  5280629  5280631
5280641  5280643  5280647  5280661  5280703  5280713  5280733  5280773  5280791  5280799
5280809  5280817  5280827  5280851  5280853  5280857  5280883  5280887  5280901  5280907
5280911  5280937  5280949  5280983  5281019  5281021  5281049  5281057  5281097  5281117
5281123  5281139  5281147  5281151  5281153  5281163  5281201  5281247  5281273  5281337
5281361  5281369  5281379  5281403  5281429  5281433  5281447  5281457  5281459  5281489
5281499  5281511  5281547  5281597  5281613  5281631  5281643  5281649  5281657  5281663
5281667  5281669  5281673  5281681  5281693  5281711  5281751  5281763  5281817  5281823
5281853  5281879  5281891  5281897  5281919  5281921  5281937  5281949  5281979  5281993
5281999  5282023  5282029  5282099  5282107  5282111  5282129  5282141  5282143  5282159
5282219  5282227  5282243  5282273  5282279  5282281  5282297  5282327  5282339  5282363
5282371  5282383  5282441  5282443  5282449  5282477  5282491  5282503  5282509  5282521
5282531  5282533  5282567  5282573  5282587  5282609  5282621  5282623  5282633  5282653
5282657  5282671  5282677  5282689  5282707  5282713  5282729  5282737  5282743  5282747
5282777  5282789  5282821  5282831  5282833  5282861  5282873  5282887  5282899  5282909
5282923  5282929  5282933  5282947  5282983  5282999  5283001  5283011  5283041  5283043
5283059  5283067  5283071  5283079  5283101  5283139  5283143  5283167  5283233  5283241
5283253  5283263  5283269  5283329  5283347  5283359  5283389  5283401  5283409  5283427
5283431  5283449  5283457  5283469  5283479  5283497  5283503  5283527  5283559  5283569
5283601  5283631  5283647  5283683  5283701  5283731  5283781  5283791  5283809  5283827
5283847  5283851  5283877  5283913  5283937  5283961  5283973  5283979  5283983  5283989
5284001  5284021  5284031  5284079  5284087  5284091  5284117  5284129  5284151  5284157
5284171  5284183  5284187  5284189  5284193  5284271  5284277  5284283  5284291  5284309
5284327  5284339  5284373  5284387  5284393  5284417  5284423  5284427  5284439  5284469
5284481  5284493  5284507  5284511  5284523  5284537  5284541  5284579  5284607  5284619
5284627  5284639  5284649  5284651  5284661  5284667  5284681  5284703  5284709  5284751
5284753  5284781  5284819  5284879  5284891  5284921  5284927  5284957  5284967  5284987
5284991  5284999  5285053  5285057  5285099  5285129  5285131  5285141  5285143  5285177
5285183  5285201  5285209  5285219  5285227  5285237  5285243  5285251  5285263  5285281
5285297  5285299  5285309  5285327  5285347  5285387  5285389  5285417  5285461  5285471
5285473  5285509  5285513  5285537  5285551  5285587  5285611  5285647  5285659  5285671
5285677  5285681  5285713  5285729  5285741  5285767  5285771  5285773  5285789  5285803
5285807  5285881  5285893  5285921  5285923  5285939  5285941  5285953  5285983  5285989
5286011  5286019  5286023  5286053  5286109  5286139  5286143  5286179  5286181  5286191
5286217  5286221  5286247  5286263  5286277  5286283  5286293  5286317  5286329  5286331
5286349  5286373  5286409  5286431  5286433  5286451  5286469  5286493  5286509  5286517
5286551  5286553  5286559  5286571  5286583  5286623  5286641  5286649  5286653  5286683
5286691  5286703  5286727  5286739  5286773  5286793  5286797  5286811  5286823  5286839
5286859  5286863  5286871  5286901  5286913  5286929  5286937  5286943  5286947  5286971
5287021  5287031  5287039  5287043  5287067  5287069  5287097  5287141  5287147  5287159
5287169  5287181  5287199  5287201  5287207  5287211  5287213  5287229  5287253  5287273
5287277  5287279  5287307  5287313  5287327  5287343  5287351  5287379  5287393  5287427
5287489  5287501  5287507  5287517  5287519  5287523  5287531  5287537  5287543  5287571
5287589  5287613  5287627  5287649  5287661  5287669  5287673  5287679  5287687  5287691
5287693  5287703  5287727  5287739  5287741  5287783  5287787  5287801  5287813  5287819
5287823  5287837  5287859  5287879  5287897  5287913  5287921  5287937  5287943  5287951
5287957  5287973  5287979  5287981  5287991  5288033  5288051  5288069  5288083  5288089
5288119  5288147  5288167  5288177  5288203  5288219  5288233  5288249  5288267  5288279
5288281  5288317  5288323  5288341  5288359  5288363  5288369  5288399  5288417  5288449
5288453  5288471  5288477  5288483  5288489  5288509  5288519  5288539  5288557  5288567
5288573  5288579  5288587  5288603  5288609  5288617  5288623  5288629  5288641  5288653
5288659  5288681  5288687  5288747  5288749  5288753  5288807  5288851  5288869  5288893
5288909  5288917  5288929  5288939  5288951  5288953  5288963  5288993  5289013  5289017
5289071  5289079  5289083  5289089  5289101  5289121  5289131  5289133  5289139  5289143
5289157  5289197  5289199  5289209  5289217  5289247  5289257  5289283  5289293  5289299
5289311  5289343  5289373  5289413  5289419  5289439  5289461  5289463  5289469  5289481
5289491  5289497  5289503  5289509  5289539  5289547  5289569  5289587  5289589  5289593
5289611  5289617  5289637  5289659  5289667  5289679  5289721  5289727  5289743  5289749
5289751  5289773  5289797  5289811  5289827  5289833  5289841  5289851  5289857  5289881
5289901  5289913  5289929  5289959  5289967  5289979  5290007  5290027  5290031  5290039
5290049  5290063  5290067  5290079  5290081  5290099  5290121  5290123  5290133  5290141
5290147  5290157  5290163  5290193  5290199  5290211  5290217  5290231  5290277  5290289
5290291  5290309  5290331  5290339  5290343  5290357  5290361  5290381  5290399  5290409
5290459  5290507  5290517  5290559  5290561  5290573  5290577  5290601  5290609
5290627  5290633  5290651  5290657  5290661  5290679  5290687  5290699  5290711  5290717
5290729  5290777  5290787  5290793  5290799  5290807  5290843  5290853  5290867  5290879
5290877  5290907  5290913  5290919  5290921  5290933  5290939  5290951  5290973  5290981
5290993  5290997  5291003  5291017  5291023  5291051  5291093  5291123  5291129  5291141
5291161  5291171  5291227  5291249  5291261  5291269  5291281  5291303  5291309  5291327
5291347  5291383  5291389  5291393  5291399  5291411  5291413  5291423  5291431  5291441
```

```
5291453  5291477  5291479  5291497  5291509  5291563  5291569  5291581  5291599  5291621
5291639  5291647  5291653  5291687  5291707  5291711  5291719  5291723  5291753  5291761
5291779  5291789  5291791  5291801  5291807  5291821  5291827  5291837  5291857  5291893
5291927  5291939  5291941  5291953  5291959  5291971  5291987  5292017  5292031
5292071  5292107  5292143  5292149  5292179  5292191  5292193  5292211  5292251  5292257
5292271  5292283  5292293  5292337  5292347  5292361  5292367  5292377  5292379  5292437
5292439  5292451  5292467  5292473  5292479  5292481  5292487  5292499  5292503  5292509
5292523  5292557  5292571  5292577  5292607  5292613  5292641  5292647  5292653  5292671
5292673  5292689  5292709  5292751  5292757  5292767  5292769  5292809  5292817  5292823
5292841  5292853  5292857  5292863  5292883  5292907  5292923  5292953  5292997  5293009
5293019  5293037  5293049  5293081  5293087  5293117  5293129  5293177  5293181  5293199
5293207  5293213  5293217  5293231  5293291  5293313  5293333  5293361  5293369  5293391
5293417  5293433  5293439  5293441  5293447  5293451  5293489  5293499  5293501  5293507
5293513  5293517  5293549  5293597  5293619  5293621  5293637  5293643  5293649  5293667
5293669  5293679  5293697  5293699  5293709  5293721  5293753  5293787  5293789  5293801
5293807  5293811  5293829  5293843  5293853  5293861  5293877  5293903  5293907  5293931
5293957  5293991  5293999  5294041  5294053  5294057  5294059  5294063  5294083  5294099
5294101  5294111  5294131  5294137  5294143  5294147  5294161  5294167  5294171  5294213
5294231  5294279  5294281  5294287  5294297  5294299  5294309  5294323  5294339  5294351
5294353  5294383  5294411  5294437  5294447  5294473  5294479  5294489  5294519  5294533
5294539  5294543  5294557  5294563  5294579  5294581  5294587  5294591  5294603  5294609
5294621  5294651  5294671  5294713  5294717  5294743  5294747  5294759  5294771  5294797
5294801  5294813  5294827  5294833  5294843  5294857  5294869  5294911  5294953  5294957
5294969  5294981  5295001  5295029  5295047  5295049  5295061  5295089  5295097  5295113
5295119  5295131  5295137  5295193  5295217  5295223  5295239  5295247  5295253  5295263
5295287  5295289  5295307  5295337  5295343  5295373  5295379  5295383  5295431  5295439
5295463  5295469  5295473  5295491  5295527  5295529  5295533  5295541  5295553  5295559
5295569  5295571  5295599  5295617  5295629  5295659  5295673  5295679  5295701  5295713
5295757  5295769  5295791  5295809  5295811  5295817  5295827  5295833  5295839  5295853
5295859  5295863  5295869  5295877  5295883  5295943  5295949  5295977  5295991  5296013
5296021  5296037  5296049  5296051  5296063  5296091  5296099  5296111  5296121
5296127  5296169  5296189  5296211  5296219  5296243  5296309  5296321  5296399  5296409
5296411  5296427  5296441  5296451  5296453  5296471  5296493  5296519  5296547  5296549
5296553  5296597  5296609  5296619  5296631  5296633  5296651  5296663  5296699  5296703
5296717  5296721  5296727  5296747  5296751  5296757  5296769  5296771  5296777  5296787
5296793  5296799  5296817  5296829  5296849  5296859  5296867  5296891  5296897  5296903
5296909  5296927  5296943  5296987  5296997  5297021  5297051  5297059  5297113  5297129
5297137  5297141  5297161  5297177  5297189  5297203  5297207  5297209  5297233  5297287
5297317  5297329  5297339  5297359  5297363  5297377  5297389  5297419  5297431  5297441
5297449  5297473  5297483  5297491  5297519  5297531  5297543  5297563  5297587  5297597
5297603  5297639  5297647  5297671  5297681  5297687  5297711  5297717  5297723  5297731
5297737  5297759  5297813  5297821  5297833  5297839  5297867  5297879  5297881  5297893
5297909  5297917  5297939  5297947  5297951  5298019  5298037  5298047  5298077  5298079
5298089  5298103  5298107  5298127  5298133  5298173  5298191  5298197  5298199  5298229
5298239  5298247  5298253  5298269  5298281  5298287  5298299  5298323  5298341  5298347
5298361  5298367  5298383  5298401  5298443  5298467  5298479  5298497  5298523  5298539
5298547  5298563  5298571  5298581  5298583  5298607  5298617  5298647  5298673  5298691
5298697  5298707  5298719  5298721  5298751  5298757  5298779  5298823  5298833  5298841
5298889  5298899  5298911  5298919  5298941  5298949  5298977  5298989  5298991  5299001
5299027  5299051  5299057  5299061  5299067  5299069  5299111  5299117  5299153  5299159
5299183  5299193  5299213  5299219  5299267  5299303  5299313  5299337  5299339
5299367  5299381  5299409  5299421  5299429  5299433  5299447  5299457  5299477  5299493
5299501  5299513  5299517  5299531  5299549  5299561  5299573  5299627  5299643  5299649
5299661  5299669  5299681  5299691  5299703  5299709  5299739  5299753  5299771  5299787
5299823  5299871  5299897  5299909  5299919  5299927  5299933  5299951  5299979  5299997
5300003  5300027  5300033  5300063  5300081  5300083  5300089  5300093  5300123  5300149
5300153  5300167  5300171  5300173  5300179  5300203  5300227  5300257  5300279  5300291
5300293  5300299  5300329  5300333  5300381  5300387  5300423  5300431  5300453  5300467
5300479  5300507  5300513  5300527  5300539  5300569  5300579  5300587  5300621  5300623
5300627  5300641  5300671  5300681  5300683  5300693  5300699  5300723  5300761  5300773
5300777  5300803  5300809  5300831  5300837  5300843  5300851  5300857  5300861  5300863
5300891  5300909  5300921  5300927  5300951  5300959  5300963  5300987  5300993  5301011
5301047  5301053  5301067  5301071  5301087  5301089  5301097  5301143  5301151  5301153
5301199  5301203  5301211  5301223  5301227  5301251  5301253  5301269  5301301  5301311
5301313  5301337  5301349  5301367  5301383  5301391  5301407  5301469  5301473  5301481
5301487  5301497  5301511  5301521  5301533  5301547  5301557  5301581  5301601  5301613
5301623  5301629  5301631  5301677  5301679  5301689  5301691  5301697  5301727  5301757
5301781  5301787  5301811  5301823  5301827  5301839  5301859  5301871  5301883  5301913
5301949  5301953  5301971  5301973  5301979  5301991  5302001  5302009  5302027  5302069
5302081  5302091  5302093  5302097  5302103  5302109  5302111  5302127  5302133  5302139
5302151  5302163  5302169  5302177  5302183  5302207  5302223  5302229  5302237  5302247
5302261  5302301  5302307  5302321  5302327  5302369  5302379  5302391  5302403  5302411
5302439  5302471  5302477  5302481  5302529  5302537  5302541  5302573  5302603  5302613
5302637  5302651  5302663  5302721  5302747  5302763  5302769  5302771  5302799  5302807
5302823  5302831  5302833  5302837  5302867  5302901  5302907  5302933  5302937  5302961
5302967  5302987  5302991  5303003  5303017  5303029  5303047  5303069  5303083  5303131
5303141  5303149  5303183  5303189  5303209  5303213  5303239  5303293  5303297  5303323
5303327  5303329  5303341  5303383  5303399  5303443  5303453  5303471  5303477  5303479
5303509  5303513  5303537  5303539  5303561  5303563  5303567  5303579  5303581  5303587
5303633  5303651  5303659  5303671  5303689  5303693  5303707  5303713  5303729  5303737
5303747  5303761  5303789  5303791  5303807  5303819  5303849  5303867  5303887
5303891  5303911  5303933  5303951  5303953  5303957  5303959  5303989  5303993  5303999
5304001  5304031  5304067  5304073  5304077  5304083  5304109  5304137  5304149  5304157
5304161  5304163  5304199  5304203  5304227  5304239  5304241  5304263  5304331  5304337
5304359  5304367  5304371  5304389  5304413  5304427  5304461  5304463  5304473  5304487
5304491  5304511  5304517  5304521  5304529  5304547  5304557  5304569  5304571  5304577
5304581  5304587  5304599  5304601  5304617  5304641  5304647  5304661  5304667  5304679
5304701  5304757  5304773  5304791  5304797  5304811  5304821  5304839  5304841  5304851
5304853  5304877  5304889  5304899  5304911  5304913  5304967  5304977  5304979  5304989
```

```
5305007 5305033 5305063 5305067 5305073 5305093 5305151 5305159 5305163 5305169
5305189 5305193 5305229 5305253 5305273 5305301 5305303 5305337 5305361 5305373
5305409 5305439 5305451 5305453 5305471 5305477 5305481 5305483 5305507 5305511
5305537 5305543 5305577 5305589 5305591 5305613 5305627 5305667 5305669 5305673
5305697 5305721 5305723 5305733 5305747 5305771 5305799 5305823 5305829 5305831
5305849 5305871 5305879 5305891 5305903 5305907 5305919 5305961 5305973 5305981
5305987 5305999 5306003 5306009 5306033 5306051 5306069 5306089 5306099 5306113
5306117 5306131 5306143 5306153 5306167 5306183 5306219 5306221 5306267 5306293
5306309 5306311 5306317 5306321 5306341 5306359 5306369 5306381 5306387 5306393
5306419 5306437 5306459 5306461 5306471 5306473 5306479 5306527 5306531 5306569
5306591 5306599 5306621 5306627 5306647 5306657 5306669 5306677 5306683 5306689
5306701 5306711 5306713 5306729 5306747 5306761 5306783 5306789 5306801 5306809
5306827 5306849 5306863 5306887 5306929 5306953 5306957 5306963 5306989 5307007
5307011 5307053 5307059 5307073 5307079 5307083 5307091 5307139 5307143 5307149
5307151 5307157 5307167 5307199 5307209 5307221 5307229 5307233 5307311 5307329
5307331 5307347 5307353 5307373 5307389 5307397 5307433 5307439 5307461 5307469
5307481 5307509 5307557 5307563 5307607 5307637 5307647 5307649 5307661 5307677
5307683 5307691 5307697 5307719 5307721 5307749 5307763 5307781 5307787 5307803
5307811 5307829 5307837 5307859 5307847 5307857 5307919 5307923 5307947 5307979
5308001 5308007 5308019 5308021 5308033 5308067 5308111 5308117 5308123 5308139
5308141 5308153 5308157 5308169 5308207 5308213 5308217 5308243 5308249 5308253
5308273 5308291 5308297 5308333 5308351 5308379 5308417 5308441 5308447 5308451
5308453 5308483 5308493 5308529 5308531 5308547 5308553 5308571 5308577 5308579
5308609 5308637 5308663 5308679 5308687 5308691 5308703 5308717 5308729 5308759
5308789 5308801 5308813 5308829 5308859 5308873 5308889 5308903 5308921 5308931
5308949 5308991 5308993 5309011 5309023 5309027 5309033 5309039 5309041 5309047
5309053 5309069 5309077 5309107 5309111 5309123 5309137 5309141 5309179 5309191
5309201 5309207 5309243 5309263 5309279 5309329 5309333 5309357 5309387 5309413
5309441 5309443 5309477 5309483 5309533 5309539 5309559 5309599 5309659 5309663
5309693 5309713 5309719 5309747 5309749 5309767 5309783 5309789 5309807 5309957
5309839 5309861 5309881 5309883 5309921 5309923 5309957
5309963 5309971 5309977 5309999 5310029 5310037 5310049 5310061 5310119 5310121
5310127 5310133 5310157 5310163 5310181 5310187 5310191 5310247 5310271 5310287
5310289 5310293 5310313 5310317 5310343 5310379 5310427 5310439 5310449
5310463 5310467 5310491 5310497 5310523 5310527 5310533 5310551 5310559 5310593
5310611 5310637 5310667 5310707 5310727 5310737 5310743 5310757 5310763 5310791
5310803 5310841 5310863 5310911 5310913 5310931 5310959 5310961 5310967 5310979
5310983 5311027 5311057 5311063 5311067 5311129 5311139 5311151 5311169 5311171
5311217 5311219 5311237 5311247 5311277 5311301 5311303 5311307 5311337 5311351
5311363 5311381 5311391 5311409 5311417 5311441 5311487 5311499 5311511 5311543
5311547 5311561 5311567 5311577 5311589 5311601 5311651 5311661 5311703 5311759
5311771 5311777 5311783 5311793 5311841 5311847 5311877 5311879 5311883 5311903
5311909 5311921 5311931 5311951 5311993 5312023 5312031 5312071 5312089 5312093
5312101 5312107 5312117 5312141 5312147 5312159 5312161 5312171 5312173 5312179
5312207 5312213 5312221 5312227 5312231 5312233 5312261 5312273 5312303 5312309
5312317 5312323 5312353 5312357 5312369 5312371 5312387 5312393 5312453 5312459
5312467 5312473 5312479 5312491 5312507 5312509 5312519 5312557 5312579 5312591
5312611 5312617 5312623 5312641 5312651 5312663 5312669 5312689 5312737
5312777 5312803 5312807 5312809 5312819 5312831 5312851 5312869 5312897 5312911
5312929 5312933 5312939 5312947 5312953 5312963 5312971 5312999 5313041 5313043
5313053 5313083 5313131 5313169 5313173 5313181 5313199 5313221 5313227
5313233 5313239 5313241 5313247 5313251 5313263 5313277 5313317 5313323 5313353
5313361 5313377 5313379 5313403 5313433 5313443 5313449 5313457 5313463 5313523
5313541 5313551 5313601 5313629 5313631 5313647 5313653 5313661 5313677 5313683
5313689 5313731 5313739 5313751 5313761 5313767 5313769 5313797 5313821 5313823
5313839 5313857 5313881 5313883 5313907 5313929 5313949 5313967 5314003 5314007
5314009 5314019 5314021 5314027 5314033 5314037 5314073 5314087 5314103 5314117
5314121 5314123 5314139 5314147 5314159 5314171 5314201 5314207 5314213 5314229
5314247 5314249 5314271 5314301 5314303 5314391 5314399 5314411 5314417 5314429
5314447 5314459 5314487 5314489 5314501 5314537 5314571 5314579 5314597 5314601
5314613 5314637 5314649 5314651 5314657 5314663 5314667 5314669 5314691 5314709
5314711 5314741 5314753 5314763 5314769 5314781 5314783 5314811 5314819 5314873
5314951 5314961 5314987 5314993 5315021 5315039 5315069 5315083 5315099 5315143
5315147 5315153 5315173 5315179 5315197 5315209 5315213 5315227 5315239 5315243
5315263 5315279 5315287 5315293 5315329 5315333 5315377 5315399 5315411 5315417
5315419 5315447 5315449 5315467 5315473 5315483 5315491 5315533 5315537 5315551
5315561 5315581 5315591 5315621 5315647 5315669 5315689 5315701 5315707 5315719
5315743 5315749 5315767 5315797 5315809 5315819 5315833 5315837 5315849
5315897 5315909 5315957 5315963 5315969 5315977 5315987 5315993 5316001 5316007
5316023 5316037 5316061 5316077 5316083 5316107 5316109 5316111 5316127
5316131 5316149 5316161 5316163 5316173 5316187 5316203 5316209 5316229 5316253
5316277 5316287 5316299 5316301 5316307 5316323 5316331 5316341 5316343 5316349
5316379 5316397 5316401 5316433 5316457 5316497 5316503 5316557 5316569 5316583
5316587 5316607 5316613 5316617 5316643 5316653 5316659 5316673 5316677 5316679
5316697 5316709 5316719 5316737 5316739 5316761 5316769 5316799 5316811
5316823 5316847 5316881 5316893 5316901 5316917 5316923 5316929 5316959 5316973
5317007 5317019 5317031 5317043 5317049 5317051 5317057 5317061 5317069 5317087
5317099 5317111 5317133 5317153 5317171 5317177 5317181 5317199 5317211 5317217
5317231 5317259 5317267 5317271 5317303 5317327 5317339 5317357 5317369 5317391
5317451 5317453 5317517 5317519 5317537 5317547 5317601 5317619 5317639 5317679
5317703 5317733 5317757 5317769 5317799 5317801 5317813 5317841 5317849 5317859
5317901 5317903 5317913 5317931 5317943 5317951 5317969 5317979 5317981 5317997
5317999 5318023 5318029 5318039 5318051 5318057 5318063 5318077 5318087 5318099
5318141 5318149 5318171 5318213 5318237 5318239 5318251 5318273 5318293 5318303
5318311 5318317 5318321 5318333 5318351 5318363 5318431 5318441 5318447 5318459
5318471 5318483 5318503 5318519 5318531 5318549 5318563 5318581 5318587 5318591
5318641 5318653 5318667 5318689 5318693 5318711 5318717 5318737 5318741 5318743
5318749 5318759 5318767 5318779 5318813 5318843 5318851 5318857 5318867 5318869
5318881 5318891 5318893 5318897 5318899 5318903 5318923 5318927 5318933 5318953
```

5318959 5318969 5318981 5319007 5319019 5319029 5319043 5319059 5319089 5319121
5319161 5319169 5319191 5319203 5319211 5319227 5319241 5319247 5319257 5319269
5319271 5319287 5319289 5319311 5319313 5319337 5319341 5319359 5319421 5319427
5319481 5319493 5319497 5319511 5319529 5319547 5319571 5319577 5319661 5319679
5319683 5319689 5319697 5319707 5319737 5319757 5319761 5319767 5319773 5319799
5319841 5319851 5319859 5319869 5319893 5319911 5319913 5319949 5319953 5319967
5319989 5320027 5320033 5320039 5320069 5320093 5320103 5320129 5320141 5320169
5320187 5320213 5320223 5320229 5320279 5320297 5320307 5320309 5320319 5320321
5320327 5320349 5320351 5320363 5320373 5320387 5320409 5320421 5320423 5320451
5320487 5320493 5320501 5320583 5320591 5320621 5320631 5320633 5320639 5320657
5320661 5320673 5320697 5320699 5320709 5320727 5320771 5320801 5320841 5320849
5320853 5320879 5320883 5320921 5320927 5320937 5320951 5320957 5320999 5321009
5321023 5321087 5321101 5321111 5321143 5321161 5321171 5321177 5321179 5321191
5321227 5321263 5321299 5321317 5321333 5321339 5321347 5321353 5321363 5321383
5321389 5321417 5321419 5321423 5321443 5321467 5321473 5321483 5321497 5321507
5321593 5321597 5321611 5321621 5321633 5321639 5321647 5321651 5321683 5321689
5321713 5321737 5321749 5321753 5321779 5321803 5321837 5321839 5321851 5321873
5321879 5321891 5321903 5321959 5321963 5321983 5322007 5322013 5322017 5322019
5322029 5322041 5322047 5322059 5322061 5322077 5322127 5322133 5322157 5322179
5322193 5322197 5322199 5322203 5322217 5322221 5322227 5322253 5322257 5322259
5322263 5322271 5322277 5322301 5322307 5322323 5322353 5322371 5322379 5322389
5322403 5322409 5322431 5322461 5322491 5322509 5322511 5322517 5322521 5322523
5322533 5322539 5322553 5322563 5322589 5322617 5322623 5322643 5322659 5322671
5322673 5322701 5322721 5322739 5322749 5322761 5322763 5322829 5322839 5322847
5322851 5322881 5322883 5322943 5322953 5322971 5322991 5322997 5323007 5323027
5323061 5323063 5323067 5323081 5323093 5323139 5323141 5323147 5323151 5323169
5323177 5323181 5323187 5323229 5323231 5323243 5323259 5323273 5323277 5323291
5323309 5323321 5323343 5323369 5323403 5323421 5323427 5323441 5323453 5323463
5323469 5323471 5323541 5323547 5323579 5323583 5323613 5323627 5323657 5323693
5323697 5323699 5323711 5323739 5323751 5323757 5323763 5323777 5323783 5323789
5323823 5323837 5323841 5323853 5323859 5323867 5323921 5323939 5323943 5323949
5324051 5324057 5324071 5324087 5324129 5324147 5324149 5324153 5324159 5324171
5324177 5324183 5324191 5324227 5324239 5324251 5324257 5324261 5324273 5324287
5324353 5324357 5324377 5324381 5324393 5324399 5324419 5324437 5324441 5324453
5324471 5324483 5324491 5324497 5324509 5324531 5324549 5324551 5324563 5324581
5324597 5324609 5324623 5324639 5324659 5324687 5324741 5324743 5324747 5324777
5324773 5324789 5324801 5324809 5324831 5324833 5324843 5324863 5324867 5324881
5324887 5324897 5324903 5324909 5324923 5324933 5324953 5324987 5324989 5324999
5325013 5325037 5325059 5325079 5325083 5325101 5325109 5325139 5325143 5325157
5325169 5325179 5325181 5325191 5325209 5325217 5325223 5325247 5325289 5325293
5325319 5325323 5325337 5325347 5325349 5325371 5325389 5325401 5325407 5325431
5325433 5325451 5325479 5325499 5325503 5325511 5325527 5325533 5325547 5325553
5325559 5325571 5325587 5325623 5325659 5325689 5325701 5325703 5325713 5325727
5325731 5325737 5325751 5325767 5325791 5325809 5325823 5325829 5325839 5325841
5325847 5325863 5325869 5325907 5325919 5325953 5325961 5325997 5326003 5326019
5326037 5326043 5326051 5326073 5326081 5326091 5326127 5326157 5326159 5326163
5326171 5326177 5326199 5326201 5326229 5326241 5326247 5326249 5326291 5326301
5326309 5326331 5326339 5326361 5326393 5326397 5326411 5326421 5326427 5326429
5326493 5326499 5326523 5326571 5326583 5326609 5326667 5326681 5326687 5326709
5326723 5326753 5326759 5326771 5326793 5326817 5326819 5326837 5326847 5326889
5326901 5326903 5326921 5326931 5326943 5326957 5326963 5327017 5327041 5327081
5327093 5327107 5327111 5327131 5327173 5327183 5327221 5327243 5327251 5327291
5327303 5327317 5327323 5327327 5327339 5327347 5327359 5327363 5327369 5327383
5327389 5327393 5327411 5327419 5327449 5327461 5327473 5327489 5327501 5327527
5327537 5327551 5327587 5327599 5327617 5327653 5327659 5327671 5327683 5327689
5327701 5327711 5327713 5327717 5327723 5327737 5327747 5327767 5327797 5327813
5327821 5327831 5327843 5327849 5327857 5327863 5327869 5327879 5327887 5327891
5327893 5327897 5327899 5327929 5327947 5327951 5328007 5328017
5328023 5328047 5328049 5328077 5328079 5328101 5328119 5328121 5328149 5328161
5328217 5328221 5328229 5328233 5328241 5328251 5328263 5328277 5328317 5328329
5328331 5328347 5328353 5328359 5328391 5328397 5328403 5328409 5328413 5328451
5328487 5328511 5328527 5328551 5328553 5328563 5328581 5328619 5328641 5328671
5328677 5328727 5328731 5328733 5328749 5328761 5328767 5328773 5328833 5328839
5328857 5328859 5328863 5328877 5328913 5328989 5328997 5329003 5329013 5329019
5329043 5329061 5329099 5329141 5329151 5329153 5329157 5329171 5329187 5329199
5329217 5329229 5329237 5329249 5329267 5329271 5329273 5329319 5329321 5329343
5329351 5329397 5329453 5329459 5329469 5329501 5329507 5329531 5329543 5329547
5329559 5329567 5329589 5329601 5329603 5329609 5329651 5329661 5329663 5329693
5329699 5329741 5329759 5329769 5329771 5329781 5329787 5329801 5329811 5329829
5329837 5329843 5329867 5329873 5329889 5329897 5329901 5329903 5329913 5329927
5329931 5329967 5329981 5329999 5330023 5330033 5330069 5330107 5330111 5330131
5330137 5330141 5330153 5330159 5330161 5330179 5330189 5330191 5330201 5330207
5330219 5330239 5330243 5330249 5330251 5330293 5330309 5330321 5330327 5330359
5330383 5330399 5330443 5330447 5330449 5330459 5330471 5330483 5330489 5330491
5330513 5330527 5330531 5330551 5330557 5330579 5330597 5330603 5330629 5330657
5330669 5330681 5330711 5330713 5330719 5330737 5330749 5330761 5330797 5330803
5330813 5330821 5330837 5330839 5330869 5330879 5330909 5330921 5330929 5330947
5330953 5330957 5330981 5330987 5331019 5331031 5331043 5331049 5331081 5331127
5331143 5331167 5331169 5331199 5331203 5331211 5331223 5331233 5331247 5331259
5331317 5331371 5331379 5331401 5331407 5331433 5331439 5331449 5331463 5331467
5331479 5331493 5331499 5331511 5331541 5331553 5331559 5331577 5331581 5331593
5331617 5331619 5331649 5331661 5331691 5331713 5331719 5331721 5331731 5331751
5331773 5331779 5331787 5331797 5331803 5331817 5331839 5331857 5331869 5331881
5331899 5331919 5331923 5331941 5331971 5331983 5332037 5332039 5332049 5332051
5332069 5332073 5332081 5332111 5332121 5332123 5332127 5332157 5332183
5332189 5332211 5332213 5332241 5332247 5332273 5332309 5332321 5332333 5332363
5332367 5332409 5332417 5332423 5332429 5332469 5332471 5332489 5332513 5332519
5332531 5332541 5332553 5332567 5332601 5332609 5332627 5332633 5332643 5332661
5332669 5332687 5332697 5332709 5332721 5332753 5332759 5332841 5332843 5332853

```
5332861 5332889 5332907 5332919 5332933 5332937 5332967 5332973 5332979 5332991
5333011 5333017 5333021 5333039 5333057 5333059 5333063 5333077 5333093 5333101
5333113 5333117 5333123 5333131 5333149 5333173 5333177 5333183 5333203 5333219
5333227 5333233 5333269 5333311 5333327 5333329 5333343 5333347 5333353 5333371
5333387 5333407 5333429 5333437 5333441 5333459 5333467 5333473 5333483 5333501
5333533 5333543 5333557 5333617 5333621 5333683 5333687 5333689 5333693 5333707
5333717 5333729 5333743 5333747 5333749 5333771 5333791 5333827 5333831 5333837
5333857 5333897 5333917 5333921 5333929 5333959 5333969 5333981 5334011 5334047
5334089 5334101 5334103 5334143 5334149 5334157 5334167 5334181 5334187 5334211
5334227 5334233 5334239 5334247 5334257 5334281 5334283 5334293 5334299 5334313
5334323 5334331 5334337 5334361 5334409 5334437 5334467 5334499 5334509 5334523
5334533 5334557 5334599 5334601 5334629 5334631 5334651 5334661
5334671 5334673 5334677 5334683 5334691 5334701 5334733 5334751 5334757 5334761
5334773 5334799 5334817 5334851 5334859 5334863 5334887 5334893 5334899
5334907 5334911 5334929 5334937 5334943 5334997 5335003 5335021 5335027 5335037
5335039 5335051 5335061 5335081 5335117 5335129 5335133 5335151 5335189 5335271
5335273 5335279 5335301 5335303 5335307 5335313 5335339 5335361 5335367 5335381
5335387 5335403 5335417 5335439 5335459 5335469 5335529 5335531 5335549 5335559
5335591 5335597 5335601 5335607 5335613 5335619 5335621 5335633 5335657
5335661 5335667 5335691 5335717 5335723 5335753 5335763 5335777 5335801 5335829
5335831 5335849 5335879 5335919 5335961 5335963 5335991 5336003 5336021
5336033 5336039 5336041 5336047 5336053 5336057 5336101 5336117 5336119 5336129
5336141 5336143 5336179 5336183 5336209 5336231 5336237 5336267 5336269 5336281
5336291 5336297 5336323 5336329 5336347 5336369 5336381 5336393 5336447 5336467
5336477 5336479 5336489 5336497 5336501 5336509 5336563 5336579 5336599 5336629
5336641 5336659 5336671 5336689 5336693 5336711 5336717 5336719 5336741 5336753
5336761 5336789 5336797 5336801 5336813 5336831 5336833 5336887 5336911 5336953
5336971 5336987 5336993 5337023 5337049 5337061 5337067 5337077 5337083 5337089
5337107 5337169 5337181 5337193 5337209 5337217 5337307 5337313 5337341 5337349
5337359 5337373 5337377 5337389 5337401 5337407 5337413 5337433 5337453 5337463
5337467 5337491 5337523 5337533 5337539 5337551 5337557 5337559 5337571 5337599
5337623 5337659 5337691 5337697 5337701 5337721 5337733 5337737 5337751 5337763
5337791 5337799 5337811 5337853 5337889 5337911 5337923 5337929 5337947 5337961
5337967 5337973 5337989 5337991 5338009 5338013 5338019 5338033 5338043 5338079
5338097 5338103 5338121 5338127 5338129 5338133 5338141 5338163 5338189 5338199
5338211 5338237 5338243 5338273 5338283 5338301 5338313 5338327 5338331 5338343
5338351 5338367 5338393 5338409 5338427 5338433 5338441 5338447 5338451 5338453
5338469 5338483 5338499 5338547 5338549 5338577 5338609 5338631 5338633 5338649
5338657 5338667 5338681 5338717 5338721 5338747 5338757 5338763 5338787 5338793
5338811 5338831 5338877 5338919 5338939 5338951 5338997 5339017 5339039 5339051
5339053 5339077 5339083 5339093 5339101 5339107 5339119 5339123 5339149 5339177
5339179 5339189 5339221 5339227 5339233 5339237 5339239 5339249 5339251 5339261
5339263 5339287 5339323 5339311 5339387 5339443 5339447 5339497 5339527
5339539 5339561 5339563 5339569 5339573 5339599 5339603 5339617 5339629 5339641
5339669 5339671 5339687 5339693 5339701 5339707 5339723 5339743 5339759 5339771
5339773 5339791 5339797 5339809 5339827 5339861 5339863 5339891 5339897 5339899
5339903 5339987 5339993 5340017 5340037 5340059 5340067 5340073 5340077 5340103
5340109 5340119 5340143 5340151 5340157 5340181 5340191 5340221 5340229 5340233
5340239 5340253 5340259 5340287 5340289 5340317 5340331 5340341 5340343 5340359
5340383 5340389 5340409 5340421 5340427 5340443 5340449 5340451 5340481 5340487
5340523 5340541 5340547 5340571 5340589 5340613 5340641 5340659 5340661
5340667 5340679 5340689 5340707 5340743 5340749 5340763 5340781 5340787 5340793
5340799 5340809 5340817 5340871 5340883 5340893 5340943 5340949 5340971 5340989
5341003 5341013 5341019 5341031 5341051 5341057 5341067 5341103 5341121 5341123
5341153 5341163 5341169 5341177 5341187 5341199 5341229 5341241 5341253 5341277
5341279 5341291 5341319 5341339 5341361 5341363 5341367 5341373 5341379 5341381
5341387 5341403 5341421 5341429 5341433 5341463 5341559 5341571 5341577 5341591
5341619 5341627 5341649 5341651 5341667 5341669 5341729 5341741
5341751 5341759 5341769 5341781 5341783 5341811 5341823 5341841 5341867 5341871
5341877 5341891 5341939 5341943 5341979 5341993 5342011 5342017 5342039 5342087
5342089 5342101 5342123 5342153 5342159 5342167 5342179 5342201 5342219 5342221
5342237 5342251 5342257 5342263 5342297 5342299 5342303 5342317 5342327 5342329
5342333 5342353 5342377 5342387 5342399 5342431 5342459 5342473 5342483 5342489
5342503 5342521 5342543 5342551 5342567 5342569 5342593 5342599 5342639 5342657
5342683 5342717 5342719 5342737 5342741 5342747 5342749 5342761 5342783 5342789
5342801 5342803 5342809 5342851 5342861 5342891 5342903 5342917 5342921 5342927
5342957 5342993 5342999 5343011 5343029 5343073 5343103 5343113 5343119 5343127
5343131 5343139 5343157 5343167 5343179 5343187 5343193 5343197 5343209 5343229
5343241 5343251 5343263 5343277 5343311 5343341 5343343 5343347 5343367 5343379
5343391 5343397 5343419 5343463 5343467 5343469 5343493 5343497 5343509 5343517
5343529 5343551 5343581 5343589 5343599 5343601 5343631 5343641 5343647 5343671
5343683 5343691 5343697 5343703 5343707 5343713 5343721 5343727 5343757 5343761
5343777 5343787 5343803 5343841 5343893 5343907 5343929 5343941 5343949 5343953
5343979 5343983 5344007 5344013 5344037 5344039 5344049 5344051 5344057 5344061
5344081 5344117 5344139 5344151 5344181 5344189 5344201 5344217 5344231 5344233
5344247 5344249 5344253 5344259 5344267 5344277 5344289 5344291 5344331 5344333
5344351 5344421 5344457 5344459 5344499 5344531 5344553 5344583 5344589 5344601
5344627 5344639 5344649 5344663 5344697 5344711 5344723 5344727 5344733 5344739
5344769 5344777 5344813 5344847 5344849 5344853 5344861 5344873 5344879 5344907
5344973 5344977 5345017 5345083 5345107 5345141 5345143 5345147 5345173 5345181
5345203 5345227 5345231 5345243 5345257 5345261 5345267 5345273 5345281 5345297
5345311 5345317 5345323 5345359 5345363 5345371 5345383 5345387 5345393 5345401
5345411 5345413 5345419 5345443 5345467 5345471 5345489 5345513 5345537 5345563
5345567 5345569 5345581 5345611 5345617 5345629 5345647 5345653 5345663 5345677
5345689 5345699 5345741 5345759 5345761 5345771 5345777 5345789 5345819 5345839
5345843 5345861 5345881 5345887 5345891 5345903 5345909 5345927 5345929 5345933
5345941 5345953 5345957 5345983 5345987 5345999 5346013 5346023 5346037
5346053 5346059 5346067 5346071 5346073 5346083 5346127 5346137 5346139 5346149
5346157 5346169 5346181 5346199 5346227 5346247 5346259 5346283 5346287 5346307
```

```
5346317  5346323  5346329  5346343  5346361  5346409  5346413  5346427  5346431  5346479
5346487  5346493  5346541  5346547  5346571  5346599  5346613  5346617  5346623  5346631
5346647  5346661  5346689  5346697  5346709  5346713  5346727  5346743  5346751  5346763
5346779  5346791  5346793  5346863  5346887  5346883  5346899  5346899  5346911  5346919
5346941  5346967  5346989  5346997  5347003  5347009  5347021  5347033  5347051  5347057
5347087  5347091  5347099  5347103  5347123  5347127  5347157  5347183  5347211  5347241
5347259  5347271  5347291  5347301  5347313  5347327  5347361  5347403  5347409  5347411
5347421  5347423  5347483  5347487  5347501  5347553  5347591  5347619  5347621  5347631
5347637  5347651  5347663  5347669  5347681  5347729  5347751  5347777  5347787  5347789
5347807  5347817  5347847  5347889  5347897  5347961  5347973  5347981  5347997  5348009
5348041  5348059  5348087  5348111  5348131  5348153  5348159  5348197  5348201  5348227
5348237  5348243  5348249  5348257  5348261  5348263  5348281  5348293  5348309  5348323
5348333  5348363  5348381  5348393  5348401  5348407  5348423  5348429  5348449  5348467
5348479  5348507  5348531  5348533  5348549  5348561  5348569  5348587  5348597  5348621
5348669  5348689  5348711  5348713  5348743  5348797  5348807  5348809  5348839  5348869
5348879  5348887  5348909  5348923  5348933  5348947  5348953  5348969  5349007  5349017
5349049  5349073  5349077  5349083  5349109  5349121  5349161  5349187  5349199  5349199
5349209  5349217  5349233  5349247  5349257  5349277  5349283  5349287  5349299  5349341
5349371  5349401  5349413  5349437  5349451  5349457  5349479  5349503  5349521  5349527
5349529  5349541  5349607  5349613  5349623  5349629  5349649  5349671  5349689  5349691
5349727  5349733  5349739  5349769  5349787  5349791  5349797  5349847  5349853  5349857
5349881  5349889  5349899  5349901  5349919  5349937  5349947  5349983  5349989  5349991
5349997  5350021  5350031  5350067  5350139  5350157  5350159  5350183  5350187  5350193
5350199  5350201  5350217  5350231  5350253  5350271  5350277  5350309  5350333  5350337
5350349  5350357  5350363  5350391  5350399  5350417  5350463  5350481  5350487  5350511
5350517  5350523  5350531  5350537  5350561  5350573  5350601  5350603  5350613  5350633
5350649  5350673  5350691  5350729  5350753  5350757  5350781  5350831  5350843  5350861
5350871  5350883  5350897  5350901  5350931  5350967  5350979  5351009  5351011  5351041
5351053  5351077  5351113  5351131  5351147  5351153  5351173  5351201  5351227  5351239
5351257  5351263  5351267  5351287  5351299  5351321  5351329  5351351  5351383  5351389
5351459  5351469  5351441  5351459  5351461  5351503  5351509  5351513  5351519  5351527
5351531  5351543  5351551  5351579  5351581  5351603  5351609  5351611  5351657  5351669
5351677  5351681  5351683  5351693  5351699  5351701  5351729  5351741  5351761  5351783
5351803  5351807  5351839  5351851  5351861  5351869  5351873  5351881  5351891  5351947
5351953  5351963  5351971  5352001  5352007  5352023  5352029  5352041  5352043  5352049
5352071  5352097  5352107  5352121  5352131  5352133  5352153  5352157  5352163  5352187  5352197
5352199  5352203  5352209  5352239  5352257  5352271  5352283  5352289  5352299  5352301
5352317  5352337  5352341  5352343  5352349  5352359  5352401  5352409  5352419  5352439
5352449  5352463  5352481  5352533  5352541  5352551  5352593  5352643  5352647  5352649
5352653  5352691  5352701  5352703  5352707  5352731  5352779  5352821  5352833  5352847
5352911  5352913  5352913  5352937  5352953  5352959  5352967  5352973  5352989  5352989
5353021  5353031  5353037  5353067  5353069  5353087  5353091  5353093  5353097  5353109
5353121  5353151  5353207  5353211  5353213  5353223  5353259  5353267  5353279  5353291
5353321  5353339  5353343  5353357  5353363  5353393  5353399  5353423  5353433  5353463
5353499  5353529  5353541  5353553  5353559  5353571  5353597  5353609  5353633  5353637
5353639  5353643  5353681  5353689  5353693  5353717  5353727  5353729  5353757  5353811
5353819  5353841  5353847  5353849  5353883  5353889  5353913  5353927  5353949  5353969
5353981  5353987  5353993  5354003  5354023  5354047  5354051  5354057  5354071  5354087
5354093  5354117  5354119  5354123  5354131  5354179  5354203  5354207  5354213  5354221
5354243  5354291  5354311  5354341  5354353  5354359  5354369  5354411  5354429  5354443
5354449  5354467  5354491  5354501  5354509  5354513  5354533  5354543  5354551  5354563
5354567  5354581  5354597  5354617  5354633  5354639  5354651  5354659  5354681  5354683
5354729  5354737  5354743  5354769  5354779  5354791  5354797  5354803  5354807  5354809
5354849  5354861  5354873  5354917  5354927  5354933  5354953  5354963  5354977  5354981
5354989  5355011  5355019  5355023  5355059  5355071  5355083  5355101  5355107  5355139
5355151  5355167  5355199  5355197  5355199  5355211  5355257  5355271  5355277  5355299
5355307  5355319  5355341  5355367  5355407  5355419  5355421  5355431  5355433  5355439
5355443  5355451  5355479  5355487  5355503  5355551  5355563  5355599  5355577  5355589
5355593  5355613  5355643  5355667  5355683  5355689  5355709  5355733  5355737  5355761
5355793  5355797  5355811  5355817  5355827  5355829  5355841  5355851  5355863  5355869
5355877  5355881  5355887  5355893  5355899  5355919  5355947  5355949  5355991  5356007
5356019  5356051  5356061  5356063  5356067  5356093  5356111  5356129  5356133  5356147
5356159  5356163  5356187  5356189  5356193  5356201  5356223  5356249  5356259  5356283
5356301  5356303  5356321  5356327  5356331  5356357  5356399  5356409  5356427  5356451
5356469  5356487  5356489  5356501  5356511  5356517  5356529  5356531  5356561  5356567
5356577  5356579  5356607  5356621  5356661  5356693  5356697  5356709  5356711  5356739
5356783  5356789  5356817  5356847  5356849  5356867  5356873  5356877  5356889  5356913
5356943  5356951  5356963  5356979  5357003  5357039  5357041  5357059  5357063  5357071
5357087  5357123  5357147  5357167  5357171  5357173  5357197  5357207  5357237  5357239
5357249  5357299  5357309  5357351  5357353  5357371  5357381  5357423  5357437  5357441
5357467  5357479  5357503  5357519  5357531  5357537  5357557  5357581  5357587  5357603
5357609  5357629  5357633  5357641  5357657  5357683  5357687  5357707  5357713  5357719
5357777  5357797  5357831  5357851  5357857  5357879  5357887  5357893  5357903  5357909
5357959  5357969  5357971  5357977  5357993  5357999  5358013  5358029  5358037  5358053
5358061  5358083  5358109  5358131  5358137  5358139  5358169  5358173  5358181  5358227
5358263  5358271  5358289  5358307  5358317  5358341  5358343  5358391  5358401  5358403
5358407  5358421  5358433  5358449  5358469  5358497  5358499  5358503  5358523  5358539
5358541  5358569  5358581  5358607  5358631  5358641  5358643  5358679  5358697  5358709
5358713  5358733  5358737  5358739  5358751  5358763  5358797  5358809  5358811  5358827
5358833  5358851  5358869  5358889  5358917  5358929  5358937  5358943  5358953  5358967
5358973  5359027  5359037  5359051  5359087  5359139  5359157  5359163  5359183  5359217
5359223  5359231  5359247  5359271  5359279  5359283  5359327  5359351  5359357  5359379
5359427  5359433  5359447  5359451  5359469  5359481  5359489  5359499  5359501  5359537
5359547  5359553  5359591  5359589  5359609  5359633  5359657  5359663  5359681  5359721
5359727  5359741  5359747  5359763  5359769  5359771  5359789  5359793  5359801  5359813
5359817  5359819  5359831  5359841  5359853  5359859  5359873  5359877  5359901  5359903
5359909  5359961  5359987  5360023  5360027  5360029  5360039  5360051  5360077  5360101
5360111  5360119  5360129  5360143  5360161  5360177  5360183  5360191  5360213  5360221
5360231  5360233  5360239  5360263  5360269  5360281  5360339  5360351  5360353  5360359
```

```
5360393  5360401  5360419  5360431  5360437  5360461  5360479  5360503  5360507  5360519
5360521  5360557  5360561  5360591  5360599  5360617  5360623  5360639  5360653  5360657
5360669  5360687  5360689  5360701  5360711  5360723  5360731  5360753  5360759  5360783
5360801  5360827  5360837  5360843  5360857  5360879  5360881  5360903  5360921
5360941  5360963  5360977  5360981  5360987  5361007  5361017  5361023  5361029  5361043
5361049  5361061  5361073  5361121  5361127  5361131  5361157  5361203  5361217  5361227
5361241  5361247  5361269  5361289  5361311  5361319  5361331  5361353  5361359  5361361
5361373  5361379  5361397  5361403  5361413  5361451  5361457  5361463  5361479  5361539
5361547  5361569  5361571  5361593  5361623  5361637  5361641  5361659  5361661  5361673
5361677  5361701  5361703  5361709  5361739  5361751  5361757  5361767  5361773  5361779
5361793  5361803  5361821  5361827  5361833  5361847  5361887  5361893  5361899  5361907
5361913  5361931  5361947  5361959  5361973  5361997  5362033  5362051  5362073  5362079
5362087  5362109  5362111  5362117  5362121  5362141  5362153  5362177  5362207  5362213
5362219  5362271  5362297  5362309  5362337  5362363  5362391  5362403  5362433  5362439
5362457  5362501  5362523  5362529  5362543  5362549  5362583  5362601  5362607  5362619
5362627  5362639  5362663  5362697  5362711  5362727  5362729  5362751  5362771  5362789
5362793  5362823  5362853  5362857  5362897  5362919  5362943  5362949  5362967  5362991
5362993  5363011  5363027  5363047  5363063  5363069  5363077  5363081  5363131  5363147
5363167  5363179  5363207  5363213  5363219  5363221  5363243  5363257  5363273  5363283
5363297  5363321  5363357  5363387  5363429  5363431  5363437  5363443  5363459  5363461
5363473  5363503  5363507  5363509  5363549  5363569  5363587  5363621  5363627  5363629
5363639  5363641  5363693  5363707  5363711  5363723  5363731  5363737  5363741  5363767
5363773  5363797  5363801  5363843  5363849  5363861  5363887  5363923  5363933  5363977
5363983  5364013  5364019  5364031  5364067  5364089  5364091  5364097  5364109  5364127
5364143  5364169  5364173  5364181  5364193  5364199  5364239  5364241  5364257  5364269
5364301  5364329  5364331  5364377  5364383  5364389  5364397  5364407  5364421  5364441
5364433  5364461  5364473  5364487  5364511  5364521  5364553  5364559  5364613  5364629
5364647  5364649  5364679  5364683  5364701  5364719  5364731  5364761  5364769  5364791
5364823  5364839  5364851  5364881  5364883  5364889  5364899  5364923  5364941  5364943
5364949  5364959  5364977  5364991  5365001  5365007  5365027  5365033  5365039  5365051
5365079  5365091  5365093  5365103  5365109  5365121  5365147  5365169  5365189  5365193
5365223  5365229  5365231  5365237  5365253  5365267  5365289  5365309  5365343  5365351
5365357  5365403  5365433  5365441  5365453  5365487  5365513  5365517  5365531  5365553
5365559  5365631  5365643  5365649  5365651  5365673  5365681  5365691  5365741  5365751
5365769  5365799  5365807  5365813  5365819  5365823  5365837  5365853  5365889  5365901
5365909  5365949  5365951  5365981  5366003  5366017  5366021  5366027  5366047  5366063
5366089  5366093  5366143  5366149  5366159  5366161  5366167  5366177  5366183  5366191
5366209  5366219  5366243  5366269  5366279  5366299  5366311  5366323  5366327  5366359
5366377  5366399  5366401  5366411  5366419  5366437  5366447  5366453  5366461  5366467
5366497  5366513  5366539  5366561  5366587  5366593  5366623  5366657  5366663  5366671
5366681  5366723  5366729  5366737  5366743  5366749  5366761  5366771  5366773  5366791
5366807  5366839  5366857  5366861  5366869  5366891  5366903  5366969  5366983  5366989
5367017  5367031  5367067  5367077  5367091  5367157  5367163  5367191  5367199  5367203
5367221  5367239  5367251  5367277  5367287  5367293  5367317  5367319  5367337  5367347
5367379  5367403  5367413  5367419  5367421  5367431  5367491  5367493  5367511  5367521
5367539  5367569  5367577  5367587  5367601  5367623  5367641  5367667  5367683  5367707
5367721  5367727  5367731  5367737  5367749  5367751  5367773  5367779  5367781  5367821
5367829  5367841  5367851  5367853  5367877  5367889  5367907  5367911  5367931  5367949
5367961  5367977  5367979  5368001  5368003  5368019  5368021  5368037  5368043  5368063
5368067  5368081  5368091  5368123  5368133  5368147  5368151  5368169  5368189  5368193
5368217  5368229  5368261  5368267  5368289  5368309  5368327  5368331  5368333  5368339
5368369  5368373  5368397  5368399  5368403  5368409  5368411  5368439  5368457  5368459
5368471  5368477  5368483  5368541  5368547  5368579  5368607  5368609  5368633  5368661
5368703  5368739  5368751  5368771  5368813  5368817  5368829  5368861  5368871  5368877
5368879  5368897  5368901  5368903  5368907  5368927  5368933  5368981  5368997  5368999
5369009  5369041  5369053  5369069  5369083  5369087  5369109  5369121  5369129
5369137  5369149  5369183  5369197  5369207  5369209  5369249  5369251  5369279  5369291
5369311  5369339  5369341  5369347  5369387  5369423  5369443  5369461  5369471  5369473
5369489  5369491  5369503  5369527  5369537  5369543  5369549  5369561  5369579  5369593
5369597  5369599  5369621  5369627  5369681  5369713  5369719  5369731  5369743  5369753
5369759  5369779  5369783  5369809  5369857  5369863  5369869  5369887  5369911  5369929
5369939  5369957  5369963  5369981  5369999  5370019  5370041  5370049  5370059  5370061
5370073  5370077  5370107  5370137  5370163  5370187  5370241  5370259  5370269  5370289
5370301  5370319  5370329  5370353  5370359  5370367  5370371  5370389  5370403  5370433
5370461  5370503  5370517  5370557  5370577  5370581  5370613  5370619  5370637  5370667
5370671  5370679  5370689  5370721  5370731  5370733  5370751  5370773  5370779  5370797
5370803  5370817  5370851  5370857  5370881  5370889  5370899  5370913  5370941  5370961
5370971  5370991  5371007  5371021  5371033  5371039  5371081  5371097  5371109  5371117
5371139  5371159  5371169  5371187  5371199  5371217  5371231  5371237  5371273  5371279
5371283  5371291  5371297  5371321  5371367  5371403  5371423  5371453  5371469  5371519
5371529  5371543  5371571  5371631  5371657  5371669  5371679  5371687  5371693  5371727
5371739  5371747  5371753  5371777  5371781  5371783  5371801  5371819  5371831  5371837
5371841  5371853  5371879  5371909  5371913  5371937  5371963  5371967  5371979  5371981
5372011  5372023  5372039  5372063  5372077  5372099  5372113  5372123  5372137  5372173
5372177  5372183  5372203  5372233  5372243  5372249  5372267  5372273  5372299  5372303
5372309  5372321  5372329  5372333  5372347  5372351  5372371  5372399  5372401  5372413
5372417  5372443  5372449  5372467  5372473  5372483  5372491  5372503  5372509  5372519
5372537  5372551  5372567  5372597  5372603  5372621  5372651  5372677  5372697  5372699
5372723  5372753  5372761  5372771  5372803  5372813  5372821  5372831  5372879  5372929
5372933  5372947  5372957  5372963  5372971  5372977  5372987  5373031  5373059  5373061
5373101  5373113  5373119  5373127  5373131  5373133  5373163  5373167  5373169  5373211
5373217  5373229  5373233  5373239  5373253  5373259  5373281  5373287  5373289  5373293
5373331  5373341  5373383  5373391  5373397  5373403  5373413  5373427  5373443  5373451
5373469  5373491  5373499  5373517  5373521  5373527  5373587  5373593  5373607  5373611
5373653  5373689  5373691  5373701  5373707  5373721  5373727  5373733  5373737  5373761
5373773  5373791  5373793  5373803  5373821  5373833  5373847  5373857  5373859  5373883
5373889  5373923  5373931  5373971  5373997  5374007  5374009  5374021  5374043  5374063
5374069  5374073  5374079  5374121  5374141  5374151  5374153  5374163  5374177  5374181
5374199  5374211  5374217  5374219  5374277  5374279  5374297  5374301  5374307  5374319
```

```
5374331  5374337  5374339  5374349  5374379  5374409  5374427  5374429  5374451  5374459
5374489  5374507  5374517  5374519  5374529  5374547  5374553  5374559  5374573  5374597
5374609  5374637  5374651  5374661  5374693  5374697  5374727  5374741  5374757  5374769
5374781  5374793  5374819  5374861  5374883  5374903  5374909  5374927  5374951  5374973
5374987  5375003  5375011  5375017  5375033  5375039  5375047  5375053  5375099  5375107
5375113  5375143  5375171  5375173  5375177  5375203  5375219  5375221  5375257  5375267
5375273  5375287  5375291  5375299  5375327  5375371  5375389  5375393  5375401  5375407
5375413  5375429  5375441  5375443  5375453  5375459  5375479  5375483  5375497  5375507
5375521  5375533  5375567  5375581  5375597  5375599  5375603  5375609  5375639  5375641
5375653  5375659  5375663  5375681  5375683  5375687  5375707  5375717  5375729  5375753
5375761  5375779  5375807  5375809  5375831  5375857  5375891  5375899  5375911  5375941
5375947  5375957  5375971  5375977  5375999  5376011  5376023  5376047  5376073  5376083
5376101  5376127  5376143  5376157  5376167  5376179  5376193  5376197  5376209  5376251
5376253  5376263  5376269  5376271  5376277  5376311  5376313  5376323  5376337  5376341
5376353  5376379  5376389  5376391  5376407  5376421  5376443  5376461  5376473  5376499
5376517  5376521  5376529  5376541  5376551  5376557  5376559  5376577  5376583  5376589
5376593  5376599  5376619  5376647  5376649  5376673  5376689  5376713  5376719  5376727
5376739  5376769  5376773  5376793  5376809  5376827  5376853  5376869  5376883  5376893
5376907  5376923  5376929  5376953  5376979  5376983  5376997  5377007  5377037
5377039  5377051  5377061  5377067  5377081  5377087  5377103  5377111  5377121  5377153
5377159  5377181  5377187  5377231  5377237  5377243  5377289  5377301  5377303  5377313
5377343  5377357  5377363  5377367  5377369  5377373  5377381  5377391  5377397  5377417
5377439  5377529  5377549  5377591  5377597  5377613  5377637  5377643  5377657  5377667
5377679  5377711  5377727  5377747  5377769  5377781  5377807  5377819  5377843  5377861
5377871  5377877  5377891  5377907  5377919  5377937  5377961  5377979  5377991  5377997
5378029  5378033  5378057  5378063  5378071  5378077  5378089  5378101  5378111  5378119
5378143  5378147  5378161  5378173  5378201  5378203  5378207  5378213  5378227  5378231
5378237  5378267  5378299  5378377  5378383  5378393  5378411  5378423  5378437  5378441
5378447  5378473  5378489  5378497  5378507  5378519  5378521  5378533  5378551  5378561
5378563  5378587  5378609  5378657  5378669  5378677  5378683  5378689  5378699  5378701
5378707  5378719  5378731  5378819  5378861  5378869  5378899  5378909  5378911  5378921
5378927  5378929  5378939  5378951  5378959  5378963  5378993  5379001  5379019  5379029
5379037  5379043  5379047  5379053  5379061  5379083  5379091  5379113  5379131  5379149
5379167  5379203  5379221  5379233  5379247  5379251  5379277  5379281  5379287  5379359
5379377  5379379  5379383  5379397  5379403  5379419  5379431  5379433  5379449  5379499
5379503  5379533  5379557  5379559  5379581  5379607  5379611  5379613  5379629  5379637
5379643  5379691  5379727  5379739  5379749  5379769  5379791  5379809  5379823  5379827
5379851  5379893  5379901  5379923  5379931  5379943  5379947  5379971  5380003  5380009
5380049  5380057  5380079  5380093  5380103  5380121  5380147  5380153  5380159  5380181
5380187  5380213  5380223  5380237  5380247  5380253  5380303  5380327  5380337  5380343
5380351  5380369  5380373  5380393  5380409  5380423  5380447  5380499  5380511  5380611
5380519  5380549  5380559  5380579  5380603  5380621  5380637  5380649  5380681  5380691
5380699  5380723  5380729  5380751  5380777  5380781  5380811  5380831  5380841  5380849
5380867  5380883  5380909  5380937  5380943  5380951  5380987  5381017  5381023  5381041
5381053  5381059  5381069  5381071  5381081  5381083  5381093  5381111  5381113  5381141
5381183  5381203  5381219  5381227  5381251  5381261  5381263  5381273  5381281  5381293
5381297  5381329  5381347  5381353  5381377  5381413  5381417  5381423  5381437  5381447
5381459  5381477  5381479  5381491  5381521  5381543  5381561  5381573  5381581  5381599
5381627  5381653  5381669  5381683  5381689  5381699  5381711  5381713  5381723  5381743
5381749  5381767  5381773  5381777  5381797  5381813  5381819  5381861  5381863  5381867
5381881  5381891  5381899  5381917  5381927  5381939  5381951  5381963  5381989
5382001  5382011  5382037  5382049  5382079  5382101  5382103  5382107  5382109  5382119
5382151  5382173  5382211  5382229  5382233  5382241  5382257  5382259  5382271  5382281
5382283  5382287  5382323  5382329  5382337  5382341  5382347  5382359  5382361  5382379
5382383  5382401  5382407  5382413  5382449  5382463  5382469  5382473  5382479  5382493
5382527  5382541  5382547  5382563  5382569  5382589  5382599  5382613  5382617  5382647
5382653  5382673  5382683  5382691  5382721  5382731  5382737  5382739  5382779  5382781
5382787  5382841  5382857  5382887  5382889  5382899  5382907  5382913  5382917
5382919  5382929  5382961  5382967  5382973  5382991  5383031  5383039  5383069  5383073
5383111  5383123  5383129  5383151  5383159  5383171  5383187  5383193  5383201  5383211
5383223  5383229  5383247  5383253  5383267  5383303  5383321  5383351  5383361  5383363
5383381  5383387  5383393  5383397  5383409  5383421  5383439  5383451  5383453  5383459
5383507  5383513  5383529  5383549  5383559  5383571  5383583  5383591  5383601  5383607
5383627  5383649  5383661  5383663  5383673  5383681  5383723  5383753  5383757  5383787
5383811  5383843  5383847  5383853  5383871  5383943  5383949  5383967  5383993  5383999
5384003  5384017  5384021  5384033  5384039  5384051  5384059  5384063  5384069  5384077
5384081  5384101  5384107  5384117  5384123  5384147  5384167  5384177  5384191  5384219
5384221  5384263  5384303  5384311  5384329  5384333  5384339  5384341  5384363  5384371
5384383  5384387  5384389  5384437  5384441  5384471  5384491  5384497  5384501  5384513
5384537  5384549  5384557  5384579  5384593  5384609  5384611  5384623  5384627  5384651
5384671  5384677  5384683  5384693  5384707  5384713  5384777  5384779  5384833  5384843
5384849  5384851  5384861  5384867  5384881  5384887  5384891  5384947  5384969  5384983
5384987  5384993  5385007  5385043  5385049  5385053  5385067  5385077  5385089  5385131
5385143  5385179  5385187  5385199  5385217  5385229  5385253  5385269  5385287  5385319
5385337  5385349  5385361  5385371  5385377  5385409  5385431  5385437  5385459  5385463
5385469  5385487  5385511  5385517  5385521  5385547  5385557  5385593  5385613  5385641
5385643  5385647  5385659  5385671  5385691  5385727  5385761  5385763  5385769  5385781
5385811  5385817  5385823  5385827  5385829  5385839  5385859  5385893  5385899  5385937
5385959  5385997  5386021  5386039  5386049  5386057  5386061  5386081  5386097  5386103
5386123  5386133  5386151  5386181  5386189  5386193  5386217  5386237  5386307  5386319
5386351  5386357  5386387  5386421  5386471  5386477  5386517  5386543  5386553  5386559
5386561  5386573  5386631  5386639  5386649  5386651  5386667  5386687  5386729  5386753
5386769  5386859  5386873  5386879  5386883  5386891  5386921  5386951  5386957  5386961
5386967  5386981  5386993  5387009  5387017  5387021  5387023  5387033  5387059  5387071
5387077  5387099  5387101  5387111  5387117  5387143  5387153  5387159  5387167  5387171
5387177  5387189  5387191  5387197  5387201  5387233  5387257  5387293  5387297  5387303
5387321  5387339  5387339  5387353  5387381  5387383  5387387  5387399  5387413  5387429
5387443  5387461  5387479  5387489  5387509  5387519  5387539  5387561  5387567  5387579
5387593  5387597  5387611  5387617  5387647  5387651  5387653  5387677  5387689  5387713
```

```
5387717 5387719 5387729 5387731 5387737 5387741 5387747 5387749 5387783 5387791
5387803 5387807 5387813 5387843 5387867 5387873 5387891 5387909 5387917 5387923
5387951 5387983 5387999 5388007 5388011 5388013 5388023 5388041 5388043 5388091
5388101 5388107 5388121 5388137 5388143 5388151 5388169 5388193 5388241 5388247
5388281 5388289 5388311 5388319 5388329 5388377 5388391 5388407 5388433 5388479
5388491 5388521 5388547 5388553 5388611 5388619 5388623 5388673 5388689 5388707
5388709 5388727 5388763 5388767 5388769 5388797 5388811 5388819 5388833 5388839
5388853 5388869 5388871 5388893 5388899 5388907 5388919 5388931 5388937 5388953
5388961 5388997 5389003 5389019 5389031 5389049 5389073 5389117 5389121 5389129
5389171 5389183 5389213 5389231 5389243 5389249 5389253 5389261 5389271 5389297
5389303 5389313 5389333 5389343 5389361 5389367 5389379 5389387 5389399 5389403
5389427 5389441 5389451 5389453 5389487 5389507 5389519 5389529 5389541
5389543 5389619 5389627 5389639 5389649 5389693 5389721 5389739 5389763 5389781
5389807 5389817 5389831 5389837 5389847 5389849 5389871 5389873 5389907 5389931
5389963 5389997 5390017 5390023 5390039 5390041 5390051 5390059 5390087 5390131
5390141 5390149 5390171 5390183 5390191 5390219 5390223 5390237 5390239 5390267
5390279 5390291 5390293 5390323 5390327 5390353 5390381 5390389 5390443 5390449
5390453 5390467 5390501 5390503 5390521 5390531 5390537 5390543 5390551 5390587
5390599 5390617 5390629 5390647 5390657 5390659 5390669 5390677 5390681
5390687 5390701 5390713 5390719 5390743 5390747 5390761 5390773 5390783 5390797
5390821 5390857 5390873 5390893 5390923 5390939 5390971 5390991 5391017 5391019
5391037 5391047 5391073 5391083 5391097 5391149 5391157 5391173 5391181 5391209
5391247 5391257 5391259 5391263 5391293 5391311 5391313 5391341 5391349 5391367
5391389 5391401 5391413 5391437 5391439 5391443 5391457 5391461 5391487 5391509
5391517 5391521 5391539 5391553 5391559 5391583 5391587 5391619 5391643 5391647
5391653 5391667 5391679 5391689 5391697 5391713 5391719 5391721 5391733 5391761
5391791 5391797 5391803 5391817 5391823 5391857 5391889 5391937 5391961 5391977
5391979 5391983 5391989 5392001 5392003 5392007 5392019 5392027 5392081 5392099
5392129 5392139 5392141 5392151 5392193 5392213 5392223 5392229 5392249 5392267
5392271 5392301 5392307 5392313 5392351 5392369 5392381 5392391 5392393 5392397
5392403 5392411 5392423 5392441 5392469 5392477 5392489 5392493 5392531 5392537
5392549 5392559 5392571 5392573 5392577 5392609 5392627 5392657 5392661 5392669
5392679 5392687 5392691 5392703 5392711 5392799 5392817 5392819 5392823 5392837
5392843 5392847 5392901 5392957 5392963 5392967 5392973 5392987 5392991
5393033 5393041 5393053 5393077 5393111 5393123 5393147 5393153 5393173 5393177
5393191 5393209 5393261 5393273 5393291 5393317 5393327 5393337 5393351 5393357
5393387 5393393 5393417 5393419 5393441 5393461 5393503 5393537 5393581 5393593
5393629 5393639 5393663 5393677 5393693 5393711 5393723 5393737 5393741 5393761
5393779 5393809 5393813 5393819 5393833 5393849 5393887 5393893 5393903 5393909
5393911 5393917 5393939 5393951 5393959 5393987 5394061 5394089 5394091 5394097
5394131 5394139 5394149 5394163 5394197 5394227 5394229 5394239
5394251 5394269 5394283 5394289 5394299 5394349 5394353 5394383 5394391 5394401
5394407 5394437 5394439 5394463 5394499 5394503 5394539 5394541 5394569 5394577
5394583 5394607 5394611 5394629 5394643 5394671 5394679 5394709 5394721 5394731
5394749 5394757 5394761 5394769 5394787 5394799 5394839 5394847 5394863 5394869
5394877 5394889 5394931 5394937 5394941 5394943 5394971 5394979 5394997 5395021
5395057 5395063 5395097 5395099 5395121 5395127 5395151 5395153 5395163 5395199
5395207 5395213 5395217 5395277 5395279 5395289 5395331 5395337 5395343 5395349
5395367 5395387 5395399 5395417 5395427 5395433 5395483 5395493 5395499 5395517
5395529 5395531 5395541 5395543 5395561 5395571 5395573 5395589 5395651 5395661
5395667 5395669 5395679 5395693 5395703 5395717 5395721 5395729 5395751 5395757
5395763 5395801 5395811 5395813 5395837 5395843 5395879 5395883 5395921 5395967
5395991 5395993 5396003 5396009 5396011 5396063 5396107 5396137 5396147 5396173
5396177 5396179 5396189 5396203 5396219 5396221 5396267 5396299 5396341 5396351
5396353 5396359 5396393 5396431 5396453 5396477 5396491 5396507 5396509 5396519
5396533 5396537 5396551 5396557 5396563 5396571 5396593 5396617 5396621 5396623
5396641 5396647 5396659 5396663 5396669 5396683 5396689 5396711 5396717 5396719
5396723 5396737 5396771 5396777 5396819 5396861 5396863 5396869 5396903 5396921
5396933 5396957 5396959 5396977 5396981 5397001 5397011 5397013 5397037 5397047
5397071 5397089 5397101 5397107 5397113 5397127 5397163 5397173 5397179 5397181
5397221 5397229 5397247 5397251 5397283 5397299 5397323 5397377 5397391 5397397
5397409 5397443 5397473 5397493 5397499 5397521 5397529 5397569 5397599 5397629
5397647 5397649 5397673 5397697 5397701 5397703 5397713 5397719 5397731 5397737
5397757 5397781 5397793 5397803 5397811 5397841 5397853 5397863 5397871 5397877
5397907 5397923 5397929 5397943 5397947 5397949 5397961 5397971 5397979 5398037
5398039 5398067 5398069 5398093 5398139 5398171 5398181 5398187 5398199 5398207
5398213 5398219 5398241 5398249 5398259 5398271 5398297 5398301 5398303 5398313
5398319 5398331 5398339 5398357 5398361 5398363 5398369 5398381 5398409 5398427
5398447 5398487 5398493 5398499 5398501 5398507 5398513 5398529 5398531 5398543
5398567 5398573 5398577 5398579 5398597 5398697 5398709 5398733 5398747 5398751
5398763 5398807 5398823 5398837 5398849 5398873 5398889 5398891 5398909 5398919
5398933 5398949 5398961 5398969 5398993 5398999 5399011 5399029 5399039 5399041
5399071 5399083 5399131 5399161 5399189 5399197 5399201 5399213 5399221
5399231 5399237 5399243 5399257 5399263 5399281 5399291 5399321 5399323 5399333
5399351 5399377 5399389 5399393 5399417 5399419 5399431 5399441 5399453 5399477
5399507 5399531 5399543 5399567 5399579 5399593 5399599 5399617 5399623 5399627
5399633 5399651 5399677 5399707 5399711 5399747 5399749 5399753 5399777 5399789
5399833 5399833 5399839 5399861 5399869 5399899 5399981 5399983 5399929 5399939
5399941 5399993 5400001 5400019 5400023 5400037 5400053 5400071 5400079 5400089
5400091 5400097 5400121 5400127 5400137 5400209 5400221 5400257 5400259 5400287
5400299 5400301 5400319 5400323 5400337 5400349 5400359 5400419 5400443 5400457
5400511 5400517 5400523 5400553 5400559 5400581 5400587 5400589 5400649 5400673
5400701 5400709 5400721 5400739 5400743 5400761 5400763 5400793 5400797 5400799
5400821 5400823 5400827 5400833 5400839 5400847 5400877 5400881 5400949 5400953
5400961 5400973 5400979 5401003 5401013 5401027 5401043 5401049 5401063 5401079
5401093 5401117 5401133 5401141 5401147 5401153 5401169 5401171 5401211
5401213 5401237 5401241 5401243 5401247 5401253 5401267 5401307 5401313 5401327
5401373 5401387 5401397 5401433 5401439 5401447 5401469 5401483 5401493 5401507
5401553 5401559 5401603 5401633 5401661 5401687 5401727 5401763 5401769 5401787
```

```
5401793 5401807 5401817 5401819 5401829 5401841 5401853 5401861 5401867 5401897
5401901 5401951 5401969 5401973 5401993 5401999 5402003 5402011 5402021 5402051
5402057 5402063 5402069 5402077 5402083 5402087 5402093 5402113 5402123 5402129
5402147 5402179 5402183 5402203 5402239 5402297 5402303 5402317 5402347 5402351
5402357 5402359 5402377 5402393 5402429 5402431 5402437 5402471 5402491 5402519
5402521 5402533 5402543 5402561 5402581 5402597 5402599 5402623 5402633 5402647
5402681 5402687 5402701 5402737 5402741 5402759 5402819 5402843 5402849 5402867
5402879 5402909 5402933 5402977 5403007 5403017 5403061 5403089 5403107 5403109
5403133 5403149 5403157 5403169 5403247 5403257 5403259 5403283 5403301 5403317
5403323 5403329 5403361 5403379 5403389 5403401 5403427 5403451 5403479 5403481
5403487 5403491 5403493 5403511 5403523 5403527 5403529 5403539 5403553 5403571
5403577 5403583 5403589 5403611 5403631 5403647 5403649 5403653 5403659 5403661
5403667 5403683 5403701 5403709 5403719 5403743 5403817 5403823 5403829 5403833
5403851 5403859 5403863 5403877 5403901 5403917 5403949 5403973 5403989 5403997
5404031 5404033 5404067 5404073 5404093 5404099 5404123 5404127 5404129 5404141
5404177 5404187 5404219 5404229 5404253 5404279 5404291 5404297 5404313 5404319
5404327 5404339 5404349 5404363 5404367 5404381 5404393 5404403 5404433 5404439
5404481 5404501 5404537 5404559 5404561 5404573 5404603 5404673 5404687 5404699
5404709 5404717 5404741 5404753 5404769 5404771 5404807 5404811 5404829 5404831
5404837 5404853 5404879 5404897 5404909 5404921 5404961 5404979 5404981 5405003
5405009 5405011 5405021 5405033 5405041 5405077 5405083 5405093 5405111 5405117
5405119 5405123 5405137 5405173 5405189 5405221 5405233 5405249 5405251 5405261
5405287 5405327 5405333 5405341 5405357 5405381 5405447 5405459 5405467 5405471
5405479 5405503 5405509 5405527 5405539 5405579 5405591 5405599 5405641 5405669
5405681 5405717 5405767 5405773 5405783 5405789 5405791 5405797 5405819 5405821
5405837 5405839 5405843 5405857 5405863 5405867 5405887 5405921 5405923 5405969
5405971 5405999 5406007 5406019 5406041 5406043 5406067 5406083 5406091 5406103
5406109 5406131 5406133 5406139 5406197 5406199 5406211 5406217 5406257 5406281
5406283 5406293 5406343 5406361 5406377 5406397 5406407 5406421 5406439 5406463
5406481 5406487 5406503 5406529 5406539 5406553 5406563 5406589 5406593 5406619
5406623 5406641 5406647 5406649 5406671 5406677 5406707 5406719 5406733 5406749
5406757 5406761 5406809 5406823 5406827 5406851 5406859 5406881 5406889 5406911
5406917 5406931 5406941 5406953 5406971 5406977 5406983 5406991 5407033 5407043
5407049 5407063 5407091 5407097 5407099 5407109 5407111 5407117 5407133 5407141
5407151 5407177 5407187 5407189 5407211 5407243 5407247 5407249 5407261 5407271
5407319 5407327 5407387 5407331 5407333 5407349 5407387 5407399 5407403 5407421
5407429 5407433 5407447 5407463 5407469 5407487 5407511 5407529 5407541 5407561
5407583 5407631 5407639 5407651 5407669 5407687 5407693 5407739 5407741 5407747
5407781 5407789 5407793 5407813 5407823 5407861 5407879 5407889 5407903 5407931
5407937 5407939 5407943 5408003 5408017 5408021 5408047 5408063 5408083 5408089
5408093 5408107 5408111 5408113 5408119 5408129 5408131 5408191 5408201 5408213
5408231 5408233 5408309 5408311 5408323 5408341 5408357 5408383 5408387 5408393
5408423 5408437 5408467 5408489 5408509 5408531 5408537 5408561 5408569 5408573
5408581 5408591 5408609 5408617 5408639 5408647 5408653 5408659 5408671 5408701
5408717 5408719 5408773 5408779 5408791 5408801 5408813 5408827 5408831 5408833
5408857 5408869 5408881 5408899 5408903 5408917 5408947 5408959 5408981
5408987 5408989 5408999 5409017 5409031 5409049 5409059 5409101 5409119 5409133
5409137 5409149 5409161 5409169 5409181 5409199 5409203 5409241 5409259 5409263
5409269 5409293 5409317 5409323 5409337 5409353 5409361 5409403 5409409 5409413
5409421 5409427 5409461 5409479 5409487 5409493 5409517 5409527 5409539 5409557
5409571 5409583 5409589 5409611 5409629 5409647 5409671 5409697 5409707 5409713
5409721 5409751 5409773 5409793 5409799 5409847 5409913 5409931 5409941 5409953
5409967 5409977 5410007 5410021 5410033 5410057 5410061 5410099 5410109 5410121
5410127 5410201 5410253 5410259 5410277 5410283 5410289 5410291 5410309 5410331
5410351 5410357 5410367 5410373 5410381 5410387 5410393 5410409 5410417 5410439
5410441 5410453 5410463 5410507 5410511 5410513 5410519 5410549 5410567 5410571
5410591 5410597 5410619 5410663 5410667 5410703 5410723 5410739 5410747
5410751 5410753 5410759 5410787 5410793 5410799 5410813 5410831 5410837
5410871 5410897 5410901 5410903 5410919 5410927 5410931 5410939 5410943 5410961
5410963 5410973 5410997 5411011 5411017 5411027 5411033 5411039 5411047 5411051
5411053 5411059 5411069 5411071 5411093 5411101 5411149 5411167 5411171
5411177 5411183 5411227 5411239 5411281 5411291 5411299 5411317 5411323 5411327
5411347 5411369 5411377 5411381 5411477 5411503 5411513 5411521 5411537 5411543
5411551 5411557 5411569 5411573 5411617 5411621 5411629 5411641 5411699 5411717
5411743 5411753 5411761 5411767 5411771 5411801 5411807 5411821 5411837 5411839
5411863 5411867 5411869 5411881 5411897 5411927 5411971 5411977 5411993 5412019
5412037 5412047 5412049 5412091 5412133 5412217 5412227 5412229 5412257 5412263
5412269 5412271 5412289 5412331 5412343 5412349 5412353 5412371 5412377 5412391
5412419 5412437 5412467 5412479 5412481 5412493 5412497 5412529 5412551 5412553
5412571 5412581 5412607 5412623 5412629 5412689 5412703 5412721 5412761 5412773
5412787 5412791 5412793 5412811 5412839 5412859 5412881 5412887 5412899
5412917 5412923 5412931 5412947 5412949 5412961 5412973 5412983 5413013 5413033
5413091 5413097 5413103 5413117 5413123 5413151 5413171 5413181 5413183
5413193 5413217 5413223 5413229 5413241 5413249 5413273 5413277 5413301 5413333
5413337 5413357 5413391 5413439 5413453 5413469 5413477 5413489
5413493 5413511 5413519 5413543 5413549 5413553 5413591 5413609 5413621 5413631
5413637 5413643 5413687 5413693 5413697 5413699 5413741 5413777 5413813 5413817
5413847 5413853 5413873 5413909 5413937 5413957 5413987 5414011 5414033
5414051 5414053 5414063 5414077 5414081 5414083 5414089 5414111 5414113 5414147
5414153 5414159 5414161 5414179 5414197 5414207 5414209 5414231 5414237 5414239
5414261 5414263 5414273 5414281 5414287 5414291 5414293 5414303 5414323
5414327 5414341 5414359 5414399 5414413 5414441 5414473 5414477 5414537
5414557 5414567 5414569 5414593 5414599 5414609 5414657 5414681 5414693 5414699
5414719 5414723 5414741 5414749 5414767 5414771 5414777 5414803 5414807 5414819
5414833 5414853 5414881 5414963 5414999 5415013 5415037 5415043
5415071 5415077 5415101 5415103 5415121 5415131 5415139 5415149 5415161 5415167
5415187 5415191 5415203 5415227 5415233 5415259 5415271 5415337
5415341 5415343 5415353 5415391 5415451 5415457 5415467 5415479 5415499
5415517 5415521 5415523 5415533 5415541 5415563 5415577 5415581 5415583 5415601
```

```
5415617  5415659  5415679  5415689  5415691  5415719  5415733  5415743  5415749  5415769
5415791  5415829  5415841  5415853  5415859  5415871  5415881  5415901  5415913  5415919
5415929  5415937  5415941  5415947  5415967  5415973  5415983  5415997  5416009  5416027
5416031  5416039  5416043  5416057  5416087  5416157  5416193  5416199  5416207  5416211
5416231  5416241  5416253  5416267  5416277  5416291  5416297  5416303  5416309  5416357
5416363  5416379  5416399  5416403  5416427  5416459  5416471  5416483  5416487  5416493
5416507  5416513  5416517  5416531  5416549  5416573  5416589  5416603  5416639  5416651
5416679  5416681  5416699  5416709  5416717  5416721  5416751  5416781  5416783  5416811
5416841  5416871  5416889  5416907  5416927  5416949  5416987  5416991  5416993  5417021
5417023  5417039  5417053  5417057  5417063  5417099  5417123  5417129  5417131  5417143
5417179  5417189  5417201  5417221  5417231  5417233  5417249  5417273  5417297  5417323
5417329  5417359  5417369  5417381  5417383  5417387  5417389  5417393  5417411  5417417
5417431  5417437  5417459  5417479  5417497  5417507  5417521  5417551  5417567  5417579
5417597  5417681  5417683  5417689  5417701  5417707  5417723  5417743  5417759  5417761
5417771  5417773  5417791  5417801  5417807  5417827  5417833  5417851  5417887  5417897
5417933  5417953  5417977  5417989  5417999  5418013  5418037  5418047  5418079  5418143
5418163  5418167  5418181  5418221  5418229  5418233  5418247  5418251  5418253  5418277
5418289  5418293  5418299  5418313  5418341  5418353  5418367  5418377  5418407  5418419
5418431  5418433  5418443  5418451  5418493  5418503  5418551  5418557  5418599
5418617  5418643  5418659  5418697  5418701  5418703  5418719  5418739  5418757  5418757
5418797  5418799  5418851  5418859  5418877  5418883  5418901  5418913  5418947  5418949
5418977  5418991  5419013  5419019  5419021  5419033  5419049  5419061  5419097  5419157
5419181  5419189  5419207  5419213  5419291  5419307  5419369  5419373  5419387  5419391
5419399  5419439  5419441  5419457  5419493  5419499  5419507  5419511  5419517
5419553  5419567  5419573  5419597  5419613  5419619  5419627  5419663  5419691  5419703
5419709  5419721  5419741  5419747  5419759  5419783  5419801  5419811  5419829  5419837
5419853  5419859  5419867  5419877  5419891  5419907  5419933  5419943  5419949  5419961
5419969  5419987  5420003  5420017  5420029  5420039  5420053  5420057  5420083  5420089
5420101  5420117  5420123  5420131  5420137  5420143  5420147  5420171  5420179
5420213  5420227  5420231  5420267  5420273  5420291  5420293  5420309  5420321  5420347
5420413  5420417  5420431  5420473  5420483  5420509  5420531  5420539  5420543
5420549  5420551  5420573  5420579  5420587  5420621  5420627  5420633  5420669  5420677
5420683  5420711  5420717  5420729  5420731  5420747  5420783  5420803  5420819  5420827
5420867  5420873  5420879  5420917  5420923  5420927  5420929  5420951  5420963
5420969  5420983  5421007  5421019  5421043  5421047  5421071  5421089  5421103  5421107
5421161  5421191  5421193  5421197  5421209  5421263  5421287  5421323  5421329
5421337  5421341  5421343  5421371  5421407  5421413  5421421  5421433  5421443  5421457
5421467  5421511  5421527  5421539  5421541  5421547  5421557  5421571  5421587  5421599
5421607  5421641  5421649  5421653  5421659  5421667  5421673  5421679  5421709  5421719
5421733  5421737  5421739  5421743  5421749  5421751  5421763  5421803  5421833  5421839
5421887  5421893  5421907  5421919  5421947  5422003  5422013  5422019  5422037  5422051
5422063  5422073  5422097  5422129  5422139  5422169  5422177  5422187  5422189  5422211
5422223  5422237  5422247  5422267  5422283  5422289  5422297  5422321  5422327
5422357  5422369  5422379  5422381  5422393  5422399  5422421  5422441  5422451  5422453
5422463  5422493  5422499  5422517  5422553  5422567  5422577  5422583  5422603  5422607
5422621  5422661  5422663  5422673  5422699  5422709  5422777  5422789  5422793
5422817  5422841  5422853  5422873  5422877  5422883  5422891  5422903  5422927  5422933
5422939  5422943  5422969  5422973  5423003  5423021  5423023  5423039  5423057  5423071
5423123  5423161  5423167  5423177  5423179  5423191  5423207  5423237  5423267  5423279
5423291  5423311  5423317  5423321  5423329  5423359  5423371  5423399  5423401  5423441
5423479  5423489  5423503  5423507  5423519  5423533  5423549  5423557  5423563
5423567  5423573  5423597  5423611  5423617  5423623  5423651  5423657  5423669  5423687
5423689  5423701  5423741  5423771  5423773  5423779  5423807  5423813  5423819  5423839
5423843  5423857  5423863  5423881  5423897  5423909  5423921  5423947  5423959  5423963
5423981  5423983  5423989  5424011  5424017  5424019  5424031  5424053  5424079  5424103
5424109  5424121  5424127  5424157  5424161  5424203  5424217  5424233  5424257  5424271
5424281  5424301  5424313  5424319  5424359  5424371  5424403  5424409  5424449  5424451
5424457  5424469  5424487  5424509  5424511  5424553  5424563  5424569  5424577  5424589
5424593  5424611  5424641  5424647  5424667  5424691  5424697  5424719  5424733  5424737
5424739  5424743  5424763  5424799  5424847  5424869  5424871  5424877  5424883  5424889
5424911  5424929  5424949  5424959  5424961  5424967  5424983  5425003  5425019  5425067
5425081  5425087  5425099  5425111  5425153  5425187  5425201  5425207  5425219  5425223
5425237  5425247  5425249  5425271  5425283  5425297  5425327  5425331  5425333  5425339
5425369  5425373  5425379  5425391  5425411  5425457  5425471  5425477  5425513  5425517
5425559  5425561  5425573  5425591  5425597  5425603  5425613  5425661  5425709
5425711  5425729  5425733  5425741  5425747  5425751  5425753  5425757  5425759  5425787
5425801  5425831  5425841  5425853  5425877  5425879  5425909  5425943  5425951  5425967
5425991  5425993  5426051  5426093  5426101  5426117  5426123  5426131  5426173  5426177
5426189  5426207  5426221  5426231  5426237  5426243  5426249  5426251  5426257  5426261
5426327  5426339  5426353  5426357  5426359  5426363  5426371  5426387  5426411  5426437
5426453  5426461  5426467  5426483  5426489  5426503  5426507  5426513  5426527  5426539
5426549  5426563  5426569  5426579  5426611  5426627  5426633  5426651  5426657  5426677
5426683  5426713  5426717  5426737  5426749  5426807  5426809  5426819  5426843
5426849  5426887  5426899  5426903  5426909  5426917  5426921  5426947  5426959  5426963
5426969  5426983  5427017  5427061  5427113  5427127  5427133  5427167  5427203  5427209
5427223  5427229  5427251  5427259  5427281  5427283  5427329  5427337  5427341  5427349
5427371  5427377  5427397  5427413  5427421  5427431  5427439  5427473  5427481  5427497
5427551  5427557  5427577  5427593  5427629  5427637  5427649  5427661  5427671  5427679
5427757  5427767  5427781  5427809  5427827  5427833  5427857  5427869  5427887  5427893
5427899  5427907  5427911  5427923  5427943  5427973  5428013  5428037  5428039
5428051  5428099  5428103  5428109  5428127  5428141  5428153  5428187  5428211  5428229
5428231  5428237  5428261  5428271  5428279  5428289  5428301  5428303  5428331  5428343
5428349  5428387  5428393  5428399  5428403  5428421  5428427  5428429  5428463  5428469
5428477  5428487  5428513  5428519  5428543  5428561  5428571  5428607  5428609  5428613
5428657  5428663  5428671  5428673  5428679  5428691  5428693  5428697  5428721  5428723
5428727  5428739  5428747  5428777  5428783  5428807  5428811  5428823  5428837  5428847
5428853  5428867  5428881  5428901  5428909  5428921  5428957  5428961  5428981  5429059
5429063  5429071  5429087  5429093  5429107  5429129  5429131  5429141  5429143  5429147
5429153  5429191  5429209  5429213  5429243  5429251  5429297  5429321  5429323  5429339
```

```
5429353  5429401  5429423  5429453  5429471  5429483  5429527  5429533  5429539  5429551
5429561  5429569  5429597  5429609  5429621  5429629  5429651  5429657  5429701  5429707
5429719  5429729  5429731  5429741  5429759  5429773  5429779  5429789  5429803  5429807
5429833  5429849  5429869  5429887  5429891  5429899  5429923  5429981  5429993  5430011
5430013  5430023  5430043  5430049  5430059  5430071  5430077  5430079  5430097  5430107
5430121  5430127  5430137  5430167  5430211  5430233  5430241  5430247  5430287  5430289
5430307  5430311  5430317  5430329  5430331  5430349  5430353  5430367  5430377  5430389
5430391  5430401  5430407  5430421  5430431  5430443  5430449  5430493  5430541  5430547
5430559  5430583  5430589  5430613  5430619  5430629  5430661  5430663  5430671  5430679
5430683  5430721  5430727  5430731  5430757  5430767  5430791  5430793  5430811  5430833
5430839  5430851  5430883  5430889  5430899  5430907  5430913  5430923  5430937  5430949
5430959  5430961  5431021  5431037  5431043  5431057  5431067  5431121  5431123  5431141
5431159  5431183  5431187  5431219  5431241  5431249  5431277  5431291  5431297  5431303
5431331  5431337  5431339  5431369  5431399  5431441  5431469  5431507  5431523  5431529
5431537  5431561  5431567  5431577  5431583  5431597  5431609  5431627  5431661  5431691
5431697  5431733  5431763  5431771  5431799  5431801  5431807  5431813  5431817  5431819
5431831  5431843  5431847  5431861  5431873  5431939  5431949  5431957  5431969  5431973
5432017  5432033  5432039  5432047  5432051  5432059  5432087  5432107  5432143  5432153
5432171  5432179  5432183  5432191  5432201  5432221  5432227  5432239  5432261  5432311
5432321  5432327  5432351  5432363  5432369  5432407  5432411  5432417  5432419  5432431
5432443  5432489  5432507  5432519  5432521  5432549  5432551  5432569  5432579  5432591
5432597  5432621  5432629  5432633  5432641  5432681  5432699  5432717  5432729  5432731
5432743  5432783  5432797  5432813  5432839  5432857  5432881  5432893  5432923  5432929
5432957  5432971  5432981  5432983  5433017  5433049  5433061  5433073  5433079  5433089
5433101  5433119  5433137  5433151  5433157  5433167  5433223  5433227  5433229  5433269
5433271  5433287  5433289  5433293  5433301  5433343  5433347  5433391  5433403  5433419
5433427  5433431  5433473  5433479  5433511  5433517  5433521  5433553  5433569  5433577
5433599  5433619  5433629  5433647  5433667  5433671  5433683  5433691  5433707  5433713
5433731  5433737  5433739  5433763  5433787  5433797  5433803  5433809  5433823  5433833
5433839  5433887  5433889  5433893  5433907  5433917  5433929  5433937  5433973  5433979
5433983  5433997  5434001  5434007  5434033  5434043  5434061  5434087  5434097  5434109
5434111  5434123  5434129  5434147  5434151  5434157  5434159  5434189  5434213  5434229
5434243  5434321  5434333  5434337  5434343  5434349  5434357  5434409  5434421  5434447
5434453  5434459  5434501  5434529  5434531  5434537  5434573  5434603  5434633  5434643
5434651  5434661  5434669  5434691  5434697  5434717  5434771  5434823  5434829  5434841
5434859  5434867  5434873  5434907  5434937  5434981  5434993  5434999  5435009  5435011
5435029  5435047  5435057  5435063  5435077  5435081  5435117  5435123  5435147  5435173
5435231  5435233  5435237  5435251  5435299  5435303  5435333  5435357  5435363  5435377
5435389  5435399  5435401  5435431  5435467  5435477  5435513  5435519  5435533  5435543
5435569  5435603  5435609  5435621  5435629  5435641  5435663  5435681  5435701  5435711
5435723  5435737  5435741  5435743  5435747  5435791  5435803  5435827  5435851  5435863
5435891  5435897  5435909  5435953  5435959  5435987  5436001  5436007  5436047  5436059
5436089  5436113  5436127  5436131  5436139  5436163  5436187  5436217  5436229  5436241
5436247  5436269  5436271  5436281  5436283  5436287  5436289  5436293  5436307  5436323
5436331  5436341  5436391  5436397  5436407  5436419  5436461  5436467  5436469  5436479
5436493  5436499  5436511  5436547  5436551  5436569  5436577  5436623  5436637  5436643
5436647  5436653  5436667  5436709  5436721  5436731  5436733  5436737  5436757  5436773
5436779  5436797  5436799  5436803  5436829  5436839  5436841  5436853  5436863  5436881
5436883  5436917  5436919  5436943  5436961  5436971  5436979  5436989  5437001  5437013
5437031  5437037  5437043  5437063  5437079  5437139  5437151  5437153  5437163  5437169
5437171  5437189  5437193  5437199  5437207  5437241  5437253  5437273  5437291  5437301
5437303  5437309  5437339  5437343  5437351  5437373  5437387  5437391  5437403  5437459
5437463  5437469  5437507  5437511  5437547  5437567  5437573  5437577  5437583  5437589
5437609  5437613  5437639  5437643  5437699  5437711  5437717  5437721  5437753  5437771
5437777  5437793  5437799  5437801  5437813  5437849  5437889  5437897  5437903  5437907
5437919  5437937  5437951  5437973  5437979  5437999  5438023  5438029  5438033
5438071  5438093  5438099  5438101  5438107  5438129  5438131  5438137  5438141  5438159
5438177  5438179  5438183  5438219  5438227  5438231  5438233  5438263  5438269  5438273
5438309  5438311  5438347  5438353  5438357  5438359  5438369  5438401  5438429  5438437
5438479  5438483  5438497  5438501  5438549  5438551  5438569  5438581  5438599  5438611
5438627  5438639  5438651  5438663  5438669  5438707  5438717  5438723  5438753  5438767
5438777  5438779  5438791  5438801  5438809  5438821  5438831  5438903  5438969  5438987
5439013  5439041  5439047  5439053  5439067  5439139  5439163  5439173  5439191  5439197
5439221  5439223  5439227  5439233  5439253  5439257  5439277  5439281  5439299  5439331
5439341  5439349  5439359  5439361  5439383  5439389  5439391  5439409  5439419  5439433
5439461  5439463  5439469  5439509  5439521  5439527  5439547  5439563  5439583  5439607
5439613  5439619  5439641  5439647  5439653  5439667  5439689  5439697  5439727  5439743
5439767  5439781  5439793  5439803  5439809  5439817  5439821  5439823  5439829  5439853
5439869  5439883  5439899  5439913  5439943  5439953  5439979  5439991  5439997  5440007
5440003  5440013  5440027  5440049  5440067  5440087  5440103  5440111  5440117  5440181
5440189  5440217  5440223  5440229  5440241  5440247  5440273  5440301  5440307  5440319
5440339  5440343  5440361  5440363  5440381  5440387  5440399  5440411  5440417  5440427
5440447  5440453  5440499  5440507  5440511  5440537  5440545  5440571  5440573  5440607
5440619  5440621  5440637  5440639  5440657  5440703  5440709  5440723  5440751  5440753
5440759  5440781  5440793  5440819  5440829  5440847  5440849  5440871  5440873  5440889
5440891  5440931  5440937  5440957  5440991  5440993  5440997  5441047  5441053  5441081
5441083  5441123  5441129  5441131  5441141  5441167  5441197  5441209  5441221  5441279
5441291  5441311  5441321  5441327  5441329  5441341  5441407  5441413  5441419  5441433
5441453  5441477  5441483  5441489  5441507  5441533  5441551  5441573  5441591  5441617
5441621  5441633  5441641  5441651  5441659  5441663  5441671  5441713  5441743  5441759
5441773  5441783  5441789  5441827  5441831  5441837  5441851  5441857  5441861  5441867
5441873  5441899  5441903  5441959  5441963  5441977  5442011  5442049  5442067  5442089
5442097  5442109  5442121  5442149  5442179  5442187  5442197  5442233  5442247
5442253  5442257  5442263  5442277  5442287  5442289  5442301  5442317  5442319  5442347
5442361  5442383  5442427  5442449  5442457  5442461  5442491  5442509  5442511  5442527
5442529  5442539  5442571  5442581  5442629  5442637  5442641  5442653  5442659  5442667
5442673  5442727  5442751  5442781  5442817  5442859  5442893  5442901  5442917  5442937
5442947  5442971  5442979  5442989  5443051  5443103  5443121  5443127  5443159  5443169
5443171  5443183  5443187  5443219  5443231  5443279  5443289  5443297  5443301  5443303
```

```
5443363 5443369 5443393 5443397 5443409 5443423 5443429 5443439 5443441 5443453
5443469 5443511 5443531 5443541 5443547 5443567 5443583 5443609 5443639 5443643
5443649 5443651 5443667 5443673 5443727 5443729 5443733 5443741 5443759 5443771
5443831 5443849 5443873 5443877 5443891 5443901 5443903 5443913 5443943 5443973
5443981 5443987 5443993 5444059 5444111 5444113 5444129 5444149 5444161 5444167
5444177 5444191 5444207 5444221 5444237 5444249 5444287 5444293 5444297 5444321
5444323 5444347 5444357 5444371 5444381 5444401 5444407 5444419 5444429 5444447
5444449 5444473 5444479 5444497 5444501 5444519 5444533 5444557 5444567 5444581
5444591 5444597 5444599 5444611 5444627 5444633 5444639 5444651 5444653 5444671
5444687 5444693 5444729 5444731 5444737 5444741 5444771 5444797 5444801 5444807
5444827 5444843 5444861 5444863 5444867 5444891 5444893 5444897 5444911 5444927
5444941 5444969 5445007 5445019 5445029 5445053 5445067 5445071 5445073 5445079
5445103 5445107 5445113 5445161 5445163 5445173 5445197 5445199 5445217 5445221
5445239 5445257 5445263 5445269 5445311 5445329 5445331 5445353 5445371 5445383
5445403 5445413 5445421 5445431 5445439 5445449 5445463 5445469 5445481 5445493
5445527 5445529 5445541 5445577 5445589 5445607 5445631 5445659 5445679 5445683
5445689 5445709 5445719 5445721 5445757 5445773 5445787 5445833 5445857 5445889
5445893 5445911 5445929 5445931 5445953 5445959 5446003 5446043 5446057 5446073
5446081 5446127 5446139 5446163 5446183 5446201 5446237 5446241 5446249 5446253
5446271 5446277 5446279 5446283 5446291 5446327 5446351 5446361 5446373 5446379
5446387 5446391 5446417 5446429 5446451 5446489 5446499 5446517 5446523 5446531
5446541 5446591 5446619 5446633 5446667 5446687 5446697 5446717 5446723 5446739
5446741 5446759 5446789 5446799 5446811 5446823 5446871 5446879 5446897 5446921
5446927 5446937 5446943 5446963 5446967 5446999 5447017 5447051 5447063 5447069
5447077 5447081 5447083 5447087 5447119 5447131 5447161 5447171 5447173 5447179
5447201 5447203 5447209 5447231 5447249 5447269 5447279 5447303 5447311 5447317
5447339 5447341 5447353 5447401 5447417 5447443 5447459 5447461 5447489 5447501
5447503 5447513 5447521 5447543 5447579 5447581 5447587 5447593 5447639 5447653
5447657 5447669 5447671 5447719 5447753 5447777 5447789 5447791 5447797 5447801
5447807 5447821 5447831 5447857 5447861 5447867 5447873 5447879 5447899 5447903
5447921 5447933 5447951 5447963 5447977 5447983 5447989 5448011 5448013 5448049
5448059 5448061 5448067 5448071 5448073 5448089 5448101 5448103 5448127 5448133
5448137 5448167 5448169 5448221 5448253 5448277 5448283 5448293 5448319 5448323
5448341 5448379 5448397 5448403 5448407 5448413 5448437 5448451 5448461 5448463
5448479 5448481 5448503 5448511 5448523 5448577 5448589 5448617 5448629 5448671
5448673 5448679 5448689 5448713 5448719 5448733 5448739 5448743 5448749 5448767
5448787 5448791 5448797 5448809 5448853 5448869 5448881 5448887 5448889 5448899
5448923 5448929 5448979 5449001 5449007 5449021 5449049 5449099 5449111 5449117
5449123 5449151 5449153 5449159 5449193 5449201 5449247 5449259 5449289 5449291
5449319 5449349 5449357 5449369 5449373 5449391 5449393 5449399 5449429 5449441
5449453 5449487 5449489 5449511 5449529 5449541 5449553 5449567 5449601 5449607
5449621 5449667 5449687 5449721 5449727 5449739 5449753 5449757 5449783 5449793
5449811 5449823 5449837 5449853 5449861 5449867 5449893 5449901 5449907 5449909
5449931 5449943 5449957 5449987 5450021 5450023 5450033 5450041 5450069 5450087
5450099 5450101 5450111 5450113 5450117 5450119 5450129 5450143 5450147 5450153
5450161 5450189 5450197 5450213 5450219 5450227 5450239 5450257 5450267
5450273 5450281 5450299 5450303 5450309 5450311 5450323 5450339 5450351 5450363
5450369 5450377 5450381 5450437 5450441 5450477 5450483 5450491 5450503 5450509
5450519 5450531 5450537 5450539 5450593 5450611 5450617 5450629 5450633 5450671
5450677 5450681 5450689 5450707 5450717 5450719 5450737 5450749 5450773 5450801
5450813 5450821 5450843 5450903 5450917 5450923 5450933 5450941 5450957 5450959
5450969 5450971 5450987 5450989 5451001 5451029 5451049 5451059 5451077 5451091
5451097 5451113 5451137 5451139 5451151 5451241 5451263 5451269 5451283 5451287
5451289 5451293 5451301 5451307 5451311 5451317 5451323 5451343 5451349 5451361
5451371 5451431 5451473 5451493 5451503 5451547 5451557 5451559 5451587 5451599
5451601 5451619 5451643 5451673 5451683 5451697 5451701 5451703 5451709 5451731
5451737 5451751 5451763 5451769 5451779 5451791 5451793 5451799 5451833 5451847
5451871 5451889 5451931 5451937 5451949 5451961 5452009 5452033 5452037
5452039 5452043 5452067 5452093 5452103 5452123 5452159 5452169 5452171 5452193
5452199 5452201 5452211 5452217 5452231 5452267 5452327 5452331 5452339 5452409
5452417 5452439 5452483 5452523 5452543 5452547 5452571 5452591 5452619 5452649
5452651 5452663 5452691 5452703 5452709 5452723 5452747 5452781 5452789 5452793
5452813 5452823 5452849 5452861 5452879 5452883 5452891 5452897 5452907 5452933
5452961 5453003 5453009 5453029 5453033 5453053 5453059 5453069 5453083 5453087
5453089 5453099 5453101 5453111 5453113 5453143 5453167 5453191 5453219 5453233
5453237 5453249 5453257 5453281 5453309 5453317 5453341 5453353 5453359 5453401
5453407 5453411 5453417 5453423 5453453 5453471 5453501 5453509 5453519 5453521
5453531 5453573 5453579 5453593 5453603 5453629 5453641 5453659 5453687 5453699
5453713 5453729 5453731 5453771 5453801 5453803 5453809 5453813 5453839 5453843
5453857 5453873 5453879 5453881 5453891 5453939 5453941 5453947 5453971
5453977 5453983 5453989 5453999 5454011 5454017 5454041 5454061 5454079 5454089
5454103 5454131 5454167 5454181 5454217 5454223 5454227 5454247 5454257 5454299
5454307 5454313 5454329 5454343 5454347 5454377 5454401 5454413 5454431 5454449
5454451 5454457 5454461 5454479 5454497 5454529 5454541 5454557 5454563 5454613
5454641 5454643 5454649 5454689 5454719 5454731 5454751 5454793 5454809 5454811
5454817 5454829 5454877 5454893 5454913 5454923 5454931 5454949 5454973 5454997
5455049 5455057 5455063 5455067 5455097 5455129 5455133 5455139 5455141 5455157
5455193 5455213 5455259 5455267 5455309 5455319 5455321 5455327 5455357 5455361
5455369 5455379 5455397 5455399 5455403 5455423 5455441 5455459 5455469 5455481
5455493 5455511 5455523 5455537 5455543 5455557 5455561 5455573 5455579
5455591 5455607 5455621 5455627 5455631 5455643 5455727 5455729 5455733 5455763
5455771 5455787 5455837 5455841 5455847 5455859 5455867 5455897 5455913 5455921
5455949 5455951 5456039 5456051 5456053 5456063 5456071 5456081 5456107
5456111 5456117 5456149 5456159 5456179 5456197 5456203 5456207 5456237 5456273
5456317 5456327 5456329 5456333 5456351 5456357 5456369 5456377 5456387 5456393
5456411 5456417 5456419 5456447 5456449 5456453 5456467 5456471 5456513 5456533
5456537 5456551 5456557 5456569 5456579 5456587 5456597 5456603 5456663 5456699
5456701 5456707 5456729 5456753 5456761 5456771 5456777 5456783 5456791
5456807 5456821 5456839 5456861 5456863 5456873 5456879 5456897 5456903 5456917
```

```
5456921 5456951 5456953 5456981 5456993 5457007 5457013 5457071 5457073 5457079
5457091 5457103 5457113 5457139 5457143 5457157 5457169 5457181 5457229 5457239
5457253 5457293 5457337 5457341 5457343 5457359 5457377 5457383 5457421 5457433
5457449 5457451 5457467 5457497 5457523 5457533 5457547 5457577 5457583 5457587
5457607 5457623 5457637 5457653 5457659 5457667 5457671 5457679 5457691 5457701
5457703 5457709 5457719 5457743 5457773 5457811 5457817 5457821 5457839 5457857
5457869 5457871 5457917 5457919 5457931 5457967 5457971 5458001 5458009 5458027
5458049 5458051 5458067 5458069 5458081 5458091 5458121 5458147 5458151 5458169
5458171 5458181 5458183 5458213 5458223 5458231 5458237 5458253 5458259 5458261
5458303 5458319 5458331 5458357 5458363 5458367 5458373 5458379 5458399 5458421
5458441 5458451 5458457 5458469 5458471 5458477 5458483 5458487 5458489 5458501
5458507 5458543 5458553 5458559 5458571 5458577 5458597 5458601 5458631 5458633
5458667 5458679 5458723 5458771 5458793 5458799 5458811 5458823 5458847 5458861
5458877 5458879 5458907 5458919 5458933 5458939 5458967 5458969 5458991 5459009
5459011 5459021 5459029 5459071 5459081 5459087 5459101 5459117 5459161 5459173
5459177 5459189 5459197 5459281 5459297 5459347 5459357 5459401 5459413 5459441
5459449 5459459 5459497 5459507 5459513 5459521 5459537 5459539 5459551 5459563
5459599 5459621 5459647 5459651 5459653 5459677 5459681 5459711 5459719 5459723
5459747 5459749 5459759 5459761 5459789 5459791 5459819 5459827 5459863 5459867
5459869 5459879 5459887 5459891 5459903 5459911 5459921 5459939 5459953 5459957
5459977 5459981 5459983 5460017 5460023 5460029 5460041 5460061 5460071 5460073
5460079 5460083 5460101 5460107 5460109 5460139 5460157 5460167 5460173 5460197
5460229 5460233 5460251 5460263 5460331 5460341 5460359 5460419 5460437 5460443
5460449 5460457 5460461 5460491 5460493 5460523 5460529 5460541 5460547 5460551
5460577 5460583 5460599 5460607 5460629 5460647 5460661 5460691 5460703 5460709
5460713 5460727 5460737 5460769 5460779 5460797 5460799 5460811 5460817 5460839
5460841 5460853 5460869 5460877 5460899 5460901 5460907 5460919 5460943 5460971
5460979 5461021 5461031 5461069 5461073 5461081 5461087 5461109 5461117 5461121
5461123 5461139 5461153 5461213 5461229 5461243 5461271 5461273 5461277 5461283
5461289 5461331 5461333 5461343 5461361 5461397 5461399 5461409 5461411 5461441
5461451 5461457 5461481 5461499 5461523 5461543 5461567 5461613 5461619 5461627
5461637 5461669 5461699 5461711 5461723 5461739 5461763 5461789 5461801 5461849
5461853 5461861 5461871 5461891 5461909 5461919 5461931 5461937 5461957 5461991
5461993 5461997 5461999 5462003 5462033 5462057 5462059 5462071 5462087 5462089
5462111 5462131 5462137 5462141 5462153 5462159 5462173 5462189 5462203 5462209
5462213 5462239 5462257 5462267 5462269 5462299 5462311 5462341 5462357 5462363
5462377 5462437 5462441 5462447 5462449 5462453 5462461 5462467 5462473 5462497
5462537 5462539 5462549 5462573 5462581 5462599 5462617 5462623 5462629 5462641
5462647 5462659 5462683 5462687 5462689 5462719 5462767 5462777 5462783 5462803
5462819 5462827 5462837 5462843 5462867 5462879 5462911 5462917 5462923 5462927
5462957 5462959 5462981 5462993 5462999 5463011 5463019 5463023 5463041 5463043
5463053 5463061 5463077 5463079 5463091 5463119 5463131 5463163 5463169 5463179
5463181 5463217 5463257 5463287 5463319 5463329 5463361 5463377 5463389
5463391 5463439 5463461 5463463 5463467 5463473 5463481 5463487 5463499 5463503
5463509 5463547 5463553 5463569 5463589 5463593 5463599 5463671 5463677 5463683
5463713 5463721 5463743 5463751 5463767 5463791 5463793 5463833 5463839 5463853
5463869 5463893 5463961 5464003 5464007 5464009 5464013 5464031 5464033 5464037
5464057 5464063 5464127 5464163 5464171 5464177 5464181 5464183 5464187 5464211
5464223 5464243 5464273 5464289 5464307 5464313 5464321 5464331 5464369 5464399
5464411 5464441 5464463 5464469 5464477 5464489 5464513 5464523 5464541 5464551
5464553 5464559 5464573 5464577 5464579 5464601 5464619 5464621 5464647 5464651
5464661 5464663 5464681 5464687 5464703 5464717 5464729 5464747 5464759 5464787
5464813 5464817 5464829 5464861 5464891 5464909 5464967 5464981 5465003
5465039 5465059 5465069 5465071 5465081 5465101 5465107 5465147 5465149 5465153
5465183 5465197 5465219 5465221 5465231 5465249 5465261 5465267 5465281 5465297
5465303 5465309 5465323 5465333 5465351 5465353 5465357 5465359 5465377 5465387
5465389 5465419 5465431 5465443 5465449 5465461 5465477 5465491 5465497 5465503
5465527 5465531 5465549 5465561 5465563 5465573 5465581 5465591 5465599 5465611
5465617 5465623 5465627 5465671 5465693 5465741 5465777 5465791 5465813 5465821
5465849 5465851 5465861 5465903 5465909 5465963 5465969 5465983 5465987 5466017
5466029 5466059 5466067 5466073 5466103 5466127 5466193 5466211 5466217 5466233
5466257 5466259 5466277 5466283 5466287 5466301 5466311 5466337 5466347 5466359
5466379 5466397 5466403 5466427 5466431 5466449 5466497 5466511 5466521 5466533
5466541 5466569 5466577 5466589 5466599 5466607 5466613 5466619 5466631 5466667
5466679 5466683 5466689 5466691 5466701 5466733 5466767 5466781 5466829 5466859
5466869 5466907 5466941 5466949 5466953 5466971 5466983 5466997 5467019 5467027
5467057 5467093 5467097 5467141 5467153 5467159 5467207 5467219 5467229 5467243
5467271 5467303 5467313 5467327 5467337 5467339 5467349 5467351 5467367 5467373
5467381 5467403 5467411 5467487 5467499 5467513 5467529 5467541 5467577 5467597
5467621 5467663 5467667 5467681 5467697 5467711 5467717 5467729 5467733
5467739 5467741 5467753 5467769 5467799 5467817 5467831 5467841 5467849 5467867
5467871 5467879 5467901 5467907 5467927 5467939 5467993 5468003 5468017 5468041
5468051 5468083 5468093 5468107 5468117 5468131 5468137 5468147 5468149 5468159
5468171 5468201 5468209 5468231 5468233 5468251 5468261 5468263 5468299 5468311
5468317 5468363 5468377 5468383 5468387 5468413 5468431 5468447 5468483 5468513
5468527 5468557 5468581 5468587 5468597 5468609 5468627 5468669 5468689 5468693
5468707 5468717 5468737 5468753 5468759 5468761 5468773 5468797 5468807 5468809
5468821 5468839 5468851 5468891 5468893 5468899 5468921 5468923 5468929 5468971
5468977 5468993 5468999 5469043 5469047 5469071 5469073 5469089 5469109 5469133
5469137 5469161 5469181 5469203 5469259 5469263 5469271 5469281 5469287 5469301
5469319 5469323 5469337 5469341 5469353 5469389 5469413 5469421 5469439 5469463
5469467 5469481 5469493 5469517 5469551 5469553 5469559 5469571 5469613 5469619
5469647 5469689 5469697 5469707 5469727 5469743 5469749 5469773 5469781 5469787
5469803 5469823 5469829 5469839 5469887 5469889 5469899 5469917 5469923 5469941
5469943 5469953 5469973 5469983 5470013 5470063 5470079 5470093 5470111 5470151
5470163 5470169 5470177 5470187 5470219 5470247 5470249 5470259 5470307 5470313
5470321 5470351 5470369 5470373 5470391 5470393 5470403 5470411 5470447 5470453
5470457 5470489 5470511 5470519 5470529 5470567 5470609 5470627 5470631 5470643
5470679 5470681 5470721 5470723 5470733 5470771 5470781 5470793 5470799 5470811
```

```
5470831  5470853  5470877  5470909  5470943  5470951  5470961  5470963  5470967  5470981
5471003  5471009  5471041  5471071  5471077  5471083  5471101  5471117  5471177
5471197  5471201  5471203  5471231  5471233  5471237  5471269  5471299  5471321  5471329
5471339  5471359  5471371  5471377  5471387  5471393  5471413  5471419  5471437  5471503
5471507  5471509  5471527  5471533  5471551  5471567  5471579  5471591  5471629  5471647
5471651  5471657  5471663  5471681  5471699  5471701  5471731  5471759  5471771  5471783
5471789  5471803  5471827  5471831  5471833  5471849  5471857  5471887  5471897
5471911  5471927  5471929  5471933  5471969  5471989  5471993  5472017  5472023  5472031
5472037  5472053  5472109  5472143  5472157  5472161  5472167  5472169  5472193
5472199  5472221  5472227  5472239  5472277  5472293  5472307  5472319  5472331  5472347
5472349  5472373  5472403  5472421  5472443  5472451  5472457  5472469  5472473  5472497
5472499  5472527  5472529  5472541  5472547  5472583  5472587  5472611  5472613  5472629
5472631  5472637  5472641  5472659  5472671  5472673  5472679  5472683  5472697  5472763
5472769  5472799  5472809  5472823  5472839  5472853  5472881  5472913  5472917  5472941
5472949  5472953  5472959  5472977  5472983  5472989  5472991  5473001  5473033  5473043
5473067  5473073  5473087  5473109  5473147  5473183  5473187  5473189  5473207  5473219
5473229  5473261  5473271  5473301  5473309  5473313  5473327  5473331  5473361  5473399
5473409  5473417  5473423  5473441  5473483  5473511  5473519  5473529  5473537  5473543
5473549  5473571  5473597  5473627  5473631  5473661  5473679  5473687  5473693  5473697
5473709  5473723  5473733  5473739  5473757  5473781  5473789  5473801  5473841  5473849
5473861  5473877  5473879  5473883  5473889  5473907  5473921  5473969  5473987  5473991
5473997  5474003  5474041  5474047  5474083  5474087  5474107  5474129  5474143  5474167
5474173  5474179  5474191  5474213  5474297  5474303  5474309  5474311  5474333  5474341
5474363  5474377  5474387  5474401  5474411  5474429  5474449  5474453  5474461  5474467
5474473  5474477  5474519  5474531  5474543  5474549  5474563  5474587  5474611  5474617
5474627  5474647  5474671  5474687  5474699  5474719  5474767  5474789  5474809  5474813
5474839  5474849  5474857  5474863  5474893  5474921  5474947  5474951  5474977  5474981
5474999  5475011  5475031  5475047  5475089  5475091  5475101  5475103  5475121  5475137
5475143  5475157  5475193  5475199  5475203  5475227  5475247  5475289  5475293  5475329
5475331  5475347  5475361  5475367  5475389  5475409  5475433  5475443  5475473  5475497
5475517  5475521  5475523  5475529  5475539  5475557  5475563  5475571  5475637  5475643
5475653  5475671  5475677  5475697  5475703  5475707  5475719  5475721  5475737  5475739
5475773  5475791  5475797  5475823  5475839  5475851  5475881  5475937  5475961  5475973
5475979  5475991  5475997  5476019  5476039  5476061  5476069  5476073  5476087  5476103
5476109  5476117  5476127  5476169  5476213  5476217  5476223  5476249  5476267  5476279
5476283  5476309  5476327  5476337  5476343  5476349  5476381  5476391  5476421  5476433
5476441  5476451  5476459  5476469  5476477  5476483  5476489  5476511  5476531  5476547
5476577  5476591  5476619  5476633  5476663  5476673  5476687  5476697  5476699  5476721
5476747  5476753  5476787  5476799  5476811  5476813  5476817  5476831  5476837  5476843
5476847  5476859  5476901  5476909  5476931  5476937  5476943  5476951  5476973  5477033
5477041  5477047  5477081  5477083  5477089  5477093  5477107  5477119  5477137  5477159
5477161  5477189  5477209  5477233  5477237  5477267  5477279  5477287  5477293  5477309
5477323  5477341  5477347  5477363  5477371  5477387  5477399  5477401  5477413  5477429
5477447  5477467  5477471  5477489  5477513  5477539  5477543  5477581  5477599  5477627
5477629  5477663  5477677  5477729  5477741  5477743  5477777  5477779  5477783  5477789
5477809  5477819  5477821  5477837  5477867  5477897  5477929  5477947  5477959  5477963
5477971  5478001  5478007  5478019  5478037  5478043  5478047  5478073  5478107  5478113
5478167  5478169  5478181  5478197  5478211  5478223  5478241  5478299  5478311  5478337
5478371  5478383  5478397  5478401  5478433  5478457  5478497  5478503  5478509
5478527  5478541  5478547  5478559  5478569  5478589  5478611  5478617  5478637  5478643
5478677  5478703  5478713  5478719  5478731  5478773  5478779  5478787  5478817  5478827
5478839  5478841  5478877  5478881  5478911  5478937  5478989  5479007  5479013  5479027
5479063  5479073  5479093  5479123  5479127  5479139  5479169  5479171  5479211  5479223
5479247  5479249  5479297  5479301  5479319  5479379  5479387  5479403  5479421  5479427
5479469  5479489  5479493  5479501  5479517  5479531  5479541  5479547  5479549  5479583
5479597  5479603  5479631  5479633  5479667  5479673  5479687  5479697  5479711  5479739
5479751  5479759  5479783  5479787  5479801  5479807  5479823  5479841  5479853  5479867
5479889  5479919  5479921  5479931  5479939  5479951  5479987  5480009  5480017  5480021
5480023  5480029  5480053  5480063  5480077  5480081  5480089  5480117  5480119  5480129
5480143  5480173  5480201  5480207  5480213  5480231  5480249  5480269  5480287
5480291  5480297  5480311  5480327  5480381  5480383  5480389  5480401  5480413  5480437
5480441  5480471  5480473  5480483  5480491  5480539  5480543  5480557  5480567  5480591
5480599  5480609  5480611  5480617  5480627  5480633  5480639  5480653  5480669  5480689
5480711  5480723  5480731  5480743  5480771  5480777  5480809  5480821  5480837
5480841  5480857  5480869  5480889  5480927  5480929  5480933  5480947
5480957  5480963  5480977  5480983  5480989  5481011  5481013  5481019  5481023  5481037
5481053  5481067  5481083  5481097  5481103  5481109  5481121  5481137  5481173  5481209
5481211  5481227  5481241  5481251  5481299  5481317  5481323  5481349  5481353  5481397
5481401  5481407  5481409  5481431  5481461  5481473  5481491  5481499  5481523  5481529
5481533  5481583  5481607  5481611  5481617  5481629  5481647  5481649  5481653  5481677
5481689  5481713  5481727  5481733  5481757  5481767  5481799  5481811  5481821  5481829
5481857  5481869  5481877  5481893  5481907  5481913  5481961  5481967  5481989  5482019
5482039  5482049  5482063  5482079  5482093  5482097  5482111  5482121  5482129  5482153
5482163  5482181  5482193  5482207  5482223  5482237  5482249  5482261  5482291  5482297
5482331  5482333  5482361  5482369  5482391  5482403  5482423  5482427  5482429  5482447
5482453  5482459  5482471  5482493  5482523  5482531  5482541  5482553  5482571  5482627
5482637  5482657  5482663  5482669  5482699  5482703  5482733  5482747  5482781  5482783
5482817  5482843  5482847  5482853  5482859  5482907  5482913  5482927  5482969
5482979  5483017  5483021  5483041  5483069  5483081  5483087  5483089  5483147  5483173
5483183  5483209  5483227  5483243  5483251  5483273  5483281  5483293  5483297  5483321
5483339  5483341  5483371  5483389  5483393  5483399  5483417  5483431  5483441  5483449
5483461  5483477  5483501  5483509  5483521  5483531  5483567  5483579  5483587  5483603
5483623  5483629  5483633  5483651  5483657  5483663  5483669  5483671  5483693  5483711
5483713  5483719  5483759  5483771  5483773  5483831  5483851  5483861  5483879  5483909
5483917  5483939  5483957  5483971  5483977  5483983  5483999  5484019  5484041
5484043  5484049  5484067  5484079  5484131  5484133  5484137  5484139  5484163  5484187
5484191  5484203  5484233  5484287  5484299  5484301  5484307  5484329  5484337  5484343
5484371  5484379  5484389  5484397  5484403  5484431  5484433  5484439  5484469  5484487
5484503  5484533  5484569  5484593  5484623  5484631  5484643  5484653  5484697  5484707
```

```
5484719 5484751 5484757 5484763 5484767 5484797 5484847 5484851 5484859 5484887
5484893 5484911 5484929 5484949 5484953 5484979 5485057 5485061 5485087 5485093
5485111 5485121 5485153 5485157 5485163 5485177 5485187 5485189 5485211 5485217
5485231 5485241 5485261 5485273 5485297 5485301 5485307 5485313 5485331 5485351
5485369 5485393 5485397 5485399 5485409 5485421 5485427 5485429 5485451 5485453
5485457 5485483 5485489 5485499 5485537 5485541 5485559 5485561 5485589 5485591
5485603 5485607 5485619 5485621 5485633 5485637 5485651 5485691 5485703 5485741
5485757 5485763 5485769 5485787 5485801 5485807 5485817 5485819 5485847 5485867
5485873 5485903 5485919 5485939 5485969 5485993 5485999 5486009 5486011 5486021
5486057 5486059 5486077 5486111 5486119 5486137 5486141 5486147 5486203 5486207
5486209 5486267 5486293 5486303 5486309 5486311 5486339 5486347 5486353 5486381
5486387 5486389 5486407 5486419 5486447 5486449 5486477 5486501 5486509 5486519
5486531 5486557 5486561 5486599 5486603 5486617 5486641 5486681 5486683 5486711
5486717 5486731 5486737 5486759 5486773 5486777 5486807 5486813 5486821 5486837
5486849 5486851 5486861 5486879 5486891 5486909 5486911 5486927 5486947 5486977
5486983 5487019 5487023 5487043 5487049 5487077 5487091 5487161 5487173 5487221
5487247 5487253 5487259 5487263 5487301 5487323 5487343 5487347 5487353 5487373
5487397 5487401 5487407 5487451 5487457 5487463 5487483 5487497 5487509 5487511
5487539 5487551 5487611 5487631 5487659 5487667 5487683 5487689 5487697 5487701
5487707 5487761 5487763 5487773 5487791 5487799 5487841 5487851 5487857 5487883
5487901 5487913 5487917 5487919 5487929 5487947 5487959 5487967 5488001 5488027
5488031 5488039 5488057 5488061 5488073 5488081 5488103 5488111 5488139 5488141
5488159 5488177 5488181 5488193 5488199 5488243 5488267 5488289 5488303 5488313
5488339 5488349 5488361 5488381 5488387 5488393 5488403 5488409 5488423 5488429
5488447 5488459 5488489 5488529 5488531 5488537 5488579 5488589 5488591 5488601
5488607 5488657 5488661 5488667 5488669 5488709 5488729 5488741 5488753 5488757
5488759 5488783 5488787 5488823 5488831 5488837 5488843 5488849 5488867 5488871
5488921 5488937 5488949 5488961 5488969 5488979 5488981 5488991 5488997 5489009
5489021 5489041 5489061 5489137 5489161 5489167 5489171 5489173 5489221 5489227
5489261 5489269 5489273 5489279 5489287 5489299 5489311 5489333 5489339 5489383
5489389 5489399 5489411 5489413 5489443 5489501 5489513 5489551 5489557 5489569
5489593 5489597 5489629 5489639 5489683 5489699 5489711 5489717 5489719 5489723
5489747 5489749 5489807 5489831 5489837 5489843 5489867 5489873 5489881 5489921
5489927 5489959 5489971 5489977 5489983 5489987 5489989 5489999 5490011 5490013
5490041 5490053 5490059 5490073 5490101 5490137 5490151 5490161 5490227 5490229
5490241 5490293 5490299 5490301 5490313 5490343 5490377 5490383 5490389 5490403
5490391 5490409 5490413 5490451 5490517 5490539 5490553 5490571 5490593 5490607
5490613 5490631 5490647 5490649 5490673 5490697 5490701 5490739 5490743 5490769
5490781 5490787 5490803 5490809 5490811 5490833 5490839 5490857 5490871 5490883
5490913 5490923 5490931 5490941 5490967 5490973 5491001 5491039 5491081 5491091
5491117 5491139 5491141 5491163 5491217 5491219 5491223 5491231 5491259 5491261
5491271 5491301 5491303 5491313 5491349 5491351 5491373 5491393 5491439 5491477
5491481 5491483 5491501 5491511 5491523 5491531 5491547 5491553 5491559 5491579
5491597 5491609 5491613 5491631 5491639 5491657 5491709 5491723 5491727 5491729
5491753 5491763 5491771 5491777 5491781 5491793 5491813 5491819 5491841 5491847
5491859 5491883 5491907 5491939 5491943 5491951 5491957 5491961 5491973 5491979
5491999 5492033 5492051 5492059 5492087 5492093 5492099 5492111 5492117 5492141
5492143 5492153 5492161 5492167 5492171 5492189 5492209 5492219 5492287 5492293
5492297 5492299 5492351 5492371 5492381 5492393 5492407 5492413 5492471 5492477
5492491 5492507 5492527 5492551 5492563 5492567 5492573 5492579 5492609 5492621
5492639 5492657 5492677 5492701 5492731 5492737 5492771 5492779 5492783 5492789
5492801 5492821 5492827 5492833 5492869 5492891 5492897 5492917 5492939 5492953
5493001 5493011 5493041 5493049 5493053 5493073 5493097 5493101 5493119 5493127
5493133 5493157 5493167 5493179 5493181 5493197 5493203 5493211 5493217 5493239
5493253 5493277 5493283 5493287 5493307 5493317 5493349 5493361 5493377 5493391
5493403 5493409 5493421 5493443 5493473 5493493 5493497 5493511 5493529 5493539
5493559 5493583 5493611 5493647 5493661 5493707 5493743 5493749 5493751 5493773
5493781 5493791 5493811 5493823 5493827 5493857 5493863 5493883 5493899 5493911
5493923 5493931 5493937 5493949 5493967 5493977 5493989 5493991 5493997 5494003
5494007 5494031 5494057 5494061 5494063 5494091 5494103 5494109 5494121 5494127
5494157 5494163 5494169 5494183 5494187 5494189 5494207 5494219 5494243 5494261
5494267 5494273 5494277 5494283 5494289 5494297 5494301 5494339 5494361 5494367
5494381 5494387 5494429 5494459 5494481 5494483 5494487 5494507 5494513 5494547
5494549 5494571 5494579 5494597 5494607 5494613 5494633 5494639 5494649 5494661
5494679 5494681 5494693 5494711 5494747 5494777 5494787 5494789 5494793 5494807
5494813 5494823 5494829 5494837 5494883 5494897 5494913 5494969 5494991 5494997
5495027 5495033 5495051 5495053 5495069 5495081 5495111 5495117 5495141 5495159
5495167 5495173 5495177 5495179 5495227 5495249 5495263 5495279 5495291 5495299
5495323 5495333 5495363 5495383 5495387 5495419 5495447 5495449 5495473 5495489
5495509 5495521 5495527 5495531 5495543 5495549 5495557 5495561 5495563 5495591
5495603 5495629 5495639 5495653 5495657 5495669 5495687 5495717 5495719 5495723
5495741 5495747 5495753 5495759 5495767 5495779 5495797 5495813 5495821 5495887
5495891 5495929 5495933 5495969 5495989 5495999 5496013 5496031 5496041
5496059 5496089 5496121 5496157 5496191 5496193 5496203 5496223 5496247 5496251
5496277 5496299 5496307 5496317 5496329 5496347 5496349 5496353 5496371 5496397
5496409 5496431 5496443 5496451 5496467 5496473 5496481 5496493 5496571 5496581
5496587 5496599 5496611 5496619 5496653 5496677 5496679 5496713 5496731 5496737
5496779 5496781 5496787 5496809 5496823 5496857 5496859 5496913 5496919 5496923
5496937 5496943 5496949 5496961 5496983 5497003 5497021 5497027 5497031 5497039
5497043 5497081 5497091 5497117 5497123 5497133 5497147 5497159 5497181 5497223
5497229 5497231 5497237 5497241 5497243 5497267 5497277 5497279 5497291 5497301
5497343 5497351 5497361 5497397 5497433 5497463 5497469 5497493 5497519 5497523
5497573 5497577 5497643 5497651 5497663 5497691 5497693 5497697 5497711 5497721
5497753 5497763 5497771 5497799 5497823 5497829 5497861 5497871 5497873 5497879
5497889 5497901 5497909 5497927 5497931 5497949 5497963 5497969 5497979
5497993 5498039 5498047 5498083 5498099 5498117 5498131 5498149 5498161 5498177
5498179 5498189 5498203 5498209 5498257 5498261 5498279 5498291 5498303 5498309
5498329 5498333 5498341 5498351 5498359 5498399 5498401 5498411 5498413 5498417
5498431 5498443 5498447 5498461 5498473 5498477 5498491 5498527 5498557 5498561
```

```
5498573  5498609  5498617  5498627  5498641  5498651  5498653  5498663  5498707  5498729
5498747  5498767  5498783  5498789  5498807  5498819  5498827  5498839  5498849  5498851
5498887  5498917  5498921  5498929  5498947  5498963  5498981  5498993  5499019  5499023
5499031  5499049  5499061  5499071  5499073  5499077  5499079  5499101  5499103  5499107
5499127  5499157  5499181  5499187  5499191  5499203  5499209  5499217  5499233  5499259
5499283  5499287  5499311  5499337  5499343  5499367  5499383  5499397  5499401  5499407
5499409  5499437  5499443  5499467  5499509  5499547  5499563  5499581  5499587  5499671
5499673  5499677  5499701  5499709  5499719  5499727  5499733  5499749  5499761  5499779
5499787  5499817  5499839  5499841  5499841  5499853  5499877  5499881  5499887  5499889
5499913  5499919  5499929  5499931  5499941  5499943  5499953  5499961  5499971  5499973  5499979
5500003  5500009  5500021  5500067  5500073  5500123  5500141  5500153  5500171  5500193
5500211  5500223  5500241  5500247  5500277  5500279  5500283  5500301  5500321  5500373
5500379  5500387  5500403  5500433  5500463  5500471  5500483  5500507  5500513  5500529
5500543  5500567  5500591  5500597  5500613  5500637  5500643  5500667  5500669  5500681
5500697  5500717  5500721  5500723  5500757  5500787  5500801  5500811  5500819  5500829
5500837  5500871  5500879  5500969  5500987  5500993  5501003  5501017
5501057  5501059  5501077  5501099  5501107  5501129  5501141  5501143  5501159  5501173
5501189  5501201  5501231  5501233  5501273  5501281  5501299  5501341  5501351  5501359
5501371  5501381  5501389  5501399  5501401  5501411  5501423  5501443  5501449  5501467
5501473  5501501  5501519  5501533  5501537  5501543  5501563  5501569  5501579  5501593
5501609  5501647  5501653  5501681  5501687  5501701  5501707  5501723  5501729  5501731
5501777  5501779  5501801  5501813  5501819  5501827  5501843  5501879  5501921  5501933
5501939  5501941  5501953  5501959  5501971  5501981  5501989  5502041  5502043  5502059
5502071  5502103  5502109  5502127  5502179  5502181  5502187  5502193  5502197  5502209
5502239  5502251  5502269  5502293  5502311  5502349  5502353  5502377  5502389  5502397
5502401  5502403  5502437  5502439  5502449  5502461  5502463  5502479  5502481  5502493
5502499  5502527  5502551  5502557  5502559  5502583  5502617  5502649  5502659  5502671
5502691  5502709  5502743  5502793  5502811  5502821  5502851  5502857  5502859  5502863
5502877  5502881  5502919  5502929  5502949  5502961  5502967  5503021  5503031  5503033
5503039  5503051  5503063  5503067  5503081  5503093  5503109  5503123  5503129  5503133
5503171  5503181  5503193  5503207  5503229  5503241  5503249  5503259  5503271  5503273
5503297  5503319  5503339  5503349  5503363  5503373  5503391  5503403  5503409  5503411
5503429  5503451  5503457  5503469  5503499  5503507  5503517  5503541  5503549  5503567
5503571  5503577  5503609  5503621  5503657  5503661  5503721  5503723  5503727  5503741
5503753  5503763  5503769  5503783  5503789  5503807  5503811  5503837  5503843  5503853
5503859  5503867  5503873  5503889  5503907  5503919  5503921  5503951  5503987  5503999
5504017  5504033  5504041  5504063  5504077  5504089  5504099  5504111  5504131  5504201
5504207  5504237  5504269  5504293  5504321  5504333  5504339  5504351  5504353  5504363
5504371  5504381  5504407  5504431  5504441  5504449  5504497  5504501  5504503  5504557
5504563  5504581  5504647  5504657  5504663  5504669  5504671  5504713  5504717  5504743
5504761  5504773  5504789  5504791  5504839  5504869  5504881  5504893  5504899  5504959
5504987  5505001  5505023  5505037  5505053  5505061  5505083  5505109  5505121
5505133  5505139  5505151  5505167  5505179  5505187  5505191  5505209  5505217  5505223
5505239  5505287  5505289  5505293  5505299  5505301  5505317  5505337  5505343  5505347
5505359  5505361  5505371  5505377  5505391  5505397  5505403  5505413  5505427  5505449
5505527  5505541  5505547  5505551  5505593  5505601  5505613  5505641  5505653  5505667
5505673  5505683  5505691  5505697  5505707  5505713  5505719  5505727  5505743  5505749
5505751  5505769  5505779  5505781  5505793  5505803  5505811  5505869  5505881  5505883
5505889  5505919  5505923  5505949  5505959  5505961  5505967  5505989  5506001  5506019
5506037  5506049  5506051  5506073  5506091  5506099  5506103  5506129  5506139  5506141
5506159  5506169  5506199  5506231  5506271  5506273  5506297  5506301  5506307  5506309
5506337  5506343  5506363  5506381  5506387  5506421  5506427  5506429  5506439  5506471
5506477  5506481  5506507  5506511  5506513  5506559  5506573  5506583  5506597  5506601
5506619  5506651  5506679  5506681  5506687  5506717  5506727  5506733  5506769  5506771
5506787  5506807  5506811  5506817  5506843  5506873  5506909  5506937  5506939  5506951
5506961  5506969  5507009  5507023  5507027  5507039  5507069  5507077  5507081  5507087
5507107  5507111  5507123  5507137  5507147  5507171  5507179  5507209  5507219  5507233
5507261  5507267  5507291  5507297  5507309  5507317  5507323  5507353  5507363
5507377  5507393  5507401  5507417  5507441  5507449  5507459  5507461  5507471  5507497
5507503  5507519  5507531  5507539  5507543  5507617  5507639  5507647  5507657  5507659
5507669  5507699  5507729  5507731  5507737  5507753  5507759  5507771  5507773  5507791
5507807  5507809  5507837  5507849  5507893  5507903  5507917  5507969  5507989  5507993
5508001  5508023  5508047  5508059  5508073  5508077  5508101  5508103  5508127  5508143
5508149  5508163  5508169  5508179  5508203  5508229  5508241  5508263  5508277  5508287
5508313  5508341  5508379  5508383  5508397  5508401  5508469  5508497  5508511  5508551
5508553  5508563  5508571  5508583  5508589  5508599  5508649  5508667  5508683  5508703
5508721  5508733  5508739  5508757  5508761  5508779  5508787  5508791  5508827  5508847
5508851  5508871  5508887  5508913  5508929  5508931  5508947  5508949  5508953  5508991
5509001  5509027  5509033  5509039  5509051  5509057  5509067  5509073  5509079  5509081
5509087  5509099  5509111  5509151  5509177  5509201  5509241  5509249  5509267  5509277
5509307  5509313  5509327  5509331  5509349  5509363  5509379  5509393  5509409  5509417
5509423  5509429  5509433  5509451  5509453  5509549  5509561  5509577  5509589  5509619
5509631  5509643  5509657  5509687  5509709  5509711  5509741  5509759  5509769  5509783
5509859  5509863  5509883  5509897  5509919  5509939  5509979  5509997  5510009  5510017
5510027  5510047  5510051  5510083  5510093  5510101  5510117  5510119  5510123  5510137
5510143  5510173  5510177  5510189  5510207  5510237  5510249  5510303  5510311  5510339
5510341  5510347  5510353  5510369  5510371  5510383  5510389  5510413  5510429  5510471
5510489  5510507  5510537  5510539  5510563  5510573  5510581  5510587  5510597  5510611
5510629  5510633  5510647  5510651  5510693  5510699  5510711  5510719  5510753  5510759
5510761  5510773  5510849  5510881  5510903  5510909  5510917  5510959  5510997  5510999
5511001  5511017  5511019  5511029  5511041  5511049  5511061  5511071  5511133  5511137
5511151  5511157  5511161  5511169  5511203  5511223  5511251  5511263  5511271
5511287  5511293  5511299  5511307  5511313  5511347  5511377  5511403  5511431  5511433
5511461  5511491  5511497  5511509  5511511  5511529  5511547  5511581  5511599  5511601
5511631  5511641  5511683  5511713  5511731  5511739  5511741  5511749  5511761  5511773
5511809  5511811  5511817  5511829  5511833  5511851  5511871  5511901  5511907  5511929
5511937  5511941  5511947  5511949  5511967  5511971  5511977  5511983  5511997  5512007
5512009  5512043  5512049  5512051  5512099  5512103  5512121  5512123  5512183  5512187
5512189  5512229  5512231  5512237  5512271  5512307  5512321  5512343  5512357  5512361
```

```
5512391  5512399  5512421  5512447  5512459  5512483  5512531  5512537  5512561  5512579
5512589  5512609  5512613  5512621  5512627  5512649  5512657  5512669  5512687  5512691
5512721  5512723  5512733  5512739  5512763  5512781  5512877  5512909  5512919  5512951
5512957  5512967  5512999  5513003  5513029  5513063  5513089  5513093  5513107  5513129
5513143  5513191  5513201  5513203  5513227  5513237  5513239  5513243  5513267  5513273
5513293  5513303  5513317  5513323  5513341  5513351  5513359  5513371  5513377  5513419
5513437  5513449  5513513  5513527  5513531  5513533  5513539  5513549  5513551  5513569
5513579  5513587  5513611  5513623  5513663  5513671  5513681  5513687  5513723  5513731
5513779  5513821  5513843  5513863  5513873  5513887  5513891  5513917  5513923  5513927
5513929  5513941  5513947  5513953  5513987  5514007  5514013  5514023  5514053  5514077
5514079  5514083  5514097  5514107  5514133  5514139  5514149  5514163  5514193  5514209
5514211  5514241  5514247  5514251  5514253  5514281  5514293  5514323  5514329  5514337
5514343  5514349  5514367  5514371  5514391  5514401  5514403  5514433  5514451  5514469
5514473  5514521  5514533  5514539  5514563  5514571  5514577  5514581  5514601  5514643
5514653  5514659  5514667  5514689  5514697  5514709  5514713  5514737  5514757  5514763
5514781  5514797  5514823  5514833  5514863  5514881  5514893  5514913  5514941  5514947
5514979  5514983  5514989  5514991  5515001  5515019  5515031  5515039  5515043  5515061
5515079  5515087  5515091  5515093  5515099  5515141  5515151  5515163  5515177  5515189
5515199  5515207  5515217  5515219  5515243  5515271  5515273  5515313  5515319  5515333
5515357  5515397  5515399  5515421  5515439  5515441  5515451  5515457  5515501  5515513
5515541  5515579  5515589  5515603  5515619  5515621  5515637  5515649  5515651  5515669
5515673  5515691  5515693  5515703  5515709  5515717  5515721  5515723  5515729  5515787
5515789  5515801  5515813  5515817  5515819  5515823  5515841  5515877  5515897  5515903
5515921  5515927  5515943  5515949  5515963  5515981  5516009  5516011  5516029  5516053
5516057  5516059  5516089  5516107  5516123  5516149  5516167  5516179  5516209  5516221
5516237  5516261  5516267  5516281  5516393  5516411  5516453  5516461  5516471  5516643
5516477  5516501  5516507  5516521  5516549  5516561  5516587  5516603  5516617  5516627
5516633  5516639  5516647  5516659  5516689  5516701  5516723  5516759  5516767  5516801
5516809  5516827  5516879  5516893  5516899  5516909  5516911  5516933  5516939  5516957
5516963  5516983  5517013  5517053  5517059  5517067  5517073  5517077  5517089  5517091
5517131  5517133  5517139  5517151  5517167  5517173  5517191  5517209  5517227  5517257
5517269  5517271  5517293  5517307  5517311  5517313  5517319  5517371  5517397  5517409
5517419  5517427  5517431  5517433  5517437  5517461  5517497  5517509  5517521  5517527
5517553  5517557  5517587  5517599  5517637  5517641  5517643  5517649  5517653  5517661
5517667  5517679  5517683  5517697  5517727  5517749  5517751  5517763  5517767  5517779
5517823  5517833  5517839  5517871  5517887  5517893  5517901  5517909  5517931  5517943
5517947  5517959  5517971  5517973  5517977  5517991  5518001  5518021  5518043  5518099
5518109  5518111  5518127  5518133  5518141  5518157  5518159  5518171  5518241  5518259
5518273  5518297  5518301  5518339  5518351  5518397  5518399  5518423  5518433  5518453
5518463  5518501  5518507  5518511  5518517  5518537  5518543  5518547  5518549  5518553
5518567  5518627  5518633  5518673  5518687  5518817  5518819  5518831  5518841  5518847
5518859  5518913  5518927  5518937  5518951  5518967  5519029  5519047  5519081  5519083
5519117  5519119  5519123  5519131  5519153  5519159  5519191  5519197  5519207  5519243
5519249  5519263  5519279  5519299  5519303  5519321  5519359  5519363  5519387  5519389
5519429  5519447  5519453  5519477  5519489  5519531  5519567  5519597  5519617  5519629
5519639  5519641  5519653  5519659  5519677  5519693  5519699  5519719  5519737  5519753
5519797  5519803  5519819  5519879  5519881  5519887  5519893  5519903  5519909  5519933
5519989  5520001  5520007  5520017  5520029  5520049  5520059  5520071  5520083  5520101
5520113  5520131  5520157  5520169  5520191  5520233  5520259  5520269  5520271  5520287
5520293  5520323  5520329  5520337  5520371  5520373  5520377  5520401  5520421  5520457
5520467  5520499  5520509  5520521  5520551  5520553  5520569  5520577  5520589  5520607
5520623  5520629  5520637  5520649  5520653  5520673  5520677  5520703  5520707  5520709
5520721  5520751  5520763  5520769  5520791  5520797  5520799  5520803  5520839  5520859
5520863  5520877  5520901  5520913  5520919  5520923  5520929  5520947  5520953  5520967
5521003  5521051  5521057  5521097  5521099  5521111  5521121  5521129  5521133  5521147
5521181  5521191  5521207  5521211  5521213  5521249  5521253  5521259  5521261  5521283
5521289  5521297  5521301  5521309  5521361  5521363  5521391  5521393  5521427  5521463
5521489  5521499  5521543  5521553  5521559  5521561  5521567  5521573  5521589  5521591
5521597  5521603  5521631  5521643  5521657  5521661  5521667  5521669  5521693  5521697
5521709  5521721  5521729  5521783  5521801  5521807  5521819  5521891  5521927  5521963
5521981  5521993  5522009  5522039  5522057  5522063  5522071  5522117  5522119  5522131
5522137  5522173  5522177  5522191  5522203  5522219  5522233  5522243  5522261  5522273
5522281  5522291  5522299  5522303  5522311  5522327  5522339  5522347  5522351  5522353
5522389  5522393  5522411  5522417  5522431  5522443  5522471  5522479  5522519  5522527
5522563  5522611  5522617  5522677  5522707  5522761  5522779  5522801  5522809  5522819
5522821  5522827  5522833  5522837  5522851  5522861  5522873  5522893  5522897  5522899
5522911  5522917  5522927  5522941  5522947  5522999  5523029  5523031  5523061  5523097
5523109  5523131  5523157  5523173  5523211  5523223  5523227  5523229  5523247  5523257
5523269  5523293  5523313  5523341  5523359  5523361  5523373  5523383  5523407  5523409
5523437  5523457  5523481  5523491  5523493  5523499  5523503  5523517  5523527  5523541
5523559  5523563  5523569  5523571  5523599  5523629  5523631  5523641  5523647  5523653
5523689  5523719  5523751  5523773  5523799  5523803  5523809  5523811  5523821  5523839
5523857  5523883  5523901  5523913  5523919  5523943  5523967  5524027  5524039  5524049
5524061  5524067  5524069  5524073  5524087  5524091  5524093  5524147  5524157  5524159
5524171  5524187  5524213  5524219  5524247  5524249  5524261  5524271  5524273  5524279
5524283  5524313  5524331  5524357  5524361  5524367  5524369  5524399  5524403  5524423
5524469  5524481  5524483  5524489  5524501  5524513  5524523  5524543  5524553  5524601
5524633  5524639  5524681  5524691  5524697  5524699  5524747  5524759  5524777  5524781
5524793  5524811  5524823  5524843  5524867  5524889  5524891  5524901  5524903  5524907
5524919  5524933  5524949  5524957  5524973  5524999  5525041  5525053  5525059  5525071
5525081  5525087  5525089  5525131  5525137  5525141  5525147  5525171  5525183  5525189
5525203  5525213  5525231  5525239  5525251  5525269  5525279  5525287  5525293  5525327
5525329  5525363  5525417  5525453  5525467  5525473  5525477  5525479  5525491  5525501
5525519  5525549  5525581  5525591  5525603  5525623  5525651  5525659  5525669  5525671
5525701  5525753  5525771  5525777  5525791  5525797  5525803  5525809  5525831  5525869
5525917  5525953  5525981  5526019  5526041  5526043  5526077  5526083  5526089  5526097
5526107  5526109  5526113  5526121  5526127  5526133  5526137  5526161  5526179  5526193
5526217  5526239  5526251  5526263  5526281  5526289  5526331  5526337  5526347  5526383
5526407  5526413  5526421  5526439  5526481  5526487  5526529  5526533  5526551  5526553
```

```
5526583 5526593 5526607 5526613 5526623 5526643 5526679 5526691 5526743 5526767
5526799 5526823 5526839 5526869 5526881 5526883 5526901 5526931 5526947 5526977
5526979 5527001 5527003 5527007 5527009 5527013 5527019 5527069 5527079 5527099
5527103 5527117 5527121 5527147 5527163 5527189 5527213 5527237 5527241 5527243
5527253 5527259 5527307 5527339 5527367 5527391 5527399 5527411 5527439 5527441
5527447 5527451 5527463 5527469 5527477 5527481 5527531 5527547 5527549 5527573
5527589 5527591 5527597 5527609 5527619 5527631 5527649 5527663 5527667 5527673
5527721 5527733 5527747 5527787 5527801 5527829 5527849 5527853 5527861 5527877
5527901 5527909 5527913 5527919 5527929 5527931 5527939 5527957 5527961 5527967
5527979 5527987 5528011 5528023 5528041 5528051 5528053 5528063 5528101 5528141
5528147 5528161 5528167 5528177 5528189 5528227 5528231 5528251 5528267 5528279
5528287 5528387 5528389 5528401 5528407 5528431 5528443 5528461 5528489 5528513
5528527 5528543 5528581 5528603 5528609 5528623 5528641 5528659 5528669 5528681
5528687 5528701 5528707 5528711 5528737 5528741 5528759 5528767 5528771 5528779
5528827 5528837 5528849 5528851 5528863 5528899 5528917 5528921 5528923 5528933
5528969 5528989 5529001 5529023 5529037 5529047 5529061 5529077 5529079 5529089
5529091 5529109 5529113 5529149 5529179 5529187 5529193 5529229 5529283 5529287
5529319 5529341 5529347 5529367 5529427 5529451 5529463 5529473 5529497 5529509
5529521 5529523 5529529 5529541 5529571 5529581 5529611 5529617 5529619 5529631
5529647 5529661 5529673 5529701 5529739 5529767 5529787 5529791 5529803 5529809
5529827 5529841 5529857 5529859 5529863 5529877 5529883 5529889 5529899 5529911
5529929 5529941 5529949 5529971 5530001 5530027 5530033 5530043 5530061 5530069
5530087 5530123 5530141 5530163 5530169 5530181 5530201 5530211 5530241 5530243
5530277 5530303 5530309 5530331 5530339 5530351 5530363 5530429 5530439 5530477
5530487 5530489 5530517 5530519 5530529 5530541 5530543 5530571 5530573 5530589
5530621 5530663 5530667 5530673 5530697 5530739 5530751 5530781 5530799 5530813
5530823 5530841 5530849 5530853 5530867 5530891 5530901 5530939 5530963 5530981
5530999 5531021 5531039 5531041 5531059 5531081 5531087 5531089 5531107 5531117
5531129 5531131 5531149 5531159 5531161 5531173 5531209 5531221 5531243 5531263
5531291 5531311 5531321 5531347 5531353 5531359 5531363 5531371 5531437 5531441
5531459 5531473 5531483 5531497 5531507 5531509 5531521 5531531 5531549 5531593
5531599 5531621 5531623 5531627 5531633 5531639 5531651 5531657 5531677 5531693
5531711 5531719 5531723 5531777 5531797 5531809 5531819 5531849 5531861 5531873
5531887 5531893 5531927 5532019 5532031 5532049 5532053 5532067 5532071 5532083
5532091 5532103 5532113 5532143 5532161 5532169 5532179 5532181 5532223 5532227
5532239 5532269 5532271 5532281 5532283 5532311 5532313 5532341 5532343 5532349
5532377 5532389 5532403 5532409 5532421 5532427 5532433 5532437 5532467 5532469
5532487 5532491 5532551 5532557 5532559 5532563 5532577 5532587 5532613 5532619
5532623 5532641 5532643 5532661 5532677 5532689 5532691 5532727 5532739 5532757
5532763 5532833 5532841 5532847 5532859 5532907 5532937 5532941 5532979 5533013
5533037 5533039 5533043 5533049 5533063 5533067 5533103 5533141 5533163 5533181
5533189 5533193 5533207 5533217 5533223 5533261 5533273 5533277 5533289 5533301
5533303 5533331 5533337 5533343 5533349 5533373 5533391 5533393 5533421 5533439
5533441 5533447 5533459 5533471 5533477 5533511 5533523 5533529 5533537 5533543
5533553 5533573 5533589 5533613 5533621 5533631 5533637 5533651 5533657 5533663
5533673 5533679 5533681 5533691 5533709 5533739 5533741 5533763 5533793 5533817
5533819 5533837 5533849 5533861 5533901 5533909 5533919 5533937 5533939 5533943
5533973 5533973 5534003 5534017 5534051 5534059 5534063 5534069 5534073 5534077
5534107 5534117 5534131 5534159 5534167 5534171 5534209 5534227 5534251 5534261
5534281 5534311 5534317 5534323 5534341 5534351 5534359 5534363 5534381 5534383
5534387 5534393 5534411 5534413 5534429 5534483 5534489 5534519 5534527 5534539
5534569 5534587 5534593 5534597 5534611 5534623 5534629 5534653 5534671 5534677
5534729 5534759 5534761 5534773 5534783 5534797 5534807 5534813 5534827 5534839
5534863 5534869 5534873 5534891 5534897 5534899 5534923 5534929 5534939 5534951
5534953 5534993 5535007 5535011 5535017 5535031 5535037 5535053 5535059 5535067
5535073 5535077 5535091 5535097 5535121 5535133 5535139 5535151 5535169 5535181
5535191 5535193 5535199 5535221 5535223 5535239 5535241 5535247 5535253 5535269
5535281 5535301 5535307 5535337 5535367 5535377 5535379 5535389 5535401 5535427
5535437 5535443 5535449 5535457 5535463 5535469 5535493 5535511 5535521 5535539
5535547 5535559 5535589 5535599 5535611 5535619 5535623 5535637 5535653 5535661
5535683 5535703 5535713 5535731 5535743 5535749 5535769 5535773 5535787 5535797
5535841 5535853 5535857 5535869 5535877 5535913 5535917 5535919 5535923 5535947
5535967 5535991 5536019 5536043 5536061 5536079 5536103 5536109 5536117 5536151
5536159 5536213 5536249 5536253 5536301 5536309 5536319 5536331 5536337 5536343
5536357 5536369 5536381 5536387 5536397 5536403 5536409 5536417 5536463 5536471
5536481 5536483 5536499 5536511 5536523 5536529 5536541 5536547 5536549 5536549
5536567 5536579 5536589 5536603 5536613 5536627 5536639 5536669 5536673 5536711
5536757 5536789 5536807 5536829 5536837 5536871 5536877 5536883 5536897 5536901
5536903 5536907 5536931 5536933 5536943 5537011 5537027 5537029 5537033 5537083
5537093 5537101 5537111 5537131 5537149 5537159 5537201 5537221 5537243 5537249
5537261 5537263 5537267 5537297 5537317 5537351 5537353 5537369 5537377 5537381
5537401 5537423 5537431 5537443 5537447 5537453 5537471 5537479 5537489 5537509
5537533 5537551 5537593 5537603 5537611 5537629 5537639 5537647 5537657 5537689
5537713 5537731 5537737 5537743 5537761 5537771 5537783 5537789 5537837 5537839
5537849 5537863 5537879 5537881 5537891 5537893 5537897 5537941 5537947 5537953
5537957 5537981 5538011 5538031 5538037 5538041 5538053 5538059 5538079 5538083
5538097 5538103 5538109 5538131 5538149 5538161 5538167 5538179 5538191 5538199
5538223 5538233 5538241 5538257 5538259 5538263 5538283 5538289 5538301 5538331
5538359 5538361 5538371 5538431 5538451 5538473 5538487 5538509 5538523 5538541
5538551 5538569 5538571 5538581 5538647 5538661 5538667 5538679 5538683 5538691
5538703 5538707 5538721 5538727 5538749 5538763 5538853 5538857 5538859 5538877
5538887 5538893 5538901 5538919 5538931 5538943 5538947 5538989 5539019 5539033
5539057 5539063 5539081 5539123 5539129 5539181 5539187 5539199 5539211 5539231
5539249 5539253 5539267 5539273 5539277 5539309 5539327 5539361 5539363 5539367
5539397 5539403 5539409 5539427 5539439 5539477 5539531 5539537 5539553 5539571
5539577 5539579 5539591 5539601 5539631 5539657 5539661 5539663 5539673 5539727
5539753 5539799 5539801 5539817 5539829 5539847 5539861 5539873 5539883 5539889
5539901 5539903 5539907 5539913 5539921 5539927 5539949 5539967 5539981 5539997
5539999 5540023 5540027 5540057 5540063 5540069 5540083 5540099 5540107 5540111
```

```
5540137 5540141 5540173 5540177 5540179 5540221 5540237 5540239 5540243 5540251
5540257 5540273 5540279 5540281 5540287 5540299 5540321 5540347 5540357 5540377
5540387 5540393 5540411 5540441 5540443 5540449 5540459 5540471 5540489 5540497
5540519 5540531 5540573 5540581 5540597 5540603 5540611 5540641 5540659 5540683
5540701 5540707 5540741 5540753 5540767 5540771 5540789 5540791 5540803 5540807
5540819 5540839 5540849 5540869 5540879 5540891 5540921 5540933 5540939 5540993
5541013 5541037 5541077 5541079 5541121 5541127 5541143 5541149 5541187 5541251
5541287 5541299 5541311 5541317 5541353 5541373 5541377 5541383 5541397 5541421
5541427 5541433 5541443 5541449 5541461 5541469 5541499 5541517 5541533 5541577
5541583 5541587 5541607 5541611 5541617 5541619 5541631 5541671 5541713 5541719
5541721 5541737 5541793 5541799 5541841 5541853 5541857 5541869 5541931 5541947
5541959 5541973 5541979 5542001 5542003 5542013 5542021 5542027 5542063 5542079
5542109 5542127 5542139 5542151 5542169 5542177 5542223 5542237 5542249 5542259
5542309 5542321 5542351 5542367 5542387 5542409 5542417 5542423 5542429 5542447
5542457 5542477 5542499 5542507 5542513 5542529 5542531 5542549 5542553 5542597
5542619 5542627 5542633 5542673 5542679 5542703 5542717 5542721 5542723 5542729
5542753 5542777 5542783 5542787 5542811 5542819 5542853 5542907 5542909 5542937
5542939 5542961 5542967 5542993 5543029 5543033 5543051 5543053 5543063 5543099
5543101 5543107 5543119 5543129 5543143 5543149 5543171 5543191 5543201 5543221
5543243 5543249 5543261 5543297 5543333 5543339 5543387 5543399 5543407 5543443
5543449 5543477 5543491 5543507 5543533 5543537 5543579 5543591 5543597 5543617
5543623 5543701 5543711 5543719 5543729 5543749 5543753 5543771 5543779 5543831
5543833 5543873 5543903 5543917 5543927 5543929 5543939 5543963 5543971 5543977
5543981 5544001 5544031 5544047 5544079 5544101 5544103 5544109 5544137 5544139
5544163 5544179 5544221 5544223 5544239 5544241 5544247 5544281 5544283 5544337
5544347 5544349 5544353 5544361 5544373 5544401 5544421 5544437 5544479 5544493
5544509 5544521 5544529 5544547 5544557 5544559 5544577 5544607 5544613 5544619
5544631 5544641 5544653 5544659 5544667 5544673 5544677 5544683 5544689 5544743
5544757 5544767 5544779 5544793 5544809 5544821 5544859 5544911 5544923 5544949
5544953 5544971 5544977 5544983 5544989 5545021 5545027 5545037 5545049 5545069
5545073 5545081 5545087 5545091 5545109 5545117 5545123 5545193 5545219 5545223
5545229 5545273 5545339 5545357 5545367 5545399 5545403 5545411 5545433 5545439
5545447 5545453 5545459 5545481 5545487 5545493 5545499 5545513 5545531 5545543
5545567 5545609 5545627 5545637 5545643 5545649 5545681 5545697 5545733 5545741
5545751 5545759 5545789 5545801 5545831 5545843 5545849 5545871 5545877 5545889
5545901 5545909 5545913 5545933 5545987 5545997 5545999 5546027 5546039 5546053
5546069 5546071 5546077 5546083 5546089 5546129 5546161 5546173 5546201 5546209
5546249 5546251 5546273 5546287 5546293 5546377 5546389 5546393 5546399 5546419
5546459 5546479 5546483 5546491 5546509 5546533 5546543 5546561 5546587 5546599
5546621 5546623 5546647 5546663 5546677 5546687 5546711 5546713 5546741 5546753
5546771 5546789 5546833 5546837 5546843 5546867 5546869 5546897 5546903 5546911
5546921 5546941 5546953 5546963 5546971 5546977 5546999 5547001 5547007 5547011
5547019 5547089 5547133 5547167 5547169 5547187 5547193 5547211 5547247 5547251
5547257 5547263 5547277 5547293 5547317 5547319 5547329 5547359 5547371 5547391
5547397 5547403 5547431 5547433 5547467 5547499 5547511 5547547 5547557 5547569
5547583 5547599 5547611 5547631 5547691 5547697 5547701 5547709 5547713 5547733
5547749 5547757 5547769 5547779 5547827 5547847 5547851 5547863 5547877 5547887
5547901 5547911 5547923 5547931 5547953 5547959 5547973 5548007 5548013 5548027
5548043 5548063 5548087 5548099 5548141 5548157 5548159 5548177 5548189 5548211
5548217 5548237 5548253 5548259 5548297 5548321 5548331 5548339 5548351 5548369
5548379 5548421 5548423 5548453 5548457 5548469 5548493 5548519 5548531 5548547
5548549 5548559 5548573 5548583 5548601 5548603 5548607 5548619 5548649 5548651
5548661 5548693 5548709 5548733 5548759 5548769 5548771 5548787 5548789 5548793
5548801 5548811 5548813 5548841 5548843 5548847 5548859 5548861 5548871 5548897
5548937 5548951 5548967 5548973 5548979 5548993 5548997 5548999 5549017 5549023
5549051 5549053 5549059 5549069 5549087 5549101 5549111 5549113 5549119 5549129
5549143 5549183 5549189 5549209 5549213 5549221 5549249 5549251 5549261 5549263
5549281 5549303 5549339 5549377 5549381 5549393 5549413 5549437 5549447 5549483
5549561 5549569 5549587 5549591 5549611 5549617 5549657 5549659 5549669 5549681
5549689 5549707 5549711 5549737 5549749 5549771 5549777 5549779 5549813 5549839
5549879 5549891 5549893 5549897 5549909 5549927 5549941 5549977 5549993 5550011
5550019 5550029 5550059 5550073 5550113 5550121 5550133 5550137 5550151 5550157
5550161 5550169 5550179 5550187 5550191 5550203 5550217 5550229 5550257 5550287
5550301 5550317 5550323 5550341 5550379 5550401 5550403 5550427 5550431 5550439
5550443 5550463 5550469 5550491 5550497 5550529 5550541 5550547 5550553 5550557
5550563 5550577 5550583 5550647 5550683 5550689 5550719 5550733 5550739 5550763
5550821 5550833 5550871 5550877 5550917 5550929 5550947 5550967 5550973 5550991
5550997 5551003 5551037 5551057 5551069 5551079 5551087 5551099 5551109 5551111
5551121 5551157 5551159 5551187 5551193 5551237 5551241 5551279 5551283 5551307
5551321 5551339 5551359 5551361 5551417 5551423 5551433 5551453 5551459
5551463 5551489 5551501 5551529 5551531 5551583 5551589 5551603 5551607 5551627
5551633 5551643 5551669 5551699 5551709 5551729 5551753 5551757 5551783 5551801
5551807 5551829 5551831 5551837 5551853 5551867 5551873 5551879 5551919 5551921
5551927 5551937 5551939 5551951 5551957 5551967 5551981 5551999 5552003 5552011
5552017 5552023 5552101 5552111 5552147 5552153 5552171 5552189 5552191 5552201
5552207 5552219 5552221 5552231 5552233 5552263 5552303 5552321 5552329 5552341
5552363 5552381 5552411 5552419 5552447 5552497 5552501 5552509 5552539 5552581
5552593 5552609 5552611 5552629 5552641 5552663 5552669 5552711 5552713 5552737
5552741 5552773 5552779 5552791 5552797 5552809 5552819 5552843 5552857 5552861
5552927 5552941 5552947 5552957 5552971 5553011 5553029 5553059 5553083
5553091 5553103 5553109 5553113 5553133 5553137 5553151 5553157 5553173 5553179
5553199 5553209 5553211 5553227 5553241 5553253 5553259 5553269 5553277 5553299
5553307 5553311 5553313 5553319 5553337 5553349 5553389 5553391 5553397 5553421
5553437 5553461 5553469 5553497 5553503 5553521 5553539 5553547 5553571 5553593
5553601 5553631 5553641 5553671 5553683 5553721 5553727 5553733 5553739 5553773
5553791 5553797 5553799 5553803 5553809 5553827 5553829 5553839 5553853 5553857
5553881 5553887 5553893 5553907 5553949 5553953 5553967 5553979 5554013 5554039
5554057 5554067 5554079 5554093 5554103 5554139 5554141 5554151 5554163 5554169
5554183 5554187 5554193 5554207 5554231 5554249 5554321 5554331 5554333 5554349
```

```
5554357  5554361  5554387  5554397  5554421  5554433  5554459  5554469  5554489  5554499
5554513  5554519  5554537  5554547  5554553  5554567  5554583  5554603  5554607  5554613
5554621  5554663  5554729  5554739  5554751  5554763  5554831  5554849  5554867  5554889
5554919  5554931  5554943  5554951  5554993  5555009  5555021  5555023  5555047  5555057
5555059  5555083  5555117  5555149  5555177  5555183  5555189  5555191  5555197  5555219
5555233  5555237  5555267  5555321  5555323  5555339  5555357  5555369  5555387  5555401
5555431  5555491  5555497  5555507  5555509  5555527  5555567  5555591  5555609  5555611
5555629  5555633  5555639  5555653  5555677  5555681  5555689  5555699  5555701  5555723
5555747  5555777  5555807  5555813  5555827  5555843  5555861  5555863  5555873  5555897
5555929  5555983  5555989  5555993  5556017  5556071  5556077  5556079  5556091  5556107
5556121  5556137  5556143  5556167  5556169  5556191  5556193  5556209  5556211  5556217
5556233  5556251  5556259  5556283  5556289  5556311  5556319  5556329  5556337  5556367
5556373  5556391  5556407  5556413  5556427  5556431  5556437  5556449  5556469  5556479
5556517  5556521  5556527  5556539  5556557  5556559  5556619  5556643  5556653  5556659
5556667  5556703  5556709  5556713  5556743  5556751  5556757  5556769  5556791  5556821
5556851  5556877  5556907  5556931  5556959  5556983  5557031  5557037  5557043  5557051
5557061  5557073  5557093  5557117  5557133  5557163  5557169  5557171  5557213  5557229
5557231  5557247  5557261  5557267  5557297  5557309  5557313  5557333  5557361  5557369
5557379  5557399  5557403  5557411  5557439  5557441  5557457  5557469  5557477  5557483
5557499  5557501  5557523  5557537  5557547  5557553  5557561  5557579  5557613  5557619
5557627  5557631  5557661  5557663  5557723  5557751  5557753  5557757  5557781  5557787
5557813  5557817  5557819  5557843  5557847  5557873  5557883  5557889  5557907  5557931
5557933  5557949  5557969  5557987  5557991  5557999  5558009  5558023  5558041  5558081
5558087  5558101  5558117  5558123  5558143  5558191  5558209  5558219  5558221
5558233  5558239  5558243  5558257  5558281  5558297  5558323  5558353  5558359  5558363
5558369  5558389  5558407  5558417  5558429  5558447  5558453  5558467  5558483
5558513  5558533  5558537  5558551  5558557  5558563  5558569  5558591  5558599  5558603
5558627  5558647  5558669  5558687  5558689  5558699  5558713  5558717  5558753  5558771
5558783  5558837  5558863  5558867  5558879  5558933  5558941  5558947  5558953  5558957
5558977  5558999  5559007  5559079  5559107  5559121  5559131  5559133  5559181  5559209
5559227  5559233  5559251  5559259  5559293  5559311  5559317  5559331  5559347  5559373
5559383  5559401  5559413  5559431  5559443  5559451  5559473  5559481  5559517  5559523
5559529  5559553  5559569  5559577  5559581  5559611  5559623  5559643  5559649  5559691
5559703  5559707  5559733  5559739  5559773  5559781  5559809  5559811
5559817  5559821  5559823  5559839  5559847  5559877  5559889  5559907  5559923  5559929
5559937  5559947  5559979  5560001  5560007  5560019  5560031  5560039  5560057  5560063
5560069  5560073  5560109  5560117  5560123  5560127  5560157  5560169  5560171  5560193
5560213  5560229  5560231  5560237  5560267  5560271  5560279  5560301  5560327  5560339
5560351  5560361  5560363  5560367  5560381  5560409  5560421  5560433  5560447  5560463
5560487  5560493  5560519  5560537  5560567  5560571  5560579  5560589  5560591  5560613
5560637  5560679  5560703  5560729  5560741  5560759  5560769  5560771  5560781
5560801  5560859  5560861  5560879  5560883  5560903  5560931  5560957  5561029  5561041
5561051  5561077  5561089  5561099  5561119  5561123  5561141  5561189  5561207  5561209
5561219  5561221  5561263  5561299  5561321  5561333  5561341  5561371  5561383  5561389
5561393  5561401  5561419  5561429  5561441  5561443  5561447  5561459  5561461  5561467
5561483  5561497  5561513  5561519  5561531  5561537  5561579  5561593  5561597  5561599
5561627  5561629  5561639  5561641  5561657  5561659  5561687  5561693  5561701  5561713
5561719  5561779  5561819  5561821  5561849  5561863  5561869  5561879  5561891
5561893  5561903  5561911  5561917  5561947  5561953  5561971  5561977  5561981  5561993
5561999  5562047  5562059  5562071  5562083  5562091  5562097  5562119  5562127  5562131
5562133  5562143  5562157  5562169  5562197  5562203  5562209  5562217  5562239  5562241
5562253  5562257  5562283  5562317  5562329  5562341  5562397  5562419  5562433  5562439
5562449  5562457  5562499  5562503  5562517  5562551  5562559  5562563  5562581
5562607  5562643  5562703  5562709  5562749  5562761  5562769  5562793  5562829  5562863
5562871  5562881  5562883  5562899  5562901  5562923  5562929  5562971  5562989  5563013
5563021  5563031  5563049  5563057  5563069  5563081  5563087  5563091  5563093  5563109
5563121  5563127  5563153  5563163  5563183  5563223  5563231  5563247  5563277  5563307
5563319  5563321  5563361  5563367  5563373  5563379  5563381  5563387  5563391  5563399
5563483  5563487  5563501  5563513  5563517  5563583  5563589  5563603  5563619  5563643
5563651  5563661  5563669  5563673  5563697  5563699  5563703  5563711  5563721  5563729
5563757  5563763  5563771  5563799  5563819  5563829  5563843  5563919  5563927  5563933
5563951  5563991  5564003  5564029  5564033  5564047  5564051  5564059  5564077  5564089
5564147  5564161  5564177  5564179  5564249  5564261  5564267  5564269  5564297  5564323
5564333  5564347  5564381  5564387  5564453  5564477  5564497  5564509  5564513  5564527
5564539  5564563  5564579  5564591  5564609  5564617  5564621  5564633  5564639  5564651
5564687  5564693  5564711  5564719  5564747  5564761  5564773  5564791  5564809  5564813
5564833  5564849  5564851  5564869  5564879  5564887  5564927  5564957  5564981  5565019
5565023  5565029  5565031  5565047  5565061  5565073  5565083  5565097  5565101  5565121
5565127  5565139  5565163  5565169  5565173  5565211  5565227  5565229  5565247  5565251
5565257  5565269  5565283  5565311  5565319  5565323  5565331  5565367  5565377  5565383
5565397  5565401  5565449  5565467  5565473  5565481  5565491  5565509  5565551  5565607
5565611  5565641  5565643  5565667  5565673  5565691  5565697  5565713  5565719  5565733
5565737  5565743  5565773  5565809  5565821  5565827  5565829  5565853  5565871  5565887
5565907  5565913  5565979  5565983  5565991  5565997  5566003  5566013  5566027  5566073
5566087  5566091  5566109  5566111  5566117  5566129  5566133  5566147  5566153  5566163
5566181  5566199  5566241  5566271  5566273  5566291  5566331  5566333  5566339  5566343
5566357  5566367  5566387  5566397  5566399  5566403  5566409  5566423  5566439  5566441
5566481  5566489  5566499  5566501  5566511  5566523  5566541  5566543  5566553  5566569
5566567  5566571  5566597  5566607  5566619  5566657  5566661  5566663  5566669  5566681
5566697  5566703  5566741  5566747  5566751  5566777  5566783  5566787  5566801  5566807
5566843  5566849  5566853  5566879  5566901  5566919  5566969  5566987  5566991  5566993
5566997  5567033  5567071  5567113  5567117  5567119  5567123  5567129  5567137  5567141
5567161  5567183  5567203  5567207  5567239  5567249  5567251  5567257  5567273  5567297
5567327  5567329  5567351  5567363  5567389  5567407  5567461  5567467  5567489  5567503
5567519  5567533  5567537  5567539  5567561  5567563  5567567  5567579  5567581  5567593
5567599  5567609  5567621  5567647  5567651  5567663  5567669  5567701  5567711  5567713
5567743  5567747  5567753  5567773  5567801  5567803  5567819  5567831  5567839  5567843
5567867  5567873  5567899  5567911  5567953  5567963  5567987  5568023  5568053  5568097
5568109  5568119  5568133  5568149  5568151  5568161  5568179  5568181  5568187  5568193
```

```
5568209  5568229  5568239  5568253  5568257  5568259  5568271  5568287  5568307  5568331
5568337  5568359  5568373  5568383  5568391  5568397  5568403  5568439  5568481  5568487
5568523  5568529  5568547  5568559  5568581  5568587  5568613  5568637  5568643  5568649
5568677  5568683  5568709  5568721  5568727  5568733  5568781  5568791  5568799  5568809
5568811  5568817  5568821  5568847  5568851  5568853  5568859  5568917  5568931  5568961
5568971  5568977  5569001  5569009  5569019  5569021  5569049  5569063  5569079  5569087
5569093  5569099  5569103  5569111  5569121  5569163  5569199  5569211  5569219  5569229
5569253  5569259  5569271  5569273  5569279  5569297  5569301  5569303  5569309  5569327
5569379  5569391  5569393  5569397  5569411  5569433  5569441  5569463  5569477  5569499
5569507  5569511  5569517  5569559  5569567  5569583  5569585  5569601  5569609  5569621
5569651  5569667  5569673  5569687  5569741  5569757  5569763  5569771  5569783  5569799
5569807  5569853  5569859  5569903  5569939  5569957  5569987  5569997  5570003  5570007
5570029  5570039  5570057  5570063  5570069  5570083  5570087  5570107  5570113  5570129
5570153  5570161  5570197  5570207  5570221  5570231  5570267  5570269  5570281  5570293
5570303  5570311  5570329  5570333  5570351  5570371  5570377  5570413  5570417  5570423
5570429  5570431  5570437  5570449  5570489  5570491  5570497  5570501  5570503  5570519
5570533  5570567  5570597  5570633  5570647  5570651  5570681  5570687  5570699  5570701
5570707  5570717  5570723  5570729  5570737  5570749  5570767  5570771  5570783  5570791
5570801  5570821  5570827  5570833  5570861  5570867  5570879  5570891  5570909  5570911
5570923  5570927  5570941  5570959  5570977  5570993  5571023  5571029  5571031  5571067
5571073  5571077  5571089  5571091  5571107  5571113  5571131  5571143  5571149  5571151
5571179  5571187  5571211  5571229  5571233  5571271  5571283  5571323  5571337  5571343
5571347  5571353  5571407  5571409  5571431  5571437  5571457  5571473  5571479  5571481
5571487  5571491  5571493  5571523  5571539  5571607  5571623  5571637  5571649  5571659
5571673  5571677  5571689  5571697  5571721  5571739  5571763  5571781  5571809  5571833
5571851  5571887  5571889  5571899  5571913  5571913  5571919  5571931  5571947  5571953
5571961  5571977  5571989  5572001  5572013  5572027  5572037  5572057  5572067  5572079
5572081  5572097  5572109  5572117  5572121  5572123  5572129  5572139  5572159  5572211
5572253  5572283  5572297  5572313  5572319  5572331  5572339  5572363  5572429  5572439
5572471  5572477  5572487  5572493  5572507  5572517  5572519  5572559  5572561  5572571
5572621  5572631  5572639  5572663  5572673  5572687  5572691  5572709  5572717  5572729
5572733  5572751  5572759  5572769  5572771  5572793  5572817  5572823  5572883  5572907
5572921  5572939  5572949  5572951  5572961  5572967  5572979  5572981  5572997  5573011
5573027  5573053  5573063  5573069  5573083  5573111  5573123  5573129  5573147  5573159
5573179  5573221  5573231  5573237  5573257  5573303  5573311  5573333  5573339  5573353
5573357  5573363  5573377  5573389  5573413  5573461  5573471  5573473  5573489  5573507
5573527  5573549  5573551  5573563  5573573  5573587  5573599  5573609  5573621  5573641
5573681  5573681  5573693  5573723  5573731  5573747  5573749  5573769  5573779  5573801
5573809  5573833  5573839  5573849  5573917  5573927  5573929  5573947  5573969  5573989
5573993  5573999  5574001  5574043  5574067  5574077  5574083  5574091  5574109  5574131
5574137  5574187  5574209  5574229  5574253  5574307  5574311  5574313  5574343  5574347
5574367  5574427  5574431  5574433  5574469  5574473  5574479  5574523  5574551  5574557
5574559  5574631  5574643  5574659  5574697  5574703  5574713  5574719  5574721  5574731
5574743  5574773  5574787  5574799  5574841  5574853  5574857  5574883  5574887  5574917
5574953  5574971  5574977  5574979  5575001  5575007  5575019  5575043  5575051  5575067
5575069  5575091  5575111  5575117  5575121  5575147  5575169  5575181  5575183  5575237
5575243  5575247  5575259  5575261  5575277  5575309  5575351  5575357  5575369  5575387
5575391  5575397  5575399  5575403  5575421  5575447  5575483  5575487  5575517  5575519
5575523  5575529  5575543  5575553  5575561  5575579  5575589  5575597  5575601  5575613
5575621  5575639  5575651  5575693  5575697  5575709  5575723  5575747  5575771  5575777
5575783  5575811  5575819  5575837  5575841  5575861  5575879  5575891  5575901  5575903
5575951  5575957  5575961  5575981  5575991  5576009  5576047  5576099  5576107  5576167
5576171  5576173  5576201  5576203  5576213  5576237  5576257  5576261  5576273  5576299
5576303  5576321  5576353  5576359  5576371  5576377  5576383  5576399  5576401  5576407
5576413  5576489  5576491  5576507  5576537  5576551  5576563  5576573  5576579  5576591
5576647  5576653  5576657  5576693  5576699  5576759  5576773  5576777  5576783  5576789
5576839  5576849  5576881  5576887  5576891  5576897  5576911  5576929  5576933  5576939
5576959  5576983  5576999  5577023  5577041  5577049  5577059  5577073  5577079  5577083
5577149  5577191  5577197  5577199  5577217  5577223  5577239  5577277  5577287  5577301
5577311  5577337  5577359  5577361  5577379  5577389  5577437  5577449  5577457  5577493
5577497  5577499  5577521  5577527  5577529  5577577  5577601  5577619  5577623  5577643
5577673  5577679  5577709  5577727  5577731  5577749  5577769  5577797  5577821  5577823
5577827  5577833  5577839  5577851  5577959  5577977  5577991  5577997  5578031  5578043
5578049  5578073  5578081  5578087  5578093  5578117  5578123  5578127  5578141  5578151
5578163  5578187  5578189  5578201  5578241  5578277  5578291  5578319  5578327  5578369
5578387  5578421  5578429  5578439  5578451  5578483  5578523  5578549  5578553  5578577
5578589  5578613  5578619  5578631  5578637  5578663  5578717  5578753  5578757  5578763
5578813  5578831  5578847  5578849  5578861  5578921  5578931  5578943  5578987
5579017  5579033  5579053  5579069  5579071  5579089  5579129  5579131  5579137  5579153
5579173  5579183  5579191  5579221  5579227  5579261  5579263  5579269  5579279  5579297
5579347  5579351  5579359  5579377  5579381  5579401  5579419  5579429  5579443  5579447
5579459  5579461  5579477  5579507  5579527  5579549  5579557  5579569  5579573  5579579
5579591  5579617  5579627  5579633  5579641  5579657  5579663  5579669  5579671  5579701
5579713  5579737  5579741  5579747  5579771  5579773  5579789  5579801  5579831  5579837
5579839  5579857  5579879  5579881  5579909  5579909  5579921  5579923  5579941  5579953
5579957  5579963  5579983  5579993  5580011  5580013  5580019  5580023  5580041  5580061
5580073  5580079  5580083  5580089  5580101  5580121  5580137  5580143  5580163  5580181
5580227  5580247  5580257  5580259  5580269  5580271  5580293  5580299  5580307  5580343
5580347  5580349  5580353  5580359  5580361  5580373  5580391  5580401  5580409  5580457
5580479  5580493  5580517  5580521  5580541  5580563  5580569  5580581  5580587  5580593
5580613  5580637  5580649  5580667  5580677  5580721  5580727  5580767  5580769  5580781
5580787  5580791  5580833  5580857  5580863  5580871  5580877  5580893  5580901  5580907
5580917  5580919  5580929  5580931  5580977  5580979  5581001  5581027  5581061  5581067
5581091  5581129  5581133  5581141  5581171  5581181  5581201  5581217  5581229  5581259
5581309  5581313  5581337  5581343  5581351  5581363  5581379  5581393  5581397
5581403  5581447  5581451  5581463  5581469  5581489  5581493  5581531  5581547  5581549
5581553  5581591  5581603  5581613  5581619  5581633  5581637  5581651  5581679  5581691
5581711  5581727  5581733  5581739  5581747  5581759  5581769  5581817  5581819  5581841
5581843  5581853  5581871  5581897  5581937  5581963  5581969  5581973  5582009  5582011
```

```
5582021 5582023 5582033 5582089 5582099 5582111 5582117 5582141 5582147 5582173
5582177 5582207 5582209 5582231 5582251 5582267 5582281 5582287 5582299 5582351
5582363 5582407 5582411 5582419 5582431 5582453 5582483 5582501 5582503 5582513
5582527 5582531 5582569 5582609 5582617 5582623 5582651 5582677 5582699 5582711
5582723 5582737 5582771 5582777 5582803 5582807 5582833 5582839 5582867 5582873
5582879 5582891 5582917 5582921 5582933 5582947 5582959 5582971 5582999 5583001
5583013 5583023 5583031 5583037 5583091 5583107 5583119 5583133 5583139 5583143
5583173 5583187 5583197 5583199 5583203 5583211 5583287 5583289 5583299 5583329
5583349 5583353 5583371 5583373 5583377 5583407 5583419 5583427 5583433 5583451
5583499 5583509 5583517 5583521 5583533 5583541 5583569 5583601 5583619 5583623
5583637 5583649 5583671 5583673 5583691 5583727 5583731 5583737 5583761 5583763
5583791 5583797 5583811 5583821 5583833 5583841 5583857 5583869 5583887 5583889
5583899 5583901 5583911 5583923 5583943 5583947 5583953 5583959 5584021 5584039
5584049 5584057 5584067 5584091 5584097 5584129 5584141 5584169 5584181
5584199 5584207 5584237 5584253 5584259 5584261 5584277 5584283 5584289 5584297
5584303 5584307 5584339 5584343 5584357 5584361 5584379 5584417 5584421 5584441
5584463 5584471 5584503 5584507 5584511 5584529 5584549 5584567 5584577 5584583
5584609 5584633 5584643 5584673 5584697 5584703 5584717 5584723 5584729 5584739
5584741 5584751 5584757 5584771 5584781 5584801 5584807 5584819 5584847 5584871
5584877 5584889 5584903 5584913 5584921 5584933 5584937 5584939 5585003 5585009
5585029 5585059 5585071 5585077 5585089 5585119 5585123 5585137 5585149 5585161
5585171 5585179 5585189 5585201 5585213 5585219 5585233 5585273 5585287 5585291
5585309 5585311 5585317 5585347 5585369 5585383 5585423 5585443 5585453 5585473
5585497 5585501 5585513 5585543 5585561 5585579 5585597 5585599 5585623 5585633
5585647 5585653 5585663 5585683 5585693 5585737 5585759 5585761 5585771 5585807
5585813 5585821 5585863 5585933 5585947 5585959 5585969 5585977 5585989 5586023
5586029 5586037 5586043 5586059 5586071 5586073 5586083 5586089 5586103 5586109
5586121 5586131 5586151 5586181 5586227 5586239 5586277 5586281 5586283 5586289
5586307 5586311 5586337 5586341 5586361 5586391 5586403 5586419 5586433
5586439 5586463 5586487 5586569 5586583 5586587 5586599 5586611 5586629 5586671
5586709 5586719 5586731 5586733 5586739 5586743 5586751 5586767 5586781 5586787
5586793 5586799 5586803 5586809 5586853 5586871 5586877 5586881 5586883 5586943
5586961 5586967 5586983 5586991 5587003 5587073 5587079 5587097 5587129 5587139
5587147 5587171 5587181 5587187 5587189 5587199 5587249 5587261 5587277 5587279
5587301 5587327 5587369 5587391 5587397 5587403 5587411 5587423 5587427 5587429
5587447 5587451 5587457 5587469 5587489 5587499 5587507 5587513 5587523 5587531
5587537 5587541 5587553 5587567 5587583 5587601 5587607 5587609 5587613 5587627
5587669 5587693 5587697 5587709 5587717 5587723 5587753 5587789 5587793 5587811
5587823 5587837 5587847 5587859 5587889 5587907 5587909 5587927 5587943 5587969
5587973 5587991 5587993 5588021 5588069 5588083 5588111 5588113 5588123 5588131
5588137 5588171 5588173 5588179 5588227 5588239 5588243 5588279 5588281 5588357
5588371 5588383 5588411 5588417 5588437 5588459 5588467 5588477 5588483 5588491
5588501 5588521 5588533 5588551 5588571 5588617 5588621 5588647 5588651
5588663 5588683 5588707 5588719 5588741 5588743 5588749 5588761 5588771 5588783
5588789 5588837 5588857 5588861 5588923 5588927 5588929 5588941 5588969 5589007
5589019 5589127 5589131 5589149 5589163 5589167 5589169 5589197 5589217
5589223 5589229 5589251 5589263 5589281 5589293 5589317 5589347 5589349 5589383
5589449 5589493 5589511 5589557 5589581 5589587 5589593 5589611 5589631
5589659 5589677 5589697 5589733 5589739 5589763 5589767 5589769 5589791 5589797
5589811 5589833 5589853 5589887 5589893 5589907 5589911 5589919 5589929 5589931
5589937 5589949 5589959 5589973 5589977 5590019 5590037 5590049 5590051 5590087
5590097 5590103 5590111 5590177 5590181 5590183 5590187 5590201 5590213 5590241
5590271 5590303 5590307 5590337 5590339 5590363 5590381 5590421 5590423
5590439 5590471 5590483 5590499 5590513 5590537 5590549 5590561 5590567 5590573
5590583 5590597 5590601 5590619 5590657 5590699 5590709 5590723 5590729 5590759
5590763 5590787 5590799 5590813 5590831 5590861 5590863 5590869 5590873 5590877
5590889 5590913 5590919 5590931 5590957 5590961 5590969 5590973 5590987 5591009
5591029 5591039 5591041 5591061 5591101 5591123
5591137 5591197 5591207 5591213 5591221 5591227 5591233 5591269 5591273 5591281
5591297 5591309 5591359 5591401 5591407 5591413 5591431 5591437 5591459 5591471
5591479 5591483 5591497 5591503 5591513 5591557 5591569 5591587 5591609 5591611
5591617 5591653 5591671 5591689 5591717 5591741 5591743 5591771 5591777 5591779
5591801 5591813 5591819 5591837 5591863 5591881 5591891 5591897 5591899
5591903 5591917 5591933 5591941 5591969 5591987 5592001 5592007 5592011 5592043
5592047 5592049 5592071 5592073 5592089 5592101 5592127 5592131 5592149
5592163 5592187 5592199 5592227 5592247 5592281 5592299 5592313 5592319
5592343 5592373 5592407 5592437 5592449 5592467 5592469 5592481 5592487 5592511
5592527 5592533 5592547 5592581 5592641 5592659 5592667 5592683 5592731
5592733 5592757 5592761 5592767 5592781 5592791 5592799 5592817 5592823 5592827
5592833 5592869 5592871 5592877 5592893 5592913 5592919 5592941 5592991 5593009
5593039 5593043 5593069 5593073 5593079 5593099 5593109 5593123 5593127 5593129
5593171 5593177 5593183 5593199 5593219 5593229 5593241 5593243 5593267 5593297
5593319 5593321 5593337 5593339 5593349 5593351 5593363 5593373 5593381 5593403
5593409 5593411 5593463 5593477 5593487 5593501 5593513 5593519 5593529 5593537
5593541 5593559 5593583 5593591 5593633 5593649 5593667 5593681 5593703 5593717
5593727 5593729 5593751 5593759 5593787 5593789 5593793 5593801 5593811 5593829
5593837 5593843 5593859 5593871 5593873 5593891 5593909 5593921 5593933 5593937
5593993 5594009 5594011 5594023 5594027 5594051 5594053 5594111 5594123
5594131 5594153 5594159 5594191 5594219 5594233 5594261 5594263 5594279 5594293
5594311 5594357 5594389 5594423 5594441 5594443 5594467 5594471
5594483 5594489 5594507 5594509 5594527 5594591 5594597 5594599 5594621 5594623
5594639 5594657 5594671 5594689 5594713 5594723 5594741 5594747 5594749 5594753
5594761 5594777 5594779 5594791 5594803 5594821 5594837 5594843 5594867 5594899
5594903 5594909 5594917 5594929 5594933 5594959 5595043 5595047 5595059 5595061
5595119 5595133 5595151 5595179 5595181 5595197 5595223 5595241 5595257 5595277
5595281 5595307 5595313 5595319 5595349 5595389 5595409 5595413 5595419 5595427
5595443 5595449 5595451 5595467 5595479 5595487 5595539 5595557 5595587 5595589
5595599 5595613 5595617 5595631 5595643 5595683 5595691 5595731 5595743 5595749
5595763 5595781 5595787 5595817 5595827 5595829 5595847 5595859 5595881 5595883
```

```
5595893  5595901  5595913  5595929  5595949  5595971  5595979  5595983  5596021  5596033
5596037  5596057  5596067  5596081  5596103  5596121  5596133  5596147  5596163  5596181
5596183  5596187  5596193  5596223  5596229  5596237  5596249  5596259  5596267  5596277
5596301  5596307  5596319  5596343  5596351  5596369  5596373  5596397  5596403  5596411
5596463  5596471  5596483  5596489  5596499  5596529  5596561  5596601  5596603  5596627
5596637  5596639  5596649  5596651  5596667  5596673  5596727  5596729  5596733  5596741
5596781  5596813  5596817  5596819  5596831  5596841  5596847  5596897  5596907  5596937
5596949  5596973  5596991  5596999  5597023  5597047  5597051  5597057  5597099  5597149
5597159  5597161  5597167  5597201  5597209  5597219  5597231  5597243  5597281  5597297
5597309  5597311  5597351  5597363  5597407  5597411  5597413  5597461  5597467  5597479
5597497  5597503  5597549  5597561  5597563  5597587  5597597  5597633  5597651  5597659
5597663  5597677  5597687  5597699  5597719  5597737  5597749  5597759  5597797  5597803
5597819  5597821  5597831  5597843  5597849  5597863  5597873  5597897  5597927  5597939
5597941  5597953  5597959  5597971  5597987  5598001  5598013  5598059  5598067  5598071
5598077  5598091  5598119  5598139  5598157  5598163  5598167  5598193  5598199  5598221
5598233  5598251  5598277  5598283  5598289  5598301  5598317  5598323  5598343  5598371
5598379  5598431  5598449  5598469  5598473  5598487  5598497  5598517  5598533
5598539  5598553  5598577  5598611  5598617  5598623  5598629  5598667  5598679  5598689
5598709  5598713  5598727  5598739  5598767  5598793  5598823  5598829  5598833  5598861
5598841  5598871  5598883  5598889  5598907  5598917  5598947  5598949  5598953  5598961
5598979  5598997  5599019  5599021  5599043  5599081  5599093  5599109  5599147  5599169
5599177  5599193  5599201  5599207  5599219  5599229  5599241  5599249  5599261  5599289
5599301  5599367  5599369  5599379  5599381  5599423  5599427  5599457  5599459  5599463
5599481  5599483  5599501  5599507  5599537  5599549  5599567  5599571  5599577  5599591
5599637  5599651  5599663  5599667  5599669  5599679  5599687  5599703  5599709  5599717
5599723  5599733  5599751  5599771  5599777  5599799  5599807  5599823  5599829  5599831
5599859  5599873  5599877  5599921  5599939  5599943  5599949  5599961  5599967  5599973
5599981  5599999  5600027  5600029  5600039  5600047  5600069  5600083  5600087  5600099
5600107  5600113  5600131  5600143  5600159  5600173  5600237  5600239  5600249  5600261
5600279  5600297  5600299  5600303  5600333  5600359  5600369  5600407  5600411  5600443
5600447  5600453  5600461  5600501  5600527  5600533  5600537  5600549  5600557  5600561
5600587  5600629  5600657  5600659  5600671  5600711  5600717  5600729  5600737  5600743
5600809  5600813  5600867  5600873  5600897  5600899  5600909  5600921  5600951  5600957
5600963  5600989  5600993  5601017  5601061  5601083  5601107  5601139  5601149  5601151
5601161  5601163  5601191  5601227  5601229  5601247  5601251  5601269  5601293  5601307
5601317  5601329  5601361  5601367  5601373  5601377  5601383  5601389  5601391  5601433
5601451  5601469  5601493  5601499  5601503  5601511  5601527  5601593  5601613  5601641
5601643  5601667  5601677  5601697  5601703  5601737  5601767  5601779  5601781  5601787
5601833  5601853  5601859  5601877  5601883  5601887  5601889  5601907  5601923  5601943
5602001  5602007  5602021  5602031  5602033  5602039  5602063  5602099  5602111  5602139
5602151  5602183  5602187  5602189  5602193  5602213  5602227  5602241  5602243  5602253
5602277  5602291  5602309  5602327  5602357  5602381  5602393  5602403  5602411  5602439
5602451  5602489  5602507  5602517  5602523  5602529  5602543  5602559  5602561  5602567
5602573  5602579  5602591  5602613  5602631  5602643  5602657  5602669  5602679  5602693
5602697  5602703  5602711  5602721  5602747  5602769  5602781  5602783  5602811  5602813
5602819  5602871  5602897  5602901  5602931  5602939  5602973  5602991  5602999  5603023
5603027  5603051  5603063  5603069  5603077  5603083  5603111  5603131  5603159  5603161
5603189  5603203  5603207  5603209  5603231  5603239  5603267  5603291  5603341  5603383
5603419  5603441  5603447  5603449  5603497  5603501  5603503  5603519  5603551  5603567
5603569  5603597  5603599  5603603  5603617  5603623  5603627  5603629  5603657  5603677
5603701  5603711  5603729  5603737  5603747  5603753  5603771  5603779  5603781  5603831
5603861  5603867  5603869  5603891  5603903  5603929  5603933  5603957  5603971  5604007
5604013  5604029  5604037  5604043  5604073  5604091  5604097  5604113  5604119  5604121
5604143  5604173  5604199  5604223  5604229  5604239  5604251  5604281  5604289  5604301
5604307  5604329  5604359  5604367  5604451  5604481  5604493  5604499  5604517  5604523
5604559  5604589  5604607  5604623  5604629  5604631  5604653  5604661  5604689  5604719
5604727  5604737  5604763  5604799  5604817  5604827  5604839  5604853  5604881  5604887
5604923  5604931  5604947  5604959  5604997  5605037  5605043  5605051
5605099  5605111  5605147  5605163  5605181  5605183  5605217  5605253  5605283  5605331
5605337  5605343  5605349  5605357  5605367  5605387  5605423  5605429  5605433  5605441
5605447  5605459  5605471  5605477  5605489  5605493  5605499  5605553  5605559  5605619
5605661  5605667  5605673  5605679  5605681  5605687  5605697  5605709  5605711  5605739
5605753  5605763  5605771  5605777  5605783  5605799  5605811  5605819  5605849  5605873
5605871  5605877  5605891  5605909  5605913  5605927  5605939  5605949  5605991  5606011
5606033  5606047  5606057  5606093  5606099  5606119  5606137  5606173  5606179  5606189
5606191  5606261  5606267  5606281  5606303  5606323  5606329  5606333  5606339  5606347
5606353  5606369  5606389  5606399  5606417  5606431  5606441  5606453  5606477  5606509
5606519  5606533  5606537  5606543  5606561  5606581  5606591  5606603  5606621  5606681
5606707  5606723  5606749  5606759  5606789  5606801  5606803  5606807  5606833  5606849
5606857  5606863  5606893  5606921  5606927  5606929  5606971  5606977  5606989  5607023
5607031  5607047  5607061  5607073  5607097  5607113  5607131  5607137  5607149  5607167
5607169  5607191  5607197  5607209  5607227  5607233  5607247  5607253  5607257  5607271
5607281  5607289  5607293  5607323  5607361  5607379  5607389  5607391  5607401  5607403
5607409  5607439  5607443  5607457  5607463  5607479  5607487  5607493  5607517  5607541
5607551  5607571  5607577  5607583  5607593  5607599  5607601  5607619  5607631  5607647
5607649  5607659  5607661  5607691  5607703  5607709  5607713  5607731  5607733  5607737
5607751  5607779  5607827  5607839  5607853  5607859  5607871  5607881  5607893  5607911
5607961  5607971  5607977  5608007  5608013  5608033  5608037  5608089  5608091
5608121  5608123  5608139  5608151  5608153  5608171  5608177  5608199  5608217  5608237
5608243  5608259  5608277  5608307  5608321  5608327  5608331  5608357  5608367  5608403
5608409  5608451  5608469  5608483  5608507  5608531  5608541  5608549  5608567  5608579
5608597  5608601  5608609  5608621  5608627  5608639  5608661  5608697  5608699  5608703
5608721  5608723  5608727  5608741  5608747  5608751  5608753  5608769  5608811
5608853  5608859  5608871  5608873  5608879  5608901  5608903  5608913  5608931  5608951
5608969  5609053  5609069  5609077  5609083  5609111  5609113  5609117  5609129  5609141
5609143  5609183  5609203  5609231  5609243  5609257  5609281  5609291  5609293  5609321
5609347  5609353  5609369  5609381  5609399  5609407  5609411  5609423  5609431
5609437  5609449  5609459  5609491  5609501  5609521  5609531  5609587  5609627  5609633
5609647  5609657  5609663  5609683  5609713  5609719  5609741  5609761  5609777  5609783
```

```
5609797   5609803   5609809   5609827   5609833   5609837   5609839   5609867   5609911   5609917
5609927   5609939   5609951   5609957   5609993   5610023   5610029   5610043   5610049   5610089
5610097   5610107   5610113   5610131   5610139   5610151   5610161   5610173   5610191   5610193
5610197   5610203   5610211   5610233   5610277   5610313   5610359   5610361   5610389   5610401
5610419   5610433   5610439   5610443   5610461   5610463   5610467   5610469   5610497   5610499
5610503   5610509   5610541   5610571   5610581   5610587   5610593   5610607   5610611   5610613
5610617   5610637   5610641   5610653   5610677   5610743   5610749   5610763   5610767   5610793
5610797   5610821   5610823   5610851   5610863   5610877   5610881   5610887   5610929   5610937
5610953   5610967   5610977   5610991   5611019   5611043   5611051   5611069   5611079   5611091
5611117   5611121   5611127   5611141   5611147   5611157   5611169   5611223   5611231   5611253
5611259   5611271   5611273   5611303   5611321   5611351   5611357   5611369   5611391   5611399
5611423   5611433   5611439   5611447   5611453   5611469   5611477   5611493   5611511   5611519
5611553   5611579   5611591   5611603   5611621   5611637   5611643   5611663   5611681   5611687
5611699   5611709   5611721   5611759   5611763   5611789   5611807   5611813   5611831   5611841
5611843   5611849   5611867   5611871   5611873   5611913   5611933   5611937   5611951   5611981
5611997   5612029   5612063   5612077   5612107   5612111   5612137   5612141   5612143   5612149
5612177   5612179   5612213   5612221   5612237   5612249   5612263   5612281   5612287   5612291
5612303   5612309   5612311   5612339   5612357   5612381   5612393   5612407   5612423   5612441
5612447   5612461   5612491   5612501   5612507   5612513   5612521   5612527   5612539   5612557
5612569   5612587   5612591   5612609   5612627   5612653   5612699   5612723   5612731   5612741
5612749   5612801   5612807   5612813   5612819   5612837   5612857   5612861   5612879   5612909
5612911   5612927   5612933   5612947   5612951   5612983   5612987   5613031   5613079   5613089
5613103   5613107   5613109   5613161   5613169   5613217   5613259   5613287   5613313   5613317
5613329   5613337   5613347   5613407   5613431   5613457   5613463   5613467   5613469   5613499
5613533   5613547   5613551   5613563   5613571   5613581   5613583   5613589   5613611   5613623
5613637   5613667   5613691   5613701   5613709   5613719   5613731   5613737   5613739   5613763
5613767   5613787   5613799   5613833   5613851   5613857   5613869   5613887   5613889   5613901
5613917   5613929   5613943   5613967   5613991   5614043   5614051   5614057   5614061   5614067
5614073   5614079   5614087   5614111   5614129   5614151   5614153   5614157   5614159   5614201
5614223   5614247   5614283   5614319   5614321   5614327   5614333   5614337   5614339   5614351
5614421   5614447   5614459   5614463   5614523   5614547   5614549   5614579   5614589   5614597
5614657   5614673   5614681   5614703   5614717   5614727   5614729   5614781   5614789   5614831
5614841   5614883   5614891   5614919   5614927   5614933   5614957   5614963   5614993   5615011
5615017   5615023   5615047   5615063   5615081   5615101   5615107   5615131   5615149   5615153
5615167   5615179   5615189   5615201   5615213   5615221   5615261   5615263   5615273   5615303
5615333   5615341   5615347   5615383   5615387   5615411   5615417   5615429   5615437   5615459
5615479   5615497   5615503   5615521   5615537   5615549   5615551   5615563   5615579   5615587
5615609   5615629   5615639   5615641   5615651   5615653   5615669   5615683   5615689   5615699
5615713   5615717   5615723   5615737   5615741   5615747   5615777   5615791   5615803   5615833
5615851   5615861   5615881   5615891   5615917   5615923   5615947   5615957   5615969   5615977
5616011   5616019   5616097   5616113   5616131   5616133   5616161   5616181   5616197   5616199
5616211   5616217   5616223   5616241   5616253   5616271   5616277   5616283   5616287   5616293
5616319   5616329   5616353   5616367   5616379   5616383   5616389   5616407   5616427   5616431
5616433   5616437   5616449   5616469   5616473   5616553   5616557   5616587   5616593   5616601
5616629   5616643   5616659   5616671   5616679   5616707   5616719   5616733   5616757   5616769
5616827   5616833   5616857   5616869   5616883   5616893   5616907   5616911   5616917   5616937
5616967   5616997   5617009   5617013   5617033   5617043   5617067   5617091   5617093   5617109
5617121   5617163   5617181   5617187   5617189   5617193   5617207   5617211   5617237   5617247
5617253   5617291   5617301   5617333   5617349   5617363   5617373   5617421   5617427   5617441
5617457   5617459   5617499   5617511   5617537   5617553   5617613   5617627   5617637   5617639
5617643   5617657   5617679   5617687   5617691   5617693   5617699   5617709   5617739   5617741
5617757   5617771   5617783   5617813   5617817   5617831   5617867   5617877   5617879   5617889
5617897   5617903   5617933   5617961   5617981   5617987   5617999   5618009   5618027   5618029
5618077   5618087   5618089   5618111   5618113   5618131   5618147   5618149   5618183   5618201
5618203   5618209   5618219   5618269   5618287   5618293   5618309   5618311   5618317   5618321
5618323   5618351   5618363   5618377   5618383   5618387   5618429   5618441   5618461   5618479
5618491   5618497   5618537   5618539   5618549   5618567   5618573   5618579   5618581   5618597
5618611   5618633   5618671   5618707   5618713   5618729   5618759   5618777   5618819   5618827
5618839   5618849   5618863   5618881   5618903   5618909   5618911   5618929   5618941   5618957
5618981   5619001   5619037   5619043   5619071   5619073   5619077   5619109   5619139   5619143
5619167   5619169   5619181   5619203   5619217   5619221   5619233   5619241   5619247   5619253
5619281   5619287   5619311   5619323   5619343   5619379   5619389   5619391   5619413   5619443
5619451   5619473   5619487   5619511   5619517   5619527   5619529   5619547   5619553   5619557
5619589   5619599   5619617   5619619   5619637   5619667   5619683   5619701   5619703   5619709
5619739   5619781   5619787   5619827   5619851   5619857   5619919   5619923   5619937   5619941
5619949   5619973   5619983   5620001   5620003   5620009   5620037   5620039   5620061   5620079
5620091   5620103   5620127   5620159   5620169   5620177   5620201   5620247   5620271   5620273
5620283   5620327   5620339   5620369   5620397   5620427   5620451   5620453   5620457   5620469
5620481   5620493   5620499   5620513   5620529   5620543   5620547   5620583   5620609   5620627
5620669   5620689   5620709   5620721   5620787   5620793   5620799   5620801   5620807   5620837
5620841   5620861   5620883   5620891   5620907   5620913   5620933   5620957   5620961   5620963
5620969   5620981   5620987   5620991   5620997   5621023   5621027   5621029   5621051   5621081
5621113   5621117   5621159   5621173   5621183   5621189   5621191   5621197   5621221   5621243
5621249   5621267   5621281   5621303   5621309   5621311   5621327   5621383   5621417   5621419
5621423   5621437   5621441   5621467   5621471   5621479   5621489   5621491   5621503   5621513
5621597   5621599   5621617   5621653   5621687   5621731   5621753   5621767   5621771   5621779
5621809   5621813   5621827   5621857   5621873   5621899   5621921   5621927   5621939   5621953
5621983   5621989   5622007   5622011   5622047   5622059   5622077   5622079   5622103   5622107
5622137   5622167   5622181   5622203   5622247   5622251   5622263   5622301   5622311   5622313
5622319   5622341   5622349   5622391   5622401   5622413   5622443   5622451   5622457   5622473
5622479   5622481   5622497   5622521   5622527   5622559   5622571   5622583   5622587   5622593
5622599   5622601   5622623   5622653   5622691   5622709   5622713   5622719   5622731   5622761
5622763   5622769   5622821   5622829   5622847   5622857   5622871   5622877   5622887   5622899
5622901   5622941   5622943   5622949   5622959   5622961   5622977   5623003   5623021   5623043
5623081   5623087   5623099   5623103   5623133   5623159   5623169   5623193   5623199   5623207
5623213   5623217   5623229   5623279   5623283   5623291   5623301   5623309   5623327   5623351
5623367   5623393   5623403   5623421   5623451   5623463   5623469   5623483   5623507   5623517
5623531   5623537   5623543   5623547   5623561   5623567   5623571   5623573   5623577   5623591
5623609   5623619   5623621   5623627   5623649   5623727   5623747   5623771   5623789   5623811
```

5623823	5623843	5623853	5623859	5623949	5623951	5623967	5623979	5624023	5624033
5624039	5624041	5624053	5624071	5624083	5624117	5624137	5624141	5624147	5624149
5624183	5624189	5624191	5624207	5624219	5624221	5624243	5624249	5624251	5624273
5624279	5624287	5624317	5624327	5624341	5624369	5624389	5624401	5624417	5624441
5624447	5624459	5624461	5624471	5624473	5624477	5624483	5624527	5624543	5624557
5624561	5624573	5624587	5624611	5624617	5624621	5624651	5624653	5624657	5624677
5624687	5624693	5624713	5624743	5624761	5624783	5624789	5624797	5624803	5624821
5624849	5624881	5624891	5624911	5624917	5624929	5624939	5624947	5624951	5624953
5624963	5624989	5625017	5625029	5625031	5625047	5625071	5625091	5625149	5625157
5625187	5625223	5625233	5625239	5625247	5625251	5625281	5625313	5625331	5625341
5625407	5625421	5625427	5625437	5625439	5625457	5625461	5625493	5625509	5625553
5625563	5625637	5625649	5625667	5625673	5625701	5625707	5625713	5625721	
5625727	5625749	5625769	5625773	5625811	5625857	5625863	5625877	5625937	5625941
5625957	5626001	5626009	5626013	5626021	5626039	5626043	5626051	5626069	5626079
5626129	5626141	5626151	5626171	5626177	5626189	5626193	5626207	5626211	5626217
5626219	5626259	5626267	5626273	5626277	5626289	5626333	5626339	5626343	5626349
5626351	5626363	5626367	5626373	5626391	5626393	5626399	5626429	5626441	5626447
5626499	5626549	5626561	5626567	5626571	5626573	5626583	5626589	5626591	5626601
5626619	5626631	5626633	5626637	5626657	5626669	5626703	5626729	5626741	5626757
5626769	5626807	5626837	5626853	5626867	5626871	5626877	5626879	5626891	5626897
5626909	5626921	5626939	5626961	5626967	5626969	5626979	5626987	5626991	5627009
5627029	5627047	5627053	5627057	5627077	5627081	5627099	5627101	5627143	5627147
5627161	5627177	5627179	5627191	5627197	5627207	5627231	5627257	5627267	5627269
5627327	5627393	5627423	5627437	5627443	5627449	5627467	5627473	5627491	5627509
5627519	5627533	5627543	5627551	5627579	5627599	5627603	5627621	5627627	5627641
5627669	5627681	5627689	5627717	5627719	5627729	5627747	5627753	5627761	5627767
5627773	5627777	5627803	5627813	5627849	5627861	5627873	5627887	5627899	5627903
5627917	5627977	5627983	5627987	5627989	5628041	5628061	5628079	5628089	5628101
5628113	5628127	5628131	5628137	5628151	5628157	5628239	5628247	5628251	5628257
5628277	5628281	5628283	5628289	5628319	5628331	5628341	5628361	5628367	5628379
5628397	5628421	5628431	5628437	5628443	5628451	5628457	5628461	5628473	5628481
5628499	5628509	5628517	5628533	5628569	5628589	5628593	5628599	5628611	5628613
5628631	5628647	5628661	5628703	5628713	5628719	5628739	5628757	5628793	5628797
5628839	5628841	5628863	5628877	5628913	5628923	5628937	5628967	5628991	
5629003	5629009	5629061	5629079	5629081	5629097	5629109	5629121	5629133	5629147
5629157	5629199	5629207	5629213	5629223	5629229	5629279	5629307	5629313	5629333
5629357	5629387	5629399	5629417	5629441	5629493	5629553	5629571	5629579	5629583
5629609	5629621	5629627	5629649	5629651	5629697	5629699	5629709	5629727	5629747
5629753	5629763	5629769	5629781	5629787	5629823	5629829	5629843	5629847	5629853
5629859	5629867	5629889	5629913	5629919	5629933	5629937	5629951	5629961	5629991
5629993	5630017	5630021	5630029	5630039	5630047	5630069	5630129	5630159	5630167
5630201	5630203	5630227	5630267	5630269	5630279	5630309	5630329	5630333	5630347
5630351	5630353	5630357	5630363	5630369	5630381	5630411	5630419	5630431	5630467
5630477	5630497	5630501	5630503	5630507	5630533	5630539	5630551	5630591	5630617
5630627	5630629	5630633	5630657	5630659	5630663	5630671	5630693	5630719	5630743
5630749	5630759	5630761	5630767	5630777	5630789	5630813	5630827	5630839	5630857
5630861	5630869	5630887	5630917	5630921	5630923	5630953	5630987	5631007	5631013
5631037	5631061	5631071	5631077	5631087	5631107	5631121	5631169	5631173	5631179
5631187	5631193	5631203	5631209	5631221	5631257	5631259	5631271	5631281	5631287
5631299	5631317	5631341	5631349	5631361	5631383	5631401	5631413	5631421	5631427
5631443	5631499	5631523	5631533	5631541	5631569	5631583	5631589	5631599	5631601
5631623	5631629	5631671	5631679	5631683	5631697	5631701	5631707	5631737	5631751
5631761	5631763	5631767	5631781	5631793	5631813	5631823	5631841	5631851	5631889
5631893	5631911	5631943	5631949	5631973	5631979	5631991	5632001	5632007	5632019
5632021	5632027	5632043	5632073	5632093	5632127	5632163	5632181	5632201	5632247
5632267	5632271	5632273	5632283	5632301	5632327	5632387	5632391	5632419	5632439
5632453	5632477	5632519	5632541	5632567	5632573	5632579	5632597	5632603	
5632609	5632637	5632639	5632651	5632667	5632709	5632717	5632733	5632741	5632747
5632751	5632777	5632799	5632807	5632817	5632819	5632829	5632841	5632853	5632859
5632883	5632889	5632909	5632919	5632943	5632969	5632973	5632981	5632993	5633009
5633027	5633039	5633051	5633057	5633059	5633087	5633107	5633119	5633141	5633149
5633153	5633161	5633189	5633219	5633231	5633237	5633249	5633269	5633297	5633311
5633333	5633347	5633363	5633371	5633417	5633437	5633461	5633471	5633479	5633501
5633503	5633513	5633521	5633539	5633543	5633549	5633587	5633591	5633623	5633651
5633699	5633701	5633711	5633717	5633729	5633737	5633753	5633759	5633807	5633813
5633821	5633833	5633867	5633869	5633893	5633923	5633939	5633959	5633977	5633981
5634001	5634007	5634019	5634023	5634029	5634037	5634049	5634061	5634071	5634073
5634107	5634113	5634131	5634151	5634163	5634193	5634217	5634221	5634227	
5634229	5634257	5634269	5634283	5634311	5634329	5634337	5634341	5634373	5634403
5634427	5634443	5634449	5634479	5634481	5634491	5634493	5634511	5634521	5634553
5634557	5634569	5634581	5634611	5634617	5634623	5634637	5634641	5634649	5634661
5634719	5634721	5634731	5634749	5634751	5634779	5634799	5634809	5634817	5634823
5634847	5634851	5634859	5634869	5634883	5634919	5634929	5634945	5634983	5635033
5635037	5635043	5635051	5635103	5635127	5635141	5635151	5635171	5635183	5635187
5635219	5635237	5635243	5635247	5635249	5635261	5635271	5635277	5635283	5635291
5635297	5635321	5635337	5635349	5635361	5635373	5635387	5635393	5635411	5635417
5635429	5635447	5635453	5635493	5635499	5635501	5635519	5635523	5635547	5635549
5635561	5635589	5635601	5635613	5635633	5635661	5635681	5635687	5635697	5635711
5635717	5635727	5635733	5635801	5635807	5635811	5635843	5635849	5635853	5635871
5635873	5635921	5635957	5635961	5635963	5635979	5635999	5636003	5636009	5636039
5636047	5636069	5636077	5636123	5636131	5636149	5636153	5636161	5636171	5636177
5636201	5636207	5636233	5636249	5636251	5636261	5636273	5636291	5636359	5636363
5636383	5636399	5636419	5636437	5636453	5636467	5636471	5636539	5636551	5636567
5636581	5636593	5636621	5636627	5636629	5636651	5636669	5636671	5636677	5636681
5636689	5636693	5636731	5636747	5636773	5636783	5636789	5636791	5636821	5636831
5636849	5636893	5636899	5636923	5636927	5636929	5636957	5636959	5636963	5636971
5636989	5637007	5637011	5637019	5637041	5637043	5637059	5637067	5637101	
5637103	5637109	5637127	5637143	5637161	5637169	5637173	5637221	5637263	5637271
5637299	5637301	5637341	5637347	5637367	5637383	5637389	5637407	5637427	5637439

```
5637469  5637473  5637479  5637481  5637493  5637521  5637563  5637587  5637631  5637637
5637641  5637647  5637689  5637707  5637733  5637743  5637767  5637811  5637817  5637823
5637833  5637839  5637857  5637871  5637881  5637893  5637899  5637913  5637917  5637953
5637959  5637997  5638019  5638021  5638037  5638043  5638051  5638057  5638103  5638111
5638121  5638133  5638141  5638147  5638159  5638163  5638177  5638183  5638207  5638219
5638223  5638229  5638247  5638253  5638277  5638313  5638327  5638349  5638351  5638357
5638363  5638379  5638397  5638411  5638429  5638433  5638489  5638517  5638531  5638537
5638601  5638603  5638613  5638631  5638639  5638643  5638651  5638663  5638691  5638709
5638751  5638753  5638769  5638777  5638799  5638811  5638817  5638823  5638857  5638871
5638873  5638939  5638949  5638957  5638961  5638967  5639003  5639009  5639027  5639069
5639083  5639167  5639171  5639173  5639191  5639197  5639213  5639243  5639261  5639273
5639287  5639327  5639357  5639377  5639399  5639411  5639453  5639467  5639479  5639489
5639497  5639507  5639521  5639527  5639533  5639549  5639567  5639581  5639587  5639593
5639609  5639611  5639617  5639693  5639707  5639723  5639729  5639741  5639749  5639759
5639773  5639797  5639813  5639831  5639839  5639857  5639867  5639927  5639929  5639939
5639969  5639981  5639983  5639989  5640031  5640043  5640059  5640067  5640071  5640079
5640119  5640149  5640163  5640211  5640251  5640253  5640281  5640287  5640293
5640331  5640337  5640343  5640347  5640361  5640367  5640373  5640377  5640389  5640403
5640449  5640457  5640461  5640463  5640527  5640533  5640541  5640559  5640599
5640619  5640623  5640629  5640643  5640659  5640671  5640673  5640683  5640689  5640709
5640721  5640769  5640779  5640781  5640823  5640829  5640857  5640879
5640881  5640883  5640917  5640919  5640953  5640961  5640989  5641019  5641033  5641061
5641079  5641121  5641123  5641133  5641159  5641169  5641171  5641189  5641201  5641217
5641241  5641243  5641277  5641291  5641301  5641303  5641327  5641343  5641369  5641379
5641381  5641387  5641393  5641421  5641429  5641453  5641459  5641529  5641541  5641547
5641553  5641577  5641607  5641633  5641661  5641679  5641681  5641687  5641709  5641711
5641781  5641787  5641793  5641819  5641837  5641843  5641847  5641859  5641861  5641897
5641931  5641939  5641997  5642017  5642027  5642033  5642041  5642053  5642057  5642059
5642083  5642099  5642191  5642227  5642233  5642239  5642251  5642261  5642267  5642281
5642293  5642309  5642311  5642321  5642323  5642359  5642363  5642369  5642381  5642387
5642401  5642407  5642459  5642477  5642479  5642489  5642509  5642513  5642531  5642591
5642597  5642599  5642627  5642629  5642633  5642641  5642653  5642669  5642687  5642699
5642711  5642717  5642729  5642743  5642783  5642801  5642803  5642839  5642851  5642863
5642873  5642909  5642911  5642947  5642969  5642977  5642999  5643041  5643047  5643059
5643089  5643091  5643103  5643109  5643137  5643161  5643163  5643181  5643217  5643221
5643227  5643241  5643259  5643263  5643301  5643307  5643317  5643329  5643331  5643347
5643373  5643383  5643389  5643413  5643427  5643479  5643503  5643509  5643529  5643553
5643563  5643569  5643571  5643587  5643593  5643601  5643607  5643613  5643623  5643641
5643653  5643667  5643683  5643709  5643727  5643733  5643769  5643787  5643797  5643821
5643851  5643857  5643877  5643919  5643923  5643961  5643973  5644021  5644027  5644031
5644033  5644043  5644061  5644073  5644087  5644103  5644109  5644127  5644157  5644169
5644181  5644193  5644207  5644213  5644217  5644259  5644267  5644283  5644319  5644321
5644351  5644363  5644367  5644369  5644399  5644409  5644417  5644421  5644439
5644477  5644487  5644517  5644523  5644547  5644601  5644607  5644627  5644643  5644657
5644673  5644679  5644687  5644693  5644699  5644703  5644711  5644733  5644741  5644777
5644781  5644801  5644813  5644829  5644849  5644889  5644907  5644919  5644927  5644931
5644939  5644963  5644967  5644981  5644987  5644993  5645011  5645047  5645063  5645077
5645089  5645093  5645099  5645113  5645119  5645137  5645161  5645177  5645191  5645203
5645239  5645243  5645251  5645257  5645273  5645279  5645291  5645293  5645323  5645329
5645333  5645347  5645383  5645407  5645447  5645473  5645483  5645491  5645501  5645539
5645551  5645569  5645573  5645579  5645609  5645623  5645639  5645657  5645671  5645677
5645681  5645693  5645699  5645701  5645711  5645713  5645723  5645729  5645779  5645851
5645881  5645891  5645903  5645911  5645917  5645947  5645951  5645957  5646019  5646049
5646073  5646107  5646119  5646127  5646131  5646229  5646239  5646269  5646281  5646317
5646323  5646341  5646349  5646379  5646383  5646391  5646409  5646419  5646449  5646451
5646517  5646521  5646539  5646541  5646551  5646577  5646581  5646593  5646617  5646637
5646647  5646649  5646659  5646671  5646679  5646689  5646691  5646749  5646757  5646763
5646791  5646811  5646821  5646859  5646869  5646877  5646881  5646887  5646899  5646917
5646919  5646943  5646959  5646973  5646997  5647001  5647007  5647021  5647027  5647039
5647069  5647087  5647091  5647093  5647129  5647163  5647171  5647189  5647193  5647219
5647223  5647231  5647241  5647253  5647261  5647267  5647307  5647321  5647333  5647337
5647339  5647357  5647361  5647409  5647457  5647471  5647483  5647493  5647501  5647507
5647511  5647513  5647517  5647559  5647561  5647567  5647573  5647589  5647591  5647601
5647613  5647633  5647637  5647639  5647651  5647667  5647669  5647699  5647729  5647771
5647801  5647813  5647823  5647841  5647843  5647861  5647897  5647907  5647909  5647913
5647919  5647933  5647951  5647963  5647969  5647981  5647991  5648009  5648017  5648023
5648039  5648047  5648057  5648059  5648077  5648117  5648141  5648183  5648189  5648191
5648197  5648219  5648221  5648239  5648273  5648281  5648297  5648329  5648333  5648341
5648347  5648371  5648393  5648411  5648429  5648449  5648459  5648473  5648477  5648519
5648527  5648561  5648597  5648651  5648663  5648669  5648677  5648683  5648711  5648717
5648729  5648749  5648761  5648767  5648771  5648779  5648791  5648801  5648803  5648809
5648843  5648873  5648891  5648893  5648911  5648927  5648999  5649001  5649011  5649019
5649047  5649067  5649079  5649101  5649121  5649157  5649167  5649181  5649187  5649221
5649307  5649311  5649317  5649367  5649401  5649433  5649437  5649439  5649451  5649473
5649481  5649487  5649493  5649521  5649547  5649557  5649563  5649569  5649587  5649599
5649619  5649647  5649649  5649667  5649673  5649701  5649733  5649739  5649757  5649769
5649779  5649793  5649799  5649817  5649827  5649829  5649851  5649871  5649877  5649883
5649901  5649907  5649911  5649913  5649949  5649953  5649977  5649991  5650009  5650013
5650027  5650031  5650033  5650039  5650063  5650081  5650097  5650121  5650133  5650187
5650189  5650193  5650213  5650219  5650223  5650231  5650279  5650283  5650297  5650303
5650313  5650321  5650361  5650363  5650373  5650397  5650417  5650427  5650453  5650457
5650487  5650499  5650507  5650517  5650537  5650549  5650553  5650573  5650583  5650591
5650609  5650627  5650637  5650643  5650651  5650691  5650693  5650703  5650741  5650747
5650753  5650769  5650781  5650787  5650789  5650793  5650811  5650823  5650829  5650837
5650859  5650861  5650867  5650871  5650927  5650937  5650993  5651011  5651039  5651059
5651069  5651099  5651131  5651137  5651141  5651161  5651171  5651183  5651237  5651251
5651257  5651263  5651273  5651279  5651281  5651291  5651297  5651299  5651309  5651311
5651329  5651333  5651369  5651377  5651389  5651407  5651413  5651431  5651449  5651453
5651461  5651473  5651479  5651501  5651509  5651519  5651539  5651557  5651561  5651573
```

```
5651593  5651603  5651617  5651621  5651623  5651707  5651717  5651729  5651731  5651741
5651743  5651747  5651749  5651771  5651773  5651801  5651831  5651851  5651869  5651887
5651917  5651923  5651927  5651941  5651953  5651969  5651981  5651983  5651999  5652011
5652019  5652029  5652067  5652091  5652103  5652107  5652113  5652121  5652149  5652161
5652193  5652203  5652271  5652277  5652289  5652293  5652299  5652341  5652349  5652401
5652403  5652421  5652431  5652469  5652499  5652511  5652533  5652539  5652541  5652553
5652583  5652617  5652623  5652649  5652683  5652701  5652719  5652727  5652761  5652799
5652817  5652833  5652847  5652853  5652863  5652887  5652923  5652929  5652947  5652953
5652961  5652989  5653001  5653007  5653049  5653073  5653097  5653103  5653111  5653133
5653157  5653169  5653177  5653181  5653183  5653189  5653201  5653211  5653223  5653237
5653247  5653261  5653283  5653313  5653381  5653387  5653399  5653411  5653421  5653433
5653441  5653493  5653499  5653519  5653523  5653537  5653589  5653601  5653603  5653633
5653643  5653649  5653657  5653679  5653691  5653709  5653723  5653751  5653757  5653759
5653763  5653783  5653787  5653799  5653807  5653819  5653841  5653861  5653867  5653871
5653909  5653919  5653931  5653937  5653957  5653993  5654017  5654071  5654083  5654087
5654123  5654137  5654161  5654171  5654177  5654179  5654189  5654203  5654213  5654219
5654221  5654249  5654263  5654281  5654287  5654293  5654309  5654323  5654357  5654359
5654393  5654417  5654423  5654447  5654477  5654479  5654483  5654503  5654513  5654521
5654531  5654549  5654567  5654569  5654581  5654641  5654651  5654657  5654689  5654713
5654717  5654731  5654743  5654749  5654767  5654773  5654777  5654783  5654807  5654813
5654819  5654827  5654839  5654861  5654881  5654911  5654917  5654921  5654933  5654939
5654947  5654953  5655019  5655031  5655037  5655049  5655071  5655077  5655107  5655109
5655119  5655131  5655137  5655157  5655163  5655173  5655211  5655227  5655233  5655241
5655257  5655283  5655301  5655313  5655323  5655329  5655347  5655359  5655367  5655379
5655409  5655439  5655443  5655449  5655451  5655467  5655469  5655473  5655491  5655511
5655523  5655527  5655541  5655569  5655577  5655583  5655589  5655599  5655607  5655619
5655623  5655641  5655649  5655659  5655721  5655731  5655739  5655743  5655757  5655791
5655823  5655851  5655877  5655887  5655893  5655911  5655929  5655941  5655943  5655961
5655997  5656003  5656031  5656037  5656093  5656097  5656099  5656109  5656111  5656117
5656139  5656141  5656171  5656181  5656193  5656253  5656283  5656297  5656307  5656379
5656381  5656397  5656411  5656423  5656439  5656463  5656481  5656489  5656493  5656549
5656559  5656577  5656603  5656619  5656621  5656649  5656691  5656723  5656727  5656757
5656759  5656789  5656799  5656817  5656823  5656829  5656837  5656921  5656933  5656949
5656969  5656997  5656999  5657021  5657027  5657033  5657051  5657053  5657063  5657077
5657081  5657129  5657131  5657143  5657147  5657153  5657173  5657177  5657207  5657251
5657261  5657297  5657299  5657317  5657321  5657329  5657347  5657359  5657387  5657389
5657417  5657423  5657429  5657441  5657461  5657489  5657503  5657513  5657551  5657599
5657623  5657627  5657629  5657657  5657671  5657683  5657693  5657699  5657711  5657731
5657749  5657761  5657767  5657789  5657831  5657837  5657851  5657867  5657881  5657887
5657921  5657941  5657969  5657989  5657999  5658007  5658031  5658043  5658047  5658071
5658073  5658097  5658109  5658113  5658119  5658131  5658137  5658139  5658187  5658223
5658251  5658259  5658269  5658281  5658307  5658329  5658343  5658379  5658383  5658397
5658403  5658407  5658463  5658469  5658473  5658479  5658491  5658493  5658503  5658547
5658557  5658559  5658571  5658577  5658589  5658593  5658613  5658623  5658643  5658649
5658673  5658677  5658707  5658721  5658733  5658761  5658769  5658781  5658791  5658823
5658839  5658859  5658889  5658893  5658899  5658949  5658959  5658967  5658977  5658997
5659001  5659009  5659013  5659037  5659051  5659057  5659063  5659067  5659091  5659097
5659099  5659111  5659117  5659141  5659163  5659177  5659183  5659193  5659201  5659211
5659229  5659237  5659259  5659279  5659307  5659319  5659343  5659363  5659373  5659399
5659417  5659441  5659447  5659469  5659477  5659513  5659543  5659547  5659559  5659567
5659597  5659603  5659609  5659627  5659651  5659663  5659721  5659723  5659729  5659751
5659781  5659783  5659813  5659837  5659847  5659859  5659873  5659877  5659879  5659883
5659897  5659919  5659921  5659931  5659937  5659943  5659957  5659987  5659993  5660003
5660033  5660059  5660071  5660087  5660101  5660147  5660153  5660177  5660189  5660203
5660209  5660243  5660273  5660279  5660293  5660299  5660327  5660341  5660359  5660363
5660381  5660393  5660411  5660443  5660449  5660471  5660491  5660503  5660513  5660521
5660527  5660531  5660561  5660579  5660581  5660591  5660623  5660653  5660657  5660663
5660717  5660723  5660731  5660749  5660761  5660789  5660797  5660801  5660807  5660833
5660843  5660867  5660869  5660899  5660923  5660927  5660929  5660933  5660951  5660971
5660987  5660989  5660999  5661001  5661041  5661067  5661083  5661113  5661121  5661141
5661163  5661167  5661169  5661179  5661191  5661203  5661209  5661217  5661247  5661277
5661281  5661283  5661287  5661311  5661317  5661319  5661343  5661367  5661389  5661401
5661419  5661421  5661451  5661457  5661497  5661503  5661517  5661521  5661529  5661547
5661559  5661587  5661589  5661613  5661631  5661637  5661647  5661653  5661659  5661673
5661683  5661713  5661727  5661739  5661743  5661779  5661781  5661787  5661811  5661823
5661839  5661893  5661899  5661907  5661911  5661923  5661941  5661961  5661973  5661991
5662039  5662049  5662051  5662087  5662093  5662109  5662121  5662123  5662159  5662169
5662201  5662211  5662229  5662249  5662253  5662273  5662277  5662297  5662313  5662331
5662351  5662357  5662373  5662381  5662409  5662421  5662451  5662471  5662477  5662487
5662499  5662523  5662529  5662561  5662567  5662597  5662609  5662619  5662637  5662663
5662681  5662697  5662729  5662733  5662757  5662759  5662781  5662793  5662823  5662831
5662843  5662847  5662849  5662861  5662873  5662883  5662897  5662903  5662913  5662919
5662927  5662933  5662963  5662967  5663011  5663017  5663039  5663051
5663059  5663069  5663071  5663081  5663089  5663093  5663101  5663107  5663123  5663131
5663153  5663201  5663219  5663239  5663263  5663269  5663293  5663303  5663321  5663327
5663347  5663353  5663369  5663377  5663389  5663393  5663407  5663417  5663419  5663429
5663459  5663467  5663477  5663491  5663503  5663513  5663519  5663521  5663549  5663561
5663569  5663579  5663591  5663597  5663611  5663657  5663689  5663759  5663783  5663803
5663807  5663821  5663887  5663893  5663897  5663909  5663929  5663953  5663969  5663989
5663993  5664011  5664013  5664031  5664053  5664067  5664083  5664091  5664101  5664107
5664151  5664157  5664173  5664199  5664203  5664209  5664257  5664271  5664287  5664301
5664311  5664313  5664359  5664377  5664397  5664401  5664419  5664427  5664431  5664443
5664467  5664479  5664493  5664497  5664499  5664511  5664523  5664563  5664611  5664623
5664629  5664653  5664671  5664697  5664707  5664719  5664731  5664779  5664797  5664809
5664817  5664823  5664829  5664851  5664931  5664941  5664943  5664977  5664979  5664991
5665013  5665027  5665039  5665043  5665069  5665073  5665081  5665109  5665123  5665151
5665159  5665183  5665189  5665193  5665213  5665217  5665243  5665259  5665273  5665277
5665313  5665349  5665351  5665367  5665381  5665399  5665417  5665433  5665441  5665447
5665459  5665463  5665483  5665507  5665519  5665531  5665537  5665549  5665559  5665571
```

```
5665579  5665601  5665609  5665631  5665661  5665687  5665691  5665703  5665733  5665747
5665783  5665787  5665797  5665837  5665853  5665883  5665903  5665937  5665949  5665967
5665969  5665993  5665997  5666021  5666051  5666053  5666093  5666131  5666181  5666191
5666197  5666203  5666209  5666233  5666249  5666251  5666261  5666263  5666267  5666279
5666317  5666341  5666347  5666377  5666383  5666387  5666393  5666407  5666417  5666431
5666443  5666447  5666467  5666483  5666489  5666501  5666519  5666527  5666539  5666561
5666599  5666621  5666623  5666641  5666677  5666681  5666701  5666711  5666737  5666767
5666777  5666783  5666789  5666819  5666821  5666833  5666849  5666873  5666887  5666911
5666939  5666951  5666953  5666963  5666971  5666981  5666987  5667029  5667047  5667071
5667089  5667091  5667097  5667113  5667133  5667173  5667197  5667199  5667217  5667241
5667247  5667281  5667283  5667287  5667293  5667313  5667317  5667359  5667367  5667371
5667373  5667379  5667421  5667427  5667437  5667461  5667503  5667517  5667523  5667547
5667593  5667601  5667611  5667631  5667667  5667679  5667689  5667691  5667703  5667709
5667737  5667769  5667773  5667803  5667841  5667853  5667863  5667869  5667901  5667911
5667917  5667931  5667941  5667971  5667973  5667983  5667989  5667997  5668027  5668037
5668049  5668063  5668073  5668129  5668139  5668151  5668163  5668177  5668211  5668237
5668241  5668249  5668279  5668283  5668301  5668309  5668339  5668343  5668357  5668387
5668433  5668447  5668451  5668469  5668471  5668477  5668483  5668489  5668493  5668513
5668519  5668563  5668571  5668573  5668583  5668591  5668609  5668627  5668639  5668673
5668681  5668687  5668699  5668727  5668757  5668759  5668771  5668801  5668813  5668823
5668829  5668867  5668903  5668909  5668919  5668951  5668963  5668997  5669021  5669023
5669051  5669089  5669099  5669129  5669159  5669189  5669203  5669207  5669221  5669243
5669263  5669267  5669273  5669291  5669309  5669317  5669327  5669333  5669371  5669387
5669423  5669437  5669441  5669479  5669501  5669513  5669537  5669539  5669561  5669579
5669611  5669617  5669623  5669627  5669639  5669659  5669663  5669681  5669693  5669711
5669731  5669747  5669759  5669773  5669777  5669791  5669801  5669803  5669821
5669827  5669831  5669861  5669863  5669879  5669893  5669903  5669929  5669933  5669947
5669953  5669969  5669971  5669977  5670031  5670053  5670059  5670089  5670097  5670103
5670149  5670157  5670173  5670193  5670199  5670209  5670229  5670257  5670263  5670307
5670323  5670331  5670337  5670349  5670359  5670373  5670391  5670403  5670419  5670433
5670439  5670451  5670461  5670473  5670479  5670481  5670487  5670491  5670527  5670529
5670547  5670593  5670611  5670619  5670641  5670649  5670653  5670661  5670671  5670697
5670701  5670703  5670757  5670779  5670787  5670803  5670823  5670827  5670829  5670839
5670851  5670853  5670869  5670887  5670937  5670941  5670961  5670979  5670989  5671019
5671033  5671091  5671093  5671097  5671111  5671117  5671147  5671181  5671199  5671207
5671213  5671241  5671261  5671277  5671279  5671361  5671381  5671403  5671411  5671417
5671427  5671429  5671451  5671499  5671507  5671511  5671513  5671517  5671553  5671573
5671579  5671609  5671613  5671621  5671649  5671669  5671681  5671697  5671717  5671739
5671741  5671753  5671763  5671769  5671789  5671793  5671801  5671807  5671811  5671837
5671859  5671871  5671877  5671921  5671927  5671949  5671957  5671969  5671979  5671987
5671993  5672011  5672021  5672057  5672071  5672111  5672123  5672131  5672141  5672143
5672167  5672179  5672189  5672231  5672239  5672263  5672267  5672291  5672299  5672311
5672321  5672327  5672333  5672341  5672351  5672353  5672363  5672369  5672377  5672389
5672399  5672413  5672423  5672449  5672453  5672461  5672501  5672531  5672533  5672539
5672549  5672551  5672561  5672591  5672599  5672609  5672627  5672629  5672633  5672663
5672669  5672677  5672707  5672721  5672767  5672809  5672813  5672827  5672831
5672833  5672837  5672857  5672869  5672873  5672879  5672923  5672929  5672959  5672977
5672983  5672993  5672999  5673011  5673013  5673023  5673029  5673037  5673043  5673079
5673089  5673097  5673149  5673163  5673179  5673181  5673233  5673259  5673281  5673287
5673319  5673329  5673361  5673373  5673383  5673401  5673407  5673413  5673431  5673443
5673449  5673557  5673587  5673601  5673623  5673637  5673643  5673649  5673653  5673659
5673673  5673677  5673683  5673719  5673727  5673737  5673739  5673743  5673757  5673781
5673827  5673851  5673883  5673901  5673907  5673911  5673929  5673947  5673953  5673959
5673973  5673991  5674033  5674049  5674091  5674093  5674117  5674133  5674177  5674181
5674183  5674199  5674219  5674223  5674231  5674241  5674247  5674259  5674267  5674289
5674309  5674337  5674351  5674381  5674411  5674421  5674439  5674453  5674463  5674489
5674507  5674511  5674547  5674589  5674601  5674607  5674621  5674631  5674661  5674663
5674693  5674703  5674717  5674723  5674759  5674783  5674819  5674831  5674847  5674873
5674897  5674909  5674913  5674927  5674931  5674937  5674961  5674969  5674987  5674993
5675017  5675027  5675029  5675063  5675069  5675071  5675083  5675107  5675119  5675141
5675143  5675147  5675149  5675177  5675191  5675207  5675221  5675233  5675237  5675279
5675287  5675311  5675317  5675333  5675339  5675347  5675359  5675363  5675377  5675381
5675389  5675401  5675407  5675419  5675429  5675443  5675447  5675473  5675489  5675491
5675513  5675519  5675539  5675543  5675557  5675563  5675587  5675591  5675599  5675633
5675639  5675653  5675711  5675713  5675723  5675729  5675731  5675749  5675801  5675827
5675833  5675843  5675849  5675869  5675881  5675893  5675903  5675933  5675959  5675981
5675983  5675987  5675993  5676001  5676017  5676031  5676037  5676053  5676067  5676089
5676107  5676109  5676127  5676137  5676157  5676179  5676191  5676211  5676217  5676271
5676277  5676313  5676367  5676371  5676401  5676403  5676427  5676439  5676467  5676493
5676499  5676523  5676551  5676557  5676563  5676569  5676571  5676617  5676641  5676647
5676659  5676661  5676667  5676679  5676719  5676733  5676739  5676757  5676761  5676767
5676787  5676823  5676833  5676841  5676851  5676857  5676863  5676887  5676889  5676893
5676919  5676941  5676943  5676961  5676981  5677003  5677013  5677037  5677057
5677073  5677079  5677081  5677097  5677121  5677129  5677163  5677187  5677193  5677207
5677211  5677213  5677223  5677249  5677253  5677261  5677279  5677289  5677327  5677339
5677349  5677363  5677367  5677403  5677423  5677457  5677489  5677517  5677537  5677543
5677549  5677559  5677571  5677583  5677589  5677601  5677603  5677621  5677663  5677667
5677691  5677699  5677703  5677709  5677723  5677729  5677739  5677753  5677801  5677807
5677817  5677843  5677853  5677873  5677891  5677897  5677913  5677937  5677957  5677963
5677993  5678003  5678039  5678041  5678069  5678077  5678129  5678143  5678149
5678173  5678191  5678203  5678209  5678227  5678243  5678269  5678273  5678293  5678327
5678329  5678339  5678341  5678347  5678411  5678419  5678423  5678437  5678471  5678483
5678489  5678507  5678521  5678531  5678581  5678593  5678609  5678627  5678641  5678669
5678713  5678737  5678767  5678773  5678779  5678789  5678807  5678821  5678831  5678839
5678843  5678851  5678883  5678899  5678903  5678923  5678941  5678947  5678957  5678989
5678993  5679013  5679017  5679029  5679031  5679101  5679103  5679127  5679131  5679143
5679199  5679211  5679221  5679251  5679259  5679263  5679269  5679299  5679319
5679337  5679341  5679371  5679383  5679391  5679407  5679419  5679431  5679449  5679451
5679467  5679481  5679511  5679521  5679539  5679559  5679571  5679577  5679589  5679593
```

```
5679601  5679617  5679623  5679637  5679673  5679677  5679691  5679701  5679721  5679749
5679769  5679829  5679847  5679899  5679923  5679941  5679943  5679953  5679967  5679977
5679979  5679983  5680001  5680007  5680009  5680019  5680049  5680067  5680079  5680097
5680111  5680133  5680151  5680153  5680163  5680177  5680187  5680189  5680211  5680229
5680231  5680237  5680243  5680249  5680253  5680289  5680319  5680357  5680361  5680369
5680393  5680403  5680453  5680459  5680483  5680489  5680501  5680559  5680613  5680621
5680627  5680643  5680667  5680679  5680681  5680691  5680709  5680733  5680739  5680751
5680783  5680789  5680799  5680813  5680823  5680841  5680847  5680861  5680877  5680891
5680901  5680921  5680963  5681003  5681033  5681059  5681089  5681119  5681141  5681167
5681177  5681191  5681201  5681227  5681231  5681237  5681243  5681279  5681293  5681297
5681309  5681311  5681317  5681327  5681369  5681381  5681413  5681447  5681449  5681453
5681471  5681497  5681503  5681509  5681521  5681531  5681561  5681567  5681579  5681603
5681617  5681623  5681629  5681647  5681693  5681699  5681707  5681717  5681729  5681737
5681743  5681761  5681777  5681803  5681861  5681869  5681899  5681911  5681933  5681939
5681947  5681981  5681983  5682011  5682023  5682031  5682041  5682049  5682073  5682091
5682109  5682119  5682137  5682143  5682151  5682161  5682167  5682217  5682221  5682223
5682239  5682251  5682293  5682319  5682329  5682353  5682371  5682373  5682379  5682401
5682409  5682419  5682451  5682461  5682503  5682529  5682553  5682569  5682581  5682631
5682643  5682647  5682659  5682661  5682667  5682671  5682673  5682689  5682697  5682701
5682731  5682763  5682773  5682779  5682791  5682797  5682829  5682839  5682841  5682851
5682893  5682899  5682907  5682931  5682953  5682961  5682973  5682979  5682983  5682997
5683003  5683037  5683061  5683063  5683081  5683087  5683121  5683127  5683129  5683189
5683213  5683283  5683289  5683291  5683303  5683313  5683319  5683343  5683351  5683357
5683361  5683367  5683387  5683421  5683427  5683453  5683463  5683471  5683481  5683487
5683499  5683501  5683537  5683547  5683549  5683577  5683583  5683609  5683619  5683637
5683651  5683673  5683687  5683703  5683721  5683751  5683753  5683771  5683781  5683801
5683817  5683823  5683841  5683859  5683889  5683901  5683949  5683957  5683961  5683963
5683981  5683987  5684011  5684017  5684033  5684057  5684071  5684083  5684099  5684101
5684111  5684113  5684123  5684131  5684141  5684149  5684167  5684183  5684209  5684233
5684257  5684269  5684279  5684311  5684323  5684353  5684383  5684387  5684389  5684411
5684417  5684423  5684431  5684449  5684459  5684489  5684521  5684533  5684537  5684561
5684693  5684617  5684633  5684639  5684641  5684659  5684663  5684669  5684671  5684699
5684713  5684737  5684741  5684747  5684759  5684771  5684837  5684839  5684849  5684863
5684867  5684881  5684891  5684909  5684927  5684929  5684941  5684947  5684963  5684969
5684981  5684983  5685023  5685037  5685049  5685061  5685067  5685083  5685103  5685137
5685149  5685179  5685203  5685221  5685227  5685241  5685283  5685287  5685311  5685319
5685341  5685343  5685349  5685371  5685373  5685377  5685397  5685403  5685413  5685451
5685481  5685487  5685499  5685523  5685529  5685539  5685557  5685569  5685601  5685607
5685613  5685619  5685643  5685649  5685661  5685677  5685683  5685689  5685697  5685733
5685739  5685763  5685773  5685781  5685791  5685809  5685829  5685833  5685857  5685859
5685863  5685887  5685887  5685961  5685971  5686003  5686063  5686067  5686091  5686099
5686127  5686133  5686139  5686141  5686147  5686151  5686157  5686159  5686169  5686181
5686193  5686217  5686229  5686253  5686259  5686297  5686309  5686333  5686397  5686399
5686403  5686411  5686427  5686433  5686441  5686487  5686501  5686507  5686519  5686531
5686537  5686573  5686591  5686601  5686607  5686613  5686631  5686633  5686649  5686669
5686673  5686691  5686693  5686711  5686717  5686739  5686759  5686763  5686787  5686817
5686829  5686843  5686853  5686861  5686867  5686873  5686921  5686931  5686949  5686963
5686979  5686991  5686997  5687009  5687021  5687053  5687063  5687081  5687089  5687093
5687107  5687111  5687119  5687179  5687191  5687237  5687239  5687249  5687261  5687267
5687273  5687303  5687317  5687369  5687387  5687389  5687413  5687419  5687431  5687449
5687453  5687459  5687471  5687491  5687497  5687501  5687531  5687551  5687599  5687609
5687651  5687657  5687687  5687699  5687711  5687743  5687761  5687767  5687771  5687791
5687813  5687827  5687833  5687837  5687839  5687861  5687863  5687867  5687873  5687887
5687917  5687951  5687959  5687977  5687993  5687999  5688037  5688041  5688043  5688071
5688077  5688091  5688127  5688139  5688143  5688167  5688191  5688247  5688259  5688281
5688313  5688317  5688329  5688359  5688401  5688409  5688443  5688461  5688479  5688493
5688497  5688499  5688503  5688509  5688511  5688517  5688539  5688541  5688547  5688559
5688569  5688577  5688607  5688653  5688667  5688679  5688689  5688701  5688719  5688743
5688757  5688773  5688803  5688811  5688821  5688827  5688871  5688883  5688887  5688899
5688911  5688913  5688919  5688929  5688941  5688971  5688979  5688983  5688989  5688997
5689007  5689039  5689087  5689091  5689097  5689111  5689121  5689127  5689129  5689139
5689141  5689153  5689183  5689207  5689241  5689247  5689289  5689309  5689351  5689361
5689363  5689369  5689381  5689403  5689457  5689483  5689499  5689507  5689513  5689517
5689549  5689591  5689613  5689637  5689639  5689643  5689657  5689661  5689703  5689741
5689753  5689757  5689787  5689793  5689799  5689811  5689813  5689819  5689843  5689847
5689861  5689877  5689891  5689933  5689967  5689973  5689991  5690023  5690051  5690057
5690059  5690071  5690077  5690099  5690129  5690159  5690171  5690197  5690203  5690207
5690213  5690249  5690261  5690273  5690297  5690299  5690303  5690317  5690323  5690339
5690357  5690371  5690381  5690383  5690413  5690429  5690471  5690473  5690483  5690497
5690501  5690527  5690533  5690537  5690539  5690543  5690551  5690561  5690593  5690599
5690611  5690617  5690621  5690623  5690627  5690651  5690669  5690687  5690689  5690693
5690717  5690719  5690723  5690731  5690753  5690761  5690777  5690791  5690813  5690827
5690833  5690837  5690851  5690867  5690881  5690897  5690901  5690917  5690929  5690941
5690953  5690957  5690969  5690977  5690983  5690987  5691001  5691029  5691041  5691043
5691053  5691071  5691079  5691083  5691109  5691113  5691121  5691131  5691137  5691139
5691149  5691151  5691167  5691173  5691187  5691211  5691247  5691253  5691263  5691269
5691293  5691319  5691349  5691359  5691403  5691409  5691421  5691457  5691463  5691467
5691487  5691493  5691499  5691509  5691529  5691533  5691541  5691547  5691551  5691563
5691577  5691601  5691613  5691619  5691641  5691667  5691689  5691691  5691701  5691709
5691739  5691757  5691761  5691793  5691799  5691823  5691827  5691869  5691877  5691893
5691899  5691913  5691919  5691929  5691943  5691947  5691977  5692007  5692009  5692031
5692051  5692061  5692067  5692097  5692103  5692121  5692129  5692133  5692157  5692171
5692177  5692199  5692243  5692249  5692279  5692289  5692301  5692319  5692327  5692363
5692367  5692391  5692397  5692403  5692411  5692441  5692471  5692541  5692559  5692573
5692591  5692597  5692643  5692649  5692657  5692667  5692669  5692693  5692699  5692717
5692751  5692763  5692769  5692777  5692801  5692811  5692823  5692853  5692859  5692861
5692877  5692879  5692901  5692927  5692949  5692957  5692963  5693021  5693033  5693047
5693081  5693089  5693117  5693123  5693131  5693171  5693173  5693189  5693201  5693203
5693209  5693231  5693263  5693287  5693297  5693299  5693327  5693333  5693339  5693353
```

```
5693357  5693371  5693399  5693411  5693417  5693431  5693461  5693503  5693509  5693539
5693543  5693549  5693563  5693573  5693591  5693617  5693621  5693641  5693647  5693651
5693659  5693663  5693669  5693683  5693707  5693713  5693729  5693741  5693747  5693771
5693797  5693813  5693837  5693839  5693851  5693881  5693887  5693899  5693917  5693921
5693959  5693969  5693971  5693993  5693999  5694011  5694019  5694037  5694043  5694047
5694067  5694071  5694109  5694113  5694119  5694137  5694151  5694163  5694187  5694197
5694209  5694217  5694239  5694259  5694277  5694313  5694323  5694329  5694331  5694337
5694341  5694347  5694389  5694391  5694407  5694427  5694431  5694443  5694499  5694517
5694539  5694569  5694581  5694649  5694659  5694671  5694673  5694709  5694719  5694727
5694743  5694761  5694763  5694769  5694841  5694883  5694893  5694901  5694907  5694919
5694971  5694989  5695013  5695033  5695069  5695091  5695097  5695111  5695133  5695139
5695159  5695163  5695171  5695177  5695229  5695253  5695259  5695271  5695273  5695279
5695297  5695301  5695303  5695309  5695321  5695367  5695379  5695381  5695399  5695409
5695411  5695439  5695451  5695457  5695463  5695471  5695477  5695483  5695499  5695531
5695619  5695621  5695633  5695639  5695667  5695681  5695721  5695727  5695741  5695747
5695757  5695769  5695777  5695783  5695787  5695813  5695819  5695829  5695831  5695841
5695849  5695853  5695889  5695903  5695933  5695959  5695961  5695967  5695981  5696017
5696021  5696027  5696057  5696063  5696101  5696107  5696123  5696129  5696147  5696153
5696161  5696177  5696183  5696191  5696221  5696227  5696239  5696279  5696291  5696293
5696321  5696329  5696347  5696351  5696357  5696381  5696389  5696393  5696399  5696423
5696429  5696437  5696459  5696461  5696477  5696489  5696491  5696497  5696503  5696531
5696533  5696549  5696569  5696629  5696633  5696641  5696651  5696659  5696671  5696681
5696693  5696707  5696711  5696723  5696737  5696741  5696753  5696759  5696767  5696771
5696783  5696791  5696813  5696849  5696861  5696891  5696897  5696923  5696953  5696959
5696983  5696987  5697047  5697049  5697053  5697061  5697071  5697127  5697161  5697173
5697179  5697191  5697221  5697247  5697257  5697269  5697277  5697287  5697301  5697317
5697323  5697331  5697343  5697379  5697383  5697403  5697421  5697443  5697451  5697463
5697467  5697487  5697493  5697509  5697529  5697547  5697551  5697563  5697581  5697599
5697617  5697619  5697631  5697641  5697661  5697673  5697677  5697697  5697709  5697719
5697743  5697751  5697761  5697793  5697829  5697841  5697851  5697863  5697883  5697899
5697911  5697917  5697919  5697931  5697943  5697953  5697983  5698003  5698013  5698031
5698039  5698051  5698073  5698093  5698097  5698151  5698153  5698159  5698163  5698169
5698171  5698183  5698211  5698219  5698223  5698229  5698243  5698249  5698261  5698267
5698289  5698313  5698331  5698339  5698351  5698361  5698367  5698379  5698391  5698393
5698439  5698463  5698493  5698501  5698523  5698543  5698547  5698571  5698573  5698577
5698579  5698591  5698603  5698607  5698639  5698691  5698717  5698739  5698741  5698753
5698769  5698783  5698807  5698811  5698813  5698817  5698829  5698831  5698837  5698843
5698853  5698883  5698907  5698921  5698933  5698939  5698949  5698951  5698967  5698997
5699011  5699017  5699021  5699027  5699033  5699039  5699053  5699081  5699117  5699119
5699137  5699153  5699159  5699161  5699191  5699203  5699207  5699227  5699231  5699237
5699261  5699269  5699311  5699357  5699359  5699363  5699371  5699389  5699431  5699467
5699479  5699497  5699503  5699557  5699587  5699593  5699599  5699609  5699627  5699647
5699669  5699713  5699717  5699723  5699731  5699741  5699761  5699773  5699789  5699807
5699819  5699821  5699839  5699851  5699857  5699873  5699899  5699909  5699923  5699927
5699933  5699963  5699971  5699983  5699987  5699989  5700007  5700031  5700041  5700047
5700053  5700061  5700073  5700089  5700091  5700131  5700139  5700157  5700173  5700179
5700181  5700193  5700221  5700229  5700239  5700259  5700263  5700283  5700307  5700341
5700347  5700349  5700367  5700391  5700397  5700419  5700421  5700439  5700451  5700473
5700493  5700533  5700547  5700571  5700577  5700581  5700601  5700623  5700631  5700637
5700659  5700671  5700679  5700691  5700713  5700731  5700767  5700769  5700781  5700823
5700833  5700847  5700857  5700859  5700883  5700887  5700911  5700913  5700943  5700949
5700973  5700991  5701013  5701019  5701037  5701043  5701049  5701061  5701093  5701123
5701133  5701169  5701177  5701207  5701211  5701249  5701253  5701259  5701261  5701271
5701291  5701301  5701321  5701357  5701361  5701379  5701391  5701393  5701403  5701417
5701637  5701639  5701643  5701649  5701651  5701669  5701679  5701693  5701727  5701733
5701739  5701741  5701763  5701781  5701789  5701807  5701831  5701837  5701847  5701849
5701873  5701877  5701889  5701897  5701909  5701931  5701933  5701979  5701981  5701991
5702003  5702023  5702027  5702029  5702041  5702057  5702063  5702129  5702131  5702143
5702153  5702159  5702161  5702201  5702227  5702231  5702237  5702267  5702287  5702297
5702353  5702363  5702381  5702387  5702401  5702407  5702449  5702453  5702471  5702479
5702483  5702503  5702539  5702563  5702569  5702581  5702591  5702611  5702623  5702639
5702663  5702693  5702737  5702759  5702777  5702819  5702843  5702857  5702861  5702867
5702897  5702911  5702923  5702927  5702929  5702941  5702947  5702969  5702981  5703001
5703017  5703023  5703029  5703037  5703077  5703091  5703127  5703151  5703157  5703161
5703197  5703199  5703221  5703233  5703239  5703251  5703259  5703263  5703281  5703283
5703289  5703293  5703301  5703307  5703311  5703319  5703323  5703329  5703337  5703361
5703367  5703371  5703377  5703407  5703409  5703427  5703431  5703437  5703463  5703479
5703493  5703499  5703521  5703527  5703557  5703559  5703583  5703611  5703623  5703631
5703641  5703679  5703689  5703713  5703727  5703739  5703751  5703757  5703787  5703791
5703811  5703851  5703889  5703899  5703917  5703989  5703991  5704003  5704007  5704033
5704057  5704081  5704087  5704103  5704109  5704121  5704141  5704157  5704159  5704187
5704189  5704201  5704241  5704247  5704267  5704273  5704291  5704319  5704331  5704339
5704357  5704373  5704393  5704397  5704409  5704441  5704451  5704463  5704481  5704487
5704499  5704513  5704547  5704583  5704591  5704603  5704607  5704609  5704613  5704667
5704631  5704649  5704661  5704709  5704717  5704729  5704747  5704757  5704789  5704801
5704819  5704823  5704841  5704847  5704859  5704873  5704889  5704891  5704913  5704949
5704957  5704969  5704987  5704991  5704999  5705033  5705039  5705057  5705069  5705071
5705093  5705107  5705113  5705137  5705153  5705159  5705177  5705179  5705201  5705213
5705237  5705239  5705243  5705279  5705281  5705299  5705303  5705309  5705321  5705327
5705341  5705417  5705419  5705423  5705467  5705527  5705543  5705569  5705573  5705597
5705599  5705603  5705621  5705629  5705671  5705699  5705731  5705737  5705741  5705783
5705789  5705803  5705809  5705827  5705849  5705857  5705867  5705873  5705879  5705939
5705957  5705969  5705977  5705981  5706013  5706017  5706031  5706049  5706053  5706079
5706083  5706121  5706131  5706163  5706193  5706221  5706269  5706287  5706299  5706307
5706313  5706319  5706329  5706331  5706343  5706353  5706377  5706383  5706391  5706397
5706409  5706419  5706427  5706443  5706469  5706497  5706529  5706541  5706581  5706583
5706637  5706641  5706643  5706647  5706653  5706661  5706671  5706677  5706683
5706689  5706709  5706721  5706731  5706773  5706791  5706797  5706853  5706863  5706887
```

```
5706901  5706907  5706919  5706931  5706937  5706949  5706959  5706971  5706979  5707001
5707027  5707033  5707043  5707061  5707073  5707133  5707157  5707183  5707231  5707237
5707249  5707259  5707279  5707301  5707307  5707309  5707319  5707357  5707397  5707399
5707447  5707451  5707453  5707459  5707463  5707469  5707501  5707523  5707547  5707549
5707553  5707571  5707573  5707591  5707607  5707613  5707679  5707711  5707721  5707747
5707753  5707759  5707763  5707781  5707811  5707817  5707843  5707853  5707861  5707883
5707901  5707907  5707921  5707939  5707963  5707967  5707969  5708011  5708029  5708033
5708057  5708069  5708077  5708081  5708083  5708093  5708161  5708167  5708173  5708179
5708203  5708231  5708233  5708237  5708251  5708279  5708357  5708359  5708377  5708383
5708399  5708401  5708429  5708431  5708453  5708473  5708501  5708533  5708539  5708543
5708579  5708603  5708609  5708627  5708639  5708641  5708671  5708687  5708701  5708707
5708711  5708779  5708783  5708803  5708831  5708839  5708861  5708887  5708891  5708893
5708903  5708909  5708933  5708939  5708953  5708971  5708977  5708999  5709007  5709013
5709019  5709029  5709061  5709071  5709073  5709089  5709091  5709097  5709103  5709149
5709163  5709169  5709217  5709269  5709281  5709287  5709289  5709293  5709299  5709307
5709349  5709377  5709397  5709421  5709437  5709479  5709493  5709523  5709527  5709533
5709541  5709547  5709559  5709593  5709601  5709623  5709629  5709643  5709647  5709659
5709667  5709677  5709679  5709689  5709719  5709721  5709751  5709757  5709779  5709787
5709799  5709811  5709817  5709857  5709863  5709887  5709901  5709917  5709923  5709929
5709953  5710021  5710031  5710037  5710039  5710043  5710087  5710097  5710109  5710123
5710139  5710163  5710189  5710207  5710219  5710223  5710261  5710333  5710337  5710349
5710363  5710373  5710387  5710391  5710399  5710403  5710409  5710429  5710457  5710493
5710511  5710513  5710517  5710531  5710567  5710631  5710667  5710699  5710711  5710721
5710729  5710741  5710751  5710753  5710769  5710781  5710799  5710801  5710813  5710819
5710823  5710841  5710847  5710853  5710871  5710897  5710919  5710927  5710933  5710937
5710961  5710973  5710979  5710993  5711029  5711051  5711071  5711081  5711087  5711089
5711113  5711149  5711171  5711179  5711197  5711203  5711213  5711257  5711261  5711287
5711297  5711323  5711327  5711351  5711399  5711401  5711411  5711413  5711417  5711437
5711467  5711477  5711483  5711501  5711509  5711527  5711539  5711543  5711551  5711557
5711591  5711597  5711603  5711623  5711627  5711663  5711681  5711747  5711759  5711773
5711777  5711807  5711809  5711821  5711831  5711851  5711861  5711899  5711903  5711911
5711917  5711921  5711933  5711939  5711963  5711971  5711987  5712011  5712013  5712041
5712059  5712061  5712121  5712139  5712149  5712151  5712167  5712169  5712173  5712193
5712199  5712209  5712229  5712241  5712247  5712271  5712283  5712299  5712313  5712323
5712341  5712347  5712359  5712361  5712367  5712373  5712383  5712389  5712431  5712451
5712457  5712479  5712491  5712523  5712529  5712583  5712601  5712611  5712613  5712617
5712631  5712647  5712659  5712677  5712683  5712703  5712713  5712719  5712737  5712743
5712757  5712769  5712823  5712829  5712859  5712869  5712887  5712893  5712919  5712929
5712943  5712953  5712961  5712983  5712989  5713007  5713013  5713049  5713061  5713067
5713069  5713093  5713117  5713121  5713151  5713153  5713159  5713163  5713171  5713181
5713217  5713219  5713229  5713231  5713249  5713259  5713283  5713289  5713297  5713327
5713333  5713369  5713399  5713403  5713427  5713439  5713447  5713457  5713459  5713481
5713507  5713511  5713529  5713531  5713537  5713541  5713549  5713553  5713597  5713601
5713607  5713613  5713633  5713663  5713681  5713709  5713723  5713733  5713739  5713753
5713759  5713769  5713777  5713781  5713787  5713789  5713811  5713843  5713847  5713891
5713901  5713909  5713919  5713933  5713937  5713943  5713949  5713963  5713993  5714029
5714063  5714069  5714077  5714081  5714083  5714087  5714099  5714101  5714123  5714153
5714167  5714171  5714197  5714207  5714249  5714309  5714311  5714321  5714339  5714347
5714353  5714369  5714377  5714389  5714393  5714411  5714417  5714453  5714461  5714483
5714491  5714503  5714507  5714519  5714521  5714531  5714581  5714587  5714591  5714609
5714627  5714641  5714647  5714671  5714689  5714699  5714701  5714747  5714759  5714783
5714803  5714837  5714843  5714851  5714857  5714869  5714893  5714959  5714963  5714987
5715011  5715023  5715037  5715041  5715049  5715053  5715071  5715089  5715091  5715121
5715133  5715163  5715169  5715187  5715209  5715211  5715217  5715221  5715239  5715251
5715299  5715319  5715323  5715329  5715343  5715373  5715379  5715403  5715433  5715449
5715461  5715469  5715473  5715481  5715487  5715497  5715499  5715527  5715547  5715557
5715583  5715601  5715617  5715631  5715641  5715643  5715673  5715683  5715701  5715719
5715727  5715733  5715737  5715739  5715763  5715767  5715793  5715817  5715823  5715839
5715841  5715863  5715901  5715949  5715989  5715991  5716003  5716013  5716021  5716031
5716037  5716043  5716049  5716091  5716133  5716141  5716147  5716153  5716157  5716171
5716181  5716211  5716223  5716231  5716253  5716273  5716289  5716303  5716309  5716327
5716363  5716367  5716379  5716387  5716391  5716409  5716429  5716433  5716441  5716453
5716483  5716517  5716553  5716561  5716583  5716591  5716597  5716619  5716621  5716631
5716639  5716649  5716681  5716691  5716693  5716699  5716717  5716727  5716729  5716757
5716771  5716787  5716801  5716813  5716819  5716829  5716847  5716871  5716897  5716901
5716937  5716943  5716961  5716987  5717021  5717029  5717053  5717059  5717069  5717077
5717111  5717143  5717149  5717161  5717183  5717189  5717191  5717207  5717213  5717227
5717249  5717251  5717281  5717291  5717293  5717297  5717303  5717329  5717339  5717353
5717399  5717401  5717419  5717431  5717441  5717447  5717489  5717521  5717533  5717549
5717563  5717567  5717599  5717603  5717623  5717629  5717641  5717653  5717681  5717683
5717707  5717741  5717743  5717771  5717773  5717809  5717827  5717837  5717849  5717851
5717861  5717863  5717891  5717893  5717899  5717909  5717927  5717939  5717947  5717951
5717963  5717977  5718023  5718029  5718047  5718059  5718061  5718071  5718073  5718101
5718109  5718113  5718121  5718131  5718149  5718151  5718157  5718179  5718211  5718217
5718233  5718241  5718253  5718263  5718277  5718287  5718289  5718301  5718343  5718367
5718379  5718403  5718407  5718413  5718431  5718437  5718439  5718469  5718497  5718499
5718523  5718551  5718569  5718577  5718589  5718593  5718623  5718641  5718649  5718659
5718667  5718673  5718679  5718701  5718703  5718709  5718737  5718763  5718767  5718773
5718793  5718799  5718809  5718827  5718847  5718863  5718899  5718901  5718959  5718971
5718983  5718989  5718991  5719001  5719009  5719013  5719033  5719069  5719073  5719079
5719081  5719099  5719117  5719151  5719163  5719183  5719199  5719211  5719223  5719237
5719243  5719253  5719261  5719267  5719277  5719279  5719291  5719297  5719303  5719333
5719367  5719369  5719381  5719391  5719397  5719403  5719453  5719457  5719481  5719499
5719523  5719561  5719603  5719607  5719619  5719621  5719657  5719661  5719673  5719687
5719691  5719697  5719771  5719783  5719807  5719823  5719829  5719843  5719849  5719859
5719897  5719913  5719921  5719937  5719943  5719949  5719957  5719963  5720017  5720053
5720063  5720087  5720093  5720101  5720107  5720129  5720137  5720147  5720171  5720189
5720201  5720203  5720223  5720243  5720249  5720291  5720293  5720321  5720329  5720369
5720371  5720389  5720401  5720413  5720423  5720431  5720441  5720447  5720471  5720479
```

```
5720531  5720543  5720567  5720579  5720597  5720621  5720657  5720707  5720711  5720731
5720747  5720753  5720761  5720773  5720777  5720783  5720807  5720809  5720821  5720837
5720839  5720863  5720893  5720909  5720927  5720971  5720987  5720999  5721011  5721013
5721029  5721031  5721041  5721047  5721059  5721113  5721119  5721127  5721139  5721151
5721161  5721179  5721203  5721211  5721241  5721269  5721271  5721281  5721307  5721343
5721349  5721371  5721389  5721409  5721431  5721433  5721437  5721461  5721479  5721481
5721493  5721517  5721523  5721539  5721557  5721563  5721589  5721593  5721601  5721619
5721631  5721649  5721659  5721689  5721691  5721697  5721713  5721719  5721743  5721757
5721767  5721797  5721817  5721823  5721829  5721839  5721841  5721851  5721853
5721889  5721901  5721913  5721929  5721931  5721941  5721943  5721971  5722007  5722069
5722099  5722111  5722117  5722133  5722141  5722153  5722177  5722181  5722187  5722201
5722219  5722243  5722261  5722267  5722271  5722273  5722279  5722291  5722303  5722307
5722313  5722333  5722337  5722361  5722369  5722373  5722399  5722427  5722429  5722459
5722487  5722499  5722501  5722511  5722513  5722517  5722547  5722567  5722573  5722603
5722621  5722637  5722649  5722697  5722729  5722733  5722757  5722763  5722771  5722793
5722799  5722841  5722853  5722859  5722867  5722877  5722891  5722909  5722943  5722949
5722957  5722979  5722991  5723017  5723023  5723057  5723077  5723083  5723087  5723119
5723129  5723131  5723147  5723173  5723183  5723209  5723219  5723233  5723269  5723281
5723287  5723293  5723299  5723303  5723317  5723327  5723363  5723369  5723383  5723387
5723423  5723461  5723479  5723483  5723491  5723507  5723539  5723593  5723621  5723633
5723639  5723659  5723681  5723719  5723737  5723779  5723819  5723821  5723833  5723843
5723867  5723869  5723891  5723897  5723899  5723999  5724001  5724007  5724013  5724023
5724097  5724101  5724109  5724113  5724127  5724137  5724139  5724143  5724151  5724157
5724163  5724193  5724197  5724209  5724211  5724221  5724247  5724253  5724269  5724283
5724287  5724311  5724317  5724319  5724331  5724349  5724373  5724403  5724421  5724443
5724449  5724479  5724503  5724527  5724533  5724541  5724559  5724581  5724611  5724613
5724661  5724679  5724683  5724727  5724731  5724737  5724749  5724787  5724793  5724799
5724809  5724811  5724841  5724847  5724853  5724857  5724877  5724883  5724931  5724941
5724967  5724989  5724991  5724997  5725001  5725009  5725021  5725081  5725087  5725129
5725133  5725157  5725163  5725169  5725193  5725201  5725241  5725253  5725259  5725273
5725283  5725303  5725331  5725333  5725339  5725361  5725393  5725409  5725439  5725461
5725453  5725457  5725469  5725471  5725477  5725501  5725507  5725519  5725523  5725543
5725547  5725613  5725627  5725663  5725679  5725693  5725697  5725717  5725721  5725729
5725739  5725747  5725759  5725763  5725777  5725799  5725801  5725807  5725829  5725843
5725849  5725871  5725883  5725913  5725927  5725943  5725981  5726023  5726069  5726111
5726113  5726129  5726143  5726153  5726159  5726179  5726191  5726209  5726213  5726249
5726251  5726257  5726269  5726291  5726293  5726309  5726321  5726323  5726341  5726359
5726387  5726393  5726407  5726411  5726447  5726459  5726477  5726507  5726519  5726521
5726531  5726549  5726561  5726587  5726627  5726629  5726639  5726663  5726683  5726687
5726689  5726711  5726713  5726729  5726761  5726767  5726779  5726797  5726803  5726813
5726827  5726837  5726843  5726857  5726867  5726879  5726881  5726887
5726893  5726933  5726957  5727013  5727017  5727019  5727031  5727047  5727049  5727053
5727077  5727089  5727101  5727103  5727121  5727133  5727149  5727199  5727209  5727221
5727223  5727251  5727269  5727277  5727287  5727289  5727301  5727313  5727347  5727349
5727367  5727377  5727401  5727409  5727427  5727431  5727433  5727443  5727461  5727481
5727497  5727503  5727509  5727523  5727539  5727571  5727583  5727613  5727647  5727649
5727671  5727677  5727697  5727707  5727719  5727739  5727751  5727767  5727781  5727791
5727803  5727809  5727907  5727917  5727919  5727923  5727971  5727973  5727979
5727991  5728001  5728027  5728043  5728049  5728057  5728061  5728103  5728147  5728153
5728181  5728189  5728199  5728207  5728223  5728231  5728241  5728243  5728271  5728279
5728297  5728301  5728319  5728363  5728379  5728391  5728409  5728441  5728447  5728453
5728477  5728517  5728523  5728543  5728553  5728559  5728579  5728621  5728627  5728651
5728661  5728691  5728721  5728727  5728729  5728733  5728739  5728741  5728753  5728757
5728763  5728781  5728859  5728867  5728871  5728873  5728883  5728897  5728913  5728939
5728991  5728997  5729021  5729039  5729041  5729057  5729083  5729099  5729123  5729131
5729137  5729147  5729167  5729173  5729183  5729189  5729201  5729233  5729239
5729263  5729329  5729341  5729359  5729377  5729417  5729419  5729447  5729453  5729483
5729489  5729491  5729557  5729567  5729579  5729593  5729597  5729609  5729657
5729683  5729701  5729729  5729741  5729747  5729767  5729797  5729821  5729827  5729839
5729851  5729863  5729869  5729881  5729897  5729921  5729929  5729951  5729953  5729959
5730007  5730031  5730047  5730061  5730073  5730089  5730097  5730103  5730121  5730143
5730149  5730163  5730181  5730211  5730217  5730247  5730251  5730253  5730269  5730293
5730311  5730317  5730331  5730337  5730341  5730349  5730353  5730379  5730383  5730397
5730407  5730451  5730497  5730509  5730521  5730539  5730559  5730563  5730589  5730607
5730611  5730619  5730631  5730643  5730667  5730701  5730709  5730713  5730721  5730763
5730737  5730743  5730763  5730773  5730779  5730793  5730811  5730821  5730833  5730839
5730863  5730869  5730871  5730883  5730899  5730931  5730961  5730983  5731013  5731079
5731081  5731087  5731103  5731097  5731123  5731139  5731147  5731151  5731153  5731177
5731207  5731259  5731277  5731279  5731283  5731289  5731291  5731309  5731339  5731351
5731361  5731391  5731403  5731417  5731421  5731423  5731433  5731441  5731463  5731469
5731471  5731487  5731519  5731541  5731543  5731549  5731571  5731573  5731591  5731619
5731639  5731651  5731657  5731667  5731679  5731681  5731709  5731717  5731723  5731729
5731751  5731777  5731793  5731799  5731801  5731811  5731823  5731829  5731837  5731861
5731877  5731889  5731919  5731949  5731951  5731963  5731967  5731981  5732011  5732017
5732039  5732047  5732059  5732071  5732081  5732113  5732131  5732137  5732141  5732143
5732147  5732149  5732171  5732189  5732197  5732203  5732219  5732239  5732249  5732257
5732273  5732297  5732317  5732323  5732329  5732341  5732347  5732351  5732371  5732387
5732393  5732407  5732437  5732447  5732501  5732513  5732527  5732537  5732539  5732549
5732591  5732599  5732627  5732647  5732677  5732711  5732729  5732747  5732789  5732801
5732809  5732819  5732843  5732869  5732917  5732921  5732929  5732933  5732941  5732983
5732999  5733001  5733019  5733031  5733053  5733103  5733121  5733157  5733173  5733209
5733223  5733239  5733241  5733263  5733283  5733309  5733311  5733323  5733337  5733367
5733373  5733401  5733449  5733461  5733499  5733517  5733521  5733523  5733527  5733529
5733551  5733569  5733613  5733617  5733643  5733661  5733691  5733703  5733713  5733719
5733737  5733751  5733769  5733773  5733799  5733803  5733821  5733823  5733829  5733857
5733881  5733887  5733919  5733929  5733941  5733943  5733971  5733983  5733997  5734021
5734051  5734081  5734087  5734097  5734103  5734121  5734133  5734171  5734207  5734217
5734231  5734243  5734271  5734277  5734283  5734343  5734357  5734439  5734459  5734471
5734481  5734493  5734507  5734511  5734513  5734541  5734571  5734579  5734591  5734601
```

```
5734607 5734621 5734643 5734669 5734681 5734691 5734693 5734697 5734699 5734709
5734727 5734733 5734747 5734801 5734823 5734849 5734871 5734873 5734891 5734901
5734909 5734913 5734919 5734921 5734943 5734973 5734997 5735003 5735029 5735033
5735047 5735057 5735063 5735087 5735129 5735153 5735179 5735189 5735201 5735221
5735251 5735263 5735287 5735291 5735357 5735369 5735393 5735413 5735419 5735423
5735461 5735467 5735489 5735507 5735519 5735581 5735599 5735603 5735617 5735623
5735627 5735633 5735659 5735677 5735693 5735699 5735711 5735729 5735731 5735747
5735753 5735759 5735771 5735791 5735797 5735801 5735827 5735831 5735857 5735861
5735869 5735879 5735893 5735903 5735909 5735923 5735959 5735963 5735981 5736001
5736007 5736011 5736067 5736079 5736083 5736091 5736149 5736151 5736167 5736169
5736193 5736197 5736217 5736251 5736281 5736301 5736307 5736323 5736337 5736371
5736431 5736439 5736481 5736487 5736503 5736509 5736527 5736541 5736547 5736551
5736553 5736557 5736569 5736571 5736589 5736593 5736611 5736659 5736691 5736697
5736707 5736713 5736733 5736737 5736763 5736781 5736793 5736823 5736833 5736839
5736859 5736869 5736881 5736911 5736919 5736979 5737021 5737027 5737037 5737049
5737057 5737073 5737153 5737169 5737181 5737187 5737213 5737229 5737241
5737247 5737271 5737283 5737321 5737343 5737351 5737357 5737363 5737379 5737393
5737397 5737399 5737421 5737427 5737429 5737451 5737469 5737471 5737481 5737493
5737513 5737531 5737549 5737559 5737579 5737583 5737597 5737607 5737631 5737637
5737643 5737703 5737717 5737729 5737751 5737757 5737769 5737783 5737793 5737811
5737817 5737889 5737951 5737961 5737973 5737999 5738009 5738011 5738023 5738041
5738077 5738093 5738101 5738107 5738119 5738123 5738147 5738153 5738167 5738177
5738207 5738251 5738263 5738267 5738269 5738279 5738297 5738329 5738347 5738351
5738353 5738377 5738419 5738449 5738471 5738497 5738501 5738521 5738527 5738531
5738533 5738539 5738543 5738573 5738581 5738587 5738591 5738599 5738611 5738633
5738641 5738683 5738687 5738693 5738699 5738713 5738743 5738767 5738801 5738827
5738833 5738849 5738861 5738867 5738903 5738927 5738939 5738947 5738951 5738981
5739011 5739017 5739031 5739049 5739053 5739073 5739089 5739091 5739101 5739103
5739109 5739127 5739131 5739133 5739161 5739169 5739179 5739191 5739193 5739203
5739229 5739233 5739269 5739281 5739301 5739323 5739347 5739389 5739401 5739407
5739413 5739431 5739439 5739451 5739473 5739491 5739541 5739553 5739563 5739571
5739583 5739589 5739607 5739637 5739641 5739649 5739667 5739677 5739703 5739707
5739731 5739739 5739749 5739779 5739791 5739793 5739803 5739817 5739821 5739827
5739841 5739859 5739869 5739887 5739901 5739907 5739913 5739947 5739971 5739973
5739977 5739983 5740001 5740043 5740073 5740079 5740081 5740093 5740099 5740103
5740117 5740129 5740139 5740159 5740181 5740183 5740193 5740213 5740253 5740277
5740297 5740303 5740307 5740309 5740321 5740327 5740333 5740349 5740367 5740387
5740393 5740417 5740429 5740453 5740459 5740477 5740481 5740507 5740517
5740519 5740571 5740583 5740597 5740607 5740613 5740619 5740633 5740643 5740663
5740681 5740687 5740699 5740723 5740727 5740741 5740783 5740789 5740799 5740829
5740853 5740873 5740879 5740897 5740919 5740937 5740949 5740967 5740979 5740991
5740997 5741033 5741039 5741051 5741063 5741081 5741089 5741093 5741149 5741201
5741209 5741213 5741227 5741233 5741261 5741279 5741303 5741311 5741321 5741339
5741341 5741369 5741383 5741387 5741389 5741419 5741423 5741443 5741453 5741459
5741509 5741531 5741537 5741569 5741573 5741579 5741587 5741609 5741611 5741621
5741689 5741693 5741707 5741711 5741713 5741737 5741741 5741753 5741759 5741761
5741803 5741831 5741839 5741843 5741873 5741887 5741893 5741917 5741947 5741963
5741969 5741987 5741999 5742007 5742041 5742049 5742053 5742083 5742089 5742103
5742133 5742137 5742167 5742169 5742181 5742193 5742197 5742211 5742221 5742227
5742239 5742257 5742259 5742271 5742281 5742283 5742287 5742361 5742367 5742371
5742383 5742397 5742403 5742421 5742439 5742461 5742467 5742469 5742509 5742523
5742563 5742577 5742599 5742619 5742623 5742631 5742641 5742643 5742673 5742679
5742683 5742689 5742701 5742703 5742707 5742713 5742727 5742743 5742749 5742791
5742799 5742809 5742811 5742833 5742851 5742859 5742871 5742887 5742929 5742937
5742973 5743007 5743009 5743021 5743033 5743051 5743057 5743061 5743069 5743097
5743099 5743121 5743139 5743147 5743201 5743207 5743219 5743253 5743279 5743289
5743291 5743313 5743337 5743343 5743349 5743357 5743369 5743373 5743393 5743411
5743417 5743457 5743459 5743469 5743471 5743477 5743481 5743483 5743489 5743499
5743513 5743519 5743597 5743601 5743607 5743613 5743627 5743651 5743667 5743691
5743697 5743733 5743741 5743747 5743763 5743789 5743799 5743817 5743819 5743831
5743861 5743877 5743879 5743883 5743901 5743939 5743961 5743963 5743967 5743987
5744003 5744017 5744029 5744077 5744093 5744107 5744131 5744143 5744153 5744161
5744171 5744177 5744197 5744201 5744203 5744231 5744239 5744261 5744267 5744279
5744311 5744329 5744339 5744353 5744371 5744377 5744429 5744447 5744461 5744467
5744477 5744507 5744527 5744561 5744569 5744587 5744597 5744603 5744621 5744659
5744663 5744677 5744693 5744699 5744701 5744719 5744729 5744737 5744741 5744749
5744773 5744777 5744803 5744833 5744863 5744867 5744899 5744903 5744911 5744941
5744957 5744971 5744983 5745017 5745023 5745053 5745059 5745071 5745079 5745109
5745119 5745197 5745203 5745211 5745221 5745231 5745263 5745293 5745307 5745347
5745349 5745379 5745403 5745409 5745419 5745431 5745461 5745463 5745491 5745517
5745521 5745539 5745557 5745559 5745563 5745569 5745583 5745599 5745629 5745631
5745647 5745659 5745671 5745673 5745679 5745689 5745697 5745713 5745731 5745743
5745787 5745823 5745827 5745869 5745871 5745877 5745893 5745911 5745931 5745941
5745947 5745953 5745967 5745977 5745979 5745997 5746001 5746033 5746057 5746087
5746093 5746123 5746127 5746157 5746199 5746217 5746231 5746249 5746271 5746283
5746291 5746309 5746319 5746337 5746373 5746397 5746409 5746421 5746427 5746441
5746451 5746453 5746457 5746471 5746511 5746537 5746567 5746583 5746591 5746603
5746613 5746639 5746651 5746673 5746691 5746693 5746703 5746753 5746771 5746787
5746789 5746801 5746817 5746889 5746903 5746913 5746927 5746957 5746963 5746973
5747023 5747029 5747051 5747057 5747069 5747083 5747089 5747107 5747111 5747117
5747123 5747129 5747141 5747143 5747149 5747179 5747201 5747221 5747227 5747239
5747279 5747281 5747303 5747323 5747333 5747341 5747351 5747383 5747387 5747389
5747393 5747407 5747419 5747449 5747459 5747477 5747491 5747537 5747549 5747551
5747563 5747593 5747611 5747629 5747647 5747657 5747669 5747699 5747701 5747737
5747743 5747759 5747773 5747783 5747833 5747837 5747843 5747849 5747857 5747879
5747881 5747909 5747923 5747977 5747983 5747993 5748007 5748019 5748031 5748037
5748047 5748049 5748059 5748073 5748079 5748097 5748103 5748107 5748139 5748143
5748167 5748173 5748187 5748199 5748217 5748233 5748251 5748269 5748287 5748313
5748341 5748349 5748371 5748377 5748403 5748427 5748437 5748451 5748461 5748473
```

```
5748481  5748503  5748517  5748529  5748553  5748557  5748559  5748563  5748571  5748577
5748619  5748661  5748679  5748683  5748707  5748719  5748731  5748763  5748767  5748803
5748817  5748851  5748859  5748863  5748877  5748881  5748889  5748893  5748913  5748923
5748929  5748937  5748947  5748959  5748961  5748973  5748983  5748997  5749013  5749027
5749033  5749091  5749127  5749141  5749157  5749169  5749193  5749201  5749231  5749243
5749253  5749259  5749273  5749283  5749297  5749351  5749361  5749397  5749409  5749411
5749427  5749441  5749501  5749507  5749529  5749531  5749547  5749561  5749577
5749589  5749603  5749607  5749619  5749631  5749633  5749637  5749649  5749661  5749691
5749693  5749703  5749729  5749759  5749771  5749781  5749831  5749841  5749847
5749867  5749871  5749879  5749883  5749897  5749901  5749903  5749907  5749943  5749949
5749957  5749967  5749981  5749987  5749993  5749999  5750047  5750051  5750057  5750071
5750083  5750093  5750099  5750113  5750117  5750119  5750153  5750167  5750191  5750197
5750203  5750237  5750249  5750263  5750279  5750333  5750351  5750359  5750363  5750377
5750389  5750399  5750441  5750443  5750449  5750509  5750527  5750561  5750581  5750603
5750617  5750623  5750639  5750669  5750681  5750707  5750737  5750747  5750791  5750807
5750809  5750827  5750837  5750861  5750869  5750881  5750887  5750893  5750911  5750917
5750933  5750957  5750993  5751001  5751007  5751023  5751037  5751043  5751047  5751059
5751073  5751101  5751103  5751107  5751113  5751149  5751157  5751197  5751199  5751203
5751209  5751217  5751223  5751247  5751259  5751271  5751283  5751301  5751307  5751329
5751341  5751349  5751359  5751373  5751377  5751407  5751413  5751419  5751443  5751463
5751467  5751479  5751503  5751517  5751527  5751531  5751607  5751611  5751617  5751631
5751643  5751653  5751659  5751673  5751677  5751701  5751727  5751791  5751799  5751841
5751853  5751857  5751859  5751871  5751877  5751881  5751887  5751901  5751913  5751919
5751929  5751937  5751943  5751961  5751971  5751989  5751997  5752031  5752091  5752099
5752111  5752127  5752129  5752141  5752147  5752157  5752163  5752169  5752199  5752223
5752247  5752261  5752301  5752303  5752319  5752321  5752339  5752343  5752363  5752379
5752381  5752387  5752403  5752489  5752499  5752519  5752531  5752547  5752561  5752589
5752601  5752609  5752631  5752661  5752667  5752679  5752697  5752699  5752711  5752739
5752757  5752771  5752781  5752787  5752823  5752853  5752881  5752907  5752937  5752939
5752961  5752993  5753009  5753051  5753053  5753063  5753087  5753113  5753117  5753119
5753131  5753141  5753179  5753183  5753207  5753213  5753221  5753249  5753273  5753291
5753299  5753323  5753329  5753351  5753353  5753369  5753387  5753399  5753401  5753413
5753417  5753431  5753441  5753453  5753467  5753479  5753483  5753509  5753533  5753549
5753551  5753557  5753563  5753591  5753603  5753609  5753617  5753639  5753647  5753659
5753663  5753669  5753677  5753681  5753717  5753719  5753723  5753731  5753743  5753747
5753767  5753777  5753801  5753819  5753821  5753831  5753843  5753851  5753897  5753927
5753929  5753953  5753971  5753983  5753999  5754013  5754031  5754043  5754059  5754061
5754097  5754103  5754107  5754113  5754149  5754167  5754187  5754197  5754233  5754241
5754247  5754289  5754311  5754317  5754341  5754349  5754373  5754377  5754379  5754407
5754409  5754431  5754443  5754451  5754457  5754467  5754481  5754491  5754493  5754503
5754523  5754547  5754571  5754589  5754607  5754613  5754629  5754631  5754641  5754643
5754659  5754689  5754691  5754709  5754757  5754767  5754769  5754773  5754779  5754799
5754803  5754811  5754817  5754863  5754887  5754893  5754901  5754907  5754911  5754937
5754979  5754989  5754997  5755019  5755031  5755033  5755049  5755051  5755069  5755073
5755133  5755147  5755151  5755153  5755159  5755171  5755187  5755207  5755219  5755237
5755261  5755297  5755307  5755319  5755349  5755357  5755361  5755381  5755433  5755441
5755459  5755483  5755489  5755517  5755531  5755559  5755567  5755577  5755579  5755583
5755649  5755657  5755663  5755691  5755709  5755733  5755753  5755787  5755811  5755817
5755823  5755859  5755907  5755909  5755921  5755931  5755933  5755951  5755973  5755999
5756011  5756017  5756027  5756059  5756063  5756083  5756087  5756089  5756119  5756131
5756147  5756161  5756189  5756197  5756203  5756207  5756209  5756213  5756227  5756237
5756243  5756263  5756287  5756321  5756341  5756347  5756351  5756357  5756363  5756369
5756389  5756447  5756459  5756477  5756501  5756521  5756579  5756581  5756593  5756599
5756623  5756627  5756633  5756717  5756741  5756743  5756749  5756789  5756801  5756833
5756837  5756843  5756857  5756887  5756903  5756939  5756951  5756953  5756957  5756977
5756987  5757001  5757023  5757029  5757049  5757071  5757079  5757091  5757121  5757127
5757131  5757137  5757139  5757173  5757181  5757217  5757221  5757223  5757229  5757239
5757251  5757253  5757259  5757263  5757277  5757281  5757287  5757293  5757317  5757331
5757379  5757403  5757421  5757449  5757467  5757469  5757473  5757481  5757491  5757497
5757523  5757539  5757541  5757553  5757559  5757569  5757593  5757611  5757617  5757623
5757701  5757721  5757727  5757733  5757737  5757767  5757809  5757811  5757821  5757827
5757901  5757907  5757919  5757929  5757943  5757949  5757967  5757989  5758003  5758031
5758061  5758069  5758097  5758099  5758117  5758133  5758139  5758169  5758177  5758229
5758237  5758243  5758253  5758267  5758279  5758283  5758297  5758321  5758381  5758411
5758433  5758439  5758447  5758451  5758469  5758477  5758481  5758513  5758523  5758537
5758549  5758589  5758601  5758607  5758619  5758637  5758639  5758667  5758679  5758681
5758721  5758723  5758741  5758757  5758771  5758811  5758817  5758829  5758853  5758867
5758889  5758913  5758933  5758943  5758987  5759003  5759009  5759011  5759059
5759077  5759093  5759099  5759111  5759123  5759191  5759203  5759213  5759219  5759249
5759251  5759261  5759267  5759317  5759321  5759339  5759353  5759357  5759359  5759381
5759399  5759401  5759417  5759423  5759431  5759441  5759473  5759477  5759483  5759491
5759503  5759519  5759539  5759543  5759581  5759587  5759597  5759599  5759629  5759647
5759687  5759693  5759713  5759759  5759771  5759779  5759783  5759791  5759797  5759801
5759833  5759837  5759839  5759843  5759851  5759857  5759903  5759911  5759927  5759933
5759953  5759981  5760011  5760071  5760091  5760101  5760103  5760107  5760119  5760121
5760133  5760137  5760163  5760193  5760217  5760233  5760247  5760259  5760269  5760277
5760289  5760311  5760343  5760371  5760383  5760427  5760431  5760437  5760497  5760509
5760523  5760527  5760543  5760551  5760571  5760611  5760613  5760619  5760631  5760659
5760661  5760679  5760691  5760707  5760719  5760749  5760767  5760803  5760817  5760827
5760829  5760877  5760883  5760899  5760907  5760913  5760949  5760959  5760961
5760973  5760983  5761001  5761003  5761027  5761043  5761057  5761061  5761069  5761081
5761127  5761139  5761157  5761163  5761187  5761193  5761219  5761229  5761253  5761271
5761277  5761289  5761297  5761321  5761331  5761337  5761367  5761373  5761387  5761403
5761417  5761421  5761423  5761433  5761439  5761447  5761451  5761463  5761489  5761493
5761499  5761501  5761507  5761537  5761543  5761559  5761601  5761619  5761621  5761633
5761649  5761673  5761687  5761729  5761741  5761783  5761801  5761813  5761837  5761841
5761861  5761879  5761901  5761909  5761913  5761919  5761927  5761991  5761993  5762011
5762027  5762033  5762041  5762077  5762087  5762089  5762123  5762131  5762137  5762143
5762161  5762173  5762177  5762179  5762203  5762219  5762221  5762231  5762233  5762261
```

```
5762287  5762293  5762299  5762321  5762333  5762347  5762359  5762381  5762411  5762413
5762429  5762437  5762459  5762461  5762501  5762513  5762521  5762557  5762597  5762611
5762641  5762651  5762657  5762663  5762689  5762723  5762741  5762749  5762759  5762777
5762831  5762843  5762863  5762891  5762917  5762927  5762941  5762969  5763011  5763013
5763019  5763047  5763059  5763067  5763071  5763073  5763077  5763089  5763143  5763151
5763181  5763229  5763253  5763293  5763299  5763319  5763343  5763347  5763349  5763361
5763371  5763413  5763421  5763467  5763481  5763491  5763497  5763503  5763521  5763529
5763553  5763557  5763577  5763587  5763617  5763619  5763647  5763649  5763673  5763679
5763683  5763689  5763691  5763733  5763743  5763773  5763781  5763787  5763817  5763827
5763839  5763853  5763871  5763889  5763893  5763917  5763929  5763931  5763937  5763959
5763991  5764009  5764013  5764019  5764027  5764061  5764063  5764079  5764081  5764091
5764097  5764103  5764111  5764117  5764133  5764147  5764151  5764217  5764229  5764249
5764259  5764271  5764289  5764303  5764349  5764351  5764379  5764387  5764397  5764399
5764459  5764471  5764501  5764511  5764523  5764531  5764541  5764567  5764579  5764589
5764607  5764609  5764621  5764643  5764663  5764687  5764699  5764721  5764739  5764741
5764763  5764783  5764793  5764799  5764817  5764841  5764873  5764877  5764897  5764903
5764907  5764909  5764943  5764951  5764963  5765003  5765009  5765033  5765041  5765063
5765069  5765077  5765083  5765087  5765093  5765143  5765167  5765191  5765209  5765213
5765231  5765233  5765237  5765269  5765273  5765317  5765323  5765327  5765351  5765401
5765407  5765423  5765449  5765453  5765471  5765491  5765497  5765503  5765521  5765561
5765563  5765579  5765603  5765611  5765623  5765647  5765653  5765671  5765681  5765699
5765701  5765729  5765731  5765779  5765791  5765831  5765833  5765843  5765849  5765857
5765861  5765863  5765869  5765887  5765891  5765933  5765951  5765957  5765959  5766017
5766023  5766037  5766053  5766071  5766083  5766091  5766107  5766109  5766113  5766119
5766121  5766133  5766143  5766161  5766203  5766239  5766287  5766301  5766311  5766317
5766323  5766361  5766373  5766379  5766421  5766433  5766457  5766463  5766469  5766643
5766493  5766499  5766581  5766599  5766611  5766613  5766619  5766641  5766659  5766667
5766701  5766703  5766707  5766727  5766743  5766749  5766779  5766799  5766811  5766829
5766851  5766913  5766919  5766973  5766977  5766989  5766991  5767007  5767039  5767049
5767057  5767061  5767087  5767093  5767109  5767129  5767169  5767171  5767187  5767189
5767207  5767213  5767217  5767247  5767253  5767283  5767297  5767303  5767313  5767331
5767339  5767351  5767357  5767379  5767381  5767397  5767409  5767423  5767439  5767441
5767453  5767477  5767481  5767483  5767493  5767499  5767501  5767529  5767577  5767589
5767603  5767631  5767637  5767649  5767669  5767673  5767681  5767721  5767739  5767789
5767841  5767847  5767873  5767877  5767903  5767943  5767961  5767997  5767999  5768011
5768033  5768047  5768057  5768069  5768089  5768093  5768123  5768137  5768141  5768143
5768159  5768173  5768183  5768197  5768207  5768233  5768317  5768327  5768369  5768383
5768393  5768401  5768443  5768471  5768473  5768479  5768507  5768513  5768519  5768527
5768531  5768549  5768551  5768557  5768569  5768591  5768599  5768629  5768641  5768663
5768669  5768671  5768677  5768689  5768701  5768731  5768747  5768753  5768779  5768783
5768801  5768803  5768809  5768857  5768863  5768869  5768887  5768889  5768909  5768911
5768957  5768977  5768981  5768993  5769017  5769037  5769041  5769047  5769053  5769073
5769089  5769121  5769143  5769149  5769161  5769199  5769241  5769287  5769311  5769329
5769359  5769367  5769383  5769403  5769419  5769457  5769461  5769469  5769493  5769499
5769541  5769553  5769557  5769581  5769583  5769587  5769649  5769653  5769677  5769691
5769703  5769713  5769719  5769721  5769769  5769791  5769809  5769821  5769833  5769833
5769853  5769857  5769871  5769877  5769887  5769899  5769917  5769943  5769949  5770001
5770003  5770027  5770027  5770031  5770073  5770097  5770103  5770109  5770111  5770117
5770147  5770153  5770183  5770249  5770253  5770267  5770273  5770277  5770279  5770291
5770321  5770343  5770367  5770379  5770393  5770399  5770411  5770439  5770459  5770469
5770477  5770487  5770489  5770511  5770517  5770529  5770537  5770543  5770553  5770559
5770573  5770579  5770601  5770607  5770649  5770651  5770657  5770673  5770697  5770703
5770717  5770727  5770747  5770757  5770759  5770771  5770789  5770811  5770819  5770829
5770841  5770859  5770879  5770903  5770931  5770949  5770979  5770981  5770993  5771057
5771063  5771081  5771089  5771111  5771131  5771167  5771173  5771237  5771251  5771257
5771263  5771267  5771281  5771287  5771291  5771299  5771303  5771309  5771323  5771327
5771351  5771357  5771369  5771387  5771401  5771411  5771461  5771501  5771527  5771543
5771567  5771569  5771587  5771603  5771617  5771627  5771639  5771641  5771663  5771671
5771677  5771681  5771683  5771707  5771723  5771743  5771747  5771749  5771767  5771771
5771833  5771837  5771851  5771861  5771863  5771869  5771879  5771893  5771897  5771951
5771981  5771989  5772007  5772043  5772047  5772059  5772077  5772079  5772097  5772101
5772113  5772119  5772121  5772139  5772157  5772161  5772167  5772187  5772199  5772203
5772209  5772227  5772233  5772269  5772281  5772289  5772301  5772307  5772311  5772317
5772337  5772341  5772343  5772353  5772359  5772391  5772397  5772413  5772427  5772433
5772443  5772457  5772461  5772463  5772467  5772497  5772499  5772509  5772511  5772527
5772539  5772551  5772553  5772581  5772589  5772617  5772631  5772643  5772661  5772709
5772719  5772721  5772731  5772763  5772773  5772799  5772803  5772817  5772829  5772847
5772859  5772863  5772889  5772953  5772961  5772983  5772989  5772997  5773003  5773021
5773049  5773063  5773067  5773109  5773121  5773127  5773129  5773133  5773139  5773199
5773213  5773219  5773249  5773259  5773267  5773279  5773331  5773363  5773367  5773373
5773379  5773393  5773423  5773429  5773447  5773451  5773477  5773501  5773513  5773541
5773543  5773553  5773561  5773577  5773583  5773597  5773631  5773679  5773687  5773709
5773741  5773751  5773763  5773769  5773771  5773793  5773811  5773819  5773837  5773849
5773861  5773877  5773879  5773883  5773913  5773919  5773939  5773969  5773991  5774017
5774023  5774047  5774051  5774059  5774099  5774113  5774117  5774123  5774129  5774141
5774143  5774147  5774149  5774159  5774177  5774179  5774207  5774273  5774287  5774291
5774299  5774323  5774369  5774371  5774387  5774411  5774429  5774453  5774471  5774497
5774521  5774539  5774551  5774559  5774581  5774591  5774597  5774641  5774669  5774699
5774851  5774893  5774911  5774939  5774953  5774963  5774981  5774983  5774987  5775017
5775037  5775041  5775043  5775059  5775061  5775067  5775101  5775127  5775149  5775191
5775197  5775239  5775241  5775271  5775337  5775349  5775401  5775403  5775409  5775421
5775431  5775439  5775443  5775457  5775481  5775499  5775521  5775527  5775551  5775557
5775571  5775587  5775613  5775617  5775661  5775667  5775673  5775683  5775697  5775701
5775709  5775713  5775739  5775751  5775799  5775821  5775839  5775841  5775851  5775853
5775857  5775863  5775881  5775883  5775893  5775899  5775929  5775947  5775961  5775983
5775989  5775997  5776021  5776027  5776037  5776049  5776079  5776081  5776091  5776093
5776099  5776103  5776109  5776117  5776123  5776129  5776163  5776193  5776201  5776207
5776217  5776241  5776259  5776279  5776301  5776321  5776333  5776357  5776387  5776429
```

```
5776439   5776451   5776453   5776457   5776483   5776579   5776591   5776601   5776607   5776619
5776649   5776679   5776721   5776759   5776783   5776811   5776831   5776853   5776861   5776891
5776873   5776877   5776909   5776913   5776919   5776949   5776951   5776963   5776987   5776993
5776999   5777017   5777021   5777047   5777077   5777089   5777111   5777113   5777131   5777137
5777171   5777173   5777183   5777201   5777227   5777237   5777279   5777309   5777323   5777353
5777363   5777407   5777423   5777459   5777461   5777479   5777489   5777491   5777509   5777521
5777533   5777537   5777543   5777549   5777557   5777573   5777593   5777621   5777627   5777633
5777657   5777677   5777711   5777719   5777743   5777747   5777771   5777789   5777797   5777819
5777833   5777857   5777869   5777887   5777903   5777911   5777917   5777927   5777939   5777951
5777963   5777971   5777983   5777987   5778001   5778041   5778043   5778053   5778061   5778077
5778137   5778151   5778161   5778173   5778217   5778229   5778233   5778251   5778259   5778263
5778277   5778287   5778301   5778319   5778329   5778341   5778349   5778361   5778371   5778391
5778407   5778427   5778433   5778439   5778449   5778467   5778491   5778517   5778529   5778551
5778571   5778611   5778629   5778631   5778649   5778653   5778659   5778671   5778673   5778733
5778737   5778757   5778763   5778767   5778769   5778779   5778821   5778847   5778887   5778893
5778931   5778943   5778953   5778973   5779001   5779009   5779043   5779061   5779063   5779069
5779093   5779117   5779121   5779127   5779139   5779153   5779181   5779183   5779199   5779217
5779231   5779253   5779271   5779297   5779307   5779331   5779339   5779343   5779349   5779387
5779399   5779429   5779441   5779447   5779451   5779457   5779493   5779513   5779517   5779537
5779573   5779577   5779583   5779607   5779633   5779649   5779661   5779663   5779681   5779687
5779691   5779717   5779723   5779727   5779769   5779793   5779799   5779841   5779843   5779849
5779867   5779901   5779913   5779967   5779993   5779999   5780087   5780111   5780147   5780179
5780191   5780197   5780207   5780209   5780219   5780227   5780231   5780249   5780261   5780267
5780273   5780287   5780293   5780297   5780317   5780329   5780347   5780387   5780393   5780417
5780419   5780443   5780491   5780507   5780513   5780519   5780531   5780569   5780587   5780603
5780609   5780611   5780623   5780627   5780633   5780681   5780683   5780689   5780699   5780711
5780737   5780743   5780759   5780771   5780779   5780783   5780809   5780821   5780837   5780851
5780857   5780881   5780893   5780923   5780927   5780933   5780939   5780987   5781007   5781011
5781029   5781053   5781059   5781067   5781077   5781091   5781101   5781107   5781131   5781133
5781143   5781151   5781169   5781239   5781247   5781253   5781271   5781277   5781289   5781311
5781313   5781319   5781331   5781371   5781383   5781409   5781431   5781437   5781439   5781441
5781443   5781467   5781499   5781539   5781541   5781553   5781569   5781571   5781599   5781613
5781623   5781637   5781653   5781661   5781689   5781691   5781709   5781733   5781749   5781791
5781793   5781803   5781829   5781847   5781857   5781859   5781869   5781889   5781901   5781911
5781961   5781977   5782001   5782013   5782031   5782037   5782043   5782093   5782103   5782109
5782121   5782157   5782163   5782171   5782181   5782187   5782199   5782201   5782207   5782211
5782219   5782277   5782279   5782291   5782297   5782307   5782319   5782321   5782333   5782349
5782367   5782369   5782379   5782391   5782393   5782409   5782411   5782433   5782451   5782463
5782477   5782489   5782519   5782529   5782547   5782561   5782577   5782603   5782607   5782627
5782639   5782643   5782657   5782663   5782697   5782717   5782753   5782759   5782787   5782793
5782801   5782807   5782853   5782891   5782921   5782939   5782949   5782951   5782969   5782981
5782993   5783017   5783023   5783033   5783039   5783047   5783053   5783069   5783101   5783119
5783123   5783153   5783171   5783177   5783203   5783207   5783233   5783249   5783251   5783269
5783273   5783287   5783323   5783363   5783369   5783381   5783387   5783389   5783399   5783419
5783443   5783461   5783473   5783497   5783509   5783513   5783539   5783549   5783551   5783579
5783677   5783693   5783719   5783737   5783749   5783761   5783779   5783807   5783821   5783839
5783851   5783861   5783891   5783903   5783917   5783941   5783969   5783983   5784001   5784007
5784019   5784047   5784061   5784067   5784071   5784083   5784089   5784091   5784133   5784139
5784161   5784179   5784209   5784211   5784221   5784223   5784257   5784263   5784269   5784271
5784283   5784319   5784323   5784343   5784349   5784391   5784407   5784409   5784421   5784439
5784461   5784463   5784479   5784497   5784503   5784509   5784529   5784557   5784563   5784577
5784589   5784599   5784613   5784629   5784637   5784671   5784673   5784719   5784749   5784761
5784767   5784781   5784787   5784841   5784853   5784869   5784871   5784889   5784913   5784923
5784929   5784931   5784959   5784967   5784973   5784991   5785001   5785019   5785027   5785051
5785067   5785069   5785079   5785081   5785093   5785097   5785103   5785147   5785193   5785207
5785229   5785271   5785331   5785337   5785379   5785391   5785399   5785411   5785421   5785441
5785433   5785447   5785463   5785477   5785501   5785511   5785513   5785523   5785537   5785541
5785543   5785553   5785589   5785601   5785621   5785643   5785657   5785669   5785691   5785711
5785721   5785757   5785771   5785777   5785783   5785799   5785807   5785837   5785853   5785859
5785873   5785889   5785891   5785973   5785991   5785999   5786017   5786083   5786093   5786113
5786129   5786141   5786159   5786173   5786177   5786213   5786227   5786237   5786257   5786269
5786281   5786293   5786309   5786327   5786329   5786351   5786353   5786359   5786369   5786377
5786387   5786411   5786413   5786419   5786441   5786447   5786461   5786479   5786503   5786509
5786527   5786537   5786551   5786563   5786567   5786569   5786587   5786591   5786603   5786609
5786611   5786629   5786657   5786707   5786761   5786797   5786813   5786827   5786839   5786861
5786867   5786899   5786917   5786927   5786947   5786959   5786971   5786981   5786999   5787013
5787071   5787079   5787091   5787101   5787107   5787121   5787143   5787149   5787151   5787163
5787167   5787169   5787179   5787181   5787193   5787203   5787209   5787217   5787247   5787277
5787317   5787319   5787347   5787349   5787371   5787373   5787389   5787391   5787409   5787427
5787433   5787443   5787473   5787493   5787531   5787541   5787563   5787631   5787637   5787703
5787713   5787739   5787751   5787763   5787767   5787773   5787779   5787781   5787797   5787823
5787827   5787829   5787833   5787851   5787869   5787883   5787889   5787919   5787949   5787961
5787983   5788001   5788003   5788037   5788043   5788051   5788067   5788117   5788121   5788127
5788129   5788147   5788151   5788193   5788201   5788207   5788213   5788241   5788247   5788259
5788267   5788271   5788297   5788301   5788303   5788327   5788357   5788373   5788403   5788423
5788427   5788439   5788441   5788457   5788463   5788477   5788481   5788499   5788513   5788529
5788543   5788553   5788583   5788589   5788609   5788621   5788631   5788639   5788693   5788697
5788729   5788763   5788787   5788793   5788811   5788829   5788837   5788841   5788873   5788877
5788919   5788921   5788931   5788949   5788963   5788967   5788987   5789029   5789059   5789071
5789081   5789089   5789107   5789111   5789117   5789141   5789143   5789153   5789177   5789191
5789221   5789227   5789233   5789249   5789263   5789291   5789309   5789341   5789347   5789359
5789363   5789383   5789423   5789437   5789453   5789461   5789479   5789513   5789519   5789533
5789551   5789573   5789587   5789599   5789617   5789627   5789657   5789659   5789677   5789681
5789683   5789711   5789731   5789743   5789747   5789759   5789779   5789857   5789863   5789869
5789881   5789891   5789893   5789899   5789909   5789921   5789929   5789933   5789947   5789957
5789969   5789981   5789999   5790011   5790017   5790023   5790067   5790077   5790097   5790101
5790119   5790139   5790157   5790203   5790209   5790223   5790247   5790271   5790277   5790299
5790313   5790349   5790359   5790361   5790373   5790377   5790419   5790427   5790439   5790451
5790469   5790481   5790487   5790527   5790529   5790539   5790563   5790569   5790571   5790581
```

5790599 5790613 5790623 5790643 5790667 5790677 5790683 5790703 5790709 5790739
5790781 5790793 5790797 5790799 5790809 5790847 5790857 5790859 5790887 5790899
5790919 5790943 5790949 5790959 5790971 5790979 5791007 5791013 5791057 5791081
5791091 5791109 5791133 5791153 5791171 5791189 5791207 5791211 5791217 5791229
5791231 5791241 5791249 5791307 5791337 5791361 5791367 5791391 5791397 5791403
5791417 5791427 5791463 5791483 5791493 5791517 5791531 5791549 5791567 5791609
5791633 5791649 5791661 5791673 5791717 5791741 5791757 5791759 5791769 5791771
5791811 5791813 5791817 5791829 5791843 5791847 5791859 5791871 5791873 5791897
5791901 5791913 5791921 5791927 5791931 5791937 5791939 5791963 5791987 5791993
5792023 5792027 5792051 5792063 5792069 5792081 5792099 5792107 5792117 5792153
5792167 5792173 5792177 5792179 5792203 5792219 5792221 5792263 5792273 5792279
5792299 5792309 5792323 5792329 5792333 5792383 5792407 5792417 5792419 5792429
5792441 5792447 5792453 5792459 5792467 5792483 5792491 5792513 5792537 5792551
5792557 5792569 5792581 5792639 5792641 5792651 5792671 5792681 5792713 5792737
5792747 5792789 5792791 5792807 5792821 5792827 5792861 5792863 5792867 5792879
5792881 5792893 5792909 5792923 5792933 5792947 5792959 5792981 5792993 5793019
5793031 5793041 5793077 5793091 5793113 5793133 5793163 5793169 5793181 5793191
5793197 5793223 5793253 5793283 5793299 5793313 5793323 5793329 5793371 5793383
5793391 5793409 5793439 5793443 5793449 5793451 5793467 5793479 5793503 5793511
5793517 5793521 5793523 5793527 5793547 5793553 5793577 5793581 5793607 5793611
5793653 5793661 5793667 5793673 5793679 5793701 5793743 5793757 5793761 5793779
5793847 5793871 5793883 5793899 5793911 5793913 5793939 5793971 5793979 5794001
5794003 5794007 5794027 5794037 5794043 5794099 5794109 5794123 5794133 5794169
5794181 5794193 5794199 5794211 5794219 5794231 5794249 5794253 5794267 5794273
5794279 5794307 5794319 5794343 5794357 5794391 5794417 5794423 5794457 5794469
5794483 5794507 5794511 5794513 5794517 5794541 5794559 5794561 5794609 5794627
5794631 5794669 5794697 5794699 5794703 5794709 5794717 5794721 5794727 5794741
5794757 5794769 5794777 5794783 5794787 5794801 5794819 5794843 5794847 5794849
5794889 5794891 5794907 5794913 5794937 5794951 5794961 5794969 5794993 5795017
5795021 5795059 5795081 5795087 5795107 5795123 5795159 5795161 5795191 5795197
5795213 5795221 5795261 5795263 5795267 5795291 5795329 5795353 5795369 5795381
5795407 5795423 5795507 5795527 5795533 5795579 5795593 5795611 5795633 5795651
5795663 5795681 5795693 5795723 5795743 5795749 5795753 5795767 5795771 5795773
5795813 5795819 5795849 5795851 5795857 5795887 5795897 5795903 5795911 5795917
5795957 5795971 5795987 5796001 5796029 5796053 5796061 5796071 5796073 5796097
5796137 5796157 5796169 5796173 5796191 5796209 5796223 5796229 5796233 5796247
5796251 5796313 5796319 5796347 5796353 5796361 5796367 5796377 5796397 5796431
5796487 5796493 5796503 5796517 5796521 5796551 5796589 5796599 5796601 5796611
5796629 5796631 5796641 5796669 5796673 5796683 5796697 5796709 5796731 5796733
5796797 5796811 5796821 5796823 5796829 5796841 5796859 5796863 5796893 5796913
5796929 5796953 5796977 5796991 5797009 5797019 5797021 5797037 5797049 5797061
5797063 5797111 5797117 5797133 5797139 5797157 5797159 5797177 5797189 5797199
5797201 5797213 5797229 5797241 5797243 5797247 5797283 5797307 5797321 5797327
5797339 5797369 5797373 5797387 5797397 5797409 5797417 5797427 5797433 5797439
5797469 5797481 5797483 5797487 5797507 5797531 5797537 5797543 5797553 5797559
5797579 5797607 5797609 5797619 5797643 5797657 5797661 5797669 5797741 5797751
5797763 5797783 5797801 5797811 5797859 5797903 5797919 5797927 5797943 5797951
5797993 5798017 5798027 5798033 5798063 5798087 5798099 5798101 5798119 5798123
5798137 5798141 5798153 5798161 5798183 5798189 5798197 5798201 5798203 5798213
5798227 5798257 5798267 5798269 5798279 5798281 5798291 5798311 5798327 5798339
5798371 5798389 5798413 5798417 5798431 5798447 5798449 5798453 5798467 5798483
5798489 5798503 5798537 5798539 5798543 5798549 5798567 5798621 5798623 5798627
5798699 5798711 5798729 5798761 5798773 5798791 5798801 5798803 5798809 5798827
5798831 5798839 5798867 5798893 5798929 5798939 5798957 5798959 5798981 5798983
5798987 5798993 5799007 5799011 5799019 5799041 5799083 5799097 5799103 5799113
5799119 5799149 5799179 5799181 5799191 5799203 5799223 5799257 5799259 5799301
5799307 5799317 5799323 5799337 5799341 5799359 5799361 5799401 5799439 5799481
5799487 5799509 5799517 5799529 5799551 5799553 5799557 5799569 5799571 5799583
5799589 5799613 5799637 5799649 5799679 5799691 5799707 5799767 5799793 5799799
5799803 5799811 5799841 5799851 5799853 5799869 5799929 5799931 5799947 5799953
5799961 5799977 5799991 5800019 5800021 5800027 5800037 5800049 5800057 5800079
5800139 5800159 5800189 5800237 5800241 5800243 5800279 5800283 5800297 5800303
5800321 5800343 5800357 5800367 5800369 5800381 5800387 5800433 5800477 5800481
5800489 5800537 5800547 5800559 5800573 5800579 5800591 5800603 5800637 5800661
5800687 5800699 5800709 5800727 5800759 5800777 5800801 5800831 5800843 5800867
5800889 5800919 5800943 5800969 5800973 5800981 5800987 5800997 5801011 5801027
5801041 5801051 5801053 5801071 5801093 5801113 5801141 5801149 5801171 5801183
5801203 5801227 5801239 5801273 5801291 5801303 5801311 5801317 5801347
5801357 5801381 5801399 5801401 5801407 5801423 5801429 5801449 5801461 5801483
5801501 5801503 5801507 5801513 5801519 5801531 5801561 5801567 5801591 5801599
5801629 5801657 5801671 5801683 5801687 5801699 5801701 5801713 5801717 5801723
5801729 5801737 5801749 5801753 5801797 5801843 5801849 5801863 5801881 5801891
5801899 5801909 5801921 5801941 5801953 5801959 5801969 5801977 5801987
5801989 5802023 5802037 5802047 5802073 5802077 5802089 5802101 5802107 5802131
5802143 5802149 5802157 5802161 5802169 5802221 5802227 5802271 5802283 5802323
5802331 5802337 5802341 5802359 5802373 5802409 5802413 5802421 5802431 5802449
5802469 5802481 5802499 5802521 5802527 5802539 5802547 5802583 5802623 5802653
5802659 5802701 5802703 5802743 5802751 5802773 5802791 5802793
5802829 5802851 5802887 5802913 5802947 5802997 5803003 5803013 5803019 5803027
5803033 5803079 5803087 5803093 5803121 5803163 5803177 5803201 5803207 5803229
5803241 5803247 5803249 5803253 5803267 5803283 5803297 5803309 5803313 5803321
5803349 5803351 5803361 5803373 5803381 5803387 5803411 5803433 5803439 5803453
5803459 5803471 5803489 5803517 5803543 5803549 5803559 5803597 5803619 5803639
5803657 5803661 5803687 5803697 5803729 5803739 5803747 5803757 5803769 5803781
5803807 5803823 5803859 5803867 5803877 5803879 5803883 5803891
5803901 5803907 5803927 5803933 5803937 5803939 5803943 5803951 5803961 5803969
5803979 5803991 5803999 5804017 5804023 5804033 5804041 5804053 5804059 5804069
5804081 5804087 5804093 5804129 5804137 5804159 5804173 5804203 5804207 5804221
5804261 5804297 5804311 5804317 5804339 5804341 5804353 5804371 5804377 5804413

```
5804423  5804431  5804473  5804483  5804509  5804521  5804543  5804563  5804573  5804581
5804609  5804621  5804639  5804651  5804653  5804663  5804677  5804693  5804707  5804737
5804749  5804759  5804767  5804783  5804797  5804807  5804831  5804849  5804873  5804879
5804881  5804927  5804941  5804971  5804983  5804987  5804989  5805011  5805053  5805061
5805073  5805077  5805097  5805113  5805119  5805161  5805167  5805193  5805227  5805229
5805251  5805253  5805257  5805259  5805287  5805341  5805343  5805367  5805377  5805383
5805391  5805403  5805413  5805419  5805439  5805467  5805479  5805491  5805493  5805509
5805511  5805521  5805523  5805529  5805539  5805577  5805589  5805593  5805623  5805629
5805671  5805689  5805691  5805719  5805733  5805743  5805749  5805809  5805841  5805847
5805851  5805853  5805859  5805869  5805871  5805889  5805893  5805907  5805911  5805941
5805953  5805967  5805973  5805977  5805997  5806033  5806043  5806049  5806067  5806069
5806081  5806109  5806111  5806117  5806121  5806123  5806139  5806147  5806159  5806217
5806237  5806243  5806253  5806259  5806289  5806301  5806319  5806337  5806349  5806357
5806369  5806387  5806391  5806397  5806429  5806441  5806453  5806477  5806481  5806487
5806513  5806523  5806531  5806547  5806561  5806613  5806637  5806643  5806657  5806687
5806727  5806729  5806739  5806747  5806769  5806771  5806781  5806807  5806813  5806841
5806861  5806883  5806901  5806907  5806909  5806937  5806961  5806981  5806987  5806993
5807029  5807069  5807071  5807101  5807111  5807119  5807147  5807159  5807167  5807171
5807173  5807209  5807213  5807227  5807233  5807239  5807257  5807267  5807299  5807327
5807357  5807401  5807413  5807423  5807467  5807479  5807497  5807507  5807513  5807533
5807539  5807561  5807579  5807603  5807617  5807621  5807647  5807651  5807653  5807657
5807663  5807671  5807677  5807701  5807717  5807719  5807723  5807731  5807741  5807771
5807777  5807797  5807827  5807831  5807849  5807869  5807887  5807903  5807929  5807941
5807947  5807957  5807959  5807969  5807981  5808007  5808017  5808037  5808041  5808059
5808073  5808083  5808097  5808107  5808113  5808157  5808161  5808193  5808211  5808221
5808227  5808239  5808241  5808247  5808269  5808277  5808287  5808293  5808301  5808329
5808331  5808337  5808349  5808367  5808379  5808403  5808419  5808421  5808487  5808493
5808499  5808521  5808527  5808541  5808553  5808557  5808571  5808601  5808617  5808631
5808643  5808653  5808689  5808697  5808701  5808707  5808731  5808739  5808743  5808767
5808773  5808779  5808797  5808799  5808809  5808841  5808863  5808899  5808919  5808931
5808947  5808973  5808983  5808989  5809031  5809033  5809051  5809093  5809103
5809109  5809123  5809129  5809151  5809159  5809201  5809207  5809229  5809241  5809283
5809289  5809313  5809327  5809357  5809387  5809399  5809403  5809411  5809439  5809451
5809469  5809477  5809499  5809511  5809549  5809567  5809571  5809589  5809607  5809613
5809619  5809627  5809633  5809651  5809663  5809667  5809681  5809693  5809711  5809721
5809723  5809729  5809747  5809753  5809757  5809829  5809847  5809849  5809861  5809871
5809873  5809883  5809891  5809931  5809939  5809943  5809949  5810011  5810023  5810071
5810081  5810087  5810111  5810137  5810149  5810159  5810171  5810177  5810183  5810197
5810201  5810251  5810263  5810267  5810279  5810291  5810297  5810303  5810309  5810317
5810323  5810327  5810341  5810351  5810359  5810381  5810383  5810401  5810407  5810419
5810437  5810471  5810477  5810489  5810507  5810521  5810531  5810533  5810537  5810557
5810587  5810593  5810603  5810611  5810621  5810639  5810647  5810653  5810659  5810683
5810689  5810699  5810731  5810741  5810771  5810773  5810801  5810803  5810863  5810869
5810953  5810983  5810989  5810993  5811007  5811011  5811061  5811073  5811083  5811089
5811101  5811119  5811121  5811163  5811187  5811191  5811227  5811241  5811301  5811307
5811313  5811343  5811347  5811349  5811373  5811383  5811389  5811391  5811401  5811413
5811419  5811431  5811437  5811461  5811469  5811497  5811517  5811521  5811527  5811529
5811599  5811607  5811643  5811649  5811661  5811667  5811727  5811731  5811733  5811761
5811769  5811779  5811797  5811811  5811823  5811829  5811833  5811863  5811889  5811899
5811907  5811917  5811931  5811937  5811959  5811961  5811979  5812013  5812057  5812063
5812073  5812087  5812111  5812117  5812127  5812129  5812199  5812217  5812223  5812231
5812237  5812243  5812253  5812259  5812277  5812319  5812327  5812343  5812361  5812363
5812369  5812379  5812397  5812403  5812421  5812427  5812463  5812483  5812493  5812517
5812523  5812549  5812559  5812571  5812577  5812579  5812619  5812633  5812649  5812661
5812687  5812711  5812733  5812801  5812823  5812837  5812843  5812867  5812883  5812889
5812907  5812927  5812931  5812943  5812957  5812981  5812991  5812999  5813009
5813023  5813051  5813053  5813077  5813123  5813131  5813141  5813147  5813149  5813153
5813191  5813233  5813251  5813263  5813281  5813309  5813323  5813333  5813341
5813347  5813407  5813419  5813429  5813441  5813443  5813527  5813537  5813567  5813573
5813579  5813593  5813603  5813611  5813617  5813627  5813663  5813723  5813749  5813761
5813767  5813783  5813789  5813803  5813807  5813827  5813861  5813879  5813887  5813893
5813903  5813989  5813993  5814001  5814043  5814071  5814077  5814079  5814089  5814091
5814113  5814121  5814131  5814139  5814161  5814167  5814199  5814203  5814223  5814227
5814257  5814287  5814301  5814311  5814313  5814317  5814343  5814349  5814353  5814371
5814397  5814401  5814421  5814433  5814449  5814467  5814481  5814491  5814499
5814521  5814533  5814541  5814547  5814559  5814563  5814569  5814583  5814619  5814623
5814643  5814647  5814673  5814707  5814713  5814727  5814737  5814749  5814751  5814769
5814797  5814803  5814811  5814821  5814827  5814839  5814841  5814857
5814899  5814911  5814923  5814937  5814967  5814983  5815009  5815013  5815027  5815039
5815057  5815079  5815081  5815087  5815097  5815127  5815133  5815141  5815151  5815163
5815177  5815181  5815189  5815211  5815219  5815223  5815231  5815291  5815307  5815331
5815333  5815361  5815379  5815417  5815421  5815423  5815487  5815489  5815517  5815519
5815529  5815541  5815543  5815559  5815591  5815603  5815627  5815651  5815661  5815687
5815699  5815721  5815723  5815739  5815753  5815769  5815781  5815783  5815811  5815813
5815847  5815861  5815867  5815903  5815907  5815937  5815951  5815961  5815963  5815967
5815981  5816009  5816021  5816029  5816047  5816077  5816089  5816093  5816113  5816117
5816123  5816143  5816183  5816191  5816201  5816207  5816221  5816233  5816243  5816257
5816267  5816303  5816333  5816339  5816341  5816347  5816387  5816399  5816407  5816463
5816467  5816477  5816483  5816491  5816507  5816521  5816549  5816563  5816581  5816597
5816609  5816611  5816639  5816647  5816651  5816683  5816687  5816689  5816731  5816749
5816753  5816801  5816813  5816821  5816851  5816879  5816891  5816897  5816917  5816927
5816971  5816989  5817001  5817037  5817041  5817047  5817061  5817073  5817107  5817113
5817167  5817191  5817199  5817209  5817233  5817239  5817263  5817283  5817293  5817299
5817319  5817347  5817377  5817379  5817389  5817397  5817403  5817437  5817467  5817503
5817517  5817533  5817563  5817569  5817571  5817583  5817593  5817601  5817641
5817649  5817653  5817671  5817673  5817683  5817703  5817733  5817751  5817767  5817803
5817829  5817853  5817869  5817887  5817899  5817907  5817913  5817937  5817947  5817967
5818013  5818061  5818073  5818081  5818117  5818121  5818129  5818133  5818151  5818159
5818193  5818229  5818231  5818247  5818249  5818259  5818277  5818279  5818283  5818289
```

5818321	5818331	5818343	5818381	5818391	5818399	5818409	5818411	5818457	5818469
5818487	5818493	5818511	5818513	5818523	5818543	5818559	5818601	5818613	5818619
5818621	5818633	5818643	5818651	5818697	5818721	5818723	5818727	5818733	5818819
5818823	5818847	5818853	5818859	5818871	5818873	5818907	5818949	5818951	5818963
5818987	5818991	5818999	5819003	5819039	5819057	5819063	5819071	5819081	5819113
5819123	5819129	5819131	5819141	5819153	5819159	5819167	5819179	5819189	5819221
5819237	5819239	5819243	5819269	5819279	5819291	5819293	5819327	5819353	5819369
5819381	5819393	5819441	5819467	5819477	5819479	5819501	5819503	5819507	5819531
5819543	5819549	5819551	5819557	5819563	5819647	5819651	5819659	5819669	5819677
5819683	5819689	5819699	5819717	5819741	5819773	5819777	5819789	5819813	5819857
5819867	5819873	5819881	5819929	5819939	5819959	5819969	5819987	5819999	5820011
5820037	5820041	5820049	5820079	5820119	5820121	5820131	5820149	5820187	5820197
5820229	5820233	5820247	5820277	5820299	5820313	5820323	5820337	5820349	5820361
5820371	5820377	5820383	5820389	5820421	5820431	5820469	5820473	5820481	5820487
5820497	5820499	5820533	5820539	5820553	5820569	5820571	5820583	5820589	5820599
5820611	5820623	5820629	5820637	5820667	5820671	5820673	5820697	5820713	5820739
5820751	5820757	5820761	5820769	5820797	5820823	5820827	5820833	5820847	5820853
5820869	5820883	5820887	5820917	5820923	5820929	5820943	5820959	5820977	5821003
5821007	5821009	5821019	5821033	5821037	5821051	5821063	5821069	5821097	5821129
5821159	5821171	5821177	5821183	5821213	5821229	5821237	5821243	5821271	5821289
5821301	5821313	5821331	5821339	5821349	5821357	5821367	5821393	5821423	5821441
5821447	5821451	5821499	5821511	5821559	5821567	5821577	5821591	5821597	5821603
5821637	5821639	5821643	5821687	5821693	5821729	5821759	5821789	5821793	5821817
5821841	5821853	5821859	5821889	5821897	5821909	5821919	5821931	5821951	5821957
5821979	5822021	5822027	5822077	5822081	5822083	5822093	5822101	5822111	5822129
5822137	5822147	5822149	5822153	5822207	5822239	5822249	5822251	5822269	5822273
5822317	5822351	5822371	5822387	5822419	5822423	5822441	5822459	5822461	5822471
5822477	5822489	5822491	5822521	5822539	5822561	5822567	5822573	5822599	5822603
5822623	5822627	5822669	5822681	5822701	5822717	5822723	5822731	5822741	5822743
5822767	5822807	5822821	5822827	5822867	5822897	5822917	5822963	5822969	5822981
5822983	5822989	5823001	5823019	5823029	5823053	5823067	5823073	5823091	5823119
5823131	5823143	5823149	5823179	5823187	5823193	5823211	5823221	5823227	5823239
5823247	5823263	5823277	5823281	5823289	5823317	5823341	5823373	5823379	5823409
5823413	5823421	5823437	5823449	5823463	5823473	5823497	5823509	5823523	5823527
5823539	5823547	5823553	5823563	5823569	5823611	5823641	5823659	5823667	5823739
5823743	5823749	5823757	5823767	5823773	5823793	5823821	5823859	5823869	5823871
5823887	5823889	5823913	5823931	5823943	5823947	5823967	5823971	5823989	5824003
5824019	5824031	5824043	5824069	5824073	5824079	5824111	5824141	5824151	5824199
5824211	5824271	5824277	5824297	5824309	5824321	5824327	5824333	5824349	5824363
5824369	5824409	5824417	5824453	5824457	5824471	5824477	5824493	5824499	5824513
5824529	5824571	5824573	5824631	5824639	5824649	5824667	5824673	5824703	5824717
5824723	5824739	5824751	5824761	5824789	5824813	5824831	5824837	5824843	5824867
5824883	5824919	5824921	5824939	5824967	5824979	5825009	5825041	5825051	5825059
5825063	5825107	5825111	5825161	5825173	5825207	5825213	5825221	5825231	5825251
5825257	5825291	5825293	5825297	5825311	5825333	5825353	5825359	5825399	5825431
5825437	5825447	5825497	5825503	5825513	5825527	5825557	5825563	5825569	5825581
5825591	5825593	5825627	5825641	5825653	5825669	5825671	5825681	5825711	5825741
5825749	5825753	5825767	5825773	5825777	5825797	5825803	5825819	5825843	5825879
5825891	5825899	5825903	5825947	5825957	5825959	5825971	5825993	5825999	5826001
5826127	5826133	5826137	5826157	5826169	5826173	5826193	5826251	5826259	5826263
5826277	5826281	5826299	5826311	5826313	5826319	5826341	5826389	5826391	5826397
5826413	5826421	5826433	5826437	5826451	5826493	5826497	5826503	5826533	5826539
5826547	5826577	5826599	5826643	5826671	5826677	5826679	5826701	5826721	5826739
5826763	5826811	5826827	5826833	5826841	5826851	5826893	5826911	5826913	5826949
5826959	5826967	5826991	5827001	5827007	5827037	5827049	5827051	5827099	5827103
5827109	5827117	5827169	5827177	5827189	5827193	5827223	5827229	5827259	5827267
5827279	5827301	5827307	5827309	5827321	5827333	5827337	5827343	5827351	5827361
5827373	5827399	5827417	5827427	5827429	5827439	5827499	5827511	5827519	5827531
5827559	5827561	5827573	5827589	5827603	5827639	5827643	5827681	5827687	5827691
5827697	5827709	5827711	5827729	5827777	5827823	5827831	5827847	5827849	5827867
5827873	5827931	5827937	5827949	5827963	5827967	5827973	5827979	5827999	5828023
5828033	5828057	5828077	5828087	5828099	5828107	5828149	5828153	5828167	5828189
5828209	5828219	5828227	5828233	5828237	5828239	5828257	5828281	5828287	5828299
5828309	5828353	5828363	5828369	5828371	5828377	5828401	5828441	5828443	5828447
5828479	5828483	5828491	5828513	5828561	5828567	5828587	5828593	5828617	5828621
5828629	5828663	5828677	5828701	5828723	5828741	5828749	5828759	5828761	5828789
5828791	5828803	5828813	5828833	5828843	5828863	5828897	5828917	5828941	5828947
5828957	5828981	5828983	5828989	5829001	5829041	5829049	5829059	5829071	5829119
5829121	5829127	5829137	5829139	5829149	5829157	5829167	5829169	5829191	5829199
5829223	5829227	5829247	5829251	5829277	5829287	5829301	5829323	5829349	5829353
5829361	5829391	5829401	5829403	5829413	5829433	5829451	5829463	5829529	5829533
5829539	5829559	5829569	5829583	5829601	5829641	5829661	5829679	5829701	5829721
5829727	5829743	5829773	5829779	5829809	5829839	5829847	5829869	5829899	5829911
5829917	5829919	5829931	5829937	5829961	5829973	5830001	5830007	5830039	5830049
5830051	5830057	5830061	5830079	5830087	5830091	5830129	5830151	5830163	5830177
5830183	5830193	5830213	5830219	5830229	5830249	5830259	5830271	5830277	5830313
5830333	5830343	5830369	5830373	5830381	5830393	5830403	5830411	5830453	5830457
5830459	5830483	5830493	5830547	5830577	5830579	5830589	5830603	5830607	5830613
5830621	5830631	5830639	5830691	5830703	5830709	5830717	5830763	5830787	5830789
5830801	5830819	5830823	5830849	5830859	5830861	5830871	5830873	5830877	5830879
5830879	5830907	5830919	5830921	5830963	5830987	5831009	5831041	5831047	5831053
5831057	5831087	5831093	5831123	5831129	5831141	5831183	5831197	5831239	5831249
5831251	5831257	5831261	5831269	5831281	5831303	5831321	5831363	5831381	5831387
5831401	5831509	5831513	5831519	5831521	5831557	5831597	5831603	5831611	5831621
5831633	5831647	5831653	5831659	5831669	5831671	5831677	5831687	5831699	5831723
5831729	5831753	5831759	5831767	5831773	5831779	5831797	5831801	5831831	5831843
5831863	5831887	5831893	5831899	5831909	5831911	5831921	5831927	5831933	5831933
5831939	5831951	5831957	5831971	5831981	5831983	5832007	5832019	5832049	5832053
5832097	5832109	5832121	5832131	5832143	5832157	5832163	5832181	5832187	5832217

```
5832257 5832287 5832289 5832293 5832313 5832329 5832331 5832353 5832361 5832389
5832397 5832403 5832419 5832427 5832439 5832461 5832467 5832473 5832499 5832503
5832523 5832527 5832529 5832553 5832571 5832583 5832587 5832599 5832611 5832613
5832623 5832641 5832647 5832679 5832709 5832713 5832719 5832763 5832767 5832769
5832779 5832781 5832803 5832839 5832847 5832941 5832977 5832997 5833001 5833063
5833067 5833097 5833103 5833109 5833169 5833181 5833187 5833207 5833229 5833241
5833253 5833277 5833349 5833393 5833403 5833409 5833411 5833433 5833441 5833453
5833459 5833463 5833481 5833493 5833537 5833547 5833591 5833609 5833631 5833693
5833717 5833721 5833739 5833759 5833769 5833777 5833783 5833787 5833813 5833819
5833829 5833837 5833847 5833879 5833889 5833909 5833943 5833951 5833967 5833991
5834011 5834021 5834027 5834033 5834041 5834051 5834053 5834057 5834069 5834089
5834099 5834117 5834119 5834131 5834167 5834183 5834189 5834201 5834207 5834209
5834219 5834243 5834261 5834267 5834287 5834291 5834299 5834317 5834321 5834327
5834329 5834351 5834357 5834363 5834371 5834377 5834401 5834407 5834431 5834441
5834459 5834461 5834473 5834497 5834503 5834513 5834531 5834551 5834557 5834579
5834593 5834599 5834623 5834629 5834657 5834659 5834677 5834683 5834701 5834797
5834809 5834821 5834831 5834867 5834891 5834903 5834947 5834947 5834953 5834977
5834987 5834999 5835001 5835007 5835013 5835043 5835059 5835101 5835103 5835113
5835127 5835139 5835157 5835163 5835173 5835197 5835209 5835211 5835217 5835227
5835239 5835251 5835253 5835257 5835281 5835283 5835289 5835311 5835329 5835341
5835343 5835371 5835383 5835421 5835439 5835449 5835461 5835469 5835497 5835509
5835521 5835551 5835553 5835569 5835581 5835601 5835611 5835615 5835619 5835691
5835701 5835761 5835769 5835773 5835787 5835803 5835821 5835827 5835833 5835853
5835871 5835923 5835953 5835959 5835961 5835971 5836007 5836009 5836013
5836027 5836067 5836069 5836079 5836081 5836087 5836093 5836177 5836183 5836189
5836217 5836223 5836241 5836247 5836291 5836349 5836351 5836357 5836379 5836381
5836399 5836403 5836409 5836421 5836427 5836429 5836447 5836451 5836459 5836499
5836543 5836547 5836583 5836613 5836631 5836657 5836669 5836673 5836717 5836723
5836739 5836741 5836751 5836771 5836799 5836807 5836813 5836823 5836829 5836889
5836903 5836927 5836931 5836937 5836939 5836951 5836969 5836997 5837003 5837017
5837053 5837063 5837081 5837087 5837099 5837119 5837131 5837173 5837189 5837191
5837201 5837219 5837233 5837257 5837263 5837281 5837287 5837297 5837309 5837311
5837317 5837387 5837399 5837501 5837521 5837537 5837543 5837567 5837593 5837597
5837603 5837609 5837627 5837633 5837651 5837677 5837687 5837717 5837719 5837773
5837803 5837831 5837849 5837879 5837891 5837893 5837899 5837939 5837947 5837963
5837977 5837989 5837999 5838017 5838043 5838047 5838071 5838083 5838097 5838101
5838163 5838167 5838197 5838211 5838221 5838223 5838229 5838233 5838247 5838253
5838257 5838271 5838299 5838307 5838319 5838331 5838353 5838373 5838379 5838383
5838397 5838409 5838419 5838431 5838433 5838439 5838449 5838451 5838479 5838499
5838551 5838557 5838587 5838589 5838593 5838607 5838617 5838631 5838641 5838659
5838661 5838689 5838691 5838697 5838713 5838727 5838731 5838751 5838779 5838787
5838797 5838887 5838907 5838913 5838919 5838929 5838949 5838953 5838971 5838977
5838991 5838997 5839037 5839039 5839073 5839087 5839091 5839147 5839151 5839181
5839187 5839219 5839231 5839259 5839283 5839291 5839307 5839319 5839339 5839363
5839367 5839373 5839387 5839397 5839409 5839417 5839433 5839453 5839481 5839511
5839513 5839523 5839531 5839541 5839543 5839553 5839567 5839571 5839573 5839577
5839579 5839597 5839627 5839633 5839637 5839649 5839657 5839661 5839667 5839681
5839693 5839697 5839709 5839711 5839741 5839751 5839829 5839837 5839843 5839901
5839903 5839909 5839919 5839931 5839937 5839949 5839979 5840039 5840041 5840047
5840077 5840083 5840089 5840099 5840101 5840113 5840119 5840161 5840213 5840251
5840287 5840291 5840293 5840297 5840309 5840311 5840347 5840371 5840399
5840411 5840423 5840449 5840473 5840477 5840489 5840507 5840509 5840521 5840539
5840563 5840593 5840609 5840609 5840633 5840663 5840669 5840671 5840677
5840683 5840693 5840699 5840701 5840713 5840719 5840743 5840749 5840753 5840761
5840767 5840773 5840777 5840789 5840801 5840851 5840867 5840869 5840881 5840899
5840903 5840909 5840951 5840953 5840963 5840969 5840987 5841001 5841007 5841013
5841053 5841067 5841097 5841107 5841109 5841131 5841169 5841179 5841203 5841211
5841239 5841263 5841281 5841293 5841317 5841323 5841371 5841373 5841377
5841389 5841397 5841401 5841443 5841461 5841463 5841467 5841469 5841481 5841487
5841509 5841559 5841571 5841581 5841587 5841601 5841611 5841617 5841629 5841707
5841743 5841751 5841779 5841791 5841799 5841821 5841859 5841883 5841907 5841961
5841989 5841991 5842013 5842027 5842051 5842087 5842097 5842099 5842103 5842157
5842159 5842163 5842171 5842181 5842183 5842201 5842211 5842213 5842223 5842231
5842247 5842261 5842267 5842283 5842289 5842301 5842327 5842387 5842393 5842399
5842451 5842457 5842471 5842493 5842511 5842531 5842537 5842553 5842567 5842589
5842607 5842631 5842657 5842673 5842687 5842691 5842703 5842723 5842769
5842777 5842799 5842813 5842819 5842831 5842841 5842867 5842871 5842873 5842877
5842901 5842909 5842931 5842957 5842961 5842979 5842991 5842993 5842997
5843009 5843017 5843023 5843039 5843041 5843063 5843083 5843093 5843099 5843111
5843113 5843147 5843161 5843171 5843179 5843191 5843213 5843231 5843267 5843281
5843287 5843309 5843323 5843329 5843339 5843347 5843363 5843389 5843401 5843429
5843441 5843477 5843483 5843489 5843491 5843501 5843503 5843533 5843543 5843561
5843567 5843603 5843609 5843639 5843641 5843647 5843653 5843671 5843683 5843687
5843693 5843701 5843707 5843711 5843731 5843737 5843749 5843753 5843809 5843821
5843837 5843843 5843857 5843881 5843897 5843951 5843953 5843969 5843989 5844029
5844031 5844037 5844043 5844049 5844053 5844061 5844101 5844103 5844119 5844131
5844133 5844143 5844149 5844169 5844193 5844203 5844211 5844217 5844221 5844269
5844281 5844299 5844301 5844313 5844317 5844329 5844331 5844361 5844367 5844383
5844389 5844439 5844451 5844463 5844493 5844511 5844539 5844547 5844549 5844559
5844613 5844637 5844677 5844679 5844697 5844701 5844721 5844731 5844733 5844763
5844787 5844809 5844851 5844859 5844869 5844871 5844899 5844901 5844931 5844961
5844983 5844997 5845009 5845039 5845069 5845079 5845087 5845097 5845111 5845117
5845139 5845159 5845171 5845193 5845309 5845319 5845321 5845339 5845349 5845373
5845387 5845403 5845417 5845421 5845451 5845457 5845459 5845481 5845501 5845523
5845557 5845573 5845583 5845589 5845591 5845601 5845627 5845651 5845681 5845699
5845709 5845751 5845753 5845771 5845781 5845783 5845793 5845799 5845823 5845859
5845871 5845887 5845891 5845919 5845967 5845969 5845991 5845993 5846021 5846047
5846051 5846083 5846089 5846101 5846107 5846123 5846131 5846153 5846161 5846171
5846173 5846207 5846221 5846233 5846261 5846263 5846273 5846279 5846293 5846297
```

```
5846299  5846303  5846327  5846329  5846339  5846359  5846381  5846389  5846411  5846413
5846417  5846441  5846443  5846447  5846459  5846461  5846473  5846501  5846513  5846537
5846539  5846557  5846563  5846567  5846573  5846579  5846591  5846597  5846609  5846627
5846653  5846663  5846681  5846683  5846689  5846717  5846747  5846773  5846791  5846809
5846821  5846831  5846849  5846857  5846873  5846891  5846903  5846917  5846933  5846957
5846977  5846983  5846987  5846989  5846993  5847019  5847029  5847043  5847047  5847053
5847089  5847103  5847109  5847113  5847137  5847139  5847143  5847161  5847169  5847181
5847187  5847199  5847203  5847239  5847263  5847271  5847301  5847323  5847341  5847349
5847353  5847397  5847403  5847419  5847427  5847463  5847467  5847481  5847487  5847493
5847503  5847509  5847511  5847529  5847533  5847539  5847557  5847577  5847581  5847587
5847593  5847617  5847641  5847661  5847671  5847679  5847683  5847689  5847691  5847701
5847703  5847713  5847731  5847749  5847761  5847767  5847769  5847797  5847823  5847833
5847841  5847851  5847857  5847883  5847889  5847899  5847913  5847917  5847979  5847997
5848039  5848061  5848099  5848123  5848127  5848159  5848189  5848211  5848259  5848273
5848303  5848307  5848309  5848313  5848319  5848321  5848327  5848361  5848369  5848373
5848379  5848397  5848433  5848441  5848471  5848487  5848489  5848501  5848511  5848519
5848537  5848547  5848567  5848571  5848589  5848597  5848639  5848651  5848673  5848679
5848681  5848699  5848723  5848747  5848763  5848781  5848783  5848819  5848823  5848837
5848853  5848859  5848861  5848883  5848893  5848907  5848933  5848939  5848943  5848951
5848961  5848963  5849023  5849029  5849059  5849087  5849089  5849099  5849113  5849117
5849119  5849149  5849171  5849177  5849191  5849203  5849227  5849231  5849237  5849269
5849317  5849323  5849341  5849353  5849381  5849401  5849407  5849413  5849423  5849431
5849461  5849471  5849491  5849497  5849507  5849551  5849579  5849603  5849621  5849633
5849647  5849651  5849653  5849681  5849687  5849693  5849699  5849719  5849741  5849749
5849801  5849803  5849813  5849821  5849863  5849867  5849869  5849911  5849933  5849939
5849941  5849947  5849969  5849993  5850049  5850113  5850121  5850127  5850149  5850161
5850179  5850191  5850209  5850217  5850241  5850259  5850307  5850319  5850323  5850337
5850343  5850359  5850367  5850379  5850391  5850437  5850443  5850457  5850469  5850473
5850479  5850491  5850527  5850529  5850539  5850541  5850557  5850563  5850569  5850583
5850631  5850643  5850667  5850673  5850679  5850683  5850751  5850769  5850781  5850787
5850791  5850811  5850827  5850833  5850857  5850883  5850893  5850899  5850913  5850979
5850989  5850997  5851003  5851007  5851051  5851063  5851093  5851103  5851117  5851123
5851141  5851159  5851163  5851189  5851193  5851199  5851201  5851249  5851277  5851283
5851309  5851319  5851333  5851337  5851367  5851369  5851387  5851403  5851409  5851421
5851423  5851427  5851429  5851441  5851457  5851459  5851463  5851471  5851477  5851481
5851493  5851507  5851511  5851523  5851541  5851543  5851589  5851597  5851603  5851613
5851619  5851627  5851673  5851691  5851693  5851697  5851709  5851711  5851717  5851733
5851759  5851787  5851789  5851801  5851831  5851837  5851841  5851843  5851849  5851871
5851873  5851877  5851897  5851907  5851919  5851921  5851969  5851991  5852009  5852023
5852027  5852069  5852123  5852129  5852153  5852159  5852167  5852183  5852201  5852213
5852219  5852227  5852237  5852239  5852251  5852263  5852291  5852293  5852303  5852333
5852347  5852359  5852377  5852389  5852423  5852443  5852447  5852449  5852467  5852477
5852479  5852501  5852527  5852531  5852569  5852591  5852593  5852597  5852621  5852653
5852657  5852659  5852663  5852669  5852677  5852681  5852683  5852699  5852711  5852713
5852719  5852747  5852753  5852761  5852797  5852801  5852807  5852827  5852857  5852881
5852887  5852923  5852927  5852933  5852939  5852941  5852963  5852989  5852999  5853047
5853059  5853101  5853131  5853137  5853149  5853173  5853217  5853223  5853227  5853233
5853241  5853269  5853277  5853289  5853307  5853319  5853343  5853383  5853391  5853403
5853433  5853443  5853467  5853481  5853487  5853509  5853541  5853553  5853581  5853583
5853587  5853607  5853623  5853641  5853643  5853647  5853667  5853677  5853697  5853751
5853779  5853791  5853833  5853839  5853877  5853889  5853893  5853901  5853917  5853923
5853931  5853949  5853971  5853989  5854003  5854031  5854049  5854067  5854081  5854087
5854091  5854099  5854129  5854141  5854169  5854187  5854207  5854243  5854271  5854283
5854297  5854309  5854313  5854339  5854357  5854361  5854369  5854391  5854403  5854423
5854439  5854481  5854483  5854487  5854507  5854523  5854529  5854543  5854561  5854577
5854601  5854619  5854631  5854633  5854663  5854669  5854697  5854699  5854711  5854727
5854729  5854741  5854757  5854777  5854787  5854789  5854799  5854801  5854813  5854859
5854867  5854883  5854889  5854909  5854957  5854993  5854999  5855023  5855029  5855033
5855093  5855099  5855107  5855141  5855149  5855159  5855167  5855183  5855189  5855203
5855209  5855233  5855237  5855263  5855279  5855309  5855341  5855347  5855357  5855383
5855393  5855417  5855437  5855441  5855513  5855483  5855489  5855499  5855513  5855527
5855533  5855537  5855539  5855557  5855581  5855587  5855623  5855699  5855719  5855723
5855737  5855747  5855749  5855753  5855761  5855771  5855779  5855797  5855833  5855851
5855873  5855887  5855891  5855897  5855903  5855909  5855911  5855921  5855951  5855957
5855963  5855977  5855981  5856013  5856029  5856043  5856073  5856079  5856089  5856091
5856107  5856113  5856121  5856131  5856139  5856167  5856187  5856197  5856229  5856239
5856287  5856337  5856353  5856377  5856379  5856401  5856407  5856413  5856419  5856439
5856443  5856467  5856469  5856479  5856491  5856493  5856497  5856509  5856527  5856547
5856589  5856601  5856607  5856661  5856689  5856691  5856703  5856707  5856709  5856713
5856749  5856751  5856761  5856791  5856797  5856833  5856839  5856847  5856853  5856899
5856911  5856913  5856919  5856931  5856967  5857031  5857057  5857067  5857081  5857097
5857099  5857147  5857177  5857183  5857193  5857237  5857259  5857279  5857283  5857303
5857307  5857309  5857337  5857349  5857351  5857361  5857381  5857399  5857409  5857451
5857457  5857459  5857463  5857487  5857493  5857499  5857519  5857531  5857549  5857561
5857583  5857601  5857619  5857627  5857633  5857661  5857669  5857699  5857717  5857727
5857759  5857763  5857783  5857829  5857849  5857861  5857879  5857883  5857897  5857903
5857921  5857937  5857961  5857967  5857981  5857991  5858003  5858009  5858093  5858113
5858131  5858149  5858187  5858201  5858219  5858227  5858239  5858243  5858263  5858267
5858269  5858291  5858297  5858311  5858317  5858341  5858351  5858371  5858407  5858417
5858429  5858431  5858453  5858459  5858483  5858497  5858519  5858533  5858539  5858563
5858579  5858581  5858599  5858627  5858639  5858647  5858651  5858687  5858689  5858701
5858717  5858731  5858753  5858773  5858791  5858803  5858807  5858833  5858843  5858857
5858873  5858891  5858927  5858933  5858947  5858983  5858999  5859017  5859019  5859037
5859041  5859071  5859107  5859109  5859143  5859167  5859179  5859211  5859221  5859241
5859299  5859311  5859317  5859347  5859367  5859379  5859383  5859401  5859409  5859437
5859439  5859487  5859533  5859541  5859547  5859569  5859593  5859613  5859617  5859629
5859643  5859661  5859677  5859691  5859697  5859727  5859757  5859787  5859793  5859803
5859817  5859829  5859859  5859869  5859877  5859941  5859947  5859967  5859969  5859977
5859991  5860033  5860039  5860079  5860091  5860109  5860123  5860133  5860139  5860163
```

```
5860177  5860181  5860187  5860199  5860207  5860213  5860229  5860241  5860243  5860247
5860249  5860259  5860273  5860277  5860297  5860301  5860313  5860321  5860343  5860363
5860373  5860399  5860403  5860433  5860441  5860451  5860501  5860507  5860511  5860537
5860559  5860567  5860573  5860577  5860579  5860609  5860627  5860637  5860651  5860661
5860667  5860681  5860709  5860717  5860747  5860753  5860769  5860781  5860787  5860807
5860843  5860847  5860849  5860861  5860867  5860889  5860901  5860919  5860927  5860969
5860973  5860993  5861003  5861027  5861033  5861057  5861069  5861081  5861099  5861123
5861129  5861153  5861171  5861179  5861183  5861189  5861203  5861221  5861231  5861239
5861249  5861267  5861279  5861299  5861309  5861321  5861347  5861351  5861371  5861381
5861407  5861411  5861437  5861461  5861467  5861497  5861501  5861507  5861539  5861579
5861593  5861621  5861623  5861663  5861677  5861701  5861707  5861731  5861749  5861761
5861767  5861773  5861787  5861789  5861813  5861837  5861851  5861881  5861929  5861951
5861963  5862011  5862023  5862029  5862053  5862083  5862113  5862121  5862133  5862137
5862149  5862167  5862173  5862179  5862187  5862211  5862239  5862253  5862287  5862293
5862313  5862349  5862361  5862371  5862377  5862397  5862419  5862421  5862443  5862449
5862473  5862497  5862509  5862517  5862529  5862547  5862559  5862599  5862601  5862617
5862667  5862673  5862679  5862691  5862709  5862713  5862763  5862767  5862787  5862799
5862821  5862833  5862847  5862929  5862931  5862973  5863009  5863027  5863043  5863049
5863051  5863073  5863111  5863129  5863139  5863159  5863199  5863211  5863213  5863217
5863261  5863271  5863303  5863313  5863327  5863331  5863349  5863373  5863379  5863411
5863421  5863441  5863469  5863499  5863511  5863513  5863519  5863531  5863541  5863567
5863573  5863577  5863591  5863601  5863621  5863631  5863633  5863651  5863667  5863679
5863699  5863703  5863709  5863727  5863729  5863733  5863751  5863763  5863769  5863789
5863801  5863807  5863811  5863817  5863831  5863841  5863843  5863853  5863859  5863877
5863889  5863903  5863927  5863939  5863981  5863987  5864009  5864021  5864029  5864063
5864071  5864077  5864081  5864101  5864153  5864171  5864173  5864197  5864203  5864207
5864213  5864233  5864263  5864279  5864281  5864311  5864317  5864321  5864347  5864401
5864413  5864429  5864431  5864437  5864449  5864459  5864489  5864497  5864501  5864513
5864533  5864557  5864561  5864567  5864569  5864603  5864623  5864627  5864629  5864633
5864657  5864669  5864687  5864713  5864731  5864737  5864753  5864773  5864783  5864791
5864819  5864849  5864857  5864861  5864869  5864891  5864909  5864917  5864933
5864993  5865019  5865031  5865043  5865059  5865061  5865103  5865121  5865133  5865137
5865143  5865151  5865179  5865191  5865193  5865199  5865227  5865257  5865259  5865283
5865347  5865389  5865391  5865403  5865407  5865431  5865439  5865467  5865473  5865487
5865533  5865551  5865571  5865599  5865611  5865641  5865653  5865679  5865703  5865707
5865709  5865719  5865733  5865751  5865757  5865773  5865779  5865803  5865809  5865817
5865823  5865841  5865863  5865887  5865919  5865941  5865947  5865961  5865967  5865971
5865973  5865983  5866001  5866013  5866019  5866031  5866039  5866043  5866057  5866067
5866073  5866097  5866109  5866123  5866129  5866141  5866151  5866177  5866213  5866243
5866247  5866249  5866261  5866277  5866291  5866327  5866351  5866363  5866369  5866373
5866379  5866417  5866423  5866451  5866457  5866519  5866533  5866577  5866607  5866631
5866661  5866691  5866699  5866709  5866711  5866723  5866727  5866747  5866759  5866769
5866793  5866799  5866807  5866811  5866823  5866837  5866841  5866849  5866867  5866871
5866891  5866897  5866951  5866957  5867003  5867009  5867011  5867027  5867033  5867063
5867087  5867089  5867101  5867107  5867111  5867119  5867129  5867149  5867161  5867179
5867207  5867237  5867293  5867297  5867311  5867317  5867321  5867327  5867347
5867357  5867377  5867399  5867417  5867419  5867429  5867443  5867467  5867473  5867489
5867509  5867531  5867539  5867549  5867557  5867569  5867581  5867591  5867593  5867597
5867623  5867647  5867671  5867707  5867717  5867731  5867747  5867749  5867761  5867767
5867777  5867791  5867803  5867857  5867861  5867891  5867893  5867899  5867929  5867933
5867951  5867957  5867969  5867989  5867993  5868019  5868073  5868083  5868101
5868103  5868127  5868133  5868143  5868193  5868211  5868217  5868223  5868241  5868257
5868263  5868271  5868277  5868293  5868301  5868307  5868347  5868361  5868377  5868461
5868479  5868487  5868509  5868521  5868523  5868529  5868539  5868557  5868581  5868593
5868601  5868613  5868619  5868623  5868649  5868677  5868721  5868761  5868767  5868803
5868809  5868833  5868869  5868883  5868899  5868901  5868953  5868959  5868971  5869001
5869007  5869033  5869067  5869069  5869079  5869091  5869093  5869099  5869103  5869111
5869121  5869139  5869151  5869153  5869159  5869169  5869181  5869229  5869243  5869277
5869289  5869319  5869337  5869343  5869349  5869351  5869361  5869363  5869399  5869411
5869417  5869427  5869429  5869433  5869441  5869453  5869469  5869477  5869489  5869517
5869561  5869579  5869597  5869609  5869627  5869657  5869663  5869667  5869673  5869679
5869691  5869739  5869741  5869751  5869763  5869769  5869781  5869837  5869859  5869891
5869933  5869949  5869959  5869987  5869997  5870017  5870021  5870023  5870027
5870041  5870057  5870077  5870089  5870099  5870101  5870113  5870141  5870143  5870167
5870171  5870197  5870201  5870243  5870251  5870273  5870299  5870303  5870311  5870327
5870329  5870357  5870363  5870393  5870407  5870419  5870429  5870437  5870467  5870471
5870477  5870509  5870533  5870549  5870561  5870573  5870581  5870591  5870603  5870611
5870621  5870633  5870659  5870693  5870701  5870713  5870719  5870737  5870759  5870779
5870783  5870801  5870803  5870807  5870857  5870881  5870923  5870927  5870939  5870959
5870987  5870993  5870999  5871013  5871017  5871023  5871037  5871071  5871109  5871113
5871139  5871161  5871163  5871167  5871179  5871211  5871223  5871259  5871301  5871319
5871343  5871353  5871373  5871377  5871391  5871403  5871407  5871421  5871451  5871457
5871461  5871479  5871529  5871533  5871539  5871557  5871559  5871563  5871571
5871577  5871581  5871599  5871611  5871631  5871661  5871673  5871707  5871709  5871713
5871727  5871731  5871743  5871763  5871769  5871787  5871797  5871823  5871829  5871841
5871871  5871881  5871907  5871911  5871917  5871959  5871961  5871973  5872003  5872019
5872033  5872067  5872079  5872091  5872103  5872109  5872117  5872127  5872147  5872151
5872171  5872187  5872213  5872249  5872253  5872261  5872289  5872303  5872313  5872319
5872331  5872343  5872357  5872369  5872379  5872397  5872403  5872417  5872421  5872439
5872441  5872457  5872459  5872507  5872511  5872513  5872523  5872543  5872549  5872561
5872571  5872579  5872583  5872589  5872597  5872627  5872651  5872661  5872663  5872673
5872681  5872687  5872693  5872709  5872739  5872787  5872793  5872807  5872813  5872817
5872839  5872873  5872879  5872921  5872941  5872963  5872979  5872983  5872991  5872931
5872943  5872961  5872969  5872987  5872991  5873003  5873009  5873011  5873039  5873057
5873083  5873107  5873117  5873159  5873173  5873201  5873207  5873217
5873239  5873243  5873249  5873267  5873281  5873293  5873297  5873311  5873323  5873359
5873419  5873423  5873437  5873471  5873473  5873479  5873501  5873503  5873519  5873521
5873561  5873587  5873591  5873611  5873677  5873711  5873719  5873741  5873753  5873761
5873767  5873801  5873807  5873837  5873851  5873897  5873899  5873941  5873951  5873953
```

```
5873971 5874007 5874017 5874023 5874041 5874049 5874103 5874133 5874137 5874139
5874151 5874161 5874179 5874199 5874227 5874229 5874251 5874263 5874277 5874293
5874301 5874331 5874347 5874371 5874397 5874403 5874419 5874431 5874481 5874497
5874509 5874563 5874607 5874641 5874643 5874647 5874653 5874709 5874721 5874731
5874751 5874769 5874787 5874793 5874829 5874833 5874839 5874853 5874863 5874871
5874881 5874889 5874899 5874917 5874923 5874937 5874941 5874977 5875003 5875021
5875031 5875033 5875063 5875087 5875109 5875117 5875159 5875169 5875171 5875187
5875211 5875231 5875249 5875273 5875291 5875301 5875333 5875343 5875349 5875361
5875367 5875369 5875403 5875409 5875417 5875433 5875439 5875451 5875469 5875501
5875531 5875547 5875549 5875553 5875577 5875589 5875609 5875613 5875619 5875621
5875627 5875631 5875643 5875657 5875663 5875687 5875721 5875729 5875757 5875763
5875781 5875811 5875813 5875817 5875847 5875861 5875867 5875901 5875913 5875937
5875939 5875943 5875973 5875979 5875981 5876011 5876021 5876023 5876029 5876041
5876051 5876053 5876071 5876077 5876083 5876089 5876107 5876131 5876137 5876147
5876153 5876177 5876179 5876197 5876207 5876219 5876231 5876239 5876249 5876309
5876323 5876327 5876371 5876383 5876389 5876393 5876399 5876401 5876443 5876447
5876501 5876513 5876579 5876593 5876597 5876609 5876621 5876627 5876641 5876677
5876683 5876687 5876699 5876729 5876743 5876797 5876807 5876809 5876839 5876867
5876869 5876881 5876903 5876911 5876929 5876933 5876947 5876963 5876971 5876977
5876989 5876993 5876999 5877013 5877031 5877041 5877103 5877127 5877143 5877149
5877161 5877181 5877187 5877211 5877229 5877233 5877239 5877247 5877253 5877269
5877299 5877301 5877323 5877331 5877341 5877349 5877353 5877367 5877371 5877407
5877419 5877439 5877481 5877499 5877503 5877511 5877523 5877527 5877551 5877559
5877583 5877587 5877601 5877629 5877659 5877661 5877671 5877689 5877701 5877737
5877763 5877769 5877779 5877791 5877793 5877797 5877829 5877841 5877853 5877871
5877881 5877913 5877917 5877929 5877947 5877953 5877959 5877967 5877979 5877983
5878007 5878009 5878027 5878051 5878063 5878069 5878091 5878109 5878121 5878123
5878139 5878219 5878241 5878247 5878289 5878333 5878343 5878349 5878399 5878403
5878417 5878421 5878451 5878463 5878489 5878493 5878507 5878511 5878517 5878529
5878541 5878553 5878559 5878571 5878591 5878603 5878633 5878637 5878661 5878673
5878679 5878681 5878693 5878709 5878721 5878723 5878739 5878751 5878799 5878811
5878837 5878849 5878877 5878927 5878963 5878969 5878981 5878993 5879009 5879011
5879017 5879021 5879023 5879033 5879039 5879077 5879087 5879123 5879177 5879197
5879207 5879213 5879231 5879239 5879239 5879273 5879333 5879339 5879353 5879369
5879381 5879383 5879387 5879407 5879413 5879437 5879473 5879479 5879483 5879507
5879521 5879537 5879539 5879557 5879593 5879597 5879611 5879617 5879623 5879647
5879659 5879669 5879681 5879693 5879711 5879749 5879761 5879791 5879813 5879821
5879831 5879833 5879857 5879869 5879957 5879959 5879983 5880023 5880031 5880037
5880041 5880047 5880053 5880059 5880067 5880073 5880103 5880109 5880137 5880143
5880163 5880169 5880187 5880209 5880229 5880233 5880241 5880263 5880269 5880271
5880307 5880323 5880349 5880361 5880377 5880397 5880401 5880409 5880437 5880449
5880463 5880493 5880503 5880529 5880541 5880547 5880587 5880601 5880619 5880629
5880631 5880643 5880653 5880697 5880713 5880727 5880737 5880739 5880751 5880757
5880767 5880769 5880773 5880811 5880821 5880829 5880841 5880851 5880857 5880863
5880883 5880887 5880907 5880911 5880913 5880923 5880947 5880967 5881003 5881009
5881019 5881021 5881033 5881037 5881069 5881079 5881087 5881093 5881097 5881111
5881159 5881177 5881189 5881217 5881219 5881231 5881237 5881247 5881277 5881319
5881339 5881349 5881367 5881373 5881397 5881417 5881423 5881429 5881441 5881457
5881459 5881487 5881501 5881511 5881517 5881523 5881543 5881567 5881597 5881607
5881633 5881637 5881639 5881649 5881657 5881699 5881703 5881709 5881717 5881727
5881739 5881759 5881783 5881793 5881801 5881807 5881823 5881831 5881873 5881879
5881913 5881919 5881969 5881973 5881979 5881991 5881999 5882011 5882027 5882053
5882057 5882059 5882083 5882101 5882123 5882141 5882143 5882159 5882171 5882179
5882189 5882197 5882203 5882207 5882213 5882231 5882237 5882243 5882249 5882257
5882263 5882287 5882309 5882321 5882329 5882333 5882339 5882347 5882351 5882353
5882363 5882377 5882407 5882423 5882431 5882459 5882479 5882489 5882501 5882509
5882531 5882537 5882579 5882581 5882587 5882603 5882623 5882627 5882651 5882659
5882677 5882689 5882717 5882729 5882743 5882749 5882771 5882783 5882797 5882819
5882827 5882857 5882861 5882879 5882881 5882887 5882923 5882927 5882939 5882941
5882971 5882977 5882983 5882993 5882999 5883001 5883019 5883029 5883077 5883083
5883089 5883091 5883107 5883109 5883113 5883121 5883127 5883133 5883151 5883169
5883221 5883233 5883271 5883277 5883281 5883301 5883323 5883347 5883359 5883379
5883391 5883401 5883403 5883419 5883431 5883439 5883443 5883457 5883467 5883473
5883487 5883503 5883509 5883569 5883587 5883593 5883599 5883641 5883643 5883659
5883667 5883671 5883677 5883679 5883719 5883721 5883737 5883803 5883821 5883827
5883847 5883881 5883919 5883947 5883961 5883967 5883971 5883973 5883979 5884001
5884003 5884027 5884049 5884051 5884061 5884063 5884069 5884097 5884103 5884133
5884139 5884169 5884171 5884181 5884201 5884217 5884237 5884253 5884271
5884289 5884309 5884313 5884321 5884331 5884337 5884349 5884379 5884393 5884427
5884429 5884453 5884469 5884511 5884523 5884531 5884559 5884577 5884589 5884633
5884639 5884649 5884663 5884673 5884687 5884691 5884717 5884721 5884727 5884741
5884751 5884759 5884777 5884787 5884793 5884807 5884817 5884819 5884829 5884841
5884861 5884867 5884871 5884877 5884907 5884909 5884919 5884939 5884943 5884951
5884969 5884973 5884993 5884997 5885029 5885051 5885059 5885081 5885083 5885093
5885123 5885129 5885137 5885141 5885147 5885177 5885189 5885203 5885207 5885227
5885233 5885239 5885249 5885267 5885311 5885323 5885353 5885359 5885377 5885389
5885431 5885449 5885483 5885501 5885507 5885513 5885531 5885533 5885543 5885599
5885623 5885647 5885653 5885713 5885717 5885731 5885741 5885743 5885777 5885783
5885807 5885821 5885827 5885833 5885843 5885879 5885881 5885897 5885903 5885909
5885911 5885933 5885981 5885983 5885993 5886007 5886011 5886019 5886031 5886037
5886059 5886061 5886121 5886149 5886157 5886169 5886191 5886239 5886241 5886259
5886263 5886269 5886271 5886281 5886289 5886341 5886359 5886383 5886407 5886427
5886451 5886457 5886469 5886473 5886481 5886487 5886499 5886521 5886533 5886541
5886547 5886581 5886611 5886613 5886631 5886649 5886653 5886659 5886667 5886677
5886679 5886691 5886701 5886719 5886721 5886757 5886761 5886767 5886787 5886799
5886851 5886857 5886871 5886887 5886889 5886901 5886911 5886929 5886943 5886953
5886967 5886989 5886997 5887003 5887031 5887039 5887043 5887051 5887061
5887069 5887097 5887109 5887121 5887127 5887129 5887153 5887157 5887163 5887183
5887213 5887229 5887243 5887279 5887289 5887307 5887327 5887351 5887367 5887381
```

```
5887393  5887421  5887447  5887451  5887459  5887463  5887487  5887507  5887513  5887529
5887543  5887573  5887577  5887589  5887591  5887597  5887601  5887621  5887631  5887649
5887691  5887711  5887733  5887741  5887751  5887753  5887757  5887769  5887801  5887807
5887811  5887867  5887879  5887909  5887927  5887939  5887963  5887993  5888009  5888011
5888021  5888039  5888053  5888059  5888083  5888087  5888089  5888093  5888117  5888167
5888173  5888177  5888203  5888219  5888221  5888227  5888231  5888261  5888263  5888287
5888321  5888359  5888369  5888383  5888411  5888431  5888453  5888471  5888497  5888501
5888521  5888539  5888557  5888573  5888593  5888611  5888627  5888633  5888639  5888657
5888693  5888717  5888719  5888737  5888741  5888873  5888881  5888887  5888899  5888903
5888923  5888929  5888951  5888963  5888969  5888999  5889011  5889017  5889019  5889029
5889043  5889049  5889073  5889077  5889097  5889109  5889113  5889119  5889131  5889139
5889167  5889187  5889211  5889239  5889251  5889263  5889269  5889271  5889277  5889283
5889313  5889319  5889341  5889347  5889383  5889419  5889451  5889461  5889467  5889469
5889491  5889517  5889539  5889547  5889551  5889553  5889577  5889607  5889619  5889649
5889661  5889671  5889683  5889703  5889707  5889727  5889739  5889787  5889809  5889811
5889833  5889853  5889857  5889869  5889881  5889887  5889889  5889893  5889913  5889953
5889959  5889971  5889979  5889991  5890013  5890051  5890061  5890081  5890111  5890117
5890121  5890123  5890189  5890193  5890207  5890223  5890237  5890267  5890301  5890303
5890307  5890337  5890349  5890397  5890447  5890459  5890471  5890481  5890493  5890531
5890537  5890541  5890543  5890559  5890561  5890583  5890601  5890607  5890609  5890637
5890639  5890663  5890667  5890679  5890693  5890747  5890751  5890777  5890813  5890849
5890853  5890873  5890883  5890889  5890903  5890979  5890981  5890987  5891009  5891021
5891047  5891051  5891077  5891087  5891113  5891117  5891131  5891141  5891143  5891153
5891161  5891203  5891213  5891219  5891227  5891233  5891261  5891279  5891293  5891297
5891317  5891323  5891357  5891359  5891363  5891371  5891383  5891393  5891407  5891419
5891443  5891447  5891449  5891453  5891467  5891471  5891477  5891491  5891501  5891507
5891521  5891531  5891569  5891573  5891579  5891597  5891617  5891623  5891629  5891663
5891687  5891759  5891761  5891773  5891783  5891789  5891797  5891803  5891813  5891839
5891849  5891863  5891867  5891939  5891971  5891981  5891983  5891993  5891999  5892001
5892011  5892023  5892043  5892059  5892091  5892113  5892121  5892127  5892137  5892193
5892197  5892199  5892203  5892277  5892283  5892311  5892323  5892331  5892371  5892377
5892379  5892391  5892401  5892409  5892427  5892433  5892443  5892457  5892461  5892493
5892521  5892529  5892533  5892547  5892559  5892571  5892581  5892599  5892617  5892619
5892637  5892683  5892701  5892703  5892707  5892709  5892721  5892739  5892749  5892767
5892791  5892823  5892827  5892833  5892839  5892841  5892889  5892937  5892941  5892947
5892959  5892973  5892977  5892989  5893049  5893051  5893057  5893079  5893081  5893087
5893081  5893087  5893091  5893093  5893103  5893117  5893127  5893141  5893171  5893201
5893231  5893241  5893243  5893247  5893273  5893319  5893331  5893337  5893343  5893357
5893367  5893369  5893399  5893403  5893411  5893417  5893421  5893423  5893457  5893493
5893507  5893513  5893519  5893529  5893549  5893571  5893609  5893621  5893633  5893661
5893673  5893691  5893709  5893721  5893733  5893799  5893807  5893837  5893859  5893861
5893871  5893879  5893891  5893897  5893907  5893919  5893939  5893961  5893963  5893973
5893997  5894033  5894039  5894051  5894071  5894081  5894099  5894101  5894107  5894111
5894143  5894149  5894153  5894167  5894177  5894179  5894209  5894249  5894263  5894267
5894293  5894303  5894321  5894323  5894327  5894333  5894347  5894353  5894363  5894377
5894401  5894431  5894441  5894477  5894479  5894533  5894543  5894561  5894591  5894641
5894653  5894659  5894671  5894683  5894701  5894711  5894717  5894719  5894723  5894761
5894773  5894783  5894789  5894797  5894813  5894839  5894849  5894873  5894891  5894893
5894899  5894927  5894947  5894953  5894957  5894983  5895011  5895017  5895023  5895037
5895041  5895049  5895077  5895079  5895089  5895119  5895143  5895151  5895157  5895161
5895167  5895179  5895181  5895203  5895229  5895233  5895251  5895283  5895293  5895299
5895319  5895341  5895347  5895353  5895359  5895367  5895371  5895389  5895401  5895403
5895419  5895427  5895443  5895479  5895499  5895503  5895509  5895511  5895517  5895523
5895541  5895557  5895559  5895581  5895607  5895629  5895641  5895647  5895679  5895689
5895697  5895707  5895731  5895733  5895737  5895761  5895763  5895767  5895793  5895809
5895817  5895863  5895883  5895893  5895899  5895907  5895931  5895941  5895943  5895949
5895959  5895971  5896003  5896043  5896049  5896057  5896123  5896129  5896133  5896139
5896151  5896153  5896181  5896183  5896207  5896217  5896243  5896259  5896271  5896327
5896301  5896307  5896313  5896379  5896391  5896421  5896427  5896459  5896463  5896493
5896507  5896523  5896537  5896567  5896591  5896601  5896609  5896613  5896691  5896699
5896711  5896747  5896769  5896771  5896777  5896811  5896819  5896823  5896829  5896867
5896843  5896927  5896951  5896963  5896981  5896987  5897033  5897041  5897057  5897069
5897093  5897107  5897117  5897119  5897123  5897167  5897173  5897183  5897197  5897199
5897209  5897219  5897251  5897261  5897267  5897279  5897291  5897299  5897303  5897327
5897329  5897341  5897377  5897387  5897389  5897413  5897417  5897443  5897447  5897449
5897477  5897497  5897531  5897537  5897539  5897561  5897599  5897609  5897611  5897621
5897627  5897641  5897653  5897669  5897707  5897711  5897761  5897767  5897807  5897813
5897819  5897831  5897833  5897839  5897851  5897869  5897911  5897917  5897921  5897953
5897977  5897981  5897989  5898001  5898023  5898043  5898047  5898071  5898121  5898131
5898163  5898169  5898197  5898199  5898209  5898253  5898257  5898259  5898283  5898287
5898293  5898307  5898311  5898313  5898323  5898329  5898331  5898349  5898367  5898413
5898421  5898433  5898437  5898443  5898457  5898469  5898509  5898521  5898533  5898539
5898593  5898601  5898617  5898623  5898637  5898689  5898691  5898733  5898749  5898757
5898817  5898821  5898839  5898853  5898859  5898931  5898967  5898973  5898979  5898989
5899013  5899043  5899073  5899079  5899081  5899087  5899099  5899163  5899171  5899181
5899183  5899193  5899199  5899211  5899217  5899241  5899259  5899261  5899273  5899279
5899307  5899321  5899337  5899343  5899363  5899373  5899379  5899381  5899409  5899427
5899429  5899451  5899489  5899501  5899507  5899529  5899541  5899547  5899559  5899561
5899567  5899573  5899591  5899601  5899627  5899639  5899651  5899657  5899669  5899681
5899693  5899711  5899739  5899759  5899763  5899783  5899807  5899813  5899837  5899849
5899853  5899877  5899919  5899931  5899967  5899973  5899979  5899991  5899997  5900047
5900093  5900109  5900111  5900113  5900123  5900183  5900189  5900191  5900197
5900227  5900231  5900243  5900263  5900281  5900287  5900291  5900299  5900303  5900329
5900381  5900383  5900399  5900407  5900423  5900441  5900459  5900467  5900473  5900519
5900539  5900551  5900567  5900569  5900593  5900617  5900633  5900641  5900657  5900677
5900681  5900701  5900707  5900711  5900731  5900743  5900753  5900771  5900779  5900813
5900831  5900833  5900863  5900879  5900893  5900911  5900941  5900953  5900959  5900969
5900971  5900981  5900987  5901031  5901043  5901047  5901061  5901083  5901097  5901109
5901113  5901131  5901163  5901173  5901187  5901209  5901223  5901251  5901257  5901263
```

```
5901289  5901299  5901331  5901341  5901347  5901349  5901353  5901359  5901403  5901407
5901421  5901433  5901437  5901481  5901487  5901503  5901509  5901521  5901527  5901541
5901551  5901557  5901569  5901607  5901617  5901619  5901629  5901631  5901653  5901659
5901667  5901671  5901677  5901697  5901739  5901751  5901757  5901767  5901781  5901821
5901851  5901859  5901871  5901887  5901893  5901901  5901919  5901971  5902019  5902021
5902031  5902033  5902037  5902063  5902081  5902087  5902093  5902139  5902147  5902151
5902157  5902181  5902187  5902201  5902219  5902249  5902261  5902289  5902291  5902321
5902333  5902363  5902367  5902373  5902387  5902397  5902411  5902423  5902433  5902447
5902471  5902487  5902489  5902517  5902549  5902571  5902601  5902607  5902609  5902613
5902619  5902627  5902639  5902649  5902661  5902669  5902693  5902703  5902733  5902753
5902759  5902783  5902807  5902823  5902829  5902837  5902843  5902861  5902879  5902903
5902907  5902931  5902987  5903021  5903039  5903041  5903081  5903099  5903119  5903137
5903141  5903143  5903159  5903171  5903173  5903189  5903197  5903201  5903251  5903257
5903263  5903311  5903321  5903329  5903333  5903351  5903353  5903389  5903393  5903399
5903411  5903413  5903419  5903431  5903441  5903449  5903453  5903473  5903483  5903489
5903503  5903507  5903533  5903537  5903543  5903563  5903567  5903587  5903593  5903603
5903621  5903627  5903629  5903633  5903687  5903693  5903761  5903789  5903809  5903837
5903867  5903869  5903897  5903899  5903921  5903941  5903969  5903977  5904013  5904089
5904097  5904121  5904133  5904149  5904161  5904163  5904179  5904209  5904211  5904221
5904233  5904247  5904257  5904263  5904271  5904319  5904323  5904329  5904337  5904341
5904347  5904361  5904377  5904391  5904397  5904403  5904407  5904419  5904427  5904433
5904439  5904461  5904463  5904499  5904511  5904517  5904541  5904557  5904607  5904623
5904683  5904707  5904727  5904737  5904749  5904761  5904781  5904791  5904827  5904853
5904863  5904901  5904907  5904917  5904923  5904929  5904931  5904937  5904959  5904961
5904979  5905007  5905021  5905027  5905037  5905049  5905051  5905057  5905063  5905073
5905091  5905099  5905117  5905121  5905153  5905177  5905187  5905213  5905217  5905243
5905247  5905253  5905279  5905297  5905301  5905309  5905331  5905351  5905381  5905387
5905391  5905399  5905423  5905433  5905439  5905441  5905463  5905483  5905499  5905507
5905513  5905519  5905547  5905553  5905569  5905609  5905619  5905643  5905657  5905667
5905673  5905703  5905727  5905769  5905771  5905787  5905793  5905813  5905831  5905847
5905877  5905883  5905891  5905897  5905931  5905943  5905967  5905981  5906003  5906011
5906029  5906041  5906071  5906083  5906099  5906113  5906137  5906141  5906143  5906167
5906189  5906221  5906231  5906237  5906261  5906269  5906279  5906291  5906297  5906309
5906311  5906323  5906371  5906441  5906449  5906489  5906539  5906557  5906603  5906611
5906629  5906683  5906687  5906707  5906711  5906713  5906723  5906731  5906737  5906743
5906753  5906759  5906773  5906779  5906801  5906809  5906839  5906843  5906867  5906869
5906881  5906893  5906899  5906933  5906951  5906959  5906977  5907001  5907017  5907023
5907049  5907061  5907071  5907073  5907089  5907103  5907107  5907127  5907133  5907137
5907163  5907169  5907191  5907199  5907217  5907227  5907259  5907263  5907277  5907281
5907287  5907299  5907311  5907331  5907337  5907353  5907371  5907373  5907401  5907409
5907427  5907437  5907443  5907467  5907479  5907497  5907521  5907533  5907547  5907557
5907563  5907581  5907589  5907607  5907617  5907631  5907673  5907683  5907703  5907739
5907749  5907761  5907767  5907773  5907779  5907799  5907809  5907829  5907871  5907877
5907883  5907907  5907943  5907953  5907961  5907973  5907983  5907989  5907991  5908003
5908037  5908043  5908051  5908081  5908093  5908121  5908151  5908159  5908169  5908187
5908207  5908213  5908237  5908241  5908247  5908249  5908303  5908327  5908337  5908339
5908351  5908361  5908379  5908393  5908403  5908423  5908439  5908451  5908453  5908457
5908459  5908471  5908477  5908499  5908517  5908519  5908559  5908577  5908589  5908603
5908607  5908619  5908649  5908667  5908697  5908703  5908711  5908717  5908733  5908739
5908783  5908787  5908807  5908811  5908849  5908871  5908873  5908891  5908897  5908901
5908921  5908927  5908933  5908957  5908993  5909021  5909039  5909041  5909053  5909087
5909089  5909093  5909119  5909147  5909153  5909173  5909179  5909231  5909237  5909249
5909261  5909273  5909287  5909297  5909303  5909317  5909383  5909389  5909411  5909429
5909473  5909479  5909483  5909509  5909549  5909567  5909581  5909587  5909599  5909621
5909647  5909663  5909669  5909671  5909681  5909737  5909749  5909759  5909767  5909777
5909789  5909797  5909807  5909819  5909821  5909833  5909837  5909843  5909879  5909887
5909903  5909909  5909927  5909957  5909983  5909987  5909993  5910029  5910041  5910053
5910059  5910097  5910127  5910133  5910143  5910161  5910173  5910251  5910277  5910283
5910293  5910301  5910313  5910319  5910323  5910337  5910341  5910353  5910361  5910371
5910389  5910397  5910413  5910427  5910433  5910467  5910469  5910493  5910521  5910523
5910529  5910533  5910547  5910551  5910559  5910581  5910599  5910607  5910617  5910623
5910637  5910647  5910659  5910703  5910721  5910727  5910731  5910733  5910761  5910769
5910803  5910811  5910829  5910841  5910857  5910901  5910907  5910911  5910913  5910943
5910953  5910967  5910973  5910991  5910997  5911027  5911039  5911051  5911057  5911063
5911079  5911091  5911097  5911123  5911127  5911153  5911163  5911181  5911183  5911193
5911201  5911211  5911229  5911267  5911289  5911309  5911313  5911319  5911351  5911357
5911361  5911417  5911439  5911463  5911481  5911487  5911501  5911513  5911523  5911537
5911547  5911547  5911553  5911559  5911579  5911589  5911651  5911657  5911663  5911681
5911709  5911721  5911729  5911739  5911747  5911751  5911759  5911777  5911781  5911811
5911817  5911819  5911831  5911871  5911877  5911883  5911901  5911921  5911931  5911933
5911951  5911963  5911973  5911981  5911987  5911993  5912017  5912029  5912033  5912057
5912089  5912111  5912117  5912183  5912189  5912239  5912251  5912261  5912279  5912293
5912321  5912327  5912329  5912353  5912369  5912377  5912381  5912393  5912429  5912437
5912461  5912483  5912507  5912527  5912531  5912539  5912579  5912581  5912593  5912603
5912609  5912657  5912659  5912663  5912681  5912689  5912693  5912701  5912717  5912727
5912749  5912761  5912773  5912813  5912827  5912831  5912833  5912861  5912867  5912873
5912899  5912903  5912917  5912939  5912983  5912987  5912999  5913031  5913041
5913049  5913067  5913097  5913109  5913121  5913133  5913163  5913179  5913181  5913191
5913197  5913203  5913221  5913223  5913233  5913241  5913251  5913253  5913269  5913283
5913289  5913293  5913319  5913337  5913367  5913371  5913373  5913379  5913409
5913421  5913431  5913437  5913443  5913463  5913473  5913497  5913499  5913517  5913521
5913527  5913533  5913559  5913563  5913601  5913631  5913643  5913679  5913703
5913707  5913727  5913757  5913763  5913797  5913823  5913857  5913863  5913893  5913907
5913911  5913913  5913917  5913923  5913931  5913937  5913953  5913979  5914003  5914021
5914039  5914049  5914061  5914063  5914067  5914093  5914121  5914123  5914141  5914159
5914163  5914171  5914189  5914193  5914199  5914201  5914247  5914261  5914267  5914277
5914303  5914321  5914327  5914333  5914343  5914357  5914369  5914393  5914409  5914411
5914421  5914423  5914447  5914457  5914477  5914483  5914501  5914511  5914553
5914591  5914609  5914627  5914717  5914723  5914739  5914751  5914763  5914787  5914789
```

```
5914801  5914807  5914813  5914817  5914819  5914873  5914879  5914889  5914897  5914919
5914921  5914991  5914999  5915003  5915033  5915047  5915051  5915057  5915069  5915083
5915087  5915093  5915113  5915131  5915149  5915183  5915191  5915197  5915219  5915233
5915237  5915293  5915297  5915323  5915339  5915341  5915359  5915401  5915417  5915419
5915431  5915443  5915447  5915453  5915477  5915491  5915501  5915509  5915519  5915543
5915551  5915557  5915573  5915587  5915621  5915683  5915717  5915731  5915737  5915743
5915773  5915803  5915809  5915831  5915839  5915851  5915857  5915863  5915867  5915869
5915887  5915891  5915911  5915929  5915939  5915951  5915957  5915969  5915977  5915999
5916007  5916023  5916047  5916061  5916077  5916089  5916101  5916109  5916143  5916149
5916151  5916161  5916173  5916179  5916191  5916199  5916227  5916233  5916247  5916269
5916271  5916299  5916307  5916311  5916349  5916367  5916401  5916419  5916433  5916437
5916439  5916457  5916481  5916503  5916511  5916517  5916529  5916539  5916557  5916583
5916593  5916601  5916613  5916623  5916637  5916649  5916661  5916683  5916719  5916721
5916739  5916763  5916767  5916769  5916797  5916839  5916851  5916853  5916871  5916881
5916907  5916919  5916931  5916941  5916943  5916949  5916959  5916979  5916991  5917007
5917013  5917039  5917099  5917103  5917117  5917123  5917127  5917157  5917181  5917201
5917213  5917229  5917231  5917259  5917267  5917271  5917277  5917297  5917313  5917321
5917349  5917361  5917367  5917381  5917393  5917403  5917423  5917451  5917459  5917477
5917481  5917511  5917517  5917519  5917543  5917567  5917577  5917619  5917627  5917631
5917633  5917661  5917673  5917687  5917727  5917729  5917741  5917757  5917771  5917781
5917783  5917823  5917829  5917837  5917843  5917859  5917861  5917871  5917883  5917897
5917903  5917907  5917913  5917963  5918009  5918021  5918027  5918051  5918053  5918083
5918093  5918111  5918119  5918123  5918147  5918161  5918167  5918173  5918191
5918207  5918221  5918239  5918243  5918251  5918273  5918279  5918293  5918299
5918317  5918321  5918323  5918371  5918377  5918387  5918389  5918399  5918401  5918413
5918417  5918441  5918447  5918461  5918501  5918509  5918527  5918531  5918573  5918599
5918603  5918623  5918657  5918681  5918683  5918687  5918699  5918723  5918741  5918753
5918777  5918789  5918863  5918867  5918879  5918909  5918921  5918933  5918947  5918953
5918977  5918999  5919031  5919041  5919061  5919071  5919091  5919097  5919107  5919131
5919139  5919157  5919181  5919191  5919197  5919229  5919253  5919269  5919271  5919283
5919289  5919367  5919373  5919377  5919429  5919433  5919449  5919469  5919489  5919493
5919499  5919547  5919559  5919577  5919581  5919607  5919611  5919629  5919631  5919673
5919679  5919691  5919713  5919721  5919733  5919737  5919743  5919751  5919761  5919779
5919787  5919817  5919829  5919833  5919863  5919869  5919877  5919911  5919923  5919929
5919931  5919937  5919959  5919971  5920003  5920043  5920049  5920069  5920091  5920099
5920121  5920127  5920139  5920151  5920157  5920169  5920171  5920207  5920219  5920241
5920247  5920249  5920253  5920273  5920279  5920289  5920303  5920309  5920319  5920351
5920357  5920363  5920367  5920391  5920399  5920423  5920429  5920433  5920463  5920469
5920483  5920487  5920489  5920501  5920511  5920513  5920529  5920549  5920561  5920567
5920633  5920657  5920667  5920679  5920693  5920711  5920741  5920757  5920787  5920801
5920853  5920877  5920891  5920909  5920921  5920931  5920939  5920949
5920961  5920979  5920997  5921009  5921011  5921039  5921089  5921101  5921119  5921131
5921159  5921173  5921177  5921231  5921233  5921239  5921257  5921263  5921269  5921291
5921297  5921309  5921317  5921351  5921353  5921359  5921371  5921411  5921413  5921431
5921459  5921473  5921477  5921479  5921501  5921533  5921543  5921549  5921561  5921599
5921639  5921677  5921683  5921689  5921717  5921737  5921759  5921789  5921791
5921807  5921809  5921869  5921891  5921893  5921957  5921959  5921989  5922013  5922019
5922029  5922031  5922067  5922071  5922073  5922083  5922097  5922107  5922113  5922127
5922143  5922151  5922157  5922173  5922179  5922187  5922221  5922223  5922227  5922229
5922251  5922253  5922269  5922283  5922289  5922311  5922317  5922349  5922353  5922359
5922383  5922419  5922421  5922427  5922437  5922461  5922463  5922473  5922481  5922487
5922493  5922503  5922533  5922541  5922577  5922593  5922617  5922619  5922629  5922649
5922667  5922671  5922677  5922713  5922743  5922771  5922773  5922779  5922781  5922793
5922811  5922823  5922827  5922841  5922853  5922857  5922859  5922877  5922881  5922883
5922887  5922911  5922913  5922941  5922971  5922979  5922991  5923009  5923019  5923031
5923041  5923061  5923067  5923087  5923097  5923133  5923189  5923223  5923237  5923241
5923243  5923261  5923271  5923297  5923319  5923321  5923331  5923343  5923369  5923433
5923471  5923493  5923501  5923507  5923513  5923517  5923523  5923529  5923553  5923571
5923591  5923597  5923609  5923669  5923679  5923681  5923691  5923699  5923711  5923727
5923733  5923741  5923783  5923787  5923829  5923843  5923847  5923849  5923889  5923901
5923913  5923919  5923933  5923937  5923961  5923979  5923997  5924009  5924011  5924053
5924063  5924111  5924117  5924119  5924129  5924141  5924159  5924161  5924173  5924189
5924203  5924221  5924231  5924263  5924267  5924293  5924307  5924327  5924331  5924339
5924351  5924383  5924407  5924417  5924437  5924467  5924489  5924507  5924509  5924519
5924531  5924537  5924539  5924543  5924573  5924587  5924617  5924647  5924657  5924693
5924707  5924717  5924719  5924749  5924759  5924767  5924771  5924783  5924791  5924833
5924843  5924851  5924881  5924939  5924953  5924969  5924977  5924981  5924983  5924987
5925001  5925041  5925043  5925083  5925097  5925107  5925109  5925119  5925133  5925137
5925151  5925167  5925173  5925181  5925203  5925209  5925211  5925223  5925229  5925239
5925253  5925277  5925289  5925313  5925317  5925319  5925331  5925341  5925343  5925373
5925377  5925383  5925389  5925419  5925427  5925449  5925461  5925463  5925497  5925499
5925509  5925551  5925583  5925593  5925611  5925613  5925641  5925643  5925659  5925677
5925683  5925691  5925727  5925749  5925757  5925761  5925797  5925817  5925823  5925839
5925841  5925847  5925863  5925943  5925961  5925971  5925989  5926007  5926033  5926049
5926051  5926057  5926069  5926073  5926079  5926087  5926093  5926103  5926113  5926127
5926133  5926139  5926147  5926169  5926171  5926187  5926189  5926199  5926223  5926229
5926231  5926247  5926259  5926273  5926307  5926313  5926337  5926381  5926397  5926399
5926429  5926447  5926457  5926463  5926477  5926519  5926541  5926567  5926601  5926607
5926621  5926637  5926639  5926649  5926703  5926721  5926729  5926741  5926751  5926763
5926769  5926783  5926793  5926853  5926873  5926889  5926891  5926903  5926927  5926951
5926967  5926979  5927003  5927017  5927027  5927039  5927057  5927059  5927087  5927137
5927143  5927147  5927177  5927179  5927213  5927239  5927263  5927267  5927269  5927321
5927323  5927333  5927351  5927371  5927393  5927401  5927413  5927419  5927443  5927447
5927473  5927477  5927483  5927501  5927503  5927531  5927539  5927549  5927561  5927567
5927587  5927591  5927617  5927627  5927633  5927661  5927689  5927699  5927707  5927711
5927717  5927723  5927729  5927731  5927741  5927743  5927749  5927759  5927773  5927809
5927833  5927837  5927843  5927897  5927921  5927941  5927989  5928031  5928047  5928049
5928059  5928061  5928071  5928073  5928079  5928107  5928119  5928173  5928187  5928193
5928199  5928229  5928253  5928259  5928271  5928277  5928289  5928311  5928331  5928337
```

5928341 5928343 5928353 5928389 5928413 5928451 5928479 5928493 5928523 5928553
5928617 5928623 5928647 5928653 5928683 5928701 5928707 5928709 5928751 5928757
5928761 5928787 5928803 5928821 5928823 5928827 5928829 5928833 5928899 5928907
5928911 5928919 5928959 5928961 5928983 5929019 5929037 5929043 5929061
5929067 5929117 5929127 5929129 5929169 5929171 5929177 5929181 5929201 5929207
5929211 5929283 5929289 5929291 5929303 5929307 5929309 5929321 5929327 5929333
5929393 5929403 5929409 5929411 5929421 5929439 5929457 5929459 5929477 5929487
5929489 5929493 5929523 5929529 5929531 5929537 5929579 5929591 5929597 5929613
5929621 5929631 5929633 5929639 5929643 5929663 5929667 5929687 5929697 5929723
5929747 5929817 5929841 5929853 5929873 5929907 5929909 5929933 5929939 5929951
5929961 5929967 5929999 5930017 5930039 5930053 5930063 5930069 5930077 5930081
5930143 5930167 5930179 5930201 5930203 5930227 5930231 5930233 5930279 5930303
5930317 5930333 5930339 5930347 5930369 5930381 5930383 5930401 5930423 5930437
5930443 5930479 5930497 5930513 5930521 5930531 5930537 5930539 5930591 5930597
5930623 5930629 5930633 5930651 5930653 5930657 5930663 5930669 5930681 5930707
5930719 5930731 5930737 5930747 5930759 5930777 5930791 5930809 5930833 5930839
5930887 5930893 5930917 5930921 5930923 5930927 5930929 5930957 5930963 5931043
5931047 5931077 5931089 5931139 5931143 5931157 5931169 5931179 5931193 5931203
5931223 5931293 5931301 5931307 5931311 5931313 5931319 5931337 5931349 5931371
5931379 5931383 5931391 5931449 5931467 5931491 5931503 5931517 5931529 5931533
5931559 5931637 5931641 5931649 5931661 5931691 5931697 5931713 5931749 5931797
5931799 5931829 5931833 5931847 5931859 5931869 5931899 5931901 5931923 5931941
5931949 5931967 5931977 5931983 5932013 5932019 5932027 5932049 5932057 5932061
5932063 5932081 5932097 5932109 5932111 5932127 5932139 5932141 5932159 5932177
5932181 5932193 5932217 5932231 5932243 5932271 5932279 5932307 5932309 5932319
5932349 5932357 5932361 5932363 5932369 5932373 5932379 5932393 5932403 5932411
5932417 5932429 5932441 5932447 5932453 5932457 5932477 5932483 5932489 5932499
5932517 5932523 5932561 5932567 5932571 5932573 5932583 5932601 5932631 5932657
5932673 5932681 5932699 5932709 5932721 5932723 5932747 5932777 5932793 5932837
5932867 5932889 5932891 5932897 5932909 5932933 5932939 5932943 5932967 5933027
5933041 5933071 5933077 5933093 5933101 5933129 5933131 5933151 5933171 5933173
5933177 5933189 5933201 5933203 5933219 5933237 5933251 5933273 5933303 5933351
5933387 5933401 5933407 5933419 5933423 5933437 5933449 5933461 5933467 5933489
5933497 5933503 5933507 5933519 5933533 5933537 5933539 5933549 5933573 5933581
5933591 5933593 5933623 5933639 5933647 5933657 5933687 5933693 5933713 5933749
5933761 5933773 5933779 5933783 5933791 5933831 5933843 5933849 5933857 5933867
5933869 5933887 5933903 5933987 5934001 5934017 5934031 5934041 5934059 5934083
5934091 5934107 5934119 5934121 5934127 5934133 5934163 5934197 5934199 5934209
5934211 5934221 5934239 5934281 5934311 5934317 5934323 5934337 5934347
5934349 5934359 5934407 5934413 5934427 5934469 5934493 5934497 5934503 5934527
5934553 5934563 5934571 5934601 5934611 5934619 5934661 5934663 5934673 5934697
5934701 5934739 5934769 5934779 5934823 5934829 5934833 5934839 5934873 5934881
5934899 5934913 5934949 5934953 5934959 5934967 5934979 5934983 5934991 5935003
5935051 5935067 5935079 5935093 5935109 5935123 5935129 5935147 5935151 5935177
5935199 5935211 5935213 5935249 5935271 5935273 5935313 5935327 5935339 5935373
5935393 5935399 5935409 5935421 5935447 5935451 5935453 5935469 5935471 5935481
5935487 5935493 5935511 5935513 5935561 5935571 5935603 5935609 5935621 5935627
5935639 5935649 5935661 5935667 5935673 5935697 5935711 5935739 5935747 5935759
5935781 5935789 5935793 5935801 5935829 5935837 5935843 5935859 5935861 5935877
5935879 5935883 5935889 5935901 5935913 5935927 5935933 5935967 5935987 5935991
5936017 5936059 5936069 5936081 5936087 5936137 5936141 5936153 5936171 5936191
5936197 5936207 5936209 5936219 5936233 5936251 5936261 5936269 5936311 5936321
5936339 5936351 5936353 5936419 5936453 5936479 5936501 5936509 5936563 5936627
5936629 5936647 5936653 5936657 5936659 5936663 5936701 5936713 5936729 5936747
5936813 5936831 5936837 5936849 5936857 5936891 5936897 5936933 5936939 5936963
5936969 5936977 5937011 5937037 5937047 5937077 5937103 5937137 5937143 5937149
5937157 5937161 5937167 5937179 5937209 5937223 5937227 5937241 5937247 5937263
5937271 5937277 5937287 5937293 5937341 5937361 5937389 5937401 5937419 5937433
5937439 5937469 5937493 5937499 5937509 5937521 5937527 5937541 5937551 5937553
5937559 5937577 5937587 5937593 5937629 5937653 5937667 5937677 5937683
5937697 5937707 5937731 5937739 5937761 5937791 5937817 5937851 5937853 5937857
5937859 5937863 5937889 5937901 5937917 5937931 5937949 5937959 5937977 5937983
5938001 5938003 5938007 5938021 5938057 5938063 5938073 5938087 5938091 5938103
5938111 5938123 5938133 5938147 5938159 5938181 5938183 5938187 5938213 5938217
5938223 5938237 5938267 5938307 5938319 5938327 5938333 5938337 5938349 5938357
5938363 5938367 5938379 5938421 5938441 5938459 5938501 5938523 5938529 5938553
5938589 5938609 5938613 5938643 5938663 5938711 5938739 5938741 5938747 5938771
5938781 5938783 5938787 5938789 5938841 5938843 5938847 5938861 5938897
5938903 5938909 5938913 5938931 5938957 5938993 5939009 5939023 5939033 5939051
5939057 5939071 5939093 5939099 5939107 5939111 5939119 5939123 5939149 5939171
5939179 5939209 5939257 5939261 5939303 5939317 5939333 5939347 5939369 5939371
5939411 5939429 5939431 5939447 5939449 5939459 5939473 5939491 5939501 5939503
5939513 5939537 5939539 5939561 5939581 5939623 5939651 5939653 5939669 5939743
5939767 5939777 5939779 5939797 5939803 5939807 5939831 5939833 5939839 5939849
5939863 5939881 5939883 5939897 5939903 5939929 5939959 5939981 5939993 5940007
5940037 5940043 5940047 5940097 5940101 5940131 5940133 5940139 5940161 5940167
5940169 5940197 5940199 5940211 5940223 5940271 5940289 5940307 5940323 5940343
5940359 5940379 5940383 5940397 5940401 5940439 5940449 5940469 5940503
5940541 5940547 5940551 5940553 5940569 5940577 5940581 5940587 5940593 5940617
5940619 5940653 5940655 5940743 5940763 5940767 5940791 5940797 5940799
5940811 5940829 5940833 5940841 5940881 5940889 5940899 5940931 5940953 5940983
5940989 5940997 5941003 5941021 5941031 5941043 5941049 5941051 5941081 5941087
5941099 5941121 5941139 5941147 5941151 5941171 5941207 5941213 5941219 5941231
5941249 5941253 5941261 5941283 5941289 5941297 5941307 5941321 5941333 5941361
5941379 5941387 5941391 5941393 5941399 5941447 5941451 5941469 5941487 5941489
5941501 5941561 5941589 5941601 5941609 5941633 5941643 5941651 5941657 5941709
5941711 5941759 5941763 5941769 5941841 5941847 5941849 5941853 5941877 5941913
5941921 5941933 5941937 5941951 5941961 5941973 5942009 5942011 5942017 5942021
5942023 5942047 5942077 5942081 5942099 5942107 5942113 5942137 5942141 5942147

```
5942149  5942159  5942161  5942177  5942191  5942207  5942221  5942227  5942239  5942243
5942249  5942267  5942309  5942329  5942347  5942357  5942369  5942399  5942407  5942429
5942467  5942509  5942513  5942543  5942549  5942561  5942569  5942597  5942603  5942609
5942623  5942647  5942653  5942669  5942683  5942689  5942701  5942719  5942747  5942749
5942777  5942863  5942873  5942879  5942891  5942897  5942939  5942957  5942969  5942971
5943001  5943023  5943031  5943037  5943043  5943053  5943061  5943071  5943079  5943083
5943089  5943097  5943107  5943109  5943127  5943139  5943151  5943167  5943187  5943191
5943193  5943239  5943281  5943299  5943307  5943313  5943317  5943323  5943341  5943373
5943397  5943419  5943437  5943439  5943449  5943467  5943493  5943517  5943527  5943551
5943559  5943563  5943577  5943583  5943607  5943611  5943617  5943629  5943653  5943671
5943689  5943701  5943703  5943737  5943757  5943781  5943793  5943797  5943803  5943809
5943823  5943841  5943851  5943853  5943887  5943919  5943923  5943929  5943937  5943943
5943953  5943961  5943983  5944007  5944009  5944021  5944061  5944069  5944079  5944117
5944129  5944163  5944181  5944187  5944193  5944229  5944241  5944243  5944247  5944273
5944291  5944313  5944331  5944349  5944357  5944361  5944369  5944381  5944403  5944409
5944469  5944481  5944483  5944487  5944541  5944553  5944559  5944573  5944579  5944597
5944619  5944637  5944661  5944669  5944691  5944693  5944703  5944711  5944723  5944789
5944811  5944819  5944837  5944867  5944871  5944907  5944909  5944919  5944921  5944931
5944937  5944943  5944949  5944973  5944993  5945039  5945059  5945089  5945129  5945141
5945153  5945161  5945213  5945221  5945231  5945237  5945267  5945279  5945281  5945299
5945311  5945321  5945333  5945351  5945353  5945413  5945449  5945473  5945479  5945483
5945497  5945501  5945509  5945531  5945573  5945581  5945587  5945591  5945659  5945671
5945677  5945713  5945717  5945729  5945741  5945743  5945761  5945773  5945813  5945833
5945839  5945851  5945857  5945867  5945873  5945883  5945909  5945941  5945977  5945981
5945999  5946007  5946019  5946023  5946041  5946043  5946047  5946053  5946067  5946089
5946103  5946119  5946139  5946163  5946181  5946217  5946223  5946253  5946289  5946301
5946313  5946323  5946329  5946337  5946349  5946371  5946377  5946401  5946407  5946431
5946461  5946469  5946497  5946509  5946511  5946541  5946569  5946571  5946593  5946607
5946623  5946641  5946649  5946659  5946667  5946671  5946683  5946691  5946697  5946709
5946727  5946737  5946749  5946767  5946793  5946797  5946869  5946877  5946887  5946893
5946929  5946959  5946979  5947027  5947043  5947061  5947079  5947099  5947103  5947147
5947153  5947159  5947163  5947177  5947181  5947189  5947211  5947223  5947241  5947243
5947261  5947267  5947273  5947327  5947351  5947379  5947391  5947397  5947411  5947423
5947429  5947441  5947451  5947453  5947463  5947477  5947481  5947489  5947493  5947499
5947519  5947559  5947573  5947577  5947597  5947651  5947661  5947663  5947679  5947687
5947693  5947699  5947723  5947727  5947729  5947759  5947769  5947771  5947783  5947847
5947853  5947867  5947873  5947891  5947901  5947951  5947957  5947973  5947979  5947999
5948003  5948027  5948051  5948069  5948101  5948119  5948123  5948141  5948143  5948149
5948153  5948209  5948221  5948263  5948269  5948281  5948291  5948297  5948303  5948303
5948323  5948333  5948347  5948357  5948363  5948381  5948389  5948399  5948407  5948413
5948417  5948429  5948431  5948443  5948447  5948483  5948507  5948519  5948533
5948549  5948563  5948581  5948587  5948609  5948627  5948633  5948639  5948641  5948681
5948689  5948699  5948711  5948713  5948753  5948777  5948791  5948821  5948851  5948867
5948909  5948939  5948959  5948983  5949017  5949037  5949043  5949049  5949067  5949079
5949101  5949127  5949137  5949143  5949149  5949169  5949173  5949211  5949217  5949227
5949239  5949247  5949259  5949269  5949277  5949283  5949287  5949311  5949313  5949319
5949331  5949343  5949347  5949349  5949397  5949407  5949431  5949457  5949481  5949511
5949529  5949539  5949557  5949583  5949599  5949623  5949653  5949673  5949703  5949721
5949743  5949751  5949763  5949791  5949803  5949821  5949857  5949877  5949887  5949919
5949929  5949971  5950003  5950019  5950027  5950057  5950067  5950079  5950093  5950103
5950117  5950141  5950159  5950177  5950181  5950193  5950199  5950253  5950267
5950277  5950279  5950283  5950291  5950313  5950319  5950333  5950339  5950349  5950369
5950379  5950393  5950397  5950433  5950463  5950487  5950499  5950513  5950523  5950547
5950559  5950573  5950577  5950579  5950589  5950603  5950621  5950627  5950631  5950639
5950643  5950649  5950657  5950661  5950669  5950709  5950751  5950753  5950783  5950823
5950831  5950837  5950843  5950871  5950877  5950897  5950921  5950927  5950943
5950949  5950957  5950963  5951051  5951063  5951081  5951107  5951137  5951147  5951159
5951189  5951203  5951219  5951263  5951269  5951303  5951321  5951333  5951353  5951357
5951401  5951419  5951441  5951453  5951459  5951489  5951521  5951531  5951537  5951551
5951557  5951591  5951599  5951609  5951611  5951633  5951663  5951669  5951689  5951749
5951761  5951767  5951789  5951791  5951797  5951801  5951833  5951839  5951843  5951849
5951861  5951867  5951879  5951893  5951903  5951923  5951947  5951951  5951983  5951987
5951993  5952007  5952041  5952071  5952077  5952083  5952113  5952131  5952137  5952151
5952157  5952161  5952169  5952181  5952209  5952241  5952253  5952259  5952277  5952281
5952283  5952293  5952299  5952307  5952311  5952343  5952367  5952371  5952379  5952383
5952389  5952391  5952407  5952433  5952437  5952487  5952493  5952547  5952553  5952559
5952577  5952593  5952613  5952629  5952631  5952673  5952689  5952697  5952721  5952763
5952769  5952781  5952797  5952799  5952803  5952809  5952811  5952823  5952827  5952841
5952847  5952889  5952901  5952911  5952949  5952959  5952971  5952977  5952979  5952983
5953019  5953027  5953039  5953069  5953081  5953093  5953097  5953109  5953117  5953133
5953139  5953141  5953153  5953169  5953183  5953187  5953219  5953229  5953237  5953267
5953301  5953319  5953351  5953399  5953427  5953487  5953459  5953463  5953679  5953511
5953523  5953567  5953589  5953603  5953637  5953639  5953657  5953667  5953679  5953691
5953693  5953699  5953721  5953751  5953793  5953799  5953853  5953873  5953879  5953889
5953921  5953939  5953943  5953949  5953951  5953963  5953991  5953999  5954009  5954021
5954023  5954041  5954071  5954093  5954111  5954129  5954147  5954153  5954177  5954191
5954197  5954213  5954219  5954231  5954237  5954257  5954261  5954269  5954287  5954293
5954297  5954303  5954317  5954321  5954329  5954371  5954381  5954407  5954411  5954413
5954441  5954461  5954479  5954489  5954513  5954519  5954563  5954569  5954579  5954587
5954591  5954593  5954609  5954623  5954633  5954647  5954653  5954681  5954731  5954749
5954789  5954797  5954801  5954803  5954827  5954843  5954849  5954873  5954917  5954933
5954939  5954951  5954957  5954969  5954989  5955011  5955013  5955023  5955029  5955031
5955041  5955067  5955071  5955073  5955107  5955119  5955139  5955149  5955181  5955197
5955211  5955221  5955241  5955259  5955281  5955307  5955311  5955329  5955331  5955337
5955343  5955347  5955359  5955359  5955361  5955403  5955419  5955421  5955431  5955437
5955487  5955497  5955517  5955529  5955533  5955539  5955541  5955553  5955583  5955611
5955617  5955623  5955647  5955671  5955709  5955737  5955743  5955749  5955773  5955821
5955823  5955839  5955841  5955863  5955877  5955883  5955923  5955931  5955959  5956003
5956007  5956031  5956037  5956073  5956129  5956133  5956141  5956151  5956157  5956187
```

```
5956189  5956199  5956207  5956211  5956213  5956219  5956229  5956259  5956277  5956337
5956351  5956361  5956373  5956393  5956399  5956417  5956421  5956429  5956459  5956493
5956507  5956537  5956541  5956543  5956549  5956591  5956607  5956627  5956663  5956669
5956697  5956739  5956751  5956759  5956763  5956771  5956787  5956789  5956801  5956807
5956831  5956843  5956913  5956927  5956933  5956943  5956957  5956967  5956997  5957009
5957027  5957033  5957047  5957059  5957071  5957087  5957117  5957129  5957137  5957141
5957143  5957167  5957173  5957179  5957197  5957201  5957219  5957221  5957227  5957249
5957251  5957257  5957261  5957269  5957291  5957309  5957339  5957387  5957389  5957411
5957459  5957509  5957513  5957527  5957563  5957591  5957617  5957639  5957641  5957663
5957671  5957689  5957711  5957723  5957729  5957737  5957741  5957753  5957771  5957801
5957821  5957839  5957843  5957857  5957881  5957899  5957911  5957933  5957953  5957969
5957971  5957981  5958047  5958061  5958067  5958089  5958097  5958131  5958133  5958163
5958179  5958181  5958193  5958217  5958247  5958257  5958263  5958269  5958289  5958299
5958301  5958317  5958319  5958349  5958367  5958371  5958389  5958401  5958431  5958437
5958439  5958451  5958473  5958499  5958503  5958521  5958527  5958569  5958577  5958583
5958607  5958643  5958671  5958683  5958691  5958709  5958749  5958751  5958763  5958767
5958773  5958781  5958787  5958839  5958853  5958871  5958877  5958881  5958889  5958893
5958923  5958929  5958947  5958971  5959039  5959043  5959067  5959073  5959081  5959087
5959111  5959127  5959133  5959147  5959153  5959189  5959193  5959199  5959211  5959237
5959253  5959259  5959279  5959307  5959313  5959319  5959339  5959361  5959381  5959397
5959399  5959403  5959411  5959423  5959427  5959433  5959487  5959489  5959511  5959519
5959543  5959549  5959567  5959589  5959601  5959607  5959619  5959633  5959661  5959663
5959687  5959721  5959727  5959739  5959747  5959763  5959771  5959799  5959813  5959817
5959831  5959853  5959867  5959871  5959879  5959937  5959949  5959957  5959963  5959969
5959973  5960027  5960041  5960077  5960083  5960089  5960099  5960113  5960137  5960159
5960173  5960179  5960203  5960261  5960267  5960287  5960309  5960323  5960329  5960333
5960347  5960389  5960413  5960429  5960431  5960443  5960453  5960483  5960501  5960503
5960527  5960543  5960599  5960627  5960639  5960671  5960683  5960701  5960707  5960719
5960723  5960729  5960753  5960767  5960777  5960791  5960797  5960803  5960807  5960809
5960821  5960827  5960831  5960833  5960849  5960861  5960881  5960891  5960909  5960917
5960951  5960971  5960993  5961001  5961017  5961049  5961091  5961097  5961119
5961127  5961149  5961157  5961167  5961173  5961199  5961217  5961223  5961233  5961239
5961259  5961283  5961287  5961289  5961299  5961311  5961313  5961337  5961343  5961349
5961353  5961379  5961401  5961409  5961427  5961447  5961457  5961463  5961481  5961491
5961499  5961503  5961511  5961533  5961539  5961547  5961569  5961581  5961583  5961587
5961643  5961647  5961653  5961689  5961707  5961721  5961731  5961737  5961751  5961757
5961779  5961793  5961797  5961833  5961859  5961863  5961869  5961881  5961887  5961919
5961931  5961971  5961979  5962001  5962027  5962031  5962039  5962043  5962063  5962093
5962109  5962123  5962133  5962153  5962157  5962171  5962183  5962193  5962207  5962241
5962259  5962277  5962283  5962289  5962331  5962379  5962381  5962387  5962391  5962399
5962417  5962433  5962441  5962459  5962477  5962499  5962519  5962547  5962549  5962573
5962577  5962591  5962601  5962613  5962643  5962673  5962679  5962709  5962711  5962721
5962729  5962741  5962763  5962769  5962771  5962783  5962787  5962823  5962837  5962849
5962867  5962907  5962909  5962919  5962949  5962967  5962973  5963011  5963021  5963047
5963051  5963053  5963059  5963119  5963147  5963149  5963159  5963173  5963203  5963213
5963227  5963249  5963257  5963263  5963317  5963341  5963351  5963381  5963411  5963423
5963449  5963459  5963471  5963479  5963519  5963527  5963537  5963557  5963561  5963569
5963579  5963599  5963609  5963611  5963621  5963641  5963653  5963669  5963677  5963707
5963729  5963731  5963761  5963773  5963791  5963809  5963813  5963827  5963833  5963843
5963857  5963869  5963899  5963911  5963927  5963933  5963939  5963981  5963989  5964001
5964017  5964019  5964041  5964083  5964097  5964103  5964113  5964149  5964163  5964181
5964187  5964191  5964197  5964209  5964223  5964241  5964247  5964293  5964313  5964341
5964359  5964373  5964377  5964391  5964419  5964443  5964457  5964473  5964481  5964503
5964523  5964527  5964529  5964533  5964551  5964559  5964593  5964599  5964631  5964653
5964661  5964677  5964683  5964697  5964701  5964709  5964719  5964731  5964743  5964767
5964793  5964811  5964839  5964857  5964863  5964877  5964883  5964887  5964919  5964941
5964947  5964949  5964979  5964983  5964997  5965009  5965013  5965019  5965021  5965067
5965093  5965123  5965139  5965163  5965171  5965247  5965273  5965279  5965301  5965307
5965319  5965321  5965327  5965331  5965343  5965397  5965409  5965417  5965429  5965439
5965447  5965469  5965483  5965489  5965493  5965501  5965507  5965511  5965537  5965573
5965643  5965649  5965651  5965669  5965693  5965697  5965699  5965709  5965721  5965723
5965727  5965781  5965783  5965789  5965807  5965819  5965831  5965847  5965849  5965853
5965857  5965877  5965907  5965933  5965961  5965979  5966011  5966017  5966029  5966041
5966047  5966063  5966087  5966101  5966113  5966117  5966143  5966153  5966183  5966189
5966239  5966243  5966273  5966281  5966299  5966309  5966339  5966341  5966347  5966351
5966357  5966377  5966381  5966383  5966393  5966413  5966419  5966459  5966483  5966491
5966497  5966501  5966503  5966531  5966533  5966537  5966549  5966557  5966561  5966563
5966573  5966579  5966599  5966629  5966651  5966659  5966669  5966693  5966699  5966717
5966773  5966797  5966803  5966839  5966843  5966861  5966887  5966921  5966923  5966929
5966963  5966971  5966993  5966999  5967019  5967029  5967037  5967043  5967061  5967079
5967109  5967133  5967151  5967161  5967163  5967179  5967193  5967251  5967253  5967271
5967277  5967287  5967293  5967317  5967341  5967347  5967433  5967439  5967461  5967487
5967499  5967503  5967517  5967547  5967553  5967571  5967589  5967601  5967631  5967667
5967679  5967737  5967743  5967749  5967803  5967809  5967839  5967851  5967877  5967887
5967889  5967893  5967917  5967931  5967937  5967947  5967977  5967979  5967991  5968007
5968009  5968019  5968021  5968031  5968043  5968049  5968051  5968087  5968091  5968093
5968097  5968103  5968121  5968133  5968141  5968163  5968181  5968199  5968217  5968219
5968231  5968253  5968267  5968279  5968307  5968367  5968379  5968409  5968439  5968453
5968463  5968471  5968481  5968549  5968583  5968591  5968601  5968609  5968621  5968643
5968681  5968711  5968723  5968741  5968759  5968783  5968801  5968811  5968813  5968817
5968843  5968849  5968883  5968889  5968901  5968909  5968927  5968939  5968961  5968973
5968981  5968987  5968993  5968997  5969009  5969027  5969053  5969063  5969107  5969123
5969129  5969147  5969153  5969177  5969179  5969221  5969233  5969237  5969239  5969263
5969269  5969279  5969309  5969333  5969347  5969357  5969393  5969407  5969413  5969417
5969437  5969449  5969461  5969473  5969497  5969507  5969519  5969531  5969569  5969573
5969597  5969651  5969653  5969657  5969669  5969681  5969729  5969741  5969753  5969773
5969779  5969809  5969813  5969827  5969833  5969861  5969863  5969897  5969921  5969927
5969939  5969947  5969959  5969993  5970001  5970017  5970023  5970037  5970053  5970067
5970071  5970089  5970101  5970119  5970121  5970127  5970137  5970157  5970191  5970193
```

```
5970203  5970221  5970227  5970241  5970277  5970287  5970299  5970301  5970329  5970337
5970347  5970359  5970373  5970443  5970449  5970487  5970499  5970509  5970511  5970533
5970557  5970563  5970577  5970589  5970599  5970649  5970661  5970673  5970677  5970697
5970703  5970721  5970733  5970763  5970773  5970779  5970787  5970793  5970799  5970803
5970827  5970847  5970857  5970901  5970919  5970967  5970983  5970989  5971001  5971027
5971061  5971067  5971081  5971087  5971093  5971123  5971151  5971157  5971193  5971243
5971253  5971279  5971289  5971307  5971309  5971321  5971337  5971379  5971391  5971409
5971411  5971429  5971439  5971447  5971451  5971463  5971481  5971487  5971489  5971507
5971517  5971519  5971543  5971547  5971549  5971577  5971591  5971613  5971627  5971639
5971657  5971663  5971673  5971699  5971703  5971723  5971759  5971781  5971793  5971799
5971807  5971813  5971841  5971873  5971877  5971919  5971939  5971951  5971993  5972003
5972009  5972017  5972051  5972053  5972063  5972077  5972107  5972129  5972147  5972209
5972257  5972261  5972279  5972293  5972297  5972303  5972311  5972339  5972357  5972363
5972377  5972381  5972383  5972443  5972453  5972501  5972507  5972509  5972513  5972537
5972557  5972563  5972567  5972611  5972647  5972653  5972671  5972689  5972699  5972719
5972723  5972737  5972741  5972749  5972767  5972773  5972779  5972803  5972851  5972881
5972903  5972909  5972917  5972957  5972959  5972999  5973013  5973029  5973041  5973053
5973083  5973119  5973131  5973133  5973139  5973151  5973161  5973179  5973197  5973223
5973257  5973263  5973287  5973311  5973313  5973323  5973329  5973343  5973347  5973349
5973361  5973367  5973389  5973403  5973433  5973437  5973439  5973463  5973481  5973497
5973503  5973509  5973521  5973523  5973533  5973553  5973563  5973571  5973587  5973589
5973599  5973601  5973637  5973673  5973679  5973701  5973707  5973713  5973719  5973763
5973811  5973829  5973853  5973881  5973883  5973889  5973893  5973911  5973937  5973943
5973949  5973973  5973991  5974009  5974019  5974027  5974039  5974063  5974079  5974093
5974097  5974109  5974121  5974127  5974139  5974141  5974187  5974193  5974211  5974223
5974237  5974249  5974271  5974301  5974313  5974333  5974337  5974343  5974363  5974369
5974387  5974403  5974421  5974459  5974469  5974471  5974477  5974487  5974499  5974511
5974543  5974547  5974583  5974627  5974669  5974693  5974697  5974699  5974711  5974747
5974757  5974763  5974777  5974789  5974799  5974811  5974817  5974823  5974853  5974861
5974877  5974879  5974897  5974933  5974937  5974961  5974999  5975017  5975023  5975029
5975051  5975071  5975089  5975111  5975117  5975161  5975171  5975173  5975191  5975197
5975209  5975227  5975257  5975267  5975287  5975293  5975311  5975317  5975341  5975351
5975369  5975393  5975401  5975413  5975441  5975447  5975503  5975509  5975513  5975521
5975527  5975539  5975597  5975617  5975659  5975677  5975681  5975689  5975701  5975713
5975773  5975807  5975813  5975819  5975831  5975863  5975869  5975881  5975887  5975897
5975903  5975911  5975923  5975951  5975953  5975969  5976007  5976017  5976023  5976029
5976031  5976049  5976071  5976079  5976181  5976193  5976209  5976221  5976281  5976301
5976319  5976323  5976329  5976331  5976337  5976359  5976403  5976409  5976413  5976419
5976449  5976463  5976491  5976497  5976541  5976547  5976557  5976563  5976569  5976577
5976599  5976637  5976653  5976679  5976701  5976713  5976727  5976749  5976787  5976791
5976793  5976821  5976823  5976881  5976889  5976917  5976923  5976931  5976947  5976953
5976959  5976961  5976967  5977009  5977019  5977031  5977051  5977057  5977073  5977121
5977159  5977199  5977211  5977247  5977253  5977259  5977261  5977273  5977289  5977297
5977303  5977331  5977333  5977337  5977339  5977351  5977357  5977379  5977397  5977409
5977429  5977453  5977469  5977471  5977487  5977501  5977511  5977547  5977549  5977603
5977607  5977613  5977619  5977627  5977639  5977649  5977651  5977663  5977667  5977679
5977681  5977687  5977691  5977717  5977733  5977739  5977747  5977753  5977801  5977843
5977847  5977849  5977859  5977871  5977877  5977889  5977899  5977901  5977921  5977943
5977949  5977957  5977963  5977969  5977981  5977991  5977997  5978003  5978047  5978051
5978059  5978069  5978083  5978117  5978131  5978143  5978149  5978153  5978171  5978177
5978213  5978221  5978227  5978233  5978239  5978243  5978261  5978267  5978279  5978309
5978311  5978317  5978341  5978363  5978377  5978389  5978393  5978417  5978449  5978461
5978471  5978507  5978513  5978527  5978537  5978563  5978603  5978617  5978633  5978639
5978653  5978657  5978659  5978663  5978681  5978683  5978699  5978701  5978723  5978737
5978783  5978801  5978803  5978809  5978813  5978821  5978831  5978851  5978857  5978887
5978891  5978909  5978911  5978933  5978993  5979007  5979023  5979041  5979049  5979059
5979067  5979079  5979097  5979131  5979143  5979151  5979173  5979179  5979203  5979209
5979229  5979269  5979271  5979277  5979283  5979313  5979331  5979341  5979361  5979367
5979377  5979383  5979397  5979401  5979409  5979437  5979443  5979469  5979527  5979551
5979581  5979583  5979593  5979613  5979629  5979653  5979679  5979689  5979703  5979707
5979731  5979749  5979761  5979773  5979781  5979797  5979811  5979823  5979859  5979893
5979899  5979917  5979929  5979943  5979947  5979949  5979959  5979979  5979983  5979991
5980021  5980033  5980081  5980099  5980111  5980127  5980129  5980151  5980171
5980189  5980201  5980223  5980229  5980237  5980267  5980279  5980291  5980319  5980321
5980333  5980339  5980363  5980367  5980393  5980433  5980439  5980453  5980477  5980493
5980517  5980519  5980531  5980561  5980567  5980589  5980591  5980607  5980619  5980631
5980661  5980669  5980673  5980691  5980693  5980747  5980781  5980829  5980859  5980903
5980921  5980967  5980981  5981021  5981033  5981051  5981069  5981071  5981077
5981099  5981123  5981137  5981141  5981149  5981159  5981167  5981177  5981179  5981189
5981191  5981197  5981201  5981207  5981237  5981317  5981323  5981341  5981347  5981351
5981359  5981363  5981377  5981387  5981411  5981431  5981441  5981471  5981483  5981489
5981491  5981533  5981539  5981567  5981579  5981609  5981629  5981641  5981659  5981663
5981669  5981681  5981683  5981707  5981711  5981719  5981749  5981797  5981813  5981819
5981851  5981867  5981873  5981879  5981887  5981891  5981939  5981947  5981971  5981993
5982007  5982037  5982043  5982071  5982121  5982127  5982173  5982191  5982217  5982227
5982233  5982239  5982241  5982257  5982293  5982307  5982329  5982341  5982371  5982373
5982401  5982407  5982413  5982523  5982527  5982551  5982563  5982577  5982601  5982607
5982611  5982637  5982661  5982689  5982709  5982727  5982731  5982733  5982751  5982763
5982773  5982791  5982803  5982811  5982817  5982833  5982839  5982841  5982869  5982877
5982881  5982883  5982931  5982943  5982947  5982953  5982971  5982973  5982993  5983009
5983027  5983037  5983051  5983067  5983069  5983091  5983121  5983127  5983129  5983141
5983169  5983181  5983183  5983213  5983231  5983247  5983259  5983267  5983277  5983283
5983297  5983331  5983339  5983357  5983361  5983363  5983391  5983399  5983421  5983441
5983447  5983451  5983459  5983489  5983511  5983517  5983531  5983577  5983583  5983597
5983619  5983631  5983661  5983669  5983693  5983699  5983723  5983781  5983793  5983801
5983807  5983829  5983849  5983853  5983877  5983903  5983907  5983919  5983921  5983927
5983931  5983969  5983997  5984021  5984053  5984057  5984059  5984101  5984131  5984137
5984159  5984201  5984203  5984207  5984213  5984227  5984233  5984257  5984261  5984263
5984299  5984309  5984327  5984339  5984371  5984387  5984399  5984453  5984471  5984477
```

```
5984479  5984497  5984501  5984509  5984513  5984521  5984533  5984543  5984567  5984569
5984579  5984591  5984597  5984599  5984659  5984681  5984687  5984711  5984717  5984747
5984749  5984773  5984777  5984821  5984837  5984843  5984851  5984857  5984879  5984903
5984911  5984921  5984929  5984939  5984941  5984947  5984959  5984963  5984971
5984977  5984987  5985011  5985013  5985029  5985053  5985059  5985061  5985073  5985103
5985143  5985151  5985169  5985179  5985193  5985211  5985233  5985251  5985257  5985269
5985283  5985289  5985307  5985337  5985341  5985347  5985349  5985389  5985401  5985407
5985431  5985439  5985461  5985481  5985493  5985533  5985541  5985559  5985583  5985589
5985611  5985647  5985653  5985659  5985671  5985673  5985677  5985689  5985691
5985709  5985719  5985739  5985743  5985761  5985799  5985809  5985827  5985829  5985841
5985871  5985899  5985913  5985923  5985929  5985943  5985983  5985997  5986009  5986021
5986027  5986031  5986033  5986037  5986093  5986103  5986111  5986117  5986147  5986153
5986157  5986163  5986177  5986207  5986231  5986237  5986271  5986291  5986303  5986327
5986333  5986339  5986381  5986391  5986427  5986429  5986433  5986447  5986471  5986481
5986483  5986523  5986537  5986559  5986571  5986579  5986583  5986597  5986609  5986613
5986619  5986621  5986663  5986679  5986727  5986733  5986753  5986759  5986769  5986777
5986793  5986817  5986819  5986823  5986829  5986867  5986879  5986889  5986891  5986901
5986921  5986927  5986931  5986951  5986961  5986979  5986987  5986991  5986993  5986997
5987029  5987057  5987083  5987101  5987129  5987141  5987159  5987167  5987183  5987221
5987227  5987231  5987239  5987243  5987249  5987257  5987263  5987273  5987339  5987341
5987347  5987389  5987393  5987411  5987419  5987437  5987441  5987447  5987461  5987467
5987473  5987477  5987483  5987503  5987539  5987549  5987551  5987561  5987563  5987573
5987593  5987609  5987627  5987629  5987633  5987651  5987677  5987687  5987693  5987701
5987719  5987731  5987749  5987759  5987767  5987771  5987777  5987789  5987803  5987819
5987873  5987897  5987899  5987903  5987911  5987921  5987953  5987959  5987977  5988001
5988011  5988013  5988019  5988061  5988067  5988079  5988083  5988113  5988139  5988163
5988167  5988193  5988197  5988217  5988221  5988251  5988253  5988271  5988289  5988293
5988319  5988331  5988343  5988347  5988361  5988371  5988379  5988421  5988427  5988443
5988461  5988467  5988497  5988511  5988517  5988557  5988571  5988589  5988617  5988659
5988679  5988691  5988733  5988737  5988769  5988791  5988793  5988817  5988833  5988839
5988869  5988883  5988923  5988943  5988967  5988989  5988991  5989001  5989007
5989013  5989019  5989021  5989043  5989057  5989099  5989127  5989171  5989183  5989241
5989259  5989271  5989273  5989297  5989307  5989309  5989327  5989349  5989367  5989381
5989409  5989429  5989439  5989463  5989469  5989481  5989483  5989493  5989517  5989537
5989547  5989561  5989589  5989601  5989609  5989619  5989639  5989663  5989667  5989673
5989681  5989691  5989699  5989703  5989721  5989751  5989787  5989793  5989801  5989811
5989817  5989829  5989843  5989853  5989871  5989873  5989889  5989897  5989903  5989909
5989931  5989939  5989999  5990011  5990081  5990101  5990119  5990129  5990147  5990177  5990183
5990191  5990203  5990213  5990221  5990233  5990249  5990251  5990293  5990297  5990311
5990317  5990353  5990357  5990363  5990371  5990381  5990389  5990401  5990417  5990423
5990437  5990441  5990461  5990473  5990513  5990519  5990521  5990549  5990561
5990563  5990581  5990597  5990629  5990651  5990653  5990659  5990669  5990687  5990693
5990711  5990713  5990723  5990729  5990731  5990737  5990759  5990771  5990779  5990813
5990821  5990861  5990863  5990867  5990893  5990903  5990911  5990917  5990977  5991031
5991047  5991059  5991071  5991101  5991103  5991107  5991113  5991131  5991149  5991169
5991187  5991217  5991221  5991229  5991239  5991241  5991253  5991257  5991263  5991311
5991343  5991367  5991379  5991389  5991397  5991413  5991443  5991449  5991451  5991457
5991473  5991533  5991541  5991551  5991553  5991563  5991571  5991589  5991641  5991653
5991659  5991677  5991709  5991721  5991731  5991757  5991779  5991823  5991827  5991829
5991833  5991841  5991851  5991857  5991883  5991899  5991901  5991907  5991943  5991949
5991961  5991967  5991977  5991989  5991991  5992003  5992013  5992031  5992033
5992073  5992097  5992111  5992153  5992157  5992169  5992199  5992223  5992237  5992247
5992267  5992271  5992289  5992291  5992297  5992303  5992307  5992309  5992319  5992361
5992379  5992403  5992411  5992421  5992463  5992501  5992529  5992537  5992559  5992603
5992639  5992667  5992669  5992691  5992697  5992717  5992747  5992751  5992759  5992783
5992793  5992859  5992901  5992907  5992933  5992969  5993023  5993047  5993059  5993089
5993101  5993107  5993123  5993131  5993167  5993173  5993191  5993201  5993209  5993213
5993219  5993233  5993237  5993249  5993291  5993321  5993327  5993329  5993353  5993357
5993359  5993387  5993411  5993413  5993419  5993423  5993431  5993473  5993483  5993521
5993539  5993543  5993549  5993551  5993557  5993579  5993591  5993597  5993599
5993609  5993621  5993623  5993627  5993653  5993671  5993693  5993699  5993711  5993719
5993723  5993761  5993783  5993791  5993837  5993849  5993927  5993941  5993947  5993959
5993969  5993993  5994041  5994049  5994073  5994083  5994089  5994091  5994133  5994143
5994151  5994169  5994179  5994181  5994187  5994199  5994203  5994221  5994229  5994269
5994301  5994337  5994347  5994361  5994371  5994379  5994403  5994431  5994447  5994449
5994473  5994491  5994511  5994517  5994529  5994551  5994553  5994589  5994607  5994613
5994617  5994631  5994641  5994647  5994649  5994661  5994679  5994701  5994707  5994719
5994739  5994767  5994797  5994809  5994829  5994839  5994847  5994853  5994869  5994871
5994887  5994943  5994949  5994971  5995009  5995021  5995037  5995043  5995063  5995069
5995079  5995081  5995091  5995117  5995123  5995151  5995163  5995177  5995181  5995211
5995217  5995219  5995243  5995277  5995309  5995331  5995337  5995343  5995349  5995397
5995399  5995411  5995427  5995439  5995481  5995513  5995523  5995541  5995573  5995579
5995589  5995597  5995603  5995609  5995631  5995651  5995669  5995687  5995727
5995729  5995777  5995783  5995817  5995819  5995853  5995867  5995901  5995933  5995949
5995967  5995973  5995991  5995999  5996009  5996027  5996033  5996041  5996047  5996083
5996093  5996099  5996101  5996129  5996131  5996143  5996149  5996167  5996171  5996231
5996233  5996251  5996273  5996311  5996323  5996327  5996329  5996339  5996357  5996371
5996407  5996437  5996477  5996489  5996509  5996519  5996521  5996527  5996539  5996561
5996587  5996603  5996611  5996621  5996633  5996657  5996677  5996681  5996687  5996719
5996729  5996741  5996759  5996789  5996797  5996807  5996809  5996839  5996899  5996911
5996953  5997001  5997031  5997041  5997083  5997091  5997097  5997119  5997151  5997161
5997163  5997191  5997197  5997203  5997221  5997223  5997301  5997307  5997317  5997347
5997349  5997359  5997361  5997373  5997377  5997419  5997421  5997437  5997463  5997469
5997487  5997517  5997553  5997571  5997599  5997611  5997613  5997631  5997637  5997643
5997647  5997659  5997683  5997689  5997713  5997721  5997731  5997743  5997781  5997791
5997839  5997841  5997847  5997853  5997869  5997877  5997883  5997919  5997961  5997967
5998001  5998007  5998037  5998039  5998051  5998061  5998073  5998079  5998081  5998103
5998121  5998133  5998141  5998171  5998207  5998211  5998217  5998253  5998261  5998277
5998303  5998339  5998351  5998361  5998367  5998373  5998387  5998393  5998409  5998417
```

```
5998427 5998439 5998451 5998459 5998481 5998513 5998537 5998541 5998567 5998579
5998583 5998609 5998613 5998627 5998639 5998651 5998667 5998673 5998687 5998691
5998697 5998703 5998709 5998721 5998723 5998757 5998763 5998793 5998799 5998843
5998859 5998871 5998873 5998891 5998901 5998907 5998913 5998919 5998933 5998957
5998987 5999009 5999053 5999083 5999107 5999129 5999137 5999171 5999173 5999177
5999183 5999197 5999207 5999209 5999233 5999237 5999261 5999263 5999267 5999303
5999309 5999311 5999327 5999341 5999347 5999377 5999387 5999393 5999417 5999423
5999449 5999471 5999479 5999519 5999537 5999551 5999561 5999563 5999569 5999593
5999599 5999603 5999627 5999629 5999633 5999639 5999663 5999677 5999681 5999699
5999717 5999729 5999731 5999737 5999743 5999767 5999779 5999831 5999863 5999869
5999881 5999909 5999911 5999921 5999923 5999927 5999933 5999947 5999993 6000011
6000023 6000041 6000047 6000053 6000061 6000073 6000091 6000093 6000109 6000119
6000121 6000149 6000157 6000173 6000191 6000199 6000221 6000229 6000233 6000271
6000277 6000283 6000301 6000307 6000317 6000343 6000377 6000389 6000403
6000427 6000431 6000457 6000479 6000481 6000503 6000529 6000551 6000557 6000565
6000571 6000581 6000611 6000619 6000641 6000653 6000679 6000703 6000733 6000773
6000793 6000803 6000809 6000821 6000823 6000829 6000853 6000857 6000859 6000889
6000893 6000899 6000937 6000961 6000977 6001013 6001019 6001033 6001043 6001049
6001063 6001069 6001087 6001109 6001147 6001189 6001201 6001207 6001249
6001253 6001271 6001277 6001291 6001297 6001339 6001343 6001351 6001427 6001433
6001439 6001447 6001453 6001469 6001483 6001517 6001531 6001547 6001577 6001601
6001609 6001613 6001627 6001669 6001673 6001679 6001717 6001727 6001741 6001747
6001757 6001763 6001789 6001819 6001829 6001903 6001907 6001909 6001921 6001937
6001939 6001981 6001991 6001997 6002033 6002047 6002053 6002063 6002083 6002089
6002093 6002111 6002123 6002131 6002137 6002153 6002179 6002201 6002203 6002209
6002237 6002239 6002257 6002273 6002281 6002291 6002357 6002363 6002369 6002371
6002383 6002387 6002389 6002429 6002431 6002453 6002467 6002489 6002509 6002519
6002527 6002539 6002573 6002599 6002603 6002617 6002627 6002629 6002641 6002653
6002669 6002677 6002693 6002707 6002723 6002729 6002741 6002767 6002849 6002861
6002869 6002881 6002891 6002903 6002911 6002951 6002987 6003001 6003007 6003043
6003047 6003059 6003077 6003079 6003083 6003093 6003113 6003143 6003197 6003199
6003211 6003223 6003241 6003247 6003251 6003281 6003293 6003313 6003323 6003331
6003341 6003379 6003407 6003409 6003419 6003443 6003497 6003511 6003521 6003527
6003539 6003581 6003607 6003623 6003643 6003649 6003659 6003661 6003703 6003727
6003757 6003761 6003769 6003793 6003797 6003821 6003853 6003857 6003859 6003871
6003883 6003887 6003889 6003901 6003913 6003929 6003931 6003947 6003967 6003983
6003997 6004001 6004007 6004013 6004021 6004067 6004069 6004087 6004093 6004121
6004139 6004153 6004157 6004217 6004231 6004241 6004259 6004277 6004283 6004289
6004301 6004307 6004309 6004321 6004331 6004333 6004337 6004343 6004351 6004367
6004373 6004379 6004387 6004393 6004429 6004459 6004463 6004499 6004507
6004517 6004543 6004549 6004561 6004567 6004571 6004577 6004601 6004631 6004637
6004639 6004651 6004699 6004727 6004729 6004751 6004759 6004763 6004777 6004781
6004783 6004787 6004799 6004811 6004813 6004837 6004877 6004889 6004897 6004901
6004903 6004949 6004951 6004963 6004981 6004987 6004991 6005011 6005039 6005101
6005107 6005113 6005141 6005149 6005177 6005183 6005191 6005201 6005203 6005213
6005287 6005297 6005303 6005309 6005327 6005339 6005341 6005357 6005371 6005381
6005383 6005401 6005429 6005443 6005459 6005477 6005497 6005533 6005569 6005579
6005591 6005603 6005627 6005647 6005651 6005663 6005687 6005717 6005719 6005749
6005759 6005789 6005849 6005851 6005861 6005863 6005869 6005887 6005891 6005893
6005897 6005899 6005903 6005911 6005917 6005927 6005953 6006029 6006031 6006047
6006053 6006067 6006073 6006079 6006089 6006097 6006127 6006137 6006141 6006163
6006229 6006233 6006241 6006251 6006257 6006269 6006293 6006313 6006359 6006361
6006383 6006389 6006391 6006409 6006421 6006431 6006433 6006439 6006479 6006503
6006503 6006529 6006547 6006551 6006557 6006563 6006569 6006599 6006601 6006619
6006631 6006643 6006667 6006673 6006677 6006697 6006757 6006761 6006769 6006779
6006817 6006851 6006859 6006883 6006893 6006911 6006941 6006943 6006953
6006961 6006991 6007003 6007037 6007051 6007091 6007093 6007109 6007123 6007151
6007159 6007181 6007187 6007189 6007207 6007217 6007223 6007231 6007247 6007271
6007277 6007297 6007303 6007333 6007349 6007367 6007369 6007373 6007387 6007403
6007427 6007429 6007433 6007447 6007459 6007471 6007483 6007489 6007513 6007517
6007537 6007541 6007559 6007567 6007597 6007601 6007609 6007619 6007621 6007627
6007643 6007649 6007657 6007663 6007693 6007697 6007711 6007717 6007721 6007723
6007739 6007741 6007759 6007769 6007787 6007789 6007861 6007867 6007877 6007879
6007891 6007907 6007913 6007927 6007931 6007961 6007979 6007999 6008033 6008039
6008059 6008063 6008077 6008081 6008087 6008111 6008113 6008131 6008143 6008153
6008173 6008201 6008207 6008227 6008231 6008251 6008257 6008281 6008333 6008357
6008363 6008369 6008377 6008381 6008399 6008437 6008447 6008449 6008461 6008477
6008489 6008491 6008507 6008521 6008533 6008609 6008617 6008677 6008687 6008707
6008719 6008729 6008749 6008753 6008759 6008789 6008791 6008797 6008813 6008833
6008857 6008867 6008881 6008887 6008897 6008941 6008953 6008969 6008971
6008983 6008987 6008993 6009011 6009037 6009067 6009089 6009103 6009127 6009167
6009253 6009271 6009307 6009317 6009323 6009331 6009337 6009343 6009359 6009361
6009383 6009397 6009401 6009407 6009413 6009431 6009461 6009469 6009491 6009499
6009533 6009539 6009541 6009557 6009569 6009571 6009581 6009587 6009589 6009593
6009599 6009611 6009613 6009623 6009631 6009667 6009683 6009709 6009713 6009727
6009733 6009737 6009761 6009791 6009797 6009811 6009841 6009851 6009853 6009859
6009863 6009881 6009893 6009901 6009911 6009919 6009929 6009961 6009977 6009979
6010009 6010033 6010039 6010051 6010087 6010091 6010093 6010097 6010111 6010157
6010159 6010171 6010189 6010201 6010211 6010229 6010237 6010261 6010307 6010343
6010351 6010379 6010393 6010421 6010427 6010447 6010451 6010481 6010483
6010489 6010523 6010547 6010549 6010573 6010591 6010597 6010603 6010619 6010633
6010643 6010649 6010661 6010663 6010679 6010681 6010691 6010717 6010721 6010727
6010729 6010759 6010769 6010787 6010811 6010837 6010847 6010853 6010867 6010883
6010891 6010903 6010919 6010933 6010937 6010957 6010967 6010997 6011017 6011029
6011051 6011077 6011111 6011113 6011141 6011143 6011171 6011209 6011213 6011219
6011221 6011233 6011267 6011287 6011293 6011309 6011311 6011321 6011329 6011351
6011359 6011363 6011377 6011399 6011413 6011417 6011449 6011471 6011483 6011491
6011513 6011519 6011521 6011531 6011539 6011549 6011569 6011573 6011587 6011597
6011609 6011617 6011627 6011639 6011647 6011653 6011699 6011711 6011741 6011749
```

```
6011767 6011779 6011807 6011813 6011851 6011867 6011869 6011879 6011899 6011933
6011969 6012011 6012029 6012043 6012089 6012091 6012103 6012119 6012121 6012179
6012191 6012211 6012229 6012239 6012257 6012263 6012283 6012313 6012317 6012319
6012323 6012329 6012337 6012371 6012401 6012403 6012439 6012467 6012473 6012491
6012497 6012511 6012533 6012547 6012551 6012553 6012583 6012613 6012619 6012659
6012673 6012689 6012697 6012703 6012719 6012731 6012763 6012779 6012803 6012827
6012847 6012857 6012859 6012893 6012899 6013013 6013027 6013081 6013109 6013123
6013141 6013151 6013153 6013157 6013159 6013181 6013187 6013199 6013211 6013213
6013247 6013261 6013283 6013303 6013309 6013313 6013331 6013333 6013369 6013379
6013387 6013409 6013453 6013459 6013471 6013489 6013493 6013517 6013523 6013531
6013537 6013541 6013547 6013561 6013583 6013591 6013627 6013691 6013703 6013723
6013727 6013729 6013739 6013753 6013781 6013793 6013829 6013841 6013849 6013867
6013871 6013883 6013897 6013901 6013919 6013927 6013949 6013951 6013961 6013981
6013993 6014009 6014011 6014027 6014053 6014081 6014083 6014101 6014111 6014117
6014119 6014123 6014131 6014137 6014147 6014159 6014161 6014219 6014233 6014237
6014269 6014287 6014299 6014321 6014347 6014357 6014369 6014381 6014419
6014423 6014443 6014467 6014473 6014483 6014497 6014509 6014521 6014557 6014563
6014573 6014581 6014597 6014627 6014633 6014639 6014641 6014647 6014653 6014663
6014677 6014681 6014699 6014717 6014737 6014777 6014807 6014843 6014857 6014867
6014881 6014893 6014903 6014909 6014929 6014941 6014951 6014971 6014999 6015007
6015011 6015017 6015047 6015083 6015089 6015091 6015131 6015169 6015197 6015199
6015203 6015211 6015221 6015223 6015239 6015277 6015287 6015301 6015311 6015319
6015337 6015353 6015403 6015407 6015413 6015431 6015437 6015439 6015469 6015481
6015511 6015521 6015523 6015539 6015551 6015563 6015587 6015593 6015619 6015623
6015629 6015641 6015683 6015697 6015701 6015703 6015721 6015733 6015749 6015791
6015797 6015803 6015833 6015839 6015851 6015853 6015883 6015907 6015917 6015931
6015967 6015979 6015983 6016009 6016013 6016019 6016033 6016039 6016057 6016063
6016067 6016091 6016093 6016097 6016099 6016111 6016123 6016177 6016211 6016229
6016273 6016301 6016303 6016313 6016319 6016321 6016357 6016391 6016429 6016447
6016457 6016513 6016519 6016523 6016529 6016541 6016579 6016583 6016609 6016649
6016669 6016679 6016687 6016729 6016739 6016741 6016757 6016771 6016789 6016811
6016817 6016831 6016837 6016841 6016847 6016853 6016859 6016921 6016937 6016957
6016973 6016991 6016993 6016999 6017003 6017009 6017021 6017027 6017041 6017057
6017059 6017071 6017093 6017107 6017111 6017117 6017149 6017153 6017159 6017183
6017189 6017213 6017257 6017267 6017309 6017369 6017381 6017399 6017411 6017419
6017437 6017457 6017477 6017483 6017489 6017491 6017497 6017521 6017527 6017537
6017579 6017581 6017593 6017597 6017603 6017621 6017629 6017633 6017639 6017647
6017657 6017701 6017719 6017729 6017731 6017741 6017773 6017777 6017827 6017831
6017849 6017863 6017887 6017897 6017899 6017903 6017909 6017923 6017929 6017951
6017971 6017987 6017989 6018029 6018037 6018043 6018083 6018107 6018127 6018137
6018143 6018191 6018197 6018223 6018239 6018241 6018253 6018263 6018277 6018293
6018301 6018317 6018329 6018347 6018367 6018373 6018377 6018401 6018427 6018469
6018473 6018487 6018499 6018503 6018539 6018541 6018563 6018569 6018577 6018583
6018587 6018589 6018613 6018659 6018671 6018673 6018703 6018707 6018713 6018757
6018769 6018781 6018787 6018791 6018797 6018823 6018829 6018853 6018869 6018913
6018919 6018937 6018949 6018959 6018967 6018973 6019001 6019009 6019019 6019021
6019061 6019063 6019073 6019081 6019103 6019187 6019193 6019199 6019201 6019267
6019283 6019289 6019331 6019339 6019367 6019379 6019381 6019393 6019417 6019421
6019459 6019469 6019471 6019483 6019511 6019553 6019571 6019589 6019597 6019603
6019609 6019627 6019633 6019639 6019667 6019669 6019679 6019681 6019691 6019697
6019757 6019771 6019781 6019787 6019801 6019817 6019823 6019837 6019861 6019889
6019891 6019913 6019919 6019931 6019967 6019973 6019987 6019991 6020039 6020051
6020059 6020087 6020099 6020117 6020137 6020143 6020167 6020173 6020177 6020221
6020251 6020257 6020263 6020269 6020279 6020281 6020291 6020297 6020299 6020309
6020327 6020341 6020351 6020401 6020423 6020447 6020449 6020459 6020471 6020477
6020491 6020519 6020551 6020557 6020579 6020591 6020617 6020621 6020627 6020647
6020681 6020699 6020717 6020723 6020741 6020759 6020801 6020831 6020843 6020867
6020879 6020899 6020909 6020921 6020923 6020947 6020969 6020977 6020983
6020999 6021007 6021011 6021017 6021019 6021053 6021073 6021079 6021083 6021091
6021109 6021139 6021181 6021199 6021203 6021209 6021227 6021263 6021289 6021319
6021359 6021373 6021397 6021403 6021437 6021467 6021479 6021497 6021511 6021517
6021523 6021529 6021557 6021559 6021569 6021571 6021577 6021583 6021601 6021623
6021637 6021641 6021649 6021661 6021667 6021679 6021683 6021749 6021751 6021761
6021773 6021809 6021811 6021823 6021833 6021839 6021863 6021877 6021881 6021887
6021901 6021907 6021943 6021949 6021991 6021997 6022057 6022061 6022073 6022087
6022117 6022123 6022127 6022129 6022147 6022171 6022223 6022229 6022271 6022273
6022283 6022319 6022321 6022381 6022391 6022399 6022409 6022441 6022447 6022477
6022483 6022493 6022501 6022507 6022519 6022547 6022553 6022559 6022567 6022571
6022579 6022589 6022603 6022609 6022631 6022637 6022651 6022663 6022699 6022703
6022727 6022733 6022739 6022741 6022747 6022759 6022763 6022769 6022771 6022781
6022799 6022801 6022843 6022847 6022853 6022873 6022883 6022889 6022901 6022921
6022927 6022949 6022969 6022993 6022999 6023029 6023047 6023051 6023071 6023077
6023083 6023093 6023107 6023111 6023123 6023141 6023153 6023159 6023161 6023203
6023221 6023243 6023257 6023273 6023279 6023299 6023327 6023333 6023357 6023359
6023363 6023371 6023383 6023461 6023467 6023509 6023527 6023533 6023557 6023581
6023587 6023599 6023621 6023629 6023639 6023651 6023653 6023657 6023659 6023663
6023683 6023701 6023707 6023713 6023747 6023767 6023777 6023783 6023789 6023791
6023803 6023807 6023813 6023819 6023863 6023879 6023881 6023911 6023923 6023929
6023947 6023957 6023971 6024017 6024019 6024041 6024043 6024047 6024049 6024071
6024097 6024107 6024119 6024127 6024169 6024179 6024191 6024209 6024259 6024283
6024371 6024391 6024401 6024419 6024433 6024449 6024467 6024479 6024493 6024497
6024503 6024521 6024533 6024553 6024569 6024583 6024587 6024589 6024593 6024607
6024611 6024637 6024659 6024661 6024671 6024679 6024701 6024703 6024719 6024731
6024737 6024769 6024797 6024803 6024833 6024853 6024857 6024869 6024877 6024899
6024901 6024911 6024923 6024947 6024929 6024949 6024983 6025001 6025009 6025013
6025037 6025079 6025087 6025091 6025099 6025111 6025121 6025133 6025163 6025171
6025181 6025207 6025213 6025247 6025269 6025291 6025297 6025307 6025321 6025343
6025351 6025363 6025373 6025381 6025399 6025421 6025441 6025451 6025457 6025469
6025507 6025529 6025549 6025571 6025577 6025583 6025589 6025597 6025613 6025627
```

```
6025631 6025637 6025661 6025673 6025681 6025693 6025697 6025703 6025711 6025727
6025741 6025751 6025753 6025759 6025771 6025777 6025781 6025801 6025813 6025829
6025849 6025889 6025909 6025933 6025937 6025961 6025967 6025969 6025979 6025991
6026017 6026071 6026081 6026087 6026089 6026099 6026107 6026123 6026159 6026179
6026191 6026197 6026203 6026213 6026231 6026233 6026243 6026257 6026261 6026263
6026269 6026281 6026291 6026297 6026309 6026323 6026327 6026333 6026341 6026351
6026389 6026411 6026413 6026417 6026429 6026441 6026453 6026521 6026543 6026557
6026563 6026567 6026609 6026611 6026627 6026641 6026663 6026677 6026711 6026723
6026737 6026747 6026749 6026753 6026827 6026843 6026873 6026887 6026889 6026929
6026939 6026947 6026957 6026981 6026987 6027013 6027017 6027019 6027023 6027037
6027053 6027059 6027067 6027071 6027079 6027083 6027089 6027097 6027101 6027143
6027149 6027167 6027187 6027191 6027221 6027223 6027247 6027269 6027277 6027283
6027383 6027407 6027409 6027419 6027443 6027487 6027517 6027523 6027529 6027601
6027607 6027613 6027641 6027647 6027649 6027653 6027661 6027667 6027689 6027691
6027713 6027719 6027727 6027739 6027751 6027757 6027761 6027767 6027773 6027803
6027811 6027821 6027823 6027851 6027887 6027893 6027907 6027941 6027949 6027961
6027977 6028019 6028031 6028039 6028049 6028051 6028063 6028069 6028097 6028103
6028109 6028123 6028129 6028147 6028157 6028171 6028177 6028193 6028219 6028247
6028261 6028279 6028283 6028289 6028303 6028313 6028327 6028331 6028343 6028349
6028357 6028367 6028381 6028403 6028417 6028423 6028427 6028457 6028469 6028483
6028493 6028511 6028513 6028537 6028571 6028577 6028579 6028597 6028609 6028613
6028629 6028637 6028639 6028651 6028667 6028699 6028703 6028721 6028747 6028793
6028801 6028807 6028811 6028837 6028853 6028873 6028879 6028907 6028933 6028969
6029003 6029017 6029021 6029029 6029041 6029047 6029053 6029063 6029081 6029087
6029119 6029123 6029131 6029147 6029161 6029171 6029183 6029209 6029273 6029281
6029299 6029329 6029363 6029371 6029377 6029383 6029389 6029431 6029447 6029449
6029467 6029497 6029521 6029561 6029563 6029591 6029603 6029609 6029641 6029659
6029671 6029687 6029689 6029719 6029743 6029759 6029791 6029797 6029809 6029813
6029831 6029843 6029861 6029891 6029919 6029921 6029923 6029939 6029953 6029963
6029981 6029987 6030023 6030029 6030041 6030043 6030077 6030083 6030091 6030103
6030107 6030109 6030113 6030119 6030127 6030137 6030161 6030181 6030197 6030247
6030259 6030263 6030281 6030313 6030317 6030361 6030379 6030383 6030397 6030419
6030421 6030433 6030473 6030481 6030491 6030503 6030517 6030533 6030539 6030569
6030599 6030611 6030641 6030653 6030669 6030677 6030679 6030691 6030721 6030727
6030743 6030751 6030757 6030763 6030769 6030779 6030797 6030799 6030821 6030823
6030839 6030851 6030859 6030883 6030901 6030919 6030929 6030949 6031001 6031031
6031049 6031063 6031099 6031117 6031133 6031153 6031171 6031177 6031183 6031199
6031211 6031213 6031219 6031229 6031247 6031261 6031283 6031301 6031321 6031327
6031339 6031409 6031411 6031423 6031429 6031433 6031439 6031471 6031477 6031499
6031513 6031517 6031547 6031561 6031591 6031603 6031637 6031657 6031661 6031673
6031679 6031709 6031717 6031723 6031757 6031789 6031793 6031799 6031801 6031811
6031843 6031847 6031849 6031853 6031871 6031891 6031897 6031903 6031931 6031937
6031979 6032009 6032017 6032021 6032041 6032051 6032057 6032069 6032111 6032129
6032149 6032167 6032171 6032179 6032251 6032269 6032283 6032303 6032311 6032317
6032359 6032363 6032393 6032413 6032437 6032459 6032483 6032489 6032491 6032503
6032531 6032539 6032567 6032581 6032597 6032639 6032641 6032651 6032723 6032729
6032743 6032749 6032777 6032791 6032797 6032801 6032821 6032833 6032869 6032891
6032951 6032959 6032963 6033023 6033031 6033037 6033047 6033049 6033091 6033101
6033103 6033133 6033143 6033169 6033179 6033193 6033197 6033211 6033227 6033229
6033239 6033253 6033263 6033299 6033319 6033329 6033341 6033347 6033371 6033397
6033403 6033407 6033427 6033451 6033491 6033493 6033527 6033541 6033557 6033563
6033581 6033593 6033607 6033611 6033619 6033641 6033647 6033661 6033673 6033707
6033737 6033739 6033743 6033761 6033763 6033787 6033811 6033821 6033823 6033857
6033883 6033893 6033901 6033931 6033947 6033959 6034037 6034081 6034109 6034121
6034123 6034139 6034141 6034159 6034177 6034207 6034213 6034241 6034247 6034393
6034397 6034403 6034411 6034423 6034459 6034481 6034493 6034499 6034529 6034537
6034549 6034583 6034591 6034601 6034607 6034621 6034657 6034687 6034703 6034727
6034741 6034751 6034771 6034781 6034849 6034867 6034883 6034937 6034939 6034957
6034967 6034969 6034979 6034997 6035021 6035023 6035069 6035087 6035089 6035101
6035137 6035143 6035147 6035189 6035191 6035201 6035207 6035209 6035251 6035291
6035299 6035311 6035321 6035327 6035347 6035353 6035377 6035417 6035423 6035429
6035431 6035461 6035473 6035501 6035531 6035539 6035573 6035581 6035611 6035633
6035647 6035707 6035719 6035723 6035737 6035747 6035761 6035779 6035789 6035801
6035803 6035831 6035839 6035849 6035899 6035933 6035951 6035957 6035971 6035987
6035989 6035993 6035999 6036001 6036013 6036067 6036073 6036101 6036103 6036127
6036187 6036197 6036203 6036221 6036269 6036271 6036293 6036301 6036313 6036323
6036337 6036361 6036367 6036397 6036409 6036421 6036427 6036487 6036497 6036551
6036559 6036571 6036577 6036607 6036617 6036637 6036659 6036677 6036697 6036713
6036721 6036731 6036739 6036757 6036769 6036803 6036817 6036857 6036869 6036907
6036923 6036929 6036949 6036969 6036967 6036973 6036979 6036983 6036991 6036997
6037001 6037007 6037039 6037043 6037051 6037061 6037069 6037093 6037111 6037147
6037153 6037189 6037211 6037223 6037237 6037271 6037277 6037301 6037309 6037313
6037379 6037387 6037391 6037393 6037399 6037403 6037429 6037441 6037463 6037487
6037489 6037511 6037513 6037531 6037541 6037543 6037547 6037553 6037583 6037589
6037613 6037621 6037631 6037639 6037643 6037657 6037699 6037703 6037709 6037711
6037723 6037739 6037741 6037747 6037781 6037793 6037817 6037819 6037831 6037861
6037909 6037939 6037943 6037957 6037981 6037987 6038023 6038033 6038041 6038047
6038051 6038057 6038069 6038089 6038093 6038099 6038113 6038129 6038161
6038173 6038191 6038203 6038233 6038239 6038287 6038297 6038303 6038311 6038317
6038321 6038327 6038359 6038393 6038407 6038429 6038441 6038471 6038477 6038503
6038507 6038531 6038537 6038551 6038563 6038597 6038611 6038623 6038629 6038653
6038657 6038671 6038677 6038717 6038731 6038783 6038803 6038819 6038843 6038863
6038887 6038897 6038917 6038951 6039001 6039037 6039067 6039073
6039083 6039091 6039101 6039107 6039109 6039139 6039149 6039151 6039157 6039193
6039197 6039211 6039223 6039227 6039239 6039247 6039263 6039329 6039343 6039347
6039349 6039367 6039373 6039391 6039413 6039421 6039443 6039463 6039487 6039491
6039559 6039563 6039577 6039589 6039601 6039659 6039667 6039673 6039679 6039697
6039727 6039749 6039763 6039767 6039773 6039779 6039797 6039809 6039821 6039841
6039851 6039863 6039871 6039877 6039881 6039883 6039893 6039907 6039911 6039937
```

```
6039941  6039959  6039977  6040019  6040061  6040063  6040109  6040141  6040147  6040171
6040187  6040211  6040231  6040241  6040249  6040267  6040277  6040289  6040301  6040313
6040327  6040337  6040343  6040351  6040367  6040369  6040373  6040379  6040387  6040409
6040417  6040429  6040451  6040477  6040493  6040547  6040549  6040561  6040579  6040607
6040621  6040631  6040633  6040637  6040649  6040663  6040667  6040673  6040679  6040681
6040687  6040693  6040703  6040711  6040721  6040733  6040739  6040747  6040759  6040777
6040799  6040807  6040813  6040819  6040829  6040843  6040887  6040901  6040949  6040963
6040997  6041003  6041023  6041033  6041041  6041089  6041129  6041153  6041159  6041197
6041207  6041267  6041281  6041291  6041303  6041317  6041351  6041353  6041363  6041369
6041377  6041381  6041383  6041401  6041419  6041437  6041447  6041489  6041491  6041507
6041509  6041513  6041531  6041549  6041551  6041569  6041573  6041593  6041597  6041641
6041669  6041689  6041701  6041713  6041723  6041729  6041731  6041747  6041759  6041809
6041843  6041857  6041873  6041879  6041881  6041891  6041909  6041911  6041927  6041929
6041933  6041951  6041977  6041983  6042007  6042041  6042061  6042079  6042103  6042107
6042109  6042139  6042143  6042149  6042163  6042173  6042181  6042203  6042217  6042221
6042229  6042263  6042269  6042277  6042287  6042319  6042331  6042349  6042373  6042383
6042401  6042409  6042451  6042479  6042481  6042493  6042499  6042511  6042521  6042523
6042557  6042559  6042563  6042571  6042577  6042601  6042607  6042671  6042677  6042683
6042697  6042719  6042727  6042731  6042733  6042749  6042763  6042781  6042791  6042793
6042811  6042821  6042823  6042847  6042853  6042887  6042913  6042917  6042929  6042937
6042943  6042983  6042989  6043001  6043019  6043073  6043097  6043111  6043117  6043123
6043129  6043139  6043151  6043153  6043157  6043187  6043217  6043231  6043243  6043259
6043267  6043351  6043361  6043363  6043379  6043393  6043399  6043403  6043417  6043439
6043459  6043487  6043489  6043493  6043519  6043529  6043553  6043559  6043561  6043573
6043603  6043613  6043621  6043649  6043657  6043669  6043747  6043753  6043757  6043759
6043781  6043799  6043801  6043831  6043837  6043841  6043847  6043879  6043883  6043903
6043943  6043949  6043967  6043979  6043981  6043991  6044011  6044021  6044023  6044047
6044069  6044081  6044089  6044099  6044107  6044117  6044141  6044149  6044183  6044189
6044191  6044219  6044221  6044237  6044249  6044251  6044321  6044347  6044351  6044359
6044371  6044399  6044407  6044453  6044461  6044477  6044497  6044513  6044531  6044569
6044573  6044581  6044627  6044629  6044663  6044669  6044677  6044683  6044713  6044729
6044737  6044747  6044767  6044771  6044777  6044827  6044849  6044867  6044883  6044891
6044893  6044903  6044923  6044957  6044981  6044989  6044993  6045019  6045037  6045041
6045043  6045049  6045071  6045077  6045089  6045101  6045103  6045107  6045133  6045167
6045191  6045223  6045227  6045269  6045301  6045313  6045323  6045329  6045337  6045373
6045397  6045407  6045419  6045443  6045461  6045463  6045493  6045497  6045509  6045517
6045521  6045547  6045569  6045577  6045583  6045593  6045617  6045623  6045631  6045661
6045679  6045701  6045709  6045731  6045749  6045769  6045779  6045797  6045799  6045811
6045841  6045847  6045881  6045883  6045887  6045917  6045937  6045953  6045959  6045989
6046003  6046021  6046031  6046049  6046063  6046069  6046087  6046093  6046109  6046189
6046193  6046211  6046213  6046219  6046223  6046231  6046253  6046267  6046279  6046283
6046331  6046349  6046363  6046387  6046461  6046477  6046483  6046489  6046511  6046561
6046591  6046603  6046609  6046613  6046619  6046657  6046669  6046697  6046709  6046727
6046751  6046753  6046759  6046771  6046783  6046793  6046801  6046813  6046837  6046853
6046871  6046889  6046913  6046919  6046933  6046987  6047003  6047009  6047023  6047033
6047071  6047089  6047099  6047117  6047143  6047147  6047177  6047191  6047207  6047221
6047231  6047267  6047287  6047299  6047303  6047311  6047329  6047347  6047351  6047369
6047423  6047497  6047513  6047519  6047521  6047543  6047549  6047557  6047579  6047599
6047603  6047609  6047611  6047651  6047653  6047663  6047669  6047683  6047699  6047707
6047729  6047731  6047737  6047771  6047773  6047791  6047837  6047843  6047857  6047891
6047897  6047929  6047933  6047941  6047957  6047959  6047969  6047999  6048013  6048067
6048071  6048109  6048113  6048167  6048181  6048187  6048191  6048199  6048221  6048233
6048247  6048257  6048271  6048281  6048299  6048313  6048407  6048409  6048431  6048439
6048457  6048467  6048473  6048487  6048499  6048521  6048541  6048547  6048569  6048611
6048613  6048619  6048641  6048659  6048661  6048667  6048671  6048673  6048683  6048697
6048709  6048727  6048747  6048769  6048773  6048829  6048841  6048899  6048901  6048919
6048949  6048967  6048971  6048979  6048989  6048997  6049007  6049013  6049033  6049037
6049067  6049073  6049079  6049091  6049097  6049133  6049151  6049171  6049177  6049223
6049237  6049243  6049259  6049319  6049327  6049333  6049343  6049357  6049409  6049411
6049423  6049441  6049451  6049457  6049481  6049489  6049507  6049517  6049531  6049567
6049573  6049607  6049613  6049633  6049639  6049643  6049651  6049679  6049709  6049717
6049721  6049727  6049753  6049763  6049781  6049811  6049817  6049819  6049831  6049843
6049871  6049877  6049889  6049891  6049913  6049931  6049933  6049963  6049993  6049997
6050017  6050039  6050047  6050059  6050063  6050069  6050087  6050089  6050137  6050141
6050159  6050171  6050201  6050207  6050221  6050237  6050269  6050293  6050327  6050333
6050339  6050347  6050353  6050371  6050377  6050381  6050389  6050393  6050413  6050431
6050441  6050477  6050489  6050491  6050501  6050503  6050507  6050543  6050563  6050567
6050581  6050591  6050599  6050609  6050621  6050641  6050669  6050687  6050713  6050717
6050719  6050731  6050747  6050749  6050753  6050761  6050767  6050791  6050801  6050839
6050881  6050893  6050899  6050927  6050953  6050959  6050969  6050977  6051007  6051013
6051029  6051041  6051061  6051077  6051079  6051103  6051113  6051119  6051123  6051131
6051161  6051181  6051187  6051197  6051209  6051211  6051223  6051233  6051247  6051257
6051271  6051289  6051299  6051301  6051307  6051317  6051319  6051341  6051349  6051361
6051379  6051403  6051407  6051413  6051421  6051457  6051497  6051499  6051503  6051511
6051523  6051527  6051533  6051581  6051583  6051587  6051601  6051607  6051611  6051623
6051629  6051631  6051649  6051653  6051667  6051679  6051739  6051743  6051761  6051763
6051769  6051781  6051791  6051797  6051803  6051821  6051869  6051883  6051917  6051959
6051961  6051977  6052003  6052031  6052061  6052073  6052087  6052091  6052103  6052117
6052139  6052147  6052157  6052159  6052171  6052181  6052261  6052273  6052283  6052301
6052303  6052313  6052327  6052337  6052339  6052351  6052369  6052373  6052399  6052421
6052429  6052433  6052463  6052483  6052489  6052499  6052511  6052517  6052531  6052567
6052573  6052577  6052591  6052597  6052601  6052639  6052643  6052667  6052681  6052687
6052691  6052729  6052763  6052771  6052807  6052819  6052831  6052853  6052859  6052861
6052873  6052903  6052927  6052951  6052973  6053011  6053027  6053041  6053051  6053053
6053081  6053093  6053101  6053111  6053129  6053143  6053147  6053167  6053227  6053231
6053251  6053263  6053269  6053279  6053287  6053291  6053303  6053317  6053323  6053329
6053353  6053357  6053407  6053447  6053461  6053477  6053483  6053491  6053519  6053521
6053543  6053549  6053561  6053563  6053599  6053603  6053617  6053627  6053633  6053639
6053687  6053693  6053699  6053737  6053743  6053753  6053759  6053777  6053783  6053797
```

```
6053809 6053821 6053843 6053881 6053891 6053909 6053911 6053923 6053933 6053941
6053947 6053981 6053987 6054001 6054017 6054029 6054071 6054079 6054089 6054107
6054119 6054133 6054157 6054197 6054203 6054229 6054247 6054263 6054277 6054281
6054283 6054287 6054289 6054299 6054319 6054341 6054353 6054361 6054379 6054437
6054457 6054463 6054479 6054487 6054491 6054527 6054539 6054551 6054553 6054557
6054563 6054571 6054583 6054599 6054613 6054617 6054619 6054637 6054661 6054679
6054683 6054691 6054709 6054721 6054733 6054739 6054751 6054779 6054817 6054821
6054833 6054877 6054899 6054929 6054931 6054947 6054967 6055001 6055037 6055079
6055081 6055097 6055103 6055109 6055139 6055163 6055169 6055193 6055201 6055207
6055219 6055223 6055297 6055307 6055321 6055327 6055337 6055363 6055369 6055373
6055381 6055397 6055453 6055477 6055493 6055507 6055513 6055523 6055541 6055579
6055591 6055603 6055619 6055627 6055631 6055639 6055667 6055669 6055681 6055697
6055703 6055711 6055729 6055747 6055759 6055771 6055781 6055787 6055789 6055793
6055799 6055801 6055843 6055849 6055853 6055871 6055873 6055883 6055891 6055909
6055913 6055919 6055949 6055957 6055967 6055979 6055993 6056023 6056027 6056033
6056053 6056059 6056111 6056119 6056159 6056177 6056179 6056201 6056203 6056207
6056209 6056213 6056241 6056243 6056251 6056287 6056293 6056311 6056317 6056329
6056353 6056357 6056381 6056387 6056399 6056411 6056431 6056443 6056473 6056543
6056549 6056569 6056581 6056639 6056651 6056653 6056657 6056663 6056669 6056671
6056707 6056711 6056723 6056731 6056747 6056753 6056767 6056773 6056833 6056837
6056857 6056887 6056891 6056899 6056929 6056933 6056951 6056957 6056959
6056989 6056993 6057013 6057017 6057019 6057061 6057097 6057113 6057133 6057137
6057157 6057169 6057173 6057179 6057187 6057193 6057197 6057199 6057209 6057221
6057241 6057251 6057263 6057277 6057319 6057329 6057343 6057379 6057391 6057419
6057427 6057437 6057449 6057451 6057461 6057473 6057497 6057509 6057511 6057521
6057551 6057563 6057581 6057587 6057619 6057643 6057659 6057683 6057697 6057721
6057731 6057743 6057749 6057757 6057787 6057841 6057859 6057871 6057917 6057929
6057937 6057977 6057991 6058007 6058033 6058049 6058057 6058097 6058099 6058109
6058123 6058127 6058147 6058163 6058183 6058189 6058193 6058211 6058219 6058243
6058289 6058301 6058331 6058333 6058369 6058373 6058379 6058421 6058439 6058457
6058469 6058513 6058519 6058531 6058541 6058543 6058553 6058583 6058597 6058603
6058607 6058621 6058631 6058649 6058667 6058669 6058673 6058691 6058697 6058727
6058763 6058799 6058807 6058813 6058823 6058831 6058837 6058841 6058847 6058879
6058901 6058903 6058907 6058931 6058933 6058937 6058957 6058961 6058963 6058989
6058993 6059003 6059017 6059023 6059029 6059033 6059041 6059047 6059059 6059071
6059107 6059117 6059147 6059153 6059171 6059197 6059237 6059239 6059243 6059269
6059321 6059323 6059341 6059369 6059377 6059393 6059401 6059407 6059467 6059483
6059489 6059491 6059503 6059507 6059509 6059519 6059549 6059563 6059587 6059611
6059623 6059639 6059653 6059693 6059707 6059719 6059723 6059737 6059761
6059771 6059773 6059777 6059789 6059821 6059839 6059863 6059887 6059891 6059903
6059909 6059941 6059953 6059957 6059981 6060013 6060037 6060049 6060053
6060071 6060091 6060113 6060137 6060149 6060151 6060181 6060203 6060233 6060281
6060287 6060319 6060337 6060359 6060361 6060367 6060371 6060401 6060433 6060437
6060443 6060473 6060479 6060491 6060511 6060521 6060547 6060581 6060583
6060599 6060641 6060667 6060689 6060737 6060749 6060751 6060757 6060781 6060809
6060853 6060863 6060869 6060911 6060949 6060953 6060961 6060991 6061001 6061031
6061039 6061043 6061067 6061091 6061123 6061141 6061157 6061169 6061183 6061189
6061201 6061217 6061243 6061267 6061271 6061283 6061301 6061309 6061327 6061331
6061339 6061343 6061369 6061379 6061403 6061411 6061421 6061427 6061439 6061441
6061459 6061463 6061487 6061499 6061507 6061511 6061519 6061529 6061541 6061553
6061579 6061597 6061601 6061661 6061669 6061687 6061697 6061711 6061723
6061729 6061751 6061777 6061813 6061829 6061849 6061883 6061897 6061921 6061967
6061987 6062003 6062029 6062039 6062053 6062099 6062101 6062129 6062153 6062213
6062249 6062257 6062263 6062279 6062291 6062321 6062327 6062333 6062341 6062347
6062359 6062393 6062417 6062423 6062429 6062443 6062449 6062461 6062467 6062491
6062503 6062519 6062521 6062523 6062543 6062579 6062603 6062621 6062627 6062681
6062717 6062741 6062743 6062747 6062753 6062759 6062773 6062803 6062807 6062809
6062831 6062839 6062867 6062873 6062891 6062911 6062923 6062971 6062977 6062981
6062983 6062989 6062993 6063089 6063091 6063097 6063133 6063143 6063149 6063163
6063181 6063193 6063199 6063221 6063251 6063263 6063287 6063289 6063293 6063313
6063347 6063377 6063389 6063391 6063419 6063427 6063439 6063457 6063469 6063479
6063493 6063503 6063511 6063539 6063553 6063587 6063601 6063619 6063647 6063649
6063653 6063667 6063683 6063689 6063703 6063709 6063721 6063751 6063769 6063773
6063791 6063839 6063877 6063887 6063899 6063901 6063913 6063931 6063943 6063947
6063979 6064001 6064007 6064013 6064027 6064033 6064049 6064061 6064099 6064117
6064129 6064139 6064159 6064199 6064213 6064217 6064231 6064241 6064259 6064273
6064307 6064309 6064319 6064339 6064349 6064369 6064381 6064397 6064417 6064423
6064447 6064453 6064459 6064463 6064469 6064483 6064499 6064511 6064523 6064543
6064547 6064577 6064627 6064637 6064649 6064657 6064661 6064673 6064693 6064703
6064717 6064771 6064783 6064789 6064813 6064829 6064841 6064873 6064879 6064897
6064921 6064951 6064957 6064963 6064967 6064979 6064991 6064997 6065029 6065051
6065053 6065069 6065071 6065093 6065117 6065149 6065153 6065159 6065167 6065177
6065183 6065197 6065203 6065219 6065221 6065233 6065239 6065249 6065281 6065287
6065329 6065333 6065341 6065357 6065359 6065363 6065369 6065387 6065407 6065461
6065467 6065483 6065489 6065513 6065561 6065573 6065593 6065597 6065603 6065621
6065639 6065687 6065707 6065713 6065747 6065771 6065777 6065791 6065809 6065819
6065831 6065861 6065869 6065887 6065929 6065963 6065989 6065993 6066007 6066029
6066031 6066037 6066041 6066061 6066077 6066079 6066083 6066097 6066101 6066119
6066157 6066163 6066197 6066199 6066239 6066241 6066257 6066259 6066271 6066293
6066317 6066341 6066383 6066407 6066413 6066443 6066449 6066469 6066517 6066521
6066523 6066527 6066551 6066581 6066583 6066587 6066589 6066611 6066617 6066623
6066629 6066659 6066661 6066673 6066679 6066707 6066743 6066761 6066769 6066787
6066799 6066817 6066821 6066839 6066859 6066869 6066881 6066889 6066941 6066959
6066967 6066971 6066989 6066997 6067013 6067037 6067067 6067073 6067081 6067097
6067109 6067111 6067123 6067141 6067153 6067157 6067169 6067181 6067199 6067207
6067231 6067261 6067273 6067333 6067357 6067361 6067363 6067367 6067379 6067381
6067393 6067417 6067447 6067471 6067499 6067511 6067543 6067547 6067577 6067597
6067613 6067627 6067643 6067651 6067681 6067693 6067729 6067739
6067799 6067801 6067807 6067823 6067829 6067843 6067849 6067881 6067903 6067907
```

```
6067913 6067927 6067939 6067949 6067969 6067993 6068003 6068009 6068089 6068093
6068119 6068137 6068173 6068189 6068197 6068233 6068243 6068267 6068273 6068317
6068351 6068393 6068399 6068411 6068431 6068437 6068443 6068459 6068471 6068477
6068479 6068483 6068497 6068501 6068519 6068537 6068549 6068551 6068561 6068567
6068597 6068599 6068603 6068617 6068651 6068669 6068693 6068717 6068723 6068747
6068753 6068819 6068827 6068833 6068857 6068873 6068893 6068897 6068899 6068921
6068957 6068971 6069023 6069029 6069047 6069059 6069067 6069071 6069097 6069101
6069121 6069127 6069137 6069139 6069163 6069197 6069199 6069241 6069247 6069253
6069257 6069269 6069311 6069331 6069367 6069403 6069419 6069433 6069449 6069449
6069461 6069487 6069509 6069529 6069551 6069559 6069563 6069601 6069611 6069619
6069641 6069643 6069647 6069659 6069673 6069689 6069691 6069709 6069727 6069737
6069757 6069761 6069781 6069793 6069803 6069823 6069827 6069839 6069841 6069851
6069853 6069857 6069863 6069871 6069913 6069941 6069971 6069977 6069983 6069989
6069997 6070007 6070013 6070027 6070073 6070087 6070093 6070117 6070121 6070151
6070159 6070187 6070189 6070199 6070223 6070231 6070237 6070243 6070271 6070279
6070289 6070297 6070307 6070313 6070373 6070387 6070417 6070433 6070447 6070453
6070457 6070469 6070487 6070489 6070499 6070507 6070529 6070543 6070573 6070577
6070579 6070591 6070613 6070621 6070651 6070679 6070693 6070711 6070723 6070741
6070759 6070763 6070769 6070777 6070789 6070811 6070837 6070879 6070901 6070907
6070927 6070969 6070979 6071003 6071017 6071027 6071029 6071047 6071059 6071069
6071077 6071081 6071099 6071101 6071113 6071137 6071161 6071173 6071189 6071207
6071231 6071243 6071249 6071251 6071267 6071297 6071311 6071323 6071369 6071371
6071383 6071399 6071407 6071419 6071437 6071447 6071449 6071453 6071479 6071503
6071509 6071519 6071531 6071537 6071543 6071551 6071561 6071579 6071581 6071591
6071617 6071623 6071641 6071647 6071651 6071657 6071671 6071677 6071683 6071687
6071693 6071711 6071717 6071761 6071777 6071783 6071797 6071803 6071837 6071851
6071893 6071911 6071917 6071927 6071951 6071969 6071971 6071983 6071993 6071999
6072029 6072037 6072041 6072047 6072089 6072091 6072097 6072109 6072119 6072149
6072151 6072167 6072169 6072173 6072211 6072233 6072293 6072301 6072307 6072317
6072323 6072337 6072347 6072361 6072371 6072377 6072379 6072389 6072421 6072427
6072431 6072461 6072467 6072481 6072487 6072509 6072511 6072527 6072557 6072569
6072601 6072613 6072617 6072623 6072641 6072643 6072673 6072707 6072721 6072739
6072743 6072817 6072821 6072841 6072863 6072887 6072889 6072901 6072907 6072923
6072953 6072973 6073003 6073021 6073031 6073033 6073037 6073051 6073057 6073061
6073079 6073121 6073147 6073157 6073159 6073169 6073181 6073183 6073201 6073211
6073237 6073247 6073259 6073273 6073307 6073321 6073339 6073373 6073399 6073421
6073423 6073451 6073493 6073523 6073531 6073537 6073547 6073549 6073567 6073577
6073583 6073603 6073619 6073643 6073651 6073657 6073663 6073667 6073693 6073721
6073723 6073733 6073741 6073813 6073829 6073843 6073867 6073871 6073877 6073889
6073891 6073927 6073933 6073943 6073961 6073967 6073999 6074011 6074041 6074063
6074087 6074119 6074149 6074177 6074209 6074239 6074251 6074261 6074279
6074317 6074329 6074347 6074353 6074359 6074363 6074381 6074399 6074417 6074429
6074447 6074449 6074473 6074477 6074483 6074501 6074503 6074513 6074527 6074531
6074533 6074539 6074561 6074569 6074573 6074587 6074591 6074603 6074611 6074617
6074633 6074647 6074669 6074693 6074707 6074713 6074741 6074753 6074779 6074821
6074857 6074909 6074917 6074923 6074941 6074963 6074969 6074983 6074989 6075029
6075031 6075071 6075077 6075089 6075107 6075109 6075119 6075131 6075187 6075191
6075211 6075217 6075221 6075253 6075263 6075281 6075301 6075313 6075317 6075331
6075343 6075347 6075367 6075371 6075373 6075379 6075389 6075397 6075403 6075431
6075457 6075467 6075469 6075479 6075521 6075523 6075527 6075533 6075557 6075569
6075577 6075581 6075583 6075593 6075607 6075617 6075631 6075637 6075673 6075679
6075689 6075697 6075701 6075709 6075739 6075757 6075767 6075793 6075799 6075803
6075809 6075847 6075893 6075929 6075931 6075947 6075959 6076001 6076003 6076013
6076033 6076043 6076069 6076099 6076121 6076139 6076141 6076153 6076183 6076193
6076223 6076229 6076237 6076247 6076249 6076267 6076277 6076303 6076307 6076309
6076321 6076331 6076337 6076339 6076363 6076379 6076381 6076417 6076453 6076493
6076501 6076519 6076537 6076541 6076571 6076579 6076591 6076597 6076607 6076613
6076619 6076627 6076643 6076649 6076661 6076673 6076687 6076703 6076709 6076753
6076781 6076783 6076787 6076799 6076813 6076817 6076841 6076849 6076883 6076891
6076907 6076919 6076933 6076937 6076943 6076949 6076981 6077039 6077051 6077063
6077081 6077117 6077119 6077167 6077173 6077179 6077189 6077191 6077237 6077249
6077257 6077293 6077299 6077311 6077329 6077371 6077411 6077441 6077453 6077459
6077507 6077527 6077557 6077567 6077573 6077579 6077611 6077629 6077639 6077641
6077677 6077683 6077693 6077713 6077719 6077723 6077737 6077741 6077759 6077809
6077821 6077833 6077837 6077861 6077867 6077903 6077909 6077947 6077971 6077983
6077999 6078011 6078029 6078047 6078071 6078073 6078091 6078103 6078143 6078151
6078169 6078217 6078221 6078227 6078251 6078253 6078283 6078287 6078301 6078329
6078337 6078353 6078361 6078377 6078389 6078407 6078409 6078419 6078421
6078427 6078439 6078451 6078473 6078481 6078493 6078521 6078529 6078539 6078547
6078551 6078559 6078577 6078581 6078587 6078599 6078617 6078629 6078641 6078643
6078649 6078659 6078679 6078691 6078713 6078731 6078733 6078749 6078763 6078791
6078797 6078823 6078851 6078859 6078869 6078881 6078889 6078899 6078901 6078937
6078983 6079037 6079043 6079079 6079097 6079127 6079133 6079141 6079147 6079159
6079181 6079201 6079219 6079237 6079243 6079267 6079273 6079279 6079303 6079313
6079327 6079351 6079361 6079391 6079411 6079427 6079453 6079459 6079481 6079483
6079499 6079519 6079547 6079553 6079571 6079583 6079607 6079631 6079637 6079651
6079657 6079663 6079673 6079699 6079709 6079747 6079757 6079783 6079793 6079811
6079819 6079823 6079861 6079883 6079903 6079907 6079933 6079939 6079949 6079961
6079963 6079979 6079991 6079993 6080003 6080017 6080021 6080023 6080051 6080059
6080069 6080131 6080141 6080147 6080153 6080161 6080201 6080213 6080261 6080267
6080279 6080281 6080287 6080311 6080353 6080357 6080381 6080413 6080429 6080443
6080461 6080507 6080519 6080537 6080549 6080561 6080567 6080573
6080597 6080609 6080621 6080623 6080677 6080689 6080693 6080699 6080707 6080731
6080761 6080771 6080797 6080831 6080857 6080873 6080881 6080897 6080909 6080911
6080927 6080933 6080939 6080943 6080957 6080959 6081013 6081043 6081059 6081073
6081091 6081113 6081139 6081143 6081181 6081199 6081203 6081211 6081217 6081227
6081233 6081247 6081259 6081263 6081289 6081319 6081323 6081331 6081337
6081343 6081347 6081353 6081371 6081401 6081403 6081409 6081451 6081457 6081479
6081497 6081521 6081583 6081599 6081601 6081613 6081617 6081629 6081671 6081679
```

```
6081707  6081731  6081737  6081739  6081743  6081749  6081763  6081787  6081799  6081809
6081811  6081853  6081857  6081871  6081893  6081961  6081989  6082001  6082003  6082007
6082057  6082061  6082079  6082081  6082099  6082103  6082123  6082151  6082177  6082183
6082211  6082217  6082247  6082259  6082267  6082273  6082283  6082301  6082303  6082313
6082339  6082343  6082367  6082381  6082397  6082399  6082409  6082421  6082429  6082441
6082457  6082471  6082477  6082561  6082567  6082589  6082597  6082607  6082613  6082619
6082631  6082633  6082639  6082667  6082669  6082691  6082711  6082751  6082819  6082877
6082891  6082939  6082943  6082961  6083009  6083023  6083041  6083053  6083071  6083083
6083087  6083089  6083113  6083123  6083141  6083171  6083177  6083191  6083213  6083219
6083221  6083227  6083251  6083269  6083299  6083303  6083321  6083333  6083377  6083381
6083383  6083387  6083411  6083437  6083443  6083479  6083491  6083507  6083513  6083527
6083531  6083543  6083551  6083573  6083579  6083599  6083611  6083641  6083647  6083659
6083669  6083677  6083687  6083689  6083723  6083729  6083761  6083767  6083789  6083797
6083809  6083813  6083837  6083839  6083849  6083897  6083899  6083911  6083921  6083927
6083963  6083969  6083993  6083999  6084007  6084017  6084019  6084037  6084073  6084097
6084147  6084157  6084163  6084173  6084179  6084191  6084193  6084209  6084233  6084269
6084289  6084293  6084319  6084361  6084367  6084383  6084409  6084437  6084451  6084467
6084473  6084497  6084499  6084509  6084571  6084599  6084601  6084619  6084641  6084643
6084665  6084671  6084679  6084703  6084781  6084787  6084829  6084839  6084853  6084889
6084893  6084899  6084901  6084919  6084941  6084943  6084961  6084977  6085103  6085109
6085111  6085139  6085151  6085153  6085159  6085171  6085181  6085193  6085199  6085213
6085223  6085229  6085243  6085283  6085327  6085333  6085357  6085397  6085433  6085441
6085561  6085571  6085577  6085591  6085601  6085627  6085631  6085633  6085663  6085669
6085691  6085697  6085699  6085721  6085741  6085759  6085769  6085789  6085799  6085819
6085843  6085861  6085897  6085901  6085927  6085943  6085987  6085991  6086009  6086011
6086029  6086057  6086063  6086117  6086123  6086131  6086147  6086173  6086183  6086189
6086209  6086219  6086231  6086243  6086273  6086279  6086281  6086287  6086299  6086309
6086321  6086351  6086371  6086383  6086387  6086401  6086413  6086417  6086429  6086449
6086461  6086471  6086497  6086503  6086539  6086543  6086567  6086569  6086599  6086623
6086657  6086677  6086701  6086711  6086719  6086747  6086753  6086767  6086777  6086807
6086809  6086827  6086831  6086837  6086851  6086869  6086879  6086893  6086903  6086921
6086929  6086933  6086939  6086947  6086953  6086963  6086989  6086999  6087023  6087031
6087073  6087077  6087079  6087083  6087101  6087113  6087121  6087127  6087161  6087167
6087181  6087217  6087223  6087233  6087247  6087259  6087269  6087283  6087287  6087293
6087307  6087313  6087349  6087383  6087401  6087407  6087409  6087427  6087437  6087449
6087457  6087463  6087493  6087509  6087533  6087539  6087583  6087589  6087643  6087659
6087667  6087671  6087673  6087691  6087707  6087787  6087791  6087793  6087827  6087833
6087853  6087857  6087859  6087871  6087881  6087889  6087911  6087929  6087931  6087947
6087953  6087959  6087971  6087973  6088001  6088009  6088013  6088039  6088063  6088067
6088079  6088087  6088097  6088099  6088109  6088111  6088129  6088139  6088141  6088153
6088157  6088171  6088207  6088211  6088219  6088237  6088249  6088259  6088301  6088337
6088343  6088351  6088361  6088373  6088393  6088403  6088421  6088429  6088441  6088457
6088477  6088483  6088513  6088517  6088529  6088543  6088547  6088549  6088559  6088561
6088597  6088613  6088627  6088633  6088661  6088673  6088681  6088699  6088723  6088727
6088729  6088739  6088751  6088763  6088769  6088777  6088781  6088793  6088801  6088807
6088861  6088867  6088877  6088879  6088889  6088909  6088933  6088937  6088947  6088949
6088967  6089023  6089047  6089087  6089093  6089107  6089131  6089137  6089147  6089207
6089219  6089221  6089233  6089243  6089261  6089267  6089287  6089309  6089341  6089351
6089371  6089381  6089387  6089389  6089431  6089437  6089453  6089459  6089471  6089483
6089491  6089509  6089521  6089533  6089537  6089539  6089543  6089581  6089591  6089597
6089609  6089651  6089659  6089693  6089731  6089737  6089739  6089761  6089767  6089807
6089827  6089833  6089849  6089851  6089869  6089903  6089911  6089929  6089953  6089957
6089983  6089999  6090001  6090011  6090023  6090053  6090067  6090103  6090109  6090121
6090137  6090143  6090173  6090209  6090223  6090251  6090257  6090269  6090277  6090289
6090299  6090349  6090373  6090379  6090397  6090421  6090433  6090449  6090481  6090491
6090499  6090503  6090517  6090523  6090527  6090529  6090541  6090559  6090569  6090571
6090577  6090599  6090611  6090613  6090647  6090661  6090671  6090677  6090691  6090701
6090709  6090737  6090739  6090751  6090757  6090781  6090791  6090797  6090803  6090809
6090823  6090839  6090859  6090863  6090869  6090881  6090923  6090941  6090949  6091027
6091031  6091103  6091109  6091207  6091213  6091223  6091243  6091259  6091271  6091279
6091291  6091307  6091313  6091331  6091357  6091367  6091387  6091391  6091409  6091433
6091447  6091451  6091483  6091487  6091489  6091511  6091513  6091517  6091541  6091597
6091607  6091621  6091633  6091637  6091639  6091649  6091663  6091669  6091699  6091703
6091727  6091733  6091741  6091747  6091751  6091753  6091807  6091819  6091823  6091829
6091843  6091847  6091861  6091867  6091879  6091931  6091937  6091957  6091973  6091991
6091997  6092011  6092029  6092041  6092057  6092077  6092081  6092083  6092101  6092113
6092123  6092143  6092147  6092159  6092173  6092183  6092189  6092227  6092237  6092249
6092269  6092287  6092299  6092311  6092329  6092353  6092357  6092363  6092371  6092441
6092467  6092479  6092491  6092503  6092533  6092557  6092561  6092573  6092591  6092599
6092609  6092629  6092633  6092659  6092663  6092683  6092689  6092693  6092701  6092729
6092731  6092747  6092761  6092767  6092791  6092797  6092809  6092831  6092837  6092843
6092897  6092903  6092909  6092917  6092927  6092951  6092959  6092963  6092993  6093011
6093041  6093071  6093077  6093083  6093097  6093121  6093151  6093163  6093173  6093179
6093187  6093193  6093211  6093223  6093247  6093287  6093313  6093337  6093371  6093389
6093403  6093467  6093481  6093491  6093499  6093511  6093553  6093561  6093577  6093601
6093629  6093631  6093671  6093709  6093713  6093719  6093721  6093733  6093739  6093743
6093749  6093761  6093767  6093779  6093809  6093811  6093817  6093853  6093869  6093881
6093911  6093931  6093947  6093991  6094009  6094013  6094019  6094021  6094027  6094043
6094069  6094087  6094091  6094111  6094141  6094157  6094181  6094183  6094189  6094213
6094217  6094223  6094229  6094247  6094267  6094301  6094303  6094337  6094343  6094357
6094373  6094391  6094393  6094397  6094411  6094481  6094489  6094493  6094567  6094579
6094591  6094601  6094633  6094651  6094657  6094729  6094747  6094757  6094807  6094849
6094861  6094867  6094873  6094883  6094889  6094903  6094909  6094919  6094927  6094943
6094969  6094981  6095021  6095039  6095051  6095071  6095077  6095083  6095093  6095119
6095147  6095149  6095153  6095203  6095209  6095227  6095233  6095239  6095261  6095263
6095291  6095317  6095321  6095329  6095339  6095359  6095363  6095381  6095393  6095407
6095413  6095431  6095449  6095473  6095489  6095497  6095543  6095549  6095581  6095587
6095591  6095611  6095627  6095639  6095647  6095667  6095671  6095693  6095717  6095729
6095731  6095737  6095743  6095753  6095767  6095773  6095777  6095797  6095801  6095807
```

```
6095819 6095833 6095879 6095891 6095893 6095909 6095917 6095927 6095951 6095959
6095977 6095987 6096049 6096053 6096059 6096071 6096107 6096109 6096137 6096161
6096163 6096187 6096191 6096197 6096199 6096241 6096247 6096257 6096269 6096271
6096289 6096313 6096317 6096329 6096373 6096383 6096407 6096427 6096437 6096439
6096457 6096469 6096481 6096487 6096499 6096521 6096593 6096617 6096619 6096631
6096653 6096661 6096683 6096703 6096709 6096719 6096721 6096733 6096751 6096773
6096787 6096809 6096821 6096833 6096859 6096877 6096899 6096901 6096907 6096913
6096917 6096943 6096949 6096991 6096997 6097019 6097031 6097057 6097079 6097103
6097109 6097121 6097127 6097153 6097171 6097177 6097183 6097187 6097199 6097207
6097211 6097213 6097219 6097241 6097243 6097253 6097261 6097283 6097303 6097307
6097313 6097319 6097331 6097361 6097363 6097381 6097411 6097417 6097439 6097463
6097501 6097519 6097547 6097573 6097579 6097631 6097633 6097649 6097661 6097681
6097687 6097699 6097717 6097753 6097757 6097759 6097789 6097813 6097867 6097877
6097907 6097913 6097937 6097943 6097963 6097969 6097991 6097997 6098003 6098009
6098011 6098017 6098039 6098047 6098051 6098083 6098101 6098117 6098137 6098143
6098153 6098167 6098181 6098191 6098237 6098249 6098263 6098269 6098311 6098327
6098341 6098357 6098363 6098371 6098383 6098401 6098429 6098447 6098467 6098471
6098479 6098483 6098501 6098513 6098531 6098539 6098549 6098557 6098567 6098581
6098623 6098629 6098633 6098663 6098669 6098717 6098733 6098759 6098761 6098779
6098783 6098789 6098797 6098831 6098837 6098839 6098843 6098849 6098857 6098863
6098891 6098899 6098927 6098929 6098941 6098947 6098951 6098959 6098977 6098999
6099001 6099011 6099029 6099053 6099059 6099083 6099091 6099097 6099109 6099127
6099139 6099161 6099167 6099179 6099199 6099217 6099221 6099227 6099239 6099257
6099271 6099307 6099319 6099349 6099371 6099389 6099391 6099407 6099409 6099419
6099427 6099433 6099493 6099497 6099503 6099521 6099523 6099547 6099559 6099563
6099571 6099601 6099619 6099629 6099631 6099637 6099641 6099649 6099659 6099697
6099701 6099713 6099721 6099727 6099733 6099767 6099829 6099859 6099871 6099883
6099887 6099917 6099941 6099959 6099979 6099983 6100001 6100013 6100019 6100027
6100043 6100049 6100051 6100067 6100091 6100111 6100117 6100123 6100139 6100147
6100163 6100169 6100181 6100189 6100201 6100207 6100217 6100223 6100253 6100261
6100307 6100319 6100321 6100333 6100337 6100351 6100357 6100379 6100429 6100439
6100483 6100489 6100511 6100517 6100519 6100529 6100559 6100561 6100579 6100613
6100667 6100673 6100697 6100709 6100723 6100733 6100771 6100781 6100799 6100813
6100823 6100847 6100859 6100867 6100873 6100877 6100879 6100889 6100901 6100903
6100907 6100931 6100949 6100961 6100973 6100981 6100987 6100993 6101027 6101047
6101077 6101083 6101089 6101093 6101111 6101119 6101129 6101149 6101167 6101171
6101213 6101219 6101237 6101269 6101297 6101311 6101321 6101357 6101369 6101393
6101429 6101441 6101443 6101449 6101467 6101471 6101507 6101531 6101549 6101551
6101561 6101593 6101597 6101609 6101621 6101639 6101651 6101653 6101663 6101669
6101671 6101677 6101701 6101729 6101741 6101747 6101749 6101773 6101783 6101789
6101791 6101807 6101813 6101819 6101853 6101867 6101873 6101889 6101903 6101917
6101941 6101959 6101993 6102007 6102023 6102043 6102073 6102079 6102101 6102139
6102149 6102157 6102169 6102179 6102181 6102191 6102203 6102233 6102247 6102251
6102253 6102263 6102301 6102307 6102323 6102353 6102377 6102403 6102407 6102419
6102449 6102457 6102479 6102487 6102491 6102497 6102511 6102533 6102559 6102571
6102589 6102599 6102617 6102619 6102631 6102703 6102709 6102739 6102749 6102757
6102763 6102769 6102773 6102787 6102793 6102821 6102823 6102851 6102869 6102871
6102893 6102911 6102913 6102917 6102919 6102923 6102931 6102953 6102977 6103007
6103057 6103067 6103087 6103093 6103099 6103103 6103117 6103121 6103133 6103169
6103171 6103177 6103183 6103193 6103217 6103241 6103271 6103277 6103283 6103327
6103333 6103367 6103381 6103393 6103397 6103403 6103423 6103439 6103453 6103451
6103453 6103481 6103511 6103519 6103523 6103583 6103627 6103637 6103649 6103667
6103679 6103681 6103687 6103703 6103739 6103751 6103759 6103771 6103789 6103817
6103819 6103829 6103831 6103841 6103847 6103849 6103859 6103913 6103939 6103943
6103961 6103987 6104009 6104023 6104047 6104051 6104057 6104099 6104129 6104141
6104143 6104159 6104167 6104171 6104183 6104201 6104221 6104227 6104233 6104261
6104279 6104281 6104291 6104321 6104347 6104353 6104363 6104369 6104389 6104393
6104419 6104431 6104447 6104467 6104473 6104533 6104537 6104563 6104569 6104573
6104597 6104617 6104621 6104627 6104629 6104639 6104641 6104647 6104653 6104663
6104687 6104701 6104713 6104767 6104807 6104827 6104831 6104837 6104849 6104851
6104869 6104927 6104929 6104939 6104951 6104953 6104957 6104999 6105007 6105013
6105049 6105079 6105089 6105101 6105149 6105161 6105163 6105179 6105181 6105191
6105217 6105223 6105247 6105257 6105263 6105293 6105301 6105317 6105367 6105371
6105377 6105389 6105391 6105439 6105443 6105467 6105469 6105487 6105521 6105553
6105569 6105571 6105577 6105587 6105611 6105623 6105641 6105661 6105683 6105709
6105713 6105719 6105721 6105727 6105767 6105769 6105773 6105809 6105811 6105823
6105829 6105877 6105889 6105893 6105899 6105919 6105937 6105947 6105949 6105959
6105997 6106003 6106057 6106081 6106091 6106097 6106123 6106127 6106141 6106151
6106189 6106207 6106223 6106241 6106249 6106271 6106273 6106279 6106297 6106319
6106337 6106343 6106351 6106363 6106403 6106421 6106423 6106427 6106459 6106481
6106483 6106487 6106489 6106511 6106531 6106549 6106589 6106609 6106637 6106643
6106673 6106679 6106691 6106693 6106729 6106741 6106747 6106787 6106801 6106823
6106873 6106879 6106883 6106889 6106897 6106921 6106939 6106993 6106997 6107009
6107011 6107021 6107041 6107047 6107053 6107083 6107119 6107173 6107177 6107209
6107219 6107221 6107249 6107273 6107287 6107291 6107293 6107317 6107327 6107329
6107347 6107359 6107363 6107383 6107393 6107459 6107461 6107501 6107513 6107567
6107579 6107587 6107593 6107599 6107609 6107617 6107623 6107657 6107671 6107681
6107687 6107699 6107717 6107741 6107769 6107809 6107819 6107821 6107831 6107833
6107851 6107861 6107867 6107897 6107909 6107939 6107953 6107971 6107977 6107999
6108007 6108013 6108019 6108079 6108103 6108131 6108143 6108149 6108161
6108169 6108173 6108191 6108217 6108227 6108229 6108247 6108269 6108283 6108307
6108313 6108341 6108353 6108373 6108391 6108397 6108407 6108413 6108437 6108439
6108461 6108463 6108497 6108499 6108511 6108521 6108533 6108541 6108607 6108617
6108653 6108677 6108679 6108689 6108691 6108743 6108749 6108761 6108779 6108787
6108793 6108841 6108847 6108853 6108857 6108863 6108887 6108889 6108913 6108929
6108941 6108943 6108979 6108983 6108989 6108997 6109003 6109009 6109021 6109031
6109039 6109043 6109057 6109067 6109073 6109087 6109093 6109133 6109141 6109183
6109217 6109219 6109223 6109231 6109249 6109253 6109277 6109289 6109291
6109303 6109321 6109331 6109339 6109349 6109357 6109399 6109417 6109423 6109427
```

6109429 6109457 6109471 6109501 6109567 6109601 6109603 6109637 6109639 6109643
6109657 6109667 6109669 6109673 6109703 6109711 6109717 6109723 6109751 6109769
6109799 6109813 6109819 6109837 6109867 6109871 6109877 6109889 6109891 6109903
6109907 6109937 6109951 6109967 6109979 6109991 6109993 6109997 6110003 6110009
6110011 6110053 6110057 6110081 6110087 6110101 6110119 6110129 6110179 6110201
6110207 6110219 6110261 6110263 6110297 6110311 6110339 6110347 6110369 6110371
6110383 6110393 6110411 6110443 6110471 6110477 6110483 6110501 6110509 6110519
6110521 6110527 6110549 6110551 6110563 6110567 6110569 6110581 6110593 6110623
6110683 6110711 6110717 6110719 6110747 6110749 6110777 6110789 6110827 6110831
6110843 6110861 6110933 6110941 6110969 6110971 6110977 6110981 6110983 6111011
6111013 6111023 6111029 6111047 6111071 6111073 6111089 6111139 6111151 6111167
6111181 6111191 6111197 6111221 6111227 6111229 6111233 6111241 6111251 6111263
6111283 6111317 6111349 6111383 6111389 6111403 6111437 6111439 6111463 6111493
6111499 6111503 6111509 6111527 6111577 6111587 6111593 6111601 6111607 6111613
6111617 6111643 6111647 6111649 6111659 6111661 6111667 6111671 6111683 6111689
6111709 6111713 6111727 6111737 6111757 6111769 6111793 6111797 6111803 6111811
6111821 6111839 6111877 6111881 6111913 6111943 6111967 6111971 6111979 6111983
6112003 6112009 6112039 6112049 6112079 6112081 6112103 6112109 6112121 6112147
6112153 6112159 6112187 6112199 6112213 6112229 6112241 6112259 6112277 6112279
6112339 6112349 6112361 6112391 6112409 6112423 6112439 6112441 6112451 6112453
6112501 6112541 6112553 6112583 6112597 6112643 6112657 6112681 6112703 6112709
6112721 6112723 6112739 6112747 6112763 6112789 6112793 6112811 6112819 6112831
6112849 6112907 6112919 6112937 6112943 6112949 6112969 6112973 6112987 6113011
6113021 6113027 6113039 6113053 6113069 6113071 6113087 6113111 6113123 6113137
6113161 6113189 6113197 6113201 6113207 6113209 6113213 6113273 6113279 6113297
6113299 6113309 6113329 6113333 6113339 6113357 6113363 6113407 6113453 6113467
6113491 6113507 6113509 6113539 6113579 6113587 6113593 6113609 6113623 6113663
6113669 6113671 6113689 6113711 6113729 6113741 6113743 6113753 6113803 6113827
6113831 6113857 6113883 6113909 6113913 6113923 6113927 6113941 6113959 6113963
6113971 6113981 6114001 6114019 6114049 6114061 6114077 6114083 6114149 6114151
6114167 6114179 6114187 6114209 6114217 6114233 6114253 6114259 6114263 6114281
6114323 6114349 6114379 6114391 6114397 6114401 6114403 6114419 6114463 6114473
6114497 6114517 6114539 6114541 6114547 6114551 6114593 6114607 6114623 6114629
6114649 6114671 6114677 6114697 6114707 6114727 6114739 6114761 6114763 6114767
6114799 6114817 6114821 6114833 6114869 6114877 6114881 6114887 6114907 6114919
6114929 6114989 6115001 6115003 6115037 6115061 6115063 6115069 6115097 6115099
6115103 6115111 6115127 6115139 6115141 6115147 6115163 6115183 6115199 6115229
6115237 6115253 6115261 6115267 6115289 6115297 6115313 6115327 6115337 6115363
6115367 6115379 6115387 6115391 6115399 6115411 6115423 6115441 6115489 6115507
6115513 6115531 6115537 6115541 6115547 6115561 6115579 6115639 6115643 6115661
6115667 6115679 6115691 6115717 6115741 6115783 6115787 6115807 6115819 6115843
6115849 6115859 6115871 6115873 6115877 6115909 6115919 6115927 6115931 6115951
6115973 6115979 6116009 6116023 6116027 6116029 6116051 6116053 6116057 6116111
6116113 6116161 6116167 6116177 6116189 6116197 6116219 6116237 6116239 6116261
6116263 6116267 6116273 6116281 6116291 6116293 6116323 6116371 6116381 6116401
6116443 6116489 6116491 6116567 6116573 6116603 6116623 6116629 6116633 6116647
6116657 6116659 6116683 6116687 6116699 6116711 6116713 6116717 6116731 6116771
6116779 6116797 6116801 6116807 6116813 6116833 6116843 6116867 6116921 6116927
6116933 6116947 6116953 6116963 6116977 6116987 6116989 6117037 6117053 6117071
6117073 6117079 6117091 6117109 6117131 6117151 6117169 6117193 6117197 6117203
6117239 6117253 6117269 6117281 6117299 6117311 6117337 6117341 6117343 6117361
6117367 6117383 6117389 6117401 6117403 6117409 6117437 6117451 6117491 6117541
6117557 6117581 6117583 6117599 6117607 6117613 6117641 6117647 6117649 6117667
6117689 6117697 6117721 6117743 6117763 6117767 6117779 6117781 6117817 6117821
6117823 6117833 6117851 6117863 6117883 6117893 6117899 6117901 6117919 6117929
6117941 6117959 6117967 6117983 6118001 6118003 6118027 6118031 6118087 6118111
6118139 6118157 6118163 6118183 6118187 6118199 6118219 6118223 6118237 6118261
6118289 6118291 6118297 6118309 6118327 6118337 6118339 6118381 6118403 6118421
6118423 6118429 6118433 6118481 6118493 6118499 6118517 6118537 6118547 6118559
6118561 6118571 6118573 6118591 6118597 6118613 6118631 6118643 6118649 6118699
6118711 6118729 6118747 6118751 6118753 6118763 6118823 6118891 6118927 6118967
6118979 6118999 6119011 6119021 6119033 6119041 6119053 6119077 6119089 6119107
6119119 6119123 6119131 6119137 6119143 6119149 6119153 6119161 6119189 6119233
6119249 6119257 6119293 6119297 6119299 6119317 6119329 6119383 6119401 6119417
6119423 6119441 6119453 6119479 6119483 6119497 6119521 6119527 6119543 6119549
6119569 6119573 6119583 6119593 6119599 6119611 6119629 6119639 6119647 6119669
6119671 6119681 6119683 6119699 6119719 6119731 6119777 6119797 6119801 6119819
6119821 6119833 6119851 6119887 6119921 6119933 6119959 6119969 6119977 6120007
6120013 6120083 6120097 6120151 6120167 6120173 6120197 6120203 6120217 6120227
6120229 6120251 6120253 6120259 6120269 6120311 6120329 6120347 6120349 6120371
6120377 6120379 6120427 6120437 6120449 6120467 6120497 6120509 6120523 6120529
6120533 6120559 6120563 6120581 6120589 6120607 6120637 6120689 6120703 6120707
6120727 6120739 6120761 6120773 6120781 6120787 6120809 6120823 6120853 6120859
6120883 6120887 6120889 6120893 6120911 6120929 6120949 6120971 6120997 6121057
6121067 6121091 6121099 6121109 6121121 6121201 6121223 6121231 6121253 6121261
6121319 6121337 6121369 6121397 6121403 6121417 6121429 6121433 6121441 6121457
6121463 6121469 6121471 6121481 6121487 6121501 6121517 6121537 6121541 6121543
6121567 6121579 6121607 6121627 6121637 6121651 6121673 6121679 6121681 6121721
6121727 6121733 6121747 6121771 6121793 6121799 6121807 6121847 6121861 6121873
6121879 6121889 6121883 6121889 6121919 6121931 6121939 6121943 6121949
6121957 6122029 6122033 6122041 6122059 6122063 6122087 6122089 6122101 6122107
6122167 6122177 6122201 6122213 6122251 6122273 6122287 6122293 6122309 6122323
6122327 6122339 6122341 6122359 6122381 6122411 6122419 6122447 6122449 6122461
6122477 6122483 6122513 6122521 6122537 6122569 6122581 6122609 6122621 6122651
6122659 6122663 6122671 6122681 6122707 6122713 6122747 6122759 6122777 6122791
6122801 6122803 6122819 6122849 6122863 6122867 6122881 6122917 6122927 6122939
6122947 6122971 6122983 6122999 6123001 6123011 6123017 6123023 6123059 6123067
6123127 6123133 6123163 6123191 6123193 6123199 6123203 6123223 6123233 6123239
6123251 6123259 6123277 6123283 6123287 6123317 6123353 6123361 6123401 6123409

```
6123413  6123427  6123443  6123449  6123487  6123493  6123499  6123517  6123563  6123571
6123613  6123617  6123619  6123629  6123631  6123641  6123653  6123683  6123703  6123713
6123721  6123737  6123739  6123743  6123749  6123781  6123797  6123829  6123841  6123863
6123869  6123877  6123881  6123889  6123913  6123917  6123937  6123941  6123967  6123977
6123979  6124007  6124009  6124021  6124109  6124121  6124163  6124169  6124207  6124219
6124229  6124231  6124253  6124271  6124273  6124291  6124297  6124303  6124319  6124331
6124367  6124379  6124397  6124411  6124421  6124427  6124439  6124451  6124477  6124501
6124507  6124513  6124529  6124541  6124543  6124589  6124609  6124649  6124663  6124667
6124681  6124691  6124717  6124751  6124753  6124793  6124801  6124817  6124823  6124837
6124847  6124873  6124883  6124889  6124901  6124907  6124933  6124961  6124991  6124997
6125023  6125029  6125057  6125089  6125123  6125137  6125143  6125159  6125173  6125183
6125191  6125213  6125227  6125233  6125243  6125257  6125261  6125267  6125269  6125279
6125281  6125297  6125303  6125309  6125323  6125333  6125363  6125381  6125417  6125443
6125447  6125459  6125489  6125563  6125573  6125579  6125599  6125653  6125663  6125671
6125689  6125701  6125711  6125741  6125747  6125753  6125761  6125773  6125783  6125789
6125807  6125813  6125849  6125863  6125881  6125887  6125891  6125893  6125927  6125939
6125947  6125957  6125969  6126017  6126019  6126023  6126031  6126041  6126067  6126079
6126083  6126089  6126091  6126139  6126149  6126161  6126181  6126187  6126191  6126203
6126209  6126271  6126277  6126293  6126299  6126311  6126317  6126347  6126359  6126391
6126427  6126431  6126457  6126467  6126473  6126481  6126541  6126551  6126553  6126577
6126581  6126587  6126629  6126649  6126677  6126689  6126691  6126697  6126709  6126727
6126733  6126751  6126787  6126821  6126823  6126829  6126839  6126847  6126877  6126881
6126893  6126907  6126929  6126931  6126937  6126961  6126971  6127019  6127067  6127073
6127117  6127153  6127159  6127169  6127183  6127211  6127213  6127241  6127273  6127279
6127283  6127307  6127313  6127321  6127337  6127357  6127379  6127391  6127399  6127403
6127417  6127421  6127423  6127447  6127483  6127493  6127501  6127523  6127529  6127549
6127559  6127567  6127577  6127579  6127603  6127609  6127631  6127643  6127661  6127669
6127679  6127687  6127691  6127697  6127703  6127711  6127717  6127733  6127757  6127763
6127777  6127789  6127831  6127841  6127859  6127889  6127897  6127909  6127931  6127949
6127963  6127967  6127969  6127993  6128011  6128029  6128039  6128053  6128063  6128069
6128107  6128113  6128137  6128141  6128149  6128159  6128167  6128183  6128197  6128201
6128207  6128237  6128257  6128299  6128303  6128321  6128341  6128351  6128387  6128411
6128413  6128417  6128459  6128461  6128467  6128477  6128491  6128501  6128503  6128509
6128513  6128531  6128539  6128567  6128581  6128587  6128597  6128611  6128623  6128651
6128663  6128693  6128723  6128729  6128737  6128767  6128777  6128779  6128783  6128813
6128819  6128821  6128851  6128921  6128923  6128929  6128951  6128953  6128957  6128977
6128987  6129029  6129043  6129059  6129073  6129083  6129089  6129107  6129113  6129119
6129133  6129143  6129157  6129181  6129187  6129199  6129209  6129257  6129269  6129271
6129287  6129311  6129313  6129323  6129329  6129379  6129407  6129421  6129433  6129439
6129449  6129481  6129491  6129493  6129511  6129547  6129553  6129577  6129581  6129583
6129587  6129611  6129619  6129631  6129637  6129649  6129653  6129659  6129667  6129677
6129713  6129731  6129743  6129769  6129803  6129811  6129857  6129863  6129899  6129919
6129947  6129953  6129961  6129967  6129973  6130021  6130043  6130067  6130097  6130099
6130129  6130133  6130151  6130153  6130169  6130171  6130177  6130199  6130249  6130253
6130261  6130273  6130301  6130337  6130373  6130391  6130393  6130427  6130439  6130441
6130459  6130469  6130477  6130499  6130517  6130541  6130543  6130547  6130549  6130603
6130609  6130661  6130667  6130679  6130697  6130699  6130703  6130717  6130739  6130741
6130753  6130763  6130769  6130781  6130783  6130807  6130819  6130823  6130849  6130907
6130951  6130967  6130973  6130979  6130981  6130997  6131039  6131057  6131077  6131089
6131119  6131131  6131189  6131219  6131239  6131297  6131303  6131309  6131311  6131329
6131351  6131353  6131369  6131387  6131393  6131399  6131401  6131423  6131431  6131443
6131453  6131473  6131491  6131507  6131527  6131533  6131549  6131551  6131561  6131597
6131621  6131627  6131641  6131651  6131663  6131669  6131681  6131683  6131753  6131759
6131771  6131821  6131857  6131863  6131887  6131891  6131911  6131921  6131947  6131953
6131977  6131981  6131989  6131999  6132029  6132037  6132089  6132103  6132107  6132109
6132127  6132131  6132143  6132149  6132151  6132167  6132169  6132179  6132221  6132229
6132233  6132239  6132271  6132281  6132299  6132317  6132319  6132337  6132349  6132353
6132377  6132403  6132431  6132439  6132473  6132479  6132481  6132509  6132523  6132551
6132569  6132571  6132587  6132593  6132647  6132653  6132661  6132671  6132673  6132751
6132769  6132773  6132779  6132781  6132799  6132809  6132811  6132817  6132827  6132829
6132851  6132857  6132871  6132883  6132887  6132911  6132923  6132967  6133003  6133013
6133031  6133033  6133037  6133069  6133093  6133117  6133129  6133139  6133151  6133159
6133163  6133177  6133187  6133189  6133199  6133207  6133223  6133261  6133271  6133273
6133279  6133291  6133331  6133339  6133343  6133349  6133373  6133411  6133429  6133441
6133483  6133487  6133493  6133499  6133537  6133573  6133579  6133591  6133607  6133643
6133657  6133661  6133669  6133727  6133769  6133781  6133811  6133837  6133843  6133867
6133871  6133873  6133891  6133913  6133921  6133927  6133937  6133943  6133961  6133987
6133993  6133999  6134003  6134021  6134069  6134071  6134083  6134101  6134129  6134137
6134143  6134153  6134159  6134197  6134213  6134231  6134237  6134257  6134269  6134279
6134309  6134327  6134339  6134357  6134363  6134369  6134419  6134441  6134449  6134483
6134519  6134521  6134533  6134551  6134561  6134567  6134593  6134617  6134641  6134651
6134659  6134699  6134743  6134749  6134759  6134797  6134801  6134809  6134833  6134837
6134839  6134851  6134857  6134881  6134893  6134911  6134917  6134923  6134927  6134941
6134963  6134969  6134981  6134983  6135023  6135029  6135047  6135049  6135053  6135131
6135133  6135161  6135163  6135167  6135187  6135191  6135203  6135209  6135221  6135223
6135251  6135253  6135289  6135293  6135299  6135329  6135331  6135341  6135343  6135359
6135383  6135397  6135421  6135433  6135463  6135473  6135491  6135509  6135523  6135533
6135539  6135553  6135581  6135593  6135611  6135637  6135643  6135653  6135667  6135677
6135683  6135707  6135721  6135743  6135781  6135797  6135839  6135859  6135881  6135887
6135889  6135893  6135901  6135919  6135931  6135947  6135953  6135973  6135977  6135979
6136003  6136073  6136079  6136087  6136111  6136121  6136127  6136153  6136157  6136189
6136211  6136213  6136217  6136219  6136231  6136237  6136243  6136271  6136301  6136309
6136321  6136327  6136349  6136363  6136379  6136391  6136399  6136441  6136451  6136477
6136517  6136519  6136523  6136547  6136549  6136577  6136619  6136621  6136631  6136651
6136673  6136679  6136681  6136693  6136703  6136717  6136721  6136723  6136733  6136751
6136807  6136841  6136873  6136877  6136901  6136919  6136927  6136939  6136967  6136979
6136993  6136997  6137011  6137023  6137041  6137059  6137069  6137077  6137081  6137123
6137137  6137177  6137179  6137191  6137203  6137233  6137279  6137303  6137309  6137317
6137333  6137353  6137363  6137371  6137387  6137423  6137441  6137447  6137477  6137491
```

```
6137497 6137501 6137503 6137533 6137557 6137563 6137567 6137569 6137587 6137591
6137603 6137609 6137623 6137633 6137639 6137641 6137653 6137687 6137689 6137693
6137701 6137713 6137717 6137749 6137753 6137797 6137801 6137809 6137827 6137837
6137839 6137861 6137909 6137917 6137951 6137959 6137981 6137993 6138019 6138023
6138113 6138127 6138131 6138149 6138161 6138179 6138191 6138193 6138211 6138239
6138271 6138277 6138281 6138299 6138313 6138331 6138347 6138367 6138371 6138383
6138409 6138413 6138427 6138437 6138439 6138443 6138449 6138467 6138469 6138481
6138523 6138557 6138563 6138569 6138571 6138593 6138599 6138611 6138647 6138659
6138661 6138667 6138673 6138689 6138709 6138739 6138779 6138787 6138793
6138823 6138827 6138841 6138859 6138863 6138871 6138877 6138883 6138893 6138901
6138947 6138983 6138991 6139019 6139027 6139031 6139037 6139051 6139061 6139073
6139099 6139103 6139117 6139121 6139123 6139139 6139141 6139201 6139219 6139241
6139249 6139253 6139279 6139283 6139297 6139303 6139319 6139351 6139369 6139379
6139391 6139417 6139423 6139453 6139493 6139513 6139517 6139531 6139547 6139559
6139579 6139591 6139613 6139663 6139673 6139681 6139687 6139691 6139697 6139699
6139733 6139739 6139741 6139753 6139787 6139789 6139849 6139853
6139871 6139883 6139897 6139901 6139921 6139937 6139949 6139951 6139961 6139979
6139993 6139999 6140023 6140041 6140051 6140053 6140087 6140107 6140129 6140137
6140153 6140171 6140191 6140207 6140219 6140227 6140231 6140243 6140269 6140273
6140279 6140291 6140339 6140353 6140359 6140369 6140389 6140411 6140419 6140429
6140441 6140461 6140467 6140473 6140521 6140531 6140539 6140549 6140567 6140569
6140579 6140581 6140593 6140647 6140653 6140657 6140671 6140707 6140711 6140753
6140767 6140773 6140777 6140789 6140803 6140807 6140843 6140851 6140863 6140903
6140909 6140923 6140929 6140947 6140957 6140983 6140989 6140999 6141013 6141017
6141041 6141049 6141059 6141061 6141071 6141077 6141137 6141173 6141203 6141209
6141229 6141257 6141263 6141277 6141281 6141323 6141337 6141341 6141347 6141397
6141407 6141409 6141433 6141439 6141449 6141463 6141467 6141469 6141491 6141493
6141497 6141521 6141559 6141599 6141601 6141613 6141659 6141661 6141671 6141679
6141691 6141727 6141739 6141757 6141761 6141763 6141791 6141797 6141809 6141827
6141833 6141853 6141857 6141859 6141887 6141893 6141899 6141977 6141983 6142033
6142057 6142063 6142079 6142109 6142141 6142153 6142177 6142189 6142207 6142211
6142231 6142237 6142243 6142261 6142267 6142277 6142291 6142303 6142307 6142327
6142343 6142349 6142351 6142361 6142363 6142373 6142387 6142391 6142397 6142441
6142463 6142469 6142483 6142489 6142501 6142523 6142547 6142573 6142589 6142603
6142613 6142649 6142651 6142663 6142687 6142727 6142739 6142783 6142813 6142819
6142837 6142841 6142879 6142897 6142949 6142951 6142957 6142963 6142973 6142987
6142993 6143003 6143063 6143083 6143087 6143113 6143141 6143149 6143167 6143197
6143219 6143227 6143233 6143237 6143243 6143279 6143287 6143303 6143309 6143311
6143339 6143353 6143359 6143381 6143387 6143393 6143407 6143413 6143437 6143483
6143497 6143509 6143513 6143519 6143521 6143531 6143537 6143569 6143573 6143587
6143597 6143603 6143609 6143617 6143629 6143639 6143651 6143663 6143671 6143693
6143713 6143741 6143779 6143791 6143803 6143807 6143827 6143861 6143927 6143941
6143957 6143999 6144007 6144029 6144037 6144041 6144043 6144071 6144079
6144091 6144113 6144119 6144121 6144161 6144211 6144223 6144247 6144253 6144283
6144311 6144323 6144349 6144371 6144373 6144377 6144379 6144389 6144403 6144409
6144421 6144461 6144487 6144493 6144499 6144517 6144527 6144529 6144539 6144557
6144563 6144583 6144647 6144653 6144679 6144707 6144709 6144751 6144763 6144799
6144821 6144833 6144863 6144869 6144881 6144893 6144899 6144907 6144909 6144911
6144959 6144967 6144977 6144989 6144991 6145019 6145031 6145057 6145081 6145123
6145159 6145171 6145199 6145229 6145231 6145261 6145273 6145277 6145291 6145327
6145339 6145343 6145351 6145357 6145369 6145387 6145397 6145411 6145421 6145427
6145429 6145457 6145481 6145511 6145519 6145523 6145537 6145543 6145553
6145583 6145597 6145609 6145621 6145631 6145637 6145649 6145661 6145693 6145699
6145703 6145723 6145729 6145753 6145787 6145793 6145801 6145817 6145829 6145849
6145877 6145879 6145889 6145903 6145913 6145927 6145961 6145981 6146003 6146011
6146053 6146059 6146069 6146071 6146081 6146087 6146093 6146099 6146117 6146141
6146159 6146167 6146191 6146213 6146227 6146249 6146281 6146297 6146303 6146341
6146369 6146407 6146417 6146449 6146453 6146461 6146467 6146473 6146489 6146501
6146507 6146531 6146533 6146593 6146603 6146611 6146627 6146629 6146659 6146663
6146677 6146687 6146713 6146729 6146743 6146771 6146783 6146849 6146869 6146873
6146879 6146891 6146923 6146939 6146969 6146971 6146981 6146983 6147017 6147023
6147041 6147073 6147077 6147079 6147131 6147133 6147139 6147161 6147179 6147199
6147221 6147223 6147247 6147263 6147277 6147287 6147307 6147347 6147359 6147373
6147377 6147389 6147419 6147443 6147487 6147503 6147521 6147527 6147541 6147551
6147563 6147577 6147599 6147607 6147611 6147613 6147619 6147653 6147721
6147737 6147749 6147751 6147767 6147781 6147787 6147793 6147821 6147847 6147851
6147857 6147881 6147917 6147937 6147941 6147949 6147959 6147979 6147983 6147997
6148009 6148057 6148069 6148091 6148123 6148127 6148139 6148141 6148147 6148193
6148243 6148249 6148273 6148283 6148297 6148301 6148309 6148313 6148349 6148361
6148367 6148369 6148393 6148403 6148409 6148411 6148427 6148459 6148463 6148487
6148489 6148501 6148507 6148511 6148531 6148537 6148547 6148559 6148579 6148589
6148601 6148603 6148607 6148619 6148621 6148627 6148631 6148643 6148651 6148661
6148673 6148691 6148713 6148721 6148759 6148777 6148789 6148801 6148823 6148883
6148859 6148897 6148931 6148937 6148973 6148991 6148999 6149021 6149023 6149041
6149047 6149063 6149083 6149093 6149147 6149161 6149167 6149197 6149207
6149233 6149237 6149243 6149251 6149263 6149267 6149287 6149309 6149317 6149321
6149323 6149329 6149333 6149357 6149371 6149383 6149389 6149399 6149411 6149417
6149443 6149459 6149477 6149489 6149491 6149501 6149503 6149543 6149551 6149557
6149599 6149603 6149617 6149623 6149669 6149681 6149683 6149707 6149723 6149761
6149771 6149779 6149783 6149791 6149797 6149839 6149851 6149863 6149873 6149879
6149887 6149893 6149909 6149911 6149917 6149929 6149963 6149981 6149987 6150007
6150013 6150019 6150037 6150043 6150049 6150061 6150077 6150083 6150097 6150113
6150119 6150127 6150139 6150149 6150163 6150191 6150211 6150227 6150239 6150257
6150259 6150271 6150283 6150289 6150293 6150299 6150301 6150317 6150343 6150377
6150409 6150421 6150437 6150457 6150503 6150511 6150527 6150539 6150551 6150559
6150577 6150589 6150643 6150649 6150653 6150707 6150713 6150733 6150743 6150797
6150811 6150817 6150847 6150853 6150863 6150877 6150883 6150889 6150901
6150919 6150941 6150961 6150971 6150997 6151007 6151027 6151037 6151039 6151049
6151063 6151073 6151081 6151091 6151129 6151133 6151141 6151151 6151153 6151157
```

```
6151181  6151183  6151217  6151241  6151247  6151253  6151267  6151273  6151291  6151303
6151349  6151351  6151357  6151391  6151427  6151477  6151507  6151513  6151529  6151531
6151543  6151553  6151559  6151577  6151597  6151661  6151669  6151679  6151697  6151699
6151721  6151727  6151729  6151757  6151771  6151777  6151793  6151811  6151813  6151819
6151843  6151853  6151867  6151883  6151903  6151907  6151931  6151939  6151961  6151969
6151987  6152039  6152057  6152071  6152077  6152093  6152117  6152123  6152131  6152161
6152189  6152191  6152203  6152207  6152227  6152231  6152233  6152239  6152243  6152269
6152273  6152281  6152369  6152383  6152389  6152401  6152407  6152411  6152417  6152449
6152459  6152467  6152479  6152491  6152519  6152527  6152537  6152563  6152581  6152593
6152621  6152633  6152639  6152651  6152687  6152701  6152719  6152743  6152749  6152771
6152777  6152779  6152791  6152801  6152803  6152851  6152857  6152863  6152869  6152879
6152893  6152899  6152921  6152947  6152953  6152957  6152969  6152977  6152981  6153013
6153019  6153041  6153047  6153053  6153061  6153067  6153071  6153101  6153107  6153109
6153127  6153139  6153149  6153151  6153163  6153181  6153187  6153197  6153209  6153229
6153233  6153263  6153271  6153281  6153311  6153313  6153317  6153319  6153331  6153349
6153361  6153379  6153383  6153409  6153421  6153431  6153451  6153461  6153467  6153487
6153491  6153493  6153503  6153509  6153557  6153559  6153577  6153599  6153611  6153613
6153647  6153683  6153709  6153737  6153781  6153793  6153799  6153809  6153817  6153821
6153839  6153871  6153899  6153911  6153919  6153923  6153943  6154007  6154009  6154013
6154019  6154033  6154073  6154103  6154111  6154163  6154171  6154189  6154217  6154259
6154273  6154277  6154279  6154301  6154333  6154339  6154361  6154381  6154403  6154433
6154441  6154453  6154457  6154471  6154487  6154507  6154517  6154529  6154531  6154541
6154549  6154567  6154579  6154591  6154597  6154601  6154619  6154627  6154649  6154657
6154661  6154667  6154669  6154711  6154721  6154723  6154751  6154769  6154787  6154789
6154793  6154807  6154817  6154831  6154843  6154847  6154853  6154909  6154927  6154933
6154991  6155009  6155029  6155033  6155077  6155087  6155113  6155129  6155137  6155179
6155239  6155249  6155257  6155263  6155299  6155311  6155351  6155353  6155417  6155419
6155423  6155437  6155447  6155459  6155483  6155489  6155497  6155519  6155531  6155537
6155549  6155551  6155561  6155573  6155593  6155599  6155621  6155641  6155687  6155689
6155711  6155713  6155761  6155767  6155777  6155783  6155839  6155857  6155873  6155899
6155939  6155957  6155969  6155971  6155977  6155983  6155987  6156037  6156047  6156049
6156067  6156079  6156089  6156103  6156113  6156131  6156169  6156173  6156179  6156187
6156221  6156229  6156257  6156263  6156281  6156289  6156313  6156317  6156331  6156343
6156349  6156373  6156379  6156407  6156443  6156487  6156509  6156523  6156539  6156583
6156599  6156629  6156637  6156641  6156659  6156713  6156719  6156721  6156739  6156767
6156781  6156793  6156811  6156823  6156853  6156877  6156901  6156919  6156923  6156937
6156959  6156967  6156971  6156973  6156977  6156979  6156989  6157001  6157013  6157033
6157051  6157079  6157097  6157103  6157139  6157147  6157153  6157163  6157171  6157183
6157187  6157199  6157201  6157211  6157219  6157271  6157289  6157297  6157303  6157337
6157343  6157351  6157363  6157369  6157397  6157427  6157447  6157453  6157469  6157493
6157507  6157511  6157513  6157549  6157559  6157573  6157597  6157603  6157607  6157609
6157637  6157639  6157661  6157663  6157673  6157681  6157717  6157727  6157741  6157751
6157763  6157777  6157793  6157819  6157841  6157847  6157861  6157883  6157891  6157897
6157909  6157937  6157939  6157969  6157973  6157979  6157993  6158003  6158041  6158059
6158069  6158083  6158093  6158099  6158101  6158107  6158149  6158167  6158183  6158189
6158197  6158213  6158221  6158231  6158249  6158263  6158279  6158291  6158293  6158297
6158309  6158311  6158333  6158381  6158389  6158393  6158407  6158483  6158501  6158507
6158521  6158527  6158531  6158543  6158557  6158563  6158681  6158689  6158699  6158723
6158729  6158767  6158771  6158783  6158797  6158843  6158857  6158861  6158923  6158939
6158941  6158969  6159007  6159011  6159031  6159073  6159079  6159103  6159113  6159121
6159133  6159137  6159161  6159167  6159181  6159189  6159199  6159203  6159217  6159221
6159247  6159299  6159311  6159313  6159317  6159323  6159337  6159367  6159379  6159407
6159443  6159451  6159467  6159473  6159487  6159493  6159499  6159509  6159523  6159529
6159533  6159539  6159547  6159557  6159563  6159577  6159583  6159589  6159613  6159617
6159619  6159623  6159641  6159677  6159689  6159691  6159697  6159701  6159721  6159757
6159787  6159817  6159827  6159833  6159847  6159851  6159869  6159893  6159943  6159947
6159953  6159983  6159991  6159997  6160003  6160027  6160039  6160043  6160073  6160079
6160109  6160111  6160139  6160157  6160167  6160163  6160169  6160211  6160229  6160247
6160277  6160303  6160321  6160331  6160333  6160339  6160361  6160379  6160381  6160391
6160393  6160403  6160423  6160433  6160439  6160447  6160489  6160507  6160513  6160529
6160549  6160559  6160589  6160591  6160597  6160601  6160607  6160621  6160633  6160639
6160663  6160699  6160709  6160733  6160747  6160771  6160793  6160811  6160813  6160823
6160831  6160853  6160867  6160871  6160907  6160937  6160949  6160961  6160967  6160969
6160993  6161003  6161009  6161017  6161039  6161041  6161063  6161081  6161107  6161117
6161143  6161147  6161159  6161161  6161179  6161189  6161201  6161209  6161213  6161249
6161257  6161269  6161279  6161329  6161333  6161347  6161383  6161413  6161417  6161431
6161437  6161459  6161471  6161473  6161479  6161483  6161489  6161501  6161503  6161509
6161527  6161579  6161581  6161609  6161629  6161641  6161651  6161663  6161693  6161761
6161819  6161873  6161899  6161917  6161927  6161929  6161941  6161951  6161959  6161993
6162001  6162043  6162059  6162071  6162077  6162113  6162127  6162131  6162139  6162157
6162179  6162197  6162199  6162209  6162223  6162241  6162263  6162283  6162307  6162319
6162323  6162329  6162337  6162349  6162379  6162391  6162437  6162439  6162473  6162487
6162493  6162511  6162523  6162539  6162547  6162557  6162571  6162577  6162581  6162589
6162599  6162601  6162613  6162623  6162641  6162659  6162743  6162749  6162809  6162817
6162829  6162841  6162847  6162881  6162883  6162887  6162931  6162941  6162943  6163007
6163009  6163021  6163037  6163039  6163043  6163097  6163123  6163139  6163151  6163153
6163159  6163169  6163177  6163181  6163189  6163207  6163217  6163249  6163271  6163279
6163291  6163301  6163303  6163309  6163321  6163351  6163357  6163361  6163373  6163387
6163411  6163433  6163441  6163453  6163483  6163499  6163511  6163541  6163567  6163579
6163583  6163589  6163601  6163603  6163607  6163643  6163649  6163679  6163693  6163697
6163711  6163739  6163753  6163757  6163769  6163783  6163813  6163819  6163837  6163849
6163879  6163889  6163891  6163903  6163957  6163991  6164017  6164021  6164027  6164029
6164033  6164077  6164083  6164099  6164101  6164117  6164129  6164141  6164159  6164167
6164173  6164177  6164203  6164209  6164243  6164267  6164293  6164329  6164359  6164369
6164371  6164383  6164399  6164419  6164429  6164461  6164491  6164503  6164507  6164513
6164519  6164537  6164549  6164551  6164563  6164579  6164611  6164623  6164633  6164647
6164651  6164657  6164677  6164689  6164701  6164731  6164749  6164771  6164773  6164779
6164783  6164803  6164813  6164819  6164827  6164833  6164839  6164869  6164887  6164891
6164929  6164971  6164981  6165007  6165017  6165031  6165053  6165059  6165077  6165083
```

```
6165097 6165109 6165113 6165121 6165191 6165217 6165221 6165227 6165251 6165259
6165277 6165283 6165307 6165349 6165359 6165377 6165391 6165409 6165431 6165461
6165463 6165479 6165491 6165499 6165527 6165529 6165553 6165563 6165581 6165583
6165589 6165629 6165637 6165653 6165689 6165701 6165707 6165737 6165739 6165751
6165763 6165827 6165829 6165833 6165839 6165857 6165881 6165911 6165919 6165923
6165947 6165953 6165979 6165997 6166037 6166049 6166057 6166081 6166099 6166103
6166109 6166123 6166129 6166133 6166159 6166163 6166169 6166207 6166213 6166219
6166247 6166249 6166261 6166271 6166273 6166289 6166327 6166333 6166339 6166351
6166361 6166367 6166379 6166403 6166409 6166417 6166451 6166471 6166477 6166483
6166487 6166519 6166549 6166571 6166577 6166591 6166609 6166637 6166639 6166669
6166681 6166703 6166711 6166717 6166723 6166751 6166777 6166789 6166813 6166837
6166841 6166843 6166871 6166877 6166883 6166889 6166891 6166907 6166913 6166943
6166973 6166981 6166987 6166997 6166999 6167009 6167023 6167033 6167041 6167069
6167081 6167089 6167101 6167129 6167137 6167167 6167173 6167177 6167207 6167221
6167251 6167257 6167269 6167281 6167299 6167303 6167309 6167327 6167333 6167341
6167347 6167351 6167353 6167377 6167383 6167407 6167411 6167429 6167443 6167453
6167461 6167471 6167503 6167509 6167521 6167531 6167561 6167563 6167573 6167597
6167621 6167627 6167639 6167659 6167677 6167687 6167731 6167773 6167779 6167783
6167809 6167827 6167831 6167839 6167849 6167867 6167887 6167891 6167911 6167921
6167927 6167929 6167947 6167971 6168013 6168023 6168031 6168053 6168061 6168073
6168077 6168079 6168089 6168091 6168109 6168121 6168131 6168143 6168167 6168181
6168187 6168223 6168247 6168251 6168277 6168313 6168317 6168341 6168353 6168359
6168367 6168377 6168401 6168413 6168457 6168469 6168497 6168499 6168523 6168527
6168553 6168563 6168581 6168587 6168599 6168601 6168607 6168611 6168629 6168647
6168649 6168667 6168683 6168689 6168691 6168709 6168713 6168731 6168779 6168781
6168821 6168881 6168893 6168923 6168931 6168949 6168971 6168989 6168997 6169013
6169019 6169021 6169027 6169039 6169049 6169057 6169063 6169087 6169123 6169127
6169133 6169139 6169193 6169201 6169231 6169259 6169301 6169309 6169321 6169327
6169333 6169337 6169349 6169363 6169369 6169379 6169399 6169409 6169421 6169439
6169441 6169447 6169463 6169469 6169477 6169483 6169507 6169517 6169523 6169529
6169531 6169591 6169609 6169619 6169627 6169649 6169679 6169693 6169711 6169729
6169733 6169753 6169763 6169781 6169789 6169811 6169847 6169859 6169871 6169883
6169897 6169901 6169907 6169909 6169921 6169931 6169937 6169949 6169973 6169981
6169987 6169993 6170029 6170057 6170093 6170107 6170123
6170159 6170173 6170221 6170251 6170317 6170327 6170341 6170357 6170363 6170387
6170389 6170407 6170413 6170429 6170431 6170441 6170447 6170449 6170477 6170491
6170501 6170503 6170557 6170561 6170579 6170587 6170639 6170641 6170651 6170653
6170657 6170663 6170713 6170719 6170743 6170753 6170761 6170783 6170819 6170837
6170861 6170893 6170911 6170921 6170929 6170933 6170947 6170977 6170981 6171001
6171031 6171037 6171047 6171049 6171073 6171089 6171091 6171097 6171101 6171149
6171163 6171167 6171203 6171227 6171233 6171239 6171247 6171251 6171271
6171281 6171293 6171301 6171329 6171331 6171353 6171359 6171377 6171397 6171413
6171427 6171463 6171467 6171469 6171491 6171509 6171589 6171593 6171611 6171619
6171623 6171643 6171647 6171679 6171701 6171703 6171707 6171719 6171727 6171743
6171749 6171761 6171773 6171793 6171829 6171857 6171881 6171887 6171911 6171917
6171923 6171967 6172003 6172043 6172051 6172063 6172079 6172097 6172109 6172123
6172147 6172183 6172213 6172217 6172247 6172249 6172259 6172267 6172277 6172279
6172291 6172337 6172363 6172367 6172373 6172381 6172393 6172409 6172421 6172477
6172489 6172493 6172499 6172519 6172531 6172541 6172553 6172559 6172571 6172577
6172603 6172609 6172619 6172637 6172657 6172667 6172697 6172709 6172711 6172721
6172741 6172753 6172759 6172787 6172799 6172801 6172847 6172861 6172877 6172889
6172897 6172909 6172913 6172927 6172931 6172949 6172987 6173003 6173009 6173047
6173051 6173059 6173071 6173093 6173137 6173147 6173149 6173171 6173183 6173197
6173207 6173239 6173243 6173249 6173257 6173327 6173341 6173353 6173359 6173369
6173393 6173417 6173437 6173441 6173449 6173459 6173473 6173483 6173501 6173513
6173527 6173539 6173551 6173569 6173593 6173603 6173621 6173641 6173647 6173653
6173677 6173731 6173753 6173767 6173773 6173777 6173809 6173813 6173833 6173837
6173861 6173863 6173887 6173891 6173927 6173939 6173957 6174001 6174011 6174017
6174083 6174101 6174109 6174131 6174137 6174139 6174151 6174163 6174167 6174191
6174229 6174253 6174257 6174271 6174293 6174299 6174307 6174317 6174331 6174347
6174379 6174391 6174431 6174439 6174461 6174463 6174473 6174479 6174503 6174517
6174533 6174547 6174569 6174577 6174583 6174599 6174631 6174643 6174697 6174703
6174713 6174737 6174743 6174769 6174781 6174793 6174809 6174811 6174821 6174823
6174827 6174841 6174869 6174899 6174913 6174919 6174989 6174991 6175021 6175027
6175033 6175067 6175069 6175123 6175129 6175139 6175151 6175153 6175157 6175163
6175181 6175207 6175217 6175219 6175223 6175229 6175237 6175243 6175259 6175261
6175271 6175303 6175313 6175319 6175333 6175349 6175363 6175373 6175381 6175391
6175409 6175423 6175427 6175439 6175457 6175487 6175501 6175517 6175529
6175577 6175583 6175619 6175643 6175657 6175681 6175691 6175693 6175711 6175717
6175721 6175739 6175751 6175769 6175787 6175837 6175843 6175853 6175861 6175867
6175889 6175903 6175921 6175951 6175973 6175979 6175987 6175991 6175997 6176011
6176033 6176039 6176041 6176057 6176059 6176063 6176069 6176119 6176173 6176201
6176207 6176221 6176231 6176237 6176239 6176293 6176323 6176327 6176329 6176377
6176407 6176413 6176419 6176437 6176473 6176549 6176551 6176557 6176561 6176587
6176591 6176617 6176647 6176671 6176683 6176689 6176701 6176707 6176713 6176717
6176741 6176747 6176783 6176801 6176803 6176809 6176813 6176827 6176837 6176839
6176861 6176869 6176917 6176927 6176941 6176953 6176959 6176981 6176983 6176999
6177007 6177011 6177023 6177049 6177053 6177107 6177151 6177161 6177167 6177181
6177191 6177209 6177221 6177229 6177233 6177263 6177289 6177293 6177331 6177383
6177389 6177397 6177403 6177419 6177427 6177449 6177461 6177481 6177499 6177503
6177533 6177541 6177559 6177569 6177581 6177599 6177617 6177629 6177637 6177643
6177671 6177673 6177701 6177707 6177739 6177763 6177797 6177803 6177807 6177821
6177883 6177887 6177889 6177893 6177901 6177929 6177937 6177947 6177967 6177971
6177973 6177979 6177989 6177991 6178057 6178061 6178087 6178093 6178129 6178153
6178181 6178187 6178201 6178213 6178219 6178241 6178243 6178267 6178273 6178301
6178309 6178313 6178321 6178339 6178343 6178357 6178379 6178391 6178397
6178399 6178433 6178441 6178451 6178481 6178483 6178493 6178561 6178567 6178597
6178607 6178619 6178631 6178639 6178643 6178663 6178691 6178693 6178699 6178717
6178721 6178723 6178747 6178759 6178831 6178847 6178853 6178859 6178891 6178903
```

```
6178937  6178957  6178969  6178981  6179021  6179023  6179053  6179081  6179083  6179087
6179099  6179113  6179153  6179171  6179183  6179189  6179197  6179207  6179213  6179221
6179227  6179269  6179273  6179287  6179293  6179297  6179309  6179311  6179317  6179321
6179353  6179399  6179413  6179417  6179431  6179441  6179461  6179473  6179489  6179507
6179519  6179533  6179539  6179549  6179567  6179597  6179623  6179647  6179681  6179683
6179699  6179707  6179713  6179717  6179741  6179749  6179753  6179759  6179779  6179783
6179791  6179821  6179861  6179863  6179903  6179941  6179969  6179981  6179989  6180001
6180007  6180019  6180029  6180037  6180047  6180049  6180059  6180127  6180131  6180133
6180143  6180157  6180179  6180193  6180199  6180203  6180233  6180241  6180259  6180271
6180283  6180289  6180319  6180329  6180331  6180341  6180379  6180389  6180397  6180413
6180497  6180511  6180521  6180527  6180533  6180539  6180541  6180557  6180589  6180599
6180611  6180617  6180649  6180653  6180659  6180661  6180667  6180679  6180689  6180731
6180737  6180751  6180773  6180793  6180827  6180841  6180847  6180869  6180901  6180907
6180919  6180929  6180953  6180989  6180991  6181001  6181009  6181027  6181033  6181057
6181079  6181103  6181127  6181141  6181151  6181169  6181187  6181223  6181229  6181249
6181261  6181271  6181277  6181291  6181297  6181349  6181361  6181363  6181391
6181423  6181433  6181451  6181477  6181531  6181573  6181579  6181589  6181601  6181613
6181619  6181633  6181639  6181649  6181657  6181699  6181739  6181753  6181787  6181811
6181831  6181841  6181873  6181913  6181919  6181921  6181933  6181937  6181943  6181949
6181969  6181993  6182039  6182047  6182053  6182069  6182081  6182083  6182093  6182107
6182131  6182149  6182161  6182171  6182179  6182221  6182227  6182243  6182251  6182257
6182261  6182263  6182269  6182287  6182317  6182321  6182327  6182347  6182359  6182387
6182389  6182401  6182413  6182459  6182483  6182531  6182537  6182549  6182557  6182573
6182623  6182639  6182641  6182647  6182717  6182723  6182767  6182783  6182789  6182797
6182819  6182863  6182873  6182879  6182909  6182921  6182971  6182977  6182989  6182993
6183007  6183011  6183017  6183029  6183049  6183059  6183077  6183091  6183103  6183127
6183157  6183161  6183217  6183241  6183269  6183301  6183347  6183349  6183361  6183371
6183391  6183413  6183421  6183431  6183449  6183451  6183469  6183487  6183491  6183517
6183559  6183571  6183581  6183589  6183599  6183623  6183629  6183643  6183659  6183691
6183703  6183713  6183761  6183823  6183829  6183839  6183857  6183871  6183889  6183893
6183917  6183929  6183977  6183979  6184001  6184019  6184037  6184067  6184091  6184099
6184109  6184111  6184121  6184127  6184133  6184147  6184169  6184181  6184183  6184187
6184201  6184219  6184229  6184237  6184259  6184261  6184267  6184273  6184289  6184319
6184327  6184349  6184393  6184403  6184417  6184441  6184457  6184463  6184471  6184483
6184499  6184537  6184547  6184559  6184601  6184609  6184613  6184637  6184639  6184643
6184667  6184657  6184667  6184669  6184679  6184681  6184687  6184693  6184747  6184757
6184799  6184811  6184813  6184847  6184853  6184873  6184909  6184931  6184933  6184939
6184963  6184967  6185021  6185041  6185057  6185063  6185099  6185107  6185131  6185143
6185159  6185171  6185173  6185177  6185189  6185191  6185197  6185251  6185261  6185273
6185293  6185299  6185303  6185353  6185357  6185359  6185369  6185407  6185419  6185429
6185441  6185453  6185477  6185483  6185503  6185527  6185533  6185537  6185539  6185561
6185567  6185573  6185579  6185587  6185611  6185617  6185633  6185651  6185677  6185701
6185713  6185719  6185723  6185731  6185759  6185761  6185813  6185831  6185857  6185863
6185867  6185891  6185897  6185941  6185989  6186007  6186029  6186041  6186049  6186053
6186083  6186119  6186133  6186151  6186157  6186161  6186163  6186197  6186217  6186233
6186259  6186263  6186269  6186277  6186347  6186353  6186359  6186371  6186377  6186407
6186413  6186461  6186463  6186493  6186497  6186503  6186527  6186629  6186581  6186611
6186667  6186619  6186641  6186667  6186671  6186673  6186679  6186703  6186707  6186709
6186749  6186767  6186779  6186781  6186811  6186821  6186833  6186853  6186857  6186871
6186877  6186907  6186911  6186953  6186959  6186967  6186979  6187003  6187007  6187019
6187037  6187039  6187067  6187079  6187087  6187147  6187163  6187189  6187199  6187211
6187219  6187231  6187241  6187277  6187289  6187301  6187309  6187319  6187327  6187333
6187343  6187367  6187393  6187427  6187451  6187453  6187457  6187459  6187463  6187477
6187487  6187499  6187501  6187537  6187549  6187561  6187583  6187607  6187633  6187637
6187639  6187661  6187663  6187681  6187717  6187729  6187739  6187747  6187751  6187757
6187771  6187799  6187837  6187849  6187859  6187871  6187873  6187889  6187891  6187901
6187963  6187981  6188009  6188011  6188029  6188033  6188057  6188059  6188071  6188093
6188113  6188123  6188179  6188191  6188207  6188223  6188239  6188249  6188263  6188283
6188297  6188317  6188341  6188359  6188363  6188393  6188401  6188407  6188411  6188477
6188491  6188521  6188531  6188551  6188597  6188617  6188641  6188647  6188661  6188683
6188717  6188759  6188761  6188779  6188789  6188797  6188821  6188833  6188843  6188861
6188873  6188881  6188887  6188893  6188929  6188981  6188983  6188993  6189017  6189019
6189023  6189031  6189067  6189077  6189083  6189089  6189103  6189107  6189109  6189113
6189137  6189143  6189163  6189191  6189199  6189203  6189217  6189221  6189223  6189229
6189233  6189247  6189251  6189257  6189299  6189341  6189353  6189361  6189389  6189419
6189431  6189433  6189481  6189503  6189509  6189511  6189517  6189529  6189539  6189541
6189551  6189563  6189569  6189577  6189593  6189607  6189613  6189637  6189643  6189653
6189671  6189697  6189713  6189719  6189727  6189769  6189791  6189793  6189803  6189857
6189901  6189913  6189917  6189961  6189971  6189973  6189977  6189983  6190003  6190007
6190033  6190043  6190061  6190069  6190073  6190081  6190109  6190123  6190127  6190141
6190147  6190153  6190169  6190187  6190199  6190259  6190267  6190273  6190291  6190309
6190313  6190319  6190337  6190343  6190351  6190367  6190411  6190423  6190439  6190441
6190451  6190469  6190487  6190489  6190571  6190589  6190621  6190627  6190651  6190661
6190697  6190727  6190747  6190763  6190781  6190783  6190799  6190819  6190823  6190837
6190843  6190853  6190859  6190871  6190897  6190937  6190959  6190963  6190969  6190973
6190991  6190999  6191051  6191069  6191083  6191137  6191147  6191153  6191197  6191201
6191221  6191243  6191257  6191279  6191291  6191299  6191323  6191363  6191371  6191389
6191411  6191443  6191461  6191483  6191489  6191491  6191501  6191539  6191567  6191579
6191593  6191597  6191611  6191629  6191659  6191677  6191681  6191687  6191693  6191711
6191719  6191737  6191741  6191743  6191747  6191767  6191803  6191813  6191821  6191833
6191837  6191849  6191897  6191903  6191947  6191951  6191959  6192023  6192031  6192047
6192071  6192077  6192113  6192127  6192133  6192143  6192161  6192163  6192187  6192211
6192229  6192253  6192259  6192269  6192289  6192299  6192317  6192331  6192337  6192349
6192377  6192379  6192409  6192413  6192419  6192449  6192493  6192509  6192521  6192523
6192541  6192569  6192583  6192601  6192611  6192619  6192629  6192671  6192697  6192707
6192749  6192779  6192799  6192821  6192853  6192869  6192871  6192883  6192899  6192937
6192961  6192971  6193001  6193007  6193013  6193027  6193043  6193051  6193063  6193067
6193073  6193093  6193123  6193129  6193133  6193157  6193181  6193189  6193193
6193223  6193249  6193301  6193303  6193307  6193309  6193339  6193351  6193361  6193367
```

```
6193381  6193399  6193427  6193441  6193469  6193471  6193507  6193553  6193571  6193609
6193631  6193651  6193657  6193667  6193669  6193673  6193687  6193697  6193711  6193717
6193771  6193783  6193787  6193793  6193799  6193813  6193819  6193823  6193843  6193853
6193861  6193871  6193897  6193901  6193931  6193963  6193973  6193987  6193991  6194029
6194033  6194039  6194051  6194053  6194093  6194099  6194113  6194117  6194119  6194131
6194147  6194159  6194161  6194179  6194183  6194189  6194191  6194213  6194219  6194261
6194267  6194299  6194303  6194329  6194347  6194359  6194387  6194393  6194413  6194449
6194467  6194479  6194483  6194509  6194519  6194543  6194549  6194557  6194563  6194569
6194581  6194591  6194609  6194621  6194663  6194701  6194723  6194743  6194803  6194807
6194819  6194827  6194831  6194833  6194849  6194857  6194861  6194863  6194869  6194879
6194891  6194911  6194921  6194927  6194939  6194959  6194971  6194983  6194989  6195001
6195017  6195019  6195029  6195031  6195041  6195043  6195061  6195097  6195103  6195109
6195113  6195143  6195149  6195151  6195173  6195181  6195251  6195281  6195283  6195323
6195337  6195341  6195353  6195401  6195419  6195421  6195439  6195461  6195479  6195481
6195517  6195521  6195547  6195559  6195601  6195617  6195619  6195641  6195661  6195697
6195713  6195731  6195737  6195743  6195757  6195773  6195779  6195781  6195799  6195817
6195829  6195859  6195863  6195883  6195889  6195911  6195923  6195957  6195971  6195991
6195997  6196009  6196019  6196027  6196031  6196037  6196067  6196079  6196081  6196097
6196103  6196117  6196123  6196153  6196159  6196163  6196189  6196193  6196243  6196247
6196273  6196277  6196291  6196297  6196321  6196327  6196363  6196369  6196387  6196391
6196397  6196409  6196417  6196423  6196439  6196469  6196471  6196493  6196507  6196513
6196529  6196537  6196549  6196571  6196607  6196643  6196669  6196703  6196709  6196727
6196733  6196739  6196741  6196747  6196753  6196769  6196777  6196783  6196787  6196819
6196843  6196847  6196849  6196871  6196877  6196901  6196909  6196933  6196937  6196943
6196961  6196973  6196991  6196999  6197011  6197017  6197047  6197053  6197071  6197077
6197089  6197099  6197123  6197137  6197153  6197161  6197171  6197207  6197209  6197227
6197239  6197251  6197263  6197267  6197293  6197309  6197311  6197339  6197351  6197353
6197381  6197383  6197431  6197447  6197459  6197483  6197497  6197507  6197563  6197599
6197617  6197641  6197647  6197651  6197669  6197671  6197687  6197689  6197717  6197731
6197753  6197771  6197791  6197801  6197813  6197827  6197831  6197869  6197881  6197887
6197897  6197899  6197903  6197921  6197927  6197941  6197951  6197959  6197963  6197999
6198019  6198037  6198053  6198061  6198107  6198119  6198131  6198139  6198151  6198167
6198169  6198187  6198193  6198209  6198221  6198223  6198239  6198259  6198281  6198289
6198299  6198307  6198317  6198323  6198329  6198331  6198341  6198359  6198377  6198391
6198443  6198449  6198457  6198463  6198497  6198529  6198551  6198553  6198559  6198571
6198587  6198593  6198601  6198611  6198631  6198641  6198663  6198671  6198677  6198679
6198683  6198691  6198697  6198713  6198719  6198733  6198737  6198757  6198767  6198793
6198809  6198817  6198823  6198833  6198851  6198859  6198889  6198901  6198911  6198917
6198919  6198989  6199007  6199013  6199027  6199031  6199043  6199057  6199093  6199099
6199133  6199153  6199183  6199201  6199211  6199229  6199231  6199273  6199283  6199321
6199327  6199331  6199337  6199363  6199381  6199399  6199409  6199429  6199433  6199451
6199469  6199483  6199499  6199511  6199517  6199547  6199549  6199553  6199559  6199579
6199601  6199619  6199631  6199637  6199639  6199663  6199691  6199693  6199709  6199727
6199729  6199751  6199763  6199771  6199777  6199799  6199807  6199819  6199847  6199859
6199873  6199877  6199889  6199891  6199927  6199957  6199981  6199987  6200003  6200027
6200059  6200063  6200071  6200081  6200107  6200111  6200141  6200149  6200167  6200171
6200191  6200219  6200221  6200231  6200237  6200239  6200261  6200269  6200273  6200281
6200297  6200303  6200309  6200321  6200323  6200333  6200339  6200347  6200351  6200353
6200371  6200399  6200443  6200459  6200503  6200507  6200539  6200549  6200561  6200567
6200581  6200603  6200609  6200617  6200627  6200653  6200659  6200741  6200749  6200771
6200791  6200807  6200861  6200863  6200891  6200893  6200921  6200923  6200939  6200951
6200981  6200989  6201037  6201043  6201047  6201059  6201061  6201067  6201103  6201109
6201149  6201161  6201187  6201193  6201203  6201229  6201253  6201259  6201281  6201287
6201289  6201301  6201323  6201347  6201361  6201367  6201383  6201397  6201401  6201439
6201449  6201451  6201473  6201479  6201491  6201493  6201497  6201499  6201521  6201523
6201539  6201551  6201589  6201599  6201641  6201647  6201649  6201683  6201691  6201709
6201731  6201739  6201781  6201799  6201817  6201823  6201851  6201863  6201869  6201883
6201887  6201893  6201907  6201917  6201929  6201941  6201967  6201983  6202013  6202033
6202043  6202057  6202061  6202067  6202087  6202103  6202117  6202121  6202129  6202159
6202177  6202237  6202243  6202247  6202253  6202271  6202283  6202291  6202349  6202367
6202373  6202393  6202397  6202403  6202409  6202411  6202429  6202447  6202451  6202453
6202459  6202481  6202487  6202519  6202523  6202561  6202577  6202583  6202589  6202601
6202613  6202619  6202633  6202649  6202657  6202661  6202681  6202687  6202699  6202711
6202733  6202741  6202747  6202751  6202753  6202769  6202771  6202783  6202799  6202817
6202831  6202837  6202853  6202877  6202891  6202901  6202907  6202979  6202991  6202993
6203003  6203023  6203027  6203047  6203059  6203089  6203143  6203203  6203221  6203223
6203237  6203251  6203287  6203293  6203297  6203311  6203357  6203359  6203369  6203371
6203377  6203387  6203411  6203429  6203459  6203473  6203479  6203501  6203513  6203543
6203563  6203573  6203579  6203609  6203621  6203641  6203663  6203693  6203699  6203707
6203741  6203749  6203773  6203779  6203789  6203801  6203803  6203819  6203831  6203837
6203849  6203863  6203881  6203887  6203903  6203917  6203927  6203959  6203971  6203983
6204017  6204019  6204059  6204071  6204097  6204103  6204113  6204119  6204131  6204151
6204157  6204179  6204229  6204259  6204281  6204287  6204301  6204311  6204313  6204323
6204353  6204377  6204379  6204383  6204391  6204397  6204409  6204413  6204421  6204437
6204461  6204467  6204479  6204511  6204533  6204547  6204563  6204577  6204613  6204629
6204661  6204683  6204701  6204703  6204719  6204721  6204727  6204749  6204769  6204827
6204829  6204851  6204889  6204901  6204911  6204923  6204941  6204953  6204967  6204973
6204977  6205007  6205013  6205021  6205033  6205079  6205091  6205097  6205109  6205117
6205123  6205139  6205151  6205183  6205189  6205237  6205253  6205271  6205273  6205279
6205291  6205313  6205319  6205321  6205327  6205349  6205351  6205369  6205411  6205427
6205429  6205439  6205453  6205477  6205481  6205501  6205517  6205519  6205523  6205531
6205543  6205547  6205559  6205579  6205583  6205597  6205643  6205649  6205651  6205669
6205709  6205711  6205747  6205753  6205777  6205783  6205807  6205813  6205817  6205819
6205831  6205861  6205879  6205891  6205931  6205937  6205943  6205967  6206017  6206051
6206069  6206077  6206089  6206111  6206117  6206119  6206153  6206177  6206191  6206197
6206227  6206257  6206273  6206287  6206327  6206329  6206341  6206357  6206371  6206383
6206393  6206413  6206423  6206429  6206437  6206449  6206461  6206503  6206507  6206509
6206531  6206549  6206561  6206579  6206653  6206693  6206701  6206719  6206737  6206747
6206779  6206791  6206797  6206801  6206833  6206839  6206869  6206903  6206909  6206917
```

```
6206923  6206929  6206953  6206969  6206983  6206999  6207001  6207013  6207017  6207029
6207041  6207043  6207101  6207107  6207119  6207133  6207137  6207139  6207143  6207163
6207181  6207197  6207199  6207209  6207211  6207241  6207259  6207269  6207283  6207287
6207301  6207367  6207371  6207389  6207403  6207419  6207427  6207473  6207491  6207517
6207569  6207577  6207587  6207599  6207611  6207613  6207629  6207671  6207673  6207689
6207727  6207739  6207779  6207793  6207809  6207821  6207829  6207863  6207869  6207893
6207931  6207947  6207973  6207977  6207989  6207991  6207997  6208021  6208067  6208087
6208093  6208099  6208109  6208121  6208127  6208159  6208199  6208207  6208217  6208219
6208243  6208249  6208259  6208303  6208309  6208327  6208331  6208337  6208351  6208357
6208379  6208387  6208403  6208427  6208441  6208457  6208471  6208513  6208537  6208541
6208547  6208561  6208583  6208591  6208603  6208607  6208613  6208619  6208627  6208633
6208651  6208661  6208663  6208691  6208693  6208717  6208721  6208733  6208759  6208771
6208793  6208799  6208817  6208819  6208831  6208861  6208913  6208949  6209009  6209017
6209023  6209039  6209041  6209051  6209053  6209087  6209089  6209111  6209117  6209173
6209179  6209183  6209191  6209201  6209213  6209239  6209249  6209279  6209297  6209299
6209309  6209341  6209351  6209353  6209381  6209383  6209407  6209419  6209429  6209431
6209443  6209449  6209461  6209473  6209503  6209513  6209521  6209527  6209537  6209543
6209551  6209569  6209591  6209597  6209603  6209629  6209633  6209647  6209663  6209669
6209681  6209717  6209719  6209729  6209773  6209779  6209803  6209807  6209831  6209837
6209867  6209893  6209897  6209909  6209911  6209921  6209923  6209933  6209939  6209963
6209971  6209989  6210011  6210041  6210053  6210059  6210067  6210097  6210101  6210167
6210203  6210209  6210221  6210223  6210241  6210247  6210277  6210289  6210301  6210307
6210319  6210353  6210377  6210383  6210401  6210409  6210419  6210433  6210443  6210461
6210467  6210481  6210497  6210499  6210539  6210551  6210569  6210577  6210599  6210613
6210623  6210637  6210643  6210671  6210689  6210691  6210697  6210707  6210719  6210731
6210749  6210751  6210779  6210817  6210821  6210829  6210839  6210847  6210863  6210887
6210889  6210907  6210923  6210949  6210979  6210983  6210991  6211019  6211027  6211033
6211039  6211057  6211061  6211091  6211159  6211187  6211223  6211237  6211241  6211259
6211279  6211291  6211297  6211321  6211349  6211367  6211397  6211421  6211427  6211451
6211453  6211489  6211507  6211553  6211559  6211573  6211609  6211619  6211631  6211657
6211669  6211703  6211729  6211747  6211753  6211757  6211763  6211769  6211781  6211831
6211853  6211867  6211871  6211897  6211901  6211903  6211927  6211937  6211939  6211957
6211963  6211973  6211981  6212009  6212053  6212113  6212117  6212147  6212153  6212159
6212161  6212201  6212203  6212243  6212267  6212273  6212299  6212321  6212347  6212357
6212359  6212363  6212377  6212383  6212387  6212389  6212407  6212417  6212471  6212483
6212489  6212491  6212533  6212543  6212551  6212561  6212587  6212621  6212669  6212671
6212681  6212711  6212747  6212749  6212761  6212777  6212807  6212809  6212821  6212831
6212839  6212851  6212881  6212893  6212917  6212923  6212951  6212953  6212971  6212993
6213029  6213037  6213043  6213073  6213083  6213089  6213091  6213101  6213107  6213121
6213127  6213149  6213157  6213173  6213203  6213223  6213239  6213253  6213257  6213287
6213301  6213307  6213329  6213331  6213341  6213343  6213367  6213391  6213401  6213407
6213413  6213433  6213443  6213479  6213491  6213503  6213523  6213527  6213533  6213563
6213593  6213601  6213607  6213617  6213637  6213659  6213679  6213689  6213719  6213731
6213737  6213751  6213769  6213787  6213791  6213793  6213797  6213799  6213827  6213839
6213869  6213899  6213913  6213947  6213953  6213997  6214031  6214037  6214051  6214073
6214099  6214123  6214139  6214157  6214171  6214177  6214181  6214211  6214223  6214267
6214283  6214309  6214319  6214321  6214331  6214339  6214357  6214361  6214363  6214399
6214421  6214433  6214441  6214447  6214471  6214487  6214511  6214519  6214541  6214543
6214573  6214591  6214597  6214627  6214651  6214687  6214699  6214751  6214753  6214757
6214777  6214783  6214799  6214801  6214811  6214837  6214841  6214907  6214931  6214933
6214937  6214981  6214993  6215017  6215021  6215023  6215039  6215051  6215057  6215063
6215089  6215093  6215101  6215141  6215171  6215173  6215189  6215191  6215201  6215203
6215213  6215227  6215249  6215273  6215281  6215317  6215333  6215347  6215357  6215369
6215381  6215393  6215401  6215423  6215431  6215441  6215449  6215453  6215459  6215467
6215471  6215491  6215501  6215533  6215551  6215579  6215597  6215611  6215617  6215623
6215639  6215647  6215653  6215669  6215701  6215719  6215771  6215789  6215813  6215851
6215861  6215873  6215917  6215921  6215929  6215933  6215959  6215971  6215987  6216011
6216013  6216019  6216029  6216031  6216047  6216061  6216071  6216073  6216103  6216107
6216109  6216139  6216149  6216191  6216227  6216229  6216239  6216251  6216253  6216257
6216277  6216281  6216283  6216293  6216307  6216311  6216341  6216349  6216367  6216377
6216389  6216403  6216421  6216437  6216479  6216499  6216503  6216541  6216557  6216569
6216599  6216697  6216719  6216731  6216733  6216751  6216757  6216761  6216773  6216779
6216797  6216823  6216829  6216841  6216887  6216893  6216913  6216929  6216943  6216961
6216967  6216979  6216989  6217027  6217037  6217039  6217051  6217067  6217091  6217097
6217103  6217151  6217157  6217177  6217229  6217231  6217249  6217259  6217261  6217279
6217283  6217297  6217307  6217319  6217381  6217411  6217441  6217457  6217481  6217493
6217543  6217633  6217637  6217643  6217649  6217657  6217681  6217697  6217709  6217711
6217721  6217741  6217747  6217777  6217789  6217811  6217817  6217831  6217859  6217867
6217873  6217879  6217901  6217927  6217931  6217933  6217943  6217963  6217993  6217999
6218021  6218033  6218057  6218059  6218083  6218089  6218099  6218117  6218143  6218159
6218161  6218189  6218207  6218221  6218227  6218231  6218237  6218269  6218291  6218297
6218323  6218351  6218357  6218363  6218369  6218417  6218431  6218449  6218477  6218489
6218539  6218581  6218599  6218603  6218621  6218623  6218647  6218657  6218669  6218683
6218687  6218689  6218713  6218741  6218749  6218759  6218827  6218837  6218867  6218881
6218887  6218897  6218917  6218929  6218951  6218981  6218987  6219001  6219041  6219043
6219049  6219077  6219091  6219097  6219113  6219121  6219139  6219149  6219173  6219197
6219203  6219209  6219211  6219221  6219233  6219271  6219287  6219319  6219359  6219371
6219379  6219383  6219419  6219443  6219457  6219503  6219509  6219541  6219547  6219583
6219617  6219643  6219667  6219679  6219701  6219727  6219757  6219779  6219781  6219793
6219797  6219803  6219847  6219853  6219887  6219893  6219913  6219919  6219923  6219941
6219953  6219971  6219989  6219991  6220001  6220003  6220043  6220061  6220063  6220073
6220091  6220099  6220117  6220129  6220141  6220157  6220169  6220177  6220187  6220199
6220217  6220229  6220237  6220241  6220259  6220261  6220271  6220289  6220307  6220321
6220339  6220343  6220349  6220369  6220387  6220399  6220411  6220421  6220433  6220447
6220457  6220463  6220469  6220517  6220519  6220567  6220579  6220631  6220633  6220639
6220651  6220661  6220673  6220693  6220723  6220727  6220729  6220751  6220757  6220777
6220813  6220817  6220829  6220831  6220849  6220871  6220897  6220927  6220937  6220943
6220979  6221003  6221009  6221023  6221027  6221041  6221071  6221077  6221081  6221093
6221101  6221107  6221119  6221123  6221147  6221153  6221161  6221177  6221179  6221183
```

```
6221191 6221203 6221209 6221213 6221231 6221239 6221263 6221273 6221287 6221309
6221311 6221317 6221377 6221429 6221459 6221471 6221489 6221497 6221539 6221543
6221549 6221557 6221561 6221563 6221591 6221629 6221639 6221647 6221651 6221671
6221693 6221749 6221767 6221771 6221773 6221819 6221827 6221833 6221837 6221849
6221867 6221869 6221879 6221909 6221927 6221933 6221951 6221953 6221977 6221981
6221989 6222011 6222049 6222053 6222059 6222071 6222077 6222113 6222149 6222163
6222169 6222173 6222191 6222193 6222197 6222217 6222233 6222241 6222263 6222287
6222299 6222313 6222319 6222341 6222343 6222353 6222361 6222373 6222383 6222407
6222419 6222421 6222449 6222451 6222457 6222467 6222473 6222479 6222497 6222499
6222523 6222533 6222551 6222607 6222641 6222679 6222707 6222743 6222757 6222761
6222763 6222767 6222781 6222817 6222829 6222869 6222877 6222883 6222947 6222959
6222967 6222977 6222991 6223001 6223057 6223069 6223073 6223099 6223109 6223111
6223117 6223121 6223171 6223181 6223187 6223193 6223201 6223211 6223247 6223253
6223277 6223291 6223319 6223331 6223333 6223337 6223351 6223387 6223391 6223397
6223439 6223463 6223471 6223489 6223531 6223549 6223561 6223577 6223579 6223601
6223627 6223667 6223669 6223673 6223687 6223727 6223739 6223741 6223747 6223757
6223771 6223781 6223783 6223811 6223817 6223873 6223897 6223909 6223933
6223937 6223939 6223957 6223967 6223993 6223999 6224011 6224017 6224033 6224041
6224051 6224059 6224063 6224081 6224089 6224093 6224101 6224131 6224137 6224171
6224189 6224201 6224213 6224221 6224243 6224249 6224263 6224269 6224279 6224287
6224353 6224359 6224369 6224377 6224401 6224411 6224417 6224423 6224429 6224437
6224447 6224461 6224483 6224503 6224507 6224509 6224527 6224573 6224611 6224627
6224629 6224639 6224653 6224657 6224671 6224681 6224683 6224689 6224693 6224717
6224747 6224753 6224759 6224767 6224851 6224861 6224861 6224891 6224909 6224921
6224923 6224971 6224983 6224987 6225001 6225007 6225013 6225029 6225097 6225119
6225137 6225181 6225211 6225223 6225299 6225313 6225319 6225353 6225377
6225379 6225391 6225409 6225449 6225469 6225487 6225523 6225529 6225533 6225547
6225551 6225607 6225619 6225623 6225647 6225649 6225677 6225679 6225697 6225701
6225719 6225733 6225763 6225767 6225773 6225781 6225797 6225803 6225827 6225829
6225839 6225851 6225871 6225889 6225899 6225917 6225931 6225941 6225979 6225983
6226007 6226019 6226021 6226049 6226067 6226127 6226141 6226159 6226163 6226177
6226201 6226229 6226273 6226277 6226279 6226291 6226303 6226313 6226321 6226343
6226349 6226361 6226379 6226391 6226393 6226417 6226427 6226439 6226457 6226469
6226477 6226481 6226499 6226523 6226559 6226589 6226603 6226609 6226613 6226621
6226631 6226643 6226663 6226673 6226687 6226729 6226733 6226741 6226747 6226757
6226769 6226799 6226807 6226817 6226861 6226867 6226901 6226903 6226907 6226921
6226931 6226933 6226963 6226993 6227027 6227029 6227033 6227057 6227069 6227099
6227101 6227107 6227113 6227149 6227161 6227183 6227189 6227201 6227209 6227233
6227239 6227261 6227267 6227297 6227323 6227329 6227363 6227369 6227371 6227387
6227393 6227399 6227401 6227437 6227443 6227461 6227471 6227477 6227521 6227527
6227563 6227567 6227569 6227579 6227587 6227591 6227603 6227633 6227651
6227653 6227657 6227671 6227677 6227701 6227707 6227713 6227731 6227737 6227743
6227747 6227773 6227783 6227821 6227833 6227861 6227867 6227873 6227891 6227909
6227911 6227927 6227939 6227959 6227971 6227987 6227989 6227999 6228007 6228031
6228037 6228041 6228059 6228073 6228091 6228121 6228139 6228203 6228223 6228227
6228251 6228263 6228311 6228317 6228329 6228337 6228353 6228361 6228373
6228389 6228413 6228449 6228457 6228463 6228473 6228493 6228499 6228503 6228539
6228553 6228583 6228589 6228611 6228623 6228631 6228659 6228667 6228671 6228683
6228709 6228721 6228731 6228743 6228773 6228779 6228787 6228793 6228797 6228809
6228821 6228829 6228841 6228847 6228853 6228857 6228869 6228877 6228889 6228907
6228917 6228947 6228949 6228961 6228983 6228991 6229033 6229073 6229079 6229081
6229087 6229099 6229103 6229117 6229129 6229133 6229141 6229151 6229177 6229183
6229187 6229193 6229213 6229231 6229247 6229261 6229303 6229319 6229339 6229369
6229373 6229393 6229409 6229439 6229441 6229451 6229471 6229501 6229507 6229513
6229523 6229529 6229547 6229583 6229589 6229591 6229621 6229627 6229649 6229661
6229723 6229789 6229793 6229799 6229813 6229823 6229829 6229843 6229877
6229889 6229907 6229913 6229921 6229933 6229943 6229957 6230017 6230047 6230053
6230057 6230069 6230123 6230131 6230153 6230167 6230173 6230209 6230221
6230251 6230291 6230303 6230311 6230317 6230351 6230359 6230369 6230383 6230429
6230443 6230501 6230507 6230527 6230533 6230557 6230579 6230599 6230617 6230629
6230633 6230663 6230671 6230681 6230683 6230699 6230711 6230759 6230761 6230771
6230797 6230821 6230827 6230831 6230849 6230863 6230869 6230881 6230899 6230909
6230921 6230927 6230929 6230947 6230957 6230971 6230977 6230981 6231007 6231011
6231037 6231053 6231073 6231097 6231101 6231109 6231131 6231149 6231151 6231187
6231209 6231223 6231227 6231241 6231301 6231347 6231349 6231361 6231371 6231383
6231419 6231427 6231437 6231439 6231451 6231461 6231481 6231493 6231497 6231523
6231529 6231553 6231559 6231569 6231587 6231613 6231623 6231629 6231637 6231647
6231661 6231679 6231691 6231697 6231703 6231721 6231733 6231749 6231767 6231803
6231833 6231851 6231853 6231887 6231893 6231913 6231949 6232043 6232049
6232067 6232087 6232097 6232099 6232159 6232199 6232201 6232277 6232279 6232297
6232321 6232327 6232337 6232339 6232349 6232351 6232357 6232363 6232367 6232393
6232397 6232409 6232411 6232417 6232423 6232433 6232439 6232441 6232459 6232469
6232487 6232493 6232531 6232543 6232561 6232573 6232619 6232649 6232657 6232663
6232669 6232679 6232753 6232757 6232763 6232771 6232781 6232783 6232789 6232799
6232801 6232823 6232849 6232859 6232867 6232889 6232897 6232907 6232927
6232939 6232951 6232981 6232987 6232991 6232997 6233039 6233047 6233063 6233119
6233137 6233141 6233147 6233153 6233167 6233191 6233221 6233239 6233257 6233267
6233327 6233329 6233333 6233341 6233377 6233389 6233393 6233399 6233401 6233411
6233429 6233473 6233477 6233497 6233503 6233531 6233533 6233561 6233567 6233593
6233603 6233659 6233667 6233683 6233687 6233693 6233699 6233719 6233737 6233743
6233749 6233761 6233771 6233779 6233789 6233791 6233803 6233809 6233831 6233833
6233863 6233867 6233873 6233879 6233893 6233921 6233923 6233933 6233959 6233963
6233971 6234001 6234029 6234031 6234061 6234077 6234079 6234089 6234113 6234133
6234143 6234169 6234181 6234197 6234199 6234203 6234211 6234233 6234247 6234253
6234259 6234321 6234331 6234343 6234367 6234373 6234377 6234407 6234469 6234491
6234509 6234511 6234517 6234523 6234559 6234619 6234637 6234643 6234649 6234653
6234659 6234661 6234671 6234673 6234677 6234703 6234713 6234719 6234721 6234731
6234737 6234743 6234757 6234763 6234779 6234803 6234821 6234827 6234841 6234859
6234883 6234889 6234901 6234919 6234923 6234959 6234979 6234989 6235013 6235027
```

```
6235037 6235049 6235051 6235057 6235069 6235081 6235111 6235121 6235133 6235147
6235153 6235181 6235189 6235193 6235219 6235223 6235241 6235283 6235289 6235331
6235337 6235357 6235367 6235373 6235381 6235399 6235417 6235423 6235457 6235459
6235483 6235487 6235513 6235519 6235529 6235531 6235543 6235561 6235577 6235597
6235601 6235627 6235643 6235657 6235661 6235673 6235699 6235703 6235727 6235739
6235741 6235751 6235771 6235777 6235793 6235807 6235837 6235843 6235877 6235909
6235939 6235949 6235961 6235973 6235997 6236011 6236029 6236051 6236057 6236071
6236089 6236099 6236137 6236179 6236201 6236203 6236207 6236231 6236249 6236267
6236299 6236303 6236309 6236323 6236327 6236353 6236369 6236393 6236411 6236413
6236423 6236437 6236443 6236453 6236459 6236507 6236509 6236521 6236533 6236557
6236623 6236627 6236639 6236647 6236687 6236689 6236717 6236719 6236743 6236761
6236771 6236801 6236819 6236833 6236899 6236903 6236911 6236917 6236927 6236929
6236939 6236941 6236953 6236957 6236969 6236981 6236999 6237013 6237017 6237019
6237061 6237083 6237103 6237109 6237131 6237167 6237191 6237211 6237221 6237223
6237227 6237239 6237251 6237277 6237281 6237313 6237331 6237353 6237373 6237379
6237383 6237397 6237409 6237431 6237443 6237449 6237467 6237493 6237503 6237509
6237527 6237547 6237557 6237599 6237629 6237641 6237667 6237689 6237701 6237739
6237769 6237773 6237787 6237809 6237811 6237817 6237877 6237911 6237937 6237943
6237949 6238009 6238013 6238033 6238039 6238051 6238073 6238079 6238087 6238091
6238121 6238123 6238147 6238151 6238157 6238159 6238171 6238241 6238249 6238261
6238279 6238283 6238291 6238301 6238307 6238319 6238321 6238333 6238369 6238373
6238381 6238411 6238423 6238429 6238433 6238457 6238469 6238489 6238493 6238513
6238559 6238579 6238591 6238597 6238649 6238651 6238663 6238667 6238679 6238693
6238703 6238721 6238723 6238751 6238759 6238777 6238787 6238801 6238823 6238831
6238873 6238891 6238907 6238909 6238931 6238933 6238937 6238951 6238961 6238987
6239033 6239053 6239071 6239081 6239099 6239113 6239131 6239143 6239197 6239209
6239227 6239231 6239243 6239281 6239327 6239333 6239351 6239369 6239381 6239393
6239411 6239413 6239419 6239423 6239447 6239449 6239461 6239473 6239489 6239501
6239533 6239537 6239539 6239557 6239567 6239599 6239603 6239617 6239627 6239659
6239677 6239683 6239699 6239707 6239759 6239789 6239797 6239801 6239813 6239819
6239837 6239839 6239887 6239921 6239927 6239941 6239951 6239953 6239957 6240001
6240007 6240011 6240019 6240041 6240053 6240079 6240089 6240097 6240103 6240109
6240121 6240149 6240163 6240177 6240181 6240187 6240193 6240197 6240211 6240233
6240251 6240257 6240263 6240277 6240287 6240293 6240319 6240329 6240349 6240373
6240401 6240407 6240419 6240431 6240463 6240473 6240491 6240499 6240503 6240523
6240527 6240587 6240589 6240631 6240671 6240691 6240701 6240737 6240743 6240749
6240757 6240791 6240799 6240811 6240821 6240823 6240841 6240847 6240851 6240869
6240893 6240917 6240967 6240991 6241009 6241021 6241031 6241033 6241061
6241097 6241111 6241127 6241129 6241141 6241153 6241171 6241181 6241187 6241201
6241217 6241219 6241229 6241241 6241243 6241247 6241259 6241267 6241289 6241297
6241331 6241343 6241387 6241399 6241421 6241441 6241451 6241457 6241463 6241483
6241511 6241513 6241523 6241537 6241559 6241589 6241603 6241619 6241621 6241643
6241649 6241661 6241663 6241673 6241679 6241687 6241691 6241693 6241721 6241723
6241733 6241777 6241783 6241793 6241801 6241811 6241831 6241841 6241847 6241871
6241883 6241897 6241913 6241957 6241967 6241979 6241987 6241997 6241999 6242003
6242017 6242021 6242029 6242087 6242113 6242143 6242149 6242153 6242161 6242207
6242219 6242237 6242239 6242261 6242263 6242363 6242387 6242413 6242437 6242443
6242473 6242479 6242497 6242503 6242527 6242531 6242573 6242581 6242597 6242609
6242633 6242657 6242669 6242671 6242693 6242713 6242759 6242771 6242779 6242809
6242813 6242837 6242869 6242889 6242897 6242909
6242921 6242941 6242981 6242987 6243007 6243043 6243049 6243071 6243073 6243079
6243109 6243157 6243161 6243163 6243187 6243197 6243239 6243247 6243257 6243277
6243287 6243313 6243317 6243319 6243353 6243359 6243361 6243371 6243379 6243383
6243407 6243409 6243443 6243451 6243469 6243473 6243481 6243487 6243553 6243563
6243577 6243583 6243623 6243631 6243659 6243661 6243667 6243673 6243683 6243689
6243691 6243703 6243707 6243749 6243773 6243779 6243781 6243791 6243817 6243823
6243859 6243863 6243869 6243871 6243893 6243907 6243929 6243943 6243967 6244003
6244031 6244033 6244039 6244061 6244079 6244093 6244099 6244153 6244171 6244187
6244207 6244213 6244229 6244241 6244261 6244289 6244307 6244313 6244327 6244349
6244351 6244391 6244429 6244439 6244451 6244471 6244487 6244489 6244519 6244531
6244573 6244577 6244591 6244603 6244607 6244621 6244643 6244649 6244691 6244699
6244727 6244741 6244747 6244757 6244769 6244789 6244793 6244811 6244817 6244829
6244859 6244867 6244873 6244883 6244889 6244951 6244969 6245011 6245017 6245023
6245039 6245047 6245051 6245087 6245101 6245111 6245123 6245153 6245177 6245189
6245201 6245203 6245249 6245251 6245257 6245293 6245311 6245321 6245329 6245333
6245339 6245381 6245383 6245387 6245401 6245413 6245431 6245453 6245497 6245507
6245513 6245521 6245549 6245557 6245567 6245587 6245593 6245597 6245599 6245609
6245651 6245669 6245677 6245683 6245717 6245731 6245741 6245761 6245779 6245791
6245803 6245821 6245831 6245873 6245887 6245909 6245923 6245929 6245947 6245951
6245957 6245959 6245963 6245969 6245989 6246017 6246029 6246043 6246047 6246061
6246077 6246091 6246127 6246131 6246151 6246161 6246181 6246187 6246197 6246199
6246203 6246239 6246257 6246277 6246313 6246319 6246337 6246341 6246353 6246371
6246379 6246403 6246413 6246431 6246437 6246439 6246503 6246517 6246523 6246533
6246577 6246589 6246601 6246619 6246623 6246671 6246677 6246689 6246697 6246761
6246781 6246787 6246791 6246797 6246811 6246833 6246859 6246881 6246889 6246907
6246931 6246941 6246943 6246967 6246983 6247001 6247019 6247061 6247069 6247079
6247081 6247103 6247127 6247159 6247183 6247201 6247229 6247231 6247243 6247247
6247253 6247261 6247271 6247273 6247277 6247289 6247309 6247321 6247343 6247369
6247379 6247387 6247403 6247411 6247433 6247453 6247463 6247471 6247477 6247519
6247529 6247537 6247541 6247543 6247547 6247573 6247583 6247601 6247609 6247613
6247667 6247691 6247727 6247733 6247739 6247777 6247781 6247811 6247819 6247831
6247841 6247849 6247853 6247859 6247861 6247887 6247909 6247919 6247937 6247987
6247999 6248023 6248057 6248059 6248069 6248089 6248119 6248149 6248161 6248167
6248171 6248191 6248233 6248239 6248243 6248251 6248257 6248261 6248269 6248303
6248327 6248377 6248399 6248461 6248471 6248483 6248519 6248521 6248551 6248563
6248579 6248591 6248609 6248611 6248633 6248651 6248653 6248677 6248689 6248699
6248719 6248729 6248731 6248743 6248771 6248773 6248789 6248797 6248807 6248813
6248839 6248857 6248881 6248899 6248941 6248953 6248959 6248969 6248999 6249029
6249059 6249101 6249107 6249127 6249151 6249161 6249193 6249211 6249223 6249227
```

```
6249247 6249281 6249323 6249359 6249361 6249379 6249391 6249403 6249407 6249409
6249433 6249443 6249473 6249479 6249497 6249517 6249521 6249539 6249547 6249553
6249563 6249571 6249619 6249647 6249653 6249667 6249673 6249679 6249697 6249701
6249713 6249743 6249751 6249757 6249773 6249791 6249809 6249821 6249823 6249833
6249839 6249851 6249871 6249883 6249889 6249899 6249907 6249913 6249923 6249949
6249953 6249959 6249967 6249973 6249979 6249989 6250009 6250039 6250087 6250091
6250099 6250117 6250129 6250147 6250157 6250171 6250199 6250207 6250217 6250247
6250249 6250253 6250261 6250301 6250303 6250331 6250337 6250357 6250367 6250393
6250397 6250417 6250421 6250423 6250427 6250451 6250459 6250469 6250477
6250493 6250507 6250513 6250537 6250547 6250553 6250579 6250591 6250597 6250633
6250649 6250681 6250697 6250703 6250711 6250723 6250729 6250759 6250787 6250799
6250801 6250807 6250831 6250837 6250843 6250861 6250877 6250879 6250889 6250903
6250919 6250949 6250957 6250961 6250987 6250999 6251017 6251023 6251051 6251071
6251117 6251123 6251129 6251137 6251149 6251159 6251177 6251183 6251207 6251233
6251237 6251263 6251279 6251339 6251347 6251351 6251369 6251387 6251417 6251431
6251459 6251467 6251519 6251521 6251527 6251533 6251537 6251543 6251573 6251579
6251587 6251591 6251599 6251629 6251633 6251659 6251669 6251671 6251681 6251683
6251711 6251717 6251731 6251737 6251743 6251759 6251761 6251771 6251783 6251789
6251797 6251821 6251831 6251851 6251857 6251873 6251881 6251887 6251909
6251911 6251953 6251963 6251977 6251989 6252011 6252017 6252019 6252031 6252059
6252091 6252097 6252101 6252109 6252119 6252143 6252151 6252163 6252227 6252229
6252247 6252341 6252347 6252391 6252401 6252419 6252427 6252443 6252451 6252461
6252469 6252497 6252503 6252509 6252511 6252529 6252557 6252559 6252611 6252709
6252733 6252751 6252769 6252791 6252823 6252847 6252853 6252871 6252877 6252901
6252937 6252943 6252959 6252989 6253001 6253019 6253057 6253063 6253069 6253073
6253123 6253129 6253133 6253139 6253141 6253151 6253157 6253207 6253211 6253243
6253267 6253271 6253301 6253319 6253321 6253327 6253339 6253349 6253367 6253391
6253409 6253411 6253441 6253463 6253477 6253483 6253517 6253519 6253543 6253549
6253563 6253571 6253573 6253627 6253653 6253669 6253673 6253693 6253697
6253699 6253711 6253727 6253729 6253733 6253747 6253783 6253787 6253789 6253813
6253817 6253843 6253859 6253873 6253889 6253891 6253901 6253937 6253939 6253957
6253969 6253979 6253991 6253993 6254009 6254023 6254041 6254051 6254063 6254069
6254107 6254117 6254141 6254153 6254179 6254203 6254207 6254233 6254239 6254267
6254273 6254279 6254291 6254293 6254309 6254323 6254327 6254329 6254357 6254359
6254377 6254389 6254399 6254407 6254411 6254441 6254447 6254449 6254483 6254489
6254491 6254497 6254503 6254527 6254533 6254547 6254561 6254579 6254593 6254617
6254621 6254639 6254641 6254681 6254683 6254687 6254693 6254701 6254707 6254741
6254761 6254771 6254783 6254789 6254863 6254867 6254901 6254903 6254917 6254921
6254939 6254953 6254987 6254993 6255013 6255061 6255071 6255157 6255163 6255173
6255181 6255203 6255209 6255217 6255229 6255259 6255281 6255307 6255343 6255349
6255377 6255383 6255391 6255409 6255419 6255421 6255437 6255463 6255481 6255497
6255527 6255533 6255547 6255577 6255581 6255607 6255629 6255631 6255649 6255661
6255671 6255679 6255713 6255719 6255737 6255751 6255761 6255787 6255791 6255797
6255803 6255827 6255833 6255859 6255901 6255913 6255919 6255929 6255937 6255943
6255989 6256013 6256021 6256031 6256037 6256043 6256049 6256057 6256087 6256091
6256093 6256109 6256121 6256127 6256139 6256169 6256171 6256177 6256193 6256223
6256277 6256297 6256309 6256331 6256333 6256337 6256351 6256363 6256381 6256409
6256421 6256427 6256469 6256487 6256501 6256511 6256531 6256541 6256553 6256571
6256573 6256583 6256631 6256633 6256639 6256651 6256669 6256673 6256693 6256727
6256729 6256739 6256741 6256751 6256753 6256769 6256771 6256793 6256819 6256843
6256853 6256883 6256907 6256919 6256933 6256937 6256949 6256951 6256981 6256993
6257029 6257047 6257057 6257077 6257087 6257089 6257093 6257101 6257123 6257129
6257143 6257161 6257171 6257189 6257203 6257227 6257239 6257249 6257261 6257267
6257281 6257299 6257347 6257371 6257387 6257389 6257399 6257429 6257431 6257473
6257483 6257491 6257497 6257507 6257509 6257519 6257521 6257527 6257539 6257557
6257579 6257609 6257617 6257611 6257617 6257623 6257653 6257663 6257677 6257711
6257723 6257759 6257767 6257777 6257791 6257803 6257813 6257831 6257861 6257873
6257879 6257891 6257899 6257903 6257917 6257947 6257957 6257957 6257963 6257969
6257981 6258013 6258029 6258037 6258041 6258067 6258073 6258079 6258089 6258107
6258127 6258137 6258157 6258167 6258181 6258209 6258221 6258233 6258247 6258271
6258299 6258313 6258331 6258347 6258361 6258387 6258389 6258401 6258409 6258419
6258443 6258457 6258463 6258481 6258503 6258517 6258541 6258547 6258557 6258563
6258583 6258631 6258647 6258649 6258653 6258677 6258689 6258697 6258701 6258727
6258757 6258767 6258793 6258803 6258817 6258821 6258851 6258853 6258859 6258877
6258881 6258899 6258911 6258919 6258953 6258971 6258977 6258977 6259003 6259039
6259063 6259081 6259109 6259129 6259139 6259153 6259159 6259177 6259193 6259199
6259217 6259219 6259237 6259259 6259283 6259291 6259301 6259307 6259333 6259367
6259373 6259397 6259453 6259457 6259469 6259471 6259537 6259547 6259571 6259579
6259651 6259681 6259691 6259709 6259727 6259733 6259739 6259741 6259753 6259763
6259783 6259793 6259801 6259807 6259817 6259831 6259843 6259867 6259871
6259889 6259901 6259907 6259909 6259931 6259973 6260017 6260021 6260041 6260057
6260083 6260099 6260129 6260153 6260161 6260179 6260183 6260207 6260231 6260239
6260251 6260269 6260273 6260297 6260299 6260321 6260323 6260339 6260377 6260381
6260383 6260389 6260411 6260453 6260459 6260461 6260467 6260479 6260483 6260497
6260503 6260509 6260521 6260587 6260591 6260593 6260599 6260603 6260629 6260717
6260753 6260767 6260783 6260797 6260801 6260803 6260827 6260867 6260869 6260873
6260893 6260909 6260911 6260923 6260927 6260941 6260951 6260957 6260959 6260963
6260989 6261001 6261023 6261041 6261077 6261097 6261107 6261109 6261121
6261173 6261181 6261191 6261193 6261197 6261247 6261289 6261301 6261371 6261373
6261377 6261379 6261383 6261391 6261401 6261447 6261539 6261551 6261571
6261581 6261587 6261601 6261623 6261637 6261649 6261677 6261683 6261691 6261707
6261719 6261737 6261743 6261751 6261777 6261787 6261799 6261809 6261817 6261821
6261823 6261839 6261841 6261851 6261863 6261869 6261877 6261901 6261919 6261947
6261949 6261953 6261973 6261977 6262007 6262027 6262043 6262079 6262111 6262117
6262127 6262147 6262169 6262211 6262241 6262247 6262261 6262283 6262301 6262337
6262339 6262349 6262357 6262363 6262369 6262379 6262387 6262393 6262397 6262411
6262429 6262439 6262441 6262453 6262489 6262513 6262519 6262537 6262541
6262547 6262559 6262561 6262577 6262621 6262631 6262643 6262679 6262721 6262727
6262733 6262741 6262757 6262759 6262769 6262771 6262777 6262787 6262801 6262829
```

```
6262847 6262849 6262859 6262897 6262901 6262903 6262933 6262939 6262943 6262967
6262973 6263011 6263039 6263051 6263057 6263069 6263071 6263099 6263137 6263161
6263171 6263183 6263189 6263207 6263233 6263237 6263239 6263261 6263269 6263281
6263287 6263303 6263311 6263317 6263339 6263351 6263359 6263363 6263371 6263377
6263393 6263399 6263417 6263437 6263441 6263489 6263501 6263527 6263539 6263557
6263561 6263563 6263573 6263591 6263641 6263651 6263657 6263671 6263683 6263689
6263707 6263729 6263753 6263759 6263773 6263779 6263783 6263809 6263821 6263827
6263839 6263849 6263869 6263879 6263941 6263963 6263987 6263993 6264001 6264023
6264043 6264061 6264079 6264107 6264127 6264133 6264149 6264161 6264169 6264173
6264179 6264187 6264199 6264217 6264221 6264241 6264277 6264287 6264311 6264329
6264331 6264341 6264343 6264353 6264361 6264367 6264371 6264373 6264383 6264389
6264409 6264413 6264421 6264437 6264439 6264481 6264497 6264499 6264523 6264527
6264539 6264553 6264569 6264571 6264593 6264611 6264613 6264617 6264631 6264637
6264673 6264689 6264703 6264733 6264751 6264773 6264781 6264793 6264829 6264859
6264887 6264913 6264917 6264919 6264931 6264943 6264983 6264997 6265001 6265019
6265067 6265093 6265097 6265109 6265123 6265139 6265153 6265157 6265187 6265201
6265213 6265243 6265261 6265267 6265271 6265283 6265309 6265319 6265351 6265381
6265393 6265417 6265423 6265439 6265477 6265481 6265489 6265507 6265513 6265529
6265531 6265547 6265549 6265559 6265561 6265601 6265657 6265667 6265681 6265697
6265709 6265723 6265733 6265747 6265757 6265771 6265781 6265783 6265789 6265811
6265849 6265873 6265879 6265901 6265921 6265933 6265949 6265951 6265967 6265997
6266009 6266011 6266023 6266033 6266107 6266129 6266147 6266159 6266167 6266171
6266191 6266203 6266207 6266237 6266269 6266279 6266287 6266321 6266329 6266363
6266413 6266423 6266437 6266441 6266453 6266459 6266467 6266471 6266479 6266483
6266497 6266503 6266521 6266527 6266543 6266549 6266587 6266593 6266609 6266621
6266629 6266657 6266677 6266683 6266731 6266759 6266779 6266783 6266837 6266849
6266873 6266927 6266947 6266951 6266963 6267007 6267011 6267013 6267031 6267047
6267049 6267059 6267061 6267071 6267077 6267083 6267119 6267133 6267139 6267181
6267193 6267221 6267223 6267227 6267251 6267253 6267257 6267329 6267339 6267341
6267347 6267361 6267367 6267377 6267389 6267419 6267491 6267517 6267529 6267533
6267539 6267589 6267619 6267643 6267659 6267671 6267719 6267731 6267733 6267743
6267761 6267769 6267773 6267787 6267791 6267803 6267817 6267823 6267841 6267851
6267889 6267893 6267901 6267907 6267913 6267923 6267941 6267971 6267977 6267979
6268013 6268021 6268027 6268037 6268049 6268057 6268063 6268091 6268099 6268109
6268111 6268117 6268127 6268159 6268183 6268187 6268201 6268247 6268279 6268289
6268303 6268313 6268331 6268333 6268369 6268373 6268387 6268391 6268403 6268433
6268439 6268441 6268459 6268517 6268523 6268589 6268601 6268609 6268621 6268637
6268643 6268649 6268657 6268663 6268687 6268693 6268711 6268723 6268747 6268751
6268763 6268781 6268807 6268849 6268883 6268891 6268897 6268939 6268943 6268957
6268963 6268967 6268973 6268979 6268981 6268987 6268991 6269033 6269047 6269051
6269057 6269063 6269093 6269099 6269113 6269119 6269147 6269149 6269223 6269231
6269233 6269251 6269261 6269273 6269279 6269293 6269303 6269339 6269381 6269383
6269437 6269441 6269477 6269479 6269489 6269491 6269503 6269509 6269521 6269537
6269551 6269569 6269573 6269581 6269611 6269623 6269629 6269647 6269663 6269689
6269699 6269707 6269717 6269749 6269759 6269773 6269801 6269807 6269819 6269827
6269831 6269839 6269849 6269881 6269891 6269909 6269917 6269947 6269953 6269961
6269969 6269971 6269987 6270001 6270013 6270023 6270037 6270041 6270049 6270067
6270073 6270083 6270101 6270113 6270137 6270157 6270163 6270167 6270169 6270193
6270197 6270211 6270221 6270227 6270239 6270241 6270269 6270281 6270289 6270301
6270347 6270359 6270391 6270419 6270457 6270479 6270487 6270527 6270529 6270533
6270547 6270553 6270601 6270611 6270613 6270629 6270631 6270701 6270713 6270727
6270749 6270751 6270767 6270769 6270793 6270799 6270809 6270821 6270829 6270833
6270857 6270877 6270883 6270889 6270911 6270923 6270947 6270961 6270967 6271037
6271039 6271043 6271049 6271063 6271081 6271091 6271123 6271127 6271129 6271151
6271171 6271189 6271193 6271219 6271247 6271259 6271271 6271289 6271297 6271301
6271303 6271327 6271333 6271367 6271373 6271379 6271381 6271403 6271417 6271477
6271513 6271519 6271561 6271583 6271597 6271609 6271621 6271631 6271651 6271667
6271673 6271697 6271711 6271721 6271739 6271747 6271757 6271763 6271777 6271787
6271789 6271807 6271817 6271841 6271849 6271871 6271873 6271891 6271897 6271933
6271943 6271961 6271973 6271987 6272017 6272027 6272029 6272051 6272107 6272141
6272143 6272153 6272171 6272173 6272183 6272191 6272209 6272213 6272219 6272243
6272257 6272263 6272267 6272297 6272333 6272341 6272347 6272359 6272369 6272401
6272417 6272419 6272429 6272459 6272471 6272477 6272501 6272503 6272531 6272533
6272543 6272551 6272557 6272579 6272611 6272627 6272639 6272659 6272663 6272681
6272683 6272689 6272723 6272731 6272737 6272753 6272759 6272801 6272839 6272857
6272863 6272867 6272873 6272879 6272887 6272897 6272899 6272927 6272933 6272941
6272947 6272971 6272977 6272999 6273011 6273023 6273031 6273037 6273053 6273061
6273073 6273083 6273101 6273121 6273139 6273151 6273161 6273167 6273199 6273217
6273229 6273233 6273247 6273257 6273263 6273271 6273299 6273307 6273329 6273331
6273353 6273359 6273373 6273433 6273479 6273481 6273523 6273559 6273589 6273655
6273569 6273593 6273611 6273623 6273637 6273643 6273649 6273661 6273677 6273691
6273703 6273763 6273767 6273793 6273797 6273821 6273823 6273847 6273881 6273893
6273907 6273937 6274027 6274031 6274049 6274061 6274091 6274109 6274111 6274117
6274133 6274187 6274211 6274217 6274223 6274231 6274249 6274267 6274283 6274291
6274297 6274337 6274361 6274397 6274409 6274459 6274481 6274523 6274529 6274531
6274549 6274553 6274577 6274601 6274633 6274661 6274663 6274673 6274687 6274703
6274729 6274747 6274753 6274757 6274771 6274783 6274787 6274789 6274799 6274813
6274823 6274831 6274841 6274843 6274847 6274859 6274871 6274877 6274931 6274937
6274949 6274951 6274969 6274973 6274981 6274993 6275053 6275077 6275081 6275083
6275099 6275171 6275141 6275161 6275167 6275177 6275179 6275189 6275209 6275219
6275233 6275257 6275267 6275273 6275279 6275303 6275309 6275317 6275323 6275327
6275341 6275371 6275407 6275411 6275441 6275449 6275473 6275483 6275509 6275519
6275531 6275539 6275543 6275557 6275579 6275587 6275597 6275603 6275611 6275623
6275627 6275641 6275651 6275699 6275701 6275707 6275729 6275743 6275749 6275777
6275821 6275827 6275887 6275891 6275933 6275939 6275953 6275959 6276019 6276047
6276059 6276073 6276097 6276119 6276131 6276139 6276143 6276161 6276163 6276169
6276181 6276227 6276233 6276253 6276269 6276271 6276293 6276301 6276307 6276311
6276317 6276343 6276371 6276407 6276433 6276437 6276449 6276461 6276463 6276469
6276481 6276497 6276509 6276527 6276533 6276541 6276563 6276583 6276607 6276623
```

```
6276637 6276671 6276701 6276719 6276733 6276749 6276763 6276779 6276793 6276799
6276817 6276827 6276841 6276871 6276877 6276901 6276931 6276979 6276997 6277001
6277009 6277027 6277043 6277067 6277093 6277111 6277123 6277133 6277151 6277169
6277171 6277177 6277189 6277211 6277213 6277237 6277241 6277291 6277303 6277307
6277319 6277333 6277339 6277357 6277361 6277393 6277409 6277417 6277421 6277433
6277451 6277487 6277499 6277501 6277507 6277511 6277553 6277559 6277567 6277591
6277603 6277631 6277639 6277669 6277703 6277721 6277727 6277763 6277769 6277783
6277787 6277823 6277829 6277849 6277861 6277867 6277889 6277897 6277907 6277933
6277939 6277987 6278003 6278021 6278023 6278029 6278047 6278053 6278087 6278099
6278137 6278143 6278147 6278177 6278179 6278231 6278243 6278267 6278309 6278329
6278339 6278351 6278353 6278381 6278407 6278411 6278449 6278479 6278497 6278501
6278507 6278513 6278521 6278527 6278537 6278543 6278557 6278561 6278579 6278581
6278621 6278663 6278681 6278687 6278707 6278717 6278749 6278801 6278807 6278809
6278813 6278821 6278827 6278843 6278851 6278879 6278897 6278927 6278929 6278939
6278941 6278953 6278971 6279029 6279041 6279043 6279067 6279083 6279089 6279107
6279127 6279131 6279151 6279181 6279187 6279197 6279227 6279257 6279263 6279289
6279319 6279323 6279347 6279353 6279359 6279373 6279389 6279397 6279421 6279431
6279439 6279451 6279461 6279463 6279467 6279479 6279503 6279541 6279551 6279569
6279617 6279629 6279643 6279649 6279653 6279673 6279703 6279723 6279731 6279733
6279739 6279743 6279773 6279781 6279797 6279803 6279809 6279827 6279839 6279841
6279853 6279859 6279893 6279907 6279941 6279961 6279983 6279991 6279997 6280003
6280007 6280031 6280033 6280039 6280067 6280091 6280139 6280147 6280189 6280199
6280207 6280213 6280229 6280231 6280237 6280243 6280247 6280273 6280283 6280289
6280291 6280297 6280303 6280319 6280333 6280367 6280397 6280399 6280433 6280523
6280441 6280453 6280457 6280481 6280487 6280489 6280493 6280511 6280517 6280523
6280567 6280577 6280591 6280601 6280607 6280661 6280663 6280699 6280717 6280739
6280741 6280759 6280763 6280777 6280789 6280801 6280843 6280853 6280867 6280877
6280889 6280919 6280927 6280933 6280943 6280949 6280957 6280979 6280991 6281017
6281021 6281027 6281029 6281059 6281063 6281069 6281071 6281087 6281101 6281113
6281117 6281123 6281129 6281131 6281137 6281141 6281161 6281173 6281213 6281237
6281239 6281257 6281263 6281269 6281273 6281281 6281287 6281309 6281321 6281329
6281339 6281351 6281377 6281383 6281459 6281477 6281479 6281489 6281491 6281501
6281519 6281537 6281567 6281573 6281579 6281591 6281621 6281629 6281633 6281641
6281657 6281659 6281663 6281669 6281683 6281701 6281707 6281711 6281729 6281767
6281791 6281797 6281819 6281839 6281909 6281917 6281923 6281927 6281929 6281941
6281953 6281969 6281981 6281983 6282019 6282043 6282071 6282079 6282109 6282113
6282131 6282137 6282139 6282167 6282173 6282191 6282203 6282209 6282233 6282233
6282251 6282259 6282271 6282277 6282313 6282323 6282337 6282347 6282361 6282371
6282377 6282391 6282413 6282457 6282481 6282487 6282499 6282533 6282547 6282557
6282569 6282581 6282607 6282613 6282659 6282671 6282701 6282709 6282737 6282743
6282761 6282767 6282797 6282803 6282811 6282823 6282847 6282853 6282889 6282893
6282929 6282931 6282943 6282961 6282967 6282971 6282989 6283001 6283009 6283019
6283021 6283051 6283093 6283099 6283141 6283157 6283159 6283171 6283177 6283201
6283213 6283219 6283223 6283241 6283247 6283253 6283259 6283267 6283273 6283279
6283307 6283331 6283337 6283351 6283363 6283367 6283379 6283391 6283397 6283399
6283447 6283457 6283463 6283481 6283493 6283507 6283561 6283567 6283573 6283583
6283597 6283601 6283603 6283631 6283637 6283649 6283663 6283679 6283687 6283703
6283751 6283763 6283769 6283787 6283799 6283811 6283831 6283841 6283843 6283861
6283873 6283903 6283909 6283919 6283933 6283943 6283961 6283967 6283973 6283987
6284011 6284017 6284077 6284081 6284093 6284123 6284137 6284143 6284147 6284189
6284197 6284209 6284241 6284261 6284279 6284297 6284347 6284353 6284389 6284393
6284401 6284429 6284437 6284449 6284461 6284471 6284479 6284489 6284491 6284507
6284513 6284519 6284527 6284539 6284549 6284563 6284567 6284569 6284587 6284609
6284627 6284633 6284669 6284683 6284693 6284701 6284717 6284731 6284737 6284741
6284743 6284749 6284753 6284777 6284807 6284821 6284827 6284897 6284903 6284933
6284963 6285007 6285011 6285031 6285043 6285047 6285077 6285107 6285137 6285151
6285179 6285193 6285221 6285241 6285247 6285271 6285277 6285289 6285299 6285311
6285313 6285317 6285347 6285361 6285397 6285401 6285457 6285469 6285473 6285481
6285491 6285493 6285497 6285527 6285541 6285553 6285557 6285569 6285581 6285589
6285593 6285607 6285613 6285659 6285661 6285667 6285691 6285737 6285749 6285761
6285787 6285791 6285841 6285847 6285883 6285887 6285889 6285899 6285907 6285911
6285931 6285947 6285973 6285977 6286009 6286013 6286019 6286043 6286051 6286057
6286067 6286081 6286097 6286099 6286117 6286129 6286157 6286177 6286219 6286223
6286229 6286253 6286271 6286289 6286309 6286327 6286331 6286339 6286351 6286361
6286367 6286403 6286433 6286451 6286457 6286487 6286499 6286507 6286513 6286517
6286531 6286547 6286561 6286597 6286601 6286603 6286619 6286661 6286681 6286691
6286697 6286711 6286723 6286733 6286759 6286783 6286801 6286829 6286849 6286867
6286873 6286909 6286933 6286969 6286909 6286927 6286933 6287009 6287033 6287051
6287089 6287101 6287107 6287111 6287117 6287137 6287153 6287173 6287179 6287189
6287191 6287201 6287243 6287251 6287261 6287273 6287311 6287317 6287321 6287329
6287363 6287371 6287377 6287381 6287419 6287431 6287459 6287483 6287497 6287507
6287509 6287543 6287551 6287573 6287581 6287587 6287591 6287597 6287599 6287609
6287621 6287627 6287639 6287647 6287713 6287731 6287741 6287753 6287767 6287767
6287777 6287783 6287789 6287821 6287837 6287849 6287861 6287873 6287881 6287887
6287893 6287903 6287921 6287923 6287927 6287929 6287959 6287969 6288053 6288059
6288077 6288089 6288103 6288119 6288137 6288167 6288169 6288173 6288179 6288197
6288199 6288209 6288229 6288241 6288287 6288299 6288301 6288311 6288313 6288323
6288343 6288349 6288353 6288379 6288391 6288427 6288463 6288493 6288509 6288511
6288517 6288559 6288571 6288587 6288613 6288617 6288619 6288643 6288649 6288701
6288727 6288743 6288749 6288761 6288769 6288773 6288781 6288787 6288797 6288809
6288811 6288817 6288833 6288857 6288881 6288889 6288899 6288907 6288923 6288937
6288941 6288977 6288979 6288983 6289021 6289037 6289079 6289091 6289121 6289123
6289147 6289163 6289229 6289237 6289253 6289289 6289313 6289343 6289379 6289397
6289411 6289417 6289429 6289447 6289453 6289463 6289469 6289471 6289477 6289483
6289499 6289501 6289529 6289531 6289537 6289579 6289601 6289631 6289663 6289697
6289709 6289727 6289729 6289733 6289757 6289783 6289799 6289837 6289841 6289849
6289853 6289861 6289867 6289883 6289903 6289909 6289939 6289957 6289967 6289973
6289981 6289991 6289999 6290003 6290021 6290029 6290047 6290077 6290101 6290113
6290143 6290147 6290149 6290177 6290213 6290243 6290257 6290269 6290279 6290309
```

```
6290327 6290351 6290359 6290363 6290369 6290377 6290413 6290441 6290443 6290467
6290497 6290567 6290573 6290587 6290611 6290617 6290633 6290657 6290677 6290681
6290693 6290699 6290701 6290743 6290749 6290759 6290761 6290783 6290789 6290797
6290803 6290821 6290827 6290839 6290873 6290887 6290899 6290909 6290951 6290953
6290959 6290971 6291011 6291041 6291059 6291079 6291119 6291133 6291149 6291157
6291161 6291169 6291179 6291191 6291209 6291211 6291217 6291247 6291253 6291269
6291277 6291293 6291301 6291319 6291331 6291353 6291403 6291421 6291431
6291437 6291449 6291469 6291487 6291503 6291511 6291529 6291533 6291539 6291563
6291569 6291587 6291599 6291611 6291619 6291653 6291689 6291697 6291709 6291713
6291721 6291757 6291763 6291767 6291773 6291781 6291821 6291827 6291833 6291839
6291847 6291851 6291863 6291881 6291893 6291899 6291911 6291931 6291941 6291947
6291959 6291973 6291991 6292007 6292009 6292049 6292051 6292063 6292073 6292079
6292081 6292129 6292177 6292201 6292241 6292267 6292283 6292309 6292327 6292339
6292343 6292361 6292367 6292417 6292421 6292427 6292441 6292453 6292457 6292471
6292483 6292493 6292511 6292513 6292519 6292541 6292543 6292589 6292607 6292613
6292621 6292661 6292711 6292733 6292753 6292757 6292787 6292807 6292813 6292817
6292831 6292859 6292861 6292879 6292901 6292919 6292927 6292973 6292981 6293011
6293017 6293039 6293057 6293059 6293081 6293113 6293137 6293153 6293171 6293173
6293201 6293207 6293239 6293249 6293251 6293269 6293291 6293297 6293299 6293311
6293359 6293363 6293387 6293393 6293423 6293429 6293447 6293449 6293473 6293477
6293479 6293533 6293561 6293569 6293597 6293603 6293647 6293669 6293681 6293687
6293699 6293719 6293747 6293753 6293767 6293801 6293809 6293821 6293827 6293843
6293849 6293857 6293863 6293873 6293879 6293891 6293939 6293977 6293981 6293999
6294007 6294011 6294031 6294037 6294049 6294077 6294083 6294089 6294091 6294137
6294143 6294151 6294161 6294217 6294241 6294251 6294269 6294283 6294289 6294293
6294307 6294311 6294313 6294317 6294359 6294367 6294373 6294389 6294391 6294413
6294451 6294461 6294467 6294473 6294481 6294487 6294499 6294503 6294511 6294527
6294553 6294557 6294577 6294593 6294599 6294649 6294667 6294671 6294677 6294683
6294697 6294707 6294713 6294721 6294733 6294749 6294751 6294779 6294791 6294797
6294809 6294839 6294857 6294877 6294889 6294923 6294929 6294941 6294971 6294973
6294979 6294983 6294989 6294991 6295019 6295033 6295043 6295063 6295087 6295097
6295103 6295109 6295129 6295141 6295147 6295183 6295189 6295193 6295207 6295231
6295249 6295259 6295271 6295277 6295279 6295283 6295309 6295313 6295337 6295363
6295381 6295409 6295417 6295433 6295451 6295469 6295481 6295483 6295489 6295493
6295507 6295519 6295567 6295571 6295577 6295579 6295637 6295651 6295657 6295687
6295693 6295717 6295741 6295769 6295777 6295787 6295801 6295811 6295829 6295841
6295847 6295873 6295879 6295903 6295907 6295909 6295943 6295963 6295999 6296009
6296027 6296033 6296039 6296041 6296053 6296071 6296099 6296107 6296113 6296117
6296119 6296141 6296153 6296159 6296183 6296197 6296203 6296233 6296281 6296321
6296333 6296357 6296363 6296369 6296371 6296377 6296387 6296399 6296413 6296419
6296431 6296489 6296491 6296497 6296513 6296519 6296531 6296557 6296569 6296573
6296597 6296599 6296611 6296617 6296639 6296651 6296659 6296663 6296669 6296671
6296701 6296707 6296713 6296723 6296729 6296737 6296747 6296789 6296819 6296827
6296831 6296833 6296867 6296869 6296891 6296911 6296921 6296947 6296951 6296959
6296977 6296989 6297023 6297029 6297043 6297059 6297073 6297077 6297103 6297131
6297133 6297163 6297173 6297209 6297211 6297217 6297223 6297229 6297233 6297241
6297253 6297281 6297283 6297323 6297367 6297383 6297409 6297419 6297481 6297503
6297509 6297517 6297527 6297541 6297547 6297581 6297583 6297587 6297589 6297593
6297617 6297623 6297647 6297649 6297677 6297679 6297689 6297713 6297749 6297751
6297761 6297763 6297779 6297787 6297793 6297817 6297827 6297853 6297869 6297899
6297931 6297947 6297961 6297971 6297979 6297983 6297997 6298003 6298009 6298031
6298037 6298069 6298079 6298091 6298099 6298111 6298121 6298147 6298153 6298163
6298181 6298183 6298199 6298207 6298213 6298217 6298219 6298231 6298241 6298267
6298283 6298319 6298321 6298337 6298351 6298387 6298393 6298417 6298421 6298447
6298451 6298459 6298463 6298477 6298493 6298531 6298541 6298559 6298571 6298577
6298583 6298609 6298613 6298627 6298639 6298651 6298657 6298661 6298667 6298697
6298717 6298723 6298727 6298751 6298753 6298793 6298801 6298807 6298811
6298837 6298841 6298847 6298883 6298909 6298913 6298933 6298937 6298949
6298961 6298969 6298973 6299053 6299057 6299071 6299087 6299093 6299131 6299141
6299143 6299147 6299149 6299179 6299221 6299239 6299291 6299303 6299353 6299357
6299369 6299383 6299387 6299413 6299429 6299443 6299453 6299459 6299473 6299483
6299497 6299519 6299521 6299567 6299591 6299599 6299611 6299627 6299653 6299663
6299669 6299693 6299701 6299719 6299729 6299737 6299749 6299767 6299771 6299791
6299803 6299819 6299831 6299837 6299857 6299899 6299929 6299933 6299941 6299957
6299977 6299983 6299987 6300011 6300017 6300023 6300029 6300061 6300063 6300077
6300103 6300109 6300121 6300127 6300131 6300143 6300157 6300169 6300179 6300181
6300193 6300199 6300241 6300277 6300299 6300311 6300313 6300331 6300341 6300373
6300383 6300431 6300443 6300449 6300451 6300467 6300473 6300499 6300509 6300529
6300559 6300563 6300589 6300599 6300601 6300607 6300617 6300631 6300641 6300649
6300667 6300677 6300709 6300713 6300737 6300739 6300793 6300821 6300823 6300857
6300887 6300923 6300941 6300947 6300953 6300971 6300991 6301007 6301039 6301049
6301051 6301069 6301073 6301109 6301121 6301129 6301147 6301157 6301159 6301187
6301189 6301193 6301199 6301201 6301213 6301291 6301297 6301303 6301307 6301319
6301327 6301357 6301363 6301391 6301397 6301423 6301447 6301457 6301459 6301469
6301481 6301487 6301501 6301511 6301513 6301523 6301531 6301549 6301553 6301567
6301621 6301637 6301639 6301667 6301681 6301697 6301703 6301709 6301717 6301721
6301723 6301739 6301759 6301777 6301817 6301829 6301837 6301847 6301853 6301861
6301891 6301907 6301913 6301927 6301957 6301963 6301969 6301973 6302003 6302011
6302033 6302047 6302057 6302059 6302063 6302081 6302113 6302117 6302141 6302143
6302147 6302159 6302171 6302213 6302249 6302293 6302311 6302323 6302327 6302339
6302341 6302347 6302353 6302369 6302377 6302419 6302423 6302431 6302441 6302449
6302473 6302477 6302519 6302521 6302531 6302533 6302539 6302573 6302587 6302603
6302609 6302651 6302663 6302671 6302683 6302689 6302701 6302711 6302717 6302719
6302729 6302731 6302753 6302789 6302797 6302833 6302837 6302867 6302899 6302917
6302929 6302941 6302957 6302969 6302981 6302993 6303001 6303007 6303023
6303043 6303071 6303091 6303097 6303113 6303119 6303133 6303139 6303151 6303163
6303197 6303211 6303221 6303229 6303239 6303251 6303257 6303281 6303287 6303301
6303317 6303337 6303347 6303371 6303377 6303389 6303397 6303419 6303433 6303461
6303467 6303487 6303491 6303503 6303523 6303529 6303533 6303551 6303553 6303559
```

```
6303581  6303599  6303607  6303629  6303641  6303667  6303733  6303761  6303779  6303799
6303809  6303823  6303827  6303833  6303841  6303853  6303883  6303887  6303901  6303919
6303937  6303967  6303971  6303977  6303989  6304003  6304007  6304009  6304013  6304043
6304057  6304067  6304147  6304159  6304163  6304169  6304189  6304211  6304213  6304217
6304241  6304247  6304267  6304271  6304301  6304307  6304343  6304349  6304357  6304379
6304481  6304387  6304421  6304427  6304429  6304453  6304477  6304483  6304511  6304517
6304583  6304589  6304601  6304607  6304619  6304631  6304651  6304663  6304667  6304673
6304679  6304699  6304741  6304769  6304787  6304817  6304847  6304853  6304867  6304897
6304927  6304973  6304993  6304999  6305009  6305023  6305029  6305041  6305063
6305071  6305081  6305087  6305107  6305111  6305119  6305129  6305141  6305149  6305171
6305177  6305203  6305231  6305237  6305239  6305263  6305309  6305311  6305333  6305339
6305347  6305353  6305363  6305393  6305401  6305407  6305413  6305417  6305443  6305449
6305459  6305461  6305471  6305479  6305489  6305491  6305501  6305527  6305573  6305599
6305603  6305627  6305647  6305659  6305669  6305681  6305693  6305707  6305711  6305729
6305737  6305791  6305801  6305809  6305837  6305843  6305857  6305867  6305869  6305903
6305909  6305939  6305983  6305987  6306029  6306049  6306059  6306061  6306077  6306109
6306121  6306151  6306173  6306187  6306193  6306197  6306199  6306211  6306263  6306277
6306283  6306341  6306343  6306353  6306359  6306373  6306379  6306383  6306401  6306403
6306409  6306457  6306463  6306467  6306479  6306481  6306511  6306529  6306551  6306557
6306563  6306571  6306581  6306593  6306617  6306647  6306667  6306673  6306679  6306697
6306709  6306721  6306731  6306737  6306739  6306787  6306791  6306809  6306821  6306827
6306829  6306863  6306887  6306893  6306913  6306931  6306943  6306953  6306961  6306967
6306997  6307009  6307033  6307039  6307099  6307121  6307177  6307193  6307219  6307237
6307241  6307247  6307261  6307303  6307309  6307331  6307333  6307351  6307363  6307381
6307387  6307397  6307409  6307417  6307429  6307453  6307489  6307507  6307517  6307531
6307537  6307549  6307559  6307571  6307573  6307577  6307621  6307633  6307657  6307661
6307673  6307687  6307739  6307771  6307783  6307793  6307811  6307817  6307831  6307841
6307883  6307897  6307909  6307921  6307979  6308017  6308021  6308023  6308033  6308039
6308041  6308047  6308059  6308077  6308087  6308089  6308129  6308147  6308153  6308189
6308191  6308243  6308257  6308273  6308287  6308297  6308311  6308317  6308321  6308329
6308333  6308347  6308369  6308449  6308459  6308461  6308483  6308501  6308521  6308527
6308569  6308639  6308641  6308651  6308663  6308671  6308719  6308723  6308737  6308761
6308773  6308801  6308837  6308851  6308867  6308881  6308891  6308947  6308959  6308971
6308983  6308993  6308999  6309013  6309031  6309047  6309053  6309073  6309103  6309109
6309113  6309133  6309143  6309161  6309181  6309187  6309209  6309217  6309221  6309223
6309239  6309271  6309287  6309313  6309343  6309371  6309377  6309389  6309437  6309439
6309473  6309481  6309497  6309503  6309509  6309517  6309529  6309547  6309551  6309593
6309599  6309619  6309623  6309629  6309631  6309661  6309671  6309679  6309727  6309731
6309757  6309763  6309769  6309781  6309817  6309827  6309851  6309857  6309881
6309887  6309911  6309913  6309917  6309923  6309931  6309959  6309973  6309997  6310039
6310049  6310061  6310069  6310093  6310097  6310123  6310133  6310151  6310153
6310163  6310169  6310181  6310201  6310217  6310229  6310243  6310273  6310277  6310279
6310289  6310319  6310327  6310333  6310363  6310411  6310427  6310439  6310451  6310457
6310459  6310477  6310481  6310483  6310517  6310523  6310531  6310543  6310547  6310583
6310589  6310607  6310613  6310627  6310669  6310673  6310687  6310709  6310727  6310741
6310769  6310771  6310781  6310789  6310807  6310819  6310841  6310847  6310849  6310879
6310897  6310919  6310921  6310939  6310943  6310963  6311023  6311047  6311051  6311057
6311093  6311099  6311117  6311147  6311159  6311161  6311167  6311189  6311191  6311203
6311219  6311251  6311297  6311303  6311309  6311311  6311317  6311323  6311329  6311351
6311353  6311359  6311377  6311381  6311387  6311413  6311419  6311429  6311441  6311479
6311483  6311509  6311521  6311537  6311563  6311567  6311597  6311623  6311633  6311639
6311659  6311689  6311707  6311713  6311759  6311779  6311801  6311807  6311873  6311881
6311891  6311923  6311939  6311953  6311957  6311983  6311989  6312017  6312023  6312029
6312041  6312043  6312071  6312133  6312139  6312157  6312181  6312191  6312217  6312221
6312259  6312269  6312283  6312301  6312323  6312329  6312349  6312377  6312379  6312409
6312431  6312521  6312547  6312571  6312577  6312583  6312589  6312599  6312613  6312619
6312637  6312641  6312659  6312667  6312689  6312703  6312727  6312739  6312751  6312773
6312781  6312799  6312847  6312851  6312853  6312863  6312869  6312913  6312931  6312937
6312947  6312949  6312979  6312983  6312991  6313007  6313009  6313019  6313031  6313033
6313067  6313079  6313117  6313121  6313129  6313141  6313147  6313183  6313189  6313231
6313253  6313267  6313309  6313327  6313337  6313361  6313379  6313397  6313399
6313427  6313451  6313457  6313459  6313469  6313481  6313493  6313499  6313507  6313513
6313583  6313589  6313597  6313621  6313639  6313669  6313691  6313693  6313709  6313711
6313721  6313751  6313777  6313781  6313787  6313829  6313831  6313861  6313889  6313913
6313921  6313949  6313961  6313969  6313997  6314039  6314051  6314057  6314081  6314093
6314107  6314129  6314183  6314197  6314201  6314207  6314219  6314221  6314263  6314279
6314291  6314299  6314339  6314377  6314389  6314393  6314447  6314501  6314543  6314563
6314569  6314611  6314617  6314641  6314647  6314653  6314677  6314681  6314687  6314699
6314713  6314717  6314761  6314773  6314801  6314809  6314831  6314839  6314863  6314881
6314887  6314899  6314911  6314921  6314963  6314983  6314993  6315017  6315031
6315037  6315059  6315073  6315077  6315083  6315091  6315121  6315131  6315139  6315151
6315161  6315167  6315191  6315209  6315217  6315223  6315251  6315259  6315293  6315307
6315311  6315341  6315371  6315373  6315377  6315383  6315389  6315403  6315433  6315451
6315469  6315473  6315479  6315481  6315503  6315511  6315527  6315541  6315557  6315559
6315571  6315577  6315601  6315607  6315611  6315613  6315629  6315637  6315667  6315671
6315677  6315691  6315697  6315709  6315713  6315737  6315769  6315779  6315781  6315791
6315839  6315871  6315899  6315901  6315917  6315919  6315929  6315941  6315943  6315949
6315971  6315977  6315979  6315983  6315989  6316003  6316019  6316031  6316039  6316067
6316069  6316073  6316109  6316117  6316139  6316147  6316153  6316199  6316207  6316213
6316229  6316273  6316279  6316309  6316319  6316339  6316351  6316393  6316423  6316433
6316451  6316463  6316477  6316483  6316517  6316523  6316537  6316543  6316649  6316663
6316669  6316679  6316703  6316727  6316757  6316769  6316801  6316811  6316823  6316837
6316861  6316889  6316897  6316913  6316939  6316957  6316967  6316969  6317011  6317021
6317027  6317029  6317033  6317053  6317057  6317119  6317141  6317147  6317159  6317191
6317197  6317219  6317231  6317237  6317243  6317261  6317293  6317327  6317351  6317357
6317369  6317371  6317383  6317401  6317407  6317413  6317429  6317471  6317473  6317477
6317483  6317503  6317527  6317533  6317537  6317569  6317581  6317611  6317627  6317657
6317669  6317677  6317681  6317683  6317699  6317719  6317743  6317767  6317771  6317783
```

```
6317789 6317803 6317807 6317821 6317849 6317873 6317887 6317923 6317929 6317933
6317951 6317957 6317963 6318001 6318007 6318019 6318061 6318071 6318073 6318107
6318131 6318139 6318149 6318161 6318181 6318187 6318211 6318227 6318229 6318233
6318239 6318253 6318269 6318281 6318283 6318287 6318311 6318331 6318349 6318353
6318391 6318409 6318419 6318421 6318427 6318439 6318467 6318493 6318497 6318511
6318547 6318553 6318589 6318593 6318617 6318619 6318623 6318667 6318673 6318701
6318709 6318737 6318743 6318751 6318757 6318791 6318799 6318803 6318833 6318857
6318877 6318881 6318889 6318901 6318913 6318919 6318931 6318937 6318943 6318967
6318989 6319003 6319037 6319057 6319091 6319111 6319127 6319163 6319177 6319211
6319219 6319277 6319279 6319297 6319301 6319307 6319333 6319337 6319351 6319363
6319387 6319403 6319429 6319433 6319441 6319451 6319463 6319471 6319483 6319499
6319513 6319551 6319553 6319559 6319583 6319589 6319591 6319603 6319613 6319633
6319657 6319669 6319679 6319681 6319693 6319697 6319727 6319757 6319769 6319787
6319793 6319813 6319823 6319847 6319861 6319867 6319889 6319891 6319897 6319927
6319961 6319981 6319993 6320003 6320023 6320033 6320051 6320053 6320059 6320071
6320077 6320099 6320121 6320117 6320129 6320131 6320159 6320189 6320219 6320227
6320233 6320261 6320263 6320287 6320291 6320297 6320299 6320317 6320323 6320329
6320333 6320359 6320371 6320417 6320459 6320477 6320507 6320551 6320563 6320569
6320581 6320593 6320603 6320623 6320627 6320641 6320687 6320689 6320723 6320731
6320777 6320779 6320803 6320813 6320827 6320843 6320849 6320891 6320893 6320903
6320911 6320921 6320947 6320953 6320959 6320971 6320987 6320989 6320999 6321013
6321017 6321023 6321037 6321041 6321071 6321079 6321089 6321097 6321121 6321131
6321137 6321157 6321163 6321169 6321173 6321181 6321193 6321209 6321221 6321223
6321253 6321277 6321307 6321323 6321353 6321361 6321373 6321377 6321379 6321401
6321407 6321409 6321443 6321457 6321461 6321479 6321493 6321521 6321563 6321577
6321599 6321611 6321643 6321647 6321677 6321683 6321701 6321703 6321713 6321719
6321751 6321767 6321793 6321811 6321823 6321853 6321863 6321871 6321883 6321901
6321907 6321947 6321961 6321983 6322009 6322013 6322021 6322049 6322067 6322073
6322091 6322093 6322123 6322123 6322163 6322259 6322271 6322279 6322313 6322331
6322343 6322361 6322387 6322391 6322397 6322403 6322411 6322451 6322469 6322489
6322501 6322513 6322549 6322553 6322559 6322571 6322627 6322633 6322637 6322639
6322643 6322661 6322681 6322699 6322703 6322709 6322717 6322727 6322739 6322747
6322753 6322777 6322807 6322831 6322859 6322867 6322871 6322879 6322889 6322891
6322909 6322969 6322973 6323003 6323011 6323027 6323033 6323063 6323087 6323111
6323147 6323153 6323171 6323173 6323179 6323197 6323209 6323227 6323237 6323281
6323293 6323299 6323327 6323329 6323347 6323351 6323353 6323357 6323399 6323407
6323419 6323431 6323441 6323453 6323467 6323477 6323491 6323497 6323519 6323557
6323567 6323573 6323579 6323587 6323617 6323651 6323657 6323663 6323671 6323693
6323699 6323719 6323741 6323743 6323747 6323753 6323761 6323767 6323773 6323791
6323839 6323843 6323851 6323861 6323869 6323879 6323887 6323909 6323923 6323927
6323939 6323951 6323981 6324023 6324037 6324049 6324061 6324067 6324079 6324091
6324091 6324107 6324113 6324137 6324167 6324191 6324203 6324223 6324239 6324247
6324257 6324277 6324313 6324337 6324347 6324371 6324377 6324401 6324403 6324413
6324427 6324433 6324443 6324463 6324469 6324481 6324491 6324529 6324533 6324547
6324551 6324553 6324557 6324559 6324601 6324611 6324613 6324641 6324653 6324667
6324679 6324689 6324709 6324737 6324761 6324779 6324797 6324809 6324821 6324823
6324847 6324881 6324883 6324911 6324919 6324953 6324959 6324971 6325021 6325031
6325049 6325051 6325087 6325093 6325097 6325117 6325129 6325169 6325183 6325201
6325217 6325223 6325229 6325237 6325243 6325279 6325283 6325301 6325303 6325313
6325321 6325339 6325349 6325367 6325387 6325441 6325447 6325453 6325471 6325481
6325493 6325507 6325511 6325549 6325559 6325607 6325619 6325633 6325691 6325699
6325703 6325721 6325747 6325757 6325763 6325771 6325783 6325807 6325811 6325817
6325831 6325861 6325887 6325901 6325903 6325909 6325919 6325937 6325967 6325987
6325981 6325987 6325999 6326017 6326041 6326053 6326063 6326087 6326119 6326123
6326129 6326137 6326141 6326143 6326167 6326179 6326189 6326191 6326197 6326213
6326233 6326237 6326273 6326279 6326293 6326339 6326351 6326377 6326381 6326389
6326443 6326459 6326497 6326513 6326521 6326527 6326543 6326549 6326561 6326581
6326591 6326599 6326603 6326627 6326641 6326651 6326659 6326681 6326699 6326707
6326729 6326767 6326779 6326809 6326813 6326849 6326857 6326861 6326869 6326893
6326897 6326911 6326923 6326927 6326933 6326951 6326953 6326963 6327009 6327067
6327073 6327089 6327091 6327107 6327109 6327121 6327127 6327143 6327151 6327157
6327163 6327203 6327227 6327229 6327239 6327241 6327253 6327271 6327287 6327301
6327313 6327331 6327359 6327371 6327389 6327397 6327401 6327421 6327457 6327473
6327479 6327491 6327509 6327523 6327527 6327533 6327569 6327593 6327611 6327613
6327631 6327641 6327649 6327707 6327709 6327721 6327743 6327749 6327773 6327787
6327781 6327793 6327803 6327833 6327847 6327857 6327869 6327877 6327889
6327901 6327907 6327913 6327943 6327947 6327973 6327977 6327983 6327991 6328019
6328027 6328031 6328067 6328099 6328103 6328109 6328141 6328171 6328193 6328207
6328229 6328237 6328249 6328261 6328291 6328319 6328327 6328331 6328337 6328363
6328367 6328411 6328429 6328489 6328529 6328541 6328601 6328603 6328613 6328627
6328631 6328633 6328639 6328643 6328661 6328669 6328687 6328711 6328723 6328733
6328771 6328781 6328787 6328789 6328793 6328831 6328837 6328849 6328853
6328877 6328897 6328909 6328939 6328951 6328967 6328997 6329003 6329077 6329111
6329119 6329137 6329143 6329149 6329171 6329201 6329203 6329227 6329231 6329233
6329269 6329291 6329311 6329317 6329327 6329339 6329341 6329353 6329359 6329369
6329377 6329387 6329417 6329431 6329447 6329459 6329473 6329489 6329501 6329503
6329507 6329509 6329567 6329573 6329581 6329597 6329647 6329651 6329657 6329671
6329677 6329681 6329683 6329689 6329699 6329707 6329711 6329723 6329731 6329749
6329753 6329759 6329777 6329837 6329857 6329879 6329887 6329891 6329893 6329927
6329963 6329993 6330017 6330019 6330029 6330041 6330043 6330053 6330063 6330067
6330109 6330119 6330131 6330133 6330139 6330143 6330151 6330157 6330187 6330193
6330217 6330223 6330229 6330253 6330257 6330263 6330283 6330299 6330319 6330329
6330343 6330353 6330371 6330391 6330407 6330413 6330419 6330421 6330449 6330461
6330473 6330491 6330509 6330521 6330529 6330547 6330551 6330557 6330559 6330581
6330617 6330619 6330631 6330679 6330683 6330697 6330703 6330707 6330719 6330733
6330739 6330767 6330799 6330809 6330827 6330839 6330859 6330881 6330887 6330901
6330923 6330931 6330941 6330967 6331001 6331043 6331057 6331063 6331067 6331069
6331081 6331109 6331133 6331147 6331151 6331153 6331183 6331189 6331207 6331249
6331253 6331267 6331289 6331291 6331301 6331319 6331321 6331333 6331337 6331379
```

```
6331399 6331411 6331439 6331447 6331469 6331517 6331519 6331529 6331537 6331543
6331547 6331571 6331573 6331603 6331607 6331609 6331669 6331679 6331691 6331723
6331733 6331757 6331763 6331783 6331789 6331817 6331823 6331849 6331859 6331873
6331903 6331951 6331957 6331979 6332009 6332021 6332033 6332047 6332059 6332077
6332089 6332099 6332101 6332113 6332119 6332129 6332159 6332167 6332197 6332201
6332213 6332219 6332243 6332269 6332297 6332299 6332311 6332317 6332341 6332363
6332369 6332393 6332399 6332413 6332437 6332441 6332477 6332503 6332507 6332539
6332549 6332563 6332591 6332603 6332611 6332621 6332629 6332657 6332663 6332693
6332699 6332723 6332741 6332747 6332761 6332771 6332803 6332849 6332861 6332863
6332867 6332869 6332881 6332899 6332923 6332927 6332939 6332951 6332971 6333013
6333017 6333029 6333043 6333053 6333059 6333071 6333077 6333079 6333101 6333113
6333121 6333127 6333139 6333157 6333181 6333191 6333221 6333233 6333277 6333287
6333293 6333307 6333317 6333337 6333359 6333361 6333389 6333419 6333449 6333451
6333461 6333463 6333511 6333521 6333529 6333559 6333601 6333619 6333643 6333653
6333683 6333727 6333731 6333737 6333749 6333757 6333787 6333793 6333799 6333907
6333923 6333931 6333937 6333959 6333961 6334007 6334019 6334033 6334037 6334051
6334061 6334073 6334121 6334127 6334147 6334169 6334187 6334231 6334241 6334249
6334259 6334291 6334297 6334309 6334327 6334333 6334399 6334411 6334439 6334463
6334481 6334501 6334513 6334547 6334561 6334567 6334577 6334579 6334607 6334621
6334639 6334651 6334661 6334663 6334697 6334703 6334709 6334723 6334747 6334751
6334763 6334781 6334813 6334837 6334841 6334859 6334871 6334873 6334877 6334879
6334891 6334907 6334919 6334921 6334927 6334969 6334981 6334987 6334997 6335011
6335027 6335039 6335041 6335047 6335053 6335059 6335071 6335081 6335171 6335183
6335201 6335213 6335239 6335257 6335261 6335267 6335309 6335317 6335359 6335387
6335393 6335411 6335423 6335429 6335431 6335449 6335467 6335477 6335513 6335519
6335533 6335551 6335573 6335579 6335591 6335599 6335617 6335627 6335669 6335677
6335701 6335711 6335729 6335731 6335737 6335761 6335767 6335773 6335783 6335807
6335837 6335851 6335863 6335867 6335869 6335893 6335897 6335899 6335909 6335939
6335941 6335947 6335977 6335987 6335983 6336013 6336041 6336067 6336073 6336079
6336091 6336103 6336133 6336149 6336163 6336167 6336193 6336217 6336221 6336227
6336233 6336241 6336259 6336271 6336283 6336289 6336301 6336311 6336313 6336347
6336349 6336371 6336373 6336389 6336403 6336409 6336419 6336439 6336467 6336487
6336503 6336553 6336559 6336571 6336599 6336623 6336641 6336643 6336667 6336683
6336697 6336713 6336721 6336727 6336739 6336763 6336773 6336791 6336797 6336829
6336853 6336857 6336893 6336907 6336917 6336943 6336949 6336973 6336977 6337021
6337031 6337049 6337063 6337069 6337099 6337103 6337129 6337139 6337169 6337181
6337183 6337217 6337223 6337231 6337267 6337271 6337273 6337321 6337327 6337333
6337381 6337403 6337439 6337451 6337453 6337517 6337523 6337537 6337541 6337543
6337561 6337579 6337589 6337607 6337633 6337637 6337663 6337679 6337699 6337703
6337729 6337759 6337763 6337777 6337783 6337789 6337801 6337819 6337823 6337829
6337847 6337861 6337871 6337873 6337879 6337897 6337901 6337907 6337913 6337939
6337943 6337967 6337987 6337993 6338009 6338011 6338021 6338027 6338029 6338047
6338069 6338107 6338113 6338117 6338119 6338131 6338141 6338147 6338183 6338197
6338203 6338207 6338209 6338221 6338239 6338257 6338281 6338287 6338309 6338333
6338347 6338357 6338377 6338393 6338411 6338413 6338417 6338471 6338473 6338483
6338513 6338531 6338537 6338557 6338599 6338609 6338611 6338621 6338653 6338701
6338707 6338719 6338741 6338743 6338753 6338767 6338771 6338789 6338831 6338833
6338851 6338873 6338879 6338903 6338947 6338953 6338957 6338963 6338971 6338993
6338999 6339029 6339037 6339041 6339043 6339061 6339077 6339083 6339119 6339121
6339149 6339161 6339167 6339209 6339227 6339253 6339257 6339259 6339269 6339287
6339299 6339323 6339349 6339391 6339449 6339461 6339493 6339497 6339511 6339551
6339577 6339583 6339611 6339631 6339637 6339647 6339653 6339677 6339679 6339703
6339709 6339721 6339757 6339761 6339769 6339799 6339811 6339847 6339869 6339899
6339911 6339919 6339937 6339947 6339989 6340013 6340021 6340039 6340043 6340063
6340069 6340109 6340127 6340189 6340193 6340219 6340237 6340247 6340261 6340267
6340273 6340297 6340343 6340361 6340379 6340381 6340391 6340403 6340409 6340423
6340429 6340457 6340463 6340483 6340501 6340519 6340567 6340573 6340597 6340637
6340657 6340669 6340673 6340687 6340721 6340739 6340757 6340787 6340811 6340843
6340861 6340871 6340877 6340883 6340891 6340897 6340903 6340913 6340921 6340931
6340963 6341039 6341057 6341059 6341063 6341087 6341107 6341131 6341141 6341149
6341177 6341191 6341197 6341201 6341207 6341213 6341219 6341243 6341249 6341263
6341273 6341297 6341299 6341311 6341341 6341351 6341369 6341407 6341411 6341417
6341441 6341443 6341473 6341477 6341491 6341501 6341509 6341519 6341521 6341539
6341549 6341551 6341563 6341591 6341603 6341641 6341653 6341659 6341669 6341677
6341737 6341759 6341771 6341779 6341801 6341827 6341831 6341843 6341857
6341861 6341879 6341893 6341903 6341939 6341963 6341971 6342013 6342023 6342031
6342047 6342053 6342079 6342101 6342107 6342137 6342157 6342163 6342169 6342179
6342191 6342209 6342221 6342239 6342251 6342277 6342289 6342293 6342307 6342317
6342337 6342341 6342361 6342373 6342379 6342389 6342419 6342443 6342461 6342467
6342473 6342487 6342499 6342517 6342521 6342527 6342529 6342533 6342551
6342587 6342593 6342647 6342667 6342671 6342691 6342731 6342737 6342757 6342767
6342769 6342773 6342797 6342839 6342857 6342877 6342883 6342907 6342911 6342923
6342929 6342949 6342971 6342977 6342993 6342997 6343019 6343033 6343039 6343063
6343097 6343133 6343153 6343163 6343177 6343187 6343201 6343213 6343217 6343219
6343247 6343277 6343279 6343291 6343319 6343327 6343339 6343367 6343387 6343399
6343409 6343417 6343429 6343433 6343439 6343453 6343457 6343459 6343483 6343537
6343553 6343591 6343609 6343619 6343633 6343639 6343651 6343667 6343693 6343723
6343741 6343751 6343759 6343769 6343789 6343793 6343801 6343811 6343819 6343847
6343849 6343859 6343861 6343877 6343879 6343901 6343903 6343927 6343949 6343957
6343979 6343993 6344003 6344017 6344027 6344033 6344087 6344147 6344161 6344171
6344189 6344207 6344209 6344227 6344237 6344249 6344257 6344267 6344269 6344291
6344311 6344321 6344323 6344341 6344363 6344369 6344399 6344407 6344413 6344441
6344467 6344473 6344509 6344557 6344579 6344581 6344599 6344609 6344617 6344623
6344641 6344647 6344659 6344669 6344687 6344729 6344747 6344759 6344761 6344771
6344777 6344809 6344813 6344827 6344843 6344851 6344857 6344909 6344911 6344929
6344957 6344963 6344983 6345007 6345011 6345041 6345067 6345091 6345127 6345133
6345137 6345139 6345149 6345179 6345181 6345187 6345197 6345253 6345257 6345271
6345293 6345299 6345307 6345323 6345337 6345343 6345347 6345377 6345407 6345449
6345431 6345439 6345457 6345481 6345491 6345497 6345533 6345541 6345551 6345617
```

```
6345629  6345659  6345673  6345683  6345701  6345721  6345737  6345739  6345749  6345763
6345803  6345821  6345827  6345839  6345851  6345853  6345877  6345883  6345887  6345919
6345923  6345949  6345971  6345973  6346003  6346009  6346037  6346111  6346127  6346141
6346163  6346177  6346181  6346187  6346199  6346201  6346211  6346213  6346231  6346237
6346243  6346297  6346303  6346313  6346337  6346339  6346381  6346387  6346391  6346397
6346409  6346427  6346433  6346463  6346469  6346489  6346493  6346519  6346523  6346553
6346579  6346583  6346609  6346631  6346633  6346651  6346663  6346667  6346727  6346733
6346751  6346771  6346777  6346783  6346787  6346789  6346793  6346801  6346811  6346859
6346877  6346883  6346891  6346897  6346957  6346973  6346987  6346999  6347009  6347023
6347059  6347177  6347183  6347189  6347203  6347221  6347261  6347269  6347309  6347321
6347339  6347371  6347377  6347381  6347447  6347483  6347521  6347527  6347567  6347611
6347623  6347639  6347641  6347657  6347659  6347669  6347687  6347689  6347707  6347753
6347771  6347791  6347797  6347801  6347819  6347827  6347849  6347879  6347903  6347909
6347921  6347927  6347941  6347947  6347959  6347983  6348011  6348019  6348029  6348037
6348059  6348061  6348073  6348101  6348107  6348113  6348119  6348137  6348143  6348151
6348179  6348233  6348239  6348241  6348247  6348257  6348263  6348271  6348283  6348289
6348301  6348311  6348343  6348371  6348373  6348383  6348389  6348401  6348439  6348449
6348467  6348469  6348473  6348479  6348523  6348533  6348541  6348569  6348623  6348647
6348673  6348689  6348691  6348703  6348721  6348739  6348751  6348761  6348763  6348773
6348781  6348787  6348799  6348827  6348829  6348847  6348863  6348877  6348887  6348889
6348899  6348913  6348917  6348971  6348977  6348997  6349001  6349003  6349009  6349037
6349043  6349051  6349069  6349073  6349087  6349093  6349099  6349129  6349139  6349153
6349157  6349169  6349181  6349199  6349223  6349253  6349261  6349267  6349271  6349283
6349297  6349303  6349331  6349333  6349361  6349373  6349379  6349391  6349393  6349397
6349433  6349481  6349501  6349529  6349531  6349537  6349543  6349549  6349561  6349589
6349621  6349631  6349643  6349649  6349663  6349691  6349697  6349703  6349709  6349723
6349727  6349741  6349751  6349787  6349843  6349859  6349879  6349897  6349913  6349919
6349921  6349951  6349961  6349969  6349997  6350011  6350017  6350021  6350041  6350063
6350083  6350107  6350119  6350131  6350137  6350143  6350167  6350169  6350171  6350191
6350209  6350219  6350221  6350233  6350249  6350251  6350263  6350269  6350287  6350291
6350293  6350297  6350329  6350341  6350353  6350411  6350419  6350423  6350431  6350441
6350459  6350471  6350479  6350483  6350501  6350549  6350563  6350621  6350633  6350647
6350651  6350653  6350677  6350699  6350719  6350759  6350761  6350801  6350833  6350837
6350867  6350873  6350887  6350891  6350899  6350917  6350923  6350933  6350957  6350963
6350983  6350987  6350989  6351017  6351019  6351031  6351089  6351097  6351113  6351127
6351181  6351211  6351221  6351223  6351229  6351253  6351271  6351277  6351283  6351287
6351299  6351313  6351329  6351379  6351403  6351431  6351461  6351469  6351479  6351481
6351509  6351517  6351547  6351563  6351571  6351581  6351601  6351607  6351613  6351619
6351629  6351649  6351671  6351673  6351677  6351743  6351767  6351769  6351781  6351809
6351847  6351853  6351857  6351859  6351889  6351893  6351911  6351913  6351929  6351937
6351959  6351969  6351987  6351997  6351973  6352001  6352013  6352039  6352051  6352079
6352081  6352091  6352109  6352121  6352139  6352147  6352183  6352201  6352219  6352243
6352259  6352267  6352297  6352309  6352331  6352343  6352361  6352391  6352399  6352429
6352453  6352477  6352487  6352547  6352573  6352603  6352607  6352609  6352637  6352639
6352651  6352657  6352673  6352681  6352693  6352729  6352741  6352763  6352771  6352813
6352817  6352831  6352837  6352879  6352933  6352979  6352987  6352993  6353003  6353021
6353027  6353029  6353033  6353051  6353071  6353093  6353099  6353111  6353153  6353161
6353167  6353173  6353213  6353219  6353227  6353231  6353261  6353279  6353299  6353317
6353341  6353351  6353363  6353377  6353383  6353387  6353411  6353437  6353441  6353449
6353453  6353471  6353489  6353491  6353513  6353519  6353521  6353527  6353531  6353561
6353569  6353573  6353579  6353591  6353617  6353629  6353653  6353687  6353689  6353707
6353713  6353717  6353731  6353741  6353759  6353779  6353783  6353827  6353833  6353857
6353863  6353873  6353909  6353933  6353959  6353989  6354001  6354013  6354017  6354043
6354059  6354077  6354083  6354091  6354097  6354109  6354119  6354133  6354149  6354167
6354169  6354181  6354203  6354217  6354251  6354263  6354289  6354301  6354307  6354317
6354319  6354331  6354389  6354391  6354421  6354427  6354433  6354437  6354443  6354449
6354457  6354461  6354479  6354487  6354503  6354527  6354529  6354539  6354547  6354559
6354589  6354599  6354619  6354641  6354643  6354703  6354709  6354727  6354743  6354757
6354773  6354793  6354811  6354827  6354847  6354853  6354871  6354913  6354937  6354947
6354967  6354977  6354983  6354989  6355001  6355039  6355049  6355073  6355079  6355081
6355087  6355103  6355121  6355133  6355169  6355171  6355187  6355189  6355201  6355213
6355243  6355247  6355259  6355301  6355309  6355333  6355373  6355381  6355441  6355447
6355487  6355493  6355507  6355511  6355513  6355523  6355543  6355549  6355561  6355577
6355597  6355607  6355621  6355631  6355667  6355673  6355711  6355733  6355759  6355777
6355781  6355793  6355819  6355879  6355903  6355913  6355933  6355949  6355963  6355997
6356003  6356033  6356039  6356041  6356071  6356081  6356083  6356087  6356093  6356099
6356101  6356123  6356149  6356153  6356159  6356171  6356173  6356179  6356213  6356219
6356239  6356243  6356263  6356297  6356309  6356321  6356323  6356347  6356377  6356387
6356401  6356407  6356437  6356443  6356461  6356479  6356503  6356531  6356543  6356551
6356557  6356569  6356573  6356587  6356591  6356593  6356611  6356617  6356639  6356641
6356653  6356699  6356737  6356741  6356747  6356783  6356789  6356803  6356821  6356869
6356879  6356881  6356897  6356921  6356923  6356941  6356957  6356969  6356971  6356981
6356983  6357011  6357017  6357019  6357023  6357047  6357067  6357083  6357097  6357101
6357107  6357121  6357157  6357179  6357193  6357199  6357203  6357217  6357233  6357287
6357289  6357301  6357311  6357313  6357317  6357331  6357347  6357349  6357353  6357397
6357413  6357431  6357433  6357479  6357503  6357529  6357539  6357557  6357569  6357587
6357607  6357623  6357629  6357653  6357661  6357667  6357691  6357713  6357731  6357751
6357811  6357817  6357839  6357853  6357859  6357877  6357887  6357889  6357911  6357929
6357941  6357943  6357947  6357961  6357971  6357977  6357991  6357997  6358003  6358013
6358021  6358031  6358057  6358061  6358069  6358073  6358123  6358127  6358129  6358139
6358147  6358151  6358169  6358181  6358211  6358223  6358229  6358237  6358267  6358271
6358273  6358283  6358291  6358333  6358351  6358361  6358409  6358411  6358433  6358439
6358477  6358481  6358507  6358523  6358529  6358537  6358549  6358553  6358573  6358577
6358591  6358613  6358619  6358621  6358661  6358669  6358679  6358721  6358747  6358753
6358777  6358829  6358837  6358839  6358887  6358901  6358921  6358927  6358943  6358981
6358991  6358997  6359011  6359039  6359047  6359057  6359083  6359107  6359113  6359131
6359137  6359159  6359179  6359203  6359219  6359231  6359233  6359237  6359239  6359251
6359261  6359279  6359299  6359303  6359341  6359347  6359351  6359359  6359383  6359393
6359401  6359407  6359453  6359461  6359467  6359473  6359489  6359491  6359501  6359531
```

```
6359533 6359537 6359609 6359621 6359627 6359659 6359693 6359723 6359777 6359783
6359789 6359803 6359807 6359839 6359897 6359909 6359911 6359917 6359957 6359963
6359981 6359987 6360031 6360083 6360103 6360113 6360127 6360131 6360143 6360149
6360157 6360161 6360169 6360191 6360199 6360209 6360217 6360247 6360253 6360281
6360283 6360293 6360317 6360323 6360331 6360349 6360379 6360391 6360413 6360427
6360433 6360437 6360449 6360451 6360461 6360469 6360503 6360509 6360547 6360551
6360553 6360569 6360593 6360619 6360623 6360631 6360647 6360659 6360721 6360727
6360743 6360787 6360799 6360817 6360833 6360841 6360847 6360853 6360899 6360923
6360931 6360943 6360989 6361013 6361031 6361039 6361073 6361079 6361127 6361139
6361171 6361189 6361193 6361207 6361217 6361241 6361261 6361279 6361297 6361301
6361307 6361331 6361343 6361351 6361361 6361367 6361379 6361423 6361427 6361429
6361457 6361477 6361493 6361499 6361517 6361573 6361609 6361627 6361651 6361657
6361661 6361679 6361699 6361711 6361739 6361741 6361763 6361783 6361799 6361801
6361829 6361837 6361841 6361871 6361879 6361919 6361963 6361973 6361981 6361997
6362009 6362021 6362071 6362087 6362089 6362141 6362149 6362171 6362177 6362189
6362201 6362203 6362219 6362227 6362231 6362263 6362287 6362299 6362311 6362341
6362357 6362371 6362399 6362407 6362429 6362441 6362443 6362453 6362479 6362519
6362561 6362569 6362591 6362593 6362617 6362621 6362623 6362633 6362639 6362659
6362669 6362677 6362711 6362723 6362729 6362731 6362761 6362771 6362791 6362819
6362833 6362857 6362887 6362911 6362921 6362953 6362957 6362999 6363013 6363023
6363041 6363047 6363059 6363061 6363067 6363073 6363079 6363089 6363107 6363109
6363131 6363139 6363163 6363169 6363179 6363187 6363193 6363199 6363221 6363289
6363293 6363299 6363307 6363319 6363349 6363359 6363373 6363421 6363439 6363449
6363451 6363481 6363493 6363503 6363509 6363523 6363541 6363583 6363601 6363607
6363619 6363647 6363653 6363671 6363701 6363713 6363737 6363739 6363743 6363761
6363769 6363817 6363823 6363829 6363839 6363881 6363883 6363887 6363901 6363911
6363913 6363919 6363923 6363937 6363949 6363977 6363991 6363997 6364013 6364019
6364049 6364063 6364117 6364133 6364159 6364177 6364199 6364201 6364217 6364231
6364247 6364249 6364271 6364279 6364291 6364339 6364343 6364349 6364381 6364433
6364441 6364447 6364451 6364483 6364493 6364513 6364529 6364541 6364549 6364571
6364573 6364591 6364621 6364627 6364637 6364663 6364693 6364717 6364723 6364727
6364733 6364739 6364741 6364747 6364751 6364759 6364763 6364781 6364789 6364807
6364811 6364819 6364847 6364879 6364901 6364909 6364913 6364921 6364927 6364957
6364961 6365003 6365011 6365033 6365039 6365053 6365059 6365063 6365071 6365081
6365083 6365111 6365153 6365173 6365197 6365231 6365263 6365269 6365279 6365299
6365311 6365321 6365329 6365339 6365341 6365357 6365371 6365377 6365383 6365393
6365407 6365417 6365423 6365441 6365449 6365453 6365479 6365483 6365507 6365521
6365543 6365561 6365563 6365581 6365651 6365657 6365663 6365669 6365699 6365717
6365723 6365731 6365753 6365759 6365767 6365773 6365791 6365797 6365809 6365857
6365861 6365869 6365897 6365911 6365959 6365977 6365987 6366001 6366023 6366037
6366047 6366053 6366071 6366077 6366089 6366133 6366137 6366149 6366161 6366163
6366169 6366187 6366203 6366223 6366229 6366247 6366251 6366263 6366281 6366289
6366299 6366317 6366319 6366329 6366337 6366359 6366361 6366381 6366419 6366433
6366461 6366473 6366487 6366523 6366557 6366571 6366583 6366587 6366589 6366593
6366629 6366643 6366649 6366671 6366683 6366697 6366707 6366719 6366743 6366751
6366779 6366781 6366803 6366827 6366859 6366869 6366889 6366901 6366911 6366913
6366917 6366937 6366947 6366953 6366977 6366989 6367001 6367003 6367007 6367019
6367057 6367063 6367069 6367079 6367087 6367091 6367099 6367111 6367157 6367169
6367181 6367187 6367213 6367243 6367247 6367267 6367289 6367301 6367303 6367331
6367379 6367391 6367393 6367409 6367433 6367507 6367523 6367531 6367547 6367553
6367561 6367591 6367597 6367601 6367633 6367643 6367651 6367667 6367681 6367703
6367709 6367723 6367727 6367771 6367787 6367789 6367807 6367841 6367847 6367853
6367859 6367871 6367873 6367883 6367901 6367903 6367909 6367937 6367951 6367967
6367981 6367993 6368027 6368029 6368053 6368069 6368071 6368083 6368129 6368137
6368143 6368177 6368179 6368189 6368207 6368209 6368221 6368231 6368233 6368239
6368267 6368279 6368291 6368293 6368311 6368317 6368333 6368357 6368389 6368393
6368413 6368431 6368437 6368441 6368443 6368449 6368459 6368471 6368501 6368521
6368581 6368587 6368601 6368627 6368647 6368711 6368741 6368753 6368759 6368767
6368779 6368833 6368867 6368881 6368917 6368927 6368977 6368983 6369001 6369007
6369023 6369049 6369073 6369127 6369131 6369149 6369151 6369163 6369173 6369239
6369269 6369283 6369301 6369317 6369343 6369359 6369371 6369379 6369383 6369401
6369403 6369409 6369449 6369479 6369497 6369499 6369511 6369523 6369529 6369553
6369557 6369563 6369569 6369619 6369631 6369643 6369667 6369697 6369703 6369707
6369709 6369733 6369773 6369793 6369799 6369823 6369841 6369859 6369883 6369889
6369901 6369929 6369947 6369949 6369971 6369983 6369989 6369991 6370003 6370007
6370027 6370037 6370043 6370061 6370079 6370099 6370127 6370141 6370157 6370163
6370181 6370183 6370207 6370219 6370249 6370261 6370271 6370277 6370307 6370313
6370337 6370361 6370387 6370391 6370411 6370477 6370487 6370501 6370513 6370519
6370523 6370537 6370541 6370543 6370571 6370583 6370603 6370619 6370627 6370667
6370739 6370769 6370781 6370799 6370811 6370849 6370853 6370873 6370891 6370913
6370921 6370933 6370943 6370951 6370957 6370961 6370967 6370999 6371003 6371011
6371021 6371033 6371041 6371051 6371063 6371081 6371083 6371087 6371111 6371117
6371119 6371129 6371237 6371249 6371257 6371263 6371293 6371303 6371333 6371347
6371371 6371401 6371537 6371539 6371557 6371579 6371581 6371591 6371623 6371627
6371641 6371653 6371671 6371681 6371699 6371723 6371737 6371747 6371749 6371777
6371791 6371797 6371809 6371843 6371857 6371861 6371867 6371873 6371879 6371917
6371921 6371927 6371929 6371947 6371977 6371983 6371987 6372001 6372013 6372043
6372053 6372073 6372101 6372131 6372139 6372167 6372193 6372211 6372217 6372253
6372259 6372271 6372287 6372293 6372313 6372319 6372323 6372337 6372347 6372361
6372371 6372407 6372419 6372481 6372503 6372511 6372517 6372521 6372529 6372533
6372539 6372563 6372593 6372617 6372623 6372647 6372659 6372697 6372719 6372727
6372749 6372781 6372869 6372881 6372911 6372913 6372929 6372967 6372979 6372983
6373021 6373033 6373039 6373049 6373051 6373057 6373061 6373063 6373067 6373099
6373111 6373123 6373187 6373193 6373207 6373217 6373223 6373229 6373253 6373261
6373267 6373271 6373273 6373291 6373307 6373309 6373319 6373333 6373337 6373363
6373387 6373391 6373397 6373399 6373421 6373459 6373469 6373481 6373501 6373511
6373517 6373571 6373603 6373613 6373637 6373639 6373663 6373673 6373687 6373699
6373709 6373733 6373747 6373769 6373781 6373813 6373831 6373837 6373859 6373867
6373877 6373897 6373903 6373907 6373909 6373931 6373943 6373973 6373979 6373981
```

```
6374021 6374029 6374033 6374041 6374051 6374057 6374077 6374087 6374089 6374117
6374129 6374131 6374149 6374153 6374213 6374219 6374293 6374297 6374299 6374339
6374341 6374351 6374353 6374383 6374399 6374477 6374491 6374503 6374509 6374513
6374527 6374539 6374551 6374569 6374573 6374651 6374659 6374689 6374699 6374701
6374717 6374759 6374761 6374777 6374783 6374789 6374791 6374821 6374831 6374833
6374843 6374873 6374903 6374911 6374917 6374923 6374941 6374947 6374959 6374971
6374987 6375023 6375037 6375043 6375053 6375067 6375073 6375077 6375079 6375091
6375097 6375107 6375133 6375139 6375143 6375151 6375191 6375197 6375199 6375217
6375233 6375253 6375269 6375277 6375283 6375287 6375307 6375311 6375319 6375361
6375401 6375403 6375427 6375437 6375449 6375451 6375517 6375521 6375539 6375547
6375557 6375571 6375617 6375631 6375637 6375643 6375647 6375667 6375671 6375701
6375751 6375757 6375763 6375767 6375769 6375823 6375829 6375841 6375851 6375931
6375937 6375947 6375949 6375959 6375961 6375983 6375989 6376021 6376031 6376043
6376057 6376079 6376081 6376093 6376121 6376127 6376133 6376177 6376191 6376193
6376303 6376333 6376339 6376351 6376369 6376373 6376387 6376393 6376399 6376423
6376429 6376441 6376453 6376459 6376471 6376481 6376493 6376499 6376501 6376507
6376541 6376553 6376577 6376597 6376613 6376621 6376633 6376637 6376639 6376651
6376673 6376679 6376739 6376763 6376787 6376789 6376813 6376829 6376841 6376847
6376873 6376883 6376889 6376891 6376919 6376933 6376969 6376991 6376999 6377009
6377047 6377069 6377081 6377113 6377153 6377167 6377177 6377191 6377197 6377221
6377257 6377269 6377297 6377321 6377323 6377339 6377389 6377401 6377411 6377447
6377453 6377461 6377467 6377519 6377549 6377551 6377573 6377587 6377603 6377617
6377621 6377633 6377639 6377641 6377689 6377713 6377741 6377747 6377753 6377773
6377779 6377783 6377807 6377821 6377843 6377887 6377943 6377951 6377953
6377957 6377963 6377981 6377983 6377993 6378011 6378037 6378079 6378101 6378103
6378109 6378121 6378131 6378133 6378137 6378139 6378181 6378209 6378217 6378241
6378257 6378271 6378277 6378287 6378311 6378331 6378341 6378367 6378371 6378389
6378397 6378401 6378403 6378409 6378487 6378503 6378517 6378551 6378557 6378563
6378607 6378611 6378629 6378703 6378721 6378731 6378733 6378761 6378767 6378781
6378787 6378847 6378863 6378871 6378877 6378881 6378907 6378913 6378919 6378923
6378937 6378947 6378973 6378979 6378989 6379001 6379049 6379081 6379091 6379111
6379123 6379129 6379141 6379151 6379181 6379201 6379223 6379237 6379247 6379249
6379259 6379277 6379283 6379327 6379379 6379409 6379411 6379423 6379427 6379433
6379453 6379469 6379481 6379501 6379517 6379519 6379531 6379537 6379547 6379553
6379601 6379613 6379619 6379621 6379691 6379693 6379699 6379753 6379759 6379817
6379819 6379829 6379837 6379843 6379853 6379859 6379861 6379873 6379887 6379897
6379909 6379927 6379931 6379937 6379951 6379963 6379999 6380027 6380053 6380057
6380063 6380071 6380081 6380107 6380111 6380149 6380161 6380167 6380183 6380189
6380221 6380233 6380237 6380249 6380251 6380263 6380267 6380279 6380281 6380347
6380351 6380357 6380401 6380443 6380449 6380467 6380471 6380483 6380497 6380503
6380509 6380519 6380527 6380531 6380567 6380573 6380581 6380597 6380623 6380629
6380639 6380657 6380659 6380663 6380681 6380741 6380749 6380819 6380837
6380849 6380863 6380873 6380897 6380923 6380929 6380939 6380963 6380971 6380977
6380989 6380993 6380999 6381007 6381031 6381047 6381059 6381077 6381101 6381127
6381139 6381191 6381209 6381217 6381227 6381241 6381251 6381299 6381313 6381317
6381337 6381343 6381371 6381379 6381407 6381437 6381457 6381461 6381467 6381469
6381481 6381491 6381497 6381503 6381509 6381523 6381547 6381559 6381563 6381569
6381577 6381581 6381589 6381607 6381611 6381619 6381643 6381659 6381667 6381671
6381679 6381689 6381703 6381719 6381737 6381761 6381799 6381811 6381821 6381829
6381847 6381863 6381899 6381911 6381913 6381941 6381961 6381979 6382007 6382039
6382049 6382069 6382073 6382087 6382097 6382099 6382111 6382121 6382133 6382139
6382141 6382147 6382151 6382153 6382193 6382199 6382213 6382217 6382253 6382283
6382289 6382297 6382303 6382307 6382319 6382367 6382379 6382381 6382393 6382399
6382421 6382433 6382469 6382501 6382513 6382517 6382529 6382543 6382547 6382549
6382583 6382589 6382637 6382643 6382681 6382699 6382711 6382751 6382763 6382787
6382793 6382801 6382811 6382819 6382823 6382847 6382921 6382927 6382933 6382951
6382969 6383021 6383051 6383053 6383057 6383063 6383071 6383081 6383087 6383093
6383119 6383123 6383137 6383141 6383171 6383191 6383197 6383227 6383233 6383239
6383261 6383287 6383317 6383329 6383341 6383353 6383359 6383371 6383407 6383417
6383431 6383453 6383459 6383471 6383521 6383537 6383549 6383557 6383593 6383599
6383603 6383609 6383617 6383621 6383651 6383701 6383731 6383749 6383771 6383801
6383807 6383809 6383831 6383843 6383851 6383863 6383887 6383893 6383899 6383917
6383933 6383939 6383953 6383957 6383969 6383983 6383989 6383999 6384013 6384067
6384071 6384101 6384113 6384121 6384127 6384139 6384143 6384173 6384181 6384187
6384193 6384211 6384269 6384283 6384289 6384319 6384349 6384353 6384359
6384439 6384463 6384467 6384487 6384491 6384493 6384509 6384523 6384529 6384541
6384559 6384563 6384569 6384617 6384619 6384629 6384647 6384689 6384691 6384709
6384737 6384739 6384773 6384787 6384793 6384811 6384821 6384827 6384841 6384863
6384881 6384883 6384907 6384913 6384919 6384929 6384943 6384953 6384991 6385009
6385021 6385037 6385061 6385063 6385087 6385117 6385129 6385151 6385177 6385187
6385193 6385213 6385231 6385259 6385261 6385271 6385289 6385303 6385339
6385343 6385369 6385391 6385397 6385399 6385403 6385427 6385429 6385447 6385453
6385469 6385471 6385487 6385537 6385553 6385567 6385583 6385601 6385609 6385619
6385733 6385739 6385741 6385751 6385781 6385849 6385853 6385859 6385871 6385877
6385879 6385891 6385901 6385909 6385933 6385943 6385987 6385993 6385997 6386011
6386021 6386027 6386041 6386057 6386063 6386069 6386099 6386117 6386143 6386153
6386161 6386173 6386197 6386207 6386209 6386221 6386227 6386257 6386291 6386323
6386327 6386333 6386357 6386363 6386371 6386377 6386417 6386431 6386453 6386533
6386483 6386491 6386519 6386531 6386557 6386561 6386579 6386593 6386621 6386623
6386669 6386683 6386687 6386711 6386731 6386773 6386777 6386791
6386819 6386839 6386923 6386953 6386959 6386981 6387001 6387013 6387037 6387041
6387061 6387067 6387079 6387109 6387131 6387179 6387187 6387193 6387217 6387259
6387289 6387301 6387313 6387317 6387323 6387379 6387383 6387413 6387449 6387463
6387487 6387499 6387503 6387523 6387527 6387533 6387539 6387541 6387559 6387611
6387637 6387649 6387653 6387673 6387697 6387707 6387709 6387739 6387757
6387761 6387803 6387811 6387827 6387853 6387863 6387877 6387881 6387883 6387893
6387907 6387919 6387949 6387961 6387977 6388021 6388027 6388051 6388061 6388069
6388121 6388189 6388211 6388219 6388253 6388259 6388267 6388271 6388289 6388297
6388337 6388339 6388373 6388391 6388399 6388409 6388429 6388433 6388441 6388453
```

```
6388463  6388471  6388483  6388507  6388523  6388559  6388597  6388601  6388607  6388619
6388621  6388633  6388637  6388667  6388691  6388751  6388771  6388777  6388783  6388819
6388829  6388853  6388859  6388861  6388867  6388881  6388891  6388909  6388913  6388927  6388939
6388951  6388973  6388979  6388981  6389017  6389021  6389041  6389083  6389087  6389113
6389137  6389167  6389171  6389177  6389189  6389209  6389213  6389237  6389249
6389267  6389281  6389303  6389333  6389351  6389353  6389363  6389371  6389387  6389393
6389407  6389417  6389431  6389443  6389447  6389473  6389479  6389489  6389519
6389527  6389531  6389623  6389629  6389683  6389687  6389701  6389711  6389717  6389729
6389731  6389737  6389749  6389767  6389771  6389777  6389783  6389797  6389819
6389821  6389849  6389861  6389879  6389881  6389897  6389899  6389917  6389941  6389953
6389959  6389963  6389983  6389989  6389993  6390001  6390029  6390031  6390047  6390053
6390107  6390119  6390127  6390161  6390173  6390199  6390211  6390227  6390239  6390257
6390281  6390313  6390337  6390367  6390379  6390401  6390407  6390409  6390413  6390427
6390431  6390443  6390463  6390499  6390533  6390541  6390551  6390563  6390569  6390577
6390583  6390611  6390641  6390653  6390679  6390689  6390697  6390719  6390721  6390733
6390749  6390763  6390799  6390829  6390847  6390851  6390871  6390883  6390887  6390893
6390907  6390947  6390949  6390953  6390971  6391009  6391043  6391061  6391069
6391093  6391117  6391123  6391127  6391129  6391157  6391181  6391183  6391193  6391199
6391241  6391243  6391247  6391261  6391267  6391319  6391321  6391327  6391373  6391379
6391387  6391409  6391421  6391453  6391457  6391471  6391499  6391501  6391523  6391537
6391547  6391559  6391589  6391597  6391601  6391607  6391663  6391667  6391669  6391699
6391727  6391729  6391757  6391789  6391799  6391817  6391837  6391841  6391877
6391897  6391901  6391927  6391933  6391939  6391963  6391991  6392003  6392011  6392027
6392041  6392053  6392081  6392117  6392123  6392131  6392143  6392147  6392167
6392173  6392207  6392233  6392263  6392299  6392311  6392327  6392333  6392339  6392359
6392387  6392389  6392401  6392429  6392447  6392461  6392497  6392513  6392521  6392539
6392543  6392563  6392567  6392587  6392623  6392651  6392657  6392677  6392699  6392707
6392717  6392747  6392777  6392779  6392783  6392803  6392809  6392819  6392839  6392857
6392863  6392879  6392889  6392921  6392951  6392989  6392999  6393029  6393047  6393059
6393061  6393067  6393077  6393083  6393091  6393097  6393109  6393131  6393169  6393203
6393209  6393217  6393229  6393251  6393259  6393283  6393293  6393301  6393319  6393353
6393383  6393397  6393403  6393421  6393433  6393449  6393461  6393467  6393469  6393473
6393503  6393509  6393529  6393577  6393587  6393599  6393617  6393619  6393623  6393641
6393661  6393691  6393731  6393733  6393749  6393757  6393767  6393769  6393773  6393787
6393791  6393797  6393809  6393811  6393817  6393841  6393847  6393857  6393869  6393911
6393913  6393917  6393941  6393943  6393953  6393983  6394009  6394043  6394093  6394097
6394099  6394103  6394117  6394121  6394133  6394147  6394151  6394163  6394177  6394183
6394211  6394217  6394231  6394247  6394249  6394273  6394313  6394321  6394357  6394373
6394433  6394439  6394441  6394457  6394459  6394477  6394481  6394501  6394513
6394517  6394543  6394559  6394571  6394579  6394603  6394607  6394627  6394637  6394643
6394651  6394657  6394709  6394723  6394733  6394741  6394763  6394781  6394789  6394799
6394807  6394823  6394837  6394847  6394853  6394859  6394879  6394909  6394933  6394957
6394967  6394981  6395047  6395063  6395071  6395087  6395101  6395119  6395141  6395171
6395189  6395201  6395203  6395209  6395227  6395231  6395237  6395239  6395299  6395317
6395327  6395359  6395369  6395377  6395387  6395407  6395437  6395443  6395447  6395471
6395483  6395489  6395503  6395509  6395513  6395531  6395539  6395567  6395581  6395611
6395639  6395651  6395657  6395663  6395671  6395677  6395681  6395699  6395707  6395729
6395743  6395797  6395801  6395803  6395819  6395833  6395839  6395861  6395867  6395869
6395891  6395903  6395929  6395941  6395947  6395953  6395969  6395971  6395981  6396053
6396073  6396113  6396133  6396151  6396167  6396191  6396223  6396239  6396241  6396259
6396281  6396307  6396347  6396349  6396361  6396373  6396389  6396409  6396433  6396463
6396469  6396491  6396541  6396547  6396569  6396581  6396583  6396589  6396613  6396619
6396631  6396659  6396661  6396679  6396683  6396701  6396703  6396707  6396751  6396773
6396799  6396827  6396833  6396847  6396851  6396853  6396857  6396869  6396877  6396911
6396937  6396953  6396961  6396983  6396989  6396997  6397003  6397007  6397019  6397031
6397033  6397051  6397073  6397079  6397099  6397103  6397109  6397121  6397133  6397147
6397211  6397213  6397229  6397273  6397283  6397291  6397301  6397327  6397331  6397343
6397351  6397373  6397387  6397397  6397399  6397421  6397451  6397453  6397463  6397493
6397511  6397529  6397549  6397553  6397571  6397579  6397591  6397607  6397609  6397631
6397649  6397667  6397691  6397693  6397697  6397717  6397733  6397751  6397759  6397771
6397817  6397823  6397837  6397843  6397883  6397889  6397891  6397903  6397921  6397949
6397957  6397961  6397981  6397991  6397999  6398017  6398057  6398081  6398083  6398111
6398113  6398129  6398141  6398149  6398159  6398167  6398177  6398179  6398201  6398207
6398237  6398243  6398261  6398267  6398281  6398291  6398297  6398303  6398317  6398339
6398389  6398417  6398429  6398437  6398453  6398461  6398467  6398471  6398479  6398519
6398537  6398543  6398551  6398563  6398569  6398593  6398597  6398599  6398621  6398629
6398633  6398671  6398723  6398729  6398731  6398737  6398753  6398759  6398767  6398789
6398797  6398809  6398863  6398867  6398881  6398883  6398867
6398929  6398933  6398941  6398981  6398983  6398999  6399007  6399013  6399023  6399031
6399049  6399059  6399109  6399119  6399131  6399137  6399139  6399161  6399193  6399209
6399251  6399269  6399277  6399311  6399319  6399331  6399347  6399377  6399391  6399397
6399427  6399433  6399457  6399467  6399509  6399511  6399521  6399527  6399541  6399551
6399577  6399581  6399583  6399587  6399611  6399629  6399643  6399677  6399683  6399689
6399707  6399709  6399719  6399737  6399739  6399761  6399793  6399797  6399817  6399821
6399829  6399847  6399917  6399929  6399931  6399947  6399961  6399971
6400013  6400019  6400033  6400091  6400099  6400117  6400123  6400139  6400151  6400159
6400183  6400189  6400193  6400201  6400231  6400241  6400253  6400259  6400349  6400357
6400363  6400367  6400369  6400391  6400403  6400411  6400423  6400451  6400453  6400489
6400531  6400543  6400591  6400607  6400621  6400627  6400637  6400655  6400697  6400717
6400753  6400759  6400763  6400799  6400813  6400837  6400843  6400883  6400921
6400939  6400951  6400957  6400981  6400987  6401011  6401029  6401033  6401069  6401093
6401117  6401123  6401149  6401179  6401183  6401191  6401203  6401249  6401267  6401273
6401293  6401303  6401327  6401341  6401357  6401363  6401377  6401387  6401389  6401399
6401411  6401413  6401419  6401459  6401467  6401471  6401477  6401497  6401509  6401533
6401547  6401557  6401569  6401579  6401587  6401609  6401621  6401669  6401687  6401713
6401719  6401723  6401749  6401761  6401771  6401827  6401831  6401849  6401867  6401869
6401887  6401891  6401893  6401921  6401929  6401933  6401939  6401959  6401963  6401971
6401977  6401987  6402001  6402007  6402041  6402049  6402059  6402061  6402079  6402091
6402139  6402157  6402161  6402163  6402167  6402169  6402181  6402203  6402247  6402269
```

```
6402271 6402287 6402311 6402323 6402329 6402379 6402391 6402401 6402413 6402433
6402439 6402457 6402493 6402527 6402541 6402547 6402577 6402581 6402593 6402619
6402629 6402631 6402653 6402661 6402701 6402719 6402731 6402733 6402751 6402779
6402787 6402817 6402839 6402841 6402859 6402883 6402889 6402899 6402911 6402929
6402937 6402941 6402953 6402967 6402971 6402973 6403003 6403021 6403031 6403051
6403063 6403127 6403141 6403151 6403153 6403157 6403181 6403193 6403219 6403273
6403279 6403297 6403303 6403321 6403333 6403343 6403351 6403363 6403379 6403381
6403387 6403393 6403417 6403429 6403433 6403451 6403469 6403489 6403493 6403511
6403571 6403601 6403643 6403651 6403681 6403687 6403711 6403723 6403739 6403757
6403769 6403811 6403847 6403853 6403877 6403889 6403907 6403921 6403939 6403967
6403973 6403979 6403981 6403993 6404003 6404009 6404017 6404023 6404059 6404063
6404089 6404117 6404131 6404137 6404141 6404161 6404171 6404179 6404191 6404227
6404239 6404243 6404249 6404261 6404263 6404269 6404297 6404303 6404317 6404341
6404347 6404353 6404357 6404369 6404381 6404401 6404407 6404449 6404473 6404477
6404521 6404527 6404551 6404581 6404591 6404599 6404611 6404623 6404639 6404647
6404659 6404669 6404677 6404683 6404689 6404701 6404711 6404719 6404743
6404753 6404771 6404773 6404777 6404779 6404789 6404791 6404809 6404819 6404837
6404873 6404917 6404921 6404927 6404929 6404987 6405011 6405013 6405023 6405029
6405031 6405043 6405053 6405059 6405067 6405079 6405089 6405101 6405131 6405137
6405149 6405163 6405169 6405187 6405221 6405263 6405271 6405283 6405331 6405353
6405367 6405391 6405397 6405457 6405461 6405463 6405473 6405517 6405517 6405533
6405541 6405547 6405559 6405577 6405587 6405593 6405629 6405643 6405647 6405649
6405653 6405701 6405703 6405727 6405731 6405733 6405743 6405761 6405767 6405797
6405811 6405827 6405829 6405877 6405889 6405901 6405911 6405913 6405929 6405941
6405943 6405979 6405989 6406051 6406067 6406079 6406087 6406109 6406111 6406123
6406151 6406177 6406193 6406199 6406219 6406247 6406307 6406313 6406321 6406343
6406369 6406381 6406427 6406447 6406457 6406483 6406493 6406507 6406529 6406549
6406571 6406573 6406577 6406579 6406601 6406639 6406643 6406657 6406679 6406681
6406691 6406717 6406721 6406727 6406747 6406759 6406787 6406789 6406793 6406823
6406831 6406847 6406849 6406861 6406867 6406877 6406879 6406913 6406919 6406931
6406951 6406973 6406993 6407003 6407017 6407039 6407069 6407077
6407099 6407119 6407131 6407189 6407197 6407201 6407209 6407227 6407239 6407251
6407263 6407279 6407293 6407299 6407309 6407333 6407371 6407393 6407417 6407431
6407441 6407449 6407461 6407491 6407497 6407507 6407519 6407551 6407561 6407563
6407567 6407573 6407591 6407671 6407701 6407741 6407749 6407773 6407809 6407831
6407833 6407851 6407857 6407873 6407879 6407881 6407893 6407897 6407899 6407923
6407941 6407953 6407971 6407981 6408023 6408029 6408047 6408091 6408097 6408113
6408119 6408131 6408137 6408163 6408169 6408173 6408197 6408209 6408211
6408223 6408253 6408257 6408277 6408299 6408313 6408323 6408331 6408359 6408407
6408427 6408443 6408461 6408469 6408481 6408487 6408503 6408517 6408533 6408553
6408581 6408593 6408631 6408637 6408653 6408691 6408709 6408713 6408749 6408769
6408791 6408793 6408799 6408811 6408823 6408839 6408841 6408851 6408859 6408869
6408877 6408901 6408907 6408931 6408923 6408929 6408931 6408953 6408977 6408991
6409003 6409009 6409027 6409031 6409037 6409043 6409063 6409093 6409097 6409127
6409133 6409141 6409163 6409189 6409201 6409217 6409223 6409253 6409267 6409297
6409303 6409307 6409321 6409339 6409363 6409367 6409369 6409373 6409379 6409393
6409397 6409409 6409471 6409483 6409511 6409523 6409549 6409577 6409589 6409603
6409607 6409633 6409643 6409651 6409673 6409679 6409681 6409693 6409703 6409721
6409747 6409751 6409757 6409807 6409849 6409883 6409889 6409913 6409933 6409943
6410009 6410023 6410029 6410059 6410081 6410111 6410113 6410119 6410137 6410147
6410161 6410171 6410179 6410221 6410231 6410237 6410249 6410251 6410267 6410269
6410279 6410303 6410317 6410321 6410333 6410357 6410401 6410413 6410423 6410431
6410441 6410447 6410449 6410497 6410507 6410531 6410549 6410557 6410561 6410563
6410587 6410609 6410623 6410639 6410647 6410669 6410681 6410687 6410689 6410693
6410699 6410713 6410743 6410749 6410777 6410783 6410797 6410821 6410843 6410851
6410857 6410863 6410883 6410891 6410897 6410909 6410939 6410947 6410959 6410969
6410977 6410981 6410993 6411011 6411019 6411049 6411073 6411103 6411121 6411131
6411137 6411143 6411149 6411157 6411187 6411191 6411221 6411239 6411241 6411259
6411263 6411269 6411289 6411299 6411331 6411337 6411359 6411373 6411421 6411437
6411439 6411467 6411469 6411521 6411529 6411541 6411557 6411571 6411593 6411661
6411673 6411701 6411709 6411749 6411751 6411763 6411791 6411793 6411799 6411829
6411851 6411869 6411883 6411901 6411953 6411961 6411971 6411973 6411997 6412013
6412019 6412067 6412097 6412121 6412127 6412141 6412157 6412171 6412181 6412199
6412207 6412249 6412261 6412267 6412271 6412283 6412313 6412321 6412327 6412333
6412339 6412363 6412387 6412409 6412421 6412429 6412447 6412453 6412457 6412459
6412493 6412499 6412531 6412541 6412543 6412589 6412603 6412613 6412619 6412643
6412657 6412661 6412669 6412739 6412759 6412781 6412787 6412801 6412807 6412871
6412873 6412889 6412897 6412919 6412929 6412969 6412981 6412993 6412997 6413003
6413023 6413041 6413047 6413083 6413101 6413111 6413117 6413129 6413153 6413167
6413177 6413189 6413191 6413201 6413213 6413219 6413243 6413273 6413287 6413333
6413339 6413377 6413383 6413387 6413401 6413411 6413413 6413419 6413467 6413483
6413489 6413503 6413509 6413513 6413531 6413551 6413569 6413591 6413593 6413597
6413609 6413651 6413653 6413663 6413699 6413711 6413741 6413779 6413783 6413789
6413801 6413809 6413821 6413857 6413863 6413873 6413899 6413903 6413951 6413983
6414013 6414019 6414041 6414071 6414073 6414091 6414103 6414127 6414131 6414143
6414173 6414193 6414269 6414281 6414293 6414311 6414313 6414341 6414349 6414361
6414377 6414383 6414391 6414403 6414407 6414413 6414451 6414461 6414467 6414479
6414503 6414511 6414547 6414557 6414581 6414587 6414589 6414601 6414619 6414623
6414641 6414659 6414673 6414689 6414703 6414719 6414731 6414739 6414767 6414773
6414787 6414803 6414809 6414827 6414839 6414847 6414883 6414917 6414929
6414937 6414959 6414973 6415007 6415009 6415051 6415081 6415093 6415099 6415121
6415133 6415139 6415159 6415169 6415193 6415219 6415237 6415243 6415249 6415271
6415291 6415301 6415303 6415337 6415361 6415363 6415373 6415391 6415411 6415417
6415427 6415429 6415433 6415439 6415441 6415447 6415457 6415501 6415529 6415567
6415571 6415589 6415603 6415649 6415657 6415679 6415687 6415691 6415693 6415697
6415727 6415733 6415753 6415771 6415789 6415807 6415813 6415819 6415831 6415841
6415859 6415861 6415883 6415891 6415943 6415951 6415957 6415961 6415979 6415999
6416071 6416087 6416117 6416153 6416161 6416177 6416197 6416203 6416209 6416219
6416237 6416239 6416251 6416257 6416273 6416303 6416317 6416321 6416329 6416363
```

```
6416369  6416381  6416383  6416413  6416419  6416437  6416447  6416477  6416489  6416491
6416507  6416513  6416521  6416523  6416537  6416539  6416567  6416573  6416593  6416611
6416629  6416653  6416677  6416689  6416723  6416741  6416749  6416759  6416777  6416779
6416789  6416807  6416819  6416827  6416831  6416843  6416867  6416887  6416903  6416923
6416953  6416959  6416981  6416987  6416999  6417001  6417011  6417013  6417029  6417043
6417049  6417067  6417077  6417083  6417113  6417121  6417127  6417133  6417137  6417179
6417227  6417233  6417247  6417251  6417263  6417287  6417319  6417343  6417353  6417373
6417379  6417401  6417413  6417431  6417451  6417457  6417479  6417487  6417553  6417563
6417569  6417571  6417577  6417583  6417599  6417623  6417629  6417659  6417661  6417673
6417679  6417683  6417703  6417731  6417737  6417739  6417743  6417767  6417779  6417841
6417847  6417869  6417889  6417911  6417919  6417923  6417937  6417947  6418031  6418037
6418043  6418091  6418103  6418117  6418123  6418133  6418171  6418177  6418189  6418201
6418207  6418213  6418229  6418253  6418259  6418261  6418267  6418277  6418283  6418289
6418303  6418319  6418327  6418331  6418339  6418351  6418361  6418369  6418381  6418387
6418397  6418417  6418429  6418439  6418487  6418493  6418499  6418507  6418543  6418579
6418583  6418663  6418693  6418703  6418717  6418721  6418733  6418747  6418757  6418759
6418799  6418813  6418873  6418913  6418927  6418933  6418943  6418949  6418967  6418981
6418991  6419003  6419009  6419011  6419029  6419033  6419051  6419053  6419059  6419071
6419087  6419107  6419111  6419113  6419117  6419129  6419173  6419209  6419221  6419227
6419233  6419239  6419249  6419261  6419267  6419291  6419293  6419297  6419299  6419311
6419327  6419339  6419407  6419419  6419423  6419431  6419443  6419447  6419467  6419503
6419521  6419561  6419563  6419593  6419597  6419627  6419629  6419653  6419663  6419669
6419671  6419687  6419689  6419711  6419717  6419729  6419741  6419767  6419797  6419807
6419813  6419843  6419851  6419879  6419899  6419909  6419911  6419927  6419953  6419969
6419971  6419983  6419989  6420023  6420031  6420041  6420053  6420061  6420077  6420079
6420103  6420109  6420173  6420199  6420221  6420259  6420307  6420343  6420353  6420377
6420383  6420389  6420391  6420413  6420431  6420437  6420451  6420457  6420467  6420487
6420511  6420523  6420587  6420599  6420683  6420697  6420707  6420709  6420731  6420737
6420763  6420767  6420789  6420807  6420809  6420833  6420851  6420853  6420857  6420877
6420881  6420893  6420899  6420901  6420907  6420913  6420959  6420961  6420971  6420989
6420991  6421001  6421013  6421021  6421039  6421049  6421067  6421073  6421099  6421111
6421127  6421139  6421141  6421157  6421159  6421201  6421211  6421231  6421237  6421243
6421249  6421271  6421279  6421339  6421343  6421351  6421361  6421367  6421369  6421403
6421411  6421421  6421477  6421507  6421511  6421523  6421559  6421561  6421567  6421573
6421579  6421589  6421637  6421643  6421697  6421703  6421721  6421729  6421739  6421759
6421763  6421777  6421781  6421783  6421787  6421799  6421817  6421841  6421843  6421873
6421901  6421907  6421913  6421931  6421967  6421997  6422011  6422023  6422027  6422041
6422051  6422071  6422077  6422081  6422089  6422111  6422113  6422167  6422183  6422189
6422203  6422261  6422333  6422337  6422357  6422371  6422387  6422407  6422417  6422431
6422441  6422443  6422453  6422459  6422473  6422477  6422501  6422509  6422519  6422531
6422539  6422557  6422561  6422567  6422569  6422579  6422599  6422639  6422641  6422657
6422677  6422701  6422711  6422729  6422761  6422779  6422803  6422813  6422837  6422849
6422903  6422909  6422929  6422939  6422947  6422959  6422981  6422989  6422993  6423013
6423029  6423047  6423119  6423149  6423167  6423173  6423191  6423203  6423217
6423227  6423247  6423257  6423269  6423281  6423283  6423289  6423301  6423337  6423367
6423377  6423401  6423407  6423409  6423449  6423481  6423493  6423497  6423503  6423517
6423523  6423551  6423553  6423559  6423581  6423589  6423611  6423623  6423629  6423643
6423649  6423661  6423673  6423707  6423721  6423731  6423737  6423749  6423751  6423763
6423779  6423797  6423799  6423803  6423811  6423821  6423827  6423853  6423863  6423883
6423889  6423917  6423929  6423947  6423953  6423997  6424001  6424013  6424031  6424057
6424069  6424087  6424109  6424111  6424123  6424129  6424141  6424177  6424193  6424217
6424237  6424241  6424277  6424279  6424309  6424343  6424357  6424361  6424373  6424381
6424423  6424447  6424463  6424469  6424507  6424513  6424529  6424531  6424541  6424547
6424553  6424609  6424619  6424637  6424661  6424669  6424681  6424699  6424723  6424727
6424753  6424757  6424771  6424783  6424799  6424801  6424807  6424811  6424837  6424871
6424877  6424879  6424883  6424897  6424903  6424909  6424919  6424927  6424933  6424937
6424961  6424969  6424973  6424993  6425011  6425033  6425063  6425071  6425077  6425101
6425117  6425143  6425171  6425179  6425207  6425213  6425219  6425227  6425239
6425267  6425329  6425333  6425347  6425351  6425359  6425369  6425381  6425399  6425411
6425413  6425423  6425467  6425483  6425491  6425509  6425521  6425527  6425543  6425567
6425593  6425597  6425599  6425621  6425641  6425647  6425651  6425663  6425687  6425693
6425701  6425707  6425719  6425737  6425761  6425789  6425833  6425863  6425869  6425899
6425911  6425917  6425927  6425929  6425941  6425957  6425987  6425989  6425999  6426001
6426011  6426019  6426041  6426071  6426113  6426149  6426157  6426163  6426181  6426227
6426229  6426241  6426247  6426257  6426311  6426317  6426349  6426359  6426367  6426377
6426379  6426383  6426397  6426401  6426403  6426421  6426437  6426443  6426461  6426473
6426491  6426509  6426523  6426557  6426559  6426569  6426583  6426587  6426593  6426599
6426611  6426613  6426631  6426653  6426659  6426669  6426689  6426713  6426757  6426781  6426793
6426809  6426851  6426853  6426859  6426869  6426877  6426881  6426907  6426911  6426919
6426923  6426947  6426967  6426971  6426983  6426989  6427007  6427039  6427061  6427079
6427087  6427117  6427121  6427171  6427193  6427219  6427247  6427249  6427259  6427273
6427277  6427331  6427349  6427367  6427433  6427439  6427441  6427459  6427471  6427483
6427489  6427493  6427507  6427517  6427537  6427543  6427573  6427583  6427591  6427607
6427613  6427639  6427651  6427657  6427661  6427667  6427679  6427703  6427709  6427721
6427727  6427739  6427783  6427789  6427793  6427807  6427831  6427891  6427907  6427931
6427951  6427957  6427963  6427969  6427979  6427987  6428011  6428029  6428033  6428041
6428083  6428087  6428117  6428131  6428141  6428153  6428171  6428173  6428189  6428197
6428207  6428263  6428281  6428291  6428311  6428323  6428369  6428393  6428399  6428407
6428419  6428447  6428473  6428489  6428551  6428573  6428623  6428627  6428647  6428651
6428671  6428693  6428731  6428743  6428761  6428777  6428789  6428791  6428803
6428809  6428813  6428819  6428827  6428833  6428857  6428879  6428921  6428957  6428963
6428969  6428971  6428987  6429019  6429047  6429089  6429103  6429107  6429109  6429139
6429149  6429151  6429161  6429173  6429187  6429191  6429193  6429197  6429221  6429223
6429323  6429337  6429341  6429343  6429347  6429359  6429373  6429389  6429413  6429419
6429427  6429433  6429439  6429457  6429463  6429481  6429487  6429509  6429529  6429539
6429541  6429551  6429557  6429571  6429613  6429641  6429649  6429659  6429671  6429691
6429697  6429701  6429707  6429727  6429739  6429763  6429769  6429779  6429799  6429869
6429877  6429881  6429887  6429931  6429937  6429947  6429953  6429977  6430003  6430027
6430069  6430079  6430111  6430157  6430159  6430163  6430169  6430183  6430201  6430219
```

```
6430223 6430231 6430241 6430247 6430253 6430261 6430283 6430289 6430309 6430313
6430321 6430327 6430343 6430381 6430427 6430429 6430433 6430439 6430441 6430451
6430453 6430477 6430499 6430511 6430519 6430561 6430579 6430597 6430621 6430661
6430667 6430687 6430747 6430751 6430763 6430769 6430793 6430799 6430819 6430829
6430841 6430847 6430849 6430883 6430901 6430903 6430927 6430937 6430969 6430997
6431017 6431039 6431093 6431141 6431171 6431189 6431207 6431213 6431221 6431233
6431239 6431261 6431273 6431297 6431309 6431323 6431351 6431363 6431387 6431401
6431429 6431431 6431437 6431441 6431461 6431471 6431483 6431501 6431507 6431549
6431561 6431563 6431569 6431573 6431597 6431641 6431663 6431681 6431683 6431687
6431693 6431699 6431701 6431713 6431723 6431749 6431801 6431807 6431833 6431839
6431851 6431857 6431863 6431869 6431891 6431951 6431963 6431977 6431987 6431993
6432011 6432017 6432037 6432047 6432053 6432061 6432071 6432077 6432079 6432109
6432131 6432149 6432163 6432187 6432193 6432227 6432263 6432269 6432281 6432289
6432301 6432329 6432331 6432347 6432383 6432397 6432401 6432421 6432427 6432457
6432509 6432527 6432533 6432551 6432563 6432599 6432607 6432611 6432619 6432623
6432631 6432637 6432649 6432691 6432707 6432721 6432739 6432743 6432799 6432827
6432863 6432869 6432889 6432901 6432913 6432917 6432949 6432961 6432989 6432991
6433003 6433019 6433043 6433057 6433061 6433067 6433069 6433093 6433103 6433111
6433129 6433159 6433181 6433199 6433201 6433211 6433237 6433241 6433249 6433253
6433291 6433303 6433319 6433333 6433369 6433379 6433387 6433393 6433403 6433409
6433421 6433519 6433529 6433547 6433549 6433561 6433591 6433613 6433619 6433631
6433643 6433699 6433711 6433733 6433741 6433747 6433751 6433753 6433759 6433781
6433787 6433793 6433831 6433841 6433909 6433927 6433937 6433963 6433981 6433991
6434011 6434033 6434039 6434053 6434059 6434063 6434069 6434083 6434093 6434111
6434117 6434123 6434137 6434167 6434173 6434191 6434209 6434251 6434287 6434297
6434299 6434303 6434321 6434371 6434377 6434383 6434401 6434429 6434431 6434441
6434447 6434489 6434531 6434537 6434567 6434569 6434579 6434621 6434627 6434647
6434651 6434657 6434669 6434683 6434699 6434713 6434759 6434767 6434773 6434833
6434843 6434849 6434899 6434919 6434921 6434927 6434933 6434947 6434969 6434983
6435001 6435019 6435029 6435031 6435043 6435049 6435059 6435067 6435083 6435089
6435097 6435109 6435119 6435127 6435133 6435139 6435169 6435173 6435179 6435277
6435293 6435311 6435329 6435343 6435353 6435371 6435379 6435413 6435431 6435449
6435467 6435479 6435487 6435491 6435493 6435497 6435529 6435563 6435581 6435599
6435601 6435613 6435617 6435629 6435643 6435691 6435697 6435713 6435719 6435721
6435731 6435733 6435739 6435763 6435797 6435833 6435841 6435907 6435917 6435973
6435983 6435991 6435997 6436007 6436009 6436019 6436033 6436037 6436043 6436061
6436063 6436091 6436093 6436103 6436121 6436147 6436151 6436153 6436201 6436207
6436211 6436223 6436237 6436271 6436279 6436291 6436301 6436327 6436351 6436361
6436379 6436447 6436457 6436507 6436511 6436531 6436543 6436553 6436571 6436583
6436589 6436597 6436613 6436643 6436657 6436663 6436667 6436699 6436709 6436739
6436751 6436769 6436817 6436847 6436879 6436889 6436909 6436919 6436939 6436973
6436993 6437021 6437027 6437047 6437051 6437059 6437069 6437071 6437083 6437099
6437107 6437131 6437141 6437173 6437177 6437183 6437201 6437239 6437279 6437303
6437317 6437329 6437363 6437383 6437393 6437413 6437423 6437443 6437477 6437489
6437521 6437527 6437531 6437537 6437551 6437567 6437569 6437579 6437581 6437597
6437657 6437663 6437671 6437689 6437693 6437699 6437701 6437707 6437719 6437737
6437749 6437773 6437777 6437791 6437807 6437813 6437839 6437881 6437887 6437909
6437923 6437929 6437933 6437957 6437969 6437983 6438007 6438031 6438059 6438077
6438079 6438101 6438109 6438143 6438151 6438161 6438163 6438167 6438191 6438193
6438197 6438199 6438241 6438251 6438253 6438269 6438307 6438331 6438343 6438361
6438373 6438379 6438391 6438403 6438409 6438419 6438431 6438457 6438463 6438539
6438547 6438557 6438571 6438581 6438583 6438617 6438637 6438647 6438659 6438661
6438721 6438727 6438749 6438799 6438809 6438833 6438871 6438877 6438881 6438889
6438893 6438911 6438923 6438931 6438959 6438961 6438973 6438983 6438997 6439001
6439003 6439007 6439021 6439033 6439049 6439051 6439063 6439067 6439123 6439127
6439133 6439159 6439163 6439171 6439177 6439187 6439217 6439227 6439259 6439273
6439291 6439313 6439327 6439331 6439357 6439397 6439427 6439439 6439451 6439469
6439483 6439493 6439507 6439513 6439519 6439541 6439547 6439557 6439577 6439607
6439619 6439639 6439679 6439681 6439703 6439717 6439729 6439751 6439759 6439777
6439819 6439837 6439903 6439919 6439921 6439933 6439949 6439969 6439997 6440003
6440011 6440029 6440039 6440099 6440111 6440119 6440131 6440141 6440143
6440149 6440171 6440177 6440179 6440191 6440201 6440249 6440303 6440311 6440327
6440341 6440351 6440359 6440383 6440389 6440393 6440419 6440429 6440431 6440443
6440453 6440459 6440471 6440477 6440491 6440513 6440519 6440537 6440543 6440549
6440561 6440579 6440587 6440661 6440667 6440683 6440699 6440723 6440737 6440747
6440771 6440779 6440783 6440789 6440803 6440809 6440821 6440831 6440837 6440881
6440891 6440893 6440933 6440939 6440947 6440953 6440969 6440983 6440999 6441031
6441041 6441053 6441077 6441101 6441109 6441119 6441131 6441157 6441163 6441199
6441229 6441241 6441257 6441269 6441299 6441307 6441319 6441343 6441349 6441353
6441359 6441371 6441377 6441389 6441427 6441433 6441439 6441467 6441477 6441481
6441497 6441499 6441511 6441527 6441557 6441559 6441563 6441569 6441571 6441577
6441601 6441607 6441629 6441637 6441647 6441653 6441697 6441709 6441733 6441749
6441763 6441833 6441839 6441847 6441871 6441877 6441889 6441899 6441901 6441907
6441917 6441949 6441977 6441989 6442003 6442021 6442039 6442049 6442057 6442063
6442081 6442103 6442109 6442123 6442127 6442129 6442153 6442169 6442223 6442237
6442259 6442279 6442283 6442301 6442307 6442339 6442343 6442351 6442357 6442361
6442367 6442399 6442427 6442433 6442459 6442481 6442493 6442531 6442559 6442567
6442571 6442573 6442591 6442613 6442633 6442661 6442673 6442691 6442697 6442703
6442721 6442763 6442771 6442801 6442811 6442817 6442831 6442841 6442853 6442861
6442871 6442873 6442879 6442883 6442889 6442937 6442949 6442971 6442981 6442993
6442999 6443011 6443081 6443083 6443111 6443117 6443131 6443159 6443167 6443231
6443287 6443293 6443329 6443351 6443377 6443383 6443389 6443399 6443407 6443417
6443429 6443447 6443461 6443463 6443471 6443483 6443501 6443537 6443543 6443551
6443557 6443573 6443579 6443621 6443639 6443677 6443719 6443737 6443743 6443779
6443791 6443797 6443837 6443839 6443863 6443873 6443893 6443897 6443903 6443909
6443911 6443917 6443947 6443953 6443959 6443963 6443977 6443981 6443999 6444017
6444019 6444041 6444043 6444049 6444079 6444083 6444121 6444161 6444167 6444169
6444181 6444197 6444199 6444233 6444259 6444271 6444299 6444313 6444329 6444337
6444353 6444371 6444391 6444413 6444437 6444443 6444481 6444491 6444517 6444521
```

6444533 6444541 6444551 6444569 6444587 6444601 6444611 6444619 6444631 6444637
6444653 6444671 6444677 6444679 6444689 6444703 6444707 6444719 6444727 6444731
6444733 6444787 6444791 6444799 6444803 6444827 6444839 6444847 6444859 6444863
6444871 6444937 6444941 6444943 6444953 6444961 6444967 6444973 6444979 6445003
6445051 6445079 6445093 6445099 6445147 6445151 6445169 6445177 6445189 6445213
6445217 6445223 6445247 6445259 6445319 6445381 6445391 6445393 6445403 6445409
6445433 6445441 6445447 6445457 6445459 6445463 6445493 6445501 6445529 6445547
6445559 6445577 6445597 6445619 6445639 6445661 6445711 6445723 6445729 6445739
6445741 6445753 6445757 6445793 6445811 6445823 6445841 6445849 6445853 6445871
6445919 6445937 6445939 6445951 6445961 6445981 6445991 6445993 6446017 6446021
6446023 6446051 6446057 6446101 6446107 6446129 6446131 6446147 6446159 6446183
6446189 6446203 6446221 6446227 6446239 6446243 6446257 6446267 6446269 6446287
6446299 6446347 6446351 6446353 6446387 6446413 6446437 6446459 6446477 6446483
6446507 6446513 6446533 6446569 6446591 6446593 6446599 6446611 6446623 6446633
6446651 6446653 6446659 6446669 6446711 6446731 6446767 6446771 6446777 6446789
6446801 6446851 6446863 6446929 6446939 6446971 6446981 6446987 6447017 6447031
6447047 6447059 6447073 6447109 6447113 6447121 6447149 6447167 6447173 6447179
6447187 6447197 6447229 6447239 6447253 6447257 6447271 6447277 6447283 6447293
6447317 6447323 6447391 6447407 6447421 6447443 6447449 6447457 6447533 6447547
6447557 6447569 6447577 6447629 6447643 6447647 6447653 6447671 6447673 6447691
6447733 6447737 6447757 6447767 6447769 6447781 6447787 6447817 6447829 6447839
6447841 6447853 6447899 6447919 6447923 6447929 6447943 6447967 6447983 6447989
6447997 6448003 6448009 6448019 6448061 6448069 6448081 6448103 6448133 6448157
6448207 6448223 6448231 6448241 6448243 6448271 6448289 6448297 6448307 6448319
6448327 6448333 6448339 6448361 6448363 6448369 6448373 6448381 6448399 6448427
6448451 6448483 6448489 6448511 6448517 6448529 6448531 6448537 6448553 6448567
6448573 6448597 6448609 6448621 6448633 6448639 6448681 6448699 6448781 6448787
6448789 6448807 6448811 6448853 6448861 6448889 6448903 6448907 6448909 6448913
6448927 6448973 6448979 6449021 6449033 6449041 6449071 6449081 6449083 6449087
6449099 6449117 6449123 6449141 6449159 6449161 6449173 6449197 6449213 6449237
6449243 6449257 6449309 6449321 6449329 6449351 6449363 6449419 6449419 6449431
6449437 6449447 6449449 6449473 6449479 6449483 6449489 6449491 6449537 6449617
6449659 6449671 6449693 6449719 6449731 6449743 6449753 6449761 6449777 6449791
6449827 6449831 6449837 6449887 6449893 6449899 6449903 6449909 6449909 6449917
6449921 6449923 6450007 6450011 6450019 6450029 6450049 6450083 6450091 6450107
6450109 6450131 6450133 6450167 6450181 6450193 6450211 6450217 6450221 6450229
6450251 6450277 6450287 6450299 6450307 6450313 6450317 6450319 6450331 6450337
6450341 6450347 6450349 6450391 6450413 6450427 6450439 6450467 6450487 6450491
6450503 6450527 6450539 6450541 6450553 6450583 6450593 6450611 6450629 6450637
6450641 6450679 6450707 6450727 6450733 6450737 6450749 6450751 6450757 6450761
6450793 6450799 6450841 6450863 6450877 6450881 6450893 6450901 6450907 6450907
6450929 6450931 6450943 6450949 6450953 6451019 6451031 6451033 6451087 6451091
6451097 6451099 6451111 6451117 6451121 6451139 6451147 6451163 6451169 6451171
6451183 6451189 6451217 6451217 6451223 6451231 6451259 6451261 6451271 6451297
6451301 6451307 6451321 6451331 6451337 6451349 6451387 6451397 6451399 6451433
6451439 6451451 6451481 6451499 6451513 6451541 6451547 6451559 6451561 6451561
6451573 6451609 6451633 6451649 6451657 6451691 6451723 6451733 6451759 6451769
6451793 6451807 6451843 6451847 6451853 6451859 6451871 6451873 6451889 6451897
6451919 6451927 6451931 6451933 6451943 6451967 6451987 6451997 6452011 6452053
6452071 6452099 6452101 6452111 6452119 6452137 6452141 6452189 6452203 6452221
6452261 6452261 6452291 6452311 6452321 6452323 6452339 6452357 6452359 6452363
6452377 6452387 6452389 6452423 6452429 6452431 6452447 6452461 6452477 6452497
6452513 6452521 6452561 6452629 6452657 6452671 6452687 6452711 6452729 6452737
6452753 6452759 6452777 6452779 6452783 6452801 6452807 6452813 6452821 6452827
6452839 6452851 6452863 6452869 6452879 6452893 6452899 6452917 6452933 6452969
6453011 6453023 6453037 6453043 6453049 6453061 6453067 6453071 6453077 6453089
6453101 6453107 6453131 6453137 6453163 6453173 6453197 6453199 6453221 6453247
6453253 6453263 6453329 6453329 6453347 6453367 6453379 6453389 6453427 6453431
6453443 6453451 6453463 6453467 6453493 6453497 6453511 6453529 6453533 6453541
6453571 6453647 6453649 6453661 6453677 6453679 6453697 6453703 6453721 6453737
6453767 6453773 6453779 6453793 6453809 6453817 6453871 6453883 6453893 6453929
6453943 6453949 6453973 6453989 6454009 6454031 6454039 6454051 6454073 6454079
6454093 6454109 6454121 6454127 6454141 6454157 6454159 6454199 6454213 6454223
6454241 6454297 6454303 6454307 6454337 6454361 6454363 6454367 6454387 6454403
6454411 6454439 6454451 6454453 6454489 6454517 6454519 6454523 6454529 6454549
6454571 6454583 6454597 6454619 6454621 6454627 6454633 6454639 6454649 6454663
6454667 6454709 6454729 6454739 6454751 6454757 6454759 6454769 6454783 6454787
6454801 6454807 6454843 6454873 6454901 6454907 6454957 6454961 6454957 6454961
6454969 6454979 6454991 6454997 6455017 6455047 6455063 6455093 6455101 6455129
6455153 6455167 6455173 6455191 6455201 6455209 6455219 6455221 6455233 6455261
6455263 6455297 6455329 6455357 6455363 6455377 6455381 6455399 6455519 6455531
6455441 6455443 6455467 6455473 6455521 6455539 6455543 6455557 6455567 6455587
6455593 6455623 6455639 6455677 6455681 6455689 6455707 6455717 6455741 6455747
6455749 6455773 6455789 6455831 6455833 6455837 6455857 6455863 6455879 6455881
6455899 6455923 6455929 6455947 6455963 6456001 6456007 6456011 6456041 6456071
6456083 6456113 6456119 6456137 6456161 6456173 6456199 6456221 6456239 6456253
6456259 6456271 6456283 6456287 6456313 6456323 6456337 6456361 6456367 6456383
6456391 6456403 6456419 6456421 6456427 6456449 6456467 6456469 6456499 6456509
6456511 6456521 6456529 6456539 6456551 6456559 6456563 6456577 6456607 6456613
6456623 6456641 6456661 6456679 6456691 6456727 6456731 6456733 6456739 6456743
6456757 6456781 6456797 6456809 6456823 6456851 6456871 6456881 6456887 6456893
6456899 6456929 6456943 6456949 6456971 6456977 6457007 6457013 6457027 6457079
6457091 6457097 6457109 6457123 6457163 6457183 6457247 6457249 6457261 6457271
6457279 6457291 6457307 6457313 6457337 6457357 6457391 6457417 6457421 6457441
6457453 6457489 6457531 6457543 6457553 6457589 6457601 6457613 6457621 6457631
6457657 6457667 6457669 6457681 6457699 6457729 6457741 6457747 6457757 6457811
6457831 6457859 6457861 6457877 6457879 6457921 6457933 6457939 6457949 6457987
6457991 6458003 6458021 6458059 6458069 6458071 6458087 6458093 6458117 6458159
6458161 6458167 6458183 6458189 6458227 6458267 6458269 6458293 6458297 6458321

```
6458327  6458339  6458341  6458371  6458393  6458399  6458407  6458437  6458449  6458477
6458483  6458513  6458563  6458587  6458597  6458603  6458629  6458681  6458687
6458713  6458717  6458731  6458737  6458773  6458779  6458783  6458797  6458801  6458813
6458843  6458869  6458897  6458907  6458911  6458923  6458953  6458957  6458981  6458989
6459029  6459049  6459091  6459097  6459109  6459121  6459149  6459157  6459169
6459197  6459203  6459223  6459227  6459239  6459247  6459281  6459283  6459287  6459307
6459311  6459317  6459319  6459329  6459359  6459361  6459391  6459407  6459421  6459437
6459443  6459457  6459491  6459493  6459499  6459511  6459533  6459553  6459559  6459569
6459577  6459581  6459613  6459617  6459623  6459631  6459637  6459659  6459679  6459683
6459701  6459703  6459707  6459731  6459743  6459767  6459773  6459787  6459797  6459823
6459833  6459841  6459863  6459877  6459883  6459899  6459907  6459913  6459923  6459979
6459991  6460031  6460037  6460039  6460043  6460093  6460141  6460147  6460169  6460189
6460199  6460213  6460231  6460241  6460249  6460261  6460283  6460331  6460351  6460367
6460379  6460423  6460439  6460453  6460457  6460463  6460477  6460481  6460499  6460523
6460529  6460543  6460547  6460567  6460577  6460579  6460583  6460603  6460613  6460651
6460673  6460687  6460691  6460709  6460711  6460717  6460721  6460747  6460759  6460781
6460801  6460819  6460843  6460871  6460891  6460897  6460919  6460963  6460967
6461017  6461023  6461027  6461041  6461047  6461089  6461093  6461099  6461107  6461123
6461129  6461131  6461141  6461167  6461199  6461201  6461209  6461219  6461233  6461243
6461249  6461261  6461263  6461269  6461317  6461333  6461341  6461353  6461359  6461369
6461383  6461393  6461401  6461407  6461417  6461437  6461443  6461471  6461509  6461527
6461531  6461537  6461549  6461561  6461563  6461573  6461617  6461627  6461657  6461713
6461737  6461753  6461759  6461761  6461773  6461779  6461783  6461801  6461803  6461821
6461831  6461839  6461869  6461891  6461893  6461899  6461941  6461947  6461951  6461953
6461999  6462017  6462031  6462037  6462047  6462059  6462061  6462097  6462101  6462107
6462119  6462163  6462199  6462221  6462233  6462251  6462259  6462263  6462271  6462289
6462301  6462307  6462319  6462367  6462373  6462377  6462403  6462409  6462419  6462439
6462473  6462487  6462541  6462559  6462569  6462571  6462587  6462593  6462607  6462647
6462667  6462671  6462689  6462691  6462697  6462713  6462727  6462739  6462751  6462769
6462803  6462811  6462851  6462877  6462881  6462893  6462947  6462997  6463001  6463003
6463031  6463073  6463081  6463099  6463103  6463109  6463129  6463139  6463151  6463169
6463183  6463189  6463231  6463243  6463267  6463279  6463307  6463309  6463337  6463381
6463399  6463421  6463441  6463463  6463489  6463507  6463537  6463571  6463573  6463577
6463601  6463603  6463637  6463643  6463649  6463651  6463661  6463669  6463673  6463687
6463693  6463703  6463727  6463739  6463741  6463753  6463771  6463777  6463811  6463823
6463837  6463871  6463879  6463883  6463901  6463907  6463909  6463949  6463969  6463973
6463979  6463991  6463999  6464021  6464041  6464057  6464083  6464111  6464113  6464137
6464141  6464153  6464167  6464179  6464197  6464201  6464203  6464207  6464209  6464221
6464261  6464273  6464281  6464287  6464299  6464317  6464323  6464329  6464377  6464387
6464401  6464411  6464413  6464431  6464483  6464501  6464509  6464519  6464531  6464533
6464537  6464551  6464561  6464567  6464609  6464611  6464639  6464687  6464713  6464723
6464729  6464741  6464747  6464753  6464797  6464813  6464819  6464827  6464831  6464849
6464851  6464873  6464881  6464903  6464923  6464933  6464951  6464971  6464977
6464989  6465013  6465023  6465061  6465077  6465097  6465101  6465127  6465131  6465133
6465163  6465181  6465197  6465203  6465223  6465229  6465233  6465257  6465271  6465293
6465317  6465337  6465373  6465383  6465409  6465419  6465467  6465469  6465493  6465497
6465499  6465527  6465533  6465539  6465551  6465581  6465587  6465601  6465607  6465623
6465653  6465671  6465677  6465703  6465707  6465733  6465739  6465779  6465791  6465803
6465821  6465839  6465847  6465853  6465859  6465883  6465911  6465917  6465929  6465937
6465941  6465959  6465997  6466037  6466051  6466063  6466067  6466081  6466123  6466127
6466129  6466133  6466147  6466177  6466193  6466219  6466241  6466247  6466249  6466261
6466277  6466279  6466283  6466301  6466303  6466309  6466319  6466349  6466351  6466363
6466367  6466393  6466399  6466417  6466429  6466433  6466457  6466463  6466487  6466489
6466501  6466529  6466531  6466543  6466547  6466591  6466597  6466627  6466633  6466661
6466679  6466709  6466711  6466717  6466723  6466729  6466771  6466781  6466787  6466799
6466819  6466843  6466847  6466853  6466883  6466921  6466937  6466951  6466969  6466991
6467033  6467093  6467099  6467137  6467141  6467147  6467161  6467171  6467183  6467207
6467213  6467231  6467233  6467249  6467257  6467269  6467273  6467287  6467291  6467317
6467323  6467371  6467387  6467413  6467423  6467441  6467453  6467459  6467471  6467477
6467479  6467491  6467507  6467533  6467557  6467597  6467611  6467621  6467653  6467663
6467683  6467689  6467693  6467723  6467731  6467753  6467767  6467789  6467801  6467819
6467821  6467827  6467849  6467861  6467869  6467917  6467927  6467947  6467953  6467969
6467971  6467977  6468001  6468023  6468031  6468053  6468061  6468079  6468089  6468149
6468167  6468179  6468191  6468197  6468223  6468269  6468271  6468277  6468289  6468317
6468323  6468349  6468373  6468383  6468389  6468391  6468401  6468403  6468409  6468419
6468437  6468443  6468461  6468463  6468481  6468509  6468541  6468559  6468577  6468593
6468613  6468617  6468629  6468641  6468647  6468661  6468667  6468691  6468697  6468767
6468793  6468811  6468817  6468829  6468847  6468853  6468883  6468887  6468907  6468967
6468971  6468977  6468983  6468997  6469031  6469039  6469069  6469081  6469087  6469091
6469093  6469157  6469159  6469171  6469189  6469193  6469217  6469219  6469241  6469247
6469303  6469313  6469343  6469357  6469373  6469381  6469391  6469399  6469423  6469427
6469429  6469439  6469457  6469501  6469511  6469517  6469531  6469559  6469577  6469579
6469637  6469649  6469667  6469699  6469703  6469753  6469781  6469787  6469807  6469811
6469837  6469847  6469849  6469867  6469891  6469919  6469921  6469943  6469949  6469951
6469961  6469963  6469993  6470003  6470029  6470039  6470053  6470069  6470083  6470119
6470129  6470141  6470147  6470171  6470201  6470213  6470231  6470249  6470263  6470273
6470297  6470327  6470341  6470369  6470371  6470377  6470411  6470417  6470419  6470423
6470437  6470467  6470473  6470491  6470531  6470543  6470549  6470551  6470561  6470573
6470593  6470627  6470641  6470677  6470687  6470689  6470701  6470729  6470731  6470753
6470759  6470771  6470801  6470831  6470837  6470839  6470861  6470873  6470879  6470897
6470899  6470903  6470951  6470953  6470983  6470987  6471013  6471019  6471037  6471053
6471103  6471107  6471121  6471131  6471133  6471137  6471139  6471151  6471163  6471167
6471173  6471187  6471193  6471233  6471251  6471259  6471277  6471287  6471313
6471319  6471323  6471331  6471347  6471359  6471391  6471401  6471431  6471433  6471449
6471461  6471473  6471499  6471503  6471511  6471541  6471547  6471583  6471617  6471643
6471649  6471667  6471677  6471691  6471733  6471737  6471749  6471791  6471797  6471811
6471821  6471827  6471877  6471889  6471893  6471919  6471953  6471967  6471977  6472007
6472009  6472021  6472049  6472061  6472079  6472097  6472099  6472111  6472139  6472157
6472159  6472163  6472171  6472187  6472199  6472237  6472247  6472259  6472261  6472309
```

```
6472337  6472351  6472357  6472363  6472381  6472387  6472421  6472429  6472457  6472463
6472469  6472471  6472513  6472523  6472561  6472577  6472601  6472603  6472619  6472621
6472633  6472643  6472667  6472679  6472721  6472723  6472757  6472777  6472783  6472789
6472859  6472871  6472887  6472909  6472927  6472931  6472933  6472951  6472967  6472987
6472993  6472997  6473009  6473011  6473029  6473041  6473057  6473069  6473099  6473147
6473149  6473197  6473231  6473239  6473251  6473279  6473287  6473297  6473321  6473323
6473329  6473333  6473347  6473353  6473399  6473407  6473437  6473443  6473461  6473477
6473479  6473491  6473543  6473561  6473569  6473591  6473609  6473629  6473633  6473659
6473671  6473681  6473689  6473711  6473723  6473743  6473749  6473801  6473807  6473843
6473861  6473867  6473881  6473891  6473903  6473911  6473953  6473963  6473977  6473981
6474007  6474019  6474049  6474053  6474077  6474101  6474103  6474119  6474137  6474173
6474227  6474233  6474241  6474253  6474311  6474313  6474317  6474329  6474341
6474343  6474353  6474361  6474389  6474397  6474401  6474407  6474409  6474439  6474449
6474451  6474473  6474487  6474493  6474499  6474509  6474557  6474577  6474613  6474619
6474623  6474631  6474641  6474659  6474697  6474701  6474731  6474737  6474751  6474791
6474803  6474821  6474823  6474827  6474829  6474833  6474857  6474883  6474887  6474893
6474911  6474929  6474931  6474959  6474973  6475019  6475043  6475057  6475061
6475087  6475097  6475103  6475127  6475153  6475159  6475163  6475177  6475223  6475247
6475267  6475277  6475279  6475289  6475291  6475307  6475321  6475387  6475457  6475459
6475463  6475471  6475493  6475517  6475529  6475537  6475543  6475571  6475583  6475597
6475619  6475631  6475643  6475649  6475669  6475681  6475687  6475717  6475739  6475741
6475753  6475771  6475783  6475829  6475831  6475837  6475841  6475879  6475883  6475897
6475901  6475913  6475939  6475951  6475957  6475967  6475969  6476003  6476009  6476027
6476039  6476069  6476081  6476089  6476137  6476159  6476161  6476191  6476209  6476213
6476219  6476227  6476233  6476257  6476293  6476297  6476329  6476333  6476339  6476347
6476357  6476377  6476383  6476387  6476417  6476419  6476429  6476447  6476467  6476471
6476497  6476513  6476543  6476557  6476563  6476581  6476611  6476621  6476641  6476651
6476669  6476681  6476683  6476693  6476699  6476749  6476753  6476783  6476791  6476809
6476837  6476839  6476849  6476851  6476857  6476867  6476879  6476917  6476933  6476941
6476959  6476963  6476969  6477011  6477013  6477019  6477049  6477059  6477083  6477089
6477101  6477113  6477143  6477151  6477161  6477169  6477181  6477193  6477199
6477203  6477227  6477241  6477253  6477269  6477277  6477281  6477299  6477301  6477307
6477337  6477343  6477371  6477377  6477379  6477397  6477409  6477413  6477439  6477463
6477487  6477491  6477503  6477533  6477577  6477589  6477599  6477623  6477637  6477641
6477671  6477677  6477683  6477703  6477707  6477721  6477739  6477767  6477769  6477781
6477811  6477829  6477841  6477857  6477871  6477879  6477929  6477931  6477949  6477967
6477971  6477983  6478009  6478013  6478027  6478033  6478061  6478103  6478117  6478187
6478193  6478201  6478229  6478267  6478273  6478279  6478301  6478313  6478363  6478379
6478421  6478429  6478447  6478453  6478457  6478463  6478469  6478471  6478481  6478489
6478499  6478501  6478519  6478543  6478559  6478567  6478579  6478583  6478603  6478607
6478631  6478673  6478723  6478729  6478733  6478757  6478763  6478777  6478781  6478793
6478831  6478841  6478883  6478891  6478931  6478937  6478949  6478951  6478961  6478973
6478991  6478999  6479021  6479041  6479047  6479059  6479089  6479113  6479119
6479131  6479147  6479149  6479153  6479167  6479173  6479191  6479269  6479299  6479311
6479327  6479351  6479357  6479387  6479401  6479411  6479423  6479461  6479471  6479489
6479509  6479521  6479549  6479569  6479587  6479593  6479609  6479617  6479633  6479647
6479657  6479663  6479701  6479729  6479743  6479747  6479791  6479801  6479807  6479827
6479831  6479897  6479903  6479917  6479923  6479929  6479933  6479953  6479959  6479989
6479999  6480011  6480017  6480049  6480053  6480107  6480109  6480113  6480127  6480139
6480163  6480167  6480191  6480193  6480223  6480233  6480239  6480251  6480259  6480263
6480269  6480289  6480301  6480329  6480359  6480367  6480373  6480389  6480403  6480413
6480421  6480491  6480497  6480499  6480533  6480541  6480547  6480563  6480599  6480613
6480631  6480637  6480707  6480739  6480751  6480781  6480811  6480827  6480847  6480859
6480907  6480913  6480931  6480941  6480959  6480967  6480979  6480989  6480997  6481019
6481021  6481037  6481039  6481051  6481073  6481087  6481121  6481127  6481141  6481169
6481171  6481177  6481183  6481187  6481207  6481217  6481219  6481243  6481259  6481273
6481289  6481303  6481313  6481339  6481367  6481381  6481393  6481417  6481427  6481439
6481457  6481463  6481477  6481499  6481543  6481571  6481583  6481591  6481609  6481619
6481627  6481639  6481667  6481669  6481693  6481711  6481729  6481747  6481751  6481753
6481757  6481763  6481789  6481807  6481823  6481829  6481841  6481843  6481861  6481873
6481927  6481931  6481939  6481957  6481961  6481963  6481991  6481997  6481999  6482009
6482017  6482023  6482033  6482041  6482053  6482057  6482071  6482081  6482089  6482101
6482129  6482149  6482171  6482197  6482209  6482221  6482227  6482233  6482239
6482243  6482257  6482261  6482269  6482299  6482351  6482369  6482393  6482407  6482417
6482431  6482447  6482459  6482467  6482479  6482501  6482521  6482537  6482561  6482579
6482587  6482599  6482603  6482611  6482621  6482639  6482657  6482669  6482699  6482701
6482737  6482741  6482753  6482767  6482779  6482783  6482789  6482837  6482867  6482891
6482909  6482929  6482947  6482989  6483011  6483017  6483031  6483053  6483077
6483091  6483101  6483109  6483131  6483143  6483163  6483193  6483209  6483233  6483241
6483271  6483277  6483283  6483287  6483299  6483311  6483317  6483343  6483359  6483391
6483403  6483413  6483419  6483457  6483461  6483469  6483479  6483481  6483527  6483563
6483593  6483599  6483611  6483643  6483667  6483671  6483679  6483683  6483689  6483709
6483713  6483721  6483727  6483761  6483773  6483787  6483793  6483803  6483809  6483823
6483833  6483839  6483857  6483871  6483887  6483889  6483913  6483931  6483937  6483941
6483949  6483967  6483989  6484001  6484003  6484019  6484031  6484057  6484061
6484063  6484067  6484069  6484087  6484097  6484103  6484129  6484133  6484169  6484207
6484243  6484249  6484253  6484267  6484297  6484319  6484333  6484337  6484343  6484351
6484381  6484397  6484403  6484409  6484427  6484433  6484441  6484447  6484477  6484553
6484561  6484579  6484609  6484613  6484619  6484627  6484651  6484669  6484691  6484703
6484711  6484717  6484721  6484733  6484763  6484799  6484801  6484823  6484831  6484853
6484861  6484889  6484897  6484901  6484913  6484931  6484979  6484981  6484987  6484999
6485021  6485029  6485033  6485053  6485081  6485113  6485117  6485119  6485123  6485147
6485153  6485207  6485209  6485233  6485243  6485261  6485291  6485329  6485387
6485407  6485419  6485429  6485431  6485447  6485461  6485477  6485489  6485491  6485497
6485527  6485543  6485579  6485587  6485599  6485629  6485657  6485659  6485681  6485683
6485719  6485729  6485741  6485771  6485803  6485833  6485837  6485849  6485863  6485867
6485881  6485923  6485939  6485951  6485971  6485987  6486001  6486041  6486043  6486079
6486083  6486089  6486101  6486107  6486121  6486127  6486131  6486133  6486143  6486149
6486209  6486217  6486247  6486251  6486257  6486281  6486287  6486301  6486307  6486349
```

```
6486377  6486379  6486407  6486427  6486439  6486443  6486461  6486463  6486479  6486499
6486547  6486553  6486559  6486563  6486577  6486589  6486629  6486647  6486653  6486671
6486677  6486709  6486737  6486751  6486761  6486763  6486787  6486791  6486793  6486797
6486811  6486839  6486841  6486869  6486889  6486899  6486919  6486929  6486941  6486947
6486959  6486973  6487001  6487003  6487027  6487049  6487051  6487067  6487073  6487079
6487123  6487157  6487181  6487223  6487259  6487267  6487279  6487297  6487301  6487337
6487373  6487381  6487391  6487399  6487427  6487441  6487487  6487501  6487511  6487519
6487549  6487567  6487577  6487643  6487667  6487687  6487751  6487753  6487757  6487763
6487807  6487813  6487837  6487841  6487847  6487849  6487879  6487903  6487919  6487933
6487939  6487951  6487979  6487991  6487993  6488003  6488023  6488071  6488089  6488107
6488123  6488129  6488137  6488147  6488149  6488179  6488201  6488239  6488243  6488249
6488263  6488267  6488281  6488297  6488309  6488311  6488327  6488333  6488353  6488371
6488389  6488401  6488411  6488413  6488423  6488429  6488453  6488501  6488527  6488533
6488539  6488551  6488563  6488567  6488591  6488609  6488617  6488623  6488627  6488639
6488681  6488683  6488687  6488693  6488719  6488767  6488777  6488791  6488809  6488819
6488831  6488851  6488869  6488887  6488893  6488939  6488941  6488959  6488969  6488971
6488987  6489083  6489101  6489107  6489113  6489143  6489163  6489179  6489209  6489211
6489221  6489227  6489253  6489271  6489277  6489293  6489299  6489311  6489313  6489331
6489341  6489349  6489361  6489367  6489389  6489401  6489409  6489421  6489433  6489449
6489451  6489463  6489487  6489491  6489499  6489551  6489557  6489559  6489569  6489577
6489599  6489601  6489629  6489641  6489647  6489653  6489667  6489671  6489677  6489683
6489709  6489719  6489779  6489781  6489793  6489803  6489809  6489839  6489859  6489863
6489877  6489883  6489893  6489913  6489949  6489953  6489983  6489991  6490007  6490027
6490031  6490037  6490063  6490079  6490093  6490109  6490111  6490123  6490139  6490151
6490189  6490193  6490201  6490213  6490219  6490247  6490271  6490273  6490303  6490313
6490321  6490331  6490333  6490369  6490373  6490391  6490409  6490411  6490417  6490427
6490483  6490487  6490507  6490511  6490541  6490567  6490591  6490597  6490613  6490643
6490661  6490663  6490667  6490691  6490699  6490709  6490711  6490717  6490733  6490739
6490769  6490777  6490793  6490801  6490817  6490831  6490877  6490879  6490903  6490907
6490909  6490921  6490927  6490931  6490937  6490943  6490961  6490969  6490973  6490999
6491011  6491039  6491047  6491081  6491101  6491117  6491119  6491131  6491137  6491153
6491159  6491167  6491189  6491207  6491213  6491227  6491231  6491257  6491299  6491333
6491377  6491411  6491413  6491417  6491449  6491461  6491477  6491533  6491549  6491557
6491561  6491623  6491627  6491651  6491657  6491659  6491663  6491669  6491677  6491689
6491701  6491707  6491729  6491731  6491747  6491759  6491783  6491813  6491833  6491857
6491861  6491873  6491893  6491897  6491923  6491929  6491951  6491971  6491991  6491993
6492007  6492029  6492043  6492061  6492067  6492071  6492103  6492121  6492133  6492137
6492139  6492163  6492173  6492191  6492223  6492253  6492257  6492271  6492287  6492323
6492329  6492331  6492337  6492373  6492383  6492389  6492397  6492403  6492407  6492443
6492449  6492467  6492503  6492511  6492523  6492557  6492569  6492571  6492581  6492593
6492611  6492631  6492643  6492677  6492679  6492683  6492709  6492727  6492749  6492751
6492763  6492809  6492821  6492833  6492847  6492887  6492911  6492953  6492961  6492991
6493001  6493027  6493033  6493063  6493073  6493087  6493139  6493141  6493147  6493169
6493177  6493183  6493217  6493219  6493237  6493259  6493261  6493273  6493283  6493297
6493309  6493321  6493343  6493349  6493367  6493373  6493381  6493397  6493433  6493441
6493451  6493463  6493469  6493493  6493517  6493523  6493547  6493561  6493603  6493607
6493631  6493667  6493673  6493679  6493681  6493699  6493741  6493769  6493793  6493819
6493829  6493831  6493853  6493909  6493913  6493919  6493933  6493957  6493969  6494021
6494039  6494041  6494069  6494101  6494167  6494171  6494177  6494179  6494183  6494197
6494209  6494237  6494239  6494251  6494261  6494263  6494273  6494281  6494287  6494297
6494311  6494317  6494321  6494339  6494363  6494387  6494393  6494417  6494443  6494473
6494489  6494491  6494503  6494513  6494539  6494549  6494611  6494623  6494627  6494633
6494641  6494651  6494659  6494689  6494693  6494707  6494711  6494729  6494743  6494749
6494771  6494773  6494777  6494783  6494821  6494837  6494857  6494861  6494863  6494881
6494909  6494911  6494921  6494951  6494959  6494981  6494987  6494989  6495011  6495031
6495067  6495079  6495103  6495109  6495121  6495157  6495163  6495197  6495211  6495227
6495263  6495319  6495323  6495367  6495371  6495383  6495389  6495409  6495421  6495431
6495443  6495457  6495481  6495491  6495509  6495527  6495529  6495539  6495563  6495569
6495571  6495607  6495641  6495653  6495659  6495661  6495667  6495677  6495679  6495721
6495737  6495761  6495773  6495779  6495791  6495793  6495803  6495809  6495847  6495871
6495889  6495919  6495941  6495943  6495947  6495949  6495991  6495997  6496001  6496027
6496037  6496067  6496079  6496109  6496117  6496121  6496123  6496151  6496153  6496169
6496181  6496211  6496223  6496247  6496277  6496279  6496283  6496289  6496307  6496333
6496337  6496339  6496351  6496361  6496379  6496417  6496433  6496459  6496467  6496487
6496517  6496531  6496543  6496547  6496559  6496583  6496591  6496597  6496621  6496627
6496631  6496643  6496661  6496663  6496717  6496729  6496747  6496759  6496799  6496807
6496811  6496837  6496843  6496849  6496859  6496871  6496883  6496891  6496909  6496937
6496943  6496981  6497003  6497033  6497053  6497059  6497083  6497087  6497123
6497129  6497143  6497159  6497167  6497173  6497177  6497203  6497209  6497243  6497261
6497263  6497269  6497291  6497299  6497303  6497317  6497329  6497347  6497369  6497377
6497389  6497399  6497441  6497453  6497461  6497471  6497483  6497497  6497509  6497539
6497581  6497591  6497683  6497713  6497717  6497737  6497761  6497779  6497807  6497809
6497819  6497831  6497837  6497851  6497857  6497863  6497873  6497899  6497917  6497921
6497923  6497929  6497957  6497969  6497989  6498007  6498013  6498017  6498043  6498067
6498077  6498091  6498101  6498103  6498109  6498113  6498161  6498169  6498181
6498197  6498211  6498221  6498223  6498227  6498229  6498281  6498287  6498299  6498307
6498311  6498341  6498343  6498353  6498379  6498419  6498473  6498487  6498491  6498497
6498509  6498511  6498521  6498553  6498563  6498571  6498577  6498629  6498659  6498671
6498683  6498707  6498721  6498727  6498731  6498733  6498761  6498763  6498769  6498773
6498797  6498803  6498823  6498827  6498829  6498839  6498847  6498853  6498901  6498907
6498923  6498937  6498941  6498959  6498979  6499037  6499039  6499061  6499079  6499081
6499111  6499147  6499169  6499177  6499183  6499187  6499189  6499193  6499211  6499217
6499247  6499289  6499307  6499331  6499333  6499351  6499357  6499369  6499373  6499379
6499391  6499397  6499399  6499439  6499453  6499459  6499483  6499513  6499517  6499523
6499541  6499549  6499573  6499601  6499631  6499637  6499647  6499651  6499663  6499673
6499681  6499699  6499709  6499721  6499723  6499747  6499793  6499841  6499859  6499861
6499879  6499897  6499903  6499939  6499943  6499949  6499991  6500003  6500023  6500029
6500059  6500063  6500077  6500093  6500101  6500113  6500149  6500159  6500161  6500167
6500177  6500183  6500203  6500209  6500231  6500233  6500243  6500251  6500257  6500279
```

```
6500281  6500287  6500309  6500317  6500323  6500327  6500339  6500369  6500371  6500387
6500401  6500441  6500447  6500449  6500453  6500491  6500497  6500519  6500531  6500537
6500539  6500563  6500569  6500573  6500581  6500597  6500621  6500633  6500677  6500687
6500693  6500729  6500737  6500759  6500761  6500771  6500779  6500801  6500807  6500839
6500849  6500861  6500873  6500887  6500903  6500939  6500941  6500951  6500969  6500971
6500981  6501007  6501029  6501031  6501049  6501073  6501091  6501109  6501113  6501149
6501179  6501217  6501221  6501239  6501241  6501251  6501263  6501277  6501281  6501283
6501301  6501311  6501337  6501343  6501349  6501367  6501379  6501389  6501403  6501409
6501419  6501421  6501431  6501487  6501491  6501513  6501569  6501587  6501589  6501601
6501611  6501631  6501637  6501647  6501689  6501697  6501707  6501721  6501727  6501731
6501749  6501757  6501773  6501791  6501793  6501797  6501799  6501809  6501823  6501827
6501863  6501889  6501947  6501983  6501991  6502039  6502049  6502079  6502099  6502117
6502127  6502129  6502141  6502147  6502151  6502163  6502187  6502193  6502207  6502229
6502241  6502247  6502259  6502267  6502271  6502277  6502289  6502291  6502297  6502337
6502339  6502367  6502373  6502423  6502439  6502453  6502471  6502487  6502501  6502519
6502543  6502547  6502553  6502571  6502577  6502603  6502609  6502627  6502631  6502633
6502637  6502649  6502663  6502667  6502669  6502673  6502679  6502681  6502697  6502703
6502733  6502739  6502753  6502759  6502799  6502817  6502829  6502849  6502877  6502879
6502889  6502919  6502927  6502939  6502941  6502973  6502987  6502999  6503011
6503033  6503041  6503069  6503093  6503099  6503113  6503137  6503143  6503173  6503179
6503239  6503269  6503281  6503303  6503309  6503311  6503347  6503369  6503381
6503389  6503407  6503417  6503423  6503443  6503447  6503473  6503477  6503501  6503507
6503513  6503533  6503557  6503587  6503591  6503593  6503597  6503599  6503603  6503611
6503617  6503633  6503647  6503663  6503669  6503677  6503711  6503713  6503737  6503771
6503803  6503807  6503837  6503839  6503851  6503857  6503869  6503923  6503927  6503957
6503969  6503977  6504011  6504037  6504041  6504049  6504053  6504059  6504067  6504077
6504083  6504103  6504109  6504131  6504133  6504143  6504181  6504187  6504191  6504233
6504257  6504259  6504263  6504269  6504343  6504359  6504361  6504367  6504397  6504401
6504419  6504457  6504467  6504493  6504499  6504503  6504539  6504571  6504577  6504583
6504587  6504599  6504611  6504629  6504647  6504669  6504677  6504683  6504697  6504737
6504749  6504763  6504769  6504803  6504853  6504877  6504881  6504889  6504899  6504907
6504913  6504923  6504977  6504983  6505003  6505013  6505027  6505043  6505063  6505069
6505117  6505123  6505141  6505153  6505181  6505189  6505199  6505211  6505243  6505267
6505283  6505307  6505327  6505333  6505337  6505351  6505357  6505361  6505363  6505393
6505409  6505453  6505469  6505501  6505507  6505519  6505537  6505547  6505549  6505559
6505607  6505621  6505627  6505643  6505649  6505663  6505669  6505703  6505717  6505783
6505799  6505823  6505841  6505859  6505861  6505867  6505931  6505937  6505949  6505973
6505991  6505997  6506023  6506039  6506051  6506057  6506089  6506099  6506111  6506141
6506147  6506161  6506177  6506183  6506197  6506207  6506209  6506219  6506231  6506243
6506261  6506299  6506323  6506327  6506329  6506347  6506363  6506371  6506387  6506389
6506399  6506429  6506441  6506473  6506483  6506491  6506557  6506581  6506587  6506611
6506657  6506693  6506707  6506719  6506779  6506789  6506813  6506881  6506887  6506891
6506893  6506897  6506921  6506959  6506961  6506963  6507023  6507031  6507037
6507047  6507071  6507077  6507097  6507119  6507121  6507143  6507157  6507161  6507167
6507173  6507199  6507203  6507211  6507217  6507239  6507251  6507269  6507271  6507307
6507317  6507323  6507337  6507341  6507343  6507359  6507373  6507407  6507421
6507463  6507469  6507511  6507517  6507521  6507533  6507539  6507569  6507587  6507619
6507623  6507649  6507661  6507673  6507691  6507701  6507707  6507727  6507757  6507763
6507773  6507793  6507833  6507859  6507871  6507881  6507901  6507913  6507953  6507959
6507961  6507979  6507989  6507997  6508003  6508027  6508031  6508039  6508049  6508079
6508081  6508091  6508097  6508131  6508133  6508139  6508141  6508147  6508163  6508181
6508193  6508199  6508207  6508237  6508247  6508253  6508259  6508277  6508283  6508301
6508309  6508343  6508361  6508363  6508367  6508387  6508421  6508429  6508483  6508493
6508511  6508549  6508561  6508571  6508577  6508589  6508651  6508657  6508661  6508699
6508727  6508741  6508751  6508757  6508763  6508769  6508787  6508813  6508819  6508823
6508871  6508891  6508907  6508921  6508937  6508949  6508951  6508969  6508979  6509017
6509033  6509093  6509123  6509143  6509177  6509179  6509189  6509197  6509203  6509213
6509219  6509221  6509233  6509257  6509263  6509273  6509309  6509341  6509357  6509387
6509389  6509417  6509429  6509449  6509491  6509501  6509507  6509527  6509537  6509557
6509563  6509567  6509579  6509603  6509617  6509677  6509681  6509683  6509687  6509689
6509707  6509719  6509749  6509771  6509779  6509791  6509803  6509809  6509819  6509821
6509843  6509863  6509869  6509873  6509903  6509941  6509947  6509953  6509977  6510011
6510019  6510037  6510047  6510073  6510079  6510107  6510109  6510131  6510139  6510143
6510151  6510191  6510193  6510197  6510199  6510209  6510211  6510221  6510223  6510227
6510247  6510263  6510277  6510281  6510313  6510367  6510373  6510397  6510421  6510433
6510443  6510451  6510463  6510479  6510481  6510499  6510523  6510533  6510563  6510571
6510577  6510583  6510593  6510611  6510613  6510641  6510649  6510659  6510661  6510671
6510697  6510701  6510727  6510731  6510793  6510799  6510821  6510839  6510857  6510869
6510883  6510887  6510919  6510929  6510953  6510967  6511003  6511007  6511013  6511019
6511027  6511031  6511033  6511049  6511073  6511111  6511121  6511133  6511159  6511171
6511229  6511237  6511247  6511273  6511291  6511301  6511303  6511321  6511327  6511331
6511363  6511367  6511387  6511411  6511469  6511487  6511489  6511499  6511501  6511523
6511537  6511541  6511543  6511559  6511577  6511597  6511601  6511621  6511649  6511669
6511711  6511717  6511721  6511723  6511727  6511751  6511759  6511781  6511787  6511789
6511801  6511807  6511871  6511909  6511937  6511961  6511997  6512027  6512039  6512047
6512053  6512069  6512081  6512083  6512087  6512089  6512101  6512119  6512137  6512147
6512159  6512161  6512171  6512183  6512189  6512213  6512227  6512251  6512279  6512281
6512291  6512293  6512321  6512323  6512329  6512347  6512351  6512353  6512371  6512413
6512417  6512419  6512431  6512437  6512447  6512453  6512477  6512489  6512491  6512509
6512521  6512533  6512537  6512579  6512593  6512603  6512609  6512633  6512647  6512659
6512663  6512699  6512711  6512713  6512719  6512729  6512731  6512741  6512747  6512767
6512771  6512773  6512797  6512807  6512813  6512861  6512879  6512899  6512903  6512911
6512917  6512929  6512977  6513019  6513041  6513053  6513079  6513103  6513107  6513113
6513121  6513127  6513173  6513179  6513191  6513211  6513229  6513239  6513281  6513289
6513293  6513319  6513323  6513341  6513361  6513373  6513407  6513413  6513427  6513457
6513461  6513473  6513497  6513553  6513569  6513581  6513587  6513593  6513613  6513649
6513653  6513671  6513673  6513691  6513707  6513709  6513733  6513743  6513779  6513803
6513809  6513817  6513847  6513869  6513877  6513889  6513901  6513911  6513917  6513919
6513929  6513931  6513953  6513973  6514003  6514021  6514031  6514049  6514051  6514069
```

```
6514073  6514091  6514099  6514117  6514127  6514139  6514141  6514147  6514159  6514187
6514201  6514253  6514259  6514289  6514297  6514303  6514307  6514327  6514381  6514427
6514489  6514507  6514537  6514559  6514567  6514579  6514591  6514597  6514609  6514633
6514637  6514639  6514649  6514657  6514687  6514699  6514751  6514759  6514769  6514793
6514817  6514829  6514843  6514883  6514897  6514933  6514939  6514951  6514969  6514979
6514993  6515009  6515017  6515021  6515027  6515057  6515087  6515099  6515129  6515153
6515183  6515189  6515203  6515261  6515287  6515297  6515303  6515329  6515387  6515407
6515413  6515419  6515473  6515479  6515497  6515501  6515503  6515513  6515521  6515527
6515543  6515557  6515567  6515609  6515623  6515627  6515659  6515659  6515669  6515671
6515687  6515701  6515711  6515723  6515731  6515753  6515791  6515827  6515863  6515867
6515881  6515893  6515897  6515909  6515941  6515953  6515963  6516001  6516011  6516017
6516023  6516043  6516047  6516073  6516079  6516113  6516119  6516121  6516149  6516161
6516163  6516187  6516197  6516227  6516229  6516233  6516239  6516241  6516269  6516281
6516299  6516317  6516319  6516331  6516359  6516379  6516401  6516421  6516431  6516437
6516439  6516463  6516467  6516469  6516481  6516511  6516527  6516539  6516553  6516571
6516583  6516611  6516617  6516623  6516647  6516649  6516667  6516673  6516701  6516703
6516739  6516743  6516761  6516767  6516781  6516787  6516833  6516859  6516871  6516883
6516893  6516901  6516907  6516919  6516931  6516941  6516949  6516959  6516971  6516977
6516989  6516997  6517003  6517033  6517061  6517079  6517097  6517107  6517117  6517127
6517129  6517169  6517177  6517183  6517187  6517193  6517201  6517213  6517249  6517261
6517283  6517289  6517309  6517321  6517331  6517339  6517369  6517391  6517393  6517411
6517447  6517481  6517499  6517507  6517517  6517519  6517523  6517529  6517543  6517561
6517573  6517583  6517597  6517603  6517607  6517633  6517649  6517673  6517699  6517711
6517733  6517739  6517747  6517751  6517757  6517759  6517787  6517799  6517801  6517831
6517853  6517867  6517877  6517891  6517921  6517933  6517937  6517963  6517981  6517997
6517999  6518003  6518023  6518047  6518051  6518077  6518081  6518107  6518111  6518121
6518129  6518137  6518147  6518173  6518209  6518227  6518263  6518279  6518299  6518321
6518341  6518381  6518411  6518419  6518431  6518441  6518443  6518459  6518461  6518489
6518503  6518507  6518537  6518557  6518593  6518593  6518621  6518647  6518651  6518657
6518669  6518693  6518731  6518747  6518749  6518753  6518777  6518779  6518789  6518791
6518801  6518807  6518819  6518839  6518873  6518879  6518891  6518893  6518923  6518947
6518989  6519011  6519017  6519049  6519059  6519061  6519091  6519127  6519133  6519157
6519169  6519193  6519209  6519217  6519257  6519259  6519277  6519283  6519307  6519329
6519341  6519343  6519361  6519367  6519391  6519397  6519421  6519427  6519463  6519509
6519529  6519547  6519553  6519563  6519571  6519587  6519593  6519607  6519613  6519647
6519673  6519683  6519719  6519757  6519763  6519767  6519787  6519803  6519829  6519841
6519871  6519883  6519893  6519917  6519941  6519973  6519977  6519979  6519991  6520057
6520067  6520069  6520079  6520081  6520093  6520117  6520127  6520139  6520147  6520153
6520183  6520201  6520207  6520223  6520253  6520277  6520279  6520289  6520309  6520313
6520321  6520343  6520379  6520387  6520403  6520411  6520417  6520421  6520441  6520453
6520457  6520471  6520483  6520487  6520499  6520511  6520513  6520519  6520541  6520567
6520573  6520589  6520597  6520609  6520691  6520693  6520699  6520727  6520747  6520771
6520777  6520793  6520817  6520823  6520831  6520837  6520847  6520867  6520883  6520903
6520919  6520939  6520949  6520951  6520957  6520963  6520973  6520981  6520999  6521003
6521023  6521041  6521057  6521059  6521071  6521077  6521087  6521089  6521101  6521107
6521111  6521131  6521153  6521197  6521209  6521243  6521257  6521269  6521293  6521303
6521321  6521363  6521369  6521381  6521399  6521401  6521441  6521477  6521479  6521497
6521513  6521521  6521527  6521531  6521533  6521561  6521587  6521677  6521689  6521699
6521717  6521737  6521759  6521773  6521783  6521789  6521791  6521813  6521821  6521833
6521843  6521899  6521909  6521923  6521929  6521947  6521951  6521987  6522001  6522007
6522011  6522017  6522023  6522031  6522053  6522083  6522151  6522167  6522199  6522209
6522227  6522253  6522287  6522293  6522311  6522337  6522343  6522353  6522367  6522371
6522379  6522413  6522421  6522427  6522437  6522449  6522469  6522487  6522497  6522499
6522539  6522563  6522569  6522583  6522587  6522599  6522601  6522629  6522641  6522661
6522667  6522673  6522683  6522727  6522739  6522743  6522749  6522751  6522779  6522787
6522809  6522811  6522851  6522877  6522899  6522911  6522931  6522937  6522949  6522953
6522979  6523001  6523003  6523031  6523037  6523039  6523043  6523079  6523091  6523103
6523117  6523133  6523163  6523171  6523183  6523199  6523201  6523243  6523247  6523249
6523259  6523277  6523313  6523337  6523339  6523343  6523357  6523373  6523381  6523477
6523493  6523511  6523549  6523567  6523577  6523607  6523613  6523619  6523661  6523663
6523681  6523703  6523721  6523739  6523747  6523757  6523763  6523787  6523799  6523813
6523819  6523837  6523841  6523843  6523861  6523871  6523873  6523939  6523943  6523963
6523969  6524009  6524017  6524027  6524029  6524033  6524041  6524071  6524081  6524093
6524113  6524129  6524137  6524183  6524191  6524197  6524213  6524227  6524251  6524267
6524269  6524293  6524299  6524303  6524327  6524333  6524389  6524407  6524411  6524417
6524423  6524431  6524447  6524471  6524473  6524489  6524503  6524509  6524513  6524537
6524563  6524569  6524579  6524591  6524599  6524603  6524611  6524627  6524629  6524647
6524653  6524659  6524669  6524697  6524737  6524747  6524773  6524783  6524789  6524803
6524807  6524831  6524851  6524873  6524891  6524933  6524941  6524951  6524953  6524977
6524981  6524983  6524993  6525007  6525047  6525049  6525073  6525083  6525089  6525107
6525119  6525149  6525179  6525187  6525193  6525217  6525257  6525301  6525349  6525361
6525367  6525371  6525373  6525427  6525443  6525457  6525499  6525511  6525517  6525521
6525529  6525553  6525559  6525581  6525587  6525611  6525613  6525639  6525643  6525647
6525661  6525677  6525691  6525703  6525707  6525751  6525763  6525781  6525787  6525793
6525811  6525817  6525821  6525839  6525853  6525877  6525887  6525901  6525907  6525917
6525919  6525923  6525947  6525971  6525973  6525979  6525991  6526033  6526057  6526061
6526087  6526123  6526141  6526159  6526187  6526199  6526217  6526229  6526231  6526237
6526241  6526277  6526297  6526301  6526307  6526309  6526313  6526343  6526379  6526409
6526423  6526463  6526469  6526483  6526489  6526501  6526511  6526529  6526547  6526571
6526601  6526607  6526627  6526643  6526651  6526667  6526699  6526739  6526777  6526781
6526783  6526789  6526799  6526847  6526867  6526873  6526879  6526889  6526909  6526967
6526969  6526973  6526981  6526991  6527021  6527039  6527047  6527063  6527069  6527083
6527119  6527123  6527137  6527141  6527173  6527177  6527197  6527199  6527207  6527237
6527249  6527251  6527263  6527273  6527309  6527383  6527401  6527413  6527447  6527467
6527471  6527497  6527509  6527531  6527537  6527539  6527551  6527557  6527567  6527597
6527603  6527617  6527623  6527627  6527629  6527641  6527663  6527681  6527687  6527693
6527723  6527737  6527789  6527803  6527827  6527869  6527891  6527893  6527921  6527977
6528013  6528023  6528031  6528043  6528047  6528089  6528091  6528101  6528107  6528121
6528133  6528139  6528157  6528167  6528209  6528233  6528257  6528271  6528283  6528287
```

```
6528299  6528331  6528367  6528371  6528373  6528377  6528397  6528407  6528421  6528469
6528479  6528497  6528499  6528503  6528517  6528541  6528559  6528581  6528583  6528589
6528601  6528607  6528617  6528623  6528637  6528649  6528653  6528659  6528671  6528673
6528677  6528679  6528703  6528707  6528719  6528737  6528749  6528751  6528791  6528793
6528811  6528829  6528839  6528853  6528869  6528871  6528883  6528887  6528917  6528923
6528937  6528959  6528961  6528971  6528979  6529021  6529043  6529051  6529073  6529087
6529097  6529109  6529121  6529153  6529157  6529169  6529177  6529183  6529223  6529261
6529267  6529319  6529337  6529349  6529357  6529363  6529387  6529399  6529403  6529409
6529423  6529463  6529469  6529487  6529489  6529511  6529517  6529519  6529529  6529541
6529543  6529571  6529573  6529577  6529591  6529603  6529613  6529651  6529661  6529667
6529681  6529697  6529709  6529763  6529771  6529781  6529793  6529801  6529811  6529813
6529823  6529829  6529847  6529849  6529877  6529879  6529927  6529949  6529951  6529967
6529969  6529973  6529979  6529981  6529987  6530003  6530011  6530047  6530059  6530063
6530071  6530087  6530107  6530177  6530189  6530203  6530221  6530257  6530309  6530323
6530333  6530339  6530341  6530347  6530351  6530387  6530399  6530401  6530417  6530437
6530443  6530473  6530483  6530519  6530561  6530581  6530591  6530617  6530621  6530659
6530663  6530681  6530683  6530687  6530707  6530717  6530753  6530773  6530779  6530789
6530803  6530807  6530809  6530831  6530861  6530879  6530891  6530893  6530899  6530903
6530911  6530929  6530933  6530947  6530957  6530971  6530989  6530999  6531029  6531053
6531059  6531071  6531089  6531097  6531101  6531113  6531121  6531131  6531139  6531181
6531191  6531199  6531211  6531221  6531233  6531251  6531253  6531289  6531319  6531323
6531373  6531377  6531391  6531401  6531403  6531407  6531419  6531431  6531433  6531457
6531461  6531463  6531479  6531487  6531491  6531509  6531521  6531523  6531527  6531533
6531557  6531593  6531599  6531617  6531619  6531643  6531653  6531673  6531683  6531703
6531709  6531719  6531761  6531769  6531779  6531781  6531797  6531857  6531887  6531907
6531951  6531971  6531983  6532003  6532007  6532037  6532049  6532051  6532073  6532081
6532093  6532117  6532121  6532129  6532159  6532171  6532177  6532189  6532223  6532231
6532241  6532249  6532283  6532291  6532319  6532327  6532343  6532367  6532381  6532397
6532399  6532423  6532439  6532441  6532459  6532469  6532481  6532507  6532531  6532541
6532543  6532549  6532553  6532601  6532649  6532651  6532693  6532699  6532733  6532739
6532763  6532769  6532783  6532807  6532829  6532849  6532881  6532891  6532901  6532907
6532919  6532937  6532961  6532987  6532991  6533003  6533027  6533029  6533057  6533071
6533077  6533089  6533113  6533123  6533143  6533147  6533159  6533167  6533209  6533213
6533239  6533251  6533273  6533297  6533299  6533339  6533347  6533383  6533411  6533437
6533453  6533459  6533477  6533479  6533489  6533503  6533509  6533561  6533567  6533603
6533617  6533623  6533641  6533647  6533651  6533669  6533689  6533699  6533707  6533717
6533743  6533749  6533759  6533783  6533803  6533809  6533819  6533833  6533851  6533873
6533911  6533939  6533951  6533977  6533981  6533983  6534013  6534049  6534071  6534083
6534109  6534131  6534133  6534173  6534191  6534197  6534247  6534257  6534281  6534287
6534289  6534299  6534313  6534329  6534331  6534337  6534349  6534361  6534379  6534389
6534419  6534433  6534439  6534467  6534481  6534487  6534509  6534523  6534547  6534569
6534589  6534601  6534611  6534617  6534631  6534679  6534701  6534709  6534713  6534743
6534751  6534757  6534791  6534799  6534823  6534859  6534883  6534901  6534907  6534929
6534937  6534943  6535019  6535027  6535049  6535057  6535073  6535091  6535093  6535099
6535163  6535187  6535189  6535201  6535213  6535219  6535223  6535229  6535241  6535279
6535301  6535343  6535349  6535369  6535387  6535391  6535457  6535493  6535511  6535517
6535541  6535549  6535553  6535561  6535577  6535603  6535619  6535631  6535651  6535663
6535673  6535681  6535691  6535693  6535709  6535741  6535747  6535751  6535787  6535799
6535819  6535831  6535847  6535853  6535861  6535873  6535891  6535897  6535901  6535927
6535987  6535993  6535999  6536003  6536029  6536039  6536059  6536063  6536077  6536081
6536083  6536111  6536141  6536191  6536203  6536219  6536227  6536239  6536251  6536267
6536269  6536293  6536297  6536311  6536317  6536329  6536359  6536363  6536371  6536377
6536389  6536423  6536441  6536461  6536477  6536479  6536489  6536503  6536527  6536557
6536561  6536573  6536581  6536591  6536597  6536603  6536609  6536611  6536617  6536633
6536659  6536693  6536707  6536723  6536729  6536743  6536759  6536767  6536771  6536773
6536797  6536801  6536813  6536837  6536843  6536851  6536863  6536869  6536879  6536897
6536911  6536921  6536947  6537019  6537029  6537053  6537059  6537067  6537079  6537109
6537131  6537137  6537143  6537169  6537173  6537191  6537199  6537203  6537211  6537217
6537227  6537239  6537283  6537287  6537301  6537319  6537331  6537337  6537341  6537347
6537353  6537361  6537397  6537403  6537407  6537437  6537439  6537457  6537511  6537521
6537523  6537541  6537547  6537563  6537569  6537599  6537611  6537649  6537667  6537679
6537697  6537701  6537733  6537757  6537781  6537787  6537799  6537821  6537859  6537899
6537907  6537941  6537943  6537977  6537989  6537991  6537997  6538001  6538009  6538019
6538043  6538057  6538069  6538073  6538111  6538127  6538139  6538151  6538157  6538171
6538201  6538211  6538219  6538267  6538289  6538297  6538309  6538313  6538331  6538351
6538373  6538403  6538409  6538423  6538429  6538447  6538453  6538457  6538459  6538487
6538507  6538517  6538531  6538549  6538559  6538561  6538573  6538577  6538607  6538621
6538669  6538681  6538703  6538711  6538723  6538747  6538757  6538771  6538783  6538789
6538813  6538817  6538837  6538843  6538853  6538859  6538879  6538927  6538937  6538963
6538979  6538991  6538997  6539003  6539023  6539041  6539051  6539057  6539081  6539083
6539111  6539119  6539129  6539149  6539167  6539177  6539191  6539201  6539209  6539243
6539263  6539293  6539317  6539327  6539347  6539353  6539359  6539369  6539371  6539387
6539421  6539443  6539473  6539497  6539513  6539531  6539537  6539539  6539551  6539557
6539579  6539581  6539593  6539647  6539671  6539681  6539707  6539717  6539719  6539777
6539801  6539807  6539831  6539833  6539839  6539867  6539873  6539893  6539917  6539927
6539959  6539963  6539983  6539989  6540007  6540013  6540029  6540067  6540103  6540133
6540139  6540169  6540181  6540187  6540217  6540239  6540241  6540251  6540269  6540277
6540299  6540301  6540311  6540323  6540329  6540337  6540383  6540409  6540487  6540499
6540421  6540431  6540433  6540451  6540467  6540493  6540511  6540539  6540557  6540587
6540593  6540619  6540623  6540637  6540643  6540673  6540679  6540691  6540717  6540739
6540827  6540829  6540841  6540857  6540871  6540893  6540899  6540913  6540949  6540953
6540967  6540977  6540983  6541021  6541033  6541049  6541057  6541061  6541069  6541079
6541081  6541097  6541103  6541109  6541123  6541151  6541163  6541183  6541229  6541247
6541253  6541261  6541291  6541309  6541321  6541333  6541343  6541351  6541363  6541373
6541393  6541429  6541433  6541439  6541441  6541447  6541487  6541511  6541517  6541519
6541523  6541541  6541571  6541597  6541609  6541621  6541663  6541687  6541693  6541699
6541723  6541739  6541741  6541751  6541763  6541771  6541807  6541819  6541831  6541841
6541877  6541879  6541901  6541903  6541921  6541937  6541939  6541973  6541981  6541993
6541999  6542021  6542077  6542089  6542101  6542113  6542117  6542119  6542131  6542141
```

```
6542171  6542201  6542219  6542243  6542257  6542279  6542287  6542293  6542299  6542339
6542351  6542357  6542369  6542381  6542387  6542401  6542413  6542423  6542443  6542453
6542461  6542489  6542491  6542513  6542527  6542531  6542537  6542551  6542561  6542609
6542611  6542621  6542633  6542647  6542681  6542689  6542693  6542699  6542713  6542717
6542737  6542743  6542749  6542779  6542791  6542801  6542803  6542827  6542843  6542857
6542867  6542927  6542929  6542933  6542959  6542989  6542993  6543001  6543007  6543029
6543059  6543073  6543101  6543127  6543169  6543179  6543193  6543203  6543223  6543233
6543259  6543269  6543301  6543307  6543323  6543337  6543343  6543347  6543359  6543367
6543373  6543377  6543389  6543403  6543443  6543451  6543457  6543461  6543479  6543497
6543499  6543503  6543517  6543533  6543541  6543577  6543583  6543587  6543599  6543613
6543617  6543629  6543643  6543659  6543671  6543679  6543683  6543701  6543731  6543737
6543739  6543767  6543769  6543773  6543781  6543787  6543833  6543853  6543871  6543877
6543893  6543907  6543947  6543973  6543989  6544003  6544009  6544039  6544049  6544063
6544117  6544157  6544163  6544171  6544177  6544207  6544217  6544243  6544261  6544277
6544309  6544313  6544333  6544357  6544393  6544399  6544403  6544411  6544423  6544427
6544429  6544451  6544453  6544481  6544487  6544547  6544579  6544589  6544619  6544631
6544639  6544649  6544651  6544663  6544667  6544739  6544753  6544757  6544787  6544801
6544831  6544841  6544843  6544849  6544861  6544883  6544907  6544919  6544927  6544943
6545003  6545027  6545053  6545059  6545081  6545089  6545111  6545167  6545171  6545191
6545197  6545219  6545243  6545249  6545257  6545261  6545293  6545303  6545321  6545347
6545351  6545353  6545377  6545381  6545423  6545437  6545467  6545471  6545477  6545489
6545509  6545531  6545537  6545543  6545563  6545569  6545573  6545579  6545587  6545599
6545603  6545621  6545641  6545653  6545687  6545689  6545701  6545711  6545713  6545717
6545729  6545741  6545771  6545789  6545809  6545813  6545821  6545827  6545839  6545857
6545863  6545879  6545881  6545887  6545893  6545897  6545923  6545941  6545947  6545953
6545963  6545989  6545993  6546041  6546049  6546061  6546079  6546097  6546107  6546119
6546131  6546149  6546167  6546181  6546223  6546229  6546251  6546259  6546263  6546269
6546289  6546307  6546311  6546313  6546349  6546359  6546361  6546389  6546403  6546409
6546437  6546443  6546451  6546461  6546473  6546509  6546539  6546541  6546557  6546571
6546587  6546599  6546607  6546643  6546647  6546667  6546671  6546689  6546733  6546767
6546769  6546803  6546823  6546829  6546847  6546851  6546857  6546889  6546893  6546923
6546937  6546941  6546961  6546979  6546997  6547007  6547027  6547031  6547033  6547049
6547081  6547087  6547103  6547109  6547117  6547129  6547141  6547181  6547183  6547199
6547207  6547213  6547217  6547253  6547271  6547279  6547291  6547319  6547327  6547337
6547349  6547351  6547369  6547391  6547399  6547423  6547427  6547447  6547459  6547469
6547477  6547493  6547517  6547529  6547553  6547561  6547579  6547613  6547627  6547637
6547661  6547687  6547693  6547733  6547747  6547753  6547759  6547769  6547781  6547811
6547817  6547829  6547831  6547841  6547859  6547861  6547867  6547897  6547909  6547943
6547967  6547973  6547979  6548023  6548029  6548033  6548051  6548057  6548071  6548093
6548107  6548131  6548147  6548153  6548177  6548207  6548239  6548251  6548263  6548291
6548299  6548303  6548323  6548327  6548359  6548359  6548411  6548441  6548447  6548453
6548459  6548489  6548497  6548539  6548573  6548579  6548603  6548609  6548623  6548639
6548653  6548669  6548681  6548687  6548701  6548743  6548753  6548779  6548797  6548803
6548819  6548833  6548837  6548849  6548873  6548881  6548897  6548909  6548911
6548929  6548947  6548953  6548957  6548981  6548989  6548999  6549017  6549019  6549031
6549061  6549071  6549077  6549079  6549119  6549133  6549139  6549161  6549173  6549187
6549197  6549223  6549241  6549247  6549251  6549269  6549271  6549311  6549313  6549353
6549383  6549391  6549467  6549479  6549493  6549511  6549523  6549551  6549583  6549589
6549601  6549611  6549617  6549619  6549671  6549677  6549689  6549707  6549721  6549727
6549761  6549769  6549787  6549797  6549817  6549839  6549857  6549859  6549877  6549901
6549923  6549931  6549937  6549979  6549979  6550001  6550007  6550013  6550031  6550043
6550057  6550067  6550081  6550091  6550099  6550109  6550123  6550129  6550157  6550163
6550169  6550177  6550183  6550199  6550211  6550213  6550223  6550261  6550267  6550289
6550303  6550337  6550361  6550367  6550403  6550409  6550417  6550471  6550499  6550501
6550513  6550519  6550547  6550553  6550631  6550639  6550651  6550669  6550679  6550741
6550757  6550771  6550783  6550793  6550799  6550811  6550823  6550847  6550879  6550891
6550913  6550919  6550927  6550963  6550981  6551011  6551047  6551057  6551063  6551081
6551087  6551117  6551141  6551161  6551173  6551177  6551191  6551213  6551231  6551249
6551291  6551299  6551353  6551387  6551393  6551407  6551411  6551417  6551423  6551429
6551497  6551533  6551563  6551569  6551581  6551591  6551603  6551639  6551653  6551689
6551693  6551719  6551731  6551737  6551747  6551791  6551801  6551821  6551833  6551843
6551861  6551879  6551887  6551899  6551917  6551921  6551947  6551957  6551959  6551983
6551989  6552001  6552011  6552047  6552053  6552061  6552083  6552097  6552101  6552113
6552121  6552149  6552151  6552163  6552167  6552179  6552187  6552197  6552199  6552209
6552229  6552233  6552239  6552277  6552307  6552313  6552323  6552331  6552341  6552349
6552353  6552373  6552379  6552391  6552419  6552421  6552431  6552433  6552449  6552457
6552467  6552479  6552503  6552527  6552529  6552541  6552547  6552593  6552619  6552629
6552647  6552671  6552673  6552691  6552697  6552719  6552731  6552773  6552781  6552797
6552817  6552829  6552841  6552851  6552859  6552863  6552883  6552901  6552919  6552937
6552961  6552979  6553003  6553009  6553021  6553037  6553039  6553049  6553061  6553111
6553117  6553123  6553139  6553147  6553187  6553213  6553219  6553231  6553241  6553273
6553277  6553297  6553303  6553319  6553331  6553343  6553357  6553361  6553363  6553373
6553387  6553441  6553447  6553451  6553453  6553487  6553489  6553511  6553541  6553567
6553571  6553577  6553621  6553663  6553733  6553769  6553777  6553793  6553801  6553817
6553889  6553903  6553909  6553933  6553949  6553951  6553957  6553961  6553969  6553979
6554021  6554059  6554083  6554101  6554123  6554147  6554153  6554173  6554201  6554213
6554239  6554243  6554269  6554281  6554309  6554329  6554341  6554357  6554371  6554381
6554399  6554413  6554419  6554437  6554441  6554453  6554459  6554461  6554481  6554501
6554519  6554521  6554531  6554539  6554557  6554567  6554579  6554599  6554617  6554621
6554623  6554653  6554657  6554663  6554683  6554687  6554689  6554699  6554731
6554767  6554771  6554773  6554777  6554789  6554813  6554827  6554831  6554833  6554837
6554869  6554897  6554897  6554909  6554921  6554941  6554971  6554983  6555007  6555011
6555041  6555067  6555083  6555089  6555097  6555103  6555119  6555139  6555169  6555173
6555223  6555233  6555239  6555271  6555281  6555301  6555317  6555337  6555343  6555349
6555377  6555383  6555389  6555397  6555403  6555407  6555413  6555427  6555433  6555443
6555457  6555463  6555491  6555503  6555541  6555547  6555581  6555611  6555649  6555671
6555677  6555683  6555691  6555707  6555709  6555719  6555733  6555751  6555767  6555781
6555797  6555803  6555821  6555833  6555839  6555907  6555917  6555929  6555959  6555961
6555971  6556003  6556013  6556019  6556027  6556031  6556037  6556049  6556061  6556063
```

```
6556079 6556111 6556201 6556223 6556243 6556267 6556301 6556331 6556367 6556369
6556393 6556397 6556399 6556421 6556439 6556483 6556489 6556507 6556513 6556519
6556559 6556567 6556601 6556603 6556607 6556609 6556621 6556631 6556643 6556651
6556657 6556673 6556699 6556709 6556723 6556727 6556741 6556757 6556777 6556783
6556799 6556831 6556861 6556937 6556961 6556969 6556973 6556993 6556999 6557003
6557041 6557059 6557077 6557081 6557099 6557101 6557123 6557153 6557167 6557179
6557183 6557191 6557203 6557207 6557233 6557279 6557293 6557303 6557333 6557339
6557351 6557363 6557381 6557401 6557407 6557423 6557429 6557459 6557471 6557479
6557513 6557519 6557521 6557533 6557557 6557569 6557623 6557651 6557657 6557659
6557671 6557687 6557689 6557693 6557723 6557731 6557753 6557777 6557797 6557807
6557813 6557819 6557839 6557861 6557867 6557939 6557963 6557977 6557981 6558007
6558011 6558017 6558029 6558037 6558067 6558077 6558119 6558121 6558127 6558133
6558163 6558169 6558179 6558187 6558193 6558217 6558229 6558241 6558269 6558271
6558283 6558301 6558313 6558323 6558337 6558353 6558359 6558371 6558373 6558389
6558449 6558457 6558467 6558469 6558479 6558491 6558493 6558511 6558523 6558547
6558581 6558589 6558593 6558599 6558619 6558623 6558641 6558659 6558683 6558689
6558707 6558733 6558737 6558751 6558791 6558793 6558809 6558823 6558829 6558847
6558883 6558899 6558911 6558913 6558917 6558931 6558941 6558961 6558973 6558983
6558997 6559001 6559019 6559037 6559067 6559079 6559081 6559109 6559141 6559151
6559153 6559159 6559171 6559181 6559187 6559219 6559253 6559261 6559277 6559279
6559337 6559339 6559363 6559369 6559373 6559379 6559381 6559409 6559447 6559451
6559457 6559489 6559493 6559519 6559523 6559529 6559547 6559583 6559613 6559627
6559633 6559639 6559643 6559661 6559667 6559673 6559687 6559691 6559699 6559703
6559717 6559727 6559733 6559741 6559747 6559759 6559781 6559783 6559793 6559801
6559823 6559831 6559843 6559859 6559867 6559871 6559873 6559897 6559901 6559907
6559939 6559957 6559963 6559981 6560017 6560027 6560039 6560053 6560069
6560093 6560117 6560131 6560143 6560159 6560161 6560227 6560231 6560243 6560299
6560303 6560327 6560341 6560347 6560357 6560371 6560413 6560417 6560429 6560431
6560447 6560459 6560461 6560479 6560503 6560509 6560513 6560531 6560537 6560551
6560579 6560597 6560599 6560627 6560633 6560647 6560651 6560663 6560669 6560677
6560689 6560717 6560731 6560737 6560753 6560767 6560783 6560797 6560821 6560843
6560849 6560857 6560867 6560881 6560891 6560921 6560927 6560941 6560959 6560971
6560987 6560993 6560999 6561001 6561007 6561011 6561013 6561017 6561019 6561073
6561089 6561091 6561097 6561103 6561127 6561143 6561151 6561161 6561193 6561197
6561199 6561209 6561223 6561259 6561277 6561281 6561283 6561287 6561293 6561307
6561311 6561319 6561383 6561427 6561437 6561461 6561481 6561493 6561497 6561521
6561539 6561547 6561551 6561557 6561589 6561613 6561619 6561629 6561637 6561649
6561673 6561679 6561683 6561697 6561719 6561727 6561761 6561767 6561781 6561787
6561791 6561809 6561827 6561833 6561857 6561871 6561883 6561887 6561911 6561937
6561941 6561943 6561991 6562001 6562021 6562037 6562057 6562069 6562079 6562097
6562123 6562133 6562139 6562141 6562169 6562177 6562211 6562243 6562261
6562271 6562279 6562307 6562331 6562333 6562351 6562363 6562373 6562397 6562399
6562463 6562477 6562489 6562519 6562541 6562547 6562553 6562559 6562571 6562573
6562597 6562603 6562637 6562643 6562651 6562679 6562681 6562687 6562691 6562723
6562741 6562753 6562763 6562769 6562783 6562813 6562823 6562849 6562859 6562861
6562909 6562921 6562933 6562943 6562973 6562987 6562991 6563017 6563021 6563087
6563093 6563107 6563129 6563147 6563159 6563177 6563191 6563203 6563209 6563261
6563269 6563287 6563327 6563371 6563383 6563407 6563419 6563437 6563443 6563461
6563507 6563509 6563519 6563527 6563549 6563551 6563561 6563587 6563591 6563611
6563621 6563629 6563633 6563639 6563659 6563663 6563677 6563693 6563729 6563743
6563771 6563779 6563801 6563803 6563833 6563857 6563863 6563929 6563933
6563939 6563957 6563981 6563983 6564001 6564007 6564011 6564043 6564053 6564071
6564073 6564113 6564127 6564143 6564167 6564169 6564197 6564203 6564211
6564241 6564247 6564287 6564289 6564301 6564317 6564319 6564323 6564359 6564401
6564409 6564419 6564449 6564457 6564461 6564511 6564521 6564539 6564563 6564583
6564587 6564611 6564647 6564661 6564667 6564677 6564707 6564749 6564763 6564769
6564773 6564781 6564793 6564809 6564827 6564847 6564917 6564919 6564967 6564973
6564977 6564983 6564997 6565019 6565037 6565063 6565093 6565099 6565123 6565133
6565159 6565171 6565193 6565231 6565249 6565259 6565277 6565291 6565309 6565313
6565319 6565331 6565333 6565367 6565379 6565381 6565399 6565409 6565411 6565421
6565439 6565463 6565487 6565499 6565501 6565543 6565561 6565567 6565609 6565633
6565661 6565681 6565709 6565711 6565717 6565721 6565729 6565739 6565747 6565753
6565777 6565807 6565829 6565847 6565873 6565877 6565901 6565903 6565907 6565913
6565921 6565957 6565967 6565973 6565981 6565987 6565991 6566003 6566033 6566069
6566071 6566083 6566089 6566171 6566177 6566199 6566227 6566237 6566249
6566251 6566291 6566297 6566299 6566303 6566309 6566311 6566333 6566359 6566363
6566377 6566387 6566393 6566407 6566453 6566479 6566489 6566503 6566507 6566551
6566563 6566587 6566591 6566597 6566599 6566621 6566629 6566657 6566663 6566701
6566713 6566741 6566767 6566773 6566779 6566783 6566809 6566827 6566849 6566851
6566869 6566883 6566893 6566899 6566909 6566921 6566927 6566939 6566957 6566969
6566977 6566993 6567013 6567017 6567023 6567031 6567047 6567073 6567091 6567109
6567131 6567149 6567157 6567163 6567173 6567181 6567193 6567203 6567227 6567229
6567269 6567271 6567307 6567343 6567367 6567391 6567401 6567403 6567409
6567413 6567437 6567479 6567511 6567527 6567529 6567557 6567563 6567607 6567641
6567647 6567653 6567683 6567709 6567721 6567731 6567751 6567761 6567779 6567781
6567839 6567851 6567859 6567871 6567881 6567887 6567893 6567937 6567941 6567961
6567971 6568027 6568031 6568043 6568049 6568061 6568073 6568097 6568099 6568127
6568141 6568151 6568153 6568183 6568189 6568193 6568201 6568217 6568223 6568229
6568259 6568267 6568279 6568339 6568381 6568399 6568403 6568417 6568439 6568447
6568451 6568453 6568459 6568469 6568483 6568493 6568517 6568519 6568543 6568553
6568561 6568589 6568591 6568603 6568609 6568633 6568643 6568649 6568657 6568669
6568687 6568691 6568693 6568697 6568717 6568729 6568737 6568799 6568801 6568811
6568829 6568841 6568853 6568867 6568901 6568909 6568957 6568967 6568973
6568999 6569009 6569011 6569023 6569027 6569039 6569047 6569083 6569093 6569107
6569111 6569137 6569161 6569183 6569203 6569209 6569219 6569249 6569263 6569267
6569291 6569347 6569371 6569377 6569413 6569441 6569449 6569483 6569491 6569543
6569579 6569581 6569593 6569603 6569623 6569627 6569653 6569657 6569659 6569677
6569681 6569723 6569729 6569741 6569791 6569807 6569809 6569813 6569867 6569869
6569897 6569917 6569929 6569951 6569957 6569971 6569987 6569993 6569999 6570001
```

```
6570049 6570077 6570089 6570097 6570103 6570131 6570139 6570149 6570169 6570191
6570199 6570227 6570229 6570241 6570253 6570259 6570283 6570287 6570301 6570307
6570323 6570337 6570359 6570379 6570407 6570413 6570437 6570439 6570451 6570457
6570461 6570469 6570503 6570521 6570527 6570539 6570581 6570587 6570589 6570593
6570601 6570631 6570643 6570649 6570661 6570677 6570691 6570703 6570727 6570731
6570749 6570769 6570779 6570797 6570841 6570869 6570871 6570881 6570899 6570901
6570917 6570919 6570923 6570943 6570953 6570961 6571013 6571021 6571051 6571057
6571069 6571073 6571079 6571087 6571109 6571127 6571133 6571151 6571153 6571171
6571183 6571189 6571199 6571219 6571223 6571247 6571249 6571259 6571267 6571271
6571291 6571309 6571319 6571337 6571393 6571421 6571441 6571447 6571451 6571471
6571489 6571519 6571529 6571553 6571559 6571573 6571589 6571633 6571651 6571657
6571687 6571693 6571703 6571711 6571729 6571759 6571771 6571787 6571793 6571811
6571861 6571867 6571871 6571879 6571883 6571889 6571921 6571987 6571993 6572003
6572011 6572029 6572039 6572087 6572099 6572129 6572131 6572141 6572143 6572147
6572161 6572191 6572197 6572243 6572281 6572287 6572297 6572303 6572317 6572351
6572369 6572381 6572389 6572393 6572413 6572417 6572431 6572437 6572441 6572453
6572459 6572471 6572483 6572497 6572513 6572543 6572597 6572617 6572627 6572677
6572681 6572707 6572711 6572723 6572729 6572737 6572743 6572747 6572749 6572759
6572773 6572801 6572831 6572843 6572857 6572887 6572921 6572927 6572941 6572957
6572957 6572959 6572971 6572977 6572983 6572989 6573041 6573071 6573103 6573121
6573143 6573167 6573173 6573179 6573197 6573223 6573233 6573257 6573263 6573311
6573341 6573349 6573409 6573419 6573443 6573461 6573491 6573493 6573499 6573521
6573527 6573529 6573533 6573547 6573551 6573559 6573583 6573617 6573631 6573641
6573659 6573661 6573667 6573689 6573701 6573703 6573709 6573719 6573733 6573747
6573779 6573793 6573799 6573821 6573841 6573851 6573863 6573877 6573881 6573887
6573893 6573907 6573911 6573913 6573949 6573967 6573971 6573979 6573997 6574003
6574033 6574037 6574069 6574079 6574081 6574093 6574109 6574111 6574129 6574157
6574177 6574207 6574231 6574259 6574273 6574319 6574331 6574333 6574349 6574357
6574423 6574433 6574441 6574457 6574471 6574483 6574487 6574507 6574517 6574523
6574541 6574559 6574577 6574583 6574613 6574639 6574649 6574661 6574669 6574681
6574693 6574727 6574739 6574751 6574769 6574787 6574843 6574847 6574853 6574861
6574873 6574879 6574889 6574921 6574927 6574943 6574949 6574963 6574973 6574979
6575029 6575059 6575071 6575077 6575081 6575099 6575111 6575113 6575123 6575143
6575147 6575161 6575227 6575237 6575279 6575281 6575299 6575321 6575333 6575341
6575351 6575353 6575363 6575377 6575399 6575411 6575423 6575453 6575467 6575479
6575481 6575497 6575507 6575521 6575537 6575563 6575567 6575573 6575579 6575593
6575641 6575669 6575671 6575687 6575693 6575711 6575717 6575731 6575749 6575783
6575791 6575797 6575839 6575851 6575857 6575873 6575879 6575887 6575893
6575897 6575917 6575927 6575929 6575969 6575981 6575993 6576001 6576013 6576023
6576041 6576043 6576049 6576067 6576077 6576083 6576131 6576133 6576139 6576149
6576151 6576179 6576203 6576221 6576259 6576271 6576289 6576293 6576307 6576313
6576319 6576329 6576341 6576347 6576389 6576407 6576419 6576431 6576439 6576461
6576469 6576473 6576511 6576529 6576539 6576547 6576571 6576587 6576589 6576599
6576601 6576613 6576617 6576631 6576667 6576673 6576683 6576701 6576709 6576719
6576737 6576763 6576767 6576797 6576809 6576839 6576847 6576853 6576863 6576883
6576931 6576967 6577013 6577027 6577033 6577037 6577049 6577061 6577073 6577091
6577093 6577127 6577163 6577187 6577199 6577217 6577273 6577297 6577309 6577313
6577327 6577331 6577381 6577399 6577427 6577429 6577469 6577481 6577489 6577499
6577513 6577523 6577531 6577541 6577559 6577561 6577579 6577583 6577607 6577621
6577631 6577643 6577651 6577661 6577663 6577679 6577699 6577709 6577717 6577729
6577757 6577763 6577783 6577787 6577789 6577799 6577801 6577817 6577847 6577871
6577873 6577891 6577913 6577943 6577951 6578003 6578017 6578051 6578053 6578063
6578101 6578111 6578129 6578137 6578147 6578171 6578177 6578189 6578197 6578203
6578213 6578227 6578263 6578281 6578287 6578291 6578309 6578311 6578333 6578339
6578359 6578381 6578393 6578399 6578431 6578461 6578513 6578557 6578581 6578587
6578591 6578597 6578633 6578639 6578651 6578653 6578657 6578659 6578669 6578717
6578743 6578749 6578753 6578777 6578801 6578821 6578837 6578839 6578849 6578857
6578863 6578867 6578899 6578927 6578963 6578977 6578987 6579019 6579047
6579077 6579113 6579137 6579163 6579179 6579193 6579211 6579217 6579227 6579247
6579253 6579257 6579281 6579283 6579319 6579337 6579341 6579359 6579373 6579379
6579401 6579407 6579421 6579439 6579479 6579487 6579539 6579553 6579571 6579589
6579593 6579623 6579631 6579637 6579647 6579653 6579667 6579701 6579707 6579733
6579761 6579767 6579779 6579787 6579829 6579883 6579889 6579899 6579907
6579913 6579917 6579919 6579929 6579941 6579959 6579961 6579977 6580019 6580031
6580039 6580051 6580069 6580073 6580081 6580087 6580097 6580159 6580163 6580169
6580181 6580193 6580237 6580243 6580283 6580291 6580297 6580331 6580337 6580363
6580373 6580397 6580417 6580433 6580451 6580471 6580481 6580499 6580501 6580529
6580537 6580543 6580573 6580579 6580583 6580597 6580627 6580633 6580643
6580661 6580663 6580667 6580681 6580687 6580697 6580727 6580729 6580733 6580753
6580757 6580813 6580817 6580837 6580841 6580843 6580891 6580901 6580913
6580943 6580961 6580991 6580997 6581009 6581017 6581027 6581039 6581041 6581051
6581077 6581111 6581119 6581123 6581131 6581137 6581143 6581149 6581161 6581171
6581177 6581189 6581191 6581221 6581251 6581291 6581297 6581299 6581317 6581321
6581327 6581339 6581357 6581369 6581371 6581387 6581401 6581413 6581423 6581437
6581441 6581447 6581483 6581501 6581503 6581507 6581557 6581563 6581591 6581599
6581609 6581621 6581633 6581683 6581719 6581761 6581767 6581779 6581807 6581831
6581837 6581843 6581849 6581851 6581857 6581909 6581921 6581929 6581959 6581963
6581969 6581977 6581987 6581989 6582001 6582007 6582011 6582019 6582047 6582061
6582073 6582089 6582091 6582097 6582119 6582127 6582133 6582143 6582167 6582187
6582193 6582211 6582221 6582223 6582253 6582259 6582287 6582293 6582307
6582313 6582343 6582353 6582431 6582437 6582461 6582463 6582467 6582469 6582479
6582487 6582497 6582503 6582523 6582551 6582557 6582581 6582593 6582599 6582643
6582649 6582661 6582677 6582691 6582701 6582727 6582731 6582733 6582749 6582767
6582769 6582787 6582799 6582803 6582811 6582839 6582841 6582847 6582857 6582871
6582883 6582941 6582997 6583009 6583019 6583021 6583051 6583061 6583069
6583103 6583111 6583117 6583121 6583123 6583127 6583133 6583141 6583189 6583193
6583201 6583207 6583211 6583229 6583231 6583249 6583271 6583277 6583321 6583327
6583331 6583349 6583351 6583361 6583363 6583391 6583393 6583399 6583433 6583453
6583463 6583469 6583523 6583529 6583531 6583537 6583561 6583567 6583571 6583637
```

```
6583649  6583663  6583691  6583693  6583699  6583721  6583729  6583741  6583757  6583763
6583769  6583771  6583789  6583793  6583813  6583831  6583847  6583849  6583853  6583867
6583897  6583909  6583919  6583933  6583949  6583963  6583991  6584009  6584021  6584027
6584029  6584033  6584041  6584057  6584063  6584087  6584093  6584099  6584101  6584107
6584119  6584159  6584173  6584197  6584213  6584251  6584269  6584293  6584311  6584329
6584339  6584353  6584359  6584377  6584399  6584411  6584447  6584449  6584471  6584489
6584497  6584503  6584549  6584579  6584587  6584609  6584629  6584663  6584671  6584681
6584701  6584707  6584713  6584717  6584749  6584759  6584761  6584771  6584789  6584791
6584833  6584857  6584863  6584867  6584917  6584939  6584951  6584953  6584957
6584983  6584987  6584999  6585013  6585023  6585031  6585053  6585067  6585071  6585079
6585097  6585169  6585181  6585193  6585211  6585221  6585251  6585253  6585259  6585263
6585269  6585277  6585283  6585287  6585289  6585329  6585347  6585367  6585373  6585421
6585431  6585433  6585437  6585451  6585473  6585479  6585517  6585539  6585559  6585569
6585577  6585583  6585587  6585617  6585629  6585641  6585643  6585653  6585661  6585673
6585721  6585737  6585769  6585773  6585791  6585793  6585809  6585823  6585853  6585863
6585869  6585877  6585881  6585941  6585983  6586039  6586049  6586051  6586067  6586087
6586091  6586121  6586147  6586163  6586187  6586189  6586193  6586201  6586207  6586213
6586241  6586243  6586271  6586319  6586337  6586339  6586357  6586373  6586379  6586387
6586399  6586417  6586421  6586423  6586453  6586493  6586501  6586507  6586519  6586523
6586529  6586561  6586577  6586589  6586603  6586637  6586639  6586649  6586661  6586687
6586693  6586709  6586739  6586753  6586757  6586781  6586817  6586829  6586831  6586847
6586861  6586873  6586889  6586891  6586903  6586913  6586919  6586927  6586961  6586991
6586997  6587011  6587033  6587047  6587051  6587057  6587069  6587111  6587123  6587137
6587149  6587153  6587171  6587201  6587219  6587233  6587263  6587267  6587293  6587311
6587323  6587327  6587351  6587353  6587359  6587377  6587389  6587393  6587401  6587417
6587419  6587431  6587459  6587467  6587479  6587489  6587491  6587533  6587549  6587569
6587579  6587587  6587599  6587629  6587657  6587689  6587701  6587743  6587773  6587783
6587797  6587807  6587809  6587831  6587837  6587863  6587873  6587879  6587899  6587923
6587947  6587951  6587963  6587981  6587989  6588007  6588011  6588067  6588083  6588107
6588119  6588139  6588149  6588173  6588199  6588203  6588209  6588223  6588233  6588251
6588277  6588289  6588313  6588341  6588343  6588349  6588383  6588389  6588397  6588409
6588433  6588437  6588443  6588473  6588487  6588509  6588551  6588563  6588599  6588613
6588619  6588629  6588653  6588683  6588689  6588721  6588731  6588733  6588767  6588773
6588779  6588781  6588817  6588851  6588853  6588863  6588893  6588899  6588899  6588931
6588947  6588973  6588983  6589021  6589031  6589039  6589043  6589057  6589091  6589097
6589103  6589111  6589117  6589123  6589127  6589147  6589171  6589189  6589207  6589221
6589229  6589237  6589243  6589273  6589279  6589283  6589291  6589301  6589313  6589321
6589327  6589337  6589393  6589411  6589417  6589433  6589459  6589463  6589481  6589493
6589511  6589519  6589529  6589547  6589549  6589567  6589571  6589579  6589607  6589657
6589669  6589703  6589717  6589733  6589747  6589787  6589819  6589831  6589841  6589883
6589901  6589909  6589963  6589969  6589981  6589993  6589997  6590027  6590039  6590041
6590063  6590069  6590071  6590081  6590099  6590119  6590141  6590159  6590161  6590189
6590191  6590201  6590209  6590239  6590261  6590263  6590317  6590327  6590341  6590347
6590357  6590413  6590429  6590459  6590461  6590483  6590531  6590533  6590557  6590593
6590609  6590621  6590629  6590641  6590651  6590671  6590677  6590711  6590737  6590783
6590797  6590807  6590813  6590839  6590869  6590899  6590927  6590937  6590939  6590971
6590993  6591031  6591059  6591061  6591077  6591089  6591163  6591181  6591191  6591197
6591223  6591229  6591253  6591269  6591281  6591287  6591293  6591329  6591349  6591367
6591373  6591401  6591419  6591433  6591443  6591457  6591463  6591469  6591481  6591491
6591493  6591509  6591517  6591553  6591577  6591581  6591583  6591617  6591619  6591643
6591647  6591649  6591653  6591659  6591667  6591671  6591679  6591707  6591713  6591719
6591737  6591743  6591749  6591757  6591763  6591779  6591791  6591799  6591811  6591821
6591833  6591847  6591863  6591881  6591887  6591889  6591899  6591913  6591941  6591953
6591989  6592009  6592037  6592043  6592111  6592121  6592123  6592133  6592147  6592151
6592171  6592219  6592241  6592249  6592291  6592321  6592343  6592351  6592357  6592363
6592387  6592393  6592403  6592423  6592427  6592433  6592451  6592501  6592507  6592517
6592561  6592567  6592571  6592589  6592603  6592609  6592613  6592633  6592661  6592669
6592673  6592693  6592693  6592727  6592741  6592753  6592763  6592769  6592777  6592783
6592813  6592823  6592843  6592871  6592879  6592891  6592897  6592903  6592931  6592933
6592961  6592967  6592997  6593009  6593021  6593023  6593039  6593089  6593143  6593149
6593177  6593183  6593219  6593227  6593231  6593243  6593267  6593299  6593311  6593317
6593329  6593351  6593357  6593369  6593371  6593401  6593407  6593413  6593417  6593423
6593443  6593449  6593453  6593473  6593507  6593533  6593563  6593591  6593593  6593599
6593611  6593621  6593633  6593647  6593689  6593693  6593707  6593723  6593729  6593747
6593767  6593777  6593809  6593833  6593837  6593857  6593861  6593863  6593887  6593897
6593911  6593927  6593929  6593941  6593953  6593981  6594023  6594037  6594043  6594047
6594059  6594109  6594127  6594131  6594139  6594143  6594151  6594191  6594193  6594229
6594233  6594239  6594239  6594241  6594319  6594331  6594337  6594347  6594359  6594361
6594377  6594389  6594403  6594407  6594421  6594431  6594439  6594449  6594449  6594451
6594457  6594461  6594529  6594541  6594557  6594559  6594611  6594619  6594649  6594677
6594697  6594713  6594719  6594733  6594751  6594761  6594787  6594799  6594821  6594823
6594839  6594857  6594869  6594883  6594911  6594943  6595007  6595009  6595021  6595027
6595037  6595049  6595051  6595067  6595091  6595103  6595111  6595117  6595123  6595129
6595153  6595163  6595177  6595207  6595217  6595229  6595231  6595241  6595243  6595271
6595289  6595313  6595333  6595349  6595367  6595397  6595409  6595417  6595423  6595453
6595487  6595493  6595513  6595517  6595559  6595571  6595573  6595577  6595579  6595597
6595601  6595607  6595619  6595627  6595661  6595703  6595763  6595781  6595859  6595861
6595867  6595873  6595877  6595897  6595921  6595937  6595951  6595953  6596033  6596053
6596063  6596069  6596077  6596089  6596143  6596167  6596171  6596179  6596189  6596197
6596231  6596257  6596267  6596299  6596321  6596339  6596341  6596351  6596383  6596389
6596399  6596407  6596431  6596437  6596441  6596461  6596467  6596483  6596489  6596503
6596513  6596533  6596549  6596573  6596581  6596609  6596617  6596627  6596633  6596641
6596647  6596701  6596719  6596729  6596741  6596749  6596771  6596783  6596797  6596809
6596839  6596869  6596879  6596881  6596897  6596899  6596903  6596911  6596917  6596927
6596951  6596957  6596961  6596987  6596999  6597011  6597017  6597091  6597101  6597131
6597133  6597163  6597167  6597179  6597193  6597197  6597209  6597221  6597223  6597233
6597247  6597257  6597263  6597271  6597307  6597323  6597347  6597373  6597379  6597397
6597401  6597407  6597431  6597463  6597467  6597469  6597499  6597517  6597551  6597583
6597589  6597593  6597601  6597629  6597641  6597673  6597677  6597707  6597739  6597779
```

```
6597781  6597827  6597847  6597859  6597889  6597893  6597931  6597949  6597953  6597967
6597971  6597973  6597977  6598013  6598019  6598021  6598063  6598069  6598087  6598103
6598117  6598127  6598139  6598153  6598157  6598169  6598199  6598201  6598211  6598219
6598223  6598237  6598271  6598279  6598289  6598303  6598313  6598343  6598349  6598357
6598387  6598411  6598421  6598429  6598433  6598439  6598481  6598507  6598517  6598517
6598523  6598541  6598547  6598561  6598589  6598597  6598621  6598639  6598649  6598661
6598667  6598673  6598679  6598721  6598733  6598741  6598759  6598777  6598799  6598807
6598817  6598819  6598829  6598841  6598843  6598849  6598853  6598903  6598927  6598931
6598951  6598961  6598967  6598993  6598997  6599003  6599011  6599053  6599059  6599071
6599113  6599119  6599123  6599141  6599161  6599191  6599207  6599221  6599227  6599231
6599267  6599287  6599293  6599297  6599309  6599323  6599347  6599363  6599389  6599393
6599399  6599429  6599449  6599477  6599491  6599513  6599533  6599557  6599561  6599569
6599573  6599591  6599603  6599609  6599611  6599627  6599639  6599687  6599699  6599713
6599717  6599743  6599753  6599759  6599779  6599797  6599819  6599833  6599839  6599861
6599891  6599899  6599921  6599951  6599953  6599959  6599963  6599981  6599987  6600001
6600031  6600043  6600053  6600067  6600071  6600101  6600107  6600109  6600119  6600133
6600157  6600169  6600211  6600221  6600227  6600229  6600247  6600259  6600263  6600281
6600299  6600323  6600331  6600367  6600421  6600431  6600439  6600449  6600491  6600493
6600497  6600499  6600533  6600557  6600589  6600593  6600611  6600617  6600623  6600667
6600677  6600679  6600691  6600707  6600721  6600731  6600757  6600761  6600787  6600791
6600823  6600829  6600899  6600901  6600917  6600943  6600949  6600953  6600989  6601013
6601019  6601031  6601033  6601039  6601061  6601081  6601093  6601129  6601157  6601159
6601163  6601169  6601201  6601211  6601213  6601223  6601247  6601261  6601277  6601279
6601307  6601313  6601339  6601349  6601363  6601381  6601393  6601411  6601433  6601447
6601459  6601501  6601513  6601519  6601523  6601549  6601561  6601601  6601631  6601633
6601649  6601669  6601691  6601703  6601717  6601739  6601757  6601769  6601781  6601783
6601787  6601789  6601807  6601811  6601813  6601817  6601843  6601849  6601883  6601891
6601909  6601921  6601927  6601961  6601993  6601997  6601999  6602003  6602023  6602027
6602059  6602087  6602093  6602119  6602129  6602147  6602149  6602161  6602201  6602203
6602207  6602209  6602237  6602257  6602261  6602303  6602327  6602347  6602363  6602371
6602377  6602383  6602389  6602399  6602413  6602417  6602423  6602429  6602437  6602447
6602461  6602467  6602501  6602509  6602549  6602551  6602573  6602591  6602593  6602627
6602653  6602663  6602669  6602683  6602689  6602707  6602711  6602737  6602753  6602767
6602789  6602797  6602819  6602831  6602833  6602839  6602899  6602957  6602963  6602993
6603007  6603011  6603017  6603029  6603043  6603049  6603053  6603059  6603083  6603137
6603151  6603161  6603167  6603169  6603211  6603229  6603283  6603299  6603307  6603313
6603343  6603349  6603371  6603383  6603391  6603407  6603413  6603437  6603439  6603449
6603451  6603479  6603491  6603511  6603517  6603523  6603529  6603557  6603581  6603593
6603617  6603629  6603647  6603671  6603703  6603731  6603733  6603743  6603749  6603761
6603763  6603787  6603791  6603827  6603869  6603893  6603907  6603913  6603917  6603937
6603943  6603953  6603979  6603991  6603997  6604009  6604021  6604027  6604033  6604049
6604057  6604063  6604097  6604099  6604133  6604181  6604183  6604187  6604217  6604231
6604249  6604291  6604303  6604309  6604319  6604331  6604357  6604369  6604379  6604387
6604397  6604399  6604421  6604469  6604471  6604561  6604573  6604579  6604583  6604603
6604607  6604639  6604651  6604667  6604673  6604681  6604691  6604699  6604709  6604727
6604733  6604751  6604753  6604771  6604783  6604811  6604817  6604847  6604859  6604861
6604867  6604877  6604883  6604901  6604903  6604943  6604973  6604987  6605023  6605029
6605033  6605041  6605049  6605107  6605119  6605149  6605153  6605167  6605171  6605191
6605219  6605237  6605257  6605267  6605281  6605297  6605303  6605309  6605311  6605321
6605327  6605341  6605363  6605371  6605377  6605381  6605399  6605411  6605429  6605437
6605441  6605477  6605477  6605479  6605513  6605519  6605527  6605561  6605563  6605579
6605587  6605593  6605653  6605657  6605663  6605693  6605701  6605717  6605737  6605747
6605791  6605801  6605813  6605827  6605831  6605849  6605857  6605891  6605903  6605909
6605917  6605933  6605941  6605947  6605953  6605969  6605971  6605983  6605987  6606011
6606023  6606031  6606077  6606097  6606101  6606109  6606121  6606139  6606143  6606157
6606161  6606169  6606181  6606191  6606209  6606223  6606247  6606263  6606269  6606283
6606293  6606307  6606323  6606329  6606331  6606343  6606389  6606409  6606419  6606437
6606443  6606463  6606469  6606473  6606487  6606493  6606521  6606527  6606541  6606581
6606629  6606631  6606637  6606641  6606647  6606653  6606673  6606679  6606731  6606739
6606749  6606779  6606811  6606827  6606833  6606839  6606877  6606893  6606913  6606917
6606923  6606953  6606959  6606967  6606973  6606991  6607009  6607019  6607037  6607039
6607063  6607121  6607151  6607163  6607177  6607199  6607207  6607229  6607241  6607243
6607261  6607283  6607291  6607297  6607301  6607343  6607361  6607369  6607379  6607409
6607439  6607487  6607493  6607501  6607529  6607537  6607567  6607591  6607597  6607613
6607631  6607663  6607673  6607697  6607709  6607717  6607721  6607729  6607751  6607813
6607819  6607829  6607837  6607841  6607889  6607939  6607949  6607957  6607961
6607963  6607967  6607981  6608003  6608047  6608051  6608071  6608083  6608099  6608117
6608123  6608131  6608137  6608141  6608149  6608167  6608207  6608209  6608221  6608227
6608243  6608263  6608269  6608279  6608281  6608293  6608321  6608323  6608351  6608387
6608417  6608419  6608423  6608431  6608473  6608479  6608489  6608507  6608519  6608527
6608573  6608603  6608621  6608633  6608639  6608647  6608653  6608683  6608729  6608737
6608741  6608747  6608761  6608783  6608807  6608809  6608821  6608837  6608851  6608857
6608863  6608867  6608881  6608911  6608929  6608939  6608951  6608981  6608993  6609007
6609011  6609019  6609023  6609049  6609089  6609101  6609139  6609149  6609179  6609181
6609191  6609221  6609223  6609227  6609283  6609247  6609263  6609271  6609287  6609299
6609301  6609307  6609313  6609331  6609341  6609353  6609409  6609437  6609439  6609443
6609457  6609467  6609503  6609517  6609523  6609553  6609571  6609601  6609607  6609649
6609661  6609667  6609679  6609689  6609737  6609761  6609769  6609781  6609793  6609797
6609803  6609833  6609847  6609859  6609877  6609881  6609893  6609971  6609973  6609989
6610049  6610063  6610067  6610069  6610091  6610103  6610111  6610117  6610133  6610141
6610151  6610159  6610169  6610181  6610187  6610189  6610199  6610217  6610237  6610249
6610273  6610283  6610321  6610337  6610343  6610379  6610393  6610397  6610411  6610427
6610441  6610451  6610459  6610469  6610489  6610493  6610507  6610511  6610517  6610529
6610559  6610561  6610573  6610589  6610601  6610607  6610609  6610619  6610621  6610673
6610687  6610699  6610711  6610733  6610759  6610763  6610783  6610787  6610789  6610801
6610817  6610819  6610853  6610859  6610861  6610883  6610907  6610937  6610939  6610951
6610991  6610999  6611027  6611039  6611041  6611057  6611071  6611081  6611141  6611149
6611179  6611191  6611219  6611237  6611303  6611321  6611323  6611329  6611347  6611369
6611383  6611389  6611393  6611399  6611413  6611417  6611441  6611447  6611461  6611489
```

```
6611491 6611497 6611503 6611509 6611519 6611533 6611573 6611593 6611597 6611611
6611621 6611629 6611651 6611653 6611659 6611663 6611699 6611707 6611777 6611807
6611821 6611849 6611873 6611881 6611893 6611921 6611923 6611933 6611951 6611989
6611993 6612013 6612041 6612061 6612079 6612097 6612119 6612127 6612143 6612149
6612161 6612169 6612181 6612187 6612197 6612223 6612241 6612257 6612271 6612299
6612311 6612313 6612341 6612391 6612401 6612427 6612449 6612451 6612457 6612467
6612469 6612479 6612481 6612491 6612499 6612539 6612547 6612563 6612577 6612581
6612601 6612607 6612623 6612629 6612653 6612659 6612673 6612679 6612691 6612701
6612721 6612731 6612733 6612791 6612811 6612857 6612871 6612877 6612883 6612887
6612911 6612913 6612919 6612929 6612953 6612959 6612961 6612971 6612979 6613001
6613003 6613021 6613027 6613031 6613037 6613039 6613043 6613069 6613081 6613091
6613109 6613111 6613129 6613141 6613151 6613157 6613163 6613183 6613207 6613219
6613223 6613231 6613237 6613253 6613267 6613283 6613297 6613301 6613307 6613319
6613331 6613333 6613337 6613339 6613361 6613429 6613433 6613471 6613483 6613507
6613517 6613543 6613567 6613573 6613589 6613591 6613597 6613601 6613603 6613619
6613631 6613753 6613781 6613807 6613823 6613829 6613853 6613879 6613883 6613891
6613913 6613927 6613973 6613979 6613987 6614017 6614053 6614063 6614089
6614093 6614119 6614123 6614137 6614141 6614143 6614149 6614159 6614177 6614183
6614189 6614197 6614203 6614221 6614249 6614269 6614273 6614323 6614327 6614339
6614341 6614371 6614393 6614401 6614423 6614429 6614437 6614449 6614467 6614471
6614473 6614477 6614507 6614533 6614537 6614539 6614579 6614609 6614611 6614617
6614623 6614651 6614677 6614693 6614701 6614711 6614719 6614737 6614759 6614791
6614801 6614833 6614863 6614879 6614891 6614893 6614911 6614939 6614947 6614957
6614963 6615013 6615019 6615031 6615043 6615047 6615067 6615071 6615079 6615113
6615127 6615131 6615143 6615157 6615179 6615181 6615199 6615221 6615229 6615233
6615241 6615251 6615263 6615269 6615289 6615299 6615311 6615317 6615353 6615361
6615377 6615443 6615449 6615463 6615487 6615491 6615503 6615523 6615529 6615541
6615547 6615551 6615571 6615577 6615589 6615613 6615641 6615643 6615649 6615659
6615671 6615677 6615727 6615733 6615751 6615757 6615769 6615773 6615787 6615809
6615853 6615887 6615899 6615911 6615913 6615919 6615943 6615967 6615977 6615979
6616003 6616021 6616033 6616069 6616073 6616087 6616117 6616139 6616151 6616163
6616189 6616217 6616219 6616223 6616231 6616271 6616283 6616289 6616297 6616301
6616339 6616343 6616381 6616391 6616397 6616399 6616403 6616447 6616469 6616471
6616481 6616483 6616499 6616513 6616517 6616523 6616529 6616531 6616537 6616543
6616549 6616567 6616583 6616591 6616601 6616607 6616637 6616651 6616657 6616667
6616681 6616697 6616717 6616751 6616759 6616763 6616777 6616781 6616783 6616787
6616789 6616837 6616861 6616871 6616873 6616879 6616931 6616991 6616993 6617003
6617011 6617053 6617057 6617071 6617087 6617159 6617161 6617173 6617183 6617189
6617197 6617257 6617293 6617323 6617327 6617329 6617357 6617363 6617371 6617383
6617407 6617411 6617431 6617449 6617467 6617473 6617483 6617489 6617497 6617503
6617521 6617531 6617543 6617557 6617563 6617579 6617581 6617599 6617603 6617627
6617693 6617701 6617711 6617747 6617753 6617761 6617789 6617797 6617803 6617827
6617837 6617861 6617867 6617873 6617893 6617917 6617921 6617939 6617953 6617957
6617969 6617983 6617987 6617993 6618013 6618037 6618041 6618047 6618077 6618103
6618109 6618113 6618127 6618169 6618191 6618197 6618203 6618217 6618223 6618229
6618233 6618239 6618247 6618277 6618281 6618299 6618323 6618349 6618401 6618413
6618419 6618421 6618433 6618463 6618487 6618497 6618499 6618509 6618511 6618529
6618533 6618551 6618553 6618569 6618581 6618617 6618653 6618659 6618701 6618713
6618727 6618737 6618739 6618751 6618761 6618769 6618809 6618811 6618823 6618827
6618839 6618851 6618853 6618901 6618907 6618919 6618923 6618929 6618949 6618959
6618971 6618979 6618991 6619021 6619031 6619043 6619051 6619073 6619079 6619091
6619099 6619111 6619139 6619141 6619157 6619159 6619169 6619211 6619219 6619229
6619231 6619253 6619289 6619303 6619343 6619357 6619363 6619369 6619381 6619441
6619451 6619471 6619493 6619507 6619513 6619519 6619589 6619609 6619643 6619649
6619651 6619673 6619687 6619693 6619747 6619751 6619757 6619759 6619777 6619799
6619813 6619829 6619849 6619861 6619871 6619889 6619927 6619931 6619933 6619937
6619967 6619981 6620011 6620017 6620027 6620039 6620057 6620059 6620083 6620101
6620171 6620183 6620209 6620231 6620261 6620281 6620287 6620291 6620309 6620351
6620353 6620357 6620363 6620371 6620387 6620399 6620401 6620407 6620423 6620441
6620461 6620489 6620501 6620503 6620507 6620519 6620587 6620597 6620611 6620617
6620629 6620681 6620689 6620693 6620699 6620717 6620741 6620771 6620777 6620791
6620807 6620819 6620833 6620851 6620861 6620863 6620869 6620899 6620927 6620947
6620951 6620953 6620981 6621029 6621061 6621071 6621103 6621119 6621127 6621211
6621151 6621163 6621191 6621233 6621239 6621281 6621283 6621287 6621289 6621311
6621331 6621337 6621341 6621353 6621359 6621361 6621371 6621379 6621413 6621421
6621451 6621463 6621487 6621527 6621529 6621533 6621553 6621607 6621649
6621691 6621707 6621731 6621749 6621751 6621809 6621827 6621829 6621833 6621841
6621851 6621883 6621911 6621929 6621931 6621943 6621949 6621961 6621991
6621997 6622009 6622019 6622037 6622069 6622081 6622097 6622111 6622151 6622153
6622157 6622177 6622193 6622199 6622211 6622223 6622303 6622307 6622309 6622339
6622349 6622373 6622379 6622391 6622423 6622457 6622489 6622493 6622501 6622523
6622531 6622541 6622547 6622601 6622619 6622631 6622661 6622663 6622703 6622711
6622729 6622753 6622763 6622787 6622789 6622799 6622801 6622813 6622823 6622829
6622859 6622867 6622897 6622907 6622939 6622961 6622981 6622997 6622999 6623009
6623021 6623033 6623041 6623059 6623087 6623101 6623117 6623131 6623159
6623171 6623173 6623203 6623213 6623231 6623237 6623261 6623273 6623297 6623303
6623311 6623321 6623327 6623341 6623369 6623371 6623389 6623401 6623411 6623413
6623417 6623423 6623459 6623467 6623521 6623531 6623549 6623581 6623611 6623707
6623711 6623719 6623737 6623741 6623759 6623789 6623791 6623797 6623809 6623819
6623833 6623857 6623873 6623879 6623959 6623963
6624017 6624031 6624041 6624043 6624047 6624061 6624077 6624127 6624143 6624197
6624199 6624259 6624269 6624307 6624337 6624353 6624377 6624379 6624413 6624427
6624433 6624439 6624463 6624469 6624473 6624481 6624487 6624503 6624533 6624547
6624551 6624581 6624589 6624599 6624613 6624619 6624641 6624659 6624671 6624721
6624727 6624733 6624739 6624757 6624763 6624769 6624773 6624799 6624803 6624817
6624833 6624859 6624899 6624923 6624931 6624941 6624953 6624971 6624973 6625001
6625007 6625033 6625039 6625043 6625061 6625093 6625117 6625123 6625141 6625147
6625153 6625163 6625181 6625193 6625207 6625237 6625247 6625273 6625301 6625321
6625343 6625349 6625361 6625363 6625373 6625379 6625387 6625417 6625447 6625453
```

```
6625459  6625481  6625501  6625511  6625513  6625519  6625571  6625573  6625579  6625603
6625607  6625613  6625621  6625639  6625667  6625669  6625673  6625687  6625693  6625709
6625747  6625769  6625777  6625781  6625789  6625819  6625823  6625841  6625859  6625873
6625907  6625921  6625939  6625943  6625979  6625987  6626029  6626069  6626077  6626083
6626089  6626129  6626143  6626161  6626173  6626177  6626183  6626227  6626267  6626303
6626309  6626329  6626341  6626351  6626377  6626381  6626407  6626423  6626443  6626453
6626513  6626531  6626551  6626561  6626563  6626569  6626579  6626593  6626597  6626603
6626621  6626623  6626639  6626647  6626657  6626677  6626693  6626699  6626701  6626713
6626723  6626729  6626743  6626747  6626779  6626797  6626833  6626849  6626861  6626863
6626881  6626887  6626941  6626947  6626981  6626989  6626999  6627001  6627017  6627043
6627077  6627083  6627097  6627113  6627119  6627139  6627157  6627163  6627169  6627191
6627193  6627217  6627251  6627253  6627287  6627319  6627343  6627347  6627349  6627359
6627373  6627377  6627391  6627407  6627431  6627443  6627479  6627493  6627497  6627503
6627553  6627557  6627581  6627587  6627601  6627617  6627623  6627629  6627661  6627667
6627679  6627697  6627701  6627727  6627737  6627757  6627767  6627793  6627811  6627821
6627851  6627853  6627857  6627869  6627877  6627899  6627911  6627917  6627949  6627989
6627991  6628007  6628033  6628051  6628057  6628073  6628087  6628099  6628103  6628123
6628133  6628159  6628177  6628189  6628201  6628247  6628253  6628261  6628267  6628277
6628289  6628309  6628313  6628357  6628367  6628373  6628379  6628403  6628409  6628411
6628417  6628421  6628423  6628477  6628483  6628499  6628537  6628541  6628553  6628561
6628571  6628607  6628613  6628621  6628651  6628667  6628673  6628679  6628711
6628717  6628723  6628729  6628753  6628781  6628813  6628819  6628847  6628859  6628877
6628879  6628943  6628981  6629033  6629039  6629041  6629059  6629101  6629107  6629111
6629113  6629141  6629149  6629173  6629191  6629213  6629219  6629237  6629239
6629251  6629279  6629281  6629291  6629317  6629323  6629333  6629351  6629369  6629377
6629383  6629387  6629393  6629407  6629411  6629437  6629471  6629477  6629479  6629509
6629551  6629561  6629563  6629573  6629591  6629593  6629617  6629627  6629647  6629683
6629687  6629713  6629729  6629731  6629737  6629747  6629761  6629807  6629873  6629891
6629897  6629921  6629923  6629927  6629941  6629963  6629969  6630011  6630023  6630037
6630061  6630089  6630097  6630101  6630103  6630121  6630131  6630137  6630157  6630163
6630167  6630191  6630203  6630223  6630227  6630229  6630257  6630269  6630277  6630287
6630293  6630313  6630319  6630359  6630367  6630409  6630433  6630457  6630461  6630467
6630499  6630523  6630539  6630541  6630551  6630553  6630583  6630587  6630599  6630607
6630641  6630653  6630661  6630691  6630709  6630737  6630749  6630769  6630773
6630779  6630803  6630817  6630839  6630847  6630851  6630853  6630859  6630887  6630907
6630913  6630919  6630961  6630979  6630983  6631021  6631033  6631039  6631063  6631067
6631081  6631109  6631129  6631147  6631151  6631189  6631193  6631213  6631223  6631237
6631271  6631279  6631321  6631327  6631333  6631367  6631369  6631379  6631409  6631421
6631447  6631477  6631483  6631501  6631553  6631571  6631579  6631591  6631607  6631619
6631637  6631643  6631661  6631663  6631679  6631693  6631697  6631699  6631721  6631733
6631739  6631763  6631789  6631871  6631883  6631901  6631903  6631907  6631909  6631913
6631939  6631951  6631979  6631993  6631997  6632009  6632051  6632063  6632113  6632117
6632141  6632149  6632167  6632177  6632203  6632207  6632221  6632231  6632237  6632239
6632251  6632267  6632291  6632299  6632317  6632333  6632359  6632377  6632389  6632393
6632401  6632413  6632429  6632459  6632467  6632477  6632491  6632519  6632537  6632573
6632599  6632617  6632623  6632627  6632651  6632683  6632699  6632701  6632711  6632723
6632777  6632789  6632797  6632803  6632807  6632819  6632837  6632849  6632887  6632911
6632921  6632981  6633001  6633007  6633013  6633017  6633019  6633031  6633047  6633089
6633091  6633119  6633139  6633149  6633161  6633173  6633181  6633191  6633197  6633229
6633241  6633283  6633293  6633301  6633343  6633353  6633371  6633391  6633421  6633433
6633449  6633461  6633463  6633467  6633479  6633491  6633493  6633503  6633511
6633569  6633577  6633589  6633593  6633607  6633643  6633647  6633661  6633667  6633701
6633719  6633727  6633749  6633773  6633787  6633839  6633853  6633857  6633877  6633889
6633899  6633917  6633931  6633947  6633967  6634009  6634013  6634039  6634049  6634079
6634081  6634091  6634109  6634151  6634171  6634219  6634223  6634231  6634237  6634241
6634297  6634307  6634319  6634337  6634339  6634357  6634361  6634391  6634423  6634429
6634447  6634451  6634469  6634517  6634519  6634531  6634547  6634549  6634559  6634571
6634583  6634597  6634613  6634619  6634627  6634631  6634633  6634637  6634643  6634673
6634711  6634717  6634739  6634759  6634769  6634783  6634799  6634829  6634841  6634853
6634871  6634889  6634891  6634921  6634931  6634949  6634967  6635003  6635011  6635033
6635051  6635053  6635087  6635089  6635093  6635129  6635137  6635143  6635179  6635221
6635231  6635243  6635249  6635261  6635263  6635267  6635309  6635311  6635323  6635327
6635353  6635359  6635407  6635467  6635513  6635521  6635527  6635539  6635549  6635561
6635597  6635609  6635611  6635621  6635633  6635659  6635663  6635669  6635677  6635683
6635689  6635719  6635723  6635737  6635749  6635777  6635791  6635813  6635821  6635843
6635857  6635861  6635879  6635887  6635897  6635903  6635917  6635927  6635947  6635957
6635963  6636011  6636017  6636023  6636037  6636059  6636083  6636101  6636109  6636127
6636169  6636173  6636181  6636199  6636221  6636229  6636269  6636293  6636317  6636337
6636359  6636433  6636457  6636467  6636479  6636493  6636523  6636527  6636557  6636559
6636571  6636589  6636593  6636611  6636661  6636667  6636689  6636701  6636709  6636767
6636769  6636779  6636781  6636797  6636803  6636809  6636827  6636863  6636887  6636913
6636923  6636937  6636943  6636961  6636979  6636989  6637003  6637049  6637063  6637067
6637073  6637091  6637109  6637117  6637139  6637153  6637159  6637177  6637181
6637187  6637223  6637229  6637237  6637249  6637273  6637277  6637283  6637291  6637297
6637303  6637307  6637313  6637321  6637339  6637357  6637369  6637373  6637399  6637439
6637447  6637453  6637487  6637571  6637583  6637591  6637601  6637621  6637637  6637643
6637649  6637651  6637679  6637681  6637691  6637693  6637703  6637711  6637717  6637721
6637727  6637739  6637811  6637819  6637843  6637847  6637853  6637877  6637903  6637919
6637921  6637931  6637933  6637949  6637957  6637979  6637987  6637997  6638017  6638029
6638057  6638069  6638101  6638131  6638141  6638147  6638153  6638167  6638179  6638221
6638227  6638231  6638249  6638251  6638263  6638273  6638299  6638321  6638339  6638341
6638363  6638369  6638377  6638393  6638407  6638459  6638473  6638491  6638497  6638509
6638519  6638531  6638549  6638579  6638591  6638603  6638617  6638627  6638633  6638647
6638669  6638689  6638701  6638741  6638773  6638791  6638803  6638851  6638893  6638903
6638911  6638953  6638977  6639001  6639011  6639013  6639041  6639047  6639049  6639067
6639077  6639107  6639109  6639119  6639209  6639223  6639233  6639251  6639263  6639287
6639293  6639307  6639313  6639331  6639337  6639349  6639377  6639383  6639389  6639407
6639439  6639449  6639467  6639481  6639497  6639509  6639511  6639527  6639533  6639547
6639593  6639601  6639629  6639631  6639641  6639653  6639679  6639697  6639719  6639739
```

```
6639757  6639769  6639799  6639803  6639817  6639823  6639833  6639839  6639851  6639863
6639881  6639889  6639907  6639929  6639937  6639943  6639959  6640003  6640009  6640021
6640027  6640061  6640069  6640079  6640091  6640093  6640111  6640121  6640129  6640157
6640163  6640181  6640213  6640223  6640241  6640271  6640297  6640321  6640327  6640331
6640339  6640349  6640369  6640373  6640393  6640397  6640409  6640411  6640429  6640441
6640451  6640453  6640463  6640477  6640493  6640499  6640511  6640547  6640549  6640553
6640567  6640577  6640589  6640597  6640631  6640639  6640651  6640657  6640663  6640679
6640687  6640757  6640759  6640769  6640793  6640807  6640817  6640831  6640841  6640849
6640889  6640891  6640901  6640903  6640927  6640939  6640967  6640979  6640987  6640993
6641021  6641027  6641039  6641077  6641083  6641143  6641149  6641153  6641177  6641179
6641183  6641197  6641231  6641249  6641263  6641267  6641287  6641291  6641329  6641333
6641351  6641353  6641357  6641359  6641381  6641387  6641399  6641419  6641449  6641473
6641477  6641489  6641491  6641501  6641513  6641519  6641527  6641561  6641563  6641567
6641573  6641587  6641633  6641669  6641671  6641683  6641693  6641699  6641707
6641717  6641729  6641753  6641771  6641797  6641809  6641813  6641821  6641827  6641839
6641851  6641861  6641903  6641953  6641969  6641977  6641983  6642007  6642023
6642067  6642071  6642079  6642089  6642109  6642127  6642137  6642143  6642149  6642151
6642169  6642187  6642211  6642281  6642283  6642289  6642299  6642301  6642319  6642329
6642341  6642347  6642353  6642371  6642373  6642379  6642403  6642409  6642431  6642439
6642487  6642497  6642521  6642523  6642539  6642551  6642553  6642593  6642613  6642619
6642637  6642659  6642707  6642709  6642763  6642793  6642803  6642817  6642829  6642847
6642863  6642877  6642887  6642893  6642907  6642917  6642919  6642991  6642997  6643019
6643033  6643051  6643057  6643069  6643097  6643111  6643123  6643127  6643129  6643139
6643151  6643181  6643201  6643211  6643213  6643229  6643249  6643261  6643283  6643289
6643303  6643319  6643321  6643333  6643337  6643361  6643381  6643411  6643423  6643453
6643489  6643499  6643499  6643513  6643537  6643589  6643607  6643633  6643649  6643667
6643687  6643691  6643699  6643723  6643729  6643733  6643739  6643781  6643789  6643807
6643811  6643823  6643829  6643837  6643843  6643859  6643883  6643891  6643907  6643909
6643919  6643969  6643981  6643993  6643999  6644023  6644047  6644069  6644081  6644087
6644101  6644111  6644123  6644147  6644149  6644153  6644159  6644177  6644191  6644227
6644269  6644273  6644293  6644299  6644311  6644327  6644359  6644371  6644377  6644381
6644389  6644413  6644431  6644441  6644459  6644483  6644503  6644527  6644543  6644543
6644549  6644551  6644579  6644581  6644587  6644621  6644647  6644681  6644717  6644753
6644761  6644789  6644801  6644837  6644863  6644873  6644879  6644887  6644903
6644933  6644959  6644969  6644983  6645013  6645019  6645047  6645049  6645059  6645071
6645073  6645083  6645131  6645139  6645149  6645151  6645161  6645169  6645187  6645209
6645211  6645217  6645227  6645259  6645293  6645313  6645319  6645329  6645341  6645389
6645391  6645461  6645467  6645469  6645479  6645491  6645493  6645517  6645547  6645557
6645571  6645577  6645593  6645601  6645619  6645637  6645641  6645677  6645679  6645697
6645713  6645721  6645739  6645757  6645787  6645799  6645803  6645817  6645823  6645833
6645851  6645857  6645881  6645883  6645907  6645911  6645917  6645923  6645943
6645949  6645971  6645979  6645983  6646001  6646019  6646039  6646049  6646153  6646163
6646193  6646207  6646217  6646231  6646247  6646259  6646271  6646309  6646313  6646319
6646331  6646357  6646361  6646363  6646373  6646399  6646403  6646417  6646423  6646429
6646477  6646511  6646513  6646543  6646559  6646573  6646579  6646613  6646657  6646663
6646669  6646687  6646697  6646699  6646769  6646777  6646781  6646819  6646831  6646837
6646859  6646867  6646873  6646877  6646883  6646891  6646907  6646919  6646921  6646933
6646951  6646957  6646967  6646973  6647009  6647029  6647033  6647041  6647059  6647077
6647089  6647099  6647107  6647111  6647129  6647141  6647167  6647189  6647191  6647209
6647213  6647219  6647227  6647239  6647243  6647269  6647273  6647279  6647287  6647317
6647339  6647363  6647369  6647393  6647401  6647411  6647447  6647489  6647497  6647519
6647521  6647551  6647569  6647573  6647579  6647581  6647593  6647623  6647647  6647653
6647657  6647681  6647717  6647741  6647743  6647747  6647761  6647779  6647783  6647791
6647813  6647831  6647869  6647887  6647899  6647909  6647911  6647917  6647923  6647939
6647947  6647951  6647959  6647983  6647987  6648001  6648007  6648023  6648053  6648067
6648073  6648079  6648091  6648097  6648133  6648143  6648203  6648251
6648259  6648269  6648287  6648307  6648331  6648371  6648401  6648407  6648409  6648413
6648431  6648457  6648461  6648491  6648503  6648517  6648571  6648583  6648599  6648623
6648637  6648647  6648661  6648701  6648713  6648731  6648737  6648749  6648757  6648773
6648791  6648809  6648823  6648839  6648859  6648877  6648979  6648991  6648997
6649007  6649063  6649073  6649099  6649103  6649117  6649127  6649141  6649151  6649163
6649189  6649199  6649229  6649249  6649267  6649271  6649273  6649289  6649319  6649333
6649337  6649367  6649387  6649393  6649399  6649403  6649417  6649441  6649453  6649481
6649483  6649547  6649571  6649579  6649583  6649589  6649609  6649627  6649631  6649633
6649661  6649691  6649693  6649723  6649733  6649801  6649823  6649837  6649849  6649859
6649861  6649871  6649883  6649891  6649901  6649919  6649999  6650003  6650011  6650041
6650051  6650071  6650093  6650099  6650131  6650153  6650207  6650233  6650239  6650257
6650263  6650279  6650309  6650327  6650333  6650339  6650351  6650393  6650431  6650443
6650459  6650467  6650503  6650507  6650521  6650531  6650533  6650557  6650561  6650591
6650597  6650603  6650659  6650669  6650671  6650687  6650701  6650717  6650729  6650731
6650737  6650797  6650801  6650821  6650827  6650837  6650843  6650849  6650867  6650869
6650909  6650911  6650929  6650971  6650993  6651049  6651053  6651077  6651091  6651101
6651107  6651119  6651133  6651149  6651167  6651181  6651187  6651217  6651221
6651223  6651251  6651277  6651317  6651319  6651343  6651361  6651367  6651377  6651397
6651401  6651413  6651427  6651433  6651457  6651467  6651473  6651479  6651497  6651503
6651517  6651521  6651523  6651571  6651583  6651587  6651647  6651649  6651661  6651679
6651683  6651707  6651727  6651773  6651791  6651793  6651809  6651839  6651847  6651851
6651857  6651901  6651907  6651923  6651941  6651959  6652001  6652021  6652031  6652039
6652081  6652091  6652097  6652103  6652141  6652153  6652157  6652159  6652171  6652181
6652183  6652187  6652199  6652207  6652211  6652213  6652231  6652241  6652249  6652273
6652279  6652301  6652307  6652319  6652343  6652351  6652381  6652391  6652409  6652411
6652421  6652433  6652451  6652457  6652463  6652501  6652553  6652579  6652621
6652643  6652651  6652673  6652697  6652703  6652733  6652739  6652741  6652747  6652753
6652757  6652787  6652799  6652801  6652813  6652823  6652829  6652837  6652853  6652871
6652901  6652927  6652937  6652949  6652951  6652963  6652969  6652973  6652979  6652993
6653011  6653027  6653039  6653057  6653077  6653099  6653107  6653117  6653123  6653159
6653183  6653219  6653221  6653243  6653299  6653329  6653351  6653389  6653399  6653411
6653429  6653467  6653483  6653501  6653533  6653573  6653587  6653593  6653627  6653641
6653653  6653659  6653683  6653701  6653707  6653711  6653723  6653761  6653771  6653797
```

```
6653813 6653827 6653833 6653839 6653869 6653873 6653879 6653887 6653891 6653897
6653917 6653921 6653939 6653957 6653989 6653993 6654007 6654017 6654019 6654029
6654031 6654041 6654059 6654071 6654073 6654113 6654127 6654143 6654173 6654211
6654217 6654229 6654251 6654269 6654281 6654289 6654299 6654317 6654331 6654353
6654391 6654443 6654451 6654481 6654493 6654509 6654517 6654533 6654539 6654547
6654563 6654577 6654581 6654643 6654647 6654649 6654653 6654679 6654737 6654743
6654749 6654761 6654773 6654779 6654821 6654829 6654847 6654859 6654877 6654887
6654913 6654919 6654937 6654941 6654943 6654953 6654961 6654971 6654979 6655001
6655003 6655009 6655037 6655057 6655063 6655069 6655087 6655091 6655093 6655097
6655133 6655169 6655199 6655237 6655249 6655261 6655273 6655289 6655307 6655309
6655321 6655333 6655343 6655351 6655367 6655373 6655379 6655393 6655403 6655409
6655423 6655531 6655541 6655543 6655547 6655549 6655577 6655591 6655603 6655631
6655633 6655637 6655639 6655651 6655661 6655667 6655673 6655723 6655729 6655739
6655751 6655769 6655801 6655837 6655879 6655889 6655897 6655903 6655907 6655919
6655931 6655937 6655951 6655997 6656003 6656009 6656011 6656059 6656071 6656077
6656101 6656123 6656171 6656183 6656201 6656239 6656257 6656261 6656291 6656311
6656339 6656347 6656371 6656387 6656393 6656437 6656449 6656459 6656471 6656483
6656497 6656527 6656539 6656543 6656549 6656561 6656569 6656597 6656603 6656621
6656623 6656627 6656647 6656669 6656711 6656737 6656743 6656753 6656759 6656779
6656807 6656833 6656857 6656861 6656879 6656887 6656891 6656893 6656899 6656917
6656927 6656963 6656967 6656977 6656981 6656987 6657017 6657019 6657023 6657041
6657061 6657067 6657073 6657103 6657107 6657109 6657179 6657191 6657193 6657223
6657257 6657263 6657283 6657311 6657349 6657359 6657367 6657377 6657379 6657407
6657437 6657449 6657451 6657461 6657473 6657517 6657533 6657571 6657583 6657587
6657593 6657613 6657631 6657661 6657667 6657671 6657697 6657709 6657731 6657751
6657769 6657773 6657779 6657799 6657811 6657851 6657853 6657881
6657887 6657919 6657929 6657947 6657953 6657979 6657997 6658007 6658013 6658027
6658049 6658051 6658079 6658097 6658103 6658121 6658129 6658153 6658159 6658181
6658193 6658243 6658279 6658283 6658321 6658331 6658361 6658367 6658369
6658411 6658427 6658453 6658469 6658471 6658501 6658511 6658541 6658573 6658609
6658637 6658649 6658667 6658697 6658711 6658723 6658787 6658793 6658823
6658837 6658843 6658859 6658871 6658903 6658909 6658921 6658961 6658969 6658997
6658999 6659021 6659027 6659033 6659041 6659057 6659077 6659089 6659111 6659113
6659201 6659207 6659209 6659227 6659231 6659249 6659243 6659249 6659267 6659293
6659293 6659321 6659333 6659353 6659363 6659369 6659377 6659399 6659413 6659417
6659437 6659441 6659447 6659491 6659501 6659561 6659567 6659579 6659591 6659623
6659663 6659677 6659683 6659687 6659689 6659693 6659713 6659749 6659773 6659777
6659803 6659813 6659833 6659843 6659893 6659921 6659929 6659941 6659957 6659977
6660011 6660023 6660029 6660061 6660091 6660103 6660109 6660113 6660119 6660161
6660191 6660193 6660197 6660211 6660217 6660221 6660233 6660239 6660287 6660293
6660299 6660307 6660337 6660347 6660349 6660359 6660371 6660377 6660389 6660391
6660397 6660419 6660421 6660427 6660473 6660499 6660503 6660509 6660523 6660551
6660553 6660557 6660587 6660601 6660613 6660649 6660677 6660679 6660707 6660721
6660733 6660751 6660763 6660781 6660791 6660799 6660809 6660859 6660911 6660919
6660931 6660937 6660943 6660949 6660959 6660967 6660977 6661013 6661021 6661037
6661049 6661069 6661079 6661091 6661103 6661111 6661117 6661141 6661157 6661189
6661211 6661217 6661223 6661231 6661243 6661273 6661279 6661301 6661307 6661313
6661327 6661337 6661349 6661367 6661379 6661409 6661423 6661429 6661439 6661441
6661477 6661493 6661511 6661547 6661549 6661553 6661583 6661597 6661601 6661643
6661649 6661661 6661687 6661691 6661693 6661709 6661727 6661741 6661747 6661751
6661757 6661771 6661777 6661783 6661849 6661873 6661883 6661891 6661901 6661933
6661957 6661987 6661997 6662003 6662009 6662041 6662059 6662063 6662069 6662077
6662087 6662093 6662099 6662101 6662137 6662171 6662177 6662191 6662197 6662209
6662231 6662233 6662281 6662309 6662329 6662333 6662347 6662353 6662371
6662393 6662399 6662401 6662417 6662437 6662449 6662477 6662507 6662531 6662533
6662543 6662561 6662563 6662567 6662581 6662633 6662641 6662651 6662671 6662707
6662717 6662723 6662741 6662743 6662753 6662771 6662809 6662813 6662839 6662857
6662879 6662881 6662891 6662911 6662941 6662947 6662959 6662987 6662989
6662993 6663029 6663043 6663067 6663073 6663079 6663089 6663103 6663121 6663179
6663191 6663193 6663203 6663227 6663229 6663257 6663289 6663299 6663311 6663317
6663329 6663347 6663383 6663389 6663407 6663431 6663451 6663469 6663487 6663493
6663499 6663511 6663523 6663539 6663557 6663593 6663599 6663611 6663617 6663647
6663653 6663673 6663731 6663739 6663749 6663751 6663763 6663793 6663809 6663827
6663829 6663841 6663857 6663863 6663869 6663893 6663901 6663907 6663911 6663941
6663961 6663971 6664019 6664027 6664069 6664087 6664093 6664103 6664121 6664139
6664159 6664169 6664199 6664201 6664213 6664223 6664237 6664261 6664277 6664279
6664309 6664321 6664351 6664381 6664387 6664417 6664429 6664447 6664453 6664481
6664501 6664513 6664517 6664523 6664529 6664531 6664543 6664547 6664571 6664607
6664631 6664643 6664657 6664661 6664667 6664711 6664717 6664729 6664739 6664753
6664759 6664769 6664771 6664787 6664789 6664811 6664831 6664843 6664859 6664877
6664891 6664937 6664939 6664951 6664961 6664979 6664997 6665011 6665017 6665047
6665051 6665059 6665063 6665077 6665081 6665089 6665111 6665123 6665159 6665167
6665179 6665201 6665213 6665231 6665237 6665249 6665261 6665297 6665317 6665339
6665353 6665359 6665363 6665369 6665383 6665413 6665437 6665497 6665537 6665539
6665567 6665573 6665591 6665597 6665611 6665623 6665627 6665639 6665669 6665671
6665689 6665707 6665719 6665741 6665773 6665777 6665797 6665801 6665803 6665831
6665839 6665843 6665861 6665873 6665881 6665909 6665917 6665927 6665947 6665951
6665959 6665987 6666001 6666029 6666047 6666059 6666061 6666097 6666133 6666137
6666157 6666167 6666173 6666203 6666223 6666229 6666239 6666241 6666269 6666337
6666347 6666353 6666379 6666383 6666391 6666437 6666449 6666467 6666479 6666487
6666509 6666523 6666547 6666551 6666563 6666577 6666589 6666593 6666599 6666613
6666661 6666679 6666683 6666689 6666719 6666761 6666769 6666791 6666793 6666797
6666833 6666841 6666883 6666931 6666937 6666943 6666949 6666977 6666991 6667019
6667027 6667039 6667049 6667061 6667069 6667127 6667147 6667151 6667153 6667159
6667169 6667181 6667183 6667207 6667223 6667229 6667253 6667259 6667261 6667273
6667291 6667301 6667321 6667327 6667337 6667343 6667369 6667393 6667399 6667403
6667429 6667439 6667457 6667471 6667481 6667487 6667523 6667541 6667589 6667597
6667607 6667637 6667643 6667657 6667669 6667673 6667693 6667711 6667721 6667729
6667741 6667753 6667781 6667813 6667819 6667853 6667867 6667873 6667889 6667891
```

```
6667897 6667909 6667931 6667933 6667949 6667951 6667979 6667981 6668021 6668027
6668033 6668047 6668059 6668083 6668113 6668119 6668149 6668161 6668181 6668203
6668209 6668213 6668237 6668257 6668269 6668273 6668341 6668351 6668353 6668359
6668377 6668381 6668419 6668423 6668429 6668447 6668461 6668507 6668509 6668531
6668537 6668549 6668567 6668603 6668611 6668617 6668659 6668687 6668699 6668707
6668713 6668719 6668723 6668731 6668737 6668747 6668759 6668789 6668807 6668821
6668833 6668839 6668869 6668881 6668887 6668903 6668911 6668939 6668953 6668971
6668953 6668957 6668969 6669007 6669017 6669029 6669053 6669059 6669067 6669071
6669097 6669119 6669121 6669137 6669161 6669163 6669197 6669199 6669233 6669239
6669251 6669269 6669281 6669293 6669331 6669337 6669349 6669367 6669401 6669409
6669413 6669451 6669463 6669469 6669473 6669493 6669503 6669521 6669541 6669547
6669587 6669617 6669643 6669647 6669653 6669671 6669673 6669683 6669697 6669709
6669769 6669781 6669809 6669827 6669847 6669853 6669857 6669863 6669869 6669877
6669881 6669889 6669907 6669947 6669959 6669961 6669973 6669983 6670019 6670033
6670039 6670043 6670067 6670073 6670109 6670187 6670199 6670201 6670211 6670231
6670243 6670259 6670267 6670271 6670291 6670297 6670303 6670309 6670327 6670351
6670369 6670373 6670403 6670423 6670427 6670429 6670451 6670457 6670513 6670537
6670553 6670583 6670603 6670607 6670637 6670649 6670661 6670687 6670717 6670751
6670753 6670771 6670799 6670801 6670819 6670831 6670837 6670847 6670849 6670883
6670901 6670903 6670933 6670967 6670973 6671003 6671009 6671017 6671047 6671051
6671059 6671083 6671099 6671111 6671113 6671153 6671167 6671201 6671239 6671243
6671263 6671281 6671309 6671323 6671341 6671377 6671381 6671383 6671389 6671411
6671443 6671447 6671453 6671459 6671461 6671501 6671503 6671513 6671519 6671549
6671551 6671569 6671573 6671591 6671593 6671597 6671617 6671627 6671647 6671663
6671669 6671671 6671677 6671681 6671683 6671713 6671719 6671723 6671747 6671767
6671801 6671809 6671823 6671839 6671881 6671889 6671893 6671921 6671947 6671957
6671963 6671969 6671989 6672013 6672019 6672067 6672077 6672089 6672101 6672137
6672157 6672179 6672187 6672191 6672229 6672257 6672269 6672283 6672301 6672307
6672319 6672331 6672359 6672389 6672397 6672433 6672467 6672473 6672493 6672503
6672527 6672529 6672557 6672559 6672563 6672569 6672571 6672623 6672661 6672671
6672683 6672703 6672749 6672761 6672769 6672773 6672779 6672797 6672803 6672817
6672863 6672877 6672881 6672889 6672899 6672917 6672923 6672931 6672943 6672947
6672977 6672979 6672997 6673021 6673031 6673033 6673081 6673097 6673109 6673111
6673141 6673159 6673169 6673187 6673193 6673223 6673273 6673279 6673319 6673321
6673327 6673363 6673369 6673379 6673391 6673397 6673399 6673409 6673411 6673421
6673453 6673477 6673493 6673501 6673507 6673517 6673523 6673543 6673547 6673553
6673559 6673591 6673607 6673609 6673613 6673627 6673631 6673633 6673637 6673687
6673691 6673699 6673717 6673739 6673753 6673757 6673759 6673763 6673789 6673847
6673861 6673867 6673889 6673951 6673963 6673969 6673981 6673991 6673993 6674009
6674011 6674029 6674039 6674051 6674053 6674069 6674093 6674123 6674177 6674189
6674197 6674201 6674203 6674219 6674233 6674243 6674249 6674273 6674281 6674287
6674293 6674299 6674309 6674323 6674357 6674359 6674369 6674399 6674401 6674407
6674413 6674429 6674441 6674443 6674461 6674483 6674527 6674533 6674537 6674539
6674561 6674573 6674599 6674617 6674621 6674651 6674671 6674683 6674711 6674741
6674747 6674749 6674771 6674779 6674791 6674809 6674813 6674821 6674839 6674881
6674891 6674903 6674917 6674929 6674953 6674963 6674971 6675007 6675029 6675043
6675073 6675077 6675079 6675091 6675103 6675107 6675113 6675127 6675131 6675161
6675181 6675209 6675211 6675223 6675233 6675241 6675299 6675301 6675331 6675343
6675377 6675379 6675391 6675397 6675433 6675463 6675523 6675527 6675541 6675547
6675563 6675569 6675587 6675601 6675649 6675653 6675667 6675671 6675709 6675719
6675733 6675749 6675763 6675769 6675787 6675803 6675811 6675817 6675839 6675857
6675863 6675869 6675899 6675913 6675919 6675931 6675953 6675959 6675961 6676001
6676013 6676057 6676081 6676091 6676093 6676099 6676123 6676139 6676171 6676199
6676213 6676217 6676231 6676247 6676259 6676261 6676273 6676301 6676321 6676331
6676333 6676339 6676387 6676433 6676441 6676447 6676451 6676457 6676471 6676519
6676559 6676573 6676609 6676651 6676661 6676667 6676669 6676697 6676711 6676717
6676721 6676729 6676741 6676753 6676763 6676777 6676793 6676823 6676829 6676837
6676861 6676871 6676883 6676889 6676913 6676927 6676949 6676979 6676991 6677017
6677029 6677071 6677087 6677123 6677129 6677147 6677171 6677173 6677179 6677191
6677213 6677233 6677239 6677261 6677269 6677273 6677299 6677309 6677327 6677329
6677341 6677351 6677357 6677389 6677393 6677399 6677401 6677423 6677459 6677467
6677471 6677477 6677491 6677527 6677537 6677543 6677579 6677597 6677611 6677623
6677641 6677663 6677677 6677707 6677729 6677747 6677761 6677777 6677779 6677789
6677809 6677813 6677831 6677837 6677851 6677861 6677887 6677893 6677897 6677903
6677921 6677941 6677959 6677969 6677971 6678017 6678037 6678079 6678109 6678141
6678143 6678157 6678173 6678197 6678209 6678227 6678233 6678247 6678271 6678281
6678289 6678313 6678317 6678383 6678401 6678421 6678431 6678437 6678457 6678461
6678491 6678499 6678509 6678521 6678523 6678577 6678593 6678629 6678641 6678647
6678667 6678691 6678701 6678703 6678713 6678743 6678751 6678767 6678779 6678797
6678799 6678817 6678839 6678851 6678853 6678871 6678877 6678883 6678911 6678929
6678967 6678979 6679009 6679031 6679063 6679067 6679087 6679097 6679103 6679121
6679133 6679139 6679157 6679159 6679171 6679199 6679237 6679247 6679271 6679273
6679289 6679303 6679307 6679313 6679327 6679339 6679349 6679363 6679369 6679373
6679381 6679391 6679397 6679423 6679451 6679459 6679471 6679481 6679513 6679523
6679531 6679553 6679571 6679579 6679613 6679619 6679639 6679661 6679667 6679681
6679693 6679723 6679747 6679763 6679789 6679801 6679807 6679823 6679853 6679901
6679919 6679931 6679949 6679951 6679957 6679979 6679993 6679999 6680021 6680027
6680029 6680033 6680053 6680059 6680069 6680081 6680087 6680111 6680119 6680123
6680137 6680147 6680183 6680203 6680227 6680249 6680273 6680287 6680321 6680329
6680339 6680341 6680357 6680389 6680413 6680431 6680441 6680449 6680497 6680519
6680521 6680539 6680543 6680549 6680551 6680561 6680563 6680567 6680579 6680621
6680651 6680657 6680659 6680699 6680731 6680743 6680789 6680797 6680851 6680873
6680923 6680939 6680941 6680959 6680969 6680977 6680981 6680987 6681001 6681013
6681019 6681023 6681041 6681067 6681071 6681133 6681137 6681139 6681161 6681167
6681193 6681197 6681203 6681209 6681239 6681287 6681329 6681359 6681361 6681377
6681403 6681419 6681421 6681427 6681439 6681443 6681481 6681487 6681491 6681511
6681529 6681539 6681541 6681547 6681557 6681581 6681589 6681637 6681671 6681677
6681679 6681683 6681721 6681733 6681751 6681761 6681781 6681791 6681817 6681839
6681847 6681877 6681887 6681889 6681923 6681929 6681931 6681947 6681949 6681953
```

```
6681959  6681967  6681971  6681979  6681989  6682007  6682009  6682021  6682051  6682063
6682069  6682087  6682097  6682099  6682103  6682133  6682141  6682153  6682183  6682211
6682219  6682223  6682231  6682253  6682279  6682283  6682289  6682301  6682327  6682337
6682349  6682363  6682369  6682393  6682409  6682421  6682439  6682447  6682483  6682561
6682573  6682583  6682597  6682603  6682609  6682693  6682721  6682729  6682747  6682769
6682783  6682787  6682801  6682843  6682849  6682859  6682861  6682901  6682909  6682913
6682943  6682957  6682961  6682969  6682999  6683029  6683059  6683111  6683119  6683129
6683143  6683161  6683167  6683177  6683207  6683213  6683233  6683249  6683251  6683267
6683291  6683293  6683351  6683357  6683359  6683381  6683387  6683401  6683407  6683423
6683429  6683449  6683471  6683477  6683483  6683491  6683519  6683527  6683531  6683549
6683557  6683581  6683609  6683627  6683641  6683689  6683711  6683723  6683749  6683759
6683767  6683797  6683821  6683827  6683851  6683867  6683903  6683921  6683927  6683947
6683951  6683977  6683981  6683993  6684001  6684019  6684023  6684037  6684047  6684059
6684061  6684089  6684091  6684101  6684103  6684109  6684133  6684151  6684163  6684193
6684203  6684229  6684233  6684253  6684259  6684277  6684299  6684341  6684343  6684361
6684373  6684443  6684449  6684473  6684493  6684497  6684527  6684541  6684551  6684569
6684577  6684583  6684593  6684607  6684647  6684647  6684659  6684673  6684677  6684707
6684719  6684749  6684773  6684779  6684781  6684817  6684833  6684869  6684907  6684911
6684913  6684949  6684971  6684983  6684991  6685001  6685013  6685027  6685031  6685033
6685037  6685043  6685117  6685127  6685141  6685163  6685201  6685247  6685303  6685307
6685331  6685351  6685363  6685379  6685391  6685409  6685447  6685477  6685487  6685489
6685499  6685507  6685517  6685519  6685529  6685541  6685543  6685577  6685603  6685619
6685621  6685633  6685643  6685667  6685669  6685673  6685687  6685697  6685711  6685717
6685741  6685751  6685753  6685759  6685781  6685787  6685789  6685807  6685813  6685823
6685837  6685843  6685859  6685867  6685907  6685927  6685933  6685961  6685963  6685969
6686041  6686047  6686051  6686093  6686107  6686167  6686177  6686191  6686203  6686213
6686221  6686227  6686237  6686243  6686263  6686279  6686299  6686311  6686333  6686341
6686357  6686363  6686413  6686419  6686437  6686447  6686453  6686467  6686479  6686489
6686507  6686509  6686527  6686539  6686569  6686591  6686611  6686653  6686663  6686681
6686699  6686711  6686717  6686723  6686747  6686761  6686773  6686777  6686783  6686789
6686843  6686861  6686881  6686893  6686907  6686921  6686941  6686947  6686983  6686987
6687011  6687013  6687017  6687049  6687077  6687097  6687127  6687133  6687143  6687167
6687173  6687199  6687209  6687229  6687251  6687283  6687293  6687323  6687353  6687367
6687379  6687383  6687389  6687391  6687427  6687437  6687451  6687463  6687497  6687521
6687523  6687529  6687533  6687539  6687557  6687589  6687617  6687623  6687631  6687689
6687701  6687757  6687761  6687763  6687767  6687773  6687781  6687803  6687809  6687823
6687853  6687869  6687881  6687931  6687973  6687983  6688001  6688013  6688027  6688049
6688051  6688069  6688079  6688093  6688103  6688109  6688111  6688117  6688127  6688151
6688153  6688211  6688217  6688267  6688273  6688301  6688307  6688309  6688313  6688337
6688351  6688387  6688393  6688411  6688421  6688433  6688457  6688471  6688481  6688499
6688501  6688519  6688537  6688559  6688573  6688579  6688631  6688633  6688639  6688651
6688657  6688663  6688673  6688691  6688723  6688727  6688757  6688783  6688789  6688793
6688807  6688813  6688831  6688849  6688853  6688859  6688907  6688909  6688919  6688933
6688943  6688967  6688999  6689029  6689047  6689069  6689099  6689101  6689117  6689131
6689141  6689147  6689153  6689171  6689203  6689233  6689237  6689239  6689257  6689281
6689303  6689317  6689323  6689327  6689339  6689351  6689359  6689363  6689377  6689383
6689399  6689413  6689429  6689491  6689497  6689503  6689537  6689561  6689567  6689581
6689587  6689591  6689593  6689611  6689623  6689629  6689659  6689681  6689689  6689699
6689701  6689719  6689723  6689741  6689773  6689779  6689791  6689797  6689801  6689821
6689869  6689873  6689909  6689971  6689989  6689999  6690001  6690029  6690059  6690067
6690107  6690119  6690143  6690149  6690169  6690179  6690199  6690221  6690227
6690239  6690247  6690251  6690269  6690283  6690319  6690323  6690331  6690347  6690353
6690361  6690373  6690379  6690427  6690433  6690473  6690479  6690517  6690557  6690559
6690569  6690577  6690583  6690587  6690601  6690611  6690623  6690643  6690647  6690689
6690701  6690703  6690721  6690737  6690743  6690767  6690787  6690797  6690829  6690847
6690863  6690881  6690889  6690923  6690941  6690949  6690991  6690997
6691007  6691019  6691037  6691039  6691049  6691051  6691057  6691073  6691079  6691093
6691099  6691129  6691147  6691163  6691169  6691171  6691177  6691193  6691207  6691219
6691231  6691259  6691277  6691301  6691309  6691331  6691337  6691361  6691369  6691397
6691403  6691411  6691423  6691427  6691457  6691463  6691471  6691481  6691483  6691493
6691501  6691507  6691513  6691519  6691541  6691577  6691613  6691631  6691637  6691661
6691687  6691697  6691723  6691771  6691777  6691793  6691799  6691801  6691843  6691859
6691891  6691903  6691943  6691969  6691981  6691987  6692017  6692029  6692051  6692053
6692071  6692083  6692087  6692093  6692099  6692107  6692111  6692117  6692131  6692141
6692167  6692173  6692183  6692197  6692209  6692261  6692263  6692267  6692269  6692281
6692297  6692299  6692303  6692317  6692341  6692347  6692353  6692383  6692393  6692419
6692423  6692431  6692437  6692443  6692461  6692473  6692479  6692501  6692507  6692513
6692549  6692551  6692557  6692573  6692593  6692603  6692663  6692669  6692669  6692677
6692689  6692723  6692729  6692759  6692767  6692771  6692809  6692813  6692827  6692843
6692863  6692867  6692897  6692909  6692923  6692929  6692953  6693013  6693059  6693061
6693083  6693101  6693107  6693133  6693143  6693163  6693217  6693227  6693277  6693289
6693307  6693311  6693319  6693331  6693341  6693343  6693353  6693361  6693397  6693413
6693419  6693431  6693439  6693451  6693457  6693473  6693481  6693487  6693497  6693503
6693517  6693539  6693541  6693569  6693571  6693593  6693607  6693611  6693623  6693629
6693637  6693641  6693647  6693669  6693689  6693697  6693703  6693721  6693761  6693773
6693821  6693829  6693839  6693887  6693901  6693913  6693917  6693931  6693941  6693949
6693961  6693991  6693997  6694001  6694013  6694019  6694021  6694087  6694091  6694097
6694111  6694133  6694117  6694183  6694211  6694217  6694229  6694249  6694253  6694267
6694307  6694309  6694333  6694339  6694349  6694361  6694367  6694393  6694399  6694409
6694411  6694433  6694463  6694469  6694477  6694511  6694537  6694561  6694643  6694663
6694673  6694687  6694693  6694703  6694711  6694747  6694763  6694769  6694823  6694829
6694837  6694861  6694871  6694879  6694901  6694913  6694937  6694949  6694979  6694981
6694993  6694999  6694999  6695021  6695041  6695069  6695071  6695081  6695111  6695131
6695149  6695153  6695159  6695167  6695207  6695219  6695233  6695237  6695257  6695281
6695321  6695333  6695389  6695393  6695407  6695413  6695417  6695429  6695431  6695441
6695453  6695459  6695489  6695503  6695509  6695537  6695539  6695561  6695617  6695627
6695629  6695639  6695641  6695651  6695653  6695681  6695687  6695699  6695701  6695707
6695713  6695729  6695743  6695747  6695863  6695869  6695873  6695891  6695903  6695933
6695947  6695951  6695959  6695981  6695987  6695993  6696023  6696049  6696061  6696077
```

```
6696083 6696091 6696101 6696103 6696127 6696143 6696163 6696169 6696229 6696233
6696241 6696253 6696257 6696259 6696281 6696293 6696307 6696331 6696337 6696343
6696353 6696359 6696373 6696377 6696383 6696451 6696463 6696479 6696491 6696517
6696553 6696577 6696581 6696587 6696601 6696617 6696619 6696637 6696643 6696661
6696671 6696673 6696707 6696743 6696757 6696773 6696779 6696787 6696799 6696829
6696839 6696853 6696857 6696869 6696871 6696917 6696919 6696923 6696953 6696959
6697043 6697049 6697081 6697087 6697109 6697127 6697153 6697157 6697169
6697189 6697193 6697199 6697213 6697219 6697241 6697277 6697279 6697283 6697297
6697307 6697319 6697321 6697331 6697343 6697357 6697363 6697381 6697399 6697403
6697423 6697429 6697441 6697459 6697477 6697487 6697489 6697499 6697511 6697529
6697549 6697553 6697567 6697573 6697589 6697591 6697597 6697619 6697651 6697657
6697661 6697667 6697681 6697693 6697721 6697727 6697741 6697751 6697759 6697763
6697771 6697799 6697837 6697841 6697843 6697877 6697897 6697921 6697939 6697967
6697973 6697979 6698033 6698039 6698053 6698063 6698071 6698099 6698143
6698149 6698189 6698207 6698231 6698233 6698281 6698291 6698303 6698309 6698311
6698339 6698381 6698383 6698389 6698413 6698429 6698441 6698467 6698477 6698491
6698501 6698509 6698533 6698551 6698557 6698567 6698569 6698579 6698597 6698599
6698611 6698633 6698651 6698677 6698687 6698689 6698729 6698737 6698743 6698749
6698761 6698767 6698771 6698777 6698803 6698807 6698831 6698897 6698899 6698903
6698953 6698977 6698981 6698987 6699059 6699061 6699067 6699073 6699089 6699097
6699101 6699103 6699151 6699167 6699197 6699211 6699221 6699227 6699247 6699269
6699281 6699293 6699307 6699311 6699337 6699349 6699361 6699367 6699389 6699401
6699421 6699439 6699481 6699491 6699541 6699577 6699599 6699607 6699611 6699613
6699617 6699619 6699643 6699703 6699727 6699743 6699757 6699767 6699779 6699793
6699817 6699821 6699827 6699839 6699857 6699859 6699871 6699881 6699893 6699907
6699919 6699929 6699941 6699947 6699949 6699961 6699977 6700007 6700033 6700039
6700063 6700079 6700087 6700093 6700129 6700147 6700157 6700163 6700171 6700231
6700237 6700249 6700271 6700277 6700279 6700321 6700327 6700387 6700399 6700403
6700409 6700411 6700417 6700489 6700493 6700501 6700517 6700553 6700579 6700583
6700607 6700609 6700621 6700637 6700651 6700657 6700691 6700693 6700697 6700699
6700709 6700717 6700723 6700739 6700741 6700777 6700783 6700831 6700849 6700879
6700891 6700919 6700921 6700933 6700937 6700957 6700961 6700973 6700987 6700997
6701003 6701021 6701029 6701039 6701069 6701083 6701131 6701141 6701143 6701147
6701159 6701197 6701207 6701221 6701251 6701263 6701269 6701287 6701309 6701311
6701323 6701339 6701341 6701347 6701353 6701369 6701377 6701381 6701393 6701411
6701413 6701437 6701447 6701459 6701467 6701483 6701537 6701603 6701609 6701627
6701641 6701693 6701701 6701707 6701713 6701729 6701741 6701749 6701753 6701759
6701771 6701801 6701803 6701831 6701837 6701843 6701861 6701867 6701873 6701881
6701923 6701941 6701953 6701957 6701971 6701977 6702011 6702037 6702043 6702049
6702053 6702067 6702089 6702119 6702139 6702149 6702181 6702191 6702197 6702209
6702239 6702257 6702263 6702271 6702287 6702299 6702317 6702343 6702347 6702359
6702379 6702413 6702427 6702431 6702457 6702463 6702469 6702473 6702503 6702517
6702533 6702547 6702559 6702571 6702583 6702599 6702617 6702653 6702667 6702671
6702691 6702713 6702733 6702749 6702757 6702769 6702779 6702791 6702823 6702827
6702833 6702841 6702847 6702869 6702887 6702893 6702907 6702919 6702923 6702929
6702979 6703001 6703009 6703019 6703043 6703057 6703061 6703087 6703111 6703127
6703129 6703133 6703153 6703159 6703199 6703217 6703241 6703247 6703261 6703271
6703297 6703309 6703337 6703349 6703357 6703363 6703381 6703393 6703397 6703427
6703451 6703453 6703483 6703507 6703513 6703579 6703589 6703591 6703597 6703621
6703633 6703651 6703679 6703687 6703691 6703709 6703721 6703759 6703783 6703799
6703841 6703847 6703867 6703877 6703883 6703889 6703913 6703927 6703937
6703943 6703973 6703981 6703997 6703999 6704003 6704011 6704021 6704051 6704081
6704099 6704119 6704143 6704149 6704161 6704179 6704209 6704213 6704237 6704261
6704267 6704297 6704309 6704333 6704377 6704413 6704417 6704429 6704471 6704479
6704483 6704497 6704507 6704519 6704521 6704531 6704557 6704567 6704611 6704617
6704641 6704653 6704669 6704671 6704717 6704729 6704741 6704759 6704779 6704791
6704801 6704813 6704821 6704837 6704839 6704843 6704857 6704869 6704903 6704909
6704921 6704923 6704927 6704969 6705001 6705019 6705031 6705037 6705053 6705071
6705077 6705079 6705091 6705109 6705113 6705133 6705143 6705163 6705211 6705227
6705229 6705247 6705277 6705287 6705299 6705323 6705329 6705341 6705359 6705367
6705371 6705373 6705389 6705449 6705469 6705481 6705511 6705539 6705541 6705553
6705557 6705563 6705593 6705617 6705619 6705649 6705659 6705661 6705697 6705731
6705733 6705749 6705767 6705773 6705779 6705793 6705799 6705817 6705821 6705823
6705851 6705859 6705887 6705899 6705911 6705977 6705997 6706003 6706009 6706019
6706033 6706057 6706067 6706081 6706099 6706103 6706111 6706121 6706129
6706153 6706169 6706181 6706187 6706207 6706223 6706229 6706243 6706253 6706267
6706277 6706303 6706319 6706321 6706327 6706331 6706339 6706351 6706367 6706369
6706379 6706387 6706393 6706397 6706421 6706423 6706459 6706463 6706481 6706519
6706529 6706537 6706543 6706549 6706573 6706591 6706597 6706613 6706621 6706631
6706669 6706681 6706699 6706709 6706727 6706741 6706747 6706751 6706771 6706781
6706793 6706811 6706841 6706849 6706907 6706927 6706939 6706957 6706969 6707017
6707047 6707083 6707087 6707111 6707117 6707119 6707123 6707131 6707137 6707143
6707153 6707159 6707161 6707177 6707201 6707219 6707243 6707263 6707273 6707279
6707291 6707293 6707339 6707357 6707359 6707369 6707387 6707411 6707413 6707429
6707447 6707461 6707483 6707489 6707507 6707531 6707539 6707543 6707549 6707557
6707573 6707581 6707587 6707599 6707629 6707633 6707677 6707681 6707689 6707717
6707731 6707747 6707783 6707801 6707803 6707807 6707819 6707821 6707851 6707863
6707879 6707891 6707917 6707929 6707933 6707947 6707963 6707971 6707993 6707999
6708017 6708061 6708067 6708071 6708089 6708113 6708179 6708181 6708199 6708209
6708227 6708253 6708259 6708271 6708277 6708281 6708283 6708337 6708343 6708347
6708371 6708397 6708409 6708413 6708437 6708439 6708497 6708503 6708517 6708563
6708587 6708589 6708607 6708613 6708619 6708631 6708649 6708661 6708673 6708677
6708701 6708721 6708739 6708749 6708781 6708787 6708791 6708797 6708809 6708823
6708839 6708851 6708853 6708857 6708859 6708869 6708883 6708901 6708907 6708913
6708929 6708937 6708943 6708959 6708967 6708971 6708983 6709009 6709019 6709049
6709057 6709069 6709091 6709093 6709133 6709159 6709163 6709177 6709181 6709187
6709189 6709201 6709253 6709273 6709289 6709309 6709331 6709349 6709369 6709379
6709387 6709397 6709463 6709487 6709501 6709511 6709513 6709519 6709529 6709541
6709553 6709561 6709597 6709607 6709613 6709627 6709631 6709663 6709687 6709693
```

```
6709699  6709711  6709723  6709727  6709751  6709757  6709783  6709789  6709823  6709837
6709841  6709867  6709873  6709877  6709889  6709891  6709921  6709949  6709957  6709961
6709973  6709979  6710009  6710027  6710029  6710047  6710071  6710083  6710153  6710159
6710161  6710191  6710203  6710219  6710243  6710261  6710267  6710269  6710303  6710317
6710321  6710329  6710369  6710371  6710377  6710381  6710399  6710419  6710437  6710441
6710443  6710449  6710471  6710521  6710533  6710567  6710569  6710609  6710617  6710621
6710657  6710667  6710659  6710677  6710723  6710729  6710747  6710761  6710771  6710783
6710791  6710797  6710827  6710833  6710863  6710887  6710897  6710909  6710927  6710929
6710947  6710969  6710983  6711011  6711017  6711031  6711043  6711071  6711077  6711079
6711113  6711119  6711121  6711137  6711149  6711157  6711163  6711169  6711179  6711197
6711217  6711227  6711233  6711241  6711251  6711253  6711301  6711307  6711317  6711343
6711371  6711391  6711421  6711431  6711437  6711449  6711451  6711473  6711491  6711511
6711521  6711533  6711539  6711571  6711581  6711587  6711637  6711641  6711643  6711667
6711671  6711697  6711703  6711707  6711713  6711739  6711749  6711773  6711797  6711811
6711833  6711853  6711863  6711869  6711877  6711937  6711949  6711953  6711967  6711977
6711983  6711989  6712007  6712019  6712033  6712037  6712051  6712061  6712129  6712141
6712193  6712243  6712249  6712259  6712267  6712271  6712283  6712289  6712333  6712351
6712361  6712367  6712373  6712417  6712421  6712441  6712451  6712457  6712463  6712471
6712483  6712487  6712499  6712513  6712579  6712591  6712631  6712639  6712661  6712669
6712697  6712721  6712723  6712729  6712751  6712753  6712787  6712789  6712817  6712831
6712847  6712879  6712903  6712913  6712921  6712933  6712939  6712997  6713017  6713027
6713029  6713039  6713051  6713059  6713087  6713089  6713101  6713107  6713129  6713149
6713173  6713177  6713191  6713219  6713221  6713257  6713261  6713279  6713321  6713323
6713363  6713383  6713389  6713393  6713407  6713417  6713431  6713489  6713491  6713507
6713513  6713533  6713549  6713569  6713573  6713579  6713617  6713647  6713653  6713671
6713683  6713699  6713711  6713717  6713731  6713741  6713747  6713767  6713779  6713789
6713797  6713803  6713851  6713857  6713867  6713899  6713911  6713921  6713923  6713947
6713951  6713969  6713981  6713989  6714007  6714013  6714017  6714041  6714047  6714053
6714067  6714097  6714079  6714107  6714151  6714157  6714161  6714173  6714181  6714187
6714193  6714217  6714221  6714241  6714251  6714263  6714311  6714317  6714319  6714329
6714343  6714349  6714403  6714431  6714443  6714479  6714481  6714497  6714503  6714511
6714523  6714527  6714559  6714563  6714577  6714583  6714599  6714601  6714607  6714637
6714647  6714671  6714679  6714703  6714707  6714709  6714713  6714739  6714787  6714793
6714821  6714823  6714833  6714853  6714893  6714899  6714913  6714931  6714943  6714947
6714977  6714989  6714991  6715001  6715039  6715061  6715067  6715073  6715081  6715087
6715097  6715123  6715129  6715141  6715157  6715171  6715193  6715201  6715217  6715223
6715231  6715249  6715253  6715271  6715273  6715277  6715279  6715297  6715301  6715309
6715337  6715339  6715351  6715367  6715403  6715409  6715421  6715441  6715469  6715481
6715483  6715523  6715567  6715573  6715589  6715627  6715637  6715649  6715679  6715691
6715699  6715717  6715727  6715739  6715769  6715771  6715801  6715811  6715823  6715831
6715837  6715847  6715859  6715861  6715889  6715897  6715903  6715913  6715921  6715937
6715957  6715963  6715967  6715979  6715991  6715993  6715997  6715999  6716009  6716011
6716053  6716077  6716093  6716113  6716117  6716137  6716153  6716191  6716201  6716209
6716221  6716257  6716267  6716287  6716293  6716327  6716363  6716393  6716401  6716417
6716431  6716447  6716453  6716459  6716461  6716477  6716533  6716539  6716551  6716569
6716627  6716639  6716651  6716653  6716681  6716687  6716693  6716701  6716761  6716767
6716791  6716797  6716821  6716837  6716867  6716873  6716891  6716909  6716917  6716923
6716929  6716953  6716977  6716993  6717001  6717031  6717037  6717047  6717077  6717079
6717083  6717101  6717103  6717119  6717131  6717143  6717149  6717169  6717181  6717197
6717223  6717229  6717281  6717301  6717307  6717323  6717341  6717349  6717383  6717391
6717401  6717407  6717413  6717419  6717427  6717433  6717457  6717479  6717493  6717497
6717509  6717517  6717551  6717553  6717577  6717593  6717619  6717629  6717649  6717653
6717671  6717673  6717701  6717709  6717713  6717769  6717787  6717791  6717797  6717829
6717833  6717853  6717859  6717877  6717881  6717899  6717947  6717959  6717961  6718003
6718021  6718031  6718067  6718087  6718099  6718163  6718171  6718193  6718199  6718211
6718223  6718241  6718253  6718259  6718273  6718303  6718319  6718331  6718337  6718339
6718367  6718379  6718391  6718399  6718441  6718447  6718469  6718471  6718477  6718483
6718487  6718489  6718493  6718499  6718541  6718561  6718567  6718573  6718583  6718589
6718667  6718687  6718721  6718727  6718741  6718759  6718763  6718771  6718781  6718787
6718819  6718853  6718889  6718897  6718919  6718937  6718939  6718963  6718997  6719003
6719017  6719077  6719107  6719107  6719113  6719117  6719143  6719149  6719159  6719161
6719177  6719183  6719221  6719231  6719299  6719303  6719327  6719341  6719347  6719353
6719357  6719359  6719371  6719413  6719423  6719441  6719477  6719491  6719501  6719509
6719527  6719563  6719593  6719621  6719623  6719627  6719639  6719693  6719701  6719719
6719729  6719759  6719789  6719809  6719813  6719827  6719837  6719849  6719869  6719873
6719893  6719897  6719917  6719969  6719983  6719989  6720011  6720047  6720059  6720089
6720143  6720157  6720173  6720179  6720191  6720227  6720229  6720239  6720251  6720271
6720283  6720289  6720299  6720323  6720331  6720353  6720361  6720367  6720377  6720383
6720403  6720407  6720409  6720437  6720443  6720473  6720481  6720499  6720503  6720517
6720533  6720553  6720589  6720601  6720607  6720617  6720619  6720629  6720667  6720673
6720683  6720691  6720697  6720719  6720731  6720739  6720743  6720751  6720773  6720811
6720817  6720821  6720823  6720841  6720887  6720911  6720929  6720941  6720947  6721009
6721019  6721051  6721061  6721093  6721109  6721123  6721133  6721147  6721153  6721157
6721159  6721177  6721181  6721189  6721199  6721207  6721213  6721219  6721237  6721259
6721277  6721283  6721289  6721303  6721331  6721333  6721343  6721361  6721367  6721381
6721387  6721411  6721427  6721433  6721439  6721447  6721469  6721483  6721487  6721489
6721501  6721523  6721541  6721549  6721553  6721567  6721571  6721577  6721609  6721661
6721667  6721669  6721691  6721711  6721723  6721733  6721739  6721747  6721751  6721769
6721787  6721789  6721843  6721849  6721859  6721861  6721867  6721879  6721927  6721943
6721951  6721961  6721969  6721973  6721993  6721999  6722039  6722057  6722063  6722069
6722117  6722129  6722137  6722153  6722161  6722173  6722207  6722239  6722263  6722273
6722291  6722321  6722329  6722341  6722377  6722393  6722399  6722411  6722413  6722423
6722473  6722477  6722479  6722537  6722539  6722549  6722557  6722563  6722581  6722587
6722593  6722603  6722623  6722657  6722659  6722669  6722687  6722689  6722717  6722719
6722741  6722743  6722747  6722759  6722761  6722767  6722791  6722797  6722801  6722819
6722839  6722843  6722857  6722861  6722869  6722879  6722899  6722909  6722929  6722957
6722987  6723023  6723037  6723049  6723053  6723071  6723077  6723089  6723091  6723113
6723121  6723127  6723163  6723181  6723193  6723217  6723251  6723257  6723259  6723271
6723289  6723293  6723323  6723329  6723349  6723371  6723403  6723427  6723439  6723443
```

```
6723461  6723499  6723503  6723533  6723539  6723571  6723583  6723589  6723593  6723617
6723623  6723637  6723641  6723643  6723667  6723697  6723709  6723719  6723727  6723733
6723757  6723763  6723767  6723779  6723799  6723803  6723863  6723881  6723901  6723907
6723917  6723949  6723979  6724007  6724013  6724021  6724033  6724037  6724051
6724063  6724093  6724111  6724139  6724169  6724177  6724189  6724219  6724229  6724247
6724253  6724261  6724283  6724301  6724307  6724351  6724357  6724373  6724379  6724387
6724439  6724453  6724463  6724477  6724507  6724511  6724583  6724591  6724603  6724609
6724621  6724631  6724637  6724649  6724709  6724721  6724747  6724759  6724769  6724771
6724789  6724793  6724801  6724829  6724831  6724847  6724853  6724859  6724871  6724873
6724889  6724903  6724931  6724933  6724937  6724951  6724981  6724987  6724999  6725021
6725027  6725051  6725063  6725077  6725093  6725099  6725101  6725113  6725119  6725123
6725141  6725143  6725153  6725161  6725167  6725197  6725219  6725239  6725249  6725261
6725273  6725281  6725309  6725317  6725339  6725347  6725363  6725377  6725399  6725401
6725423  6725429  6725437  6725441  6725443  6725473  6725479  6725491  6725497  6725513
6725519  6725531  6725533  6725549  6725597  6725611  6725633  6725657  6725687  6725717
6725731  6725737  6725743  6725827  6725833  6725839  6725843  6725861  6725879  6725881
6725891  6725899  6725909  6725911  6725923  6725951  6725963  6725969  6725987  6726023
6726053  6726073  6726079  6726107  6726131  6726151  6726157  6726179  6726191  6726221
6726227  6726229  6726233  6726241  6726257  6726299  6726329  6726367  6726383  6726397
6726427  6726431  6726481  6726487  6726493  6726497  6726523  6726529  6726539  6726547
6726571  6726581  6726607  6726623  6726647  6726667  6726689  6726697  6726737  6726739
6726749  6726761  6726763  6726773  6726793  6726799  6726821  6726947  6726949  6726953
6726961  6726989  6726991  6727009  6727013  6727027  6727069  6727073  6727079  6727099
6727139  6727163  6727171  6727181  6727187  6727199  6727207  6727213  6727249  6727267
6727271  6727283  6727297  6727319  6727337  6727351  6727361  6727363  6727379  6727397
6727417  6727423  6727433  6727447  6727481  6727493  6727517  6727519  6727541  6727543
6727547  6727549  6727559  6727579  6727583  6727601  6727603  6727619  6727621  6727657
6727663  6727667  6727703  6727717  6727741  6727769  6727771  6727781  6727783  6727789
6727793  6727811  6727817  6727847  6727867  6727871  6727879  6727927  6727943  6727949
6727967  6727993  6728009  6728011  6728027  6728041  6728047  6728083  6728101  6728123
6728129  6728131  6728149  6728171  6728177  6728179  6728201  6728221  6728231  6728251
6728257  6728273  6728279  6728321  6728327  6728347  6728369  6728383  6728399  6728401
6728437  6728441  6728467  6728503  6728521  6728531  6728539  6728543  6728563  6728569
6728591  6728639  6728653  6728663  6728713  6728723  6728731  6728749  6728759  6728801
6728809  6728833  6728837  6728861  6728873  6728881  6728947  6728963  6728977  6729007
6729017  6729053  6729061  6729083  6729089  6729109  6729137  6729157  6729169  6729193
6729197  6729209  6729223  6729241  6729257  6729259  6729269  6729313  6729329  6729341
6729347  6729361  6729377  6729383  6729389  6729419  6729427  6729461  6729469  6729473
6729487  6729493  6729497  6729509  6729517  6729521  6729533  6729571  6729587  6729589
6729607  6729631  6729643  6729647  6729659  6729661  6729677  6729683  6729691  6729719
6729721  6729727  6729787  6729791  6729799  6729821  6729829  6729847  6729871  6729901
6729911  6729991  6730033  6730037  6730043  6730049  6730051  6730067  6730093  6730121
6730153  6730159  6730177  6730187  6730201  6730211  6730253  6730261  6730271  6730277
6730279  6730289  6730319  6730327  6730331  6730333  6730343  6730357  6730369  6730391
6730463  6730469  6730481  6730483  6730501  6730531  6730547  6730561  6730571  6730583
6730597  6730609  6730613  6730637  6730663  6730667  6730681  6730687  6730699  6730709
6730727  6730771  6730783  6730811  6730849  6730903  6730907  6730909  6730939  6730949
6730951  6730961  6730967  6730979  6730991  6730993  6731009  6731017  6731027  6731029
6731033  6731041  6731047  6731059  6731063  6731069  6731083  6731107  6731113  6731117
6731171  6731183  6731239  6731267  6731273  6731279  6731281  6731311  6731323  6731327
6731363  6731401  6731407  6731437  6731449  6731467  6731471  6731489  6731497  6731537
6731539  6731561  6731563  6731579  6731591  6731597  6731611  6731623  6731633  6731639
6731651  6731657  6731707  6731713  6731717  6731729  6731759  6731773  6731783  6731797
6731821  6731843  6731849  6731869  6731903  6731927  6731941  6731957  6731981  6731993
6732029  6732041  6732059  6732097  6732107  6732127  6732151  6732157  6732163  6732179
6732181  6732191  6732197  6732247  6732269  6732281  6732283  6732293  6732311  6732337
6732343  6732347  6732359  6732373  6732449  6732461  6732469  6732497  6732503  6732511
6732521  6732529  6732541  6732563  6732577  6732589  6732599  6732613  6732619  6732623
6732647  6732659  6732679  6732683  6732689  6732701  6732709  6732751  6732773  6732787
6732793  6732809  6732823  6732827  6732851  6732857  6732889  6732893  6732899  6732907
6732919  6732931  6732937  6732949  6732953  6732967  6733009  6733033  6733073  6733093
6733099  6733109  6733121  6733123  6733127  6733141  6733147  6733151  6733171  6733187
6733193  6733211  6733221  6733229  6733247  6733253  6733261  6733271  6733283  6733289
6733291  6733313  6733351  6733357  6733369  6733379  6733393  6733439  6733453  6733469
6733511  6733579  6733609  6733613  6733627  6733633  6733637  6733663  6733669  6733681
6733709  6733721  6733747  6733777  6733787  6733807  6733813  6733817  6733823  6733841
6733861  6733879  6733891  6733897  6733901  6733907  6733919  6733927  6733957  6733997
6734011  6734017  6734029  6734033  6734047  6734053  6734059  6734069  6734081  6734093
6734141  6734149  6734173  6734179  6734183  6734191  6734213  6734249  6734257  6734267
6734281  6734297  6734309  6734327  6734369  6734381  6734383  6734401  6734443  6734447
6734459  6734477  6734479  6734491  6734503  6734521  6734543  6734573  6734593  6734597
6734599  6734603  6734627  6734633  6734647  6734681  6734713  6734729  6734731  6734753
6734779  6734803  6734813  6734831  6734879  6734881  6734891  6734903  6734921  6734947
6734939  6734951  6734969  6734977  6734993  6735011  6735013  6735017  6735019  6735037
6735049  6735089  6735097  6735107  6735151  6735161  6735173  6735181  6735217  6735229
6735271  6735283  6735301  6735307  6735319  6735341  6735347  6735359  6735373  6735397
6735403  6735413  6735427  6735433  6735467  6735493  6735497  6735503  6735529  6735539
6735571  6735581  6735601  6735613  6735623  6735643  6735647  6735653  6735661  6735667
6735679  6735727  6735731  6735733  6735749  6735761  6735763  6735811  6735829  6735847
6735863  6735871  6735887  6735901  6735913  6735919  6735923  6735943  6735947  6735973
6735977  6736003  6736019  6736027  6736039  6736061  6736069  6736111  6736117  6736123
6736129  6736157  6736189  6736211  6736243  6736253  6736271  6736273  6736283  6736297
6736309  6736333  6736339  6736351  6736361  6736417  6736441  6736451  6736453
6736481  6736487  6736489  6736511  6736519  6736523  6736531  6736537  6736547  6736549
6736603  6736633  6736643  6736663  6736687  6736727  6736733  6736739  6736759  6736771
6736799  6736817  6736819  6736823  6736831  6736837  6736841  6736859  6736897  6736927
6736931  6736943  6736973  6736987  6736991  6737009  6737021  6737057  6737063  6737099
6737123  6737131  6737141  6737147  6737149  6737177  6737207  6737231  6737233  6737239
6737257  6737273  6737299  6737303  6737317  6737327  6737347  6737351  6737371  6737383
```

```
6737411  6737417  6737429  6737443  6737449  6737473  6737503  6737513  6737527  6737531
6737557  6737581  6737611  6737639  6737651  6737659  6737669  6737671  6737677  6737701
6737707  6737719  6737767  6737777  6737789  6737791  6737803  6737807  6737821  6737833
6737839  6737849  6737891  6737893  6737903  6737921  6737953  6737963  6737987  6738007
6738031  6738047  6738059  6738079  6738089  6738091  6738131  6738133  6738139  6738163
6738169  6738187  6738197  6738203  6738223  6738233  6738269  6738301  6738317  6738337
6738349  6738359  6738373  6738383  6738419  6738427  6738451  6738461  6738481  6738491
6738499  6738503  6738533  6738541  6738553  6738623  6738631  6738649  6738689  6738727
6738751  6738757  6738761  6738763  6738799  6738827  6738857  6738877  6738887  6738889
6738899  6738913  6738929  6738943  6738959  6738961  6738971  6738973  6739009  6739037
6739043  6739063  6739067  6739147  6739151  6739153  6739177  6739193  6739199  6739231
6739267  6739273  6739279  6739289  6739297  6739301  6739303  6739309  6739331  6739333
6739363  6739373  6739387  6739409  6739417  6739423  6739451  6739459  6739477  6739487
6739501  6739541  6739543  6739549  6739559  6739573  6739591  6739627  6739643  6739709
6739723  6739751  6739771  6739783  6739793  6739801  6739807  6739877  6739903  6739913
6739921  6739963  6739969  6739979  6739981  6739987  6740021  6740023  6740029  6740077
6740087  6740089  6740099  6740131  6740137  6740141  6740161  6740171  6740183  6740189
6740191  6740197  6740273  6740297  6740341  6740351  6740369  6740387  6740389  6740399
6740407  6740429  6740443  6740471  6740473  6740477  6740491  6740501  6740507
6740519  6740543  6740597  6740647  6740651  6740659  6740707  6740711  6740719  6740737
6740743  6740759  6740761  6740807  6740813  6740819  6740827  6740831  6740843  6740849
6740861  6740869  6740873  6740879  6740897  6740917  6740941  6740969  6740971  6740977
6740989  6740999  6741019  6741023  6741037  6741089  6741101  6741103  6741113  6741151
6741173  6741221  6741223  6741227  6741233  6741263  6741269  6741313  6741337  6741341
6741347  6741373  6741419  6741421  6741431  6741433  6741439  6741443  6741451  6741463
6741481  6741487  6741491  6741533  6741551  6741557  6741563  6741569  6741577  6741587
6741613  6741617  6741619  6741641  6741689  6741701  6741703  6741719  6741767  6741793
6741799  6741853  6741857  6741859  6741869  6741883  6741887  6741899  6741901  6741913
6741929  6741937  6741953  6741961  6741991  6742003  6742017  6742067  6742091  6742117
6742171  6742189  6742193  6742199  6742201  6742213  6742237  6742249  6742259  6742279
6742313  6742349  6742361  6742363  6742369  6742423  6742443  6742441  6742451  6742459
6742481  6742493  6742507  6742517  6742553  6742559  6742577  6742643  6742649  6742651
6742691  6742699  6742709  6742733  6742753  6742763  6742781  6742783  6742807  6742817
6742859  6742889  6742913  6742921  6742951  6742961  6742969  6742997  6743017  6743053
6743059  6743069  6743111  6743129  6743153  6743159  6743161  6743171  6743173  6743189
6743197  6743239  6743249  6743257  6743267  6743273  6743279  6743281  6743291  6743323
6743327  6743333  6743353  6743357  6743369  6743371  6743381  6743431  6743437  6743447
6743449  6743453  6743459  6743491  6743533  6743563  6743579  6743603  6743609  6743629
6743663  6743683  6743687  6743699  6743717  6743729  6743753  6743767  6743777  6743783
6743801  6743809  6743831  6743843  6743851  6743873  6743887  6743923  6743927  6743929
6743941  6743987  6744007  6744013  6744041  6744071  6744079  6744097  6744137  6744139
6744161  6744169  6744181  6744191  6744203  6744209  6744217  6744229  6744233  6744239
6744253  6744263  6744271  6744277  6744289  6744293  6744299  6744301  6744307  6744319
6744347  6744371  6744383  6744389  6744403  6744407  6744431  6744433  6744469  6744473
6744499  6744511  6744523  6744527  6744539  6744557  6744571  6744581  6744583  6744611
6744613  6744653  6744659  6744667  6744757  6744769  6744779  6744781  6744817  6744827
6744847  6744889  6744893  6744901  6744931  6744961  6744967  6744973  6744977  6744979
6745009  6745021  6745027  6745031  6745051  6745061  6745069  6745121  6745129
6745147  6745159  6745169  6745181  6745183  6745199  6745201  6745229  6745231  6745241
6745261  6745267  6745289  6745301  6745307  6745331  6745357  6745369  6745391  6745397
6745421  6745439  6745451  6745457  6745483  6745499  6745511  6745517  6745523  6745553
6745559  6745579  6745597  6745621  6745633  6745643  6745657  6745663  6745667  6745679
6745691  6745709  6745751  6745763  6745801  6745811  6745829  6745841  6745873  6745897
6745903  6745909  6745913  6745919  6745927  6745939  6745943  6745961  6745979  6745997
6746039  6746041  6746053  6746057  6746063  6746101  6746137  6746147  6746171  6746209
6746219  6746231  6746249  6746261  6746281  6746293  6746303  6746339  6746353  6746359
6746371  6746381  6746393  6746401  6746449  6746461  6746471  6746479  6746483  6746503
6746513  6746527  6746533  6746549  6746557  6746581  6746599  6746609  6746611  6746627
6746639  6746651  6746669  6746681  6746683  6746713  6746717  6746723  6746737  6746771
6746777  6746813  6746819  6746849  6746851  6746863  6746903  6746947  6746959  6746963
6746969  6746983  6746989  6747007  6747017  6747019  6747023  6747031  6747043  6747049
6747107  6747127  6747163  6747187  6747193  6747229  6747233  6747239  6747241  6747253
6747263  6747281  6747289  6747331  6747347  6747353  6747359  6747371  6747373  6747379
6747397  6747407  6747421  6747467  6747509  6747511  6747523  6747529  6747541  6747547
6747551  6747557  6747571  6747577  6747581  6747583  6747589  6747599  6747607  6747617
6747619  6747667  6747707  6747721  6747731  6747733  6747761  6747773  6747779  6747781
6747803  6747823  6747833  6747847  6747857  6747877  6747887  6747899  6747953  6747959
6747971  6747973  6747989  6748009  6748043  6748051  6748087  6748117  6748127  6748141
6748151  6748153  6748163  6748187  6748207  6748229  6748253  6748267  6748277  6748279
6748309  6748321  6748327  6748333  6748343  6748351  6748367  6748373  6748381  6748397
6748409  6748411  6748433  6748447  6748451  6748459  6748487  6748493  6748501  6748523
6748529  6748531  6748571  6748583  6748627  6748633  6748639  6748673  6748691  6748771
6748783  6748787  6748789  6748799  6748823  6748849  6748871  6748883  6748897  6748901
6748927  6748939  6748943  6748981  6748999  6749003  6749027  6749033  6749053  6749081
6749087  6749107  6749117  6749129  6749131  6749159  6749173  6749177  6749191  6749203
6749209  6749213  6749261  6749263  6749279  6749291  6749293  6749299  6749321  6749329
6749359  6749371  6749381  6749383  6749399  6749401  6749411  6749437  6749443  6749447
6749531  6749563  6749569  6749593  6749621  6749627  6749657  6749669  6749719
6749747  6749759  6749761  6749767  6749783  6749801  6749803  6749819  6749843  6749861
6749887  6749903  6749917  6749927  6749933  6749947  6749959  6750001  6750019  6750053
6750059  6750067  6750103  6750113  6750167  6750193  6750203  6750209  6750217  6750221
6750223  6750229  6750251  6750253  6750259  6750329  6750397  6750407  6750409  6750413
6750437  6750439  6750461  6750481  6750487  6750511  6750551  6750553  6750559  6750571
6750577  6750593  6750607  6750617  6750631  6750637  6750647  6750659  6750671  6750673
6750701  6750703  6750713  6750727  6750781  6750791  6750797  6750817  6750827
6750829  6750841  6750847  6750851  6750859  6750869  6750907  6750911  6750923  6750943
6750973  6751001  6751009  6751021  6751027  6751037  6751049  6751067  6751079  6751081
6751109  6751111  6751117  6751123  6751153  6751169  6751181  6751189  6751231  6751243
6751253  6751267  6751271  6751291  6751307  6751313  6751337  6751373  6751391  6751399
```

```
6751439  6751453  6751457  6751487  6751513  6751529  6751543  6751553  6751561  6751571
6751573  6751651  6751681  6751687  6751711  6751727  6751729  6751733  6751739  6751747
6751793  6751799  6751813  6751819  6751837  6751847  6751853  6751861  6751883  6751889
6751891  6751909  6751919  6751931  6751933  6751939  6751957  6751963  6751981  6751991
6751993  6752027  6752033  6752063  6752071  6752101  6752117  6752131  6752159  6752173
6752177  6752189  6752191  6752197  6752219  6752231  6752237  6752257  6752279  6752287
6752293  6752297  6752309  6752321  6752329  6752351  6752357  6752377  6752381  6752387
6752393  6752399  6752401  6752407  6752479  6752489  6752503  6752509  6752521  6752533
6752539  6752617  6752623  6752747  6752749  6752789  6752803  6752807  6752813  6752827
6752831  6752857  6752861  6752887  6752891  6752897  6752899  6752909  6752951  6752953
6752957  6753001  6753013  6753031  6753059  6753067  6753077  6753119  6753161  6753169
6753179  6753209  6753251  6753281  6753293  6753311  6753323  6753347  6753349  6753353
6753359  6753389  6753391  6753407  6753413  6753427  6753457  6753469  6753497  6753517
6753521  6753529  6753547  6753563  6753581  6753583  6753589  6753599  6753611  6753613
6753619  6753679  6753707  6753727  6753739  6753757  6753767  6753779  6753821  6753823
6753827  6753829  6753833  6753841  6753847  6753883  6753893  6753917  6753919  6753937
6753941  6753953  6753977  6754009  6754031  6754037  6754039  6754051  6754057  6754073
6754087  6754141  6754147  6754169  6754171  6754183  6754199  6754211  6754213  6754243
6754271  6754283  6754289  6754331  6754339  6754343  6754351  6754357  6754369  6754393
6754409  6754411  6754441  6754453  6754459  6754487  6754493  6754513  6754523  6754537
6754543  6754547  6754549  6754567  6754597  6754603  6754607  6754667  6754669  6754673
6754679  6754681  6754697  6754703  6754721  6754723  6754751  6754771  6754799  6754817
6754829  6754837  6754849  6754871  6754877  6754879  6754889  6754961  6754973  6754987
6754991  6755029  6755039  6755041  6755071  6755081  6755083  6755093  6755107  6755113
6755129  6755143  6755149  6755159  6755167  6755191  6755227  6755237  6755249  6755267
6755269  6755291  6755297  6755299  6755311  6755321  6755351  6755363  6755377  6755381
6755383  6755389  6755401  6755407  6755417  6755449  6755459  6755473  6755503  6755509
6755513  6755519  6755549  6755557  6755561  6755563  6755599  6755603  6755641  6755653
6755657  6755663  6755699  6755713  6755717  6755741  6755761  6755779  6755797  6755821
6755893  6755897  6755909  6755971  6755977  6755981  6755989  6755999  6756017  6756023
6756037  6756053  6756091  6756097  6756131  6756133  6756137  6756161  6756173  6756179
6756199  6756209  6756241  6756251  6756263  6756329  6756331  6756353  6756359  6756367
6756371  6756377  6756397  6756401  6756403  6756413  6756439  6756469  6756479  6756487
6756499  6756511  6756521  6756523  6756539  6756551  6756553  6756557  6756577  6756593
6756611  6756619  6756671  6756679  6756683  6756689  6756691  6756709  6756799  6756817
6756823  6756833  6756847  6756851  6756859  6756863  6756881  6756889  6756899  6756901
6756941  6756961  6756979  6756983  6756991  6757021  6757033  6757057  6757067  6757073
6757133  6757139  6757159  6757181  6757229  6757241  6757243  6757249  6757271  6757277
6757327  6757339  6757343  6757351  6757363  6757367  6757393  6757409  6757427  6757433
6757441  6757451  6757453  6757463  6757477  6757481  6757501  6757507  6757511  6757523
6757529  6757547  6757573  6757589  6757601  6757603  6757627  6757637  6757657  6757669
6757679  6757693  6757759  6757813  6757819  6757843  6757847  6757853  6757867  6757873
6757889  6757913  6757921  6757937  6757951  6757963  6757967  6757973  6757979  6757981
6757987  6758023  6758029  6758039  6758047  6758069  6758077  6758107  6758111  6758117
6758137  6758149  6758179  6758183  6758201  6758207  6758209  6758233  6758237  6758261
6758291  6758293  6758303  6758321  6758351  6758369  6758377  6758407  6758429  6758431
6758447  6758449  6758473  6758483  6758489  6758501  6758513  6758533  6758539  6758567
6758579  6758593  6758659  6758723  6758743  6758747  6758761  6758767  6758771  6758777
6758779  6758821  6758831  6758833  6758839  6758867  6758879  6758881  6758887  6758909
6758923  6758951  6758953  6758957  6758959  6758977  6758989  6759017  6759019  6759029
6759031  6759043  6759061  6759089  6759091  6759101  6759107  6759113  6759119  6759139
6759157  6759167  6759187  6759191  6759229  6759239  6759241  6759257  6759281  6759317
6759341  6759343  6759359  6759367  6759371  6759377  6759397  6759427  6759449  6759451
6759463  6759479  6759481  6759491  6759499  6759503  6759517  6759527  6759551  6759569
6759583  6759589  6759601  6759619  6759647  6759667  6759671  6759679  6759691  6759703
6759707  6759713  6759743  6759811  6759821  6759847  6759887  6759889  6759899  6759911
6759917  6759943  6759947  6759967  6759971  6759979  6759983  6759989  6760001  6760003
6760007  6760009  6760037  6760051  6760079  6760093  6760111  6760129  6760133  6760141
6760147  6760157  6760163  6760177  6760189  6760213  6760217  6760231  6760241  6760249
6760253  6760261  6760283  6760319  6760343  6760357  6760363  6760379  6760399  6760423
6760427  6760471  6760477  6760483  6760489  6760493  6760499  6760541  6760547  6760553
6760619  6760639  6760669  6760687  6760693  6760703  6760711  6760717  6760727  6760753
6760771  6760783  6760789  6760801  6760807  6760841  6760861  6760867  6760889  6760907
6760909  6760921  6760937  6760939  6760969  6760991  6761003  6761033  6761059  6761101
6761107  6761123  6761143  6761159  6761197  6761203  6761213  6761219  6761223  6761233
6761239  6761273  6761281  6761299  6761311  6761323  6761347  6761387  6761399  6761407
6761411  6761453  6761477  6761483  6761497  6761527  6761537  6761539  6761551  6761567
6761569  6761603  6761633  6761699  6761717  6761723  6761759  6761779  6761803  6761819
6761873  6761897  6761921  6761939  6761941  6761947  6761957  6761981  6761983  6762001
6762011  6762013  6762071  6762097  6762113  6762121  6762127  6762139  6762143  6762147
6762149  6762169  6762179  6762181  6762221  6762257  6762269  6762317  6762319  6762337
6762361  6762367  6762373  6762439  6762443  6762449  6762463  6762467  6762473  6762491
6762517  6762533  6762541  6762551  6762559  6762571  6762607  6762611  6762629  6762649
6762673  6762677  6762697  6762751  6762773  6762797  6762839  6762871  6762881  6762883
6762893  6762901  6762941  6762949  6762979  6763013  6763037  6763039  6763049  6763063
6763067  6763087  6763129  6763147  6763153  6763189  6763213  6763217  6763223  6763241
6763243  6763249  6763261  6763283  6763303  6763307  6763313  6763321  6763343  6763349
6763369  6763381  6763387  6763423  6763429  6763447  6763451  6763453  6763459  6763481
6763507  6763511  6763573  6763579  6763591  6763597  6763607  6763613  6763621  6763649
6763657  6763663  6763681  6763693  6763709  6763721  6763747  6763751  6763759  6763763
6763769  6763787  6763793  6763831  6763837  6763847  6763849  6763853  6763871  6763877
6763891  6763903  6763931  6763987  6763993  6763999  6764003  6764039  6764041  6764053
6764077  6764083  6764111  6764137  6764161  6764179  6764183  6764189  6764227  6764239
6764281  6764299  6764309  6764311  6764327  6764333  6764339  6764341  6764353  6764357
6764371  6764393  6764411  6764441  6764477  6764503  6764531  6764551  6764557  6764567
6764573  6764579  6764581  6764587  6764591  6764621  6764633  6764671  6764707  6764711
6764729  6764753  6764767  6764773  6764777  6764831  6764833  6764873  6764887  6764897
6764899  6764903  6764939  6764941  6764977  6764981  6764993  6765019  6765023  6765067
6765089  6765103  6765107  6765113  6765127  6765131  6765139  6765169  6765173  6765179
```

```
6765181 6765211 6765217 6765221 6765257 6765263 6765299 6765301 6765307 6765329
6765361 6765379 6765389 6765391 6765401 6765419 6765431 6765433 6765443 6765461
6765467 6765523 6765527 6765553 6765559 6765569 6765587 6765607 6765617 6765623
6765631 6765673 6765683 6765743 6765751 6765763 6765769 6765799 6765809 6765817
6765823 6765893 6765901 6765917 6765923 6765929 6765947 6765959 6765977 6765991
6766003 6766027 6766031 6766037 6766049 6766127 6766141 6766169 6766171 6766183
6766211 6766217 6766219 6766231 6766237 6766241 6766259 6766267 6766273 6766283
6766313 6766321 6766369 6766399 6766411 6766423 6766447 6766469 6766477 6766499
6766511 6766519 6766579 6766583 6766601 6766607 6766631 6766661 6766691 6766699
6766703 6766751 6766757 6766777 6766789 6766801 6766811 6766843 6766861 6766871
6766883 6766891 6766909 6766931 6766943 6766951 6766979 6767017 6767029 6767051
6767053 6767069 6767119 6767143 6767153 6767161 6767177 6767191 6767197 6767213
6767251 6767273 6767281 6767291 6767311 6767317 6767333 6767347 6767351 6767417
6767437 6767447 6767461 6767489 6767491 6767531 6767533 6767557 6767561 6767567
6767569 6767599 6767609 6767639 6767647 6767653 6767687 6767689 6767731 6767741
6767749 6767753 6767797 6767801 6767807 6767837 6767843 6767863 6767867 6767869
6767881 6767897 6767927 6767963 6767977 6767983 6768001 6768029 6768043 6768053
6768079 6768089 6768109 6768127 6768131 6768149 6768163 6768191 6768197 6768221
6768257 6768263 6768269 6768271 6768277 6768283 6768337 6768353 6768367 6768383
6768409 6768413 6768449 6768469 6768473 6768481 6768491 6768493 6768523 6768547
6768557 6768569 6768583 6768589 6768607 6768631 6768637 6768653 6768659 6768661
6768667 6768679 6768689 6768691 6768701 6768709 6768721 6768761 6768781 6768793
6768821 6768829 6768833 6768859 6768887 6768889 6768911 6768917 6768947 6768961
6768991 6769003 6769013 6769019 6769051 6769079 6769099 6769127 6769157 6769171
6769177 6769181 6769193 6769201 6769229 6769237 6769241 6769271 6769277 6769283
6769289 6769297 6769303 6769313 6769327 6769331 6769351 6769379 6769391 6769403
6769421 6769423 6769459 6769463 6769471 6769487 6769489 6769547 6769549 6769559
6769579 6769583 6769591 6769639 6769649 6769661 6769669 6769691 6769699 6769703
6769733 6769759 6769769 6769771 6769793 6769799 6769813 6769817 6769831 6769897
6769901 6769913 6769937 6769951 6769957 6769969 6769991 6770011 6770033 6770039
6770047 6770053 6770069 6770081 6770089 6770111 6770117 6770123 6770143 6770161
6770173 6770189 6770201 6770237 6770249 6770279 6770287 6770321 6770353 6770359
6770363 6770383 6770389 6770419 6770429 6770447 6770459 6770501 6770507 6770509
6770527 6770549 6770557 6770563 6770581 6770587 6770597 6770609 6770611 6770653
6770657 6770683 6770713 6770719 6770723 6770767 6770789 6770801 6770807 6770837
6770839 6770851 6770861 6770873 6770887 6770903 6770921 6770941 6770977 6770987
6771001 6771041 6771059 6771071 6771077 6771091 6771097 6771101 6771103 6771119
6771137 6771139 6771143 6771161 6771173 6771187 6771197 6771203 6771211 6771217
6771251 6771263 6771283 6771307 6771311 6771319 6771367 6771379 6771383 6771397
6771409 6771419 6771421 6771451 6771469 6771487 6771493 6771533 6771539 6771551
6771563 6771571 6771577 6771631 6771641 6771649 6771673 6771689 6771701 6771707
6771719 6771799 6771803 6771871 6771883 6771911 6771917 6771937 6771943 6771953
6771971 6771979 6772013 6772033 6772039 6772049 6772063 6772067 6772081 6772121
6772123 6772127 6772133 6772163 6772201 6772211 6772223 6772237 6772243 6772309
6772313 6772319 6772333 6772343 6772357 6772387 6772391 6772397 6772411 6772459
6772463 6772471 6772481 6772483 6772537 6772541 6772547 6772609 6772643 6772651
6772657 6772673 6772679 6772687 6772691 6772697 6772723 6772729 6772751 6772763
6772771 6772789 6772793 6772819 6772837 6772853 6772859 6772897 6772929 6772939
6772951 6772967 6772981 6772991 6773003 6773033 6773047 6773069 6773083 6773087
6773099 6773111 6773131 6773147 6773149 6773171 6773189 6773203 6773209 6773213
6773237 6773243 6773251 6773279 6773287 6773297 6773303 6773329 6773357 6773359
6773387 6773401 6773411 6773423 6773441 6773467 6773483 6773491 6773509 6773527
6773537 6773539 6773551 6773567 6773579 6773581 6773603 6773621 6773629 6773639
6773647 6773659 6773681 6773729 6773783 6773797 6773807 6773821 6773827 6773843
6773857 6773863 6773869 6773881 6773911 6773917 6773929 6773941 6773951 6773953
6773959 6773999 6774017 6774059 6774073 6774077 6774083 6774101 6774133 6774149
6774179 6774191 6774217 6774221 6774223 6774247 6774289 6774319 6774331 6774343
6774353 6774379 6774389 6774401 6774409 6774421 6774433 6774451 6774457 6774479
6774503 6774527 6774529 6774539 6774541 6774587 6774601 6774623 6774631 6774637
6774643 6774671 6774683 6774731 6774743 6774763 6774767 6774797 6774809 6774821
6774827 6774829 6774871 6774877 6774883 6774899 6774931 6774941 6774953 6774983
6774991 6774997 6775007 6775051 6775063 6775099 6775117 6775121 6775157 6775169
6775177 6775193 6775201 6775211 6775217 6775247 6775253 6775261 6775273 6775337
6775369 6775387 6775393 6775399 6775427 6775429 6775441 6775463 6775471 6775493
6775513 6775519 6775529 6775541 6775579 6775583 6775591 6775603 6775607 6775627
6775633 6775663 6775667 6775693 6775709 6775721 6775733 6775781 6775801 6775807
6775817 6775829 6775861 6775919 6775927 6775931 6775969 6775981 6775987 6776009
6776023 6776039 6776041 6776051 6776087 6776089 6776101 6776111 6776117 6776123
6776153 6776167 6776171 6776173 6776207 6776233 6776243 6776249 6776257 6776269
6776279 6776281 6776303 6776333 6776347 6776351 6776413 6776449 6776461 6776477
6776479 6776491 6776501 6776503 6776519 6776537 6776543 6776573 6776599 6776611
6776617 6776621 6776629 6776641 6776677 6776683 6776689 6776713 6776717 6776741
6776753 6776771 6776773 6776779 6776813 6776873 6776879 6776911 6776921 6776933
6776947 6776963 6776969 6776971 6777007 6777011 6777041 6777047 6777049 6777061
6777073 6777079 6777101 6777103 6777137 6777149 6777151 6777181 6777191 6777217
6777227 6777229 6777241 6777263 6777289 6777299 6777307 6777317 6777349 6777367
6777413 6777443 6777451 6777461 6777467 6777469 6777493 6777497 6777517 6777521
6777559 6777569 6777583 6777599 6777601 6777607 6777613 6777629 6777637 6777691
6777707 6777733 6777739 6777769 6777803 6777811 6777829 6777839 6777923 6777931
6777943 6777949 6777959 6777971 6777989 6778021 6778027 6778033 6778039 6778043
6778049 6778061 6778063 6778073 6778099 6778111 6778127 6778147 6778153 6778183
6778201 6778207 6778217 6778229 6778237 6778241 6778249 6778267 6778271 6778273
6778283 6778297 6778301 6778319 6778331 6778351 6778373 6778397 6778403 6778417
6778423 6778433 6778439 6778463 6778469 6778483 6778517 6778543 6778559 6778567
6778579 6778589 6778621 6778631 6778643 6778661 6778691 6778703 6778727 6778741
6778769 6778777 6778799 6778823 6778829 6778831 6778841 6778861 6778921 6778927
6778939 6778943 6778949 6778963 6778973 6779023 6779027 6779033 6779093 6779099
6779131 6779147 6779153 6779161 6779183 6779189 6779197 6779203 6779207 6779231
6779239 6779249 6779281 6779299 6779303 6779321 6779323 6779347 6779393 6779441
```

```
6779449 6779453 6779459 6779467 6779491 6779497 6779501 6779519 6779537 6779557
6779567 6779581 6779587 6779611 6779629 6779639 6779653 6779657 6779671 6779683
6779693 6779711 6779743 6779771 6779777 6779783 6779791 6779803 6779807 6779833
6779837 6779849 6779863 6779911 6779921 6779951 6779953 6779987 6779999 6780013
6780019 6780031 6780049 6780073 6780077 6780083 6780097 6780119 6780133 6780143
6780157 6780217 6780223 6780233 6780247 6780251 6780253 6780259 6780271 6780299
6780307 6780317 6780329 6780379 6780383 6780407 6780419 6780421 6780427 6780439
6780443 6780463 6780479 6780481 6780503 6780517 6780551 6780581 6780611 6780619
6780623 6780629 6780679 6780707 6780743 6780757 6780769 6780817 6780827 6780833
6780857 6780859 6780863 6780871 6780881 6780901 6780913 6780931 6780941 6780959
6780973 6780989 6781007 6781009 6781013 6781037 6781051 6781063 6781087 6781091
6781097 6781109 6781111 6781121 6781127 6781129 6781133 6781141 6781153 6781163
6781169 6781193 6781223 6781231 6781253 6781303 6781319 6781321 6781337 6781381
6781387 6781391 6781399 6781409 6781433 6781457 6781493 6781501 6781531 6781543
6781547 6781549 6781559 6781603 6781609 6781633 6781661 6781667 6781699 6781729
6781763 6781799 6781813 6781823 6781843 6781867 6781891 6781897 6781939 6781961
6781967 6782021 6782029 6782051 6782057 6782059 6782077 6782081 6782093 6782123
6782129 6782159 6782177 6782197 6782231 6782239 6782249 6782257 6782287 6782291
6782299 6782311 6782329 6782333 6782339 6782351 6782381 6782431 6782437 6782441
6782443 6782509 6782543 6782561 6782579 6782597 6782603 6782621 6782627 6782641
6782663 6782669 6782683 6782687 6782717 6782719 6782749 6782759 6782761 6782767
6782771 6782801 6782807 6782821 6782827 6782833 6782869 6782903 6782911 6782921
6782929 6782933 6782939 6782959 6782969 6782977 6783011 6783031 6783047 6783067
6783083 6783089 6783097 6783107 6783131 6783143 6783149 6783151 6783169 6783193
6783211 6783223 6783239 6783241 6783253 6783263 6783299 6783317 6783331 6783353
6783421 6783433 6783449 6783457 6783461 6783467 6783481 6783521 6783529 6783533
6783583 6783607 6783611 6783613 6783619 6783641 6783653 6783661 6783677 6783701
6783713 6783719 6783727 6783739 6783743 6783769 6783773 6783787 6783797 6783853
6783857 6783859 6783869 6783889 6783877 6783929 6783937 6783949 6783971
6783991 6784013 6784021 6784033 6784039 6784049 6784073 6784081 6784087 6784091
6784093 6784111 6784123 6784157 6784163 6784177 6784189 6784199 6784201 6784243
6784247 6784249 6784259 6784291 6784303 6784313 6784321 6784361 6784363 6784373
6784399 6784409 6784429 6784433 6784447 6784457 6784489 6784499 6784523 6784573
6784597 6784601 6784619 6784627 6784643 6784667 6784697 6784699 6784703 6784711
6784733 6784769 6784777 6784783 6784787 6784807 6784849 6784871 6784907 6784913
6784933 6784937 6784961 6784997 6785003 6785017 6785021 6785029 6785039 6785047
6785081 6785111 6785117 6785173 6785179 6785183 6785189 6785197 6785209 6785263
6785269 6785279 6785287 6785293 6785341 6785347 6785351 6785369 6785417 6785419
6785453 6785461 6785463 6785477 6785501 6785503 6785539 6785557 6785561 6785573
6785591 6785593 6785599 6785617 6785629 6785651 6785671 6785707 6785729 6785731
6785741 6785761 6785773 6785783 6785791 6785843 6785893 6785899 6785917 6785923
6785929 6785939 6785953 6785963 6785969 6786037 6786041 6786049 6786053 6786061
6786083 6786103 6786107 6786137 6786139 6786149 6786181 6786187 6786209 6786253
6786257 6786259 6786277 6786293 6786323 6786341 6786347 6786359 6786371 6786391
6786407 6786413 6786457 6786467 6786469 6786473 6786509 6786511 6786529 6786539
6786547 6786557 6786581 6786589 6786643 6786649 6786683 6786691 6786707 6786709
6786719 6786721 6786727 6786749 6786751 6786761 6786797 6786821 6786833 6786839
6786869 6786877 6786887 6786889 6786917 6786919 6786929 6786937 6786943 6787019
6787031 6787037 6787049 6787061 6787069 6787087 6787091 6787133 6787141 6787147
6787211 6787213 6787273 6787279 6787289 6787343 6787349 6787367 6787393 6787399
6787439 6787441 6787453 6787457 6787493 6787499 6787507 6787513 6787519 6787577
6787589 6787603 6787609 6787619 6787631 6787633 6787637 6787639 6787643 6787663
6787709 6787717 6787721 6787733 6787741 6787747 6787751 6787771 6787799 6787801
6787841 6787849 6787867 6787871 6787873 6787889 6787901 6787933 6787951 6787961
6788021 6788053 6788063 6788087 6788099 6788107 6788123 6788129 6788137 6788143
6788147 6788153 6788179 6788183 6788207 6788237 6788251 6788267 6788273 6788323
6788333 6788357 6788387 6788393 6788413 6788417 6788429 6788437 6788443 6788447
6788459 6788469 6788477 6788521 6788527 6788557 6788563 6788569 6788591 6788609
6788609 6788647 6788651 6788669 6788687 6788689 6788699 6788731 6788737 6788741
6788759 6788773 6788777 6788801 6788839 6788861 6788863 6788869 6788879 6788891
6788897 6788911 6788939 6788959 6788963 6788981 6788983 6788989 6789037
6789047 6789059 6789077 6789089 6789121 6789143 6789157 6789191 6789199 6789203
6789269 6789281 6789287 6789319 6789323 6789359 6789371 6789373 6789383 6789397
6789401 6789407 6789421 6789427 6789469 6789473 6789481 6789493 6789499 6789521
6789529 6789553 6789557 6789617 6789619 6789637 6789701 6789737 6789763 6789773
6789793 6789901 6789929 6789931 6789941 6789947 6789967 6789977 6789983 6790009
6790033 6790067 6790073 6790081 6790099 6790111 6790141 6790153 6790159 6790169
6790171 6790181 6790183 6790187 6790219 6790237 6790247 6790253 6790261 6790349
6790363 6790409 6790411 6790471 6790501 6790523 6790529 6790549 6790559 6790561
6790571 6790579 6790583 6790631 6790649 6790691 6790697 6790717 6790741 6790753
6790759 6790793 6790799 6790801 6790807 6790831 6790853 6790859 6790867 6790871
6790879 6790897 6790913 6790921 6790933 6790951 6790963 6790981 6790997 6791009
6791101 6791103 6791107 6791111 6791149 6791207 6791219 6791231 6791237 6791287
6791297 6791299 6791311 6791333 6791353 6791383 6791399 6791429 6791437 6791441
6791459 6791467 6791471 6791503 6791513 6791537 6791563 6791567 6791591 6791593
6791599 6791623 6791677 6791689 6791699 6791711 6791731 6791753 6791767 6791777
6791779 6791783 6791803 6791819 6791861 6791881 6791933 6791963 6791971 6791999
6792001 6792011 6792013 6792083 6792089 6792143 6792157 6792161 6792169 6792171
6792187 6792209 6792211 6792217 6792221 6792223 6792239 6792241 6792251 6792271
6792281 6792307 6792311 6792331 6792337 6792397 6792403 6792407 6792419 6792421
6792437 6792449 6792473 6792491 6792509 6792517 6792529 6792547 6792559 6792601
6792607 6792629 6792631 6792679 6792691 6792697 6792701 6792727 6792733 6792739
6792763 6792781 6792811 6792829 6792857 6792859 6792881 6792883 6792893 6792901
6792917 6792923 6792943 6792949 6792959 6792967 6792977 6792983 6792997 6793001
6793019 6793019 6793043 6793093 6793099 6793117 6793121 6793133 6793141 6793147
6793153 6793177 6793181 6793223 6793231 6793243 6793253 6793261 6793273 6793277
6793321 6793343 6793363 6793373 6793379 6793399 6793403 6793411 6793417 6793463
6793477 6793481 6793483 6793499 6793517 6793531 6793541 6793543 6793559 6793561
6793573 6793609 6793649 6793651 6793663 6793667 6793669 6793687 6793691 6793711
```

```
6793723  6793739  6793771  6793781  6793807  6793837  6793841  6793847  6793873  6793877
6793951  6793961  6793973  6794023  6794063  6794071  6794089  6794093  6794107  6794111
6794113  6794173  6794209  6794213  6794231  6794243  6794279  6794311  6794317  6794327
6794341  6794357  6794369  6794401  6794413  6794423  6794449  6794467  6794471  6794477
6794483  6794503  6794507  6794521  6794539  6794551  6794597  6794633  6794639  6794651
6794657  6794687  6794693  6794699  6794701  6794707  6794719  6794741  6794773  6794779
6794813  6794819  6794857  6794863  6794873  6794891  6794899  6794911  6794927  6794929
6794933  6794987  6794993  6794999  6795001  6795007  6795011  6795023  6795031  6795037
6795043  6795067  6795071  6795079  6795083  6795137  6795157  6795163  6795199  6795203
6795211  6795221  6795227  6795233  6795259  6795263  6795277  6795311  6795391  6795413
6795421  6795433  6795469  6795491  6795493  6795499  6795527  6795533  6795539  6795553
6795587  6795617  6795619  6795629  6795637  6795647  6795667  6795671  6795689  6795697
6795703  6795721  6795751  6795757  6795779  6795781  6795793  6795821  6795829  6795847
6795853  6795857  6795883  6795941  6795953  6795967  6795983  6795989  6795991  6796067
6796087  6796103  6796117  6796147  6796157  6796171  6796177  6796187  6796199  6796213
6796241  6796261  6796297  6796313  6796393  6796417  6796421  6796429  6796453  6796457
6796463  6796487  6796507  6796511  6796541  6796553  6796571  6796577  6796591  6796597
6796631  6796633  6796637  6796639  6796649  6796679  6796703  6796711  6796729  6796763
6796771  6796819  6796831  6796847  6796849  6796861  6796871  6796877  6796883  6796919
6796931  6796969  6796973  6796987  6797009  6797017  6797023  6797027  6797033  6797051
6797057  6797069  6797111  6797123  6797129  6797137  6797143  6797173  6797177  6797201
6797209  6797221  6797227  6797237  6797251  6797257  6797261  6797293  6797299  6797317
6797321  6797333  6797347  6797353  6797363  6797369  6797387  6797419  6797423  6797429
6797447  6797477  6797503  6797507  6797509  6797533  6797537  6797543  6797551  6797561
6797579  6797591  6797639  6797647  6797669  6797683  6797701  6797729  6797737  6797743
6797767  6797809  6797821  6797849  6797863  6797873  6797891  6797927  6797933  6797951
6797957  6797963  6797981  6797993  6798017  6798019  6798049  6798053  6798059  6798089
6798097  6798101  6798107  6798131  6798137  6798139  6798161  6798167  6798191  6798199
6798203  6798223  6798227  6798247  6798293  6798299  6798313  6798329  6798347  6798349
6798353  6798359  6798373  6798377  6798391  6798397  6798401  6798413  6798431  6798433
6798457  6798527  6798551  6798607  6798611  6798619  6798643  6798647  6798653  6798679
6798683  6798689  6798697  6798719  6798739  6798761  6798763  6798797  6798809  6798817
6798821  6798829  6798853  6798863  6798901  6798917  6798923  6798931  6798937  6798947
6798949  6798971  6798991  6799003  6799033  6799043  6799049  6799057  6799069  6799081
6799103  6799109  6799123  6799127  6799139  6799141  6799151  6799159  6799181  6799183
6799189  6799223  6799249  6799267  6799291  6799297  6799301  6799313  6799327  6799343
6799363  6799367  6799391  6799433  6799459  6799469  6799477  6799483  6799489  6799501
6799517  6799561  6799579  6799589  6799591  6799613  6799619  6799621  6799657  6799669
6799679  6799687  6799699  6799729  6799753  6799759  6799769  6799781  6799783  6799799
6799801  6799811  6799831  6799861  6799889  6799901  6799907  6799921  6799937  6799979
6799993  6799999  6800033  6800047  6800069  6800071  6800077  6800089  6800093  6800099
6800113  6800117  6800147  6800161  6800177  6800191  6800201  6800231  6800251  6800257
6800279  6800291  6800293  6800317  6800329  6800333  6800359  6800393  6800411  6800419
6800429  6800441  6800473  6800491  6800503  6800513  6800531  6800533  6800581  6800609
6800621  6800623  6800639  6800641  6800653  6800657  6800669  6800671  6800683  6800699
6800719  6800737  6800743  6800777  6800791  6800809  6800821  6800839  6800861  6800869
6800891  6800903  6800929  6800999  6801001  6801023  6801049  6801061  6801079  6801089
6801101  6801143  6801187  6801199  6801211  6801217  6801227  6801247  6801253  6801271
6801281  6801299  6801313  6801329  6801383  6801391  6801401  6801407  6801433  6801467
6801499  6801521  6801523  6801541  6801551  6801559  6801577  6801607  6801637  6801653
6801703  6801713  6801717  6801731  6801733  6801757  6801761  6801763  6801779  6801787
6801797  6801833  6801877  6801889  6801919  6801923  6801937  6801947  6801953  6801959
6801961  6802001  6802011  6802027  6802031  6802039  6802063  6802093  6802111  6802121
6802123  6802129  6802139  6802141  6802157  6802177  6802183  6802189  6802207  6802217
6802219  6802231  6802259  6802267  6802277  6802283  6802291  6802307  6802321  6802331
6802337  6802343  6802373  6802379  6802409  6802427  6802441  6802447  6802459  6802469
6802483  6802493  6802507  6802511  6802519  6802529  6802541  6802553  6802571  6802573
6802583  6802591  6802613  6802619  6802633  6802637  6802667  6802673  6802681  6802693
6802721  6802727  6802751  6802753  6802777  6802787  6802793  6802801  6802819  6802823
6802837  6802883  6802891  6802909  6802937  6802949  6802951  6802993  6802997  6803011
6803033  6803051  6803053  6803059  6803063  6803099  6803107  6803117  6803119  6803129
6803141  6803143  6803161  6803177  6803201  6803207  6803219  6803233  6803257  6803287
6803323  6803327  6803339  6803347  6803351  6803399  6803411  6803431  6803437  6803441
6803471  6803473  6803491  6803497  6803509  6803521  6803543  6803551  6803591  6803623
6803669  6803683  6803701  6803711  6803743  6803773  6803801  6803807  6803851  6803869
6803887  6803891  6803903  6803941  6803947  6803977  6803983  6803987  6804011  6804013
6804043  6804047  6804059  6804079  6804089  6804103  6804121  6804137  6804163  6804173
6804209  6804227  6804253  6804287  6804311  6804313  6804341  6804353  6804361  6804487
6804373  6804377  6804397  6804409  6804419  6804431  6804433  6804443  6804463  6804487
6804491  6804493  6804503  6804509  6804517  6804557  6804563  6804571  6804583  6804649
6804661  6804683  6804689  6804697  6804701  6804727  6804739  6804751  6804767  6804797
6804799  6804839  6804857  6804859  6804871  6804887  6804899  6804911  6804943  6804949
6804953  6804997  6805013  6805037  6805061  6805063  6805069  6805109  6805121  6805157
6805159  6805163  6805181  6805243  6805273  6805283  6805289  6805327  6805333  6805339
6805349  6805367  6805369  6805397  6805411  6805427  6805429  6805433  6805441  6805453
6805471  6805483  6805489  6805499  6805501  6805507  6805529  6805537  6805541  6805543
6805573  6805577  6805597  6805607  6805609  6805619  6805621  6805639  6805649  6805663
6805679  6805681  6805693  6805699  6805727  6805753  6805787  6805789  6805829  6805853
6805871  6805879  6805913  6805937  6805943  6805987  6805991  6806017  6806021  6806027
6806029  6806053  6806071  6806077  6806099  6806111  6806147  6806179  6806201  6806203
6806221  6806231  6806243  6806251  6806257  6806263  6806311  6806279  6806309  6806357
6806363  6806381  6806383  6806407  6806411  6806431  6806467  6806473  6806479  6806509
6806521  6806537  6806539  6806543  6806573  6806603  6806609  6806621  6806633  6806651
6806669  6806671  6806687  6806711  6806729  6806743  6806777  6806791  6806797  6806801
6806803  6806833  6806867  6806893  6806903  6806923  6806939  6806957  6806971
6806977  6806981  6806993  6807013  6807061  6807067  6807077  6807091  6807121  6807127
6807131  6807137  6807139  6807181  6807217  6807221  6807239  6807253  6807277  6807313
6807319  6807329  6807331  6807337  6807341  6807347  6807349  6807389  6807391  6807397
6807407  6807419  6807457  6807467  6807473  6807499  6807511  6807523  6807571  6807589
```

514

```
6807601 6807607 6807613 6807629 6807637 6807641 6807649 6807653 6807659 6807683
6807707 6807709 6807727 6807733 6807739 6807767 6807781 6807799 6807821 6807841
6807847 6807863 6807869 6807883 6807887 6807901 6807919 6807923 6807961 6807971
6807979 6808001 6808013 6808019 6808049 6808057 6808073 6808079 6808093 6808097
6808103 6808159 6808171 6808181 6808223 6808229 6808237 6808247 6808267 6808273
6808397 6808409 6808421 6808427 6808429 6808447 6808471 6808519 6808523 6808531
6808537 6808547 6808559 6808601 6808603 6808639 6808643 6808651 6808667 6808699
6808709 6808717 6808733 6808787 6808793 6808801 6808811 6808817 6808861 6808873
6808883 6808889 6808909 6808913 6808927 6808969 6808979 6809029 6809063 6809137
6809141 6809149 6809167 6809189 6809191 6809203 6809207 6809213 6809251 6809261
6809279 6809323 6809347 6809371 6809377 6809389 6809393 6809423 6809459 6809483
6809507 6809527 6809531 6809533 6809549 6809597 6809611 6809617 6809629 6809641
6809653 6809669 6809683 6809687 6809701 6809713 6809717 6809743 6809753 6809767
6809779 6809797 6809807 6809833 6809849 6809851 6809893 6809899 6809899 6809903
6809921 6809927 6809981 6809989 6810019 6810029 6810043 6810053 6810071 6810073
6810091 6810103 6810119 6810131 6810143 6810161 6810169 6810179 6810187 6810203
6810247 6810263 6810269 6810281 6810289 6810299 6810301 6810313 6810337 6810367
6810371 6810373 6810403 6810409 6810431 6810437 6810449 6810451 6810457 6810473
6810481 6810497 6810509 6810527 6810539 6810541 6810571 6810577 6810613 6810631
6810653 6810673 6810677 6810703 6810707 6810719 6810743 6810763 6810767 6810773
6810779 6810799 6810803 6810809 6810841 6810877 6810893 6810907 6810913 6810919
6810943 6810983 6810989 6811003 6811031 6811037 6811061 6811069 6811073 6811097
6811109 6811111 6811117 6811121 6811127 6811141 6811213 6811223 6811247 6811249
6811267 6811279 6811303 6811309 6811313 6811319 6811327 6811331 6811333 6811361
6811369 6811393 6811397 6811403 6811423 6811439 6811451 6811457 6811463 6811471
6811477 6811489 6811517 6811579 6811583 6811591 6811601 6811603 6811619 6811621
6811627 6811639 6811667 6811681 6811697 6811729 6811733 6811741 6811751 6811789
6811799 6811801 6811813 6811829 6811843 6811853 6811867 6811873 6811877 6811879
6811891 6811913 6811919 6811921 6811939 6811943 6811949 6811967 6811993 6811997
6812009 6812021 6812077 6812161 6812167 6812171 6812177 6812207 6812231 6812233
6812339 6812341 6812353 6812363 6812371 6812381 6812383 6812401 6812411 6812413
6812417 6812441 6812453 6812459 6812471 6812479 6812483 6812513 6812527 6812537
6812539 6812549 6812573 6812581 6812629 6812633 6812693 6812711 6812719 6812731
6812759 6812783 6812803 6812809 6812821 6812833 6812837 6812857 6812867 6812879
6812891 6812909 6812933 6812957 6812959 6812983 6812987 6813007 6813013 6813031
6813041 6813061 6813071 6813091 6813101 6813113 6813127 6813137 6813139 6813181
6813193 6813199 6813227 6813239 6813269 6813293 6813299 6813349 6813353 6813361
6813371 6813403 6813409 6813473 6813487 6813491 6813509 6813511 6813529 6813539
6813559 6813577 6813581 6813593 6813613 6813629 6813649 6813659 6813673 6813683
6813689 6813691 6813701 6813713 6813739 6813797 6813817 6813847 6813853 6813857
6813881 6813887 6813899 6813901 6813943 6813949 6813973 6813977 6814001 6814009
6814019 6814021 6814037 6814057 6814061 6814063 6814069 6814091 6814097 6814099
6814117 6814123 6814133 6814139 6814147 6814151 6814183 6814189 6814219 6814231
6814237 6814259 6814261 6814267 6814273 6814277 6814289 6814309 6814343 6814361
6814363 6814373 6814387 6814393 6814397 6814411 6814429 6814453 6814459 6814519
6814523 6814537 6814543 6814547 6814553 6814573 6814579 6814609 6814627 6814631
6814649 6814663 6814679 6814729 6814741 6814763 6814783 6814849 6814853 6814861
6814879 6814933 6814957 6814961 6814991 6814999 6815021 6815033 6815041
6815051 6815057 6815059 6815063 6815069 6815099 6815101 6815117 6815131 6815161
6815227 6815231 6815233 6815293 6815297 6815311 6815321 6815327 6815399 6815447
6815461 6815467 6815491 6815507 6815513 6815533 6815561 6815573 6815593 6815597
6815603 6815639 6815651 6815671 6815689 6815693 6815701 6815719 6815723 6815729
6815741 6815749 6815777 6815789 6815803 6815833 6815839 6815849 6815863 6815867
6815869 6815891 6815903 6815909 6815911 6815923 6815951 6815969 6815971 6816011
6816013 6816049 6816067 6816107 6816109 6816113 6816137 6816149 6816151 6816157
6816163 6816169 6816179 6816233 6816239 6816253 6816263 6816281 6816301 6816331
6816361 6816367 6816401 6816413 6816427 6816431 6816449 6816461 6816493 6816503
6816517 6816527 6816561 6816581 6816587 6816613 6816617 6816629 6816631 6816659
6816679 6816703 6816721 6816731 6816737 6816743 6816757 6816787 6816829 6816841
6816851 6816853 6816871 6816889 6816907 6816911 6816937 6816967 6816973 6817007
6817009 6817033 6817051 6817081 6817093 6817099 6817103 6817121 6817157 6817163
6817171 6817211 6817243 6817259 6817271 6817297 6817301 6817309 6817313 6817319
6817331 6817379 6817387 6817387 6817429 6817457 6817469 6817471 6817477 6817483
6817501 6817511 6817519 6817529 6817553 6817567 6817571 6817589 6817597 6817619
6817631 6817651 6817661 6817669 6817687 6817709 6817717 6817739 6817747 6817777
6817807 6817819 6817823 6817829 6817843 6817859 6817873 6817891 6817897 6817927
6817949 6817957 6817963 6817991 6817999 6818011 6818041 6818057 6818069 6818083
6818107 6818113 6818137 6818159 6818167 6818179 6818183 6818191 6818197
6818221 6818239 6818257 6818261 6818263 6818267 6818293 6818297 6818303 6818333
6818347 6818363 6818401 6818407 6818429 6818437 6818447 6818459 6818489 6818491
6818507 6818527 6818561 6818573 6818579 6818593 6818597 6818621 6818629 6818653
6818677 6818719 6818731 6818737 6818743 6818771 6818783 6818797 6818803 6818827
6818831 6818837 6818843 6818843 6818849 6818863 6818869 6818873 6818893 6818899
6818939 6818941 6818947 6818953 6818969 6818993 6819013 6819019 6819037 6819041
6819049 6819067 6819077 6819083 6819097 6819103 6819107 6819121 6819191 6819199
6819203 6819209 6819221 6819229 6819289 6819299 6819313 6819341 6819343 6819353
6819361 6819377 6819383 6819389 6819401 6819403 6819443 6819481 6819493 6819503
6819511 6819521 6819539 6819541 6819557 6819583 6819623 6819629 6819641 6819649
6819667 6819679 6819719 6819749 6819767 6819781 6819797 6819829 6819847 6819851
6819887 6819893 6819913 6819931 6819949 6819977 6820001 6820007 6820013
6820019 6820039 6820057 6820061 6820067 6820087 6820097 6820103 6820109 6820117
6820127 6820129 6820139 6820141 6820147 6820157 6820169 6820181 6820207 6820211
6820241 6820267 6820277 6820283 6820291 6820339 6820367 6820369 6820393 6820421
6820433 6820441 6820483 6820493 6820511 6820537 6820547 6820559 6820573 6820579
6820607 6820633 6820643 6820663 6820711 6820721 6820727 6820733 6820739 6820741
6820769 6820783 6820817 6820823 6820841 6820873 6820897 6820909 6820921 6820937
6820951 6820967 6820973 6820991 6820993 6820999 6821011 6821021 6821077 6821083
6821099 6821107 6821117 6821141 6821159 6821161 6821173 6821197 6821201 6821207
6821231 6821239 6821249 6821257 6821261 6821263 6821281 6821291 6821303 6821383
```

6821389	6821393	6821401	6821407	6821443	6821461	6821473	6821491	6821497	6821509
6821531	6821537	6821543	6821561	6821567	6821597	6821599	6821611	6821623	6821629
6821663	6821669	6821671	6821677	6821693	6821701	6821707	6821723	6821747	6821753
6821791	6821803	6821809	6821819	6821827	6821831	6821833	6821839	6821851	6821863
6821897	6821911	6821921	6821933	6821959	6821963	6822017	6822043	6822061	6822089
6822091	6822131	6822133	6822143	6822161	6822173	6822187	6822199	6822209	6822217
6822269	6822271	6822289	6822323	6822353	6822371	6822373	6822377	6822401	6822481
6822493	6822533	6822581	6822589	6822619	6822623	6822631	6822659	6822703	6822709
6822713	6822719	6822721	6822727	6822757	6822773	6822779	6822793	6822817	6822839
6822889	6822901	6822913	6822929	6822931	6822953	6822971	6822983	6822989	6823013
6823021	6823027	6823039	6823043	6823049	6823051	6823057	6823067	6823081	6823121
6823123	6823127	6823139	6823163	6823169	6823177	6823183	6823189	6823199	6823241
6823247	6823253	6823259	6823351	6823373	6823391	6823423	6823447	6823457	6823463
6823469	6823471	6823501	6823543	6823549	6823561	6823567	6823573	6823657	6823693
6823699	6823703	6823721	6823757	6823759	6823771	6823777	6823781	6823819	6823823
6823829	6823877	6823879	6823889	6823891	6823931	6823933	6823963	6823991	6824003
6824039	6824093	6824101	6824141	6824149	6824161	6824197	6824203	6824219	6824269
6824281	6824297	6824299	6824329	6824341	6824357	6824359	6824369	6824393	6824413
6824423	6824443	6824453	6824463	6824499	6824473	6824499	6824507	6824527	6824561
6824569	6824611	6824617	6824639	6824641	6824663	6824669	6824717	6824723	6824749
6824759	6824771	6824777	6824791	6824801	6824809	6824833	6824869	6824891	6824897
6824899	6824903	6824911	6824927	6824959	6824977	6824981	6825001	6825019	6825037
6825067	6825079	6825097	6825101	6825127	6825151	6825167	6825193	6825197	6825233
6825241	6825251	6825257	6825289	6825307	6825323	6825331	6825349	6825359	6825367
6825383	6825397	6825407	6825419	6825437	6825439	6825451	6825461	6825463	6825509
6825541	6825569	6825583	6825587	6825589	6825613	6825629	6825661	6825683	6825697
6825703	6825737	6825739	6825743	6825757	6825761	6825773	6825781	6825787	6825799
6825811	6825827	6825829	6825877	6825881	6825901	6825911	6825919	6825943	6825947
6825953	6825971	6825977	6825979	6825989	6826007	6826051	6826063	6826067	6826069
6826081	6826087	6826097	6826103	6826133	6826159	6826271	6826289	6826291	6826307
6826319	6826321	6826349	6826357	6826361	6826381	6826399	6826403	6826409	6826411
6826427	6826433	6826439	6826441	6826451	6826471	6826481	6826499	6826507	6826511
6826543	6826553	6826583	6826591	6826597	6826601	6826621	6826657	6826709	6826739
6826747	6826751	6826769	6826783	6826801	6826811	6826823	6826829	6826849	6826867
6826873	6826901	6826903	6826933	6826969	6826973	6826991	6826993	6827011	6827017
6827027	6827053	6827057	6827069	6827071	6827077	6827083	6827087	6827131	6827141
6827143	6827167	6827189	6827201	6827231	6827237	6827243	6827273	6827281	6827287
6827299	6827309	6827311	6827321	6827333	6827363	6827377	6827399	6827413	6827449
6827453	6827467	6827473	6827503	6827507	6827519	6827521	6827531	6827543	6827551
6827567	6827603	6827629	6827633	6827671	6827683	6827687	6827699	6827729	6827747
6827759	6827797	6827801	6827837	6827839	6827867	6827881	6827911	6827917	6827927
6827923	6827939	6827969	6827981	6827983	6827993	6828023	6828053	6828061	6828071
6828077	6828083	6828089	6828103	6828109	6828131	6828139	6828167	6828187	6828193
6828197	6828259	6828293	6828299	6828317	6828323	6828329	6828331	6828377	6828383
6828389	6828397	6828403	6828413	6828433	6828449	6828457	6828487	6828499	6828517
6828527	6828543	6828599	6828607	6828617	6828623	6828641	6828667	6828727	6828737
6828739	6828743	6828749	6828751	6828761	6828763	6828779	6828821	6828827	6828853
6828863	6828869	6828889	6828893	6828911	6828937	6828971	6828973	6828989	6829033
6829049	6829051	6829057	6829063	6829093	6829111	6829129	6829139	6829159	6829169
6829187	6829213	6829259	6829267	6829271	6829279	6829283	6829301	6829327	6829337
6829351	6829363	6829373	6829391	6829397	6829439	6829441	6829447	6829451	6829453
6829457	6829483	6829507	6829513	6829547	6829549	6829567	6829583	6829601	6829609
6829619	6829637	6829649	6829651	6829681	6829687	6829717	6829729	6829751	6829763
6829777	6829783	6829811	6829817	6829897	6829931	6829939	6829957	6829967	6829981
6829997	6830009	6830023	6830027	6830029	6830041	6830053	6830071	6830081	6830093
6830111	6830143	6830147	6830171	6830191	6830221	6830227	6830251	6830253	6830297
6830303	6830339	6830347	6830359	6830377	6830407	6830423	6830429	6830431	6830479
6830497	6830501	6830503	6830513	6830521	6830531	6830539	6830567	6830569	6830591
6830611	6830623	6830627	6830647	6830669	6830699	6830729	6830741	6830743	6830777
6830783	6830797	6830833	6830869	6830897	6830909	6830917	6830939	6830947	6830951
6830959	6831007	6831029	6831043	6831047	6831061	6831091	6831107	6831113	6831131
6831151	6831157	6831163	6831173	6831221	6831233	6831239	6831247	6831259	6831271
6831277	6831301	6831311	6831313	6831343	6831359	6831361	6831371	6831397	6831401
6831427	6831449	6831463	6831479	6831491	6831499	6831523	6831533	6831553	6831557
6831577	6831581	6831593	6831599	6831611	6831631	6831653	6831661	6831703	6831709
6831719	6831751	6831761	6831767	6831821	6831827	6831829	6831857	6831863	6831889
6831899	6831911	6831919	6831941	6831971	6831991	6832003	6832009	6832027	6832031
6832037	6832069	6832073	6832099	6832103	6832151	6832159	6832187	6832193	6832201
6832211	6832213	6832223	6832237	6832247	6832253	6832277	6832291	6832303	6832321
6832349	6832361	6832367	6832379	6832387	6832411	6832417	6832421	6832451	6832519
6832523	6832537	6832559	6832597	6832621	6832627	6832649	6832663	6832667	6832669
6832687	6832697	6832703	6832717	6832729	6832733	6832739	6832747	6832783	6832801
6832811	6832831	6832841	6832843	6832867	6832871	6832877	6832879	6832897	6832921
6832939	6832949	6832957	6832979	6832993	6833011	6833023	6833039	6833059	6833069
6833081	6833083	6833089	6833107	6833117	6833137	6833143	6833147	6833207	6833209
6833221	6833243	6833257	6833261	6833273	6833287	6833291	6833297	6833317	6833363
6833399	6833401	6833413	6833443	6833467	6833479	6833527	6833539	6833543	6833549
6833573	6833591	6833621	6833653	6833663	6833669	6833681	6833693	6833699	6833707
6833713	6833719	6833731	6833773	6833777	6833791	6833797	6833803	6833843	6833851
6833899	6833909	6833927	6833933	6833951	6833983	6833993	6833999	6834001	
6834007	6834031	6834073	6834077	6834083	6834089	6834131	6834133	6834143	6834173
6834193	6834199	6834209	6834241	6834263	6834271	6834277	6834287	6834293	6834301
6834313	6834371	6834397	6834407	6834419	6834439	6834449	6834497	6834511	6834533
6834551	6834557	6834559	6834563	6834587	6834593	6834613	6834617	6834631	6834637
6834643	6834647	6834661	6834671	6834679	6834689	6834701	6834739	6834761	6834797
6834829	6834853	6834913	6834931	6834937	6834941	6834943	6834959	6834991	6835007
6835009	6835019	6835033	6835043	6835051	6835061	6835093	6835109	6835177	6835181
6835201	6835217	6835219	6835223	6835249	6835253	6835259	6835261	6835277	6835313
6835319	6835321	6835331	6835337	6835363	6835369	6835373	6835379	6835391	6835399

```
6835447  6835457  6835487  6835489  6835519  6835537  6835571  6835583  6835589  6835597
6835601  6835627  6835637  6835657  6835663  6835691  6835729  6835783  6835813  6835817
6835837  6835883  6835891  6835901  6835931  6835979  6836003  6836017  6836021  6836033
6836047  6836051  6836101  6836111  6836113  6836131  6836149  6836171  6836173  6836177
6836191  6836201  6836237  6836243  6836279  6836281  6836293  6836309  6836317  6836321
6836327  6836339  6836341  6836351  6836369  6836407  6836411  6836477  6836483  6836503
6836513  6836521  6836539  6836549  6836563  6836579  6836587  6836591  6836597  6836603
6836623  6836633  6836651  6836653  6836659  6836671  6836677  6836693  6836701  6836707
6836729  6836741  6836777  6836783  6836857  6836867  6836969  6836981  6836983  6836987
6837001  6837029  6837031  6837041  6837067  6837079  6837101  6837109  6837113  6837139
6837151  6837161  6837167  6837199  6837203  6837209  6837217  6837221  6837223  6837251
6837269  6837287  6837317  6837319  6837323  6837343  6837353  6837367  6837377  6837379
6837401  6837409  6837421  6837437  6837443  6837487  6837499  6837521  6837557  6837581
6837613  6837617  6837619  6837631  6837641  6837643  6837653  6837667  6837683  6837697
6837703  6837713  6837751  6837767  6837769  6837773  6837799  6837833  6837841  6837847
6837863  6837869  6837899  6837907  6837913  6837931  6837937  6837973  6837977  6838001
6838019  6838033  6838037  6838079  6838099  6838123  6838133  6838141  6838151
6838163  6838177  6838187  6838193  6838201  6838207  6838213  6838217  6838241  6838261
6838343  6838357  6838367  6838387  6838399  6838411  6838417  6838441  6838457  6838487
6838511  6838523  6838529  6838541  6838549  6838553  6838561  6838571  6838583  6838589
6838603  6838621  6838633  6838681  6838687  6838703  6838729  6838739  6838801  6838807
6838831  6838837  6838847  6838861  6838883  6838919  6838921  6838927  6838943  6838957
6838963  6839011  6839029  6839047  6839051  6839071  6839089  6839093  6839113  6839123
6839149  6839153  6839197  6839207  6839213  6839233  6839237  6839263  6839269  6839281
6839311  6839323  6839351  6839369  6839377  6839387  6839401  6839419  6839429  6839461
6839467  6839471  6839489  6839507  6839513  6839527  6839557  6839587  6839629  6839659
6839663  6839669  6839683  6839689  6839713  6839719  6839771  6839801  6839803  6839837
6839843  6839849  6839851  6839873  6839879  6839891  6839893  6839897  6839923  6839939
6839971  6839983  6840013  6840017  6840049  6840061  6840073  6840083  6840091  6840109
6840157  6840161  6840167  6840179  6840187  6840199  6840203  6840221  6840241  6840257
6840263  6840271  6840289  6840293  6840299  6840313  6840331  6840349  6840353  6840359
6840371  6840377  6840413  6840439  6840461  6840469  6840473  6840497  6840527  6840541
6840557  6840577  6840583  6840619  6840643  6840649  6840653  6840661  6840721  6840737
6840761  6840793  6840797  6840811  6840871  6840929  6840941  6840979  6840983
6840989  6840997  6841019  6841027  6841031  6841039  6841057  6841061  6841091  6841117
6841139  6841181  6841183  6841199  6841207  6841217  6841223  6841229  6841243  6841277
6841279  6841283  6841291  6841309  6841319  6841339  6841379  6841381  6841397  6841409
6841423  6841427  6841433  6841451  6841453  6841517  6841537  6841543  6841561  6841573
6841609  6841663  6841673  6841727  6841733  6841739  6841759  6841763  6841777  6841801
6841829  6841831  6841889  6841897  6841907  6841921  6841927  6841949  6841951  6841963
6841987  6841993  6842021  6842023  6842047  6842051  6842081  6842083  6842093  6842113
6842131  6842137  6842149  6842159  6842167  6842179  6842189  6842197  6842207  6842219
6842221  6842233  6842243  6842249  6842267  6842273  6842281  6842317  6842417  6842321
6842327  6842333  6842357  6842359  6842369  6842383  6842387  6842399  6842417  6842441
6842443  6842453  6842467  6842497  6842501  6842503  6842557  6842567  6842573  6842581
6842593  6842597  6842609  6842611  6842617  6842621  6842629  6842639  6842651  6842681
6842701  6842729  6842741  6842779  6842783  6842807  6842813  6842819  6842821  6842827
6842853  6842861  6842873  6842881  6842893  6842923  6842929  6842963
6842981  6843007  6843017  6843019  6843037  6843049  6843071  6843073  6843103  6843107
6843127  6843131  6843143  6843181  6843203  6843241  6843257  6843283  6843289  6843293
6843311  6843323  6843329  6843359  6843371  6843373  6843377  6843379  6843427  6843437
6843451  6843461  6843479  6843491  6843497  6843509  6843511  6843521  6843539  6843547
6843559  6843583  6843593  6843607  6843637  6843643  6843671  6843689  6843703
6843709  6843757  6843799  6843803  6843821  6843829  6843841  6843869  6843899  6843917
6843919  6843937  6843953  6843961  6843989  6843997  6844027  6844031  6844039  6844043
6844051  6844067  6844069  6844091  6844099  6844111  6844121  6844127  6844129  6844141
6844151  6844163  6844193  6844231  6844249  6844289  6844303  6844307  6844309
6844339  6844349  6844373  6844379  6844403  6844433  6844441  6844447  6844451  6844463
6844477  6844483  6844507  6844517  6844543  6844549  6844559  6844567  6844571  6844573
6844597  6844601  6844603  6844631  6844633  6844637  6844687  6844703  6844709
6844757  6844763  6844771  6844801  6844813  6844843  6844853  6844861  6844907  6844913
6844967  6844969  6844987  6845009  6845011  6845029  6845057  6845063  6845081  6845087
6845117  6845161  6845171  6845177  6845207  6845219  6845227  6845231  6845261
6845287  6845303  6845317  6845341  6845347  6845351  6845353  6845369  6845381  6845383
6845413  6845417  6845519  6845561  6845563  6845609  6845621  6845633  6845659
6845687  6845693  6845701  6845717  6845723  6845767  6845779  6845803  6845807  6845809
6845819  6845821  6845843  6845869  6845873  6845897  6845911  6845921  6845939  6845941
6845953  6845959  6845981  6845983  6846017  6846029  6846031  6846079  6846097  6846107
6846131  6846143  6846149  6846187  6846193  6846209  6846211  6846227  6846241  6846247
6846263  6846271  6846277  6846283  6846293  6846313  6846337  6846361  6846379
6846383  6846391  6846397  6846409  6846431  6846439  6846461  6846473  6846491  6846509
6846533  6846577  6846583  6846599  6846607  6846611  6846641  6846647  6846649  6846673
6846691  6846697  6846703  6846727  6846731  6846757  6846787  6846803  6846809  6846811
6846817  6846839  6846841  6846881  6846899  6846907  6846923  6846941  6846947  6846949
6846967  6846979  6846991  6847003  6847033  6847081  6847091  6847121  6847147
6847153  6847157  6847213  6847223  6847237  6847283  6847301  6847319  6847349  6847367
6847381  6847387  6847403  6847409  6847439  6847471  6847487  6847499  6847507  6847573
6847579  6847591  6847597  6847609  6847649  6847663  6847681  6847691  6847693  6847723
6847727  6847739  6847747  6847781  6847783  6847801  6847811  6847817  6847829  6847831
6847837  6847843  6847871  6847873  6847903  6847937  6847949  6847969  6847979  6848027
6848029  6848047  6848063  6848087  6848099  6848111  6848131  6848141  6848167  6848197
6848213  6848269  6848291  6848329  6848333  6848339  6848351  6848357  6848371  6848377
6848383  6848389  6848449  6848453  6848459  6848473  6848477  6848483  6848509  6848521
6848537  6848563  6848581  6848609  6848617  6848623  6848627  6848629  6848657  6848659
6848701  6848711  6848717  6848731  6848789  6848791  6848821  6848833  6848867
6848867  6848869  6848903  6848929  6848939  6848951  6848953  6848957  6848969  6849061
6849071  6849103  6849119  6849131  6849151  6849229  6849247  6849277  6849281  6849287
6849289  6849301  6849313  6849347  6849373  6849389  6849407  6849413  6849421  6849463
6849467  6849473  6849497  6849499  6849509  6849527  6849541  6849559  6849569  6849581
```

```
6849593 6849617 6849637 6849659 6849673 6849677 6849683 6849697 6849701 6849727
6849737 6849757 6849767 6849769 6849799 6849851 6849871 6849881 6849893 6849917
6849919 6849923 6849949 6849971 6849991 6850007 6850049 6850057 6850087 6850097
6850139 6850141 6850153 6850183 6850187 6850189 6850211 6850213 6850223 6850229
6850243 6850267 6850271 6850273 6850289 6850309 6850331 6850339 6850369 6850379
6850421 6850429 6850451 6850463 6850471 6850477 6850489 6850511 6850531 6850553
6850559 6850589 6850601 6850603 6850607 6850637 6850639 6850651 6850663 6850681
6850691 6850693 6850703 6850709 6850741 6850747 6850751 6850769 6850787 6850793
6850807 6850829 6850843 6850853 6850897 6850901 6850913 6850927 6850937 6850967
6850997 6850999 6851023 6851057 6851063 6851071 6851081 6851101 6851107 6851111
6851113 6851129 6851149 6851167 6851177 6851189 6851213 6851231 6851239 6851249
6851261 6851293 6851311 6851333 6851347 6851407 6851437 6851441 6851443 6851461
6851479 6851483 6851489 6851497 6851503 6851513 6851543 6851557 6851563 6851573
6851587 6851597 6851599 6851617 6851639 6851653 6851659 6851683 6851687 6851717
6851737 6851753 6851759 6851773 6851783 6851791 6851807 6851821 6851827 6851839
6851863 6851963 6851987 6852019 6852047 6852059 6852061 6852073 6852077 6852089
6852101 6852127 6852133 6852151 6852161 6852163 6852169 6852187 6852193 6852203
6852227 6852239 6852247 6852259 6852277 6852301 6852311 6852337 6852341 6852359
6852379 6852389 6852401 6852421 6852427 6852431 6852473 6852481 6852499 6852523
6852541 6852569 6852607 6852611 6852619 6852623 6852631 6852641 6852653 6852661
6852691 6852701 6852709 6852719 6852739 6852743 6852757 6852773 6852779 6852799
6852803 6852809 6852821 6852823 6852871 6852883 6852907 6852913 6852917 6852947
6852971 6852973 6852997 6853001 6853031 6853043 6853051 6853081 6853097 6853123
6853127 6853169 6853181 6853183 6853199 6853213 6853219 6853247 6853279 6853321
6853339 6853351 6853369 6853391 6853409 6853421 6853423 6853447 6853463 6853477
6853489 6853501 6853523 6853529 6853531 6853537 6853543 6853549 6853577 6853591
6853603 6853607 6853619 6853633 6853643 6853663 6853667 6853709 6853711 6853733
6853753 6853783 6853787 6853807 6853817 6853823 6853829 6853837 6853841 6853877
6853879 6853901 6853921 6853937 6853939 6853949 6853967 6853969 6853981 6853993
6853997 6853999 6854027 6854053 6854059 6854083 6854101 6854123 6854147 6854153
6854171 6854173 6854209 6854219 6854233 6854249 6854251 6854297 6854303 6854321
6854333 6854347 6854359 6854369 6854371 6854401 6854413 6854423 6854429 6854453
6854461 6854479 6854489 6854531 6854557 6854563 6854579 6854581 6854623 6854629
6854641 6854647 6854671 6854677 6854681 6854707 6854711 6854717 6854737 6854761
6854789 6854803 6854807 6854819 6854833 6854857 6854863 6854867 6854873 6854891
6854921 6854941 6854951 6854963 6854977 6854983 6854987 6854993 6855007 6855019
6855031 6855041 6855059 6855071 6855089 6855113 6855133 6855137 6855139 6855157
6855161 6855187 6855197 6855203 6855217 6855221 6855227 6855229 6855253 6855283
6855293 6855307 6855313 6855319 6855353 6855377 6855379 6855419 6855441 6855449
6855461 6855463 6855479 6855481 6855491 6855493 6855529 6855593 6855631 6855643
6855659 6855669 6855671 6855677 6855683 6855691 6855697 6855707 6855757 6855763
6855769 6855787 6855799 6855809 6855829 6855869 6855887 6855889 6855899 6855911
6855923 6855931 6855967 6855971 6856009 6856019 6856037 6856039 6856051 6856079
6856103 6856111 6856121 6856123 6856127 6856141 6856153 6856159 6856181 6856189
6856229 6856243 6856247 6856249 6856261 6856271 6856273 6856279 6856357 6856387
6856391 6856403 6856411 6856429 6856459 6856463 6856469 6856477 6856483 6856517
6856523 6856529 6856537 6856543 6856561 6856573 6856589 6856601 6856613 6856621
6856631 6856663 6856669 6856693 6856697 6856723 6856757 6856771 6856781 6856819
6856841 6856873 6856897 6856901 6856919 6856931 6856937 6856973 6856999 6857003
6857023 6857033 6857041 6857047 6857051 6857057 6857063 6857093 6857101 6857117
6857141 6857143 6857161 6857177 6857189 6857203 6857219 6857269 6857281 6857297
6857303 6857317 6857329 6857353 6857359 6857387 6857407 6857419 6857429 6857449
6857453 6857467 6857471 6857489 6857497 6857503 6857507 6857527 6857533 6857549
6857551 6857567 6857569 6857581 6857593 6857621 6857639 6857671 6857687 6857699
6857707 6857713 6857729 6857743 6857759 6857777 6857779 6857801 6857821 6857831
6857849 6857881 6857907 6857957 6857959 6857969 6857971 6857989 6858013 6858017
6858043 6858077 6858091 6858097 6858109 6858119 6858139 6858149 6858167 6858179
6858233 6858263 6858289 6858307 6858329 6858331 6858349 6858353 6858403 6858407
6858427 6858433 6858443 6858469 6858473 6858479 6858491 6858499 6858517 6858581
6858613 6858617 6858637 6858647 6858661 6858673 6858679 6858689 6858697 6858707
6858721 6858737 6858749 6858751 6858793 6858823 6858827 6858869 6858893 6858923
6858937 6858947 6858953 6858979 6858983 6858989 6858997 6859003 6859009 6859031
6859033 6859063 6859067 6859081 6859087 6859093 6859103 6859123 6859159 6859169
6859183 6859199 6859217 6859241 6859249 6859253 6859271 6859289 6859309 6859327
6859337 6859367 6859379 6859387 6859409 6859417 6859421 6859429 6859441 6859469
6859471 6859481 6859493 6859499 6859507 6859519 6859537 6859547 6859561 6859571
6859577 6859607 6859609 6859621 6859667 6859679 6859691 6859693 6859709 6859717
6859739 6859739 6859757 6859781 6859813 6859841 6859847 6859861 6859873 6859901
6859933 6859939 6859943 6859961 6859967 6859973 6859981 6859991 6860011 6860023
6860047 6860069 6860071 6860093 6860099 6860111 6860143 6860171 6860179 6860213
6860237 6860239 6860251 6860257 6860297 6860303 6860317 6860323 6860341 6860353
6860389 6860419 6860437 6860453 6860471 6860473 6860551 6860561 6860563 6860573
6860587 6860591 6860653 6860663 6860671 6860677 6860687 6860681 6860683 6860701
6860719 6860747 6860753 6860773 6860783 6860803 6860807 6860813 6860837 6860839
6860851 6860857 6860889 6860897 6860929 6860963 6860977 6860989 6860999 6861011
6861017 6861053 6861067 6861073 6861077 6861079 6861083 6861091 6861103 6861119
6861121 6861133 6861157 6861163 6861187 6861191 6861203 6861241 6861263 6861271
6861307 6861311 6861329 6861333 6861367 6861377 6861379 6861409 6861419 6861431
6861427 6861431 6861461 6861469 6861479 6861493 6861497 6861499 6861559 6861581
6861583 6861601 6861613 6861623 6861629 6861691 6861697 6861733 6861737 6861769
6861773 6861791 6861809 6861817 6861821 6861823 6861847 6861851 6861913 6861923
6861947 6861949 6861971 6861973 6861977 6861997 6862001 6862003 6862007 6862039
6862043 6862049 6862061 6862087 6862103 6862111 6862127 6862133 6862139 6862147
6862159 6862171 6862199 6862201 6862213 6862217 6862223 6862259 6862267 6862277
6862307 6862319 6862333 6862337 6862343 6862367 6862369 6862381 6862393 6862397
6862403 6862409 6862417 6862421 6862433 6862447 6862451 6862469 6862481 6862483
6862489 6862507 6862529 6862547 6862571 6862573 6862601 6862607 6862613 6862631
6862643 6862693 6862711 6862727 6862753 6862759 6862771 6862777 6862783 6862831
6862841 6862859 6862897 6862903 6862943 6862963 6862969 6862979 6862981 6862991
```

```
6863027  6863029  6863063  6863071  6863099  6863107  6863117  6863119  6863137  6863141
6863147  6863149  6863159  6863173  6863243  6863249  6863251  6863261  6863303  6863309
6863317  6863323  6863327  6863333  6863347  6863371  6863377  6863383  6863419  6863443
6863449  6863471  6863477  6863489  6863501  6863509  6863513  6863561  6863567  6863581
6863587  6863603  6863629  6863651  6863653  6863663  6863669  6863711  6863723  6863737
6863771  6863797  6863819  6863827  6863849  6863861  6863873  6863881  6863887  6863891
6863893  6863897  6863993  6863953  6863957  6863993  6864019  6864031  6864043  6864059
6864079  6864089  6864101  6864127  6864131  6864139  6864167  6864173  6864181  6864191
6864199  6864211  6864233  6864239  6864241  6864251  6864257  6864259  6864283  6864287
6864307  6864317  6864323  6864331  6864383  6864427  6864437  6864443  6864449  6864461
6864479  6864497  6864521  6864523  6864541  6864553  6864581  6864587  6864601  6864607
6864623  6864629  6864653  6864673  6864661  6864691  6864713  6864769  6864779  6864811
6864839  6864841  6864853  6864881  6864911  6864937  6864941  6864953  6864973  6864983
6864997  6865007  6865009  6865031  6865039  6865049  6865051  6865057  6865073  6865087
6865121  6865129  6865169  6865211  6865231  6865267  6865277  6865279  6865303  6865319
6865343  6865351  6865357  6865361  6865363  6865381  6865393  6865451  6865459  6865483
6865499  6865513  6865519  6865531  6865543  6865553  6865559  6865561  6865571  6865591
6865597  6865613  6865643  6865657  6865667  6865679  6865693  6865697  6865709  6865711
6865717  6865759  6865763  6865769  6865847  6865861  6865867  6865907  6865919  6865921
6865927  6865931  6865949  6865961  6865967  6865997  6866003  6866017  6866021  6866039
6866047  6866051  6866059  6866071  6866077  6866129  6866131  6866137  6866143  6866149
6866173  6866177  6866191  6866257  6866263  6866273  6866287  6866291  6866329  6866357
6866381  6866383  6866389  6866411  6866413  6866437  6866449  6866459  6866471  6866473
6866513  6866549  6866551  6866609  6866621  6866633  6866647  6866659  6866663  6866677
6866681  6866683  6866693  6866723  6866729  6866731  6866749  6866767  6866773  6866777
6866789  6866791  6866801  6866819  6866837  6866843  6866863  6866879  6866887  6866907
6866933  6866957  6866969  6866983  6866987  6866989  6867001  6867019  6867043  6867053
6867059  6867061  6867067  6867073  6867079  6867097  6867103  6867121  6867137  6867139
6867149  6867181  6867199  6867221  6867239  6867247  6867251  6867281  6867307  6867323
6867331  6867347  6867361  6867373  6867383  6867389  6867407  6867437  6867449  6867451
6867463  6867467  6867473  6867529  6867551  6867557  6867571  6867587  6867589  6867599
6867613  6867629  6867649  6867667  6867733  6867739  6867743  6867761  6867769  6867799
6867821  6867841  6867871  6867907  6867923  6867941  6867967  6867989  6867997  6868021
6868039  6868061  6868067  6868073  6868079  6868093  6868109  6868117  6868123  6868133
6868163  6868189  6868193  6868201  6868207  6868229  6868231  6868241  6868243  6868247
6868297  6868307  6868319  6868363  6868373  6868387  6868403  6868423  6868427  6868457
6868489  6868507  6868517  6868523  6868529  6868531  6868549  6868553  6868571  6868579
6868583  6868597  6868613  6868649  6868681  6868699  6868703  6868727  6868739  6868759
6868781  6868801  6868811  6868817  6868819  6868843  6868859  6868891  6868877  6868881
6868889  6868891  6868903  6868913  6868921  6868987  6868991  6868999  6869021  6869029
6869039  6869047  6869053  6869101  6869113  6869183  6869189  6869237  6869257  6869267
6869273  6869299  6869327  6869333  6869371  6869389  6869399  6869407  6869413  6869437
6869441  6869459  6869461  6869521  6869543  6869561  6869563  6869573  6869593  6869623
6869627  6869633  6869647  6869671  6869677  6869689  6869699  6869713  6869719  6869729
6869741  6869743  6869749  6869777  6869789  6869803  6869813  6869833  6869857  6869861
6869869  6869909  6869927  6869953  6869959  6869969  6869977  6869987  6870011  6870029
6870041  6870043  6870053  6870107  6870119  6870151  6870167  6870179  6870181
6870233  6870263  6870277  6870317  6870377  6870389  6870401  6870403  6870421  6870433
6870449  6870467  6870473  6870481  6870503  6870509  6870527  6870553  6870559  6870653
6870673  6870679  6870683  6870691  6870697  6870701  6870707  6870713  6870733  6870751
6870757  6870779  6870781  6870797  6870803  6870811  6870817  6870847  6870869  6870893
6870911  6870931  6870943  6871001  6871003  6871019  6871031  6871037  6871049  6871061
6871087  6871097  6871121  6871127  6871133  6871147  6871169  6871171  6871177  6871201
6871211  6871253  6871261  6871283  6871301  6871327  6871351  6871399  6871421  6871441
6871471  6871481  6871507  6871511  6871547  6871561  6871567  6871573  6871583  6871639
6871651  6871661  6871679  6871681  6871699  6871703  6871717  6871759  6871763  6871791
6871793  6871807  6871829  6871831  6871841  6871849  6871897  6871913  6871933  6871979
6871981  6872017  6872023  6872071  6872081  6872087  6872113  6872119  6872137  6872141
6872171  6872179  6872189  6872197  6872207  6872219  6872231  6872237  6872251  6872273
6872287  6872291  6872311  6872329  6872363  6872381  6872419  6872431  6872477  6872479
6872501  6872513  6872521  6872581  6872603  6872609  6872611  6872617  6872627  6872629
6872633  6872651  6872683  6872689  6872693  6872759  6872779  6872783  6872807  6872821
6872849  6872869  6872869  6872891  6872893  6872897  6872909  6872911  6872933  6872939
6872941  6872959  6872963  6873001  6873007  6873011  6873017  6873019  6873037  6873043
6873059  6873071  6873089  6873091  6873107  6873109  6873121  6873131  6873137  6873143
6873161  6873173  6873187  6873211  6873257  6873277  6873283  6873301
6873311  6873331  6873337  6873371  6873397  6873403  6873407  6873437  6873467  6873473
6873521  6873523  6873533  6873563  6873571  6873577  6873583  6873613  6873641  6873653
6873673  6873683  6873697  6873707  6873719  6873721  6873743  6873751  6873767  6873781
6873791  6873799  6873821  6873827  6873829  6873833  6873863  6873871  6873901  6873929
6873943  6873949  6873961  6874003  6874013  6874039  6874061  6874111  6874121  6874139
6874159  6874163  6874177  6874187  6874201  6874207  6874211  6874213  6874223  6874229
6874243  6874261  6874279  6874297  6874319  6874331  6874339  6874349  6874369  6874379
6874381  6874397  6874423  6874451  6874459  6874499  6874507  6874531  6874573  6874583
6874597  6874603  6874607  6874619  6874633  6874657  6874667  6874687  6874727  6874733
6874753  6874771  6874781  6874787  6874799  6874823  6874837  6874841  6874843  6874871
6874877  6874909  6874913  6874927  6874939  6874949  6874961  6874981  6874991  6874993
6874997  6875023  6875027  6875041  6875047  6875053  6875101  6875119  6875129  6875153
6875159  6875189  6875203  6875221  6875237  6875269  6875279  6875299  6875311  6875333
6875353  6875387  6875389  6875419  6875423  6875431  6875441  6875449  6875461  6875483
6875513  6875543  6875567  6875573  6875579  6875591  6875593  6875621  6875623  6875717
6875723  6875731  6875749  6875753  6875767  6875779  6875807  6875819  6875833  6875839
6875851  6875861  6875923  6875933  6875941  6875951  6875963  6875977  6875983  6875993
6876029  6876031  6876049  6876071  6876073  6876091  6876097  6876101  6876113  6876131
6876169  6876179  6876187  6876217  6876223  6876227  6876251  6876253  6876257
6876263  6876293  6876307  6876319  6876323  6876329  6876343  6876349  6876361  6876377
6876403  6876409  6876433  6876439  6876491  6876503  6876533  6876539  6876581  6876587
6876593  6876599  6876601  6876607  6876629  6876631  6876659  6876677  6876731  6876767
6876769  6876773  6876781  6876791  6876809  6876811  6876817  6876827  6876829  6876833
```

6876851 6876853 6876869 6876901 6876937 6876943 6876949 6876953 6876979 6876983
6877043 6877051 6877109 6877219 6877223 6877229 6877237 6877249 6877261 6877271
6877307 6877327 6877331 6877361 6877399 6877421 6877427 6877433 6877441 6877447
6877471 6877477 6877489 6877501 6877513 6877579 6877583 6877603 6877609 6877613
6877649 6877657 6877679 6877681 6877693 6877697 6877711 6877723 6877729 6877763
6877771 6877789 6877799 6877817 6877837 6877847 6877883 6877889 6877891 6877907
6877919 6877921 6877957 6877963 6877993 6878023 6878029 6878033 6878059 6878071
6878077 6878083 6878087 6878089 6878093 6878099 6878107 6878129 6878141 6878143
6878167 6878203 6878233 6878269 6878273 6878321 6878341 6878351 6878363 6878369
6878371 6878383 6878401 6878407 6878413 6878429 6878453 6878467 6878479 6878491
6878519 6878527 6878533 6878567 6878569 6878579 6878593 6878603 6878617 6878623
6878639 6878647 6878657 6878671 6878699 6878731 6878737 6878743 6878749 6878759
6878777 6878789 6878797 6878803 6878813 6878821 6878827 6878831 6878843 6878849
6878867 6878891 6878903 6878917 6878951 6878953 6878959 6878981 6878983 6879013
6879017 6879023 6879049 6879073 6879079 6879113 6879133 6879163 6879193 6879227
6879253 6879259 6879263 6879307 6879319 6879329 6879331 6879361 6879371 6879419
6879421 6879443 6879451 6879469 6879487 6879491 6879511 6879533 6879541 6879581
6879589 6879643 6879661 6879671 6879673 6879683 6879797 6879811 6879823 6879839
6879857 6879869 6879893 6879913 6879941 6879947 6879949 6879959 6879969 6879973
6879997 6880009 6880021 6880051 6880057 6880061 6880063 6880073 6880099 6880123
6880127 6880141 6880157 6880183 6880193 6880229 6880241 6880249 6880259 6880267
6880271 6880273 6880303 6880319 6880327 6880331 6880369 6880411 6880417 6880429
6880439 6880441 6880477 6880487 6880493 6880507 6880541 6880547 6880561 6880589
6880591 6880609 6880613 6880633 6880637 6880649 6880651 6880673 6880691 6880693
6880721 6880771 6880777 6880781 6880787 6880789 6880807 6880837 6880871 6880873
6880877 6880879 6880891 6880931 6880943 6880963 6880997 6881003 6881009 6881023
6881027 6881041 6881047 6881057 6881081 6881087 6881093 6881113 6881123 6881131
6881167 6881183 6881191 6881197 6881239 6881257 6881261 6881263 6881269 6881291
6881321 6881339 6881341 6881351 6881353 6881359 6881383 6881387 6881389 6881417
6881429 6881437 6881443 6881461 6881489 6881507 6881509 6881513 6881551 6881579
6881603 6881639 6881653 6881657 6881663 6881683 6881713 6881731 6881759 6881773
6881803 6881839 6881843 6881851 6881869 6881873 6881893 6881939 6881947 6881951
6881977 6881981 6881989 6881993 6881999 6882011 6882049 6882067 6882079 6882089
6882091 6882097 6882131 6882149 6882167 6882181 6882191 6882287 6882289 6882311
6882319 6882329 6882353 6882361 6882373 6882377 6882397 6882419 6882431 6882439
6882457 6882461 6882479 6882487 6882493 6882517 6882523 6882529 6882553 6882581
6882583 6882593 6882607 6882611 6882613 6882641 6882643 6882647 6882653 6882677
6882679 6882683 6882697 6882761 6882767 6882779 6882787 6882791 6882797 6882803
6882817 6882823 6882833 6882839 6882887 6882897 6882907 6882917 6882919 6882923
6882937 6882949 6882971 6882979 6882991 6883007 6883027 6883069 6883091 6883099
6883127 6883153 6883159 6883189 6883199 6883213 6883259 6883267 6883297 6883307
6883309 6883313 6883337 6883343 6883361 6883381 6883391 6883399 6883403 6883427
6883447 6883451 6883477 6883489 6883523 6883537 6883543 6883549 6883553 6883559
6883561 6883571 6883577 6883607 6883627 6883649 6883661 6883673 6883687 6883703
6883711 6883717 6883729 6883733 6883753 6883763 6883783 6883841 6883867 6883873
6883897 6883927 6883931 6883951 6884027 6884029 6884039 6884041 6884051 6884057
6884063 6884069 6884081 6884083 6884093 6884123 6884147 6884149 6884159 6884173
6884191 6884197 6884203 6884209 6884221 6884237 6884243 6884279 6884321 6884323
6884333 6884341 6884357 6884359 6884369 6884389 6884393 6884401 6884431 6884447
6884453 6884459 6884483 6884489 6884491 6884497 6884509 6884539 6884599 6884611
6884617 6884641 6884649 6884653 6884681 6884693 6884699 6884737 6884741
6884743 6884747 6884749 6884777 6884789 6884791 6884831 6884833 6884863 6884869
6884893 6884939 6884947 6884959 6884977 6884989 6884993 6885001 6885019 6885023
6885029 6885041 6885091 6885097 6885127 6885139 6885143 6885161 6885167 6885173
6885199 6885217 6885233 6885251 6885259 6885269 6885313 6885331 6885337 6885371
6885377 6885401 6885407 6885409 6885413 6885419 6885443 6885451 6885457 6885479
6885481 6885511 6885517 6885539 6885551 6885553 6885583 6885587 6885617 6885623
6885631 6885647 6885649 6885667 6885677 6885679 6885691 6885709 6885743 6885761
6885779 6885797 6885821 6885883 6885889 6885899 6885913 6885917 6885941 6885973
6886027 6886043 6886069 6886081 6886091 6886109 6886133 6886141 6886147 6886153
6886171 6886211 6886213 6886283 6886291 6886301 6886331 6886349 6886357 6886367
6886387 6886423 6886441 6886447 6886457 6886469 6886471 6886489 6886501 6886519
6886541 6886549 6886567 6886571 6886577 6886589 6886597 6886609 6886613 6886639
6886643 6886673 6886679 6886727 6886739 6886753 6886757 6886771 6886783 6886799
6886807 6886813 6886843 6886861 6886883 6886897 6886907 6886921 6886933 6886937
6886963 6886967 6886969 6886973 6886981 6887059 6887077 6887093 6887113 6887137
6887147 6887149 6887161 6887171 6887183 6887201 6887219 6887249 6887273 6887339
6887341 6887351 6887357 6887381 6887389 6887393 6887411 6887417 6887429 6887437
6887453 6887473 6887479 6887501 6887527 6887599 6887609 6887627 6887663 6887677
6887681 6887753 6887759 6887767 6887789 6887791 6887807 6887813 6887821 6887831
6887843 6887851 6887863 6887893 6887917 6887927 6887929 6887953 6888019 6888053
6888097 6888103 6888113 6888139 6888143 6888151 6888157 6888163 6888173 6888187
6888197 6888199 6888209 6888221 6888229 6888257 6888263 6888269 6888289 6888311
6888359 6888377 6888379 6888389 6888391 6888397 6888407 6888437 6888439 6888467
6888487 6888521 6888551 6888559 6888571 6888577 6888599 6888613 6888619 6888641
6888647 6888653 6888667 6888671 6888677 6888683 6888709 6888719 6888731 6888733
6888737 6888793 6888809 6888829 6888839 6888841 6888857 6888877 6888941 6888953
6888967 6888971 6888989 6888997 6889009 6889013 6889019 6889027 6889031 6889049
6889079 6889081 6889087 6889133 6889147 6889151 6889171 6889193 6889217 6889219
6889241 6889247 6889261 6889273 6889283 6889297 6889321 6889339 6889357
6889367 6889373 6889391 6889411 6889427 6889433 6889451 6889453 6889481 6889483
6889499 6889529 6889537 6889541 6889549 6889613 6889621 6889637 6889639 6889643
6889661 6889679 6889703 6889717 6889721 6889739 6889741 6889759 6889789 6889793
6889823 6889853 6889859 6889873 6889891 6889901 6889921 6889931 6889937 6889963
6889969 6889997 6890017 6890033 6890047 6890063 6890077 6890101 6890111 6890123
6890161 6890167 6890171 6890183 6890209 6890227 6890231 6890237 6890239 6890243
6890249 6890263 6890269 6890309 6890327 6890353 6890413 6890437 6890447 6890453
6890497 6890503 6890519 6890531 6890537 6890539 6890549 6890569 6890581 6890591
6890633 6890641 6890651 6890657 6890659 6890671 6890677 6890683 6890687 6890699

```
6890701  6890713  6890753  6890761  6890789  6890791  6890801  6890809  6890813  6890833
6890837  6890861  6890957  6890969  6891011  6891013  6891019  6891029  6891041  6891061
6891077  6891107  6891119  6891133  6891149  6891161  6891169  6891173  6891179  6891193
6891211  6891217  6891251  6891277  6891289  6891291  6891317  6891323  6891337  6891383
6891413  6891427  6891457  6891461  6891487  6891491  6891499  6891503  6891527  6891529
6891539  6891541  6891551  6891557  6891587  6891593  6891601  6891607  6891617  6891629
6891631  6891637  6891673  6891691  6891713  6891721  6891727  6891733  6891769  6891793
6891823  6891869  6891883  6891887  6891901  6891917  6891931  6891943  6891949  6891971
6891979  6891991  6892001  6892007  6892009  6892031  6892051  6892057  6892069  6892073
6892091  6892097  6892099  6892103  6892133  6892159  6892181  6892187  6892201  6892211
6892217  6892219  6892229  6892241  6892243  6892253  6892267  6892271  6892273  6892289
6892313  6892337  6892351  6892363  6892367  6892381  6892393  6892477  6892489  6892499
6892519  6892549  6892553  6892559  6892579  6892583  6892601  6892603  6892621  6892631
6892643  6892651  6892669  6892727  6892729  6892741  6892777  6892799  6892813  6892849
6892859  6892861  6892867  6892891  6892913  6892937  6892957  6892993  6893009  6893011
6893057  6893059  6893083  6893087  6893119  6893167  6893189  6893197  6893203  6893221
6893239  6893251  6893267  6893273  6893291  6893311  6893321  6893357  6893363
6893389  6893401  6893417  6893423  6893431  6893437  6893441  6893473  6893527  6893533
6893543  6893567  6893573  6893611  6893623  6893639  6893641  6893647  6893651  6893659
6893669  6893681  6893707  6893753  6893839  6893867  6893879  6893911  6893917  6893921
6893933  6893987  6894001  6894011  6894023  6894049  6894053  6894067  6894077  6894079
6894103  6894119  6894127  6894133  6894143  6894149  6894157  6894161  6894179  6894203
6894211  6894241  6894259  6894263  6894269  6894301  6894317  6894323  6894337  6894343
6894421  6894427  6894439  6894463  6894479  6894487  6894499  6894521  6894529  6894541
6894553  6894557  6894581  6894593  6894607  6894619  6894623  6894637  6894649  6894697
6894731  6894743  6894751  6894757  6894761  6894763  6894773  6894781  6894791  6894821
6894827  6894859  6894863  6894869  6894887  6894949  6894959  6894971  6894977  6894983
6894991  6894997  6895001  6895003  6895019  6895033  6895039  6895087  6895099  6895111
6895121  6895123  6895139  6895159  6895169  6895223  6895249  6895253  6895267  6895279
6895289  6895297  6895303  6895327  6895337  6895349  6895363  6895367  6895381  6895393
6895397  6895403  6895411  6895451  6895471  6895481  6895487  6895517  6895519
6895529  6895531  6895583  6895619  6895639  6895643  6895657  6895661  6895663  6895687
6895739  6895753  6895769  6895771  6895787  6895807  6895813  6895817  6895849  6895853
6895871  6895873  6895901  6895907  6895927  6895943  6895951  6895957
6895961  6895963  6895969  6895991  6896003  6896009  6896011  6896053  6896063  6896089
6896117  6896129  6896143  6896173  6896177  6896261  6896269  6896273  6896293  6896303
6896311  6896317  6896327  6896347  6896363  6896371  6896399  6896423  6896429  6896447
6896453  6896459  6896473  6896479  6896489  6896501  6896507  6896531  6896551  6896557
6896597  6896627  6896629  6896647  6896653  6896657  6896683  6896707  6896723  6896737
6896741  6896759  6896761  6896767  6896783  6896789  6896807  6896831  6896833  6896887
6896893  6896909  6896947  6896959  6896963  6896969  6896977  6896999  6897073  6897083
6897091  6897101  6897103  6897119  6897151  6897173  6897199  6897211  6897271  6897299
6897347  6897353  6897403  6897409  6897413  6897431  6897463  6897487  6897491  6897509
6897521  6897523  6897533  6897547  6897557  6897571  6897599  6897607  6897637  6897641
6897643  6897659  6897689  6897691  6897719  6897739  6897743  6897797  6897811  6897823
6897827  6897857  6897877  6897883  6897887  6897901  6897929  6897949  6897991
6898009  6898019  6898033  6898037  6898051  6898069  6898081  6898097  6898117  6898139
6898163  6898181  6898187  6898231  6898247  6898249  6898267  6898271  6898279  6898313
6898319  6898327  6898357  6898363  6898417  6898483  6898511  6898531  6898547
6898553  6898571  6898579  6898601  6898609  6898621  6898627  6898637  6898663  6898667
6898739  6898741  6898751  6898769  6898777  6898799  6898807  6898813  6898817  6898819
6898823  6898841  6898861  6898867  6898883  6898891  6898901  6898907  6898921  6898949
6898967  6898973  6898981  6898993  6899023  6899027  6899069  6899077  6899099  6899117
6899201  6899219  6899227  6899231  6899251  6899281  6899293  6899309  6899317  6899323
6899327  6899339  6899351  6899371  6899383  6899423  6899429  6899443  6899447  6899461
6899483  6899491  6899507  6899509  6899533  6899537  6899551  6899561  6899573  6899579
6899587  6899597  6899617  6899657  6899663  6899687  6899719  6899749  6899777  6899779
6899791  6899801  6899803  6899819  6899863  6899881  6899891  6899899  6899923  6899947
6899951  6899969  6899989  6900001  6900053  6900067  6900077  6900083  6900121  6900149
6900151  6900203  6900209  6900221  6900233  6900281  6900293  6900301  6900337  6900359
6900367  6900379  6900403  6900407  6900409  6900427  6900433  6900449  6900469  6900479
6900497  6900499  6900527  6900533  6900559  6900563  6900577  6900599  6900601
6900613  6900643  6900659  6900679  6900689  6900727  6900731  6900739  6900767  6900787
6900791  6900821  6900823  6900841  6900847  6900853  6900863  6900877  6900889  6900911
6900913  6900917  6900919  6900923  6900937  6900947  6900961  6900967  6900973  6900977
6901007  6901033  6901049  6901061  6901073  6901087  6901091  6901109  6901163  6901187
6901207  6901241  6901253  6901261  6901273  6901291  6901331  6901369  6901379  6901381
6901387  6901397  6901399  6901417  6901429  6901441  6901451  6901459  6901463  6901511
6901513  6901523  6901529  6901547  6901589  6901591  6901597  6901613  6901637  6901651
6901673  6901691  6901699  6901751  6901753  6901777  6901781  6901789  6901799  6901823
6901837  6901849  6901859  6901889  6901891  6901897  6901901  6901907  6901919  6901957
6902003  6902011  6902033  6902053  6902083  6902101  6902107  6902113  6902131  6902141
6902171  6902179  6902183  6902213  6902219  6902237  6902257  6902293  6902297  6902303
6902321  6902341  6902353  6902359  6902381  6902393  6902417  6902431  6902437  6902447
6902479  6902503  6902523  6902537  6902543  6902557  6902591  6902627  6902633  6902657
6902659  6902671  6902689  6902711  6902717  6902741  6902759  6902767  6902789  6902803
6902813  6902827  6902849  6902851  6902881  6902893  6902897  6902911  6902923  6902927
6902933  6902939  6902971  6902983  6902989  6903007  6903041  6903067  6903089  6903103
6903109  6903121  6903161  6903167  6903179  6903191  6903209  6903217  6903227  6903271
6903301  6903311  6903317  6903331  6903341  6903353  6903367  6903371  6903383  6903389
6903397  6903419  6903437  6903439  6903443  6903461  6903467  6903503  6903529  6903563
6903577  6903599  6903601  6903623  6903643  6903647  6903679  6903737  6903739  6903773
6903811  6903901  6903913  6903937  6903977  6904033  6904039  6904063  6904067  6904081
6904097  6904099  6904109  6904129  6904133  6904171  6904181  6904207  6904217  6904229
6904231  6904241  6904279  6904309  6904321  6904333  6904367  6904369  6904379  6904421
6904427  6904433  6904463  6904483  6904487  6904501  6904507  6904519  6904561  6904571
6904591  6904613  6904627  6904631  6904633  6904637  6904643  6904649  6904691  6904693
6904721  6904727  6904747  6904757  6904763  6904789  6904801  6904831  6904883  6904901
6904913  6904921  6904927  6904943  6904957  6904973  6904979  6904981  6904993  6905011
```

```
6905027 6905029 6905039 6905053 6905057 6905071 6905123 6905137 6905149 6905167
6905191 6905201 6905203 6905207 6905231 6905263 6905237 6905263 6905291 6905293
6905299 6905323 6905329 6905357 6905363 6905377 6905399 6905401 6905407 6905411
6905443 6905449 6905453 6905461 6905473 6905491 6905513 6905533 6905573 6905579
6905597 6905611 6905629 6905651 6905669 6905677 6905699 6905707 6905713 6905729
6905737 6905771 6905779 6905783 6905803 6905807 6905827 6905831 6905837 6905863
6905867 6905869 6905881 6905923 6905947 6905971 6905981 6906007 6906017 6906041
6906043 6906061 6906071 6906073 6906079 6906103 6906143 6906157 6906167 6906169
6906173 6906203 6906209 6906217 6906223 6906229 6906247 6906257 6906269 6906283
6906313 6906323 6906343 6906401 6906407 6906421 6906461 6906467 6906469 6906499
6906511 6906527 6906541 6906551 6906569 6906577 6906593 6906631 6906637 6906649
6906661 6906677 6906689 6906719 6906761 6906763 6906793 6906797 6906803 6906817
6906821 6906833 6906853 6906857 6906859 6906881 6906883 6906917 6906919 6906931
6906941 6906943 6906973 6906989 6906997 6907001 6907007 6907027 6907031 6907037
6907039 6907063 6907111 6907139 6907157 6907183 6907211 6907217 6907223 6907247
6907259 6907297 6907309 6907319 6907349 6907361 6907363 6907367 6907399 6907409
6907427 6907441 6907463 6907501 6907517 6907531 6907541 6907553 6907561 6907591
6907609 6907619 6907631 6907643 6907673 6907679 6907711 6907723 6907727 6907739
6907741 6907753 6907781 6907793 6907799 6907819 6907843 6907853 6907867
6907877 6907891 6907909 6907949 6907969 6907987 6908017 6908021 6908047 6908059
6908081 6908101 6908117 6908149 6908183 6908203 6908207 6908249 6908263 6908281
6908287 6908309 6908329 6908357 6908359 6908383 6908387 6908393 6908399 6908411
6908413 6908431 6908453 6908507 6908521 6908527 6908537 6908557 6908569 6908581
6908597 6908599 6908611 6908621 6908633 6908651 6908653 6908687 6908711 6908717
6908729 6908743 6908771 6908777 6908779 6908789 6908801 6908807 6908813 6908827
6908831 6908833 6908867 6908887 6908893 6908897 6908917 6908929 6908969 6908971
6908983 6908999 6909011 6909013 6909017 6909037 6909041 6909053 6909059 6909109
6909113 6909127 6909151 6909167 6909173 6909247 6909257 6909263 6909271 6909281
6909289 6909299 6909317 6909319 6909323 6909341 6909347 6909359 6909379 6909389
6909391 6909437 6909439 6909449 6909457 6909467 6909473 6909493 6909503 6909533
6909547 6909563 6909571 6909583 6909587 6909613 6909629 6909641 6909647 6909659
6909677 6909709 6909719 6909751 6909761 6909787 6909817 6909823 6909827 6909841
6909887 6909899 6909907 6909919 6909923 6909941 6909949 6909967 6909983 6909997
6910027 6910069 6910073 6910103 6910121 6910133 6910147 6910159 6910187 6910201
6910237 6910249 6910261 6910271 6910291 6910301 6910333 6910361 6910369 6910403
6910411 6910429 6910459 6910441 6910499 6910513 6910523 6910529 6910537
6910597 6910637 6910639 6910679 6910697 6910703 6910733 6910747 6910759 6910763
6910777 6910781 6910801 6910807 6910819 6910853 6910867 6910901 6910909 6910913
6910921 6910931 6910951 6910963 6910979 6910979 6910997 6911029 6911033 6911053
6911057 6911059 6911081 6911087 6911101 6911131 6911141 6911183 6911189 6911207
6911221 6911227 6911249 6911257 6911263 6911273 6911279 6911291 6911321 6911323
6911371 6911381 6911389 6911407 6911413 6911423 6911441 6911447 6911461 6911507
6911539 6911549 6911561 6911579 6911587 6911591 6911603 6911621 6911627 6911633
6911647 6911683 6911693 6911701 6911719 6911731 6911743 6911759 6911761 6911771
6911797 6911819 6911833 6911837 6911857 6911873 6911887 6911897 6911899 6911917
6911939 6911941 6911969 6911987 6912011 6912019 6912023 6912049 6912071
6912089 6912091 6912131 6912133 6912173 6912187 6912203 6912211 6912223 6912253
6912271 6912277 6912281 6912299 6912329 6912359 6912361 6912407 6912461 6912463
6912487 6912497 6912517 6912539 6912547 6912569 6912583 6912593 6912611 6912613
6912623 6912649 6912677 6912683 6912707 6912709 6912733 6912757 6912769 6912779
6912797 6912833 6912869 6912911 6912929 6912943 6912953 6912959 6912967 6912977
6912989 6913003 6913009 6913013 6913019 6913021 6913073 6913079 6913111 6913121
6913129 6913139 6913141 6913171 6913177 6913189 6913201 6913213 6913229 6913259
6913273 6913301 6913331 6913337 6913351 6913367 6913381 6913393 6913421 6913429
6913433 6913447 6913457 6913469 6913471 6913507 6913519 6913523 6913531 6913541
6913573 6913603 6913607 6913631 6913649 6913661 6913693 6913703 6913723 6913727
6913733 6913741 6913759 6913763 6913793 6913799 6913807 6913813 6913831 6913847
6913859 6913877 6913889 6913897 6913943 6913957 6913969 6913987 6913993 6913997
6914003 6914021 6914059 6914069 6914077 6914101 6914111 6914113 6914129 6914137
6914161 6914177 6914213 6914251 6914263 6914279 6914293 6914339 6914351 6914353
6914371 6914377 6914429 6914429 6914431 6914459 6914471 6914473 6914543 6914569
6914587 6914599 6914603 6914641 6914657 6914659 6914683 6914711 6914717 6914723
6914729 6914759 6914771 6914783 6914807 6914821 6914861 6914863 6914909
6914923 6914933 6914939 6914951 6914981 6914989 6915011 6915043 6915053 6915061
6915067 6915091 6915119 6915121 6915127 6915149 6915151 6915173 6915179 6915191
6915193 6915197 6915199 6915247 6915269 6915289 6915299 6915319 6915367 6915371
6915407 6915431 6915451 6915457 6915463 6915473 6915497 6915499 6915521 6915529
6915541 6915551 6915589 6915607 6915619 6915661 6915683 6915703 6915737 6915743
6915763 6915817 6915823 6915827 6915841 6915851 6915863 6915869 6915871 6915901
6915907 6915911 6915973 6915967 6915983 6916001 6916027 6916033 6916051
6916073 6916081 6916099 6916103 6916109 6916121 6916153 6916187 6916199 6916243
6916277 6916289 6916291 6916303 6916313 6916319 6916333 6916337 6916339 6916387
6916397 6916409 6916411 6916439 6916451 6916463 6916489 6916493 6916517 6916519
6916543 6916549 6916561 6916571 6916573 6916601 6916619 6916633 6916673 6916681
6916691 6916697 6916711 6916727 6916769 6916771 6916787 6916799 6916829 6916837
6916873 6916883 6916919 6916933 6916939 6916957 6916961 6916963 6917021 6917047
6917063 6917081 6917093 6917107 6917111 6917143 6917149 6917153 6917173 6917177
6917179 6917191 6917201 6917221 6917243 6917279 6917293 6917297 6917299 6917327
6917329 6917353 6917357 6917359 6917381 6917431 6917441 6917473 6917489 6917497
6917513 6917531 6917543 6917551 6917567 6917579 6917593 6917611 6917621 6917629
6917633 6917663 6917693 6917707 6917723 6917731 6917737 6917753 6917761 6917773
6917783 6917791 6917803 6917821 6917831 6917839 6917857 6917879 6917893 6917899
6917923 6917941 6917947 6917959 6917983 6917993 6918001 6918011 6918013 6918017
6918019 6918029 6918047 6918061 6918083 6918091 6918103 6918127 6918161 6918173
6918179 6918187 6918203 6918221 6918229 6918253 6918257 6918271 6918277 6918287
6918323 6918341 6918343 6918347 6918349 6918361 6918383 6918389 6918391 6918397
6918403 6918409 6918419 6918427 6918433 6918449 6918467 6918481 6918491 6918521
6918533 6918551 6918553 6918577 6918581 6918599 6918619 6918623 6918647 6918649
6918689 6918731 6918739 6918749 6918761 6918763 6918799 6918827 6918839 6918851
```

```
6918853  6918943  6918953  6918959  6918973  6918979  6918997  6919009  6919019  6919039
6919043  6919061  6919069  6919093  6919109  6919117  6919141  6919177  6919181  6919189
6919223  6919229  6919247  6919261  6919271  6919277  6919279  6919303  6919307  6919327
6919331  6919361  6919379  6919397  6919399  6919421  6919427  6919433  6919441  6919453
6919463  6919469  6919489  6919499  6919501  6919511  6919519  6919537  6919543  6919547
6919567  6919607  6919613  6919639  6919651  6919673  6919681  6919687  6919691  6919699
6919721  6919723  6919751  6919753  6919769  6919807  6919817  6919853  6919879  6919897
6919903  6919907  6919909  6919919  6919937  6919943  6919963  6919967  6919973  6919981
6919993  6920041  6920059  6920093  6920101  6920129  6920131  6920149  6920169  6920201
6920203  6920219  6920227  6920257  6920273  6920279  6920293  6920297  6920311  6920323
6920339  6920341  6920371  6920383  6920387  6920399  6920423  6920429  6920449  6920453
6920477  6920483  6920489  6920509  6920521  6920569  6920587  6920597  6920629  6920651
6920681  6920707  6920741  6920761  6920773  6920791  6920801  6920803  6920827  6920831
6920833  6920869  6920909  6920917  6920939  6920941  6920951  6920983  6920987  6921007
6921017  6921037  6921041  6921043  6921077  6921097  6921107  6921127  6921133  6921139
6921157  6921179  6921181  6921197  6921209  6921221  6921223  6921247  6921281  6921283
6921317  6921319  6921337  6921347  6921353  6921433  6921437  6921443  6921447  6921449
6921451  6921493  6921503  6921511  6921521  6921527  6921547  6921571  6921583  6921599
6921613  6921637  6921653  6921671  6921709  6921727  6921749  6921763  6921779  6921791
6921793  6921847  6921857  6921869  6921877  6921883  6921917  6921949  6921961  6922001
6922007  6922033  6922037  6922051  6922081  6922087  6922127  6922129  6922141  6922147
6922169  6922187  6922189  6922193  6922207  6922229  6922231  6922261  6922273  6922297
6922309  6922319  6922343  6922369  6922381  6922397  6922427  6922457  6922469  6922477
6922483  6922499  6922501  6922523  6922541  6922547  6922577  6922603  6922607  6922633
6922637  6922639  6922649  6922661  6922667  6922673  6922679  6922693  6922697  6922709
6922739  6922759  6922763  6922787  6922801  6922813  6922841  6922847  6922879  6922901
6922907  6922921  6922933  6922943  6922969  6922999  6923003  6923009  6923017  6923027
6923039  6923047  6923057  6923071  6923089  6923117  6923123  6923149  6923197  6923209
6923243  6923249  6923263  6923303  6923309  6923321  6923327  6923341  6923347  6923363
6923377  6923381  6923417  6923419  6923459  6923461  6923479  6923503  6923533  6923537
6923563  6923593  6923627  6923669  6923671  6923673  6923681  6923687  6923701  6923717
6923723  6923737  6923747  6923753  6923767  6923783  6923821  6923869  6923887  6923893
6923909  6923911  6923929  6923971  6924013  6924019  6924023  6924031  6924041  6924053
6924059  6924089  6924097  6924101  6924107  6924119  6924131  6924139  6924149  6924319
6924163  6924193  6924221  6924223  6924233  6924241  6924251  6924263  6924277  6924319
6924331  6924343  6924403  6924409  6924413  6924427  6924431  6924433  6924451  6924479
6924487  6924523  6924551  6924553  6924581  6924583  6924629  6924641  6924667  6924739
6924761  6924787  6924829  6924833  6924847  6924857  6924887  6924893  6924901  6924917
6924947  6924961  6924991  6925003  6925019  6925049  6925057  6925067  6925099  6925109
6925111  6925123  6925151  6925153  6925157  6925159  6925199  6925201  6925211  6925249
6925283  6925301  6925319  6925333  6925337  6925349  6925393  6925421  6925423  6925439
6925441  6925447  6925453  6925483  6925517  6925531  6925547  6925559  6925561  6925563
6925571  6925573  6925601  6925609  6925619  6925631  6925643  6925649  6925661  6925663
6925673  6925717  6925727  6925733  6925777  6925781  6925799  6925811  6925813  6925819
6925847  6925889  6925901  6925909  6925931  6925949  6925957  6925973  6925999  6926011
6926039  6926057  6926081  6926083  6926107  6926111  6926119  6926131  6926137  6926149
6926173  6926177  6926207  6926209  6926239  6926251  6926261  6926291  6926321  6926347
6926351  6926357  6926399  6926419  6926443  6926461  6926471  6926501  6926551  6926567
6926573  6926581  6926587  6926599  6926617  6926627  6926629  6926639  6926651  6926669
6926687  6926693  6926743  6926761  6926771  6926779  6926783  6926791  6926797  6926809
6926833  6926851  6926863  6926869  6926891  6926893  6926947  6926951  6926961  6926987
6927017  6927023  6927079  6927083  6927091  6927101  6927113  6927119  6927127  6927133
6927139  6927169  6927181  6927227  6927247  6927281  6927293  6927329  6927373  6927391
6927407  6927421  6927461  6927497  6927509  6927511  6927521  6927523  6927559  6927563
6927581  6927611  6927631  6927637  6927667  6927689  6927703  6927719  6927731  6927743
6927757  6927793  6927797  6927803  6927821  6927827  6927829  6927841  6927863  6927871
6927887  6927889  6927901  6927971  6927979  6927997  6928003  6928021  6928043  6928049
6928073  6928079  6928091  6928099  6928111  6928133  6928151  6928157  6928171  6928219
6928237  6928241  6928247  6928249  6928261  6928279  6928301  6928307  6928309  6928347
6928349  6928409  6928417  6928421  6928423  6928457  6928487  6928489  6928511  6928513
6928517  6928529  6928541  6928609  6928619  6928643  6928661  6928667  6928679  6928699
6928703  6928729  6928759  6928763  6928771  6928777  6928781  6928793  6928811  6928813
6928829  6928847  6928887  6928897  6928931  6928951  6928969  6928973  6929009  6929019
6929023  6929033  6929071  6929077  6929093  6929099  6929107  6929113  6929147  6929159
6929161  6929189  6929191  6929201  6929203  6929267  6929317  6929333  6929339  6929359
6929381  6929401  6929413  6929423  6929431  6929437  6929441  6929443  6929453  6929467
6929479  6929497  6929513  6929519  6929537  6929551  6929561  6929563  6929569  6929581
6929621  6929641  6929651  6929659  6929701  6929707  6929717  6929723  6929729  6929759
6929789  6929809  6929827  6929887  6929891  6929899  6929903  6929917  6929921  6929929
6929939  6929941  6929953  6929981  6929983  6930023  6930031  6930037  6930047  6930067
6930071  6930073  6930089  6930113  6930127  6930151  6930167  6930173  6930191  6930223
6930233  6930241  6930257  6930277  6930281  6930299  6930311  6930323  6930367  6930379
6930389  6930409  6930431  6930461  6930463  6930481  6930499  6930503  6930523  6930527
6930529  6930541  6930551  6930557  6930563  6930569  6930587  6930589  6930593  6930601
6930607  6930619  6930641  6930643  6930653  6930661  6930673  6930719  6930727  6930731
6930769  6930779  6930793  6930811  6930851  6930853  6930857  6930929  6930947  6930961
6930977  6931007  6931013  6931049  6931069  6931097  6931103  6931117  6931129  6931147
6931155  6931157  6931159  6931163  6931187  6931193  6931207  6931229  6931237  6931273
6931283  6931297  6931313  6931339  6931361  6931363  6931373  6931387  6931391  6931403
6931411  6931429  6931441  6931451  6931453  6931481  6931511  6931537  6931541  6931549
6931553  6931559  6931571  6931627  6931633  6931649  6931651  6931657  6931679  6931721
6931723  6931777  6931807  6931831  6931853  6931871  6931877  6931919  6931961  6931997
6932033  6932047  6932053  6932083  6932089  6932111  6932117  6932161  6932163  6932171
6932179  6932197  6932213  6932221  6932231  6932267  6932281  6932287  6932293  6932297
6932309  6932327  6932333  6932339  6932371  6932377  6932381  6932411  6932459  6932461
6932483  6932489  6932531  6932533  6932543  6932581  6932599  6932603  6932609  6932633
6932659  6932669  6932693  6932707  6932743  6932749  6932759  6932767  6932773  6932791
6932819  6932831  6932837  6932857  6932897  6932909  6932911  6932917  6932921  6932941
6932953  6932969  6932971  6932999  6933007  6933013  6933041  6933049  6933061  6933067
```

```
6933071  6933083  6933131  6933137  6933167  6933169  6933197  6933203  6933209  6933211
6933253  6933257  6933287  6933307  6933323  6933337  6933343  6933371  6933379  6933383
6933397  6933401  6933403  6933427  6933431  6933439  6933473  6933481  6933517  6933527
6933529  6933533  6933539  6933547  6933559  6933601  6933607  6933617  6933623  6933631
6933659  6933683  6933701  6933713  6933721  6933749  6933767  6933779  6933781  6933791
6933799  6933821  6933827  6933853  6933859  6933869  6933877  6933887  6933893  6933947
6933959  6933967  6933991  6934003  6934021  6934033  6934091  6934097  6934099  6934121
6934127  6934129  6934139  6934157  6934159  6934163  6934171  6934189  6934217  6934241
6934243  6934261  6934267  6934271  6934303  6934321  6934331  6934337  6934363  6934379
6934381  6934387  6934391  6934397  6934409  6934423  6934441  6934469  6934507  6934513
6934517  6934537  6934547  6934549  6934579  6934591  6934621  6934633  6934667  6934673
6934687  6934693  6934717  6934723  6934727  6934751  6934757  6934769  6934771  6934787
6934789  6934817  6934819  6934831  6934841  6934859  6934871  6934901  6934903  6934933
6934957  6934999  6935003  6935011  6935029  6935053  6935081  6935087  6935107  6935111
6935113  6935119  6935129  6935143  6935153  6935177  6935183  6935197  6935233  6935239
6935251  6935261  6935281  6935287  6935293  6935297  6935309  6935329  6935333  6935339
6935353  6935363  6935393  6935407  6935409  6935431  6935453  6935459  6935471  6935479
6935483  6935491  6935497  6935501  6935543  6935587  6935623  6935629  6935671  6935689
6935699  6935717  6935749  6935807  6935809  6935839  6935849  6935861  6935879  6935891
6935897  6935911  6935921  6935927  6935941  6935977  6935989  6935993  6936001  6936023
6936031  6936043  6936067  6936077  6936091  6936151  6936199  6936211  6936247  6936253
6936263  6936283  6936299  6936301  6936313  6936337  6936361  6936367  6936403  6936407
6936431  6936451  6936469  6936473  6936499  6936509  6936511  6936541  6936551  6936557
6936563  6936569  6936607  6936619  6936623  6936637  6936641  6936659  6936661  6936673
6936701  6936707  6936719  6936733  6936739  6936751  6936757  6936773  6936779  6936793
6936821  6936827  6936841  6936847  6936851  6936857  6936863  6936883  6936907  6936953
6936959  6936967  6936973  6936977  6936989  6936991  6936997  6937009  6937027  6937037
6937081  6937111  6937123  6937157  6937163  6937169  6937171  6937193  6937213  6937253
6937267  6937297  6937303  6937307  6937313  6937337  6937357  6937363  6937369  6937373
6937379  6937417  6937423  6937433  6937439  6937457  6937493  6937501  6937519  6937561
6937573  6937607  6937613  6937621  6937627  6937661  6937709  6937727  6937729  6937739
6937747  6937813  6937829  6937837  6937841  6937877  6937913  6937919  6937931  6937937
6937939  6937943  6937949  6937951  6937961  6937963  6937967  6937969  6938003  6938011
6938027  6938039  6938069  6938081  6938089  6938101  6938131  6938147  6938161  6938167
6938189  6938207  6938209  6938213  6938231  6938237  6938251  6938257  6938263  6938291
6938303  6938309  6938339  6938357  6938359  6938377  6938381  6938383  6938417  6938419
6938423  6938429  6938441  6938443  6938447  6938461  6938467  6938497  6938509  6938527
6938531  6938557  6938579  6938621  6938623  6938651  6938653  6938671  6938681  6938719
6938731  6938749  6938773  6938777  6938789  6938791  6938797  6938803  6938817  6938819
6938821  6938837  6938849  6938851  6938861  6938891  6938909  6938923  6938951  6938969
6938977  6938993  6938999  6939011  6939029  6939061  6939067  6939083  6939103  6939137
6939139  6939143  6939151  6939173  6939181  6939193  6939223  6939227  6939277  6939301
6939337  6939341  6939347  6939367  6939437  6939467  6939473  6939487  6939509  6939511
6939529  6939533  6939551  6939563  6939571  6939589  6939601  6939623  6939643  6939649
6939677  6939679  6939697  6939733  6939743  6939749  6939761  6939797  6939799  6939817
6939833  6939887  6939901  6939923  6939937  6939941  6939943  6939967  6940007  6940027
6940033  6940049  6940057  6940069  6940091  6940099  6940103  6940123  6940147  6940177
6940189  6940207  6940217  6940223  6940261  6940277  6940279  6940289  6940331  6940361
6940379  6940391  6940399  6940421  6940423  6940441  6940477  6940513  6940561  6940589
6940639  6940651  6940663  6940679  6940691  6940697  6940711  6940723  6940729  6940741
6940753  6940771  6940781  6940783  6940823  6940841  6940853  6940873  6940891  6940907
6940919  6940939  6940943  6940951  6940961  6940987  6940991  6941003  6941057  6941087
6941093  6941107  6941111  6941113  6941119  6941149  6941153  6941159  6941167  6941171
6941183  6941191  6941201  6941203  6941257  6941293  6941299  6941309  6941317  6941323
6941339  6941369  6941381  6941387  6941413  6941419  6941437  6941443  6941449  6941453
6941471  6941483  6941503  6941507  6941509  6941549  6941567  6941581  6941591  6941603
6941633  6941639  6941657  6941659  6941687  6941713  6941719  6941731  6941743  6941749
6941771  6941773  6941777  6941801  6941807  6941813  6941843  6941873  6941917  6941939
6941941  6941951  6941953  6941969  6941981  6942031  6942073  6942119  6942121  6942149
6942179  6942197  6942209  6942211  6942217  6942241  6942263  6942269  6942293  6942301
6942329  6942337  6942359  6942361  6942367  6942371  6942379  6942401  6942419  6942431
6942433  6942469  6942491  6942493  6942497  6942499  6942521  6942541  6942547  6942553
6942563  6942577  6942583  6942601  6942631  6942673  6942679  6942703  6942713  6942721
6942751  6942769  6942779  6942781  6942787  6942797  6942799  6942821  6942827  6942857
6942883  6942907  6942917  6942931  6942967  6942983  6942989  6942997  6943003  6943007
6943067  6943091  6943129  6943141  6943147  6943177  6943187  6943193  6943207  6943213
6943219  6943241  6943243  6943247  6943271  6943283  6943289  6943319  6943351  6943397
6943399  6943403  6943421  6943427  6943439  6943459  6943481  6943483  6943487  6943501
6943523  6943529  6943543  6943567  6943579  6943591  6943603  6943613  6943619  6943661
6943669  6943681  6943711  6943747  6943751  6943763  6943771  6943777  6943787  6943793
6943819  6943837  6943877  6943889  6943897  6943903  6943913  6943919  6943991  6944009
6944011  6944017  6944051  6944059  6944083  6944089  6944111  6944149  6944159  6944209
6944227  6944237  6944239  6944257  6944263  6944269  6944291  6944299  6944303  6944309
6944317  6944387  6944429  6944437  6944461  6944467  6944471  6944489  6944501  6944507
6944513  6944549  6944573  6944599  6944603  6944627  6944657  6944669  6944681  6944699
6944701  6944731  6944737  6944753  6944761  6944771  6944779  6944783  6944803  6944809
6944813  6944851  6944869  6944881  6944893  6944953  6944957  6944983  6944999  6945017
6945047  6945053  6945077  6945083  6945091  6945097  6945109  6945119  6945121  6945131
6945139  6945161  6945167  6945179  6945193  6945199  6945217  6945223  6945251  6945283
6945313  6945329  6945347  6945361  6945397  6945437  6945457  6945473  6945481  6945509
6945511  6945527  6945541  6945551  6945553  6945557  6945559  6945577  6945607  6945611
6945623  6945637  6945641  6945671  6945683  6945709  6945713  6945733  6945739  6945749
6945779  6945803  6945817  6945857  6945881  6945911  6945929  6945941  6945947  6945949
6945959  6946003  6946019  6946061  6946063  6946087  6946111  6946117  6946157  6946171
6946189  6946193  6946211  6946213  6946241  6946273  6946279  6946301  6946321  6946327
6946337  6946363  6946393  6946411  6946439  6946441  6946447  6946451  6946463  6946487
6946501  6946531  6946559  6946613  6946633  6946637  6946651  6946661  6946669  6946703
6946729  6946757  6946769  6946781  6946783  6946801  6946817  6946831  6946843  6946845
6946847  6946867  6946889  6946903  6946909  6946939  6946949  6946963  6946969  6946987
```

```
6946991  6946993  6946997  6947011  6947021  6947051  6947053  6947063  6947071  6947077
6947089  6947099  6947111  6947147  6947167  6947177  6947197  6947207  6947221  6947233
6947249  6947257  6947261  6947263  6947273  6947299  6947321  6947329  6947363  6947383
6947389  6947401  6947411  6947417  6947419  6947459  6947471  6947477  6947489  6947513
6947519  6947531  6947539  6947557  6947561  6947581  6947593  6947609  6947621  6947641
6947651  6947653  6947669  6947693  6947719  6947723  6947729  6947741  6947753  6947761
6947777  6947783  6947803  6947821  6947851  6947861  6947867  6947873  6947879  6947881
6947893  6947903  6947911  6947923  6947947  6947953  6947957  6947959  6948041  6948049
6948077  6948079  6948113  6948113  6948143  6948163  6948173  6948191  6948203  6948209
6948211  6948217  6948233  6948239  6948251  6948283  6948289  6948299  6948301  6948307
6948343  6948367  6948373  6948377  6948379  6948391  6948397  6948419  6948437  6948439
6948443  6948467  6948479  6948481  6948517  6948521  6948523  6948569  6948581  6948583
6948593  6948611  6948629  6948647  6948649  6948659  6948679  6948701  6948713  6948727
6948731  6948763  6948779  6948787  6948791  6948793  6948847  6948871  6948911  6948923
6948941  6948947  6948973  6948979  6949001  6949021  6949057  6949069  6949087  6949097
6949121  6949127  6949139  6949147  6949199  6949207  6949219  6949223  6949247  6949259
6949297  6949309  6949321  6949331  6949333  6949337  6949339  6949343  6949361  6949399
6949417  6949429  6949457  6949469  6949471  6949477  6949483  6949489  6949517  6949529
6949571  6949577  6949597  6949603  6949609  6949627  6949633  6949639  6949661  6949697
6949711  6949721  6949727  6949741  6949751  6949769  6949777  6949783  6949793  6949799
6949823  6949853  6949897  6949907  6949909  6949927  6949931  6949967  6949981  6949993
6950057  6950081  6950089  6950101  6950149  6950159  6950179  6950189  6950201  6950221
6950239  6950243  6950249  6950267  6950269  6950303  6950311  6950323  6950351  6950353
6950369  6950381  6950389  6950423  6950431  6950453  6950491  6950507  6950519  6950521
6950527  6950557  6950591  6950617  6950639  6950641  6950651  6950653  6950659  6950663
6950677  6950683  6950693  6950717  6950747  6950753  6950777  6950813  6950819  6950833
6950843  6950869  6950883  6950887  6950893  6950927  6950929  6950947  6950959  6950963
6951013  6951023  6951029  6951031  6951047  6951053  6951059  6951071  6951101  6951103
6951121  6951137  6951143  6951149  6951151  6951157  6951173  6951179  6951187  6951199
6951209  6951233  6951247  6951277  6951293  6951319  6951323  6951341  6951349  6951379
6951383  6951391  6951403  6951431  6951433  6951443  6951463  6951467  6951479  6951481
6951491  6951541  6951547  6951551  6951559  6951563  6951583  6951613  6951617  6951641
6951643  6951649  6951697  6951713  6951733  6951751  6951757  6951761  6951799  6951811
6951821  6951829  6951839  6951871  6951877  6951883  6951899  6951913  6951941  6951943
6951953  6951961  6951977  6951983  6951991  6952013  6952019  6952051  6952061  6952067
6952073  6952093  6952097  6952103  6952123  6952139  6952159  6952177  6952207  6952213
6952217  6952223  6952241  6952243  6952261  6952289  6952291  6952313  6952331  6952333
6952343  6952349  6952357  6952367  6952403  6952409  6952427  6952433  6952441  6952457
6952459  6952481  6952511  6952531  6952549  6952571  6952579  6952607  6952639  6952667
6952679  6952691  6952709  6952717  6952723  6952741  6952747  6952789  6952801  6952807
6952811  6952819  6952849  6952853  6952859  6952867  6952873  6952909  6952921  6952937
6952961  6952987  6952991  6952997  6952999  6953029  6953033  6953053  6953071  6953081
6953099  6953113  6953117  6953129  6953131  6953137  6953147  6953171  6953173  6953179
6953201  6953203  6953213  6953239  6953249  6953267  6953273  6953279  6953281  6953293
6953311  6953333  6953341  6953347  6953351  6953371  6953407  6953413  6953423  6953431
6953483  6953497  6953503  6953519  6953537  6953543  6953581  6953587  6953599  6953621
6953627  6953647  6953651  6953671  6953689  6953693  6953699  6953711  6953717  6953719
6953767  6953773  6953777  6953783  6953789  6953801  6953803  6953813  6953819  6953851
6953879  6953893  6953897  6953899  6953911  6953941  6953957  6953959  6953963  6953977
6953993  6954023  6954049  6954083  6954107  6954121  6954127  6954149  6954191  6954197
6954203  6954217  6954223  6954239  6954253  6954263  6954293  6954307  6954313  6954317
6954319  6954341  6954383  6954391  6954401  6954407  6954419  6954421  6954439  6954443
6954463  6954503  6954511  6954517  6954553  6954583  6954593  6954611  6954613  6954697
6954709  6954733  6954737  6954749  6954781  6954791  6954797  6954799  6954823  6954839
6954841  6954859  6954877  6954889  6954971  6954977  6955009  6955021  6955027  6955033
6955051  6955061  6955063  6955073  6955093  6955127  6955153  6955187  6955213  6955217
6955219  6955229  6955237  6955241  6955271  6955301  6955307  6955309  6955313  6955327
6955333  6955357  6955369  6955381  6955393  6955411  6955427  6955433  6955457  6955477
6955517  6955523  6955537  6955547  6955549  6955573  6955583  6955589  6955603  6955607
6955633  6955639  6955643  6955661  6955673  6955721  6955727  6955733  6955763  6955777
6955789  6955801  6955807  6955813  6955831  6955841  6955849  6955877  6955877  6955933
6955939  6955943  6955979  6956021  6956057  6956063  6956093  6956099  6956107  6956123
6956129  6956203  6956237  6956249  6956251  6956263  6956273  6956291  6956321  6956353
6956371  6956377  6956387  6956399  6956401  6956437  6956441  6956461  6956471  6956473
6956531  6956539  6956561  6956563  6956567  6956581  6956597  6956639  6956647  6956659
6956671  6956683  6956687  6956693  6956701  6956711  6956731  6956737  6956767  6956797
6956809  6956837  6956857  6956861  6956891  6956909  6956923  6956953  6956969  6957001
6957037  6957043  6957091  6957101  6957107  6957121  6957127  6957133  6957149
6957169  6957179  6957229  6957253  6957259  6957283  6957311  6957317  6957319  6957337
6957343  6957359  6957371  6957373  6957389  6957407  6957427  6957463  6957473  6957491
6957493  6957497  6957527  6957571  6957583  6957611  6957619  6957623  6957631  6957653
6957689  6957737  6957757  6957791  6957809  6957829  6957851  6957859  6957869  6957901
6957917  6957943  6957967  6957989  6957997  6958001  6958019  6958031  6958033  6958051
6958067  6958073  6958099  6958111  6958157  6958169  6958177  6958181  6958187  6958207
6958243  6958247  6958261  6958277  6958319  6958337  6958339  6958349  6958361  6958363
6958379  6958409  6958411  6958429  6958439  6958447  6958481  6958487  6958507  6958513
6958537  6958547  6958571  6958573  6958591  6958619  6958621  6958649  6958667  6958801
6958813  6958817  6958823  6958829  6958837  6958841  6958891  6958901  6958909  6958937
6958951  6958957  6959003  6959027  6959033  6959083  6959093  6959119  6959123  6959153
6959167  6959209  6959213  6959233  6959237  6959257  6959261  6959279  6959287  6959297
6959327  6959369  6959371  6959423  6959437  6959471  6959497  6959509  6959521  6959543
6959549  6959569  6959573  6959597  6959621  6959651  6959671  6959677  6959683  6959707
6959723  6959753  6959761  6959767  6959789  6959803  6959831  6959861  6959863  6959867
6959881  6959891  6959921  6959929  6959941  6959951  6959957  6959969  6959983  6959989
6959999  6960001  6960017  6960049  6960073  6960077  6960091  6960103  6960113  6960127
6960133  6960139  6960167  6960169  6960193  6960197  6960199  6960211  6960223  6960227
6960241  6960269  6960271  6960287  6960299  6960301  6960307  6960311  6960313  6960341
6960347  6960353  6960379  6960383  6960389  6960419  6960427  6960433  6960439  6960449
6960487  6960511  6960521  6960533  6960571  6960587  6960673  6960683  6960713  6960719
```

```
6960731  6960739  6960763  6960787  6960791  6960799  6960809  6960823  6960827  6960851
6960853  6960869  6960887  6960901  6960917  6960923  6960929  6960937  6960953  6960971
6960977  6961013  6961027  6961037  6961039  6961043  6961063  6961117  6961121  6961133
6961147  6961151  6961153  6961159  6961169  6961181  6961187  6961231  6961271  6961289
6961303  6961309  6961321  6961327  6961373  6961379  6961393  6961403  6961417  6961447
6961463  6961511  6961519  6961529  6961531  6961541  6961547  6961573  6961579  6961583
6961601  6961607  6961609  6961613  6961649  6961673  6961681  6961697  6961699  6961739
6961751  6961753  6961777  6961813  6961849  6961853  6961879  6961897  6961907  6961909
6961919  6961931  6961951  6961963  6961967  6961979  6962003  6962009  6962029  6962041
6962057  6962069  6962071  6962107  6962147  6962149  6962159  6962167  6962183  6962209
6962237  6962279  6962281  6962297  6962311  6962359  6962377  6962393  6962419  6962429
6962437  6962441  6962443  6962447  6962467  6962471  6962551  6962561  6962567  6962587
6962591  6962617  6962633  6962647  6962651  6962671  6962677  6962687  6962701  6962713
6962719  6962777  6962779  6962783  6962801  6962807  6962819  6962821  6962831  6962833
6962849  6962863  6962867  6962869  6962887  6962933  6962957  6962971  6962999  6963007
6963017  6963023  6963031  6963037  6963049  6963053  6963083  6963113  6963133  6963137
6963157  6963163  6963167  6963169  6963179  6963199  6963221  6963233  6963241  6963259
6963269  6963301  6963331  6963337  6963347  6963371  6963373  6963391  6963401  6963409
6963413  6963419  6963427  6963433  6963487  6963491  6963497  6963527  6963553  6963563
6963569  6963587  6963589  6963611  6963673  6963701  6963703  6963707  6963739  6963763
6963773  6963793  6963797  6963811  6963839  6963877  6963883  6963889  6963907  6963919
6963923  6963941  6963953  6963961  6963967  6963989  6964003  6964007  6964021  6964073
6964081  6964099  6964109  6964117  6964123  6964157  6964159  6964211  6964213  6964231
6964247  6964249  6964259  6964261  6964277  6964289  6964291  6964313  6964343  6964351
6964361  6964381  6964387  6964421  6964427  6964453  6964457  6964459  6964471  6964481
6964493  6964499  6964511  6964549  6964567  6964579  6964591  6964597  6964609  6964619
6964627  6964631  6964649  6964651  6964663  6964691  6964693  6964703  6964709  6964723
6964729  6964733  6964751  6964759  6964777  6964787  6964799  6964813  6964817  6964819
6964823  6964829  6964831  6964837  6964871  6964879  6964897  6964907  6964921  6964931
6964933  6964939  6964949  6964961  6964973  6965027  6965047  6965059  6965081  6965083
6965089  6965093  6965099  6965131  6965201  6965219  6965221  6965227  6965237  6965239
6965243  6965261  6965281  6965311  6965317  6965323  6965327  6965333  6965339  6965341
6965347  6965369  6965377  6965383  6965411  6965417  6965459  6965507  6965537  6965549
6965591  6965603  6965617  6965627  6965681  6965701  6965753  6965759  6965779  6965797
6965809  6965831  6965857  6965867  6965873  6965891  6965897  6965909  6965911  6965921
6965939  6965947  6965963  6965977  6966007  6966019  6966031  6966049  6966053  6966059
6966109  6966149  6966151  6966163  6966173  6966203  6966221  6966233  6966241  6966257
6966319  6966329  6966341  6966353  6966359  6966361  6966367  6966419  6966431  6966437
6966461  6966469  6966523  6966527  6966529  6966551  6966569  6966613  6966623  6966629
6966643  6966647  6966649  6966689  6966697  6966703  6966737  6966803  6966809  6966811
6966823  6966829  6966851  6966853  6966881  6966887  6966899  6966913  6966919  6966929
6966941  6966943  6966961  6966979  6966983  6966997  6967019  6967039  6967043  6967057
6967099  6967117  6967123  6967151  6967223  6967231  6967249  6967271  6967273  6967307
6967309  6967313  6967351  6967361  6967423  6967427  6967439  6967447  6967451  6967463
6967469  6967483  6967517  6967523  6967549  6967553  6967559  6967561  6967573  6967577
6967589  6967613  6967619  6967621  6967633  6967657  6967669  6967673  6967679  6967691
6967717  6967757  6967769  6967771  6967787  6967789  6967811  6967819  6967823  6967837
6967861  6967897  6967903  6967937  6967949  6967967  6967981  6967993  6967997  6967999
6968009  6968023  6968029  6968047  6968051  6968063  6968111  6968119  6968123  6968141
6968179  6968183  6968257  6968263  6968303  6968327  6968347  6968359  6968399  6968407
6968417  6968443  6968447  6968461  6968473  6968491  6968501  6968503  6968509  6968531
6968539  6968551  6968557  6968561  6968567  6968569  6968587  6968629  6968659  6968677
6968683  6968693  6968723  6968749  6968791  6968809  6968821  6968849  6968869  6968873
6968887  6968891  6968909  6968911  6968921  6968933  6968939  6968947  6968957  6968981
6968989  6968993  6968999  6969013  6969047  6969089  6969097  6969107  6969121  6969173
6969191  6969217  6969229  6969247  6969293  6969343  6969349  6969359  6969373  6969401
6969421  6969449  6969461  6969463  6969481  6969491  6969499  6969503  6969527  6969563
6969587  6969607  6969619  6969629  6969647  6969661  6969671  6969673  6969689  6969691
6969733  6969757  6969791  6969793  6969803  6969811  6969817  6969829  6969839  6969841
6969869  6969883  6969899  6969901  6969917  6969923  6969931  6969971  6969973  6970013
6970037  6970039  6970049  6970069  6970099  6970157  6970247  6970253  6970267
6970273  6970277  6970279  6970291  6970297  6970303  6970307  6970309  6970331  6970339
6970349  6970351  6970361  6970387  6970417  6970447  6970463  6970471  6970477  6970487
6970499  6970519  6970543  6970547  6970553  6970571  6970603  6970619  6970627  6970637
6970681  6970693  6970741  6970751  6970793  6970801  6970811  6970813  6970829  6970841
6970849  6970879  6970889  6970907  6970961  6970973  6970981  6971009  6971017  6971033
6971051  6971053  6971057  6971089  6971101  6971113  6971123  6971131  6971137  6971161
6971177  6971183  6971201  6971219  6971221  6971227  6971243  6971257  6971287  6971297
6971299  6971303  6971317  6971333  6971351  6971357  6971383  6971389  6971399  6971401
6971431  6971441  6971453  6971467  6971473  6971477  6971509  6971539  6971543  6971579
6971603  6971609  6971611  6971641  6971647  6971659  6971669  6971677  6971693  6971707
6971711  6971729  6971747  6971753  6971777  6971791  6971827  6971837  6971857  6971863
6971893  6971897  6971903  6971911  6971959  6971963  6971981  6972001  6972019
6972029  6972037  6972041  6972061  6972071  6972079  6972127  6972233  6972253  6972269
6972281  6972293  6972307  6972311  6972313  6972319  6972359  6972389  6972401  6972451
6972467  6972491  6972509  6972517  6972547  6972569  6972571  6972593  6972607  6972617
6972629  6972631  6972643  6972649  6972659  6972661  6972683  6972689  6972709  6972739
6972743  6972781  6972787  6972793  6972811  6972859  6972863
6972871  6972877  6972893  6972899  6972961  6973003  6973007  6973069  6973073  6973081
6973091  6973103  6973121  6973139  6973147  6973193  6973201  6973207
6973223  6973229  6973231  6973259  6973271  6973273  6973277  6973289  6973319  6973333
6973381  6973391  6973397  6973423  6973429  6973441  6973453  6973489  6973517  6973529
6973573  6973579  6973583  6973591  6973597  6973609  6973613  6973619  6973639  6973651
6973657  6973663  6973679  6973699  6973709  6973721  6973727  6973739  6973787  6973801
6973819  6973831  6973843  6973847  6973861  6973867  6973883  6973897  6973913
6973919  6973921  6973933  6973957  6973973  6973987  6973999  6974017  6974053  6974057
6974081  6974089  6974137  6974171  6974173  6974179  6974251  6974257  6974321  6974329
6974333  6974339  6974351  6974371  6974399  6974417  6974419  6974423  6974431  6974447
6974453  6974467  6974477  6974479  6974483  6974489  6974491  6974503  6974507  6974509
```

```
6974519  6974521  6974531  6974563  6974609  6974623  6974629  6974647  6974651  6974657
6974683  6974687  6974689  6974711  6974731  6974741  6974749  6974789  6974791  6974809
6974837  6974857  6974861  6974867  6974887  6974897  6974899  6974909  6974917  6974939
6974963  6974983  6974999  6975053  6975061  6975079  6975091  6975097  6975103  6975107
6975119  6975121  6975127  6975139  6975193  6975209  6975211  6975229  6975239  6975247
6975281  6975313  6975323  6975329  6975343  6975349  6975359  6975361  6975373  6975379
6975401  6975407  6975427  6975433  6975461  6975467  6975481  6975497  6975523  6975539
6975581  6975583  6975587  6975611  6975613  6975623  6975643  6975653  6975659  6975697
6975707  6975719  6975743  6975769  6975791  6975799  6975803  6975827  6975833  6975841
6975883  6975887  6975889  6975919  6975929  6975971  6976033  6976051  6976093  6976111
6976117  6976121  6976127  6976139  6976157  6976169  6976181  6976217  6976223  6976243
6976259  6976261  6976267  6976279  6976289  6976301  6976309  6976331  6976349  6976369
6976379  6976381  6976393  6976421  6976423  6976433  6976441  6976471  6976483  6976517
6976523  6976547  6976561  6976577  6976589  6976637  6976661  6976679  6976693  6976699
6976729  6976747  6976771  6976787  6976861  6976873  6976877  6976903  6976939  6976951
6976961  6976993  6977017  6977029  6977041  6977057  6977059  6977071  6977101  6977107
6977141  6977147  6977153  6977167  6977171  6977181  6977183  6977207  6977213  6977219
6977221  6977227  6977231  6977239  6977251  6977261  6977281  6977287  6977297  6977317
6977329  6977331  6977381  6977393  6977407  6977419  6977431  6977461  6977471  6977483
6977489  6977491  6977527  6977569  6977587  6977611  6977623  6977639  6977681  6977683
6977687  6977699  6977723  6977741  6977743  6977767  6977797  6977813  6977827  6977843
6977891  6977897  6977903  6977923  6977969  6978001  6978011  6978019  6978031  6978047
6978061  6978091  6978113  6978133  6978173  6978199  6978221  6978227  6978247
6978253  6978281  6978287  6978319  6978371  6978383  6978421  6978431  6978437  6978451
6978463  6978467  6978469  6978481  6978511  6978547  6978593  6978613  6978617  6978641
6978649  6978659  6978677  6978703  6978707  6978709  6978739  6978743  6978749  6978761
6978779  6978793  6978809  6978841  6978869  6978877  6978883  6978901  6978911  6978919
6978929  6978931  6978941  6978973  6978991  6979001  6979003  6979009  6979013  6979033
6979057  6979067  6979093  6979117  6979139  6979153  6979187  6979207  6979223  6979237
6979241  6979249  6979261  6979267  6979277  6979279  6979303  6979361  6979363  6979381
6979391  6979393  6979429  6979439  6979463  6979477  6979481  6979487  6979493  6979507
6979519  6979529  6979543  6979561  6979573  6979579  6979663  6979667  6979697  6979699
6979703  6979727  6979733  6979769  6979771  6979781  6979789  6979801  6979831  6979853
6979871  6979883  6979891  6979901  6979913  6979919  6979937  6979943  6979957  6979961
6979967  6980021  6980027  6980069  6980089  6980101  6980117  6980137  6980159  6980167
6980173  6980179  6980191  6980221  6980227  6980257  6980263  6980269
6980273  6980279  6980317  6980327  6980341  6980357  6980371  6980399  6980401  6980417
6980419  6980423  6980443  6980453  6980461  6980497  6980509  6980521  6980527  6980551
6980587  6980593  6980611  6980621  6980629  6980641  6980647  6980669  6980681
6980711  6980717  6980731  6980737  6980777  6980833  6980849  6980899  6980903  6980927
6980929  6980969  6980977  6981011  6981043  6981053  6981059  6981061  6981103  6981133
6981157  6981181  6981211  6981229  6981251  6981263  6981277  6981283  6981287  6981301
6981313  6981323  6981329  6981349  6981367  6981371  6981391  6981409  6981421  6981433
6981463  6981483  6981497  6981503  6981539  6981551  6981563  6981593  6981599  6981613
6981619  6981631  6981659  6981661  6981671  6981697  6981703  6981731  6981739  6981749
6981757  6981791  6981823  6981829  6981841  6981847  6981853  6981859  6981889  6981943
6981959  6981967  6981973  6981977  6981983  6982009  6982021  6982033  6982049  6982051
6982057  6982081  6982093  6982111  6982147  6982153  6982163  6982181  6982193  6982207
6982219  6982229  6982247  6982279  6982319  6982343  6982357  6982369  6982397  6982403
6982411  6982421  6982429  6982457  6982463  6982489  6982531  6982537  6982553  6982561
6982567  6982571  6982579  6982583  6982601  6982607  6982621  6982627  6982643  6982691
6982721  6982741  6982763  6982783  6982793  6982817  6982819  6982831  6982849  6982879
6982901  6982907  6982951  6982957  6982979  6982981  6982991  6982999  6983003  6983017
6983021  6983023  6983033  6983057  6983077  6983087  6983101  6983111  6983129  6983143
6983147  6983189  6983231  6983233  6983257  6983261  6983281  6983309  6983323  6983357
6983359  6983377  6983381  6983387  6983421  6983431  6983437  6983497  6983531  6983567
6983579  6983593  6983597  6983609  6983629  6983657  6983671  6983677  6983699  6983723
6983729  6983731  6983737  6983747  6983797  6983803  6983807  6983843  6983947
6983953  6983971  6983987  6983993  6984023  6984031  6984053  6984071  6984079  6984101
6984139  6984143  6984149  6984151  6984163  6984167  6984169  6984179  6984193  6984209
6984239  6984253  6984277  6984283  6984301  6984319  6984323  6984337  6984347  6984349
6984353  6984371  6984409  6984437  6984449  6984463  6984487  6984511  6984521  6984541
6984547  6984559  6984581  6984587  6984613  6984629  6984689  6984697  6984707  6984721
6984727  6984743  6984751  6984779  6984793  6984797  6984881  6984907  6984917  6984931
6984937  6984941  6984949  6984953  6984959  6984961  6984979  6984983  6984997  6985001
6985009  6985021  6985037  6985073  6985081  6985133  6985157  6985159  6985183  6985213
6985229  6985243  6985247  6985301  6985309  6985327  6985361  6985367  6985373
6985397  6985403  6985421  6985427  6985439  6985441  6985481  6985499  6985513
6985519  6985523  6985553  6985579  6985603  6985609  6985631  6985639  6985679  6985681
6985687  6985697  6985717  6985753  6985763  6985789  6985799  6985829  6985831  6985841
6985871  6985883  6985907  6985931  6985961  6985967  6985969  6985973  6985981  6986011
6986047  6986087  6986093  6986101  6986117  6986123  6986171  6986197  6986219  6986257
6986261  6986297  6986299  6986311  6986321  6986323  6986327  6986333  6986341  6986383
6986389  6986401  6986423  6986431  6986437  6986449  6986453  6986489  6986491  6986519
6986521  6986533  6986537  6986543  6986569  6986587  6986591  6986627  6986647  6986669
6986671  6986689  6986713  6986717  6986719  6986723  6986729  6986731  6986753  6986761
6986773  6986783  6986789  6986801  6986807  6986849  6986869  6986887  6986891  6986909
6986911  6986977  6986989  6987031  6987037  6987047  6987053  6987077  6987083  6987091
6987103  6987107  6987109  6987139  6987163  6987203  6987241  6987247  6987251  6987257
6987263  6987271  6987293  6987359  6987373  6987397  6987403  6987419  6987427  6987433
6987451  6987473  6987499  6987509  6987511  6987517  6987523  6987529  6987551  6987557
6987583  6987593  6987601  6987613  6987619  6987661  6987677  6987683  6987703  6987707
6987713  6987719  6987727  6987737  6987767  6987769  6987793  6987797  6987817
6987821  6987823  6987847  6987863  6987907  6987923  6987941  6987943  6987949  6987971
6987979  6987983  6988039  6988049  6988057  6988073  6988123  6988127  6988133  6988141
6988169  6988193  6988199  6988211  6988213  6988243  6988253  6988271  6988273  6988307
6988313  6988321  6988357  6988367  6988379  6988417  6988427  6988439  6988451  6988453
6988463  6988483  6988511  6988537  6988543  6988549  6988567  6988589  6988603  6988607
6988621  6988627  6988643  6988669  6988691  6988763  6988769  6988771  6988777  6988799
```

```
6988811  6988829  6988841  6988847  6988871  6988873  6988879  6988907  6988909  6988931
6988939  6988991  6988999  6989009  6989039  6989063  6989071  6989107  6989111  6989113
6989119  6989123  6989137  6989153  6989183  6989219  6989233  6989237  6989249  6989267
6989273  6989287  6989293  6989303  6989327  6989341  6989351  6989357  6989369  6989383
6989387  6989419  6989429  6989443  6989449  6989459  6989461  6989491  6989497  6989501
6989509  6989519  6989537  6989573  6989579  6989581  6989599  6989617  6989627  6989651
6989657  6989669  6989687  6989713  6989729  6989743  6989761  6989791  6989809  6989813
6989819  6989821  6989833  6989869  6989921  6989923  6989933  6989947  6989959  6989963
6989987  6990001  6990017  6990019  6990041  6990059  6990107  6990161  6990187  6990199
6990227  6990241  6990251  6990253  6990259  6990289  6990307  6990317  6990323  6990331
6990337  6990341  6990353  6990359  6990371  6990419  6990427  6990439  6990463  6990493
6990517  6990527  6990547  6990559  6990563  6990611  6990617  6990619  6990629  6990667
6990673  6990677  6990679  6990691  6990701  6990703  6990721  6990749  6990751  6990761
6990799  6990821  6990829  6990839  6990853  6990857  6990871  6990881  6990889  6990901
6990911  6990913  6990923  6990953  6990959  6990967  6991003  6991013  6991043  6991091
6991093  6991099  6991111  6991129  6991133  6991147  6991253  6991277  6991289  6991319
6991363  6991381  6991417  6991427  6991447  6991459  6991463  6991493  6991511  6991513
6991531  6991541  6991549  6991553  6991571  6991577  6991597  6991603  6991613  6991619
6991657  6991667  6991687  6991693  6991711  6991723  6991729  6991741  6991783  6991799
6991819  6991823  6991841  6991847  6991877  6991889  6991903  6991939  6991951  6991967
6991969  6991973  6991979  6991991  6991993  6991997  6992039  6992047  6992059  6992119
6992137  6992147  6992177  6992189  6992191  6992201  6992231  6992233  6992257
6992261  6992269  6992317  6992333  6992339  6992347  6992351  6992353  6992383  6992407
6992417  6992429  6992443  6992467  6992471  6992507  6992543  6992569  6992581
6992599  6992651  6992653  6992681  6992693  6992731  6992737  6992749  6992753  6992803
6992807  6992809  6992813  6992849  6992879  6992903  6992917  6992927  6992941  6992957
6992959  6992971  6992981  6992983  6993043  6993061  6993067  6993071  6993079  6993131
6993149  6993163  6993167  6993169  6993187  6993221  6993257  6993269  6993277  6993281
6993293  6993299  6993319  6993323  6993367  6993401  6993421  6993451  6993461  6993479
6993499  6993517  6993523  6993533  6993551  6993557  6993559  6993583  6993593  6993599
6993607  6993667  6993671  6993673  6993677  6993689  6993719  6993733  6993737  6993751
6993769  6993773  6993781  6993787  6993799  6993823  6993839  6993853  6993869  6993893
6993913  6993937  6993979  6994007  6994019  6994027  6994049  6994051  6994103  6994111
6994121  6994151  6994153  6994159  6994171  6994177  6994181  6994187  6994201  6994213
6994219  6994237  6994279  6994289  6994291  6994297  6994301  6994303  6994319  6994333
6994363  6994373  6994387  6994409  6994411  6994417  6994433  6994447  6994457  6994459
6994469  6994487  6994511  6994529  6994549  6994567  6994577  6994579  6994583  6994601
6994607  6994613  6994621  6994649  6994661  6994693  6994703  6994711  6994727  6994751
6994759  6994811  6994817  6994843  6994847  6994859  6994873  6994891  6994903  6994913
6994919  6994927  6994951  6994987  6994997  6995017  6995029  6995047  6995069  6995071
6995077  6995089  6995101  6995113  6995117  6995123  6995137  6995147  6995161  6995171
6995179  6995189  6995207  6995227  6995231  6995267  6995281  6995309  6995333  6995341
6995353  6995383  6995389  6995393  6995399  6995407  6995411  6995431  6995497  6995501
6995503  6995509  6995533  6995539  6995557  6995567  6995617  6995623  6995647  6995683
6995693  6995711  6995719  6995753  6995759  6995761  6995777  6995803  6995837  6995839
6995851  6995861  6995899  6995909  6995927  6995941  6995951  6995957  6995977  6995983
6995999  6996001  6996007  6996019  6996037  6996079  6996083  6996089  6996097  6996103
6996109  6996133  6996137  6996149  6996167  6996181  6996191  6996203  6996211  6996217
6996233  6996239  6996257  6996271  6996277  6996289  6996307  6996349  6996377  6996419
6996433  6996461  6996491  6996499  6996523  6996529  6996559  6996611  6996629  6996631
6996643  6996653  6996679  6996701  6996709  6996713  6996721  6996733  6996739  6996823
6996839  6996851  6996907  6996923  6996947  6996961  6996967  6996989  6997021  6997043
6997057  6997063  6997069  6997087  6997093  6997097  6997117  6997139  6997147  6997153
6997157  6997163  6997171  6997201  6997213  6997229  6997231  6997253  6997259  6997273
6997283  6997303  6997307  6997321  6997327  6997343  6997349  6997357  6997363  6997369
6997373  6997379  6997411  6997457  6997469  6997499  6997513  6997531  6997559  6997579
6997597  6997603  6997607  6997609  6997619  6997621  6997631  6997633  6997649  6997651
6997657  6997663  6997687  6997733  6997747  6997789  6997807  6997817  6997841  6997843
6997849  6997867  6997873  6997891  6997901  6997927  6997937  6997967  6998009  6998029
6998039  6998051  6998053  6998059  6998063  6998087  6998093  6998107  6998111  6998113
6998153  6998161  6998171  6998177  6998191  6998197  6998209  6998221  6998261  6998267
6998269  6998287  6998297  6998353  6998357  6998377  6998389  6998393  6998401  6998419
6998423  6998447  6998449  6998461  6998471  6998473  6998489  6998501  6998533  6998561
6998581  6998603  6998617  6998623  6998627  6998681  6998687  6998711  6998737  6998749
6998767  6998779  6998833  6998837  6998851  6998857  6998861  6998863  6998869  6998909
6998921  6998933  6998939  6998941  6998983  6998989  6999007  6999017  6999023  6999037
6999059  6999071  6999073  6999077  6999103  6999131  6999143  6999169  6999173  6999203
6999241  6999263  6999271  6999281  6999283  6999299  6999341  6999361  6999367  6999373
6999379  6999389  6999409  6999413  6999431  6999449  6999457  6999463  6999481  6999491
6999493  6999523  6999533  6999539  6999547  6999589  6999599  6999611  6999647  6999661
6999673  6999703  6999721  6999731  6999749  6999781  6999799  6999821  6999823  6999829
6999857  6999877  6999899  6999911  6999929  6999973  6999989  6999997  7000003  7000009
7000033  7000057  7000061  7000069  7000087  7000109  7000121  7000127  7000129  7000157
7000163  7000171  7000181  7000219  7000241  7000249  7000267  7000297  7000309  7000313
7000333  7000337  7000351  7000373  7000391  7000429  7000459  7000517  7000519  7000523
7000541  7000573  7000577  7000589  7000619  7000633  7000657  7000661  7000663  7000673
7000703  7000727  7000739  7000751  7000757  7000793  7000811  7000831  7000841  7000849
7000913  7000943  7000969  7001003  7001011  7001021  7001041  7001047  7001051  7001069
7001077  7001083  7001087  7001089  7001107  7001123  7001213  7001221  7001233  7001237
7001249  7001273  7001279  7001287  7001311  7001317  7001327  7001343  7001347  7001359
7001369  7001377  7001387  7001411  7001413  7001429  7001431  7001437  7001479  7001507
7001513  7001537  7001581  7001587  7001597  7001639  7001653  7001663  7001669  7001681
7001689  7001713  7001723  7001767  7001779  7001783  7001803  7001831  7001851  7001879
7001887  7001893  7001921  7001923  7001927  7001999  7002019  7002029  7002041  7002053
7002059  7002067  7002071  7002101  7002109  7002131  7002157  7002161  7002167  7002197
7002199  7002217  7002221  7002223  7002227  7002257  7002293  7002319  7002337  7002353
7002367  7002377  7002383  7002397  7002409  7002433  7002439  7002449  7002451  7002491
7002529  7002539  7002551  7002581  7002587  7002599  7002613  7002629  7002631  7002637
7002641  7002673  7002689  7002701  7002703  7002713  7002719  7002733  7002781  7002791
```

```
7002803  7002823  7002839  7002871  7002881  7002883  7002889  7002899  7002917  7002973
7002979  7002991  7003021  7003057  7003079  7003081  7003091  7003093  7003097  7003103
7003111  7003121  7003127  7003163  7003189  7003207  7003223  7003231  7003273  7003289
7003313  7003327  7003351  7003357  7003361  7003379  7003393  7003411  7003421  7003463
7003487  7003537  7003543  7003561  7003573  7003589  7003603  7003639  7003651  7003657
7003679  7003687  7003697  7003721  7003727  7003729  7003739  7003741  7003757  7003769
7003771  7003781  7003783  7003807  7003811  7003849  7003859  7003879  7003889  7003901
7003933  7003939  7003943  7003957  7003961  7003963  7003991  7003999  7004009  7004057
7004059  7004069  7004077  7004083  7004087  7004093  7004099  7004111  7004117  7004143
7004149  7004159  7004189  7004191  7004197  7004201  7004237  7004243  7004279  7004281
7004297  7004329  7004339  7004353  7004383  7004401  7004429  7004441  7004461  7004471
7004477  7004497  7004509  7004513  7004593  7004603  7004609  7004611  7004623  7004633
7004651  7004677  7004681  7004713  7004717  7004737  7004741  7004759  7004771  7004797
7004843  7004873  7004887  7004897  7004909  7004911  7004941  7005013  7005017  7005023
7005059  7005077  7005107  7005113  7005121  7005127  7005151  7005161  7005181  7005197
7005199  7005203  7005227  7005239  7005277  7005293  7005331  7005347  7005359  7005371
7005373  7005391  7005403  7005419  7005421  7005451  7005463  7005511  7005521  7005527
7005529  7005541  7005569  7005571  7005613  7005619  7005637  7005643  7005673  7005697
7005703  7005727  7005743  7005763  7005767  7005787  7005809  7005821  7005827  7005847
7005863  7005877  7005899  7005917  7005931  7005941  7005953  7005959  7005979  7005983
7005997  7006063  7006133  7006141  7006147  7006157  7006171  7006177  7006183  7006187
7006189  7006201  7006211  7006247  7006289  7006297  7006303  7006319  7006331  7006343
7006361  7006379  7006381  7006393  7006423  7006451  7006457  7006477  7006481  7006637
7006541  7006553  7006561  7006577  7006607  7006621  7006627  7006633  7006639  7006667
7006679  7006693  7006709  7006723  7006729  7006733  7006751  7006757  7006787  7006799
7006817  7006823  7006829  7006843  7006849  7006871  7006891  7006903  7006933  7006963
7006969  7006981  7006997  7006999  7007003  7007027  7007041  7007069  7007071  7007081
7007083  7007087  7007101  7007107  7007113  7007137  7007149  7007159  7007173  7007177
7007191  7007227  7007267  7007303  7007309  7007311  7007317  7007347  7007353  7007369
7007389  7007401  7007411  7007419  7007423  7007437  7007449  7007459  7007461  7007471
7007477  7007491  7007503  7007509  7007527  7007563  7007569  7007579  7007603  7007633
7007729  7007779  7007783  7007797  7007809  7007813  7007831  7007857  7007867  7007873
7007899  7007909  7007933  7007947  7007951  7007969  7007977  7007983  7007989  7007993
7008013  7008019  7008037  7008041  7008047  7008091  7008101  7008103  7008119  7008121
7008143  7008151  7008163  7008173  7008181  7008191  7008203  7008247  7008251  7008259
7008317  7008319  7008329  7008341  7008361  7008413  7008427  7008451  7008457  7008461
7008467  7008479  7008493  7008523  7008557  7008559  7008563  7008569  7008601  7008611
7008619  7008653  7008671  7008679  7008707  7008713  7008751  7008761  7008763  7008779
7008817  7008851  7008853  7008857  7008887  7008889  7008891  7008901  7008917  7008943
7008977  7009001  7009019  7009031  7009099  7009111  7009133  7009139  7009147  7009159
7009183  7009199  7009201  7009217  7009231  7009279  7009291  7009297  7009307  7009313
7009337  7009349  7009351  7009361  7009363  7009393  7009397  7009399  7009421  7009427
7009447  7009469  7009477  7009481  7009487  7009493  7009507  7009517  7009543  7009547
7009553  7009577  7009601  7009603  7009609  7009637  7009643  7009657  7009663  7009669
7009699  7009711  7009757  7009773  7009777  7009799  7009801  7009823  7009859  7009867
7009889  7009897  7009921  7009969  7009979  7009991  7009997  7010011  7010021  7010023
7010033  7010041  7010051  7010089  7010099  7010111  7010119  7010197  7010209  7010219
7010231  7010281  7010291  7010293  7010317  7010323  7010329  7010347  7010351  7010357
7010359  7010417  7010447  7010453  7010459  7010483  7010491  7010503  7010513  7010537
7010543  7010551  7010569  7010573  7010581  7010603  7010621  7010651  7010657  7010659
7010671  7010687  7010693  7010719  7010759  7010803  7010821  7010831  7010833  7010863
7010879  7010891  7010909  7010917  7010921  7010923  7010951  7010957  7010963  7010977
7011001  7011023  7011031  7011049  7011073  7011079  7011083  7011143  7011181  7011187
7011223  7011229  7011233  7011253  7011283  7011307  7011353  7011377  7011379  7011439
7011479  7011491  7011503  7011547  7011553  7011559  7011593  7011607  7011637  7011647
7011659  7011661  7011671  7011677  7011713  7011731  7011733  7011743  7011749  7011761
7011799  7011811  7011827  7011853  7011877  7011887  7011913  7011919  7011937  7011947
7012001  7012003  7012009  7012013  7012063  7012067  7012069  7012099  7012111  7012141
7012151  7012157  7012193  7012199  7012223  7012241  7012249  7012253  7012261  7012267
7012283  7012319  7012331  7012333  7012337  7012363  7012367  7012373  7012391  7012393
7012409  7012429  7012469  7012471  7012477  7012487  7012507  7012529  7012543  7012547
7012571  7012583  7012613  7012627  7012657  7012661  7012669  7012679  7012697  7012703
7012771  7012777  7012781  7012787  7012797  7012807  7012829  7012847  7012849  7012853
7012877  7012903  7012921  7012937  7012949  7012963  7012969  7012979  7012981  7013029
7013053  7013057  7013063  7013077  7013093  7013117  7013131  7013141  7013143  7013159
7013179  7013203  7013213  7013219  7013243  7013263  7013267  7013269  7013297  7013311
7013317  7013327  7013351  7013371  7013381  7013393  7013407  7013423  7013431  7013443
7013453  7013473  7013477  7013483  7013491  7013521  7013549  7013557  7013561  7013581
7013623  7013653  7013659  7013723  7013729  7013731  7013759  7013771  7013807  7013863
7013887  7013899  7013921  7013927  7013971  7014037  7014043  7014061  7014071  7014073
7014107  7014113  7014121  7014131  7014151  7014187  7014191  7014193  7014209  7014257
7014269  7014283  7014299  7014311  7014313  7014323  7014347  7014367  7014373  7014377
7014383  7014389  7014409  7014419  7014437  7014457  7014467  7014481  7014503  7014509
7014521  7014533  7014541  7014577  7014583  7014611  7014613  7014617  7014619  7014641
7014653  7014671  7014677  7014691  7014739  7014751  7014757  7014767  7014769  7014803
7014809  7014841  7014851  7014859  7014869  7014877  7014881  7014899  7014929  7014947
7014979  7014983  7014989  7014991  7015003  7015039  7015049  7015087  7015097  7015109
7015111  7015139  7015213  7015259  7015273  7015301  7015343  7015363  7015399  7015417
7015423  7015429  7015457  7015479  7015487  7015499  7015501  7015507  7015511  7015523
7015531  7015537  7015553  7015559  7015571  7015583  7015597  7015609  7015627  7015649
7015661  7015691  7015699  7015711  7015717  7015721  7015733  7015739  7015777  7015787
7015817  7015819  7015823  7015891  7015927  7015933  7015949  7015969  7015973  7016011
7016017  7016029  7016041  7016047  7016059  7016063  7016071  7016077  7016083  7016099
7016101  7016117  7016131  7016147  7016153  7016179  7016201  7016213  7016237  7016279
7016287  7016333  7016341  7016363  7016381  7016389  7016413  7016423  7016431  7016437
7016467  7016473  7016479  7016483  7016497  7016501  7016507  7016519  7016531  7016533
7016539  7016561  7016599  7016609  7016629  7016641  7016663  7016683  7016731  7016741
7016743  7016747  7016749  7016759  7016777  7016803  7016809  7016831  7016837  7016873
7016879  7016887  7016899  7016921  7016923  7016941  7016963  7016981  7016983  7017007
```

```
7017029 7017071 7017079 7017083 7017089 7017097 7017113 7017119 7017133 7017151
7017163 7017203 7017211 7017221 7017223 7017229 7017233 7017239 7017281 7017293
7017301 7017317 7017319 7017331 7017347 7017389 7017419 7017431 7017467 7017473
7017487 7017497 7017499 7017503 7017511 7017533 7017541 7017547 7017559 7017589
7017607 7017611 7017613 7017641 7017653 7017667 7017671 7017697 7017701 7017761
7017763 7017767 7017793 7017799 7017817 7017823 7017833 7017839 7017851 7017869
7017887 7017911 7017919 7017937 7017947 7017953 7017977 7017979 7018019 7018021
7018043 7018061 7018069 7018079 7018097 7018129 7018139 7018169 7018171 7018177
7018189 7018199 7018213 7018259 7018267 7018301 7018303 7018321 7018343 7018351
7018357 7018367 7018379 7018387 7018409 7018423 7018441 7018447 7018457 7018469
7018471 7018481 7018499 7018511 7018513 7018541 7018547 7018549 7018553 7018573
7018577 7018579 7018607 7018633 7018639 7018673 7018691 7018709 7018747 7018751
7018763 7018777 7018799 7018801 7018811 7018813 7018829 7018867 7018871 7018883
7018897 7018901 7018931 7018939 7018951 7018969 7018981 7018997 7019003 7019021
7019029 7019041 7019057 7019069 7019081 7019101 7019119 7019123 7019137 7019149
7019153 7019203 7019219 7019231 7019239 7019263 7019279 7019291 7019297 7019321
7019329 7019377 7019429 7019471 7019473 7019483 7019489 7019503 7019533 7019549
7019561 7019563 7019567 7019587 7019611 7019633 7019641 7019689 7019729 7019731
7019741 7019767 7019773 7019777 7019783 7019801 7019833 7019849 7019851 7019863
7019867 7019893 7019923 7019939 7019951 7019953 7019993 7020023 7020029 7020073
7020077 7020103 7020107 7020109 7020113 7020119 7020131 7020161 7020173 7020187
7020197 7020199 7020227 7020239 7020257 7020271 7020287 7020289 7020301 7020311
7020317 7020319 7020323 7020331 7020341 7020347 7020361 7020379 7020397 7020413
7020427 7020449 7020457 7020463 7020479 7020487 7020499 7020509 7020511 7020529
7020547 7020593 7020613 7020619 7020623 7020641 7020647 7020649 7020667 7020679
7020691 7020701 7020707 7020737 7020743 7020749 7020757 7020781 7020791 7020821
7020829 7020877 7020889 7020901 7020913 7020931 7020953 7020971 7020991 7021033
7021057 7021073 7021081 7021111 7021117 7021139 7021163 7021199 7021211 7021229
7021237 7021249 7021253 7021309 7021319 7021321 7021331 7021361 7021363 7021367
7021381 7021423 7021433 7021439 7021457 7021489 7021501 7021519 7021541 7021543
7021549 7021559 7021571 7021577 7021589 7021607 7021627 7021643 7021657 7021691
7021711 7021723 7021759 7021769 7021789 7021843 7021853 7021879 7021913 7021939
7021951 7021979 7021981 7021997 7021999 7022033 7022051 7022063 7022083 7022087
7022101 7022117 7022123 7022131 7022143 7022149 7022161 7022177 7022179 7022219
7022233 7022237 7022269 7022273 7022293 7022297 7022329 7022333 7022339 7022347
7022371 7022411 7022441 7022443 7022467 7022507 7022531 7022549 7022551
7022569 7022573 7022591 7022597 7022621 7022627 7022629 7022641 7022651 7022663
7022671 7022677 7022737 7022753 7022777 7022789 7022791 7022831 7022839 7022857
7022861 7022887 7022891 7022893 7022941 7022969 7022971 7022987 7022993 7022999
7023001 7023011 7023043 7023053 7023059 7023067 7023089 7023097 7023109 7023131
7023139 7023151 7023157 7023169 7023173 7023187 7023209 7023221 7023223 7023251
7023271 7023283 7023287 7023299 7023323 7023347 7023353 7023361 7023371 7023383
7023421 7023427 7023433 7023461 7023469 7023473 7023517 7023529 7023551 7023563
7023581 7023589 7023593 7023617 7023619 7023623 7023629 7023631 7023637 7023647
7023683 7023721 7023739 7023767 7023799 7023823 7023847 7023857 7023869 7023881
7023923 7023937 7023943 7023983 7024021 7024051 7024057 7024081 7024097
7024109 7024123 7024163 7024181 7024183 7024189 7024217 7024231 7024253 7024261
7024267 7024273 7024289 7024301 7024309 7024313 7024387 7024393 7024411 7024421
7024441 7024463 7024469 7024477 7024513 7024517 7024529 7024531 7024541 7024543
7024579 7024597 7024607 7024627 7024691 7024727 7024733 7024739 7024741 7024753
7024763 7024769 7024793 7024799 7024807 7024819 7024847 7024877 7024891 7024907
7024933 7024937 7024939 7024957 7024967 7024987 7024999 7025027 7025059 7025069
7025077 7025087 7025093 7025101 7025107 7025111 7025113 7025129 7025141 7025149
7025167 7025173 7025177 7025197 7025209 7025219 7025243 7025287 7025303 7025311
7025329 7025339 7025387 7025407 7025429 7025467 7025479 7025483 7025489 7025507
7025509 7025531 7025533 7025563 7025567 7025587 7025591 7025617 7025621 7025633
7025639 7025651 7025653 7025657 7025659 7025713 7025723 7025737 7025783 7025791
7025827 7025831 7025861 7025869 7025881 7025891 7025903 7025957 7025969 7025987
7026007 7026013 7026043 7026053 7026059 7026073 7026079 7026121 7026127 7026139
7026167 7026169 7026179 7026197 7026203 7026209 7026233 7026241 7026259 7026277
7026289 7026301 7026307 7026343 7026347 7026377 7026379 7026391 7026421 7026443
7026463 7026473 7026493 7026499 7026517 7026521 7026527 7026533 7026541 7026577
7026619 7026623 7026629 7026631 7026647 7026653 7026667 7026669 7026731 7026737
7026743 7026749 7026769 7026791 7026809 7026821 7026823 7026847 7026853 7026857
7026871 7026881 7026883 7026919 7026973 7026997 7027021 7027043 7027057 7027061
7027063 7027099 7027109 7027117 7027133 7027147 7027159 7027201 7027207 7027211
7027219 7027243 7027253 7027303 7027327 7027333 7027369 7027379 7027403 7027451
7027453 7027457 7027459 7027469 7027481 7027547 7027567 7027571 7027577 7027589
7027591 7027621 7027633 7027649 7027679 7027703 7027711 7027717 7027721 7027723
7027729 7027759 7027771 7027807 7027819 7027837 7027849 7027873 7027879 7027901
7027907 7027913 7027921 7027927 7027931 7027939 7027961 7027973 7027981 7027991
7028011 7028017 7028027 7028029 7028033 7028057 7028059 7028069 7028093 7028101
7028107 7028111 7028137 7028141 7028167 7028173 7028183 7028201 7028209 7028213
7028243 7028249 7028267 7028269 7028279 7028297 7028299 7028311 7028323 7028339
7028341 7028377 7028381 7028389 7028401 7028407 7028431 7028447 7028459
7028467 7028473 7028477 7028519 7028533 7028563 7028569 7028573 7028579 7028591
7028627 7028657 7028663 7028669 7028677 7028683 7028687 7028699 7028711 7028719
7028741 7028761 7028767 7028771 7028797 7028831 7028839 7028843 7028849 7028851
7028873 7028881 7028887 7028891 7028921 7028941 7028947 7028963 7028977 7029013
7029017 7029023 7029073 7029079 7029089 7029101 7029103 7029133 7029137 7029161
7029173 7029181 7029203 7029227 7029233 7029241 7029257 7029263 7029287 7029293
7029307 7029317 7029331 7029359 7029403 7029427 7029479 7029521 7029527 7029541
7029587 7029599 7029611 7029637 7029641 7029661 7029689 7029691 7029709 7029713
7029719 7029731 7029749 7029767 7029779 7029787 7029797 7029809 7029811 7029817
7029821 7029833 7029863 7029877 7029899 7029917 7029929 7029937 7029947 7029961
7030013 7030033 7030039 7030063 7030091 7030097 7030099 7030117 7030123 7030141
7030159 7030193 7030217 7030237 7030313 7030319 7030343 7030351 7030357 7030363
7030379 7030403 7030421 7030423 7030427 7030451 7030453 7030477 7030487 7030489
7030501 7030523 7030531 7030549 7030561 7030577 7030579 7030603 7030613 7030631
```

```
7030637  7030643  7030669  7030687  7030691  7030697  7030717  7030729  7030753  7030757
7030783  7030787  7030811  7030823  7030841  7030873  7030897  7030937  7030943  7030951
7030957  7030981  7030993  7030997  7031023  7031039  7031041  7031051  7031071  7031107
7031111  7031113  7031173  7031177  7031191  7031209  7031243  7031257  7031281  7031293
7031309  7031333  7031347  7031357  7031359  7031363  7031371  7031383  7031393  7031411
7031417  7031419  7031429  7031441  7031461  7031467  7031471  7031473  7031477  7031483
7031503  7031509  7031527  7031533  7031551  7031567  7031573  7031597  7031599  7031603
7031621  7031639  7031641  7031671  7031681  7031737  7031743  7031749  7031753  7031771
7031807  7031819  7031837  7031839  7031861  7031867  7031909  7031939  7031977  7031989
7032013  7032029  7032037  7032041  7032049  7032059  7032079  7032083  7032107  7032121
7032127  7032131  7032167  7032191  7032217  7032229  7032247  7032251  7032283  7032313
7032317  7032359  7032367  7032383  7032391  7032397  7032409  7032437  7032463  7032481
7032497  7032499  7032551  7032569  7032581  7032583  7032589  7032617  7032647  7032653
7032667  7032671  7032677  7032709  7032749  7032787  7032799  7032803  7032829  7032863
7032881  7032889  7032899  7032901  7032911  7032913  7032919  7032929  7032931  7032937
7032947  7032959  7032973  7033031  7033049  7033067  7033069  7033093  7033111  7033151
7033163  7033177  7033199  7033207  7033231  7033237  7033241  7033253  7033267  7033289
7033303  7033321  7033333  7033339  7033357  7033379  7033391  7033421  7033451  7033493
7033501  7033513  7033517  7033547  7033549  7033553  7033601  7033603  7033619  7033627
7033633  7033651  7033657  7033679  7033681  7033703  7033721  7033723  7033729  7033751
7033771  7033787  7033799  7033813  7033823  7033847  7033853  7033877  7033891  7033909
7033927  7033951  7033963  7033967  7033987  7033997  7034003  7034011  7034017  7034023
7034029  7034063  7034077  7034087  7034099  7034119  7034143  7034147  7034171  7034173
7034191  7034219  7034221  7034233  7034249  7034267  7034281  7034299  7034309  7034317
7034323  7034341  7034369  7034371  7034381  7034383  7034429  7034437  7034441  7034449
7034473  7034479  7034491  7034497  7034519  7034563  7034567  7034593  7034603  7034611
7034627  7034639  7034641  7034647  7034653  7034663  7034669  7034681  7034683  7034701
7034717  7034723  7034749  7034761  7034767  7034771  7034779  7034837  7034851  7034857
7034887  7034891  7034899  7034971  7034977  7034999  7035001  7035011  7035037  7035053
7035107  7035151  7035173  7035211  7035221  7035227  7035239  7035251  7035253  7035257
7035269  7035293  7035299  7035307  7035311  7035341  7035367  7035389  7035403  7035409
7035421  7035437  7035449  7035451  7035463  7035473  7035499  7035517  7035527  7035533
7035541  7035547  7035551  7035563  7035577  7035593  7035607  7035629  7035647  7035649
7035659  7035683  7035709  7035713  7035727  7035731  7035733  7035751  7035757  7035799
7035823  7035839  7035851  7035863  7035869  7035881  7035911  7035913  7035971  7035979
7035989  7036021  7036049  7036087  7036097  7036103  7036109  7036123  7036129  7036177
7036187  7036193  7036199  7036207  7036247  7036259  7036261  7036301  7036303  7036307
7036331  7036339  7036343  7036361  7036363  7036373  7036387  7036409  7036423  7036493
7036499  7036501  7036529  7036559  7036573  7036577  7036591  7036637  7036661  7036681
7036703  7036709  7036717  7036741  7036769  7036801  7036807  7036811  7036817  7036819
7036829  7036847  7036867  7036889  7036891  7036901  7036903  7036921  7036933  7036957
7036961  7036979  7036987  7037003  7037029  7037033  7037039  7037071  7037089  7037101
7037123  7037159  7037161  7037171  7037183  7037203  7037207  7037209  7037221  7037231
7037243  7037249  7037267  7037291  7037323  7037347  7037351  7037369  7037383  7037389
7037417  7037453  7037489  7037521  7037531  7037551  7037573  7037587  7037593  7037629
7037647  7037671  7037683  7037687  7037689  7037699  7037707  7037729  7037791  7037831
7037843  7037861  7037867  7037879  7037893  7037897  7037903  7037909  7037917  7037929
7037957  7037963  7037969  7037993  7038001  7038013  7038043  7038047  7038049  7038061
7038067  7038071  7038077  7038079  7038089  7038107  7038121  7038127  7038133  7038167
7038179  7038181  7038191  7038193  7038211  7038247  7038259  7038263  7038277  7038281
7038319  7038331  7038359  7038389  7038397  7038401  7038407  7038419  7038461  7038463
7038469  7038491  7038497  7038509  7038533  7038539  7038553  7038557  7038571  7038583
7038599  7038617  7038623  7038631  7038659  7038671  7038679  7038701  7038709  7038719
7038751  7038763  7038803  7038841  7038853  7038859  7038929  7038931  7038937  7038947
7038959  7039001  7039013  7039027  7039031  7039093  7039103  7039117  7039121  7039129
7039133  7039159  7039169  7039181  7039183  7039187  7039211  7039223  7039243  7039247
7039259  7039261  7039273  7039283  7039321  7039327  7039363  7039381  7039399  7039429
7039433  7039447  7039457  7039477  7039493  7039507  7039517  7039531  7039537  7039559
7039567  7039603  7039607  7039667  7039673  7039691  7039693  7039699  7039727  7039763
7039777  7039783  7039789  7039829  7039841  7039843  7039847  7039849  7039867  7039873
7039889  7039913  7039919  7039943  7039957  7039961  7039973  7039979  7040009  7040011
7040021  7040041  7040053  7040063  7040081  7040113  7040129  7040171  7040179  7040183
7040197  7040213  7040221  7040263  7040269  7040281  7040287  7040321  7040353  7040381
7040387  7040389  7040413  7040443  7040477  7040483  7040513  7040521  7040543  7040549
7040557  7040563  7040569  7040597  7040623  7040629  7040633  7040639  7040651  7040653
7040687  7040711  7040713  7040723  7040731  7040743  7040749  7040791  7040797  7040827
7040837  7040843  7040861  7040867  7040893  7040897  7040899  7040903  7040909  7040911
7040943  7040947  7040953  7040963  7040981  7040983  7040987  7040993  7041011  7041049
7041071  7041091  7041101  7041107  7041109  7041127  7041157  7041161  7041163  7041193
7041227  7041233  7041241  7041253  7041259  7041263  7041271  7041311  7041317  7041319
7041337  7041341  7041367  7041373  7041401  7041407  7041409  7041439  7041449  7041467
7041469  7041479  7041487  7041491  7041523  7041539  7041547  7041569  7041623  7041631
7041641  7041649  7041679  7041701  7041707  7041721  7041731  7041781  7041787  7041817
7041829  7041847  7041863  7041871  7041883  7041899  7041907  7041911  7041941  7041943
7041949  7041953  7041967  7041971  7041977  7042001  7042031  7042033  7042043  7042051
7042069  7042073  7042081  7042093  7042121  7042129  7042183  7042193  7042207  7042219
7042229  7042253  7042271  7042291  7042319  7042327  7042337  7042349  7042367  7042379
7042391  7042421  7042423  7042457  7042459  7042493  7042501  7042517  7042523  7042559
7042589  7042601  7042603  7042619  7042631  7042639  7042643  7042649  7042681  7042723
7042727  7042747  7042753  7042769  7042781  7042801  7042823  7042829  7042843  7042873
7042883  7042907  7042933  7042949  7042961  7042993  7043017  7043041  7043063  7043077
7043123  7043137  7043147  7043159  7043161  7043171  7043173  7043189  7043191  7043203
7043213  7043233  7043237  7043251  7043263  7043273  7043291  7043299  7043339  7043369
7043383  7043401  7043411  7043441  7043447  7043459  7043473  7043483  7043503  7043521
7043527  7043537  7043539  7043557  7043563  7043567  7043573  7043633  7043657  7043669
7043671  7043713  7043717  7043747  7043767  7043783  7043791  7043807  7043821  7043863
7043887  7043909  7043941  7043947  7043969  7043987  7044017  7044019  7044029  7044061
7044073  7044077  7044091  7044101  7044109  7044133  7044139  7044157  7044173  7044181
7044197  7044199  7044203  7044209  7044211  7044221  7044229  7044253  7044259  7044299
```

7044329	7044337	7044391	7044397	7044413	7044449	7044451	7044469	7044487	7044493
7044503	7044517	7044529	7044539	7044547	7044553	7044589	7044623	7044629	7044637
7044641	7044643	7044679	7044703	7044721	7044731	7044757	7044761	7044769	7044797
7044803	7044811	7044827	7044857	7044859	7044871	7044881	7044889	7044901	7044931
7044943	7044949	7044959	7044977	7044979	7045007	7045009	7045033	7045037	7045039
7045081	7045109	7045111	7045127	7045139	7045177	7045189	7045193	7045223	7045243
7045279	7045301	7045309	7045331	7045373	7045387	7045391	7045393	7045403	7045411
7045427	7045453	7045469	7045487	7045517	7045537	7045541	7045547	7045553	7045589
7045601	7045607	7045627	7045631	7045639	7045657	7045669	7045673	7045681	7045691
7045693	7045697	7045699	7045739	7045757	7045777	7045781	7045783	7045807	7045813
7045823	7045849	7045859	7045867	7045877	7045879	7045901	7045919	7045949	7045963
7045967	7045991	7045999	7046029	7046059	7046069	7046071	7046107	7046129	7046147
7046161	7046167	7046173	7046183	7046201	7046203	7046213	7046227	7046251	7046261
7046309	7046339	7046363	7046387	7046407	7046411	7046443	7046447	7046461	
7046489	7046491	7046497	7046503	7046519	7046521	7046561	7046573	7046581	7046597
7046609	7046639	7046647	7046691	7046707	7046713	7046719	7046723	7046729	7046731
7046737	7046749	7046771	7046791	7046803	7046807	7046833	7046839	7046843	7046861
7046863	7046911	7046917	7046927	7046981	7046987	7046989	7046999	7047011	7047031
7047041	7047049	7047059	7047083	7047091	7047097	7047107	7047113	7047151	7047169
7047179	7047181	7047191	7047211	7047239	7047241	7047263	7047277	7047283	7047289
7047301	7047311	7047317	7047331	7047343	7047371	7047379	7047419	7047421	7047431
7047433	7047451	7047457	7047473	7047487	7047539	7047541	7047553	7047559	7047577
7047587	7047589	7047617	7047619	7047629	7047653	7047659	7047671	7047701	7047713
7047731	7047737	7047739	7047749	7047751	7047773	7047787	7047823	7047839	7047851
7047857	7047863	7047883	7047893	7047907	7047919	7047947	7047967	7047973	7047977
7048003	7048007	7048009	7048021	7048037	7048039	7048043	7048061	7048127	7048133
7048141	7048157	7048163	7048207	7048211	7048213	7048271	7048303	7048309	7048343
7048397	7048399	7048403	7048409	7048441	7048451	7048469	7048477	7048493	7048499
7048519	7048549	7048567	7048571	7048579	7048583	7048589	7048621	7048631	7048633
7048673	7048697	7048709	7048721	7048729	7048747	7048763	7048771	7048777	7048781
7048799	7048801	7048859	7048883	7048913	7048957	7048967	7048973	7049039	
7049047	7049111	7049113	7049123	7049131	7049149	7049153	7049167	7049173	7049191
7049197	7049213	7049219	7049239	7049269	7049297	7049303	7049311	7049333	7049347
7049353	7049363	7049381	7049401	7049411	7049449	7049453	7049461	7049473	7049479
7049489	7049501	7049507	7049521	7049527	7049531	7049563	7049579	7049591	7049597
7049599	7049621	7049633	7049657	7049659	7049677	7049681	7049687	7049701	7049717
7049759	7049761	7049773	7049789	7049821	7049839	7049843	7049857	7049879	7049899
7049921	7049947	7049971	7049993	7050013	7050031	7050037	7050049	7050061	7050067
7050077	7050079	7050089	7050107	7050133	7050187	7050191	7050193	7050217	7050227
7050271	7050287	7050293	7050301	7050353	7050391	7050403	7050467	7050499	7050521
7050553	7050557	7050569	7050583	7050587	7050599	7050613	7050619	7050623	7050629
7050679	7050689	7050697	7050707	7050721	7050731	7050737	7050761	7050781	7050787
7050793	7050817	7050859	7050863	7050871	7050877	7050889	7050899	7050917	7050931
7050941	7050947	7050959	7050977	7050983	7050991	7051001	7051003	7051007	7051019
7051049	7051061	7051069	7051091	7051103	7051111	7051123	7051129	7051151	7051153
7051157	7051189	7051199	7051207	7051211	7051249	7051259	7051283	7051327	7051333
7051361	7051367	7051391	7051393	7051397	7051399	7051411	7051427	7051433	7051453
7051459	7051463	7051469	7051523	7051567	7051607	7051633	7051643	7051673	7051687
7051697	7051711	7051721	7051729	7051741	7051757	7051769	7051771	7051841	7051853
7051859	7051879	7051883	7051897	7051903	7051931	7051937	7051939	7051943	7051949
7051981	7051987	7052011	7052029	7052033	7052057	7052069	7052083	7052107	7052113
7052141	7052147	7052197	7052207	7052231	7052273	7052281	7052321	7052323	7052327
7052333	7052341	7052351	7052371	7052377	7052389	7052411	7052417	7052429	7052431
7052483	7052489	7052497	7052503	7052519	7052543	7052557	7052561	7052581	7052599
7052609	7052611	7052699	7052707	7052723	7052737	7052741	7052753	7052809	7052813
7052827	7052833	7052873	7052891	7052917	7052921	7052939	7052951	7052953	
7052957	7052987	7052993	7053001	7053029	7053031	7053049	7053127	7053197	7053217
7053223	7053229	7053239	7053253	7053269	7053287	7053301	7053307	7053323	
7053329	7053331	7053349	7053359	7053367	7053379	7053401	7053407	7053437	7053443
7053451	7053463	7053481	7053493	7053533	7053551	7053577	7053581	7053587	7053593
7053601	7053653	7053667	7053679	7053689	7053703	7053721	7053727	7053733	7053773
7053797	7053817	7053869	7053877	7053899	7053911	7053971	7053973	7054001	7054007
7054039	7054043	7054049	7054057	7054067	7054079	7054093	7054097	7054121	7054127
7054129	7054139	7054171	7054181	7054199	7054207	7054213	7054249	7054259	7054273
7054283	7054297	7054319	7054361	7054381	7054387	7054409	7054417	7054427	7054433
7054441	7054447	7054493	7054499	7054513	7054543	7054591	7054601	7054613	7054633
7054637	7054651	7054657	7054661	7054669	7054687	7054693	7054699	7054727	7054741
7054759	7054769	7054771	7054781	7054783	7054787	7054799	7054811	7054819	7054823
7054849	7054867	7054877	7054891	7054897	7054919	7054961	7054963	7054981	7054987
7055003	7055021	7055047	7055071	7055093	7055107	7055117	7055141	7055143	7055159
7055177	7055183	7055189	7055203	7055219	7055263	7055281	7055287	7055291	7055303
7055309	7055317	7055329	7055339	7055353	7055369	7055371	7055407	7055429	7055437
7055449	7055453	7055471	7055491	7055509	7055513	7055533	7055537	7055563	7055599
7055611	7055617	7055627	7055647	7055651	7055677	7055699	7055701	7055723	7055743	7055749
7055761	7055771	7055773	7055803	7055819	7055857	7055899	7055933	7055953	7055989
7056013	7056017	7056029	7056031	7056061	7056067	7056083	7056121	7056167	7056197
7056211	7056227	7056229	7056281	7056289	7056293	7056311	7056317	7056323	7056347
7056349	7056383	7056403	7056407	7056409	7056421	7056451	7056457	7056463	7056481
7056487	7056503	7056509	7056521	7056523	7056557	7056563	7056571	7056593	7056611
7056617	7056631	7056661	7056667	7056689	7056697	7056701	7056703	7056713	7056719
7056727	7056779	7056793	7056799	7056811	7056817	7056821	7056827	7056851	7056857
7056893	7056937	7056941	7056943	7056949	7057013	7057027	7057033	7057051	
7057069	7057081	7057103	7057123	7057133	7057139	7057153	7057157	7057201	7057229
7057247	7057249	7057279	7057283	7057291	7057301	7057319	7057327	7057331	7057333
7057339	7057361	7057373	7057381	7057409	7057441	7057459	7057487	7057489	7057507
7057537	7057549	7057559	7057591	7057637	7057649	7057651	7057667	7057693	7057697
7057709	7057717	7057723	7057741	7057769	7057793	7057811	7057871	7057879	7057889
7057901	7057903	7057931	7057937	7057951	7057961	7057997	7058021	7058047	7058053
7058059	7058069	7058081	7058089	7058141	7058143	7058153	7058159	7058197	7058209

```
7058221 7058239 7058243 7058251 7058257 7058267 7058287 7058341 7058357 7058393
7058419 7058431 7058449 7058459 7058461 7058473 7058497 7058521 7058531 7058537
7058543 7058551 7058561 7058567 7058581 7058591 7058609 7058627 7058641 7058647
7058659 7058713 7058717 7058719 7058741 7058743 7058759 7058761 7058783 7058813
7058827 7058879 7058903 7058921 7058939 7058951 7058957 7058963 7058969 7058983
7058993 7059007 7059037 7059043 7059047 7059049 7059061 7059077 7059113 7059121
7059133 7059149 7059161 7059163 7059179 7059211 7059251 7059253 7059263 7059271
7059277 7059281 7059307 7059313 7059323 7059359 7059373 7059379 7059407 7059419
7059433 7059443 7059461 7059463 7059487 7059491 7059529 7059587 7059589 7059593
7059617 7059623 7059629 7059631 7059683 7059691 7059707 7059719 7059727 7059733
7059737 7059739 7059751 7059761 7059791 7059863 7059883 7059893 7059911 7059931
7059937 7059953 7060013 7060037 7060043 7060051 7060061 7060069 7060073 7060087
7060093 7060111 7060139 7060187 7060217 7060223 7060231 7060237 7060243 7060247
7060279 7060327 7060357 7060367 7060373 7060399 7060411 7060429 7060439 7060441
7060463 7060483 7060489 7060511 7060513 7060523 7060531 7060549 7060553 7060631
7060639 7060657 7060667 7060681 7060699 7060709 7060741 7060751 7060759 7060771
7060787 7060789 7060813 7060817 7060841 7060847 7060853 7060861 7060871 7060877
7060909 7060919 7060973 7061009 7061017 7061029 7061039 7061051 7061077 7061083
7061101 7061111 7061167 7061189 7061203 7061221 7061237 7061267 7061269 7061279
7061281 7061303 7061311 7061333 7061381 7061393 7061399 7061401 7061419 7061429
7061449 7061473 7061479 7061489 7061501 7061513 7061563 7061567 7061569 7061591
7061603 7061627 7061629 7061633 7061641 7061657 7061671 7061689 7061693 7061701
7061737 7061767 7061771 7061777 7061807 7061827 7061833 7061837 7061849 7061861
7061869 7061917 7061941 7061969 7061981 7061983 7062007 7062049 7062071 7062073
7062101 7062113 7062149 7062199 7062287 7062313 7062323 7062329 7062337 7062353
7062371 7062383 7062413 7062427 7062479 7062493 7062521 7062527 7062529 7062533
7062551 7062557 7062569 7062571 7062581 7062593 7062611 7062659 7062673 7062691
7062703 7062721 7062739 7062751 7062767 7062779 7062787 7062821 7062827 7062859
7062877 7062907 7062911 7062919 7062941 7062943 7063013 7063039 7063097 7063099
7063103 7063123 7063157 7063169 7063171 7063201 7063213 7063229 7063241 7063247
7063253 7063267 7063271 7063321 7063333 7063339 7063349 7063361 7063367 7063403
7063429 7063447 7063451 7063457 7063477 7063487 7063493 7063499 7063513 7063523
7063543 7063571 7063579 7063591 7063597 7063601 7063631 7063703 7063709 7063717
7063723 7063729 7063741 7063747 7063751 7063757 7063769 7063799 7063807 7063817
7063853 7063873 7063897 7063919 7063957 7063981 7064039 7064089 7064111 7064149
7064171 7064173 7064179 7064191 7064201 7064203 7064207 7064221 7064237 7064261
7064263 7064293 7064297 7064303 7064329 7064347 7064357 7064359 7064389 7064419
7064441 7064459 7064479 7064501 7064509 7064527 7064539 7064549 7064557 7064567
7064569 7064579 7064591 7064609 7064627 7064633 7064663 7064663 7064671 7064687
7064689 7064693 7064753 7064767 7064773 7064779 7064791 7064797 7064819 7064831
7064861 7064881 7064889 7064923 7064947 7064947 7064957 7064971 7064977 7065007
7065031 7065041 7065089 7065101 7065127 7065143 7065167 7065173 7065193 7065211
7065221 7065229 7065239 7065257 7065263 7065277 7065293 7065329 7065343 7065367
7065371 7065389 7065403 7065413 7065419 7065433 7065437 7065459 7065467 7065469
7065497 7065503 7065533 7065547 7065559 7065563 7065581 7065601 7065607 7065629
7065637 7065649 7065671 7065673 7065679 7065683 7065689 7065703 7065733 7065749
7065767 7065769 7065791 7065797 7065809 7065811 7065833 7065841 7065847 7065871
7065881 7065911 7065941 7065943 7065953 7065973 7065983 7066019 7066069 7066079
7066091 7066093 7066097 7066117 7066183 7066187 7066207 7066249 7066259 7066261
7066273 7066277 7066303 7066321 7066337 7066351 7066379 7066393 7066399 7066429
7066449 7066453 7066463 7066469 7066483 7066487 7066523 7066541 7066561 7066567
7066571 7066573 7066639 7066643 7066699 7066721 7066723 7066739 7066771 7066777
7066799 7066837 7066847 7066859 7066909 7066931 7066937 7066973 7066979 7066987
7067017 7067063 7067077 7067089 7067117 7067131 7067143 7067147 7067149 7067153
7067161 7067209 7067237 7067239 7067251 7067303 7067309 7067311 7067317 7067341
7067363 7067369 7067381 7067381 7067429 7067443 7067471 7067477 7067483 7067491
7067513 7067519 7067527 7067537 7067611 7067617 7067623 7067651 7067663 7067681
7067689 7067707 7067713 7067729 7067737 7067747 7067761 7067779 7067789 7067833
7067839 7067861 7067873 7067881 7067899 7067911 7067917 7067927 7067939 7067959
7067987 7068007 7068013 7068049 7068059 7068071 7068077 7068101 7068137 7068143
7068157 7068161 7068167 7068179 7068181 7068203 7068223 7068227 7068287 7068301
7068329 7068331 7068343 7068349 7068353 7068389 7068421 7068463 7068511 7068533
7068539 7068559 7068563 7068569 7068571 7068577 7068599 7068601 7068623 7068637
7068653 7068661 7068667 7068673 7068697 7068707 7068749 7068767 7068773 7068781
7068791 7068793 7068823 7068829 7068839 7068857 7068869 7068871 7068911 7068917
7068959 7068983 7069009 7069019 7069037 7069061 7069067 7069079 7069081
7069099 7069141 7069151 7069187 7069207 7069219 7069267 7069291 7069313 7069357
7069369 7069373 7069409 7069423 7069429 7069451 7069471 7069477 7069481 7069499
7069523 7069529 7069549 7069571 7069583 7069607 7069609 7069613 7069661 7069663
7069681 7069687 7069721 7069771 7069781 7069801 7069847 7069861 7069873 7069883
7069889 7069897 7069921 7069949 7069973 7069987 7070003 7070009 7070027 7070047
7070053 7070057 7070059 7070087 7070093 7070099 7070111 7070117 7070143 7070149
7070153 7070179 7070191 7070197 7070207 7070209 7070213 7070221 7070227
7070243 7070267 7070291 7070311 7070333 7070341 7070347 7070353 7070363 7070377
7070381 7070389 7070417 7070423 7070431 7070467 7070477 7070507 7070537 7070543
7070551 7070581 7070599 7070611 7070627 7070639 7070653 7070681 7070689 7070731
7070741 7070743 7070747 7070761 7070779 7070801 7070813 7070849 7070863 7070873
7070879 7070893 7070917 7070923 7070933 7070951 7070953 7070957 7070971 7070977
7070993 7071013 7071017 7071023 7071047 7071061 7071073 7071079 7071083 7071121
7071149 7071151 7071187 7071191 7071199 7071217 7071227 7071241 7071257 7071263
7071283 7071299 7071341 7071343 7071353 7071359 7071367 7071409 7071413 7071431
7071433 7071443 7071451 7071457 7071461 7071497 7071499 7071509 7071521 7071587
7071599 7071601 7071607 7071611 7071613 7071619 7071637 7071661 7071697 7071703
7071719 7071739 7071763 7071767 7071769 7071797 7071809 7071817 7071821 7071839
7071859 7071883 7071889 7071901 7071907 7071923 7071943 7071959 7071989 7071991
7071997 7072003 7072007 7072031 7072033 7072057 7072073 7072127 7072129 7072133
7072151 7072171 7072183 7072193 7072243 7072277 7072321 7072337 7072343 7072349
7072363 7072369 7072397 7072399 7072411 7072421 7072441 7072447 7072487 7072501
7072517 7072531 7072537 7072543 7072547 7072553 7072567 7072573 7072577 7072589
```

```
7072591  7072601  7072603  7072613  7072621  7072631  7072649  7072657  7072669  7072673
7072699  7072771  7072777  7072801  7072811  7072823  7072831  7072841  7072853  7072873
7072909  7072913  7072927  7072943  7072963  7072981  7072987  7072993  7073023  7073039
7073041  7073069  7073089  7073137  7073147  7073159  7073201  7073203  7073219  7073237
7073243  7073249  7073267  7073273  7073281  7073317  7073323  7073329  7073347  7073369
7073383  7073387  7073399  7073441  7073459  7073467  7073471  7073483  7073501  7073503
7073527  7073533  7073557  7073579  7073597  7073653  7073657  7073699  7073701  7073707
7073741  7073747  7073753  7073761  7073789  7073813  7073821  7073827  7073839  7073851
7073861  7073863  7073867  7073873  7073879  7073917  7073959  7073981  7074013  7074019
7074047  7074049  7074071  7074077  7074083  7074097  7074101  7074121  7074157  7074163
7074167  7074187  7074191  7074203  7074217  7074233  7074247  7074253  7074257  7074313
7074337  7074341  7074359  7074367  7074373  7074391  7074401  7074407  7074433  7074443
7074451  7074469  7074481  7074491  7074523  7074527  7074539  7074563  7074569  7074607
7074623  7074629  7074643  7074647  7074677  7074679  7074701  7074709  7074713  7074757
7074763  7074779  7074797  7074799  7074827  7074829  7074853  7074883  7074887  7074901
7074911  7074923  7074931  7074943  7074959  7074971  7075021  7075027  7075039  7075067
7075073  7075093  7075097  7075141  7075147  7075157  7075183  7075199  7075231  7075241
7075259  7075273  7075279  7075301  7075303  7075337  7075351  7075357  7075361  7075373
7075423  7075433  7075459  7075469  7075483  7075487  7075529  7075597  7075603  7075613
7075633  7075637  7075643  7075661  7075687  7075699  7075741  7075759  7075763  7075777
7075807  7075813  7075819  7075829  7075837  7075841  7075853  7075867  7075877  7075879
7075883  7075907  7075909  7075919  7075921  7075933  7075949  7075969  7075979  7076009
7076033  7076051  7076057  7076077  7076089  7076093  7076099  7076107  7076119  7076137
7076141  7076143  7076177  7076191  7076197  7076207  7076221  7076263  7076281  7076317
7076327  7076393  7076413  7076429  7076431  7076453  7076501  7076521  7076533  7076543
7076581  7076603  7076611  7076621  7076647  7076651  7076669  7076677  7076687  7076701
7076717  7076737  7076749  7076753  7076761  7076791  7076803  7076807  7076809  7076813
7076827  7076833  7076857  7076863  7076869  7076903  7076921  7076933  7076941  7076963
7076969  7076999  7077041  7077061  7077071  7077079  7077113  7077127  7077137  7077149
7077157  7077163  7077167  7077181  7077197  7077199  7077211  7077221  7077223  7077229
7077251  7077263  7077289  7077299  7077311  7077313  7077347  7077349  7077359  7077361
7077377  7077391  7077409  7077419  7077437  7077449  7077467  7077487  7077509  7077527
7077599  7077601  7077611  7077613  7077617  7077667  7077677  7077691  7077727  7077731
7077737  7077739  7077743  7077751  7077761  7077781  7077787  7077793  7077803  7077809
7077821  7077853  7077857  7077877  7077883  7077893  7077901  7077907  7077911  7077923
7077971  7078009  7078033  7078039  7078073  7078079  7078111  7078121  7078129  7078147
7078151  7078177  7078189  7078213  7078219  7078237  7078271  7078277  7078283  7078301
7078303  7078333  7078339  7078343  7078369  7078373  7078387  7078391  7078397  7078399
7078439  7078471  7078481  7078493  7078537  7078559  7078567  7078597  7078667  7078693
7078699  7078711  7078723  7078739  7078759  7078763  7078777  7078781  7078823  7078829
7078843  7078873  7078899  7078873  7078889  7078901  7078907  7078921  7078921  7078931
7078933  7078949  7078957  7078969  7078979  7078991  7079003  7079041  7079053  7079069
7079071  7079081  7079119  7079159  7079203  7079209  7079221  7079231  7079243  7079249
7079251  7079257  7079279  7079291  7079299  7079309  7079311  7079323  7079329  7079353
7079363  7079417  7079431  7079447  7079459  7079473  7079489  7079491  7079507  7079521
7079539  7079549  7079557  7079573  7079591  7079603  7079627  7079641  7079663  7079669
7079671  7079707  7079711  7079713  7079717  7079719  7079767  7079771  7079773  7079783
7079833  7079867  7079879  7079953  7079977  7079981  7080001  7080011  7080043  7080071
7080077  7080097  7080107  7080119  7080131  7080133  7080169  7080173  7080181  7080193
7080233  7080247  7080257  7080259  7080277  7080289  7080317  7080329  7080383  7080391
7080401  7080433  7080439  7080443  7080461  7080487  7080523  7080547  7080569  7080583
7080589  7080599  7080613  7080683  7080701  7080713  7080739  7080769  7080791  7080793
7080809  7080817  7080833  7080839  7080869  7080889  7080881  7080889  7080893
7080907  7080923  7080937  7080947  7080991  7081001  7081021  7081049  7081093  7081099
7081117  7081157  7081169  7081181  7081183  7081187  7081189  7081199  7081201  7081213
7081241  7081247  7081253  7081267  7081279  7081337  7081339  7081351  7081379  7081387
7081411  7081427  7081439  7081441  7081457  7081499  7081553  7081573  7081577  7081579
7081589  7081603  7081619  7081637  7081649  7081663  7081709  7081727  7081747  7081751
7081757  7081759  7081783  7081787  7081831  7081847  7081849  7081853  7081859  7081871
7081891  7081897  7081903  7081909  7081931  7081933  7081937  7081961  7081973  7082011
7082017  7082021  7082029  7082063  7082069  7082071  7082087  7082093  7082099  7082107
7082111  7082123  7082191  7082197  7082209  7082219  7082227  7082233  7082237  7082249
7082311  7082323  7082329  7082333  7082371  7082377  7082389  7082399  7082431  7082461
7082479  7082507  7082519  7082561  7082563  7082567  7082599  7082629  7082657  7082671
7082701  7082723  7082737  7082753  7082807  7082809  7082813  7082833  7082837  7082857
7082861  7082899  7082909  7082921  7082923  7082927  7082941  7082951  7082963  7082981
7082983  7082987  7082993  7083017  7083049  7083053  7083071  7083107  7083113  7083121
7083133  7083151  7083157  7083187  7083191  7083211  7083227  7083247  7083269  7083277
7083289  7083331  7083341  7083343  7083353  7083361  7083367  7083383  7083389  7083431
7083449  7083463  7083487  7083497  7083499  7083521  7083533  7083541  7083547  7083551
7083581  7083589  7083607  7083641  7083667  7083673  7083689  7083697  7083707  7083719
7083737  7083757  7083763  7083767  7083809  7083823  7083871  7083877  7083893  7083911
7083943  7083943  7083959  7083961  7083971  7084043  7084061  7084067  7084073  7084097
7084109  7084117  7084123  7084141  7084153  7084163  7084171  7084193  7084243  7084249
7084261  7084271  7084277  7084327  7084331  7084333  7084361  7084369  7084387  7084403
7084417  7084421  7084423  7084433  7084453  7084459  7084463  7084471  7084477  7084499
7084531  7084537  7084541  7084547  7084559  7084591  7084603  7084607  7084643  7084687
7084697  7084703  7084717  7084741  7084757  7084807  7084811  7084813  7084817  7084843
7084849  7084859  7084867  7084879  7084901  7084907  7084919  7084927  7084951  7084991
7084993  7085003  7085017  7085041  7085047  7085051  7085053  7085059  7085069  7085083
7085101  7085123  7085137  7085147  7085149  7085231  7085237  7085249  7085257  7085261
7085279  7085293  7085339  7085341  7085359  7085371  7085399  7085417  7085437  7085443
7085459  7085467  7085501  7085509  7085521  7085531  7085543  7085563  7085569  7085581
7085629  7085653  7085681  7085713  7085731  7085737  7085779  7085783  7085797  7085801
7085809  7085839  7085843  7085849  7085873  7085933  7085951  7085963  7085971  7085983
7085999  7086029  7086041  7086061  7086067  7086083  7086089  7086097  7086103  7086109
7086113  7086119  7086133  7086169  7086173  7086193  7086217  7086239  7086241  7086251
7086257  7086283  7086293  7086307  7086319  7086341  7086347  7086361  7086367  7086371
7086377  7086397  7086407  7086421  7086427  7086437  7086451  7086479  7086493  7086511
```

```
7086517  7086551  7086557  7086571  7086587  7086593  7086617  7086619  7086659  7086661
7086679  7086689  7086719  7086731  7086749  7086763  7086811  7086839  7086881  7086889
7086899  7086907  7086923  7086929  7086949  7086971  7086983  7086997  7087027  7087039
7087043  7087063  7087081  7087097  7087099  7087103  7087109  7087117  7087123  7087207
7087229  7087237  7087261  7087273  7087277  7087307  7087309  7087331  7087349  7087357
7087369  7087391  7087393  7087411  7087429  7087439  7087481  7087501  7087511  7087517
7087543  7087567  7087583  7087601  7087603  7087631  7087667  7087669  7087681  7087697
7087723  7087727  7087753  7087771  7087799  7087807  7087813  7087853  7087867  7087879
7087889  7087891  7087901  7087907  7087921  7087937  7087973  7087987  7087999
7088009  7088021  7088041  7088047  7088069  7088087  7088089  7088111  7088149  7088171
7088173  7088177  7088183  7088189  7088231  7088233  7088293  7088297  7088299  7088309
7088321  7088339  7088351  7088353  7088359  7088401  7088407  7088447  7088461  7088467
7088479  7088489  7088537  7088551  7088561  7088581  7088611  7088629  7088647  7088659
7088671  7088687  7088693  7088699  7088717  7088737  7088743  7088821  7088827  7088833
7088849  7088891  7088897  7088903  7088911  7088923  7088927  7088929  7088933  7088953
7088971  7089001  7089007  7089011  7089031  7089041  7089059  7089067  7089073  7089091
7089107  7089127  7089133  7089143  7089157  7089161  7089167  7089169  7089179  7089193
7089209  7089211  7089217  7089239  7089241  7089287  7089301  7089307  7089319  7089343
7089353  7089361  7089373  7089377  7089403  7089409  7089419  7089431  7089441  7089443
7089461  7089463  7089517  7089529  7089539  7089559  7089571  7089581  7089583  7089587
7089619  7089637  7089661  7089673  7089683  7089701  7089707  7089737  7089743  7089757
7089767  7089769  7089779  7089781  7089787  7089821  7089857  7089877  7089881  7089889
7089893  7089913  7089931  7089937  7089941  7089991  7090001  7090009  7090043  7090063
7090067  7090079  7090087  7090093  7090117  7090121  7090129  7090133  7090147  7090151
7090157  7090163  7090169  7090177  7090183  7090201  7090219  7090229  7090231  7090247
7090261  7090267  7090327  7090331  7090333  7090387  7090397  7090403  7090427  7090429
7090451  7090469  7090481  7090483  7090511  7090519  7090549  7090583  7090597  7090613
7090619  7090631  7090639  7090651  7090673  7090687  7090691  7090697  7090747  7090771
7090793  7090801  7090813  7090859  7090861  7090871  7090873  7090901  7090931  7090957
7090981  7091003  7091017  7091027  7091039  7091041  7091053  7091069  7091083  7091099
7091113  7091129  7091137  7091143  7091171  7091191  7091197  7091209  7091213  7091233
7091239  7091251  7091263  7091297  7091303  7091317  7091323  7091333  7091339  7091353
7091377  7091411  7091419  7091449  7091471  7091473  7091489  7091507  7091509  7091519
7091527  7091537  7091543  7091549  7091587  7091599  7091621  7091627  7091633  7091663
7091671  7091681  7091683  7091701  7091713  7091717  7091719  7091723  7091743  7091779
7091813  7091831  7091837  7091857  7091879  7091881  7091899  7091911  7091927  7091933
7091939  7091951  7091957  7091999  7092047  7092053  7092091  7092097  7092109  7092131
7092157  7092167  7092193  7092203  7092223  7092259  7092307  7092311  7092313
7092367  7092431  7092439  7092457  7092479  7092497  7092511  7092539  7092571  7092577
7092581  7092593  7092601  7092647  7092649  7092661  7092667  7092691  7092731  7092749
7092751  7092773  7092779  7092781  7092793  7092811  7092881  7092911  7092913  7092983
7092989  7093001  7093003  7093007  7093013  7093049  7093057  7093067  7093091  7093109
7093111  7093117  7093127  7093147  7093153  7093181  7093201  7093217  7093249  7093277
7093279  7093291  7093297  7093321  7093343  7093391  7093433  7093439  7093447  7093459
7093469  7093501  7093531  7093547  7093553  7093561  7093577  7093579  7093589  7093601
7093621  7093627  7093633  7093643  7093651  7093667  7093673  7093703  7093711  7093717
7093727  7093739  7093763  7093769  7093771  7093787  7093813  7093819  7093831  7093837
7093841  7093883  7093903  7093907  7093909  7093949  7093979  7093987  7094023  7094029
7094041  7094057  7094063  7094069  7094077  7094111  7094119  7094137  7094141  7094147
7094149  7094159  7094173  7094177  7094179  7094203  7094231  7094233  7094251  7094293
7094303  7094369  7094371  7094377  7094383  7094411  7094413  7094449  7094477  7094489
7094519  7094539  7094551  7094579  7094587  7094597  7094611  7094621  7094669  7094671
7094683  7094719  7094749  7094761  7094779  7094807  7094827  7094839  7094851  7094863
7094869  7094881  7094887  7094891  7094897  7094909  7094921  7094993  7095007  7095013
7095029  7095031  7095041  7095059  7095061  7095079  7095119  7095133  7095161  7095181
7095197  7095199  7095203  7095217  7095241  7095271  7095287  7095289  7095299  7095313
7095323  7095359  7095371  7095377  7095437  7095457  7095467  7095479  7095503  7095509
7095521  7095551  7095589  7095611  7095619  7095631  7095643  7095667  7095677  7095679
7095689  7095713  7095727  7095733  7095757  7095761  7095833  7095853  7095857  7095883
7095889  7095899  7095917  7095961  7095967  7095973  7096049  7096051  7096057  7096073
7096079  7096091  7096099  7096109  7096127  7096129  7096147  7096153  7096163  7096169
7096181  7096183  7096211  7096249  7096261  7096283  7096307  7096319  7096337  7096339
7096357  7096363  7096399  7096409  7096421  7096447  7096451  7096457  7096459  7096469
7096477  7096499  7096517  7096543  7096553  7096571  7096601  7096643  7096651  7096657
7096681  7096693  7096699  7096717  7096741  7096751  7096757  7096759  7096777  7096783
7096787  7096853  7096867  7096877  7096879  7096889  7096891  7096897  7096907  7096951
7096961  7096981  7096993  7096997  7097033  7097063  7097093  7097113  7097117  7097119
7097131  7097147  7097153  7097159  7097161  7097173  7097197  7097213  7097227  7097239
7097267  7097269  7097273  7097291  7097297  7097323  7097341  7097353  7097359  7097383
7097399  7097401  7097429  7097443  7097459  7097471  7097473  7097521  7097531  7097549
7097591  7097603  7097647  7097681  7097683  7097689  7097693  7097723  7097737  7097749
7097767  7097801  7097803  7097807  7097809  7097819  7097861  7097873  7097921  7097929
7097939  7097957  7097983  7097989  7097999  7098019  7098031  7098037  7098041  7098079
7098097  7098109  7098121  7098137  7098141  7098151  7098167  7098187  7098193  7098199
7098203  7098227  7098229  7098263  7098277  7098281  7098283  7098307  7098313  7098319
7098323  7098331  7098337  7098353  7098379  7098383  7098391  7098431  7098439  7098463
7098491  7098493  7098499  7098521  7098541  7098577  7098589  7098599  7098607  7098613
7098629  7098653  7098667  7098671  7098677  7098691  7098713  7098731  7098737
7098769  7098797  7098829  7098841  7098853  7098859  7098887  7098893  7098899  7098901
7098937  7098941  7098943  7098947  7098953  7098967  7098977  7098983  7099007  7099039
7099051  7099063  7099087  7099091  7099123  7099163  7099181  7099193  7099199  7099201
7099207  7099223  7099231  7099237  7099271  7099283  7099307  7099321  7099327  7099357
7099409  7099439  7099453  7099457  7099459  7099507  7099511  7099537  7099541
7099549  7099553  7099583  7099627  7099633  7099643  7099657  7099691  7099733  7099739
7099793  7099799  7099811  7099817  7099823  7099843  7099853  7099871  7099877  7099913
7099927  7099949  7099957  7099969  7099991  7100003  7100017  7100029  7100059  7100063
7100081  7100083  7100089  7100111  7100113  7100121  7100141  7100143  7100161  7100173
7100179  7100183  7100221  7100227  7100231  7100239  7100267  7100279  7100293  7100309
7100311  7100321  7100323  7100329  7100363  7100371  7100377  7100381  7100383  7100419
```

```
7100453  7100477  7100479  7100501  7100521  7100531  7100557  7100579  7100617  7100641
7100647  7100651  7100657  7100659  7100669  7100671  7100677  7100683  7100689  7100693
7100711  7100759  7100761  7100773  7100791  7100809  7100833  7100837  7100839  7100843
7100857  7100867  7100879  7100897  7100909  7100921  7100941  7100957  7100959  7100963
7100971  7100981  7100983  7100987  7100999  7101001  7101037  7101047  7101067  7101091
7101097  7101137  7101161  7101163  7101169  7101179  7101187  7101197  7101229  7101233
7101239  7101247  7101253  7101271  7101287  7101313  7101329  7101337  7101377  7101401
7101431  7101439  7101443  7101463  7101469  7101473  7101481  7101499  7101509  7101533
7101557  7101593  7101599  7101623  7101637  7101643  7101671  7101673  7101683  7101691
7101709  7101719  7101737  7101739  7101761  7101769  7101797  7101811  7101827  7101847
7101851  7101893  7101907  7101949  7101989  7102001  7102031  7102033  7102057  7102079
7102091  7102093  7102099  7102103  7102127  7102153  7102157  7102171  7102177  7102213
7102223  7102229  7102231  7102241  7102247  7102253  7102273  7102279  7102297  7102301
7102313  7102321  7102349  7102357  7102367  7102369  7102373  7102387  7102397  7102411
7102457  7102463  7102489  7102519  7102531  7102573  7102577  7102591  7102609  7102633
7102643  7102649  7102661  7102663  7102679  7102703  7102721  7102741  7102757  7102759
7102763  7102801  7102807  7102817  7102819  7102829  7102847  7102859  7102867  7102873
7102897  7102919  7102933  7102939  7102961  7102967  7102987  7103009  7103029  7103077
7103081  7103101  7103137  7103141  7103143  7103147  7103153  7103171  7103177  7103183
7103227  7103249  7103269  7103279  7103281  7103303  7103333  7103339  7103363  7103387
7103401  7103417  7103429  7103441  7103461  7103477  7103489  7103497  7103507  7103513
7103531  7103539  7103561  7103599  7103611  7103617  7103647  7103651  7103683  7103687
7103689  7103693  7103699  7103731  7103771  7103791  7103801  7103819  7103821  7103827
7103839  7103843  7103851  7103879  7103881  7103897  7103903  7103911  7103923  7103933
7103939  7103953  7103959  7103969  7103981  7104001  7104023  7104059  7104061  7104089
7104103  7104107  7104109  7104127  7104133  7104143  7104179  7104199  7104221  7104241
7104257  7104269  7104277  7104281  7104311  7104319  7104323  7104329  7104341  7104353
7104359  7104389  7104397  7104413  7104437  7104443  7104451  7104463  7104467  7104509
7104533  7104563  7104569  7104583  7104599  7104607  7104619  7104653  7104659  7104667
7104697  7104709  7104719  7104737  7104743  7104749  7104751  7104763  7104821  7104829
7104833  7104887  7104889  7104893  7104919  7104941  7104949  7104961  7104967  7104973
7104989  7104991  7105001  7105027  7105051  7105061  7105067  7105081  7105093  7105117
7105129  7105141  7105151  7105157  7105159  7105207  7105213  7105223  7105243  7105247
7105253  7105289  7105313  7105331  7105361  7105379  7105421  7105477  7105481  7105489
7105499  7105513  7105529  7105573  7105583  7105589  7105613  7105627  7105673  7105697
7105699  7105717  7105723  7105729  7105753  7105741  7105759  7105771  7105807  7105831
7105837  7105843  7105853  7105859  7105907  7105927  7105933  7105991  7105993  7106003
7106041  7106069  7106083  7106089  7106101  7106117  7106147  7106167  7106179  7106201
7106219  7106227  7106237  7106249  7106251  7106261  7106273  7106299  7106303  7106369
7106371  7106389  7106419  7106423  7106431  7106441  7106443  7106497  7106501  7106503
7106531  7106549  7106573  7106579  7106581  7106591  7106597  7106621  7106633  7106669
7106647  7106651  7106669  7106677  7106681  7106707  7106753  7106773  7106777  7106783
7106797  7106819  7106831  7106851  7106857  7106861  7106863  7106903  7106921  7106933
7106941  7106947  7106951  7106959  7106987  7106999  7107031  7107043  7107097  7107109
7107119  7107131  7107137  7107157  7107179  7107187  7107203  7107211  7107229  7107239
7107251  7107259  7107263  7107271  7107281  7107329  7107337  7107371  7107383  7107409
7107421  7107431  7107433  7107461  7107469  7107509  7107511  7107521  7107533  7107557
7107559  7107571  7107593  7107619  7107623  7107631  7107643  7107647  7107677  7107701
7107703  7107707  7107757  7107769  7107797  7107803  7107817  7107827  7107833  7107847
7107889  7107899  7107923  7107949  7107953  7107967  7107973  7107979  7108001  7108009
7108061  7108121  7108141  7108151  7108169  7108177  7108187  7108243  7108249  7108253
7108259  7108273  7108289  7108303  7108313  7108349  7108399  7108411  7108429  7108463
7108469  7108471  7108487  7108511  7108523  7108529  7108537  7108553  7108573  7108583
7108613  7108637  7108639  7108643  7108649  7108663  7108681  7108687  7108693  7108709
7108711  7108721  7108723  7108763  7108807  7108811  7108819  7108823  7108853  7108859
7108861  7108883  7108887  7108931  7108963  7108967  7108979  7108993  7108999  7109027
7109041  7109051  7109057  7109071  7109083  7109099  7109101  7109107  7109119  7109171
7109183  7109191  7109197  7109201  7109257  7109269  7109273  7109293  7109309  7109317
7109327  7109339  7109351  7109353  7109371  7109381  7109387  7109407  7109423  7109429
7109449  7109467  7109471  7109483  7109497  7109503  7109527  7109551  7109561  7109567
7109569  7109623  7109639  7109653  7109659  7109671  7109681  7109731  7109747  7109779
7109789  7109801  7109803  7109807  7109821  7109827  7109849  7109887  7109899  7109903
7109917  7109911  7109923  7109929  7109941  7109953  7109969  7109983  7110001  7110049
7110053  7110083  7110091  7110101  7110119  7110157  7110167  7110203  7110209  7110217
7110239  7110263  7110277  7110317  7110319  7110329  7110347  7110353  7110379  7110413
7110449  7110451  7110457  7110487  7110491  7110497  7110511  7110559  7110569  7110577
7110581  7110601  7110619  7110637  7110647  7110659  7110661  7110673  7110683  7110689
7110707  7110737  7110757  7110791  7110797  7110809  7110839  7110847  7110853  7110871
7110877  7110889  7110907  7110923  7110949  7110989  7110991  7111007  7111019  7111021
7111031  7111033  7111057  7111087  7111099  7111103  7111123  7111127  7111157  7111193
7111199  7111207  7111213  7111243  7111271  7111277  7111303  7111331  7111337  7111399
7111411  7111417  7111427  7111463  7111477  7111499  7111519  7111537  7111549  7111561
7111589  7111603  7111607  7111639  7111649  7111651  7111667  7111697  7111703  7111721
7111747  7111751  7111759  7111771  7111777  7111789  7111799  7111837  7111843  7111861
7111877  7111889  7111903  7111913  7111957  7111963  7111981  7111987  7111997  7112003
7112009  7112011  7112041  7112059  7112089  7112111  7112153  7112167  7112191  7112201
7112227  7112233  7112249  7112263  7112297  7112351  7112377  7112389  7112411  7112429
7112431  7112437  7112447  7112461  7112467  7112503  7112507  7112513  7112531  7112551
7112561  7112563  7112603  7112657  7112659  7112663  7112683  7112687  7112689  7112701
7112711  7112713  7112717  7112731  7112741  7112747  7112753  7112761  7112779  7112823
7112849  7112887  7112909  7112927  7112939  7112951  7112983  7112999  7113023  7113037
7113053  7113061  7113097  7113101  7113109  7113133  7113137  7113151  7113173  7113179
7113181  7113203  7113209  7113221  7113299  7113311  7113313  7113319  7113341  7113343
7113373  7113383  7113437  7113461  7113493  7113517  7113527  7113553  7113559  7113563
7113569  7113593  7113611  7113641  7113661  7113677  7113679  7113683  7113697  7113719
7113721  7113727  7113749  7113751  7113763  7113767  7113773  7113781  7113793  7113817
7113823  7113839  7113851  7113857  7113889  7113893  7113907  7113913  7113917  7113937
7113941  7113943  7113983  7113989  7114039  7114057  7114067  7114087  7114091  7114117
7114123  7114139  7114147  7114157  7114169  7114171  7114181  7114213  7114231  7114241
```

```
7114277 7114297 7114301 7114319 7114351 7114357 7114363 7114391 7114399 7114403
7114409 7114423 7114427 7114433 7114451 7114453 7114463 7114477 7114487 7114489
7114501 7114553 7114573 7114577 7114579 7114621 7114643 7114649 7114669 7114673
7114699 7114703 7114711 7114727 7114729 7114733 7114753 7114763 7114777 7114817
7114837 7114859 7114867 7114883 7114897 7114937 7114951 7114957 7114963 7114973
7114997 7114999 7115011 7115041 7115051 7115057 7115093 7115107 7115111 7115117
7115153 7115159 7115161 7115183 7115191 7115203 7115209 7115219 7115221 7115233
7115243 7115249 7115279 7115281 7115309 7115327 7115347 7115351 7115357 7115363
7115387 7115389 7115417 7115473 7115477 7115483 7115501 7115513 7115539 7115561
7115567 7115593 7115611 7115617 7115627 7115651 7115657 7115681 7115687 7115737
7115743 7115749 7115777 7115791 7115807 7115819 7115873 7115879 7115881 7115887
7115891 7115893 7115903 7115921 7115959 7115963 7115971 7115981 7115987 7115989
7116023 7116059 7116061 7116071 7116079 7116119 7116121 7116133 7116139 7116209
7116229 7116253 7116287 7116289 7116299 7116301 7116311 7116323 7116331 7116341
7116349 7116367 7116379 7116409 7116419 7116427 7116433 7116437 7116509 7116511
7116533 7116559 7116563 7116581 7116619 7116631 7116647 7116649 7116667 7116679
7116689 7116709 7116737 7116749 7116751 7116779 7116799 7116847 7116869 7116871
7116877 7116899 7116911 7116943 7116983 7116997 7117007 7117021 7117027 7117037
7117057 7117081 7117087 7117109 7117129 7117133 7117141 7117147 7117171 7117177
7117183 7117193 7117199 7117277 7117291 7117303 7117337 7117387 7117417 7117421
7117433 7117447 7117459 7117483 7117501 7117519 7117567 7117589 7117613 7117637
7117639 7117657 7117667 7117697 7117703 7117717 7117729 7117753 7117769 7117823
7117841 7117843 7117861 7117867 7117871 7117889 7117897 7117921 7117927 7117931
7117939 7117967 7117973 7117987 7118077 7118081 7118093 7118099 7118101 7118107
7118113 7118117 7118119 7118123 7118159 7118161 7118183 7118191 7118203 7118207
7118213 7118219 7118231 7118239 7118261 7118317 7118333 7118341 7118381 7118387
7118399 7118411 7118413 7118443 7118459 7118473 7118491 7118497 7118513 7118519
7118591 7118627 7118663 7118669 7118677 7118687 7118701 7118719 7118737 7118791
7118803 7118807 7118857 7118861 7118893 7118897 7118921 7118963 7118987
7119011 7119061 7119067 7119103 7119109 7119131 7119139 7119149 7119169 7119173
7119193 7119247 7119253 7119271 7119283 7119289 7119293 7119317 7119323
7119337 7119341 7119347 7119349 7119403 7119407 7119439 7119449 7119473 7119517
7119521 7119523 7119533 7119557 7119569 7119611 7119613 7119653 7119709 7119713
7119727 7119743 7119751 7119779 7119797 7119803 7119817 7119829 7119881 7119899
7119901 7119919 7119929 7119941 7119977 7119979 7120007 7120013 7120031 7120037
7120039 7120063 7120097 7120121 7120123 7120147 7120153 7120159 7120163 7120177
7120181 7120187 7120189 7120213 7120219 7120237 7120277 7120279 7120303 7120319
7120361 7120367 7120369 7120381 7120387 7120411 7120417 7120423 7120447 7120471
7120481 7120489 7120523 7120537 7120541 7120543 7120567 7120571 7120579 7120583
7120621 7120657 7120679 7120697 7120723 7120727 7120733 7120741 7120781 7120783
7120811 7120837 7120847 7120871 7120873 7120879 7120891 7120903 7120907 7120913
7120933 7120963 7120969 7120987 7120999 7121021 7121033 7121071 7121089 7121137
7121141 7121161 7121173 7121203 7121209 7121263 7121267 7121321 7121339 7121341
7121347 7121357 7121377 7121399 7121407 7121417 7121437 7121441 7121473 7121489
7121503 7121509 7121519 7121533 7121539 7121573 7121579 7121591 7121593 7121603
7121629 7121669 7121683 7121687 7121693 7121701 7121707 7121711 7121717 7121731
7121761 7121767 7121773 7121801 7121809 7121819 7121833 7121839 7121867 7121879
7121921 7121923 7121993 7121999 7122001 7122007 7122013 7122029 7122041 7122053
7122061 7122079 7122091 7122103 7122107 7122109 7122119 7122121 7122149 7122179
7122187 7122209 7122253 7122257 7122263 7122289 7122293 7122307 7122319 7122331
7122361 7122373 7122377 7122407 7122413 7122443 7122449 7122457 7122469 7122491
7122497 7122509 7122517 7122551 7122559 7122593 7122607 7122623 7122637 7122641
7122667 7122679 7122691 7122697 7122721 7122733 7122743 7122749 7122757 7122761
7122763 7122769 7122781 7122793 7122799 7122809 7122859 7122887 7122953 7122961
7122989 7123003 7123021 7123027 7123037 7123057 7123063 7123073 7123093 7123099
7123117 7123159 7123177 7123199 7123201 7123213 7123223 7123229 7123231 7123279
7123297 7123301 7123313 7123327 7123331 7123339 7123343 7123379 7123409 7123411
7123421 7123427 7123447 7123453 7123469 7123481 7123489 7123511 7123513 7123547
7123549 7123579 7123591 7123607 7123619 7123657 7123661 7123679 7123691 7123693
7123703 7123729 7123733 7123747 7123751 7123771 7123793 7123847 7123849 7123861
7123877 7123891 7123903 7123957 7123981 7124009 7124023 7124041 7124057 7124081
7124083 7124087 7124093 7124099 7124123 7124147 7124171 7124179 7124231 7124233
7124261 7124269 7124279 7124287 7124291 7124311 7124321 7124329 7124333
7124339 7124347 7124357 7124393 7124413 7124417 7124431 7124437 7124443 7124477
7124483 7124519 7124521 7124527 7124543 7124561 7124569 7124591 7124597 7124603
7124629 7124651 7124653 7124657 7124669 7124701 7124707 7124731 7124743 7124759
7124771 7124783 7124801 7124833 7124839 7124851 7124869 7124879 7124891 7124903
7124911 7124977 7124987 7124993 7125037 7125043 7125047 7125049 7125061 7125067
7125077 7125113 7125121 7125169 7125187 7125197 7125199 7125203 7125263 7125269
7125277 7125281 7125299 7125337 7125353 7125359 7125379 7125407 7125413 7125421
7125463 7125473 7125527 7125553 7125583 7125611 7125617 7125649 7125661 7125673
7125683 7125689 7125707 7125731 7125743 7125751 7125761 7125787 7125803 7125809
7125821 7125827 7125829 7125847 7125863 7125869 7125887 7125889 7125901 7125947
7125949 7125971 7125973 7125983 7126069 7126109 7126123 7126127 7126153 7126157
7126181 7126183 7126201 7126243 7126253 7126277 7126279 7126289 7126291 7126313
7126331 7126363 7126367 7126381 7126393 7126429 7126439 7126453 7126507 7126517
7126543 7126549 7126583 7126591 7126597 7126601 7126627 7126631 7126633 7126649
7126699 7126703 7126727 7126733 7126739 7126769 7126811 7126817 7126841 7126871
7126883 7126891 7126897 7126901 7126943 7126979 7126981 7126997 7127009 7127027
7127039 7127053 7127077 7127083 7127089 7127129 7127137 7127161 7127173 7127177
7127201 7127203 7127231 7127251 7127257 7127287 7127311 7127327 7127333 7127339
7127353 7127357 7127363 7127371 7127383 7127431 7127441 7127443 7127467 7127473
7127479 7127513 7127567 7127581 7127587 7127623 7127629 7127633 7127639 7127651
7127663 7127689 7127711 7127719 7127753 7127767 7127779 7127797 7127803 7127819
7127893 7127929 7127963 7127971 7127977 7127987 7127993 7128007 7128031 7128077
7128101 7128139 7128167 7128181 7128193 7128221 7128223 7128227 7128259 7128269
7128281 7128293 7128307 7128347 7128353 7128361 7128391 7128427 7128437 7128463
7128467 7128493 7128503 7128509 7128529 7128533 7128581 7128587 7128601 7128617
7128619 7128647 7128673 7128691 7128697 7128701 7128703 7128707 7128727 7128739
```

```
7128749 7128761 7128767 7128799 7128817 7128833 7128907 7128931 7128943 7128949
7128973 7128991 7128997 7129027 7129037 7129061 7129079 7129081 7129091 7129093
7129117 7129127 7129159 7129183 7129207 7129211 7129217 7129219 7129229 7129231
7129247 7129249 7129259 7129261 7129267 7129277 7129301 7129321 7129337 7129361
7129373 7129387 7129417 7129439 7129453 7129469 7129481 7129483 7129519 7129543
7129559 7129561 7129583 7129589 7129601 7129637 7129651 7129673 7129687 7129711
7129729 7129781 7129819 7129831 7129847 7129861 7129877 7130003 7130009 7130029
7130051 7130063 7130083 7130113 7130117 7130119 7130141 7130147 7130153 7130171
7130173 7130177 7130197 7130213 7130231 7130237 7130239 7130243 7130251 7130267
7130329 7130359 7130363 7130393 7130407 7130411 7130423 7130441 7130449 7130471
7130479 7130489 7130509 7130533 7130537 7130551 7130573 7130579 7130687 7130707
7130729 7130731 7130737 7130749 7130789 7130791 7130797 7130807 7130813 7130861
7130863 7130867 7130869 7130881 7130891 7130911 7130933 7130941 7130951 7130957
7130993 7131001 7131017 7131037 7131049 7131053 7131119 7131133 7131139 7131191
7131193 7131199 7131217 7131259 7131281 7131301 7131323 7131329 7131337 7131349
7131353 7131359 7131373 7131379 7131407 7131433 7131437 7131461 7131469 7131503
7131511 7131533 7131569 7131577 7131583 7131601 7131613 7131623 7131629
7131647 7131661 7131689 7131701 7131703 7131727 7131779 7131793 7131797 7131841
7131847 7131853 7131869 7131877 7131889 7131899 7131923 7131947 7131967 7131977
7131983 7131989 7132019 7132031 7132043 7132063 7132091 7132117 7132121 7132123
7132127 7132141 7132159 7132171 7132187 7132189 7132211 7132241 7132243 7132249
7132259 7132261 7132267 7132283 7132291 7132309 7132327 7132337 7132373 7132381
7132393 7132397 7132417 7132421 7132423 7132427 7132459 7132487 7132493 7132523
7132529 7132577 7132583 7132593 7132603 7132627 7132649 7132651 7132661 7132681
7132693 7132703 7132709 7132751 7132781 7132813 7132841 7132849 7132859 7132871
7132891 7132901 7132907 7132919 7132933 7132943 7132949 7132973 7132987 7132997
7133033 7133107 7133117 7133129 7133167 7133171 7133177 7133201 7133207 7133219
7133233 7133239 7133257 7133281 7133293 7133297 7133339 7133363 7133393 7133411
7133443 7133447 7133459 7133479 7133509 7133521 7133527 7133537 7133551 7133561
7133587 7133593 7133597 7133603 7133647 7133663 7133701 7133719 7133729 7133771
7133809 7133821 7133827 7133831 7133837 7133839 7133843 7133849 7133851 7133857
7133869 7133879 7133881 7133891 7133899 7133921 7133927 7133939 7133957 7133963
7133969 7133983 7134031 7134079 7134091 7134107 7134109 7134119 7134131 7134137
7134143 7134157 7134181 7134199 7134223 7134233 7134251 7134263 7134307 7134311
7134317 7134331 7134341 7134353 7134397 7134409 7134427 7134437 7134467 7134497
7134503 7134511 7134527 7134583 7134593 7134601 7134643 7134661 7134663 7134737
7134739 7134767 7134769 7134773 7134791 7134793 7134817 7134833 7134851 7134857
7134859 7134877 7134887 7134893 7134923 7134949 7134973 7134977 7134979 7134989
7135001 7135021 7135027 7135061 7135069 7135099 7135103 7135123 7135133 7135153
7135169 7135171 7135181 7135199 7135207 7135217 7135229 7135237 7135253 7135259
7135277 7135309 7135319 7135321 7135327 7135343 7135351 7135379 7135391 7135423
7135441 7135459 7135483 7135489 7135511 7135547 7135553 7135559 7135573 7135577
7135591 7135607 7135613 7135619 7135633 7135643 7135669 7135691 7135717 7135741
7135747 7135757 7135771 7135781 7135813 7135831 7135847 7135853 7135861 7135871
7135883 7135889 7135901 7135907 7135913 7135939 7135949 7135967 7136021 7136023
7136027 7136033 7136047 7136069 7136071 7136081 7136083 7136089 7136099 7136111
7136123 7136131 7136161 7136167 7136177 7136179 7136201 7136203 7136221 7136249
7136309 7136317 7136369 7136377 7136383 7136401 7136429 7136431 7136443 7136461
7136471 7136473 7136477 7136483 7136489 7136491 7136497 7136537 7136539 7136543
7136567 7136593 7136599 7136611 7136627 7136659 7136663 7136681 7136711 7136729
7136743 7136771 7136791 7136797 7136807 7136863 7136867 7136873 7136879 7136887
7136897 7136917 7136971 7137001 7137029 7137043 7137047 7137071 7137073 7137077
7137083 7137101 7137121 7137131 7137149 7137167 7137181 7137191 7137203 7137209
7137259 7137287 7137301 7137311 7137313 7137343 7137359 7137371 7137379 7137397
7137421 7137437 7137439 7137463 7137491 7137517 7137553 7137583 7137587 7137589
7137593 7137601 7137617 7137623 7137631 7137653 7137677 7137703 7137733 7137737
7137743 7137763 7137769 7137817 7137827 7137829 7137833 7137839 7137847 7137853
7137859 7137877 7137913 7137947 7137961 7137989 7138009 7138039 7138049 7138069
7138121 7138123 7138169 7138177 7138193 7138207 7138217 7138237 7138273 7138279
7138297 7138309 7138331 7138337 7138343 7138363 7138367 7138393 7138399 7138409
7138489 7138513 7138541 7138561 7138577 7138603 7138613 7138619 7138631 7138639
7138643 7138673 7138693 7138697 7138723 7138741 7138751 7138753 7138771 7138777
7138787 7138799 7138801 7138811 7138819 7138829 7138841 7138849 7138853 7138867
7138883 7138919 7138931 7138949 7138973 7138981 7138987 7139009 7139023 7139071
7139089 7139101 7139123 7139189 7139219 7139273 7139287 7139299 7139311 7139323
7139329 7139351 7139357 7139401 7139437 7139449 7139513 7139519 7139521 7139527
7139543 7139567 7139569 7139581 7139603 7139621 7139659 7139663 7139701 7139731
7139753 7139777 7139809 7139833 7139861 7139897 7139913 7139917 7139933
7139939 7139947 7139971 7139999 7140011 7140031 7140041 7140047 7140053 7140059
7140071 7140079 7140083 7140101 7140113 7140127 7140157 7140163 7140167 7140169
7140173 7140209 7140227 7140247 7140251 7140253 7140271 7140277 7140283 7140299
7140307 7140311 7140317 7140347 7140359 7140361 7140379 7140383 7140401 7140403
7140433 7140439 7140443 7140457 7140473 7140479 7140487 7140499 7140547 7140563
7140611 7140643 7140647 7140671 7140673 7140677 7140689 7140701 7140733 7140767
7140769 7140779 7140797 7140803 7140811 7140823 7140841 7140853 7140857 7140863
7140883 7140899 7140911 7140923 7140937 7140949 7140953 7140961 7140977 7140983
7140997 7141007 7141009 7141021 7141033 7141049 7141051 7141103 7141117 7141153
7141159 7141177 7141181 7141187 7141219 7141231 7141291 7141307 7141319 7141349
7141357 7141361 7141369 7141391 7141417 7141427 7141429 7141441 7141451 7141457
7141471 7141489 7141531 7141567 7141573 7141577 7141601 7141621 7141637 7141639
7141643 7141657 7141669 7141691 7141699 7141709 7141723 7141733 7141759 7141769
7141781 7141787 7141807 7141829 7141843 7141867 7141889 7141903 7141907 7141919
7141931 7141933 7141943 7141949 7141951 7141957 7141963 7141969 7141973 7141991
7142011 7142027 7142039 7142053 7142111 7142117 7142129 7142141 7142173 7142189
7142203 7142209 7142263 7142269 7142293 7142299 7142321 7142341 7142371 7142383
7142413 7142419 7142437 7142479 7142483 7142501 7142503 7142507 7142519 7142521
7142557 7142563 7142593 7142609 7142621 7142623 7142633 7142659 7142699 7142713
7142743 7142749 7142783 7142791 7142809 7142819 7142833 7142851 7142869 7142881
7142893 7142899 7142909 7142923 7142929 7142939 7142951 7142957 7142959 7142981
```

```
7142987  7143001  7143007  7143049  7143053  7143067  7143079  7143083  7143089  7143119
7143121  7143127  7143133  7143139  7143163  7143173  7143187  7143211  7143217  7143223
7143233  7143263  7143277  7143313  7143319  7143341  7143347  7143377  7143379  7143391
7143397  7143401  7143413  7143419  7143421  7143439  7143443  7143457  7143467  7143469
7143491  7143517  7143529  7143557  7143569  7143581  7143589  7143613  7143637  7143667
7143673  7143679  7143683  7143691  7143709  7143737  7143739  7143743  7143749  7143761
7143767  7143797  7143821  7143841  7143883  7143887  7143911  7143931  7143959  7143967
7143979  7143989  7144001  7144021  7144031  7144037  7144051  7144061  7144129  7144153
7144201  7144211  7144217  7144223  7144231  7144289  7144307  7144327  7144331  7144339
7144351  7144363  7144387  7144409  7144429  7144433  7144447  7144451  7144477  7144483
7144691  7144717  7144721  7144757  7144769  7144793  7144843  7144853  7144859  7144861
7144873  7144903  7144967  7144979  7144999  7145003  7145011  7145041  7145051  7145063
7145069  7145071  7145087  7145101  7145129  7145137  7145153  7145161  7145179  7145183
7145189  7145191  7145209  7145231  7145233  7145239  7145251  7145291  7145377  7145393
7145399  7145417  7145443  7145473  7145503  7145507  7145527  7145533  7145557  7145563
7145587  7145591  7145597  7145599  7145609  7145623  7145641  7145647  7145651  7145669
7145681  7145689  7145693  7145701  7145707  7145731  7145737  7145759  7145813  7145819
7145821  7145839  7145863  7145867  7145917  7145923  7145947  7145951  7145953  7145969
7145981  7145987  7145993  7146023  7146047  7146049  7146059  7146091  7146133  7146157
7146173  7146193  7146197  7146199  7146203  7146241  7146263  7146277  7146283  7146311
7146313  7146379  7146389  7146401  7146437  7146463  7146497  7146521  7146539  7146559
7146553  7146571  7146589  7146593  7146619  7146649  7146677  7146683  7146691  7146697
7146701  7146703  7146707  7146719  7146739  7146743  7146757  7146761  7146779  7146787
7146791  7146827  7146829  7146857  7146871  7146889  7146929  7146941  7146947  7146949
7146959  7146973  7147001  7147003  7147033  7147037  7147039  7147093  7147109  7147117
7147121  7147139  7147169  7147183  7147193  7147219  7147223  7147237  7147247  7147397
7147403  7147423  7147451  7147471  7147507  7147523  7147529  7147537  7147541  7147559
7147573  7147583  7147597  7147603  7147607  7147643  7147663  7147681  7147691  7147703
7147709  7147747  7147757  7147759  7147787  7147807  7147813  7147823  7147831  7147849
7147859  7147873  7147879  7147883  7147913  7147927  7147961  7147967  7147969  7147979
7147991  7147997  7148023  7148051  7148069  7148081  7148129  7148131  7148149  7148153
7148171  7148201  7148203  7148243  7148261  7148287  7148291  7148299  7148311  7148341
7148357  7148387  7148399  7148419  7148429  7148461  7148489  7148497  7148501  7148513
7148521  7148597  7148611  7148629  7148633  7148657  7148663  7148683  7148717  7148737
7148749  7148753  7148759  7148809  7148839  7148849  7148893  7148899  7148917
7148923  7148927  7148951  7148987  7148989  7149007  7149013  7149019  7149041  7149049
7149053  7149059  7149097  7149143  7149161  7149193  7149209  7149221  7149227  7149239
7149253  7149257  7149271  7149277  7149347  7149349  7149353  7149361  7149379  7149403
7149407  7149409  7149413  7149433  7149449  7149463  7149479  7149497  7149509  7149511
7149521  7149523  7149533  7149551  7149557  7149559  7149563  7149581  7149589  7149599
7149601  7149613  7149617  7149641  7149671  7149677  7149691  7149713  7149731  7149733
7149761  7149767  7149799  7149811  7149817  7149823  7149827  7149829  7149841  7149851
7149899  7149907  7149929  7149943  7149959  7149971  7149983  7150007  7150009  7150019
7150027  7150103  7150123  7150133  7150147  7150189  7150193  7150207  7150219  7150223
7150249  7150259  7150279  7150313  7150331  7150333  7150343  7150357  7150379  7150393
7150399  7150417  7150459  7150469  7150477  7150483  7150499  7150519  7150529  7150543
7150567  7150589  7150613  7150639  7150643  7150651  7150673  7150681  7150691  7150729
7150747  7150757  7150763  7150799  7150807  7150811  7150817  7150831  7150837
7150841  7150851  7150867  7150873  7150961  7150963  7150967  7151009  7151017  7151021
7151041  7151051  7151057  7151059  7151063  7151083  7151093  7151113  7151141  7151143
7151147  7151149  7151167  7151189  7151219  7151227  7151267  7151273  7151279  7151281
7151327  7151329  7151341  7151357  7151369  7151377  7151399  7151401  7151447  7151453
7151489  7151503  7151531  7151533  7151549  7151561  7151569  7151609  7151621  7151623
7151653  7151659  7151663  7151687  7151699  7151707  7151723  7151741  7151779  7151797
7151801  7151819  7151831  7151839  7151843  7151857  7151869  7151887  7151891  7151897
7151909  7151927  7151933  7151939  7151953  7151981  7151983  7152007  7152023  7152031
7152071  7152073  7152083  7152097  7152139  7152143  7152161  7152169  7152181  7152203
7152221  7152239  7152247  7152251  7152263  7152269  7152283  7152323  7152329  7152331
7152337  7152347  7152349  7152367  7152373  7152389  7152391  7152407  7152419  7152447
7152499  7152527  7152547  7152557  7152559  7152571  7152583  7152619  7152623  7152641
7152643  7152653  7152667  7152671  7152697  7152703  7152751  7152779  7152791  7152823
7152829  7152851  7152863  7152889  7152913  7152923  7152941  7152947  7152961  7152967
7152973  7152991  7153049  7153067  7153103  7153109  7153117  7153129  7153151  7153187
7153193  7153199  7153217  7153261  7153297  7153303  7153309  7153313  7153319  7153339
7153369  7153381  7153387  7153397  7153403  7153411  7153423  7153427  7153429  7153457
7153501  7153507  7153513  7153567  7153579  7153589  7153607  7153631  7153637  7153649
7153669  7153673  7153681  7153693  7153697  7153711  7153733  7153763  7153771  7153789
7153801  7153829  7153837  7153843  7153849  7153871  7153873  7153877  7153891  7153921
7153961  7153969  7154023  7154027  7154047  7154101  7154107  7154123  7154137
7154167  7154177  7154183  7154207  7154221  7154227  7154237  7154239  7154243  7154261
7154267  7154269  7154309  7154321  7154353  7154401  7154433  7154443  7154471  7154479
7154491  7154527  7154549  7154557  7154573  7154591  7154597  7154627  7154639  7154681
7154687  7154699  7154701  7154713  7154717  7154723  7154737  7154759  7154783  7154789
7154837  7154839  7154879  7154911  7154923  7154929  7154933  7154971  7154981  7154993
7154999  7155019  7155037  7155041  7155059  7155061  7155067  7155073  7155091  7155121
7155149  7155151  7155193  7155209  7155217  7155271  7155287  7155289  7155293  7155331
7155341  7155359  7155367  7155383  7155391  7155397  7155403  7155409  7155413  7155439
7155479  7155503  7155509  7155517  7155527  7155529  7155539  7155559  7155601  7155611
7155649  7155653  7155671  7155677  7155751  7155769  7155809  7155821  7155851  7155881
7155887  7155917  7155919  7155943  7155961  7155977  7155983  7155991  7156001  7156033
7156043  7156049  7156063  7156067  7156073  7156091  7156109  7156111  7156183  7156187
7156199  7156213  7156229  7156231  7156271  7156277  7156291  7156307  7156309  7156327
7156333  7156339  7156349  7156351  7156367  7156379  7156393  7156397  7156411  7156441
7156463  7156517  7156529  7156553  7156561  7156571  7156573  7156601  7156603  7156607
7156621  7156627  7156631  7156663  7156697  7156717  7156727  7156741  7156769  7156771
7156777  7156781  7156783  7156811  7156817  7156819  7156829  7156843  7156861  7156883
7156907  7156913  7156927  7156967  7156969  7156973  7156987  7156991  7156999  7157009
```

```
7157011 7157023 7157027 7157039 7157041 7157047 7157089 7157093 7157099 7157107
7157131 7157201 7157219 7157237 7157239 7157257 7157261 7157263 7157273 7157299
7157303 7157341 7157377 7157387 7157389 7157401 7157407 7157417 7157429 7157443
7157477 7157483 7157503 7157587 7157603 7157609 7157611 7157627 7157653 7157659
7157681 7157701 7157713 7157719 7157729 7157741 7157747 7157749 7157797 7157803
7157827 7157849 7157863 7157873 7157879 7157881 7157893 7157897 7157933 7157963
7157981 7157987 7157999 7158013 7158017 7158023 7158059 7158061 7158089 7158097
7158119 7158133 7158163 7158197 7158199 7158223 7158227 7158247 7158257 7158271
7158317 7158329 7158337 7158367 7158379 7158391 7158409 7158449 7158461 7158467
7158469 7158491 7158493 7158509 7158517 7158527 7158539 7158553 7158583 7158587
7158607 7158629 7158631 7158637 7158659 7158673 7158689 7158691 7158703 7158707
7158709 7158713 7158719 7158721 7158733 7158761 7158787 7158791 7158803 7158817
7158821 7158829 7158847 7158857 7158881 7158919 7158937 7158947 7158959 7158961
7158967 7158971 7158983 7158997 7159013 7159039 7159063 7159073 7159079 7159099
7159111 7159147 7159157 7159169 7159213 7159223 7159231 7159247 7159303 7159307
7159309 7159319 7159337 7159343 7159349 7159367 7159381 7159421 7159429 7159459
7159469 7159487 7159489 7159501 7159507 7159511 7159513 7159517 7159519 7159541
7159583 7159589 7159597 7159609 7159627 7159657 7159661 7159673 7159681 7159699
7159741 7159777 7159787 7159799 7159811 7159813 7159837 7159843 7159891 7159921
7159927 7159931 7159937 7159939 7159949 7159963 7159987 7160003 7160011 7160033
7160051 7160053 7160057 7160081 7160099 7160113 7160123 7160147 7160149 7160177
7160189 7160227 7160347 7160369 7160381 7160389 7160401 7160407 7160437 7160441
7160449 7160467 7160507 7160533 7160539 7160551 7160557 7160561 7160581 7160599
7160603 7160623 7160669 7160683 7160693 7160711 7160717 7160731 7160743 7160801
7160821 7160827 7160861 7160887 7160899 7160917 7160921 7160939 7160947 7160963
7160971 7160977 7160983 7160987 7161013 7161023 7161047 7161071 7161103 7161107
7161109 7161137 7161139 7161151 7161179 7161197 7161223 7161229 7161251 7161269
7161277 7161293 7161299 7161317 7161331 7161337 7161359 7161379 7161421 7161433
7161443 7161449 7161457 7161467 7161493 7161503 7161509 7161547 7161559 7161569
7161577 7161599 7161619 7161629 7161653 7161667 7161673 7161703 7161751 7161761
7161769 7161773 7161787 7161793 7161823 7161851 7161853 7161857 7161859 7161863
7161877 7161887 7161929 7161937 7161971 7161991 7161997 7162007 7162009 7162021
7162033 7162073 7162087 7162093 7162109 7162171 7162229 7162237 7162241 7162247
7162273 7162289 7162303 7162307 7162339 7162403 7162439 7162469 7162513 7162523
7162549 7162583 7162609 7162613 7162619 7162633 7162667 7162679 7162697 7162699
7162703 7162711 7162733 7162747 7162751 7162759 7162781 7162783 7162807 7162843
7162849 7162853 7162861 7162871 7162873 7162889 7162907 7162919 7162921 7162931
7162951 7162963 7162993 7162997 7162999 7163011 7163017 7163033 7163041 7163053
7163059 7163113 7163147 7163173 7163179 7163197 7163213 7163227 7163251 7163267
7163269 7163279 7163287 7163297 7163309 7163339 7163347 7163357 7163363 7163383
7163393 7163407 7163423 7163447 7163461 7163501 7163503 7163509 7163537 7163539
7163623 7163633 7163659 7163669 7163677 7163683 7163711 7163713 7163719 7163729
7163731 7163747 7163773 7163777 7163797 7163803 7163809 7163831 7163869 7163873
7163909 7163911 7163917 7163927 7163941 7163951 7163983 7163993 7164011 7164019
7164029 7164037 7164043 7164071 7164077 7164107 7164119 7164127 7164137 7164139
7164151 7164167 7164173 7164203 7164239 7164251 7164253 7164263 7164307 7164319
7164329 7164331 7164413 7164433 7164491 7164499 7164527 7164529 7164533 7164541
7164551 7164557 7164559 7164571 7164581 7164583 7164587 7164623 7164629 7164631
7164649 7164673 7164697 7164713 7164719 7164721 7164733 7164737 7164757 7164761
7164763 7164793 7164797 7164847 7164853 7164863 7164887 7164889 7164893 7164917
7164923 7164929 7164931 7164953 7165003 7165021 7165027 7165043 7165049 7165049
7165051 7165057 7165069 7165079 7165091 7165097 7165139 7165187 7165189 7165199
7165253 7165267 7165273 7165289 7165321 7165339 7165343 7165363 7165387 7165399
7165409 7165421 7165423 7165427 7165463 7165471 7165493 7165519 7165541 7165553
7165567 7165577 7165579 7165597 7165601 7165621 7165633 7165661 7165663 7165699
7165729 7165733 7165757 7165777 7165783 7165787 7165859 7165883 7165889 7165909
7165913 7165933 7165943 7165973 7165979 7165981 7165997 7166057 7166063 7166099
7166113 7166141 7166143 7166147 7166149 7166153 7166167 7166171 7166209 7166221
7166227 7166233 7166261 7166279 7166297 7166321 7166339 7166353 7166371 7166377
7166389 7166407 7166413 7166417 7166443 7166447 7166459 7166461 7166479 7166491
7166507 7166531 7166543 7166561 7166563 7166569 7166581 7166597 7166603 7166609
7166633 7166647 7166659 7166689 7166693 7166699 7166729 7166749 7166771 7166773
7166791 7166813 7166827 7166833 7166839 7166851 7166867 7166891 7166897 7166899
7166909 7166941 7166963 7166969 7166977 7166987 7166989 7166993 7167001 7167019
7167029 7167059 7167101 7167103 7167119 7167151 7167157 7167163 7167187 7167211
7167221 7167227 7167239 7167241 7167253 7167287 7167289 7167301 7167323 7167331
7167343 7167361 7167367 7167373 7167409 7167431 7167463 7167469 7167481 7167491
7167509 7167527 7167551 7167571 7167607 7167613 7167619 7167623 7167647 7167673
7167701 7167707 7167737 7167739 7167757 7167767 7167791 7167841 7167871 7167887
7167911 7167917 7167967 7167991 7168001 7168069 7168093 7168097 7168159 7168163
7168177 7168181 7168193 7168211 7168219 7168243 7168267 7168277 7168279 7168283
7168289 7168297 7168313 7168319 7168331 7168333 7168349 7168351 7168361 7168379
7168391 7168411 7168459 7168477 7168489 7168493 7168507 7168517 7168541 7168547
7168561 7168583 7168589 7168613 7168619 7168631 7168649 7168661 7168669 7168691
7168703 7168729 7168739 7168739 7168741 7168751 7168789 7168813 7168817 7168841
7168853 7168859 7168873 7168877 7168897 7168901 7168907 7168919 7168921 7168927
7168943 7168949 7168963 7168969 7168981 7168991 7168999 7169017 7169021 7169033
7169047 7169101 7169131 7169159 7169161 7169167 7169199 7169221 7169233 7169243
7169249 7169273 7169311 7169317 7169369 7169411 7169413 7169429 7169447 7169471
7169489 7169501 7169551 7169557 7169581 7169599 7169609 7169611 7169627 7169633
7169647 7169653 7169663 7169671 7169677 7169689 7169713 7169741 7169753 7169779
7169809 7169819 7169831 7169837 7169843 7169849 7169861 7169887 7169909 7169923
7169927 7169941 7169947 7169977 7169983 7169993 7170013 7170017 7170019 7170041
7170067 7170071 7170103 7170113 7170127 7170161 7170173 7170197 7170199 7170253
7170257 7170259 7170263 7170271 7170299 7170313 7170343 7170377 7170403 7170419
7170421 7170431 7170439 7170451 7170469 7170489 7170539 7170577 7170601 7170607
7170643 7170665 7170671 7170673 7170679 7170689 7170721 7170731 7170739 7170749
7170763 7170767 7170769 7170773 7170781 7170791 7170797 7170803 7170811 7170829
7170833 7170851 7170869 7170881 7170883 7170887 7170901 7170907 7170949 7170959
```

7170967 7170971 7170983 7171019 7171049 7171051 7171057 7171063 7171069 7171079
7171097 7171103 7171111 7171133 7171139 7171159 7171181 7171183 7171201 7171217
7171223 7171237 7171249 7171259 7171267 7171279 7171291 7171327 7171337 7171357
7171387 7171393 7171397 7171429 7171441 7171453 7171471 7171499 7171513 7171529
7171553 7171573 7171579 7171621 7171651 7171657 7171663 7171667 7171689 7171691
7171711 7171741 7171751 7171753 7171783 7171789 7171793 7171799 7171811 7171847
7171849 7171861 7171891 7171933 7171937 7171939 7171951 7171979 7171991 7171997
7172003 7172029 7172093 7172107 7172131 7172167 7172189 7172201 7172219 7172237
7172267 7172287 7172311 7172327 7172369 7172383 7172387 7172411 7172423 7172447
7172467 7172479 7172497 7172507 7172549 7172567 7172569 7172587 7172591 7172597
7172603 7172617 7172639 7172677 7172681 7172707 7172719 7172723 7172729 7172731
7172791 7172797 7172839 7172843 7172863 7172881 7172897 7172911 7172923 7172927
7172939 7172969 7172989 7172993 7173017 7173029 7173071 7173083 7173091 7173097
7173137 7173139 7173143 7173149 7173157 7173191 7173193 7173209 7173233 7173239
7173251 7173277 7173293 7173347 7173349 7173377 7173379 7173409 7173433 7173479
7173503 7173533 7173547 7173559 7173571 7173577 7173581 7173589 7173599 7173611
7173613 7173619 7173629 7173653 7173689 7173703 7173721 7173737 7173739 7173743
7173781 7173787 7173799 7173809 7173821 7173823 7173853 7173857 7173863 7173877
7173889 7173899 7173913 7173917 7173919 7173923 7173931 7173941 7173977 7173979
7174007 7174009 7174021 7174043 7174061 7174073 7174093 7174109 7174117 7174129
7174147 7174157 7174171 7174177 7174199 7174231 7174241 7174247 7174253 7174301
7174313 7174331 7174369 7174373 7174399 7174403 7174417 7174439 7174441 7174471
7174481 7174501 7174523 7174529 7174589 7174591 7174613 7174619 7174627 7174639
7174649 7174681 7174693 7174703 7174711 7174721 7174747 7174751 7174753 7174777
7174787 7174793 7174801 7174807 7174819 7174823 7174841 7174883 7174889 7174891
7174907 7174927 7174933 7174949 7174967 7174987 7174991 7174997 7175033 7175039
7175053 7175059 7175107 7175117 7175153 7175159 7175191 7175197 7175219 7175239
7175249 7175251 7175261 7175279 7175303 7175317 7175323 7175327 7175351 7175359
7175417 7175437 7175449 7175459 7175461 7175501 7175503 7175549 7175551 7175561
7175569 7175587 7175591 7175593 7175611 7175629 7175647 7175653 7175657 7175677
7175687 7175699 7175761 7175783 7175813 7175821 7175843 7175873 7175941 7175953
7175957 7175983 7176011 7176019 7176047 7176089 7176121 7176133 7176179 7176181
7176203 7176241 7176259 7176269 7176277 7176317 7176331 7176343 7176349 7176371
7176419 7176457 7176461 7176473 7176479 7176497 7176511 7176527 7176551 7176629
7176683 7176691 7176707 7176721 7176733 7176773 7176781 7176823 7176863 7176881
7176901 7176929 7176971 7176979 7176997 7177013 7177031 7177033 7177039 7177061
7177063 7177067 7177069 7177103 7177109 7177133 7177139 7177147 7177153 7177201
7177217 7177237 7177243 7177253 7177267 7177271 7177273 7177327 7177343 7177351
7177367 7177381 7177393 7177397 7177411 7177427 7177441 7177463 7177481 7177531
7177537 7177601 7177609 7177613 7177619 7177627 7177637 7177657 7177661 7177663
7177669 7177673 7177691 7177693 7177697 7177711 7177717 7177733 7177739 7177783
7177811 7177823 7177837 7177853 7177879 7177921 7177979 7177987 7177997 7178011
7178021 7178023 7178027 7178057 7178069 7178071 7178077 7178107 7178113 7178137
7178141 7178159 7178189 7178201 7178203 7178209 7178221 7178243 7178251 7178261
7178273 7178287 7178293 7178299 7178351 7178363 7178387 7178393 7178401 7178411
7178417 7178443 7178449 7178459 7178467 7178477 7178489 7178531 7178537 7178609
7178617 7178621 7178623 7178627 7178653 7178657 7178659 7178687 7178693 7178719
7178723 7178729 7178741 7178749 7178767 7178771 7178779 7178819 7178833 7178837
7178839 7178869 7178909 7178917 7178939 7178953 7178957 7178971 7178987 7179001
7179019 7179041 7179043 7179047 7179071 7179077 7179079 7179091 7179097 7179101
7179127 7179143 7179157 7179217 7179233 7179239 7179241 7179247 7179301 7179343
7179373 7179377 7179413 7179421 7179439 7179461 7179467 7179479 7179481 7179493
7179521 7179527 7179547 7179553 7179607 7179619 7179629 7179643 7179647 7179671
7179677 7179707 7179709 7179737 7179743 7179779 7179803 7179811 7179827 7179829
7179833 7179859 7179889 7179911 7179919 7179923 7179937 7179943 7179947 7179971
7179983 7180009 7180031 7180039 7180051 7180067 7180079 7180087 7180091 7180093
7180099 7180169 7180177 7180193 7180223 7180259 7180279 7180291 7180297 7180319
7180321 7180333 7180337 7180339 7180351 7180363 7180391 7180399 7180421 7180427
7180483 7180489 7180507 7180513 7180543 7180549 7180567 7180573 7180583 7180597
7180633 7180643 7180673 7180697 7180703 7180717 7180721 7180729 7180739 7180741
7180751 7180759 7180769 7180793 7180799 7180819 7180829 7180843 7180861 7180883
7180889 7180897 7180903 7180909 7180931 7180969 7180973 7181017 7181033 7181039
7181051 7181063 7181087 7181093 7181099 7181113 7181131 7181147 7181149 7181159
7181171 7181173 7181189 7181197 7181203 7181227 7181231 7181249 7181257 7181309
7181323 7181371 7181381 7181399 7181423 7181431 7181443 7181453 7181477 7181479
7181507 7181513 7181527 7181533 7181549 7181567 7181597 7181609 7181611 7181621
7181623 7181641 7181687 7181689 7181693 7181717 7181719 7181729 7181747 7181761
7181827 7181831 7181843 7181849 7181851 7181861 7181869 7181873 7181889 7181891
7181897 7181963 7181971 7181983 7182001 7182047 7182061 7182067 7182089 7182101
7182113 7182121 7182137 7182139 7182151 7182157 7182193 7182221 7182223 7182271
7182281 7182283 7182299 7182317 7182353 7182367 7182377 7182433 7182451 7182473
7182529 7182541 7182563 7182583 7182629 7182649 7182661 7182671 7182683 7182697
7182701 7182709 7182727 7182743 7182751 7182757 7182767 7182797 7182809 7182827
7182829 7182853 7182859 7182863 7182883 7182899 7182943 7182971 7182997 7183049
7183063 7183067 7183081 7183093 7183109 7183139 7183201 7183207 7183219 7183223
7183237 7183243 7183261 7183277 7183301 7183313 7183327 7183331 7183373 7183403
7183409 7183411 7183453 7183459 7183471 7183483 7183511 7183531 7183541 7183559
7183591 7183609 7183633 7183637 7183643 7183667 7183679 7183681 7183699 7183703
7183717 7183721 7183727 7183739 7183769 7183783 7183801 7183811 7183837 7183853
7183859 7183907 7183927 7183933 7183963 7183973 7183987 7184011 7184041 7184057
7184059 7184063 7184077 7184113 7184117 7184129 7184137 7184159 7184197 7184207
7184213 7184249 7184269 7184273 7184291 7184341 7184349 7184351 7184363 7184369
7184377 7184381 7184383 7184399 7184407 7184423 7184447 7184453 7184459 7184461
7184473 7184479 7184501 7184531 7184537 7184539 7184543 7184581 7184621 7184629
7184633 7184647 7184651 7184669 7184677 7184699 7184701 7184713 7184753 7184773
7184783 7184789 7184797 7184833 7184851 7184857 7184861 7184867 7184873 7184917
7184921 7184923 7184939 7184977 7184981 7185019 7185029 7185037 7185041 7185043
7185047 7185053 7185083 7185091 7185109 7185119 7185121 7185133 7185137 7185151
7185161 7185163 7185179 7185187 7185193 7185221 7185247

7185253 7185307 7185319 7185323 7185337 7185341 7185349 7185391 7185403 7185421
7185427 7185449 7185473 7185491 7185517 7185523 7185559 7185571 7185623 7185641
7185643 7185677 7185719 7185727 7185757 7185767 7185779 7185833 7185863 7185869
7185887 7185889 7185907 7185911 7185929 7185931 7185943 7185961 7185967 7185973
7185979 7185989 7186007 7186033 7186037 7186093 7186129 7186133 7186147 7186163
7186169 7186183 7186187 7186279 7186297 7186301 7186303 7186307 7186331 7186337
7186343 7186367 7186369 7186391 7186397 7186423 7186433 7186457 7186463 7186469
7186477 7186481 7186489 7186499 7186523 7186537 7186559 7186561 7186583 7186589
7186607 7186663 7186643 7186651 7186657 7186667 7186679 7186681 7186703 7186759
7186771 7186799 7186813 7186831 7186841 7186847 7186859 7186877 7186897 7186901
7186909 7186919 7186951 7186973 7186981 7186987 7186999 7187027 7187051 7187077
7187087 7187093 7187113 7187119 7187129 7187153 7187161 7187189 7187197 7187207
7187221 7187227 7187233 7187251 7187267 7187269 7187281 7187317 7187333 7187347
7187363 7187393 7187399 7187417 7187459 7187461 7187471 7187473 7187497 7187503
7187581 7187599 7187627 7187641 7187647 7187683 7187743 7187759 7187767 7187771
7187773 7187777 7187779 7187783 7187801 7187857 7187861 7187881 7187897 7187933
7187941 7187951 7187963 7187981 7187987 7187989 7187993 7188007 7188011 7188017
7188031 7188037 7188047 7188109 7188113 7188119 7188149 7188151 7188157 7188163
7188173 7188191 7188193 7188197 7188221 7188227 7188241 7188277 7188281
7188287 7188329 7188341 7188347 7188361 7188371 7188413 7188431 7188437 7188449
7188451 7188457 7188481 7188499 7188523 7188541 7188553 7188557 7188563 7188583
7188613 7188689 7188691 7188703 7188733 7188743 7188757 7188787 7188793 7188809
7188833 7188847 7188871 7188889 7188893 7188901 7188913 7188917 7188919 7188953
7188991 7189003 7189027 7189037 7189081 7189097 7189103 7189123 7189151 7189157
7189159 7189207 7189253 7189267 7189289 7189307 7189319 7189321 7189333 7189339
7189421 7189423 7189439 7189459 7189463 7189513 7189519 7189537 7189541 7189549
7189561 7189571 7189573 7189577 7189591 7189603 7189607 7189627 7189649 7189661
7189667 7189669 7189717 7189727 7189739 7189747 7189751 7189757 7189781 7189783
7189849 7189859 7189867 7189873 7189879 7189907 7189921 7189933 7189939 7189943
7189993 7190003 7190021 7190023 7190039 7190063 7190081 7190087 7190119 7190123
7190137 7190177 7190179 7190213 7190219 7190243 7190263 7190273 7190279 7190299
7190311 7190317 7190353 7190363 7190369 7190377 7190413 7190423 7190429 7190437
7190441 7190471 7190479 7190489 7190527 7190537 7190567 7190581 7190593 7190597
7190611 7190633 7190647 7190657 7190663 7190693 7190699 7190737 7190749 7190773
7190783 7190801 7190803 7190837 7190851 7190857 7190891 7190893 7190917 7190921
7190929 7190941 7190947 7190957 7190969 7190971 7190999 7191001 7191007 7191029
7191049 7191053 7191059 7191077 7191127 7191131 7191161 7191167 7191169 7191179
7191181 7191193 7191211 7191241 7191251 7191281 7191293 7191299 7191319 7191343
7191347 7191383 7191403 7191407 7191413 7191419 7191421 7191439 7191461 7191469
7191487 7191491 7191511 7191533 7191539 7191551 7191581 7191589 7191593 7191599
7191601 7191641 7191647 7191649 7191689 7191703 7191757 7191761 7191763 7191827
7191829 7191841 7191853 7191857 7191859 7191869 7191881 7191889 7191911 7191931
7191953 7191959 7191967 7191983 7191991 7191997 7192019 7192021 7192027 7192039
7192043 7192057 7192067 7192079 7192091 7192103 7192111 7192121 7192151 7192183
7192187 7192201 7192231 7192243 7192247 7192301 7192303 7192313 7192321 7192331
7192333 7192349 7192373 7192417 7192429 7192439 7192441 7192447 7192459 7192483
7192489 7192501 7192529 7192543 7192553 7192561 7192573 7192579 7192643 7192657
7192681 7192709 7192711 7192727 7192741 7192771 7192777 7192793 7192807 7192847
7192873 7192877 7192883 7192897 7192901 7192903 7192931 7192979 7192981 7193009
7193051 7193063 7193071 7193093 7193101 7193113 7193117 7193149 7193171 7193177
7193203 7193231 7193257 7193297 7193299 7193309 7193323 7193357 7193371 7193377
7193383 7193387 7193393 7193401 7193437 7193441 7193449 7193497 7193509 7193521
7193579 7193587 7193591 7193611 7193621 7193661 7193671 7193709 7193737 7193739
7193731 7193749 7193783 7193789 7193807 7193833 7193861 7193899 7193903 7193971
7193981 7193987 7194013 7194023 7194041 7194053 7194067 7194071 7194079 7194107
7194113 7194119 7194151 7194163 7194181 7194221 7194227 7194251 7194269 7194289
7194307 7194323 7194347 7194353 7194361 7194367 7194403 7194419 7194427 7194433
7194487 7194491 7194497 7194503 7194529 7194563 7194599 7194611 7194647 7194659
7194667 7194679 7194701 7194703 7194727 7194731 7194739 7194751 7194773 7194799
7194809 7194833 7194841 7194857 7194877 7194881 7194899 7194907 7194917 7194919
7194923 7194959 7194973 7194989 7194997 7195003 7195037 7195039 7195051 7195079
7195087 7195141 7195151 7195157 7195163 7195189 7195217 7195247 7195249 7195259
7195261 7195283 7195289 7195291 7195303 7195313 7195327 7195337 7195351 7195361
7195367 7195373 7195387 7195411 7195423 7195453 7195457 7195469 7195493 7195511
7195523 7195549 7195571 7195579 7195597 7195667 7195679 7195681 7195687 7195691
7195697 7195717 7195729 7195753 7195759 7195789 7195807 7195823 7195847 7195897
7195907 7195933 7195939 7195949 7195963 7195967 7195997 7196009 7196011 7196023
7196047 7196087 7196099 7196107 7196131 7196141 7196159 7196173 7196177 7196191
7196209 7196227 7196237 7196243 7196251 7196261 7196291 7196297 7196303 7196317
7196323 7196327 7196339 7196341 7196359 7196363 7196369 7196377 7196381 7196417
7196467 7196477 7196479 7196513 7196521 7196553 7196561 7196569 7196591 7196603
7196617 7196621 7196633 7196639 7196641 7196647 7196653 7196659 7196701 7196731
7196753 7196767 7196789 7196803 7196869 7196881 7196887 7196909 7196941
7196951 7196989 7196993 7197011 7197019 7197023 7197031 7197041 7197049 7197061
7197079 7197089 7197101 7197107 7197119 7197131 7197139 7197209 7197221 7197227
7197259 7197283 7197287 7197299 7197313 7197349 7197353 7197389 7197391 7197397
7197401 7197419 7197431 7197433 7197457 7197461 7197467 7197503 7197517 7197527
7197529 7197557 7197571 7197583 7197601 7197607 7197663 7197683 7197731 7197733
7197739 7197779 7197791 7197793 7197803 7197809 7197833 7197847 7197857 7197863
7197881 7197893 7197907 7197923 7197929 7197937 7197961 7197977 7198013 7198039
7198043 7198067 7198073 7198099 7198109 7198133 7198141 7198151 7198153 7198159
7198181 7198187 7198199 7198223 7198237 7198267 7198271 7198277 7198297 7198343
7198363 7198369 7198403 7198421 7198423 7198447 7198481 7198483 7198523
7198537 7198553 7198561 7198571 7198579 7198589 7198601 7198613 7198621 7198643
7198689 7198691 7198693 7198721 7198771 7198783 7198799 7198811 7198813 7198847
7198879 7198883 7198897 7198907 7198909 7198963 7198969 7198987 7198999 7199009
7199011 7199021 7199029 7199039 7199051 7199057 7199063 7199077 7199089 7199107
7199111 7199113 7199147 7199167 7199173 7199183 7199197 7199219 7199261 7199263
7199267 7199323 7199327 7199359 7199369 7199371 7199377 7199383 7199389 7199407

```
7199411  7199417  7199419  7199429  7199431  7199441  7199443  7199519  7199527  7199539
7199561  7199567  7199579  7199603  7199609  7199617  7199623  7199639  7199659  7199663
7199681  7199683  7199701  7199707  7199729  7199737  7199747  7199749  7199767  7199807
7199809  7199813  7199839  7199861  7199869  7199909  7199911  7199921  7199957  7200007
7200023  7200043  7200047  7200059  7200073  7200097  7200101  7200121  7200131  7200143
7200157  7200187  7200191  7200203  7200211  7200217  7200223  7200227  7200229  7200233
7200239  7200241  7200253  7200269  7200283  7200287  7200313  7200317  7200331  7200337
7200343  7200377  7200397  7200409  7200443  7200451  7200467  7200481  7200493  7200511
7200517  7200521  7200551  7200553  7200559  7200569  7200619  7200629  7200643  7200659
7200701  7200703  7200719  7200733  7200751  7200763  7200769  7200803  7200811  7200821
7200859  7200887  7200889  7200899  7200913  7200923  7200937  7200971  7200983  7201031
7201037  7201049  7201063  7201091  7201097  7201099  7201109  7201123  7201147  7201153
7201157  7201189  7201211  7201237  7201241  7201267  7201279  7201297  7201307  7201351
7201357  7201423  7201427  7201429  7201457  7201499  7201531  7201543  7201547  7201573
7201577  7201583  7201619  7201631  7201633  7201637  7201639  7201651  7201673  7201687
7201697  7201699  7201709  7201751  7201759  7201793  7201801  7201811  7201813  7201823
7201847  7201861  7201867  7201871  7201919  7201927  7201949  7201963  7201973  7201979
7201981  7201991  7202003  7202017  7202021  7202051  7202053  7202057  7202077  7202093
7202099  7202119  7202131  7202149  7202177  7202201  7202219  7202269  7202287  7202291
7202303  7202317  7202357  7202359  7202369  7202401  7202413  7202417  7202431  7202467
7202471  7202477  7202513  7202561  7202579  7202597  7202599  7202621  7202627  7202639
7202641  7202651  7202659  7202669  7202683  7202693  7202711  7202717  7202761  7202803
7202813  7202857  7202861  7202869  7202903  7202927  7202963  7202977  7202981  7202999
7203023  7203041  7203043  7203061  7203073  7203089  7203101  7203149  7203151  7203187
7203193  7203227  7203233  7203239  7203241  7203247  7203263  7203289  7203293  7203319
7203341  7203349  7203353  7203367  7203379  7203401  7203407  7203409  7203431  7203433
7203437  7203467  7203473  7203479  7203481  7203491  7203503  7203509  7203517  7203523
7203541  7203583  7203593  7203607  7203611  7203613  7203617  7203649  7203667  7203683
7203689  7203697  7203739  7203743  7203769  7203797  7203799  7203839  7203851  7203857
7203881  7203883  7203887  7203901  7203913  7203929  7203941  7203943  7203949  7203961
7203979  7204003  7204009  7204013  7204031  7204033  7204051  7204061  7204079  7204103
7204117  7204123  7204133  7204147  7204163  7204189  7204193  7204201  7204261  7204271
7204273  7204279  7204289  7204333  7204339  7204391  7204403  7204423  7204427  7204471
7204501  7204507  7204513  7204517  7204523  7204531  7204567  7204579  7204609  7204619
7204621  7204697  7204699  7204733  7204739  7204759  7204777  7204783  7204793  7204801
7204811  7204823  7204829  7204831  7204849  7204853  7204859  7204861  7204891  7204913
7204919  7204921  7204943  7204949  7204987  7204997  7205039  7205041  7205069  7205087
7205111  7205119  7205167  7205171  7205179  7205183  7205189  7205203  7205213  7205243
7205249  7205309  7205321  7205327  7205329  7205333  7205339  7205347  7205357  7205383
7205437  7205461  7205477  7205483  7205507  7205521  7205531  7205533  7205537  7205551
7205557  7205563  7205587  7205629  7205641  7205657  7205687  7205743  7205753  7205761
7205771  7205797  7205813  7205819  7205843  7205851  7205893  7205911  7205929  7205941
7205963  7205971  7206019  7206053  7206097  7206103  7206109  7206127  7206131  7206191
7206197  7206203  7206223  7206233  7206247  7206259  7206289  7206307  7206313  7206323
7206347  7206359  7206391  7206403  7206431  7206443  7206449  7206469  7206473  7206509
7206517  7206523  7206533  7206541  7206547  7206581  7206593  7206607  7206629  7206631
7206649  7206677  7206697  7206701  7206737  7206739  7206743  7206767  7206769  7206811
7206817  7206821  7206841  7206847  7206907  7206917  7206919  7206943  7206949  7206959
7206961  7206977  7207001  7207009  7207019  7207033  7207037  7207043  7207049  7207069
7207087  7207093  7207129  7207141  7207147  7207153  7207163  7207169  7207171  7207181
7207223  7207229  7207231  7207237  7207243  7207247  7207297  7207301  7207331  7207339
7207351  7207367  7207379  7207393  7207411  7207427  7207481  7207493  7207511  7207561
7207597  7207619  7207621  7207633  7207649  7207657  7207661  7207667  7207687  7207691
7207693  7207709  7207729  7207757  7207769  7207771  7207799  7207829  7207831  7207861
7207867  7207877  7207883  7207891  7207909  7207919  7207957  7207987  7207997  7208059
7208099  7208107  7208129  7208141  7208143  7208147  7208161  7208171  7208189  7208209
7208281  7208297  7208317  7208347  7208351  7208363  7208381  7208389  7208413  7208419
7208449  7208473  7208489  7208491  7208507  7208519  7208521  7208533  7208557  7208569
7208573  7208603  7208611  7208623  7208627  7208653  7208659  7208693  7208699  7208711
7208717  7208723  7208753  7208759  7208779  7208807  7208827  7208837  7208869  7208879
7208881  7208893  7208899  7208909  7208917  7208941  7208951  7208977  7208983  7209011
7209031  7209091  7209109  7209119  7209121  7209157  7209179  7209187  7209199  7209211
7209229  7209233  7209239  7209247  7209259  7209271  7209277  7209311  7209347  7209359
7209361  7209383  7209421  7209427  7209439  7209451  7209457  7209467  7209491  7209523
7209533  7209539  7209541  7209551  7209589  7209599  7209611  7209613  7209637  7209641
7209647  7209667  7209673  7209679  7209689  7209703  7209731  7209737  7209757  7209779
7209781  7209793  7209823  7209827  7209841  7209863  7209871  7209877  7209889  7209919
7209947  7210001  7210031  7210037  7210043  7210061  7210117  7210123  7210169  7210187
7210207  7210237  7210243  7210249  7210267  7210277  7210297  7210319  7210327  7210337
7210349  7210361  7210373  7210403  7210421  7210433  7210451  7210453  7210457  7210471
7210529  7210537  7210549  7210561  7210573  7210591  7210603  7210639  7210657  7210663
7210667  7210681  7210699  7210717  7210729  7210733  7210739  7210751  7210757  7210759
7210781  7210807  7210811  7210877  7210897  7210901  7210909  7210939  7210943  7210949
7210963  7210969  7210991  7210997  7210999  7211011  7211027  7211033  7211063  7211081
7211093  7211107  7211119  7211129  7211131  7211147  7211173  7211177  7211201  7211231
7211249  7211261  7211273  7211287  7211291  7211297  7211311  7211329  7211333  7211341
7211353  7211363  7211371  7211377  7211381  7211429  7211447  7211483  7211509  7211513
7211521  7211527  7211537  7211569  7211591  7211593  7211599  7211639  7211641  7211651
7211653  7211663  7211713  7211717  7211741  7211753  7211761  7211783  7211801  7211803
7211807  7211843  7211861  7211863  7211873  7211889  7211899  7211909  7211921  7211977
7211993  7212011  7212013  7212019  7212059  7212061  7212083  7212157  7212169  7212173
7212193  7212209  7212211  7212239  7212253  7212259  7212263  7212277  7212311  7212319
7212323  7212341  7212353  7212371  7212377  7212379  7212383  7212389  7212397  7212487
7212493  7212497  7212509  7212523  7212529  7212551  7212577  7212599  7212637  7212661
7212703  7212719  7212721  7212727  7212757  7212767  7212769  7212773  7212791  7212797
7212833  7212839  7212841  7212859  7212871  7212893  7212899  7212917  7212943  7212971
7212973  7212979  7212983  7213009  7213021  7213033  7213061  7213069  7213079  7213081
7213091  7213097  7213123  7213133  7213139  7213169  7213177  7213201  7213223  7213229
7213243  7213273  7213277  7213279  7213291  7213303  7213307  7213309  7213313  7213337
```

```
7213343  7213351  7213391  7213397  7213441  7213469  7213471  7213477  7213487  7213541
7213543  7213553  7213561  7213567  7213571  7213601  7213603  7213621  7213639  7213667
7213681  7213699  7213709  7213747  7213751  7213769  7213771  7213781  7213819  7213841
7213847  7213849  7213859  7213861  7213897  7213903  7213919  7213937  7214023  7214027
7214029  7214059  7214063  7214099  7214101  7214131  7214143  7214161  7214173  7214177
7214183  7214191  7214197  7214257  7214269  7214279  7214293  7214299  7214303  7214323
7214369  7214377  7214393  7214399  7214423  7214437  7214447  7214503  7214507  7214513
7214521  7214527  7214549  7214551  7214573  7214611  7214633  7214639  7214651  7214657
7214671  7214717  7214747  7214771  7214773  7214791  7214843  7214861  7214863  7214873
7214887  7214917  7214947  7214951  7214959  7214983  7214989  7215001  7215007  7215011
7215053  7215059  7215067  7215119  7215121  7215127  7215133  7215167  7215179  7215199
7215209  7215217  7215223  7215227  7215239  7215277  7215283  7215301  7215323  7215347
7215401  7215413  7215419  7215427  7215433  7215437  7215449  7215451  7215457  7215479
7215499  7215503  7215547  7215553  7215557  7215601  7215643  7215647  7215661  7215671
7215679  7215697  7215709  7215739  7215749  7215779  7215797  7215811  7215821  7215827
7215829  7215869  7215893  7215899  7215911  7215919  7215941  7215961  7215979  7216009
7216037  7216049  7216061  7216063  7216081  7216091  7216129  7216141  7216151  7216159
7216163  7216169  7216193  7216199  7216213  7216241  7216247  7216277  7216291  7216301
7216309  7216343  7216351  7216357  7216367  7216373  7216403  7216421  7216423  7216439
7216453  7216471  7216493  7216507  7216513  7216537  7216543  7216567  7216577  7216589
7216597  7216609  7216613  7216631  7216633  7216661  7216663  7216667  7216673  7216691
7216711  7216717  7216723  7216757  7216763  7216787  7216799  7216801  7216837  7216879
7216889  7216919  7216927  7216931  7216967  7216973  7216981  7216987  7216997  7217033
7217047  7217059  7217071  7217081  7217123  7217137  7217149  7217159  7217167  7217191
7217213  7217219  7217237  7217251  7217267  7217279  7217281  7217323  7217339  7217369
7217407  7217417  7217429  7217527  7217557  7217563  7217569  7217579  7217591  7217603
7217611  7217629  7217657  7217659  7217671  7217687  7217713  7217719  7217731  7217747
7217753  7217759  7217767  7217779  7217783  7217797  7217801  7217807  7217831  7217863
7217887  7217893  7217909  7217939  7217941  7217953  7217963  7218019  7218049  7218053
7218059  7218083  7218121  7218139  7218143  7218161  7218179  7218181  7218193  7218199
7218209  7218221  7218227  7218247  7218259  7218269  7218311  7218317  7218331  7218349
7218371  7218391  7218397  7218403  7218433  7218439  7218451  7218457  7218469  7218479
7218503  7218529  7218551  7218559  7218569  7218577  7218581  7218599  7218623  7218637
7218649  7218661  7218677  7218697  7218713  7218721  7218749  7218763  7218769  7218787
7218791  7218793  7218817  7218821  7218839  7218853  7218859  7218889  7218899  7218907
7218919  7218929  7218947  7218973  7218977  7218979  7218983  7218987  7219007  7219013
7219019  7219021  7219073  7219081  7219109  7219111  7219129  7219133  7219139  7219213
7219241  7219253  7219273  7219283  7219307  7219327  7219337  7219343  7219361  7219391
7219427  7219469  7219483  7219507  7219519  7219523  7219561  7219603  7219643  7219661
7219669  7219673  7219687  7219703  7219727  7219739  7219741  7219757  7219801  7219831
7219841  7219843  7219859  7219871  7219879  7219903  7219913  7219939  7219963  7219973
7219997  7220027  7220033  7220089  7220107  7220111  7220113  7220123  7220131  7220149
7220153  7220167  7220177  7220201  7220219  7220231  7220237  7220249  7220261  7220263
7220299  7220347  7220371  7220377  7220383  7220407  7220417  7220441  7220443  7220453
7220483  7220491  7220497  7220519  7220531  7220557  7220569  7220573  7220581  7220611
7220621  7220671  7220677  7220693  7220701  7220711  7220713  7220729  7220743  7220747
7220761  7220789  7220803  7220821  7220849  7220867  7220891  7220897  7220921  7220933
7220953  7220977  7220981  7220999  7221013  7221017  7221037  7221041  7221077  7221079
7221089  7221101  7221131  7221143  7221157  7221161  7221163  7221169  7221173  7221199
7221251  7221257  7221259  7221281  7221283  7221293  7221299  7221301  7221307  7221353
7221367  7221373  7221391  7221439  7221449  7221457  7221499  7221509  7221523  7221547
7221569  7221587  7221589  7221611  7221619  7221629  7221631  7221649  7221661  7221689
7221707  7221733  7221737  7221743  7221749  7221757  7221769  7221779  7221811  7221829
7221847  7221859  7221869  7221871  7221911  7221917  7221937  7221953  7221961  7221967
7221983  7222001  7222009  7222021  7222031  7222037  7222043  7222063  7222087  7222091
7222097  7222099  7222121  7222123  7222129  7222153  7222155  7222177  7222181  7222183
7222199  7222219  7222279  7222291  7222321  7222343  7222357  7222361  7222373  7222379
7222427  7222429  7222493  7222499  7222507  7222511  7222549  7222559  7222561  7222571
7222573  7222591  7222609  7222613  7222627  7222643  7222661  7222673  7222687  7222723
7222729  7222757  7222763  7222771  7222781  7222799  7222811  7222823  7222849  7222903
7222931  7222937  7222939  7222981  7222991  7223017  7223023  7223039  7223053  7223087
7223119  7223123  7223137  7223143  7223159  7223171  7223179  7223189  7223191  7223197
7223201  7223221  7223239  7223243  7223261  7223267  7223303  7223323  7223369  7223417
7223443  7223467  7223483  7223497  7223519  7223533  7223537  7223543  7223549  7223551
7223563  7223603  7223609  7223627  7223641  7223647  7223659  7223683  7223701  7223707
7223717  7223719  7223729  7223731  7223737  7223747  7223761  7223767  7223773  7223791
7223807  7223809  7223833  7223851  7223893  7223897  7223911  7223921  7223941  7223959
7223981  7223999  7224029  7224073  7224089  7224097  7224101  7224109  7224121  7224127
7224131  7224143  7224149  7224181  7224197  7224211  7224221  7224233  7224251  7224281
7224289  7224311  7224341  7224359  7224367  7224379  7224391  7224401  7224407  7224419
7224431  7224433  7224443  7224449  7224479  7224493  7224499  7224517  7224521  7224551
7224557  7224577  7224601  7224611  7224641  7224647  7224661  7224667  7224671  7224673
7224689  7224697  7224709  7224743  7224751  7224761  7224773  7224809  7224823  7224839
7224869  7224911  7224923  7224937  7224941  7224947  7225007  7225019  7225033  7225037
7225039  7225063  7225069  7225091  7225123  7225133  7225177  7225189  7225193  7225217
7225241  7225271  7225277  7225279  7225303  7225327  7225349  7225363  7225373  7225403
7225417  7225429  7225441  7225469  7225483  7225487  7225489  7225513  7225531  7225541
7225571  7225579  7225583  7225601  7225607  7225651  7225661  7225667  7225679  7225709
7225711  7225723  7225739  7225747  7225781  7225783  7225793  7225807  7225811  7225819
7225831  7225837  7225853  7225879  7225913  7225931  7225949  7225951  7225957
7225973  7225987  7225997  7226027  7226057  7226059  7226077  7226081  7226083  7226101
7226111  7226119  7226123  7226159  7226183  7226189  7226201  7226227  7226267  7226269
7226281  7226321  7226333  7226341  7226357  7226363  7226369  7226371  7226381  7226431
7226437  7226447  7226467  7226491  7226501  7226509  7226519  7226521  7226563  7226567
7226573  7226587  7226617  7226629  7226633  7226641  7226683  7226771  7226699
7226741  7226753  7226759  7226831  7226833  7226839  7226903  7226909  7226917  7226929
7226941  7226951  7226953  7226959  7226981  7226987  7226993  7227007  7227013  7227041
7227047  7227071  7227109  7227127  7227131  7227137  7227167  7227197  7227211  7227229
7227251  7227287  7227289  7227301  7227317  7227343  7227377  7227379  7227403  7227419
```

```
7227449 7227457 7227461 7227527 7227541 7227547 7227551 7227667 7227679 7227683
7227713 7227719 7227721 7227739 7227751 7227793 7227797 7227799 7227811 7227817
7227823 7227859 7227877 7227881 7227887 7227937 7227943 7227953 7227967 7227971
7227973 7227977 7228021 7228033 7228093 7228121 7228129 7228147 7228153 7228183
7228201 7228211 7228217 7228223 7228229 7228237 7228253 7228321 7228373 7228391
7228393 7228399 7228411 7228427 7228433 7228447 7228471 7228477 7228483 7228499
7228517 7228523 7228547 7228567 7228577 7228591 7228609 7228619 7228631 7228651
7228657 7228681 7228691 7228699 7228703 7228717 7228729 7228733 7228747 7228769
7228783 7228789 7228811 7228817 7228853 7228861 7228867 7228883 7228889 7228891
7228909 7228913 7228933 7228939 7228943 7228951 7228979 7228981 7228999 7229003
7229009 7229011 7229021 7229039 7229059 7229069 7229077 7229129 7229137 7229141
7229143 7229191 7229197 7229219 7229239 7229279 7229281 7229297 7229333 7229347
7229377 7229419 7229441 7229449 7229459 7229473 7229477 7229513 7229531 7229569
7229581 7229591 7229609 7229611 7229617 7229623 7229639 7229687 7229707 7229711
7229713 7229741 7229753 7229771 7229791 7229809 7229813 7229857 7229867 7229897
7229909 7229939 7229941 7229951 7229953 7229969 7230023 7230043 7230053 7230061
7230071 7230103 7230109 7230121 7230131 7230137 7230163 7230173 7230199 7230221
7230229 7230239 7230277 7230299 7230319 7230323 7230331 7230479 7230481 7230511
7230521 7230563 7230571 7230581 7230611 7230617 7230647 7230649 7230653 7230673
7230677 7230701 7230709 7230731 7230749 7230761 7230767 7230787 7230827 7230851
7230857 7230859 7230871 7230911 7230929 7230943 7230961 7230991 7231013 7231019
7231027 7231031 7231033 7231051 7231057 7231073 7231117 7231127 7231139 7231141
7231151 7231157 7231163 7231183 7231187 7231193 7231199 7231201 7231219 7231247
7231261 7231283 7231291 7231309 7231319 7231333 7231369 7231397 7231403 7231429
7231459 7231487 7231501 7231537 7231559 7231583 7231607 7231633 7231657 7231663
7231669 7231709 7231741 7231751 7231769 7231771 7231781 7231787 7231793 7231801
7231813 7231831 7231849 7231853 7231871 7231879 7231883 7231907 7231943 7231957
7231963 7231967 7231969 7231979 7231981 7231997 7232003 7232011 7232053 7232059
7232111 7232153 7232167 7232171 7232209 7232227 7232231 7232233 7232243 7232249
7232261 7232341 7232363 7232377 7232383 7232389 7232411 7232413 7232431 7232443
7232453 7232503 7232527 7232543 7232549 7232551 7232569 7232573 7232581 7232623
7232627 7232639 7232647 7232657 7232663 7232669 7232671 7232707 7232713 7232737
7232759 7232761 7232779 7232789 7232801 7232807 7232809 7232839 7232873 7232887
7232891 7232893 7232899 7232909 7232917 7232947 7232993 7233001 7233011 7233029
7233047 7233049 7233071 7233077 7233089 7233101 7233103 7233139 7233169 7233173
7233181 7233217 7233229 7233257 7233263 7233277 7233283 7233287 7233299 7233311
7233329 7233337 7233371 7233377 7233397 7233407 7233419 7233437 7233439 7233481
7233487 7233511 7233529 7233559 7233593 7233607 7233617 7233637 7233641 7233647
7233669 7233683 7233689 7233701 7233703 7233719 7233727 7233739 7233749 7233767
7233773 7233791 7233827 7233829 7233869 7233871 7233883 7233887 7233893 7233899
7233901 7233913 7233953 7233971 7233979 7233991 7234001 7234063 7234069 7234091
7234093 7234111 7234141 7234151 7234153 7234159 7234169 7234177 7234181 7234211
7234243 7234289 7234303 7234309 7234313 7234319 7234321 7234349 7234361 7234387
7234391 7234399 7234433 7234453 7234457 7234471 7234477 7234481 7234483 7234511
7234517 7234541 7234547 7234589 7234597 7234609 7234613 7234637 7234651 7234679
7234681 7234691 7234693 7234709 7234723 7234729 7234739 7234753 7234771 7234781
7234813 7234817 7234831 7234841 7234847 7234849 7234853 7234859 7234897 7234937
7234951 7234961 7234973 7234987 7235009 7235071 7235101 7235153 7235167 7235177
7235191 7235201 7235203 7235209 7235237 7235273 7235279 7235281 7235299 7235323
7235339 7235341 7235351 7235383 7235419 7235477 7235479 7235483 7235497 7235513
7235533 7235537 7235551 7235573 7235581 7235597 7235623 7235653 7235663 7235671
7235699 7235707 7235737 7235743 7235749 7235771 7235783 7235797 7235807 7235821
7235843 7235861 7235873 7235939 7235947 7235951 7235953 7235957 7235959 7235983
7236001 7236011 7236013 7236043 7236121 7236133 7236161 7236193 7236197 7236209
7236211 7236217 7236223 7236241 7236269 7236289 7236293 7236301 7236311 7236319
7236331 7236343 7236353 7236367 7236371 7236389 7236403 7236413 7236419 7236431
7236443 7236487 7236499 7236503 7236529 7236539 7236617 7236643 7236683 7236703
7236707 7236721 7236727 7236767 7236773 7236797 7236809 7236811 7236821 7236829
7236851 7236877 7236893 7236899 7236937 7236947 7236949 7236961 7237003 7237007
7237031 7237039 7237057 7237067 7237091 7237093 7237103 7237127 7237129 7237133
7237141 7237151 7237169 7237183 7237193 7237207 7237247 7237253 7237259 7237277
7237283 7237297 7237301 7237303 7237331 7237333 7237339 7237343 7237367 7237369
7237397 7237409 7237421 7237453 7237457 7237469 7237481 7237487 7237493 7237513
7237519 7237523 7237547 7237553 7237561 7237567 7237579 7237609 7237621 7237639
7237661 7237673 7237697 7237723 7237729 7237739 7237753 7237757 7237777 7237781
7237817 7237819 7237823 7237837 7237873 7237897 7237949 7237961 7237969 7237987
7238041 7238057 7238071 7238089 7238093 7238113 7238129 7238131 7238149 7238167
7238191 7238207 7238267 7238269 7238293 7238299 7238303 7238339 7238351 7238377
7238381 7238383 7238389 7238401 7238419 7238467 7238503 7238507 7238519 7238527
7238551 7238573 7238579 7238587 7238599 7238633 7238653 7238659 7238683 7238701
7238711 7238743 7238761 7238773 7238783 7238797 7238827 7238831 7238863 7238879
7238897 7238909 7238911 7238927 7238941 7238953 7238969 7238977 7238983 7238999
7239031 7239047 7239061 7239073 7239101 7239107 7239109 7239131 7239139
7239143 7239157 7239163 7239173 7239187 7239233 7239251 7239289 7239293 7239311
7239317 7239347 7239371 7239389 7239391 7239409 7239413 7239443 7239469 7239487
7239497 7239499 7239517 7239521 7239539 7239559 7239563 7239577 7239581 7239587
7239643 7239649 7239653 7239667 7239691 7239719 7239721 7239751 7239823 7239839
7239847 7239851 7239863 7239889 7239913 7239919 7239923 7239961
7239979 7240001 7240031 7240033 7240063 7240069 7240073 7240091 7240097 7240109
7240117 7240133 7240153 7240153 7240157 7240183 7240187 7240201 7240241 7240243
7240253 7240279 7240291 7240301 7240309 7240319 7240333 7240361 7240381 7240393
7240403 7240411 7240439 7240447 7240481 7240523 7240529 7240531 7240549 7240553
7240573 7240579 7240603 7240613 7240627 7240631 7240637 7240643 7240663 7240669
7240687 7240693 7240721 7240733 7240741 7240769 7240787 7240799 7240811 7240841
7240847 7240853 7240873 7240883 7240897 7240901 7240907 7240921 7240973
7240991 7241009 7241027 7241029 7241041 7241053 7241063 7241083 7241093 7241111
7241131 7241137 7241141 7241173 7241177 7241183 7241189 7241207 7241257 7241263
7241279 7241281 7241291 7241317 7241347 7241357 7241363 7241393 7241441 7241447
7241453 7241459 7241471 7241491 7241497 7241513 7241519 7241537 7241551 7241567
```

```
7241579 7241581 7241617 7241623 7241627 7241657 7241671 7241699 7241701 7241723
7241743 7241747 7241753 7241771 7241797 7241891 7241903 7241911 7241947 7241951
7241959 7241977 7241989 7242007 7242023 7242029 7242043 7242049 7242061 7242077
7242091 7242101 7242113 7242133 7242139 7242143 7242149 7242181 7242203 7242233
7242241 7242247 7242259 7242271 7242307 7242329 7242337 7242341 7242349 7242359
7242379 7242383 7242409 7242419 7242449 7242451 7242457 7242479 7242481 7242511
7242523 7242551 7242569 7242589 7242593 7242601 7242617 7242637 7242643 7242649
7242661 7242673 7242679 7242707 7242727 7242733 7242737 7242751 7242793 7242803
7242839 7242847 7242853 7242863 7242887 7242943 7242947 7242967 7242979 7243001
7243007 7243021 7243109 7243111 7243129 7243147 7243153 7243163 7243189 7243213
7243259 7243261 7243267 7243277 7243289 7243297 7243339 7243381 7243387 7243391
7243399 7243403 7243409 7243421 7243441 7243451 7243469 7243471 7243477 7243487
7243517 7243519 7243529 7243531 7243549 7243573 7243583 7243627 7243631 7243667
7243673 7243697 7243711 7243721 7243741 7243763 7243771 7243777 7243787 7243837
7243849 7243861 7243867 7243871 7243877 7243879 7243889 7243891 7243903 7243927
7243931 7243937 7243949 7243967 7243979 7243993 7244017 7244047 7244053 7244077
7244087 7244089 7244099 7244117 7244131 7244141 7244143 7244161 7244179 7244183
7244189 7244191 7244233 7244243 7244257 7244269 7244273 7244291 7244311 7244351
7244353 7244357 7244371 7244383 7244389 7244399 7244407 7244437 7244441 7244443
7244449 7244507 7244513 7244521 7244539 7244557 7244569 7244579 7244591 7244599
7244621 7244647 7244651 7244687 7244707 7244717 7244723 7244753 7244761 7244767
7244773 7244789 7244791 7244803 7244813 7244849 7244857 7244921 7244927 7244953
7244957 7244959 7244999 7245001 7245019 7245059 7245071 7245127 7245143 7245167
7245181 7245197 7245209 7245239 7245241 7245257 7245263 7245283 7245307 7245311
7245317 7245353 7245361 7245373 7245409 7245439 7245461 7245467 7245499 7245503
7245509 7245521 7245523 7245533 7245551 7245571 7245583 7245619 7245671 7245677
7245701 7245703 7245709 7245739 7245743 7245751 7245769 7245779 7245787 7245809
7245829 7245863 7245869 7245871 7245877 7245881 7245883 7245919 7245923 7245929
7245937 7245941 7245949 7245991 7246039 7246051 7246069 7246079 7246091 7246093
7246123 7246133 7246139 7246159 7246171 7246177 7246181 7246193 7246207 7246229
7246243 7246249 7246279 7246307 7246313 7246333 7246363 7246367 7246387 7246397
7246417 7246427 7246453 7246483 7246501 7246513 7246523 7246537 7246553 7246559
7246609 7246643 7246663 7246667 7246691 7246693 7246699 7246711 7246717 7246727
7246753 7246763 7246819 7246823 7246843 7246867 7246871 7246891 7246903 7246927
7246933 7246949 7246951 7246969 7246991 7246997 7247011 7247021 7247033 7247057
7247069 7247077 7247089 7247099 7247101 7247137 7247159 7247179 7247213 7247237
7247243 7247249 7247257 7247267 7247269 7247281 7247291 7247293 7247297 7247327
7247333 7247351 7247363 7247371 7247377 7247393 7247399 7247407 7247411 7247441
7247453 7247479 7247497 7247533 7247543 7247551 7247557 7247561 7247567 7247573
7247579 7247587 7247623 7247629 7247641 7247663 7247687 7247699 7247701 7247717
7247719 7247731 7247741 7247753 7247761 7247839 7247843 7247881 7247897 7247927
7247953 7247969 7247971 7247983 7248019 7248049 7248053 7248077 7248083 7248089
7248113 7248119 7248167 7248179 7248191 7248193 7248211 7248217 7248223 7248229
7248233 7248251 7248277 7248299 7248313 7248317 7248323 7248343 7248359 7248377
7248379 7248401 7248407 7248413 7248457 7248469 7248497 7248503 7248517 7248551
7248581 7248587 7248599 7248601 7248607 7248643 7248653 7248667 7248697 7248719
7248727 7248737 7248739 7248751 7248793 7248821 7248833 7248881 7248893 7248949
7248959 7248977 7248991 7249001 7249007 7249019 7249027 7249031 7249049 7249091
7249093 7249097 7249111 7249129 7249141 7249183 7249211 7249213 7249223 7249237
7249247 7249261 7249283 7249331 7249337 7249339 7249343 7249349 7249369 7249379
7249387 7249397 7249399 7249427 7249441 7249457 7249483 7249493 7249511 7249513
7249523 7249537 7249549 7249553 7249573 7249589 7249591 7249603 7249631 7249643
7249657 7249663 7249709 7249717 7249727 7249729 7249733 7249747 7249763 7249829
7249831 7249841 7249867 7249873 7249889 7249897 7249901 7249919 7249927 7249937
7249943 7249961 7249981 7249997 7250011 7250017 7250021 7250027 7250051 7250053
7250059 7250069 7250099 7250119 7250123 7250161 7250183 7250189 7250197 7250209
7250219 7250231 7250237 7250239 7250263 7250281 7250291 7250293 7250297 7250323
7250339 7250363 7250389 7250393 7250401 7250407 7250413 7250423 7250429 7250491
7250501 7250519 7250527 7250561 7250599 7250629 7250669 7250671 7250693 7250701
7250707 7250717 7250759 7250777 7250791 7250801 7250833 7250839 7250843 7250861
7250863 7250879 7250897 7250921 7250939 7250987 7251011 7251031 7251037 7251053
7251059 7251071 7251091 7251143 7251157 7251169 7251199 7251221 7251227 7251239
7251269 7251311 7251313 7251317 7251329 7251337 7251341 7251379 7251389 7251397
7251481 7251487 7251523 7251529 7251557 7251577 7251599 7251617 7251637 7251691
7251701 7251703 7251709 7251719 7251721 7251731 7251733 7251757 7251773 7251779
7251781 7251791 7251823 7251833 7251847 7251851 7251857 7251883 7251887 7251899
7251919 7251929 7251941 7251947 7251949 7251961 7251973 7251983 7251989 7251997
7252019 7252027 7252031 7252051 7252057 7252073 7252087 7252151 7252169 7252181
7252187 7252207 7252237 7252253 7252303 7252327 7252363 7252373 7252381 7252393
7252409 7252411 7252417 7252447 7252459 7252463 7252499 7252501 7252513 7252517
7252519 7252529 7252559 7252571 7252601 7252607 7252631 7252633 7252649 7252657
7252669 7252733 7252771 7252783 7252801 7252807 7252837 7252867 7252879 7252907
7252909 7252937 7252957 7252963 7252967 7252979 7252991 7253009 7253017 7253053
7253063 7253089 7253093 7253107 7253123 7253137 7253167 7253173 7253177 7253179
7253189 7253201 7253261 7253263 7253293 7253321 7253329 7253333 7253347 7253359
7253381 7253387 7253399 7253419 7253429 7253447 7253461 7253471 7253479 7253483
7253507 7253513 7253531 7253537 7253539 7253581 7253593 7253599 7253639 7253641
7253647 7253657 7253669 7253699 7253707 7253711 7253723 7253773 7253777 7253789
7253819 7253833 7253837 7253861 7253879 7253881 7253893 7253899 7253903 7253927
7253941 7253957 7253959 7254001 7254011 7254041 7254043 7254047 7254073 7254077
7254097 7254101 7254119 7254127 7254133 7254167 7254173 7254179 7254193 7254199
7254211 7254259 7254281 7254307 7254319 7254323 7254337 7254343 7254347 7254349
7254383 7254389 7254397 7254419 7254421 7254451 7254469 7254473 7254509 7254517
7254539 7254551 7254557 7254571 7254593 7254601 7254617 7254619 7254623 7254629
7254673 7254679 7254703 7254719 7254743 7254749 7254761 7254803 7254847 7254857
7254881 7254887 7254893 7254977 7254983 7255007 7255009 7255019 7255021 7255037
7255043 7255057 7255067 7255069 7255081 7255099 7255103 7255121 7255151 7255153
7255159 7255163 7255181 7255187 7255201 7255211 7255231 7255247 7255253 7255267
7255301 7255357 7255403 7255453 7255459 7255463 7255477 7255487 7255489 7255499
```

```
7255513  7255529  7255609  7255621  7255627  7255639  7255681  7255693  7255709  7255711
7255723  7255727  7255733  7255757  7255763  7255763  7255799  7255817  7255841  7255847
7255867  7255883  7255901  7255909  7255951  7255961  7255979  7255993  7255999  7256023
7256027  7256047  7256087  7256089  7256099  7256111  7256113  7256141  7256147  7256149
7256153  7256173  7256203  7256209  7256213  7256251  7256257  7256261  7256287  7256311
7256321  7256341  7256357  7256363  7256369  7256393  7256401  7256497  7256503  7256519
7256527  7256531  7256533  7256539  7256581  7256591  7256593  7256609  7256611  7256617
7256629  7256657  7256681  7256693  7256719  7256737  7256741  7256771  7256779  7256791
7256827  7256849  7256903  7256911  7256947  7256999  7257001  7257013  7257017  7257023
7257037  7257043  7257073  7257077  7257083  7257091  7257097  7257127  7257137  7257139
7257157  7257179  7257227  7257241  7257247  7257253  7257281  7257293  7257311  7257323
7257361  7257389  7257401  7257409  7257421  7257431  7257463  7257469  7257491  7257517
7257527  7257529  7257553  7257559  7257571  7257577  7257629  7257659  7257667  7257707
7257709  7257721  7257739  7257749  7257773  7257781  7257797  7257799  7257821  7257823
7257839  7257847  7257851  7257853  7257863  7257893  7257907  7257911  7257941  7257947
7257989  7258001  7258007  7258021  7258049  7258063  7258067  7258073  7258079  7258081
7258093  7258109  7258129  7258169  7258187  7258211  7258243  7258261  7258291  7258313
7258319  7258331  7258333  7258343  7258373  7258387  7258411  7258417  7258421  7258469
7258477  7258483  7258487  7258519  7258571  7258583  7258631  7258651  7258661  7258673
7258709  7258747  7258753  7258789  7258807  7258831  7258837  7258861  7258871  7258877
7258883  7258897  7258921  7258943  7258957  7258963  7258967  7258973  7259003  7259011
7259027  7259041  7259059  7259069  7259081  7259089  7259101  7259117  7259137  7259167
7259267  7259279  7259297  7259299  7259327  7259347  7259359  7259407  7259423  7259431
7259443  7259449  7259453  7259477  7259489  7259491  7259507  7259519  7259533  7259557
7259563  7259597  7259621  7259633  7259639  7259677  7259689  7259711  7259713  7259717
7259723  7259737  7259741  7259753  7259783  7259801  7259803  7259809  7259839  7259849
7259851  7259869  7259897  7259899  7259909  7259933  7259971  7259977  7259999  7260007
7260023  7260031  7260049  7260059  7260067  7260079  7260083  7260089  7260119  7260133
7260181  7260191  7260199  7260199  7260217  7260221  7260229  7260269  7260277  7260283
7260287  7260301  7260307  7260313  7260329  7260347  7260349  7260371  7260373  7260397
7260401  7260427  7260431  7260439  7260443  7260457  7260493  7260511  7260521  7260529
7260551  7260553  7260559  7260563  7260569  7260601  7260611  7260613  7260619  7260667
7260689  7260691  7260697  7260703  7260713  7260719  7260739  7260767  7260787  7260791
7260797  7260821  7260823  7260839  7260859  7260901  7260941  7260959  7260961
7261003  7261027  7261039  7261061  7261063  7261069  7261073  7261081  7261087  7261153
7261157  7261183  7261187  7261207  7261231  7261271  7261279  7261283  7261291  7261313
7261337  7261349  7261357  7261369  7261381  7261391  7261403  7261433  7261447  7261451
7261459  7261481  7261483  7261511  7261523  7261531  7261561  7261577  7261607  7261613
7261627  7261637  7261651  7261663  7261667  7261679  7261691  7261699  7261739  7261747
7261757  7261763  7261783  7261789  7261801  7261817  7261823  7261841  7261847  7261871
7261909  7261921  7261927  7261939  7261949  7261963  7261973  7261979  7261981  7261999
7262023  7262039  7262051  7262071  7262081  7262117  7262131  7262149  7262173  7262191
7262201  7262243  7262257  7262261  7262291  7262303  7262309  7262347  7262357  7262419
7262429  7262443  7262459  7262461  7262467  7262473  7262483  7262501  7262513  7262531
7262533  7262569  7262597  7262603  7262609  7262639  7262653  7262659  7262669  7262677
7262719  7262729  7262737  7262753  7262797  7262819  7262821  7262833  7262837  7262851
7262861  7262873  7262891  7262909  7262923  7262933  7262939  7262947  7262953  7263013
7263031  7263037  7263043  7263049  7263101  7263103  7263107  7263127  7263143  7263161
7263163  7263197  7263203  7263227  7263241  7263287  7263293  7263299  7263307  7263317
7263323  7263337  7263341  7263343  7263353  7263367  7263383  7263391  7263401  7263407
7263419  7263419  7263439  7263463  7263467  7263493  7263523  7263551  7263559  7263563
7263583  7263589  7263593  7263611  7263623  7263629  7263637  7263673  7263677  7263679
7263727  7263731  7263749  7263787  7263793  7263799  7263821  7263829  7263857  7263859
7263863  7263887  7263901  7263917  7263931  7263937  7263953  7263959  7263967  7263973
7263983  7263989  7264003  7264009  7264043  7264069  7264111  7264121  7264141  7264171
7264183  7264189  7264193  7264211  7264217  7264267  7264277  7264319  7264351
7264363  7264373  7264379  7264381  7264391  7264393  7264399  7264489  7264501  7264511
7264513  7264531  7264553  7264577  7264583  7264589  7264591  7264597  7264601  7264613
7264637  7264643  7264651  7264679  7264717  7264723  7264727  7264739  7264759  7264787
7264799  7264801  7264811  7264813  7264823  7264841  7264871  7264889  7264903  7264927
7264937  7264963  7264991  7264997  7265003  7265017  7265023  7265047  7265057  7265101
7265107  7265131  7265147  7265149  7265149  7265207  7265221  7265227  7265231  7265243
7265249  7265281  7265287  7265303  7265317  7265329  7265333  7265339  7265347  7265369
7265371  7265381  7265473  7265491  7265507  7265509  7265513  7265519  7265537  7265549
7265593  7265603  7265623  7265633  7265651  7265659  7265663  7265701  7265707  7265711
7265729  7265759  7265761  7265779  7265807  7265813  7265837  7265857  7265887  7265899
7265911  7265917  7265933  7265963  7265971  7265981  7265983  7265989  7266001  7266019
7266031  7266047  7266067  7266071  7266073  7266079  7266101  7266109  7266139  7266163
7266169  7266187  7266197  7266221  7266223  7266251  7266253  7266299  7266313
7266349  7266403  7266407  7266419  7266421  7266433  7266449  7266451  7266461  7266481
7266491  7266509  7266557  7266601  7266653  7266661  7266673  7266697  7266709  7266713
7266719  7266737  7266751  7266773  7266817  7266823  7266829  7266839  7266851  7266859
7266877  7266893  7266923  7266929  7266947  7266979  7267009  7267019  7267021  7267031
7267033  7267049  7267061  7267069  7267079  7267087  7267097  7267111  7267121  7267123
7267147  7267153  7267163  7267171  7267181  7267193  7267213  7267217  7267219  7267229
7267243  7267259  7267297  7267303  7267349  7267363  7267391  7267399  7267411  7267417
7267433  7267441  7267451  7267453  7267457  7267459  7267493  7267499  7267511  7267529
7267565  7267571  7267583  7267591  7267597  7267613  7267621  7267627  7267639  7267669
7267717  7267739  7267753  7267769  7267787  7267811  7267831  7267849  7267877  7267889
7267901  7267907  7267933  7267961  7267991  7268003  7268017  7268039  7268081
7268087  7268101  7268117  7268119  7268141  7268143  7268153  7268159  7268201  7268213
7268267  7268297  7268321  7268323  7268329  7268347  7268351  7268383  7268399  7268411
7268423  7268441  7268453  7268467  7268497  7268509  7268533  7268549  7268551  7268561
7268563  7268567  7268581  7268593  7268633  7268641  7268693  7268717  7268743  7268747
7268749  7268777  7268783  7268803  7268819  7268827  7268857  7268881  7268903  7268923
7268953  7268969  7268971  7268981  7268999  7269007  7269023  7269043  7269061  7269079
7269089  7269133  7269137  7269139  7269151  7269167  7269181  7269203  7269209  7269233
7269239  7269247  7269281  7269289  7269293  7269307  7269347  7269371  7269373  7269439
7269461  7269481  7269487  7269491  7269511  7269527  7269529  7269539  7269569  7269589
```

7269601	7269611	7269641	7269643	7269667	7269671	7269683	7269697	7269719	7269733
7269737	7269763	7269781	7269793	7269811	7269827	7269853	7269869	7269893	7269929
7269937	7269949	7269953	7269959	7269971	7269991	7270009	7270031	7270057	7270061
7270091	7270099	7270121	7270127	7270147	7270171	7270181	7270189	7270253	7270259
7270267	7270309	7270327	7270343	7270349	7270379	7270391	7270411	7270421	7270447
7270451	7270457	7270481	7270493	7270517	7270519	7270547	7270567	7270573	7270579
7270591	7270609	7270621	7270643	7270649	7270661	7270663	7270693	7270721	7270733
7270751	7270763	7270789	7270807	7270811	7270819	7270831	7270843	7270847	7270859
7270871	7270891	7270903	7270919	7270931	7270933	7270937	7270969	7270987	7270993
7270997	7271003	7271009	7271027	7271057	7271111	7271113	7271137	7271177	7271183
7271191	7271213	7271221	7271233	7271237	7271273	7271279	7271317	7271321	7271387
7271413	7271477	7271479	7271483	7271497	7271501	7271503	7271513	7271521	7271531
7271533	7271543	7271557	7271569	7271587	7271591	7271599	7271609	7271617	7271629
7271651	7271669	7271683	7271689	7271723	7271731	7271777	7271783	7271791	7271821
7271839	7271843	7271867	7271881	7271897	7271911	7271917	7271921	7271939	7271963
7271969	7271977	7271987	7271989	7272007	7272049	7272059	7272061	7272119	7272121
7272131	7272137	7272143	7272149	7272151	7272173	7272179	7272191	7272217	7272227
7272229	7272257	7272283	7272319	7272337	7272361	7272367	7272373	7272409	7272427
7272431	7272437	7272449	7272491	7272493	7272509	7272511	7272527	7272557	7272563
7272581	7272593	7272599	7272637	7272641	7272647	7272659	7272673	7272677	7272679
7272689	7272691	7272697	7272721	7272737	7272751	7272767	7272779	7272791	7272799
7272803	7272809	7272829	7272833	7272841	7272869	7272883	7272887	7272907	7272911
7272929	7272943	7272971	7273001	7273033	7273039	7273061	7273069	7273073	7273087
7273099	7273151	7273159	7273177	7273187	7273199	7273237	7273241	7273249	7273283
7273289	7273303	7273309	7273337	7273363	7273367	7273379	7273393	7273411	7273429
7273463	7273477	7273481	7273489	7273507	7273529	7273547	7273583	7273597	7273601
7273619	7273627	7273633	7273639	7273661	7273663	7273691	7273711	7273723	7273759
7273771	7273801	7273811	7273817	7273829	7273843	7273901	7273913	7273921	7273927
7273951	7273961	7273991	7273993	7273997	7273999	7274053	7274063	7274081	7274087
7274101	7274107	7274117	7274129	7274153	7274159	7274171	7274173	7274177	7274191
7274213	7274251	7274263	7274269	7274291	7274327	7274339	7274341	7274347	7274357
7274383	7274401	7274411	7274413	7274431	7274437	7274441	7274461	7274467	7274479
7274489	7274513	7274537	7274543	7274569	7274591	7274629	7274639	7274651	7274653
7274699	7274711	7274717	7274719	7274767	7274779	7274789	7274819	7274851	7274857
7274879	7274887	7274893	7274951	7274957	7275001	7275007	7275011	7275017	7275019
7275077	7275091	7275161	7275181	7275187	7275193	7275197	7275209	7275211	7275217
7275221	7275227	7275239	7275263	7275283	7275311	7275313	7275353	7275361	7275377
7275379	7275391	7275397	7275403	7275427	7275431	7275451	7275479	7275487	7275497
7275503	7275511	7275529	7275533	7275551	7275563	7275571	7275589	7275599	7275601
7275623	7275629	7275637	7275673	7275707	7275713	7275721	7275733	7275739	7275743
7275757	7275769	7275773	7275809	7275811	7275823	7275833	7275857	7275869	7275883
7275911	7275923	7275937	7275943	7275967	7275971	7275973	7275977	7276001	7276007
7276021	7276039	7276043	7276063	7276081	7276097	7276099	7276121	7276123	7276127
7276163	7276169	7276177	7276189	7276193	7276219	7276223	7276271	7276277	7276279
7276333	7276337	7276363	7276369	7276387	7276397	7276403	7276427	7276429	7276433
7276447	7276463	7276471	7276517	7276559	7276597	7276609	7276631	7276637	7276699
7276727	7276733	7276739	7276771	7276777	7276781	7276813	7276837	7276849	7276853
7276877	7276879	7276889	7276897	7276903	7276931	7276957	7276979	7276987	7277009
7277021	7277027	7277063	7277069	7277077	7277093	7277099	7277141	7277147	7277183
7277189	7277201	7277203	7277279	7277293	7277299	7277317	7277321	7277327	7277329
7277341	7277351	7277371	7277381	7277423	7277441	7277489	7277503	7277519	7277531
7277533	7277537	7277549	7277573	7277593	7277597	7277609	7277617	7277639	7277651
7277657	7277659	7277663	7277681	7277687	7277719	7277723	7277731	7277737	7277759
7277761	7277783	7277833	7277843	7277857	7277861	7277873	7277891	7277899	7277909
7277929	7277947	7277953	7277981	7277987	7277993	7278001	7278017	7278031	7278041
7278053	7278059	7278067	7278071	7278107	7278133	7278151	7278157	7278199	7278209
7278239	7278241	7278251	7278253	7278259	7278263	7278269	7278343	7278347	7278377
7278379	7278389	7278407	7278421	7278473	7278527	7278541	7278547	7278653	7278571
7278587	7278599	7278613	7278617	7278619	7278641	7278643	7278647	7278659	7278721
7278727	7278773	7278779	7278781	7278793	7278811	7278827	7278829	7278841	7278847
7278857	7278883	7278917	7278949	7278959	7278961	7279003	7279037	7279039	7279057
7279061	7279067	7279117	7279157	7279177	7279187	7279199	7279211	7279229	7279231
7279241	7279249	7279253	7279267	7279273	7279301	7279309	7279333	7279351	7279369
7279379	7279411	7279421	7279429	7279439	7279457	7279463	7279471	7279499	7279507
7279529	7279541	7279543	7279549	7279567	7279579	7279607	7279631	7279669	7279687
7279691	7279729	7279733	7279759	7279763	7279813	7279817	7279829	7279849	7279879
7279897	7279931	7279939	7279963	7279969	7279981	7279997	7279999	7280011	7280033
7280051	7280081	7280089	7280093	7280099	7280101	7280113	7280129	7280137	7280149
7280183	7280197	7280263	7280279	7280291	7280293	7280309	7280311	7280323	7280341
7280393	7280393	7280417	7280461	7280491	7280503	7280513	7280521	7280531	7280549
7280563	7280569	7280579	7280593	7280599	7280617	7280621	7280633	7280639	7280671
7280687	7280701	7280731	7280737	7280747	7280771	7280807	7280809	7280831	7280863
7280869	7280881	7280891	7280927	7280941	7280951	7280953	7280993	7281011	7281031
7281077	7281089	7281097	7281103	7281167	7281181	7281203	7281223	7281229	7281247
7281251	7281257	7281277	7281283	7281289	7281301	7281353	7281401	7281403	7281437
7281451	7281467	7281473	7281487	7281517	7281539	7281557	7281587	7281629	7281649
7281653	7281679	7281707	7281709	7281737	7281739	7281751	7281767	7281773	7281787
7281803	7281853	7281863	7281877	7281881	7281889	7281893	7281913	7281917	7281919
7281941	7281943	7281947	7281977	7282003	7282019	7282027	7282057	7282063	7282087
7282097	7282109	7282123	7282127	7282129	7282151	7282153	7282157	7282169	7282183
7282213	7282217	7282259	7282267	7282271	7282279	7282291	7282309	7282333	7282361
7282367	7282391	7282397	7282411	7282423	7282459	7282463	7282481	7282487	7282501
7282507	7282519	7282537	7282559	7282573	7282577	7282589	7282591	7282601	7282619
7282621	7282657	7282661	7282679	7282739	7282753	7282763	7282771	7282777	7282787
7282801	7282811	7282813	7282819	7282823	7282831	7282843	7282853	7282883	7282903
7282939	7282943	7282981	7282997	7282999	7283041	7283071	7283077	7283093	7283113
7283119	7283131	7283141	7283149	7283173	7283219	7283231	7283257	7283273	7283291
7283299	7283303	7283317	7283351	7283399	7283401	7283407	7283411	7283417	7283431
7283443	7283447	7283459	7283513	7283533	7283537	7283539	7283569	7283579	7283587

```
7283603 7283623 7283651 7283657 7283659 7283693 7283699 7283711 7283719 7283723
7283741 7283747 7283753 7283761 7283777 7283789 7283797 7283807 7283833 7283839
7283863 7283873 7283891 7283909 7283921 7283929 7283933 7283951 7283953 7283989
7283999 7284023 7284029 7284073 7284113 7284119 7284131 7284149 7284181 7284187
7284197 7284217 7284223 7284229 7284241 7284253 7284257 7284259 7284293 7284341
7284367 7284371 7284377 7284401 7284413 7284419 7284421 7284443 7284463 7284493
7284499 7284521 7284527 7284533 7284569 7284617 7284623 7284631 7284647 7284649
7284689 7284749 7284769 7284799 7284811 7284817 7284821 7284833 7284853 7284869
7284877 7284899 7284941 7284943 7284971 7284973 7285001 7285007 7285049 7285067
7285081 7285099 7285127 7285133 7285139 7285147 7285199 7285219 7285237 7285241
7285247 7285253 7285277 7285283 7285339 7285349 7285373 7285387 7285391 7285393
7285427 7285429 7285441 7285463 7285483 7285501 7285507 7285519 7285529 7285541
7285543 7285547 7285591 7285601 7285613 7285631 7285643 7285661 7285679 7285697
7285703 7285711 7285723 7285727 7285739 7285753 7285771 7285787 7285813 7285819
7285841 7285847 7285849 7285879 7285891 7285897 7285903 7285907 7285919 7285973
7285981 7285997 7286011 7286033 7286053 7286099 7286107 7286113 7286119 7286129
7286131 7286137 7286159 7286171 7286173 7286189 7286197 7286219 7286243 7286261
7286297 7286311 7286339 7286347 7286369 7286381 7286399 7286413 7286417 7286429
7286437 7286449 7286483 7286497 7286501 7286537 7286603 7286621 7286681 7286683
7286687 7286689 7286701 7286707 7286777 7286779 7286803 7286809 7286813 7286831
7286843 7286849 7286857 7286887 7286921 7286947 7286963 7286969 7286989 7287001
7287017 7287019 7287029 7287037 7287043 7287047 7287061 7287083 7287097 7287103
7287107 7287131 7287193 7287199 7287211 7287229 7287233 7287277 7287281 7287289
7287331 7287337 7287359 7287361 7287367 7287383 7287433 7287437 7287451 7287457
7287473 7287493 7287499 7287547 7287551 7287563 7287569 7287571 7287601 7287607
7287617 7287629 7287647 7287677 7287691 7287701 7287703 7287727 7287733 7287743
7287751 7287767 7287799 7287817 7287851 7287859 7287899 7287911 7287919 7287947
7287953 7287979 7287983 7287991 7287997 7288013 7288031 7288049 7288051 7288063
7288103 7288109 7288111 7288123 7288129 7288157 7288159 7288163 7288181 7288213
7288231 7288271 7288273 7288277 7288301 7288331 7288339 7288349 7288357 7288361
7288397 7288399 7288423 7288429 7288433 7288439 7288451 7288459 7288471 7288481
7288499 7288511 7288517 7288531 7288553 7288559 7288577 7288583 7288591 7288601
7288607 7288637 7288639 7288643 7288649 7288651 7288661 7288691 7288703 7288711
7288727 7288739 7288753 7288759 7288763 7288817 7288819 7288823 7288843 7288869
7288877 7288891 7288909 7288927 7288933 7288949 7288969 7288979 7288993 7289003
7289017 7289033 7289041 7289047 7289057 7289071 7289077 7289081 7289083 7289099
7289119 7289129 7289167 7289203 7289213 7289221 7289239 7289279 7289281 7289287
7289323 7289327 7289339 7289341 7289363 7289377 7289423 7289437 7289441 7289449
7289467 7289479 7289507 7289519 7289531 7289543 7289587 7289599 7289603 7289609
7289621 7289657 7289663 7289669 7289687 7289693 7289713 7289729 7289731 7289741
7289767 7289771 7289773 7289813 7289819 7289837 7289857 7289861 7289911 7289917
7289921 7289959 7289987 7289993 7290001 7290037 7290043 7290061 7290077 7290089
7290119 7290121 7290187 7290191 7290193 7290233 7290271 7290289 7290307 7290317
7290323 7290341 7290347 7290359 7290373 7290377 7290389 7290391 7290401 7290409
7290403 7290449 7290463 7290469 7290511 7290523 7290527 7290529 7290533 7290541
7290551 7290553 7290557 7290589 7290601 7290641 7290643 7290653 7290691 7290697
7290721 7290749 7290757 7290769 7290799 7290809 7290821 7290853 7290863 7290883
7290893 7290947 7290949 7290971 7290979 7290991 7291001 7291033 7291049 7291073
7291091 7291103 7291111 7291121 7291129 7291133 7291139 7291159 7291177 7291187
7291211 7291217 7291241 7291247 7291259 7291261 7291303 7291309 7291321 7291327
7291357 7291363 7291367 7291411 7291423 7291429 7291447 7291457 7291469 7291477
7291489 7291507 7291519 7291547 7291567 7291577 7291597 7291601 7291607 7291619
7291631 7291643 7291663 7291693 7291703 7291717 7291723 7291769 7291813 7291819
7291829 7291831 7291871 7291883 7291901 7291903 7291919 7291927 7291931 7291939
7291969 7291979 7291981 7292011 7292023 7292039 7292041 7292053 7292059 7292063
7292083 7292093 7292101 7292107 7292113 7292149 7292177 7292183 7292203 7292221
7292227 7292237 7292239 7292251 7292267 7292273 7292279 7292287 7292291 7292317
7292353 7292359 7292381 7292401 7292407 7292431 7292479 7292491 7292497 7292501
7292513 7292521 7292531 7292563 7292573 7292581 7292591 7292651 7292653 7292669
7292687 7292693 7292707 7292729 7292731 7292759 7292767 7292777 7292797 7292819
7292821 7292837 7292839 7292851 7292867 7292869 7292917 7292933 7292969 7292981
7292993 7293023 7293059 7293067 7293071 7293073 7293079 7293089 7293157 7293179
7293197 7293199 7293217 7293233 7293257 7293271 7293281 7293311 7293331 7293337
7293353 7293371 7293373 7293379 7293389 7293409 7293431 7293437 7293439 7293443
7293457 7293467 7293487 7293491 7293497 7293509 7293523 7293547 7293569 7293571
7293577 7293607 7293619 7293623 7293641 7293653 7293659 7293667 7293679 7293683
7293707 7293719 7293763 7293827 7293851 7293863 7293883 7293899 7293907 7293911
7293919 7293931 7293943 7293971 7293973 7293983 7293999 7294003 7294097 7294117
7294121 7294127 7294129 7294141 7294163 7294169 7294193 7294201 7294213 7294237
7294267 7294279 7294333 7294349 7294361 7294373 7294409 7294421 7294453 7294459
7294543 7294559 7294571 7294577 7294601 7294603 7294619 7294633 7294643 7294657
7294681 7294687 7294697 7294699 7294709 7294711 7294723 7294733 7294753 7294783
7294799 7294811 7294849 7294871 7294873 7294897 7294913 7294943 7294949 7295003
7295017 7295033 7295047 7295053 7295059 7295081 7295083 7295087 7295111 7295131
7295143 7295177 7295191 7295201 7295203 7295213 7295219 7295231 7295243 7295279
7295287 7295303 7295317 7295377 7295381 7295383 7295399 7295461 7295471 7295473
7295543 7295551 7295557 7295569 7295579 7295611 7295621 7295647 7295657 7295671
7295683 7295689 7295699 7295719 7295723 7295731 7295759 7295771 7295777 7295779
7295797 7295803 7295809 7295833 7295837 7295843 7295863 7295921 7295923 7295933
7295963 7295983 7295987 7295989 7296001 7296011 7296013 7296017 7296041 7296053
7296059 7296061 7296089 7296097 7296101 7296103 7296119 7296127 7296161 7296167
7296181 7296187 7296193 7296217 7296239 7296241 7296259 7296293 7296299 7296301
7296329 7296379 7296403 7296407 7296413 7296427 7296449 7296481 7296491 7296493
7296521 7296529 7296547 7296557 7296571 7296581 7296593 7296617 7296629 7296643
7296649 7296671 7296673 7296691 7296697 7296701 7296739 7296743 7296761 7296763
7296767 7296781 7296803 7296827 7296841 7296851 7296853 7296857 7296869 7296871
7296907 7296917 7296937 7296941 7296953 7296959 7296973 7296979 7296983 7297027
7297033 7297051 7297091 7297099 7297109 7297117 7297123 7297127 7297133 7297181
7297189 7297231 7297237 7297243 7297253 7297271 7297291 7297321 7297333 7297379
```

7297397 7297421 7297429 7297453 7297457 7297481 7297483 7297489 7297559 7297561
7297567 7297571 7297583 7297603 7297627 7297637 7297649 7297669 7297681 7297711
7297747 7297753 7297781 7297789 7297813 7297837 7297847 7297861 7297867 7297889
7297891 7297897 7297921 7297931 7297933 7297963 7297967 7297973 7297993 7298017
7298059 7298069 7298077 7298087 7298131 7298143 7298167 7298173 7298177 7298191
7298197 7298201 7298209 7298231 7298233 7298281 7298297 7298323 7298339 7298381
7298387 7298393 7298399 7298407 7298437 7298441 7298443 7298453 7298479 7298483
7298497 7298503 7298507 7298591 7298597 7298611 7298617 7298639 7298647 7298663
7298699 7298719 7298741 7298803 7298827 7298839 7298849 7298867 7298891 7298897
7298903 7298909 7298911 7298939 7298947 7298957 7298971 7298989 7298999 7299011
7299023 7299041 7299049 7299079 7299091 7299109 7299113 7299133 7299143 7299151
7299163 7299179 7299203 7299209 7299217 7299233 7299247 7299251 7299289 7299317
7299359 7299367 7299407 7299427 7299431 7299437 7299463 7299469 7299493 7299499
7299527 7299529 7299557 7299563 7299577 7299587 7299623 7299631 7299673 7299689
7299703 7299707 7299709 7299769 7299779 7299791 7299797 7299821 7299823 7299889
7299907 7299923 7299937 7299949 7299959 7299961 7300001 7300003 7300037 7300043
7300049 7300079 7300109 7300127 7300133 7300169 7300171 7300187 7300207 7300213
7300231 7300243 7300261 7300277 7300301 7300303 7300333 7300339 7300357 7300367
7300399 7300409 7300417 7300441 7300451 7300457 7300459 7300477 7300481 7300487
7300523 7300529 7300543 7300549 7300571 7300577 7300619 7300621 7300639 7300649
7300673 7300751 7300753 7300801 7300819 7300831 7300861 7300901 7300919 7300963
7300967 7300981 7300991 7301033 7301039 7301071 7301081 7301087 7301123 7301131
7301137 7301159 7301179 7301183 7301197 7301209 7301221 7301249 7301257 7301291
7301299 7301311 7301323 7301341 7301353 7301363 7301369 7301389 7301401 7301423
7301431 7301473 7301477 7301479 7301507 7301513 7301519 7301537 7301561 7301563
7301587 7301597 7301621 7301633 7301641 7301677 7301699 7301717 7301729 7301737
7301743 7301753 7301783 7301803 7301807 7301821 7301831 7301849 7301851 7301893
7301897 7301923 7301927 7301929 7301933 7301951 7301981 7301989 7301999 7302013
7302037 7302047 7302079 7302101 7302103 7302107 7302149 7302151 7302179 7302187
7302241 7302259 7302271 7302301 7302307 7302311 7302313 7302319 7302331 7302349
7302377 7302443 7302457 7302467 7302473 7302487 7302509 7302553 7302583 7302587
7302599 7302601 7302613 7302619 7302629 7302641 7302667 7302677 7302683 7302709
7302731 7302739 7302749 7302761 7302767 7302773 7302781 7302787 7302791 7302793
7302829 7302833 7302871 7302901 7302917 7302929 7302931 7302941 7302943 7303003
7303031 7303061 7303063 7303069 7303091 7303111 7303117 7303129 7303133 7303141
7303147 7303151 7303159 7303181 7303211 7303243 7303279 7303291 7303297 7303301
7303339 7303349 7303357 7303369 7303403 7303423 7303441 7303451 7303463 7303481
7303493 7303511 7303519 7303547 7303561 7303567 7303573 7303633 7303651 7303663
7303687 7303691 7303711 7303717 7303729 7303739 7303757 7303783 7303789 7303819
7303823 7303843 7303861 7303889 7303909 7303913 7303921 7303939 7303943 7303951
7303973 7303979 7303991 7303993 7304009 7304051 7304053 7304057 7304081 7304107
7304117 7304123 7304131 7304137 7304149 7304159 7304173 7304183 7304257 7304279
7304287 7304291 7304309 7304327 7304329 7304333 7304357 7304359 7304383 7304387
7304389 7304393 7304399 7304431 7304443 7304447 7304449 7304483 7304527 7304537
7304587 7304597 7304603 7304621 7304653 7304669 7304681 7304699 7304701 7304707
7304719 7304729 7304753 7304789 7304821 7304837 7304851 7304879 7304887
7304903 7304909 7304939 7304963 7304971 7304981 7304989 7304993 7305041 7305047
7305049 7305061 7305073 7305097 7305161 7305217 7305239 7305241 7305269 7305293
7305301 7305307 7305323 7305343 7305371 7305373 7305377 7305379 7305383 7305407
7305409 7305413 7305437 7305449 7305457 7305469 7305499 7305509 7305511 7305517
7305521 7305523 7305547 7305569 7305581 7305583 7305587 7305601 7305607 7305611
7305637 7305643 7305647 7305653 7305669 7305673 7305691 7305707 7305731 7305751
7305757 7305763 7305791 7305797 7305817 7305827 7305839 7305871 7305901 7305923
7305959 7305989 7306007 7306021 7306027 7306063 7306069 7306081 7306093 7306097
7306121 7306129 7306151 7306177 7306207 7306213 7306217 7306223 7306237 7306267
7306301 7306303 7306339 7306337 7306339 7306363 7306367 7306373 7306381 7306423
7306471 7306489 7306499 7306531 7306543 7306553 7306567 7306589 7306609 7306613
7306661 7306679 7306687 7306699 7306711 7306729 7306771 7306781 7306799 7306807
7306829 7306837 7306841 7306853 7306877 7306883 7306891 7306909 7306931 7306933
7306961 7306967 7306987 7306993 7307009 7307011 7307017 7307051 7307063 7307089
7307099 7307147 7307189 7307203 7307207 7307213 7307219 7307239 7307273 7307299
7307303 7307309 7307323 7307329 7307359 7307383 7307387 7307393 7307401 7307411
7307441 7307449 7307459 7307477 7307483 7307497 7307527 7307543 7307551 7307557
7307561 7307581 7307593 7307621 7307627 7307633 7307659 7307669 7307683 7307719
7307731 7307741 7307749 7307771 7307777 7307803 7307819 7307821 7307827 7307831
7307849 7307857 7307863 7307869 7307873 7307897 7307929 7307939 7307941 7307969
7307987 7308001 7308013 7308019 7308031 7308047 7308073 7308121 7308137 7308173
7308221 7308239 7308241 7308247 7308251 7308253 7308263 7308269 7308289 7308307
7308311 7308313 7308337 7308347 7308361 7308401 7308403 7308437 7308439 7308451
7308463 7308473 7308491 7308523 7308569 7308577 7308583 7308601 7308611 7308629
7308643 7308649 7308671 7308683 7308689 7308703 7308709 7308713 7308739 7308751
7308767 7308773 7308781 7308803 7308809 7308817 7308893 7308907 7308913 7308919
7308941 7308949 7308967 7308971 7308991 7309013 7309019 7309021 7309063 7309163
7309051 7309079 7309117 7309121 7309123 7309139 7309151 7309153 7309157 7309163
7309171 7309187 7309207 7309217 7309219 7309223 7309249 7309261 7309279 7309297
7309301 7309307 7309321 7309343 7309369 7309373 7309391 7309403 7309427 7309529
7309567 7309579 7309619 7309637 7309639 7309651 7309697 7309723 7309741 7309747
7309751 7309787 7309801 7309811 7309859 7309877 7309879
7309903 7309921 7309933 7309987 7310011 7310027 7310029 7310033 7310063 7310071
7310087 7310123 7310137 7310161 7310167 7310189 7310197 7310213 7310227 7310257
7310263 7310299 7310311 7310351 7310353 7310399 7310411 7310417 7310419 7310431
7310441 7310447 7310467 7310483 7310489 7310491 7310507 7310509 7310543 7310551
7310579 7310593 7310603 7310621 7310627 7310651 7310671 7310701 7310707 7310747
7310753 7310773 7310783 7310819 7310827 7310843 7310851 7310857 7310869 7310893
7310899 7310917 7310921 7310959 7310981 7310993 7311011 7311047 7311091
7311113 7311119 7311121 7311127 7311149 7311199 7311209 7311211 7311223 7311253
7311259 7311287 7311313 7311323 7311329 7311341 7311347 7311349 7311373 7311383
7311413 7311431 7311449 7311463 7311467 7311497 7311583 7311587 7311593 7311659
7311673 7311679 7311701 7311709 7311737 7311779 7311797 7311803 7311809 7311823

```
7311833 7311839 7311859 7311883 7311893 7311937 7311943 7311949 7311959 7311991
7312007 7312013 7312037 7312061 7312069 7312079 7312087 7312099 7312103 7312127
7312133 7312139 7312141 7312153 7312157 7312171 7312177 7312231 7312237 7312243
7312267 7312271 7312297 7312301 7312339 7312381 7312387 7312399 7312411 7312427
7312439 7312441 7312453 7312469 7312489 7312493 7312517 7312531 7312541 7312561
7312583 7312631 7312633 7312639 7312681 7312693 7312699 7312751 7312757 7312759
7312819 7312831 7312841 7312859 7312861 7312867 7312909 7312913 7312933 7312957
7312961 7312969 7312979 7312997 7313063 7313083 7313113 7313123 7313143 7313167
7313183 7313203 7313221 7313239 7313261 7313291 7313297 7313323 7313381 7313389
7313393 7313401 7313407 7313419 7313429 7313441 7313443 7313447 7313459 7313503
7313513 7313543 7313561 7313567 7313611 7313617 7313633 7313641 7313659 7313671
7313693 7313707 7313729 7313749 7313759 7313773 7313777 7313809 7313819 7313833
7313837 7313849 7313857 7313863 7313869 7313881 7313903 7313951 7313953 7313981
7313983 7314037 7314067 7314071 7314077 7314079 7314101 7314127 7314137 7314143
7314163 7314173 7314193 7314211 7314217 7314239 7314269 7314313 7314317 7314331
7314337 7314353 7314361 7314397 7314401 7314421 7314431 7314443 7314499 7314509
7314511 7314533 7314547 7314557 7314577 7314589 7314599 7314611 7314617 7314631
7314649 7314653 7314661 7314679 7314683 7314719 7314731 7314733 7314779 7314781
7314793 7314803 7314823 7314833 7314869 7314871 7314877 7314883 7314887 7314907
7314911 7314919 7314941 7314949 7314953 7314961 7314971 7314973 7315001 7315003
7315013 7315027 7315067 7315093 7315141 7315169 7315207 7315213 7315223 7315229
7315249 7315271 7315309 7315313 7315333 7315339 7315367 7315379 7315391 7315397
7315417 7315421 7315447 7315459 7315463 7315471 7315487 7315489 7315499 7315543
7315571 7315579 7315601 7315619 7315621 7315631 7315657 7315667 7315673 7315687
7315727 7315739 7315747 7315757 7315793 7315807 7315811 7315813 7315829 7315843
7315849 7315853 7315877 7315883 7315901 7315921 7315939 7315949 7315951 7315963
7315981 7315991 7316009 7316017 7316021 7316027 7316039 7316041 7316077 7316107
7316119 7316129 7316131 7316143 7316167 7316191 7316203 7316213 7316227 7316233
7316249 7316251 7316263 7316291 7316293 7316297 7316299 7316317 7316329 7316339
7316371 7316389 7316429 7316431 7316447 7316453 7316459 7316471 7316473 7316483
7316509 7316513 7316521 7316549 7316557 7316567 7316587 7316591 7316593 7316611
7316627 7316641 7316657 7316663 7316693 7316707 7316711 7316719 7316723 7316741
7316747 7316761 7316791 7316797 7316801 7316831 7316833 7316849 7316857 7316867
7316873 7316887 7316893 7316909 7316917 7316927 7316929 7316941 7316951 7316971
7316977 7317029 7317041 7317043 7317053 7317067 7317073 7317091 7317097 7317103
7317119 7317131 7317133 7317139 7317143 7317161 7317169 7317173 7317179 7317187
7317203 7317253 7317283 7317329 7317347 7317371 7317391 7317397 7317407 7317433
7317437 7317487 7317493 7317503 7317511 7317517 7317523 7317547 7317553 7317577
7317587 7317617 7317619 7317631 7317637 7317647 7317659 7317661 7317689 7317719
7317731 7317781 7317787 7317797 7317809 7317833 7317839 7317851 7317859 7317881
7317911 7317929 7317943 7317947 7318009 7318013 7318019 7318033 7318037 7318049
7318061 7318067 7318093 7318099 7318159 7318189 7318247 7318271 7318273 7318303
7318307 7318309 7318319 7318321 7318327 7318349 7318361 7318363 7318379 7318397
7318429 7318453 7318457 7318499 7318513 7318523 7318529 7318543 7318601 7318613
7318627 7318631 7318681 7318723 7318733 7318739 7318757 7318769 7318777 7318813
7318861 7318867 7318889 7318903 7318919 7318921 7318931 7318943 7318967 7318973
7318979 7319003 7319017 7319041 7319057 7319063 7319071 7319087 7319089 7319099
7319119 7319173 7319201 7319203 7319219 7319227 7319233 7319239 7319243 7319251
7319287 7319309 7319321 7319371 7319381 7319383 7319387 7319393 7319437 7319467
7319479 7319483 7319509 7319531 7319551 7319561 7319569 7319581 7319597 7319621
7319623 7319633 7319657 7319659 7319699 7319713 7319737 7319739 7319743 7319779
7319789 7319791 7319849 7319857 7319863 7319867 7319869 7319881 7319891 7319909
7319941 7319947 7319971 7319987 7320011 7320023 7320033 7320037 7320041 7320067
7320077 7320083 7320091 7320101 7320119 7320121 7320127 7320133 7320169 7320197
7320199 7320211 7320239 7320241 7320259 7320311 7320317 7320337 7320343 7320347
7320359 7320403 7320409 7320419 7320437 7320451 7320461 7320473 7320497 7320503
7320527 7320541 7320553 7320589 7320617 7320623 7320637 7320653 7320667 7320679
7320697 7320701 7320721 7320737 7320749 7320763 7320773 7320787 7320799 7320811
7320821 7320823 7320827 7320853 7320883 7320941 7320949 7320959 7320961 7320979
7320983 7320997 7321003 7321007 7321031 7321043 7321063 7321073 7321081 7321091
7321103 7321109 7321117 7321121 7321123 7321129 7321147 7321151 7321163 7321183
7321189 7321201 7321207 7321217 7321219 7321231 7321241 7321267 7321277 7321319
7321357 7321361 7321393 7321399 7321439 7321451 7321453 7321469 7321507 7321523
7321541 7321583 7321619 7321621 7321627 7321661 7321663 7321687 7321697 7321703
7321709 7321729 7321753 7321757 7321789 7321813 7321829 7321837 7321861 7321877
7321919 7321927 7321943 7321969 7321987 7322023 7322033 7322069 7322071 7322111
7322113 7322129 7322131 7322137 7322153 7322173 7322179 7322213 7322219 7322221
7322233 7322251 7322261 7322269 7322299 7322309 7322351 7322389 7322401 7322407
7322437 7322489 7322521 7322531 7322537 7322551 7322561 7322569 7322593 7322611
7322617 7322621 7322663 7322669 7322677 7322681 7322683 7322743 7322753 7322779
7322797 7322807 7322813 7322827 7322837 7322839 7322873 7322891 7322893 7322897
7322911 7322921 7322927 7322933 7322963 7322981 7323013 7323053 7323089 7323137
7323149 7323157 7323161 7323163 7323179 7323181 7323203 7323229 7323259 7323289
7323313 7323317 7323319 7323331 7323353 7323359 7323367 7323377 7323391 7323397
7323421 7323439 7323469 7323473 7323479 7323499 7323509 7323523 7323527 7323533
7323557 7323571 7323577 7323581 7323623 7323647 7323661 7323731 7323733 7323737
7323763 7323773 7323779 7323793 7323839 7323851 7323857 7323859 7323881 7323917
7323929 7323931 7323937 7323941 7323947 7323977 7323997 7324007 7324013 7324027
7324033 7324069 7324073 7324081 7324103 7324111 7324133 7324171 7324223 7324237
7324267 7324271 7324307 7324313 7324337 7324349 7324351 7324357 7324379 7324381
7324403 7324411 7324417 7324423 7324439 7324451 7324459 7324469 7324477 7324487
7324517 7324531 7324549 7324561 7324571 7324579 7324589 7324591 7324607 7324613
7324619 7324651 7324661 7324703 7324717 7324721 7324727 7324753 7324763 7324769
7324771 7324777 7324783 7324799 7324817 7324831 7324843 7324847 7324871 7324873
7324901 7324931 7324939 7324949 7324951 7324957 7324963 7324969 7325029 7325053
7325069 7325099 7325119 7325137 7325159 7325191 7325209 7325231 7325239 7325243
7325267 7325273 7325281 7325321 7325333 7325341 7325363 7325399 7325407 7325411
7325413 7325443 7325447 7325449 7325459 7325471 7325473 7325491 7325503 7325509
7325531 7325533 7325543 7325557 7325587 7325627 7325629 7325653 7325671 7325683
```

```
7325693 7325723 7325729 7325761 7325767 7325779 7325797 7325803 7325807 7325837
7325881 7325897 7325909 7325947 7325957 7325959 7325977 7325987 7326017 7326019
7326041 7326047 7326071 7326079 7326083 7326101 7326107 7326139 7326157 7326173
7326197 7326203 7326239 7326247 7326257 7326271 7326289 7326301 7326307 7326311
7326317 7326359 7326401 7326409 7326427 7326433 7326461 7326467 7326491 7326497
7326511 7326547 7326559 7326593 7326607 7326617 7326619 7326661 7326691 7326713
7326721 7326731 7326733 7326743 7326749 7326827 7326833 7326841 7326853 7326883
7326887 7326889 7326901 7326911 7326923 7326931 7326967 7326997 7327009 7327031
7327037 7327043 7327057 7327093 7327109 7327121 7327127 7327129 7327181 7327183
7327211 7327219 7327237 7327241 7327249 7327261 7327279 7327297 7327319 7327337
7327361 7327367 7327393 7327399 7327403 7327417 7327427 7327447 7327451 7327469
7327511 7327513 7327543 7327571 7327583 7327601 7327603 7327613 7327627 7327657
7327679 7327693 7327699 7327703 7327709 7327721 7327751 7327763 7327769 7327781
7327843 7327847 7327861 7327871 7327877 7327897 7327909 7327921 7327933 7327949
7327963 7327967 7327973 7328011 7328021 7328023 7328029 7328033 7328051 7328077
7328117 7328131 7328149 7328161 7328177 7328197 7328201 7328231 7328239 7328249
7328263 7328291 7328303 7328333 7328351 7328353 7328359 7328383 7328401 7328413
7328423 7328429 7328437 7328441 7328443 7328473 7328491 7328501 7328521 7328539
7328551 7328591 7328609 7328621 7328647 7328669 7328693 7328719 7328747 7328749
7328753 7328771 7328773 7328777 7328779 7328801 7328807 7328821 7328831 7328837
7328843 7328879 7328891 7328899 7328903 7328939 7328941 7328953 7328957 7329013
7329031 7329059 7329073 7329097 7329103 7329107 7329109 7329121 7329131 7329139
7329151 7329163 7329167 7329169 7329173 7329181 7329187 7329209 7329229 7329241
7329247 7329251 7329263 7329271 7329297 7329313 7329353 7329359 7329403 7329407
7329409 7329461 7329473 7329503 7329559 7329587 7329593 7329613 7329653 7329659
7329661 7329677 7329713 7329719 7329731 7329743 7329761 7329769 7329781 7329793
7329809 7329841 7329851 7329853 7329899 7329937 7329961 7329967 7329977 7329989
7330013 7330019 7330027 7330039 7330049 7330051 7330097 7330117 7330121 7330153
7330157 7330163 7330171 7330177 7330207 7330223 7330241 7330259 7330289 7330303
7330363 7330373 7330391 7330439 7330457 7330471 7330481 7330493 7330501 7330517
7330541 7330559 7330571 7330579 7330607 7330619 7330627 7330633 7330667 7330669
7330693 7330703 7330711 7330717 7330747 7330753 7330781 7330783 7330831 7330837
7330889 7330901 7330909 7330913 7330931 7330933 7330943 7330993 7331011 7331021
7331033 7331039 7331047 7331053 7331059 7331083 7331111 7331147 7331167 7331173
7331179 7331183 7331189 7331213 7331237 7331249 7331293 7331299 7331309 7331323
7331339 7331347 7331353 7331377 7331381 7331383 7331393 7331413 7331431 7331447
7331453 7331477 7331479 7331501 7331509 7331537 7331557 7331561 7331563 7331581
7331591 7331627 7331633 7331647 7331657 7331683 7331689 7331711 7331719 7331761
7331771 7331789 7331813 7331839 7331881 7331887 7331889 7331921 7331923 7331969
7331999 7332001 7332023 7332029 7332037 7332077 7332079 7332113 7332121 7332131
7332161 7332181 7332187 7332191 7332203 7332209 7332257 7332289 7332301 7332313
7332319 7332341 7332349 7332361 7332373 7332379 7332407 7332419 7332421 7332427
7332433 7332487 7332503 7332509 7332511 7332541 7332551 7332569 7332581 7332583
7332601 7332629 7332641 7332659 7332691 7332707 7332713 7332733 7332751 7332779
7332811 7332821 7332847 7332863 7332877 7332887 7332901 7332943 7332947 7332953
7332959 7332971 7332991 7333003 7333033 7333037 7333043 7333049 7333057 7333061
7333099 7333129 7333147 7333153 7333189 7333211 7333231 7333243 7333247 7333253
7333279 7333303 7333321 7333327 7333337 7333357 7333367 7333369 7333387 7333393
7333397 7333423 7333427 7333429 7333441 7333463 7333483 7333489 7333493 7333657
7333709 7333717 7333741 7333751 7333771 7333789 7333831 7333853 7333883 7333891
7333901 7333933 7333961 7333979 7333999 7334023 7334027 7334051 7334059 7334069
7334077 7334081 7334099 7334111 7334137 7334147 7334161 7334179 7334189 7334207
7334219 7334269 7334273 7334287 7334291 7334333 7334347 7334357 7334359 7334363
7334387 7334389 7334407 7334413 7334417 7334441 7334443 7334489 7334521 7334533
7334549 7334567 7334581 7334609 7334611 7334623 7334647 7334653 7334659 7334687
7334689 7334699 7334711 7334713 7334731 7334749 7334753 7334759 7334771 7334783
7334809 7334813 7334827 7334839 7334851 7334857 7334863 7334869 7334881 7334903
7334989 7335019 7335047 7335059 7335061 7335079 7335089 7335101 7335103 7335161
7335179 7335193 7335217 7335221 7335239 7335247 7335257 7335277 7335281 7335283
7335299 7335301 7335319 7335331 7335343 7335353 7335379 7335389 7335403 7335407
7335409 7335421 7335439 7335467 7335481 7335487 7335533 7335541 7335547 7335553
7335563 7335569 7335589 7335593 7335611 7335613 7335617 7335641 7335659 7335661
7335667 7335673 7335683 7335701 7335707 7335709 7335733 7335743 7335751 7335787
7335793 7335803 7335833 7335851 7335863 7335907 7335917 7335931 7335941 7335943
7335947 7335949 7335961 7335967 7335971 7335973 7335983 7335997 7336037 7336039
7336079 7336081 7336093 7336097 7336099 7336127 7336169 7336267 7336279 7336289
7336297 7336309 7336327 7336349 7336369 7336387 7336403 7336421 7336423 7336447
7336457 7336481 7336513 7336529 7336561 7336577 7336601 7336607 7336613 7336627
7336633 7336657 7336661 7336687 7336691 7336699 7336711 7336727 7336729 7336733
7336759 7336781 7336787 7336799 7336807 7336829 7336859 7336873 7336891 7336919
7336921 7336933 7336963 7337003 7337009 7337017 7337039 7337041 7337053 7337089
7337101 7337107 7337153 7337221 7337227 7337269 7337279 7337327 7337333 7337339
7337357 7337381 7337413 7337419 7337459 7337467 7337497 7337503 7337509 7337521
7337567 7337569 7337633 7337641 7337651 7337663 7337677 7337683 7337689 7337699
7337717 7337723 7337749 7337767 7337777 7337789 7337791 7337809 7337831 7337839
7337843 7337861 7337879 7337909 7337929 7337959 7337983 7337987 7338011 7338013
7338031 7338043 7338059 7338061 7338077 7338109 7338119 7338137 7338181 7338211
7338217 7338241 7338263 7338269 7338293 7338299 7338301 7338307 7338343 7338367
7338371 7338379 7338389 7338391 7338431 7338493 7338497 7338511 7338521 7338557
7338607 7338619 7338623 7338629 7338641 7338689 7338719 7338757 7338787 7338797
7338803 7338823 7338829 7338869 7338871 7338887 7338889 7338901 7338907 7338931
7338967 7339027 7339043 7339049 7339051 7339081 7339091 7339141 7339151 7339159
7339183 7339193 7339217 7339229 7339243 7339249 7339253 7339303 7339307 7339309
7339313 7339333 7339361 7339363 7339373 7339391 7339397 7339403 7339411 7339417
7339421 7339433 7339447 7339469 7339477 7339487 7339489 7339511 7339513 7339543
7339559 7339571 7339583 7339603 7339609 7339621 7339667 7339721 7339729 7339751
7339753 7339763 7339769 7339781 7339793 7339823 7339837 7339841 7339847 7339859
7339867 7339897 7339957 7339961 7339991 7339999 7340009 7340033 7340071 7340083
```

```
7340101  7340117  7340119  7340147  7340153  7340159  7340167  7340183  7340227  7340231
7340233  7340237  7340293  7340257  7340269  7340293  7340297  7340299  7340309  7340317
7340329  7340357  7340363  7340383  7340419  7340483  7340527  7340537  7340539  7340569
7340581  7340591  7340621  7340633  7340639  7340647  7340653  7340687  7340693  7340699
7340713  7340717  7340731  7340743  7340779  7340803  7340813  7340833  7340843  7340867
7340869  7340873  7340881  7340891  7340899  7340929  7340939  7340951  7341001  7341023
7341029  7341043  7341067  7341073  7341077  7341097  7341121  7341137  7341143  7341149
7341157  7341197  7341199  7341227  7341241  7341247  7341293  7341349  7341359  7341361
7341413  7341427  7341443  7341449  7341457  7341461  7341463  7341491  7341493  7341517
7341539  7341557  7341559  7341571  7341617  7341629  7341647  7341667  7341673  7341689
7341767  7341769  7341779  7341781  7341811  7341827  7341857  7341871  7341881  7341889
7341907  7341937  7341941  7341953  7341979  7341989  7342003  7342007  7342031  7342033
7342051  7342057  7342067  7342081  7342087  7342099  7342103  7342109  7342117  7342123
7342163  7342177  7342183  7342187  7342193  7342201  7342211  7342213  7342253  7342261
7342271  7342297  7342301  7342331  7342343  7342369  7342393  7342409  7342421  7342441
7342457  7342459  7342469  7342471  7342477  7342483  7342501  7342507  7342513  7342523
7342537  7342549  7342583  7342603  7342633  7342643  7342659  7342693  7342703  7342729
7342757  7342787  7342799  7342807  7342817  7342831  7342837  7342843  7342847  7342849
7342859  7342883  7342903  7342913  7342967  7343009  7343023  7343027  7343037  7343041
7343051  7343053  7343087  7343107  7343111  7343159  7343173  7343183  7343207  7343213
7343227  7343243  7343263  7343321  7343333  7343359  7343381  7343383  7343389  7343393
7343429  7343449  7343471  7343489  7343527  7343543  7343587  7343599  7343617
7343653  7343663  7343681  7343689  7343701  7343719  7343737  7343741  7343771  7343827
7343837  7343863  7343893  7343909  7343951  7343953  7343971  7343977  7343981  7344011
7344041  7344121  7344149  7344193  7344223  7344247  7344251  7344257  7344269  7344287
7344307  7344313  7344319  7344331  7344347  7344349  7344367  7344397  7344409  7344419
7344439  7344451  7344481  7344487  7344503  7344517  7344539  7344541  7344553  7344563
7344577  7344593  7344599  7344637  7344647  7344653  7344677  7344679  7344683  7344713
7344721  7344739  7344761  7344763  7344767  7344809  7344817  7344823  7344829  7344839
7344853  7344893  7344941  7344973  7344977  7344983  7344991  7345007  7345031  7345043
7345049  7345057  7345067  7345069  7345097  7345103  7345123  7345127  7345133  7345141
7345147  7345181  7345189  7345199  7345201  7345213  7345223  7345243  7345249  7345271
7345291  7345313  7345319  7345321  7345337  7345363  7345423  7345433  7345451  7345453
7345463  7345469  7345477  7345483  7345501  7345517  7345549  7345607  7345627  7345631
7345661  7345699  7345711  7345727  7345739  7345757  7345777  7345783  7345801
7345817  7345823  7345859  7345861  7345889  7345909  7345931  7345937  7345957
7345963  7345967  7345979  7346069  7346071  7346083  7346107  7346111  7346113  7346117
7346123  7346137  7346153  7346161  7346167  7346173  7346189  7346191  7346197  7346201
7346219  7346221  7346231  7346233  7346237  7346281  7346303  7346333  7346341  7346347
7346371  7346459  7346467  7346477  7346527  7346531  7346551  7346557  7346623  7346627
7346641  7346653  7346687  7346693  7346699  7346707  7346709  7346761  7346767  7346803
7346813  7346819  7346827  7346837  7346869  7346879  7346891  7346897  7346909  7346917
7346929  7346951  7346953  7347037  7347047  7347059  7347073  7347107  7347113  7347133
7347139  7347149  7347157  7347161  7347163  7347187  7347199  7347203  7347209
7347229  7347233  7347239  7347251  7347253  7347259  7347271  7347313  7347359  7347371
7347391  7347407  7347437  7347449  7347491  7347503  7347517  7347521  7347533
7347559  7347563  7347601  7347619  7347629  7347631  7347647  7347667  7347709  7347731
7347749  7347827  7347841  7347859  7347881  7347911  7347913  7347943  7347947  7347953
7347959  7347983  7348001  7348007  7348013  7348021  7348043  7348067  7348087  7348111
7348127  7348139  7348151  7348153  7348157  7348169  7348171  7348177  7348181  7348207
7348221  7348241  7348259  7348261  7348279  7348283  7348321  7348347  7348351
7348357  7348361  7348373  7348379  7348387  7348409  7348417  7348423  7348447  7348469
7348489  7348499  7348507  7348511  7348541  7348559  7348577  7348597  7348603  7348613
7348631  7348633  7348637  7348639  7348651  7348667  7348669  7348697  7348711  7348721
7348727  7348739  7348751  7348787  7348793  7348807  7348823  7348843  7348849  7348883
7348897  7348907  7348909  7348921  7348931  7348941  7348961  7348981  7348987  7349003
7349021  7349039  7349047  7349057  7349059  7349071  7349101  7349119  7349123  7349141
7349149  7349161  7349171  7349183  7349191  7349233  7349239  7349311  7349323  7349339
7349357  7349369  7349393  7349413  7349471  7349473  7349477  7349483  7349497  7349501
7349513  7349527  7349533  7349539  7349609  7349611  7349621  7349647  7349651  7349677
7349687  7349711  7349737  7349743  7349753  7349801  7349809  7349879  7349893  7349897
7349911  7349917  7349921  7349957  7349959  7349983  7349989  7350011  7350023  7350059
7350071  7350089  7350107  7350121  7350127  7350143  7350149  7350157  7350173  7350209
7350221  7350257  7350263  7350281  7350293  7350313  7350353  7350361  7350373  7350401
7350407  7350419  7350433  7350437  7350449  7350467  7350481  7350493  7350509  7350523
7350527  7350533  7350557  7350571  7350611  7350619  7350631  7350641  7350653  7350677
7350691  7350703  7350773  7350779  7350781  7350799  7350809  7350829  7350841  7350857
7350877  7350883  7350899  7350947  7350983  7351031  7351033  7351073  7351079  7351087
7351093  7351103  7351109  7351111  7351117  7351121  7351147  7351163  7351189  7351207
7351217  7351219  7351227  7351261  7351273  7351277  7351313  7351343  7351349  7351363
7351369  7351373  7351391  7351397  7351403  7351427  7351439  7351447  7351469  7351481
7351523  7351541  7351579  7351583  7351601  7351607  7351609  7351627  7351637  7351679
7351691  7351699  7351717  7351733  7351739  7351753  7351763  7351777  7351783  7351801
7351807  7351823  7351829  7351847  7351853  7351909  7351913  7351943  7351957  7351963
7351969  7351987  7352017  7352027  7352029  7352047  7352063  7352071  7352083  7352089
7352099  7352117  7352129  7352131  7352141  7352179  7352197  7352231  7352251  7352273
7352287  7352299  7352321  7352333  7352339  7352353  7352369  7352393  7352417  7352419
7352431  7352437  7352447  7352461  7352473  7352491  7352507  7352519  7352537  7352561
7352567  7352581  7352599  7352621  7352627  7352629  7352651  7352659  7352671  7352701
7352707  7352713  7352749  7352759  7352777  7352803  7352809  7352819  7352827  7352833
7352869  7352881  7352909  7352923  7352929  7352951  7352953  7352963  7352977  7352987
7352999  7353007  7353011  7353029  7353079  7353089  7353097  7353109  7353113  7353127
7353131  7353149  7353179  7353193  7353221  7353223  7353233  7353251  7353253  7353259
7353271  7353287  7353289  7353329  7353341  7353373  7353377  7353389  7353407  7353413
7353431  7353439  7353457  7353461  7353481  7353497  7353527  7353539  7353553  7353569
7353581  7353601  7353613  7353641  7353659  7353679  7353751  7353769  7353811  7353821
7353883  7353889  7353901  7353943  7353953  7353959  7353961  7354001  7354019
7354021  7354027  7354033  7354063  7354069  7354079  7354091  7354111  7354133  7354141
7354147  7354163  7354169  7354177  7354199  7354201  7354219  7354241  7354253  7354261
```

```
7354267 7354271 7354279 7354283 7354289 7354307 7354309 7354327 7354357 7354367
7354423 7354427 7354433 7354447 7354481 7354483 7354493 7354499 7354519 7354537
7354559 7354609 7354631 7354639 7354643 7354649 7354667 7354679 7354681 7354751
7354769 7354807 7354807 7354811 7354813 7354817 7354821 7354873 7354877 7354879
7354883 7354891 7354903 7354913 7354927 7354933 7354937 7354939 7354973 7354981
7355011 7355017 7355039 7355093 7355141 7355143 7355149 7355167 7355177 7355189
7355191 7355207 7355213 7355221 7355233 7355263 7355269 7355273 7355281 7355303
7355311 7355317 7355323 7355329 7355347 7355363 7355417 7355431 7355437 7355443
7355477 7355479 7355497 7355503 7355507 7355521 7355533 7355549 7355553 7355581
7355591 7355599 7355609 7355627 7355629 7355633 7355651 7355657 7355669 7355693
7355723 7355749 7355767 7355771 7355779 7355819 7355857 7355861 7355867 7355893
7355903 7355911 7355947 7355987 7355989 7356001 7356023 7356031 7356041 7356049
7356071 7356073 7356077 7356079 7356091 7356103 7356109 7356119 7356149 7356191
7356199 7356203 7356247 7356253 7356259 7356263 7356277 7356313 7356361 7356367
7356403 7356407 7356409 7356421 7356431 7356457 7356463 7356467 7356469 7356493
7356497 7356499 7356511 7356521 7356541 7356551 7356611 7356623 7356647 7356689
7356697 7356707 7356709 7356719 7356731 7356761 7356779 7356787 7356793 7356799
7356809 7356823 7356847 7356859 7356883 7356907 7356911 7356929 7356931 7356953
7356977 7356989 7356991 7356997 7357001 7357003 7357057 7357067 7357087 7357093
7357111 7357127 7357169 7357183 7357193 7357211 7357219 7357223 7357247 7357289
7357307 7357321 7357367 7357373 7357403 7357411 7357417 7357421 7357433 7357433
7357457 7357459 7357463 7357499 7357529 7357531 7357577 7357589 7357621 7357639
7357643 7357661 7357667 7357673 7357681 7357699 7357703 7357711 7357729 7357747
7357771 7357789 7357811 7357829 7357837 7357841 7357843 7357871 7357879 7357891
7357913 7357939 7357963 7357979 7357993 7358009 7358017 7358027 7358047 7358063
7358077 7358081 7358089 7358101 7358107 7358123 7358159 7358177 7358189 7358201
7358207 7358231 7358233 7358251 7358269 7358279 7358287 7358291 7358293 7358341
7358353 7358357 7358359 7358363 7358371 7358383 7358389 7358411 7358419 7358437
7358471 7358479 7358503 7358509 7358513 7358581 7358599 7358627 7358641 7358647
7358669 7358693 7358707 7358723 7358731 7358809 7358843 7358851 7358861 7358867
7358881 7358887 7358893 7358941 7358951 7358969 7358971 7358983 7358987 7358999
7359007 7359013 7359031 7359067 7359083 7359091 7359151 7359161 7359173 7359179
7359197 7359211 7359217 7359257 7359277 7359323 7359343 7359371 7359383 7359389
7359397 7359409 7359427 7359437 7359461 7359463 7359497 7359509 7359511 7359551
7359581 7359587 7359607 7359629 7359637 7359643 7359661 7359673 7359713 7359727
7359731 7359761 7359763 7359787 7359791 7359809 7359811 7359817 7359829 7359851
7359853 7359887 7359893 7359907 7359917 7359941 7359949 7359959 7359967 7360013
7360027 7360063 7360091 7360097 7360103 7360121 7360123 7360141 7360147 7360159
7360169 7360183 7360259 7360261 7360269 7360273 7360307 7360309 7360363 7360381
7360411 7360459 7360469 7360471 7360477 7360487 7360489 7360501 7360513 7360531
7360579 7360583 7360589 7360597 7360673 7360679 7360681 7360709 7360717 7360723
7360729 7360739 7360741 7360753 7360757 7360763 7360807 7360819 7360823 7360831
7360847 7360861 7360883 7360907 7360921 7360937 7360957 7360963 7360967 7360973
7360987 7360993 7361009 7361027 7361033 7361063 7361069 7361071 7361083 7361129
7361131 7361143 7361149 7361161 7361171 7361177 7361191 7361197 7361203 7361231
7361239 7361257 7361267 7361287 7361293 7361309 7361327 7361359 7361363 7361369
7361377 7361381 7361399 7361407 7361413 7361423 7361429 7361437 7361441 7361461
7361467 7361503 7361507 7361521 7361537 7361551 7361597 7361609 7361617 7361623
7361639 7361659 7361671 7361677 7361699 7361701 7361741 7361743 7361749 7361801
7361803 7361819 7361821 7361839 7361881 7361891 7361897 7361923 7361929 7361951
7361953 7361957 7361971 7361989 7361993 7361999 7362011 7362023 7362031 7362041
7362049 7362059 7362067 7362107 7362133 7362181 7362227 7362233 7362263 7362281
7362287 7362293 7362301 7362319 7362353 7362373 7362391 7362401 7362419 7362427
7362437 7362457 7362463 7362473 7362497 7362499 7362541 7362559 7362569 7362577
7362587 7362613 7362617 7362637 7362643 7362653 7362659 7362701 7362713 7362767
7362769 7362809 7362827 7362871 7362893 7362907 7362917 7362923 7362941 7362977
7362997 7363003 7363009 7363039 7363049 7363061 7363063 7363073 7363123 7363163
7363171 7363177 7363183 7363201 7363207 7363217 7363219 7363229 7363271 7363297
7363309 7363319 7363327 7363357 7363373 7363387 7363403 7363409 7363439 7363441
7363451 7363453 7363459 7363463 7363487 7363513 7363579 7363589 7363619 7363627
7363639 7363673 7363679 7363691 7363693 7363717 7363721 7363739 7363747 7363751
7363753 7363781 7363789 7363799 7363813 7363823 7363877 7363897 7363901 7363919
7363921 7363973 7363991 7363997 7364003 7364017 7364023 7364033 7364041 7364047
7364059 7364069 7364083 7364087 7364099 7364113 7364131 7364141 7364219 7364233
7364293 7364299 7364303 7364311 7364317 7364339 7364351 7364377 7364407 7364429
7364447 7364471 7364479 7364527 7364537 7364541 7364563 7364569 7364583 7364593
7364611 7364627 7364641 7364657 7364663 7364671 7364677 7364681 7364683 7364699
7364711 7364743 7364767 7364771 7364779 7364821 7364859 7364861 7364909 7364923
7364939 7364963 7364971 7364977 7364993 7364999 7365019 7365047 7365049 7365053
7365119 7365121 7365133 7365139 7365143 7365161 7365173 7365181 7365247 7365269
7365277 7365283 7365289 7365299 7365311 7365317 7365343 7365361 7365367 7365389
7365401 7365419 7365431 7365439 7365443 7365461 7365487 7365493 7365499 7365529
7365557 7365563 7365577 7365593 7365637 7365647 7365649 7365661 7365667 7365697
7365713 7365751 7365767 7365791 7365803 7365823 7365833 7365847 7365871 7365899
7365929 7365949 7365959 7365961 7365979 7365983 7365989 7366013 7366033 7366043
7366063 7366067 7366069 7366081 7366109 7366123 7366147 7366153 7366159 7366193
7366199 7366217 7366223 7366259 7366267 7366273 7366291 7366301 7366309 7366339
7366349 7366361 7366369 7366379 7366393 7366397 7366399 7366411 7366429 7366447
7366487 7366507 7366529 7366531 7366553 7366573 7366577 7366591 7366603 7366607
7366613 7366621 7366633 7366661 7366669 7366687 7366703 7366721 7366753 7366759
7366769 7366789 7366817 7366819 7366823 7366847 7366873 7366883 7366897 7366903
7366913 7366939 7366943 7366949 7366951 7366979 7366981 7366991 7366993 7366999
7367011 7367021 7367023 7367037 7367039 7367041 7367149 7367161 7367171 7367183
7367197 7367207 7367221 7367237 7367263 7367267 7367287 7367293 7367333 7367351
7367357 7367377 7367387 7367401 7367407 7367411 7367447 7367453 7367467 7367471
7367473 7367483 7367489 7367513 7367527 7367531 7367587 7367609 7367621 7367627
7367639 7367669 7367747 7367753 7367761 7367779 7367807 7367809 7367813 7367821
7367887 7367893 7367911 7367929 7367947 7367951 7367959 7367977 7367989 7367999
7368013 7368017 7368037 7368041 7368077 7368079 7368083 7368091 7368103 7368107
```

```
7368149  7368197  7368209  7368223  7368227  7368241  7368247  7368281  7368287  7368289
7368301  7368313  7368323  7368337  7368353  7368367  7368377  7368379  7368433  7368443
7368461  7368467  7368499  7368511  7368527  7368551  7368583  7368601  7368623  7368629
7368631  7368653  7368659  7368689  7368709  7368719  7368721  7368737  7368743  7368787
7368791  7368811  7368817  7368833  7368853  7368857  7368863  7368869
7368899  7368913  7368931  7368943  7368967  7369001  7369003  7369013  7369051  7369073
7369081  7369097  7369099  7369121  7369123  7369127  7369133  7369151  7369171  7369183
7369189  7369231  7369237  7369247  7369249  7369259  7369261  7369267  7369273  7369291
7369301  7369309  7369331  7369333  7369337  7369339  7369387  7369399  7369421  7369441
7369447  7369457  7369477  7369519  7369529  7369541  7369551  7369633  7369639  7369643
7369651  7369657  7369679  7369693  7369699  7369711  7369751  7369759  7369763  7369801
7369841  7369849  7369883  7369889  7369903  7369939  7369949  7369951  7369961  7369969
7369981  7369991  7370003  7370029  7370057  7370059  7370087  7370101  7370123  7370131
7370137  7370161  7370171  7370183  7370213  7370227  7370239  7370261  7370269  7370291
7370303  7370323  7370353  7370359  7370369  7370381  7370393  7370417  7370431  7370443
7370491  7370507  7370509  7370533  7370543  7370563  7370579  7370609  7370617  7370633
7370641  7370647  7370719  7370731  7370747  7370749  7370771  7370791  7370827  7370849
7370873  7370887  7370893  7370899  7370903  7370921  7370983  7371019  7371037  7371061
7371097  7371113  7371121  7371131  7371137  7371157  7371163  7371167  7371173  7371193
7371197  7371223  7371227  7371257  7371269  7371277  7371311  7371341  7371389  7371391
7371409  7371437  7371443  7371451  7371457  7371491  7371509  7371571  7371577  7371589
7371593  7371631  7371641  7371643  7371647  7371649  7371653  7371673  7371697  7371731
7371733  7371743  7371751  7371773  7371787  7371797  7371803  7371817  7371821  7371827
7371839  7371869  7371883  7371901  7371913  7371941  7371953  7371967  7371989  7372009
7372037  7372063  7372069  7372093  7372103  7372111  7372117  7372147  7372151  7372159
7372163  7372187  7372217  7372219  7372229  7372241  7372243  7372283  7372301  7372303
7372319  7372357  7372369  7372411  7372429  7372439  7372447  7372481  7372487  7372499
7372523  7372553  7372571  7372591  7372601  7372619  7372633  7372639  7372649  7372667
7372721  7372753  7372787  7372861  7372867  7372919  7372921  7372933  7372943  7372957
7372961  7372987  7372993  7372997  7373011  7373017  7373033  7373039  7373057  7373059
7373063  7373077  7373099  7373123  7373129  7373147  7373161  7373183  7373209  7373213
7373227  7373231  7373237  7373243  7373251  7373269  7373287  7373293  7373299  7373321
7373351  7373357  7373369  7373411  7373447  7373449  7373459  7373479  7373489  7373491
7373503  7373507  7373521  7373537  7373543  7373549  7373573  7373579  7373591  7373599
7373603  7373609  7373617  7373621  7373633  7373651  7373659  7373701  7373711  7373719
7373749  7373771  7373789  7373791  7373797  7373813  7373831  7373851  7373857  7373887
7373893  7373911  7373921  7373923  7373983  7373987  7373999  7374011  7374013  7374019
7374023  7374043  7374067  7374077  7374083  7374127  7374151  7374161  7374163  7374167
7374173  7374179  7374193  7374197  7374247  7374251  7374259  7374271  7374281  7374287
7374293  7374307  7374317  7374331  7374361  7374377  7374391  7374403  7374407  7374427
7374443  7374449  7374461  7374463  7374511  7374539  7374569  7374589  7374599  7374607
7374611  7374643  7374649  7374659  7374667  7374673  7374677  7374691  7374707  7374709
7374727  7374739  7374749  7374751  7374767  7374769  7374779  7374797  7374811  7374853
7374863  7374873  7374883  7374893  7374929  7374943  7374947  7374953  7374967  7374989
7375009  7375013  7375037  7375057  7375073  7375079  7375091  7375183  7375187  7375213
7375217  7375223  7375243  7375253  7375273  7375283  7375339  7375343  7375349  7375393
7375411  7375421  7375429  7375441  7375447  7375471  7375481  7375513  7375517  7375547
7375549  7375559  7375573  7375579  7375583  7375597  7375601  7375609  7375619  7375631
7375663  7375681  7375721  7375729  7375751  7375763  7375769  7375787  7375789  7375793
7375811  7375813  7375817  7375843  7375867  7375871  7375873  7375883  7375981  7375997
7375999  7376021  7376027  7376029  7376041  7376051  7376069  7376071  7376087  7376101
7376107  7376111  7376141  7376143  7376153  7376167  7376189  7376191  7376207  7376219
7376279  7376297  7376311  7376323  7376329  7376339  7376359  7376363  7376371  7376377
7376387  7376407  7376417  7376423  7376441  7376443  7376449  7376489  7376497  7376507
7376513  7376533  7376539  7376561  7376563  7376569  7376573  7376599  7376627  7376651
7376659  7376683  7376689  7376713  7376773  7376797  7376833  7376849  7376851  7376857
7376867  7376879  7376899  7376917  7376923  7376953  7376981  7376983  7377053  7377061
7377077  7377103  7377109  7377119  7377131  7377137  7377143  7377151  7377191  7377203
7377211  7377221  7377233  7377241  7377259  7377277  7377283  7377311  7377317  7377361
7377367  7377373  7377443  7377463  7377481  7377493  7377497  7377521  7377533  7377551
7377569  7377577  7377583  7377589  7377593  7377607  7377611  7377613  7377631  7377647
7377649  7377661  7377673  7377683  7377697  7377701  7377739  7377749  7377751  7377761
7377791  7377793  7377817  7377841  7377857  7377859  7377899  7377943  7377949  7378027
7378039  7378043  7378057  7378067  7378079  7378081  7378087  7378097  7378117  7378121
7378123  7378141  7378157  7378159  7378211  7378219  7378229  7378243  7378271  7378291
7378297  7378307  7378333  7378337  7378339  7378361  7378369  7378373  7378379  7378387
7378421  7378439  7378447  7378453  7378457  7378463  7378513  7378531  7378541  7378543
7378549  7378571  7378597  7378601  7378603  7378627  7378639  7378661  7378687  7378691
7378711  7378739  7378741  7378771  7378781  7378793  7378807  7378829  7378841  7378849
7378853  7378871  7378879  7378909  7378919  7378937  7378951  7378979  7378981  7378993
7378997  7379027  7379063  7379069  7379077  7379083  7379107  7379117  7379123  7379129
7379131  7379167  7379171  7379213  7379237  7379249  7379263  7379287  7379291  7379327
7379347  7379357  7379387  7379399  7379401  7379413  7379419  7379431  7379441  7379453
7379461  7379483  7379501  7379503  7379507  7379569  7379591  7379599  7379629  7379639
7379677  7379681  7379689  7379707  7379731  7379747  7379753  7379759  7379797  7379807
7379843  7379851  7379861  7379873  7379929  7379941  7379947  7379951  7380031  7380067
7380073  7380083  7380089  7380103  7380157  7380161  7380167  7380179  7380189  7380199
7380209  7380223  7380229  7380257  7380271  7380283  7380293  7380301  7380311  7380319
7380361  7380371  7380389  7380403  7380419  7380421  7380463  7380467  7380469  7380473
7380479  7380481  7380491  7380509  7380517  7380523  7380547  7380557  7380589  7380599
7380619  7380623  7380641  7380643  7380661  7380673  7380679  7380689  7380691
7380701  7380713  7380719  7380731  7380743  7380757  7380767  7380773  7380781  7380799
7380805  7380869  7380887  7380889  7380913  7380917  7380931  7380937  7380977  7380997
7381067  7381097  7381117  7381123  7381141  7381159  7381163  7381169  7381211  7381217
7381259  7381261  7381267  7381277  7381279  7381301  7381303  7381343  7381411  7381433
7381447  7381453  7381483  7381501  7381511  7381531  7381547  7381601  7381607  7381613
7381639  7381651  7381663  7381691  7381711  7381721  7381729  7381733  7381739  7381741
7381753  7381789  7381819  7381831  7381837  7381841  7381849  7381877  7381879  7381889
7381897  7381909  7381931  7381943  7381949  7381963  7381967  7382003  7382017  7382033
```

```
7382047 7382077 7382087 7382093 7382099 7382119 7382143 7382171 7382189 7382201
7382209 7382227 7382237 7382321 7382339 7382357 7382363 7382377 7382387 7382399
7382407 7382411 7382413 7382449 7382467 7382477 7382489 7382491 7382521 7382527
7382537 7382549 7382561 7382567 7382579 7382581 7382593 7382597 7382633 7382653
7382657 7382671 7382677 7382689 7382717 7382719 7382737 7382761 7382779 7382783
7382819 7382821 7382833 7382857 7382863 7382873 7382899 7382951 7382957 7382959
7382983 7382987 7382989 7383007 7383011 7383031 7383037 7383041 7383073 7383097
7383109 7383113 7383127 7383137 7383149 7383163 7383179 7383193 7383209 7383217
7383221 7383223 7383227 7383241 7383269 7383281 7383283 7383289 7383317 7383323
7383329 7383347 7383359 7383367 7383373 7383413 7383421 7383433 7383449 7383469
7383473 7383479 7383511 7383521 7383527 7383547 7383557 7383587 7383599 7383631
7383637 7383641 7383671 7383689 7383697 7383709 7383721 7383751 7383767 7383773
7383809 7383811 7383823 7383829 7383833 7383839 7383847 7383853 7383863 7383923
7383973 7383997 7384019 7384021 7384033 7384049 7384061 7384079 7384087 7384093
7384099 7384121 7384129 7384147 7384187 7384189 7384193 7384229 7384243 7384253
7384277 7384297 7384301 7384303 7384343 7384393 7384397 7384411 7384439 7384441
7384451 7384457 7384463 7384469 7384471 7384493 7384501 7384523 7384547 7384549
7384561 7384567 7384577 7384591 7384627 7384651 7384667 7384697 7384709 7384733
7384739 7384747 7384757 7384799 7384801 7384813 7384847 7384877 7384903 7384921
7384933 7384943 7385009 7385011 7385017 7385029 7385039 7385057 7385069 7385083
7385101 7385107 7385117 7385137 7385153 7385159 7385171 7385219 7385233 7385267
7385269 7385291 7385299 7385351 7385359 7385363 7385381 7385407 7385419 7385447
7385449 7385467 7385489 7385503 7385519 7385527 7385557 7385569 7385579 7385591
7385597 7385639 7385641 7385647 7385659 7385663 7385669 7385683 7385687 7385743
7385759 7385761 7385767 7385771 7385801 7385831 7385839 7385849 7385869 7385881
7385897 7385953 7385969 7385999 7386011 7386023 7386031 7386053 7386061 7386073
7386089 7386149 7386157 7386179 7386187 7386209 7386227 7386229 7386241 7386257
7386293 7386311 7386319 7386361 7386367 7386373 7386391 7386413 7386443 7386469
7386481 7386493 7386523 7386529 7386571 7386593 7386607 7386637 7386641 7386667
7386713 7386719 7386739 7386761 7386767 7386779 7386803 7386809 7386811 7386833
7386871 7386893 7386901 7386937 7386947 7386961 7386967 7387019 7387031 7387033
7387043 7387073 7387091 7387103 7387109 7387111 7387139 7387147 7387157 7387169
7387187 7387201 7387217 7387223 7387243 7387253 7387277 7387291 7387349 7387361
7387363 7387411 7387417 7387441 7387453 7387459 7387543 7387553 7387559 7387573
7387613 7387631 7387643 7387651 7387657 7387661 7387691 7387733 7387759 7387799
7387813 7387817 7387871 7387909 7387927 7387943 7387957 7387967 7387969 7387973
7387987 7387993 7388009 7388021 7388027 7388033 7388057 7388089 7388099 7388167
7388191 7388201 7388203 7388209 7388219 7388231 7388237 7388287 7388299 7388309
7388327 7388341 7388351 7388357 7388363 7388369 7388371 7388377 7388429 7388431
7388441 7388443 7388449 7388461 7388467 7388477 7388483 7388519 7388527 7388551
7388573 7388593 7388603 7388617 7388621 7388639 7388653 7388669 7388683 7388699
7388723 7388737 7388741 7388749 7388753 7388779 7388803 7388813 7388831 7388837
7388839 7388851 7388861 7388873 7388893 7388921 7388923 7388933 7388959 7388981
7388993 7389013 7389023 7389029 7389037 7389079 7389091 7389103 7389121 7389127
7389131 7389139 7389149 7389181 7389197 7389209 7389223 7389247 7389257 7389259
7389269 7389281 7389289 7389331 7389353 7389383 7389397 7389401 7389433 7389443
7389451 7389469 7389491 7389493 7389541 7389589 7389607 7389619 7389623 7389637
7389649 7389659 7389661 7389703 7389709 7389721 7389757 7389761 7389769 7389779
7389787 7389791 7389793 7389817 7389839 7389871 7389901 7389913 7389929 7389959
7389961 7389971 7389989 7390007 7390013 7390021 7390027 7390039 7390043 7390051
7390057 7390079 7390081 7390111 7390151 7390201 7390217 7390219 7390231 7390261
7390277 7390283 7390289 7390321 7390349 7390351 7390379 7390381 7390391 7390423
7390451 7390457 7390459 7390469 7390477 7390483 7390499 7390507 7390519 7390531
7390541 7390547 7390553 7390561 7390573 7390633 7390651 7390667 7390673 7390693
7390723 7390729 7390759 7390763 7390771 7390777 7390813 7390819 7390907 7390913
7390921 7390931 7390951 7390967 7390973 7390979 7390987 7390993 7391011 7391017
7391053 7391071 7391077 7391081 7391093 7391099 7391101 7391117 7391123 7391129
7391147 7391149 7391159 7391179 7391261 7391269 7391291 7391333 7391339 7391353
7391381 7391387 7391393 7391401 7391407 7391429 7391473 7391519 7391543 7391567
7391581 7391599 7391621 7391623 7391653 7391663 7391689 7391693 7391701 7391759
7391773 7391777 7391789 7391803 7391807 7391819 7391827 7391831 7391863 7391873
7391899 7391911 7391927 7391929 7391939 7391941 7391953 7391983 7391999 7392017
7392029 7392101 7392103 7392137 7392139 7392149 7392157 7392179 7392181 7392191
7392211 7392239 7392241 7392247 7392257 7392293 7392313 7392317 7392323 7392367
7392373 7392377 7392403 7392409 7392443 7392467 7392503 7392527 7392533 7392547
7392551 7392559 7392611 7392617 7392629 7392631 7392647 7392701 7392719 7392761
7392779 7392793 7392823 7392839 7392851 7392871 7392907 7392937 7392949 7392953
7392967 7392991 7393003 7393013 7393019 7393027 7393039 7393063 7393069 7393091
7393093 7393103 7393117 7393121 7393123 7393171 7393187 7393201 7393207 7393219
7393259 7393273 7393279 7393297 7393313 7393333 7393343 7393357 7393363 7393369
7393411 7393417 7393433 7393459 7393471 7393483 7393537 7393543 7393567 7393573
7393577 7393609 7393613 7393621 7393643 7393663 7393667 7393681 7393697 7393733
7393739 7393751 7393777 7393781 7393783 7393873 7393877 7393883 7393891 7393897
7393901 7393913 7393921 7393931 7393933 7393957 7394029 7394041 7394047 7394081
7394111 7394129 7394131 7394137 7394141 7394143 7394171 7394203 7394239 7394249
7394279 7394281 7394297 7394347 7394351 7394353 7394357 7394377 7394417 7394419
7394459 7394467 7394483 7394489 7394503 7394509 7394521 7394531 7394533 7394549
7394551 7394599 7394627 7394687 7394701 7394713 7394729 7394731 7394741 7394749
7394759 7394767 7394773 7394809 7394831 7394837 7394867 7394869 7394873 7394879
7394897 7394909 7394919 7394941 7394963 7394977 7394987 7395007 7395013 7395023
7395043 7395049 7395061 7395067 7395071 7395127 7395139 7395163 7395169 7395197
7395209 7395229 7395233 7395239 7395253 7395257 7395263 7395287 7395299 7395307
7395341 7395359 7395373 7395379 7395413 7395419 7395467 7395469 7395491 7395541
7395547 7395559 7395569 7395587 7395589 7395593 7395601 7395607 7395637 7395649
7395677 7395683 7395749 7395757 7395767 7395781 7395793 7395797 7395803 7395807
7395809 7395821 7395847 7395851 7395859 7395917 7395919 7395931 7395943 7395961
7396001 7396007 7396009 7396019 7396021 7396027 7396033 7396091 7396127 7396171
7396223 7396229 7396237 7396243 7396253 7396267 7396273 7396289 7396297 7396303
7396307 7396369 7396373 7396381 7396397 7396399 7396423 7396439 7396447 7396463
```

```
7396469  7396481  7396483  7396511  7396517  7396553  7396577  7396591  7396601  7396619
7396621  7396657  7396661  7396663  7396667  7396673  7396679  7396699  7396721  7396723
7396729  7396747  7396783  7396793  7396801  7396841  7396843  7396847  7396859  7396897
7396901  7396913  7396951  7396967  7396969  7396973  7396981  7397009  7397063
7397069  7397083  7397087  7397101  7397107  7397113  7397119  7397141  7397147  7397171
7397183  7397219  7397267  7397279  7397293  7397303  7397321  7397347  7397353  7397381
7397393  7397399  7397443  7397461  7397473  7397483  7397491  7397501  7397527
7397539  7397549  7397557  7397609  7397617  7397629  7397633  7397647  7397699  7397711
7397713  7397729  7397773  7397777  7397801  7397851  7397857  7397861  7397867
7397869  7397879  7397909  7397911  7397921  7397953  7397981  7397993  7398007  7398023
7398037  7398047  7398067  7398089  7398091  7398109  7398121  7398133  7398191  7398197
7398199  7398211  7398227  7398229  7398241  7398253  7398329  7398343  7398359  7398361
7398389  7398397  7398403  7398421  7398427  7398431  7398439  7398473  7398493  7398529
7398539  7398563  7398569  7398577  7398583  7398613  7398647  7398653  7398661  7398667
7398701  7398731  7398763  7398793  7398803  7398817  7398823  7398827  7398829  7398883
7398887  7398899  7398913  7398929  7398931  7398949  7398953  7398971  7399003  7399009
7399027  7399033  7399039  7399043  7399057  7399079  7399103  7399153  7399181  7399237
7399241  7399243  7399283  7399289  7399291  7399309  7399313  7399319  7399331  7399339
7399373  7399391  7399409  7399411  7399433  7399439  7399459  7399463  7399477  7399529
7399577  7399591  7399597  7399619  7399627  7399631  7399643  7399649  7399661  7399663
7399687  7399697  7399703  7399723  7399751  7399753  7399771  7399783  7399789  7399811
7399831  7399837  7399841  7399853  7399867  7399883  7399897  7399907  7399933
7399961  7399993  7400011  7400021  7400023  7400051  7400069  7400077  7400123  7400137
7400147  7400153  7400189  7400203  7400207  7400209  7400243  7400251  7400269  7400279
7400293  7400297  7400299  7400303  7400317  7400347  7400369  7400381  7400399  7400453
7400461  7400467  7400473  7400489  7400501  7400507  7400527  7400531  7400551  7400567
7400579  7400587  7400621  7400647  7400651  7400663  7400683  7400711  7400717  7400719
7400737  7400741  7400803  7400807  7400821  7400837  7400839  7400863  7400873  7400879
7400891  7400893  7400903  7400923  7400927  7400989  7400993  7401041  7401047  7401049
7401071  7401077  7401091  7401109  7401131  7401133  7401139  7401143  7401167  7401181
7401187  7401211  7401227  7401263  7401283  7401287  7401311  7401319  7401323  7401337
7401347  7401349  7401353  7401367  7401379  7401403  7401413  7401479  7401497  7401521
7401533  7401539  7401553  7401571  7401577  7401599  7401617  7401619  7401623  7401629
7401637  7401649  7401667  7401703  7401707  7401721  7401731  7401767  7401769  7401781
7401787  7401799  7401803  7401809  7401827  7401841  7401871  7401899  7401907  7401917
7401937  7401943  7401949  7401991  7402007  7402009  7402037  7402049  7402051  7402061
7402097  7402103  7402147  7402169  7402201  7402207  7402217  7402223  7402231  7402237
7402253  7402303  7402309  7402313  7402349  7402363  7402399  7402403  7402433  7402441
7402471  7402489  7402501  7402519  7402523  7402541  7402559  7402561  7402613  7402631
7402649  7402693  7402709  7402721  7402739  7402741  7402771  7402781  7402783  7402841
7402867  7402873  7402891  7402921  7402933  7402937  7402949  7402961  7402963
7402979  7402981  7403023  7403029  7403047  7403051  7403089  7403101  7403113  7403117
7403119  7403129  7403131  7403153  7403167  7403183  7403191  7403197  7403213  7403233
7403239  7403243  7403281  7403317  7403321  7403339
7403359  7403371  7403419  7403423  7403453  7403471  7403479  7403527  7403531  7403533
7403549  7403569  7403573  7403593  7403629  7403633  7403639  7403707  7403717  7403771
7403791  7403797  7403807  7403813  7403819  7403827  7403839  7403843  7403887  7403897
7403899  7403909  7403917  7403923  7403927  7403931  7403971  7404029  7404031  7404037
7404073  7404083  7404101  7404161  7404203  7404211  7404223  7404247  7404253  7404263
7404289  7404307  7404337  7404343  7404359  7404379  7404389  7404409  7404421  7404431
7404437  7404451  7404457  7404461  7404491  7404493  7404499  7404517  7404563  7404569
7404581  7404611  7404637  7404647  7404653  7404659  7404731  7404743  7404757  7404767
7404769  7404779  7404811  7404823  7404829  7404833  7404841  7404863  7404869  7404871
7404899  7404923  7404931  7404961  7404977  7404983  7404997  7405007  7405009  7405049
7405061  7405127  7405129  7405141  7405163  7405199  7405247  7405259  7405303  7405361
7405369  7405397  7405399  7405429  7405451  7405477  7405483  7405487  7405501  7405507
7405511  7405529  7405537  7405547  7405571  7405613  7405627  7405633  7405639  7405663
7405667  7405679  7405691  7405709  7405729  7405733  7405757  7405771  7405799  7405813
7405831  7405859  7405861  7405891  7405901  7405903  7405913  7405927  7405943  7405961
7405963  7405967  7405973  7405997  7406011  7406017  7406041  7406057  7406099  7406111
7406131  7406137  7406161  7406197  7406233  7406251  7406261  7406291  7406297  7406309
7406323  7406341  7406351  7406353  7406383  7406387  7406411  7406417  7406423  7406453
7406461  7406471  7406473  7406479  7406537  7406563  7406569  7406573  7406579  7406587
7406603  7406639  7406677  7406699  7406719  7406723  7406731  7406741  7406743  7406753
7406779  7406807  7406843  7406881  7406891  7406899  7406921  7406929  7406947
7406953  7406957  7406963  7406969  7406981  7406983  7407007  7407013  7407041  7407061
7407073  7407077  7407079  7407083  7407097  7407107  7407139  7407143  7407181  7407187
7407229  7407241  7407269  7407271  7407287  7407293  7407299  7407307  7407311
7407329  7407349  7407373  7407401  7407431  7407443  7407457  7407479  7407493  7407497
7407523  7407527  7407529  7407551  7407571  7407581  7407601  7407611  7407637  7407641
7407649  7407661  7407671  7407677  7407683  7407689  7407703  7407713  7407761  7407781
7407797  7407859  7407871  7407887  7407889  7407893  7407899  7407949  7407979  7408007
7408057  7408061  7408087  7408097  7408117  7408127  7408129  7408133  7408147
7408151  7408171  7408183  7408189  7408199  7408207  7408213  7408229  7408241  7408279
7408301  7408307  7408321  7408333  7408343  7408361  7408363  7408367  7408409  7408459
7408477  7408487  7408523  7408559  7408567  7408589  7408603  7408649  7408669  7408679
7408703  7408733  7408757  7408777  7408781  7408789  7408813  7408853  7408861  7408883
7408901  7408909  7408913  7408931  7408937  7408997  7409009  7409011  7409021
7409041  7409047  7409113  7409119  7409131  7409147  7409153  7409159  7409191  7409249
7409251  7409261  7409267  7409273  7409291  7409293  7409299  7409309  7409317  7409333
7409351  7409357  7409359  7409377  7409387  7409393  7409407  7409431  7409477  7409483
7409497  7409531  7409533  7409537  7409543  7409551  7409579  7409599  7409617  7409629
7409669  7409737  7409747  7409767  7409777  7409783  7409813  7409821  7409837
7409839  7409851  7409861  7409863  7409891  7409893  7409903  7409911  7409917  7409921
7409947  7409989  7410017  7410031  7410037  7410041  7410047  7410083  7410103  7410127
7410131  7410149  7410187  7410191  7410203  7410239  7410241  7410253  7410259  7410281
7410287  7410289  7410307  7410329  7410353  7410367  7410371  7410379  7410383  7410409
7410413  7410433  7410451  7410493  7410497  7410517  7410523  7410527  7410553  7410563
7410569  7410607  7410617  7410629  7410647  7410659  7410661  7410719  7410727  7410731
```

```
7410737 7410743 7410757 7410773 7410797 7410811 7410833 7410847 7410857 7410859
7410877 7410883 7410889 7410919 7410961 7410971 7410973 7410983 7411003 7411013
7411021 7411039 7411067 7411081 7411087 7411123 7411171 7411189 7411199 7411207
7411213 7411223 7411247 7411253 7411291 7411301 7411307 7411309 7411321 7411333
7411343 7411367 7411381 7411399 7411423 7411429 7411457 7411483 7411513 7411517
7411519 7411531 7411553 7411583 7411597 7411601 7411667 7411669 7411687 7411699
7411709 7411739 7411751 7411771 7411801 7411823 7411829 7411841 7411871 7411879
7411889 7411913 7411969 7411973 7411979 7411981 7412057 7412059 7412113 7412117
7412123 7412159 7412161 7412177 7412179 7412183 7412191 7412213 7412227 7412229
7412263 7412269 7412287 7412309 7412341 7412351 7412381 7412389 7412393 7412399
7412443 7412467 7412477 7412497 7412507 7412533 7412539 7412549 7412557 7412563
7412579 7412591 7412593 7412597 7412611 7412621 7412623 7412653 7412681 7412683
7412707 7412723 7412729 7412771 7412773 7412789 7412791 7412843 7412849 7412857
7412879 7412891 7412917 7412921 7412929 7412941 7412953 7412957 7412971 7413001
7413011 7413017 7413019 7413023 7413041 7413047 7413053 7413073 7413079 7413083
7413089 7413101 7413127 7413143 7413151 7413167 7413187 7413191 7413221 7413229
7413233 7413239 7413257 7413271 7413277 7413319 7413331 7413359 7413379 7413443
7413449 7413457 7413463 7413467 7413487 7413493 7413499 7413503 7413533 7413551
7413559 7413563 7413577 7413583 7413599 7413641 7413677 7413689 7413691 7413713
7413737 7413761 7413803 7413811 7413839 7413851 7413859 7413869 7413871 7413877
7413893 7413899 7413919 7413977 7413979 7413983 7413997 7414003 7414007 7414021
7414037 7414039 7414049 7414051 7414061 7414067 7414079 7414087 7414093 7414129
7414151 7414157 7414163 7414181 7414201 7414217 7414219 7414241 7414273 7414321
7414331 7414357 7414369 7414373 7414403 7414411 7414417 7414439 7414483 7414513
7414523 7414529 7414531 7414543 7414573 7414597 7414609 7414613 7414621 7414637
7414643 7414651 7414663 7414681 7414689 7414699 7414709 7414711 7414739 7414741
7414783 7414787 7414789 7414793 7414801 7414817 7414819 7414843 7414853 7414879
7414889 7414903 7414909 7414931 7414933 7414937 7414969 7414987 7414991 7414999
7415003 7415017 7415029 7415053 7415087 7415101 7415111 7415119 7415123 7415147
7415153 7415159 7415171 7415183 7415197 7415201 7415209 7415227 7415251 7415257
7415321 7415323 7415327 7415333 7415347 7415363 7415371 7415423 7415437 7415477
7415483 7415489 7415501 7415509 7415543 7415557 7415593 7415599 7415609 7415623
7415633 7415641 7415647 7415659 7415663 7415699 7415701 7415713 7415717 7415741
7415743 7415753 7415773 7415783 7415797 7415803 7415819 7415827 7415839 7415857
7415861 7415869 7415899 7415917 7415929 7415939 7415963 7415971 7415977 7415981
7415997 7416001 7416007 7416043 7416047 7416049 7416091 7416109 7416139 7416151
7416179 7416187 7416191 7416193 7416229 7416247 7416259 7416287 7416307 7416313
7416341 7416349 7416361 7416371 7416377 7416379 7416421 7416443 7416463 7416467
7416473 7416481 7416499 7416559 7416571 7416583 7416587 7416659 7416671 7416677
7416679 7416749 7416751 7416791 7416809 7416823 7416839 7416841 7416847 7416869
7416889 7416917 7416931 7416961 7416977 7416991 7417009 7417021 7417037 7417061
7417093 7417097 7417099 7417121 7417141 7417169 7417177 7417213 7417217 7417237
7417259 7417261 7417273 7417307 7417309 7417313 7417331 7417337 7417357 7417373
7417393 7417411 7417439 7417447 7417453 7417481 7417507 7417511 7417513 7417517
7417519 7417549 7417577 7417607 7417609 7417621 7417633 7417643 7417673 7417691
7417693 7417717 7417747 7417757 7417759 7417769 7417789 7417829 7417849 7417853
7417859 7417873 7417877 7417901 7417909 7417987 7418003 7418023 7418051 7418071
7418077 7418087 7418107 7418141 7418153 7418183 7418209 7418219 7418233 7418237
7418261 7418309 7418311 7418347 7418371 7418377 7418387 7418419 7418423 7418447
7418449 7418459 7418473 7418491 7418497 7418501 7418503 7418507 7418539 7418557
7418591 7418599 7418603 7418639 7418669 7418689 7418699 7418707 7418711 7418729
7418731 7418737 7418767 7418779 7418791 7418813 7418839 7418849 7418863 7418869
7418893 7418899 7418927 7418933 7418941 7418947 7419007 7419019 7419029 7419031
7419037 7419043 7419047 7419067 7419077 7419079 7419103 7419107 7419109 7419119
7419131 7419143 7419151 7419161 7419163 7419169 7419173 7419187 7419197 7419221
7419227 7419299 7419301 7419337 7419341 7419353 7419383 7419407 7419413 7419421
7419431 7419437 7419439 7419457 7419469 7419553 7419569 7419583 7419623 7419637
7419641 7419649 7419673 7419677 7419689 7419691 7419697 7419719 7419743 7419751
7419761 7419767 7419773 7419787 7419799 7419809 7419851 7419889 7419913 7419931
7419967 7419983 7419991 7420001 7420003 7420009 7420033 7420043 7420069 7420073
7420079 7420097 7420111 7420121 7420141 7420157 7420169 7420181 7420187 7420199
7420207 7420213 7420243 7420261 7420277 7420289 7420307 7420333 7420337 7420339
7420363 7420397 7420409 7420411 7420447 7420459 7420463 7420481 7420493 7420499
7420519 7420529 7420531 7420537 7420561 7420573 7420577 7420579 7420591 7420601
7420613 7420643 7420661 7420681 7420691 7420703 7420709 7420727 7420729 7420733
7420739 7420741 7420753 7420769 7420801 7420807 7420813 7420837 7420883 7420913
7420921 7420939 7420943 7420951 7420969 7421003 7421009 7421017 7421021 7421033
7421083 7421093 7421101 7421131 7421137 7421143 7421173 7421207 7421213 7421237
7421251 7421257 7421261 7421263 7421329 7421357 7421363 7421371 7421383 7421437
7421471 7421489 7421509 7421539 7421563 7421569 7421587 7421633 7421641 7421677
7421681 7421683 7421693 7421717 7421759 7421773 7421797 7421807 7421831 7421833
7421849 7421851 7421857 7421863 7421891 7421923 7421963 7421987 7421993 7422001
7422011 7422017 7422049 7422061 7422071 7422083 7422091 7422097 7422131 7422143
7422167 7422199 7422203 7422211 7422221 7422223 7422227 7422229 7422253 7422263
7422277 7422281 7422301 7422313 7422323 7422341 7422379 7422383 7422391 7422397
7422403 7422409 7422413 7422431 7422433 7422449 7422469 7422473 7422479 7422487
7422497 7422539 7422551 7422589 7422641 7422643 7422647 7422683 7422691 7422719
7422743 7422781 7422827 7422839 7422841 7422871 7422887 7422893 7422913 7422937
7422949 7422959 7423007 7423019 7423027 7423037 7423049 7423057 7423069 7423079
7423103 7423109 7423111 7423153 7423187 7423193 7423211 7423231 7423249 7423253
7423261 7423267 7423301 7423307 7423327 7423331 7423343 7423349 7423363 7423369
7423379 7423387 7423417 7423453 7423463 7423487 7423489 7423499 7423511 7423513
7423541 7423607 7423609 7423621 7423631 7423673 7423693 7423711 7423723 7423727
7423751 7423753 7423783 7423799 7423807 7423841 7423847 7423859 7423873 7423879
7423903 7423909 7423929 7423949 7423951 7423967 7423969 7423981 7423991 7424017
7424023 7424033 7424051 7424063 7424071 7424083 7424107 7424119 7424141 7424149
7424201 7424233 7424243 7424273 7424279 7424299 7424363 7424369 7424381 7424401
7424413 7424419 7424437 7424467 7424507 7424513 7424533 7424537 7424539 7424569
7424579 7424581 7424617 7424629 7424633 7424663 7424693 7424701 7424707 7424719
```

```
7424723  7424761  7424789  7424797  7424849  7424861  7424887  7424897  7424909  7424927
7424933  7424951  7424959  7424983  7424993  7424999  7425023  7425037  7425043  7425053
7425083  7425133  7425149  7425157  7425161  7425169  7425179  7425191  7425193  7425199
7425203  7425227  7425233  7425239  7425259  7425281  7425307  7425329  7425331  7425349
7425361  7425377  7425391  7425401  7425403  7425437  7425443  7425449  7425463  7425503
7425529  7425533  7425547  7425553  7425557  7425571  7425581  7425601  7425611  7425623
7425631  7425661  7425667  7425683  7425689  7425703  7425707  7425721  7425731  7425739
7425749  7425773  7425809  7425829  7425839  7425841  7425857  7425877  7425881  7425911
7425919  7425931  7425959  7425967  7425973  7425983  7426031  7426039  7426051  7426063
7426073  7426087  7426091  7426099  7426109  7426129  7426151  7426157  7426163  7426183
7426187  7426189  7426193  7426219  7426231  7426253  7426261  7426273  7426277  7426301
7426319  7426333  7426351  7426357  7426361  7426373  7426379  7426411  7426421  7426451
7426457  7426477  7426483  7426537  7426541  7426543  7426547  7426583  7426589  7426597
7426613  7426621  7426649  7426651  7426667  7426669  7426673  7426681  7426687  7426691
7426693  7426709  7426721  7426733  7426747  7426789  7426817  7426823  7426849  7426873
7426877  7426901  7426931  7426957  7426963  7426981  7427009  7427023  7427029  7427033
7427041  7427051  7427053  7427083  7427099  7427117  7427131  7427141  7427149  7427159
7427209  7427221  7427281  7427323  7427327  7427339  7427353  7427443  7427447  7427449
7427467  7427477  7427479  7427503  7427533  7427561  7427573  7427591  7427593  7427611
7427617  7427663  7427699  7427731  7427731  7427737  7427779  7427789  7427809  7427813
7427867  7427869  7427887  7427891  7427899  7427921  7427933  7427939  7427947  7427951
7427957  7427977  7428007  7428013  7428017  7428019  7428037  7428067  7428079
7428119  7428151  7428173  7428191  7428203  7428217  7428227  7428271  7428283  7428301
7428307  7428341  7428349  7428383  7428389  7428399  7428401  7428409  7428413  7428419
7428431  7428433  7428457  7428461  7428469  7428521  7428529  7428539  7428571  7428581
7428587  7428593  7428599  7428649  7428653  7428671  7428683  7428691  7428697  7428703
7428713  7428731  7428737  7428761  7428767  7428781  7428803  7428821  7428833  7428859
7428877  7428887  7428899  7428917  7428929  7428937  7428997  7429001  7429003  7429013
7429021  7429031  7429039  7429087  7429091  7429109  7429111  7429151  7429157  7429183
7429199  7429211  7429223  7429231  7429271  7429273  7429277  7429291  7429313  7429319
7429343  7429363  7429379  7429421  7429439  7429441  7429451  7429463  7429469  7429517
7429523  7429531  7429547  7429559  7429573  7429577  7429607  7429633  7429649  7429673
7429679  7429687  7429729  7429757  7429777  7429783  7429837  7429843  7429879  7429883
7429907  7429913  7429951  7429963  7429999  7430003  7430023  7430039  7430041  7430051
7430053  7430057  7430069  7430107  7430113  7430117  7430131  7430141  7430147  7430149
7430153  7430161  7430167  7430179  7430201  7430209  7430237  7430239  7430251  7430263
7430279  7430281  7430299  7430329  7430333  7430341  7430383  7430393  7430419  7430429
7430447  7430453  7430459  7430477  7430537  7430557  7430561  7430567  7430569  7430611
7430617  7430623  7430629  7430651  7430663  7430667  7430707  7430711  7430737
7430777  7430783  7430791  7430803  7430807  7430809  7430831  7430893  7430923  7430939
7430947  7430981  7430987  7431013  7431019  7431031  7431049  7431089  7431097  7431107
7431119  7431143  7431157  7431167  7431169  7431173  7431199  7431211  7431247  7431253
7431269  7431271  7431283  7431331  7431343  7431353  7431367  7431377  7431379  7431419
7431447  7431449  7431467  7431481  7431491  7431493  7431497  7431503  7431517  7431521
7431551  7431563  7431577  7431583  7431587  7431617  7431637  7431643  7431649  7431689
7431719  7431727  7431731  7431751  7431757  7431769  7431773  7431779  7431791  7431797
7431799  7431821  7431833  7431871  7431881  7431889  7431923  7431929  7431937  7431959
7431961  7431973  7431979  7431989  7431997  7432003  7432027  7432037  7432081  7432093
7432099  7432127  7432129  7432141  7432147  7432177  7432181  7432231  7432261  7432273
7432277  7432279  7432307  7432309  7432319  7432331  7432391  7432409  7432457  7432459
7432471  7432483  7432487  7432499  7432501  7432517  7432543  7432571  7432573  7432619
7432639  7432651  7432693  7432751  7432753  7432759  7432769  7432793  7432807  7432823
7432853  7432871  7432877  7432883  7432889  7432891  7432907  7432921  7432939  7432951
7432973  7432981  7432987  7432993  7433011  7433017  7433021  7433039  7433051  7433053
7433057  7433059  7433093  7433119  7433141  7433143  7433159  7433171  7433213  7433219
7433227  7433269  7433299  7433317  7433323  7433339  7433357  7433359  7433381
7433429  7433431  7433441  7433497  7433501  7433507  7433509  7433519  7433527  7433533
7433537  7433549  7433593  7433609  7433639  7433653  7433659  7433681  7433683  7433689
7433719  7433737  7433747  7433749  7433753  7433843  7433861  7433863  7433869  7433873
7433891  7433897  7433927  7433953  7433957  7433971  7433989  7433999  7434001  7434013
7434041  7434047  7434071  7434103  7434109  7434113  7434143  7434169  7434181  7434223
7434241  7434269  7434283  7434311  7434337  7434341  7434347  7434367  7434397  7434409
7434419  7434431  7434433  7434443  7434461  7434463  7434499  7434503  7434517  7434523
7434551  7434569  7434587  7434599  7434607  7434613  7434641  7434659  7434683  7434697
7434703  7434709  7434731  7434733  7434737  7434799  7434803  7434821  7434851  7434857
7434859  7434877  7434887  7434901  7434949  7434989  7434997  7435013  7435019
7435027  7435031  7435033  7435067  7435081  7435093  7435097  7435111  7435117  7435139
7435151  7435157  7435159  7435163  7435177  7435193  7435199  7435247  7435277  7435291
7435303  7435331  7435349  7435361  7435369  7435399  7435411  7435451  7435453  7435457
7435471  7435499  7435501  7435531  7435553  7435577  7435583  7435591  7435609  7435619
7435621  7435633  7435639  7435657  7435663  7435667  7435709  7435733  7435763  7435789
7435793  7435807  7435819  7435843  7435867  7435873  7435891  7435903  7435907  7435913
7435921  7435931  7435933  7435951  7435957  7435963  7435979  7435997  7436027
7436069  7436071  7436081  7436111  7436113  7436131  7436137  7436141  7436147  7436161
7436171  7436227  7436257  7436269  7436279  7436287  7436309  7436323  7436339  7436347
7436369  7436389  7436399  7436411  7436423  7436447  7436453  7436459  7436479  7436489
7436491  7436509  7436587  7436591  7436609  7436629  7436647  7436707  7436713  7436719
7436777  7436783  7436833  7436839  7436881  7436887  7436899  7436921  7436941
7436971  7436983  7436987  7437029  7437047  7437061  7437071  7437077  7437083  7437091
7437103  7437121  7437149  7437161  7437163  7437191  7437217  7437293  7437299  7437301
7437329  7437361  7437371  7437373  7437383  7437389  7437401  7437413  7437431  7437457
7437461  7437491  7437497  7437499  7437503  7437511  7437553  7437557  7437587  7437589
7437611  7437623  7437631  7437637  7437697  7437701  7437707  7437709  7437739
7437743  7437757  7437761  7437779  7437803  7437887  7437917  7437971  7437973
7438001  7438033  7438037  7438091  7438099  7438117  7438127  7438153  7438169  7438213
7438217  7438219  7438241  7438247  7438271  7438289  7438309  7438331  7438337  7438339
7438349  7438363  7438373  7438381  7438399  7438423  7438427  7438433  7438439  7438447
7438463  7438477  7438489  7438493  7438511  7438513  7438547  7438567  7438597  7438619
7438621  7438631  7438663  7438687  7438693  7438721  7438727  7438759  7438777  7438787
```

```
7438789 7438793 7438801 7438807 7438829 7438841 7438891 7438901 7438909 7438927
7438931 7438939 7438967 7438973 7438987 7438997 7439023 7439053 7439059 7439083
7439087 7439093 7439099 7439111 7439147 7439153 7439161 7439177 7439191 7439197
7439209 7439213 7439219 7439231 7439233 7439269 7439273 7439297 7439323 7439339
7439347 7439371 7439401 7439407 7439417 7439423 7439449 7439459 7439477 7439501
7439527 7439543 7439561 7439567 7439569 7439623 7439639 7439647 7439651 7439669
7439671 7439681 7439687 7439699 7439717 7439749 7439767 7439791 7439801 7439813
7439827 7439843 7439851 7439857 7439867 7439909 7439917 7439933 7439951 7439953
7439977 7440011 7440047 7440049 7440061 7440089 7440091 7440107 7440113 7440127
7440151 7440163 7440187 7440221 7440227 7440263 7440289 7440317 7440319 7440347
7440383 7440397 7440409 7440413 7440421 7440427 7440437 7440467 7440469 7440481
7440491 7440529 7440539 7440547 7440583 7440593 7440619 7440637 7440649 7440659
7440689 7440691 7440703 7440709 7440731 7440739 7440749 7440757 7440767 7440779
7440821 7440857 7440859 7440869 7440893 7440943 7440947 7440997 7441003
7441009 7441037 7441039 7441061 7441067 7441073 7441097 7441099 7441111 7441123
7441127 7441151 7441153 7441157 7441177 7441183 7441219 7441229 7441237 7441243
7441261 7441283 7441289 7441319 7441339 7441349 7441363 7441367 7441381 7441387
7441391 7441409 7441411 7441417 7441471 7441513 7441523 7441561 7441583 7441591
7441601 7441607 7441619 7441633 7441639 7441657 7441663 7441667 7441669 7441691
7441739 7441747 7441751 7441769 7441771 7441793 7441823 7441831 7441849 7441867
7441871 7441877 7441883 7441897 7441909 7441927 7441961 7441963 7441969 7441981
7441997 7441999 7442023 7442047 7442081 7442093 7442117 7442119 7442137 7442147
7442153 7442161 7442189 7442203 7442213 7442231 7442233 7442249 7442333 7442339
7442341 7442371 7442377 7442381 7442399 7442431 7442453 7442459 7442467 7442489
7442507 7442521 7442551 7442557 7442563 7442621 7442627 7442653 7442657 7442663
7442681 7442749 7442767 7442783 7442797 7442801 7442823 7442843 7442863 7442867
7442881 7442887 7442893 7442917 7442933 7442947 7442951 7442959 7442969 7442983
7442987 7442989 7443011 7443013 7443043 7443047 7443067 7443077 7443083 7443091
7443109 7443113 7443119 7443133 7443157 7443167 7443173 7443199 7443203 7443209
7443211 7443221 7443223 7443239 7443259 7443277 7443287 7443313 7443323 7443349
7443367 7443377 7443389 7443407 7443413 7443419 7443431 7443451 7443473 7443481
7443487 7443493 7443539 7443563 7443571 7443577 7443587 7443607 7443613 7443629
7443643 7443679 7443727 7443757 7443803 7443809 7443811 7443823 7443833 7443889
7443899 7443911 7443941 7443949 7443959 7443979 7444027 7444033 7444043 7444049
7444081 7444093 7444109 7444153 7444159 7444163 7444183 7444193 7444201 7444223
7444231 7444243 7444253 7444267 7444273 7444277 7444301 7444313 7444319
7444331 7444343 7444357 7444361 7444369 7444397 7444399 7444403 7444427 7444429
7444439 7444441 7444457 7444477 7444483 7444499 7444529 7444559 7444579 7444597
7444601 7444621 7444627 7444631 7444639 7444643 7444649 7444651 7444669 7444673
7444687 7444721 7444727 7444729 7444757 7444771 7444781 7444799 7444813 7444823
7444841 7444859 7444873 7444883 7444889 7444937 7444947 7444949 7444961
7444961 7444981 7444993 7445003 7445023 7445047 7445159 7445161 7445173 7445189
7445203 7445219 7445237 7445279 7445287 7445293 7445299 7445309 7445311 7445323
7445327 7445369 7445377 7445393 7445437 7445441 7445443 7445461 7445467 7445479
7445519 7445521 7445527 7445531 7445551 7445569 7445593 7445597 7445639 7445653
7445687 7445689 7445707 7445719 7445729 7445731 7445749 7445759 7445761 7445771
7445773 7445803 7445831 7445839 7445857 7445869 7445873 7445897 7445939 7445941
7445959 7445989 7445993 7446001 7446053 7446067 7446071 7446079 7446083 7446097
7446121 7446149 7446151 7446167 7446191 7446211 7446223 7446239 7446247 7446253
7446259 7446269 7446277 7446317 7446337 7446343 7446349 7446367 7446377 7446407
7446419 7446421 7446431 7446443 7446463 7446469 7446487 7446557 7446589 7446601
7446617 7446623 7446631 7446643 7446679 7446709 7446739 7446743 7446763 7446773
7446793 7446839 7446853 7446883 7446889 7446911 7446931 7446941 7446947 7446961
7446979 7447007 7447019 7447021 7447043 7447049 7447051 7447057 7447061 7447067
7447073 7447079 7447081 7447087 7447091 7447109 7447123 7447133 7447151 7447163
7447201 7447211 7447217 7447243 7447247 7447267 7447277 7447289 7447303 7447313
7447333 7447357 7447361 7447399 7447417 7447439 7447459 7447483 7447493 7447499
7447501 7447523 7447529 7447537 7447541 7447549 7447589 7447597 7447631 7447637
7447651 7447669 7447681 7447697 7447703 7447721 7447763 7447771 7447777 7447789
7447799 7447801 7447813 7447877 7447879 7447889 7447903 7447919 7447933 7447939
7447961 7447963 7447991 7447997 7448003 7448017 7448027 7448047 7448053 7448059
7448069 7448071 7448081 7448083 7448087 7448093 7448107 7448131 7448141 7448149
7448167 7448179 7448269 7448291 7448293 7448303 7448331 7448333 7448351 7448387
7448407 7448453 7448471 7448473 7448477 7448479 7448489 7448491 7448501 7448509
7448521 7448537 7448543 7448557 7448561 7448569 7448579 7448599 7448603 7448629
7448633 7448641 7448647 7448657 7448663 7448687 7448689 7448699 7448713 7448717
7448719 7448723 7448743 7448797 7448813 7448821 7448863 7448867 7448887 7448923
7448953 7448971 7449011 7449017 7449023 7449037 7449047 7449059 7449067 7449103
7449133 7449151 7449181 7449187 7449193 7449199 7449209 7449223 7449227 7449229
7449241 7449271 7449287 7449289 7449301 7449307 7449313 7449319 7449329 7449341
7449353 7449367 7449373 7449397 7449461 7449473 7449487 7449509 7449511 7449523
7449581 7449613 7449619 7449623 7449643 7449667 7449679 7449683 7449721 7449731
7449737 7449749 7449773 7449787 7449809 7449811 7449821 7449823 7449847 7449853
7449857 7449863 7449877 7449941 7449971 7449973 7449979 7450007 7450021 7450031
7450039 7450043 7450067 7450073 7450099 7450117 7450123 7450127 7450139 7450169
7450171 7450181 7450193 7450211 7450213 7450231 7450249 7450277 7450291 7450297
7450349 7450351 7450409 7450427 7450463 7450501 7450507 7450511 7450519 7450523
7450537 7450543 7450549 7450559 7450577 7450589 7450609 7450637 7450673 7450693
7450699 7450721 7450747 7450763 7450787 7450789 7450823 7450829 7450837 7450843
7450859 7450867 7450889 7450901 7450909 7450921 7450931 7450969 7450987 7451009
7451033 7451071 7451161 7451167 7451177 7451179 7451189 7451203 7451209 7451221
7451261 7451263 7451267 7451273 7451281 7451309 7451317 7451351 7451369 7451387
7451399 7451413 7451417 7451419 7451441 7451449 7451461 7451471 7451473 7451551
7451557 7451581 7451597 7451603 7451617 7451623 7451669 7451671 7451677 7451681
7451693 7451699 7451711 7451713 7451723 7451777 7451789 7451809 7451813 7451849
7451861 7451867 7451879 7451891 7451893 7451909 7451957 7451963 7451981 7451987
7451993 7452007 7452013 7452017 7452019 7452077 7452079 7452091 7452127 7452143
7452157 7452163 7452169 7452191 7452223 7452271 7452293 7452301 7452311 7452317
7452323 7452329 7452337 7452377 7452397 7452407 7452433 7452451 7452457 7452469
```

7452479 7452491 7452499 7452509 7452521 7452527 7452547 7452559 7452563 7452569
7452583 7452587 7452619 7452659 7452673 7452691 7452719 7452727 7452751 7452773
7452787 7452791 7452811 7452827 7452829 7452833 7452839 7452859 7452869 7452877
7452901 7452917 7452923 7452961 7452967 7452979 7453003 7453007 7453009 7453027
7453031 7453049 7453063 7453067 7453079 7453133 7453181 7453223 7453241 7453247
7453253 7453297 7453309 7453321 7453343 7453363 7453409 7453421 7453441 7453447
7453451 7453471 7453477 7453487 7453499 7453517 7453553 7453561 7453573 7453583
7453601 7453603 7453637 7453639 7453657 7453697 7453703 7453709 7453723 7453753
7453799 7453807 7453829 7453843 7453847 7453861 7453879 7453891 7453933 7453961
7453967 7453987 7453991 7454021 7454053 7454063 7454071 7454081 7454101 7454107
7454113 7454129 7454149 7454173 7454191 7454201 7454207 7454243 7454257 7454269
7454273 7454281 7454297 7454303 7454309 7454311 7454357 7454387 7454389 7454399
7454411 7454413 7454423 7454467 7454471 7454521 7454533 7454563 7454611 7454639
7454641 7454651 7454701 7454731 7454753 7454767 7454779 7454791 7454807 7454809
7454851 7454861 7454869 7454879 7454899 7454903 7454933 7454947 7454957 7454969
7454971 7454983 7455017 7455029 7455031 7455053 7455067 7455073 7455083 7455101
7455103 7455109 7455121 7455179 7455193 7455223 7455257 7455269 7455307 7455373
7455379 7455431 7455433 7455443 7455479 7455493 7455499 7455527 7455533 7455541
7455551 7455577 7455583 7455587 7455589 7455599 7455601 7455629 7455631 7455649
7455659 7455667 7455671 7455683 7455691 7455737 7455739 7455743 7455769 7455803
7455823 7455829 7455863 7455893 7455901 7455913 7455937 7455947 7455949 7455977
7455983 7455991 7455997 7456003 7456021 7456039 7456051 7456061 7456063 7456121
7456159 7456171 7456177 7456181 7456187 7456231 7456237 7456247 7456249 7456259
7456261 7456271 7456279 7456283 7456289 7456291 7456321 7456327 7456333 7456357
7456373 7456381 7456429 7456433 7456441 7456459 7456481 7456483 7456507 7456511
7456513 7456549 7456583 7456601 7456609 7456613 7456619 7456621 7456639 7456663
7456667 7456733 7456739 7456747 7456751 7456769 7456783 7456811 7456837 7456843
7456859 7456861 7456901 7456907 7456909 7456921 7456963 7456997 7457011 7457053
7457071 7457077 7457111 7457113 7457123 7457133 7457137 7457141 7457159 7457171
7457179 7457231 7457243 7457257 7457269 7457273 7457279 7457287 7457299 7457309
7457323 7457347 7457357 7457371 7457419 7457477 7457479 7457503 7457561 7457573
7457581 7457587 7457591 7457603 7457621 7457629 7457641 7457647 7457687 7457689
7457693 7457707 7457711 7457717 7457731 7457759 7457771 7457797 7457803 7457833
7457839 7457867 7457881 7457909 7457927 7457929 7457953 7457987 7457997 7457999
7458029 7458047 7458067 7458083 7458103 7458119 7458137 7458151 7458167 7458169
7458173 7458179 7458193 7458211 7458229 7458263 7458271 7458281 7458299 7458313
7458379 7458389 7458403 7458419 7458421 7458443 7458449 7458487 7458499 7458511
7458523 7458527 7458533 7458551 7458559 7458587 7458589 7458593 7458611 7458613
7458623 7458643 7458667 7458683 7458707 7458797 7458809 7458827 7458833 7458883
7458889 7458907 7458917 7458931 7458949 7458953 7458959 7458989 7458991 7459013
7459027 7459033 7459037 7459057 7459069 7459079 7459087 7459093 7459097 7459121
7459139 7459147 7459159 7459169 7459181 7459183 7459201 7459211 7459247 7459261
7459279 7459297 7459301 7459321 7459349 7459367 7459373 7459399 7459421 7459433
7459451 7459477 7459479 7459493 7459531 7459559 7459577 7459601 7459603 7459619
7459637 7459649 7459667 7459679 7459693 7459703 7459709 7459717 7459721 7459801
7459811 7459813 7459831 7459841 7459867 7459883 7459897 7459907 7459937 7459967
7459997 7459999 7460003 7460017 7460039 7460053 7460071 7460077 7460087 7460111
7460129 7460143 7460149 7460191 7460197 7460203 7460209 7460231 7460251 7460261
7460291 7460317 7460329 7460351 7460419 7460423 7460437 7460449 7460459 7460461
7460471 7460477 7460489 7460503 7460507 7460513 7460611 7460617 7460623 7460641
7460653 7460657 7460669 7460683 7460693 7460699 7460731 7460737 7460741 7460753
7460771 7460777 7460779 7460813 7460833 7460837 7460851 7460857 7460861 7460879
7460881 7460891 7460897 7460927 7460951 7460983 7460989 7461007 7461017 7461019
7461029 7461031 7461043 7461073 7461089 7461101 7461121 7461127 7461169 7461193
7461211 7461247 7461299 7461329 7461343 7461353 7461371 7461397 7461401 7461469
7461479 7461491 7461527 7461529 7461557 7461563 7461569 7461599 7461611 7461647
7461653 7461667 7461677 7461689 7461697 7461757 7461761 7461763 7461781 7461809
7461847 7461869 7461941 7461943 7461983 7462033 7462043 7462057 7462111 7462127
7462151 7462157 7462159 7462199 7462223 7462229 7462243 7462277 7462319 7462321
7462333 7462381 7462387 7462391 7462397 7462457 7462463 7462471 7462487 7462513
7462523 7462529 7462547 7462549 7462579 7462583 7462589 7462591 7462601 7462619
7462621 7462627 7462639 7462691 7462703 7462727 7462747 7462751 7462753 7462769
7462799 7462817 7462823 7462841 7462843 7462849 7462853 7462907 7462913 7462919
7462921 7462927 7462957 7462967 7462979 7462981 7462997 7462999 7463021 7463039
7463041 7463059 7463077 7463081 7463101 7463147 7463149 7463171 7463191 7463207
7463213 7463227 7463231 7463249 7463279 7463297 7463317 7463321 7463329 7463341
7463347 7463359 7463363 7463377 7463387 7463399 7463413 7463429 7463453 7463461
7463497 7463501 7463509 7463549 7463551 7463563 7463567 7463579 7463581 7463657
7463669 7463671 7463693 7463699 7463723 7463737 7463747 7463761 7463773 7463783
7463791 7463801 7463803 7463809 7463843 7463873 7463879 7463881 7463887 7463921
7463923 7463947 7463953 7463959 7463971 7464007 7464013 7464019 7464059 7464073
7464113 7464137 7464179 7464187 7464199 7464217 7464227 7464229 7464239 7464253
7464263 7464271 7464289 7464313 7464329 7464371 7464407 7464409 7464421 7464433
7464461 7464463 7464517 7464529 7464533 7464551 7464553 7464557 7464559 7464563
7464577 7464593 7464617 7464623 7464703 7464731 7464749 7464763 7464767 7464799
7464823 7464833 7464839 7464841 7464851 7464859 7464871 7464881 7464883 7464889
7464901 7464913 7464923 7464943 7464959 7464979 7465013 7465027 7465039 7465063
7465097 7465099 7465109 7465111 7465121 7465127 7465169 7465189 7465219 7465243
7465291 7465303 7465307 7465313 7465331 7465333 7465343 7465357 7465369 7465373
7465387 7465399 7465429 7465439 7465481 7465483 7465487 7465489 7465511 7465529
7465573 7465583 7465603 7465631 7465657 7465663 7465681 7465687 7465693 7465697
7465723 7465741 7465747 7465751 7465753 7465763 7465769 7465793 7465831 7465837
7465857 7465867 7465891 7465937 7465957 7465959 7466003 7466093 7466101 7466131
7466149 7466159 7466167 7466189 7466201 7466209 7466231 7466233 7466243 7466287
7466293 7466323 7466359 7466377 7466401 7466419 7466423 7466429 7466441 7466447
7466453 7466471 7466483 7466491 7466531 7466549 7466579 7466581 7466593 7466611
7466647 7466653 7466671 7466699 7466713 7466729 7466731 7466741 7466747 7466759
7466773 7466807 7466813 7466819 7466831 7466839 7466861 7466873 7466887 7466917
7466959 7466969 7466989 7467023 7467037 7467049 7467059 7467073 7467107 7467121

```
7467127  7467137  7467139  7467143  7467151  7467167  7467169  7467197  7467221  7467253
7467259  7467281  7467307  7467347  7467401  7467409  7467431  7467443  7467457  7467469
7467487  7467503  7467511  7467563  7467611  7467631  7467659  7467661  7467667  7467671
7467697  7467721  7467737  7467751  7467763  7467773  7467793  7467799  7467841  7467857
7467871  7467881  7467899  7467907  7467959  7467979  7467989  7467991  7467997  7468001
7468009  7468037  7468039  7468061  7468063  7468067  7468093  7468103  7468129  7468147
7468157  7468183  7468187  7468189  7468199  7468207  7468211  7468213  7468229  7468249
7468259  7468313  7468319  7468337  7468367  7468381  7468393  7468403  7468429  7468451
7468453  7468459  7468507  7468523  7468529  7468543  7468547  7468567  7468597  7468607
7468619  7468651  7468663  7468667  7468679  7468693  7468697  7468711  7468733  7468753
7468759  7468771  7468781  7468787  7468793  7468801  7468807  7468819  7468841  7468871
7468891  7468927  7468943  7468973  7468991  7468999  7469009  7469017  7469027  7469039
7469053  7469081  7469083  7469101  7469107  7469113  7469117  7469123  7469159  7469177
7469179  7469183  7469207  7469243  7469249  7469279  7469303  7469309  7469311  7469317
7469347  7469351  7469353  7469359  7469369  7469387  7469393  7469431  7469447  7469453
7469461  7469507  7469521  7469537  7469591  7469593  7469599  7469653  7469669  7469669
7469741  7469753  7469771  7469773  7469789  7469797  7469807  7469837  7469843  7469857
7469881  7469887  7469899  7469911  7469921  7469923  7469933  7469939  7469941  7469947
7469951  7469993  7470007  7470079  7470103  7470107  7470137  7470143  7470149  7470179
7470181  7470187  7470223  7470233  7470247  7470255  7470257  7470271  7470283  7470301
7470311  7470329  7470367  7470383  7470389  7470391  7470427  7470443  7470457  7470461
7470467  7470479  7470481  7470499  7470511  7470527  7470611  7470613  7470623  7470637
7470641  7470643  7470647  7470677  7470689  7470703  7470709  7470713  7470761  7470763
7470767  7470773  7470809  7470811  7470821  7470823  7470839  7470851  7470887  7470889
7470919  7470941  7470961  7470977  7470989  7471033  7471049  7471081  7471099  7471127
7471133  7471147  7471157  7471171  7471193  7471213  7471249  7471271  7471291  7471301
7471309  7471339  7471349  7471361  7471367  7471369  7471391  7471393  7471417  7471423
7471439  7471441  7471501  7471511  7471549  7471561  7471571  7471591  7471601  7471603
7471621  7471649  7471679  7471691  7471733  7471771  7471801  7471811  7471831  7471873
7471889  7471897  7471913  7471931  7471939  7471943  7471957  7471967  7471973  7471979
7471991  7471999  7472011  7472051  7472063  7472089  7472123  7472161  7472167  7472177
7472189  7472191  7472221  7472237  7472243  7472273  7472293  7472321  7472323  7472359
7472369  7472383  7472419  7472429  7472431  7472449  7472461  7472489  7472513  7472533
7472579  7472587  7472603  7472609  7472611  7472617  7472627  7472659  7472693  7472737
7472747  7472761  7472771  7472819  7472827  7472849  7472863  7472867  7472869  7472873
7472893  7472903  7472921  7472929  7472951  7472989  7473007  7473017  7473031  7473041
7473101  7473119  7473121  7473127  7473143  7473173  7473203  7473209  7473211  7473227
7473233  7473253  7473259  7473281  7473287  7473299  7473307  7473311  7473313  7473317
7473331  7473337  7473341  7473359  7473373  7473377  7473383  7473391  7473397  7473451
7473461  7473463  7473467  7473491  7473493  7473509  7473541  7473553  7473581  7473607
7473617  7473623  7473679  7473709  7473731  7473733  7473743  7473779  7473797  7473811
7473833  7473839  7473841  7473871  7473887  7473913  7473923  7473929  7473937  7473979
7474001  7474003  7474009  7474031  7474063  7474073  7474079  7474097  7474109  7474121
7474123  7474153  7474171  7474183  7474189  7474211  7474213  7474223  7474267  7474273
7474283  7474289  7474301  7474307  7474321  7474343  7474361  7474367  7474381  7474387
7474393  7474409  7474417  7474421  7474443  7474459  7474463  7474469  7474477  7474483
7474499  7474501  7474507  7474553  7474559  7474567  7474573  7474591  7474603  7474631
7474633  7474661  7474673  7474681  7474693  7474711  7474717  7474759  7474783  7474799
7474801  7474807  7474823  7474829  7474867  7474871  7474877  7474887  7474903  7474933
7474939  7474949  7474967  7474969  7474979  7475009  7475029  7475033  7475047  7475057
7475071  7475081  7475089  7475101  7475107  7475129  7475137  7475141  7475159  7475179
7475197  7475201  7475213  7475233  7475261  7475263  7475267  7475287  7475317  7475327
7475333  7475357  7475381  7475383  7475387  7475389  7475411  7475441  7475453  7475459
7475467  7475473  7475509  7475521  7475527  7475537  7475543  7475551  7475581  7475599
7475603  7475609  7475617  7475623  7475627  7475639  7475641  7475647  7475651  7475687
7475701  7475723  7475737  7475747  7475749  7475761  7475771  7475789  7475807  7475827
7475861  7475891  7475917  7475921  7475933  7475947  7475957  7475959  7475999  7476013
7476017  7476019  7476043  7476047  7476071  7476083  7476137  7476143  7476151  7476167
7476211  7476247  7476251  7476263  7476283  7476289  7476307  7476319  7476341  7476349
7476353  7476377  7476383  7476397  7476409  7476433  7476437  7476439  7476451  7476467
7476493  7476499  7476527  7476529  7476559  7476569  7476589  7476593  7476607  7476613
7476641  7476643  7476653  7476659  7476661  7476683  7476691  7476697  7476739  7476743
7476767  7476773  7476779  7476793  7476803  7476829  7476841  7476851  7476853  7476877
7476919  7476941  7476947  7476961  7476971  7477007  7477021  7477031  7477037  7477069
7477103  7477109  7477111  7477117  7477121  7477123  7477147  7477159  7477163  7477177
7477181  7477189  7477193  7477243  7477259  7477289  7477303  7477307  7477321  7477339
7477357  7477361  7477391  7477403  7477409  7477427  7477451  7477453  7477471  7477493
7477499  7477511  7477517  7477523  7477543  7477573  7477577  7477627  7477643  7477651
7477661  7477667  7477711  7477733  7477741  7477751  7477777  7477781  7477787  7477801
7477817  7477831  7477861  7477889  7477919  7477927  7477961  7477979  7477991  7477993
7477997  7477999  7478017  7478069  7478089  7478111  7478117  7478129  7478131  7478137
7478189  7478203  7478209  7478257  7478269  7478279  7478287  7478293  7478299  7478327
7478333  7478357  7478363  7478369  7478371  7478389  7478407  7478411  7478413  7478423
7478447  7478467  7478479  7478507  7478543  7478563  7478567  7478573  7478579  7478587
7478621  7478629  7478633  7478661  7478677  7478683  7478701  7478707  7478717  7478729
7478743  7478753  7478767  7478771  7478791  7478813  7478831  7478869  7478873  7478893
7478941  7478959  7478971  7478983  7479001  7479019  7479037  7479053  7479061  7479089
7479113  7479127  7479137  7479161  7479191  7479203  7479223  7479229  7479233  7479257
7479259  7479281  7479289  7479299  7479341  7479349  7479391  7479397  7479421  7479427
7479431  7479467  7479469  7479487  7479491  7479497  7479503  7479517  7479539  7479547
7479557  7479599  7479601  7479611  7479617  7479629  7479631  7479683  7479691  7479697
7479701  7479727  7479733  7479737  7479743  7479803  7479811  7479817  7479821  7479839
7479841  7479851  7479859  7479887  7479911  7479929  7479931  7479937  7479971  7480013
7480027  7480069  7480093  7480111  7480127  7480147  7480157  7480159  7480171  7480177
7480181  7480199  7480219  7480223  7480249  7480259  7480271  7480283  7480301  7480307
7480339  7480351  7480397  7480411  7480441  7480457  7480481  7480511  7480513  7480519
7480591  7480597  7480601  7480607  7480619  7480639  7480651  7480657  7480673  7480679
7480687  7480721  7480723  7480729  7480741  7480757  7480763  7480769  7480783  7480793
7480817  7480829  7480831  7480853  7480861  7480903  7480909  7480933  7480937  7481009
```

```
7481021 7481051 7481083 7481087 7481093 7481107 7481143 7481167 7481179 7481191
7481197 7481203 7481209 7481219 7481249 7481263 7481281 7481291 7481293 7481297
7481317 7481339 7481351 7481359 7481381 7481387 7481389 7481401 7481407 7481491
7481503 7481531 7481543 7481549 7481563 7481567 7481587 7481599 7481603 7481609
7481629 7481653 7481701 7481713 7481723 7481753 7481759 7481779 7481783 7481809
7481857 7481861 7481879 7481911 7481917 7481927 7481933 7481939 7481983 7481987
7481993 7482001 7482017 7482037 7482053 7482089 7482113 7482119 7482121 7482157
7482161 7482173 7482179 7482217 7482221 7482239 7482263 7482269 7482283 7482287
7482311 7482313 7482317 7482323 7482331 7482347 7482389 7482407 7482421 7482451
7482469 7482479 7482539 7482569 7482577 7482583 7482611 7482647 7482649 7482653
7482661 7482679 7482689 7482691 7482697 7482701 7482733 7482743 7482757 7482767
7482779 7482781 7482799 7482821 7482829 7482857 7482859 7482863 7482877
7482883 7482901 7482949 7482961 7482983 7483001 7483013 7483019 7483037 7483039
7483057 7483079 7483109 7483127 7483141 7483153 7483159 7483171 7483237 7483241
7483243 7483253 7483271 7483277 7483309 7483313 7483319 7483327 7483337 7483339
7483373 7483379 7483391 7483403 7483423 7483447 7483457 7483477 7483559 7483561
7483577 7483601 7483603 7483627 7483643 7483659 7483661 7483681 7483691
7483733 7483747 7483781 7483783 7483787 7483789 7483813 7483829 7483837 7483843
7483867 7483871 7483913 7483933 7483939 7483969 7483979 7483981 7483991
7484003 7484011 7484023 7484041 7484047 7484089 7484093 7484111 7484129 7484149
7484159 7484189 7484251 7484261 7484287 7484293 7484297 7484303 7484311 7484317
7484333 7484341 7484357 7484363 7484371 7484377 7484383 7484401 7484413 7484429
7484431 7484441 7484473 7484483 7484489 7484513 7484551 7484557 7484567 7484579
7484593 7484599 7484657 7484699 7484707 7484723 7484731 7484747 7484779 7484783
7484801 7484809 7484833 7484839 7484843 7484861 7484899 7484923 7484927 7484933
7484941 7484963 7485019 7485047 7485061 7485073 7485077 7485089 7485091 7485131
7485133 7485187 7485193 7485197 7485227 7485251 7485263 7485293 7485299 7485301
7485337 7485341 7485367 7485377 7485383 7485391 7485403 7485427 7485437 7485561
7485469 7485473 7485479 7485497 7485503 7485529 7485551 7485571 7485623 7485631
7485637 7485641 7485659 7485679 7485689 7485691 7485697 7485707 7485713 7485721
7485727 7485749 7485757 7485809 7485811 7485823 7485837 7485851 7485869 7485889
7485893 7485901 7485941 7485949 7485953 7485997 7486009 7486013 7486033 7486043
7486051 7486079 7486093 7486139 7486163 7486187 7486189 7486217 7486243 7486253
7486261 7486279 7486289 7486309 7486319 7486327 7486337 7486357 7486373 7486393
7486411 7486417 7486421 7486439 7486441 7486459 7486463 7486471 7486481 7486499
7486529 7486537 7486561 7486567 7486571 7486573 7486603 7486607 7486631 7486649
7486673 7486693 7486711 7486729 7486733 7486747 7486763 7486793 7486819 7486823
7486847 7486867 7486873 7486877 7486907 7486933 7486951 7486961 7486979 7486981
7487047 7487057 7487069 7487087 7487107 7487113 7487119 7487131 7487149 7487171
7487177 7487189 7487243 7487261 7487269 7487281 7487287 7487299 7487321 7487329
7487339 7487341 7487369 7487371 7487377 7487393 7487401 7487407 7487413 7487419
7487437 7487449 7487453 7487503 7487507 7487549 7487573 7487591 7487593 7487603
7487611 7487621 7487639 7487651 7487657 7487677 7487687 7487723 7487737 7487741
7487743 7487747 7487759 7487761 7487783 7487797 7487813 7487819 7487827 7487839
7487863 7487911 7487917 7487923 7487927 7487941 7487969 7487989 7488017 7488031
7488053 7488059 7488067 7488079 7488101 7488127 7488137 7488163 7488227 7488233
7488259 7488263 7488269 7488277 7488289 7488307 7488311 7488323 7488361 7488373
7488379 7488401 7488419 7488427 7488431 7488433 7488473 7488479 7488499 7488511
7488527 7488539 7488553 7488571 7488581 7488589 7488617 7488629 7488643 7488659
7488667 7488671 7488673 7488683 7488707 7488713 7488737 7488739 7488769 7488779
7488797 7488829 7488863 7488881 7488937 7488947 7488973 7488991 7489033 7489043
7489051 7489067 7489093 7489103 7489117 7489123 7489127 7489171 7489177 7489189
7489201 7489213 7489241 7489243 7489253 7489303 7489351 7489357 7489387 7489393
7489399 7489423 7489457 7489463 7489481 7489501 7489523 7489529 7489541 7489549
7489561 7489567 7489579 7489607 7489609 7489619 7489633 7489649 7489681 7489709
7489711 7489721 7489733 7489739 7489787 7489789 7489829 7489841 7489847 7489849
7489871 7489913 7489919 7489931 7489939 7489943 7489949 7489957 7489981 7489987
7490023 7490029 7490051 7490089 7490099 7490101 7490113 7490141 7490143 7490159
7490179 7490191 7490209 7490221 7490233 7490239 7490257 7490297 7490303 7490309
7490363 7490369 7490377 7490401 7490407 7490411 7490419 7490423 7490443 7490453
7490459 7490491 7490519 7490537 7490551 7490573 7490597 7490599 7490611 7490629
7490647 7490653 7490683 7490723 7490737 7490759 7490767 7490771 7490783 7490797
7490803 7490827 7490839 7490851 7490869 7490927 7490981 7491007 7491049
7491059 7491061 7491089 7491091 7491137 7491161 7491167 7491199 7491217 7491221
7491223 7491229 7491241 7491247 7491257 7491259 7491269 7491287 7491299 7491311
7491313 7491343 7491347 7491361 7491371 7491389 7491401 7491439 7491449 7491457
7491467 7491469 7491493 7491551 7491557 7491559 7491607 7491619 7491623 7491641
7491647 7491667 7491689 7491691 7491697 7491727 7491733 7491749 7491763 7491779
7491791 7491811 7491821 7491823 7491839 7491851 7491853 7491893 7491901 7491907
7491923 7491929 7491937 7491943 7491949 7491973 7492031 7492057 7492097 7492103
7492127 7492153 7492157 7492249 7492253 7492267 7492307 7492313 7492343 7492361
7492369 7492391 7492423 7492477 7492481 7492487 7492519 7492523 7492531 7492547
7492553 7492561 7492567 7492591 7492609 7492657 7492673 7492697 7492703 7492711
7492717 7492741 7492747 7492753 7492757 7492777 7492781 7492799 7492819 7492831
7492841 7492853 7492867 7492869 7492909 7492921 7492943 7493029 7493033 7493053
7493063 7493077 7493081 7493093 7493099 7493111 7493117 7493159 7493237 7493249
7493251 7493261 7493263 7493287 7493293 7493303 7493329 7493333 7493341 7493357
7493363 7493371 7493383 7493389 7493399 7493401 7493417 7493419 7493443
7493449 7493461 7493471 7493491 7493527 7493587 7493597 7493621 7493623 7493627
7493639 7493671 7493701 7493729 7493737 7493747 7493777 7493807 7493811 7493831
7493833 7493839 7493851 7493867 7493879 7493881 7493891 7493903 7493917
7493921 7493947 7494001 7494023 7494029 7494031 7494049 7494073 7494101 7494119
7494131 7494139 7494163 7494181 7494203 7494217 7494257 7494269 7494271 7494287
7494329 7494337 7494367 7494371 7494373 7494401 7494407 7494413 7494437 7494439
7494449 7494469 7494491 7494497 7494517 7494523 7494563 7494587 7494623 7494631
7494661 7494679 7494703 7494719 7494733 7494737 7494743 7494749 7494763 7494869
7494871 7494881 7494917 7494919 7494953 7494959 7495003 7495013 7495039 7495049
7495051 7495069 7495073 7495097 7495121 7495153 7495193 7495199 7495247 7495289
7495303 7495307 7495321 7495339 7495361 7495379 7495381 7495387 7495393 7495409
```

```
7495429  7495463  7495469  7495511  7495531  7495573  7495577  7495591  7495597  7495637
7495639  7495679  7495687  7495703  7495711  7495727  7495739  7495771  7495777  7495783
7495811  7495837  7495841  7495849  7495879  7495883  7495903  7495909  7495913  7495931
7495973  7495981  7495991  7495993  7496011  7496029  7496053  7496057  7496059  7496087
7496117  7496143  7496149  7496173  7496189  7496191  7496227  7496243  7496249  7496287
7496299  7496323  7496347  7496369  7496407  7496449  7496483  7496497  7496501  7496519
7496537  7496539  7496543  7496549  7496557  7496579  7496581  7496603  7496623  7496627
7496639  7496651  7496653  7496701  7496719  7496729  7496743  7496767  7496771  7496791
7496807  7496821  7496833  7496843  7496851  7496857  7496861  7496893  7496899  7496917
7496933  7496939  7496959  7496971  7496987  7496989  7497019  7497023  7497029  7497031
7497043  7497053  7497059  7497067  7497073  7497089  7497101  7497107  7497121  7497143
7497157  7497181  7497209  7497223  7497253  7497263  7497293  7497311  7497313  7497349
7497353  7497377  7497397  7497401  7497407  7497409  7497431  7497439  7497467  7497499
7497509  7497541  7497557  7497587  7497593  7497601  7497641  7497649  7497703  7497709
7497727  7497733  7497739  7497767  7497797  7497817  7497821  7497823  7497827  7497859
7497869  7497871  7497881  7497883  7497887  7497907  7497911  7497943  7497961  7497967
7498009  7498019  7498031  7498033  7498067  7498093  7498109  7498111  7498151  7498157
7498159  7498189  7498199  7498201  7498229  7498237  7498247  7498273  7498289  7498291
7498301  7498313  7498319  7498321  7498363  7498417  7498423  7498429  7498459  7498471
7498481  7498499  7498507  7498511  7498537  7498549  7498553  7498577  7498583  7498609
7498637  7498643  7498663  7498693  7498697  7498703  7498721  7498739  7498741  7498747
7498763  7498769  7498781  7498783  7498789  7498831  7498861  7498867  7498871  7498879
7498903  7498927  7498937  7498957  7498961  7498979  7498987  7498999  7499027  7499029
7499039  7499069  7499083  7499111  7499119  7499131  7499137  7499147  7499153  7499161
7499171  7499183  7499201  7499203  7499207  7499209  7499231  7499237  7499249  7499251
7499257  7499263  7499287  7499291  7499321  7499333  7499347  7499369  7499381  7499389
7499411  7499413  7499441  7499483  7499491  7499507  7499519  7499537  7499539  7499543
7499561  7499579  7499627  7499651  7499663  7499677  7499683  7499689  7499693  7499729
7499747  7499749  7499753  7499773  7499809  7499819  7499849  7499867  7499887  7499969
7499981  7500013  7500029  7500049  7500061  7500071  7500091  7500113  7500121  7500127
7500169  7500197  7500203  7500217  7500221  7500223  7500271  7500293  7500313  7500319
7500347  7500373  7500397  7500407  7500413  7500439  7500443  7500457  7500463  7500491
7500539  7500547  7500557  7500569  7500607  7500631  7500641  7500673  7500679  7500707
7500709  7500721  7500739  7500749  7500767  7500781  7500797  7500799  7500803  7500811
7500817  7500833  7500841  7500863  7500881  7500901  7500917  7500919  7500923  7500943
7500949  7500979  7500979  7501003  7501027  7501031  7501033  7501061  7501069  7501103
7501141  7501147  7501157  7501159  7501189  7501211  7501217  7501297  7501309  7501313
7501339  7501367  7501379  7501391  7501433  7501441  7501451  7501463  7501511  7501513
7501537  7501541  7501579  7501583  7501601  7501609  7501643  7501649  7501687  7501687
7501693  7501723  7501727  7501733  7501757  7501759  7501771  7501801  7501817  7501843
7501849  7501859  7501867  7501873  7501889  7501891  7501937  7501939  7501951  7501961
7501987  7501993  7501997  7502003  7502029  7502051  7502107  7502111  7502113  7502119
7502129  7502153  7502171  7502177  7502189  7502197  7502227  7502237  7502249  7502251
7502267  7502273  7502291  7502293  7502323  7502333  7502353  7502377  7502399  7502413
7502431  7502441  7502461  7502477  7502479  7502483  7502533  7502557  7502567  7502603
7502609  7502629  7502633  7502639  7502653  7502681  7502687  7502689  7502707  7502711
7502717  7502723  7502753  7502771  7502791  7502801  7502813  7502819  7502821  7502827
7502843  7502849  7502857  7502863  7502879  7502881  7502917  7502983  7503017  7503019
7503029  7503049  7503059  7503077  7503107  7503109  7503149  7503163  7503203  7503211
7503227  7503253  7503317  7503343  7503361  7503383  7503389  7503401  7503407  7503413
7503469  7503521  7503527  7503553  7503577  7503599  7503607  7503619  7503649  7503659
7503667  7503677  7503701  7503703  7503731  7503737  7503739  7503751  7503757  7503761
7503763  7503787  7503809  7503833  7503863  7503869  7503877  7503929  7503931  7503941
7503949  7503959  7503961  7503967  7503971  7503983  7503989  7504009  7504019  7504027
7504039  7504043  7504051  7504093  7504097  7504099  7504103  7504109  7504117  7504153
7504163  7504169  7504171  7504241  7504249  7504253  7504291  7504307  7504309  7504313
7504319  7504331  7504339  7504369  7504379  7504381  7504421  7504423  7504439  7504457
7504459  7504481  7504501  7504507  7504513  7504529  7504543  7504561  7504589  7504613
7504643  7504663  7504691  7504703  7504711  7504727  7504729  7504733  7504751  7504781
7504787  7504789  7504799  7504807  7504817  7504841  7504897  7504901  7504909  7504957
7504961  7504967  7504979  7504993  7505011  7505021  7505023  7505033  7505051  7505053
7505063  7505077  7505081  7505089  7505129  7505149  7505159  7505161  7505207  7505219
7505221  7505227  7505233  7505243  7505249  7505297  7505299  7505321  7505341  7505357
7505359  7505389  7505417  7505423  7505431  7505447  7505453  7505467  7505471  7505479
7505539  7505543  7505549  7505557  7505579  7505581  7505587  7505591  7505593  7505611
7505633  7505639  7505647  7505657  7505669  7505677  7505681  7505717  7505723  7505731
7505737  7505753  7505761  7505767  7505801  7505821  7505833  7505837  7505863  7505873
7505881  7505909  7505923  7505929  7505941  7505977  7506011  7506029  7506043  7506071
7506089  7506097  7506113  7506133  7506137  7506143  7506179  7506181  7506203  7506217
7506221  7506241  7506253  7506259  7506263  7506277  7506281  7506287  7506293  7506329
7506341  7506379  7506397  7506407  7506419  7506439  7506509  7506547  7506581  7506593
7506601  7506637  7506647  7506661  7506677  7506701  7506739  7506757  7506773  7506791
7506797  7506803  7506823  7506827  7506827  7506857  7506907  7506913  7506923  7506931
7506959  7507021  7507037  7507051  7507057  7507099  7507103  7507127  7507153  7507163
7507211  7507231  7507271  7507273  7507277  7507289  7507309  7507333  7507369  7507373
7507399  7507403  7507429  7507459  7507471  7507481  7507517  7507537  7507543  7507547
7507553  7507561  7507579  7507597  7507613  7507627  7507649  7507657  7507711  7507751
7507763  7507769  7507771  7507777  7507783  7507789  7507813  7507837  7507847  7507849
7507853  7507883  7507889  7507891  7507901  7507919  7507933  7507937  7507939  7507963
7507967  7507991  7507993  7508009  7508041  7508047  7508057  7508069  7508093  7508141
7508147  7508161  7508167  7508183  7508191  7508197  7508201  7508209  7508227  7508233
7508243  7508251  7508257  7508309  7508341  7508353  7508357  7508377  7508381  7508383
7508393  7508437  7508443  7508467  7508503  7508507  7508533  7508569  7508573
7508581  7508587  7508609  7508647  7508659  7508671  7508689  7508693  7508701  7508717
7508729  7508749  7508759  7508771  7508791  7508797  7508801  7508843  7508869  7508887
7508903  7508909  7508911  7508923  7508929  7508947  7508953  7508981  7508993  7509001
7509013  7509023  7509041  7509043  7509059  7509071  7509077  7509083  7509091  7509101
7509157  7509169  7509179  7509181  7509209  7509211  7509217  7509233  7509239  7509241
7509251  7509253  7509263  7509269  7509301  7509311  7509317  7509323  7509349  7509361
```

```
7509379 7509401 7509407 7509419 7509487 7509499 7509559 7509571 7509577 7509589
7509611 7509629 7509647 7509679 7509709 7509713 7509721 7509727 7509739 7509743
7509787 7509793 7509839 7509851 7509917 7509919 7509949 7510033 7510067 7510081
7510109 7510117 7510127 7510133 7510147 7510163 7510183 7510189 7510193 7510201
7510207 7510249 7510253 7510267 7510273 7510343 7510357 7510367 7510369 7510387
7510403 7510429 7510439 7510441 7510483 7510487 7510493 7510511 7510543 7510561
7510579 7510603 7510619 7510669 7510687 7510709 7510729 7510733 7510801 7510813
7510817 7510847 7510859 7510873 7510879 7510933 7510969 7510973 7510999 7511011
7511027 7511033 7511039 7511047 7511057 7511071 7511123 7511129 7511149 7511167
7511173 7511183 7511191 7511191 7511209 7511219 7511227 7511233 7511243 7511267
7511281 7511291 7511341 7511347 7511381 7511419 7511423 7511431 7511443 7511453
7511461 7511473 7511477 7511513 7511519 7511533 7511549 7511561 7511563 7511591
7511597 7511599 7511611 7511633 7511659 7511663 7511701 7511717 7511719 7511737
7511761 7511767 7511789 7511813 7511837 7511843 7511857 7511891 7511947 7511969
7511981 7511989 7511993 7512019 7512023 7512041 7512047 7512083 7512097 7512101
7512119 7512173 7512187 7512209 7512217 7512289 7512311 7512319 7512343 7512377
7512383 7512403 7512409 7512437 7512469 7512493 7512497 7512563 7512569 7512587
7512599 7512601 7512611 7512613 7512641 7512667 7512671 7512677 7512679 7512709
7512721 7512727 7512731 7512737 7512749 7512751 7512763 7512773 7512779 7512781
7512797 7512851 7512853 7512859 7512863 7512893 7512907 7512913 7512919 7512931
7512977 7512991 7513021 7513039 7513057 7513063 7513073 7513123 7513139 7513141
7513147 7513153 7513171 7513199 7513213 7513223 7513229 7513267 7513277 7513283
7513321 7513327 7513343 7513351 7513357 7513361 7513391 7513393 7513397 7513403
7513411 7513423 7513427 7513459 7513477 7513481 7513529 7513543 7513547 7513559
7513567 7513573 7513577 7513579 7513589 7513601 7513603 7513613 7513633 7513637
7513661 7513669 7513679 7513703 7513729 7513733 7513763 7513771 7513787 7513799
7513819 7513823 7513837 7513867 7513879 7513889 7513897 7513901
7513931 7513951 7513967 7513973 7513981 7513991 7513999 7514009 7514011 7514033
7514047 7514057 7514099 7514113 7514147 7514149 7514167 7514189 7514231 7514233
7514237 7514249 7514257 7514267 7514279 7514281 7514321 7514327 7514341 7514371
7514411 7514413 7514447 7514449 7514467 7514471 7514477 7514489 7514543 7514581
7514597 7514623 7514627 7514641 7514659 7514669 7514701 7514713 7514719 7514743
7514779 7514791 7514797 7514807 7514821 7514827 7514851 7514869 7514873 7514887
7514917 7514929 7514963 7514977 7514993 7515019 7515041 7515047 7515061 7515073
7515121 7515133 7515143 7515149 7515161 7515163 7515197 7515199 7515217 7515229
7515247 7515251 7515281 7515283 7515307 7515311 7515331 7515337 7515367 7515373
7515397 7515407 7515413 7515419 7515461 7515481 7515491 7515493 7515499 7515523
7515527 7515533 7515593 7515617 7515619 7515623 7515637 7515647 7515661 7515689
7515691 7515719 7515721 7515731 7515757 7515763 7515791 7515797 7515799 7515803
7515821 7515883 7515889 7515913 7515923 7515929 7515931 7515947 7515967 7515971
7515973 7515979 7516049 7516051 7516063 7516081 7516087 7516097 7516121 7516151
7516181 7516183 7516189 7516211 7516213 7516247 7516259 7516283 7516303 7516321
7516337 7516351 7516361 7516373 7516391 7516393 7516409 7516417 7516427 7516451
7516463 7516471 7516493 7516547 7516573 7516583 7516589 7516633 7516657 7516681
7516687 7516693 7516711 7516721 7516739 7516741 7516753 7516781 7516793 7516801
7516807 7516819 7516843 7516853 7516867 7516871 7516877 7516879 7516889 7516891
7516897 7516903 7516909 7516919 7516921 7516933 7516939 7516963 7516987 7516991
7517033 7517047 7517057 7517089 7517117 7517123 7517129 7517137 7517143 7517161
7517183 7517189 7517201 7517231 7517239 7517243 7517273 7517287 7517291 7517311
7517347 7517353 7517357 7517371 7517381 7517387 7517399 7517413 7517423 7517429
7517431 7517443 7517453 7517479 7517491 7517533 7517539 7517557 7517567 7517581
7517591 7517599 7517611 7517617 7517633 7517639 7517651 7517659 7517663 7517669
7517677 7517681 7517687 7517707 7517729 7517737 7517747 7517753 7517761 7517773
7517789 7517813 7517827 7517831 7517833 7517843 7517857 7517899 7517921 7517953
7517963 7517971 7517981 7518001 7518023 7518031 7518041 7518109 7518113 7518127
7518157 7518169 7518187 7518191 7518241 7518253 7518283 7518307 7518317 7518323
7518331 7518347 7518359 7518361 7518383 7518431 7518463 7518473 7518481 7518491
7518499 7518503 7518517 7518529 7518571 7518587 7518601 7518619 7518629 7518671
7518727 7518751 7518767 7518773 7518803 7518821 7518853 7518869 7518871 7518877
7518893 7518961 7518977 7518989 7519009 7519063 7519067 7519069 7519093 7519121
7519123 7519139 7519157 7519159 7519181 7519189 7519217 7519223 7519261 7519271
7519273 7519297 7519313 7519331 7519333 7519339 7519363 7519411 7519417 7519451
7519489 7519491 7519493 7519499 7519507 7519513 7519517 7519529 7519541 7519553
7519579 7519591 7519607 7519637 7519667 7519691 7519697 7519703 7519741 7519747
7519777 7519789 7519807 7519817 7519871 7519891 7519901 7519907 7519913 7519943
7519987 7519997 7519999 7520017 7520027 7520063 7520083 7520087 7520099 7520111
7520113 7520173 7520189 7520203 7520207 7520209 7520221 7520267 7520297 7520311
7520347 7520351 7520389 7520407 7520417 7520419 7520437 7520459 7520467 7520479
7520501 7520503 7520543 7520551 7520567 7520573 7520581 7520587 7520593 7520603
7520621 7520627 7520633 7520659 7520663 7520677 7520687 7520707 7520719 7520729
7520759 7520791 7520797 7520809 7520837 7520861 7520867 7520881 7520899
7520911 7520921 7520927 7520969 7520993 7521013 7521049 7521053 7521061 7521079
7521113 7521119 7521149 7521197 7521203 7521209 7521221 7521229 7521233 7521247
7521257 7521271 7521277 7521281 7521287 7521307 7521317 7521329 7521331 7521341
7521343 7521347 7521373 7521383 7521407 7521421 7521433 7521439 7521443 7521467
7521533 7521539 7521541 7521559 7521581 7521583 7521593 7521607 7521617 7521641
7521649 7521659 7521691 7521719 7521721 7521743 7521791 7521793 7521821 7521823
7521859 7521869 7521881 7521887 7521893 7521911 7521931 7521937 7521949 7521977
7521979 7522003 7522037 7522061 7522069 7522079 7522091 7522103 7522111 7522159
7522169 7522171 7522187 7522201 7522217 7522221 7522241 7522261 7522267 7522283
7522289 7522321 7522327 7522331 7522351 7522363 7522387 7522391 7522409 7522439
7522451 7522453 7522469 7522519 7522531 7522573 7522579 7522597 7522609 7522621
7522631 7522643 7522741 7522747 7522751 7522759 7522769 7522787 7522793 7522799
7522813 7522829 7522843 7522847 7522901 7522927 7522973 7522981 7522997 7523011
7523023 7523039 7523041 7523051 7523053 7523077 7523083 7523101 7523137 7523141
7523147 7523177 7523179 7523189 7523239 7523261 7523279 7523281 7523293 7523303
7523309 7523311 7523317 7523357 7523381 7523387 7523419 7523443 7523471 7523479
7523531 7523533 7523539 7523561 7523567 7523569 7523573 7523587 7523651
7523671 7523689 7523693 7523699 7523717 7523729 7523767 7523771 7523777 7523819
```

```
7523821  7523849  7523863  7523909  7523927  7523939  7523953  7523969  7523977  7523993
7524017  7524029  7524031  7524071  7524107  7524119  7524131  7524151  7524169  7524191
7524203  7524221  7524229  7524233  7524259  7524271  7524317  7524343  7524383  7524397
7524403  7524409  7524449  7524457  7524467  7524469  7524479  7524493  7524499  7524511
7524521  7524541  7524553  7524593  7524619  7524631  7524641  7524667  7524677  7524679
7524701  7524707  7524709  7524719  7524721  7524733  7524739  7524757  7524763  7524773
7524799  7524859  7524859  7524883  7524889  7524911  7524917  7524929  7524941  7524943
7524967  7524973  7524983  7524997  7525003  7525013  7525027  7525051  7525061  7525073
7525081  7525109  7525127  7525151  7525153  7525213  7525247  7525249  7525261  7525291
7525307  7525313  7525333  7525363  7525367  7525369  7525381  7525403  7525411  7525423
7525429  7525433  7525451  7525457  7525493  7525513  7525517  7525519  7525571  7525579
7525589  7525601  7525613  7525633  7525657  7525709  7525723  7525741  7525751  7525759
7525783  7525823  7525867  7525891  7525907  7525943  7525961  7525967  7525979  7526003
7526011  7526039  7526041  7526047  7526089  7526111  7526117  7526143  7526153  7526171
7526179  7526201  7526219  7526231  7526237  7526243  7526249  7526263  7526269  7526279
7526297  7526317  7526339  7526347  7526377  7526381  7526443  7526447  7526501  7526507
7526509  7526537  7526549  7526557  7526569  7526593  7526611  7526633  7526647  7526653
7526663  7526683  7526749  7526789  7526791  7526833  7526837  7526843  7526861  7526879
7526881  7526899  7526941  7526963  7526993  7527011  7527029  7527053  7527061  7527071
7527077  7527083  7527089  7527109  7527127  7527139  7527151  7527181  7527229  7527251
7527253  7527257  7527259  7527283  7527293  7527307  7527329  7527341  7527347  7527367
7527419  7527433  7527437  7527449  7527467  7527497  7527523  7527551  7527571  7527577
7527589  7527599  7527607  7527677  7527683  7527697  7527701  7527713  7527727  7527731
7527763  7527769  7527797  7527841  7527853  7527911  7527913  7527931  7527941  7527953
7527977  7528007  7528021  7528033  7528043  7528063  7528091  7528097  7528111  7528121
7528141  7528151  7528207  7528211  7528217  7528219  7528231  7528249  7528273  7528289
7528309  7528357  7528363  7528387  7528393  7528403  7528453  7528457  7528471  7528489
7528517  7528519  7528529  7528531  7528537  7528553  7528607  7528639  7528663  7528667
7528669  7528679  7528699  7528721  7528733  7528747  7528757  7528783  7528793  7528799
7528811  7528817  7528837  7528853  7528867  7528879  7528891  7528903  7528907  7528933
7528949  7528973  7528979  7528983  7529003  7529017  7529033  7529051  7529059  7529083
7529087  7529089  7529099  7529101  7529107  7529129  7529131  7529161  7529173  7529177
7529189  7529201  7529209  7529219  7529227  7529231  7529243  7529261  7529267  7529287
7529297  7529309  7529323  7529359  7529369  7529371  7529381  7529387  7529399  7529401
7529471  7529519  7529573  7529603  7529617  7529659  7529663  7529693  7529699  7529707
7529713  7529737  7529741  7529747  7529761  7529771  7529783  7529791  7529801  7529813
7529831  7529857  7529867  7529881  7529887  7529891  7529903  7529923  7529933  7529939
7529941  7529959  7529971  7529983  7529987  7529999  7530007  7530059  7530067  7530071
7530073  7530077  7530091  7530097  7530113  7530119  7530121  7530139  7530151  7530157
7530161  7530209  7530217  7530239  7530283  7530301  7530307  7530317  7530319  7530323
7530329  7530349  7530353  7530377  7530421  7530431  7530449  7530451  7530463  7530491
7530493  7530503  7530529  7530533  7530539  7530559  7530563  7530569  7530571  7530577
7530587  7530617  7530619  7530629  7530641  7530671  7530689  7530697  7530703  7530713
7530727  7530739  7530751  7530769  7530781  7530791  7530827  7530829  7530841  7530851
7530883  7530889  7530893  7530911  7530931  7530947  7530953  7530961  7530967  7531019
7531031  7531037  7531057  7531061  7531079  7531099  7531127  7531151  7531157  7531211
7531217  7531231  7531241  7531253  7531283  7531297  7531319  7531343  7531351  7531367
7531369  7531397  7531399  7531417  7531423  7531451  7531453  7531457  7531477  7531499
7531501  7531519  7531541  7531567  7531571  7531597  7531637  7531639  7531651  7531681
7531687  7531691  7531709  7531717  7531721  7531739  7531747  7531753  7531807  7531813
7531829  7531839  7531841  7531859  7531861  7531871  7531877  7531897  7531913  7531919
7531933  7531943  7531957  7531991  7532011  7532023  7532027  7532029  7532033  7532059
7532089  7532131  7532137  7532141  7532149  7532153  7532171  7532209  7532221  7532249
7532251  7532297  7532299  7532323  7532347  7532381  7532383  7532407  7532419  7532419
7532443  7532449  7532453  7532501  7532507  7532509  7532521  7532527  7532533  7532537
7532573  7532579  7532617  7532621  7532633  7532639  7532647  7532653  7532669  7532687
7532711  7532741  7532771  7532773  7532813  7532821  7532839  7532929  7532933  7532957
7532977  7532981  7532999  7533007  7533037  7533047  7533067  7533077  7533079  7533131
7533137  7533151  7533161  7533181  7533187  7533191  7533199  7533209  7533221  7533223
7533247  7533269  7533271  7533289  7533293  7533319  7533343  7533349  7533377  7533389
7533391  7533433  7533451  7533457  7533469  7533511  7533521  7533551  7533553  7533563
7533571  7533577  7533593  7533611  7533619  7533629  7533637  7533641  7533653  7533667
7533689  7533727  7533731  7533733  7533749  7533751  7533781  7533787  7533793  7533803
7533809  7533821  7533833  7533853  7533859  7533917  7533947  7533979  7533983  7533991
7534019  7534027  7534057  7534061  7534063  7534067  7534069  7534081  7534099  7534103
7534157  7534169  7534183  7534193  7534243  7534249  7534253  7534259  7534277  7534291
7534301  7534327  7534337  7534361  7534367  7534369  7534381  7534391  7534433  7534441
7534463  7534481  7534489  7534493  7534511  7534601  7534603  7534607  7534609  7534627
7534649  7534673  7534699  7534721  7534729  7534741  7534789  7534799  7534801  7534817
7534819  7534837  7534871  7534883  7534889  7534897  7534907  7534921  7534931  7534937
7534979  7534991  7534997  7535027  7535069  7535071  7535083  7535089  7535093  7535107
7535113  7535167  7535183  7535197  7535239  7535243  7535287  7535323  7535401  7535413
7535459  7535461  7535477  7535483  7535501  7535503  7535519  7535527  7535551  7535551
7535569  7535587  7535599  7535603  7535617  7535623  7535629  7535659  7535663  7535669
7535681  7535683  7535701  7535713  7535729  7535741  7535747  7535767  7535771  7535783
7535791  7535797  7535807  7535809  7535813  7535849  7535851  7535861  7535887  7535917
7535921  7535953  7535963  7535971  7535999  7536013  7536031  7536059  7536073  7536077
7536091  7536119  7536127  7536149  7536167  7536187  7536241  7536281  7536289  7536337
7536343  7536349  7536371  7536383  7536391  7536401  7536409  7536421  7536427  7536443
7536461  7536467  7536499  7536509  7536511  7536517  7536523  7536527  7536541  7536577
7536583  7536589  7536637  7536647  7536667  7536677  7536707  7536757  7536769  7536773
7536811  7536821  7536827  7536829  7536833  7536853  7536857  7536869  7536871  7536883
7536887  7536917  7536929  7536941  7536949  7536959  7536961  7536979  7537003  7537007
7537009  7537027  7537037  7537043  7537063  7537067  7537087  7537093  7537097  7537109
7537121  7537133  7537151  7537181  7537193  7537207  7537223  7537237  7537253  7537259
7537291  7537297  7537331  7537333  7537337  7537339  7537373  7537421  7537441  7537451
7537483  7537489  7537493  7537507  7537559  7537561  7537571  7537589  7537591  7537637
7537639  7537657  7537669  7537687  7537697  7537703  7537711  7537723  7537729  7537741
7537763  7537793  7537799  7537807  7537837  7537841  7537861  7537897  7537903  7537913
```

```
7537939 7537949 7537963 7538009 7538039 7538081 7538087 7538093 7538099 7538147
7538159 7538203 7538221 7538233 7538251 7538303 7538341 7538359 7538423 7538449
7538473 7538477 7538483 7538501 7538513 7538519 7538527 7538533 7538543 7538551
7538591 7538603 7538617 7538647 7538651 7538683 7538693 7538719 7538731 7538737
7538747 7538759 7538761 7538771 7538813 7538827 7538849 7538857 7538863 7538887
7538893 7538903 7538933 7538959 7538969 7538987 7538989 7539001 7539011 7539017
7539019 7539023 7539031 7539047 7539053 7539073 7539089 7539127 7539137 7539149
7539151 7539179 7539199 7539253 7539283 7539299 7539307 7539341 7539349 7539373
7539383 7539397 7539401 7539431 7539439 7539451 7539481 7539487 7539529 7539533
7539557 7539563 7539583 7539589 7539593 7539629 7539641 7539643 7539671 7539673
7539677 7539709 7539731 7539737 7539743 7539757 7539761 7539767 7539773 7539793
7539799 7539809 7539821 7539869 7539871 7539877 7539893 7539899 7539919 7539923
7539943 7539949 7539977 7539989 7540009 7540019 7540051 7540063 7540079 7540081
7540103 7540111 7540133 7540139 7540147 7540157 7540171 7540189 7540199 7540219
7540237 7540241 7540277 7540289 7540327 7540349 7540369 7540391 7540399 7540411
7540439 7540441 7540447 7540451 7540453 7540457 7540459 7540499 7540501 7540517
7540529 7540541 7540567 7540583 7540601 7540651 7540661 7540691 7540699 7540717
7540721 7540751 7540763 7540769 7540801 7540807 7540823 7540831 7540837 7540861
7540873 7540901 7540903 7540909 7540913 7540919 7540921 7540931 7540943 7540969
7540991 7540993 7540997 7541021 7541041 7541057 7541063 7541069 7541077 7541087
7541099 7541111 7541129 7541141 7541147 7541159 7541179 7541201 7541213 7541227
7541231 7541239 7541249 7541257 7541273 7541279 7541293 7541299 7541311 7541327
7541329 7541333 7541371 7541381 7541389 7541399 7541431 7541437 7541441 7541477
7541509 7541531 7541533 7541579 7541603 7541617 7541623 7541627 7541647 7541669
7541671 7541683 7541701 7541717 7541719 7541731 7541767 7541777 7541783 7541789
7541791 7541839 7541843 7541851 7541867 7541869 7541873 7541881 7541903 7541921
7541923 7541927 7541929 7541951 7541957 7541981 7541983 7542013 7542019 7542023
7542047 7542049 7542053 7542077 7542097 7542103 7542121 7542131 7542133 7542163
7542167 7542181 7542187 7542253 7542277 7542289 7542313 7542317 7542341 7542347
7542389 7542439 7542461 7542463 7542481 7542533 7542541 7542547 7542553 7542569
7542593 7542599 7542629 7542653 7542707 7542719 7542721 7542727 7542749 7542761
7542763 7542767 7542797 7542823 7542851 7542853 7542859 7542869 7542877 7542901
7542923 7542947 7542967 7542971 7542979 7542989 7542991 7543001 7543007 7543009
7543021 7543043 7543049 7543069 7543073 7543097 7543117 7543141 7543147 7543169
7543177 7543181 7543183 7543201 7543213 7543231 7543243 7543259 7543271 7543273
7543279 7543351 7543363 7543381 7543409 7543429 7543439 7543441 7543499 7543511
7543531 7543561 7543577 7543579 7543603 7543639 7543643 7543651 7543661 7543709
7543717 7543751 7543759 7543763 7543769 7543777 7543807 7543813 7543831 7543843
7543849 7543853 7543859 7543901 7543909 7543931 7543957 7543961 7543979 7544027
7544057 7544063 7544077 7544081 7544093 7544099 7544113 7544137 7544143 7544149
7544167 7544203 7544227 7544233 7544237 7544269 7544281 7544291 7544323 7544347
7544363 7544429 7544431 7544443 7544461 7544491 7544519 7544521 7544543 7544557
7544561 7544567 7544573 7544587 7544591 7544609 7544627 7544629 7544657 7544699
7544701 7544723 7544731 7544777 7544791 7544819 7544827 7544833 7544837 7544839
7544857 7544869 7544879 7544899 7544939 7544941 7544947 7544963 7544981 7544983
7544993 7545007 7545011 7545023 7545037 7545047 7545067 7545079 7545113 7545119
7545137 7545143 7545157 7545163 7545169 7545193 7545217 7545221 7545233 7545247
7545257 7545269 7545277 7545283 7545287 7545289 7545313 7545341 7545359 7545361
7545367 7545443 7545463 7545479 7545487 7545497 7545529 7545547 7545563 7545737
7545581 7545589 7545611 7545631 7545647 7545649 7545653 7545689 7545697 7545737
7545749 7545751 7545781 7545787 7545799 7545827 7545833 7545847 7545899 7545911
7545913 7545917 7545919 7545931 7545949 7545953 7545997 7546031 7546037 7546057
7546067 7546069 7546141 7546151 7546153 7546157 7546183 7546207 7546223 7546241
7546243 7546247 7546271 7546289 7546303 7546307 7546313 7546321 7546327 7546333
7546373 7546381 7546391 7546393 7546421 7546471 7546481 7546489 7546499 7546523
7546529 7546531 7546541 7546571 7546579 7546607 7546613 7546639 7546673 7546681
7546687 7546703 7546711 7546717 7546729 7546739 7546741 7546751 7546753 7546769
7546771 7546789 7546811 7546841 7546871 7546883 7546901 7546969 7546991 7547003
7547011 7547017 7547021 7547053 7547077 7547083 7547093
7547117 7547129 7547143 7547159 7547171 7547173 7547179 7547191 7547203 7547209
7547219 7547233 7547249 7547263 7547299 7547329 7547341 7547357 7547377 7547399
7547411 7547429 7547431 7547437 7547443 7547479 7547497 7547509 7547521 7547537
7547549 7547563 7547587 7547633 7547641 7547647 7547671 7547699 7547717 7547719
7547723 7547753 7547759 7547773 7547803 7547809 7547843 7547851 7547857 7547867
7547909 7547927 7547971 7547987 7547989 7547993 7548007 7548011 7548031 7548043
7548067 7548077 7548083 7548113 7548157 7548169 7548173 7548181 7548193 7548217
7548227 7548241 7548257 7548271 7548293 7548311 7548319 7548353 7548379 7548383
7548389 7548397 7548413 7548427 7548433 7548451 7548461 7548467 7548473 7548487
7548523 7548533 7548539 7548553 7548557 7548571 7548581 7548587 7548589 7548599
7548617 7548647 7548659 7548677 7548683 7548701 7548707 7548727 7548763 7548803
7548817 7548829 7548839 7548847 7548859 7548869 7548883 7548907 7548911 7548917
7548929 7548941 7548953 7548971 7548977 7549001 7549039 7549049 7549063 7549067
7549079 7549097 7549121 7549127 7549141 7549153 7549159 7549169 7549181 7549189
7549211 7549249 7549253 7549271 7549277 7549291 7549331 7549349 7549357 7549363
7549391 7549393 7549427 7549429 7549439 7549459 7549481 7549489 7549537 7549559
7549567 7549571 7549573 7549583 7549601 7549609 7549613 7549621 7549637 7549651
7549687 7549693 7549697 7549721 7549741 7549753 7549757 7549777 7549799 7549847
7549877 7549907 7549931 7549963 7549967 7549991 7549999 7550017 7550047 7550071
7550083 7550089 7550099 7550113 7550117 7550119 7550131 7550149 7550173 7550177
7550203 7550243 7550251 7550269 7550293 7550303 7550311 7550351 7550357 7550377
7550381 7550401 7550443 7550449 7550461 7550483 7550513 7550537 7550563 7550573
7550579 7550591 7550617 7550629 7550677 7550707 7550713 7550729 7550731 7550747
7550783 7550789 7550791 7550797 7550801 7550819 7550863 7550867 7550869 7550891
7550909 7550911 7550927 7550947 7550951 7550953 7550957 7550981 7550987 7550989
7551001 7551013 7551017 7551041 7551053 7551119 7551083 7551119 7551121 7551127
7551133 7551149 7551157 7551163 7551169 7551191 7551209 7551211 7551217 7551263
7551287 7551317 7551319 7551329 7551331 7551343 7551371 7551407 7551409 7551413
7551419 7551433 7551457 7551461 7551491 7551497 7551499 7551517 7551527 7551529
7551541 7551581 7551647 7551653 7551671 7551673 7551679 7551697 7551707 7551743
```

```
7551769 7551781 7551787 7551793 7551799 7551827 7551829 7551853 7551877 7551883
7551899 7551937 7551967 7551979 7551989 7551991 7551997 7552001 7552021 7552031
7552043 7552049 7552067 7552079 7552081 7552091 7552109 7552121 7552123 7552169
7552183 7552187 7552201 7552243 7552247 7552261 7552271 7552277 7552297 7552327
7552343 7552351 7552387 7552397 7552409 7552417 7552453 7552463 7552469 7552511
7552513 7552529 7552537 7552541 7552549 7552577 7552583 7552591 7552603 7552609
7552613 7552619 7552621 7552627 7552663 7552667 7552691 7552693 7552723 7552729
7552757 7552771 7552781 7552793 7552801 7552829 7552849 7552859 7552889 7552891
7552927 7552939 7552943 7552957 7552967 7552997 7553009 7553011 7553017 7553027
7553047 7553059 7553123 7553129 7553173 7553191 7553197 7553207 7553209 7553267
7553281 7553309 7553327 7553333 7553339 7553387 7553411 7553419 7553437 7553449
7553459 7553467 7553479 7553503 7553521 7553531 7553549 7553573 7553597 7553599
7553603 7553617 7553639 7553653 7553669 7553671 7553687 7553713 7553731 7553737
7553779 7553783 7553803 7553807 7553837 7553869 7553893 7553921 7553927 7553929
7553951 7553971 7553977 7553993 7554017 7554047 7554061 7554083 7554089 7554091
7554101 7554109 7554133 7554167 7554193 7554203 7554223 7554247 7554251 7554277
7554289 7554293 7554299 7554311 7554319 7554331 7554353 7554367 7554467 7554487
7554493 7554499 7554509 7554517 7554523 7554527 7554539 7554563 7554583 7554601
7554641 7554653 7554671 7554689 7554709 7554721 7554727 7554739 7554791 7554809
7554821 7554823 7554839 7554847 7554863 7554871 7554889 7554893 7554929 7554941
7554959 7554961 7554973 7554977 7555001 7555003 7555013 7555043 7555049 7555069
7555073 7555081 7555091 7555129 7555133 7555151 7555159 7555169 7555183 7555189
7555199 7555211 7555243 7555271 7555291 7555313 7555319 7555321 7555333 7555337
7555349 7555367 7555393 7555421 7555423 7555469 7555517 7555529 7555549 7555571
7555601 7555637 7555649 7555651 7555679 7555693 7555703 7555721 7555741 7555759
7555763 7555783 7555789 7555819 7555829 7555841 7555843 7555879 7555883 7555897
7555903 7555907 7555927 7555943 7555981 7555991 7555993 7556027 7556039 7556047
7556069 7556083 7556093 7556099 7556117 7556137 7556141 7556173 7556201 7556231
7556239 7556257 7556267 7556287 7556291 7556309 7556323 7556333 7556359 7556363
7556387 7556411 7556413 7556431 7556441 7556453 7556477 7556491 7556503 7556513
7556531 7556539 7556573 7556579 7556597 7556609 7556611 7556629 7556639 7556641
7556651 7556657 7556663 7556683 7556693 7556701 7556711 7556713 7556767 7556797
7556803 7556807 7556821 7556831 7556893 7556909 7556929 7556947 7556951 7556957
7556971 7556979 7556987 7556999 7557019 7557029 7557031 7557047 7557049 7557059
7557071 7557073 7557091 7557113 7557127 7557157 7557167 7557181 7557191 7557203
7557227 7557239 7557241 7557281 7557283 7557289 7557343 7557373 7557413 7557427
7557437 7557439 7557443 7557449 7557457 7557463 7557479 7557493 7557499 7557523
7557541 7557587 7557601 7557623 7557659 7557691 7557703 7557713 7557743 7557749
7557751 7557761 7557773 7557787 7557793 7557799 7557811 7557827 7557829 7557833
7557857 7557859 7557863 7557871 7557887 7557937 7557941 7557943 7557967 7557971
7557973 7557983 7557989 7557997 7558043 7558049 7558051 7558087 7558091 7558097
7558121 7558129 7558157 7558189 7558193 7558207 7558223 7558247 7558267 7558279
7558289 7558297 7558301 7558303 7558339 7558349 7558351 7558367 7558393 7558417
7558429 7558469 7558477 7558511 7558517 7558519 7558541 7558553 7558597 7558643
7558687 7558709 7558711 7558717 7558721 7558761 7558769 7558813 7558843 7558871
7558877 7558891 7558933 7558939 7558949 7558961 7558981 7558987 7558989 7559011
7559023 7559029 7559051 7559081 7559117 7559119 7559147 7559161 7559171 7559173
7559177 7559191 7559197 7559221 7559239 7559243 7559267 7559287 7559291 7559297
7559311 7559317 7559323 7559333 7559347 7559353 7559371 7559399 7559411 7559417
7559423 7559467 7559471 7559521 7559551 7559561 7559569 7559593 7559599 7559603
7559609 7559623 7559627 7559639 7559641 7559647 7559659 7559681 7559683 7559711
7559719 7559731 7559737 7559759 7559767 7559789 7559819 7559821 7559831 7559837
7559863 7559887 7559911 7559933 7559941 7559947 7559957 7559983 7559989 7559997
7559989 7559999 7560013 7560023 7560029 7560061 7560107 7560109 7560167 7560191
7560193 7560211 7560227 7560239 7560313 7560331 7560361 7560367 7560383 7560407
7560433 7560439 7560451 7560457 7560463 7560473 7560493 7560517 7560521 7560533
7560541 7560547 7560569 7560571 7560587 7560599 7560601 7560643 7560659 7560661
7560667 7560697 7560701 7560703 7560731 7560737 7560757 7560779 7560799 7560809
7560811 7560823 7560827 7560857 7560863 7560871 7560881 7560887 7560923 7560929
7560947 7560977 7560983 7560989 7561007 7561009 7561013 7561019 7561063 7561067
7561091 7561093 7561123 7561157 7561187 7561193 7561207 7561231 7561271 7561289
7561291 7561331 7561349 7561361 7561363 7561391 7561397 7561409 7561417 7561423
7561459 7561469 7561471 7561483 7561517 7561531 7561537 7561573 7561633 7561681
7561691 7561699 7561709 7561751 7561789 7561793 7561811 7561843 7561849 7561901
7561903 7561909 7561913 7561919 7561921 7561969 7561993 7562021 7562041 7562053
7562077 7562099 7562111 7562119 7562123 7562129 7562141 7562167 7562189 7562201
7562221 7562227 7562251 7562257 7562273 7562279 7562287 7562293 7562309 7562329
7562333 7562341 7562351 7562369 7562381 7562407 7562413 7562441 7562447 7562449
7562461 7562473 7562483 7562497 7562519 7562521 7562557 7562567 7562641 7562657
7562663 7562683 7562693 7562701 7562717 7562743 7562771 7562777 7562801 7562803
7562809 7562827 7562831 7562833 7562839 7562857 7562861 7562869 7562879 7562887
7562897 7562917 7562921 7562923 7562927 7562987 7562999 7563001 7563013 7563029
7563071 7563097 7563107 7563139 7563169 7563173 7563191 7563233 7563239 7563277
7563289 7563293 7563299 7563301 7563319 7563323 7563331 7563337 7563379 7563397
7563427 7563431 7563433 7563497 7563499 7563511 7563553 7563563 7563581
7563583 7563593 7563601 7563607 7563629 7563631 7563643 7563649 7563667 7563679
7563709 7563719 7563761 7563763 7563779 7563811 7563821 7563833 7563839 7563841
7563883 7563887 7563901 7563911 7563917 7563943 7563949 7563953 7563971 7563973
7563979 7563989 7564009 7564019 7564057 7564091 7564097 7564129 7564159 7564163
7564177 7564211 7564229 7564231 7564301 7564313 7564357 7564363 7564373 7564379
7564397 7564421 7564429 7564457 7564471 7564477 7564499 7564511 7564523 7564573
7564591 7564619 7564649 7564657 7564673 7564681 7564691 7564693 7564727 7564747
7564757 7564759 7564763 7564789 7564819 7564859 7564861 7564867 7564877 7564891
7564913 7564919 7564939 7564981 7565029 7565053 7565071 7565081 7565083 7565093
7565113 7565123 7565149 7565161 7565189 7565191 7565303 7565347 7565387 7565417
7565419 7565423 7565447 7565461 7565479 7565483 7565489 7565497 7565513 7565531
7565539 7565563 7565567 7565599 7565603 7565617 7565627 7565633 7565653 7565669
7565671 7565687 7565711 7565729 7565737 7565741 7565749 7565777 7565783 7565813
7565821 7565837 7565869 7565881 7565911 7565917 7565923 7565927 7565941 7565947
```

```
7565951  7565959  7566007  7566029  7566043  7566059  7566061  7566073  7566079  7566113
7566131  7566133  7566193  7566203  7566211  7566217  7566239  7566253  7566281  7566331
7566341  7566347  7566353  7566359  7566371  7566397  7566407  7566413  7566421  7566431
7566443  7566451  7566457  7566497  7566527  7566553  7566589  7566599  7566619  7566641
7566659  7566703  7566737  7566739  7566749  7566781  7566799  7566803  7566841  7566877
7566893  7566899  7566901  7566917  7566971  7566973  7566983  7567009  7567013  7567019
7567031  7567033  7567039  7567061  7567081  7567099  7567121  7567123  7567151  7567169
7567171  7567201  7567211  7567213  7567249  7567267  7567279  7567291  7567309  7567319
7567321  7567327  7567333  7567349  7567369  7567387  7567409  7567433  7567447  7567459
7567471  7567481  7567487  7567531  7567537  7567591  7567597  7567603  7567619  7567631
7567639  7567661  7567663  7567709  7567793  7567801  7567823  7567831  7567841  7567853
7567867  7567883  7567913  7567919  7567933  7567991  7568021  7568039  7568047
7568051  7568053  7568059  7568063  7568069  7568083  7568089  7568161  7568177  7568201
7568207  7568257  7568261  7568303  7568329  7568339  7568369  7568381  7568389  7568399
7568419  7568423  7568489  7568497  7568501  7568503  7568527  7568531  7568537  7568549
7568569  7568581  7568591  7568611  7568629  7568647  7568651  7568663  7568699  7568719
7568741  7568747  7568761  7568767  7568777  7568801  7568809  7568849  7568857  7568879
7568917  7568921  7568947  7568959  7568963  7568987  7568993  7568999  7569013  7569017
7569031  7569043  7569071  7569079  7569083  7569091  7569101  7569103  7569119
7569143  7569157  7569167  7569173  7569179  7569181  7569187  7569197  7569217  7569241
7569251  7569271  7569281  7569283  7569293  7569299  7569313  7569343  7569347  7569383
7569389  7569409  7569427  7569431  7569439  7569449  7569451  7569469  7569473
7569481  7569503  7569509  7569511  7569533  7569547  7569599  7569613  7569629  7569631
7569649  7569659  7569671  7569697  7569703  7569713  7569721  7569739  7569787  7569791
7569799  7569817  7569823  7569827  7569833  7569839  7569851  7569857  7569869  7569893
7569907  7569911  7569931  7569971  7569979  7569997  7570007  7570009  7570019
7570033  7570061  7570063  7570067  7570093  7570103  7570111  7570141  7570183  7570201
7570207  7570217  7570259  7570261  7570267  7570271  7570273  7570291  7570309  7570327
7570331  7570369  7570373  7570391  7570399  7570439  7570463  7570477  7570481  7570487
7570489  7570501  7570523  7570529  7570543  7570553  7570561  7570567  7570583  7570601
7570613  7570631  7570663  7570669  7570699  7570703  7570723  7570747  7570749  7570793
7570819  7570837  7570847  7570867  7570877  7570897  7570921  7570931  7570961  7570973
7570991  7570993  7571009  7571017  7571021  7571023  7571029  7571033  7571041  7571077
7571087  7571147  7571149  7571153  7571159  7571167  7571173  7571203  7571231  7571269
7571297  7571299  7571303  7571309  7571323  7571351  7571357  7571383  7571387  7571401
7571419  7571423  7571437  7571441  7571453  7571461  7571491  7571537  7571539  7571549
7571563  7571567  7571573  7571587  7571591  7571611  7571617  7571651  7571687  7571689
7571699  7571701  7571731  7571743  7571771  7571777  7571803  7571819  7571821  7571833
7571849  7571857  7571891  7571909  7571911  7571933  7571957  7571989  7572043  7572067
7572073  7572077  7572109  7572137  7572181  7572211  7572223  7572233  7572247  7572263
7572289  7572337  7572347  7572371  7572373  7572391  7572403  7572427  7572437  7572449
7572503  7572529  7572563  7572613  7572637  7572641  7572661  7572673  7572689  7572707
7572713  7572739  7572749  7572751  7572767  7572779  7572791  7572793  7572833  7572863
7572881  7572889  7572899  7572907  7572919  7572937  7572941  7572949  7572977  7572989
7572991  7572997  7573009  7573037  7573043  7573051  7573057  7573087  7573091  7573133
7573213  7573217  7573243  7573249  7573253  7573261  7573297  7573327  7573351
7573367  7573387  7573403  7573409  7573427  7573451  7573471  7573477  7573481  7573507
7573519  7573537  7573543  7573589  7573591  7573597  7573607  7573639  7573673  7573679
7573691  7573697  7573729  7573733  7573751  7573759  7573763  7573801  7573817  7573829
7573847  7573849  7573871  7573873  7573883  7573903  7573921  7573931  7573933  7573939
7573949  7573987  7573991  7574023  7574029  7574033  7574041  7574087  7574101  7574111
7574123  7574143  7574173  7574183  7574207  7574221  7574239  7574251  7574269  7574317
7574341  7574353  7574387  7574393  7574443  7574449  7574467  7574471  7574477  7574491
7574507  7574531  7574533  7574549  7574569  7574617  7574647  7574683  7574687  7574717
7574719  7574747  7574759  7574761  7574767  7574783  7574789  7574803  7574807  7574821
7574839  7574891  7574893  7574921  7574927  7574947  7574969  7574971  7574993  7574999
7575019  7575049  7575059  7575077  7575103  7575109  7575133  7575179  7575193  7575209
7575223  7575229  7575233  7575277  7575289  7575307  7575311  7575329  7575371  7575383
7575401  7575461  7575473  7575481  7575511  7575527  7575559  7575569  7575571  7575577
7575587  7575593  7575619  7575637  7575643  7575647  7575653  7575691  7575703  7575709
7575739  7575779  7575781  7575791  7575793  7575803  7575833  7575853  7575877  7575881
7575899  7575923  7575929  7575937  7575949  7575973  7576027  7576043  7576057  7576073
7576081  7576087  7576099  7576109  7576133  7576181  7576187  7576199  7576207
7576211  7576229  7576243  7576253  7576273  7576301  7576319  7576321  7576333  7576351
7576357  7576381  7576399  7576411  7576433  7576463  7576477  7576483  7576487  7576529
7576531  7576559  7576567  7576571  7576607  7576609  7576619  7576651  7576661  7576669
7576691  7576697  7576703  7576711  7576733  7576753  7576757  7576769  7576843  7576847
7576853  7576861  7576883  7576931  7576949  7576973  7576981  7576997  7577027  7577041
7577047  7577057  7577069  7577071  7577077  7577081  7577093  7577099  7577107  7577117
7577123  7577137  7577147  7577177  7577183  7577197  7577209  7577243  7577263  7577279
7577287  7577309  7577321  7577329  7577351  7577363  7577369  7577389  7577407  7577459
7577467  7577491  7577501  7577509  7577513  7577527  7577551  7577567  7577593  7577629
7577639  7577653  7577657  7577659  7577663  7577689  7577701  7577723  7577749  7577753
7577771  7577777  7577807  7577809  7577831  7577849  7577861  7577909  7577923  7577953
7578001  7578013  7578029  7578037  7578041  7578047  7578049  7578059  7578079  7578089
7578097  7578101  7578113  7578121  7578143  7578161  7578163  7578173  7578187  7578199
7578223  7578227  7578239  7578257  7578269  7578271  7578281  7578287  7578301  7578331
7578343  7578407  7578427  7578479  7578503  7578521  7578533  7578551  7578553  7578559
7578607  7578619  7578643  7578677  7578679  7578691  7578709  7578721  7578731  7578733
7578749  7578751  7578763  7578803  7578811  7578817  7578829  7578833  7578859  7578877
7578899  7578913  7578919  7578959  7578971  7579001  7579003  7579027  7579069  7579073
7579087  7579109  7579111  7579123  7579139  7579163  7579171  7579193  7579207  7579261
7579279  7579307  7579333  7579349  7579357  7579367  7579373  7579387  7579391
7579417  7579427  7579441  7579457  7579471  7579493  7579513  7579541  7579543  7579571
7579573  7579577  7579591  7579601  7579619  7579631  7579633  7579639  7579657  7579679
7579697  7579699  7579703  7579721  7579769  7579771  7579801  7579823  7579829  7579837
7579861  7579867  7579937  7579973  7580009  7580017  7580021  7580047  7580051  7580057
7580059  7580071  7580081  7580093  7580119  7580123  7580149  7580161  7580171  7580197
7580239  7580257  7580263  7580269  7580299  7580303  7580311  7580329  7580357  7580359
```

```
7580371 7580381 7580383 7580387 7580389 7580401 7580423 7580437 7580459 7580483
7580509 7580519 7580527 7580533 7580561 7580567 7580569 7580579 7580591 7580627
7580663 7580669 7580681 7580701 7580707 7580711 7580717 7580723 7580737 7580743
7580747 7580767 7580773 7580801 7580813 7580821 7580879 7580887 7580891 7580917
7580933 7580939 7580999 7581001 7581017 7581037 7581043 7581047 7581061 7581073
7581089 7581103 7581113 7581127 7581131 7581149 7581157 7581163 7581179 7581253
7581289 7581311 7581313 7581317 7581341 7581347 7581349 7581389 7581403 7581407
7581461 7581463 7581479 7581481 7581487 7581493 7581517 7581527 7581529 7581533
7581599 7581601 7581611 7581641 7581647 7581649 7581659 7581667 7581671 7581683
7581733 7581737 7581793 7581823 7581839 7581841 7581851 7581859 7581901 7581911
7581919 7581923 7581941 7581943 7581947 7581953 7581989 7581997 7582009 7582013
7582049 7582063 7582093 7582109 7582123 7582219 7582229 7582231 7582243 7582277
7582283 7582327 7582363 7582381 7582403 7582409 7582429 7582453 7582489 7582511
7582517 7582529 7582537 7582541 7582559 7582567 7582607 7582613 7582649 7582661
7582681 7582699 7582703 7582721 7582733 7582747 7582787 7582807 7582811 7582819
7582823 7582829 7582853 7582873 7582903 7582907 7582937 7582987 7582997 7582999
7583011 7583029 7583053 7583083 7583109 7583111 7583117 7583119 7583137 7583143
7583153 7583171 7583203 7583209 7583227 7583243 7583263 7583267 7583287 7583327
7583333 7583383 7583431 7583449 7583467 7583501 7583503 7583507 7583509 7583529
7583531 7583533 7583539 7583567 7583573 7583579 7583599 7583617 7583621 7583633
7583651 7583657 7583659 7583669 7583689 7583699 7583707 7583711 7583713 7583749
7583753 7583759 7583773 7583789 7583791 7583803 7583827 7583833 7583837 7583879
7583881 7583899 7583963 7583969 7583977 7583981 7584013 7584041 7584067 7584107
7584121 7584133 7584151 7584161 7584163 7584217 7584233 7584253 7584259 7584263
7584271 7584281 7584289 7584293 7584299 7584323 7584337 7584359 7584361 7584373
7584389 7584407 7584413 7584427 7584449 7584461 7584463 7584487 7584517 7584539
7584541 7584559 7584569 7584571 7584581 7584587 7584589 7584613 7584617 7584637
7584701 7584749 7584757 7584761 7584793 7584799 7584803 7584809 7584851 7584893
7584901 7584931 7584937 7584947 7584949 7584961 7584977 7584991 7585013 7585021
7585051 7585057 7585079 7585087 7585103 7585117 7585129 7585133 7585139 7585163
7585181 7585223 7585261 7585273 7585301 7585309 7585321 7585363 7585367 7585373
7585379 7585387 7585393 7585397 7585429 7585433 7585439 7585447 7585463 7585499
7585511 7585517 7585549 7585573 7585597 7585603 7585609 7585631 7585639 7585657
7585687 7585741 7585763 7585771 7585789 7585813 7585843 7585867 7585871 7585873
7585909 7585913 7585967 7585969 7585987 7586003 7586011 7586027 7586039 7586057
7586077 7586119 7586123 7586141 7586167 7586171 7586177 7586191 7586219 7586231
7586239 7586303 7586311 7586321 7586347 7586363 7586393 7586399 7586401 7586419
7586479 7586483 7586497 7586507 7586531 7586543 7586549 7586581 7586587 7586597
7586609 7586629 7586639 7586651 7586659 7586687 7586699 7586737 7586741 7586767
7586771 7586779 7586783 7586797 7586801 7586809 7586819 7586827 7586837 7586857
7586863 7586867 7586903 7586939 7586959 7586993 7587001 7587007 7587011 7587017
7587031 7587043 7587053 7587059 7587071 7587089 7587103 7587121 7587133 7587191
7587199 7587227 7587233 7587247 7587259 7587269 7587277 7587301 7587317 7587329
7587367 7587373 7587379 7587383 7587407 7587413 7587421 7587431 7587443 7587449
7587451 7587469 7587497 7587499 7587509 7587511 7587521 7587563 7587581 7587617
7587623 7587637 7587641 7587659 7587667 7587673 7587689 7587703 7587709 7587731
7587733 7587739 7587743 7587751 7587757 7587761 7587773 7587779 7587787 7587791
7587793 7587799 7587803 7587809 7587863 7587883 7587887 7587917 7587919 7587941
7587961 7587977 7587991 7588003 7588013 7588027 7588033 7588039 7588057 7588067
7588073 7588093 7588099 7588117 7588129 7588151 7588153 7588159 7588199 7588241
7588249 7588279 7588297 7588303 7588309 7588331 7588337 7588349 7588351 7588387
7588393 7588411 7588417 7588447 7588453 7588457 7588463 7588481 7588499 7588501
7588507 7588519 7588523 7588561 7588591 7588627 7588687 7588697 7588703 7588709
7588723 7588727 7588751 7588793 7588829 7588843 7588853 7588877 7588879 7588891
7588897 7588927 7588951 7588957 7588963 7588979 7589009 7589047 7589051 7589053
7589077 7589081 7589083 7589129 7589159 7589171 7589173 7589177 7589201 7589207
7589209 7589221 7589233 7589243 7589269 7589273 7589279 7589317 7589353 7589357
7589363 7589369 7589381 7589383 7589401 7589423 7589473 7589489 7589507 7589521
7589557 7589573 7589587 7589597 7589611 7589623 7589627 7589639 7589641 7589651
7589671 7589677 7589707 7589723 7589731 7589783 7589809 7589821 7589833 7589843
7589849 7589863 7589867 7589883 7589899 7589903 7589951 7589963 7589969 7589993
7589999 7590001 7590013 7590019 7590031 7590053 7590061 7590067 7590073 7590103
7590119 7590127 7590157 7590197 7590221 7590223 7590227 7590277 7590281 7590293
7590301 7590311 7590353 7590361 7590377 7590383 7590389 7590461 7590463 7590487
7590493 7590503 7590509 7590523 7590571 7590581 7590589 7590593 7590623 7590643
7590659 7590673 7590679 7590689 7590701 7590703 7590733 7590743 7590757 7590787
7590811 7590827 7590839 7590841 7590871 7590887 7590889 7590893 7590941 7590949
7590967 7590971 7591007 7591039 7591043 7591079 7591093 7591139 7591141
7591159 7591169 7591183 7591193 7591217 7591229 7591237 7591247 7591271 7591277
7591289 7591291 7591303 7591313 7591361 7591369 7591387 7591411 7591427 7591439
7591447 7591457 7591459 7591481 7591483 7591499 7591501 7591513 7591531 7591547
7591553 7591603 7591609 7591631 7591637 7591643 7591657 7591687 7591711 7591721
7591723 7591729 7591751 7591759 7591799 7591819 7591841 7591873 7591889 7591907
7591937 7591981 7592003 7592023 7592029 7592033 7592063 7592071 7592087 7592089
7592107 7592119 7592159 7592161 7592173 7592201 7592203 7592227 7592237 7592261
7592279 7592309 7592311 7592317 7592329 7592341 7592359 7592383 7592393 7592401
7592423 7592471 7592477 7592479 7592483 7592513 7592537 7592539 7592549 7592561
7592567 7592573 7592579 7592633 7592653 7592713 7592719 7592729 7592747 7592759
7592773 7592777 7592779 7592789 7592801 7592821 7592839 7592843 7592873 7592899
7592903 7592933 7592941 7592957 7592969 7592987 7592993 7593007 7593011 7593023
7593119 7593127 7593133 7593137 7593139 7593163 7593167 7593191 7593211 7593221
7593247 7593253 7593259 7593277 7593301 7593307 7593317 7593319 7593329 7593343
7593347 7593349 7593353 7593371 7593403 7593409 7593433 7593479 7593491 7593497
7593517 7593527 7593529 7593539 7593541 7593557 7593571 7593589 7593613 7593617
7593623 7593637 7593643 7593647 7593659 7593661 7593689 7593701 7593721 7593827
7593727 7593731 7593767 7593779 7593793 7593799 7593809 7593811 7593823 7593827
7593871 7593881 7593889 7593913 7593953 7593959 7593961 7593967 7593973 7593983
7593997 7594003 7594009 7594021 7594049 7594057 7594079 7594123 7594141 7594157
7594159 7594183 7594193 7594199 7594207 7594241 7594253 7594271 7594283 7594289
```

```
7594337  7594339  7594397  7594399  7594403  7594441  7594453  7594481  7594487  7594501
7594513  7594519  7594537  7594541  7594567  7594571  7594603  7594619  7594633  7594663
7594667  7594673  7594681  7594687  7594693  7594709  7594751  7594759  7594771  7594787
7594819  7594841  7594859  7594861  7594877  7594901  7594913  7594933  7594943  7594949
7594957  7594973  7594997  7594999  7595017  7595023  7595033  7595057  7595087  7595089
7595111  7595113  7595123  7595131  7595167  7595173  7595179  7595183  7595191  7595207
7595227  7595239  7595251  7595281  7595309  7595333  7595339  7595351  7595353  7595369
7595387  7595407  7595411  7595429  7595443  7595453  7595461  7595473  7595479  7595491
7595519  7595557  7595561  7595569  7595587  7595629  7595633  7595639  7595657  7595663
7595671  7595677  7595761  7595813  7595827  7595843  7595849  7595867  7595873  7595881
7595891  7595909  7595927  7595969  7595971  7595977  7596007  7596011  7596019  7596031
7596041  7596047  7596091  7596097  7596107  7596139  7596157  7596203  7596217  7596221
7596227  7596241  7596247  7596283  7596299  7596313  7596341  7596343  7596373  7596377
7596383  7596397  7596431  7596443  7596451  7596473  7596493  7596497  7596541  7596551
7596553  7596557  7596571  7596577  7596583  7596587  7596593  7596607  7596613  7596619
7596623  7596629  7596653  7596691  7596697  7596703  7596727  7596731  7596733  7596769
7596791  7596793  7596833  7596839  7596851  7596857  7596859  7596887  7596937
7596947  7596983  7597003  7597021  7597027  7597039  7597049  7597067  7597069  7597081
7597087  7597091  7597133  7597137  7597141  7597151  7597171  7597189  7597211  7597231
7597273  7597277  7597301  7597309  7597313  7597327  7597339  7597349  7597357  7597393
7597399  7597411  7597417  7597427  7597433  7597441  7597459  7597481  7597483  7597493
7597501  7597531  7597537  7597547  7597553  7597561  7597631  7597643  7597651  7597661
7597717  7597729  7597753  7597757  7597763  7597769  7597823  7597829  7597847  7597859
7597873  7597901  7597949  7597951  7597979  7598033  7598047  7598051  7598053  7598077
7598083  7598089  7598111  7598113  7598117  7598159  7598179  7598189  7598191  7598219
7598231  7598237  7598249  7598251  7598263  7598287  7598323  7598341  7598359  7598389
7598399  7598411  7598429  7598447  7598453  7598467  7598477  7598483  7598501  7598509
7598519  7598531  7598543  7598593  7598597  7598599  7598611  7598621  7598641  7598681
7598687  7598693  7598699  7598707  7598741  7598749  7598753  7598771  7598797  7598827
7598837  7598839  7598849  7598863  7598867  7598869  7598873  7598893  7598959  7599029
7599037  7599041  7599043  7599047  7599049  7599071  7599079  7599091  7599121  7599127
7599143  7599157  7599161  7599167  7599169  7599173  7599181  7599191  7599203  7599239
7599257  7599281  7599283  7599287  7599301  7599311  7599313  7599337  7599349  7599367
7599379  7599401  7599413  7599419  7599451  7599457  7599481  7599497  7599509  7599533
7599539  7599551  7599577  7599593  7599607  7599623  7599661  7599673  7599707  7599749
7599751  7599773  7599793  7599797  7599817  7599841  7599847  7599857  7599859  7599871
7599889  7599919  7599941  7599971  7599989  7600013  7600031  7600039  7600067  7600069
7600079  7600093  7600141  7600157  7600163  7600169  7600181  7600183  7600193  7600199
7600217  7600231  7600259  7600273  7600277  7600289  7600297  7600303  7600319  7600331
7600339  7600357  7600391  7600403  7600421  7600423  7600427  7600433  7600451  7600459
7600469  7600471  7600499  7600517  7600543  7600561  7600573  7600597  7600601  7600613
7600631  7600633  7600667  7600727  7600729  7600757  7600771  7600777  7600807
7600811  7600829  7600837  7600843  7600849  7600861  7600883  7600907  7600913  7600927
7600933  7600991  7600993  7601039  7601051  7601053  7601059  7601081  7601089
7601093  7601117  7601119  7601123  7601131  7601137  7601141  7601177  7601183  7601213
7601249  7601257  7601287  7601303  7601323  7601327  7601353  7601369  7601371  7601413
7601423  7601443  7601453  7601467  7601483  7601507  7601519  7601521  7601543  7601597
7601621  7601641  7601647  7601651  7601681  7601689  7601701  7601731  7601749  7601777
7601779  7601791  7601801  7601807  7601809  7601833  7601837  7601861  7601879  7601897
7601903  7601929  7601947  7601953  7601963  7601989  7602011  7602017  7602047  7602059
7602079  7602107  7602137  7602143  7602151  7602187  7602191  7602193  7602211  7602233
7602251  7602253  7602269  7602277  7602307  7602311  7602313  7602319  7602359  7602367
7602377  7602389  7602401  7602403  7602421  7602433  7602449  7602461  7602481  7602487
7602499  7602503  7602509  7602521  7602523  7602547  7602577  7602593  7602619  7602629
7602631  7602643  7602653  7602677  7602697  7602703  7602709  7602733  7602737  7602743
7602769  7602773  7602779  7602817  7602823  7602841  7602863  7602899  7602913  7602929
7602937  7602943  7602997  7603007  7603027  7603033  7603051  7603061  7603069  7603111
7603121  7603147  7603157  7603159  7603171  7603201  7603213  7603223  7603231  7603259
7603279  7603283  7603289  7603333  7603367  7603397  7603399  7603417  7603429  7603441
7603451  7603457  7603459  7603493  7603499  7603511  7603517  7603529  7603559  7603567
7603577  7603601  7603627  7603669  7603687  7603691  7603703  7603721  7603723  7603789
7603793  7603831  7603837  7603853  7603867  7603891  7603903  7603909  7603931  7603957
7603969  7603993  7604017  7604027  7604033  7604057  7604059  7604081  7604087
7604101  7604131  7604137  7604159  7604173  7604197  7604213  7604231  7604239  7604243
7604279  7604309  7604327  7604347  7604357  7604369  7604371  7604381  7604407  7604411
7604437  7604447  7604449  7604473  7604479  7604489  7604497  7604501  7604521  7604533
7604549  7604563  7604581  7604587  7604659  7604669  7604671  7604683  7604689  7604711
7604717  7604719  7604759  7604767  7604771  7604801  7604819  7604843  7604867
7604879  7604893  7604903  7604911  7604939  7604953  7604957  7604963  7604977  7604983
7604999  7605011  7605029  7605061  7605071  7605089  7605113  7605119  7605121  7605127
7605133  7605151  7605179  7605193  7605197  7605209  7605217  7605223  7605229  7605233
7605271  7605287  7605289  7605293  7605331  7605349  7605379  7605383  7605397  7605413
7605421  7605427  7605431  7605457  7605463  7605469  7605473  7605487  7605497  7605517
7605523  7605527  7605557  7605593  7605601  7605607  7605641  7605671  7605677  7605679
7605707  7605713  7605721  7605727  7605737  7605751  7605769  7605779  7605791  7605799
7605803  7605809  7605821  7605839  7605841  7605853  7605887  7605929  7605959  7605967
7605971  7606009  7606019  7606051  7606063  7606097  7606111  7606121  7606139  7606147
7606153  7606171  7606177  7606211  7606217  7606229  7606231  7606237  7606243  7606271
7606283  7606297  7606303  7606321  7606331  7606337  7606343  7606373  7606387  7606393
7606397  7606409  7606421  7606451  7606471  7606477  7606481  7606499  7606559  7606561
7606579  7606597  7606603  7606609  7606619  7606661  7606663  7606679  7606681  7606691
7606733  7606789  7606799  7606801  7606817  7606843  7606847  7606849  7606877  7606901
7606913  7606967  7606969  7606981  7606987  7607021  7607029  7607069  7607071  7607081
7607107  7607123  7607137  7607141  7607161  7607167  7607179  7607189  7607203  7607207
7607209  7607221  7607231  7607233  7607261  7607267  7607269  7607291  7607293  7607297
7607317  7607357  7607359  7607363  7607387  7607393  7607417  7607423  7607441  7607443
7607447  7607489  7607491  7607497  7607507  7607521  7607527  7607557  7607627  7607629
7607669  7607671  7607693  7607701  7607707  7607729  7607753  7607759  7607777  7607813
7607827  7607839  7607849  7607869  7607879  7607881  7607893  7607909  7607911  7607921
```

```
7607933 7607939 7607983 7608017 7608043 7608049 7608053 7608077 7608079 7608131
7608143 7608157 7608169 7608187 7608221 7608233 7608241 7608257 7608259 7608269
7608281 7608311 7608323 7608371 7608383 7608409 7608413 7608427 7608439 7608457
7608467 7608473 7608487 7608499 7608509 7608511 7608529 7608551 7608553 7608577
7608589 7608599 7608613 7608631 7608641 7608649 7608659 7608661 7608703 7608709
7608719 7608737 7608743 7608749 7608751 7608761 7608773 7608779 7608793 7608829
7608833 7608841 7608847 7608851 7608889 7608901 7608907 7608941 7608943 7608947
7608973 7608977 7609001 7609031 7609033 7609039 7609057 7609073 7609099 7609103
7609153 7609193 7609207 7609211 7609213 7609219 7609241 7609243 7609271 7609279
7609321 7609333 7609337 7609373 7609417 7609423 7609451 7609453 7609463 7609471
7609487 7609493 7609501 7609529 7609541 7609543 7609577 7609607 7609627 7609639
7609669 7609661 7609669 7609673 7609681 7609691 7609699 7609769 7609781 7609799
7609807 7609813 7609831 7609837 7609841 7609843 7609871 7609891 7609907 7609909
7609957 7609963 7610003 7610009 7610041 7610063 7610077 7610081 7610107 7610117
7610129 7610131 7610143 7610179 7610189 7610201 7610231 7610243 7610257 7610293
7610303 7610311 7610333 7610341 7610347 7610359 7610363 7610371 7610377 7610387
7610399 7610409 7610483 7610497 7610501 7610503 7610513 7610521 7610563 7610573
7610599 7610609 7610627 7610639 7610651 7610671 7610689 7610693 7610741 7610749
7610783 7610807 7610809 7610819 7610821 7610839 7610843 7610857 7610873 7610879
7610921 7610923 7610927 7610929 7610947 7610971 7610989 7611007 7611041 7611047
7611061 7611101 7611113 7611119 7611127 7611139 7611157 7611161 7611167 7611169
7611179 7611187 7611209 7611211 7611217 7611239 7611269 7611283 7611287 7611293
7611313 7611353 7611371 7611377 7611379 7611389 7611407 7611421 7611431 7611437
7611449 7611463 7611469 7611479 7611497 7611521 7611553 7611557 7611581 7611589
7611607 7611613 7611661 7611673 7611713 7611719 7611743 7611787 7611809 7611823
7611841 7611853 7611859 7611889 7611917 7611931 7611941 7611977 7611997 7612037
7612043 7612051 7612063 7612079 7612091 7612097 7612117 7612127 7612153
7612169 7612193 7612201 7612207 7612211 7612219 7612223 7612229 7612273 7612289
7612291 7612307 7612313 7612321 7612327 7612351 7612399 7612403 7612427 7612441
7612457 7612469 7612487 7612489 7612531 7612537 7612547 7612601 7612603 7612621
7612643 7612663 7612723 7612727 7612751 7612769 7612771 7612777 7612783 7612789
7612799 7612831 7612837 7612841 7612859 7612873 7612879 7612883 7612897 7612903
7612907 7612909 7612937 7612961 7612963 7612981 7612987 7613017 7613033 7613057
7613063 7613071 7613101 7613131 7613141 7613147 7613153 7613159 7613171 7613209
7613233 7613251 7613261 7613267 7613273 7613329 7613339 7613369 7613377 7613381
7613387 7613461 7613497 7613519 7613533 7613539 7613579 7613581 7613629 7613647
7613651 7613653 7613677 7613701 7613707 7613717 7613719 7613729 7613779 7613791
7613797 7613803 7613819 7613831 7613843 7613849 7613867 7613923 7613981 7613999
7614007 7614017 7614067 7614071 7614083 7614091 7614097 7614107 7614121 7614137
7614143 7614163 7614169 7614179 7614197 7614199 7614223 7614239 7614259 7614263
7614293 7614331 7614361 7614371 7614391 7614401 7614427 7614433 7614463 7614469
7614493 7614511 7614527 7614547 7614553 7614571 7614601 7614613 7614619 7614647
7614661 7614667 7614683 7614689 7614697 7614701 7614707 7614709 7614773 7614811
7614833 7614847 7614911 7614947 7614967 7614983 7615009 7615037 7615039 7615043
7615051 7615061 7615073 7615079 7615103 7615109 7615123 7615147 7615159 7615163
7615177 7615187 7615207 7615211 7615249 7615261 7615319 7615331 7615351 7615357
7615379 7615417 7615441 7615459 7615471 7615477 7615481 7615483 7615519 7615547
7615549 7615571 7615577 7615583 7615589 7615607 7615649 7615669 7615697 7615723
7615733 7615757 7615763 7615767 7615781 7615807 7615877 7615879 7615931 7615961
7615963 7615981 7615991 7615999 7616003 7616027 7616039 7616041 7616053 7616057
7616069 7616123 7616137 7616143 7616179 7616213 7616239 7616249 7616261 7616263
7616267 7616281 7616291 7616293 7616333 7616347 7616377 7616393 7616407 7616423
7616431 7616443 7616469 7616503 7616509 7616513 7616533 7616551 7616563 7616573
7616599 7616621 7616659 7616677 7616689 7616699 7616711 7616717 7616729 7616737
7616767 7616771 7616797 7616803 7616831 7616837 7616839 7616863 7616881 7616897
7616899 7616911 7616923 7616957 7616971 7616977 7616989 7617007 7617009 7617019
7617031 7617047 7617083 7617091 7617109 7617133 7617143 7617151 7617161 7617179
7617191 7617199 7617221 7617251 7617263 7617277 7617283 7617293 7617299 7617317
7617341 7617353 7617359 7617361 7617367 7617397 7617403 7617419 7617427 7617433
7617451 7617473 7617503 7617509 7617527 7617529 7617553 7617557 7617559 7617563
7617569 7617583 7617593 7617601 7617607 7617679 7617697 7617719 7617763 7617773
7617809 7617829 7617851 7617859 7617877 7617881 7617889 7617913 7617931 7617941
7617949 7617959 7617979 7617977 7618001 7618019 7618019 7618027 7618073 7618103
7618147 7618151 7618153 7618201 7618211 7618217 7618223 7618231 7618241 7618243
7618249 7618301 7618319 7618327 7618357 7618367 7618381 7618393 7618399 7618409
7618423 7618427 7618441 7618447 7618459 7618517 7618537 7618547 7618549 7618607
7618609 7618613 7618621 7618649 7618651 7618657 7618679 7618687 7618691 7618711
7618757 7618769 7618789 7618811 7618823 7618859 7618861 7618883 7618889 7618913
7618921 7618927 7618931 7618951 7618969 7618973 7619011 7619021 7619047 7619069
7619089 7619099 7619107 7619119 7619147 7619167 7619177 7619191 7619197 7619207
7619237 7619263 7619267 7619291 7619321 7619329 7619341 7619357 7619377 7619389
7619393 7619411 7619419 7619473 7619497 7619503 7619527 7619533 7619537 7619543
7619581 7619597 7619603 7619609 7619617 7619653 7619659 7619683 7619699 7619713
7619747 7619749 7619753 7619767 7619771 7619783 7619789 7619797 7619827 7619839
7619861 7619867 7619881 7619897 7619903 7619917 7619921 7619999 7620013 7620023
7620049 7620101 7620143 7620161 7620167 7620169 7620191 7620227 7620241 7620247
7620259 7620271 7620289 7620293 7620323 7620329 7620343 7620373 7620391 7620407
7620421 7620427 7620443 7620449 7620461 7620469 7620491 7620497 7620523 7620527
7620541 7620559 7620593 7620619 7620671 7620673 7620677 7620703 7620733 7620737
7620749 7620757 7620787 7620839 7620863 7620869 7620871 7620883 7620887 7620911
7620931 7620941 7620959 7620979 7621037 7621043 7621057 7621079 7621087 7621093
7621099 7621111 7621123 7621177 7621181 7621189 7621213 7621217 7621249 7621259
7621399 7621409 7621417 7621421 7621433 7621463 7621483 7621507 7621513 7621517
7621541 7621543 7621547 7621573 7621583 7621609 7621619 7621633 7621639 7621643
7621673 7621681 7621687 7621703 7621723 7621759 7621769 7621799 7621813 7621837
7621843 7621883 7621891 7621903 7621909 7621919 7621927 7621961 7621981 7621997
7622053 7622057 7622081 7622093 7622101 7622113 7622123 7622141 7622143 7622179
7622201 7622203 7622213 7622231 7622257 7622267 7622281 7622291 7622317 7622339
7622353 7622371 7622399 7622411 7622423 7622429 7622431 7622449 7622491 7622519
```

```
7622561  7622581  7622611  7622617  7622627  7622633  7622639  7622663  7622669  7622677
7622689  7622711  7622717  7622731  7622753  7622767  7622779  7622837  7622863  7622873
7622891  7622897  7622917  7622941  7622983  7623013  7623017  7623023  7623029  7623037
7623067  7623079  7623101  7623107  7623113  7623127  7623137  7623163  7623167  7623173
7623197  7623211  7623227  7623229  7623247  7623251  7623257  7623269  7623271  7623289
7623311  7623323  7623337  7623349  7623359  7623367  7623377  7623397  7623403  7623409
7623437  7623439  7623457  7623479  7623481  7623493  7623523  7623529  7623559  7623589
7623593  7623611  7623619  7623647  7623653  7623661  7623689  7623709  7623713  7623727
7623779  7623809  7623817  7623851  7623859  7623893  7623899  7623907  7623911  7623919
7623929  7623947  7623953  7623977  7623983  7624003  7624009  7624021  7624027  7624033
7624037  7624061  7624081  7624087  7624091  7624093  7624117  7624121  7624139  7624151
7624189  7624217  7624219  7624229  7624231  7624241  7624261  7624271  7624273  7624277
7624291  7624307  7624327  7624333  7624349  7624403  7624411  7624423  7624427  7624429
7624433  7624439  7624457  7624471  7624531  7624537  7624549  7624559  7624571  7624577
7624579  7624597  7624601  7624607  7624609  7624613  7624649  7624657  7624663  7624679
7624691  7624711  7624723  7624733  7624741  7624759  7624769  7624783  7624807  7624819
7624829  7624831  7624847  7624861  7624867  7624873  7624913  7624919  7624921  7624931
7624949  7624957  7624963  7624973  7625003  7625011  7625017  7625021  7625041  7625077
7625089  7625113  7625119  7625143  7625171  7625209  7625227  7625249  7625257  7625273
7625281  7625291  7625297  7625309  7625323  7625339  7625341  7625357  7625363  7625369
7625377  7625389  7625393  7625417  7625419  7625437  7625477  7625483  7625509  7625543
7625551  7625561  7625591  7625599  7625603  7625617  7625621  7625677  7625687  7625689
7625699  7625701  7625729  7625731  7625743  7625747  7625771  7625777  7625789  7625801
7625819  7625837  7625851  7625867  7625899  7625923  7625939  7625941  7625951  7625957
7626023  7626029  7626061  7626071  7626077  7626083  7626097  7626119  7626127  7626137
7626139  7626167  7626197  7626221  7626233  7626247  7626253  7626259  7626299  7626301
7626313  7626337  7626369  7626371  7626373  7626397  7626401  7626407  7626413  7626469
7626473  7626481  7626503  7626511  7626539  7626559  7626569  7626583  7626587  7626599
7626601  7626613  7626629  7626631  7626637  7626649  7626667  7626691  7626701  7626719
7626721  7626743  7626757  7626763  7626793  7626799  7626803  7626833  7626851  7626881
7626887  7626889  7626893  7626901  7626929  7626947  7626959  7626977  7626979  7626991
7627003  7627023  7627027  7627063  7627091  7627093  7627111  7627121  7627127  7627129
7627141  7627153  7627157  7627187  7627199  7627223  7627229  7627231  7627241  7627247
7627273  7627289  7627307  7627309  7627327  7627331  7627351  7627357  7627381  7627393
7627423  7627429  7627447  7627453  7627523  7627537  7627541  7627547  7627549  7627573
7627589  7627591  7627597  7627603  7627619  7627637  7627649  7627663  7627691  7627703
7627717  7627729  7627733  7627751  7627799  7627811  7627817  7627819  7627831  7627847
7627853  7627889  7627913  7627931  7627943  7627969  7627979  7627981  7628011  7628021
7628039  7628041  7628069  7628081  7628083  7628107  7628119  7628129  7628143
7628171  7628183  7628191  7628197  7628209  7628221  7628251  7628293  7628317  7628321
7628323  7628333  7628339  7628347  7628377  7628389  7628399  7628407  7628417  7628437
7628441  7628471  7628483  7628497  7628513  7628521  7628527  7628561  7628567  7628581
7628591  7628603  7628609  7628627  7628629  7628657  7628659  7628681  7628689  7628717
7628723  7628741  7628773  7628807  7628809  7628837  7628839  7628867  7628897  7628909
7628917  7628927  7628947  7628963  7628981  7628987  7629029  7629043  7629071  7629079
7629091  7629121  7629133  7629137  7629143  7629161  7629173  7629179  7629187  7629191
7629199  7629217  7629221  7629263  7629283  7629299  7629301  7629329  7629359  7629371
7629487  7629493  7629497  7629521  7629527  7629529  7629539  7629547  7629569  7629607
7629623  7629631  7629637  7629683  7629691  7629701  7629707  7629737  7629749  7629757
7629781  7629799  7629841  7629847  7629851  7629863  7629883  7629901  7629911  7629913
7629917  7629949  7629959  7629961  7629967  7629993  7629999  7630009  7630019  7630037
7630067  7630069  7630079  7630081  7630087  7630111  7630159  7630163  7630171  7630199
7630201  7630211  7630213  7630241  7630243  7630253  7630261  7630279  7630289  7630291
7630303  7630321  7630333  7630349  7630367  7630369  7630379  7630421  7630423  7630453
7630459  7630477  7630487  7630499  7630523  7630559  7630573  7630577  7630589  7630607
7630613  7630639  7630643  7630657  7630663  7630709  7630717  7630751  7630757
7630789  7630793  7630811  7630813  7630817  7630829  7630849  7630891  7630901  7630907
7630921  7630927  7630939  7630979  7630999  7631021  7631051  7631077  7631083  7631123
7631131  7631149  7631191  7631209  7631231  7631251  7631279  7631329  7631341  7631357
7631359  7631381  7631383  7631397  7631401  7631411  7631441  7631461  7631489  7631537
7631561  7631563  7631567  7631583  7631599  7631609  7631633  7631641  7631677  7631693
7631737  7631761  7631779  7631783  7631801  7631803  7631831  7631851  7631857  7631881
7631891  7631909  7631917  7631951  7631957  7631969  7631971  7631999  7632007  7632011
7632013  7632043  7632047  7632049  7632059  7632083  7632089  7632143  7632151  7632161
7632179  7632187  7632211  7632217  7632221  7632239  7632253  7632263  7632271  7632311
7632329  7632347  7632353  7632367  7632379  7632447  7632487  7632497  7632511  7632517
7632533  7632563  7632593  7632607  7632613  7632617  7632641  7632649  7632673  7632679
7632697  7632701  7632719  7632721  7632731  7632733  7632797  7632809  7632817
7632853  7632871  7632883  7632971  7633009  7633039  7633091  7633103  7633111  7633123
7633147  7633163  7633181  7633237  7633253  7633259  7633267  7633291  7633303  7633321
7633337  7633349  7633363  7633369  7633393  7633399  7633409  7633459  7633489  7633517
7633519  7633523  7633531  7633541  7633543  7633547  7633559  7633567  7633579  7633603
7633621  7633627  7633679  7633733  7633751  7633753  7633793  7633807  7633817  7633819
7633841  7633859  7633897  7633903  7633909  7633921  7633937  7633939  7633949  7633957
7633963  7633979  7633981  7633987  7634009  7634021  7634027  7634041  7634057  7634083
7634087  7634093  7634111  7634113  7634119  7634141  7634147  7634149  7634161  7634189
7634203  7634243  7634281  7634293  7634299  7634327  7634353  7634357  7634359  7634369
7634381  7634387  7634447  7634441  7634443  7634467  7634477  7634519  7634547  7634557
7634563  7634567  7634573  7634593  7634603  7634623  7634629  7634647  7634657  7634677
7634719  7634723  7634729  7634741  7634749  7634807  7634831  7634849  7634863
7634867  7634899  7634911  7634923  7634927  7634929  7634933  7634953  7634969  7634993
7634999  7635029  7635031  7635049  7635053  7635059  7635077  7635079  7635101  7635139
7635151  7635157  7635167  7635179  7635181  7635191  7635217  7635223  7635239  7635259
7635263  7635281  7635293  7635311  7635317  7635319  7635337  7635343  7635347  7635349
7635377  7635391  7635403  7635443  7635449  7635461  7635469  7635491  7635503  7635539
7635557  7635583  7635619  7635629  7635631  7635647  7635689  7635697  7635707  7635757
7635773  7635779  7635781  7635791  7635809  7635821  7635857  7635899  7635911  7635959
7635973  7635997  7636003  7636007  7636021  7636037  7636049  7636051  7636067  7636073
7636093  7636099  7636117  7636133  7636147  7636159  7636177  7636229  7636267  7636273
```

```
7636303 7636313 7636331 7636337 7636339 7636351 7636357 7636361 7636379 7636381
7636397 7636403 7636411 7636441 7636477 7636481 7636487 7636493 7636511 7636561
7636579 7636583 7636597 7636627 7636661 7636663 7636669 7636703 7636709 7636721
7636751 7636771 7636777 7636781 7636787 7636789 7636793 7636807 7636813 7636829
7636873 7636931 7636949 7636957 7636963 7636997 7636999 7637011 7637033 7637053
7637057 7637083 7637093 7637117 7637143 7637153 7637199 7637213 7637243 7637249
7637251 7637291 7637323 7637327 7637341 7637351 7637363 7637381 7637401 7637407
7637419 7637423 7637447 7637467 7637473 7637477 7637533 7637537 7637543 7637549
7637551 7637561 7637569 7637599 7637611 7637629 7637647 7637659 7637681 7637711
7637719 7637741 7637779 7637797 7637803 7637807 7637813 7637827 7637831 7637857
7637941 7637953 7637969 7637977 7638011 7638023 7638031 7638053 7638061 7638073
7638077 7638089 7638143 7638149 7638167 7638173 7638227 7638229 7638233 7638269
7638271 7638283 7638289 7638313 7638331 7638347 7638373 7638383 7638401 7638403
7638473 7638497 7638503 7638509 7638517 7638523 7638541 7638557 7638569 7638577
7638601 7638619 7638641 7638643 7638689 7638707 7638721 7638727 7638733 7638767
7638773 7638791 7638823 7638853 7638859 7638877 7638881 7638889 7638901 7638929
7638937 7638941 7638947 7638971 7638973 7638979 7638997 7639031 7639037 7639067
7639111 7639117 7639123 7639127 7639147 7639153 7639189 7639193 7639199 7639217
7639249 7639253 7639259 7639271 7639277 7639283 7639307 7639309 7639319 7639327
7639339 7639363 7639369 7639397 7639399 7639417 7639421 7639433 7639449 7639481
7639487 7639549 7639573 7639589 7639601 7639603 7639607 7639633 7639637 7639663
7639699 7639717 7639721 7639727 7639739 7639759 7639771 7639799 7639831 7639859
7639873 7639883 7639913 7639921 7639927 7639993 7639997 7639999 7640023 7640029
7640047 7640053 7640069 7640131 7640141 7640161 7640173 7640177 7640183 7640219
7640221 7640249 7640263 7640279 7640287 7640329 7640333 7640341 7640351 7640357
7640359 7640363 7640371 7640377 7640411 7640419 7640443 7640453 7640471 7640483
7640519 7640579 7640617 7640621 7640681 7640683 7640707 7640723 7640749 7640767
7640771 7640777 7640821 7640827 7640861 7640873 7640879 7640887 7640903 7640909
7640929 7640933 7640987 7640989 7640999 7641001 7641013 7641017 7641061
7641071 7641077 7641079 7641103 7641107 7641113 7641121 7641131 7641133 7641197
7641223 7641241 7641251 7641253 7641259 7641281 7641289 7641313 7641317 7641323
7641329 7641341 7641353 7641367 7641371 7641373 7641377 7641379 7641383 7641427
7641437 7641461 7641479 7641493 7641509 7641511 7641527 7641533 7641611 7641637
7641649 7641661 7641677 7641679 7641691 7641709 7641737 7641791 7641793 7641811
7641817 7641839 7641847 7641863 7641883 7641913 7641923 7641937 7641941 7641947
7641961 7641967 7641973 7641979 7641983 7641989 7642007 7642013 7642039 7642043
7642069 7642111 7642121 7642127 7642133 7642139 7642157 7642169 7642171 7642181
7642183 7642241 7642249 7642253 7642267 7642273 7642301 7642321 7642331 7642343
7642361 7642373 7642403 7642487 7642493 7642499 7642501 7642513 7642543 7642561
7642567 7642577 7642619 7642627 7642669 7642681 7642711 7642729 7642781 7642783
7642787 7642813 7642831 7642837 7642847 7642859 7642861 7642871
7642913 7642931 7642939 7642963 7643017 7643021 7643023 7643029 7643033 7643039
7643057 7643059 7643063 7643123 7643131 7643137 7643161 7643191 7643197 7643203
7643213 7643219 7643227 7643249 7643257 7643287 7643297 7643347 7643351 7643357
7643359 7643371 7643381 7643393 7643399 7643411 7643413 7643417 7643431 7643473
7643533 7643539 7643543 7643593 7643609 7643621 7643633 7643663 7643677
7643683 7643687 7643707 7643717 7643731 7643737 7643747 7643767 7643807 7643813
7643827 7643861 7643869 7643879 7643893 7643899 7643927 7643937 7643953 7643957
7643959 7643969 7644001 7644017 7644019 7644029 7644037 7644041 7644047 7644053
7644059 7644071 7644079 7644083 7644103 7644107 7644157 7644167 7644193 7644199
7644223 7644229 7644253 7644269 7644281 7644293 7644317 7644347 7644353 7644367
7644389 7644391 7644421 7644431 7644433 7644449 7644467 7644489 7644521
7644523 7644529 7644541 7644547 7644551 7644587 7644599 7644601 7644617 7644691
7644709 7644739 7644797 7644799 7644803 7644843 7644853 7644887 7644899 7644907
7644913 7644919 7644937 7644953 7644961 7644991 7644997 7645007 7645061 7645073
7645117 7645159 7645171 7645219 7645237 7645283 7645289 7645301 7645307 7645327
7645331 7645333 7645343 7645387 7645403 7645411 7645423 7645433 7645447 7645483
7645487 7645489 7645501 7645507 7645513 7645523 7645577 7645579 7645601 7645607
7645661 7645663 7645667 7645669 7645681 7645691 7645697 7645709 7645739 7645753
7645783 7645789 7645817 7645837 7645843 7645853 7645861 7645889 7645909 7645943
7645991 7645999 7646011 7646017 7646027 7646029 7646033 7646047 7646059
7646071 7646083 7646099 7646117 7646123 7646129 7646137 7646147 7646153 7646179
7646183 7646201 7646231 7646263 7646279 7646293 7646297 7646299 7646321
7646323 7646329 7646351 7646369 7646393 7646423 7646437 7646453 7646461 7646473
7646479 7646497 7646501 7646503 7646519 7646567 7646581 7646641 7646659
7646663 7646671 7646687 7646699 7646711 7646729 7646731 7646747 7646761 7646789
7646803 7646831 7646843 7646861 7646887 7646897 7646909 7646921 7646953 7646959
7646993 7647001 7647019 7647023 7647037 7647041 7647061 7647071 7647091 7647103
7647149 7647151 7647181 7647191 7647193 7647221 7647227 7647259 7647319 7647337
7647347 7647373 7647377 7647391 7647397 7647427 7647439 7647457 7647461 7647463
7647469 7647487 7647491 7647499 7647517 7647527 7647539 7647571 7647583 7647587
7647589 7647599 7647613 7647617 7647643 7647659 7647667 7647683 7647691 7647701
7647733 7647743 7647749 7647763 7647781 7647791 7647789 7647839 7647877 7647883
7647889 7647901 7647923 7647931 7647949 7647973 7647989 7648001 7648009 7648019
7648027 7648031 7648057 7648061 7648073 7648093 7648097 7648163 7648171 7648177
7648183 7648211 7648217 7648219 7648237 7648243 7648261 7648309 7648313 7648327
7648331 7648337 7648343 7648349 7648369 7648387 7648391 7648411 7648439 7648441
7648447 7648463 7648481 7648493 7648499 7648513 7648523 7648549 7648559 7648609
7648633 7648637 7648643 7648649 7648687 7648703 7648727 7648747 7648757 7648763
7648777 7648789 7648813 7648841 7648847 7648871 7648891 7648897 7648913
7648931 7648939 7648943 7648951 7648967 7648981 7648987 7649003 7649009 7649021
7649023 7649029 7649063 7649071 7649113 7649137 7649143 7649177 7649209 7649231
7649237 7649241 7649251 7649261 7649263 7649273 7649311 7649347 7649353 7649377
7649393 7649413 7649431 7649459 7649471 7649479 7649499 7649513
7649539 7649557 7649561 7649567 7649573 7649599 7649617 7649641 7649651 7649671
7649689 7649693 7649737 7649749 7649783 7649791 7649797 7649801 7649833 7649849
7649867 7649879 7649887 7649897 7649899 7649933 7649953 7649959 7649969 7649977
7650011 7650023 7650031 7650047 7650077 7650121 7650197 7650199 7650239 7650241
7650257 7650263 7650277 7650299 7650301 7650311 7650317 7650319 7650337 7650343
```

```
7650347 7650361 7650367 7650373 7650389 7650413 7650451 7650457 7650479 7650499
7650541 7650547 7650551 7650553 7650563 7650593 7650611 7650623 7650631 7650647
7650653 7650683 7650701 7650719 7650733 7650739 7650757 7650761 7650763 7650791
7650817 7650827 7650847 7650883 7650917 7650919 7650941 7650949 7650959 7650961
7651009 7651013 7651043 7651073 7651087 7651093 7651097 7651103 7651121 7651151
7651153 7651159 7651187 7651211 7651219 7651261 7651277 7651289 7651339 7651373
7651403 7651421 7651477 7651499 7651507 7651517 7651529 7651537 7651541 7651559
7651573 7651591 7651603 7651607 7651613 7651619 7651627 7651639 7651643 7651673
7651681 7651723 7651739 7651747 7651753 7651759 7651771 7651783 7651793 7651817
7651829 7651849 7651867 7651873 7651879 7651907 7651913 7651949 7651951 7651961
7651993 7651999 7652011 7652017 7652053 7652059 7652083 7652111 7652119 7652129
7652171 7652189 7652191 7652207 7652213 7652219 7652251 7652273 7652287 7652291
7652297 7652321 7652347 7652357 7652369 7652387 7652401 7652413 7652417 7652423
7652453 7652471 7652483 7652501 7652503 7652509 7652521 7652531 7652543 7652551
7652569 7652641 7652647 7652657 7652677 7652693 7652717 7652731 7652761 7652779
7652783 7652819 7652837 7652857 7652863 7652881 7652891 7652917 7652921 7652929
7652947 7652959 7652987 7652989 7652997 7653007 7653017 7653031 7653047 7653049
7653053 7653083 7653091 7653103 7653119 7653157 7653193 7653211 7653229 7653251
7653259 7653263 7653271 7653277 7653293 7653299 7653301 7653307 7653313 7653323
7653329 7653353 7653367 7653391 7653403 7653427 7653431 7653439 7653449 7653467
7653509 7653517 7653533 7653551 7653557 7653577 7653601 7653623 7653631 7653649
7653661 7653671 7653673 7653691 7653697 7653707 7653727 7653749 7653761 7653781
7653797 7653799 7653803 7653847 7653901 7653953 7653959 7653967 7654001 7654007
7654019 7654037 7654051 7654067 7654069 7654081 7654109 7654121 7654133 7654139
7654189 7654211 7654217 7654223 7654237 7654243 7654253 7654259 7654271 7654277
7654291 7654319 7654337 7654349 7654357 7654363 7654379 7654391 7654399 7654411
7654429 7654441 7654457 7654477 7654481 7654499 7654513 7654529 7654541 7654567
7654571 7654627 7654649 7654679 7654681 7654687 7654693 7654697 7654729 7654763
7654769 7654771 7654793 7654807 7654813 7654831 7654847 7654859 7654867 7654873
7654897 7654901 7654909 7654919 7654939 7654973 7655003 7655017 7655023 7655027
7655051 7655057 7655071 7655107 7655183 7655201 7655203 7655213 7655227 7655231
7655237 7655239 7655257 7655273 7655279 7655281 7655299 7655303 7655311 7655341
7655363 7655369 7655377 7655381 7655383 7655387 7655413 7655429 7655443 7655467
7655489 7655503 7655519 7655521 7655533 7655569 7655579 7655587 7655597 7655611
7655639 7655647 7655657 7655693 7655701 7655719 7655723 7655737 7655759 7655761
7655777 7655779 7655789 7655801 7655821 7655833 7655839 7655881 7655891 7655897
7655939 7655953 7656007 7656041 7656043 7656059 7656073 7656097 7656109 7656133
7656149 7656161 7656211 7656247 7656281 7656301 7656323 7656331 7656379 7656413
7656431 7656437 7656457 7656469 7656497 7656499 7656527 7656529 7656533 7656577
7656589 7656611 7656619 7656637 7656641 7656643 7656653 7656661 7656673 7656679
7656689 7656697 7656713 7656731 7656763 7656787 7656809 7656821 7656823 7656839
7656863 7656877 7656893 7656931 7656941 7656947 7656949 7656959 7656989 7656991
7657003 7657007 7657009 7657049 7657061 7657103 7657109 7657121 7657127 7657159
7657253 7657271 7657289 7657291 7657297 7657303 7657313 7657333 7657339 7657357
7657379 7657423 7657427 7657511 7657519 7657523 7657541 7657543 7657561 7657571
7657579 7657591 7657607 7657609 7657613 7657679 7657687 7657691 7657709 7657717
7657721 7657723 7657751 7657777 7657789 7657807 7657813 7657831 7657841 7657849
7657861 7657877 7657891 7657901 7657907 7657933 7657963 7657967 7657987 7657997
7658009 7658017 7658071 7658081 7658087 7658089 7658099 7658113 7658137 7658173
7658201 7658207 7658213 7658237 7658249 7658269 7658281 7658293 7658309 7658317
7658323 7658351 7658363 7658369 7658383 7658393 7658401 7658419 7658459 7658461
7658467 7658473 7658491 7658507 7658531 7658579 7658587 7658591 7658597 7658621
7658627 7658633 7658641 7658647 7658657 7658663 7658669 7658671 7658681 7658683
7658689 7658713 7658723 7658737 7658743 7658779 7658831 7658867 7658869 7658879
7658899 7658921 7658927 7658933 7658939 7658947 7658951 7658969 7659011 7659013
7659017 7659019 7659053 7659059 7659079 7659097 7659101 7659107 7659137 7659143
7659149 7659187 7659199 7659209 7659227 7659241 7659247 7659257 7659271 7659283
7659329 7659347 7659361 7659383 7659419 7659427 7659467 7659493 7659499 7659517
7659521 7659541 7659563 7659569 7659577 7659581 7659583 7659599 7659601 7659611
7659623 7659647 7659721 7659727 7659737 7659749 7659787 7659791 7659803 7659811
7659853 7659887 7659889 7659893 7659901 7659917 7659923 7659929 7659937 7659991
7659997 7660001 7660027 7660039 7660057 7660061 7660067 7660087 7660099 7660129
7660139 7660181 7660199 7660207 7660223 7660231 7660243 7660271 7660291 7660297
7660307 7660309 7660339 7660349 7660361 7660397 7660409 7660417 7660423 7660427
7660459 7660469 7660507 7660529 7660531 7660559 7660561 7660573 7660589 7660603
7660607 7660621 7660643 7660649 7660699 7660703 7660711 7660717 7660721 7660729
7660747 7660753 7660787 7660801 7660811 7660823 7660841 7660871 7660883 7660889
7660907 7660943 7660967 7660969 7660993 7661029 7661039 7661053 7661057 7661077
7661081 7661083 7661089 7661099 7661111 7661119 7661189 7661197 7661207 7661221
7661233 7661239 7661279 7661281 7661293 7661299 7661317 7661321 7661333 7661347
7661393 7661399 7661411 7661471 7661473 7661483 7661491 7661497 7661531 7661567
7661581 7661603 7661639 7661663 7661671 7661677 7661707 7661723 7661741 7661749
7661771 7661789 7661803 7661821 7661827 7661831 7661833 7661837 7661851 7661881
7661897 7661903 7661939 7661947 7661963 7661981 7661989 7661993 7662001 7662023
7662029 7662047 7662077 7662079 7662089 7662091 7662103 7662139 7662143 7662169
7662173 7662211 7662217 7662227 7662241 7662247 7662307 7662313 7662329 7662331
7662337 7662353 7662371 7662397 7662401 7662407 7662419 7662433 7662451 7662463
7662469 7662481 7662493 7662517 7662621 7662629 7662647 7662659 7662667 7662701
7662751 7662761 7662773 7662803 7662827 7662847 7662877 7662913 7662917 7662929
7663009 7663049 7663063 7663069 7663081 7663087 7663093 7663109 7663127 7663133
7663147 7663153 7663157 7663171 7663177 7663189 7663193 7663207 7663211 7663223
7663241 7663261 7663267 7663273 7663283 7663297 7663319 7663343 7663349 7663361
7663367 7663373 7663387 7663399 7663421 7663427 7663459 7663471 7663489 7663499
7663501 7663507 7663529 7663567 7663633 7663637 7663693 7663697 7663709 7663729
7663739 7663741 7663751 7663769 7663781 7663793 7663813 7663823 7663829 7663871
7663907 7663927 7663951 7663967 7663969 7663993 7664009 7664021 7664023 7664029
7664047 7664053 7664077 7664123 7664147 7664177 7664179 7664203 7664219 7664227
7664231 7664249 7664273 7664281 7664309 7664311 7664329 7664341 7664351 7664357
7664369 7664407 7664453 7664477 7664483 7664507 7664519
```

```
7664537  7664549  7664551  7664557  7664561  7664563  7664597  7664611  7664627  7664633
7664641  7664651  7664653  7664669  7664687  7664717  7664737  7664753  7664791  7664803
7664821  7664849  7664851  7664863  7664873  7664887  7664929  7664933  7664939  7664953
7664963  7664971  7664983  7665017  7665023  7665061  7665071  7665083  7665101  7665107
7665127  7665131  7665143  7665149  7665167  7665191  7665197  7665239  7665247  7665257
7665271  7665311  7665313  7665347  7665353  7665389  7665397  7665407  7665431  7665439
7665451  7665461  7665491  7665503  7665517  7665527  7665533  7665547  7665557  7665571
7665583  7665613  7665641  7665667  7665703  7665731  7665733  7665737  7665743  7665751
7665769  7665781  7665787  7665821  7665829  7665851  7665859  7665863  7665881  7665899
7665907  7665913  7665953  7665967  7665979  7666003  7666013  7666027  7666037  7666039
7666069  7666091  7666093  7666103  7666117  7666151  7666157  7666159  7666163  7666171
7666181  7666213  7666247  7666249  7666261  7666273  7666277  7666279  7666313  7666333
7666349  7666357  7666381  7666409  7666423  7666433  7666453  7666459  7666487  7666493
7666501  7666531  7666543  7666553  7666559  7666573  7666583  7666591  7666597  7666619
7666621  7666639  7666661  7666667  7666669  7666693  7666699  7666717  7666741  7666787
7666819  7666849  7666853  7666859  7666903  7666909  7666913  7666973  7666993  7666999
7667003  7667021  7667047  7667053  7667057  7667069  7667111  7667113  7667129  7667147
7667159  7667173  7667183  7667207  7667237  7667243  7667267  7667269  7667293  7667329
7667333  7667377  7667381  7667383  7667417  7667449  7667453  7667461  7667467  7667477
7667483  7667519  7667531  7667537  7667551  7667567  7667599  7667603  7667609  7667641
7667651  7667677  7667707  7667711  7667713  7667719  7667729  7667747  7667749  7667767
7667771  7667783  7667791  7667801  7667827  7667839  7667857  7667873  7667893  7667903
7667911  7667923  7667953  7667971  7667999  7668007  7668019  7668029  7668049  7668079
7668091  7668113  7668137  7668149  7668161  7668197  7668203  7668231  7668257  7668281
7668299  7668313  7668337  7668389  7668391  7668403  7668421  7668433  7668449  7668467
7668481  7668527  7668541  7668559  7668587  7668589  7668601  7668611  7668613  7668629
7668631  7668653  7668667  7668671  7668677  7668691  7668697  7668701  7668707  7668709
7668757  7668823  7668827  7668833  7668839  7668851  7668877  7668883  7668889  7668893
7668901  7668911  7668919  7668937  7668977  7669001  7669003  7669019  7669033  7669043
7669049  7669063  7669069  7669087  7669163  7669169  7669171  7669177  7669213  7669231
7669247  7669267  7669273  7669279  7669301  7669303  7669309  7669339  7669367  7669393
7669411  7669421  7669429  7669447  7669451  7669457  7669463  7669489  7669517  7669547
7669549  7669553  7669561  7669579  7669589  7669663  7669667  7669681  7669687  7669699
7669721  7669723  7669751  7669759  7669777  7669793  7669811  7669813  7669817  7669819
7669843  7669847  7669859  7669877  7669943  7669951  7669967  7669979  7670021  7670023
7670027  7670083  7670087  7670141  7670147  7670153  7670161  7670171  7670191  7670197
7670203  7670207  7670231  7670233  7670249  7670251  7670261  7670269  7670303  7670317
7670363  7670381  7670389  7670393  7670401  7670441  7670461  7670473  7670489  7670491
7670501  7670503  7670527  7670539  7670543  7670561  7670573  7670639  7670653  7670693
7670701  7670711  7670713  7670749  7670771  7670797  7670801  7670807  7670809  7670827
7670833  7670837  7670843  7670869  7670879  7670881  7670903  7670941  7670947  7670963
7670969  7670987  7670989  7671017  7671023  7671049  7671089  7671091  7671101  7671113
7671143  7671149  7671163  7671179  7671187  7671217  7671227  7671241  7671263  7671277
7671289  7671319  7671343  7671359  7671361  7671371  7671373  7671407  7671413  7671451
7671463  7671467  7671473  7671487  7671493  7671509  7671511  7671523  7671541  7671553
7671569  7671571  7671577  7671583  7671637  7671679  7671721  7671731  7671733  7671737
7671751  7671757  7671779  7671791  7671799  7671809  7671817  7671821  7671893  7671899
7671901  7671907  7671929  7671941  7671959  7671967  7671971  7671977  7672003  7672009
7672013  7672019  7672033  7672039  7672057  7672073  7672099  7672109  7672111  7672123
7672127  7672141  7672163  7672169  7672177  7672199  7672201  7672229  7672241  7672261
7672267  7672307  7672319  7672337  7672359  7672349  7672391  7672417  7672429  7672487
7672493  7672507  7672513  7672529  7672541  7672543  7672549  7672571  7672589  7672597
7672631  7672663  7672657  7672663  7672669  7672697  7672711  7672739  7672741  7672759
7672783  7672787  7672793  7672799  7672853  7672859  7672867  7672879  7672883  7672901
7672909  7672913  7672927  7672937  7672943  7672981  7672993  7672999  7673011  7673047
7673051  7673059  7673143  7673119  7673143  7673167  7673179  7673209  7673219  7673227
7673231  7673243  7673261  7673269  7673279  7673297  7673311  7673317  7673327  7673333
7673357  7673383  7673387  7673401  7673423  7673431  7673453  7673489  7673503  7673509
7673521  7673527  7673531  7673537  7673539  7673543  7673569  7673581  7673597  7673621
7673791  7673801  7673819  7673843  7673903  7673917  7673959  7673969  7673977  7673989
7673993  7673999  7674001  7674031  7674047  7674049  7674091  7674101  7674109  7674131
7674137  7674179  7674181  7674197  7674209  7674223  7674269  7674287  7674311  7674323
7674353  7674367  7674377  7674379  7674389  7674413  7674419  7674431  7674437  7674439
7674451  7674467  7674481  7674487  7674521  7674523  7674533  7674551  7674553  7674587
7674619  7674629  7674673  7674691  7674697  7674707  7674713  7674721  7674731  7674743
7674767  7674773  7674781  7674809  7674829  7674869  7674881  7674883  7674899  7674911
7674971  7674977  7675009  7675013  7675023  7675049  7675067  7675099  7675103  7675121
7675141  7675193  7675207  7675219  7675229  7675247  7675267  7675273  7675289  7675303
7675309  7675331  7675337  7675351  7675357  7675363  7675427  7675433  7675469  7675471
7675477  7675489  7675511  7675553  7675567  7675571  7675579  7675589  7675621  7675637
7675649  7675669  7675673  7675727  7675729  7675741  7675747  7675763  7675769  7675771
7675793  7675847  7675853  7675873  7675931  7675939  7675949  7675957  7675961  7675991
7675999  7676021  7676041  7676083  7676113  7676173  7676177  7676191  7676233  7676243
7676269  7676293  7676297  7676311  7676321  7676341  7676359  7676363  7676371  7676377
7676419  7676447  7676477  7676491  7676507  7676519  7676527  7676531  7676563  7676567
7676569  7676579  7676593  7676597  7676609  7676611  7676621  7676633  7676671  7676699
7676719  7676741  7676783  7676791  7676803  7676807  7676819  7676821  7676827  7676849
7676857  7676861  7676887  7676923  7676939  7676947  7676957  7676959  7676971  7676987
7676989  7677001  7677011  7677029  7677031  7677049  7677053  7677067  7677071  7677073
7677079  7677097  7677113  7677151  7677161  7677169  7677179  7677203  7677211  7677223
7677227  7677253  7677269  7677281  7677283  7677323  7677359  7677379  7677409  7677413
7677433  7677437  7677487  7677503  7677511  7677533  7677569  7677581  7677587  7677589
7677599  7677601  7677613  7677623  7677661  7677673  7677679  7677713  7677751  7677757
7677793  7677797  7677799  7677809  7677811  7677821  7677889  7677893  7677903  7677911
7677937  7677959  7677961  7677973  7677991  7678003  7678031  7678043  7678051  7678087
7678091  7678093  7678171  7678183  7678189  7678211  7678217  7678273  7678283  7678291
7678309  7678313  7678327  7678331  7678361  7678367  7678379  7678387  7678397  7678403
7678409  7678453  7678459  7678477  7678507  7678511  7678513  7678523  7678571  7678589
```

```
7678597  7678609  7678613  7678621  7678631  7678633  7678637  7678661  7678663  7678667
7678681  7678709  7678733  7678751  7678771  7678787  7678789  7678817  7678841  7678859
7678861  7678873  7678889  7678927  7678933  7678961  7678963  7678967  7678999  7679003
7679039  7679081  7679099  7679101  7679123  7679129  7679149  7679153  7679197  7679201
7679207  7679213  7679233  7679267  7679281  7679299  7679317  7679323  7679383  7679389
7679429  7679437  7679443  7679459  7679467  7679479  7679491  7679509  7679513  7679521
7679557  7679561  7679569  7679627  7679653  7679687  7679689  7679701  7679713  7679719
7679747  7679761  7679773  7679797  7679827  7679849  7679873  7679879  7679911  7679921
7679923  7679927  7679951  7679957  7679963  7679977  7679981  7679989  7680017  7680019
7680037  7680059  7680067  7680103  7680119  7680131  7680149  7680173  7680181  7680191
7680217  7680247  7680251  7680259  7680269  7680287  7680289  7680293  7680329  7680341
7680377  7680383  7680419  7680437  7680469  7680479  7680493  7680509  7680523  7680527
7680539  7680553  7680559  7680581  7680613  7680637  7680649  7680667  7680671  7680677
7680691  7680697  7680727  7680733  7680763  7680779  7680791  7680809  7680811  7680847
7680859  7680863  7680877  7680887  7680929  7680973  7680979  7680989  7681007  7681013
7681021  7681031  7681039  7681109  7681123  7681147  7681153  7681169  7681199  7681213
7681231  7681243  7681249  7681307  7681337  7681357  7681361  7681363  7681367  7681369
7681403  7681409  7681411  7681487  7681489  7681493  7681507  7681511  7681519  7681537
7681543  7681573  7681577  7681589  7681591  7681613  7681631  7681651  7681657  7681691
7681693  7681711  7681753  7681763  7681771  7681783  7681787  7681789  7681799  7681811
7681813  7681819  7681837  7681867  7681879  7681889  7681937  7681939  7681969  7681991
7682021  7682029  7682053  7682057  7682083  7682089  7682093  7682107  7682111  7682117
7682119  7682149  7682159  7682173  7682189  7682201  7682219  7682221  7682237  7682239
7682261  7682281  7682309  7682321  7682329  7682333  7682341  7682359  7682369  7682377
7682383  7682387  7682393  7682399  7682417  7682431  7682471  7682489  7682491  7682527
7682533  7682551  7682557  7682581  7682629  7682639  7682641  7682659  7682683  7682687
7682693  7682711  7682737  7682743  7682749  7682771  7682789  7682809  7682813  7682819
7682833  7682837  7682849  7682869  7682879  7682881  7682891  7682893  7682911  7682923
7682951  7682977  7682993  7683017  7683029  7683037  7683041  7683047  7683077  7683089
7683101  7683107  7683131  7683233  7683241  7683253  7683259  7683271  7683287  7683293
7683307  7683317  7683341  7683343  7683367  7683409  7683413  7683431  7683479  7683497
7683517  7683527  7683539  7683547  7683553  7683583  7683593  7683601  7683617  7683649
7683663  7683673  7683707  7683719  7683721  7683727  7683749  7683757  7683773  7683787
7683821  7683829  7683859  7683931  7683939  7683943  7683967  7683989  7684007
7684009  7684021  7684087  7684091  7684133  7684147  7684169  7684207  7684211  7684213
7684247  7684253  7684267  7684273  7684283  7684301  7684319  7684361  7684367  7684381
7684399  7684403  7684421  7684423  7684429  7684441  7684447  7684477  7684483  7684489
7684519  7684529  7684549  7684583  7684603  7684619  7684639  7684661  7684667  7684669
7684673  7684693  7684709  7684711  7684751  7684757  7684763  7684769  7684771  7684777
7684793  7684801  7684813  7684819  7684837  7684871  7684877  7684889  7684891  7684903
7684939  7684951  7684973  7684997  7685021  7685023  7685033  7685047  7685057  7685077
7685107  7685129  7685137  7685141  7685143  7685149  7685189  7685201  7685231  7685257
7685269  7685297  7685341  7685351  7685383  7685387  7685389  7685401  7685423  7685429
7685437  7685459  7685467  7685497  7685501  7685521  7685527  7685543  7685549  7685593
7685627  7685641  7685647  7685651  7685653  7685663  7685669  7685681  7685687  7685693
7685701  7685707  7685719  7685729  7685759  7685761  7685767  7685789  7685791  7685801
7685807  7685809  7685827  7685833  7685849  7685851  7685857  7685879  7685891  7685893
7685903  7685911  7685941  7686011  7686017  7686037  7686053  7686067  7686083  7686101
7686103  7686139  7686143  7686149  7686157  7686179  7686181  7686187  7686191  7686199
7686221  7686223  7686257  7686271  7686277  7686319  7686323  7686331  7686391  7686443
7686449  7686541  7686589  7686593  7686617  7686619  7686631  7686649  7686689  7686691
7686719  7686727  7686733  7686739  7686751  7686817  7686821  7686851  7686857  7686859
7686863  7686869  7686871  7686883  7686911  7686919  7686923  7686947  7686953
7686979  7686983  7687003  7687013  7687021  7687061  7687063  7687073  7687079  7687081
7687087  7687093  7687103  7687123  7687133  7687139  7687181  7687217  7687219  7687223
7687237  7687261  7687271  7687283  7687289  7687297  7687321  7687327  7687331  7687387
7687399  7687409  7687439  7687447  7687483  7687487  7687499  7687501  7687517  7687573
7687579  7687607  7687619  7687627  7687637  7687651  7687663  7687699  7687711  7687717
7687733  7687739  7687741  7687763  7687777  7687793  7687811  7687829  7687831  7687847
7687853  7687861  7687873  7687919  7687921  7687937  7687943  7687949  7687963  7687991
7687993  7688011  7688017  7688039  7688047  7688071  7688077  7688101  7688117  7688129
7688143  7688159  7688171  7688173  7688189  7688209  7688237  7688243  7688273  7688297
7688299  7688309  7688321  7688327  7688333  7688389  7688399  7688413  7688419  7688431
7688449  7688459  7688491  7688497  7688503  7688537  7688543  7688561  7688581  7688591
7688627  7688663  7688671  7688677  7688687  7688727  7688731  7688753  7688789  7688797
7688809  7688839  7688843  7688861  7688881  7688887  7688893  7688921  7688929  7688951
7688957  7688963  7688971  7688983  7688999  7689043  7689047  7689103  7689109  7689119
7689137  7689139  7689193  7689197  7689211  7689221  7689223  7689239  7689257
7689299  7689301  7689323  7689343  7689359  7689391  7689397  7689401  7689419  7689467
7689497  7689499  7689503  7689527  7689533  7689557  7689571  7689607  7689629  7689631
7689653  7689667  7689707  7689713  7689719  7689739  7689743  7689761  7689779  7689793
7689817  7689827  7689833  7689839  7689859  7689863  7689881  7689911  7689917  7689923
7689931  7689937  7689949  7689961  7689971  7689973  7690013  7690021  7690031
7690051  7690061  7690091  7690099  7690129  7690157  7690159  7690169  7690181  7690259
7690261  7690271  7690283  7690297  7690301  7690313  7690321  7690343  7690357  7690379
7690391  7690399  7690433  7690439  7690457  7690483  7690519  7690537  7690541
7690549  7690559  7690567  7690583  7690589  7690603  7690607  7690609  7690619  7690621
7690637  7690643  7690651  7690663  7690691  7690693  7690699  7690703  7690721  7690733
7690741  7690807  7690831  7690843  7690849  7690861  7690867  7690873  7690897  7690927
7690951  7690961  7690967  7690973  7690981  7691017  7691027  7691041  7691051  7691059
7691071  7691083  7691129  7691137  7691147  7691171  7691179  7691183  7691197  7691209
7691213  7691261  7691329  7691339  7691347  7691357  7691377  7691381  7691389  7691401
7691419  7691443  7691473  7691479  7691483  7691491  7691507  7691557  7691569  7691603
7691617  7691623  7691639  7691659  7691669  7691707  7691741  7691743  7691773  7691777
7691779  7691839  7691851  7691861  7691863  7691891  7691897  7691919  7691931
7691933  7691951  7691977  7692001  7692019  7692037  7692043  7692053  7692079  7692089
7692101  7692103  7692121  7692127  7692137  7692149  7692193  7692233  7692241  7692253
7692257  7692271  7692277  7692287  7692301  7692323  7692329  7692331  7692341  7692343
7692389  7692407  7692409  7692437  7692439  7692469  7692491  7692533  7692539  7692541
```

```
7692547 7692577 7692583 7692589 7692599 7692611 7692617 7692623 7692647 7692661
7692683 7692691 7692697 7692719 7692731 7692733 7692757 7692767 7692799 7692809
7692821 7692827 7692847 7692851 7692863 7692869 7692887 7692889 7692901 7692911
7692943 7692977 7692983 7693009 7693031 7693039 7693057 7693067 7693073 7693079
7693093 7693097 7693123 7693159 7693181 7693183 7693211 7693223 7693243 7693267
7693291 7693297 7693303 7693313 7693327 7693331 7693349 7693351 7693369 7693393
7693403 7693417 7693453 7693459 7693481 7693493 7693507 7693513 7693529 7693531
7693577 7693583 7693589 7693597 7693619 7693633 7693643 7693667 7693681 7693687
7693703 7693709 7693717 7693739 7693757 7693769 7693771 7693793 7693801 7693837
7693867 7693909 7693919 7693927 7693951 7693963 7693967 7693999 7694003 7694009
7694021 7694051 7694111 7694117 7694123 7694143 7694147 7694153 7694173 7694189
7694209 7694233 7694237 7694243 7694279 7694287 7694303 7694311 7694321 7694327
7694329 7694339 7694369 7694383 7694389 7694431 7694437 7694459 7694497 7694501
7694527 7694539 7694543 7694567 7694569 7694579 7694633 7694647 7694651 7694663
7694669 7694671 7694683 7694689 7694737 7694747 7694833 7694861 7694881 7694891
7694917 7694923 7694933 7694971 7694977 7694987 7694993 7695007 7695011 7695043
7695049 7695097 7695109 7695113 7695137 7695159 7695197 7695199 7695207 7695221
7695227 7695239 7695241 7695253 7695257 7695269 7695293 7695299 7695307 7695313
7695319 7695329 7695341 7695343 7695349 7695379 7695421 7695461 7695463 7695481
7695487 7695491 7695503 7695517 7695521 7695539 7695557 7695599 7695601 7695613
7695617 7695629 7695637 7695641 7695661 7695671 7695683 7695697 7695707 7695739
7695749 7695763 7695769 7695791 7695797 7695833 7695859 7695871 7695881 7695887
7695913 7695929 7695937 7695949 7695959 7695973 7695977 7695979 7696021 7696033
7696063 7696079 7696103 7696123 7696127 7696133 7696141 7696177 7696181 7696193
7696201 7696207 7696211 7696217 7696219 7696229 7696243 7696303 7696321 7696343
7696361 7696363 7696369 7696411 7696433 7696457 7696477 7696483 7696489 7696511
7696531 7696537 7696573 7696583 7696657 7696669 7696679 7696681 7696693 7696709
7696721 7696739 7696747 7696753 7696763 7696811 7696823 7696841 7696849 7696859
7696867 7696873 7696877 7696879 7696933 7696951 7696967 7696979 7696993 7697003
7697009 7697017 7697029 7697057 7697059 7697099 7697113 7697119 7697153 7697159
7697177 7697189 7697219 7697221 7697257 7697273 7697279 7697281 7697303 7697309
7697321 7697351 7697357 7697363 7697399 7697401 7697453 7697461 7697477 7697483
7697497 7697507 7697509 7697533 7697539 7697551 7697567 7697581 7697593 7697611
7697623 7697633 7697639 7697653 7697693 7697713 7697741 7697759 7697761 7697771
7697803 7697819 7697843 7697849 7697857 7697863 7697881 7697909 7697929 7697947
7697969 7697971 7697993 7698007 7698029 7698043 7698049 7698101 7698113 7698121
7698133 7698151 7698157 7698179 7698193 7698241 7698259 7698269 7698277 7698289
7698319 7698337 7698349 7698371 7698373 7698377 7698403 7698413 7698437 7698443
7698451 7698461 7698469 7698487 7698521 7698527 7698533 7698541 7698547 7698591
7698631 7698641 7698643 7698679 7698703 7698707 7698709 7698731 7698737 7698791
7698797 7698829 7698853 7698863 7698869 7698893 7698913 7698917 7698931 7698933
7698937 7698961 7698973 7698991 7699057 7699061 7699063 7699073 7699099 7699141
7699157 7699189 7699207 7699213 7699229 7699231 7699243 7699247 7699259 7699271
7699291 7699333 7699337 7699343 7699357 7699369 7699379 7699387 7699397 7699403
7699409 7699423 7699499 7699511 7699519 7699547 7699553 7699561 7699567 7699591
7699597 7699607 7699609 7699633 7699639 7699649 7699673 7699697 7699717 7699721
7699723 7699729 7699739 7699753 7699777 7699781 7699789 7699801 7699823 7699829
7699837 7699849 7699879 7699891 7699897 7699919 7699931 7699961 7699973 7699981
7700071 7700081 7700117 7700131 7700179 7700207 7700233 7700237 7700249 7700257
7700261 7700279 7700281 7700291 7700293 7700299 7700309 7700321 7700327 7700347
7700351 7700387 7700389 7700393 7700419 7700437 7700467 7700471 7700479 7700489
7700501 7700509 7700513 7700519 7700531 7700557 7700587 7700599 7700603 7700629
7700639 7700647 7700659 7700687 7700717 7700723 7700729 7700753 7700789 7700807
7700831 7700839 7700879 7700911 7700923 7700933 7700939 7700941 7700963 7700969
7700977 7701011 7701013 7701019 7701049 7701053 7701073 7701103 7701107 7701131
7701163 7701167 7701191 7701223 7701227 7701229 7701247 7701263 7701283 7701307
7701313 7701319 7701347 7701409 7701451 7701497 7701503 7701511 7701521 7701523
7701541 7701557 7701569 7701571 7701581 7701599 7701607 7701611 7701623 7701643
7701647 7701649 7701689 7701713 7701721 7701761 7701763 7701767 7701769 7701779
7701797 7701817 7701823 7701829 7701847 7701853 7701871 7701877 7701893 7701917
7701923 7701931 7701961 7701977 7701979 7701983 7701989 7701997 7702001 7702063
7702069 7702073 7702099 7702103 7702111 7702127 7702141 7702153 7702199 7702213
7702243 7702259 7702271 7702297 7702319 7702333 7702349 7702363 7702379 7702397
7702399 7702427 7702433 7702451 7702459 7702469 7702507 7702511 7702517 7702529
7702559 7702561 7702567 7702571 7702573 7702687 7702727 7702729 7702757 7702763
7702781 7702801 7702811 7702829 7702831 7702837 7702841 7702843 7702889 7702901
7702909 7702913 7702949 7702969 7702987 7702997 7703011 7703021 7703027 7703029
7703041 7703071 7703107 7703131 7703153 7703161 7703173 7703219 7703231 7703233
7703237 7703239 7703249 7703257 7703273 7703281 7703309 7703317 7703351 7703383
7703387 7703389 7703411 7703419 7703447 7703461 7703467 7703491 7703513 7703537
7703539 7703581 7703587 7703609 7703621 7703639 7703653 7703671 7703681 7703701
7703711 7703719 7703741 7703743 7703749 7703753 7703767 7703791 7703809 7703851
7703939 7703951 7703953 7703957 7703963 7703999 7704007 7704013 7704017 7704041
7704049 7704071 7704083 7704097 7704119 7704121 7704127 7704131 7704163 7704173
7704217 7704233 7704271 7704289 7704299 7704311 7704331 7704341 7704407 7704409
7704421 7704449 7704457 7704467 7704499 7704511 7704527 7704533 7704539 7704551
7704559 7704577 7704581 7704617 7704623 7704629 7704661 7704667 7704677 7704713
7704731 7704737 7704773 7704787 7704803 7704841 7704863 7704871 7704877 7704887
7704911 7704913 7704919 7704929 7704941 7704943 7704953 7704959 7705003 7705031
7705037 7705043 7705057 7705073 7705079 7705091 7705129 7705153 7705157 7705169
7705183 7705211 7705219 7705249 7705283 7705297 7705303 7705307 7705331 7705333
7705339 7705363 7705367 7705409 7705427 7705433 7705441 7705519 7705567 7705591
7705597 7705601 7705609 7705651 7705669 7705679 7705693 7705699 7705721 7705741
7705757 7705769 7705783 7705787 7705799 7705837 7705847 7705853 7705861 7705883
7705903 7705921 7705927 7705933 7705937 7705961 7705993 7706003 7706047 7706051
7706059 7706063 7706071 7706087 7706119 7706143 7706161 7706177 7706201 7706203
7706221 7706227 7706239 7706317 7706327 7706329 7706333 7706341 7706393 7706399
7706459 7706473 7706497 7706509 7706513 7706519 7706527 7706539 7706551 7706561
7706579 7706591 7706617 7706641 7706669 7706681 7706701 7706717 7706719 7706749
```

```
7706753 7706759 7706789 7706807 7706821 7706833 7706843 7706851 7706857 7706869
7706873 7706887 7706903 7706921 7706929 7707023 7707043 7707053 7707061 7707067
7707097 7707113 7707157 7707163 7707187 7707199 7707223 7707233 7707241 7707253
7707269 7707283 7707353 7707377 7707383 7707397 7707431 7707439 7707473 7707481
7707487 7707509 7707517 7707541 7707569 7707571 7707587 7707607 7707643 7707659
7707677 7707697 7707709 7707719 7707727 7707761 7707767 7707769 7707773 7707779
7707797 7707811 7707839 7707857 7707883 7707907 7707923 7707943 7707979 7707991
7708003 7708007 7708009 7708027 7708037 7708039 7708049 7708061 7708067 7708081
7708087 7708093 7708117 7708133 7708139 7708147 7708177 7708189 7708193 7708199
7708213 7708237 7708241 7708249 7708271 7708273 7708279 7708301 7708303 7708307
7708313 7708331 7708333 7708397 7708411 7708439 7708447 7708453 7708457 7708483
7708499 7708501 7708507 7708529 7708573 7708607 7708621 7708627 7708651 7708669
7708711 7708717 7708721 7708777 7708781 7708783 7708823 7708847 7708849 7708859
7708879 7708891 7708901 7708907 7708919 7708937 7708949 7708969 7708991 7709011
7709017 7709033 7709047 7709059 7709063 7709069 7709089 7709113 7709131 7709153
7709161 7709197 7709213 7709227 7709257 7709263 7709267 7709287 7709291 7709293
7709309 7709323 7709329 7709369 7709371 7709417 7709419 7709441 7709453 7709479
7709501 7709519 7709521 7709557 7709561 7709567 7709587 7709609 7709617 7709629
7709659 7709683 7709693 7709699 7709711 7709717 7709719 7709771 7709783 7709813
7709827 7709843 7709861 7709869 7709879 7709881 7709887 7709903 7709921 7709929
7709951 7709957 7710007 7710013 7710071 7710089 7710107 7710127 7710133 7710139
7710149 7710161 7710167 7710169 7710193 7710233 7710247 7710251 7710253 7710277
7710301 7710323 7710331 7710343 7710349 7710361 7710377 7710421 7710449 7710473
7710481 7710511 7710539 7710553 7710559 7710569 7710581 7710587 7710611 7710613
7710629 7710641 7710667 7710701 7710709 7710719 7710733 7710739 7710743 7710757
7710761 7710767 7710797 7710799 7710817 7710823 7710851 7710853 7710863 7710893
7710907 7710947 7710977 7711001 7711009 7711019 7711031 7711057 7711069 7711079
7711087 7711103 7711127 7711139 7711159 7711181 7711189 7711201 7711211 7711229
7711259 7711261 7711267 7711271 7711273 7711309 7711339 7711349 7711351 7711357
7711373 7711391 7711399 7711409 7711433 7711439 7711441 7711453 7711469 7711471
7711519 7711537 7711541 7711573 7711579 7711589 7711603 7711607 7711609 7711637
7711643 7711661 7711667 7711687 7711689 7711703 7711723 7711733 7711741 7711747
7711751 7711757 7711763 7711783 7711789 7711817 7711819 7711841 7711843 7711849
7711861 7711889 7711903 7711909 7711927 7711933 7711943 7711981 7711987 7712011
7712027 7712041 7712051 7712063 7712071 7712099 7712123 7712161 7712171 7712207
7712209 7712213 7712219 7712249 7712267 7712269 7712281 7712297 7712321 7712323
7712359 7712381 7712399 7712431 7712479 7712483 7712501 7712503 7712527 7712531
7712557 7712563 7712581 7712587 7712597 7712603 7712623 7712641 7712699 7712701
7712711 7712729 7712737 7712741 7712767 7712773 7712777 7712807 7712813 7712819
7712821 7712833 7712857 7712891 7712897 7712899 7712921 7712923 7712933 7712959
7712977 7712987 7712989 7713047 7713071 7713077 7713089 7713109 7713127 7713133
7713137 7713157 7713161 7713163 7713179 7713187 7713191 7713193 7713197 7713263
7713281 7713317 7713397 7713401 7713413 7713443 7713479 7713491 7713539 7713547
7713569 7713571 7713577 7713611 7713613 7713659 7713661 7713689 7713697 7713701
7713707 7713709 7713721 7713743 7713749 7713757 7713799 7713817 7713841 7713847
7713859 7713907 7713919 7713941 7713961 7713967 7713997 7714001 7714033 7714061
7714067 7714099 7714111 7714117 7714123 7714127 7714139 7714153 7714159 7714183
7714193 7714207 7714211 7714219 7714229 7714237 7714249 7714283 7714303 7714307
7714327 7714349 7714367 7714387 7714393 7714409 7714417 7714423 7714451 7714471
7714477 7714489 7714517 7714523 7714541 7714543 7714559 7714561 7714571 7714573
7714613 7714621 7714631 7714643 7714649 7714661 7714669 7714687 7714697 7714699
7714739 7714747 7714757 7714799 7714801 7714843 7714871 7714873 7714879 7714891
7714897 7714921 7714943 7714951 7714963 7714997 7714999 7715027 7715033 7715053
7715069 7715077 7715101 7715177 7715179 7715261 7715287 7715291 7715293
7715299 7715317 7715333 7715359 7715381 7715401 7715423 7715453 7715459 7715471
7715483 7715549 7715551 7715563 7715579 7715593 7715611 7715629 7715633 7715657
7715681 7715689 7715699 7715713 7715723 7715737 7715759 7715761 7715777 7715797
7715801 7715803 7715809 7715821 7715837 7715857 7715861 7715863 7715887 7715889
7715891 7715927 7715933 7715959 7715969 7715989 7715999 7716019 7716053 7716089
7716103 7716119 7716127 7716143 7716151 7716161 7716169 7716187 7716199 7716229
7716271 7716277 7716281 7716329 7716341 7716343 7716353 7716367 7716377 7716383
7716391 7716409 7716421 7716463 7716473 7716491 7716497 7716503 7716517 7716539
7716547 7716557 7716559 7716563 7716571 7716587 7716607 7716619 7716629 7716637
7716673 7716689 7716701 7716713 7716721 7716743 7716763 7716767 7716773 7716809
7716811 7716829 7716833 7716847 7716881 7716889 7716893 7716899 7716913 7716941
7716953 7716967 7716971 7716991 7717001 7717007 7717009 7717013 7717033 7717037
7717043 7717063 7717117 7717147 7717153 7717159 7717183 7717187 7717189 7717207
7717231 7717247 7717313 7717321 7717331 7717343 7717373 7717379 7717387 7717399
7717403 7717427 7717429 7717433 7717483 7717499 7717513 7717519 7717547 7717579
7717607 7717631 7717651 7717679 7717681 7717709 7717727 7717733 7717751 7717763
7717783 7717789 7717837 7717859 7717873 7717883 7717889 7717891 7717901 7717907
7717909 7717937 7717939 7717951 7717981 7717993 7718003 7718057 7718083 7718093
7718107 7718111 7718129 7718131 7718143 7718159 7718173 7718177 7718189 7718201
7718219 7718251 7718257 7718279 7718297 7718299 7718309 7718327 7718329 7718341
7718369 7718393 7718401 7718407 7718413 7718423 7718449 7718461 7718471 7718483
7718519 7718551 7718563 7718567 7718569 7718587 7718621 7718653 7718671 7718677
7718687 7718707 7718713 7718719 7718729 7718743 7718747 7718749 7718771 7718773
7718791 7718803 7718813 7718839 7718861 7718863 7718881 7718887 7718939 7718941
7718981 7718993 7719067 7719109 7719119 7719121 7719157 7719167 7719181 7719197
7719203 7719209 7719211 7719221 7719227 7719247 7719253 7719259 7719269 7719281
7719289 7719311 7719319 7719323 7719337 7719353 7719359 7719373 7719379 7719389
7719401 7719407 7719419 7719427 7719443 7719451 7719457 7719473 7719487 7719497
7719511 7719557 7719631 7719667 7719689 7719721 7719727 7719739 7719763 7719769
7719773 7719787 7719793 7719799 7719809 7719827 7719841 7719869 7719883 7719889
7719893 7719917 7719923 7719937 7719967 7719979 7719997 7720001 7720021 7720039
7720049 7720051 7720067 7720081 7720093 7720103 7720109 7720121 7720123 7720151
7720171 7720183 7720187 7720189 7720201 7720211 7720241 7720247 7720283 7720313
7720319 7720331 7720337 7720357 7720369 7720373 7720381 7720393 7720399 7720429
7720439 7720451 7720481 7720487 7720507 7720529 7720561 7720589 7720597 7720619
```

7720621	7720633	7720637	7720639	7720649	7720667	7720673	7720697	7720717	7720721
7720723	7720729	7720759	7720813	7720819	7720841	7720849	7720861	7720871	7720877
7720903	7720943	7720949	7720957	7720967	7720969	7721003	7721023	7721029	7721053
7721057	7721059	7721069	7721071	7721101	7721117	7721143	7721149	7721167	7721173
7721191	7721249	7721251	7721267	7721269	7721293	7721303	7721339	7721347	7721359
7721369	7721377	7721393	7721401	7721423	7721437	7721459	7721477	7721479	7721501
7721521	7721611	7721671	7721711	7721713	7721717	7721761	7721827	7721837	7721843
7721849	7721873	7721891	7721911	7721921	7721947	7721953	7721963	7721969	7721977
7721993	7722017	7722041	7722049	7722061	7722067	7722107	7722119	7722139	7722163
7722167	7722179	7722191	7722217	7722229	7722251	7722257	7722269	7722271	7722277
7722283	7722287	7722331	7722343	7722349	7722361	7722367	7722371	7722373	7722383
7722397	7722401	7722409	7722419	7722431	7722443	7722447	7722449	7722527	7722551
7722557	7722563	7722571	7722623	7722629	7722643	7722647	7722653	7722667	7722679
7722691	7722707	7722731	7722739	7722749	7722761	7722769	7722773	7722791	7722823
7722829	7722833	7722839	7722851	7722857	7722877	7722919	7722931	7722941	7722943
7722983	7723003	7723007	7723013	7723039	7723081	7723097	7723099	7723127	7723169
7723201	7723207	7723217	7723231	7723241	7723267	7723279	7723283	7723297	7723337
7723349	7723351	7723357	7723361	7723363	7723379	7723381	7723403	7723411	7723439
7723447	7723453	7723459	7723477	7723493	7723501	7723511	7723517	7723537	7723543
7723549	7723553	7723567	7723579	7723589	7723603	7723609	7723613	7723643	7723679
7723697	7723721	7723733	7723753	7723777	7723783	7723811	7723817	7723829	7723841
7723843	7723853	7723871	7723907	7723913	7723927	7723939	7723943	7723957	7723973
7723979	7723997	7723999	7724033	7724039	7724099	7724107	7724111	7724117	7724131
7724191	7724201	7724257	7724261	7724263	7724281	7724293	7724323	7724329	7724331
7724419	7724447	7724449	7724459	7724461	7724473	7724513	7724531	7724539	7724543
7724551	7724593	7724597	7724599	7724609	7724617	7724627	7724663	7724683	7724723
7724737	7724741	7724747	7724753	7724771	7724777	7724791	7724807	7724819	7724831
7724837	7724839	7724861	7724869	7724879	7724881	7724891	7724957	7724999	7725017
7725023	7725031	7725043	7725071	7725073	7725127	7725131	7725143	7725149	7725161
7725181	7725199	7725239	7725241	7725269	7725271	7725287	7725299	7725307	7725317
7725323	7725329	7725349	7725373	7725407	7725409	7725427	7725433	7725449	7725469
7725503	7725511	7725521	7725527	7725559	7725611	7725649	7725669	7725689	7725709
7725713	7725733	7725787	7725797	7725821	7725857	7725869	7725877	7725881	7725911
7725937	7725947	7725959	7725967	7725997	7726003	7726009	7726013	7726051	7726057
7726063	7726073	7726079	7726087	7726123	7726129	7726139	7726157	7726193	7726207
7726237	7726261	7726273	7726297	7726307	7726309	7726319	7726333	7726337	7726343
7726349	7726379	7726391	7726423	7726427	7726447	7726469	7726489	7726531	7726547
7726549	7726561	7726567	7726571	7726633	7726637	7726661	7726669	7726679	7726739
7726769	7726777	7726783	7726793	7726801	7726813	7726837	7726889	7726897	7726903
7726907	7726913	7726921	7726933	7726973	7727003	7727009	7727017	7727033	7727047
7727059	7727063	7727081	7727087	7727099	7727101	7727107	7727113	7727131	7727189
7727201	7727221	7727233	7727267	7727273	7727303	7727309	7727323	7727329	7727351
7727353	7727359	7727371	7727381	7727387	7727389	7727447	7727459	7727477	7727479
7727491	7727501	7727507	7727519	7727521	7727567	7727581	7727593	7727597	7727633
7727653	7727677	7727689	7727777	7727779	7727789	7727807	7727827	7727869	7727887
7727903	7727921	7727947	7727953	7727969	7727971	7727989	7728031	7728043	7728053
7728067	7728103	7728109	7728121	7728139	7728167	7728179	7728191	7728197	7728199
7728211	7728221	7728271	7728293	7728311	7728317	7728337	7728341	7728349	7728359
7728361	7728367	7728373	7728389	7728397	7728401	7728403	7728439	7728443	7728451
7728463	7728527	7728533	7728551	7728571	7728599	7728601	7728613	7728631	7728647
7728673	7728689	7728697	7728701	7728709	7728739	7728757	7728769	7728797	7728803
7728841	7728857	7728871	7728907	7728923	7728983	7729003	7729019	7729031	7729037
7729039	7729049	7729063	7729069	7729079	7729091	7729097	7729123	7729147	7729151
7729153	7729157	7729247	7729259	7729277	7729289	7729301	7729327	7729331	7729343
7729349	7729363	7729367	7729369	7729391	7729433	7729451	7729471	7729481	7729487
7729507	7729537	7729549	7729567	7729583	7729591	7729613	7729619	7729621	7729643
7729661	7729663	7729669	7729693	7729697	7729717	7729721	7729753	7729759	7729763
7729823	7729829	7729831	7729837	7729847	7729861	7729867	7729889	7729901	7729919
7729933	7729937	7729957	7729963	7729973	7729993	7729999	7730033	7730057	7730101
7730111	7730113	7730123	7730167	7730167	7730197	7730201	7730213	7730243	7730249
7730279	7730287	7730293	7730297	7730311	7730339	7730341	7730383	7730413	7730417
7730423	7730431	7730453	7730479	7730491	7730519	7730531	7730533	7730539	7730561
7730573	7730579	7730621	7730623	7730651	7730677	7730683	7730719	7730731	7730753
7730759	7730761	7730771	7730797	7730809	7730819	7730881	7730887	7730893	7730897
7730911	7730911	7730917	7730923	7730953	7730959	7730963	7730981	7730993	7731011
7731029	7731037	7731067	7731089	7731091	7731103	7731127	7731131	7731133	7731137
7731169	7731179	7731193	7731203	7731239	7731259	7731281	7731299	7731337	7731401
7731421	7731433	7731439	7731457	7731463	7731491	7731497	7731511	7731517	7731523
7731527	7731541	7731569	7731571	7731593	7731629	7731667	7731671	7731707	7731721
7731743	7731767	7731797	7731817	7731827	7731839	7731851	7731863	7731877	7731881
7731883	7731943	7731949	7731961	7732019	7732027	7732037	7732061	7732063	7732091
7732103	7732121	7732129	7732147	7732169	7732171	7732181	7732189	7732199	7732211
7732213	7732261	7732279	7732289	7732321	7732327	7732337	7732339	7732343	7732391
7732427	7732451	7732457	7732469	7732471	7732489	7732493	7732499	7732511	7732523
7732553	7732567	7732579	7732583	7732591	7732597	7732607	7732631	7732633	7732651
7732667	7732679	7732687	7732693	7732727	7732729	7732771	7732789	7732801	7732811
7732847	7732849	7732877	7732891	7732961	7732973	7732993	7733021	7733041	7733069
7733087	7733093	7733123	7733161	7733179	7733183	7733197	7733233	7733251	7733281
7733287	7733293	7733303	7733311	7733321	7733329	7733347	7733357	7733377	7733393
7733413	7733423	7733431	7733447	7733471	7733501	7733567	7733573	7733581	7733597
7733599	7733611	7733647	7733653	7733669	7733683	7733699	7733701	7733711	7733717
7733723	7733771	7733797	7733809	7733837	7733867	7733879	7733881	7733903	7733909
7733939	7733941	7733951	7733983	7733993	7734029	7734091	7734119	7734127	7734137
7734161	7734169	7734193	7734203	7734211	7734217	7734227	7734229	7734239	7734241
7734247	7734257	7734301	7734317	7734341	7734347	7734359	7734383	7734401	7734403
7734409	7734437	7734451	7734457	7734497	7734523	7734581	7734589	7734607	7734637
7734659	7734667	7734689	7734697	7734703	7734707	7734719	7734721	7734731	7734761
7734787	7734791	7734799	7734803	7734811	7734821	7734823	7734827	7734831	7734863
7734869	7734893	7734911	7734913	7734941	7734943	7734971	7734973	7734997	7735009

```
7735043 7735081 7735097 7735099 7735103 7735111 7735121 7735129 7735163 7735171
7735181 7735193 7735219 7735241 7735243 7735249 7735253 7735267 7735271 7735279
7735283 7735303 7735319 7735327 7735333 7735361 7735363 7735369 7735381 7735393
7735421 7735439 7735457 7735463 7735487 7735499 7735513 7735531 7735537 7735543
7735573 7735577 7735583 7735597 7735631 7735661 7735669 7735687 7735699 7735703
7735711 7735733 7735747 7735781 7735787 7735789 7735807 7735811 7735813 7735823
7735841 7735877 7735891 7735909 7735913 7735919 7735927 7735939 7735967 7735977
7735999 7736009 7736023 7736033 7736063 7736077 7736083 7736101 7736111 7736123
7736149 7736159 7736161 7736189 7736213 7736263 7736269 7736273 7736327 7736369
7736381 7736383 7736389 7736461 7736473 7736501 7736507 7736537 7736543 7736551
7736567 7736587 7736593 7736621 7736627 7736633 7736647 7736653 7736723 7736749
7736753 7736761 7736777 7736783 7736831 7736843 7736867 7736873 7736891 7736893
7736951 7736977 7737001 7737007 7737017 7737029 7737031 7737043 7737049 7737071
7737101 7737137 7737143 7737167 7737173 7737203 7737209 7737211 7737217 7737239
7737241 7737263 7737293 7737299 7737337 7737341 7737409 7737413 7737419 7737451
7737487 7737529 7737539 7737547 7737557 7737607 7737619 7737647 7737659 7737671
7737677 7737689 7737701 7737733 7737739 7737761 7737767 7737803 7737811 7737827
7737833 7737859 7737929 7737967 7737973 7738001 7738037 7738061 7738063 7738067
7738091 7738109 7738121 7738123 7738141 7738153 7738169 7738177 7738193 7738201
7738207 7738223 7738229 7738231 7738243 7738259 7738261 7738267 7738271 7738303
7738309 7738319 7738321 7738337 7738343 7738351 7738391 7738397 7738411 7738427
7738429 7738441 7738447 7738483 7738487 7738501 7738537 7738543 7738559 7738589
7738607 7738663 7738693 7738697 7738711 7738727 7738729 7738733 7738739 7738771
7738777 7738781 7738789 7738799 7738813 7738823 7738849 7738867 7738877 7738889
7738937 7738943 7738967 7738981 7738987 7739033 7739047 7739051 7739101 7739117
7739167 7739177 7739189 7739191 7739197 7739227 7739231 7739261 7739273 7739279
7739311 7739321 7739323 7739341 7739353 7739359 7739363 7739383 7739411 7739419
7739449 7739453 7739461 7739509 7739519 7739521 7739531 7739581 7739587 7739597
7739603 7739609 7739621 7739647 7739671 7739677 7739687 7739689 7739713 7739737
7739759 7739779 7739789 7739803 7739843 7739887 7739903 7739911 7739917 7739929
7739951 7739959 7739969 7740001 7740023 7740037 7740077 7740091 7740097 7740119
7740127 7740133 7740137 7740143 7740149 7740157 7740169 7740179 7740191 7740203
7740217 7740221 7740233 7740251 7740281 7740307 7740319 7740323 7740371 7740377
7740379 7740407 7740413 7740433 7740451 7740461 7740463 7740517 7740521 7740533
7740541 7740547 7740563 7740569 7740587 7740599 7740611 7740641 7740643 7740647
7740653 7740671 7740727 7740739 7740743 7740749 7740751 7740757 7740773 7740779
7740781 7740791 7740833 7740851 7740871 7740907 7740913 7740983 7740991 7741007
7741009 7741043 7741051 7741061 7741067 7741073 7741079 7741081 7741093 7741099
7741121 7741141 7741147 7741157 7741159 7741163 7741193 7741207 7741241 7741243
7741249 7741259 7741267 7741277 7741297 7741301 7741367 7741369 7741387 7741397
7741403 7741427 7741441 7741451 7741469 7741483 7741541 7741543 7741561 7741603
7741633 7741663 7741703 7741709 7741711 7741717 7741729 7741757 7741781 7741807
7741819 7741841 7741859 7741871 7741879 7741933 7741963 7741967 7741997 7741999
7742003 7742017 7742023 7742027 7742029 7742041 7742069 7742087 7742093 7742113
7742129 7742131 7742143 7742149 7742171 7742179 7742183 7742197 7742209 7742221
7742239 7742299 7742309 7742321 7742341 7742353 7742387 7742401 7742411 7742417
7742419 7742437 7742447 7742459 7742461 7742477 7742521 7742533 7742549 7742561
7742569 7742573 7742593 7742641 7742677 7742687 7742689 7742699 7742723 7742737
7742759 7742771 7742807 7742843 7742887 7742923 7742941 7742947 7742957 7742993
7743031 7743049 7743077 7743079 7743097 7743119 7743121 7743133 7743167 7743179
7743181 7743191 7743193 7743199 7743209 7743217 7743221 7743223 7743233 7743371
7743389 7743403 7743409 7743419 7743427 7743443 7743457 7743467 7743481 7743487
7743497 7743503 7743511 7743529 7743557 7743559 7743563 7743577 7743581 7743587
7743599 7743611 7743613 7743647 7743661 7743683 7743727 7743731 7743737 7743779
7743781 7743797 7743821 7743833 7743851 7743859 7743863 7743871 7743881 7743907
7743919 7743937 7743941 7743949 7743991 7744007 7744019 7744021 7744043 7744057
7744081 7744091 7744127 7744151 7744159 7744193 7744207 7744213 7744223 7744249
7744259 7744271 7744273 7744277 7744301 7744313 7744357 7744369 7744379 7744391
7744393 7744403 7744409 7744423 7744427 7744439 7744441 7744453 7744459 7744487
7744489 7744501 7744523 7744547 7744549 7744603 7744631 7744651 7744657 7744669
7744717 7744733 7744739 7744757 7744783 7744817 7744829 7744831 7744883 7744889
7744901 7744903 7744921 7744927 7744931 7744939 7744949 7744963 7744991 7744993
7745011 7745029 7745033 7745039 7745041 7745051 7745077 7745119 7745123 7745131
7745147 7745161 7745189 7745207 7745263 7745299 7745323 7745341 7745363 7745377
7745399 7745417 7745429 7745447 7745537 7745539 7745561 7745587 7745593 7745651
7745653 7745657 7745663 7745671 7745701 7745743 7745747 7745767 7745789 7745807
7745819 7745827 7745833 7745849 7745851 7745869 7745873 7745893 7745911 7745951
7745953 7745971 7745989 7746017 7746019 7746031 7746047 7746049 7746059 7746073
7746083 7746097 7746107 7746113 7746119 7746127 7746131 7746133 7746163 7746173
7746181 7746191 7746197 7746217 7746227 7746241 7746247 7746301 7746337 7746341
7746353 7746367 7746413 7746419 7746439 7746449 7746457 7746461 7746491 7746511
7746553 7746569 7746593 7746617 7746689 7746691 7746701 7746719 7746721 7746763
7746773 7746779 7746793 7746811 7746839 7746847 7746853 7746863 7746913 7746943
7746953 7746967 7746983 7746989 7746997 7747001 7747013 7747027 7747037 7747039
7747081 7747093 7747109 7747123 7747153 7747211 7747217 7747219 7747247 7747249
7747273 7747279 7747301 7747309 7747367 7747373 7747423 7747429 7747463 7747477
7747499 7747511 7747513 7747517 7747543 7747561 7747567 7747589 7747601 7747603
7747633 7747643 7747673 7747693 7747723 7747739 7747771 7747787 7747807 7747833
7747841 7747853 7747867 7747871 7747891 7747907 7747913 7747919 7747931 7747933
7747963 7747979 7747981 7748003 7748009 7748011 7748021 7748051 7748063 7748077
7748093 7748099 7748113 7748129 7748177 7748189 7748197 7748201 7748203 7748227
7748239 7748261 7748267 7748269 7748287 7748291 7748317 7748339 7748341 7748347
7748359 7748387 7748407 7748449 7748453 7748459 7748479 7748509 7748527 7748537
7748551 7748563 7748579 7748591 7748593 7748603 7748623 7748627 7748659 7748669
7748681 7748683 7748687 7748707 7748711 7748717 7748737 7748761 7748773 7748779
7748801 7748803 7748809 7748813 7748831 7748837 7748863 7748879 7748893 7748899
7748911 7748921 7748927 7748929 7748969 7748981 7749029 7749037 7749067 7749109
7749113 7749121 7749149 7749173 7749193 7749197 7749199 7749227 7749241 7749251
7749253 7749271 7749277 7749281 7749299 7749307 7749337 7749353 7749361 7749377
```

7749383	7749403	7749439	7749449	7749457	7749463	7749479	7749487	7749491	7749493
7749499	7749517	7749527	7749559	7749571	7749593	7749611	7749661	7749673	7749691
7749727	7749737	7749751	7749767	7749769	7749799	7749803	7749839	7749869	7749887
7749913	7749941	7749947	7749949	7749961	7749997	7750003	7750021	7750051	7750069
7750087	7750097	7750109	7750121	7750139	7750187	7750201	7750213	7750229	7750231
7750247	7750273	7750313	7750339	7750343	7750361	7750373	7750381	7750399	7750409
7750433	7750439	7750459	7750481	7750507	7750513	7750529	7750549	7750559	7750577
7750579	7750583	7750597	7750661	7750669	7750693	7750709	7750711	7750733	7750739
7750741	7750753	7750807	7750867	7750891	7750901	7750913	7750943	7750949	7750969
7750987	7750991	7751011	7751021	7751039	7751047	7751063	7751077	7751089	7751101
7751111	7751113	7751119	7751123	7751143	7751153	7751179	7751189	7751203	7751239
7751251	7751267	7751273	7751279	7751281	7751321	7751327	7751347	7751351	7751357
7751363	7751441	7751467	7751477	7751489	7751503	7751531	7751543	7751551	7751573
7751587	7751591	7751593	7751599	7751617	7751629	7751669	7751683	7751693	7751701
7751741	7751749	7751761	7751771	7751789	7751827	7751831	7751839	7751921	7751923
7751927	7751963	7751969	7751977	7751987	7752007	7752013	7752029	7752037	7752047
7752061	7752067	7752079	7752103	7752109	7752121	7752131	7752137	7752161	7752163
7752179	7752181	7752197	7752211	7752223	7752229	7752253	7752259	7752271	7752281
7752293	7752313	7752317	7752319	7752331	7752343	7752373	7752377	7752379	7752383
7752389	7752401	7752413	7752421	7752431	7752463	7752473	7752517	7752529	7752539
7752557	7752571	7752581	7752583	7752601	7752607	7752623	7752643	7752653	7752677
7752683	7752691	7752709	7752713	7752743	7752749	7752751	7752761	7752763	7752803
7752827	7752839	7752847	7752851	7752853	7752859	7752887	7752911	7752923	7752929
7752937	7752959	7752961	7752971	7752989	7752991	7753033	7753049	7753079	7753087
7753099	7753117	7753127	7753133	7753153	7753157	7753171	7753177	7753181	7753183
7753189	7753247	7753289	7753301	7753303	7753321	7753337	7753357	7753363	7753393
7753409	7753429	7753439	7753451	7753453	7753481	7753489	7753517	7753523	7753561
7753567	7753579	7753583	7753589	7753619	7753621	7753663	7753667	7753673	7753679
7753787	7753799	7753849	7753873	7753883	7753891	7753897	7753901	7753903	7753909
7753931	7753939	7753973	7754003	7754009	7754011	7754017	7754077	7754081	7754113
7754119	7754141	7754167	7754189	7754203	7754209	7754237	7754249	7754251	7754269
7754273	7754291	7754293	7754321	7754323	7754347	7754353	7754419	7754437	7754443
7754447	7754479	7754507	7754563	7754573	7754581	7754599	7754609	7754639	7754651
7754653	7754683	7754689	7754711	7754713	7754723	7754729	7754741	7754777	7754797
7754809	7754821	7754827	7754843	7754891	7754893	7754897	7754899	7754911	7754927
7754947	7754951	7754963	7754969	7754987	7755017	7755029	7755031	7755067	7755079
7755091	7755107	7755131	7755133	7755149	7755157	7755161	7755197	7755199	7755203
7755233	7755263	7755277	7755283	7755289	7755323	7755337	7755353	7755359	7755361
7755379	7755409	7755413	7755421	7755427	7755481	7755497	7755521	7755547	7755551
7755563	7755569	7755571	7755581	7755613	7755617	7755619	7755637	7755641	7755653
7755659	7755691	7755697	7755721	7755767	7755773	7755779	7755793	7755809	7755811
7755821	7755823	7755833	7755841	7755851	7755877	7755889	7755907	7755959	7755973
7755989	7756013	7756019	7756033	7756043	7756057	7756069	7756139	7756157	7756163
7756193	7756223	7756241	7756247	7756279	7756283	7756321	7756349	7756361	7756367
7756373	7756381	7756387	7756409	7756429	7756499	7756501	7756519	7756559	7756591
7756597	7756627	7756631	7756633	7756669	7756687	7756703	7756733	7756753	7756757
7756781	7756783	7756787	7756841	7756849	7756871	7756897	7756909	7756919	7756933
7756937	7756951	7756961	7756967	7756999	7757011	7757017	7757023	7757041	7757047
7757051	7757063	7757069	7757081	7757093	7757119	7757131	7757137	7757171	7757207
7757221	7757231	7757237	7757251	7757257	7757293	7757311	7757341	7757353	7757363
7757401	7757411	7757419	7757437	7757441	7757443	7757447	7757467	7757473	7757483
7757513	7757521	7757537	7757543	7757551	7757579	7757597	7757599	7757609	7757611
7757621	7757623	7757653	7757677	7757683	7757699	7757707	7757713	7757723	7757731
7757741	7757747	7757779	7757791	7757803	7757807	7757809	7757861	7757873	7757887
7757891	7757903	7757977	7757987	7757999	7758011	7758019	7758043	7758053	7758071
7758073	7758083	7758089	7758097	7758133	7758139	7758151	7758161	7758181	7758187
7758209	7758227	7758253	7758263	7758313	7758329	7758343	7758371	7758433	7758437
7758461	7758461	7758473	7758503	7758523	7758551	7758577	7758607	7758629	7758643
7758671	7758679	7758683	7758697	7758701	7758727	7758731	7758733	7758743	7758769
7758781	7758787	7758853	7758857	7758869	7758871	7758899	7758911	7758917	7758929
7758977	7758983	7758991	7758997	7759007	7759009	7759013	7759039	7759043	7759051
7759057	7759079	7759099	7759111	7759151	7759177	7759187	7759189	7759229	7759231
7759237	7759249	7759309	7759313	7759343	7759351	7759357	7759379	7759387	7759393
7759457	7759469	7759483	7759489	7759513	7759547	7759589	7759639	7759649	7759663
7759669	7759691	7759699	7759721	7759723	7759777	7759789	7759811	7759813	7759831
7759853	7759859	7759861	7759877	7759879	7759883	7759891	7759897	7759943	7759981
7759987	7759991	7760017	7760021	7760033	7760057	7760059	7760063	7760089	7760107
7760117	7760149	7760171	7760173	7760183	7760191	7760213	7760243	7760257	7760273
7760281	7760287	7760297	7760321	7760327	7760387	7760393	7760399	7760413	7760437
7760443	7760471	7760479	7760497	7760507	7760561	7760563	7760567	7760579	7760609
7760611	7760617	7760647	7760663	7760671	7760693	7760717	7760743	7760747	7760761
7760803	7760807	7760813	7760827	7760839	7760887	7760897	7760927	7760933	7760971
7760983	7760989	7760999	7761001	7761007	7761023	7761029	7761059	7761071	7761077
7761107	7761121	7761133	7761151	7761167	7761181	7761211	7761217	7761233	7761239
7761283	7761289	7761293	7761301	7761307	7761311	7761317	7761323	7761331	7761353
7761361	7761389	7761407	7761409	7761421	7761427	7761437	7761451	7761487	7761491
7761493	7761499	7761539	7761577	7761581	7761583	7761599	7761613	7761617	7761643
7761661	7761679	7761697	7761703	7761731	7761739	7761769	7761799	7761799	7761967
7761839	7761847	7761851	7761889	7761907	7761913	7761917	7761947	7761953	7761967
7761989	7762021	7762031	7762061	7762091	7762093	7762103	7762129	7762133	7762141
7762187	7762199	7762207	7762213	7762229	7762259	7762277	7762289	7762291	7762297
7762301	7762331	7762333	7762351	7762357	7762373	7762397	7762423	7762427	7762429
7762439	7762451	7762463	7762483	7762487	7762499	7762511	7762537	7762543	7762589
7762597	7762603	7762607	7762609	7762627	7762639	7762673	7762681	7762709	7762717
7762721	7762723	7762739	7762757	7762763	7762771	7762787	7762859	7762863	7762877
7762903	7762913	7762949	7762967	7762991	7763003	7763009	7763047	7763053	7763083
7763099	7763111	7763123	7763137	7763183	7763221	7763269	7763291	7763293	7763297
7763311	7763317	7763389	7763401	7763411	7763429	7763449	7763461	7763467	7763471
7763501	7763513	7763519	7763537	7763549	7763551	7763557	7763597	7763629	7763641

```
7763669  7763683  7763687  7763689  7763729  7763731  7763741  7763753  7763771  7763773
7763797  7763803  7763809  7763827  7763839  7763843  7763863  7763867  7763881  7763923
7763929  7763933  7763939  7763947  7763953  7763957  7763963  7763983  7763993  7763999
7764007  7764011  7764013  7764049  7764059  7764073  7764077  7764079  7764101  7764131
7764139  7764151  7764181  7764187  7764193  7764221  7764247  7764283  7764287  7764299
7764313  7764329  7764349  7764371  7764377  7764389  7764391  7764403  7764437  7764439
7764443  7764451  7764469  7764479  7764509  7764511  7764517  7764527  7764599  7764607
7764611  7764613  7764641  7764643  7764661  7764667  7764677  7764683  7764707  7764727
7764739  7764761  7764769  7764797  7764803  7764839  7764847  7764851  7764877  7764881
7764893  7764943  7764959  7764979  7765001  7765003  7765013  7765019  7765103  7765111
7765123  7765133  7765151  7765169  7765181  7765193  7765201  7765207  7765211  7765213
7765249  7765259  7765267  7765279  7765291  7765309  7765313  7765321  7765337  7765343
7765391  7765393  7765399  7765411  7765489  7765493  7765519  7765553  7765567  7765579
7765603  7765627  7765643  7765673  7765711  7765721  7765733  7765781  7765783  7765829
7765837  7765847  7765853  7765859  7765861  7765883  7765913  7765921  7765943  7765949
7765963  7765969  7765987  7766009  7766021  7766039  7766053  7766071  7766107  7766153
7766201  7766221  7766237  7766243  7766267  7766279  7766293  7766309  7766321  7766323
7766329  7766371  7766389  7766401  7766413  7766417  7766419  7766441  7766443  7766449
7766453  7766483  7766491  7766503  7766527  7766533  7766537  7766587  7766599  7766621
7766657  7766659  7766711  7766713  7766729  7766741  7766743  7766749  7766767  7766777
7766791  7766813  7766827  7766849  7766851  7766861  7766879  7766881  7766897  7766911
7766933  7766951  7766959  7766963  7766971  7767007  7767017  7767037  7767049  7767083
7767103  7767107  7767139  7767167  7767197  7767217  7767229  7767239  7767241  7767247
7767293  7767301  7767343  7767349  7767401  7767421  7767427  7767433  7767443  7767457
7767479  7767493  7767497  7767499  7767503  7767533  7767541  7767547  7767553  7767559
7767569  7767631  7767647  7767659  7767689  7767703  7767709  7767719  7767731  7767757
7767769  7767787  7767797  7767811  7767869  7767883  7767899  7767917  7767919  7767931
7767953  7767961  7767967  7767973  7767989  7768001  7768049  7768069  7768081  7768087
7768109  7768121  7768129  7768139  7768141  7768171  7768177  7768193  7768223  7768237
7768247  7768249  7768253  7768331  7768333  7768349  7768357  7768361  7768379  7768381
7768403  7768447  7768449  7768459  7768487  7768499  7768547  7768561  7768567  7768577
7768591  7768597  7768601  7768613  7768619  7768627  7768669  7768699  7768703  7768729
7768751  7768753  7768759  7768763  7768769  7768811  7768843  7768877  7768889  7768907
7768921  7768961  7768979  7768987  7768997  7769029  7769057  7769059  7769087  7769141
7769219  7769243  7769261  7769263  7769273  7769287  7769291  7769327  7769329  7769339
7769351  7769383  7769389  7769401  7769417  7769431  7769441  7769471  7769507  7769513
7769549  7769569  7769579  7769633  7769639  7769647  7769669  7769693  7769701  7769717
7769737  7769759  7769761  7769771  7769813  7769819  7769831  7769849  7769857  7769891
7769893  7769897  7769911  7769947  7770001  7770013  7770017  7770023  7770041  7770053
7770073  7770089  7770097  7770101  7770109  7770121  7770131  7770151  7770157  7770163
7770167  7770179  7770187  7770223  7770227  7770247  7770253  7770281  7770293  7770299
7770313  7770319  7770337  7770341  7770391  7770403  7770439  7770457  7770461  7770467
7770473  7770509  7770523  7770551  7770559  7770577  7770583  7770599  7770613  7770617
7770643  7770667  7770673  7770691  7770731  7770733  7770743  7770761  7770769  7770773
7770779  7770781  7770787  7770793  7770799  7770809  7770859  7770871  7770877  7770899
7770901  7770911  7770929  7770953  7770991  7771009  7771013  7771031  7771039  7771061
7771063  7771081  7771087  7771103  7771109  7771139  7771177  7771187  7771189  7771201
7771219  7771237  7771241  7771271  7771277  7771307  7771411  7771429  7771441  7771451
7771457  7771459  7771469  7771471  7771481  7771487  7771523  7771529  7771537  7771541
7771553  7771559  7771571  7771609  7771619  7771633  7771637  7771639  7771649  7771651
7771661  7771667  7771693  7771697  7771711  7771717  7771721  7771727  7771733  7771787
7771811  7771823  7771843  7771859  7771877  7771891  7771903  7771909  7771943  7771957
7771963  7771993  7771997  7772021  7772047  7772053  7772057  7772059  7772101  7772113
7772117  7772123  7772131  7772143  7772173  7772189  7772209  7772221  7772251  7772263
7772267  7772279  7772309  7772333  7772339  7772341  7772353  7772389  7772393  7772399
7772417  7772431  7772447  7772449  7772461  7772473  7772507  7772509  7772521  7772543
7772561  7772591  7772617  7772629  7772641  7772663  7772669  7772711  7772747  7772753
7772761  7772771  7772773  7772777  7772789  7772797  7772833  7772839  7772857  7772861
7772879  7772917  7772929  7772951  7772953  7772959  7772977  7772983  7773013  7773037
7773043  7773053  7773083  7773089  7773107  7773119  7773121  7773133  7773163  7773167
7773173  7773179  7773187  7773193  7773197  7773209  7773211  7773217  7773251  7773253
7773257  7773317  7773319  7773323  7773331  7773347  7773361  7773371  7773391  7773401
7773419  7773431  7773439  7773449  7773463  7773473  7773481  7773487  7773499  7773503
7773511  7773523  7773569  7773581  7773587  7773593  7773599  7773611  7773613  7773617
7773673  7773739  7773749  7773761  7773763  7773767  7773803  7773833  7773851  7773859
7773877  7773889  7773893  7773911  7773917  7773919  7773929  7773949  7773967  7773973
7773979  7774007  7774031  7774037  7774043  7774057  7774079  7774103  7774121  7774127
7774141  7774147  7774151  7774159  7774163  7774171  7774183  7774189  7774201  7774213
7774229  7774231  7774237  7774279  7774301  7774303  7774307  7774309  7774313  7774331
7774343  7774367  7774381  7774399  7774433  7774463  7774471  7774499  7774519  7774531
7774541  7774549  7774567  7774577  7774579  7774597  7774601  7774603  7774609  7774631
7774651  7774703  7774709  7774721  7774751  7774777  7774783  7774799  7774807  7774829
7774849  7774853  7774889  7774891  7774903  7774913  7774939  7774957  7774973  7774979
7774979  7774993  7775023  7775029  7775039  7775051  7775071  7775077  7775087  7775099
7775179  7775213  7775221  7775231  7775269  7775279  7775293  7775309  7775323  7775329
7775347  7775377  7775399  7775401  7775429  7775459  7775461  7775473  7775479  7775497
7775501  7775507  7775519  7775533  7775543  7775549  7775569  7775597  7775623  7775627
7775639  7775641  7775657  7775701  7775717  7775737  7775753  7775759  7775827  7775843
7775861  7775879  7775881  7775893  7775903  7775969  7775981  7776059  7776061  7776079
7776127  7776143  7776151  7776173  7776203  7776211  7776239  7776269  7776283  7776287
7776289  7776311  7776313  7776331  7776371  7776383  7776389  7776403  7776409  7776413
7776427  7776451  7776469  7776473  7776541  7776551  7776569  7776583  7776589  7776607
7776619  7776631  7776641  7776649  7776673  7776683  7776709  7776749  7776751  7776779
7776787  7776799  7776889  7776907  7776913  7776929  7776931  7776941  7776971  7776983
7777009  7777031  7777093  7777103  7777123  7777139  7777171  7777193  7777223  7777229
7777241  7777261  7777267  7777271  7777283  7777291  7777337  7777361  7777369  7777397
7777409  7777421  7777447  7777463  7777487  7777489  7777499  7777501  7777537  7777543
7777573  7777579  7777589  7777603  7777613  7777643  7777663  7777667  7777673  7777709
7777727  7777753  7777769  7777801  7777811  7777813  7777843  7777849  7777853  7777867
```

```
7777873  7777879  7777919  7777943  7777951  7777967  7777981  7777997  7778033  7778039
7778041  7778051  7778059  7778063  7778081  7778083  7778101  7778123  7778137  7778149
7778153  7778159  7778167  7778189  7778203  7778213  7778237  7778269  7778273  7778279
7778291  7778317  7778321  7778327  7778339  7778389  7778413  7778417  7778423  7778431
7778447  7778461  7778471  7778483  7778509  7778539  7778549  7778557  7778591  7778593
7778611  7778627  7778629  7778647  7778671  7778713  7778731  7778747  7778753  7778759
7778773  7778777  7778779  7778783  7778791  7778801  7778839  7778891  7778921  7778929
7778933  7778941  7778951  7778957  7778959  7778963  7778983  7779019  7779041  7779049
7779071  7779077  7779097  7779103  7779127  7779137  7779157  7779197  7779203  7779241
7779253  7779263  7779283  7779293  7779301  7779311  7779347  7779349  7779371  7779377
7779383  7779389  7779397  7779403  7779427  7779433  7779461  7779469  7779479  7779491
7779521  7779529  7779547  7779587  7779593  7779601  7779613  7779617  7779623  7779631
7779641  7779677  7779679  7779701  7779713  7779719  7779763  7779787  7779809  7779833
7779847  7779869  7779881  7779883  7779887  7779907  7779913  7779943  7779979  7779991
7779997  7780007  7780013  7780043  7780061  7780081  7780117  7780127  7780133  7780151
7780159  7780181  7780183  7780189  7780193  7780217  7780219  7780229  7780231  7780243
7780259  7780261  7780277  7780307  7780309  7780321  7780327  7780333  7780351  7780369
7780387  7780391  7780403  7780429  7780459  7780477  7780499  7780511  7780523  7780537
7780541  7780547  7780561  7780567  7780573  7780579  7780583  7780589  7780621  7780637
7780639  7780649  7780651  7780657  7780667  7780691  7780699  7780711  7780727  7780741
7780757  7780769  7780811  7780873  7780889  7780891  7780901  7780919  7780921  7780963
7780999  7781023  7781027  7781029  7781057  7781101  7781113  7781117  7781119  7781159
7781161  7781197  7781231  7781239  7781261  7781287  7781297  7781299  7781311  7781321
7781327  7781329  7781353  7781357  7781369  7781377  7781413  7781441  7781453  7781467
7781491  7781503  7781533  7781539  7781549  7781551  7781561  7781573  7781591  7781603
7781611  7781617  7781623  7781629  7781639  7781647  7781663  7781689  7781701  7781723
7781731  7781777  7781779  7781819  7781821  7781857  7781861  7781863  7781881  7781897
7781909  7781927  7781929  7781933  7781957  7781987  7781989  7781993  7782013  7782017
7782029  7782037  7782067  7782113  7782127  7782133  7782157  7782161  7782167  7782199
7782227  7782263  7782283  7782287  7782289  7782301  7782337  7782377  7782403  7782443
7782449  7782451  7782473  7782479  7782493  7782499  7782503  7782521  7782529  7782553
7782569  7782587  7782629  7782641  7782659  7782689  7782703  7782707  7782713  7782727
7782737  7782739  7782769  7782773  7782779  7782781  7782793  7782811  7782823  7782847
7782851  7782877  7782881  7782883  7782911  7782917  7782937  7782979  7783007  7783021
7783037  7783057  7783081  7783109  7783117  7783123  7783133  7783147  7783163  7783169
7783207  7783211  7783213  7783231  7783241  7783249  7783267  7783277  7783291  7783309
7783319  7783343  7783379  7783409  7783411  7783427  7783459  7783463  7783471  7783507
7783519  7783541  7783547  7783549  7783609  7783619  7783621  7783631  7783649  7783651
7783669  7783691  7783723  7783733  7783751  7783753  7783757  7783777  7783781  7783793
7783819  7783829  7783837  7783843  7783847  7783849  7783873  7783877  7783879  7783921
7783927  7783967  7783987  7784009  7784033  7784039  7784159  7784177  7784221  7784233
7784237  7784303  7784323  7784339  7784341  7784353  7784389  7784407  7784459  7784461
7784473  7784479  7784527  7784549  7784561  7784573  7784593  7784611  7784617  7784633
7784639  7784659  7784669  7784687  7784701  7784713  7784723  7784729  7784743  7784747
7784761  7784771  7784779  7784783  7784807  7784809  7784831  7784857  7784863  7784867
7784869  7784891  7784921  7784923  7784941  7784951  7784977  7784981  7784983  7784999
7784993  7785013  7785067  7785077  7785083  7785103  7785131  7785161  7785179  7785209
7785257  7785259  7785277  7785289  7785319  7785341  7785343  7785347  7785359  7785389
7785391  7785403  7785413  7785457  7785469  7785487  7785493  7785499  7785521  7785539
7785551  7785563  7785571  7785593  7785607  7785653  7785671  7785683  7785731  7785737
7785749  7785793  7785803  7785821  7785823  7785851  7785853  7785863  7785871  7785887
7785907  7785913  7785917  7785971  7785977  7785997  7786019  7786027  7786043  7786063
7786091  7786099  7786117  7786127  7786151  7786157  7786159  7786189  7786201  7786231
7786241  7786249  7786267  7786279  7786309  7786367  7786417  7786421  7786451  7786463
7786511  7786547  7786553  7786567  7786573  7786577  7786579  7786609  7786619  7786657
7786661  7786693  7786721  7786733  7786739  7786763  7786787  7786829  7786847  7786861
7786871  7786873  7786907  7786927  7786957  7786967  7786981  7787009  7787011  7787023
7787047  7787081  7787083  7787111  7787123  7787137  7787141  7787147  7787149  7787161
7787183  7787189  7787239  7787291  7787303  7787323  7787327  7787333  7787347  7787371
7787389  7787413  7787441  7787453  7787471  7787503  7787519  7787537  7787551  7787561
7787569  7787579  7787597  7787609  7787623  7787627  7787629  7787657  7787677  7787699
7787707  7787719  7787749  7787761  7787771  7787779  7787803  7787833  7787837  7787849
7787861  7787881  7787911  7787951  7787957  7787959  7787963  7787971  7787981  7787987
7787999  7788017  7788029  7788047  7788083  7788089  7788097  7788101  7788103  7788113
7788133  7788149  7788181  7788199  7788247  7788259  7788307  7788311  7788317  7788349
7788353  7788367  7788427  7788439  7788457  7788481  7788493  7788497  7788523  7788527
7788577  7788581  7788593  7788607  7788619  7788631  7788653  7788667  7788679  7788691
7788701  7788707  7788709  7788763  7788769  7788779  7788787  7788821  7788853  7788857
7788871  7788883  7788889  7788919  7788929  7788931  7788953  7788983  7788997  7789021
7789073  7789079  7789099  7789123  7789141  7789147  7789181  7789189  7789193  7789211
7789217  7789253  7789261  7789267  7789289  7789333  7789337  7789343  7789363  7789367
7789393  7789399  7789403  7789447  7789459  7789469  7789489  7789501  7789531  7789541
7789559  7789567  7789583  7789589  7789597  7789609  7789619  7789627  7789657  7789669
7789687  7789703  7789729  7789739  7789741  7789759  7789813  7789819  7789823  7789841
7789849  7789871  7789879  7789913  7789919  7789931  7789949  7789963  7789967  7789979
7789987  7789997  7790047  7790051  7790087  7790089  7790093  7790117  7790119  7790129
7790137  7790143  7790147  7790149  7790161  7790173  7790197  7790201  7790219  7790243
7790273  7790327  7790329  7790347  7790359  7790401  7790407  7790411  7790423  7790443
7790459  7790477  7790501  7790507  7790567  7790569  7790581  7790591  7790593  7790597
7790621  7790623  7790639  7790669  7790677  7790681  7790687  7790689  7790719  7790723
7790729  7790791  7790801  7790803  7790819  7790833  7790843  7790857  7790863  7790873
7790897  7790899  7790903  7790917  7790929  7790953  7790989  7791001  7791037  7791073
7791097  7791101  7791109  7791139  7791233  7791239  7791247  7791257  7791269  7791283
7791313  7791337  7791373  7791379  7791383  7791391  7791403  7791431  7791437  7791451
7791467  7791473  7791493  7791499  7791527  7791529  7791551  7791569  7791587  7791607
7791617  7791629  7791673  7791677  7791697  7791709  7791727  7791731  7791737  7791739
7791743  7791761  7791781  7791787  7791799  7791829  7791851  7791853  7791857  7791877
7791907  7791911  7791929  7791961  7791977  7792003  7792021  7792051  7792121  7792133
7792139  7792151  7792153  7792157  7792181  7792207  7792297  7792303  7792313  7792319
```

```
7792327 7792333 7792349 7792357 7792361 7792363 7792373 7792397 7792399 7792429
7792457 7792471 7792513 7792549 7792559 7792601 7792627 7792649 7792651 7792669
7792693 7792709 7792711 7792723 7792739 7792769 7792777 7792781 7792789 7792801
7792843 7792859 7792861 7792891 7792913 7792931 7792937 7792951 7792957 7792963
7792999 7793003 7793033 7793041 7793047 7793057 7793063 7793081 7793087 7793111
7793143 7793153 7793161 7793171 7793197 7793207 7793209 7793213 7793231 7793237
7793281 7793311 7793333 7793339 7793341 7793351 7793353 7793371 7793393 7793411
7793413 7793417 7793447 7793459 7793473 7793483 7793501 7793503 7793509 7793521
7793561 7793581 7793603 7793623 7793647 7793651 7793657 7793671 7793677 7793683
7793719 7793729 7793749 7793759 7793761 7793777 7793831 7793833 7793843 7793873
7793893 7793897 7793917 7793921 7793957 7793969 7793983 7793999 7794019 7794023
7794049 7794053 7794071 7794089 7794119 7794121 7794131 7794133 7794139 7794173
7794209 7794221 7794229 7794239 7794247 7794251 7794253 7794257 7794277 7794287
7794289 7794307 7794323 7794329 7794343 7794349 7794373 7794379 7794407 7794421
7794439 7794443 7794461 7794463 7794467 7794491 7794509 7794511 7794529 7794557
7794559 7794569 7794571 7794607 7794643 7794701 7794737 7794751 7794781 7794799
7794803 7794811 7794817 7794821 7794833 7794841 7794853 7794863 7794929 7794947
7794949 7794971 7794977 7795031 7795033 7795069 7795103 7795121 7795141 7795153
7795157 7795189 7795217 7795219 7795223 7795237 7795247 7795253 7795261 7795273
7795309 7795313 7795331 7795343 7795357 7795363 7795369 7795379 7795397 7795423
7795429 7795439 7795441 7795499 7795507 7795511 7795549 7795559 7795573 7795603
7795639 7795637 7795649 7795661 7795687 7795709 7795721 7795747 7795759 7795763
7795769 7795807 7795811 7795813 7795819 7795831 7795859 7795883 7795897 7795901
7795927 7795933 7795939 7795961 7795993 7795999 7796003 7796017 7796021 7796039
7796059 7796069 7796071 7796101 7796111 7796119 7796123 7796147 7796153 7796161
7796177 7796179 7796189 7796207 7796231 7796249 7796263 7796309 7796323 7796339
7796363 7796377 7796401 7796423 7796449 7796461 7796491 7796497 7796507 7796513
7796521 7796527 7796539 7796549 7796561 7796567 7796573 7796587 7796597 7796599
7796611 7796623 7796639 7796641 7796653 7796687 7796699 7796713 7796741 7796759
7796797 7796801 7796843 7796849 7796851 7796869 7796881 7796917 7796923 7796939
7796947 7796951 7796963 7796981 7796993 7797017 7797043 7797071 7797077 7797109
7797131 7797133 7797137 7797157 7797173 7797199 7797211 7797227 7797241
7797247 7797281 7797287 7797311 7797313 7797323 7797359 7797389 7797401 7797451
7797463 7797481 7797487 7797511 7797521 7797541 7797547 7797551 7797553 7797563
7797583 7797589 7797593 7797599 7797623 7797631 7797653 7797659 7797683 7797697
7797701 7797721 7797737 7797743 7797763 7797793 7797799 7797841 7797877 7797887
7797899 7797901 7797919 7797953 7797983 7797991 7797997 7798069 7798073 7798097
7798103 7798111 7798163 7798171 7798199 7798201 7798249 7798253 7798279 7798289
7798313 7798333 7798337 7798369 7798397 7798411 7798421 7798457 7798463 7798489
7798499 7798501 7798537 7798547 7798559 7798591 7798603 7798613 7798619 7798621
7798627 7798649 7798657 7798669 7798673 7798717 7798727 7798729 7798741 7798751
7798753 7798783 7798793 7798799 7798807 7798811 7798831 7798837 7798859 7798877
7798891 7798907 7798919 7798927 7798933 7798939 7798951 7798957 7798961 7798963
7798969 7798991 7798997 7799017 7799023 7799027 7799041 7799069 7799089 7799111
7799131 7799153 7799167 7799171 7799189 7799201 7799203 7799213 7799251 7799257
7799299 7799303 7799327 7799333 7799339 7799377 7799417 7799423 7799431 7799453
7799459 7799501 7799503 7799513 7799527 7799543 7799573 7799581 7799587 7799611
7799621 7799653 7799657 7799669 7799683 7799689 7799699 7799723 7799731 7799761
7799767 7799789 7799797 7799809 7799837 7799843 7799849 7799863 7799883 7799903
7799929 7799951 7799971 7799999 7800017 7800029 7800041 7800047 7800053 7800077
7800083 7800097 7800103 7800111 7800119 7800137 7800139 7800179 7800181 7800187
7800211 7800259 7800271 7800281 7800307 7800311 7800323 7800337 7800347 7800349
7800371 7800383 7800389 7800409 7800413 7800479 7800491 7800511 7800521 7800547
7800553 7800571 7800577 7800613 7800629 7800647 7800649 7800733 7800769 7800781
7800791 7800799 7800817 7800827 7800839 7800851 7800869 7800883 7800889 7800901
7800941 7800953 7800959 7800967 7800979 7800997 7801007 7801019 7801033 7801037
7801051 7801063 7801067 7801069 7801081 7801093 7801099 7801121 7801141 7801159
7801169 7801207 7801219 7801223 7801231 7801237 7801247 7801259 7801289 7801307
7801333 7801337 7801349 7801363 7801373 7801379 7801427 7801459 7801463 7801471
7801489 7801523 7801567 7801597 7801627 7801631 7801637 7801649 7801663 7801679
7801697 7801699 7801721 7801727 7801753 7801757 7801769 7801811 7801813 7801833
7801823 7801867 7801879 7801883 7801897 7801903 7801907 7801919 7801921 7801933
7801939 7801943 7801973 7801979 7801993 7801999 7802009 7802017 7802029 7802051
7802059 7802107 7802117 7802161 7802191 7802203 7802213 7802231 7802233 7802237
7802239 7802251 7802281 7802299 7802323 7802339 7802357 7802381 7802387 7802401
7802413 7802419 7802437 7802441 7802447 7802453 7802477 7802513 7802539 7802549
7802551 7802563 7802621 7802657 7802659 7802699 7802701 7802791 7802801 7802803
7802869 7802889 7802929 7802941 7802953 7802959 7803011 7803023 7803037
7803083 7803097 7803143 7803149 7803151 7803193 7803203 7803217 7803223 7803239
7803241 7803247 7803251 7803259 7803283 7803317 7803329 7803331 7803343 7803353
7803373 7803379 7803401 7803437 7803443 7803449 7803451 7803461 7803491 7803611
7803613 7803619 7803643 7803659 7803673 7803689 7803701 7803703 7803709 7803721
7803749 7803751 7803767 7803793 7803797 7803811 7803827 7803839 7803853 7803881
7803883 7803907 7803937 7803949 7803953 7803973 7803977 7803979 7803997 7804007
7804009 7804019 7804039 7804051 7804057 7804081 7804099 7804123 7804141 7804163
7804171 7804187 7804201 7804229 7804243 7804261 7804267 7804271 7804283 7804289
7804297 7804327 7804333 7804339 7804351 7804369 7804387 7804403 7804417 7804439
7804441 7804453 7804463 7804469 7804481 7804501 7804519 7804553 7804561 7804597
7804607 7804609 7804631 7804633 7804639 7804651 7804661 7804673 7804681 7804703
7804721 7804723 7804733 7804757 7804759 7804787 7804789 7804793 7804807 7804813
7804829 7804849 7804871 7804873 7804879 7804913 7804949 7804957 7804987 7805009
7805041 7805053 7805069 7805081 7805093 7805099 7805107 7805117 7805123 7805131
7805137 7805141 7805153 7805173 7805177 7805197 7805201 7805207 7805209 7805221
7805269 7805297 7805323 7805327 7805353 7805359 7805383 7805387 7805393 7805401
7805419 7805429 7805449 7805453 7805461 7805467 7805471 7805477 7805503 7805507
7805509 7805519 7805537 7805549 7805591 7805593 7805617 7805627 7805639 7805647
7805657 7805683 7805689 7805719 7805729 7805741 7805767 7805783 7805797 7805821
7805851 7805879 7805887 7805891 7805909 7805921 7805929 7805939 7805957 7805981
7805983 7806013 7806047 7806049 7806059 7806151 7806157 7806163 7806187 7806193
```

```
7806217  7806221  7806229  7806241  7806257  7806287  7806289  7806311  7806313  7806319
7806329  7806341  7806343  7806347  7806373  7806377  7806419  7806431  7806433  7806437
7806439  7806479  7806493  7806497  7806503  7806509  7806551  7806577  7806599  7806611
7806619  7806661  7806647  7806661  7806709  7806751  7806787  7806797  7806803  7806809
7806811  7806833  7806863  7806871  7806881  7806917  7806919  7806943  7806973  7806977
7806979  7806983  7807001  7807013  7807027  7807031  7807039  7807049  7807067  7807087
7807103  7807127  7807141  7807147  7807181  7807193  7807201  7807223  7807243  7807273
7807291  7807313  7807321  7807339  7807361  7807379  7807399  7807421  7807427  7807439
7807441  7807463  7807487  7807489  7807517  7807519  7807531  7807543  7807549  7807601
7807637  7807643  7807673  7807697  7807717  7807721  7807729  7807739  7807747  7807759
7807771  7807783  7807823  7807829  7807843  7807859  7807901  7807903  7807927  7807937
7807951  7807963  7807967  7807991  7808011  7808023  7808029  7808033  7808039  7808051
7808093  7808131  7808149  7808161  7808167  7808173  7808191  7808197  7808231  7808239
7808243  7808257  7808267  7808309  7808329  7808347  7808371  7808399  7808401  7808407
7808429  7808441  7808459  7808461  7808467  7808483  7808501  7808503  7808513  7808519
7808527  7808579  7808599  7808617  7808623  7808629  7808657  7808681  7808687  7808693
7808699  7808711  7808747  7808767  7808777  7808789  7808803  7808821  7808833  7808837
7808839  7808873  7808893  7808897  7808921  7808951  7808953  7808963  7808971  7808989
7809049  7809079  7809089  7809107  7809143  7809157  7809177  7809191  7809199  7809203
7809211  7809223  7809253  7809343  7809349  7809353  7809377  7809383  7809413  7809433
7809449  7809463  7809469  7809491  7809499  7809509  7809517  7809533  7809541  7809547
7809559  7809583  7809601  7809667  7809679  7809689  7809691  7809697  7809713  7809727
7809731  7809733  7809751  7809791  7809793  7809797  7809821  7809829  7809847  7809859
7809863  7809869  7809881  7809889  7809911  7809913  7809917  7809941  7809947  7809959
7809983  7810001  7810039  7810043  7810057  7810063  7810067  7810069  7810073  7810079
7810091  7810097  7810111  7810139  7810141  7810147  7810169  7810183  7810189  7810199
7810207  7810211  7810223  7810237  7810241  7810291  7810301  7810321  7810333  7810339
7810381  7810399  7810421  7810427  7810433  7810457  7810511  7810529  7810553  7810559
7810591  7810609  7810619  7810637  7810643  7810661  7810681  7810697  7810703  7810711
7810717  7810721  7810739  7810753  7810783  7810801  7810807  7810819  7810841  7810877
7810879  7810909  7810931  7810987  7810991  7811017  7811029  7811057  7811059  7811077
7811081  7811117  7811129  7811131  7811171  7811173  7811189  7811201  7811203  7811249
7811281  7811303  7811311  7811333  7811339  7811341  7811357  7811359  7811369  7811393
7811407  7811429  7811437  7811497  7811521  7811539  7811543  7811549  7811561  7811563
7811567  7811579  7811591  7811593  7811611  7811621  7811663  7811669  7811693  7811747
7811813  7811819  7811821  7811833  7811861  7811879  7811893  7811899  7811911  7811941
7811953  7811957  7811971  7811977  7811981  7812001  7812023  7812037  7812067  7812071
7812109  7812113  7812121  7812127  7812137  7812169  7812179  7812191  7812221  7812227
7812239  7812247  7812289  7812307  7812313  7812319  7812323  7812347  7812349  7812361
7812377  7812379  7812407  7812421  7812449  7812457  7812461  7812463  7812487  7812491
7812499  7812521  7812523  7812529  7812551  7812557  7812559  7812569  7812577  7812599
7812601  7812611  7812613  7812647  7812689  7812691  7812703  7812719  7812731  7812733
7812767  7812787  7812797  7812821  7812829  7812841  7812851  7812881  7812887  7812901
7812907  7812923  7812929  7812943  7812947  7812953  7812967  7812983  7813007  7813019
7813027  7813037  7813061  7813067  7813073  7813087  7813103  7813109  7813111  7813129
7813133  7813153  7813177  7813181  7813213  7813241  7813243  7813249  7813277  7813279
7813291  7813297  7813301  7813303  7813331  7813343  7813349  7813361  7813363  7813367
7813369  7813397  7813417  7813423  7813433  7813439  7813451  7813453  7813469  7813471
7813483  7813511  7813513  7813517  7813613  7813633  7813639  7813649  7813651  7813661
7813669  7813691  7813699  7813711  7813717  7813723  7813753  7813759  7813777  7813781
7813787  7813801  7813823  7813849  7813853  7813879  7813907  7813909  7813933  7813937
7813957  7813973  7813979  7813987  7814011  7814087  7814117  7814119  7814159  7814171
7814179  7814207  7814221  7814239  7814249  7814251  7814291  7814293  7814297  7814299
7814309  7814321  7814341  7814371  7814381  7814393  7814411  7814413  7814489  7814501
7814557  7814561  7814563  7814581  7814593  7814623  7814627  7814633  7814647  7814663
7814669  7814683  7814689  7814707  7814717  7814743  7814749  7814767  7814773  7814783
7814791  7814797  7814809  7814819  7814837  7814843  7814857  7814861  7814867  7814879
7814897  7814921  7814923  7814927  7814941  7814943  7814951  7814981  7815013  7815043
7815047  7815091  7815097  7815127  7815151  7815163  7815169  7815253  7815263  7815281
7815287  7815337  7815341  7815371  7815373  7815397  7815421  7815443  7815463  7815491
7815499  7815523  7815527  7815557  7815559  7815623  7815629  7815641  7815659  7815667
7815673  7815701  7815719  7815721  7815727  7815737  7815763  7815779  7815781  7815793
7815799  7815811  7815817  7815823  7815839  7815851  7815887  7815919  7815943  7815947
7815989  7816001  7816007  7816009  7816033  7816057  7816079  7816091  7816103  7816111
7816121  7816157  7816169  7816189  7816217  7816219  7816253  7816267  7816271  7816273
7816279  7816301  7816321  7816327  7816331  7816409  7816423  7816427  7816439  7816463
7816477  7816511  7816513  7816519  7816531  7816541  7816547  7816561  7816579  7816597
7816607  7816637  7816643  7816649  7816661  7816667  7816673  7816687  7816703  7816709
7816727  7816729  7816759  7816777  7816789  7816799  7816807  7816843  7816859  7816877
7816883  7816891  7816913  7816933  7816981  7816997  7817003  7817009  7817011  7817021
7817041  7817071  7817077  7817081  7817107  7817111  7817143  7817179  7817191  7817197
7817213  7817219  7817233  7817237  7817261  7817267  7817279  7817311  7817353  7817387
7817393  7817419  7817443  7817449  7817461  7817473  7817479  7817483  7817489  7817503
7817507  7817573  7817587  7817599  7817609  7817639  7817681  7817743  7817749  7817809
7817813  7817819  7817827  7817837  7817863  7817867  7817879  7817889  7817893  7817903
7817939  7817941  7817951  7817963  7817991  7818001  7818037  7818049  7818053  7818067
7818071  7818127  7818133  7818191  7818221  7818233  7818269  7818287  7818311  7818323
7818337  7818347  7818353  7818361  7818379  7818397  7818451  7818457  7818463  7818467
7818469  7818563  7818599  7818607  7818617  7818631  7818637  7818649  7818653  7818667
7818677  7818697  7818731  7818761  7818799  7818821  7818829  7818859  7818869  7818871
7818887  7818907  7818949  7818953  7818961  7818971  7818973  7818977  7818989  7819033
7819043  7819079  7819087  7819109  7819111  7819121  7819129  7819139  7819153  7819157
7819169  7819171  7819177  7819187  7819193  7819219  7819237  7819243  7819271  7819297
7819309  7819313  7819327  7819351  7819391  7819417  7819423  7819429  7819457  7819459
7819481  7819489  7819501  7819519  7819571  7819577  7819579  7819601  7819619  7819627
7819631  7819639  7819661  7819681  7819703  7819717  7819721  7819733  7819741  7819751
7819753  7819787  7819789  7819831  7819853  7819873  7819883  7819921  7819927  7819951
7819969  7819993  7819997  7820003  7820063  7820083  7820089  7820093  7820101  7820107
7820123  7820143  7820147  7820149  7820159  7820171  7820231  7820243  7820249  7820257
```

```
7820269  7820287  7820297  7820303  7820317  7820321  7820347  7820359  7820369  7820389
7820399  7820411  7820429  7820479  7820507  7820551  7820573  7820581  7820591  7820597
7820599  7820611  7820623  7820639  7820669  7820671  7820677  7820693  7820699  7820719
7820783  7820803  7820821  7820881  7820887  7820927  7820929  7820947  7820957  7820963
7820971  7820983  7820991  7821017  7821019  7821031  7821043  7821059  7821067  7821091
7821101  7821133  7821167  7821169  7821181  7821197  7821211  7821221  7821239  7821257
7821277  7821287  7821299  7821301  7821323  7821353  7821361  7821367  7821371  7821383
7821397  7821413  7821419  7821427  7821461  7821469  7821487  7821493  7821497  7821509
7821523  7821563  7821589  7821601  7821607  7821629  7821631  7821637  7821643  7821661
7821697  7821701  7821719  7821721  7821733  7821757  7821761  7821767  7821769  7821791
7821797  7821799  7821811  7821823  7821833  7821841  7821859  7821893  7821907  7821917
7821937  7821941  7821959  7821971  7821991  7822007  7822019  7822033  7822037  7822039
7822109  7822117  7822151  7822187  7822189  7822201  7822223  7822237  7822247  7822271
7822291  7822327  7822333  7822337  7822361  7822379  7822387  7822391  7822417  7822427
7822439  7822519  7822531  7822537  7822543  7822559  7822561  7822589  7822597  7822613
7822621  7822627  7822657  7822679  7822687  7822693  7822723  7822729  7822733  7822739
7822741  7822769  7822831  7822847  7822849  7822879  7822891  7822897  7822931  7822933
7822951  7822961  7822963  7822979  7822981  7823017  7823027  7823029  7823051  7823071
7823083  7823089  7823093  7823099  7823113  7823131  7823141  7823143  7823161  7823183
7823201  7823203  7823219  7823227  7823237  7823239  7823261  7823267  7823279  7823293
7823303  7823323  7823351  7823357  7823369  7823371  7823407  7823411  7823423  7823429
7823437  7823471  7823477  7823503  7823513  7823527  7823537  7823597  7823603  7823609
7823617  7823633  7823653  7823671  7823681  7823731  7823737  7823747  7823759  7823771
7823773  7823779  7823789  7823797  7823819  7823831  7823833  7823869  7823891  7823897
7823899  7823903  7823951  7823969  7823971  7823993  7824001  7824013  7824017  7824023
7824053  7824077  7824107  7824109  7824119  7824127  7824133  7824169  7824191  7824197
7824203  7824211  7824217  7824221  7824251  7824253  7824277  7824281  7824293  7824329
7824331  7824361  7824379  7824407  7824433  7824457  7824469  7824497  7824517  7824527
7824529  7824541  7824559  7824587  7824611  7824647  7824671  7824673  7824683  7824703
7824721  7824731  7824749  7824763  7824767  7824781  7824823  7824829  7824833  7824841
7824881  7824907  7824919  7824923  7824937  7824953  7824961  7824977  7825003  7825021
7825057  7825091  7825121  7825133  7825189  7825193  7825199  7825217  7825247  7825249
7825261  7825327  7825333  7825369  7825373  7825403  7825409  7825417  7825421  7825429
7825459  7825469  7825481  7825483  7825487  7825501  7825523  7825529  7825553  7825591
7825607  7825619  7825633  7825637  7825639  7825651  7825687  7825703  7825709  7825717
7825723  7825747  7825757  7825789  7825813  7825823  7825847  7825849  7825861  7825889
7825903  7825921  7825943  7825949  7825973  7825991  7825997  7825999  7826023  7826047
7826099  7826101  7826107  7826123  7826183  7826191  7826197  7826207  7826227  7826261
7826281  7826303  7826327  7826339  7826359  7826369  7826383  7826411  7826419  7826437
7826447  7826459  7826513  7826521  7826551  7826561  7826569  7826587  7826597  7826603
7826627  7826653  7826677  7826683  7826699  7826701  7826711  7826713  7826737  7826743
7826773  7826801  7826807  7826809  7826837  7826843  7826887  7826899  7827019  7827037
7827049  7827059  7827067  7827101  7827109  7827139  7827151  7827167  7827173  7827217
7827227  7827247  7827253  7827257  7827271  7827299  7827301  7827307  7827317  7827329
7827331  7827343  7827349  7827359  7827377  7827403  7827431  7827437  7827493  7827509
7827527  7827529  7827539  7827541  7827569  7827577  7827587  7827607  7827619  7827637
7827661  7827671  7827713  7827719  7827727  7827773  7827793  7827823  7827857  7827877
7827881  7827893  7827901  7827913  7827917  7827931  7827949  7827959  7827971  7827983
7828033  7828039  7828043  7828087  7828091  7828099  7828111  7828123  7828129  7828141
7828147  7828157  7828187  7828199  7828217  7828237  7828243  7828277  7828283  7828291
7828319  7828343  7828357  7828369  7828391  7828393  7828397  7828411  7828421  7828447
7828453  7828501  7828507  7828511  7828519  7828543  7828547  7828553  7828559  7828573
7828603  7828607  7828621  7828631  7828667  7828669  7828699  7828729  7828747  7828781
7828783  7828841  7828853  7828879  7828913  7828921  7828937  7828939  7828943  7828963
7828987  7828999  7829011  7829021  7829023  7829047  7829051  7829057  7829071  7829077
7829093  7829111  7829149  7829179  7829183  7829201  7829203  7829207  7829219  7829221
7829233  7829243  7829249  7829251  7829291  7829293  7829317  7829321  7829351  7829357
7829369  7829377  7829389  7829399  7829417  7829429  7829467  7829489  7829509  7829513
7829519  7829527  7829543  7829551  7829557  7829573  7829581  7829587  7829593  7829603
7829617  7829629  7829671  7829711  7829719  7829737  7829779  7829791  7829837  7829851
7829869  7829873  7829923  7829933  7829963  7830007  7830037  7830041  7830043  7830077
7830101  7830103  7830113  7830127  7830157  7830161  7830169  7830187  7830191  7830209
7830211  7830239  7830269  7830271  7830283  7830289  7830293  7830307  7830323  7830349
7830359  7830371  7830437  7830457  7830481  7830503  7830521  7830547  7830577  7830587
7830593  7830607  7830611  7830617  7830619  7830653  7830671  7830701  7830703  7830707
7830721  7830731  7830737  7830763  7830821  7830827  7830847  7830853  7830881  7830883
7830913  7830917  7830919  7830923  7830937  7830961  7830973  7830989  7831039  7831069
7831099  7831081  7831099  7831111  7831141  7831157  7831163  7831171  7831177  7831203
7831231  7831253  7831259  7831261  7831267  7831279  7831283  7831297  7831301  7831303
7831319  7831337  7831357  7831379  7831381  7831387  7831391  7831403  7831409  7831423
7831463  7831471  7831477  7831487  7831493  7831501  7831511  7831517  7831559  7831567
7831583  7831613  7831627  7831639  7831643  7831669  7831673  7831693  7831699  7831717
7831739  7831741  7831763  7831793  7831813  7831837  7831847  7831853  7831897  7831903
7831919  7831921  7831927  7831949  7831997  7832003  7832021  7832023  7832039  7832093
7832101  7832113  7832131  7832141  7832159  7832173  7832177  7832203  7832249  7832261
7832263  7832281  7832299  7832317  7832327  7832371  7832381  7832387  7832401  7832411
7832437  7832509  7832527  7832533  7832543  7832551  7832557  7832569  7832633  7832647
7832659  7832687  7832689  7832723  7832743  7832749  7832771  7832779  7832843  7832873
7832893  7832897  7832911  7832939  7832941  7832947  7832963  7832969  7832977  7832983
7832989  7832999  7833043  7833061  7833083  7833109  7833113  7833121  7833131  7833143
7833151  7833167  7833191  7833197  7833251  7833269  7833289  7833299  7833313  7833323
7833341  7833361  7833367  7833383  7833389  7833391  7833401  7833461  7833473  7833479
7833493  7833517  7833563  7833589  7833599  7833601  7833619  7833641  7833647  7833649
7833653  7833659  7833671  7833673  7833701  7833737  7833769  7833781  7833809  7833827
7833851  7833853  7833883  7833887  7833893  7833907  7833953  7833967  7833971  7833977
7833989  7834027  7834037  7834039  7834051  7834091  7834097  7834111  7834117  7834153
7834199  7834201  7834207  7834217  7834259  7834273  7834279  7834303  7834313  7834357
7834361  7834363  7834367  7834373  7834381  7834427  7834429  7834447  7834459  7834487
7834499  7834529  7834543  7834573  7834583  7834591  7834597  7834621  7834627  7834633
```

```
7834663  7834679  7834699  7834709  7834711  7834721  7834747  7834763  7834769  7834781
7834817  7834819  7834823  7834837  7834877  7834889  7834891  7834903  7834907  7834919
7834933  7834949  7834961  7834963  7834969  7834991  7834993  7835021  7835027  7835039
7835053  7835057  7835089  7835119  7835129  7835143  7835153  7835173  7835189  7835209
7835251  7835257  7835263  7835279  7835287  7835297  7835339  7835357  7835363  7835371
7835381  7835383  7835407  7835411  7835413  7835431  7835437  7835447  7835459  7835461
7835483  7835491  7835497  7835501  7835507  7835537  7835549  7835593  7835599  7835603
7835609  7835621  7835629  7835647  7835651  7835669  7835677  7835741  7835743  7835753
7835767  7835791  7835803  7835819  7835857  7835873  7835881  7835903  7835909  7835911
7835917  7835957  7835959  7835977  7835983  7836007  7836013  7836041  7836047  7836067
7836079  7836091  7836107  7836139  7836161  7836163  7836173  7836181  7836217  7836221
7836223  7836229  7836251  7836259  7836271  7836269  7836347  7836349  7836373  7836377
7836401  7836407  7836419  7836427  7836431  7836457  7836469  7836481  7836497  7836509
7836523  7836529  7836559  7836559  7836593  7836613  7836649  7836659  7836667  7836679
7836709  7836713  7836737  7836761  7836791  7836823  7836841  7836883  7836887  7836947
7836967  7836971  7836979  7837003  7837009  7837013  7837021  7837031  7837033  7837069
7837091  7837121  7837127  7837133  7837169  7837171  7837199  7837211  7837213  7837231
7837241  7837261  7837267  7837301  7837321  7837331  7837343  7837351  7837363  7837369
7837381  7837393  7837397  7837409  7837429  7837441  7837443  7837517  7837541  7837553
7837559  7837573  7837603  7837631  7837639  7837649  7837657  7837679  7837691  7837703
7837717  7837721  7837723  7837759  7837763  7837769  7837783  7837807  7837813  7837831
7837883  7837889  7837897  7837913  7837919  7837931  7837943  7837967  7837983  7837987
7837993  7838021  7838023  7838029  7838041  7838053  7838057  7838063  7838069  7838107
7838113  7838119  7838137  7838153  7838167  7838177  7838179  7838183  7838213  7838219
7838221  7838261  7838273  7838287  7838291  7838293  7838321  7838333  7838351  7838371
7838387  7838407  7838429  7838447  7838461  7838477  7838489  7838491  7838527  7838533
7838543  7838557  7838569  7838587  7838591  7838641  7838651  7838657  7838669  7838687
7838689  7838723  7838731  7838737  7838759  7838767  7838797  7838807  7838839  7838851
7838879  7838891  7838893  7838951  7838969  7839011  7839017  7839037  7839043  7839047
7839059  7839089  7839103  7839107  7839121  7839131  7839137  7839151  7839157  7839163
7839173  7839179  7839197  7839199  7839211  7839233  7839253  7839263  7839269  7839281
7839289  7839313  7839319  7839331  7839347  7839353  7839361  7839371  7839379  7839401
7839421  7839427  7839451  7839463  7839473  7839479  7839493  7839509  7839511  7839539
7839547  7839563  7839581  7839589  7839613  7839617  7839641  7839649  7839679  7839691
7839697  7839709  7839719  7839731  7839763  7839779  7839787  7839809  7839817  7839823
7839833  7839847  7839857  7839877  7839883  7839911  7839959  7839961  7840013  7840031
7840037  7840057  7840067  7840073  7840081  7840153  7840159  7840163  7840169  7840177
7840199  7840207  7840253  7840267  7840271  7840289  7840291  7840297  7840351  7840363
7840367  7840381  7840409  7840431  7840433  7840439  7840461  7840499  7840507  7840517
7840523  7840537  7840561  7840589  7840603  7840627  7840649  7840667  7840691  7840699
7840709  7840727  7840733  7840771  7840783  7840823  7840837  7840841  7840849  7840867
7840871  7840891  7840909  7840913  7840949  7840967  7840969  7840981  7840997  7841021
7841023  7841033  7841083  7841089  7841117  7841143  7841153  7841161  7841173  7841177
7841201  7841219  7841221  7841231  7841263  7841341  7841347  7841359  7841363  7841377
7841381  7841399  7841401  7841411  7841429  7841467  7841473  7841497  7841501  7841507
7841531  7841557  7841563  7841567  7841599  7841627  7841651  7841657  7841671  7841677
7841693  7841707  7841711  7841719  7841731  7841759  7841773  7841789  7841797  7841807
7841839  7841843  7841849  7841863  7841893  7841921  7841929  7841957  7841959  7841969
7841971  7841983  7841987  7841989  7842013  7842031  7842047  7842059  7842061  7842067
7842073  7842097  7842119  7842127  7842139  7842143  7842167  7842199  7842203  7842217
7842227  7842229  7842239  7842257  7842259  7842271  7842277  7842281  7842293  7842299
7842323  7842337  7842361  7842371  7842403  7842427  7842431  7842433  7842437  7842451
7842481  7842493  7842503  7842511  7842529  7842533  7842553  7842559  7842607  7842617
7842619  7842643  7842677  7842697  7842713  7842719  7842733  7842761  7842773  7842787
7842803  7842823  7842827  7842833  7842851  7842859  7842871  7842881  7842917  7842943
7842949  7842973  7843009  7843019  7843027  7843037  7843039  7843049  7843051  7843057
7843063  7843097  7843111  7843123  7843127  7843151  7843189  7843201  7843229  7843237
7843247  7843271  7843291  7843309  7843321  7843331  7843343  7843351  7843361  7843439
7843453  7843463  7843469  7843471  7843487  7843513  7843567  7843573  7843597  7843607
7843609  7843639  7843643  7843657  7843663  7843679  7843687  7843691  7843697  7843699
7843709  7843721  7843727  7843733  7843739  7843747  7843753  7843763  7843793  7843799
7843819  7843853  7843861  7843879  7843883  7843907  7843939  7843951  7843981  7843999
7844027  7844041  7844059  7844069  7844087  7844101  7844111  7844119  7844129  7844141
7844153  7844167  7844183  7844197  7844233  7844237  7844251  7844257  7844269  7844273
7844281  7844303  7844329  7844341  7844351  7844383  7844387  7844393  7844401  7844423
7844437  7844443  7844453  7844467  7844521  7844537  7844567  7844591  7844593  7844597
7844623  7844651  7844657  7844671  7844687  7844693  7844713  7844717  7844729  7844731
7844741  7844773  7844801  7844807  7844813  7844821  7844831  7844833  7844849  7844867
7844869  7844887  7844897  7844933  7844951  7844957  7844959  7844983  7844987  7845011
7845037  7845059  7845067  7845107  7845121  7845127  7845137  7845151  7845169  7845181
7845203  7845209  7845241  7845259  7845269  7845293  7845301  7845317  7845329  7845349
7845361  7845367  7845371  7845373  7845379  7845389  7845401  7845403  7845413  7845437
7845451  7845463  7845491  7845521  7845547  7845559  7845581  7845583  7845587  7845611
7845623  7845641  7845647  7845667  7845671  7845683  7845701  7845709  7845731  7845743
7845763  7845779  7845791  7845793  7845797  7845811  7845833  7845839  7845889  7845899
7845913  7845931  7845947  7845949  7845977  7845991  7846001  7846063  7846099  7846103
7846117  7846159  7846171  7846199  7846207  7846217  7846229  7846249  7846261  7846271
7846273  7846277  7846283  7846309  7846337  7846343  7846357  7846403  7846409  7846439
7846451  7846463  7846483  7846493  7846513  7846523  7846541  7846543  7846547  7846549
7846561  7846577  7846633  7846637  7846649  7846667  7846679  7846691  7846693  7846739
7846757  7846759  7846763  7846771  7846777  7846789  7846799  7846807  7846819  7846831
7846847  7846873  7846889  7846901  7846913  7846919  7846921  7846939  7846961  7846963
7847003  7847011  7847029  7847033  7847039  7847051  7847083  7847089  7847111  7847137
7847141  7847153  7847159  7847179  7847239  7847243  7847249  7847267  7847269  7847291
7847299  7847311  7847317  7847321  7847327  7847351  7847363  7847369  7847377  7847407
7847423  7847431  7847443  7847447  7847459  7847461  7847471  7847473  7847479  7847491
7847501  7847503  7847507  7847519  7847533  7847579  7847597  7847611  7847633  7847639
7847641  7847647  7847677  7847689  7847699  7847713  7847759  7847783  7847797  7847803
7847813  7847821  7847839  7847857  7847881  7847909  7847927  7847941  7847977  7847981
```

```
7847993  7848023  7848041  7848073  7848089  7848091  7848103  7848119  7848131  7848133
7848149  7848151  7848163  7848167  7848209  7848227  7848229  7848233  7848251  7848259
7848263  7848307  7848331  7848377  7848391  7848409  7848419  7848437  7848457  7848469
7848479  7848481  7848493  7848559  7848569  7848601  7848629  7848637  7848649  7848667
7848689  7848719  7848733  7848739  7848749  7848761  7848769  7848779  7848787  7848791
7848839  7848851  7848871  7848877  7848889  7848899  7848923  7848943  7848959  7848961
7848977  7849001  7849007  7849027  7849031  7849043  7849073  7849099  7849123  7849133
7849181  7849211  7849243  7849267  7849273  7849277  7849313  7849351  7849363
7849367  7849379  7849397  7849399  7849403  7849421  7849453  7849483  7849493  7849507
7849549  7849553  7849561  7849579  7849609  7849637  7849643  7849649  7849657  7849729
7849781  7849783  7849811  7849813  7849817  7849837  7849847  7849879  7849931  7849943
7849949  7849967  7849991  7849999  7850033  7850041  7850047  7850053  7850077  7850083
7850111  7850119  7850131  7850149  7850177  7850191  7850197  7850231  7850233  7850239
7850261  7850267  7850279  7850281  7850317  7850333  7850357  7850371  7850407  7850411
7850419  7850431  7850443  7850459  7850461  7850473  7850489  7850509  7850537  7850539
7850543  7850587  7850593  7850603  7850627  7850653  7850663  7850669  7850671  7850701
7850707  7850729  7850747  7850789  7850839  7850849  7850861  7850881  7850891  7850903
7850917  7850929  7850939  7850951  7850963  7850987  7851001  7851007  7851031  7851037
7851043  7851061  7851091  7851101  7851113  7851121  7851143  7851157  7851191  7851197
7851227  7851253  7851287  7851293  7851301  7851317  7851323  7851329  7851341  7851343
7851359  7851383  7851409  7851419  7851439  7851443  7851449  7851451  7851457  7851461
7851479  7851509  7851517  7851523  7851563  7851583  7851593  7851601  7851611  7851619
7851629  7851643  7851647  7851653  7851667  7851691  7851707  7851709  7851713  7851719
7851751  7851761  7851803  7851827  7851863  7851871  7851887  7851919  7851923  7851937
7851941  7851967  7851973  7851979  7851989  7852001  7852037  7852051  7852057  7852063
7852067  7852087  7852093  7852123  7852129  7852153  7852171  7852183  7852211  7852217
7852219  7852241  7852253  7852261  7852267  7852277  7852289  7852303  7852307  7852309
7852319  7852349  7852373  7852421  7852433  7852457  7852459  7852489  7852513  7852541
7852543  7852553  7852571  7852577  7852597  7852609  7852613  7852633  7852651  7852661
7852711  7852717  7852721  7852727  7852751  7852777  7852811  7852877  7852903  7852919
7852921  7852927  7852931  7852937  7852967  7852973  7852979  7852981  7852987  7852993
7853039  7853059  7853071  7853081  7853101  7853119  7853129  7853147  7853173  7853179
7853203  7853221  7853231  7853233  7853249  7853257  7853291  7853333  7853357  7853383
7853389  7853393  7853399  7853401  7853407  7853437  7853453  7853491  7853497  7853501
7853513  7853551  7853561  7853569  7853579  7853597  7853621  7853623  7853687  7853701
7853717  7853719  7853723  7853737  7853753  7853759  7853773  7853803  7853831  7853873
7853887  7853921  7853927  7853929  7853957  7853959  7853977  7853987  7853999  7854023
7854031  7854037  7854043  7854047  7854089  7854097  7854127  7854131  7854151  7854169
7854179  7854199  7854211  7854227  7854241  7854269  7854271  7854313  7854317  7854359
7854361  7854383  7854401  7854403  7854409  7854433  7854437  7854443  7854449  7854461
7854479  7854487  7854503  7854533  7854541  7854551  7854557  7854559  7854571  7854577
7854589  7854599  7854601  7854607  7854617  7854631  7854641  7854643  7854667  7854683
7854689  7854703  7854757  7854761  7854773  7854797  7854817  7854829  7854839  7854851
7854859  7854863  7854877  7854887  7854893  7854949  7854953  7854967  7854991  7855009
7855033  7855061  7855079  7855087  7855091  7855093  7855097  7855103  7855109  7855163
7855217  7855223  7855249  7855261  7855271  7855273  7855297  7855301  7855321  7855333
7855339  7855349  7855357  7855381  7855399  7855403  7855423  7855427  7855447  7855453
7855469  7855483  7855487  7855517  7855537  7855543  7855567  7855571  7855583  7855591
7855597  7855609  7855613  7855633  7855637  7855651  7855667  7855669  7855693  7855697
7855703  7855709  7855711  7855747  7855777  7855829  7855843  7855849  7855871  7855889
7855907  7855931  7855973  7856011  7856039  7856053  7856059  7856089  7856161  7856197
7856203  7856207  7856213  7856231  7856249  7856257  7856269  7856279  7856293  7856311
7856327  7856399  7856411  7856413  7856417  7856441  7856447  7856467  7856483  7856503
7856507  7856579  7856587  7856591  7856603  7856663  7856687  7856713  7856741  7856743
7856759  7856801  7856803  7856819  7856843  7856851  7856867  7856881  7856887  7856909
7856911  7856921  7856939  7856957  7856963  7856969  7857001  7857011  7857019  7857067
7857071  7857079  7857107  7857137  7857163  7857169  7857211  7857233  7857263  7857271
7857277  7857287  7857293  7857301  7857313  7857337  7857359  7857371  7857373  7857389
7857397  7857401  7857403  7857407  7857457  7857461  7857481  7857503  7857523  7857529
7857533  7857541  7857557  7857569  7857571  7857581  7857589  7857607  7857611  7857613
7857643  7857649  7857671  7857673  7857683  7857709  7857719  7857737  7857781  7857799
7857803  7857823  7857853  7857917  7857943  7857947  7857953  7857979  7857989  7858003
7858009  7858013  7858027  7858049  7858073  7858079  7858093  7858099  7858127
7858129  7858141  7858181  7858211  7858223  7858237  7858307  7858309  7858337  7858339
7858349  7858373  7858427  7858439  7858441  7858463  7858481  7858483  7858537
7858547  7858549  7858561  7858577  7858579  7858583  7858589  7858597  7858601  7858639
7858651  7858687  7858693  7858733  7858771  7858783  7858793  7858817  7858819  7858831
7858849  7858861  7858867  7858889  7858891  7858897  7858901  7858909  7858927  7858931
7858937  7858957  7858973  7858979  7858987  7858993  7858997  7859017  7859023  7859039
7859041  7859053  7859063  7859069  7859081  7859099  7859119  7859129  7859147  7859149
7859161  7859171  7859191  7859221  7859233  7859297  7859311  7859329  7859333  7859339
7859347  7859359  7859363  7859419  7859431  7859441  7859447  7859513  7859531  7859549
7859573  7859581  7859591  7859603  7859617  7859623  7859639  7859641  7859699  7859717
7859723  7859737  7859773  7859777  7859779  7859791  7859801  7859809  7859849  7859861
7859879  7859923  7859981  7859989  7860011  7860029  7860031  7860049  7860079  7860107
7860109  7860133  7860163  7860187  7860191  7860199  7860211  7860217  7860241  7860253
7860283  7860289  7860299  7860323  7860331  7860337  7860343  7860353  7860361  7860371
7860389  7860401  7860407  7860439  7860451  7860467  7860469  7860533  7860553  7860557
7860563  7860581  7860617  7860631  7860659  7860673  7860689  7860691  7860707  7860719
7860731  7860751  7860767  7860781  7860791  7860799  7860821  7860823  7860829
7860841  7860863  7860877  7860893  7860901  7860911  7860913  7860961  7860967  7860989
7860991  7861027  7861031  7861033  7861037  7861039  7861093  7861099  7861109  7861111
7861127  7861141  7861153  7861159  7861181  7861201  7861207  7861223  7861229
7861241  7861289  7861309  7861319  7861339  7861351  7861363  7861367  7861391  7861393
7861409  7861411  7861417  7861489  7861493  7861499  7861519  7861547  7861577  7861583
7861591  7861613  7861657  7861669  7861673  7861717  7861727  7861747  7861757  7861781
7861783  7861787  7861793  7861807  7861811  7861823  7861829  7861849  7861853  7861897
7861907  7861933  7861951  7861957  7861969  7861999  7862011  7862017  7862047  7862053
7862059  7862081  7862083  7862087  7862111  7862131  7862137  7862147  7862149  7862209
```

```
7862213 7862233 7862237 7862263 7862273 7862287 7862303 7862321 7862339 7862357
7862359 7862363 7862377 7862417 7862423 7862429 7862441 7862453 7862479 7862513
7862521 7862539 7862557 7862579 7862597 7862609 7862639 7862641 7862669 7862707
7862719 7862731 7862737 7862797 7862801 7862819 7862831 7862843 7862863 7862867
7862887 7862893 7862909 7862923 7862927 7862963 7862977 7862983 7863001
7863007 7863019 7863029 7863041 7863047 7863059 7863067 7863101 7863127 7863143
7863161 7863211 7863227 7863253 7863257 7863259 7863269 7863293 7863301 7863307
7863311 7863313 7863347 7863353 7863377 7863391 7863403 7863407 7863433 7863439
7863467 7863497 7863509 7863521 7863533 7863547 7863551 7863563 7863577 7863593
7863601 7863613 7863619 7863637 7863641 7863643 7863671 7863679 7863683 7863689
7863719 7863731 7863733 7863749 7863761 7863763 7863767 7863803 7863811 7863829
7863833 7863851 7863881 7863931 7863941 7863949 7863971 7863997 7864019 7864027
7864033 7864037 7864057 7864063 7864067 7864069 7864093 7864117 7864121 7864123
7864127 7864147 7864151 7864159 7864187 7864201 7864243 7864247 7864253 7864277
7864291 7864301 7864331 7864361 7864379 7864391 7864397 7864403 7864411 7864427
7864433 7864447 7864471 7864477 7864501 7864573 7864589 7864621 7864627 7864639
7864673 7864697 7864699 7864711 7864721 7864777 7864789 7864799 7864811 7864817
7864819 7864823 7864837 7864867 7864903 7864939 7864949 7864951 7864957 7864991
7865009 7865017 7865023 7865047 7865059 7865083 7865111 7865131 7865159 7865171
7865257 7865261 7865267 7865269 7865281 7865303 7865311 7865327 7865353 7865357
7865383 7865393 7865443 7865453 7865461 7865483 7865489 7865503 7865519 7865527
7865551 7865569 7865573 7865617 7865623 7865629 7865651 7865657 7865687 7865707
7865749 7865771 7865773 7865789 7865807 7865831 7865833 7865881 7865929 7865933
7865959 7865983 7866017 7866029 7866037 7866041 7866059 7866077 7866091 7866097
7866107 7866127 7866139 7866151 7866167 7866169 7866179 7866191 7866193 7866227
7866239 7866251 7866259 7866263 7866277 7866289 7866307 7866329 7866347 7866349
7866389 7866431 7866457 7866473 7866479 7866493 7866497 7866503 7866517 7866539
7866541 7866557 7866559 7866571 7866611 7866637 7866643 7866659 7866673 7866679
7866689 7866701 7866707 7866709 7866731 7866739 7866751 7866769 7866773 7866791
7866811 7866827 7866841 7866847 7866863 7866889 7866923 7866941 7866959 7866967
7866973 7866997 7867009 7867019 7867021 7867049 7867061 7867063 7867083 7867103
7867133 7867183 7867213 7867247 7867253 7867271 7867291 7867309 7867313 7867337
7867351 7867361 7867369 7867393 7867411 7867441 7867469 7867493 7867513 7867543
7867571 7867581 7867619 7867637 7867649 7867669 7867681 7867687 7867693 7867717
7867789 7867793 7867813 7867823 7867837 7867879 7867891 7867897 7867901 7867913
7867921 7867931 7867967 7867973 7867987 7867999 7868027 7868051 7868053 7868057
7868083 7868089 7868099 7868111 7868131 7868137 7868153 7868191 7868209 7868219
7868233 7868293 7868339 7868353 7868359 7868363 7868381 7868423 7868431 7868437
7868447 7868449 7868453 7868477 7868491 7868503 7868521 7868537 7868551 7868561
7868563 7868587 7868591 7868593 7868617 7868621 7868629 7868633 7868647 7868677
7868687 7868689 7868711 7868713 7868719 7868741 7868747 7868759 7868779 7868789
7868801 7868813 7868821 7868849 7868851 7868897 7868923 7868933 7868969 7868999
7869023 7869031 7869041 7869053 7869067 7869077 7869091 7869107 7869131 7869157
7869161 7869167 7869187 7869193 7869203 7869221 7869227 7869229 7869241 7869247
7869259 7869307 7869343 7869359 7869371 7869403 7869413 7869431 7869451 7869457
7869467 7869481 7869497 7869517 7869523 7869551 7869571 7869577 7869593 7869607
7869637 7869661 7869679 7869683 7869709 7869713 7869721 7869739 7869751 7869761
7869767 7869769 7869779 7869791 7869871 7869881 7869889 7869899 7869919 7869923
7869931 7869941 7870007 7870013 7870019 7870081 7870091 7870097 7870139 7870141
7870147 7870157 7870183 7870193 7870207 7870211 7870229 7870231 7870241 7870243
7870277 7870283 7870321 7870327 7870361 7870363 7870367 7870391 7870399 7870409
7870411 7870417 7870433 7870453 7870459 7870481 7870487 7870493 7870519 7870523
7870547 7870549 7870561 7870589 7870601 7870619 7870633 7870651 7870657 7870661
7870679 7870697 7870699 7870717 7870721 7870739 7870817 7870823 7870867 7870879
7870897 7870903 7870909 7870937 7870943 7870957 7871029 7871053 7871063 7871077
7871081 7871113 7871141 7871159 7871183 7871191 7871197 7871203 7871207 7871219
7871243 7871251 7871261 7871287 7871291 7871293 7871299 7871317 7871329 7871341
7871351 7871387 7871389 7871393 7871411 7871429 7871443 7871449 7871473 7871477
7871483 7871503 7871519 7871573 7871579 7871581 7871593 7871597 7871599 7871621
7871627 7871651 7871671 7871707 7871711 7871723 7871729 7871741 7871749 7871761
7871767 7871771 7871791 7871799 7871807 7871813 7871821 7871827 7871837 7871863
7871873 7871887 7871893 7871917 7871933 7871939 7871953 7871971 7871977 7871993
7872001 7872003 7872017 7872103 7872107 7872119 7872127 7872131 7872149 7872181
7872191 7872217 7872223 7872239 7872269 7872283 7872313 7872323 7872329 7872341
7872353 7872367 7872391 7872413 7872437 7872439 7872443 7872521 7872541 7872559
7872577 7872583 7872611 7872619 7872629 7872637 7872643 7872653 7872661 7872671
7872677 7872679 7872731 7872757 7872763 7872793 7872797 7872803 7872817 7872863
7872869 7872871 7872883 7872919 7872929 7872937 7872947 7873001 7873009 7873027
7873031 7873067 7873069 7873093 7873133 7873147 7873157 7873183 7873213 7873223
7873273 7873279 7873289 7873301 7873321 7873351 7873357 7873367 7873379 7873387
7873399 7873409 7873417 7873421 7873433 7873447 7873451 7873457 7873469 7873477
7873483 7873507 7873511 7873513 7873531 7873553 7873559 7873573 7873589 7873603
7873631 7873633 7873651 7873661 7873699 7873717 7873739 7873753 7873757 7873759
7873787 7873799 7873823 7873841 7873849 7873871 7873897 7873903 7873913 7873937
7873951 7873973 7873979 7874011 7874033 7874039 7874047 7874057 7874059 7874071
7874089 7874099 7874101 7874107 7874123 7874129 7874131 7874147 7874149 7874161
7874177 7874183 7874201 7874219 7874221 7874233 7874261 7874297 7874311 7874323
7874327 7874329 7874351 7874359 7874387 7874393 7874401 7874407 7874411 7874413
7874423 7874431 7874467 7874479 7874497 7874507 7874513 7874561 7874591 7874609
7874617 7874627 7874653 7874677 7874743 7874749 7874753 7874761 7874777 7874819
7874827 7874849 7874851 7874861 7874887 7874929 7874939 7874959 7874981 7874983
7875013 7875017 7875031 7875047 7875059 7875061 7875067 7875073 7875079 7875089
7875137 7875163 7875169 7875181 7875187 7875193 7875227 7875287 7875293 7875299
7875317 7875331 7875341 7875347 7875349 7875377 7875389 7875401 7875409 7875419
7875421 7875449 7875451 7875467 7875551 7875563 7875583 7875611 7875619 7875631
7875653 7875661 7875667 7875697 7875701 7875713 7875727 7875739 7875793 7875797
7875799 7875827 7875841 7875869 7875871 7875911 7875919 7875961 7875971 7875983
7876003 7876007 7876031 7876069 7876091 7876103 7876111 7876123 7876147 7876207
7876217 7876237 7876247 7876261 7876273 7876291 7876331 7876339 7876343 7876357
```

```
7876361 7876367 7876369 7876397 7876399 7876403 7876409 7876417 7876433 7876447
7876459 7876471 7876483 7876493 7876501 7876529 7876567 7876579 7876607 7876643
7876663 7876679 7876717 7876727 7876733 7876753 7876769 7876789 7876801 7876823
7876829 7876837 7876859 7876907 7876927 7876937 7876969 7876987 7876993 7876997
7877047 7877053 7877057 7877071 7877081 7877099 7877101 7877119 7877143 7877147
7877159 7877167 7877179 7877197 7877203 7877291 7877323 7877329 7877333 7877351
7877369 7877377 7877383 7877399 7877407 7877437 7877491 7877509 7877561 7877587
7877591 7877593 7877599 7877629 7877669 7877677 7877687 7877693 7877711 7877731
7877741 7877743 7877747 7877759 7877773 7877777 7877791 7877797 7877803 7877809
7877819 7877839 7877843 7877861 7877873 7877917 7877923 7877939 7877957 7877971
7877981 7877993 7878007 7878011 7878019 7878023 7878037 7878043 7878047 7878071
7878097 7878139 7878163 7878181 7878197 7878229 7878239 7878251 7878257 7878271
7878289 7878301 7878313 7878317 7878319 7878323 7878337 7878341 7878347 7878359
7878383 7878391 7878413 7878419 7878421 7878427 7878439 7878461 7878487 7878491
7878511 7878527 7878551 7878553 7878569 7878571 7878613 7878641 7878643 7878649
7878653 7878677 7878697 7878709 7878713 7878721 7878763 7878791 7878797 7878809
7878823 7878841 7878853 7878859 7878869 7878877 7878887 7878911 7878917 7878947
7878961 7878967 7878979 7878989 7879021 7879051 7879061 7879073 7879099 7879103
7879147 7879153 7879163 7879169 7879181 7879199 7879219 7879237 7879247 7879253
7879303 7879307 7879321 7879327 7879343 7879369 7879379 7879393 7879411 7879423
7879427 7879447 7879453 7879463 7879477 7879481 7879489 7879499 7879507 7879511
7879513 7879523 7879527 7879541 7879559 7879577 7879579 7879589 7879609 7879637
7879679 7879723 7879727 7879733 7879741 7879747 7879757 7879783 7879799 7879841
7879843 7879847 7879849 7879871 7879897 7879901 7879931 7879979 7879999 7880009
7880011 7880017 7880021 7880063 7880111 7880113 7880123 7880143 7880153 7880177
7880179 7880189 7880207 7880209 7880227 7880233 7880239 7880251 7880261 7880263
7880267 7880273 7880287 7880291 7880317 7880321 7880347 7880351 7880359 7880387
7880393 7880413 7880437 7880441 7880447 7880449 7880471 7880531 7880533 7880549
7880557 7880627 7880641 7880659 7880671 7880693 7880713 7880737 7880749 7880753
7880771 7880777 7880783 7880791 7880797 7880827 7880849 7880857 7880863 7880869
7880879 7880891 7880903 7880909 7880947 7880969 7880989 7881023 7881031 7881059
7881073 7881077 7881079 7881089 7881113 7881151 7881163 7881173 7881179 7881187
7881193 7881221 7881227 7881229 7881241 7881253 7881271 7881281 7881287 7881317
7881323 7881329 7881331 7881337 7881373 7881487 7881491 7881499 7881509 7881521
7881527 7881569 7881581 7881583 7881589 7881613 7881619 7881647 7881689 7881701
7881721 7881739 7881743 7881767 7881791 7881803 7881817 7881859 7881889
7881901 7881911 7881917 7881919 7881959 7881961 7881971 7881977 7881983 7882003
7882009 7882013 7882027 7882037 7882051 7882097 7882099 7882111 7882129 7882177
7882181 7882183 7882187 7882211 7882219 7882243 7882247 7882253 7882267 7882289
7882297 7882309 7882333 7882361 7882367 7882423 7882451 7882453 7882471 7882489
7882529 7882571 7882597 7882601 7882607 7882621 7882627 7882661 7882673 7882681
7882691 7882697 7882709 7882727 7882729 7882733 7882741 7882753 7882789 7882801
7882807 7882811 7882837 7882841 7882871 7882873 7882877 7882879 7882907 7882909
7882939 7882943 7882957 7882991 7882999 7883009 7883023 7883027 7883033 7883039
7883047 7883063 7883077 7883101 7883129 7883131 7883137 7883149 7883159 7883177
7883191 7883203 7883209 7883237 7883261 7883297 7883299 7883303 7883321 7883327
7883329 7883333 7883341 7883377 7883383 7883387 7883399 7883419 7883429 7883431
7883443 7883459 7883467 7883497 7883507 7883509 7883567 7883581 7883587 7883599
7883609 7883611 7883633 7883657 7883677 7883683 7883693 7883713 7883717 7883741
7883753 7883761 7883773 7883789 7883819 7883831 7883839 7883851 7883873 7883891
7883899 7883933 7883983 7884029 7884047 7884049 7884059 7884077 7884103 7884113
7884119 7884127 7884131 7884133 7884167 7884197 7884223 7884263 7884269 7884299
7884313 7884319 7884329 7884353 7884403 7884407 7884431 7884467 7884517 7884521
7884529 7884553 7884559 7884577 7884593 7884623 7884631 7884647 7884649 7884661
7884683 7884689 7884691 7884713 7884727 7884731 7884739 7884809 7884823 7884827
7884851 7884853 7884869 7884871 7884887 7884893 7884901 7884907 7884913
7884967 7884973 7884979 7884983 7885051 7885061 7885063 7885081 7885091 7885099
7885103 7885123 7885147 7885153 7885177 7885193 7885201 7885217 7885219 7885223
7885259 7885261 7885289 7885301 7885307 7885321 7885349 7885351 7885357 7885369
7885379 7885391 7885411 7885447 7885453 7885457 7885483 7885511 7885517 7885523
7885547 7885567 7885621 7885643 7885649 7885681 7885693 7885723 7885733 7885781
7885789 7885819 7885837 7885861 7885879 7885901 7885903 7885919 7885961 7885963
7885973 7885993 7886051 7886077 7886093 7886111 7886129 7886161 7886167 7886169
7886191 7886213 7886233 7886237 7886257 7886261 7886287 7886293 7886297 7886321
7886323 7886341 7886357 7886363 7886393 7886399 7886407 7886423 7886441 7886497
7886519 7886533 7886591 7886597 7886603 7886621 7886633 7886639 7886663
7886687 7886689 7886693 7886699 7886717 7886731 7886777 7886783 7886789 7886797
7886819 7886821 7886833 7886867 7886899 7886903 7886911 7886917 7886939 7886947
7886959 7886987 7887001 7887037 7887041 7887053 7887083 7887097 7887149 7887151
7887157 7887161 7887169 7887181 7887221 7887247 7887251 7887259 7887263 7887311
7887317 7887323 7887329 7887359 7887403 7887409 7887421 7887427 7887469 7887479
7887487 7887491 7887497 7887499 7887511 7887521 7887557 7887559 7887599 7887601
7887611 7887629 7887631 7887647 7887653 7887661 7887707 7887721 7887743 7887757
7887767 7887773 7887809 7887811 7887821 7887823 7887851 7887871 7887883 7887889
7887923 7887941 7887947 7887953 7887959 7887989 7888007 7888009 7888019 7888033
7888037 7888039 7888063 7888073 7888081 7888099 7888117 7888157 7888163 7888169
7888183 7888189 7888207 7888213 7888217 7888219 7888247 7888259 7888271 7888273
7888297 7888301 7888303 7888327 7888343 7888367 7888369 7888373 7888381 7888399
7888411 7888421 7888423 7888429 7888451 7888469 7888483 7888499 7888519 7888541
7888547 7888567 7888571 7888583 7888589 7888607 7888613 7888619 7888637 7888649
7888669 7888721 7888729 7888757 7888759 7888801 7888817 7888843 7888847 7888877
7888883 7888919 7888921 7888981 7888987 7888999 7889017 7889033 7889039 7889041
7889051 7889053 7889059 7889083 7889089 7889111 7889149 7889239 7889243 7889249
7889257 7889281 7889291 7889293 7889341 7889347 7889383 7889423 7889443 7889459
7889461 7889471 7889491 7889499 7889521 7889533 7889543 7889549 7889551 7889569
7889603 7889627 7889639 7889641 7889659 7889663 7889669 7889677 7889681 7889701
7889723 7889729 7889741 7889771 7889789 7889797 7889803 7889821 7889831 7889837
7889863 7889873 7889881 7889891 7889909 7889927 7889929 7889953 7889957 7889977
7890013 7890041 7890049 7890061 7890067 7890083 7890097 7890119 7890137 7890143
```

```
7890161  7890191  7890209  7890217  7890251  7890299  7890307  7890319  7890331  7890343
7890347  7890373  7890391  7890413  7890427  7890437  7890439  7890479  7890503  7890511
7890517  7890539  7890551  7890557  7890563  7890569  7890607  7890611  7890661  7890683
7890691  7890713  7890733  7890739  7890749  7890763  7890769  7890787  7890797  7890811
7890847  7890851  7890859  7890881  7890913  7890919  7890923  7890943  7890959  7890979
7890989  7890991  7890997  7891031  7891033  7891067  7891069  7891123  7891141  7891151
7891171  7891181  7891183  7891187  7891207  7891211  7891217  7891237  7891259  7891271
7891283  7891297  7891307  7891313  7891361  7891379  7891381  7891421  7891423  7891439
7891463  7891469  7891483  7891493  7891523  7891537  7891549  7891589  7891591  7891603
7891613  7891649  7891651  7891673  7891703  7891717  7891727  7891739  7891769  7891777
7891787  7891801  7891813  7891847  7891853  7891861  7891867  7891901  7891909  7891913
7891951  7891969  7891979  7891981  7891987  7891991  7892009  7892023  7892051  7892057
7892069  7892077  7892107  7892111  7892149  7892153  7892173  7892189  7892207  7892219
7892251  7892257  7892279  7892293  7892299  7892303  7892309  7892323  7892327  7892329
7892341  7892347  7892393  7892413  7892419  7892441  7892449  7892453  7892461  7892477
7892491  7892503  7892513  7892527  7892531  7892537  7892551  7892557  7892567  7892579
7892597  7892603  7892617  7892627  7892659  7892681  7892699  7892713  7892723  7892741
7892789  7892791  7892827  7892831  7892849  7892873  7892891  7892897  7892917  7892939
7892953  7893007  7893013  7893019  7893031  7893043  7893047  7893077  7893089
7893091  7893097  7893101  7893107  7893139  7893161  7893169  7893187  7893211  7893269
7893289  7893311  7893317  7893323  7893331  7893359  7893367  7893371  7893373  7893397
7893409  7893427  7893451  7893503  7893511  7893517  7893521  7893527  7893533  7893581
7893619  7893629  7893631  7893637  7893643  7893647  7893649  7893653  7893673  7893707
7893727  7893779  7893793  7893833  7893863  7893883  7893943  7893989  7893997
7894021  7894027  7894039  7894043  7894087  7894091  7894093  7894097  7894121  7894123
7894127  7894153  7894157  7894207  7894217  7894219  7894247  7894301  7894303  7894321
7894333  7894349  7894363  7894387  7894417  7894433  7894457  7894489  7894547  7894573
7894577  7894619  7894631  7894639  7894643  7894651  7894657  7894661  7894669  7894687
7894697  7894717  7894723  7894741  7894751  7894759  7894763  7894771  7894787  7894793
7894807  7894829  7894841  7894871  7894883  7894897  7894907  7894921  7894961  7894969
7894973  7894981  7894993  7895009  7895029  7895033  7895057  7895071  7895077  7895081
7895087  7895093  7895113  7895117  7895131  7895149  7895159  7895179  7895183  7895207
7895227  7895269  7895281  7895299  7895309  7895311  7895333  7895351  7895353  7895383
7895387  7895441  7895443  7895449  7895477  7895491  7895513  7895521  7895527  7895549
7895561  7895579  7895581  7895597  7895603  7895609  7895611  7895623  7895651  7895653
7895663  7895681  7895683  7895711  7895729  7895747  7895759  7895777  7895791  7895807
7895809  7895827  7895857  7895929  7895959  7895977  7895989  7895999  7896011  7896043
7896071  7896089  7896139  7896157  7896179  7896181  7896197  7896233  7896241  7896263
7896271  7896297  7896283  7896299  7896307  7896331  7896341  7896349  7896353  7896373
7896379  7896397  7896401  7896409  7896431  7896433  7896437  7896443  7896481  7896491
7896527  7896529  7896541  7896547  7896569  7896587  7896593  7896631  7896689  7896709
7896719  7896731  7896743  7896767  7896769  7896773  7896781  7896793  7896803  7896809
7896827  7896829  7896859  7896871  7896883  7896899  7896901  7896937  7896949  7896979
7896991  7896997  7897003  7897013  7897031  7897037  7897049  7897063  7897147  7897177
7897181  7897207  7897247  7897261  7897271  7897283  7897321  7897339  7897387  7897397
7897403  7897411  7897453  7897471  7897481  7897499  7897517  7897531  7897553  7897577
7897601  7897607  7897619  7897621  7897633  7897649  7897661  7897663  7897667  7897691
7897697  7897723  7897727  7897751  7897783  7897807  7897817  7897819  7897847  7897849
7897861  7897873  7897907  7897951  7897957  7897961  7897987  7897999  7898029  7898069
7898071  7898123  7898141  7898159  7898171  7898203  7898213  7898221  7898239  7898263
7898287  7898291  7898299  7898309  7898311  7898323  7898333  7898339  7898347  7898377
7898393  7898413  7898417  7898447  7898477  7898479  7898519  7898531  7898533  7898543
7898549  7898551  7898567  7898593  7898603  7898621  7898641  7898663  7898669  7898687
7898731  7898741  7898747  7898753  7898767  7898789  7898791  7898801  7898809  7898843
7898857  7898873  7898879  7898887  7898899  7898909  7898921  7898923  7898929  7898939
7898981  7898983  7898993  7899011  7899029  7899037  7899053  7899071  7899083  7899113
7899127  7899137  7899161  7899163  7899179  7899197  7899211  7899217  7899239  7899253
7899301  7899319  7899343  7899349  7899361  7899371  7899391  7899413  7899443  7899457
7899467  7899473  7899481  7899499  7899523  7899539  7899553  7899559  7899581  7899587
7899589  7899607  7899623  7899641  7899643  7899677  7899701  7899719  7899733  7899743
7899751  7899779  7899797  7899811  7899817  7899821  7899851  7899859  7899863  7899887
7899911  7899929  7899949  7899967  7899979  7899989  7900001  7900007  7900033  7900043
7900073  7900091  7900103  7900117  7900163  7900177  7900187  7900199  7900213  7900229
7900231  7900253  7900273  7900283  7900301  7900303  7900337  7900349  7900357  7900363
7900369  7900411  7900421  7900457  7900481  7900531  7900547  7900549  7900583  7900609
7900663  7900679  7900709  7900757  7900759  7900769  7900787  7900793  7900807  7900811
7900813  7900817  7900829  7900859  7900873  7900883  7900889  7900909  7900931  7900967
7900969  7900993  7901041  7901057  7901071  7901087  7901119  7901149  7901161  7901171
7901183  7901191  7901197  7901203  7901251  7901261  7901273  7901281  7901287  7901291
7901303  7901353  7901371  7901381  7901389  7901401  7901407  7901419  7901423  7901437
7901441  7901459  7901477  7901483  7901507  7901521  7901539  7901563  7901567  7901591
7901599  7901603  7901669  7901671  7901713  7901741  7901743  7901759  7901767  7901783
7901797  7901819  7901837  7901861  7901893  7901897  7901899  7901909  7901947  7901983
7901989  7902017  7902019  7902029  7902061  7902073  7902079  7902101  7902109  7902131
7902137  7902143  7902151  7902163  7902191  7902227  7902253  7902259  7902269  7902277
7902287  7902329  7902343  7902359  7902383  7902421  7902437  7902443  7902511  7902523
7902527  7902553  7902581  7902589  7902599  7902617  7902619  7902649  7902659  7902673
7902701  7902707  7902749  7902757  7902767  7902779  7902787  7902809  7902833  7902863
7902871  7902893  7902899  7902919  7902931  7902949  7902959  7902997  7903001  7903009
7903033  7903043  7903057  7903061  7903067  7903073  7903139  7903141  7903151  7903213
7903241  7903277  7903279  7903303  7903319  7903331  7903339  7903349  7903367  7903369
7903391  7903417  7903439  7903471  7903517  7903531  7903541  7903547  7903579  7903613
7903633  7903669  7903703  7903711  7903717  7903723  7903741  7903757  7903801  7903807
7903811  7903813  7903859  7903877  7903891  7903897  7903937  7903991  7903993  7903999
7904009  7904063  7904069  7904087  7904093  7904119  7904123  7904161  7904177  7904207
7904263  7904279  7904291  7904297  7904297  7904311  7904317  7904321  7904333  7904363
7904381  7904417  7904419  7904423  7904453  7904467  7904471  7904483  7904509  7904521
7904527  7904531  7904557  7904573  7904581  7904587  7904591  7904621  7904629  7904639
7904651  7904653  7904657  7904669  7904683  7904707  7904719  7904723  7904731  7904753
```

```
7904773  7904843  7904857  7904863  7904867  7904873  7904887  7904903  7904947  7904957
7904959  7904987  7904993  7904999  7905043  7905047  7905049  7905059  7905061  7905067
7905089  7905091  7905113  7905137  7905143  7905151  7905167  7905179  7905193  7905223
7905229  7905239  7905253  7905257  7905269  7905277  7905343  7905379  7905407  7905419
7905431  7905439  7905449  7905467  7905479  7905509  7905529  7905551  7905553  7905563
7905571  7905607  7905619  7905631  7905669  7905671  7905707  7905727  7905739  7905757
7905761  7905763  7905769  7905787  7905797  7905803  7905809  7905817  7905829  7905839
7905847  7905853  7905869  7905889  7905929  7905949  7905967  7905979  7905983  7905991
7906001  7906013  7906021  7906039  7906051  7906069  7906081  7906099  7906117  7906127
7906163  7906189  7906193  7906211  7906229  7906237  7906247  7906253  7906267  7906277
7906279  7906289  7906291  7906307  7906361  7906369  7906391  7906397  7906403  7906417
7906427  7906433  7906463  7906471  7906501  7906523  7906529  7906541  7906543  7906559
7906571  7906601  7906621  7906627  7906667  7906697  7906709  7906721  7906729  7906741
7906753  7906757  7906771  7906781  7906783  7906799  7906807  7906817  7906823  7906841
7906859  7906889  7906897  7906901  7906909  7906919  7906939  7906957  7906961  7906981
7906993  7906999  7907033  7907047  7907069  7907071  7907083  7907117  7907131  7907143
7907153  7907167  7907171  7907183  7907213  7907231  7907257  7907267  7907269  7907297
7907299  7907309  7907323  7907351  7907353  7907359  7907371  7907411  7907429  7907437
7907447  7907453  7907459  7907461  7907467  7907489  7907507  7907513  7907521  7907527
7907531  7907563  7907569  7907587  7907597  7907639  7907651  7907671  7907687  7907689
7907701  7907717  7907723  7907741  7907747  7907761  7907773  7907813  7907827  7907833
7907863  7907881  7907899  7907927  7907953  7907959  7907983  7907989  7908011  7908023
7908029  7908053  7908083  7908091  7908107  7908139  7908143  7908149  7908151  7908167
7908169  7908181  7908203  7908217  7908221  7908233  7908239  7908287  7908293  7908311
7908319  7908353  7908359  7908371  7908403  7908409  7908413  7908437  7908463  7908469
7908487  7908493  7908497  7908499  7908529  7908533  7908569  7908581  7908623  7908647
7908653  7908697  7908707  7908709  7908721  7908739  7908743  7908763  7908767  7908799
7908809  7908811  7908829  7908853  7908871  7908877  7908889  7908899  7908911  7908917
7908919  7908977  7908991  7909003  7909021  7909043  7909049  7909051  7909067  7909081
7909087  7909091  7909103  7909117  7909133  7909159  7909183  7909193  7909219  7909259
7909271  7909273  7909303  7909313  7909337  7909357  7909381  7909393  7909397  7909399
7909399  7909409  7909423  7909439  7909441  7909457  7909459  7909469  7909483  7909487
7909507  7909511  7909513  7909523  7909541  7909553  7909589  7909591  7909609  7909633
7909637  7909639  7909673  7909691  7909703  7909711  7909729  7909739  7909751  7909753
7909799  7909801  7909829  7909841  7909849  7909859  7909873  7909903  7909919  7909921
7909937  7909939  7909943  7909949  7909987  7910003  7910009  7910029  7910039  7910047
7910057  7910081  7910107  7910129  7910153  7910159  7910233  7910249  7910257  7910263
7910281  7910311  7910317  7910333  7910381  7910393  7910407  7910411  7910443  7910453
7910471  7910473  7910519  7910531  7910537  7910561  7910579  7910599  7910633  7910653
7910657  7910659  7910671  7910687  7910719  7910731  7910741  7910789  7910801  7910803
7910809  7910849  7910887  7910911  7910923  7910927  7910941  7910951  7910953  7910971
7910977  7910989  7911037  7911047  7911053  7911067  7911077  7911089  7911109  7911119
7911143  7911161  7911173  7911179  7911187  7911193  7911199  7911209  7911217  7911227
7911301  7911313  7911331  7911347  7911349  7911359  7911361  7911367  7911373  7911383
7911413  7911433  7911457  7911503  7911523  7911539  7911551  7911571  7911583  7911623
7911641  7911653  7911669  7911677  7911679  7911683  7911713  7911763  7911767  7911779
7911781  7911797  7911803  7911823  7911859  7911881  7911899  7911907  7911971  7911989
7911997  7912013  7912031  7912033  7912039  7912061  7912067  7912081  7912103  7912133
7912159  7912171  7912181  7912199  7912213  7912217  7912237  7912277  7912279  7912283
7912291  7912319  7912321  7912343  7912349  7912351  7912363  7912433  7912451  7912477
7912507  7912511  7912517  7912519  7912523  7912537  7912547  7912571  7912577  7912579
7912589  7912603  7912651  7912669  7912673  7912687  7912699  7912703  7912717  7912733
7912739  7912763  7912771  7912787  7912811  7912823  7912829  7912833  7912841  7912867
7912889  7912907  7912909  7912937  7912951  7912991  7912999  7913011  7913057  7913069
7913071  7913077  7913093  7913099  7913117  7913159  7913167  7913179  7913183  7913197
7913203  7913209  7913231  7913233  7913237  7913239  7913251  7913261  7913327  7913341
7913363  7913383  7913393  7913429  7913431  7913441  7913461  7913467  7913473  7913527
7913561  7913567  7913573  7913599  7913611  7913617  7913623  7913627  7913657  7913663
7913669  7913681  7913683  7913701  7913749  7913753  7913761  7913767  7913777  7913783
7913797  7913809  7913831  7913833  7913887  7913903  7913911  7913923  7913947  7913953
7913981  7913989  7914017  7914037  7914073  7914077  7914113  7914121  7914131  7914161
7914169  7914191  7914209  7914227  7914229  7914233  7914239  7914251  7914253  7914293
7914307  7914341  7914343  7914349  7914359  7914373  7914383  7914391  7914397  7914409
7914421  7914449  7914479  7914481  7914497  7914499  7914547  7914551  7914563  7914581
7914589  7914601  7914607  7914617  7914619  7914629  7914637  7914653  7914667  7914679
7914713  7914719  7914743  7914749  7914761  7914769  7914779  7914793  7914853  7914859
7914871  7914899  7914919  7914937  7914943  7914947  7914953  7914961  7914997  7915049
7915051  7915069  7915081  7915087  7915093  7915099  7915109  7915133  7915147  7915157
7915181  7915189  7915213  7915273  7915279  7915283  7915321  7915331  7915351  7915357
7915361  7915363  7915367  7915399  7915403  7915409  7915423  7915457  7915487  7915507
7915513  7915517  7915541  7915549  7915561  7915573  7915597  7915601  7915619  7915631
7915643  7915651  7915681  7915729  7915751  7915759  7915777  7915781  7915801  7915847
7915857  7915871  7915873  7915903  7915969  7915987  7916011  7916017  7916023  7916053
7916057  7916059  7916081  7916093  7916107  7916119  7916131  7916137  7916143  7916147
7916197  7916213  7916263  7916273  7916317  7916323  7916341  7916357  7916399  7916413
7916417  7916423  7916459  7916471  7916473  7916533  7916549  7916551  7916569  7916591
7916593  7916617  7916627  7916647  7916659  7916677  7916707  7916719  7916729  7916737
7916771  7916809  7916833  7916851  7916861  7916881  7916891  7916899  7916911  7916929
7916933  7916947  7916957  7916959  7916963  7917011  7917047  7917061  7917067  7917071
7917097  7917099  7917113  7917137  7917179  7917181  7917187  7917191  7917199  7917209
7917211  7917229  7917241  7917253  7917263  7917271  7917277  7917311  7917331  7917337
7917341  7917347  7917389  7917401  7917407  7917409  7917419  7917421  7917443  7917449
7917467  7917473  7917487  7917517  7917521  7917557  7917561  7917577  7917583  7917583
7917587  7917599  7917601  7917607  7917647  7917659  7917673  7917731  7917743  7917769
7917781  7917811  7917817  7917821  7917827  7917841  7917853  7917863  7917881  7917887
7917929  7917953  7917967  7917997  7918081  7918093  7918103  7918109  7918123  7918129
7918139  7918153  7918159  7918177  7918199  7918201  7918223  7918291  7918319  7918367
7918369  7918373  7918381  7918387  7918397  7918403  7918411  7918429  7918457  7918483
7918487  7918499  7918511  7918517  7918531  7918541  7918543  7918613  7918627  7918637
```

```
7918643  7918657  7918661  7918697  7918717  7918721  7918727  7918793  7918811  7918829
7918847  7918853  7918871  7918879  7918909  7918913  7918951  7918961  7918979  7918987
7919003  7919033  7919047  7919053  7919057  7919069  7919071  7919083  7919089  7919123
7919129  7919173  7919179  7919183  7919209  7919227  7919231  7919239  7919251  7919281
7919287  7919299  7919311  7919341  7919357  7919363  7919381  7919389  7919413  7919449
7919459  7919479  7919491  7919533  7919543  7919557  7919563  7919573  7919579  7919609
7919617  7919621  7919623  7919633  7919647  7919657  7919669  7919687  7919689  7919693
7919701  7919711  7919731  7919741  7919801  7919851  7919861  7919893  7919921  7919939
7919971  7919993  7920019  7920043  7920047  7920053  7920061  7920067  7920071  7920091
7920139  7920149  7920163  7920173  7920193  7920203  7920217  7920229  7920233  7920251
7920259  7920287  7920313  7920323  7920329  7920343  7920347  7920361  7920371  7920389
7920401  7920431  7920433  7920443  7920449  7920457  7920463  7920467  7920481  7920529
7920551  7920559  7920569  7920611  7920613  7920629  7920641  7920677  7920707  7920709
7920713  7920727  7920761  7920767  7920791  7920811  7920817  7920821  7920833  7920883
7920893  7920949  7920959  7921003  7921013  7921021  7921057  7921061  7921087  7921129
7921141  7921153  7921169  7921171  7921189  7921211  7921229  7921237  7921247  7921259
7921261  7921273  7921289  7921307  7921313  7921351  7921373  7921391  7921411  7921447
7921451  7921457  7921489  7921493  7921519  7921549  7921559  7921561  7921579  7921597
7921607  7921621  7921631  7921679  7921687  7921691  7921703  7921723  7921757  7921759
7921777  7921787  7921817  7921819  7921831  7921861  7921873  7921889  7921891  7921909
7921919  7921931  7921943  7921981  7921987  7921999  7922021  7922023  7922059  7922093
7922111  7922113  7922129  7922141  7922149  7922171  7922177  7922197  7922203  7922207
7922209  7922219  7922227  7922231  7922261  7922269  7922293  7922303  7922309  7922311
7922347  7922351  7922371  7922399  7922401  7922413  7922441  7922443  7922483  7922491
7922501  7922503  7922507  7922531  7922567  7922569  7922587  7922591  7922627  7922653
7922689  7922693  7922711  7922723  7922767  7922779  7922801  7922809  7922813  7922821
7922851  7922891  7922903  7922911  7922923  7922939  7922947  7922953  7922987  7923001
7923043  7923049  7923059  7923067  7923079  7923131  7923161  7923187  7923191  7923193
7923199  7923211  7923239  7923257  7923269  7923271  7923277  7923281  7923299  7923301
7923313  7923337  7923371  7923379  7923397  7923427  7923449  7923451  7923469  7923491
7923497  7923499  7923521  7923527  7923563  7923607  7923611  7923613  7923623  7923647
7923667  7923679  7923691  7923719  7923731  7923733  7923737  7923749  7923763  7923781
7923787  7923803  7923823  7923827  7923847  7923857  7923863  7923869  7923907  7923917
7923953  7923959  7923967  7923991  7924009  7924013  7924019  7924039  7924043  7924051
7924061  7924067  7924069  7924073  7924079  7924109  7924123  7924141  7924177  7924181
7924183  7924187  7924199  7924201  7924211  7924229  7924237  7924243  7924271  7924289
7924307  7924309  7924373  7924393  7924403  7924417  7924421  7924429  7924457  7924487
7924531  7924541  7924589  7924597  7924607  7924639  7924643  7924681  7924711  7924733
7924739  7924759  7924769  7924783  7924799  7924817  7924877  7924879  7924883  7924901
7924913  7924921  7924967  7924981  7924991  7925017  7925053  7925073  7925083  7925101
7925123  7925173  7925209  7925227  7925237  7925257  7925263  7925273  7925279  7925321
7925327  7925329  7925339  7925347  7925353  7925377  7925389  7925453  7925471  7925503
7925509  7925513  7925521  7925531  7925543  7925551  7925557  7925609  7925611  7925627
7925629  7925651  7925663  7925681  7925693  7925699  7925711  7925719  7925737  7925741
7925759  7925761  7925783  7925789  7925837  7925843  7925849  7925851  7925857  7925867
7925873  7925891  7925917  7925959  7925969  7925977  7925989  7926041  7926047  7926067
7926071  7926091  7926109  7926151  7926169  7926179  7926181  7926187  7926229  7926241
7926257  7926271  7926277  7926293  7926311  7926323  7926343  7926383  7926389  7926419
7926431  7926449  7926463  7926469  7926487  7926493  7926497  7926509  7926517  7926563
7926587  7926593  7926601  7926617  7926619  7926643  7926647  7926649  7926661  7926671
7926673  7926701  7926707  7926713  7926719  7926727  7926757  7926761  7926799  7926803
7926823  7926847  7926859  7926869  7926883  7926887  7926907  7926911  7926923  7926943
7926953  7926967  7926977  7927013  7927027  7927037  7927039  7927043  7927057  7927069
7927091  7927099  7927109  7927159  7927163  7927169  7927177  7927201  7927207  7927211
7927217  7927223  7927229  7927259  7927277  7927279  7927301  7927307  7927327  7927343
7927357  7927393  7927397  7927421  7927429  7927441  7927459  7927471  7927483  7927487
7927489  7927511  7927531  7927553  7927573  7927589  7927607  7927639  7927649  7927669
7927681  7927697  7927739  7927747  7927753  7927757  7927811  7927823  7927841  7927849
7927859  7927891  7927919  7927937  7927943  7927979  7927999  7928003  7928021  7928023
7928059  7928083  7928099  7928117  7928131  7928147  7928153  7928161  7928183  7928189
7928191  7928201  7928257  7928267  7928269  7928303  7928309  7928317  7928329  7928351
7928363  7928369  7928407  7928411  7928423  7928441  7928461  7928497  7928507  7928527
7928533  7928549  7928563  7928573  7928581  7928587  7928617  7928623  7928651  7928671
7928689  7928717  7928761  7928797  7928801  7928821  7928831  7928849  7928857  7928863
7928881  7928897  7928903  7928911  7928923  7928927  7928929  7928933  7928939  7928941
7928969  7929007  7929013  7929017  7929079  7929083  7929101  7929133  7929139  7929143
7929167  7929197  7929199  7929217  7929253  7929263  7929269  7929287  7929301  7929307
7929343  7929347  7929349  7929367  7929371  7929401  7929413  7929431  7929443  7929469
7929473  7929491  7929527  7929547  7929563  7929577  7929589  7929613  7929617  7929619
7929673  7929683  7929703  7929709  7929739  7929743  7929749  7929763  7929773
7929797  7929799  7929827  7929829  7929833  7929863  7929869  7929899  7929907  7929937
7929949  7929953  7929979  7929983  7929997  7930003  7930031  7930037  7930057  7930093
7930121  7930123  7930133  7930151  7930159  7930229  7930243  7930267  7930271  7930283
7930289  7930291  7930297  7930303  7930319  7930333  7930339  7930387  7930393  7930397
7930399  7930409  7930411  7930421  7930457  7930463  7930471  7930529  7930537  7930553
7930579  7930591  7930597  7930649  7930651  7930661  7930673  7930693  7930709  7930757
7930759  7930799  7930807  7930829  7930841  7930849  7930859  7930861  7930903  7930907
7930933  7930943  7931003  7931017  7931041  7931101  7931117  7931137  7931141  7931149
7931173  7931177  7931179  7931207  7931233  7931249  7931263  7931267  7931269  7931293
7931347  7931351  7931353  7931369  7931383  7931411  7931423  7931437  7931449  7931453
7931459  7931461  7931467  7931477  7931501  7931507  7931509  7931513  7931519  7931533
7931597  7931611  7931621  7931633  7931659  7931699  7931713  7931719  7931731  7931771
7931773  7931779  7931789  7931813  7931831  7931857  7931863  7931867  7931883  7931893
7931921  7931923  7931953  7931977  7932011  7932031  7932037  7932053  7932083  7932103
7932151  7932157  7932161  7932179  7932193  7932203  7932209  7932241  7932247  7932259
7932269  7932271  7932277  7932289  7932307  7932317  7932347  7932371  7932377  7932403
7932433  7932451  7932461  7932473  7932479  7932499  7932503  7932517  7932521  7932527
7932553  7932571  7932577  7932581  7932593  7932601  7932607  7932619  7932629  7932637
7932647  7932653  7932679  7932697  7932703  7932781  7932787  7932791  7932797  7932809
```

```
7932811  7932817  7932839  7932851  7932853  7932857  7932871  7932887  7932889  7932893
7932913  7932917  7932919  7932923  7932949  7932961  7932971  7932973  7933021  7933039
7933061  7933069  7933073  7933099  7933109  7933139  7933151  7933157  7933171  7933181
7933201  7933231  7933243  7933273  7933283  7933291  7933313  7933319  7933361  7933363
7933379  7933397  7933399  7933447  7933451  7933463  7933481  7933487  7933511  7933531
7933547  7933573  7933589  7933591  7933609  7933619  7933633  7933661  7933693  7933711
7933769  7933771  7933777  7933813  7933823  7933829  7933837  7933841  7933867  7933897
7933903  7933909  7933927  7933957  7934009  7934027  7934029  7934063  7934089  7934093
7934099  7934119  7934123  7934131  7934137  7934141  7934159  7934167  7934177
7934183  7934203  7934221  7934239  7934249  7934263  7934273  7934281  7934293  7934323
7934363  7934369  7934383  7934387  7934389  7934413  7934417  7934441  7934449  7934467
7934483  7934491  7934501  7934513  7934519  7934527  7934557  7934587  7934593
7934627  7934651  7934653  7934657  7934659  7934669  7934737  7934741  7934749  7934779
7934803  7934807  7934821  7934831  7934867  7934917  7934921  7934923  7934929  7934957
7934959  7934981  7934987  7934999  7935041  7935047  7935061  7935071  7935113  7935119
7935127  7935133  7935143  7935157  7935197  7935203  7935229  7935259  7935269  7935271
7935283  7935289  7935359  7935383  7935397  7935401  7935409  7935439  7935443  7935449
7935463  7935467  7935491  7935497  7935511  7935539  7935553  7935563  7935569  7935601
7935619  7935623  7935661  7935679  7935701  7935703  7935709  7935727  7935761  7935791
7935799  7935833  7935839  7935847  7935853  7935887  7935899  7935931  7935947  7935953
7935959  7935971  7935979  7936009  7936043  7936051  7936063  7936069  7936079  7936109
7936139  7936141  7936153  7936163  7936177  7936183  7936207  7936223  7936231  7936259
7936289  7936303  7936333  7936349  7936367  7936421  7936429  7936441  7936477  7936519
7936529  7936531  7936567  7936571  7936583  7936597  7936613  7936631  7936667  7936673
7936723  7936727  7936751  7936757  7936763  7936769  7936801  7936823  7936829  7936847
7936867  7936879  7936891  7936913  7936949  7936963  7936967  7936969  7936979  7936987
7936997  7937057  7937063  7937087  7937089  7937101  7937107  7937123  7937141  7937177
7937179  7937183  7937191  7937201  7937243  7937261  7937263  7937273  7937291  7937297
7937299  7937311  7937339  7937357  7937359  7937389  7937399  7937431  7937441  7937443
7937467  7937473  7937483  7937491  7937533  7937549  7937551  7937563  7937569  7937591
7937597  7937621  7937639  7937659  7937681  7937693  7937701  7937711  7937719  7937731
7937749  7937753  7937771  7937777  7937791  7937819  7937837  7937857  7937879  7937899
7937903  7937927  7937933  7937939  7937981  7937983  7937987  7938023  7938041  7938053
7938061  7938071  7938079  7938089  7938109  7938121  7938127  7938149  7938163  7938173
7938179  7938193  7938211  7938233  7938241  7938247  7938251  7938311  7938317  7938349
7938397  7938407  7938443  7938457  7938481  7938503  7938517  7938527  7938529  7938551
7938563  7938569  7938583  7938607  7938641  7938649  7938727  7938761  7938767  7938773
7938787  7938803  7938811  7938839  7938851  7938857  7938859  7938877  7938893  7938907
7938919  7938929  7938977  7938991  7939027  7939037  7939039  7939049  7939053  7939057
7939081  7939091  7939103  7939147  7939157  7939171  7939177  7939189  7939213  7939223
7939229  7939237  7939241  7939249  7939259  7939273  7939279  7939303  7939313  7939319
7939339  7939361  7939367  7939387  7939403  7939409  7939411  7939447  7939499  7939523
7939543  7939573  7939583  7939597  7939619  7939621  7939637  7939643  7939661  7939693
7939709  7939727  7939733  7939753  7939769  7939781  7939787  7939817
7939829  7939831  7939837  7939847  7939849  7939861  7939909  7939931  7939933  7939949
7939951  7939963  7939991  7940001  7940017  7940021  7940047  7940063  7940069  7940077
7940087  7940147  7940159  7940197  7940209  7940239  7940243  7940249  7940269  7940293
7940327  7940329  7940341  7940353  7940357  7940381  7940383  7940393  7940399
7940417  7940419  7940437  7940447  7940467  7940473  7940483  7940503  7940507  7940521
7940539  7940549  7940567  7940591  7940627  7940629  7940641  7940663  7940707  7940719
7940747  7940761  7940763  7940783  7940789  7940813  7940833  7940851  7940857  7940893
7940927  7940963  7940971  7940981  7941007  7941019  7941061  7941083  7941097  7941103
7941119  7941121  7941139  7941161  7941173  7941211  7941229  7941247  7941257  7941277
7941281  7941287  7941299  7941319  7941343  7941359  7941377  7941379  7941383  7941391
7941419  7941457  7941469  7941473  7941481  7941497  7941503  7941517  7941539  7941547
7941581  7941599  7941607  7941623  7941641  7941649  7941667  7941671  7941697  7941701
7941707  7941709  7941719  7941721  7941751  7941761  7941767  7941779  7941781  7941803
7941827  7941833  7941851  7941883  7941917  7941937  7941959  7941961  7941977  7941991
7942003  7942031  7942063  7942091  7942097  7942117  7942163  7942177  7942211  7942219
7942223  7942243  7942267  7942279  7942303  7942307  7942313  7942331  7942343  7942357
7942369  7942373  7942379  7942387  7942411  7942427  7942447  7942469  7942471  7942477
7942481  7942499  7942507  7942511  7942523  7942537  7942559  7942579  7942601  7942609
7942663  7942667  7942691  7942729  7942733  7942747  7942769  7942789  7942819
7942829  7942861  7942867  7942903  7942919  7942967  7942973  7942997  7942999  7943059
7943077  7943081  7943087  7943093  7943107  7943113  7943127  7943137  7943147  7943167
7943171  7943179  7943207  7943209  7943227  7943231  7943239  7943249  7943263  7943279
7943291  7943293  7943297  7943317  7943321  7943333  7943357  7943363  7943399  7943407
7943431  7943443  7943449  7943459  7943473  7943491  7943497  7943513  7943531  7943543
7943557  7943563  7943569  7943591  7943597  7943599  7943629  7943713  7943731  7943737
7943753  7943773  7943783  7943787  7943801  7943807  7943833  7943851
7943861  7943891  7943911  7943917  7943921  7943927  7943951  7943983  7944017  7944019
7944047  7944059  7944061  7944067  7944089  7944103  7944113  7944133  7944143  7944149
7944163  7944169  7944191  7944199  7944197  7944227  7944241  7944259  7944281
7944301  7944317  7944341  7944353  7944373  7944437  7944439  7944443  7944481  7944487
7944523  7944533  7944553  7944571  7944577  7944581  7944589  7944631  7944653  7944667
7944707  7944721  7944731  7944733  7944737  7944769  7944787  7944791  7944799  7944841
7944851  7944877  7944887  7944919  7944929  7944931  7944943  7944953  7944961  7944991
7945031  7945033  7945037  7945039  7945057  7945073  7945079  7945081  7945087  7945099
7945123  7945129  7945139  7945151  7945163  7945169  7945181  7945187  7945193  7945199
7945213  7945219  7945229  7945237  7945241  7945243  7945261  7945277  7945279  7945291
7945309  7945313  7945319  7945321  7945361  7945381  7945387  7945423  7945429  7945451
7945481  7945489  7945519  7945537  7945541  7945547  7945559  7945573  7945621  7945633
7945661  7945687  7945697  7945699  7945709  7945711  7945727  7945733  7945757  7945789
7945801  7945811  7945843  7945849  7945897  7945909  7945937  7945957  7945963  7945967
7945969  7945979  7945981  7946023  7946039  7946049  7946051  7946063  7946069  7946093
7946119  7946129  7946153  7946167  7946177  7946189  7946233  7946303  7946321  7946353
7946359  7946369  7946387  7946417  7946441  7946473  7946479  7946483  7946489  7946501
7946507  7946513  7946537  7946539  7946557  7946567  7946581  7946621  7946623  7946629
7946639  7946641  7946657  7946663  7946671  7946681  7946683  7946699  7946711  7946717
```

```
7946737 7946747 7946777 7946791 7946801 7946821 7946833 7946839 7946843 7946857
7946903 7946909 7946927 7946929 7946941 7946947 7946969 7947011 7947013 7947053
7947059 7947061 7947083 7947091 7947097 7947133 7947151 7947157 7947169 7947197
7947221 7947227 7947229 7947257 7947271 7947283 7947287 7947293 7947323 7947337
7947343 7947349 7947361 7947409 7947427 7947431 7947461 7947469 7947487 7947493
7947521 7947539 7947553 7947587 7947601 7947613 7947631 7947649 7947661 7947677
7947679 7947683 7947691 7947703 7947707 7947739 7947761 7947767 7947799 7947803
7947839 7947851 7947869 7947899 7947917 7947931 7947937 7947941 7947971 7947977
7947983 7948019 7948033 7948037 7948049 7948063 7948069 7948079 7948091 7948093
7948103 7948147 7948151 7948153 7948177 7948181 7948189 7948207 7948223 7948247
7948261 7948267 7948279 7948309 7948351 7948373 7948393 7948429 7948433 7948453
7948477 7948487 7948511 7948513 7948519 7948529 7948541 7948543 7948553 7948561
7948583 7948597 7948609 7948637 7948643 7948651 7948667 7948691 7948723 7948757
7948763 7948769 7948817 7948841 7948861 7948867 7948873 7948879 7948883 7948907
7948931 7948939 7948943 7948951 7948981 7948991 7948999 7949009 7949017 7949083
7949101 7949111 7949119 7949141 7949143 7949167 7949171 7949233 7949269 7949273
7949297 7949299 7949303 7949309 7949317 7949323 7949327 7949369 7949397 7949399
7949401 7949411 7949443 7949497 7949503 7949507 7949519 7949537 7949563 7949573
7949593 7949633 7949639 7949647 7949653 7949697 7949681 7949723 7949731 7949737
7949759 7949791 7949801 7949803 7949813 7949833 7949839 7949861 7949873 7949891
7949899 7949933 7950001 7950109 7950119 7950121 7950127 7950139 7950143 7950179
7950197 7950209 7950223 7950251 7950253 7950277 7950307 7950311 7950317 7950343
7950347 7950359 7950361 7950377 7950391 7950403 7950409 7950413 7950419 7950431
7950451 7950457 7950461 7950463 7950469 7950497 7950499 7950511 7950529 7950533
7950541 7950559 7950563 7950587 7950589 7950599 7950623 7950641 7950667 7950707
7950737 7950739 7950749 7950769 7950779 7950791 7950827 7950853 7950857 7950863
7950871 7950881 7950889 7950913 7950919 7950931 7950937 7950947 7950953 7950961
7950979 7950991 7950997 7951033 7951039 7951049 7951051 7951067 7951081 7951103
7951127 7951157 7951183 7951193 7951201 7951211 7951213 7951243 7951247 7951297
7951301 7951327 7951331 7951351 7951357 7951387 7951397 7951403 7951453 7951459
7951477 7951523 7951561 7951571 7951577 7951589 7951621 7951639 7951667 7951679
7951681 7951687 7951693 7951711 7951729 7951751 7951753 7951807 7951819 7951847
7951849 7951897 7951901 7951913 7951949 7951967 7951969 7951973 7952011 7952041
7952047 7952059 7952069 7952081 7952083 7952099 7952117 7952123 7952129 7952171
7952183 7952233 7952249 7952267 7952309 7952333 7952363 7952369 7952389 7952407
7952419 7952423 7952443 7952453 7952471 7952473 7952489 7952501 7952533 7952537
7952573 7952587 7952591 7952599 7952603 7952611 7952627 7952629 7952657 7952677
7952683 7952689 7952701 7952761 7952767 7952797 7952803 7952831 7952843 7952869
7952897 7952909 7952921 7952929 7952953 7952969 7952993 7952999 7953007 7953061
7953073 7953079 7953083 7953089 7953091 7953097 7953107 7953109 7953133 7953157
7953217 7953247 7953251 7953269 7953271 7953289 7953299 7953301 7953311 7953313
7953347 7953359 7953371 7953373 7953389 7953427 7953487 7953493 7953497 7953499
7953509 7953527 7953529 7953541 7953553 7953559 7953563 7953593 7953611 7953619
7953661 7953677 7953679 7953689 7953691 7953707 7953721 7953727 7953781 7953793
7953797 7953811 7953821 7953833 7953863 7953871 7953899 7953901 7953919 7953923
7953931 7953971 7954003 7954013 7954031 7954039 7954069 7954099 7954117 7954127
7954151 7954213 7954231 7954253 7954277 7954279 7954301 7954313 7954319 7954333
7954337 7954361 7954379 7954393 7954423 7954459 7954469 7954477 7954523 7954537
7954543 7954571 7954607 7954621 7954649 7954651 7954721 7954763 7954777 7954781
7954783 7954799 7954801 7954811 7954813 7954819 7954867 7954907 7954927 7954931
7954937 7954979 7954993 7955009 7955011 7955039 7955047 7955053 7955083 7955093
7955113 7955117 7955159 7955177 7955183 7955191 7955203 7955209 7955239 7955273
7955279 7955323 7955327 7955329 7955351 7955359 7955377 7955393 7955399 7955417
7955449 7955461 7955489 7955491 7955527 7955543 7955551 7955567 7955569 7955573
7955579 7955581 7955587 7955603 7955627 7955639 7955687 7955693 7955707 7955719
7955741 7955767 7955789 7955791 7955797 7955807 7955863 7955869 7955879 7955887
7955891 7955897 7955911 7955917 7955923 7955929 7955963 7956031 7956043 7956061
7956077 7956089 7956101 7956103 7956139 7956149 7956163 7956211 7956259 7956283
7956287 7956293 7956329 7956349 7956373 7956379 7956401 7956407 7956409 7956427
7956437 7956467 7956503 7956521 7956523 7956587 7956589 7956593 7956601 7956631
7956661 7956667 7956671 7956703 7956709 7956727 7956737 7956743 7956761 7956769
7956791 7956797 7956803 7956821 7956847 7956857 7956859 7956889 7956913 7956947
7956967 7956979 7956983 7956989 7957013 7957039 7957069 7957091 7957099 7957129
7957151 7957177 7957189 7957211 7957217 7957237 7957249 7957253 7957259 7957273
7957283 7957291 7957319 7957337 7957349 7957351 7957361 7957381 7957387 7957393
7957423 7957427 7957441 7957463 7957493 7957501 7957519 7957531 7957577 7957597
7957601 7957603 7957613 7957619 7957667 7957673 7957681 7957699 7957721 7957727
7957739 7957769 7957771 7957787 7957801 7957837 7957847 7957867 7957871 7957879
7957909 7957951 7957973 7957987 7957991 7958009 7958011 7958021 7958029 7958033
7958039 7958047 7958063 7958077 7958099 7958143 7958183 7958189 7958213 7958231
7958257 7958263 7958281 7958309 7958317 7958371 7958399 7958407 7958429 7958443
7958459 7958471 7958521 7958527 7958563 7958591 7958593 7958597 7958617 7958623
7958627 7958641 7958689 7958693 7958749 7958761 7958773 7958791 7958807 7958831
7958833 7958837 7958843 7958849 7958857 7958861 7958869 7958893 7958917 7958921
7958927 7958983 7958987 7959011 7959019 7959023 7959031 7959037 7959067 7959073
7959089 7959151 7959163 7959187 7959191 7959199 7959209 7959221 7959227
7959239 7959241 7959251 7959269 7959283 7959307 7959319 7959323 7959331 7959337
7959373 7959401 7959421 7959473 7959491 7959493 7959503 7959517 7959521 7959527
7959577 7959583 7959599 7959649 7959661 7959673 7959703 7959713 7959719 7959761
7959793 7959799 7959821 7959823 7959827 7959851 7959857 7959869 7959871 7959883
7959907 7959929 7959937 7959971 7959983 7959997 7960003 7960009 7960013 7960019
7960021 7960033 7960037 7960039 7960067 7960079 7960081 7960129 7960133 7960151
7960153 7960157 7960159 7960163 7960171 7960177 7960189 7960201 7960207 7960213
7960223 7960237 7960241 7960243 7960261 7960279 7960283 7960313 7960327 7960333
7960349 7960361 7960363 7960399 7960417 7960429 7960451 7960453 7960481 7960523
7960541 7960543 7960549 7960559 7960567 7960571 7960609 7960619 7960621 7960637
7960643 7960651 7960679 7960681 7960697 7960699 7960717 7960763 7960787 7960789
7960793 7960801 7960837 7960853 7960903 7960969 7960991 7961003 7961021 7961029
7961069 7961087 7961101 7961119 7961131 7961137 7961143 7961147 7961227 7961231
```

```
7961267  7961279  7961281  7961299  7961333  7961347  7961353  7961357  7961363  7961411
7961413  7961417  7961441  7961449  7961461  7961477  7961479  7961489  7961497  7961509
7961521  7961533  7961539  7961557  7961561  7961563  7961567  7961617  7961621  7961651
7961669  7961693  7961711  7961717  7961719  7961743  7961783  7961803  7961809  7961827
7961839  7961879  7961881  7961929  7961939  7961951  7961953  7961957  7961959  7961981
7961999  7962013  7962041  7962047  7962091  7962127  7962139  7962151  7962161  7962167
7962193  7962203  7962293  7962247  7962271  7962277  7962293  7962313  7962359  7962377
7962389  7962397  7962401  7962403  7962419  7962421  7962433  7962467  7962469  7962491
7962497  7962499  7962503  7962517  7962527  7962541  7962551  7962571  7962583  7962593
7962607  7962637  7962641  7962677  7962701  7962707  7962719  7962743  7962751  7962769
7962781  7962797  7962809  7962811  7962847  7962859  7962887  7962917  7962923  7962931
7962943  7962947  7962961  7962989  7963003  7963009  7963013  7963031  7963049  7963057
7963073  7963079  7963099  7963117  7963141  7963159  7963199  7963217  7963229  7963231
7963237  7963247  7963253  7963271  7963297  7963301  7963321  7963343  7963349  7963369
7963379  7963391  7963393  7963411  7963433  7963441  7963469  7963481  7963493  7963499
7963507  7963513  7963517  7963519  7963523  7963537  7963561  7963567  7963577  7963591
7963607  7963607  7963663  7963693  7963723  7963757  7963763  7963783  7963801  7963847
7963849  7963859  7963873  7963909  7963919  7963937  7963961  7963981  7964023  7964029
7964039  7964051  7964053  7964071  7964093  7964113  7964129  7964137  7964147  7964149
7964161  7964167  7964207  7964237  7964251  7964263  7964273  7964311  7964329  7964339
7964377  7964387  7964393  7964413  7964423  7964441  7964443  7964459  7964471  7964549
7964569  7964569  7964603  7964609  7964611  7964623  7964633  7964651  7964683  7964689
7964707  7964711  7964713  7964717  7964729  7964741  7964753  7964779  7964791  7964807
7964813  7964833  7964863  7964881  7964897  7964909  7964921  7964939  7964941  7964977
7964981  7964987  7965007  7965037  7965049  7965071  7965073  7965079  7965091  7965127
7965131  7965151  7965173  7965229  7965241  7965247  7965253  7965263  7965271  7965281
7965283  7965289  7965329  7965361  7965371  7965379  7965403  7965407  7965409  7965421
7965457  7965467  7965473  7965479  7965487  7965497  7965499  7965527  7965547  7965557
7965577  7965599  7965623  7965637  7965641  7965653  7965677  7965719  7965721  7965743
7965757  7965761  7965779  7965781  7965787  7965799  7965803  7965863  7965871  7965907
7965941  7965949  7966001  7966009  7966019  7966031  7966061  7966103  7966117  7966141
7966157  7966199  7966207  7966219  7966237  7966247  7966253  7966261  7966267  7966279
7966333  7966351  7966363  7966379  7966381  7966391  7966393  7966397  7966403  7966429
7966451  7966463  7966493  7966499  7966499  7966549  7966559  7966571  7966573  7966603
7966627  7966633  7966663  7966691  7966703  7966723  7966747  7966759  7966781  7966787
7966807  7966817  7966831  7966843  7966853  7966867  7966873  7966879  7966897  7966939
7966943  7966949  7966979  7967009  7967021  7967041  7967051  7967053  7967081  7967107
7967117  7967143  7967209  7967221  7967227  7967231  7967249  7967261  7967263  7967273
7967303  7967317  7967329  7967347  7967357  7967381  7967383  7967389  7967417  7967423
7967429  7967459  7967461  7967497  7967521  7967569  7967579  7967621  7967623  7967627
7967657  7967681  7967689  7967711  7967723  7967741  7967749  7967753  7967777  7967797
7967803  7967819  7967831  7967851  7967879  7967893  7967909  7967923  7967933  7967941
7967963  7967989  7968001  7968007  7968017  7968031  7968043  7968101  7968113  7968133
7968151  7968157  7968167  7968199  7968203  7968217  7968229  7968299  7968307  7968313
7968319  7968341  7968347  7968349  7968379  7968409  7968413  7968449  7968463  7968469
7968479  7968487  7968503  7968523  7968539  7968551  7968577  7968593  7968617  7968641
7968661  7968673  7968679  7968683  7968689  7968691  7968703  7968743  7968749  7968757
7968761  7968769  7968773  7968791  7968811  7968817  7968853  7968859  7968871  7968893
7968911  7968941  7968959  7969019  7969033  7969043  7969051  7969057  7969069  7969103
7969121  7969183  7969187  7969193  7969217  7969219  7969231  7969267  7969279  7969309
7969321  7969333  7969333  7969349  7969361  7969363  7969373  7969391  7969397  7969399
7969439  7969453  7969463  7969469  7969499  7969513  7969517  7969547  7969561  7969571
7969597  7969601  7969603  7969609  7969627  7969639  7969657  7969667  7969673  7969723
7969727  7969729  7969739  7969747  7969771  7969781  7969783  7969807  7969813  7969823
7969849  7969853  7969877  7969901  7969943  7969961  7969967  7969979  7969993  7969999
7970021  7970023  7970033  7970047  7970051  7970057  7970071  7970089  7970107  7970141
7970143  7970153  7970173  7970191  7970203  7970219  7970227  7970257  7970267  7970269
7970279  7970293  7970309  7970311  7970327  7970353  7970357  7970371  7970377  7970471
7970477  7970491  7970497  7970507  7970509  7970533  7970539  7970549  7970551  7970561
7970579  7970591  7970597  7970653  7970657  7970659  7970693  7970701  7970731  7970761
7970771  7970783  7970801  7970821  7970827  7970849  7970869  7970881  7970887  7970917
7970927  7970951  7970983  7970987  7970993  7971017  7971031  7971091  7971101  7971109
7971137  7971149  7971157  7971199  7971209  7971217  7971221  7971239  7971251  7971263
7971269  7971281  7971307  7971311  7971323  7971331  7971347  7971373  7971389  7971401
7971413  7971443  7971461  7971493  7971499  7971503  7971563  7971577  7971611  7971617
7971637  7971679  7971683  7971701  7971707  7971709  7971713  7971721  7971737  7971739
7971757  7971763  7971787  7971833  7971851  7971853  7971871  7971881  7971911  7971913
7971919  7971959  7971973  7972009  7972033  7972043  7972049  7972051  7972061  7972087
7972103  7972121  7972141  7972147  7972183  7972189  7972193  7972199  7972219  7972231
7972253  7972271  7972277  7972291  7972297  7972309  7972339  7972351  7972357  7972373
7972387  7972411  7972417  7972429  7972451  7972453  7972499  7972511  7972553  7972577
7972579  7972583  7972589  7972603  7972619  7972621  7972633  7972663  7972667  7972669
7972689  7972691  7972693  7972733  7972739  7972753  7972763  7972771  7972777  7972781
7972817  7972831  7972849  7972879  7972889  7972903  7972907  7972957  7972963  7972967
7972969  7973047  7973089  7973101  7973117  7973123  7973129  7973131  7973137  7973143
7973159  7973159  7973171  7973183  7973191  7973209  7973213  7973219  7973227  7973237
7973239  7973269  7973281  7973299  7973309  7973321  7973327  7973351  7973353  7973363
7973377  7973401  7973411  7973419  7973423  7973431  7973443  7973453  7973461  7973473
7973477  7973489  7973509  7973519  7973543  7973591  7973627  7973653  7973659  7973681
7973687  7973689  7973701  7973723  7973741  7973767  7973773  7973807  7973813  7973837
7973881  7973899  7973921  7973929  7973941  7973971  7974017  7974041  7974061  7974073
7974107  7974137  7974143  7974149  7974179  7974191  7974199  7974209  7974227  7974229
7974243  7974251  7974259  7974269  7974287  7974289  7974293  7974299  7974361  7974371
7974401  7974403  7974413  7974419  7974437  7974451  7974481  7974493  7974511  7974587
7974599  7974601  7974607  7974611  7974613  7974641  7974643  7974653  7974677  7974709
7974727  7974731  7974779  7974803  7974821  7974829  7974833  7974893  7974899  7974917
7974919  7974929  7974937  7974961  7974977  7974991  7975013  7975021  7975027  7975039
7975063  7975067  7975073  7975103  7975109  7975111  7975133  7975139  7975147  7975169
7975171  7975189  7975199  7975213  7975229  7975237  7975241  7975267  7975271  7975291
```

```
7975309 7975321 7975327 7975337 7975343 7975351 7975369 7975399 7975417 7975423
7975433 7975439 7975447 7975483 7975507 7975519 7975531 7975543 7975559 7975577
7975619 7975633 7975637 7975651 7975691 7975717 7975739 7975741 7975777 7975817
7975837 7975843 7975861 7975883 7975889 7975921 7975937 7975943 7975949 7975973
7975987 7975997 7976047 7976057 7976063 7976081 7976093 7976117 7976123 7976141
7976153 7976159 7976161 7976173 7976183 7976203 7976209 7976231 7976233 7976249
7976261 7976279 7976303 7976317 7976321 7976327 7976329 7976347 7976357 7976359
7976369 7976389 7976399 7976401 7976413 7976429 7976461 7976467 7976477 7976483
7976513 7976533 7976563 7976567 7976593 7976603 7976609 7976611 7976627 7976651
7976663 7976693 7976701 7976707 7976753 7976767 7976807 7976809 7976831 7976833
7976849 7976861 7976869 7976873 7976897 7976911 7976923 7976939 7976963 7976971
7976987 7976993 7977019 7977043 7977049 7977119 7977133 7977139 7977143 7977149
7977157 7977161 7977187 7977191 7977197 7977209 7977217 7977227 7977241 7977253
7977259 7977271 7977287 7977289 7977293 7977353 7977433 7977443 7977457 7977503
7977517 7977521 7977551 7977553 7977559 7977569 7977577 7977583 7977589 7977611
7977617 7977643 7977649 7977653 7977677 7977679 7977707 7977713 7977721 7977727
7977731 7977737 7977779 7977787 7977793 7977797 7977799 7977817 7977841 7977857
7977863 7977869 7977883 7977887 7977899 7977923 7977961 7977971 7977989 7977997
7978021 7978063 7978099 7978169 7978181 7978189 7978193 7978207 7978211 7978237
7978247 7978279 7978301 7978307 7978319 7978331 7978337 7978339 7978343 7978367
7978379 7978381 7978403 7978409 7978429 7978441 7978459 7978463 7978471 7978519
7978547 7978577 7978603 7978609 7978637 7978639 7978657 7978667 7978679 7978699
7978709 7978721 7978753 7978757 7978771 7978777 7978781 7978783 7978793 7978807
7978819 7978837 7978847 7978849 7978871 7978877 7978889 7978903 7978913 7978937
7978961 7978979 7978981 7979009 7979021 7979057 7979063 7979071 7979113 7979129
7979131 7979141 7979173 7979189 7979197 7979201 7979243 7979249 7979261 7979267
7979281 7979287 7979351 7979353 7979357 7979423 7979441 7979453 7979479 7979497
7979501 7979533 7979549 7979561 7979567 7979581 7979599 7979623 7979663 7979687
7979693 7979717 7979737 7979771 7979773 7979779 7979813 7979819 7979821 7979833
7979857 7979863 7979891 7979893 7979911 7979921 7979957 7979969 7980013 7980029
7980031 7980041 7980047 7980059 7980061 7980067 7980101 7980121 7980143 7980151
7980179 7980221 7980227 7980239 7980251 7980283 7980289 7980311 7980319 7980331
7980341 7980353 7980373 7980383 7980391 7980403 7980409 7980431 7980439 7980443
7980451 7980473 7980491 7980509 7980529 7980587 7980593 7980601 7980617 7980629
7980673 7980677 7980683 7980689 7980697 7980727 7980751 7980761 7980787 7980811
7980821 7980859 7980881 7980911 7980923 7980953 7980983 7980997 7981013 7981021
7981033 7981037 7981049 7981067 7981087 7981123 7981139 7981147 7981151 7981189
7981223 7981231 7981247 7981283 7981289 7981297 7981319 7981321 7981327 7981331
7981333 7981339 7981397 7981411 7981417 7981433 7981447 7981453 7981471 7981481
7981487 7981507 7981513 7981537 7981553 7981591 7981627 7981639 7981661 7981711
7981717 7981783 7981793 7981801 7981807 7981811 7981817 7981819 7981837 7981847
7981859 7981867 7981871 7981877 7981889 7981907 7981927 7981937 7981949 7981999
7982017 7982021 7982053 7982059 7982063 7982083 7982087 7982101 7982111 7982123
7982137 7982141 7982153 7982201 7982203 7982209 7982237 7982257 7982267 7982297
7982323 7982327 7982329 7982423 7982461 7982473 7982483 7982509 7982539 7982543
7982561 7982567 7982609 7982629 7982651 7982671 7982683 7982693 7982699 7982729
7982749 7982761 7982773 7982783 7982789 7982791 7982797 7982851 7982867 7982879
7982893 7982899 7982927 7982941 7982951 7982957 7982959 7982963 7982969 7982971
7982977 7982981 7982999 7983037 7983043 7983049 7983109 7983119 7983121 7983133
7983161 7983167 7983179 7983181 7983223 7983229 7983247 7983257 7983259 7983299
7983301 7983307 7983329 7983331 7983359 7983361 7983383 7983419 7983433 7983449
7983457 7983463 7983473 7983511 7983517 7983529 7983539 7983541 7983551 7983571
7983581 7983583 7983589 7983593 7983611 7983617 7983631 7983637 7983673 7983683
7983697 7983707 7983721 7983733 7983739 7983751 7983757 7983763 7983793 7983797
7983803 7983809 7983827 7983841 7983851 7983869 7983883 7983893 7983901 7983919
7983929 7983947 7983953 7983959 7983979 7984001 7984003 7984027 7984037 7984121
7984127 7984129 7984133 7984147 7984153 7984159 7984181 7984183 7984201 7984253
7984259 7984261 7984331 7984337 7984349 7984357 7984387 7984399 7984409 7984421
7984423 7984429 7984433 7984439 7984513 7984523 7984531 7984547 7984553 7984573
7984583 7984601 7984621 7984631 7984633 7984643 7984649 7984651 7984673 7984681
7984687 7984721 7984723 7984759 7984787 7984789 7984793 7984829 7984891 7984897
7984901 7984903 7984931 7984939 7984957 7985009 7985017 7985023 7985039 7985041
7985069 7985077 7985093 7985099 7985101 7985123 7985141 7985147 7985171 7985203
7985221 7985227 7985239 7985249 7985267 7985279 7985287 7985293 7985297 7985309
7985311 7985323 7985381 7985387 7985389 7985413 7985423 7985429 7985431 7985437
7985489 7985501 7985503 7985521 7985561 7985581 7985587 7985603 7985617 7985641
7985647 7985657 7985683 7985711 7985713 7985729 7985737 7985741 7985743 7985749
7985771 7985777 7985779 7985839 7985843 7985851 7985893 7985897 7985927 7985959
7985983 7986001 7986007 7986019 7986029 7986047 7986053 7986071 7986079 7986091
7986113 7986133 7986161 7986163 7986179 7986197 7986203 7986211 7986217 7986229
7986233 7986241 7986259 7986269 7986317 7986331 7986353 7986361 7986371 7986389
7986401 7986439 7986457 7986463 7986529 7986553 7986557 7986581 7986599 7986607
7986611 7986619 7986637 7986643 7986659 7986661 7986679 7986683 7986697 7986701
7986721 7986731 7986739 7986743 7986749 7986751 7986761 7986767 7986779 7986799
7986817 7986827 7986869 7986893 7986907 7986917 7986947 7986959 7986969 7986997
7987009 7987013 7987019 7987027 7987037 7987043 7987051 7987069 7987081 7987099
7987123 7987129 7987139 7987223 7987241 7987247 7987249 7987253 7987289 7987307
7987313 7987319 7987327 7987351 7987363 7987373 7987387 7987393 7987403 7987423
7987439 7987457 7987459 7987477 7987481 7987487 7987531 7987537 7987541 7987559
7987561 7987589 7987591 7987607 7987613 7987627 7987649 7987663 7987669 7987687
7987699 7987703 7987717 7987729 7987751 7987757 7987781 7987799 7987813 7987823
7987843 7987867 7987883 7987897 7987901 7987921 7987957 7988009 7988033 7988063
7988081 7988089 7988093 7988117 7988129 7988131 7988177 7988203 7988219 7988221
7988237 7988251 7988257 7988273 7988293 7988339 7988347 7988381 7988389 7988413
7988437 7988441 7988443 7988459 7988473 7988479 7988503 7988507 7988527 7988537
7988557 7988573 7988579 7988587 7988597 7988599 7988627 7988639 7988641 7988663
7988689 7988711 7988713 7988723 7988741 7988749 7988753 7988767 7988789 7988801
7988803 7988819 7988821 7988839 7988857 7988899 7988923 7988971 7988977 7988983
7988993 7989011 7989067 7989071 7989083 7989143 7989169 7989173 7989187 7989197
```

```
7989199  7989203  7989221  7989251  7989323  7989341  7989343  7989407  7989409  7989419
7989427  7989431  7989461  7989463  7989467  7989469  7989491  7989493  7989511  7989517
7989523  7989563  7989571  7989589  7989593  7989601  7989613  7989617  7989637  7989649
7989679  7989713  7989749  7989757  7989767  7989769  7989851  7989857  7989869  7989907
7989929  7989973  7990001  7990057  7990063  7990067  7990079  7990091  7990093  7990111
7990163  7990183  7990231  7990237  7990249  7990259  7990273  7990277  7990291  7990319
7990337  7990349  7990363  7990373  7990379  7990427  7990441  7990471  7990481  7990519
7990559  7990579  7990589  7990597  7990639  7990643  7990649  7990667  7990669  7990673
7990709  7990711  7990751  7990789  7990813  7990823  7990847  7990877  7990891  7990897
7990907  7990909  7990919  7990933  7990937  7990951  7990993  7990999  7991017  7991033
7991047  7991057  7991059  7991083  7991089  7991099  7991101  7991107  7991119  7991129
7991147  7991167  7991177  7991209  7991217  7991219  7991231  7991233  7991239  7991251  7991257
7991303  7991311  7991329  7991339  7991341  7991369  7991407  7991437  7991441  7991447
7991453  7991471  7991483  7991531  7991537  7991563  7991569  7991573  7991579  7991591
7991623  7991629  7991639  7991653  7991657  7991701  7991713  7991743  7991747  7991749
7991759  7991773  7991777  7991779  7991803  7991839  7991857  7991869  7991891  7991897
7991939  7991941  7991947  7991953  7991957  7991981  7991993  7991999  7992011  7992031
7992041  7992059  7992073  7992077  7992107  7992137  7992143  7992181  7992221  7992223
7992239  7992251  7992263  7992277  7992311  7992337  7992343  7992349  7992373  7992401
7992419  7992421  7992463  7992493  7992503  7992511  7992527  7992571  7992577  7992583
7992613  7992617  7992619  7992659  7992689  7992701  7992727  7992739  7992763  7992767
7992781  7992791  7992821  7992847  7992857  7992869  7992871  7992881  7992923  7992973
7993021  7993057  7993061  7993093  7993099  7993103  7993127  7993157  7993169  7993171
7993177  7993187  7993199  7993201  7993207  7993211  7993217  7993229  7993231  7993273
7993277  7993283  7993289  7993309  7993327  7993331  7993361  7993367  7993421  7993423
7993439  7993459  7993493  7993499  7993511  7993523  7993529  7993537  7993543  7993559
7993577  7993651  7993663  7993679  7993681  7993693  7993697  7993709  7993717  7993721
7993747  7993759  7993781  7993787  7993801  7993823  7993841  7993849  7993871  7993883
7993897  7993907  7993913  7993957  7993963  7993967  7993987  7994017  7994023  7994033
7994039  7994059  7994071  7994081  7994083  7994093  7994113  7994137  7994153  7994159
7994171  7994177  7994191  7994197  7994213  7994237  7994263  7994279  7994281  7994299
7994309  7994321  7994341  7994347  7994351  7994377  7994407  7994443  7994447  7994461
7994489  7994491  7994513  7994521  7994527  7994557  7994617  7994647  7994659  7994663
7994669  7994681  7994699  7994711  7994729  7994759  7994761  7994803  7994827  7994867
7994873  7994881  7994897  7994927  7994941  7994969  7994971  7994977  7994999  7995011
7995017  7995023  7995047  7995073  7995107  7995109  7995131  7995157  7995161  7995173
7995187  7995199  7995203  7995233  7995263  7995269  7995277  7995301  7995319  7995341
7995349  7995373  7995391  7995397  7995413  7995431  7995437  7995443  7995461  7995479
7995509  7995529  7995553  7995557  7995563  7995567  7995577  7995587  7995607  7995629
7995643  7995653  7995679  7995683  7995727  7995749  7995761  7995769  7995773  7995791
7995809  7995817  7995821  7995839  7995863  7995877  7995901  7995907  7995917  7995929
7995931  7995937  7995991  7996031  7996049  7996061  7996073  7996081  7996097  7996099
7996133  7996187  7996193  7996231  7996243  7996259  7996277  7996309  7996319  7996333
7996337  7996363  7996367  7996369  7996381  7996423  7996463  7996487  7996501  7996519
7996537  7996559  7996577  7996589  7996591  7996601  7996607  7996619  7996631  7996649
7996661  7996669  7996687  7996691  7996697  7996711  7996727  7996733  7996741  7996787
7996789  7996823  7996843  7996867  7996871  7996873  7996889  7996903  7996913  7996951
7996957  7996969  7996973  7996981  7996993  7996997  7997029  7997047  7997051  7997057
7997071  7997083  7997113  7997131  7997141  7997147  7997153  7997159  7997167
7997201  7997203  7997207  7997219  7997237  7997239  7997251  7997257  7997303  7997323
7997333  7997351  7997357  7997377  7997387  7997389  7997393  7997447  7997471  7997477
7997489  7997519  7997543  7997551  7997557  7997579  7997581  7997621  7997623  7997663
7997677  7997683  7997711  7997713  7997729  7997741  7997749  7997769  7997777  7997789
7997831  7997833  7997839  7997867  7997903  7997933  7997947  7997959  7997971  7997989
7998013  7998019  7998047  7998049  7998059  7998061  7998073  7998077  7998091  7998101
7998119  7998139  7998167  7998169  7998223  7998269  7998293  7998307  7998337  7998349
7998379  7998383  7998409  7998421  7998437  7998443  7998451  7998481  7998491  7998509
7998511  7998521  7998533  7998539  7998547  7998553  7998569  7998593  7998629  7998631
7998637  7998643  7998659  7998667  7998673  7998691  7998701  7998703  7998719  7998743
7998763  7998769  7998773  7998797  7998803  7998827  7998839  7998847  7998853  7998863
7998937  7998941  7998953  7998967  7998971  7998979  7999051  7999081  7999087  7999151
7999177  7999207  7999241  7999249  7999283  7999297  7999319  7999339  7999351  7999379
7999393  7999403  7999417  7999451  7999463  7999481  7999487  7999501  7999507  7999531
7999543  7999547  7999573  7999577  7999613  7999637  7999669  7999681  7999709  7999711
7999727  7999753  7999757  7999759  7999769  7999781  7999787  7999793  7999811  7999813
7999847  7999909  7999913  7999919  7999921  7999963  7999993  8000009  8000017  8000023
8000033  8000051  8000053  8000063  8000071  8000087  8000099  8000101  8000117  8000119
8000141  8000171  8000173  8000189  8000219  8000221  8000231  8000261  8000309  8000323
8000339  8000357  8000359  8000401  8000407  8000411  8000413  8000431  8000437  8000441
8000479  8000507  8000519  8000533  8000543  8000561  8000579  8000599  8000609  8000611
8000627  8000633  8000651  8000677  8000683  8000689  8000719  8000747  8000749  8000753
8000771  8000789  8000791  8000801  8000807  8000809  8000819  8000831  8000869  8000879
8000887  8000891  8000893  8000899  8000921  8000947  8000953  8000963  8000977
8000981  8000983  8000989  8001029  8001047  8001107  8001157  8001163  8001173  8001179
8001197  8001229  8001241  8001247  8001269  8001277  8001281  8001289  8001293  8001307
8001347  8001359  8001491  8001517  8001533  8001541  8001551  8001559  8001571  8001589
8001599  8001607  8001619  8001647  8001659  8001661  8001667  8001727  8001737  8001739
8001779  8001787  8001811  8001823  8001839  8001841  8001857  8001859  8001863  8001871
8001893  8001899  8001911  8001949  8001971  8001991  8002003  8002009  8002013  8002051
8002067  8002069  8002073  8002103  8002117  8002151  8002177  8002193  8002199  8002201
8002219  8002243  8002259  8002261  8002271  8002277  8002283  8002297  8002303  8002349
8002381  8002399  8002409  8002411  8002441  8002493  8002507  8002513  8002517  8002543
8002559  8002573  8002627  8002639  8002649  8002663  8002679  8002691  8002697  8002721
8002741  8002747  8002751  8002759  8002769  8002783  8002793  8002823  8002829  8002837
8002843  8002847  8002921  8002961  8002987  8003027  8003029  8003033  8003041  8003059
8003069  8003071  8003087  8003089  8003111  8003119  8003143  8003167  8003197  8003201
8003227  8003231  8003251  8003257  8003263  8003273  8003297  8003309  8003381  8003419
8003423  8003431  8003459  8003483  8003491  8003497  8003509  8003521  8003531  8003537
8003539  8003561  8003573  8003587  8003591  8003629  8003641  8003657  8003659  8003663
```

```
8003669  8003687  8003717  8003741  8003777  8003813  8003819  8003843  8003857  8003861
8003867  8003869  8003873  8003893  8003899  8003909  8003927  8003981  8003987  8004011
8004013  8004047  8004067  8004071  8004079  8004083  8004091  8004097  8004103  8004119
8004121  8004133  8004151  8004163  8004179  8004181  8004193  8004211  8004221  8004223
8004257  8004259  8004277  8004281  8004313  8004383  8004401  8004413  8004419  8004427
8004443  8004449  8004457  8004463  8004487  8004511  8004547  8004559  8004583  8004613
8004629  8004631  8004649  8004653  8004673  8004677  8004679  8004697  8004709  8004743
8004781  8004797  8004803  8004817  8004823  8004853  8004869  8004877  8004889  8004901
8004911  8004917  8004949  8004973  8004979  8005003  8005007  8005027  8005051  8005097
8005103  8005117  8005121  8005133  8005139  8005141  8005169  8005183  8005187  8005211
8005241  8005243  8005271  8005301  8005337  8005339  8005343  8005367  8005379  8005391
8005397  8005411  8005423  8005429  8005483  8005493  8005499  8005511  8005519  8005523
8005531  8005549  8005559  8005573  8005603  8005643  8005649  8005663  8005667  8005681
8005693  8005717  8005721  8005729  8005757  8005799  8005819  8005831  8005841  8005853
8005873  8005891  8005903  8005913  8005927  8005957  8006003  8006017  8006039  8006057
8006077  8006081  8006083  8006101  8006107  8006137  8006149  8006177  8006179  8006203
8006209  8006221  8006237  8006279  8006281  8006287  8006329  8006333  8006347  8006363
8006387  8006437  8006441  8006443  8006447  8006459  8006483  8006513  8006549  8006561
8006563  8006569  8006597  8006611  8006623  8006629  8006633  8006641  8006651  8006683
8006699  8006749  8006753  8006797  8006819  8006821  8006827  8006857  8006861  8006863
8006891  8006893  8006899  8006903  8006909  8006939  8006941  8006989  8007001  8007011
8007019  8007047  8007053  8007071  8007089  8007091  8007121  8007127  8007143  8007173
8007193  8007199  8007211  8007229  8007271  8007283  8007299  8007313  8007319  8007353
8007359  8007383  8007401  8007403  8007407  8007413  8007431  8007449  8007463  8007487
8007491  8007497  8007499  8007541  8007551  8007553  8007557  8007581  8007599  8007613
8007617  8007631  8007647  8007667  8007673  8007679  8007689  8007691  8007709  8007733
8007743  8007781  8007803  8007809  8007821  8007829  8007851  8007859  8007869  8007871
8007917  8007931  8007943  8007991  8008009  8008081  8008093  8008103  8008109  8008123
8008127  8008157  8008159  8008181  8008211  8008229  8008237  8008249  8008267  8008279
8008289  8008313  8008327  8008331  8008337  8008349  8008369  8008373  8008381  8008387
8008409  8008453  8008523  8008529  8008537  8008541  8008549  8008573  8008579  8008589
8008597  8008603  8008607  8008619  8008631  8008643  8008667  8008673  8008691  8008697
8008703  8008733  8008739  8008769  8008771  8008789  8008799  8008801  8008811  8008829
8008831  8008841  8008859  8008867  8008877  8008907  8008933  8008951  8008961  8008967
8009003  8009009  8009011  8009033  8009039  8009059  8009081  8009087  8009093  8009119
8009123  8009143  8009147  8009149  8009161  8009167  8009179  8009219  8009231  8009233
8009237  8009291  8009293  8009303  8009321  8009347  8009369  8009389  8009399  8009453
8009459  8009461  8009467  8009513  8009537  8009549  8009557  8009569  8009579  8009591
8009593  8009609  8009611  8009623  8009627  8009629  8009707  8009747  8009759  8009761
8009767  8009789  8009831  8009843  8009861  8009863  8009893  8009927  8009929  8009951
8009959  8009977  8009987  8009999  8010011  8010029  8010031  8010109  8010113  8010131
8010137  8010139  8010143  8010151  8010157  8010161  8010173  8010181  8010199  8010203
8010221  8010239  8010251  8010263  8010313  8010323  8010361  8010391  8010397  8010403
8010407  8010421  8010437  8010449  8010461  8010481  8010487  8010503  8010547  8010557
8010589  8010593  8010631  8010643  8010661  8010707  8010713  8010749  8010809  8010817
8010839  8010841  8010853  8010869  8010883  8010887  8010889  8010901  8010929  8010953
8010967  8010973  8011007  8011013  8011021  8011039  8011067  8011127  8011139  8011169
8011177  8011183  8011187  8011207  8011247  8011253  8011259  8011261  8011271  8011273
8011303  8011319  8011343  8011357  8011363  8011379  8011387  8011397  8011439  8011477
8011481  8011517  8011529  8011561  8011571  8011583  8011589  8011621  8011643  8011651
8011693  8011697  8011727  8011739  8011747  8011763  8011781  8011789  8011819  8011841
8011847  8011849  8011891  8011921  8011937  8011951  8011961  8011967  8011973  8011979
8011999  8012003  8012021  8012029  8012057  8012077  8012087  8012107  8012113  8012131
8012143  8012161  8012201  8012203  8012209  8012227  8012269  8012299  8012317  8012341
8012351  8012359  8012363  8012369  8012371  8012383  8012399  8012401  8012429  8012437
8012449  8012453  8012467  8012479  8012483  8012519  8012531  8012549  8012551  8012561
8012573  8012617  8012621  8012639  8012647  8012659  8012681  8012687  8012707  8012713
8012723  8012789  8012791  8012801  8012819  8012839  8012857  8012863  8012881  8012887
8012897  8012923  8012929  8012941  8012951  8012957  8012959  8012987  8013013  8013029
8013043  8013101  8013107  8013119  8013121  8013151  8013157  8013233  8013259  8013263
8013281  8013287  8013323  8013329  8013371  8013373  8013377  8013391  8013403  8013433
8013449  8013451  8013457  8013463  8013479  8013487  8013521  8013539  8013581  8013587
8013589  8013601  8013619  8013623  8013659  8013679  8013689  8013697  8013701  8013703
8013727  8013743  8013757  8013769  8013799  8013809  8013857  8013869  8013871  8013883
8013893  8013917  8013949  8013977  8013989  8014001  8014033  8014037  8014049  8014057
8014079  8014093  8014103  8014117  8014129  8014141  8014177  8014199  8014207  8014243
8014247  8014261  8014271  8014301  8014343  8014351  8014381  8014403  8014421  8014427
8014453  8014477  8014481  8014493  8014519  8014529  8014537  8014541  8014549  8014553
8014579  8014583  8014613  8014631  8014663  8014679  8014687  8014703  8014723  8014733
8014777  8014793  8014801  8014807  8014841  8014847  8014891  8014907  8014921  8014927
8014943  8014949  8014961  8014987  8014999  8015011  8015023  8015039  8015053  8015069
8015087  8015089  8015101  8015129  8015141  8015167  8015179  8015221  8015233  8015269
8015291  8015297  8015299  8015303  8015311  8015317  8015341  8015363  8015369  8015383
8015387  8015389  8015443  8015489  8015507  8015509  8015519  8015531  8015543  8015591
8015599  8015603  8015611  8015621  8015627  8015653  8015659  8015699  8015719  8015723
8015737  8015741  8015743  8015747  8015771  8015783  8015797  8015809  8015837  8015849
8015863  8015867  8015921  8015923  8015927  8015941  8015957  8015981  8015989  8016023
8016031  8016037  8016049  8016059  8016089  8016097  8016109  8016133  8016139  8016149
8016191  8016221  8016247  8016257  8016287  8016289  8016293  8016313  8016331  8016343
8016353  8016373  8016403  8016413  8016419  8016433  8016467  8016479  8016487  8016493
8016511  8016527  8016529  8016551  8016553  8016563  8016587  8016599  8016611  8016637
8016643  8016661  8016677  8016703  8016713  8016733  8016737  8016763  8016769  8016779
8016781  8016793  8016797  8016839  8016851  8016863  8016907  8016913  8016923  8016937
8016991  8017001  8017039  8017057  8017063  8017091  8017111  8017117  8017159  8017171
8017187  8017201  8017223  8017241  8017267  8017283  8017301  8017327  8017343  8017349
8017351  8017357  8017423  8017439  8017441  8017447  8017453  8017459  8017483  8017531
8017549  8017553  8017571  8017573  8017579  8017609  8017613  8017619  8017643  8017649
8017661  8017697  8017721  8017739  8017741  8017769  8017781  8017783  8017811  8017819
8017843  8017853  8017873  8017879  8017903  8017927  8017939  8017951  8017967  8017969
```

```
8017979 8017987 8017991 8017993 8018027 8018029 8018039 8018047 8018069 8018071
8018089 8018107 8018177 8018183 8018189 8018207 8018221 8018273 8018279 8018281
8018291 8018299 8018303 8018327 8018333 8018347 8018369 8018383 8018419 8018443
8018449 8018453 8018477 8018497 8018501 8018519 8018557 8018561 8018567 8018573
8018599 8018609 8018629 8018639 8018671 8018701 8018719 8018767 8018783 8018807
8018837 8018851 8018861 8018887 8018891 8018909 8018911 8018921 8018929 8018947
8018963 8018981 8019001 8019013 8019023 8019041 8019043 8019071 8019073 8019079
8019091 8019119 8019131 8019169 8019181 8019191 8019217 8019227 8019233 8019247
8019251 8019259 8019289 8019293 8019307 8019337 8019353 8019397 8019413 8019439
8019449 8019481 8019509 8019511 8019541 8019553 8019581 8019587 8019611 8019619
8019643 8019647 8019667 8019679 8019719 8019721 8019727 8019769 8019773 8019779
8019821 8019827 8019839 8019871 8019877 8019911 8019931 8019953 8019959 8019961
8019983 8019989 8019997 8020003 8020007 8020027 8020043 8020049 8020069 8020121
8020151 8020183 8020237 8020241 8020247 8020249 8020253 8020273 8020303 8020333
8020339 8020343 8020357 8020361 8020381 8020387 8020393 8020423 8020429 8020433
8020457 8020499 8020517 8020553 8020567 8020577 8020589 8020631 8020643 8020669
8020673 8020681 8020687 8020693 8020697 8020699 8020703 8020709 8020751 8020757
8020763 8020781 8020783 8020801 8020867 8020891 8020913 8020921 8020927 8020931
8020933 8020963 8020993 8021003 8021009 8021011 8021017 8021029 8021041 8021047
8021053 8021063 8021077 8021099 8021113 8021129 8021131 8021147 8021159 8021171
8021191 8021231 8021239 8021257 8021269 8021291 8021323 8021327 8021333 8021339
8021347 8021353 8021359 8021381 8021383 8021389 8021413 8021471 8021539 8021567
8021579 8021593 8021597 8021627 8021639 8021647 8021669 8021677 8021681 8021729
8021737 8021747 8021749 8021753 8021759 8021771 8021789 8021791 8021801 8021821
8021831 8021833 8021851 8021863 8021869 8021873 8021887 8021911 8021939 8021941
8021969 8021989 8021999 8022017 8022029 8022041 8022061 8022071 8022083 8022089
8022097 8022103 8022109 8022121 8022137 8022139 8022143 8022151 8022163 8022169
8022173 8022227 8022247 8022251 8022257 8022281 8022307 8022323 8022353 8022359
8022367 8022373 8022403 8022409 8022437 8022457 8022491 8022493 8022517 8022523
8022527 8022551 8022563 8022569 8022613 8022629 8022667 8022671 8022683 8022689
8022709 8022739 8022743 8022779 8022797 8022803 8022809 8022823 8022829 8022841
8022869 8022877 8022901 8022943 8022961 8023009 8023013 8023019 8023027 8023033
8023039 8023063 8023091 8023123 8023139 8023151 8023153 8023157 8023189 8023217
8023231 8023237 8023243 8023247 8023259 8023273 8023277 8023289 8023363 8023369
8023387 8023403 8023409 8023423 8023439 8023441 8023471 8023493 8023523 8023553
8023559 8023579 8023583 8023591 8023601 8023627 8023651 8023661 8023663 8023667
8023669 8023739 8023747 8023759 8023777 8023787 8023811 8023819 8023831 8023837
8023861 8023877 8023889 8023901 8023957 8023969 8023979 8023991 8023993 8023999
8024047 8024057 8024063 8024077 8024089 8024117 8024129 8024161 8024167 8024189
8024239 8024249 8024279 8024281 8024293 8024321 8024333 8024353 8024363 8024371
8024383 8024399 8024407 8024417 8024431 8024437 8024453 8024509 8024521 8024537
8024543 8024563 8024573 8024579 8024591 8024603 8024623 8024641 8024647 8024659
8024683 8024701 8024711 8024729 8024743 8024761 8024771 8024773 8024777 8024813
8024831 8024837 8024839 8024843 8024857 8024869 8024873 8024879 8024881 8024911
8024923 8024927 8024941 8024959 8024987 8025013 8025019 8025067 8025089 8025097
8025103 8025119 8025161 8025167 8025169 8025181 8025211 8025233 8025253 8025271
8025293 8025301 8025317 8025331 8025341 8025349 8025361 8025371 8025379 8025389
8025421 8025439 8025449 8025469 8025473 8025487 8025491 8025503 8025509 8025517
8025527 8025533 8025553 8025557 8025569 8025601 8025607 8025613 8025623 8025653
8025659 8025671 8025679 8025691 8025697 8025701 8025713 8025727 8025739 8025761
8025793 8025803 8025881 8025889 8025893 8025917 8025967 8025973 8026013 8026027
8026087 8026093 8026097 8026099 8026111 8026121 8026129 8026133 8026141 8026157
8026169 8026171 8026199 8026217 8026223 8026231 8026253 8026289 8026297 8026307
8026309 8026313 8026327 8026357 8026387 8026411 8026429 8026451 8026453 8026477
8026483 8026507 8026511 8026541 8026559 8026561 8026583 8026597 8026619 8026631
8026633 8026661 8026669 8026673 8026699 8026723 8026727 8026741 8026751 8026769
8026787 8026789 8026813 8026829 8026831 8026849 8026877 8026901 8026913 8026919
8026933 8026937 8026961 8026969 8026973 8026979 8026981 8027007 8027011 8027017
8027029 8027053 8027059 8027093 8027141 8027147 8027191 8027209 8027211 8027237
8027249 8027251 8027273 8027303 8027309 8027317 8027339 8027381 8027423 8027491
8027497 8027501 8027507 8027563 8027587 8027609 8027611 8027629 8027639 8027641
8027651 8027653 8027659 8027683 8027687 8027699 8027807 8027813 8027819 8027821
8027827 8027837 8027839 8027849 8027863 8027881 8027891 8027911 8027933 8027939
8027941 8027969 8028019 8028037 8028043 8028061 8028077 8028107 8028109 8028113
8028121 8028151 8028179 8028193 8028227 8028247 8028259 8028263 8028277 8028289
8028299 8028343 8028347 8028361 8028367 8028373 8028379 8028407 8028413 8028439
8028443 8028463 8028479 8028491 8028521 8028523 8028529 8028547 8028551 8028557
8028577 8028619 8028649 8028693 8028703 8028707 8028719 8028731 8028733 8028739
8028749 8028767 8028781 8028791 8028799 8028809 8028827 8028833 8028851 8028857
8028889 8028919 8028923 8028931 8028949 8028961 8028973 8028993 8028997 8029009
8029019 8029061 8029069 8029081 8029097 8029157 8029187 8029211 8029243 8029249
8029271 8029291 8029309 8029327 8029331 8029361 8029363 8029391 8029393 8029421
8029471 8029493 8029501 8029513 8029517 8029529 8029537 8029577 8029579 8029583
8029591 8029597 8029631 8029633 8029643 8029649 8029663 8029673 8029717 8029739
8029751 8029771 8029793 8029811 8029823 8029843 8029859 8029867
8029909 8029943 8029969 8029993 8030021 8030039 8030041 8030047 8030053 8030081
8030089 8030093 8030107 8030117 8030123 8030131 8030149 8030153 8030227 8030233
8030237 8030249 8030257 8030291 8030299 8030353 8030371 8030387 8030411 8030413
8030417 8030423 8030437 8030441 8030461 8030497 8030513 8030531 8030557 8030567
8030591 8030599 8030609 8030623 8030663 8030683 8030717 8030741 8030753
8030761 8030773 8030777 8030819 8030849 8030873 8030879 8030917 8030927 8030929
8030963 8030969 8031007 8031017 8031019 8031033 8031097 8031119 8031123
8031181 8031187 8031227 8031253 8031269 8031299 8031323 8031337 8031341 8031343
8031349 8031371 8031379 8031403 8031409 8031421 8031431 8031437 8031451 8031467
8031469 8031473 8031523 8031557 8031563 8031581 8031587 8031589 8031593
8031619 8031641 8031643 8031671 8031677 8031703 8031719 8031731 8031763 8031767
8031773 8031781 8031787 8031797 8031799 8031817 8031833 8031857 8031911 8031913
8031929 8031937 8031943 8031953 8031967 8031977 8031979 8032001 8032019 8032039
8032049 8032051 8032061 8032067 8032103 8032121 8032133 8032163 8032223 8032229
```

8032247 8032273 8032291 8032303 8032327 8032337 8032361 8032363 8032397 8032399
8032411 8032439 8032471 8032481 8032489 8032511 8032513 8032567 8032571 8032579
8032613 8032621 8032637 8032639 8032643 8032669 8032691 8032699 8032729 8032741
8032769 8032781 8032807 8032859 8032879 8032883 8032889 8032903 8032931 8032939
8032943 8032967 8032987 8033009 8033017 8033021 8033023 8033041 8033071 8033117
8033119 8033159 8033161 8033167 8033173 8033177 8033183 8033209 8033213 8033243
8033281 8033293 8033327 8033339 8033359 8033383 8033419 8033429 8033461 8033471
8033479 8033483 8033491 8033497 8033539 8033573 8033587 8033591 8033593 8033621
8033629 8033657 8033659 8033671 8033689 8033717 8033719 8033749 8033759 8033777
8033791 8033797 8033807 8033813 8033821 8033849 8033873 8033891 8033933 8033939
8033951 8033989 8034023 8034031 8034043 8034049 8034067 8034079 8034083 8034097
8034101 8034113 8034121 8034137 8034157 8034167 8034181 8034193 8034209 8034241
8034253 8034263 8034277 8034287 8034311 8034331 8034347 8034373 8034437 8034451
8034461 8034469 8034491 8034503 8034547 8034553 8034563 8034569 8034589 8034601
8034619 8034629 8034671 8034683 8034703 8034709 8034749 8034757 8034781 8034787
8034799 8034821 8034833 8034839 8034847 8034869 8034877 8034881 8034899 8034907
8034911 8034919 8034973 8034977 8034989 8034991 8034997 8035003 8035007 8035021
8035051 8035061 8035063 8035087 8035099 8035121 8035129 8035177 8035193 8035201
8035207 8035213 8035229 8035241 8035249 8035259 8035273 8035301 8035337 8035343
8035351 8035361 8035369 8035427 8035457 8035463 8035477 8035483 8035501 8035507
8035519 8035529 8035553 8035597 8035607 8035609 8035667 8035693 8035733 8035759
8035787 8035793 8035799 8035823 8035829 8035831 8035841 8035861 8035889 8035903
8035927 8035939 8035949 8035961 8035967 8035991 8035997 8035999 8036003 8036011
8036051 8036071 8036081 8036101 8036137 8036153 8036167 8036209 8036233 8036239
8036261 8036279 8036299 8036311 8036317 8036321 8036341 8036381 8036401 8036417
8036429 8036459 8036467 8036473 8036503 8036507 8036519 8036521 8036527 8036531
8036537 8036569 8036579 8036599 8036621 8036629 8036681 8036701 8036711 8036723
8036731 8036747 8036771 8036797 8036813 8036827 8036837 8036849 8036863 8036879
8036887 8036893 8036909 8036939 8036947 8036957 8036983 8036989 8036993 8036999
8037023 8037049 8037053 8037059 8037067 8037077 8037101 8037131 8037137 8037151
8037163 8037167 8037181 8037187 8037191 8037229 8037233 8037269 8037307 8037313
8037317 8037319 8037347 8037377 8037383 8037391 8037409 8037439 8037461 8037529
8037559 8037569 8037571 8037581 8037593 8037641 8037643 8037647 8037661 8037683
8037691 8037707 8037713 8037721 8037737 8037739 8037749 8037751 8037781 8037793
8037829 8037847 8037851 8037899 8037919 8037937 8037941 8037943 8037961 8037973
8038003 8038027 8038061 8038097 8038111 8038117 8038141 8038193 8038227 8038253
8038259 8038271 8038279 8038313 8038319 8038343 8038379 8038409 8038441 8038451
8038453 8038469 8038483 8038507 8038531 8038543 8038559 8038561 8038571 8038601
8038609 8038627 8038631 8038649 8038651 8038663 8038697 8038717 8038757 8038759
8038769 8038783 8038819 8038831 8038837 8038867 8038873 8038883 8038897 8038907
8038913 8038931 8038967 8038981 8038991 8039051 8039063 8039081 8039107 8039123
8039149 8039153 8039173 8039183 8039189 8039201 8039203 8039219 8039221 8039233
8039257 8039287 8039309 8039333 8039359 8039363 8039377 8039393 8039431 8039441
8039461 8039497 8039501 8039533 8039539 8039561 8039569 8039587 8039599 8039639
8039653 8039671 8039677 8039683 8039711 8039737 8039741 8039749 8039761 8039771
8039783 8039789 8039791 8039797 8039803 8039807 8039833 8039849 8039851 8039879
8039897 8039923 8039939 8039947 8039951 8039959 8039971 8039981 8039987 8040013
8040017 8040029 8040037 8040049 8040073 8040089 8040091 8040121 8040157 8040169
8040217 8040229 8040239 8040247 8040257 8040311 8040323 8040341 8040367 8040379
8040391 8040407 8040413 8040421 8040437 8040443 8040449 8040457 8040463 8040467
8040481 8040491 8040493 8040499 8040503 8040517 8040523 8040559 8040583 8040587
8040589 8040601 8040607 8040623 8040631 8040647 8040653 8040661 8040671 8040689
8040691 8040701 8040707 8040709 8040727 8040757 8040763 8040787 8040793 8040811
8040827 8040829 8040839 8040853 8040863 8040889 8040899 8040919 8040931 8040937
8040947 8041003 8041027 8041037 8041057 8041067 8041079 8041087 8041093 8041097
8041127 8041133 8041147 8041151 8041177 8041181 8041219 8041249 8041261 8041303
8041333 8041379 8041399 8041403 8041457 8041463 8041471 8041477 8041483 8041499
8041511 8041547 8041549 8041571 8041577 8041589 8041597 8041609 8041619 8041643
8041667 8041669 8041681 8041703 8041711 8041717 8041723 8041727 8041739 8041757
8041771 8041783 8041801 8041811 8041837 8041853 8041861 8041879 8041889 8041897
8041907 8041967 8041991 8041993 8042009 8042017 8042033 8042053 8042059 8042063
8042081 8042093 8042101 8042147 8042159 8042183 8042189 8042197 8042201 8042213
8042239 8042267 8042303 8042317 8042329 8042351 8042371 8042389 8042393 8042407
8042413 8042443 8042449 8042471 8042473 8042477 8042509 8042521 8042533 8042543
8042563 8042569 8042603 8042611 8042621 8042623 8042633 8042641 8042647 8042659
8042669 8042693 8042701 8042707 8042711 8042729 8042737 8042761 8042767 8042777
8042779 8042807 8042813 8042843 8042861 8042863 8042897 8042917 8042959 8042977
8043017 8043029 8043041 8043059 8043073 8043089 8043103 8043151 8043163 8043181
8043187 8043199 8043239 8043253 8043263 8043271 8043323 8043331 8043341 8043349
8043361 8043367 8043401 8043433 8043449 8043457 8043461 8043463 8043481 8043487
8043557 8043559 8043571 8043587 8043589 8043611 8043649 8043683 8043693 8043697
8043713 8043733 8043743 8043769 8043773 8043781 8043809 8043851 8043869 8043877
8043899 8043923 8043929 8043949 8043977 8043979 8043983 8044013 8044019 8044021
8044027 8044033 8044037 8044039 8044051 8044061 8044067 8044073 8044079 8044103
8044109 8044123 8044129 8044171 8044189 8044193 8044217 8044243 8044249 8044259
8044261 8044271 8044291 8044297 8044303 8044313 8044331 8044343 8044363 8044373
8044409 8044423 8044427 8044447 8044453 8044493 8044507 8044529 8044559 8044601
8044607 8044613 8044627 8044633 8044667 8044679 8044681 8044691 8044693 8044697
8044703 8044747 8044759 8044763 8044769 8044783 8044787 8044789 8044823 8044843
8044853 8044867 8044877 8044879 8044921 8044931 8044937 8044951 8044987 8044991
8044997 8045003 8045017 8045047 8045053 8045071 8045077 8045099 8045117 8045119
8045137 8045153 8045173 8045179 8045183 8045197 8045203 8045207 8045221 8045249
8045287 8045321 8045327 8045329 8045339 8045353 8045381 8045393 8045419 8045447
8045483 8045489 8045503 8045509 8045519 8045533 8045537 8045567 8045579 8045581
8045593 8045603 8045621 8045623 8045629 8045657 8045659 8045663 8045669 8045671
8045701 8045729 8045747 8045753 8045767 8045783 8045801 8045809 8045819 8045827
8045857 8045861 8045887 8045897 8045903 8045923 8045927 8045951 8045953 8045969
8045971 8046001 8046013 8046023 8046029 8046041 8046043 8046061 8046107 8046109
8046119 8046121 8046161 8046187 8046191 8046197 8046221 8046239 8046277 8046281

```
8046299  8046331  8046347  8046371  8046397  8046419  8046433  8046487  8046497  8046523
8046551  8046553  8046581  8046589  8046607  8046611  8046613  8046631  8046637  8046653
8046667  8046691  8046697  8046713  8046733  8046737  8046743  8046751  8046761  8046769
8046791  8046811  8046817  8046827  8046839  8046869  8046881  8046889  8046911  8046931
8046943  8046953  8046989  8046991  8047003  8047027  8047031  8047037  8047057  8047097
8047129  8047133  8047139  8047141  8047157  8047159  8047189  8047261  8047267  8047271
8047327  8047331  8047337  8047339  8047343  8047381  8047397  8047399  8047451  8047453
8047483  8047489  8047513  8047519  8047561  8047601  8047643  8047649  8047657  8047687
8047691  8047709  8047711  8047727  8047729  8047771  8047801  8047807  8047829  8047843
8047873  8047883  8047889  8047903  8047909  8047939  8047957  8047969  8048017  8048057
8048059  8048069  8048071  8048081  8048083  8048099  8048101  8048113  8048119  8048141
8048147  8048179  8048197  8048207  8048269  8048273  8048297  8048303  8048309  8048313
8048333  8048363  8048389  8048393  8048461  8048473  8048477  8048483  8048507  8048539
8048567  8048581  8048627  8048629  8048639  8048653  8048657  8048659  8048671  8048687
8048699  8048707  8048713  8048717  8048731  8048737  8048743  8048779  8048801  8048813
8048819  8048849  8048851  8048881  8048897  8048923  8048941  8048969  8048981  8049001
8049023  8049049  8049031  8049061  8049077  8049089  8049101  8049113  8049137  8049169
8049187  8049221  8049227  8049229  8049247  8049253  8049259  8049263  8049271  8049317
8049373  8049383  8049401  8049403  8049413  8049467  8049469  8049473  8049479  8049487
8049523  8049533  8049593  8049607  8049611  8049703  8049719  8049731  8049751  8049773
8049779  8049803  8049829  8049841  8049851  8049859  8049869  8049871  8049883  8049887
8049889  8049913  8049947  8049949  8049953  8049967  8049989  8049997  8050001  8050013
8050039  8050043  8050093  8050103  8050151  8050157  8050177  8050183  8050187  8050213
8050241  8050261  8050267  8050271  8050279  8050291  8050307  8050327  8050351  8050379
8050381  8050387  8050397  8050409  8050411  8050439  8050457  8050481  8050499  8050517
8050543  8050577  8050579  8050591  8050633  8050663  8050687  8050697  8050703  8050711
8050717  8050729  8050739  8050807  8050817  8050829  8050831  8050873  8050891  8050919
8050937  8050949  8050957  8050961  8050967  8050981  8050993  8050997  8051011  8051033
8051051  8051063  8051077  8051093  8051101  8051123  8051143  8051167  8051171  8051203
8051209  8051213  8051221  8051257  8051261  8051273  8051279  8051339  8051369  8051371
8051377  8051401  8051447  8051453  8051501  8051509  8051543  8051551  8051561  8051567
8051609  8051623  8051639  8051651  8051657  8051663  8051669  8051677  8051713  8051717
8051731  8051783  8051803  8051807  8051831  8051833  8051837  8051851  8051881  8051893
8051921  8051947  8051959  8051963  8051969  8052007  8052013  8052017  8052019  8052043
8052049  8052073  8052089  8052103  8052133  8052167  8052173  8052179  8052193  8052211
8052217  8052229  8052241  8052251  8052259  8052263  8052269  8052293  8052299  8052311
8052313  8052349  8052353  8052361  8052367  8052389  8052397  8052413  8052431  8052433
8052479  8052487  8052491  8052511  8052521  8052587  8052601  8052619  8052623  8052641
8052647  8052659  8052683  8052731  8052763  8052773  8052787  8052817  8052823  8052841
8052853  8052857  8052881  8052887  8052893  8052929  8052937  8052949  8052953  8052971
8052983  8052991  8053007  8053009  8053043  8053051  8053061  8053063  8053073  8053079
8053091  8053099  8053103  8053109  8053117  8053127  8053139  8053147  8053153  8053183
8053187  8053193  8053217  8053219  8053249  8053259  8053267  8053303  8053313  8053327
8053337  8053349  8053351  8053363  8053369  8053373  8053379  8053399  8053417  8053421
8053429  8053439  8053469  8053477  8053483  8053489  8053499  8053537  8053541  8053543
8053553  8053567  8053571  8053603  8053607  8053613  8053621  8053627  8053649  8053651
8053687  8053693  8053751  8053757  8053763  8053781  8053807  8053817  8053847  8053861
8053889  8053921  8053931  8053949  8053961  8053973  8053987  8054021  8054023  8054069
8054087  8054089  8054099  8054113  8054147  8054171  8054177  8054191  8054199  8054231
8054239  8054261  8054281  8054297  8054323  8054341  8054369  8054377  8054383  8054399
8054407  8054441  8054443  8054471  8054477  8054483  8054507  8054509  8054521  8054533
8054551  8054581  8054587  8054593  8054597  8054609  8054647  8054659  8054671  8054693
8054713  8054729  8054731  8054741  8054743  8054771  8054833  8054869  8054881  8054903
8054927  8054929  8054939  8054951  8054999  8055007  8055013  8055049  8055101  8055109
8055119  8055121  8055143  8055149  8055167  8055169  8055193  8055197  8055227  8055247
8055251  8055293  8055317  8055337  8055349  8055361  8055371  8055379  8055403  8055407
8055409  8055413  8055461  8055469  8055473  8055493  8055499  8055503  8055511  8055517
8055521  8055571  8055581  8055587  8055613  8055617  8055631  8055647  8055661  8055673
8055701  8055703  8055713  8055779  8055781  8055787  8055793  8055809  8055811  8055851
8055857  8055869  8055871  8055889  8055893  8055917  8055937  8055959  8055961  8055979
8056021  8056033  8056039  8056043  8056051  8056067  8056099  8056123  8056127  8056151
8056163  8056177  8056193  8056199  8056201  8056211  8056219  8056231  8056241  8056259
8056261  8056267  8056271  8056277  8056289  8056291  8056297  8056309  8056313  8056327
8056333  8056337  8056339  8056357  8056379  8056381  8056393  8056409  8056423  8056429
8056439  8056469  8056481  8056493  8056501  8056507  8056511  8056537  8056553  8056567
8056591  8056597  8056603  8056619  8056637  8056649  8056661  8056673  8056679  8056681
8056687  8056721  8056733  8056747  8056771  8056777  8056799  8056801  8056823  8056837
8056843  8056859  8056869  8056879  8056883  8056889  8056943  8056949  8056957  8056991
8057003  8057011  8057017  8057029  8057047  8057057  8057087  8057089  8057123  8057141
8057143  8057177  8057183  8057191  8057221  8057227  8057237  8057243  8057267  8057281
8057321  8057323  8057339  8057347  8057359  8057393  8057411  8057419  8057449  8057459
8057471  8057503  8057513  8057549  8057561  8057573  8057591  8057597  8057603  8057611
8057627  8057629  8057639  8057657  8057663  8057669  8057671  8057683  8057701  8057713
8057747  8057761  8057773  8057809  8057827  8057837  8057851  8057867  8057873  8057893
8057927  8057947  8057953  8057977  8057989  8058013  8058019  8058041  8058049  8058059
8058091  8058101  8058133  8058139  8058179  8058191  8058199  8058209  8058227  8058293
8058311  8058319  8058353  8058359  8058373  8058377  8058383  8058403  8058409  8058431
8058437  8058439  8058497  8058499  8058503  8058511  8058521  8058529  8058539  8058569
8058577  8058581  8058593  8058599  8058601  8058619  8058623  8058643  8058647  8058691
8058707  8058733  8058769  8058779  8058797  8058829  8058847  8058851  8058877  8058881
8058887  8058899  8058917  8058929  8058937  8059033  8059049  8059061  8059063
8059067  8059069  8059087  8059123  8059151  8059153  8059157  8059169  8059171  8059193
8059199  8059213  8059243  8059267  8059279  8059283  8059291  8059297  8059307  8059313
8059333  8059367  8059369  8059379  8059391  8059393  8059399  8059409  8059417  8059427
8059433  8059489  8059511  8059517  8059529  8059531  8059537  8059543  8059589  8059603
8059643  8059661  8059669  8059693  8059697  8059741  8059759  8059789  8059829  8059837
8059841  8059859  8059879  8059937  8059939  8059943  8059949  8059967  8059981  8060027
8060053  8060069  8060099  8060147  8060153  8060179  8060197  8060201  8060207  8060209
8060219  8060233  8060251  8060257  8060263  8060267  8060287  8060317  8060321  8060333
```

```
8060369  8060383  8060387  8060401  8060443  8060461  8060489  8060491  8060497  8060519
8060539  8060551  8060573  8060581  8060593  8060597  8060599  8060609  8060653  8060671
8060681  8060683  8060699  8060779  8060791  8060803  8060813  8060821  8060827  8060849
8060861  8060863  8060867  8060881  8060891  8060939  8060947  8060953  8060957  8060963
8061007  8061013  8061019  8061037  8061041  8061061  8061103  8061107  8061121  8061143
8061169  8061173  8061181  8061191  8061223  8061289  8061323  8061331  8061337  8061341
8061343  8061359  8061371  8061401  8061407  8061409  8061413  8061419  8061421  8061467
8061481  8061499  8061503  8061509  8061527  8061539  8061593  8061607  8061611  8061619
8061629  8061653  8061659  8061667  8061679  8061721  8061727  8061731  8061733  8061737
8061743  8061761  8061763  8061773  8061787  8061839  8061841  8061847  8061877  8061881
8061899  8061923  8061929  8061931  8061997  8062001  8062003  8062007  8062009  8062013
8062037  8062057  8062069  8062073  8062079  8062091  8062111  8062169  8062181  8062183
8062207  8062231  8062237  8062247  8062253  8062273  8062277  8062303  8062321  8062357
8062361  8062367  8062381  8062391  8062399  8062433  8062451  8062459  8062463  8062477
8062501  8062507  8062513  8062529  8062541  8062583  8062589  8062597  8062601  8062603
8062643  8062651  8062679  8062721  8062727  8062751  8062753  8062757  8062787  8062793
8062799  8062823  8062843  8062853  8062867  8062871  8062877  8062907  8062909  8062921
8062933  8062963  8062969  8062979  8062987  8062993  8062997  8063017  8063051  8063053
8063089  8063093  8063123  8063147  8063161  8063171  8063173  8063177  8063191
8063197  8063203  8063221  8063227  8063233  8063243  8063269  8063309  8063323  8063329
8063339  8063359  8063371  8063381  8063401  8063411  8063417  8063437  8063453  8063459
8063477  8063509  8063527  8063557  8063563  8063569  8063597  8063599  8063633  8063641
8063647  8063681  8063701  8063723  8063753  8063761  8063789  8063821  8063851  8063873
8063879  8063911  8063917  8063927  8063959  8063963  8063971  8063981  8063987
8063989  8064011  8064013  8064041  8064097  8064107  8064127  8064149  8064157  8064169
8064193  8064223  8064257  8064271  8064293  8064299  8064313  8064319  8064347  8064361
8064367  8064377  8064391  8064431  8064449  8064461  8064473  8064499  8064517  8064527
8064571  8064587  8064601  8064653  8064671  8064673  8064691  8064701  8064713  8064737
8064739  8064757  8064761  8064773  8064781  8064787  8064799  8064809  8064827  8064839
8064841  8064863  8064883  8064893  8064907  8064941  8064943  8064971  8064977  8065007
8065009  8065033  8065051  8065067  8065073  8065081  8065093  8065117  8065121  8065129
8065133  8065171  8065201  8065229  8065243  8065279  8065283  8065289  8065319  8065373
8065391  8065399  8065417  8065423  8065439  8065441  8065457  8065459  8065471  8065483
8065489  8065507  8065511  8065517  8065523  8065573  8065579  8065583  8065613  8065619
8065627  8065637  8065649  8065679  8065693  8065711  8065721  8065723  8065727  8065751
8065777  8065781  8065789  8065793  8065819  8065829  8065853  8065867  8065877  8065879
8065901  8065907  8065909  8065931  8065957  8065987  8066027  8066039  8066057  8066059
8066083  8066087  8066099  8066129  8066141  8066153  8066161  8066171  8066173  8066207
8066209  8066243  8066251  8066273  8066287  8066291  8066329  8066339  8066341  8066351
8066369  8066389  8066411  8066419  8066497  8066501  8066533  8066543  8066549  8066557
8066561  8066581  8066593  8066677  8066683  8066689  8066717  8066749  8066753  8066761
8066771  8066797  8066827  8066879  8066881  8066897  8066909  8066923  8066969  8066977
8067023  8067047  8067053  8067079  8067083  8067097  8067113  8067139  8067149  8067151
8067179  8067203  8067209  8067217  8067239  8067253  8067259  8067263  8067271  8067277
8067281  8067287  8067313  8067329  8067337  8067341  8067377  8067379  8067383  8067407
8067413  8067431  8067461  8067467  8067491  8067497  8067511  8067547  8067551  8067557
8067569  8067581  8067599  8067613  8067629  8067643  8067667  8067679  8067727  8067737
8067749  8067751  8067757  8067767  8067769  8067803  8067811  8067817  8067821  8067823
8067827  8067841  8067847  8067863  8067881  8067883  8067947  8067949  8067953  8067959
8067991  8068019  8068063  8068069  8068079  8068127  8068139  8068163  8068171  8068199
8068213  8068223  8068241  8068283  8068297  8068301  8068303  8068327  8068367  8068373
8068397  8068399  8068433  8068441  8068447  8068451  8068453  8068457  8068481  8068493
8068519  8068573  8068579  8068589  8068633  8068681  8068703  8068717  8068729  8068769
8068771  8068777  8068793  8068817  8068831  8068843  8068847  8068861  8068867  8068871
8068903  8068933  8068961  8068967  8068969  8069041  8069057  8069063  8069069  8069077
8069081  8069093  8069099  8069107  8069119  8069143  8069147  8069153  8069189  8069213
8069231  8069261  8069267  8069291  8069311  8069351  8069353  8069359  8069377  8069381
8069417  8069431  8069459  8069469  8069473  8069483  8069491  8069531  8069533  8069539
8069561  8069587  8069599  8069603  8069651  8069671  8069683  8069687  8069693  8069717
8069749  8069753  8069777  8069779  8069783  8069791  8069797  8069861  8069863  8069879
8069899  8069911  8069921  8069953  8069977  8069983  8070011  8070037  8070043  8070061
8070067  8070113  8070119  8070133  8070157  8070169  8070187  8070191  8070211  8070221
8070241  8070289  8070299  8070301  8070319  8070331  8070371  8070379  8070389  8070397
8070407  8070409  8070437  8070443  8070449  8070457  8070463  8070467  8070473
8070487  8070521  8070523  8070527  8070589  8070599  8070617  8070637  8070653  8070659
8070683  8070701  8070707  8070709  8070721  8070731  8070737  8070739  8070743  8070749
8070781  8070817  8070827  8070851  8070857  8070859  8070863  8070871  8070889  8070901
8070911  8070913  8070917  8070919  8070929  8070967  8070989  8071009  8071033  8071043
8071061  8071097  8071103  8071109  8071111  8071127  8071139  8071153  8071159  8071171
8071177  8071187  8071201  8071223  8071237  8071249  8071267  8071307  8071319
8071363  8071369  8071373  8071381  8071387  8071411  8071417  8071421  8071429  8071457
8071463  8071489  8071507  8071517  8071519  8071601  8071603  8071619  8071621  8071631
8071633  8071663  8071669  8071709  8071727  8071757  8071783  8071799  8071807  8071823
8071859  8071897  8071901  8071907  8071933  8071937  8071981  8072027  8072041  8072087
8072101  8072107  8072111  8072117  8072123  8072137  8072143  8072159  8072167  8072171
8072173  8072189  8072209  8072219  8072221  8072257  8072269  8072291  8072293  8072303
8072329  8072357  8072417  8072423  8072429  8072447  8072453  8072461  8072489  8072503
8072507  8072513  8072521  8072551  8072573  8072591  8072593  8072599  8072621  8072633
8072639  8072641  8072657  8072677  8072689  8072693  8072707  8072717  8072737  8072749
8072761  8072791  8072797  8072809  8072821  8072837  8072843  8072881  8072903  8072921
8072957  8072971  8072983  8073001  8073041  8073053  8073073  8073077  8073083  8073103
8073127  8073133  8073139  8073151  8073193  8073199  8073203  8073229  8073239  8073277
8073287  8073313  8073319  8073323  8073337  8073341  8073349  8073353  8073367  8073371
8073389  8073413  8073431  8073451  8073467  8073473  8073491  8073503  8073523  8073539
8073557  8073577  8073587  8073607  8073641  8073647  8073749  8073763  8073787  8073799
8073811  8073817  8073829  8073847  8073859  8073869  8073887  8073889  8073893  8073911
8073931  8073941  8073959  8073979  8074009  8074013  8074057  8074097  8074111  8074117
8074123  8074139  8074147  8074159  8074207  8074211  8074217  8074247  8074249  8074277
8074289  8074301  8074309  8074349  8074351  8074379  8074397  8074421  8074427  8074463
```

```
8074481 8074483 8074501 8074523 8074529 8074537 8074543 8074559 8074567 8074589
8074637 8074657 8074687 8074697 8074699 8074723 8074739 8074747 8074777 8074783
8074811 8074831 8074837 8074861 8074873 8074877 8074903 8074931 8074933 8074967
8074993 8074999 8075003 8075009 8075029 8075033 8075083 8075107 8075129 8075131
8075141 8075147 8075149 8075167 8075173 8075203 8075219 8075261 8075267
8075281 8075293 8075299 8075339 8075341 8075429 8075449 8075471 8075491 8075497
8075519 8075521 8075533 8075537 8075539 8075563 8075579 8075591 8075597 8075623
8075633 8075687 8075689 8075693 8075719 8075747 8075773 8075777 8075789 8075801
8075819 8075827 8075839 8075843 8075849 8075857 8075863 8075887 8075909 8075911
8075927 8075939 8075957 8075989 8075993 8075999 8076011 8076031 8076041 8076077
8076119 8076157 8076191 8076199 8076203 8076227 8076319 8076329 8076331 8076347
8076353 8076371 8076379 8076403 8076437 8076443 8076457 8076491 8076503 8076517
8076521 8076553 8076557 8076571 8076599 8076623 8076637 8076641 8076643 8076701
8076707 8076721 8076727 8076737 8076743 8076769 8076773 8076779 8076781 8076787
8076797 8076799 8076811 8076821 8076823 8076911 8076941 8076953 8076961 8076973
8076977 8076983 8077001 8077007 8077037 8077049 8077079 8077129 8077133 8077169
8077171 8077183 8077189 8077207 8077213 8077217 8077247 8077259 8077271
8077339 8077357 8077379 8077387 8077403 8077409 8077417 8077427 8077463 8077471
8077529 8077541 8077583 8077607 8077621 8077633 8077649 8077661 8077673
8077687 8077691 8077709 8077711 8077723 8077753 8077757 8077789 8077799 8077847
8077871 8077891 8077897 8077903 8077913 8077919 8077939 8077967 8077969 8077973
8078003 8078017 8078027 8078029 8078033 8078051 8078053 8078069 8078071 8078087
8078113 8078131 8078143 8078177 8078183 8078201 8078209 8078237 8078243 8078251
8078261 8078297 8078299 8078341 8078347 8078351 8078387 8078429 8078431 8078437
8078459 8078467 8078471 8078489 8078491 8078503 8078527 8078531 8078533 8078537
8078579 8078611 8078627 8078647 8078663 8078669 8078671 8078677 8078699 8078701
8078747 8078761 8078767 8078827 8078831 8078867 8078897 8078899 8078909 8078921
8078923 8078951 8078981 8078989 8078999 8079007 8079041 8079059 8079073 8079077
8079083 8079101 8079107 8079119 8079121 8079133 8079193 8079229 8079241
8079257 8079263 8079271 8079287 8079289 8079299 8079307 8079341 8079343 8079353
8079397 8079413 8079451 8079457 8079473 8079481 8079493 8079497 8079521
8079527 8079529 8079551 8079563 8079581 8079649 8079667 8079679 8079703 8079707
8079761 8079763 8079767 8079779 8079787 8079791 8079803 8079821 8079833 8079847
8079853 8079857 8079883 8079889 8079917 8079943 8079977 8079983 8079989 8080027
8080063 8080069 8080081 8080139 8080147 8080159 8080201 8080223 8080229 8080271
8080273 8080277 8080283 8080309 8080313 8080343 8080363 8080379 8080411 8080417
8080421 8080441 8080451 8080459 8080477 8080481 8080483 8080493 8080507 8080537
8080561 8080591 8080601 8080607 8080621 8080651 8080679 8080693 8080727 8080733
8080759 8080769 8080777 8080781 8080789 8080797 8080823 8080847 8080859 8080901
8080903 8080907 8080927 8080931 8080939 8080951 8080957 8080993 8080999 8081009
8081011 8081041 8081057 8081063 8081077 8081083 8081093 8081113 8081123 8081153
8081197 8081221 8081237 8081263 8081267 8081287 8081299 8081323 8081351 8081357
8081383 8081399 8081419 8081471 8081497 8081501 8081519 8081527 8081537 8081539
8081543 8081561 8081569 8081573 8081581 8081629 8081641 8081653 8081657 8081659
8081663 8081699 8081713 8081719 8081737 8081747 8081753 8081771 8081787 8081803
8081813 8081833 8081837 8081839 8081849 8081929 8081963 8081971 8082013 8082017
8082037 8082077 8082079 8082127 8082161 8082199 8082211 8082229 8082247 8082251
8082257 8082287 8082301 8082311 8082313 8082337 8082343 8082359 8082379 8082383
8082397 8082401 8082419 8082421 8082461 8082521 8082527 8082533 8082541 8082559
8082563 8082611 8082629 8082631 8082653 8082691 8082749 8082751 8082773 8082787
8082797 8082799 8082827 8082857 8082859 8082869 8082881 8082889 8082929
8082911 8082931 8082937 8083001 8083021 8083063 8083073 8083087 8083091 8083111
8083123 8083129 8083139 8083147 8083213 8083223 8083253 8083259 8083289 8083291
8083297 8083321 8083357 8083367 8083391 8083393 8083409 8083447 8083451 8083457
8083477 8083541 8083561 8083567 8083571 8083589 8083597 8083609 8083627 8083633
8083637 8083639 8083643 8083657 8083661 8083679 8083703 8083709 8083711 8083739
8083753 8083763 8083769 8083799 8083807 8083811 8083841 8083849 8083861 8083877
8083897 8083919 8083961 8083967 8083979 8083997 8084023 8084033 8084049
8084159 8084173 8084179 8084189 8084207 8084213 8084221 8084227 8084261 8084281
8084309 8084317 8084327 8084341 8084353 8084371 8084383 8084393 8084399 8084407
8084411 8084413 8084429 8084437 8084441 8084467 8084471 8084501 8084509 8084579
8084581 8084597 8084603 8084617 8084621 8084627 8084641 8084647 8084663 8084669
8084701 8084717 8084723 8084729 8084737 8084761 8084767 8084771 8084801 8084803
8084837 8084863 8084873 8084917 8084929 8084941 8084959 8084977 8085019 8085023
8085031 8085043 8085053 8085071 8085073 8085083 8085101 8085107 8085109 8085137
8085157 8085163 8085169 8085173 8085179 8085197 8085199 8085223 8085227
8085239 8085257 8085281 8085307 8085313 8085331 8085347 8085379 8085433 8085437
8085449 8085469 8085499 8085503 8085509 8085529 8085547 8085563 8085569 8085599
8085613 8085617 8085619 8085643 8085653 8085667 8085683 8085691 8085743 8085787
8085793 8085817 8085827 8085851 8085861 8085893 8085911 8085919 8085929
8085953 8086003 8086007 8086031 8086049 8086063 8086129 8086139 8086181 8086187
8086207 8086213 8086223 8086249 8086277 8086289 8086291 8086321 8086349 8086357
8086391 8086399 8086411 8086417 8086453 8086469 8086489 8086513 8086517
8086523 8086531 8086541 8086549 8086579 8086583 8086591 8086597 8086613 8086627
8086643 8086657 8086669 8086681 8086693 8086699 8086703 8086733 8086751 8086769
8086783 8086787 8086801 8086811 8086843 8086847 8086861 8086873 8086879 8086889
8086891 8086901 8086907 8086927 8086931 8086937 8086943 8086999 8087003 8087017
8087059 8087069 8087077 8087081 8087089 8087129 8087137 8087153 8087203 8087207
8087239 8087263 8087267 8087269 8087281 8087333 8087351 8087353 8087363 8087371
8087383 8087389 8087413 8087449 8087477 8087479 8087489 8087507 8087557 8087561
8087591 8087617 8087627 8087633 8087647 8087659 8087669 8087687 8087689 8087693
8087707 8087731 8087753 8087773 8087797 8087813 8087819 8087861 8087873 8087879
8087887 8087917 8087921 8087951 8087953 8087969 8087983 8088001 8088011 8088037
8088043 8088061 8088079 8088083 8088109 8088121 8088131 8088137 8088139 8088149
8088161 8088191 8088211 8088217 8088221 8088247 8088259 8088293 8088323 8088329
8088331 8088349 8088359 8088373 8088389 8088397 8088401 8088407 8088449 8088463
8088467 8088469 8088497 8088499 8088523 8088527 8088541 8088557 8088569 8088581
8088589 8088611 8088631 8088637 8088643 8088649 8088667 8088671 8088679 8088721
8088727 8088739 8088749 8088761 8088791 8088809 8088811 8088833 8088853 8088863
```

```
8088869 8088877 8088881 8088929 8088937 8088947 8088953 8088973 8089001 8089007
8089009 8089033 8089043 8089049 8089063 8089087 8089129 8089139 8089141 8089157
8089181 8089187 8089219 8089247 8089253 8089303 8089321 8089327 8089339 8089351
8089369 8089387 8089391 8089397 8089409 8089451 8089457 8089483 8089493 8089511
8089531 8089541 8089553 8089559 8089561 8089591 8089597 8089619 8089639 8089673
8089681 8089691 8089693 8089727 8089769 8089789 8089793 8089799 8089817 8089819
8089843 8089849 8089901 8089919 8089931 8089937 8089967 8090041 8090057 8090081
8090083 8090099 8090107 8090119 8090123 8090141 8090171 8090197 8090209 8090213
8090231 8090233 8090239 8090267 8090279 8090293 8090297 8090353 8090363 8090387
8090393 8090413 8090437 8090441 8090443 8090497 8090539 8090573 8090581 8090603
8090629 8090639 8090647 8090651 8090671 8090683 8090689 8090699 8090701 8090711
8090717 8090741 8090749 8090777 8090801 8090813 8090843 8090851 8090879 8090891
8090897 8090911 8090933 8090939 8090989 8090993 8091001 8091007 8091023 8091047
8091059 8091077 8091091 8091107 8091119 8091143 8091151 8091173 8091221 8091241
8091277 8091289 8091361 8091367 8091409 8091427 8091431 8091443 8091451 8091481
8091491 8091509 8091521 8091529 8091533 8091547 8091553 8091557 8091569 8091571
8091583 8091617 8091679 8091683 8091689 8091703 8091731 8091751 8091763 8091767
8091773 8091803 8091821 8091829 8091871 8091877 8091901 8091907 8091913 8091931
8091959 8091973 8091991 8092003 8092009 8092033 8092039 8092069 8092103 8092109
8092111 8092121 8092141 8092177 8092243 8092267 8092277 8092291 8092361 8092369
8092393 8092397 8092429 8092433 8092439 8092451 8092463 8092477 8092489 8092501
8092541 8092547 8092549 8092577 8092589 8092627 8092633 8092657 8092661 8092699
8092709 8092723 8092739 8092741 8092759 8092801 8092811 8092817 8092831 8092871
8092897 8092913 8092919 8092921 8092927 8092939 8092963 8092967 8092979 8092991
8093011 8093017 8093023 8093027 8093083 8093093 8093119 8093123 8093143 8093191
8093209 8093213 8093227 8093237 8093249 8093251 8093273 8093287 8093303 8093333
8093341 8093347 8093357 8093363 8093369 8093429 8093473 8093483 8093509 8093537
8093543 8093551 8093557 8093567 8093593 8093597 8093599 8093611 8093621 8093623
8093627 8093631 8093647 8093651 8093669 8093671 8093689 8093699 8093707 8093711
8093719 8093731 8093737 8093779 8093803 8093807 8093809 8093873 8093893 8093947
8093963 8093977 8093983 8093993 8094017 8094043 8094059 8094061 8094067 8094089
8094101 8094113 8094169 8094181 8094211 8094223 8094253 8094257 8094259 8094263
8094271 8094299 8094311 8094341 8094347 8094353 8094391 8094407 8094421 8094439
8094487 8094491 8094521 8094523 8094539 8094547 8094557 8094563 8094571 8094587
8094607 8094631 8094641 8094659 8094673 8094679 8094719 8094731 8094773 8094797
8094797 8094809 8094811 8094829 8094833 8094847 8094901 8094919 8094929 8094967
8094997 8095013 8095027 8095033 8095039 8095063 8095093 8095097 8095151 8095177
8095181 8095183 8095187 8095201 8095211 8095231 8095237 8095253 8095259 8095271
8095289 8095291 8095301 8095303 8095313 8095343 8095357 8095369 8095393 8095397
8095411 8095427 8095429 8095441 8095459 8095469 8095487 8095531 8095541 8095547
8095561 8095589 8095597 8095601 8095603 8095613 8095631 8095639 8095661 8095667
8095673 8095679 8095687 8095699 8095709 8095733 8095783 8095799 8095807 8095831
8095847 8095873 8095877 8095889 8095907 8095937 8095939 8095951 8095963 8095973
8095979 8095987 8096003 8096009 8096041 8096087 8096107 8096113 8096117 8096119
8096129 8096141 8096149 8096159 8096171 8096183 8096189 8096197 8096203 8096219
8096273 8096293 8096317 8096323 8096329 8096339 8096351 8096353 8096381 8096383
8096441 8096449 8096479 8096509 8096519 8096533 8096593 8096609 8096633 8096653
8096657 8096719 8096729 8096731 8096779 8096783 8096807 8096813 8096819 8096827
8096833 8096839 8096849 8096873 8096903 8096917 8096923 8096939 8096951 8096993
8096999 8097007 8097031 8097071 8097077 8097091 8097137 8097143 8097161 8097163
8097203 8097217 8097227 8097229 8097247 8097259 8097277 8097289 8097307 8097319
8097343 8097347 8097361 8097371 8097431 8097437 8097469 8097493 8097517 8097521
8097527 8097539 8097571 8097581 8097599 8097601 8097613 8097637 8097643 8097697
8097721 8097731 8097767 8097779 8097823 8097833 8097839 8097871 8097893 8097917
8097941 8097961 8097977 8097983 8098007 8098039 8098043 8098049 8098067 8098073
8098091 8098133 8098141 8098157 8098159 8098187 8098193 8098201 8098213 8098219
8098243 8098253 8098261 8098283 8098291 8098367 8098379 8098411 8098417 8098423
8098457 8098459 8098469 8098487 8098529 8098537 8098561 8098567 8098619 8098621
8098637 8098661 8098667 8098669 8098687 8098697 8098709 8098729 8098747 8098763
8098789 8098793 8098799 8098837 8098861 8098883 8098897 8098903 8098913 8098927
8098931 8098933 8098939 8098943 8098957 8098963 8098969 8098991 8099011 8099023
8099071 8099081 8099083 8099141 8099167 8099173 8099219 8099227 8099249 8099251
8099257 8099279 8099281 8099347 8099353 8099363 8099383 8099387 8099393 8099411
8099419 8099431 8099447 8099449 8099477 8099503 8099521 8099527 8099537 8099543
8099549 8099551 8099561 8099573 8099603 8099617 8099621 8099627 8099629 8099639
8099653 8099659 8099683 8099713 8099723 8099731 8099747 8099761 8099771 8099797
8099821 8099827 8099843 8099849 8099863 8099873 8099879 8099891 8099921 8099963
8099969 8099981 8099993 8099999 8100073 8100091 8100097 8100133 8100139 8100167
8100173 8100181 8100203 8100217 8100227 8100241 8100259 8100263 8100283 8100343
8100349 8100353 8100359 8100371 8100377 8100401 8100413 8100419 8100437 8100457
8100481 8100487 8100511 8100529 8100539 8100557 8100569 8100583 8100607 8100629
8100637 8100643 8100661 8100667 8100671 8100689 8100709 8100713 8100731 8100767
8100793 8100803 8100831 8100871 8100881 8100893 8100919 8100931 8100943 8100977
8100979 8101019 8101021 8101031 8101033 8101057 8101081 8101097 8101117 8101127
8101133 8101147 8101151 8101183 8101217 8101241 8101253 8101271 8101273 8101283
8101297 8101319 8101339 8101351 8101363 8101369 8101393 8101397 8101399 8101459
8101463 8101481 8101487 8101493 8101517 8101549 8101567 8101591 8101607 8101637
8101651 8101661 8101669 8101699 8101721 8101729 8101747 8101777 8101781 8101783
8101787 8101789 8101799 8101801 8101811 8101823 8101831 8101859 8101867 8101871
8101901 8101903 8101909 8101913 8101963 8101967 8101981 8101997 8102009 8102041
8102053 8102063 8102089 8102111 8102117 8102137 8102167 8102177 8102221 8102257
8102287 8102291 8102309 8102323 8102351 8102357 8102363 8102383 8102389 8102399
8102407 8102431 8102441 8102453 8102459 8102537 8102561 8102579 8102581 8102597
8102609 8102639 8102657 8102669 8102681 8102713 8102723 8102737 8102747 8102777
8102821 8102849 8102851 8102867 8102879 8102903 8102921 8102929 8102933 8102959
8102971 8103019 8103023 8103031 8103071 8103079 8103083 8103091 8103097 8103127
8103149 8103157 8103163 8103187 8103229 8103233 8103239 8103289 8103299 8103311
8103313 8103323 8103349 8103353 8103391 8103397 8103401 8103409 8103419 8103421
8103427 8103437 8103439 8103451 8103457 8103461 8103497 8103503 8103523 8103547
```

8103553 8103559 8103581 8103619 8103631 8103637 8103643 8103653 8103661 8103721
8103749 8103757 8103761 8103763 8103769 8103779 8103811 8103817 8103841 8103853
8103857 8103863 8103923 8103941 8103947 8103967 8103971 8103983 8104007 8104039
8104067 8104097 8104099 8104111 8104123 8104133 8104141 8104169 8104199 8104207
8104219 8104231 8104249 8104289 8104297 8104301 8104307 8104309 8104331 8104337
8104363 8104381 8104403 8104409 8104451 8104457 8104463 8104483 8104549 8104553
8104559 8104561 8104571 8104573 8104619 8104639 8104667 8104683 8104687 8104741
8104751 8104753 8104793 8104799 8104823 8104829 8104843 8104853 8104861 8104909
8104927 8104933 8104991 8105017 8105021 8105047 8105051 8105059 8105063 8105081
8105087 8105099 8105129 8105179 8105189 8105219 8105221 8105231 8105261 8105281
8105303 8105329 8105333 8105341 8105347 8105359 8105369 8105399 8105401 8105423
8105437 8105441 8105443 8105473 8105483 8105491 8105509 8105519 8105551 8105557
8105561 8105563 8105599 8105621 8105633 8105639 8105653 8105677 8105693 8105707
8105731 8105737 8105743 8105771 8105789 8105813 8105869 8105893 8105897
8105899 8105921 8105927 8105941 8105983 8106001 8106011 8106017 8106019 8106041
8106053 8106073 8106079 8106083 8106089 8106101 8106157 8106173 8106181 8106199
8106211 8106253 8106257 8106271 8106277 8106289 8106299 8106313 8106337
8106349 8106377 8106379 8106389 8106391 8106401 8106421 8106443 8106463 8106491
8106503 8106523 8106529 8106533 8106583 8106587 8106599 8106601 8106611 8106617
8106629 8106647 8106677 8106691 8106697 8106751 8106757 8106767 8106797 8106803
8106817 8106871 8106873 8106893 8106907 8106913 8106947 8106991 8106997 8107003
8107019 8107031 8107051 8107097 8107103 8107111 8107117 8107123 8107133 8107139
8107157 8107159 8107193 8107199 8107207 8107219 8107223 8107237 8107241 8107261
8107271 8107279 8107289 8107303 8107313 8107331 8107361 8107369 8107387 8107417
8107423 8107441 8107483 8107493 8107499 8107511 8107531 8107543 8107549 8107577
8107591 8107601 8107609 8107613 8107621 8107651 8107669 8107679 8107717 8107739
8107741 8107769 8107787 8107789 8107817 8107823 8107831 8107867 8107877 8107903
8107919 8107943 8107949 8107961 8107973 8107999 8108011 8108047 8108083 8108137
8108147 8108159 8108161 8108171 8108173 8108207 8108237 8108239 8108279 8108293
8108297 8108333 8108341 8108357 8108363 8108389 8108423 8108479 8108501 8108531
8108533 8108537 8108539 8108561 8108563 8108593 8108641 8108651 8108657 8108671
8108689 8108699 8108713 8108731 8108741 8108743 8108747 8108753 8108759 8108773
8108803 8108827 8108831 8108861 8108869 8108899 8108911 8108917 8108921 8108923
8108929 8108963 8108999 8109001 8109007 8109061 8109071 8109083 8109089
8109091 8109097 8109107 8109109 8109131 8109139 8109149 8109151 8109163 8109173
8109191 8109203 8109217 8109229 8109247 8109251 8109263 8109301 8109307 8109319
8109329 8109337 8109341 8109359 8109397 8109419 8109421 8109433 8109443 8109457
8109461 8109467 8109481 8109503 8109511 8109529 8109533 8109539 8109551 8109553
8109557 8109581 8109617 8109649 8109659 8109679 8109683 8109701 8109719 8109733
8109743 8109749 8109779 8109793 8109797 8109853 8109859 8109883 8109887 8109917
8109967 8109971 8109973 8110009 8110033 8110043 8110097 8110103 8110129 8110153
8110163 8110181 8110183 8110211 8110213 8110231 8110253 8110301 8110327 8110331
8110337 8110339 8110381 8110387 8110393 8110409 8110423 8110441 8110447 8110457
8110469 8110489 8110507 8110541 8110577 8110589 8110591 8110607 8110631 8110637
8110639 8110667 8110673 8110679 8110681 8110699 8110721 8110723 8110727 8110741
8110783 8110787 8110813 8110831 8110841 8110847 8110859 8110873 8110897
8110901 8110903 8110909 8110919 8110939 8110997 8111011 8111021 8111053 8111083
8111093 8111101 8111123 8111149 8111161 8111171 8111189 8111239 8111263 8111269
8111273 8111281 8111287 8111291 8111303 8111333 8111339 8111377 8111393 8111413
8111417 8111419 8111447 8111459 8111471 8111501 8111513 8111527 8111531 8111539
8111581 8111599 8111603 8111611 8111639 8111657 8111659 8111681 8111693
8111707 8111711 8111717 8111723 8111729 8111731 8111747 8111759 8111767 8111783
8111791 8111849 8111903 8111911 8111923 8111947 8111953 8111977 8111981 8112001
8112011 8112019 8112023 8112029 8112037 8112047 8112061 8112073 8112089 8112103
8112109 8112119 8112133 8112151 8112161 8112187 8112191 8112193 8112211 8112227
8112229 8112277 8112283 8112319 8112331 8112367 8112371 8112397 8112407 8112413
8112443 8112463 8112469 8112473 8112493 8112497 8112521 8112527 8112539 8112569
8112581 8112613 8112619 8112649 8112653 8112667 8112679 8112683 8112691 8112703
8112707 8112737 8112743 8112749 8112787 8112799 8112803 8112821 8112851 8112857
8112911 8112919 8112941 8112947 8112959 8112967 8112971 8112977 8112989 8112991
8113037 8113067 8113109 8113153 8113163 8113211 8113213 8113271 8113279 8113297
8113307 8113321 8113331 8113337 8113349 8113363 8113387 8113421 8113447 8113451
8113453 8113459 8113477 8113487 8113519 8113529 8113543 8113559 8113571 8113597
8113601 8113631 8113639 8113643 8113663 8113669 8113673 8113681 8113691 8113711
8113727 8113753 8113771 8113783 8113789 8113829 8113837 8113843 8113867 8113883
8113927 8113961 8113967 8113979 8113993 8113999 8114021 8114039 8114053 8114059
8114089 8114107 8114111 8114129 8114149 8114177 8114179 8114201 8114203 8114207
8114213 8114263 8114279 8114291 8114333 8114347 8114369 8114371 8114383 8114429
8114453 8114473 8114479 8114489 8114531 8114537 8114551 8114563 8114567 8114611
8114633 8114641 8114669 8114677 8114707 8114719 8114741 8114749 8114759 8114783
8114807 8114819 8114833 8114851 8114857 8114861 8114863 8114893 8114947 8114971
8115011 8115049 8115053 8115083 8115101 8115119 8115131 8115167 8115169 8115179
8115181 8115187 8115197 8115203 8115209 8115227 8115259 8115277 8115293 8115313
8115383 8115403 8115407 8115421 8115431 8115439 8115463 8115467 8115479
8115529 8115533 8115539 8115551 8115553 8115557 8115571 8115577 8115587 8115593
8115649 8115659 8115661 8115671 8115673 8115683 8115703 8115713 8115721 8115733
8115761 8115763 8115791 8115799 8115829 8115841 8115847 8115857 8115883 8115889
8115937 8115959 8115973 8115977 8115997 8116001 8116013 8116019 8116037 8116051
8116063 8116093 8116103 8116109 8116117 8116127 8116133 8116139 8116169 8116181
8116187 8116193 8116219 8116231 8116243 8116253 8116267 8116279 8116301 8116307
8116333 8116337 8116351 8116369 8116373 8116399 8116411 8116421 8116441 8116457
8116469 8116481 8116489 8116499 8116501 8116519 8116523 8116541 8116543 8116547
8116561 8116567 8116601 8116609 8116621 8116643 8116681 8116741 8116747 8116753
8116763 8116783 8116793 8116799 8116813 8116817 8116841 8116847 8116877 8116909
8116921 8116961 8116963 8116967 8116993 8117017 8117027 8117059 8117069 8117077
8117093 8117099 8117101 8117111 8117119 8117141 8117147 8117149 8117167 8117173
8117189 8117191 8117201 8117203 8117243 8117261 8117267 8117287 8117353 8117377
8117383 8117401 8117407 8117429 8117437 8117479 8117491 8117507 8117509 8117513
8117521 8117537 8117561 8117569 8117573 8117611 8117621 8117657 8117663 8117671

```
8117717  8117719  8117729  8117737  8117743  8117761  8117771  8117783  8117831  8117839
8117843  8117849  8117867  8117881  8117899  8117903  8117929  8117933  8117947  8117951
8117969  8118023  8118043  8118049  8118083  8118101  8118107  8118109  8118137  8118139
8118157  8118161  8118179  8118181  8118191  8118193  8118199  8118217  8118233  8118239
8118251  8118329  8118337  8118343  8118359  8118391  8118413  8118433  8118493  8118499
8118511  8118527  8118553  8118569  8118581  8118587  8118589  8118599  8118601  8118611
8118619  8118623  8118629  8118641  8118653  8118661  8118669  8118709  8118727  8118731
8118739  8118767  8118791  8118823  8118829  8118853  8118857  8118863  8118883  8118919
8118949  8118953  8118973  8118991  8119009  8119037  8119051  8119057  8119079  8119093
8119151  8119157  8119187  8119201  8119211  8119231  8119247  8119259  8119273  8119313
8119337  8119339  8119343  8119361  8119367  8119369  8119379  8119417  8119429  8119439
8119451  8119469  8119471  8119477  8119493  8119499  8119537  8119549  8119567  8119577
8119603  8119607  8119627  8119633  8119637  8119651  8119679  8119697  8119711  8119721
8119753  8119777  8119781  8119789  8119823  8119831  8119873  8119879  8119901  8119907
8119919  8119921  8119939  8119981  8119987  8119997  8120023  8120027  8120039  8120051
8120069  8120071  8120113  8120117  8120129  8120153  8120179  8120207  8120209  8120213
8120243  8120251  8120263  8120269  8120317  8120363  8120369  8120383  8120393  8120459
8120461  8120477  8120479  8120491  8120527  8120531  8120561  8120573  8120591  8120597
8120599  8120617  8120641  8120653  8120659  8120677  8120683  8120687  8120699  8120711
8120719  8120731  8120737  8120741  8120759  8120773  8120779  8120789  8120807  8120837
8120839  8120843  8120867  8120873  8120887  8120891  8120921  8120933  8120941  8120953
8121011  8121013  8121049  8121059  8121067  8121079  8121089  8121097  8121103  8121119
8121199  8121209  8121283  8121293  8121299  8121307  8121319  8121331  8121371  8121383
8121397  8121401  8121419  8121431  8121433  8121439  8121499  8121521  8121541  8121557
8121559  8121577  8121587  8121613  8121623  8121629  8121643  8121671  8121677  8121679
8121689  8121697  8121709  8121727  8121739  8121749  8121793  8121811  8121821  8121823
8121847  8121851  8121871  8121877  8121887  8121889  8121901  8121923  8121947  8121959
8121973  8121983  8121991  8122003  8122007  8122021  8122027  8122043  8122057  8122061
8122067  8122097  8122099  8122123  8122133  8122157  8122171  8122181  8122183  8122193
8122201  8122207  8122237  8122241  8122249  8122273  8122307  8122337  8122339  8122357
8122369  8122397  8122417  8122421  8122501  8122537  8122561  8122579  8122591  8122601
8122603  8122619  8122643  8122649  8122669  8122679  8122687  8122693  8122729  8122733
8122739  8122757  8122759  8122769  8122781  8122799  8122819  8122843  8122847  8122903
8122909  8122921  8122927  8122931  8122951  8122969  8123053  8123069  8123077  8123083
8123123  8123183  8123189  8123191  8123197  8123233  8123237  8123243  8123251  8123261
8123267  8123273  8123287  8123303  8123321  8123327  8123341  8123351  8123359  8123377
8123383  8123389  8123407  8123411  8123417  8123447  8123449  8123471  8123473  8123477
8123483  8123543  8123551  8123573  8123587  8123593  8123597  8123627  8123639  8123657
8123693  8123719  8123729  8123737  8123747  8123771  8123779  8123789  8123837  8123851
8123867  8123873  8123881  8123897  8123917  8123933  8123959  8123971  8123987  8123989
8124007  8124013  8124019  8124023  8124029  8124043  8124047  8124071  8124073  8124101
8124107  8124131  8124143  8124157  8124161  8124167  8124169  8124173  8124199  8124209
8124217  8124223  8124239  8124247  8124251  8124257  8124287  8124293  8124299  8124301
8124307  8124323  8124329  8124341  8124367  8124397  8124401  8124421  8124427  8124433
8124443  8124461  8124469  8124481  8124491  8124499  8124503  8124517  8124527  8124539
8124551  8124563  8124569  8124581  8124583  8124629  8124637  8124643  8124659  8124671
8124673  8124679  8124703  8124709  8124731  8124757  8124763  8124769  8124791  8124797
8124803  8124839  8124863  8124869  8124877  8124887  8124917  8124923  8124931  8124947
8124983  8125009  8125021  8125037  8125081  8125087  8125097  8125109  8125123  8125127
8125153  8125177  8125181  8125189  8125199  8125207  8125211  8125223  8125231  8125253
8125267  8125301  8125309  8125319  8125321  8125343  8125363  8125367  8125373  8125391
8125427  8125457  8125499  8125511  8125517  8125519  8125529  8125531  8125543  8125547
8125549  8125561  8125571  8125573  8125577  8125583  8125631  8125639  8125669  8125697
8125723  8125729  8125757  8125759  8125781  8125811  8125823  8125837  8125867  8125883
8125921  8125927  8125933  8125951  8125973  8125987  8125991  8126009  8126029  8126057
8126071  8126087  8126093  8126099  8126101  8126117  8126137  8126143  8126147  8126149
8126161  8126179  8126189  8126197  8126201  8126203  8126213  8126219  8126227  8126233
8126257  8126263  8126297  8126303  8126333  8126401  8126407  8126411  8126423  8126431
8126449  8126453  8126473  8126479  8126491  8126513  8126519  8126533  8126537  8126539
8126581  8126593  8126617  8126647  8126653  8126707  8126711  8126747  8126749  8126773
8126777  8126819  8126821  8126863  8126869  8126879  8126887  8126891  8126893  8126917
8126953  8126959  8126983  8127001  8127023  8127029  8127083  8127089  8127101  8127103
8127107  8127121  8127127  8127131  8127169  8127181  8127199  8127209  8127227  8127253
8127247  8127253  8127263  8127271  8127289  8127293  8127311  8127313  8127319  8127331
8127341  8127397  8127403  8127409  8127433  8127437  8127451  8127461  8127463  8127467
8127491  8127517  8127529  8127541  8127551  8127557  8127577  8127589  8127593  8127617
8127641  8127653  8127659  8127667  8127689  8127697  8127719  8127737  8127761  8127793
8127811  8127829  8127841  8127847  8127863  8127871  8127883  8127919  8127923  8127929
8127937  8127961  8127979  8127997  8128013  8128019  8128037  8128051  8128061  8128063
8128069  8128111  8128117  8128129  8128147  8128171  8128187  8128213  8128217  8128243
8128249  8128259  8128319  8128357  8128369  8128403  8128411  8128423  8128441  8128501
8128511  8128513  8128543  8128579  8128633  8128639  8128649  8128651  8128667  8128691
8128693  8128723  8128733  8128741  8128753  8128759  8128781  8128801  8128807  8128819
8128829  8128871  8128877  8128919  8128931  8128949  8128957  8128969  8129027  8129039
8129047  8129057  8129081  8129113  8129117  8129123  8129129  8129141  8129153  8129183
8129201  8129203  8129221  8129227  8129243  8129249  8129263  8129267  8129273  8129323
8129339  8129351  8129371  8129399  8129411  8129413  8129431  8129453  8129477  8129479
8129489  8129501  8129507  8129509  8129567  8129629  8129633  8129647  8129659  8129683
8129707  8129743  8129761  8129783  8129801  8129819  8129837  8129839  8129873  8129903
8129909  8129917  8129921  8129923  8129939  8129963  8129999  8130007  8130071  8130077
8130113  8130137  8130149  8130169  8130191  8130193  8130251  8130299  8130313  8130319
8130329  8130337  8130361  8130373  8130391  8130427  8130439  8130449  8130509  8130547
8130553  8130581  8130583  8130589  8130593  8130599  8130611  8130631  8130673  8130697
8130721  8130737  8130757  8130761  8130767  8130769  8130779  8130791  8130797  8130809
8130821  8130839  8130851  8130853  8130869  8130877  8130883  8130901  8130907  8130911
8130931  8130943  8130949  8130973  8130977  8130989  8131003  8131033  8131051  8131091
8131093  8131111  8131127  8131139  8131147  8131153  8131159  8131177  8131229  8131237
8131241  8131271  8131309  8131327  8131337  8131349  8131363  8131369  8131399  8131421
8131463  8131469  8131477  8131481  8131493  8131499  8131507  8131511  8131523  8131553
```

```
8131567  8131573  8131577  8131583  8131603  8131609  8131621  8131633  8131637  8131657
8131667  8131681  8131691  8131693  8131699  8131733  8131741  8131757  8131769  8131777
8131807  8131853  8131873  8131901  8131927  8131931  8131939  8131957  8131961  8131969
8131993  8131997  8131999  8132011  8132017  8132027  8132039  8132051  8132077  8132083
8132099  8132101  8132177  8132219  8132221  8132281  8132287  8132291  8132329  8132347
8132351  8132389  8132401  8132429  8132431  8132471  8132483  8132491  8132503  8132521
8132543  8132549  8132561  8132567  8132591  8132603  8132617  8132629  8132653  8132659
8132669  8132687  8132689  8132693  8132701  8132713  8132743  8132759  8132843  8132849
8132879  8132899  8132911  8132923  8132951  8132989  8133017  8133019  8133023  8133031
8133043  8133049  8133101  8133107  8133109  8133119  8133127  8133133  8133143  8133163
8133187  8133199  8133233  8133241  8133247  8133277  8133289  8133317  8133341  8133347
8133371  8133379  8133383  8133403  8133413  8133431  8133449  8133469  8133481  8133511
8133527  8133529  8133533  8133569  8133589  8133607  8133611  8133613  8133617  8133623
8133641  8133707  8133731  8133737  8133757  8133779  8133791  8133809  8133841  8133869
8133877  8133883  8133893  8133901  8133913  8133929  8133943  8133947  8133953  8133967
8133971  8133989  8134003  8134039  8134051  8134057  8134073  8134099  8134103  8134127
8134151  8134163  8134187  8134193  8134201  8134229  8134303  8134349  8134363  8134367
8134391  8134417  8134429  8134453  8134457  8134459  8134481  8134501  8134513  8134543
8134547  8134549  8134573  8134589  8134597  8134613  8134627  8134639  8134657  8134661
8134691  8134699  8134723  8134727  8134733  8134739  8134759  8134781  8134799  8134813
8134849  8134871  8134873  8134897  8134943  8134949  8134957  8134961  8134963  8134981
8134991  8135003  8135011  8135033  8135053  8135063  8135069  8135081  8135093  8135131
8135137  8135147  8135159  8135177  8135189  8135191  8135201  8135203  8135221  8135243
8135273  8135279  8135311  8135329  8135359  8135381  8135383  8135389  8135417  8135429
8135441  8135443  8135459  8135461  8135467  8135473  8135489  8135497  8135521  8135551
8135563  8135581  8135593  8135599  8135623  8135627  8135641  8135713  8135759  8135773
8135789  8135797  8135801  8135821  8135833  8135839  8135861  8135873  8135891  8135899
8135927  8135947  8135957  8135983  8136053  8136059  8136061  8136067  8136077  8136091
8136097  8136133  8136137  8136143  8136151  8136157  8136169  8136197  8136203  8136221
8136223  8136259  8136281  8136283  8136307  8136341  8136343  8136347  8136367  8136377
8136383  8136391  8136397  8136433  8136437  8136461  8136463  8136467  8136487  8136497
8136521  8136551  8136563  8136571  8136577  8136629  8136637  8136649  8136677  8136679
8136683  8136701  8136743  8136833  8136857  8136859  8136881  8136889  8136893  8136899
8136913  8136943  8136967  8136977  8136991  8137007  8137013  8137021  8137027  8137043
8137069  8137117  8137121  8137127  8137133  8137141  8137183  8137189  8137211  8137219
8137223  8137231  8137247  8137273  8137289  8137291  8137303  8137333  8137361  8137379
8137387  8137397  8137411  8137417  8137421  8137463  8137501  8137513  8137517  8137559
8137573  8137609  8137631  8137651  8137691  8137697  8137733  8137763  8137783  8137813
8137819  8137853  8137861  8137867  8137889  8137897  8137919  8137931  8137957  8137979
8137981  8137999  8138063  8138083  8138107  8138111  8138129  8138149  8138197  8138201
8138209  8138219  8138227  8138239  8138243  8138279  8138323  8138363  8138371  8138387
8138413  8138443  8138467  8138477  8138489  8138497  8138509  8138513  8138539  8138549
8138561  8138569  8138579  8138629  8138639  8138651  8138657  8138671  8138677  8138687
8138693  8138717  8138729  8138737  8138743  8138747  8138761  8138773  8138789  8138807
8138861  8138863  8138881  8138891  8138909  8138947  8138981  8138983  8138993  8139013
8139017  8139031  8139059  8139067  8139071  8139113  8139119  8139127  8139137  8139151
8139203  8139211  8139221  8139251  8139253  8139283  8139301  8139331  8139337  8139359
8139377  8139403  8139407  8139409  8139421  8139431  8139451  8139457  8139473  8139479
8139487  8139497  8139529  8139533  8139541  8139553  8139563  8139569  8139589  8139611
8139641  8139661  8139683  8139707  8139709  8139743  8139767  8139773  8139797  8139829
8139869  8139871  8139913  8139919  8139959  8139973  8139983  8139997  8140001  8140009
8140043  8140051  8140061  8140063  8140087  8140103  8140109  8140117  8140123  8140133
8140147  8140159  8140163  8140177  8140211  8140247  8140261  8140291  8140313  8140339
8140343  8140351  8140361  8140369  8140381  8140393  8140409  8140411  8140421  8140439
8140441  8140519  8140523  8140529  8140537  8140553  8140571  8140577  8140589  8140609
8140661  8140663  8140669  8140681  8140687  8140711  8140763  8140771  8140829  8140823
8140831  8140843  8140849  8140897  8140907  8140927  8140961  8140963  8140981  8140991
8141027  8141039  8141041  8141059  8141071  8141087  8141093  8141117  8141129  8141131
8141137  8141143  8141153  8141167  8141183  8141197  8141209  8141213  8141227  8141261
8141267  8141327  8141339  8141363  8141377  8141401  8141407  8141423  8141449  8141459
8141461  8141473  8141477  8141527  8141531  8141533  8141569  8141597  8141599  8141603
8141611  8141659  8141677  8141681  8141689  8141723  8141729  8141741  8141753  8141767
8141789  8141797  8141801  8141803  8141831  8141849  8141851  8141869  8141873  8141879
8141891  8141893  8141911  8141957  8141971  8141981  8141993  8141999  8142037  8142049
8142077  8142103  8142107  8142131  8142137  8142151  8142157  8142221  8142229  8142247
8142271  8142287  8142289  8142307  8142311  8142319  8142349  8142353  8142389  8142397
8142401  8142467  8142487  8142503  8142509  8142517  8142527  8142557  8142569  8142581
8142599  8142619  8142637  8142653  8142671  8142683  8142727  8142731  8142733  8142749
8142751  8142769  8142787  8142791  8142793  8142803  8142809  8142817  8142821  8142833
8142839  8142853  8142857  8142907  8142917  8142929  8142971  8143007  8143013  8143019
8143033  8143043  8143097  8143129  8143141  8143147  8143151  8143159  8143169  8143183
8143199  8143207  8143231  8143237  8143271  8143273  8143277  8143309  8143313  8143319
8143337  8143339  8143351  8143427  8143453  8143463  8143501  8143537  8143601  8143613
8143627  8143637  8143651  8143657  8143687  8143721  8143741  8143753  8143763  8143769
8143781  8143787  8143801  8143819  8143823  8143841  8143847  8143853  8143859  8143907
8143921  8143931  8143937  8143939  8143987  8143997  8143999  8144009  8144011  8144029
8144039  8144053  8144057  8144069  8144083  8144111  8144137  8144161  8144167  8144219
8144221  8144233  8144247  8144261  8144263  8144267  8144291  8144327  8144341  8144359
8144387  8144393  8144399  8144429  8144441  8144443  8144449  8144459  8144467  8144497
8144531  8144557  8144561  8144567  8144569  8144579  8144593  8144627  8144639  8144641
8144651  8144671  8144687  8144693  8144743  8144753  8144761  8144777  8144791  8144803
8144827  8144833  8144837  8144839  8144849  8144861  8144879  8144893  8144897  8144923
8144933  8144951  8144957  8144963  8144999  8145001  8145031  8145043  8145047  8145073
8145113  8145133  8145139  8145149  8145169  8145173  8145209  8145211  8145223  8145239
8145253  8145283  8145299  8145323  8145337  8145349  8145367  8145407  8145419  8145437
8145443  8145457  8145463  8145479  8145541  8145563  8145569  8145581  8145583  8145629
8145637  8145647  8145649  8145671  8145673  8145689  8145691  8145707  8145713  8145727
8145733  8145743  8145773  8145811  8145827  8145833  8145853  8145859  8145871  8145911
8145919  8145937  8145971  8146007  8146067  8146091  8146109  8146133  8146169  8146183
```

```
8146223  8146291  8146309  8146339  8146343  8146363  8146387  8146399  8146409  8146423
8146429  8146433  8146441  8146447  8146483  8146493  8146507  8146511  8146529  8146571
8146591  8146603  8146609  8146627  8146631  8146637  8146639  8146657  8146673  8146679
8146681  8146703  8146711  8146751  8146781  8146811  8146819  8146843  8146843  8146867
8146907  8146913  8146937  8146949  8146967  8146969  8147039  8147047  8147053  8147059
8147071  8147093  8147101  8147123  8147137  8147147  8147159  8147189  8147261  8147291
8147299  8147303  8147317  8147323  8147341  8147351  8147357  8147387  8147393  8147407
8147417  8147443  8147449  8147483  8147509  8147519  8147533  8147537  8147549  8147551
8147567  8147611  8147617  8147621  8147627  8147647  8147653  8147663  8147677  8147687
8147693  8147717  8147759  8147791  8147813  8147833  8147837  8147857  8147863  8147891
8147899  8147917  8147921  8147933  8147963  8147977  8147983  8147987  8147999  8148013
8148047  8148059  8148073  8148079  8148089  8148137  8148181  8148191  8148209  8148211
8148221  8148229  8148263  8148277  8148289  8148311  8148341  8148347  8148367  8148373
8148401  8148407  8148421  8148467  8148487  8148493  8148499  8148521  8148527  8148541
8148551  8148557  8148571  8148589  8148631  8148641  8148671  8148683  8148703
8148713  8148727  8148733  8148737  8148743  8148757  8148779  8148793  8148809  8148821
8148827  8148839  8148841  8148871  8148911  8148919  8148937  8148947  8148977  8148979
8149003  8149007  8149027  8149079  8149109  8149111  8149123  8149129  8149147  8149151
8149177  8149181  8149237  8149243  8149247  8149259  8149279  8149301  8149303  8149313
8149331  8149343  8149363  8149367  8149369  8149381  8149457  8149459  8149481  8149483
8149487  8149517  8149543  8149553  8149571  8149577  8149591  8149601  8149607  8149619
8149627  8149633  8149639  8149663  8149699  8149703  8149721  8149723  8149733  8149741
8149759  8149763  8149769  8149777  8149789  8149831  8149849  8149859  8149861  8149873
8149891  8149901  8149907  8149913  8149927  8149937  8149949  8149951  8149979  8149991
8150011  8150017  8150029  8150033  8150047  8150057  8150059  8150071  8150099  8150111
8150137  8150141  8150159  8150173  8150209  8150237  8150243  8150269  8150273  8150279
8150281  8150291  8150309  8150321  8150333  8150357  8150369  8150371  8150383  8150399
8150413  8150419  8150447  8150453  8150459  8150473  8150477  8150491  8150503  8150539
8150561  8150591  8150609  8150621  8150629  8150647  8150651  8150657  8150663  8150687
8150707  8150713  8150731  8150741  8150743  8150761  8150771  8150773  8150789  8150819
8150839  8150851  8150869  8150893  8150903  8150921  8150929  8150953  8150971  8150977
8151023  8151043  8151049  8151053  8151079  8151083  8151097  8151113  8151119  8151139
8151149  8151151  8151161  8151167  8151173  8151179  8151191  8151193  8151197  8151203
8151217  8151229  8151259  8151271  8151281  8151289  8151301  8151329  8151337  8151371
8151379  8151383  8151391  8151397  8151401  8151427  8151431  8151463  8151469  8151487
8151511  8151527  8151541  8151547  8151569  8151571  8151607  8151623  8151629  8151631
8151659  8151673  8151701  8151719  8151733  8151751  8151763  8151799  8151809  8151827
8151841  8151859  8151881  8151887  8151901  8151917  8151937  8151943  8151953  8151961
8151967  8151991  8152021  8152031  8152033  8152093  8152181  8152187  8152201  8152213
8152217  8152253  8152267  8152283  8152303  8152357  8152363  8152369  8152379  8152409
8152427  8152429  8152447  8152457  8152471  8152477  8152519  8152549  8152579  8152591
8152601  8152609  8152621  8152631  8152633  8152637  8152643  8152663  8152681  8152693
8152699  8152709  8152747  8152751  8152763  8152801  8152813  8152817  8152819  8152883
8152889  8152901  8152909  8152927  8152931  8152933  8152961  8152993  8152997  8153003
8153009  8153011  8153021  8153027  8153039  8153053  8153069  8153083  8153099  8153113
8153153  8153177  8153179  8153191  8153207  8153213  8153237  8153267  8153287  8153329
8153333  8153347  8153371  8153381  8153399  8153401  8153417  8153447  8153449  8153471
8153473  8153479  8153491  8153521  8153539  8153543  8153567  8153581  8153597  8153609
8153681  8153683  8153731  8153737  8153759  8153771  8153773  8153779  8153791  8153797
8153813  8153819  8153851  8153857  8153861  8153867  8153903  8153933  8153939  8153941
8153953  8153989  8153993  8154007  8154019  8154031  8154043  8154061  8154071
8154073  8154127  8154131  8154163  8154199  8154217  8154221  8154229  8154253  8154257
8154277  8154283  8154299  8154313  8154317  8154343  8154347  8154371  8154379  8154383
8154403  8154427  8154431  8154469  8154473  8154511  8154529  8154557  8154569  8154571
8154583  8154599  8154623  8154631  8154647  8154659  8154677  8154683  8154691  8154697
8154749  8154761  8154779  8154787  8154799  8154823  8154827  8154851  8154863  8154869
8154877  8154893  8154929  8154931  8154947  8154961  8154967  8154973  8154977  8154983
8155001  8155013  8155027  8155031  8155033  8155067  8155073  8155093  8155099  8155141
8155171  8155183  8155193  8155229  8155243  8155261  8155267  8155283  8155289  8155297
8155309  8155319  8155321  8155339  8155349  8155369  8155391  8155421  8155451  8155453
8155457  8155471  8155493  8155507  8155513  8155523  8155531  8155561  8155591  8155607
8155613  8155621  8155657  8155669  8155673  8155687  8155717  8155727  8155729  8155751
8155753  8155787  8155793  8155817  8155831  8155837  8155859  8155887  8155909  8155913
8155943  8155949  8155967  8155981  8155999  8156003  8156009  8156017  8156023  8156063
8156077  8156081  8156129  8156147  8156153  8156167  8156173  8156177  8156179  8156189
8156231  8156233  8156251  8156257  8156297  8156299  8156303  8156341  8156347  8156359
8156383  8156387  8156389  8156429  8156437  8156461  8156471  8156497  8156501  8156507
8156527  8156537  8156543  8156557  8156591  8156593  8156609  8156641  8156653  8156669
8156699  8156723  8156749  8156767  8156773  8156779  8156807  8156849  8156857  8156867
8156893  8156903  8156933  8156963  8156969  8156989  8157001  8157007  8157011  8157013
8157029  8157031  8157041  8157043  8157047  8157053  8157067  8157077  8157101  8157109
8157113  8157133  8157169  8157181  8157187  8157197  8157211  8157221  8157223  8157241
8157257  8157271  8157293  8157299  8157301  8157311  8157313  8157329  8157343  8157379
8157421  8157431  8157463  8157481  8157491  8157503  8157509  8157521  8157533  8157547
8157553  8157559  8157581  8157587  8157599  8157629  8157641  8157673  8157679  8157683
8157701  8157727  8157731  8157749  8157757  8157767  8157769  8157803  8157817  8157827
8157833  8157839  8157857  8157869  8157949  8157959  8157979  8158013  8158021  8158027
8158061  8158063  8158097  8158103  8158109  8158127  8158133  8158187  8158211  8158217
8158223  8158229  8158243  8158259  8158279  8158289  8158291  8158331  8158333  8158373
8158387  8158411  8158421  8158439  8158441  8158457  8158471  8158489  8158499  8158511
8158517  8158529  8158531  8158547  8158561  8158603  8158613  8158621  8158649  8158663
8158669  8158727  8158729  8158751  8158757  8158763  8158769  8158781  8158783  8158789
8158837  8158841  8158867  8158879  8158919  8158967  8158987  8159009  8159017  8159029
8159033  8159069  8159093  8159101  8159117  8159131  8159143  8159183  8159197  8159209
8159213  8159219  8159233  8159243  8159251  8159311  8159321  8159339  8159363  8159377
8159383  8159399  8159419  8159423  8159441  8159443  8159467  8159477  8159483  8159521
8159561  8159563  8159611  8159621  8159639  8159651  8159653  8159669  8159663  8159681
8159731  8159743  8159747  8159771  8159773  8159791  8159807  8159819  8159821  8159839
8159923  8159939  8159941  8159947  8159951  8159953  8159971  8159993  8160011  8160041
```

```
8160043  8160059  8160071  8160077  8160079  8160083  8160127  8160133  8160137  8160149
8160157  8160179  8160181  8160197  8160199  8160209  8160211  8160227  8160247  8160259
8160287  8160293  8160307  8160337  8160371  8160379  8160401  8160407  8160413  8160421
8160433  8160437  8160473  8160479  8160491  8160547  8160553  8160577  8160589  8160601
8160613  8160617  8160631  8160637  8160673  8160727  8160739  8160749  8160769  8160773
8160827  8160839  8160851  8160913  8160917  8160923  8160931  8160941  8160947  8160959
8160961  8160989  8160991  8161001  8161031  8161039  8161063  8161073  8161081  8161121
8161183  8161187  8161193  8161213  8161243  8161249  8161259  8161261  8161273  8161319
8161333  8161381  8161403  8161427  8161429  8161451  8161453  8161477  8161487  8161493
8161511  8161519  8161537  8161579  8161589  8161591  8161607  8161627  8161631  8161661
8161667  8161669  8161687  8161753  8161763  8161807  8161817  8161831  8161837  8161843
8161859  8161889  8161903  8161913  8161931  8161939  8161943  8161949  8161957  8161961
8161969  8161981  8161991  8161997  8161999  8162009  8162017  8162027  8162041  8162047
8162051  8162059  8162069  8162081  8162111  8162123  8162149  8162179  8162183  8162197
8162213  8162233  8162243  8162251  8162299  8162317  8162333  8162339  8162347  8162351
8162353  8162411  8162437  8162467  8162489  8162491  8162501  8162509  8162513  8162521
8162563  8162599  8162603  8162611  8162617  8162621  8162629  8162633  8162653  8162663
8162699  8162701  8162711  8162743  8162747  8162773  8162779  8162789  8162797  8162809
8162831  8162849  8162851  8162857  8162863  8162887  8162893  8162897  8162899  8162929
8162939  8162969  8162971  8162981  8162983  8163017  8163019  8163031  8163037  8163047
8163049  8163107  8163109  8163121  8163131  8163139  8163143  8163191  8163193  8163227
8163241  8163251  8163271  8163283  8163313  8163319  8163329  8163359  8163401  8163427
8163457  8163473  8163479  8163487  8163497  8163503  8163539  8163541  8163557  8163563
8163583  8163599  8163607  8163613  8163629  8163637  8163641  8163647  8163709  8163713
8163737  8163739  8163769  8163803  8163817  8163821  8163823  8163829  8163833  8163839
8163847  8163871  8163917  8163923  8163929  8163971  8163983  8163989  8163997  8164003
8164027  8164031  8164033  8164069  8164073  8164099  8164111  8164127  8164141  8164147
8164159  8164183  8164201  8164213  8164217  8164249  8164259  8164291  8164297  8164307
8164327  8164339  8164349  8164397  8164441  8164451  8164469  8164477  8164523  8164529
8164543  8164549  8164567  8164577  8164579  8164601  8164603  8164613  8164619  8164621
8164643  8164657  8164669  8164691  8164693  8164697  8164733  8164759  8164799  8164801
8164817  8164841  8164847  8164859  8164861  8164907  8164909  8164939  8164943  8164967
8164973  8164987  8164991  8164993  8165011  8165029  8165039  8165077  8165093  8165107
8165111  8165149  8165221  8165239  8165249  8165303  8165309  8165317  8165323  8165329
8165341  8165347  8165351  8165359  8165371  8165387  8165393  8165401  8165407  8165411
8165429  8165447  8165467  8165471  8165473  8165503  8165527  8165533  8165537  8165539
8165543  8165569  8165581  8165609  8165629  8165653  8165671  8165681  8165701  8165711
8165723  8165753  8165761  8165767  8165779  8165809  8165813  8165867  8165873  8165879
8165881  8165903  8165909  8165917  8165939  8165957  8165977  8166007  8166019  8166031
8166047  8166049  8166061  8166071  8166073  8166077  8166079  8166083  8166097  8166107
8166209  8166211  8166217  8166229  8166269  8166271  8166283  8166289  8166317  8166331
8166337  8166359  8166383  8166401  8166407  8166439  8166451  8166461  8166469  8166553
8166559  8166577  8166581  8166589  8166593  8166601  8166649  8166659  8166727  8166731
8166737  8166757  8166773  8166793  8166797  8166799  8166841  8166853  8166887  8166911
8166923  8166937  8166943  8166959  8166967  8166997  8167007  8167039  8167051  8167057
8167063  8167069  8167073  8167079  8167087  8167091  8167111  8167147  8167151  8167189
8167199  8167213  8167217  8167219  8167253  8167267  8167307  8167319  8167337  8167373
8167381  8167387  8167391  8167399  8167403  8167409  8167427  8167433  8167447  8167451
8167483  8167493  8167499  8167513  8167517  8167541  8167543  8167559  8167561  8167571
8167583  8167597  8167603  8167637  8167673  8167699  8167703  8167711  8167727  8167729
8167771  8167811  8167823  8167843  8167847  8167867  8167909  8167919  8167927  8167993
8168011  8168023  8168063  8168071  8168089  8168099  8168101  8168117  8168161  8168179
8168207  8168257  8168269  8168287  8168299  8168333  8168341  8168357  8168359  8168371
8168411  8168429  8168437  8168441  8168533  8168539  8168549  8168561  8168579  8168591
8168599  8168603  8168617  8168623  8168669  8168681  8168683  8168729  8168791  8168801
8168819  8168833  8168873  8168911  8168921  8168939  8168947  8168983  8168989
8169001  8169013  8169017  8169019  8169041  8169067  8169079  8169101  8169103  8169113
8169121  8169131  8169137  8169143  8169157  8169179  8169191  8169229  8169241  8169247
8169253  8169263  8169277  8169283  8169289  8169313  8169319  8169353  8169379  8169383
8169391  8169409  8169419  8169431  8169433  8169457  8169463  8169467  8169481  8169509
8169517  8169541  8169559  8169583  8169589  8169599  8169611  8169617  8169653  8169661
8169691  8169731  8169767  8169817  8169823  8169827  8169839  8169841  8169881  8169893
8169901  8169919  8169923  8169929  8169937  8169961  8169971  8169983  8169989  8170009
8170031  8170039  8170093  8170139  8170153  8170163  8170177  8170187  8170189  8170207
8170223  8170231  8170241  8170243  8170297  8170307  8170369  8170381  8170397  8170441
8170447  8170457  8170469  8170471  8170483  8170501  8170507  8170511  8170529  8170537
8170541  8170549  8170567  8170571  8170579  8170607  8170619  8170649  8170697  8170699
8170709  8170711  8170777  8170781  8170787  8170793  8170807  8170831  8170847  8170859
8170871  8170873  8170901  8170907  8170909  8170913  8170933  8170937  8170961  8170973
8170991  8170993  8171017  8171029  8171039  8171047  8171057  8171071  8171081  8171089
8171129  8171131  8171153  8171173  8171201  8171213  8171221  8171227  8171231  8171263
8171287  8171297  8171327  8171347  8171399  8171431  8171437  8171447  8171459  8171473
8171479  8171497  8171549  8171563  8171573  8171629  8171659  8171687  8171689
8171701  8171717  8171731  8171741  8171759  8171791  8171803  8171827  8171837  8171851
8171861  8171873  8171893  8171897  8171899  8171909  8171921  8171927  8171939  8171953
8171963  8171971  8171983  8171993  8172013  8172023  8172037  8172049  8172077  8172083
8172089  8172091  8172103  8172119  8172137  8172139  8172167  8172179  8172181  8172209
8172211  8172233  8172253  8172293  8172319  8172341  8172349  8172371  8172389  8172391
8172419  8172443  8172467  8172469  8172473  8172481  8172487  8172491  8172497  8172511
8172517  8172539  8172557  8172559  8172583  8172589  8172607  8172611  8172673  8172677
8172683  8172691  8172701  8172707  8172713  8172821  8172833  8172839  8172847  8172911
8172917  8172919  8172943  8172953  8172973  8172979  8172991  8173001  8173003  8173019
8173021  8173049  8173051  8173079  8173091  8173117  8173127  8173163  8173169  8173199
8173201  8173219  8173229  8173237  8173267  8173351  8173387  8173423  8173427  8173453
8173471  8173489  8173499  8173513  8173519  8173523  8173537  8173547  8173567  8173597
8173643  8173663  8173673  8173681  8173687  8173691  8173699  8173709  8173729  8173751
8173769  8173783  8173807  8173811  8173859  8173861  8173871  8173903  8173927  8173937
8173943  8173951  8174011  8174021  8174041  8174053  8174063  8174087  8174107  8174113
8174167  8174189  8174203  8174207  8174219  8174251  8174261  8174267  8174281  8174291
```

8174329 8174363 8174371 8174401 8174417 8174431 8174437 8174461 8174471 8174473
8174477 8174513 8174527 8174563 8174567 8174581 8174597 8174599 8174611 8174623
8174629 8174681 8174689 8174701 8174711 8174713 8174717 8174741 8174767 8174783
8174797 8174813 8174861 8174893 8174911 8174953 8174963 8174983 8174987 8175001
8175017 8175019 8175029 8175047 8175053 8175059 8175061 8175067 8175077 8175107
8175131 8175137 8175161 8175163 8175169 8175173 8175241 8175253 8175311 8175313
8175319 8175331 8175337 8175341 8175347 8175353 8175367 8175379 8175383 8175389
8175397 8175439 8175449 8175457 8175463 8175469 8175493 8175499 8175539 8175551
8175569 8175577 8175619 8175637 8175653 8175677 8175699 8175703 8175707 8175731
8175733 8175743 8175773 8175803 8175821 8175829 8175857 8175877 8175887 8175899
8175907 8175911 8175913 8175919 8175949 8175953 8175967 8175983 8175991 8176019
8176079 8176087 8176093 8176111 8176121 8176123 8176141 8176159 8176171 8176177
8176229 8176237 8176283 8176291 8176309 8176367 8176369 8176373 8176409 8176411
8176447 8176453 8176457 8176459 8176489 8176547 8176607 8176621 8176639 8176687
8176691 8176699 8176709 8176723 8176759 8176769 8176771 8176789 8176823 8176829
8176841 8176843 8176849 8176871 8176873 8176913 8176921 8176939 8176951 8176957
8176967 8176979 8176981 8176991 8177021 8177027 8177033 8177041 8177063 8177089
8177131 8177173 8177177 8177179 8177207 8177209 8177219 8177227 8177251 8177293
8177297 8177303 8177311 8177321 8177339 8177359 8177383 8177401 8177431 8177477
8177441 8177447 8177453 8177461 8177473 8177503 8177513 8177539 8177549 8177563
8177597 8177621 8177647 8177651 8177669 8177677 8177699 8177713 8177723 8177747
8177753 8177759 8177773 8177789 8177791 8177801 8177839 8177849 8177879 8177881
8177887 8177921 8177927 8177929 8177933 8177957 8177959 8177963 8177977 8178007
8178011 8178013 8178019 8178031 8178043 8178077 8178083 8178091 8178101 8178109
8178143 8178169 8178187 8178193 8178217 8178251 8178253 8178257 8178259 8178281
8178293 8178307 8178337 8178347 8178349 8178353 8178371 8178383 8178397 8178413
8178421 8178427 8178437 8178439 8178449 8178463 8178473 8178481 8178487 8178497
8178503 8178529 8178559 8178563 8178617 8178619 8178631 8178647 8178659 8178661
8178691 8178707 8178713 8178719 8178743 8178769 8178829 8178839 8178857 8178881
8178889 8178913 8178959 8178977 8178991 8178997 8179001 8179019 8179021 8179079
8179103 8179117 8179151 8179153 8179169 8179201 8179211 8179219 8179273 8179277
8179289 8179309 8179313 8179321 8179343 8179349 8179351 8179357 8179373 8179393
8179399 8179403 8179439 8179441 8179447 8179453 8179463 8179471 8179487 8179489
8179511 8179529 8179573 8179579 8179597 8179607 8179621 8179631 8179643 8179657
8179667 8179679 8179693 8179727 8179729 8179751 8179757 8179777 8179783 8179793
8179807 8179811 8179813 8179817 8179841 8179867 8179879 8179903 8179909 8179921
8179961 8179979 8179993 8180017 8180023 8180027 8180041 8180057 8180083 8180093
8180099 8180101 8180119 8180143 8180149 8180153 8180177 8180189 8180201 8180239
8180251 8180261 8180273 8180299 8180323 8180351 8180353 8180357 8180369 8180413
8180423 8180429 8180437 8180477 8180483 8180503 8180509 8180521 8180531
8180537 8180561 8180573 8180591 8180593 8180597 8180611 8180671 8180693 8180699
8180701 8180713 8180719 8180741 8180743 8180759 8180779 8180789 8180857 8180873
8180897 8180911 8180917 8180923 8180933 8180941 8180957 8180989 8181007 8181011
8181023 8181049 8181053 8181071 8181073 8181079 8181091 8181119 8181127 8181139
8181167 8181193 8181203 8181211 8181221 8181253 8181269 8181281 8181287 8181311
8181347 8181349 8181359 8181361 8181377 8181379 8181389 8181421 8181449 8181499
8181517 8181521 8181527 8181529 8181577 8181581 8181587 8181601 8181611 8181617
8181623 8181631 8181637 8181697 8181727 8181731 8181751 8181781 8181791 8181809
8181821 8181829 8181841 8181851 8181871 8181881 8181889 8181893 8181917 8181931
8181937 8181949 8181959 8181961 8181967 8181977 8181983 8182003 8182007 8182021
8182033 8182039 8182067 8182073 8182081 8182091 8182121 8182123 8182157 8182159
8182201 8182211 8182243 8182259 8182271 8182309 8182327 8182333 8182337 8182367
8182373 8182387 8182403 8182409 8182417 8182429 8182441 8182451 8182453 8182463
8182469 8182477 8182487 8182541 8182547 8182579 8182589 8182591 8182619 8182637
8182639 8182649 8182663 8182693 8182703 8182709 8182753 8182781 8182793 8182813
8182819 8182847 8182849 8182859 8182861 8182877 8182879 8182891 8182897 8182913
8182921 8182949 8182973 8182981 8182987 8183011 8183051 8183083 8183099 8183111
8183113 8183117 8183141 8183159 8183209 8183221 8183233 8183237 8183257 8183269
8183293 8183297 8183299 8183309 8183317 8183321 8183369 8183407 8183429 8183437
8183449 8183479 8183491 8183503 8183507 8183521 8183533 8183537 8183543 8183569
8183587 8183603 8183621 8183627 8183629 8183633 8183657 8183663 8183671 8183683
8183711 8183719 8183729 8183731 8183743 8183759 8183761 8183767 8183789 8183797
8183807 8183809 8183827 8183843 8183867 8183869 8183873 8183881 8183891 8183893
8183897 8183899 8183933 8183941 8183947 8183951 8183977 8184017 8184019 8184053
8184073 8184091 8184097 8184139 8184149 8184151 8184167 8184179 8184199 8184221
8184223 8184227 8184247 8184263 8184287 8184299 8184301 8184311 8184317 8184359
8184367 8184391 8184443 8184469 8184493 8184521 8184523 8184557 8184563 8184571
8184581 8184593 8184607 8184613 8184629 8184647 8184691 8184727 8184731 8184767
8184773 8184779 8184793 8184817 8184829 8184851 8184853 8184857 8184887 8184889
8184907 8184947 8184971 8184977 8185027 8185031 8185039 8185049 8185061 8185081
8185123 8185127 8185139 8185157 8185159 8185169 8185213 8185223 8185231 8185237
8185253 8185259 8185283 8185291 8185301 8185369 8185391 8185403 8185421 8185433
8185451 8185459 8185469 8185481 8185501 8185537 8185553 8185579 8185589 8185603
8185633 8185649 8185657 8185663 8185669 8185673 8185711 8185729 8185757 8185777
8185783 8185787 8185799 8185813 8185817 8185819 8185873 8185897 8185909 8185921
8185951 8185967 8185981 8186029 8186051 8186071 8186081 8186083 8186089 8186099
8186111 8186117 8186141 8186153 8186177 8186179 8186219 8186251 8186267 8186273
8186279 8186291 8186317 8186329 8186351 8186363 8186377 8186389 8186393 8186407
8186411 8186417 8186419 8186441 8186447 8186483 8186489 8186527 8186531 8186557
8186561 8186567 8186579 8186599 8186603 8186611 8186621 8186653 8186681 8186687
8186693 8186719 8186723 8186743 8186753 8186807 8186831 8186837 8186851 8186861
8186863 8186869 8186917 8186933 8186947 8186951 8186987 8186989 8187029 8187031
8187041 8187073 8187089 8187097 8187139 8187143 8187163 8187197 8187211 8187227
8187247 8187269 8187293 8187307 8187337 8187349 8187373 8187409 8187419 8187427
8187449 8187451 8187463 8187469 8187511 8187521 8187527 8187539 8187583 8187593
8187611 8187617 8187623 8187629 8187637 8187661 8187667 8187677 8187691 8187719
8187721 8187743 8187757 8187769 8187799 8187827 8187853 8187877 8187887 8187913
8187919 8187929 8187941 8187943 8187953 8187983 8188001 8188007 8188009 8188013
8188049 8188051 8188057 8188087 8188097 8188099 8188111 8188133 8188139 8188163

```
8188181 8188223 8188231 8188249 8188261 8188291 8188307 8188321 8188331 8188333
8188357 8188363 8188399 8188409 8188421 8188423 8188451 8188459 8188489 8188493
8188513 8188519 8188547 8188559 8188567 8188597 8188613 8188657 8188693 8188703
8188717 8188721 8188723 8188757 8188769 8188793 8188799 8188819 8188841 8188861
8188913 8188931 8188937 8188949 8188967 8188987 8188993 8189003 8189009 8189011
8189021 8189033 8189039 8189047 8189059 8189063 8189101 8189119 8189123 8189131
8189141 8189161 8189191 8189197 8189227 8189231 8189243 8189249 8189261 8189263
8189267 8189287 8189297 8189309 8189317 8189333 8189347 8189369 8189387 8189411
8189443 8189453 8189471 8189473 8189483 8189491 8189501 8189509 8189521 8189537
8189539 8189561 8189567 8189579 8189581 8189591 8189603 8189639 8189641 8189663
8189681 8189683 8189711 8189743 8189761 8189773 8189777 8189789 8189833 8189837
8189899 8189917 8189927 8189939 8189941 8189947 8189957 8189959 8189963 8189981
8189999 8190011 8190029 8190031 8190041 8190067 8190097 8190113 8190131 8190157
8190163 8190179 8190187 8190211 8190223 8190227 8190233 8190257 8190331 8190359
8190367 8190397 8190401 8190407 8190449 8190467 8190473 8190487 8190491 8190493
8190509 8190563 8190571 8190593 8190601 8190607 8190647 8190661 8190667 8190697
8190701 8190751 8190823 8190827 8190839 8190859 8190863 8190877 8190887
8190893 8190899 8190901 8190907 8190943 8190947 8190953 8190979 8190983 8190997
8191049 8191069 8191091 8191123 8191129 8191133 8191181 8191189 8191193 8191217
8191259 8191277 8191279 8191283 8191291 8191307 8191321 8191333 8191343 8191357
8191363 8191387 8191423 8191441 8191493 8191511 8191529 8191537 8191607 8191609
8191613 8191633 8191639 8191643 8191691 8191697 8191699 8191727 8191753 8191783
8191811 8191817 8191819 8191829 8191847 8191849 8191853 8191867 8191877 8191903
8191913 8191921 8191969 8191991 8192003 8192033 8192039 8192081 8192089 8192099
8192111 8192141 8192143 8192159 8192167 8192201 8192237 8192257 8192267 8192269
8192299 8192321 8192341 8192357 8192383 8192411 8192423 8192441 8192447 8192449
8192473 8192479 8192491 8192507 8192533 8192551 8192557 8192599 8192627 8192653
8192641 8192647 8192671 8192677 8192683 8192699 8192771 8192783 8192803 8192809
8192813 8192837 8192861 8192881 8192887 8192893 8192923 8192927 8192939 8192953
8192969 8192981 8192983 8192999 8193001 8193023 8193041 8193067 8193079 8193103
8193113 8193127 8193131 8193137 8193139 8193173 8193193 8193197 8193209 8193247
8193253 8193257 8193259 8193281 8193307 8193319 8193343 8193397 8193403 8193407
8193413 8193443 8193461 8193469 8193491 8193509 8193527 8193529 8193551 8193569
8193571 8193587 8193599 8193611 8193623 8193629 8193649 8193667 8193671 8193697
8193701 8193707 8193719 8193733 8193737 8193751 8193781 8193791 8193793 8193803
8193817 8193851 8193859 8193877 8193907 8193929 8193961 8194007 8194063 8194127
8194129 8194139 8194159 8194183 8194213 8194217 8194229 8194237 8194243 8194247
8194259 8194267 8194271 8194283 8194337 8194349 8194363 8194367 8194369 8194387
8194393 8194399 8194409 8194411 8194429 8194457 8194471 8194481 8194517 8194519
8194541 8194583 8194597 8194631 8194651 8194661 8194691 8194721 8194727 8194759
8194763 8194777 8194787 8194841 8194859 8194861 8194883 8194889 8194903 8194931
8194933 8194937 8194939 8194951 8194961 8194981 8194987 8194997 8195009 8195017
8195021 8195059 8195087 8195101 8195111 8195113 8195119 8195179 8195189 8195227
8195267 8195269 8195273 8195287 8195293 8195303 8195321 8195329 8195339 8195347
8195351 8195393 8195399 8195423 8195431 8195461 8195483 8195489 8195497 8195527
8195543 8195569 8195573 8195587 8195617 8195639 8195647 8195651 8195657 8195689
8195699 8195711 8195713 8195729 8195741 8195767 8195773 8195779 8195801 8195807
8195809 8195839 8195849 8195917 8195923 8195947 8195953 8195959 8195969 8195977
8196007 8196017 8196029 8196031 8196061 8196077 8196109 8196113 8196127 8196137
8196157 8196173 8196217 8196233 8196247 8196259 8196301 8196313 8196319 8196343
8196347 8196361 8196379 8196389 8196401 8196421 8196437 8196443 8196469 8196479
8196481 8196491 8196497 8196511 8196523 8196557 8196563 8196571 8196577 8196599
8196607 8196613 8196623 8196641 8196649 8196653 8196667 8196689 8196701 8196709
8196719 8196739 8196757 8196779 8196787 8196817 8196823 8196827 8196833 8196883
8196887 8196899 8196911 8196917 8196919 8196931 8196953 8196959 8196967 8196971
8197001 8197003 8197019 8197031 8197069 8197081 8197091 8197099 8197141 8197153
8197159 8197183 8197193 8197199 8197201 8197271 8197279 8197297 8197327 8197331
8197339 8197381 8197403 8197429 8197471 8197487 8197489 8197507 8197537 8197543
8197549 8197559 8197571 8197573 8197577 8197603 8197619 8197627 8197687 8197699
8197741 8197747 8197753 8197771 8197789 8197799 8197801 8197817 8197823 8197829
8197837 8197901 8197921 8197933 8197967 8198009 8198011 8198017 8198023 8198027
8198041 8198059 8198083 8198087 8198107 8198117 8198147 8198191 8198219 8198221
8198249 8198261 8198269 8198303 8198317 8198363 8198371 8198381 8198389 8198459
8198467 8198479 8198501 8198507 8198521 8198551 8198587 8198611 8198627 8198639
8198651 8198669 8198683 8198689 8198693 8198713 8198717 8198753 8198759 8198783
8198789 8198791 8198797 8198803 8198807 8198809 8198831 8198843 8198863 8198891
8198917 8198951 8198959 8198963 8199001 8199007 8199029 8199077 8199091 8199101
8199133 8199137 8199143 8199157 8199161 8199179 8199181 8199187 8199229 8199239
8199251 8199271 8199277 8199341 8199343 8199349 8199353 8199361 8199371 8199379
8199383 8199391 8199409 8199413 8199419 8199427 8199449 8199461 8199463 8199473
8199493 8199497 8199509 8199511 8199553 8199557 8199563 8199571 8199589 8199599
8199613 8199623 8199629 8199637 8199641 8199649 8199673 8199677 8199679 8199689
8199703 8199767 8199781 8199787 8199791 8199809 8199827 8199853 8199857
8199869 8199883 8199901 8199907 8199913 8199931 8199941 8199943 8199979 8200007
8200013 8200037 8200061 8200079 8200091 8200109 8200141 8200147 8200177 8200183
8200211 8200217 8200219 8200271 8200289 8200303 8200321 8200327 8200363 8200391
8200403 8200411 8200427 8200433 8200441 8200447 8200459 8200463 8200529 8200537
8200541 8200559 8200561 8200589 8200631 8200663 8200667 8200669 8200679 8200691
8200721 8200739 8200741 8200769 8200789 8200847 8200853 8200877 8200879 8200883
8200921 8200979 8200991 8201009 8201033 8201071 8201101 8201111 8201153 8201159
8201183 8201197 8201213 8201233 8201239 8201251 8201257 8201299 8201311 8201321
8201339 8201341 8201351 8201357 8201371 8201377 8201419 8201441 8201449 8201467
8201489 8201507 8201509 8201513 8201527 8201541 8201551 8201563 8201573 8201579
8201587 8201603 8201621 8201647 8201663 8201689 8201729 8201747 8201771 8201773
8201797 8201801 8201807 8201813 8201819 8201821 8201839 8201857 8201861 8201873
8201881 8201891 8201903 8201911 8201929 8201933 8201951 8201957 8201969 8201971
8201981 8201987 8201989 8202013 8202023 8202031 8202043 8202059 8202067 8202071
8202097 8202127 8202137 8202149 8202179 8202193 8202221 8202253 8202263 8202277
8202367 8202371 8202373 8202407 8202409 8202413 8202427 8202431 8202443 8202457
```

```
8202461  8202463  8202479  8202497  8202521  8202533  8202589  8202613  8202629  8202647
8202659  8202673  8202683  8202703  8202709  8202713  8202767  8202787  8202793  8202797
8202811  8202833  8202839  8202847  8202871  8202893  8202907  8202913  8202919  8202949
8202967  8202977  8202983  8202989  8203001  8203021  8203073  8203081  8203087  8203103
8203109  8203133  8203147  8203187  8203199  8203213  8203241  8203243  8203253  8203267
8203271  8203289  8203291  8203297  8203303  8203309  8203319  8203331  8203337  8203339
8203343  8203361  8203373  8203379  8203409  8203451  8203453  8203457  8203483  8203511
8203543  8203577  8203619  8203633  8203651  8203661  8203691  8203703  8203717  8203729
8203733  8203757  8203771  8203777  8203787  8203831  8203859  8203873  8203879  8203883
8203901  8203903  8203907  8203963  8203967  8204003  8204017  8204033  8204041  8204067
8204093  8204101  8204111  8204113  8204167  8204171  8204177  8204191  8204221  8204233
8204239  8204267  8204281  8204297  8204299  8204311  8204359  8204369  8204389  8204423
8204431  8204473  8204479  8204501  8204507  8204513  8204527  8204531  8204569  8204587
8204597  8204611  8204617  8204621  8204627  8204657  8204687  8204719  8204737  8204741
8204747  8204759  8204773  8204783  8204809  8204843  8204849  8204851  8204891  8204899
8204921  8204929  8204957  8205011  8205013  8205023  8205037  8205047  8205059  8205061
8205073  8205077  8205079  8205097  8205103  8205121  8205137  8205143  8205163  8205179
8205187  8205191  8205199  8205221  8205233  8205251  8205259  8205287  8205311  8205313
8205361  8205391  8205403  8205409  8205427  8205433  8205437  8205443  8205461  8205467
8205487  8205497  8205523  8205529  8205553  8205559  8205569  8205581  8205599  8205623
8205643  8205653  8205667  8205671  8205677  8205727  8205737  8205773  8205787  8205797
8205817  8205829  8205833  8205839  8205859  8205881  8205887  8205893  8205913  8205931
8205941  8205949  8205973  8205983  8206013  8206021  8206039  8206057  8206061  8206069
8206073  8206091  8206097  8206111  8206117  8206123  8206129  8206139  8206141  8206169
8206171  8206181  8206183  8206199  8206201  8206207  8206229  8206243  8206279  8206337
8206339  8206343  8206403  8206409  8206411  8206439  8206447  8206463  8206477  8206511
8206531  8206559  8206571  8206577  8206589  8206603  8206619  8206621  8206633  8206643
8206663  8206669  8206691  8206703  8206729  8206741  8206777  8206787  8206789  8206799
8206817  8206829  8206831  8206843  8206853  8206871  8206873  8206889  8206901  8206907
8206927  8206931  8206943  8206951  8206963  8206967  8206969  8206981  8206987  8207009
8207027  8207041  8207047  8207051  8207057  8207071  8207117  8207153  8207161  8207189
8207191  8207197  8207207  8207237  8207249  8207273  8207327  8207333  8207347  8207359
8207363  8207369  8207371  8207383  8207393  8207399  8207429  8207471  8207477  8207483
8207497  8207501  8207513  8207519  8207531  8207561  8207569  8207579  8207581  8207587
8207627  8207663  8207699  8207707  8207743  8207767  8207789  8207827  8207851  8207861
8207873  8207879  8207893  8207897  8207909  8207911  8207917  8207959  8207971  8207989
8207999  8208001  8208023  8208037  8208041  8208049  8208061  8208071  8208091  8208107
8208113  8208143  8208157  8208181  8208197  8208199  8208251  8208253  8208271  8208281
8208283  8208287  8208311  8208349  8208353  8208359  8208377  8208383  8208427  8208439
8208443  8208449  8208553  8208601  8208619  8208647  8208649  8208667  8208721  8208727
8208731  8208749  8208751  8208757  8208763  8208787  8208797  8208803  8208821  8208859
8208877  8208881  8208883  8208887  8208901  8208911  8208913  8208917  8208919  8208929
8208947  8208961  8208971  8209009  8209031  8209037  8209043  8209063  8209081  8209099
8209109  8209129  8209133  8209151  8209171  8209193  8209211  8209213  8209217  8209231
8209237  8209241  8209261  8209277  8209297  8209303  8209339  8209343  8209363  8209379
8209391  8209429  8209433  8209483  8209489  8209493  8209499  8209559  8209561  8209571
8209609  8209633  8209681  8209693  8209703  8209709  8209723  8209741  8209763  8209769
8209777  8209787  8209829  8209837  8209841  8209847  8209849  8209867  8209891  8209907
8209931  8209933  8209947  8209961  8209973  8209991  8210017  8210053  8210063
8210077  8210087  8210093  8210107  8210117  8210123  8210129  8210131  8210141  8210159
8210171  8210179  8210183  8210197  8210239  8210249  8210309  8210311  8210317  8210351
8210353  8210387  8210399  8210401  8210437  8210441  8210453  8210459  8210483  8210491
8210497  8210519  8210533  8210561  8210599  8210621  8210627  8210639  8210647  8210651
8210659  8210663  8210669  8210681  8210723  8210729  8210749  8210767  8210777  8210789
8210791  8210801  8210803  8210809  8210819  8210827  8210833  8210837  8210887  8210911
8210927  8210933  8210987  8211011  8211013  8211019  8211043  8211103  8211109  8211121
8211127  8211139  8211163  8211167  8211169  8211191  8211197  8211227  8211331  8211349
8211353  8211361  8211367  8211383  8211389  8211397  8211403  8211421  8211433  8211457
8211461  8211479  8211499  8211503  8211509  8211523  8211563  8211583  8211601  8211607
8211613  8211631  8211641  8211659  8211673  8211677  8211689  8211701  8211719  8211737
8211739  8211751  8211757  8211769  8211773  8211787  8211803  8211809  8211821  8211829
8211871  8211877  8211883  8211893  8211899  8211919  8211949  8211953  8211961  8211977
8211991  8212019  8212021  8212063  8212067  8212091  8212093  8212109  8212147  8212157
8212163  8212189  8212213  8212277  8212283  8212291  8212333  8212363  8212367  8212381
8212397  8212439  8212453  8212471  8212487  8212493  8212511  8212517  8212549  8212553
8212583  8212591  8212609  8212637  8212661  8212667  8212681  8212691  8212697  8212703
8212723  8212759  8212801  8212811  8212837  8212847  8212849  8212873  8212877  8212879
8212891  8212901  8212907  8212913  8212931  8212951  8212961  8212969  8212973  8212987
8212991  8213033  8213053  8213059  8213063  8213069  8213071  8213089  8213123  8213131
8213147  8213167  8213173  8213189  8213207  8213221  8213267  8213273  8213279  8213291
8213311  8213321  8213333  8213347  8213353  8213399  8213411  8213417  8213423  8213437
8213441  8213459  8213479  8213497  8213503  8213531  8213549  8213581  8213591  8213603
8213627  8213629  8213633  8213659  8213671  8213677  8213693  8213717  8213743  8213747
8213761  8213789  8213797  8213813  8213819  8213851  8213869  8213879  8213893  8213897
8213951  8213969  8213971  8213983  8213987  8214007  8214029  8214071  8214091  8214097
8214103  8214113  8214127  8214149  8214169  8214181  8214209  8214211  8214223  8214253
8214257  8214263  8214293  8214301  8214307  8214313  8214317  8214319  8214329  8214343
8214359  8214377  8214379  8214389  8214439  8214457  8214461  8214467  8214469  8214509
8214527  8214529  8214533  8214539  8214541  8214571  8214581  8214589  8214599  8214601
8214623  8214643  8214667  8214683  8214691  8214697  8214709  8214727  8214737  8214769
8214779  8214781  8214793  8214799  8214827  8214889  8214901  8214911  8214923  8214929
8214949  8214953  8215001  8215043  8215057  8215061  8215079  8215099  8215133  8215153
8215157  8215171  8215187  8215237  8215247  8215253  8215283  8215303  8215313  8215327
8215343  8215349  8215367  8215379  8215387  8215397  8215399  8215411  8215453  8215469
8215507  8215511  8215513  8215523  8215547  8215549  8215579  8215601  8215633  8215637
8215673  8215681  8215693  8215699  8215717  8215783  8215789  8215793  8215799  8215829
8215841  8215843  8215849  8215861  8215877  8215897  8215951  8215957  8215969  8215973
8215993  8216003  8216017  8216057  8216063  8216099  8216101  8216107  8216111  8216123
8216137  8216149  8216161  8216179  8216231  8216269  8216293  8216297  8216317  8216347
```

```
8216353  8216371  8216387  8216407  8216437  8216447  8216459  8216471  8216473  8216477
8216489  8216503  8216521  8216539  8216557  8216561  8216573  8216597  8216603  8216609
8216641  8216647  8216669  8216671  8216693  8216717  8216723  8216731  8216737  8216743
8216777  8216783  8216801  8216809  8216821  8216833  8216839  8216843  8216863  8216893
8216921  8216927  8216939  8216951  8216969  8216977  8216983  8217007  8217017  8217023
8217029  8217047  8217073  8217089  8217091  8217113  8217133  8217169  8217193  8217197
8217199  8217203  8217221  8217227  8217229  8217241  8217271  8217277  8217299  8217301
8217311  8217323  8217331  8217347  8217359  8217373  8217379  8217383  8217427  8217437
8217439  8217467  8217479  8217523  8217529  8217551  8217607  8217623  8217631  8217653
8217661  8217667  8217679  8217689  8217691  8217721  8217757  8217767  8217793  8217827
8217841  8217871  8217887  8217893  8217929  8217931  8217947  8217949  8217967  8217973
8217983  8218009  8218027  8218057  8218073  8218087  8218099  8218109  8218139  8218141
8218187  8218201  8218207  8218229  8218253  8218277  8218307  8218319  8218333  8218351
8218369  8218381  8218391  8218423  8218433  8218439  8218447  8218451  8218459  8218481
8218489  8218499  8218537  8218541  8218543  8218549  8218589  8218597  8218619  8218663
8218669  8218681  8218703  8218723  8218729  8218741  8218753  8218781  8218783  8218801
8218817  8218831  8218853  8218897  8218913  8218961  8218993  8219009  8219011  8219021
8219023  8219033  8219047  8219051  8219053  8219087  8219131  8219137  8219171  8219179
8219203  8219207  8219213  8219221  8219227  8219243  8219269  8219317  8219327  8219329
8219339  8219353  8219357  8219401  8219411  8219423  8219429  8219447  8219459  8219509
8219521  8219527  8219569  8219591  8219593  8219597  8219623  8219641  8219657  8219711
8219719  8219747  8219777  8219779  8219791  8219819  8219839  8219851  8219879  8219881
8219899  8219903  8219909  8219917  8219941  8219969  8219983  8220013  8220089  8220097
8220101  8220109  8220139  8220143  8220169  8220193  8220203  8220211  8220221  8220229
8220271  8220281  8220283  8220287  8220313  8220337  8220341  8220379  8220389  8220391
8220397  8220409  8220419  8220461  8220481  8220493  8220497  8220517  8220523  8220551
8220557  8220577  8220581  8220631  8220649  8220689  8220691  8220713  8220727  8220731
8220733  8220743  8220767  8220791  8220799  8220803  8220851  8220853  8220881  8220887
8220899  8220923  8220929  8220931  8220937  8221009  8221021  8221027  8221061  8221063
8221069  8221111  8221139  8221177  8221211  8221219  8221223  8221229  8221249  8221253
8221261  8221267  8221273  8221277  8221313  8221321  8221331  8221337  8221349  8221391
8221403  8221427  8221439  8221453  8221463  8221469  8221487  8221513  8221537  8221561
8221567  8221573  8221579  8221583  8221589  8221597  8221621  8221627  8221651  8221657
8221669  8221689  8221721  8221739  8221747  8221751  8221753  8221763  8221823  8221831
8221841  8221847  8221859  8221891  8221903  8221919  8221921  8221937  8221949  8221963
8221981  8221991  8222009  8222047  8222057  8222059  8222069  8222089  8222111  8222119
8222131  8222141  8222143  8222147  8222153  8222183  8222213  8222239  8222243  8222257
8222303  8222323  8222351  8222353  8222363  8222369  8222377  8222393  8222413  8222419
8222437  8222447  8222449  8222453  8222479  8222483  8222491  8222519  8222549  8222563
8222567  8222587  8222597  8222609  8222623  8222681  8222693  8222701  8222717  8222737
8222749  8222779  8222783  8222807  8222813  8222821  8222853  8222887  8222899  8222911
8222923  8222941  8222947  8222957  8222959  8222969  8222987  8222989  8222999  8223013
8223043  8223077  8223079  8223107  8223113  8223119  8223133  8223157  8223169  8223179
8223197  8223199  8223217  8223251  8223253  8223289  8223317  8223331  8223337  8223353
8223367  8223407  8223421  8223451  8223469  8223473  8223491  8223497  8223499  8223541
8223569  8223577  8223601  8223653  8223659  8223667  8223679  8223701  8223703  8223727
8223737  8223749  8223863  8223871  8223877  8223881  8223883  8223893  8223899  8223967
8223977  8223989  8223991  8223997  8224031  8224043  8224057  8224061  8224079  8224091
8224121  8224123  8224157  8224163  8224171  8224189  8224211  8224219  8224259  8224261
8224289  8224291  8224297  8224301  8224303  8224319  8224369  8224417  8224421  8224439
8224441  8224449  8224499  8224507  8224519  8224529  8224537  8224543  8224561  8224571
8224591  8224609  8224631  8224633  8224637  8224669  8224673  8224681  8224709  8224729
8224747  8224751  8224763  8224781  8224789  8224793  8224807  8224831  8224847  8224861
8224877  8224897  8224903  8224913  8224919  8224933  8224963  8224981  8225003  8225029
8225039  8225101  8225117  8225149  8225153  8225171  8225177  8225201  8225207  8225257
8225293  8225311  8225333  8225351  8225377  8225381  8225407  8225429  8225431  8225471
8225491  8225519  8225527  8225533  8225551  8225573  8225579  8225593  8225597  8225629
8225641  8225669  8225677  8225687  8225699  8225731  8225747  8225761  8225783  8225813
8225827  8225831  8225849  8225863  8225873  8225929  8225939  8225941  8225947  8225963
8225983  8225999  8226013  8226017  8226037  8226041  8226083  8226089  8226091  8226103
8226109  8226133  8226137  8226143  8226161  8226187  8226209  8226271  8226293  8226299
8226307  8226331  8226353  8226389  8226391  8226409  8226431  8226451  8226499  8226503
8226509  8226529  8226539  8226541  8226553  8226577  8226583  8226593  8226599  8226611
8226629  8226637  8226641  8226649  8226653  8226697  8226719  8226731  8226733  8226767
8226769  8226781  8226809  8226821  8226857  8226899  8226941  8226947  8226949  8226971
8226973  8226989  8226991  8227003  8227007  8227033  8227049  8227067  8227069  8227081
8227091  8227103  8227117  8227127  8227159  8227189  8227207  8227217  8227229  8227237
8227259  8227273  8227279  8227291  8227309  8227321  8227339  8227363  8227379  8227381
8227391  8227393  8227403  8227411  8227421  8227423  8227451  8227469  8227477  8227487
8227489  8227501  8227547  8227553  8227559  8227573  8227591  8227601  8227607  8227621
8227633  8227649  8227651  8227657  8227669  8227673  8227691  8227697  8227699  8227729
8227753  8227759  8227777  8227781  8227787  8227789  8227799  8227811  8227819  8227829
8227837  8227861  8227871  8227883  8227889  8227937  8227939  8227943  8227957
8227987  8227993  8228009  8228021  8228029  8228041  8228047  8228063  8228071  8228111
8228117  8228123  8228131  8228147  8228161  8228173  8228183  8228189  8228191  8228201
8228263  8228267  8228293  8228327  8228333  8228347  8228377  8228401  8228417  8228419
8228447  8228449  8228461  8228497  8228513  8228543  8228551  8228557  8228569  8228573
8228579  8228581  8228587  8228593  8228603  8228651  8228723  8228747  8228777  8228797
8228813  8228821  8228827  8228863  8228879  8228893  8228897  8228903  8228947  8228951
8228959  8228989  8228993  8229017  8229019  8229031  8229073  8229077  8229079  8229103
8229107  8229131  8229149  8229157  8229161  8229163  8229181  8229187  8229191  8229253
8229269  8229283  8229293  8229313  8229317  8229323  8229329  8229373  8229401  8229407
8229433  8229439  8229443  8229461  8229511  8229541  8229553  8229569  8229619  8229623
8229629  8229631  8229701  8229731  8229737  8229743  8229763  8229779  8229797  8229821
8229829  8229833  8229857  8229887  8229863  8229901  8229913  8229931  8229943  8229957
8230003  8230037  8230049  8230063  8230081  8230109  8230121  8230127  8230139  8230153
8230199  8230223  8230253  8230267  8230279  8230291  8230301  8230309  8230331  8230349
8230351  8230357  8230379  8230399  8230427  8230429  8230433  8230447  8230459  8230471
8230483  8230511  8230513  8230517  8230543  8230561  8230583  8230603  8230609  8230637
```

```
8230639  8230643  8230679  8230681  8230697  8230723  8230727  8230753  8230769  8230777
8230799  8230813  8230829  8230853  8230877  8230887  8230889  8230891  8230949  8230959
8230967  8230973  8230979  8231021  8231087  8231107  8231137  8231143  8231147  8231159
8231177  8231219  8231221  8231227  8231231  8231239  8231287  8231291  8231297  8231299
8231303  8231317  8231329  8231339  8231341  8231347  8231357  8231369  8231387  8231393
8231411  8231413  8231423  8231437  8231449  8231459  8231467  8231471  8231473  8231479
8231491  8231507  8231537  8231549  8231557  8231567  8231581  8231593  8231633  8231651
8231659  8231681  8231683  8231747  8231749  8231753  8231777  8231779  8231827  8231849
8231887  8231891  8231917  8231929  8231933  8231947  8232001  8232017  8232041  8232043
8232083  8232109  8232113  8232121  8232127  8232151  8232179  8232181  8232197  8232227
8232239  8232251  8232277  8232281  8232311  8232337  8232347  8232359  8232361  8232373
8232383  8232401  8232439  8232449  8232451  8232493  8232503  8232509  8232517  8232527
8232533  8232541  8232547  8232557  8232559  8232563  8232569  8232571  8232583  8232593
8232613  8232659  8232667  8232691  8232703  8232727  8232733  8232739  8232769  8232773
8232797  8232817  8232821  8232857  8232859  8232863  8232869  8232881  8232883  8232899
8232929  8232941  8232953  8232971  8232977  8232979  8232989  8233003  8233021  8233031
8233033  8233039  8233091  8233111  8233133  8233139  8233153  8233163  8233171  8233201
8233207  8233261  8233279  8233331  8233349  8233367  8233369  8233397  8233399  8233409
8233411  8233417  8233427  8233447  8233453  8233469  8233487  8233501  8233523  8233541
8233549  8233567  8233571  8233583  8233613  8233637  8233639  8233649  8233663  8233679
8233681  8233691  8233699  8233703  8233711  8233723  8233739  8233759  8233781  8233787
8233801  8233811  8233843  8233847  8233867  8233873  8233877  8233891  8233903  8233909
8233913  8233937  8233949  8233961  8233993  8233997  8234033  8234059  8234063  8234081
8234089  8234101  8234119  8234123  8234141  8234147  8234167  8234183  8234203  8234209
8234243  8234257  8234263  8234279  8234293  8234297  8234309  8234311  8234321  8234357
8234363  8234389  8234393  8234411  8234417  8234419  8234497  8234503  8234519  8234531
8234549  8234587  8234593  8234599  8234641  8234671  8234687  8234701  8234711  8234761
8234773  8234789  8234803  8234813  8234839  8234857  8234867  8234893  8234899  8234909
8234921  8234929  8234951  8234977  8235013  8235047  8235049  8235067  8235083  8235091
8235103  8235107  8235131  8235163  8235187  8235209  8235229  8235239  8235247  8235251
8235263  8235281  8235287  8235307  8235313  8235323  8235329  8235371  8235377  8235413
8235431  8235433  8235443  8235457  8235473  8235499  8235517  8235551  8235589  8235593
8235631  8235637  8235653  8235673  8235697  8235709  8235727  8235737  8235743  8235757
8235781  8235791  8235809  8235827  8235859  8235881  8235883  8235893  8235923  8235947
8235967  8235989  8235991  8236003  8236009  8236021  8236027  8236031  8236057  8236061
8236069  8236073  8236099  8236103  8236117  8236133  8236141  8236157  8236169  8236181
8236219  8236229  8236259  8236271  8236309  8236321  8236337  8236343  8236379  8236387
8236399  8236433  8236439  8236441  8236447  8236451  8236477  8236499  8236541  8236567
8236583  8236589  8236603  8236637  8236643  8236649  8236673  8236717  8236729  8236733
8236741  8236751  8236757  8236763  8236771  8236799  8236801  8236817  8236831  8236843
8236867  8236871  8236873  8236883  8236919  8236933  8236939  8236961  8236973  8236981
8236999  8237011  8237029  8237063  8237071  8237077  8237081  8237083  8237111  8237113
8237137  8237153  8237171  8237191  8237213  8237237  8237261  8237263  8237287  8237293
8237297  8237303  8237309  8237311  8237321  8237323  8237329  8237357  8237377  8237387
8237417  8237429  8237441  8237461  8237477  8237497  8237513  8237527  8237533  8237543
8237561  8237617  8237627  8237629  8237681  8237683  8237687  8237693  8237699  8237701
8237729  8237753  8237767  8237777  8237783  8237821  8237839  8237869  8237881  8237891
8237899  8237903  8237921  8237923  8237951  8237969  8237981  8238011  8238023  8238029
8238053  8238067  8238101  8238121  8238151  8238169  8238179  8238203  8238227  8238247
8238283  8238287  8238299  8238337  8238361  8238371  8238389  8238397  8238437  8238443
8238481  8238493  8238541  8238553  8238563  8238613  8238619  8238683  8238709  8238719
8238743  8238751  8238767  8238781  8238787  8238809  8238817  8238823  8238847  8238859
8238877  8238883  8238887  8238907  8238953  8238961  8239003  8239019  8239031  8239039
8239051  8239069  8239079  8239093  8239097  8239117  8239139  8239151  8239157  8239159
8239171  8239177  8239193  8239199  8239207  8239223  8239229  8239247  8239249  8239261
8239303  8239307  8239349  8239367  8239403  8239411  8239417  8239421  8239423  8239447
8239457  8239481  8239489  8239499  8239501  8239513  8239519  8239529  8239537  8239547
8239571  8239601  8239603  8239607  8239619  8239631  8239639  8239667  8239669  8239687
8239717  8239723  8239733  8239753  8239759  8239771  8239783  8239801  8239823  8239843
8239871  8239877  8239879  8239921  8239927  8239967  8239969  8239997  8240027  8240033
8240041  8240077  8240081  8240083  8240093  8240119  8240131  8240143  8240161  8240171
8240173  8240179  8240213  8240227  8240231  8240249  8240269  8240273  8240329  8240333
8240339  8240341  8240363  8240383  8240399  8240431  8240447  8240483  8240501  8240537
8240539  8240543  8240587  8240621  8240627  8240629  8240633  8240663  8240671  8240681
8240711  8240717  8240719  8240731  8240741  8240753  8240759  8240779  8240797  8240803
8240807  8240809  8240841  8240857  8240861  8240867  8240873  8240879  8240909
8240929  8240957  8240963  8240983  8240989  8241001  8241007  8241019  8241091  8241097
8241113  8241131  8241137  8241139  8241143  8241173  8241223  8241227  8241229  8241263
8241271  8241281  8241301  8241313  8241329  8241349  8241361  8241367  8241371  8241377
8241391  8241397  8241407  8241419  8241427  8241433  8241463  8241479  8241487  8241503
8241511  8241523  8241529  8241551  8241559  8241577  8241587  8241589  8241593  8241601
8241647  8241661  8241671  8241677  8241703  8241721  8241749  8241781  8241791  8241803
8241847  8241851  8241859  8241899  8241907  8241911  8241913  8241931  8241941  8241949
8241973  8241979  8242007  8242021  8242037  8242043  8242049  8242051  8242079  8242081
8242097  8242109  8242121  8242141  8242159  8242183  8242207  8242217  8242243  8242261
8242277  8242279  8242301  8242309  8242327  8242337  8242361  8242363  8242411  8242439
8242457  8242459  8242469  8242519  8242529  8242537  8242547  8242567  8242571  8242607
8242609  8242631  8242639  8242667  8242679  8242687  8242693  8242697  8242723  8242727
8242733  8242777  8242783  8242811  8242847  8242849  8242859  8242867  8242877  8242889
8242919  8242933  8242937  8242957  8242961  8243023  8243033  8243041  8243063  8243069
8243083  8243099  8243101  8243107  8243149  8243159  8243167  8243201  8243203  8243219
8243227  8243231  8243239  8243251  8243281  8243297  8243327  8243329  8243353  8243363
8243381  8243383  8243393  8243423  8243429  8243441  8243497  8243509  8243513  8243531
8243533  8243537  8243579  8243581  8243603  8243611  8243617  8243633  8243647  8243681
8243687  8243693  8243707  8243713  8243731  8243749  8243761  8243791  8243813  8243819
8243839  8243843  8243849  8243857  8243863  8243869  8243897  8243899  8243909  8243927
8243947  8243953  8243957  8243971  8244001  8244013  8244053  8244079  8244083  8244113
8244139  8244161  8244163  8244169  8244179  8244191  8244199  8244209  8244221  8244263
8244277  8244287  8244293  8244311  8244329  8244331  8244343  8244389  8244391  8244407
```

```
8244409  8244463  8244469  8244491  8244503  8244517  8244527  8244553  8244559  8244563
8244569  8244583  8244589  8244611  8244619  8244629  8244631  8244669  8244679  8244683
8244697  8244701  8244707  8244739  8244757  8244763  8244781  8244793  8244799  8244811
8244827  8244829  8244857  8244883  8244893  8244911  8244937  8244941  8244947  8244959
8244989  8244997  8245001  8245033  8245037  8245057  8245091  8245123  8245129  8245147
8245177  8245199  8245217  8245219  8245231  8245241  8245243  8245249  8245267  8245273
8245319  8245343  8245409  8245417  8245421  8245441  8245451  8245453  8245481  8245499
8245507  8245513  8245519  8245547  8245571  8245577  8245579  8245621  8245631  8245649
8245667  8245673  8245693  8245711  8245747  8245751  8245759  8245777  8245789  8245807
8245837  8245843  8245877  8245883  8245921  8245927  8245957  8245973  8245997  8246023
8246039  8246047  8246059  8246081  8246083  8246101  8246113  8246129  8246131  8246143
8246201  8246221  8246233  8246243  8246263  8246267  8246281  8246363  8246369  8246389
8246393  8246417  8246419  8246423  8246461  8246467  8246471  8246477  8246503  8246509
8246533  8246587  8246599  8246621  8246629  8246639  8246647  8246653  8246663
8246677  8246681  8246723  8246729  8246743  8246789  8246803  8246809  8246813  8246827
8246839  8246867  8246879  8246897  8246929  8246939  8246947  8246951  8246981  8246993
8247077  8247089  8247101  8247103  8247199  8247203  8247221  8247229  8247233  8247241
8247247  8247251  8247257  8247293  8247319  8247341  8247359  8247361  8247373  8247377
8247391  8247413  8247427  8247451  8247487  8247509  8247517  8247553  8247557  8247583
8247599  8247641  8247647  8247661  8247697  8247713  8247739  8247763  8247769  8247773
8247791  8247821  8247853  8247859  8247887  8247923  8247947  8247949  8247973  8247991
8247997  8248013  8248021  8248027  8248039  8248049  8248057  8248061  8248063  8248067
8248069  8248081  8248087  8248091  8248117  8248127  8248133  8248157  8248183  8248187
8248211  8248249  8248277  8248301  8248307  8248313  8248321  8248327  8248363  8248369
8248379  8248381  8248391  8248397  8248403  8248423  8248459  8248483  8248501  8248507
8248517  8248531  8248543  8248577  8248637  8248649  8248663  8248687  8248693  8248699
8248711  8248727  8248729  8248739  8248741  8248763  8248769  8248841  8248861  8248873
8248879  8248897  8248901  8248921  8248949  8248957  8248987  8249009  8249023  8249041
8249053  8249057  8249071  8249081  8249089  8249093  8249119  8249123  8249149  8249161
8249177  8249179  8249183  8249191  8249207  8249303  8249309  8249327  8249333  8249357
8249359  8249383  8249389  8249411  8249429  8249431  8249459  8249489  8249491  8249497
8249519  8249531  8249533  8249537  8249551  8249567  8249587  8249597  8249599  8249611
8249621  8249623  8249687  8249699  8249707  8249711  8249713  8249719  8249723  8249783
8249797  8249809  8249827  8249837  8249881  8249909  8249921  8249977  8249993  8250011
8250019  8250037  8250059  8250071  8250079  8250089  8250103  8250107  8250113  8250131
8250133  8250157  8250167  8250173  8250191  8250251  8250257  8250259  8250269  8250293
8250317  8250323  8250329  8250343  8250349  8250373  8250391  8250397  8250419  8250439
8250443  8250461  8250479  8250481  8250493  8250497  8250509  8250547  8250569  8250607
8250631  8250637  8250643  8250653  8250659  8250673  8250691  8250707  8250713  8250727
8250751  8250787  8250793  8250811  8250817  8250833  8250857  8250863  8250871  8250911
8250919  8250937  8250941  8250953  8250961  8250989  8251013  8251027  8251031  8251039
8251049  8251097  8251121  8251151  8251153  8251157  8251183  8251189  8251207  8251219
8251249  8251253  8251267  8251277  8251289  8251337  8251343  8251349  8251351  8251357
8251361  8251379  8251387  8251403  8251421  8251427  8251429  8251483  8251489  8251493
8251501  8251513  8251541  8251561  8251583  8251591  8251597  8251601  8251603  8251651
8251667  8251709  8251717  8251723  8251741  8251751  8251753  8251781  8251807  8251819
8251823  8251843  8251849  8251877  8251907  8251913  8251937  8251939  8251949  8251951
8252017  8252033  8252059  8252093  8252129  8252149  8252183  8252197  8252203  8252219
8252227  8252249  8252297  8252303  8252311  8252339  8252351  8252359  8252371  8252381
8252383  8252399  8252411  8252459  8252509  8252533  8252539  8252549  8252551  8252557
8252567  8252597  8252623  8252641  8252659  8252681  8252687  8252711  8252737  8252747
8252753  8252759  8252771  8252779  8252801  8252807  8252809  8252879  8252891  8252899
8252903  8252917  8252941  8252953  8252957  8252971  8252977  8252989  8253029  8253031
8253053  8253061  8253071  8253079  8253083  8253101  8253149  8253173  8253187
8253199  8253221  8253227  8253281  8253293  8253299  8253337  8253359  8253373  8253383
8253397  8253431  8253461  8253473  8253491  8253499  8253521  8253523  8253541  8253577
8253607  8253611  8253617  8253667  8253671  8253673  8253689  8253691  8253697  8253703
8253737  8253761  8253787  8253793  8253799  8253829  8253851  8253853  8253863  8253887
8253911  8253913  8253919  8253929  8253937  8253943  8253953  8253977  8253989  8253991
8254013  8254019  8254049  8254073  8254097  8254121  8254139  8254177  8254193  8254223
8254229  8254249  8254271  8254283  8254291  8254297  8254307  8254319  8254369  8254373
8254381  8254391  8254397  8254403  8254423  8254429  8254439  8254457  8254507  8254511
8254541  8254549  8254553  8254559  8254577  8254579  8254613  8254627  8254633  8254651
8254669  8254691  8254693  8254699  8254709  8254747  8254787  8254801  8254837  8254849
8254853  8254859  8254871  8254889  8254901  8254933  8254951  8254963  8255029  8255057
8255077  8255087  8255089  8255123  8255129  8255131  8255147  8255171  8255179  8255197
8255213  8255239  8255243  8255249  8255257  8255287  8255323  8255363  8255399  8255407
8255411  8255417  8255419  8255447  8255449  8255453  8255479  8255501  8255509  8255521
8255549  8255561  8255563  8255567  8255587  8255617  8255629  8255647  8255657  8255669
8255701  8255707  8255711  8255713  8255717  8255771  8255783  8255791  8255803  8255831
8255837  8255857  8255869  8255881  8255903  8255909  8255917  8255939  8255963
8255977  8255983  8256007  8256019  8256029  8256037  8256041  8256071  8256091  8256107
8256109  8256139  8256173  8256197  8256221  8256223  8256229  8256233  8256251  8256253
8256257  8256299  8256307  8256337  8256341  8256361  8256383  8256389  8256403  8256427
8256433  8256449  8256463  8256491  8256511  8256541  8256569  8256581  8256607  8256613
8256617  8256629  8256643  8256653  8256673  8256691  8256719  8256727  8256749  8256751
8256779  8256823  8256863  8256889  8256907  8256929  8256961  8256973  8257003  8257009
8257043  8257057  8257157  8257163  8257169  8257177  8257211  8257219  8257237  8257243
8257259  8257261  8257307  8257309  8257313  8257321  8257339  8257349  8257351  8257357
8257363  8257367  8257409  8257423  8257429  8257433  8257451  8257471  8257499  8257519
8257531  8257537  8257553  8257577  8257583  8257589  8257607  8257637  8257643  8257673
8257679  8257681  8257693  8257703  8257709  8257757  8257787  8257789  8257813  8257829
8257841  8257859  8257871  8257889  8257961  8257967  8257973  8257987
8258009  8258017  8258051  8258083  8258093  8258099  8258101  8258111  8258123  8258137
8258143  8258147  8258177  8258197  8258203  8258207  8258213  8258227  8258233  8258249
8258269  8258273  8258281  8258287  8258303  8258321  8258333  8258351  8258377  8258381
8258389  8258401  8258441  8258443  8258461  8258473  8258477  8258479  8258489  8258539
8258543  8258557  8258561  8258567  8258573  8258599  8258611  8258641  8258687  8258689
8258713  8258717  8258737  8258743  8258759  8258797  8258813  8258819  8258837  8258843
```

```
8258867  8258891  8258893  8258903  8258911  8258951  8258953  8258959  8258969  8258983
8259007  8259019  8259037  8259061  8259067  8259071  8259077  8259089  8259101  8259109
8259137  8259143  8259179  8259187  8259197  8259203  8259269  8259271  8259301  8259337
8259353  8259379  8259389  8259401  8259421  8259463  8259479  8259481  8259487  8259497
8259499  8259521  8259527  8259551  8259557  8259571  8259607  8259631  8259649  8259659
8259683  8259701  8259703  8259743  8259767  8259787  8259791  8259799  8259817  8259833
8259859  8259871  8259877  8259887  8259907  8259929  8259973  8260009  8260019  8260027
8260033  8260039  8260051  8260061  8260067  8260073  8260097  8260111  8260123  8260127
8260201  8260223  8260261  8260267  8260271  8260277  8260309  8260327  8260337  8260339
8260349  8260387  8260397  8260403  8260433  8260457  8260489  8260493  8260501  8260513
8260523  8260541  8260547  8260619  8260627  8260643  8260667  8260669  8260697  8260711
8260723  8260771  8260799  8260807  8260823  8260829  8260843  8260871  8260873  8260883
8260919  8260937  8260939  8260943  8260961  8260999  8261017  8261023  8261041  8261107
8261111  8261147  8261161  8261171  8261177  8261233  8261243  8261251  8261261  8261263
8261293  8261327  8261339  8261353  8261359  8261369  8261381  8261399  8261411  8261419
8261441  8261443  8261453  8261467  8261479  8261501  8261509  8261521  8261551  8261567
8261573  8261621  8261641  8261647  8261651  8261653  8261689  8261749  8261783  8261809
8261819  8261833  8261843  8261857  8261879  8261893  8261909  8261917  8261933  8261969
8261993  8261999  8262019  8262031  8262041  8262043  8262047  8262053  8262061  8262077
8262101  8262109  8262113  8262157  8262161  8262173  8262179  8262181  8262193  8262227
8262253  8262257  8262259  8262263  8262277  8262311  8262343  8262347  8262349  8262367
8262379  8262383  8262427  8262431  8262437  8262467  8262479  8262481  8262487  8262491
8262509  8262517  8262533  8262547  8262559  8262571  8262599  8262601  8262613  8262619
8262623  8262637  8262677  8262691  8262719  8262743  8262757  8262769  8262809  8262811
8262823  8262827  8262829  8262841  8262857  8262869  8262889  8262913  8262937  8262949
8262977  8262979  8262983  8262997  8263033  8263063  8263097  8263147  8263153  8263169
8263183  8263223  8263237  8263249  8263291  8263301  8263313  8263331  8263357  8263369
8263373  8263379  8263433  8263441  8263471  8263483  8263501  8263511  8263523  8263531
8263553  8263571  8263573  8263583  8263589  8263597  8263621  8263627  8263631  8263643
8263657  8263663  8263667  8263679  8263709  8263733  8263769  8263771  8263781  8263789
8263799  8263823  8263859  8263889  8263897  8263901  8263909  8263951  8263961  8263973
8263979  8264027  8264033  8264059  8264099  8264119  8264141  8264147  8264167  8264171
8264231  8264233  8264239  8264281  8264293  8264309  8264317  8264327  8264353  8264369
8264387  8264401  8264407  8264419  8264423  8264437  8264441  8264447  8264467  8264513
8264537  8264551  8264587  8264591  8264593  8264611  8264689  8264713  8264723  8264731
8264749  8264777  8264783  8264819  8264831  8264833  8264869  8264887  8264899  8264909
8264911  8264917  8264923  8264939  8264953  8264957  8264959  8264999  8265017  8265041
8265107  8265121  8265137  8265139  8265151  8265157  8265161  8265167  8265197  8265199
8265227  8265233  8265239  8265259  8265289  8265293  8265311  8265329  8265343  8265359
8265371  8265379  8265407  8265419  8265427  8265431  8265443  8265449  8265457  8265463
8265473  8265511  8265539  8265557  8265617  8265619  8265629  8265637  8265659  8265679
8265701  8265713  8265731  8265737  8265743  8265769  8265773  8265787  8265793  8265811
8265821  8265833  8265877  8265889  8265919  8265973  8265977  8265979  8265989  8266001
8266003  8266043  8266061  8266067  8266079  8266081  8266091  8266099  8266109  8266129
8266151  8266163  8266187  8266211  8266217  8266229  8266241  8266253  8266309  8266319
8266331  8266337  8266339  8266351  8266373  8266411  8266417  8266439  8266457  8266477
8266487  8266513  8266519  8266561  8266567  8266571  8266579  8266597  8266613  8266633
8266663  8266697  8266703  8266723  8266751  8266759  8266807  8266829  8266837  8266849
8266859  8266861  8266889  8266891  8266897  8266931  8266939  8266949  8266961  8266963
8266997  8267003  8267009  8267029  8267041  8267047  8267069  8267087  8267101  8267107
8267123  8267167  8267179  8267201  8267209  8267227  8267251  8267263  8267267  8267333
8267339  8267341  8267351  8267353  8267383  8267393  8267443  8267447  8267459  8267471
8267503  8267521  8267533  8267543  8267549  8267561  8267579  8267591  8267647  8267657
8267659  8267663  8267671  8267681  8267711  8267719  8267747  8267789  8267801  8267807
8267837  8267839  8267851  8267887  8267891  8267951  8267953  8267981  8267999  8268023
8268031  8268037  8268067  8268077  8268079  8268149  8268151  8268157  8268179  8268187
8268203  8268209  8268223  8268229  8268241  8268263  8268283  8268301  8268317  8268331
8268343  8268349  8268383  8268389  8268397  8268419  8268433  8268493  8268497  8268499
8268517  8268527  8268539  8268541  8268563  8268577  8268607  8268619  8268641  8268653
8268679  8268691  8268697  8268713  8268739  8268751  8268761  8268763  8268779  8268803
8268823  8268829  8268833  8268859  8268863  8268889  8268893  8268899  8268907  8268913
8268917  8268941  8268947  8268979  8268989  8268991  8269013  8269043  8269049  8269061
8269087  8269091  8269103  8269109  8269111  8269117  8269127  8269139  8269141  8269171
8269187  8269189  8269211  8269229  8269231  8269243  8269271  8269273  8269279  8269291
8269297  8269309  8269319  8269333  8269337  8269363  8269369  8269399  8269409  8269411
8269423  8269439  8269447  8269451  8269477  8269487  8269493  8269507  8269511  8269517
8269519  8269559  8269567  8269589  8269601  8269619  8269663  8269687  8269691  8269711
8269739  8269753  8269757  8269763  8269819  8269841  8269843  8269873  8269891  8269897
8269909  8269931  8269967  8269991  8269993  8269999  8270021  8270027  8270029  8270033
8270039  8270047  8270057  8270063  8270077  8270153  8270201  8270209  8270219  8270221
8270231  8270237  8270239  8270281  8270299  8270303  8270309  8270323  8270359  8270417
8270419  8270429  8270461  8270467  8270477  8270489  8270513  8270519  8270527  8270531
8270533  8270557  8270599  8270609  8270617  8270623  8270671  8270677  8270693  8270699
8270711  8270737  8270761  8270767  8270791  8270803  8270813  8270819  8270839  8270849
8270881  8270897  8270903  8270923  8270939  8270953  8270963  8270981  8271019  8271041
8271047  8271049  8271059  8271077  8271103  8271113  8271161  8271167  8271169  8271181
8271227  8271257  8271259  8271271  8271281  8271301  8271317  8271323  8271331  8271371
8271377  8271391  8271407  8271443  8271457  8271493  8271499  8271509  8271511  8271521
8271533  8271547  8271569  8271581  8271587  8271607  8271611  8271617  8271643  8271647
8271721  8271727  8271737  8271773  8271793  8271803  8271811  8271817  8271829  8271839
8271841  8271847  8271871  8271883  8271889  8271941  8271943  8271959  8271983  8272057
8272067  8272073  8272091  8272093  8272097  8272129  8272153  8272171  8272177  8272189
8272219  8272241  8272247  8272261  8272267  8272273  8272301  8272309  8272321  8272333
8272343  8272351  8272357  8272403  8272409  8272441  8272457  8272463  8272483  8272493
8272513  8272531  8272541  8272553  8272597  8272603  8272609  8272613  8272633  8272661
8272673  8272681  8272697  8272699  8272703  8272711  8272723  8272733  8272751  8272757
8272763  8272769  8272787  8272819  8272853  8272861  8272879  8272883  8272909  8272933
8272937  8272949  8272951  8272963  8272969  8272973  8272997  8273047  8273051  8273119
8273129  8273137  8273143  8273197  8273231  8273257  8273263  8273299  8273327  8273333
```

```
8273389  8273411  8273413  8273437  8273443  8273449  8273453  8273467  8273477  8273479
8273527  8273539  8273549  8273579  8273593  8273599  8273609  8273623  8273627  8273647
8273651  8273653  8273659  8273693  8273711  8273719  8273753  8273761  8273773  8273779
8273789  8273791  8273801  8273827  8273831  8273879  8273899  8273921  8273933  8273953
8273959  8273963  8273971  8273981  8274011  8274023  8274029  8274037  8274041  8274047
8274059  8274061  8274073  8274083  8274107  8274109  8274113  8274131  8274137  8274143
8274157  8274229  8274239  8274247  8274271  8274281  8274283  8274313  8274317  8274323
8274379  8274401  8274403  8274437  8274439  8274449  8274463  8274493  8274499  8274509
8274521  8274527  8274547  8274559  8274611  8274653  8274669  8274667  8274677  8274689
8274703  8274713  8274719  8274727  8274751  8274793  8274803  8274811  8274817  8274839
8274841  8274863  8274881  8274883  8274901  8274911  8274913  8274919  8274941  8274949
8274977  8274983  8274997  8275019  8275027  8275037  8275067  8275093  8275097  8275117
8275133  8275159  8275177  8275181  8275187  8275213  8275229  8275249  8275259  8275271
8275283  8275291  8275301  8275303  8275343  8275369  8275381  8275391  8275403  8275409
8275417  8275439  8275451  8275453  8275459  8275471  8275493  8275511  8275513  8275523
8275541  8275559  8275567  8275571  8275573  8275577  8275601  8275613  8275633  8275649
8275703  8275711  8275717  8275723  8275733  8275763  8275783  8275793  8275819  8275873
8275879  8275903  8275987  8275997  8276017  8276029  8276057  8276063  8276071  8276087
8276111  8276117  8276131  8276141  8276143  8276173  8276189  8276201  8276207  8276227
8276231  8276273  8276311  8276327  8276329  8276341  8276351  8276363  8276369  8276431
8276441  8276447  8276491  8276509  8276519  8276531  8276537  8276539  8276551  8276563
8276591  8276599  8276617  8276627  8276669  8276693  8276701  8276713  8276743  8276777
8276797  8276819  8276831  8276833  8276857  8276867  8276869  8276881  8276887  8276893
8276899  8276903  8276921  8276923  8276953  8276993  8276999  8277001  8277019  8277023
8277043  8277047  8277083  8277097  8277119  8277149  8277163  8277167  8277173  8277193
8277211  8277221  8277229  8277257  8277271  8277299  8277323  8277329  8277343  8277359
8277361  8277377  8277391  8277427  8277439  8277461  8277469  8277473  8277481  8277491
8277509  8277547  8277553  8277587  8277601  8277611  8277617  8277637  8277653  8277671
8277683  8277697  8277701  8277707  8277719  8277757  8277767  8277809  8277811  8277851
8277853  8277881  8277889  8277923  8277943  8277949  8277967  8277991  8278001  8278013
8278017  8278037  8278043  8278073  8278097  8278111  8278141  8278159  8278199  8278211
8278247  8278261  8278279  8278297  8278301  8278307  8278313  8278327  8278339  8278363
8278373  8278393  8278411  8278421  8278477  8278481  8278511  8278549  8278553  8278559
8278561  8278577  8278583  8278603  8278619  8278631  8278637  8278649  8278651  8278657
8278663  8278681  8278687  8278693  8278709  8278729  8278763  8278783  8278789  8278793
8278799  8278801  8278811  8278817  8278841  8278849  8278867  8278883  8278931  8278937
8278943  8278951  8278961  8278969  8278973  8278987  8278999  8279023  8279027  8279053
8279093  8279107  8279113  8279147  8279203  8279207  8279209  8279213  8279233  8279237
8279281  8279291  8279317  8279329  8279353  8279377  8279389  8279399  8279407  8279423
8279461  8279489  8279533  8279539  8279543  8279549  8279569  8279597  8279627  8279633
8279639  8279641  8279651  8279653  8279657  8279669  8279671  8279683  8279699  8279729
8279741  8279743  8279771  8279837  8279857  8279881  8279899  8279917  8279923  8279933
8279959  8279963  8279983  8279987  8280011  8280043  8280047  8280049  8280053  8280127
8280133  8280149  8280157  8280169  8280187  8280197  8280199  8280247  8280263
8280277  8280281  8280287  8280289  8280331  8280353  8280359  8280367  8280373  8280397
8280407  8280431  8280439  8280449  8280451  8280469  8280487  8280491  8280497  8280499
8280509  8280511  8280521  8280557  8280571  8280583  8280593  8280607  8280619  8280653
8280677  8280703  8280707  8280721  8280737  8280739  8280743  8280749  8280761  8280763
8280787  8280791  8280799  8280817  8280821  8280841  8280911  8280917  8280929  8280949
8280959  8280967  8280971  8281003  8281019  8281043  8281067  8281073  8281099  8281129
8281157  8281171  8281199  8281201  8281223  8281237  8281249  8281291  8281313  8281319
8281367  8281373  8281379  8281381  8281387  8281391  8281393  8281411  8281423  8281439
8281457  8281459  8281463  8281477  8281487  8281517  8281531  8281547  8281571  8281573
8281577  8281579  8281591  8281597  8281639  8281643  8281687  8281709  8281751  8281753
8281789  8281799  8281811  8281813  8281831  8281837  8281859  8281879  8281927  8281943
8281979  8281981  8281993  8282003  8282039  8282063  8282083  8282107  8282129  8282137
8282159  8282171  8282189  8282201  8282203  8282227  8282237  8282249  8282269  8282279
8282291  8282297  8282317  8282327  8282341  8282357  8282377  8282401  8282411
8282419  8282437  8282441  8282453  8282467  8282497  8282513  8282567  8282569  8282581
8282623  8282627  8282629  8282633  8282639  8282671  8282683  8282693  8282713  8282717
8282731  8282753  8282761  8282767  8282773  8282809  8282821  8282831  8282837  8282843
8282851  8282873  8282887  8282891  8282903  8282941  8282959  8282969  8282987  8283001
8283043  8283049  8283053  8283061  8283083  8283089  8283101  8283109  8283161  8283181
8283193  8283203  8283217  8283257  8283263  8283269  8283281  8283287  8283329  8283349
8283361  8283371  8283377  8283397  8283433  8283439  8283461  8283463  8283481  8283493
8283503  8283521  8283547  8283551  8283559  8283581  8283593  8283629  8283637  8283683
8283689  8283697  8283713  8283719  8283721  8283731  8283733  8283757  8283761  8283767
8283787  8283799  8283809  8283817  8283857  8283859  8283871  8283889  8283901
8283929  8283949  8283971  8283973  8283997  8284007  8284033  8284051  8284061  8284063
8284069  8284093  8284097  8284103  8284123  8284127  8284141  8284153  8284181  8284183
8284193  8284201  8284207  8284217  8284229  8284231  8284273  8284277  8284303  8284307
8284319  8284363  8284373  8284379  8284391  8284417  8284427  8284433  8284447  8284453
8284469  8284477  8284481  8284487  8284489  8284519  8284537  8284541  8284547  8284553
8284567  8284579  8284597  8284607  8284613  8284621  8284637  8284649  8284663  8284667
8284687  8284693  8284699  8284709  8284739  8284823  8284841  8284849  8284873  8284877
8284879  8284883  8284889  8284891  8284937  8284949  8284951  8284961  8284963  8284979
8284987  8284999  8285021  8285023  8285027  8285051  8285059  8285063  8285071  8285087
8285089  8285093  8285107  8285177  8285183  8285191  8285201  8285227  8285231  8285237
8285243  8285257  8285269  8285293  8285317  8285323  8285363  8285377  8285383  8285393
8285399  8285411  8285461  8285471  8285491  8285507  8285509  8285513  8285527  8285531
8285533  8285549  8285551  8285581  8285591  8285593  8285597  8285603  8285611  8285617
8285621  8285639  8285657  8285659  8285687  8285723  8285789  8285791  8285831  8285833
8285839  8285857  8285869  8285873  8285887  8285899  8285903  8285933  8285941  8285947
8285983  8285993  8286001  8286029  8286037  8286097  8286101  8286107  8286121  8286133
8286149  8286163  8286169  8286193  8286203  8286209  8286211  8286221  8286247  8286251
8286253  8286281  8286283  8286287  8286349  8286379  8286433  8286437  8286461  8286511
8286541  8286569  8286571  8286583  8286671  8286673  8286683  8286689  8286713  8286731
8286743  8286767  8286791  8286809  8286821  8286857  8286881  8286913  8286937  8286947
8286977  8286979  8286989  8286991  8286997  8287067  8287079  8287091  8287093  8287099
```

```
8287117  8287121  8287141  8287159  8287171  8287229  8287271  8287273  8287283  8287309
8287327  8287339  8287343  8287351  8287361  8287373  8287403  8287421  8287427  8287469
8287481  8287493  8287507  8287523  8287537  8287549  8287561  8287607  8287679  8287693
8287711  8287717  8287723  8287729  8287793  8287801  8287813  8287817  8287831  8287837
8287847  8287859  8287861  8287871  8287883  8287921  8287991  8288011  8288017  8288023
8288029  8288041  8288057  8288069  8288081  8288083  8288099  8288107  8288141  8288167
8288177  8288179  8288183  8288213  8288249  8288263  8288311  8288321  8288339  8288361
8288353  8288411  8288417  8288419  8288447  8288453  8288459  8288473  8288477  8288479
8288521  8288531  8288543  8288557  8288569  8288587  8288593  8288597  8288627  8288633
8288647  8288653  8288669  8288681  8288689  8288729  8288737  8288743  8288803  8288831
8288849  8288857  8288869  8288881  8288893  8288897  8288899  8288923  8288927  8288933
8288957  8288977  8289023  8289031  8289053  8289079  8289101  8289103  8289119  8289139
8289143  8289161  8289191  8289247  8289271  8289277  8289313  8289349  8289367  8289383
8289401  8289403  8289409  8289419  8289433  8289451  8289461  8289469  8289487  8289521
8289527  8289539  8289551  8289577  8289581  8289587  8289607  8289623  8289647  8289649
8289653  8289703  8289731  8289751  8289763  8289767  8289817  8289847  8289857  8289877
8289881  8289899  8289901  8289917  8289949  8289997  8290043  8290063  8290069  8290081
8290103  8290127  8290129  8290133  8290151  8290153  8290229  8290273  8290277  8290291
8290297  8290309  8290319  8290363  8290369  8290393  8290397  8290409  8290411  8290421
8290427  8290453  8290459  8290463  8290481  8290489  8290507  8290523  8290531  8290559
8290561  8290567  8290591  8290613  8290619  8290643  8290657  8290661  8290663  8290691
8290729  8290769  8290771  8290811  8290817  8290819  8290831  8290837  8290861  8290889
8290901  8290903  8290907  8290921  8290927  8290939  8290943  8290967  8290987  8290991
8290999  8291009  8291029  8291033  8291039  8291047  8291069  8291081  8291083  8291089
8291099  8291111  8291113  8291117  8291159  8291207  8291209  8291221  8291233  8291237
8291243  8291249  8291263  8291281  8291299  8291333  8291341  8291357  8291399  8291401
8291407  8291443  8291483  8291509  8291519  8291527  8291531  8291551  8291557  8291573
8291609  8291623  8291639  8291653  8291659  8291671  8291677  8291681  8291687  8291711
8291713  8291729  8291741  8291743  8291749  8291779  8291807  8291813  8291831  8291839
8291879  8291893  8291909  8291929  8291939  8291947  8291953  8291981  8291989  8292001
8292017  8292023  8292043  8292047  8292071  8292079  8292091  8292101  8292103  8292133
8292187  8292203  8292217  8292247  8292293  8292301  8292307  8292331  8292337  8292343
8292353  8292359  8292367  8292419  8292451  8292461  8292491  8292503  8292527  8292547
8292557  8292629  8292643  8292649  8292659  8292667  8292671  8292677  8292689  8292707
8292737  8292761  8292763  8292803  8292859  8292887  8292901  8292913  8292917  8292919
8292941  8292943  8292959  8292967  8292979  8292983  8292997  8293003  8293007  8293039
8293049  8293057  8293073  8293079  8293121  8293141  8293171  8293223  8293231  8293237
8293283  8293289  8293303  8293319  8293321  8293339  8293349  8293361  8293393  8293423
8293429  8293451  8293459  8293469  8293471  8293477  8293487  8293511  8293577  8293591
8293613  8293619  8293627  8293631  8293651  8293673  8293687  8293699  8293717  8293751
8293757  8293759  8293763  8293783  8293801  8293819  8293829  8293847  8293853  8293877
8293889  8293903  8293921  8293933  8293939  8293979  8293993  8294009  8294021  8294123
8294159  8294171  8294173  8294183  8294189  8294197  8294201  8294213  8294233  8294239
8294263  8294303  8294309  8294311  8294339  8294347  8294357  8294359  8294369  8294381
8294411  8294413  8294437  8294459  8294471  8294483  8294491  8294501  8294509  8294543
8294569  8294579  8294593  8294603  8294611  8294641  8294653  8294707  8294729  8294731
8294749  8294753  8294779  8294809  8294821  8294837  8294851  8294857  8294863  8294879
8294893  8294911  8294941  8294959  8294971  8294999  8295037  8295047  8295061  8295097
8295101  8295107  8295109  8295113  8295121  8295127  8295137  8295139  8295163  8295169
8295179  8295211  8295239  8295241  8295251  8295263  8295271  8295293  8295317  8295347
8295349  8295373  8295379  8295403  8295449  8295467  8295481  8295491  8295493  8295503
8295527  8295557  8295563  8295583  8295587  8295589  8295607  8295611  8295619  8295629
8295649  8295671  8295673  8295697  8295701  8295737  8295743  8295751  8295787  8295811
8295839  8295841  8295849  8295851  8295857  8295863  8295897  8295901  8295907  8295919
8295921  8295953  8295961  8295967  8295971  8295977  8296069  8296081  8296087  8296097
8296133  8296139  8296147  8296167  8296169  8296181  8296193  8296199  8296213  8296219
8296247  8296259  8296271  8296273  8296283  8296333  8296339  8296363  8296367  8296373
8296381  8296397  8296411  8296417  8296429  8296447  8296513  8296517  8296553  8296571
8296577  8296579  8296591  8296627  8296649  8296657  8296693  8296699  8296703  8296709
8296723  8296733  8296751  8296781  8296789  8296819  8296823  8296831  8296853  8296879
8296889  8296891  8296913  8296919  8296921  8296927  8296943  8296973  8296999  8297011
8297017  8297027  8297059  8297063  8297099  8297123  8297137  8297141  8297143  8297171
8297197  8297249  8297269  8297279  8297321  8297329  8297339  8297351  8297353  8297369
8297413  8297431  8297437  8297441  8297459  8297473  8297501  8297519  8297537  8297543
8297563  8297573  8297587  8297591  8297609  8297617  8297633  8297659  8297669  8297689
8297693  8297711  8297713  8297719  8297747  8297761  8297789  8297797  8297831  8297873
8297881  8297909  8297941  8297977  8297981  8297999  8298001  8298019  8298029  8298047
8298067  8298071  8298077  8298119  8298127  8298131  8298149  8298163  8298187  8298209
8298221  8298223  8298229  8298247  8298259  8298287  8298293  8298313  8298337  8298347
8298361  8298373  8298427  8298443  8298467  8298473  8298487  8298509  8298529  8298539
8298541  8298547  8298559  8298583  8298593  8298617  8298629  8298659  8298661  8298673
8298683  8298691  8298707  8298709  8298721  8298733  8298749  8298751  8298779  8298781
8298803  8298811  8298817  8298847  8298911  8298923  8298937  8298943  8298949  8299001
8299007  8299013  8299037  8299073  8299091  8299099  8299121  8299127  8299147  8299153
8299157  8299169  8299259  8299283  8299303  8299309  8299321  8299331  8299367  8299381
8299411  8299427  8299439  8299441  8299453  8299463  8299483  8299493  8299513  8299547
8299549  8299567  8299583  8299591  8299607  8299639  8299649  8299651  8299663  8299667
8299673  8299679  8299703  8299717  8299741  8299763  8299769  8299783  8299787  8299793
8299891  8299919  8299931  8299933  8299939  8299969  8299981  8300009  8300041  8300057
8300069  8300077  8300101  8300129  8300137  8300141  8300147  8300167  8300183  8300191
8300197  8300213  8300239  8300261  8300269  8300273  8300317  8300323  8300353  8300371
8300377  8300381  8300389  8300393  8300417  8300423  8300431  8300441  8300443  8300477
8300497  8300503  8300519  8300521  8300531  8300557  8300569  8300597  8300603  8300659
8300671  8300683  8300687  8300689  8300711  8300731  8300741  8300749  8300753  8300771
8300783  8300797  8300801  8300813  8300827  8300833  8300837  8300863  8300869  8300881
8300893  8300899  8300909  8300911  8300917  8300921  8300927  8300933  8300959  8300977
8300993  8301011  8301017  8301023  8301031  8301037  8301053  8301067  8301103  8301121
8301133  8301143  8301169  8301179  8301199  8301217  8301257  8301259  8301263  8301269
8301277  8301289  8301301  8301313  8301329  8301353  8301361  8301379  8301401  8301421
```

```
8301437  8301463  8301467  8301481  8301547  8301571  8301581  8301599  8301611  8301619
8301637  8301641  8301659  8301677  8301679  8301691  8301701  8301703  8301709  8301731
8301739  8301757  8301823  8301851  8301857  8301869  8301877  8301883  8301901  8301911
8301947  8301961  8301983  8301991  8302013  8302027  8302043  8302061  8302123  8302153
8302157  8302159  8302169  8302181  8302193  8302211  8302219  8302247  8302267  8302277
8302309  8302313  8302321  8302351  8302367  8302391  8302403  8302417  8302423  8302447
8302457  8302493  8302499  8302501  8302523  8302529  8302537  8302571  8302577  8302583
8302589  8302603  8302633  8302673  8302687  8302703  8302709  8302711  8302717  8302733
8302751  8302759  8302769  8302781  8302799  8302813  8302831  8302843  8302871  8302891
8302949  8302963  8302967  8302991  8302993  8302997  8303003  8303017  8303027  8303041
8303047  8303051  8303063  8303081  8303101  8303111  8303117  8303131  8303143  8303167
8303179  8303189  8303201  8303203  8303213  8303219  8303221  8303249  8303261  8303263
8303287  8303291  8303303  8303333  8303341  8303411  8303441  8303447  8303459  8303467
8303479  8303501  8303509  8303539  8303543  8303549  8303557  8303587  8303597  8303609
8303623  8303653  8303681  8303683  8303693  8303717  8303723  8303749  8303777  8303783
8303791  8303821  8303839  8303843  8303849  8303857  8303861  8303863  8303903  8303909
8303923  8303929  8303941  8303957  8304061  8304091  8304103  8304133  8304151  8304167
8304193  8304209  8304223  8304229  8304251  8304259  8304271  8304281  8304301  8304337
8304343  8304371  8304379  8304389  8304397  8304419  8304421  8304433  8304437  8304467
8304481  8304503  8304557  8304599  8304607  8304617  8304629  8304641  8304671  8304677
8304707  8304713  8304733  8304739  8304757  8304763  8304773  8304797  8304809  8304827
8304839  8304841  8304883  8304887  8304889  8304913  8304917  8304937  8304943  8304949
8304953  8304973  8304979  8304997  8305009  8305021  8305039  8305051  8305081  8305091
8305097  8305103  8305133  8305159  8305177  8305181  8305183  8305207  8305217  8305243
8305267  8305273  8305307  8305313  8305327  8305343  8305357  8305361  8305403  8305433
8305459  8305481  8305487  8305499  8305519  8305529  8305541  8305543  8305567  8305573
8305589  8305597  8305669  8305681  8305697  8305709  8305711  8305729  8305733  8305753
8305769  8305777  8305811  8305813  8305849  8305859  8305873  8305883  8305889  8305901
8305931  8305951  8305987  8305993  8306027  8306029  8306041  8306063  8306069  8306071
8306099  8306117  8306119  8306131  8306143  8306147  8306153  8306161  8306201  8306227
8306237  8306261  8306273  8306279  8306293  8306299  8306323  8306369  8306377  8306393
8306407  8306423  8306429  8306449  8306453  8306461  8306471  8306479  8306483  8306491
8306509  8306513  8306521  8306533  8306581  8306587  8306603  8306609  8306621  8306647
8306651  8306653  8306677  8306681  8306687  8306699  8306717  8306741  8306773  8306803
8306821  8306867  8306873  8306891  8306911  8306927  8306951  8306957  8307001  8307007
8307017  8307043  8307049  8307077  8307139  8307151  8307157  8307179  8307193
8307223  8307239  8307241  8307251  8307283  8307307  8307319  8307323  8307331  8307359
8307361  8307413  8307437  8307443  8307469  8307487  8307491  8307493  8307521  8307547
8307571  8307583  8307631  8307641  8307661  8307667  8307683  8307709  8307751  8307787
8307791  8307797  8307809  8307823  8307841  8307857  8307863  8307881  8307913  8307919
8307931  8307961  8307977  8307983  8308021  8308033  8308043  8308063  8308103  8308133
8308163  8308177  8308219  8308231  8308241  8308243  8308247  8308259  8308271  8308277
8308343  8308367  8308369  8308373  8308409  8308423  8308429  8308463  8308477  8308481
8308483  8308493  8308499  8308501  8308507  8308511  8308537  8308541  8308571  8308579
8308583  8308591  8308637  8308649  8308669  8308693  8308697  8308709  8308723  8308739
8308747  8308753  8308759  8308763  8308789  8308823  8308841  8308879  8308891  8308919
8308921  8308931  8308939  8308943  8308973  8308981  8308991  8308997  8308999  8309009
8309011  8309033  8309037  8309123  8309143  8309149  8309153  8309159  8309173  8309227
8309261  8309291  8309293  8309297  8309303  8309339  8309369  8309381  8309387  8309401
8309437  8309443  8309453  8309467  8309473  8309491  8309503  8309507  8309527  8309533
8309537  8309551  8309557  8309563  8309579  8309591  8309599  8309611  8309629  8309633
8309641  8309659  8309677  8309687  8309701  8309713  8309759  8309761  8309771  8309779
8309803  8309849  8309869  8309881  8309909  8309963  8309989  8309999  8310007  8310031
8310047  8310073  8310097  8310131  8310149  8310151  8310157  8310173  8310191  8310193
8310233  8310251  8310259  8310271  8310287  8310293  8310299  8310307  8310343  8310361
8310371  8310377  8310389  8310397  8310409  8310427  8310431  8310441  8310461  8310469
8310503  8310527  8310529  8310551  8310593  8310611  8310623  8310629  8310641  8310647
8310661  8310667  8310677  8310683  8310689  8310691  8310703  8310713  8310719  8310749
8310767  8310781  8310787  8310803  8310833  8310851  8310859  8310871  8310899  8310919
8310931  8310941  8310947  8310959  8310971  8310979  8310989  8311003  8311021  8311031
8311099  8311111  8311117  8311183  8311187  8311201  8311217  8311231  8311241  8311243
8311253  8311267  8311279  8311291  8311297  8311309  8311319  8311321  8311327  8311357
8311361  8311393  8311399  8311409  8311447  8311451  8311469  8311481  8311519  8311543
8311547  8311549  8311571  8311573  8311591  8311601  8311609  8311613  8311649  8311663
8311687  8311697  8311711  8311729  8311733  8311739  8311781  8311801  8311811  8311817
8311871  8311883  8311883  8311907  8311909  8311957  8311981  8311991  8312033  8312093
8312113  8312119  8312137  8312147  8312153  8312159  8312173  8312179  8312189  8312191
8312197  8312207  8312209  8312219  8312233  8312237  8312243  8312251  8312257  8312267
8312273  8312281  8312321  8312327  8312347  8312351  8312363  8312377  8312383  8312389
8312411  8312413  8312417  8312419  8312441  8312461  8312483  8312497  8312501  8312503
8312527  8312537  8312539  8312567  8312587  8312593  8312599  8312611  8312651  8312657
8312663  8312669  8312693  8312713  8312737  8312789  8312849  8312851  8312903  8312911
8312921  8312947  8312951  8312957  8312971  8312977  8312979  8312981  8312987  8312989
8312999  8313001  8313029  8313043  8313077  8313101  8313113  8313133  8313161  8313181
8313199  8313229  8313247  8313251  8313257  8313259  8313269  8313353  8313359  8313377
8313413  8313433  8313443  8313449  8313457  8313463  8313479  8313509  8313533  8313541
8313551  8313553  8313563  8313581  8313587  8313589  8313619  8313637  8313647  8313661
8313667  8313671  8313677  8313707  8313719  8313733  8313737  8313763  8313791  8313803
8313847  8313869  8313871  8313883  8313889  8313911  8313913  8313917  8313919  8313931
8313941  8313953  8313961  8313979  8313989  8314049  8314067  8314069  8314073  8314099
8314121  8314157  8314181  8314183  8314199  8314223  8314277  8314279  8314289  8314297
8314333  8314337  8314357  8314363  8314367  8314373  8314379  8314391  8314399  8314403
8314409  8314433  8314457  8314459  8314487  8314507  8314531  8314567  8314573  8314577
8314591  8314601  8314613  8314643  8314651  8314679  8314681  8314711  8314771  8314777
8314807  8314843  8314871  8314897  8314903  8314907  8314927  8314931  8314939  8314949
8314979  8314981  8314991  8314993  8314997  8315009  8315053  8315063  8315081  8315089
8315107  8315113  8315137  8315143  8315149  8315201  8315221  8315231  8315239  8315249
8315267  8315273  8315317  8315323  8315327  8315341  8315353  8315371  8315387  8315393
8315399  8315413  8315429  8315441  8315467  8315477  8315507  8315509  8315513  8315543
```

```
8315551  8315561  8315599  8315603  8315609  8315611  8315651  8315689  8315701  8315707
8315729  8315731  8315767  8315773  8315789  8315807  8315809  8315821  8315831  8315887
8315927  8315969  8315971  8315987  8315999  8316001  8316047  8316089  8316103  8316131
8316151  8316163  8316173  8316181  8316193  8316199  8316211  8316221  8316289  8316293
8316299  8316307  8316337  8316353  8316377  8316419  8316421  8316437  8316449  8316457
8316467  8316479  8316491  8316493  8316523  8316541  8316559  8316569  8316577  8316611
8316617  8316619  8316641  8316647  8316653  8316677  8316691  8316701  8316709  8316739
8316743  8316751  8316799  8316811  8316821  8316829  8316839  8316853  8316857  8316863
8316887  8316899  8316947  8316967  8316989  8316991  8317009  8317013  8317069  8317093
8317121  8317157  8317213  8317223  8317241  8317247  8317259  8317271  8317273  8317277
8317297  8317303  8317339  8317367  8317373  8317381  8317417  8317423  8317427  8317429
8317433  8317453  8317457  8317483  8317487  8317511  8317523  8317531  8317549  8317553
8317571  8317601  8317609  8317657  8317663  8317669  8317691  8317741  8317747  8317753
8317781  8317787  8317807  8317843  8317861  8317871  8317891  8317909  8317949  8317999
8318027  8318047  8318059  8318069  8318071  8318077  8318113  8318129  8318161  8318173
8318179  8318197  8318227  8318231  8318237  8318239  8318243  8318263  8318267  8318279
8318281  8318291  8318293  8318327  8318329  8318339  8318347  8318353  8318357  8318381
8318411  8318413  8318417  8318419  8318467  8318477  8318489  8318507  8318533  8318537
8318543  8318549  8318581  8318591  8318603  8318641  8318647  8318657  8318659  8318669
8318683  8318689  8318693  8318699  8318701  8318707  8318711  8318759  8318809  8318813
8318837  8318839  8318867  8318897  8318917  8318927  8318951  8318971  8318977  8318983
8318987  8318993  8319029  8319037  8319041  8319049  8319071  8319083  8319089  8319109
8319121  8319127  8319133  8319161  8319163  8319209  8319211  8319217  8319221  8319247
8319257  8319263  8319271  8319277  8319281  8319293  8319313  8319319  8319331  8319343
8319373  8319379  8319391  8319401  8319407  8319419  8319427  8319431  8319481  8319497
8319499  8319503  8319527  8319529  8319533  8319541  8319557  8319559  8319581  8319617
8319659  8319677  8319691  8319697  8319719  8319733  8319757  8319791  8319803  8319821
8319833  8319841  8319847  8319863  8319869  8319877  8319881  8319889  8319923  8319937
8319943  8319947  8319959  8319997  8320001  8320033  8320051  8320057  8320061  8320063
8320073  8320087  8320093  8320097  8320111  8320159  8320177  8320211  8320219  8320229
8320267  8320289  8320313  8320373  8320379  8320381  8320387  8320393  8320409  8320451
8320453  8320469  8320471  8320519  8320541  8320547  8320567  8320591  8320601  8320603
8320619  8320657  8320681  8320693  8320717  8320729  8320747  8320777  8320783  8320789
8320811  8320813  8320817  8320831  8320847  8320849  8320853  8320859  8320861  8320903
8320919  8320943  8321003  8321011  8321029  8321039  8321081  8321111  8321119  8321123
8321141  8321153  8321161  8321171  8321213  8321227  8321249  8321273  8321281  8321293
8321309  8321311  8321321  8321323  8321359  8321389  8321393  8321429  8321503  8321507
8321519  8321527  8321539  8321543  8321549  8321557  8321591  8321603  8321611  8321627
8321657  8321683  8321723  8321743  8321779  8321783  8321801  8321809  8321813  8321843
8321851  8321861  8321881  8321897  8321903  8321941  8321977  8321983  8321987  8322001
8322023  8322029  8322121  8322141  8322187  8322191  8322211  8322233  8322239  8322241
8322253  8322257  8322269  8322277  8322283  8322287  8322289  8322313  8322317  8322329
8322341  8322359  8322371  8322383  8322397  8322403  8322409  8322439  8322451  8322467
8322491  8322529  8322533  8322541  8322557  8322569  8322581  8322593  8322637  8322647
8322661  8322679  8322683  8322689  8322719  8322731  8322733  8322737  8322751  8322761
8322773  8322799  8322807  8322841  8322863  8322871  8322883  8322907  8322917  8322929
8322947  8322967  8322989  8322997  8323009  8323027  8323031  8323043  8323069  8323099
8323103  8323109  8323151  8323153  8323163  8323169  8323177  8323201  8323213  8323229
8323243  8323247  8323253  8323291  8323297  8323339  8323363  8323373  8323379  8323391
8323397  8323439  8323457  8323481  8323487  8323499  8323517  8323537  8323541  8323571
8323603  8323613  8323619  8323643  8323649  8323681  8323741  8323751  8323753  8323759
8323771  8323787  8323789  8323793  8323817  8323823  8323831  8323849  8323859  8323867
8323873  8323883  8323891  8323933  8323937  8323949  8323951  8323963  8323967  8323979
8323981  8324023  8324039  8324051  8324053  8324059  8324077  8324083  8324143  8324167
8324171  8324191  8324201  8324207  8324219  8324227  8324231  8324269  8324287  8324333
8324347  8324401  8324411  8324419  8324447  8324453  8324471  8324473  8324483  8324497
8324513  8324557  8324567  8324621  8324623  8324627  8324633  8324663  8324699  8324749
8324759  8324773  8324777  8324791  8324801  8324803  8324807  8324839  8324879  8324881
8324887  8324893  8324923  8325007  8325013  8325029  8325041  8325047  8325061  8325067
8325071  8325073  8325089  8325113  8325131  8325151  8325179  8325193  8325217  8325227
8325269  8325277  8325283  8325307  8325367  8325377  8325403  8325433  8325437  8325467
8325491  8325503  8325509  8325511  8325521  8325539  8325547  8325587  8325589  8325599
8325601  8325613  8325619  8325623  8325649  8325661  8325671  8325677  8325689  8325719
8325769  8325773  8325797  8325803  8325809  8325833  8325841  8325853  8325893  8325899
8325907  8325923  8325943  8325997  8326001  8326007  8326027  8326033  8326051  8326057
8326061  8326063  8326079  8326091  8326111  8326127  8326163  8326193  8326223  8326231
8326261  8326267  8326273  8326289  8326301  8326303  8326319  8326327  8326387  8326399
8326411  8326421  8326429  8326463  8326465  8326469  8326499  8326511  8326523  8326553
8326589  8326601  8326603  8326607  8326609  8326613  8326657  8326673  8326697  8326711
8326727  8326763  8326781  8326789  8326793  8326811  8326823  8326853  8326859  8326861
8326867  8326919  8326931  8326939  8326949  8326963  8326979  8326987  8327021  8327047
8327051  8327069  8327101  8327113  8327117  8327129  8327177  8327191  8327227  8327233
8327237  8327239  8327243  8327261  8327269  8327279  8327287  8327299  8327303  8327359
8327381  8327383  8327393  8327401  8327411  8327441  8327443  8327471  8327483  8327503
8327513  8327521  8327531  8327533  8327549  8327563  8327581  8327593  8327609  8327651
8327677  8327687  8327689  8327699  8327717  8327743  8327779  8327827  8327831  8327857
8327861  8327881  8327887  8327983  8327993  8327999  8328007  8328013  8328029  8328031
8328041  8328053  8328083  8328091  8328097  8328107  8328109  8328121  8328127  8328161
8328169  8328209  8328211  8328217  8328227  8328233  8328239  8328253  8328311  8328319
8328337  8328343  8328361  8328377  8328389  8328401  8328409  8328413  8328427  8328443
8328449  8328451  8328493  8328511  8328527  8328547  8328557  8328571  8328577  8328583
8328611  8328629  8328637  8328659  8328667  8328673  8328679  8328689  8328701  8328731
8328743  8328751  8328769  8328839  8328841  8328847  8328851  8328871  8328877  8328889
8328899  8328913  8328919  8328923  8328941  8328949  8328961  8328977  8328979  8328989
8329037  8329043  8329063  8329067  8329073  8329091  8329093  8329103  8329121  8329129
8329141  8329157  8329187  8329193  8329213  8329241  8329247  8329253  8329267  8329309
8329313  8329327  8329333  8329361  8329379  8329393  8329397  8329411  8329423  8329441
8329471  8329493  8329501  8329537  8329553  8329567  8329577  8329589  8329597  8329603
8329637  8329661  8329691  8329693  8329709  8329747  8329759  8329819  8329823  8329829
```

```
8329837  8329859  8329891  8329901  8329903  8329907  8329913  8329927  8329939  8329969
8329987  8330009  8330027  8330039  8330053  8330059  8330081  8330087  8330111  8330137
8330167  8330207  8330213  8330237  8330239  8330299  8330353  8330363  8330369  8330383
8330389  8330401  8330407  8330411  8330423  8330437  8330467  8330479  8330507  8330521
8330549  8330557  8330563  8330591  8330603  8330617  8330639  8330659  8330677  8330689
8330701  8330753  8330771  8330779  8330789  8330827  8330837  8330851  8330857  8330893
8330923  8330929  8330947  8330963  8330983  8330989  8330999  8331007  8331019  8331047
8331061  8331097  8331131  8331137  8331163  8331181  8331203  8331209  8331217  8331223
8331227  8331263  8331269  8331287  8331289  8331291  8331307  8331317  8331347  8331371
8331397  8331409  8331413  8331431  8331473  8331493  8331509  8331523  8331527  8331539
8331571  8331593  8331599  8331607  8331629  8331641  8331647  8331667  8331679  8331689
8331691  8331749  8331761  8331767  8331811  8331857  8331871  8331877  8331881  8331889
8331907  8331923  8331943  8331977  8331997  8332007  8332021  8332043  8332073  8332081
8332099  8332111  8332133  8332139  8332169  8332171  8332213  8332217  8332223  8332231
8332237  8332249  8332267  8332277  8332283  8332297  8332319  8332327  8332339  8332351
8332361  8332403  8332409  8332427  8332529  8332531  8332537  8332543  8332547  8332549
8332559  8332561  8332579  8332613  8332651  8332663  8332673  8332679  8332691  8332699
8332729  8332759  8332763  8332777  8332789  8332817  8332823  8332829  8332837  8332843
8332847  8332859  8332861  8332867  8332879  8332897  8332913  8332921  8332937  8332939
8332967  8333033  8333047  8333051  8333069  8333071  8333113  8333119  8333131  8333167
8333183  8333197  8333231  8333239  8333257  8333261  8333279  8333309  8333323  8333329
8333363  8333371  8333387  8333401  8333407  8333431  8333441  8333447  8333453  8333459
8333471  8333489  8333531  8333557  8333579  8333581  8333593  8333599  8333603  8333623
8333629  8333651  8333657  8333671  8333683  8333687  8333707  8333729  8333737  8333747
8333749  8333779  8333803  8333807  8333821  8333839  8333861  8333891  8333911  8333957
8333987  8333999  8334013  8334019  8334041  8334043  8334047  8334101  8334101  8334173
8334187  8334241  8334259  8334269  8334283  8334299  8334307  8334311  8334323  8334343
8334367  8334377  8334379  8334383  8334413  8334433  8334449  8334457  8334461  8334481
8334493  8334497  8334509  8334527  8334553  8334563  8334569  8334581  8334587  8334617
8334631  8334661  8334701  8334707  8334713  8334719  8334721  8334751  8334757  8334773
8334779  8334791  8334829  8334841  8334847  8334889  8334899  8334919  8334929  8334959
8335003  8335007  8335031  8335043  8335057  8335073  8335081  8335087  8335097  8335099
8335123  8335153  8335157  8335183  8335189  8335237  8335241  8335273  8335279  8335289
8335297  8335337  8335387  8335409  8335417  8335427  8335447  8335451  8335463  8335487
8335489  8335519  8335529  8335531  8335543  8335549  8335553  8335567  8335571  8335577
8335583  8335597  8335609  8335633  8335643  8335703  8335709  8335721  8335727  8335739
8335741  8335753  8335771  8335781  8335793  8335799  8335837  8335849  8335853  8335879
8335883  8335903  8335909  8335991  8336011  8336017  8336047  8336057  8336059  8336071
8336087  8336093  8336101  8336113  8336131  8336147  8336173  8336183  8336197  8336201
8336213  8336227  8336267  8336291  8336297  8336299  8336329  8336333  8336347  8336357
8336387  8336411  8336413  8336467  8336479  8336491  8336501  8336513  8336519  8336533
8336569  8336591  8336593  8336597  8336599  8336617  8336621  8336639  8336651  8336663
8336677  8336683  8336701  8336747  8336753  8336767  8336771  8336777  8336789  8336849
8336873  8336893  8336917  8336921  8336927  8336941  8336957  8336963  8336983  8337013
8337019  8337023  8337031  8337061  8337071  8337079  8337103  8337127  8337137  8337149
8337151  8337167  8337179  8337187  8337209  8337221  8337223  8337229  8337269  8337281
8337289  8337319  8337323  8337331  8337347  8337379  8337383  8337421  8337451  8337457
8337491  8337499  8337509  8337517  8337607  8337611  8337619  8337629  8337643  8337647
8337653  8337689  8337709  8337727  8337731  8337773  8337811  8337817  8337859  8337863
8337869  8337881  8337887  8337893  8337899  8337919  8337947  8337971  8337991  8337997
8338009  8338021  8338037  8338049  8338067  8338073  8338079  8338091  8338103  8338111
8338123  8338139  8338147  8338153  8338171  8338181  8338199  8338219  8338237  8338241
8338247  8338261  8338271  8338289  8338301  8338303  8338307  8338333  8338339  8338361
8338367  8338373  8338387  8338409  8338417  8338423  8338481  8338523  8338537  8338553
8338559  8338601  8338613  8338637  8338643  8338651  8338667  8338669  8338709  8338751
8338763  8338793  8338817  8338819  8338829  8338849  8338859  8338871  8338873  8338877
8338933  8338943  8338961  8338963  8338987  8338991  8338999  8339017  8339039  8339057
8339063  8339077  8339117  8339131  8339159  8339167  8339203  8339239  8339273  8339281
8339297  8339321  8339339  8339399  8339407  8339411  8339413  8339437  8339449  8339453
8339489  8339491  8339519  8339521  8339533  8339543  8339561  8339563  8339581  8339587
8339599  8339621  8339623  8339627  8339629  8339657  8339663  8339677  8339693  8339701
8339711  8339717  8339729  8339743  8339761  8339767  8339801  8339819  8339831  8339857
8339887  8339907  8339909  8339939  8339941  8339957  8339971  8339983  8339987  8340041
8340043  8340049  8340061  8340071  8340091  8340119  8340121  8340127  8340131  8340161
8340169  8340173  8340187  8340223  8340247  8340257  8340301  8340307  8340317  8340337
8340341  8340349  8340401  8340403  8340419  8340433  8340443  8340473  8340509  8340517
8340529  8340533  8340593  8340611  8340613  8340623  8340637  8340641  8340679  8340691
8340721  8340733  8340749  8340781  8340793  8340803  8340811  8340817  8340821  8340833
8340841  8340847  8340851  8340853  8340877  8340887  8340911  8340961  8340967  8340977
8340989  8341001  8341013  8341027  8341051  8341063  8341117  8341121  8341129  8341153
8341187  8341211  8341213  8341217  8341259  8341261  8341303  8341309  8341313  8341337
8341349  8341351  8341363  8341369  8341379  8341381  8341393  8341397  8341427  8341451
8341453  8341457  8341477  8341481  8341499  8341507  8341517  8341523  8341537  8341559
8341561  8341591  8341601  8341603  8341631  8341643  8341649  8341657  8341667  8341721
8341727  8341757  8341769  8341777  8341789  8341813  8341831  8341841  8341843  8341859
8341873  8341877  8341891  8341897  8341913  8341919  8341943  8341961  8341967  8341973
8341979  8341981  8341987  8341997  8342011  8342017  8342029  8342051  8342093  8342101
8342119  8342137  8342141  8342143  8342149  8342153  8342167  8342179  8342183  8342203
8342219  8342239  8342251  8342267  8342293  8342303  8342329  8342333  8342339  8342351
8342357  8342377  8342381  8342407  8342431  8342437  8342447  8342483  8342507  8342519
8342531  8342549  8342561  8342567  8342569  8342573  8342617  8342647  8342651  8342669
8342681  8342687  8342693  8342759  8342779  8342791  8342809  8342821  8342827  8342837
8342839  8342879  8342933  8342939  8342947  8342959  8342971  8342993
8343029  8343037  8343047  8343053  8343059  8343079  8343091  8343119  8343121  8343133
8343143  8343169  8343173  8343199  8343211  8343221  8343233  8343239  8343253  8343263
8343289  8343301  8343317  8343323  8343341  8343343  8343353  8343359  8343373  8343383
8343403  8343407  8343431  8343469  8343479  8343499  8343523  8343529  8343571  8343589
8343593  8343613  8343653  8343659  8343667  8343703  8343781  8343791  8343809  8343857
8343859  8343877  8343887  8343899  8343911  8343941  8343943  8343947  8343961  8343971
```

```
8343989  8344001  8344013  8344043  8344057  8344067  8344069  8344087  8344099  8344117
8344121  8344123  8344139  8344151  8344153  8344157  8344159  8344163  8344169  8344187
8344213  8344253  8344283  8344289  8344313  8344319  8344327  8344337  8344367  8344387
8344403  8344481  8344493  8344507  8344513  8344541  8344577  8344597  8344601  8344621
8344627  8344631  8344667  8344681  8344697  8344717  8344733  8344759  8344793  8344799
8344811  8344829  8344867  8344871  8344873  8344891  8344913  8344927  8344961  8344979
8344993  8345023  8345027  8345033  8345039  8345041  8345083  8345087  8345089  8345101
8345119  8345153  8345167  8345171  8345173  8345177  8345189  8345191  8345203  8345219
8345279  8345291  8345299  8345303  8345321  8345333  8345339  8345353  8345357  8345371
8345377  8345399  8345413  8345423  8345429  8345431  8345459  8345473  8345489  8345501
8345549  8345581  8345599  8345621  8345633  8345651  8345663  8345669  8345723  8345737
8345747  8345761  8345767  8345773  8345791  8345801  8345809  8345819  8345833  8345839
8345891  8345917  8345923  8345927  8345951  8345969  8345971  8345983  8346011  8346029
8346047  8346049  8346077  8346097  8346101  8346103  8346157  8346181  8346197  8346209
8346211  8346227  8346241  8346251  8346253  8346311  8346319  8346341  8346353  8346361
8346367  8346379  8346383  8346389  8346407  8346413  8346421  8346427  8346431  8346433
8346449  8346469  8346487  8346517  8346521  8346551  8346607  8346617  8346619  8346623
8346641  8346647  8346649  8346703  8346713  8346721  8346727  8346743  8346761  8346763
8346787  8346791  8346797  8346799  8346803  8346817  8346823  8346829  8346839  8346853
8346869  8346883  8346889  8346901  8346913  8346931  8346937  8346959  8346977  8346979
8346991  8346997  8347007  8347021  8347037  8347049  8347069  8347081  8347093  8347123
8347133  8347139  8347147  8347151  8347217  8347243  8347249  8347253  8347267  8347271
8347303  8347309  8347319  8347333  8347337  8347343  8347349  8347351  8347369  8347373
8347433  8347483  8347487  8347501  8347511  8347513  8347523  8347531  8347571  8347579
8347589  8347609  8347657  8347699  8347721  8347741  8347747  8347753  8347777  8347813
8347817  8347831  8347849  8347879  8347907  8347909  8347921  8347939  8347957  8347979
8347981  8347987  8347991  8347993  8348017  8348029  8348077  8348089  8348107  8348117
8348129  8348147  8348159  8348177  8348191  8348213  8348227  8348231  8348243  8348261
8348293  8348299  8348303  8348339  8348341  8348359  8348383  8348387  8348413  8348423
8348437  8348443  8348477  8348519  8348531  8348533  8348537  8348539  8348551  8348567
8348573  8348603  8348611  8348617  8348629  8348633  8348651  8348671  8348687  8348689
8348699  8348731  8348737  8348759  8348773  8348777  8348797  8348843  8348849  8348863
8348869  8348881  8348891  8348903  8348909  8348911  8348927  8348929  8348947  8348969
8348971  8348981  8348983  8348993  8349007  8349041  8349043  8349049  8349067  8349109
8349119  8349139  8349157  8349163  8349169  8349197  8349203  8349217  8349223  8349241
8349251  8349269  8349277  8349301  8349311  8349337  8349347  8349359  8349371  8349389
8349403  8349433  8349487  8349511  8349541  8349553  8349557  8349559  8349577  8349581
8349587  8349599  8349613  8349631  8349637  8349641  8349659  8349701  8349707  8349743
8349787  8349791  8349793  8349799  8349821  8349829  8349877  8349887  8349893  8349899
8349919  8349931  8349953  8349977  8349983  8349997  8350031  8350037  8350061  8350079
8350099  8350103  8350117  8350141  8350151  8350157  8350193  8350201  8350217  8350247
8350249  8350259  8350261  8350267  8350283  8350297  8350301  8350319  8350343  8350373
8350393  8350399  8350457  8350469  8350483  8350583  8350597  8350607  8350613  8350619
8350669  8350691  8350697  8350739  8350751  8350763  8350777  8350787  8350831  8350841
8350843  8350871  8350877  8350889  8350897  8350933  8350939  8350957  8350963  8350967
8350973  8351009  8351017  8351023  8351033  8351071  8351087  8351099  8351107  8351111
8351113  8351117  8351129  8351141  8351149  8351171  8351173  8351177  8351201  8351207
8351209  8351227  8351261  8351281  8351293  8351339  8351341  8351347  8351351  8351353
8351363  8351411  8351423  8351429  8351443  8351459  8351467  8351489  8351501  8351513
8351527  8351531  8351533  8351561  8351597  8351633  8351639  8351663  8351669  8351699
8351701  8351719  8351731  8351747  8351753  8351767  8351771  8351789  8351807  8351813
8351821  8351839  8351851  8351881  8351891  8351909  8351911  8351923  8351939  8351951
8351953  8351969  8351977  8351983  8352007  8352031  8352037  8352061  8352079  8352089
8352101  8352103  8352119  8352133  8352139  8352161  8352173  8352187  8352199  8352221
8352241  8352247  8352251  8352257  8352293  8352301  8352307  8352341  8352347  8352353
8352359  8352367  8352391  8352403  8352413  8352437  8352439  8352451  8352467  8352469
8352481  8352497  8352517  8352529  8352541  8352577  8352581  8352583  8352601  8352629
8352679  8352709  8352727  8352731  8352737  8352769  8352803  8352809  8352821  8352829
8352863  8352881  8352893  8352901  8352923  8352931  8352941  8352943  8352947  8353021
8353049  8353063  8353067  8353097  8353099  8353109  8353123  8353129  8353133  8353151
8353153  8353183  8353201  8353207  8353243  8353259  8353313  8353333  8353339  8353343
8353361  8353427  8353441  8353459  8353517  8353519  8353529  8353547  8353561  8353589
8353607  8353621  8353637  8353643  8353649  8353661  8353687  8353699  8353703  8353717
8353729  8353747  8353753  8353801  8353819  8353837  8353843  8353847  8353859  8353861
8353937  8353951  8353967  8353979  8353993  8353999  8354023  8354041  8354051  8354057
8354069  8354077  8354113  8354131  8354161  8354171  8354183  8354197  8354199  8354207
8354209  8354237  8354251  8354257  8354279  8354287  8354303  8354323  8354347  8354351
8354363  8354369  8354371  8354387  8354389  8354419  8354449  8354461  8354477
8354483  8354491  8354503  8354539  8354551  8354557  8354569  8354587  8354603  8354651
8354657  8354669  8354677  8354683  8354713  8354729  8354789  8354791  8354807  8354849
8354869  8354887  8354897  8354947  8354953  8354963  8354971  8354977  8354989  8354993
8354999  8355001  8355013  8355031  8355043  8355073  8355077  8355091  8355131  8355133
8355173  8355199  8355223  8355227  8355239  8355251  8355253  8355271  8355299  8355323
8355329  8355341  8355343  8355359  8355367  8355379  8355401  8355407  8355419  8355439
8355469  8355533  8355547  8355553  8355563  8355583  8355617  8355623  8355661  8355667
8355671  8355689  8355691  8355713  8355731  8355749  8355779  8355817  8355827  8355883
8355917  8355929  8355931  8355961  8355967  8356001  8356003  8356009  8356013  8356021
8356037  8356057  8356063  8356093  8356099  8356123  8356153  8356171  8356213  8356217
8356241  8356247  8356261  8356289  8356297  8356301  8356303  8356331  8356343  8356349
8356363  8356393  8356399  8356417  8356421  8356423  8356489  8356499  8356507  8356511
8356531  8356549  8356559  8356591  8356597  8356619  8356631  8356633  8356651  8356679
8356681  8356697  8356721  8356729  8356739  8356769  8356781  8356837  8356849  8356853
8356861  8356867  8356871  8356879  8356889  8356919  8356961  8356969  8356991  8356993
8357003  8357033  8357039  8357051  8357053  8357057  8357087  8357099  8357123  8357143
8357171  8357177  8357197  8357201  8357203  8357233  8357269  8357281  8357287  8357347
8357389  8357417  8357429  8357467  8357471  8357483  8357491  8357501  8357509  8357537
8357543  8357567  8357599  8357603  8357611  8357621  8357627  8357633  8357641  8357651
8357677  8357683  8357707  8357711  8357719  8357731  8357749  8357753  8357773  8357827
8357831  8357837  8357873  8357903  8357917  8357927  8357933  8357957  8357971  8357977
```

```
8357983 8358019 8358029 8358059 8358083 8358109 8358143 8358167 8358173 8358179
8358197 8358227 8358239 8358241 8358247 8358253 8358277 8358283 8358299 8358307
8358323 8358331 8358359 8358377 8358379 8358397 8358419 8358421 8358439 8358463
8358473 8358479 8358491 8358521 8358529 8358563 8358569 8358599 8358607 8358619
8358643 8358653 8358661 8358667 8358671 8358673 8358677 8358703 8358731 8358737
8358739 8358767 8358787 8358797 8358799 8358811 8358817 8358827 8358839 8358859
8358863 8358877 8358881 8358893 8358923 8358941 8358953 8358983 8359007 8359009
8359037 8359067 8359073 8359081 8359093 8359103 8359133 8359177 8359201 8359207
8359217 8359229 8359249 8359271 8359277 8359283 8359289 8359331 8359343
8359349 8359387 8359391 8359513 8359517 8359541 8359579 8359621 8359633 8359679
8359697 8359717 8359723 8359763 8359783 8359811 8359831 8359861 8359873 8359889
8359907 8359919 8359921 8359927 8359933 8359951 8359957 8359961 8359963 8359969
8359979 8359993 8360003 8360081 8360083 8360087 8360129 8360147 8360203 8360213
8360221 8360227 8360239 8360249 8360263 8360267 8360281 8360291 8360309 8360347
8360353 8360371 8360377 8360383 8360389 8360411 8360419 8360479 8360489 8360503
8360509 8360579 8360581 8360629 8360657 8360683 8360687 8360717 8360743 8360767
8360771 8360773 8360801 8360809 8360867 8360897 8360899 8360921 8360941 8360951
8360959 8360987 8360997 8360999 8361011 8361043 8361047 8361053 8361071
8361097 8361137 8361139 8361151 8361179 8361191 8361203 8361211 8361233 8361257
8361277 8361293 8361313 8361319 8361329 8361359 8361377 8361389 8361403 8361449
8361491 8361557 8361589 8361601 8361611 8361623 8361631 8361641 8361677 8361679
8361701 8361707 8361709 8361721 8361733 8361751 8361761 8361763 8361779 8361803
8361809 8361833 8361851 8361853 8361901 8361907 8361917 8361937 8361953 8361961
8361967 8361979 8362021 8362027 8362031 8362049 8362091 8362097 8362103 8362117
8362127 8362139 8362163 8362169 8362199 8362231 8362297 8362303 8362331 8362349
8362357 8362391 8362397 8362399 8362423 8362427 8362447 8362457 8362463 8362477
8362493 8362537 8362559 8362561 8362573 8362583 8362619 8362631 8362649 8362687
8362727 8362733 8362747 8362751 8362763 8362771 8362801 8362813 8362819
8362843 8362853 8362867 8362897 8362903 8362931 8362951 8362967 8362973 8363009
8363023 8363071 8363081 8363093 8363119 8363123 8363129 8363143 8363153 8363183
8363189 8363197 8363209 8363219 8363231 8363239 8363261 8363279 8363297 8363323
8363351 8363353 8363387 8363413 8363431 8363471 8363483 8363533 8363561 8363567
8363569 8363573 8363581 8363617 8363627 8363653 8363669 8363671 8363681 8363689
8363701 8363717 8363737 8363753 8363777 8363787 8363807 8363821 8363851 8363867
8363879 8363903 8363917 8363939 8363941 8363969 8363981 8363989 8364011 8364023
8364043 8364067 8364071 8364077 8364101 8364107 8364173 8364193 8364197 8364217
8364227 8364229 8364233 8364241 8364247 8364281 8364311 8364319 8364329 8364359
8364361 8364379 8364431 8364443 8364457 8364509 8364523 8364539 8364563 8364583
8364589 8364593 8364611 8364613 8364623 8364647 8364649 8364689 8364691 8364703
8364721 8364739 8364751 8364767 8364773 8364781 8364793 8364821 8364827 8364859
8364871 8364877 8364899 8364911 8364913 8364929 8364931 8364949 8364973 8364977
8365001 8365039 8365057 8365061 8365081 8365087 8365099 8365121 8365157 8365163
8365171 8365193 8365223 8365229 8365243 8365283 8365303 8365327 8365333 8365387
8365391 8365397 8365403 8365417 8365421 8365447 8365457 8365463 8365471 8365477
8365481 8365493 8365501 8365519 8365523 8365551 8365559 8365561 8365613 8365633
8365661 8365699 8365711 8365739 8365741 8365759 8365769 8365771 8365783 8365793
8365807 8365829 8365837 8365843 8365867 8365883 8365897 8365901 8365913 8365933
8365943 8365957 8365961 8365963 8365969 8366003 8366069 8366087 8366093 8366101
8366117 8366119 8366129 8366131 8366147 8366161 8366167 8366191 8366203 8366207
8366227 8366257 8366263 8366269 8366279 8366287 8366321 8366341 8366353 8366359
8366389 8366401 8366447 8366459 8366461 8366489 8366573 8366591 8366599 8366609
8366629 8366647 8366663 8366681 8366717 8366719 8366723 8366741 8366753 8366767
8366777 8366787 8366791 8366843 8366851 8366861 8366881 8366903 8366927 8366933
8366957 8366959 8366977 8366989 8367017 8367031 8367053 8367059 8367083 8367089
8367091 8367103 8367113 8367119 8367133 8367169 8367173 8367197 8367221 8367223
8367251 8367253 8367299 8367301 8367329 8367343 8367361 8367371 8367379 8367389
8367397 8367517 8367521 8367523 8367533 8367539 8367559 8367571 8367577 8367589
8367641 8367643 8367659 8367673 8367677 8367679 8367683 8367707 8367719 8367727
8367743 8367767 8367769 8367787 8367803 8367817 8367829 8367841 8367851 8367857
8367881 8367913 8367937 8367949 8367959 8367991 8368007 8368033 8368043 8368057
8368069 8368079 8368081 8368091 8368103 8368111 8368123 8368169 8368193 8368201
8368209 8368219 8368229 8368237 8368247 8368249 8368259 8368271 8368289 8368291
8368307 8368319 8368331 8368337 8368351 8368361 8368421 8368433 8368439 8368457
8368489 8368499 8368517 8368561 8368567 8368579 8368595 8368597 8368601 8368603
8368621 8368637 8368643 8368669 8368739 8368741 8368747 8368781 8368817 8368819
8368831 8368837 8368847 8368861 8368891 8368901 8368931 8368951 8368957 8368963
8368979 8368991 8369003 8369021 8369029 8369057 8369069 8369077 8369089 8369111
8369143 8369161 8369167 8369183 8369199 8369203 8369213 8369227 8369233 8369269
8369279 8369281 8369299 8369303 8369311 8369323 8369341 8369351 8369353 8369359
8369381 8369399 8369407 8369419 8369441 8369461 8369499 8369509 8369521 8369527
8369531 8369533 8369579 8369587 8369609 8369629 8369639 8369657 8369663 8369687
8369701 8369731 8369743 8369759 8369771 8369773 8369791 8369819 8369833 8369849
8369869 8369891 8369897 8369903 8369909 8369927 8369929 8369941 8369947 8369989
8370049 8370053 8370133 8370143 8370151 8370157 8370161 8370181 8370211 8370223
8370247 8370269 8370281 8370293 8370311 8370347 8370353 8370379 8370391 8370407
8370433 8370457 8370463 8370487 8370491 8370499 8370517 8370521 8370529 8370553
8370569 8370587 8370611 8370617 8370631 8370673 8370679 8370721 8370757 8370787
8370793 8370797 8370823 8370833 8370871 8370877 8370881 8370883 8370889 8370911
8370941 8370959 8371007 8371009 8371037 8371049 8371061 8371063 8371067 8371081
8371109 8371117 8371127 8371133 8371141 8371159 8371193 8371199 8371211 8371249
8371273 8371331 8371351 8371357 8371367 8371373 8371387 8371399 8371409 8371411
8371427 8371481 8371487 8371501 8371507 8371513 8371529 8371537 8371547 8371589
8371613 8371619 8371631 8371639 8371679 8371703 8371729 8371733 8371739 8371751
8371763 8371777 8371813 8371819 8371861 8371897 8371901 8371903 8371907
8371919 8371921 8371927 8371999 8372029 8372051 8372053 8372059 8372081 8372083
8372137 8372153 8372173 8372191 8372219 8372227 8372233 8372237 8372261 8372291
8372317 8372321 8372327 8372359 8372383 8372411 8372417 8372423 8372453 8372467
8372473 8372477 8372491 8372501 8372519 8372543 8372549 8372557 8372563 8372579
```

8372587 8372591 8372599 8372629 8372633 8372641 8372669 8372671 8372717 8372723
8372737 8372743 8372747 8372761 8372773 8372779 8372783 8372801 8372809 8372813
8372839 8372869 8372941 8372951 8372953 8372963 8372971 8372999 8373011 8373041
8373049 8373067 8373073 8373133 8373139 8373151 8373181 8373217 8373223 8373227
8373229 8373259 8373263 8373293 8373329 8373361 8373377 8373397 8373461 8373467
8373479 8373481 8373487 8373493 8373511 8373517 8373539 8373569 8373583 8373601
8373619 8373649 8373671 8373697 8373709 8373731 8373749 8373767 8373769 8373773
8373791 8373823 8373829 8373847 8373853 8373857 8373887 8373907 8373917 8373919
8373923 8373931 8373941 8373961 8373971 8373983 8373989 8373991 8373997 8374031
8374043 8374057 8374063 8374073 8374087 8374097 8374103 8374109 8374133 8374153
8374181 8374199 8374241 8374259 8374271 8374339 8374343 8374349 8374351 8374363
8374367 8374409 8374423 8374427 8374439 8374441 8374453 8374481 8374511 8374529
8374547 8374559 8374567 8374571 8374589 8374603 8374607 8374609 8374627 8374651
8374657 8374661 8374669 8374679 8374721 8374733 8374739 8374741 8374753 8374771
8374837 8374841 8374871 8374907 8374937 8374943 8374957 8374963 8374973 8374979
8375009 8375023 8375039 8375041 8375047 8375057 8375069 8375083 8375099 8375119
8375123 8375137 8375149 8375173 8375183 8375189 8375251 8375261 8375273 8375291
8375299 8375303 8375309 8375317 8375321 8375327 8375347 8375351 8375359 8375383
8375399 8375401 8375459 8375467 8375489 8375491 8375513 8375527 8375533 8375557
8375569 8375593 8375597 8375617 8375641 8375663 8375677 8375683 8375753 8375771
8375803 8375831 8375833 8375837 8375863 8375869 8375891 8375893 8375897 8375929
8375953 8375957 8375963 8375981 8375987 8375989 8376029 8376037 8376059 8376061
8376077 8376079 8376089 8376113 8376149 8376167 8376187 8376191 8376197 8376217
8376253 8376299 8376307 8376343 8376371 8376373 8376377 8376409 8376463 8376469
8376493 8376503 8376523 8376551 8376569 8376619 8376647 8376649 8376653 8376661
8376671 8376691 8376721 8376749 8376773 8376791 8376799 8376811 8376821 8376827
8376829 8376847 8376859 8376871 8376883 8376889 8376917 8376931 8376983 8376989
8377003 8377007 8377013 8377063 8377087 8377091 8377111 8377123 8377147 8377151
8377153 8377169 8377177 8377183 8377241 8377247 8377249 8377253 8377289 8377297
8377307 8377321 8377331 8377349 8377357 8377367 8377373 8377393 8377399 8377403
8377417 8377427 8377459 8377477 8377487 8377493 8377511 8377517 8377519 8377529
8377531 8377559 8377597 8377601 8377619 8377637 8377639 8377643 8377673 8377693
8377697 8377709 8377729 8377739 8377751 8377757 8377777 8377783 8377807 8377829
8377847 8377877 8377903 8377907 8377909 8377913 8377921 8377927 8377931 8377939
8377949 8377951 8377969 8377973 8377979 8377997 8378011 8378039 8378047 8378053
8378057 8378087 8378101 8378119 8378131 8378147 8378171 8378179 8378203 8378219
8378231 8378239 8378257 8378261 8378273 8378281 8378287 8378291 8378299 8378311
8378327 8378341 8378347 8378351 8378353 8378369 8378387 8378389 8378393 8378407
8378431 8378437 8378479 8378483 8378519 8378521 8378561 8378567 8378581 8378621
8378633 8378641 8378653 8378659 8378681 8378683 8378707 8378723 8378731 8378771
8378803 8378809 8378827 8378833 8378857 8378863 8378869 8378873 8378879 8378893
8378987 8378989 8379017 8379029 8379031 8379043 8379067 8379073 8379127 8379149
8379167 8379187 8379197 8379223 8379253 8379257 8379271 8379299 8379307 8379373
8379389 8379391 8379401 8379407 8379409 8379421 8379461 8379467 8379473 8379499
8379529 8379533 8379557 8379563 8379571 8379599 8379643 8379647 8379653 8379661
8379673 8379689 8379713 8379719 8379731 8379737 8379769 8379781 8379799 8379829
8379823 8379851 8379853 8379859 8379863 8379887 8379901 8379907 8379911 8379923
8379937 8379941 8379961 8380037 8380039 8380051 8380061 8380067 8380079 8380087
8380097 8380103 8380109 8380111 8380123 8380139 8380213 8380223 8380237 8380249
8380259 8380271 8380279 8380283 8380291 8380321 8380357 8380367 8380369 8380373
8380381 8380403 8380417 8380451 8380453 8380459 8380469 8380511 8380531 8380543
8380597 8380621 8380649 8380661 8380663 8380667 8380693 8380699 8380721 8380733
8380741 8380751 8380781 8380787 8380789 8380807 8380811 8380831 8380859 8380861
8380877 8380903 8380921 8380927 8380969 8380991 8381003 8381047 8381059 8381083
8381123 8381143 8381159 8381161 8381183 8381207 8381209 8381227 8381237 8381267
8381291 8381293 8381309 8381311 8381333 8381341 8381353 8381371 8381393 8381437
8381447 8381449 8381467 8381497 8381531 8381533 8381537 8381539 8381543 8381627
8381669 8381693 8381699 8381707 8381719 8381777 8381801 8381803 8381809 8381819
8381843 8381881 8381887 8381903 8381909 8381927 8381941 8381951 8381963 8381977
8381981 8381987 8381993 8382007 8382013 8382053 8382067 8382083 8382089 8382107
8382113 8382133 8382149 8382151 8382167 8382181 8382197 8382203 8382223 8382229
8382233 8382259 8382263 8382277 8382289 8382299 8382323 8382349 8382359 8382379
8382389 8382433 8382443 8382457 8382467 8382481 8382499 8382503 8382509 8382523
8382527 8382529 8382541 8382551 8382587 8382589 8382593 8382607 8382623 8382637
8382707 8382709 8382713 8382719 8382727 8382739 8382767 8382797 8382811 8382823
8382841 8382869 8382877 8382919 8382929 8382937 8382949 8382953 8382977 8383007
8383013 8383019 8383021 8383027 8383033 8383069 8383087 8383093 8383097 8383099
8383103 8383163 8383171 8383213 8383217 8383223 8383267 8383283 8383289 8383301
8383327 8383367 8383379 8383391 8383429 8383433 8383439 8383457 8383469 8383471
8383481 8383483 8383489 8383493 8383511 8383513 8383519 8383537 8383553 8383557
8383589 8383591 8383603 8383619 8383621 8383631 8383649 8383673 8383709 8383741
8383757 8383759 8383787 8383789 8383801 8383819 8383829 8383847 8383861 8383897
8383939 8383961 8384003 8384021 8384041 8384043 8384059 8384071 8384083 8384087
8384093 8384107 8384119 8384141 8384143 8384147 8384209 8384221 8384227 8384239
8384251 8384273 8384279 8384287 8384293 8384297 8384309 8384319 8384323 8384347
8384357 8384381 8384399 8384401 8384419 8384429 8384449 8384479 8384501 8384503
8384531 8384543 8384591 8384611 8384639 8384641 8384671 8384687 8384693 8384711
8384729 8384749 8384767 8384771 8384773 8384797 8384813 8384819 8384821 8384839
8384843 8384863 8384867 8384881 8384891 8384923 8384933 8384969 8384989 8384993
8385001 8385049 8385059 8385071 8385073 8385101 8385103 8385107 8385109 8385119
8385161 8385211 8385217 8385239 8385253 8385277 8385281 8385331 8385337 8385341
8385371 8385373 8385383 8385389 8385397 8385427 8385431 8385439 8385451 8385457
8385463 8385497 8385499 8385511 8385521 8385523 8385529 8385551 8385557 8385563
8385577 8385581 8385589 8385649 8385667 8385677 8385679 8385691 8385701 8385719
8385721 8385733 8385737 8385749 8385757 8385761 8385763 8385781 8385803 8385809
8385827 8385833 8385863 8385877 8385887 8385889 8385893 8385917 8385931 8385983
8385991 8385997 8386019 8386033 8386039 8386067 8386073 8386123 8386129 8386141
8386153 8386177 8386193 8386207 8386211 8386223 8386229 8386267 8386289 8386291
8386303 8386327 8386331 8386373 8386379 8386387 8386409 8386439 8386447 8386471

8386493	8386501	8386507	8386529	8386541	8386549	8386571	8386579	8386601	8386603
8386639	8386669	8386711	8386723	8386739	8386757	8386759	8386769	8386817	8386823
8386883	8386913	8386921	8386943	8386949	8386979	8387023	8387033	8387047	8387053
8387063	8387077	8387089	8387101	8387117	8387129	8387131	8387147	8387149	8387153
8387167	8387173	8387191	8387219	8387221	8387231	8387243	8387251	8387297	8387311
8387339	8387369	8387371	8387377	8387413	8387437	8387447	8387471	8387473	8387501
8387507	8387513	8387539	8387543	8387557	8387563	8387581	8387591	8387609	8387611
8387671	8387707	8387723	8387737	8387741	8387807	8387809	8387831	8387839	8387857
8387861	8387867	8387879	8387891	8387917	8387921	8387933	8387947	8387957	8387959
8387993	8387999	8388013	8388019	8388059	8388071	8388091	8388109	8388113	8388187
8388209	8388239	8388277	8388283	8388287	8388301	8388319	8388371	8388377	8388409
8388421	8388427	8388439	8388449	8388451	8388461	8388473	8388539	8388547	8388571
8388581	8388587	8388593	8388617	8388619	8388623	8388637	8388673	8388683	8388691
8388697	8388733	8388739	8388761	8388763	8388791	8388811	8388833	8388841	8388857
8388881	8388901	8388923	8388929	8388949	8388953	8388971	8389001	8389019	8389027
8389039	8389057	8389061	8389063	8389079	8389081	8389093	8389099	8389103	8389111
8389123	8389141	8389153	8389159	8389163	8389187	8389201	8389219	8389231	8389237
8389261	8389301	8389309	8389351	8389361	8389373	8389441	8389463	8389489	8389501
8389519	8389523	8389541	8389553	8389559	8389567	8389603	8389607	8389651	8389657
8389669	8389679	8389681	8389691	8389699	8389709	8389727	8389769	8389781	8389783
8389793	8389813	8389819	8389837	8389877	8389883	8389897	8389907	8389919	8389921
8389937	8389939	8389943	8389949	8389951	8389957	8389967	8389973	8390021	8390029
8390047	8390051	8390069	8390089	8390093	8390143	8390183	8390219	8390227	8390233
8390257	8390273	8390287	8390303	8390311	8390323	8390329	8390351	8390359	8390399
8390413	8390441	8390443	8390467	8390471	8390479	8390497	8390513	8390531	8390539
8390549	8390587	8390593	8390623	8390663	8390671	8390687	8390713	8390717	8390729
8390731	8390737	8390743	8390747	8390771	8390779	8390783	8390819	8390857	8390861
8390867	8390869	8390873	8390909	8390927	8390939	8390959	8390981	8390999	8391001
8391011	8391037	8391073	8391079	8391083	8391109	8391121	8391127	8391137	8391151
8391197	8391199	8391209	8391211	8391223	8391263	8391283	8391287	8391289	8391323
8391337	8391349	8391377	8391401	8391413	8391433	8391443	8391457	8391463	8391469
8391491	8391499	8391517	8391533	8391553	8391577	8391589	8391623	8391641	8391653
8391667	8391679	8391697	8391707	8391737	8391739	8391743	8391767	8391769	8391791
8391797	8391809	8391811	8391841	8391893	8391919	8391937	8391947	8391949	8391959
8391997	8392037	8392039	8392051	8392061	8392063	8392093	8392099	8392123	8392133
8392141	8392147	8392157	8392177	8392193	8392207	8392211	8392231	8392261	8392277
8392283	8392291	8392301	8392327	8392333	8392361	8392387	8392411	8392421	8392453
8392463	8392477	8392481	8392499	8392507	8392511	8392519	8392561	8392597	8392607
8392619	8392633	8392639	8392651	8392669	8392693	8392721	8392739	8392753	8392763
8392793	8392799	8392817	8392819	8392829	8392831	8392843	8392897	8392903	8392933
8392959	8392961	8392997	8393017	8393057	8393069	8393107	8393111	8393171	8393179
8393243	8393249	8393251	8393263	8393279	8393293	8393309	8393311	8393347	8393351
8393353	8393381	8393389	8393419	8393423	8393431	8393443	8393447	8393491	8393509
8393519	8393533	8393543	8393569	8393599	8393603	8393629	8393633	8393639	8393647
8393669	8393677	8393711	8393717	8393741	8393747	8393761	8393773	8393813	8393821
8393861	8393863	8393867	8393881	8393887	8393893	8393899	8393911	8393923	8393929
8393941	8393947	8393951	8393969	8393977	8393993	8393999	8394013	8394017	8394037
8394041	8394049	8394083	8394091	8394097	8394109	8394121	8394151	8394161	8394163
8394173	8394187	8394223	8394251	8394263	8394289	8394293	8394307	8394317	8394353
8394361	8394377	8394383	8394403	8394433	8394437	8394439	8394467	8394469	8394487
8394493	8394499	8394509	8394539	8394541	8394557	8394559	8394577	8394593	8394613
8394643	8394667	8394679	8394689	8394691	8394721	8394733	8394739	8394779	8394797
8394803	8394851	8394863	8394887	8394907	8394913	8394917	8394943	8394983	8395021
8395027	8395031	8395043	8395061	8395067	8395087	8395091	8395097	8395129	8395133
8395151	8395193	8395199	8395217	8395237	8395241	8395243	8395249	8395267	8395273
8395291	8395313	8395319	8395339	8395349	8395351	8395357	8395381	8395403	8395441
8395487	8395489	8395493	8395531	8395601	8395619	8395627	8395631	8395643	8395649
8395669	8395721	8395733	8395741	8395747	8395753	8395757	8395769	8395799	8395801
8395811	8395813	8395817	8395847	8395867	8395913	8395931	8395951	8395957	8395973
8395991	8395997	8396023	8396027	8396039	8396057	8396093	8396107	8396111	8396117
8396131	8396149	8396177	8396189	8396243	8396263	8396279	8396281	8396291	8396321
8396329	8396369	8396371	8396383	8396411	8396413	8396429	8396441	8396483	8396491
8396497	8396509	8396569	8396581	8396599	8396617	8396639	8396693	8396699	8396719
8396741	8396761	8396767	8396777	8396779	8396783	8396789	8396797	8396807	8396809
8396813	8396819	8396849	8396873	8396881	8396951	8396953	8396977	8396981	8396987
8397007	8397017	8397019	8397023	8397041	8397073	8397079	8397091	8397097	8397101
8397119	8397121	8397131	8397149	8397157	8397197	8397209	8397217	8397223	8397227
8397283	8397287	8397307	8397313	8397317	8397329	8397331	8397353	8397377	8397379
8397391	8397397	8397419	8397421	8397437	8397457	8397509	8397523	8397533	8397539
8397547	8397583	8397611	8397619	8397629	8397709	8397721	8397751	8397761	8397793
8397803	8397817	8397827	8397839	8397859	8397863	8397877	8397887	8397897	8397901
8397947	8397959	8397971	8398003	8398021	8398067	8398069	8398097	8398111	8398141
8398149	8398177	8398183	8398193	8398199	8398207	8398211	8398217	8398231	8398267
8398277	8398301	8398321	8398337	8398339	8398343	8398349	8398387	8398393	8398409
8398421	8398447	8398451	8398471	8398483	8398531	8398543	8398547	8398553	8398567
8398601	8398619	8398633	8398673	8398679	8398721	8398739	8398757	8398759	8398787
8398801	8398811	8398877	8398879	8398883	8398903	8398909	8398913	8398921	8398927
8398937	8398961	8398967	8398993	8398997	8399011	8399021	8399057	8399077	8399081
8399093	8399099	8399101	8399107	8399119	8399123	8399129	8399141	8399189	8399191
8399231	8399239	8399243	8399257	8399263	8399267	8399291	8399297	8399311	8399331
8399401	8399423	8399429	8399437	8399441	8399459	8399477	8399483	8399497	8399519
8399533	8399551	8399561	8399563	8399569	8399593	8399603	8399621	8399627	8399641
8399659	8399687	8399689	8399701	8399707	8399709	8399731	8399773	8399779	8399837
8399861	8399863	8399873	8399893	8399927	8399953	8399987	8400011	8400019	8400031
8400039	8400047	8400061	8400069	8400079	8400097	8400121	8400143	8400157	8400167
8400211	8400229	8400233	8400247	8400251	8400253	8400269	8400283	8400311	8400317
8400319	8400323	8400373	8400377	8400409	8400419	8400433	8400439	8400461	8400481
8400529	8400563	8400569	8400571	8400593	8400617	8400619	8400629	8400631	8400647
8400653	8400673	8400683	8400697	8400701	8400709	8400713	8400731	8400751	8400757

```
8400761 8400797 8400811 8400823 8400829 8400841 8400851 8400853 8400883 8400901
8400919 8400937 8400943 8400967 8400971 8400979 8401013 8401027 8401033 8401037
8401051 8401061 8401087 8401117 8401121 8401147 8401153 8401157 8401193 8401199
8401201 8401207 8401219 8401241 8401243 8401259 8401273 8401277 8401291 8401301
8401303 8401313 8401321 8401339 8401357 8401361 8401381 8401397 8401409 8401411
8401427 8401429 8401447 8401457 8401513 8401529 8401531 8401537 8401543 8401559
8401573 8401633 8401637 8401639 8401661 8401681 8401699 8401703 8401709 8401717
8401721 8401741 8401759 8401763 8401769 8401787 8401801 8401807 8401873 8401901
8401907 8401919 8401963 8401973 8401993 8401999 8402027 8402033 8402039
8402041 8402057 8402077 8402099 8402111 8402159 8402179 8402183 8402197 8402221
8402279 8402309 8402311 8402327 8402357 8402363 8402371 8402399 8402413 8402419
8402453 8402473 8402477 8402479 8402491 8402497 8402507 8402509 8402531 8402543
8402561 8402593 8402609 8402623 8402627 8402629 8402633 8402651 8402657 8402683
8402687 8402711 8402717 8402747 8402749 8402791 8402803 8402831 8402833 8402857
8402861 8402917 8402951 8402963 8402969 8402971 8403029 8403053 8403061 8403067
8403079 8403089 8403091 8403121 8403133 8403167 8403179 8403217 8403221 8403223
8403247 8403259 8403277 8403289 8403323 8403331 8403337 8403383 8403391 8403419
8403431 8403481 8403509 8403517 8403557 8403583 8403587 8403599 8403623 8403641
8403677 8403679 8403683 8403691 8403709 8403721 8403727 8403761 8403779 8403803
8403817 8403827 8403841 8403853 8403869 8403917 8403931 8403943 8403959 8403977
8404013 8404021 8404111 8404127 8404141 8404183 8404189 8404219 8404237 8404241
8404243 8404247 8404259 8404283 8404301 8404313 8404337 8404339 8404343 8404351
8404381 8404387 8404411 8404427 8404433 8404463 8404469 8404489 8404531 8404553
8404597 8404603 8404619 8404639 8404673 8404679 8404703 8404717 8404741 8404771
8404777 8404787 8404789 8404807 8404819 8404849 8404871 8404873 8404901 8404927
8404939 8404951 8404969 8404993 8404997 8405003 8405029 8405063 8405077 8405101
8405149 8405153 8405183 8405197 8405203 8405207 8405209 8405219 8405227 8405233
8405261 8405263 8405269 8405297 8405329 8405333 8405347 8405377 8405393 8405407
8405417 8405431 8405461 8405471 8405473 8405479 8405483 8405489 8405491 8405503
8405513 8405519 8405567 8405587 8405591 8405609 8405627 8405629 8405647 8405651
8405669 8405689 8405711 8405713 8405723 8405759 8405773 8405777 8405807 8405843
8405849 8405851 8405863 8405899 8405921 8405951 8405977 8406001 8406043 8406049
8406059 8406061 8406071 8406077 8406089 8406103 8406127 8406161 8406173 8406191
8406193 8406221 8406253 8406283 8406287 8406337 8406367 8406439 8406473 8406479
8406481 8406509 8406527 8406529 8406539 8406547 8406553 8406577 8406583 8406631
8406637 8406649 8406667 8406689 8406719 8406737 8406773 8406779 8406787 8406791
8406793 8406809 8406817 8406829 8406841 8406847 8406901 8406917 8406919 8406941
8406967 8406971 8406977 8406991 8407001 8407037 8407067 8407073 8407079 8407099
8407109 8407111 8407123 8407129 8407141 8407151 8407159 8407171 8407183 8407199
8407211 8407229 8407237 8407249 8407261 8407271 8407283 8407297 8407307 8407309
8407331 8407349 8407363 8407379 8407381 8407387 8407391 8407409 8407423 8407433
8407439 8407453 8407459 8407471 8407513 8407523 8407573 8407579 8407591 8407613
8407643 8407649 8407657 8407667 8407699 8407723 8407753 8407757 8407771 8407837
8407849 8407871 8407879 8407907 8407909 8407943 8407951 8407959 8407961 8407967
8407969 8407981 8408003 8408009 8408017 8408039 8408053 8408069 8408083 8408093
8408111 8408117 8408129 8408131 8408137 8408143 8408189 8408227 8408233 8408237
8408261 8408273 8408293 8408297 8408327 8408329 8408333 8408339 8408341 8408357
8408371 8408377 8408399 8408401 8408429 8408437 8408447 8408461 8408513 8408537
8408549 8408563 8408573 8408597 8408599 8408623 8408641 8408663 8408677 8408683
8408689 8408707 8408711 8408713 8408747 8408767 8408791 8408801 8408819 8408831
8408837 8408867 8408891 8408893 8408923 8408941 8408959 8408971 8408977 8408989
8408993 8409019 8409041 8409047 8409061 8409073 8409097 8409119 8409127 8409133
8409173 8409179 8409187 8409227 8409239 8409263 8409281 8409307 8409319 8409353
8409377 8409383 8409403 8409409 8409413 8409433 8409437 8409439 8409473 8409481
8409491 8409493 8409497 8409523 8409529 8409581 8409593 8409601 8409613 8409617
8409637 8409671 8409689 8409691 8409719 8409721 8409829 8409839 8409857 8409871
8409889 8409899 8409931 8409941 8410001 8410013 8410033 8410057 8410079 8410081
8410097 8410099 8410109 8410117 8410139 8410151 8410153 8410183 8410187 8410201
8410229 8410231 8410271 8410279 8410301 8410313 8410343 8410349 8410351 8410397
8410399 8410421 8410429 8410439 8410459 8410463 8410471 8410487 8410489 8410511
8410531 8410537 8410543 8410583 8410607 8410613 8410643 8410651 8410679 8410681
8410691 8410723 8410739 8410763 8410769 8410793 8410799 8410811 8410813 8410819
8410849 8410859 8410861 8410921 8410943 8410991 8410999 8411009 8411017 8411021
8411023 8411033 8411059 8411069 8411071 8411089 8411111 8411119 8411149 8411171
8411197 8411201 8411231 8411233 8411237 8411267 8411269 8411287 8411297 8411317
8411327 8411329 8411339 8411341 8411371 8411383 8411387 8411393 8411407 8411419
8411443 8411467 8411477 8411483 8411489 8411521 8411539 8411551 8411563 8411567
8411573 8411587 8411593 8411597 8411603 8411621 8411677 8411681 8411693 8411713
8411723 8411759 8411761 8411791 8411797 8411849 8411869 8411873 8411911 8411969
8411971 8411981 8411993 8412017 8412023 8412031 8412049 8412077 8412101 8412109
8412119 8412121 8412137 8412139 8412143 8412149 8412163 8412167 8412169 8412221
8412223 8412241 8412251 8412259 8412277 8412281 8412289 8412311 8412317 8412329
8412347 8412367 8412379 8412401 8412409 8412451 8412461 8412479 8412487 8412493
8412499 8412527 8412529 8412533 8412539 8412553 8412617 8412623 8412629 8412643
8412673 8412683 8412707 8412709 8412769 8412793 8412799 8412809 8412823 8412851
8412853 8412857 8412881 8412883 8412889 8412923 8412961 8412967 8412973 8412979
8412983 8413001 8413007 8413021 8413037 8413043 8413051 8413057 8413073 8413087
8413099 8413109 8413133 8413151 8413157 8413187 8413201 8413211 8413243 8413247
8413271 8413289 8413291 8413309 8413313 8413373 8413403 8413411 8413417 8413439
8413463 8413477 8413499 8413511 8413519 8413543 8413549 8413553 8413597 8413609
8413619 8413631 8413649 8413661 8413663 8413687 8413693 8413721 8413723 8413729
8413739 8413747 8413777 8413781 8413807 8413829 8413831 8413841 8413843 8413849
8413859 8413921 8413957 8413981 8414009 8414011 8414023 8414027 8414039
8414057 8414069 8414083 8414117 8414137 8414141 8414171 8414177 8414191 8414213
8414233 8414243 8414257 8414293 8414309 8414311 8414347 8414353 8414381 8414383
8414387 8414443 8414449 8414453 8414479 8414531 8414533 8414537 8414543 8414557
8414561 8414579 8414617 8414621 8414641 8414647 8414657 8414699 8414723 8414737
8414743 8414753 8414761 8414773 8414797 8414807 8414831 8414837 8414839 8414851
8414867 8414869 8414897 8414899 8414911 8414957 8415023 8415031 8415037 8415049
```

```
8415053  8415059  8415061  8415067  8415083  8415089  8415091  8415101  8415103  8415109
8415137  8415139  8415151  8415163  8415193  8415241  8415257  8415259  8415293
8415301  8415331  8415343  8415359  8415361  8415383  8415403  8415413  8415419  8415427
8415431  8415439  8415467  8415467  8415469  8415497  8415503  8415509  8415541  8415553
8415557  8415577  8415581  8415587  8415599  8415611  8415637  8415653  8415661  8415691
8415703  8415709  8415733  8415739  8415763  8415767  8415793  8415809  8415857  8415863
8415889  8415893  8415919  8415941  8415959  8415991  8415997  8416007  8416013  8416019
8416021  8416049  8416081  8416087  8416099  8416123  8416129  8416141  8416147  8416171
8416189  8416223  8416249  8416253  8416267  8416273  8416301  8416313  8416327  8416333
8416349  8416361  8416363  8416381  8416391  8416393  8416403  8416451  8416481  8416483
8416511  8416561  8416567  8416591  8416621  8416627  8416637  8416651  8416657  8416663
8416669  8416673  8416693  8416697  8416721  8416747  8416769  8416799  8416813  8416817
8416879  8416937  8416951  8417021  8417029  8417033  8417051  8417063  8417069  8417077
8417081  8417131  8417173  8417147  8417153  8417173  8417203  8417231  8417237  8417243
8417267  8417273  8417327  8417347  8417351  8417359  8417377  8417393  8417401  8417449
8417489  8417503  8417527  8417579  8417593  8417623  8417641  8417657  8417659  8417677
8417681  8417683  8417703  8417699  8417711  8417719  8417729  8417749  8417791  8417807
8417821  8417891  8417911  8417921  8417963  8417971  8417987  8417993  8417999  8418001
8418013  8418017  8418037  8418037  8418041  8418049  8418071  8418089  8418097  8418101
8418103  8418107  8418119  8418127  8418133  8418139  8418169  8418173  8418197  8418199
8418209  8418221  8418237  8418233  8418251  8418259  8418271  8418283  8418313  8418317
8418331  8418337  8418341  8418343  8418359  8418373  8418379  8418409  8418413  8418457
8418469  8418481  8418493  8418503  8418511  8418521  8418547  8418559  8418563  8418581
8418589  8418601  8418623  8418643  8418659  8418661  8418673  8418677  8418719  8418779
8418797  8418803  8418847  8418857  8418863  8418901  8418913  8418923  8418929  8418937
8418941  8418979  8419039  8419049  8419067  8419069  8419079  8419087  8419121  8419141
8419181  8419183  8419207  8419231  8419237  8419249  8419277  8419283  8419297  8419303
8419319  8419331  8419343  8419351  8419361  8419363  8419373  8419381  8419399  8419417
8419423  8419429  8419441  8419447  8419457  8419459  8419469  8419511  8419513  8419519
8419531  8419547  8419549  8419553  8419559  8419571  8419591  8419597  8419613  8419651
8419661  8419727  8419751  8419759  8419783  8419813  8419843  8419861  8419867  8419877
8419919  8419927  8419933  8419967  8419987  8419993  8420009  8420051  8420119  8420123
8420149  8420171  8420183  8420197  8420207  8420221  8420233  8420239  8420261  8420263
8420273  8420281  8420311  8420317  8420327  8420351  8420393  8420407  8420413  8420441
8420443  8420449  8420453  8420483  8420509  8420519  8420521  8420543  8420563  8420569
8420597  8420603  8420651  8420653  8420669  8420677  8420681  8420749  8420771  8420773
8420801  8420821  8420827  8420833  8420837  8420843  8420869  8420887  8420891  8420897
8420903  8420917  8420927  8420939  8420953  8420957  8420959  8420969  8420977  8420983
8421041  8421067  8421079  8421079  8421143  8421167  8421173  8421187  8421191  8421209
8421227  8421229  8421241  8421251  8421403  8421407  8421419  8421463  8421487  8421493
8421509  8421529  8421547  8421557  8421559  8421563  8421577  8421587  8421619  8421641
8421653  8421697  8421701  8421709  8421713  8421727  8421733  8421737  8421757  8421773
8421779  8421793  8421799  8421821  8421823  8421827  8421839  8421857  8421877  8421901
8421911  8421923  8421929  8421961  8421971  8421983  8421989  8421991  8422019  8422027
8422033  8422039  8422061  8422067  8422079  8422133  8422153  8422181  8422201  8422213
8422217  8422223  8422231  8422237  8422241  8422243  8422247  8422279  8422303  8422307
8422313  8422333  8422357  8422387  8422399  8422411  8422451  8422457  8422459  8422471
8422481  8422489  8422493  8422501  8422511  8422553  8422549  8422559  8422571  8422573
8422597  8422627  8422649  8422691  8422703  8422723  8422727  8422741  8422747  8422751
8422763  8422783  8422787  8422811  8422831  8422859  8422867  8422873  8422877  8422879
8422913  8422927  8422993  8422993  8423027  8423029  8423057  8423071  8423111  8423113
8423117  8423153  8423167  8423179  8423201  8423209  8423231  8423249  8423257  8423263
8423269  8423281  8423321  8423323  8423329  8423333  8423353  8423357  8423377  8423407
8423419  8423423  8423447  8423461  8423473  8423477  8423507  8423549  8423563  8423603
8423617  8423621  8423651  8423663  8423671  8423683  8423699  8423711  8423729  8423731
8423759  8423777  8423791  8423797  8423801  8423803  8423867  8423879  8423887  8423893
8423903  8423923  8423927  8423929  8423953  8423999  8424019  8424023  8424029  8424041
8424047  8424067  8424071  8424077  8424089  8424103  8424109  8424121  8424131  8424137
8424151  8424179  8424193  8424209  8424211  8424287  8424289  8424293  8424307  8424319
8424341  8424341  8424349  8424359  8424389  8424397  8424407  8424439  8424443  8424457
8424487  8424497  8424499  8424539  8424569  8424589  8424593  8424599  8424623  8424659
8424667  8424677  8424683  8424697  8424701  8424727  8424763  8424769  8424817  8424841
8424853  8424869  8424883  8424887  8424917  8424919  8424973  8425057  8425097  8425103
8425111  8425133  8425169  8425171  8425177  8425181  8425187  8425237  8425243  8425253
8425279  8425289  8425309  8425321  8425327  8425331  8425423  8425427  8425433  8425447
8425453  8425519  8425537  8425553  8425577  8425589  8425621  8425657  8425663  8425667
8425673  8425679  8425687  8425691  8425717  8425741  8425777  8425799  8425811  8425841
8425847  8425861  8425883  8425877  8425883  8425891  8425909  8425913  8425919  8425927
8425939  8425943  8425997  8426009  8426021  8426023  8426039  8426059  8426087  8426107
8426123  8426147  8426149  8426161  8426179  8426183  8426189  8426221  8426227  8426261
8426263  8426287  8426381  8426393  8426399  8426413  8426419  8426449  8426461  8426477
8426497  8426503  8426507  8426521  8426527  8426549  8426563  8426567  8426569  8426591
8426599  8426603  8426669  8426647  8426661  8426669  8426701  8426731  8426767  8426797
8426801  8426819  8426827  8426863  8426893  8426897  8426903  8426939  8426953  8426969
8426983  8426989  8427031  8427043  8427049  8427077  8427103  8427109  8427113  8427161
8427163  8427173  8427191  8427217  8427233  8427247  8427271  8427283  8427299  8427311
8427323  8427337  8427401  8427403  8427413  8427437  8427439  8427449  8427467  8427481
8427491  8427521  8427533  8427539  8427557  8427569  8427581  8427599  8427607  8427647
8427667  8427701  8427707  8427721  8427739  8427751  8427761  8427779  8427781  8427787
8427791  8427803  8427831  8427841  8427851  8427907  8427911  8427929  8427931  8427941
8427953  8427961  8427977  8428003  8428031  8428037  8428061  8428081  8428099  8428139
8428157  8428159  8428163  8428169  8428171  8428201  8428213  8428237  8428289  8428291
8428297  8428307  8428313  8428319  8428333  8428337  8428351  8428363  8428391  8428393
8428403  8428417  8428421  8428423  8428439  8428471  8428477  8428487  8428501  8428513
8428531  8428547  8428591  8428601  8428613  8428631  8428633  8428661  8428663  8428687
8428691  8428697  8428703  8428709  8428729  8428759  8428769  8428789  8428793  8428811
8428867  8428873  8428891  8428897  8428909  8428943  8428949  8428967  8428969  8429011
8429051  8429089  8429123  8429131  8429143  8429147  8429167  8429171  8429189  8429209
8429233  8429243  8429249  8429257  8429329  8429341  8429411  8429423  8429429  8429437
```

```
8429453  8429479  8429503  8429527  8429539  8429573  8429579  8429581  8429587  8429593
8429609  8429621  8429627  8429639  8429657  8429669  8429689  8429693  8429699  8429717
8429731  8429741  8429761  8429767  8429789  8429797  8429831  8429833  8429851  8429867
8429893  8429917  8429947  8429957  8429959  8429963  8430013  8430031  8430041  8430049
8430067  8430073  8430089  8430137  8430143  8430151  8430203  8430217  8430251  8430263
8430299  8430311  8430341  8430349  8430353  8430377  8430391  8430427  8430439  8430449
8430467  8430473  8430479  8430491  8430493  8430511  8430517  8430529  8430577  8430599
8430613  8430649  8430659  8430679  8430683  8430689  8430701  8430713  8430727  8430731
8430739  8430757  8430769  8430787  8430803  8430833  8430893  8430913  8430937  8430941
8431013  8431021  8431051  8431061  8431063  8431067  8431069  8431097  8431103  8431109
8431123  8431127  8431169  8431211  8431243  8431289  8431327  8431331  8431351  8431369
8431393  8431417  8431441  8431447  8431453  8431469  8431487  8431499  8431519  8431529
8431543  8431559  8431567  8431583  8431589  8431607  8431627  8431637  8431651  8431667
8431673  8431679  8431697  8431723  8431729  8431733  8431739  8431751  8431769  8431793
8431799  8431811  8431817  8431831  8431849  8431861  8431897  8431901  8431903  8431909
8431931  8431933  8431963  8431979  8431981  8431987  8431993  8432003  8432033  8432057
8432071  8432087  8432089  8432117  8432147  8432161  8432167  8432197  8432201  8432231
8432239  8432251  8432261  8432267  8432269  8432297  8432309  8432311  8432321  8432327
8432387  8432401  8432407  8432441  8432443  8432453  8432461  8432471  8432477  8432497
8432509  8432521  8432531  8432537  8432573  8432581  8432587  8432617  8432621  8432623
8432647  8432653  8432659  8432681  8432689  8432719  8432737  8432747  8432759  8432783
8432791  8432797  8432807  8432813  8432819  8432843  8432849  8432861  8432873  8432909
8432917  8432923  8432933  8432951  8432959  8432981  8432987  8432993  8433011  8433043
8433059  8433079  8433101  8433107  8433109  8433119  8433121  8433133  8433143  8433193
8433211  8433233  8433247  8433253  8433259  8433263  8433319  8433367  8433407  8433409
8433443  8433463  8433493  8433497  8433517  8433527  8433559  8433613  8433619
8433631  8433641  8433661  8433671  8433673  8433697  8433703  8433707  8433769  8433779
8433787  8433797  8433839  8433863  8433869  8433871  8433899  8433913  8433917  8433941
8433947  8433959  8433973  8434003  8434007  8434021  8434027  8434037  8434079  8434087
8434141  8434171  8434177  8434189  8434199  8434213  8434219  8434243  8434253  8434259
8434289  8434297  8434337  8434351  8434357  8434379  8434399  8434403  8434427  8434453  8434477
8434501  8434513  8434523  8434607  8434609  8434637  8434691  8434693  8434733  8434753
8434763  8434787  8434793  8434799  8434819  8434823  8434843  8434847  8434861  8434891
8434901  8434903  8434943  8434957  8434963  8434967  8434991  8434999  8435047  8435051
8435057  8435071  8435081  8435083  8435117  8435129  8435159  8435173  8435191  8435197
8435209  8435237  8435243  8435257  8435261  8435269  8435291  8435293  8435303  8435309
8435311  8435333  8435341  8435347  8435351  8435359  8435377  8435389  8435431  8435437
8435459  8435473  8435477  8435489  8435521  8435527  8435551  8435561  8435573  8435579
8435591  8435599  8435633  8435659  8435681  8435711  8435729  8435731  8435741  8435743
8435747  8435759  8435797  8435821  8435827  8435831  8435849  8435887  8435891  8435899
8435929  8435939  8435941  8435951  8435969  8435971  8436017  8436023  8436031  8436047
8436067  8436073  8436079  8436083  8436137  8436143  8436151  8436167  8436179  8436191
8436217  8436271  8436277  8436287  8436293  8436319  8436353  8436367  8436397  8436401
8436409  8436431  8436451  8436457  8436473  8436479  8436499  8436503  8436509  8436517
8436541  8436569  8436581  8436599  8436601  8436613  8436671  8436679  8436689  8436713
8436731  8436739  8436749  8436751  8436763  8436781  8436797  8436809  8436821  8436877
8436889  8436899  8436907  8436917  8436937  8436949  8436959  8436977  8436979  8436983
8436997  8437063  8437069  8437081  8437087  8437127  8437129  8437133  8437153  8437171
8437181  8437183  8437201  8437211  8437213  8437217  8437223  8437241  8437259  8437291
8437307  8437309  8437327  8437357  8437367  8437379  8437391  8437399  8437409  8437411
8437421  8437433  8437447  8437453  8437489  8437493  8437519  8437529  8437537  8437543
8437553  8437601  8437609  8437621  8437631  8437669  8437727  8437733  8437771  8437777
8437783  8437789  8437837  8437861  8437879  8437883  8437889  8437901  8437903  8437909
8437931  8437939  8437943  8437951  8437969  8437973  8437991  8438011  8438041  8438083
8438093  8438099  8438117  8438119  8438123  8438141  8438161  8438173  8438201  8438207
8438281  8438303  8438323  8438327  8438329  8438351  8438359  8438371  8438377  8438387
8438399  8438407  8438429  8438459  8438467  8438473  8438483  8438503  8438513  8438519
8438531  8438533  8438567  8438587  8438609  8438629  8438653  8438657  8438659  8438663
8438699  8438741  8438753  8438761  8438779  8438813  8438863  8438909  8438917  8438921
8438929  8438951  8438957  8438959  8438977  8438981  8439007  8439043  8439049  8439061
8439073  8439103  8439133  8439143  8439149  8439163  8439187  8439199  8439209  8439217
8439241  8439251  8439269  8439271  8439281  8439307  8439323  8439341  8439383  8439437
8439443  8439449  8439467  8439469  8439479  8439499  8439503  8439517  8439547  8439569
8439577  8439581  8439583  8439601  8439617  8439619  8439637  8439647  8439659  8439707
8439709  8439713  8439721  8439751  8439763  8439791  8439817  8439859  8439887  8439901
8439901  8439947  8439953  8439961  8439989  8440031  8440037  8440043  8440063  8440097
8440139  8440147  8440183  8440193  8440207  8440231  8440249  8440259  8440291  8440319
8440321  8440331  8440343  8440357  8440361  8440373  8440391  8440423  8440429  8440441
8440457  8440499  8440507  8440511  8440529  8440559  8440561  8440567  8440571  8440577
8440591  8440603  8440613  8440637  8440639  8440667  8440669  8440673  8440703  8440739
8440787  8440799  8440811  8440813  8440819  8440841  8440853  8440877  8440889  8440907
8440919  8440961  8440963  8440969  8440973  8440979  8441009  8441011  8441033  8441057
8441077  8441087  8441089  8441099  8441101  8441107  8441137  8441221  8441227  8441243
8441249  8441273  8441311  8441327  8441347  8441359  8441369  8441399  8441413  8441423
8441431  8441497  8441519  8441527  8441539  8441557  8441569  8441603  8441617  8441633
8441651  8441663  8441669  8441677  8441701  8441731  8441737  8441749  8441761  8441767
8441789  8441791  8441801  8441821  8441831  8441837  8441857  8441863  8441869  8441969
8442011  8442029  8442043  8442079  8442089  8442097  8442107  8442121  8442131
8442151  8442157  8442167  8442221  8442223  8442229  8442263  8442271  8442299  8442337
8442349  8442359  8442367  8442373  8442389  8442419  8442437  8442439  8442457  8442481
8442521  8442559  8442607  8442641  8442647  8442653  8442667  8442671  8442673  8442689
8442713  8442767  8442769  8442779  8442781  8442793  8442803  8442839  8442869  8442883
8442901  8442923  8442937  8442947  8442971  8442979  8442997  8443037  8443063  8443069
8443073  8443079  8443091  8443109  8443117  8443121  8443151  8443159  8443177  8443187
8443189  8443199  8443213  8443229  8443243  8443261  8443291  8443301  8443319  8443327
8443349  8443361  8443367  8443397  8443433  8443453  8443489  8443517  8443529  8443531
8443571  8443573  8443583  8443607  8443613  8443621  8443627  8443637  8443639  8443649
8443651  8443703  8443709  8443711  8443717  8443739  8443751  8443759  8443763  8443777
8443819  8443913  8443927  8443937  8443949  8443969  8443993  8444003  8444027  8444041
```

```
8444057  8444063  8444083  8444123  8444147  8444159  8444203  8444207  8444213  8444273
8444279  8444281  8444287  8444299  8444309  8444323  8444327  8444351  8444353  8444363
8444407  8444411  8444419  8444467  8444477  8444507  8444527  8444549  8444555  8444561
8444573  8444581  8444591  8444593  8444599  8444609  8444629  8444663  8444671  8444687
8444701  8444707  8444719  8444731  8444773  8444783  8444789  8444809  8444831  8444851
8444923  8444929  8444941  8444951  8444957  8444981  8444983  8445013  8445029  8445049
8445079  8445089  8445097  8445109  8445137  8445161  8445251  8445259  8445271  8445343
8445377  8445419  8445421  8445427  8445433  8445449  8445457  8445473  8445517  8445523
8445527  8445529  8445599  8445601  8445607  8445629  8445643  8445649  8445659  8445677
8445683  8445707  8445727  8445737  8445739  8445751  8445769  8445781  8445797  8445799
8445841  8445847  8445851  8445859  8445863  8445893  8445907  8445911  8445917  8445929
8445949  8445961  8445967  8445971  8445973  8445977  8445979  8446001  8446019  8446063
8446073  8446079  8446091  8446117  8446153  8446159  8446177  8446183  8446199  8446201
8446223  8446237  8446247  8446253  8446261  8446283  8446303  8446351  8446391  8446409
8446421  8446429  8446441  8446481  8446513  8446517  8446549  8446567  8446591  8446597
8446639  8446649  8446667  8446679  8446709  8446717  8446741  8446747  8446751  8446777
8446783  8446813  8446829  8446843  8446873  8446883  8446919  8446939  8446949  8446961
8446967  8446979  8447029  8447041  8447053  8447057  8447059  8447069  8447081  8447093
8447111  8447129  8447141  8447161  8447171  8447177  8447183  8447203  8447209  8447213
8447227  8447237  8447251  8447287  8447303  8447311  8447377  8447389  8447399  8447401
8447423  8447429  8447431  8447437  8447441  8447471  8447477  8447489  8447501  8447503
8447549  8447573  8447591  8447603  8447611  8447627  8447641  8447653  8447683  8447687
8447689  8447701  8447711  8447713  8447731  8447743  8447771  8447783  8447809  8447819
8447839  8447843  8447847  8447849  8447851  8447861  8447893  8447897  8447899  8447911
8447917  8447939  8447947  8447977  8447981  8447987  8448007  8448017  8448043  8448047
8448049  8448053  8448067  8448079  8448101  8448131  8448137  8448157  8448161  8448191
8448197  8448227  8448233  8448239  8448277  8448287  8448311  8448313  8448343  8448397
8448403  8448413  8448431  8448437  8448443  8448457  8448463  8448493  8448527  8448551
8448553  8448563  8448577  8448589  8448593  8448607  8448611  8448619  8448667  8448689
8448701  8448703  8448719  8448721  8448733  8448757  8448761  8448763  8448793  8448799
8448821  8448841  8448851  8448861  8448871  8448881  8448931  8448959  8449013  8449097
8449099  8449117  8449139  8449141  8449159  8449223  8449249  8449253  8449271  8449277
8449327  8449333  8449361  8449373  8449387  8449409  8449417  8449421  8449423  8449429
8449439  8449451  8449477  8449481  8449489  8449499  8449513  8449517  8449523  8449541
8449549  8449591  8449607  8449627  8449667  8449673  8449681  8449687  8449699  8449711
8449729  8449739  8449747  8449751  8449769  8449807  8449829  8449841  8449853  8449859
8449907  8449913  8449943  8449957  8449967  8449979  8449999  8450009  8450021  8450063
8450069  8450087  8450089  8450149  8450153  8450159  8450179  8450201  8450203  8450209
8450243  8450279  8450287  8450291  8450327  8450341  8450363  8450369  8450371  8450381
8450399  8450419  8450423  8450441  8450447  8450471  8450483  8450521  8450537  8450557
8450579  8450597  8450599  8450609  8450623  8450627  8450641  8450653  8450669  8450681
8450713  8450719  8450749  8450779  8450791  8450809  8450821  8450857  8450863  8450873
8450881  8450899  8450947  8450951  8450957  8450963  8450969  8450987  8451007  8451013
8451019  8451041  8451073  8451077  8451083  8451089  8451109  8451161  8451169  8451187
8451199  8451217  8451239  8451241  8451259  8451269  8451271  8451293  8451323  8451353
8451379  8451389  8451407  8451413  8451427  8451439  8451449  8451451  8451461  8451473
8451481  8451491  8451517  8451551  8451571  8451589  8451613  8451631  8451647  8451659
8451683  8451719  8451739  8451743  8451749  8451763  8451767  8451791  8451797  8451811
8451829  8451851  8451853  8451881  8451887  8451889  8451893  8451899  8451929  8451931
8451953  8451967  8451991  8452001  8452007  8452019  8452033  8452051  8452091  8452097
8452133  8452141  8452189  8452193  8452211  8452217  8452229  8452237  8452259  8452267
8452271  8452277  8452291  8452303  8452307  8452351  8452363  8452373  8452403  8452439
8452441  8452453  8452469  8452481  8452529  8452531  8452537  8452567  8452571  8452579
8452603  8452649  8452667  8452681  8452693  8452699  8452711  8452721  8452727  8452733
8452751  8452771  8452781  8452783  8452789  8452793  8452819  8452877  8452879  8452907
8452931  8452933  8452957  8452967  8452973  8452981  8452999  8453021  8453041  8453051
8453089  8453099  8453113  8453117  8453141  8453143  8453147  8453153  8453161  8453177
8453201  8453219  8453227  8453231  8453273  8453281  8453317  8453329  8453363  8453377
8453381  8453383  8453399  8453411  8453477  8453479  8453509  8453513  8453527  8453531
8453567  8453569  8453597  8453603  8453611  8453629  8453639  8453657  8453663  8453681
8453693  8453701  8453711  8453729  8453737  8453741  8453759  8453773  8453789  8453791
8453821  8453849  8453873  8453897  8453909  8453923  8453927  8453941  8453957  8453969
8453971  8453983  8453987  8453989  8453999  8454011  8454013  8454023  8454029  8454053
8454067  8454079  8454139  8454143  8454191  8454197  8454209  8454211  8454217  8454223
8454239  8454247  8454269  8454307  8454331  8454361  8454371  8454379  8454403  8454411
8454431  8454461  8454493  8454503  8454527  8454533  8454541  8454547  8454577  8454581
8454587  8454619  8454623  8454637  8454653  8454673  8454697  8454713  8454727  8454737
8454739  8454749  8454757  8454767  8454793  8454799  8454829  8454839  8454841  8454883
8454889  8454917  8454923  8454937  8454947  8454959  8455063  8455091  8455093  8455121
8455123  8455141  8455147  8455151  8455163  8455169  8455189  8455193  8455207  8455217
8455241  8455243  8455259  8455261  8455297  8455301  8455339  8455357  8455387  8455397
8455411  8455427  8455429  8455439  8455453  8455463  8455481  8455483  8455487  8455493
8455507  8455543  8455561  8455583  8455597  8455621  8455631  8455633  8455639  8455661
8455669  8455679  8455691  8455729  8455747  8455751  8455753  8455793  8455807  8455813
8455819  8455831  8455841  8455861  8455879  8455883  8455891  8455897  8455903  8455913
8455981  8456009  8456011  8456027  8456033  8456039  8456053  8456069  8456113  8456131
8456141  8456153  8456167  8456179  8456183  8456207  8456213  8456221  8456233  8456263
8456303  8456333  8456339  8456347  8456353  8456359  8456389  8456417  8456419  8456467
8456473  8456489  8456507  8456519  8456527  8456543  8456551  8456561  8456573  8456579
8456587  8456593  8456611  8456639  8456641  8456659  8456717  8456731  8456753  8456761
8456771  8456797  8456809  8456827  8456849  8456867  8456879  8456887  8456891  8456927
8456969  8456989  8456999  8457019  8457037  8457049  8457061  8457073  8457103  8457107
8457131  8457151  8457179  8457181  8457217  8457221  8457233  8457247  8457251  8457271
8457277  8457287  8457329  8457367  8457377  8457391  8457401  8457443  8457457  8457461
8457479  8457481  8457487  8457499  8457511  8457523  8457529  8457539  8457563  8457577
8457593  8457599  8457607  8457623  8457643  8457649  8457677  8457727  8457731  8457739
8457749  8457751  8457781  8457803  8457809  8457811  8457847  8457851  8457863  8457881
8457887  8457893  8457901  8457923  8457973  8457989  8458001  8458003  8458007  8458019
8458039  8458067  8458069  8458081  8458091  8458103  8458117  8458123  8458139  8458141
```

```
8458171 8458183 8458187 8458189 8458193 8458253 8458271 8458297 8458313 8458337
8458369 8458391 8458393 8458397 8458403 8458409 8458427 8458433 8458441 8458493
8458501 8458507 8458519 8458577 8458579 8458601 8458603 8458621 8458627 8458631
8458651 8458657 8458663 8458679 8458721 8458739 8458757 8458759 8458783 8458789
8458799 8458811 8458823 8458837 8458847 8458861 8458867 8458873 8458883 8458897
8458909 8458913 8458921 8458949 8458969 8458973 8458987 8458991 8458993 8459023
8459027 8459029 8459069 8459093 8459119 8459131 8459141 8459173 8459179 8459189
8459197 8459233 8459263 8459281 8459299 8459327 8459357 8459359 8459369 8459371
8459393 8459413 8459417 8459441 8459461 8459471 8459501 8459509 8459533 8459567
8459573 8459593 8459603 8459611 8459629 8459641 8459651 8459657 8459723 8459729
8459747 8459767 8459783 8459797 8459809 8459813 8459821 8459827 8459831 8459839
8459879 8459903 8459911 8459917 8459933 8459987 8460007 8460017 8460041 8460059
8460061 8460079 8460091 8460097 8460103 8460119 8460143 8460191 8460209 8460217
8460223 8460239 8460247 8460281 8460307 8460311 8460313 8460367 8460371 8460401
8460409 8460433 8460479 8460493 8460499 8460503 8460511 8460521 8460533 8460539
8460563 8460581 8460583 8460587 8460589 8460593 8460601 8460623 8460653 8460671
8460677 8460701 8460707 8460731 8460743 8460763 8460769 8460797 8460817 8460869
8460877 8460899 8460931 8460943 8460967 8460997 8461003 8461007 8461009 8461021
8461039 8461043 8461091 8461097 8461147 8461157 8461169 8461177 8461183 8461231
8461241 8461247 8461267 8461279 8461333 8461339 8461361 8461373 8461379 8461391
8461399 8461423 8461429 8461451 8461459 8461463 8461469 8461471 8461483 8461489
8461507 8461511 8461513 8461549 8461571 8461577 8461613 8461627 8461633 8461637
8461639 8461643 8461657 8461693 8461697 8461711 8461727 8461757 8461777 8461787
8461793 8461807 8461811 8461813 8461877 8461891 8461909 8461913 8461951 8461961
8461979 8461991 8462017 8462023 8462029 8462053 8462059 8462063 8462071 8462081
8462093 8462099 8462117 8462131 8462147 8462161 8462177 8462189 8462213 8462221
8462249 8462263 8462291 8462323 8462329 8462339 8462369 8462371 8462383 8462393
8462417 8462423 8462437 8462449 8462477 8462479 8462497 8462527 8462537 8462557
8462567 8462579 8462593 8462609 8462639 8462723 8462747 8462749 8462761 8462767
8462777 8462801 8462807 8462813 8462819 8462833 8462843 8462879 8462893 8462897
8462903 8462911 8462917 8462953 8462981 8462989 8463023 8463029 8463043 8463061
8463067 8463083 8463089 8463107 8463139 8463163 8463167 8463187 8463193 8463211
8463223 8463233 8463251 8463253 8463281 8463283 8463289 8463313 8463353 8463383
8463391 8463397 8463409 8463419 8463457 8463461 8463487 8463529 8463551 8463557
8463617 8463649 8463667 8463673 8463757 8463761 8463769 8463799 8463803 8463821
8463827 8463857 8463859 8463869 8463877 8463887 8463893 8463913 8463919 8463937
8463947 8463979 8464007 8464019 8464031 8464033 8464037 8464073 8464109 8464111
8464117 8464133 8464193 8464213 8464223 8464229 8464237 8464241 8464273 8464307
8464331 8464343 8464361 8464363 8464369 8464387 8464397 8464403 8464409 8464441
8464447 8464451 8464493 8464513 8464517 8464571 8464583 8464591 8464597 8464627
8464639 8464661 8464681 8464693 8464697 8464699 8464711 8464721 8464727
8464739 8464741 8464763 8464769 8464777 8464783 8464811 8464817 8464837 8464867
8464871 8464873 8464889 8464903 8464913 8464957 8464979 8464991 8464993 8465003
8465033 8465053 8465059 8465101 8465131 8465183 8465207 8465209 8465221 8465243
8465251 8465257 8465273 8465297 8465329 8465333 8465339 8465363 8465377 8465381
8465399 8465407 8465423 8465437 8465459 8465461 8465503 8465533 8465537 8465581
8465603 8465617 8465623 8465627 8465657 8465663 8465669 8465671 8465683 8465713
8465741 8465747 8465753 8465761 8465783 8465789 8465791 8465819 8465833 8465839
8465861 8465867 8465893 8465903 8465927 8465929 8465939 8465957 8465959 8465971
8466013 8466019 8466037 8466041 8466043 8466079 8466091 8466103 8466121 8466179
8466181 8466203 8466209 8466223 8466229 8466247 8466259 8466281 8466307 8466319
8466361 8466389 8466401 8466407 8466413 8466421 8466427 8466431 8466433 8466443
8466473 8466487 8466499 8466529 8466547 8466551 8466569 8466583 8466587 8466593
8466611 8466671 8466683 8466701 8466707 8466713 8466719 8466767 8466827 8466851
8466859 8466889 8466917 8466919 8466943 8466947 8466961 8466979 8467007 8467009
8467021 8467049 8467093 8467099 8467111 8467157 8467169 8467171 8467181 8467183
8467189 8467201 8467211 8467213 8467253 8467271 8467297 8467307 8467357 8467399
8467409 8467477 8467493 8467499 8467523 8467541 8467553 8467579 8467583 8467601
8467609 8467631 8467633 8467637 8467639 8467699 8467721 8467729 8467759 8467763
8467769 8467777 8467793 8467801 8467817 8467843 8467889 8467891 8467897 8467903
8467951 8467999 8468011 8468041 8468077 8468123 8468137 8468149 8468171 8468179
8468183 8468221 8468237 8468249 8468267 8468269 8468279 8468293 8468303 8468309
8468323 8468353 8468371 8468399 8468401 8468419 8468429 8468437 8468441 8468459
8468461 8468477 8468483 8468491 8468503 8468519 8468521 8468527 8468561 8468587
8468627 8468639 8468641 8468687 8468693 8468717 8468723 8468731 8468753 8468767
8468773 8468777 8468821 8468839 8468849 8468857 8468887 8468903 8468917
8468947 8468963 8469007 8469017 8469023 8469049 8469061 8469089 8469091 8469113
8469119 8469121 8469127 8469133 8469161 8469173 8469187 8469233 8469239 8469271
8469283 8469287 8469319 8469343 8469367 8469379 8469397 8469401 8469407 8469427
8469431 8469449 8469473 8469481 8469491 8469523 8469547 8469551 8469577 8469583
8469599 8469619 8469623 8469631 8469641 8469647 8469677 8469691 8469701 8469709
8469733 8469737 8469767 8469779 8469809 8469817 8469833 8469841 8469847 8469869
8469871 8469889 8469929 8469949 8469973 8469997 8470031 8470039
8470057 8470061 8470069 8470081 8470109 8470123 8470139 8470153 8470159 8470169
8470171 8470201 8470213 8470237 8470247 8470261 8470283 8470289 8470303 8470309
8470339 8470351 8470381 8470393 8470421 8470433 8470439 8470487 8470489 8470493
8470507 8470531 8470537 8470543 8470547 8470549 8470589 8470597 8470661 8470663
8470673 8470681 8470711 8470729 8470747 8470757 8470771 8470783 8470801 8470829
8470837 8470841 8470859 8470867 8470873 8470883 8470907 8470919 8470927 8471053
8471069 8471079 8471087 8471137 8471147 8471159 8471167 8471179 8471201 8471209
8471213 8471227 8471263 8471269 8471293 8471303 8471317 8471347 8471357 8471363
8471381 8471399 8471447 8471453 8471459 8471479 8471503 8471527 8471531 8471539
8471569 8471581 8471597 8471611 8471621 8471623 8471641 8471653 8471677 8471699
8471713 8471717 8471747 8471753 8471759 8471767 8471803 8471809 8471819 8471839
8471849 8471863 8471909 8471917 8471921 8471923 8471941 8471963 8472007 8472011
8472017 8472047 8472049 8472053 8472109 8472127 8472133 8472151 8472169 8472179
8472193 8472203 8472221 8472259 8472293 8472301 8472319 8472337 8472383 8472407
8472427 8472433 8472463 8472469 8472479 8472481 8472493 8472509 8472523 8472539
8472547 8472559 8472571 8472589 8472617 8472623 8472631 8472649 8472661 8472683
```

```
8472701  8472707  8472713  8472721  8472733  8472743  8472767  8472787  8472797  8472799
8472847  8472857  8472859  8472869  8472881  8472899  8472911  8472923  8472941  8472943
8472977  8472983  8473001  8473027  8473043  8473051  8473097  8473099  8473117  8473141
8473147  8473151  8473169  8473181  8473189  8473217  8473219  8473243  8473247  8473273
8473277  8473321  8473337  8473343  8473349  8473351  8473369  8473391  8473427  8473433
8473457  8473459  8473471  8473483  8473523  8473529  8473559  8473573  8473589  8473603
8473607  8473609  8473627  8473631  8473643  8473649  8473657  8473679  8473697  8473721
8473723  8473739  8473741  8473763  8473781  8473793  8473807  8473811  8473813  8473831
8473841  8473873  8473883  8473889  8473897  8473901  8473903  8473909  8473919  8473951
8473991  8474021  8474023  8474027  8474047  8474083  8474107  8474149  8474153  8474159
8474161  8474173  8474183  8474201  8474231  8474237  8474267  8474273  8474299  8474317
8474321  8474353  8474357  8474359  8474363  8474371  8474387  8474407  8474447  8474461
8474503  8474509  8474537  8474561  8474581  8474597  8474611  8474621  8474623  8474633
8474651  8474657  8474663  8474689  8474707  8474717  8474723  8474731  8474747  8474761
8474771  8474777  8474797  8474801  8474803  8474821  8474831  8474849  8474863  8474903
8474911  8474923  8474927  8474929  8474951  8474981  8475013  8475037  8475067  8475119
8475139  8475169  8475191  8475193  8475217  8475223  8475239  8475253  8475263  8475277
8475289  8475301  8475317  8475319  8475323  8475329  8475361  8475371  8475377  8475391
8475413  8475419  8475421  8475427  8475451  8475461  8475473  8475487  8475491  8475521
8475547  8475563  8475581  8475589  8475613  8475619  8475637  8475641  8475647  8475671
8475689  8475697  8475713  8475721  8475739  8475757  8475769  8475787  8475793  8475821
8475827  8475833  8475871  8475899  8475931  8475941  8475947  8475991  8476001
8476009  8476063  8476073  8476079  8476099  8476157  8476159  8476177  8476189  8476199
8476231  8476241  8476253  8476277  8476301  8476333  8476357  8476373  8476379  8476399
8476427  8476483  8476493  8476511  8476529  8476543  8476549  8476553  8476571  8476583
8476607  8476649  8476667  8476681  8476691  8476697  8476703  8476711  8476723  8476747
8476751  8476757  8476763  8476799  8476801  8476807  8476813  8476817  8476823  8476843
8476849  8476883  8476889  8476933  8476957  8476991  8477009  8477011  8477017  8477047
8477071  8477081  8477089  8477099  8477111  8477113  8477129  8477137  8477147  8477159
8477197  8477207  8477219  8477243  8477263  8477267  8477269  8477281  8477299  8477303
8477311  8477323  8477327  8477341  8477389  8477393  8477419  8477431  8477449  8477453
8477459  8477461  8477473  8477507  8477561  8477587  8477617  8477633  8477671  8477681
8477687  8477701  8477737  8477741  8477761  8477767  8477771  8477779  8477783  8477789
8477803  8477867  8477887  8477891  8477893  8477929  8477941  8477957  8477983  8477999
8478013  8478017  8478031  8478037  8478049  8478061  8478083  8478101  8478109  8478131
8478133  8478137  8478141  8478163  8478167  8478187  8478209  8478259  8478263  8478269
8478271  8478287  8478317  8478319  8478361  8478383  8478391  8478433  8478493  8478497
8478511  8478521  8478523  8478539  8478551  8478553  8478571  8478581  8478599  8478601
8478619  8478623  8478629  8478641  8478653  8478667  8478671  8478689  8478709  8478719
8478727  8478737  8478739  8478751  8478791  8478797  8478803  8478823  8478829  8478851
8478853  8478859  8478863  8478889  8478893  8478907  8478929  8478947  8478961  8478989
8479007  8479013  8479043  8479057  8479109  8479117  8479123  8479153  8479171  8479193
8479199  8479217  8479259  8479267  8479271  8479291  8479309  8479313  8479321  8479349
8479357  8479381  8479403  8479477  8479479  8479511  8479531  8479547  8479553
8479561  8479573  8479591  8479609  8479619  8479621  8479631  8479649  8479699  8479703
8479717  8479733  8479741  8479747  8479769  8479777  8479799  8479813  8479817  8479819
8479829  8479853  8479883  8479903  8479937  8479943  8479949  8479951  8479963  8479967
8479979  8479981  8480033  8480047  8480051  8480063  8480089  8480107  8480111  8480113
8480117  8480149  8480167  8480177  8480179  8480183  8480207  8480221  8480231  8480233
8480239  8480243  8480249  8480273  8480279  8480291  8480293  8480321  8480323  8480347
8480357  8480369  8480431  8480447  8480471  8480489  8480509  8480513  8480531
8480533  8480567  8480581  8480597  8480599  8480609  8480611  8480617  8480621  8480623
8480651  8480663  8480677  8480683  8480687  8480699  8480741  8480753  8480777  8480803
8480819  8480827  8480833  8480839  8480851  8480863  8480873  8480903  8480911  8480929
8480939  8480959  8480971  8480981  8480987  8481059  8481101  8481107  8481119  8481127
8481131  8481133  8481139  8481149  8481157  8481169  8481173  8481211  8481223  8481247
8481269  8481287  8481289  8481293  8481299  8481307  8481313  8481331  8481371  8481373
8481377  8481397  8481409  8481413  8481437  8481461  8481469  8481481  8481493  8481497
8481509  8481511  8481559  8481593  8481607  8481637  8481661  8481673  8481689  8481701
8481709  8481713  8481727  8481743  8481773  8481787  8481791  8481799  8481877  8481881
8481901  8481911  8481913  8481973  8481983  8482027  8482039  8482049  8482063  8482069
8482073  8482087  8482091  8482169  8482207  8482217  8482219  8482241  8482247  8482259
8482261  8482277  8482289  8482291  8482319  8482333  8482343  8482373  8482387  8482391
8482403  8482447  8482451  8482459  8482549  8482559  8482577  8482589  8482601  8482619
8482633  8482637  8482651  8482681  8482723  8482751  8482757  8482769  8482781  8482787
8482807  8482823  8482829  8482891  8482897  8482907  8482913  8482919  8482921  8482931
8482939  8482951  8482967  8482973  8482979  8483003  8483011  8483081  8483089  8483093
8483117  8483131  8483141  8483179  8483191  8483201  8483203  8483207  8483227  8483231
8483261  8483273  8483287  8483311  8483317  8483327  8483333  8483369  8483381  8483383
8483417  8483437  8483467  8483477  8483479  8483507  8483509  8483521  8483533  8483537
8483539  8483567  8483581  8483593  8483603  8483609  8483611  8483617  8483621  8483639
8483653  8483659  8483687  8483723  8483729  8483743  8483759  8483773  8483777  8483779
8483789  8483807  8483831  8483837  8483851  8483879  8483897  8483903  8483929  8483933
8483947  8483963  8483971  8483977  8484001  8484031  8484041  8484043  8484053  8484061
8484083  8484097  8484107  8484121  8484131  8484149  8484167  8484169  8484181  8484191
8484227  8484239  8484251  8484271  8484283  8484319  8484323  8484337  8484347  8484349
8484353  8484361  8484383  8484397  8484403  8484407  8484449  8484467  8484563  8484569
8484577  8484587  8484589  8484601  8484661  8484667  8484689  8484691  8484701  8484703
8484709  8484727  8484757  8484761  8484767  8484797  8484799  8484809  8484829  8484851
8484857  8484871  8484901  8484913  8484937  8484961  8485003  8485019  8485021  8485027
8485031  8485063  8485069  8485079  8485093  8485123  8485129  8485133  8485151  8485163
8485177  8485181  8485187  8485199  8485201  8485219  8485223  8485231  8485241  8485249
8485259  8485271  8485273  8485277  8485303  8485307  8485323  8485387  8485389  8485391
8485403  8485409  8485417  8485441  8485453  8485471  8485481  8485489  8485507  8485511
8485517  8485579  8485583  8485591  8485613  8485619  8485639  8485667  8485679  8485681
8485721  8485727  8485733  8485753  8485769  8485801  8485817  8485831  8485843  8485859
8485877  8485889  8485891  8485903  8485927  8485931  8485949  8485963  8485969  8485973
8485979  8486039  8486041  8486047  8486069  8486081  8486083  8486117  8486119  8486129
8486167  8486197  8486207  8486227  8486243  8486249  8486263  8486279  8486297  8486339
```

```
8486347 8486353 8486371 8486377 8486399 8486419 8486447 8486453 8486459 8486507
8486537 8486539 8486581 8486603 8486617 8486623 8486629 8486641 8486657 8486659
8486663 8486707 8486717 8486719 8486741 8486759 8486771 8486783 8486809 8486827
8486851 8486857 8486873 8486903 8486917 8486941 8486983 8486987 8486993 8487001
8487019 8487047 8487071 8487079 8487103 8487121 8487137 8487139 8487163 8487173
8487181 8487191 8487197 8487217 8487221 8487223 8487229 8487239 8487293 8487313
8487329 8487337 8487341 8487371 8487373 8487377 8487379 8487389 8487419 8487421
8487527 8487551 8487569 8487571 8487587 8487593 8487613 8487617 8487631 8487649
8487653 8487671 8487701 8487719 8487751 8487793 8487797 8487821 8487823 8487827
8487859 8487863 8487881 8487887 8487907 8487937 8487949 8487953 8487959 8488013
8488027 8488031 8488033 8488037 8488061 8488063 8488087 8488091 8488093 8488169
8488171 8488177 8488199 8488201 8488217 8488229 8488289 8488301 8488339 8488349
8488379 8488391 8488397 8488411 8488433 8488477 8488481 8488499 8488511 8488523
8488531 8488537 8488583 8488589 8488609 8488621 8488663 8488691 8488709 8488721
8488751 8488783 8488829 8488841 8488849 8488853 8488859 8488867 8488871 8488891
8488901 8488913 8488919 8488939 8488969 8488981 8488993 8489003 8489011 8489023
8489027 8489053 8489113 8489123 8489161 8489167 8489183 8489191 8489197 8489207
8489213 8489227 8489251 8489263 8489267 8489269 8489311 8489329 8489339 8489347
8489357 8489413 8489417 8489423 8489441 8489449 8489473 8489483 8489513 8489521
8489527 8489543 8489581 8489587 8489597 8489603 8489623 8489633 8489639 8489641
8489651 8489659 8489729 8489743 8489777 8489807 8489813 8489839 8489843 8489849
8489857 8489861 8489863 8489867 8489891 8489917 8489927 8489933 8489947 8489951
8489969 8490019 8490023 8490043 8490047 8490071 8490073 8490101 8490107 8490121
8490133 8490143 8490179 8490217 8490233 8490247 8490253 8490271 8490281 8490323
8490341 8490379 8490389 8490401 8490413 8490421 8490439 8490457 8490487 8490491
8490499 8490539 8490541 8490553 8490563 8490571 8490583 8490589 8490593 8490613
8490617 8490619 8490623 8490637 8490661 8490673 8490721 8490761 8490763 8490787
8490791 8490793 8490799 8490827 8490829 8490877 8490893 8490899 8490901 8490913
8490917 8490919 8490941 8490947 8490949 8491001 8491033 8491037 8491051 8491061
8491069 8491073 8491097 8491099 8491121 8491127 8491151 8491169 8491181 8491193
8491207 8491237 8491247 8491267 8491277 8491297 8491319 8491321 8491331 8491333
8491337 8491363 8491369 8491391 8491409 8491411 8491429 8491451 8491453 8491471
8491487 8491507 8491541 8491543 8491547 8491559 8491583 8491589 8491591 8491621
8491643 8491663 8491667 8491673 8491697 8491711 8491723 8491733 8491741 8491753
8491801 8491817 8491829 8491831 8491897 8491919 8491921 8491933 8491943 8491949
8491963 8491969 8492039 8492053 8492093 8492111 8492119 8492123 8492153 8492161
8492179 8492189 8492201 8492249 8492251 8492261 8492303 8492321 8492329 8492369
8492377 8492399 8492413 8492417 8492423 8492437 8492441 8492459 8492461 8492489
8492501 8492507 8492513 8492521 8492533 8492557 8492567 8492569 8492591 8492593
8492597 8492611 8492623 8492633 8492651 8492657 8492683 8492689 8492713 8492717
8492749 8492777 8492797 8492831 8492849 8492857 8492881 8492899 8492903 8492917
8492921 8492927 8492929 8492959 8492963 8492971 8492993 8492999 8493007 8493031
8493073 8493077 8493103 8493127 8493139 8493151 8493157 8493179 8493203 8493257
8493281 8493283 8493293 8493311 8493341 8493367 8493377 8493413 8493427 8493431
8493439 8493449 8493451 8493469 8493487 8493493 8493497 8493503 8493559 8493631
8493637 8493661 8493671 8493697 8493707 8493713 8493731 8493737 8493743 8493763
8493773 8493799 8493803 8493811 8493827 8493841 8493853 8493869 8493883 8493899
8493913 8493937 8493941 8493949 8493959 8493967 8493973 8493977 8493983 8493997
8494019 8494021 8494027 8494037 8494039 8494051 8494063 8494069 8494081 8494099
8494133 8494139 8494147 8494181 8494219 8494231 8494243 8494247 8494253 8494267
8494301 8494313 8494331 8494333 8494351 8494391 8494399 8494439 8494447 8494457
8494459 8494483 8494487 8494523 8494547 8494553 8494559 8494573 8494583 8494597
8494627 8494657 8494663 8494669 8494687 8494699 8494711 8494721 8494727 8494753
8494757 8494769 8494813 8494817 8494823 8494841 8494853 8494897 8494901 8494909
8494939 8494943 8494963 8494973 8494979 8494987 8495029 8495041 8495059 8495063
8495093 8495099 8495101 8495117 8495129 8495141 8495177 8495183 8495191 8495203
8495243 8495251 8495269 8495273 8495321 8495327 8495329 8495341 8495369 8495387
8495407 8495429 8495447 8495449 8495471 8495477 8495497 8495503 8495549 8495561
8495573 8495593 8495609 8495621 8495623 8495629 8495657 8495659 8495677 8495683
8495701 8495731 8495737 8495761 8495783 8495803 8495807 8495849 8495863 8495873
8495887 8495899 8495923 8495933 8495951 8495957 8495959 8495989 8495999 8496001
8496011 8496013 8496017 8496041 8496067 8496079 8496083 8496091 8496109 8496119
8496151 8496193 8496227 8496239 8496247 8496259 8496281 8496343 8496349 8496359
8496403 8496419 8496431 8496437 8496443 8496469 8496479 8496491 8496493 8496503
8496517 8496533 8496539 8496541 8496547 8496571 8496581 8496611 8496661 8496673
8496679 8496713 8496721 8496727 8496731 8496749 8496769 8496773 8496823 8496833
8496841 8496853 8496869 8496871 8496893 8496941 8496949 8496967 8496973 8496979
8497031 8497033 8497037 8497039 8497057 8497091 8497133 8497147 8497157 8497163
8497169 8497207 8497213 8497217 8497219 8497243 8497249 8497259 8497283 8497289
8497303 8497337 8497339 8497343 8497369 8497387 8497403 8497417 8497421 8497429
8497451 8497469 8497507 8497519 8497523 8497561 8497571 8497583 8497607 8497639
8497651 8497661 8497681 8497717 8497757 8497759 8497771 8497817 8497823 8497843
8497849 8497859 8497867 8497873 8497897 8497913 8497927 8497963 8497969 8497991
8498051 8498053 8498071 8498081 8498089 8498099 8498137 8498141 8498143 8498153
8498159 8498167 8498173 8498177 8498233 8498239 8498257 8498297 8498299 8498323
8498327 8498333 8498341 8498353 8498359 8498389 8498401 8498407 8498417 8498423
8498429 8498437 8498449 8498467 8498471 8498473 8498489 8498509 8498519 8498527
8498543 8498549 8498551 8498561 8498573 8498591 8498593 8498647 8498663 8498669
8498671 8498683 8498687 8498701 8498723 8498731 8498761 8498779 8498801 8498837
8498873 8498911 8498953 8498957 8498969 8498977 8498989 8498999 8499037 8499041
8499047 8499077 8499083 8499089 8499097 8499103 8499143 8499193 8499203 8499209
8499223 8499229 8499277 8499287 8499311 8499329 8499367 8499377 8499383 8499389
8499409 8499461 8499503 8499511 8499541 8499571 8499577 8499583 8499589 8499641
8499653 8499661 8499683 8499703 8499727 8499731 8499739 8499763 8499773 8499839
8499851 8499877 8499899 8499917 8499941 8499947 8499971 8499977 8499999 8500007
8500021 8500027 8500057 8500061 8500067 8500069 8500081 8500099 8500109 8500117
8500127 8500139 8500157 8500159 8500181 8500183 8500211 8500213 8500229 8500249
8500259 8500309 8500313 8500337 8500361 8500381 8500399 8500403 8500421 8500433
8500447 8500483 8500517 8500519 8500529 8500549 8500573 8500577 8500579 8500607
```

8500621 8500633 8500643 8500673 8500691 8500699 8500703 8500711 8500729 8500753
8500757 8500781 8500783 8500819 8500841 8500859 8500871 8500873 8500879 8500881
8500903 8500907 8500931 8500951 8500957 8500963 8500967 8501011 8501023 8501029
8501033 8501039 8501067 8501117 8501123 8501159 8501183 8501201 8501209 8501221
8501239 8501243 8501267 8501293 8501323 8501351 8501357 8501399 8501431 8501443
8501447 8501459 8501461 8501477 8501489 8501497 8501543 8501551 8501557 8501561
8501567 8501579 8501609 8501617 8501627 8501639 8501641 8501663 8501671 8501681
8501693 8501711 8501729 8501737 8501767 8501777 8501813 8501821 8501837 8501839
8501849 8501861 8501869 8501893 8501923 8501951 8501993 8502041 8502049 8502061
8502073 8502097 8502103 8502121 8502127 8502161 8502181 8502187 8502251 8502287
8502301 8502311 8502317 8502343 8502349 8502353 8502359 8502371 8502379 8502391
8502409 8502449 8502467 8502469 8502493 8502497 8502503 8502509 8502553 8502577
8502581 8502583 8502589 8502619 8502643 8502661 8502677 8502707 8502719 8502727
8502733 8502743 8502749 8502751 8502757 8502787 8502797 8502799 8502803 8502811
8502827 8502841 8502853 8502881 8502883 8502913 8502917 8502929 8502931 8502943
8502947 8502953 8502997 8503039 8503057 8503063 8503067 8503073 8503087 8503091
8503093 8503109 8503133 8503141 8503147 8503163 8503189 8503211 8503219 8503223
8503237 8503273 8503283 8503289 8503309 8503321 8503337 8503357 8503361 8503403
8503421 8503423 8503427 8503447 8503471 8503477 8503483 8503489 8503499 8503501
8503513 8503529 8503531 8503559 8503609 8503631 8503643 8503657 8503681 8503711
8503717 8503751 8503777 8503787 8503799 8503819 8503829 8503837 8503871 8503879
8503907 8503919 8503967 8503973 8503991 8503993 8504021 8504051 8504053 8504057
8504081 8504129 8504143 8504183 8504189 8504203 8504231 8504257 8504291 8504297
8504299 8504303 8504317 8504341 8504347 8504357 8504359 8504393 8504399 8504417
8504423 8504449 8504459 8504477 8504501 8504513 8504527 8504543 8504559 8504563
8504567 8504579 8504581 8504591 8504597 8504599 8504653 8504659 8504693 8504729
8504759 8504767 8504789 8504807 8504849 8504887 8504891 8504893 8504933 8504941
8504953 8504971 8504983 8504987 8505001 8505023 8505031 8505037 8505053 8505059
8505071 8505089 8505113 8505127 8505137 8505187 8505197 8505209 8505221 8505229
8505247 8505257 8505269 8505283 8505313 8505337 8505347 8505359 8505361 8505373
8505391 8505401 8505403 8505433 8505451 8505461 8505467 8505473 8505481 8505487
8505509 8505517 8505527 8505533 8505547 8505551 8505569 8505577 8505619 8505631
8505643 8505647 8505649 8505667 8505691 8505709 8505719 8505727 8505767 8505769
8505793 8505799 8505811 8505821 8505823 8505841 8505859 8505881 8505907 8505941
8505943 8505949 8505979 8505989 8506031 8506039 8506051 8506063 8506081 8506087
8506093 8506117 8506153 8506163 8506181 8506213 8506219 8506271 8506279 8506291
8506313 8506327 8506331 8506339 8506349 8506361 8506363 8506373 8506391 8506403
8506423 8506427 8506441 8506501 8506507 8506513 8506517 8506543 8506549 8506571
8506643 8506649 8506651 8506703 8506717 8506759 8506777 8506787 8506801 8506811
8506829 8506843 8506847 8506867 8506907 8506921 8506933 8506937 8506951 8506963
8506973 8507017 8507029 8507039 8507053 8507069 8507081 8507087 8507099 8507101
8507137 8507159 8507167 8507173 8507197 8507207 8507209 8507221 8507267 8507281
8507321 8507357 8507363 8507371 8507407 8507419 8507461 8507467 8507479 8507483
8507537 8507549 8507561 8507591 8507617 8507627 8507647 8507651 8507659 8507689
8507711 8507729 8507753 8507761 8507783 8507789 8507791 8507797 8507809 8507831
8507833 8507843 8507879 8507881 8507887 8507897 8507899 8507909 8507911 8507921
8507929 8507957 8507959 8508011 8508013 8508053 8508061 8508083 8508089 8508103
8508127 8508151 8508169 8508173 8508179 8508191 8508193 8508209 8508217 8508251
8508277 8508287 8508289 8508293 8508323 8508337 8508343 8508373 8508389 8508391
8508403 8508421 8508433 8508469 8508473 8508491 8508509 8508527 8508529 8508547
8508553 8508559 8508583 8508589 8508593 8508611 8508613 8508623 8508671 8508679
8508691 8508719 8508733 8508737 8508749 8508757 8508761 8508767 8508769 8508793
8508809 8508811 8508841 8508881 8508893 8508917 8508923 8508931 8508949 8508967
8508989 8509009 8509031 8509037 8509043 8509049 8509063 8509069 8509079 8509087
8509091 8509121 8509133 8509147 8509183 8509199 8509211 8509219 8509229 8509247
8509261 8509301 8509303 8509331 8509339 8509349 8509363 8509373 8509387 8509403
8509451 8509453 8509483 8509489 8509507 8509513 8509541 8509547 8509573 8509577
8509583 8509597 8509601 8509607 8509619 8509649 8509661 8509681 8509703 8509727
8509751 8509763 8509769 8509783 8509799 8509811 8509849 8509861 8509873 8509883
8509901 8509909 8509933 8509937 8509939 8509973 8509981 8509987 8509999 8510009
8510011 8510017 8510039 8510057 8510059 8510071 8510129 8510147 8510167 8510179
8510191 8510237 8510287 8510317 8510323 8510339 8510351 8510357 8510401 8510419
8510429 8510441 8510443 8510479 8510497 8510501 8510507 8510519 8510527 8510531
8510539 8510609 8510617 8510627 8510639 8510641 8510653 8510669 8510701 8510707
8510729 8510743 8510753 8510767 8510797 8510819 8510839 8510849 8510921 8510923
8510933 8510959 8510969 8510977 8510987 8511001 8511011 8511017 8511023 8511037
8511043 8511049 8511053 8511059 8511079 8511091 8511121 8511131 8511157 8511161
8511187 8511193 8511197 8511223 8511229 8511247 8511253 8511287 8511301 8511317
8511319 8511331 8511353 8511361 8511367 8511383 8511439 8511457 8511491 8511497
8511511 8511521 8511523 8511527 8511557 8511571 8511589 8511599 8511617 8511619
8511631 8511637 8511647 8511649 8511683 8511689 8511691 8511731 8511787 8511793
8511799 8511803 8511809 8511821 8511857 8511859 8511907 8511911 8511913 8511929
8511931 8511941 8511953 8511973 8511983 8511991 8512003 8512033 8512039 8512043
8512067 8512079 8512081 8512111 8512117 8512129 8512169 8512181 8512187 8512193
8512201 8512219 8512267 8512271 8512307 8512313 8512337 8512351 8512363 8512391
8512411 8512421 8512423 8512433 8512451 8512453 8512523 8512531 8512547 8512549
8512561 8512571 8512577 8512607 8512633 8512639 8512643 8512663 8512709 8512717
8512723 8512739 8512759 8512771 8512787 8512793 8512799 8512831 8512837 8512841
8512853 8512859 8512877 8512883 8512891 8512901 8512909 8512919 8512981 8512991
8512993 8513023 8513033 8513069 8513077 8513111 8513129 8513137 8513143 8513147
8513171 8513173 8513177 8513179 8513201 8513207 8513233 8513237 8513257 8513291
8513321 8513339 8513341 8513347 8513357 8513359 8513389 8513429 8513431 8513459
8513467 8513497 8513507 8513509 8513513 8513521 8513537 8513551 8513563 8513579
8513597 8513629 8513633 8513647 8513677 8513683 8513693 8513731 8513783 8513797
8513801 8513803 8513819 8513839 8513861 8513863 8513893 8513899 8513927 8513929
8513941 8513951 8513969 8513971 8513977 8513987 8513993 8514013 8514029 8514041
8514049 8514073 8514131 8514133 8514137 8514157 8514169 8514173 8514179 8514193
8514203 8514227 8514239 8514241 8514251 8514257 8514277 8514343 8514353 8514361
8514377 8514409 8514419 8514463 8514469 8514479 8514481 8514497 8514509 8514521

```
8514523  8514529  8514547  8514557  8514599  8514601  8514619  8514683  8514691  8514697
8514707  8514743  8514749  8514787  8514791  8514797  8514823  8514833  8514871  8514881
8514901  8514911  8514923  8514941  8514949  8515063  8515081  8515123  8515127  8515141
8515153  8515159  8515207  8515229  8515237  8515277  8515289  8515301  8515303  8515307
8515321  8515361  8515369  8515373  8515379  8515391  8515433  8515447  8515471  8515511
8515519  8515541  8515561  8515597  8515621  8515627  8515631  8515649  8515651  8515673
8515679  8515687  8515697  8515699  8515711  8515721  8515723  8515747  8515757  8515769
8515813  8515847  8515853  8515867  8515877  8515889  8515891  8515907  8515909  8515931
8515939  8515951  8515967  8515993  8515999  8516029  8516051  8516059  8516077  8516083
8516153  8516159  8516173  8516177  8516197  8516213  8516251  8516273  8516297  8516323
8516329  8516341  8516357  8516363  8516407  8516419  8516429  8516467  8516477  8516483
8516489  8516491  8516513  8516527  8516533  8516539  8516567  8516569  8516581  8516597
8516611  8516621  8516639  8516653  8516657  8516659  8516701  8516707  8516737  8516741
8516743  8516773  8516797  8516803  8516819  8516843  8516857  8516863  8516867  8516873
8516887  8516899  8516927  8516951  8516957  8516987  8517023  8517029  8517031  8517037
8517049  8517071  8517077  8517083  8517121  8517127  8517137  8517163  8517169  8517191
8517193  8517203  8517233  8517253  8517269  8517277  8517319  8517331  8517349  8517359
8517401  8517403  8517409  8517413  8517419  8517433  8517449  8517461  8517469  8517479
8517497  8517499  8517517  8517541  8517547  8517557  8517563  8517571  8517581  8517583
8517589  8517599  8517611  8517617  8517631  8517661  8517671  8517727  8517737  8517767
8517779  8517787  8517823  8517863  8517877  8517893  8517907  8517919  8517937  8517983
8517991  8518009  8518019  8518021  8518033  8518039  8518049  8518051  8518067  8518079
8518091  8518109  8518121  8518157  8518183  8518189  8518219  8518231  8518261  8518277
8518291  8518331  8518339  8518351  8518357  8518369  8518387  8518417  8518427  8518439
8518451  8518481  8518483  8518493  8518501  8518507  8518519  8518541  8518567  8518577
8518603  8518607  8518613  8518619  8518639  8518661  8518667  8518681  8518709
8518723  8518729  8518733  8518739  8518747  8518771  8518781  8518787  8518801  8518841
8518847  8518883  8518889  8518907  8518931  8518933  8518963  8518969  8518981  8518997
8518999  8519009  8519041  8519051  8519053  8519081  8519089  8519111  8519143  8519207
8519209  8519221  8519237  8519257  8519263  8519279  8519299  8519317  8519351  8519377
8519383  8519387  8519393  8519411  8519471  8519473  8519477  8519479  8519491  8519551
8519569  8519587  8519603  8519617  8519647  8519681  8519711  8519717  8519723  8519743
8519747  8519773  8519783  8519789  8519813  8519827  8519837  8519843  8519857  8519869
8519887  8519899  8519911  8519933  8519957  8519963  8519971  8519983  8519989
8520007  8520011  8520023  8520041  8520079  8520091  8520103  8520107  8520139  8520157
8520163  8520181  8520191  8520241  8520269  8520289  8520293  8520307  8520311  8520329
8520331  8520353  8520359  8520389  8520401  8520409  8520427  8520431  8520433  8520437
8520481  8520503  8520509  8520521  8520527  8520571  8520613  8520623  8520647  8520653
8520679  8520709  8520713  8520719  8520737  8520739  8520749  8520761  8520793  8520803
8520821  8520829  8520851  8520887  8520901  8520913  8520929  8520943  8520947  8520973
8520979  8521003  8521013  8521021  8521061  8521069  8521091  8521103  8521111  8521129
8521133  8521141  8521171  8521189  8521213  8521223  8521229  8521231  8521237  8521243
8521259  8521283  8521297  8521321  8521327  8521343  8521391  8521397  8521411  8521417
8521427  8521451  8521453  8521501  8521561  8521567  8521577  8521589  8521603  8521613
8521619  8521631  8521649  8521687  8521699  8521703  8521739  8521759  8521763  8521781
8521787  8521789  8521813  8521819  8521829  8521831  8521841  8521867  8521871  8521907
8521939  8521949  8521963  8521999  8522009  8522021  8522039  8522047  8522113  8522119
8522141  8522147  8522149  8522159  8522161  8522197  8522207  8522209  8522221  8522233
8522237  8522251  8522281  8522291  8522309  8522341  8522363  8522401  8522407  8522411
8522413  8522419  8522429  8522461  8522473  8522477  8522497  8522509  8522513  8522533
8522537  8522561  8522567  8522603  8522623  8522639  8522641  8522663  8522669  8522671
8522681  8522699  8522707  8522713  8522741  8522743  8522749  8522777  8522779  8522791
8522803  8522809  8522863  8522909  8522939  8522951  8522959  8522989  8522999  8523007
8523017  8523029  8523043  8523049  8523083  8523091  8523101  8523113  8523127  8523131
8523139  8523143  8523149  8523173  8523211  8523223  8523227  8523259  8523287  8523311
8523313  8523323  8523329  8523349  8523391  8523397  8523413  8523421  8523439  8523461
8523467  8523499  8523509  8523517  8523521  8523523  8523527  8523587  8523601  8523607
8523611  8523617  8523629  8523631  8523637  8523643  8523659  8523661  8523679  8523689
8523701  8523707  8523719  8523721  8523733  8523743  8523769  8523773  8523787  8523793
8523821  8523841  8523877  8523881  8523899  8523917  8523959  8523973  8523979  8524013
8524037  8524049  8524073  8524079  8524091  8524111  8524193  8524207  8524213  8524247
8524253  8524267  8524273  8524279  8524291  8524297  8524303  8524333  8524339  8524357
8524391  8524423  8524427  8524441  8524487  8524489  8524499  8524507  8524511  8524543
8524547  8524553  8524561  8524591  8524603  8524609  8524613  8524631  8524639  8524643
8524657  8524669  8524699  8524709  8524717  8524723  8524727  8524729  8524739  8524741
8524777  8524799  8524801  8524807  8524819  8524823  8524853  8524877  8524889  8524897
8524909  8524931  8524949  8524951  8524963  8524979  8524981  8524987  8524993  8525017
8525029  8525047  8525071  8525113  8525117  8525119  8525131  8525141  8525149  8525161
8525191  8525201  8525213  8525227  8525239  8525261  8525263  8525291  8525329  8525351
8525371  8525401  8525411  8525431  8525459  8525477  8525497  8525501  8525521  8525557
8525579  8525593  8525599  8525603  8525669  8525689  8525701  8525707  8525711  8525723
8525729  8525731  8525747  8525749  8525761  8525771  8525773  8525779  8525791  8525809
8525831  8525833  8525849  8525861  8525863  8525879  8525887  8525897  8525969  8525971
8525981  8525983  8525989  8526013  8526017  8526053  8526059  8526071  8526097  8526101
8526107  8526127  8526143  8526151  8526173  8526179  8526191  8526211  8526247  8526251
8526253  8526257  8526277  8526281  8526283  8526359  8526373  8526389  8526403  8526409
8526439  8526449  8526451  8526499  8526527  8526533  8526541  8526559  8526563  8526569
8526577  8526601  8526607  8526631  8526671  8526691  8526709  8526719  8526733  8526737
8526769  8526773  8526779  8526781  8526797  8526863  8526871  8526901  8526913  8526919
8526929  8526941  8526949  8526971  8526977  8527009  8527021  8527027  8527033  8527037
8527039  8527049  8527087  8527097  8527109  8527147  8527159  8527177  8527193  8527213
8527229  8527231  8527237  8527243  8527261  8527271  8527283  8527289  8527301  8527331
8527361  8527369  8527391  8527399  8527403  8527417  8527429  8527433  8527439  8527451
8527469  8527471  8527481  8527487  8527499  8527513  8527529  8527543  8527601  8527609
8527613  8527619  8527627  8527643  8527661  8527663  8527681  8527691  8527699  8527741
8527763  8527777  8527781  8527807  8527817  8527819  8527837  8527843  8527847  8527853
8527867  8527873  8527901  8527913  8527921  8527927  8527951  8527991  8528021  8528029
8528057  8528063  8528087  8528111  8528141  8528159  8528171  8528173  8528183  8528209
8528213  8528243  8528257  8528281  8528309  8528353  8528357  8528383  8528411  8528417
```

```
8528461  8528467  8528483  8528489  8528519  8528551  8528557  8528563  8528567  8528599
8528609  8528633  8528657  8528671  8528683  8528687  8528693  8528717  8528783  8528789
8528797  8528843  8528867  8528873  8528879  8528887  8528893  8528903  8528911  8528969
8528977  8528983  8529023  8529041  8529047  8529049  8529089  8529091  8529097  8529109
8529139  8529173  8529197  8529221  8529229  8529259  8529281  8529293  8529299  8529317
8529361  8529373  8529383  8529397  8529403  8529413  8529439  8529473  8529559  8529601
8529611  8529617  8529623  8529641  8529643  8529649  8529659  8529673  8529679  8529707
8529749  8529751  8529761  8529769  8529779  8529809  8529811  8529821  8529823  8529847
8529853  8529863  8529877  8529919  8529923  8529931  8529949  8529959  8530001  8530003
8530007  8530037  8530051  8530063  8530099  8530103  8530117  8530121  8530127  8530133
8530213  8530219  8530229  8530237  8530241  8530253  8530261  8530273  8530283  8530289
8530307  8530351  8530367  8530391  8530409  8530427  8530441  8530451  8530523  8530531
8530537  8530541  8530567  8530591  8530597  8530619  8530637  8530693  8530699  8530733
8530759  8530771  8530799  8530801  8530807  8530811  8530817  8530849  8530891  8530897
8530913  8530927  8530939  8531009  8531021  8531023  8531051  8531063  8531099  8531101
8531129  8531141  8531153  8531189  8531197  8531203  8531207  8531213  8531219  8531221
8531227  8531233  8531267  8531269  8531279  8531287  8531309  8531317  8531333
8531339  8531359  8531371  8531381  8531389  8531407  8531429  8531443  8531461  8531473
8531477  8531483  8531489  8531507  8531531  8531533  8531543  8531561  8531609  8531617
8531639  8531647  8531659  8531683  8531687  8531693  8531707  8531711  8531717  8531749
8531767  8531801  8531821  8531833  8531849  8531879  8531881  8531903  8531911  8531923
8531933  8531947  8532019  8532031  8532071  8532127  8532133  8532137  8532157  8532169
8532179  8532191  8532221  8532229  8532233  8532247  8532257  8532259  8532269  8532281
8532289  8532299  8532301  8532319  8532323  8532331  8532343  8532371  8532413  8532421
8532437  8532439  8532443  8532449  8532457  8532473  8532541  8532547  8532569  8532571
8532593  8532631  8532637  8532659  8532679  8532707  8532737  8532739  8532761  8532773
8532779  8532787  8532809  8532817  8532833  8532889  8532893  8532899  8532911  8532913
8532917  8532941  8532943  8532971  8532973  8532983  8533001  8533009  8533061  8533067
8533073  8533079  8533097  8533103  8533123  8533139  8533141  8533169  8533183  8533211
8533237  8533267  8533297  8533309  8533333  8533361  8533363  8533387  8533397  8533411
8533429  8533433  8533457  8533513  8533517  8533531  8533537  8533543  8533549  8533559
8533601  8533619  8533639  8533663  8533669  8533673  8533697  8533729  8533739  8533741
8533751  8533753  8533757  8533783  8533787  8533799  8533829  8533841  8533849  8533853
8533871  8533879  8533883  8533891  8533913  8533933  8533951  8533979  8533981  8534003
8534011  8534023  8534041  8534047  8534069  8534089  8534101  8534107  8534131  8534137
8534147  8534177  8534179  8534189  8534203  8534209  8534243  8534261  8534297
8534303  8534329  8534341  8534347  8534353  8534359  8534371  8534377  8534387  8534411
8534419  8534423  8534429  8534441  8534443  8534447  8534467  8534473  8534489  8534509
8534521  8534543  8534549  8534567  8534569  8534573  8534593  8534621  8534627  8534639
8534651  8534657  8534681  8534699  8534707  8534717  8534741  8534759  8534789  8534791
8534849  8534861  8534873  8534891  8534917  8534921  8534927  8534947  8534957  8534959
8534983  8534989  8534993  8535029  8535031  8535061  8535083  8535089  8535091  8535097
8535119  8535157  8535179  8535209  8535211  8535223  8535253  8535259  8535269  8535287
8535337  8535347  8535349  8535361  8535403  8535413  8535431  8535433  8535437  8535469
8535473  8535487  8535523  8535533  8535539  8535551  8535559  8535587  8535607  8535613
8535661  8535673  8535677  8535689  8535701  8535719  8535721  8535727  8535739  8535743
8535767  8535781  8535847  8535869  8535911  8535929  8535931  8535949  8535977  8535983
8535991  8536007  8536037  8536043  8536069  8536081  8536101  8536103  8536153  8536169  8536183
8536201  8536219  8536223  8536249  8536267  8536271  8536273  8536277  8536313  8536321
8536343  8536351  8536357  8536361  8536379  8536387  8536399  8536417  8536441  8536457
8536459  8536471  8536477  8536511  8536513  8536531  8536571  8536573  8536579  8536631
8536637  8536673  8536699  8536709  8536711  8536721  8536727  8536729  8536739  8536753
8536777  8536783  8536793  8536807  8536831  8536869  8536883  8536903  8536921  8536961
8536993  8536999  8537003  8537027  8537041  8537051  8537083  8537093  8537101  8537153
8537159  8537167  8537173  8537197  8537201  8537203  8537219  8537237  8537239  8537267
8537303  8537317  8537323  8537329  8537357  8537381  8537387  8537407  8537411  8537413
8537437  8537443  8537447  8537467  8537497  8537527  8537533  8537539  8537549  8537561
8537563  8537603  8537651  8537657  8537671  8537699  8537731  8537747  8537759  8537801
8537839  8537857  8537873  8537911  8537923  8537933  8537957  8537959  8537981  8537983
8538017  8538031  8538053  8538071  8538073  8538077  8538107  8538143  8538149  8538193
8538223  8538227  8538259  8538263  8538269  8538281  8538317  8538319  8538331  8538347
8538367  8538371  8538377  8538401  8538419  8538433  8538457  8538461  8538469  8538511
8538529  8538533  8538587  8538599  8538611  8538613  8538617  8538637  8538653  8538659
8538667  8538679  8538683  8538689  8538697  8538703  8538713  8538721  8538767  8538779
8538781  8538793  8538797  8538833  8538839  8538851  8538853  8538869  8538889  8538931
8538941  8538967  8538977  8538979  8538991  8538997  8539033  8539039  8539051  8539057
8539061  8539067  8539087  8539093  8539121  8539147  8539163  8539171  8539177  8539183
8539199  8539213  8539259  8539273  8539277  8539301  8539313  8539337  8539343  8539361
8539373  8539393  8539397  8539409  8539429  8539441  8539471  8539507  8539537  8539547
8539561  8539567  8539591  8539631  8539669  8539673  8539679  8539691  8539747  8539771
8539781  8539807  8539813  8539829  8539847  8539889  8539901  8539903  8539907  8539913
8539919  8539961  8539997  8540003  8540009  8540011  8540027  8540033  8540047  8540053
8540083  8540087  8540089  8540099  8540111  8540113  8540117  8540141  8540143  8540167
8540179  8540219  8540227  8540237  8540243  8540281  8540293  8540327  8540333  8540339
8540347  8540353  8540381  8540387  8540393  8540401  8540431  8540461  8540479  8540501
8540503  8540507  8540509  8540513  8540527  8540533  8540537  8540551  8540563  8540569
8540573  8540621  8540629  8540639  8540683  8540689  8540713  8540723  8540729  8540731
8540737  8540743  8540759  8540771  8540773  8540801  8540809  8540839  8540849  8540867
8540869  8540891  8540893  8540921  8540933  8540941  8540971  8540977  8540989  8540999
8541007  8541011  8541023  8541041  8541053  8541067  8541101  8541121  8541139  8541149
8541163  8541173  8541179  8541199  8541217  8541233  8541251  8541277  8541289  8541301
8541307  8541319  8541347  8541353  8541359  8541367  8541373  8541389  8541397  8541409
8541473  8541479  8541499  8541503  8541509  8541517  8541521  8541551  8541553  8541587
8541679  8541691  8541707  8541713  8541721  8541737  8541749  8541751  8541823  8541881
8541889  8541941  8541943  8541959  8541971  8541983  8541991  8541997  8542043  8542057
8542067  8542069  8542129  8542133  8542139  8542141  8542151  8542189  8542201  8542243
8542253  8542273  8542291  8542321  8542333  8542351  8542357  8542363  8542367  8542409
8542411  8542421  8542427  8542451  8542459  8542463  8542481  8542493  8542519
8542529  8542531  8542537  8542549  8542553  8542561  8542601  8542603  8542621  8542631
```

```
8542643  8542663  8542711  8542747  8542769  8542771  8542777  8542811  8542817  8542847
8542873  8542879  8542927  8542943  8542973  8542979  8542999  8543009  8543069  8543071
8543077  8543083  8543089  8543099  8543113  8543131  8543137  8543147  8543149  8543153
8543167  8543177  8543191  8543207  8543257  8543261  8543267  8543279  8543309  8543317
8543323  8543329  8543341  8543347  8543363  8543387  8543389  8543399  8543413  8543443
8543453  8543459  8543461  8543471  8543473  8543527  8543543  8543551  8543567  8543573
8543609  8543617  8543641  8543651  8543657  8543681  8543683  8543687  8543699  8543723
8543729  8543753  8543779  8543791  8543803  8543807  8543819  8543827  8543831  8543839
8543861  8543881  8543903  8543923  8543957  8543963  8543969  8543999  8544001  8544007
8544037  8544049  8544059  8544071  8544073  8544079  8544121  8544131  8544157  8544161
8544163  8544169  8544197  8544199  8544223  8544253  8544287  8544301  8544307  8544317
8544329  8544337  8544379  8544383  8544391  8544397  8544413  8544427  8544449  8544451
8544457  8544491  8544493  8544527  8544539  8544541  8544551  8544593  8544617  8544629
8544649  8544671  8544709  8544733  8544751  8544773  8544797  8544803  8544839  8544841
8544853  8544859  8544953  8544971  8544973  8544997  8545007  8545049  8545051  8545073
8545087  8545091  8545109  8545123  8545139  8545151  8545153  8545177  8545183  8545217
8545249  8545279  8545283  8545291  8545301  8545319  8545321  8545331  8545333  8545337
8545357  8545387  8545417  8545447  8545451  8545463  8545469  8545477  8545491  8545499
8545529  8545541  8545571  8545613  8545637  8545643  8545651  8545661  8545667  8545699
8545717  8545721  8545729  8545759  8545787  8545813  8545829  8545837  8545841  8545843
8545907  8545909  8545937  8545939  8545961  8545967  8545993  8546017  8546023  8546059
8546093  8546107  8546117  8546119  8546123  8546129  8546171  8546201  8546227  8546243
8546249  8546267  8546273  8546287  8546311  8546381  8546383  8546389  8546407  8546413
8546423  8546429  8546431  8546437  8546441  8546443  8546459  8546467  8546477  8546497
8546507  8546521  8546537  8546539  8546543  8546611  8546623  8546627  8546633  8546647
8546651  8546653  8546663  8546683  8546687  8546689  8546717  8546743  8546749  8546761
8546779  8546803  8546807  8546831  8546843  8546899  8546911  8546927  8546929  8546933
8546947  8546953  8546959  8546969  8546999  8547029  8547031  8547079  8547109  8547113
8547157  8547171  8547179  8547197  8547211  8547223  8547233  8547241  8547251  8547269
8547317  8547353  8547361  8547377  8547403  8547419  8547437  8547463  8547491  8547493
8547499  8547509  8547521  8547523  8547541  8547593  8547601  8547631  8547641  8547653
8547667  8547673  8547677  8547767  8547809  8547817  8547829  8547839  8547857  8547863
8547871  8547887  8547899  8547901  8547907  8547911  8547919  8547941  8547947  8547949
8547983  8548003  8548009  8548039  8548063  8548079  8548091  8548109  8548121  8548129
8548151  8548159  8548171  8548181  8548193  8548201  8548223  8548231  8548237  8548247
8548273  8548277  8548283  8548291  8548303  8548321  8548327  8548339  8548363  8548367
8548409  8548411  8548429  8548447  8548453  8548469  8548483  8548487  8548489  8548523
8548559  8548567  8548583  8548609  8548619  8548621  8548627  8548643  8548681  8548693
8548697  8548721  8548733  8548747  8548759  8548769  8548781  8548817  8548829  8548831
8548843  8548849  8548853  8548913  8548927  8548933  8548949  8548987  8549027  8549071
8549117  8549129  8549137  8549153  8549201  8549243  8549263  8549291  8549293  8549329
8549339  8549371  8549383  8549413  8549417  8549503  8549507  8549531  8549539  8549543
8549557  8549573  8549579  8549591  8549599  8549609  8549641  8549663  8549683  8549711
8549719  8549773  8549777  8549789  8549797  8549837  8549857  8549881  8549887  8549903
8549909  8549921  8549941  8549969  8550001  8550007  8550011  8550023  8550037  8550053
8550107  8550109  8550161  8550169  8550197  8550211  8550229  8550251  8550253  8550301
8550313  8550329  8550341  8550349  8550359  8550379  8550397  8550413  8550419  8550449
8550461  8550469  8550481  8550517  8550547  8550557  8550571  8550583  8550611  8550613
8550617  8550623  8550653  8550667  8550671  8550683  8550697  8550727  8550739  8550769
8550781  8550791  8550793  8550799  8550803  8550821  8550827  8550859  8550869  8550877
8550887  8550889  8550907  8550943  8550973  8550977  8550989  8550991  8551019  8551043
8551057  8551061  8551063  8551069  8551079  8551087  8551091  8551097  8551099  8551139
8551157  8551171  8551189  8551211  8551219  8551223  8551243  8551253  8551271  8551297
8551303  8551307  8551313  8551337  8551351  8551373  8551379  8551393  8551397  8551409
8551421  8551427  8551441  8551447  8551451  8551457  8551481  8551483  8551489  8551507
8551511  8551523  8551531  8551537  8551541  8551553  8551579  8551591  8551601  8551639
8551667  8551687  8551721  8551733  8551759  8551769  8551783  8551787  8551789  8551819
8551831  8551849  8551853  8551871  8551889  8551891  8551931  8551937  8551981  8551993
8551997  8552039  8552057  8552059  8552077  8552101  8552107  8552111  8552119  8552123
8552161  8552177  8552191  8552213  8552221  8552233  8552263  8552267  8552279  8552281
8552287  8552293  8552339  8552347  8552351  8552353  8552359  8552363  8552381  8552429
8552437  8552443  8552459  8552471  8552473  8552491  8552501  8552503  8552519  8552521
8552539  8552549  8552563  8552567  8552591  8552623  8552629  8552647  8552653  8552659
8552671  8552681  8552689  8552707  8552737  8552741  8552771  8552779  8552801  8552813
8552833  8552851  8552861  8552867  8552881  8552897  8552909  8552911  8552923  8552927
8552939  8552953  8552959  8553007  8553029  8553043  8553073  8553101  8553113  8553119
8553137  8553143  8553163  8553187  8553199  8553221  8553229  8553247  8553269  8553271
8553277  8553283  8553301  8553313  8553337  8553361  8553367  8553373  8553403  8553437
8553449  8553451  8553469  8553487  8553491  8553497  8553527  8553529  8553541  8553547
8553563  8553569  8553581  8553593  8553599  8553607  8553619  8553673  8553679  8553683
8553691  8553719  8553733  8553749  8553757  8553767  8553773  8553793  8553803  8553817
8553821  8553827  8553833  8553851  8553877  8553911  8553913  8553929  8553949  8553959
8553967  8553973  8553989  8554019  8554027  8554031  8554049  8554079  8554081  8554093
8554099  8554103  8554121  8554127  8554153  8554157  8554163  8554177  8554187  8554193
8554223  8554243  8554261  8554267  8554277  8554279  8554283  8554297  8554309  8554327
8554361  8554373  8554379  8554387  8554393  8554421  8554453  8554471  8554487  8554489
8554501  8554523  8554529  8554547  8554607  8554619  8554633  8554639  8554649  8554669
8554687  8554697  8554707  8554717  8554747  8554751  8554771  8554787  8554789  8554817
8554829  8554837  8554849  8554867  8554877  8554901  8554907  8554939  8554951  8554957
8554969  8554979  8554981  8554993  8554999  8555021  8555047  8555051  8555123  8555143
8555153  8555159  8555171  8555191  8555221  8555227  8555279  8555291  8555317  8555321
8555353  8555359  8555389  8555441  8555447  8555461  8555467  8555507  8555543  8555549
8555557  8555587  8555611  8555623  8555629  8555633  8555639  8555683  8555693  8555711
8555717  8555749  8555759  8555761  8555773  8555791  8555801  8555803  8555809  8555831
8555861  8555873  8555881  8555887  8555891  8555903  8555929  8555933  8555951  8555959
8555999  8556001  8556007  8556017  8556059  8556071  8556089  8556091  8556133  8556157
8556181  8556187  8556199  8556203  8556211  8556241  8556271  8556277  8556319  8556323
8556347  8556349  8556419  8556463  8556467  8556511  8556521  8556523  8556557  8556563
8556571  8556629  8556641  8556649  8556671  8556697  8556739  8556749  8556761  8556791
```

```
8556817  8556839  8556853  8556869  8556887  8556893  8556907  8556923  8556937  8556941
8556949  8556959  8557007  8557013  8557033  8557057  8557061  8557063  8557067  8557079
8557091  8557093  8557121  8557123  8557139  8557169  8557181  8557189  8557193  8557207
8557223  8557229  8557253  8557267  8557303  8557309  8557319  8557363  8557399  8557411
8557421  8557447  8557459  8557463  8557469  8557489  8557529  8557531  8557547  8557553
8557567  8557573  8557589  8557607  8557609  8557649  8557691  8557711  8557721  8557723
8557727  8557729  8557763  8557777  8557781  8557793  8557799  8557819  8557853  8557859
8557867  8557897  8557907  8557921  8557931  8557933  8557937  8557981  8557993  8558003
8558027  8558029  8558041  8558053  8558087  8558101  8558107  8558119  8558159  8558171
8558233  8558261  8558273  8558287  8558309  8558311  8558321  8558399  8558413  8558423
8558441  8558443  8558453  8558471  8558477  8558479  8558489  8558491  8558503  8558521
8558549  8558551  8558587  8558603  8558611  8558629  8558651  8558659  8558681  8558687
8558689  8558713  8558723  8558731  8558743  8558749  8558761  8558777  8558779  8558813
8558827  8558833  8558843  8558861  8558867  8558881  8558887  8558897  8558899  8558929
8558933  8558941  8558999  8559011  8559017  8559073  8559079  8559091  8559113  8559127
8559137  8559149  8559157  8559179  8559181  8559223  8559227  8559233  8559259  8559269
8559277  8559301  8559361  8559371  8559373  8559389  8559391  8559401  8559431  8559433
8559479  8559487  8559491  8559511  8559533  8559539  8559559  8559563  8559569  8559583
8559589  8559599  8559613  8559631  8559713  8559767  8559773  8559799  8559827  8559829
8559833  8559869  8559877  8559917  8559949  8559983  8559989  8560001  8560007  8560009
8560031  8560049  8560073  8560087  8560093  8560099  8560159  8560169  8560217  8560219
8560229  8560289  8560299  8560301  8560303  8560319  8560327  8560337  8560373  8560403
8560411  8560417  8560421  8560427  8560441  8560451  8560463  8560493  8560499  8560529
8560543  8560549  8560609  8560631  8560633  8560661  8560663  8560687  8560691  8560693
8560711  8560729  8560733  8560753  8560763  8560787  8560793  8560813  8560817  8560823
8560831  8560859  8560879  8560883  8560891  8560907  8560933  8560957  8560961  8561011
8561017  8561027  8561041  8561057  8561071  8561089  8561099  8561101  8561107  8561117
8561131  8561159  8561213  8561237  8561263  8561269  8561279  8561281  8561297  8561299
8561321  8561339  8561341  8561347  8561383  8561407  8561417  8561437  8561447  8561471
8561477  8561479  8561503  8561537  8561551  8561569  8561573  8561603  8561627  8561633
8561701  8561713  8561731  8561737  8561741  8561801  8561803  8561807  8561809  8561857
8561867  8561869  8561887  8561893  8561909  8561939  8561953  8561963  8562023  8562041
8562061  8562077  8562079  8562083  8562121  8562137  8562149  8562167  8562193  8562199
8562251  8562263  8562269  8562283  8562311  8562313  8562329  8562343  8562353  8562361
8562377  8562383  8562397  8562401  8562403  8562409  8562419  8562431  8562457  8562473
8562523  8562527  8562551  8562557  8562581  8562599  8562607  8562613  8562629  8562641
8562643  8562649  8562661  8562683  8562689  8562703  8562707  8562709  8562737  8562751
8562767  8562769  8562773  8562791  8562797  8562803  8562821  8562857  8562887  8562899
8562941  8562943  8562979  8562991  8563001  8563003  8563007  8563031  8563039  8563043
8563067  8563073  8563081  8563109  8563117  8563123  8563141  8563171  8563183  8563187
8563271  8563271  8563277  8563277  8563283  8563307  8563309  8563351  8563397  8563403
8563421  8563463  8563481  8563501  8563517  8563519  8563537  8563553  8563559  8563571
8563589  8563619  8563627  8563637  8563693  8563697  8563717  8563727  8563741  8563747
8563757  8563769  8563771  8563783  8563811  8563817  8563831  8563853  8563859  8563861
8563883  8563901  8563939  8563969  8563987  8564053  8564063  8564071  8564089  8564099
8564113  8564123  8564147  8564167  8564177  8564191  8564197  8564221  8564273  8564291
8564299  8564317  8564321  8564329  8564333  8564341  8564351  8564357  8564359  8564407
8564419  8564431  8564467  8564471  8564503  8564527  8564537  8564551  8564557  8564593
8564597  8564653  8564681  8564713  8564729  8564741  8564749  8564767  8564789  8564791
8564813  8564819  8564833  8564837  8564861  8564863  8564867  8564891  8564909  8564939
8564981  8564987  8565031  8565047  8565049  8565077  8565097  8565107  8565113  8565119
8565203  8565209  8565211  8565217  8565281  8565283  8565289  8565301  8565307  8565317
8565343  8565373  8565379  8565397  8565419  8565439  8565451  8565461  8565509  8565539
8565577  8565581  8565589  8565593  8565619  8565629  8565631  8565673  8565677  8565691
8565707  8565721  8565727  8565731  8565737  8565743  8565787  8565829  8565847  8565853
8565857  8565881  8565917  8565929  8565971  8565989  8566001  8566003  8566009  8566021
8566027  8566031  8566037  8566043  8566109  8566111  8566121  8566123  8566157  8566163
8566177  8566193  8566211  8566213  8566237  8566247  8566279  8566289  8566297  8566301
8566303  8566307  8566319  8566357  8566399  8566409  8566427  8566451  8566469  8566489
8566507  8566543  8566559  8566583  8566601  8566609  8566619  8566627  8566631  8566639
8566651  8566667  8566673  8566697  8566703  8566729  8566771  8566781  8566783  8566799
8566801  8566813  8566823  8566837  8566849  8566897  8566907  8566913  8566949  8566981
8567003  8567033  8567047  8567057  8567059  8567101  8567107  8567131  8567161  8567173
8567179  8567197  8567203  8567219  8567243  8567257  8567261  8567281  8567297  8567311
8567341  8567399  8567411  8567417  8567453  8567513  8567539  8567549  8567561  8567591
8567617  8567619  8567627  8567653  8567681  8567693  8567701  8567717  8567723  8567737
8567743  8567747  8567761  8567809  8567827  8567833  8567851  8567857  8567861  8567863
8567869  8567899  8567903  8567929  8567939  8567953  8567957  8567969  8567987  8567989
8568011  8568019  8568023  8568041  8568047  8568061  8568071  8568073  8568097  8568101
8568113  8568149  8568169  8568179  8568181  8568191  8568221  8568227  8568251  8568271
8568281  8568283  8568319  8568337  8568353  8568379  8568383  8568401  8568403  8568407
8568409  8568433  8568463  8568473  8568491  8568509  8568529  8568541  8568557  8568559
8568583  8568611  8568619  8568643  8568647  8568649  8568661  8568683  8568691  8568701
8568709  8568733  8568737  8568743  8568757  8568761  8568767  8568773  8568787  8568823
8568839  8568851  8568869  8568907  8568913  8568947  8568961  8568979  8569013  8569021
8569031  8569039  8569049  8569063  8569069  8569079  8569081  8569111  8569117  8569147
8569153  8569159  8569189  8569193  8569201  8569229  8569273  8569277  8569283  8569289
8569313  8569321  8569331  8569339  8569349  8569357  8569381  8569387  8569417  8569433
8569441  8569447  8569453  8569469  8569481  8569493  8569499  8569511  8569541  8569553
8569559  8569567  8569571  8569577  8569591  8569619  8569633  8569637  8569663  8569669
8569679  8569699  8569711  8569727  8569747  8569763  8569787  8569793  8569801  8569811
8569871  8569879  8569937  8569949  8569963  8569987  8569991  8570011  8570021  8570041
8570069  8570101  8570107  8570123  8570129  8570137  8570161  8570203  8570207  8570209
8570231  8570267  8570269  8570279  8570293  8570299  8570357  8570371  8570383  8570389
8570411  8570437  8570447  8570449  8570461  8570479  8570483  8570489  8570491  8570509
8570537  8570563  8570587  8570621  8570633  8570641  8570647  8570659  8570671  8570677
8570687  8570701  8570719  8570761  8570797  8570813  8570819  8570827  8570831  8570867
8570869  8570899  8570909  8570923  8570951  8570953  8570963  8570977  8570981  8570983
8570987  8570999  8571011  8571023  8571041  8571047  8571053  8571067  8571083  8571089
```

```
8571113  8571119  8571137  8571151  8571169  8571181  8571197  8571229  8571253  8571259
8571271  8571287  8571289  8571301  8571307  8571317  8571347  8571359  8571361  8571391
8571401  8571403  8571427  8571439  8571467  8571473  8571481  8571487  8571509  8571529
8571533  8571539  8571551  8571581  8571601  8571643  8571649  8571653  8571671  8571677
8571683  8571691  8571701  8571707  8571727  8571751  8571767  8571799  8571803  8571809
8571811  8571839  8571851  8571853  8571863  8571881  8571917  8571919  8571929  8571947
8571967  8571973  8572009  8572033  8572073  8572079  8572099  8572111  8572117  8572121
8572127  8572133  8572141  8572163  8572217  8572219  8572229  8572237  8572241  8572243
8572253  8572279  8572309  8572331  8572339  8572349  8572367  8572387  8572397  8572411
8572427  8572433  8572451  8572483  8572507  8572511  8572517  8572541  8572549  8572589
8572621  8572633  8572639  8572643  8572651  8572657  8572673  8572679  8572693  8572699
8572727  8572783  8572799  8572807  8572829  8572831  8572841  8572853  8572871  8572903
8572961  8573003  8573017  8573023  8573027  8573041  8573051  8573053  8573077  8573101
8573107  8573111  8573167  8573189  8573207  8573209  8573221  8573239  8573249  8573251
8573261  8573269  8573293  8573303  8573309  8573353  8573363  8573377  8573393  8573399
8573401  8573413  8573419  8573429  8573431  8573437  8573441  8573443  8573447  8573449
8573471  8573479  8573497  8573501  8573507  8573519  8573533  8573561  8573567  8573573
8573623  8573657  8573671  8573683  8573689  8573713  8573717  8573723  8573737  8573743
8573749  8573753  8573759  8573767  8573771  8573783  8573801  8573809  8573827  8573843
8573849  8573869  8573951  8573953  8573987  8574019  8574037  8574061  8574067  8574077
8574079  8574089  8574133  8574161  8574179  8574199  8574211  8574229  8574253  8574271
8574277  8574283  8574311  8574323  8574337  8574353  8574359  8574367  8574373  8574403
8574413  8574427  8574437  8574439  8574463  8574473  8574479  8574497  8574521  8574523
8574541  8574547  8574557  8574571  8574623  8574649  8574661  8574667  8574679  8574689
8574721  8574737  8574743  8574751  8574763  8574767  8574809  8574823  8574847  8574857
8574859  8574877  8574887  8574899  8574911  8574959  8574961  8574971  8574977  8574983
8574991  8575013  8575031  8575033  8575037  8575057  8575069  8575079  8575093  8575117
8575121  8575141  8575169  8575181  8575187  8575199  8575201  8575207  8575211  8575219
8575247  8575321  8575331  8575337  8575339  8575351  8575393  8575409  8575423  8575439
8575459  8575487  8575493  8575543  8575547  8575577  8575579  8575603  8575613  8575627
8575649  8575657  8575663  8575703  8575727  8575733  8575739  8575741  8575751  8575759
8575829  8575841  8575873  8575901  8575913  8575937  8575969  8575981  8575991  8575997
8576017  8576021  8576027  8576077  8576081  8576107  8576111  8576123  8576131  8576147
8576153  8576159  8576203  8576207  8576219  8576233  8576261  8576273  8576311  8576317
8576327  8576329  8576333  8576363  8576383  8576387  8576411  8576441  8576443  8576453
8576459  8576461  8576507  8576509  8576521  8576531  8576549  8576567  8576569  8576573
8576591  8576593  8576597  8576599  8576609  8576621  8576627  8576629  8576641  8576647
8576761  8576767  8576791  8576797  8576807  8576839  8576849  8576861  8576867  8576903
8576927  8576929  8576941  8576947  8576957  8576969  8577001  8577017  8577029  8577053
8577073  8577089  8577103  8577133  8577161  8577169  8577181  8577187  8577193  8577209
8577251  8577259  8577263  8577293  8577307  8577313  8577329  8577337  8577343  8577353
8577397  8577403  8577449  8577463  8577473  8577521  8577529  8577557  8577563  8577589
8577593  8577601  8577617  8577623  8577629  8577631  8577671  8577677  8577727  8577739
8577743  8577757  8577761  8577763  8577773  8577787  8577799  8577817  8577847  8577853
8577871  8577883  8577893  8577901  8577929  8577931  8577977  8577983  8577991  8578019
8578021  8578033  8578039  8578049  8578067  8578091  8578093  8578099  8578109  8578121
8578123  8578127  8578147  8578181  8578189  8578223  8578231  8578237  8578243  8578249
8578321  8578327  8578331  8578343  8578363  8578397  8578417  8578439  8578447  8578469
8578463  8578477  8578513  8578567  8578571  8578589  8578607  8578639  8578651  8578667
8578681  8578697  8578699  8578711  8578729  8578733  8578771  8578781  8578789  8578807
8578811  8578819  8578831  8578879  8578883  8578891  8578901  8578903  8578907  8578919
8578943  8578949  8578981  8578991  8578993  8579003  8579071  8579093  8579107  8579111
8579113  8579117  8579141  8579159  8579167  8579173  8579183  8579191  8579201  8579251
8579287  8579297  8579303  8579309  8579341  8579353  8579357  8579399  8579411  8579419
8579443  8579491  8579503  8579513  8579531  8579533  8579561  8579573  8579633  8579639
8579651  8579663  8579687  8579699  8579731  8579743  8579749  8579761  8579789  8579807
8579821  8579869  8579873  8579881  8579903  8579929  8579939  8579963  8579981
8579999  8580023  8580031  8580037  8580043  8580071  8580073  8580079  8580097  8580101
8580113  8580133  8580151  8580167  8580217  8580227  8580233  8580241  8580251  8580287
8580289  8580301  8580353  8580389  8580391  8580409  8580413  8580431  8580469  8580479
8580487  8580497  8580499  8580503  8580511  8580527  8580553  8580557  8580569  8580581
8580601  8580613  8580617  8580643  8580653  8580697  8580713  8580731  8580739  8580751
8580763  8580773  8580787  8580791  8580821  8580829  8580833  8580841  8580851  8580853
8580857  8580883  8580899  8580917  8580919  8580953  8580959  8580967  8580977  8580983
8580997  8581007  8581021  8581043  8581049  8581051  8581087  8581099  8581117  8581147
8581163  8581169  8581171  8581189  8581193  8581201  8581211  8581241  8581247  8581253
8581267  8581289  8581337  8581343  8581351  8581367  8581399  8581403  8581411  8581429
8581457  8581471  8581499  8581501  8581511  8581519  8581523  8581567  8581577  8581591
8581607  8581613  8581621  8581631  8581633  8581681  8581693  8581717  8581723  8581733
8581739  8581747  8581759  8581789  8581799  8581819  8581843  8581847  8581861  8581927
8581931  8581933  8581943  8581961  8581973  8581981  8582017  8582023  8582027  8582051
8582083  8582111  8582137  8582143  8582159  8582177  8582179  8582183  8582191  8582201
8582207  8582209  8582213  8582221  8582293  8582303  8582309  8582311  8582339  8582369
8582383  8582389  8582411  8582417  8582419  8582423  8582447  8582461  8582491  8582543
8582593  8582597  8582617  8582641  8582659  8582663  8582687  8582711  8582713  8582723
8582731  8582741  8582747  8582759  8582771  8582801  8582803  8582831  8582837  8582857
8582863  8582867  8582891  8582921  8582963  8582969  8582971  8583013  8583019  8583059
8583061  8583073  8583077  8583083  8583109  8583131  8583137  8583139  8583151  8583167
8583203  8583221  8583233  8583241  8583247  8583259  8583277  8583287  8583313  8583343
8583353  8583361  8583397  8583401  8583457  8583479  8583481  8583503  8583511  8583527
8583529  8583539  8583541  8583569  8583581  8583599  8583613  8583629  8583713  8583779
8583781  8583791  8583833  8583847  8583871  8583893  8583907  8583919  8583923  8583937
8583941  8583947  8583977  8583979  8583989  8584001  8584007  8584013  8584019  8584073
8584097  8584151  8584157  8584183  8584187  8584189  8584193  8584217  8584229  8584231
8584243  8584249  8584253  8584273  8584291  8584309  8584327  8584339  8584343  8584351
8584393  8584399  8584417  8584421  8584423  8584519  8584529  8584531  8584547  8584549
8584567  8584577  8584577  8584579  8584619  8584633  8584657  8584663  8584679  8584733
8584739  8584747  8584753  8584757  8584759  8584787  8584811  8584817  8584837  8584853
```

```
8584859  8584883  8584909  8584921  8584937  8584943  8584951  8584967  8584987  8585021
8585039  8585053  8585069  8585077  8585081  8585111  8585173  8585177  8585191  8585209
8585237  8585243  8585261  8585287  8585293  8585333  8585387  8585389  8585399  8585429
8585431  8585449  8585477  8585497  8585501  8585513  8585531  8585539  8585569  8585611
8585617  8585623  8585639  8585651  8585657  8585669  8585671  8585713  8585719  8585743
8585747  8585789  8585803  8585807  8585839  8585873  8585879  8585881  8585893  8585921
8585963  8585981  8585989  8586013  8586031  8586073  8586077  8586103  8586121  8586131
8586143  8586167  8586181  8586191  8586209  8586239  8586247  8586269  8586301  8586307
8586311  8586317  8586323  8586341  8586353  8586367  8586373  8586419  8586427  8586439
8586443  8586463  8586467  8586481  8586491  8586493  8586497  8586511  8586533  8586559
8586563  8586577  8586587  8586593  8586619  8586623  8586629  8586637  8586647  8586661
8586667  8586679  8586691  8586709  8586719  8586733  8586737  8586761  8586769  8586791
8586793  8586829  8586847  8586859  8586863  8586869  8586883  8586899  8586913  8586937
8586959  8586967  8586979  8587039  8587043  8587087  8587109  8587123  8587127  8587147
8587207  8587231  8587247  8587253  8587283  8587289  8587301  8587309  8587321  8587333
8587351  8587357  8587361  8587399  8587421  8587459  8587471  8587493  8587529  8587531
8587541  8587543  8587549  8587561  8587577  8587583  8587597  8587609  8587619  8587633
8587687  8587693  8587697  8587723  8587751  8587757  8587769  8587801  8587807  8587841
8587849  8587861  8587871  8587889  8587897  8587937  8587949  8587963  8588017  8588029
8588059  8588071  8588087  8588143  8588149  8588159  8588161  8588189  8588191  8588207
8588221  8588227  8588249  8588257  8588273  8588291  8588299  8588341  8588381  8588389
8588423  8588429  8588431  8588473  8588479  8588497  8588501  8588521  8588527  8588533
8588539  8588543  8588549  8588563  8588579  8588623  8588647  8588651  8588659  8588677
8588681  8588707  8588717  8588719  8588761  8588771  8588813  8588819  8588831  8588837
8588849  8588851  8588897  8588903  8588911  8588917  8588929  8588947  8588971  8589001
8589011  8589013  8589037  8589041  8589073  8589101  8589149  8589157  8589167  8589173
8589179  8589181  8589193  8589209  8589223  8589241  8589247  8589289  8589299  8589319
8589323  8589331  8589337  8589341  8589359  8589401  8589431  8589473  8589487  8589491
8589517  8589521  8589523  8589533  8589547  8589563  8589569  8589583  8589589  8589613
8589619  8589629  8589631  8589677  8589683  8589689  8589733  8589739  8589769  8589773
8589797  8589839  8589857  8589859  8589871  8589877  8589901  8589923  8589929  8589943
8589953  8589961  8589967  8589989  8589991  8590009  8590073  8590111  8590121  8590139
8590159  8590163  8590171  8590189  8590199  8590207  8590217  8590243  8590249  8590273
8590289  8590291  8590301  8590333  8590357  8590363  8590367  8590391  8590427  8590433
8590469  8590471  8590487  8590501  8590507  8590513  8590529  8590531  8590537  8590553
8590573  8590591  8590597  8590633  8590643  8590657  8590663  8590693  8590703  8590711
8590721  8590723  8590727  8590733  8590741  8590759  8590783  8590789  8590811  8590837
8590877  8590889  8590909  8590913  8590949  8590951  8590957  8590963  8590969  8590987
8590991  8590997  8591039  8591041  8591087  8591113  8591117  8591119  8591129  8591131
8591183  8591227  8591237  8591251  8591257  8591291  8591293  8591299  8591311  8591327
8591369  8591377  8591381  8591389  8591419  8591431  8591441  8591449  8591467  8591483
8591501  8591507  8591519  8591533  8591543  8591549  8591563  8591573  8591587  8591593
8591599  8591603  8591617  8591623  8591633  8591663  8591683  8591689  8591711  8591717
8591741  8591771  8591773  8591809  8591813  8591827  8591833  8591887  8591899  8591909
8591927  8591941  8591963  8592043  8592049  8592061  8592079  8592097  8592109  8592121
8592127  8592151  8592169  8592193  8592197  8592203  8592209  8592253  8592257  8592299
8592343  8592377  8592401  8592431  8592443  8592461  8592481  8592499  8592509  8592511
8592523  8592533  8592539  8592559  8592581  8592589  8592637  8592641  8592653  8592659
8592677  8592691  8592697  8592709  8592719  8592743  8592763  8592791  8592809  8592833
8592851  8592863  8592889  8592893  8592901  8592911  8592923  8592929  8592931  8592949
8592989  8592997  8593001  8593021  8593027  8593033  8593037  8593043  8593087  8593097
8593103  8593121  8593127  8593129  8593147  8593153  8593157  8593159  8593171  8593183
8593199  8593223  8593229  8593243  8593289  8593297  8593303  8593307  8593331  8593349
8593369  8593379  8593391  8593423  8593471  8593511  8593531  8593549  8593591  8593597
8593609  8593631  8593639  8593667  8593703  8593747  8593759  8593771  8593777  8593799
8593813  8593817  8593829  8593841  8593843  8593847  8593901  8593931  8593933  8593937
8593939  8593943  8593951  8593957  8593961  8593979  8594009  8594017  8594029  8594059
8594081  8594083  8594093  8594123  8594129  8594213  8594219  8594227  8594233  8594263
8594269  8594357  8594359  8594371  8594407  8594413  8594419  8594429  8594431  8594449
8594477  8594507  8594549  8594557  8594563  8594581  8594587  8594591  8594603  8594623
8594627  8594659  8594681  8594683  8594687  8594689  8594699  8594713  8594723  8594731
8594737  8594743  8594753  8594771  8594777  8594791  8594837  8594857  8594863  8594891
8594917  8594921  8594923  8594951  8595001  8595007  8595017  8595019  8595023  8595127
8595133  8595143  8595151  8595173  8595187  8595221  8595253  8595259  8595269  8595283
8595287  8595289  8595311  8595329  8595347  8595371  8595383  8595409  8595443  8595451
8595469  8595493  8595511  8595539  8595541  8595547  8595551  8595553  8595577  8595589
8595599  8595607  8595611  8595623  8595637  8595667  8595673  8595683  8595703  8595731
8595737  8595749  8595751  8595779  8595781  8595787  8595793  8595817  8595833  8595841
8595857  8595889  8595893  8595941  8595943  8595947  8595967  8596031  8596039  8596057
8596097  8596109  8596121  8596121  8596127  8596153  8596157  8596171  8596187  8596193
8596199  8596201  8596213  8596223  8596283  8596297  8596333  8596369  8596381  8596387
8596397  8596403  8596409  8596439  8596453  8596459  8596463  8596513  8596519  8596529
8596537  8596561  8596571  8596573  8596583  8596589  8596597  8596619  8596631  8596637
8596649  8596657  8596663  8596667  8596727  8596729  8596739  8596741  8596793  8596807
8596811  8596813  8596823  8596829  8596843  8596877  8596879  8596897  8596901  8596909
8596943  8596961  8596967  8596969  8596979  8596981  8596997  8597023  8597027  8597041
8597047  8597051  8597059  8597081  8597093  8597111  8597117  8597123  8597143  8597159
8597179  8597203  8597213  8597219  8597227  8597263  8597293  8597297  8597299  8597317
8597321  8597339  8597341  8597353  8597363  8597371  8597417  8597471  8597473  8597521
8597527  8597531  8597551  8597587  8597591  8597599  8597621  8597623  8597629  8597663
8597647  8597651  8597669  8597707  8597723  8597737  8597753  8597759  8597773  8597783
8597821  8597839  8597843  8597857  8597863  8597873  8597879  8597947  8597969  8597977
8597989  8597993  8597999  8598001  8598061  8598071  8598101  8598119  8598143  8598167
8598169  8598179  8598197  8598221  8598307  8598341  8598347  8598353  8598361  8598367
8598383  8598391  8598427  8598437  8598511  8598523  8598547  8598553  8598571  8598589
8598593  8598599  8598613  8598647  8598649  8598661  8598673  8598677  8598691  8598701
8598781  8598797  8598809  8598817  8598829  8598851  8598857  8598859  8598869  8598893
8598899  8598917  8598937  8598973  8598977  8598983  8599013  8599021  8599027  8599037
8599061  8599067  8599069  8599081  8599111  8599117  8599141  8599159  8599163  8599169
```

8599193 8599211 8599219 8599223 8599243 8599271 8599273 8599289 8599301 8599319
8599333 8599363 8599379 8599397 8599403 8599411 8599439 8599453 8599469 8599471
8599489 8599519 8599541 8599553 8599559 8599561 8599567 8599579 8599583 8599589
8599607 8599649 8599667 8599673 8599687 8599691 8599693 8599771 8599793 8599817
8599819 8599823 8599849 8599867 8599891 8599897 8599961 8599967 8599993 8600023
8600029 8600041 8600047 8600063 8600071 8600089 8600093 8600099 8600101 8600143
8600161 8600171 8600213 8600219 8600231 8600233 8600239 8600309 8600323 8600341
8600359 8600393 8600399 8600411 8600437 8600461 8600467 8600477 8600491 8600497
8600509 8600519 8600533 8600549 8600587 8600591 8600593 8600621 8600629 8600633
8600639 8600677 8600701 8600717 8600719 8600741 8600743 8600747 8600777 8600783
8600789 8600807 8600819 8600881 8600897 8600899 8600923 8600941 8600947 8600957
8600959 8600971 8601013 8601029 8601037 8601077 8601083 8601097 8601101 8601107
8601113 8601121 8601143 8601157 8601163 8601169 8601191 8601209 8601233 8601253
8601277 8601289 8601293 8601331 8601343 8601361 8601389 8601391 8601401 8601421
8601443 8601449 8601457 8601491 8601499 8601503 8601511 8601557 8601569 8601581
8601587 8601629 8601631 8601641 8601647 8601653 8601667 8601683 8601689 8601707
8601727 8601739 8601743 8601767 8601773 8601821 8601823 8601869 8601877 8601883
8601907 8601917 8601937 8601947 8601961 8601979 8601991 8601997 8602001 8602007
8602031 8602039 8602043 8602049 8602109 8602151 8602157 8602177 8602199 8602201
8602211 8602213 8602219 8602273 8602301 8602303 8602313 8602339 8602343 8602379
8602381 8602397 8602409 8602417 8602439 8602471 8602481 8602487 8602507 8602511
8602519 8602543 8602549 8602567 8602631 8602637 8602673 8602679 8602691 8602703
8602729 8602751 8602753 8602757 8602777 8602787 8602807 8602817 8602823 8602837
8602873 8602931 8602933 8602949 8602961 8602987 8603009 8603017 8603041 8603047
8603051 8603057 8603087 8603093 8603099 8603131 8603137 8603167 8603183 8603201
8603233 8603237 8603239 8603249 8603251 8603263 8603267 8603293 8603297 8603299
8603341 8603347 8603369 8603381 8603389 8603393 8603407 8603429 8603453 8603467
8603471 8603477 8603489 8603509 8603521 8603533 8603579 8603591 8603593 8603597
8603603 8603611 8603657 8603663 8603677 8603681 8603689 8603701 8603711 8603729
8603731 8603753 8603767 8603779 8603797 8603813 8603831 8603839 8603843 8603893
8603927 8603951 8603953 8603963 8604059 8604067 8604077 8604083 8604107 8604119
8604151 8604157 8604161 8604203 8604209 8604221 8604223 8604241 8604259 8604269
8604287 8604293 8604307 8604317 8604319 8604347 8604353 8604371 8604373 8604403
8604413 8604467 8604469 8604481 8604487 8604509 8604529 8604539 8604551 8604593
8604613 8604623 8604641 8604643 8604647 8604649 8604667 8604689 8604697 8604707
8604733 8604749 8604751 8604767 8604769 8604779 8604781 8604797 8604809 8604811
8604823 8604863 8604913 8604943 8604961 8604977 8604983 8604991 8605001 8605019
8605057 8605061 8605147 8605153 8605159 8605169 8605171 8605187 8605211 8605217
8605229 8605231 8605237 8605241 8605273 8605297 8605307 8605319 8605361 8605369
8605379 8605403 8605411 8605433 8605447 8605463 8605469 8605481 8605501 8605511
8605529 8605543 8605561 8605567 8605577 8605601 8605607 8605609 8605637 8605691
8605733 8605789 8605801 8605811 8605813 8605823 8605829 8605843 8605853 8605871
8605873 8605913 8605931 8605939 8605963 8605997 8605999 8606041 8606047 8606051
8606053 8606077 8606093 8606137 8606173 8606179 8606197 8606201 8606219 8606261
8606263 8606281 8606287 8606293 8606309 8606327 8606329 8606341 8606363 8606387
8606401 8606413 8606431 8606441 8606443 8606447 8606453 8606491 8606501 8606509
8606527 8606537 8606557 8606599 8606603 8606621 8606657 8606693 8606729 8606737
8606779 8606789 8606797 8606827 8606839 8606863 8606869 8606893 8606909 8606911
8606929 8606957 8606959 8606963 8606999 8607023 8607029 8607043 8607059 8607061
8607073 8607077 8607103 8607139 8607163 8607167 8607173 8607191 8607197 8607217
8607223 8607227 8607233 8607241 8607257 8607271 8607281 8607293 8607307 8607329
8607341 8607343 8607371 8607373 8607377 8607383 8607397 8607407 8607409 8607413
8607427 8607433 8607449 8607463 8607479 8607481 8607539 8607563 8607583 8607587
8607601 8607629 8607631 8607637 8607653 8607659 8607667 8607673 8607689 8607713
8607733 8607737 8607749 8607769 8607803 8607821 8607871 8607883 8607887 8607901
8607913 8607917 8607943 8607947 8607991 8607997 8608009 8608027 8608037 8608079
8608081 8608091 8608133 8608147 8608163 8608183 8608217 8608231 8608241 8608247
8608261 8608291 8608321 8608333 8608357 8608373 8608399 8608423 8608427 8608429
8608451 8608487 8608489 8608507 8608529 8608543 8608549 8608553 8608571 8608573
8608583 8608591 8608597 8608603 8608609 8608619 8608627 8608667 8608673 8608727
8608751 8608759 8608771 8608777 8608799 8608801 8608823 8608829 8608837 8608841
8608861 8608871 8608879 8608889 8608891 8608907 8608909 8608913 8608931 8608973
8609023 8609063 8609077 8609087 8609093 8609099 8609119 8609129 8609137 8609149
8609173 8609207 8609239 8609257 8609269 8609273 8609281 8609287 8609297 8609309
8609323 8609333 8609347 8609353 8609371 8609411 8609431 8609441 8609443 8609449
8609459 8609473 8609477 8609483 8609501 8609533 8609563 8609569 8609581 8609591
8609597 8609609 8609611 8609617 8609621 8609639 8609647 8609651 8609663 8609669
8609677 8609683 8609687 8609719 8609729 8609753 8609773 8609791 8609813 8609819
8609833 8609849 8609879 8609891 8609899 8609911 8609917 8609927 8609963 8609987
8609999 8610001 8610061 8610067 8610101 8610113 8610137 8610139 8610167 8610169
8610197 8610209 8610227 8610229 8610247 8610269 8610293 8610299 8610311 8610319
8610323 8610331 8610341 8610359 8610367 8610373 8610377 8610379 8610389 8610403
8610409 8610431 8610443 8610461 8610463 8610479 8610509 8610521 8610523 8610557
8610559 8610583 8610599 8610601 8610607 8610617 8610643 8610649 8610659 8610731
8610737 8610739 8610803 8610827 8610829 8610851 8610863 8610871 8610881 8610893
8610913 8610919 8610937 8610961 8610997 8611003 8611033 8611037 8611063 8611117
8611133 8611139 8611147 8611151 8611181 8611201 8611219 8611247 8611249 8611261
8611283 8611297 8611301 8611303 8611307 8611321 8611331 8611349 8611357 8611381
8611399 8611403 8611411 8611423 8611433 8611439 8611441 8611487 8611501 8611523
8611529 8611531 8611549 8611573 8611577 8611601 8611613 8611619 8611633 8611643
8611663 8611667 8611679 8611697 8611703 8611709 8611721 8611723 8611783 8611789
8611793 8611819 8611829 8611847 8611849 8611859 8611873 8611879 8611891 8611903
8611961 8611969 8611987 8611991 8612011 8612033 8612059 8612057 8612059 8612089
8612099 8612119 8612167 8612209 8612221 8612243 8612293 8612299 8612311 8612347
8612399 8612411 8612413 8612423 8612437 8612473 8612479 8612497 8612503 8612531
8612581 8612627 8612629 8612633 8612641 8612653 8612663 8612671 8612683 8612687
8612689 8612701 8612707 8612711 8612713 8612729 8612731 8612743 8612753 8612767
8612777 8612801 8612831 8612837 8612839 8612861 8612873 8612903 8612927 8612941
8612957 8612959 8612969 8612983 8613001 8613019 8613041 8613043 8613047 8613089

```
8613091  8613107  8613127  8613149  8613161  8613181  8613211  8613221  8613229  8613281
8613299  8613323  8613329  8613347  8613349  8613379  8613391  8613421  8613427  8613439
8613457  8613461  8613463  8613481  8613529  8613547  8613559  8613571  8613617  8613623
8613677  8613701  8613733  8613739  8613743  8613751  8613757  8613797  8613809  8613811
8613817  8613827  8613851  8613853  8613863  8613887  8613893  8613911  8613929  8613947
8613953  8613959  8613961  8613967  8614003  8614009  8614031  8614051  8614079  8614093
8614117  8614129  8614157  8614159  8614171  8614181  8614231  8614253  8614261
8614273  8614297  8614313  8614327  8614337  8614357  8614369  8614381  8614409  8614439
8614453  8614477  8614483  8614499  8614513  8614517  8614519  8614547  8614549  8614553
8614561  8614579  8614601  8614609  8614637  8614651  8614681  8614693  8614717  8614729
8614757  8614759  8614777  8614783  8614787  8614789  8614829  8614831  8614841  8614849
8614867  8614873  8614883  8614889  8614901  8614913  8614939  8614951  8614967  8614973
8614979  8614987  8615017  8615051  8615063  8615083  8615099  8615137  8615149  8615161
8615177  8615197  8615219  8615231  8615237  8615261  8615267  8615273  8615279  8615287
8615323  8615333  8615377  8615389  8615423  8615461  8615471  8615473  8615479  8615491
8615507  8615513  8615527  8615539  8615543  8615567  8615587  8615591  8615623  8615653
8615657  8615703  8615707  8615723  8615749  8615757  8615771  8615791  8615809  8615833
8615879  8615881  8615891  8615917  8615941  8615963  8615983  8615989  8616011  8616019
8616029  8616037  8616043  8616071  8616089  8616131  8616149  8616151  8616169  8616173
8616187  8616197  8616199  8616203  8616217  8616221  8616241  8616247  8616271  8616281
8616299  8616319  8616323  8616337  8616353  8616371  8616373  8616379  8616397  8616407
8616431  8616457  8616493  8616499  8616527  8616533  8616541  8616547  8616563  8616599
8616653  8616661  8616679  8616689  8616691  8616703  8616719  8616721  8616733  8616757
8616763  8616767  8616809  8616821  8616827  8616833  8616859  8616869  8616887
8616901  8616911  8616913  8616917  8616919  8616947  8616989  8616991  8616997  8617001
8617073  8617097  8617129  8617153  8617171  8617177  8617187  8617201  8617207
8617211  8617237  8617253  8617261  8617277  8617291  8617313  8617319  8617327  8617333
8617361  8617373  8617381  8617391  8617397  8617417  8617439  8617447  8617513  8617519
8617523  8617547  8617549  8617561  8617627  8617681  8617699  8617703  8617753  8617769
8617787  8617799  8617823  8617837  8617871  8617877  8617927  8617933  8617943  8617949
8617991  8617993  8618021  8618033  8618041  8618047  8618059  8618063  8618083  8618087
8618089  8618107  8618119  8618131  8618147  8618149  8618173  8618213  8618221  8618237
8618243  8618251  8618257  8618273  8618287  8618293  8618297  8618317  8618327  8618329
8618339  8618377  8618387  8618413  8618429  8618443  8618479  8618483  8618501  8618557
8618567  8618581  8618591  8618593  8618639  8618681  8618683  8618689  8618699  8618737
8618747  8618749  8618759  8618783  8618789  8618809  8618833  8618851  8618861  8618867
8618879  8618893  8618917  8618923  8618933  8618959  8618999  8619031  8619041  8619053
8619059  8619067  8619071  8619077  8619097  8619101  8619131  8619151  8619157  8619167
8619197  8619199  8619211  8619223  8619229  8619241  8619263  8619269  8619343  8619353
8619397  8619421  8619427  8619431  8619433  8619437  8619439  8619461  8619469  8619473
8619491  8619509  8619511  8619539  8619551  8619587  8619593  8619601  8619623  8619649
8619661  8619683  8619713  8619719  8619773  8619791  8619797  8619811  8619817  8619857
8619859  8619883  8619893  8619937  8619943  8619977  8619997  8620043  8620049  8620063
8620069  8620109  8620111  8620121  8620133  8620141  8620151  8620159  8620187  8620189
8620211  8620217  8620219  8620231  8620259  8620267  8620277  8620289  8620307  8620327
8620349  8620361  8620369  8620393  8620429  8620499  8620529  8620543  8620553  8620567
8620571  8620589  8620603  8620621  8620631  8620637  8620639  8620663  8620673  8620687
8620691  8620721  8620723  8620727  8620739  8620747  8620757  8620841  8620847  8620861
8620873  8620897  8620943  8620949  8620951  8620973  8620993  8621009  8621017  8621047
8621051  8621077  8621083  8621087  8621089  8621101  8621143  8621147  8621153  8621183
8621189  8621201  8621209  8621213  8621237  8621241  8621281  8621299  8621309  8621339
8621377  8621411  8621413  8621429  8621443  8621453  8621467  8621477  8621479  8621491
8621511  8621581  8621609  8621617  8621623  8621653  8621677  8621681  8621693  8621707
8621747  8621757  8621773  8621779  8621797  8621819  8621827  8621831  8621851  8621857
8621861  8621863  8621867  8621869  8621897  8621911  8621927  8621933  8621939  8621947
8621959  8621971  8621983  8621989  8622001  8622007  8622011  8622017  8622023  8622051
8622071  8622113  8622127  8622137  8622191  8622209  8622223  8622241  8622287  8622293
8622301  8622307  8622323  8622331  8622337  8622343  8622353  8622359  8622373  8622379
8622391  8622413  8622421  8622461  8622463  8622469  8622473  8622487  8622491  8622499
8622511  8622521  8622529  8622563  8622577  8622611  8622683  8622707  8622721  8622763
8622767  8622781  8622793  8622811  8622841  8622847  8622853  8622857  8622871  8622877
8622883  8622923  8622959  8622973  8622983  8623003  8623019  8623031  8623033  8623037
8623039  8623051  8623061  8623067  8623073  8623081  8623103  8623123  8623141  8623193
8623213  8623247  8623249  8623253  8623261  8623291  8623319  8623339  8623357  8623393
8623409  8623423  8623429  8623519  8623523  8623529  8623547  8623579  8623583  8623603
8623619  8623621  8623639  8623651  8623661  8623679  8623687  8623717  8623721  8623729
8623751  8623757  8623763  8623787  8623793  8623799  8623801  8623807  8623831  8623843
8623847  8623883  8623897  8623903  8623939  8623957  8623963  8623969  8624003  8624009
8624017  8624023  8624027  8624051  8624059  8624101  8624111  8624129  8624131  8624137
8624141  8624153  8624163  8624177  8624179  8624183  8624191  8624201  8624221  8624237
8624243  8624249  8624251  8624267  8624311  8624323  8624327  8624353  8624383  8624393
8624449  8624459  8624477  8624503  8624507  8624573  8624599  8624617  8624621  8624633
8624669  8624677  8624713  8624717  8624753  8624771  8624773  8624807  8624847  8624873
8624881  8624887  8624921  8624929  8624953  8624981  8624999  8625007  8625011  8625013
8625053  8625059  8625073  8625077  8625083  8625091  8625119  8625121  8625131  8625173
8625187  8625191  8625203  8625229  8625233  8625247  8625263  8625289  8625301  8625311
8625313  8625317  8625343  8625349  8625359  8625431  8625451  8625467  8625479  8625493
8625509  8625517  8625521  8625527  8625541  8625553  8625559  8625587  8625599  8625637
8625641  8625649  8625689  8625707  8625709  8625733  8625787  8625809  8625811  8625821
8625823  8625853  8625889  8625901  8625913  8625959  8625961  8625973  8625979  8625983
8625997  8626001  8626043  8626061  8626063  8626067  8626099  8626103  8626109  8626129
8626139  8626141  8626159  8626169  8626181  8626199  8626237  8626243  8626249  8626271
8626283  8626297  8626301  8626349  8626391  8626417  8626421  8626459  8626481  8626487
8626493  8626507  8626517  8626529  8626549  8626577  8626603  8626613  8626621  8626643
8626669  8626691  8626699  8626727  8626733  8626747  8626763  8626777  8626801  8626811
8626819  8626823  8626831  8626841  8626847  8626861  8626901  8626903  8626927  8626999
8627029  8627033  8627051  8627057  8627081  8627111  8627119  8627141  8627147  8627149
8627153  8627161  8627167  8627173  8627191  8627243  8627251  8627257  8627299  8627321
8627329  8627341  8627351  8627357  8627363  8627371  8627417  8627429  8627431  8627441
```

643

```
8627447  8627467  8627473  8627497  8627503  8627513  8627527  8627533  8627561  8627569
8627573  8627581  8627603  8627609  8627611  8627617  8627627  8627629  8627681  8627693
8627699  8627701  8627713  8627741  8627777  8627807  8627809  8627813  8627833  8627851
8627867  8627893  8627897  8627903  8627909  8627911  8627939  8627947  8627953  8627977
8627987  8628007  8628017  8628019  8628031  8628049  8628077  8628097  8628107  8628121
8628131  8628149  8628157  8628161  8628173  8628181  8628187  8628203  8628233  8628271
8628293  8628349  8628353  8628359  8628377  8628383  8628407  8628421  8628443  8628449
8628463  8628479  8628481  8628493  8628547  8628551  8628553  8628601  8628623  8628629
8628643  8628647  8628661  8628677  8628709  8628727  8628751  8628773  8628779  8628787
8628791  8628799  8628811  8628847  8628857  8628859  8628883  8628889  8628899  8628913
8628923  8628937  8628967  8628973  8629003  8629009  8629063  8629073  8629079  8629087
8629109  8629123  8629139  8629141  8629157  8629169  8629171  8629193  8629199  8629213
8629241  8629279  8629297  8629333  8629343  8629349  8629409  8629429  8629433  8629441
8629447  8629483  8629507  8629561  8629583  8629597  8629613  8629637  8629651  8629661
8629679  8629681  8629711  8629739  8629763  8629771  8629813  8629823  8629847  8629867
8629883  8629889  8629891  8629909  8629927  8629949  8629961  8629963  8629981  8630003
8630029  8630071  8630113  8630117  8630159  8630163  8630173  8630179  8630191  8630197
8630201  8630207  8630231  8630239  8630243  8630249  8630269  8630291  8630311  8630387
8630417  8630443  8630449  8630477  8630483  8630491  8630519  8630591  8630593  8630599
8630639  8630641  8630647  8630653  8630663  8630669  8630683  8630737  8630749  8630759
8630771  8630779  8630789  8630813  8630821  8630833  8630837  8630851  8630857  8630861
8630899  8630903  8630929  8630971  8630983  8631001  8631011  8631017  8631023  8631037
8631041  8631083  8631097  8631109  8631151  8631167  8631191  8631193  8631199  8631229
8631247  8631251  8631269  8631277  8631283  8631307  8631319  8631331  8631341  8631367
8631373  8631379  8631391  8631401  8631451  8631479  8631499  8631517  8631533  8631569
8631599  8631611  8631617  8631629  8631659  8631673  8631713  8631737  8631743  8631769
8631781  8631787  8631803  8631823  8631851  8631881  8631893  8631899  8631907  8631911
8631943  8631977  8631979  8632003  8632009  8632027  8632069  8632081  8632087  8632103
8632123  8632133  8632139  8632157  8632187  8632219  8632223  8632237  8632279  8632297
8632303  8632313  8632333  8632357  8632361  8632363  8632367  8632381  8632387  8632391
8632399  8632411  8632423  8632451  8632453  8632457  8632487  8632489  8632493  8632513
8632523  8632529  8632531  8632573  8632579  8632597  8632609  8632621  8632649  8632661
8632667  8632699  8632717  8632727  8632759  8632777  8632801  8632817  8632829  8632831
8632891  8632901  8632927  8632931  8632933  8632937  8632979  8633021  8633029  8633047
8633063  8633069  8633111  8633113  8633137  8633143  8633167  8633189  8633231  8633237
8633279  8633281  8633311  8633323  8633327  8633347  8633363  8633371  8633377  8633381
8633389  8633413  8633423  8633431  8633453  8633459  8633461  8633489  8633551  8633567
8633633  8633641  8633659  8633663  8633683  8633699  8633701  8633711  8633719  8633731
8633747  8633767  8633777  8633827  8633843  8633857  8633861  8633869  8633893  8633897
8633899  8633921  8633939  8633941  8633951  8633957  8633959  8633971  8633981  8633983
8634009  8634053  8634077  8634107  8634133  8634137  8634139  8634161  8634163  8634169
8634173  8634179  8634203  8634211  8634233  8634251  8634253  8634259  8634299  8634347
8634359  8634371  8634383  8634391  8634397  8634413  8634421  8634427  8634449  8634467
8634469  8634481  8634497  8634503  8634517  8634539  8634551  8634557  8634581  8634617
8634629  8634667  8634671  8634677  8634679  8634697  8634713  8634751  8634761  8634767
8634803  8634811  8634823  8634839  8634841  8634859  8634863  8634881  8634883  8634883
8634889  8634907  8634917  8634947  8634961  8634971  8635021  8635043  8635049  8635057
8635061  8635073  8635087  8635093  8635117  8635141  8635163  8635199  8635219  8635241
8635259  8635261  8635273  8635279  8635283  8635313  8635321  8635351  8635381  8635409
8635423  8635433  8635441  8635469  8635477  8635513  8635531  8635553  8635559  8635567
8635579  8635607  8635621  8635631  8635637  8635657  8635663  8635667  8635673  8635687
8635699  8635717  8635723  8635729  8635777  8635811  8635817  8635849  8635853  8635867
8635883  8635897  8635919  8635927  8635933  8635951  8635967  8635969  8635981  8635999
8636021  8636039  8636057  8636081  8636083  8636087  8636093  8636107  8636123  8636129
8636137  8636141  8636167  8636219  8636237  8636239  8636261  8636263  8636269  8636347
8636377  8636387  8636389  8636423  8636449  8636473  8636491  8636513  8636521  8636533
8636539  8636543  8636549  8636581  8636587  8636591  8636599  8636603  8636627  8636633
8636647  8636671  8636689  8636701  8636713  8636737  8636741  8636759  8636779  8636791
8636801  8636819  8636839  8636857  8636869  8636893  8636899  8636909  8636911  8636917
8636921  8636923  8636959  8636987  8636989  8637007  8637017  8637053  8637059  8637061
8637067  8637091  8637103  8637107  8637119  8637131  8637133  8637151  8637163  8637179
8637203  8637227  8637247  8637253  8637257  8637263  8637289  8637301  8637311  8637319
8637323  8637337  8637341  8637373  8637379  8637447  8637449  8637451  8637467  8637481
8637491  8637493  8637509  8637521  8637523  8637527  8637611  8637617  8637619  8637637
8637641  8637667  8637697  8637701  8637749  8637779  8637787  8637791  8637821  8637829
8637847  8637869  8637929  8637943  8637959  8638001  8638013  8638033  8638039  8638043
8638051  8638061  8638067  8638117  8638121  8638139  8638151  8638183  8638187  8638199
8638207  8638213  8638219  8638229  8638237  8638241  8638247  8638277  8638283  8638291
8638319  8638327  8638337  8638339  8638349  8638373  8638379  8638381  8638403  8638411
8638447  8638451  8638453  8638457  8638463  8638471  8638477  8638481  8638517  8638543
8638583  8638621  8638627  8638633  8638661  8638687  8638691  8638697  8638727  8638733
8638807  8638843  8638849  8638853  8638867  8638891  8638909  8638933  8638937  8638951
8638967  8638991  8638997  8639009  8639011  8639027  8639051  8639063  8639089  8639107
8639119  8639123  8639131  8639143  8639149  8639153  8639161  8639171  8639177  8639207
8639219  8639227  8639249  8639251  8639261  8639263  8639273  8639291  8639299  8639347
8639363  8639381  8639401  8639413  8639441  8639443  8639453  8639459  8639461  8639507
8639531  8639539  8639549  8639551  8639563  8639567  8639591  8639597  8639599  8639639
8639647  8639663  8639711  8639713  8639747  8639749  8639753  8639773  8639779  8639797
8639803  8639809  8639819  8639837  8639849  8639863  8639899  8639903  8639909  8639921
8639923  8639951  8639977  8639987  8640001  8640013  8640017  8640059  8640109  8640133
8640161  8640169  8640187  8640197  8640211  8640221  8640241  8640251  8640259  8640263
8640287  8640329  8640337  8640349  8640391  8640407  8640409  8640419  8640427  8640439
8640451  8640481  8640493  8640503  8640547  8640553  8640559  8640587  8640601  8640679
8640683  8640689  8640691  8640701  8640703  8640707  8640713  8640719  8640733  8640739
8640761  8640767  8640781  8640787  8640799  8640811  8640823  8640859  8640871  8640883
8640887  8640889  8640911  8640949  8640967  8640977  8641007  8641063  8641079  8641093
8641097  8641133  8641147  8641187  8641211  8641231  8641247  8641249  8641273  8641289
8641301  8641309  8641319  8641327  8641331  8641349  8641351  8641361  8641421  8641429
8641433  8641453  8641469  8641471  8641513  8641517  8641519  8641541  8641543  8641547
```

```
8641571 8641603 8641613 8641621 8641631 8641643 8641651 8641669 8641673 8641697
8641709 8641733 8641741 8641747 8641781 8641783 8641807 8641817 8641819 8641873
8641883 8641891 8641909 8641949 8641957 8641987 8641991 8642003 8642027 8642033
8642057 8642059 8642063 8642077 8642099 8642107 8642111 8642119 8642141 8642147
8642173 8642189 8642197 8642237 8642281 8642303 8642329 8642383 8642429
8642449 8642453 8642467 8642489 8642507 8642509 8642519 8642533 8642567 8642581
8642591 8642633 8642651 8642723 8642747 8642761 8642773 8642819 8642839 8642849
8642857 8642861 8642863 8642897 8642903 8642911 8642927 8642939 8642947 8642951
8642989 8643013 8643023 8643053 8643059 8643077 8643083 8643091 8643109 8643121
8643133 8643137 8643143 8643149 8643181 8643197 8643199 8643209 8643211 8643223
8643281 8643287 8643307 8643317 8643337 8643343 8643359 8643367 8643409 8643433
8643443 8643457 8643487 8643521 8643527 8643539 8643563 8643577 8643587 8643589
8643619 8643631 8643647 8643671 8643673 8643697 8643707 8643721 8643749 8643757
8643779 8643787 8643797 8643821 8643839 8643851 8643889 8643893 8643919 8643923
8643941 8643953 8643959 8643991 8643997 8644019 8644049 8644057 8644061 8644081
8644091 8644123 8644147 8644157 8644171 8644187 8644213 8644231 8644243 8644253
8644261 8644301 8644327 8644331 8644397 8644439 8644451 8644453 8644457 8644477
8644499 8644501 8644507 8644511 8644529 8644553 8644607 8644609 8644633 8644651
8644661 8644679 8644703 8644723 8644729 8644751 8644771 8644781 8644799 8644843
8644861 8644873 8644903 8644913 8644919 8644927 8644949 8644957 8644963 8644991
8645009 8645011 8645023 8645029 8645047 8645053 8645071 8645081 8645113 8645123
8645141 8645179 8645237 8645239 8645243 8645257 8645261 8645267 8645269 8645281
8645293 8645327 8645341 8645353 8645359 8645381 8645407 8645431 8645443 8645449
8645477 8645491 8645543 8645579 8645587 8645597 8645617 8645633 8645647 8645653
8645657 8645669 8645687 8645719 8645729 8645759 8645761 8645773 8645789 8645803
8645849 8645863 8645887 8645899 8645927 8645941 8645971 8645981 8646017 8646059
8646061 8646103 8646107 8646119 8646163 8646181 8646221 8646223 8646227 8646233
8646247 8646257 8646259 8646269 8646277 8646293 8646299 8646317 8646329 8646361
8646377 8646389 8646401 8646403 8646457 8646479 8646487 8646497 8646503 8646511
8646529 8646559 8646571 8646581 8646607 8646667 8646683 8646707 8646709 8646719
8646721 8646751 8646779 8646793 8646817 8646821 8646823 8646851 8646853 8646889
8646899 8646929 8646943 8646947 8646949 8646961 8646971 8647007 8647021 8647027
8647031 8647043 8647061 8647063 8647091 8647123 8647127 8647129 8647139 8647157
8647181 8647183 8647193 8647229 8647231 8647253 8647273 8647277 8647349 8647367
8647369 8647391 8647393 8647409 8647411 8647417 8647447 8647459 8647469 8647501
8647511 8647531 8647537 8647567 8647579 8647589 8647657 8647697 8647699 8647711
8647739 8647753 8647759 8647783 8647801 8647817 8647819 8647823 8647879 8647889
8647897 8647913 8647927 8647937 8647949 8647963 8647967 8647979 8647993 8647997
8648033 8648083 8648093 8648099 8648111 8648113 8648131 8648149 8648179 8648191
8648221 8648239 8648251 8648267 8648317 8648323 8648333 8648347 8648369 8648371
8648389 8648413 8648447 8648459 8648501 8648513 8648531 8648533 8648537 8648543
8648551 8648557 8648677 8648687 8648701 8648729 8648737 8648741 8648747 8648749
8648779 8648791 8648797 8648813 8648831 8648833 8648837 8648839 8648863 8648867
8648879 8648881 8648921 8648923 8648929 8648953 8649001 8649023 8649029 8649049
8649061 8649071 8649079 8649103 8649187 8649191 8649197 8649211 8649227 8649239
8649241 8649253 8649283 8649293 8649299 8649317 8649323 8649331 8649343 8649349
8649353 8649367 8649371 8649383 8649391 8649409 8649419 8649451 8649463 8649467
8649469 8649479 8649491 8649517 8649521 8649533 8649581 8649611 8649623 8649629
8649637 8649661 8649671 8649677 8649689 8649691 8649703 8649721 8649757 8649761
8649763 8649791 8649793 8649803 8649847 8649853 8649857 8649869 8649871 8649881
8649887 8649911 8649929 8649937 8649967 8649973 8650003 8650027 8650039 8650051
8650087 8650121 8650123 8650129 8650141 8650151 8650153 8650189 8650211 8650217
8650219 8650223 8650253 8650259 8650283 8650307 8650309 8650319 8650321 8650361
8650391 8650409 8650423 8650429 8650451 8650459 8650463 8650487 8650511 8650517
8650531 8650541 8650559 8650561 8650583 8650597 8650627 8650633 8650651 8650657
8650667 8650669 8650673 8650687 8650703 8650709 8650721 8650723 8650727 8650763
8650777 8650793 8650799 8650813 8650849 8650879 8650897 8650919 8650927 8650979
8650981 8650997 8651009 8651017 8651039 8651047 8651051 8651063 8651117 8651119
8651141 8651143 8651161 8651179 8651189 8651191 8651207 8651231 8651233 8651239
8651261 8651267 8651281 8651297 8651311 8651323 8651329 8651353 8651359 8651389
8651399 8651429 8651437 8651443 8651459 8651501 8651507 8651537 8651543 8651549
8651579 8651581 8651603 8651609 8651627 8651639 8651647 8651663 8651683 8651689
8651693 8651711 8651717 8651723 8651737 8651771 8651791 8651803 8651857 8651869
8651891 8651893 8651917 8651939 8651941 8651953 8651959 8651977 8651999 8652013
8652023 8652029 8652037 8652041 8652047 8652053 8652079 8652097 8652101 8652139
8652143 8652151 8652187 8652211 8652223 8652227 8652229 8652253 8652257 8652263
8652283 8652299 8652349 8652359 8652361 8652373 8652389 8652401 8652403 8652407
8652433 8652461 8652463 8652493 8652551 8652563 8652571 8652587 8652593 8652601
8652613 8652629 8652641 8652647 8652659 8652661 8652697 8652703 8652731 8652767
8652773 8652781 8652793 8652797 8652803 8652821 8652823 8652827 8652863 8652887
8652913 8652929 8652947 8652971 8652979 8652997 8653031 8653063 8653081 8653087
8653093 8653103 8653111 8653121 8653147 8653157 8653163 8653171 8653199 8653207
8653219 8653231 8653237 8653241 8653243 8653259 8653261 8653279 8653283 8653297
8653319 8653327 8653343 8653361 8653373 8653453 8653457 8653487 8653517 8653529
8653537 8653549 8653553 8653591 8653609 8653613 8653627 8653651 8653657 8653669
8653679 8653691 8653699 8653703 8653709 8653717 8653741 8653763 8653769 8653789
8653807 8653811 8653817 8653847 8653859 8653877 8653889 8653891 8653903 8653937
8653963 8654011 8654017 8654021 8654027 8654029 8654033 8654039 8654047 8654057
8654089 8654099 8654111 8654117 8654123 8654147 8654171 8654183 8654201 8654221
8654231 8654237 8654249 8654257 8654281 8654287 8654299 8654333 8654339 8654351
8654357 8654381 8654389 8654431 8654447 8654453 8654461 8654467 8654483 8654489
8654521 8654543 8654563 8654573 8654579 8654609 8654617 8654621 8654641 8654663
8654689 8654713 8654729 8654749 8654753 8654759 8654761 8654771 8654773 8654803
8654809 8654837 8654839 8654873 8654897 8654917 8654941 8654959 8654981 8655007
8655011 8655029 8655037 8655041 8655047 8655071 8655103 8655149 8655167 8655173
8655197 8655211 8655217 8655259 8655263 8655287 8655307 8655313 8655331 8655343
8655349 8655371 8655401 8655403 8655421 8655433 8655457 8655497 8655527 8655611
8655623 8655629 8655631 8655637 8655641 8655649 8655653 8655671 8655677 8655679
8655701 8655707 8655719 8655721 8655733 8655739 8655749 8655761 8655769 8655809
```

```
8655841  8655859  8655869  8655877  8655883  8655901  8655917  8655919  8655923  8655937
8655953  8655967  8655991  8656019  8656031  8656033  8656057  8656069  8656079  8656091
8656093  8656097  8656117  8656129  8656133  8656147  8656159  8656163  8656169  8656171
8656177  8656189  8656231  8656253  8656273  8656279  8656283  8656313  8656321  8656339
8656357  8656363  8656367  8656369  8656379  8656393  8656399  8656411  8656423  8656433
8656463  8656469  8656477  8656481  8656493  8656499  8656511  8656517  8656523  8656537
8656547  8656561  8656573  8656577  8656589  8656603  8656667  8656691  8656721  8656727
8656729  8656733  8656759  8656787  8656801  8656807  8656829  8656831  8656847  8656849
8656871  8656891  8656897  8656903  8656919  8656933  8656939  8656969  8657009  8657017
8657021  8657041  8657053  8657069  8657111  8657123  8657161  8657221  8657237  8657239
8657249  8657291  8657309  8657323  8657333  8657357  8657377  8657381  8657387  8657423
8657431  8657449  8657461  8657503  8657513  8657533  8657557  8657563  8657567  8657569
8657611  8657629  8657633  8657639  8657651  8657681  8657687  8657699  8657723  8657731
8657767  8657771  8657783  8657801  8657827  8657833  8657849  8657851  8657881  8657903
8657923  8657927  8657933  8657969  8657983  8658017  8658043  8658059  8658101  8658103
8658107  8658109  8658137  8658161  8658193  8658203  8658217  8658233  8658277  8658289
8658313  8658323  8658329  8658371  8658383  8658413  8658431  8658469  8658493  8658527
8658553  8658569  8658571  8658577  8658581  8658583  8658589  8658613  8658619  8658653
8658659  8658673  8658677  8658679  8658697  8658709  8658739  8658757  8658773  8658829
8658847  8658873  8658877  8658887  8658893  8658911  8658919  8658931  8658941  8658943
8658959  8658961  8658977  8658983  8658989  8658997  8659009  8659019  8659037  8659043
8659051  8659061  8659067  8659097  8659099  8659121  8659153  8659181  8659207  8659219
8659223  8659243  8659279  8659289  8659309  8659351  8659363  8659381  8659393  8659423
8659457  8659463  8659471  8659501  8659513  8659531  8659537  8659543  8659559  8659589
8659601  8659627  8659631  8659643  8659663  8659667  8659669  8659691  8659711  8659741
8659747  8659769  8659793  8659811  8659837  8659867  8659873  8659909  8659913  8659921
8659927  8659939  8659949  8659957  8659997  8659999  8660033  8660039  8660051  8660053
8660077  8660081  8660087  8660107  8660161  8660177  8660189  8660203  8660221  8660227
8660233  8660263  8660269  8660287  8660291  8660297  8660339  8660369  8660381  8660383
8660387  8660401  8660413  8660419  8660423  8660437  8660461  8660467  8660503  8660507
8660527  8660537  8660539  8660543  8660569  8660579  8660609  8660611  8660623  8660653
8660657  8660671  8660681  8660683  8660689  8660693  8660699  8660723  8660741  8660747
8660753  8660767  8660797  8660819  8660863  8660887  8660891  8660909  8660921  8660929
8660933  8660947  8660969  8660983  8660987  8661001  8661043  8661047  8661049  8661061
8661089  8661119  8661137  8661161  8661173  8661181  8661193  8661197  8661203  8661217
8661223  8661239  8661241  8661251  8661253  8661281  8661311  8661353  8661383  8661407
8661413  8661427  8661437  8661439  8661461  8661469  8661479  8661487  8661491  8661509
8661529  8661553  8661557  8661571  8661577  8661581  8661623  8661629  8661641  8661643
8661673  8661683  8661689  8661703  8661707  8661727  8661733  8661743  8661767  8661769
8661799  8661839  8661841  8661871  8661881  8661883  8661889  8661899  8661901  8661941
8661943  8661953  8661977  8661997  8662009  8662019  8662021  8662037  8662057  8662079
8662091  8662109  8662127  8662133  8662151  8662153  8662169  8662177  8662181  8662189
8662201  8662217  8662219  8662223  8662243  8662249  8662259  8662273  8662279  8662319
8662327  8662337  8662349  8662363  8662397  8662411  8662441  8662447  8662453  8662471
8662481  8662483  8662487  8662517  8662531  8662541  8662553  8662579  8662583  8662597
8662649  8662657  8662729  8662747  8662751  8662769  8662783  8662799  8662807  8662811
8662831  8662853  8662859  8662867  8662889  8662891  8662939  8662943  8662963  8662987
8662991  8663003  8663023  8663071  8663089  8663093  8663099  8663101  8663117  8663119
8663153  8663209  8663261  8663273  8663279  8663309  8663311  8663357  8663401  8663437
8663441  8663461  8663467  8663471  8663497  8663503  8663507  8663509  8663519  8663521
8663537  8663579  8663593  8663609  8663621  8663653  8663687  8663701  8663719  8663741
8663777  8663797  8663803  8663807  8663819  8663821  8663827  8663861  8663869  8663899
8663923  8663959  8663969  8663987  8664023  8664037  8664043  8664053  8664107  8664109
8664157  8664181  8664193  8664223  8664259  8664311  8664317  8664329  8664367  8664377
8664389  8664413  8664419  8664421  8664427  8664431  8664433  8664451  8664473  8664517
8664527  8664539  8664559  8664553  8664581  8664613  8664661  8664671  8664701  8664703
8664731  8664739  8664743  8664757  8664787  8664791  8664847  8664857  8664863  8664869
8664871  8664907  8664941  8664947  8664949  8664959  8664961  8664977  8664979  8664991
8665021  8665031  8665039  8665073  8665099  8665109  8665123  8665147  8665157  8665193
8665201  8665207  8665219  8665253  8665259  8665277  8665303  8665313  8665333  8665357
8665361  8665369  8665373  8665409  8665429  8665441  8665451  8665469  8665471  8665499
8665541  8665543  8665561  8665567  8665571  8665583  8665603  8665619  8665633  8665649
8665651  8665667  8665703  8665717  8665777  8665799  8665817  8665849  8665873  8665889
8665897  8665913  8665931  8665933  8665939  8665949  8665967  8665973  8665991  8665999
8666017  8666023  8666027  8666051  8666057  8666059  8666069  8666093  8666137  8666153
8666159  8666167  8666173  8666183  8666201  8666219  8666237  8666269  8666291  8666323
8666327  8666347  8666351  8666369  8666381  8666387  8666393  8666417  8666419  8666431
8666443  8666459  8666477  8666479  8666491  8666501  8666513  8666519  8666533  8666543
8666591  8666597  8666627  8666681  8666683  8666711  8666747  8666767  8666773  8666783
8666797  8666807  8666809  8666839  8666849  8666863  8666881  8666891  8666917  8666939
8666953  8666989  8666993  8667079  8667103  8667121  8667137  8667151  8667167  8667179
8667227  8667257  8667271  8667289  8667299  8667301  8667313  8667319  8667349  8667371
8667377  8667403  8667413  8667421  8667427  8667431  8667457  8667497  8667511  8667521
8667539  8667559  8667563  8667601  8667611  8667613  8667641  8667653  8667661  8667677
8667689  8667697  8667707  8667721  8667727  8667733  8667793  8667807  8667809  8667821
8667829  8667847  8667863  8667871  8667899  8667907  8667913  8667929  8667931  8667949
8667961  8667973  8667979  8668001  8668031  8668043  8668057  8668061  8668063  8668067
8668073  8668081  8668111  8668133  8668151  8668157  8668193  8668201  8668207
8668267  8668273  8668279  8668301  8668349  8668357  8668367  8668369  8668379  8668381
8668403  8668421  8668423  8668459  8668483  8668489  8668501  8668519  8668523  8668547
8668549  8668553  8668571  8668577  8668609  8668613  8668637  8668643  8668687  8668697
8668711  8668721  8668739  8668741  8668763  8668783  8668799  8668801  8668813  8668817
8668831  8668837  8668873  8668889  8668901  8668951  8668967  8668973  8668993
8669027  8669041  8669071  8669083  8669107  8669113  8669117  8669123  8669159  8669179
8669189  8669207  8669233  8669237  8669249  8669249  8669251  8669279  8669293  8669317
8669329  8669333  8669341  8669351  8669389  8669393  8669399  8669411  8669417  8669443
8669447  8669477  8669483  8669489  8669501  8669513  8669527  8669543  8669593  8669611
8669621  8669623  8669627  8669629  8669651  8669657  8669669  8669671  8669701  8669767
8669777  8669821  8669831  8669861  8669879  8669893  8669897  8669911  8669923  8669929
```

```
8669939  8669963  8669981  8669989  8669993  8670007  8670029  8670031  8670037  8670041
8670071  8670089  8670107  8670127  8670157  8670191  8670197  8670239  8670257  8670281
8670301  8670313  8670331  8670353  8670371  8670373  8670397  8670407  8670433  8670451
8670481  8670491  8670499  8670503  8670509  8670523  8670533  8670551  8670553  8670559
8670583  8670589  8670611  8670619  8670637  8670653  8670667  8670679  8670703  8670709
8670713  8670743  8670751  8670773  8670791  8670811  8670863  8670869  8670887  8670919
8670941  8670943  8670947  8670989  8670997  8671007  8671009  8671031  8671051  8671057
8671063  8671067  8671097  8671099  8671127  8671133  8671147  8671151  8671177  8671193
8671219  8671231  8671249  8671291  8671307  8671321  8671331  8671339  8671361  8671363
8671367  8671381  8671393  8671409  8671427  8671441  8671447  8671457  8671463  8671469
8671471  8671499  8671501  8671511  8671517  8671519  8671549  8671573  8671583  8671589
8671631  8671633  8671639  8671669  8671697  8671709  8671711  8671721  8671739  8671769
8671811  8671837  8671907  8671919  8671937  8671967  8671979  8671981  8671987  8671991
8672003  8672047  8672063  8672087  8672099  8672101  8672117  8672161  8672177  8672201
8672203  8672207  8672239  8672263  8672267  8672273  8672297  8672333  8672347  8672353
8672381  8672387  8672407  8672423  8672429  8672441  8672471  8672483  8672501  8672509
8672513  8672519  8672527  8672539  8672551  8672561  8672563  8672597  8672621  8672639
8672641  8672647  8672659  8672687  8672707  8672723  8672731  8672767  8672773  8672779
8672789  8672791  8672801  8672819  8672821  8672831  8672861  8672869  8672891  8672899
8672927  8672933  8672947  8672953  8672969  8673011  8673019  8673029  8673037  8673073
8673097  8673107  8673109  8673113  8673121  8673127  8673131  8673157  8673167  8673187
8673199  8673209  8673221  8673271  8673293  8673341  8673347  8673359  8673361  8673373
8673377  8673389  8673419  8673421  8673433  8673463  8673499  8673517  8673547  8673569
8673571  8673593  8673601  8673611  8673677  8673683  8673703  8673727  8673761  8673781
8673817  8673839  8673877  8673901  8673911  8673913  8673923  8673941  8673953  8673989
8673997  8674009  8674037  8674049  8674069  8674087  8674091  8674109  8674177  8674187
8674213  8674249  8674271  8674307  8674321  8674331  8674339  8674343  8674349  8674361
8674397  8674399  8674409  8674447  8674453  8674483  8674489  8674499  8674511  8674531
8674537  8674543  8674553  8674571  8674577  8674619  8674667  8674681  8674693  8674727
8674759  8674769  8674781  8674793  8674819  8674859  8674867  8674889  8674891  8674901
8674921  8674927  8674937  8674961  8675003  8675011  8675021  8675027  8675033  8675047
8675053  8675059  8675099  8675111  8675113  8675137  8675189  8675197  8675221  8675297
8675309  8675311  8675323  8675327  8675341  8675357  8675371  8675377  8675383  8675399
8675413  8675441  8675449  8675453  8675503  8675509  8675521  8675573  8675591  8675621
8675651  8675671  8675677  8675699  8675743  8675749  8675767  8675813  8675833  8675839
8675857  8675861  8675869  8675879  8675893  8675903  8675911  8675921  8675923  8676013
8676029  8676043  8676049  8676053  8676061  8676071  8676079  8676089  8676119  8676131
8676139  8676163  8676169  8676181  8676197  8676209  8676211  8676223  8676229  8676251
8676257  8676263  8676281  8676287  8676301  8676319  8676337  8676361  8676377  8676383
8676397  8676401  8676431  8676449  8676467  8676487  8676517  8676527  8676533  8676541
8676587  8676601  8676631  8676641  8676643  8676659  8676691  8676719  8676721  8676743
8676751  8676757  8676769  8676779  8676781  8676799  8676821  8676827  8676847  8676883
8676893  8676937  8676949  8676971  8676973  8676991  8677027  8677037  8677043  8677051
8677057  8677079  8677121  8677127  8677139  8677171  8677181  8677223  8677247  8677261
8677267  8677283  8677289  8677327  8677343  8677367  8677387  8677391  8677393  8677397
8677399  8677453  8677457  8677477  8677481  8677483  8677511  8677553  8677577  8677607
8677651  8677663  8677681  8677723  8677727  8677759  8677763  8677771  8677829  8677841
8677847  8677883  8677891  8677951  8677961  8677967  8677979  8677993  8678011  8678027
8678029  8678039  8678051  8678053  8678057  8678063  8678069  8678081  8678083  8678093
8678113  8678129  8678141  8678147  8678149  8678161  8678179  8678203  8678213  8678237
8678311  8678323  8678333  8678339  8678353  8678359  8678363  8678393  8678399  8678447
8678473  8678507  8678519  8678557  8678581  8678587  8678599  8678603  8678639  8678669
8678671  8678693  8678699  8678701  8678707  8678713  8678741  8678749  8678753  8678759
8678773  8678777  8678779  8678783  8678821  8678833  8678851  8678863  8678893  8678899
8678903  8678927  8678933  8678939  8678941  8678947  8678951  8678963  8679037  8679059
8679071  8679079  8679109  8679137  8679179  8679193  8679199  8679217  8679221  8679271
8679277  8679289  8679311  8679347  8679353  8679373  8679379  8679397  8679427  8679449
8679457  8679499  8679527  8679529  8679551  8679557  8679581  8679607  8679617  8679641
8679677  8679709  8679739  8679743  8679767  8679791  8679841  8679871  8679883  8679887
8679899  8679943  8679953  8679971  8679973  8679991  8680003  8680027  8680033  8680037
8680043  8680073  8680099  8680103  8680121  8680153  8680157  8680171  8680187  8680201
8680213  8680219  8680229  8680249  8680267  8680277  8680297  8680303  8680307  8680313
8680327  8680337  8680369  8680379  8680409  8680417  8680439  8680471  8680481
8680501  8680513  8680543  8680559  8680583  8680601  8680613  8680619  8680631  8680669
8680691  8680697  8680699  8680717  8680723  8680733  8680741  8680753  8680769  8680781
8680801  8680811  8680813  8680823  8680871  8680901  8680907  8680909  8680921  8680939
8680951  8680993  8681003  8681009  8681021  8681047  8681059  8681077  8681089  8681111
8681117  8681129  8681131  8681159  8681177  8681191  8681207  8681213  8681221  8681243
8681251  8681263  8681287  8681291  8681311  8681317  8681341  8681357  8681359  8681363
8681369  8681377  8681401  8681429  8681447  8681467  8681473  8681483  8681489  8681503
8681507  8681513  8681539  8681549  8681567  8681579  8681587  8681623  8681639  8681663
8681669  8681693  8681707  8681731  8681737  8681779  8681789  8681821  8681831  8681837
8681851  8681857  8681899  8681923  8681941  8681957  8681969  8681977  8681989  8681999
8682007  8682041  8682043  8682067  8682097  8682127  8682133  8682143  8682181  8682199
8682203  8682209  8682211  8682229  8682239  8682241  8682251  8682253  8682269  8682277
8682299  8682319  8682343  8682391  8682403  8682409  8682413  8682433  8682437  8682467
8682473  8682481  8682493  8682533  8682551  8682559  8682577  8682587  8682589  8682659
8682671  8682691  8682701  8682719  8682721  8682727  8682743  8682749  8682757  8682763
8682841  8682851  8682871  8682887  8682893  8682911  8682959  8682991  8683001  8683009
8683013  8683027  8683063  8683091  8683097  8683153  8683159  8683163
8683183  8683187  8683189  8683201  8683217  8683219  8683223  8683231  8683237  8683249
8683253  8683261  8683303  8683307  8683309  8683319  8683321  8683327  8683331  8683393
8683427  8683439  8683453  8683459  8683483  8683511  8683517  8683523  8683529  8683531
8683541  8683553  8683603  8683607  8683613  8683637  8683639  8683657  8683663  8683681
8683687  8683691  8683693  8683699  8683723  8683729  8683757  8683769  8683781  8683783
8683793  8683823  8683853  8683877  8683897  8683907  8683933  8683943  8684003  8684009
8684023  8684029  8684047  8684051  8684069  8684077  8684089  8684099  8684107  8684111
8684131  8684147  8684171  8684173  8684177  8684189  8684201  8684213  8684231  8684243
8684257  8684261  8684267  8684279  8684329  8684341  8684359  8684407  8684411  8684419
```

```
8684437  8684461  8684471  8684479  8684483  8684503  8684513  8684521  8684537  8684573
8684587  8684597  8684629  8684657  8684693  8684699  8684713  8684747  8684759  8684761
8684771  8684783  8684789  8684821  8684831  8684861  8684873  8684903  8684911  8684939
8684941  8684947  8684959  8684981  8684983  8685013  8685031  8685041  8685043  8685073
8685077  8685107  8685151  8685161  8685167  8685197  8685199  8685211  8685227  8685251
8685253  8685263  8685289  8685311  8685319  8685323  8685367  8685371  8685373  8685377
8685379  8685407  8685409  8685463  8685473  8685493  8685517  8685539  8685557  8685569
8685571  8685577  8685583  8685601  8685619  8685629  8685631  8685637  8685653  8685659
8685661  8685667  8685683  8685709  8685731  8685737  8685739  8685749  8685751  8685763
8685767  8685769  8685791  8685847  8685857  8685863  8685893  8685913  8685917  8685923
8685949  8685953  8685961  8685967  8685979  8686001  8686003  8686049  8686087  8686103
8686121  8686123  8686127  8686141  8686147  8686159  8686163  8686177  8686187  8686189
8686193  8686207  8686213  8686241  8686259  8686273  8686277  8686291  8686297  8686309
8686313  8686361  8686369  8686373  8686397  8686409  8686421  8686459  8686463  8686471
8686487  8686499  8686501  8686529  8686567  8686589  8686651  8686661  8686669  8686679
8686687  8686703  8686721  8686729  8686807  8686829  8686841  8686877  8686883  8686889
8686901  8686961  8686981  8686999  8687027  8687069  8687087  8687089  8687093  8687117
8687131  8687141  8687149  8687171  8687183  8687197  8687207  8687209  8687213  8687227
8687233  8687249  8687291  8687299  8687303  8687309  8687317  8687321  8687359  8687363
8687369  8687381  8687383  8687387  8687401  8687423  8687429  8687453  8687461  8687467
8687477  8687479  8687513  8687521  8687587  8687599  8687603  8687641  8687659  8687669
8687671  8687687  8687699  8687713  8687729  8687759  8687771  8687797  8687827  8687883
8687879  8687881  8687891  8687911  8687923  8687929  8687953  8687963  8687981  8687983
8687993  8688011  8688013  8688059  8688067  8688077  8688083  8688101  8688109  8688133
8688143  8688157  8688161  8688167  8688203  8688209  8688221  8688259  8688271  8688283
8688287  8688299  8688311  8688349  8688353  8688397  8688409  8688437  8688469  8688497
8688521  8688527  8688551  8688553  8688557  8688569  8688571  8688577  8688583  8688593
8688601  8688607  8688611  8688613  8688629  8688671  8688697  8688703  8688707  8688739
8688787  8688791  8688809  8688817  8688829  8688863  8688919  8688943  8688961  8688991
8688997  8689033  8689039  8689063  8689069  8689097  8689111  8689129  8689133  8689141
8689169  8689181  8689217  8689223  8689243  8689249  8689259  8689273  8689279  8689283
8689301  8689309  8689319  8689321  8689349  8689399  8689433  8689451  8689453  8689463
8689481  8689489  8689493  8689529  8689537  8689543  8689553  8689573  8689591  8689609
8689627  8689643  8689649  8689657  8689661  8689673  8689687  8689711  8689727  8689729
8689753  8689777  8689799  8689817  8689823  8689841  8689843  8689853  8689943  8689949
8689957  8689969  8689979  8689981  8689987  8689997  8690041  8690063  8690069  8690089
8690093  8690117  8690119  8690173  8690177  8690191  8690203  8690221  8690267  8690291
8690293  8690303  8690317  8690333  8690351  8690359  8690371  8690377  8690387  8690399
8690411  8690443  8690453  8690477  8690489  8690531  8690551  8690557  8690567  8690593
8690599  8690603  8690611  8690639  8690659  8690663  8690677  8690683  8690713  8690741
8690767  8690783  8690789  8690797  8690813  8690821  8690867  8690869  8690917  8690921
8690947  8690951  8690953  8690959  8690963  8690971  8691019  8691043  8691091  8691101
8691119  8691127  8691157  8691167  8691187  8691209  8691211  8691223  8691229  8691239
8691247  8691251  8691269  8691281  8691299  8691313  8691359  8691367  8691373  8691383
8691391  8691407  8691413  8691433  8691451  8691469  8691479  8691481  8691497  8691509
8691541  8691581  8691583  8691587  8691589  8691593  8691623  8691643  8691653  8691667
8691673  8691689  8691731  8691733  8691751  8691763  8691799  8691803  8691827  8691833
8691853  8691883  8691901  8691921  8691923  8691937  8691941  8691961  8691971  8691973
8691979  8692001  8692027  8692043  8692051  8692069  8692093  8692097  8692109  8692127
8692169  8692181  8692207  8692217  8692223  8692237  8692249  8692259  8692279  8692283
8692289  8692297  8692309  8692319  8692331  8692339  8692351  8692393  8692403  8692417
8692421  8692427  8692429  8692433  8692441  8692469  8692483  8692487  8692499  8692571
8692577  8692589  8692591  8692609  8692637  8692657  8692667  8692681  8692687  8692693
8692703  8692711  8692727  8692759  8692793  8692799  8692807  8692819  8692829  8692841
8692877  8692889  8692907  8692909  8692961  8692963  8692973  8692987  8692991  8693021
8693033  8693071  8693093  8693117  8693131  8693159  8693161  8693173  8693197  8693207
8693213  8693227  8693231  8693233  8693257  8693263  8693281  8693309  8693323  8693327
8693339  8693369  8693381  8693387  8693401  8693407  8693441  8693459  8693467  8693491
8693521  8693549  8693551  8693567  8693617  8693623  8693627  8693639  8693653  8693677
8693687  8693689  8693693  8693743  8693753  8693759  8693767  8693771  8693801  8693813
8693837  8693891  8693911  8693947  8693957  8693947  8693957  8693969  8693983
8694017  8694019  8694031  8694047  8694073  8694079  8694083  8694097  8694109  8694131
8694197  8694211  8694221  8694233  8694239  8694241  8694247  8694281  8694313  8694317
8694319  8694331  8694341  8694347  8694379  8694397  8694449  8694451  8694479  8694481
8694527  8694541  8694551  8694607  8694613  8694641  8694649  8694683  8694689  8694691
8694709  8694727  8694733  8694739  8694767  8694793  8694797  8694823  8694839  8694841
8694857  8694869  8694899  8694941  8694947  8694967  8694971  8694991  8695009  8695013
8695019  8695051  8695061  8695069  8695079  8695117  8695121  8695129  8695133  8695139
8695147  8695151  8695171  8695187  8695199  8695201  8695207  8695213  8695223  8695277
8695301  8695303  8695319  8695343  8695373  8695399  8695411  8695433  8695457  8695501
8695513  8695529  8695543  8695549  8695571  8695573  8695591  8695601  8695639  8695651
8695663  8695667  8695681  8695723  8695727  8695747  8695769  8695807  8695837  8695849
8695859  8695879  8695889  8695927  8695931  8695937  8695949  8695957  8695961  8695991
8696021  8696029  8696041  8696063  8696113  8696123  8696137  8696153  8696161  8696179
8696183  8696189  8696203  8696209  8696227  8696239  8696249  8696251  8696263  8696267
8696273  8696309  8696321  8696371  8696377  8696381  8696383  8696407  8696411  8696419
8696431  8696437  8696459  8696473  8696483  8696521  8696531  8696561  8696573  8696581
8696603  8696609  8696617  8696627  8696629  8696651  8696663  8696671  8696689  8696693
8696711  8696713  8696749  8696759  8696761  8696767  8696771  8696791  8696837  8696867
8696893  8696903  8696917  8696939  8696951  8696977  8696983  8696993  8696999  8697037
8697049  8697061  8697089  8697097  8697103  8697107  8697113  8697127  8697133  8697163
8697233  8697239  8697253  8697263  8697277  8697301  8697313  8697343  8697379  8697389
8697407  8697433  8697499  8697503  8697509  8697511  8697531  8697539  8697551  8697587
8697599  8697607  8697613  8697641  8697673  8697683  8697691  8697697  8697707  8697769
8697779  8697791  8697797  8697803  8697809  8697811  8697823  8697833  8697851  8697859
8697869  8697889  8697901  8697919  8697937  8697943  8697947  8697967  8697971  8697973
8697977  8698009  8698037  8698049  8698061  8698093  8698097  8698111  8698121  8698133
8698153  8698187  8698189  8698213  8698223  8698229  8698241  8698253  8698297  8698343
8698363  8698369  8698397  8698399  8698421  8698451  8698457  8698493  8698499  8698517
```

```
8698549  8698553  8698559  8698597  8698603  8698621  8698633  8698639  8698643  8698673
8698681  8698699  8698727  8698757  8698763  8698777  8698787  8698801  8698813  8698861
8698831  8698841  8698861  8698871  8698899  8698931  8698933  8698939  8698961  8698969
8698973  8698997  8699039  8699051  8699063  8699069  8699077  8699113  8699143  8699161
8699167  8699179  8699219  8699227  8699233  8699237  8699239  8699263  8699269  8699279
8699293  8699297  8699309  8699311  8699351  8699381  8699387  8699389  8699413  8699419
8699423  8699443  8699489  8699501  8699513  8699519  8699533  8699539  8699557  8699567
8699573  8699611  8699633  8699641  8699669  8699723  8699731  8699753  8699771  8699807
8699813  8699827  8699851  8699857  8699879  8699893  8699917  8699923  8699947  8699953
8699959  8699981  8699993  8700001  8700007  8700011  8700019  8700031  8700037
8700047  8700059  8700071  8700079  8700113  8700121  8700161  8700169  8700193  8700239
8700253  8700257  8700281  8700283  8700287  8700299  8700353  8700361  8700383  8700401
8700407  8700421  8700431  8700449  8700457  8700467  8700473  8700511  8700521  8700529
8700539  8700547  8700563  8700581  8700589  8700599  8700649  8700697  8700709  8700721
8700751  8700767  8700773  8700793  8700799  8700817  8700827  8700833  8700869  8700871
8700893  8700911  8700931  8700941  8700947  8700953  8701001  8701009  8701013  8701027
8701039  8701057  8701067  8701081  8701117  8701123  8701141  8701163  8701177  8701193
8701207  8701211  8701243  8701267  8701271  8701279  8701289  8701309  8701321  8701349
8701367  8701391  8701403  8701409  8701423  8701447  8701457  8701477  8701489  8701493
8701499  8701507  8701519  8701529  8701531  8701559  8701571  8701577  8701621  8701631
8701643  8701657  8701703  8701709  8701723  8701729  8701741  8701747  8701757  8701789
8701811  8701813  8701853  8701871  8701873  8701877  8701883  8701907  8701921  8701933
8701949  8701951  8701961  8701991  8701997  8701999  8702009  8702051  8702063  8702093
8702107  8702131  8702137  8702149  8702159  8702173  8702179  8702189  8702207  8702231
8702251  8702279  8702311  8702327  8702329  8702333  8702341  8702359  8702371  8702387
8702411  8702431  8702459  8702483  8702489  8702497  8702503  8702539  8702543  8702557
8702569  8702587  8702591  8702593  8702597  8702647  8702663  8702689  8702693  8702699
8702731  8702747  8702753  8702777  8702803  8702819  8702821  8702833  8702839  8702843
8702879  8702959  8702989  8702999  8703001  8703041  8703047  8703061  8703089  8703091
8703113  8703119  8703137  8703139  8703151  8703173  8703181  8703241  8703257  8703283
8703287  8703293  8703301  8703307  8703347  8703353  8703377  8703379  8703389  8703403
8703427  8703481  8703491  8703493  8703511  8703523  8703533  8703551  8703581  8703589
8703593  8703613  8703619  8703623  8703631  8703641  8703659  8703661  8703719  8703743
8703781  8703787  8703811  8703817  8703823  8703829  8703833  8703841  8703853  8703859
8703889  8703899  8703911  8703943  8703971  8704027  8704049  8704067  8704117  8704121
8704123  8704159  8704169  8704183  8704193  8704219  8704229  8704253  8704279  8704303
8704309  8704313  8704331  8704351  8704369  8704403  8704417  8704433  8704481  8704499
8704513  8704523  8704547  8704559  8704567  8704589  8704601  8704607  8704609  8704613
8704621  8704651  8704687  8704691  8704699  8704711  8704721  8704723  8704757  8704777
8704783  8704811  8704837  8704853  8704889  8704897  8704903  8704909  8704921  8704937
8704951  8704967  8704973  8704979  8704981  8705009  8705029  8705033  8705041  8705051
8705057  8705069  8705077  8705087  8705093  8705111  8705149  8705159  8705167  8705171
8705183  8705219  8705237  8705261  8705269  8705297  8705299  8705311  8705351  8705369
8705383  8705399  8705419  8705429  8705441  8705443  8705449  8705453  8705461  8705467
8705483  8705491  8705507  8705519  8705527  8705531  8705549  8705551  8705561  8705573
8705611  8705617  8705639  8705657  8705681  8705689  8705729  8705747  8705759  8705773
8705777  8705791  8705803  8705831  8705843  8705861  8705881  8705903  8705911  8705923
8705941  8705959  8705969  8705999  8706001  8706007  8706011  8706013  8706059  8706073
8706079  8706101  8706107  8706149  8706163  8706169  8706197  8706221  8706239  8706241
8706251  8706277  8706283  8706287  8706289  8706323  8706337  8706349  8706361  8706367
8706371  8706403  8706407  8706413  8706419  8706457  8706461  8706463  8706479  8706497
8706527  8706547  8706553  8706557  8706569  8706587  8706611  8706613  8706647  8706667
8706671  8706707  8706727  8706743  8706751  8706791  8706793  8706823  8706829  8706833
8706853  8706869  8706871  8706881  8706937  8706947  8706953  8706961  8706967  8706979
8706983  8707003  8707007  8707021  8707031  8707037  8707057  8707091  8707093  8707103
8707123  8707147  8707159  8707183  8707189  8707207  8707219  8707241  8707273  8707277
8707289  8707327  8707333  8707343  8707351  8707357  8707379  8707393  8707421  8707429
8707477  8707537  8707579  8707591  8707603  8707607  8707631  8707649  8707651  8707661
8707669  8707687  8707697  8707711  8707747  8707753  8707763  8707781  8707793  8707817
8707837  8707841  8707843  8707861  8707873  8707877  8707879  8707883  8707903  8707939
8707969  8707997  8707999  8708003  8708017  8708039  8708069  8708071  8708081  8708087
8708093  8708101  8708129  8708143  8708153  8708159  8708173  8708197  8708201  8708261
8708269  8708291  8708339  8708387  8708393  8708411  8708423  8708429  8708449  8708461
8708501  8708507  8708509  8708519  8708521  8708527  8708537  8708591  8708611  8708617
8708621  8708627  8708639  8708657  8708663  8708701  8708717  8708731  8708741  8708803
8708807  8708831  8708839  8708893  8708911  8708963  8708969  8708971  8709007  8709059
8709067  8709079  8709121  8709133  8709139  8709149  8709187  8709191  8709221  8709229
8709257  8709271  8709289  8709299  8709301  8709313  8709317  8709361  8709373  8709377
8709383  8709431  8709443  8709461  8709469  8709509  8709527  8709553  8709563  8709587
8709611  8709647  8709653  8709677  8709697  8709713  8709719  8709721  8709731  8709737
8709751  8709781  8709793  8709817  8709821  8709839  8709871  8709913  8709919  8709929
8709931  8709941  8709959  8709971  8709973  8709979  8709991  8710021  8710033  8710043
8710057  8710061  8710109  8710127  8710147  8710193  8710213  8710241  8710243  8710249
8710253  8710271  8710277  8710279  8710301  8710313  8710333  8710337  8710343  8710357
8710393  8710397  8710421  8710423  8710441  8710459  8710483  8710487  8710523  8710529
8710547  8710567  8710571  8710589  8710609  8710621  8710627  8710631  8710633  8710649
8710679  8710687  8710693  8710699  8710703  8710717  8710727  8710729  8710733  8710747
8710771  8710781  8710829  8710847  8710903  8710909  8710913  8710939  8710957  8710963
8710967  8710973  8710979  8711009  8711011  8711033  8711051  8711071  8711081  8711083
8711159  8711137  8711141  8711159  8711161  8711179  8711189  8711237  8711267  8711333
8711347  8711357  8711359  8711363  8711377  8711383  8711389  8711399  8711401  8711447
8711467  8711489  8711491  8711501  8711533  8711543  8711551  8711561  8711569  8711603
8711617  8711621  8711627  8711653  8711657  8711669  8711683  8711707  8711719  8711737
8711741  8711743  8711749  8711767  8711777  8711783  8711797  8711821  8711849  8711851
8711863  8711867  8711869  8711887  8711897  8711921  8711933  8711951  8711953  8711971
8711987  8712017  8712019  8712029  8712059  8712091  8712113  8712133  8712149  8712157
8712163  8712167  8712169  8712173  8712181  8712227  8712229  8712233  8712257  8712259
8712269  8712281  8712287  8712293  8712307  8712311  8712323  8712337  8712349  8712367
8712371  8712373  8712397  8712421  8712491  8712497  8712523  8712533  8712547  8712577
```

```
8712601  8712611  8712629  8712661  8712677  8712701  8712709  8712713  8712727  8712749
8712751  8712757  8712761  8712779  8712793  8712827  8712859  8712863  8712919  8712931
8712973  8712997  8713007  8713009  8713013  8713037  8713043  8713051  8713069  8713087
8713109  8713121  8713123  8713127  8713141  8713157  8713181  8713193  8713213  8713217
8713249  8713261  8713291  8713303  8713307  8713319  8713339  8713349  8713363  8713373
8713399  8713403  8713421  8713429  8713433  8713447  8713451  8713459  8713487  8713513
8713519  8713531  8713547  8713553  8713567  8713577  8713583  8713591  8713603  8713631
8713643  8713693  8713699  8713709  8713721  8713763  8713781  8713807  8713811  8713813
8713823  8713867  8713879  8713897  8713919  8713927  8713931  8713933  8713961  8714003
8714009  8714021  8714023  8714039  8714051  8714053  8714063  8714071  8714077  8714107
8714117  8714119  8714161  8714177  8714197  8714213  8714231  8714261  8714267  8714269
8714281  8714287  8714291  8714311  8714323  8714333  8714339  8714341  8714357  8714393
8714417  8714429  8714437  8714449  8714467  8714473  8714491  8714507  8714551  8714567
8714581  8714593  8714609  8714639  8714669  8714683  8714701  8714729  8714731  8714743
8714773  8714779  8714789  8714821  8714857  8714873  8714903  8714921  8714941  8714947
8714957  8714963  8714983  8714989  8715011  8715013  8715019  8715023  8715029  8715041
8715059  8715079  8715103  8715107  8715143  8715151  8715181  8715191  8715193  8715209
8715233  8715263  8715269  8715323  8715337  8715347  8715349  8715361  8715383  8715401
8715403  8715409  8715431  8715449  8715491  8715523  8715559  8715587  8715589  8715601
8715617  8715647  8715649  8715653  8715659  8715667  8715671  8715673  8715697  8715703
8715709  8715719  8715731  8715761  8715769  8715779  8715787  8715793  8715841  8715877
8715881  8715887  8715901  8715907  8715937  8715947  8715961  8715977  8715989  8716007
8716013  8716021  8716027  8716039  8716061  8716063  8716069  8716109  8716151  8716159
8716163  8716181  8716187  8716207  8716217  8716219  8716237  8716243  8716249  8716271
8716283  8716289  8716373  8716381  8716429  8716439  8716441  8716447  8716451  8716453
8716469  8716489  8716531  8716553  8716567  8716579  8716583  8716613  8716619  8716627
8716639  8716661  8716663  8716679  8716691  8716693  8716703  8716709  8716727  8716753
8716759  8716769  8716783  8716817  8716819  8716843  8716853  8716861  8716889  8716891
8716919  8716943  8716957  8716969  8716999  8717011  8717021  8717041  8717113  8717117
8717119  8717123  8717131  8717171  8717201  8717213  8717239  8717263  8717273  8717287
8717323  8717329  8717341  8717353  8717389  8717393  8717491  8717509  8717521  8717531
8717551  8717557  8717563  8717591  8717623  8717633  8717677  8717689  8717717  8717741
8717743  8717747  8717749  8717767  8717773  8717783  8717791  8717803  8717809  8717843
8717857  8717861  8717867  8717869  8717873  8717881  8717909  8717927  8717939  8717959
8717963  8717981  8717987  8717993  8717999  8718007  8718011  8718013  8718043  8718089
8718091  8718097  8718103  8718109  8718113  8718163  8718191  8718197  8718217  8718221
8718247  8718251  8718271  8718277  8718301  8718313  8718343  8718349  8718377  8718401
8718407  8718419  8718427  8718431  8718439  8718461  8718469  8718487  8718491  8718503
8718539  8718571  8718581  8718601  8718649  8718673  8718709  8718727  8718733  8718737
8718757  8718779  8718793  8718797  8718799  8718803  8718811  8718823  8718833  8718839
8718851  8718859  8718869  8718877  8718881  8718887  8718907  8718917  8718949  8718953
8718973  8719003  8719021  8719031  8719037  8719049  8719057  8719099  8719127  8719133
8719141  8719159  8719163  8719177  8719187  8719199  8719211  8719213  8719219  8719223
8719253  8719261  8719273  8719289  8719301  8719303  8719307  8719327  8719349  8719367
8719379  8719391  8719421  8719441  8719483  8719519  8719541  8719549  8719567  8719573
8719577  8719591  8719603  8719661  8719663  8719681  8719699  8719703  8719747  8719771
8719801  8719813  8719817  8719819  8719831  8719847  8719873  8719903  8719939  8719943
8719951  8719961  8719987  8719999  8720027  8720057  8720071  8720081  8720087  8720111
8720113  8720119  8720137  8720161  8720171  8720177  8720189  8720191  8720227  8720233
8720281  8720311  8720317  8720321  8720339  8720347  8720389  8720407  8720417  8720429
8720431  8720447  8720471  8720477  8720479  8720483  8720489  8720497  8720513  8720531
8720533  8720557  8720581  8720597  8720617  8720623  8720627  8720629  8720671  8720681
8720687  8720689  8720693  8720707  8720713  8720729  8720771  8720773  8720783  8720797
8720807  8720809  8720819  8720837  8720839  8720891  8720911  8720941  8720947  8720953
8720969  8720977  8721029  8721043  8721049  8721061  8721077  8721079  8721101  8721121
8721157  8721191  8721197  8721239  8721253  8721259  8721269  8721281  8721299  8721311
8721313  8721329  8721359  8721371  8721379  8721403  8721413  8721443  8721467  8721469
8721473  8721481  8721487  8721499  8721511  8721533  8721539  8721541  8721599  8721607
8721617  8721631  8721667  8721673  8721701  8721737  8721749  8721763  8721773  8721851
8721877  8721883  8721907  8721913  8721917  8721929  8721941  8721989  8721997  8722001
8722009  8722019  8722027  8722033  8722079  8722081  8722093  8722097  8722099  8722117
8722123  8722169  8722171  8722187  8722193  8722211  8722223  8722237  8722283  8722291
8722297  8722303  8722331  8722333  8722339  8722361  8722367  8722391  8722393  8722409
8722423  8722429  8722447  8722459  8722471  8722477  8722499  8722517  8722541  8722603
8722607  8722613  8722621  8722631  8722643  8722661  8722673  8722711  8722739  8722757
8722789  8722799  8722829  8722841  8722859  8722877  8722891  8722913  8722949  8722969
8722981  8722991  8722993  8722999  8723017  8723041  8723047  8723053  8723063  8723081
8723089  8723107  8723123  8723137  8723149  8723191  8723203  8723213  8723243  8723263
8723311  8723317  8723321  8723347  8723353  8723359  8723387  8723399  8723419  8723423
8723437  8723441  8723459  8723479  8723483  8723497  8723521  8723531  8723551  8723569
8723593  8723609  8723639  8723653  8723677  8723707  8723731  8723789  8723807  8723821
8723833  8723851  8723879  8723887  8723893  8723899  8723903  8723909  8723921  8723929
8723933  8723947  8723951  8723977  8723987  8723993  8724013  8724071  8724073  8724101
8724127  8724139  8724143  8724161  8724169  8724181  8724223  8724241  8724253  8724259
8724263  8724269  8724283  8724293  8724301  8724311  8724319  8724323  8724329  8724347
8724371  8724377  8724421  8724441  8724461  8724467  8724479  8724481  8724493  8724497
8724511  8724559  8724589  8724601  8724619  8724631  8724641  8724643  8724649  8724697
8724713  8724719  8724721  8724739  8724787  8724799  8724803  8724827  8724847  8724871
8724883  8724929  8724943  8724949  8724967  8724983  8725021  8725037  8725039  8725051
8725091  8725099  8725103  8725111  8725133  8725139  8725141  8725147  8725153  8725159
8725177  8725183  8725207  8725217  8725219  8725243  8725253  8725279  8725307  8725319
8725357  8725361  8725363  8725391  8725397  8725399  8725421  8725429  8725459  8725463
8725481  8725489  8725499  8725511  8725523  8725531  8725547  8725567  8725571  8725609
8725621  8725627  8725631  8725643  8725657  8725669  8725681  8725699  8725733  8725757
8725799  8725813  8725817  8725823  8725831  8725841  8725877  8725931  8725949  8725961
8725963  8725979  8725989  8725991  8725999  8726017  8726021  8726027  8726051  8726063
8726087  8726093  8726101  8726141  8726143  8726197  8726203  8726209  8726227  8726239
8726243  8726257  8726273  8726323  8726329  8726351  8726357  8726359  8726363  8726381
8726383  8726401  8726447  8726449  8726461  8726467  8726479  8726507  8726521  8726527
```

```
8726533  8726569  8726573  8726587  8726611  8726633  8726647  8726671  8726677  8726687
8726699  8726713  8726723  8726737  8726759  8726761  8726777  8726789  8726801  8726803
8726849  8726863  8726873  8726917  8726923  8726953  8726957  8726969  8726983  8726987
8726989  8727031  8727049  8727053  8727067  8727083  8727091  8727109  8727113  8727119
8727149  8727157  8727161  8727163  8727179  8727197  8727211  8727247  8727263  8727269
8727283  8727287  8727317  8727343  8727349  8727359  8727413  8727427  8727431  8727451
8727493  8727497  8727529  8727539  8727569  8727577  8727583  8727599  8727601  8727611
8727619  8727623  8727643  8727659  8727673  8727689  8727701  8727727  8727731  8727757
8727767  8727773  8727779  8727791  8727809  8727857  8727871  8727899  8727907  8727913
8727931  8727937  8727989  8728037  8728073  8728079  8728129  8728147  8728169  8728193
8728207  8728211  8728241  8728261  8728273  8728289  8728303  8728309  8728331  8728373
8728381  8728387  8728397  8728427  8728457  8728471  8728481  8728483  8728513  8728549
8728571  8728579  8728591  8728597  8728607  8728609  8728627  8728649  8728663  8728679
8728691  8728711  8728717  8728721  8728757  8728787  8728807  8728823  8728849  8728883
8728897  8728901  8728903  8728921  8728927  8728943  8728963  8728969  8728987  8729033
8729051  8729053  8729057  8729059  8729081  8729093  8729099  8729107  8729117  8729131
8729141  8729173  8729179  8729183  8729191  8729207  8729219  8729221  8729239  8729243
8729249  8729291  8729309  8729317  8729323  8729327  8729333  8729389  8729401  8729411
8729461  8729467  8729491  8729543  8729557  8729563  8729593  8729603  8729621  8729629
8729641  8729647  8729659  8729681  8729689  8729711  8729717  8729729  8729767  8729801
8729821  8729837  8729839  8729849  8729867  8729869  8729881  8729887  8729923  8729939
8729977  8729983  8729999  8730013  8730049  8730067  8730077  8730083  8730091  8730103
8730149  8730151  8730157  8730181  8730229  8730257  8730263  8730269  8730283  8730287
8730307  8730311  8730331  8730341  8730343  8730349  8730353  8730377  8730467  8730473
8730487  8730511  8730517  8730529  8730559  8730577  8730583  8730607  8730611  8730619
8730629  8730649  8730661  8730691  8730697  8730737  8730781  8730793  8730797  8730803
8730847  8730851  8730857  8730859  8730863  8730881  8730889  8730893  8730901  8730913
8730919  8730929  8730947  8730949  8730977  8730983  8731027  8731031  8731039  8731069
8731097  8731103  8731109  8731111  8731139  8731141  8731153  8731187  8731201  8731211
8731213  8731231  8731249  8731277  8731301  8731309  8731313  8731321  8731339  8731343
8731363  8731369  8731381  8731417  8731427  8731433  8731447  8731477  8731493  8731501
8731511  8731529  8731531  8731571  8731579  8731607  8731609  8731627  8731637  8731643
8731661  8731673  8731687  8731699  8731711  8731721  8731757  8731763  8731777  8731783
8731787  8731817  8731819  8731831  8731859  8731861  8731867  8731873  8731901  8731907
8731913  8731937  8731939  8731951  8731979  8731981  8731991  8731993  8732023  8732027
8732029  8732047  8732051  8732071  8732081  8732093  8732117  8732123  8732137  8732159
8732189  8732197  8732201  8732209  8732239  8732257  8732261  8732291  8732299  8732309
8732351  8732363  8732369  8732371  8732411  8732417  8732429  8732431  8732447  8732461
8732473  8732489  8732501  8732551  8732573  8732593  8732599  8732627  8732639  8732641
8732653  8732677  8732687  8732719  8732743  8732749  8732797  8732807  8732819  8732831
8732833  8732839  8732861  8732869  8732879  8732887  8732921  8732923  8732957  8732963
8732993  8733001  8733017  8733047  8733059  8733083  8733107  8733113  8733119  8733133
8733143  8733149  8733157  8733161  8733163  8733173  8733247  8733251  8733259  8733271
8733281  8733301  8733321  8733323  8733337  8733383  8733389  8733391  8733397  8733401
8733419  8733433  8733463  8733467  8733479  8733511  8733541  8733547  8733551  8733617
8733619  8733649  8733677  8733691  8733701  8733707  8733709  8733713  8733719  8733731
8733737  8733743  8733811  8733821  8733827  8733833  8733839  8733871  8733889  8733899
8733929  8733941  8733979  8734001  8734013  8734021  8734027  8734051  8734069  8734079
8734093  8734147  8734153  8734169  8734199  8734211  8734213  8734223  8734237  8734247
8734259  8734283  8734351  8734361  8734367  8734373  8734387  8734393  8734403  8734417
8734441  8734451  8734469  8734483  8734501  8734507  8734511  8734513  8734519  8734543
8734571  8734573  8734577  8734603  8734613  8734639  8734643  8734697  8734729  8734741
8734757  8734769  8734801  8734807  8734819  8734823  8734841  8734853  8734883  8734919
8734981  8734993  8735011  8735029  8735039  8735047  8735113  8735137  8735179  8735183
8735197  8735249  8735291  8735299  8735339  8735341  8735347  8735359  8735371  8735413
8735417  8735429  8735443  8735449  8735453  8735479  8735509  8735537  8735549  8735557
8735563  8735581  8735609  8735621  8735633  8735677  8735681  8735711  8735743  8735761
8735777  8735789  8735809  8735813  8735821  8735827  8735849  8735851  8735861  8735879
8735891  8735897  8735933  8735941  8735971  8736001  8736037  8736041  8736059  8736061
8736073  8736089  8736097  8736109  8736127  8736139  8736173  8736179  8736187  8736191
8736199  8736209  8736223  8736263  8736323  8736341  8736367  8736401  8736433  8736449
8736461  8736463  8736473  8736503  8736509  8736529  8736547  8736583  8736593  8736617
8736631  8736647  8736653  8736659  8736667  8736683  8736701  8736703  8736719  8736727
8736781  8736787  8736799  8736809  8736817  8736853  8736881  8736883  8736899  8736907
8736911  8736919  8736943  8736989  8737021  8737039  8737049  8737061  8737063  8737067
8737073  8737097  8737111  8737117  8737129  8737139  8737153  8737177  8737193  8737199
8737237  8737243  8737247  8737249  8737271  8737277  8737301  8737343  8737349  8737357
8737373  8737423  8737427  8737433  8737453  8737479  8737541  8737613  8737649  8737501
8737523  8737529  8737543  8737571  8737577  8737583  8737591  8737627  8737657  8737667
8737669  8737693  8737697  8737699  8737709  8737717  8737741  8737763  8737783  8737789
8737801  8737829  8737843  8737849  8737867  8737871  8737873  8737921  8737933  8737943
8737979  8738011  8738033  8738047  8738053  8738071  8738083  8738087  8738089  8738101
8738123  8738129  8738161  8738201  8738209  8738227  8738231  8738239  8738263  8738273
8738281  8738293  8738299  8738333  8738339  8738351  8738363  8738377  8738383  8738399
8738407  8738437  8738447  8738449  8738473  8738491  8738507  8738533  8738539  8738567
8738579  8738581  8738591  8738641  8738659  8738671  8738707  8738711  8738713  8738729
8738759  8738767  8738783  8738801  8738809  8738813  8738837  8738839  8738843  8738881
8738929  8738957  8738963  8739001  8739007  8739023  8739053  8739079  8739097  8739113
8739119  8739127  8739163  8739167  8739169  8739187  8739193  8739197  8739209  8739281
8739299  8739331  8739337  8739349  8739359  8739389  8739391  8739397  8739431  8739433
8739463  8739481  8739491  8739499  8739503  8739529  8739583  8739607  8739617  8739619
8739637  8739667  8739671  8739673  8739713  8739721  8739739  8739749  8739767  8739769
8739803  8739811  8739821  8739823  8739827  8739851  8739869  8739871  8739883  8739899
8739911  8739917  8739919  8739937  8739953  8739961  8739967  8740003  8740037  8740087
8740097  8740111  8740117  8740129  8740139  8740157  8740163  8740169  8740183  8740187
8740219  8740273  8740289  8740301  8740321  8740327  8740331  8740337  8740367  8740373
8740387  8740393  8740411  8740427  8740429  8740447  8740453  8740493  8740517  8740519
8740531  8740541  8740559  8740561  8740577  8740579  8740591  8740603  8740607  8740643
8740649  8740657  8740679  8740681  8740727  8740757  8740763  8740783  8740789  8740793
```

```
8740799  8740807  8740841  8740859  8740867  8740871  8740891  8740939  8740951  8740993
8740999  8741041  8741053  8741071  8741099  8741119  8741123  8741129  8741137  8741141
8741143  8741147  8741149  8741153  8741191  8741203  8741231  8741233  8741251  8741269
8741279  8741303  8741309  8741321  8741329  8741347  8741353  8741363  8741371  8741393
8741401  8741431  8741437  8741459  8741471  8741479  8741503  8741521  8741533  8741563
8741609  8741639  8741641  8741683  8741687  8741699  8741741  8741743  8741749  8741753
8741779  8741797  8741801  8741813  8741839  8741861  8741867  8741911  8741923  8741933
8741947  8741951  8741977  8741983  8741987  8741989  8742011  8742037  8742059  8742067
8742077  8742103  8742121  8742133  8742157  8742161  8742169  8742187  8742193  8742197
8742259  8742263  8742313  8742317  8742347  8742353  8742359  8742367  8742379  8742401
8742421  8742449  8742463  8742469  8742493  8742497  8742499  8742511  8742529  8742541
8742551  8742571  8742577  8742623  8742637  8742653  8742673  8742677  8742689  8742739
8742779  8742787  8742817  8742821  8742847  8742857  8742887  8742917  8742919  8742931
8742941  8742973  8742977  8742997  8743001  8743019  8743027  8743037  8743043  8743067
8743079  8743087  8743099  8743103  8743121  8743139  8743169  8743213  8743261  8743277
8743279  8743309  8743327  8743331  8743349  8743367  8743379  8743393  8743409  8743411
8743417  8743421  8743441  8743453  8743459  8743489  8743499  8743513  8743531  8743547
8743549  8743561  8743571  8743583  8743589  8743597  8743621  8743633  8743639  8743673
8743681  8743711  8743717  8743733  8743747  8743753  8743769  8743771  8743807  8743817
8743837  8743843  8743853  8743879  8743883  8743901  8743913  8743919  8743937  8743963
8743981  8743991  8743997  8744003  8744023  8744033  8744041  8744063  8744081  8744083
8744101  8744129  8744143  8744149  8744189  8744191  8744207  8744227  8744233  8744243
8744261  8744269  8744297  8744317  8744413  8744419  8744423  8744447  8744459  8744467
8744497  8744507  8744513  8744537  8744551  8744557  8744563  8744599  8744611  8744627
8744663  8744683  8744707  8744711  8744717  8744737  8744819  8744831  8744833  8744837
8744843  8744861  8744887  8744891  8744903  8744909  8744917  8744927  8744929  8744941
8744951  8744969  8745017  8745019  8745031  8745067  8745071  8745097  8745101  8745119
8745133  8745161  8745169  8745199  8745203  8745223  8745227  8745239  8745241  8745299
8745307  8745311  8745329  8745343  8745353  8745367  8745419  8745437  8745449  8745493
8745523  8745547  8745551  8745553  8745749  8745767  8745799  8745817  8745827  8745829
8745857  8745881  8745889  8745917  8745923  8745929  8745991  8746009  8746037  8746063
8746069  8746093  8746117  8746193  8746207  8746223  8746229  8746237  8746259  8746261
8746267  8746271  8746303  8746323  8746351  8746357  8746369  8746379  8746391  8746399
8746427  8746447  8746453  8746459  8746469  8746513  8746519  8746609  8746637  8746651
8746679  8746697  8746709  8746723  8746733  8746753  8746757  8746799  8746807  8746811
8746813  8746819  8746847  8746849  8746861  8746873  8746879  8746919  8746921  8746937
8746939  8746949  8746957  8746963  8746967  8746979  8746999  8747041  8747071  8747083
8747093  8747111  8747149  8747159  8747171  8747191  8747213  8747243  8747251  8747257
8747261  8747273  8747327  8747329  8747381  8747407  8747419  8747423  8747441  8747471
8747483  8747489  8747513  8747527  8747539  8747561  8747573  8747579  8747603  8747617
8747623  8747653  8747677  8747689  8747701  8747723  8747737  8747743  8747747  8747759
8747777  8747789  8747803  8747807  8747819  8747831  8747857  8747863  8747891  8747903
8747917  8747927  8747929  8747933  8747941  8747957  8747971  8747987  8748001  8748011
8748017  8748031  8748043  8748097  8748109  8748137  8748143  8748161  8748167  8748191
8748199  8748203  8748209  8748263  8748277  8748281  8748287  8748323  8748329  8748331
8748359  8748361  8748367  8748403  8748413  8748419  8748431  8748463  8748469  8748473
8748499  8748503  8748563  8748581  8748583  8748587  8748589  8748599  8748601  8748643
8748647  8748653  8748673  8748709  8748713  8748731  8748739  8748743  8748767  8748787
8748811  8748821  8748827  8748841  8748847  8748853  8748877  8748881  8748889  8748893
8748953  8748973  8748979  8748989  8748991  8749001  8749007  8749019  8749049  8749087
8749121  8749127  8749133  8749141  8749151  8749163  8749199  8749207  8749219  8749229
8749243  8749309  8749331  8749337  8749343  8749357  8749417  8749421  8749423  8749439
8749451  8749457  8749469  8749549  8749571  8749579  8749589  8749603  8749607  8749613
8749627  8749651  8749669  8749733  8749751  8749753  8749771  8749787  8749789  8749813
8749817  8749837  8749891  8749897  8749903  8749933  8749947  8749957  8749981  8749991
8750011  8750017  8750033  8750039  8750047  8750069  8750101  8750107  8750123  8750171
8750177  8750191  8750197  8750227  8750233  8750239  8750243  8750249  8750293  8750309
8750321  8750333  8750341  8750347  8750351  8750363  8750369  8750377  8750387  8750429
8750447  8750453  8750471  8750479  8750491  8750501  8750509  8750519  8750527  8750531
8750549  8750551  8750591  8750639  8750641  8750657  8750689  8750701  8750713  8750719
8750737  8750761  8750771  8750783  8750809  8750831  8750843  8750857  8750867  8750873
8750881  8750891  8750893  8750921  8750923  8750933  8750941  8750947  8750957  8750969
8751007  8751013  8751037  8751079  8751089  8751091  8751097  8751101  8751139  8751143
8751151  8751157  8751173  8751181  8751221  8751233  8751251  8751257  8751289  8751319
8751329  8751341  8751349  8751367  8751371  8751401  8751427  8751439  8751451  8751461
8751467  8751469  8751493  8751503  8751527  8751557  8751563  8751577  8751593  8751599
8751619  8751629  8751667  8751671  8751727  8751733  8751739  8751749  8751767  8751773
8751781  8751803  8751817  8751829  8751839  8751859  8751863  8751871  8751887  8751907
8751931  8751949  8751973  8752031  8752033  8752039  8752057  8752063  8752067  8752123
8752129  8752153  8752157  8752181  8752187  8752201  8752207  8752231  8752253  8752273
8752291  8752309  8752321  8752327  8752339  8752361  8752379  8752417  8752421  8752427
8752441  8752477  8752507  8752511  8752531  8752537  8752543  8752553  8752561  8752567
8752573  8752613  8752619  8752643  8752651  8752657  8752697  8752717  8752741  8752769
8752771  8752781  8752801  8752817  8752823  8752847  8752853  8752871  8752897  8752993
8753021  8753023  8753047  8753051  8753071  8753077  8753083  8753089  8753119  8753141
8753149  8753153  8753161  8753177  8753189  8753197  8753203  8753207  8753219  8753231
8753257  8753267  8753291  8753293  8753359  8753369  8753401  8753441  8753443  8753449
8753461  8753489  8753513  8753531  8753539  8753557  8753567  8753573  8753579  8753581
8753587  8753603  8753651  8753659  8753663  8753669  8753707  8753713  8753741  8753743
8753747  8753791  8753809  8753821  8753839  8753879  8753887  8753893  8753903  8753947
8753971  8753977  8753981  8753989  8753999  8754013  8754017  8754029  8754037  8754061
8754071  8754077  8754091  8754101  8754107  8754131  8754157  8754181  8754199  8754257
8754281  8754289  8754301  8754313  8754349  8754367  8754373  8754397  8754401  8754451
8754461  8754469  8754523  8754539  8754549  8754583  8754587  8754623  8754631  8754653
8754667  8754703  8754721  8754731  8754751  8754773  8754787  8754869  8754871  8754883
8754913  8754917  8754919  8754931  8754959  8754971  8754979  8755001  8755027  8755031
8755049  8755063  8755073  8755079  8755121  8755141  8755177  8755189  8755217  8755231
8755247  8755267  8755277  8755283  8755291  8755297  8755319  8755321  8755337  8755339
```

```
8755343  8755349  8755379  8755381  8755393  8755399  8755451  8755469  8755499  8755501
8755517  8755529  8755559  8755601  8755603  8755613  8755619  8755639  8755667  8755699
8755711  8755723  8755729  8755741  8755781  8755811  8755819  8755823  8755841  8755849
8755853  8755889  8755891  8755913  8755921  8755937  8755951  8755963  8755973  8755991
8755997  8756009  8756021  8756039  8756051  8756063  8756089  8756101  8756107  8756113
8756117  8756119  8756129  8756149  8756159  8756201  8756203  8756213  8756221  8756233
8756239  8756263  8756299  8756317  8756323  8756333  8756357  8756381  8756393  8756401
8756413  8756437  8756441  8756459  8756471  8756507  8756509  8756519  8756533  8756551
8756557  8756567  8756591  8756593  8756609  8756623  8756633  8756653  8756659  8756669
8756677  8756687  8756689  8756707  8756771  8756789  8756807  8756837  8756843  8756897
8756939  8756941  8756947  8756953  8756959  8756963  8756971  8756981  8756983  8756999
8757013  8757019  8757029  8757037  8757041  8757053  8757059  8757061  8757083  8757107
8757109  8757113  8757121  8757127  8757131  8757143  8757173  8757179  8757187  8757191
8757209  8757223  8757253  8757263  8757269  8757277  8757289  8757341  8757373  8757377
8757379  8757389  8757409  8757473  8757487  8757517  8757523  8757527  8757563  8757569
8757571  8757599  8757643  8757659  8757691  8757701  8757713  8757719  8757757  8757769
8757799  8757809  8757817  8757821  8757829  8757851  8757857  8757877  8757893  8757919
8757943  8757961  8758003  8758007  8758049  8758067  8758081  8758093  8758103  8758117
8758129  8758157  8758171  8758187  8758199  8758201  8758219  8758229  8758279  8758289
8758313  8758327  8758333  8758339  8758361  8758391  8758427  8758429  8758433  8758447
8758457  8758459  8758481  8758483  8758499  8758501  8758507  8758511  8758513  8758537
8758549  8758573  8758577  8758583  8758597  8758637  8758661  8758669  8758697  8758721
8758733  8758747  8758777  8758781  8758787  8758793  8758801  8758819  8758823  8758847
8758861  8758877  8758879  8758889  8758891  8758901  8758903  8758921  8758931  8758933
8758951  8758979  8758987  8758993  8759033  8759039  8759059  8759077  8759087  8759089
8759123  8759137  8759141  8759161  8759167  8759183  8759207  8759221  8759273  8759279
8759287  8759299  8759327  8759339  8759347  8759351  8759353  8759363  8759371  8759393
8759407  8759419  8759423  8759459  8759467  8759503  8759507  8759521  8759531  8759579
8759581  8759591  8759603  8759657  8759677  8759689  8759693  8759731  8759749  8759759
8759761  8759771  8759797  8759819  8759837  8759843  8759851  8759867  8759869  8759897
8759899  8759921  8759951  8759953  8759977  8760029  8760041  8760061  8760067  8760071
8760091  8760107  8760113  8760119  8760127  8760131  8760139  8760161  8760163  8760187
8760209  8760223  8760229  8760239  8760247  8760281  8760289  8760293  8760299  8760307
8760337  8760341  8760373  8760391  8760403  8760419  8760421  8760449  8760461  8760463
8760467  8760469  8760481  8760487  8760503  8760517  8760533  8760553  8760571  8760607
8760613  8760623  8760629  8760641  8760649  8760667  8760671  8760673  8760701  8760721
8760727  8760743  8760779  8760781  8760799  8760809  8760811  8760833  8760877  8760883
8760901  8760911  8760923  8760959  8760977  8760991  8761007  8761009  8761019  8761037
8761079  8761099  8761117  8761133  8761139  8761141  8761153  8761157  8761169  8761177
8761213  8761237  8761243  8761253  8761279  8761289  8761297  8761303  8761327  8761339
8761429  8761433  8761439  8761453  8761457  8761463  8761469  8761507  8761517  8761531
8761537  8761547  8761601  8761619  8761631  8761633  8761639  8761691  8761703  8761721
8761733  8761751  8761763  8761789  8761807  8761843  8761847  8761849  8761853  8761867
8761877  8761889  8761903  8761939  8761943  8761957  8761967  8761993  8761997  8761999
8762023  8762027  8762041  8762051  8762063  8762099  8762129  8762141  8762179  8762189
8762203  8762213  8762219  8762231  8762261  8762269  8762311  8762353  8762357  8762389
8762399  8762407  8762441  8762447  8762449  8762473  8762483  8762489  8762513  8762521
8762549  8762557  8762569  8762573  8762597  8762603  8762617  8762627  8762639  8762647
8762651  8762653  8762671  8762683  8762687  8762731  8762737  8762773  8762777  8762783
8762797  8762813  8762827  8762849  8762867  8762893  8762903  8762911  8762921  8762947
8762951  8762953  8762989  8763019  8763031  8763059  8763067  8763101  8763107  8763119
8763121  8763187  8763203  8763229  8763239  8763241  8763277  8763283  8763289  8763301
8763311  8763319  8763331  8763341  8763353  8763361  8763367  8763371  8763373  8763379
8763383  8763397  8763409  8763439  8763457  8763473  8763499  8763509  8763511  8763527
8763553  8763569  8763571  8763581  8763589  8763611  8763613  8763637  8763641  8763649
8763671  8763679  8763691  8763737  8763749  8763763  8763771  8763803  8763817  8763827
8763841  8763847  8763863  8763877  8763893  8763901  8763907  8763967  8763971  8763973
8763977  8763983  8764001  8764009  8764013  8764033  8764039  8764087  8764117  8764121
8764139  8764141  8764183  8764193  8764207  8764229  8764237  8764247  8764253  8764277
8764309  8764319  8764321  8764331  8764361  8764387  8764423  8764429  8764433  8764439
8764469  8764487  8764499  8764501  8764507  8764519  8764573  8764577  8764579  8764589
8764601  8764621  8764687  8764703  8764711  8764751  8764753  8764759  8764781  8764787
8764807  8764829  8764831  8764859  8764889  8764897  8764919  8764927  8764931  8764933
8764937  8764961  8764963  8765011  8765027  8765039  8765051  8765059  8765063  8765089
8765101  8765117  8765131  8765143  8765161  8765173  8765177  8765179  8765191  8765203
8765209  8765243  8765261  8765269  8765291  8765293  8765321  8765357  8765371  8765377
8765401  8765417  8765423  8765429  8765437  8765473  8765483  8765501  8765503  8765539
8765551  8765579  8765597  8765611  8765629  8765657  8765711  8765741  8765747  8765753
8765789  8765797  8765837  8765849  8765857  8765881  8765927  8765957  8765969  8765971
8765983  8765989  8765993  8766007  8766029  8766031  8766047  8766073  8766089  8766113
8766119  8766133  8766137  8766143  8766187  8766193  8766209  8766217  8766223  8766229
8766269  8766283  8766293  8766301  8766311  8766337  8766343  8766383  8766413  8766419
8766431  8766437  8766449  8766451  8766463  8766469  8766503  8766517  8766523  8766533
8766557  8766559  8766587  8766599  8766601  8766673  8766689  8766691  8766701  8766721
8766727  8766811  8766827  8766829  8766833  8766851  8766881  8766889  8766911  8766931
8766929  8766941  8766943  8766949  8766959  8766977  8766997  8767001  8767007  8767021
8767061  8767067  8767069  8767093  8767111  8767127  8767169  8767219  8767243  8767249
8767267  8767271  8767289  8767321  8767337  8767349  8767361  8767387  8767391  8767397
8767403  8767433  8767453  8767471  8767501  8767511  8767537  8767543  8767547  8767559
8767567  8767573  8767579  8767609  8767621  8767639  8767643  8767673  8767679  8767697
8767711  8767753  8767757  8767763  8767769  8767771  8767777  8767799  8767841  8767849
8767867  8767877  8767883  8767907  8767919  8767921  8767939  8767943  8767951  8767963
8767979  8768017  8768021  8768027  8768029  8768033  8768041  8768051  8768057  8768059
8768077  8768093  8768119  8768153  8768171  8768197  8768213  8768231  8768233  8768251
8768261  8768269  8768281  8768317  8768327  8768339  8768341  8768351  8768377  8768387
8768401  8768407  8768423  8768437  8768453  8768467  8768471  8768477  8768483  8768503
8768531  8768533  8768561  8768563  8768579  8768581  8768587  8768597  8768609  8768621
8768647  8768653  8768657  8768693  8768707  8768717  8768729  8768737  8768779  8768789
8768801  8768803  8768813  8768843  8768887  8768891  8768909  8768917  8768953  8768983
```

```
8768987  8769011  8769041  8769043  8769071  8769083  8769109  8769113  8769133  8769143
8769151  8769157  8769217  8769239  8769247  8769253  8769283  8769287  8769301  8769349
8769353  8769361  8769379  8769403  8769413  8769443  8769451  8769457  8769461  8769473
8769491  8769493  8769499  8769503  8769517  8769529  8769547  8769577  8769581  8769587
8769599  8769617  8769623  8769641  8769653  8769661  8769667  8769679  8769737  8769757
8769767  8769779  8769797  8769799  8769809  8769821  8769829  8769833  8769847  8769853
8769883  8769899  8769907  8769911  8769913  8769961  8769967  8769973  8769983  8770007
8770009  8770033  8770037  8770063  8770081  8770109  8770121  8770159  8770169  8770171
8770189  8770193  8770213  8770217  8770219  8770253  8770273  8770277  8770297  8770301
8770309  8770313  8770357  8770379  8770423  8770451  8770477  8770481  8770547  8770561
8770607  8770621  8770633  8770661  8770681  8770687  8770703  8770709  8770771  8770777
8770823  8770831  8770841  8770849  8770873  8770891  8770901  8770907  8770939  8770943
8770967  8770973  8770987  8771017  8771029  8771033  8771041  8771051  8771069  8771071
8771107  8771123  8771149  8771159  8771177  8771207  8771219  8771227  8771239  8771261
8771263  8771267  8771327  8771333  8771351  8771363  8771381  8771383  8771401  8771423
8771429  8771431  8771437  8771443  8771459  8771489  8771491  8771501  8771549  8771551
8771569  8771591  8771593  8771599  8771603  8771621  8771639  8771641  8771647  8771669
8771681  8771683  8771723  8771743  8771767  8771783  8771797  8771857  8771869  8771887
8771897  8771941  8771953  8771969  8771981  8772011  8772013  8772031  8772037  8772067
8772079  8772089  8772139  8772149  8772157  8772161  8772173  8772209  8772229  8772233
8772241  8772251  8772259  8772299  8772307  8772317  8772329  8772347  8772371  8772419
8772427  8772437  8772443  8772479  8772481  8772523  8772551  8772553  8772563  8772581
8772619  8772649  8772653  8772667  8772679  8772727  8772733  8772739  8772749  8772763
8772767  8772773  8772781  8772791  8772809  8772839  8772847  8772853  8772857  8772859
8772917  8772923  8772937  8772941  8772947  8772977  8772979  8772983  8772991  8773007
8773019  8773021  8773027  8773073  8773091  8773103  8773111  8773133  8773147  8773151
8773153  8773157  8773159  8773199  8773211  8773223  8773253  8773273  8773319  8773321
8773339  8773351  8773357  8773379  8773393  8773439  8773469  8773481  8773483  8773487
8773517  8773543  8773559  8773561  8773571  8773577  8773579  8773607  8773619  8773637
8773657  8773669  8773697  8773727  8773729  8773733  8773757  8773759  8773771  8773781
8773783  8773799  8773823  8773859  8773861  8773871  8773873  8773883  8773903  8773907
8773927  8773937  8773951  8773969  8773981  8773997  8774009  8774011  8774033  8774039
8774047  8774053  8774071  8774083  8774093  8774113  8774131  8774137  8774141  8774149
8774177  8774191  8774221  8774239  8774273  8774299  8774317  8774341  8774351  8774399
8774419  8774429  8774483  8774489  8774497  8774509  8774531  8774543  8774551  8774611
8774639  8774659  8774663  8774671  8774683  8774693  8774719  8774723  8774741  8774747
8774783  8774803  8774813  8774837  8774851  8774863  8774869  8774897  8774917  8774921
8774929  8774933  8774939  8774951  8774959  8774989  8774993  8774999  8775001  8775047
8775073  8775089  8775127  8775149  8775161  8775163  8775199  8775233  8775269  8775287
8775301  8775329  8775331  8775343  8775367  8775373  8775407  8775409  8775413  8775419
8775439  8775457  8775461  8775463  8775469  8775499  8775523  8775527  8775539  8775541
8775551  8775583  8775589  8775607  8775629  8775631  8775647  8775659  8775677  8775691
8775709  8775721  8775731  8775733  8775737  8775743  8775749  8775761  8775773  8775797
8775863  8775937  8775941  8775947  8775953  8775971  8775973  8775979  8775989  8775997
8776013  8776021  8776037  8776039  8776051  8776121  8776151  8776181  8776211  8776213
8776219  8776223  8776231  8776277  8776291  8776297  8776349  8776367  8776373  8776387
8776393  8776399  8776421  8776447  8776459  8776483  8776507  8776513  8776519  8776529
8776541  8776543  8776553  8776561  8776567  8776577  8776609  8776633  8776637  8776667
8776673  8776681  8776693  8776697  8776699  8776721  8776739  8776753  8776759  8776769
8776783  8776787  8776819  8776849  8776891  8776897  8776909  8776919  8776931  8776969
8776987  8776991  8776997  8777011  8777033  8777047  8777051  8777077  8777081  8777101
8777113  8777141  8777149  8777173  8777189  8777231  8777243  8777257  8777267  8777281
8777303  8777339  8777357  8777381  8777407  8777497  8777519  8777521  8777533  8777543
8777551  8777569  8777581  8777591  8777617  8777641  8777647  8777663  8777669  8777683
8777689  8777693  8777707  8777723  8777759  8777771  8777779  8777819  8777837  8777851
8777869  8777897  8777911  8777947  8777971  8777999  8778013  8778023  8778041  8778043
8778061  8778101  8778131  8778167  8778191  8778241  8778269  8778293  8778299  8778313
8778353  8778359  8778379  8778383  8778389  8778391  8778421  8778431  8778461  8778463
8778467  8778499  8778521  8778527  8778547  8778557  8778569  8778577  8778593  8778607
8778629  8778641  8778643  8778667  8778701  8778713  8778719  8778727  8778739  8778769
8778799  8778829  8778839  8778881  8778883  8778899  8778901  8778947  8778997  8779013
8779019  8779037  8779051  8779061  8779063  8779073  8779087  8779091  8779117  8779139
8779151  8779153  8779163  8779171  8779189  8779201  8779213  8779217  8779237  8779241
8779247  8779313  8779319  8779321  8779391  8779403  8779409  8779451  8779469  8779481
8779493  8779513  8779517  8779523  8779549  8779607  8779621  8779703  8779711  8779717
8779723  8779753  8779787  8779801  8779807  8779819  8779831  8779853  8779867  8779873
8779877  8779879  8779907  8779909  8779933  8779937  8779943  8779961  8779993  8780017
8780021  8780081  8780087  8780111  8780113  8780131  8780153  8780159  8780171  8780173
8780183  8780201  8780207  8780237  8780249  8780251  8780263  8780281  8780287  8780309
8780311  8780323  8780327  8780329  8780339  8780363  8780371  8780377  8780383  8780389
8780393  8780419  8780423  8780459  8780509  8780521  8780531  8780543  8780561  8780573
8780593  8780617  8780663  8780677  8780689  8780699  8780701  8780711  8780743  8780747
8780749  8780773  8780791  8780813  8780833  8780851  8780861  8780867  8780873  8780879
8780887  8780909  8780923  8780977  8780999  8781013  8781023  8781037  8781043  8781049
8781053  8781077  8781079  8781083  8781107  8781109  8781131  8781137  8781181  8781191
8781233  8781259  8781263  8781271  8781293  8781301  8781319  8781337  8781341  8781347
8781349  8781359  8781371  8781373  8781379  8781397  8781407  8781413  8781419  8781449
8781457  8781487  8781497  8781499  8781511  8781547  8781551  8781559  8781583
8781593  8781599  8781601  8781611  8781631  8781637  8781659  8781683  8781709  8781713
8781727  8781739  8781763  8781767  8781769  8781793  8781797  8781853  8781859  8781863
8781869  8781889  8781893  8781907  8781917  8781931  8781937  8781953  8781967  8782001
8782049  8782057  8782097  8782117  8782121  8782127  8782129  8782139  8782141  8782181
8782211  8782229  8782243  8782261  8782289  8782307  8782309  8782321  8782337  8782369
8782381  8782391  8782399  8782429  8782439  8782441  8782463  8782513  8782519  8782531
8782537  8782547  8782549  8782559  8782589  8782601  8782607  8782637  8782639  8782643
8782649  8782661  8782717  8782723  8782729  8782747  8782759  8782777  8782783  8782817
8782819  8782847  8782861  8782867  8782871  8782877  8782903  8782909  8782919  8782927
8782957  8782967  8782973  8782981  8783009  8783017  8783029  8783039  8783041  8783053
8783057  8783063  8783069  8783077  8783113  8783123  8783129  8783147  8783161  8783167
```

```
8783183  8783191  8783209  8783227  8783239  8783249  8783251  8783267  8783279  8783293
8783303  8783353  8783371  8783399  8783417  8783429  8783431  8783449  8783459  8783473
8783479  8783483  8783513  8783521  8783527  8783557  8783561  8783563  8783587  8783591
8783609  8783617  8783627  8783629  8783647  8783659  8783669  8783683  8783759  8783771
8783791  8783843  8783851  8783857  8783891  8783893  8783903  8783921  8783933  8783959
8783969  8783987  8783989  8784001  8784007  8784031  8784073  8784077  8784079  8784101
8784103  8784107  8784161  8784197  8784203  8784221  8784227  8784239  8784241  8784263
8784277  8784301  8784311  8784313  8784317  8784323  8784329  8784331  8784337  8784343
8784397  8784401  8784407  8784431  8784443  8784449  8784469  8784487  8784491  8784497
8784509  8784511  8784533  8784547  8784553  8784557  8784583  8784613  8784623  8784641
8784647  8784649  8784653  8784667  8784719  8784731  8784739  8784751  8784757  8784761
8784779  8784833  8784847  8784863  8784877  8784887  8784889  8784899  8784907  8784917
8784929  8784949  8784953  8784961  8784983  8785001  8785003  8785009  8785013  8785027
8785033  8785061  8785067  8785069  8785079  8785093  8785109  8785123  8785157  8785171
8785177  8785181  8785187  8785199  8785223  8785261  8785267  8785297  8785303  8785313
8785349  8785397  8785409  8785417  8785421  8785423  8785433  8785453  8785489  8785501
8785507  8785519  8785541  8785547  8785571  8785573  8785589  8785607  8785649  8785661
8785681  8785691  8785697  8785783  8785789  8785801  8785837  8785841  8785853  8785871
8785883  8785897  8785913  8785937  8785943  8785951  8785963  8785981  8785993  8786009
8786017  8786021  8786047  8786053  8786077  8786087  8786119  8786123  8786149  8786153
8786171  8786201  8786231  8786269  8786273  8786359  8786363  8786369  8786377  8786389
8786413  8786419  8786429  8786431  8786441  8786443  8786473  8786513  8786521  8786527
8786537  8786543  8786593  8786597  8786611  8786639  8786641  8786651  8786677  8786689
8786707  8786719  8786779  8786809  8786831  8786839  8786861  8786863  8786879  8786887
8786893  8786903  8786917  8786927  8786951  8786957  8786963  8787001  8787017  8787041
8787049  8787061  8787089  8787109  8787131  8787157  8787187  8787193  8787199  8787209
8787211  8787217  8787223  8787227  8787263  8787269  8787281  8787287  8787299  8787301
8787307  8787323  8787341  8787343  8787371  8787391  8787409  8787413  8787431  8787491
8787497  8787503  8787529  8787547  8787553  8787563  8787577  8787607  8787617  8787629
8787643  8787661  8787673  8787683  8787697  8787703  8787733  8787739  8787743  8787749
8787763  8787773  8787797  8787799  8787809  8787811  8787829  8787839  8787847  8787853
8787859  8787887  8787893  8787901  8787917  8787941  8787971  8787979  8788007  8788027
8788037  8788057  8788079  8788081  8788121  8788141  8788147  8788151  8788163  8788181
8788187  8788193  8788217  8788223  8788243  8788267  8788319  8788321  8788327  8788387
8788399  8788433  8788441  8788447  8788477  8788487  8788511  8788517  8788523  8788597
8788603  8788607  8788627  8788639  8788651  8788657  8788667  8788669  8788673  8788723
8788729  8788757  8788771  8788777  8788799  8788823  8788861  8788891  8788907  8788909
8788931  8788939  8788951  8788957  8788973  8788979  8788991  8789009  8789021  8789041
8789057  8789101  8789111  8789113  8789189  8789201  8789203  8789227  8789251  8789279
8789281  8789309  8789311  8789321  8789327  8789359  8789369  8789371  8789393  8789401
8789411  8789447  8789453  8789477  8789483  8789497  8789507  8789531  8789557  8789569
8789579  8789593  8789597  8789623  8789653  8789681  8789687  8789689  8789699  8789713
8789719  8789747  8789773  8789821  8789827  8789843  8789897  8789899  8789909  8789923
8789927  8789939  8789941  8789953  8789981  8789983  8789989  8790007  8790077  8790079
8790083  8790107  8790137  8790151  8790167  8790169  8790191  8790193  8790227  8790247
8790289  8790307  8790323  8790403  8790413  8790473  8790487  8790517  8790539
8790541  8790557  8790583  8790589  8790599  8790647  8790653  8790667  8790671  8790679
8790689  8790703  8790707  8790721  8790757  8790781  8790811  8790839  8790841  8790871
8790889  8790907  8790911  8790917  8790919  8790923  8790937  8790953  8790967  8790983
8791009  8791019  8791051  8791063  8791093  8791103  8791109  8791121  8791169  8791183
8791187  8791219  8791229  8791247  8791249  8791253  8791273  8791283  8791297  8791327
8791369  8791373  8791411  8791421  8791423  8791429  8791457  8791469  8791477  8791487
8791493  8791537  8791561  8791571  8791591  8791603  8791637  8791639
8791667  8791697  8791709  8791721  8791733  8791751  8791759  8791781  8791787  8791793
8791801  8791847  8791891  8791933  8791987  8792027  8792039  8792059  8792087  8792099
8792101  8792123  8792129  8792131  8792137  8792197  8792207  8792237  8792261  8792263
8792291  8792293  8792299  8792317  8792321  8792323  8792351  8792387  8792393  8792401
8792419  8792429  8792447  8792449  8792453  8792467  8792473  8792503  8792513  8792549
8792551  8792599  8792603  8792617  8792627  8792657  8792669  8792671  8792677  8792681
8792699  8792761  8792783  8792813  8792821  8792837  8792843  8792857  8792891  8792897
8792899  8792909  8792911  8792929  8792957  8792963  8792977  8792981  8792989  8793019
8793023  8793041  8793047  8793053  8793073  8793079  8793101  8793121  8793133  8793149
8793163  8793167  8793173  8793193  8793209  8793221  8793227  8793247  8793251  8793259
8793271  8793287  8793307  8793329  8793347  8793349  8793373  8793391  8793397  8793431
8793439  8793461  8793469  8793479  8793481  8793487  8793493  8793503  8793509  8793511
8793517  8793541  8793571  8793593  8793623  8793643  8793649  8793667  8793671  8793689
8793691  8793703  8793737  8793749  8793761  8793779  8793839  8793857  8793859  8793871
8793881  8793991  8793997  8794003  8794007  8794031  8794033  8794081  8794087
8794139  8794153  8794157  8794183  8794189  8794193  8794241  8794249  8794259  8794267
8794307  8794327  8794333  8794351  8794367  8794387  8794393  8794399  8794411  8794439
8794463  8794489  8794477  8794501  8794507  8794523  8794543  8794547  8794561  8794571
8794573  8794589  8794603  8794613  8794619  8794631  8794673  8794697  8794703  8794757
8794771  8794811  8794837  8794867  8794909  8794913  8794921  8794927  8794931
8794943  8794949  8794963  8794997  8794999  8795029  8795047  8795057  8795077  8795089
8795093  8795099  8795107  8795123  8795167  8795183  8795201  8795219  8795221  8795231
8795249  8795287  8795299  8795327  8795329  8795377  8795387  8795393  8795399  8795411
8795429  8795431  8795441  8795467  8795473  8795483  8795489  8795491  8795519  8795557
8795561  8795573  8795609  8795617  8795621  8795629  8795641  8795687  8795711  8795747
8795753  8795767  8795791  8795797  8795833  8795849  8795861  8795887  8795911  8795921
8795929  8795947  8796001  8796049  8796071  8796091  8796093  8796101  8796113  8796127
8796131  8796163  8796167  8796169  8796173  8796187  8796197  8796199  8796217  8796233
8796241  8796253  8796283  8796287  8796301  8796323  8796331  8796349  8796353  8796371
8796419  8796439  8796451  8796481  8796499  8796503  8796511  8796521  8796523
8796527  8796533  8796547  8796581  8796583  8796587  8796611  8796617  8796629  8796637
8796647  8796659  8796679  8796691  8796709  8796721  8796727  8796743  8796757  8796761
8796763  8796817  8796847  8796859  8796863  8796869  8796881  8796911  8796923  8796929
8796941  8796961  8797003  8797021  8797049  8797051  8797079  8797081  8797111  8797153
8797169  8797183  8797199  8797207  8797289  8797291  8797297  8797307  8797331  8797337
8797343  8797363  8797387  8797391  8797421  8797423  8797441  8797447  8797457  8797487
```

```
8797489 8797501 8797511 8797541 8797543 8797553 8797559 8797571 8797577 8797597
8797639 8797669 8797673 8797709 8797771 8797777 8797781 8797783 8797787 8797849
8797853 8797871 8797907 8797909 8797939 8797949 8797961 8797967 8797979 8798011
8798047 8798057 8798063 8798077 8798081 8798087 8798093 8798113 8798131 8798137
8798143 8798147 8798161 8798171 8798173 8798201 8798219 8798221 8798233 8798243
8798263 8798269 8798287 8798323 8798329 8798347 8798357 8798369 8798381 8798393
8798407 8798417 8798431 8798459 8798473 8798483 8798509 8798527 8798549 8798567
8798597 8798623 8798633 8798651 8798683 8798749 8798759 8798771 8798813 8798821
8798827 8798831 8798837 8798849 8798851 8798863 8798869 8798891 8798893 8798963
8798983 8798987 8798989 8799001 8799017 8799023 8799029 8799031 8799073 8799097
8799137 8799173 8799227 8799233 8799239 8799247 8799253 8799269 8799277 8799281
8799283 8799331 8799389 8799403 8799463 8799487 8799491 8799503 8799509 8799517
8799521 8799529 8799533 8799551 8799587 8799601 8799607 8799611 8799613 8799617
8799619 8799671 8799683 8799689 8799701 8799719 8799733 8799737 8799751 8799757
8799779 8799781 8799851 8799853 8799883 8799887 8799899 8799911 8799913 8799919
8799929 8799941 8799949 8799971 8799977 8799997 8800009 8800019 8800037 8800049
8800069 8800087 8800111 8800123 8800123 8800147 8800151 8800153 8800159
8800201 8800213 8800247 8800261 8800273 8800291 8800301 8800303 8800307 8800331
8800343 8800349 8800357 8800361 8800391 8800397 8800403 8800411 8800459 8800483
8800489 8800501 8800511 8800523 8800529 8800537 8800541 8800579 8800619 8800657
8800721 8800777 8800787 8800793 8800801 8800829 8800867 8800877 8800889 8800901
8800903 8800963 8800997 8800999 8801003 8801011 8801033 8801057 8801059
8801069 8801083 8801129 8801137 8801147 8801159 8801209 8801213 8801269 8801293
8801327 8801329 8801333 8801357 8801371 8801381 8801399 8801437 8801447 8801459
8801467 8801473 8801483 8801491 8801501 8801519 8801521 8801531 8801543 8801557
8801581 8801599 8801623 8801633 8801707 8801711 8801717 8801729 8801743 8801773
8801791 8801803 8801843 8801851 8801867 8801879 8801911 8801917 8801951 8801953
8801963 8801977 8801981 8801983 8801987 8801999 8802007 8802029 8802037 8802061
8802091 8802097 8802161 8802179 8802181 8802191 8802197 8802203 8802217 8802221
8802223 8802253 8802257 8802281 8802289 8802317 8802323 8802329 8802359 8802371
8802373 8802383 8802397 8802421 8802433 8802439 8802461 8802467 8802511 8802517
8802523 8802533 8802539 8802553 8802571 8802589 8802593 8802637 8802679 8802681
8802697 8802701 8802749 8802763 8802769 8802779 8802797 8802803 8802809 8802811
8802817 8802841 8802869 8802877 8802883 8802931 8802949 8802953 8802961 8803001
8803013 8803027 8803057 8803097 8803103 8803111 8803121 8803129 8803159 8803169
8803177 8803183 8803189 8803199 8803231 8803237 8803253 8803283 8803303 8803343
8803351 8803363 8803369 8803387 8803391 8803393 8803409 8803423 8803453 8803469
8803471 8803481 8803493 8803507 8803511 8803537 8803547 8803573 8803577 8803579
8803589 8803591 8803601 8803621 8803649 8803657 8803667 8803679 8803699 8803759
8803789 8803799 8803801 8803811 8803819 8803829 8803877 8803901 8803903 8803913
8803931 8803937 8803957 8803967 8803981 8803987 8804017 8804027 8804051 8804077
8804111 8804123 8804129 8804141 8804149 8804153 8804161 8804167 8804171 8804177
8804179 8804183 8804209 8804219 8804231 8804233 8804251 8804267 8804273 8804287
8804291 8804297 8804303 8804321 8804329 8804333 8804333 8804359 8804387 8804417
8804437 8804449 8804461 8804479 8804491 8804513 8804533 8804539 8804567 8804569
8804591 8804611 8804617 8804633 8804647 8804669 8804683 8804689 8804707 8804729
8804737 8804743 8804797 8804813 8804833 8804843 8804849 8804867 8804869 8804891
8804897 8804941 8804947 8804953 8804959 8804969 8804987 8804993 8805011 8805029
8805091 8805109 8805157 8805163 8805169 8805189 8805197 8805211 8805217 8805253
8805257 8805287 8805301 8805323 8805359 8805383 8805397 8805437 8805449 8805451
8805463 8805487 8805509 8805521 8805523 8805617 8805623 8805631 8805637 8805649
8805653 8805661 8805707 8805773 8805781 8805817 8805827 8805851 8805859 8805869
8805913 8805931 8805947 8805959 8805961 8805971 8805997 8806019 8806027 8806043
8806069 8806073 8806081 8806087 8806093 8806117 8806121 8806129 8806141 8806183
8806199 8806211 8806241 8806243 8806247 8806261 8806277 8806297 8806313 8806327
8806331 8806337 8806351 8806363 8806373 8806379 8806393 8806403 8806417 8806439
8806451 8806487 8806537 8806543 8806559 8806579 8806583 8806591 8806597 8806607
8806613 8806657 8806667 8806669 8806711 8806741 8806757 8806781 8806801 8806829
8806843 8806859 8806879 8806891 8806991 8807021 8807033 8807041 8807059 8807077
8807129 8807159 8807177 8807219 8807233 8807263 8807269 8807273 8807297 8807311
8807341 8807353 8807371 8807401 8807417 8807419 8807437 8807453 8807467 8807483
8807489 8807521 8807549 8807563 8807567 8807573 8807587 8807599 8807609 8807629
8807639 8807651 8807663 8807671 8807681 8807693 8807723 8807731 8807749 8807759
8807779 8807783 8807801 8807803 8807807 8807861 8807863 8807879 8807881 8807893
8807899 8807917 8807951 8807957 8807959 8807969 8807971 8807977 8807987 8807993
8808029 8808073 8808091 8808097 8808101 8808139 8808143 8808157 8808179 8808187
8808203 8808211 8808221 8808259 8808269 8808299 8808301 8808307 8808353 8808361
8808383 8808389 8808413 8808427 8808439 8808451 8808467 8808491 8808497 8808511
8808521 8808539 8808551 8808559 8808577 8808581 8808587 8808607 8808623 8808629
8808643 8808649 8808671 8808673 8808733 8808739 8808763 8808773 8808781 8808829
8808841 8808859 8808853 8808893 8808901 8808967 8809001 8809013 8809037 8809049
8809051 8809057 8809061 8809063 8809067 8809091 8809117 8809121 8809123 8809139
8809153 8809159 8809187 8809259 8809277 8809279 8809291 8809303 8809319 8809337
8809373 8809379 8809387 8809393 8809429 8809439 8809447 8809457 8809459 8809469
8809477 8809499 8809513 8809543 8809561 8809571 8809573 8809613 8809627 8809639
8809651 8809687 8809709 8809721 8809729 8809739 8809739 8809769 8809771 8809781
8809789 8809817 8809837 8809841 8809847 8809861 8809877 8809891 8809903 8809919
8809937 8809949 8809967 8809973 8809991 8809993 8810003 8810027 8810041 8810051
8810077 8810083 8810089 8810093 8810099 8810101 8810111 8810119 8810147 8810161
8810183 8810189 8810239 8810261 8810279 8810309 8810323 8810341 8810353 8810359
8810363 8810383 8810393 8810401 8810407 8810423 8810441 8810447 8810467 8810491
8810563 8810591 8810609 8810617 8810663 8810671 8810687 8810713 8810729 8810741
8810749 8810759 8810807 8810821 8810839 8810849 8810861 8810873 8810891
8810897 8810903 8810939 8810951 8810957 8810959 8810987 8810993 8810999 8811007
8811017 8811059 8811067 8811113 8811163 8811167 8811199 8811211 8811221 8811227
8811247 8811251 8811281 8811301 8811329 8811337 8811359 8811373 8811391 8811437
8811443 8811449 8811463 8811469 8811479 8811487 8811499 8811541 8811601 8811631
8811637 8811643 8811653 8811659 8811667 8811707 8811721 8811731 8811743 8811749
8811769 8811779 8811787 8811799 8811851 8811917 8811937 8811949 8811961 8811973
```

656

```
8811997  8812003  8812019  8812021  8812043  8812061  8812099  8812109  8812117  8812123
8812127  8812147  8812207  8812211  8812231  8812241  8812249  8812267  8812303  8812313
8812319  8812357  8812361  8812369  8812387  8812393  8812411  8812439  8812457  8812459
8812471  8812537  8812543  8812571  8812589  8812597  8812669  8812673  8812679  8812693
8812753  8812801  8812809  8812831  8812847  8812873  8812877  8812879  8812883  8812891
8812901  8812907  8812913  8812939  8812943  8812949  8812961  8812967  8812981  8812997
8813009  8813011  8813029  8813039  8813041  8813053  8813059  8813069  8813081  8813107
8813143  8813149  8813153  8813171  8813221  8813227  8813249  8813251  8813257  8813261
8813263  8813267  8813279  8813281  8813291  8813353  8813383  8813407  8813447  8813471
8813489  8813501  8813503  8813513  8813527  8813533  8813543  8813557  8813569  8813627
8813639  8813653  8813671  8813683  8813689  8813699  8813713  8813723  8813737  8813743
8813747  8813771  8813773  8813789  8813821  8813867  8813873  8813879  8813897  8813921
8813923  8813933  8813963  8813969  8813971  8813983  8813993  8814017  8814031  8814089
8814101  8814121  8814133  8814149  8814151  8814163  8814167  8814191  8814217  8814227
8814229  8814241  8814257  8814263  8814283  8814287  8814301  8814331  8814341  8814343
8814361  8814373  8814397  8814401  8814409  8814413  8814419  8814433  8814457  8814469
8814479  8814493  8814511  8814529  8814539  8814547  8814563  8814569  8814577  8814593
8814599  8814607  8814643  8814647  8814661  8814667  8814671  8814679  8814697  8814703
8814733  8814739  8814749  8814779  8814787  8814797  8814809  8814821  8814833  8814851
8814853  8814893  8814901  8814913  8814919  8814929  8814931  8814941  8814983  8815007
8815021  8815063  8815097  8815111  8815117  8815127  8815151  8815189  8815193  8815201
8815207  8815211  8815237  8815267  8815277  8815283  8815291  8815307  8815309  8815321
8815337  8815343  8815349  8815363  8815379  8815397  8815403  8815421  8815427  8815489
8815549  8815567  8815577  8815579  8815589  8815591  8815607  8815613  8815621  8815637
8815663  8815759  8815769  8815777  8815787  8815789  8815799  8815801  8815819  8815823
8815853  8815889  8815897  8815909  8815949  8815951  8815973  8816053  8816063  8816083
8816117  8816123  8816191  8816201  8816207  8816219  8816221  8816231  8816237  8816243
8816263  8816267  8816273  8816281  8816303  8816309  8816317  8816347  8816351  8816359
8816447  8816449  8816461  8816473  8816501  8816519  8816531  8816537  8816543  8816573
8816579  8816611  8816623  8816629  8816641  8816651  8816653  8816671  8816701  8816711
8816723  8816747  8816749  8816771  8816789  8816791  8816807  8816809  8816827  8816837
8816861  8816869  8816891  8816911  8816917  8816933  8816939  8816959  8816987  8817023
8817031  8817047  8817049  8817071  8817077  8817089  8817103  8817163  8817191  8817209
8817227  8817241  8817247  8817251  8817253  8817283  8817287  8817293  8817301  8817307
8817313  8817323  8817329  8817331  8817353  8817371  8817377  8817383  8817409  8817437
8817439  8817443  8817449  8817469  8817481  8817493  8817511  8817541  8817553  8817559
8817563  8817593  8817607  8817619  8817629  8817649  8817661  8817689  8817701  8817751
8817761  8817779  8817791  8817817  8817821  8817839  8817847  8817863  8817871  8817923
8817931  8817959  8817973  8818009  8818013  8818027  8818037  8818057  8818063  8818067
8818097  8818133  8818141  8818151  8818153  8818163  8818207  8818211  8818231  8818253
8818259  8818273  8818283  8818289  8818297  8818307  8818309  8818333  8818357  8818373
8818379  8818409  8818417  8818423  8818471  8818507  8818531  8818541  8818549  8818559
8818571  8818651  8818669  8818673  8818681  8818703  8818727  8818759  8818763  8818811
8818819  8818879  8818891  8818897  8818933  8818961  8818969  8818991  8819003  8819011
8819023  8819087  8819089  8819113  8819117  8819119  8819131  8819137  8819149  8819183
8819191  8819201  8819207  8819227  8819269  8819273  8819303  8819329  8819351  8819381
8819383  8819389  8819423  8819449  8819453  8819467  8819471  8819491  8819501  8819507
8819513  8819527  8819533  8819539  8819543  8819561  8819609  8819611  8819621  8819647
8819659  8819729  8819737  8819761  8819791  8819809  8819813  8819843  8819869  8819893
8819897  8819911  8819917  8819959  8819977  8819999  8820001  8820013  8820029  8820041
8820073  8820083  8820121  8820137  8820139  8820143  8820169  8820181  8820187  8820193
8820221  8820223  8820257  8820269  8820283  8820299  8820347  8820367  8820373  8820377
8820397  8820421  8820451  8820473  8820479  8820481  8820499  8820509  8820529  8820563
8820577  8820589  8820593  8820601  8820619  8820649  8820697  8820733  8820743  8820761
8820767  8820793  8820803  8820811  8820821  8820829  8820839  8820853  8820857  8820859
8820869  8820881  8820887  8820907  8820919  8820923  8820947  8820961  8820971  8821003
8821009  8821013  8821049  8821067  8821091  8821093  8821103  8821129  8821139  8821151
8821193  8821201  8821223  8821231  8821237  8821243  8821291  8821297  8821303  8821313
8821327  8821343  8821343  8821361  8821363  8821367  8821387  8821399  8821427  8821457
8821507  8821511  8821517  8821523  8821543  8821573  8821583  8821633  8821661  8821663
8821727  8821727  8821733  8821777  8821783  8821807  8821817  8821819  8821867  8821877
8821889  8821919  8821927  8821951  8821961  8821973  8821979  8821991  8821999  8822017
8822027  8822029  8822057  8822063  8822069  8822071  8822101  8822111  8822129  8822159
8822161  8822171  8822183  8822189  8822227  8822237  8822239  8822263  8822279  8822291
8822299  8822347  8822377  8822413  8822423  8822431  8822459  8822533  8822537  8822551
8822581  8822587  8822591  8822599  8822617  8822621  8822623  8822629  8822633  8822647
8822657  8822717  8822743  8822767  8822797  8822833  8822839  8822843  8822851  8822867
8822893  8822903  8822911  8822923  8822939  8822951  8822953  8822969  8822977  8822987
8822993  8823013  8823019  8823043  8823097  8823107  8823137  8823151  8823161  8823167
8823181  8823233  8823253  8823257  8823271  8823293  8823301  8823307  8823317  8823343
8823359  8823359  8823361  8823377  8823389  8823401  8823407  8823413  8823439  8823443
8823601  8823611  8823613  8823637  8823653  8823691  8823707  8823709  8823713  8823719
8823751  8823769  8823791  8823803  8823823  8823839  8823851  8823853  8823883  8823911
8823949  8823977  8824027  8824043  8824051  8824103  8824133  8824147  8824169  8824201
8824219  8824229  8824247  8824247  8824253  8824259  8824273  8824279  8824301  8824327
8824351  8824357  8824363  8824393  8824421  8824423  8824427  8824441  8824457  8824457
8824469  8824481  8824489  8824511  8824523  8824549  8824561  8824577  8824583  8824601
8824603  8824619  8824633  8824639  8824667  8824679  8824681  8824691  8824727  8824733
8824741  8824747  8824757  8824793  8824811  8824817  8824831  8824841  8824843  8824859
8824877  8824883  8824891  8824901  8824957  8824969  8824979  8824997  8824999  8825021
8825027  8825041  8825051  8825059  8825071  8825081  8825107  8825119  8825149  8825153
8825171  8825183  8825197  8825207  8825213  8825231  8825233  8825239  8825263  8825269
8825281  8825287  8825293  8825321  8825407  8825437  8825447  8825459  8825461  8825471
8825477  8825489  8825501  8825503  8825539  8825543  8825549  8825561  8825563  8825569
8825581  8825591  8825617  8825623  8825651  8825653  8825659  8825689  8825711  8825743
8825749  8825753  8825777  8825779  8825819  8825821  8825837  8825851  8825857  8825867
8825881  8825891  8825893  8825897  8825903  8825909  8825911  8825963  8825969  8825981
8826011  8826019  8826023  8826047  8826061  8826067  8826071  8826073  8826079  8826107
```

657

```
8826131  8826133  8826157  8826161  8826163  8826187  8826197  8826217  8826221  8826229
8826253  8826263  8826277  8826283  8826331  8826371  8826401  8826407  8826421  8826427
8826437  8826443  8826463  8826473  8826479  8826497  8826511  8826523  8826529  8826539
8826541  8826547  8826551  8826581  8826589  8826593  8826607  8826617  8826637  8826667
8826677  8826691  8826703  8826721  8826731  8826737  8826743  8826787  8826793  8826803
8826809  8826821  8826823  8826833  8826863  8826877  8826889  8826899  8826919  8826943
8826947  8826949  8826953  8826959  8826977  8827003  8827031  8827037  8827051  8827057
8827061  8827079  8827081  8827099  8827103  8827111  8827121  8827123  8827139  8827151
8827237  8827243  8827253  8827261  8827271  8827279  8827319  8827327  8827337  8827363
8827367  8827387  8827391  8827411  8827417  8827433  8827459  8827487  8827517  8827541
8827543  8827547  8827549  8827579  8827603  8827613  8827649  8827667  8827691  8827711
8827727  8827729  8827739  8827769  8827781  8827783  8827807  8827823  8827843  8827877
8827891  8827909  8827937  8827939  8827967  8827969  8827979  8828003  8828009  8828041
8828059  8828063  8828077  8828119  8828123  8828167  8828191  8828203  8828227  8828269
8828279  8828291  8828317  8828327  8828359  8828371  8828381  8828387  8828411  8828419
8828431  8828447  8828467  8828471  8828473  8828497  8828503  8828507  8828509  8828513
8828539  8828543  8828549  8828563  8828609  8828629  8828639  8828641  8828663  8828669
8828683  8828689  8828719  8828723  8828741  8828747  8828753  8828777  8828801  8828857
8828861  8828879  8828917  8828923  8828927  8828929  8828951  8828971  8828983  8828993
8829019  8829031  8829047  8829049  8829071  8829077  8829101  8829113  8829143  8829151
8829157  8829169  8829179  8829187  8829229  8829241  8829257  8829259  8829287  8829313
8829329  8829349  8829371  8829383  8829397  8829413  8829437  8829449  8829479  8829487
8829503  8829551  8829559  8829571  8829581  8829599  8829617  8829629  8829649  8829673
8829713  8829721  8829731  8829757  8829767  8829781  8829803  8829827  8829839  8829841
8829857  8829869  8829871  8829917  8829923  8829971  8829973  8829983  8829991  8830033
8830037  8830051  8830069  8830103  8830147  8830163  8830189  8830243  8830247  8830267
8830271  8830273  8830279  8830291  8830357  8830369  8830373  8830379  8830391  8830397
8830441  8830477  8830487  8830517  8830537  8830553  8830559  8830571  8830583  8830637
8830639  8830651  8830663  8830681  8830693  8830697  8830709  8830711  8830721  8830729
8830739  8830741  8830813  8830823  8830859  8830879  8830891  8830897  8830907  8830931
8830937  8830957  8830961  8830999  8831003  8831021  8831027  8831033  8831047  8831059
8831089  8831099  8831107  8831111  8831161  8831183  8831189  8831191  8831201  8831209
8831213  8831233  8831237  8831239  8831261  8831269  8831281  8831299  8831309  8831351
8831353  8831357  8831369  8831387  8831393  8831401  8831413  8831429  8831479  8831509
8831513  8831527  8831569  8831587  8831593  8831633  8831663  8831699  8831717  8831729
8831749  8831773  8831783  8831791  8831821  8831831  8831833  8831861  8831881  8831897
8831909  8831923  8831929  8831951  8831957  8831969  8831971  8831981  8831983  8831987
8831989  8832001  8832029  8832049  8832053  8832067  8832127  8832137  8832149  8832181
8832203  8832209  8832223  8832227  8832289  8832311  8832337  8832377  8832389  8832403
8832407  8832431  8832451  8832479  8832487  8832491  8832493  8832497  8832517  8832521
8832541  8832553  8832557  8832581  8832583  8832623  8832631  8832641  8832643  8832647
8832653  8832661  8832679  8832683  8832689  8832709  8832721  8832727  8832749  8832773
8832779  8832793  8832839  8832847  8832881  8832883  8832893  8832913  8832919  8832959
8832961  8833003  8833049  8833051  8833061  8833063  8833091  8833101  8833117  8833169
8833193  8833211  8833229  8833241  8833243  8833247  8833249  8833261  8833277  8833289
8833337  8833379  8833393  8833399  8833427  8833439  8833477  8833483  8833493  8833501
8833507  8833519  8833529  8833547  8833567  8833571  8833597  8833609  8833631  8833663
8833673  8833681  8833703  8833709  8833717  8833751  8833753  8833757  8833789  8833793
8833823  8833849  8833871  8833889  8833933  8833961  8833969  8833973  8834029  8834041
8834087  8834117  8834131  8834149  8834153  8834179  8834191  8834209  8834213  8834219
8834249  8834263  8834269  8834281  8834291  8834303  8834321  8834363  8834383  8834389
8834443  8834477  8834489  8834513  8834519  8834537  8834549  8834561  8834587  8834627
8834629  8834671  8834689  8834699  8834711  8834717  8834741  8834759  8834779  8834789
8834797  8834827  8834831  8834843  8834851  8834873  8834893  8834899  8834911  8834927
8834933  8834939  8834957  8834963  8834983  8834989  8834999  8835007  8835023  8835077
8835103  8835109  8835137  8835143  8835157  8835163  8835221  8835241  8835269  8835271
8835287  8835293  8835313  8835317  8835319  8835329  8835331  8835353  8835367  8835371
8835373  8835397  8835419  8835467  8835481  8835487  8835493  8835499  8835503  8835523
8835539  8835553  8835559  8835569  8835571  8835613  8835679  8835689  8835707  8835709
8835751  8835763  8835773  8835797  8835811  8835823  8835833  8835863  8835881  8835889
8835901  8835947  8835949  8835973  8835991  8836013  8836019  8836031  8836043  8836049
8836049  8836063  8836103  8836123  8836129  8836151  8836171  8836183  8836207  8836211
8836249  8836283  8836307  8836309  8836327  8836337  8836351  8836357  8836367  8836391
8836397  8836403  8836417  8836427  8836433  8836441  8836453  8836459  8836483  8836507
8836523  8836571  8836573  8836609  8836621  8836657  8836661  8836667  8836727  8836741
8836757  8836759  8836783  8836811  8836813  8836819  8836859  8836871  8836879  8836897
8836903  8836907  8836943  8836951  8836979  8836981  8836999  8837011  8837027  8837053
8837057  8837089  8837111  8837113  8837119  8837123  8837137  8837149  8837159  8837183
8837189  8837209  8837219  8837243  8837249  8837251  8837287  8837293  8837303  8837321
8837327  8837329  8837341  8837347  8837351  8837357  8837377  8837401  8837417  8837419
8837429  8837443  8837447  8837461  8837471  8837513  8837519  8837531  8837533  8837539
8837557  8837567  8837593  8837597  8837623  8837657  8837659  8837677  8837683  8837707
8837729  8837737  8837753  8837771  8837813  8837827  8837861  8837867  8837893  8837897
8837921  8837929  8837951  8837987  8837989  8837993  8837999  8838013  8838017  8838019
8838043  8838077  8838101  8838103  8838119  8838133  8838161  8838199  8838217  8838257
8838289  8838299  8838337  8838343  8838353  8838367  8838383  8838391  8838407  8838413
8838433  8838443  8838451  8838457  8838481  8838539  8838541  8838551  8838569  8838617
8838637  8838653  8838677  8838727  8838733  8838761  8838769  8838803  8838833  8838853
8838859  8838883  8838901  8838917  8838953  8838959  8838979  8838989  8839007  8839021
8839027  8839043  8839049  8839069  8839079  8839093  8839111  8839139  8839141  8839177
8839183  8839211  8839249  8839253  8839267  8839273  8839277  8839279  8839297  8839301
8839307  8839331  8839333  8839339  8839343  8839349  8839361  8839367  8839373  8839387
8839409  8839423  8839459  8839483  8839529  8839531  8839543  8839601  8839631  8839637
8839667  8839669  8839687  8839703  8839729  8839739  8839757  8839763  8839771  8839783
8839799  8839801  8839819  8839829  8839837  8839841  8839857  8839877  8839903  8839907
8839927  8839931  8839933  8839951  8839967  8840057  8840093  8840113  8840123  8840129
8840131  8840141  8840159  8840171  8840173  8840191  8840201  8840207  8840213
8840231  8840243  8840287  8840309  8840317  8840333  8840341  8840369  8840393  8840401
8840407  8840411  8840417  8840431  8840437  8840443  8840467  8840477  8840497  8840509
```

```
8840551  8840569  8840581  8840591  8840599  8840609  8840627  8840647  8840659  8840683
8840687  8840701  8840749  8840753  8840759  8840761  8840773  8840779  8840857  8840863
8840869  8840879  8840893  8840917  8840927  8840939  8840959  8840963  8840977  8840987
8840999  8841017  8841031  8841043  8841073  8841083  8841097  8841167  8841179  8841181
8841191  8841197  8841221  8841227  8841247  8841263  8841331  8841337  8841367  8841383
8841389  8841431  8841449  8841451  8841463  8841467  8841473  8841487  8841493  8841509
8841529  8841629  8841643  8841653  8841659  8841661  8841673  8841697  8841709  8841719
8841733  8841739  8841743  8841757  8841787  8841817  8841823  8841827  8841871  8841881
8841941  8841947  8841949  8841953  8841967  8841983  8841991  8841997  8842007  8842027
8842033  8842039  8842069  8842079  8842103  8842109  8842123  8842151  8842177  8842199
8842213  8842217  8842231  8842243  8842259  8842279  8842291  8842307  8842313  8842319
8842349  8842387  8842399  8842403  8842453  8842487  8842489  8842523  8842541  8842579
8842591  8842607  8842609  8842633  8842637  8842643  8842661  8842697  8842699  8842747
8842753  8842783  8842793  8842807  8842831  8842871  8842877  8842919  8842927  8842931
8842937  8842949  8842957  8842969  8842973  8843011  8843047  8843053  8843059  8843071
8843089  8843101  8843141  8843183  8843269  8843273  8843287  8843291  8843297  8843309
8843323  8843369  8843371  8843377  8843381  8843389  8843399  8843411  8843441  8843447
8843501  8843503  8843507  8843539  8843551  8843557  8843561  8843563  8843573  8843591
8843603  8843631  8843641  8843647  8843669  8843671  8843677  8843699  8843701  8843713
8843729  8843771  8843789  8843827  8843867  8843881  8843903  8843909  8843917  8843993
8844001  8844007  8844013  8844047  8844049  8844053  8844071  8844089  8844091  8844103
8844107  8844113  8844127  8844133  8844181  8844191  8844223  8844229  8844239  8844263
8844271  8844289  8844307  8844313  8844323  8844347  8844349  8844361  8844371  8844373
8844377  8844379  8844389  8844401  8844421  8844457  8844463  8844467  8844469  8844499
8844547  8844559  8844571  8844593  8844613  8844629  8844653  8844659  8844677  8844691
8844697  8844701  8844721  8844733  8844767  8844769  8844779  8844853  8844859  8844863
8844877  8844881  8844911  8844929  8844931  8844943  8844991  8845003  8845021  8845027
8845033  8845063  8845069  8845073  8845079  8845099  8845129  8845141  8845147  8845157
8845163  8845171  8845181  8845189  8845201  8845211  8845231  8845237  8845247  8845267
8845297  8845303  8845307  8845327  8845349  8845357  8845373  8845387  8845391  8845399
8845451  8845453  8845477  8845517  8845519  8845531  8845567  8845589  8845597  8845601
8845607  8845619  8845637  8845657  8845673  8845687  8845691  8845699  8845703  8845723
8845789  8845813  8845817  8845829  8845853  8845861  8845897  8845901  8845937  8845951
8846023  8846027  8846063  8846081  8846083  8846087  8846093  8846111  8846141  8846143
8846207  8846209  8846221  8846231  8846251  8846263  8846291  8846309  8846317  8846323
8846353  8846371  8846393  8846399  8846413  8846423  8846429  8846437  8846449  8846459
8846471  8846483  8846507  8846521  8846527  8846543  8846557  8846581  8846599  8846627
8846641  8846659  8846683  8846713  8846729  8846731  8846741  8846753  8846759  8846779
8846807  8846809  8846821  8846833  8846839  8846861  8846879  8846899  8846909  8846923
8846963  8846977  8846983  8847023  8847029  8847031  8847043  8847061  8847067  8847071
8847077  8847127  8847133  8847143  8847161  8847169  8847193  8847229  8847247  8847253
8847271  8847277  8847281  8847287  8847301  8847353  8847359  8847373  8847383  8847389
8847409  8847413  8847427  8847439  8847451  8847457  8847469  8847473  8847481  8847491
8847511  8847529  8847533  8847539  8847547  8847557  8847563  8847569  8847577  8847589
8847593  8847607  8847613  8847647  8847653  8847659  8847689  8847691  8847719  8847731
8847733  8847743  8847751  8847793  8847799  8847859  8847869  8847877  8847887  8847889
8847899  8847907  8847911  8847913  8847919  8847941  8847967  8847991  8847997  8848027
8848057  8848061  8848093  8848097  8848121  8848127  8848139  8848141  8848159  8848163
8848181  8848183  8848187  8848193  8848199  8848201  8848247  8848271  8848283  8848309
8848327  8848337  8848349  8848351  8848373  8848379  8848391  8848429  8848453  8848459
8848487  8848493  8848501  8848529  8848571  8848577  8848589  8848607  8848613  8848621
8848633  8848667  8848703  8848709  8848717  8848739  8848759  8848769  8848771  8848783
8848811  8848817  8848837  8848871  8848887  8848897  8848901  8848923  8848949  8848969
8849021  8849047  8849063  8849077  8849081  8849083  8849111  8849119  8849131  8849173
8849177  8849189  8849201  8849219  8849237  8849249  8849257  8849261  8849287  8849297
8849303  8849363  8849371  8849381  8849387  8849389  8849413  8849417  8849429  8849441
8849447  8849461  8849473  8849483  8849521  8849531  8849567  8849579  8849591  8849597
8849627  8849647  8849661  8849681  8849747  8849767  8849783  8849791  8849803  8849833
8849837  8849851  8849857  8849861  8849879  8849899  8849903  8849921  8849969  8849977
8849987  8849999  8850001  8850007  8850011  8850019  8850031  8850073  8850089  8850113
8850151  8850157  8850167  8850187  8850197  8850203  8850209  8850211  8850263
8850271  8850293  8850329  8850343  8850349  8850379  8850403  8850419  8850433  8850461
8850463  8850487  8850497  8850509  8850521  8850533  8850559  8850577  8850587  8850601
8850613  8850641  8850661  8850671  8850773  8850797  8850811  8850839  8850847  8850857
8850859  8850869  8850937  8850949  8850973  8850977  8851009  8851043  8851057  8851069
8851091  8851097  8851111  8851123  8851133  8851187  8851211  8851223  8851229  8851243
8851253  8851267  8851307  8851309  8851313  8851319  8851331  8851333  8851363  8851379
8851387  8851393  8851429  8851439  8851457  8851471  8851487  8851489  8851517  8851529
8851553  8851567  8851597  8851603  8851627  8851631  8851637  8851639  8851657  8851669
8851691  8851697  8851721  8851723  8851727  8851751  8851763  8851793  8851807  8851813
8851831  8851837  8851841  8851847  8851861  8851877  8851879  8851889  8851897  8851919
8851939  8851949  8851961  8851963  8852009  8852057  8852059  8852069  8852071  8852093
8852141  8852147  8852153  8852159  8852161  8852177  8852197  8852201  8852203  8852227
8852231  8852243  8852251  8852273  8852293  8852323  8852339  8852353  8852357  8852377
8852411  8852413  8852429  8852443  8852449  8852471  8852477  8852479  8852513  8852567
8852593  8852611  8852617  8852629  8852633  8852647  8852663  8852681  8852687  8852707
8852719  8852729  8852737  8852791  8852807  8852813  8852827  8852867  8852881  8852923
8852939  8852941  8852947  8852951  8852981  8852989  8853001  8853017  8853079  8853109
8853139  8853151  8853157  8853167  8853181  8853191  8853193  8853217  8853223  8853233
8853239  8853241  8853263  8853269  8853289  8853329  8853337  8853347  8853359  8853371
8853389  8853391  8853401  8853407  8853409  8853419  8853421  8853433  8853443  8853457
8853463  8853469  8853473  8853511  8853521  8853529  8853541  8853547  8853553  8853577
8853587  8853589  8853641  8853661  8853673  8853683  8853697  8853731  8853737  8853739
8853749  8853763  8853797  8853799  8853847  8853851  8853863  8853893  8853917  8853937
8853947  8853973  8854007  8854031  8854037  8854039  8854049  8854061  8854067  8854081
8854121  8854123  8854129  8854151  8854163  8854169  8854177  8854199  8854207  8854217
8854231  8854249  8854253  8854267  8854273  8854303  8854337  8854369  8854381  8854387
8854409  8854411  8854423  8854453  8854463  8854487  8854493  8854553  8854579  8854607
8854613  8854621  8854631  8854639  8854667  8854669  8854679  8854687  8854691  8854693
```

```
8854697  8854723  8854733  8854751  8854757  8854759  8854777  8854789  8854799  8854829
8854837  8854849  8854843  8854883  8854919  8854927  8854949  8854961  8854981  8854987
8854991  8854997  8855003  8855009  8855027  8855039  8855047  8855053  8855059  8855087
8855089  8855101  8855111  8855123  8855137  8855149  8855167  8855183  8855239  8855257
8855261  8855267  8855279  8855281  8855359  8855389  8855401  8855423  8855447  8855461
8855477  8855479  8855503  8855507  8855533  8855537  8855563  8855569  8855573  8855593
8855597  8855669  8855687  8855689  8855719  8855747  8855771  8855773  8855779  8855857
8855867  8855887  8855911  8855921  8855927  8855939  8855941  8855981  8856019  8856037
8856053  8856073  8856079  8856101  8856103  8856121  8856131  8856179  8856181  8856187
8856227  8856233  8856241  8856251  8856259  8856293  8856307  8856317  8856329  8856361
8856377  8856427  8856437  8856443  8856457  8856487  8856503  8856557  8856559  8856569
8856593  8856613  8856637  8856649  8856689  8856703  8856713  8856721  8856733  8856761
8856763  8856767  8856787  8856829  8856833  8856877  8856901  8856929  8856959  8856971
8856997  8857003  8857027  8857031  8857039  8857049  8857063  8857067  8857091  8857111
8857127  8857133  8857157  8857159  8857181  8857217  8857253  8857259  8857273  8857283
8857301  8857367  8857379  8857399  8857411  8857421  8857447  8857451  8857483  8857487
8857489  8857501  8857523  8857529  8857531  8857543  8857621  8857637  8857643  8857649
8857669  8857687  8857721  8857727  8857733  8857753  8857757  8857759  8857777  8857787
8857817  8857831  8857841  8857853  8857873  8857879  8857883  8857907  8857913  8857973
8857999  8858023  8858027  8858029  8858093  8858107  8858141  8858149  8858153  8858203
8858233  8858249  8858257  8858273  8858287  8858293  8858299  8858303  8858323  8858327
8858329  8858347  8858357  8858431  8858441  8858449  8858453  8858461  8858471  8858483
8858489  8858527  8858569  8858573  8858587  8858593  8858621  8858627  8858677  8858711
8858713  8858723  8858743  8858753  8858767  8858779  8858783  8858797  8858813  8858821
8858881  8858923  8858951  8858953  8858957  8858987  8859029  8859031  8859041  8859049
8859083  8859089  8859101  8859127  8859131  8859143  8859197  8859203  8859223  8859229
8859233  8859271  8859283  8859289  8859299  8859307  8859373  8859421  8859437  8859463
8859467  8859479  8859481  8859497  8859511  8859541  8859551  8859559  8859581  8859589
8859607  8859637  8859659  8859671  8859673  8859691  8859709  8859733  8859743  8859749
8859787  8859793  8859811  8859817  8859827  8859841  8859857  8859863  8859887  8859889
8859911  8859913  8859919  8859943  8859953  8859967  8859973  8859989  8859997  8860003
8860031  8860069  8860073  8860081  8860097  8860121  8860123  8860127  8860139  8860151
8860157  8860171  8860177  8860183  8860219  8860231  8860259  8860261  8860273  8860297
8860301  8860307  8860309  8860343  8860351  8860361  8860363  8860367  8860429  8860463
8860471  8860477  8860547  8860567  8860571  8860597  8860601  8860603  8860619  8860627
8860639  8860651  8860661  8860673  8860703  8860739  8860771  8860793  8860807  8860811
8860837  8860849  8860861  8860867  8860883  8860889  8860909  8860913  8860931  8860933
8860939  8860949  8860963  8860993  8861059  8861089  8861113  8861117  8861119  8861137
8861143  8861147  8861159  8861173  8861191  8861213  8861227  8861231  8861243  8861249
8861261  8861263  8861273  8861291  8861309  8861383  8861393  8861401  8861423  8861473
8861491  8861497  8861513  8861519  8861533  8861557  8861561  8861563  8861597  8861609
8861627  8861659  8861663  8861683  8861701  8861707  8861711  8861717  8861719  8861729
8861747  8861767  8861773  8861779  8861807  8861813  8861837  8861851  8861857  8861861
8861869  8861873  8861887  8861891  8861893  8861903  8861911  8861921  8861927  8861929
8861987  8861989  8862013  8862031  8862041  8862053  8862079  8862097  8862137  8862163
8862167  8862173  8862181  8862221  8862229  8862233  8862239  8862241  8862247  8862323
8862349  8862391  8862397  8862409  8862421  8862431  8862443  8862467  8862479  8862481
8862509  8862517  8862527  8862541  8862547  8862563  8862571  8862577  8862583  8862611
8862619  8862631  8862641  8862673  8862677  8862691  8862697  8862757  8862769  8862781
8862787  8862809  8862817  8862877  8862881  8862883  8862901  8862907  8862923  8862977
8862983  8862991  8863007  8863013  8863037  8863051  8863109  8863123  8863147  8863163
8863199  8863201  8863207  8863219  8863237  8863249  8863259  8863319  8863331  8863333
8863343  8863373  8863399  8863423  8863429  8863433  8863447  8863453  8863469  8863471
8863493  8863499  8863501  8863513  8863529  8863537  8863567  8863573  8863577  8863619
8863639  8863643  8863651  8863661  8863663  8863691  8863697  8863703  8863781  8863787
8863801  8863807  8863837  8863867  8863907  8863963  8863969  8863973  8863993  8863997
8863999  8864003  8864029  8864041  8864081  8864099  8864117  8864147  8864161  8864179
8864189  8864231  8864239  8864243  8864249  8864267  8864291  8864299  8864329  8864333
8864351  8864371  8864381  8864399  8864411  8864417  8864461  8864477  8864491  8864503
8864509  8864521  8864549  8864561  8864587  8864641  8864663  8864731  8864741  8864747
8864759  8864761  8864767  8864771  8864797  8864813  8864851  8864879  8864881
8864893  8864899  8864903  8864917  8864929  8864953  8864969  8864987  8864993  8865011
8865013  8865019  8865029  8865067  8865083  8865113  8865137  8865139  8865149  8865167
8865179  8865203  8865209  8865289  8865293  8865299  8865317  8865331  8865341  8865359
8865371  8865377  8865391  8865397  8865401  8865403  8865413  8865421  8865427  8865431
8865443  8865487  8865497  8865499  8865581  8865583  8865601  8865613  8865683  8865707
8865719  8865737  8865749  8865763  8865797  8865803  8865809  8865821  8865827  8865847
8865859  8865877  8865911  8865919  8865929  8865953  8865973  8865991  8866003  8866007
8866019  8866057  8866079  8866087  8866097  8866111  8866139  8866147  8866157  8866159
8866171  8866189  8866259  8866283  8866303  8866313  8866337  8866391  8866397  8866399
8866427  8866433  8866439  8866441  8866453  8866457  8866463  8866513  8866567  8866573
8866577  8866591  8866601  8866603  8866609  8866621  8866633  8866657  8866667  8866679
8866709  8866733  8866751  8866801  8866811  8866817  8866829  8866861  8866873  8866903
8866909  8866919  8866931  8866943  8866951  8866967  8866993  8867003  8867063  8867071
8867099  8867107  8867153  8867179  8867189  8867191  8867207  8867231  8867233  8867269
8867273  8867279  8867291  8867293  8867303  8867311  8867321  8867323  8867381  8867393
8867399  8867423  8867429  8867459  8867473  8867479  8867501  8867527  8867539  8867549
8867563  8867587  8867597  8867609  8867633  8867647  8867657  8867669  8867701  8867711
8867731  8867743  8867773  8867779  8867791  8867797  8867843  8867861  8867869  8867893
8867909  8867917  8867923  8867959  8867977  8867993  8868011  8868017  8868047  8868071
8868089  8868091  8868107  8868109  8868137  8868149  8868151  8868161  8868173  8868217
8868247  8868253  8868319  8868323  8868329  8868337  8868359  8868361  8868367  8868389
8868401  8868443  8868451  8868463  8868469  8868473  8868479  8868521  8868523  8868527
8868529  8868533  8868553  8868581  8868599  8868631  8868647  8868653  8868689  8868701
8868719  8868721  8868733  8868737  8868767  8868803  8868841  8868859  8868887  8868893
8868907  8868919  8868931  8868943  8868949  8868971  8869009  8869037  8869039  8869043
8869061  8869109  8869127  8869129  8869141  8869153  8869169  8869171  8869177  8869187
8869213  8869241  8869247  8869253  8869277  8869279  8869321  8869349  8869351  8869361
8869363  8869369  8869373  8869387  8869397  8869423  8869429  8869453  8869459  8869477
```

```
8869499  8869507  8869547  8869577  8869579  8869591  8869607  8869633  8869649  8869669
8869673  8869681  8869687  8869703  8869711  8869717  8869727  8869741  8869747  8869759
8869771  8869781  8869799  8869837  8869843  8869859  8869873  8869901  8869909
8869919  8869951  8869957  8870003  8870009  8870021  8870053  8870129  8870149  8870153
8870167  8870179  8870261  8870273  8870287  8870333  8870353  8870369  8870377  8870383
8870399  8870401  8870423  8870429  8870431  8870443  8870467  8870471  8870483  8870489
8870497  8870503  8870507  8870509  8870551  8870567  8870573  8870593  8870627  8870633
8870647  8870671  8870683  8870689  8870711  8870737  8870749  8870761  8870779  8870783
8870819  8870833  8870837  8870863  8870879  8870881  8870899  8870909  8870947  8870951
8870959  8870987  8870993  8870999  8871019  8871041  8871089  8871091  8871097  8871101
8871103  8871113  8871139  8871143  8871151  8871167  8871173  8871199  8871209  8871217
8871223  8871241  8871251  8871257  8871259  8871277  8871337  8871341  8871349  8871371
8871389  8871409  8871427  8871449  8871503  8871509  8871547  8871553  8871571  8871587
8871589  8871607  8871623  8871641  8871661  8871677  8871683  8871697  8871701  8871719
8871757  8871761  8871769  8871781  8871799  8871833  8871847  8871853  8871869  8871871
8871887  8871893  8871899  8871931  8871991  8872001  8872009  8872037  8872051  8872063
8872067  8872091  8872099  8872103  8872121  8872133  8872139  8872153  8872177  8872189
8872211  8872217  8872219  8872223  8872261  8872271  8872291  8872301  8872309  8872313
8872327  8872337  8872343  8872349  8872363  8872387  8872393  8872429  8872447  8872459
8872471  8872477  8872481  8872483  8872537  8872559  8872573  8872583  8872621  8872631
8872649  8872673  8872679  8872693  8872697  8872723  8872739  8872741  8872751  8872771
8872781  8872819  8872837  8872849  8872891  8872901  8872907  8872909  8872937  8872939
8872957  8872967  8872973  8872979  8872991  8872993  8873017  8873021  8873027  8873041
8873047  8873071  8873087  8873089  8873107  8873119  8873129  8873149  8873191  8873219
8873233  8873251  8873257  8873273  8873299  8873309  8873317  8873321  8873327  8873329
8873387  8873401  8873407  8873411  8873429  8873453  8873461  8873477  8873489  8873497
8873519  8873531  8873537  8873539  8873549  8873563  8873573  8873591  8873597  8873611
8873629  8873639  8873663  8873687  8873701  8873707  8873713  8873723  8873743  8873749
8873771  8873773  8873783  8873801  8873803  8873819  8873827  8873849  8873869  8873897
8873903  8873927  8873933  8873939  8873951  8873989  8874011  8874037  8874049  8874053
8874079  8874109  8874113  8874133  8874137  8874139  8874143  8874157  8874167  8874169
8874181  8874199  8874227  8874233  8874241  8874253  8874263  8874269  8874287  8874293
8874301  8874317  8874331  8874353  8874419  8874461  8874497  8874499  8874533  8874557
8874559  8874563  8874581  8874599  8874631  8874637  8874643  8874647  8874659  8874661
8874673  8874689  8874703  8874713  8874743  8874751  8874763  8874779  8874791  8874809
8874847  8874863  8874883  8874911  8874913  8874917  8874937  8874949  8874953  8874977
8874989  8875001  8875039  8875051  8875093  8875123  8875127  8875129  8875159  8875183
8875211  8875231  8875249  8875253  8875277  8875283  8875297  8875303  8875313  8875319
8875351  8875369  8875379  8875409  8875417  8875453  8875457  8875469  8875463  8875469
8875481  8875487  8875499  8875511  8875541  8875591  8875609  8875619  8875651  8875661
8875667  8875739  8875747  8875753  8875777  8875787  8875817  8875829  8875859  8875871
8875891  8875939  8875969  8875973  8876003  8876033  8876039  8876051  8876053  8876081
8876083  8876089  8876099  8876107  8876149  8876239  8876267  8876297  8876299  8876327
8876341  8876347  8876353  8876383  8876393  8876419  8876423  8876443  8876449  8876471
8876473  8876479  8876501  8876503  8876531  8876557  8876563  8876579  8876603  8876611
8876627  8876653  8876657  8876663  8876683  8876687  8876701  8876707  8876719  8876729
8876759  8876773  8876797  8876801  8876831  8876863  8876867  8876887  8876893  8876899
8876911  8876921  8876927  8876939  8876983  8876999  8877013  8877053  8877061  8877073
8877083  8877091  8877097  8877109  8877119  8877131  8877133  8877137  8877163  8877181
8877217  8877223  8877227  8877229  8877233  8877257  8877259  8877283  8877293  8877329
8877331  8877347  8877409  8877413  8877419  8877461  8877481  8877497  8877499  8877511
8877527  8877581  8877593  8877599  8877601  8877611  8877623  8877629  8877637  8877647
8877653  8877667  8877677  8877679  8877691  8877697  8877703  8877707  8877719  8877727
8877733  8877767  8877787  8877809  8877821  8877829  8877833  8877851  8877881  8877889
8877899  8877919  8877923  8877937  8877943  8877989  8878003  8878007  8878019  8878033
8878043  8878049  8878057  8878061  8878087  8878151  8878153  8878157  8878201  8878213
8878223  8878229  8878241  8878249  8878271  8878273  8878277  8878279  8878283  8878319
8878327  8878343  8878349  8878381  8878393  8878411  8878417  8878421  8878423  8878433
8878477  8878517  8878531  8878537  8878543  8878549  8878561  8878601  8878603  8878609
8878627  8878633  8878637  8878657  8878663  8878687  8878691  8878693  8878711  8878789
8878799  8878823  8878849  8878861  8878867  8878873  8878921  8878949  8878963  8878973
8878979  8878997  8878999  8879021  8879069  8879077  8879111  8879119  8879131  8879153
8879159  8879161  8879177  8879179  8879183  8879197  8879207  8879231  8879243  8879261
8879267  8879279  8879281  8879291  8879293  8879341  8879359  8879369  8879393  8879401
8879417  8879447  8879489  8879503  8879537  8879551  8879581  8879623  8879641  8879659
8879681  8879687  8879701  8879719  8879723  8879743  8879747  8879749  8879753  8879777
8879791  8879807  8879809  8879813  8879861  8879869  8879911  8879957  8879971  8879987
8879993  8879999  8880007  8880023  8880029  8880073  8880089  8880101  8880107
8880143  8880161  8880173  8880187  8880191  8880211  8880233  8880241  8880269  8880271
8880281  8880283  8880337  8880371  8880379  8880431  8880433  8880439  8880451  8880457
8880463  8880479  8880491  8880499  8880517  8880527  8880533  8880541  8880551  8880569
8880577  8880587  8880593  8880623  8880637  8880643  8880653  8880667  8880671  8880689
8880709  8880713  8880719  8880743  8880761  8880809  8880811  8880853  8880871
8880877  8880889  8880901  8880913  8880959  8881027  8881039  8881057  8881069  8881087
8881099  8881111  8881121  8881129  8881141  8881183  8881199  8881207  8881217  8881219
8881231  8881241  8881273  8881277  8881291  8881357  8881363  8881391  8881393  8881403
8881501  8881507  8881513  8881529  8881547  8881549  8881553  8881583  8881589  8881601
8881651  8881663  8881681  8881711  8881751  8881753  8881771  8881777  8881781  8881787
8881799  8881811  8881819  8881853  8881861  8881879  8881909  8881921  8881969  8881991
8881997  8882009  8882017  8882021  8882047  8882051  8882057  8882119  8882131  8882141
8882147  8882161  8882173  8882191  8882203  8882219  8882221  8882233  8882261  8882297
8882303  8882311  8882317  8882327  8882353  8882369  8882383  8882407  8882417  8882437
8882441  8882453  8882473  8882491  8882513  8882561  8882579  8882603  8882611  8882651
8882677  8882683  8882689  8882693  8882711  8882749  8882777  8882779  8882803  8882813
8882821  8882827  8882831  8882843  8882851  8882873  8882879  8882893  8882911  8882921
8882941  8882963  8882971  8882977  8882987  8882989  8882999  8883041  8883053  8883059
8883067  8883079  8883103  8883107  8883131  8883137  8883157  8883181  8883209  8883229
8883239  8883257  8883263  8883271  8883283  8883319  8883349  8883361  8883379  8883389
8883397  8883403  8883409  8883419  8883421  8883437  8883439  8883473  8883487  8883493
```

```
8883527 8883557 8883569 8883587 8883607 8883617 8883631 8883649 8883683 8883691
8883703 8883751 8883767 8883779 8883793 8883803 8883817 8883821 8883883 8883937
8883971 8883977 8883991 8883997 8884009 8884021 8884037 8884067 8884079 8884091
8884123 8884129 8884147 8884151 8884163 8884177 8884243 8884277 8884283 8884297
8884303 8884339 8884349 8884357 8884361 8884391 8884409 8884427 8884433 8884463
8884453 8884483 8884511 8884541 8884607 8884619 8884621 8884627 8884649 8884651
8884679 8884717 8884769 8884783 8884807 8884849 8884859 8884871 8884873 8884907
8884943 8884949 8884979 8885017 8885029 8885039 8885059 8885083 8885087 8885113
8885117 8885119 8885159 8885161 8885167 8885171 8885183 8885197 8885207 8885221
8885231 8885243 8885249 8885263 8885267 8885269 8885287 8885299 8885309 8885311
8885323 8885333 8885347 8885377 8885389 8885411 8885413 8885423 8885447 8885449
8885467 8885497 8885507 8885519 8885531 8885533 8885551 8885557 8885573 8885603
8885641 8885647 8885663 8885689 8885699 8885717 8885719 8885743 8885761 8885771
8885777 8885783 8885801 8885831 8885837 8885839 8885857 8885869 8885923 8885941
8885959 8886011 8886013 8886023 8886041 8886061 8886067 8886077 8886089 8886107
8886109 8886113 8886133 8886161 8886169 8886173 8886187 8886193 8886239 8886247
8886287 8886301 8886307 8886313 8886329 8886331 8886347 8886379 8886389 8886391
8886407 8886421 8886439 8886467 8886469 8886481 8886497 8886503 8886511 8886517
8886523 8886539 8886551 8886569 8886599 8886601 8886607 8886611 8886617 8886629
8886637 8886649 8886653 8886667 8886701 8886707 8886721 8886781 8886793 8886799
8886811 8886817 8886821 8886827 8886833 8886841 8886859 8886877 8886883 8886929
8886931 8886949 8886959 8886961 8886967 8886973 8887001 8887013 8887031 8887051
8887061 8887063 8887103 8887127 8887129 8887133 8887139 8887159 8887163 8887169
8887213 8887217 8887247 8887259 8887267 8887271 8887301 8887321 8887331 8887367
8887381 8887387 8887393 8887397 8887399 8887423 8887441 8887493 8887513 8887519
8887523 8887537 8887547 8887553 8887597 8887609 8887621 8887631 8887633 8887657
8887661 8887663 8887667 8887679 8887691 8887699 8887721 8887727 8887757 8887759
8887777 8887817 8887849 8887861 8887871 8887873 8887897 8887903 8887919 8887961
8887981 8888003 8888017 8888023 8888027 8888039 8888063 8888071 8888083 8888107
8888119 8888129 8888137 8888147 8888167 8888183 8888197 8888213 8888233 8888293
8888309 8888323 8888329 8888339 8888357 8888359 8888381 8888389 8888417 8888437
8888441 8888449 8888459 8888461 8888479 8888489 8888491 8888497 8888507 8888521
8888531 8888549 8888563 8888609 8888629 8888641 8888651 8888657 8888669 8888701
8888731 8888749 8888753 8888767 8888771 8888791 8888801 8888813 8888821 8888839
8888849 8888851 8888861 8888927 8888933 8888939 8888947 8888951 8888953 8888959
8888989 8889007 8889019 8889031 8889143 8889149 8889151 8889187 8889193 8889203
8889229 8889233 8889263 8889301 8889323 8889329 8889337 8889401 8889403 8889407
8889427 8889479 8889499 8889527 8889539 8889557 8889563 8889571 8889581 8889607
8889659 8889679 8889719 8889757 8889779 8889781 8889821 8889833 8889851 8889871
8889877 8889883 8889889 8889893 8889941 8889971 8889973 8889977 8890039 8890051
8890069 8890073 8890093 8890103 8890109 8890117 8890129 8890187 8890223 8890229
8890241 8890243 8890247 8890267 8890283 8890291 8890307 8890361 8890363 8890373
8890403 8890411 8890421 8890429 8890447 8890457 8890463 8890513 8890529 8890543
8890589 8890601 8890603 8890621 8890633 8890639 8890657 8890667 8890669 8890709
8890741 8890747 8890757 8890759 8890781 8890793 8890799 8890801 8890823 8890829
8890837 8890919 8890963 8890969 8890997 8891009 8891033 8891053 8891059
8891083 8891093 8891147 8891149 8891167 8891171 8891191 8891231 8891237 8891243
8891249 8891261 8891279 8891291 8891293 8891303 8891339 8891341 8891347 8891387
8891417 8891419 8891431 8891461 8891471 8891477 8891479 8891539 8891549 8891551 8891557
8891579 8891591 8891611 8891621 8891627 8891633 8891657 8891689 8891693 8891741
8891747 8891783 8891797 8891809 8891837 8891843 8891851 8891879 8891881 8891891
8891899 8891921 8891923 8891929 8891983 8891999 8892001 8892011 8892029 8892041
8892049 8892073 8892077 8892097 8892101 8892109 8892119 8892127 8892131 8892137
8892157 8892179 8892187 8892193 8892197 8892217 8892223 8892263 8892277 8892337
8892347 8892379 8892391 8892409 8892427 8892431 8892439 8892451 8892461 8892487
8892491 8892493 8892497 8892509 8892517 8892553 8892557 8892577 8892599 8892601
8892607 8892623 8892661 8892671 8892677 8892721 8892727 8892733 8892749 8892773
8892781 8892799 8892827 8892847 8892857 8892883 8892889 8892907 8892991 8893009
8893013 8893021 8893039 8893043 8893051 8893099 8893103 8893139
8893153 8893177 8893189 8893211 8893219 8893223 8893229 8893237 8893243 8893253
8893259 8893271 8893279 8893289 8893309 8893319 8893321 8893327 8893331 8893361
8893393 8893399 8893403 8893421 8893427 8893457 8893471 8893477 8893487 8893523
8893541 8893553 8893589 8893603 8893607 8893609 8893613 8893627 8893649 8893697
8893751 8893789 8893793 8893799 8893817 8893823 8893831 8893851 8893853 8893867
8893879 8893883 8893889 8893897 8893901 8893921 8893943 8893961 8893967 8893979
8893987 8894003 8894021 8894029 8894059 8894063 8894107 8894141 8894167 8894173
8894189 8894201 8894209 8894219 8894243 8894251 8894267 8894269 8894279 8894287
8894311 8894321 8894323 8894339 8894351 8894357 8894377 8894381 8894401 8894419
8894423 8894429 8894443 8894447 8894461 8894477 8894497 8894533 8894563 8894573
8894597 8894617 8894623 8894647 8894657 8894659 8894681 8894701 8894707 8894713
8894729 8894741 8894761 8894773 8894777 8894783 8894789 8894807 8894819 8894839
8894843 8894857 8894887 8894933 8894939 8894947 8894981 8894993 8895011 8895013
8895037 8895049 8895067 8895071 8895091 8895113 8895143 8895169 8895179 8895197
8895209 8895221 8895223 8895239 8895251 8895277 8895307 8895311 8895347 8895349
8895353 8895379 8895407 8895413 8895421 8895427 8895451 8895493 8895511 8895517
8895521 8895527 8895529 8895559 8895571 8895587 8895611 8895613 8895631 8895683
8895697 8895701 8895703 8895727 8895751 8895767 8895769 8895827 8895829 8895839
8895851 8895869 8895877 8895881 8895889 8895899 8895911 8895919 8895959 8895983
8895989 8896001 8896003 8896031 8896061 8896067 8896073 8896093 8896109 8896133
8896171 8896177 8896183 8896211 8896249 8896259 8896273 8896289 8896309 8896319
8896333 8896337 8896339 8896361 8896397 8896403 8896441 8896451 8896453 8896483
8896487 8896507 8896519 8896543 8896619 8896621 8896651 8896673 8896681 8896691
8896709 8896711 8896747 8896759 8896781 8896793 8896801 8896813 8896841 8896843
8896847 8896861 8896873 8896891 8896903 8896913 8896919 8896931 8896981 8896991
8897011 8897017 8897039 8897047 8897099 8897129 8897143 8897153 8897183 8897209
8897221 8897227 8897233 8897249 8897261 8897267 8897293 8897299 8897309 8897311
8897321 8897323 8897327 8897359 8897381 8897387 8897401 8897407 8897423 8897437
8897467 8897503 8897509 8897513 8897543 8897557 8897569 8897591 8897621 8897627
8897633 8897639 8897641 8897653 8897671 8897677 8897687 8897729 8897771 8897773
```

```
8897813  8897821  8897831  8897839  8897857  8897869  8897881  8897921  8897929  8897939
8897951  8897963  8897969  8897989  8898017  8898031  8898047  8898053  8898059  8898073
8898077  8898083  8898103  8898133  8898139  8898143  8898151  8898163  8898179  8898193
8898199  8898221  8898229  8898233  8898257  8898283  8898301  8898311  8898313  8898317
8898319  8898341  8898343  8898367  8898391  8898419  8898443  8898467  8898521  8898523
8898529  8898551  8898553  8898569  8898629  8898653  8898671  8898691  8898697  8898709
8898719  8898733  8898749  8898751  8898761  8898779  8898787  8898809  8898811  8898823
8898887  8898913  8898931  8898937  8898941  8898943  8898949  8898971  8898977  8898997
8899013  8899019  8899031  8899057  8899061  8899067  8899073  8899117  8899123  8899127
8899157  8899171  8899181  8899193  8899213  8899217  8899243  8899249  8899307  8899333
8899339  8899361  8899399  8899411  8899417  8899421  8899439  8899441  8899447  8899453
8899463  8899469  8899477  8899481  8899489  8899531  8899537  8899571  8899603  8899609
8899613  8899633  8899651  8899663  8899691  8899711  8899727  8899783  8899799  8899801
8899819  8899831  8899837  8899843  8899853  8899867  8899909  8899927  8899937  8899949
8899987  8899997  8900029  8900039  8900051  8900053  8900093  8900123  8900159  8900161
8900179  8900201  8900207  8900251  8900257  8900261  8900273  8900279  8900291  8900293
8900323  8900351  8900353  8900399  8900407  8900413  8900431  8900447  8900459  8900473
8900483  8900513  8900579  8900603  8900641  8900669  8900713  8900737  8900761  8900783
8900789  8900803  8900807  8900821  8900849  8900861  8900863  8900869  8900887  8900891
8900893  8900909  8900923  8900929  8900939  8900953  8900959  8900971  8900981  8901019
8901031  8901041  8901089  8901091  8901097  8901103  8901107  8901119  8901121  8901227
8901239  8901259  8901281  8901293  8901307  8901323  8901337  8901383  8901397  8901413
8901461  8901467  8901493  8901499  8901511  8901533  8901577  8901587  8901599  8901611
8901617  8901631  8901643  8901649  8901653  8901679  8901689  8901701  8901749  8901751
8901773  8901779  8901803  8901853  8901857  8901877  8901881  8901887  8901889  8901911
8901923  8901947  8901953  8902001  8902007  8902009  8902037  8902063  8902093  8902109
8902111  8902121  8902133  8902141  8902151  8902183  8902189  8902199  8902211  8902249
8902261  8902297  8902337  8902351  8902379  8902381  8902417  8902429  8902433  8902447
8902457  8902471  8902483  8902489  8902499  8902501  8902513  8902547  8902567  8902609
8902637  8902639  8902643  8902651  8902657  8902661  8902667  8902711  8902717  8902727
8902769  8902783  8902799  8902807  8902837  8902853  8902867  8902871  8902877  8902879
8902969  8902973  8902979  8902987  8902991  8903017  8903023  8903033
8903071  8903101  8903129  8903131  8903177  8903179  8903183  8903201  8903207  8903233
8903239  8903243  8903249  8903269  8903309  8903317  8903323  8903333  8903353  8903357
8903387  8903407  8903431  8903441  8903443  8903473  8903491  8903497  8903509
8903561  8903583  8903593  8903641  8903663  8903681  8903689  8903693  8903707  8903753
8903759  8903771  8903773  8903777  8903813  8903819  8903833  8903849  8903863  8903887
8903891  8903893  8903959  8904023  8904043  8904067  8904079  8904113  8904127  8904143
8904163  8904173  8904193  8904199  8904239  8904253  8904263  8904299  8904317  8904341
8904359  8904373  8904377  8904403  8904431  8904437  8904439  8904443  8904451  8904487
8904491  8904499  8904509  8904523  8904541  8904557  8904587  8904601  8904631  8904677
8904691  8904733  8904737  8904767  8904773  8904799  8904809  8904817  8904823  8904839
8904851  8904869  8904871  8904899  8904911  8904919  8904937  8904947  8904953  8904989
8905003  8905009  8905021  8905031  8905063  8905079  8905097  8905109  8905111  8905139
8905147  8905151  8905177  8905181  8905187  8905189  8905199  8905321  8905327  8905361
8905397  8905423  8905427  8905441  8905447  8905499  8905517  8905529  8905543  8905549
8905571  8905579  8905583  8905597  8905613  8905619  8905657  8905679  8905681  8905691
8905693  8905703  8905723  8905747  8905759  8905777  8905801  8905811  8905823  8905843
8905903  8905903  8905913  8905933  8905957  8905997  8906017  8906033  8906071  8906087
8906089  8906111  8906123  8906137  8906153  8906179  8906189  8906197  8906237  8906239
8906251  8906257  8906263  8906273  8906291  8906327  8906329  8906333  8906347  8906353
8906357  8906369  8906399  8906407  8906411  8906413  8906423  8906437  8906441  8906489
8906501  8906519  8906533  8906537  8906561  8906587  8906591  8906593  8906617  8906627
8906629  8906659  8906663  8906669  8906701  8906707  8906713  8906747  8906753  8906761
8906771  8906783  8906789  8906797  8906837  8906851  8906869  8906893  8906897  8906921
8906927  8906939  8906941  8906959  8906969  8907007  8907011  8907061  8907077  8907113
8907161  8907169  8907179  8907193  8907203  8907211  8907221  8907229  8907271  8907277
8907287  8907293  8907307  8907313  8907317  8907319  8907331  8907359  8907361  8907377
8907389  8907391  8907427  8907443  8907467  8907469  8907497  8907511  8907517  8907539
8907557  8907593  8907623  8907631  8907659  8907671  8907673  8907683  8907697  8907719
8907733  8907737  8907781  8907793  8907799  8907839  8907841  8907847  8907853  8907883
8907889  8907893  8907911  8907917  8907919  8907929  8907937  8907989  8908001  8908007
8908021  8908033  8908037  8908057  8908063  8908087  8908091  8908103  8908121
8908127  8908139  8908147  8908183  8908201  8908217  8908223  8908261  8908271  8908313
8908327  8908331  8908363  8908373  8908411  8908421  8908433  8908457  8908463  8908477
8908483  8908507  8908513  8908517  8908519  8908541  8908563  8908589  8908591  8908619
8908621  8908637  8908667  8908673  8908681  8908693  8908703  8908721  8908723  8908727
8908733  8908741  8908769  8908793  8908817  8908819  8908877  8908883  8908903
8908937  8908943  8908951  8908979  8908987  8909023  8909029  8909039  8909051  8909083
8909099  8909101  8909143  8909149  8909161  8909171  8909189  8909209  8909227  8909237
8909239  8909249  8909261  8909281  8909287  8909291  8909297  8909317  8909321  8909323
8909359  8909387  8909389  8909393  8909401  8909437  8909449  8909473  8909491  8909497
8909501  8909503  8909539  8909567  8909573  8909591  8909609  8909611  8909647  8909653
8909707  8909713  8909731  8909737  8909749  8909759  8909773  8909779  8909807  8909821
8909863  8909867  8909881  8909899  8909903  8909909  8909941  8909963  8909983  8910001
8910017  8910043  8910049  8910053  8910067  8910079  8910089  8910101  8910103  8910127
8910137  8910149  8910151  8910157  8910169  8910179  8910199  8910203  8910233  8910241
8910247  8910257  8910271  8910277  8910281  8910283  8910289  8910301  8910311  8910347
8910379  8910409  8910437  8910439  8910443  8910463  8910469  8910481  8910497  8910509
8910527  8910529  8910557  8910581  8910607  8910659  8910667  8910679  8910689  8910691
8910709  8910719  8910749  8910757  8910763  8910767  8910771  8910773  8910833  8910877
8910887  8910893  8910911  8910929  8910949  8910971  8910973  8910977  8910989  8911031
8911061  8911061  8911103  8911087  8911093  8911103  8911141  8911169  8911201  8911219
8911223  8911237  8911241  8911271  8911283  8911297  8911313  8911319  8911321  8911333
8911369  8911379  8911433  8911453  8911471  8911489  8911493  8911499  8911501  8911517
8911523  8911531  8911547  8911549  8911571  8911583  8911607  8911619  8911631  8911633
8911667  8911697  8911739  8911759  8911781  8911789  8911829  8911841  8911843  8911853
8911901  8911907  8911909  8911919  8911933  8911963  8911967  8911979  8911997  8912011
8912021  8912023  8912053  8912087  8912107  8912147  8912173  8912177  8912203  8912207
```

```
8912209  8912213  8912219  8912237  8912243  8912269  8912279  8912297  8912303  8912317
8912333  8912347  8912353  8912357  8912359  8912381  8912383  8912389  8912399  8912401
8912411  8912447  8912459  8912489  8912509  8912537  8912551  8912591  8912609  8912627
8912663  8912669  8912681  8912689  8912699  8912711  8912713  8912723  8912731  8912741
8912749  8912791  8912801  8912833  8912863  8912887  8912921  8912927  8912929  8912941
8912963  8912971  8912977  8912989  8912999  8913013  8913019  8913043  8913053  8913067
8913103  8913119  8913139  8913143  8913161  8913173  8913181  8913187  8913197  8913199
8913239  8913283  8913293  8913323  8913347  8913349  8913391  8913403  8913407  8913419
8913433  8913473  8913481  8913497  8913521  8913529  8913539  8913547  8913551  8913557
8913563  8913587  8913589  8913623  8913677  8913683  8913689  8913703  8913713  8913721
8913727  8913731  8913733  8913739  8913743  8913761  8913767  8913787  8913791  8913803
8913847  8913871  8913887  8913889  8913893  8913901  8913917  8913923  8913941  8913953
8913977  8914007  8914027  8914033  8914043  8914051  8914079  8914099  8914109  8914127
8914141  8914153  8914181  8914183  8914187  8914189  8914247  8914253  8914259  8914291
8914319  8914331  8914403  8914427  8914463  8914471  8914481  8914483  8914519  8914531
8914567  8914573  8914583  8914621  8914637  8914649  8914651  8914673  8914679  8914709
8914721  8914729  8914733  8914739  8914757  8914771  8914799  8914811  8914837  8914847
8914849  8914853  8914877  8914879  8914883  8914897  8914921  8914937  8914951  8914957
8914963  8914981  8914993  8915003  8915029  8915069  8915083  8915119  8915129  8915131
8915141  8915143  8915149  8915167  8915171  8915177  8915213  8915243  8915281  8915297
8915299  8915303  8915311  8915339  8915341  8915359  8915363  8915377  8915393  8915407
8915411  8915419  8915443  8915447  8915449  8915461  8915519  8915521  8915537  8915539
8915551  8915591  8915593  8915597  8915639  8915671  8915677  8915681  8915707  8915717
8915719  8915723  8915741  8915747  8915761  8915801  8915831  8915839  8915843  8915867
8915869  8915897  8915917  8915953  8915981  8915993  8915999  8916029  8916043  8916049
8916067  8916077  8916107  8916121  8916151  8916161  8916163  8916181  8916191  8916197
8916199  8916217  8916233  8916239  8916329  8916331  8916361  8916367  8916379  8916389
8916403  8916419  8916421  8916443  8916451  8916461  8916463  8916469  8916487  8916503
8916521  8916539  8916541  8916559  8916563  8916569  8916581  8916587  8916599  8916629
8916641  8916671  8916673  8916679  8916689  8916727  8916737  8916749  8916779  8916827
8916839  8916841  8916863  8916881  8916899  8916911  8916913  8916923  8916931  8916977
8917001  8917009  8917021  8917033  8917043  8917063  8917067  8917109  8917127  8917141
8917151  8917159  8917187  8917199  8917219  8917229  8917247  8917253  8917309  8917339
8917351  8917361  8917369  8917373  8917393  8917397  8917411  8917423  8917453  8917463
8917523  8917663  8917679  8917681  8917691  8917693  8917697  8917709  8917717  8917729
8917747  8917763  8917771  8917781  8917789  8917793  8917817  8917829  8917837  8917841
8917849  8917871  8917873  8917879  8917891  8917903  8917907  8917913  8917927  8917949
8917963  8917991  8918003  8918023  8918029  8918059  8918069  8918099  8918113  8918123
8918131  8918141  8918171  8918177  8918207  8918209  8918237  8918269  8918293  8918311
8918333  8918347  8918407  8918417  8918419  8918453  8918473  8918477  8918479  8918509
8918519  8918521  8918527  8918561  8918597  8918621  8918639  8918653  8918677  8918713
8918717  8918729  8918743  8918753  8918773  8918797  8918821  8918827  8918831  8918843
8918849  8918857  8918869  8918891  8918909  8918911  8918927  8918929  8918933  8918939
8918947  8918953  8918983  8918989  8919011  8919019  8919023  8919061  8919073  8919077
8919121  8919133  8919139  8919149  8919161  8919167  8919173  8919187  8919191  8919211
8919223  8919259  8919277  8919283  8919293  8919299  8919301  8919319  8919343  8919347
8919349  8919371  8919389  8919401  8919403  8919431  8919437  8919451  8919461  8919487
8919497  8919503  8919527  8919539  8919541  8919551  8919557  8919571  8919583  8919593
8919623  8919629  8919649  8919671  8919689  8919737  8919767  8919803  8919809  8919817
8919839  8919851  8919853  8919857  8919871  8919887  8919893  8919899  8919901  8919913
8919931  8919941  8919959  8919979  8919989  8920003  8920027  8920031  8920039  8920057
8920069  8920097  8920103  8920123  8920129  8920141  8920147  8920169  8920181  8920199
8920201  8920243  8920277  8920279  8920321  8920337  8920391  8920403  8920423  8920433
8920463  8920489  8920517  8920531  8920537  8920543  8920547  8920567  8920609  8920649
8920679  8920687  8920693  8920721  8920729  8920753  8920763  8920771  8920783  8920817
8920837  8920853  8920867  8920889  8920927  8920939  8920977  8920981
8920999  8921021  8921053  8921063  8921069  8921071  8921123  8921131  8921161  8921173
8921179  8921197  8921207  8921239  8921249  8921261  8921267  8921287  8921321  8921333
8921359  8921371  8921377  8921383  8921387  8921389  8921417  8921441  8921453  8921461
8921467  8921569  8921573  8921581  8921599  8921603  8921609  8921629  8921639  8921663
8921669  8921701  8921729  8921741  8921761  8921771  8921777  8921779  8921791  8921833
8921837  8921863  8921867  8921873  8921911  8921917  8921951  8921959  8921989  8922013
8922019  8922041  8922047  8922049  8922083  8922097  8922103  8922107  8922139  8922149
8922163  8922187  8922209  8922211  8922223  8922233  8922241  8922247  8922257  8922259
8922281  8922283  8922289  8922299  8922301  8922307  8922311  8922313  8922337  8922349
8922359  8922377  8922383  8922421  8922427  8922443  8922449  8922469  8922479  8922521
8922523  8922539  8922547  8922553  8922559  8922577  8922601  8922607  8922611  8922649
8922659  8922677  8922701  8922703  8922731  8922733  8922737  8922743  8922763  8922779
8922791  8922811  8922817  8922829  8922833  8922847  8922869  8922877  8922917  8922931
8922937  8922959  8922967  8923003  8923007  8923021  8923049  8923063  8923069  8923073
8923087  8923093  8923099  8923121  8923157  8923171  8923177  8923193  8923207  8923223
8923259  8923267  8923309  8923339  8923357  8923367  8923391  8923427  8923457  8923463
8923469  8923477  8923501  8923511  8923531  8923571  8923601  8923603  8923631  8923651
8923637  8923639  8923643  8923669  8923679  8923727  8923729  8923781  8923801  8923807
8923813  8923819  8923829  8923841  8923847  8923883  8923891  8923897  8923913  8923921
8923933  8923951  8923961  8923969  8923987  8923991  8924011  8924017  8924029  8924033
8924039  8924059  8924081  8924089  8924131  8924137  8924171  8924189  8924213  8924287
8924309  8924327  8924329  8924341  8924369  8924387  8924389  8924411  8924441  8924449
8924453  8924477  8924479  8924491  8924519  8924527  8924533  8924537  8924543  8924579
8924581  8924603  8924611  8924633  8924639  8924651  8924681  8924687  8924701  8924719
8924731  8924743  8924749  8924777  8924801  8924803  8924809  8924819  8924821  8924879
8924887  8924893  8924911  8924917  8924933  8924941  8924963  8924969  8924987  8924999
8925001  8925013  8925019  8925023  8925031  8925043  8925047  8925061  8925083  8925097
8925109  8925113  8925131  8925149  8925181  8925211  8925223  8925233  8925263  8925277
8925281  8925283  8925299  8925313  8925317  8925377  8925401  8925407  8925419  8925437
8925439  8925443  8925457  8925463  8925487  8925509  8925523  8925529  8925557  8925559
8925563  8925569  8925583  8925599  8925617  8925643  8925661  8925691  8925701  8925713
8925727  8925739  8925767  8925773  8925781  8925793  8925797  8925803  8925809  8925827
8925841  8925853  8925883  8925887  8925913  8925967  8925971  8925977  8925979  8925989
```

```
8926013 8926019 8926031 8926033 8926039 8926061 8926079 8926081 8926091 8926097
8926111 8926123 8926129 8926133 8926147 8926189 8926201 8926217 8926237 8926243
8926271 8926273 8926283 8926301 8926319 8926331 8926339 8926349 8926363 8926387
8926391 8926417 8926427 8926439 8926451 8926453 8926457 8926459 8926501 8926517
8926529 8926571 8926573 8926591 8926597 8926607 8926609 8926613 8926681 8926699
8926711 8926721 8926781 8926811 8926817 8926823 8926859 8926873 8926891 8926927
8926933 8926937 8926943 8926961 8926967 8926993 8926999 8927063 8927069 8927077
8927111 8927141 8927143 8927153 8927203 8927213 8927221 8927239 8927263 8927279
8927293 8927297 8927309 8927311 8927333 8927341 8927353 8927357 8927383 8927407
8927423 8927441 8927453 8927461 8927483 8927489 8927497 8927521 8927537 8927539
8927543 8927551 8927561 8927579 8927593 8927623 8927629 8927641 8927647 8927687
8927689 8927707 8927713 8927717 8927741 8927761 8927803 8927813 8927833 8927851
8927881 8927909 8927927 8927957 8927959 8927981 8928001 8928041 8928053 8928067
8928079 8928083 8928089 8928091 8928107 8928121 8928131 8928149 8928151 8928169
8928173 8928191 8928193 8928203 8928223 8928239 8928253 8928263 8928277 8928289
8928313 8928319 8928329 8928371 8928389 8928407 8928419 8928421 8928431 8928457
8928511 8928523 8928547 8928551 8928571 8928583 8928593 8928599 8928643 8928653
8928671 8928679 8928683 8928707 8928709 8928719 8928721 8928749 8928767 8928769
8928779 8928797 8928811 8928847 8928851 8928863 8928869 8928929 8928971 8928979
8929003 8929007 8929009 8929033 8929051 8929073 8929087 8929093 8929111 8929117
8929127 8929139 8929163 8929169 8929177 8929189 8929211 8929213 8929229 8929231
8929253 8929289 8929307 8929331 8929339 8929343 8929367 8929381 8929391 8929399
8929409 8929439 8929447 8929463 8929517 8929537 8929549 8929553 8929561 8929567
8929597 8929603 8929621 8929631 8929667 8929673 8929733 8929763 8929769 8929783
8929799 8929807 8929849 8929873 8929897 8929909 8929919 8929927 8929931 8929933
8929937 8929951 8929967 8929969 8930011 8930021 8930027 8930029 8930059 8930069
8930093 8930101 8930107 8930123 8930143 8930179 8930183 8930189 8930213 8930227
8930227 8930249 8930267 8930293 8930297 8930351 8930353 8930413 8930419 8930429
8930459 8930473 8930483 8930501 8930507 8930549 8930557 8930567 8930569 8930591
8930599 8930629 8930639 8930651 8930681 8930683 8930707 8930749 8930783 8930809
8930813 8930833 8930839 8930849 8930863 8930879 8930881 8930891 8930897 8930917
8930941 8930947 8930951 8930959 8930981 8930983 8931017 8931037 8931067 8931073
8931079 8931089 8931113 8931119 8931149 8931163 8931179 8931211 8931277 8931283
8931287 8931289 8931313 8931343 8931353 8931359 8931367 8931421 8931431 8931493
8931497 8931509 8931523 8931583 8931617 8931631 8931649 8931667 8931673 8931677
8931683 8931697 8931709 8931731 8931737 8931757 8931779 8931799 8931827 8931863
8931869 8931877 8931907 8931929 8931941 8931947 8931961 8931983 8931997 8932009
8932031 8932043 8932097 8932111 8932117 8932139 8932141 8932159 8932181 8932193
8932199 8932213 8932241 8932271 8932277 8932289 8932321 8932367 8932369 8932381
8932447 8932453 8932457 8932481 8932501 8932523 8932529 8932589 8932591 8932597
8932601 8932613 8932621 8932631 8932639 8932669 8932687 8932727 8932733 8932739
8932747 8932751 8932753 8932757 8932771 8932787 8932801 8932813 8932817 8932823
8932849 8932883 8932921 8932927 8932933 8932951 8932967 8932981 8932999 8933011
8933017 8933027 8933047 8933117 8933123 8933137 8933153 8933159 8933179 8933191
8933209 8933227 8933231 8933233 8933251 8933257 8933263 8933273 8933297 8933299
8933303 8933329 8933339 8933369 8933387 8933413 8933417 8933423 8933429 8933437
8933443 8933447 8933471 8933489 8933497 8933501 8933503 8933513 8933563 8933567
8933569 8933621 8933623 8933641 8933651 8933657 8933671 8933677 8933681 8933699
8933737 8933741 8933747 8933767 8933773 8933779 8933791 8933801 8933803 8933831
8933849 8933851 8933861 8933887 8933917 8933927 8933929 8933963 8933989 8934017
8934019 8934043 8934071 8934073 8934083 8934127 8934137 8934139 8934173 8934223
8934227 8934229 8934253 8934257 8934259 8934271 8934283 8934287 8934301 8934307
8934319 8934391 8934413 8934421 8934439 8934451 8934461 8934463 8934467 8934473
8934481 8934491 8934509 8934521 8934533 8934553 8934587 8934589 8934623 8934631
8934637 8934659 8934721 8934733 8934743 8934773 8934791 8934803 8934817 8934823
8934829 8934869 8934889 8934907 8934923 8934953 8934983
8935009 8935021 8935039 8935049 8935051 8935079 8935133 8935139 8935153 8935177
8935193 8935207 8935229 8935231 8935237 8935243 8935259 8935291 8935307 8935313
8935327 8935331 8935343 8935361 8935363 8935391 8935397 8935411 8935439 8935457
8935469 8935481 8935517 8935541 8935573 8935583 8935601 8935603 8935607 8935613
8935627 8935631 8935637 8935651 8935691 8935699 8935733 8935739 8935763 8935777
8935793 8935811 8935813 8935819 8935831 8935841 8935879 8935889 8935919 8935921
8935933 8935943 8935957 8935987 8936009 8936017 8936021 8936027 8936041 8936069
8936071 8936077 8936087 8936107 8936119 8936141 8936159 8936173 8936183 8936197
8936209 8936219 8936231 8936233 8936261 8936287 8936293 8936311 8936329 8936341
8936357 8936371 8936377 8936387 8936399 8936413 8936419 8936429 8936467 8936471
8936491 8936507 8936519 8936531 8936537 8936563 8936617 8936621 8936623 8936651
8936657 8936659 8936663 8936731 8936737 8936743 8936749 8936771 8936777 8936791
8936797 8936827 8936833 8936887 8936947 8936953 8936969 8936971 8936981 8936989
8937013 8937029 8937031 8937037 8937067 8937079 8937101 8937107 8937109 8937119
8937151 8937157 8937161 8937167 8937193 8937209 8937211 8937233 8937241 8937263
8937281 8937311 8937323 8937343 8937361 8937367 8937373 8937377 8937437 8937451
8937457 8937491 8937493 8937503 8937521 8937527 8937557 8937559 8937569 8937583
8937587 8937613 8937623 8937667 8937697 8937701 8937707 8937727 8937751 8937763
8937769 8937787 8937791 8937811 8937833 8937857 8937881 8937893 8937917 8937919
8937931 8937947 8937949 8937953 8937983 8937997 8938009 8938019 8938049 8938051
8938057 8938081 8938093 8938103 8938121 8938129 8938157 8938159 8938183 8938207
8938217 8938219 8938229 8938231 8938247 8938253 8938271 8938273 8938301 8938309
8938331 8938333 8938381 8938427 8938429 8938469 8938471 8938477 8938511 8938541
8938543 8938561 8938577 8938627 8938637 8938663 8938667 8938669 8938679 8938681
8938693 8938729 8938739 8938799 8938801 8938807 8938817 8938823 8938843 8938849
8938859 8938871 8938901 8938903 8938921 8938933 8938961 8938997 8938999 8939003
8939023 8939027 8939039 8939041 8939053 8939057 8939131 8939159 8939167 8939173
8939179 8939197 8939219 8939233 8939243 8939257 8939299 8939303 8939321 8939323
8939339 8939347 8939363 8939383 8939389 8939393 8939407 8939419 8939431 8939471
8939521 8939531 8939537 8939549 8939551 8939587 8939591 8939597 8939699
8939701 8939731 8939759 8939789 8939803 8939809 8939831 8939849 8939863 8939891
8939921 8939923 8939929 8939933 8939947 8939951 8939963 8939969 8939971 8939989
8939993 8940007 8940017 8940023 8940037 8940049 8940053 8940083 8940097 8940109
```

```
8940119  8940131  8940143  8940157  8940161  8940163  8940167  8940187  8940227  8940229
8940247  8940251  8940263  8940271  8940287  8940301  8940311  8940313  8940319  8940359
8940367  8940397  8940427  8940433  8940457  8940461  8940479  8940499  8940523  8940539
8940541  8940553  8940563  8940571  8940593  8940601  8940611  8940649  8940707  8940719
8940727  8940731  8940769  8940779  8940809  8940839  8940863  8940889  8940913  8940917
8940923  8940931  8940973  8940977  8940979  8940991  8941021  8941057  8941061  8941067
8941091  8941109  8941117  8941123  8941129  8941147  8941151  8941171  8941189  8941249
8941271  8941277  8941279  8941297  8941301  8941313  8941333  8941349  8941357  8941369
8941397  8941399  8941417  8941447  8941451  8941459  8941469  8941477  8941487  8941519
8941523  8941553  8941573  8941589  8941607  8941637  8941651  8941661  8941663  8941693
8941727  8941759  8941781  8941783  8941817  8941819  8941859  8941861  8941873  8941897
8941903  8941921  8941927  8941973  8941993  8942039  8942041  8942051  8942071  8942081
8942083  8942111  8942117  8942137  8942149  8942159  8942177  8942207  8942233  8942243
8942257  8942261  8942299  8942309  8942317  8942321  8942327  8942341  8942347  8942359
8942363  8942383  8942393  8942413  8942443  8942447  8942467  8942473  8942491  8942501
8942509  8942569  8942587  8942599  8942611  8942623  8942651  8942671  8942741  8942761
8942771  8942779  8942803  8942821  8942851  8942873  8942881  8942891  8942909  8942951
8942963  8942971  8942981  8942993  8943007  8943013  8943023  8943047  8943059  8943073
8943079  8943127  8943133  8943199  8943203  8943229  8943299  8943313  8943317  8943323
8943329  8943331  8943359  8943367  8943401  8943413  8943419  8943437  8943439  8943457
8943461  8943463  8943523  8943533  8943551  8943553  8943563  8943569  8943601  8943607
8943653  8943667  8943673  8943679  8943689  8943707  8943709  8943719  8943743  8943761
8943769  8943773  8943787  8943791  8943797  8943811  8943817  8943829  8943833  8943859
8943901  8943911  8943917  8943923  8943937  8943943  8943953  8943971  8944009  8944051
8944069  8944073  8944099  8944123  8944127  8944153  8944181  8944189  8944207  8944249
8944253  8944259  8944279  8944291  8944297  8944303  8944349  8944357  8944361  8944409
8944427  8944469  8944487  8944489  8944513  8944517  8944533  8944541  8944553  8944561
8944571  8944583  8944591  8944597  8944603  8944609  8944643  8944679  8944681  8944693
8944699  8944739  8944759  8944777  8944853  8944883  8944889  8944919  8944927  8944937
8944939  8944973  8945003  8945033  8945039  8945047  8945051  8945063  8945071  8945099
8945117  8945119  8945147  8945149  8945171  8945173  8945177  8945191  8945207  8945221
8945263  8945273  8945309  8945323  8945327  8945351  8945353  8945381  8945401  8945429
8945441  8945449  8945471  8945477  8945483  8945501  8945549  8945579  8945581  8945593
8945609  8945611  8945617  8945627  8945641  8945663  8945669  8945683  8945707  8945719
8945747  8945759  8945771  8945779  8945809  8945813  8945819  8945821  8945837  8945851
8945869  8945879  8945939  8945947  8945957  8945953  8945969  8945983  8945999  8946001
8946031  8946037  8946043  8946061  8946083  8946089  8946101  8946137  8946139  8946151
8946173  8946187  8946209  8946211  8946221  8946247  8946251  8946253  8946281  8946293
8946313  8946317  8946337  8946367  8946373  8946391  8946409  8946461  8946481  8946491
8946493  8946499  8946503  8946521  8946527  8946533  8946541  8946557  8946589  8946593
8946629  8946647  8946659  8946673  8946697  8946713  8946719  8946727  8946737  8946757
8946767  8946787  8946797  8946799  8946827  8946851  8946857  8946869  8946887  8946893
8946911  8946919  8946991  8947009  8947021  8947027  8947031  8947039  8947063  8947067
8947111  8947121  8947123  8947153  8947171  8947177  8947181  8947193  8947201  8947217
8947319  8947331  8947339  8947361  8947369  8947417  8947441  8947459  8947469  8947481
8947487  8947501  8947511  8947517  8947567  8947577  8947579  8947583  8947591  8947597
8947639  8947643  8947657  8947669  8947681  8947699  8947703  8947709  8947721  8947723
8947751  8947753  8947769  8947789  8947801  8947817  8947819  8947823  8947837  8947843
8947853  8947889  8947891  8947903  8947951  8947973  8947987  8947997  8948021  8948041
8948053  8948063  8948077  8948083  8948087  8948099  8948101  8948111  8948123  8948143
8948161  8948179  8948207  8948227  8948231  8948237  8948263  8948279  8948309  8948323
8948333  8948369  8948371  8948383  8948393  8948417  8948419  8948431  8948441  8948473
8948503  8948507  8948509  8948519  8948539  8948543  8948549  8948581  8948591  8948609
8948623  8948629  8948669  8948671  8948689  8948711  8948759  8948789  8948803  8948813
8948827  8948837  8948869  8948887  8948893  8948897  8948899  8948917  8948921  8948939
8948957  8948969  8948971  8948999  8949013  8949037  8949067  8949071  8949077  8949097
8949113  8949131  8949151  8949167  8949181  8949213  8949253  8949299  8949331  8949341
8949379  8949419  8949427  8949433  8949443  8949469  8949481  8949503  8949517  8949761
8949557  8949559  8949601  8949617  8949631  8949637  8949649  8949679  8949757  8949761
8949781  8949791  8949797  8949823  8949839  8949869  8949883  8949911  8949923  8949937
8949947  8949953  8949959  8949961  8949991  8950001  8950027  8950037  8950043  8950049
8950087  8950091  8950129  8950133  8950157  8950169  8950199  8950213  8950217
8950247  8950267  8950303  8950309  8950339  8950363  8950369  8950373  8950393  8950399
8950421  8950429  8950453  8950489  8950507  8950511  8950543  8950547  8950549  8950553
8950583  8950607  8950609  8950639  8950649  8950673  8950681  8950709  8950741  8950759
8950769  8950783  8950787  8950793  8950807  8950813  8950817  8950829  8950849  8950853
8950873  8950883  8950889  8950897  8950901  8950913  8950951  8950967  8950973  8950987
8951023  8951039  8951051  8951081  8951113  8951119  8951123  8951141  8951149
8951153  8951171  8951177  8951207  8951213  8951221  8951249  8951251  8951263  8951269
8951273  8951287  8951309  8951317  8951321  8951339  8951387  8951389  8951399  8951417
8951419  8951441  8951477  8951543  8951549  8951557  8951563  8951581  8951587  8951599
8951629  8951651  8951659  8951687  8951693  8951699  8951711  8951729  8951737  8951779
8951791  8951819  8951821  8951827  8951837  8951851  8951857  8951861  8951863
8951867  8951879  8951897  8951903  8951909  8951939  8951947  8951959  8951989  8952001
8952007  8952023  8952067  8952089  8952091  8952101  8952107  8952109  8952121  8952133
8952143  8952157  8952161  8952179  8952193  8952197  8952233  8952239  8952241  8952259
8952277  8952289  8952311  8952323  8952341  8952347  8952431  8952457  8952467  8952469
8952479  8952481  8952487  8952499  8952509  8952511  8952529  8952533  8952547  8952569
8952613  8952623  8952641  8952649  8952673  8952679  8952683  8952689  8952721  8952731
8952733  8952767  8952791  8952799  8952817  8952821  8952841  8952859  8952869  8952899
8952907  8952929  8952949  8952953  8952959  8952973  8953013  8953019  8953057  8953093
8953099  8953111  8953121  8953157  8953177  8953181  8953183  8953193  8953207  8953229
8953247  8953267  8953289  8953291  8953303  8953319  8953349  8953367  8953387  8953393
8953403  8953409  8953423  8953429  8953433  8953487  8953499  8953501  8953517  8953531
8953537  8953631  8953639  8953643  8953691  8953697  8953709  8953723  8953727  8953729
8953733  8953757  8953771  8953783  8953793  8953801  8953811  8953853  8953859  8953871
8953891  8953897  8953913  8953927  8953943  8953993  8953999  8954021  8954027  8954041
8954051  8954059  8954063  8954083  8954089  8954093  8954131  8954161  8954171  8954177
8954213  8954221  8954227  8954261  8954273  8954287  8954311  8954317  8954321  8954329
```

```
8954347  8954369  8954401  8954419  8954437  8954447  8954467  8954471  8954479  8954497
8954501  8954507  8954513  8954527  8954531  8954573  8954593  8954599  8954609  8954639
8954641  8954663  8954713  8954747  8954773  8954779  8954789  8954791  8954807  8954831
8954849  8954857  8954867  8954899  8954917  8954921  8954929  8954951  8954977  8954987
8955053  8955083  8955103  8955109  8955131  8955139  8955143  8955157  8955181  8955241
8955253  8955259  8955263  8955281  8955283  8955293  8955299  8955307  8955371  8955389
8955407  8955431  8955439  8955449  8955493  8955511  8955539  8955547  8955563  8955581
8955587  8955599  8955619  8955623  8955629  8955637  8955643  8955673  8955701  8955703
8955721  8955731  8955733  8955757  8955761  8955769  8955773  8955797  8955833  8955839
8955841  8955853  8955871  8955883  8955893  8955899  8955929  8955937  8955967  8955971
8955977  8955979  8956001  8956021  8956063  8956069  8956097  8956121  8956133  8956139
8956147  8956217  8956219  8956231  8956237  8956243  8956247  8956249  8956253  8956261
8956291  8956307  8956333  8956351  8956369  8956397  8956403  8956411  8956457  8956459
8956463  8956471  8956481  8956483  8956487  8956517  8956531  8956537  8956547  8956559
8956567  8956609  8956631  8956643  8956663  8956681  8956699  8956723  8956757  8956789
8956817  8956823  8956859  8956879  8956889  8956891  8956897  8956903  8956933  8956939
8956951  8957009  8957063  8957083  8957093  8957107  8957129  8957131
8957141  8957153  8957167  8957231  8957243  8957251  8957269  8957309  8957359  8957381
8957383  8957407  8957413  8957447  8957449  8957461  8957467  8957479  8957489  8957513
8957537  8957539  8957551  8957561  8957563  8957567  8957579  8957591  8957593  8957621
8957629  8957651  8957653  8957671  8957681  8957693  8957743  8957749  8957771  8957821
8957843  8957887  8957889  8957917  8957957  8957977  8957983  8957989  8958011  8958067
8958073  8958077  8958083  8958097  8958119  8958121  8958143  8958149  8958161  8958193
8958203  8958217  8958227  8958311  8958331  8958343  8958353  8958407  8958409  8958449
8958479  8958493  8958497  8958517  8958553  8958563  8958583  8958611  8958641  8958647
8958667  8958683  8958701  8958727  8958731  8958739  8958743  8958757  8958769  8958793
8958797  8958809  8958839  8958851  8958857  8958863  8958871  8958877  8958883  8958947
8958953  8958997  8959001  8959021  8959063  8959073  8959081  8959109  8959133  8959141
8959147  8959157  8959163  8959169  8959183  8959199  8959207  8959219  8959229  8959273
8959303  8959333  8959337  8959343  8959367  8959369  8959373  8959387  8959409  8959411
8959421  8959427  8959429  8959451  8959463  8959493  8959499  8959529  8959537  8959603  8959667
8959711  8959729  8959739  8959759  8959763  8959777  8959787  8959789  8959807  8959823
8959829  8959879  8959891  8959913  8959921  8959931  8959981  8959991  8959997  8959999
8960011  8960047  8960053  8960057  8960089  8960113  8960117  8960123  8960137  8960167
8960177  8960183  8960213  8960227  8960243  8960249  8960257  8960261  8960291  8960293
8960299  8960311  8960321  8960323  8960353  8960359  8960387  8960443  8960447  8960453
8960467  8960477  8960489  8960527  8960557  8960573  8960587  8960603  8960617  8960669
8960689  8960701  8960713  8960729  8960737  8960741  8960747  8960753  8960773  8960789
8960801  8960803  8960807  8960861  8960863  8960867  8960887  8960893  8960909  8960923
8960933  8960977  8960983  8961019  8961031  8961037  8961041  8961047  8961061  8961079
8961101  8961109  8961131  8961133  8961137  8961149  8961209  8961221  8961223  8961257
8961269  8961299  8961301  8961311  8961341  8961347  8961353  8961373  8961383  8961391
8961401  8961409  8961419  8961439  8961473  8961479  8961487  8961497  8961509  8961527
8961583  8961619  8961661  8961671  8961679  8961707  8961709  8961713  8961731  8961751
8961763  8961767  8961779  8961791  8961793  8961809  8961811  8961851  8961859  8961889
8961893  8961943  8961959  8961961  8961983  8961989  8962003  8962013  8962027  8962039
8962081  8962097  8962127  8962139  8962169  8962183  8962207  8962237  8962253  8962279
8962309  8962321  8962337  8962367  8962381  8962411  8962453  8962493  8962511  8962529
8962531  8962561  8962573  8962579  8962601  8962607  8962633  8962643  8962693  8962697
8962729  8962741  8962781  8962799  8962819  8962823  8962861  8962871  8962873  8962879
8962901  8962931  8962979  8962997  8963021  8963033  8963081  8963083  8963093
8963099  8963107  8963147  8963161  8963167  8963173  8963177  8963191  8963197  8963203
8963237  8963239  8963249  8963257  8963281  8963299  8963347  8963351  8963377  8963429
8963431  8963473  8963483  8963501  8963503  8963551  8963561  8963579  8963593  8963599
8963609  8963621  8963623  8963627  8963653  8963677  8963683  8963701  8963719  8963723
8963741  8963753  8963761  8963771  8963791  8963797  8963803  8963807  8963827  8963831
8963849  8963861  8963869  8963873  8963891  8963897  8963923  8963939  8963957  8963959
8963993  8964013  8964019  8964023  8964049  8964079  8964097  8964107  8964113
8964119  8964121  8964127  8964149  8964191  8964211  8964217  8964223  8964251  8964259
8964289  8964299  8964311  8964313  8964331  8964337  8964349  8964359  8964379  8964383
8964391  8964407  8964413  8964419  8964441  8964433  8964463  8964467  8964469
8964479  8964497  8964517  8964521  8964541  8964547  8964563  8964569  8964577  8964583
8964587  8964601  8964607  8964623  8964647  8964667  8964677  8964701  8964721  8964731
8964737  8964793  8964817  8964821  8964853  8964877  8964887  8964889  8964919  8964929
8964947  8964953  8964961  8965007  8965013  8965039  8965049  8965051  8965087  8965091
8965097  8965127  8965213  8965153  8965189  8965217  8965267  8965279
8965289  8965291  8965301  8965303  8965309  8965351  8965357  8965367  8965381  8965393
8965399  8965403  8965447  8965487  8965499  8965513  8965529  8965559  8965589  8965591
8965609  8965643  8965651  8965657  8965661  8965679  8965687  8965709  8965717  8965721
8965753  8965763  8965781  8965787  8965829  8965867  8965903  8965907  8965939  8965961
8965969  8965981  8965991  8966011  8966057  8966077  8966101  8966107  8966117  8966129
8966137  8966149  8966179  8966183  8966203  8966219  8966227  8966257  8966267  8966299
8966303  8966311  8966333  8966339  8966341  8966357  8966359  8966369  8966383  8966387
8966411  8966443  8966453  8966479  8966501  8966561  8966567  8966569  8966591  8966603
8966609  8966621  8966623  8966627  8966641  8966653  8966669  8966681  8966687  8966693
8966717  8966729  8966759  8966779  8966807  8966813  8966821  8966831  8966851  8966869
8966873  8966891  8966897  8966899  8966927  8966959  8966963  8966977  8966999  8967001
8967011  8967037  8967043  8967073  8967097  8967113  8967149  8967169  8967173  8967191
8967193  8967199  8967223  8967241  8967251  8967253  8967269  8967281  8967311  8967317
8967319  8967323  8967353  8967377  8967383  8967389  8967391  8967407  8967419
8967457  8967503  8967533  8967557  8967571  8967593  8967611  8967659  8967667  8967697
8967713  8967719  8967731  8967737  8967743  8967767  8967799  8967809  8967811  8967853
8967859  8967899  8967911  8967913  8967919  8967947  8967961  8967967  8967991  8968033
8968049  8968051  8968103  8968109  8968111  8968121  8968139  8968153  8968181  8968187
8968189  8968199  8968213  8968237  8968241  8968243  8968273  8968283  8968301  8968303
8968339  8968357  8968363  8968373  8968387  8968397  8968409  8968417  8968433  8968439
8968499  8968567  8968573  8968591  8968601  8968637  8968651  8968657  8968693  8968721
8968727  8968733  8968759  8968783  8968789  8968793  8968823  8968829  8968831  8968871
8968879  8968907  8968913  8968937  8968943  8968957  8968987  8969017  8969029  8969039
```

```
8969041  8969053  8969087  8969099  8969101  8969117  8969131  8969143  8969171  8969179
8969189  8969203  8969221  8969231  8969237  8969263  8969293  8969309  8969321  8969347
8969351  8969393  8969407  8969417  8969419  8969473  8969479  8969483  8969579  8969617
8969647  8969657  8969663  8969683  8969689  8969707  8969713  8969717  8969731  8969771
8969777  8969783  8969789  8969791  8969803  8969813  8969887  8969899  8969921  8969923
8969959  8969971  8969993  8970007  8970011  8970037  8970041  8970047  8970089  8970097
8970119  8970121  8970133  8970139  8970163  8970217  8970229  8970263  8970281  8970289
8970293  8970319  8970329  8970331  8970341  8970361  8970389  8970421  8970427  8970433
8970443  8970449  8970473  8970491  8970497  8970499  8970503  8970547  8970583  8970587
8970593  8970601  8970607  8970629  8970649  8970653  8970659  8970671  8970673  8970691
8970707  8970737  8970757  8970763  8970769  8970791  8970799  8970803  8970821  8970827
8970839  8970877  8970883  8970887  8970901  8970919  8970953  8970959  8970971  8971007
8971033  8971037  8971049  8971091  8971117  8971129  8971139  8971147  8971163  8971177
8971181  8971213  8971217  8971229  8971241  8971243  8971271  8971283  8971297  8971321
8971337  8971351  8971379  8971381  8971397  8971399  8971421  8971441  8971447  8971471
8971483  8971499  8971511  8971559  8971561  8971583  8971601  8971619  8971637  8971639
8971657  8971663  8971687  8971691  8971693  8971709  8971727  8971747  8971751  8971757
8971777  8971789  8971799  8971811  8971813  8971849  8971873  8971883  8971913  8971939
8971943  8971969  8971973  8971979  8972023  8972053  8972069  8972081  8972083  8972101
8972129  8972137  8972147  8972177  8972191  8972203  8972207  8972219  8972221  8972261
8972263  8972273  8972279  8972287  8972291  8972297  8972303  8972309  8972371  8972407
8972449  8972473  8972489  8972501  8972567  8972569  8972591  8972603  8972627  8972647
8972657  8972669  8972701  8972749  8972797  8972801  8972813  8972827  8972837  8972839
8972849  8972863  8972869  8972879  8972903  8972933  8972947  8972963  8972969  8972983
8972993  8973001  8973007  8973023  8973049  8973061  8973067  8973071  8973101  8973103
8973113  8973121  8973131  8973163  8973199  8973221  8973241  8973259  8973269  8973311
8973317  8973323  8973329  8973343  8973347  8973389  8973401  8973407  8973409  8973413
8973421  8973493  8973509  8973521  8973533  8973551  8973563  8973577  8973581  8973593
8973617  8973659  8973661  8973667  8973691  8973697  8973709  8973737  8973751  8973763
8973791  8973803  8973821  8973857  8973859  8973863  8973889  8973901  8973919  8973931
8973961  8973967  8974001  8974019  8974033  8974037  8974051  8974067  8974087  8974093
8974103  8974111  8974123  8974127  8974129  8974139  8974151  8974169  8974177  8974193
8974219  8974223  8974241  8974271  8974279  8974363  8974391  8974409  8974429  8974447
8974451  8974481  8974499  8974507  8974519  8974529  8974579  8974597  8974607  8974627
8974661  8974663  8974673  8974681  8974703  8974711  8974723  8974741  8974751  8974769
8974789  8974811  8974829  8974843  8974877  8974913  8974937  8974969  8974981  8974993
8975009  8975033  8975041  8975047  8975059  8975063  8975101  8975117  8975143  8975147
8975159  8975171  8975173  8975189  8975191  8975227  8975237  8975243  8975293  8975311
8975327  8975333  8975339  8975341  8975363  8975377  8975381  8975389  8975437  8975441
8975453  8975459  8975489  8975501  8975503  8975531  8975539  8975579  8975621  8975633
8975639  8975641  8975651  8975653  8975669  8975689  8975703  8975713  8975717  8975723
8975767  8975783  8975797  8975803  8975821  8975839  8975887  8975899  8975903  8975933
8975947  8975951  8975963  8975987  8976001  8976029  8976031  8976043  8976047  8976053
8976061  8976067  8976073  8976091  8976127  8976137  8976157  8976169  8976179  8976197
8976223  8976229  8976257  8976263  8976271  8976277  8976281  8976287  8976301  8976349
8976353  8976361  8976397  8976403  8976413  8976421  8976431  8976439  8976449  8976467
8976469  8976479  8976491  8976503  8976521  8976529  8976547  8976559  8976587  8976589
8976619  8976659  8976677  8976707  8976713  8976719  8976749  8976757  8976767  8976787
8976811  8976823  8976839  8976841  8976853  8976861  8976889  8976893  8976907  8976931
8976937  8976941  8976967  8976971  8976997  8977013  8977021  8977039  8977049  8977069
8977091  8977097  8977099  8977117  8977159  8977201  8977217  8977223  8977229  8977247
8977261  8977271  8977277  8977279  8977303  8977307  8977313  8977333  8977369  8977379
8977433  8977439  8977459  8977471  8977477  8977523  8977541  8977571  8977589  8977597
8977603  8977607  8977651  8977663  8977673  8977679  8977681  8977687  8977699  8977721
8977741  8977763  8977807  8977831  8977867  8977873  8977883  8977901  8977909  8977949
8977951  8977957  8977961  8978059  8978063  8978069  8978071  8978093  8978117  8978129
8978171  8978173  8978183  8978191  8978237  8978239  8978243  8978273  8978287  8978297
8978311  8978323  8978327  8978351  8978353  8978369  8978377  8978381  8978449  8978471
8978479  8978489  8978503  8978539  8978573  8978617  8978633  8978639  8978663  8978687
8978689  8978699  8978707  8978743  8978759  8978779  8978803  8978807  8978813  8978821
8978831  8978863  8978869  8978891  8978909  8978911  8978923  8978953  8978969  8978971
8978989  8979007  8979011  8979013  8979029  8979059  8979071  8979097  8979107  8979137
8979149  8979163  8979169  8979199  8979211  8979221  8979233  8979251  8979259  8979263
8979293  8979317  8979329  8979331  8979337  8979353  8979359  8979371  8979379  8979409
8979427  8979431  8979433  8979461  8979479  8979497  8979569  8979577  8979599  8979611
8979617  8979629  8979653  8979661  8979671  8979701  8979703  8979709  8979721  8979731
8979767  8979781  8979787  8979797  8979811  8979827  8979847  8979857  8979881  8979889
8979923  8979973  8979983  8980003  8980007  8980031  8980061  8980067  8980079  8980087
8980093  8980109  8980133  8980171  8980177  8980187  8980219  8980229  8980253  8980259
8980277  8980289  8980313  8980319  8980333  8980339  8980417  8980429  8980441  8980451
8980469  8980493  8980501  8980523  8980541  8980547  8980549  8980571  8980579  8980583
8980589  8980591  8980627  8980637  8980663  8980667  8980687  8980703  8980729  8980733
8980739  8980753  8980757  8980789  8980813  8980823  8980841  8980859  8980883  8980891
8980897  8980931  8980943  8980963  8980987  8980991  8980997  8981057  8981087  8981099
8981101  8981107  8981111  8981113  8981123  8981143  8981153  8981177  8981179  8981191
8981233  8981249  8981251  8981261  8981267  8981279  8981299  8981303  8981311  8981317
8981341  8981359  8981363  8981377  8981383  8981411  8981437  8981447  8981459  8981461
8981563  8981573  8981597  8981611  8981617  8981633  8981647  8981657  8981659  8981689
8981717  8981743  8981767  8981773  8981783  8981801  8981807  8981809  8981827  8981837
8981839  8981867  8981873  8981879  8981887  8981897  8981921  8981923  8981939  8981957
8981977  8981981  8981989  8982007  8982013  8982019  8982023  8982037  8982053  8982073
8982089  8982091  8982107  8982109  8982119  8982143  8982151  8982173  8982187  8982191
8982209  8982229  8982241  8982247  8982293  8982317  8982331  8982349  8982353  8982359
8982361  8982367  8982371  8982419  8982427  8982437  8982439  8982461  8982469  8982473
8982517  8982521  8982541  8982551  8982553  8982559  8982619  8982629  8982643  8982697
8982713  8982737  8982751  8982769  8982773  8982821  8982847  8982863  8982871  8982881
8982887  8982889  8982893  8982899  8982907  8982913  8982923  8982929  8982947  8982973
8982989  8983027  8983031  8983049  8983057  8983081  8983099  8983151  8983187  8983189
8983199  8983201  8983207  8983217  8983229  8983231  8983237  8983241  8983253  8983279
```

8983283	8983297	8983309	8983343	8983349	8983391	8983411	8983421	8983423	8983433
8983493	8983511	8983519	8983529	8983537	8983549	8983577	8983607	8983619	8983621
8983631	8983661	8983669	8983687	8983693	8983699	8983703	8983729	8983759	8983783
8983787	8983811	8983813	8983841	8983847	8983883	8983901	8983907	8983913	8983937
8983943	8983951	8983981	8983991	8983993	8983999	8984021	8984029	8984077	8984089
8984149	8984159	8984167	8984179	8984197	8984201	8984219	8984221	8984243	8984251
8984257	8984267	8984273	8984293	8984299	8984309	8984341	8984351	8984363	8984369
8984399	8984407	8984441	8984471	8984477	8984489	8984491	8984497	8984509	8984531
8984539	8984557	8984593	8984609	8984611	8984623	8984641	8984669	8984671	8984707
8984711	8984753	8984771	8984783	8984791	8984803	8984813	8984827	8984839	8984861
8984879	8984903	8984923	8984951	8984957	8984981	8985001	8985007	8985017	8985023
8985091	8985103	8985113	8985139	8985149	8985161	8985167	8985181	8985187	8985211
8985217	8985241	8985247	8985253	8985259	8985269	8985281	8985283	8985289	8985293
8985307	8985311	8985313	8985337	8985349	8985373	8985391	8985451	8985463	8985467
8985481	8985517	8985541	8985577	8985589	8985593	8985607	8985611	8985653	8985659
8985661	8985671	8985677	8985719	8985721	8985733	8985751	8985763	8985773	8985787
8985799	8985811	8985817	8985833	8985863	8985881	8985913	8985923	8985937	8985947
8985953	8985959	8985989	8985997	8986039	8986057	8986073	8986091	8986121	8986127
8986151	8986163	8986193	8986199	8986213	8986223	8986247	8986253	8986277	8986283
8986303	8986333	8986361	8986363	8986379	8986381	8986391	8986403	8986409	
8986423	8986451	8986457	8986477	8986499	8986507	8986511	8986513	8986531	8986547
8986573	8986657	8986669	8986673	8986687	8986697	8986717	8986739	8986751	8986787
8986793	8986799	8986801	8986841	8986843	8986849	8986877	8986883	8986891	8986903
8986909	8986919	8986921	8986927	8986933	8986937	8986949	8986963	8986987	8987023
8987029	8987047	8987093	8987107	8987113	8987137	8987149	8987161	8987183	8987197
8987207	8987213	8987219	8987221	8987243	8987269	8987287	8987291	8987299	8987311
8987327	8987347	8987351	8987353	8987357	8987371	8987383	8987389	8987401	8987417
8987443	8987449	8987467	8987483	8987497	8987501	8987507	8987519	8987527	8987567
8987579	8987591	8987603	8987609	8987621	8987623	8987639	8987653	8987659	8987689
8987711	8987723	8987749	8987753	8987761	8987777	8987789	8987791	8987807	8987809
8987851	8987911	8987921	8987933	8987939	8987947	8987959	8987981	8988013	8988017
8988029	8988037	8988043	8988079	8988113	8988131	8988149	8988163	8988191	8988209
8988227	8988229	8988241	8988253	8988263	8988277	8988281	8988337	8988367	8988391
8988401	8988437	8988443	8988449	8988451	8988503	8988509	8988517	8988523	8988557
8988569	8988571	8988583	8988587	8988601	8988611	8988613	8988619	8988643	8988649
8988659	8988689	8988701	8988751	8988757	8988761	8988769	8988773	8988781	8988809
8988821	8988829	8988839	8988871	8988877	8988887	8988901	8988943	8988949	8988979
8988989	8988997	8989007	8989027	8989051	8989061	8989069	8989081	8989103	8989117
8989133	8989139	8989153	8989199	8989207	8989229	8989231	8989237	8989241	8989329
8989273	8989301	8989313	8989369	8989399	8989459	8989469	8989493	8989499	8989511
8989517	8989553	8989567	8989571	8989577	8989579	8989601	8989609	8989621	8989627
8989637	8989639	8989661	8989667	8989691	8989697	8989699	8989703	8989723	
8989733	8989741	8989759	8989763	8989781	8989789	8989817	8989837	8989861	8989867
8989873	8989919	8989921	8989973	8989999	8990011	8990027	8990039	8990041	8990063
8990081	8990083	8990099	8990101	8990123	8990141	8990143	8990147	8990153	8990183
8990209	8990239	8990257	8990321	8990339	8990347	8990353	8990407	8990411	8990413
8990441	8990459	8990497	8990533	8990543	8990563	8990567	8990573	8990581	
8990587	8990617	8990623	8990669	8990687	8990693	8990719	8990731	8990747	8990777
8990791	8990803	8990831	8990843	8990873	8990887	8990929	8990939	8990981	
8991001	8991007	8991029	8991041	8991067	8991077	8991089	8991097	8991127	8991139
8991149	8991163	8991167	8991197	8991223	8991239	8991251	8991253	8991289	8991293
8991299	8991319	8991347	8991361	8991371	8991377	8991379	8991383	8991401	8991431
8991439	8991443	8991449	8991517	8991529	8991533	8991539	8991553	8991559	8991599
8991607	8991611	8991613	8991637	8991649	8991667	8991679	8991713	8991739	8991743
8991757	8991761	8991779	8991799	8991823	8991839	8991893	8991901	8991967	8991973
8991977	8991989	8991991	8992007	8992019	8992069	8992091	8992121	8992129	8992141
8992153	8992157	8992183	8992189	8992199	8992211	8992219	8992229	8992231	8992259
8992279	8992283	8992297	8992307	8992331	8992343	8992397	8992411	8992421	8992441
8992483	8992493	8992499	8992519	8992531	8992549	8992553	8992561	8992583	8992619
8992631	8992637	8992661	8992663	8992691	8992693	8992699	8992703	8992717	8992723
8992729	8992741	8992769	8992771	8992777	8992811	8992831	8992861	8992877	8992889
8992897	8992901	8992903	8992913	8992927	8992937	8992979	8992993	8992999	8993003
8993011	8993041	8993053	8993057	8993071	8993087	8993143	8993147	8993167	8993191
8993197	8993233	8993249	8993261	8993267	8993269	8993273	8993287	8993297	8993329
8993333	8993351	8993363	8993371	8993377	8993399	8993401	8993417	8993419	8993443
8993447	8993449	8993471	8993489	8993507	8993531	8993533	8993563	8993573	8993587
8993599	8993603	8993609	8993681	8993687	8993693	8993723	8993737	8993749	8993753
8993771	8993773	8993791	8993807	8993827	8993839	8993861	8993863	8993869	8993891
8993909	8993921	8993941	8993951	8993977	8993981	8994017	8994053		
8994077	8994091	8994101	8994103	8994109	8994121	8994133	8994157	8994169	8994191
8994197	8994199	8994233	8994283	8994299	8994317	8994347	8994383	8994407	8994413
8994463	8994473	8994481	8994487	8994497	8994509	8994533	8994563	8994569	8994593
8994599	8994613	8994631	8994637	8994641	8994647	8994653	8994659	8994677	8994707
8994721	8994731	8994767	8994779	8994781	8994833	8994851	8994857	8994859	8994871
8994883	8994889	8994893	8994899	8994911	8994943	8995003	8995013	8995027	8995039
8995069	8995073	8995079	8995097	8995109	8995111	8995123	8995163	8995187	8995211
8995223	8995229	8995247	8995253	8995267	8995289	8995297	8995309	8995313	8995331
8995333	8995339	8995351	8995373	8995381	8995387	8995391	8995411	8995447	8995451
8995453	8995513	8995529	8995543	8995559	8995561	8995573	8995579	8995583	8995603
8995619	8995631	8995681	8995709	8995741	8995751	8995757	8995787	8995799	8995801
8995813	8995823	8995837	8995841	8995843	8995849	8995867	8995871	8995937	8995939
8995957	8995963	8995981	8995993	8995997	8996011	8996017	8996027	8996033	8996041
8996047	8996083	8996087	8996089	8996093	8996131	8996149	8996153	8996161	8996191
8996201	8996203	8996233	8996303	8996311	8996321	8996327	8996333	8996357	8996359
8996371	8996389	8996401	8996419	8996431	8996437	8996521	8996527	8996539	8996543
8996549	8996551	8996563	8996567	8996569	8996573	8996579	8996609	8996627	8996629
8996639	8996651	8996681	8996711	8996717	8996759	8996797	8996831	8996833	8996837
8996843	8996849	8996857	8996863	8996879	8996891	8996903	8996941	8996963	8996971
8996983	8996993	8997007	8997011	8997017	8997059	8997083	8997101	8997103	8997113

8997119	8997139	8997167	8997217	8997239	8997259	8997293	8997299	8997311	8997319
8997341	8997343	8997353	8997407	8997413	8997421	8997451	8997457	8997463	8997487
8997503	8997517	8997529	8997551	8997553	8997587	8997601	8997613	8997647	8997649
8997661	8997671	8997701	8997713	8997721	8997733	8997767	8997797	8997803	8997847
8997869	8997871	8997881	8997883	8997889	8997931	8997941	8997943	8997953	8997971
8997973	8997979	8998061	8998063	8998109	8998139	8998159	8998169	8998177	8998189
8998211	8998243	8998247	8998261	8998271	8998307	8998333	8998349	8998351	8998357
8998361	8998373	8998391	8998397	8998411	8998417	8998421	8998427	8998433	8998447
8998471	8998487	8998489	8998519	8998547	8998553	8998579	8998603	8998607	8998643
8998651	8998657	8998663	8998673	8998687	8998709	8998747	8998757	8998771	8998793
8998813	8998823	8998861	8998877	8998883	8998889	8998901	8998919	8998921	8998963
8998987	8998991	8999009	8999033	8999047	8999051	8999059	8999087	8999099	8999101
8999113	8999143	8999161	8999183	8999189	8999197	8999203	8999209	8999219	8999257
8999299	8999303	8999311	8999317	8999323	8999327	8999339	8999359	8999381	8999383
8999387	8999401	8999411	8999423	8999429	8999437	8999461	8999467	8999489	8999491
8999503	8999519	8999527	8999567	8999581	8999609	8999651	8999671	8999687	8999699
8999707	8999737	8999741	8999761	8999777	8999789	8999813	8999819	8999839	
8999849	8999867	8999897	8999899	8999927	8999957	8999971	8999981	8999993	9000011
9000041	9000049	9000059	9000067	9000119	9000127	9000143	9000163	9000193	9000203
9000209	9000217	9000223	9000253	9000269	9000283	9000289	9000317	9000331	9000349
9000377	9000379	9000403	9000427	9000451	9000461	9000473	9000487	9000499	9000517
9000569	9000577	9000601	9000637	9000683	9000703	9000709	9000721	9000743	9000767
9000773	9000779	9000781	9000787	9000791	9000793	9000809	9000821	9000839	9000841
9000877	9000899	9000907	9000913	9000931	9000961	9000983	9000989	9000997	9001001
9001033	9001039	9001063	9001093	9001121	9001163	9001169	9001171	9001189	9001199
9001219	9001229	9001243	9001259	9001277	9001283	9001301	9001337	9001351	9001387
9001417	9001429	9001463	9001481	9001493	9001507	9001511	9001519	9001523	9001561
9001621	9001627	9001667	9001691	9001723	9001739	9001747	9001769	9001781	9001793
9001799	9001829	9001843	9001897	9001933	9001961	9001963	9001969	9001987	9001999
9002003	9002009	9002011	9002023	9002033	9002041	9002047	9002087	9002107	9002113
9002171	9002233	9002249	9002251	9002293	9002311	9002317	9002339	9002341	9002347
9002363	9002377	9002393	9002449	9002467	9002489	9002501	9002519	9002533	9002549
9002569	9002621	9002629	9002641	9002663	9002671	9002689	9002701	9002717	9002779
9002801	9002813	9002831	9002839	9002849	9002863	9002879	9002893	9002909	9002923
9002969	9002977	9002993	9003023	9003031	9003061	9003083	9003103	9003133	9003187
9003191	9003193	9003209	9003221	9003227	9003233	9003263	9003271	9003277	9003343
9003347	9003349	9003377	9003403	9003409	9003431	9003437	9003487	9003497	9003517
9003529	9003583	9003607	9003613	9003619	9003647	9003667	9003689	9003703	9003707
9003713	9003719	9003721	9003749	9003767	9003773	9003779	9003803	9003809	9003817
9003821	9003859	9003871	9003877	9003889	9003901	9003959	9003977	9003997	9004013
9004019	9004031	9004057	9004069	9004087	9004091	9004097	9004103	9004111	9004147
9004189	9004231	9004249	9004267	9004277	9004301	9004319	9004327	9004343	9004349
9004351	9004361	9004367	9004399	9004451	9004459	9004469	9004481	9004507	9004511
9004519	9004531	9004561	9004591	9004591	9004603	9004621	9004627	9004643	9004649
9004669	9004687	9004691	9004711	9004739	9004741	9004771	9004811	9004829	9004843
9004889	9004901	9004907	9004909	9004921	9004927	9004939	9004943	9004969	9004991
9004999	9005011	9005021	9005027	9005039	9005041	9005047	9005057	9005081	9005089
9005093	9005099	9005119	9005149	9005173	9005179	9005197	9005201	9005219	9005233
9005237	9005267	9005279	9005299	9005327	9005329	9005371	9005387	9005401	9005429
9005473	9005497	9005509	9005519	9005539	9005543	9005551	9005561	9005621	9005657
9005663	9005693	9005713	9005723	9005729	9005741	9005743	9005783	9005839	9005849
9005873	9005879	9005881	9005897	9005917	9005923	9005947	9005977	9005989	9006013
9006031	9006043	9006061	9006071	9006077	9006139	9006157	9006163	9006169	9006181
9006191	9006197	9006199	9006203	9006253	9006289	9006293	9006313	9006359	9006373
9006377	9006391	9006397	9006419	9006433	9006457	9006493	9006499	9006509	9006581
9006587	9006601	9006611	9006623	9006631	9006649	9006653	9006659	9006671	9006677
9006707	9006749	9006769	9006793	9006797	9006853	9006859	9006863	9006883	9006919
9006929	9006937	9006953	9006971	9006973	9006983	9007001	9007039	9007043	9007049
9007051	9007087	9007111	9007123	9007151	9007157	9007171	9007177	9007181	9007183
9007189	9007211	9007213	9007223	9007231	9007241	9007259	9007261	9007277	9007289
9007291	9007303	9007309	9007319	9007333	9007351	9007357	9007363	9007373	9007393
9007441	9007457	9007477	9007499	9007507	9007529	9007541	9007549	9007553	9007567
9007571	9007573	9007619	9007627	9007631	9007633	9007643	9007657	9007679	9007703
9007709	9007717	9007727	9007753	9007759	9007771	9007781	9007783	9007793	9007811
9007849	9007853	9007861	9007877	9007883	9007891	9007903	9007913	9007939	9007961
9007979	9007991	9007993	9008023	9008029	9008059	9008063	9008101	9008117	9008119
9008123	9008141	9008171	9008177	9008213	9008221	9008231	9008243	9008269	9008281
9008303	9008309	9008359	9008369	9008381	9008393	9008423	9008431	9008497	9008557
9008581	9008599	9008633	9008639	9008687	9008707	9008731	9008761	9008767	9008771
9008773	9008777	9008803	9008809	9008837	9008843	9008863	9008873	9008899	9008911
9008921	9008927	9008933	9008947	9008969	9008981	9009017	9009023	9009041	9009061
9009083	9009103	9009107	9009157	9009163	9009179	9009191	9009199	9009223	9009229
9009277	9009281	9009331	9009347	9009349	9009367	9009379	9009391	9009409	9009419
9009443	9009487	9009509	9009521	9009527	9009551	9009593	9009601	9009631	9009647
9009659	9009673	9009683	9009697	9009727	9009739	9009751	9009769	9009773	9009811
9009827	9009839	9009851	9009893	9009901	9009929	9009941	9009943	9009961	9009977
9009989	9009991	9010003	9010007	9010031	9010033	9010063	9010081	9010087	9010103
9010121	9010139	9010207	9010219	9010241	9010247	9010279	9010291	9010301	9010307
9010381	9010399	9010409	9010423	9010433	9010439	9010451	9010453	9010471	9010481
9010501	9010531	9010559	9010567	9010633	9010637	9010667	9010711	9010717	9010741
9010751	9010759	9010787	9010829	9010843	9010847	9010849	9010853	9010873	9010877
9010879	9010889	9010891	9010907	9010913	9010927	9010933	9010949	9010973	9010979
9010993	9011029	9011053	9011059	9011069	9011077	9011081	9011099	9011117	9011143
9011159	9011183	9011201	9011213	9011221	9011237	9011251	9011269	9011273	9011279
9011281	9011287	9011333	9011341	9011407	9011417	9011419	9011459	9011501	9011507
9011521	9011531	9011543	9011549	9011551	9011579	9011593	9011617	9011623	9011627
9011633	9011659	9011671	9011687	9011689	9011693	9011707	9011711	9011747	9011753
9011771	9011803	9011843	9011857	9011867	9011869	9011881	9011903	9011939	9011987
9012001	9012007	9012013	9012037	9012043	9012049	9012071	9012077	9012097	9012121

```
9012131 9012149 9012181 9012187 9012217 9012239 9012247 9012253 9012259 9012277
9012281 9012293 9012299 9012313 9012319 9012337 9012383 9012401 9012449 9012463
9012467 9012529 9012539 9012547 9012551 9012559 9012583 9012583 9012587 9012589
9012611 9012617 9012623 9012629 9012637 9012659 9012667 9012691 9012697 9012709
9012761 9012769 9012791 9012797 9012833 9012841 9012869 9012889 9012893 9012911
9012923 9012943 9012961 9012967 9012977 9012979 9013019 9013027 9013051 9013057
9013061 9013097 9013117 9013129 9013223 9013231 9013243 9013271 9013283 9013289
9013313 9013321 9013327 9013351 9013369 9013387 9013393 9013409 9013423 9013439
9013441 9013453 9013463 9013483 9013507 9013513 9013523 9013541 9013547 9013561
9013597 9013603 9013639 9013649 9013673 9013687 9013691 9013699 9013729 9013747
9013811 9013813 9013817 9013853 9013871 9013889 9013937 9013957 9013969 9013993
9013997 9014003 9014017 9014021 9014023 9014039 9014059 9014077 9014101 9014107
9014111 9014119 9014141 9014143 9014167 9014171 9014179 9014207 9014209 9014221
9014237 9014249 9014279 9014281 9014287 9014309 9014323 9014353 9014371 9014387
9014393 9014407 9014443 9014449 9014479 9014483 9014507 9014513 9014527 9014591
9014609 9014623 9014639 9014653 9014659 9014693 9014699 9014701 9014767 9014773
9014807 9014809 9014813 9014839 9014861 9014891 9014897 9014903 9014909
9014921 9014923 9014953 9014963 9014983 9015001 9015029 9015047 9015059 9015089
9015091 9015109 9015119 9015131 9015133 9015137 9015169 9015173 9015179 9015187
9015197 9015199 9015217 9015229 9015233 9015257 9015263 9015271 9015283 9015301
9015343 9015359 9015371 9015421 9015431 9015439 9015463 9015467 9015497 9015511
9015521 9015533 9015547 9015553 9015577 9015581 9015583 9015599 9015619 9015631
9015647 9015649 9015653 9015659 9015673 9015689 9015691 9015703 9015707 9015803
9015821 9015847 9015863 9015889 9015911 9015913 9015943 9015949 9015953 9015991
9016027 9016037 9016043 9016061 9016067 9016079 9016087 9016121 9016177 9016193
9016199 9016223 9016237 9016277 9016289 9016291 9016297 9016327 9016363 9016367
9016411 9016421 9016457 9016463 9016481 9016499 9016523 9016543 9016547 9016561
9016571 9016577 9016603 9016607 9016643 9016649 9016687 9016703 9016717 9016727
9016757 9016769 9016801 9016841 9016901 9016921 9016949 9016957 9016961 9016967
9017027 9017051 9017053 9017083 9017087 9017093 9017101 9017111 9017117 9017119
9017137 9017161 9017167 9017189 9017201 9017207 9017209 9017221 9017227 9017237
9017263 9017269 9017291 9017317 9017339 9017353 9017363 9017377 9017387 9017389
9017413 9017423 9017431 9017441 9017443 9017453 9017479 9017537 9017543 9017549
9017627 9017651 9017681 9017689 9017693 9017707 9017711 9017717 9017719 9017741
9017759 9017773 9017777 9017797 9017819 9017821 9017839 9017849 9017857 9017861
9017881 9017891 9017893 9017941 9017947 9017969 9017977 9018011 9018013 9018019
9018049 9018059 9018071 9018077 9018127 9018131 9018161 9018169 9018193 9018221
9018223 9018227 9018257 9018263 9018307 9018337 9018341 9018353 9018367 9018379
9018409 9018413 9018421 9018431 9018473 9018479 9018487 9018511 9018547 9018571
9018587 9018589 9018601 9018617 9018629 9018661 9018671 9018677 9018679 9018683
9018703 9018727 9018733 9018743 9018761 9018781 9018791 9018809 9018817 9018827
9018853 9018871 9018887 9018899 9018907 9018929 9018941 9018973 9018979 9018983
9018991 9019001 9019007 9019019 9019039 9019067 9019081 9019093 9019097 9019099
9019117 9019141 9019147 9019177 9019181 9019229 9019247 9019249 9019259 9019291
9019327 9019331 9019363 9019393 9019421 9019429 9019447 9019457 9019459 9019463
9019489 9019499 9019523 9019529 9019553 9019567 9019573 9019579 9019583
9019589 9019597 9019613 9019651 9019679 9019687 9019691 9019697 9019709 9019711
9019753 9019763 9019771 9019781 9019789 9019793 9019799 9019831 9019847 9019867
9019891 9019909 9019937 9019939 9019949 9019963 9019973 9019987 9020003 9020027
9020029 9020051 9020057 9020069 9020083 9020107 9020113 9020147 9020159 9020173
9020177 9020201 9020203 9020227 9020233 9020243 9020279 9020281 9020293 9020309
9020317 9020329 9020339 9020371 9020413 9020419 9020437 9020447 9020467 9020477
9020483 9020503 9020507 9020509 9020519 9020527 9020549 9020551 9020567 9020587
9020617 9020633 9020639 9020657 9020681 9020699 9020707 9020717 9020719 9020747
9020789 9020797 9020819 9020821 9020831 9020857 9020873 9020881 9020887 9020917
9020929 9020941 9020983 9020987 9020989 9020993 9021043 9021071 9021113
9021119 9021127 9021137 9021149 9021151 9021161 9021179 9021197 9021211 9021223
9021241 9021251 9021253 9021269 9021281 9021283 9021317 9021323 9021329 9021347
9021361 9021379 9021401 9021427 9021433 9021449 9021457 9021511 9021541 9021547
9021553 9021557 9021569 9021601 9021619 9021641 9021647 9021703 9021707 9021709
9021731 9021737 9021739 9021769 9021833 9021847 9021863 9021869 9021877 9021893
9021907 9021923 9021931 9021937 9021949 9021967 9021977 9022001 9022061 9022081
9022109 9022127 9022129 9022159 9022163 9022193 9022201 9022297 9022301 9022309
9022313 9022361 9022367 9022381 9022399 9022411 9022439 9022441 9022471 9022477
9022483 9022493 9022513 9022523 9022537 9022547 9022579 9022589 9022591 9022603
9022613 9022621 9022627 9022679 9022723 9022753 9022759 9022763 9022781 9022787
9022789 9022807 9022817 9022841 9022861 9022883 9022913 9022933 9022939 9022961
9022997 9022997 9023009 9023011 9023017 9023029 9023051 9023057 9023071
9023083 9023093 9023099 9023101 9023111 9023117 9023123 9023137 9023159 9023167
9023171 9023173 9023207 9023213 9023221 9023237 9023251 9023269 9023297 9023299
9023323 9023327 9023341 9023363 9023369 9023381 9023419 9023431 9023473 9023479
9023489 9023491 9023501 9023533 9023543 9023551 9023559 9023561 9023579 9023587
9023591 9023629 9023639 9023647 9023657 9023683 9023699 9023713 9023723 9023737
9023747 9023789 9023801 9023809 9023827 9023831 9023867 9023869 9023891 9023897
9023899 9023909 9023947 9023983 9023999 9024011 9024013 9024049 9024077 9024079
9024121 9024137 9024181 9024209 9024217 9024233 9024271 9024277 9024299
9024311 9024347 9024359 9024371 9024397 9024403 9024409 9024413 9024419 9024427
9024439 9024473 9024527 9024541 9024553 9024557 9024577 9024593 9024599 9024607
9024641 9024649 9024667 9024679 9024703 9024731 9024733 9024737 9024749 9024779
9024793 9024823 9024863 9024871 9024931 9024959 9024973 9024979 9024989 9025013
9025021 9025031 9025073 9025097 9025099 9025109 9025111 9025117 9025139 9025157
9025183 9025187 9025201 9025213 9025231 9025241 9025243 9025267 9025271 9025273
9025301 9025319 9025327 9025333 9025339 9025391 9025397 9025417 9025441 9025451
9025463 9025477 9025517 9025519 9025537 9025543 9025547 9025553 9025561 9025573
9025609 9025613 9025651 9025661 9025663 9025727 9025777 9025789 9025801 9025811
9025813 9025837 9025853 9025859 9025883 9025889 9025901 9025909 9025937 9025943
9025957 9025979 9025999 9026029 9026041 9026057 9026063 9026071 9026077 9026081
9026111 9026119 9026123 9026131 9026179 9026203 9026249 9026257 9026263 9026267
9026287 9026309 9026317 9026341 9026357 9026359 9026429 9026447 9026449 9026509
```

```
9026513 9026527 9026531 9026543 9026551 9026561 9026573 9026581 9026593 9026623
9026639 9026657 9026669 9026663 9026681 9026687 9026747 9026761 9026783 9026807
9026819 9026863 9026873 9026887 9026891 9026893 9026903 9026933 9026959 9026987
9027043 9027049 9027061 9027089 9027097 9027101 9027127 9027133 9027167 9027173
9027191 9027199 9027217 9027259 9027283 9027301 9027307 9027311 9027353 9027373
9027407 9027419 9027427 9027433 9027443 9027461 9027467 9027509 9027511 9027517
9027533 9027539 9027547 9027553 9027559 9027587 9027611 9027637 9027643 9027653
9027673 9027703 9027757 9027779 9027791 9027803 9027829 9027839 9027877 9027881
9027923 9027929 9027943 9027947 9027959 9027973 9028007 9028009 9028013 9028067
9028069 9028079 9028091 9028109 9028141 9028181 9028231 9028247 9028267 9028273
9028291 9028297 9028337 9028373 9028381 9028387 9028399 9028403 9028423 9028429
9028433 9028499 9028501 9028507 9028519 9028529 9028531 9028543 9028571 9028589
9028609 9028619 9028631 9028633 9028637 9028699 9028741 9028757 9028759 9028763
9028787 9028801 9028807 9028847 9028861 9028867 9028871 9028883 9028891 9028919
9028927 9028931 9028969 9028973 9028991 9028997 9029003 9029017 9029071 9029081
9029093 9029099 9029107 9029113 9029129 9029131 9029171 9029173 9029191 9029197
9029201 9029203 9029219 9029231 9029243 9029291 9029303 9029309 9029327 9029341
9029357 9029393 9029399 9029417 9029429 9029477 9029479 9029497 9029513 9029519
9029539 9029543 9029551 9029561 9029563 9029597 9029599 9029609 9029627 9029651
9029689 9029707 9029719 9029723 9029729 9029743 9029747 9029753 9029789 9029803
9029809 9029849 9029861 9029879 9029893 9029899 9029903 9029929 9029947 9029953
9029971 9030001 9030017 9030019 9030031 9030041 9030071 9030079 9030089 9030101
9030121 9030143 9030163 9030181 9030199 9030211 9030239 9030293 9030313 9030347
9030353 9030361 9030389 9030391 9030401 9030407 9030431 9030457 9030487 9030509
9030523 9030557 9030577 9030583 9030601 9030607 9030613 9030647 9030653 9030661
9030683 9030709 9030733 9030739 9030751 9030761 9030767 9030781 9030793 9030811
9030823 9030839 9030859 9030869 9030877 9030883 9030887 9030899 9030911 9030929
9030941 9030943 9030949 9030971 9030979 9031021 9031027 9031051 9031067 9031069
9031091 9031103 9031109 9031153 9031163 9031171 9031181 9031207 9031229 9031259
9031279 9031283 9031291 9031309 9031331 9031339 9031343 9031361 9031381 9031391
9031409 9031427 9031457 9031481 9031489 9031493 9031501 9031511 9031531 9031537
9031541 9031579 9031597 9031609 9031613 9031619 9031637 9031639 9031657 9031681
9031699 9031703 9031717 9031727 9031747 9031787 9031793 9031807 9031831 9031837
9031853 9031871 9031873 9031901 9031903 9031909 9031927 9031969 9032003 9032017
9032029 9032039 9032041 9032047 9032059 9032099 9032119 9032141 9032167 9032171
9032189 9032197 9032227 9032249 9032267 9032269 9032291 9032297 9032299 9032339
9032347 9032357 9032381 9032393 9032437 9032449 9032459 9032461 9032473 9032479
9032483 9032489 9032497 9032539 9032567 9032579 9032599 9032609 9032633 9032663
9032671 9032689 9032713 9032719 9032731 9032741 9032753 9032761 9032783 9032839
9032857 9032887 9032911 9032929 9032981 9032983 9032987 9032993 9033019 9033023
9033029 9033049 9033083 9033109 9033119 9033133 9033143 9033163 9033173 9033187
9033191 9033229 9033253 9033257 9033287 9033317 9033331 9033337 9033359 9033361
9033371 9033389 9033391 9033419 9033421 9033449 9033467 9033491 9033499 9033509
9033523 9033527 9033533 9033539 9033547 9033599 9033601 9033611 9033649 9033659
9033671 9033697 9033701 9033709 9033719 9033757 9033769 9033793 9033799 9033839
9033841 9033847 9033853 9033859 9033863 9033889 9033907 9033923 9033929 9033931
9033943 9033967 9033979 9033991 9034007 9034033 9034037 9034043 9034073 9034087
9034093 9034097 9034121 9034127 9034133 9034163 9034169 9034189 9034219 9034271
9034273 9034303 9034307 9034351 9034357 9034369 9034393 9034397 9034409 9034411
9034427 9034447 9034451 9034453 9034471 9034477 9034489 9034499 9034507 9034511
9034513 9034559 9034567 9034577 9034591 9034621 9034639 9034651 9034691 9034691
9034693 9034721 9034723 9034741 9034757 9034777 9034789 9034807 9034813 9034841
9034843 9034853 9034877 9034943 9034957 9034969 9034997 9034999 9035003 9035009
9035027 9035029 9035063 9035071 9035077 9035093 9035101 9035107 9035111 9035171
9035183 9035207 9035239 9035249 9035267 9035321 9035329 9035333 9035357 9035399
9035459 9035471 9035479 9035489 9035497 9035513 9035519 9035563 9035569 9035591
9035603 9035627 9035641 9035657 9035683 9035693 9035699 9035707 9035723 9035729
9035759 9035771 9035777 9035779 9035801 9035809 9035833 9035837 9035839 9035861
9035879 9035899 9035921 9035927 9035933 9035947 9035951 9036007 9036047 9036059
9036073 9036091 9036101 9036107 9036121 9036133 9036143 9036151 9036179 9036187
9036253 9036281 9036311 9036317 9036329 9036331 9036337 9036347 9036373 9036373
9036421 9036463 9036481 9036509 9036541 9036581 9036583 9036589 9036613 9036619
9036637 9036653 9036683 9036689 9036697 9036721 9036733 9036739 9036749 9036767
9036803 9036817 9036821 9036823 9036827 9036847 9036857 9036887 9036901 9036941
9036947 9036959 9036997 9037043 9037051 9037057 9037069 9037073 9037079 9037087
9037099 9037169 9037201 9037219 9037243 9037247 9037253 9037271 9037277 9037279
9037283 9037309 9037313 9037381 9037397 9037403 9037409 9037433 9037451 9037453
9037463 9037477 9037481 9037487 9037499 9037537 9037543 9037573 9037601 9037603
9037631 9037649 9037663 9037667 9037669 9037681 9037687 9037703 9037723 9037733
9037739 9037747 9037751 9037759 9037789 9037793 9037799 9037801 9037807 9037811
9037817 9037841 9037843 9037849 9037867 9037871 9037883 9037891 9037907 9037909
9037927 9037933 9037949 9037961 9037979 9037981 9037991 9038021 9038023 9038059
9038069 9038077 9038123 9038189 9038219 9038221 9038231 9038257 9038273 9038317
9038347 9038369 9038377 9038399 9038411 9038423 9038437 9038443 9038467 9038473
9038479 9038483 9038503 9038507 9038527 9038537 9038539 9038551 9038569 9038581
9038599 9038629 9038657 9038671 9038681 9038683 9038707 9038723 9038773 9038789
9038831 9038857 9038867 9038873 9038879 9038881 9038891 9038893 9038921 9038969
9039007 9039049 9039059 9039061 9039067 9039071 9039083 9039091 9039109 9039119
9039143 9039157 9039167 9039169 9039179 9039221 9039227 9039287 9039301 9039319
9039323 9039347 9039353 9039377 9039379 9039389 9039403 9039419 9039431 9039469
9039487 9039493 9039523 9039533 9039551 9039559 9039571 9039593 9039607 9039617
9039623 9039629 9039637 9039643 9039659 9039673 9039689 9039691 9039727 9039781
9039827 9039893 9039907 9039913 9039931 9039959 9039983 9039997 9040001 9040007
9040021 9040033 9040043 9040061 9040063 9040079 9040093 9040117 9040123 9040153
9040159 9040169 9040177 9040183 9040193 9040201 9040223 9040231 9040237 9040249
9040253 9040259 9040271 9040279 9040307 9040331 9040397 9040399 9040411 9040417
9040429 9040439 9040453 9040457 9040463 9040477 9040487 9040517 9040529 9040553
9040567 9040571 9040573 9040589 9040597 9040601 9040631 9040639 9040693 9040711
9040723 9040727 9040739 9040741 9040777 9040799 9040819 9040849 9040853 9040859
```

```
9040861 9040877 9040883 9040891 9040897 9040907 9040919 9040931 9040937 9040939
9040943 9040949 9040961 9040963 9041023 9041027 9041029 9041063 9041077 9041083
9041129 9041141 9041143 9041173 9041189 9041203 9041261 9041267 9041281 9041287
9041293 9041311 9041327 9041339 9041341 9041371 9041377 9041401 9041453 9041479
9041497 9041521 9041551 9041563 9041581 9041611 9041623 9041633 9041657 9041693
9041713 9041723 9041741 9041759 9041761 9041789 9041797 9041861 9041867 9041869
9041873 9041887 9041889 9041917 9041933 9041941 9041947 9041951 9041953 9041971
9041993 9042029 9042037 9042053 9042067 9042107 9042109 9042127 9042179 9042221
9042223 9042239 9042251 9042307 9042331 9042337 9042349 9042353 9042391 9042401
9042409 9042413 9042433 9042443 9042491 9042493 9042503 9042511 9042529 9042533
9042547 9042557 9042563 9042569 9042619 9042637 9042641 9042647 9042707 9042713
9042739 9042743 9042757 9042769 9042779 9042797 9042829 9042877 9042881 9042889
9042907 9042931 9042949 9042953 9042977 9043003 9043007 9043009 9043033 9043037
9043039 9043049 9043079 9043081 9043087 9043093 9043109 9043121 9043123 9043127
9043159 9043169 9043171 9043187 9043211 9043241 9043261 9043267 9043271 9043291
9043361 9043381 9043387 9043409 9043421 9043427 9043451 9043471 9043477 9043481
9043499 9043513 9043547 9043553 9043571 9043591 9043607 9043613 9043649 9043681
9043687 9043691 9043703 9043721 9043733 9043789 9043817 9043819 9043823 9043849
9043871 9043877 9043883 9043891 9043919 9043927 9043939 9043963 9043967
9043987 9043997 9044003 9044011 9044023 9044029 9044047 9044053 9044059 9044099
9044107 9044111 9044117 9044137 9044159 9044177 9044179 9044197 9044227 9044237
9044249 9044251 9044279 9044303 9044309 9044339 9044363 9044369 9044401 9044417
9044461 9044471 9044479 9044509 9044521 9044537 9044557 9044573 9044579 9044597
9044599 9044647 9044669 9044671 9044677 9044683 9044699 9044701 9044719 9044729
9044767 9044771 9044801 9044807 9044831 9044837 9044843 9044863 9044879 9044891
9044939 9044941 9044951 9044977 9044989 9044993 9044999 9045011 9045017 9045053
9045061 9045073 9045079 9045089 9045107 9045119 9045137 9045143 9045161 9045163
9045191 9045193 9045199 9045209 9045217 9045229 9045247 9045251 9045277 9045299
9045313 9045307 9045317 9045367 9045383 9045389 9045391 9045409 9045431
9045473 9045493 9045497 9045551 9045557 9045559 9045571 9045587 9045599 9045607
9045611 9045637 9045643 9045677 9045679 9045689 9045697 9045713 9045719 9045727
9045733 9045749 9045779 9045809 9045811 9045823 9045837 9045851 9045857 9045859
9045901 9045913 9045917 9045931 9045937 9045947 9045977 9045979 9045983 9045991
9046001 9046021 9046031 9046067 9046069 9046073 9046097 9046111 9046151 9046157
9046189 9046207 9046217 9046243 9046249 9046277 9046283 9046307 9046309 9046313
9046319 9046339 9046391 9046393 9046399 9046403 9046409 9046447 9046449 9046459
9046487 9046523 9046547 9046571 9046589 9046621 9046627 9046633 9046643 9046649
9046651 9046693 9046711 9046721 9046733 9046757 9046777 9046781 9046789 9046819
9046837 9046841 9046861 9046871 9046879 9046897 9046903 9046909 9046913 9046949
9046951 9046967 9046979 9046987 9046997 9047011 9047023 9047029 9047039 9047041
9047053 9047057 9047063 9047089 9047113 9047123 9047149 9047161 9047167 9047201
9047209 9047219 9047221 9047231 9047273 9047279 9047293 9047299 9047309 9047321
9047323 9047341 9047387 9047393 9047399 9047413 9047447 9047503 9047509 9047513
9047527 9047537 9047543 9047557 9047569 9047603 9047611 9047627 9047639 9047659
9047677 9047707 9047719 9047729 9047741 9047749 9047761 9047821 9047833 9047837
9047849 9047851 9047873 9047879 9047897 9047903 9047907 9047911 9047917 9047953
9047957 9047959 9047963 9047999 9048031 9048037 9048043 9048049 9048077 9048157
9048163 9048197 9048209 9048217 9048253 9048289 9048329 9048337 9048343 9048349
9048379 9048443 9048469 9048491 9048509 9048511 9048521 9048527 9048583 9048593
9048601 9048631 9048643 9048647 9048659 9048661 9048673 9048703 9048763 9048773
9048797 9048803 9048829 9048833 9048881 9048887 9048889 9048911 9048917 9048929
9048937 9048943 9048973 9048983 9048989 9049003 9049013 9049031 9049037 9049109
9049121 9049133 9049147 9049177 9049193 9049199 9049211 9049231 9049237 9049259
9049277 9049283 9049291 9049351 9049357 9049409 9049433 9049441 9049463 9049471
9049483 9049493 9049517 9049519 9049531 9049541 9049543 9049549 9049553 9049583
9049619 9049631 9049633 9049657 9049669 9049699 9049717 9049727
9049753 9049783 9049801 9049811 9049829 9049837 9049841 9049847 9049849 9049877
9049913 9049939 9049961 9049969 9049973 9049987 9050039 9050051 9050077 9050087
9050123 9050183 9050189 9050191 9050203 9050207 9050219 9050239 9050267 9050287
9050297 9050303 9050317 9050323 9050329 9050347 9050359 9050369 9050383 9050413
9050419 9050449 9050473 9050491 9050497 9050501 9050519 9050521 9050527 9050539
9050557 9050563 9050599 9050609 9050653 9050663 9050687 9050731 9050747 9050827
9050831 9050843 9050861 9050869 9050879 9050911 9050939 9050947 9050957
9050981 9050989 9051017 9051019 9051047 9051059 9051061 9051071 9051079 9051137
9051139 9051221 9051253 9051257 9051269 9051313 9051323 9051337 9051359 9051373
9051379 9051403 9051407 9051433 9051437 9051481 9051487 9051523 9051563 9051587
9051593 9051613 9051617 9051697 9051737 9051751 9051761 9051787 9051827 9051841
9051859 9051863 9051881 9051883 9051919 9051929 9051947 9051967 9051983 9051989
9052009 9052033 9052039 9052049 9052051 9052061 9052067 9052081 9052117 9052129
9052139 9052159 9052181 9052207 9052223 9052237 9052243 9052249 9052259 9052301
9052319 9052333 9052343 9052367 9052369 9052387 9052391 9052411 9052423 9052427
9052441 9052451 9052469 9052487 9052499 9052507 9052541 9052577 9052579 9052591
9052609 9052613 9052627 9052649 9052663 9052691 9052697 9052699
9052733 9052739 9052751 9052787 9052801 9052819 9052829 9052853 9052859 9052871
9052907 9052909 9052937 9052943 9052951 9052969 9053003 9053021 9053029 9053041
9053047 9053111 9053117 9053119 9053141 9053153 9053159 9053171 9053179 9053201
9053227 9053243 9053257 9053267 9053269 9053273 9053287 9053293 9053309 9053311
9053323 9053331 9053381 9053411 9053413 9053459 9053461 9053483 9053501 9053531
9053543 9053587 9053593 9053599 9053663 9053683 9053699 9053711 9053731 9053749
9053753 9053761 9053773 9053791 9053797 9053813 9053819 9053827 9053851 9053857
9053873 9053893 9053897 9053909 9053917 9053921 9053929 9053959 9053969 9053983
9053987 9054007 9054029 9054049 9054053 9054091 9054103 9054109 9054137 9054167
9054181 9054191 9054197 9054223 9054259 9054277 9054281 9054329 9054359 9054371
9054377 9054389 9054391 9054401 9054403 9054407 9054439 9054443 9054473 9054499
9054533 9054569 9054607 9054629 9054631 9054649 9054653 9054667 9054673
9054707 9054713 9054763 9054769 9054781 9054797 9054839 9054911 9054919 9054937
9054959 9054961 9054971 9054977 9054979 9055003 9055019 9055021 9055027 9055037
9055043 9055049 9055061 9055063 9055087 9055091 9055099 9055129 9055133 9055141
9055147 9055157 9055159 9055171 9055181 9055183 9055187 9055201 9055213 9055223
```

```
9055231 9055247 9055259 9055283 9055297 9055309 9055313 9055331 9055391 9055429
9055439 9055463 9055477 9055507 9055523 9055561 9055567 9055589 9055591 9055601
9055663 9055667 9055681 9055687 9055699 9055729 9055759 9055763 9055769 9055771
9055777 9055811 9055831 9055873 9055889 9055901 9055903 9055927 9055931 9055939
9055993 9056023 9056041 9056051 9056081 9056093 9056107 9056119 9056129 9056137
9056143 9056153 9056167 9056171 9056183 9056191 9056197 9056209 9056221 9056233
9056237 9056279 9056297 9056303 9056317 9056321 9056329 9056339 9056363 9056387
9056389 9056401 9056413 9056417 9056419 9056429 9056431 9056447 9056471 9056473
9056479 9056507 9056573 9056581 9056623 9056627 9056629 9056633 9056651 9056653
9056657 9056669 9056683 9056713 9056717 9056737 9056783 9056819 9056843 9056909
9056953 9056959 9056969 9057001 9057017 9057049 9057067 9057079 9057109 9057121
9057143 9057151 9057161 9057163 9057197 9057199 9057227 9057247 9057289 9057299
9057313 9057337 9057343 9057359 9057371 9057397 9057401 9057403 9057407 9057427
9057431 9057439 9057449 9057467 9057491 9057493 9057497 9057533 9057539 9057553
9057557 9057571 9057577 9057589 9057593 9057667 9057689 9057701 9057703 9057709
9057731 9057743 9057749 9057779 9057799 9057817 9057833 9057847 9057869 9057899
9057901 9057943 9057949 9057959 9057973 9057977 9057979 9058001 9058013 9058033
9058057 9058087 9058099 9058111 9058139 9058141 9058163 9058187 9058201 9058241
9058243 9058249 9058267 9058271 9058277 9058279 9058363 9058367 9058381 9058383
9058397 9058409 9058463 9058471 9058523 9058531 9058549 9058559 9058591 9058613
9058631 9058667 9058669 9058691 9058729 9058741 9058771 9058811 9058823 9058831
9058837 9058843 9058859 9058879 9058891 9058901 9058957 9058963 9058979 9058981
9058999 9059021 9059027 9059053 9059059 9059087 9059093 9059101 9059123 9059153
9059173 9059177 9059179 9059207 9059209 9059251 9059269 9059279 9059287 9059299
9059311 9059329 9059341 9059353 9059357 9059359 9059363 9059381 9059383 9059389
9059417 9059437 9059443 9059461 9059467 9059489 9059497 9059503 9059551 9059563
9059573 9059581 9059587 9059621 9059639 9059643 9059683 9059689 9059693 9059699
9059711 9059717 9059731 9059737 9059747 9059749 9059761 9059779 9059819 9059851
9059867 9059887 9059891 9059903 9059909 9059923 9059951 9059959 9059969 9059989
9060013 9060041 9060043 9060047 9060061 9060067 9060071 9060089 9060109 9060113
9060173 9060179 9060193 9060203 9060223 9060253 9060257 9060281 9060299 9060319
9060323 9060349 9060377 9060379 9060409 9060419 9060461 9060481 9060497 9060503
9060547 9060553 9060559 9060563 9060581 9060593 9060607 9060617 9060619 9060629
9060647 9060661 9060683 9060691 9060697 9060703 9060743 9060749 9060761 9060791
9060803 9060809 9060817 9060829 9060841 9060851 9060869 9060871 9060899 9060907
9060911 9060943 9060971 9060991 9061009 9061033 9061097 9061099 9061109 9061111
9061121 9061133 9061141 9061163 9061181 9061223 9061229 9061237 9061249 9061259
9061267 9061307 9061313 9061319 9061321 9061343 9061363 9061387 9061421 9061441
9061447 9061453 9061457 9061469 9061483 9061513 9061523 9061531 9061571 9061573
9061589 9061621 9061627 9061667 9061669 9061673 9061693 9061699 9061711 9061721
9061739 9061763 9061767 9061771 9061783 9061807 9061847 9061859 9061907 9061919
9061939 9061957 9061973 9061981 9061991 9061999 9062017 9062029 9062033 9062057
9062059 9062089 9062093 9062101 9062111 9062113 9062129 9062143 9062153 9062159
9062177 9062203 9062231 9062243 9062279 9062281 9062303 9062321 9062351 9062359
9062393 9062401 9062407 9062423 9062429 9062441 9062453 9062477 9062491 9062503
9062507 9062519 9062527 9062539 9062597 9062617 9062623 9062663 9062689 9062699
9062719 9062737 9062741 9062777 9062789 9062797 9062803 9062821 9062839 9062843
9062861 9062863 9062903 9062909 9062917 9062957 9062969 9062983 9063013 9063029
9063037 9063059 9063077 9063097 9063107 9063121 9063149 9063161 9063179 9063197
9063211 9063233 9063269 9063277 9063281 9063317 9063331 9063349 9063367 9063401
9063407 9063413 9063421 9063427 9063443 9063451 9063463 9063487 9063491 9063529
9063547 9063553 9063569 9063581 9063599 9063611 9063623 9063661 9063667 9063697
9063701 9063707 9063713 9063731 9063739 9063751 9063781 9063787 9063793 9063797
9063833 9063851 9063869 9063871 9063877 9063881 9063889 9063913 9063917 9063919
9063949 9063953 9063959 9063973 9063991 9064019 9064031 9064039 9064063 9064079
9064087 9064109 9064129 9064161 9064163 9064169 9064177 9064193 9064199 9064241
9064301 9064303 9064313 9064343 9064411 9064421 9064423 9064427 9064439 9064441
9064457 9064459 9064469 9064481 9064571 9064579 9064589 9064591 9064597 9064603
9064613 9064633 9064639 9064651 9064663 9064673 9064751 9064753 9064801 9064817
9064823 9064837 9064841 9064871 9064877 9064897 9064901 9064903 9064943 9064949
9064969 9064981 9064987 9064997 9064999 9065003 9065009 9065057 9065083 9065093
9065099 9065101 9065107 9065123 9065129 9065137 9065143 9065179 9065207 9065239
9065257 9065263 9065269 9065293 9065297 9065317 9065327 9065363 9065367 9065383
9065401 9065411 9065417 9065443 9065449 9065461 9065467 9065477 9065479 9065503
9065513 9065521 9065531 9065533 9065543 9065591 9065627 9065653 9065669 9065677
9065681 9065687 9065723 9065729 9065737 9065753 9065801 9065809 9065867 9065891
9065899 9065923 9065939 9065963 9066011 9066019 9066041 9066047 9066091 9066131
9066133 9066139 9066143 9066181 9066193 9066199 9066251 9066257 9066269 9066271
9066307 9066313 9066319 9066359 9066361 9066367 9066383 9066391 9066397 9066413
9066433 9066437 9066451 9066469 9066481 9066503 9066557 9066569 9066571 9066581
9066599 9066637 9066661 9066669 9066653 9066677 9066683 9066691 9066709 9066713
9066719 9066721 9066727 9066731 9066737 9066749 9066767 9066779 9066803 9066809
9066877 9066901 9066909 9066983 9067013 9067021 9067031 9067049 9067057 9067087
9067117 9067127 9067133 9067141 9067147 9067153 9067189 9067207 9067211 9067213
9067229 9067241 9067243 9067249 9067259 9067277 9067321 9067361 9067393 9067397
9067417 9067423 9067439 9067441 9067447 9067483 9067489 9067507 9067523 9067529
9067547 9067561 9067567 9067571 9067573 9067607 9067609 9067621 9067631 9067637
9067649 9067687 9067697 9067733 9067741 9067751 9067759 9067777 9067781 9067817
9067829 9067831 9067837 9067843 9067873 9067879 9067889 9067897 9067901 9067909
9067913 9067937 9067963 9068009 9068023 9068039 9068041 9068047 9068053 9068069
9068099 9068117 9068119 9068131 9068159 9068161 9068177 9068183 9068207 9068209
9068209 9068237 9068273 9068287 9068309 9068317 9068347 9068351 9068393 9068401
9068413 9068471 9068483 9068513 9068519 9068533 9068563 9068569 9068585 9068571
9068581 9068597 9068611 9068623 9068639 9068659 9068669 9068711 9068753 9068767
9068827 9068849 9068861 9068867 9068879 9068887 9068903 9068907 9068983 9068989
9068921 9068929 9068933 9068971 9068977 9068981 9068987 9068993 9069013 9069017
9069037 9069097 9069101 9069103 9069113 9069131 9069133 9069139 9069149 9069163
9069169 9069191 9069217 9069227 9069233 9069239 9069287 9069299 9069311 9069317
9069341 9069349 9069353 9069371 9069377 9069397 9069407 9069433 9069439 9069443
```

```
9069461  9069503  9069583  9069623  9069647  9069661  9069667  9069673  9069677  9069703
9069713  9069727  9069761  9069793  9069799  9069829  9069829  9069833  9069839  9069869
9069877  9069883  9069913  9069917  9069923  9069941  9069961  9069967  9069971  9069989
9070001  9070007  9070043  9070057  9070063  9070067  9070097  9070123  9070133  9070153
9070169  9070223  9070253  9070279  9070297  9070319  9070331  9070337  9070339  9070351
9070357  9070363  9070381  9070403  9070409  9070423  9070447  9070459  9070499  9070519
9070547  9070559  9070573  9070583  9070597  9070609  9070627  9070637  9070643  9070667
9070669  9070681  9070687  9070697  9070727  9070729  9070739  9070751  9070753  9070759
9070769  9070777  9070783  9070793  9070813  9070819  9070829  9070861  9070891  9070913
9070933  9070951  9070973  9070981  9071009  9071071  9071077  9071099  9071119  9071129
9071137  9071143  9071201  9071203  9071207  9071213  9071219  9071221  9071233  9071263
9071267  9071347  9071351  9071369  9071383  9071393  9071399  9071429  9071431  9071441
9071443  9071459  9071467  9071471  9071479  9071497  9071501  9071507  9071521  9071551
9071563  9071593  9071597  9071603  9071609  9071633  9071677  9071687  9071707  9071767
9071773  9071779  9071791  9071801  9071819  9071827  9071831  9071833  9071837  9071849
9071861  9071879  9071903  9071917  9071939  9071969  9071971  9071977  9071989  9072031
9072043  9072059  9072071  9072079  9072083  9072109  9072127  9072191  9072199  9072227
9072229  9072247  9072299  9072311  9072317  9072337  9072359  9072361  9072383  9072421
9072433  9072449  9072463  9072467  9072473  9072517  9072523  9072541  9072587  9072589
9072601  9072629  9072631  9072643  9072653  9072673  9072689  9072727  9072731  9072757
9072761  9072769  9072793  9072797  9072799  9072827  9072859  9072893  9072901  9072919
9072923  9072949  9072967  9072983  9072989  9072991  9072997  9073003  9073033  9073039
9073067  9073091  9073093  9073117  9073147  9073153  9073193  9073199  9073213  9073217
9073219  9073231  9073249  9073289  9073307  9073313  9073319  9073321  9073327  9073357
9073367  9073369  9073381  9073429  9073451  9073457  9073459  9073489  9073499  9073511
9073517  9073531  9073553  9073573  9073577  9073591  9073601  9073619  9073637  9073657
9073663  9073703  9073709  9073747  9073777  9073783  9073789  9073819  9073853  9073873
9073879  9073913  9073919  9073927  9073931  9073957  9073993  9074003  9074027  9074033
9074053  9074057  9074069  9074081  9074083  9074089  9074111  9074123  9074147  9074189
9074207  9074231  9074269  9074291  9074309  9074321  9074323  9074327  9074339  9074341
9074347  9074357  9074363  9074371  9074389  9074393  9074423  9074437  9074441  9074459
9074467  9074519  9074521  9074561  9074567  9074579  9074603  9074621  9074633  9074683
9074687  9074693  9074701  9074711  9074771  9074783  9074789  9074803  9074827  9074839
9074843  9074851  9074861  9074867  9074873  9074881  9074887  9074911  9074929  9074959
9074987  9074993  9075019  9075037  9075043  9075049  9075097  9075119  9075163  9075191
9075197  9075259  9075307  9075329  9075359  9075361  9075373  9075377  9075379  9075383
9075403  9075421  9075427  9075461  9075491  9075503  9075511  9075523  9075533  9075541
9075551  9075571  9075581  9075587  9075601  9075617  9075679  9075683  9075697  9075713
9075733  9075761  9075769  9075779  9075797  9075799  9075809  9075827  9075851  9075853
9075889  9075907  9075917  9075931  9075971  9075973  9075991  9076009  9076033  9076117
9076121  9076127  9076153  9076183  9076187  9076201  9076213  9076229  9076241  9076247
9076253  9076259  9076271  9076279  9076297  9076307  9076343  9076367  9076399
9076451  9076481  9076517  9076519  9076531  9076541  9076549  9076579  9076609  9076637
9076643  9076663  9076667  9076673  9076693  9076709  9076723  9076733  9076777  9076799
9076801  9076811  9076819  9076829  9076841  9076849  9076871  9076883  9076897  9076901
9076909  9076933  9076961  9076967  9076993  9077023  9077027  9077059  9077063  9077119
9077149  9077153  9077161  9077183  9077191  9077197  9077207  9077213  9077219  9077221
9077239  9077267  9077273  9077281  9077293  9077297  9077311  9077323  9077329  9077333
9077347  9077351  9077381  9077399  9077401  9077407  9077413  9077417  9077423  9077489
9077491  9077501  9077521  9077531  9077539  9077557  9077561  9077581  9077587  9077591
9077597  9077599  9077639  9077647  9077669  9077689  9077713  9077723  9077729  9077737
9077741  9077749  9077759  9077767  9077771  9077777  9077807  9077819  9077821  9077843
9077857  9077863  9077869  9077891  9077903  9077923  9077927  9077963  9077977  9077993
9078037  9078053  9078059  9078109  9078137  9078149  9078151  9078161  9078217  9078227
9078233  9078241  9078253  9078259  9078263  9078281  9078301  9078313  9078367  9078397
9078403  9078413  9078439  9078449  9078451  9078463  9078467  9078469  9078539  9078541
9078577  9078581  9078607  9078613  9078617  9078631  9078673  9078679  9078683  9078709
9078733  9078737  9078739  9078749  9078761  9078781  9078821  9078851  9078857  9078863
9078869  9078887  9078919  9078929  9078931  9078961  9078973  9079013  9079027  9079051
9079061  9079067  9079069  9079073  9079079  9079087  9079099  9079111  9079151  9079183
9079199  9079223  9079243  9079253  9079277  9079303  9079331  9079337  9079339  9079361
9079379  9079381  9079387  9079429  9079463  9079481  9079487  9079517  9079529  9079531
9079537  9079571  9079607  9079627  9079643  9079669  9079673  9079723  9079727  9079757
9079769  9079771  9079793  9079823  9079841  9079861  9079867  9079901  9079909  9079969
9079979  9079997  9080021  9080039  9080069  9080077  9080087  9080089  9080107  9080129
9080131  9080143  9080153  9080167  9080173  9080177  9080189  9080213  9080231  9080237
9080257  9080263  9080273  9080293  9080299  9080333  9080371  9080381  9080387  9080413
9080417  9080441  9080459  9080471  9080473  9080479  9080501  9080531  9080563  9080573
9080579  9080587  9080593  9080623  9080629  9080641  9080657  9080663  9080677  9080693
9080707  9080717  9080719  9080777  9080779  9080801  9080821  9080831  9080833  9080927
9080963  9080969  9080977  9081001  9081071  9081091  9081101  9081119  9081133  9081143
9081151  9081161  9081173  9081181  9081203  9081211  9081223  9081227  9081257  9081269
9081277  9081307  9081321  9081323  9081341  9081353  9081409  9081421  9081427  9081433
9081461  9081463  9081467  9081469  9081473  9081491  9081509  9081517  9081533  9081547
9081559  9081577  9081599  9081607  9081637  9081659  9081661  9081703  9081707  9081713
9081739  9081769  9081773  9081781  9081797  9081799  9081817  9081833  9081847  9081881
9081883  9081887  9081889  9081931  9081949  9081967  9081971  9081973  9081991  9082049
9082061  9082067  9082069  9082081  9082091  9082093  9082103  9082111  9082127  9082153
9082187  9082189  9082193  9082211  9082219  9082243  9082253  9082259  9082261  9082273
9082277  9082289  9082303  9082313  9082363  9082379  9082397  9082429  9082433  9082439
9082457  9082459  9082483  9082511  9082529  9082531  9082537  9082543  9082547  9082561
9082571  9082583  9082613  9082657  9082669  9082679  9082681  9082687  9082691  9082693
9082727  9082729  9082747  9082751  9082757  9082761  9082781  9082793  9082813  9082823
9082831  9082841  9082859  9082877  9082889  9082901  9082903  9082919  9082943  9082949
9082967  9082979  9082993  9083021  9083023  9083027  9083029  9083033  9083047  9083057
9083069  9083077  9083121  9083131  9083141  9083143  9083149  9083153  9083201  9083203
9083281  9083303  9083357  9083359  9083369  9083381  9083383  9083401  9083407  9083411
9083441  9083443  9083453  9083461  9083471  9083479  9083513  9083519  9083521  9083533
9083561  9083563  9083579  9083587  9083629  9083639  9083647  9083663  9083681  9083717
```

```
9083741  9083747  9083771  9083779  9083783  9083791  9083801  9083803  9083807  9083813
9083821  9083849  9083857  9083891  9083897  9083909  9083911  9083939  9083959  9083969
9083983  9083993  9084007  9084037  9084043  9084073  9084077  9084079  9084107  9084133
9084139  9084143  9084161  9084211  9084217  9084233  9084281  9084323  9084331  9084343
9084347  9084349  9084373  9084391  9084401  9084419  9084431  9084431  9084461  9084469
9084473  9084503  9084529  9084539  9084557  9084587  9084589  9084611  9084619  9084637
9084667  9084671  9084689  9084697  9084707  9084709  9084727  9084781  9084799  9084811
9084833  9084857  9084863  9084871  9084877  9084899  9084941  9084961  9084989  9084991
9085001  9085007  9085019  9085039  9085073  9085081  9085099  9085103  9085121  9085127
9085129  9085151  9085163  9085171  9085229  9085241  9085261  9085277  9085283  9085289
9085291  9085309  9085337  9085339  9085357  9085397  9085399  9085409  9085423  9085471
9085481  9085493  9085499  9085543  9085547  9085561  9085567  9085577  9085603  9085607
9085627  9085649  9085651  9085663  9085673  9085693  9085717  9085751  9085763  9085777
9085793  9085829  9085841  9085847  9085851  9085919  9085957  9085963  9085981  9085987
9086039  9086057  9086101  9086107  9086113  9086117  9086149  9086167  9086179  9086191
9086197  9086213  9086227  9086239  9086243  9086261  9086269  9086299  9086321  9086327
9086353  9086401  9086411  9086417  9086437  9086447  9086453  9086471  9086477  9086489
9086507  9086513  9086521  9086533  9086537  9086563  9086593  9086611  9086629  9086639
9086647  9086663  9086677  9086681  9086683  9086699  9086711  9086713  9086729  9086747
9086783  9086801  9086827  9086837  9086843  9086849  9086851  9086873  9086879  9086881
9086887  9086897  9086927  9086929  9086963  9086981  9086983  9087017  9087049  9087053
9087079  9087083  9087097  9087103  9087107  9087119  9087131  9087157  9087161  9087181
9087191  9087193  9087203  9087217  9087223  9087227  9087229  9087241  9087257  9087269
9087307  9087313  9087343  9087359  9087373  9087389  9087391  9087409  9087427  9087431
9087437  9087451  9087479  9087493  9087509  9087511  9087541  9087563  9087581  9087629
9087641  9087647  9087667  9087671  9087703  9087713  9087761  9087763  9087769  9087781
9087797  9087811  9087839  9087847  9087853  9087893  9087899  9087901  9087913  9087917
9087931  9087941  9087943  9087961  9088031  9088033  9088039  9088087  9088091  9088097
9088103  9088139  9088141  9088147  9088153  9088159  9088181  9088193  9088229  9088231
9088241  9088271  9088279  9088307  9088333  9088337  9088357  9088369  9088379  9088423
9088433  9088447  9088481  9088507  9088543  9088559  9088561  9088577  9088579  9088589
9088603  9088613  9088619  9088621  9088633  9088679  9088697  9088699  9088711  9088733
9088741  9088759  9088763  9088771  9088787  9088789  9088801  9088831  9088837  9088843
9088847  9088873  9088883  9088903  9088909  9088913  9088943  9088957  9088967  9088987
9088993  9089021  9089051  9089053  9089057  9089077  9089123  9089131  9089137  9089141
9089147  9089159  9089177  9089219  9089229  9089243  9089251  9089261  9089279  9089281
9089317  9089321  9089323  9089357  9089371  9089387  9089389  9089419  9089461  9089473
9089477  9089497  9089501  9089513  9089527  9089533  9089551  9089567  9089569  9089573
9089609  9089623  9089629  9089651  9089653  9089687  9089693  9089699  9089701  9089711
9089719  9089737  9089767  9089783  9089791  9089803  9089831  9089863  9089879  9089891
9089893  9089903  9089913  9089921  9089929  9089947  9089981  9089989  9090007  9090013
9090017  9090023  9090041  9090061  9090127  9090131  9090139  9090173  9090181  9090203
9090217  9090229  9090241  9090247  9090251  9090259  9090331  9090353  9090377  9090391
9090407  9090437  9090449  9090463  9090503  9090509  9090517  9090527  9090539  9090547
9090551  9090583  9090611  9090623  9090629  9090649  9090671  9090689  9090691  9090701
9090703  9090749  9090751  9090793  9090811  9090821  9090847  9090853  9090857
9090859  9090871  9090901  9090919  9090947  9090953  9090973  9090989  9091009  9091021
9091051  9091057  9091067  9091079  9091099  9091109  9091127  9091151  9091157  9091207
9091213  9091219  9091223  9091259  9091267  9091273  9091289  9091331  9091333  9091343
9091373  9091387  9091391  9091429  9091441  9091451  9091477  9091483  9091513  9091541
9091543  9091553  9091561  9091591  9091597  9091609  9091613  9091631  9091637  9091657
9091679  9091729  9091741  9091759  9091769  9091777  9091783  9091807  9091813  9091829
9091843  9091871  9091879  9091891  9091909  9091921  9091939  9091961  9091997  9092003
9092011  9092053  9092063  9092071  9092081  9092087  9092113  9092117  9092131  9092137
9092143  9092177  9092179  9092183  9092191  9092219  9092227  9092231  9092257  9092261
9092299  9092333  9092353  9092359  9092371  9092381  9092387  9092437  9092449  9092471
9092527  9092533  9092543  9092557  9092561  9092563  9092581  9092591  9092593  9092617
9092647  9092653  9092711  9092717  9092723  9092789  9092791  9092833  9092851  9092873
9092891  9092893  9092911  9092933  9092947  9092971  9092987  9092989  9092999  9093017
9093061  9093089  9093109  9093121  9093127  9093143  9093151  9093163  9093169  9093197
9093239  9093251  9093289  9093299  9093311  9093313  9093353  9093373  9093389  9093407
9093421  9093437  9093439  9093463  9093473  9093481  9093503  9093523  9093529  9093547
9093551  9093583  9093587  9093593  9093599  9093629  9093631  9093641  9093659  9093661
9093713  9093719  9093727  9093739  9093787  9093803  9093817  9093839  9093853  9093857
9093869  9093871  9093919  9093937  9093961  9093991  9094009  9094049  9094069  9094093
9094123  9094153  9094159  9094181  9094207  9094213  9094219  9094229  9094237  9094247
9094289  9094291  9094297  9094321  9094357  9094363  9094373  9094387  9094399  9094403
9094409  9094417  9094441  9094469  9094493  9094511  9094517  9094529  9094537  9094549
9094571  9094583  9094601  9094607  9094639  9094649  9094663  9094669  9094691  9094693
9094697  9094703  9094721  9094727  9094753  9094759  9094769  9094807  9094819  9094823
9094831  9094837  9094843  9094849  9094861  9094871  9094903  9094913  9094919  9094927
9094957  9094961  9094979  9094991  9094993  9095041  9095077  9095087  9095089  9095113
9095117  9095123  9095131  9095137  9095147  9095179  9095201  9095213  9095267  9095269
9095279  9095297  9095309  9095311  9095347  9095351  9095363  9095371  9095417  9095423
9095441  9095447  9095453  9095477  9095479  9095491  9095503  9095519  9095521  9095543
9095551  9095579  9095591  9095609  9095627  9095657  9095659  9095683  9095729  9095773
9095777  9095791  9095819  9095831  9095837  9095843  9095857  9095899  9095909  9095917
9095923  9095929  9095939  9096011  9096013  9096029  9096047  9096049  9096077  9096083
9096097  9096107  9096127  9096149  9096151  9096163  9096181  9096203  9096209
9096221  9096229  9096253  9096257  9096277  9096281  9096289  9096313  9096341
9096359  9096397  9096407  9096419  9096433  9096481  9096499  9096511  9096533  9096559
9096583  9096587  9096589  9096623  9096631  9096643  9096667  9096677  9096697  9096713
9096721  9096727  9096743  9096781  9096811  9096817  9096821  9096823  9096827  9096883
9096881  9096889  9096911  9096917  9096947  9096977  9096979  9097003  9097009  9097021
9097069  9097073  9097093  9097111  9097129  9097141  9097147  9097169  9097177  9097183
9097201  9097223  9097267  9097279  9097303  9097307  9097349  9097369  9097427  9097453
9097457  9097469  9097537  9097573  9097577  9097579  9097589  9097591  9097633  9097651
9097667  9097691  9097709  9097717  9097721  9097733  9097757  9097769  9097799  9097813
9097817  9097831  9097841  9097853  9097861  9097867  9097871  9097883  9097919  9097939
```

```
9097961  9097981  9097987  9097999  9098003  9098029  9098059  9098071  9098099  9098101
9098107  9098113  9098129  9098143  9098147  9098161  9098183  9098191  9098233  9098237
9098261  9098293  9098303  9098311  9098347  9098357  9098393  9098423  9098447  9098459
9098461  9098471  9098477  9098513  9098521  9098527  9098569  9098591  9098603  9098627
9098657  9098659  9098693  9098741  9098743  9098753  9098773  9098783  9098809  9098827
9098833  9098861  9098897  9098911  9098923  9098941  9098963  9098977  9098981  9099017
9099037  9099047  9099067  9099113  9099121  9099133  9099137  9099161  9099179  9099193
9099197  9099217  9099227  9099229  9099257  9099263  9099269  9099287  9099317  9099323
9099331  9099353  9099361  9099379  9099383  9099397  9099401  9099427  9099439  9099443
9099451  9099469  9099479  9099487  9099491  9099527  9099547  9099583  9099589  9099593
9099611  9099659  9099661  9099683  9099691  9099719  9099721  9099731  9099737  9099751
9099763  9099767  9099791  9099793  9099799  9099809  9099821  9099829  9099847  9099863
9099869  9099887  9099889  9099899  9099901  9099907  9099929  9099943  9099949  9099953
9099967  9099989  9100009  9100033  9100051  9100061  9100067  9100079  9100099  9100103
9100109  9100121  9100129  9100159  9100193  9100211  9100271  9100279  9100303  9100309
9100313  9100327  9100349  9100367  9100381  9100417  9100447  9100459  9100489  9100501
9100513  9100523  9100537  9100541  9100547  9100561  9100583  9100591  9100603  9100613
9100621  9100669  9100673  9100687  9100697  9100699  9100703  9100711  9100717  9100727
9100733  9100739  9100787  9100813  9100843  9100849  9100859  9100877  9100891  9100901
9100919  9100937  9100951  9100961  9100969  9100991  9101003  9101023  9101039  9101087
9101089  9101093  9101117  9101119  9101143  9101153  9101159  9101167  9101177  9101189
9101207  9101231  9101237  9101249  9101263  9101269  9101293  9101317  9101327  9101329
9101377  9101381  9101401  9101441  9101453  9101461  9101471  9101473  9101489  9101539
9101623  9101633  9101639  9101657  9101671  9101689  9101699  9101707  9101711  9101717
9101731  9101747  9101759  9101777  9101789  9101791  9101797  9101803  9101819  9101831
9101839  9101843  9101857  9101861  9101867  9101881  9101887  9101891  9101899  9101903
9101909  9101921  9101923  9101929  9101933  9101977  9101999  9102047  9102053  9102091
9102097  9102101  9102109  9102131  9102139  9102179  9102187  9102193  9102199  9102209
9102229  9102241  9102277  9102307  9102323  9102337  9102341  9102367  9102377  9102397
9102403  9102421  9102439  9102449  9102523  9102529  9102547  9102557  9102571  9102581
9102593  9102647  9102661  9102673  9102677  9102689  9102719  9102739  9102749  9102757
9102763  9102773  9102787  9102817  9102829  9102883  9102887  9102889  9102893  9102901
9102911  9102923  9102937  9102949  9102953  9102991  9102997  9103019  9103021  9103049
9103063  9103067  9103069  9103079  9103093  9103099  9103111  9103117  9103139  9103141
9103153  9103183  9103247  9103253  9103267  9103273  9103277  9103291  9103301  9103307
9103309  9103327  9103343  9103349  9103351  9103379  9103397  9103399  9103417  9103421
9103441  9103447  9103459  9103463  9103481  9103499  9103531  9103537  9103541  9103609
9103649  9103657  9103669  9103673  9103693  9103697  9103747  9103753  9103769  9103771
9103777  9103799  9103807  9103817  9103819  9103841  9103847  9103859  9103867  9103873
9103901  9103909  9103921  9103943  9103949  9103951  9103973  9103981  9104033  9104047
9104063  9104087  9104101  9104111  9104143  9104153  9104167  9104177  9104203  9104209
9104213  9104219  9104233  9104267  9104279  9104281  9104321  9104327  9104351  9104357
9104371  9104383  9104399  9104411  9104413  9104423  9104437  9104453  9104461  9104507
9104509  9104531  9104539  9104551  9104561  9104567  9104581  9104597  9104617  9104621
9104647  9104651  9104657  9104659  9104687  9104723  9104759  9104773  9104783  9104791
9104801  9104807  9104833  9104873  9104881  9104897  9104899  9104947  9104983  9104989
9105001  9105023  9105053  9105077  9105113  9105119  9105133  9105137  9105139  9105179
9105181  9105203  9105209  9105223  9105247  9105277  9105281  9105301  9105337  9105361
9105377  9105419  9105433  9105457  9105463  9105469  9105491  9105511  9105521  9105553
9105583  9105611  9105641  9105671  9105683  9105689  9105709  9105713  9105721  9105743
9105749  9105779  9105787  9105791  9105793  9105823  9105839  9105841  9105851  9105853
9105881  9105893  9105911  9105917  9105937  9105949  9105973  9106003  9106007  9106039
9106043  9106061  9106063  9106079  9106081  9106099  9106103  9106117  9106121  9106151
9106159  9106189  9106193  9106199  9106211  9106217  9106231  9106241  9106283  9106289
9106313  9106337  9106351  9106381  9106397  9106399  9106417  9106429  9106481  9106499
9106501  9106523  9106553  9106561  9106589  9106607  9106613  9106621  9106627  9106633
9106649  9106661  9106693  9106717  9106723  9106729  9106739  9106759  9106763  9106771
9106787  9106793  9106807  9106813  9106817  9106819  9106859  9106891  9106907  9106931
9106939  9106943  9106949  9106997  9107027  9107051  9107081  9107083  9107089  9107107
9107123  9107159  9107167  9107173  9107177  9107179  9107191  9107209  9107221  9107269
9107279  9107303  9107317  9107321  9107323  9107369  9107381  9107389  9107401  9107411
9107429  9107447  9107489  9107503  9107509  9107531  9107591  9107599  9107603  9107611
9107627  9107629  9107639  9107647  9107663  9107671  9107689  9107717  9107719  9107723
9107729  9107731  9107741  9107743  9107773  9107797  9107807  9107837  9107843  9107881
9107899  9107909  9107941  9107999  9108061  9108067  9108091  9108133  9108157  9108167
9108193  9108199  9108227  9108241  9108263  9108269  9108293  9108331  9108419  9108427
9108431  9108433  9108439  9108443  9108457  9108461  9108469  9108487  9108493  9108497
9108499  9108509  9108511  9108521  9108557  9108559  9108563  9108569  9108587  9108607
9108629  9108677  9108679  9108691  9108709  9108727  9108731  9108751  9108763  9108767
9108769  9108791  9108797  9108859  9108877  9108893  9108901  9108917  9108941  9108973
9108977  9109019  9109027  9109031  9109039  9109049  9109059  9109129  9109153  9109157
9109169  9109181  9109183  9109201  9109207  9109223  9109259  9109271  9109279  9109301
9109351  9109361  9109369  9109427  9109439  9109459  9109469  9109483  9109519  9109537
9109547  9109553  9109571  9109577  9109579  9109591  9109613  9109619  9109627  9109649
9109651  9109687  9109697  9109703  9109717  9109729  9109757  9109781  9109783  9109811
9109813  9109843  9109883  9109927  9109957  9109967  9109979  9109993  9109999  9110039
9110051  9110071  9110119  9110141  9110161  9110183  9110197  9110203  9110221  9110237
9110267  9110279  9110287  9110293  9110303  9110357  9110371  9110417  9110429  9110447
9110467  9110471  9110483  9110489  9110501  9110513  9110551  9110561  9110573  9110579
9110581  9110597  9110609  9110617  9110627  9110639  9110641  9110677  9110681  9110687
9110693  9110707  9110713  9110719  9110723  9110741  9110771  9110779  9110813  9110819
9110821  9110831  9110837  9110873  9110923  9110939  9110953  9110971  9110977  9110987
9110989  9111001  9111007  9111023  9111079  9111083  9111101  9111103  9111329  9111161
9111163  9111173  9111199  9111229  9111233  9111247  9111253  9111257  9111281  9111329
9111331  9111341  9111463  9111457  9111461  9111463  9111497  9111503  9111511  9111517
9111521  9111523  9111527  9111533  9111559  9111563  9111581  9111587  9111593  9111629
9111649  9111667  9111673  9111691  9111709  9111719  9111727  9111757  9111803  9111821
9111827  9111853  9111857  9111859  9111871  9111877  9111899  9111911  9111929  9111959
9111961  9112043  9112049  9112091  9112121  9112133  9112141  9112157  9112193  9112223
```

9112231 9112247 9112261 9112283 9112309 9112319 9112331 9112333 9112339 9112349
9112361 9112387 9112399 9112403 9112427 9112463 9112483 9112489 9112507 9112511
9112529 9112541 9112559 9112591 9112613 9112639 9112643 9112651 9112657 9112679
9112709 9112717 9112721 9112759 9112769 9112771 9112781 9112787 9112793 9112823
9112843 9112849 9112889 9112919 9112949 9112993 9112997 9113011 9113017
9113051 9113059 9113087 9113089 9113107 9113113 9113147 9113161 9113171 9113189
9113227 9113243 9113249 9113263 9113323 9113383 9113399 9113413 9113431 9113501
9113551 9113557 9113561 9113591 9113593 9113609 9113617 9113633 9113639 9113719
9113737 9113759 9113771 9113779 9113791 9113833 9113837 9113843 9113851
9113861 9113869 9113873 9113879 9113891 9113899 9113903 9113927 9113941 9113959
9113963 9113983 9113987 9113999 9114011 9114029 9114041 9114047 9114059 9114073
9114101 9114103 9114109 9114121 9114137 9114163 9114197 9114221 9114239 9114257
9114263 9114271 9114283 9114293 9114311 9114317 9114331 9114337 9114353 9114377
9114383 9114421 9114449 9114461 9114481 9114487 9114491 9114503 9114517 9114541
9114551 9114577 9114583 9114593 9114607 9114619 9114631 9114641 9114643 9114673
9114683 9114709 9114719 9114773 9114793 9114817 9114841 9114857 9114893 9114901
9114929 9114943 9114953 9114967 9114971 9114991 9115013 9115033 9115049 9115069
9115091 9115109 9115121 9115129 9115151 9115159 9115177 9115181 9115189 9115201
9115207 9115229 9115237 9115241 9115259 9115261 9115273 9115277 9115279 9115297
9115303 9115331 9115339 9115399 9115427 9115439 9115471 9115501 9115507 9115511
9115529 9115537 9115549 9115633 9115637 9115663 9115669 9115693 9115709 9115739
9115741 9115753 9115789 9115861 9115879 9115907 9115919 9115943 9115993 9115999
9116033 9116039 9116059 9116083 9116089 9116099 9116111 9116113 9116147 9116161
9116197 9116203 9116207 9116213 9116243 9116249 9116269 9116273 9116281 9116287
9116299 9116339 9116357 9116381 9116383 9116399 9116407 9116417 9116423 9116461
9116491 9116531 9116557 9116587 9116609 9116617 9116629 9116663 9116707 9116729
9116747 9116749 9116761 9116773 9116813 9116819 9116831 9116843 9116851 9116867
9116873 9116881 9116917 9116923 9116929 9116951 9116957 9116959 9116971 9116977
9116983 9117011 9117029 9117037 9117041 9117061 9117067 9117077 9117109 9117137
9117139 9117187 9117191 9117209 9117221 9117257 9117263 9117289 9117299 9117331
9117337 9117341 9117343 9117391 9117401 9117403 9117443 9117463 9117497 9117509
9117517 9117527 9117529 9117551 9117553 9117557 9117569 9117599 9117601 9117613
9117649 9117653 9117659 9117673 9117679 9117697 9117707 9117721 9117727 9117733
9117737 9117743 9117769 9117781 9117809 9117811 9117827 9117841 9117847 9117851
9117863 9117877 9117883 9117887 9117893 9117917 9117923 9117931 9117971 9117973
9118019 9118027 9118049 9118063 9118091 9118111 9118117 9118127 9118129 9118133
9118147 9118163 9118181 9118183 9118223 9118253 9118283 9118301 9118303 9118313
9118321 9118349 9118387 9118397 9118411 9118427 9118481 9118493 9118541 9118553
9118559 9118573 9118589 9118607 9118609 9118621 9118631 9118691 9118699 9118721
9118751 9118757 9118763 9118771 9118793 9118807 9118819 9118853 9118859 9118871
9118877 9118887 9118903 9118927 9118931 9118979 9118997 9119023 9119051 9119059
9119093 9119101 9119113 9119129 9119147 9119153 9119161 9119167 9119171 9119197
9119203 9119219 9119249 9119251 9119263 9119273 9119287 9119333 9119351 9119359
9119377 9119389 9119399 9119401 9119417 9119419 9119471 9119479 9119491 9119519
9119521 9119533 9119567 9119587 9119597 9119603 9119609 9119623 9119629 9119641
9119647 9119653 9119699 9119713 9119729 9119731 9119749 9119767 9119779 9119783
9119801 9119809 9119813 9119819 9119849 9119861 9119863 9119897 9119899 9119909
9119933 9119941 9119951 9119977 9119987 9119989 9120011 9120017 9120073 9120077
9120079 9120091 9120101 9120103 9120119 9120127 9120149 9120151 9120193 9120197
9120203 9120217 9120233 9120253 9120263 9120269 9120271 9120277 9120283 9120301
9120311 9120329 9120337 9120367 9120403 9120421 9120427 9120473 9120487 9120493
9120497 9120511 9120521 9120533 9120563 9120571 9120599 9120607 9120623 9120641
9120647 9120649 9120667 9120677 9120691 9120701 9120739 9120743 9120757 9120791
9120799 9120803 9120821 9120829 9120871 9120887 9120889 9120941 9120967 9120971
9120989 9120997 9121003 9121009 9121019 9121033 9121043 9121067 9121081 9121097
9121153 9121171 9121183 9121193 9121199 9121207 9121213 9121241 9121249 9121279
9121291 9121327 9121331 9121339 9121361 9121379 9121397 9121403 9121433 9121439
9121493 9121523 9121529 9121559 9121561 9121601 9121621 9121627 9121649 9121663
9121667 9121681 9121687 9121703 9121727 9121733 9121751 9121753 9121769 9121787
9121799 9121829 9121837 9121841 9121859 9121897 9121909 9121951 9121963 9121993
9121999 9122021 9122023 9122027 9122039 9122077 9122083 9122137 9122143 9122159
9122161 9122207 9122231 9122257 9122263 9122279 9122287 9122291 9122297 9122341
9122381 9122383 9122389 9122417 9122429 9122453 9122471 9122473 9122483 9122497
9122507 9122543 9122551 9122569 9122593 9122599 9122629 9122657 9122669 9122671
9122723 9122741 9122749 9122759 9122803 9122821 9122833 9122851 9122929 9122933
9122957 9122963 9122969 9122989 9123013 9123017 9123031 9123041 9123061 9123073
9123089 9123109 9123133 9123137 9123143 9123161 9123167 9123193 9123199 9123239
9123251 9123263 9123293 9123307 9123329 9123337 9123379 9123403 9123421 9123437
9123461 9123463 9123469 9123481 9123493 9123503 9123511 9123533 9123557 9123559
9123619 9123623 9123643 9123659 9123677 9123683 9123707 9123721 9123739 9123761
9123767 9123769 9123787 9123797 9123799 9123823 9123833 9123841 9123871 9123887
9123901 9123923 9123943 9123949 9123967 9123979 9124001 9124007 9124021 9124043
9124057 9124069 9124079 9124081 9124117 9124133 9124151 9124153 9124177 9124187
9124201 9124207 9124229 9124243 9124249 9124277 9124279 9124289 9124301 9124309
9124327 9124331 9124361 9124373 9124397 9124403 9124417 9124457 9124463 9124481
9124519 9124523 9124553 9124559 9124651 9124669 9124691 9124727 9124777 9124793
9124799 9124811 9124861 9124897 9124939 9124967 9124981 9124993 9125009 9125021
9125023 9125029 9125033 9125057 9125069 9125071 9125087 9125101 9125113 9125131
9125143 9125147 9125161 9125167 9125177 9125197 9125201 9125203 9125239 9125261
9125279 9125293 9125309 9125317 9125321 9125323 9125341 9125351 9125359 9125387
9125393 9125419 9125423 9125449 9125461 9125483 9125497 9125507 9125509 9125513
9125521 9125531 9125561 9125573 9125581 9125609 9125621 9125639 9125659 9125671
9125713 9125729 9125747 9125771 9125773 9125777 9125797 9125801 9125819 9125863
9125867 9125887 9125891 9125899 9125927 9125951 9125953 9125959 9125969 9125983
9125989 9125999 9126011 9126043 9126077 9126083 9126107 9126133 9126151 9126163
9126167 9126181 9126197 9126199 9126203 9126223 9126233 9126287 9126301 9126311
9126349 9126353 9126361 9126367 9126379 9126389 9126401 9126407 9126421 9126473
9126487 9126497 9126499 9126511 9126527 9126541 9126571 9126587 9126613 9126643
9126647 9126659 9126661 9126703 9126713 9126743 9126749 9126751 9126757 9126787

```
9126797  9126809  9126829  9126833  9126847  9126853  9126869  9126877  9126907  9126913
9126919  9126947  9126959  9126983  9126991  9127043  9127061  9127091  9127093  9127099
9127103  9127169  9127187  9127189  9127193  9127213  9127219  9127231  9127267  9127291
9127303  9127319  9127331  9127337  9127357  9127367  9127463  9127499  9127507  9127519
9127523  9127529  9127537  9127553  9127561  9127579  9127583  9127597  9127621  9127627
9127631  9127633  9127637  9127639  9127667  9127669  9127681  9127693  9127697  9127709
9127717  9127753  9127777  9127787  9127813  9127817  9127873  9127883  9127891  9127901
9127903  9127913  9127927  9127933  9127939  9127957  9128003  9128017  9128023  9128029
9128047  9128051  9128057  9128087  9128089  9128123  9128129  9128131  9128153  9128177
9128209  9128219  9128237  9128239  9128267  9128297  9128299  9128311  9128323  9128377
9128407  9128411  9128419  9128443  9128453  9128461  9128501  9128503  9128521  9128557
9128563  9128579  9128597  9128617  9128629  9128653  9128659  9128681  9128689  9128701
9128719  9128737  9128741  9128747  9128789  9128803  9128807  9128827  9128831  9128837
9128843  9128851  9128863  9128909  9128923  9128927  9128929  9128957  9128969  9128981
9128989  9129013  9129023  9129031  9129041  9129049  9129061  9129067  9129073  9129149
9129151  9129167  9129181  9129193  9129203  9129257  9129277  9129293  9129299  9129301
9129331  9129377  9129401  9129437  9129457  9129473  9129499  9129509  9129553  9129563
9129569  9129581  9129607  9129613  9129619  9129641  9129647  9129683  9129739  9129761
9129767  9129773  9129811  9129847  9129851  9129853  9129877  9129883  9129929  9129947
9129943  9129947  9129959  9129979  9129997  9130007  9130019  9130031  9130063  9130067
9130081  9130111  9130117  9130123  9130133  9130141  9130153  9130201  9130211  9130217
9130237  9130259  9130283  9130301  9130321  9130339  9130351  9130357  9130423  9130463
9130477  9130481  9130483  9130519  9130543  9130553  9130567  9130573  9130613  9130619
9130633  9130651  9130657  9130661  9130669  9130691  9130729  9130733  9130757  9130783
9130789  9130799  9130801  9130817  9130829  9130841  9130859  9130867  9130871  9130879
9130889  9130903  9130937  9130939  9130943  9130967  9130991  9131009  9131011  9131021
9131033  9131041  9131117  9131123  9131131  9131189  9131209  9131219  9131231  9131237
9131263  9131279  9131293  9131303  9131321  9131333  9131347  9131359  9131383  9131387
9131389  9131399  9131429  9131443  9131471  9131477  9131501  9131509  9131543  9131579
9131587  9131593  9131599  9131611  9131641  9131651  9131653  9131659  9131663  9131687
9131747  9131767  9131777  9131779  9131783  9131791  9131797  9131803  9131809  9131813
9131821  9131831  9131849  9131891  9131917  9131923  9131929  9131939  9131957  9131977
9131987  9132001  9132031  9132041  9132047  9132049  9132089  9132113  9132119  9132121
9132131  9132157  9132169  9132203  9132209  9132229  9132251  9132257  9132269  9132313
9132317  9132323  9132337  9132341  9132353  9132367  9132391  9132397  9132421  9132427
9132457  9132491  9132499  9132503  9132511  9132527  9132577  9132611  9132619  9132649
9132653  9132661  9132667  9132691  9132719  9132731  9132733  9132743  9132751  9132769
9132797  9132803  9132829  9132833  9132839  9132853  9132857  9132887  9132889  9132917
9132919  9132923  9132931  9132973  9132979  9132983  9132989  9132997  9133021  9133031
9133073  9133099  9133123  9133151  9133153  9133171  9133183  9133211  9133213  9133217
9133247  9133261  9133279  9133291  9133303  9133307  9133309  9133337  9133349  9133351
9133361  9133363  9133381  9133391  9133393  9133409  9133417  9133477  9133483  9133489
9133519  9133559  9133567  9133571  9133589  9133603  9133633  9133667  9133669  9133681
9133697  9133717  9133723  9133739  9133757  9133763  9133769  9133771  9133801  9133807
9133823  9133837  9133847  9133853  9133897  9133907  9133951  9133961  9133987  9133991
9133997  9134009  9134011  9134023  9134029  9134033  9134063  9134077  9134087  9134089
9134093  9134113  9134131  9134161  9134207  9134249  9134261  9134291  9134317  9134327
9134347  9134351  9134369  9134371  9134387  9134407  9134441  9134471  9134479  9134501
9134509  9134537  9134539  9134561  9134617  9134633  9134639  9134669  9134701  9134711
9134717  9134737  9134747  9134753  9134767  9134803  9134809  9134821  9134837  9134843
9134869  9134903  9134947  9134959  9134969  9134999  9135013  9135017  9135031  9135043
9135079  9135083  9135097  9135107  9135109  9135121  9135127  9135149  9135199  9135211
9135233  9135253  9135263  9135271  9135277  9135281  9135283  9135289  9135311  9135317
9135331  9135353  9135361  9135389  9135391  9135397  9135403  9135407  9135419  9135431
9135433  9135449  9135461  9135521  9135527  9135541  9135563  9135569  9135589  9135593
9135601  9135629  9135639  9135653  9135671  9135677  9135701  9135703  9135757  9135799
9135811  9135829  9135839  9135857  9135859  9135881  9135883  9135901  9135911  9135913
9135923  9135949  9135961  9135977  9136009  9136027  9136051  9136063  9136079  9136109
9136111  9136147  9136159  9136177  9136181  9136199  9136201  9136213  9136217  9136219
9136229  9136241  9136261  9136273  9136277  9136279  9136297  9136307  9136319  9136349
9136367  9136417  9136441  9136453  9136459  9136487  9136499  9136513  9136529  9136529
9136573  9136577  9136579  9136583  9136591  9136613  9136637  9136643  9136657  9136679
9136691  9136693  9136703  9136709  9136717  9136741  9136747  9136781  9136793  9136807
9136811  9136823  9136843  9136849  9136861  9136873  9136877  9136879  9136901  9136921
9136937  9136951  9136961  9136969  9136993  9137021  9137047  9137053  9137077  9137087
9137099  9137101  9137111  9137131  9137159  9137173  9137179  9137197  9137201  9137213
9137239  9137251  9137267  9137273  9137287  9137339  9137353  9137419  9137437  9137441
9137459  9137473  9137501  9137503  9137521  9137533  9137539  9137563  9137567  9137573
9137593  9137621  9137641  9137657  9137659  9137669  9137683  9137699  9137701  9137707
9137729  9137731  9137741  9137759  9137767  9137809  9137827  9137833  9137837  9137873
9137893  9137899  9137911  9137941  9137951  9137981  9138007  9138029  9138043  9138047
9138049  9138071  9138083  9138091  9138119  9138131  9138133  9138137  9138139  9138169
9138179  9138193  9138209  9138229  9138247  9138251  9138271  9138281  9138289  9138293
9138323  9138329  9138341  9138343  9138347  9138413  9138421  9138427  9138433  9138439
9138443  9138463  9138491  9138511  9138517  9138523  9138527  9138533  9138541  9138553
9138587  9138589  9138607  9138637  9138697  9138719  9138721  9138739  9138749  9138757
9138803  9138839  9138847  9138851  9138853  9138863  9138917  9138929  9138931  9138947
9138967  9138991  9139021  9139033  9139051  9139059  9139069  9139093  9139099  9139153
9139181  9139201  9139219  9139231  9139237  9139253  9139271  9139279  9139283  9139289
9139297  9139309  9139313  9139343  9139363  9139367  9139369  9139391  9139393  9139397
9139439  9139453  9139457  9139463  9139469  9139483  9139517  9139519  9139531  9139547
9139567  9139583  9139601  9139609  9139639  9139649  9139651  9139661  9139687  9139709
9139723  9139751  9139759  9139769  9139771  9139783  9139787  9139789  9139807  9139811
9139841  9139853  9139861  9139873  9139883  9139927  9139943  9139973  9139981  9139987
9140003  9140011  9140029  9140059  9140081  9140093  9140099  9140119  9140129  9140143
9140149  9140167  9140189  9140227  9140239  9140267  9140279  9140281  9140291  9140297
9140303  9140321  9140347  9140353  9140359  9140363  9140377  9140393  9140401  9140429
9140437  9140447  9140449  9140459  9140473  9140477  9140479  9140489  9140491  9140497
9140519  9140533  9140557  9140563  9140569  9140587  9140623  9140627  9140633  9140641
```

```
9140669  9140671  9140711  9140717  9140749  9140783  9140797  9140809  9140851  9140861
9140863  9140893  9140899  9140921  9140933  9140953  9140977  9141007  9141023  9141029
9141031  9141089  9141127  9141149  9141151  9141161  9141163  9141193  9141199  9141221
9141229  9141247  9141259  9141263  9141269  9141271  9141287  9141317  9141343  9141367
9141397  9141403  9141421  9141437  9141443  9141469  9141481  9141491  9141533  9141541
9141569  9141577  9141581  9141589  9141593  9141607  9141623  9141659  9141661  9141667
9141673  9141677  9141689  9141697  9141707  9141731  9141751  9141761  9141763  9141779
9141809  9141817  9141823  9141851  9141871  9141883  9141901  9141911  9141919  9141943
9141947  9141961  9142013  9142019  9142033  9142037  9142061  9142069  9142087  9142093
9142099  9142103  9142151  9142171  9142207  9142229  9142283  9142297  9142313  9142321
9142327  9142333  9142361  9142369  9142373  9142391  9142411  9142423  9142429  9142499
9142501  9142517  9142519  9142543  9142547  9142561  9142571  9142577  9142633  9142643
9142691  9142697  9142711  9142723  9142729  9142733  9142747  9142813  9142831  9142843
9142849  9142873  9142901  9142909  9142919  9142921  9142927  9142949  9142963  9142981
9142993  9142997  9143011  9143023  9143063  9143081  9143117  9143119  9143137  9143179
9143203  9143221  9143273  9143279  9143291  9143293  9143327  9143339  9143341  9143347
9143353  9143373  9143383  9143411  9143437  9143483  9143509  9143513  9143527  9143531
9143549  9143567  9143573  9143587  9143591  9143597  9143599  9143611  9143623  9143633
9143657  9143663  9143681  9143689  9143713  9143723  9143737  9143749  9143753  9143767
9143777  9143789  9143801  9143809  9143819  9143831  9143843  9143867  9143881  9143887
9143891  9143917  9143923  9143933  9143969  9143971  9143983  9143987  9143999  9144001
9144007  9144029  9144043  9144049  9144059  9144067  9144131  9144167  9144169  9144173
9144197  9144209  9144221  9144229  9144253  9144257  9144259  9144277  9144281  9144293
9144307  9144313  9144323  9144341  9144347  9144383  9144389  9144391  9144397  9144403
9144413  9144427  9144431  9144433  9144437  9144467  9144493  9144511  9144563  9144581
9144617  9144631  9144677  9144679  9144689  9144697  9144701  9144727  9144739  9144749
9144761  9144769  9144787  9144797  9144799  9144829  9144851  9144861  9144881  9144893
9144899  9144901  9144911  9144913  9144917  9145033  9145039  9145049  9145051  9145057
9145067  9145069  9145109  9145117  9145127  9145139  9145151  9145153  9145159  9145163
9145187  9145219  9145229  9145243  9145249  9145259  9145291  9145313  9145319  9145321
9145333  9145349  9145351  9145379  9145447  9145457  9145459  9145463  9145489  9145519
9145561  9145571  9145597  9145601  9145613  9145637  9145663  9145667  9145673  9145693
9145699  9145739  9145753  9145781  9145811  9145823  9145831  9145867  9145883  9145889
9145891  9145901  9145921  9145937  9145943  9145957  9145963  9145967  9145987  9146009
9146021  9146041  9146063  9146069  9146099  9146101  9146113  9146117  9146167  9146177
9146183  9146197  9146213  9146273  9146303  9146309  9146311  9146327  9146359  9146381
9146393  9146411  9146443  9146447  9146461  9146477  9146491  9146509  9146539  9146549
9146563  9146569  9146587  9146591  9146609  9146611  9146633  9146647  9146651  9146671
9146677  9146689  9146693  9146707  9146713  9146723  9146729  9146737  9146751  9146759
9146783  9146789  9146869  9146873  9146897  9146903  9146933  9146957  9146959  9146971
9146981  9146983  9146987  9146989  9146993  9147007  9147013  9147023  9147043  9147053
9147097  9147101  9147137  9147161  9147163  9147199  9147253  9147283  9147287  9147293
9147311  9147367  9147373  9147421  9147431  9147487  9147497  9147503  9147521  9147527
9147529  9147537  9147553  9147571  9147587  9147601  9147613  9147643  9147659  9147661
9147667  9147707  9147727  9147737  9147763  9147781  9147811  9147823  9147833  9147839
9147857  9147869  9147871  9147881  9147889  9147893  9147899  9147907  9147913  9147947
9147953  9147967  9147977  9148001  9148003  9148019  9148031  9148037  9148099  9148133
9148169  9148199  9148241  9148267  9148309  9148331  9148333  9148351  9148387  9148423
9148459  9148463  9148471  9148487  9148501  9148523  9148537  9148553  9148561  9148589
9148591  9148609  9148613  9148619  9148631  9148639  9148673  9148679  9148693  9148729
9148739  9148757  9148817  9148829  9148831  9148849  9148927  9148957  9148961  9148991
9149011  9149029  9149053  9149057  9149087  9149093  9149099  9149113  9149141  9149143
9149149  9149167  9149177  9149219  9149221  9149233  9149243  9149251  9149267  9149293
9149341  9149359  9149363  9149401  9149419  9149447  9149449  9149477  9149479  9149501
9149509  9149527  9149533  9149563  9149579  9149599  9149603  9149611  9149627  9149629
9149633  9149639  9149663  9149687  9149711  9149717  9149729  9149737  9149759  9149783
9149801  9149807  9149809  9149813  9149827  9149831  9149843  9149851  9149857  9149869
9149873  9149909  9149923  9149947  9149951  9149977  9149981  9149989  9150019  9150041
9150083  9150091  9150121  9150139  9150149  9150161  9150173  9150181  9150187  9150209
9150227  9150241  9150247  9150259  9150263  9150277  9150299  9150311  9150313  9150329
9150347  9150353  9150371  9150373  9150377  9150413  9150451  9150461  9150467  9150497
9150517  9150523  9150563  9150569  9150577  9150587  9150613  9150637  9150653  9150703
9150719  9150737  9150773  9150851  9150871  9150887  9150893  9150899  9150901  9150907
9150917  9150919  9150929  9150943  9150991  9150997  9151003  9151007  9151013  9151031
9151039  9151067  9151073  9151081  9151097  9151147  9151183  9151193  9151199  9151201
9151213  9151237  9151243  9151273  9151279  9151283  9151291  9151297  9151301  9151319
9151333  9151339  9151349  9151357  9151381  9151391  9151397  9151409  9151411  9151451
9151459  9151507  9151523  9151537  9151553  9151573  9151577  9151583  9151607  9151609
9151613  9151619  9151633  9151643  9151717  9151721  9151741  9151759  9151771  9151777
9151783  9151801  9151823  9151841  9151843  9151847  9151871  9151927  9151931  9151943
9151949  9151957  9151963  9151969  9151993  9151997  9152009  9152051  9152057  9152063
9152089  9152111  9152123  9152131  9152149  9152153  9152173  9152179  9152189  9152201
9152237  9152279  9152291  9152293  9152303  9152323  9152353  9152369  9152383  9152393
9152417  9152453  9152461  9152489  9152491  9152497  9152527  9152531  9152543  9152557
9152567  9152569  9152581  9152587  9152599  9152617  9152641  9152677  9152687  9152701
9152723  9152743  9152761  9152779  9152789  9152791  9152797  9152809  9152831  9152837
9152863  9152879  9152903  9152909  9152933  9152947  9152977  9152981  9152993  9152999
9153007  9153031  9153037  9153043  9153049  9153061  9153073  9153077  9153119  9153121
9153139  9153161  9153163  9153173  9153197  9153227  9153239  9153311  9153337  9153341
9153343  9153349  9153377  9153409  9153433  9153439  9153451  9153491  9153499  9153509
9153511  9153527  9153581  9153593  9153623  9153631  9153637  9153659  9153671  9153689
9153691  9153733  9153737  9153761  9153799  9153811  9153853  9153857  9153863  9153869
9153913  9153923  9153941  9153943  9153961  9153971  9153983  9153997  9154013  9154027
9154039  9154043  9154091  9154099  9154151  9154157  9154163  9154231  9154247  9154267
9154289  9154291  9154297  9154303  9154307  9154309  9154361  9154367  9154421  9154427
9154463  9154487  9154493  9154501  9154507  9154543  9154547  9154549  9154553  9154591
9154631  9154681  9154693  9154729  9154771  9154777  9154781  9154793  9154837  9154841
9154879  9154883  9154909  9154913  9154927  9154933  9154939  9154961  9154963  9154967
9154969  9154991  9154997  9155009  9155011  9155023  9155051  9155053  9155057  9155077
```

```
9155099  9155101  9155117  9155119  9155123  9155143  9155183  9155189  9155227  9155233
9155239  9155257  9155287  9155291  9155297  9155309  9155339  9155351  9155411  9155413
9155417  9155477  9155527  9155543  9155581  9155593  9155609  9155611  9155621  9155623
9155659  9155683  9155693  9155719  9155723  9155737  9155743  9155747  9155749  9155753
9155759  9155789  9155807  9155821  9155837  9155857  9155869  9155897  9155933  9155941
9155963  9155977  9155987  9155999  9156071  9156073  9156101  9156127  9156137  9156143
9156163  9156167  9156193  9156197  9156209  9156221  9156239  9156241  9156263  9156281
9156307  9156331  9156341  9156359  9156379  9156383  9156403  9156437  9156449  9156473
9156479  9156481  9156487  9156529  9156533  9156541  9156551  9156577  9156583  9156593
9156607  9156611  9156619  9156629  9156647  9156661  9156673  9156677  9156683  9156701
9156743  9156781  9156787  9156793  9156821  9156839  9156853  9156857  9156887  9156923
9156989  9157003  9157007  9157021  9157051  9157073  9157087  9157123  9157139  9157157
9157201  9157219  9157223  9157229  9157231  9157249  9157273  9157283  9157321  9157387
9157399  9157439  9157451  9157453  9157471  9157483  9157513  9157529  9157541  9157549
9157553  9157571  9157573  9157579  9157583  9157609  9157613  9157619  9157661  9157661
9157663  9157669  9157691  9157693  9157717  9157721  9157723  9157727  9157769  9157783
9157789  9157807  9157847  9157873  9157901  9157909  9157931  9157949  9157957  9157981
9157969  9158003  9158027  9158059  9158081  9158089  9158119  9158159  9158161  9158167
9158197  9158207  9158213  9158221  9158231  9158243  9158251  9158263  9158267  9158273
9158309  9158329  9158339  9158353  9158363  9158381  9158389  9158407  9158411  9158417
9158459  9158473  9158483  9158489  9158491  9158497  9158509  9158521  9158543  9158593
9158599  9158651  9158663  9158701  9158711  9158713  9158717  9158777  9158783  9158789
9158791  9158797  9158803  9158813  9158827  9158873  9158911  9158923  9158927  9158939
9158953  9158977  9158993  9158999  9159001  9159013  9159049  9159053  9159061  9159067
9159077  9159097  9159103  9159109  9159119  9159131  9159149  9159169  9159191  9159203
9159217  9159233  9159247  9159259  9159263  9159281  9159287  9159289  9159317  9159329
9159347  9159361  9159377  9159421  9159427  9159443  9159453  9159457  9159469  9159487
9159499  9159511  9159533  9159541  9159547  9159551  9159569  9159581  9159599  9159641
9159643  9159649  9159659  9159739  9159751  9159823  9159827  9159833  9159847  9159859
9159863  9159869  9159901  9159907  9159977  9160007  9160009  9160031  9160057  9160061
9160069  9160087  9160091  9160103  9160121  9160139  9160181  9160183  9160189  9160213
9160219  9160241  9160243  9160273  9160289  9160313  9160321  9160339  9160351  9160357
9160363  9160369  9160379  9160381  9160387  9160409  9160421  9160429  9160439  9160471
9160477  9160483  9160499  9160513  9160519  9160537  9160579  9160621  9160643  9160649
9160661  9160663  9160691  9160721  9160727  9160729  9160741  9160751  9160757  9160769
9160771  9160783  9160787  9160819  9160829  9160847  9160889  9160913  9160939  9160973
9161051  9161057  9161083  9161093  9161101  9161137  9161143  9161149  9161161  9161167
9161171  9161177  9161179  9161183  9161203  9161219  9161239  9161261  9161263  9161293
9161297  9161353  9161371  9161377  9161387  9161389  9161413  9161431  9161437  9161441
9161473  9161483  9161497  9161501  9161531  9161543  9161557  9161597  9161611  9161639
9161641  9161671  9161681  9161693  9161707  9161717  9161723  9161729  9161753  9161791
9161807  9161809  9161837  9161839  9161869  9161891  9161897  9161899  9161909  9161917
9161923  9161939  9161959  9161987  9161993  9162001  9162007  9162037  9162059  9162091
9162137  9162151  9162191  9162193  9162203  9162221  9162233  9162247  9162281  9162299
9162301  9162319  9162331  9162343  9162353  9162359  9162367  9162467  9162469  9162493
9162547  9162553  9162563  9162581  9162583  9162589  9162611  9162613  9162623  9162653
9162661  9162679  9162683  9162689  9162709  9162737  9162739  9162761  9162773  9162787
9162823  9162833  9162841  9162851  9162863  9162893  9162899  9162919  9162929  9162961
9163003  9163009  9163027  9163031  9163069  9163079  9163081  9163103  9163127  9163139
9163169  9163199  9163243  9163249  9163267  9163279  9163313  9163369  9163381  9163397
9163403  9163409  9163411  9163417  9163423  9163439  9163463  9163477  9163537  9163559
9163571  9163573  9163577  9163589  9163621  9163633  9163639  9163699  9163711  9163717
9163723  9163727  9163733  9163741  9163747  9163769  9163771  9163789  9163813  9163829
9163837  9163873  9163897  9163927  9163937  9163943  9163967  9163981  9163997
9164011  9164021  9164027  9164047  9164069  9164083  9164147  9164167  9164171  9164179
9164191  9164231  9164249  9164273  9164291  9164297  9164299  9164303  9164317  9164333
9164359  9164369  9164383  9164387  9164401  9164417  9164423  9164429  9164431  9164471
9164473  9164489  9164501  9164503  9164521  9164527  9164531  9164563  9164587  9164591
9164627  9164651  9164663  9164677  9164681  9164731  9164759  9164767  9164773  9164791
9164839  9164843  9164861  9164873  9164917  9164923  9164927  9164929  9164941  9164951
9164959  9165007  9165041  9165053  9165061  9165071  9165083  9165097  9165137  9165151
9165157  9165173  9165179  9165199  9165203  9165217  9165241  9165251  9165253  9165257
9165259  9165271  9165283  9165301  9165313  9165323  9165341  9165347  9165349  9165379
9165419  9165439  9165451  9165469  9165511  9165547  9165551  9165577  9165599  9165613
9165617  9165623  9165631  9165643  9165647  9165679  9165683  9165691  9165719  9165757
9165781  9165791  9165797  9165803  9165811  9165823  9165829  9165833  9165841  9165853
9165857  9165859  9165869  9165883  9165901  9165911  9165913  9165917  9165929  9165931
9165977  9165997  9166019  9166039  9166057  9166061  9166093  9166109  9166123  9166127
9166141  9166159  9166187  9166211  9166217  9166219  9166229  9166231  9166237  9166243
9166273  9166277  9166301  9166309  9166319  9166321  9166327  9166361  9166387  9166393
9166427  9166429  9166441  9166477  9166481  9166499  9166511  9166517  9166529  9166567
9166571  9166589  9166601  9166609  9166613  9166643  9166649  9166667  9166681  9166687
9166693  9166709  9166727  9166747  9166753  9166763  9166777  9166789  9166819  9166823
9166837  9166841  9166847  9166849  9166853  9166867  9166879  9166891  9166909  9166931
9166943  9166951  9166967  9166973  9166981  9167003  9167017  9167027  9167047  9167051
9167069  9167077  9167113  9167143  9167167  9167203  9167269  9167287  9167297  9167311
9167321  9167341  9167371  9167381  9167383  9167419  9167423  9167429  9167441  9167489
9167513  9167531  9167533  9167549  9167551  9167579  9167603  9167611  9167617  9167621
9167651  9167657  9167687  9167689  9167699  9167771  9167779  9167791  9167797  9167813
9167819  9167827  9167839  9167923  9167933  9167959  9167989  9167999  9168001  9168011
9168031  9168043  9168059  9168067  9168077  9168109  9168167  9168169  9168171  9168181
9168209  9168217  9168221  9168233  9168251  9168259  9168293  9168319  9168349  9168359
9168371  9168391  9168403  9168407  9168409  9168413  9168427  9168433  9168449  9168463
9168487  9168499  9168521  9168557  9168571  9168623  9168631  9168647  9168671  9168673
9168689  9168701  9168721  9168737  9168739  9168767  9168769  9168793  9168799  9168823
9168833  9168853  9168889  9168911  9168941  9168961  9168979  9168983  9168997
9169003  9169021  9169037  9169049  9169063  9169073  9169099  9169109  9169129  9169141
9169201  9169207  9169217  9169241  9169243  9169261  9169283  9169291  9169301  9169319
9169331  9169333  9169339  9169351  9169357  9169373  9169379  9169399  9169411  9169417
```

9169421 9169429 9169439 9169441 9169471 9169493 9169499 9169513 9169529 9169561
9169577 9169619 9169631 9169637 9169649 9169661 9169669 9169679 9169711 9169717
9169733 9169739 9169753 9169763 9169789 9169807 9169819 9169861 9169871 9169877
9169889 9169921 9169933 9169967 9169999 9170011 9170023 9170033 9170039 9170047
9170059 9170071 9170081 9170087 9170111 9170129 9170143 9170149 9170171 9170173
9170197 9170201 9170209 9170233 9170237 9170257 9170263 9170269 9170281 9170297
9170299 9170341 9170363 9170377 9170383 9170401 9170411 9170417 9170423 9170437
9170443 9170449 9170453 9170459 9170489 9170519 9170533 9170549 9170569 9170611
9170617 9170621 9170627 9170657 9170713 9170717 9170723 9170729 9170737 9170743
9170779 9170807 9170809 9170851 9170881 9170899 9170927 9170929 9170957 9170983
9171013 9171049 9171061 9171119 9171131 9171229 9171233 9171259 9171263 9171269
9171307 9171311 9171317 9171343 9171353 9171367 9171401 9171431 9171467 9171497
9171527 9171581 9171593 9171601 9171607 9171611 9171649 9171677 9171683 9171689
9171707 9171713 9171731 9171751 9171763 9171769 9171787 9171797 9171803 9171829
9171853 9171881 9171887 9171907 9171913 9171919 9171923 9171937 9171947 9171961
9171971 9171977 9171983 9171989 9171991 9171997 9172039 9172043 9172049 9172057
9172087 9172133 9172153 9172157 9172159 9172183 9172211 9172217 9172237 9172243
9172259 9172271 9172279 9172297 9172343 9172349 9172351 9172363 9172391 9172399
9172403 9172409 9172433 9172441 9172451 9172463 9172481 9172483 9172531 9172547
9172577 9172591 9172609 9172637 9172663 9172679 9172693 9172721 9172727 9172739
9172747 9172759 9172771 9172777 9172783 9172811 9172817 9172831 9172841 9172861
9172873 9172913 9172949 9172957 9172967 9172981 9173011 9173023 9173041 9173051
9173057 9173071 9173093 9173111 9173137 9173161 9173173 9173209 9173231 9173237
9173249 9173267 9173273 9173279 9173287 9173291 9173317 9173321 9173323 9173327
9173341 9173347 9173357 9173369 9173377 9173393 9173441 9173459 9173471 9173473
9173509 9173531 9173533 9173543 9173569 9173579 9173587 9173597 9173603 9173609
9173617 9173629 9173641 9173653 9173683 9173719 9173753 9173771 9173777 9173797
9173819 9173867 9173881 9173887 9173893 9173917 9173951 9173953 9173959 9174001
9174029 9174041 9174043 9174089 9174091 9174097 9174103 9174149 9174157 9174197
9174227 9174251 9174281 9174299 9174311 9174317 9174329 9174331 9174337 9174371
9174383 9174391 9174413 9174433 9174449 9174457 9174463 9174521 9174533 9174547
9174563 9174569 9174589 9174601 9174617 9174619 9174623 9174637 9174647 9174689
9174703 9174707 9174719 9174721 9174749 9174751 9174761 9174787 9174793 9174797
9174821 9174839 9174871 9174887 9174889 9174901 9174937 9174943 9174947
9174959 9174983 9175013 9175037 9175057 9175063 9175073 9175079 9175093 9175123
9175171 9175207 9175217 9175219 9175241 9175249 9175273 9175279 9175289 9175319
9175337 9175351 9175403 9175417 9175421 9175429 9175447 9175451 9175457 9175471
9175477 9175501 9175541 9175561 9175577 9175591 9175601 9175619 9175637 9175657
9175693 9175697 9175711 9175723 9175753 9175787 9175789 9175823 9175843 9175847
9175871 9175883 9175891 9175913 9175921 9175931 9175949 9175967 9175973 9175979
9175981 9175987 9176003 9176009 9176017 9176023 9176029 9176053 9176059 9176099
9176117 9176129 9176137 9176147 9176159 9176161 9176171 9176177 9176191 9176207
9176249 9176269 9176273 9176339 9176347 9176351 9176353 9176359 9176369 9176371
9176381 9176389 9176393 9176429 9176443 9176459 9176507 9176509 9176513 9176533
9176543 9176551 9176567 9176581 9176593 9176599 9176603 9176621 9176647 9176659
9176689 9176693 9176711 9176749 9176771 9176773 9176803 9176809 9176813 9176831
9176857 9176861 9176863 9176887 9176911 9176917 9176939 9176953 9176969 9176971
9177001 9177011 9177013 9177031 9177041 9177043 9177067 9177083 9177089 9177097
9177107 9177139 9177143 9177169 9177187 9177199 9177211 9177239 9177241 9177251
9177257 9177269 9177277 9177293 9177307 9177319 9177347 9177353 9177367 9177373
9177431 9177439 9177451 9177479 9177491 9177499 9177503 9177523 9177527 9177547
9177583 9177587 9177599 9177607 9177611 9177617 9177697 9177709 9177733 9177761
9177781 9177787 9177793 9177811 9177827 9177853 9177869 9177881 9177899 9177901
9177923 9177929 9177937 9177941 9177979 9177997 9178027 9178051 9178061 9178067
9178069 9178073 9178151 9178157 9178171 9178177 9178187 9178189 9178229 9178231
9178259 9178261 9178277 9178313 9178319 9178327 9178333 9178361 9178373 9178399
9178409 9178423 9178439 9178441 9178451 9178459 9178483 9178493 9178513 9178523
9178537 9178579 9178591 9178597 9178607 9178613 9178619 9178621 9178643 9178649
9178669 9178681 9178709 9178717 9178723 9178733 9178739 9178747 9178751 9178753
9178769 9178783 9178787 9178789 9178831 9178867 9178889 9178937 9178943 9178973
9178979 9178987 9178991 9179003 9179011 9179021 9179029 9179057 9179101 9179111
9179113 9179129 9179141 9179153 9179171 9179189 9179197 9179213 9179227 9179237
9179249 9179263 9179267 9179281 9179297 9179309 9179311 9179333 9179347 9179363
9179389 9179407 9179419 9179431 9179453 9179459 9179477 9179479 9179483 9179491
9179497 9179509 9179537 9179539 9179557 9179561 9179579 9179581 9179591 9179593
9179647 9179693 9179713 9179761 9179767 9179791 9179801 9179809 9179827 9179837
9179839 9179843 9179857 9179861 9179867 9179873 9179887 9179897 9179909 9179927
9179953 9179963 9179971 9180001 9180019 9180029 9180043 9180053 9180071 9180079
9180091 9180109 9180121 9180131 9180137 9180161 9180167 9180191 9180239 9180251
9180257 9180263 9180277 9180299 9180319 9180331 9180359 9180361 9180377 9180383
9180421 9180469 9180481 9180497 9180499 9180503 9180571 9180583 9180631 9180641
9180653 9180659 9180671 9180727 9180737 9180753 9180763 9180767 9180859
9180883 9180917 9180967 9180989 9181013 9181019 9181021 9181033
9181057 9181063 9181079 9181087 9181093 9181097 9181099 9181103 9181127 9181129
9181141 9181181 9181187 9181189 9181201 9181213 9181219 9181247 9181261 9181279
9181303 9181321 9181327 9181357 9181379 9181387 9181391 9181409 9181421 9181433
9181441 9181451 9181453 9181481 9181511 9181519 9181553 9181573 9181597 9181619
9181621 9181631 9181633 9181651 9181657 9181691 9181703 9181727 9181763
9181771 9181787 9181789 9181793 9181817 9181849 9181871 9181891 9181901 9181937
9181961 9181979 9181981 9181987 9182003 9182021 9182027 9182039 9182053 9182077
9182081 9182093 9182101 9182113 9182123 9182137 9182153 9182171 9182233 9182281
9182287 9182309 9182323 9182387 9182389 9182447 9182449 9182507 9182519 9182527
9182557 9182561 9182573 9182581 9182599 9182609 9182611 9182627 9182639 9182651
9182653 9182687 9182711 9182713 9182717 9182731 9182741 9182777 9182783 9182801
9182807 9182843 9182863 9182891 9182903 9182963 9182977 9182981 9183011
9183017 9183029 9183047 9183073 9183079 9183101 9183103 9183113 9183121 9183127
9183131 9183143 9183149 9183157 9183193 9183199 9183217 9183241 9183263 9183311
9183323 9183329 9183331 9183341 9183373 9183389 9183407 9183413 9183431 9183439
9183457 9183481 9183487 9183491 9183523 9183529 9183541 9183557 9183571 9183589

```
9183613  9183641  9183649  9183653  9183661  9183679  9183709  9183737  9183761  9183767
9183793  9183799  9183803  9183817  9183827  9183841  9183851  9183871  9183883  9183899
9183907  9183931  9183949  9183989  9183991  9184009  9184027  9184037  9184067  9184073
9184079  9184093  9184111  9184127  9184139  9184151  9184157  9184171  9184181  9184207
9184243  9184249  9184283  9184309  9184321  9184361  9184367  9184381  9184393  9184421
9184433  9184453  9184457  9184459  9184477  9184481  9184493  9184501  9184523  9184537
9184583  9184597  9184601  9184603  9184661  9184663  9184673  9184691  9184717  9184727
9184729  9184759  9184781  9184783  9184801  9184817  9184823  9184837  9184841  9184849
9184853  9184867  9184883  9184921  9184939  9184949  9184951  9184969  9184993  9185039
9185051  9185081  9185087  9185123  9185149  9185153  9185159  9185161  9185171  9185173
9185177  9185191  9185237  9185261  9185291  9185299  9185311  9185317  9185329  9185339
9185347  9185387  9185399  9185401  9185443  9185447  9185453  9185471  9185497  9185507
9185513  9185521  9185549  9185551  9185557  9185573  9185591  9185621  9185623  9185653
9185669  9185689  9185699  9185711  9185719  9185723  9185741  9185749  9185753  9185773
9185791  9185819  9185833  9185857  9185863  9185867  9185881  9185893  9185921  9185941
9185959  9185971  9185977  9185983  9185989  9186017  9186043  9186053  9186059  9186071
9186077  9186083  9186161  9186167  9186179  9186181  9186209  9186217  9186251
9186257  9186259  9186263  9186277  9186299  9186311  9186319  9186379  9186389  9186403
9186413  9186421  9186427  9186433  9186439  9186461  9186487  9186497  9186521  9186547
9186553  9186559  9186577  9186587  9186589  9186599  9186623  9186677  9186691  9186719
9186739  9186763  9186769  9186781  9186797  9186803  9186811  9186833  9186857  9186869
9186871  9186883  9186929  9186971  9187001  9187007  9187037  9187039  9187049  9187069
9187081  9187091  9187093  9187103  9187109  9187117  9187141  9187153  9187159  9187163
9187177  9187183  9187201  9187207  9187223  9187237  9187247  9187249  9187261  9187267
9187273  9187289  9187313  9187331  9187333  9187351  9187369  9187397  9187411  9187417
9187427  9187441  9187447  9187457  9187459  9187481  9187499  9187517  9187523  9187537
9187543  9187547  9187609  9187639  9187679  9187721  9187723  9187727  9187733  9187753
9187781  9187847  9187861  9187901  9187903  9187907  9187933  9187943  9187957  9187967
9187993  9188009  9188021  9188033  9188057  9188107  9188117  9188119  9188149  9188189
9188219  9188243  9188281  9188297  9188299  9188303  9188327  9188341  9188351  9188353
9188371  9188393  9188401  9188407  9188423  9188441  9188461  9188467  9188479  9188503
9188539  9188593  9188603  9188611  9188623  9188629  9188639  9188659  9188701  9188717
9188731  9188743  9188747  9188783  9188791  9188801  9188807  9188813  9188869  9188887
9188897  9188903  9188917  9188929  9188947  9188953  9189007  9189023
9189031  9189041  9189049  9189067  9189071  9189077  9189079  9189091  9189097  9189107
9189119  9189127  9189133  9189137  9189139  9189157  9189181  9189199  9189211
9189221  9189227  9189239  9189247  9189263  9189269  9189329  9189343  9189353  9189377
9189379  9189391  9189413  9189419  9189421  9189457  9189461  9189497  9189527  9189529
9189533  9189563  9189577  9189599  9189619  9189623  9189637  9189643  9189647  9189667
9189689  9189701  9189703  9189731  9189737  9189757  9189767  9189793  9189797  9189827
9189871  9189881  9189883  9189923  9189937  9189941  9189951  9189959  9189989  9189997
9190001  9190033  9190037  9190057  9190073  9190079  9190121  9190127  9190157  9190163
9190201  9190211  9190231  9190249  9190301  9190331  9190339  9190343  9190351  9190367
9190373  9190411  9190463  9190487  9190513  9190529  9190537  9190543  9190561  9190579
9190603  9190613  9190633  9190669  9190681  9190703  9190711  9190717  9190721  9190723
9190751  9190757  9190789  9190799  9190801  9190807  9190817  9190861  9190871  9190873
9190891  9190913  9190933  9190963  9190997  9191009  9191023  9191047  9191051  9191069
9191071  9191089  9191107  9191141  9191153  9191167  9191177  9191201  9191227  9191233
9191243  9191249  9191263  9191267  9191279  9191309  9191311  9191323  9191333  9191381
9191389  9191393  9191417  9191423  9191431  9191437  9191491  9191519  9191527  9191537
9191549  9191561  9191563  9191569  9191591  9191599  9191627  9191639  9191647  9191657
9191659  9191671  9191711  9191771  9191773  9191783  9191821  9191827  9191863  9191867
9191891  9191893  9191899  9191933  9191957  9191969  9191971  9191977  9191983  9191989
9191993  9192013  9192017  9192037  9192041  9192047  9192061  9192091  9192097  9192103
9192107  9192109  9192137  9192149  9192229  9192247  9192269  9192277  9192301  9192319
9192339  9192343  9192347  9192389  9192413  9192419  9192431  9192439  9192451  9192493
9192503  9192509  9192511  9192541  9192551  9192559  9192577  9192587  9192607  9192619
9192643  9192653  9192661  9192679  9192697  9192707  9192727  9192749  9192763  9192773
9192779  9192793  9192803  9192811  9192823  9192851  9192857  9192877  9192881  9192917
9192929  9192949  9192959  9192961  9192973  9192977  9193027  9193033  9193069  9193091
9193103  9193157  9193181  9193189  9193193  9193229  9193231  9193241  9193253  9193259
9193297  9193339  9193343  9193351  9193361  9193381  9193409  9193411  9193417  9193421
9193441  9193463  9193487  9193489  9193523  9193531  9193543  9193559  9193571  9193573
9193607  9193627  9193633  9193637  9193643  9193669  9193687  9193699  9193703  9193741
9193781  9193819  9193831  9193837  9193843  9193867  9193897  9193901  9193913  9193927
9193931  9193939  9193969  9193979  9194021  9194023  9194033  9194063  9194071  9194083
9194113  9194137  9194153  9194179  9194183  9194191  9194203  9194231  9194249  9194261
9194267  9194279  9194329  9194359  9194377  9194401  9194407  9194417  9194441
9194443  9194453  9194473  9194483  9194489  9194527  9194531  9194539  9194551  9194567
9194587  9194593  9194597  9194623  9194629  9194639  9194659  9194663  9194677  9194767
9194771  9194789  9194797  9194821  9194837  9194839  9194851  9194869  9194881  9194897
9194903  9194929  9194951  9194971  9195041  9195049  9195083  9195097  9195133  9195143
9195157  9195161  9195181  9195191  9195211  9195217  9195223  9195253  9195257  9195287
9195289  9195293  9195311  9195353  9195359  9195371  9195383  9195397  9195401  9195427
9195451  9195457  9195467  9195491  9195509  9195517  9195533  9195539  9195541  9195551
9195559  9195569  9195587  9195611  9195619  9195629  9195631  9195671  9195673
9195701  9195709  9195727  9195731  9195743  9195751  9195757  9195761  9195779  9195787
9195821  9195839  9195859  9195889  9195899  9195911  9195913  9195941
9195947  9195983  9196001  9196007  9196009  9196049  9196063  9196081  9196087  9196093
9196127  9196139  9196141  9196163  9196169  9196183  9196207  9196217  9196223  9196241
9196249  9196267  9196273  9196283  9196289  9196301  9196309  9196333  9196339  9196351
9196357  9196373  9196403  9196409  9196441  9196457  9196463  9196477  9196511  9196531
9196549  9196571  9196591  9196597  9196601  9196633  9196639  9196661  9196679
9196697  9196699  9196721  9196753  9196763  9196771  9196777  9196783  9196807  9196823
9196877  9196887  9196907  9196919  9196933  9196939  9196961  9196963  9196981  9197003
9197009  9197011  9197021  9197039  9197047  9197057  9197059  9197063  9197077  9197081
9197129  9197131  9197207  9197233  9197239  9197257  9197261  9197267  9197281  9197317
9197329  9197341  9197347  9197351  9197369  9197381  9197389  9197429  9197449  9197453
9197473  9197509  9197533  9197537  9197543  9197549  9197579  9197593  9197599  9197603
```

```
9197609  9197623  9197633  9197647  9197651  9197659  9197681  9197711  9197717  9197753
9197761  9197777  9197791  9197819  9197849  9197869  9197873  9197879  9197897  9197911
9197921  9197983  9197989  9198019  9198083  9198107  9198113  9198151  9198157  9198169
9198197  9198199  9198257  9198269  9198281  9198331  9198341  9198347  9198353  9198359
9198379  9198383  9198403  9198407  9198433  9198437  9198439  9198443  9198457  9198461
9198463  9198487  9198503  9198509  9198557  9198559  9198569  9198571  9198577  9198587
9198589  9198611  9198613  9198647  9198659  9198667  9198677  9198691  9198697  9198703
9198727  9198743  9198767  9198779  9198799  9198817  9198823  9198851  9198859  9198863
9198901  9198911  9198913  9198941  9198961  9199007  9199009  9199019  9199027  9199037
9199039  9199063  9199067  9199079  9199081  9199087  9199093  9199109  9199117  9199121
9199123  9199153  9199163  9199171  9199187  9199207  9199247  9199259  9199279  9199331
9199391  9199417  9199423  9199427  9199469  9199501  9199523  9199543  9199559
9199573  9199579  9199627  9199633  9199649  9199661  9199711  9199727  9199739  9199741
9199759  9199789  9199823  9199831  9199843  9199849  9199859  9199871  9199889  9199891
9199909  9199913  9199919  9199937  9199987  9199991  9199997  9200017  9200021  9200027
9200029  9200033  9200053  9200057  9200071  9200089  9200119  9200137  9200141  9200167
9200171  9200183  9200227  9200249  9200267  9200287  9200293  9200327  9200329  9200333
9200341  9200369  9200377  9200381  9200407  9200413  9200423  9200431  9200449  9200461
9200489  9200561  9200563  9200567  9200591  9200593  9200599  9200603  9200623  9200647
9200651  9200663  9200669  9200683  9200699  9200717  9200761  9200771  9200803  9200837
9200879  9200881  9200923  9200929  9200941  9200951  9200953  9200963  9200969  9200977
9200981  9201007  9201013  9201041  9201053  9201067  9201089  9201113  9201119  9201121
9201133  9201151  9201161  9201169  9201211  9201217  9201221  9201253  9201259  9201281
9201287  9201307  9201317  9201337  9201341  9201391  9201407  9201421  9201427  9201433
9201461  9201481  9201503  9201509  9201547  9201551  9201593  9201601  9201611  9201623
9201631  9201653  9201677  9201727  9201733  9201749  9201763  9201767  9201769  9201779
9201821  9201827  9201877  9201883  9201901  9201919  9201923  9201949  9201953  9201971
9201991  9202013  9202051  9202057  9202073  9202079  9202087  9202121  9202147  9202183
9202199  9202223  9202229  9202243  9202261  9202267  9202279  9202313  9202339  9202351
9202373  9202379  9202411  9202421  9202429  9202447  9202451  9202463  9202477  9202489
9202493  9202519  9202537  9202561  9202577  9202579  9202591  9202597  9202601  9202621
9202637  9202649  9202667  9202679  9202693  9202703  9202709  9202717  9202747  9202769
9202847  9202861  9202871  9202873  9202883  9202937  9202961  9202981  9202993  9203003
9203039  9203041  9203071  9203099  9203101  9203111  9203119  9203141  9203149  9203189
9203191  9203209  9203213  9203251  9203287  9203303  9203317  9203347  9203357  9203371
9203387  9203413  9203437  9203459  9203471  9203521  9203561  9203567  9203569  9203617
9203627  9203641  9203653  9203671  9203687  9203707  9203729  9203731  9203743  9203791
9203839  9203891  9203897  9203899  9203917  9203947  9203951  9203959  9203969  9203983
9204007  9204023  9204043  9204061  9204073  9204077  9204101  9204127  9204129  9204133
9204137  9204203  9204257  9204269  9204271  9204289  9204311  9204313  9204319  9204331
9204337  9204343  9204353  9204383  9204407  9204409  9204449  9204467  9204479  9204491
9204499  9204509  9204523  9204557  9204581  9204583  9204589  9204593  9204659  9204673
9204677  9204691  9204697  9204703  9204707  9204731  9204733  9204739  9204743  9204751
9204757  9204763  9204821  9204827  9204829  9204857  9204859  9204883  9204887  9204901
9204913  9204953  9204959  9204983  9204989  9205013  9205019  9205043  9205051  9205061
9205069  9205073  9205123  9205153  9205187  9205223  9205237  9205243  9205249  9205271
9205277  9205303  9205307  9205309  9205321  9205349  9205379  9205393  9205409  9205423
9205429  9205439  9205453  9205459  9205487  9205507  9205513  9205523  9205579  9205583
9205601  9205631  9205639  9205649  9205697  9205717  9205739  9205753  9205769  9205783
9205793  9205883  9205897  9205909  9205919  9205943  9205951  9205961  9205969  9205981
9206011  9206023  9206053  9206069  9206083  9206117  9206123  9206143  9206159  9206161
9206167  9206179  9206189  9206191  9206207  9206213  9206221  9206227  9206237  9206261
9206291  9206321  9206359  9206363  9206389  9206399  9206413  9206437  9206447  9206459
9206479  9206497  9206521  9206531  9206539  9206551  9206567  9206569  9206573  9206627
9206629  9206633  9206651  9206657  9206663  9206677  9206699  9206711  9206713  9206723
9206731  9206737  9206749  9206753  9206761  9206767  9206777  9206789  9206797  9206801
9206803  9206851  9206863  9206867  9206909  9206917  9206947  9206959  9206983  9206987
9206993  9207017  9207053  9207071  9207089  9207091  9207097  9207101  9207103  9207109
9207131  9207137  9207151  9207167  9207173  9207197  9207227  9207257  9207259  9207277
9207287  9207293  9207307  9207311  9207323  9207349  9207379  9207389  9207397  9207409
9207437  9207449  9207467  9207469  9207503  9207551  9207577  9207593  9207607  9207617
9207619  9207641  9207677  9207683  9207689  9207697  9207701  9207721  9207733  9207763
9207769  9207773  9207787  9207823  9207827  9207833  9207841  9207853  9207871  9207901
9207917  9207941  9207943  9207959  9207997  9208007  9208009  9208037  9208039  9208049
9208057  9208081  9208123  9208151  9208159  9208187  9208201  9208219  9208229  9208247
9208249  9208253  9208259  9208261  9208267  9208289  9208291  9208337  9208387  9208417
9208453  9208481  9208489  9208531  9208553  9208561  9208571  9208583  9208603  9208613
9208627  9208637  9208649  9208669  9208699  9208721  9208733  9208739  9208753  9208783
9208789  9208811  9208813  9208817  9208831  9208853  9208873  9208879  9208931  9208937
9208961  9208973  9208981  9208999  9209017  9209027  9209029  9209047  9209059  9209069
9209089  9209107  9209113  9209117  9209141  9209147  9209173  9209191  9209203  9209219
9209237  9209261  9209273  9209279  9209287  9209293  9209303  9209323  9209329  9209341
9209401  9209429  9209437  9209467  9209489  9209491  9209503  9209531  9209561  9209569
9209579  9209587  9209593  9209621  9209639  9209647  9209701  9209731  9209747  9209771
9209803  9209807  9209819  9209831  9209833  9209843  9209857  9209861  9209881  9209897
9209909  9209917  9209957  9209983  9209999  9210013  9210017  9210029  9210031  9210037
9210059  9210067  9210119  9210121  9210133  9210161  9210169  9210203  9210221  9210233
9210241  9210251  9210259  9210263  9210283  9210301  9210323  9210349  9210359  9210367
9210389  9210437  9210457  9210463  9210473  9210533  9210559  9210563  9210571  9210581
9210587  9210589  9210613  9210653  9210673  9210679  9210683  9210697  9210701  9210703
9210709  9210713  9210727  9210749  9210757  9210769  9210781  9210791  9210793  9210809
9210811  9210841  9210853  9210857  9210869  9210871  9210911  9210917  9210931  9210941
9210961  9210973  9210979  9210983  9210997  9211051  9211087  9211117  9211133  9211141
9211171  9211177  9211199  9211207  9211231  9211249  9211253  9211259  9211273  9211289
9211291  9211303  9211337  9211369  9211379  9211387  9211403  9211441  9211451  9211459
9211463  9211471  9211487  9211507  9211513  9211529  9211567  9211571  9211583  9211597
9211667  9211673  9211679  9211711  9211717  9211723  9211733  9211747  9211759  9211781
9211823  9211831  9211837  9211849  9211861  9211889  9211913  9211919  9211949  9211957
9211973  9211987  9211997  9211999  9212009  9212033  9212041  9212059  9212069  9212081
```

```
9212107  9212117  9212129  9212153  9212171  9212197  9212209  9212219  9212233  9212237
9212243  9212251  9212263  9212267  9212293  9212303  9212309  9212323  9212327  9212347
9212377  9212383  9212387  9212389  9212429  9212447  9212461  9212477  9212491  9212507
9212531  9212537  9212543  9212561  9212563  9212573  9212639  9212641  9212669  9212681
9212683  9212699  9212711  9212713  9212767  9212767  9212773  9212783  9212809  9212821
9212849  9212851  9212869  9212887  9212911  9212927  9212933  9212939  9212953  9212977
9212989  9212993  9212999  9213011  9213019  9213023  9213047  9213067  9213073  9213079
9213089  9213101  9213131  9213143  9213161  9213163  9213181  9213199  9213203  9213209
9213221  9213227  9213283  9213299  9213307  9213311  9213313  9213319  9213341  9213349
9213353  9213383  9213401  9213419  9213431  9213433  9213437  9213497  9213511  9213517
9213527  9213559  9213563  9213571  9213583  9213587  9213601  9213637  9213641  9213647
9213683  9213697  9213733  9213749  9213751  9213761  9213767  9213791  9213797  9213821
9213829  9213839  9213857  9213863  9213871  9213923  9213937  9213947  9213979  9214001
9214027  9214033  9214039  9214061  9214063  9214067  9214109  9214123  9214151  9214181
9214189  9214201  9214211  9214253  9214267  9214301  9214307  9214313  9214319  9214327
9214333  9214339  9214343  9214351  9214363  9214367  9214393  9214423  9214433  9214441
9214501  9214507  9214511  9214531  9214537  9214567  9214583  9214603  9214609  9214613
9214631  9214637  9214649  9214661  9214687  9214693  9214703  9214729  9214747  9214759
9214769  9214783  9214787  9214819  9214823  9214831  9214841  9214847  9214859  9214861
9214871  9214883  9214889  9214897  9214913  9214957  9214987  9215023  9215027  9215039
9215047  9215051  9215081  9215137  9215159  9215231  9215233  9215237  9215251  9215293
9215299  9215317  9215333  9215347  9215351  9215419  9215441  9215449  9215461  9215467
9215471  9215473  9215477  9215483  9215497  9215509  9215597  9215603  9215639  9215641
9215651  9215653  9215669  9215699  9215753  9215777  9215797  9215809  9215821  9215827
9215831  9215837  9215879  9215891  9215909  9215911  9215933  9215951  9215953  9215963
9215971  9216019  9216029  9216037  9216049  9216101  9216107  9216133  9216139  9216157
9216161  9216191  9216199  9216239  9216241  9216247  9216253  9216257  9216281  9216283
9216299  9216301  9216343  9216359  9216373  9216391  9216409  9216419  9216433  9216437
9216443  9216451  9216481  9216521  9216523  9216527  9216547  9216593  9216611  9216631
9216661  9216689  9216707  9216719  9216731  9216733  9216787  9216793  9216797  9216799
9216833  9216847  9216853  9216869  9216913  9216943  9216947  9216973  9216979  9217001
9217003  9217031  9217051  9217069  9217073  9217079  9217097  9217121  9217129
9217141  9217163  9217171  9217189  9217193  9217207  9217211  9217237  9217277  9217303
9217309  9217321  9217339  9217343  9217381  9217387  9217421  9217423  9217427  9217441
9217471  9217517  9217531  9217541  9217561  9217567  9217577  9217583  9217589  9217631
9217657  9217667  9217669  9217673  9217697  9217711  9217721  9217727  9217739  9217759
9217763  9217777  9217801  9217807  9217811  9217829  9217837  9217843  9217877  9217883
9217909  9217931  9217933  9217951  9217973  9217979  9217981  9218017  9218023  9218047
9218051  9218087  9218089  9218107  9218117  9218119  9218123  9218141  9218161  9218177
9218189  9218197  9218207  9218213  9218257  9218263  9218269  9218281  9218303  9218309
9218323  9218327  9218347  9218357  9218383  9218393  9218441  9218453  9218459  9218483
9218497  9218507  9218519  9218527  9218537  9218543  9218551  9218557  9218581  9218623
9218633  9218647  9218683  9218689  9218771  9218773  9218821  9218827  9218831  9218843
9218861  9218881  9218917  9218953  9218969  9218983  9218987  9219011  9219017  9219053
9219079  9219107  9219131  9219139  9219167  9219169  9219173  9219211  9219229  9219239
9219241  9219247  9219263  9219271  9219277  9219289  9219293  9219299  9219323  9219337
9219341  9219347  9219367  9219373  9219377  9219409  9219433  9219449  9219451  9219461
9219467  9219499  9219523  9219589  9219611  9219631  9219641  9219653  9219659  9219667
9219671  9219701  9219703  9219733  9219739  9219751  9219757  9219779  9219787  9219799
9219823  9219841  9219851  9219863  9219877  9219907  9219913  9219923  9219929  9219953
9219961  9219979  9220019  9220031  9220049  9220061  9220091  9220093  9220097  9220109
9220117  9220147  9220151  9220157  9220163  9220181  9220207  9220213  9220219  9220241
9220243  9220247  9220249  9220261  9220279  9220283  9220291  9220303  9220313  9220331
9220369  9220399  9220403  9220427  9220429  9220439  9220441  9220451  9220459  9220481
9220483  9220487  9220501  9220537  9220559  9220573  9220583  9220591  9220597  9220621
9220633  9220639  9220649  9220669  9220693  9220709  9220711  9220721  9220751  9220759
9220763  9220787  9220793  9220847  9220867  9220873  9220879  9220891  9220951
9220957  9220969  9221011  9221027  9221033  9221039  9221041  9221057  9221077  9221083
9221087  9221131  9221161  9221171  9221189  9221203  9221207  9221227  9221231  9221237
9221249  9221257  9221297  9221341  9221357  9221371  9221389  9221423  9221453  9221467
9221501  9221503  9221519  9221567  9221617  9221647  9221657  9221659  9221683  9221687
9221711  9221713  9221717  9221741  9221747  9221753  9221777  9221789  9221801  9221809
9221819  9221831  9221833  9221857  9221867  9221879  9221893  9221921  9221923  9221929
9221941  9221951  9221957  9221959  9221983  9221987  9221999  9222001  9222013  9222061
9222079  9222133  9222137  9222173  9222179  9222193  9222197  9222217  9222229  9222247
9222271  9222281  9222289  9222307  9222323  9222341  9222383  9222419  9222431
9222443  9222461  9222487  9222491  9222503  9222527  9222541  9222553  9222569  9222589
9222607  9222623  9222637  9222641  9222649  9222659  9222671  9222673  9222691  9222709
9222713  9222727  9222737  9222739  9222757  9222767  9222781  9222791  9222797  9222799
9222887  9222907  9222911  9222919  9222937  9222979  9222989  9223001  9223003  9223009
9223033  9223063  9223091  9223103  9223111  9223121  9223133  9223141  9223157  9223169
9223177  9223183  9223187  9223211  9223229  9223241  9223259  9223271  9223289  9223297
9223307  9223309  9223321  9223351  9223373  9223387  9223393  9223427  9223429  9223441
9223453  9223481  9223517  9223519  9223549  9223559  9223561  9223567  9223573  9223583
9223597  9223601  9223603  9223637  9223649  9223661  9223679  9223733  9223751  9223757
9223763  9223777  9223783  9223817  9223847  9223853  9223859  9223867  9223889  9223909
9223919  9223927  9223931  9223939  9223969  9223997  9224009  9224029  9224053  9224069
9224093  9224099  9224123  9224147  9224153  9224161  9224167  9224191  9224197  9224239
9224261  9224263  9224269  9224273  9224297  9224321  9224323  9224351  9224381  9224393
9224399  9224437  9224447  9224461  9224483  9224497  9224503  9224513  9224521  9224573
9224609  9224629  9224647  9224653  9224669  9224681  9224687  9224689  9224711  9224717
9224731  9224753  9224773  9224777  9224819  9224837  9224843  9224851  9224857  9224867
9224893  9224911  9224923  9224929  9224947  9224953  9224957  9224969  9224983  9224993
9225023  9225031  9225077  9225079  9225107  9225119  9225133  9225143  9225179  9225191
9225211  9225217  9225221  9225269  9225283  9225289  9225319  9225329  9225331  9225343
9225353  9225361  9225371  9225397  9225421  9225439  9225449  9225467  9225487  9225493
9225497  9225499  9225539  9225547  9225563  9225589  9225613  9225649  9225703  9225709
9225719  9225731  9225739  9225757  9225761  9225803  9225809  9225859  9225871  9225877
9225911  9225919  9225929  9225947  9225971  9225977  9225989  9226027  9226033  9226051
```

```
9226069  9226093  9226099  9226109  9226141  9226159  9226163  9226171  9226177  9226183
9226193  9226207  9226211  9226213  9226247  9226253  9226297  9226307  9226319  9226339
9226351  9226367  9226387  9226391  9226411  9226421  9226439  9226447  9226453  9226493
9226507  9226531  9226537  9226549  9226559  9226573  9226577  9226601  9226603  9226619
9226661  9226667  9226673  9226687  9226697  9226709  9226739  9226753  9226757  9226759
9226769  9226781  9226787  9226793  9226817  9226831  9226859  9226873  9226879  9226883
9226907  9226939  9226957  9226961  9226991  9226999  9227003  9227021  9227041  9227051
9227063  9227083  9227093  9227111  9227129  9227131  9227143  9227149  9227159  9227161
9227203  9227213  9227221  9227227  9227233  9227261  9227297  9227299  9227321  9227329
9227357  9227371  9227381  9227389  9227443  9227479  9227497  9227527  9227563  9227579
9227587  9227591  9227611  9227627  9227633  9227639  9227641  9227683  9227717  9227723
9227731  9227741  9227767  9227791  9227797  9227809  9227849  9227851  9227861  9227879
9227891  9227917  9227921  9227927  9227969  9227983  9228031  9228041  9228047  9228073
9228097  9228103  9228139  9228151  9228169  9228181  9228203  9228209  9228211  9228217
9228223  9228251  9228257  9228259  9228277  9228283  9228287  9228301  9228311  9228337
9228341  9228343  9228361  9228377  9228383  9228389  9228391  9228397  9228419  9228449
9228523  9228553  9228559  9228561  9228563  9228589  9228599  9228601  9228627  9228631
9228689  9228691  9228719  9228743  9228749  9228763  9228767  9228787  9228811  9228827
9228829  9228833  9228881  9228887  9228899  9228907  9228937  9228959  9228971  9228983
9228991  9228997  9229007  9229013  9229027  9229037  9229057  9229069  9229091  9229093
9229111  9229123  9229153  9229177  9229189  9229201  9229237  9229247  9229267  9229277
9229291  9229309  9229331  9229349  9229369  9229373  9229393  9229397  9229399  9229403
9229411  9229427  9229433  9229439  9229457  9229489  9229513  9229523  9229529  9229603
9229607  9229621  9229651  9229663  9229667  9229669  9229673  9229679  9229699  9229709
9229711  9229721  9229741  9229751  9229757  9229769  9229789  9229799  9229823  9229889
9229931  9229939  9229943  9229949  9229951  9229967  9229973  9230009  9230021  9230027
9230051  9230063  9230077  9230083  9230113  9230119  9230161  9230171  9230173  9230183
9230191  9230203  9230209  9230227  9230231  9230239  9230267  9230291  9230297  9230317
9230327  9230329  9230341  9230357  9230363  9230369  9230407  9230411  9230437  9230443
9230449  9230461  9230477  9230483  9230489  9230519  9230537  9230549  9230579  9230587
9230593  9230623  9230629  9230633  9230651  9230687  9230707  9230717  9230737  9230743
9230773  9230803  9230807  9230821  9230867  9230869  9230873  9230891  9230911  9230917
9230927  9230929  9230953  9230959  9230971  9230987  9230999  9231029  9231031  9231049
9231067  9231091  9231113  9231133  9231139  9231143  9231203  9231217  9231247  9231253
9231281  9231293  9231301  9231307  9231311  9231329  9231331  9231371  9231373  9231379
9231401  9231419  9231427  9231451  9231457  9231479  9231569  9231571  9231577  9231619
9231623  9231631  9231637  9231641  9231647  9231659  9231661  9231689  9231721  9231727
9231737  9231751  9231791  9231793  9231821  9231823  9231829  9231839  9231851  9231869
9231899  9231913  9231919  9231953  9231979  9231983  9232021  9232049  9232051  9232073
9232103  9232117  9232127  9232147  9232193  9232217  9232219  9232231  9232243  9232253
9232259  9232313  9232319  9232337  9232373  9232381  9232397  9232429  9232459  9232463
9232471  9232477  9232481  9232507  9232543  9232549  9232579  9232589  9232603  9232607
9232631  9232661  9232669  9232673  9232681  9232693  9232703  9232711  9232753  9232757
9232763  9232781  9232793  9232807  9232829  9232843  9232849  9232877  9232889  9232901
9232907  9232919  9232931  9232939  9232957  9232961  9232987  9233039  9233041  9233047
9233093  9233099  9233111  9233123  9233167  9233171  9233173  9233189  9233201  9233207
9233209  9233219  9233233  9233243  9233267  9233269  9233293  9233299  9233303  9233311
9233317  9233321  9233407  9233417  9233437  9233447  9233453  9233459  9233489  9233507
9233561  9233579  9233591  9233611  9233657  9233659  9233671  9233681  9233689  9233701
9233711  9233729  9233743  9233759  9233767  9233773  9233821  9233837  9233849  9233869
9233881  9233899  9233923  9233927  9233929  9233951  9233969  9234013  9234037  9234041
9234067  9234079  9234089  9234101  9234107  9234131  9234139  9234161  9234163  9234223
9234227  9234229  9234257  9234263  9234271  9234283  9234287  9234299  9234353  9234359
9234367  9234391  9234403  9234413  9234457  9234469  9234479  9234487  9234493  9234509
9234517  9234521  9234529  9234539  9234581  9234601  9234613  9234619  9234623  9234647
9234649  9234679  9234697  9234717  9234727  9234747  9234751  9234761  9234763  9234767
9234803  9234853  9234917  9234919  9234923  9234943  9234947  9234949  9234959  9234971
9234977  9234989  9234991  9234997  9235003  9235019  9235049  9235053  9235057  9235061
9235123  9235133  9235141  9235201  9235207  9235223  9235229  9235309  9235319  9235333
9235363  9235367  9235381  9235433  9235483  9235487  9235507  9235511  9235519  9235529
9235531  9235549  9235553  9235559  9235561  9235591  9235637  9235649  9235651  9235663
9235693  9235697  9235703  9235711  9235739  9235747  9235753  9235781  9235819  9235823
9235857  9235867  9235871  9235901  9235921  9235931  9235943  9235979  9235987  9235997
9235999  9236021  9236023  9236057  9236077  9236081  9236089  9236093  9236119  9236131
9236137  9236141  9236167  9236173  9236191  9236197  9236203  9236207  9236231  9236251
9236263  9236291  9236303  9236309  9236327  9236341  9236351  9236369  9236371  9236399
9236431  9236441  9236449  9236453  9236477  9236483  9236497  9236503  9236531  9236537
9236567  9236621  9236651  9236657  9236663  9236671  9236699  9236707  9236713  9236723
9236737  9236741  9236749  9236779  9236783  9236789  9236813  9236867  9236879  9236881
9236897  9236911  9236921  9236923  9236963  9237017  9237031  9237037  9237049  9237061
9237073  9237113  9237121  9237149  9237181  9237187  9237197  9237199  9237227  9237253
9237257  9237281  9237299  9237301  9237331  9237343  9237353  9237377  9237419  9237433
9237461  9237469  9237479  9237517  9237533  9237539  9237541  9237551  9237581  9237593
9237611  9237617  9237643  9237649  9237661  9237677  9237691  9237703  9237713  9237737
9237769  9237799  9237821  9237829  9237869  9237871  9237887  9237889  9237913  9237923
9237929  9237959  9237961  9238001  9238007  9238013  9238039  9238057  9238063  9238069
9238081  9238087  9238109  9238121  9238129  9238133  9238171  9238189  9238193  9238231
9238241  9238261  9238277  9238291  9238297  9238301  9238303  9238319  9238459  9238481
9238391  9238399  9238409  9238423  9238457  9238459  9238477  9238499  9238519  9238529
9238553  9238561  9238577  9238597  9238609  9238613  9238627  9238631  9238637  9238681
9238687  9238699  9238703  9238721  9238739  9238741  9238753  9238759  9238763  9238771
9238777  9238787  9238799  9238811  9238819  9238841  9238897  9238903  9238909  9238919
9238951  9238967  9238981  9239033  9239039  9239053  9239071  9239089  9239107  9239117
9239137  9239141  9239161  9239171  9239189  9239201  9239207  9239221  9239231  9239239
9239249  9239257  9239291  9239303  9239323  9239327  9239359  9239383  9239387  9239423
9239467  9239471  9239513  9239521  9239563  9239579  9239591  9239597  9239611  9239623
9239663  9239689  9239693  9239701  9239707  9239729  9239743  9239753  9239759  9239773
9239803  9239837  9239843  9239849  9239863  9239873  9239887  9239933  9239939  9239941
9239963  9239977  9239987  9239999  9240001  9240013  9240017  9240019  9240029  9240053
```

```
9240107  9240113  9240131  9240151  9240157  9240169  9240173  9240221  9240223  9240229
9240281  9240311  9240337  9240359  9240377  9240383  9240409  9240421  9240431  9240433
9240461  9240467  9240509  9240523  9240601  9240607  9240617  9240619  9240629  9240643
9240667  9240683  9240689  9240701  9240727  9240731  9240739  9240767  9240769  9240797
9240817  9240827  9240839  9240857  9240893  9240919  9240923  9240929  9240947  9240953
9240961  9240967  9240983  9240989  9240991  9241021  9241039  9241079  9241091  9241097
9241103  9241121  9241123  9241151  9241181  9241213  9241223  9241237  9241249  9241261
9241273  9241301  9241313  9241327  9241333  9241339  9241357  9241367  9241369  9241373
9241381  9241403  9241411  9241433  9241447  9241457  9241471  9241549  9241553  9241559
9241567  9241571  9241579  9241643  9241669  9241681  9241709  9241711  9241717  9241723
9241747  9241777  9241787  9241811  9241831  9241853  9241871  9241877  9241879  9241889
9241901  9241907  9241957  9241963  9241993  9242003  9242017  9242029  9242053  9242059
9242069  9242081  9242111  9242117  9242137  9242143  9242153  9242183  9242197  9242209
9242231  9242239  9242243  9242279  9242323  9242327  9242333  9242347  9242353  9242357
9242381  9242393  9242399  9242413  9242419  9242423  9242459  9242461  9242473  9242477
9242479  9242483  9242501  9242539  9242581  9242587  9242627  9242633  9242641  9242657
9242663  9242687  9242689  9242693  9242699  9242707  9242719  9242729  9242731  9242741
9242791  9242819  9242833  9242837  9242843  9242887  9242897  9242923  9242957  9242971
9242983  9243001  9243011  9243049  9243071  9243077  9243089  9243097  9243103  9243107
9243131  9243133  9243167  9243181  9243197  9243209  9243211  9243259  9243281  9243293
9243307  9243317  9243319  9243337  9243341  9243371  9243383  9243389  9243407  9243433
9243439  9243457  9243467  9243469  9243473  9243497  9243499  9243503  9243523  9243551
9243583  9243607  9243613  9243649  9243653  9243659  9243679  9243683  9243691  9243713
9243743  9243761  9243781  9243791  9243799  9243833  9243841  9243847  9243877  9243881
9243887  9243929  9243931  9243947  9243967  9243977  9243979  9243989  9243991  9244009
9244021  9244031  9244049  9244093  9244099  9244111  9244133  9244171  9244177  9244199
9244211  9244217  9244223  9244237  9244309  9244337  9244351  9244357  9244369  9244373
9244381  9244387  9244421  9244423  9244439  9244451  9244453  9244483  9244513  9244517
9244523  9244531  9244537  9244553  9244577  9244579  9244607  9244667  9244681  9244747
9244757  9244771  9244777  9244799  9244819  9244841  9244867  9244877  9244903  9244909
9244927  9244933  9244951  9244969  9244979  9244987  9244993  9244999  9245017  9245087
9245101  9245107  9245141  9245189  9245233  9245251  9245263  9245309  9245311  9245317
9245339  9245371  9245413  9245437  9245441  9245443  9245447  9245491  9245503  9245507
9245513  9245557  9245591  9245611  9245617  9245627  9245653  9245659  9245689  9245711
9245729  9245741  9245759  9245777  9245791  9245813  9245851  9245911  9245921  9245927
9245947  9245959  9245963  9245969  9245987  9246007  9246019  9246031  9246037  9246047
9246053  9246071  9246097  9246131  9246151  9246163  9246199  9246227  9246229  9246233
9246287  9246301  9246323  9246329  9246343  9246353  9246359  9246371  9246379  9246403
9246427  9246439  9246467  9246473  9246491  9246551  9246553  9246557  9246569  9246571
9246577  9246593  9246599  9246617  9246631  9246637  9246647  9246661  9246683  9246701
9246703  9246709  9246761  9246767  9246779  9246803  9246821  9246841  9246847  9246859
9246869  9246877  9246889  9246899  9246907  9246917  9246931  9246949  9246967  9246971
9246973  9247009  9247019  9247033  9247057  9247079  9247087  9247123  9247157  9247169
9247171  9247177  9247211  9247283  9247289  9247307  9247339  9247349  9247351  9247361
9247379  9247397  9247409  9247423  9247463  9247477  9247489  9247501  9247519  9247529
9247543  9247577  9247577  9247583  9247597  9247603  9247613  9247619  9247621  9247663
9247687  9247691  9247727  9247739  9247741  9247751  9247757  9247769  9247787  9247793
9247801  9247829  9247831  9247853  9247877  9247879  9247907  9247913  9247921  9247933
9247937  9247939  9247969  9247993  9247999  9248009  9248011  9248059  9248069  9248081
9248089  9248101  9248111  9248123  9248147  9248159  9248171  9248189  9248201  9248219
9248243  9248263  9248269  9248281  9248287  9248289  9248333  9248339  9248347  9248359
9248363  9248377  9248431  9248467  9248501  9248513  9248537  9248539  9248543  9248549
9248563  9248621  9248639  9248641  9248647  9248653  9248677  9248683  9248689  9248693
9248699  9248719  9248761  9248767  9248803  9248843  9248851  9248861  9248879  9248887
9248893  9248929  9248933  9248947  9248963  9248971  9248983  9249041  9249073  9249077
9249103  9249113  9249131  9249157  9249161  9249167  9249193  9249209  9249211  9249217
9249221  9249263  9249269  9249287  9249293  9249299  9249301  9249323  9249337  9249353
9249367  9249379  9249391  9249403  9249407  9249419  9249421  9249431  9249433  9249481
9249497  9249511  9249529  9249533  9249571  9249587  9249589  9249623  9249661  9249671
9249689  9249701  9249707  9249731  9249733  9249739  9249763  9249767  9249781  9249787
9249797  9249803  9249839  9249847  9249871  9249881  9249893  9249899  9249907  9249913
9249923  9249937  9249943  9249959  9249967  9249971  9249983  9250009  9250013  9250039
9250061  9250097  9250123  9250127  9250139  9250177  9250181  9250229  9250231  9250237
9250243  9250247  9250273  9250279  9250309  9250331  9250337  9250343  9250349  9250361
9250387  9250403  9250427  9250429  9250441  9250447  9250453  9250459  9250463  9250469
9250513  9250537  9250561  9250573  9250583  9250607  9250609  9250611  9250627  9250639
9250643  9250649  9250667  9250693  9250697  9250699  9250723  9250727  9250733  9250751
9250753  9250763  9250781  9250819  9250823  9250837  9250849  9250867  9250877  9250883
9250897  9250903  9250909  9250921  9250937  9250949  9250951  9250957  9250981  9250993
9251003  9251017  9251027  9251059  9251161  9251167  9251173  9251183  9251189  9251201
9251219  9251227  9251239  9251273  9251279  9251323  9251329  9251353  9251387  9251399
9251401  9251413  9251419  9251447  9251449  9251479  9251483  9251491  9251503  9251507
9251531  9251533  9251549  9251581  9251597  9251603  9251617  9251629  9251647  9251657
9251659  9251663  9251677  9251699  9251719  9251771  9251821  9251831  9251843  9251863
9251873  9251881  9251897  9251909  9251933  9251941  9251951  9251971  9251999  9252007
9252011  9252013  9252041  9252079  9252143  9252149  9252161  9252169  9252209  9252241
9252251  9252281  9252283  9252311  9252319  9252323  9252329  9252337  9252343  9252349
9252359  9252361  9252367  9252377  9252379  9252389  9252409  9252413  9252427  9252431
9252433  9252457  9252473  9252497  9252517  9252521  9252547  9252571  9252577  9252583
9252587  9252589  9252599  9252619  9252623  9252629  9252637  9252667  9252679  9252721
9252773  9252781  9252787  9252809  9252821  9252847  9252857  9252863  9252883  9252917
9252931  9252949  9252953  9252959  9252961  9252977  9253007  9253043  9253051  9253073
9253081  9253087  9253099  9253103  9253163  9253177  9253187  9253193  9253207  9253243
9253259  9253267  9253297  9253319  9253333  9253351  9253357  9253373  9253379  9253381
9253393  9253397  9253451  9253463  9253467  9253483  9253493  9253511  9253537  9253549
9253561  9253579  9253603  9253609  9253633  9253649  9253669  9253679  9253687  9253693
9253711  9253723  9253789  9253807  9253847  9253873  9253879  9253891  9253957  9253963
9254009  9254023  9254029  9254053  9254057  9254059  9254093  9254111  9254149  9254153
9254177  9254183  9254191  9254227  9254237  9254243  9254261  9254263  9254281  9254291
```

```
9254299 9254317 9254351 9254359 9254369 9254381 9254411 9254449 9254459 9254473
9254507 9254513 9254549 9254569 9254593 9254599 9254603 9254611 9254627 9254633
9254657 9254659 9254677 9254689 9254747 9254789 9254821 9254831 9254879 9254891
9254897 9254899 9254923 9254939 9254963 9254983 9254989 9255007 9255023 9255041
9255047 9255067 9255079 9255083 9255101 9255119 9255137 9255139 9255161 9255163
9255167 9255173 9255181 9255203 9255221 9255227 9255241 9255289 9255319 9255331
9255349 9255353 9255383 9255397 9255409 9255427 9255431 9255457 9255461 9255479
9255503 9255509 9255511 9255523 9255529 9255601 9255613 9255619 9255647 9255677
9255691 9255737 9255739 9255749 9255751 9255767 9255811 9255817 9255853 9255881
9255893 9255919 9255919 9255931 9255941 9255947 9255971 9255977 9255989 9255991
9255997 9256033 9256063 9256069 9256099 9256103 9256111 9256147 9256151 9256153
9256183 9256187 9256207 9256213 9256217 9256229 9256237 9256271 9256277 9256297
9256319 9256337 9256343 9256361 9256367 9256399 9256411 9256417 9256441 9256469
9256493 9256501 9256523 9256531 9256537 9256561 9256571 9256573 9256589 9256601
9256651 9256657 9256661 9256669 9256673 9256703 9256729 9256733 9256747 9256757
9256763 9256769 9256777 9256799 9256813 9256831 9256837 9256873 9256901 9256937
9256943 9256957 9256963 9256969 9256981 9256987 9256991 9256999 9257011 9257023
9257029 9257069 9257071 9257081 9257093 9257099 9257111 9257117 9257141 9257153
9257173 9257179 9257207 9257219 9257233 9257243 9257249 9257257 9257263 9257273
9257279 9257291 9257317 9257321 9257329 9257359 9257393 9257419 9257429 9257441
9257447 9257459 9257461 9257471 9257473 9257483 9257489 9257491 9257497 9257509
9257527 9257551 9257557 9257587 9257597 9257603 9257627 9257629 9257657 9257663
9257671 9257681 9257683 9257687 9257711 9257713 9257723 9257767 9257791 9257797
9257803 9257813 9257821 9257827 9257837 9257839 9257849 9257861 9257879 9257893
9257917 9257939 9257951 9257953 9257981 9257999 9258001 9258019 9258023 9258037
9258043 9258083 9258091 9258097 9258113 9258157 9258191 9258209 9258229 9258253
9258269 9258281 9258289 9258299 9258341 9258349 9258391 9258407 9258419 9258433
9258439 9258449 9258451 9258463 9258467 9258481 9258503 9258521 9258527 9258541
9258551 9258559 9258593 9258607 9258617 9258629 9258653 9258679 9258701 9258703
9258707 9258731 9258791 9258793 9258827 9258841 9258869 9258919 9258923 9258959
9258961 9258971 9258983 9259013 9259027 9259051 9259057 9259073 9259109 9259121
9259123 9259163 9259171 9259177 9259193 9259267 9259291 9259301 9259303 9259309
9259321 9259357 9259379 9259387 9259429 9259433 9259447 9259451 9259457 9259463
9259487 9259493 9259499 9259507 9259513 9259531 9259553 9259567 9259571 9259589
9259619 9259667 9259681 9259711 9259721 9259751 9259753 9259759 9259801 9259819
9259829 9259837 9259841 9259847 9259853 9259889 9259909 9259927 9259931 9259933
9259937 9259963 9260023 9260039 9260051 9260057 9260071 9260113 9260117 9260129
9260131 9260149 9260159 9260161 9260197 9260203 9260231 9260263 9260267 9260281
9260287 9260327 9260347 9260369 9260399 9260401 9260411 9260417 9260431 9260441
9260443 9260453 9260477 9260477 9260479 9260491 9260497 9260501 9260549 9260567
9260569 9260611 9260621 9260633 9260639 9260659 9260663 9260677 9260681 9260699
9260753 9260777 9260803 9260827 9260857 9260861 9260873 9260887 9260893 9260899
9260921 9260939 9260963 9261013 9261023 9261041 9261059 9261089 9261101 9261103
9261127 9261143 9261163 9261173 9261181 9261191 9261193 9261199 9261229 9261233
9261293 9261299 9261331 9261361 9261391 9261409 9261443 9261457 9261487 9261521
9261533 9261541 9261547 9261557 9261559 9261601 9261619 9261631 9261647 9261671
9261673 9261677 9261689 9261713 9261731 9261751 9261757 9261793 9261799 9261829
9261869 9261907 9261929 9261943 9261947 9262007 9262009 9262051 9262061 9262073
9262079 9262091 9262103 9262109 9262117 9262129 9262171 9262181 9262193 9262199
9262217 9262249 9262259 9262277 9262283 9262289 9262343 9262361 9262387 9262391
9262411 9262427 9262441 9262453 9262457 9262483 9262489 9262507 9262541 9262553
9262567 9262573 9262577 9262613 9262639 9262661 9262697 9262703 9262733 9262741
9262753 9262763 9262777 9262783 9262787 9262819 9262837 9262849 9262867 9262871
9262889 9262961 9262963 9262991 9262993 9263003 9263041 9263047 9263063 9263077
9263081 9263083 9263087 9263117 9263131 9263143 9263153 9263159 9263161 9263167
9263173 9263179 9263207 9263231 9263237 9263239 9263269 9263297 9263331 9263337
9263363 9263369 9263407 9263437 9263489 9263491 9263509 9263537 9263539 9263567
9263587 9263599 9263647 9263651 9263669 9263677 9263689 9263693 9263707 9263741
9263753 9263809 9263819 9263831 9263843 9263851 9263857 9263869 9263873 9263939
9263951 9263957 9263971 9263981 9263983 9263987 9263999 9264007 9264037 9264041
9264061 9264067 9264103 9264109 9264127 9264139 9264163 9264169 9264199 9264223
9264247 9264263 9264271 9264317 9264329 9264349 9264389 9264391 9264397 9264403
9264407 9264449 9264461 9264481 9264491 9264517 9264527 9264529 9264547 9264557
9264583 9264587 9264599 9264611 9264613 9264617 9264623 9264631 9264667
9264683 9264707 9264721 9264743 9264751 9264769 9264793 9264797 9264803 9264817
9264821 9264839 9264881 9264887 9264919 9264941 9264967 9264971 9264991 9265013
9265019 9265037 9265043 9265049 9265073 9265079 9265099 9265127 9265147 9265159
9265171 9265177 9265211 9265213 9265259 9265261 9265271 9265273 9265279 9265283
9265307 9265309 9265387 9265393 9265397 9265411 9265423 9265433 9265453 9265453
9265463 9265469 9265517 9265519 9265541 9265547 9265579 9265589 9265603 9265609
9265637 9265657 9265679 9265691 9265709 9265723 9265741 9265759 9265771 9265783
9265801 9265843 9265847 9265859 9265889 9265903 9265943 9265957 9265967 9265979
9265999 9266011 9266019 9266039 9266063 9266077 9266087 9266111 9266137 9266141
9266143 9266183 9266197 9266219 9266221 9266233 9266237 9266239 9266267 9266291
9266311 9266333 9266353 9266381 9266393 9266407 9266419 9266429 9266431 9266483
9266497 9266501 9266503 9266527 9266531 9266557 9266563 9266597 9266639 9266641
9266659 9266729 9266731 9266753 9266767 9266771 9266773 9266783 9266827 9266843
9266857 9266897 9266899 9266903 9266941 9266951 9266977 9266989 9267029 9267031
9267061 9267067 9267073 9267101 9267113 9267119 9267121 9267127 9267149 9267157
9267169 9267179 9267187 9267217 9267241 9267263 9267299 9267301 9267311 9267341
9267347 9267359 9267361 9267371 9267389 9267407 9267449 9267491 9267493 9267509
9267521 9267523 9267529 9267539 9267541 9267563 9267581 9267593 9267607 9267613
9267619 9267623 9267637 9267647 9267653 9267679 9267683 9267707 9267721 9267761
9267767 9267773 9267787 9267823 9267829 9267887 9267917 9267959 9267983 9267989
9268001 9268013 9268031 9268033 9268037 9268073 9268087 9268109 9268121
9268123 9268141 9268151 9268159 9268211 9268261 9268267 9268271 9268277 9268291
9268307 9268309 9268319 9268321 9268339 9268387 9268397 9268403 9268421 9268423
9268443 9268459 9268489 9268513 9268543 9268547 9268559 9268573 9268577 9268627
9268631 9268639 9268663 9268673 9268681 9268691 9268709 9268711 9268739 9268741
```

```
9268811  9268813  9268817  9268873  9268877  9268879  9268891  9268901  9268921  9268939
9268943  9268949  9268957  9268997  9268999  9269041  9269053  9269081  9269087  9269119
9269147  9269153  9269159  9269171  9269177  9269189  9269213  9269237  9269243  9269257
9269269  9269287  9269291  9269297  9269311  9269333  9269339  9269353  9269371  9269389
9269419  9269453  9269459  9269479  9269461  9269479  9269489  9269509  9269543  9269563
9269581  9269591  9269599  9269609  9269629  9269633  9269653  9269657  9269671  9269677
9269693  9269699  9269707  9269719  9269761  9269773  9269779  9269783  9269797  9269801
9269807  9269833  9269839  9269849  9269861  9269867  9269893  9269921  9269933  9269941
9269959  9269969  9269971  9270007  9270011  9270029  9270047  9270061  9270101  9270113
9270143  9270167  9270179  9270199  9270203  9270211  9270221  9270263  9270269  9270281
9270293  9270301  9270307  9270323  9270361  9270367  9270377  9270383  9270397  9270409
9270419  9270427  9270431  9270433  9270463  9270467  9270473  9270497  9270511  9270523
9270529  9270539  9270553  9270557  9270563  9270577  9270637  9270647  9270697  9270733
9270743  9270769  9270773  9270791  9270809  9270823  9270827  9270853  9270881  9270889
9270893  9270901  9270931  9270941  9270971  9270973  9270977  9271021  9271051  9271057
9271061  9271063  9271081  9271091  9271099  9271111  9271121  9271123  9271151  9271153
9271169  9271193  9271217  9271253  9271261  9271279  9271291  9271309  9271313  9271337
9271403  9271421  9271429  9271441  9271447  9271459  9271469  9271481  9271489  9271499
9271513  9271517  9271529  9271543  9271583  9271597  9271617  9271651  9271667  9271679
9271687  9271693  9271711  9271721  9271727  9271729  9271733  9271739  9271741  9271747
9271771  9271807  9271837  9271841  9271849  9271859  9271861  9271877  9271879  9271891
9271903  9271907  9271937  9271963  9271991  9272017  9272033  9272041  9272101  9272129
9272147  9272167  9272173  9272177  9272189  9272201  9272203  9272213  9272231  9272239
9272279  9272339  9272353  9272357  9272359  9272363  9272371  9272401  9272411  9272413
9272423  9272447  9272479  9272537  9272539  9272569  9272579  9272587  9272603  9272609
9272621  9272623  9272647  9272687  9272713  9272773  9272777  9272797  9272801  9272819
9272831  9272833  9272849  9272863  9272873  9272899  9272927  9272947  9272951  9272983
9273013  9273029  9273031  9273049  9273059  9273067  9273073  9273133  9273161  9273179
9273181  9273191  9273203  9273217  9273227  9273287  9273289  9273293  9273307  9273317
9273323  9273353  9273373  9273377  9273379  9273391  9273419  9273431  9273437  9273461
9273469  9273479  9273487  9273497  9273499  9273527  9273541  9273553  9273581  9273587
9273637  9273659  9273689  9273703  9273713  9273739  9273757  9273763  9273773  9273793
9273799  9273809  9273821  9273841  9273851  9273871  9273893  9273907  9273923  9273931
9273947  9273961  9273973  9273983  9274003  9274019  9274039  9274049  9274051  9274063
9274079  9274081  9274093  9274103  9274117  9274141  9274157  9274183  9274189  9274217
9274247  9274253  9274273  9274277  9274319  9274327  9274351  9274373  9274399  9274409
9274411  9274453  9274459  9274471  9274481  9274511  9274513  9274553  9274561  9274579
9274583  9274597  9274619  9274631  9274637  9274663  9274667  9274687  9274691  9274697
9274709  9274711  9274721  9274739  9274747  9274781  9274787  9274789  9274813  9274861
9274871  9274879  9274883  9274939  9274949  9274961  9274987  9274997  9274999  9275009
9275023  9275029  9275033  9275039  9275083  9275093  9275111  9275117  9275119  9275209
9275219  9275257  9275261  9275281  9275297  9275317  9275339  9275341  9275377  9275381
9275393  9275423  9275429  9275443  9275473  9275543  9275561  9275569  9275579  9275593
9275597  9275611  9275633  9275671  9275677  9275683  9275687  9275701  9275731  9275753
9275759  9275767  9275797  9275801  9275807  9275821  9275837  9275839  9275867  9275869
9275879  9275939  9275951  9275983  9275989  9275993  9276017  9276019  9276023  9276073
9276097  9276119  9276121  9276149  9276173  9276181  9276187  9276191  9276229  9276247
9276251  9276257  9276269  9276277  9276287  9276301  9276353  9276359  9276367  9276391
9276403  9276419  9276439  9276469  9276473  9276481  9276497  9276499  9276517  9276523
9276539  9276557  9276563  9276569  9276581  9276583  9276637  9276649  9276671  9276689
9276727  9276739  9276763  9276791  9276811  9276821  9276847  9276851  9276853  9276857
9276859  9276871  9276877  9276893  9276923  9276977  9276979  9276989  9276991  9277031
9277039  9277043  9277069  9277097  9277109  9277127  9277139  9277141  9277157  9277183
9277199  9277201  9277217  9277241  9277243  9277253  9277267  9277297  9277309  9277327
9277363  9277369  9277381  9277397  9277399  9277403  9277421  9277451  9277483  9277501
9277511  9277521  9277537  9277547  9277549  9277553  9277559  9277607  9277613  9277621
9277663  9277669  9277693  9277727  9277729  9277747  9277769  9277771  9277799  9277819
9277831  9277843  9277859  9277867  9277913  9277921  9277951  9277967  9277973  9277979
9277991  9278029  9278033  9278041  9278053  9278069  9278117  9278119  9278149  9278167
9278197  9278201  9278221  9278249  9278257  9278263  9278267  9278279  9278309  9278323
9278329  9278333  9278363  9278369  9278383  9278429  9278449  9278459  9278479  9278483
9278491  9278513  9278531  9278539  9278557  9278573  9278597  9278609  9278611  9278623
9278639  9278681  9278699  9278713  9278723  9278743  9278767  9278791  9278809  9278837
9278849  9278879  9278887  9278891  9278909  9278911  9278917  9278921  9278947  9278953
9278963  9278987  9278993  9279007  9279029  9279037  9279041  9279071  9279077  9279089
9279113  9279139  9279157  9279169  9279191  9279197  9279211  9279227  9279233  9279241
9279269  9279289  9279301  9279313  9279329  9279337  9279359  9279367  9279371  9279377
9279401  9279437  9279451  9279481  9279493  9279527  9279551  9279553  9279559  9279583
9279587  9279601  9279607  9279617  9279631  9279643  9279659  9279661  9279703  9279709
9279731  9279737  9279749  9279761  9279769  9279793  9279811  9279863  9279877  9279887
9279889  9279901  9279911  9279917  9279931  9279937  9279953  9279973  9279983  9280001
9280027  9280043  9280049  9280069  9280091  9280097  9280099  9280121  9280123  9280163
9280199  9280211  9280241  9280267  9280277  9280279  9280289  9280301  9280321  9280387
9280393  9280399  9280409  9280421  9280429  9280457  9280471  9280483  9280507  9280511
9280519  9280529  9280541  9280543  9280547  9280549  9280559  9280571  9280603  9280627
9280631  9280633  9280651  9280679  9280693  9280703  9280717  9280729  9280751  9280757
9280771  9280781  9280787  9280823  9280829  9280837  9280847  9280849  9280871  9280879
9280897  9280903  9280919  9280927  9280933  9280939  9280951  9280979  9281003  9281011
9281017  9281071  9281081  9281093  9281119  9281123  9281171  9281179  9281197  9281273
9281281  9281297  9281299  9281323  9281399  9281407  9281417  9281423  9281449  9281453
9281477  9281491  9281497  9281521  9281527  9281549  9281567  9281603  9281611  9281647
9281651  9281659  9281663  9281669  9281689  9281737  9281749  9281771  9281773  9281809
9281843  9281849  9281869  9281889  9281873  9281891  9281899  9281951  9281953  9281959
9281963  9281971  9281977  9281999  9282011  9282019  9282029  9282037  9282061  9282083
9282103  9282131  9282137  9282149  9282151  9282157  9282173  9282191  9282193  9282197
9282209  9282211  9282239  9282269  9282283  9282307  9282319  9282337  9282341  9282373
9282379  9282389  9282397  9282401  9282419  9282437  9282439  9282451  9282457  9282467
9282491  9282503  9282577  9282587  9282589  9282613  9282631  9282643  9282673  9282677
9282701  9282739  9282743  9282751  9282781  9282787  9282817  9282827  9282839  9282863
```

```
9282877 9282881 9282907 9282943 9283031 9283033 9283049 9283061 9283069 9283093
9283117 9283129 9283133 9283159 9283171 9283177 9283181 9283187 9283193 9283201
9283223 9283247 9283259 9283271 9283273 9283279 9283303 9283327 9283331 9283349
9283357 9283403 9283409 9283423 9283429 9283433 9283447 9283541 9283543 9283583
9283607 9283643 9283667 9283669 9283691 9283693 9283711 9283727 9283733 9283739
9283759 9283763 9283801 9283811 9283823 9283831 9283847 9283861 9283867 9283873
9283907 9283909 9283919 9283943 9283961 9283969 9283993 9284029 9284039 9284047
9284059 9284071 9284083 9284113 9284117 9284129 9284153 9284183 9284201 9284207
9284237 9284243 9284267 9284269 9284273 9284279 9284281 9284309 9284311 9284323
9284371 9284377 9284393 9284399 9284423 9284449 9284453 9284459 9284477 9284501
9284543 9284557 9284563 9284609 9284623 9284641 9284677 9284683 9284707 9284713
9284773 9284789 9284813 9284827 9284831 9284833 9284851 9284857 9284867
9284879 9284917 9284921 9284923 9284929 9284953 9284963 9284971 9284987 9284999
9285011 9285013 9285047 9285049 9285161 9285173 9285181 9285193 9285197 9285203
9285209 9285217 9285239 9285253 9285257 9285259 9285277 9285299 9285313 9285343
9285371 9285379 9285391 9285401 9285403 9285407 9285413 9285421 9285427 9285439
9285457 9285469 9285487 9285489 9285503 9285509 9285569 9285571 9285589
9285607 9285613 9285643 9285659 9285671 9285677 9285691 9285697 9285733 9285751
9285763 9285797 9285799 9285811 9285821 9285841 9285911 9285917 9285919 9285929
9285949 9285953 9285959 9285973 9285977 9286009 9286021 9286027 9286033 9286073
9286093 9286129 9286139 9286141 9286153 9286169 9286219 9286259 9286261 9286279
9286309 9286327 9286363 9286379 9286399 9286429 9286439 9286441 9286447 9286463
9286469 9286477 9286499 9286507 9286517 9286523 9286531 9286547 9286559 9286561
9286619 9286631 9286643 9286657 9286663 9286799 9286807 9286817 9286829
9286831 9286843 9286847 9286859 9286897 9286903 9286919 9286943 9286957 9286961
9286969 9286997 9286999 9287027 9287041 9287053 9287063 9287081 9287087 9287099
9287107 9287123 9287141 9287167 9287177 9287203 9287227 9287231 9287237 9287261
9287263 9287293 9287303 9287329 9287363 9287381 9287413 9287429 9287437 9287471
9287483 9287489 9287497 9287501 9287519 9287521 9287539 9287543 9287567 9287573
9287591 9287639 9287651 9287659 9287737 9287749 9287813 9287821 9287833 9287849
9287857 9287869 9287881 9287939 9287947 9287977 9287987 9287989 9288023 9288049
9288053 9288077 9288089 9288121 9288151 9288179 9288199 9288211 9288233 9288241
9288259 9288269 9288271 9288319 9288329 9288337 9288347 9288361 9288401 9288413
9288421 9288449 9288451 9288467 9288479 9288529 9288533 9288553 9288557 9288571
9288581 9288589 9288599 9288649 9288659 9288661 9288677 9288683 9288691 9288703
9288709 9288733 9288743 9288767 9288781 9288791 9288793 9288823 9288853 9288857
9288883 9288893 9288913 9288949 9288971 9288973 9288977 9289009 9289013 9289037
9289039 9289061 9289069 9289073 9289099 9289103 9289129 9289139 9289153 9289187
9289199 9289211 9289223 9289253 9289319 9289321 9289337 9289339 9289351 9289381
9289387 9289393 9289417 9289433 9289451 9289457 9289459 9289471 9289481 9289487
9289517 9289523 9289529 9289547 9289549 9289561 9289571 9289573 9289589 9289601
9289607 9289619 9289639 9289661 9289663 9289733 9289757 9289771 9289781 9289793
9289807 9289811 9289817 9289829 9289867 9289897 9289913 9289919 9289933 9289937
9289979 9289991 9290003 9290009 9290033 9290039 9290077 9290101 9290123
9290131 9290147 9290167 9290181 9290209 9290227 9290233 9290243 9290249 9290251
9290257 9290269 9290329 9290339 9290363 9290371 9290387 9290399 9290417
9290419 9290447 9290461 9290467 9290473 9290507 9290509 9290539 9290543 9290573
9290581 9290587 9290591 9290599 9290609 9290657 9290681 9290683 9290761 9290773
9290803 9290843 9290863 9290893 9290903 9290921 9290923 9290947 9290987
9290999 9291013 9291031 9291047 9291071 9291077 9291083 9291097 9291109 9291119
9291127 9291137 9291151 9291167 9291169 9291179 9291211 9291251 9291263 9291277
9291283 9291307 9291319 9291343 9291371 9291389 9291391 9291407 9291419 9291421
9291433 9291439 9291449 9291467 9291479 9291481 9291521 9291523 9291539 9291553
9291613 9291617 9291631 9291641 9291643 9291647 9291649 9291671 9291691 9291719
9291721 9291749 9291757 9291781 9291811 9291829 9291859 9291869 9291937 9291941
9291967 9292001 9292021 9292037 9292039 9292051 9292057 9292091 9292097 9292117
9292169 9292177 9292189 9292193 9292211 9292259 9292279 9292321 9292333 9292337
9292357 9292381 9292397 9292399 9292411 9292453 9292457 9292471 9292477 9292487
9292537 9292541 9292553 9292589 9292603 9292627 9292631 9292639 9292643 9292663
9292669 9292709 9292711 9292741 9292753 9292771 9292783 9292837 9292841 9292853
9292867 9292879 9292939 9292949 9292961 9292999 9293003 9293017 9293029 9293051
9293059 9293069 9293093 9293107 9293129 9293159 9293161 9293171 9293177 9293209
9293213 9293227 9293239 9293243 9293269 9293287 9293303 9293309 9293321 9293329
9293341 9293353 9293363 9293371 9293393 9293399 9293419 9293423 9293443 9293447
9293467 9293483 9293491 9293519 9293539 9293551 9293561 9293563 9293567 9293573
9293579 9293591 9293629 9293657 9293663 9293723 9293729 9293731 9293737 9293741
9293743 9293749 9293761 9293773 9293783 9293789 9293803 9293819 9293873 9293881
9293887 9293923 9293927 9293939 9293941 9293953 9293959 9293969 9293981 9294011
9294013 9294023 9294031 9294049 9294071 9294073 9294083 9294101 9294107 9294179
9294193 9294199 9294209 9294247 9294283 9294293 9294317 9294343 9294347 9294349
9294361 9294367 9294371 9294409 9294419 9294421 9294463 9294473 9294479 9294489
9294497 9294499 9294517 9294521 9294547 9294611 9294613 9294643 9294671 9294689
9294697 9294707 9294713 9294721 9294739 9294763 9294773 9294793 9294799 9294809
9294821 9294827 9294833 9294847 9294851 9294853 9294889 9294899 9294907 9294911
9294913 9294941 9294959 9294973 9295001 9295007 9295019 9295021 9295043
9295063 9295079 9295081 9295093 9295147 9295157 9295159 9295201 9295207 9295213
9295217 9295271 9295301 9295303 9295327 9295337 9295357 9295361 9295393 9295417
9295453 9295483 9295529 9295537 9295543 9295553 9295589 9295591 9295597 9295603
9295609 9295619 9295633 9295639 9295661 9295669 9295679 9295681 9295687 9295709
9295717 9295739 9295757 9295783 9295787 9295789 9295799 9295823 9295831 9295849
9295901 9295907 9295919 9295927 9295931 9295963 9295969 9295999 9296029 9296033
9296051 9296069 9296081 9296087 9296107 9296123 9296129 9296143 9296173 9296179
9296191 9296197 9296207 9296227 9296251 9296281 9296293 9296303 9296321 9296333
9296351 9296369 9296387 9296407 9296431 9296437 9296489 9296537 9296561 9296563
9296579 9296587 9296591 9296593 9296611 9296633 9296653 9296701 9296753 9296759
9296767 9296779 9296801 9296803 9296809 9296839 9296857 9296863 9296867 9296893
9296897 9296921 9296923 9296971 9296981 9296983 9297017 9297019 9297047 9297053
9297059 9297091 9297097 9297103 9297109 9297131 9297133 9297143 9297149 9297157
9297163 9297199 9297203 9297209 9297217 9297227 9297229 9297247 9297257 9297259
```

```
9297263  9297269  9297271  9297311  9297319  9297329  9297341  9297347  9297361  9297367
9297377  9297401  9297461  9297467  9297469  9297473  9297481  9297511  9297521  9297569
9297583  9297599  9297601  9297637  9297641  9297643  9297649  9297653  9297671  9297677
9297713  9297721  9297731  9297733  9297781  9297787  9297823  9297829  9297853  9297881
9297887  9297889  9297907  9297931  9297943  9297971  9297983  9298039  9298043  9298073
9298111  9298117  9298153  9298181  9298189  9298213  9298217  9298243  9298253  9298259
9298271  9298283  9298301  9298307  9298313  9298319  9298321  9298351  9298369  9298381
9298397  9298403  9298409  9298427  9298441  9298447  9298451  9298483  9298489  9298493
9298501  9298591  9298603  9298607  9298649  9298651  9298687  9298697  9298699  9298703
9298717  9298721  9298741  9298747  9298753  9298769  9298777  9298781  9298801  9298811
9298819  9298829  9298859  9298889  9298897  9298909  9298957  9298963  9298967  9298973
9298979  9299021  9299029  9299063  9299089  9299141  9299159  9299161  9299179  9299183
9299197  9299201  9299203  9299207  9299219  9299233  9299243  9299261  9299317  9299347
9299351  9299359  9299363  9299369  9299377  9299387  9299419  9299431  9299441  9299443
9299447  9299449  9299483  9299489  9299491  9299501  9299503  9299513  9299519  9299551
9299557  9299593  9299603  9299611  9299621  9299627  9299657  9299669  9299671  9299711
9299723  9299747  9299761  9299789  9299791  9299813  9299819  9299827  9299831  9299837
9299861  9299891  9299909  9299921  9299933  9299957  9299977  9300001  9300007  9300017
9300023  9300043  9300047  9300079  9300103  9300143  9300149  9300157  9300191  9300199
9300223  9300227  9300287  9300293  9300301  9300359  9300373  9300409  9300437  9300451
9300461  9300497  9300517  9300521  9300539  9300541  9300559  9300569  9300587  9300593
9300611  9300623  9300637  9300647  9300659  9300667  9300703  9300719  9300721  9300737
9300757  9300773  9300779  9300791  9300799  9300803  9300817  9300821  9300827  9300833
9300839  9300847  9300859  9300883  9300911  9300919  9300959  9300983  9300997  9301001
9301009  9301031  9301043  9301081  9301121  9301139  9301157  9301169  9301181  9301211
9301217  9301247  9301267  9301277  9301283  9301289  9301309  9301339  9301349  9301351
9301367  9301387  9301417  9301423  9301451  9301471  9301477  9301493  9301511
9301517  9301529  9301549  9301577  9301609  9301613  9301619  9301651  9301661  9301667
9301673  9301679  9301681  9301687  9301693  9301709  9301739  9301753  9301757  9301769
9301801  9301807  9301813  9301819  9301823  9301841  9301843  9301847  9301883  9301909
9301931  9301939  9301949  9301967  9301973  9301987  9301991  9302003  9302023  9302057
9302063  9302071  9302081  9302089  9302101  9302113  9302123  9302131  9302141  9302149
9302159  9302177  9302197  9302231  9302257  9302261  9302269  9302291  9302299  9302303
9302309  9302323  9302333  9302341  9302351  9302393  9302399  9302411  9302413  9302431
9302443  9302459  9302467  9302483  9302521  9302539  9302543  9302549  9302551  9302563
9302599  9302611  9302627  9302639  9302641  9302669  9302677  9302681  9302693  9302717
9302731  9302743  9302753  9302771  9302801  9302819  9302861  9302863  9302869  9302897
9302911  9302963  9302983  9302987  9303001  9303011  9303013  9303031  9303053  9303089
9303101  9303121  9303137  9303163  9303181  9303197  9303209  9303223  9303241  9303251
9303253  9303257  9303263  9303289  9303319  9303341  9303347  9303353  9303373  9303377
9303397  9303439  9303467  9303479  9303487  9303491  9303499  9303517  9303587  9303589
9303611  9303643  9303649  9303663  9303677  9303691  9303703  9303731  9303733  9303773
9303823  9303839  9303851  9303857  9303859  9303869  9303881  9303907  9303919  9303929
9303941  9303961  9303967  9304027  9304043  9304051  9304073  9304103  9304109  9304177
9304181  9304193  9304201  9304273  9304277  9304283  9304301  9304303  9304313  9304333
9304343  9304367  9304369  9304381  9304387  9304409  9304411  9304429  9304453  9304481
9304487  9304511  9304523  9304553  9304571  9304573  9304583  9304591  9304609  9304639
9304657  9304697  9304717  9304721  9304763  9304777  9304781  9304783  9304787  9304793
9304807  9304819  9304849  9304877  9304891  9304931  9304937  9304943  9304951
9304961  9304963  9304973  9304993  9305057  9305059  9305063  9305083  9305089  9305111
9305141  9305183  9305207  9305209  9305227  9305267  9305281  9305287  9305293
9305297  9305299  9305333  9305339  9305353  9305371  9305381  9305393  9305399  9305419
9305449  9305453  9305479  9305503  9305509  9305521  9305531  9305551  9305557  9305561
9305591  9305609  9305617  9305623  9305627  9305629  9305651  9305693  9305701  9305707
9305717  9305743  9305761  9305771  9305773  9305789  9305809  9305819  9305867  9305887
9305969  9305971  9305993  9306001  9306023  9306049  9306079  9306097  9306113  9306119
9306127  9306131  9306133  9306151  9306173  9306197  9306223  9306229  9306239  9306263
9306287  9306289  9306307  9306313  9306317  9306373  9306379  9306383  9306403  9306449
9306461  9306503  9306511  9306553  9306571  9306581  9306589  9306607  9306617  9306643
9306659  9306673  9306683  9306691  9306733  9306749  9306757  9306761  9306779  9306797
9306841  9306889  9306907  9306931  9306971  9306991  9307003  9307013  9307061  9307063
9307087  9307097  9307121  9307127  9307139  9307141  9307153  9307159  9307163  9307189
9307219  9307223  9307229  9307253  9307261  9307271  9307273  9307303  9307339  9307343
9307357  9307367  9307373  9307379  9307391  9307423  9307447  9307477  9307513  9307553
9307559  9307589  9307607  9307633  9307667  9307673  9307679  9307691  9307699  9307717
9307729  9307733  9307741  9307747  9307751  9307759  9307763  9307793  9307819  9307897
9307901  9307931  9307937  9307943  9307997  9307999  9308009  9308041  9308069  9308087
9308099  9308111  9308117  9308141  9308161  9308177  9308203  9308227  9308237  9308249
9308249  9308267  9308269  9308281  9308291  9308293  9308311  9308323  9308329
9308357  9308393  9308437  9308471  9308473  9308479  9308513  9308521  9308527  9308531
9308543  9308557  9308561  9308567  9308573  9308581  9308591  9308603  9308609  9308617
9308627  9308641  9308647  9308653  9308659  9308671  9308693  9308701  9308723  9308737
9308749  9308753  9308837  9308851  9308861  9308869  9308881  9308897  9308909  9308921
9308939  9308947  9309007  9309017  9309019  9309061  9309071  9309077  9309103  9309119
9309137  9309151  9309191  9309193  9309211  9309241  9309257  9309277  9309299  9309317
9309323  9309329  9309341  9309347  9309359  9309361  9309367  9309379  9309383  9309389
9309407  9309413  9309437  9309451  9309467  9309479  9309491  9309511  9309569  9309571
9309577  9309593  9309613  9309653  9309661  9309673  9309679  9309691  9309697
9309709  9309719  9309721  9309737  9309739  9309743  9309793  9309809  9309847  9309869
9309893  9309907  9309919  9309929  9309941  9309961  9309983  9310001  9310087
9310111  9310121  9310123  9310129  9310151  9310153  9310163  9310181  9310187  9310211
9310219  9310241  9310267  9310291  9310297  9310303  9310307  9310309  9310333  9310337
9310349  9310393  9310451  9310481  9310501  9310507  9310517  9310523  9310529
9310541  9310573  9310591  9310597  9310619  9310663  9310667  9310681  9310733  9310753
9310759  9310771  9310783  9310823  9310831  9310843  9310871  9310877  9310879  9310901
9310921  9310927  9310937  9310949  9310957  9310981  9310991  9310993  9310999  9311009
9311017  9311041  9311063  9311069  9311111  9311119  9311131  9311143  9311149  9311167
9311171  9311173  9311179  9311207  9311221  9311227  9311231  9311249  9311279  9311287
9311327  9311329  9311371  9311381  9311399  9311413  9311429  9311431  9311443  9311453
```

```
9311473  9311483  9311503  9311537  9311567  9311569  9311587  9311591  9311609  9311657
9311663  9311677  9311681  9311683  9311689  9311707  9311713  9311719  9311723  9311737
9311741  9311747  9311773  9311789  9311791  9311837  9311867  9311893  9311899  9311917
9311923  9311933  9311963  9311977  9311989  9312013  9312031  9312067  9312089  9312119
9312131  9312137  9312151  9312167  9312179  9312181  9312187  9312211  9312229  9312241
9312253  9312287  9312313  9312323  9312343  9312349  9312361  9312377  9312389  9312403
9312437  9312449  9312461  9312469  9312473  9312487  9312491  9312497  9312547  9312551
9312559  9312581  9312593  9312601  9312637  9312643  9312647  9312671  9312673  9312697
9312707  9312727  9312731  9312733  9312739  9312749  9312761  9312767  9312773  9312791
9312817  9312827  9312839  9312841  9312859  9312881  9312883  9312887  9312899  9312913
9312917  9312949  9312967  9312997  9313009  9313013  9313033  9313043  9313063  9313079
9313099  9313103  9313111  9313163  9313169  9313217  9313219  9313253  9313259  9313277
9313279  9313301  9313303  9313313  9313333  9313349  9313391  9313393  9313427  9313429
9313441  9313463  9313471  9313481  9313483  9313487  9313511  9313523  9313561  9313589
9313613  9313621  9313627  9313631  9313639  9313651  9313673  9313687  9313699  9313721
9313747  9313771  9313789  9313817  9313823  9313853  9313861  9313883  9313897  9313921
9313949  9313957  9313969  9313991  9314003  9314023  9314033  9314059  9314083  9314087
9314089  9314099  9314111  9314141  9314189  9314209  9314233  9314267  9314293  9314299
9314303  9314311  9314323  9314329  9314363  9314381  9314399  9314401  9314441  9314447
9314449  9314483  9314489  9314527  9314537  9314549  9314551  9314573  9314587  9314603
9314621  9314629  9314633  9314677  9314681  9314699  9314707  9314719  9314729  9314741
9314777  9314779  9314783  9314791  9314797  9314801  9314819  9314821  9314857  9314867
9314881  9314917  9314923  9314939  9314941  9314947  9314953  9314983  9314999  9315001
9315029  9315037  9315067  9315079  9315101  9315109  9315143  9315169  9315181  9315191
9315199  9315223  9315239  9315247  9315277  9315289  9315307  9315329  9315343  9315347
9315359  9315367  9315419  9315421  9315433  9315461  9315497  9315499  9315517  9315521
9315547  9315557  9315571  9315587  9315599  9315611  9315619  9315623  9315637  9315661
9315673  9315689  9315701  9315703  9315707  9315721  9315731  9315751  9315763  9315767
9315769  9315781  9315799  9315809  9315811  9315827  9315883  9315889  9315893  9315899
9315913  9315959  9315967  9315973  9315991  9316007  9316009  9316033  9316037  9316057
9316067  9316093  9316117  9316129  9316141  9316147  9316189  9316201  9316207  9316211
9316231  9316243  9316259  9316273  9316297  9316319  9316331  9316343  9316369  9316379
9316397  9316451  9316457  9316519  9316547  9316577  9316607  9316621  9316639  9316661
9316687  9316693  9316757  9316759  9316777  9316781  9316823  9316831  9316837  9316861
9316873  9316877  9316891  9316903  9316907  9316913  9316919  9316921  9316943  9316961
9316967  9317017  9317057  9317059  9317083  9317089  9317123  9317137  9317159  9317177
9317179  9317213  9317219  9317227  9317237  9317257  9317263  9317279  9317281  9317299
9317333  9317359  9317383  9317387  9317389  9317419  9317443  9317459  9317471  9317491
9317519  9317551  9317563  9317591  9317593  9317597  9317617  9317621  9317629  9317653
9317681  9317687  9317731  9317743  9317761  9317767  9317779  9317801  9317831  9317839
9317843  9317849  9317851  9317853  9317887  9317909  9317911  9317941  9318017  9318031
9318041  9318103  9318109  9318121  9318131  9318137  9318139  9318157  9318163  9318167
9318209  9318271  9318313  9318343  9318347  9318349  9318359  9318391  9318403  9318409
9318451  9318451  9318457  9318461  9318467  9318469  9318481  9318503  9318511  9318527
9318539  9318553  9318581  9318583  9318613  9318623  9318641  9318671  9318677  9318707
9318713  9318731  9318763  9318769  9318779  9318809  9318811  9318823  9318833  9318853
9318893  9318899  9318913  9318973  9318983  9318989  9319001  9319007  9319021  9319027
9319033  9319039  9319067  9319069  9319073  9319087  9319091  9319099  9319103  9319181
9319183  9319187  9319241  9319243  9319249  9319307  9319309  9319319  9319333  9319351
9319357  9319381  9319403  9319447  9319477  9319487  9319493  9319501  9319547  9319549
9319559  9319567  9319571  9319589  9319619  9319627  9319631  9319657  9319693  9319697
9319703  9319721  9319753  9319781  9319787  9319789  9319829  9319831  9319847  9319889
9319897  9319943  9319951  9319963  9319969  9319979  9320009  9320023  9320053  9320093
9320111  9320123  9320141  9320159  9320167  9320191  9320231  9320239  9320249  9320261
9320273  9320287  9320291  9320309  9320321  9320323  9320327  9320329  9320357  9320371
9320387  9320401  9320419  9320453  9320459  9320461  9320477  9320533  9320537  9320561
9320569  9320587  9320593  9320599  9320627  9320639  9320671  9320683  9320719  9320741
9320749  9320783  9320797  9320807  9320833  9320851  9320873  9320891  9320921  9320939
9320989  9321023  9321029  9321041  9321047  9321061  9321073  9321089  9321097  9321101
9321113  9321121  9321127  9321139  9321161  9321167  9321199  9321251  9321259  9321283
9321307  9321311  9321313  9321331  9321341  9321379  9321401  9321407  9321437  9321451
9321467  9321503  9321517  9321523  9321541  9321547  9321553  9321563  9321569  9321577
9321581  9321619  9321629  9321649  9321677  9321679  9321691  9321701  9321703  9321713
9321721  9321751  9321779  9321791  9321811  9321821  9321827  9321833  9321853  9321857
9321863  9321869  9321901  9321919  9321929  9321937  9321943  9321973  9322009  9322031
9322037  9322051  9322109  9322169  9322201  9322219  9322231  9322241  9322249  9322277
9322279  9322301  9322333  9322349  9322367  9322373  9322393  9322399  9322471  9322493
9322501  9322507  9322517  9322549  9322583  9322609  9322619  9322627  9322637  9322661
9322679  9322693  9322699  9322739  9322741  9322769  9322799  9322801  9322811  9322823
9322829  9322861  9322883  9322921  9322931  9322933  9322969  9322979  9322991  9322993
9322997  9323009  9323023  9323047  9323051  9323063  9323077  9323099  9323101  9323107
9323137  9323159  9323161  9323173  9323183  9323201  9323203  9323221  9323227  9323233
9323263  9323267  9323309  9323311  9323317  9323329  9323339  9323381  9323383  9323393
9323399  9323417  9323449  9323459  9323477  9323513  9323527  9323537  9323539  9323549
9323557  9323563  9323569  9323581  9323603  9323609  9323617  9323641  9323669  9323681
9323683  9323689  9323693  9323723  9323749  9323753  9323773  9323801  9323827  9323833
9323849  9323857  9323863  9323893  9323903  9323929  9323953  9323983  9323987  9323989
9324013  9324019  9324031  9324053  9324061  9324101  9324113  9324121  9324171  9324173
9324197  9324199  9324209  9324221  9324229  9324239  9324241  9324247  9324253  9324257
9324463  9324473  9324503  9324541  9324547  9324559  9324563  9324571  9324587  9324599
9324613  9324617  9324641  9324677  9324691  9324697  9324739  9324743  9324751  9324761
9324787  9324803  9324817  9324827  9324853  9324877  9324881  9324907  9324911  9324929
9324949  9324989  9325003  9325021  9325033  9325039  9325049  9325087  9325091  9325111
9325123  9325139  9325159  9325171  9325177  9325181  9325207  9325213  9325237  9325241
9325243  9325249  9325259  9325271  9325291  9325313  9325319  9325357  9325361  9325391
9325399  9325417  9325427  9325439  9325457  9325487  9325489  9325499  9325507  9325543
9325553  9325579  9325583  9325601  9325627  9325661  9325703  9325709  9325753  9325763
9325769  9325793  9325807  9325817  9325829  9325847  9325853  9325861  9325867  9325873
```

```
9325889  9325891  9325913  9325919  9325937  9325949  9325951  9325973  9325997  9326011
9326027  9326033  9326041  9326077  9326087  9326089  9326101  9326113  9326117  9326137
9326153  9326167  9326173  9326203  9326237  9326249  9326263  9326267  9326269  9326279
9326281  9326287  9326297  9326309  9326323  9326329  9326363  9326389  9326419  9326423
9326501  9326507  9326509  9326519  9326531  9326561  9326563  9326573  9326593  9326621
9326623  9326641  9326651  9326677  9326687  9326689  9326711  9326729  9326741  9326767
9326797  9326851  9326857  9326861  9326903  9326917  9326921  9326927  9326963  9326969
9326971  9326981  9327089  9327113  9327127  9327139  9327151  9327161  9327181  9327193
9327209  9327211  9327217  9327247  9327257  9327277  9327281  9327323  9327337  9327343
9327361  9327389  9327401  9327427  9327469  9327481  9327491  9327503  9327529  9327533
9327551  9327553  9327583  9327599  9327601  9327607  9327631  9327649  9327671  9327691
9327697  9327701  9327709  9327739  9327743  9327749  9327751  9327757  9327779  9327793
9327797  9327817  9327833  9327839  9327853  9327863  9327887  9327889  9327907  9327953
9327961  9327973  9328003  9328009  9328027  9328049  9328093  9328103  9328127  9328129
9328157  9328201  9328211  9328213  9328219  9328229  9328237  9328247  9328261  9328273
9328289  9328301  9328307  9328321  9328331  9328369  9328381  9328391  9328433  9328439
9328441  9328447  9328457  9328471  9328481  9328499  9328507  9328519  9328537  9328567
9328577  9328589  9328591  9328603  9328643  9328687  9328703  9328723  9328729  9328747
9328763  9328789  9328793  9328811  9328817  9328831  9328849  9328859  9328883  9328967
9328973  9328997  9328999  9329003  9329011  9329051  9329059  9329063  9329071  9329081
9329101  9329129  9329149  9329153  9329161  9329179  9329207  9329227  9329239  9329249
9329251  9329267  9329273  9329297  9329303  9329317  9329377  9329381  9329389  9329407
9329417  9329429  9329443  9329477  9329479  9329501  9329521  9329527  9329531  9329533
9329539  9329597  9329623  9329629  9329633  9329647  9329681  9329687  9329693  9329707
9329759  9329773  9329783  9329807  9329861  9329867  9329869  9329891  9329899  9329939
9329953  9329963  9329981  9329987  9329989  9329993  9330029  9330047  9330053  9330089
9330091  9330103  9330107  9330119  9330149  9330151  9330239  9330289  9330337  9330359
9330361  9330367  9330371  9330379  9330383  9330389  9330397  9330407  9330413  9330427
9330469  9330533  9330551  9330557  9330593  9330619  9330647  9330649  9330679  9330689
9330701  9330707  9330751  9330757  9330829  9330833  9330851  9330857  9330877  9330887
9330901  9330913  9330917  9330929  9330947  9330961  9330991  9331001  9331009  9331013
9331019  9331057  9331061  9331073  9331097  9331099  9331103  9331111  9331117  9331121
9331151  9331159  9331183  9331199  9331211  9331241  9331247  9331253  9331297  9331319
9331321  9331331  9331349  9331367  9331369  9331391  9331393  9331397  9331409  9331429
9331433  9331457  9331463  9331471  9331493  9331501  9331507  9331513  9331519  9331541
9331547  9331573  9331613  9331627  9331639  9331643  9331661  9331667  9331669  9331711
9331741  9331747  9331753  9331769  9331771  9331783  9331787  9331789  9331801  9331811
9331843  9331877  9331891  9331909  9331919  9331921  9331957  9331967  9331999  9332003
9332017  9332039  9332093  9332107  9332111  9332119  9332131  9332137  9332149  9332189
9332203  9332231  9332263  9332339  9332347  9332353  9332359  9332369  9332383  9332423
9332447  9332459  9332489  9332513  9332527  9332563  9332569  9332579  9332593  9332597
9332623  9332627  9332633  9332669  9332671  9332683  9332699  9332723  9332747  9332749
9332753  9332759  9332761  9332777  9332801  9332803  9332821  9332887  9332893  9332909
9332927  9332941  9332951  9332957  9332959  9332987  9333001  9333007  9333011  9333013
9333029  9333031  9333043  9333059  9333067  9333083  9333089  9333097  9333109  9333113
9333131  9333143  9333169  9333197  9333209  9333229  9333241  9333251  9333257  9333271
9333283  9333293  9333319  9333349  9333367  9333371  9333383  9333397  9333407  9333409
9333413  9333473  9333479  9333481  9333487  9333517  9333521  9333529  9333539  9333547
9333553  9333557  9333581  9333637  9333647  9333659  9333661  9333677  9333737  9333739
9333743  9333749  9333767  9333781  9333787  9333803  9333817  9333827  9333829  9333847
9333851  9333893  9333917  9333941  9333943  9334001  9334009  9334033  9334049  9334051
9334079  9334081  9334103  9334123  9334141  9334147  9334163  9334177  9334219  9334243
9334271  9334277  9334279  9334289  9334337  9334357  9334363  9334387  9334393  9334399
9334417  9334421  9334427  9334447  9334459  9334463  9334469  9334477  9334489  9334499
9334499  9334517  9334537  9334553  9334571  9334603  9334609  9334613  9334621  9334631
9334657  9334639  9334691  9334697  9334709  9334733  9334739  9334747  9334771  9334807
9334861  9334873  9334889  9334903  9334931  9334933  9334939  9334957  9334961  9334967
9334979  9334993  9335041  9335063  9335089  9335111  9335113  9335119  9335141  9335143
9335147  9335189  9335201  9335203  9335219  9335233  9335267  9335323  9335357  9335399
9335411  9335461  9335471  9335483  9335489  9335497  9335503  9335519  9335537  9335549
9335561  9335587  9335597  9335609  9335621  9335647  9335653  9335659  9335699  9335759
9335779  9335789  9335831  9335849  9335863  9335869  9335881  9335899  9335917  9335933
9335971  9335993  9336001  9336007  9336013  9336017  9336029  9336059  9336079  9336083
9336097  9336143  9336149  9336157  9336167  9336169  9336193  9336199  9336209  9336241
9336251  9336253  9336259  9336263  9336293  9336307  9336311  9336317  9336323  9336331
9336343  9336359  9336361  9336373  9336401  9336403  9336407  9336419  9336433  9336449
9336493  9336511  9336527  9336557  9336583  9336589  9336623  9336629  9336661  9336667
9336683  9336697  9336703  9336707  9336727  9336739  9336749  9336769  9336829  9336853
9336863  9336883  9336911  9336917  9336959  9336979  9336989  9337001  9337007  9337021
9337033  9337039  9337093  9337099  9337109  9337117  9337121  9337127  9337171  9337193
9337213  9337219  9337243  9337249  9337253  9337291  9337297  9337313  9337319  9337337
9337343  9337351  9337373  9337411  9337429  9337439  9337441  9337457  9337459  9337469
9337477  9337501  9337547  9337553  9337567  9337577  9337597  9337619  9337621  9337633
9337637  9337639  9337651  9337661  9337663  9337667  9337673  9337693  9337711  9337717
9337733  9337763  9337777  9337807  9337813  9337831  9337843  9337891  9337897  9337901
9337903  9337907  9337927  9337943  9337957  9337961  9337963  9337973  9338011  9338033
9338039  9338051  9338053  9338059  9338071  9338111  9338137  9338141  9338143  9338179
9338191  9338213  9338221  9338237  9338243  9338257  9338269  9338279  9338281  9338297
9338309  9338311  9338317  9338327  9338339  9338363  9338369  9338387  9338401  9338411
9338449  9338453  9338479  9338489  9338509  9338513  9338573  9338579  9338591  9338593
9338603  9338617  9338629  9338647  9338663  9338677  9338683  9338687  9338699  9338711
9338731  9338737  9338741  9338753  9338779  9338803  9338809  9338821  9338839  9338863
9338881  9338893  9338933  9338969  9338983  9339023  9339047  9339053  9339061  9339107
9339119  9339139  9339151  9339163  9339181  9339191  9339193  9339217  9339227  9339259
9339263  9339293  9339313  9339359  9339361  9339367  9339371  9339373  9339391  9339397
9339413  9339433  9339439  9339457  9339467  9339509  9339521  9339559  9339569  9339581
9339593  9339601  9339611  9339619  9339623  9339661  9339689  9339719  9339721  9339727
9339739  9339761  9339763  9339787  9339791  9339821  9339823  9339833  9339857  9339871
9339917  9339971  9339973  9339977  9340003  9340013  9340061  9340069  9340081  9340109
```

```
9340127  9340129  9340147  9340171  9340181  9340183  9340189  9340193  9340211  9340213
9340273  9340297  9340301  9340307  9340367  9340411  9340427  9340433  9340447  9340459
9340481  9340501  9340511  9340577  9340627  9340637  9340657  9340673  9340679  9340699
9340729  9340741  9340777  9340787  9340819  9340841  9340843  9340897  9340901  9340937
9340943  9340949  9340957  9340963  9340999  9341023  9341047  9341051  9341077  9341081
9341083  9341093  9341117  9341159  9341201  9341221  9341249  9341281  9341287  9341291
9341309  9341333  9341359  9341377  9341413  9341429  9341441  9341443  9341459  9341461
9341489  9341503  9341531  9341533  9341561  9341581  9341593  9341599  9341617  9341623
9341639  9341659  9341663  9341681  9341713  9341729  9341747  9341771  9341777  9341803
9341821  9341837  9341851  9341869  9341897  9341911  9341929  9341947  9341957  9341963
9341989  9341999  9342007  9342013  9342037  9342041  9342043  9342077  9342079  9342083
9342103  9342107  9342127  9342133  9342161  9342169  9342181  9342199  9342217
9342239  9342269  9342283  9342287  9342293  9342313  9342323  9342341  9342353  9342371
9342373  9342391  9342457  9342479  9342511  9342517  9342523  9342533  9342539  9342559
9342583  9342587  9342589  9342617  9342631  9342637  9342647  9342659  9342689  9342691
9342701  9342703  9342713  9342731  9342743  9342763  9342769  9342779  9342791  9342799
9342857  9342863  9342871  9342881  9342917  9342929  9342947  9343001  9343021  9343043
9343049  9343057  9343069  9343073  9343091  9343097  9343099  9343109  9343111  9343123
9343127  9343157  9343199  9343219  9343223  9343247  9343261  9343283  9343289  9343297
9343303  9343333  9343337  9343349  9343357  9343381  9343403  9343447  9343457  9343469
9343471  9343501  9343507  9343511  9343571  9343577  9343583  9343603  9343627  9343637
9343639  9343643  9343657  9343661  9343673  9343703  9343723  9343751  9343757  9343759
9343783  9343787  9343793  9343849  9343879  9343909  9343937  9343951  9343967  9343969
9343981  9343993  9344011  9344039  9344053  9344077  9344147  9344149  9344161  9344171
9344173  9344191  9344197  9344207  9344213  9344261  9344281  9344297  9344311  9344317
9344323  9344327  9344329  9344341  9344347  9344353  9344429  9344431  9344437  9344471
9344473  9344477  9344497  9344501  9344507  9344513  9344519  9344527  9344537  9344539
9344549  9344551  9344563  9344567  9344569  9344581  9344591  9344603  9344639  9344659
9344663  9344667  9344677  9344707  9344723  9344743  9344749  9344771  9344779  9344813
9344837  9344851  9344879  9344891  9344899  9344927  9344971  9344977  9345001  9345023
9345029  9345067  9345073  9345079  9345097  9345103  9345113  9345143  9345157  9345161
9345197  9345209  9345269  9345277  9345289  9345299  9345313  9345341  9345367  9345377
9345403  9345419  9345421  9345431  9345449  9345451  9345481  9345493  9345503  9345547
9345559  9345593  9345599  9345607  9345619  9345641  9345643  9345647  9345667  9345683
9345689  9345691  9345697  9345709  9345757  9345773  9345781  9345811  9345839  9345851
9345857  9345881  9345887  9345893  9345899  9345901  9345907  9345913  9345923  9345953
9345961  9345983  9345989  9346009  9346019  9346037  9346063  9346079  9346087  9346109
9346123  9346147  9346171  9346187  9346193  9346201  9346213  9346217  9346223  9346229
9346247  9346289  9346291  9346301  9346307  9346313  9346327  9346331  9346333  9346339
9346361  9346387  9346397  9346399  9346417  9346427  9346429  9346451  9346471  9346501
9346507  9346517  9346541  9346553  9346559  9346577  9346619  9346627  9346639  9346643
9346657  9346661  9346663  9346693  9346697  9346723  9346739  9346741  9346759  9346783
9346789  9346793  9346807  9346837  9346849  9346853  9346861  9346871  9346873  9346891
9346907  9346913  9346927  9346973  9346979  9346999  9347011  9347029  9347031  9347033
9347071  9347081  9347083  9347101  9347111  9347141  9347159  9347189  9347197  9347203
9347227  9347231  9347257  9347279  9347293  9347321  9347323  9347341  9347357  9347381
9347417  9347419  9347423  9347441  9347477  9347497  9347509  9347521  9347531  9347539
9347567  9347573  9347587  9347593  9347609  9347621  9347629  9347659  9347669  9347693
9347707  9347747  9347801  9347827  9347839  9347851  9347873  9347879  9347883
9347903  9347911  9347927  9347929  9347941  9347951  9347953  9347963  9347969  9347983
9347999  9348023  9348049  9348061  9348083  9348091  9348109  9348127  9348139  9348169
9348187  9348191  9348203  9348217  9348223  9348233  9348263  9348271  9348289  9348301
9348319  9348337  9348359  9348373  9348389  9348413  9348421  9348431  9348461  9348463
9348481  9348517  9348529  9348571  9348583  9348601  9348607  9348611  9348613  9348637
9348653  9348667  9348671  9348683  9348721  9348737  9348739  9348761  9348767  9348791
9348809  9348811  9348839  9348841  9348847  9348883  9348887  9348919  9348923  9348947
9348961  9348967  9348973  9349009  9349019  9349033  9349051  9349057  9349061  9349069
9349079  9349091  9349111  9349127  9349129  9349177  9349181  9349187  9349211  9349213
9349217  9349231  9349243  9349283  9349289  9349309  9349343  9349363  9349367  9349393
9349399  9349411  9349421  9349427  9349429  9349433  9349453  9349481  9349489  9349511
9349519  9349537  9349547  9349559  9349589  9349603  9349651  9349657  9349661  9349667
9349673  9349679  9349699  9349709  9349723  9349727  9349751  9349787  9349801  9349849
9349853  9349859  9349931  9349943  9349973  9349993  9349997  9350027  9350041
9350063  9350069  9350083  9350111  9350123  9350137  9350161  9350177  9350183  9350191
9350269  9350273  9350281  9350293  9350303  9350311  9350317  9350329  9350333  9350339
9350353  9350399  9350417  9350437  9350461  9350491  9350513  9350521  9350569  9350573
9350591  9350597  9350599  9350633  9350683  9350687  9350699  9350707  9350711  9350723
9350729  9350743  9350749  9350753  9350767  9350773  9350777  9350789  9350797  9350801
9350807  9350813  9350819  9350827  9350849  9350879  9350893  9350921  9350927  9350941
9350951  9350987  9351007  9351011  9351031  9351053  9351101  9351107  9351109  9351113
9351127  9351163  9351187  9351191  9351193  9351203  9351217  9351229  9351259  9351281
9351289  9351299  9351301  9351337  9351341  9351347  9351379  9351383  9351421  9351443
9351451  9351469  9351487  9351493  9351509  9351521  9351539  9351557  9351569  9351571
9351583  9351599  9351611  9351619  9351653  9351689  9351707  9351709  9351737  9351761
9351773  9351779  9351791  9351821  9351829  9351871  9351877  9351887  9351889  9351911
9351917  9351931  9351943  9351967  9352001  9352003  9352037  9352043  9352069  9352073
9352097  9352117  9352139  9352169  9352171  9352177  9352183  9352241  9352247  9352253
9352271  9352289  9352349  9352361  9352381  9352391  9352393  9352411  9352423  9352429
9352493  9352507  9352517  9352531  9352537  9352547  9352561  9352591  9352613  9352619
9352639  9352649  9352669  9352711  9352723  9352729  9352741  9352781  9352797  9352799
9352817  9352841  9352891  9352909  9352913  9352933  9352939  9352943  9352949  9353011
9353017  9353033  9353039  9353053  9353083  9353087  9353089  9353101  9353107  9353137
9353159  9353173  9353189  9353209  9353221  9353257  9353261  9353273  9353291
9353293  9353297  9353299  9353303  9353411  9353431  9353437  9353473  9353483  9353497
9353501  9353527  9353569  9353579  9353581  9353593  9353609  9353639  9353657
9353671  9353693  9353713  9353731  9353737  9353741  9353749  9353777  9353779  9353783
9353789  9353797  9353819  9353821  9353831  9353849  9353857  9353867  9353873  9353879
9353887  9353941  9353951  9353957  9353959  9353969  9353977  9354019  9354043  9354083
9354133  9354139  9354143  9354161  9354173  9354187  9354193  9354203  9354227  9354259
```

```
9354277 9354287 9354329 9354379 9354383 9354409 9354419 9354427 9354461 9354487
9354493 9354503 9354547 9354557 9354571 9354577 9354581 9354613 9354619 9354637
9354661 9354671 9354677 9354679 9354691 9354703 9354713 9354749 9354757 9354781
9354797 9354799 9354803 9354809 9354817 9354823 9354827 9354869 9354883 9354887
9354893 9354937 9354941 9354953 9354967 9354979 9354991 9355039 9355063 9355067
9355091 9355097 9355109 9355111 9355127 9355141 9355147 9355153 9355187 9355193
9355223 9355231 9355237 9355249 9355267 9355271 9355301 9355309 9355343 9355363
9355393 9355399 9355403 9355427 9355433 9355441 9355447 9355469 9355471 9355481
9355483 9355499 9355501 9355517 9355547 9355573 9355589 9355637 9355651 9355669
9355693 9355721 9355739 9355817 9355849 9355873 9355901 9355903 9355919 9355921
9355937 9355939 9355943 9355949 9355979 9355981 9355987 9355991 9355993 9356003
9356027 9356029 9356033 9356041 9356047 9356051 9356059 9356093 9356107 9356129
9356173 9356177 9356197 9356209 9356213 9356231 9356251 9356257 9356297 9356311
9356317 9356351 9356371 9356381 9356387 9356419 9356429 9356437 9356441 9356453
9356489 9356491 9356519 9356521 9356537 9356549 9356551 9356563 9356573 9356587
9356591 9356609 9356621 9356657 9356663 9356701 9356707 9356723 9356747 9356771
9356773 9356777 9356801 9356803 9356827 9356843 9356891 9356901 9356903 9356927
9356933 9356939 9356951 9356981 9356983 9356989 9356999 9357001 9357011 9357037
9357059 9357083 9357119 9357163 9357181 9357197 9357247 9357269 9357289 9357301
9357311 9357317 9357353 9357373 9357377 9357391 9357409 9357419 9357427 9357431
9357449 9357457 9357473 9357533 9357539 9357547 9357571 9357611 9357631 9357637
9357641 9357661 9357683 9357721 9357731 9357739 9357763 9357767 9357773 9357779
9357791 9357793 9357809 9357811 9357833 9357847 9357851 9357853 9357857 9357863
9357883 9357893 9357913 9357917 9357919 9357967 9358009 9358021 9358031 9358043
9358067 9358073 9358081 9358117 9358121 9358159 9358169 9358183 9358189 9358199
9358201 9358207 9358229 9358231 9358267 9358277 9358289 9358351 9358367 9358379
9358397 9358399 9358411 9358417 9358421 9358423 9358441 9358451 9358457 9358471
9358487 9358501 9358511 9358549 9358553 9358567 9358571 9358589 9358597 9358603
9358633 9358637 9358651 9358663 9358693 9358709 9358747 9358751 9358757 9358787
9358799 9358801 9358813 9358837 9358841 9358859 9358871 9358873 9358883 9358897
9358913 9358933 9358949 9358957 9358961 9358981 9358991 9359017 9359057 9359059
9359069 9359101 9359123 9359167 9359173 9359177 9359219 9359221 9359227 9359237
9359243 9359249 9359269 9359279 9359281 9359309 9359341 9359351 9359353 9359369
9359387 9359407 9359417 9359443 9359447 9359453 9359461 9359477 9359491 9359513
9359531 9359543 9359561 9359563 9359579 9359587 9359599 9359621 9359633 9359671
9359719 9359759 9359783 9359789 9359807 9359813 9359839 9359851 9359881 9359893
9359929 9359941 9359963 9359971 9359981 9359983 9360007 9360067 9360073 9360077
9360079 9360083 9360181 9360187 9360203 9360229 9360269 9360271 9360289 9360311
9360313 9360317 9360347 9360361 9360367 9360413 9360431 9360437 9360451 9360457
9360469 9360479 9360487 9360499 9360509 9360551 9360553 9360577 9360623 9360629
9360647 9360679 9360697 9360733 9360739 9360773 9360799 9360803 9360817 9360827
9360847 9360859 9360887 9360893 9360899 9360907 9360917 9360919 9360929 9360937
9360941 9360973 9360979 9360991 9361003 9361007 9361013 9361021 9361031 9361063
9361081 9361087 9361103 9361127 9361141 9361151 9361189 9361193 9361211 9361217
9361249 9361273 9361277 9361309 9361367 9361369 9361393 9361399 9361409 9361423
9361427 9361453 9361459 9361477 9361493 9361531 9361591 9361603 9361607 9361613
9361619 9361631 9361633 9361663 9361697 9361727 9361733 9361801 9361811 9361823
9361829 9361873 9361921 9361931 9361939 9361967 9361987 9361991 9361997 9362021
9362027 9362039 9362047 9362059 9362069 9362087 9362093 9362117 9362123 9362123
9362137 9362141 9362153 9362159 9362167 9362191 9362201 9362203 9362239 9362251
9362293 9362297 9362293 9362299 9362303 9362321 9362333 9362351 9362363 9362371
9362377 9362399 9362411 9362417 9362471 9362501 9362531 9362539 9362569 9362581
9362587 9362641 9362653 9362657 9362659 9362663 9362669 9362671 9362681 9362693
9362741 9362747 9362753 9362783 9362789 9362791 9362809 9362833 9362851 9362861
9362867 9362893 9362897 9362921 9362923 9362929 9362957 9362959 9362987 9362993
9363007 9363019 9363031 9363041 9363059 9363061 9363077 9363089 9363097 9363101
9363113 9363131 9363161 9363169 9363173 9363187 9363191 9363197 9363217 9363223
9363227 9363251 9363253 9363301 9363307 9363337 9363373 9363377 9363383 9363431
9363443 9363467 9363469 9363493 9363499 9363503 9363509 9363511 9363517 9363521
9363527 9363533 9363569 9363577 9363593 9363631 9363647 9363649 9363671 9363689
9363709 9363721 9363769 9363793 9363799 9363803 9363841 9363847 9363859 9363877
9363883 9363901 9363911 9363917 9363919 9363931 9363943 9363947 9363973 9364007
9364051 9364097 9364099 9364109 9364111 9364123 9364141 9364177 9364183 9364193
9364211 9364213 9364247 9364279 9364307 9364339 9364357 9364373 9364393 9364409
9364429 9364447 9364457 9364463 9364469 9364471 9364483 9364493 9364499 9364541
9364543 9364571 9364591 9364601 9364627 9364631 9364633 9364643 9364679 9364877
9364699 9364723 9364727 9364757 9364783 9364787 9364837 9364867 9364871 9364877
9364889 9364907 9364907 9364919 9364949 9364991 9364997 9365003 9365017 9365021
9365021 9365029 9365039 9365051 9365053 9365063 9365077 9365137 9365141 9365149
9365177 9365189 9365197 9365201 9365219 9365221 9365263 9365281 9365297 9365299
9365311 9365333 9365341 9365353 9365359 9365399 9365407 9365411 9365429 9365431
9365437 9365467 9365479 9365519 9365533 9365557 9365561 9365569 9365591 9365593
9365597 9365599 9365611 9365617 9365621 9365659 9365663 9365717 9365723 9365747
9365749 9365767 9365791 9365801 9365809 9365821 9365849 9365891 9365899 9365903
9365977 9366013 9366023 9366041 9366053 9366059 9366103 9366127 9366151
9366169 9366173 9366179 9366187 9366193 9366197 9366199 9366229 9366233 9366257
9366277 9366283 9366293 9366299 9366317 9366323 9366347 9366397 9366419 9366443
9366461 9366493 9366503 9366517 9366523 9366527 9366551 9366569 9366629 9366641
9366653 9366659 9366671 9366713 9366719 9366757 9366761 9366769 9366839 9366853
9366859 9366889 9366919 9366937 9366961 9366967 9366979 9366989 9366997 9367013
9367027 9367063 9367067 9367073 9367079 9367081 9367093 9367097 9367103 9367117
9367123 9367157 9367159 9367181 9367201 9367207 9367217 9367219 9367277 9367291
9367307 9367321 9367331 9367373 9367373 9367381 9367409 9367427 9367439 9367441
9367469 9367483 9367499 9367511 9367543 9367559 9367577 9367597 9367619 9367637
9367643 9367651 9367681 9367691 9367717 9367753 9367769 9367789 9367789 9367793
9367807 9367819 9367823 9367829 9367847 9367849 9367903 9367949 9367991 9367997
9368011 9368041 9368059 9368069 9368081 9368113 9368119 9368129 9368137 9368143
9368147 9368167 9368179 9368201 9368221 9368243 9368257 9368269 9368297 9368299
9368327 9368329 9368339 9368341 9368351 9368371 9368389 9368399 9368423 9368449
```

```
9368467 9368477 9368483 9368503 9368507 9368519 9368549 9368573 9368587 9368609
9368617 9368621 9368627 9368633 9368663 9368693 9368707 9368713 9368743 9368753
9368759 9368773 9368783 9368831 9368837 9368897 9368911 9368923 9368977 9368987
9368999 9369013 9369043 9369047 9369049 9369053 9369067 9369127 9369131 9369149
9369167 9369187 9369203 9369209 9369221 9369229 9369247 9369253 9369271 9369277
9369301 9369307 9369317 9369319 9369323 9369341 9369343 9369379 9369391 9369401
9369419 9369427 9369433 9369439 9369457 9369461 9369469 9369491 9369551 9369553
9369557 9369559 9369583 9369589 9369593 9369631 9369643 9369649 9369667 9369673
9369677 9369707 9369709 9369713 9369727 9369733 9369739 9369751 9369757 9369761
9369797 9369821 9369859 9369863 9369881 9369931 9369937 9369949 9369959 9369961
9369977 9369979 9369989 9370019 9370033 9370051 9370057 9370063 9370069 9370093
9370117 9370147 9370159 9370169 9370171 9370183 9370201 9370243 9370253 9370261
9370307 9370327 9370337 9370351 9370369 9370373 9370409 9370421 9370423 9370457
9370469 9370481 9370483 9370489 9370511 9370523 9370541 9370547 9370549 9370577
9370579 9370589 9370597 9370601 9370609 9370643 9370693 9370703 9370763 9370769
9370967 9370987 9370993 9371017 9371053 9371071 9371081 9371099 9371107 9371111
9371113 9371137 9371171 9371177 9371183 9371191 9371209 9371213 9371221 9371231
9371261 9371273 9371287 9371293 9371303 9371309 9371311 9371353 9371371 9371387
9371413 9371423 9371431 9371441 9371489 9371497 9371543 9371563 9371567 9371569
9371723 9371749 9371783 9371819 9371837 9371851 9371863 9371897 9371899 9371909
9371917 9371933 9371939 9371953 9371963 9371983 9372001 9372029 9372053 9372059
9372113 9372119 9372127 9372131 9372163 9372169 9372173 9372197 9372203 9372221
9372239 9372241 9372281 9372289 9372299 9372329 9372331 9372343 9372347 9372367
9372379 9372401 9372421 9372427 9372437 9372439 9372449 9372463 9372487 9372521
9372527 9372557 9372577 9372637 9372647 9372653 9372703 9372709 9372751 9372761
9372791 9372823 9372827 9372841 9372859 9372907 9372911 9372931 9372949 9372953
9372971 9372973 9372991 9373031 9373033 9373037 9373073 9373081 9373087 9373109
9373123 9373139 9373141 9373193 9373219 9373223 9373241 9373261 9373267 9373277
9373319 9373333 9373337 9373339 9373361 9373369 9373393 9373417 9373423 9373433
9373451 9373453 9373459 9373487 9373493 9373499 9373523 9373531 9373537 9373549
9373571 9373577 9373591 9373601 9373607 9373621 9373643 9373667 9373697 9373703
9373717 9373759 9373783 9373813 9373841 9373853 9373867 9373909 9373921 9373933
9373943 9373961 9373981 9373993 9374023 9374033 9374039 9374063 9374069 9374083
9374093 9374111 9374119 9374143 9374153 9374159 9374173 9374213 9374227 9374237
9374249 9374257 9374273 9374303 9374311 9374347 9374359 9374389 9374399 9374401
9374423 9374437 9374447 9374461 9374483 9374503 9374507 9374537 9374549 9374557
9374611 9374623 9374647 9374669 9374741 9374747 9374779 9374789 9374821
9374831 9374839 9374857 9374861 9374863 9374887 9374891 9374909 9374929 9374991
9374983 9374987 9375001 9375017 9375049 9375059 9375061 9375071 9375073 9375077
9375083 9375127 9375131 9375169 9375173 9375193 9375203 9375217 9375239 9375241
9375251 9375259 9375263 9375269 9375281 9375293 9375307 9375343 9375367 9375371
9375383 9375391 9375397 9375407 9375409 9375433 9375437 9375451 9375469 9375481
9375491 9375499 9375503 9375529 9375533 9375557 9375571 9375577 9375601 9375649
9375679 9375703 9375713 9375719 9375739 9375767 9375791 9375809 9375811 9375827
9375829 9375833 9375871 9375887 9375893 9375937 9375941 9375943 9375953 9375979
9375991 9375997 9376001 9376039 9376049 9376069 9376079 9376093 9376099 9376121
9376141 9376183 9376187 9376219 9376259 9376267 9376271 9376277 9376313 9376319
9376321 9376337 9376357 9376361 9376363 9376373 9376403 9376441 9376447 9376459
9376463 9376487 9376489 9376501 9376513 9376529 9376531 9376561 9376573 9376597
9376613 9376621 9376643 9376649 9376667 9376669 9376729 9376733 9376751 9376753
9376769 9376789 9376793 9376847 9376897 9376921 9376931 9376957 9377023 9377059
9377083 9377099 9377101 9377107 9377113 9377117 9377141 9377209 9377213 9377287
9377297 9377323 9377327 9377339 9377351 9377359 9377369 9377371 9377377 9377419
9377437 9377441 9377461 9377471 9377509 9377567 9377603 9377617 9377647
9377651 9377671 9377723 9377743 9377747 9377821 9377839 9377843 9377861 9377869
9377899 9377939 9377947 9377969 9377989 9377993 9378013 9378023 9378029
9378037 9378041 9378059 9378071 9378119 9378133 9378137 9378143 9378163 9378199
9378211 9378233 9378241 9378247 9378269 9378277 9378301 9378307 9378311 9378329
9378359 9378361 9378377 9378379 9378409 9378437 9378439 9378451 9378491
9378493 9378511 9378517 9378541 9378547 9378559 9378563 9378583 9378587 9378613
9378619 9378623 9378631 9378653 9378659 9378667 9378697 9378703 9378749 9378763
9378769 9378793 9378839 9378847 9378851 9378869 9378893 9378899 9378911
9378923 9378931 9378953 9378979 9378983 9379001 9379003 9379021 9379043 9379049
9379061 9379091 9379099 9379159 9379229 9379231 9379247
9379261 9379277 9379297 9379301 9379309 9379333 9379373 9379379 9379387 9379399
9379411 9379417 9379429 9379451 9379457 9379477 9379501 9379507 9379511 9379519
9379523 9379549 9379553 9379571 9379589 9379613 9379627 9379637 9379661 9379663
9379679 9379681 9379687 9379691 9379699 9379711 9379751 9379793 9379813 9379829
9379841 9379849 9379861 9379921 9379943 9379973 9379999 9380003
9380009 9380029 9380047 9380057 9380083 9380087 9380101 9380117 9380131 9380183
9380207 9380219 9380221 9380227 9380237 9380249 9380291 9380309 9380323 9380341
9380353 9380359 9380429 9380453 9380467 9380473 9380477 9380479 9380489 9380491
9380521 9380531 9380561 9380597 9380599 9380611 9380633 9380639 9380653 9380669
9380681 9380731 9380807 9380827 9380857 9380863 9380873 9380893 9380897 9380911
9380929 9380933 9380951 9380953 9380963 9380977 9381019 9381023 9381037 9381061
9381083 9381089 9381107 9381121 9381149 9381173 9381179 9381187 9381191 9381211
9381209 9381227 9381257 9381259 9381277 9381283 9381287 9381289 9381299 9381311
9381319 9381367 9381389 9381391 9381397 9381403 9381419 9381431 9381503 9381517
9381523 9381553 9381557 9381571 9381601 9381607 9381643 9381679 9381719 9381737
9381751 9381787 9381817 9381821 9381859 9381863 9381881 9381899 9381917 9381919
9381941 9381949 9381983 9381997 9382001 9382031 9382039 9382049 9382063 9382073
9382099 9382103 9382123 9382133 9382141 9382151 9382157 9382159 9382169 9382199
9382207 9382223 9382229 9382271 9382313 9382319 9382327 9382343 9382363
9382391 9382411 9382421 9382427 9382433 9382463 9382501 9382507 9382511 9382517
9382547 9382567 9382601 9382603 9382609 9382619 9382621 9382627 9382649 9382669
9382673 9382693 9382699 9382717 9382741 9382757 9382777 9382783 9382787 9382811
9382819 9382823 9382831 9382843 9382847 9382889 9382927 9382931 9382943 9382949
```

```
9382951  9382969  9383009  9383021  9383027  9383041  9383053  9383071  9383107  9383161
9383177  9383189  9383239  9383251  9383261  9383263  9383281  9383317  9383323  9383329
9383351  9383357  9383369  9383377  9383393  9383411  9383449  9383453  9383477  9383497
9383513  9383557  9383603  9383623  9383653  9383657  9383659  9383707  9383713  9383723
9383729  9383741  9383743  9383749  9383753  9383767  9383771  9383783  9383789  9383797
9383807  9383827  9383831  9383837  9383851  9383861  9383863  9383867  9383873  9383887
9383939  9383947  9383963  9383981  9383987  9383993  9384013  9384031  9384049
9384059  9384061  9384083  9384091  9384097  9384101  9384131  9384143  9384149  9384209
9384241  9384251  9384257  9384259  9384269  9384281  9384293  9384317  9384329  9384341
9384353  9384373  9384377  9384383  9384469  9384491  9384521  9384523  9384539  9384553
9384559  9384581  9384589  9384611  9384671  9384677  9384691  9384703  9384721  9384733
9384737  9384769  9384811  9384829  9384839  9384853  9384857  9384871  9384877
9384889  9384923  9384929  9384931  9384937  9384967  9384979  9384983  9384997  9385027
9385043  9385049  9385073  9385091  9385093  9385111  9385133  9385147  9385151  9385153
9385163  9385171  9385199  9385213  9385231  9385253  9385261  9385267  9385273  9385283
9385301  9385319  9385339  9385367  9385417  9385421  9385469  9385471  9385483  9385489
9385511  9385553  9385573  9385577  9385581  9385613  9385619  9385631  9385693
9385699  9385709  9385711  9385721  9385741  9385781  9385793  9385807  9385811  9385813
9385837  9385861  9385903  9385919  9385927  9385929  9385967  9385969  9385979  9385991
9385993  9386017  9386021  9386051  9386063  9386077  9386101  9386161  9386173  9386177
9386183  9386191  9386203  9386219  9386239  9386257  9386263  9386303  9386309  9386327
9386339  9386347  9386357  9386359  9386383  9386393  9386423  9386449  9386453  9386467
9386471  9386473  9386477  9386501  9386527  9386537  9386579  9386603  9386609  9386617
9386621  9386639  9386651  9386653  9386657  9386731  9386743  9386791  9386801
9386803  9386813  9386821  9386833  9386837  9386843  9386849  9386879  9386911  9386917
9386933  9386953  9386957  9386977  9386987  9386999  9387031  9387047  9387061  9387071
9387089  9387109  9387113  9387127  9387163  9387199  9387221  9387223  9387239  9387241
9387251  9387269  9387283  9387331  9387341  9387347  9387359  9387361  9387379  9387403
9387409  9387421  9387441  9387449  9387457  9387467  9387481  9387509  9387527
9387533  9387541  9387551  9387559  9387569  9387589  9387607  9387629  9387671  9387683
9387709  9387773  9387779  9387797  9387799  9387857  9387877  9387883  9387901  9387913
9387923  9387941  9387949  9387971  9387977  9387991  9387997  9388007  9388031  9388069
9388079  9388091  9388103  9388111  9388177  9388187  9388189  9388201  9388207  9388219
9388229  9388231  9388243  9388271  9388273  9388283  9388307  9388321  9388349  9388387
9388397  9388399  9388409  9388427  9388433  9388441  9388453  9388459  9388481
9388487  9388507  9388513  9388517  9388529  9388541  9388559  9388591  9388601  9388609
9388619  9388661  9388667  9388681  9388697  9388703  9388723  9388751  9388781  9388801
9388829  9388843  9388849  9388891  9388903  9388919  9388943  9388949  9388957  9388979
9388993  9388999  9389047  9389077  9389089  9389099  9389101  9389113  9389131  9389137
9389141  9389153  9389161  9389167  9389183  9389189  9389197  9389203  9389207  9389227
9389239  9389251  9389269  9389279  9389297  9389299  9389323  9389327  9389329  9389339
9389353  9389381  9389383  9389399  9389407  9389431  9389441  9389449  9389459  9389461
9389467  9389483  9389489  9389531  9389551  9389557  9389561  9389573  9389579  9389603
9389617  9389641  9389651  9389653  9389663  9389671  9389689  9389713  9389717  9389719
9389741  9389813  9389827  9389927  9389929  9389951  9389977  9389987  9390037  9390041
9390053  9390061  9390127  9390079  9390097  9390121  9390151  9390181  9390191  9390203
9390221  9390257  9390281  9390289  9390299  9390317  9390319  9390323  9390331  9390343
9390361  9390379  9390397  9390419  9390431  9390439  9390457  9390467  9390481  9390497
9390529  9390553  9390559  9390571  9390581  9390587  9390607  9390629  9390643  9390671
9390679  9390683  9390691  9390697  9390707  9390709  9390713  9390757  9390779  9390781
9390791  9390803  9390811  9390833  9390839  9390863  9390877  9390937  9390947  9390949
9390973  9391001  9391033  9391079  9391093  9391097  9391103  9391121  9391139  9391141
9391147  9391169  9391181  9391183  9391223  9391289  9391307  9391313  9391351  9391363
9391373  9391387  9391397  9391423  9391427  9391433  9391439  9391471  9391477  9391483
9391489  9391507  9391517  9391537  9391541  9391601  9391607  9391609  9391631  9391639
9391663  9391691  9391693  9391703  9391709  9391717  9391727  9391763  9391771  9391787
9391801  9391817  9391841  9391847  9391873  9391883  9391927  9391937  9391979  9392003
9392059  9392063  9392237  9392083  9392129  9392147  9392153  9392161  9392167  9392171
9392209  9392233  9392237  9392267  9392281  9392291  9392311  9392329  9392333  9392359
9392371  9392407  9392417  9392423  9392429  9392431  9392459  9392497  9392503  9392507
9392521  9392531  9392541  9392563  9392611  9392627  9392629  9392641  9392651  9392681
9392683  9392729  9392749  9392753  9392759  9392777  9392827  9392833  9392849  9392869
9392909  9392917  9392921  9392923  9392927  9392951  9392953  9392989  9393001
9393017  9393019  9393037  9393073  9393077  9393089  9393103  9393107  9393113  9393127
9393143  9393151  9393191  9393233  9393253  9393271  9393281  9393289  9393313  9393317
9393323  9393343  9393389  9393413  9393427  9393431  9393437  9393463  9393473  9393557
9393563  9393569  9393623  9393641  9393647  9393677  9393701  9393739  9393751  9393757
9393763  9393779  9393827  9393871  9393929  9393949  9393973  9393977  9393991
9394001  9394009  9394019  9394027  9394067  9394079  9394087  9394093  9394109  9394123
9394139  9394153  9394169  9394181  9394199  9394201  9394213  9394241  9394243
9394249  9394261  9394277  9394349  9394351  9394361  9394367  9394369  9394381  9394391
9394397  9394423  9394447  9394471  9394477  9394487  9394499  9394513  9394529  9394537
9394543  9394577  9394631  9394657  9394667  9394669  9394681  9394691  9394709  9394771
9394789  9394813  9394817  9394823  9394837  9394841  9394843  9394859  9394867  9394901
9394909  9394961  9394963  9394967  9394969  9394981  9394993  9394997  9395011  9395051
9395053  9395081  9395083  9395093  9395117  9395131  9395147  9395153  9395161  9395171
9395179  9395207  9395227  9395249  9395251  9395279  9395311  9395341  9395357  9395377
9395381  9395383  9395401  9395411  9395413  9395417  9395453  9395459  9395461  9395467
9395471  9395479  9395489  9395513  9395539  9395591  9395593  9395599  9395609  9395651
9395653  9395693  9395699  9395717  9395731  9395741  9395773  9395779  9395783  9395843
9395851  9395873  9395923  9395941  9395959  9395963  9395977  9395987  9396001  9396043
9396047  9396071  9396077  9396091  9396103  9396119  9396133  9396137  9396143  9396157
9396161  9396173  9396209  9396229  9396239  9396251  9396271  9396307  9396311  9396323
9396329  9396337  9396371  9396391  9396407  9396433  9396437  9396451  9396467  9396479
9396481  9396509  9396553  9396559  9396577  9396599  9396613  9396617  9396619  9396701
9396707  9396713  9396731  9396743  9396769  9396791  9396797  9396799  9396809  9396823
9396859  9396889  9396901  9396911  9396917  9396929  9396931  9396941  9396943  9396973
9397007  9397013  9397019  9397021  9397043  9397049  9397067  9397103  9397109  9397117
9397127  9397139  9397151  9397163  9397181  9397211  9397237  9397259  9397301  9397303
```

```
9397319 9397327 9397337 9397351 9397357 9397369 9397393 9397417 9397429 9397459
9397463 9397469 9397471 9397499 9397513 9397517 9397529 9397541 9397559 9397561
9397643 9397649 9397657 9397669 9397699 9397709 9397757 9397781 9397811 9397813
9397819 9397831 9397847 9397849 9397853 9397859 9397891 9397901 9397909 9397937
9397939 9397981 9398003 9398021 9398041 9398047 9398069 9398101 9398107 9398113
9398149 9398171 9398183 9398201 9398227 9398243 9398251 9398267 9398269 9398281
9398299 9398303 9398317 9398321 9398327 9398351 9398357 9398359 9398371 9398377
9398383 9398401 9398419 9398423 9398429 9398443 9398447 9398461 9398479 9398497
9398509 9398527 9398563 9398567 9398579 9398591 9398617 9398633 9398657 9398681
9398687 9398689 9398699 9398723 9398729 9398737 9398783 9398801 9398803 9398839
9398843 9398849 9398869 9398899 9398903 9398911 9398923 9398953 9398957 9398971
9398989 9398993 9399017 9399029 9399031 9399043 9399063 9399097 9399109 9399121
9399133 9399139 9399151 9399163 9399191 9399217 9399223 9399233 9399239 9399251
9399253 9399287 9399323 9399337 9399347 9399409 9399421 9399431 9399437 9399449
9399463 9399473 9399491 9399493 9399503 9399527 9399529 9399563 9399569 9399581
9399601 9399641 9399653 9399743 9399749 9399751 9399773 9399779 9399781 9399809
9399811 9399823 9399869 9399889 9399937 9399959 9399967 9399977 9399981 9399989
9400009 9400019 9400021 9400043 9400049 9400063 9400073 9400087 9400093 9400103
9400121 9400151 9400189 9400199 9400211 9400219 9400247 9400253 9400277 9400327
9400333 9400343 9400351 9400361 9400381 9400387 9400393 9400397 9400463 9400477
9400481 9400483 9400493 9400499 9400511 9400519 9400571 9400591 9400619 9400639
9400673 9400681 9400693 9400697 9400723 9400733 9400739 9400747 9400759 9400793
9400817 9400823 9400841 9400861 9400871 9400873 9400879 9400889 9400891 9400907
9400927 9400933 9400943 9400969 9400973 9400999 9401009 9401023 9401027 9401033
9401053 9401057 9401059 9401069 9401083 9401099 9401101 9401107 9401113 9401123
9401149 9401167 9401207 9401213 9401233 9401243 9401267 9401279 9401309 9401311
9401347 9401369 9401377 9401419 9401467 9401489 9401519 9401569 9401627 9401633
9401647 9401699 9401701 9401753 9401767 9401797 9401807 9401809 9401837 9401839
9401849 9401863 9401879 9401881 9401921 9401947 9401957 9401981 9402007 9402011
9402023 9402047 9402059 9402067 9402091 9402103 9402121 9402137 9402143 9402167
9402179 9402199 9402203 9402221 9402223 9402233 9402271 9402277 9402287 9402319
9402361 9402373 9402401 9402413 9402439 9402451 9402457 9402461 9402493 9402521
9402527 9402529 9402539 9402553 9402559 9402577 9402593 9402599 9402623 9402643
9402647 9402661 9402671 9402689 9402709 9402719 9402733 9402737 9402749 9402781
9402803 9402857 9402863 9402893 9402901 9402917 9402919 9402923 9402937 9402947
9402971 9402979 9402983 9402997 9403001 9403003 9403019 9403061 9403073 9403099
9403109 9403129 9403139 9403183 9403187 9403189 9403231 9403237 9403259 9403301
9403327 9403351 9403357 9403367 9403393 9403409 9403411 9403451 9403463 9403469
9403487 9403501 9403519 9403523 9403531 9403569 9403621 9403673 9403729 9403733
9403741 9403753 9403763 9403769 9403777 9403781 9403783 9403811 9403871 9403897
9403991 9403997 9404011 9404029 9404051 9404093 9404099 9404117 9404119 9404141
9404147 9404159 9404167 9404173 9404177 9404201 9404231 9404233 9404237 9404243
9404257 9404261 9404279 9404287 9404299 9404341 9404347 9404357 9404393 9404399
9404443 9404489 9404491 9404531 9404537 9404561 9404567 9404569 9404597 9404599
9404609 9404641 9404693 9404699 9404737 9404743 9404761 9404767 9404783 9404803
9404807 9404849 9404869 9404881 9404887 9404891 9404909 9404921 9404947 9404957
9404959 9404971 9404987 9405017 9405037 9405043 9405061 9405079 9405107 9405127
9405139 9405211 9405223 9405241 9405257 9405287 9405313 9405343 9405349 9405353
9405377 9405379 9405391 9405401 9405419 9405421 9405427 9405443 9405457 9405463
9405479 9405481 9405497 9405509 9405521 9405533 9405547 9405551 9405563 9405569
9405569 9405587 9405601 9405611 9405623 9405629 9405653 9405667 9405727 9405731
9405749 9405761 9405763 9405791 9405793 9405797 9405821 9405823 9405841 9405853
9405859 9405883 9405887 9405911 9405953 9405959 9405961 9405967 9405973 9405983
9405997 9406003 9406021 9406037 9406043 9406073 9406079 9406081 9406091 9406099
9406127 9406147 9406153 9406161 9406181 9406211 9406213 9406223 9406247 9406249
9406259 9406277 9406279 9406289 9406291 9406297 9406301 9406337 9406339 9406393
9406417 9406421 9406427 9406483 9406511 9406513 9406541 9406549 9406571 9406601
9406613 9406619 9406651 9406667 9406673 9406693 9406697 9406699 9406703 9406711
9406739 9406741 9406757 9406777 9406799 9406807 9406819 9406849 9406879 9406889
9406897 9406913 9406919 9406927 9406937 9406939 9406949 9406951 9406961 9406973
9406997 9407009 9407029 9407051 9407053 9407087 9407089 9407117 9407131 9407143
9407179 9407183 9407227 9407243 9407249 9407257 9407263 9407287 9407309 9407317
9407329 9407347 9407357 9407369 9407383 9407407 9407417 9407423 9407441 9407459
9407467 9407471 9407479 9407521 9407543 9407551 9407569 9407581 9407617 9407623
9407633 9407639 9407667 9407683 9407689 9407719 9407747 9407767 9407789 9407809
9407821 9407833 9407843 9407891 9407903 9407929 9407941 9407971 9408011 9408017
9408023 9408043 9408053 9408067 9408071 9408103 9408109 9408137 9408143 9408149
9408163 9408169 9408187 9408193 9408241 9408253 9408257 9408263 9408277 9408331
9408337 9408349 9408389 9408391 9408431 9408433 9408517 9408527 9408547 9408563
9408569 9408571 9408577 9408583 9408589 9408611 9408643 9408647 9408653 9408661
9408677 9408697 9408757 9408799 9408809 9408827 9408829 9408869 9408887 9408913
9408983 9409051 9409069 9409073 9409111 9409117 9409121 9409159 9409163 9409181
9409187 9409193 9409219 9409229 9409247 9409271 9409273 9409307 9409319 9409331
9409339 9409357 9409373 9409403 9409409 9409423 9409429 9409441 9409451 9409457
9409489 9409529 9409531 9409537 9409573 9409577 9409591 9409607 9409639 9409649
9409651 9409657 9409661 9409663 9409667 9409711 9409723 9409727 9409747 9409753
9409759 9409801 9409837 9409871 9409873 9409903 9409909 9409943 9409963 9409973
9410003 9410017 9410021 9410029 9410039 9410053 9410057 9410117 9410189 9410207
9410227 9410237 9410251 9410257 9410273 9410311 9410341 9410347 9410353 9410363
9410369 9410399 9410419 9410431 9410437 9410447 9410449 9410461 9410477 9410483
9410497 9410501 9410509 9410539 9410551 9410561 9410563 9410581 9410603 9410629
9410633 9410659 9410671 9410699 9410747 9410759 9410767 9410777 9410783 9410803
9410813 9410831 9410861 9410879 9410881 9410899 9410903 9410923 9410927 9410939
9410953 9410957 9410959 9410963 9410969 9410983 9411029 9411043 9411049 9411067
9411091 9411107 9411119 9411133 9411161 9411173 9411187 9411203 9411221 9411229
9411239 9411257 9411271 9411293 9411299 9411313 9411317 9411329 9411331 9411343
9411359 9411407 9411443 9411449 9411461 9411469 9411473 9411481 9411487 9411497
9411511 9411529 9411553 9411583 9411587 9411599 9411601 9411607 9411617 9411697
```

```
9411709 9411713 9411737 9411749 9411757 9411769 9411799 9411833 9411841 9411847
9411869 9411877 9411893 9411901 9411917 9411937 9411943 9411947 9411967 9411981
9411977 9411989 9412021 9412027 9412043 9412061 9412099 9412133 9412147 9412157
9412177 9412187 9412213 9412231 9412241 9412253 9412303 9412343 9412349 9412367
9412369 9412379 9412397 9412427 9412433 9412439 9412471 9412489 9412511 9412517
9412519 9412523 9412553 9412567 9412573 9412583 9412591 9412597 9412603 9412631
9412649 9412661 9412687 9412691 9412699 9412709 9412717 9412721 9412723 9412759
9412807 9412811 9412813 9412817 9412867 9412873 9412889 9412891 9412901 9412943
9412973 9412979 9412981 9412993 9413011 9413017 9413021 9413029 9413039 9413051
9413071 9413083 9413101 9413123 9413137 9413143 9413153 9413167 9413177 9413179
9413191 9413213 9413221 9413237 9413269 9413293 9413311 9413321 9413333 9413347
9413351 9413353 9413381 9413387 9413389 9413399 9413447 9413473 9413483 9413501
9413507 9413513 9413519 9413527 9413533 9413633 9413639 9413707 9413711 9413717
9413737 9413749 9413773 9413779 9413813 9413821 9413837 9413839 9413849 9413851
9413879 9413881 9413897 9413909 9413933 9413937 9413939 9413983 9413993 9414001
9414011 9414017 9414023 9414047 9414071 9414079 9414089 9414091 9414113 9414149
9414151 9414203 9414211 9414227 9414233 9414247 9414263 9414271 9414283 9414287
9414289 9414319 9414323 9414341 9414373 9414389 9414401 9414403 9414409 9414437
9414451 9414469 9414479 9414499 9414527 9414533 9414547 9414551 9414563 9414569
9414593 9414599 9414619 9414631 9414649 9414653 9414673 9414677 9414697 9414701
9414703 9414749 9414781 9414791 9414817 9414841 9414857 9414869 9414901 9414913
9414919 9414929 9414931 9414941 9414943 9414949 9414989 9414997 9415019 9415033
9415121 9415129 9415139 9415157 9415163 9415201 9415207 9415213 9415223 9415249
9415253 9415267 9415313 9415319 9415327 9415339 9415361 9415387 9415391 9415421
9415423 9415451 9415489 9415513 9415531 9415541 9415543 9415547 9415559 9415561
9415573 9415597 9415673 9415687 9415699 9415771 9415781 9415789 9415799 9415817
9415823 9415829 9415831 9415837 9415843 9415921 9415969 9416041 9416047 9416053
9416059 9416087 9416137 9416171 9416179 9416201 9416203 9416207 9416221 9416227
9416237 9416263 9416273 9416279 9416287 9416291 9416309 9416327 9416333 9416339
9416357 9416359 9416377 9416383 9416399 9416417 9416423 9416431 9416447 9416461
9416479 9416483 9416501 9416513 9416531 9416543 9416549 9416557 9416573 9416581
9416597 9416633 9416639 9416669 9416707 9416711 9416713 9416717 9416741 9416747
9416809 9416819 9416843 9416863 9416899 9416903 9416933 9416941 9416947 9416971
9416983 9417019 9417029 9417047 9417053 9417059 9417071 9417091 9417101
9417113 9417127 9417137 9417157 9417173 9417193 9417223 9417229 9417259 9417283
9417299 9417311 9417323 9417329 9417347 9417361 9417367 9417377 9417379 9417383
9417449 9417451 9417461 9417467 9417469 9417479 9417481 9417493 9417497 9417523
9417539 9417553 9417571 9417581 9417593 9417671 9417689 9417697 9417701 9417703
9417739 9417763 9417773 9417779 9417797 9417799 9417809 9417829 9417841 9417911
9417913 9417917 9417923 9417929 9417931 9417997 9418007 9418009 9418037 9418049
9418067 9418081 9418099 9418121 9418133 9418163 9418169 9418177 9418231 9418237
9418261 9418267 9418309 9418337 9418349 9418369 9418399 9418403 9418421 9418429
9418481 9418489 9418531 9418537 9418543 9418567 9418571 9418573 9418597 9418667
9418681 9418687 9418693 9418711 9418727 9418729 9418733 9418741 9418777 9418811
9418817 9418841 9418873 9418879 9418883 9418907 9418909 9418919 9418921 9418943
9418963 9418973 9418987 9419023 9419027 9419063 9419077 9419093
9419141 9419143 9419149 9419177 9419183 9419191 9419197 9419203 9419233 9419249
9419273 9419303 9419321 9419327 9419339 9419353 9419359 9419363 9419393 9419413
9419447 9419471 9419477 9419483 9419503 9419507 9419521 9419533
9419551 9419561 9419569 9419591 9419593 9419609 9419617 9419621 9419633 9419639
9419647 9419651 9419653 9419699 9419713 9419737 9419741 9419747 9419749 9419759
9419771 9419797 9419807 9419831 9419863 9419869 9419897 9419899 9419909 9419923
9419947 9419951 9419987 9420011 9420017 9420043 9420049 9420077 9420083 9420097
9420101 9420121 9420127 9420149 9420201 9420223 9420239 9420241 9420253 9420263
9420269 9420287 9420293 9420319 9420337 9420347 9420391 9420407 9420421 9420451
9420487 9420491 9420503 9420527 9420553 9420571 9420581 9420623 9420629 9420643
9420659 9420667 9420701 9420709 9420721 9420743 9420757 9420793 9420809 9420811
9420833 9420841 9420863 9420871 9420877 9420893 9420899 9420947 9420953 9420959
9420997 9421039 9421063 9421067 9421079 9421091 9421109 9421129 9421147 9421157
9421183 9421189 9421261 9421271 9421277 9421309 9421331 9421351 9421403 9421411
9421441 9421459 9421469 9421471 9421483 9421493 9421501 9421507 9421537 9421541
9421543 9421567 9421589 9421591 9421597 9421603 9421609 9421631 9421637 9421661
9421669 9421673 9421679 9421691 9421729 9421733 9421751 9421793 9421801 9421813
9421817 9421823 9421829 9421831 9421843 9421847 9421849 9421871 9421873 9421883
9421903 9421921 9421931 9421933 9421943 9421963 9421981 9422027 9422057 9422107
9422113 9422159 9422173 9422201 9422213 9422227 9422269 9422291 9422293 9422327
9422351 9422363 9422389 9422407 9422417 9422429 9422431 9422443 9422447 9422459
9422467 9422489 9422503 9422509 9422521 9422533 9422549 9422561 9422591 9422599
9422639 9422653 9422657 9422681 9422683 9422687 9422717 9422737 9422759 9422761
9422779 9422783 9422789 9422821 9422837 9422863 9422887 9422911 9422921 9422927
9422969 9422983 9423013 9423017 9423061 9423103 9423109 9423131 9423133 9423179
9423181 9423187 9423217 9423229 9423233 9423251 9423269 9423277 9423291 9423299
9423313 9423329 9423331 9423343 9423361 9423371 9423413 9423433 9423437 9423461
9423499 9423503 9423509 9423511 9423517 9423529 9423541 9423569 9423577 9423581
9423607 9423613 9423619 9423671 9423683 9423691 9423697 9423709 9423719 9423731
9423761 9423787 9423773 9423793 9423833 9423839 9423847 9423853 9423857
9423871 9423929 9423949 9423961 9423971 9423991 9424003 9424027 9424039 9424049
9424091 9424097 9424099 9424123 9424139 9424169 9424187 9424189 9424201 9424211
9424231 9424237 9424241 9424243 9424253 9424277 9424291 9424309 9424321 9424343
9424351 9424427 9424433 9424501 9424523 9424531 9424537 9424559 9424573 9424577
9424607 9424609 9424643 9424661 9424663 9424669 9424673 9424691 9424693 9424699
9424721 9424729 9424757 9424763 9424771 9424781 9424829 9424847 9424853 9424859
9424861 9424873 9424907 9424949 9424981 9424993 9424999 9425027 9425033 9425077
9425093 9425099 9425107 9425113 9425137 9425161 9425233 9425257 9425263 9425279
9425287 9425329 9425341 9425363 9425389 9425399 9425419 9425431 9425447 9425473
9425489 9425503 9425509 9425527 9425543 9425567 9425579 9425593 9425597 9425617
9425629 9425641 9425683 9425693 9425707 9425719 9425743 9425749 9425753 9425771
9425789 9425797 9425827 9425831 9425849 9425851 9425863 9425879 9425947 9425963
9426037 9426047 9426049 9426059 9426089 9426091 9426107 9426161 9426167 9426181
```

```
9426191  9426199  9426239  9426259  9426281  9426283  9426289  9426293  9426311  9426323
9426341  9426349  9426353  9426377  9426383  9426397  9426409  9426427  9426467  9426491
9426493  9426497  9426499  9426541  9426553  9426577  9426581  9426583  9426617  9426631
9426643  9426667  9426671  9426691  9426701  9426713  9426719  9426727  9426731  9426737
9426763  9426787  9426797  9426811  9426817  9426853  9426863  9426871  9426881  9426887
9426899  9426913  9426917  9426919  9426929  9426953  9426997  9427003  9427031  9427039
9427043  9427051  9427063  9427111  9427127  9427133  9427151  9427181  9427183  9427219
9427237  9427259  9427261  9427279  9427321  9427339  9427357  9427387  9427399  9427403
9427409  9427421  9427427  9427459  9427463  9427501  9427507  9427513  9427529  9427541
9427549  9427567  9427597  9427601  9427633  9427687  9427727  9427739  9427753  9427763
9427783  9427801  9427823  9427849  9427853  9427883  9427889  9427903  9427921  9427931
9427949  9427961  9427963  9427967  9427973  9427993  9427997  9428017  9428033  9428063
9428071  9428077  9428093  9428101  9428119  9428129  9428131  9428143  9428147  9428179
9428189  9428213  9428227  9428233  9428239  9428261  9428267  9428297  9428299  9428323
9428357  9428359  9428399  9428407  9428411  9428423  9428431  9428437  9428463  9428473
9428479  9428491  9428501  9428513  9428527  9428539  9428543  9428563  9428569  9428581
9428593  9428603  9428611  9428621  9428633  9428641  9428669  9428707  9428759  9428777
9428779  9428791  9428851  9428879  9428917  9428941  9428963  9428989  9429001  9429023
9429029  9429037  9429041  9429113  9429127  9429131  9429143  9429157  9429163  9429179
9429181  9429193  9429223  9429229  9429247  9429269  9429289  9429313  9429323  9429347
9429349  9429367  9429391  9429397  9429419  9429443  9429451  9429457  9429463  9429473
9429493  9429499  9429503  9429523  9429569  9429613  9429617  9429653  9429659  9429671
9429691  9429703  9429731  9429769  9429809  9429821  9429829  9429841  9429851  9429863
9429869  9429881  9429887  9429907  9429913  9429923  9429961  9429967  9429997  9430009
9430021  9430027  9430081  9430093  9430097  9430103  9430111  9430129  9430139  9430163
9430199  9430241  9430259  9430273  9430277  9430283  9430303  9430331  9430339  9430361
9430363  9430367  9430429  9430439  9430457  9430489  9430493  9430507  9430549  9430579
9430583  9430591  9430607  9430613  9430627  9430633  9430649  9430679  9430693  9430703
9430721  9430739  9430753  9430759  9430763  9430769  9430777  9430781  9430787  9430793
9430843  9430877  9430891  9430919  9430921  9430931  9430951  9430963  9430969  9430999
9431021  9431029  9431069  9431111  9431117  9431159  9431167  9431171  9431197  9431221
9431231  9431237  9431249  9431267  9431269  9431273  9431291  9431299  9431321  9431363
9431399  9431417  9431431  9431437  9431479  9431501  9431503  9431507  9431531  9431561
9431579  9431593  9431613  9431627  9431641  9431671  9431677  9431687  9431693  9431713
9431743  9431761  9431767  9431783  9431789  9431797  9431801  9431803  9431833  9431839
9431867  9431887  9431897  9431941  9431951  9431959  9431977  9432011  9432013  9432021
9432067  9432119  9432121  9432149  9432187  9432191  9432197  9432209  9432217  9432239
9432253  9432259  9432287  9432301  9432307  9432317  9432343  9432347  9432361  9432391
9432407  9432413  9432439  9432449  9432457  9432473  9432481  9432497  9432509
9432529  9432541  9432547  9432551  9432559  9432581  9432589  9432611  9432623  9432653
9432659  9432667  9432707  9432713  9432727  9432733  9432749  9432757  9432769  9432791
9432803  9432809  9432811  9432823  9432827  9432833  9432923  9432961  9432971  9432991
9433007  9433009  9433027  9433043  9433057  9433069  9433087  9433111  9433129  9433159
9433163  9433183  9433201  9433213  9433217  9433231  9433241  9433247  9433267  9433271
9433309  9433343  9433349  9433379  9433421  9433447  9433477  9433493  9433537  9433549
9433559  9433577  9433591  9433607  9433609  9433621  9433661  9433679  9433693  9433741
9433751  9433757  9433763  9433777  9433783  9433799  9433811  9433817  9433829  9433843
9433847  9433859  9433967  9433969  9433987  9434003  9434011  9434017  9434023  9434119
9434129  9434143  9434147  9434171  9434187  9434197  9434207  9434219  9434221  9434239
9434273  9434291  9434311  9434333  9434339  9434351  9434353  9434377  9434401  9434407
9434413  9434423  9434429  9434441  9434447  9434521  9434533  9434539  9434543  9434561
9434567  9434569  9434573  9434591  9434597  9434617  9434627  9434641  9434647  9434671
9434699  9434701  9434707  9434717  9434723  9434729  9434731  9434741  9434753  9434767
9434791  9434833  9434917  9434923  9434927  9434941  9434951  9434969  9434981  9434993
9435011  9435047  9435059  9435073  9435079  9435091  9435131  9435133  9435163  9435169
9435199  9435263  9435271  9435281  9435301  9435329  9435331  9435347  9435379  9435383
9435397  9435421  9435467  9435509  9435511  9435539  9435551  9435557  9435583  9435607
9435611  9435623  9435631  9435637  9435641  9435649  9435659  9435661  9435707  9435721
9435739  9435743  9435757  9435763  9435779  9435809  9435823  9435827  9435847  9435859
9435871  9435889  9435893  9435941  9435947  9435953  9435967  9435977  9436019  9436033
9436057  9436087  9436093  9436099  9436117  9436123  9436129  9436157  9436159  9436169
9436181  9436201  9436211  9436249  9436253  9436277  9436289  9436303  9436321  9436327
9436333  9436363  9436367  9436379  9436387  9436421  9436429  9436433  9436439  9436447
9436459  9436477  9436487  9436499  9436501  9436523  9436541  9436543  9436649  9436573
9436577  9436579  9436607  9436619  9436657  9436667  9436669  9436727  9436729  9436747
9436781  9436807  9436811  9436841  9436907  9436913  9436943  9436949  9436951  9436957
9436967  9436979  9436981  9436993  9437009  9437027  9437039  9437041  9437069  9437101
9437117  9437123  9437143  9437171  9437173  9437179  9437189  9437191  9437203  9437231
9437269  9437303  9437321  9437333  9437347  9437353  9437377  9437381  9437387  9437399
9437401  9437411  9437413  9437437  9437447  9437453  9437473  9437489  9437579  9437591
9437599  9437611  9437621  9437639  9437677  9437689  9437693  9437707  9437713  9437717
9437719  9437723  9437759  9437761  9437773  9437807  9437861  9437899  9437921  9437933
9437957  9437969  9437971  9437977  9437999  9438001  9438017  9438049  9438083  9438109
9438127  9438151  9438173  9438181  9438203  9438251  9438263  9438277  9438287  9438301
9438343  9438379  9438397  9438431  9438437  9438461  9438463  9438479  9438503  9438523
9438529  9438563  9438571  9438593  9438613  9438617  9438619  9438623  9438661  9438679
9438691  9438697  9438701  9438719  9438721  9438727  9438731  9438739  9438743  9438773
9438799  9438829  9438851  9438853  9438881  9438883  9438931  9438937  9438971
9438977  9438983  9439019  9439043  9439069  9439081  9439093  9439099  9439109  9439117
9439121  9439141  9439153  9439169  9439189  9439193  9439211  9439249  9439253  9439259
9439271  9439273  9439277  9439279  9439289  9439303  9439321  9439337  9439343  9439349
9439363  9439373  9439387  9439393  9439421  9439427  9439439  9439481  9439487  9439513
9439537  9439541  9439543  9439559  9439571  9439601  9439603  9439613  9439643
9439657  9439667  9439679  9439687  9439691  9439721  9439723  9439757  9439853  9439873
9439889  9439891  9439931  9439937  9439961  9439973  9439987  9440017  9440021  9440023
9440029  9440033  9440047  9440063  9440077  9440087  9440111  9440113  9440149  9440159
9440161  9440173  9440183  9440203  9440227  9440243  9440251  9440267  9440273  9440293
9440303  9440309  9440311  9440323  9440329  9440363  9440371  9440383  9440401  9440407
9440429  9440441  9440443  9440447  9440449  9440477  9440479  9440507  9440527  9440551
```

```
9440569  9440591  9440609  9440617  9440621  9440653  9440681  9440707  9440713  9440723
9440791  9440801  9440803  9440857  9440869  9440897  9440923  9440953  9440969  9440987
9440989  9440993  9440999  9441007  9441023  9441071  9441073  9441101  9441127  9441139
9441149  9441161  9441181  9441197  9441199  9441203  9441221  9441227  9441259  9441281
9441283  9441287  9441331  9441337  9441349  9441353  9441361  9441373  9441389  9441413
9441433  9441457  9441463  9441479  9441491  9441529  9441539  9441541  9441547  9441571
9441583  9441587  9441589  9441599  9441637  9441643  9441667  9441673  9441721  9441737
9441739  9441781  9441797  9441833  9441847  9441871  9441889  9441961  9441967  9441973
9441977  9441979  9441989  9442009  9442019  9442051  9442057  9442063  9442079  9442091
9442093  9442117  9442127  9442133  9442151  9442189  9442193  9442207  9442211  9442229
9442231  9442247  9442249  9442283  9442291  9442309  9442333  9442337  9442379  9442387
9442417  9442439  9442457  9442469  9442471  9442481  9442493  9442501  9442523  9442529
9442547  9442549  9442553  9442567  9442579  9442597  9442607  9442613  9442637  9442649
9442679  9442691  9442709  9442711  9442717  9442729  9442747  9442759  9442781  9442789
9442799  9442813  9442847  9442877  9442889  9442907  9442921  9442931  9442933  9442963
9442969  9443011  9443017  9443039  9443051  9443053  9443059  9443089  9443123  9443131
9443141  9443153  9443191  9443201  9443233  9443237  9443261  9443263  9443267  9443303
9443309  9443311  9443321  9443327  9443333  9443341  9443351  9443383  9443387  9443419
9443429  9443443  9443453  9443461  9443479  9443507  9443509  9443519  9443527  9443549
9443557  9443573  9443579  9443587  9443597  9443611  9443633  9443669  9443671  9443677
9443719  9443729  9443737  9443743  9443767  9443773  9443807  9443831  9443839  9443849
9443867  9443873  9443909  9443939  9443947  9443957  9443971  9443977  9444013  9444031
9444041  9444049  9444059  9444091  9444103  9444109  9444143  9444151  9444179  9444187
9444217  9444221  9444247  9444251  9444257  9444263  9444271  9444277  9444319  9444353
9444359  9444403  9444437  9444439  9444449  9444511  9444541  9444557  9444587  9444601
9444607  9444619  9444629  9444641  9444671  9444683  9444713  9444763  9444781  9444803
9444811  9444821  9444829  9444833  9444839  9444847  9444887  9444889  9444893  9444901
9444937  9444949  9444977  9444983  9445001  9445021  9445043  9445061  9445063  9445067
9445087  9445091  9445103  9445127  9445169  9445187  9445193  9445237  9445283  9445307
9445333  9445339  9445349  9445351  9445357  9445379  9445391  9445393  9445399  9445411
9445453  9445511  9445529  9445531  9445537  9445547  9445573  9445577  9445589  9445609
9445633  9445673  9445699  9445721  9445729  9445741  9445753  9445757  9445771  9445781
9445811  9445859  9445871  9445873  9445889  9445901  9445921  9445937  9445987  9445991
9445993  9446011  9446039  9446071  9446081  9446093  9446117  9446131  9446149  9446161
9446179  9446183  9446189  9446191  9446207  9446221  9446231  9446291  9446303  9446309
9446321  9446323  9446329  9446443  9446449  9446453  9446467  9446497  9446501  9446513
9446527  9446551  9446587  9446597  9446609  9446617  9446639  9446651  9446659  9446677
9446683  9446707  9446719  9446737  9446777  9446783  9446791  9446797  9446807  9446809
9446831  9446839  9446861  9446863  9446867  9446869  9446873  9446881  9446891  9446897
9446929  9446981  9446989  9446993  9446999  9447007  9447017  9447029  9447037  9447041
9447073  9447077  9447079  9447101  9447167  9447187  9447211  9447233  9447239  9447241
9447259  9447271  9447283  9447287  9447307  9447349  9447353  9447371  9447379  9447391
9447397  9447407  9447419  9447479  9447481  9447499  9447511  9447521  9447523  9447527
9447539  9447557  9447569  9447583  9447593  9447601  9447623  9447629  9447667  9447679
9447701  9447721  9447743  9447751  9447761  9447787  9447791  9447811  9447821  9447827
9447829  9447857  9447859  9447887  9447943  9447953  9447983  9448001  9448007  9448013
9448037  9448051  9448067  9448069  9448079  9448093  9448097  9448123  9448129  9448133
9448177  9448181  9448189  9448199  9448213  9448217  9448237  9448253  9448259  9448279
9448289  9448291  9448333  9448339  9448367  9448399  9448427  9448429  9448451  9448489
9448501  9448511  9448513  9448553  9448589  9448591  9448603  9448613  9448619  9448627
9448631  9448639  9448657  9448667  9448679  9448687  9448723  9448729  9448759  9448771
9448781  9448783  9448793  9448807  9448823  9448841  9448847  9448877  9448897  9448903
9448919  9448921  9448931  9448937  9448951  9448963  9448973  9448979  9449003  9449009
9449021  9449039  9449051  9449071  9449107  9449129  9449131  9449183  9449189  9449191
9449201  9449221  9449243  9449249  9449267  9449281  9449287  9449299  9449309  9449347
9449351  9449353  9449357  9449371  9449387  9449411  9449413  9449447  9449457  9449471
9449477  9449483  9449497  9449507  9449519  9449521  9449533  9449549  9449581  9449591
9449597  9449611  9449623  9449641  9449651  9449663  9449677  9449681  9449683  9449717
9449801  9449813  9449819  9449827  9449831  9449857  9449879  9449903  9449917  9449927
9449933  9449939  9449963  9449983  9449989  9450013  9450017  9450019  9450037  9450043
9450061  9450073  9450083  9450097  9450101  9450127  9450151  9450157  9450167  9450169
9450173  9450211  9450227  9450229  9450253  9450269  9450289  9450307  9450341  9450349
9450403  9450407  9450439  9450457  9450461  9450473  9450481  9450499  9450523
9450557  9450587  9450599  9450611  9450647  9450673  9450689  9450731  9450757  9450761
9450773  9450803  9450811  9450823  9450851  9450853  9450887  9450893  9450899  9450911
9450941  9450943  9450967  9450977  9451003  9451009  9451019  9451051  9451059  9451061
9451067  9451069  9451073  9451093  9451097  9451103  9451109  9451111  9451121  9451139
9451147  9451153  9451181  9451193  9451199  9451223  9451261  9451289  9451319  9451327
9451339  9451349  9451363  9451381  9451423  9451427  9451441  9451451  9451483  9451487
9451501  9451513  9451549  9451553  9451567  9451571  9451573  9451579  9451619  9451627
9451633  9451657  9451669  9451691  9451693  9451697  9451751  9451753  9451769  9451817
9451829  9451831  9451843  9451867  9451877  9451879  9451913  9451943  9451961  9451963
9451969  9451973  9451979  9452021  9452039  9452077  9452083  9452087  9452089  9452129
9452137  9452141  9452143  9452161  9452197  9452227  9452243  9452251  9452269  9452297
9452299  9452309  9452321  9452327  9452341  9452351  9452369  9452383  9452393  9452419
9452423  9452441  9452447  9452467  9452477  9452491  9452537  9452543  9452657  9452683
9452711  9452719  9452741  9452767  9452771  9452777  9452783  9452801  9452809  9452831
9452851  9452857  9452873  9452881  9452897  9452917  9452959  9453079  9453107  9453113
9453131  9453151  9453209  9453211  9453221  9453277  9453287  9453289  9453307  9453319
9453331  9453337  9453347  9453359  9453373  9453383  9453401  9453487  9453497  9453503
9453517  9453541  9453551  9453559  9453569  9453599  9453601  9453607  9453637  9453641
9453643  9453671  9453677  9453737  9453749  9453757  9453779  9453781  9453803  9453809
9453817  9453839  9453869  9453881  9453889  9453923  9453953  9453967  9453973
9453979  9453991  9454013  9454019  9454021  9454031  9454033  9454043  9454051  9454073
9454079  9454099  9454103  9454141  9454147  9454161  9454171  9454177  9454183  9454187
9454201  9454213  9454217  9454223  9454253  9454297  9454321  9454369  9454373  9454409
9454421  9454439  9454463  9454481  9454513  9454517  9454547  9454561  9454579  9454583
9454589  9454591  9454603  9454607  9454619  9454631  9454639  9454651  9454657  9454693
9454717  9454727  9454733  9454751  9454789  9454801  9454813  9454831  9454859  9454871
```

```
9454901  9454903  9454931  9454961  9454979  9454993  9454997  9455003  9455029  9455053
9455059  9455063  9455099  9455101  9455129  9455137  9455143  9455161  9455191
9455357  9455377  9455389  9455393  9455401  9455419  9455437  9455441  9455489  9455497
9455513  9455581  9455623  9455681  9455717  9455729  9455731  9455759  9455767  9455807
9455819  9455821  9455843  9455857  9455861  9455867  9455881  9455903  9455917  9455947
9455951  9455969  9456017  9456049  9456061  9456067  9456103  9456113  9456137  9456191
9456193  9456203  9456229  9456241  9456247  9456253  9456257  9456269  9456299  9456311
9456329  9456341  9456361  9456371  9456373  9456397  9456409  9456449  9456467  9456479
9456481  9456487  9456563  9456613  9456617  9456637  9456649  9456659  9456683  9456757
9456763  9456779  9456781  9456787  9456803  9456817  9456827  9456833  9456847  9456859
9456869  9456877  9456883  9456893  9456899  9456901  9456907  9456919  9456943  9456959
9456961  9456971  9456977  9456989  9457009  9457027  9457031  9457037  9457067  9457073
9457109  9457111  9457121  9457127  9457171  9457177  9457181  9457241  9457243  9457297
9457313  9457319  9457333  9457361  9457367  9457397  9457411  9457447  9457489  9457493
9457507  9457517  9457537  9457541  9457561  9457571  9457619  9457621  9457631  9457673
9457709  9457727  9457739  9457753  9457777  9457843  9457849  9457859  9457871
9457891  9457897  9457901  9457907  9457913  9457927  9457939  9457961  9457963  9457969
9458021  9458023  9458041  9458077  9458093  9458101  9458107  9458153  9458159  9458173
9458191  9458201  9458209  9458243  9458261  9458279  9458287  9458291  9458299  9458311
9458357  9458369  9458377  9458389  9458411  9458419  9458473  9458483  9458507  9458509
9458513  9458521  9458531  9458557  9458563  9458599  9458621  9458623  9458633  9458651
9458663  9458671  9458707  9458711  9458723  9458767  9458777  9458803  9458849  9458861
9458887  9458899  9458909  9458927  9458983  9458989  9459007  9459019  9459041  9459059
9459071  9459077  9459091  9459113  9459119  9459137  9459143  9459167  9459179  9459193
9459199  9459217  9459221  9459251  9459277  9459287  9459299  9459301  9459337  9459389
9459403  9459419  9459421  9459451  9459487  9459503  9459517  9459521  9459523  9459533
9459551  9459577  9459589  9459607  9459629  9459631  9459661  9459673  9459677  9459683
9459689  9459691  9459707  9459727  9459733  9459767  9459781  9459809  9459823  9459833
9459839  9459869  9459881  9459893  9459907  9459911  9459937  9459943  9459949  9459953
9459959  9460027  9460037  9460067  9460079  9460093  9460117  9460127  9460141  9460147
9460151  9460163  9460249  9460259  9460267  9460303  9460331  9460379  9460391  9460393
9460397  9460403  9460411  9460417  9460439  9460469  9460471  9460501  9460511  9460513
9460543  9460571  9460573  9460597  9460609  9460621  9460631  9460637  9460639  9460643
9460657  9460669  9460681  9460691  9460697  9460723  9460733  9460739  9460741  9460769
9460799  9460811  9460813  9460837  9460849  9460853  9460861  9460883  9460897  9460901
9460909  9460933  9460939  9460987  9461017  9461021  9461033  9461071  9461093  9461099
9461113  9461117  9461131  9461143  9461149  9461167  9461171  9461173  9461191  9461203
9461209  9461219  9461237  9461251  9461269  9461273  9461283  9461329  9461333  9461341
9461359  9461363  9461369  9461371  9461383  9461399  9461407  9461461  9461467  9461471
9461497  9461519  9461521  9461581  9461591  9461609  9461623  9461633  9461651  9461657
9461663  9461681  9461723  9461729  9461777  9461779  9461783  9461797  9461819  9461821
9461827  9461831  9461833  9461839  9461861  9461927  9461929  9461989  9462017  9462023
9462029  9462049  9462073  9462077  9462097  9462127  9462139  9462151  9462157  9462169
9462191  9462197  9462199  9462221  9462227  9462239  9462263  9462283  9462287  9462289
9462311  9462317  9462359  9462367  9462373  9462377  9462379  9462413  9462419  9462443
9462457  9462473  9462487  9462511  9462517  9462521  9462539  9462571  9462577  9462587
9462599  9462601  9462619  9462647  9462689  9462701  9462707  9462737  9462743  9462749
9462751  9462757  9462769  9462773  9462793  9462811  9462823  9462847  9462877  9462883
9462889  9462899  9462907  9462911  9462953  9462979  9462989  9463057  9463061  9463073
9463109  9463117  9463123  9463133  9463141  9463163  9463171  9463177  9463213  9463229
9463241  9463243  9463247  9463249  9463253  9463261  9463283  9463301  9463303  9463319
9463343  9463427  9463429  9463439  9463469  9463481  9463507  9463513  9463567  9463583
9463589  9463609  9463631  9463633  9463639  9463651  9463693  9463697  9463703  9463709
9463717  9463721  9463739  9463759  9463789  9463807  9463813  9463841  9463877  9463901
9463921  9463931  9463933  9463973  9463991  9463997  9464011  9464023  9464027
9464047  9464099  9464111  9464113  9464123  9464137  9464149  9464159  9464173  9464233
9464239  9464297  9464327  9464363  9464381  9464383  9464417  9464419  9464443  9464447
9464449  9464453  9464467  9464473  9464479  9464519  9464537  9464549  9464551  9464599
9464633  9464647  9464659  9464677  9464681  9464683  9464713  9464723  9464729  9464737
9464743  9464761  9464787  9464837  9464849  9464857  9464863  9464867  9464887  9464897
9464893  9464909  9464941  9464953  9464999  9465011  9465017  9465047  9465067  9465083
9465089  9465091  9465103  9465139  9465151  9465161  9465221  9465251  9465263  9465271
9465293  9465317  9465329  9465331  9465347  9465353  9465359  9465371  9465409  9465427
9465457  9465473  9465479  9465493  9465497  9465499  9465503  9465517  9465527  9465529
9465539  9465587  9465593  9465601  9465613  9465637  9465661  9465679  9465683  9465707
9465721  9465733  9465749  9465751  9465763  9465809  9465829  9465839  9465871  9465913
9465917  9465931  9465939  9465979  9466007  9466021  9466027  9466033  9466069  9466099
9466103  9466111  9466139  9466141  9466147  9466169  9466187  9466189  9466207  9466211
9466213  9466241  9466243  9466273  9466309  9466319  9466337  9466343  9466361  9466381
9466393  9466403  9466423  9466447  9466451  9466459  9466517  9466543  9466563  9466577
9466591  9466621  9466657  9466703  9466711  9466747  9466753  9466757  9466763  9466781
9466799  9466813  9466817  9466819  9466829  9466861  9466867  9466871  9466889  9466939
9466949  9466957  9466973  9466979  9466981  9466991  9466999  9467047  9467057  9467083
9467119  9467141  9467173  9467177  9467179  9467207  9467233  9467251  9467287  9467291
9467299  9467309  9467321  9467327  9467333  9467347  9467357  9467363  9467371  9467387
9467399  9467407  9467411  9467417  9467441  9467461  9467473  9467519  9467531  9467537
9467581  9467587  9467599  9467603  9467629  9467641  9467677  9467683  9467687  9467699
9467701  9467713  9467747  9467753  9467791  9467873  9467903  9467917  9467951  9467957
9467959  9467971  9467987  9467999  9468029  9468037  9468047  9468083  9468091  9468097
9468119  9468131  9468139  9468149  9468163  9468169  9468191  9468209  9468223  9468227
9468241  9468247  9468257  9468259  9468271  9468293  9468301  9468311  9468313  9468317
9468343  9468367  9468401  9468419  9468449  9468451  9468467  9468483  9468521  9468523
9468533  9468539  9468553  9468601  9468607  9468623  9468629  9468637  9468647  9468661
9468673  9468713  9468727  9468737  9468749  9468763  9468769  9468787  9468793  9468817
9468829  9468839  9468863  9468869  9468871  9468883  9468911  9468913  9468931  9468937
9468947  9468959  9468971  9468989  9468997  9469001  9469007  9469013  9469027  9469039
9469063  9469079  9469081  9469093  9469111  9469121  9469127  9469129  9469133  9469181
9469193  9469211  9469217  9469219  9469223  9469241  9469253  9469267  9469301  9469309
```

9469321 9469337 9469349 9469367 9469403 9469409 9469423 9469433 9469451 9469489
9469507 9469519 9469529 9469541 9469547 9469549 9469661 9469687 9469693 9469703
9469709 9469711 9469723 9469727 9469753 9469763 9469777 9469781 9469829 9469843
9469853 9469871 9469879 9469883 9469903 9469907 9469919 9469927 9469937 9469939
9469963 9469991 9470017 9470107 9470117 9470119 9470161 9470177 9470179 9470183
9470203 9470231 9470233 9470239 9470243 9470257 9470281 9470287 9470297 9470299
9470339 9470347 9470371 9470387 9470389 9470393 9470413 9470423 9470429 9470431
9470437 9470471 9470473 9470491 9470497 9470507 9470519 9470533 9470551 9470563
9470749 9470777 9470807 9470809 9470821 9470833 9470837 9470863 9470933 9470939
9470969 9470977 9471013 9471019 9471029 9471037 9471061 9471079 9471097 9471103
9471107 9471109 9471127 9471131 9471191 9471247 9471251 9471269 9471277 9471283
9471289 9471307 9471311 9471317 9471323 9471347 9471353 9471359 9471361 9471373
9471383 9471391 9471403 9471437 9471439 9471467 9471491 9471493 9471521 9471551
9471587 9471611 9471617 9471619 9471629 9471641 9471659 9471673 9471689 9471691
9471701 9471713 9471731 9471733 9471743 9471751 9471757 9471799 9471821 9471827
9471841 9471853 9471859 9471887 9471901 9471947 9471971 9471977
9472007 9472027 9472061 9472063 9472091 9472097 9472103 9472109 9472117 9472121
9472129 9472139 9472151 9472153 9472157 9472163 9472207 9472231 9472237 9472283
9472289 9472313 9472321 9472339 9472367 9472387 9472429 9472439 9472447 9472451
9472493 9472499 9472511 9472523 9472543 9472571 9472597 9472643 9472649 9472651
9472657 9472679 9472691 9472693 9472717 9472721 9472747 9472759 9472829 9472831
9472843 9472847 9472867 9472871 9472877 9472901 9472913 9472951 9472979 9473017
9473021 9473041 9473059 9473083 9473141 9473143 9473159 9473161 9473207 9473213
9473231 9473237 9473251 9473257 9473293 9473297 9473323 9473327 9473329 9473333
9473351 9473357 9473363 9473377 9473389 9473411 9473417 9473423 9473441 9473467
9473479 9473491 9473531 9473543 9473549 9473557 9473567 9473587 9473603 9473617
9473621 9473623 9473627 9473657 9473663 9473671 9473683 9473701 9473719 9473729
9473731 9473741 9473753 9473767 9473771 9473797 9473801 9473809 9473831 9473833
9473843 9473857 9473897 9473899 9473929 9473977 9473983 9473987 9474019 9474041
9474053 9474071 9474107 9474133 9474149 9474163 9474181 9474209 9474211 9474221
9474247 9474277 9474323 9474341 9474343 9474347 9474359 9474371 9474373 9474461
9474467 9474469 9474481 9474511 9474523 9474539 9474541 9474571 9474599 9474611
9474617 9474631 9474637 9474653 9474667 9474679 9474697 9474713 9474721
9474733 9474739 9474769 9474779 9474791 9474799 9474811 9474821 9474833 9474841
9474859 9474893 9474931 9474941 9474943 9474953 9474979 9474989 9475003 9475009 9475019
9475049 9475051 9475097 9475111 9475117 9475121 9475131 9475139 9475157 9475159
9475177 9475187 9475189 9475201 9475231 9475253 9475267 9475283 9475309 9475321
9475337 9475381 9475391 9475399 9475423 9475451 9475457 9475463 9475483 9475513
9475541 9475549 9475561 9475591 9475603 9475607 9475621 9475643 9475657 9475667
9475673 9475693 9475751 9475759 9475771 9475777 9475787 9475789 9475819 9475831
9475871 9475909 9475933 9475937 9475943 9475951 9475957 9475979 9475981 9475997
9476009 9476059 9476099 9476101 9476113 9476119 9476141 9476143 9476149 9476171
9476209 9476219 9476227 9476239 9476261 9476273 9476303 9476317 9476321 9476323
9476339 9476377 9476381 9476393 9476399 9476407 9476419 9476431 9476443 9476449
9476473 9476491 9476501 9476539 9476543 9476561 9476567 9476581 9476587 9476627
9476647 9476653 9476659 9476683 9476689 9476711 9476717 9476723 9476737 9476743
9476807 9476827 9476849 9476891 9476893 9476923 9476941 9476947 9476959 9476981
9477019 9477031 9477037 9477047 9477053 9477059 9477073 9477101 9477107
9477119 9477137 9477187 9477199 9477233 9477253 9477263 9477269 9477271 9477317
9477331 9477337 9477353 9477359 9477367 9477373 9477379 9477383 9477401
9477427 9477463 9477467 9477491 9477527 9477529 9477539 9477569 9477607 9477667
9477707 9477733 9477749 9477763 9477781 9477791 9477799 9477821 9477829 9477851
9477889 9477893 9477907 9477911 9477917 9477947 9477989 9478009 9478013 9478057
9478069 9478097 9478111 9478123 9478127 9478141 9478153 9478159 9478181 9478187
9478201 9478211 9478221 9478213 9478237 9478267 9478297 9478307 9478309 9478319
9478373 9478387 9478433 9478439 9478453 9478457 9478459 9478487 9478541 9478543
9478559 9478583 9478597 9478627 9478633 9478643 9478681 9478687 9478717 9478727
9478751 9478769 9478787 9478793 9478801 9478811 9478817 9478837 9478841 9478873
9478879 9478883 9478897 9478927 9478943 9478949 9478957 9478981 9478991 9479003
9479017 9479021 9479051 9479083 9479089 9479111 9479137 9479147 9479161 9479179
9479191 9479203 9479207 9479219 9479263 9479287 9479321 9479329 9479333 9479359
9479371 9479411 9479413 9479417 9479419 9479453 9479467 9479497 9479531 9479539
9479563 9479567 9479579 9479593 9479599 9479609 9479627 9479641 9479647 9479663
9479677 9479681 9479711 9479741 9479753 9479783 9479791 9479797 9479801 9479809
9479819 9479857 9479891 9479923 9479929 9479941 9479947 9479957 9479969 9479971
9479983 9480001 9480007 9480043 9480047 9480049 9480059 9480073 9480083 9480091
9480127 9480139 9480151 9480173 9480181 9480191 9480239 9480257 9480277 9480281
9480283 9480293 9480311 9480329 9480337 9480349 9480379 9480391 9480397 9480403
9480409 9480479 9480503 9480517 9480539 9480557 9480571 9480589 9480607 9480613
9480617 9480619 9480629 9480641 9480649 9480661 9480673 9480683 9480743 9480749
9480749 9480797 9480827 9480839 9480857 9480859 9480893 9480901 9480923 9480937
9480953 9480959 9480973 9480997 9481013 9481061 9481063
9481067 9481079 9481099 9481111 9481141 9481177 9481193 9481201 9481207 9481217
9481249 9481261 9481279 9481309 9481321 9481327 9481331 9481333 9481337 9481363
9481421 9481447 9481471 9481487 9481519 9481523 9481531 9481559 9481561 9481601
9481603 9481609 9481613 9481621 9481643 9481651 9481673 9481687 9481697 9481711
9481721 9481727 9481739 9481757 9481763 9481789 9481799 9481861 9481867 9481883
9481889 9481951 9481963 9481991 9481993 9481999 9482009 9482069 9482113 9482131
9482147 9482153 9482219 9482251 9482257 9482269 9482287 9482299
9482339 9482353 9482381 9482399 9482411 9482419 9482437 9482453 9482477 9482491
9482503 9482527 9482531 9482533 9482567 9482569 9482573 9482581 9482591 9482611
9482659 9482677 9482687 9482699 9482713 9482717 9482731 9482777 9482783
9482791 9482857 9482873 9482887 9482897 9482899 9482903 9482911 9482927 9482929
9482939 9482981 9483007 9483017 9483023 9483051 9483053 9483077 9483083
9483101 9483169 9483181 9483191 9483197 9483233 9483251 9483269 9483283 9483289
9483307 9483317 9483347 9483361 9483373 9483401 9483407 9483421 9483437 9483443
9483457 9483473 9483491 9483499 9483547 9483571 9483583 9483589 9483619 9483623
9483631 9483653 9483673 9483697 9483709 9483769 9483781 9483791 9483809 9483823

```
9483839  9483847  9483863  9483883  9483893  9483911  9483919  9483949  9483953  9483959
9484003  9484019  9484049  9484061  9484067  9484129  9484157  9484183  9484217  9484231
9484253  9484259  9484261  9484289  9484291  9484331  9484337  9484361  9484367  9484399
9484411  9484451  9484457  9484483  9484511  9484513  9484523  9484529  9484577  9484597
9484603  9484609  9484613  9484619  9484621  9484633  9484637  9484649  9484681  9484693
9484733  9484747  9484751  9484753  9484771  9484777  9484789  9484799  9484823  9484831
9484837  9484843  9484847  9484873  9484883  9484889  9484907  9484919  9484931  9484939
9484973  9485033  9485041  9485057  9485087  9485089  9485093  9485111  9485129  9485137
9485143  9485159  9485171  9485173  9485183  9485207  9485239  9485243  9485261  9485263
9485279  9485297  9485321  9485341  9485363  9485369  9485383  9485393  9485419  9485423
9485429  9485449  9485461  9485477  9485479  9485501  9485513  9485537  9485549  9485557
9485563  9485599  9485603  9485611  9485627  9485687  9485689  9485701  9485713  9485737
9485771  9485797  9485803  9485809  9485831  9485851  9485863  9485873  9485893  9485897
9485899  9485909  9485911  9485923  9485933  9485941  9485947  9485953  9485977  9485989
9485999  9486007  9486013  9486041  9486067  9486137  9486157  9486163  9486167  9486173
9486181  9486193  9486199  9486203  9486209  9486229  9486251  9486259  9486283  9486307
9486317  9486331  9486353  9486361  9486409  9486413  9486427  9486431  9486439  9486469
9486473  9486481  9486487  9486497  9486559  9486563  9486571  9486577  9486593  9486613
9486647  9486661  9486667  9486671  9486707  9486707  9486733  9486761  9486793  9486847
9486853  9486881  9486907  9486923  9486931  9486943  9486977  9486989  9486991  9487001
9487013  9487043  9487057  9487069  9487073  9487081  9487087  9487097  9487111  9487123
9487157  9487187  9487211  9487217  9487223  9487243  9487249  9487253  9487273  9487297
9487307  9487319  9487337  9487349  9487351  9487363  9487393  9487397  9487399  9487409
9487421  9487427  9487451  9487459  9487483  9487501  9487529  9487571  9487579  9487589
9487601  9487619  9487657  9487679  9487697  9487703  9487711  9487721  9487729  9487733
9487739  9487759  9487763  9487781  9487811  9487817  9487823  9487831  9487837  9487867
9487871  9487913  9487939  9487949  9487963  9487991  9487997  9487999  9488009  9488027
9488033  9488047  9488053  9488069  9488093  9488117  9488119  9488131  9488161  9488173
9488177  9488189  9488197  9488207  9488221  9488233  9488267  9488291  9488309  9488327
9488357  9488359  9488371  9488377  9488383  9488389  9488399  9488417  9488419  9488441
9488471  9488491  9488503  9488513  9488569  9488579  9488587  9488603  9488621  9488623
9488629  9488639  9488641  9488659  9488663  9488683  9488693  9488701  9488711  9488779
9488797  9488807  9488813  9488819  9488833  9488837  9488861  9488879  9488891  9488929
9488957  9488981  9488987  9489019  9489047  9489099  9489121  9489149  9489157  9489167
9489169  9489191  9489199  9489203  9489217  9489229  9489241  9489289  9489301  9489329
9489331  9489367  9489407  9489419  9489433  9489443  9489457  9489461  9489463  9489497
9489517  9489521  9489523  9489527  9489533  9489539  9489577  9489581  9489611  9489631
9489637  9489643  9489653  9489671  9489673  9489691  9489707  9489719  9489763  9489769
9489773  9489787  9489793  9489811  9489827  9489833  9489841  9489877  9489881  9489899
9489913  9489917  9489923  9489943  9489967  9489979  9490001  9490009  9490067  9490069
9490087  9490153  9490157  9490181  9490183  9490207  9490223  9490249  9490277  9490289
9490307  9490321  9490331  9490361  9490363  9490399  9490409  9490423  9490457  9490477
9490517  9490529  9490541  9490543  9490553  9490567  9490571  9490601  9490631  9490661
9490673  9490687  9490699  9490703  9490711  9490717  9490813  9490847  9490849  9490889
9490903  9490919  9490933  9490939  9490951  9490963  9490969  9491011  9491017  9491021
9491023  9491039  9491047  9491077  9491087  9491093  9491101  9491137  9491147  9491171
9491179  9491189  9491191  9491197  9491201  9491231  9491257  9491281  9491291  9491309
9491329  9491333  9491357  9491359  9491371  9491401  9491429  9491437  9491453  9491467
9491477  9491483  9491513  9491543  9491561  9491563  9491569  9491579  9491597  9491609
9491633  9491681  9491683  9491687  9491701  9491707  9491711  9491719  9491723  9491737
9491789  9491803  9491809  9491813  9491819  9491827  9491843  9491851  9491857  9491861
9491897  9491917  9491947  9491969  9491981  9491987  9492013  9492037  9492053  9492059
9492079  9492089  9492139  9492143  9492157  9492173  9492179  9492181  9492199  9492209
9492211  9492221  9492233  9492253  9492269  9492277  9492281  9492289  9492311  9492331
9492349  9492389  9492397  9492407  9492421  9492463  9492521  9492529  9492547  9492559
9492563  9492601  9492611  9492617  9492619  9492643  9492673  9492677  9492697  9492713
9492733  9492739  9492779  9492797  9492803  9492811  9492827  9492863  9492871  9492893
9492911  9492929  9492937  9492941  9492943  9492949  9492971  9492983  9492991  9493009
9493051  9493061  9493069  9493073  9493079  9493087  9493093  9493097  9493109  9493111
9493117  9493151  9493241  9493249  9493271  9493303  9493313  9493357  9493387  9493399
9493403  9493417  9493433  9493441  9493447  9493453  9493459  9493499  9493507  9493529
9493543  9493567  9493607  9493619  9493639  9493651  9493661  9493663  9493703  9493717
9493727  9493739  9493741  9493747  9493751  9493753  9493807  9493829  9493849  9493853
9493873  9493877  9493889  9493909  9493937  9493949  9493951  9493961  9493999  9494033
9494039  9494057  9494063  9494071  9494077  9494081  9494113  9494123  9494137  9494159
9494171  9494179  9494201  9494203  9494209  9494239  9494257  9494269  9494273  9494321
9494293  9494297  9494327  9494363  9494371  9494389  9494399  9494417  9494447  9494461
9494491  9494497  9494501  9494521  9494531  9494533  9494543  9494557  9494567  9494581
9494591  9494593  9494603  9494627  9494633  9494659  9494669  9494689  9494713  9494731
9494747  9494761  9494767  9494777  9494783  9494827  9494831  9494839  9494867  9494869
9494879  9494911  9494917  9494941  9494943  9494949  9494957  9494971  9494977  9494981
9495001  9495007  9495019  9495023  9495029  9495053  9495071  9495103  9495121  9495127
9495139  9495169  9495221  9495223  9495263  9495269  9495277  9495281  9495293  9495341
9495349  9495359  9495371  9495377  9495403  9495419  9495433  9495487  9495491  9495509
9495523  9495529  9495539  9495547  9495553  9495583  9495587  9495593  9495601  9495613
9495653  9495671  9495691  9495701  9495751  9495769  9495799  9495823  9495833  9495841
9495853  9495859  9495907  9495923  9495949  9495973  9496031  9496043  9496057  9496073
9496081  9496099  9496103  9496117  9496127  9496153  9496159  9496177  9496213  9496229
9496231  9496241  9496243  9496259  9496271  9496273  9496313  9496327  9496337  9496339
9496343  9496363  9496373  9496411  9496433  9496439  9496441  9496451  9496471  9496481
9496499  9496517  9496537  9496547  9496559  9496573  9496589  9496609  9496621  9496649
9496651  9496687  9496691  9496709  9496741  9496771  9496783  9496787  9496811  9496831
9496853  9496873  9496883  9496921  9497021  9497027  9497039  9497051  9497057  9497063
9497069  9497071  9497083  9497099  9497113  9497141  9497153  9497161  9497177  9497219
9497263  9497267  9497269  9497287  9497291  9497303  9497329  9497353  9497357  9497381
9497387  9497399  9497461  9497479  9497483  9497489  9497491  9497503  9497507  9497531
9497533  9497557  9497573  9497581  9497591  9497623  9497627  9497647  9497651  9497669
9497681  9497693  9497767  9497771  9497783  9497837  9497843  9497861  9497869  9497881
9497899  9497903  9497921  9497923  9497941  9497959  9497977  9498001  9498007  9498023
```

```
9498031 9498037 9498067 9498107 9498113 9498133 9498161 9498163 9498179 9498187
9498193 9498197 9498217 9498253 9498259 9498263 9498299 9498301 9498323 9498383
9498397 9498403 9498409 9498413 9498421 9498479 9498491 9498509 9498527 9498539
9498547 9498553 9498569 9498581 9498583 9498623 9498637 9498647 9498649 9498661
9498719 9498739 9498761 9498773 9498799 9498817 9498847 9498851 9498857 9498871
9498889 9498913 9498953 9498959 9498961 9498967 9499013 9499027 9499033 9499043
9499057 9499079 9499081 9499093 9499097 9499099 9499129 9499157 9499159 9499181
9499187 9499199 9499201 9499213 9499223 9499229 9499261 9499279 9499291 9499309
9499313 9499319 9499333 9499339 9499387 9499403 9499409 9499429 9499439 9499453
9499471 9499489 9499519 9499543 9499579 9499597 9499613 9499619 9499631 9499669
9499673 9499691 9499739 9499747 9499751 9499783 9499799 9499807 9499811 9499817
9499873 9499883 9499921 9499927 9499933 9499951 9499961 9499967 9500021 9500041
9500047 9500089 9500107 9500111 9500143 9500159 9500189 9500191 9500207 9500213
9500221 9500279 9500287 9500299 9500317 9500321 9500327 9500333 9500339 9500347
9500369 9500383 9500401 9500419 9500431 9500441 9500473 9500507 9500537 9500591
9500599 9500611 9500629 9500639 9500651 9500677 9500713 9500737 9500753 9500759
9500791 9500809 9500831 9500837 9500861 9500867 9500873 9500879 9500899 9500903
9500917 9500921 9500923 9500929 9500941 9500957 9500963 9500983 9500993 9500999
9501013 9501043 9501049 9501061 9501073 9501077 9501091 9501101 9501109 9501127
9501133 9501137 9501157 9501161 9501187 9501199 9501211 9501229 9501253 9501269
9501281 9501287 9501293 9501307 9501313 9501329 9501347 9501353 9501367 9501383
9501389 9501391 9501413 9501431 9501491 9501497 9501509 9501511 9501517 9501523
9501529 9501533 9501571 9501587 9501601 9501629 9501631 9501643 9501659 9501683
9501689 9501719 9501721 9501733 9501743 9501749 9501761 9501781 9501809 9501851
9501889 9501913 9501949 9501959 9501971 9501991 9502019 9502021 9502043 9502063
9502067 9502069 9502079 9502093 9502139 9502159 9502189 9502193 9502219 9502231
9502237 9502247 9502249 9502271 9502277 9502301 9502307 9502313 9502321 9502331
9502333 9502351 9502369 9502373 9502379 9502429 9502433 9502463 9502469 9502477
9502499 9502513 9502531 9502547 9502553 9502561 9502583 9502589 9502627 9502637
9502651 9502663 9502687 9502697 9502721 9502723 9502733 9502751 9502769 9502781
9502783 9502817 9502819 9502837 9502859 9502903 9502937 9502951 9502967 9502973
9503009 9503027 9503041 9503069 9503077 9503093 9503101 9503107 9503141 9503149
9503161 9503167 9503171 9503183 9503201 9503203 9503231 9503237 9503243 9503257
9503261 9503269 9503281 9503297 9503303 9503309 9503317 9503327 9503399 9503411
9503437 9503441 9503443 9503449 9503467 9503471 9503479 9503489 9503497 9503519
9503521 9503551 9503573 9503581 9503609 9503653 9503671 9503693 9503717 9503719
9503773 9503777 9503843 9503869 9503873 9503881 9503929 9503939 9503947 9503951
9503953 9503957 9503959 9503987 9503993 9504023 9504029 9504059 9504067 9504097
9504113 9504163 9504203 9504211 9504223 9504233 9504239 9504281 9504289 9504307
9504311 9504323 9504329 9504337 9504347 9504353 9504361 9504371 9504379 9504409
9504421 9504433 9504457 9504493 9504499 9504511 9504529 9504533 9504559 9504563
9504571 9504601 9504613 9504619 9504629 9504637 9504641 9504647 9504653 9504667
9504679 9504689 9504697 9504707 9504709 9504713 9504749 9504767 9504787 9504809
9504823 9504839 9504863 9504877 9504889 9504919 9504931 9504947 9504949 9504961
9504977 9504991 9505033 9505037 9505063 9505087 9505099 9505117 9505123 9505147
9505151 9505163 9505169 9505183 9505207 9505241 9505253 9505259 9505271 9505277
9505283 9505297 9505303 9505319 9505333 9505361 9505367 9505369 9505373 9505381
9505393 9505439 9505459 9505477 9505487 9505493 9505511 9505513 9505519 9505523
9505529 9505543 9505547 9505553 9505571 9505579 9505583 9505589 9505597 9505607
9505619 9505627 9505631 9505637 9505663 9505679 9505711 9505723 9505729 9505733
9505751 9505777 9505801 9505843 9505849 9505889 9505897 9505901 9505919 9505927
9505943 9505957 9505963 9505981 9506011 9506039 9506041 9506047 9506069 9506083
9506093 9506117 9506129 9506131 9506207 9506249 9506269 9506297 9506303 9506309
9506317 9506333 9506339 9506347 9506353 9506369 9506377 9506381 9506389 9506437
9506459 9506467 9506489 9506501 9506527 9506537 9506543 9506597 9506599 9506603
9506639 9506641 9506657 9506681 9506747 9506763 9506767 9506773 9506813 9506827
9506857 9506879 9506881 9506899 9506921 9506929 9506947 9506953 9506963 9506969
9507007 9507031 9507037 9507053 9507077 9507079 9507101 9507133 9507139 9507149
9507151 9507161 9507191 9507217 9507241 9507259 9507263 9507269 9507287 9507293
9507317 9507341 9507361 9507383 9507419 9507427 9507431 9507439 9507451 9507497
9507499 9507503 9507517 9507523 9507527 9507551 9507559 9507599 9507637 9507647
9507661 9507683 9507689 9507703 9507727 9507761 9507767 9507787 9507803 9507821
9507833 9507863 9507877 9507881 9507893 9507919 9507929 9507931 9507977 9507983
9507997 9508003 9508013 9508061 9508063 9508067 9508069 9508073 9508087 9508091
9508099 9508123 9508129 9508133 9508139 9508141 9508153 9508183 9508193 9508199
9508217 9508273 9508283 9508337 9508393 9508409 9508451 9508463 9508469 9508471
9508481 9508483 9508489 9508561 9508567 9508589 9508601 9508613 9508643 9508649
9508669 9508687 9508691 9508693 9508699 9508703 9508717 9508747 9508753 9508757
9508777 9508787 9508789 9508801 9508823 9508859 9508861 9508879 9508883 9508901
9508903 9508927 9508951 9508957 9508969 9508973 9508979 9508981 9508991 9508997
9509011 9509023 9509039 9509039 9509063 9509071 9509081 9509087 9509131 9509161
9509167 9509173 9509183 9509191 9509231 9509233 9509249 9509267 9509287 9509323
9509347 9509359 9509363 9509399 9509413 9509431 9509441 9509449 9509471 9509497
9509503 9509531 9509543 9509569 9509597 9509609 9509611 9509641 9509677 9509693
9509701 9509719 9509723 9509729 9509761 9509789 9509791 9509809 9509849 9509867
9509873 9509897 9509911 9509971 9509977 9509993 9510001 9510023 9510031 9510037
9510041 9510077 9510079 9510103 9510107 9510113 9510119 9510133 9510143 9510167
9510187 9510197 9510199 9510227 9510251 9510271 9510287 9510301 9510307 9510311
9510313 9510331 9510337 9510341 9510349 9510421 9510427 9510437 9510491 9510493
9510503 9510509 9510511 9510533 9510539 9510541 9510547 9510551 9510563 9510581
9510587 9510607 9510617 9510643 9510673 9510679 9510733 9510737 9510749 9510751
9510757 9510763 9510791 9510829 9510833 9510841 9510857 9510863 9510883 9510899
9510931 9510941 9510959 9510971 9510979 9510991 9511003 9511007 9511017 9511023
9511067 9511087 9511091 9511093 9511111 9511171 9511189 9511199 9511207 9511223
9511241 9511261 9511273 9511277 9511289 9511291 9511361 9511379 9511393 9511395
9511399 9511417 9511421 9511423 9511427 9511429 9511441 9511477 9511493 9511501
9511511 9511543 9511559 9511573 9511577 9511583 9511589 9511591 9511639 9511661
9511693 9511703 9511727 9511753 9511771 9511793 9511807 9511841 9511847 9511867
9511871 9511927 9511933 9511939 9511969 9512003 9512017 9512021 9512023 9512051
```

```
9512077  9512081  9512089  9512099  9512101  9512117  9512137  9512149  9512161  9512171
9512183  9512207  9512213  9512221  9512249  9512263  9512329  9512351  9512353
9512357  9512389  9512413  9512449  9512467  9512497  9512507  9512519  9512549  9512561
9512579  9512603  9512611  9512617  9512623  9512641  9512677  9512687  9512689  9512717
9512729  9512759  9512773  9512801  9512803  9512807  9512813  9512851  9512857  9512873
9512891  9512903  9512929  9512947  9512969  9512989  9513017  9513041  9513043  9513059
9513067  9513071  9513079  9513103  9513109  9513113  9513139  9513199  9513209
9513227  9513233  9513253  9513269  9513293  9513307  9513323  9513331  9513359  9513367
9513401  9513407  9513409  9513437  9513451  9513457  9513461  9513473  9513481  9513521
9513527  9513529  9513533  9513563  9513571  9513589  9513601  9513617  9513619  9513641
9513643  9513667  9513677  9513701  9513731  9513739  9513811  9513839  9513853  9513877
9513887  9513899  9513913  9513923  9513937  9513941  9513949  9513953  9513967  9513979
9513989  9514013  9514027  9514031  9514039  9514061  9514073  9514081  9514093  9514129
9514151  9514171  9514199  9514229  9514243  9514247  9514259  9514273  9514279
9514319  9514327  9514331  9514343  9514361  9514381  9514391  9514429  9514493  9514499
9514529  9514537  9514541  9514553  9514559  9514607  9514619  9514621  9514643  9514651
9514669  9514691  9514711  9514777  9514789  9514793  9514807  9514811  9514849  9514853
9514859  9514867  9514891  9514909  9514919  9514933  9514943  9514949  9514961  9514979
9515017  9515041  9515057  9515059  9515063  9515069  9515101  9515111  9515117  9515119
9515137  9515141  9515147  9515153  9515167  9515183  9515201  9515213  9515237  9515267
9515269  9515279  9515281  9515287  9515323  9515347  9515377  9515381  9515411  9515423
9515437  9515453  9515459  9515483  9515497  9515531  9515533  9515551  9515557  9515593
9515621  9515641  9515647  9515651  9515659  9515663  9515669  9515689  9515713  9515719
9515749  9515773  9515783  9515833  9515837  9515839  9515851  9515873  9515893  9515897
9515911  9515923  9515959  9515963  9515999  9516007  9516019  9516037  9516053  9516121
9516127  9516149  9516167  9516173  9516187  9516191  9516197  9516229  9516271  9516281
9516317  9516337  9516361  9516407  9516421  9516433  9516439  9516443  9516449  9516497
9516509  9516517  9516541  9516547  9516569  9516571  9516593  9516599  9516629  9516643
9516653  9516673  9516679  9516691  9516709  9516737  9516761  9516763  9516809  9516811
9516817  9516823  9516827  9516841  9516847  9516883  9516887  9516931  9516943  9516953
9516989  9517003  9517033  9517073  9517091  9517111  9517139  9517141  9517187
9517201  9517213  9517223  9517237  9517241  9517247  9517259  9517273  9517301  9517327
9517357  9517363  9517381  9517439  9517447  9517451  9517457  9517463  9517471  9517483
9517493  9517513  9517517  9517531  9517549  9517559  9517567  9517583  9517601  9517631
9517633  9517639  9517643  9517649  9517657  9517691  9517709  9517723  9517741  9517759
9517799  9517847  9517861  9517867  9517873  9517889  9517901  9517903  9517919  9517951
9517969  9517973  9517979  9517987  9518009  9518053  9518071  9518099  9518123  9518129
9518137  9518141  9518143  9518153  9518161  9518203  9518219  9518237  9518263  9518281
9518291  9518339  9518371  9518381  9518401  9518407  9518417  9518471  9518477  9518491
9518497  9518503  9518507  9518533  9518549  9518617  9518651  9518659  9518681  9518687
9518693  9518701  9518723  9518737  9518771  9518779  9518797  9518813  9518819  9518893
9518917  9518921  9518923  9518933  9518939  9518969  9519043  9519049  9519053  9519071
9519073  9519109  9519113  9519121  9519143  9519151  9519179  9519197  9519203  9519227
9519241  9519253  9519281  9519283  9519287  9519313  9519317  9519319  9519329  9519331
9519347  9519359  9519409  9519413  9519431  9519443  9519457  9519481  9519487  9519509
9519527  9519533  9519547  9519557  9519571  9519581  9519593  9519607  9519611  9519617
9519637  9519649  9519661  9519691  9519773  9519781  9519799  9519823  9519869  9519877
9519889  9519919  9519929  9519941  9519943  9519947  9519973  9520001  9520037  9520039
9520061  9520067  9520081  9520103  9520117  9520123  9520127  9520129  9520139  9520151
9520201  9520219  9520253  9520261  9520271  9520307  9520309  9520351  9520373  9520397
9520409  9520411  9520429  9520451  9520471  9520477  9520481  9520523  9520529  9520547
9520559  9520571  9520579  9520583  9520601  9520619  9520631  9520657  9520661  9520699
9520703  9520711  9520727  9520739  9520741  9520747  9520769  9520783  9520793
9520807  9520817  9520829  9520891  9520909  9520913  9520921  9520933  9520939  9520963
9521023  9521047  9521051  9521053  9521087  9521093  9521101  9521107  9521117  9521129
9521153  9521167  9521177  9521191  9521201  9521209  9521219  9521227  9521231
9521233  9521257  9521263  9521273  9521279  9521297  9521311  9521327  9521329  9521341
9521353  9521357  9521381  9521387  9521417  9521441  9521453  9521459  9521461
9521497  9521507  9521537  9521549  9521569  9521587  9521623  9521627  9521647  9521653
9521671  9521689  9521693  9521711  9521723  9521731  9521737  9521741  9521753  9521789
9521803  9521807  9521849  9521851  9521873  9521887  9521903  9521957  9521959  9522001
9522013  9522017  9522031  9522043  9522067  9522113  9522119  9522133  9522137  9522157
9522167  9522169  9522181  9522197  9522203  9522217  9522269  9522281  9522313  9522319
9522361  9522367  9522379  9522407  9522413  9522419  9522433  9522451  9522463  9522481
9522493  9522497  9522503  9522511  9522517  9522523  9522551  9522559  9522571  9522577
9522607  9522637  9522647  9522661  9522677  9522691  9522697  9522749  9522757  9522761
9522763  9522767  9522787  9522791  9522803  9522827  9522853  9522871  9522889  9522899
9522937  9522959  9522977  9523001  9523039  9523051  9523061  9523067  9523079  9523091
9523099  9523103  9523121  9523139  9523141  9523153  9523181  9523183  9523229  9523243
9523271  9523273  9523279  9523289  9523303  9523333  9523369  9523373  9523399  9523421
9523429  9523453  9523457  9523471  9523499  9523559  9523583  9523589  9523609  9523637
9523639  9523643  9523673  9523681  9523697  9523699  9523711  9523741  9523781  9523783
9523819  9523853  9523873  9523897  9523903  9523937  9523949  9523967  9523973  9523993
9523999  9524041  9524051  9524069  9524071  9524077  9524083  9524087  9524129  9524147
9524159  9524171  9524183  9524189  9524191  9524197  9524201  9524219  9524227  9524243
9524261  9524279  9524297  9524299  9524303  9524309  9524321  9524327  9524363  9524387
9524393  9524399  9524443  9524447  9524467  9524509  9524521  9524531  9524563  9524569
9524591  9524611  9524623  9524633  9524663  9524687  9524707  9524717  9524729  9524761
9524791  9524839  9524849  9524881  9524891  9524897  9524923  9524941  9524959
9524987  9524993  9525017  9525031  9525041  9525053  9525073  9525077  9525101
9525119  9525121  9525149  9525157  9525181  9525193  9525203  9525223  9525227  9525281
9525283  9525353  9525367  9525371  9525377  9525413  9525419  9525433  9525449  9525469
9525499  9525511  9525551  9525563  9525569  9525589  9525599  9525617  9525641  9525647
9525667  9525673  9525709  9525721  9525751  9525757  9525767  9525779  9525799  9525839
9525851  9525853  9525871  9525877  9525907  9525941  9525953  9525961  9525977  9525991
9526009  9526037  9526043  9526051  9526073  9526109  9526129  9526147  9526151  9526157
9526169  9526183  9526193  9526217  9526229  9526243  9526247  9526259  9526267  9526271
9526303  9526313  9526339  9526343  9526351  9526357  9526369  9526399  9526403  9526417
9526441  9526453  9526457  9526487  9526493  9526499  9526513  9526519  9526537  9526547
```

```
9526549 9526589 9526597 9526609 9526639 9526667 9526679 9526711 9526717 9526721
9526729 9526753 9526757 9526763 9526787 9526799 9526813 9526841 9526879 9526897
9526901 9526903 9526949 9526967 9526969 9526973 9526981 9526997 9527003 9527009
9527017 9527033 9527039 9527053 9527057 9527071 9527081 9527101 9527149 9527153
9527171 9527179 9527201 9527213 9527233 9527249 9527251 9527263 9527279 9527281
9527311 9527317 9527339 9527347 9527377 9527393 9527411 9527423 9527459 9527461
9527473 9527503 9527549 9527563 9527587 9527591 9527627 9527657 9527663 9527677
9527719 9527723 9527729 9527743 9527753 9527779 9527783 9527801 9527807 9527813
9527827 9527857 9527879 9527909 9527933 9527941 9527963 9527977 9527989 9528011
9528053 9528059 9528061 9528083 9528091 9528097 9528119 9528131 9528157 9528163
9528223 9528257 9528283 9528289 9528301 9528307 9528341 9528391 9528403 9528419
9528433 9528511 9528521 9528527 9528577 9528581 9528583 9528587 9528593 9528613
9528637 9528641 9528689 9528719 9528737 9528751 9528773 9528781 9528793 9528797
9528803 9528829 9528833 9528847 9528859 9528881 9528931 9528947 9528949 9529021
9529033 9529057 9529063 9529073 9529103 9529133 9529151 9529189 9529193 9529207
9529213 9529253 9529259 9529271 9529277 9529283 9529301 9529321 9529327 9529361
9529363 9529397 9529409 9529427 9529433 9529441 9529447 9529463 9529501 9529511
9529519 9529523 9529547 9529561 9529573 9529601 9529607 9529627 9529633 9529643
9529649 9529651 9529657 9529693 9529711 9529727 9529759 9529763 9529769 9529787
9529801 9529813 9529823 9529837 9529907 9529909 9529937 9529943 9529957 9529967
9529997 9530011 9530029 9530033 9530041 9530083 9530099 9530123 9530137 9530159
9530161 9530173 9530179 9530203 9530221 9530233 9530249 9530263 9530273 9530291
9530321 9530333 9530363 9530377 9530393 9530413 9530429 9530431 9530449 9530453
9530459 9530467 9530471 9530501 9530503 9530509 9530539 9530551 9530581 9530593
9530617 9530621 9530627 9530657 9530669 9530681 9530687 9530699 9530749 9530767
9530771 9530777 9530791 9530803 9530849 9530861 9530869 9530881 9530887 9530891
9530903 9530909 9530971 9530977 9530987 9531001 9531007 9531017 9531031 9531047
9531059 9531073 9531097 9531121 9531127 9531133 9531161 9531173 9531187 9531233
9531281 9531283 9531299 9531307 9531349 9531367 9531377 9531397 9531409 9531413
9531419 9531421 9531427 9531439 9531443 9531449 9531461 9531469 9531479 9531481
9531493 9531523 9531527 9531541 9531547 9531551 9531559 9531581 9531589 9531593
9531617 9531631 9531661 9531671 9531701 9531707 9531727 9531733 9531737 9531757
9531761 9531763 9531773 9531779 9531817 9531827 9531869 9531871 9531877 9531919
9531931 9531943 9531961 9531979 9531983 9532009 9532013 9532027 9532057 9532063
9532073 9532109 9532123 9532139 9532163 9532181 9532183 9532207 9532231 9532241
9532249 9532253 9532261 9532297 9532321 9532331 9532333 9532339 9532343 9532349
9532351 9532379 9532417 9532441 9532451 9532483 9532489 9532499 9532513 9532543
9532591 9532609 9532613 9532637 9532639 9532651 9532667 9532687 9532709 9532711
9532723 9532751 9532771 9532777 9532811 9532823 9532847 9532867 9532877 9532891
9532907 9532921 9532933 9532949 9532969 9532979 9533011 9533021 9533023 9533053
9533059 9533071 9533081 9533113 9533119 9533129 9533137 9533149 9533159 9533171
9533177 9533179 9533189 9533203 9533207 9533261 9533273 9533281 9533287 9533291
9533299 9533317 9533323 9533327 9533333 9533351 9533357 9533369 9533387 9533389
9533411 9533417 9533423 9533429 9533437 9533453 9533479 9533501 9533519 9533521
9533533 9533539 9533567 9533597 9533599 9533609 9533627 9533669 9533677 9533681
9533683 9533717 9533723 9533729 9533737 9533743 9533759 9533789 9533819 9533851
9533879 9533893 9533897 9533911 9533933 9533959 9533969 9533971 9533977 9534023
9534037 9534053 9534061 9534071 9534101 9534103 9534113 9534137 9534163 9534179
9534193 9534211 9534221 9534233 9534251 9534269 9534281 9534307 9534313 9534319
9534323 9534337 9534353 9534367 9534379 9534389 9534403 9534439 9534451 9534463
9534479 9534487 9534491 9534517 9534547 9534571 9534583 9534619 9534631 9534643
9534653 9534667 9534677 9534697 9534709 9534731 9534743 9534761 9534781 9534787
9534797 9534799 9534817 9534829 9534851 9534853 9534869 9534871 9534901 9534907
9534913 9534923 9534929 9534947 9534953 9534961 9534989 9534991 9535007 9535021
9535037 9535039 9535061 9535067 9535069 9535103 9535111 9535189 9535217 9535223
9535231 9535277 9535297 9535319 9535327 9535349 9535367 9535417 9535423 9535433
9535439 9535441 9535451 9535469 9535573 9535579 9535583 9535607 9535609 9535619
9535627 9535633 9535655 9535661 9535667 9535679 9535681 9535697 9535699 9535751
9535763 9535769 9535807 9535819 9535831 9535873 9535927 9535931 9535943 9535949
9535951 9535979 9536017 9536027 9536029 9536077 9536123 9536141 9536143 9536147
9536213 9536227 9536249 9536257 9536287 9536321 9536353 9536357 9536363 9536381
9536383 9536399 9536413 9536419 9536453 9536479 9536489 9536503 9536509 9536531
9536533 9536551 9536581 9536591 9536603 9536627 9536633 9536687 9536717 9536719
9536731 9536741 9536753 9536771 9536773 9536827 9536831 9536837 9536843 9536851
9536867 9536893 9536897 9536903 9536909 9536953 9536957 9536963 9536977 9536999
9537007 9537023 9537029 9537049 9537053 9537061 9537067 9537089 9537091 9537097
9537109 9537139 9537197 9537211 9537239 9537251 9537257 9537263 9537277 9537343
9537349 9537371 9537397 9537401 9537419 9537457 9537467 9537469 9537499 9537547
9537551 9537581 9537587 9537589 9537611 9537623 9537637 9537673 9537683 9537713
9537727 9537743 9537751 9537761 9537767 9537769 9537793 9537797 9537809 9537811
9537817 9537841 9537887 9537889 9537923 9537973 9537977 9537991 9538027 9538033
9538051 9538091 9538093 9538097 9538099 9538103 9538121 9538159 9538181 9538201
9538229 9538237 9538269 9538279 9538283 9538367 9538391 9538409 9538423 9538433
9538447 9538453 9538457 9538469 9538499 9538511 9538517 9538523 9538531 9538553
9538559 9538579 9538601 9538619 9538621 9538643 9538663 9538673 9538679 9538693
9538757 9538759 9538783 9538801 9538807 9538811 9538829 9538861 9538877 9538887
9538889 9538897 9538913 9538981 9538987 9539003 9539011 9539017 9539029 9539039
9539053 9539071 9539087 9539111 9539137 9539141 9539163 9539177 9539181 9539191
9539209 9539213 9539219 9539237 9539239 9539251 9539269 9539279 9539281 9539291
9539317 9539333 9539357 9539399 9539401 9539407 9539419 9539443 9539551 9539557
9539561 9539581 9539611 9539623 9539627 9539633 9539657 9539671 9539681 9539689
9539693 9539701 9539711 9539741 9539743 9539749 9539801 9539807 9539833 9539837
9539843 9539863 9539867 9539879 9539891 9539923 9539939 9539951 9539971 9539977
9539989 9539993 9540001 9540017 9540019 9540059 9540067 9540073 9540121 9540127
9540143 9540149 9540161 9540173 9540203 9540253 9540257 9540263 9540283 9540287
9540301 9540313 9540317 9540319 9540347 9540353 9540361 9540397 9540403 9540407
9540409 9540437 9540439 9540457 9540473 9540493 9540497 9540499 9540523 9540541
9540551 9540563 9540571 9540617 9540649 9540673 9540677 9540697 9540701 9540719
9540731 9540803 9540809 9540829 9540847 9540871 9540911 9540919 9540941 9540943
```

```
9540989  9540991  9540997  9541009  9541019  9541031  9541033  9541043  9541057  9541061
9541093  9541109  9541127  9541157  9541163  9541171  9541177  9541183  9541187  9541223
9541241  9541243  9541247  9541271  9541283  9541289  9541291  9541307  9541327  9541331
9541333  9541349  9541373  9541387  9541391  9541393  9541409  9541417  9541429  9541451
9541457  9541487  9541489  9541547  9541549  9541577  9541589  9541613  9541627  9541663
9541669  9541687  9541691  9541717  9541723  9541729  9541733  9541739  9541747  9541771
9541789  9541801  9541813  9541823  9541837  9541843  9541853  9541871  9541877  9541901
9541907  9541919  9541927  9541937  9541949  9541951  9541979  9541991  9541993  9541997
9541999  9542003  9542051  9542063  9542069  9542101  9542107  9542147  9542149  9542167
9542209  9542227  9542233  9542243  9542251  9542257  9542317  9542333  9542353  9542369
9542371  9542383  9542417  9542419  9542441  9542443  9542453  9542473  9542527  9542549
9542557  9542563  9542573  9542587  9542591  9542629  9542683  9542749  9542777  9542789
9542801  9542821  9542843  9542849  9542851  9542867  9542879  9542891  9542903  9542909
9542917  9542969  9542971  9542987  9542989  9542993  9543013  9543019  9543029  9543047
9543067  9543089  9543109  9543113  9543143  9543167  9543169  9543173  9543179  9543251
9543253  9543269  9543293  9543311  9543343  9543353  9543361  9543371  9543403  9543433
9543439  9543451  9543461  9543467  9543497  9543517  9543533  9543553  9543571  9543577
9543593  9543619  9543623  9543659  9543673  9543707  9543727  9543767  9543769  9543791
9543799  9543803  9543811  9543829  9543847  9543901  9543983  9543991  9543997
9544009  9544013  9544019  9544027  9544037  9544097  9544109  9544111  9544127  9544141
9544147  9544159  9544169  9544181  9544189  9544193  9544207  9544211  9544229  9544247
9544273  9544343  9544369  9544387  9544411  9544417  9544427  9544433  9544439  9544499
9544511  9544519  9544523  9544537  9544541  9544571  9544573  9544643  9544649  9544657
9544663  9544679  9544681  9544687  9544699  9544709  9544729  9544739  9544763  9544781
9544789  9544811  9544819  9544831  9544849  9544867  9544877  9544883  9544889  9544903
9544919  9544957  9544963  9544967  9544979  9544981  9544999  9545009  9545051  9545057
9545077  9545093  9545099  9545119  9545153  9545167  9545171  9545189  9545209  9545227
9545231  9545233  9545317  9545323  9545351  9545369  9545383  9545399  9545401  9545411
9545413  9545461  9545477  9545507  9545513  9545537  9545539  9545563  9545567  9545573
9545617  9545629  9545633  9545639  9545659  9545681  9545689  9545693  9545717  9545719
9545773  9545779  9545797  9545801  9545803  9545819  9545827  9545849  9545863  9545869
9545881  9545909  9545911  9545917  9545933  9545941  9545969  9545981  9546001  9546007
9546011  9546013  9546041  9546049  9546059  9546083  9546091  9546139  9546157  9546167
9546193  9546203  9546211  9546223  9546239  9546241  9546247  9546253  9546269  9546287
9546293  9546343  9546347  9546373  9546391  9546431  9546443  9546451  9546467  9546479
9546497  9546521  9546529  9546533  9546553  9546557  9546583  9546599  9546611  9546617
9546619  9546653  9546671  9546689  9546697  9546701  9546737  9546739  9546769  9546773
9546787  9546793  9546799  9546811  9546821  9546833  9546839  9546847  9546857  9546869
9546871  9546883  9546899  9546917  9546923  9546931  9546947  9546959  9546961
9546991  9547007  9547019  9547037  9547091  9547099  9547103  9547123  9547127  9547129
9547133  9547151  9547169  9547189  9547193  9547249  9547267  9547271  9547273  9547303
9547331  9547337  9547339  9547357  9547361  9547403  9547427  9547457  9547459  9547469
9547471  9547477  9547487  9547501  9547511  9547529  9547541  9547543  9547561  9547607
9547609  9547621  9547639  9547649  9547651  9547669  9547679  9547751  9547777  9547787
9547799  9547801  9547817  9547819  9547841  9547871  9547877  9547883  9547919  9547927
9547933  9547949  9547963  9547973  9547981  9548023  9548081  9548111  9548113  9548117
9548131  9548141  9548171  9548173  9548233  9548249  9548263  9548309  9548311
9548333  9548347  9548353  9548369  9548401  9548417  9548419  9548423  9548437  9548443
9548447  9548461  9548491  9548521  9548549  9548551  9548557  9548563  9548579  9548587
9548593  9548597  9548599  9548603  9548653  9548677  9548683  9548687  9548699  9548711
9548731  9548761  9548779  9548789  9548807  9548813  9548827  9548831  9548909  9548921
9548927  9548947  9548953  9548993  9548999  9549101  9549103  9549107  9549109  9549119
9549157  9549167  9549217  9549259  9549263  9549277  9549299  9549307  9549341  9549361
9549373  9549383  9549389  9549401  9549431  9549437  9549451  9549469  9549473  9549479
9549481  9549493  9549499  9549539  9549557  9549587  9549607  9549619  9549629  9549677
9549691  9549697  9549703  9549719  9549721  9549739  9549763  9549791  9549871  9549887
9549889  9549893  9549901  9549907  9549923  9549973  9549983  9550001  9550003  9550049
9550067  9550069  9550081  9550087  9550091  9550111  9550127  9550147  9550159  9550183
9550199  9550207  9550223  9550237  9550241  9550279  9550283  9550291  9550327  9550349
9550351  9550357  9550391  9550393  9550397  9550399  9550433  9550487  9550531  9550553
9550577  9550579  9550591  9550613  9550621  9550627  9550631  9550633  9550669  9550691
9550741  9550763  9550769  9550771  9550777  9550799  9550813  9550913  9550943  9550949
9550963  9550987  9550997  9550999  9551027  9551029  9551033  9551039  9551057  9551089
9551111  9551119  9551123  9551137  9551149  9551159  9551173  9551177  9551207  9551209
9551219  9551239  9551249  9551251  9551257  9551287  9551309  9551327  9551389  9551413
9551429  9551449  9551489  9551491  9551497  9551519  9551537  9551567  9551573
9551593  9551599  9551621  9551629  9551639  9551677  9551681  9551683  9551741  9551753
9551767  9551771  9551833  9551837  9551879  9551887  9551903  9551917  9551947  9551953
9551959  9551981  9551987  9552001  9552007  9552013  9552017  9552019  9552029  9552043
9552047  9552077  9552083  9552089  9552121  9552131  9552133  9552143  9552157  9552167
9552187  9552197  9552209  9552227  9552239  9552271  9552287  9552299  9552311  9552313
9552331  9552341  9552343  9552353  9552373  9552427  9552451  9552457  9552461  9552481
9552509  9552511  9552523  9552551  9552577  9552581  9552593  9552607  9552617  9552689
9552701  9552721  9552731  9552733  9552757  9552761  9552787  9552791  9552811  9552817
9552821  9552847  9552857  9552871  9552931  9552943  9552967  9552971  9552973  9552989
9553001  9553007  9553039  9553043  9553057  9553081  9553111  9553139  9553153  9553183
9553207  9553213  9553241  9553249  9553253  9553259  9553261  9553277  9553283  9553309
9553319  9553343  9553367  9553399  9553403  9553417  9553459  9553469  9553483  9553493
9553501  9553513  9553529  9553553  9553567  9553571  9553589  9553631  9553633  9553667
9553679  9553681  9553703  9553721  9553757  9553769  9553793  9553801  9553837  9553849
9553853  9553867  9553879  9553891  9553897  9553927  9553933  9553937  9553967  9553981
9553987  9553991  9553997  9554009  9554033  9554057  9554059  9554071  9554081  9554087
9554089  9554099  9554101  9554117  9554123  9554141  9554143  9554159  9554161  9554179
9554183  9554191  9554197  9554201  9554219  9554309  9554317  9554329  9554333  9554341
9554371  9554381  9554387  9554423  9554431  9554477  9554507  9554509  9554513  9554521
9554533  9554537  9554539  9554563  9554569  9554579  9554593  9554609  9554639  9554653
9554719  9554723  9554749  9554767  9554807  9554837  9554849  9554861  9554869  9554879
9554887  9554921  9554933  9554939  9554947  9554957  9554983  9554989  9555017  9555031
9555041  9555047  9555059  9555061  9555079  9555083  9555103  9555107  9555113  9555121
```

```
9555127 9555131 9555137 9555151 9555187 9555191 9555229 9555253 9555257 9555263
9555269 9555311 9555313 9555367 9555379 9555389 9555391 9555397 9555407 9555433
9555439 9555443 9555449 9555451 9555487 9555493 9555521 9555527 9555551 9555569
9555593 9555599 9555631 9555641 9555643 9555647 9555653 9555659 9555671 9555673
9555737 9555739 9555757 9555779 9555797 9555809 9555811 9555823 9555827
9555859 9555863 9555869 9555881 9555893 9555901 9555929 9555943 9555983 9555991
9556003 9556007 9556021 9556049 9556073 9556081 9556093 9556117 9556123 9556147
9556163 9556189 9556243 9556291 9556307 9556331 9556361 9556367 9556409 9556423
9556429 9556439 9556441 9556447 9556453 9556489 9556493 9556507 9556511 9556513
9556517 9556543 9556549 9556559 9556579 9556583 9556597 9556607 9556609 9556663
9556691 9556699 9556739 9556751 9556759 9556787 9556817 9556819 9556831 9556847
9556849 9556871 9556889 9556901 9556903 9556913 9556969 9556973 9556993 9557003
9557017 9557071 9557089 9557113 9557117 9557129 9557143 9557147 9557161 9557189
9557231 9557237 9557263 9557279 9557287 9557291 9557293 9557299 9557311 9557321
9557329 9557333 9557363 9557369 9557377 9557389 9557407 9557411 9557413 9557441
9557459 9557461 9557467 9557479 9557491 9557521 9557539 9557549 9557599 9557623
9557651 9557677 9557693 9557711 9557749 9557753 9557767 9557777 9557783
9557789 9557843 9557851 9557881 9557887 9557897 9557923 9557957 9557959 9557971
9557981 9557983 9557987 9557993 9558011 9558037 9558047 9558049 9558053 9558113
9558127 9558163 9558167 9558187 9558191 9558193 9558217 9558221 9558223 9558253
9558259 9558277 9558281 9558293 9558361 9558379 9558383 9558397 9558407 9558431
9558433 9558457 9558467 9558491 9558533 9558541 9558551 9558553 9558559 9558583
9558587 9558589 9558623 9558629 9558643 9558667 9558673 9558683 9558713 9558733
9558737 9558749 9558751 9558799 9558803 9558821 9558827 9558841 9558847 9558851
9558853 9558859 9558877 9558889 9558917 9558931 9558937 9558953 9558959 9558971
9558979 9559013 9559021 9559051 9559057 9559063 9559073 9559087 9559103 9559139
9559141 9559157 9559171 9559211 9559213 9559271 9559289 9559301 9559307 9559309
9559313 9559349 9559351 9559379 9559387 9559391 9559397 9559399 9559411 9559427
9559469 9559477 9559507 9559541 9559577 9559591 9559597 9559607 9559609
9559621 9559637 9559657 9559699 9559703 9559709 9559721 9559733 9559783 9559799
9559817 9559841 9559843 9559867 9559883 9559887 9559903 9559909 9559931 9559943
9559969 9559993 9559999 9560009 9560017 9560039 9560041 9560051 9560071 9560081
9560119 9560141 9560149 9560167 9560209 9560219 9560231 9560237 9560279 9560293
9560303 9560321 9560333 9560359 9560377 9560389 9560399 9560407 9560413 9560437
9560449 9560461 9560483 9560497 9560527 9560531 9560533 9560539 9560561 9560581
9560597 9560627 9560653 9560659 9560669 9560701 9560731 9560753 9560779 9560797
9560809 9560813 9560843 9560861 9560909 9560959 9560983 9561011 9561017 9561053
9561061 9561103 9561107 9561119 9561121 9561131 9561187 9561197 9561203 9561221
9561229 9561283 9561291 9561289 9561301 9561341 9561373 9561379 9561401 9561601
9561403 9561407 9561421 9561443 9561511 9561521 9561533 9561551 9561557 9561611
9561623 9561631 9561647 9561653 9561659 9561661 9561679 9561691 9561709 9561719
9561737 9561757 9561779 9561787 9561809 9561817 9561823 9561833 9561847 9561863
9561869 9561901 9561911 9561941 9561943 9561961 9561983 9561989 9561991 9562027
9562053 9562057 9562093 9562097 9562099 9562117 9562123 9562127 9562139 9562171
9562213 9562219 9562247 9562261 9562271 9562303 9562321 9562331 9562363 9562367
9562369 9562387 9562393 9562403 9562429 9562433 9562439 9562447 9562451 9562459
9562499 9562507 9562519 9562541 9562559 9562561 9562589 9562591 9562603 9562627
9562633 9562649 9562669 9562673 9562691 9562699 9562703 9562739 9562741 9562753
9562771 9562801 9562807 9562831 9562841 9562859 9562867 9562873 9562877 9562879
9562901 9562913 9562933 9562937 9562951 9562991 9562999 9563003 9563017 9563039
9563063 9563093 9563117 9563143 9563171 9563173 9563233 9563237 9563249 9563261
9563287 9563293 9563297 9563321 9563363 9563371 9563429 9563443 9563461 9563467
9563471 9563473 9563483 9563507 9563549 9563569 9563593 9563621 9563623 9563621
9563663 9563677 9563711 9563731 9563777 9563789 9563839 9563849 9563899 9563921
9563933 9563941 9563999 9564001 9564031 9564041 9564043 9564059 9564073 9564091
9564097 9564109 9564133 9564143 9564199 9564211 9564227 9564253 9564259 9564263
9564299 9564301 9564307 9564349 9564371 9564377 9564383 9564449 9564469 9564479
9564487 9564509 9564517 9564571 9564593 9564613 9564637 9564661 9564673 9564691
9564697 9564701 9564749 9564781 9564787 9564799 9564811 9564817 9564827 9564869
9564881 9564901 9564913 9564937 9564943 9564953 9564979 9565001 9565027 9565063
9565091 9565093 9565103 9565109 9565123 9565141 9565159 9565163 9565187 9565201
9565207 9565211 9565219 9565243 9565247 9565249 9565253 9565279 9565291 9565313
9565319 9565327 9565357 9565363 9565429 9565433 9565463 9565469 9565481 9565483
9565529 9565537 9565547 9565579 9565583 9565601 9565603 9565627 9565649 9565663
9565681 9565687 9565697 9565709 9565711 9565727 9565733 9565739 9565757 9565771
9565793 9565799 9565817 9565859 9565867 9565877 9565879 9565889 9565891 9565903
9565921 9565931 9565967 9565979 9565991 9566003 9566009 9566041 9566047 9566057
9566071 9566077 9566093 9566111 9566113 9566141 9566149 9566159 9566171 9566173
9566213 9566233 9566251 9566267 9566287 9566309 9566351 9566353 9566369 9566371
9566377 9566389 9566429 9566449 9566533 9566539 9566561 9566567 9566581 9566587
9566621 9566647 9566651 9566681 9566701 9566717 9566719 9566731 9566737 9566741
9566759 9566761 9566771 9566773 9566789 9566797 9566807 9566849 9566857 9566867
9566881 9566891 9566939 9566963 9566989 9566993 9567001 9567007 9567011 9567031
9567043 9567049 9567079 9567101 9567139 9567157 9567163 9567169 9567221 9567223
9567289 9567347 9567363 9567403 9567407 9567433 9567441 9567449 9567451
9567487 9567491 9567521 9567553 9567557 9567581 9567587 9567631 9567643 9567647
9567653 9567661 9567671 9567683 9567689 9567703 9567713 9567731 9567739 9567749
9567751 9567757 9567773 9567797 9567829 9567851 9567863 9567881 9567907 9567913
9567917 9567919 9567953 9567959 9567967 9567997 9568007 9568019 9568073 9568079
9568099 9568103 9568121 9568133 9568171 9568187 9568189 9568193 9568201 9568219
9568259 9568271 9568283 9568291 9568303 9568309 9568313 9568327 9568369 9568379
9568397 9568421 9568439 9568451 9568453 9568469 9568477 9568499 9568511 9568523
9568543 9568549 9568577 9568583 9568591 9568627 9568649 9568693 9568697 9568709
9568721 9568733 9568781 9568787 9568799 9568813 9568817 9568847 9568859 9568877
9568907 9568921 9568923 9568931 9568939 9568947 9568963 9568973 9568981 9569003
9569017 9569023 9569041 9569047 9569057 9569089 9569093 9569107 9569129 9569143
9569221 9569233 9569251 9569257 9569299 9569303 9569327 9569353 9569363 9569377
9569383 9569393 9569401 9569411 9569423 9569431 9569459 9569471 9569473 9569479
9569503 9569509 9569531 9569533 9569551 9569557 9569563 9569603 9569617 9569641
```

```
9569647  9569653  9569663  9569671  9569683  9569689  9569699  9569701  9569713  9569719
9569737  9569743  9569753  9569767  9569773  9569783  9569801  9569807  9569837  9569849
9569867  9569881  9569887  9569891  9569921  9569947  9569953  9569957  9569969  9570007
9570023  9570049  9570059  9570089  9570101  9570131  9570137  9570163  9570173  9570181
9570199  9570221  9570233  9570241  9570251  9570271  9570293  9570299  9570313  9570317
9570329  9570361  9570389  9570391  9570443  9570487  9570497  9570499  9570503  9570511
9570521  9570523  9570557  9570571  9570577  9570629  9570641  9570653  9570689  9570697
9570703  9570709  9570713  9570721  9570767  9570797  9570809  9570817  9570853  9570857
9570919  9570923  9570943  9570947  9570959  9570973  9570989  9570997  9571019  9571027
9571031  9571057  9571061  9571091  9571109  9571129  9571169  9571207  9571223  9571259
9571267  9571277  9571283  9571321  9571349  9571351  9571361  9571369  9571411  9571417
9571433  9571447  9571453  9571483  9571489  9571501  9571531  9571543  9571547  9571559
9571577  9571579  9571589  9571607  9571619  9571631  9571633  9571637  9571699  9571717
9571721  9571729  9571733  9571741  9571753  9571781  9571787  9571817  9571831  9571847
9571883  9571889  9571897  9571907  9571921  9571927  9571931  9571949  9571951  9571981
9571987  9571993  9571997  9571999  9572009  9572021  9572027  9572051  9572063  9572077
9572081  9572083  9572093  9572111  9572129  9572131  9572137  9572153  9572183  9572191
9572201  9572203  9572239  9572243  9572249  9572261  9572293  9572369  9572389  9572399
9572413  9572419  9572441  9572467  9572471  9572483  9572503  9572527  9572539  9572543
9572551  9572579  9572587  9572597  9572621  9572627  9572657  9572659  9572663  9572671
9572687  9572711  9572737  9572743  9572747  9572749  9572753  9572837  9572839  9572863
9572869  9572873  9572917  9572933  9572951  9572957  9572963  9572977  9572999  9573013
9573029  9573043  9573059  9573061  9573071  9573077  9573097  9573127  9573173  9573191
9573199  9573217  9573229  9573233  9573241  9573251  9573253  9573257  9573307  9573323
9573331  9573341  9573367  9573371  9573373  9573407  9573409  9573433  9573449  9573461
9573467  9573481  9573583  9573593  9573631  9573643  9573653  9573661  9573671  9573677
9573709  9573719  9573721  9573749  9573757  9573763  9573769  9573793  9573847  9573859
9573881  9573899  9573901  9573913  9573937  9573983  9574007  9574013  9574057  9574067
9574069  9574087  9574091  9574109  9574127  9574129  9574159  9574183  9574189  9574193
9574219  9574241  9574249  9574259  9574283  9574289  9574297  9574303  9574307  9574333
9574363  9574373  9574387  9574399  9574429  9574469  9574471  9574483  9574489  9574493
9574529  9574541  9574549  9574573  9574589  9574597  9574619  9574627  9574661  9574667
9574673  9574679  9574687  9574703  9574717  9574729  9574751  9574781  9574787  9574801
9574849  9574861  9574871  9574883  9574891  9574909  9574919  9574931  9574937  9574949
9574997  9575003  9575009  9575011  9575039  9575077  9575089  9575113  9575123  9575141
9575147  9575173  9575201  9575213  9575219  9575227  9575239  9575257  9575299  9575327
9575329  9575333  9575339  9575359  9575381  9575389  9575393  9575413  9575441  9575453
9575473  9575491  9575519  9575561  9575569  9575633  9575647  9575693  9575717  9575737
9575749  9575789  9575801  9575809  9575851  9575857  9575861  9575893  9575903  9575929
9575941  9575953  9575957  9575989  9575999  9576011  9576023  9576031  9576053  9576059
9576061  9576089  9576097  9576101  9576103  9576107  9576121  9576137  9576139  9576157
9576169  9576187  9576197  9576227  9576233  9576239  9576263  9576271  9576277  9576283
9576299  9576313  9576317  9576319  9576337  9576341  9576373  9576383  9576397  9576407
9576421  9576431  9576433  9576439  9576443  9576461  9576473  9576483  9576499  9576503
9576521  9576547  9576563  9576577  9576601  9576629  9576643  9576691  9576709  9576727
9576731  9576733  9576751  9576773  9576781  9576793  9576803  9576811  9576829  9576841
9576851  9576857  9576859  9576871  9576877  9576881  9576883  9576911  9576929  9576953
9576971  9576979  9577019  9577021  9577027  9577033  9577063  9577081  9577093  9577097
9577129  9577133  9577147  9577151  9577187  9577189  9577199  9577219  9577289  9577297
9577303  9577319  9577327  9577333  9577363  9577367  9577397  9577417  9577429  9577439
9577441  9577457  9577483  9577493  9577507  9577523  9577537  9577561  9577571  9577621
9577643  9577651  9577657  9577669  9577679  9577697  9577727  9577739  9577741  9577747
9577759  9577769  9577781  9577823  9577831  9577837  9577847  9577849  9577871  9577879
9577927  9577933  9577979  9577999  9578003  9578017  9578027  9578029  9578047
9578053  9578057  9578059  9578131  9578141  9578161  9578183  9578203  9578209  9578221
9578249  9578251  9578273  9578311  9578329  9578341  9578357  9578363  9578389  9578399
9578407  9578417  9578423  9578441  9578453  9578477  9578483  9578501  9578507  9578561
9578573  9578579  9578617  9578623  9578627  9578651  9578663  9578669  9578677  9578683
9578711  9578749  9578753  9578761  9578773  9578791  9578797  9578813  9578839  9578867
9578887  9578911  9578917  9578957  9578963  9578977  9578993  9578999  9579043  9579047
9579079  9579083  9579121  9579127  9579131  9579137  9579149  9579151  9579187  9579203
9579209  9579221  9579233  9579277  9579301  9579307  9579319  9579331  9579343  9579371
9579373  9579377  9579391  9579407  9579413  9579443  9579457  9579469  9579473  9579503
9579511  9579539  9579601  9579617  9579641  9579643  9579649  9579659  9579671  9579677
9579709  9579719  9579751  9579761  9579763  9579767  9579797  9579809  9579811  9579821
9579827  9579839  9579851  9579859  9579877  9579881  9579887  9579907  9579919  9579923
9579953  9579967  9580001  9580037  9580097  9580117  9580127  9580139  9580141  9580157
9580169  9580177  9580187  9580201  9580211  9580217  9580223  9580247  9580267  9580279
9580283  9580309  9580331  9580381  9580387  9580391  9580393  9580421  9580451  9580453
9580463  9580471  9580481  9580513  9580523  9580553  9580559  9580561  9580591  9580601
9580603  9580609  9580631  9580657  9580667  9580679  9580709  9580729  9580733  9580763
9580771  9580783  9580789  9580841  9580861  9580867  9580871  9580889  9580919
9580927  9580937  9580943  9580949  9581009  9581023  9581029  9581051  9581053  9581057
9581119  9581123  9581129  9581141  9581161  9581171  9581189  9581191  9581197  9581203
9581219  9581227  9581233  9581267  9581293  9581309  9581311  9581321  9581329  9581347
9581359  9581371  9581381  9581399  9581417  9581419  9581431  9581461  9581477  9581497
9581527  9581543  9581549  9581569  9581587  9581633  9581653  9581669  9581683  9581699
9581701  9581717  9581723  9581753  9581771  9581773  9581783  9581791  9581797  9581801
9581809  9581813  9581827  9581837  9581839  9581849  9581851  9581893  9581903  9581911
9581933  9581939  9581963  9581981  9581983  9581993  9582017  9582019  9582029  9582027
9582059  9582073  9582091  9582103  9582107  9582127  9582161  9582179  9582187  9582197
9582229  9582247  9582259  9582263  9582269  9582311  9582319  9582323  9582337  9582341
9582343  9582359  9582361  9582409  9582437  9582439  9582451  9582467  9582487  9582497
9582511  9582523  9582527  9582539  9582553  9582563  9582569  9582571  9582581  9582589
9582623  9582629  9582641  9582647  9582649  9582659  9582691  9582701  9582757  9582761
9582763  9582773  9582791  9582817  9582827  9582829  9582841  9582871  9582887  9582899
9582901  9582907  9582919  9582977  9583001  9583009  9583031  9583033  9583051  9583069
9583073  9583081  9583103  9583117  9583127  9583129  9583139  9583153  9583169  9583177
9583181  9583187  9583207  9583213  9583219  9583237  9583261  9583271  9583289  9583297
```

```
9583303  9583313  9583319  9583331  9583337  9583339  9583349  9583351  9583363  9583397
9583403  9583423  9583439  9583447  9583451  9583477  9583487  9583493  9583501  9583507
9583537  9583549  9583559  9583579  9583621  9583687  9583741  9583757  9583759  9583781
9583811  9583813  9583823  9583843  9583859  9583877  9583907  9583909  9583919  9583921
9583979  9583997  9584009  9584017  9584021  9584033  9584033  9584051  9584063  9584099
9584101  9584111  9584117  9584129  9584153  9584173  9584203  9584207  9584213  9584257
9584291  9584327  9584347  9584357  9584371  9584401  9584411  9584429  9584431  9584441
9584453  9584461  9584483  9584501  9584507  9584513  9584521  9584527  9584543  9584557
9584579  9584581  9584593  9584623  9584633  9584639  9584669  9584689  9584699  9584711
9584717  9584737  9584749  9584777  9584789  9584801  9584807  9584831  9584843  9584849
9584863  9584867  9584879  9584881  9584893  9584903  9584917  9584933  9584947  9584969
9585011  9585019  9585041  9585053  9585061  9585073  9585083  9585091  9585131  9585143
9585151  9585157  9585193  9585197  9585239  9585281  9585287  9585311  9585313  9585343
9585353  9585361  9585371  9585379  9585383  9585391  9585397  9585403  9585409  9585419
9585437  9585449  9585469  9585473  9585491  9585533  9585547  9585551  9585559  9585571
9585577  9585593  9585599  9585613  9585619  9585647  9585649  9585661  9585679  9585691
9585707  9585713  9585721  9585743  9585761  9585767  9585769  9585799  9585803  9585811
9585817  9585827  9585847  9585859  9585869  9585881  9585883  9585887  9585889  9585893
9585911  9585929  9585931  9585959  9585971  9585991  9586001  9586007  9586021  9586039
9586061  9586063  9586069  9586111  9586121  9586123  9586151  9586183  9586189  9586229
9586231  9586259  9586267  9586271  9586273  9586277  9586307  9586361  9586373  9586387
9586399  9586403  9586411  9586429  9586459  9586477  9586517  9586523  9586531  9586537
9586541  9586567  9586573  9586597  9586601  9586631  9586649  9586651  9586673  9586727
9586741  9586747  9586769  9586777  9586787  9586823  9586847  9586859  9586897  9586903
9586909  9586933  9586937  9586939  9586957  9586961  9586981  9586987  9586999  9587003
9587041  9587063  9587101  9587111  9587119  9587129  9587147  9587173  9587177  9587183
9587209  9587213  9587233  9587239  9587243  9587257  9587261  9587293  9587311  9587351
9587353  9587359  9587377  9587387  9587393  9587407  9587423  9587449  9587453  9587467
9587489  9587491  9587537  9587593  9587623  9587651  9587653  9587657  9587663  9587681
9587689  9587693  9587701  9587707  9587713  9587729  9587731  9587737  9587741  9587783
9587789  9587827  9587843  9587857  9587863  9587867  9587869  9587873  9587939  9587969
9588023  9588037  9588043  9588091  9588101  9588107  9588109  9588121  9588127  9588157
9588181  9588197  9588223  9588247  9588277  9588281  9588307  9588343  9588367  9588419
9588421  9588431  9588443  9588463  9588487  9588499  9588511  9588533  9588569  9588577
9588583  9588599  9588617  9588619  9588643  9588659  9588671  9588679  9588701  9588713
9588727  9588737  9588757  9588781  9588791  9588811  9588823  9588829  9588847  9588853
9588869  9588899  9588913  9588923  9588959  9588961  9588967  9588983  9588989  9589001
9589009  9589033  9589049  9589087  9589123  9589133  9589141  9589147  9589157  9589201
9589219  9589247  9589259  9589271  9589273  9589289  9589313  9589351  9589373  9589379
9589399  9589421  9589423  9589427  9589429  9589451  9589469  9589477  9589487  9589507
9589511  9589529  9589553  9589583  9589603  9589607  9589639  9589667  9589673  9589681
9589693  9589703  9589709  9589753  9589799  9589829  9589831  9589841  9589843  9589847
9589861  9589883  9589891  9589933  9589939  9589961  9589963  9589969  9589973  9589991
9589997  9590029  9590033  9590093  9590107  9590111  9590123  9590131  9590153  9590173
9590177  9590219  9590221  9590233  9590257  9590267  9590299  9590311  9590323  9590327
9590343  9590369  9590393  9590417  9590429  9590443  9590473  9590479  9590489  9590531
9590543  9590549  9590557  9590579  9590593  9590617  9590621  9590629  9590653  9590671
9590699  9590723  9590743  9590767  9590783  9590797  9590809  9590857  9590879  9590891
9590897  9590921  9590927  9590939  9590951  9590957  9590989  9591011  9591031  9591037
9591041  9591047  9591053  9591073  9591079  9591097  9591119  9591137  9591151  9591157
9591163  9591171  9591187  9591223  9591227  9591229  9591269  9591271  9591289  9591313
9591317  9591331  9591341  9591343  9591367  9591377  9591401  9591419  9591433  9591443
9591467  9591479  9591487  9591509  9591539  9591541  9591557  9591583  9591629  9591641
9591649  9591683  9591727  9591731  9591739  9591761  9591763  9591767  9591773  9591793
9591809  9591811  9591817  9591821  9591833  9591839  9591853  9591863  9591871  9591877
9591913  9591931  9591937  9591949  9591977  9591983  9591997  9592001  9592003  9592007
9592013  9592021  9592057  9592087  9592091  9592117  9592129  9592133  9592151  9592159
9592201  9592217  9592223  9592241  9592259  9592291  9592307  9592333  9592337  9592379
9592381  9592409  9592411  9592447  9592459  9592463  9592469  9592481  9592487  9592489
9592507  9592519  9592537  9592553  9592567  9592571  9592579  9592601  9592613  9592619
9592631  9592651  9592669  9592673  9592697  9592703  9592717  9592721  9592727  9592753
9592757  9592783  9592801  9592813  9592861  9592889  9592901  9592903  9592907  9592927
9592931  9592937  9592951  9593011  9593021  9593033  9593041  9593071  9593099  9593107
9593131  9593161  9593191  9593197  9593239  9593251  9593267  9593273  9593279  9593281
9593329  9593333  9593351  9593383  9593387  9593393  9593401  9593407  9593411  9593431
9593447  9593473  9593533  9593561  9593567  9593579  9593603  9593609  9593657  9593659
9593677  9593723  9593743  9593761  9593777  9593819  9593827  9593861  9593869  9593873
9593923  9593929  9593951  9593957  9593963  9594007  9594029  9594037  9594043  9594073
9594077  9594089  9594119  9594127  9594133  9594139  9594149  9594161  9594181  9594191
9594209  9594217  9594227  9594257  9594269  9594271  9594281  9594329  9594349  9594353
9594371  9594379  9594383  9594391  9594397  9594401  9594421  9594479  9594499  9594509
9594517  9594523  9594527  9594539  9594549  9594589  9594617  9594619  9594649  9594653
9594659  9594667  9594701  9594709  9594713  9594733  9594743  9594763  9594769  9594773
9594799  9594811  9594821  9594857  9594859  9594863  9594889  9594913  9594917  9594929
9594931  9594947  9594983  9594989  9595007  9595009  9595037  9595039  9595043  9595051
9595073  9595087  9595109  9595127  9595147  9595177  9595181  9595199  9595207  9595211
9595217  9595219  9595237  9595241  9595253  9595291  9595331  9595349  9595363  9595367
9595373  9595423  9595427  9595441  9595471  9595477  9595501  9595507  9595559  9595603
9595637  9595679  9595693  9595753  9595783  9595793  9595799  9595801  9595811  9595841
9595877  9595903  9595933  9595961  9595967  9596017  9596023  9596029  9596039  9596099
9596107  9596117  9596141  9596161  9596179  9596183  9596189  9596203  9596207  9596219
9596227  9596231  9596239  9596243  9596261  9596263  9596281  9596287  9596297  9596309
9596317  9596333  9596371  9596399  9596401  9596417  9596437  9596441  9596443  9596467
9596471  9596473  9596479  9596533  9596537  9596549  9596557  9596591  9596597  9596617
9596621  9596623  9596627  9596633  9596641  9596647  9596689  9596707  9596711  9596731
9596753  9596761  9596771  9596777  9596779  9596803  9596809  9596827  9596837  9596849
9596897  9596921  9596927  9596933  9596953  9596963  9596981  9597031  9597043  9597047
9597053  9597067  9597079  9597089  9597131  9597139  9597143  9597179  9597193  9597209
9597221  9597227  9597229  9597257  9597271  9597307  9597349  9597359  9597361  9597377
```

```
9597389  9597397  9597407  9597421  9597431  9597433  9597439  9597449  9597479  9597481
9597491  9597547  9597551  9597563  9597587  9597593  9597613  9597661  9597677  9597701
9597703  9597719  9597737  9597751  9597767  9597769  9597779  9597799  9597803  9597853
9597899  9597919  9597937  9597949  9597953  9597971  9597997  9598019  9598031  9598049
9598051  9598063  9598067  9598079  9598087  9598093  9598109  9598111  9598129  9598139
9598157  9598163  9598177  9598181  9598187  9598201  9598229  9598231  9598301  9598321
9598339  9598343  9598349  9598373  9598387  9598403  9598427  9598451  9598483  9598529
9598541  9598543  9598573  9598597  9598607  9598609  9598627  9598637  9598639  9598657
9598661  9598663  9598691  9598709  9598733  9598753  9598759  9598807  9598811  9598837
9598861  9598877  9598909  9598921  9598937  9598943  9598949  9598997  9599017  9599059
9599069  9599071  9599089  9599099  9599111  9599113  9599131  9599147  9599159  9599167
9599173  9599189  9599267  9599279  9599299  9599309  9599311  9599323  9599329  9599333
9599341  9599393  9599417  9599419  9599423  9599431  9599437  9599461  9599467  9599483
9599489  9599501  9599507  9599537  9599563  9599587  9599647  9599657  9599653  9599683
9599701  9599729  9599743  9599749  9599767  9599777  9599789  9599791  9599813  9599861
9599869  9599873  9599881  9599893  9599897  9599911  9599923  9599939  9599963  9599969
9599977  9600037  9600047  9600091  9600103  9600133  9600141  9600161  9600169  9600181
9600251  9600271  9600287  9600293  9600319  9600323  9600337  9600347  9600389  9600413
9600419  9600431  9600433  9600439  9600443  9600469  9600509  9600533  9600551  9600553
9600557  9600559  9600571  9600581  9600583  9600587  9600599  9600623  9600629
9600659  9600667  9600671  9600673  9600709  9600713  9600727  9600743  9600751  9600763
9600779  9600781  9600803  9600809  9600817  9600841  9600853  9600883  9600889  9600907
9600923  9600953  9600977  9600991  9601013  9601027  9601057  9601069  9601079  9601091
9601159  9601177  9601187  9601201  9601219  9601223  9601237  9601253  9601261  9601279
9601297  9601303  9601313  9601367  9601457  9601469  9601477  9601499  9601519  9601531
9601547  9601561  9601573  9601589  9601591  9601607  9601609  9601619  9601621  9601663
9601693  9601699  9601717  9601721  9601727  9601733  9601751  9601769  9601793  9601811
9601817  9601819  9601829  9601843  9601849  9601853  9601861  9601877  9601883  9601931
9601937  9601961  9601993  9601997  9602003  9602009  9602023  9602057  9602069
9602081  9602113  9602119  9602149  9602183  9602233  9602237  9602261  9602267  9602269
9602311  9602317  9602363  9602387  9602389  9602407  9602413  9602423  9602441  9602443
9602471  9602479  9602491  9602497  9602521  9602539  9602557  9602563  9602599  9602611
9602623  9602633  9602669  9602689  9602701  9602713  9602729  9602731  9602737  9602743
9602767  9602779  9602797  9602837  9602843  9602861  9602867  9602893  9602917  9602947
9602951  9602953  9602969  9602981  9603007  9603019  9603023  9603067  9603103  9603107
9603119  9603137  9603151  9603163  9603173  9603179  9603193  9603203  9603221  9603241
9603271  9603281  9603287  9603299  9603301  9603331  9603343  9603353  9603361  9603409
9603457  9603467  9603509  9603551  9603599  9603619  9603637  9603641  9603647  9603667
9603677  9603683  9603703  9603709  9603731  9603743  9603773  9603791  9603809  9603817
9603823  9603851  9603859  9603863  9603877  9603883  9603889  9603917  9603931  9603943
9603967  9603977  9604019  9604037  9604039  9604043  9604051  9604057  9604069  9604081
9604097  9604117  9604129  9604157  9604187  9604193  9604207  9604211  9604229  9604237
9604277  9604297  9604313  9604319  9604369  9604379  9604381  9604411  9604453  9604457
9604459  9604477  9604487  9604531  9604549  9604579  9604589  9604601  9604631
9604663  9604681  9604691  9604697  9604703  9604717  9604723  9604729  9604739  9604759
9604801  9604807  9604811  9604831  9604841  9604849  9604871  9604881  9604891  9604909
9604913  9604939  9604943  9604957  9604963  9604979  9604981  9604993  9605027  9605033
9605041  9605047  9605087  9605107  9605117  9605131  9605149  9605159  9605161  9605179
9605209  9605213  9605227  9605263  9605269  9605273  9605327  9605333  9605347  9605359
9605363  9605369  9605371  9605389  9605411  9605429  9605447  9605461  9605473  9605501
9605509  9605551  9605587  9605593  9605597  9605611  9605627  9605639  9605647
9605653  9605669  9605671  9605707  9605737  9605749  9605779  9605801  9605809  9605831
9605923  9605971  9605983  9605993  9606011  9606043  9606049  9606067  9606101  9606119
9606131  9606133  9606161  9606193  9606217  9606239  9606251  9606253  9606257  9606263
9606269  9606281  9606287  9606293  9606299  9606301  9606319  9606349  9606379  9606383
9606397  9606431  9606437  9606449  9606451  9606491  9606529  9606539  9606551  9606563
9606593  9606599  9606607  9606629  9606631  9606671  9606677  9606691  9606697  9606713
9606721  9606739  9606763  9606767  9606803  9606809  9606811  9606889  9606899  9606901
9606907  9606943  9606979  9606991  9607021  9607043  9607051  9607067  9607121  9607139
9607153  9607163  9607183  9607187  9607201  9607219  9607231  9607249  9607291  9607337
9607349  9607357  9607373  9607387  9607393  9607417  9607441  9607453  9607457  9607471
9607487  9607513  9607517  9607519  9607523  9607529  9607547  9607573  9607579  9607607
9607643  9607651  9607657  9607691  9607699  9607727  9607747  9607751  9607769  9607777
9607781  9607783  9607789  9607841  9607847  9607849  9607853  9607879  9607883  9607891
9607909  9607921  9607957  9607987  9608003  9608017  9608021  9608057  9608087  9608099
9608113  9608143  9608147  9608189  9608191  9608219  9608267  9608287  9608297  9608303
9608311  9608323  9608341  9608353  9608369  9608371  9608377  9608381  9608399  9608407
9608413  9608441  9608461  9608467  9608491  9608497  9608507  9608513  9608527
9608569  9608581  9608609  9608617  9608629  9608663  9608713  9608717  9608743  9608749
9608761  9608783  9608843  9608857  9608867  9608869  9608883  9608887  9608923  9608933
9608941  9608959  9608969  9608971  9608983  9608987  9609001  9609023  9609031  9609037
9609053  9609071  9609107  9609133  9609139  9609143  9609157  9609169  9609191  9609203
9609227  9609247  9609251  9609263  9609281  9609311  9609319  9609329  9609337  9609367
9609371  9609409  9609427  9609433  9609451  9609461  9609493  9609503  9609517  9609533
9609547  9609553  9609557  9609571  9609577  9609581  9609583  9609601  9609623  9609629
9609661  9609671  9609673  9609679  9609697  9609713  9609749  9609773  9609781  9609799
9609827  9609829  9609851  9609863  9609871  9609881  9609893  9609911  9609917  9609937
9609959  9610033  9610061  9610079  9610091  9610103  9610109  9610129  9610141  9610147
9610157  9610163  9610169  9610187  9610259  9610261  9610301  9610313  9610319  9610327
9610361  9610373  9610387  9610399  9610459  9610463  9610507  9610511  9610529
9610541  9610577  9610609  9610613  9610691  9610703  9610717  9610739  9610747  9610753
9610759  9610771  9610781  9610793  9610807  9610813  9610841  9610871  9610879  9610883
9610891  9610897  9610927  9610957  9610981  9611003  9611011  9611053  9611071
9611087  9611117  9611141  9611143  9611149  9611153  9611183  9611191  9611201  9611237
9611269  9611297  9611299  9611353  9611387  9611419  9611423  9611431  9611491
9611521  9611531  9611533  9611551  9611573  9611597  9611611  9611617  9611627  9611659
9611669  9611687  9611713  9611717  9611737  9611759  9611761  9611773  9611779  9611807
9611813  9611839  9611843  9611869  9611873  9611879  9611881  9611939  9611941  9611951
9611957  9611977  9611993  9612007  9612047  9612059  9612101  9612107  9612143  9612179
```

```
9612181  9612199  9612209  9612223  9612277  9612283  9612287  9612301  9612329  9612359
9612377  9612401  9612403  9612433  9612439  9612443  9612467  9612469  9612481  9612523
9612539  9612541  9612553  9612569  9612587  9612611  9612653  9612671  9612677  9612719
9612721  9612749  9612763  9612787  9612791  9612817  9612829  9612847  9612851  9612853
9612857  9612899  9612907  9612931  9612937  9612961  9612989  9613001  9613003  9613013
9613027  9613039  9613061  9613063  9613067  9613073  9613099  9613111  9613127  9613129
9613133  9613139  9613159  9613199  9613213  9613217  9613231  9613243  9613271  9613277
9613301  9613319  9613327  9613337  9613339  9613343  9613349  9613363  9613367  9613369
9613391  9613399  9613421  9613423  9613433  9613447  9613459  9613481  9613489  9613501
9613507  9613531  9613537  9613547  9613561  9613567  9613621  9613631  9613633  9613633
9613663  9613693  9613727  9613729  9613733  9613739  9613757  9613759  9613771  9613777
9613781  9613787  9613817  9613831  9613837  9613841  9613847  9613859  9613861  9613907
9613939  9613949  9613951  9613957  9613963  9613979  9613987  9614029  9614081  9614083
9614141  9614159  9614183  9614201  9614219  9614237  9614239  9614251  9614257  9614261
9614369  9614389  9614411  9614419  9614431  9614441  9614443  9614447  9614453  9614477
9614489  9614497  9614509  9614519  9614569  9614587  9614597  9614603  9614609  9614617
9614629  9614653  9614659  9614663  9614669  9614687  9614729  9614753  9614767  9614771
9614791  9614819  9614827  9614833  9614849  9614861  9614873  9614879  9614887  9614909
9614923  9614939  9614953  9614959  9614963  9614971  9614981  9614993  9615019  9615029
9615031  9615041  9615061  9615113  9615139  9615157  9615161  9615191  9615223  9615233
9615257  9615259  9615271  9615323  9615329  9615337  9615377  9615379  9615383  9615391
9615409  9615413  9615427  9615433  9615439  9615457  9615461  9615479  9615499  9615511
9615521  9615527  9615553  9615563  9615569  9615581  9615583  9615623  9615637  9615709
9615721  9615731  9615751  9615757  9615763  9615803  9615811  9615841  9615883  9615889
9615911  9615913  9615923  9615929  9615937  9615941  9615953  9615971  9615973  9615989
9616003  9616007  9616021  9616031  9616037  9616039  9616043  9616049  9616111  9616121
9616127  9616129  9616151  9616157  9616177  9616193  9616199  9616207  9616213  9616241
9616259  9616273  9616279  9616283  9616291  9616319  9616331  9616333  9616357  9616379
9616393  9616421  9616441  9616457  9616459  9616471  9616493  9616499  9616517  9616547
9616549  9616561  9616571  9616573  9616613  9616619  9616627  9616631  9616637  9616657
9616667  9616687  9616697  9616699  9616709  9616729  9616741  9616759  9616771  9616813
9616819  9616843  9616853  9616861  9616891  9616909  9616927  9616933  9616939  9616963
9616987  9616991  9617011  9617017  9617033  9617051  9617081  9617089  9617107  9617117
9617123  9617137  9617141  9617143  9617147  9617171  9617191  9617219  9617233  9617261
9617269  9617273  9617297  9617303  9617339  9617369  9617371  9617417  9617431  9617441
9617449  9617507  9617527  9617561  9617579  9617581  9617593  9617609  9617617  9617623
9617633  9617651  9617653  9617659  9617683  9617723  9617747  9617753  9617759  9617761
9617779  9617789  9617813  9617851  9617893  9617897  9617911  9617929  9617947  9617953
9617983  9617987  9617989  9617999  9618001  9618017  9618019  9618041  9618043
9618079  9618083  9618101  9618109  9618137  9618233  9618241  9618251  9618253  9618307
9618353  9618361  9618373  9618377  9618391  9618403  9618431  9618437  9618443  9618451
9618457  9618491  9618509  9618527  9618547  9618563  9618589  9618607  9618619  9618643
9618647  9618667  9618677  9618701  9618709  9618727  9618733  9618743  9618757  9618767
9618823  9618827  9618871  9618877  9618889  9618893  9618943  9618967  9619007  9619013
9619019  9619061  9619069  9619079  9619081  9619091  9619109  9619117  9619163  9619177
9619201  9619219  9619289  9619303  9619307  9619321  9619327  9619369  9619373
9619381  9619397  9619409  9619417  9619427  9619439  9619457  9619459  9619469  9619471
9619481  9619499  9619507  9619523  9619531  9619583  9619601  9619609  9619613  9619627
9619633  9619651  9619661  9619663  9619669  9619679  9619691  9619693  9619747  9619753
9619763  9619777  9619787  9619817  9619829  9619837  9619847  9619873  9619877  9619901
9619903  9619937  9619979  9619991  9619993  9620021  9620027  9620041  9620057  9620071
9620081  9620119  9620129  9620131  9620153  9620161  9620167  9620173  9620183  9620197
9620201  9620203  9620269  9620291  9620297  9620311  9620341  9620389  9620393  9620399
9620411  9620437  9620473  9620497  9620531  9620543  9620561  9620563  9620581  9620591
9620617  9620627  9620641  9620671  9620687  9620701  9620711  9620747  9620753  9620761
9620797  9620801  9620833  9620867  9620873  9620879  9620887  9620889  9620899  9620911
9620917  9620927  9620971  9620993  9621043  9621077  9621083  9621089  9621091  9621097
9621149  9621169  9621197  9621203  9621223  9621233  9621251  9621257  9621259  9621263
9621317  9621349  9621397  9621413  9621433  9621449  9621463  9621481  9621487  9621503
9621509  9621571  9621589  9621617  9621641  9621671  9621683  9621697  9621709  9621743
9621763  9621767  9621769  9621791  9621817  9621853  9621863  9621869  9621877
9621883  9621907  9621919  9621929  9621943  9621947  9621959  9621971  9621977  9621979
9622009  9622013  9622021  9622031  9622033  9622049  9622099  9622103  9622117
9622139  9622159  9622163  9622219  9622231  9622237  9622241  9622243  9622259  9622267
9622297  9622367  9622387  9622421  9622423  9622429  9622447  9622463  9622471  9622489
9622499  9622511  9622513  9622517  9622523  9622549  9622589  9622597  9622601  9622603
9622609  9622619  9622621  9622637  9622661  9622681  9622747  9622783  9622801  9622807
9622813  9622817  9622853  9622871  9622891  9622897  9622903  9622909  9622913  9622931
9622957  9622961  9622973  9622979  9623021  9623023  9623059  9623083  9623087  9623093
9623111  9623123  9623137  9623147  9623149  9623161  9623167  9623191  9623197  9623209
9623213  9623221  9623239  9623249  9623251  9623281  9623287  9623311  9623323  9623347
9623353  9623363  9623399  9623401  9623413  9623437  9623459  9623461  9623477
9623491  9623503  9623521  9623527  9623531  9623533  9623567  9623569  9623573
9623587  9623597  9623623  9623657  9623681  9623689  9623693  9623699  9623743  9623753
9623759  9623771  9623777  9623833  9623843  9623863  9623881  9623891  9623893
9623897  9623953  9623983  9623993  9624001  9624019  9624037  9624047  9624061  9624067
9624071  9624073  9624077  9624103  9624149  9624151  9624157  9624161  9624191  9624211
9624233  9624239  9624269  9624271  9624289  9624301  9624311  9624319  9624341  9624359
9624379  9624409  9624413  9624421  9624443  9624451  9624467  9624479  9624521  9624523
9624529  9624541  9624569  9624577  9624599  9624619  9624653  9624677  9624679  9624683
9624691  9624721  9624761  9624767  9624779  9624793  9624799  9624803  9624827  9624841
9624859  9624869  9624871  9624883  9624889  9624893  9624899  9624913  9624917  9624943
9624947  9624961  9625003  9625051  9625081  9625087  9625117  9625127  9625141  9625151
9625169  9625181  9625207  9625237  9625241  9625243  9625279  9625289  9625321  9625327
9625387  9625391  9625403  9625409  9625411  9625423  9625493  9625501  9625519  9625589
9625591  9625607  9625619  9625631  9625633  9625643  9625657  9625663  9625667  9625669
9625691  9625697  9625703  9625729  9625747  9625751  9625771  9625783  9625787  9625789
9625793  9625831  9625843  9625849  9625871  9625877  9625879  9625901  9625907  9625921
9625933  9625943  9625949  9625963  9625969  9625981  9625997  9626003  9626017  9626033
```

```
9626039  9626053  9626077  9626087  9626107  9626129  9626137  9626147  9626161  9626171
9626189  9626237  9626249  9626269  9626297  9626299  9626303  9626333  9626341  9626363
9626371  9626429  9626459  9626479  9626497  9626501  9626503  9626509  9626531  9626543
9626557  9626563  9626567  9626621  9626629  9626651  9626671  9626693  9626699  9626707
9626767  9626783  9626789  9626801  9626803  9626839  9626849  9626873  9626887  9626893
9626899  9626909  9626999  9627011  9627031  9627061  9627071  9627073  9627077  9627097
9627109  9627113  9627131  9627161  9627181  9627199  9627221  9627223  9627239  9627257
9627259  9627283  9627301  9627311  9627323  9627353  9627379  9627403  9627413  9627427
9627439  9627461  9627463  9627467  9627469  9627473  9627481  9627517  9627523  9627533
9627551  9627589  9627599  9627601  9627613  9627649  9627677  9627707  9627721  9627749
9627767  9627769  9627773  9627791  9627799  9627803  9627841  9627853  9627857  9627883
9627901  9627953  9627973  9627977  9627983  9628009  9628013  9628037  9628039  9628061
9628063  9628067  9628081  9628093  9628111  9628121  9628127  9628133  9628147  9628163
9628169  9628187  9628207  9628219  9628253  9628303  9628309  9628331  9628343  9628361
9628393  9628397  9628403  9628433  9628439  9628447  9628453  9628469  9628519  9628607
9628639  9628699  9628709  9628711  9628721  9628777  9628793  9628811  9628813  9628831
9628837  9628847  9628873  9628883  9628889  9628897  9628909  9628921  9628939  9628943
9628961  9628981  9629023  9629047  9629057  9629063  9629077  9629083  9629099  9629107
9629117  9629129  9629149  9629153  9629159  9629167  9629171  9629197  9629201  9629209
9629237  9629273  9629297  9629299  9629303  9629311  9629329  9629339  9629359  9629369
9629401  9629413  9629419  9629453  9629461  9629483  9629489  9629507  9629513  9629539
9629579  9629611  9629621  9629639  9629651  9629671  9629677  9629681  9629687  9629693
9629707  9629749  9629759  9629761  9629773  9629777  9629813  9629821  9629831  9629839
9629849  9629861  9629881  9629891  9629899  9629911  9629927  9629959  9629969  9629981
9629987  9629993  9630013  9630053  9630079  9630083  9630097  9630139  9630149  9630161
9630163  9630167  9630221  9630239  9630263  9630301  9630311  9630319  9630329  9630331
9630371  9630373  9630403  9630419  9630421  9630431  9630437  9630443  9630449  9630457
9630463  9630479  9630499  9630503  9630521  9630539  9630541  9630547  9630559  9630611
9630631  9630661  9630703  9630743  9630757  9630763  9630787  9630803  9630821  9630827
9630833  9630883  9630889  9630917  9630919  9630923  9630961  9630977  9630979  9630991
9631019  9631031  9631051  9631067  9631073  9631091  9631117  9631159  9631169  9631189
9631201  9631207  9631243  9631247  9631249  9631261  9631267  9631289  9631291  9631327
9631331  9631357  9631361  9631373  9631379  9631397  9631409  9631417  9631439  9631471
9631487  9631493  9631519  9631543  9631561  9631577  9631591  9631603  9631621  9631627
9631649  9631667  9631681  9631697  9631703  9631709  9631711  9631723  9631747  9631751
9631753  9631763  9631771  9631777  9631813  9631829  9631859  9631873  9631883  9631913
9631991  9631997  9632027  9632053  9632057  9632111  9632113  9632137  9632143  9632177
9632179  9632191  9632209  9632213  9632261  9632267  9632279  9632303  9632309  9632317
9632323  9632339  9632347  9632369  9632383  9632401  9632407  9632429  9632479  9632501
9632503  9632507  9632521  9632531  9632533  9632551  9632573  9632587  9632593  9632629
9632681  9632683  9632687  9632717  9632729  9632767  9632771  9632773  9632789  9632797
9632849  9632851  9632873  9632879  9632899  9632921  9632927  9632933  9632939  9632941
9632947  9632963  9632969  9632983  9633031  9633089  9633097  9633109  9633119  9633139
9633149  9633163  9633187  9633233  9633241  9633269  9633277  9633287  9633289
9633301  9633329  9633367  9633397  9633409  9633433  9633443  9633451  9633457  9633469
9633473  9633521  9633541  9633553  9633563  9633583  9633607  9633623  9633643
9633661  9633671  9633691  9633721  9633733  9633751  9633769  9633773  9633787  9633797
9633821  9633853  9633857  9633859  9633889  9633929  9633937  9633961  9633973  9633979
9633989  9634039  9634091  9634099  9634103  9634109  9634111  9634123  9634151  9634153
9634199  9634241  9634243  9634249  9634271  9634277  9634283  9634307  9634327  9634333
9634357  9634363  9634379  9634403  9634411  9634421  9634433  9634511  9634531
9634553  9634571  9634589  9634607  9634609  9634633  9634637  9634649  9634661  9634663
9634697  9634721  9634727  9634741  9634747  9634777  9634789  9634819  9634829  9634841
9634847  9634883  9634901  9634909  9634921  9634949  9634969  9634973  9634979  9634981
9634987  9634991  9634997  9635009  9635023  9635027  9635083  9635089  9635099  9635111
9635117  9635179  9635189  9635257  9635267  9635291  9635293  9635303  9635309  9635357
9635359  9635371  9635401  9635411  9635449  9635459  9635473  9635477  9635519  9635537
9635539  9635557  9635567  9635579  9635609  9635653  9635663  9635669  9635677  9635683
9635687  9635707  9635711  9635723  9635729  9635767  9635777  9635797  9635803  9635807
9635819  9635837  9635839  9635851  9635863  9635881  9635887  9635909  9635921  9635933
9635953  9635963  9635993  9636023  9636031  9636037  9636041  9636047  9636061
9636079  9636083  9636131  9636139  9636157  9636163  9636167  9636197  9636199  9636203
9636223  9636227  9636233  9636247  9636251  9636281  9636299  9636307  9636311  9636337
9636373  9636413  9636421  9636427  9636437  9636461  9636469  9636479  9636481  9636493
9636533  9636541  9636559  9636587  9636593  9636607  9636623  9636631  9636673  9636689
9636703  9636707  9636709  9636727  9636733  9636769  9636791  9636797  9636827
9636889  9636899  9636917  9636941  9636947  9636953  9636967  9636997  9637013  9637027
9637039  9637073  9637093  9637097  9637099  9637109  9637127  9637129  9637139  9637157
9637183  9637217  9637223  9637261  9637297  9637301  9637307  9637357  9637363  9637399
9637409  9637421  9637471  9637477  9637489  9637493  9637513  9637531  9637549  9637567
9637571  9637577  9637601  9637603  9637609  9637613  9637637  9637643  9637687
9637697  9637703  9637729  9637741  9637777  9637799  9637819  9637879  9637913  9637919
9637937  9637949  9637951  9637967  9637973  9637981  9637987  9638009  9638011  9638021
9638023  9638039  9638053  9638059  9638113  9638137  9638143  9638159  9638177  9638191
9638197  9638203  9638207  9638231  9638261  9638267  9638281  9638287  9638309  9638323
9638327  9638341  9638347  9638383  9638393  9638401  9638423  9638437  9638441  9638443
9638459  9638471  9638477  9638479  9638483  9638557  9638591  9638597  9638621  9638623
9638627  9638641  9638659  9638743  9638749  9638753  9638767  9638773  9638801  9638809
9638831  9638851  9638857  9638891  9638897  9638899  9638911  9638921  9638927  9638929
9638953  9638957  9639011  9639043  9639079  9639083  9639103  9639131  9639151  9639169
9639209  9639229  9639241  9639247  9639283  9639307  9639317  9639319  9639341  9639349
9639359  9639367  9639389  9639401  9639433  9639437  9639449  9639467  9639473  9639503
9639529  9639533  9639547  9639563  9639583  9639589  9639601  9639643  9639661
9639671  9639673  9639677  9639701  9639719  9639757  9639761  9639811  9639827  9639863
9639887  9639893  9639901  9639907  9639911  9639913  9639923  9639937  9639947  9639979
9639997  9640021  9640031  9640051  9640061  9640109  9640121  9640129  9640171  9640199
9640219  9640231  9640237  9640247  9640259  9640297  9640303  9640321  9640333  9640361
9640363  9640373  9640417  9640447  9640457  9640481  9640483  9640487  9640489  9640507
9640517  9640523  9640529  9640549  9640577  9640591  9640621  9640627  9640637  9640639
```

```
9640661  9640663  9640667  9640693  9640711  9640727  9640739  9640811  9640817  9640837
9640849  9640871  9640889  9640913  9640919  9640957  9640973  9640991  9640993  9640997
9641011  9641017  9641029  9641041  9641069  9641083  9641087  9641123  9641141  9641143
9641147  9641153  9641171  9641173  9641221  9641231  9641237  9641257  9641267  9641293
9641297  9641299  9641383  9641399  9641419  9641441  9641447  9641453  9641461  9641473
9641479  9641491  9641507  9641549  9641563  9641579  9641591  9641617  9641633  9641647
9641657  9641741  9641743  9641747  9641777  9641783  9641789  9641831  9641857  9641881
9641887  9641893  9641917  9641921  9641959  9641963  9641971  9641981  9641999  9642047
9642049  9642109  9642119  9642121  9642133  9642151  9642161  9642173  9642203  9642211
9642223  9642229  9642233  9642251  9642263  9642287  9642293  9642301  9642307  9642319
9642323  9642341  9642371  9642377  9642389  9642397  9642401  9642419  9642461  9642463
9642499  9642541  9642583  9642593  9642599  9642601  9642613  9642617  9642623  9642637
9642641  9642653  9642679  9642683  9642701  9642713  9642719  9642751  9642769  9642799
9642803  9642811  9642821  9642827  9642839  9642863  9642869  9642887  9642889
9642907  9642929  9642931  9642949  9642967  9642973  9642989  9642991  9643031  9643033
9643043  9643057  9643069  9643079  9643129  9643163  9643181  9643213  9643247  9643259
9643261  9643289  9643321  9643327  9643351  9643357  9643363  9643391  9643427
9643441  9643453  9643483  9643493  9643531  9643537  9643541  9643547  9643549  9643553
9643559  9643577  9643603  9643661  9643663  9643669  9643691  9643703  9643723  9643729
9643763  9643771  9643801  9643807  9643813  9643819  9643867  9643871  9643873  9643901
9643903  9643927  9643937  9643943  9643961  9643973  9644003  9644009  9644021  9644053
9644057  9644093  9644099  9644101  9644111  9644119  9644147  9644149  9644179  9644183
9644189  9644197  9644203  9644207  9644227  9644263  9644273  9644303  9644333  9644359
9644363  9644377  9644387  9644461  9644483  9644489  9644519  9644539  9644561  9644573
9644587  9644633  9644641  9644653  9644669  9644707  9644731  9644741  9644743  9644749
9644777  9644779  9644783  9644801  9644809  9644811  9644821  9644839  9644861  9644867
9644879  9644891  9644897  9644903  9644909  9644911  9644941  9644959  9644977  9644983
9645007  9645017  9645067  9645079  9645091  9645101  9645107  9645113  9645131  9645133
9645149  9645157  9645169  9645173  9645191  9645193  9645203  9645221  9645241  9645263
9645281  9645283  9645289  9645299  9645319  9645329  9645343  9645353  9645367  9645401
9645413  9645437  9645451  9645469  9645479  9645499  9645509  9645529  9645539
9645541  9645577  9645589  9645593  9645607  9645611  9645637  9645653  9645659  9645667
9645677  9645739  9645761  9645767  9645781  9645791  9645827  9645829  9645833  9645859
9645871  9645907  9645913  9645917  9645931  9645949  9645959  9646003  9646037  9646079
9646081  9646093  9646099  9646103  9646121  9646141  9646151  9646163  9646181  9646199
9646201  9646213  9646229  9646249  9646261  9646271  9646277  9646283  9646289  9646291
9646297  9646303  9646309  9646313  9646321  9646337  9646339  9646367  9646387  9646397
9646423  9646457  9646501  9646513  9646523  9646537  9646541  9646543  9646561  9646597
9646607  9646613  9646619  9646631  9646639  9646643  9646669  9646691  9646711  9646717
9646733  9646753  9646771  9646783  9646801  9646817  9646843  9646883  9646907  9646933
9646951  9646953  9646957  9646961  9646963  9646969  9646979  9646981  9646991  9646993
9646997  9647021  9647039  9647059  9647069  9647081  9647087  9647153  9647161  9647171
9647207  9647213  9647221  9647237  9647251  9647257  9647291  9647317  9647369  9647371
9647377  9647389  9647399  9647411  9647413  9647447  9647453  9647467  9647489  9647501
9647509  9647527  9647543  9647569  9647579  9647581  9647591  9647597  9647623  9647647
9647707  9647711  9647723  9647731  9647761  9647767  9647773  9647777  9647779
9647819  9647849  9647873  9647881  9647887  9647893  9647909  9647929  9647987  9648011
9648031  9648047  9648101  9648103  9648127  9648137  9648139  9648151  9648167
9648179  9648193  9648209  9648217  9648229  9648239  9648241  9648251  9648253  9648259
9648277  9648307  9648311  9648323  9648341  9648343  9648361  9648377  9648421  9648427
9648473  9648481  9648547  9648557  9648563  9648587  9648589  9648593
9648607  9648659  9648671  9648679  9648689  9648701  9648733  9648739  9648787  9648791
9648811  9648839  9648857  9648887  9648889  9648901
9648907  9648923  9648949  9648953  9648997  9649001  9649009  9649027  9649033  9649039
9649043  9649061  9649069  9649097  9649099  9649109  9649117  9649177  9649181  9649187
9649203  9649219  9649247  9649249  9649261  9649271  9649301  9649303  9649307
9649313  9649327  9649337  9649357  9649361  9649379  9649403  9649417  9649447  9649481
9649513  9649553  9649559  9649567  9649571  9649583  9649589  9649603  9649609
9649639  9649667  9649669  9649729  9649747  9649753  9649769  9649781  9649789  9649793
9649799  9649819  9649847  9649867  9649877  9649901  9649909  9649919  9649921  9649973
9649979  9649987  9650023  9650027  9650051  9650063  9650117  9650149
9650159  9650167  9650171  9650183  9650191  9650213  9650219  9650227  9650231  9650273
9650281  9650287  9650299  9650321  9650341  9650351  9650371  9650387  9650401
9650411  9650467  9650503  9650513  9650519  9650549  9650551  9650567  9650569  9650573
9650609  9650617  9650623  9650681  9650737  9650759  9650761  9650779  9650789
9650813  9650831  9650843  9650891  9650923  9650941  9650983  9650987  9650989  9651001
9651011  9651029  9651041  9651073  9651091  9651119  9651133  9651167  9651179  9651181
9651253  9651269  9651281  9651289  9651331  9651367  9651381  9651391  9651401  9651407
9651419  9651437  9651457  9651491  9651503  9651517  9651533  9651539  9651541  9651547
9651553  9651557  9651581  9651589  9651599  9651611  9651637  9651643  9651647  9651659
9651673  9651679  9651683  9651689  9651727  9651749  9651781  9651797  9651799  9651833
9651839  9651871  9651877  9651893  9651911  9651913  9651919  9651923  9651959  9651977
9651979  9652007  9652033  9652043  9652051  9652063  9652103  9652147  9652151  9652163
9652169  9652177  9652183  9652193  9652199  9652229  9652231  9652241  9652259  9652289
9652303  9652309  9652327  9652337  9652351  9652367  9652393  9652397  9652403  9652411
9652417  9652421  9652441  9652453  9652463  9652477  9652483  9652529  9652537  9652541
9652543  9652561  9652637  9652639  9652649  9652681  9652693  9652723  9652733  9652739
9652759  9652763  9652781  9652789  9652793  9652849  9652859  9652861  9652871  9652897
9652901  9652913  9652919  9652921  9652927  9652961  9652963  9653003  9653071  9653099
9653131  9653141  9653153  9653179  9653191  9653213  9653243  9653309  9653333  9653339
9653351  9653363  9653381  9653383  9653393  9653407  9653417  9653419  9653429  9653443
9653453  9653489  9653507  9653513  9653519  9653531  9653587  9653599  9653621  9653641
9653663  9653687  9653701  9653717  9653747  9653789  9653821  9653827  9653837  9653851
9653857  9653873  9653899  9653923  9653933  9653939  9653971  9653981  9653999  9654017
9654019  9654023  9654041  9654067  9654091  9654107  9654131  9654133  9654143  9654149
9654163  9654167  9654191  9654193  9654209  9654221  9654241  9654247  9654263  9654329
9654331  9654341  9654349  9654371  9654377  9654383  9654397  9654433  9654443  9654473
9654479  9654493  9654497  9654517  9654529  9654553  9654563  9654577  9654629  9654637
9654647  9654649  9654677  9654683  9654703  9654707  9654731  9654737  9654739  9654751
```

```
9654763  9654769  9654781  9654791  9654797  9654823  9654889  9654899  9654913  9654923
9654943  9654947  9654959  9654961  9654973  9654977  9654989  9655003  9655007  9655013
9655027  9655033  9655067  9655073  9655109  9655123  9655127  9655157  9655159  9655207
9655223  9655237  9655253  9655267  9655273  9655277  9655279  9655309  9655333  9655367
9655391  9655411  9655421  9655447  9655453  9655489  9655493  9655501  9655517  9655523
9655559  9655577  9655589  9655603  9655619  9655621  9655627  9655651  9655661  9655673
9655687  9655697  9655717  9655721  9655729  9655733  9655741  9655757  9655759  9655769
9655777  9655799  9655801  9655829  9655843  9655859  9655861  9655889  9655901  9655907
9655967  9655979  9655981  9655991  9656027  9656029  9656039  9656041  9656057  9656069
9656083  9656089  9656093  9656099  9656111  9656131  9656167  9656177  9656203  9656281
9656321  9656347  9656359  9656377  9656393  9656453  9656461  9656473  9656489  9656501
9656539  9656551  9656557  9656587  9656611  9656627  9656651  9656671  9656753  9656783
9656789  9656819  9656821  9656827  9656851  9656863  9656869  9656887  9656909  9656917
9656939  9656947  9656981  9657001  9657007  9657013  9657023  9657047  9657091  9657101
9657107  9657113  9657143  9657157  9657161  9657163  9657191  9657209  9657211  9657233
9657239  9657247  9657251  9657253  9657269  9657281  9657287  9657293  9657311  9657331
9657341  9657353  9657359  9657367  9657397  9657433  9657437  9657459  9657467  9657463
9657467  9657497  9657503  9657521  9657553  9657563  9657569  9657577  9657619  9657653
9657679  9657691  9657707  9657763  9657769  9657761  9657773  9657779  9657799  9657787
9657793  9657799  9657811  9657821  9657839  9657847  9657863  9657881  9657937  9657943
9657959  9657961  9658003  9658007  9658021  9658037  9658043  9658049  9658079  9658087
9658093  9658097  9658109  9658127  9658133  9658139  9658151  9658153  9658211  9658219
9658277  9658291  9658301  9658331  9658333  9658351  9658357  9658361  9658373  9658393
9658399  9658409  9658423  9658447  9658447  9658463  9658469  9658471  9658487  9658489
9658513  9658541  9658553  9658559  9658573  9658589  9658603  9658609  9658633  9658687
9658697  9658709  9658723  9658751  9658837  9658853  9658861  9658889  9658927  9658939
9658961  9658993  9659021  9659029  9659033  9659051  9659099  9659123  9659131
9659147  9659159  9659161  9659171  9659173  9659203  9659227  9659269  9659297  9659311
9659327  9659339  9659341  9659359  9659371  9659381  9659387  9659389  9659423  9659453
9659483  9659491  9659497  9659509  9659513  9659537  9659549  9659561  9659593  9659603
9659633  9659647  9659653  9659711  9659719  9659729  9659731  9659737  9659753  9659759
9659761  9659773  9659803  9659827  9659831  9659851  9659857  9659891  9659911  9659921
9659953  9659959  9659963  9659981  9659983  9659989  9660019  9660043  9660089  9660107
9660109  9660139  9660173  9660179  9660191  9660193  9660197  9660221  9660223  9660263
9660271  9660283  9660319  9660323  9660349  9660353  9660359  9660377  9660383  9660397
9660401  9660407  9660419  9660421  9660433  9660463  9660467  9660487  9660533  9660557
9660559  9660571  9660577  9660587  9660611  9660613  9660617  9660643  9660647  9660653
9660659  9660661  9660689  9660691  9660701  9660727  9660731  9660769  9660817  9660821
9660841  9660863  9660869  9660881  9660901  9660907  9660979  9661009  9661009  9661013
9661019  9661037  9661079  9661087  9661109  9661129  9661153  9661159  9661163  9661187
9661189  9661207  9661231  9661261  9661277  9661303  9661313  9661319  9661339  9661349
9661361  9661373  9661391  9661397  9661409  9661417  9661439  9661441  9661459  9661489
9661507  9661511  9661517  9661523  9661537  9661567  9661571  9661579  9661583  9661637
9661667  9661681  9661703  9661709  9661711  9661733  9661753  9661759  9661777  9661783
9661787  9661829  9661849  9661853  9661859  9661867  9661871  9661889  9661913  9661919
9661943  9661957  9661969  9661979  9661991  9662021  9662063  9662071  9662123
9662129  9662131  9662153  9662161  9662179  9662201  9662227  9662243  9662269  9662293
9662311  9662321  9662329  9662363  9662381  9662383  9662399  9662407  9662437  9662447
9662449  9662479  9662491  9662509  9662519  9662537  9662551  9662561  9662581  9662617
9662629  9662633  9662663  9662671  9662677  9662687  9662689  9662693  9662699  9662701
9662711  9662729  9662759  9662761  9662767  9662797  9662869  9662899  9662911  9662927
9662951  9662971  9662981  9663023  9663053  9663091  9663107  9663127  9663131  9663161
9663169  9663187  9663217  9663223  9663233  9663257  9663271  9663299  9663301  9663307
9663319  9663337  9663349  9663373  9663391  9663403  9663449  9663469  9663481  9663499
9663503  9663523  9663527  9663539  9663553  9663581  9663587  9663629  9663677  9663679
9663683  9663713  9663721  9663727  9663737  9663743  9663763  9663779  9663791  9663917
9663923  9663937  9663961  9663977  9664003  9664009  9664043  9664051  9664063  9664091
9664097  9664129  9664153  9664183  9664223  9664231  9664247  9664273  9664283  9664309
9664321  9664339  9664349  9664367  9664399  9664411  9664423  9664427  9664429  9664451
9664463  9664471  9664477  9664519  9664537  9664553  9664579  9664583  9664601  9664621
9664631  9664651  9664661  9664679  9664691  9664693  9664717  9664727  9664729  9664741
9664757  9664771  9664793  9664813  9664841  9664843  9664847  9664867  9664871  9664873
9664877  9664883  9664903  9664909  9664913  9664927  9664937  9664957  9664969  9664973
9664997  9665039  9665041  9665063  9665069  9665107  9665113  9665137  9665141  9665143
9665189  9665209  9665269  9665287  9665291  9665297  9665309  9665329  9665339  9665363
9665377  9665387  9665393  9665407  9665423  9665429  9665431  9665437  9665441  9665449
9665479  9665497  9665501  9665507  9665519  9665527  9665567  9665603  9665609  9665641
9665653  9665657  9665701  9665713  9665723  9665731  9665749  9665767  9665827  9665833
9665837  9665863  9665891  9665923  9665933  9665939  9665947  9665951  9665959  9665969
9665983  9665987  9665993  9666001  9666031  9666043  9666053  9666061  9666073  9666091
9666101  9666109  9666131  9666143  9666169  9666197  9666227  9666247  9666257  9666259
9666277  9666301  9666311  9666313  9666323  9666331  9666337  9666343  9666347  9666373
9666401  9666403  9666409  9666427  9666457  9666467  9666473  9666479  9666491  9666533
9666551  9666563  9666571  9666577  9666589  9666623  9666661  9666689  9666707  9666719
9666743  9666757  9666779  9666781  9666799  9666817  9666821  9666847  9666851  9666887
9666901  9666911  9666929  9666941  9666989  9667001  9667003  9667057  9667079  9667081
9667109  9667111  9667139  9667159  9667187  9667193  9667201  9667211  9667223  9667241
9667247  9667277  9667279  9667283  9667297  9667313  9667321  9667331  9667379  9667393
9667421  9667433  9667439  9667451  9667453  9667459  9667481  9667499  9667501  9667529
9667531  9667583  9667597  9667607  9667633  9667639  9667661  9667663  9667667  9667673
9667711  9667717  9667727  9667729  9667739  9667769  9667793  9667807  9667811  9667837
9667859  9667871  9667873  9667889  9667891  9667913  9667919  9667927  9667927  9667943
9667943  9667963  9667993  9667997  9668003  9668011  9668039  9668051  9668059  9668081
9668111  9668117  9668123  9668147  9668171  9668177  9668207  9668213  9668221  9668261
9668273  9668279  9668293  9668297  9668341  9668353  9668363  9668369  9668371  9668377
9668387  9668401  9668429  9668431  9668453  9668471  9668479  9668521  9668537  9668539
9668551  9668557  9668591  9668599  9668639  9668647  9668651  9668677  9668689  9668719
9668741  9668761  9668773  9668779  9668783  9668819  9668821  9668833  9668873  9668881
```

```
9668899  9668909  9668921  9668933  9668941  9668959  9668969  9668987  9668999  9669001
9669013  9669019  9669041  9669053  9669059  9669061  9669083  9669091  9669103
9669113  9669137  9669139  9669167  9669181  9669197  9669199  9669203  9669217  9669221
9669259  9669287  9669299  9669307  9669329  9669337  9669343  9669377  9669389  9669391
9669397  9669403  9669409  9669421  9669431  9669433  9669487  9669529  9669547  9669559
9669571  9669577  9669593  9669599  9669607  9669619  9669623  9669631  9669661  9669677
9669707  9669713  9669739  9669767  9669773  9669811  9669823  9669851  9669859  9669887
9669899  9669901  9669929  9669931  9669937  9669941  9669953  9669997  9670013  9670019
9670057  9670099  9670123  9670163  9670187  9670207  9670217  9670223  9670231
9670273  9670279  9670291  9670303  9670307  9670319  9670321  9670343  9670351  9670363
9670403  9670421  9670429  9670439  9670457  9670459  9670483  9670499  9670537  9670541
9670613  9670621  9670663  9670699  9670723  9670733  9670747  9670769  9670781  9670789
9670811  9670823  9670831  9670849  9670877  9670883  9670907  9670919  9670931  9670933
9670937  9670987  9670993  9671021  9671033  9671047  9671059  9671071  9671083  9671093
9671099  9671117  9671149  9671159  9671161  9671183  9671197  9671251  9671257  9671261
9671267  9671273  9671303  9671377  9671381  9671401  9671429  9671447  9671479  9671503
9671527  9671533  9671537  9671539  9671561  9671567  9671573  9671581  9671591  9671593
9671621  9671639  9671647  9671663  9671677  9671687  9671731  9671743  9671747  9671749
9671771  9671791  9671807  9671813  9671821  9671863  9671867  9671869  9671881
9671887  9671923  9671951  9671953  9671971  9672011  9672017  9672041  9672043  9672067
9672077  9672079  9672101  9672107  9672127  9672137  9672149  9672163  9672191  9672199
9672233  9672277  9672287  9672293  9672317  9672319  9672323  9672329  9672331  9672359
9672361  9672367  9672373  9672389  9672391  9672409  9672419  9672437  9672449  9672469
9672491  9672493  9672497  9672511  9672557  9672617  9672629  9672661  9672683  9672703
9672727  9672749  9672757  9672763  9672781  9672791  9672823  9672841  9672851  9672853
9672869  9672917  9672941  9672973  9673003  9673043  9673049  9673057  9673063  9673093
9673127  9673129  9673177  9673201  9673207  9673219  9673231  9673247  9673249  9673267
9673273  9673343  9673351  9673361  9673369  9673379  9673387  9673397  9673439  9673481
9673483  9673487  9673511  9673523  9673529  9673541  9673553  9673579  9673583  9673597
9673607  9673627  9673649  9673669  9673673  9673691  9673693  9673709  9673711  9673723
9673747  9673757  9673771  9673801  9673803  9673819  9673837  9673841  9673847
9673871  9673879  9673883  9673913  9673919  9673921  9673949  9673967  9673997  9673999
9674009  9674017  9674039  9674087  9674089  9674107  9674141  9674149  9674153  9674177
9674209  9674221  9674227  9674239  9674257  9674267  9674281  9674299  9674303  9674311
9674317  9674321  9674359  9674369  9674381  9674383  9674437  9674447  9674459  9674503
9674507  9674521  9674537  9674543  9674551  9674557  9674579  9674611  9674627  9674633
9674641  9674653  9674659  9674663  9674669  9674681  9674701  9674711  9674741  9674747
9674773  9674801  9674813  9674827  9674837  9674849  9674851  9674869  9674911  9674939
9674953  9674999  9675013  9675037  9675053  9675059  9675079  9675089  9675109
9675119  9675137  9675151  9675187  9675257  9675277  9675293  9675307  9675319  9675359
9675361  9675443  9675451  9675481  9675509  9675519  9675551  9675553  9675557  9675569
9675577  9675593  9675599  9675623  9675629  9675649  9675691  9675697  9675707  9675761
9675767  9675779  9675781  9675797  9675803  9675811  9675857  9675859  9675863  9675871
9675889  9675947  9675961  9675979  9675983  9676001  9676019  9676021  9676027  9676087
9676091  9676099  9676141  9676159  9676171  9676181  9676189  9676201  9676217  9676229
9676243  9676253  9676267  9676273  9676291  9676321  9676357  9676363  9676421  9676427
9676439  9676463  9676477  9676483  9676543  9676549  9676607  9676627  9676651  9676657
9676663  9676669  9676673  9676679  9676699  9676717  9676729  9676741  9676753  9676787
9676801  9676811  9676829  9676831  9676841  9676847  9676889  9676903  9676907  9676913
9676937  9676949  9676957  9676963  9676967  9676969  9676987  9676999  9677027  9677047
9677071  9677077  9677123  9677191  9677197  9677201  9677203  9677209  9677221
9677249  9677257  9677281  9677287  9677293  9677299  9677303  9677309  9677321  9677341
9677351  9677377  9677383  9677389  9677417  9677453  9677477  9677489  9677491  9677501
9677509  9677519  9677557  9677567  9677587  9677621  9677651  9677653  9677671  9677713
9677729  9677749  9677753  9677761  9677803  9677809  9677819  9677861  9677873  9677891
9677893  9677923  9677937  9677953  9677999  9678007  9678013  9678017  9678023  9678029
9678037  9678047  9678061  9678073  9678079  9678131  9678133  9678143  9678181  9678187
9678191  9678197  9678203  9678209  9678233  9678241  9678247  9678259  9678269  9678271
9678299  9678323  9678329  9678341  9678343  9678367  9678379  9678401  9678407  9678439
9678499  9678503  9678509  9678511  9678517  9678521  9678577  9678589  9678611  9678623
9678629  9678637  9678671  9678679  9678689  9678737  9678743  9678749  9678751
9678761  9678787  9678821  9678833  9678841  9678853  9678857  9678863  9678901  9678947
9678959  9678971  9678973  9678979  9679003  9679027  9679049  9679057  9679063  9679073
9679081  9679121  9679129  9679141  9679147  9679169  9679181  9679183  9679193  9679199
9679213  9679247  9679249  9679277  9679279  9679291  9679331  9679333  9679349  9679357
9679361  9679367  9679381  9679387  9679393  9679399  9679421  9679441  9679447  9679457
9679463  9679469  9679489  9679513  9679517  9679561  9679577  9679597  9679609  9679627
9679661  9679667  9679673  9679679  9679751  9679753  9679771  9679793  9679799  9679801
9679807  9679811  9679819  9679847  9679853  9679861  9679871  9679877  9679889  9679909
9679913  9679933  9679937  9679951  9679981  9680003  9680023  9680057  9680087  9680119
9680131  9680137  9680173  9680197  9680201  9680221  9680239  9680257  9680267
9680299  9680303  9680351  9680357  9680369  9680393  9680413  9680431  9680467  9680471
9680477  9680479  9680483  9680491  9680501  9680509  9680521  9680527  9680533  9680537
9680549  9680579  9680591  9680623  9680641  9680647  9680659  9680663  9680689  9680743
9680771  9680789  9680807  9680843  9680893  9680903  9680929  9680947  9680963
9680969  9680971  9680989  9681011  9681017  9681019  9681029  9681071  9681097
9681101  9681103  9681131  9681163  9681167  9681169  9681179  9681193  9681223  9681227
9681233  9681257  9681263  9681277  9681281  9681283  9681307  9681311  9681319  9681341
9681349  9681359  9681361  9681401  9681409  9681421  9681437  9681443  9681481  9681499
9681533  9681547  9681559  9681569  9681571  9681587  9681589  9681611  9681613  9681629
9681649  9681677  9681709  9681739  9681757  9681761  9681769  9681797  9681799  9681803
9681809  9681829  9681883  9681899  9681907  9681913  9681929  9681937  9681941  9681967
9681977  9681983  9681989  9682007  9682019  9682051  9682067  9682087  9682091
9682111  9682133  9682139  9682147  9682151  9682171  9682177  9682187  9682193  9682207
9682213  9682217  9682223  9682243  9682297  9682303  9682327  9682339  9682369
9682391  9682427  9682429  9682481  9682499  9682511  9682513  9682553  9682583  9682597
9682613  9682619  9682627  9682649  9682663  9682691  9682693  9682703  9682727  9682733
9682759  9682763  9682811  9682817  9682823  9682853  9682859  9682889  9682901  9682919
9682961  9682963  9682973  9682991  9682993  9682997  9683033  9683039  9683053  9683059
```

```
9683077 9683099 9683123 9683137 9683147 9683171 9683189 9683197 9683203 9683209
9683221 9683249 9683263 9683279 9683287 9683321 9683327 9683347 9683351 9683431
9683449 9683459 9683461 9683543 9683573 9683579 9683599 9683627 9683633 9683647
9683657 9683671 9683699 9683717 9683719 9683777 9683803 9683809 9683813 9683819
9683837 9683881 9683909 9683911 9683951 9683959 9683963 9683969 9683983 9684011
9684013 9684019 9684023 9684049 9684089 9684097 9684133 9684137 9684149 9684193
9684239 9684293 9684313 9684317 9684341 9684349 9684359 9684361 9684371 9684377
9684379 9684413 9684419 9684427 9684443 9684457 9684461 9684469 9684511 9684517
9684527 9684557 9684583 9684593 9684599 9684601 9684607 9684629 9684641 9684659
9684683 9684707 9684709 9684721 9684739 9684749 9684769 9684793 9684797 9684799
9684809 9684823 9684827 9684839 9684853 9684877 9684881 9684887 9684907 9684923
9684931 9684947 9684959 9684967 9684973 9685007 9685033 9685057 9685063 9685127
9685133 9685141 9685171 9685177 9685211 9685213 9685229 9685241 9685259 9685267
9685271 9685279 9685303 9685327 9685349 9685387 9685439 9685441 9685451
9685463 9685477 9685483 9685513 9685537 9685541 9685561 9685579 9685583 9685589
9685639 9685651 9685661 9685667 9685679 9685693 9685703 9685723 9685727 9685757
9685759 9685771 9685787 9685813 9685817 9685831 9685843 9685847 9685861 9685889
9685931 9685933 9685939 9685969 9685979 9685987 9685993 9685997 9686003 9686041
9686057 9686063 9686077 9686081 9686093 9686113 9686153 9686161 9686189 9686191
9686213 9686221 9686233 9686239 9686249 9686273 9686279 9686321 9686329 9686357
9686359 9686363 9686393 9686399 9686401 9686407 9686419 9686461 9686497 9686507
9686527 9686531 9686543 9686557 9686581 9686623 9686629 9686647 9686669 9686689
9686707 9686759 9686767 9686773 9686777 9686791 9686819 9686837 9686839 9686851
9686869 9686879 9686919 9686921 9686951 9686977 9687001 9687019 9687023 9687043
9687053 9687077 9687089 9687091 9687109 9687137 9687143 9687187 9687211 9687233
9687241 9687257 9687281 9687299 9687313 9687317 9687323 9687361 9687367 9687389
9687401 9687443 9687449 9687493 9687523 9687527 9687539 9687553 9687563 9687571
9687583 9687589 9687641 9687647 9687661 9687697 9687703 9687709 9687719 9687721
9687751 9687787 9687791 9687797 9687809 9687823 9687833 9687851 9687877 9687889
9687911 9687913 9687919 9687947 9687989 9688031 9688051 9688057 9688067 9688097
9688099 9688103 9688109 9688111 9688127 9688139 9688141 9688169 9688183 9688187
9688193 9688201 9688243 9688253 9688279 9688297 9688319 9688361 9688369 9688379
9688381 9688391 9688397 9688403 9688409 9688411 9688417 9688421 9688463 9688477
9688501 9688517 9688531 9688571 9688577 9688579 9688591 9688597 9688619 9688649
9688663 9688687 9688699 9688711 9688739 9688741 9688747 9688753 9688781 9688799
9688817 9688859 9688867 9688897 9688907 9688919 9688927 9688933 9688951 9688961
9688967 9688969 9688979 9688981 9689021 9689033 9689047 9689059 9689077 9689093
9689101 9689117 9689123 9689131 9689137 9689149 9689177 9689189 9689213 9689231
9689237 9689249 9689263 9689283 9689297 9689347 9689357 9689359 9689369 9689377
9689387 9689389 9689401 9689419 9689437 9689443 9689447 9689461 9689479 9689483
9689531 9689533 9689539 9689549 9689591 9689599 9689623 9689633 9689651 9689681
9689689 9689707 9689717 9689731 9689767 9689891 9689929 9689957 9689987
9689993 9690029 9690059 9690067 9690071 9690077 9690091 9690097 9690103 9690139
9690211 9690217 9690251 9690253 9690257 9690281 9690287 9690299 9690313 9690341
9690347 9690349 9690353 9690371 9690407 9690419 9690431 9690433 9690451 9690469
9690479 9690491 9690497 9690503 9690517 9690529 9690533 9690539 9690547 9690557
9690563 9690581 9690607 9690619 9690623 9690641 9690671 9690673 9690701 9690713
9690721 9690743 9690749 9690773 9690787 9690803 9690829 9690841 9690907
9691001 9691061 9691091 9691093 9691111 9691117 9691141 9691147 9691183 9691193
9691223 9691237 9691247 9691267 9691277 9691291 9691327 9691337 9691351 9691393
9691403 9691417 9691427 9691433 9691439 9691459 9691471 9691489 9691519 9691523
9691543 9691559 9691573 9691589 9691609 9691639 9691673 9691679 9691697 9691723
9691733 9691757 9691789 9691807 9691811 9691831 9691861 9691879 9691907 9691909
9691931 9691937 9691943 9691963 9691987 9691999 9692017 9692021 9692027 9692029
9692041 9692047 9692051 9692063 9692069 9692083 9692087 9692099 9692117 9692141
9692149 9692161 9692183 9692191 9692221 9692231 9692233 9692239 9692251 9692279
9692311 9692323 9692341 9692383 9692393 9692399 9692401 9692411 9692437 9692443
9692447 9692467 9692497 9692503 9692509 9692519 9692521 9692537 9692549 9692569
9692593 9692611 9692621 9692633 9692651 9692659 9692663 9692701 9692719 9692741
9692743 9692773 9692783 9692797 9692803 9692807 9692819 9692827 9692833 9692861
9692899 9692923 9692929 9692939 9692981 9692983 9692999 9693007 9693031 9693037
9693053 9693067 9693107 9693119 9693137 9693193 9693197 9693209 9693217 9693251
9693259 9693263 9693289 9693293 9693301 9693311 9693317 9693323 9693353 9693367
9693377 9693389 9693403 9693407 9693413 9693457 9693469 9693473 9693503 9693517
9693521 9693539 9693577 9693583 9693623 9693631 9693637 9693659 9693661 9693713
9693727 9693737 9693763 9693821 9693829 9693839 9693841 9693851 9693863 9693881
9693899 9693907 9693913 9693947 9693967 9693977 9693989 9693991 9694007 9694021
9694031 9694057 9694097 9694121 9694141 9694211 9694213 9694249 9694253
9694271 9694273 9694309 9694331 9694337 9694417 9694429 9694459 9694469 9694499
9694501 9694513 9694561 9694571 9694577 9694589 9694603 9694621 9694627 9694637
9694639 9694667 9694673 9694679 9694691 9694697 9694717 9694733 9694739 9694759
9694793 9694843 9694849 9694877 9694931 9694933 9694963 9694973 9694987 9694991
9695011 9695017 9695027 9695041 9695051 9695069 9695087 9695089 9695099 9695109
9695129 9695143 9695159 9695171 9695183 9695197 9695233 9695243 9695249 9695267
9695269 9695293 9695299 9695327 9695333 9695341 9695347 9695359 9695381 9695417
9695419 9695429 9695431 9695447 9695459 9695461 9695471 9695473 9695501 9695507
9695537 9695549 9695563 9695573 9695603 9695617 9695633 9695669 9695687 9695701
9695711 9695713 9695731 9695737 9695747 9695753 9695759 9695789 9695809 9695891
9695921 9695923 9695953 9695971 9695993 9696007 9696017 9696031 9696059 9696067
9696073 9696077 9696091 9696097 9696139 9696157 9696229 9696277 9696287 9696293
9696299 9696301 9696311 9696359 9696361 9696367 9696373 9696391 9696431 9696433
9696439 9696451 9696481 9696487 9696493 9696503 9696529 9696559 9696563 9696569
9696571 9696601 9696607 9696611 9696619 9696637 9696649 9696667 9696679 9696689
9696691 9696703 9696719 9696733 9696763 9696773 9696781 9696793 9696811 9696829
9696833 9696839 9696847 9696853 9696871 9696877 9696889 9696901 9696913 9696937
9696979 9696983 9697003 9697019 9697027 9697043 9697081 9697091 9697133 9697171
9697183 9697217 9697229 9697243 9697249 9697253 9697267 9697273 9697297 9697301
9697309 9697319 9697333 9697343 9697399 9697411 9697427 9697439 9697447 9697459
9697477 9697481 9697511 9697549 9697573 9697579 9697603 9697691 9697711 9697729
```

```
9697739  9697801  9697817  9697829  9697843  9697879  9697907  9697937  9697957  9697967
9697979  9697991  9698021  9698023  9698053  9698069  9698083  9698089  9698131  9698137
9698141  9698149  9698167  9698173  9698191  9698219  9698233  9698237  9698239  9698251
9698291  9698321  9698327  9698333  9698357  9698363  9698371  9698393  9698413  9698453
9698489  9698501  9698519  9698527  9698537  9698543  9698621  9698627  9698639  9698659
9698713  9698737  9698747  9698761  9698783  9698791  9698803  9698809  9698839  9698851
9698861  9698867  9698879  9698957  9698981  9699007  9699013  9699017  9699023  9699047
9699071  9699073  9699089  9699113  9699133  9699141  9699161  9699191  9699199  9699203
9699211  9699233  9699251  9699289  9699323  9699331  9699341  9699359  9699377  9699409
9699433  9699449  9699451  9699461  9699509  9699511  9699533  9699563  9699567  9699593
9699611  9699623  9699631  9699637  9699643  9699647  9699649  9699653  9699667  9699713
9699727  9699731  9699733  9699749  9699763  9699769  9699773  9699799  9699803  9699817
9699827  9699841  9699853  9699887  9699889  9699913  9699917  9699919  9699923  9699929
9699941  9699953  9699959  9699973  9700003  9700027  9700039  9700063  9700073  9700079
9700099  9700111  9700139  9700147  9700153  9700169  9700213  9700247  9700289  9700307
9700337  9700357  9700381  9700417  9700429  9700433  9700441  9700447  9700451  9700463
9700487  9700501  9700511  9700519  9700541  9700543  9700567  9700571  9700573  9700577
9700589  9700597  9700601  9700609  9700627  9700631  9700637  9700651  9700657  9700709
9700717  9700787  9700789  9700813  9700837  9700879  9700883  9700907  9700913  9700927
9700939  9700967  9700981  9701011  9701017  9701063  9701099  9701113  9701117  9701137
9701161  9701177  9701179  9701201  9701207  9701213  9701231  9701243  9701287  9701291
9701333  9701347  9701383  9701413  9701431  9701443  9701473  9701477  9701479  9701513
9701551  9701563  9701567  9701581  9701603  9701633  9701641  9701663  9701677  9701687
9701711  9701713  9701717  9701719  9701737  9701743  9701759  9701767  9701771  9701777
9701803  9701819  9701821  9701827  9701831  9701833  9701873  9701891  9701927  9701933
9701957  9701963  9701969  9701971  9701983  9701999  9702041  9702083  9702107  9702149
9702151  9702167  9702181  9702191  9702193  9702197  9702229  9702239  9702247  9702271
9702299  9702307  9702311  9702313  9702317  9702361  9702377  9702397  9702401  9702403
9702421  9702431  9702437  9702449  9702487  9702509  9702557  9702571  9702601  9702607
9702611  9702629  9702677  9702697  9702713  9702743  9702761  9702809  9702811  9702829
9702839  9702851  9702877  9702883  9702899  9702919  9702929  9702943  9702961  9702967
9702983  9703013  9703021  9703049  9703063  9703069  9703117  9703121  9703123  9703147
9703151  9703153  9703163  9703223  9703231  9703237  9703261  9703271  9703273  9703283
9703297  9703303  9703307  9703363  9703367  9703387  9703391  9703427  9703457  9703459
9703483  9703489  9703501  9703517  9703523  9703531  9703541  9703567  9703579  9703597
9703609  9703619  9703627  9703643  9703663  9703669  9703691  9703693  9703709  9703711
9703739  9703747  9703763  9703781  9703849  9703873  9703877  9703891  9703901  9703913
9703919  9703931  9703933  9703997  9704021  9704029  9704033  9704039  9704047  9704069
9704113  9704153  9704163  9704173  9704207  9704243  9704251  9704257  9704273  9704309
9704311  9704329  9704363  9704371  9704377  9704381  9704389  9704393  9704407  9704423
9704441  9704479  9704483  9704489  9704491  9704507  9704521  9704543  9704561  9704567
9704593  9704599  9704621  9704623  9704657  9704663  9704699  9704711  9704731  9704743
9704759  9704771  9704789  9704797  9704809  9704813  9704819  9704831  9704833  9704861
9704867  9704887  9704899  9704911  9704923  9704939  9704951  9704957  9705001  9705013
9705023  9705037  9705043  9705083  9705089  9705097  9705121  9705133  9705167  9705193
9705209  9705239  9705247  9705253  9705259  9705271  9705329  9705331  9705337  9705347
9705349  9705383  9705389  9705407  9705427  9705431  9705481  9705499  9705503  9705533
9705541  9705601  9705607  9705611  9705617  9705667  9705671  9705719  9705727  9705733
9705751  9705757  9705767  9705769  9705791  9705799  9705847  9705853  9705859  9705887
9705901  9705907  9705911  9705947  9705961  9705973  9705989  9705991  9706001  9706043
9706057  9706061  9706063  9706087  9706091  9706117  9706127  9706139  9706141  9706157
9706159  9706171  9706181  9706187  9706189  9706199  9706219  9706237  9706241  9706243
9706273  9706289  9706297  9706309  9706349  9706351  9706363  9706373  9706399  9706409
9706423  9706427  9706447  9706451  9706457  9706471  9706513  9706517  9706523  9706531
9706553  9706577  9706589  9706603  9706649  9706657  9706661  9706681  9706687  9706699
9706703  9706721  9706771  9706799  9706831  9706841  9706843  9706867  9706877  9706889
9706901  9706927  9706979  9706981  9706993  9707023  9707041  9707057  9707059  9707063
9707141  9707143  9707149  9707167  9707171  9707177  9707179  9707189  9707227  9707251
9707263  9707267  9707273  9707281  9707287  9707297  9707317  9707339  9707351  9707359
9707381  9707387  9707389  9707393  9707407  9707437  9707443  9707471  9707473  9707483
9707501  9707507  9707519  9707531  9707567  9707591  9707603  9707623  9707627  9707641
9707657  9707669  9707671  9707699  9707701  9707741  9707767  9707773  9707783  9707807
9707813  9707827  9707843  9707849  9707869  9707891  9707911  9707917  9707933  9707947
9707977  9707987  9707989  9708113  9708121  9708137  9708143  9708187  9708191  9708227
9708229  9708247  9708253  9708263  9708287  9708289  9708299  9708311  9708313  9708317
9708331  9708341  9708343  9708373  9708383  9708397  9708421  9708431  9708493  9708499
9708529  9708551  9708557  9708571  9708607  9708617  9708631  9708661  9708679  9708697
9708701  9708709  9708719  9708731  9708749  9708757  9708767  9708773  9708799  9708863
9708869  9708871  9708893  9708899  9708901  9708917  9708949  9708971  9708973  9708977
9708991  9709003  9709009  9709027  9709033  9709039  9709061  9709069  9709079  9709081
9709093  9709111  9709153  9709157  9709163  9709171  9709181  9709199  9709237  9709253
9709283  9709291  9709303  9709313  9709331  9709339  9709367  9709369  9709379  9709387
9709391  9709411  9709477  9709481  9709493  9709507  9709517  9709537  9709543  9709559
9709597  9709619  9709621  9709631  9709639  9709663  9709673  9709691  9709723  9709757
9709781  9709813  9709823  9709849  9709859  9709881  9709897  9709901  9709927  9709937
9709939  9709951  9709957  9709961  9709963  9709993  9710003  9710011  9710017  9710033
9710053  9710137  9710147  9710177  9710191  9710219  9710221  9710237  9710251  9710263
9710269  9710291  9710297  9710299  9710321  9710339  9710381  9710411  9710413  9710461
9710473  9710489  9710497  9710513  9710521  9710527  9710537  9710551  9710557  9710567
9710609  9710611  9710627  9710629  9710641  9710663  9710707  9710711  9710747  9710783
9710797  9710803  9710821  9710839  9710849  9710851  9710863  9710873  9710903  9710923
9710933  9710941  9710947  9710951  9710959  9710977  9710993  9711007  9711019  9711041
9711043  9711059  9711061  9711089  9711113  9711121  9711151  9711157  9711179  9711227
9711239  9711241  9711253  9711257  9711269  9711271  9711283  9711293  9711307  9711311
9711323  9711333  9711367  9711371  9711379  9711389  9711397  9711399  9711407  9711419
9711431  9711467  9711473  9711479  9711503  9711511  9711521  9711523  9711529  9711557
9711571  9711601  9711613  9711617  9711619  9711643  9711659  9711733  9711739  9711787
9711799  9711809  9711829  9711833  9711841  9711853  9711859  9711881  9711883  9711893
9711899  9711901  9711941  9711967  9711971  9711979  9711991  9712007  9712051  9712057
```

```
9712081  9712103  9712111  9712133  9712147  9712189  9712201  9712231  9712259  9712271
9712273  9712289  9712309  9712333  9712337  9712343  9712349  9712379  9712397  9712399
9712421  9712441  9712447  9712459  9712489  9712499  9712501  9712519  9712543  9712561
9712567  9712583  9712589  9712609  9712669  9712673  9712679  9712687  9712697  9712699
9712751  9712753  9712771  9712799  9712811  9712817  9712849  9712861  9712873  9712897
9712921  9712931  9712949  9712957  9712961  9712979  9712987  9713017  9713021  9713059
9713083  9713101  9713113  9713117  9713131  9713147  9713149  9713159  9713167  9713177
9713201  9713219  9713279  9713303  9713309  9713311  9713339  9713359  9713369  9713381
9713401  9713419  9713441  9713467  9713471  9713507  9713527  9713531  9713563  9713569
9713591  9713623  9713629  9713653  9713689  9713699  9713707  9713713  9713729  9713741
9713773  9713789  9713791  9713813  9713839  9713863  9713887  9713897  9713903  9713909
9713911  9713917  9713939  9713947  9713969  9713989  9714031  9714041  9714049  9714053
9714059  9714097  9714109  9714137  9714163  9714169  9714179  9714197  9714227  9714241
9714247  9714251  9714277  9714323  9714337  9714347  9714359  9714371  9714373  9714379
9714389  9714413  9714421  9714437  9714457  9714473  9714479  9714493  9714503  9714511
9714521  9714559  9714577  9714587  9714589  9714613  9714619  9714629  9714641  9714659
9714673  9714697  9714703  9714721  9714741  9714751  9714823  9714839  9714863  9714869
9714883  9714923  9714941  9714961  9714983  9715009  9715037  9715049  9715103  9715157
9715169  9715187  9715219  9715231  9715241  9715243  9715259  9715297  9715301  9715309
9715331  9715333  9715339  9715367  9715393  9715397  9715421  9715429  9715439  9715451
9715477  9715487  9715501  9715513  9715523  9715529  9715543  9715547  9715553  9715579
9715613  9715639  9715663  9715697  9715709  9715723  9715747  9715757  9715759  9715763
9715799  9715817  9715831  9715861  9715873  9715879  9715883  9715931  9715963  9715967
9715969  9715991  9716017  9716023  9716071  9716107  9716111  9716117  9716123  9716153
9716167  9716171  9716183  9716207  9716209  9716233  9716251  9716257  9716269  9716293
9716321  9716351  9716359  9716381  9716383  9716431  9716449  9716453  9716477  9716491
9716501  9716513  9716569  9716579  9716599  9716617  9716621  9716627  9716633  9716647
9716659  9716677  9716687  9716689  9716701  9716717  9716719  9716731  9716747  9716767
9716789  9716801  9716807  9716821  9716851  9716867  9716929  9716947  9716951  9716969
9717007  9717049  9717083  9717091  9717107  9717119  9717143  9717193  9717221  9717223
9717259  9717263  9717277  9717289  9717299  9717307  9717313  9717317  9717377  9717397
9717401  9717403  9717413  9717439  9717443  9717467  9717469  9717481  9717503  9717509
9717511  9717517  9717551  9717559  9717593  9717599  9717611  9717619  9717623  9717641
9717647  9717649  9717689  9717691  9717733  9717739  9717749  9717781  9717811  9717839
9717857  9717899  9717901  9717919  9717923  9717959  9717977  9717989  9717997  9718019
9718021  9718039  9718057  9718081  9718109  9718123  9718147  9718151  9718157  9718171
9718183  9718187  9718193  9718199  9718211  9718217  9718297  9718307  9718327  9718361
9718381  9718391  9718427  9718453  9718477  9718483  9718493  9718507  9718529  9718537
9718547  9718571  9718573  9718591  9718609  9718649  9718661  9718669  9718717  9718727
9718733  9718777  9718783  9718789  9718829  9718831  9718837  9718843  9718913  9718931
9718939  9718979  9718987  9718993  9718999  9719029  9719033  9719057  9719063  9719071
9719081  9719107  9719111  9719113  9719137  9719141  9719167  9719209  9719219  9719231
9719249  9719251  9719267  9719309  9719327  9719329  9719351  9719377  9719387  9719401
9719407  9719429  9719441  9719453  9719471  9719477  9719531  9719539  9719569  9719573
9719579  9719581  9719587  9719599  9719603  9719609  9719651  9719657  9719701  9719707
9719729  9719737  9719761  9719797  9719851  9719867  9719873  9719893  9719909  9719917
9719947  9719951  9719977  9719981  9719989  9720031  9720037  9720043  9720083  9720089
9720097  9720103  9720119  9720121  9720149  9720163  9720197  9720203  9720223  9720247
9720259  9720281  9720299  9720301  9720317  9720353  9720371  9720377  9720383  9720407
9720433  9720437  9720439  9720443  9720449  9720463  9720479  9720497  9720521  9720523
9720547  9720551  9720589  9720619  9720631  9720653  9720661  9720673  9720727  9720757
9720769  9720773  9720791  9720797  9720803  9720817  9720827  9720833  9720839  9720857
9720863  9720883  9720901  9720911  9720917  9720937  9720959  9721013  9721031  9721039
9721067  9721069  9721079  9721081  9721087  9721091  9721123  9721133  9721147  9721163
9721169  9721181  9721183  9721189  9721199  9721241  9721247  9721273  9721301  9721319
9721357  9721367  9721373  9721421  9721423  9721427  9721429  9721441  9721451  9721477
9721511  9721513  9721519  9721529  9721561  9721573  9721577  9721589  9721609  9721643
9721667  9721687  9721697  9721703  9721717  9721721  9721727  9721759  9721763  9721771
9721781  9721783  9721793  9721813  9721823  9721837  9721849  9721853  9721867  9721871
9721883  9721891  9721897  9721919  9721927  9721937  9721951  9721969  9721979  9721991
9722051  9722071  9722087  9722107  9722117  9722137  9722177  9722179  9722191  9722201
9722203  9722233  9722269  9722287  9722299  9722309  9722329  9722333  9722347  9722387
9722389  9722411  9722413  9722441  9722459  9722477  9722483  9722507  9722513  9722549
9722579  9722591  9722597  9722599  9722611  9722621  9722639  9722641  9722659  9722677
9722681  9722693  9722723  9722771  9722789  9722807  9722819  9722821  9722833  9722837
9722879  9722887  9722893  9722939  9722957  9722959  9722969  9722981  9723001  9723011
9723013  9723017  9723019  9723029  9723053  9723059  9723071  9723121  9723137  9723179
9723211  9723229  9723239  9723251  9723253  9723271  9723277  9723281  9723283  9723317
9723331  9723349  9723391  9723397  9723401  9723403  9723409  9723419  9723431  9723449
9723451  9723479  9723487  9723523  9723529  9723551  9723577  9723617  9723631  9723647
9723653  9723661  9723667  9723691  9723697  9723709  9723713  9723757  9723761  9723767
9723773  9723797  9723799  9723803  9723809  9723821  9723829  9723841  9723851  9723853
9723869  9723887  9723907  9723907  9723937  9723941  9723943  9723979  9723997
9724021  9724061  9724079  9724087  9724097  9724103  9724129  9724151  9724171  9724201
9724207  9724213  9724223  9724241  9724259  9724277  9724279  9724283  9724291  9724327
9724343  9724349  9724411  9724427  9724433  9724457  9724471  9724487  9724489  9724531
9724543  9724553  9724573  9724601  9724633  9724643  9724661  9724703  9724709  9724717
9724727  9724733  9724769  9724801  9724823  9724843  9724823  9724873  9724879  9724919
9724921  9724927  9724937  9724961  9724993  9725033  9725039  9725059  9725087  9725141
9725143  9725153  9725161  9725171  9725197  9725213  9725231  9725239  9725257  9725269
9725273  9725327  9725347  9725357  9725393  9725399  9725407  9725431  9725437  9725449
9725459  9725461  9725467  9725489  9725491  9725531  9725539  9725563  9725567  9725591
9725609  9725621  9725629  9725633  9725641  9725647  9725671  9725687  9725707  9725713
9725731  9725741  9725753  9725801  9725809  9725827  9725839  9725873  9725879  9725923
9725939  9725951  9725953  9725957  9725959  9726001  9726007  9726011  9726019  9726029
9726071  9726089  9726097  9726109  9726121  9726137  9726149  9726151  9726161  9726163
9726173  9726191  9726221  9726229  9726239  9726257  9726259  9726289  9726313  9726319
9726337  9726359  9726371  9726391  9726403  9726413  9726419  9726433  9726463  9726469
9726473  9726487  9726491  9726517  9726547  9726551  9726569  9726617  9726623  9726649
```

```
9726667 9726683 9726707 9726709 9726713 9726733 9726749 9726751 9726763 9726767
9726779 9726781 9726797 9726809 9726811 9726817 9726823 9726883 9726911 9726943
9726947 9726949 9726961 9726971 9726973 9726989 9726991 9727013 9727021 9727027
9727079 9727103 9727129 9727139 9727141 9727163 9727169 9727181 9727187 9727199
9727219 9727231 9727241 9727253 9727279 9727283 9727303 9727313 9727343 9727363
9727369 9727391 9727427 9727429 9727453 9727463 9727489 9727493 9727541 9727547
9727579 9727603 9727649 9727651 9727657 9727661 9727681 9727687 9727693 9727699
9727709 9727747 9727771 9727787 9727799 9727811 9727841 9727843 9727871 9727889
9727903 9727951 9727957 9727973 9727997 9727999 9728009 9728023 9728027 9728039
9728051 9728071 9728123 9728129 9728143 9728153 9728167 9728177 9728197 9728231
9728249 9728261 9728263 9728269 9728273 9728281 9728291 9728317 9728321 9728339
9728371 9728377 9728401 9728417 9728419 9728423 9728429 9728431 9728441 9728443
9728489 9728497 9728503 9728519 9728527 9728533 9728557 9728567 9728591 9728597
9728611 9728617 9728639 9728651 9728681 9728729 9728731 9728737 9728753 9728759
9728773 9728791 9728801 9728827 9728837 9728843 9728861 9728867 9728881 9728897
9728899 9728903 9728909 9728921 9728933 9728941 9729017 9729037 9729053 9729067
9729091 9729101 9729103 9729127 9729131 9729143 9729149 9729163 9729169 9729173
9729191 9729193 9729211 9729217 9729227 9729241 9729283 9729289 9729361 9729371
9729373 9729397 9729427 9729469 9729479 9729487 9729493 9729497 9729541 9729553
9729571 9729613 9729619 9729641 9729647 9729649 9729677 9729679 9729697 9729743
9729757 9729791 9729803 9729817 9729821 9729829 9729857 9729859 9729869 9729871
9729887 9729913 9729917 9729931 9729947 9729949 9729953 9729961 9729983 9729991
9730003 9730013 9730031 9730043 9730087 9730093 9730099 9730117 9730121 9730129
9730141 9730153 9730163 9730177 9730181 9730183 9730199 9730207 9730229 9730241
9730247 9730291 9730319 9730333 9730349 9730367 9730381 9730387 9730393 9730423
9730449 9730471 9730493 9730499 9730529 9730531 9730547 9730577 9730597 9730601
9730607 9730627 9730639 9730649 9730657 9730673 9730691 9730697 9730709 9730711
9730723 9730727 9730729 9730751 9730753 9730759 9730801 9730813 9730829 9730841
9730843 9730849 9730859 9730873 9730883 9730913 9730933 9730939 9730951 9730957
9730961 9730969 9730991 9730997 9731009 9731011 9731027 9731039 9731053 9731081
9731101 9731143 9731149 9731159 9731207 9731213 9731233 9731237 9731243 9731261
9731273 9731279 9731317 9731321 9731387 9731389 9731399 9731417 9731419 9731437
9731441 9731467 9731471 9731509 9731563 9731567 9731569 9731581 9731587 9731663
9731669 9731671 9731699 9731707 9731713 9731747 9731753 9731767 9731779 9731831
9731863 9731927 9731929 9731947 9731977 9731989 9732011 9732029 9732043 9732071
9732083 9732091 9732097 9732103 9732119 9732127 9732157 9732169 9732179 9732187
9732193 9732251 9732263 9732269 9732299 9732311 9732323 9732329 9732361 9732379
9732397 9732439 9732509 9732521 9732523 9732529 9732533 9732559 9732571 9732599
9732607 9732631 9732647 9732649 9732659 9732673 9732677 9732691 9732707 9732727
9732757 9732799 9732839 9732859 9732869 9732881 9732911 9732917 9732923 9732941
9732953 9732967 9732971 9732991 9733001 9733013 9733021 9733033 9733043 9733049
9733081 9733121 9733123 9733159 9733181 9733189 9733201 9733211 9733223 9733237
9733247 9733253 9733279 9733303 9733313 9733337 9733363 9733379 9733387 9733391
9733403 9733417 9733421 9733429 9733447 9733459 9733463 9733487 9733489 9733501
9733513 9733519 9733541 9733543 9733547 9733561 9733579 9733631 9733651 9733657
9733667 9733679 9733699 9733729 9733733 9733739 9733751 9733771 9733793 9733811
9733813 9733817 9733819 9733847 9733873 9733901 9733903 9733921 9733939 9733943
9733957 9733963 9733973 9734003 9734049 9734051 9734059 9734069 9734107 9734113
9734141 9734147 9734161 9734177 9734189 9734203 9734237 9734239 9734243 9734269
9734281 9734287 9734299 9734317 9734321 9734357 9734371 9734381 9734393 9734411
9734431 9734443 9734447 9734453 9734467 9734503 9734509 9734513 9734519 9734521
9734531 9734551 9734573 9734579 9734581 9734603 9734639 9734653 9734719 9734729
9734737 9734801 9734827 9734843 9734861 9734873 9734887 9734913 9734939 9734951
9734953 9734971 9735007 9735029 9735031 9735043 9735073 9735109 9735119 9735137
9735151 9735161 9735179 9735191 9735197 9735217 9735221 9735223 9735227 9735241
9735247 9735263 9735269 9735283 9735311 9735317 9735331 9735337 9735343 9735347
9735359 9735361 9735377 9735419 9735433 9735437 9735469 9735493 9735497 9735521
9735541 9735559 9735563 9735571 9735589 9735613 9735637 9735653 9735663 9735683
9735701 9735707 9735709 9735731 9735743 9735749 9735763 9735787 9735797 9735821
9735833 9735839 9735863 9735871 9735889 9735893 9735899 9735919 9735949 9735991
9736007 9736009 9736033 9736043 9736057 9736063 9736079 9736081 9736091 9736099
9736109 9736117 9736123 9736127 9736157 9736163 9736169 9736187 9736211 9736213
9736231 9736241 9736247 9736253 9736261 9736277 9736283 9736289 9736297 9736319
9736327 9736339 9736343 9736351 9736381 9736409 9736411 9736451 9736457 9736459
9736499 9736537 9736543 9736561 9736563 9736603 9736609 9736627 9736651 9736717
9736729 9736747 9736777 9736787 9736807 9736819 9736823 9736847 9736879 9736891
9736897 9736901 9736919 9736921 9736927 9736939 9736973 9736997 9737023 9737029
9737047 9737051 9737071 9737081 9737093 9737111 9737113 9737137 9737159 9737173
9737197 9737201 9737207 9737227 9737237 9737239 9737267 9737279 9737281 9737293
9737333 9737339 9737341 9737383 9737389 9737407 9737423 9737467 9737501 9737509
9737561 9737569 9737573 9737587 9737593 9737621 9737639 9737641 9737657 9737659
9737669 9737683 9737687 9737701 9737711 9737729 9737731 9737797 9737801 9737807
9737831 9737879 9737887 9737921 9737941 9737943 9737971 9737973 9737989 9738017
9738023 9738041 9738049 9738077 9738083 9738103 9738107 9738119 9738133 9738139
9738149 9738163 9738173 9738181 9738191 9738199 9738221 9738257 9738277 9738293
9738299 9738329 9738349 9738359 9738367 9738389 9738397 9738401 9738413 9738427
9738451 9738493 9738497 9738503 9738523 9738529 9738551 9738571 9738601 9738649
9738655 9738661 9738667 9738709 9738719 9738721 9738737 9738763 9738767 9738779
9738787 9738791 9738793 9738797 9738829 9738847 9738851 9738871 9738889 9738893
9738907 9738923 9738931 9738947 9738979 9738997 9739007 9739021 9739023 9739031
9739057 9739061 9739063 9739069 9739109 9739111 9739117 9739129 9739133 9739151
9739159 9739201 9739217 9739237 9739241 9739243 9739271 9739297 9739309 9739339
9739417 9739451 9739493 9739519 9739559 9739643 9739699 9739703 9739711 9739721
9739747 9739771 9739777 9739781 9739789 9739811 9739817 9739819 9739823 9739841
9739871 9739901 9739903 9739907 9739909 9739937 9739949 9739979 9740009 9740021
9740023 9740033 9740047 9740051 9740069 9740089 9740111 9740113 9740117 9740161
9740173 9740177 9740183 9740197 9740207 9740239 9740257 9740267 9740309 9740321
9740351 9740359 9740363 9740377 9740383 9740389 9740399 9740411 9740441 9740443
9740447 9740461 9740501 9740503 9740513 9740543 9740551 9740611 9740617 9740629
```

```
9740639  9740651  9740659  9740669  9740683  9740693  9740719  9740729  9740737  9740741
9740761  9740771  9740777  9740791  9740827  9740867  9740869  9740883  9740909  9740911
9740917  9740933  9740947  9740957  9740989  9740993  9741023  9741049  9741089  9741097
9741103  9741107  9741113  9741131  9741133  9741163  9741181  9741209  9741227  9741247
9741269  9741283  9741287  9741293  9741301  9741307  9741341  9741367  9741377  9741383
9741449  9741451  9741467  9741469  9741541  9741583  9741587  9741649  9741653  9741679
9741689  9741691  9741701  9741703  9741707  9741713  9741749  9741757  9741763  9741773
9741791  9741817  9741821  9741829  9741859  9741863  9741871  9741881  9741899  9741911
9741913  9741917  9741929  9741937  9741961  9742027  9742097  9742111  9742121  9742147
9742163  9742171  9742181  9742189  9742199  9742217  9742219  9742253  9742259  9742267
9742331  9742349  9742351  9742391  9742393  9742399  9742417  9742427  9742471  9742483
9742511  9742541  9742567  9742571  9742589  9742591  9742597  9742627  9742633  9742643
9742657  9742661  9742669  9742679  9742693  9742699  9742709  9742739  9742757  9742793
9742813  9742829  9742849  9742861  9742879  9742891  9742903  9742963  9742969  9743003
9743011  9743017  9743039  9743077  9743081  9743087  9743089  9743119  9743131  9743141
9743161  9743171  9743179  9743197  9743213  9743243  9743249  9743267  9743273  9743299
9743309  9743311  9743317  9743351  9743353  9743417  9743441  9743443  9743471  9743473
9743477  9743479  9743501  9743509  9743519  9743537  9743563  9743581  9743593  9743597
9743603  9743611  9743627  9743633  9743639  9743653  9743659  9743663  9743677  9743687
9743689  9743693  9743707  9743717  9743719  9743729  9743753  9743759  9743779  9743803
9743807  9743813  9743857  9743861  9743893  9743897  9743947  9743953  9743959  9743963
9743989  9744001  9744023  9744037  9744041  9744067  9744073  9744089  9744121  9744139
9744143  9744149  9744151  9744167  9744193  9744197  9744227  9744233  9744239  9744257
9744277  9744299  9744307  9744313  9744331  9744373  9744389  9744391  9744401  9744403
9744407  9744409  9744419  9744437  9744443  9744457  9744461  9744481  9744517  9744529
9744569  9744577  9744589  9744599  9744641  9744643  9744649  9744677  9744737  9744743
9744767  9744773  9744797  9744803  9744809  9744829  9744851  9744857  9744863  9744869
9744871  9744901  9744923  9744937  9744979  9744997  9745009  9745013  9745019  9745037
9745039  9745049  9745051  9745069  9745093  9745103  9745111  9745117  9745181  9745201
9745213  9745223  9745231  9745237  9745273  9745277  9745289  9745303  9745313  9745321
9745327  9745339  9745349  9745367  9745381  9745387  9745397  9745409  9745441  9745447
9745451  9745507  9745511  9745513  9745523  9745529  9745559  9745579  9745597  9745621
9745639  9745661  9745663  9745669  9745699  9745739  9745751  9745781  9745783  9745789
9745817  9745819  9745831  9745843  9745847  9745849  9745861  9745867  9745877  9745889
9745891  9745949  9745979  9745999  9746027  9746029  9746047  9746063  9746071  9746081
9746111  9746119  9746131  9746141  9746147  9746159  9746161  9746167  9746173  9746179
9746257  9746267  9746279  9746293  9746311  9746327  9746333  9746339  9746351  9746353
9746381  9746447  9746459  9746483  9746489  9746497  9746501  9746521  9746533  9746543
9746551  9746567  9746573  9746579  9746587  9746603  9746629  9746707  9746731  9746761
9746771  9746777  9746801  9746827  9746837  9746839  9746861  9746897  9746903  9746909
9746983  9746999  9747029  9747037  9747061  9747077  9747109  9747119  9747121  9747149
9747187  9747203  9747223  9747233  9747253  9747281  9747293  9747301  9747337  9747343
9747347  9747349  9747383  9747401  9747403  9747421  9747457  9747467  9747473  9747481
9747497  9747523  9747533  9747559  9747571  9747583  9747587  9747643  9747667  9747677
9747679  9747701  9747721  9747737  9747781  9747811  9747827  9747839  9747863  9747901
9747911  9747917  9747923  9747943  9747967  9747977  9748001  9748009  9748019  9748033
9748049  9748051  9748069  9748073  9748091  9748097  9748111  9748127  9748133  9748153
9748163  9748169  9748183  9748187  9748199  9748213  9748231  9748241  9748243  9748247
9748253  9748313  9748337  9748337  9748339  9748367  9748369  9748391  9748411  9748423
9748441  9748451  9748457  9748469  9748537  9748547  9748549  9748559  9748561  9748579
9748591  9748603  9748657  9748661  9748703  9748709  9748721  9748741  9748751  9748771
9748777  9748799  9748819  9748859  9748861  9748883  9748909  9748927  9748933  9748951
9748961  9748967  9748993  9748997  9749023  9749029  9749059  9749063  9749083  9749099
9749107  9749111  9749119  9749141  9749161  9749183  9749189  9749197  9749231  9749239
9749251  9749273  9749281  9749291  9749317  9749323  9749329  9749339  9749353  9749357
9749359  9749393  9749437  9749461  9749479  9749491  9749497  9749501  9749521  9749533
9749557  9749561  9749563  9749587  9749591  9749629  9749647  9749681  9749693  9749699
9749731  9749741  9749743  9749801  9749819  9749843  9749851  9749867  9749881  9749887
9749899  9749911  9749921  9749963  9749989  9750001  9750011  9750017  9750029  9750043
9750049  9750053  9750071  9750073  9750077  9750079  9750157  9750187  9750193  9750239
9750253  9750269  9750271  9750311  9750319  9750329  9750341  9750347  9750361  9750371
9750373  9750383  9750397  9750407  9750473  9750511  9750527  9750529  9750539  9750541
9750547  9750557  9750563  9750581  9750599  9750607  9750613  9750617  9750623  9750649
9750659  9750737  9750739  9750749  9750773  9750779  9750787  9750821  9750841  9750859
9750863  9750893  9750901  9750947  9750973  9750977  9750997  9751051  9751061  9751073
9751087  9751111  9751129  9751139  9751141  9751151  9751169  9751171  9751213  9751219
9751229  9751253  9751289  9751309  9751321  9751327  9751349  9751361  9751373  9751397
9751403  9751433  9751447  9751451  9751457  9751459  9751493  9751499  9751501  9751537
9751549  9751589  9751613  9751619  9751633  9751663  9751667  9751673  9751699  9751739
9751799  9751811  9751813  9751817  9751843  9751849  9751867  9751879  9751909  9751913
9751969  9751981  9751991  9751993  9752003  9752021  9752047  9752059  9752081  9752117
9752153  9752167  9752173  9752177  9752179  9752189  9752191  9752213  9752221  9752233
9752243  9752261  9752279  9752293  9752297  9752317  9752333  9752341  9752363  9752387
9752389  9752399  9752447  9752467  9752503  9752521  9752549  9752563  9752573  9752579
9752591  9752597  9752609  9752623  9752627  9752647  9752653  9752663  9752707  9752723
9752731  9752737  9752753  9752777  9752783  9752789  9752797  9752801  9752803  9752843
9752857  9752861  9752891  9752921  9752927  9752929  9752969  9752983  9752987  9752999
9753001  9753011  9753041  9753043  9753047  9753067  9753097  9753101  9753109  9753119
9753151  9753169  9753179  9753181  9753187  9753197  9753209  9753239  9753269  9753277
9753283  9753287  9753319  9753323  9753329  9753353  9753383  9753409  9753421  9753433
9753439  9753451  9753463  9753493  9753521  9753553  9753589  9753637  9753649  9753683
9753683  9753701  9753719  9753721  9753739  9753761  9753763  9753781  9753787  9753827
9753833  9753841  9753851  9753853  9753857  9753899  9753907  9753917  9753929  9753943
9753949  9753979  9753983  9754009  9754033  9754037  9754091  9754099  9754109  9754117
9754127  9754169  9754189  9754207  9754211  9754219  9754267  9754289  9754313  9754321
9754337  9754343  9754357  9754361  9754363  9754373  9754397  9754399  9754403  9754453
9754457  9754471  9754513  9754523  9754531  9754559  9754579  9754601  9754607  9754609
9754621  9754639  9754699  9754711  9754721  9754729  9754757  9754763  9754813  9754837
9754859  9754861  9754867  9754879  9754891  9754909  9754919  9754973  9754993  9755017
```

```
9755029 9755033 9755071 9755077 9755099 9755117 9755129 9755147 9755149 9755153
9755183 9755191 9755203 9755257 9755261 9755269 9755279 9755299 9755327 9755331
9755363 9755371 9755377 9755411 9755413 9755419 9755441 9755479 9755491 9755503
9755507 9755521 9755527 9755549 9755567 9755573 9755587 9755593 9755651 9755663
9755669 9755677 9755693 9755717 9755771 9755777 9755819 9755821 9755831 9755843
9755849 9755881 9755971 9755981 9755983 9756001 9756023 9756067 9756083 9756107
9756121 9756133 9756161 9756167 9756169 9756179 9756191 9756193 9756211 9756221
9756223 9756259 9756277 9756281 9756287 9756337 9756359 9756379 9756391 9756427
9756431 9756437 9756449 9756463 9756503 9756517 9756529 9756541 9756553 9756569
9756583 9756587 9756619 9756631 9756667 9756679 9756707 9756713 9756727 9756757
9756779 9756787 9756797 9756809 9756833 9756841 9756869 9756883 9756907 9756911
9756913 9756949 9756953 9756959 9756977 9756979 9757019 9757039 9757043 9757049
9757061 9757073 9757081 9757091 9757093 9757103 9757109 9757171 9757177 9757183
9757199 9757217 9757271 9757289 9757291 9757301 9757333 9757339 9757379 9757387
9757403 9757441 9757453 9757457 9757463 9757471 9757477 9757483 9757487 9757493
9757523 9757613 9757619 9757633 9757637 9757667 9757673 9757687 9757703 9757723
9757733 9757739 9757753 9757757 9757763 9757777 9757799 9757801 9757817 9757823
9757829 9757831 9757873 9757903 9757907 9757921 9757927 9757931 9757981 9757991
9758009 9758011 9758029 9758057 9758101 9758107 9758143 9758171 9758173 9758179
9758183 9758197 9758207 9758209 9758219 9758237 9758249 9758261 9758263 9758339
9758351 9758383 9758387 9758407 9758431 9758447 9758461 9758467 9758473 9758477
9758501 9758537 9758557 9758579 9758591 9758599 9758611 9758627 9758653 9758687
9758699 9758717 9758729 9758741 9758743 9758747 9758753 9758759 9758767 9758783
9758797 9758803 9758821 9758839 9758857 9758863 9758887 9758911 9758927 9758933
9758953 9758971 9758999 9759007 9759011 9759023 9759031 9759041 9759047 9759059
9759067 9759077 9759091 9759119 9759121 9759143 9759187 9759193 9759247 9759257
9759263 9759289 9759301 9759307 9759317 9759319 9759349 9759359 9759361 9759371
9759401 9759413 9759419 9759433 9759437 9759439 9759467 9759481 9759487 9759493
9759499 9759509 9759511 9759539 9759551 9759553 9759571 9759593 9759611 9759641
9759643 9759707 9759713 9759727 9759769 9759779 9759793 9759803 9759809 9759811
9759847 9759851 9759859 9759877 9759899 9759907 9759917 9759929 9759943 9759949
9759961 9759983 9759991 9760013 9760021 9760033 9760039 9760081 9760117 9760151
9760169 9760171 9760189 9760199 9760217 9760229 9760241 9760271 9760273 9760301
9760307 9760313 9760339 9760343 9760351 9760367 9760369 9760379 9760393 9760403
9760409 9760411 9760423 9760453 9760459 9760469 9760481 9760511 9760523 9760561
9760571 9760573 9760577 9760591 9760609 9760633 9760643 9760651 9760697 9760721
9760727 9760739 9760769 9760781 9760789 9760801 9760831 9760837 9760909 9760921
9760937 9760963 9760967 9760969 9760973 9760979 9760981 9760991 9761021 9761033
9761051 9761107 9761123 9761183 9761201 9761209 9761221 9761233 9761243 9761261
9761273 9761287 9761291 9761299 9761309 9761327 9761329 9761333 9761351 9761359
9761363 9761369 9761399 9761419 9761441 9761447 9761449 9761461 9761467 9761471
9761483 9761489 9761501 9761513 9761527 9761533 9761537 9761539 9761551 9761617
9761623 9761629 9761639 9761657 9761669 9761671 9761677 9761693 9761707 9761711
9761737 9761743 9761749 9761753 9761761 9761797 9761809 9761827 9761837 9761849
9761909 9761923 9761929 9761987 9762019 9762023 9762037 9762047 9762061 9762073
9762079 9762083 9762089 9762091 9762113 9762121 9762127 9762163 9762167 9762227
9762307 9762329 9762349 9762353 9762383 9762439 9762479 9762491 9762497 9762517
9762521 9762593 9762611 9762619 9762631 9762667 9762673 9762679 9762691 9762703
9762719 9762721 9762749 9762769 9762773 9762839 9762847 9762853 9762859 9762877
9762881 9762901 9762917 9762919 9762967 9763007 9763009 9763051 9763067 9763069
9763073 9763081 9763097 9763099 9763121 9763141 9763157 9763189 9763213 9763231
9763241 9763297 9763309 9763319 9763337 9763361 9763363 9763381 9763387 9763393
9763447 9763469 9763493 9763513 9763541 9763547 9763553 9763573 9763577 9763591
9763613 9763651 9763657 9763669 9763681 9763693 9763727 9763757 9763813 9763829
9763837 9763841 9763879 9763883 9763889 9763903 9763909 9763927 9763931 9763939
9763961 9763979 9763997 9764003 9764009 9764011 9764023 9764033 9764077 9764089
9764107 9764129 9764143 9764159 9764197 9764219 9764221 9764231 9764257 9764267
9764269 9764281 9764303 9764317 9764393 9764399 9764413 9764449 9764459 9764471
9764507 9764533 9764539 9764549 9764563 9764567 9764591 9764603 9764617 9764621
9764641 9764663 9764687 9764693 9764737 9764747 9764753 9764759 9764779 9764801
9764849 9764863 9764873 9764897 9764899 9764921 9764949 9764957 9764959 9764971
9764977 9764981 9765001 9765017 9765023 9765029 9765037 9765043 9765047 9765053
9765061 9765071 9765109 9765139 9765181 9765187 9765193 9765209 9765211 9765227
9765233 9765277 9765289 9765323 9765337 9765359 9765367 9765377 9765383 9765389
9765401 9765407 9765433 9765443 9765461 9765467 9765473 9765517 9765529 9765583
9765611 9765617 9765619 9765629 9765643 9765653 9765661 9765671 9765683 9765751
9765757 9765761 9765793 9765809 9765827 9765841 9765851 9765893 9765911 9765941
9765949 9765967 9765991 9766033 9766037 9766051 9766079 9766087 9766091 9766103
9766123 9766129 9766139 9766157 9766193 9766201 9766219 9766223 9766231 9766303
9766307 9766321 9766343 9766349 9766387 9766391 9766423 9766429 9766489 9766501
9766531 9766543 9766567 9766573 9766609 9766637 9766667 9766699 9766711 9766739
9766747 9766759 9766763 9766781 9766793 9766807 9766819 9766837 9766843 9766847
9766871 9766877 9766901 9766903 9766937 9766951 9766957 9766987 9766997 9767011
9767029 9767041 9767047 9767053 9767071 9767101 9767161 9767183 9767227 9767243
9767267 9767269 9767291 9767293 9767339 9767347 9767353 9767369 9767377 9767383
9767393 9767411 9767413 9767419 9767431 9767447 9767467 9767497 9767507 9767521
9767531 9767543 9767561 9767567 9767581 9767591 9767603 9767629 9767633 9767657
9767671 9767677 9767711 9767713 9767731 9767761 9767767 9767787 9767827 9767837
9767861 9767873 9767887 9767899 9767903 9767909 9767921 9767929 9767941 9767969
9767977 9767987 9767999 9768001 9768029 9768043 9768049 9768061 9768067 9768079
9768089 9768091 9768119 9768133 9768139 9768163 9768173 9768233 9768263 9768281
9768293 9768301 9768329 9768347 9768361 9768371 9768391 9768419 9768431 9768443
9768449 9768461 9768487 9768509 9768529 9768541 9768547 9768553 9768559 9768569
9768599 9768617 9768637 9768673 9768683 9768709 9768719 9768739 9768743 9768769
9768799 9768809 9768817 9768823 9768833 9768881 9768883 9768901 9768907 9768917
9768971 9768973 9769003 9769007 9769009 9769037 9769049 9769087 9769093 9769121
9769129 9769139 9769157 9769159 9769163 9769229 9769267 9769301 9769303 9769307
9769313 9769327 9769391 9769393 9769423 9769429 9769441 9769453 9769489 9769493
9769519 9769531 9769537 9769541 9769547 9769559 9769567 9769579 9769589 9769597
```

```
9769609  9769621  9769631  9769637  9769651  9769657  9769703  9769709  9769741  9769757
9769777  9769801  9769807  9769817  9769891  9769909  9769913  9769927  9769939  9769957
9769979  9769993  9770017  9770021  9770039  9770041  9770051  9770069  9770083  9770113
9770119  9770143  9770149  9770191  9770207  9770209  9770213  9770221  9770231  9770249
9770251  9770261  9770263  9770273  9770279  9770311  9770329  9770333  9770401  9770441
9770443  9770471  9770489  9770531  9770533  9770557  9770569  9770573  9770591  9770623
9770633  9770647  9770659  9770707  9770711  9770723  9770737  9770741  9770753  9770759
9770773  9770779  9770809  9770819  9770821  9770851  9770857  9770881  9770899  9770909
9770911  9770939  9770947  9770951  9770963  9771007  9771023  9771029  9771031  9771053
9771089  9771103  9771119  9771131  9771137  9771143  9771211  9771217  9771227  9771241
9771247  9771259  9771299  9771313  9771317  9771319  9771371  9771373  9771383  9771401
9771409  9771427  9771439  9771467  9771469  9771473  9771533  9771539  9771551  9771599
9771611  9771613  9771631  9771661  9771667  9771677  9771689  9771691  9771703  9771709
9771721  9771731  9771733  9771743  9771763  9771767  9771809  9771823  9771829  9771841
9771857  9771893  9771907  9771953  9771961  9771967  9771977  9771997  9772019  9772027
9772039  9772057  9772067  9772097  9772121  9772129  9772141  9772157  9772163  9772187
9772199  9772201  9772211  9772219  9772241  9772247  9772271  9772277  9772303  9772313
9772319  9772361  9772393  9772421  9772423  9772453  9772487  9772489  9772519  9772547
9772573  9772589  9772591  9772601  9772639  9772643  9772661  9772667  9772703  9772709
9772717  9772727  9772747  9772753  9772759  9772811  9772877  9772879  9772891  9772901
9772969  9772979  9772981  9773003  9773051  9773053  9773077  9773123  9773131  9773149
9773161  9773171  9773177  9773207  9773209  9773251  9773263  9773287  9773297  9773299
9773303  9773311  9773329  9773347  9773369  9773381  9773411  9773417  9773431  9773441
9773447  9773471  9773479  9773497  9773501  9773503  9773531  9773549  9773557  9773563
9773593  9773633  9773639  9773641  9773653  9773663  9773671  9773681  9773707  9773723
9773737  9773747  9773749  9773767  9773821  9773833  9773837  9773839  9773851  9773879
9773887  9773941  9773947  9773977  9773983  9773989  9773993  9774001  9774007  9774019
9774049  9774059  9774067  9774071  9774077  9774097  9774143  9774173  9774197  9774199
9774209  9774211  9774221  9774263  9774293  9774299  9774307  9774319  9774361  9774367
9774377  9774389  9774397  9774409  9774451  9774461  9774463  9774467  9774469  9774491
9774497  9774503  9774509  9774511  9774533  9774547  9774551  9774553  9774559  9774571
9774581  9774599  9774601  9774617  9774647  9774689  9774727  9774733  9774767  9774811
9774829  9774833  9774841  9774857  9774859  9774883  9774887  9774893  9774899  9774901
9774913  9774917  9774929  9774967  9774971  9774991  9775021  9775027  9775033  9775037
9775039  9775091  9775093  9775111  9775121  9775123  9775133  9775151  9775163  9775169
9775193  9775217  9775219  9775231  9775243  9775247  9775307  9775313  9775323  9775379
9775399  9775427  9775429  9775457  9775463  9775499  9775531  9775537  9775541  9775543
9775553  9775559  9775573  9775583  9775603  9775609  9775637  9775673  9775699  9775723
9775751  9775763  9775771  9775793  9775837  9775847  9775877  9775879  9775933  9775959
9775949  9775993  9776017  9776059  9776069  9776113  9776119  9776147  9776149  9776153
9776159  9776167  9776197  9776213  9776227  9776237  9776257  9776281  9776293  9776303
9776323  9776341  9776369  9776381  9776387  9776407  9776413  9776419  9776441  9776453
9776471  9776521  9776549  9776551  9776579  9776593  9776603  9776617  9776623  9776639
9776651  9776693  9776729  9776761  9776779  9776783  9776807  9776813  9776821  9776881
9776891  9776929  9776939  9776941  9776947  9776951  9776957  9776971  9776981  9776993
9777007  9777011  9777013  9777017  9777037  9777043  9777049  9777071  9777073  9777083
9777113  9777161  9777167  9777169  9777179  9777199  9777217  9777221  9777223  9777239
9777259  9777301  9777331  9777347  9777353  9777371  9777373  9777389  9777403  9777407
9777413  9777463  9777491  9777497  9777527  9777541  9777563  9777569  9777577  9777769
9777587  9777619  9777631  9777637  9777653  9777661  9777671  9777707  9777749  9777769
9777773  9777791  9777793  9777797  9777851  9777853  9777869  9777871  9777877  9777883
9777919  9777923  9777949  9777973  9777979  9778001  9778019  9778031  9778033  9778037
9778039  9778057  9778061  9778073  9778081  9778091  9778121  9778123  9778127  9778159
9778183  9778187  9778189  9778199  9778201  9778211  9778231  9778253  9778259  9778261
9778267  9778273  9778297  9778309  9778319  9778337  9778387  9778403  9778411  9778441
9778463  9778469  9778487  9778523  9778543  9778589  9778651  9778669  9778687  9778739
9778751  9778753  9778763  9778817  9778819  9778843  9778859  9778891  9778897  9778913
9778943  9778963  9778973  9778991  9778997  9779009  9779027  9779039  9779069  9779073
9779087  9779089  9779101  9779113  9779141  9779179  9779201  9779207  9779239  9779251
9779257  9779261  9779269  9779303  9779311  9779321  9779323  9779333  9779339  9779383
9779389  9779423  9779453  9779491  9779513  9779537  9779551  9779563  9779563  9779569
9779579  9779593  9779597  9779629  9779633  9779659  9779701  9779741  9779779  9779797
9779801  9779839  9779843  9779857  9779881  9779909  9779921  9779929  9779933  9779941
9779969  9779971  9779977  9779983  9779993  9780011  9780013  9780031  9780053  9780059
9780091  9780101  9780131  9780137  9780149  9780157  9780167  9780187  9780203  9780217
9780227  9780233  9780241  9780317  9780319  9780341  9780343  9780347  9780367  9780373
9780377  9780403  9780431  9780439  9780473  9780487  9780493  9780499  9780517  9780521
9780523  9780529  9780553  9780577  9780581  9780583  9780587  9780599  9780601  9780647
9780721  9780731  9780761  9780781  9780787  9780809  9780811  9780821  9780829  9780847
9780851  9780857  9780871  9780887  9780893  9780931  9780971  9780973  9780989  9781007
9781021  9781039  9781043  9781063  9781073  9781099  9781117  9781127  9781139  9781153
9781157  9781183  9781193  9781201  9781223  9781229  9781237  9781249  9781259  9781267
9781297  9781313  9781319  9781349  9781361  9781373  9781391  9781399  9781451  9781469
9781481  9781483  9781487  9781501  9781517  9781529  9781549  9781589  9781591  9781609
9781631  9781643  9781649  9781661  9781697  9781699  9781703  9781711  9781747  9781753
9781757  9781763  9781823  9781829  9781843  9781853  9781861  9781867  9781873  9781879
9781909  9781943  9781963  9781991  9781997  9782011  9782029  9782033  9782041  9782083
9782117  9782137  9782173  9782209  9782239  9782273  9782281  9782299  9782317  9782323
9782351  9782389  9782411  9782413  9782417  9782441  9782459  9782501  9782503  9782519
9782527  9782533  9782551  9782561  9782569  9782573  9782579  9782611  9782621  9782663
9782653  9782677  9782699  9782713  9782719  9782743  9782761  9782779  9782783  9782813
9782821  9782833  9782873  9782879  9782917  9782933  9782951  9782953  9782957  9782963
9782989  9783013  9783031  9783047  9783061  9783067  9783079  9783083  9783089  9783101
9783107  9783113  9783149  9783173  9783181  9783187  9783199  9783223  9783247  9783253
9783283  9783311  9783329  9783341  9783359  9783373  9783377  9783391  9783409  9783413
9783451  9783479  9783497  9783509  9783511  9783539  9783547  9783589  9783601  9783647
9783649  9783659  9783667  9783677  9783703  9783713  9783737  9783751  9783757  9783773
9783779  9783797  9783811  9783821  9783881  9783883  9783887  9783889  9783923  9783929
9783937  9783967  9783979  9783989  9784007  9784009  9784051  9784057  9784063  9784079
```

```
9784081  9784097  9784109  9784111  9784133  9784141  9784153  9784213  9784249  9784253
9784261  9784267  9784283  9784309  9784321  9784343  9784351  9784417  9784427  9784429
9784433  9784457  9784459  9784477  9784493  9784519  9784529  9784543  9784549  9784553
9784559  9784573  9784589  9784597  9784633  9784657  9784661  9784667  9784669  9784717
9784721  9784751  9784757  9784759  9784777  9784781  9784811  9784823  9784837  9784849
9784889  9784903  9784921  9784987  9784991  9785021  9785059  9785077  9785089  9785107
9785129  9785137  9785141  9785147  9785159  9785197  9785201  9785203  9785207  9785213
9785233  9785239  9785249  9785261  9785287  9785297  9785299  9785311  9785333  9785333
9785357  9785359  9785389  9785411  9785423  9785449  9785483  9785497  9785507  9785519
9785527  9785533  9785537  9785543  9785561  9785597  9785599  9785621  9785641  9785663
9785669  9785683  9785689  9785701  9785707  9785719  9785753  9785777  9785807  9785813
9785821  9785827  9785849  9785851  9785887  9785903  9785989  9786041  9786043  9786043
9786059  9786089  9786097  9786103  9786131  9786151  9786157  9786163  9786181  9786187
9786191  9786211  9786221  9786263  9786269  9786277  9786299  9786319  9786323  9786379
9786383  9786409  9786419  9786457  9786479  9786487  9786521  9786533  9786547  9786551
9786559  9786619  9786631  9786641  9786643  9786697  9786719  9786727  9786737  9786739
9786761  9786787  9786827  9786841  9786863  9786877  9786893  9786911  9786923  9786923
9786941  9786967  9786977  9786991  9787003  9787021  9787039  9787049  9787067  9787091
9787093  9787117  9787133  9787153  9787171  9787177  9787229  9787237  9787303  9787307
9787313  9787319  9787321  9787343  9787373  9787381  9787387  9787391  9787409  9787411
9787433  9787447  9787469  9787487  9787493  9787501  9787507  9787513  9787543  9787553
9787567  9787571  9787577  9787639  9787649  9787663  9787667  9787709  9787727  9787741
9787753  9787759  9787769  9787777  9787787  9787837  9787849  9787859  9787861  9787867
9787871  9787901  9787931  9787933  9787951  9787969  9787991  9787997  9788029  9788029
9788057  9788069  9788083  9788089  9788101  9788113  9788137  9788143  9788153  9788171
9788183  9788201  9788203  9788227  9788279  9788293  9788297  9788329  9788333  9788347
9788353  9788357  9788369  9788377  9788383  9788417  9788423  9788437  9788453  9788473
9788489  9788491  9788503  9788509  9788521  9788533  9788539  9788543  9788551  9788567
9788587  9788599  9788657  9788659  9788677  9788693  9788717  9788759  9788773  9788809
9788813  9788827  9788879  9788887  9788893  9788897  9788899  9788917  9788927  9788929
9788939  9788951  9788953  9788959  9788981  9789001  9789011  9789071  9789083  9789121
9789137  9789173  9789193  9789203  9789257  9789271  9789281  9789289  9789293  9789293
9789317  9789319  9789343  9789359  9789361  9789371  9789379  9789383  9789391  9789401
9789413  9789431  9789469  9789473  9789487  9789491  9789523  9789553  9789557  9789557
9789587  9789589  9789607  9789629  9789641  9789667  9789713  9789727  9789773  9789779
9789781  9789797  9789803  9789823  9789833  9789851  9789869  9789877  9789887  9789937
9789947  9789953  9789971  9789991  9790003  9790013  9790043  9790051  9790057  9790061
9790063  9790069  9790091  9790127  9790129  9790133  9790153  9790159  9790177  9790199
9790201  9790211  9790217  9790219  9790229  9790259  9790273  9790279  9790331  9790337
9790367  9790373  9790379  9790381  9790397  9790399  9790409  9790411  9790421  9790423
9790441  9790457  9790463  9790481  9790483  9790499  9790499  9790507  9790559  9790579
9790621  9790631  9790633  9790639  9790667  9790673  9790679  9790717  9790727  9790733
9790747  9790751  9790771  9790789  9790813  9790817  9790819  9790831  9790843  9790901
9790931  9790933  9790967  9790969  9790981  9790987  9791003  9791029  9791039  9791039
9791059  9791063  9791069  9791081  9791101  9791129  9791149  9791189  9791209  9791263
9791279  9791317  9791321  9791323  9791329  9791351  9791363  9791387  9791413  9791423
9791459  9791461  9791521  9791533  9791543  9791549  9791597  9791599  9791603  9791641
9791653  9791657  9791687  9791693  9791701  9791713  9791723  9791729  9791731  9791737
9791771  9791777  9791843  9791861  9791863  9791911  9791923  9791941  9791953  9791959
9791981  9792031  9792059  9792073  9792103  9792113  9792137  9792143  9792149  9792151
9792157  9792173  9792191  9792203  9792217  9792229  9792271  9792283  9792301  9792329
9792331  9792337  9792359  9792361  9792371  9792397  9792427  9792473  9792479  9792487
9792491  9792499  9792509  9792521  9792529  9792539  9792571  9792583  9792593  9792611
9792613  9792631  9792659  9792659  9792677  9792701  9792703  9792707  9792709  9792719
9792737  9792743  9792763  9792767  9792793  9792841  9792851  9792857  9792889  9792899
9792943  9792947  9792971  9792983  9793019  9793027  9793031  9793033  9793057  9793057
9793099  9793103  9793111  9793129  9793141  9793159  9793163  9793177  9793187  9793211
9793229  9793247  9793261  9793283  9793291  9793307  9793319  9793321  9793327  9793339
9793349  9793361  9793363  9793369  9793373  9793391  9793397  9793447  9793451  9793451
9793453  9793463  9793477  9793481  9793507  9793519  9793559  9793571  9793573  9793577
9793583  9793601  9793631  9793657  9793661  9793663  9793687  9793697  9793727  9793727
9793741  9793747  9793757  9793787  9793829  9793831  9793841  9793843  9793877  9793891
9793897  9793933  9793951  9793963  9793991  9794003  9794009  9794009  9794009  9794009
9794017  9794041  9794051  9794069  9794087  9794089  9794093  9794107  9794117  9794119
9794123  9794137  9794143  9794149  9794173  9794179  9794201  9794207  9794209  9794219
9794243  9794263  9794293  9794311  9794321  9794339  9794353  9794359  9794371  9794411
9794423  9794429  9794467  9794503  9794469  9794491  9794593  9794599  9794611  9794623
9794627  9794639  9794657  9794689  9794699  9794713  9794723  9794749  9794761  9794789
9794801  9794809  9794857  9794891  9794923  9794929  9794951  9794971  9794989  9795029
9795083  9795091  9795103  9795109  9795133  9795139  9795151  9795161  9795167  9795169
9795193  9795209  9795211  9795257  9795259  9795299  9795307  9795311  9795323  9795347
9795367  9795371  9795391  9795413  9795419  9795421  9795427  9795437  9795439  9795481
9795497  9795509  9795517  9795523  9795547  9795557  9795559  9795551  9795599  9795613
9795623  9795629  9795641  9795661  9795671  9795673  9795683  9795727  9795781  9795809
9795827  9795847  9795883  9795899  9795917  9795923  9795931  9795967  9795977  9795979
9796037  9796057  9796067  9796117  9796121  9796123  9796139  9796147  9796151  9796159
9796177  9796201  9796211  9796243  9796247  9796261  9796273  9796277  9796289  9796327
9796357  9796393  9796411  9796421  9796429  9796439  9796441  9796447  9796469  9796477
9796481  9796483  9796489  9796511  9796517  9796529  9796531  9796543  9796603  9796621
9796627  9796637  9796667  9796687  9796691  9796747  9796753  9796841  9796847  9796867
9796889  9796933  9796937  9796939  9796949  9796973  9796999  9797017  9797033  9797063
9797069  9797089  9797107  9797113  9797129  9797143  9797153  9797159  9797167  9797171
9797181  9797189  9797191  9797231  9797233  9797239  9797243  9797251  9797261  9797279
9797297  9797299  9797309  9797311  9797323  9797329  9797339  9797351  9797357  9797371
9797377  9797383  9797413  9797419  9797443  9797449  9797461  9797467  9797477  9797497
9797531  9797533  9797551  9797603  9797651  9797657  9797677  9797687  9797699  9797713
9797719  9797731  9797771  9797773  9797783  9797791  9797803  9797807  9797819  9797833
9797849  9797861  9797867  9797869  9797903  9797917  9797959  9797993  9797999  9798059
9798079  9798083  9798101  9798149  9798157  9798169  9798193  9798197  9798199  9798211
```

```
9798227  9798241  9798251  9798293  9798301  9798323  9798329  9798359  9798379  9798403
9798457  9798461  9798479  9798487  9798499  9798517  9798553  9798557  9798563  9798589
9798601  9798617  9798619  9798637  9798643  9798703  9798707  9798727  9798743  9798769
9798793  9798823  9798827  9798829  9798847  9798853  9798869  9798871  9798881  9798907
9798911  9798913  9798917  9798941  9798961  9798973  9799019  9799033  9799039  9799057
9799067  9799073  9799087  9799093  9799099  9799103  9799147  9799169  9799183  9799211
9799213  9799217  9799243  9799249  9799253  9799261  9799271  9799277  9799319  9799331
9799333  9799337  9799351  9799373  9799409  9799411  9799423  9799457  9799481  9799483
9799607  9799511  9799519  9799529  9799549  9799567  9799577  9799579  9799583  9799591
9799607  9799613  9799661  9799663  9799681  9799693  9799703  9799733  9799759  9799781
9799789  9799819  9799831  9799843  9799847  9799849  9799897  9799903  9799913  9799927
9799957  9799967  9799969  9799987  9799997  9800003  9800009  9800027  9800053  9800101
9800113  9800129  9800137  9800149  9800171  9800179  9800183  9800191  9800207  9800221
9800243  9800251  9800261  9800281  9800311  9800327  9800363  9800383  9800387  9800407
9800423  9800467  9800471  9800491  9800519  9800533  9800563  9800611  9800617  9800621
9800629  9800633  9800639  9800641  9800657  9800663  9800677  9800683  9800711  9800731
9800741  9800767  9800771  9800799  9800801  9800803  9800821  9800831  9800839  9800873
9800881  9800897  9800909  9800963  9801019  9801031  9801037  9801047  9801049  9801067
9801079  9801083  9801089  9801109  9801133  9801137  9801149  9801157  9801167  9801191
9801203  9801223  9801227  9801251  9801269  9801271  9801277  9801317  9801349  9801383
9801413  9801431  9801439  9801443  9801461  9801523  9801527  9801557  9801563  9801569
9801577  9801581  9801593  9801599  9801601  9801613  9801619  9801641  9801647  9801677
9801683  9801689  9801691  9801713  9801769  9801773  9801791  9801793  9801811  9801817
9801839  9801851  9801881  9801889  9801901  9801917  9801937  9801941  9801943  9801973
9801977  9801989  9801997  9802019  9802027  9802031  9802057  9802061  9802073  9802097
9802103  9802139  9802153  9802159  9802171  9802181  9802211  9802223  9802249
9802259  9802267  9802291  9802307  9802333  9802339  9802343  9802349  9802369  9802381
9802391  9802433  9802459  9802477  9802501  9802511  9802519  9802547  9802553  9802571
9802601  9802607  9802619  9802627  9802633  9802663  9802691  9802711  9802717  9802729
9802747  9802759  9802777  9802781  9802811  9802867  9802889  9802921  9802963  9802979
9802981  9802987  9803023  9803029  9803051  9803077  9803081  9803093  9803137
9803149  9803159  9803173  9803177  9803179  9803191  9803197  9803201  9803207  9803219
9803279  9803281  9803317  9803323  9803327  9803329  9803333  9803341  9803369  9803377
9803383  9803393  9803399  9803413  9803429  9803477  9803491  9803539  9803559  9803587
9803597  9803603  9803623  9803669  9803701  9803707  9803723  9803741  9803743  9803771
9803789  9803803  9803813  9803863  9803891  9803921  9803923  9803929  9803933  9803937
9803939  9803947  9803953  9803987  9803999  9804007  9804013  9804017  9804031  9804061
9804071  9804077  9804079  9804097  9804101  9804107  9804143  9804161  9804167  9804173
9804191  9804199  9804211  9804217  9804229  9804239  9804241  9804253  9804259  9804269
9804281  9804283  9804299  9804317  9804331  9804337  9804343  9804391  9804397  9804409
9804449  9804451  9804481  9804491  9804499  9804503  9804511  9804521  9804539
9804547  9804569  9804577  9804607  9804653  9804677  9804689  9804721  9804727  9804749
9804757  9804763  9804787  9804793  9804799  9804803  9804829  9804833  9804853  9804859
9804881  9804901  9804911  9804941  9804943  9804967  9804973  9804983  9804997  9805001
9805057  9805063  9805067  9805069  9805091  9805097  9805099  9805157  9805163  9805177
9805189  9805193  9805217  9805223  9805283  9805307  9805309  9805343  9805357  9805361
9805363  9805391  9805399  9805403  9805409  9805457  9805459  9805483  9805489  9805493
9805513  9805529  9805547  9805561  9805571  9805589  9805603  9805619  9805639  9805643
9805661  9805669  9805673  9805693  9805709  9805721  9805759  9805781  9805793  9805819
9805823  9805879  9805883  9805891  9805897  9805903  9805907  9805921  9805927  9805963
9805993  9805997  9806029  9806039  9806049  9806081  9806087  9806089  9806117  9806171
9806183  9806189  9806197  9806207  9806227  9806231  9806249  9806273  9806281  9806317
9806327  9806333  9806341  9806359  9806383  9806387  9806389  9806429  9806453  9806477
9806483  9806491  9806497  9806519  9806539  9806549  9806557  9806561  9806581  9806639
9806653  9806663  9806681  9806683  9806689  9806701  9806729  9806759  9806767  9806777
9806779  9806789  9806801  9806833  9806837  9806861  9806891  9806899  9806911  9806917
9806957  9806969  9806971  9806989  9807001  9807019  9807041  9807043  9807073  9807089
9807103  9807107  9807137  9807143  9807151  9807167  9807179  9807209  9807233  9807247
9807293  9807313  9807337  9807353  9807359  9807367  9807373  9807389  9807431  9807437
9807449  9807451  9807463  9807503  9807541  9807571  9807583  9807587  9807593  9807599
9807617  9807619  9807643  9807649  9807673  9807689  9807709  9807731  9807737  9807751
9807771  9807773  9807779  9807797  9807799  9807817  9807823  9807851  9807859  9807871
9807877  9807881  9807883  9807907  9807911  9807943  9807949  9807953  9807991  9808013
9808033  9808069  9808091  9808093  9808109  9808111  9808151  9808181  9808183  9808187
9808217  9808231  9808243  9808259  9808291  9808319  9808333  9808361  9808387  9808391
9808399  9808417  9808451  9808457  9808501  9808517  9808531  9808537  9808549  9808559
9808607  9808619  9808621  9808661  9808703  9808709  9808723  9808751  9808783
9808823  9808831  9808837  9808891  9808961  9808969  9808973  9809007  9809027
9809029  9809057  9809069  9809071  9809077  9809089  9809123  9809131  9809141  9809143
9809159  9809161  9809171  9809197  9809207  9809231  9809249  9809287  9809297  9809321
9809341  9809363  9809381  9809383  9809389  9809407  9809419  9809447  9809479  9809489
9809497  9809507  9809519  9809539  9809549  9809587  9809599  9809603  9809621  9809651
9809659  9809677  9809693  9809711  9809741  9809749  9809759  9809771  9809777  9809791
9809797  9809803  9809809  9809843  9809893  9809897  9809923  9809927  9809941  9809971
9810001  9810007  9810049  9810067  9810077  9810083  9810089  9810113  9810179  9810181
9810209  9810221  9810239  9810253  9810257  9810271  9810293  9810329  9810331  9810337
9810347  9810349  9810373  9810389  9810413  9810421  9810431  9810467  9810469  9810473
9810491  9810499  9810523  9810527  9810529  9810551  9810557  9810571  9810617  9810629
9810637  9810641  9810643  9810653  9810781  9810791  9810793  9810803  9810847  9810863
9810881  9810893  9810901  9810907  9810919  9810943  9810947  9810953  9810971  9810979
9810991  9811001  9811007  9811027  9811033  9811069  9811073  9811103  9811129  9811147
9811157  9811183  9811213  9811229  9811231  9811303  9811313  9811337  9811343  9811379
9811381  9811393  9811427  9811441  9811457  9811481  9811511  9811517  9811553  9811559
9811577  9811583  9811591  9811597  9811603  9811609  9811631  9811643  9811661  9811663
9811687  9811693  9811699  9811709  9811727  9811757  9811801  9811811  9811817  9811819
9811843  9811859  9811909  9811933  9811939  9811969  9811973  9811981  9812017  9812039
9812081  9812087  9812123  9812167  9812183  9812197  9812207  9812233  9812249  9812263
9812269  9812273  9812279  9812287  9812311  9812317  9812321  9812323  9812333  9812347
9812377  9812389  9812393  9812431  9812443  9812447  9812477  9812497  9812503  9812533
```

```
9812549 9812567 9812573 9812591 9812597 9812599 9812603 9812609 9812611 9812711
9812717 9812731 9812741 9812749 9812783 9812809 9812837 9812861 9812867 9812903
9812917 9812923 9812941 9812947 9812951 9812953 9812963 9812969 9812993 9813043
9813061 9813127 9813149 9813151 9813179 9813197 9813211 9813217 9813239 9813241
9813247 9813263 9813283 9813311 9813313 9813343 9813359 9813361 9813373 9813383
9813409 9813431 9813451 9813457 9813467 9813469 9813487 9813491 9813493 9813499
9813509 9813511 9813521 9813523 9813527 9813563 9813581 9813593 9813611 9813613
9813623 9813659 9813677 9813679 9813703 9813731 9813733 9813757 9813787 9813827
9813829 9813871 9813877 9813889 9813907 9813961 9813967 9813971 9813997 9814043
9814061 9814087 9814097 9814099 9814111 9814141 9814159 9814177 9814187 9814199
9814223 9814247 9814289 9814291 9814303 9814313 9814319 9814327 9814331 9814333
9814349 9814367 9814379 9814403 9814417 9814421 9814429 9814439 9814447 9814471
9814477 9814513 9814517 9814579 9814589 9814601 9814603 9814613 9814639 9814643
9814663 9814669 9814733 9814759 9814771 9814801 9814823 9814829 9814837 9814843
9814891 9814901 9814907 9814921 9814943 9814979 9814991 9814993 9815011 9815033
9815041 9815053 9815059 9815093 9815129 9815147 9815149 9815159 9815167 9815173
9815177 9815203 9815209 9815213 9815219 9815231 9815233 9815237 9815257 9815263
9815269 9815279 9815287 9815297 9815317 9815321 9815353 9815357 9815383 9815387
9815413 9815447 9815459 9815467 9815479 9815539 9815557 9815563 9815569 9815587
9815593 9815599 9815629 9815651 9815657 9815669 9815683 9815713 9815719 9815737
9815753 9815789 9815803 9815807 9815831 9815843 9815849 9815863 9815867 9815879
9815881 9815893 9815909 9815941 9815959 9815999 9816029 9816031 9816043 9816047
9816067 9816071 9816113 9816127 9816167 9816203 9816221 9816227 9816229 9816253
9816271 9816281 9816307 9816329 9816337 9816347 9816397 9816403 9816439 9816449
9816451 9816481 9816517 9816533 9816551 9816557 9816571 9816593 9816601 9816613
9816623 9816637 9816641 9816647 9816727 9816731 9816733 9816757 9816767 9816797
9816799 9816811 9816823 9816839 9816841 9816847 9816889 9816923 9816923 9816941
9816953 9816959 9816971 9816997 9817013 9817019 9817039 9817043 9817057 9817061
9817063 9817103 9817117 9817121 9817127 9817141 9817151 9817169 9817183 9817189
9817207 9817217 9817229 9817253 9817261 9817289 9817307 9817333 9817351 9817361
9817369 9817387 9817393 9817397 9817411 9817417 9817427 9817441 9817447 9817463
9817477 9817487 9817513 9817519 9817531 9817537 9817559 9817579 9817583 9817597
9817601 9817603 9817609 9817627 9817637 9817649 9817663 9817673 9817727 9817751
9817771 9817799 9817811 9817853 9817861 9817867 9817897 9817903 9817919 9817931
9817937 9817939 9817943 9817949 9817961 9817981 9817991 9818009 9818023 9818047
9818057 9818071 9818087 9818089 9818111 9818143 9818161 9818173 9818177 9818183
9818189 9818191 9818201 9818219 9818251 9818257 9818267 9818273 9818287 9818293
9818317 9818353 9818363 9818371 9818399 9818411 9818423 9818429 9818449 9818477
9818507 9818509 9818533 9818551 9818561 9818563 9818591 9818593 9818657 9818657
9818671 9818689 9818693 9818701 9818713 9818717 9818729 9818761 9818773 9818779
9818789 9818797 9818807 9818813 9818827 9818867 9818873 9818881 9818891 9818899
9818903 9818923 9818929 9818947 9818959 9818969 9819031 9819037 9819053 9819079
9819083 9819101 9819127 9819133 9819163 9819167 9819191 9819211 9819221 9819223
9819239 9819241 9819263 9819289 9819301 9819317 9819323 9819331 9819347 9819391
9819427 9819451 9819457 9819503 9819517 9819521 9819533 9819539 9819553 9819571
9819577 9819611 9819613 9819617 9819671 9819673 9819679 9819683 9819697 9819703
9819707 9819731 9819773 9819791 9819809 9819847 9819853 9819857 9819871 9819877
9819881 9819889 9819899 9819907 9819913 9819947 9819959 9819961 9819967 9820037
9820043 9820049 9820061 9820073 9820099 9820117 9820121 9820147 9820159 9820163
9820189 9820199 9820201 9820219 9820229 9820243 9820249 9820259 9820277 9820289
9820303 9820313 9820319 9820337 9820351 9820367 9820381 9820387 9820403
9820417 9820427 9820453 9820457 9820463 9820483 9820487 9820493 9820513 9820519
9820523 9820537 9820541 9820579 9820601 9820621 9820627 9820631 9820633 9820639
9820661 9820687 9820703 9820721 9820729 9820751 9820757 9820787 9820801 9820823
9820841 9820843 9820861 9820871 9820897 9820901 9820907 9820957 9820961 9820969
9820997 9821033 9821047 9821051 9821107 9821129 9821131 9821137 9821159 9821173
9821213 9821219 9821281 9821293 9821303 9821321 9821333 9821351 9821363 9821381
9821429 9821449 9821443 9821453 9821489 9821503 9821507 9821521 9821527 9821531
9821561 9821569 9821579 9821593 9821599 9821629 9821641 9821657 9821659 9821821
9821683 9821701 9821719 9821723 9821737 9821743 9821783 9821797 9821809 9821821
9821843 9821849 9821857 9821873 9821887 9821893 9821899 9821921 9821939
9821957 9822019 9822047 9822061 9822067 9822079 9822089 9822091 9822101 9822121
9822151 9822161 9822167 9822179 9822187 9822191 9822193 9822203 9822233 9822251
9822289 9822343 9822347 9822359 9822367 9822409 9822419 9822431 9822433 9822451
9822457 9822499 9822509 9822521 9822523 9822551 9822559 9822569 9822607 9822611
9822623 9822641 9822643 9822653 9822721 9822727 9822731 9822737 9822809 9822833
9822847 9822887 9822893 9822907 9822941 9822949 9822961 9822973 9823027 9823031
9823039 9823043 9823099 9823103 9823109 9823117 9823129 9823153 9823157 9823169
9823181 9823201 9823207 9823211 9823217 9823267 9823271 9823273 9823279 9823283
9823291 9823309 9823327 9823343 9823351 9823367 9823403 9823409 9823427 9823439
9823453 9823487 9823493 9823511 9823531 9823543 9823549 9823579 9823613 9823633
9823657 9823661 9823669 9823673 9823679 9823711 9823757 9823763 9823769 9823773
9823897 9823903 9823937 9823937 9823973 9824029 9824047 9824071 9824077
9824119 9824123 9824153 9824161 9824183 9824189 9824201 9824207 9824237 9824261
9824291 9824299 9824323 9824327 9824357 9824369 9824383 9824393 9824423 9824459
9824471 9824509 9824527 9824537 9824641 9824651 9824669 9824671 9824693 9824701
9824723 9824741 9824743 9824747 9824761 9824779 9824791 9824797 9824803 9824819
9824821 9824831 9824879 9824897 9824917 9824941 9824947 9824987 9824989 9825001
9825007 9825019 9825037 9825107 9825119 9825121 9825139 9825149 9825161 9825173
9825181 9825187 9825191 9825247 9825251 9825253 9825311 9825341 9825359 9825373
9825379 9825391 9825427 9825443 9825449 9825469 9825499 9825523 9825533 9825547
9825551 9825553 9825559 9825589 9825593 9825611 9825631 9825649 9825653 9825659
9825661 9825671 9825701 9825709 9825713 9825731 9825737 9825743 9825757 9825817
9825821 9825833 9825839 9825841 9825857 9825859 9825877 9825901 9825913 9825929
9825931 9825953 9825967 9825971 9826001 9826013 9826057 9826073 9826079
9826093 9826123 9826133 9826151 9826169 9826171 9826177 9826181 9826207 9826237
9826247 9826261 9826277 9826279 9826283 9826291 9826343 9826351 9826361 9826373
9826379 9826381 9826393 9826409 9826417 9826433 9826463 9826499 9826501 9826507
9826517 9826519 9826541 9826547 9826567 9826601 9826633 9826643 9826669 9826709
```

```
9826717 9826753 9826769 9826777 9826801 9826811 9826813 9826829 9826837 9826841
9826847 9826877 9826891 9826913 9826937 9826939 9826961 9826979 9826991 9827011
9827017 9827021 9827023 9827029 9827053 9827063 9827119 9827131 9827179 9827189
9827197 9827203 9827221 9827243 9827281 9827287 9827297 9827299 9827303 9827329
9827339 9827347 9827353 9827357 9827381 9827383 9827393 9827399 9827407 9827437
9827471 9827473 9827501 9827507 9827537 9827551 9827557 9827561 9827569 9827591
9827599 9827633 9827639 9827669 9827743 9827777 9827791 9827809 9827813 9827821
9827827 9827879 9827927 9827929 9827953 9827963 9827971 9827981 9827999 9828001
9828017 9828019 9828031 9828053 9828067 9828079 9828083 9828089 9828097 9828121
9828127 9828167 9828179 9828197 9828211 9828223 9828239 9828241 9828253 9828257
9828277 9828283 9828293 9828319 9828323 9828341 9828349 9828367 9828391 9828433
9828437 9828443 9828449 9828461 9828463 9828473 9828493 9828547 9828557 9828571
9828583 9828617 9828619 9828629 9828641 9828653 9828677 9828697 9828701 9828713
9828727 9828733 9828761 9828769 9828773 9828787 9828811 9828821 9828823 9828827
9828851 9828859 9828877 9828881 9828901 9828919 9828961 9828977 9828979 9828997
9829007 9829019 9829021 9829031 9829033 9829037 9829081 9829091 9829093 9829097
9829103 9829129 9829153 9829163 9829177 9829181 9829189 9829229 9829243 9829273
9829277 9829291 9829319 9829333 9829343 9829373 9829399 9829409 9829447 9829481
9829483 9829489 9829493 9829507 9829513 9829543 9829549 9829583 9829591 9829639
9829643 9829657 9829681 9829691 9829711 9829739 9829789 9829793 9829823 9829829
9829861 9829867 9829877 9829889 9829921 9829933 9829943 9829951 9829969 9829987
9829997 9829999 9830017 9830047 9830053 9830057 9830059 9830081 9830083 9830089
9830113 9830141 9830147 9830153 9830213 9830221 9830231 9830237 9830243 9830257
9830297 9830321 9830329 9830341 9830347 9830351 9830357 9830363 9830377 9830393
9830413 9830459 9830477 9830479 9830519 9830533 9830609 9830651 9830663 9830669
9830671 9830707 9830713 9830719 9830747 9830753 9830759 9830761 9830767 9830783
9830791 9830801 9830803 9830833 9830861 9830893 9830897 9830903 9830921 9830929
9830941 9830957 9830987 9831013 9831043 9831077 9831091 9831109 9831119 9831127
9831139 9831163 9831167 9831179 9831181 9831191 9831193 9831223 9831259 9831271
9831277 9831325 9831329 9831337 9831361 9831383 9831397 9831407 9831443 9831461
9831463 9831487 9831509 9831517 9831527 9831533 9831539 9831571 9831587 9831589
9831617 9831637 9831641 9831707 9831709 9831719 9831727 9831737 9831749 9831769
9831799 9831803 9831827 9831839 9831851 9831853 9831863 9831869 9831881 9831889
9831893 9831947 9831949 9831953 9832003 9832007 9832019 9832021 9832027 9832033
9832037 9832061 9832091 9832093 9832099 9832111 9832117 9832129 9832133 9832153
9832157 9832181 9832217 9832223 9832231 9832237 9832267 9832271 9832279 9832309
9832313 9832321 9832327 9832349 9832351 9832357 9832369 9832373 9832379 9832387
9832393 9832399 9832441 9832513 9832517 9832547 9832553 9832567 9832583 9832591
9832597 9832601 9832607 9832609 9832619 9832637 9832643 9832663 9832679 9832703
9832717 9832723 9832733 9832741 9832777 9832813 9832819 9832829 9832847 9832877
9832897 9832909 9832967 9832981 9833039 9833053 9833063 9833069 9833113 9833133
9833137 9833141 9833149 9833179 9833189 9833221 9833227 9833237 9833267 9833273
9833281 9833303 9833309 9833311 9833339 9833347 9833359 9833363 9833437 9833441
9833449 9833491 9833519 9833533 9833563 9833597 9833609 9833617 9833623 9833631
9833647 9833671 9833687 9833689 9833711 9833717 9833729 9833743 9833771 9833797
9833807 9833821 9833869 9833881 9833893 9833909 9833917 9833937 9833953 9833977
9833981 9834023 9834029 9834047 9834073 9834079 9834091 9834107 9834113 9834173
9834199 9834217 9834221 9834241 9834247 9834283 9834289 9834299 9834361 9834367
9834373 9834379 9834413 9834443 9834467 9834491 9834497 9834511 9834527 9834529
9834557 9834581 9834599 9834613 9834689 9834739 9834751 9834757 9834763 9834787
9834809 9834817 9834821 9834827 9834829 9834841 9834871 9834883 9834889 9834893
9834899 9834901 9834907 9834911 9834941 9834953 9834971 9834977 9834983 9835009
9835037 9835069 9835073 9835109 9835117 9835127 9835171 9835183 9835207 9835211
9835219 9835247 9835253 9835259 9835297 9835313 9835333 9835357 9835381 9835391
9835393 9835409 9835453 9835471 9835489 9835493 9835499 9835517 9835543 9835561
9835577 9835589 9835601 9835603 9835621 9835627 9835663 9835681 9835699 9835723
9835729 9835733 9835739 9835751 9835753 9835757 9835759 9835781 9835811 9835829
9835841 9835849 9835863 9835919 9835951 9835961 9835963 9835981 9835999 9836003
9836027 9836033 9836039 9836077 9836107 9836131 9836143 9836147 9836153 9836159
9836171 9836201 9836209 9836219 9836221 9836227 9836257 9836287 9836317 9836363
9836377 9836381 9836389 9836399 9836411 9836419 9836441 9836459 9836483 9836501
9836503 9836507 9836543 9836569 9836573 9836581 9836621 9836627 9836633 9836647
9836653 9836681 9836683 9836689 9836707 9836711 9836719 9836759 9836767 9836773
9836777 9836791 9836819 9836821 9836839 9836899 9836917 9836929 9836933 9836947
9836963 9836971 9836987 9836993 9837019 9837059 9837071 9837083 9837109 9837127
9837131 9837143 9837161 9837173 9837181 9837187 9837209 9837211 9837229 9837251
9837281 9837283 9837313 9837329 9837341 9837343 9837389 9837397 9837431 9837433
9837439 9837481 9837511 9837517 9837521 9837557 9837587 9837613 9837631 9837673
9837683 9837691 9837697 9837727 9837731 9837739 9837749 9837761 9837787 9837799
9837809 9837829 9837847 9837851 9837857 9837869 9837871 9837911 9837923 9837941
9837979 9837989 9838001 9838021 9838033 9838097 9838111 9838117 9838123 9838133
9838139 9838151 9838159 9838183 9838187 9838207 9838243 9838247 9838259 9838277
9838303 9838331 9838351 9838363 9838379 9838397 9838417 9838441 9838447 9838489
9838519 9838531 9838547 9838553 9838573 9838583 9838589 9838607 9838639 9838657
9838679 9838681 9838691 9838693 9838723 9838727 9838747 9838769 9838799 9838813
9838823 9838831 9838853 9838877 9838889 9838919 9838931 9838943 9838951 9838961
9838987 9838991 9838999 9839021 9839083 9839097 9839099 9839111 9839119 9839129
9839153 9839161 9839171 9839177 9839189 9839201 9839227 9839237 9839251 9839261
9839267 9839273 9839287 9839329 9839339 9839353 9839411 9839449 9839461 9839471
9839507 9839509 9839527 9839537 9839561 9839569 9839603 9839611 9839619 9839633
9839659 9839687 9839689 9839707 9839749 9839761 9839771 9839783 9839813 9839839
9839857 9839887 9839897 9839909 9839911 9839917 9839939 9839941 9839969 9839987
9839993 9840001 9840011 9840013 9840023 9840069 9840071 9840073 9840091 9840073
9840101 9840121 9840133 9840137 9840151 9840169 9840179 9840199 9840203 9840209
9840239 9840242 9840247 9840253 9840269 9840283 9840293 9840317 9840349 9840373
9840401 9840431 9840443 9840449 9840487 9840503 9840521 9840539 9840577 9840583
9840587 9840601 9840617 9840643 9840647 9840659 9840661 9840667 9840707 9840709
9840713 9840731 9840751 9840763 9840781 9840811 9840833 9840839 9840869 9840899
9840983 9840989 9841019 9841021 9841037 9841067 9841081 9841087 9841099 9841127
```

```
9841133  9841157  9841163  9841177  9841193  9841201  9841207  9841219  9841243  9841253
9841261  9841277  9841319  9841343  9841369  9841379  9841397  9841421  9841423  9841427
9841439  9841441  9841457  9841483  9841537  9841543  9841561  9841591  9841597  9841607
9841609  9841619  9841627  9841661  9841693  9841703  9841721  9841739  9841747  9841751
9841771  9841789  9841813  9841823  9841837  9841841  9841877  9841921  9841939  9841987
9842011  9842017  9842023  9842033  9842051  9842059  9842071  9842081  9842083  9842101
9842117  9842123  9842197  9842207  9842213  9842263  9842267  9842279  9842291
9842293  9842297  9842347  9842353  9842363  9842369  9842383  9842467  9842477  9842509
9842519  9842527  9842561  9842563  9842579  9842603  9842611  9842617  9842621  9842647
9842653  9842731  9842761  9842773  9842831  9842837  9842849  9842857  9842863  9842869
9842879  9842909  9842953  9842981  9843013  9843019  9843049  9843079  9843109  9843139
9843179  9843191  9843199  9843203  9843217  9843233  9843263  9843283  9843293  9843299
9843343  9843371  9843373  9843397  9843419  9843437  9843451  9843473  9843487  9843497
9843521  9843529  9843541  9843553  9843569  9843571  9843583  9843599  9843601  9843611
9843661  9843677  9843683  9843721  9843761  9843787  9843797  9843803  9843809  9843811
9843817  9843859  9843863  9843877  9843907  9843913  9843917  9843923  9843959  9843979
9843989  9843991  9844001  9844013  9844027  9844031  9844039  9844063  9844067  9844097
9844099  9844129  9844157  9844181  9844187  9844189  9844217  9844229  9844259  9844277
9844279  9844283  9844301  9844319  9844339  9844349  9844357  9844361  9844403  9844417
9844487  9844493  9844501  9844517  9844531  9844537  9844619  9844631  9844657  9844661
9844663  9844669  9844687  9844693  9844699  9844727  9844733  9844739  9844741  9844753
9844777  9844811  9844823  9844829  9844837  9844841  9844847  9844871  9844889  9844903
9844927  9844937  9844987  9844993  9845009  9845029  9845051  9845053  9845063  9845083
9845089  9845107  9845113  9845117  9845141  9845161  9845233  9845263  9845273  9845299
9845369  9845387  9845417  9845483  9845489  9845491  9845497  9845501  9845531  9845551
9845557  9845593  9845599  9845609  9845623  9845657  9845677  9845681  9845687  9845707
9845711  9845713  9845723  9845741  9845747  9845749  9845767  9845777  9845789  9845807
9845809  9845813  9845821  9845831  9845833  9845837  9845887  9845897  9845903  9845917
9845939  9845947  9845951  9845963  9845989  9845999  9846013  9846017  9846019  9846037
9846061  9846101  9846103  9846113  9846131  9846149  9846163  9846173  9846197  9846217
9846223  9846227  9846233  9846271  9846289  9846301  9846311  9846377  9846391  9846413
9846439  9846443  9846449  9846467  9846469  9846497  9846509  9846511  9846517  9846523
9846533  9846563  9846583  9846589  9846593  9846607  9846637  9846643  9846647  9846649
9846659  9846673  9846677  9846699  9846701  9846709  9846713  9846721  9846743  9846779
9846833  9846839  9846841  9846857  9846869  9846889  9846897  9846913  9846953  9846973  9846989
9847001  9847003  9847009  9847027  9847031  9847051  9847067  9847087  9847091  9847099
9847127  9847147  9847157  9847213  9847219  9847223  9847249  9847259  9847273  9847297
9847303  9847307  9847309  9847337  9847363  9847379  9847391  9847417  9847451  9847463
9847499  9847507  9847543  9847549  9847571  9847577  9847597  9847603  9847609  9847613
9847619  9847633  9847637  9847699  9847723  9847741  9847759  9847763  9847781  9847793
9847807  9847819  9847829  9847847  9847889  9847891  9847897  9847921  9847927  9847931
9847949  9847963  9847967  9847969  9847991  9847993  9847997  9848021  9848039  9848053
9848057  9848093  9848107  9848123  9848131  9848141  9848147  9848149  9848171  9848183
9848191  9848233  9848249  9848257  9848261  9848269  9848273  9848281  9848291  9848299
9848303  9848309  9848341  9848351  9848353  9848369  9848381  9848383  9848417  9848459
9848467  9848471  9848537  9848543  9848557  9848581  9848617  9848647  9848669  9848737
9848747  9848749  9848789  9848789  9848791  9848801  9848809  9848827  9848833  9848843
9848857  9848869  9848879  9848887  9848903  9848911  9848957  9848959  9848987  9849017
9849019  9849031  9849097  9849097  9849101  9849109  9849121  9849139  9849187  9849197
9849209  9849211  9849223  9849247  9849251  9849253  9849271  9849311  9849317  9849319
9849337  9849383  9849397  9849403  9849407  9849421  9849449  9849479  9849503  9849509
9849517  9849523  9849533  9849551  9849563  9849569  9849571  9849577  9849583  9849607
9849629  9849683  9849689  9849701  9849703  9849769  9849779  9849793  9849857  9849863
9849877  9849899  9849941  9849959  9849989  9850007  9850037  9850067  9850069  9850081
9850129  9850171  9850193  9850207  9850223  9850237  9850261  9850277  9850331  9850333
9850359  9850363  9850369  9850387  9850403  9850411  9850427  9850433  9850441  9850453
9850457  9850471  9850481  9850499  9850543  9850559  9850567  9850571  9850573  9850583
9850597  9850613  9850627  9850637  9850649  9850661  9850663  9850669  9850703  9850723
9850727  9850733  9850751  9850781  9850801  9850849  9850853  9850861  9850889  9850921
9850931  9850961  9850993  9851011  9851033  9851047  9851071  9851081  9851099  9851113
9851123  9851137  9851141  9851141  9851147  9851167  9851173  9851197  9851203  9851239
9851243  9851249  9851267  9851293  9851327  9851339  9851363  9851377  9851389  9851393
9851411  9851419  9851431  9851441  9851447  9851461  9851467  9851477  9851489  9851507
9851563  9851591  9851617  9851627  9851651  9851669  9851689  9851701  9851711  9851713
9851719  9851749  9851759  9851783  9851791  9851813  9851837  9851867  9851873  9851887
9851911  9851923  9851929  9851951  9851977  9851997  9852019  9852041  9852067  9852077
9852091  9852097  9852103  9852109  9852113  9852179  9852191  9852251  9852263  9852277
9852313  9852331  9852343  9852361  9852383  9852391  9852413  9852419  9852433  9852439
9852443  9852467  9852509  9852511  9852527  9852529  9852539  9852553  9852559  9852569
9852589  9852593  9852607  9852617  9852649  9852653  9852679  9852683  9852691  9852701
9852743  9852827  9852851  9852889  9852907  9852917  9852937  9852943  9852949  9852961
9852967  9852991  9853007  9853027  9853037  9853043  9853049  9853061  9853073  9853121
9853139  9853141  9853159  9853169  9853171  9853237  9853241  9853303  9853307  9853313
9853367  9853369  9853379  9853399  9853411  9853423  9853439  9853447  9853463  9853483
9853517  9853559  9853577  9853603  9853607  9853619  9853631  9853633  9853639  9853643
9853661  9853663  9853681  9853699  9853703  9853717  9853733  9853763  9853769  9853783
9853801  9853819  9853841  9853847  9853873  9853889  9853901  9853933  9853967  9853979
9853993  9854011  9854017  9854023  9854041  9854051  9854077  9854081  9854083  9854087
9854153  9854177  9854219  9854231  9854261  9854279  9854329  9854371  9854399  9854401
9854417  9854431  9854447  9854459  9854477  9854527  9854549  9854563  9854567  9854569
9854573  9854591  9854623  9854627  9854629  9854633  9854639  9854643  9854653  9854681
9854699  9854707  9854717  9854743  9854753  9854759  9854771  9854777  9854791  9854851
9854857  9854893  9854939  9854941  9854959  9854969  9854981  9854989  9855011  9855029
9855031  9855037  9855049  9855071  9855107  9855113  9855119  9855133  9855149  9855151
9855161  9855169  9855173  9855187  9855193  9855199  9855217  9855229  9855233  9855253
9855259  9855271  9855311  9855323  9855367  9855371  9855379  9855401  9855433  9855437
9855451  9855463  9855467  9855481  9855493  9855497  9855533  9855541  9855553  9855577
9855583  9855607  9855611  9855647  9855689  9855697  9855701  9855743  9855787  9855793
9855817  9855821  9855823  9855863  9855871  9855887  9855913  9855929  9855941  9855943
```

9855959 9855977 9855991 9855997 9856019 9856037 9856051 9856061 9856069 9856081
9856103 9856111 9856123 9856129 9856139 9856151 9856157 9856163 9856181 9856183
9856211 9856219 9856237 9856261 9856279 9856283 9856313 9856339 9856349 9856361
9856381 9856391 9856403 9856409 9856411 9856423 9856439 9856471 9856477 9856487
9856493 9856513 9856529 9856531 9856537 9856559 9856577 9856579 9856591 9856619
9856633 9856697 9856709 9856727 9856741 9856757 9856783 9856789 9856817 9856829
9856843 9856883 9856919 9856937 9856939 9856943 9856963 9857009 9857011 9857027
9857047 9857053 9857123 9857131 9857137 9857147 9857149 9857153 9857167 9857201
9857209 9857213 9857251 9857293 9857321 9857327 9857347 9857369 9857377
9857387 9857389 9857413 9857423 9857443 9857459 9857461 9857479 9857483 9857489
9857513 9857527 9857537 9857579 9857591 9857609 9857611 9857641 9857647 9857657
9857663 9857669 9857681 9857693 9857719 9857737 9857791 9857801 9857831 9857839
9857849 9857891 9857893 9857899 9857927 9857933 9857957 9857959 9857963 9857971
9857983 9858041 9858047 9858061 9858073 9858089 9858097 9858103 9858119 9858157
9858193 9858197 9858229 9858241 9858253 9858257 9858259 9858269 9858293 9858301
9858311 9858319 9858349 9858353 9858361 9858367 9858413 9858437 9858449 9858451
9858461 9858469 9858479 9858503 9858517 9858523 9858529 9858533 9858547 9858551
9858593 9858599 9858631 9858677 9858683 9858703 9858727 9858731 9858733 9858757
9858769 9858781 9858787 9858791 9858799 9858809 9858823 9858833 9858869 9858887
9858949 9858971 9858991 9859001 9859013 9859021 9859027 9859033 9859039 9859051
9859061 9859067 9859093 9859103 9859123 9859127 9859139 9859163 9859193 9859207
9859231 9859253 9859277 9859319 9859351 9859357 9859361 9859373 9859379 9859417
9859429 9859441 9859463 9859471 9859483 9859511 9859523 9859543 9859547 9859559
9859567 9859573 9859597 9859601 9859621 9859637 9859669 9859673 9859679 9859691
9859693 9859697 9859769 9859781 9859783 9859799 9859807 9859823 9859831 9859849
9859859 9859867 9859897 9859901 9859909 9859931 9859937 9859957 9859963 9859973
9859981 9859999 9860023 9860057 9860089 9860099 9860117 9860129 9860141 9860143
9860161 9860197 9860209 9860219 9860231 9860237 9860273 9860281 9860299 9860303
9860311 9860339 9860351 9860381 9860393 9860401 9860413 9860419 9860429 9860437
9860447 9860453 9860479 9860497 9860509 9860519 9860531 9860549 9860567 9860579
9860593 9860603 9860651 9860657 9860681 9860687 9860707 9860713 9860723 9860743
9860771 9860777 9860789 9860797 9860801 9860819 9860831 9860839 9860843 9860881
9860891 9860897 9860909 9860941 9860947 9860959 9860971 9860987 9860999 9861029
9861041 9861053 9861079 9861109 9861143 9861151 9861157 9861191 9861217 9861221
9861223 9861239 9861253 9861301 9861307 9861349 9861353 9861359 9861367 9861373
9861389 9861391 9861407 9861409 9861413 9861431 9861433 9861461 9861463 9861469
9861487 9861559 9861563 9861569 9861571 9861583 9861611 9861613 9861619 9861629
9861637 9861661 9861667 9861679 9861697 9861707 9861713 9861727 9861743 9861757
9861767 9861781 9861823 9861833 9861847 9861881 9861883 9861913 9861919 9861947
9861953 9861967 9861983 9861991 9862019 9862033 9862043 9862049 9862063 9862067
9862079 9862103 9862109 9862129 9862133 9862141 9862157 9862201 9862207 9862213
9862243 9862249 9862253 9862277 9862283 9862319 9862327 9862361 9862379 9862393
9862403 9862409 9862417 9862451 9862481 9862487 9862507 9862513 9862529 9862537
9862579 9862603 9862627 9862631 9862637 9862649 9862651 9862679 9862687 9862709
9862711 9862733 9862739 9862747 9862759 9862777 9862789 9862793 9862817 9862829
9862847 9862861 9862881 9862917 9862921 9862927 9862949 9862961 9862981 9862999
9863017 9863047 9863059 9863081 9863093 9863099 9863101 9863129 9863131 9863149
9863171 9863221 9863263 9863267 9863303 9863311 9863317 9863323 9863351 9863419
9863429 9863449 9863453 9863479 9863513 9863531 9863543 9863553 9863599
9863647 9863669 9863677 9863701 9863713 9863729 9863743 9863753 9863759 9863767
9863779 9863801 9863809 9863837 9863851 9863923 9863933 9863939 9863947 9863959
9864007 9864011 9864061 9864083 9864091 9864119 9864133 9864139 9864143 9864167
9864187 9864191 9864203 9864241 9864277 9864331 9864347 9864353 9864359 9864373
9864383 9864397 9864427 9864433 9864443 9864457 9864473 9864487 9864497 9864509
9864529 9864581 9864583 9864599 9864601 9864637 9864643 9864649 9864653 9864683
9864697 9864707 9864713 9864719 9864721 9864733 9864761 9864763 9864773 9864787
9864791 9864817 9864823 9864839 9864847 9864889 9864937 9864949 9864983 9864989
9865007 9865021 9865033 9865057 9865069 9865073 9865081 9865087 9865097 9865109
9865127 9865129 9865139 9865153 9865171 9865181 9865187 9865201 9865211 9865241
9865243 9865267 9865277 9865279 9865333 9865337 9865343 9865363 9865381 9865403
9865411 9865417 9865433 9865451 9865511 9865517 9865519 9865523 9865529 9865531
9865553 9865573 9865577 9865589 9865601 9865613 9865621 9865633 9865637 9865651
9865711 9865733 9865747 9865753 9865777 9865787 9865811 9865813 9865819 9865837
9865841 9865879 9865903 9865907 9865927 9865931 9865937 9865949 9865979 9865993
9866009 9866033 9866041 9866047 9866071 9866083 9866107 9866147 9866167 9866179
9866203 9866237 9866243 9866261 9866291 9866303 9866327 9866401 9866407 9866411
9866413 9866419 9866431 9866449 9866489 9866497 9866501 9866509 9866513
9866537 9866551 9866557 9866561 9866573 9866581 9866599 9866611 9866627 9866653
9866669 9866671 9866677 9866683 9866687 9866693 9866707 9866713 9866729 9866741
9866761 9866767 9866777 9866797 9866803 9866809 9866819 9866849 9866869 9866887
9866897 9866913 9866921 9866933 9866951 9866981 9866999 9867037 9867043 9867059
9867071 9867073 9867079 9867119 9867149 9867173 9867203 9867211 9867233 9867239
9867241 9867257 9867281 9867283 9867307 9867349 9867353 9867359 9867371 9867427
9867449 9867457 9867467 9867469 9867491 9867521 9867541 9867551 9867581 9867601
9867617 9867623 9867653 9867659 9867677 9867721 9867731 9867761 9867769 9867797
9867799 9867817 9867841 9867853 9867883 9867929 9867931 9867959 9867971 9868009
9868021 9868037 9868039 9868043 9868051 9868063 9868129 9868141 9868147 9868151
9868169 9868181 9868189 9868217 9868237 9868253 9868291 9868319 9868343 9868351
9868367 9868393 9868421 9868423 9868433 9868459 9868471 9868477 9868499 9868501
9868511 9868513 9868553 9868559 9868561 9868597 9868643 9868693 9868699 9868769
9868777 9868799 9868813 9868829 9868843 9868847 9868849 9868853 9868887 9868889
9868897 9868913 9868921 9868933 9868951 9868967 9868979 9868981 9869003 9869017
9869039 9869053 9869087 9869089 9869117 9869137 9869143 9869149 9869173 9869181
9869221 9869239 9869243 9869257 9869261 9869263 9869267 9869339 9869347 9869393
9869399 9869411 9869413 9869437 9869443 9869449 9869467 9869513 9869557 9869567
9869581 9869593 9869603 9869609 9869621 9869627 9869633 9869641 9869663 9869669
9869677 9869681 9869693 9869701 9869711 9869777 9869789 9869791 9869801 9869851
9869857 9869863 9869869 9869903 9869917 9869927 9869929 9869939 9869957 9869963
9869969 9869999 9870017 9870061 9870067 9870071 9870143 9870163 9870167 9870173

```
9870193  9870199  9870241  9870247  9870283  9870317  9870323  9870337  9870347  9870361
9870389  9870391  9870401  9870407  9870409  9870449  9870461  9870499  9870503  9870541
9870547  9870551  9870569  9870577  9870583  9870589  9870647  9870661  9870673  9870677
9870683  9870691  9870737  9870787  9870797  9870811  9870827  9870851  9870853  9870859
9870871  9870907  9870911  9870943  9870947  9870953  9870961  9870967  9870977  9870983
9871007  9871027  9871031  9871039  9871073  9871093  9871097  9871111  9871157  9871159
9871181  9871189  9871217  9871219  9871229  9871247  9871259  9871289  9871291  9871307
9871321  9871327  9871331  9871357  9871391  9871403  9871427  9871429  9871471  9871481
9871483  9871487  9871501  9871517  9871523  9871573  9871591  9871607  9871619  9871633
9871649  9871651  9871661  9871663  9871699  9871721  9871753  9871759  9871789  9871817
9871843  9871877  9871891  9871907  9871909  9871931  9871943  9871949  9871957  9871973
9871993  9872011  9872017  9872047  9872063  9872089  9872099  9872111  9872113  9872117
9872123  9872131  9872171  9872201  9872207  9872243  9872251  9872263  9872273  9872281
9872299  9872309  9872311  9872321  9872323  9872329  9872339  9872341  9872347  9872371
9872399  9872407  9872417  9872437  9872449  9872501  9872509  9872519  9872521  9872567
9872579  9872581  9872587  9872623  9872641  9872657  9872659  9872683  9872693  9872711
9872713  9872717  9872729  9872741  9872749  9872791  9872809  9872827  9872839  9872887
9872899  9872921  9872927  9872939  9872977  9872983  9873011  9873023  9873029  9873041
9873067  9873109  9873113  9873121  9873131  9873133  9873151  9873167  9873181  9873223
9873229  9873239  9873247  9873263  9873299  9873313  9873319  9873349  9873373  9873389
9873433  9873439  9873449  9873467  9873503  9873527  9873557  9873569  9873581  9873607
9873613  9873623  9873631  9873637  9873649  9873653  9873671  9873679  9873691  9873697
9873701  9873707  9873733  9873751  9873767  9873769  9873811  9873817  9873839  9873859
9873881  9873883  9873893  9873911  9873917  9873937  9873943  9873947  9873967  9873971
9873979  9874003  9874019  9874021  9874031  9874057  9874103  9874121  9874141  9874147
9874157  9874169  9874187  9874223  9874247  9874313  9874327  9874339  9874349  9874351
9874363  9874367  9874373  9874409  9874411  9874439  9874441  9874451  9874453  9874463
9874499  9874511  9874517  9874531  9874537  9874541  9874577  9874607  9874633  9874643
9874651  9874673  9874681  9874691  9874693  9874717  9874769  9874793  9874811  9874831
9874847  9874853  9874901  9874933  9874937  9874939  9874951  9874961  9874999  9875009
9875017  9875023  9875039  9875057  9875059  9875069  9875071  9875087  9875141  9875153
9875171  9875209  9875227  9875233  9875287  9875293  9875323  9875339  9875341  9875347
9875357  9875377  9875381  9875389  9875407  9875417  9875429  9875443  9875447  9875449
9875471  9875491  9875507  9875519  9875539  9875549  9875557  9875561  9875563  9875587
9875651  9875669  9875683  9875693  9875699  9875729  9875741  9875753  9875777  9875783
9875813  9875821  9875893  9875917  9875927  9875933  9875941  9875977  9875981  9876017
9876019  9876023  9876059  9876071  9876079  9876091  9876101  9876103  9876107  9876109
9876137  9876149  9876161  9876271  9876281  9876289  9876301  9876331  9876341  9876359
9876379  9876413  9876437  9876469  9876479  9876511  9876527  9876553  9876563  9876577
9876589  9876593  9876611  9876623  9876641  9876673  9876701  9876719  9876761  9876781
9876803  9876809  9876829  9876833  9876851  9876857  9876871  9876883  9876899  9876901
9876929  9876931  9876943  9876947  9876961  9877001  9877033  9877129  9877151  9877159
9877177  9877193  9877199  9877211  9877213  9877223  9877237  9877243  9877247  9877267
9877331  9877333  9877337  9877381  9877393  9877421  9877443  9877453  9877463  9877477
9877481  9877489  9877501  9877507  9877513  9877523  9877529  9877537  9877541  9877559
9877577  9877579  9877583  9877589  9877613  9877619  9877627  9877633  9877643  9877667
9877687  9877709  9877723  9877727  9877753  9877783  9877811  9877823  9877841  9877859
9877897  9877921  9877937  9877961  9877997  9878023  9878039  9878041  9878047  9878051
9878053  9878059  9878069  9878083  9878101  9878117  9878123  9878129  9878147  9878153
9878177  9878179  9878191  9878203  9878227  9878249  9878251  9878257  9878291  9878303
9878321  9878327  9878333  9878353  9878369  9878381  9878399  9878419  9878467  9878471
9878483  9878489  9878503  9878509  9878521  9878527  9878563  9878567  9878599  9878611
9878657  9878731  9878747  9878749  9878773  9878797  9878839  9878851  9878857  9878861
9878867  9878893  9878903  9878923  9878927  9878929  9879007  9879013  9879047
9879059  9879061  9879097  9879101  9879131  9879139  9879151  9879157  9879179  9879197
9879209  9879223  9879229  9879239  9879257  9879263  9879269  9879271  9879277  9879281
9879283  9879299  9879323  9879349  9879371  9879391  9879403  9879409  9879413  9879427
9879439  9879469  9879473  9879479  9879521  9879557  9879577  9879587  9879589  9879599
9879641  9879643  9879659  9879689  9879697  9879757  9879763  9879767  9879773  9879781
9879787  9879817  9879827  9879871  9879901  9879911  9879913  9879937  9879953  9879959
9879983  9879997  9880001  9880027  9880033  9880037  9880061  9880093  9880127  9880163
9880177  9880183  9880187  9880193  9880201  9880223  9880243  9880267  9880277  9880291
9880301  9880307  9880321  9880357  9880373  9880391  9880421  9880427  9880433  9880441
9880447  9880457  9880459  9880463  9880469  9880483  9880489  9880529  9880567  9880579
9880601  9880603  9880643  9880667  9880693  9880709  9880721  9880733  9880747  9880811
9880837  9880853  9880861  9880873  9880891  9880921  9880939  9880943  9880973  9880991
9880993  9881009  9881023  9881051  9881087  9881101  9881107  9881111  9881119  9881149
9881153  9881167  9881171  9881203  9881231  9881239  9881269  9881279  9881299  9881303
9881309  9881321  9881363  9881381  9881401  9881411  9881413  9881419  9881429  9881449
9881453  9881477  9881483  9881491  9881503  9881507  9881527  9881551  9881561  9881569
9881593  9881603  9881611  9881621  9881623  9881633  9881639  9881661  9881671  9881687
9881689  9881693  9881713  9881719  9881741  9881747  9881749  9881803  9881819  9881821
9881827  9881857  9881863  9881889  9881899  9881909  9881951  9881981  9881987
9881999  9882013  9882017  9882029  9882073  9882097  9882101  9882113  9882139  9882161
9882163  9882181  9882233  9882239  9882241  9882269  9882281  9882283  9882289  9882307
9882317  9882319  9882323  9882343  9882371  9882383  9882391  9882403  9882407  9882437
9882443  9882449  9882461  9882463  9882469  9882487  9882503  9882511  9882563  9882577
9882601  9882619  9882659  9882663  9882673  9882731  9882739  9882767  9882773  9882787
9882809  9882839  9882863  9882871  9882877  9882919  9882923  9882947  9882989
9883007  9883057  9883061  9883067  9883073  9883087  9883117  9883151  9883157  9883177
9883187  9883189  9883193  9883201  9883213  9883219  9883231  9883241  9883251  9883303
9883309  9883333  9883351  9883441  9883457  9883463  9883469  9883481  9883487  9883499
9883541  9883547  9883567  9883669  9883673  9883729
9883763  9883787  9883799  9883849  9883871  9883877  9883879  9883883  9883901  9883903
9883931  9883941  9883967  9884003  9884027  9884033  9884051  9884057  9884107
9884113  9884117  9884137  9884153  9884159  9884179  9884209  9884233  9884263  9884269
9884269  9884279  9884297  9884299  9884311  9884317  9884359  9884363  9884383  9884431
9884467  9884473  9884489  9884507  9884509  9884519  9884521  9884527  9884533  9884543
9884551  9884557  9884561  9884569  9884573  9884593  9884597  9884603  9884627  9884663
```

```
9884671  9884681  9884689  9884713  9884723  9884741  9884747  9884761  9884773  9884783
9884821  9884827  9884843  9884863  9884887  9884891  9884903  9884909  9884923  9884929
9884951  9884983  9884999  9885017  9885023  9885049  9885061  9885077  9885089  9885091
9885103  9885119  9885151  9885157  9885163  9885199  9885203  9885209  9885229  9885241
9885283  9885287  9885329  9885361  9885389  9885397  9885437  9885439  9885443  9885493
9885503  9885511  9885521  9885523  9885539  9885563  9885583  9885593  9885611  9885637
9885647  9885727  9885731  9885737  9885749  9885761  9885763  9885773  9885803  9885817
9885859  9885893  9885901  9885913  9885979  9885989  9886007  9886069  9886073  9886091
9886103  9886109  9886127  9886147  9886153  9886157  9886169  9886199  9886211  9886223
9886229  9886237  9886243  9886271  9886277  9886301  9886313  9886339  9886369  9886381
9886397  9886399  9886411  9886417  9886451  9886493  9886507  9886529  9886549  9886553
9886559  9886561  9886589  9886601  9886607  9886621  9886633  9886637  9886649  9886691
9886717  9886729  9886739  9886759  9886769  9886801  9886813  9886817  9886829  9886837
9886847  9886853  9886871  9886937  9886939  9886949  9886957  9886993  9886997  9887021
9887023  9887041  9887069  9887093  9887107  9887117  9887131  9887159  9887179  9887221
9887299  9887321  9887323  9887327  9887333  9887359  9887363  9887393  9887407  9887413
9887431  9887441  9887457  9887509  9887573  9887587  9887593  9887599  9887609  9887611
9887617  9887629  9887641  9887651  9887653  9887663  9887681  9887687  9887699  9887711
9887741  9887747  9887767  9887783  9887797  9887819  9887827  9887831  9887837  9887851
9887881  9887887  9887909  9887921  9887939  9887971  9887993  9888013  9888019  9888023
9888029  9888031  9888041  9888089  9888097  9888107  9888121  9888127  9888133  9888143
9888149  9888173  9888187  9888199  9888209  9888239  9888247  9888251  9888269  9888289
9888299  9888301  9888311  9888313  9888317  9888337  9888353  9888397  9888443  9888451
9888469  9888479  9888481  9888499  9888511  9888521  9888533  9888539  9888547  9888553
9888563  9888629  9888631  9888661  9888719  9888727  9888733  9888751  9888757  9888761
9888763  9888773  9888779  9888787  9888803  9888817  9888841  9888863  9888871  9888887
9888887  9888889  9888929  9888931  9888943  9888947  9888961  9888973  9888979  9888997  9889013
9889037  9889039  9889051  9889067  9889069  9889073  9889079  9889081  9889123  9889147
9889151  9889169  9889171  9889181  9889193  9889207  9889283  9889289  9889307  9889309
9889331  9889343  9889357  9889409  9889417  9889423  9889459  9889463  9889469  9889501
9889507  9889511  9889541  9889543  9889553  9889559  9889601  9889637  9889673  9889687
9889697  9889717  9889723  9889741  9889753  9889799  9889807  9889811  9889813  9889843
9889849  9889877  9889889  9889909  9889921  9889927  9889933  9889951  9889969  9889981
9889987  9890009  9890011  9890033  9890043  9890053  9890057  9890077  9890081  9890149
9890159  9890183  9890191  9890201  9890219  9890233  9890239  9890249  9890263  9890297
9890329  9890341  9890381  9890407  9890417  9890423  9890429  9890443  9890467  9890501
9890509  9890527  9890579  9890591  9890597  9890599  9890603  9890609  9890623  9890663
9890669  9890681  9890693  9890737  9890743  9890747  9890761  9890789  9890791  9890813
9890833  9890863  9890869  9890889  9890899  9890911  9890917  9890941  9890977  9890981
9890983  9890999  9891023  9891029  9891041  9891043  9891053  9891061  9891097  9891121
9891131  9891137  9891149  9891151  9891179  9891199  9891229  9891239  9891241  9891251
9891253  9891257  9891289  9891293  9891307  9891319  9891341  9891367  9891377  9891383
9891391  9891439  9891451  9891461  9891463  9891473  9891487  9891491  9891517  9891551
9891589  9891593  9891601  9891613  9891619  9891669  9891709  9891731  9891733  9891737
9891757  9891779  9891781  9891793  9891797  9891809  9891823  9891851  9891853  9891877
9891887  9891899  9891923  9891953  9891991  9891997  9892009  9892013  9892019  9892031
9892033  9892037  9892039  9892063  9892067  9892073  9892087  9892121  9892151  9892153
9892159  9892247  9892271  9892273  9892321  9892339  9892343  9892367  9892381  9892387
9892403  9892409  9892417  9892423  9892447  9892499  9892511  9892523  9892541  9892543
9892573  9892577  9892591  9892613  9892621  9892639  9892651  9892661  9892667  9892681
9892699  9892703  9892717  9892723  9892747  9892763  9892777  9892789  9892819  9892823
9892837  9892859  9892867  9892871  9892873  9892879  9892891  9892903  9892951  9892957
9893003  9893017  9893027  9893057  9893083  9893087  9893101  9893111  9893131  9893137
9893141  9893183  9893189  9893209  9893239  9893293  9893333  9893339  9893363  9893383
9893399  9893417  9893419  9893431  9893441  9893447  9893461  9893491  9893497  9893501
9893503  9893539  9893573  9893621  9893633  9893647  9893659  9893687  9893693
9893707  9893713  9893747  9893753  9893771  9893777  9893789  9893803  9893809  9893831
9893839  9893857  9893861  9893869  9893889  9893951  9893977  9894003  9894007  9894013
9894019  9894023  9894083  9894107  9894109  9894113  9894121  9894127  9894149  9894151
9894173  9894179  9894211  9894217  9894223  9894229  9894259  9894271  9894293  9894319
9894331  9894337  9894377  9894411  9894419  9894427  9894441  9894457  9894461  9894523
9894541  9894557  9894559  9894569  9894587  9894593  9894607  9894617  9894641  9894659
9894691  9894701  9894721  9894739  9894743  9894751  9894791  9894793  9894803  9894809
9894827  9894847  9894851  9894883  9894889  9894893  9894919  9894923  9894967  9894971
9894977  9894979  9895001  9895007  9895009  9895019  9895033  9895043  9895049  9895069
9895079  9895091  9895097  9895103  9895111  9895121  9895133  9895141  9895159  9895183
9895201  9895213  9895229  9895247  9895279  9895307  9895321  9895337  9895339
9895357  9895363  9895367  9895381  9895387  9895393  9895397  9895429  9895441  9895453
9895463  9895493  9895517  9895559  9895573  9895579  9895591  9895601  9895621  9895631
9895651  9895663  9895667  9895679  9895693  9895723  9895741  9895747  9895759  9895763
9895793  9895799  9895817  9895829  9895839  9895877  9895889  9895939  9895943  9895961
9895981  9895993  9896039  9896041  9896053  9896077  9896083  9896123  9896143  9896147
9896153  9896167  9896171  9896189  9896239  9896267  9896269  9896281  9896291  9896297
9896303  9896311  9896317  9896351  9896357  9896363  9896429  9896441  9896443  9896449
9896459  9896489  9896507  9896521  9896527  9896543  9896563  9896581  9896591
9896597  9896603  9896611  9896629  9896639  9896641  9896659  9896681  9896699  9896713
9896717  9896741  9896749  9896753  9896767  9896773  9896791  9896807  9896833  9896851
9896857  9896863  9896881  9896893  9896907  9896911  9896941  9896951  9896981  9896987
9896989  9897001  9897011  9897023  9897037  9897059  9897071  9897109  9897127  9897161
9897203  9897211  9897221  9897227  9897253  9897257  9897263  9897287  9897313  9897331
9897343  9897361  9897367  9897397  9897457  9897467  9897469  9897473  9897529  9897533
9897539  9897541  9897571  9897581  9897599  9897617  9897631  9897637  9897653  9897661
9897703  9897743  9897761  9897769  9897803  9897809  9897829  9897847  9897857  9897863
9897887  9897913  9897919  9897929  9897931  9897941  9897971  9897973  9897983  9898001
9898003  9898081  9898087  9898117  9898123  9898139  9898151  9898157  9898159  9898169
9898177  9898223  9898237  9898241  9898243  9898271  9898279  9898283  9898307  9898319
9898337  9898381  9898397  9898423  9898433  9898451  9898457  9898481  9898519  9898543
9898547  9898571  9898597  9898613  9898627  9898633  9898649  9898667  9898673  9898697
9898711  9898723  9898769  9898771  9898783  9898793  9898799  9898807  9898841  9898849
```

```
9898853 9898859 9898877 9898907 9898921 9898979 9899003 9899009 9899023 9899041
9899069 9899119 9899143 9899147 9899167 9899173 9899221 9899257 9899273 9899291
9899297 9899303 9899333 9899341 9899347 9899363 9899371 9899377 9899429 9899431
9899443 9899467 9899497 9899501 9899531 9899567 9899581 9899587 9899597 9899599
9899611 9899621 9899641 9899651 9899663 9899671 9899689 9899693 9899731 9899753
9899783 9899789 9899809 9899833 9899861 9899863 9899887 9899891 9899921 9899947
9899951 9899963 9899977 9899993 9899999 9900047 9900091 9900101 9900113 9900119
9900139 9900161 9900179 9900181 9900199 9900203 9900251 9900283 9900287 9900301
9900343 9900367 9900379 9900391 9900413 9900421 9900427 9900437 9900461 9900467
9900469 9900481 9900487 9900491 9900493 9900509 9900529 9900533 9900547 9900589
9900593 9900599 9900601 9900623 9900641 9900643 9900661 9900677 9900683 9900697
9900733 9900757 9900769 9900773 9900799 9900827 9900857 9900859 9900883 9900889
9900893 9900907 9900923 9900931 9900949 9900959 9901007 9901009 9901019 9901037
9901061 9901069 9901103 9901117 9901139 9901141 9901159 9901187 9901189
9901211 9901219 9901231 9901253 9901271 9901277 9901289 9901291 9901303 9901313
9901343 9901379 9901391 9901393 9901403 9901421 9901427 9901433 9901457 9901543
9901547 9901553 9901561 9901571 9901601 9901613 9901627 9901637 9901649
9901691 9901709 9901721 9901747 9901751 9901763 9901777 9901783 9901807 9901813
9901823 9901841 9901867 9901877 9901883 9901901 9901961 9901987 9901999
9902017 9902023 9902047 9902089 9902099 9902107 9902117 9902119 9902153 9902183
9902203 9902209 9902219 9902239 9902257 9902281 9902293 9902327 9902353 9902359
9902411 9902419 9902437 9902447 9902471 9902491 9902509 9902531 9902537 9902539
9902549 9902567 9902587 9902593 9902597 9902617 9902621 9902663 9902681 9902699
9902707 9902723 9902749 9902797 9902807 9902831 9902839 9902861 9902873 9902881
9902897 9902909 9902911 9902917 9902927 9902929 9902951 9902983 9902989 9903001
9903011 9903031 9903037 9903059 9903067 9903071 9903073 9903077 9903083 9903109
9903149 9903169 9903191 9903193 9903211 9903227 9903241 9903247 9903251 9903259
9903269 9903281 9903307 9903331 9903349 9903359 9903379 9903407 9903431 9903451
9903473 9903493 9903499 9903557 9903559 9903583 9903623 9903671 9903683 9903701
9903709 9903713 9903721 9903749 9903767 9903779 9903811 9903821 9903847 9903853
9903857 9903871 9903913 9903921 9903937 9903947 9903953 9903977 9903989 9904019
9904079 9904117 9904133 9904157 9904189 9904199 9904201 9904207 9904211 9904231
9904253 9904261 9904267 9904273 9904277 9904289 9904291 9904313 9904331 9904333
9904343 9904351 9904361 9904373 9904381 9904393 9904397 9904403 9904411 9904459
9904471 9904483 9904487 9904519 9904547 9904579 9904589 9904613 9904621 9904633
9904649 9904667 9904679 9904703 9904709 9904747 9904751 9904777 9904781 9904793
9904801 9904819 9904823 9904837 9904847 9904889 9904891 9904901 9904919 9904949
9904967 9904987 9905003 9905017 9905053 9905057 9905059 9905087 9905113 9905123
9905141 9905167 9905173 9905177 9905183 9905191 9905197 9905209 9905221 9905239
9905261 9905263 9905267 9905293 9905377 9905383 9905411 9905417 9905419 9905431
9905447 9905453 9905459 9905473 9905491 9905513 9905521 9905561 9905563 9905591
9905627 9905629 9905639 9905653 9905657 9905659 9905671 9905683 9905711 9905717
9905719 9905759 9905813 9905839 9905869 9905879 9905891 9905911 9905921 9905941
9905947 9905963 9905971 9905981 9905989 9905993 9906007 9906079 9906101 9906107
9906109 9906119 9906157 9906161 9906187 9906209 9906227 9906233 9906241 9906263
9906271 9906289 9906293 9906349 9906361 9906367 9906401 9906409 9906443 9906473
9906493 9906509 9906511 9906517 9906527 9906569 9906593 9906599 9906653 9906671
9906691 9906703 9906731 9906737 9906751 9906761 9906773 9906779 9906781 9906791
9906833 9906839 9906851 9906863 9906877 9906917 9906929 9906931 9906943 9906973
9906983 9906991 9907003 9907013 9907021 9907031 9907033 9907057 9907069 9907081
9907087 9907091 9907093 9907099 9907109 9907123 9907147 9907187 9907211 9907229
9907279 9907291 9907297 9907307 9907309 9907349 9907367 9907423 9907433 9907477
9907517 9907519 9907529 9907567 9907571 9907619 9907621 9907637 9907649 9907663
9907669 9907679 9907697 9907699 9907717 9907769 9907771 9907801 9907813 9907819
9907841 9907847 9907861 9907867 9907901 9907907 9907921 9907951 9907993 9908021
9908039 9908051 9908063 9908081 9908093 9908099 9908123 9908207
9908221 9908231 9908257 9908279 9908293 9908299 9908303 9908321 9908359 9908369
9908389 9908393 9908407 9908411 9908419 9908449 9908471 9908477 9908491 9908513
9908527 9908531 9908537 9908551 9908599 9908617 9908621 9908629 9908651 9908693
9908707 9908713 9908719 9908729 9908737 9908753 9908797 9908803 9908819 9908851
9908867 9908881 9908887 9908897 9908911 9908941 9908947 9908953 9908957 9909017
9909019 9909047 9909061 9909071 9909091 9909139 9909143 9909161 9909187 9909191
9909209 9909217 9909247 9909253 9909293 9909311 9909323 9909337 9909353 9909373
9909397 9909401 9909407 9909409 9909421 9909437 9909439 9909443 9909457 9909461
9909499 9909509 9909533 9909539 9909551 9909563 9909593 9909611 9909629 9909649
9909667 9909689 9909701 9909703 9909707 9909749 9909751 9909763 9909787
9909791 9909797 9909799 9909833 9909847 9909857 9909859 9909869 9909871 9909881
9909917 9909943 9909961 9909989 9910007 9910009 9910013 9910063 9910067
9910073 9910097 9910123 9910129 9910157 9910181 9910183 9910193 9910211 9910223
9910249 9910301 9910319 9910331 9910333 9910361 9910363 9910367 9910387 9910391
9910403 9910409 9910423 9910429 9910441 9910463 9910469 9910499 9910523 9910529
9910531 9910567 9910577 9910591 9910601 9910627 9910657 9910673 9910697 9910727
9910753 9910757 9910759 9910811 9910829 9910867 9910883 9910909 9910919
9910921 9910973 9910993 9911009 9911023 9911063 9911081 9911087 9911101 9911123
9911131 9911147 9911149 9911171 9911173 9911191 9911201 9911249 9911257 9911263
9911269 9911273 9911287 9911309 9911327 9911333 9911339 9911347 9911353 9911399
9911431 9911443 9911453 9911467 9911471 9911497 9911519 9911549 9911581 9911609
9911623 9911633 9911647 9911659 9911669 9911677 9911683 9911701 9911717 9911743
9911747 9911753 9911761 9911773 9911789 9911809 9911821 9911831 9911849 9911851
9911857 9911861 9911917 9911929 9911953 9911961 9911963 9912017 9912021 9912029
9912031 9912043 9912079 9912101 9912121 9912137 9912143 9912151 9912169 9912211
9912251 9912257 9912269 9912277 9912307 9912311 9912313 9912391 9912401 9912407
9912421 9912481 9912491 9912499 9912521 9912533 9912541 9912557 9912589 9912599
9912613 9912631 9912659 9912671 9912689 9912691 9912703 9912719 9912757 9912761
9912779 9912803 9912809 9912829 9912869 9912871 9912893 9912899 9912913 9912937
9912941 9912943 9912967 9912979 9913027 9913051 9913081 9913093 9913097 9913129
9913133 9913139 9913147 9913153 9913187 9913201 9913213 9913217 9913219 9913283
9913289 9913291 9913297 9913333 9913361 9913367 9913403 9913411 9913429 9913433
9913439 9913469 9913507 9913511 9913523 9913531 9913549 9913559 9913571 9913609
```

```
9913613  9913637  9913643  9913661  9913697  9913721  9913723  9913727  9913733  9913753
9913807  9913811  9913837  9913847  9913861  9913879  9913889  9913901  9913919  9913921
9913931  9913933  9913957  9913973  9913979  9913987  9913997  9914033  9914053  9914063
9914071  9914089  9914117  9914119  9914153  9914159  9914171  9914189  9914221  9914239
9914287  9914297  9914309  9914323  9914341  9914351  9914363  9914407  9914427  9914431
9914441  9914461  9914477  9914479  9914501  9914521  9914539  9914543  9914617  9914627
9914629  9914659  9914669  9914687  9914693  9914701  9914719  9914747  9914759  9914767
9914819  9914843  9914887  9914911  9914917  9914929  9914939  9914951  9914953  9914963
9914969  9914977  9914987  9915041  9915043  9915083  9915107  9915109  9915119  9915121
9915137  9915161  9915173  9915181  9915193  9915197  9915203  9915209  9915229  9915281
9915289  9915299  9915307  9915313  9915329  9915331  9915341  9915343  9915349  9915377
9915379  9915391  9915407  9915421  9915427  9915457  9915467  9915491  9915497  9915509
9915533  9915541  9915547  9915559  9915589  9915617  9915623  9915673  9915677  9915679
9915683  9915713  9915721  9915749  9915751  9915791  9915803  9915817  9915821  9915827
9915833  9915847  9915859  9915881  9915887  9915907  9915911  9915937  9915949  9915979
9915991  9916003  9916009  9916021  9916031  9916061  9916069  9916091  9916103  9916129
9916139  9916163  9916169  9916177  9916183  9916199  9916211  9916217  9916229  9916237
9916279  9916297  9916331  9916337  9916339  9916351  9916363  9916391  9916409  9916411
9916433  9916441  9916451  9916507  9916513  9916523  9916549  9916553  9916561  9916567
9916573  9916583  9916589  9916597  9916607  9916609  9916619  9916631  9916639  9916649
9916679  9916681  9916691  9916723  9916741  9916787  9916813  9916843  9916849  9916873
9916889  9916891  9916903  9916939  9916969  9916981  9917009  9917027  9917051  9917053
9917057  9917059  9917077  9917087  9917119  9917129  9917153  9917191  9917207  9917231
9917249  9917263  9917267  9917279  9917287  9917309  9917317  9917321  9917353  9917363
9917371  9917381  9917387  9917389  9917399  9917419  9917429  9917447  9917471  9917473
9917483  9917491  9917503  9917513  9917521  9917539  9917549  9917569  9917597  9917599
9917603  9917627  9917641  9917653  9917659  9917683  9917689  9917701  9917711  9917729
9917759  9917771  9917779  9917827  9917839  9917849  9917881  9917891  9917903  9917909
9917911  9917939  9917969  9917983  9917989  9918017  9918059  9918091  9918121  9918127
9918131  9918137  9918143  9918163  9918169  9918197  9918199  9918217  9918253  9918289
9918317  9918353  9918373  9918379  9918383  9918407  9918409  9918413  9918421  9918521
9918523  9918533  9918547  9918563  9918593  9918607  9918611  9918617  9918637  9918641
9918647  9918683  9918697  9918707  9918709  9918721  9918743  9918763  9918787  9918851
9918877  9918889  9918917  9918941  9918949  9918959  9918983  9918991  9919009  9919031
9919033  9919037  9919057  9919061  9919067  9919069  9919097  9919183  9919193  9919199
9919201  9919223  9919229  9919237  9919243  9919249  9919267  9919277  9919291  9919297
9919307  9919309  9919361  9919373  9919379  9919391  9919409  9919423  9919439  9919447
9919471  9919487  9919489  9919519  9919523  9919531  9919543  9919573  9919583  9919607
9919667  9919669  9919681  9919697  9919717  9919727  9919813  9919829  9919837  9919841
9919849  9919853  9919883  9919933  9919937  9919939  9919963  9919979  9919997  9920021
9920047  9920077  9920089  9920111  9920123  9920137  9920159  9920161  9920167  9920177
9920203  9920213  9920219  9920249  9920257  9920293  9920303  9920311  9920347  9920353
9920357  9920363  9920371  9920387  9920399  9920411  9920419  9920423  9920447  9920467
9920479  9920501  9920507  9920513  9920531  9920539  9920543  9920557  9920559  9920597
9920611  9920621  9920653  9920657  9920671  9920683  9920689  9920711  9920737  9920749
9920777  9920783  9920803  9920821  9920861  9920863  9920873  9920881  9920903  9920923
9920947  9920951  9920957  9920993  9921001  9921007  9921011  9921019  9921053  9921133
9921137  9921167  9921169  9921179  9921187  9921193  9921199  9921227  9921259  9921283
9921299  9921311  9921323  9921337  9921341  9921343  9921383  9921391  9921407  9921409
9921449  9921473  9921479  9921491  9921521  9921529  9921577  9921599  9921601  9921619
9921641  9921679  9921731  9921733  9921797  9921803  9921817  9921823  9921827  9921851
9921869  9921889  9921907  9921917  9921983  9921991  9921997  9922001  9922007  9922013
9922019  9922021  9922043  9922049  9922057  9922063  9922109  9922111  9922127  9922151
9922153  9922193  9922219  9922229  9922247  9922261  9922273  9922277  9922279  9922303
9922307  9922399  9922403  9922433  9922439  9922447  9922457  9922459  9922483  9922487
9922489  9922529  9922531  9922559  9922571  9922609  9922613  9922651  9922657  9922667
9922691  9922721  9922739  9922741  9922763  9922777  9922811  9922813  9922873  9922897
9922903  9922907  9922909  9922933  9922937  9922961  9922967  9922987  9923009  9923021
9923029  9923057  9923059  9923083  9923101  9923113  9923129  9923167  9923171  9923201
9923209  9923213  9923219  9923227  9923261  9923273  9923279  9923299  9923311  9923323
9923341  9923369  9923371  9923383  9923413  9923429  9923449  9923467  9923471  9923477
9923483  9923509  9923521  9923531  9923579  9923591  9923609  9923611  9923621  9923629
9923647  9923671  9923677  9923701  9923707  9923731  9923747  9923783  9923789  9923791
9923803  9923819  9923821  9923831  9923861  9923891  9923897  9923899  9923911  9923923
9923933  9923941  9923981  9923983  9923987  9923989  9923993  9924043  9924053  9924071
9924113  9924121  9924133  9924157  9924159  9924193  9924199  9924229  9924263  9924283
9924287  9924323  9924347  9924353  9924367  9924391  9924407  9924437  9924457  9924463
9924469  9924487  9924499  9924503  9924511  9924521  9924539  9924553  9924587  9924601
9924613  9924623  9924647  9924653  9924671  9924683  9924689  9924703  9924709  9924721
9924751  9924763  9924767  9924779  9924797  9924823  9924841  9924847  9924851  9924881
9924899  9924919  9924941  9924961  9924979  9924997  9925021  9925031  9925043  9925051
9925063  9925081  9925109  9925117  9925133  9925147  9925159  9925171  9925189  9925193
9925207  9925219  9925243  9925261  9925271  9925283  9925309  9925379  9925387  9925439
9925471  9925519  9925537  9925541  9925579  9925589  9925607  9925613  9925633  9925667
9925687  9925703  9925709  9925711  9925717  9925757  9925777  9925781  9925793  9925823
9925837  9925843  9925873  9925889  9925901  9925907  9925919  9925931  9925957  9925963
9925969  9925973  9925987  9925997  9926003  9926023  9926057  9926083  9926099  9926123
9926143  9926159  9926167  9926173  9926201  9926233  9926243  9926269  9926299  9926311
9926333  9926339  9926377  9926383  9926393  9926401  9926443  9926473  9926489  9926491
9926503  9926509  9926513  9926561  9926563  9926597  9926599  9926611  9926617  9926621
9926627  9926641  9926669  9926677  9926681  9926699  9926737  9926743  9926747  9926771
9926773  9926783  9926801  9926821  9926837  9926857  9926893  9926897  9926899  9926909
9926923  9926933  9926947  9926951  9926999  9927011  9927017  9927041  9927047  9927083
9927097  9927103  9927119  9927121  9927131  9927179  9927217  9927221  9927299  9927319
9927331  9927349  9927361  9927373  9927383  9927397  9927447  9927493  9927497  9927509
9927521  9927553  9927563  9927583  9927613  9927623  9927629  9927637  9927641  9927647
9927667  9927679  9927691  9927703  9927707  9927733  9927739  9927751  9927767  9927769
9927787  9927791  9927793  9927809  9927833  9927893  9927911  9927917  9927941  9927943
9927959  9927961  9927991  9928007  9928021  9928043  9928049  9928057  9928069  9928081
```

```
9928129  9928133  9928151  9928159  9928169  9928207  9928213  9928231  9928267  9928283
9928291  9928319  9928333  9928337  9928351  9928361  9928367  9928379  9928381  9928397
9928403  9928409  9928441  9928453  9928487  9928537  9928547  9928553  9928577  9928591
9928613  9928619  9928661  9928669  9928679  9928693  9928727  9928739  9928741  9928747
9928783  9928813  9928843  9928859  9928873  9928879  9928889  9928903  9928907  9928927
9928937  9928943  9928981  9928999  9929009  9929047  9929053  9929057  9929069  9929089
9929099  9929111  9929141  9929149  9929159  9929177  9929189  9929201  9929203  9929221
9929233  9929237  9929243  9929263  9929291  9929317  9929321  9929323  9929329  9929341
9929347  9929351  9929363  9929369  9929371  9929383  9929417  9929429  9929453  9929459
9929473  9929489  9929501  9929531  9929551  9929567  9929587  9929611  9929617  9929627
9929651  9929659  9929663  9929693  9929701  9929719  9929729  9929753  9929771  9929833
9929839  9929851  9929863  9929867  9929873  9929889  9929891  9929893  9929903  9929917
9929929  9929939  9929981  9929993  9929999  9930001  9930031  9930049  9930061  9930073
9930083  9930139  9930143  9930169  9930191  9930197  9930233  9930247  9930269  9930287
9930307  9930311  9930317  9930337  9930341  9930391  9930419  9930433  9930443  9930461
9930469  9930491  9930497  9930517  9930523  9930527  9930581  9930587  9930589  9930607
9930611  9930629  9930631  9930637  9930647  9930667  9930691  9930707  9930773  9930797
9930827  9930829  9930889  9930919  9930923  9930931  9930953  9930961  9930997  9931001
9931007  9931037  9931039  9931049  9931063  9931093  9931109  9931121  9931123  9931171
9931183  9931219  9931223  9931261  9931277  9931279  9931283  9931291  9931301  9931321
9931333  9931351  9931367  9931379  9931381  9931393  9931399  9931447  9931459  9931463
9931489  9931499  9931507  9931517  9931583  9931589  9931591  9931613  9931619  9931627
9931631  9931639  9931709  9931741  9931759  9931763  9931769  9931771  9931783  9931787
9931793  9931807  9931841  9931843  9931853  9931861  9931897  9931903  9931907  9931913
9931921  9931951  9932009  9932017  9932023  9932047  9932051  9932071  9932077  9932101
9932107  9932129  9932141  9932171  9932177  9932179  9932201  9932207  9932213  9932227
9932257  9932303  9932309  9932323  9932347  9932353  9932387  9932399  9932411  9932423
9932443  9932467  9932477  9932479  9932491  9932501  9932513  9932521  9932567  9932579
9932581  9932603  9932609  9932621  9932639  9932669  9932707  9932717  9932719  9932723
9932729  9932753  9932759  9932771  9932773  9932779  9932789  9932809  9932821  9932833
9932837  9932851  9932861  9932873  9932887  9932893  9932903  9932959  9932969  9932977
9932999  9933019  9933041  9933059  9933071  9933103  9933127  9933149  9933163  9933197
9933199  9933221  9933229  9933239  9933241  9933251  9933271  9933277  9933281  9933311
9933317  9933323  9933349  9933359  9933367  9933377  9933431  9933437  9933463
9933467  9933499  9933503  9933509  9933529  9933541  9933551  9933571  9933601  9933607
9933611  9933613  9933617  9933619  9933643  9933647  9933659  9933683  9933691  9933701
9933727  9933739  9933743  9933757  9933761  9933787  9933793  9933811  9933841  9933851
9933853  9933877  9933883  9933887  9933923  9933947  9933961  9933971  9933977  9933983
9933997  9934009  9934031  9934039  9934049  9934063  9934073  9934079  9934081  9934087
9934097  9934121  9934129  9934147  9934159  9934163  9934181  9934189  9934219  9934237
9934271  9934297  9934333  9934357  9934363  9934381  9934387  9934411  9934451  9934471
9934481  9934493  9934499  9934543  9934553  9934571  9934577  9934583  9934619  9934627
9934649  9934651  9934657  9934667  9934697  9934699  9934703  9934709  9934741  9934801
9934807  9934811  9934819  9934823  9934861  9934867  9934877  9934889  9934901  9934927
9934931  9934943  9934963  9934999  9935027  9935033  9935039  9935041  9935047  9935053
9935059  9935063  9935077  9935087  9935099  9935111  9935137  9935141  9935143  9935153
9935173  9935213  9935231  9935239  9935251  9935257  9935267  9935291  9935297  9935311
9935323  9935381  9935383  9935389  9935399  9935411  9935413  9935417  9935437  9935467
9935477  9935479  9935503  9935521  9935531  9935567  9935579  9935587  9935617  9935621
9935641  9935657  9935663  9935671  9935711  9935729  9935749  9935773  9935789  9935797
9935801  9935813  9935831  9935867  9935911  9935927  9935929  9935969  9935987  9936037
9936061  9936071  9936083  9936119  9936133  9936163  9936181  9936187  9936191  9936193
9936197  9936209  9936233  9936257  9936263  9936271  9936293  9936319  9936343  9936349
9936361  9936371  9936419  9936431  9936439  9936457  9936467  9936499  9936503  9936533
9936557  9936571  9936581  9936593  9936611  9936613  9936617  9936629  9936631  9936649
9936673  9936679  9936697  9936727  9936733  9936737  9936739  9936779  9936781  9936793
9936803  9936841  9936847  9936859  9936889  9936893  9936907  9936911  9936919
9936923  9936977  9937007  9937013  9937051  9937063  9937073
9937079  9937141  9937189  9937199  9937229  9937237  9937241  9937253  9937261  9937297
9937309  9937321  9937339  9937387  9937409  9937441  9937481  9937483  9937493  9937511
9937519  9937531  9937561  9937573  9937579  9937591  9937597  9937607  9937637  9937649
9937661  9937663  9937699  9937729  9937751  9937769  9937789  9937801  9937831  9937849
9937891  9937927  9937957  9937973  9937997  9938017  9938021  9938023  9938051  9938057
9938069  9938107  9938119  9938141  9938143  9938153  9938179  9938207  9938221  9938233
9938239  9938249  9938263  9938281  9938297  9938309  9938347  9938377  9938389  9938393
9938399  9938407  9938413  9938417  9938471  9938503  9938519  9938527  9938531  9938549
9938563  9938581  9938597  9938603  9938611  9938623  9938641  9938647  9938701  9938749
9938801  9938807  9938809  9938813  9938821  9938833  9938849  9938861  9938867
9938869  9938899  9938927  9938953  9938959  9938983  9938989  9938993  9939011  9939019
9939029  9939031  9939047  9939049  9939053  9939073  9939079  9939089  9939103  9939131
9939211  9939217  9939229  9939247  9939263  9939269  9939277  9939301  9939323  9939341
9939353  9939359  9939379  9939403  9939463  9939491  9939497  9939521  9939529  9939533
9939539  9939541  9939557  9939571  9939583  9939613  9939617  9939619  9939637  9939647
9939653  9939661  9939667  9939707  9939731  9939733  9939737  9939757  9939763  9939773
9939799  9939803  9939817  9939821  9939823  9939833  9939857  9939893  9939901  9939911
9939913  9939919  9939949  9939959  9939961  9940001  9940003  9940027  9940031
9940039  9940043  9940067  9940093  9940111  9940123  9940129  9940199  9940219  9940241
9940247  9940279  9940283  9940297  9940313  9940331  9940349  9940361  9940369  9940387
9940397  9940433  9940451  9940471  9940501  9940507  9940519  9940537  9940561  9940571
9940603  9940613  9940643  9940681  9940703  9940709  9940717  9940729  9940741  9940747
9940837  9940841  9940859  9940867  9940871  9940873  9940877  9940907  9940927  9940951
9940963  9941003  9941023  9941051  9941053  9941059  9941077  9941089  9941143  9941149
9941167  9941177  9941189  9941219  9941227  9941249  9941257  9941273  9941291  9941293
9941317  9941333  9941341  9941383  9941431  9941447  9941467  9941509  9941513  9941521
9941537  9941573  9941587  9941599  9941609  9941611  9941621  9941629  9941647  9941653
9941671  9941699  9941713  9941717  9941749  9941761  9941777  9941779  9941843  9941851
9941857  9941873  9941879  9941881  9941891  9941903  9941927  9941951  9941969  9941977
9942007  9942013  9942029  9942043  9942047  9942067  9942077  9942133  9942143  9942151
```

```
9942167  9942169  9942173  9942181  9942199  9942203  9942211  9942223  9942269  9942271
9942277  9942299  9942311  9942341  9942347  9942353  9942367  9942391  9942407  9942409
9942419  9942421  9942437  9942461  9942473  9942479  9942481  9942497  9942523  9942533
9942539  9942557  9942571  9942577  9942587  9942593  9942607  9942617  9942619  9942629
9942659  9942683  9942689  9942697  9942701  9942707  9942721  9942727  9942731  9942749
9942763  9942767  9942797  9942883  9942893  9942917  9942931  9942941  9943057  9943067
9943069  9943091  9943097  9943123  9943127  9943139  9943159  9943187  9943207  9943237
9943243  9943247  9943253  9943301  9943303  9943319  9943331  9943333  9943357  9943369
9943379  9943387  9943391  9943393  9943397  9943411  9943457  9943459  9943477  9943481
9943513  9943523  9943559  9943579  9943663  9943673  9943679  9943693  9943699  9943709
9943711  9943721  9943727  9943729  9943733  9943819  9943849  9943873  9943877  9943883
9943903  9943907  9943943  9943949  9943951  9943957  9943993  9944029  9944041  9944063
9944069  9944089  9944093  9944117  9944153  9944171  9944177  9944191  9944197  9944251
9944261  9944267  9944287  9944301  9944329  9944351  9944357  9944377  9944387  9944393
9944423  9944449  9944461  9944471  9944483  9944491  9944497  9944503  9944513  9944531
9944563  9944569  9944617  9944629  9944663  9944681  9944689  9944719  9944729  9944789
9944801  9944807  9944821  9944839  9944843  9944849  9944917  9944927  9944933  9944939
9944951  9944953  9945043  9945049  9945053  9945071  9945077  9945101  9945109  9945121
9945137  9945149  9945157  9945161  9945181  9945209  9945211  9945233  9945239  9945253
9945259  9945277  9945307  9945317  9945337  9945343  9945349  9945359  9945409  9945421
9945443  9945449  9945457  9945461  9945511  9945539  9945553  9945581  9945583  9945587
9945619  9945631  9945647  9945667  9945679  9945707  9945709  9945743  9945779  9945781
9945841  9945847  9945853  9945877  9945883  9945889  9945919  9945937  9945941  9945961
9945967  9945977  9945979  9945983  9945997  9946039  9946049  9946073  9946099  9946103
9946109  9946169  9946171  9946193  9946199  9946213  9946243  9946247  9946271  9946273
9946301  9946357  9946393  9946427  9946429  9946439  9946441  9946483  9946487  9946501
9946523  9946549  9946571  9946583  9946591  9946597  9946609  9946639  9946661  9946733
9946759  9946763  9946771  9946777  9946789  9946799  9946817  9946829  9946831  9946841
9946847  9946873  9946883  9946891  9946897  9946901  9946911  9946927  9946933  9946943
9946957  9946973  9946991  9946999  9947009  9947011  9947039  9947071  9947101  9947123
9947129  9947131  9947141  9947153  9947177  9947183  9947207  9947219  9947237  9947239
9947243  9947251  9947281  9947291  9947299  9947303  9947321  9947323  9947369  9947383
9947407  9947417  9947429  9947437  9947473  9947489  9947501  9947513  9947521  9947527
9947573  9947593  9947599  9947611  9947627  9947643  9947671  9947719  9947741  9947761
9947779  9947803  9947837  9947851  9947863  9947867  9947923  9947947  9947969  9947999
9948011  9948013  9948041  9948061  9948083  9948097  9948101  9948109  9948137  9948161
9948163  9948173  9948203  9948217  9948277  9948287  9948293  9948311  9948313  9948319
9948329  9948347  9948359  9948413  9948431  9948469  9948473  9948487  9948503  9948511
9948517  9948541  9948557  9948559  9948583  9948593  9948623  9948643  9948663  9948643
9948677  9948703  9948709  9948713  9948739  9948749  9948751  9948767  9948779  9948787
9948793  9948797  9948833  9948847  9948871  9948887  9948889  9948893  9948907  9948907
9948931  9948941  9948947  9948971  9948973  9948979  9949021  9949061  9949067  9949073
9949081  9949099  9949123  9949169  9949231  9949249  9949253  9949259  9949273  9949321
9949393  9949417  9949421  9949427  9949439  9949441  9949451  9949457  9949519  9949549
9949601  9949613  9949619  9949627  9949631  9949651  9949657  9949661  9949663  9949703
9949717  9949721  9949733  9949739  9949741  9949747  9949769  9949783  9949829  9949831
9949859  9949867  9949873  9949883  9949889  9949909  9949931  9949943  9949963  9949967
9950021  9950023  9950029  9950047  9950051  9950063  9950081  9950089  9950093  9950141
9950147  9950179  9950183  9950201  9950203  9950207  9950209  9950221  9950233  9950257
9950263  9950293  9950309  9950327  9950351  9950363  9950377  9950383  9950399  9950401
9950407  9950429  9950453  9950459  9950461  9950469  9950531  9950533  9950537  9950539
9950569  9950581  9950609  9950617  9950641  9950653  9950657  9950687  9950693  9950701
9950711  9950713  9950753  9950771  9950777  9950779  9950819  9950821  9950827  9950833
9950861  9950867  9950873  9950879  9950911  9950917  9950921  9950957  9950959  9950977
9950989  9951013  9951023  9951047  9951059  9951083  9951101  9951127  9951143  9951163
9951167  9951181  9951191  9951211  9951229  9951251  9951257  9951281  9951283  9951299
9951301  9951317  9951329  9951343  9951367  9951371  9951377  9951401  9951407  9951413
9951419  9951449  9951457  9951463  9951467  9951481  9951499  9951503  9951517  9951523
9951541  9951547  9951563  9951569  9951583  9951587  9951637  9951701  9951703  9951719
9951731  9951737  9951743  9951751  9951761  9951769  9951793  9951829  9951841  9951869
9951883  9951911  9951913  9951917  9951919  9952037  9952039  9952043  9952057  9952087
9952093  9952099  9952121  9952127  9952153  9952213  9952253  9952273  9952277  9952289
9952303  9952337  9952339  9952343  9952351  9952357  9952363  9952367  9952403  9952417
9952421  9952427  9952441  9952469  9952471  9952483  9952489  9952493  9952513  9952541
9952549  9952559  9952589  9952661  9952669  9952693  9952727  9952757  9952793  9952799
9952847  9952853  9952897  9952931  9952949  9952961  9952967  9952981  9952991  9953011
9953023  9953071  9953107  9953113  9953129  9953173  9953179  9953183  9953191  9953197
9953219  9953231  9953239  9953243  9953261  9953287  9953291  9953299  9953303
9953311  9953323  9953327  9953341  9953369  9953389  9953399  9953401  9953413  9953429
9953479  9953491  9953497  9953507  9953513  9953521  9953533  9953539  9953557  9953569
9953579  9953621  9953711  9953717  9953719  9953737  9953743  9953747  9953753  9953809
9953813  9953837  9953869  9953887  9953897  9953899  9953903  9953927  9953947  9953953
9954001  9954013  9954017  9954019  9954029  9954031  9954053  9954097  9954137  9954143
9954149  9954151  9954167  9954169  9954173  9954181  9954209  9954211  9954223  9954227
9954253  9954277  9954281  9954289  9954293  9954311  9954313  9954319  9954323  9954341
9954359  9954433  9954437  9954449  9954463  9954467  9954473  9954479  9954481  9954487
9954491  9954521  9954533  9954547  9954583  9954587  9954601  9954617  9954667  9954683
9954707  9954709  9954713  9954719  9954731  9954733  9954767  9954787  9954823  9954829
9954851  9954871  9954881  9954907  9954949  9954983  9954991  9955003  9955009  9955073
9955093  9955157  9955163  9955171  9955177  9955189  9955199  9955201  9955219  9955223
9955241  9955243  9955249  9955271  9955277  9955289  9955291  9955301  9955303  9955313
9955349  9955397  9955417  9955441  9955447  9955453  9955459  9955471  9955499  9955507
9955511  9955531  9955559  9955567  9955571  9955577  9955633  9955637  9955643  9955651
9955697  9955709  9955717  9955723  9955739  9955757  9955819  9955823  9955853  9955901
9955909  9955921  9955937  9955949  9956003  9956017  9956027  9956041  9956047  9956069
9956087  9956113  9956119  9956143  9956161  9956189  9956197  9956207  9956213  9956227
9956231  9956249  9956279  9956311  9956321  9956327  9956333  9956347  9956357  9956369
9956383  9956389  9956411  9956423  9956459  9956467  9956473  9956477  9956503  9956537
9956561  9956579  9956587  9956591  9956593  9956623  9956641  9956699  9956717  9956719
```

```
9956729  9956753  9956761  9956801  9956813  9956819  9956867  9956873  9956897  9956909
9956911  9956939  9956941  9956963  9956977  9956993  9957001  9957029  9957043  9957047
9957061  9957067  9957089  9957109  9957133  9957151  9957161  9957187  9957191  9957193
9957203  9957247  9957251  9957271  9957307  9957317  9957323  9957331  9957347  9957379
9957391  9957401  9957407  9957439  9957487  9957511  9957523  9957533  9957569  9957581
9957589  9957599  9957611  9957613  9957637  9957659  9957667  9957671  9957677  9957683
9957697  9957737  9957751  9957757  9957769  9957863  9957877  9957887  9957889  9957901
9957947  9957967  9957973  9957989  9958019  9958021  9958027  9958051  9958063  9958087
9958093  9958129  9958133  9958139  9958171  9958177  9958181  9958183  9958199  9958229
9958231  9958237  9958253  9958259  9958271  9958279  9958283  9958303  9958309  9958331
9958357  9958363  9958453  9958457  9958463  9958519  9958537  9958573  9958591  9958621
9958631  9958633  9958639  9958681  9958691  9958693  9958703  9958709  9958723  9958759
9958763  9958807  9958841  9958847  9958849  9958853  9958873  9958901  9958913  9958937
9958939  9958961  9958969  9958973  9958999  9959009  9959017  9959041  9959051  9959057
9959063  9959077  9959113  9959129  9959143  9959167  9959219  9959227  9959231  9959233
9959237  9959251  9959291  9959303  9959311  9959321  9959329  9959371  9959393  9959407
9959431  9959449  9959461  9959471  9959479  9959491  9959497  9959513  9959523  9959533
9959563  9959581  9959611  9959633  9959639  9959641  9959659  9959683  9959687  9959689
9959699  9959749  9959753  9959777  9959779  9959797  9959801  9959803  9959837  9959861
9959867  9959869  9959879  9959899  9959927  9959947  9959981  9959987  9960023  9960029
9960031  9960043  9960053  9960059  9960091  9960101  9960107  9960143  9960157  9960163
9960169  9960179  9960187  9960211  9960217  9960233  9960239  9960259  9960277  9960281
9960337  9960341  9960347  9960359  9960367  9960371  9960383  9960407  9960443  9960463
9960473  9960479  9960493  9960527  9960553  9960583  9960619  9960653  9960667  9960673
9960683  9960719  9960761  9960763  9960773  9960779  9960781  9960787  9960869  9960877
9960901  9960941  9960943  9960947  9960961  9960967  9960971  9960989  9961009  9961033
9961037  9961043  9961051  9961057  9961129  9961141  9961151  9961207  9961213  9961243
9961249  9961267  9961279  9961283  9961291  9961313  9961333  9961351  9961381  9961387
9961397  9961421  9961429  9961451  9961459  9961463  9961487  9961517  9961519  9961531
9961543  9961573  9961579  9961583  9961607  9961613  9961631  9961649  9961657  9961669
9961673  9961687  9961723  9961733  9961739  9961771  9961817  9961841  9961867  9961873
9961879  9961907  9961927  9961937  9961951  9961957  9961961  9961981  9962003  9962027
9962033  9962047  9962053  9962063  9962077  9962083  9962087  9962101  9962149  9962171
9962179  9962189  9962201  9962207  9962233  9962283  9962291  9962317  9962321  9962333
9962339  9962347  9962363  9962387  9962389  9962401  9962411  9962413  9962417  9962509
9962443  9962461  9962489  9962497  9962521  9962531  9962567  9962591  9962597  9962599
9962639  9962651  9962653  9962683  9962737  9962753  9962759  9962761  9962767  9962779
9962801  9962809  9962819  9962837  9962839  9962851  9962857  9962891  9962893  9962923
9962929  9962951  9962957  9962963  9962977  9962983  9962987  9962999  9963029  9963043
9963061  9963067  9963077  9963127  9963137  9963169  9963199  9963223  9963227  9963251
9963263  9963281  9963299  9963329  9963337  9963341  9963361  9963367  9963383  9963407
9963419  9963449  9963463  9963469  9963487  9963521  9963539  9963553  9963563  9963571
9963587  9963641  9963689  9963703  9963713  9963719  9963727  9963739  9963749  9963769
9963787  9963797  9963823  9963827  9963829  9963839  9963871  9963883  9963913  9963929
9963931  9963959  9963973  9963977  9963997  9964007  9964013  9964021  9964049  9964099
9964111  9964133  9964153  9964177  9964181  9964183  9964187  9964217  9964247  9964259
9964291  9964301  9964321  9964327  9964343  9964369  9964403  9964439  9964463  9964469
9964481  9964483  9964489  9964501  9964561  9964579  9964597  9964613  9964631  9964639
9964651  9964667  9964769  9964781  9964793  9964811  9964813  9964841  9964847  9964857
9964859  9964879  9964883  9964909  9964931  9964937  9964939  9964961  9964967  9964979
9965023  9965027  9965029  9965051  9965071  9965083  9965089  9965093  9965117  9965161
9965171  9965191  9965203  9965227  9965239  9965257  9965273  9965311  9965339  9965341
9965359  9965369  9965377  9965381  9965399  9965401  9965407  9965411  9965413  9965447
9965479  9965497  9965503  9965507  9965533  9965537  9965573  9965581  9965603  9965611
9965651  9965687  9965699  9965701  9965713  9965717  9965729  9965731  9965737  9965743
9965759  9965777  9965779  9965783  9965797  9965801  9965803  9965819  9965843  9965863
9965869  9965881  9965903  9965947  9965951  9965957  9965959  9966001  9966007  9966023
9966037  9966091  9966113  9966137  9966139  9966167  9966191  9966193  9966211  9966217
9966223  9966251  9966259  9966263  9966269  9966277  9966323  9966329  9966331  9966347
9966367  9966371  9966389  9966409  9966419  9966433  9966449  9966493  9966499  9966503
9966511  9966529  9966533  9966547  9966559  9966577  9966581  9966587  9966599  9966623
9966629  9966643  9966667  9966689  9966701  9966707  9966721  9966769  9966791  9966799
9966823  9966829  9966853  9966863  9966871  9966881  9966937  9966941  9966967  9966989
9966997  9967003  9967031  9967033  9967043  9967063  9967079  9967081  9967103  9967123
9967129  9967147  9967159  9967163  9967169  9967183  9967187  9967189  9967249  9967259
9967261  9967277  9967297  9967301  9967327  9967333  9967367  9967379  9967409
9967411  9967421  9967439  9967453  9967481  9967483  9967499  9967501  9967513  9967537
9967549  9967597  9967601  9967621  9967649  9967669  9967673  9967681  9967691
9967697  9967703  9967721  9967759  9967777  9967781  9967801  9967813  9967819  9967823
9967883  9967891  9967987  9968009  9968029  9968041  9968053  9968113  9968117  9968129
9968149  9968173  9968201  9968219  9968231  9968243  9968261  9968263  9968279
9968291  9968297  9968317  9968351  9968359  9968363  9968381  9968411  9968417  9968423
9968449  9968461  9968509  9968519  9968533  9968537  9968551  9968573  9968587
9968627  9968633  9968641  9968657  9968659  9968669  9968677  9968687  9968713  9968719
9968741  9968767  9968771  9968789  9968809  9968839  9968843  9968857  9968879  9968891
9968899  9968911  9968927  9968951  9968971  9969023  9969059  9969101  9969103  9969121
9969133  9969137  9969151  9969161  9969173  9969187  9969203  9969209  9969221  9969227
9969229  9969233  9969263  9969269  9969283  9969313  9969329  9969331  9969341  9969367
9969397  9969431  9969451  9969457  9969503  9969517  9969523  9969527  9969529  9969551
9969559  9969571  9969577  9969601  9969611  9969629  9969637  9969653  9969689  9969697
9969703  9969709  9969719  9969731  9969793  9969797  9969809  9969823  9969857  9969859
9969887  9969893  9969899  9969907  9969913  9969919  9969923  9969931  9969943  9969959
9970001  9970019  9970027  9970049  9970073  9970091  9970111  9970123  9970139  9970141
9970151  9970159  9970183  9970223  9970237  9970241  9970243  9970249  9970273  9970283
9970291  9970303  9970333  9970357  9970397  9970409  9970423  9970463  9970481  9970487
9970489  9970529  9970531  9970537  9970549  9970567  9970579  9970589  9970603  9970607
9970621  9970679  9970699  9970703  9970729  9970733  9970757  9970777  9970783  9970787
9970811  9970847  9970853  9970859  9970861  9970879  9970901  9970907  9970951  9970981
9971033  9971047  9971063  9971107  9971123  9971131  9971147  9971149  9971153  9971161
```

```
9971173  9971179  9971207  9971209  9971251  9971281  9971287  9971303  9971341  9971359
9971363  9971387  9971393  9971407  9971411  9971417  9971441  9971461  9971483  9971497
9971501  9971509  9971513  9971519  9971539  9971551  9971597  9971603  9971641  9971653
9971681  9971683  9971699  9971711  9971729  9971749  9971761  9971779  9971783  9971807
9971837  9971839  9971861  9971881  9971887  9971917  9971921  9971957  9971959  9971989
9971993  9972007  9972023  9972029  9972043  9972059  9972101  9972103  9972119  9972139
9972161  9972187  9972199  9972233  9972241  9972329  9972343  9972377  9972379  9972383
9972401  9972439  9972449  9972451  9972497  9972509  9972527  9972551  9972559  9972569
9972577  9972581  9972583  9972617  9972623  9972631  9972649  9972653  9972673  9972679
9972691  9972713  9972733  9972757  9972773  9972779  9972803  9972811  9972913  9972973
9972997  9973001  9973003  9973009  9973021  9973027  9973049  9973057  9973079  9973109
9973121  9973123  9973133  9973147  9973153  9973163  9973199  9973207  9973211  9973213
9973217  9973219  9973241  9973253  9973261  9973297  9973307  9973321  9973331  9973349
9973357  9973367  9973393  9973409  9973417  9973489  9973507  9973511  9973517  9973531
9973547  9973567  9973589  9973591  9973597  9973603  9973627  9973631  9973669  9973673
9973751  9973753  9973763  9973793  9973811  9973813  9973819  9973837  9973853  9973871
9973877  9973889  9973903  9973907  9973919  9973921  9973931  9973933  9973981  9974021
9974039  9974051  9974077  9974093  9974099  9974101  9974113  9974117  9974131  9974137
9974147  9974177  9974179  9974197  9974213  9974227  9974243  9974269  9974273  9974287
9974299  9974309  9974317  9974333  9974339  9974351  9974353  9974469  9974483  9974489
9974399  9974401  9974407  9974431  9974443  9974473  9974509  9974513  9974527  9974551
9974557  9974561  9974609  9974611  9974651  9974653  9974689  9974711  9974747  9974761
9974771  9974773  9974803  9974807  9974821  9974827  9974837  9974843  9974897  9974911
9974929  9974933  9974947  9974957  9974969  9974977  9974983  9975029  9975037  9975067
9975079  9975109  9975131  9975157  9975181  9975187  9975191  9975193  9975197  9975223
9975253  9975263  9975281  9975299  9975319  9975331  9975337  9975359  9975367  9975373
9975389  9975403  9975431  9975451  9975457  9975461  9975529  9975547  9975569  9975593
9975599  9975619  9975631  9975643  9975683  9975689  9975709  9975727  9975733  9975737
9975773  9975803  9975827  9975839  9975841  9975851  9975857  9975863  9975899  9975943
9975989  9976003  9976013  9976027  9976037  9976061  9976063  9976067  9976081  9976091
9976097  9976103  9976151  9976171  9976193  9976201  9976217  9976223  9976247  9976259
9976279  9976289  9976303  9976313  9976321  9976333  9976381  9976409  9976429  9976453
9976469  9976471  9976481  9976511  9976523  9976529  9976537  9976541  9976553  9976591
9976607  9976613  9976619  9976627  9976639  9976649  9976651  9976669  9976693  9976697
9976711  9976763  9976777  9976787  9976801  9976819  9976847  9976853  9976859  9976861
9976867  9976873  9976913  9976921  9976927  9976933  9976937  9977021  9977027  9977041
9977047  9977053  9977057  9977069  9977137  9977141  9977183  9977203  9977213  9977237
9977251  9977269  9977273  9977287  9977311  9977321  9977327  9977329  9977339  9977371
9977389  9977399  9977411  9977437  9977447  9977449  9977483  9977503  9977509  9977519
9977551  9977579  9977581  9977593  9977599  9977609  9977633  9977651  9977659  9977683
9977741  9977767  9977777  9977783  9977797  9977809  9977819  9977839  9977867
9977873  9977881  9977887  9977899  9977909  9977911  9977917  9977921  9977923  9977951
9977971  9977977  9977993  9977999  9978037  9978041  9978079  9978103  9978119  9978131
9978169  9978179  9978191  9978223  9978229  9978257  9978281  9978289  9978301  9978307
9978313  9978323  9978341  9978347  9978359  9978361  9978383  9978427  9978431  9978461
9978547  9978557  9978583  9978587  9978599  9978601  9978607  9978613  9978649  9978799
9978653  9978659  9978719  9978721  9978733  9978737  9978739  9978767  9978791  9978799
9978811  9978817  9978821  9978827  9978833  9978877  9978883  9978887  9978889  9978911
9978919  9978959  9978961  9979019  9979037  9979061  9979091  9979111  9979127
9979163  9979169  9979183  9979213  9979243  9979259  9979261  9979271  9979273  9979283
9979297  9979301  9979327  9979337  9979399  9979433  9979469  9979471  9979511  9979513
9979537  9979549  9979553  9979577  9979609  9979621  9979639  9979643  9979681  9979727
9979759  9979763  9979771  9979777  9979789  9979811  9979817  9979819  9979843  9979859
9979877  9979889  9979897  9979927  9979943  9979961  9979967  9979993  9980017  9980021
9980029  9980053  9980063  9980077  9980083  9980099  9980107  9980123  9980129  9980141
9980143  9980153  9980167  9980177  9980209  9980221  9980227  9980231  9980237  9980239
9980249  9980251  9980279  9980281  9980287  9980291  9980293  9980297  9980303  9980317
9980351  9980363  9980389  9980431  9980441  9980459  9980461  9980471  9980473  9980519
9980539  9980599  9980603  9980629  9980693  9980699  9980723  9980731  9980741  9980749
9980771  9980777  9980813  9980837  9980857  9980863  9980869  9980899  9980911  9980941
9980969  9980987  9981001  9981043  9981053  9981073  9981079  9981121  9981143  9981151
9981161  9981197  9981199  9981211  9981221  9981229  9981271  9981317  9981319  9981341
9981359  9981371  9981373  9981383  9981463  9981467  9981551  9981557  9981599  9981611
9981637  9981661  9981689  9981691  9981731  9981733  9981739  9981779  9981787  9981799
9981809  9981847  9981863  9981869  9981889  9981899  9981911  9981913  9981919  9981929
9981943  9982051  9982057  9982067  9982097  9982099  9982117  9982123  9982127  9982139
9982169  9982171  9982183  9982211  9982237  9982241  9982243  9982303  9982319  9982333
9982337  9982363  9982373  9982381  9982433  9982457  9982477  9982499  9982513  9982517
9982523  9982541  9982549  9982571  9982591  9982597  9982601  9982607  9982627  9982631
9982649  9982663  9982669  9982673  9982681  9982697  9982703  9982729  9982747  9982769
9982781  9982783  9982787  9982801  9982807  9982811  9982829  9982831  9982867  9982871
9982879  9982883  9982901  9982909  9982913  9982939  9982957  9982963  9982979  9982981
9983011  9983033  9983101  9983107  9983137  9983151  9983161  9983179  9983203  9983207
9983243  9983251  9983263  9983273  9983287  9983293  9983339  9983371  9983383  9983387
9983399  9983401  9983423  9983497  9983507  9983509  9983527  9983541  9983549  9983551
9983579  9983591  9983609  9983629  9983639  9983653  9983689  9983707  9983723  9983773
9983789  9983791  9983837  9983839  9983867  9983929  9983959  9983971  9983977  9983983
9983989  9983999  9984011  9984031  9984059  9984061  9984067  9984071  9984089  9984097
9984103  9984119  9984131  9984133  9984167  9984179  9984187  9984199  9984209  9984223
9984229  9984241  9984251  9984301  9984311  9984347  9984353  9984383  9984397  9984421
9984431  9984437  9984451  9984479  9984493  9984521  9984563  9984577  9984587  9984589
9984619  9984631  9984647  9984649  9984673  9984677  9984679  9984683  9984701  9984713
9984739  9984743  9984757  9984761  9984769  9984781  9984787  9984803  9984811  9984827
9984833  9984851  9984859  9984869  9984881  9984893  9984913  9984929  9984941  9984979
9984991  9985021  9985033  9985037  9985057  9985061  9985067  9985091  9985093  9985109
9985111  9985123  9985139  9985169  9985187  9985207  9985229  9985231  9985237  9985249
9985259  9985267  9985303  9985319  9985333  9985351  9985361  9985373  9985397  9985399
9985403  9985421  9985429  9985433  9985447  9985453  9985499  9985501  9985553  9985559
9985601  9985607  9985631  9985637  9985649  9985669  9985693  9985709  9985739  9985753
```

```
9985763 9985771 9985799 9985853 9985867 9985879 9985891 9985901 9985903 9985909
9985961 9985973 9985993 9986023 9986029 9986033 9986051 9986057 9986069 9986111
9986113 9986161 9986183 9986213 9986227 9986233 9986239 9986257 9986287 9986323
9986351 9986359 9986369 9986377 9986407 9986413 9986443 9986467 9986479 9986489
9986503 9986507 9986539 9986563 9986567 9986569 9986573 9986591 9986593 9986611
9986651 9986653 9986659 9986693 9986699 9986731 9986747 9986749 9986783 9986791
9986813 9986831 9986849 9986857 9986861 9986863 9986881 9986897 9986917 9986941
9986987 9986993 9987001 9987013 9987031 9987071 9987091 9987113 9987119 9987121
9987157 9987181 9987191 9987209 9987247 9987253 9987283 9987287 9987311 9987317
9987323 9987389 9987391 9987403 9987413 9987427 9987433 9987443 9987457 9987493
9987503 9987511 9987533 9987539 9987553 9987569 9987577 9987617 9987643 9987671
9987709 9987737 9987793 9987827 9987841 9987851 9987853 9987877 9987881 9987889
9987893 9987931 9987937 9987941 9987949 9987953 9987961 9987973 9987979 9988001
9988007 9988057 9988063 9988073 9988109 9988127 9988157 9988171 9988177 9988211
9988213 9988229 9988249 9988271 9988283 9988291 9988301 9988309 9988313 9988331
9988339 9988361 9988369 9988373 9988397 9988399 9988403 9988411 9988453 9988481
9988553 9988579 9988587 9988599 9988607 9988609 9988633 9988687 9988691 9988697
9988711 9988721 9988733 9988747 9988753 9988757 9988793 9988817 9988873 9988879
9988907 9988921 9988939 9988949 9988973 9988981 9988991 9989027 9989039 9989053
9989059 9989071 9989123 9989159 9989167 9989171 9989173 9989179 9989191 9989197
9989227 9989233 9989237 9989261 9989267 9989293 9989321 9989323 9989327 9989341
9989377 9989381 9989389 9989411 9989417 9989423 9989431 9989437 9989477 9989503
9989509 9989569 9989579 9989587 9989671 9989677 9989689 9989699 9989713 9989723
9989729 9989737 9989747 9989779 9989807 9989813 9989827 9989849 9989879 9989887
9989899 9989921 9989923 9989927 9989957 9990017 9990047 9990089 9990121 9990131
9990133 9990137 9990163 9990187 9990193 9990209 9990221 9990251 9990263 9990283
9990289 9990307 9990359 9990389 9990403 9990457 9990467 9990473 9990493 9990499
9990551 9990557 9990569 9990653 9990661 9990667 9990677 9990683 9990689 9990727
9990731 9990733 9990769 9990767 9990769 9990779 9990797 9990803 9990811 9990817
9990821 9990833 9990847 9990857 9990859 9990863 9990887 9990899 9990913 9990919
9990943 9990949 9990999 9991007 9991027 9991057 9991063 9991069 9991087 9991123
9991127 9991133 9991139 9991141 9991151 9991159 9991183 9991187 9991199 9991211
9991259 9991277 9991297 9991301 9991313 9991337 9991343 9991349 9991357 9991379
9991433 9991439 9991441 9991451 9991463 9991469 9991489 9991513 9991553 9991559
9991567 9991571 9991603 9991649 9991669 9991673 9991691 9991693 9991697 9991711
9991727 9991757 9991769 9991771 9991811 9991837 9991847 9991879 9991939 9991963
9991973 9991997 9992009 9992029 9992033 9992053 9992057 9992083 9992113 9992117
9992131 9992149 9992161 9992173 9992197 9992201 9992207 9992231 9992237 9992263
9992281 9992291 9992321 9992329 9992363 9992383 9992401 9992449 9992483 9992491
9992497 9992531 9992533 9992569 9992597 9992621 9992629 9992639 9992663 9992669
9992681 9992693 9992699 9992711 9992713 9992737 9992743 9992761 9992777 9992783
9992797 9992861 9992867 9992869 9992891 9992903 9992909 9992921 9992933 9992963
9993019 9993047 9993079 9993083 9993089 9993091 9993103 9993119 9993121 9993149
9993167 9993169 9993173 9993209 9993223 9993227 9993233 9993239 9993257 9993271
9993289 9993317 9993337 9993341 9993343 9993349 9993359 9993383 9993397 9993407
9993409 9993413 9993419 9993437 9993443 9993457 9993469 9993473 9993493 9993517
9993527 9993539 9993541 9993551 9993611 9993623 9993629 9993649 9993679 9993701
9993703 9993743 9993769 9993793 9993803 9993821 9993827 9993857 9993869
9993871 9993881 9993887 9993901 9993911 9993913 9993917 9993923 9993941 9993967
9993989 9994001 9994003 9994021 9994027 9994043 9994091 9994097 9994099 9994109
9994141 9994151 9994163 9994169 9994177 9994207 9994219 9994223 9994261 9994273
9994289 9994321 9994331 9994333 9994337 9994349 9994363 9994367 9994373 9994379
9994393 9994399 9994417 9994421 9994427 9994441 9994451 9994469 9994499 9994507
9994553 9994559 9994573 9994603 9994613 9994631 9994669 9994681 9994697 9994709
9994717 9994727 9994739 9994753 9994757 9994769 9994799 9994801 9994807 9994813
9994861 9994867 9994871 9994913 9994951 9995003 9995009 9995023 9995039 9995057
9995077 9995093 9995101 9995107 9995119 9995129 9995147 9995149 9995213 9995239
9995243 9995257 9995329 9995333 9995341 9995347 9995369 9995407 9995411 9995413
9995437 9995477 9995483 9995497 9995519 9995527 9995533 9995549 9995563 9995567
9995569 9995581 9995597 9995599 9995611 9995617 9995647 9995659 9995669 9995683
9995701 9995717 9995723 9995743 9995801 9995827 9995831 9995837 9995849 9995861
9995891 9995903 9995911 9995927 9995971 9995987 9995999 9996001 9996011 9996059
9996067 9996073 9996089 9996137 9996139 9996149 9996157 9996209 9996211 9996241
9996247 9996263 9996313 9996359 9996361 9996373 9996419 9996457 9996461 9996487
9996491 9996509 9996517 9996523 9996541 9996557 9996583 9996589 9996593 9996599
9996617 9996631 9996647 9996659 9996667 9996673 9996703 9996709 9996719 9996737
9996751 9996757 9996781 9996803 9996809 9996817 9996823 9996829 9996859 9996887
9996931 9996937 9996949 9996991 9997007 9997033 9997049 9997063 9997069 9997087
9997093 9997109 9997123 9997129 9997133 9997177 9997189 9997201 9997219 9997237
9997291 9997303 9997319 9997321 9997327 9997333 9997349 9997357 9997367 9997381
9997397 9997441 9997451 9997483 9997517 9997523 9997573 9997577 9997579 9997583
9997597 9997601 9997613 9997621 9997627 9997643 9997661 9997697 9997703 9997711
9997717 9997747 9997753 9997771 9997783 9997787 9997817 9997829 9997831 9997859
9997873 9997877 9997879 9997913 9997927 9997937 9997951 9997957 9997969 9997987
9997991 9997997 9998017 9998033 9998099 9998117 9998119 9998121 9998127 9998143
9998147 9998173 9998179 9998201 9998203 9998207 9998239 9998249 9998273 9998279
9998281 9998309 9998321 9998323 9998333 9998377 9998381 9998393 9998413 9998423
9998441 9998447 9998459 9998479 9998539 9998543 9998557 9998561 9998581 9998587
9998603 9998623 9998633 9998641 9998689 9998699 9998701 9998719 9998741 9998743
9998749 9998753 9998777 9998797 9998801 9998809 9998851 9998861 9998867 9998887
9998893 9998903 9998929 9998969 9998971 9998987 9999047 9999049 9999053 9999071
9999083 9999161 9999163 9999167 9999193 9999217 9999221 9999233 9999271 9999277
9999289 9999299 9999317 9999337 9999347 9999397 9999401 9999419 9999433 9999463
9999469 9999481 9999511 9999533 9999593 9999601 9999637 9999653 9999659 9999667
9999677 9999713 9999739 9999749 9999761 9999823 9999863 9999877 9999883 9999889
9999901 9999907 9999929 9999931 9999937 9999943 9999971 9999973 9999991
```

time 2:40:48.984000

www.ingramcontent.com/pod-product-compliance
Lightning Source LLC
Chambersburg PA
CBHW031809170526
45157CB00001B/6